LM 1711918 9

# The Grants Register 2021

# The Grants Register 2021

The Complete Guide to Postgraduate Funding Worldwide

Thirty-Ninth Edition

Palgrave Macmillan
Macmillan Publishers Ltd.

ISBN 978-1-349-95987-7          ISBN 978-1-349-95988-4 (eBook)
ISBN 978-1-349-95989-1 (print and electronic bundle)
https://doi.org/10.1057/978-1-349-95988-4

The Palgrave imprint is published by Springer Nature.
The registered company is Macmillan Publishers Ltd. London.

# Preface

The thirty-ninth edition of *The Grants Register* provides a detailed, accurate and comprehensive survey of awards intended for students at or above the postgraduate level, or those who require further professional or advanced vocational training.

Student numbers around the world continue to grow rapidly, and overseas study is now the first choice for many of these students. *The Grants Register* provides comprehensive, up-to-date information about the availability of, and eligibility for, non-refundable postgraduate and professional awards worldwide.

We remain grateful to the institutions which have supplied information for inclusion in this edition, and would also like to thank the International Association of Universities for continued permission to use their subject index within our Subject and Eligibility Guide to Awards.

*The Grants Register* database is updated continually in order to ensure that the information provided is the most current available. **Therefore, if your details have changed or you would like to be included for the first time, please contact the Senior Editor, at the address below.** If you wish to obtain further information relating to specific application procedures, please contact the relevant grant-awarding institution, rather than the publisher.

The Grants Register
Palgrave Macmillan
The Macmillan Campus
4 Crinan St
London
N1 9XW
United Kingdom
Tel: 144 (0)207 843 4634
Fax: 144 (0)207 843 4650
Email: Grants.Register@spi-global.com

Ruth Lefèvre
Senior Editor

For ease of use, *The Grants Register 2021* is divided into four sections:

- The Grants Register
- Subject and Eligibility Guide to Awards
- Index of Awards
- Index of Awarding Organisations

## *The Grants Register*

Information in this section is supplied directly by the awarding organisations. Entries are arranged alphabetically by name of organisation, and awards are listed alphabetically within the awarding organisation. This section includes details on subject area, eligibility, purpose, type, numbers offered, frequency, value, length of study, study establishment, country of study, and application procedure. Full contact details appear with each awarding organisation and also appended to individual awards where additional addresses are given.

---

# A

**AACR - American Association for Cancer Research**

615 Chestnut St., 17th Floor, Philadelphia, PA 19106-4404, United States of America.

**Tel:** (1) 215 440 9300
**Email:** aacr@aacr.org
**Website:** www.aacr.org/

From the simple beginning of a few scientists gathering to share information to the multifaceted organization that exists today, the growth of the AACR reflects the increasing complexity of our understanding of over 200 diseases we now know as cancer.

**AACR NextGen Grants for Transformative Cancer Research**

**Purpose:** The AACR NextGen Grants for Transformative Cancer Research represent a funding initiative to stimulate highly innovative research from young investigators. This grant mechanism is intended to promote and support creative, paradigm-shifting cancer research that may not be funded through conventional channels. It is expected that these grants will catalyze significant scientific discoveries and help talented young investigators gain scientific independence. The grants provide US\$450,000 over three years for expenses related to the research project, which may include salary and benefits of the grant recipient, postdoctoral or clinical research fellows, graduate students (including tuition costs), and research assistants, research/laboratory supplies, equipment, travel applicable to the research project, publication charges for manuscripts that pertain directly to the funded project, other research expenses, and indirect costs.

**Eligibility:** Applicants must have a doctoral degree (PhD, MD, MD/PhD, or equivalent) in a related field and not currently be a candidate for a further doctoral degree. At the start of the grant term on Nov. 1, applicants must: hold a tenure-eligible appointment (or equivalent, if institution does not follow a tenure system) at the rank of assistant professor (appointments such as research assistant professor, adjunct assistant professor, assistant professor research track, visiting professor, or instructor are not eligible; applicants that have progressed to associate professor appointments are also not eligible.); have held a tenure-eligible assistant professor appointment for less than three years (appointed on or after Nov. 1, 2017); and work at an academic, medical, or research institution anywhere in the world. If eligibility is based on a future position, the position must be confirmed at the time of submission, and CANNOT be contingent upon receiving this grant. If the future position is at a different institution than the applicant's current institution, the applicant must contact AACR's Scientific Review and Grants Administration Department (AACR's SRGA) at grants@aacr.org before submitting their Letter of Intent for information on additional verification materials/signatures that may be required. There are no citizenship or geographic requirements. However, by submitting a Letter of Intent for this grant, an applicant applying from an institution located in a country in which they are not a citizen or a permanent resident assures that their visa status will provide sufficient time to complete the project and grant term at the institution from which they applied.
**Level of Study:** Masters
**Type:** Fellowship
**Value:** US\$450,000
**Length of Study:** 3 years
**Frequency:** Annual
**Country of Study:** US
**Application Procedure:** The AACR requires applicants to complete an online Letter of Intent submission by 1 p.m. U.S. Eastern Time, Tuesday, May 5, using the proposalCENTRAL website at proposalcentral.com Program

## Subject and Eligibility Guide to Awards

Awards can be located through the Subject and Eligibility Guide to Awards. This section allows the user to find an award within a specific subject area. *The Grants Register* uses a list of subjects endorsed by the International Association of Universities (IAU), the information centre on higher education, located at UNESCO, Paris. It is further subdivided into eligibility by nationality. Thereafter, awards are listed alphabetically within their designated category, along with a page reference where full details of the award can be found.

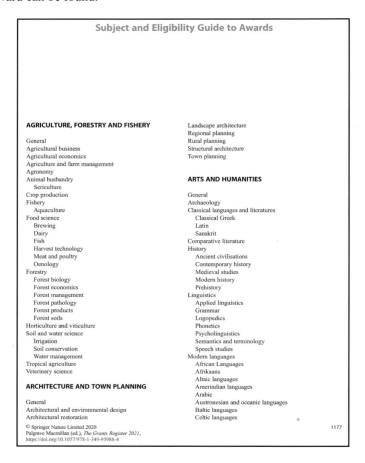

**Subject and Eligibility Guide to Awards**

**AGRICULTURE, FORESTRY AND FISHERY**

General
Agricultural business
Agricultural economics
Agriculture and farm management
Agronomy
Animal husbandry
  Sericulture
Crop production
Fishery
  Aquaculture
Food science
  Brewing
  Dairy
  Fish
  Harvest technology
  Meat and poultry
  Oenology
Forestry
  Forest biology
  Forest economics
  Forest management
  Forest pathology
  Forest products
  Forest soils
Horticulture and viticulture
Soil and water science
  Irrigation
  Soil conservation
  Water management
Tropical agriculture
Veterinary science

**ARCHITECTURE AND TOWN PLANNING**

General
Architectural and environmental design
Architectural restoration

Landscape architecture
Regional planning
Rural planning
Structural architecture
Town planning

**ARTS AND HUMANITIES**

General
Archaeology
Classical languages and literatures
  Classical Greek
  Latin
  Sanskrit
Comparative literature
History
  Ancient civilisations
  Contemporary history
  Medieval studies
  Modern history
  Prehistory
Linguistics
  Applied linguistics
  Grammar
  Logopedics
  Phonetics
  Psycholinguistics
  Semantics and terminology
  Speech studies
Modern languages
  African Languages
  Afrikaans
  Altaic languages
  Amerindian languages
  Arabic
  Austronesian and oceanic languages
  Baltic languages
  Celtic languages

1177

## Index of Awards

All awards are indexed alphabetically with a page reference.

## Index of Awarding Organisations

A complete list of all awarding organisations, with country name and page reference.

# List of Contents

# A

## AACR - American Association for Cancer Research

615 Chestnut St., 17th Floor, Philadelphia, PA 19106-4404, United States of America.

**Tel:**       (1) 215 440 9300
**Email:**    aacr@aacr.org
**Website:**  www.aacr.org/

From the simple beginning of a few scientists gathering to share information to the multifaceted organization that exists today, the growth of the AACR reflects the increasing complexity of our understanding of over 200 diseases we now know as cancer.

## AACR NextGen Grants for Transformative Cancer Research

**Purpose**: The AACR NextGen Grants for Transformative Cancer Research represent a funding initiative to stimulate highly innovative research from young investigators. This grant mechanism is intended to promote and support creative, paradigm-shifting cancer research that may not be funded through conventional channels. It is expected that these grants will catalyze significant scientific discoveries and help talented young investigators gain scientific independence. The grants provide US$450,000 over three years for expenses related to the research project, which may include salary and benefits of the grant recipient, postdoctoral or clinical research fellows, graduate students (including tuition costs), and research assistants, research/laboratory supplies, equipment, travel applicable to the research project, publication charges for manuscripts that pertain directly to the funded project, other research expenses, and indirect costs.

**Eligibility**: Applicants must have a doctoral degree (PhD, MD, MD/PhD, or equivalent) in a related field and not currently be a candidate for a further doctoral degree. At the start of the grant term on Nov. 1, applicants must: hold a tenure-eligible appointment (or equivalent, if institution does not follow a tenure system) at the rank of assistant professor (appointments such as research assistant professor, adjunct assistant professor, assistant professor research track, visiting professor, or instructor are not eligible; applicants that have progressed to associate professor appointments are also not eligible.); have held a tenure-eligible assistant professor appointment for less than three years (appointed on or after Nov. 1, 2017); and work at an academic, medical, or research institution anywhere in the world. If eligibility is based on a future position, the position must be confirmed at the time of submission, and CANNOT be contingent upon receiving this grant. If the future position is at a different institution than the applicant's current institution, the applicant must contact AACR's Scientific Review and Grants Administration Department (AACR's SRGA) at grants@aacr.org before submitting their Letter of Intent for information on additional verification materials/signatures that may be required. There are no citizenship or geographic requirements. However, by submitting a Letter of Intent for this grant, an applicant applying from an institution located in a country in which they are not a citizen or a permanent resident assures that their visa status will provide sufficient time to complete the project and grant term at the institution from which they applied.

**Level of Study**: Masters
**Type**: Fellowship
**Value**: US$450,000
**Length of Study**: 3 years
**Frequency**: Annual
**Country of Study**: US
**Application Procedure**: The AACR requires applicants to complete an online Letter of Intent submission by 1 p.m. U.S. Eastern Time, Tuesday, May 5, using the proposalCENTRAL website at proposalcentral.com Program

© Springer Nature Limited 2020
Palgrave Macmillan (ed.), *The Grants Register 2021*,
https://doi.org/10.1057/978-1-349-95988-4

Guidelines and Competitive Letter of Intent Instructions are available for download.

**Closing Date**: 5 May

**Additional Information**: proposalcentral.com/

## AACR-Bayer Stimulating Therapeutic Advances through Research Training (START) Grants

**Purpose**: Dramatic advances made in recent years towards precision medicine initiatives, biomarker and novel target identification, and high-throughput examination of genomic data, have resulted in a trove of valuable data that can inform the development of new therapeutics to combat cancer. However, to effectively harness this wealth of information and advance the discovery and development of new therapies for cancer patients, enhanced collaboration between academia and industry will be needed. The AACR-Bayer Stimulating Therapeutic Advances through Research Training (START) Grants represent an exciting and novel initiative to encourage and support such collaboration. These grants, which will provide support to postdoctoral or clinical research fellows, combines research experiences in both an academic and industry setting, following a research timeline that will be of greatest benefit to the proposed work. The training provided through this grants program will be invaluable to young investigators, by allowing fellows to attain a comprehensive research experience that will make them highly desirable to potential employers in either academic research or the pharmaceutical industry. Likewise, academic research centers and industry will benefit from the introduction of such dual-trained individuals into the field. Each fellowship provides a three-year grant of US$225,000 to support the salary and benefits of the fellow while working on a mentored cancer research project. Proposals focused on clinical research are highly encouraged. Applicants must plan to spend one year on site at a Bayer facility. One of a number of Bayer's locations are possible, at the discretion of Bayer. The year at Bayer will be determined on a case-by-case basis, and will be at a time agreed upon by the fellow, the academic supervisor, the Bayer mentor, and Bayer.

**Eligibility**: Applicants must have a doctoral degree (PhD, MD, MD/PhD, or equivalent) in a related field and not currently be a candidate for a further doctoral degree.At the start of the grant term on Nov. 1, applicants must: hold a tenure-eligible appointment (or equivalent, if institution does not follow a tenure system) at the rank of assistant professor (appointments such as research assistant professor, adjunct assistant professor, assistant professor research track, visiting professor, or instructor are not eligible; applicants that have progressed to associate professor appointments are also not eligible.); have held a tenure-eligible assistant professor appointment for less than three years (appointed on or after

Nov. 1, 2017); and work at an academic, medical, or research institution anywhere in the world. If eligibility is based on a future position, the position must be confirmed at the time of submission, and CANNOT be contingent upon receiving this grant. If the future position is at a different institution than the applicant's current institution, the applicant must contact AACR's Scientific Review and Grants Administration Department (AACR's SRGA) at grants@aacr.org before submitting their Letter of Intent for information on additional verification materials/signatures that may be required. There are no citizenship or geographic requirements. However, by submitting a Letter of Intent for this grant, an applicant applying from an institution located in a country in which they are not a citizen or a permanent resident assures that their visa status will provide sufficient time to complete the project and grant term at the institution from which they applied.

**Level of Study**: Masters

**Type**: Fellowship

**Value**: US$225,000

**Length of Study**: 3 years

**Frequency**: Annual

**Country of Study**: US

**Application Procedure**: The AACR requires applicants to submit an online application by 1:00 p.m. U.S. Eastern Time on May 26 using the proposalCENTRAL website at proposalcentral.com/. Program Guidelines and Application Instructions are available for download.

**Closing Date**: 26 May

**Additional Information**: proposalcentral.com/

## Aarhus University

Nordre Ringgade 1, DK-8000 Aarhus C, Denmark.

**Tel**:　　　　(45) 8715 0000, (45) 30 31478610
**Website**:　www.au.dk

Established in 1928, Aarhus University has since developed into a major Danish university with a strong international reputation across the entire research spectrum.

## Aarhus University Scholarships

**Purpose**: Aarhus University Scholarships are available for highly qualified non-European Union/EEA/Swiss applicants to pursue 2-year master's degree programmes

**Value**: A monthly scholarship for a maximum of 1 year and 11 months

**Country of Study**: Denmark
**Application Procedure**: All applications for Master's degree programmes at Aarhus University must be submitted online through the digital application portal
**Closing Date**: 15 March
**Additional Information**: The scholarships are awarded on the basis of the following criteria: 1. Students may apply for any English-taught Master's degree programme at Aarhus University. 2. The scholarships generally include a full tuition waiver and generally, but not always, including a monthly scholarship for a maximum of 1 year and 11 months for the duration of the degree programme. 3. The general admission requirements and application procedures and deadlines at Aarhus University apply. Prior to applying for admission, applicants are kindly asked to make themselves acquainted with the specific admission requirements for the Master's degree programmes they wish to apply for international.au.dk/education/admissions/exchange/studying-at-aarhus-university/scholarships/

**For further information contact:**

**Email**: ELKLIT@ps.au.dk

## Aaron Siskind Foundation

C/o School of Visual Arts, MFA Photography, 209 East 23rd Street, New York, NY 10010, United States of America.

**Tel**:    (1) 212 592 2363
**Email**:    info@aaronsiskind.org
**Website**:    www.aaronsiskind.org

The Foundation works to preserve and protect Aaron Siskind's artistic legacy, and foster knowledge of and appreciation of his art.

### Individual Photographer

**Purpose**: To stimulate excellence and the promise of future achievement in the photographic field
**Eligibility**: Applicants must be at least 21 years of age. Students enrolled in a college degree program are not eligible to apply. Please note: students who will graduate before the application deadline are eligible to apply. Previous IPF recipients are not currently being considered for new awards.
**Level of Study**: Postgraduate
**Type**: Fellowship or Grant
**Value**: US$15,000 each

**Frequency**: Annual
**Country of Study**: Any country
**Application Procedure**: Applications must be submitted through the Slideroom application portal at www.slideroom.com
**Closing Date**: 18 May
**Funding**: Private
**Additional Information**: aaronsiskind.org/grant.html

## Abbey Harris Mural Fund

43 Carson Road, London, SE21 8HT, United Kingdom.

**Tel**:    (44) 20 8761 7980
**Email**:    administrator@abbey.org.uk
**Website**:    www.abbey.org.uk
**Contact**:    Ms Jane Reid, Administrator

The Abbey Harris Mural Fund supports the creation of murals in public places in the United Kingdom.

### Abbey Harris Mural Fund

**Purpose**: To provide grants to artists who have been commissioned to create murals in public places or in charitable institutions in the United Kingdom
**Eligibility**: Awards are for painters and the work must be carried out in the United Kingdom. There are other restrictions
**Level of Study**: Unrestricted
**Type**: Grant
**Value**: Approx. £3,000
**Frequency**: Annual
**Country of Study**: United Kingdom
**Application Procedure**: Applicants must send for an application form, enclosing a stamped addressed envelope. Application forms can also be requested by email
**No. of awards offered**: 6
**Funding**: Private
**Contributor**: E A Abbey Memorial Trust Fund for Mural Painting in Great Britain and E Vincent Harris Fund for Mural Decoration
**No. of awards given last year**: 2
**No. of applicants last year**: 6
**Additional Information**: abbey.org.uk/about_abbey_harris

**For further information contact:**

**Email**:    contact@abbey.org.uk

## Abdul Aziz Al Ghurair Foundation For Education

### The Abdul Aziz Al Ghurair Refugee Education Fund

**Purpose**: The Abdul Aziz Al Ghurair Refugee Education Fund invites proposals for programs that explore and identify new solutions to long-standing challenges in refugee education that can improve impact at scale. The Abdul Aziz Al Ghurair Refugee Education Fund aims to equip young refugees with a pathway to sustainable livelihoods

**Eligibility**: 1. Organisations must have experience in at least one successful program with refugees (Syrian and/or Palestinian). 2. be able to demonstrate proof of concept and potential for scale; be a non-profit organisation; be registered in either Jordan and/or Lebanon or have programmes or partners based there. Other eligibility terms for this fundings are listed below. Able to demonstrate proof of concept, that the program or pilot has had significant impact and has potential to be scaled to benefit larger number of refugee youth in Jordan and/or Lebanon. 1. Be a non-profit organization, including educational institutions. The Fund will consider forprofit companies on an exceptional basis and with clear rationale. 2. Be a registered organization in either Jordan and/or Lebanon where the activities would take place or have programs or partners based in either Lebanon and/or Jordan

**Level of Study**: Professional development, Foundation programme

**Type**: Funding support

**Frequency**: Annual

**Country of Study**: Jordan

**Application Procedure**: Application form details are entitled on the below link. Kindly check the following files. www.alghurairfoundation.org/sites/default/files/The%20Abdul%20Aziz%20Al%20Ghurair%20Refugee%20Education%20Fund%20Grant%20Guidelines%20February%202019.pdf

**Closing Date**: 19 March

**Funding**: Private

**Additional Information**: www.alghurairfoundation.org/en/content/abdul-aziz-al-ghurair-refugee-education-fund-call-proposals-0

### For further information contact:

Abdulla Al Ghurair Foundation for Education, P.O.Box 6999, Dubai, UAE.

**Email**:   info@alghurairfoundation.org

## Abdus Salam International Centre for Theoretical Physics (ICTP)

Strada Costiera 11, 34151 Trieste, Italy.

**Tel**:            (39) 40 224 0111
**Email**:        sci_info@ictp.it
**Website**:     www.ictp.it
**Contact**:     May Ann Williams, Public Information Officer

The Abdus Salam International Centre for Theoretical Physics (ICTP) is an institution for research and high-level training in physics and mathematics, mainly for scientists from developing countries. It also maintains a network of associate members and federated institutes.

### Abdus Salam ICTP Fellowships

**Purpose**: To enable qualified applicants to pursue research in the fields of condensed matter physics, mathematics and high-energy physics

**Eligibility**: Open to qualified applicants of any nationality who have a PhD in physics or mathematics

**Level of Study**: Postdoctorate

**Type**: Fellowship

**Value**: Monthly stipend and round-trip expenses where applicable, and allowances according to the length of the visit

**Length of Study**: Up to 1 year

**Frequency**: Dependent on funds available

**Study Establishment**: ICTP

**Country of Study**: Italy

**Application Procedure**: Applicants must visit the ICTP website

**Closing Date**: 31 January

**Funding**: Government

**Contributor**: The Italian government, IAEA and UNESCO

### For further information contact:

**Email**:   calligar@ictp.it

## Abell Foundation

Suite 2300, 111 S. Calvert Street, Baltimore, MD 21202-6174, United States of America.

**Tel**:            (1) 410 547 1300
**Website**:     www.abell.org/

The Abell Foundation, formerly known as The A.S. Abell Company Foundation, was established on December 31, 1953 by Harry C Black, philanthropist and then chairman of the board of the A.S. Abell Company, the former publisher of The Baltimore Sun. Upon the sale of the A.S. Abell Company in 1986, the resources of the Foundation increased significantly. The Abell Foundation is the largest private foundation serving only Maryland. The Foundation has acted as an agent of change by supporting innovative, results-oriented efforts to ameliorate the systemic social, economic, and environmental challenges encountered by those living in concentrated poverty. With a unique focus on Baltimore City, Abell provides grant funding to enterprising non-profits as well as research to better inform civic conversation. It also invests in new businesses and technologies that have the potential to benefit society and build Baltimore's workforce. Since its establishment, the Abell Foundation has contributed more than US$339,000,000 to the community.

## Abell Foundation - For Small Grant Requests

**Purpose**: The Abell Foundation is dedicated to the enhancement of the quality of life in Maryland, with a focus on Baltimore City. The Foundation is committed to improving the lives of underserved populations by supporting innovative, results-oriented efforts to solve systemic social, economic, and environmental problems.
**Eligibility**: The Foundation funds nonprofit organizations located and active in Maryland. Our focus is on Baltimore City, with more than 95% of our grants being awarded to organizations in the Baltimore metropolitan area.
**Level of Study**: Masters/PhD Degree
**Type**: Grants
**Value**: Up to US$5,000
**Country of Study**: US
**Application Procedure**: For grant requests greater than US$5,000: Step 1: Letter of Inquiry. The Foundation requests that applications for new grants in excess of US$5,000 are initiated by providing a letter of inquiry. A letter of inquiry should include: Description of the project; Amount requested; Total budget: Population served. A letter of inquiry is NOT necessary if the grantee has previously applied, or if contact has been made with the President, Vice President, or relevant Program Officer first to ensure that the proposed project meets the Foundation's criteria. A letter of inquiry is also NOT necessary if the grant amount requested is US$5,000 or less. These small grants are considered on a rolling basis. Please submit your letter of inquiry by email to abell@abell.org or mail a hard copy to: Robert C. Embry, Jr., President, Abell Foundation, 111 South Calvert Street, Suite 2300, Baltimore, MD 21202. Step 2: Application, If the Foundation is interested in reviewing the project described in the letter of inquiry, the applicant will receive an invitation to complete a more detailed application. Applications should be completed online. If you do not have access to the Internet, please mail a hard copy of your application with attachments to: Robert C. Embry, Jr., President, Abell Foundation, 111 South Calvert Street, Suite 2300, Baltimore, Maryland 21202
**Closing Date**: 1 May
**Additional Information**: www.abell.org/applying-funding

### For further information contact:

**Email**: abell@abell.org

## Abell Foundation - Grant Requests Greater than $5,000

**Purpose**: The Abell Foundation is dedicated to the enhancement of the quality of life in Maryland, with a focus on Baltimore City. The Foundation is committed to improving the lives of underserved populations by supporting innovative, results-oriented efforts to solve systemic social, economic, and environmental problems.
**Eligibility**: The Foundation funds nonprofit organizations located and active in Maryland. Our focus is on Baltimore City, with more than 95% of our grants being awarded to organizations in the Baltimore metropolitan area.
**Level of Study**: Masters/PhD Degree
**Type**: Grants
**Value**: US$5,000
**Country of Study**: US
**Application Procedure**: For Grant Requests Greater than US$5,000: Step 1: Letter of Inquiry. The Foundation requests that applications for new grants in excess of US$5,000 are initiated by providing a letter of inquiry. A letter of inquiry should include: Description of the project; Amount requested; Total budget: Population served. A letter of inquiry is NOT necessary if the grantee has previously applied, or if contact has been made with the President, Vice President, or relevant Program Officer first to ensure that the proposed project meets the Foundation's criteria. A letter of inquiry is also NOT necessary if the grant amount requested is US$5,000 or less. These small grants are considered on a rolling basis. Please submit your letter of inquiry by email to abell@abell.org or mail a hard copy to: Robert C. Embry, Jr., President, Abell Foundation, 111 South Calvert Street, Suite 2300, Baltimore, MD 21202, Step 2: Application If the Foundation is interested in reviewing the project described in the letter of inquiry, the applicant will receive an invitation to complete a more detailed application. Applications should be completed online. Click here to complete a report or return to a saved application. If you do not have access to the Internet, please

mail a hard copy of your application with attachments to: Robert C. Embry, Jr., President, Abell Foundation, 111 South Calvert Street, Suite 2300, Baltimore, Maryland 21202
**Closing Date**: 1 May
**Additional Information**: www.abell.org/applying-funding

### For further information contact:

**Email**:    abell@abell.org

## Abilene Christian University

College of Business Administration, MBA Program Graduate School Office, PO Box 29140, Abilene, TX 79699, United States of America.

**Tel**:          (1) 915 674 2466
**Email**:      mbainfo@web.acu.edu
**Contact**:   MBA Admissions Officer

### Abilene Christian University National Merit Finalist or Semifinalist Scholarship

**Purpose**: Abilene Christian University offers a variety of levels of academic scholarships to incoming first-time freshmen (students entering ACU with fewer than 12 hours, excluding dual credit, AP and IB) based on academic achievements, class rank, and standardized test scores
**Eligibility**: To be eligible for this award, 1. National Merit Finalists and Semifinalist are required to list ACU as first choice with the National Merit Corporation. 2. Recipients must also participate in the Honors College by completing four honors courses within your first year. Students must complete an Honors College application as soon as he/she is awarded a scholarship
**Level of Study**: Postgraduate
**Type**: Scholarship
**Value**: US$32,020
**Frequency**: Annual
**Country of Study**: Any country
**Application Procedure**: To apply, students must apply for admission to Abilene Christian University (ACU) and provide their National Merit Certificate to the admissions office. For further information, check the below link. www.acu.edu/parents.html
**Closing Date**: 1 February
**Funding**: Private
**Additional Information**: www.unigo.com/scholarships/all/abilene-christian-university-national-merit-finalist-or-semifinalist-scholarship/1002888

### For further information contact:

1600 Campus Ct, Abilene, TX 79601, United States of America.

**Tel**:          (1) 800 460 6228
**Email**:      info@admissions.acu.edu

### Abilene Christian University Valedictorian/ Salutatorian Scholarship

**Purpose**: Abilene Christian University offers a variety of levels of academic scholarships to incoming first-time freshmen (students entering ACU with fewer than 12 hours, excluding dual credit, AP and IB) based on academic achievements
**Eligibility**: Must be a U.S citizen. Must be accepted to Abilene Christian University. Must be an incoming first year freshmen. Must have a number one or number two high school class rank. This award is for U.S students.
**Level of Study**: Postgraduate
**Type**: Scholarship
**Value**: US$1,000
**Frequency**: Annual
**Country of Study**: Any country
**Closing Date**: 1 February
**Funding**: Private
**Additional Information**: Abilene Christian University offers a variety of levels of academic scholarships to incoming first-time freshmen (students entering ACU with fewer than 12 hours, excluding dual credit, AP and IB) based on academic achievements, class rank, and standardized test scores at the time of admission. Interested students should contact ACU for additional information or visit the college website. www.unigo.com/scholarships/all/abilene-christian-university-valedictoriansalutatorian-scholarship-/1002884

### For further information contact:

Hunter Welcome Center Rm 140 ACU Box 29000 Abilene, TX 79699-9000, United States of America.

**Tel**:          (1) 800 460 6228; 325 674 2650
**Email**:      info@admissions.acu.edu

### Society for Immunotherapy of Cancer Scholarship

**Purpose**: The School of Information Technology and Computing awards scholarships in varying amounts to a select number of incoming freshmen and transfer students each year
**Eligibility**: Scholarship applicants must declare a major in Computer Science, Computer Science/Math Teaching or Digital Entertainment Technology (DET)

**Level of Study**: Graduate
**Type**: Scholarship
**Frequency**: Annual
**Country of Study**: Any country
**Application Procedure**: Application has to be processed through physical mailing address. apply.acu.edu/register/?id=3f5eee06-eddd-41c3-9d36-2dffb4f8400b
**Funding**: Private

**For further information contact:**

**Email**:    info@admissions.acu.edu

## Abraham Lincoln High School

## Abraham Lincoln High School Alumni Association

**Purpose**: The purpose of the ALHS Alumni Association Scholarship Program is to make available scholarships to Lincoln High School students who are graduating and going onto college or continuing education
**Eligibility**: 1. ALHS Alumni will award scholarships. 2. ALHS graduating seniors seeking to further his/her education by obtaining a higher degree such as AA, BA, BS, or Certificated from a Trade, Vocational School or Military Academy. 3. Applications shall be completed by the applicant together with the official transcript, recommendation(s) by faculty/staff member(s), school activities records and a personal statement by the applicant of his/her goals. 4. Applicants will be evaluated and judged on the following factors. a. Their scholastic record. b. Their activity and other evidence of leadership and character. c. Recommendations of faculty and/or staff. d. A personal statement by applicant of his/her goals must be attached together with official transcripts, school activities records and personal statement by the applicant. 5. Results of the competition will be announced in April. Judging will be done by the ALHS Alumni Association Scholarship Committee. The committee looks forward to honoring the recipients in person at the Annual Wall of Fame/Scholarship Dinner. If the recipient is unable to attend the Scholarship Dinner a family member should attend to accept the scholarship on their behalf
**Level of Study**: Postgraduate
**Type**: Funding support
**Frequency**: Annual
**Country of Study**: Any country
**Closing Date**: 20 April
**Funding**: Private
**Additional Information**: www.sfusd.edu/school/abraham-lincoln-high-school/alumni/alumni-association

**For further information contact:**

2162 24th Avenue San Francisco, CA 94116, United States of America.

**Tel**:        (1) 415 759 2700
**Email**:    scholarships@lincolnalumni.com

## Academia Resource Management (ARM)

535 East 4500 South, Suite D-120, Salt Lake City, UT 84107, United States of America.

**Tel**:        (1) 801 273 8911
**Email**:    info@armanagement.org
**Website**:   www.awu.org

Academia Resource Management (ARM) is committed to the advancement of scientific knowledge and enrichment of the academic experience. Its mission is to identify and facilitate mutually beneficial research and training endeavours among academic institutions, government agencies and private industry.

## Academia Resource Management Postgraduate Fellowship

**Purpose**: To fund postgraduate research and technology at co-operating facilities
**Level of Study**: Postgraduate
**Type**: Fellowship
**Value**: Varies
**Frequency**: Annual
**Country of Study**: United States of America
**Application Procedure**: Applicants need to submit their application form, transcripts and reference letters
**Funding**: Foundation
**Contributor**: Academia Resource Management

## Academy of Marketing Science Foundation

424 Santa Teresa Street Stanford University, Stanford, CA 94305-4015, United States of America.

**Tel**:        (1) 650 723 3054
**Email**:    ams.sba@miami.edu

**Website**:    www.ams-web.org
**Contact**:    Ms Rania Hegazi, Fellowship Administrator

Under the direction of Dr Harold W Berkman, the Academy of Marketing Science may be considered a full service scholarly professional organisation. The AMS established the Academy of Marketing Science Foundation to provide awards to marketing students, primarily at the graduate level. It is also the intention of the Foundation to provide awards for both the advancement of the teaching of marketing and for research in marketing.

## Mary Kay Doctoral Dissertation Award

**Purpose**: Sponsored by Mary Kay Inc. and the Academy of Marketing Science, doctoral candidates in marketing who have completed their dissertation
**Eligibility**: Open to individuals of any nationality
**Level of Study**: Doctorate
**Value**: the winner will receive US$600 and a one-year membership in the Academy of Marketing Science. Two runners up will receive US$500 each.
**Frequency**: Annual
**Country of Study**: Any country
**No. of awards offered**: AMS members who participate
**Closing Date**: 5 January
**No. of applicants last year**: AMS members who participate
**Additional Information**: The Academy of Marketing Science (AMS) does not fund scholarships or grants towards studies. Awards and cash prizes are presented at the AMS Annual Conference to Academy members that participated in various paper competitions cdn.ymaws.com/www.ams-web.org/resource/resmgr/2020_ac/2020_dissert_invtn.pdf

## Academy of Medical Sciences

41 Portland Place, London, W1B 1QH, United Kingdom.

**Email**:     newton-advanced@acmedsci.ac.uk
**Website**:    www.acmedsci.ac.uk

Finding the brightest and best, celebrating their achievements and harnessing their expertise for the benefit of wider society is central to our role as a National Academy.

## Daniel Turnberg Travel Fellowships

**Purpose**: This scheme aims to build research links and developing ongoing scientific collaborations between the United Kingdom and the Middle East. Daniel Turnberg Travel Fellowships give chance to undertake short-term visits to learn research techniques
**Eligibility**: Your research must fall within the broad scope of medical or bioscience research
**Level of Study**: Research
**Type**: Fellowship
**Value**: Up to £3,500 (four weeks) or up to £9,000 (three months)
**Length of Study**: Four weeks or three months
**Frequency**: Annual
**Country of Study**: United Kingdom
**Application Procedure**: Applications will need to be submitted online using the Academy's electronic Grants and Awards management system Flexi-Grant®. Please download the guidance notes from the right hand side of this page to assist you in your application. If you have any queries after referring to the guidance notes. For further details, contact turnberg.fellowships@acmedsci.ac.uk
**Closing Date**: January
**Funding**: Private
**Additional Information**: Use the below link for scholarship application. acmedsci.ac.uk/grants-and-schemes/grant-schemes/daniel-turnberg-travel-fellowship wellcome.ac. uk/funding/schemes/daniel-turnberg-travel-fellowships

### For further information contact:

The Academy of Medical Sciences, 41 Portland Place, London, W1B 1QH, United Kingdom.

**Email**:     turnberg.fellowships@acmedsci.ac.uk

## Global Challenges Research Fund Networking Grants

**Purpose**: These grants provide opportunities for researchers, drawn from a wide spectrum of disciplines and backgrounds. It helps to develop new collaborations and improve interactions between United Kingdom researchers and those in developing countries
**Eligibility**: The GCRF Networking Grants will be delivered as part of the Joint Academies Resilient Futures programme. Your application will be reviewed by Fellows across all of the partnership Academies and experts from developing or Low and Middle Income Countries (LMICs), and you will not need to attend an interview
**Level of Study**: Research
**Type**: Grant
**Value**: Awards provide up to £25,000 over a year
**Frequency**: Annual
**Country of Study**: Any country
**Application Procedure**: Applications are invited from researchers affiliated to institutions in DAC-listed countries

in collaboration with researchers within eligible United Kingdom higher education institutions (HEIs). You will need to apply for the programme using the Academy's online grant management system: Flexi-Grant. Grants cannot be used to pay for salary costs or to employ research assistants, PhD students or postdoctoral staff

**Closing Date**: 31 March
**Funding**: Private
**Additional Information**: acmedsci.ac.uk/grants-and-schemes/grant-schemes/gcrf-networking-grants

### For further information contact:

**Email**: gcrfnetworking@acmedsci.ac.uk

## Newton Advanced Fellowships

**Purpose**: Mid-career postdoctoral career-development fellowship. Available for overseas researchers from specific countries in collaboration with a researcher at a United Kingdom institution
**Eligibility**: Must have a PhD or equivalent research experience. have less than 15 years of postdoctoral experience. hold a permanent or fixed-term contract in an eligible university or research institute which must span the duration of the project. are based in one of the eligible Newton Fund partner Countries.
**Level of Study**: Postdoctorate
**Type**: Fellowship
**Value**: Salary top up of £5,000 for the overseas-based researcher and/or project leader ("the Applicant") from the partner country. Research support. Travel and subsistence. Training costs
**Length of Study**: 2 years
**Frequency**: Annual
**Country of Study**: United Kingdom
**Application Procedure**: Applications can only be submitted online using the Royal Society's electronic Grant. Application and Processing (e-GAP) system. Please download Newton Advanced Fellowship Scheme notes for guidance on applying. To find out more information about the application process and to apply please follow the link royalsociety.org/grants/schemes/newton-advanced-fellowships
**Closing Date**: 10 March
**Funding**: Government
**Contributor**: The Academy of Medical Sciences, in partnership with the Royal Society and the British Academy
**Additional Information**: We are working to include additional countries in future calls royalsociety.org/grants-schemes-awards/grants/newton-advanced-fellowships/

### For further information contact:

**Tel**: (44) 20 7451 2666

## Newton International Fellowships

**Purpose**: Early-career postdoctoral fellowship opportunity for overseas (non-United Kingdom) researchers to spend 2 years, full-time researching at a United Kingdom institution
**Eligibility**: Must have a PhD, or will have a PhD by the time the funding starts. Must have no more than 7 years of active full time postdoctoral experience at the time of application (discounting career breaks, but including teaching experience and/or time spent in industry). Must be working outside the UK. Must hold UK citizenship. Must be competent in oral and written English. Must have a clearly defined and mutually-beneficial research proposal agreed with a UK host scientist
**Level of Study**: Postdoctorate
**Type**: Fellowship
**Value**: £24,000 per annum. Research expenses. Contribution to overheads at UK host organisation
**Length of Study**: 2 years
**Frequency**: Annual
**Application Procedure**: Applications can only be submitted online using the Royal Society's electronic Grant Application and Processing (e-GAP) system. Please download Newton Advanced Fellowship Scheme notes for guidance on applying. To find out more information about the application process and to apply please follow the link royalsociety.org/grants/schemes/newton-advanced-fellowships
**Closing Date**: 26 March
**Funding**: Government
**Additional Information**: royalsociety.org/grants-schemes-awards/grants/newton-international/

### For further information contact:

**Tel**: (44) 20 7451 2666
**Email**: newton-international@acmedsci.ac.uk

## Academy of Sciences of the Czech Republic

UNESCO-ROSTE Course Institute of Microbiology Videnská 1083, CS-142 20 Prague, Czech Republic.

**Tel**: (420) 2 4752 379
**Email**: nerud@biomed.cas.cz
**Website**: www.biomed.cas.cz
**Contact**: Mr F Nerud, Director of Course

The Institute of Microbiology is one of the major biological institutes of the Academy of Sciences. Main areas of research at the Institute include biogenesis and biotechnology of natural compounds, cell and molecular microbiology, ecology, immunology, gnotobiology and autotrophic micro-organisms.

## United Nations Educational, Scientific and Cultural Organization-ROSTE Long-term Postgraduate Training Course

**Purpose**: To enable young scientists to obtain a more profound education and prepare for a research career
**Eligibility**: Open to young scientists from European countries and a limited number of students from other regions who hold an MSc, PhD or equivalent degree, and who have two-three years of practical experience in their field. Candidates should be no more than 35 years of age and should possess a good knowledge of English
**Level of Study**: Postgraduate
**Type**: Grant
**Value**: KČ 5,000 plus accommodation
**Length of Study**: 11 months
**Frequency**: Annual
**Study Establishment**: Insitute of Microbiology of the Academy of Sciences of the Czech Republic
**Country of Study**: Czech Republic
**Application Procedure**: Applicants must write for details
**No. of awards offered**: 12
**Closing Date**: 31 March
**Funding**: Government
**Contributor**: The Academy of Sciences of the Czech Republic
**No. of awards given last year**: 6
**No. of applicants last year**: 12
**Additional Information**: The course is given in co-operation with the Czech Commission for UNESCO and sponsored by the Academy of Sciences of the Czech Republic

## Acadia University

Room 214 Horton Hall, 18 University Avenue, Wolfville, NS B4P 2R6, Canada.

**Tel:**       (1) 902 585 1914
**Email:**     theresa.starratt@acadiau.ca
**Website:**   www.acadiau.ca
**Contact:**   Ms Theresa Starratt, Graduate Studies Officer-Research and Graduate Studies

Acadia University is an institution that is committed to providing a liberal education based on the highest standards. The University houses a scholarly community that aims to ensure a broadening life experience for students, faculty and staff.

## Acadia Graduate Scholarship / Acadia Graduate Teaching Assistantships

**Purpose**: To financially support students
**Eligibility**: Open to registered full-time graduate students at Acadia University. In order to be eligible for an award, students must have a GPA of not less than 3.0 in their major field in each of their last 2 years of undergraduate study
**Level of Study**: Postgraduate
**Type**: Award
**Value**: Canadian Dollars. Value can vary
**Length of Study**: 1–2 years
**Frequency**: Annual
**Study Establishment**: The Division of Research and Graduate Studies at Acadia University
**Country of Study**: Canada
**Application Procedure**: Applicants must write for details. In almost all cases, to be automatically considered for funding, applicants need to apply by 1 February of each year
**Funding**: Private
**Additional Information**: Recipients of an Acadia Graduate Teaching Assistantship should expect to undertake certain duties during the academic year (up to 10 hours per week and a maximum of 120 hours per semester) as a condition of tenure  gradstudies.acadiau.ca/tl_files/sites/gradstudies/docs/University%20Support.pdf

## Action Cancer

1 Marlborough Park, Belfast, Co Antrim BT9 6XS, Northern Ireland.

**Tel:**       (44) 28 9080 3363
**Email:**     info@actioncancer.org
**Website:**   www.actioncancer.org
**Contact:**   Caroline Hughes, Research and Evaluation Officer

Action Cancer is a Northern Ireland cancer charity that relies entirely on voluntary donations. Founded in 1973, it offers awareness and health promotion, free early-detection clinics for men and women concerned about cancer and a support service for cancer patients and their families. Action Cancer also provides funding for research at local universities.

## Action Cancer Project Grant

**Purpose**: To help researchers in Northern Ireland carry out significant cancer-related projects by contributing to salaries, the purchase of materials and equipments and to other appropriate costs

**Eligibility**: Researchers must be working in Northern Ireland

**Level of Study**: Postdoctorate

**Type**: Project grant

**Value**: Up to £45,000 per year for up to 3 years

**Length of Study**: 3 years

**Frequency**: Every 2 years

**Country of Study**: United Kingdom

**Application Procedure**: Awards are advertised in the local press in March. Applicants must submit a form, based on which a decision is taken by the Action Cancer Scientific and Research Committee, which also takes advice from external reviewers

**Closing Date**: May

**Funding**: Private

**Contributor**: Voluntary donations

### For further information contact:

**Email**:    grants@solvingkidscancer.org

## Action Medical Research

Vincent House, North Parade, West Sussex, Horsham, RH12 2DP, United Kingdom.

**Tel**:        (44) 14 0321 0406
**Email**:     applications@action.org.uk
**Website**:   www.action.org.uk

Action Medical Research is dedicated to preventing and treating disease and disability by funding vital medical research in United Kingdom-based hospitals and universities. The remit focuses on child health with an emphasis on clinical research or research at the clinical/basic interface. Research applications are judged by rigorous peer review.

### Action Medical Research Project Grants

**Subjects**: A broad spectrum of research with the objective of preventing and treating disease and disability and alleviating physical disability The remit focuses on child health to include problems affecting pregnancy, childbirth, babies, children and adolescents.

**Purpose**: To support one precisely formulated line of research

**Eligibility**: Open to researchers based in the United Kingdom. Grants are not awarded to other charities or for higher education

**Level of Study**: Unrestricted

**Type**: Project grant

**Value**: Varies

**Length of Study**: Up to 3 years, assessed annually

**Frequency**: Dependent on funds available

**Study Establishment**: Hospitals, universities and recognised research establishments in the United Kingdom

**Country of Study**: United Kingdom

**Application Procedure**: Applicants must submit a one-page outline of the project before an application form can be issued. Full details and outline proposals are available on the website

**No. of awards offered**: Varies

**Closing Date**: 20 November

**Funding**: Private, Trusts, Individuals

**Contributor**: Voluntary income

**No. of awards given last year**: 12

**No. of applicants last year**: 83 applications

### Action Medical Research Training Fellowship

**Subjects**: A broad spectrum of research with the objective of preventing and treating disease and disability and alleviating physical disability. The remit focuses on child health to include problems affecting pregnancy, childbirth, babies, children and adolescents.

**Purpose**: To support training in research techniques and methodology applied to subjects relevant to the aims of the charity.

**Eligibility**: Open to researchers based in the United Kingdom. Grants are not awarded to other charities or for higher education.

**Level of Study**: Medical graduates, clinicians, bioengineers, research nurses, physiotherapists and allied health professionals

**Type**: Research Training Fellowship

**Value**: Up to £250,000

**Length of Study**: 2 or 3 years, assessed annually

**Frequency**: Dependent on funds available

**Study Establishment**: Hospitals, universities and recognised research establishments in the UK

**Country of Study**: United Kingdom

**Application Procedure**: Applicants must submit an outline of the project and may then be invited to submit a full application. Full details are available on the website.

**No. of awards offered**: Typically 2 or 3 annually

**Funding**: Private, Trusts, Individuals

**Contributor**: Voluntary income

**No. of awards given last year**: 2 awarded

**No. of applicants last year**: 26 applications

**Additional Information**: 13 full applications invited, 10 submitted, 5 interviewed

## Adelphi University

1 South Avenue, PO BOX 701, Garden City, NY 11530-0701, United States of America.

**Tel**:        (1) 516 877 3412/3080
**Email**:      ucinfo@adelphi.edu
**Website**:    www.adelphi.edu/

Adelphi University is the oldest institution of higher education for liberal arts and sciences on Long Island.

### Adelphi University Full-Time Transfer Merit Award

**Purpose**: Adelphi University has made a substantial commitment to make the cost of attending the University more affordable through its institutional scholarship and grant programs
**Eligibility**: Eligible students will receive a letter of notification from the Scholarship Committee. After filing the FAFSA, a financial assistance summary detailing all financial aid will be mailed to the student
**Type**: Award
**Value**: Up to US$11,000 depending upon the individual's academic profile
**Frequency**: Annual
**Country of Study**: Any country
**Application Procedure**: A student must first file an admissions application and is encouraged to file the FAFSA as soon as possible after 1 January, but no later than 15 February to ensure maximum eligibility for other sources of financial aid
**Additional Information**: financial-aid.adelphi.edu/files/2018/02/2018-2019-Transfer-Scholarship-for-Full-Time-Study.pdf

#### For further information contact:

**Tel**:        (1) 516 877 3080
**Email**:      admissions@adelphi.edu

## Advance Africa

### Baxter International Foundation Grants

**Purpose**: The Baxter International Foundation offers grants to NGOs working to provide accessibility and affordability of healthcare services to disadvantaged communities around the world
**Eligibility**: NGOs need to understand Foundation priorities, besides following the application procedures carefully while submitting the proposal. Although proposals are accepted round the year, there are quarterly deadlines

**Level of Study**: Graduate
**Type**: Grant
**Frequency**: Annual
**Country of Study**: Any country
**Application Procedure**: Submit the proposal through physical communication on the below address
**Funding**: Private
**Additional Information**: www.advance-africa.com/Baxter-International-Foundation-Grants.html

#### For further information contact:

The Baxter International Foundation, One Baxter Parkway - DF2-2E, Deerfield, IL 60015, United States of America.

**Tel**:        (1) 847 948 4605
**Email**:      fdninfo@baxter.com

### Maypole Fund Grants for Women

**Purpose**: Grants from the Maypole Fund have contributed to a wide range of activities
**Eligibility**: 1. Young women's groups/individuals. 2. Activities or projects not yet started. 3. Women who do not have access to other sources of funding or whose projects find it difficult to attract funding from elsewhere. 4. Imaginative/creative activities. 5. Individual and small women's groups over larger established women's groups
**Level of Study**: Postgraduate
**Type**: Funding support
**Value**: £750
**Frequency**: Annual
**Country of Study**: Any country
**Application Procedure**: Interested applicants can download the application forms via given website. The Maypole Fund is seeking applications from women only for projects and activities for any of the following: 1. Anti-militarism. 2. Action against the arms trade. 3. Action against nuclear weapons and weapons systems. Creating a culture of peace and non-violence and the prevention of conflict and war
**Closing Date**: 30 June
**Funding**: Private
**Additional Information**: www.maypolefund.org/the-grant/

### Rudolf Steiner Foundation Seed Fund

**Purpose**: It helps in Providing Small Grants to Organizations. The Rudolf Steiner Foundation (RSF) is inviting applicants for its Seed Fund to provide small grants to organizations that offer innovative solutions to challenges in the areas of social finance, food and agriculture, education and the arts, or ecological stewardship

**Eligibility**: 1. Alignment with RSF's mission and focus areas. 2. Non-profit status: The RSF Seed Fund accepts proposals from organizations that are any of the following: 501(c)(3) tax-exempt per the IRS Fiscally sponsored with 501(c)(3) tax-exempt status per the IRS. 3. Schools or universities. 4. Non-governmental entities, Indian tribes or tribal non-profit organizations, and territorial, tribal, or unit of local government entities

**Level of Study**: Postgraduate

**Type**: Award

**Value**: US$500 - US$3,500

**Frequency**: Annual

**Country of Study**: United States of America

**Application Procedure**: Apply online. 1. Interested applicants can apply online via given website. 2. Eligible Country: United States. For more information and grant application details, see; application details, see; RSF Seed Fund - Providing Small Grants to Organizations

**Closing Date**: 20 March

**Funding**: Private

**Additional Information**: www.instrumentl.com/grants/rudolf-steiner-foundation-seed-fund-grant-programme

**For further information contact:**

1002 O'Reilly Avenue, San Francisco, CA 94129, United States of America.

**Tel**: (1) 415 561 3900
**Email**: rsf@socialfinance.org

# African Forest Forum (AFF)

The African Forest Forum, United Nations Avenue, P.O. Box 30677, Nairobi, KE 00100, Kenya.

**Tel**: (254) 207 224 000
**Email**: exec.sec@afforum.org
**Website**: www.afforum.org/

The African Forest Forum is an association of individuals with a commitment to the sustainable management, wise use and conservation of Africa's forest and tree resources for the socio-economic well-being of its peoples and for the stability and improvement of its environment.

## African Forest Forum (AFF) Research Fellowships

**Purpose**: The African Forest Forum (AFF) is a pan-African non-governmental organization with its headquarters in Nairobi, Kenya. It is an association of individuals who share the quest for and commitment to the sustainable management, use and conservation of the forest and tree resources of Africa for the socio-economic wellbeing of its people and for the stability and improvement of its environment

**Eligibility**: Applicants must meet the general eligibility criteria as well as the specific eligibility criteria. Applications that do not meet eligibility criteria will not receive further evaluation. Should have a Master's or Bachelor's degree plus two or more years of professional experience related to forestry, natural resource management, development studies, climate change and environmental studies. Please refer to the website for more information

**Level of Study**: Postgraduate

**Value**: Each fellow will receive up to AF$10,000 for research and AF$2,000 to cover cost of travel, subsistence, and accommodation while in the field including supervision

**Country of Study**: Kenya

**Application Procedure**: Check website for more details

**Closing Date**: 31 May

**Funding**: Trusts

# African Mathematics Millennium Scientific Initiative

School of Mathematics, University of Nairobi, PO Box 30197, Nairobi, GPO 00100, Kenya.

**Tel**: (254) 20 445 0934
**Email**: ammsi@uonbi.ac.ke
**Website**: www.ammsi.org
**Contact**: Professor Wandera Ogana, AMMSI Programme Director

The African Mathematics Millennium Science Initiative (AMMSI) is a distributed network of mathematics research, training and promotion throughout sub-Saharan Africa. It has five regional offices located in Botswana, Cameroon, Kenya, Nigeria and Senegal. It is a project established by the Millennium Science Initiative (MSI), administered by the Science Initiative Group (SIG). The primary goal of the MSI is to create and nurture world-class science and scientific talent in the developing world by strengthening S&T capacity through integrated programmes of research and training, planned and driven by local scientists in the field of mathematics.

## Research/Visiting Scientist Fellowships

**Purpose**: The Scientific and Technological Research Council of Turkey (TÜBITAK) grants fellowships for international scientists/researchers who would like to give workshops/conferences/lectures, or conduct R&D activities in Turkey in the fields of Natural Sciences, Engineering and Technological Sciences, Medical Sciences, Agricultural Sciences, Social Sciences and Humanities. The program aims to promote Turkey's scientific and technological collaboration with countries of the prospective fellows

**Eligibility**: Candidates should undertake research and postgraduate teaching in mathematics at any university in sub-Saharan Africa, should be a staff member at a university and hold at least a Master's degree, and should obtain an official invitation from the host institution

**Level of Study**: Postgraduate

**Type**: Fellowships

**Value**: A monthly stipend of up to US$ 3500 for Visiting Scientists on Sabbatical Leave

**Length of Study**: 1–12 months

**Application Procedure**: Application forms should be filled and submitted online. In exceptional circumstances, hard copy application forms may be obtained from the nearest AMMSI Regional Coordinator whose contact details can be found in the website

**Closing Date**: 15 September

**Additional Information**: e-bideb.tubitak.gov.tr/ royalsociety.org/~/media/grants/schemes/TUBITAK_Fellowships_visiting_scientists.pdf

### For further information contact:

**Tel**:      (254) 20 235 8569/20 445 0934
**Fax**:      (254) 20 445 0934
**Email**:    progoffice@ammsi.org

---

## African Wildlife Foundation (AWF)

PO Box 48177, Nairobi, Kenya.

**Tel**:        (254) 2 710 367
**Email**:      awfnrb@awfke.org
**Website**:    www.awf.org

The African Wildlife Foundation (AWF) has been working with the people of Africa to protect their environment since 1961. Most of AWF's staff are based in Africa, working with park managers and communities to safeguard wildlife and wilderness areas. AWF helps African nations design long-term strategies for conserving their magnificent natural treasures for all the world to enjoy.

## African Institute for Mathematical Sciences Postdoctoral Fellowship in Data Science

**Purpose**: African Institute for Mathematical Sciences (AIMS) is a pan-African network of centers of excellence

for Postgraduate education, research and outreach in mathematical sciences

**Eligibility**: Applicants should be SADC member state, and applicant should be proficient in English language with good communication skills. A relevant doctorate of high standing and developing research capability which will lead to good publications. Candidates should have a ability to tutor postgraduate students successfully work as part of an interdisciplinary team

**Level of Study**: Graduate

**Type**: Fellowship

**Value**: ZAR200–ZAR240,000 per annul, tax-free, subject to qualification and experience. Other benefits include the provision of a laptop, coverage of all cost associated with the use of HPC resource

**Frequency**: Annual

**Country of Study**: Any country

**Closing Date**: February

**Funding**: Private

**Additional Information**: scholarship-fellowship.com/aims-postdoctoral-fellowship/

### For further information contact:

**Email**:    joan@aims.ac.za

---

## After School Africa

### AfterCollege STEM Inclusion Scholarship

**Purpose**: AfterCollege has been connecting students and recent grads with employers hiring for internships and entry-level positions since it was founded in a dorm room in 1999

**Eligibility**: To be eligible for this scholarship, you must be applying with this condition. 1. Minimum 3.0 GPA. 2. Applicant must be from a group underrepresented in their field of study. 3. Underrepresented groups may be defined by: gender, race, ethnic background, disability, sexual orientation, age, socio-economic status, nationality, and other non-visible differences. 4. Quarterly deadlines: 3/31; 6/30; 9/30; 12/31. 5. Winners notified 30 days after scholarship deadline. 6. After College profiles are used as criteria to select recipients

**Level of Study**: Graduate

**Type**: Scholarship

**Value**: US$500

**Frequency**: Annual

**Country of Study**: Any country

**Application Procedure**: In order to process the scholarship application, check the website. www.aftercollege.com/company/aftercollege-inc/10/scholarship/220/?source=ur-sch-stem

**Closing Date**: 31 March

**Funding**: Private
**Additional Information**: www.unigo.com/scholarships/all/aftercollege-stem-inclusion-scholarship/1003907

### For further information contact:

After College 98 Battery Street, Suite 502 San Francisco, CA 94111, United States of America.

**Email**:　scholarships@aftercollege.com

## HKBU Fully Funded International Postgraduate Scholarship

**Purpose**: The International Postgraduate Scholarship (IPS) scheme at the HKBU School of Business is a global initiative designed to nurture business leaders, bringing together highly talented and intellectually-motivated students from around the world to one of our selected taught postgraduate programmes. Although these young achievers come from diverse backgrounds, they have all demonstrated leadership potential and have a common interest in making a difference in the world.
**Eligibility**: Scholarships are available to students from all around the world.
**Level of Study**: Postgraduate
**Type**: Scholarship
**Value**: Full tuition fee waiver and allowance (HK$100,000 = ~US$12,800)
**Application Procedure**: 1. Submit your application online to one of the 5 masters programmes listed above. Competition increases as the year progress, so we recommend starting your application early. 2. No individual application for the IPS is required.
**Closing Date**: May
**Additional Information**: www.afterschoolafrica.com/32703/hkbu-fully-funded-international-postgraduate-scholarship-ips-scheme/

## Zhengzhou University President Scholarships

**Purpose**: The scholarship aims to sponsor international postgraduate students to pursue their degree, especially the doctor degree, in Zhengzhou University
**Eligibility**: This scholarship is eligible for International Candidates. 1. Non-Chinese citizen, physically healthy, without crime record. 2. Abide by the laws and regulations of the People's Republic of China as well as regulations of ZZU. 3. Good learning attitude and academic performance.
**Level of Study**: Postgraduate
**Type**: Scholarship
**Value**: Partial tuition fee
**Length of Study**: 3–4 years
**Frequency**: Annual

**Country of Study**: China
**Application Procedure**: Applicants must fill in an application form and submit the following supporting documents: 1. Original or notarized copies of highest degree (applicants must additionally submit study certificate or employment certificate issued by the applicants' schools if the applicants are students or employed). Documents in neither Chinese nor English must be attached with a notarized Chinese or English translations. 2. Applicants for master programs must provide original or notarized copies of bachelor study transcripts, and doctoral programs bachelor and master study transcripts. Documents in neither Chinese nor English must be attached with a notarized Chinese or English translations. 3. Applicants for master programs must provide study plans of 800 words, and for doctoral programs must provide research proposal of 2,000 words written in Chinese or English. 4. Applicants for master and doctoral programs must provide two letters of recommendation from associate professors or professors respectively written in Chinese or English. 5. Applicants for programs of art must submit other documents as in the requirements of ZZU; Official test results of Chinese or English language. 6. Original or notarized copies of Foreigner Physical Examination Form and blood test reports, filled in Chinese or English. 7. Original or notarized copies of certificates of no criminal record. Documents in neither Chinese nor English must be attached with a notarized Chinese or English translations
**Closing Date**: 30 June
**Funding**: Private
**Additional Information**: www.buddy4study.com/scholarship/zhengzhou-university-president-scholarship

### For further information contact:

No.100 Science Avenue, Zhengzhou, Henan Province, People's Republic of China.

**Tel**:　　(86) 371 67780102
**Email**:　zhaochun@zzu.edu.cn

## Agency for Science, Technology and Research (A*STAR)

1 Fusionopolis Way, 20-10 Connexis North Tower, 138632, Singapore.

**Tel**:　　(65) 6826 6111
**Email**:　contact@a-star.edu.sg
**Website**:　www.a-star.edu.sg/astar

A*STAR comprises of the Biomedical Research Council (BMRC), the Science and Engineering Research Council

(SERC), Exploit Technologies Private Ltd (ETPL), the A*STAR Graduate Academy (AGA) and the Corporate Planning and Administration Division (CPAD). Both BMRC and SERC promote, support and oversee the public sector R&D research activities in Singapore.

## A*Star Graduate Scholarship

**Purpose**: A fully funded overseas post-doctoral programme, the AGS Post-Doctoral Fellowship is opened only to A*STAR Graduate Scholarship (AGS) awardees. With this fellowship, scholars may conduct post-doctoral research at a leading overseas laboratory of their choice for up to two years.
**Eligibility**: 1. Have an excellent publication records. 2. Have applied or be applying for a post-doctoral position at a top overseas university/institution. 3. Applicants working or have worked in A*STAR Research Institute should have performed well and have strong recommendations from their supervisor and Research Institute Executive Director.
**Application Procedure**: As AGS (PDF) awardees are required to serve in an A*STAR Research Institute after their post-doctoral training, AGS (PDF) applicants should identify the relevant Research Institute in which they will work during their service commitment period, and engage the Research Institute Executive Director and prospective supervisor prior to their AGS (PDF) application.
**Additional Information**: www.a-star.edu.sg/Scholarships/for-post-doctoral-studies/a-star-graduate-scholarship-(post-doc)

### For further information contact:

**Email**:    tellusmore@hq.a-star.edu.sg

## Singapore International Graduate Award (SINGA)

**Purpose**: The Singapore International Graduate Award (SINGA) is a collaboration between the Agency for Science, Technology & Research (A*STAR), the Nanyang Technological University (NTU) and the National University of Singapore (NUS). PhD training will be carried out in English at chosen lab at A*STAR Research Institutes, NTU or NUS
**Eligibility**: Open to all international students; graduates with a passion for research and excellent academic results; good skills in written and spoken English; good reports from academic referees
**Type**: Award
**Value**: The award provides support for up to 4 years of PhD studies including: Monthly stipend of S$2,000, which will be increased to S$2,500 after the passing of the Qualifying Examination. One-time airfare grant of up to S$1,500*. One-time settling-in allowance of S$1,000

**Country of Study**: Singapore
**Application Procedure**: www.a-star.edu.sg/Scholarships/For-Graduate-Studies/Singapore-International-Graduate-Award-SINGA
**Closing Date**: 1 June
**Additional Information**: For detailed information, please visit www.singa.a-star.edu.sg/ www.a-star.edu.sg/Scholarships/For-Graduate-Studies/Singapore-International-Graduate-Award-SINGA

### For further information contact:

**Email**:    singa_enquiries@hq.a-star.edu.sg

# Agilent Technology and American Association of Critical Care Nurses

3000 Minuteman Road MS210, Andover, MA 01810, United States of America.

**Tel**:        (1) 978 659 4748
**Contact**:    Ms Joan Hodges, Learning Products Manager

## Agilent Technology Critical Care Nursing Research Grant

**Purpose**: To support research in critical care nursing. Preferred topics will address information technology requirements of patient management in critical care
**Eligibility**: AACN members may apply (current registered nurse members only). Research must be undertaken in the United States of America
**Level of Study**: Postgraduate
**Type**: Other
**Value**: US$37,000
**Length of Study**: 1 year
**Frequency**: Annual
**Study Establishment**: Hospital
**Country of Study**: United States of America
**Application Procedure**: Applicants must write to the Agilent Technology address for applications
**No. of awards offered**: 22
**No. of awards given last year**: 1
**No. of applicants last year**: 22
**Additional Information**: Questions about suitability of research topics should be addressed to the AACN Research Department

### For further information contact:

**Tel**:       (1) 800 394 5995
**Email**:    research@aacn.org

## Agricultural History Society

MSU History Department, PO Box H, Mississippi State, MS 39762, United States of America.

| | |
|---|---|
| Tel: | (1) 501 569 8782/662 268 2247 |
| Email: | CSTROM@Rollins.edu |
| Website: | www.aghistorysociety.org |
| Contact: | Claire Strom, Editor, Agricultural History |

The Agricultural History Society recognizes the roles of agriculture and agri-business in shaping the political, economic, social and historical profiles of different countries worldwide. Since 1927, the Society's publication, Agricultural History, has been the international journal for the field and publishes innovative research on agricultural and rural history.

## Agriculture Awareness Grants

**Purpose**: Metro Vancouver supports agriculture awareness by providing funding grants to community organizations to educate the public about local food and agricultural production. Grants are open to non-profit organizations that meet the eligibility criteria
**Eligibility**: 1. Funding will be available to nonprofit organizations within the state of Maine or serving students within the state of Maine. 2. US$60,000 is earmarked for grants in 5 categories
**Level of Study**: Postgraduate
**Type**: Grant
**Value**: The grant request is in the range of US$500 to US$6,000. A higher score will be awarded if the Metro Vancouver cash contribution is greater than 20% of the total cash budget, so that new or smaller projects that may have a greater financial need are prioritized.
**Frequency**: Annual
**Country of Study**: Any country
**Closing Date**: 2 March
**Funding**: Private
**Additional Information**: www.metrovancouver.org/services/regional-planning/agriculture/awareness-grants/Pages/default.aspx

### For further information contact:

GrantsAlert P.O. Box 706 Newton, Catawba, NC 28658, United States of America.

**Email**: maitca@maine.gov

## Henry A Wallace Award

**Purpose**: Presented to the author of the best book on any aspect of agricultural history outside the United States. The book must be based on substantial primary research and should represent new scholarly interpretation or reinterpretation of agricultural history scholarship
**Level of Study**: Unrestricted
**Type**: Award
**Value**: US$500
**Frequency**: Annual
**Country of Study**: Any country
**Application Procedure**: Applicants must send four copies of the book of the editor. Books may be nominated by their authors, the publisher, a member of the award committee, or a member of the society
**Closing Date**: 31 December
**No. of awards given last year**: 1
**Additional Information**: Available upon request to the Society

### For further information contact:

**Email**: mikegaul@iastate.edu

# Air Force Office of Scientific Research (AFOSR)

AFOSR/PIE, 4015 Wilson Boulevard Room 713, Arlington, VA 22203-1954, United States of America.

| | |
|---|---|
| Tel: | (1) 703 696 7319 |
| Email: | info@afosr.af.mil |
| Website: | www.afosr.af.mil |
| Contact: | Dr Koto White, Chief External Programmes & Resources Interface |

The Air Force Office of Scientific Research's (AFOSR) mission is to sponsor and sustain basic research, transfer and transition research results and support Air Force goals of control and maximum utilisation of air and space.

## United States Air Force Academy/National Research Council Summer Faculty Research Program (SFFP)

**Purpose**: To provide research opportunities for qualified faculty members of United States colleges and universities at Air Force research facilities within the continental United States

**Eligibility**: Applicants must be United States citizens or permanent residents, faculty members of accredited United States of America colleges, universities or technical institutions, and have at least two years of teaching or research experience

**Level of Study**: Professional development

**Value**: Assistant professors receive US$1,250, associate professors receive US$1,450, and full professors receive US$1,650 per week

**Length of Study**: 8–12 weeks

**Frequency**: Annual

**Study Establishment**: An Air Force facility

**Country of Study**: United States of America

**Application Procedure**: Applicants must contact the National Research Council on (1) 202 334 2760

**Closing Date**: 1 November

**Funding**: Government

**Additional Information**: Please see the website www. national-academies.org/rap afsffp.sysplus.com/SFFP/about/ stipends.aspx

---

# Air-Conditioning, Heating, and Refrigeration Institute

## Air-Conditioning, Heating, and Refrigeration Institute MSc Scholarship

**Purpose**: The AHRI MSc Scholarship, sponsored by University College London (UCL), is a singular award for the United Kingdom academic year. The scholarship is administered via AHRI and is for applicants whose academic background and interests are aligned with the programmes of research at AHRI

**Eligibility**: 1. Must be permanently based in South Africa at the time of application. 2. Must hold a valid passport at the time of application. 3. Must have an Honours degree equivalent to a Bachelor (Honours) degree with Second Class Division 1 Honours or 70% in an appropriate subject. 4. The successful applicant must be in London to start their chosen course in September

**Level of Study**: Postdoctorate

**Type**: Scholarship

**Frequency**: Annual

**Country of Study**: Any country

**Closing Date**: 29 March

**Funding**: Foundation

### For further information contact:

Nelson R. Mandela School of Medicine, 3rd Floor, K-RITH Tower Building, 719 Umbilo Road, Durban, South Africa.

| | |
|---|---|
| **Tel**: | (27) 31 260 4991 |
| **Email**: | info@ahri.org |

---

# Alabama A and M University

School of Business Administration, Office of the Dean of Graduate Studies & Extended Studies, PO Box 998, Normal, AL 35762, United States of America.

| | |
|---|---|
| **Tel**: | (1) 256 851 5266 |
| **Email**: | nmurrell@aamu.edu |
| **Contact**: | MBA Admissions Officer |

## Alabama Student Assistance Program

**Purpose**: The Alabama Student Grant Program is a state student assistance program designed to provide financial assistance to residents of the State of Alabama for undergraduate study

**Eligibility**: To be eligible for an Alabama Student Grant Program award the student must: (1) Have obtained a certificate of graduation from a secondary school or the recognized equivalence of such graduation. (2) Be classified as an undergraduate student. (3) Be an Alabama resident as defined in Alabama Student Grant Program Act 90. (4) Be a citizen of the United States or in the process of becoming a citizen of the United States. (5) Be enrolled as a full-time or half-time student in an eligible program in an approved institution. (6)Applicants must have obtained a certificate of graduation from a secondary school or the recognized equivalence of such graduation. (7) Be an Alabama resident as defined in Alabama Stud and Grant Program Act 90; be a citizen of the United States or in the process of becoming a citizen of the United States

**Level of Study**: Postgraduate

**Type**: Programme grant

**Value**: US$300–US$2,500

**Frequency**: Annual

**Country of Study**: Any country

**Funding**: Private

**Additional Information**: bigfuture.collegeboard.org/scholar ships/alabama-student-assistance-program

### For further information contact:

Scholarship Committee, 100 N. Union Street P.O. Box 302000, Montgomery, AL 36104, United States of America.

| | |
|---|---|
| **Tel**: | (1) 334 242 2273 |
| **Email**: | Cheryl.Newton@ache.alabama.gov |

# Alberta Innovates Health Solutions

Suite 1500, Bell Tower, 10104-103 Avenue, Edmonton, AB T5J 4A7, Canada.

| | |
|---|---|
| **Tel**: | (1) 780 423 5727 |
| **Email**: | pamela.valentine@albertainnovates.ca |
| **Website**: | www.albertainnovates.ca |
| **Contact**: | Dr Pamela Valentine, Interim Vice-President |

Alberta Innovates Health Solutions supports a community of researchers who generate knowledge that improves the health and quality of life of Albertans and people throughout the world. The long-term commitment is to fund basic patient and health research based on international standards of excellence and carried out by new and established investigators and researchers in training.

## Alberta Heritage Foundation for Medical Research Part-Time Studentship

**Purpose**: To enable full-time degree students to continue research training on a part-time basis
**Eligibility**: Candidates must normally have been accepted into, or be currently engaged in, a full-time graduate program at an Alberta-based university in a health-related discipline leading to a Master's or doctoral degree
**Level of Study**: Doctorate, Graduate
**Type**: Studentship
**Value**: Pro-rated on full-time studentship stipend and dependent on the amount of time spent in research
**Length of Study**: 3 years, maximum
**Frequency**: Annual
**Study Establishment**: A university in Alberta
**Country of Study**: Canada
**Application Procedure**: Applicants must complete an application form
**No. of awards offered**: 1
**Closing Date**: 1 October
**Funding**: Government
**No. of awards given last year**: 1
**No. of applicants last year**: 1

### For further information contact:

**Email**: grants.health@albertainnovates.ca

## Alberta Innovates - Health Solutions Postgraduate Fellowships

**Purpose**: To provide opportunities for individuals to pursue postgraduate health-related research at an Alberta University

**Eligibility**: Open to candidates with a PhD, MD, DDS, DVM or DPharm degree. Normally, support will not be provided beyond 5 years after receipt of the PhD degree, or beyond 8 years after receipt of the MD, DDS, DVM or DPharm degrees
**Level of Study**: Postdoctorate
**Type**: Fellowship
**Value**: C$5,000 research allowance plus a stipend of C$50,000
**Length of Study**: 1 year, with a possibility of renewal for a maximum of 3 years of support
**Frequency**: Annual
**Study Establishment**: Usually at a university in Alberta
**Country of Study**: Canada
**Application Procedure**: Applicants must complete an application form. Candidates must submit, in full, the original application to the AIHS office by the deadline
**No. of awards offered**: 156
**Closing Date**: 1 October
**Funding**: Government
**No. of awards given last year**: 39
**No. of applicants last year**: 156
**Additional Information**: Please contact at grants.health@albertainnovates.ca albertainnovates.ca/programs/postgraduate-fellowships-in-health-innovation/

### For further information contact:

**Email**: Kathy.Morrison@albertainnovates.ca

## Graduate Studentships

**Purpose**: To provide opportunities for support for individuals undertaking health-related research areas in pursuit of a Master's or PhD.
**Eligibility**: Applicants must be currently enrolled in a graduate program at an Alberta University undertaking health-related research training leading to thesis-based graduate degree
**Level of Study**: Doctorate, Graduate
**Type**: Studentship
**Value**: C$30,000 stipend and a research and career development allowance of C$2,000 per year for up to 4 years (maximum of 2 years support towards a Master)
**Length of Study**: 1 year with the possibility of renewal for a maximum of 5 years of support; 2 years maximum at the masters level
**Frequency**: Annual
**Study Establishment**: A university in Alberta
**Country of Study**: Canada
**Application Procedure**: Candidates must submit, in full, the original application to the AIHS offices by the deadlines
**No. of awards offered**: 200
**Closing Date**: 1 April

**Funding**: Government
**No. of awards given last year**: 49
**No. of applicants last year**: 200
**Additional Information**: Please contact at grants.health@al bertainnovates.ca www.trophoblast.cam.ac.uk/opportunities/ studentships

**For further information contact:**

**Email**:    health@albertainnovates.ca

## Alex's Lemonade Stand Foundation

### POST Program Grants

**Subjects**: Pediatric Oncology
**Purpose**: The Pediatric Oncology Student Training (POST) Program is designed for undergraduate, graduate and medical students who have an interest in pediatric oncology research and would like to experience the field first hand. Students train with a pediatric oncology research mentor. Students may join a research project underway in a mentor's lab or begin an original investigation with the mentor.
**Eligibility**: Mentors must be ALSF grantees (past or present, including those who have previously mentored POST students), Advisory Board, or Review Board members. Mentor/mentee pair must be identified prior to submitting an application. Mentor must be active in the field of pediatric oncology research. Mentor must submit a commitment letter, plan training activities, and provide guidance during the Program period. Student must currently be enrolled in an undergraduate, graduate, or medical degree-granting program. Student does not need to be enrolled in classes over the summer. Student must be able to dedicate at least eight full consecutive weeks to the program, typically between May 1 and August 31 (dates may vary depending on the student's scheduled break). ALSF will consider only one application from any one mentor.
**Type**: Grant
**Value**: Max US$5,000
**Country of Study**: Any country
**Application Procedure**: See website for further details.
**Closing Date**: 10 February
**Additional Information**: www.alexslemonade.org/grants/ program-areas/early-career-research-programs

### RUNX1 Early Career Investigator Grants

**Subjects**: Leukemia
**Purpose**: The RUNX1 Early Career Investigator grant is a 3-year award designed to fund research in strategies leading to the development of therapies to prevent the transition from pre-leukemia to leukemia for patients with RUNX1-FPD. Collaboration and data sharing are a priority for this research program. The RUNX1 Research Program and ALSF host an annual scientific meeting that brings together grant recipients and other scientists. Grant recipients are expected to present their progress as part of the annual review.
**Eligibility**: Applicants must have an M.D., PhD or dual M.D., PhD (D.O., MBBS or equivalent) and be within 5 years of their first faculty appointment as an Assistant Professor or equivalent. Associate and Full Professors are ineligible. If still at the Instructor level, the applicant must have a commitment from the Department Chief at the time of grant submission for an Assistant Professor position within one year of receiving the award. A minimum of 75% of the applicant's time during the award period must be allocated as protected time for all research activities. This percentage of time includes both activities on this grant and the applicant's other research responsibilities. Applicants may have research grants from other funding sources during the award period, but there must be clear documentation of mechanisms to avoid scientific and budgetary overlap. Applicants must have research experience working in and a deep understanding of normal or malignant hematopoiesis and/or immunology. Applicant institutions may be based in the U.S. or outside of the U.S. Applicants need not be United States citizens. Funds must be granted to non-profit institutions or organizations. One resubmission of a previously unfunded application is allowed. Use the Resubmission section of the application to respond to the prior RRP/ALSF critique of the proposal. The response will be scored in the review process in addition to the criteria used for new applications. Resubmissions compete with new applicants for funding.
**Type**: Grant
**Value**: up to US$60,000 per year for three years.
**Length of Study**: Three years
**Country of Study**: Any country
**Application Procedure**: See website for further details.
**Closing Date**: 16 December
**Additional Information**: www.alexslemonade.org/grants/ program-areas/early-career-research-programs

## Alfred L and Constance C Wolf Aviation Fund

2060 State Highway 595, Gavilan Community, Lindrith, NM 87029, United States of America.

**Tel**:          (1) 575 774 0029
**Email**:      mail@wolf-aviation.org
**Website**:   www.wolf-aviation.org
**Contact**:   Rol Murrow, Executive Director

The Wolf Aviation Fund was established in the wills of Alfred L. and Constance C. Wolf. The Wolf Foundation hopes to help people and projects that benefit general aviation by identifying talented, worthy individuals - often working in collaboration with others - and worthwhile projects and providing them support

## Wolf Aviation Fund Grants Program

**Purpose**: To promote and support the advancement of personal air transportation by seeking and funding the most promising individuals and worthy projects which advance the field of general aviation
**Level of Study**: Postgraduate
**Type**: Grant
**Value**: Grants range in size from a few hundred dollars to a maximum of five thousand dollars
**Frequency**: Annual
**Country of Study**: Any country
**Application Procedure**: For more details please visit the website
**Closing Date**: 15 December
**Additional Information**: In preparing proposals, the foundation strongly encourages applicants to browse the Resources section and learn how to find out what kinds of grants might be available from any source and to learn in general how to properly prepare grant requests

## Alfred Toepfer Foundation

Georgsplatz 10, D-20099 Hamburg, Germany.

**Tel**: (49) 4033 4020
**Email**: mail@toepfer-fvs.de
**Website**: www.toepfer-fvs.de

## Alfred Toepfer Natural Heritage Scholarships

**Purpose**: To provide scholarships for doctoral candidates from the humanities and the social sciences who are in the final stages of research on European issues
**Eligibility**: Candidates should be no older than 30 years and should be from Central and Eastern Europe: Albania, Armenia, Azerbaijan, Belarus, Bosnia-Herzegovina, Bulgaria, Croatia, Czech Republic, Estonia, Georgia, Hungary, Kosovo, Latvia, Lithuania, Macedonia, Moldavia, Poland, Romania, Russia, Slovakia, Slovenia, Ukraine. Applicants should have a good knowledge of German. Elaborated guidelines are available on the official website.
**Level of Study**: Doctorate

**Type**: Scholarship
**Value**: €3,000
**Length of Study**: Up to 1 year
**Frequency**: Annual
**Country of Study**: Germany
**Application Procedure**: Applications have to be submitted online. 1. Online application form– that includes your Curriculum vitae, your motivation letter, the proposed programme of your study visit, and contact details of protected areas you want to visit. 2. Proof of employment
**Closing Date**: 4 May
**Contributor**: Alfred Toepfer Foundation
**Additional Information**: Available on www.toepfer-fvs.de www.youthop.com/scholarships/alfred-toepfer-natural-heritage-scholarships-2019

**For further information contact:**

**Email**: ericke@toepfer-fvs.de

## Max Brauer Award

**Purpose**: To honour personalities and institutions in the City of Hamburg for their services to the city's cultural, scientific, or intellectual life and for extraordinary impulses for the preservation of its architecture and architectural monuments, its city and landscape and renewal of the city, as well as its tradition and its customs
**Type**: Award
**Value**: €20,000
**Frequency**: Annual
**Contributor**: Alfred Toepfer Foundation in association with European school
**Additional Information**: The selection of the Preisträgerin and/or the winner is decided by the Kuratorium Max Brauer award

**For further information contact:**

**Tel**: (49) 4033 402 16
**Email**: luthe@toepfer-fvs.de

## Alzheimer's Association

225 N. Michigan Ave. Floor 17 Chicago, IL 60601, United States of America.

## Alzheimer's Association Clinician Scientist Fellowship (AACSF) Program

**Subjects**: Clinical fields that include patient contact (e.g., neurology, psychiatry, geriatrics, psychology)

**Purpose**: The Alzheimer's Association recognizes the need to support the training of clinician scientists in Alzheimer's and all other dementia. For the purpose of this program, a clinician scientist is defined as an individual already trained, licensed and practicing in a clinical field that includes patient contact (e.g., neurology, psychiatry, geriatrics, psychology) or patient-related diagnostic studies (e.g., neuropathology and radiology). Applicants who hold an M.D. or D.O. degree or applicants with a PhD who have licensure for clinical practice are eligible.

**Eligibility**: Applicant must be a clinician who is interested in an academic career in research and has completed residency for an M.D. or D.O. (i.e. any degree that allows the applicant to achieve licensure to practice medicine) or a post-doctoral fellowship (PhD) in a clinical practice field or both within the past five years. Individuals applying to the program will be accepted from individuals with full-time positions at their respective institution who are within 10 years of receiving their M.D., D.O. or PhD (or equivalent), including postdoctoral fellows through Assistant Professors. Positions higher than Assistant Professor will not be considered. Individuals who are early in their clinician scientist careers will be given priority. Proposals are strongly encouraged from individuals training in specialties of behavioral neurology and neuropathology, geriatrics with focus on dementia/cognitive disorders, geriatric psychiatry with focus on dementia/cognitive disorders or neuropsychology with focus on dementia/cognitive disorders. The applicant must be at a recognized academic institution. The Alzheimer's Association reserves the right to request additional information to confirm that the institution meets not-for-profit requirements of the Association.

**Type**: Fellowship

**Value**: Each AACSF award is limited to US$175,000. A total of US$155,000 will be awarded for costs related to the proposed research for up to three years (minimum two years) for direct and indirect costs. Requests in any given year may not exceed US$60,000 (direct and indirect costs). Indirect costs are capped at 10% (rent for laboratory/office space is expected to be covered by indirect costs paid to the institution). This is inclusive of indirect costs for the implementing institution as well as any to subcontracts. The Principal Investigator must commit up to an average of two protected days per week (40%) effort toward their research efforts during each funding year. The remaining funds, US$10,000 to the applicant and US$10,000 to the primary mentor, will be awarded upon successful completion of the three years (minimum two years). These additional funds are to be applied to sustaining ongoing research in the Alzheimer's field and will be awarded through the applicant's and mentor's institutions. Successful completion of the program includes " but is not limited to " reaching all of the demonstrable benchmarks listed. A total of US$5,000 over a three-year period (two-year minimum) may be requested for travel purposes and is not to exceed US$3,000

in one given year. A portion must be allocated to support registration and travel to the annual Alzheimer's Association International Conference® (AAIC®), as AAIC attendance is a condition of the award. If you request the full US$5,000 for two years of travel and are requesting a three-year award, you will not be able to request travel funds for one of those years.

**Length of Study**: Two to three years

**Country of Study**: Any country

**Application Procedure**: See website for further details.

**Closing Date**: 19 March

**Additional Information**: Applications from currently funded investigators (including the mentor) who are delinquent in submitting required reports and other deliverables on active grants are ineligible. Investigators (or mentors) that have previous Alzheimer's Association awards closed as 'Incomplete' are not eligible to apply. This policy will be strictly adhered to with no exceptions. www.alz.org/research/for_researchers/grants/types-of-grants

## Alzheimer's Association Clinician Scientist Fellowship to Promote Diversity (AACSF-D)

**Subjects**: Alzheimer's and all dementia research

**Purpose**: The Alzheimer's Association Clinician Scientist Fellowship to Promote Diversity is up to three years (minimum two years) and is intended to support exceptional clinician scientists who are currently underrepresented at academic institutions in clinical research training in Alzheimer's and all dementias. Applicants who hold an M.D. or D.O. degree or applicants with a PhD who have licensure for clinical practice are eligible.

**Eligibility**: Applicant must be a clinician who is interested in an academic career in research and has completed residency for an M.D. or D.O. (i.e. any degree that allows the applicant to achieve licensure to practice medicine) or a post-doctoral fellowship (PhD) in a clinical practice field or both within the past five years. Individuals applying to the program will be accepted from individuals with full-time positions at their respective institution who are within 10 years of receiving their M.D., D.O. or PhD (or equivalent), including postdoctoral fellows through Assistant Professors. Positions higher than Assistant Professor will not be considered. Individuals who are early in their clinician scientist careers will be given priority. Proposals are strongly encouraged from individuals training in specialties of behavioral neurology and neuropathology, geriatrics with focus on dementia/cognitive disorders, geriatric psychiatry with focus on dementia/cognitive disorders or neuropsychology with focus on dementia/cognitive disorders. Specific to the AACSF-D program, eligible applicants are faculty members who have been determined to be underrepresented faculty in biomedical and behavioral research on a national, international or institutional basis.

The Alzheimer's Association will require documentation to support the faculty member's underrepresented status at their institution. Applicants from the U.S. submitting to the Alzheimer's Association will be subject to the definitions as stated by the National Institutes of Health, including: Blacks and African Americans; Hispanics and Latinos; American Indians and Alaska Natives; Asian Americans, Native Hawaiians and other Pacific Islanders; Socioeconomically disadvantaged populations; Underserved rural populations; Persons with disabilities; Sexual and gender minorities. Applicants must submit a Letter of Assurance letter printed on the hiring institution letterhead with the current date, signed by an authorized institutional official (i.e. Grants and Contracts officer) that states you have been determined by your institution to be underrepresented in the above areas at the time of Letter of Intent (LOI) for verification. The Alzheimer's Association reserves the right to require additional documentation to help confirm the applicant's eligibility. Non-U.S. applicants, in addition to a Letter of Assurance, must provide official documentation from their institutional materials, such as, website, manual or other legal documentation that indicates their eligibility for this program. The applicant must be at a recognized academic institution. The Alzheimer's Association reserves the right to request additional information to confirm that the institution meets not-for-profit requirements of the Association.

**Type**: Fellowship

**Value**: Each Alzheimer's Association Clinician Scientist Fellowship to Promote Diversity is limited to US$175,000. A total of US$155,000 will be awarded for costs related to the proposed research for up to three years (minimum two years) for direct and indirect costs. Requests in any given year may not exceed US$60,000 (direct and indirect costs). Indirect costs are capped at 10% (rent for laboratory/office space is expected to be covered by indirect costs paid to the institution). This is inclusive of indirect costs for the implementing institution as well as any to subcontracts. The Principal Investigator (PI) must commit up to an average of two protected days per week (40%) effort toward their research efforts during each funding year. The remaining funds, US$10,000 to the applicant and US$10,000 to the primary mentor, will be awarded upon successful completion of the three-year program (minimum two years). These additional funds are to be applied to sustaining ongoing research in the Alzheimer's field and will be awarded through the applicant's and mentor's institutions. Successful completion of the program includes, but is not limited to, reaching all of the demonstrable benchmarks listed. A total of US$5,000 over a three-year period (minimum two years) may be requested for travel purposes and is not to exceed US$3,000 in any given year. A portion must be allocated to support registration and travel to the annual Alzheimer's Association International Conference® (AAIC®), as AAIC attendance is a condition of the award.

**Length of Study**: Two to three years
**Country of Study**: Any country
**Application Procedure**: See website for further details.
**Closing Date**: 19 March
**Additional Information**: Applications from currently funded investigators (including the mentor) who are delinquent in submitting required reports and other deliverables on active grants are ineligible. Investigators (or mentors) that have previous Alzheimer's Association awards closed as 'Incomplete' are not eligible to apply. This policy will be strictly adhered to with no exceptions. www.alz.org/research/for_researchers/grants/types-of-grants

## Alzheimer's Association Research Fellowship to Promote Diversity (AARF-D)

**Subjects**: Alzheimer's and all dementia research
**Purpose**: The Alzheimer's Association Research Fellowship to Promote Diversity is up to three years (minimum two years) and is intended to support exceptional scientist from underrepresented groups working in Alzheimer's and all other dementia research, and who are engaged in their postgraduate work (i.e. postdoctoral fellows) and before they have their first independent faculty positions (i.e. Assistant Professor) and working in diverse areas of research including basic, translational, clinical, functional and social-behavioral research.
**Eligibility**: Individuals applying to the program will be accepted from postdoctoral fellows with full-time positions at their respective institution who have less than 10 years of research experience after receipt of their terminal degree. Individuals who have a position of an Assistant Professorship or above are not eligible. Specific to the AARF-D program, eligible applicants are faculty members who have been determined to be underrepresented faculty in biomedical and behavioral research on a national, international or institutional basis. The Alzheimer's Association will require documentation to support the faculty member's underrepresented status at their institution. Applicants from the U.S. submitting to the Alzheimer's Association will be subject to the definitions as stated by the National Institutes of Health. NIH-designated U.S health disparity populations include: Blacks and African Americans; Hispanics and Latinos; American Indians and Alaska Natives; Asian Americans; Native Hawaiians and other Pacific Islanders; Socioeconomically disadvantaged populations; Underserved rural populations; Persons with disabilities; Sexual and gender minorities. Applicants must submit a Letter of Assurance letter printed on the hiring institution letterhead with the current date, signed by an authorized institutional official (i.e. Grants and Contracts officer) that states you have been determined by your institution to be underrepresented in the above areas at the time of

Letter of Intent (LOI) for verification. The Alzheimer's Association reserves the right to require additional documentation to help confirm the applicant's eligibility. Non-U.S. applicants, in addition to the letter, must provide official documentation from their institutional materials, such as website, manual or other legal documentation that indicates their eligibility for this program.

**Type**: Fellowship

**Value**: Each AARF-D award is limited to US$175,000. A total of US$155,000 will be awarded for costs related to the proposed research for up to three years (minimum two years) for direct and indirect costs. Requests in any given year may not exceed US$60,000 (direct and indirect costs). Indirect costs are capped at 10% (rent for laboratory/office space is expected to be covered by indirect costs paid to the institution). This is inclusive of indirect costs for the implementing institution as well as any to subcontracts. The Principal Investigator must commit to a 50% effort toward the proposed project each funding year. The remaining funds "US$10,000 to the applicant and US$10,000 to the primary mentor" will be awarded upon successful completion of the three years (minimum two years). These additional funds are to be applied to sustaining ongoing research in the neurodegenerative field and will be awarded through the applicant's and mentor's institutions. Successful completion of the program includes, but is not limited to, reaching all of the demonstrable benchmarks listed. A total of US$5,000 over a three-year period (minimum two years) may be requested for travel purposes and is not to exceed US$3,000 in any given year. A portion must be allocated to support registration and travel to the annual Alzheimer's Association International Conference® (AAIC®), as AAIC attendance is a condition of the award. If you request the full US$5,000 for two years of travel and are requesting a three-year award, you will not be able to request travel funds for one of those years.

**Length of Study**: Two to three years

**Country of Study**: Any country

**Application Procedure**: See website for further details.

**Closing Date**: 19 March

**Additional Information**: Applications from currently funded investigators who are delinquent in submitting required reports and other deliverables on active grants. Investigators that have previous Alzheimer' Association awards closed as 'Incomplete' are not eligible to apply without exception. This policy will be strictly adhered to with no exceptions. www.alz.org/research/for_researchers/grants/types- of-grants

## Alzheimer's Association Research Grant - New to the Field (AARG-NTF)

**Subjects**: Alzheimer's and all dementia research

**Purpose**: The Alzheimer's Association Research Grant "New to the Field (AARG" NTF) aims to fund investigators who are new to Alzheimer's or other dementias field of research. The purpose of this program is to provide independent investigators with unique expertise and apply their knowledge to Alzheimer's and all dementias.

**Eligibility**: Individuals who are new to the field of neuroscience or neurodegeneration (Alzheimer's, Parkinson's, Lewy body dementia, etc.) will be considered for this program and will need to contact the Association at grantsapp@alz.org to receive an exception prior to submitting a Letter of Intent (LOI). Investigators who have published work and/or been funded in neurodegeneration will not be eligible for this program. Please note the following: If you submit an LOI without an approved exception, your LOI will be rejected. Investigators that have published and/or have been funded in neurodegeneration will not be eligible for this program. If the applicant's institution does not have an Assistant Professor position, the letter of employment should include sufficient information to allow the Alzheimer's Association staff to evaluate the eligibility of the applicant.

**Type**: Grant

**Value**: Each AARG-NTF total award is limited to US$150,000 (direct and indirect costs) for up to three years (minimum two years). Requests may not exceed US$60,000 in any given year (direct and indirect costs). Indirect costs are capped at 10% (rent for laboratory/office space is expected to be covered by indirect costs paid to the institution). This is inclusive of indirect costs for the implementing institution as well as any to subcontracts.

**Length of Study**: Two to three years

**Country of Study**: Any country

**Application Procedure**: See website for further details.

**Closing Date**: 19 March

**Additional Information**: Applicants must be Assistant Professors or above at their respective institution. For individuals who are at non-academic institutions, please contact the Alzheimer's Association at grantsapp@alz.org, to verify your eligibility. www.alz.org/research/for_researchers/grants/types-of-grants

## Alzheimer's Association Research Grant (AARG)

**Subjects**: Alzheimer's and all dementia research

**Purpose**: The Alzheimer's Association Research Grant aims to fund investigators who are less than 15 years past their doctoral or post-residency (M.D. or D.O.). The purpose of this program is to provide newly independent investigators with funding that will allow them to develop preliminary or pilot data, to test procedures and to develop hypotheses. The intent is to support early-career development that will lay the groundwork for future research grant applications to federal or other funding entities, like the National Institutes of Health, including future proposals to the Alzheimer's Association. The Alzheimer's Association recognizes the need to increase the number of scientists from underrepresented groups in the research enterprise for Alzheimer's and other dementias. Young scientists from these groups are encouraged to apply.

**Eligibility**: Eligibility to apply for this grant competition is restricted to investigators who have less than 15 years of research experience after receipt of their terminal degree "doctorate or post-residency (M.D. or D.O.). The 15-year period applies to the date of submission of the grant application. Adjustments for career interruptions can be made. These can include, but are not limited to, family leave, military service and major illness or injury. It is the responsibility of the applicant to point out and document such interruptions within their application. Applicants must contact the Alzheimer's Association at grantsapp@alz.org regarding any possible exception prior to submitting a Letter of Intent (LOI) due to the review process; no exceptions will be made after the LOI deadline has passed. Applications to the Alzheimer's Association Research Grant (AARG) program will be accepted from postdoctoral fellows and other junior faculty members (e.g., Instructor, Research Associate Scientist, Lecturer, etc.) who can provide a letter of employment verification indicating they will have a full-time faculty position of an Assistant Professor or above by the award date should the proposal be in funding range and funded. If applicable, the letter of employment must be uploaded with the application and dated within three months from application submission date, printed on the hiring institution letterhead, signed by an authorized institutional official (i.e., Grants and Contracts officer) and must indicate that the position will be activated by the grant award date. If the anticipated position is not activated by the award date for any reason, any offer of funding will be withdrawn. There will be no exceptions. In the event your application is funded, you will be required to provide an official letter on organizational letterhead, signed by an institutional signing official, stating you have a full-time faculty position of an Assistant Professor and above. If the applicant's institution does not have an Assistant Professor position, the letter of employment should include sufficient information to allow the Alzheimer's Association staff to evaluate the eligibility of the applicant.

**Type**: Grant

**Value**: Each AARG total award is limited to US$150,000 (direct and indirect costs) for up to three years (minimum two years). Requests in any given year may not exceed US$60,000 (direct and indirect costs). Indirect costs are capped at 10% (rent for laboratory/office space is expected to be covered by indirect costs paid to the institution). This is inclusive of indirect costs for the implementing institution as well as any to subcontracts.

**Length of Study**: Two to three years

**Country of Study**: Any country

**Application Procedure**: See website for further details.

**Closing Date**: 19 March

**Additional Information**: Applicants must be Assistant Professors or above at their respective institution. For individuals who are at non-academic institutions, please contact the Alzheimer's Association at grantsapp@alz.org, to verify your eligibility. www.alz.org/research/for_researchers/grants/types-of-grants

## Alzheimer's Association Research Grant to Promote Diversity - New to the Field (AARG-D-NTF)

**Subjects**: Alzheimer's and all dementia research

**Purpose**: The Alzheimer's Association Research Grant to Promote Diversity - New to the Field award is up to three years (minimum two years) to increase the number of scientists from underrepresented groups at academic institutions in Alzheimer's and all dementia research. The AARG-D-NTF aims to fund individuals who are new to the Alzheimer's and all dementia field of research. Individuals who are new to the field of neuroscience or neurodegeneration (Alzheimer's, Parkinson's, Lewy body dementia, etc.) will be considered for this program.

**Eligibility**: Specific for the AARG-D-NTF program, eligible applicants are faculty members who have been determined to be underrepresented faculty in biomedical and behavioral research on a national, international or institutional basis. The Alzheimer's Association will require documentation to support the faculty member's underrepresented status at their institution. Applicants from the United States submitting to the Alzheimer's Association will be subject to the definitions as stated by the National Institutes of Health. NIH-designated U.S health disparity populations include: Blacks and African Americans; Hispanics and Latinos; American Indians and Alaska Natives; Asian Americans; Native Hawaiians and other Pacific Islanders; Socioeconomically disadvantaged populations; Underserved rural populations; Persons with disabilities; Sexual and gender minorities. Applicants must submit a Letter of Assurance printed on the hiring institution letterhead, signed by an authorized institutional official (i.e., Grants and Contracts officer) that states you have been determined by your institution to be underrepresented in the above areas at the time of LOI for verification. The Alzheimer's Association reserves the right to require additional documentation to help confirm the applicant's eligibility. Non-U.S. applicants, in addition to the letter, must provide official documentation from their institutional materials, such as website, manual or other legal documentation that indicates their eligibility for this program. If the applicant institution does not have an Assistant Professor position, the letter of employment should include sufficient information to allow the Alzheimer's Association staff to evaluate the eligibility of the applicant.

**Type**: Grant

**Value**: Each AARG-D-NTF award is limited to US$150,000 (direct and indirect costs) for up to three years (minimum two years). Requests may not exceed US$60,000 in any given year (direct and indirect costs). Indirect costs are capped at 10% (rent for laboratory/office space is expected to be covered by indirect costs paid to the institution). This is inclusive of indirect costs for the implementing institution as well as any to subcontracts.

**Length of Study**: Two to three years

**Country of Study**: Any country

**Application Procedure**: See website for further details.

**Closing Date**: 19 March

**Additional Information**: Applicants must be Assistant Professors or above at their respective institution. For individuals who are at non-academic institutions, please contact the Alzheimer's Association at grantsapp@alz.org, to verify your eligibility. Eligibility to apply for this grant competition is restricted to investigators who are new to the Alzheimer's and all dementia field of research. Individuals who are new to the field as defined above will need to contact the Association at grantsapp@alz.org, to receive an exception prior to submitting a Letter of Intent (LOI). If you submit an LOI without an approved exception, your LOI will be rejected. Investigators that have published and/or have been funded in neurodegeneration will not be eligible for this program. www.alz.org/research/for_researchers/grants/types-of-grants

## Alzheimer's Association Research Grant to Promote Diversity (AARG-D)

**Subjects**: Alzheimer's and all dementia research

**Purpose**: The Alzheimer's Association Research Grant to Promote Diversity (AARG-D) award is up to three years (minimum 2 years) to increase the number of scientists from underrepresented groups at academic institutions in Alzheimer's and other dementias research. The AARG-D aims to fund investigators who are less than 15 years past their doctoral or post residency (M.D. or D.O.).

**Eligibility**: Eligibility to apply for this grant competition is restricted to investigators who have less than 15 years of research experience after receipt of their terminal degree. The 15-year period applies to the date of submission of the grant application. Adjustments for career interruptions can be made. These would include, but are not limited to, family leave, military service and major illness or injury. It is the responsibility of the applicant to point out and document such interruptions within their application. Applicants must contact the Alzheimer's Association at grantsapp@alz.org regarding any possible exception prior to submitting a Letter of Intent (LOI) due to the review process; no exceptions will be made after the LOI deadline has passed. Specific for the

AARG-D program, eligible applicants are faculty members who have been determined to be underrepresented faculty in biomedical and behavioral research on a national, international or institutional basis. The Alzheimer's Association will require documentation to support the faculty member's underrepresented status at their institution. Applicants from the U.S. submitting to the Alzheimer's Association will be subject to the definitions as stated by the National Institutes of Health. NIH-designated U.S health disparity populations include: Blacks and African Americans; Hispanics and Latinos; American Indians and Alaska Natives; Asian Americans; Native Hawaiians and other Pacific Islanders; Socioeconomically disadvantaged populations; Underserved rural populations; Persons with disabilities; Sexual and gender minorities. Applicants must submit a Letter of Assurance printed on the hiring institution letterhead, signed by an authorized institutional official (i.e., Grants and Contracts officer) that states the applicant has been determined by their institution to be underrepresented in the above areas at the time of LOI for verification. The Alzheimer's Association reserves the right to require additional documentation to help confirm the applicant's eligibility. Non-U.S. applicants, in addition to the letter, must provide official documentation from their institutional materials, such as, website, manual or other legal documentation that indicates their eligibility for this program. Applications to the Alzheimer's Association Research Grant to Promote Diversity (AARG-D) program will be accepted from postdoctoral fellows and other junior faculty members (e.g. Instructor, Research Associate Scientist, Lecturer, etc.) who can provide a letter of employment verification indicating you will have a full-time faculty position of an Assistant Professor or above by the award date should the proposal be in funding range and funded. If applicable, the letter of employment must be uploaded with the application and dated within three months from application submission date, printed on the hiring institution letterhead, signed by an authorized institutional official (i.e., Grants and Contracts officer) and must indicate that the position will be activated by the grant award date. If the anticipated position is not activated by the award date for any reason, any offer of funding will be withdrawn. There will be no exceptions. In the event your application is funded, you will be required to provide an official letter on organizational letterhead, signed by an institutional signing official, stating you will have a full-time faculty position of an Assistant Professor and above. If the applicant's institution does not have an Assistant Professor position, the letter of employment should include sufficient information to allow the Alzheimer's Association staff to evaluate the eligibility of the applicant.

**Type**: Grant

**Value**: Each AARG-D award is limited to US$150,000 (direct and indirect costs) for up to three years (minimum two years). Requests may not exceed US$60,000 in any given year (direct and indirect costs). Indirect costs are capped at 10% (rent for laboratory/office space is expected to be covered by indirect costs paid to the institution). This is inclusive of indirect costs for the implementing institution as well as any to subcontracts.

**Length of Study**: Two to three years

**Country of Study**: Any country

**Application Procedure**: See website for further details.

**Closing Date**: 19 March

**Additional Information**: Applicants must be Assistant Professors or above at their respective institution. For individuals who are at non-academic institutions, please contact the Alzheimer's Association at grantsapp@alz.org, to verify your eligibility. www.alz.org/research/for_researchers/grants/ types-of-grants

## New Connections: Increasing Diversity

**Subjects**: Alzheimer's Research

**Purpose**: The fellowship is intended to support exceptional researchers who are engaged in their post-graduate work (i.e. postdoctoral fellows) and before they have their first independent faculty positions (i.e. Assistant Professor) and working in diverse areas of research, including basic, translational, clinical, functional and social-behavioral research.

**Eligibility**: Individuals applying to the AARF program will be accepted from postdoctoral fellows with full-time positions at their respective institution who have less than 10 years of research experience after receipt of their terminal degree. Individuals who have a position of an Assistant Professorship or above are not eligible. Applications from currently funded investigators who are delinquent in submitting required reports and other deliverables on active grants. Investigators that have previous Alzheimer's Association awards closed as 'Incomplete' are not eligible to apply without exception. This policy will be strictly adhered to with no exceptions.

**Type**: Fellowship

**Value**: Max. US$175,000. A total of US$155,000 will be awarded for costs related to the proposed research for up to three years (minimum two years) for direct and indirect costs. Requests in any given year may not exceed US$60,000 (direct and indirect costs) Indirect costs are capped at 10% (rent for laboratory/office space is expected to be covered by indirect costs paid to the institution). This is inclusive of indirect costs for the implementing institution as well as any to subcontracts. The Principal Investigator must commit to a 50% effort toward the proposed project each funding year. The remaining funds, US$10,000 to the applicant and US$10,000 to the primary mentor, will be awarded upon successful completion of the three years (minimum two years). These additional funds are to be applied to sustaining ongoing research in the Alzheimer's field and will be awarded through the applicant's and mentor's institutions. Successful completion of the program includes, but is not limited to, reaching all of the demonstrable benchmarks listed. A total of US$5,000 over a three-year period may

be requested for travel purposes and is not to exceed US$3,000 in any given year. A portion must be allocated to support registration and travel to the annual Alzheimer's Association International Conference® (AAIC®), as AAIC attendance is a condition of the award. If you request the full US$5,000 for two years of travel and are requesting a three-year award, you will not be able to request travel funds for one of those years.

**Length of Study**: Two to three years

**Country of Study**: Any country

**Application Procedure**: See website for further details.

**Closing Date**: 19 March

**Additional Information**: For individuals who are at non-academic institutions, please contact the Alzheimer's Association at grantsapp@alz.org, to verify your eligibility. www.alz.org/research/for_researchers/grants/types-of-grants

## Alzheimer's Australia

1 Frewin Place, Scullin, ACT 2614, Australia.

| | |
|---|---|
| **Tel**: | (61) 2 6254 4233 |
| **Email**: | secretariat@alzheimers.org.au |
| **Website**: | www.fightdementia.org.au |
| **Contact**: | Dr Mary Gray, Manager AADRF |

Alzheimer's Australia Dementia Research Foundation (AADRF) was established as the research arm of Alzheimer's Australia to provide funds and disseminate into Alzheimer's disease and other forms of dementia. AADRF provides annual research grants and a key priority is to support emerging researchers and to encourage the next generation of dementia researchers.

## Association of American Railroads Janssen Cilag Dementia Research Grant

**Purpose**: To support research into Alzheimer's disease and other types of dementia

**Eligibility**: Open to citizens of Australia or permanent residents

**Level of Study**: Postgraduate, Research

**Type**: Scholarship

**Value**: Maximum AU$20,000

**Length of Study**: 1 year

**Frequency**: Annual

**Country of Study**: Australia

**Application Procedure**: Check website for further details

**Closing Date**: 4 June

**Contributor**: Janssen Cilag Pty Ltd

**For further information contact:**

Alzheimer's Australia Research Ltd, PO Box 4019, Scullin, ACT 2614, Australia.

**Email**:    aar@alzheimers.org.au

## Association of American Railroads Rosemary Foundation Travel Project Grant-Dementia Research

**Purpose**: For undertaking research that is not fully available in Australia and is relevant to the advancement of understanding dementia
**Eligibility**: Open to citizens of Australia or permanent residents who have a degree in a discipline relevant to the field of dementia and be associated with an institute of higher learning
**Level of Study**: Postgraduate, Research
**Type**: Scholarship
**Value**: AU$10,000
**Length of Study**: 6 weeks to 3 months
**Frequency**: Annual
**Application Procedure**: Check website for further details
**Closing Date**: 4 June
**Additional Information**: The applicant must undertake to return to a position in Australia for at least 1 year after the completion of the travel

**For further information contact:**

**Email**:    aar@alzheimers.org.au

## Hunter Postgraduate Scholarship

**Purpose**: This scholarship is to encourage and support students to pursue postgraduate study at Victoria University of Wellington. The scholarship will be awarded as a fees contribution to the top ranked applicant across all disciplines who applied but does not receive a Victoria Master's by Thesis Scholarship.
**Eligibility**: All applicants who have applied and submitted an application for the Victoria Master's by Thesis Scholarship will be considered.
**Level of Study**: Masters Research; Postgraduate
**Type**: Scholarship
**Value**: Up to US$5,000 towards fees
**Length of Study**: 1 year
**Frequency**: Annual
**Application Procedure**: Check website for further details. Applications will be open from 1 September
**Closing Date**: 1 October
**Additional Information**: www.wgtn.ac.nz/scholarships/current/hunter-postgraduate-scholarship

**For further information contact:**

**Tel**:       (64) 463 5557
**Email**:    scholarships-office@vuw.ac.nz;
              pg-research@vuw.ac.nz; summer-research@vuw.ac.nz

## Rosemary Foundation Travel Grant

**Purpose**: To enable an Australian researcher to travel overseas in order to learn new techniques and/or network with international dementia research teams
**Eligibility**: Open to citizens of Australia or permanent residents and New Zealand citizens residing permanently in Australia
**Level of Study**: Doctorate, Postdoctorate, Postgraduate, Research
**Type**: Grant
**Value**: AU$15,000
**Length of Study**: 1 month
**Country of Study**: Any country
**Application Procedure**: Please check the website for details
**No. of awards offered**: 5
**Closing Date**: April
**Funding**: Foundation
**Contributor**: The Rosemary Foundation for Memory Support Inc
**No. of awards given last year**: 1
**No. of applicants last year**: 5

**For further information contact:**

**Email**:    Admin@RosaMary.org

## Alzheimer's Drug Discovery Foundation (ADDF)

57 W 57th Street, Suit 904, New York, NY 10019, United States of America.

**Tel**:       (1) 212 901 8000
**Email**:    nthakker@alzdiscovery.org
**Website**:  www.alzdiscovery.org
**Contact**:  Mr Niyati Thakker, Grants Associate

The ADDF is an affiliated public charity of the Institute for the Study of Aging (ISOA), a private foundation founded by the Estè Lauder family in 1998.

## Alzheimers Drug Discovery Foundation Grants Program

**Purpose**: This program supports studies advancing lead molecules to clinical candidate selection or building preclinical evidence in relevant animal models for repurposed/repositioned drugs.
**Eligibility**: Funding is open to researchers and clinicians worldwide
**Level of Study**: Unrestricted
**Type**: Grant
**Value**: US$150,000–US$600,000
**Length of Study**: one year
**Frequency**: Dependent on funds available
**Study Establishment**: A non-profit public foundation
**Country of Study**: Any country
**Application Procedure**: Candidates must submit a letter of intent through our online submission system at www.alzdiscovery.org
**Funding**: Government, Private, Foundation, Individuals
**No. of awards given last year**: 29
**Additional Information**: In addition to funding research activities, the foundation sponsors and/or co-sponsors conferences, scientific and medical workshops to advance knowledge on issues related to Alzheimer's disease and cognitive vitality mcgill.ca/research/files/research/listserv_addf_program_to_accelerate_clinical_trials_march2019.docx.pdf

### For further information contact:

Katarina Stojkovic, Grants Officer.

**Tel**: (1) 514 398 5184

## America–Israel Cultural Foundation (AICF)

1140 Broadway, Suite #304, New York, NY 10001, United States of America.

**Tel**: (1) 212 557 1600
**Email**: info@aicf.co.il
**Website**: www.aicf.org
**Contact**: Mr David Homan, Executive Director

The America–Israel Cultural Foundation (AICF) has been promoting and supporting the arts in Israel for over 60 years. Through its Sharett Scholarship Program, the AICF grants hundreds of study scholarships each year to Israeli students of the arts, music, dance, visual arts, film, television and theatre, mainly for studies in Israel. The AICF also provides short-term fellowships to artists and art teachers and financially supports various projects in art schools, workshops, master classes, etc.

## AICF Sharett Scholarship Program

**Purpose**: To respond to Israel's ever-evolving artistic life and the needs of her artists and institutions
**Eligibility**: Open to Israeli citizens only
**Level of Study**: Unrestricted
**Type**: Scholarship
**Value**: US$750–2,000
**Length of Study**: Varies
**Frequency**: Annual
**Country of Study**: Any country
**Application Procedure**: Applicants must complete and submit an application form with recommendations and pre-required repertoire. Application forms are available from 1 February of each year
**No. of awards offered**: 2300
**Closing Date**: February
**Funding**: Private
**Contributor**: America—Israel Cultural Foundation
**No. of awards given last year**: 1110
**No. of applicants last year**: 2300
**Additional Information**: The programme is revised on an annual basis. For more detailed information, please contact the Foundation after 1 February aicf.org/

## America-Norway Heritage Fund

Norwegian Information Service in the US, 825 Third Avenue 38th Floor, New York, NY 10022-7584, United States of America.

**Tel**: (1) 212 421 7333
**Email**: norcons@interport.net
**Website**: www.norway.org
**Contact**: Grants Management Officer

## Norwegian Emigration Fund

**Purpose**: To award scholarships to Americans for advanced or specialised studies in Norway of subjects dealing with emigration history and relations between the United States and Norway
**Eligibility**: Open to citizens and residents of the United States. The fund may also give grants to institutions in the

United States whose activities are primarily centred on the subjects mentioned

**Level of Study**: Graduate, Professional development

**Type**: Grant

**Value**: The individual grants last year were between NOK 5,000 and NOK 20,000

**Country of Study**: Norway

**Application Procedure**: Applicants must send applications to Nordmanns-Forbundet in envelopes that are clearly marked with 'Emigration Fund'

**Closing Date**: 15 February

**Additional Information**: Please see the website www.folkehogskole.no/undersider/engminnefond.html

### For further information contact:

Nordmanns-Forbundet Råhusgtgata 23 B, N-0158056, Norway.

**Tel**:       (47) 2 335 7170
**Fax**:       (47) 2 335 7175
**Email**:     norseman@online.no

## American Academy of Child and Adolescent Psychiatry

### AACAP Pilot Research Award for Attention Disorders

**Subjects**: Child and adolescent mental health

**Purpose**: To support young investigators at a critical stage, encouraging a future career in child and adolescent psychiatry research.

**Eligibility**: Candidates must be board eligible/certified in child and adolescent psychiatry, or enrolled in a child psychiatry residency or fellowship program. Candidates must have a faculty appointment in an accredited medical school or be in a fully accredited child and adolescent psychiatry clinical research or training program. At the time of application, candidates may not have more than two years of experience following graduation from residency/fellowship training. Candidates must not have any previous significant, individual research funding in the field of child and adolescent mental health. These include the following: NIMH/NIH funding (Small Grants, R-01) or similar foundation or industry research funding. Candidates who have received or are currently receiving "T32" funding support are eligible to apply. Candidates must either be AACAP members or have a membership application pending (not paid by the award) and agree to submit a poster presentation on his or her research for AACAP's 68th Annual Meeting in Atlanta, Georgia, October 25-30, 2021.

**Type**: Award

**Value**: US$15,000

**Country of Study**: Any country

**Application Procedure**: Apply online

**No. of awards offered**: Up to two

**Closing Date**: 1 April

**Additional Information**: www.aacap.org/aacap/Awards/Resident_and_ECP_Awards/AACAP_Pilot_Research_Award_for_Attention_Disorders.aspx

### AACAP Pilot Research Award for Learning Disabilities

**Subjects**: Child and adolescent mental health

**Purpose**: To support child and adolescent psychiatry fellows and junior faculty who have an interest in beginning a career in child and adolescent mental health research.

**Eligibility**: Candidates must be board eligible/certified in child and adolescent psychiatry, or enrolled in a child psychiatry residency or fellowship program. Candidates must have a faculty appointment in an accredited medical school or be in a fully accredited child and adolescent psychiatry clinical research or training program. At the time of application, candidates may not have more than two years of experience following graduation from residency/fellowship training. Candidates must not have any previous significant, individual research funding in the field of child and adolescent mental health. These include the following: NIMH/NIH Funding (Small Grants, R-01) or similar foundation or industry research funding. Candidates who have received or are currently receiving "T32" funding support are eligible to apply. Candidates must either be AACAP members or have a membership application pending (not paid by the award) and agree to submit a poster presentation on his or her research for AACAP's 68th Annual Meeting in Atlanta, Georgia, October 25-30, 2021.

**Type**: Award

**Value**: US$15,000

**Country of Study**: Any country

**Application Procedure**: Apply online

**No. of awards offered**: Up to two

**Closing Date**: 1 April

**Additional Information**: www.aacap.org/aacap/Awards/Resident_and_ECP_Awards/AACAP_Pilot_Research_Award_for_Attention_Disorders.aspx

### Pilot Research Award for General Psychiatry Residents

**Subjects**: Child and adolescent mental health

**Purpose**: To award general psychiatry residents who have an interest in beginning a career in child and adolescent mental health research.

**Eligibility**: Candidates must be enrolled in a general psychiatry residency. Candidates must not have any previous significant, individual research funding in the field of child and adolescent mental health. These include the following: NIMH/NIH funding (Small Grants, R-01) or similar foundation or industry research funding. Candidates who have received or are currently receiving "T32" funding support are eligible to apply. Candidates must either be AACAP members or have a membership application pending (not paid by the award) and agree to submit a poster presentation on his or her research for AACAP's 68th Annual Meeting in Atlanta, Georgia, October 25-30, 2021.
**Type**: Award
**Value**: US$15,000
**Country of Study**: Any country
**Application Procedure**: Apply online
**No. of awards offered**: Up to two
**Closing Date**  1 April
**Additional Information**: www.aacap.org/aacap/Awards/Res ident_and_ECP_Awards/AACAP_Pilot_Research_Award_ for_Attention_Disorders.aspx

## American Academy of Neurology (AAN)

IAC Foreign Scholarship Award Subcommittee, 1080 Montreal Avenue, St Paul, MN 55116, United States of America.

**Tel**:    (1) 612 395 1940
**Email**:    kjames@aan.com
**Website**:    www.aan.com
**Contact**:    Ms Kathleen James

## A. B. Baker Award for Lifetime Achievement in Neurologic Education

**Purpose**: To provide funding for training in neuropharmacology
**Eligibility**: Nominee should exhibit lifetime career achievements in the field of neurologic education, with an emphasis on national accomplishments. Nominee should exhibit leadership, creativity, and scholarship. Nominee's neurological education activities should include significant current or past work in the AAN. Nominations should be inclusive in regards to gender and under-represented groups. Posthumous nominations will not be accepted
**Level of Study**: Postgraduate
**Type**: Other
**Value**: The Award will consist of a minimum commitment of two years
**Frequency**: Annual
**Country of Study**: Any country

**Closing Date**: 31 December
**Funding**: Private
**Additional Information**: tools.aan.com/science/awards/? fuseaction=home.info&id=99

### For further information contact:

**Tel**:    (1) 612 623 8115
**Fax**:    (1) 612 623 3504
**Email**:    bmcdonald@aan.com

## American Academy of Pediatrics (AAP)

Division of Member Sections, 141 Northwest Point Boulevard, Elk Grove Village, IL 60007, United States of America.

**Tel**:    (1) 847 952 4926
**Email**:    membership@aap.org
**Website**:    www.aap.org
**Contact**:    Division Co-ordinator

The American Academy of Pediatrics (AAP) is an organisation of 55,000 primary care paediatricians, paediatric medical subspecialists and paediatric surgical specialists dedicated to the health, safety and well being of infants, children, adolescents and young adults.

## Advocacy Training Grants

**Purpose**: CPTI supports 4 pediatric faculty-resident pairs annually to attend the AAP Legislative Conference in Washington, DC. Following the conference, the faculty-resident pairs are required to implement an educational project in collaboration with their AAP chapter to strengthen the advocacy skills of their trainees.
**Value**: up to US$1,000
**Additional Information**: www.aap.org/en-us/advocacy-and-policy/aap-health-initiatives/CPTI/Pages/Grants.aspx

## American Academy of Pediatrics Resident Research Grants

**Purpose**: To enhance the development of research skills among physicians in paediatric training. Pediatric residents have an opportunity to initiate and completeprojects related to their professional interests through the AAP Resident Research Grant program

**Eligibility**: Open to paediatric residents in a training programme and have a definite commitment for another year of residency in a programme accredited by the Residency Review Committee for Paediatrics. Applicants must be United States or Canadian citizens or permanent residents. International medical graduates are eligible

**Type**: Research grant

**Value**: Up to US$2,000

**Length of Study**: Up to 2 years

**Frequency**: Annual

**Country of Study**: Any country

**Application Procedure**: Applications are sent automatically to AAP Residents and programme directors every year. Non members should write for details

**Funding**: Private

**Additional Information**: research.weill.cornell.edu/funding/open-submission-grants/resident-research-grant-american-academy-pediatrics

## Leonard P. Rome CATCH Visiting Professorships

**Purpose**: CPTI partners with the CATCH Program to offer this opportunity. This program promotes advocacy for children and advances the field of community pediatrics by focusing on resident education, faculty development, and community partnerships.

**Value**: US$4,500

**Additional Information**: www.aap.org/en-us/advocacy-and-policy/aap-health-initiatives/CPTI/Pages/Grants.aspx

### For further information contact:

**Tel**: (1) 630 626 6397
**Email**: jdonnelly@aap.org?

## American Alpine Club (AAC)

710 Tenth Street, Suite 100, Golden, CO 80401, United States of America.

**Tel**: (1) 303 384 0110
**Email**: getinfo@americanalpineclub.org
**Website**: www.americanalpineclub.org
**Contact**: Janet Miller, Grants Administrator

The American Alpine Club (AAC) is a national non-profit organization that has represented mountaineers and rock climbers for almost a century. AAC has been the only national climbers' organization devoted to the exploration and scientific study of high mountain elevations and polar regions of the world, and the promotion and dissemination of knowledge about the mountains and mountaineering through its meetings, publications and libraries. It is also dedicated to the conservation and preservation of mountain regions and other climbing areas and the representation of the interests and concerns of the American climbing community.

## American Alpine Club Research Grants

**Purpose**: To recognize a specific contribution to scientific endeavour germane to mountain regions and alpine research projects

**Eligibility**: Must be a graduate student or a postgraduate student. Must attend a university or a four-year college. Must not be attending high school currently. Both full-time and part-time students

**Level of Study**: Postgraduate

**Type**: Research grant

**Value**: US$1,500 and US$9,750

**Frequency**: Annual

**Country of Study**: Any country

**Application Procedure**: Applicants must call or write for application forms, which are also available from the website

**Closing Date**: 15 November

**Funding**: Private

**Contributor**: The Arthur K. Gilkey Memorial Research Fund, the R.L. Putnam Research Fund, and the Bedayn Research Fund

**Additional Information**: A report must be submitted upon completion of the project www.petersons.com/scholarship/american-alpine-club-research-grants-111_189245.aspx

### For further information contact:

710 10th St, Suite 100, Golden, CO 80401, United States of America.

**Email**: grants@americanalpineclub.org

## American Association for Cancer Research (AACR)

615 Chestnut Street, 17th Floor, Philadelphia, PA 19106-4404, United States of America.

**Tel**: (1) 215 440 9300
**Email**: aacr@aacr.org
**Website**: www.aacr.org
**Contact**: Ms Sheri Ozard, Program Co-ordinator

The American Association for Cancer Research (AACR) is a scientific society of over 17,000 laboratory and clinical cancer researchers. It was founded in 1907 to facilitate communication and dissemination of knowledge among scientists and others dedicated to the cancer problem, and to foster research in cancer and related biomedical sciences. It is also dedicated to encouraging the presentation and discussion of new and important observations in the field, fostering public education, science education and training, and advancing the understanding of cancer aetiology, prevention, diagnosis and treatment throughout the world.

## American Association for Cancer Research Anna D. Barker Basic Cancer Research Fellowship

**Purpose**: The AACR Anna D. Barker Basic Cancer Research Fellowship encourages and supports postdoctoral or clinical research fellows to establish a successful career path in cancer research. The research proposed for funding may be in any area of basic cancer research

**Eligibility**: Applicants must have a doctoral degree (including PhD, MD, DO, DC, ND, DDS, DVM, ScD, DNS, PharmD, or equivalent) in a related field and not currently be a candidate for a further doctoral degree. applicants must: 1. Hold a mentored research position with the title of postdoctoral fellow, clinical research fellow, or the equivalent. i. If eligibility is based on a future position, the position must be confirmed at the time of application and CANNOT be contingent upon receiving this grant. ii. If the future position is at a different institution than the applicant's current institution, the applicant must contact AACR's Scientific Review and Grants Administration Department (AACR's SRGA) at 28T grants@aacr.org 28T before submitting their application for information on additional verification materials/signatures that may be required. 2. Have completed their most recent doctoral degree within the past three years (i.e., degree cannot have been conferred before 1 July; the formal date of receipt of doctoral degree is the date the degree was conferred, as indicated on their diploma and/or transcript). i. Applicants with a medical degree must have completed their most recent doctoral degree or medical residency - whichever date is later - within the past three years. 3. Work under the auspices of a mentor at an academic, medical, or research institution anywhere in the world (There are no citizenship or geographic requirements. However, by submitting a Letter of Intent for this grant, an applicant applying from an institution located in a country in which they are not a citizen or a permanent resident assures that the visa status will provide sufficient time to complete the project and grant term at the institution from which they applied)
**Level of Study**: Postdoctorate
**Type**: Fellowship or Grant

**Value**: US$110,000
**Length of Study**: 2 years
**Frequency**: Dependent on funds available
**Country of Study**: Any country
**Application Procedure**: Please visit funding page for details at www.aacr.org/FUNDING/PAGES/DEFAULT.ASPX
**Closing Date**: 28 January
**Funding**: Private, Foundation
**Contributor**: AACR
**No. of awards given last year**: 2
**Additional Information**: memento.epfl.ch/event/aacr-anna-d-barker-basic-cancer-research-fellowshi/

### For further information contact:

**Email**:    grants@aacr.org

## American Association for Cancer Research Career Development Awards

**Purpose**: To support cancer research by junior faculty
**Eligibility**: Applicants must have a doctoral degree (including PhD, MD, DO, DC, ND, DDS, DVM, ScD, DNS, PharmD, or equivalent doctoral degree, or a combined clinical and research doctoral degree) in a related field and not currently be a candidate for a further doctoral or professional degree
**Level of Study**: Postdoctorate, Research
**Type**: Award
**Value**: US$50,000 per year
**Length of Study**: 2 years
**Frequency**: Annual
**Study Establishment**: Universities or research institutions
**Country of Study**: Any country
**Application Procedure**: Candidates must be nominated by a member of AACR and must be an AACR member or apply for membership by the time the application is submitted. Associate members may not be nominators. The online application is available at the AACR website. Please see the website for further details regarding eligibility at www.aacr.org/Uploads/DocumentRepository/Grants/2012_FCC_CDA_PG.rev.pdf
**No. of awards offered**: 75
**Closing Date**: 1 February
**Funding**: Private
**Contributor**: The Cancer Research and Prevention Foundation, the Susan G Komen Breast Cancer Foundation, Genentech Inc., the Pancreatic Cancer Action Network
**No. of awards given last year**: 6
**No. of applicants last year**: 75
**Additional Information**: www.aacr.org/Funding/Pages/Funding-Detail.aspx?ItemID=30

**For further information contact:**

**Tel**:      (1) 215 446 7191
**Fax**:     (1) 215 440 9372
**Email**:   grants@aacr.org

## American Association for Cancer Research Gertrude B. Elion Cancer Research Award

**Purpose**: The AACR Gertrude B. Elion Cancer Research Award represents a joint effort to encourage and support tenure-eligible junior faculty

**Eligibility**: Applicants must have a doctoral degree (including PhD, MD, DO, DC, ND, DDS, DVM, ScD, DNS, PharmD, or equivalent) in a related field and not currently be a candidate for a further doctoral degree. At the start of the grant term on 1 July, applicants must: 1. Hold a tenure-eligible appointment (or equivalent, if institution does not follow a tenure system) at the rank of assistant professor (Appointments such as research assistant professor, adjunct assistant professor, assistant professor research track, visiting professor, or instructor are not eligible. Applicants cannot be tenured or under consideration for a tenured academic position at the time of the application. Applicants that have progressed to associate professor appointments are also not eligible). i. If eligibility is based on a future position, the position must be confirmed at the time of application, and CANNOT be contingent upon receiving this grant. ii. If the future position is at a different institution than the applicant's current institution, the applicant must contact AACR's Scientific Review and Grants Administration Department (AACR's SRGA) at grants@aacr.org before submitting their application for information on additional verification materials/signatures that may be required. 2. Have completed their most recent doctoral degree within the past 11 years (i.e., degree cannot have been conferred before 1 July; the formal date of receipt of doctoral degree is the date the degree was conferred, as indicated on their diploma and/or transcript). i. Applicants with a medical degree must have completed their most recent doctoral degree or medical residency (or equivalent) - whichever date is later - within the past 11 years. 3. Work at an academic, medical, or research institution anywhere in the world. (There are no citizenship or geographic requirements. However, by submitting an application for this grant, an applicant applying from an institution located in a country in which they are not a citizen or a permanent resident assures that the visa status will provide sufficient time to complete the project and grant term at the institution from which they applied)

**Level of Study**: Postdoctorate, Research
**Type**: Grant
**Value**: US$75,000
**Length of Study**: 1 year

**Frequency**: Annual
**Study Establishment**: Universities or research institutions
**Country of Study**: Any country
**Funding**: Private
**Contributor**: GlaxoSmithKline
**No. of awards given last year**: 1
**Additional Information**: www.aacr.org/Funding/Pages/Funding-Detail.aspx?ItemID=7

**For further information contact:**

**Email**:     grants@aacr.org

## American Association for Cancer Research NextGen Grants for Transformative Cancer Research

**Purpose**: The AACR NextGen Grants for Transformative Cancer Research represent the AACR's flagship funding initiative to stimulate highly innovative research from young investigators. This grant mechanism is intended to promote and support creative, paradigm-shifting cancer research that may not be funded through conventional channels. It is expected that these grants will catalyze significant scientific discoveries and help talented young investigators gain scientific independence

**Eligibility**: Applicants must have a doctoral degree (including PhD, MD, DO, DC, ND, DDS, DVM, ScD, DNS, PharmD, or equivalent) in a related field and not currently be a candidate for a further doctoral degree. At the start of the grant term on 1 July, applicants must: 1. Hold a tenure-eligible appointment (or equivalent, if institution does not follow a tenure system) at the rank of assistant professor (appointments such as research assistant professor, adjunct assistant professor, assistant professor research track, visiting professor, or instructor are not eligible. Applicants that have progressed to associate professor appointments are also not eligible). i. If eligibility is based on a future position, the position must be confirmed at the time of submission, and CANNOT be contingent upon receiving this grant. ii. If the future position is at a different institution than the applicant's current institution, the applicant must contact AACR's Scientific Review and Grants Administration. Department (AACR's SRGA) at grants@aacr.org before submitting their Letter of Intent for information on additional verification materials/signatures that may be required. 2. Have held a tenure-eligible assistant professor appointment for no more than three years (i.e., cannot have held a tenure-eligible appointment prior to 1 July). 3. Work at an academic, medical, or research institution anywhere in the world (there are no citizenship or geographic requirements. However, by submitting a Letter of Intent for this grant, an applicant applying from an institution located in a country in which they are not a citizen or a permanent resident assures that their visa status will provide sufficient time to complete the project and grant term at the institution from which they applied)

**Level of Study**: Postdoctorate

**Type**: Grant

**Value**: US$450,000

**Length of Study**: 3 years

**Frequency**: Dependent on funds available

**Country of Study**: Any country

**Application Procedure**: Please visit our funding page for details: www.aacr.org/FUNDING/PAGES/DEFAULT.ASPX

**Funding**: Private, Foundation

**Contributor**: AACR

**No. of awards given last year**: 2

**Additional Information**: researchfunding.duke.edu/aacr-nextgen-grants-transformative-cancer-research

**For further information contact:**

**Email**:    grants@aacr.org

## American Association for Cancer Research-AstraZeneca Stimulating Therapeutic Advancements through Research Training (START) Grants

**Purpose**: Dramatic advances made in recent years towards precision medicine initiatives, biomarker and novel target identification, and high-throughput examination of genomic data, have resulted in a trove of valuable data that can inform the development of new therapeutics to combat cancer. However, to effectively harness this wealth of information and advance the discovery and development of new therapies for cancer patients, enhanced collaboration between academia and industry will be needed. The AACR-AstraZeneca Stimulating Therapeutic Advancements through Research Training (START) Grants represent an exciting new initiative to encourage and support such collaboration. This novel model, which will provide support to postdoctoral or clinical research fellows, combines research experiences in both an academic and industry setting, following a research timeline that will be of greatest benefit to the proposed work. The training provided through this grant program will be invaluable to young investigators, by allowing fellows to attain a comprehensive research experience that will make them highly desirable to potential employers in either academic research or the pharmaceutical industry. Likewise, academic research centers and industry will benefit from the introduction of such dual-trained individuals into the field **Eligibility**: APPLICANT ELIGIBILITY CRITERIA Applicants must have a doctoral degree (including PhD, MD, DO, DC, ND, DDS, DVM, ScD, DNS, PharmD, or equivalent) in a related field and not currently be a candidate for a further doctoral degree. At the start of the grant term on 1 July,

applicants must: 1. Hold a full-time, mentored research position with the title of postdoctoral fellow, clinical research fellow, or the equivalent; this position must have been held for at least one, but not more than three, years. i. If eligibility is based on a future position, the position must be confirmed at the time of application, and CANNOT be contingent upon receiving this grant. ii. If the future position is at a different institution than the applicant's current institution, the applicant must contact AACR's Scientific Review and Grants AdministrationDepartment (AACR's SRGA) at grants@aacr.org before submitting their application forinformation on additional verification materials/signatures that may be required. 2. Have completed their most recent doctoral degree within the past one to three years (i.e., degree cannot have been conferred before 1 July; the formal date of receipt ofdoctoral degree is the date the degree was conferred, as indicated on their diploma and/ortranscript). i. Applicants with a medical degree must have completed their most recent doctoraldegree or medical residency - whichever date is later - within the past three years. 3. Work under the auspices of a mentor at an academic, medical, or research institution in the United States of America (there are no citizenship requirements. However, by submitting an application for this grant, the applicant who is not a United States citizen or a permanent resident assures that the visa status will provide sufficient time to complete the project and grant term)

**Level of Study**: Postdoctorate

**Type**: Fellowship or Grant

**Value**: US$225,000

**Length of Study**: 3 years

**Frequency**: Dependent on funds available

**Country of Study**: United States of America

**Application Procedure**: Please visit funding page for details at www.aacr.org/FUNDING/PAGES/DEFAULT.ASPX

**Funding**: Private

**Contributor**: AstraZeneca

**No. of awards given last year**: 2

**Additional Information**: www.aacr.org/Funding/Pages/Funding-Detail.aspx?ItemID=73

**For further information contact:**

**Email**:    grants@aacr.org

## QuadW Foundation-AACR Fellowship for Clinical/Translational Sarcoma Research

**Purpose**: The QuadW Foundation-AACR Fellowship for Clinical/Translational Sarcoma Research represents a joint effort to encourage and support a postdoctoral or clinical research fellow to conduct translational or clinical sarcoma research and to establish a successful career path in this field **Eligibility**: Applicants must have a doctoral degree (including PhD, MD, DO, DC, ND, DDS, DVM, ScD, DNS, PharmD, or equivalent) in a related field and not currently be a candidate for a further doctoral degree. At the start of the grant term on 1 July, applicants must: 1. Hold a mentored research position with the title of postdoctoral fellow, clinical research fellow, or the equivalent. i. If eligibility is based on a future position, the position must be confirmed at the time of application and CANNOT be contingent upon receiving this grant. ii. If the future position is at a different institution than the applicant's current institution, the applicant must contact AACR's Scientific Review and Grants Administration Department (AACR's SRGA) at grants@aacr.org before submitting their application for information on additional verification materials/signatures that may be required. 2. Have completed their most recent doctoral degree within the past five years (i.e., degree cannot have been conferred before 1 July; the formal date of receipt of doctoral degree is the date the degree was conferred, as indicated on your diploma and/or transcript). i. Applicants with a medical degree must have completed their most recent doctoral degree or medical residency - whichever date is later - within the past five years. 3. Work under the auspices of a mentor at an academic, medical, or research institution anywhere in the world. (There are no citizenship or geographic requirements. However, by submitting an application for this grant, an applicant applying from an institution located in a country in which they are not a citizen or a permanent resident assures that the visa status will provide sufficient time to complete the project and grant term at the institution from which they applied)

**Level of Study**: Postdoctorate
**Type**: Fellowship or Grant
**Value**: US$55,000
**Length of Study**: 1 year
**Frequency**: Dependent on funds available
**Country of Study**: Any country
**Application Procedure**: Please visit our funding page for details www.aacr.org/FUNDING/PAGES/DEFAULT.ASPX
**Funding**: Private, Foundation
**Contributor**: QuadW Foundation
**No. of awards given last year**: 1
**Additional Information**: www.aacr.org/Funding/Pages/Funding-Detail.aspx?ItemID=12

### For further information contact:

**Email**:    grants@aacr.org

---

## American Association for the History of Nursing (AAHN)

PO Box 175, Lanoka Harbor, NJ 08734, United States of America.

**Tel**:        (1) 609 693 7250
**Email**:    aahn@aahn.org
**Website**:    www.aahn.org
**Contact**:    Executive Secretary

The American Association for the History of Nursing (AAHN) is a professional organization accessible to everyone interested in the history of nursing. Originally founded in 1978 as a historical methodology group, the Association was briefly named the International History of Nursing Society. The Association's purpose is to foster the importance of history in understanding the present and guiding the future of nursing.

### H-15 Grant

**Purpose**: The H-15 Grant is awarded to faculty members or independent researchers for proposals outlining a historical research study
**Eligibility**: Applicants must be AAHN members and hold the doctorate
**Level of Study**: Doctorate
**Type**: Award/Grant
**Value**: US$3,000
**Frequency**: Annual
**Country of Study**: Any country
**Application Procedure**: A copy of the proposal should be sent by email to grants@aahn.org
**Closing Date**: 1 April
**Funding**: Private
**No. of awards given last year**: 1
**Additional Information**: www.aahn.org/research-grants

### H 31 Pre-Doctoral Grant

**Purpose**: This grant is designed to encourage and support graduate training and historical research at the Masters and Doctoral levels. The grant will be US$2,000
**Eligibility**: Eligibility Criteria; 1. Proposals will focus on a significant question in the history of nursing. 2. The student will be enrolled in an accredited masters program or doctoral program. 3. The student will be a member of AAHN. 4. The research advisor will be doctorally prepared with scholarly activity in the field of nursing history and prior experience in guidance of research training
**Level of Study**: Doctorate
**Type**: Award/Grant
**Value**: US$2,000
**Frequency**: Annual
**Country of Study**: Any country
**Application Procedure**: Application: Form 1. Title Page. 2. Narrative (four [4] double-spaced pages, maximum). Include the following: 1. Central thesis or questions of the study. 2. Explanation of your approach to the study, identifying pertinent

secondary sources and primary sources critical to the project. 3. Any additional relevant facilities and resources. 4. Significance of the study. Attachments 1. Applicant's curriculum vitae, including education and any research publications and presentations relevant to the proposed project. 2. Letter of support from advisor. 3. Budget: Outline and itemize the budget detailing the ways you will use the award and briefly justify each item. For example: travel, purchase of equipment, copying. A copy of the proposal should be sent by email to grants@aahn.org

**Closing Date**: 1 April
**Funding**: Private
**Additional Information**: www.aahn.org/research-grants

## H-21 Grant

**Purpose**: The Eleanor Crowder Bjoring Research (H-21) Grant is awarded to senior scholars (faculty members or independent researchers) for proposals outlining a new historical research study. The grant provides US$3,000 in funding. For faculty members affiliated with an academic institution, indirect costs for Facilities and Administration (F & A) of 8% are also available. Applicants must be AAHN members, hold a research doctorate, and be the author of a published book in the field of history that is based on original research. It is expected that the research and new materials produced by the grant recipient will help ensure the growth of scholarly work focused on the history of nursing
**Eligibility**: 1. Proposals for a new historical research study in the history of nursing. 2. The scholar will be a faculty member or independent researcher who holds a research doctorate. 3. The scholar will be the author of a published book in the field of history based on original research
**Level of Study**: Doctorate
**Type**: Award/Grant
**Value**: US$3,000
**Frequency**: Annual
**Country of Study**: Any country
**Application Procedure**: A copy of the proposal should be sent by email to grants@aahn.org
**Closing Date**: 1 April
**Funding**: Private
**Additional Information**: www.aahn.org/research-grants

## American Association for Women Radiologists (AAWR)

1891 Preston White Drive, Reston, VA 20191, United States of America.

**Tel**: (1) 713 965 0566
**Email**: admin@aawr.org
**Website**: www.aawr.org

The Association was founded in 1981 to provide a forum for issues unique to women in radiology, radiation oncology and related professions; sponsor programs that promote opportunities for women; and facilitate networking among members and other professionals.

## Alice Ettinger Distinguished Achievement Award

**Purpose**: To recognize long-term contribution to radiology and to the American Association for Women Radiologists
**Eligibility**: Open to AAWR members only
**Level of Study**: Unrestricted
**Type**: Award
**Value**: Plaque
**Frequency**: Annual
**Country of Study**: Any country
**Application Procedure**: Candidates must submit a current curriculum vitae and letters of support
**Closing Date**: 30 June
**Contributor**: Membership dues
**Additional Information**: www.aawr.org/AAWR-Awards#42621451-alice-ettinger-distinguished-achievement-award

## Lucy Frank Squire Distinguished Resident Award in Diagnostic Radiology

**Purpose**: To honor a resident diagnostic radiologist on the basis of outstanding contributions to clinical care, teaching, research and/or public service
**Eligibility**: Open to candidates in the field of diagnostic radiology who are members of the AAWR as of 1 January of the year of the award
**Level of Study**: Unrestricted
**Type**: Award
**Value**: Plaque
**Frequency**: Annual
**Country of Study**: Any country
**Application Procedure**: Candidates must submit an application including a curriculum vitae, a letter of nomination and a letter of concurrence
**Closing Date**: 30 June
**Contributor**: Membership dues
**Additional Information**: Nominees will be evaluated on the basis of outstanding contributions in clinical care, teaching, research, or public service www.aawr.org/AAWR-Awards#42621452-lucy-frank-squire-distinguished-resident-award-in-diagnostic-radiology

### For further information contact:

**Email**: info@aawr.org

## American Association of Critical-Care Nurses (AACN)

101 Columbia, Aliso Viejo, CA 92656-4109, United States of America.

**Tel**:          (1) 800 899 2226
**Email**:      info@aacn.org
**Website**:   www.aacn.org
**Contact**:   Research Department

The American Association of Critical-Care Nurses (AACN) is the world's largest nursing speciality organization with approx. 68,000 members worldwide. The AACN is committed to providing the highest quality resources to maximize nurses' contributions to caring and improving the healthcare of critically ill patients and their families.

### Agilent Technologies - AACN Critical-Care Nursing Research Grant

**Purpose**: To fund research for study conducted by a critical care nurse
**Eligibility**: Principal investigators must be nurses holding current AACN membership. Investigators who have received funding from the AACN are ineligible to receive additional funding during the lifetime of their original award. They may apply for a new award when their original award obligations have been met
**Level of Study**: Research
**Type**: Grant
**Value**: US$35,000, providing US$33,000 for the research study and US$2,000 for travel expenses associated with presentations of the study findings
**Country of Study**: Any country
**Application Procedure**: Applicants must submit a completed application form and supporting materials. Details and forms are available directly from the organisation or from the website
**Closing Date**: 1 September
**Contributor**: Hewlett-Packard, Inc

### American Nurses Foundation Research Grant Program

**Purpose**: To encourage the research career development of nurses
**Eligibility**: Principal investigators must be nurses holding current AACN membership. Investigators who have received funding from the AACN are ineligible to receive additional funding during the lifetime of their original award. They may apply for a new award when their original award obligations have been met
**Level of Study**: Research
**Type**: Research grant
**Value**: Up to US$5,000 is awarded by the American Nurses Foundation
**Application Procedure**: Applicants must obtain information and application forms from the American Nurses Foundation, and should see the website for further details
**Closing Date**: 1 May
**Contributor**: The AACN
**Additional Information**: www.petersons.com/scholarship/ american-nurses-foundationnursing-research-grants-111_ 179095.aspx

### For further information contact:

The American Nurses Foundation, 600 Maryland Avenue SW, Suite 100W, Washington DC 20024, United States of America.

**Tel**:       (1) 202 651 7298
**Email**:   anf@ana.org

## American Association of Family and Consumer Sciences (AAFCS)

400 N. Columbus Street, Suite 202, Alexandria, VA 22314-2752, United States of America.

**Tel**:          (1) 703 706 4600
**Email**:      cislamd@aafcs.org
**Website**:   www.aafcs.org
**Contact**:   Ms Amy Campbell, Grants Management Officer

Founded in 1909 as the American Home Economics Association, the American Association of Family and Consumer Sciences (AAFCS) is an organisation of members dedicated to improving the quality of individual and family life through programs that educate, influence public policy, disseminate information and publish research findings. Representing nearly 16,000 professionals in the family and consumer sciences, AAFCS members include elementary, secondary and post secondary educators and administrators, co-operative extension agents and other professionals in government, business and non-profit sectors.

## American Association of Family and Consumer Sciences National Fellowships in Family and Consumer Sciences

**Purpose**: To support a student pursuing study in family and consumer sciences at the graduate level
**Eligibility**: Applicants must be current members of the AAFCS
**Level of Study**: Doctorate, Graduate, Postgraduate
**Type**: Fellowship
**Value**: US$3,000–5,000
**Frequency**: Annual
**Country of Study**: United States of America
**Application Procedure**: Applicants must apply using official AAFCS application forms. Seven copies of the completed application must be submitted. All requests for fellowship application materials must be accompanied by a fee of US$25 (non refundable)
**Closing Date**: 31 December
**Additional Information**: awards@aafcs.org higherlogic download.s3.amazonaws.com/AAFCS/1c95de14-d78f-40b8-a6ef-a1fb628c68fe/UploadedImages/awards/DSA_Nomination_Guidelines_2019_2020.pdf

## American Association of Family and Consumer Sciences New Achievers Award

**Purpose**: The programme was developed to recognise emerging professionals who have exhibited the potential for making significant contributions in or through family and consumer sciences
**Eligibility**: Any living family and consumer sciences professional who is 35 years of age or younger or who has a least three years service in the field, but no more than eight years of service to the field, and is an active member of AAFCS is eligible for consideration by a nominating group
**Type**: Award
**Value**: A desk plaque and commemorative pin
**Frequency**: Annual
**Country of Study**: Any country
**Application Procedure**: One nomination will be accepted from each nominating group. Eligible nominating groups include the AAFCS affiliates, sections and divisions, the Higher Education Unit, and the Past President Unit
**Additional Information**: www.aafcs.org/resources/recognition/fellowships

### For further information contact:

**Email**:    awards@aafcs.org

## Ethel L. Parker International Fellowship Fund

**Purpose**: To be awarded to no more than one (1) FCS graduate student from the U.S. who participates in international study or an international graduate student who studies family and consumer sciences in the U.S.
**Level of Study**: Postgraduate
**Value**: Funding includes a US$5,000 fellowship and up to US$2,500 of support for one year of AAFCS membership, International Federation of Home Economics (IFHE) Registration, AAFCS Annual Conference & IFHE travel. (reimbursable upon event participation and receipt submission).
**Additional Information**: www.aafcs.org/resources/recognition/fellowships

### For further information contact:

**Email**:    awards@aafcs.org

## Helen Strow International Fellowship Fund

**Purpose**: To be awarded to no more than one (1) international student who is working to complete a graduate degree* in family and consumer sciences in the United States.
**Level of Study**: Postgraduate
**Value**: Funding includes a US$5,000 fellowship and up to US$2,500 of support for one year of AAFCS membership, International Federation of Home Economics (IFHE) Registration, AAFCS Annual Conference & IFHE travel. (reimbursable upon event participation and receipt submission).
**Additional Information**: www.aafcs.org/resources/recognition/fellowships

### For further information contact:

**Email**:    awards@aafcs.org

## Jewell L Taylor Fellowship

**Purpose**: To support a student pursuing a degree in family and consumer sciences
**Eligibility**: Open only to United States citizens
**Level of Study**: Postgraduate
**Type**: Fellowship
**Value**: US$5,000
**Frequency**: Annual
**Country of Study**: United States of America
**Application Procedure**: Application must be made using official AAFCS application forms. Seven (7) copies of the completed application must be submitted. There is an

application fee of US$15 for AAFCS members, US$30 for non members
**Closing Date**: 31 December
**Funding**: Private
**Additional Information**: www.collegexpress.com/scholar ships/jewell-l-taylor-national-graduate-fellowship/2011825/

## Ruth O Brian Project Grant

**Eligibility**: Open to suitably qualified individuals of any nationality
**Level of Study**: Graduate, Postgraduate
**Type**: Project grant
**Value**: Up to US$5,000
**Country of Study**: Any country
**Application Procedure**: Applicants must write for details
**Closing Date**: 14 January

### For further information contact:

**Email**:    robrien@gc.cuny.edu

## American Association of Law Libraries (AALL)

105 W. Adams Street, Suite 3300, Chicago, IL 60603, United States of America.

**Tel**:         (1) 312 939 4764
**Email**:      scholarships@aall.org
**Website**:    www.aallnet.org

The American Association of Law Libraries (AALL) was founded in 1906 to promote and enhance the value of law libraries to legal and public communities, to foster the profession of law librarianship and to provide leadership in the field of legal information. Today, the AALL represents law librarians and related professionals who are affiliated with a wide range of institutions including law firms, law schools, corporate legal departments and courts, and local, state and federal government agencies.

## American Association of Law Libraries James F Connolly LexisNexis Academic and Library Solutions Scholarship

**Eligibility**: Awarded to library school graduates with law library experience who are presently attending an accredited

law school with the intention of pursuing a career as a law librarian. Preference will be given to individuals who have demonstrated an interest in government documents
**Level of Study**: Graduate
**Type**: Scholarship
**Value**: Up to US$3,000 for tuition and school-related expenses
**Frequency**: Annual
**Study Establishment**: ABA-accredited Law Schools
**Country of Study**: Any country
**Application Procedure**: Applicants must write for details or download an application form from the website
**Closing Date**: 1 April
**Additional Information**: www.encyclopedia.com/educa tion/news-and-education-magazines/american-association-law-libraries#E

### For further information contact:

53 West Jackson Boulevard, Suite 940, Chicago, IL 60604, United States of America.

**Email**:    scholarships@csulb.edu

## American Association of Law Libraries LexisNexis/ John R Johnson Memorial Scholarship Endowment

**Eligibility**: Candidates who apply for AALL educational scholarships, types I–IV, become automatically eligible to receive the LexisNexis/John R Johnson Memorial Scholarship
**Level of Study**: Graduate
**Type**: Scholarship
**Value**: Up to US$2,000 for tuition and school-related expenses
**Frequency**: Annual
**Study Establishment**: ALA-accredited library schools or ABA-Accredited Law Schools
**Country of Study**: Any country
**Application Procedure**: Applicants must write for details or download an application form from the website
**Closing Date**: 1 April
**Additional Information**: www.lifelaunchr.com/scholarship/ lexisnexis-john-r-johnson-memorial-scholarship-endowment/

## American Association of Law Libraries Scholarship (Type II)

**Purpose**: Candidates should apply for more than one scholarship when appropriate

**Eligibility**: Open to library school graduates working towards a degree in an accredited law school who have no more than 36 semester credit hours remaining before qualifying for the law degree, who have law library experience and who have the intention of pursuing a career as a law librarian. Preference is given to members of the AALL

**Level of Study**: Graduate

**Value**: Up to US$2,000 for tuition and school-related expenses

**Frequency**: Annual

**Study Establishment**: ABA-accredited law schools

**Country of Study**: Any country

**Application Procedure**: Applicants must write for details or download an application form from the website

**Closing Date**: 1 April

## American Association of Neurological Surgeons (AANS)

5550 Meadowbrook Drive, Rolling Meadows, IL 60008-3852, United States of America.

| | |
|---|---|
| **Tel**: | (1) 847 378 0500 |
| **Email**: | info@aans.org |
| **Website**: | www.aans.org |
| **Contact**: | Julie Qattrocchi, Development Coordinator |

Founded in 1931 as the Harvey Cushing Society, the American Association of Neurological Surgeons (AANS) is a scientific and educational association with more than 6,500 members worldwide. The AANS is dedicated to advancing the specialty of neurological surgery in order to provide the highest quality of neurosurgical care to the public. All active members of the AANS are certified by the American Board of Neurological Surgery, The Royal College of Physicians and Surgeons (Neurosurgery) of Canada or the Mexican Council of Neurological Surgery, AC. Neurological surgery is the medical specialty concerned with the prevention, diagnosis, treatment and rehabilitation of disorders that affect the entire nervous system including the spinal column, spinal cord, brain and peripheral nerves.

## Neurosurgery Research and Education Foundation Research Fellowship

**Purpose**: To provide training for neurosurgeons who are preparing for academic careers as clinician investigators

**Eligibility**: Open to MDs who have been accepted into, or who are in, an approved residency training programme in neurological surgery in North America

**Level of Study**: Postdoctorate

**Type**: Fellowship

**Value**: US$40,000 for a 1-year fellowship

**Length of Study**: 1–2 years

**Frequency**: Annual

**Country of Study**: Other

**Application Procedure**: Applicants must send a completed application, sponsor statement, programme director comments and letters of recommendation. Responses to questions 1–9, a curriculum vitae and photographic images must also be submitted. Applications are available at the website www.aans.org

**No. of awards offered**: 25

**Closing Date**: 31 October

**Funding**: Private

**Contributor**: Corporations and membership

**No. of awards given last year**: 5

**No. of applicants last year**: 25

**Additional Information**: Notification of awards will be made by 28 February. After notification of the award, the applicant must indicate acceptance, in writing, no later than 1 April. If unwilling to accept the award by that date, funds will be awarded to the first runner-up. A report of findings and accounting of funds will be expected at the halfway point and upon completion of the fellowship. Normally, no more than one award per year will be made to any one institution. Individuals who accept a grant from another source, NIH or private, for the same research project will become ineligible for the award. A budget must be prepared by the applicant and the sponsor indicating how the grant funds will be expended. It is the policy of the NREF to fund only direct costs involved with the research awards. This means no fringe benefits, publication costs or travel expenses. The signature representing the applicant's institution's financial officer on page four should be that of their chief financial officer or grants and contracts manager. The award will be made payable to the institution and disbursed by it according to its institutional policy research.weill.cornell.edu/funding/open-submission-grants/research-fellowship-neurosurgery-research-and-education-foundation

### For further information contact:

**Email**:    nref@aans.org

## Neurosurgery Research and Education Foundation Young Clinician Investigator Award

**Purpose**: To fund pilot studies that provide preliminary data used to strengthen applications for more permanent funding from other sources

**Eligibility**: Candidates must be neurosurgeons who are full-time faculty in teaching institutions in North America and in the early years of their careers
**Level of Study**: Postdoctorate
**Type**: Award
**Value**: 1-year research project grant of US$40,000
**Length of Study**: 1 year
**Frequency**: Annual
**Application Procedure**: Candidates must send a completed application, sponsor statement, programme director comments and letters of recommendation. Responses to questions 1–9, a curriculum vitae and photographic images must also be submitted. Applications are available at the website www. aans.org
**No. of awards offered**: 20
**Closing Date**: 31 October
**Funding**: Private
**Contributor**: Corporations and membership
**No. of awards given last year**: 3
**No. of applicants last year**: 20
**Additional Information**: Notification of awards will be made by 28 February. After notification of the award, the applicant must indicate acceptance, in writing, no later than 1 April. If unwilling to accept the award by that date, funds will be awarded to the first runner-up. A summary report and an accounting of funds will be expected upon completion of the award. Normally, no more than one award per year will be made to any one institution. Individuals who accept a grant from another source, NIH or private, for the same research project will become ineligible for the award. The award is for those budget items necessary to pursue proper research. It may be used entirely, or in part, for stipend. A budget must be prepared by the applicant and sponsor indicating how the award funds will be expended. It is the policy of the NREF to fund only direct costs involved with the research awards. This means no fringe benefits, publication costs or travel expenses www.petersons.com/scholarship/neurosurgery-research-and-education-foundation-young-clinician-investigator-award-111_169592.aspx

**For further information contact:**

**Email**:    NREF@aans.org

## William P Van Wagenen Fellowship

**Purpose**: To fund quality research in which the plan for a period abroad has been designed
**Eligibility**: All senior neurological residents in approved neurosurgery residency programs
**Level of Study**: Postdoctorate
**Type**: Travelling fellowship

**Value**: US$120,000 stipend for living and travel expenses to a foreign country for a period of 12 months. A family travel and living allowance of US$6,000 is available if spouse and/or children are accompanying the Fellow. In addition, US$15,000 of research support is available to the University, hospital or laboratory, which has agreed to sponsor the Van Wagenen Fellow. If needed, US$5,000 is available for medical insurance
**Length of Study**: 6–12 months
**Frequency**: Annual
**Country of Study**: Country of study must be different than the country of residence
**Application Procedure**: Application should be submitted with letters of reference, including one from the applicant's Program Director. A letter from the proposed sponsor and documentation of intent to pursue an academic career, while not required, will strengthen the application
**No. of awards offered**: 6
**Closing Date**: 1 October
**Funding**: Private
**Contributor**: William P Van Wagenen
**No. of awards given last year**: 1
**No. of applicants last year**: 6
**Additional Information**: By 31 December, the Chairman of the Van Wagenen Selection Committee will notify the winning applicant, who will be expected to implement the fellowship within 6 months following notification. A formal announcement of the award will be made at the Annual Meeting of the AANS. Applications and additional information regarding the William P Van Wagenen Fellowship can be located at www.aans.org researchfunding.duke.edu/william-p-van-wagenen-fellowship

**For further information contact:**

**Email**:    nref@aans.org

# American Association of University Women (AAUW)

## American Association of University Women (AAUW) American Fellowships

**Subjects**: Business
**Purpose**: Summer/Short-Term Research Publication Grants fund women, college and university faculty and independent researchers to prepare research for publication.
**Eligibility**: Available to women who are U.S. citizens or permanent residents.
**Type**: Fellowship
**Value**: The Dissertation Fellowship award is US$20,000 and covers a 12-month period beginning July 1.

**Length of Study**: One year
**Country of Study**: United States of America
**Closing Date**: 15 November
**Additional Information**: Applicants may be tenure-track, part-time, or temporary faculty, or independent scholars and researchers, either new or established. Time must be available for eight consecutive weeks of final writing, editing, and responding to issues raised in critical reviews. Funds cannot be used for undertaking research. Applicants must have received their doctorates by the application deadline. Scholars with strong publishing records should seek other funding. www.aauw.org

## American Association of University Women (AAUW) Career Development Grants

**Subjects**: Business
**Purpose**: Grants awarded to women who are preparing to re-enter the work force, changing careers, or advance their current careers, and who have five or more years since their baccalaureate degree.
**Eligibility**: Available to women who are U.S. citizens or permanent residents.
**Type**: Grant
**Value**: Grants up to US$8,000 are offered to women pursuing graduate or doctoral degrees.
**Country of Study**: United States of America
**Closing Date**: 1 December
**Additional Information**: The grants apply only to coursework; not for dissertation research or writing. www.aauw.org

## American Association of University Women (AAUW) International Fellowships

**Subjects**: Business
**Purpose**: Applicants are judged on their professional potential and on the importance of their projects to their country of origin. Upon completion of their studies, fellowship recipients must return to their home countries to pursue a professional career; preference will be given to applicants who can verify that they have a definite position awaiting them.
**Eligibility**: Available for full-time graduate or postgraduate study or research in the U.S. are awarded to women of outstanding academic ability who are not citizens or permanent residents of the U.S. Applicants must hold the equivalent of a U.S. bachelor's degree.
**Type**: Fellowship
**Value**: The Masters/First Professional Fellowship award is US$18,000 and the Doctoral Fellowship is US$20,000.

**Length of Study**: One year
**Country of Study**: United States of America
**Closing Date**: 15 December
**Additional Information**: www.aauw.org

## American Association of University Women Educational Foundation

1111 16 Street North West, Washington, DC 20036, United States of America.

| | |
|---|---|
| **Tel**: | (1) 202 785 7700 |
| **Email**: | fellowships@aauw.org |
| **Website**: | www.aauw.org |
| **Contact**: | Gloria Blackwell, Director of Fellowship |

The AAUW Educational Foundation is composed of three corporations. These are the Association, a 150,000 member organization with more than 1,500 branches nationwide that lobbies and advocates for education and equity; the AAUW Educational Foundation, which funds pioneering research on girls and education, community action projects, and fellowships and grants for outstanding women around the globe; and the AAUW Legal Advocacy Fund, which provides funds and a support system for women seeking judicial redress for sexual discrimination in higher education.

## American Association of University Women Career Development Grants

**Purpose**: To support women who hold a bachelor's degree and are preparing to advance their careers, change careers, or re-enter the work force
**Eligibility**: Primary consideration is given to women of color and women pursuing their first advanced degree or credentials in nontraditional fields
**Level of Study**: Graduate, Postgraduate
**Type**: Grant
**Value**: US$2,000–12,000 (Funds are available for tuition, fees, books, supplies, local transportation, and dependent care.)
**Length of Study**: 1 year
**Frequency**: Annual
**Closing Date**: 15 December
**No. of awards given last year**: 47
**Additional Information**: Materials sent to the Washington, DC office will be disqualified and will not be reviewed www.unigo.com/scholarships/all/aauw-career-development-grant/4362

**For further information contact:**

ACT, Inc., 101 ACT Dr., Iowa City, IA 52243, United States of America.

**Tel**:     (1) 319 337 1716 ext. 60
**Email**:   aauw@act.org

## American Association of University Women Case Support Travel Grants

**Purpose**: To enable Legal Advocacy Fund-supported plaintiffs, their lawyers, and related experts to speak at state meetings or conventions about LAF-supported cases, sex discrimination issues in the workplace and higher education, and the work of LAF
**Eligibility**: Please see website for conditions
**Level of Study**: Postgraduate, Research
**Type**: Grant
**Value**: The grant covers the speaker's travel, lodging, and meal expenses
**Frequency**: Annual
**Application Procedure**: Apply online
**Closing Date**: 15 October
**Additional Information**: Please note that materials sent to the Washington, DC office will be disqualified and will not be reviewed www.aauw.org/act/laf/travelgrant.cfm

**For further information contact:**

**Fax**:     (1) 202 463 7169
**Email**:   laf@aauw.org

## American Association of University Women Community Action Grants

**Purpose**: To provide seed money to individual women, local community-based non-profit organizations, AAUW branches and AAUW state organizations for innovative programmes or non-degree research projects that engage girls in mathematics, science and technology
**Eligibility**: Applicants must be women who are citizens or permanent residents of the United States of America. Special consideration will be given to AAUW members and AAUW branch and state applicants who seek partners for collaborative projects. Collaborators can include local schools or school districts, businesses and other community-based organizations. 2-year grants are restricted to projects focused on girls' achievement in mathematics, science or technology. Projects must involve community and school collaboration. The fund supports planning and coalition-building activities during the 1st year and implementation and evaluation the following year

**Type**: Grant
**Value**: US$2,000–7,000 (1-year grant); US$5,000–10,000 (2-year grant)
**Length of Study**: 1 or 2 years
**Frequency**: Annual
**Application Procedure**: Applicants must write for an application form, which is also available from the website
**Closing Date**: 15 January
**Funding**: Private
**Additional Information**: Please note that materials sent to the Washington, DC office will be disqualified and will not be reviewed. Two types of grant are available: 1-year grants are for short-term projects. Topic areas are unrestricted but should have a clearly defined educational activity; 2-year grants are for longer term programmes and are restricted to projects focused on K-12 girls achievement in mathematics, science and/or technology. Funds support planning activities and coalition-building during the 1st year and implementation and evaluation the following year www.aauw.org/what-we-do/educational-funding-and-awards/community-action-grants/

**For further information contact:**

**Tel**:     (1) 319 337 1716 ext. 60
**Email**:   aauw@act.org

## American Association of University Women Eleanor Roosevelt Fund Award

**Purpose**: To remove barriers to women's and girls' participation in education; to promote the value of diversity and cross-cultural communication; and to develop greater understanding of the ways women learn, think, work, and play
**Eligibility**: To be eligible for the award, projects or activities must take place within the United States and recipients or organizational representatives must reside in the United States at the time the award is given. AAUA programs are not eligible for this award
**Level of Study**: Professional development
**Type**: Award
**Value**: US$5,000 plus travel expenses to attend the AAUW National Convention
**Frequency**: Every 2 years
**Application Procedure**: Please see the website for details
**Closing Date**: 1 August
**Funding**: Private, Individuals
**No. of awards given last year**: 1
**Additional Information**: www.aauw.org/resource/eleanor-roosevelt-fund-award-nominate/

**For further information contact:**

**Tel**:   (1) 202 728 3300

## American Association of University Women International Fellowships

**Purpose**: To support full-time study or research to women who are not United States citizen or permanent residents

**Eligibility**: Have citizenship in a country other than the U.S. or possession of a nonimmigrant visa if residing in the U.S. Women who are currently, or expect to be during the fellowship year, a U.S. citizen, U.S. permanent resident, or dual citizen with the U.S. and another country are not eligible. Hold an academic degree (earned in the U.S. or abroad) equivalent to a U.S. bachelor's degree completed by 15 November 2019. Intend to devote herself full-time to the proposed academic plan during the fellowship year. Intend to return to her home country to pursue a professional career. Be proficient in English. Unless the applicant can verify that her native language is English (written statement required), that she received her secondary diploma or undergraduate degree from an English-speaking institution (transcript required), or that she will have completed one semester of full-time study in her discipline at an English-speaking college or university between November 2017 and November 2019 (transcript required), she must upload a recent ETS TOEFL* (Test of English as a Foreign Language) score (no older than November 2017). Institutional TOEFL scores and other English proficiency test scores (such as IELTS) will not be accepted. Minimum score acceptable: 550 for Paper-Based Test (TOEFL PBT); 79 for Internet-Based Test (TOEFL iBT); 60 for Revised TOEFL Paper-Delivered Test.. Master's/first professional degree and doctoral applicants must have applied by 15 November 2019, to an accredited institution of study for the period of the fellowship year and must indicate the name of the institution in the International Fellowship application.

**Level of Study**: Doctorate, Postdoctorate, Postgraduate, Professional development, MBA

**Type**: Fellowship

**Value**: US$18,000 (Master's/First Professional Degree Fellowship); US$20,000 (Doctoral Fellowship); US$30,000 (Postdoctoral Fellowship)

**Length of Study**: 1 year

**Frequency**: Annual

**Study Establishment**: Any accredited institution

**Country of Study**: United States of America

**Application Procedure**: Applicants must complete an application for each year applying. Applications must be obtained from the customer service centre or the AAUW website between 1 August and 15 December. Three letters of recommendation, transcripts and a minimum score of 550 on the Test of English as a Foreign Language (213 computer-based) are also required. Order for brochure at www.act.org/aauw/brochurerequest.html

**No. of awards offered**: 1194

**Closing Date**: 1 December

**Funding**: Foundation

**No. of awards given last year**: 36

**No. of applicants last year**: 1194

**Additional Information**: Please note that materials sent to the Washington, DC office will be disqualified and will not be reviewed www.scholars4dev.com/1877/aauw-international-fellowships-in-usa-for-women/

### For further information contact:

**Tel**:      (1) 319 337 1716 ext. 60
**Email**:   aauw@act.org

## American Association of University Women Selected Professions Fellowships

**Purpose**: To support women who intend to pursue a full-time course of study at accredited institutions during the fellowship year in one of the designated degree programs where women's participation has been low

**Eligibility**: Women candidates who intend to pursue a full-time course of study at accredited United States institutions during the fellowship year in one of the designated degree programs where women's participation traditionally has been low (see list below). Applicants must be United States citizens or permanent residents. Please check the website for further details of eligibility

**Level of Study**: Doctorate, Postdoctorate, Postgraduate

**Type**: Fellowships

**Value**: US$5,000–18,000

**Length of Study**: 1 year

**Frequency**: Annual

**Study Establishment**: Any accredited institution

**Application Procedure**: Check website for details

**Closing Date**: 10 January

**Additional Information**: Materials sent to the Washington, DC office will be disqualified and will not be reviewed www.aauw.org/what-we-do/educational-funding-and-awards/selected-professions-fellowships/

### For further information contact:

C/O ACT, Inc., P.O. Box 4030, Iowa City, IA 52243 4030, United States of America.

**Tel**:      (1) 319 337 1716 ext. 60
**Email**:   aauw@act.org

## American Australian Association (AAA)

50 Broadway, Suite 2003, New York, NY 10004, United States of America.

**Tel**:       (1) 212 338 6860
**Email**:    information@aaanyc.org

**Website**:    www.americanaustralian.org
**Contact**:    Diane Sinclair, Director of Education

The American Australian Association (AAA), founded in 1948, is the largest non-profit organization in the United States devoted to relations between the United States, Australia and New Zealand, with operations throughout the tri-state and the New England regions. Its goal is to encourage stronger ties across the Pacific, particularly in the private sector.

## AAA Graduate Education Scholarships

**Purpose**: The AAA Graduate Education Scholarships support American and Australian individuals undertaking or planning to undertake full-time Graduate level study (Masters, PhD or Postdoctoral Research) at an accredited institution in the country of the other, for a minimum of one year. The scholarships outlined below will provide support of up to US$40,000 to those in the specialty fields of Science, Technology, Engineering, Mathematics, Health, Medicine and Sustainability. Scholarship funds may be used toward travel, living, tuition and other associated educational costs.
**Eligibility**: 1. All AUS to USA applicants must be an Australian citizen or permanent resident (dual citizens or USA permanent residents are not eligible); 2. Applicants must have a formal letter of offer into the accredited institution, program or course, in the country of the other, at the time of application; 3. Applicants must be conducting research or studying within the fields supported; 4. Applicants must be studying at Graduate-level or above (Masters, PhD or Postdoctoral Research); 5. Applicants may already have commenced their studies in the USA, but must have at least one-year of full-time study left at the time of application.
**Level of Study**: Masters, PhD or Postdoctoral
**Value**: US$40,000
**Length of Study**: 1 year
**Application Procedure**: 1. High-resolution headshot & in-action study field shot (min 1MB, 300 DPI); 2. Video presentation (max 1 minute – introducing yourself & your planned research/study abroad); 3. Passport biographic page from Australia or USA; 4. Offer or acceptance letter from your host university or research supervisor, confirming your placement; 5. Academic transcripts for Graduate and/or Undergraduate study; 6. Resume (please reduce to 1-page); 7. Detailed budget outlining expenses and income throughout the year of supported study – please download and use the Graduate Education Scholarships Budget Template as a guide. This is available to download in the application portal; 8. Three referees to list in the Letter of Recommendation section. Please note: after listing, referees will be automatically contacted to complete a recommendation within the online submission form. This is not viewable to the applicant.
**Closing Date**: 15 October
**Additional Information**: www.americanaustralian.org/scholarships/education-fund/specialty-field-scholarships/

### For further information contact:

50 Broadway Suite 2003 New York, NY 10004, United States of America.

**Tel**:      (1) 212 338 6860
**Email**:    scholarships@aaanyc.org

## Sir Keith Murdoch Fellowships

**Purpose**: To facilitate intellectual interchange between Australia and the United States and create a channel for ongoing collaborative research
**Level of Study**: Graduate, Postdoctorate
**Type**: Fellowships
**Value**: Up to US$320,000
**Frequency**: Annual
**Study Establishment**: Harvard Medical, John Hopkins, MIT, Stanford Business School and Cold Spring Harbor Laboratory
**Country of Study**: United States of America
**Closing Date**: 31 October
**Contributor**: American Australian Association
**Additional Information**: ecms.adelaide.edu.au/faculty-intranet/news/list/2019/11/19/sir-keith-murdoch-fellowship-award-winner

### For further information contact:

**Email**:    jhelum.bagchi@aaanyc.org

## American Cancer Society (ACS)

1599 Clifton Road North East, Atlanta, GA 30329-4251, United States of America.

**Email**:      fellows@uicc.org
**Website**:    fellows.uicc.org
**Contact**:    Ms Brita Baker, Head of Fellowships Department

The American Cancer Society (ACS) is the largest non government fund holder of cancer research in the United States. ACS has devoted more than US$2 billion to cancer research.

## American Cancer Society International Fellowships for Beginning Investigators

**Purpose**: To foster a bi-directional flow of knowledge, experience, expertise, and innovation to and from the United States of America. To enable beginning investigators and clinicians, who are in the early stages of their careers, to carry out basic or clinical research projects and to develop, acquire and apply advanced research procedures and techniques

**Eligibility**: Eligible candidates should hold assistant professorships or similar positions at their home institutes and have a minimum of two and a maximum of 10 years of postdoctoral experience after obtaining their MD or PhD degrees or equivalents. Awards are conditional on the return of the Fellow to the home institute at the end of the Fellowship and on the availability of appropriate facilities and resources to develop the newly acquired skills. No extensions are permitted. Candidates who are already physically present at the proposed host institution whilst their applications are under consideration are not eligible

**Level of Study**: Postdoctorate

**Type**: Fellowship

**Value**: An average value of US$36,000 for travel and stipend support

**Length of Study**: 1 year

**Frequency**: Annual

**Country of Study**: United States of America

**Application Procedure**: Applicants must obtain an application form from the Fellowships department

**No. of awards offered**: 23

**Closing Date**: 1 November

**No. of awards given last year**: 9

**No. of applicants last year**: 23

**Additional Information**: No allowances are made for accompanying dependants www.caca.org.cn/system/2015/07/03/011227242.shtml

### For further information contact:

International Union Against Cancer, 3 rue Conseil-Général, CH-1205 Genève, Switzerland.

**Tel**: (1) 22 809 1840
**Fax**: (1) 22 809 1081
**Email**: fellows@uicc.ch

## American Chemical Society (ACS)

1155 16th Street, NW, Washington, DC 20036, United States of America.

**Tel**: (1) 202 872 4600
**Email**: help@acs.org

The American Chemical Society is a self-governed individual membership organization that consists of more than 160,000 members at all degree levels and in all fields of chemistry. The organization provides a broad range of opportunities for peer interaction and career development, regardless of professional or scientific interests. The program and activities conducted by ACS today are the products of a tradition of excellence in meeting member needs that dates from the Society's founding in 1876.

## Alfred Burger Award in Medicinal Chemistry

**Purpose**: To acknowledge outstanding contributions to research in medicinal chemistry

**Eligibility**: The award will be granted for outstanding contributions in the field of medicinal chemistry regardless of race, gender, age, religion, ethnicity, nationality, sexual orientation, gender expression, gender identity, presence of disabilities and educational background

**Level of Study**: Postgraduate

**Type**: Award

**Value**: The award consists of US$5,000 and a certificate. Up to US$2,500 for travel expenses to the meeting at which the award will be presented will be reimbursed

**Application Procedure**: A completed nomination form available on the website www.chemistry.org

**Closing Date**: 1 November

**Contributor**: Glaxo Smith Kline

**Additional Information**: www.acs.org/content/acs/en/funding-and-awards/awards/national/bytopic/alfred-burger-award-in-medicinal-chemistry.html

### For further information contact:

**Tel**: (1) 202 872 4575
**Fax**: (1) 202 776 8008
**Email**: awards@acs.org

## American Chemical Society Ahmed Zewail Award in Ultrafast Science and Technology

**Purpose**: To recognize outstanding and creative contributions to fundamental discoveries or inventions in ultrafast science and technology

**Eligibility**: The award will be for outstanding and creative contributions by a nominee to fundamental discoveries or inventions in ultrafast science and technology in the areas of physics, chemistry, biology, or related fields. Please see the website for further details regarding eligibility

**Level of Study**: Postgraduate

**Type**: Award

**Value**: The award will consist of US$5,000 and a certificate. Up to US$2,500 for travel expenses to the meeting at which the award will be presented will be reimbursed

**Frequency**: Annual

**Application Procedure**: See website for details

**Closing Date**: 1 November

**Funding**: Trusts

**Contributor**: Ahmed Zewail Endowment Fund

**Additional Information**: www.acs.org/content/acs/en/funding-and-awards/awards/national/bytopic/the-ahmed-zewail-award-in-ultrafast-science-and-technology.html

**For further information contact:**

**Tel**:        (1) 202 872 4575
**Fax**:       (1) 202 776 8008
**Email**:    awards@acs.org

## American Chemical Society Award for Creative Advances in Environmental Science and Technology

**Purpose**: To encourage creativity in research and technology

**Eligibility**: The award will be granted regardless of race, gender, age, religion, ethnicity, nationality, sexual orientation, gender expression, gender identity, presence of disabilities and educational background

**Level of Study**: Postgraduate

**Type**: Award

**Value**: The award consists of US$5,000 and a certificate. Up to US$2,500 for travel expenses to the meeting at which the award will be presented will be reimbursed

**Frequency**: Annual

**Application Procedure**: See the website for more details

**Closing Date**: 1 November

**Contributor**: ACS Division of Environmental Chemistry

**Additional Information**: Air Products and Chemicals, Inc www.acs.org/content/acs/en/funding-and-awards/awards/national/bytopic/acs-award-for-creative-advances-in-environmental-science-and-technology.html

**For further information contact:**

**Tel**:        (1) 202 872 4575
**Fax**:       (1) 202 776 8008
**Email**:    awards@acs.org

## American Chemical Society Award for Creative Research and Applications of Iodine Chemistry

**Purpose**: To support, promote, and motivate global research of iodine chemistry and develop its use and knowledge through applications

**Eligibility**: A nominee must have performed outstanding and creative research related to iodine chemistry or its applications. Please see the website for further details regarding eligibility

**Level of Study**: Postgraduate

**Type**: Award

**Value**: The award consists of US$10,000 and a certificate. Up to US$1,000 for travel expenses to the meeting at which the award will be presented will be reimbursed. The award is presented biennially in odd-numbered years

**Application Procedure**: A completed nomination form and curriculum vitae must be sent

**Closing Date**: 1 November

**Contributor**: Sociedad Quimica y Minera de chile S.A. (SQM S.A.)

**Additional Information**: www.acs.org/content/acs/en/funding-and-awards/awards/national/bytopic/acs-award-for-creative-research-and-applications-of-iodine-chemistry.html

**For further information contact:**

**Tel**:        (1) 202 872 4575
**Fax**:       (1) 202 776 8008
**Email**:    awards@acs.org

## American Chemical Society Award for Creative Work in Synthetic Organic Chemistry

**Purpose**: To recognize and encourage creative work in synthetic organic chemistry

**Eligibility**: A nominee must have accomplished outstanding creative work in synthetic organic chemistry that has been published. Please see website for further details regarding eligibility

**Level of Study**: Postgraduate

**Type**: Award

**Value**: The award consists of US$5,000 and a certificate. Up to US$1,000 for travel expenses to the meeting at which the award will be presented will be reimbursed

**Frequency**: Annual

**Application Procedure**: See the website for more details

**Closing Date**: 1 November

**Contributor**: The Aldrich Chemical Company, Inc

**Additional Information**: www.acs.org/content/acs/en/funding-and-awards/awards/national/bytopic/acs-award-for-creative-work-in-synthetic-organic-chemistry.html

**For further information contact:**

**Tel**:        (1) 202 872 4575
**Fax**:       (1) 202 776 8008
**Email**:    awards@acs.org

## American Chemical Society Award for Encouraging Disadvantaged Students into Careers in the Chemical Sciences

**Purpose**: To recognize significant accomplishments by individuals in stimulating students, underrepresented in the profession, to elect careers in the chemical sciences and engineering

**Eligibility**: Nominees for the award may come from any professional setting: academia, industry, government or other independent facility. Please see the website for further details regarding eligibility

**Level of Study**: Postgraduate

**Type**: Award

**Value**: The award consists of US$5,000 and a certificate. A grant of US$10,000 will be made to an academic institution, designated by the recipient, to strengthen its activities in meeting the objectives of the award. Up to US$1,500 for travel expenses to the meeting at which the award will be presented will be reimbursed

**Frequency**: Annual

**Country of Study**: United States of America

**Application Procedure**: Completed nomination and optional support forms must be submitted to the awards office

**Closing Date**: 1 November

**Contributor**: The Camille and Henry Dreyfus Foundation, Inc

**Additional Information**: www.acs.org/content/acs/en/funding-and-awards/awards/national/bytopic/acs-award-for-encouraging-disadvantaged-students-into-careers-in-the-chemical-sciences.html

### For further information contact:

**Tel**:    (1) 202 872 4575
**Fax**:    (1) 202 776 8008
**Email**:    awards@acs.org

## American Chemical Society Award for Encouraging Women into Careers in the Chemical Sciences

**Purpose**: To recognize individuals who have significantly stimulated the interests of women in chemistry

**Eligibility**: Open to candidates of all nationalities. Nominees for the award may come from any professional setting: academia, industry, government, or other independent facility

**Level of Study**: Professional development

**Type**: Award

**Value**: The award consists of US$5,000 and a certificate. A grant of US$10,000 will be made to an academic institution, designated by the recipient, to strengthen its activities in meeting the objectives of the award. Up to US$1,500 for travel expenses to the meeting at which the award will be presented will be reimbursed

**Frequency**: Annual

**Application Procedure**: For more details visit the website

**Closing Date**: 1 November

**Contributor**: The Camille and Henry Dreyfus Foundation, Inc

**Additional Information**: www.acs.org/content/acs/en/funding-and-awards/awards/national/bytopic/acs-award-for-encouraging-women-into-careers-in-the-chemical-sciences.html

### For further information contact:

**Tel**:    (1) 202 872 4575
**Fax**:    (1) 202 776 8008
**Email**:    awards@acs.org

## American Chemical Society Award in Chromatography

**Purpose**: To recognize outstanding contributions to the fields of chromatography

**Eligibility**: A nominee must have made an outstanding contribution to the fields of chromatography with particular consideration given to developments of new methods. Please see the website for further details regarding eligibility

**Level of Study**: Postgraduate

**Type**: Award

**Value**: The award consists of US$5,000 and a certificate. Up to US$2,500 for travel expenses to the meeting at which the award will be presented will be reimbursed

**Frequency**: Annual

**Application Procedure**: See the website for more details

**Closing Date**: 1 November

**Contributor**: SUPELCO, Inc

**Additional Information**: www.acs.org/content/acs/en/funding-and-awards/awards/national/bytopic/acs-award-in-chromatography.html

### For further information contact:

The Awards Office, American Chemical Society, 1155 16th Street, NW, Washington, DC 20036-4801, United States of America.

**Tel**:    (1) 202 872 4575
**Fax**:    (1) 202 776 8008
**Email**:    awards@acs.org

## American Chemical Society Award in Colloid Chemistry

**Purpose**: To recognize and encourage outstanding scientific contributions to colloid chemistry

**Eligibility**: The nominee must have made outstanding scientific contributions to colloid chemistry. The award will be granted regardless of race, gender, age, religion, ethnicity, nationality, sexual orientation, gender expression, gender identity, presence of disabilities, and educational background
**Level of Study**: Postgraduate
**Type**: Award
**Value**: The award consists of US$5,000 and a certificate. Up to US$2,500 for travel expenses to the meeting at which the award will be presented will be reimbursed
**Frequency**: Annual
**Application Procedure**: Completed nomination and optional support forms must be submitted
**Closing Date**: 1 November
**Contributor**: Colgate-Palmolive Company
**Additional Information**: www.acs.org/content/acs/en/funding-and-awards/awards/national/bytopic/acs-award-in-colloid-chemistry.html

### For further information contact:

**Tel**:     (1) 202 872 4575
**Fax**:     (1) 202 776 8008
**Email**:    awards@acs.org

## American Chemical Society National Awards

**Purpose**: To recognize premier chemical professionals in extraordinary ways
**Level of Study**: Postgraduate
**Type**: Grant
**Length of Study**: 2 years
**Frequency**: Annual
**Country of Study**: Any country
**Application Procedure**: See website for details
**Additional Information**: Inquiries concerning awards should be directed to the office of the National Awards office awards@acs.org   www.acs.org/content/acs/en/funding-and-awards/awards/national.html

### For further information contact:

**Email**:    awards@acs.org

## American Chemical Society Priestley Medal

**Purpose**: To recognize distinguished services to chemistry
**Eligibility**: Open to applicants of any nationality who may or may not be members of the Society
**Level of Study**: Doctorate
**Type**: Award
**Value**: A gold medallion, a presentation box and a certificate

**Frequency**: Annual
**Application Procedure**: Applicants must send their nominations to the ACS Board of Directors
**Closing Date**: 1 November
**Funding**: Trusts
**Contributor**: The American Chemical Society
**Additional Information**: www.acs.org/content/acs/en/funding-and-awards/awards/national/bytopic/priestley-medal.html

### For further information contact:

**Email**:    awards@acs.org

## American Chemical Society Roger Adams Award in Organic Chemistry

**Purpose**: To recognize and encourage outstanding contributions to research in organic chemistry
**Eligibility**: The award will be granted regardless of race, gender, age, religion, ethnicity, nationality, sexual orientation, gender expression, gender identity, presence of disabilities and educational background
**Type**: Award
**Value**: The award consists of a medallion and a replica, a certificate and US$25,000
**Application Procedure**: A completed nomination form must be sent as an email attachment. See the website www.chemistry.org
**Closing Date**: 1 November
**Contributor**: Organic Reactions, Inc. and Organic Synthesis, Inc
**Additional Information**: www.acs.org/content/acs/en/funding-and-awards/awards/national/bytopic/roger-adams-award-in-organic-chemistry.html

### For further information contact:

**Tel**:     (1) 202 872 4575
**Fax**:     (1) 202 776 8008
**Email**:    awards@acs.org

## American Chemical Society Stanley C. Israel Regional Award for Advancing Diversity in the Chemical Sciences

**Purpose**: To recognize individuals who have advanced diversity in the chemical sciences and significantly stimulated or fostered activities that promote inclusiveness within the region
**Eligibility**: Nominees may come from academia, industry, government, or independent entities, and may also be organizations, including ACS Local Sections and Divisions. The

nominee must have created and fostered ongoing programs or activities that result in increased numbers of persons from diverse and underrepresented minority groups, persons with disabilities, or women who participate in the chemical enterprise

**Level of Study**: Postgraduate

**Type**: Award

**Value**: The award consists of a medal and a US$1,000 grant to support and further the activities for which the award was made. The award also will include funding to cover the recipient's travel expenses to the ACS regional meeting at which the award will be presented

**Frequency**: Annual

**Application Procedure**: See website for details

**Closing Date**: 1 August

**Contributor**: ACS Committee on Minority Affairs

**Additional Information**: First deadline is for Middle Atlantic (MARM), Central (CERM), and Northwest (NORM) and second deadline is for Midwest (MWRM), Northeast (NERM), Southeastern (SERMACS), Southwest (SWRM), and Rocky Mountain (RMRM) www.acs.org/content/acs/en/funding-and-awards/awards/other/diversity/stan-israel-award.html

## For further information contact:

**Fax**:     (1) 202 776 8003

**Email**:   Diversity@acs.org

## Arthur C. Cope Scholar Awards

**Purpose**: To recognize outstanding achievement in the field of organic chemistry

**Eligibility**: The award will be granted regardless of race, gender, religion, ethnicity, nationality, sexual orientation, gender expression, gender identity, presence of disabilities and educational background. Please see the website for further details regarding eligibility

**Level of Study**: Postgraduate

**Type**: Award

**Value**: The award consists of US$5,000, a certificate, and a US$40,000 unrestricted research grant to be assigned by the recipient to any university or nonprofit institution. Up to US$2,500 for travel expenses to the fall national meeting will be reimbursed

**Frequency**: Annual

**Application Procedure**: See the website

**Closing Date**: 1 November

**Contributor**: The Arthur C. Cope Fund

**Additional Information**: www.acs.org/content/acs/en/funding-and-awards/awards/national/bytopic/arthur-cope-scholar-award.html

## For further information contact:

**Tel**:     (1) 202 872 4575

**Fax**:     (1) 202 776 8008

**Email**:   awards@acs.org

## Award in Chemical Instrumentation

**Purpose**: Conceptualization and development of unique instrumentation that has made a significant impact on the field. Demonstration of innovative use of instrumentation in chemical measurement. Stimulation of other researchers to use instrumentation in chemical measurement. Authorship of research papers or books that have had an influential role in the use of chemical instrumentation

**Eligibility**: Eligibility is not restricted to members of the Division of Analytical Chemistry. Nominees for the J. Calvin Giddings Award for Excellence in Education must, however, must have demonstrated excellence in teaching through at least five years at the time the award is presented

**Level of Study**: Postgraduate

**Type**: Grant

**Frequency**: Annual

**Country of Study**: Any country

**Application Procedure**: Apply online

**Funding**: Trusts

**Additional Information**: www.acs.org/content/acs/en/funding-and-awards/awards/national/bytopic/arthur-cope-scholar-award.html

## For further information contact:

**Email**:   miquela@sciencemanagers.com

## Award in Spectrochemical Analysis

**Purpose**: Development of novel and important instrumentation. Elucidation of fundamental events or processes important to the field. Authorship of important research papers and/or books that have had an influential role in the development of the field. role in the use of chemical instrumentation

**Eligibility**: Eligibility is not restricted to members of the Division of Analytical Chemistry. Nominees for the J. Calvin Giddings Award for Excellence in Education must, however, must have demonstrated excellence in teaching through at least five years at the time the award is presented

**Level of Study**: Postgraduate

**Type**: Award

**Value**: US$2,500

**Length of Study**: 1 year

**Frequency**: Annual

**Country of Study**: Any country

**Application Procedure**: Apply online
**Funding**: Trusts
**Additional Information**: www.acs.org/content/acs/en/funding-and-awards/awards/division/analytical/anyl-award-in-spectrochemical-analysis.html

### For further information contact:

**Email**:    miquela@sciencemanagers.com

## Ernest Guenther Award in the Chemistry of Natural Products

**Purpose**: To recognize and encourage outstanding achievements in analysis, structure elucidation and chemical synthesis of natural products
**Eligibility**: Open to all applicants
**Type**: Grant
**Value**: US$6,000, a medallion and a certificate. Up to US$2,500 for travel expenses to the meeting at which the award will be presented will be reimbursed
**Frequency**: Annual
**Application Procedure**: A completed nomination form and optional support forms must be mailed to awards@acs.org
**Closing Date**: 1 November
**Contributor**: Givaudan
**No. of awards given last year**: 1
**Additional Information**: www.acs.org/content/acs/en/funding-and-awards/awards/national/bytopic/ernest-guenther-award-in-the-chemistry-of-natural-products.html

### For further information contact:

**Tel**:      (1) 202 872 4575
**Fax**:      (1) 202 776 8008
**Email**:    awards@acs.org

## F. Albert Cotton Award in Synthetic Inorganic Chemistry

**Purpose**: To recognize distinguished work in synthetic inorganic chemistry
**Eligibility**: The award recognizes outstanding synthetic accomplishment in the field of inorganic chemistry. The award will be granted regardless of race, gender, age, religion, ethnicity, nationality, sexual orientation, gender expression, gender identity, presence of disabilities and educational background
**Level of Study**: Postgraduate
**Type**: Award
**Value**: US$5,000 and a certificate. Up to US$2,500 for travel expenses to the meeting at which the award will be presented will be reimbursed

**Frequency**: Annual
**Application Procedure**: A completed application form to be submitted as an email attachment to awards@acs.org
**Closing Date**: 1 November
**Funding**: Private
**Contributor**: F. Albert Cotton Endowment Fund
**No. of awards given last year**: 1
**Additional Information**: www.acs.org/content/acs/en/funding-and-awards/awards/national/bytopic/f-albert-cotton-award-in-synthetic-inorganic-chemistry.html

### For further information contact:

**Tel**:      (1) 202 872 4575
**Fax**:      (1) 202 776 8008
**Email**:    awards@acs.org

## Frederic Stanley Kipping Award in Silicon Chemistry

**Purpose**: To recognize distinguished contributions to the field of silicon chemistry
**Eligibility**: Open to all candidates who have contributed to the field of silicon chemistry. There are no limits on age or on nationality. A nominee must have made distinguished contributions in the field of silicon chemistry during the 10 years preceding the current nomination
**Level of Study**: Postgraduate
**Type**: Award
**Value**: US$5,000 and a certificate. Up to US$2,500 for travel expenses will be reimbursed to the spring national meeting at which the award will be presented and to the United States based Silicon Symposium to deliver an award address
**Application Procedure**: A completed nomination form to be mailed to awards@acs.org
**Closing Date**: 1 November
**Funding**: Corporation
**Contributor**: Dow Corning Corporation
**Additional Information**: www.acs.org/content/acs/en/funding-and-awards/awards/national/bytopic/frederic-stanley-kipping-award-in-silicon-chemistry.html

### For further information contact:

**Tel**:      (1) 202 872 4575
**Fax**:      (1) 202 776 8008
**Email**:    awards@acs.org

## Glenn T. Seaborg Award for Nuclear Chemistry

**Purpose**: To recognize and encourage research in nuclear and radiochemistry or their applications

**Eligibility**: Nominee must have made outstanding contributions to nuclear or radiochemistry or to their applications. The award will be granted regardless of race, gender, age, religion, ethnicity, nationality, sexual orientation, gender expression, gender identity, presence of disabilities and educational background

**Level of Study**: Postgraduate

**Type**: Award

**Value**: US$5,000 and a certificate. Up to US$2,500 for expenses to the meeting at which the award will be presented will be reimbursed

**Frequency**: Annual

**Application Procedure**: See the website

**Closing Date**: 1 November

**Contributor**: ACS Division of Nuclear Chemistry and Technology

**No. of awards given last year**: 1

**Additional Information**: www.acs.org/content/acs/en/funding-and-awards/awards/national/bytopic/glenn-t-seaborg-award-for-nuclear-chemistry.html

**For further information contact:**

Tel:       (1) 202 8721 4575
Fax:      (1) 202 776 8008
Email:   awards@acs.org

## Ipatieff Prize

**Purpose**: To recognize outstanding chemical experimental work in the field of catalysis

**Eligibility**: Open to candidates who should not have passed his or her 40th birthday on 3 April of the year in which the award is presented, and must have done outstanding chemical experimental work in the field of catalysis or high pressure. Special weight will be given to independence of thought and originality. The award may be made for investigations carried out in any country and without consideration of nationality

**Level of Study**: Postgraduate

**Type**: Prize

**Value**: The award will consist of the income from a trust fund and a certificate. The financial value of the prize may vary, but it is expected that it will be approximately US$5,000 and that it will be awarded every three years. Travel expenses related to conferment of the award will be reimbursed

**Frequency**: Every 3 years

**Country of Study**: Any country

**Application Procedure**: Contact the awards office

**Closing Date**: 1 November

**Contributor**: Ipatieff Trust Fund

**Additional Information**: Preference will be given to American chemists www.acs.org/content/acs/en/funding-and-awards/awards/national/bytopic/ipatieff-prize.html

**For further information contact:**

Tel:       (1) 202 872 4575
Email:   awards@acs.org

## Irving Langmuir Award in Chemical Physics

**Purpose**: To encourage research in chemistry and physics

**Eligibility**: A candidate must have made an outstanding contribution to chemical physics or physical chemistry within the 10 years preceding the year in which the award is made. The award will be granted without restriction, except that the recipient must be a resident of the United States and the monetary prize must be used in the United States or its possessions

**Level of Study**: Postgraduate

**Type**: Award

**Value**: US$75,000 for full Professor and scholars of equivalent accomplishment. US$50,000 for Associate Professor and equivalent. US$40,000 for Assistant Professor and equivalent

**Frequency**: Every 2 years

**Country of Study**: United States of America

**Application Procedure**: University of Texas, Austin

**Closing Date**: 1 November

**Funding**: Foundation

**Contributor**: GE Global Research and The American Chemical Society Division of Physical Chemistry

**Additional Information**: www.aps.org/programs/honors/prizes/langmuir.cfm

**For further information contact:**

Tel:       (1) 202 872 4575
Email:   awards@acs.org

## James Bryant Conant Award in High School Chemistry Teaching

**Purpose**: To recognize outstanding teachers of high school chemistry in the United States

**Eligibility**: Open to candidates who are actively engaged in the teaching of chemistry in high school. The nominee must be actively engaged in the teaching of chemistry in a high school (grades 9–12). Please see the website for further details regarding eligibility

**Level of Study**: Postgraduate

**Type**: Award

**Value**: US$5,000 and a certificate. Up to US$2,500 for travel expenses to the meeting at which the award will be presented will be reimbursed

**Frequency**: Annual

**Country of Study**: United States of America

**Application Procedure**: A completed nomination form must be submitted as an email attachment

**Closing Date**: 1 November
**Contributor**: The Thermo Fisher Scientific, Inc
**No. of awards given last year**: 1
**Additional Information**: A certificate will also be provided to the recipient's institution for display www.acs.org/content/acs/en/funding-and-awards/awards/national/bytopic/james-bryant-conant-award-in-high-school-chemistry-teaching.html

### For further information contact:

**Tel**:      (1) 202 872 4575
**Email**:    awards@acs.org

## Peter Debye Award in Physical Chemistry

**Purpose**: To encourage and reward outstanding research in physical chemistry
**Eligibility**: Open to all candidates without regard to age or nationality. Please see the website for further details regarding eligibility
**Level of Study**: Postgraduate
**Type**: Award
**Value**: US$5,000 and a certificate. Up to US$2,500 for travel expenses to the meeting at which the award will be presented will be reimbursed
**Frequency**: Annual
**Application Procedure**: A completed nominations form to be sent as an email attachment to awards@acs.org
**Closing Date**: 1 November
**Contributor**: E.I. du Pont de Nemours and Company
**No. of awards given last year**: 1
**Additional Information**: www.acs.org/content/acs/en/funding-and-awards/awards/national/bytopic/peter-debye-award-in-physical-chemistry.html

### For further information contact:

**Tel**:      (1) 202 872 4575
**Email**:    awards@acs.org

## Pfizer Graduate Travel Awards in Analytical Chemistry

**Purpose**: To provide funds for students to travel to an ACS National meeting and present the results of their research
**Eligibility**: Open to candidates who are United States citizens and permanent residents
**Level of Study**: Postgraduate
**Type**: Award
**Value**: US$1,000
**Frequency**: Annual
**Study Establishment**: Open to candidates who are United States citizens and permanent residents

**Application Procedure**: A completed application form, which may be downloaded from the website, must be sent
**Closing Date**: 21 October
**Contributor**: The Division of Analytical Chemistry of the ACS
**Additional Information**:      www.acs.org/content/acs/en/funding-and-awards/awards/division/analytical/anyl-pfizer-graduate-travel-awards-in-analytical-chemistry.html

### For further information contact:

Department of Chemistry, The College of Wooster, Wooster, OH 44691, United States of America.

**Tel**:      (1) 202 872 4575
**Email**:    awards@acs.org

# American College of Chest Physicians

## CHEST Foundation Grants

**Subjects**: Lung health
**Purpose**: The CHEST Foundation, the American College of Chest Physician's charitable foundation, champions lung health by supporting clinical research, community service, and patient education. Through CHEST Foundation-supported programs, CHEST's 20,000+ members engage in advancing the lung health of millions of patients in local communities around the world.
**Eligibility**: No restrictions on eligibility
**Type**: Grant
**Value**: Varies
**Frequency**: Annual
**Country of Study**: Any country
**Application Procedure**: Visit website for details
**Closing Date**: 6 April

# American Congress on Surveying and Mapping (ACSM)

6, Montgomery Village Avenue, Suite 403, Gaithersburg, MD 20879, United States of America.

**Tel**:       (1) 240 632 9716 ext. 109
**Email**:     ilse.genovese@acsm.net
**Website**:   www.acsm.net

The ACSM is a nonprofit association dedicated to serving the public interest and advancing the profession of surveying and mapping.

## American College of Sports Medicine Fellows Scholarship

**Purpose**: To encourage, recognize and support exceptional surveying and mapping students

**Eligibility**: Open to students with a junior or higher degree and enrolled in four-year degree programs in surveying or in closely related programs such as geomatics or surveying engineering

**Level of Study**: Graduate, Postgraduate

**Type**: Scholarship

**Value**: US$2,000

**Length of Study**: 4 years

**Frequency**: Annual

**Country of Study**: Any country

**Application Procedure**: Applicants must submit a completed application form along with proof of membership in ACSM, a complete statement indicating educational objectives, future plans of study or research, professional activities and financial need, three letters of recommendation and a complete original official transcript

**Closing Date**: 17 February

**Funding**: Corporation

**Additional Information**: Prior scholarship winners are eligible to apply in succeeding years providing all appropriate criteria are satisfied

## American Council of Learned Societies (ACLS)

633 3rd Avenue, 8th Floor between 40th & 41st Streets, New York, NY 10017-6795, United States of America.

**Tel**:        (1) 212 697 1505
**Email**:     sfisher@acls.org
**Website**:   www.acls.org

The American Council of Learned Societies (ACLS) is a private non-profit federation of 68 national scholarly organizations. The mission of the ACLS, as set forth in its Constitution is the advancement of humanistic studies in all fields of learning in the humanities and the social sciences and the maintenance and strengthening of relations among the national societies devoted to such studies.

## American Council of Learned Societies Humanities Program in Belarus, Russia and Ukraine

**Purpose**: To sustain individuals doing exemplary work, so as to assure continued future leadership in the humanities

**Eligibility**: Applicants should be involved in studies related to performing arts, ethnographic and cultural studies, gender studies, philosophy or religious studies. ACLS organizes annual regional meetings for advisers and grant recipients

**Level of Study**: Research

**Type**: Grant

**Value**: Varies

**Frequency**: Annual

**Country of Study**: Any country

**Application Procedure**: Application forms can be obtained by writing to hp@acls.org

**Closing Date**: 18 November

**Funding**: Foundation

**Additional Information**: In 2007, with the help of the Carnegie Corporation of New York and the American Council of Learned Societies, the International Association for the Humanities (IAH) was founded as an independent association of humanities scholars primarily in Belarus, Russia and Ukraine to help represent the post-Soviet region in the international scholarly community. IAH organizes a competition for short-term grants in the humanities. For further details and current competition application form, see the IAH website www.acls.org/Past-Programs/ACLS-Humanities-Program-in-Belarus-Russia-and-Ukraine

### For further information contact:

**Email**:    hp@acls.org

## American Council of Learned Societies/New York Public Library (NYPL) Fellowships

**Purpose**: To explore the rich and diverse collections of the NYPL Humanities and Social Sciences Library

**Eligibility**: be a US citizen or permanent resident. have a PhD that was conferred at least two years before the application deadline. (An established scholar who can demonstrate the equivalent of a PhD in publications and professional experience may also qualify.). have had a lapse of at least two years between the last "supported research leave" and September 1. Please see FAQ about the definition of supported research leaves and how the timing of such leaves affects eligibility.

**Level of Study**: Postdoctorate

**Type**: Fellowship

**Value**: Up to US$50,000 for full professor and equivalent, US$40,000 for associate professor and equivalent and US$30,000 for assistant professor and equivalent

**Length of Study**: 6–12 months

**Application Procedure**: Applications must be made to the ACLS Fellowship Program. Note that applications must also be made to the competition for residential fellowships administered separately by the NYPL Center for Scholars and Writers

**Additional Information**: More information about the NYPL is available at www.nypl.org www.acls.org/Competitions-and-Deadlines/ACLS-Fellowships

### For further information contact:

Center for Scholars & Writers, The New York Public Library Humanities & Social Sciences Library, Fifth Avenue & 42nd Street, New York, NY 10001, United States of America.

**Email**: csw@nypl.org

### Andrew W. Mellon Foundation/ACLS Early Career Fellowships Program Dissertation Completion Fellowships

**Purpose**: To assist graduates in the last year of their PhD dissertation writing

**Eligibility**: Open to a PhD candidate in a humanities or social science department in an American University. Applicant should not be in the degree programme for more than 6 years and the successful candidates cannot hold this fellowship after the 7th year

**Level of Study**: Doctorate

**Type**: Fellowships

**Value**: Stipend: US$35,000, plus funds for research costs of up to US$3,000 and for university fees of up toUS$5,000

**Length of Study**: 1 year

**Frequency**: Annual

**Country of Study**: United States of America

**Application Procedure**: Applicants can apply online (ofa. acls.org)

**Closing Date**: 9 November

**Contributor**: The Andrew W. Mellon Foundation

**Additional Information**: www.acls.org/programs/dcf/

### For further information contact:

**Email**: grants@acls.org

### American Council on Education (ACE)

One Dupont Circle North West, Suite 800, Washington, DC 20036-1193, United States of America.

**Tel**: (1) 202 939 9420
**Email**: fellows@ace.nche.edu
**Website**: www.acenet.edu
**Contact**: Awards Committee

The American Council on Education (ACE), founded in 1918, is the nation's umbrella higher education association. ACE is dedicated to the belief that equal educational opportunity and a strong higher education system are essential cornerstones of a democratic society. ACE is a forum for the discussion of major issues related to higher education and its potential to contribute to the quality of American life. ACE maintains both a domestic and an international agenda and seeks to advance the interests and goals of higher and adult education in a changing environment by providing leadership and advocacy on important issues representing the views of the higher and adult education community to policy makers, and offering services to its members.

### American Council on Education Fellows Program

**Purpose**: Since 1965, nearly 2,000 vice presidents, deans, department chairs, faculty, and other emerging leaders have participated in the ACE Fellows Program, a customized learning experience that enables participants to immerse themselves in the study and practice of leadership and experience the culture, policies, and decision-making processes of another institution.

**Eligibility**: Open to senior members of college faculty or mid-level staff with a minimum of five years teaching or administrative experience who show evidence of potential for senior level administration. English is the language of instruction

**Level of Study**: Professional development

**Type**: Fellowship

**Value**: The nominating institution supports the salaries and benefits. The host institution supports the seminar and travel costs of the ACE Fellows and the Council provides support for programmatic costs

**Length of Study**: 1 academic year

**Frequency**: Annual

**Study Establishment**: A host college or university

**Country of Study**: Any country

**Application Procedure**: Applicants must be nominated by the president or vice president of a college or university. Applications must be submitted with a nomination form, along with four confidential letters of reference

**Additional Information**: ACE Fellows work with a mentor, normally a president or other senior officer, at policy and practical levels. The fellowship experience is supplemented with national and regional seminars and meetings. Contact could be established only through webform www.acenet.edu/Programs-Services/Pages/Professional-Learning/ACE-Fellows-Program.aspx

### For further information contact:

**Email**: FellowsProgApp@acenet.edu

## American Council on Rural Special Education (ACRES)

West Virginia University, 509 Allen Hall, PO Box 6122, Morgantown, WV 26506-6122, United States of America.

**Tel**:        (1) 304 293 3450
**Email**:    acres-sped@mail.wvu.edu
**Website**:  acres-sped.org
**Contact**:  David Forbush, Headquarters Co-ordinator

### Alliance for Clinical Research Excellence and Safety Teacher Scholarship Award

**Purpose**: To give a rural teacher an opportunity to pursue education and training not otherwise affordable within his or her district
**Eligibility**: To be eligible for an ACRES teacher scholarship award, an individual must be: currently or recently employed by a rural school district as a certified teacher in regular or special education; working with students with disabilities or with regular education students and "retooling" for work in a special education setting; pursuing a goal of increasing skills in special education or "retooling" from a regular education to a special education career; and a citizen of the United States
**Level of Study**: Graduate
**Type**: Scholarship
**Value**: Up to US$1,000
**Length of Study**: 1 year
**Frequency**: Annual
**Country of Study**: United States of America
**Application Procedure**: Applications must consist of: a completed application form; an essay describing the opportunities and challenges of rural special education, the reason why funds are needed for the training, the plans for using the scholarship award for further education or training, and how the information gained from the education or training will be shared with other educators in rural schools; and two letters of recommendation from persons in a position to judge capabilities as a rural special educator; at least one reference must be from an individual actively involved in rural special education
**Closing Date**: 15 February
**Funding**: Private
**Additional Information**: The award will be announced at the March ACRES conference

**For further information contact:**

**Tel**:    (1) 304 293 4384

## American Diabetes Association (ADA)

1701 North Beauregard Street, Alexandria, VA 22311, United States of America.

**Tel**:        (1) 703 549 1500, ext. 2362
**Email**:    grantquestions@diabetes.org
**Website**:  professional.diabetes.org/grants

The American Diabetes Association (ADA) is the nation's leading non-profit health organization providing diabetes research information and advocacy. The mission of the organization is to prevent and cure diabetes, and to improve the lives of all people affected by diabetes. To fulfil this mission, the ADA funds research, publishes scientific findings and provides information and other services to people with diabetes, their families, healthcare professionals and the public.

### Lions Clubs International Foundation Clinical Research Grant Program

**Purpose**: To support clinical or applied research
**Eligibility**: Open to holders of an MD or PhD degree, or, in the case of other health professions, an appropriate health or science related degree. The applicant must hold a faculty level appointment or its equivalent at a research institution. The programme is intended for any investigator with or without NIH or other significant support
**Level of Study**: Postdoctorate
**Type**: Research grant
**Value**: Up to US$100,000 per year. The grants carry no commitment for overhead costs or tuition. The funds may be used for equipment, supplies, salary support or a combination of the three. The funds may not be used for the principal investigator
**Length of Study**: 3 years
**Frequency**: Annual
**Country of Study**: Any country
**Closing Date**: 1 July
**Additional Information**: This programme is part of the Lions Sightfirst Diabetic Retinopathy Research Program, funded by the Lions Club International Foundation temp. lionsclubs.org/EN/pdfs/lcif/lcif109.pdf

**For further information contact:**

**Email**:    lcif@lionsclubs.org

## Lions Clubs International Foundation Equipment Grant Program

**Purpose**: To enable investigators to purchase equipment in order to conduct clinical research projects

**Eligibility**: Open to holders of an MD or PhD degree, or, in the case of other health professions, an appropriate health- or science-related degree. The applicant must hold a faculty-level appointment at a research institution

**Level of Study**: Research

**Type**: Grant

**Value**: US$25,000 for the purchase of equipment. One payment is made in July

**Frequency**: Annual

**Country of Study**: Any country

**Application Procedure**: Applicants must submit a detailed justification of the need to purchase the equipment and an explanation of its intended use. All applications must be submitted online via the website

**Closing Date**: 15 January

**Additional Information**: This programme is part of the Lions Sightfirst Diabetic Retinopathy Research Program, funded by the Lions Club International Foundation temp. lionsclubs.org/EN/pdfs/lcif/lcif109.pdf

### For further information contact:

**Email**:    lcif@lionsclubs.org

## Lions Clubs International Foundation Training Grant Program

**Purpose**: To enable foreign investigators to visit American research institutions and receive training in clinical research and the implementation of public health programmes, eg. screening or epidemiology. The programme also aims to enable United States of America investigators to visit foreign institutions, particularly institutions in developing countries, to conduct training programmes in clinical research and implement public health programmes

**Eligibility**: Open to citizens of the United States of America who have an MD or a PhD degree, or, in the case of other health professions, an appropriate health- or science-related degree, and hold a faculty-level appointment at a United States of America research institution. The programme is also open to citizens of other countries who have an MD or a PhD degree

**Level of Study**: Research

**Value**: Up to US$40,000 per year

**Length of Study**: 2 years

**Frequency**: Annual

**Study Establishment**: An approved institution

**Country of Study**: Any country

**Application Procedure**: All applications must be submitted online via the website

**Closing Date**: 15 January

**Additional Information**: This programme is part of the Lions Sightfirst Diabetic Retinopathy Research Program, funded by the Lions Club International Foundation temp. lionsclubs.org/EN/pdfs/lcif/lcif109.pdf

### For further information contact:

**Email**:    LCIFHumanitarianPrograms@lionsclubs.org

## Pathway to Stop Diabetes Diabetes Initiator Award

**Purpose**: Pathway seeks to bring new investigators and new perspectives to diabetes research. Supporting scientists with different backgrounds and experience is critical to achieving that objective. Pathway accepts nominations for exceptional investigators with medical and scientific backgrounds who propose innovative basic, clinical, translational, behavioral, epidemiological and health services research relevant to any type of diabetes, diabetes-related disease state or complication. Pathway solicits nominations for candidates in all disciplines as applied to diabetes

**Eligibility**: Eligible applicants must currently be in research training positions (post-doctoral fellow, research fellowship) and have no more than seven years of research training following terminal doctoral degree. Applicants cannot concurrently hold an NIH K99/R00 grant.

**Level of Study**: Postdoctoral

**Type**: Award

**Value**: Up to US$100,000/year in Phase 1, Up to US$325,000/year in Phase 2

**Length of Study**: Up to 7 years

**Frequency**: Annual

**Country of Study**: United States

**Closing Date**: 14 May

**Additional Information**: professional.diabetes.org/meetings/pathway-stop-diabetes%C2%AE

## American Federation for Aging Research (AFAR)

55 West 39th Street, 16th Floor, New York, NY 10018, United States of America.

**Tel**:        (1) 212 703 9977
**Email**:    grants@afar.org

**Website**:    www.afar.org
**Contact**:    Director, Grant Programs

The American Federation for Aging Research (AFAR) is a leading non-profit organization supporting biomedical aging research. Since its founding in 1981, AFAR has provided approximately US$124 million to more than 2,600 new investigators and students conducting cutting-edge biomedical research on the aging process and age-related diseases. The important work AFAR supports leads to a better understanding of the aging process and to improvements in the health of all Americans as they age.

## American Federation for Aging Research Research Grants for Junior Faculty

**Purpose**: To help junior faculty to carry out research that will serve as the basis for longer term research efforts
**Eligibility**: Open to junior faculty with an MD or PhD degree
**Level of Study**: Postdoctorate, Research
**Type**: Research grant
**Value**: US$100,000
**Length of Study**: 1–2 years
**Frequency**: Annual
**Country of Study**: United States of America
**Application Procedure**: Applicants must complete and return the application by the annual deadline. These are available from the website
**Closing Date**: 15 December
**Funding**: Private, Foundation
**Contributor**: AFAR
**Additional Information**: Exceptions to the ten year rule may be requested for unusual circumstances by emailing an NIH-style biosketch to AFAR at grants@afar.org research. weill.cornell.edu/funding/open-submission-grants/afar-research-grants-junior-faculty-american-federation-aging

## American Federation for Aging Research/Pfizer Research Grants in Metabolic Control and Late Life Diseases

**Purpose**: To address specific areas of research that focus on the aging process and age related diseases
**Eligibility**: Applicants must be United States citizens or permanent residents
**Level of Study**: Research
**Type**: Grant

**Value**: US$60,000
**Length of Study**: 1–2 years
**Frequency**: Annual
**Country of Study**: United States of America
**Application Procedure**: Applicants must complete and return the application by the annual deadline. These are available from the website
**Closing Date**: 14 December
**Funding**: Private
**Contributor**: Pfizer Pharmaceuticals, Inc
**Additional Information**: Projects may involve basic, clinical or epidemiological research

## Diana Jacobs Kalman/AFAR Scholarships for Research in the Biology of Aging

**Purpose**: An opportunity to conduct a three-to-six-month research project focused on biomedical research in aging.
**Eligibility**: Applicants must be MD, DO, PhD, or combined degree students in good standing at a not-for-profit institution in the United States, such as universities, medical schools, hospitals, or non-government agencies. If accepted, applicants will be asked to submit a Proof of Enrollment form confirming their enrollment at a U.S. institution. Applicants who also receive NIH, NSF or DOD stipend support are eligible to receive the AFAR Scholarship, but may not hold another award or participate in another scholarship program concurrently with the Kalman/AFAR Scholarship. The research project must be carried out under the supervision of a faculty mentor
**Level of Study**: Three to six month research project
**Type**: Scholarships
**Value**: Each scholarship is US$5,000
**Length of Study**: 90 days
**Frequency**: Annual
**Application Procedure**: The full application in pdf form with instructions on all required parts is available afar.org/docs/Kalman_AFAR_Scholarship_WuFoo.pdf
**Closing Date**: 15 May
**Contributor**: The Kalman/AFAR Student Scholarships are supported by Diana Jacobs Kalman, an endowment from the former American Foundation for Aging Research, the Nicole Girard Charitable Fund of the Jewish Communal Fund, and individual contribution
**Additional Information**: www.afar.org/research/funding/afar-scholarships/

### For further information contact:

**Email**:    scholarship@afar.org

## Glenn/American Federation for Aging Research Scholarships for Research in the Biology of Aging

**Purpose**: To attract potential scientists to aging research and provide students with the opportunity to conduct a research project

**Eligibility**: Open to students completing MD or PhD degrees

**Level of Study**: Doctorate, Research

**Type**: Scholarship

**Value**: US$6,000

**Length of Study**: 3 months

**Frequency**: Annual

**Country of Study**: Any country

**Application Procedure**: Applicants should submit one original and four copies of the application and of all supporting materials, including academic transcripts from all institutions attended, Graduate Record Examination and/or MCAT scores, and a biographical sketch and endorsing letter of the designated mentor. In addition, one letter of reference is also required

**Closing Date**: 26 February

**Funding**: Private

**Contributor**: The Glenn Foundation for Medical Research

**Additional Information**: www.afar.org/research/funding/afar-scholarships/

### For further information contact:

**Email**:    info@afar.org

## Merck/American Federation for Aging Research Junior Investigator Award in Geriatric Clinical Pharmacology

**Purpose**: To help develop a cadre of physicians with a command of the emerging field of geriatric clinical pharmacology

**Eligibility**: Open to candidates who are board certified or eligible in a primary specialty having completed postdoctoral or fellowship training

**Level of Study**: Research

**Type**: Award

**Value**: US$60,000

**Length of Study**: 2 years

**Frequency**: Annual

**Country of Study**: Any country

**Application Procedure**: Applications must be submitted by an institution on behalf of the candidate. See the AFAR website for details

**Funding**: Foundation

**Contributor**: Merck Company Foundation

**Additional Information**: www.unmc.edu/media/intmed/geriatrics/pdf/2004%20AFAR%20AWARD%20PROGRAMS.pdf

## Royal Photographic Society/American Federation for Aging Research Medical Student Geriatric Scholars Program

**Purpose**: To encourage medical students, particularly budding researchers, to consider a career in academic geriatrics

**Eligibility**: Applicants must be citizens of the United States of America or permanent residents and have completed at least 1 year of medical school by the start date of the award

**Level of Study**: Doctorate

**Type**: Scholarship

**Value**: US$4,000

**Length of Study**: 8 weeks

**Frequency**: Annual

**Country of Study**: United States of America

**Application Procedure**: Applicants must complete and return the application by the annual deadline. Applications are available from the website

**Closing Date**: 6 February

**Funding**: Private

**Contributor**: Anonymous donor

**Additional Information**: www.unmc.edu/media/intmed/geriatrics/pdf/2004%20AFAR%20AWARD%20PROGRAMS.pdf

### For further information contact:

**Email**:    info@afar.org

## The Paul Beeson Career Development Awards in Aging Research for the Island of Ireland

**Purpose**: To encourage and assist the development of future leaders in the field of aging, deepen the commitment of research institutions to academic research in aging, and to expand medical research on aging

**Level of Study**: Research

**Type**: Award

**Value**: €339,390/£228,000

**Length of Study**: 3 years

**Country of Study**: Ireland

**Application Procedure**: All candidates must submit applications endorsed by the Dean of School of Medicine (or equivalent). Scholars will be required to submit a brief annual narrative report on the progress of their research and career plans

**Closing Date**: 22 January

**Funding**: Private

**Additional Information**: www.unmc.edu/media/intmed/geriatrics/pdf/2004%20AFAR%20AWARD%20PROGRAMS.pdf

### For further information contact:

**Email**:    beeson@afar.org

# American Foundation for Suicide Prevention (AFSP)

120 Wall Street, 29th Floor, New York, NY 10005, United States of America.

| | |
|---|---|
| **Tel**: | (1) 212 363 3500 |
| **Email**: | grantsmanager@afsp.org |
| **Website**: | www.afsp.org |
| **Contact**: | Carl Niedzielski, Grants Manager |

The American Foundation for Suicide Prevention (AFSP) is the only national non-profit organization exclusively dedicated to understanding and preventing suicide through research and education, and to reaching out to people with mood disorders and those affected by suicide.

## American Foundation for Suicide Prevention Distinguished Investigator Awards

**Purpose** Awarded to investigators at the level of associate professor or higher with a proven history of research in the area of suicide
**Level of Study**: Research
**Type**: Grant
**Value**: Up to US$125,000 over 2 years
**Length of Study**: 1–2 years
**Frequency**: Annual
**Country of Study**: Worldwide
**Application Procedure**: Application information at afsp.org/grants. Apply online at afsp.org/grants
**No. of awards offered**: 14
**Closing Date**: 15 November
**Funding**: Private
**No. of applicants last year**: 14
**Additional Information**: Decisions regarding awards are made in May and funding begins in October afsp.org/our-work/research/grant-information/

## Blue Sky Focus Grant

**Purpose**: Focus grants are targeted, innovative and potentially high impact studies that seek to inform and even transform suicide prevention efforts
**Eligibility**: Investigators from all academic disciplines are eligible to apply, and both basic science and applied research projects will be considered, provided that the proposed study has an essential focus on suicide or suicide prevention. Grant applications are not accepted from for-profit organizations, or from federal or state government agencies. Applications from the Veterans Administration are eligible
**Level of Study**: Research
**Type**: Research grant
**Value**: They are awarded in the amount of US$500,000 per year for a maximum of three years
**Length of Study**: 3 years
**Frequency**: Annual
**Country of Study**: Any country
**Application Procedure**: Applicants must submit a Letter of Intent by email to JHarkavyFriedman@afsp.org
**No. of awards offered**: 4
**Closing Date**: 6 December
**Funding**: Private
**No. of awards given last year**: 1
**No. of applicants last year**: 4
**Additional Information**: afsp.org/our-work/research/grant-information/the-focus-grants/

## Distinguished Investigator Grant

**Purpose**: We welcome innovative studies relevant to understanding and preventing suicide. Applications are open to biological, psychological, and sociological approaches, and we encourage multidisciplinary research. These are investigator initiated grants
**Eligibility**: Investigators from all academic disciplines are eligible to apply, and both basic science and applied research projects will be considered, provided that the proposed study has an essential focus on suicide or suicide prevention. Grant applications are not accepted from for-profit organizations, or from federal or state government agencies. Applications from the Veterans Administration are eligible
**Level of Study**: Research
**Type**: Grant
**Value**: Up to US$125,000 over 2 Years
**Length of Study**: 2 years
**Frequency**: Annual
**Country of Study**: Any country
**Application Procedure**: Applicants are instructed to apply afsp.org/our-work/research/apply-for-a-grant/
**No. of awards offered**: 9
**Closing Date**: 14 November
**Funding**: Private
**No. of awards given last year**: 3
**No. of applicants last year**: 9
**Additional Information**: afsp.org/our-work/research/grant-information/

## Linked Standard Research Grant

**Purpose**: We welcome innovative studies relevant to understanding and preventing suicide. Applications are open to biological, psychological, and sociological approaches, and we encourage multidisciplinary research. These are investigator initiated grants

**Eligibility**: Investigators from all academic disciplines are eligible to apply, and both basic science and applied research projects will be considered, provided that the proposed study has an essential focus on suicide or suicide prevention. Grant applications are not accepted from for-profit organizations, or from federal or state government agencies. Applications from the Veterans Administration are eligible

**Level of Study**: Research

**Type**: Grant

**Value**: Up to US$300,000 over 2 Years

**Length of Study**: 2 years

**Frequency**: Annual

**Country of Study**: Any country

**Application Procedure**: Applicants must submit a Letter of Intent by email to JHarkavyFriedman@afsp.org

**No. of awards offered**: 13

**Closing Date**: 14 November

**Funding**: Private

**No. of awards given last year**: 2

**No. of applicants last year**: 13

**Additional Information**: afsp.org/our-work/research/grant-information/

## Pilot Research Grant

**Purpose**: We welcome innovative studies relevant to understanding and preventing suicide. Applications are open to biological, psychological, and sociological approaches, and we encourage multidisciplinary research. These are investigator initiated grants

**Eligibility**: Investigators from all academic disciplines are eligible to apply, and both basic science and applied research projects will be considered, provided that the proposed study has an essential focus on suicide or suicide prevention. Grant applications are not accepted from for-profit organizations, or from federal or state government agencies. Applications from the Veterans Administration are eligible

**Level of Study**: Research

**Type**: Grant

**Value**: Up to US$10,000

**Length of Study**: 1–2 years

**Frequency**: Annual

**Country of Study**: Any country

**Application Procedure**: Applicants are instructed to apply afsp.org/our-work/research/apply-for-a-grant/

**No. of awards offered**: 32

**Closing Date**: 14 November

**Funding**: Private

**No. of awards given last year**: 3

**No. of applicants last year**: 32

**Additional Information**: www.thepsf.org/research/grants-program/pilot-research-grants

## For further information contact:

Weill Cornell Medicine, 2015 PSF Pilot Research Grant Recipient.

## Postdoctoral Fellowship

**Purpose**: We welcome innovative studies relevant to understanding and preventing suicide. Applications are open to biological, psychological, and sociological approaches, and we encourage multidisciplinary research. These are investigator initiated grants

**Eligibility**: Investigators from all academic disciplines are eligible to apply, and both basic science and applied research projects will be considered, provided that the proposed study has an essential focus on suicide or suicide prevention. New grantees must begin their studies within 6 months of the approved start date. Failure to begin the study within this time frame may result in withdrawal of the grant award

**Level of Study**: Postdoctorate, Research

**Type**: Grant

**Value**: Up to US$112,000 over 2 years

**Length of Study**: 2 years

**Frequency**: Annual

**Country of Study**: Any country

**Application Procedure**: Applicants are instructed to apply afsp.org/our-work/research/apply-for-a-grant/

**No. of awards offered**: 9

**Closing Date**: 14 November

**Funding**: Private

**No. of awards given last year**: 1

**No. of applicants last year**: 9

**Additional Information**: afsp.org/our-work/research/grant-information/

## Reaching 20% by 2025

**Purpose**: Focus grants are targeted, innovative and potentially high impact studies that seek to inform and even transform suicide prevention efforts

**Eligibility**: Investigators from all academic disciplines are eligible to apply, and both basic science and applied research projects will be considered, provided that the proposed study has an essential focus on suicide or suicide prevention. Grant applications are not accepted from for-profit organizations, or from federal or state government agencies. Applications from the Veterans Administration are eligible

**Level of Study**: Research

**Type**: Grant

**Value**: They are awarded in the amount of US$500,000 per year for a maximum of three years

**Length of Study**: 3 years

**Frequency**: Annual

**Country of Study**: Any country

**Application Procedure**: Applicants must submit a Letter of Intent by email to JHarkavyFriedman@afsp.org

**Closing Date**: 6 December

**Funding**: Private

**Additional Information**: cpb-us-e1.wpmucdn.com/blogs. gwu.edu/dist/e/969/files/2018/07/AFSP_2018_Focus_Grants_ Flyer-14f56ys.pdf

## Short-Term Risk Focus Grant

**Purpose**: Focus grants are targeted, innovative and potentially high impact studies that seek to inform and even transform suicide prevention efforts

**Eligibility**: Investigators from all academic disciplines are eligible to apply, and both basic science and applied research projects will be considered, provided that the proposed study has an essential focus on suicide or suicide prevention. Grant applications are not accepted from for-profit organizations, or from federal or state government agencies. Applications from the Veterans Administration are eligible

**Level of Study**: Research

**Type**: Grant

**Value**: They are awarded in the amount of US$500,000 per year for a maximum of three years

**Length of Study**: 3 years

**Frequency**: Annual

**Country of Study**: Any country

**Application Procedure**: Applicants must submit a Letter of Intent by email to JHarkavyFriedman@afsp.org

**No. of awards offered**: 1

**Closing Date**: 6 December

**Funding**: Private

**No. of awards given last year**: 1

**No. of applicants last year**: 1

**Additional Information**: cpb-us-e1.wpmucdn.com/blogs. gwu.edu/dist/e/969/files/2018/07/AFSP_2018_Focus_Grants_ Flyer-14f56ys.pdf

## Standard Research Grant

**Purpose**: We welcome innovative studies relevant to understanding and preventing suicide. Applications are open to biological, psychological, and sociological approaches, and

we encourage multidisciplinary research. These are investigator initiated grants

**Eligibility**: Investigators from all academic disciplines are eligible to apply, and both basic science and applied research projects will be considered, provided that the proposed study has an essential focus on suicide or suicide prevention. Grant applications are not accepted from for-profit organizations, or from federal or state government agencies. Applications from the Veterans Administration are eligible

**Level of Study**: Research

**Type**: Grant

**Value**: Up to US$100,000 over 2 Years

**Length of Study**: 2 years

**Frequency**: Annual

**Country of Study**: Any country

**Application Procedure**: Applicants are instructed to apply afsp.org/our-work/research/apply-for-a-grant/

**No. of awards offered**: 70

**Closing Date**: 14 November

**Funding**: Private

**No. of awards given last year**: 10

**No. of applicants last year**: 70

**Additional Information**: afsp.org/our-work/research/grant-information/

# American Foundation for Urologic Disease, Inc. (AFUD)

Research Program Division, 300 West Pratt Street Suite 401, Baltimore, MD 21202 2463, United States of America.

**Tel**:         (1) 410 689 3990

**Website**:   www.auanet.org/

**Contact**:   Grants Management Officer

The mission of the American Foundation for Urologic Disease (AFUD) is the prevention and cure of urologic diseases through the expansion of medical research and the education of the public and health care professionals concerning urologic diseases.

## National Institute of Diabetes and Digestive and Kidney Diseases (NIDDK)/AFUD Intramural Urology Research Training Program

**Purpose**: Provides an opportunity for selected individuals to complete a research project under the direction of a Senior Investigator in the Intramural Programme of NIDDK

**Eligibility**: Open to physicians who have recently completed a urology residency. Applicants must have less than five years postdoctoral experience (clinical residency training is not counted as postdoctoral research)

**Level of Study**: Postdoctorate
**Type**: Fellowship
**Value**: US$45,000–52,000 per year depending on experience
**Length of Study**: 2 years, possible extension for a further year
**Study Establishment**: Participating NIDDK laboratories
**Country of Study**: United States of America
**Application Procedure**: Applicants must submit a cover letter, curriculum vitae and three letters of recommendation. Further information available from NIDDK or the American Foundation for Urologic Disease
**Additional Information**: Further information available on request

### For further information contact:

Division of Kidney, Urology & Hematology, National Institute of Diabetes, Digestive & Kidney Diseases, Natcher Building Room 6AS13D, Bethesda, MD 20892-6600, United States of America.

**Tel**:        (1) 301 594 7717
**Fax**:       (1) 301 480 3510
**Email**:     nybergl@ep.niddk.nih.gov

## American Geophysical Union (AGU)

2000 Florida Avenue, N.W., Washington, DC 20009, United States of America.

**Tel**:        (1) 202 462 6900
**Email**:     service@agu.org
**Website**:   www.agu.org
**Contact**:   Director, Outreach and Research Support

The American Geophysical Union (AGU) is an international scientific society with more than 45,000 members, primarily research scientists, dedicated to advancing the understanding of Earth and space and making the results of the AGU's research available to the public.

## Fred. L. Scarf Award

**Purpose**: To award outstanding dissertation research that contributes directly to solar-planetary science
**Eligibility**: Open to all candidates with a PhD (or equivalent) degree
**Level of Study**: Doctorate
**Value**: US$1,000, a complimentary ticket for the SPA dinner, and a certificate

**Frequency**: Annual
**Application Procedure**: Nominations to be sent to outreach administrator at AGU
**Closing Date**: 15 April
**Contributor**: The Space Physics and Aeronomy section of AGU
**Additional Information**: Awardee will have the opportunity to deliver an invited paper on the dissertation topic at appropriate SPA session at the upcoming AGU Fall Meeting www.agu.org/Honor-and-Recognize/Honors/Section-Awards/Scarf-Award

### For further information contact:

2000 Florida Ave. NW, Washington, DC 20009, United States of America.

**Tel**:        (1) 202 462 6900
**Email**:     leadership@agu.org

## Mineral and Rock Physics Graduate Research Award

**Purpose**: The Mineral and Rock Physics Graduate Research Award is presented annually to one or more promising young scientists and recognizes outstanding contributions to the field of mineral and rock physics achieved during the honoree's PhD research. The nominee should be engaged in experimental or theoretical studies on Earth and planetary materials with the purpose of unravelling the physics and chemistry behind their origin and physical properties.
**Eligibility**: Open to students who have completed their PhD.
**Level of Study**: Doctorate
**Type**: Award
**Value**: US$500, a certificate and Announcement in Eos. Recognition at the AGU Fall Meeting during the award presentation year
**Frequency**: Annual
**Application Procedure**: A letter of nomination along with a curriculum vitae, two supporting letters and 3 reprints or preprints of the nominee's work should be sent
**Closing Date**: 15 April
**Contributor**: Mineral and Rock Physics community at AGU
**No. of awards given last year**: 2
**Additional Information**: www.agu.org/Honor-and-Recognize/Honors/Section-Awards/MRP-Graduate-Research-Award

### For further information contact:

Department of Geology and Environmental Geoscience, Northern Illinois University, Davis Hall 312, Normal Road, DeKalb, IL 60115, United States of America.

**Email**:     hwatson@niu.edu

# American Gynecological Club

## American Gynecological Club / Gynaecological Visiting Society Fellowship

**Purpose**: Through generous funding from the American Gynecological Club and the Gynaecological Visiting Society of Great Britain, the RCOG can offer up to £1,200 to an individual to visit and gain knowledge from a specific centre offering new techniques of clinical management within O&G

**Eligibility**: 1. Travel must take place within 12 months of the award being made. 2. The award may only be used for the purpose outlined in your original application. 3. A detailed report (maximum 1,000 words), including pictures if necessary, must be submitted to the RCOG Awards Administrator within eight weeks after the elective

**Level of Study**: Postdoctorate

**Type**: Fellowship

**Value**: £1,200

**Length of Study**: 1 year

**Frequency**: Annual

**Country of Study**: Any country

**Closing Date**: 31 May

**Funding**: Foundation

**Additional Information**: www.rcog.org.uk/en/careers-training/awards-grants-prizes/american-gynecological-clubgynaecological-visiting-society-fellowship/

### For further information contact:

**Email**:    awards@rcog.org.uk

# American Head and Neck Society (AHNS)

AHNS, 11300 W. Olympic Boulevard, Suite 600, Los Angeles, CA 90064, United States of America.

**Tel**:          (1) 310 437 0559
**Email**:       admin@ahns.info
**Website**:     www.headandneckcancer.org
**Contact**:     Joyce Hasper, Research Grants Enquiries

The purpose of the American Head and Neck Society (AHNS) is to promote and advance the knowledge of prevention, diagnosis, treatment and rehabilitation of neoplasms and other diseases of the head and neck.

# American Academy of Otolaryngology - Head and Neck Surgery Translational Innovator Award

**Purpose**: The purpose of this award is to support contemporary basic or clinical research focused on neoplastic disease by full time academic head and neck surgeons; to promote novel translational research preferably with biomarker ideas

**Eligibility**: Candidates for this award must be: 1. Otolaryngologist—Head and Neck surgeons, who are active members of the AAO-HNS. OR: Surgeons who are in head and neck fellowships, or have completed a head and neck surgery fellowship and are active or candidate members of the AHNS. PLEASE NOTE: Medical oncologists and radiation oncologists are not eligible to apply for this award. 2. Citizens of the United States, noncitizen nationals, or have been lawfully admitted for permanent residency at the time of application. 3. Full-time academic surgeons in faculty positions at the rank of instructor or assistant professor. 4. Hold a Doctor of Medicine (MD) degree or equivalent (DO, MBBS) from an accredited institution. 5. Have demonstrated the capacity or potential for a highly productive independent research career with an emphasis in head and neck surgical oncology

**Level of Study**: Graduate

**Type**: Award

**Value**: US$80,000 maximum (US$40,000 per year)

**Length of Study**: 24 months

**Frequency**: Annual

**Country of Study**: Any country

**Closing Date**: 1 January

**Funding**: Private

**Additional Information**: www.entnet.org/sites/default/files/uploads/PracticeManagement/Resources/_files/2020_ahns_aaohnsf_innovat_foa.pdf

### For further information contact:

AHNS, 11300 W. Olympic Blvd, Suite 600, Los Angeles, CA 90064, United States of America.

**Email**:    betty@ahns.info

## American Head and Neck Society Endocrine Research Grant

**Purpose**: Open to medical students focusing in otolaryngology, otolaryngology residents, PhDs or faculty members in otolaryngology departments

**Level of Study**: Graduate

**Type**: Research grant

**Value**: Upto US$10,000 are available per year

**Frequency**: Annual

**Country of Study**: Any country

**Closing Date**: 15 March

**Funding**: Private

**Additional Information**: www.ahns.info/ahns-endocrine-research-grants/

**For further information contact:**

**Email**:    betty@ahns.info

## American Head and Neck Society Pilot Research Grant

**Purpose**: To support students who wish to try a pilot project in head- and neck-related research

**Eligibility**: Open to residents and fellows in the junior faculty

**Level of Study**: Doctorate, Postgraduate

**Type**: Award

**Value**: US$10,000

**Length of Study**: 1 year

**Frequency**: Annual

**Study Establishment**: A university in the United States of America

**Country of Study**: United States of America

**Closing Date**: 15 December

**Funding**: Private

**Additional Information**: www.entnet.org/sites/default/files/uploads/PracticeManagement/Research/_files/2019_ahns_pilot_research_award.pdf

**For further information contact:**

**Email**:    betty@ahns.info

## American Head and Neck Society Surgeon Scientist Career Development Award (with AAOHNS)

**Purpose**: To support research in the pathogenesis, pathophysiology, diagnosis, prevention or treatment of head and neck neoplastic disease

**Eligibility**: Open to surgeons beginning a clinician-scientist career

**Level of Study**: Postdoctorate

**Type**: Award

**Value**: US$35,000 per year (non-renewable)

**Length of Study**: 2 years

**Frequency**: Annual

**Study Establishment**: A university in the United States of America

**Country of Study**: United States of America

**Application Procedure**: The grants are reviewed through the Academy CORE (combined otolaryngologic research evaluation) process

**Closing Date**: 16 January

**Funding**: Private

**Additional Information**: Applicants are requested to submit their LOI early to gain advanced access to the full application. Forms are available through American Academy of Otolaryngology CORE www.entnet.org/sites/default/files/uploads/PracticeManagement/Research/_files/2019_ahns_aaohnsf_translational_innovator_award_final.pdf

**For further information contact:**

**Email**:    pcsupport@altum.com

## American Head and Neck Society Young Investigator Award (with AAOHNS)

**Purpose**: To support research in neoplastic disease of the head and neck

**Eligibility**: Candidate must be a member of AHNS

**Level of Study**: Doctorate

**Type**: Award

**Value**: US$20,000 per year

**Length of Study**: Up to 2 years

**Frequency**: Annual

**Study Establishment**: A university in the United States of America

**Country of Study**: United States of America

**Application Procedure**: The grants are reviewed through the Academy CORE (combined otolaryngologic research evaluation) process

**Closing Date**: 15 January

**Funding**: Private

**Additional Information**: Submit your LOI early to gain advanced access to the full application. Forms are available through American Academy of Otolaryngology CORE www.entnet.org/sites/default/files/uploads/PracticeManagement/Resources/_files/2020_ahns_aaohnsf_ynginv_foa.pdf

## American Head and Neck Society-American Cyronics Society Career Development Award

**Purpose**: To facilitate research in connection with career development

**Eligibility**: Applicants must be a member or candidate member of ACS and AHNS. Applicants must be within 5 years of completion of training, and be full-time faculty member

**Level of Study**: Postgraduate

**Type**: Award

**Value**: US$40,000 per year (non-renewable)

**Length of Study**: 2 years

**Frequency**: Annual
**Study Establishment**: A university in the United States of America
**Country of Study**: United States of America
**Funding**: Private
**Additional Information**: Please check website for more details

# American Hearing Research Foundation - AHRF

275 N. York Street, Suite 201, Elmhurst, IL 60126, United States of America.

**Tel**:       (1) 630 617 5079
**Email**:     info@american-hearing.org
**Website**:   www.american-hearing.org/

At the American Hearing Research Foundation (AHRF), we recognize the boundless potential of new ideas. That's why we focus our resources on providing seed grants for novel research to better understand and overcome hearing and balance disorders of the inner ear, funding five to ten research projects each year, with an average grant of US$20,000. We also work hard to educate the public about these life-altering conditions, which are inextricably linked to people's quality of life and their ability to meet the challenges of day-to-day living. Tracing our roots back to the first-ever successful operation to restore hearing, AHRF has been making new discoveries possible for more than 60 years. Founded in 1956 by Dr. George E. Shaumbaugh, Jr., our mission is to better understand why we lose hearing and balance functions and to learn all that we can about how to preserve and restore them.

## AHRF Regular Grants

**Purpose**: AHRF typically funds six to ten regular research grants that investigate various aspects of hearing and balance disorders related to the inner ear. Grants are for US$20,000 to US$50,000 for one year of research. Grants are paid in one lump sum in January in the year after the application deadline. Priority is given to investigators early in their careers who need seed funds to generate results and data that can be used to support applications for larger grants (i.e., NIH grants) in the future. Grant funds may only be used for direct costs, including salaries of technical and supporting staff, equipment related to the research, and supplies. Note that the cost for salaries plus fringe benefits cannot be more than 80% of the direct costs. Funding may not be used for the salary of the principal investigator, travel, conference attendance, educational costs, or indirect costs. Depending on funds available, grant amounts occasionally may be adjusted at the discretion of AHRF. Our goal is to fund as many promising, novel projects as feasible

**Eligibility**: Applicants must hold an MD, PhD, AuD, or equivalent degree(s) and be associated with a university or hospital in the United States.

**Level of Study**: Masters
**Type**: Grants
**Value**: US$20,000 - US$50,000
**Frequency**: Annual
**Country of Study**: US
**Application Procedure**: Please write your application using this checklist. Please follow these guidelines carefully: Title Page (first page of proposal), Title of research project, Principal investigator name(s), Credentials, Institution name, USPS mailing address, Telephone number, Email address, Financial officer contact information, Description, Brief 2-page summary of the project, Include performance site and key personnel of project. Table of Contents, Include all first-level headings with page numbers. Detailed Budget Provide a one-year budget that includes salary for support staff (students, post-doctorate fellows, etc.), equipment and supplies. Salaries plus fringe benefits may not be more than 80% of your total direct costs. Do not include salaries for principal investigator(s), travel or conference attendance expenses, educational costs, or indirect costs (overhead). AHRF does not fund these costs. The budget should include the total amount requested. Biographical Sketch, Include contact information (USPS mailing address, telephone, email, etc.) with each investigator's biographical sketch page. List all publications (maximum of two pages), current funding, pending funding, and requested funding. Indicate what you will do if you receive overlapping funding. Letters of support from colleagues are welcome, but not required. Include any letters of support within your proposal document whenever possible. Main Body, Include specific aims of the project (body no longer than 10-15 pages at 12-point type, standard margins); background and significance; methods; and what type of subjects (human or animal), if applicable. Progress Report (For Renewal Projects Only), Indicate if you are requesting that your proposal be renewed for additional funding, which is considered on a case-by-case basis. Saving your proposal as a PDF: Save your proposal as a PDF, naming it as follows: "Yourlastname_Yourfirstname" If the PDF file is 5 MG or smaller, you can submit it via the online portal. If your PDF is larger than 5 MB, please email the PDF and application form data to Info@American-Hearing.org.

**Closing Date**: 14 August
**Additional Information**: www.american-hearing.org/research-grants/grant-process/

## Bernard & Lottie Drazin Memorial Grants

**Purpose**: AHRF offers up to five US$1,000 awards to otolaryngology residents to support research projects during their residency.

**Eligibility**: Eligibility requirements for Bernard & Lottie Drazin Memorial Grants: Applicants must be otolaryngology residents at these specific universities: Northwestern University, Loyola University Chicago, University of Illinois, University of Chicago, Rush University, Washington University, St. Louis, MO, Medical College of Wisconsin, Milwaukee, WI, Mayo Clinic, Rochester, MN, University of Miami, FL, Baylor College of Medicine, Houston, TX, Acceptable topics for the Bernard & Lottie Drazin Memorial Grants:Research topics must be related to hearing and balance disorders of the inner ear.

**Level of Study**: Masters
**Type**: Grants
**Value**: US$1,000
**Frequency**: Annual
**Country of Study**: US
**Application Procedure**: Please write your application using this checklist. Please follow these guidelines carefully: Title Page (first page of proposal), Title of research project, Principal investigator name(s), Credentials, Institution name, USPS mailing address, Telephone number, Email address, Financial officer contact information, Description, Brief 2-page summary of the project, Include performance site and key personnel of project. Table of Contents, Include all first-level headings with page numbers. Detailed Budget, Provide a one-year budget that includes salary for support staff (students, post-doctorate fellows, etc.), equipment and supplies. Salaries plus fringe benefits may not be more than 80% of your total direct costs. Do not include salaries for principal investigator(s), travel or conference attendance expenses, educational costs, or indirect costs (overhead). AHRF does not fund these costs. The budget should include the total amount requested. Biographical Sketch, Include contact information (USPS mailing address, telephone, email, etc.) with each investigator's biographical sketch page. List all publications (maximum of two pages), current funding, pending funding, and requested funding. Indicate what you will do if you receive overlapping funding. Letters of support from colleagues are welcome, but not required. Include any letters of support within your proposal document whenever possible. Main Body, Include specific aims of the project (body no longer than 10-15 pages at 12-point type, standard margins); background and significance; methods; and what type of subjects (human or animal), if applicable. Progress Report (For Renewal Projects Only), Indicate if you are requesting that your proposal be renewed for additional funding, which is considered on a case-by-case basis. Saving your proposal as a PDF: Save your proposal as a PDF, naming it as follows: "Yourlastname_Yourfirstname" If the PDF file is 5 MG or smaller, you can submit it via the online portal. If your PDF is larger than 5 MB, please email the PDF and application form data to Info@American-Hearing.org.

**Closing Date**: 14 August
**Additional Information**: www.american-hearing.org/research-grants/grant-process/

## Causes of Sudden Hearing Loss Grant

**Purpose**: This one-year grant will be offered in 2021. It will be paid in one lump sum in January. About the Grant: AHRF is matching an individual donor's contribution to provide up to US$40,000 in funding for a one-year project. This donor was affected by sudden hearing loss, in two instances 38 years apart. The donor would like to spur investigation in the field. Grant funds may only be used for direct costs, including salaries of technical and supporting staff, equipment related to the research, and supplies. Note that the cost for salaries plus fringe benefits cannot be more than 80% of the direct costs. Funding may not be used for the salary of the principal investigator, travel, conference attendance, educational costs, or indirect costs.

**Eligibility**: Applicants must hold an MD, PhD, AuD, or equivalent degree(s) and be associated with a university or hospital in the United States.

**Level of Study**: Masters
**Type**: Grants
**Value**: US$40,000
**Length of Study**: 1 year
**Frequency**: Annual
**Country of Study**: US
**Application Procedure**: Please write your application using this checklist. Please follow these guidelines carefully: Title Page (first page of proposal), Title of research project, Principal investigator name(s), Credentials, Institution name, USPS mailing address, Telephone number, Email address, Financial officer contact information, Description, Brief 2-page summary of the project, Include performance site and key personnel of project. Table of Contents, Include all first-level headings with page numbers. Detailed Budget Provide a one-year budget that includes salary for support staff (students, post-doctorate fellows, etc.), equipment and supplies. Salaries plus fringe benefits may not be more than 80% of your total direct costs. Do not include salaries for principal investigator(s), travel or conference attendance expenses, educational costs, or indirect costs (overhead). AHRF does not fund these costs. The budget should include the total amount requested. Biographical Sketch, Include contact information (USPS mailing address, telephone, email, etc.) with each investigator's biographical sketch page. List all publications (maximum of two pages), current funding, pending funding, and requested funding. Indicate what you will do if you receive overlapping funding. Letters of support from

colleagues are welcome, but not required. Include any letters of support within your proposal document whenever possible. Main Body, Include specific aims of the project (body no longer than 10-15 pages at 12-point type, standard margins); background and significance; methods; and what type of subjects (human or animal), if applicable. Progress Report (For Renewal Projects Only), Indicate if you are requesting that your proposal be renewed for additional funding, which is considered on a case-by-case basis. Saving your proposal as a PDF: Save your proposal as a PDF, naming it as follows: "Yourlastname_Yourfirstname" If the PDF file is 5 MG or smaller, you can submit it via the online portal. If your PDF is larger than 5 MB, please email the PDF and application form data to Info@American-Hearing.org.

**Closing Date**: 14 August

**Additional Information**: www.american-hearing.org/research-grants/grant-process/

## Meniere's Disease Grant

**Purpose**: AHRF occasionally awards grants specifically related to the study of Meniere's disease. The amount can range from US$20,000 to US$25,000. Meniere's research grants are paid in one lump sum in January in the year after the application deadline. These grants are supported through the fundraising efforts of run because and subsidized by AHRF.Grant funds may only be used for direct costs, including salaries of technical and supporting staff, equipment related to the research, and supplies. Note that the cost for salaries plus fringe benefits cannot be more than 80% of the direct costs. Funding may not be used for the salary of the principal investigator, travel, conference attendance, educational costs, or indirect costs.

**Eligibility**: Applicants must hold an MD, PhD, AuD, or equivalent degree(s) and be associated with a university or hospital in the United States.

**Level of Study**: Masters

**Type**: Grants

**Value**: US$20,000 - US$25,000

**Frequency**: Annual

**Country of Study**: US

**Application Procedure**: Please write your application using this checklist. Please follow these guidelines carefully: Title Page (first page of proposal), Title of research project, Principal investigator name(s), Credentials, Institution name, USPS mailing address, Telephone number, Email address, Financial officer contact information, Description, Brief 2-page summary of the project, Include performance site and key personnel of project. Table of Contents, Include all first-level headings with page numbers. Detailed Budget,Provide a one-year budget that includes salary for support staff (students, post-doctorate fellows, etc.), equipment and

supplies. Salaries plus fringe benefits may not be more than 80% of your total direct costs. Do not include salaries for principal investigator(s), travel or conference attendance expenses, educational costs, or indirect costs (overhead). AHRF does not fund these costs. The budget should include the total amount requested. Biographical Sketch, Include contact information (USPS mailing address, telephone, email, etc.) with each investigator's biographical sketch page. List all publications (maximum of two pages), current funding, pending funding, and requested funding. Indicate what you will do if you receive overlapping funding. Letters of support from colleagues are welcome, but not required. Include any letters of support within your proposal document whenever possible. Main Body, Include specific aims of the project (body no longer than 10-15 pages at 12-point type, standard margins); background and significance; methods; and what type of subjects (human or animal), if applicable. Progress Report (For Renewal Projects Only), Indicate if you are requesting that your proposal be renewed for additional funding, which is considered on a case-by-case basis., Saving your proposal as a PDF: Save your proposal as a PDF, naming it as follows: "Yourlastname_Yourfirstname" If the PDF file is 5 MG or smaller, you can submit it via the online portal. If your PDF is larger than 5 MB, please email the PDF and application form data to Info@American-Hearing.org.

**Closing Date**: 14 August

**Additional Information**: www.american-hearing.org/research-grants/grant-process/

## American Heart Association (AHA)

### AHA Postdoctoral Fellowship

**Subjects**: AHA awards are open to the array of academic and health professionals. This includes but is not limited to all academic disciplines (biology, chemistry, mathematics, technology, physics, etc.) and all health-related professions (physicians, nurses, nurse practitioners, pharmacists, dentists, physical and occupational therapists, statisticians, nutritionists, etc.). Clinical, translational, population, and basic scientists are encouraged to apply.

**Purpose**: To enhance the integrated research and clinical training of postdoctoral applicants who are not yet independent. The applicant must be embedded in an appropriate research group with the mentorship, support, and relevant scientific guidance of a research sponsor. Recognizing the unique challenges that clinicians, in particular, experience in balancing research and clinical activity, this award mechanism aims to be as flexible as possible to enable applicants to develop academic careers in research alongside fulfilling clinical service commitments.

**Eligibility**: At the time of award activation, the applicant must hold a post-baccalaureate PhD degree or equivalent, or a - doctoral-level clinical degree, such as M.D., D.O., D.V.M., Pharm.D., D.D.S., Dr.Ph, PhD in nursing, public health, or other clinical health science., or equivalent clinical health science doctoral student who seeks research training with a sponsor prior to embarking upon a research career. At the time of award activation, the awardee may not be pursuing a doctoral degree. At the time of award activation, the applicant may have no more than five years of research training or experience since obtaining a post-baccalaureate doctoral-level degree (excluding clinical training). The awardee will be expected to devote at least 80 % of full-time work either to research or to activities pursuant to independent research (instead of administrative, clinical duties that are not an integral part of the research training program, or teaching responsibilities). This award is not intended for individuals of faculty rank

**Type**: Fellowship

**Value**: Between US$50,004 and US$61,308 annual stipend depending on experience, plus health insurance, plus, US$3,000 project support

**Length of Study**: One or two years

**Frequency**: Annual

**Country of Study**: Any country

**Closing Date**: 15 August

**Additional Information**: The following designations are also eligible to apply: Pending permanent resident (any resident who has an approved I-765 form and has submitted an I-485 application with the United States Citizenship and Immigration Services). E-3 Visa - specialty occupation worker, F1 Visa - student, H1-B Visa - temporary worker in a specialty occupation, J-1 Visa - exchange visitor, O-1 Visa - temporary worker with extraordinary abilities in the sciences, TN Visa - North American Free Trade Agreement (NAFTA) professional, G-4 Visa - family member of employee of international organizations, DACA - Deferred Action for Childhood Arrivals status requires additional AHA approval to apply. Send an email to apply@heart.org with an explanation of your status and a statement of support from your sponsor. professional.heart.org/professional/ResearchPrograms/Applicat ionInformation/UCM_443314_Postdoctoral-Fellowship.jsp

## American Indian Science and Engineering Society

1630 30th Street Suite 301, Boulder, CO 80301-1014, United States of America.

**Tel**:          (1) 303 939 0023
**Email**:       ascholar@spot.colorado.edu
**Contact**:     Ms Sonya Todacheene

## Naval Sea Systems Command (NAVSEA) and Strategic Systems Programs Scholarship

**Purpose**: This scholarship is open to United States college freshmen who are American Indian, Alaskan Native, or Native Hawaiian and enrolled at a minority-serving institution (as designated by the United States Department of Education) that is ABET-accredited

**Eligibility**: Must be a US Citizen

**Level of Study**: Graduate

**Type**: Scholarship

**Value**: US$10,000

**Frequency**: Annual

**Country of Study**: Any country

**Application Procedure**: Apply online: www.unigo.com/match/register?redirecturl=https%3a%2f%2fwww.unigo.com%2fscholarships%2fby-type%2fneed-based-scholarships%2fnaval-sea-systems-command-navsea-and-strategic-systems-programs-scholarship%2f1005894

**No. of awards offered**: 1

**Closing Date**: 20 September

**Funding**: Foundation

**Additional Information**: www.smartscholar.com/scholarship/naval-sea-systems-command-navsea-and-strategic-systems-programs-scholarship/

## For further information contact:

203 N. La Salle St. Suite 1675, Chicago, IL 60601, United States of America.

**Email**:     scholarships@swe.org

## American Institute for Economic Research (AIER)

250 Division St, PO Box 1000, Great Barrington, MA 01230, United States of America.

**Tel**:         (1) 888 528 1216
**Email**:       info@aier.org
**Website**:     www.aier.org

The American Institute for Economic Research (AIER), founded in 1933, is an independent scientific educational organization. The Institute conducts scientific enquiry into general economics with a focus on monetary issues. Attention is also given to business cycle analysis and forecasting as well as monetary economics.

## American Institute for Economic Research Summer Fellowship

**Purpose**: To further the development of economic scientists

**Eligibility**: Open to graduating seniors who are entering doctoral programmes in economics, or those enrolled in doctoral programmes in economics for no longer than 2 years. The programme is not designed for those enrolling into business school

**Level of Study**: Postgraduate

**Type**: Fellowship

**Value**: US$500 weekly stipend plus room and full board

**Length of Study**: 8 weeks

**Frequency**: Annual

**Study Establishment**: AIER

**Country of Study**: United States of America

**Application Procedure**: A current resume; a writing sample; a statement explaining why you would like to be a student fellow at AIER and whether you qualify to reside on campus; an official transcript directly from your school or university; two letters of recommendation from teachers, college professors, or employers should be sent either by electronic or United States mail to the American Institute for Economic Research. Please state "Summer Fellowship Practicum" in the subject line

**No. of awards offered**: 47

**Closing Date**: 23 March

**Funding**: Private

**No. of awards given last year**: 17

**No. of applicants last year**: 47

**Additional Information**: AIER does not sponsor visa applications for foreign nationals. However, foreign nationals are welcome to apply if they are enrolled in a United States degree granting institution, have CPT or OPT, or have employment authorization in the United States drexel.edu/fellowships/search/fellowships/American_Institute_for_Economic_Research/

### For further information contact:

Summer Fellowship Program Coordinator, American Institute for Economic Research, PO Box 1000, 250 Division St, Great Barrington, MA 01230, United States of America.

**Fax**:     (1) 413 528 0103
**Email**:  internships@aier.org

## American Institute for Sri Lankan Studies (AISLS)

155 Pine Street, Belmont, MA 02478, United States of America.

**Email**:     rogersjohnd@aol.com

**Website**:   www.aisls.org
**Contact**:   John Rogers

The American Institute for Sri Lankan Studies (AISLS) was established in 1995, to foster excellence in American research and teaching on Sri Lanka, and to promote the exchange of scholars and scholarly information between the United States and Sri Lanka. The Institute serves as the professional association for United States-based scholars and other professionals who are interested in Sri Lanka.

## Fellowship Program

**Purpose**: Supports from 2 to 6 months research in Sri Lanka on topics in the social sciences, humanities, and related fields

**Eligibility**: Applicants must be United States citizens and hold a PhD or equivalent at the time they plan to begin research

**Level of Study**: Postdoctorate

**Type**: Fellowship

**Value**: A per diem of $3,700Rs/month, for a period of two to six months. Reimbursement for round trip airfare between the United States and Colombo, for an amount up to $2,000Rs. Travel must comply with the Fly America Act. Details will be provided to successful applicants.

**Length of Study**: 2 to 6 months

**Frequency**: Annual

**Country of Study**: Sri Lanka

**Application Procedure**: Questions to be addressed by the project. The approach to be taken. work done to date. work to be accomplished during the fellowship period. The applicant's competence to carry out the project. how the project addresses the criteria of the competition. a statement of other support received or being sought for the project

**Closing Date**: March

**Funding**: Government

**Contributor**: Bureau of Economic and Cultural Affairs, United States State Department

**No. of awards given last year**: 2

**Additional Information**: www.aisls.org/grants/aisls-fellowship-program/

## American Institute of Bangladesh Studies (AIBS)

B 488 Medical Sciences Center, 1300 University Ave, Madison, WI 53706, United States of America.

**Tel**:     (1) 608 265 1471
**Email**:   info@aibs.net

**Website**: www.aibs.net
**Contact**: Laura Hammond, Administrative Program Manager

The American Institute of Bangladesh Studies (AIBS) is a consortium of United States universities and colleges involved in research on Bangladesh. It strives to improve the scholarly understanding of Bangladesh culture and society in the United States and to promote educational exchange between the two countries.

## American Institute of Bangladesh Studies Junior Fellowship

**Purpose**: To improve the scholarly understanding of Bangladesh culture and society in the United States
**Eligibility**: Open to an individual member of AIBS; currently in the ABD phase of your PhD program; is in the data collection and writing stage of the dissertation, and must be United States citizen
**Level of Study**: Research
**Type**: Fellowship
**Value**: Fellowships will be equivalent to 1,150 Tk per month, plus economy Round-Trip Air Transportation (up to 2,500 Tk) via the most direct route
**Length of Study**: 2–12 months
**Frequency**: Annual
**Country of Study**: Bangladesh
**Application Procedure**: Applicants can access our online application form at www.aibs.net
**Closing Date**: 15 September
**Funding**: Government
**Contributor**: United States Department of State Bureau of Educational and Cultural Affairs through the Council of American Overseas Research Centers
**Additional Information**: Please check AIBS website www.aibs.net www.aibs.net/fellowship/junior

## American Institute of Bangladesh Studies Pre-Dissertation Fellowships

**Purpose**: The American Institute of Bangladesh Studies offers short-term grants to graduate students pursuing studies of Bangladesh funded by the United States Department of State Bureau of Educational and Cultural Affairs through the Council of American Overseas Research Centers
**Eligibility**: All applicants must be enrolled/employed at a United States academic institution and a United States citizen. Open to an individual member of AIBS and must have completed at least 1 year of graduate study in a recognized PhD granting institution and enrolled in a graduate program but not yet at the dissertation research or writing stage
**Level of Study**: Research
**Type**: Fellowship
**Value**: The award is for 3,000 Tk plus economy round trip transportation (up to 2,500 Tk) via the most direct route
**Frequency**: Annual
**Country of Study**: Bangladesh
**Application Procedure**: Applicants can access the online application at www.aibs.net
**No. of awards offered**: Varies
**Closing Date**: 15 September
**Funding**: Government
**Contributor**: United States Department of State Bureau of Educational and Cultural Affairs through the council of American Overseas Research Centres
**No. of awards given last year**: Varies
**No. of applicants last year**: Varies
**Additional Information**: Please check ABIS website (www.aibs.net www.aibs.net/fellowship/pre-dissertation)

## American Institute of Bangladesh Studies Senior Fellowship

**Purpose**: To improve the scholarly understanding of Bangladesh culture and society in the United States
**Eligibility**: Enrolled/employed/affiliated with a US or non-US academic institution (independent scholars are also welcome to apply). US Citizens. be an individual member of AIBS (click here for membership information). have a well-developed research agenda relevant to Bangladesh
**Level of Study**: Doctorate, Postdoctorate, Predoctorate, Research
**Type**: Fellowship
**Value**: 1,400 Tk per month plus research and dependent
**Length of Study**: 2–12 months
**Frequency**: Annual
**Country of Study**: Bangladesh
**Application Procedure**: Applicants can access our online application form at www.aibs.net
**No. of awards offered**: Varies
**Closing Date**: 1 March
**Funding**: Government
**Contributor**: United States department of State Bureau of Educational and Cultural Affairs through the council of American overseas research centres
**No. of awards given last year**: Varies
**No. of applicants last year**: Varies
**Additional Information**: Please check AIBS website for additional information (www.aibs.net www.aibs.net/fellowship/senior)

### For further information contact:

**Email**: sudiptaroy.aibs@gmail.com

## American Institute of Bangladesh Studies Travel Grants

**Purpose**: AIBS can provide funding for conference travel for the presentation of papers or organization of panels that include topics relevant to Bangladesh Studies at scholarly conferences

**Eligibility**: Must be a United States citizen travelling within the United States

**Level of Study**: Graduate

**Type**: Travel grant

**Value**: Up to 600 Tk for travel to conferences within the United States. International travel grants have been suspended until further notice due to budgetary constraints

**Frequency**: Annual

**Country of Study**: Bangladesh

**Application Procedure**: Please fill out online application at www.aibs.net

**Funding**: Government

**Additional Information**: Please check the AIBS website for more information www.aibs.net/node/179

## American Institute of Certified Public Accountants (AICPA)

1211 Avenue of the Americas, New York, NY 10036-8775, United States of America.

**Tel**: (1) 212 596 6200
**Email**: service@aicpa.org
**Website**: www.aicpa.org

The American Institute of Certified Public Accountants (AICPA) is a national, professional organization for all Certified Public Accountants. Its mission is to provide members with the resources, information and leadership that enable them to provide valuable services in the highest professional manner to benefit the public as well as employers and clients. In fulfilling its mission, the AICPA works with state CPA organizations and gives priority to those areas where public reliance on CPA skills is most significant.

## American Institute of Certified Public Accountants Fellowship for Minority Doctoral students

**Purpose**: To encourage practising CPAs to consider a career change to academe

**Eligibility**: 1. Open to United States citizens who hold a valid CPA certificate, and have at least five years of professional accounting experience. 2. Candidates must be accepted into or be in the process of applying to a doctoral programme in accounting at a college or university whose business administration programmes are accredited by the AACSB. 3. Applicants should have the intention to pursue an academic career in accounting in the United States. All applicants are expected to exhibit fluency in English appropriate to teaching

**Level of Study**: Doctorate

**Type**: Fellowship

**Value**: US$5,000 per year

**Length of Study**: A maximum of 3 years

**Frequency**: Annual

**Study Establishment**: A college or university whose business administration programs are accredited by the AACSB - the International Association for Management Education

**Country of Study**: United States of America

**Application Procedure**: An official academic transcript is required, in addition to references from three individuals, and the completion of an application form. Application procedure is as follows: 1. A completed application form. 2. An official academic transcript from each institution from which you have received a degree. 3. Confidential references from two individuals. 4. Visit ThisWayToCPA.com for more application requirements

**Closing Date**: 15 May

**Additional Information**: usascholarships.com/aicpa-fellowship-for-minority-doctoral-students/

## For further information contact:

**Email**: academics@aicpa.org

## American Library Association (ALA)

50 E. Huron Street, Chicago, IL 60611, United States of America.

**Tel**: (1) 800 545 2433 ext. 4274
**Email**: ala@ala.org
**Website**: www.ala.org
**Contact**: Ms Melissa Jacobsen, Manager, Prof. Dev

Each year the American Library Association (ALA) and its member units sponsor awards to honour distinguished service and foster professional growth.

## American Library Association Carroll Preston Baber Research Grant

**Purpose**: To encourage innovative research that could lead to an improvement in library services to any specified group or groups of people. The project should aim to answer a question that is of vital importance to the library community and the researchers should plan to provide documentation of the results of their work

**Eligibility**: Any ALA member may apply. The Jury would welcome projects that involve both a practicing librarian and a researcher

**Level of Study**: Unrestricted

**Type**: Research grant

**Value**: Up to US$3,000

**Length of Study**: Up to 18 months

**Frequency**: Annual

**Country of Study**: Any country

**Application Procedure**: Applicants must submit an application including a research proposal

**No. of awards offered**: 5

**Closing Date**: 12 February

**Funding**: Private

**Contributor**: Eric R Baber

**No. of awards given last year**: 1

**No. of applicants last year**: 5

**Additional Information**: The project should aim to answer a question that is of vital importance to the library community and the researchers should plan to provide documentation of the results of their work. The jury would welcome proposals that involve innovative uses of technology and proposals that involve co-operation between libraries and other agencies, or between librarians and persons in other disciplines www.ala.org/aboutala/offices/ors/orsawards/baberresearchgrant/babercarroll

**For further information contact:**

**Tel**:       (1) 312 280 4273
**Email**:   krosa@ala.org

## American Library Association John Phillip Immroth Memorial Award

**Purpose**: The John Phillip Immroth Memorial Award, presented annually, honors notable contributions to intellectual freedom and demonstrations of personal courage in defense of freedom of expression.

**Eligibility**: Open to intellectual freedom fighters. Individuals, a group of individuals or an organization are eligible for the award

**Level of Study**: Unrestricted

**Type**: Award

**Value**: US$500 plus a citation

**Frequency**: Annual

**Country of Study**: Any country

**Application Procedure**: Applicants must submit a detailed statement explaining why the nominator believes that the

nominee should receive the award. Nominations should be submitted to IFRT Staff Liaison at the ALA

**Closing Date**: 1 December

**Funding**: Private

**Contributor**: Intellectual Freedom Round Table (IFRT) of the American Library Association

**Additional Information**: www.ala.org/rt/ifrt/john-phillip-immroth-memorial-award

**For further information contact:**

American Library Association, Office for Intellectual Freedom, 50 East Huron Street, Chicago, IL 60611.

**Tel**:       (1) 312 280 4226
**Fax**:      (1) 312 280 4227
**Email**:   oif@ala.org

## American Library Association Loleta D. Fyan Grant

**Purpose**: To facilitate the development and improvement of public libraries and the services they provide

**Eligibility**: Applicants can include but are not limited to local, regional or state libraries, associations or organizations including units of the ALA, library schools or individuals

**Level of Study**: Unrestricted

**Type**: Research grant

**Value**: Up to US$5,000

**Frequency**: Annual

**Country of Study**: Any country

**Application Procedure**: Applicants must submit an application form in addition to a proposal and budget to the ALA Staff Liaison. Please do not fax or mail

**No. of awards offered**: 10

**Closing Date**: 21 December

**Funding**: Private

**No. of awards given last year**: 1

**No. of applicants last year**: 10

**Additional Information**: The project must result in the development and improvement of public libraries and the services they provide, have the potential for broader impact and application beyond meeting a specific local need, should be designed to effect changes in public library services that are innovative and responsive to the future and should be capable of completion within one year www.ala.org/aboutala/offices/ors/orsawards/fyanloletad/fyanloletad

**For further information contact:**

American Library Association, Chicago, IL 60611, United States of America.

**Tel**:       (1) 312 280 3217
**Email**:   cbourdon@ala.org

## American Library Association Miriam L Hornback Scholarship

**Purpose**: To assist an individual pursuing a Master's degree
**Eligibility**: Open to ALA or library support staff who are pursuing a Master's degree in library science and who are citizens of the United States of America or Canada
**Level of Study**: Postgraduate
**Type**: Scholarship
**Value**: US$3,000
**Frequency**: Annual
**Application Procedure**: Applicants must write for details
**Closing Date**: 1 March
**No. of awards given last year**: 2
**Additional Information**: www.ala.org/awardsgrants/miriam-l-hornback-scholarship

### For further information contact:

**Email**: klredd@ala.org

## American Library Association Shirley Olofson Memorial Awards

**Purpose**: To allow individuals to attend ALA conferences
**Eligibility**: Open to members of the ALA who are also current or potential members of the New Members Round Table. Applicants should not have attended any more than five conferences
**Level of Study**: Unrestricted
**Type**: Award
**Value**: US$1,000
**Frequency**: Annual
**Country of Study**: Any country
**Application Procedure**: Applicants must write for details. Fill out the application online
**Closing Date**: 10 December
**Contributor**: The New Members Round Table ( NMRT) and the Shirley Olofson Memorial Award Committee
**Additional Information**: www.ala.org/awardsgrants/shirley-olofson-memorial-award

## American Library Association W. David Rozkuszka Scholarship

**Purpose**: To provide financial assistance to an individual who is currently working with government documents in a library
**Eligibility**: Open to applicants currently completing a Master's programme in library science
**Level of Study**: Postgraduate
**Type**: Scholarship
**Value**: US$3,000
**Frequency**: Annual
**Country of Study**: Any country
**Application Procedure**: Applicants must write for details
**Closing Date**: 31 December
**Additional Information**: www.ala.org/awardsgrants/w-david-rozkuszka-scholarship

### For further information contact:

PO Box 515, United States of America.

**Tel**:     (1) 541 992 5461
**Email**:     asevetson@hotmail.com

## American Library Association YALSA/Baker and Taylor Conference Grant

**Purpose**: To allow young adult librarians who work directly with young adults in either a public library or a school library to attend the Annual Conference of the ALA
**Eligibility**: 1. The degree of need for additional materials for young adults. 2. The degree of the current collection's use and the specificity of examples used. 3The soundness of the rationale for the selection of materials. The quality of the description of the benefits this grant will bring to young adults.
**Level of Study**: Professional development
**Type**: Grant
**Value**: US$1,000 each
**Frequency**: Annual
**Country of Study**: Any country
**Application Procedure**: Applicants must submit applications to the Young Adult Library Services Association, ALA, by email to Nichole Gilbert at ngilbert@ala.org
**No. of awards offered**: 2
**Closing Date**: 1 December
**Additional Information**: www.ala.org/yalsa/awardsandgrants/bwi

### For further information contact:

50 E. Huron St. Chicago, IL 60611, United States of America.

**Tel**:     (1) 800 545 2433
**Email**:     YALSA@ala.org

## Dixie Electric Membership Corporation New Leaders Travel Grant

**Purpose**: To enhance professional development and improve the expertise of public librarians new to the field by making possible their attendance at major PLA professional development activities

**Eligibility**: Open to qualified public librarians, MLS, PLA member
**Level of Study**: Professional development
**Type**: Travel grant
**Value**: Plaque and travel grant of up to US$1,500 per awardee
**Frequency**: Annual
**Country of Study**: Any country
**Application Procedure**: Visit website www.pla.org
**Closing Date**: 1 December
**Funding**: Corporation
**No. of awards given last year**: 4
**Additional Information**: www.ala.org/awardsgrants/awards/48/apply

**For further information contact:**

**Email**:    jkloeppel@ala.org

## Spectrum Initiative Scholarship Program

**Purpose**: To encourage admission to an ALA recognized Master's degree programme by the four largest underrepresented minority groups
**Eligibility**: 1. be a citizen or permanent resident of the U.S. or Canada. 2. identify as American Indian/Alaska Native, Asian, Black/African American, Hispanic/Latino, Middle Eastern/North African, and/or Native Hawaiian/Other Pacific Islander. 3. be enrolled in an accredited program and begin no later than September 1st or Fall Semester. have full or part-time status.
**Level of Study**: Postgraduate
**Type**: Scholarship
**Value**: US$5,000
**Frequency**: Annual
**Country of Study**: United States of America or Canada
**Application Procedure**: Applicants must request details via fax or visit the website
**Closing Date**: 1 March
**Additional Information**: Applications accepted from mid-October to 1 March each year www.ala.org/advocacy/spectrum/apply

**For further information contact:**

**Tel**:    (1) 800 545 2433 ext 5048
**Email**:    spectrum@ala.org

## American Lung Association

1301 Pennsylvania Ave., NW, Suite 800, Washington, DC 20004, United States of America.

**Tel**:        (1) 202 785 3355
**Email**:      info@lungusa.org
**Website**:    www.lungusa.org
**Contact**:    Ms Evita Mendoza

The American Lung Association is the oldest voluntary health organization in the United States, with a National Office and constituent and affiliate associations around the country. Founded in 1904 to fight tuberculosis, the American Lung Association today fights lung disease in all its forms, with special emphasis on asthma, tobacco control and environmental health.

## Lung Health (LH) Research Dissertation Grants

**Purpose**: To provide financial assistance for Doctoral research training for dissertation research on issues relevant to lung disease
**Eligibility**: Open to citizens or permanent residents of the United States
**Level of Study**: Doctorate
**Type**: Research grant
**Value**: US$21,000 per year
**Length of Study**: 1–2 years
**Frequency**: Annual
**Country of Study**: United States of America
**Closing Date**: 20 October
**Funding**: Government, Corporation, Foundation
**Contributor**: American Lung Association
**Additional Information**: Up to US$16,000 of the award may be used for a student stipend. Funds may not be used for tuition. The award will terminate at the time the awardee is granted a doctoral degree action.lung.org/site/DocServer/2016_LH_LUNG_HEALTH_RESEARCH_DISSERTATION_GRANT_Program_.pdf?docID=36206

**For further information contact:**

Research and Program Services, American Lung Association, 14 Wall Street, 8th Floor, New York, NY 10006, United States of America.

## American Mathematical Society

201 Charles Street, Providence, RI 02904-2294, United States of America.

**Tel**:        (1) 401 455 4000
**Website**:    www.ams.org

The AMS, founded in 1888 to further the interests of mathematical research and scholarship, serves the national and international community through its publications, meetings, advocacy and other programs, which promote mathematical research, its communication and uses, encourage and promote the transmission of mathematical understanding and skills, support mathematical education at all levels, advance the status of the profession of mathematics, encouraging and facilitating full participation of all individuals, foster an awareness and appreciation of mathematics and its connections to other disciplines and everyday life.

## American Meteorological Society Centennial Fellowships in Mathematics

**Purpose**: To help mathematicians in their careers in research
**Eligibility**: The primary selection criterion for the Centennial Fellowship is the excellence of the candidate's research. Preference will be given to candidates who have not had extensive fellowship support in the past. Recipients may not hold the Centennial Fellowship concurrently with other major research award such as a Sloan fellowship, NSF Postdoctoral fellowship, or career award. Under normal circumstances, the fellowship cannot be deferred. The students of North America can apply for these scholarships. For detailed information, visit website
**Level of Study**: Research
**Type**: Fellowship
**Value**: The stipend for fellowships awarded was US$89,000, with an additional expense allowance of US$8,900
**Country of Study**: Any country
**Application Procedure**: The mode of applying is by post
**Closing Date**: 1 December
**Additional Information**: Scholarship can be taken at North America    www.ams.org/prizes-awards/paview.cgi?parent_id=11

### For further information contact:

Professional Programs Department, American Mathematical Society, 201 Charles Street, Providence, RI 02904-2213, United States of America.

**Tel**:        (1) 401 455 4096
**Email**:    development@ams.org

## American Meteorological Society (AMS)

45 Beacon Street, Boston, MA 02108-3693, United States of America.

**Tel**:        (1) 617 227 2425

**Email**:        amsinfo@ametsoc.org
**Website**:    www.ametsoc.org

The American Meteorological Society (AMS) promotes the development and dissemination of information and education on the atmospheric and related oceanic and hydrologic sciences and the advancement of their professional applications. Founded in 1919, AMS has a membership of more than 11,000 professionals, professors, students and weather enthusiasts.

## American Meteorological Society Graduate Fellowships

**Purpose**: To attract promising young scientists to prepare for careers in the atmospheric and related oceanic and hydrologic fields
**Eligibility**: 1. Entering their first year of graduate school in the fall. 2. Pursuing a degree in the atmospheric or related sciences at a US accredited institution. 3. Have a minimum grade point average of 3.25 on a 4.0-point scale. 4 U.-S. citizens or hold permanent resident status. No age restriction exists.
**Level of Study**: Graduate
**Type**: Fellowship
**Value**: US$25,000 to each recipient for a 9-month period
**Length of Study**: 9 months
**Frequency**: Annual
**Country of Study**: United States of America
**Application Procedure**: Application form should be completed and written references, official transcripts, and GRE score reports, may be sent under separate cover. Applications and written references can be sent via email to dFernandez@ametsoc.org
**Closing Date**: 13 January
**Funding**: Government, Corporation, Foundation
**Contributor**: Industry leaders and government agencies
**No. of awards given last year**: 13
**Additional Information**: The evaluation of applicants will be based on applicant's performance as an undergraduate student, including academic records, recommendations and GRE scores. Please see the website for further details www.ametsoc.org/amsstudentinfo/scholfeldocs/ www.ametsoc.org/ams/index.cfm/information-for/students/ams-scholarships-and-fellowships/ams-graduate-fellowships/

### For further information contact:

**Tel**:        (1) 617 227 2426
**Email**:    dfernandez@ametsoc.org

# American Museum of Natural History (AMNH)

Central Park West, 79th Street, New York, NY 10024-5192, United States of America.

**Tel**: (1) 212 769 5100
**Email**: yna@amnh.org
**Website**: www.amnh.org
**Contact**: Ms Maria Dixon, Office of Grants & Fellowships

For 125 years, the American Museum of Natural History (AMNH) has been one of the world's pre-eminent science and research institutions, renowned for its collections and exhibitions that illuminate millions of years of the Earth's evolution.

## American Museum of Natural History Collection Study Grants

**Purpose**: Collection Study Grants provide financial assistance to enable pre-doctoral and recent postdoctoral investigators to study the scientific collections at the American Museum of Natural History. These collections represent the fields in the divisions of Anthropology, Invertebrate Zoology, Physical Sciences, Paleontology, and Vertebrate Zoology. The visit must be arranged through and sponsored by an American Museum of Natural History curator. Projects of four days or longer are encouraged.
**Eligibility**: Open to predoctoral and recent postdoctoral investigators. The award is not available to investigators residing within daily commuting distance of the Museum
**Level of Study**: Postdoctorate, Predoctorate
**Type**: Grant
**Value**: Up to US$1,500 to support travel and subsistence while visiting the Museum
**Frequency**: Twice a year
**Study Establishment**: The Museum
**Country of Study**: United States of America
**Application Procedure**: Applicants must contact the appropriate Museum department to discuss the feasibility of the project and obtain written approval from the Chairman. A special application form is required and should be requested by name from the Office of Grants and Fellowships. A final report is also required. Application forms can be obtained from the website
**Closing Date**: May
**Additional Information**: Mammalogy, herpetology and ichthyology have one deadline date of 1 November. All other departments can submit 1 May and 1 November. Ornithology applications can be submitted two months prior to the visit and has no deadline date www.instrumentl.com/grants/amnh-collection-study-grants

### For further information contact:

**Email**: careers@amnh.org

# American Nuclear Society (ANS)

555 North Kensington Avenue, La Grange Park, IL 60526, United States of America.

**Tel**: (1) 708 352 6611
**Email**: outreach@ans.org
**Website**: www.ans.org
**Contact**: Scholarship Programme

The American Nuclear Society (ANS) is a non-profit, international, scientific and educational organization. It was established by a group of individuals who recognized the need to unify the professional activities within the diverse fields of nuclear science and technology.

## American Nuclear Society Mishima Award

**Purpose**: To recognize outstanding contributions in research
**Eligibility**: Open to candidates who may or may not be members of ANS
**Level of Study**: Postgraduate
**Type**: Award
**Value**: An engraved plaque and a monetary award
**Frequency**: Annual
**Country of Study**: Any country
**Application Procedure**: Eight sets of the nomination form and supporting materials must be submitted
**Closing Date**: 1 March
**Additional Information**: www.ans.org/honors/awards/award-mishima/

### For further information contact:

**Email**: honors@ans.org

## American Nuclear Society Utility Achievement Award

**Purpose**: To recognize professional excellence and leadership

**Eligibility**: Open to members of ANS
**Level of Study**: Postgraduate
**Type**: Award
**Value**: An engraved plaque that is presented in August each year in conjunction with the ANS
**Frequency**: Annual
**Country of Study**: Any country
**Application Procedure**: Nominations must be sent before the deadline
**Closing Date**: 30 April
**Additional Information**: www.ans.org/honors/awards/award-utilachieve/

**For further information contact:**

Center for Energy Research 460 EBU II, United States of America.

**Email**:   meetings@ans.org

## Ely M. Gelbard Graduate Scholarship

**Level of Study**: Graduate, Postgraduate
**Type**: Scholarship
**Value**: US$3,500/each
**Frequency**: Annual
**Country of Study**: Any country
**Application Procedure**: A selection committee will be established by the Mathematics and Computation Division
**Closing Date**: 1 February
**Funding**: Private
**Contributor**: Mathematics and Computation Division (MCD)
**Additional Information**: For further information, check the below link. www.ans.org/honors/scholarships/gelbard/ www.ans.org/honors/scholarships/gelbard/

**For further information contact:**

American Nuclear Society, 555 North Kensington Avenue, La Grange Park, IL 60526, United States of America.

**Tel**:       (1) 800 323 3044
**Email**:   nuclear@illinois.edu

## Henry DeWolf Smyth Nuclear Statesman Award

**Purpose**: To recognize outstanding and statesmanlike contributions to many aspects of nuclear energy activities
**Eligibility**: Open to candidates of any nationality
**Level of Study**: Postgraduate
**Type**: Award

**Value**: An engraved medal
**Country of Study**: Any country
**Application Procedure**: Nomination to be sent, see the website for further information
**Closing Date**: 28 February
**Contributor**: ANS and Nuclear Energy Institute
**Additional Information**:   www.ans.org/honors/awards/award-smyth/

**For further information contact:**

**Email**:   honors@ans.org

## John R. Lamarsh Scholarship

**Eligibility**: United States and non-United States applicants must be ANS student members enrolled in and attending an accredited institution in the United States. Academic accomplishments must be confirmed by transcript
**Value**: US$2,000
**Frequency**: Annual
**Study Establishment**: An accredited institution
**Country of Study**: United States of America
**Application Procedure**: Applications are available online at www.ans.org/honors/scholarships
**Closing Date**: 1 February
**No. of awards given last year**: 1
**Additional Information**: www.ans.org/honors/scholarships/lamarsh/

## Landis Public Communication and Education Award

**Purpose**: To award outstanding efforts in furthering public education
**Eligibility**: Open to both members and non-members of ANS
**Level of Study**: Postgraduate
**Type**: Award
**Value**: US$1,000 and an engraved plaque
**Frequency**: Annual
**Country of Study**: Any country
**Application Procedure**: Eight sets of the completed application form and supporting documents must be sent
**Closing Date**: 1 August
**Contributor**: The Landis Public Communication and Education Award
**Additional Information**:   www.ans.org/honors/awards/award-pubcomm/

**For further information contact:**

**Email**:   honors@ans.org

## Landis Young Member Engineering Achievement Award

**Purpose**: To recognize outstanding achievement in the field of engineering
**Eligibility**: Open to candidates who are members of ANS below the age of 40 years
**Level of Study**: Postgraduate
**Type**: Award
**Value**: An engraved plaque and US$2,000
**Frequency**: Annual
**Country of Study**: Any country
**Application Procedure**: Eight sets of the completed application form and supporting documents to be submitted
**Closing Date**: 1 March
**Additional Information**: www.ans.org/honors/awards/award-yngmbreng/

### For further information contact:

**Email**:    honors@ans.org

## Mark Mills Award

**Purpose**: To recognise the important contributions of the late Mark Mills to the field. Established in 1958, it is awarded to the author who submits the best original technical paper
**Eligibility**: Applicants must have been registered in a graduate degree programme in a recognised Institute of Higher Education for one year prior to the award, and a certification of this fact must be made by the faculty advisor on the nomination form. Thus, this competition is open to a graduate student completing the work on which his or her paper is based from a minimum of four months prior to the award to a maximum of 16 months prior to the award. The paper should demonstrate originality and ingenuity and should be in a form suitable for publication. A thesis is not acceptable. A paper already published or submitted for publication is eligible if nominated by the faculty adviser. A paper jointly authored is eligible if the candidate has the primary responsibility
**Level of Study**: Graduate
**Type**: Award
**Value**: An engraved plaque and US$500
**Country of Study**: Any country
**Application Procedure**: Applicants must be nominated by the student faculty adviser. Multiple nominees by one nominator, nomination of past recipients of the award, and multiple year nominations of the same paper are prohibited. Forms are available from the ANS headquarters
**Closing Date**: 1 August

**Additional Information**: www.ans.org/honors/awards/award-mills/

### For further information contact:

Honors and Awards, American Nuclear Society, 555 N. Kensington Avenue, La Grange Park, IL 60526-5535, United States of America.

**Email**:    honors@ans.org

## Mary Jane Oestmann Professional Women

**Purpose**: To recognize outstanding personal dedication by a woman
**Eligibility**: Open to female candidates who need not be members of ANS but should be affiliated with the nuclear community in some manner
**Type**: Award
**Country of Study**: Any country
**Application Procedure**: Eight sets of the nomination form and supporting documents be submitted
**Closing Date**: 1 July
**Additional Information**: www.ans.org/honors/awards/award-oestmann/

### For further information contact:

**Email**:    honors@ans.org

## Operations and Power Division Scholarship Award

**Eligibility**: United States and non-United States applicants must be ANS student members enrolled in and attending an accredited institution in the United States. Academic accomplishments must be confirmed by transcript. The OPD Scholarship is intended for an undergraduate or graduate student. Applicants: must be enrolled in a course of study leading to a degree in nuclear science or engineering at an accredited institution in the United States; must have completed a minimum of two complete academic years in a four-year nuclear science or engineering program; must be United States citizens or possess a permanent resident visa; must have intentions of working in the nuclear power industry
**Value**: US$2,500
**Frequency**: Annual
**Study Establishment**: An accredited institution
**Country of Study**: United States of America
**Application Procedure**: Applications are available online at www.ans.org/honors/scholarships
**Closing Date**: 1 February

## For further information contact:

**Email**: honors@ans.org

## Samuel Glasstone Award

**Purpose**: This award recognizes ANS student sections that have accomplished notable achievements in public service and the advancement of nuclear science and engineering. The award was established in 1969 by ANS when Dr. Samuel Glasstone contributed funds to the Society to be used specifically for an annual award to the outstanding Student Section of ANS. These reports will be used to evaluate the student sections for the secondary purpose of selecting the Samuel J. Glasstone Award recipient
**Level of Study**: Postgraduate
**Type**: Award
**Frequency**: Annual
**Country of Study**: Any country
**Closing Date**: 1 May
**Funding**: Private
**Additional Information**: www.ans.org/honors/awards/award-glasstone/

## For further information contact:

Honors and Awards American Nuclear Society 555 N. Kensington Avenue La Grange Park, IL 60526-5535, United States of America.

**Email**: ssc@ans.org

## Verne R Dapp Memorial Scholarship

**Eligibility**: Open to citizens of the United States of America or holders of a permanent resident visa who are full-time graduate students enrolled in a programme leading to an advanced degree
**Level of Study**: Graduate
**Type**: Scholarship
**Value**: US$3,000
**Frequency**: Varies
**Study Establishment**: An accredited institution
**Country of Study**: United States of America
**Application Procedure**: Applicants must submit a request for an application form that includes the name of the university the candidate will be attending, the year the candidate will be in during the Autumn of the award, the major course of study and a stamped addressed envelope. Completed applications must include a grade transcript and three confidential reference forms. Candidates must be sponsored by an ANS section, division, student branch, committee, member or organization member. Applications are available online at www.ans.org/honors/scholarships
**Closing Date**: 1 February
**Additional Information**: www.collegexpress.com/scholarships/verne-r-dapp-memorial-scholarship/544/

## American Numismatic Society (ANS)

75 Varick Street, floor 11, New York, NY 10013, United States of America.

**Tel**: (1) 212 571 4470
**Email**: wartenberg@numismatics.org
**Website**: www.numismatics.org
**Contact**: Dr Ute Wartenberg Kagan, Executive Director

The mission of the American Numismatic Society (ANS) is to be the preeminent national institution advancing the study and appreciation of coins, medals and related objects of all cultures as historical and artistic documents. It aims to do this by maintaining the foremost numismatic collection and library, supporting scholarly research and publications, and sponsoring educational and interpretative programmes for diverse audiences.

## Grants for ANS Summer Seminar in Numismatics

**Purpose**: To provide a selected number of graduate students with a deeper understanding of the contribution that this subject makes to other fields
**Eligibility**: Open to applicants who have had at least one year's graduate study at a university in the United States of America or Canada and who are students of classical studies, history, near eastern studies or other humanistic fields
**Level of Study**: Postgraduate
**Type**: Grant
**Value**: US$4,000
**Length of Study**: 9 weeks during the Summer
**Frequency**: Annual
**Study Establishment**: Museum of the American Numismatic Society
**Country of Study**: United States of America
**Application Procedure**: Applicants must write well in advance for details of the application process
**No. of awards offered**: 21
**Closing Date**: 31 July
**Funding**: Private
**No. of awards given last year**: 12

**No. of applicants last year**: 21
**Additional Information**: One or two students from overseas are usually accepted to the seminar but will not receive a grant
numismatics.org/seminar/

**For further information contact:**

**Tel**:     (1) 212 571 4470
**Email**:     community.matters@dia.govt.nz

## American Orchid Society

Fairchild Tropical Botanic Garden, 10901 Old Cutler Road, Coral Gables, FL 33156, United States of America.

**Tel**:     (1) 305 740 2010
**Email**:     theaos@aos.org
**Website**:     www.aos.org
**Contact**:     Ms Pamela S Giust, Awards Registrar

### Grants for Orchid Research

**Purpose**: To advance scientific study of orchids in every respect and to assist in the publication of scholarly and popular scientific literature on orchids
**Eligibility**: There are no eligibility restrictions
**Level of Study**: Postgraduate
**Type**: Grant
**Value**: US$500–12,000
**Length of Study**: Up to 3 years
**Frequency**: Annual
**Country of Study**: Any country
**Application Procedure**: Applicants must write for guidelines
**Closing Date**: 1 January
**Additional Information**: www.aos.org/about-us/orchid-research.aspx

**For further information contact:**

**Tel**:     (1) 561 404 2000

## American Ornithologists' Union (AOU)

MRC-116 National Museum of Natural History Smithsonian Institution, Washington, DC 20560-0116, United States of America.

**Tel**:     (1) 202 357 2051
**Email**:     aou@nmnh.si.edu

**Website**:     www.aou.org
**Contact**:     Secretary

The American Ornithologists' Union (AOU) is the oldest and largest organisation in the New World devoted to the scientific study of birds. The organisation's primary function is the publication and dissemination of ornithology research results.

### Marcia Brady Tucker Travel Award

**Purpose**: To assist student AOU members planning to give a paper to attend the annual meeting
**Eligibility**: Open to students in a relevant discipline. Applicants must be student members of the organisation and planning to present a paper or poster at the annual meeting
**Level of Study**: Unrestricted
**Type**: Travel grant
**Value**: Travel expenses. Maximum expense of US$1,000 will be given
**Frequency**: Annual
**Country of Study**: Any country
**Application Procedure**: Applicants must submit eight copies of an expanded abstract of the presentation or poster they plan to present at the meeting, a curriculum vitae and anticipated transportation costs to the Student Awards Committee
**Funding**: Private
**Additional Information**: www.collegexpress.com/scholarships/marcia-brady-tucker-travel-award/14154/

**For further information contact:**

American Ornithologists' Union, Archbold Biological Station, P.O. Box 2057, Lake Placid, FL 33862, United States of America.

## American Otological Society (AOS)

3096 Riverdale Road, The Villages, FL 32162, United States of America.

**Tel**:     (1) 352 751 0932
**Email**:     segossard@aol.com
**Website**:     www.americanotologicalsociety.org
**Contact**:     Ms Shirley Gossard, Administrator

The AOS is a society focused upon 'aural' medicine. The society's mission is to advance and promote medical and surgical otology, encouraging research in the related disciplines.

## American Otological Society Research Training Fellowships

**Purpose**: To support research
**Eligibility**: Open to physicians, residents and medical students in the United States of America and Canada
**Level of Study**: Postgraduate
**Type**: Fellowship
**Value**: Up to US$40,000 depending on position and institutional norms (US$35,000 for stipend, US$5,000 for supplies)
**Length of Study**: 1–2 years
**Frequency**: Annual
**Country of Study**: United States of America or Canada
**No. of awards offered**: 1
**Closing Date**: 31 January
**Contributor**: American Otological Society, Inc
**No. of awards given last year**: 1
**No. of applicants last year**: 1
**Additional Information**: The organization requires institutional documentation that facilities and faculty are appropriate for the requested research www.americanotologicalsociety.org/research-grants

### For further information contact:

American Otological Society, Inc, American Otological Society Research Foundation, 5830 1st St N, St Petersburg, FL 33703.

| | |
|---|---|
| **Tel**: | (1) 410 955 7381 |
| **Fax**: | (1) 410 955 0035 |
| **Email**: | jcarey@jhmi.edu |

## American Parkinson Disease Association

### Dr. George C. Cotzias Memorial Fellowship

**Subjects**: Parkinson's Disease
**Purpose**: George C. Cotzias, MD was a pathfinder in the pharmacologic exploration of brain functions and in the treatment of Parkinson's disease with levodopa. His work stimulated much of the current interest and research on neurological movement disorders. The American Parkinson Disease Association has established the Cotzias fellowship, in honor of his memory, to stimulate neurologists to follow his leadership. The goal of the Cotzias fellowship is to assist promising young neurologists in establishing careers in research, teaching and clinical services relevant to the problems, causes, prevention, diagnosis and treatment of Parkinson's disease and related neurological movement disorders.

**Eligibility**: The applicant must be a physician and a U.S. citizen or a permanent resident of the U.S. who is completing, or has completed, training in a clinical discipline concerned with disorders of the nervous system (i.e. medical neurology, child neurology, neurosurgery, neuropathology). The applicant should be an instructor or assistant professor and demonstrate a clear commitment to the goals described above. There should also be evidence that the sponsoring institution will provide the environment and support needed for career development. The applicant should be no more than 6 years beyond completion of their clinical training at the time of submission and must be sponsored by a non-profit institution in the U.S. or its territories.
**Level of Study**: Junior Faculty
**Type**: Fellowship
**Value**: US$80,000 per year
**Length of Study**: Three years
**Country of Study**: Any country
**Application Procedure**: Complete the application form. Upload as one PDF document. Description of the research proposal should not exceed six (6) pages and should consist of background, specific aims, research design, and a statement of significance for Parkinson disease research. The applicant's NIH biosketch as well as two letters of reference, one from the applicants's direct sponsor and one from a professional person with personal knowledge of the applicant's academic past and ability, should be included. The applicant should list all current and pending support, including sponsoring agency, amount and dates for awards. The application should indicate how other sponsored research complements or supplements the present proposal. The six page limit only applies to the length of the proposal, not the entire application. After the submit button is clicked, applicants can print the complete application
**Closing Date**: 14 March
**Additional Information**: Funding is not to be used for: Indirect costs; Institutional overhead; Salary for the principal investigator higher than US$75,000; Travel expenses higher than US$3,000 per year; Publication costs higher than US$1,000; Equipment costs higher than US$10,000 per year. www.apdaparkinson.org/research/research-opportunities/dr-george-c-cotzias-memorial-fellowship/

### Research Grants

**Subjects**: Parkinson's disease
**Purpose**: Research grants are intended and available for junior investigators to pursue research in Parkinson's disease.
**Eligibility**: All research scientists in the field of Parkinson's research can apply, but the selection committee will more favorably consider researchers who are new to the field of Parkinson's disease.

**Level of Study**: Junior Faculty
**Type**: Grant
**Value**: Up to US$75,000
**Country of Study**: Any country
**Application Procedure**: Complete application form. Upload as one PDF document. Description of the research proposal should not exceed three (3) pages and should consist of background, specific aims, research design, and a statement of significance for Parkinson disease research. The applicant's NIH biosketch should be included. The applicant should list all current and pending support, including sponsoring agency, amount and dates for awards. The application should indicate how other sponsored research complements or supplements the present proposal. The three page limit only applies to the length of the proposal, not the entire application. After the submit button is clicked, applicants can print the complete application.
**Closing Date**: 14 March
**Additional Information**: Funding is not to be used for: Indirect costs; Institutional overhead; Salary for the principal investigator higher than US$50,000; Travel expenses; Publication costs higher than US$1,000; Equipment costs higher than US$8,000.www.apdaparkinson.org/research/research-opportunities/grants/

## American Philosophical Association (APA)

University of Delaware, 31 Amstel Avenue, Newark, DE 19716, United States of America.

**Tel**:        (1) 212 366 5260
**Email**:    anna@amc.net
**Website**:  www.apa.udel.edu/apa
**Contact**:  Dr Anna Smith, Manager of Grantmaking Programs

The American Philosophical Association (APA) was founded in 1900 to promote the exchange of ideas among philosophers, to encourage creative and scholarly activity in philosophy, to facilitate the professional work and teaching of philosophers and to represent philosophy as a discipline.

## Frank Chapman Sharp Memorial Prize

**Purpose**: To recognise unpublished work in philosophy
**Eligibility**: Authors must be members of the APA. Undergraduate entrants must be philosophy majors (or something

close); graduate students must be enrolled in, or on leave from, a graduate program in philosophy. Manuscripts should be between 7,500 and 75,000 words (between 30 and 300 double-spaced typed pages)
**Level of Study**: Postgraduate
**Type**: Prize
**Value**: US$1,500
**Country of Study**: Any country
**Application Procedure**: Applicants must write for details or visit the website
**No. of awards offered**: 8
**Closing Date**: 15 March
**Funding**: Private
**No. of awards given last year**: 1
**No. of applicants last year**: 8
**Additional Information**: www.apaonline.org/page/sharp

### For further information contact:

University of Delaware, 31 Amstel Avenue, Newark, DE 19716, United States of America.

**Tel**:      (1) 302 831 1112
**Fax**:      (1) 302 831 8690
**Email**:    prizes@apaonline.org

## American Philosophical Society

### Phillips Fund for Native American Research

**Subjects**: Native American studies
**Purpose**: The Phillips Fund of the American Philosophical Society provides grants for research in Native American linguistics, ethnohistory, and the history of studies of Native Americans, in the continental United States and Canada. Grants are not made for projects in archaeology, ethnography, psycholinguistics, or for the preparation of pedagogical materials. The committee distinguishes ethnohistory from contemporary ethnography as the study of cultures and culture change through time. The grants are intended for such costs as travel, tapes, films, and consultants' fees but not for the purchase of books or permanent equipment or to pay income tax on the award.
**Eligibility**: The committee prefers to support the work of younger scholars who have received the doctorate. Applications are also accepted from graduate students for research on master's theses or doctoral dissertations. It is assumed that appropriate contacts and arrangements have or will be made with communities for ethical access and community guidance. The committee sometimes approves two awards to the same person within a five-year period.

**Level of Study**: Junior Faculty
**Value**: Approximately US$3000; will not exceed US$3,500
**Length of Study**: One year
**Country of Study**: United States of America
**Application Procedure**: Apply online.
**Closing Date**: May
**Additional Information**: www.amphilsoc.org/grants/phillips-fund-native-american-research

## American Physiological Society (APS)

9650 Rockville Pike, Bethesda, MD 20814-3991, United States of America.

**Tel**:       (1) 301 634 7164
**Email**:     webmaster@the-aps.org
**Website**:   www.the-aps.org
**Contact**:   Ms Linda Jean Dresser, Executive Assistant

The American Physiological Society (APS) is a non-profit scientific society devoted to fostering education, scientific research and the dissemination of information in the physiological sciences. The Society strives to play a role in the progress of science and the advancement of knowledge.

## American Physiological Society Minority Travel Fellowship Awards

**Purpose**: To increase the participation of predoctoral and postdoctoral minority students in the physiological sciences
**Eligibility**: Open to advanced predoctoral and postdoctoral students. Students in the APS Porter Physiology Development programme are also eligible. Minority faculty members at MBRS and MARC eligible institutions may also submit applications
**Level of Study**: Postdoctorate, Predoctorate
**Type**: Travel grant
**Value**: US$1,800
**Length of Study**: The duration of the conference or meeting
**Country of Study**: United States of America
**Application Procedure**: Applicants must contact the Education Office of the APS for further details
**Closing Date**: 21 November
**Contributor**: NIDDK and NIGMS
**Additional Information**: www.the-aps.org/professional-development/awards/trainees/martin-frank-diversity-travel-awards?SSO=Y

**For further information contact:**

Brooke Bruthers, Senior Program Manager, Minority Programs, American Physiological Society, 9650 Rockville Pike, Bethesda, MD 20814 United States of America.

**Tel**:       (1) 301 634 7226
**Fax**:       (1) 301 634 7098
**Email**:     education@the-aps.org

## American Psychological Association Minority Fellowship Program (APA/MFP)

Minority Fellowships Program (MFP), 750 First Street, N.E., Washington, DC 20002-4242, United States of America.

**Tel**:       (1) 800 374 2721, 202 336 5500
**Email**:     mfp@apa.org
**Website**:   www.apa.org/pi/mfp
**Contact**:   Administrative Assistant

The American Psychological Association's (APA) Minority Fellowship Program (MFP) is an innovative, comprehensive and coordinated training and career development program that promotes psychological and behavioural outcomes of ethnic minority communities. MFP is committed to increasing the number of ethnic minority professionals in the field and enhancing our understanding of the life experiences of ethnic minority communities.

## Dissertation Research Grants

**Purpose**: The purpose of the APA Science Directorate's Dissertation Research Award program is to assist science-oriented doctoral students of psychology with research costs.
**Eligibility**: 1. Funding preference is given to projects that addresses the ONS Research Priorities and/or the ONS Research Agenda. 2. Membership in ONS is not required for eligibility
**Type**: Grants, work-study (not just grants)
**Value**: Upto US$5,000 each
**Country of Study**: Any country
**Closing Date**: 1 September
**Additional Information**: www.apa.org/about/awards/scidir-dissertre

# American Psychological Foundation (APF)

## Esther Katz Rosen Fund Grants

**Subjects**: Child psychology

**Purpose**: The Ester Katz Rosen Fund was established in 1974 by a generous bequest intended to support activities related to the advancement and application of knowledge about gifted children. Rosen Fund grants: Enable and enhance development of identified gifted and talented children and adolescents. Encourage promising psychologists to continue innovative research and programs in this area.

**Eligibility**: Applicants must: Be affiliated with a school or education institution. Hold a doctoral degree from, or be a graduate student at, an accredited university for research proposals. Graduate students and early career psychologists (10 years or less postdoctoral) are encouraged to apply. APF also supports pilot projects that, if successful, would be strong candidates for support from major federal and foundation funding agencies, and 'demonstration projects' that promise to generalize broadly to other geographical areas and/or to other settings. Teaching time releases are not supported from the Rosen Fund.

**Type**: Grant

**Value**: Grant amounts range from US$1,000 to US$50,000.

**Country of Study**: United States of America

**Application Procedure**: Apply online.

**Closing Date**: 1 March

**Additional Information**: www.apa.org/apf/funding/rosen?tab=3

## F.J. McGuigan Early Career Investigator Research Grant on Understanding the Human Mind

**Subjects**: Psychology

**Purpose**: The award aims to support research that aims to address any aspect of mental function (e.g., cognition, affect, motivation) and seeks to understand the mind from both a behavioral and neural perspective.

**Eligibility**: The applicant must: Have demonstrated commitment to stated program goals. Be a psychologist or in a related field with a doctoral degree from an accredited university. Be no more than 10 years postdoctoral.

**Level of Study**: Junior Faculty

**Type**: Research grant

**Value**: US$15,000

**Length of Study**: Two years

**Frequency**: Every 2 years

**Country of Study**: United States of America

**Application Procedure**: Apply online

**Additional Information**: www.apa.org/apf/funding/mcguigan-grant-human-mind?tab=3

## John and Polly Sparks Early Career Grant for Psychologists Investigating Serious Emotional Disturbance (SED)

**Subjects**: Children's psychology

**Purpose**: The John and Polly Sparks Early Career Grant supports early career psychologists conducting research in the area of early intervention and treatment for serious emotional disturbance in children. The John and Polly Sparks Foundation partnered with APF to empower early career psychologists to produce scientifically-based research and programs that could provide models for broad-based applications across the country.

**Eligibility**: Be an early career psychologist (no more than 10 years postdoctoral with a degree from an accredited university).

**Level of Study**: Junior Faculty

**Type**: Grant

**Value**: Three grants of up to US$20,000 and one grant of up to US$19,000.

**Country of Study**: Any country

**Application Procedure**: Apply online.

**No. of awards offered**: Four

**Additional Information**: www.apa.org/apf/funding/sparks-early-career?tab=3

# American Public Power Association (APPA)

2551 Crystal Drive, Suite 1000, Arlington, VA 22202, United States of America.

**Tel**:        (1) 202 467 2942
**Email**:      DEED@PublicPower.org
**Website**:    www.PublicPower.org/DEED
**Contact**:    Ms Michele Suddleson, DEED Program Manager

The American Public Power Association (APPA), based in Washington, D.C., is the service organization for the nation's more than 2,000 community-owned electric utilities. Collectively, these utilities serve more than 47 million Americans. Its purpose is to advance the public policy interests of its members and their consumers, and provide member services to ensure adequate, reliable electricity at a reasonable price with the proper protection of the environment.

## Demonstration of Energy & Efficiency Developments (DEED) - Technical Design Project

**Purpose**: Provides funding to support the students working on a technical project of interest to electric utilities
**Eligibility**: This scholarship targets full-time college juniors and seniors, and graduate students attending a college/university or vocational school in the United States Students must be majoring in a field that could lead to a career in the public power industry. Applicants must obtain a DEED member utility to sponsor their application. An official transcript must be received by the application deadline
**Level of Study**: Doctorate, Graduate
**Type**: Scholarship
**Value**: US$5,000 plus up to US$3,000 in travel funds to share project results at APPA's Engineering & Operations Technical Conference
**Frequency**: Annual
**Country of Study**: United States of America
**Application Procedure**: If you wish to apply for a scholarship please DEED@publicpower.org
**Closing Date**: 15 October
**Funding**: Private
**Additional Information**: www.eduinreview.com/scholarships/demonstration-of-energy-efficient-developments-(deed)-technical-design-project-award-88899

### For further information contact:

**Tel**:       ( ) 202 467 2960
**Email**:   DEED@publcipower.org

## American Research Institute in Turkey (ARIT)

University of Pennsylvania Museum, 3260 South Street, Philadelphia, PA 19104-6324, United States of America.

**Tel**:       (I) 215 898 3474
**Email**:    leinwand@sas.upenn.edu
**Website**:  ccat.sas.upenn.edu/ARIT
**Contact**:  Nancy Leinwand, Executive Director

The American Research Institute in Turkey's (ARIT) aim is to support U.S based scholarly research in all fields of the humanities and social sciences in Turkey through administering fellowship programmes at the doctoral and postdoctoral level and through maintaining research centres in Ankara and Istanbul.

## BIAA – ANAMED Joint Fellowship in Heritage Studies

**Purpose**: The BIAA and ANAMED joint fellowship will support research in heritage studies, concerned with the understanding, promotion, and/or preservation of the historical and archaeological material culture of Turkey and the Black Sea region with particular reference to specific sites, monuments, or regions. Successful applicants should have an MA or PhD qualification in museology, heritage management, conservation, or a related specialization, or have appropriate and comparable professional experience in these fields.
**Eligibility**: 1. A monthly stipend calculated by Koç University each year to cover most local expenses not covered by the fellowship. 2. Accommodation at ANAMED's residential facility in the center of Beyoglu, Istanbul. 3. ANAMED provides fellows five meals per week. These include two in-house dinners a week during the academic year (excepting national and university holidays) and a meal card for three meals a week at rates set by Koç University. 4. One lowest-possible cost, economy class, round-trip airfare will be reimbursed upon the beginning of the fellowship based on a region of origin. 5. Expenses may include books, research materials, research-related travel expenses within Turkey, and/or travel expenses for the presentation of papers at academic conferences during the period of the fellow's appointment. 6. Currently available health insurance plans cover general in-patient and limited outpatient treatments, including medicines and advanced diagnostic methods.
**Level of Study**: Fellowship
**Closing Date**: 15 December
**Additional Information**: anamed.ku.edu.tr/en/fellowships/joint-fellowships/biaa-anamed-joint-fellowship-in-heritage-studies/

## Fellowships for Intensive Advanced Turkish Language Study in Istanbul, Turkey

**Purpose**: To provide full travel and fellowship to students and scholars for participation in the summer program in advanced Turkish language at Bogazici University in Istanbul
**Eligibility**: 1. Be a citizen, national, or permanent resident of the United States. 2. Be currently enrolled in an undergraduate or graduate level academic program, or be faculty. 3. Have a minimum B average in current program of study. 4. Perform at the high-intermediate level on a proficiency-based admissions examination
**Level of Study**: Graduate, Postdoctorate, Postgraduate, Predoctorate
**Type**: Fellowship
**Value**: Fellowship includes round-trip airfare to Istanbul, application and tuition fees, and a maintenance stipend

**Length of Study**: 8 weeks
**Frequency**: Annual
**Study Establishment**: Bogazici University
**Country of Study**: Turkey
**Application Procedure**: Application forms and procedure are available at the ARIT website ccat.sas.upenn.edu/ARIT
**No. of awards offered**: 65
**Closing Date**: 3 February
**Funding**: Government
**Contributor**: United States Department of Education, Fulbright-Hays Group Projects Abroad Programme
**No. of awards given last year**: 17
**No. of applicants last year**: 65
**Additional Information**: ccat.sas.upenn.edu/ARIT/ARITSummerLanguageProgram.html

**For further information contact:**

Director, Dr. Sylvia Önder, Division of Eastern Mediterranean Languages, Department of Arabic and Islamic Studies, Georgetown University, 210 North Poulton Hall, 1437 - 37th Street N.W., Washington D.C. 0007, United States of America.

**Tel**:        (1) 212 359 4913
**Fax**:        (1) 212 265 7131
**Email**:    aritfellowship@georgtown.edu

### National Endowment for the Humanities American Research Institute in Turkey-National Endowment for the Humanities Fellowships for Research in Turkey

**Purpose**: To support research on ancient, medieval or modern times
**Eligibility**: Open to scholars who have completed their formal training by the application deadline and plan to carry out research in Turkey may apply. They may be United States citizens or 3-year residents of the United States. Please consult ARIT headquarters on questions of eligibility. Advanced scholars also may apply for ARIT Fellowships in the Humanities and Social Sciences
**Level of Study**: Postdoctorate, Postgraduate, Professional development, Research
**Type**: Fellowship
**Value**: 16,800–50,400 lira
**Length of Study**: 4–12 months
**Frequency**: Annual
**Study Establishment**: Either of ARIT's two research establishments in Ankara or Istanbul
**Country of Study**: Turkey
**Application Procedure**: Applicants must submit an application form, project statement and references
**No. of awards offered**: 16

**Closing Date**: 1 November
**Funding**: Government
**Contributor**: National Endowment for the Humanities (NEH)
**No. of awards given last year**: 3
**No. of applicants last year**: 16
**Additional Information**: The hostel, research and study facilities are available at ARIT's branch centers in Istanbul and Ankara ccat.sas.upenn.edu/ARIT/NEHFellowships.html

**For further information contact:**

**Tel**:        (1) 215 898 3474
**Fax**:        (1) 215 898 0657
**Email**:    aritoffice@gmail.com

## American School of Classical Studies at Athens (ASCSA)

6-8 Charlton Street, Princeton, NJ 08540-5232, United States of America.

**Tel**:        (1) 609 683 0800
**Email**:    ascsa@ascsa.org
**Website**:  www.ascsa.edu.gr
**Contact**:  Ms Mary E Darlington, Executive Associate

Established in 1881, the American School of Classical Studies at Athens (ASCSA) offers both graduate students and scholars the opportunity to study Greek civilization, first hand, in Greece. The ASCSA supports and encourages the teaching of the archaeology, art, history, language and literature of Greece from early times to the present.

### American School of Classical Studies at Athens Advanced Fellowships

**Subjects**: Archaeology, History, Classics, Medieval Studies, Literature, Classical Philology
**Purpose**: Several fellowships for the full academic year at the School are available to students who plan to stay on or return to the School to pursue independent research, usually for their PhD dissertation. Advanced Fellowships fields awarded by the School include one each in art and architecture of antiquity, history of architecture, Mycenaean archaeology or Athenian architecture and/or archaeology, and the study of pottery; and three unrestricted as to field.
**Eligibility**: Applicants must have completed the Regular Program or one academic year (Sept. – May) as a Student Associate Member.

**Level of Study**: Doctorate, Graduate
**Type**: Fellowship
**Value**: €11,500 stipend plus fees, room and partial board (The Kress Fellowship is €15,000 plus room and partial board.)
**Length of Study**: 1 academic year
**Frequency**: Annual
**Study Establishment**: American School of Classical Studies at Athens (ASCSA)
**Country of Study**: Greece
**Application Procedure**: Applicants must complete online applications. For guidelines and application visit www. ascsa.edu.gr.
**No. of awards offered**: 5
**Closing Date**: 15 February
**Funding**: ASCSA and Kress Foundation
**No. of awards given last year**: 5
**No. of applicants last year**: 18
**Additional Information**: The fellowships include: the Edward Capps, the Doreen C Spitzer and the Eugene Vanderpool Fellowships (subject unrestricted); the Samuel H. Kress Fellowships in art and architecture in antiquity; the Gorham P Stevens Fellowship in the history of architecture; and the Homer A and Dorothy B Thompson Fellowship in the study of pottery. Ione Mylonas Shear in Mycenaean Archaeology or Athenian architecture. www.ascsa.edu.gr/fellowships-and-grants/graduate-and-postdoctoral

**For further information contact:**

**Tel**: (1) 609 683 0800

## American School of Classical Studies at Athens Fellowships

**Eligibility**: Open to graduate and well-qualified undergraduate students preparing for an advanced degree in Classical Studies or a related field. Applicants must be enrolled in a North American Institution
**Level of Study**: Graduate, Predoctorate
**Type**: Fellowship
**Value**: €11,500 stipend plus fees, room and partial board
**Length of Study**: 1 academic year
**Frequency**: Annual
**Study Establishment**: ASCSA
**Country of Study**: Greece
**Application Procedure**: Submit online application form for "Associate Membership with Fellowship", curriculum vitae, a detailed description of the project to be pursued in Greece (250-word abstract and a statement up to three pages, single spaced). Arrange for three letters of recommendation. Student applicants are required to submit scans of official academic transcripts as part of the online application.
**No. of awards offered**: 21

**Closing Date**: 15 January
**Funding**: Private
**No. of awards given last year**: 12
**No. of applicants last year**: 21
**Additional Information**: www.ascsa.edu.gr/fellowships-and-grants/postdoctoral-and-senior-scholars

**For further information contact:**

54 Souidias Street, GR-106 76 Athens, Greece.

**Tel**:     (30) 213 000 2400
**Fax**:     (30) 210 725 0584
**Email**:   Ascsa_info@ascsa.edu.gr

## American School of Classical Studies at Athens Research Fellowship in Environmental Studies

**Purpose**: To support research on studies from archaeological contexts in Greece
**Eligibility**: Doctoral candidates working on their dissertation and postdoctoral scholars with well-defined projects that can be completed during the academic year of the fellowship
**Level of Study**: Doctorate, Graduate, Postdoctorate, Postgraduate, Predoctorate
**Type**: Fellowship
**Value**: €15,500–27,000 stipend depending on seniority and experience
**Length of Study**: 1 academic year
**Frequency**: Annual
**Study Establishment**: The Malcolm H Wiener Research Laboratory for Archaeological Science, ASCSA
**Country of Study**: Greece
**Application Procedure**: Applicants must complete online applications. For guidelines and application visit www. ascsa.edu.gr
**No. of awards offered**: 8
**Closing Date**: 15 January
**Funding**: Private
**No. of awards given last year**: 1
**No. of applicants last year**: 8

## American School of Classical Studies at Athens Research Fellowship in Faunal Studies

**Purpose**: To study faunal remains from archaeological contexts in Greece
**Eligibility**: Doctoral candidates working on their dissertation and postdoctoral scholars with well-defined projects that can be completed during the academic year of the fellowship. There is no citizenship requirement

**Level of Study**: Doctorate, Graduate, Postdoctorate, Postgraduate, Predoctorate
**Type**: Fellowship
**Value**: €15,500–27,000 stipend depending on seniority and experience
**Length of Study**: 1 academic year
**Frequency**: Annual
**Study Establishment**: The Malcolm H Wiener Research Laboratory for Archaeological Science, ASCSA
**Country of Study**: Greece
**Application Procedure**: Applicants must complete online applications. For guidelines and application visit www.ascsa.edu.gr
**No. of awards offered**: 8
**Closing Date**: 15 January
**Funding**: Private
**No. of awards given last year**: 1
**No. of applicants last year**: 8

## American School of Classical Studies at Athens Research Fellowship in Geoarchaeology

**Purpose**: To support research on a geoarchaeological topic in Greece
**Eligibility**: Doctoral candidates working on their dissertation and postdoctoral scholars with well-defined projects that can be completed during the academic year of the fellowship. There is no citizenship requirement
**Level of Study**: Doctorate, Graduate, Postdoctorate, Postgraduate, Predoctorate
**Type**: Fellowship
**Value**: €15,500–27,000 stipend depending on seniority and experience
**Length of Study**: 1 academic year
**Frequency**: Annual
**Study Establishment**: The Malcolm H Wiener Research Laboratory for Archaeological Science, ASCSA
**Country of Study**: Greece
**Application Procedure**: Applicants must complete online applications. For guidelines and application visit www.ascsa.edu.gr
**No. of awards offered**: 8
**Closing Date**: 15 January
**Funding**: Private
**No. of awards given last year**: 1
**No. of applicants last year**: 8

## American School of Classical Studies at Athens Summer Sessions

**Purpose**: The two 6-week sessions are designed for those who wish to become acquainted with Greece and its antiquities, and to improve their understanding of the relationship between the monuments, landscape, and climate of the country and its history, literature and culture
**Eligibility**: Enrolment is open to graduate and advanced undergraduate students and to high school and college instructors of classics and related subjects
**Level of Study**: Graduate, Postdoctorate, Postgraduate, Professional development
**Type**: Scholarship
**Length of Study**: 6 weeks
**Frequency**: Annual
**Study Establishment**: ASCSA
**Country of Study**: Greece
**Application Procedure**: Submit the application form online by January 15. Applicants for School scholarships must review the program material on the website to learn about the requirements. High school teachers and college professors should be prepared to attach a copy of their curriculum vitae (saved as doc, docx, or pdf) to the application form. Student applicants are required to submit scans of undergraduate and graduate transcripts (unofficial are acceptable) in legible pdf format as part of the online application. Please be sure to name the file "LastnameTranscripts.pdf" (e.g. SmithTranscripts.pdf) Applicants arrange for two letters of recommendation to be submitted online by their recommenders. After you submit your online application, your recommenders will automatically be sent instructions about how to upload their recommendation. Recommendations are due January 10.
**No. of awards offered**: 83
**Closing Date**: 10 January
**Funding**: Private
**No. of awards given last year**: 13
**No. of applicants last year**: 83
**Additional Information**: www.ascsa.edu.gr/programs/summer-session

### For further information contact:

**Email**: ssapplication@ascsa.org

## Cotsen Traveling Fellowship for Research in Greece

**Subjects**: Archaeology, History, Classics, Medieval Studies.
**Purpose**: Short term travel award for senior scholars and graduate students for projects and research at the Gennadius Library.
**Eligibility**: Senior scholars (PhD holders) and graduate students of any nationality.
**Level of Study**: Doctorate, Graduate, Postdoctorate, Postgraduate

**Type**: Fellowship
**Value**: Stipend of €2,000 and School fees waived
**Length of Study**: At least 1 month in residence.
**Frequency**: Annual
**Study Establishment**: The Gennadius Library, American School of Classical Studies at Athens (ASCSA)
**Country of Study**: Greece
**Application Procedure**: Applicants must complete online applications. For guidelines and application visit www. ascsa.edu.gr.
**No. of awards offered**: 1
**Closing Date**: 15 January
**Funding**: Private
**No. of awards given last year**: 1
**No. of applicants last year**: 12
**Additional Information**: Programs Administrator, Alicia Dissinger

**For further information contact:**

**Tel:**   (1) 609 683 0800

## Cotsen Travelling Fellowship

**Purpose**: The Gennadius Library offers the Cotsen Traveling Fellowship, a short-term grant awarded each year to scholars and graduate students pursuing research topics that require the use of the Gennadeion collections
**Eligibility**: 1. Senior scholars and graduate students of any nationality. 2. School fees are waived for a maximum of two months
**Level of Study**: Postgraduate
**Type**: Fellowship
**Value**: US$2,000
**Frequency**: Annual
**Country of Study**: Any country
**Application Procedure**: 1. Submit "Associate Membership with Fellowship" application online. 2. The application should include a curriculum vitae, a letter (up to 750 words) describing the project and its relation to the Gennadius Library collections, proposed dates, a brief budget (not more than one page), and two letters of recommendation
**Closing Date**: 15 January
**Funding**: Private
**Additional Information**: www.ascsa.edu.gr/fellowships-and-grants/postdoctoral-and-senior-scholars

**For further information contact:**

ASCSA 54 Souidias Street GR-106 76 Athens, Greece.

**Email:**   application@ascsa.org

## Council of American Overseas Research Centers Multi Country Research Fellowships

**Subjects**: Graduate students/scholars in ancient studies, archaeology, classical studies, anthropology, Byzantine, post-Byzantine, Ottoman studies and modern Greek.
**Purpose**: The Multi-Country Research Fellowship supports advanced regional or trans-regional research in the humanities, social sciences, or allied natural sciences for U.S. doctoral candidates, and postdoctoral scholars. Preference will be given to candidates examining comparative and/or cross-regional research.
**Eligibility**: Applicants must be U.S. citizens; Fellowship awards will not exceed US$11,000; Funding is not available for research conducted in the U.S.; Group projects are admissible and will be evaluated as a single application. Groups should submit one (1) application for the group project and Curriculum Vitae for each member of the group. Two (2) letters of recommendation are required for the group. If awarded, a single grant of €11,000 will be issued to the group; It is not required that you be affiliated with a U.S. academic institution to apply. As long as you are a PhD candidate at an accredited university, or have already earned your PhD, you are eligible for the fellowships; PhD candidates must be ABD (all but dissertation) by May; If you have held a Multi-Country Fellowship in the past, you must wait 3 years before you are eligible to apply again.
**Level of Study**: Doctorate, Graduate, Postdoctorate, Postgraduate
**Type**: Fellowship
**Value**: up to €11,000
**Length of Study**: 90 day minimum
**Frequency**: Annual
**Study Establishment**: American School of Classical Studies at Athens (ASCSA)
**Country of Study**: Greece
**Application Procedure**: Consult CAORC website for application and deadline: www.caorc.org.
**No. of awards offered**: 8
**Funding**: Council of American Overseas Research Centers (CAORC)
**No. of awards given last year**: 1
**No. of applicants last year**: 1

## Fowler-Merle Smith Summer Scholarship for Teachers

**Subjects**: Archaeology, History, Classics, Medieval Studies
**Purpose**: To attend the ASCSA Summer Session or Summer Seminars
**Eligibility**: The Fowler Merle-Smith scholarships are for high school teachers. The scholarships are designed for teachers

who wish to become acquainted with Greece and its major monuments, and to improve their understanding of the country's landscape, history, literature, and culture from antiquity to the present.

**Level of Study**: Teachers
**Type**: Scholarship
**Value**: All Fees and €2,000 to offset the cost of international travel.
**Length of Study**: 6 weeks (Session) or 18 days (Seminar)
**Frequency**: Annual
**Study Establishment**: American School of Classical Studies at Athens (ASCSA)
**Country of Study**: Greece
**Application Procedure**: Applicants will be considered for this scholarship when they apply for the Summer Session and/or Summer Seminars. No additional forms are required. For guidelines and application visit www.ascsa.edu.gr.
**No. of awards offered**: 6
**Closing Date**: 15 January
**Funding**: Private
**No. of awards given last year**: 7
**No. of applicants last year**: 10

## Harry Bikakis Fellowship

**Subjects**: Archaeology, History, Ancient Law, Classics.
**Purpose**: To support research on ancient Greek law Greek graduate students working on excavations conducted by or affiliated with the ASCSA.
**Eligibility**: North American or Greek graduate students researching ancient Greek law or Greek graduate students working on a School excavation.
**Level of Study**: Doctorate, Graduate
**Type**: Fellowship
**Value**: A stipend of €1,875 and all School fees are waived.
**Length of Study**: Short-term
**Frequency**: Annual
**Study Establishment**: American School of Classical Studies at Athens (ASCSA)
**Country of Study**: Greece
**Application Procedure**: Applicants must complete online applications. For guidelines and application visit www.ascsa.edu.gr.
**No. of awards offered**: 1
**Closing Date**: 15 January
**Funding**: Private
**No. of awards given last year**: 1
**No. of applicants last year**: 2

## For further information contact:

**Tel**:    (1) 609 683 0800

## Jacob Hirsch Fellowship

**Subjects**: Archaeology
**Purpose**: Students who hold U.S. or Israeli citizenship, and who are PhD candidates writing their dissertations in archaeology, and early-career scholars (PhD earned within the last five years) completing a project, such as the revision of a dissertation for publication, which requires a lengthy residence in Greece.
**Eligibility**: For projects carried out in Greece; eligibility is limited to U.S. or Israeli citizens, PhD candidate writing a dissertation or recent PhD (not more than five years since the awarding of the PhD)
**Level of Study**: Doctorate, Graduate, Postdoctorate, Postgraduate
**Type**: Fellowship
**Value**: Stipend of €11,500 plus room, board and waiver of School fees.
**Length of Study**: Academic year
**Frequency**: Annual
**Study Establishment**: American School of Classical Studies at Athens (ASCSA)
**Country of Study**: Greece
**Application Procedure**: Applicants must complete online applications. For guidelines and application visit www.ascsa.edu.gr.
**No. of awards offered**: 1
**Closing Date**: 15 January
**Funding**: Private
**No. of awards given last year**: 1
**No. of applicants last year**: 6

## For further information contact:

**Tel**:    (1) 609 683 0800

## Kress Publications Fellowships

**Subjects**: Archaeology, History, Classics, Medieval Studies.
**Purpose**: Postdoctoral scholars working on assigned material from excavations at Ancient Corinth, the Athenian Agora, Lerna, and affiliated projects of the ASCSA to support research for publication of the excavated material.
**Eligibility**: Postdoctoral scholars working on assigned material from excavations at Ancient Corinth, the Athenian Agora, Lerna, and affiliated projects of the ASCSA to support research for publication of the excavated material.
**Level of Study**: Postdoctorate, postgraduate
**Type**: Fellowship
**Value**: Three months up to €100,000; Nine months up to €30,000

**Length of Study**: Minimum of three, maximum of nine months
**Frequency**: Annual
**Study Establishment**: American School of Classical Studies at Athens (ASCSA)
**Country of Study**: Greece
**Application Procedure**: Applicants must complete online applications. For guidelines and application visit www. ascsa.edu.gr.
**No. of awards offered**: Up to 3
**Closing Date**: 15 January
**Funding**: Kress Foundation
**No. of awards given last year**: 2
**No. of applicants last year**: 5

## M. Alison Frantz Fellowship in Post-Classical Studies at the Gennadius Library

**Subjects**: Late Antique through Modern Greek Studies, including but not limited to the Byzantine, Frankish, Post-Byzantine, and Ottoman periods.
**Purpose**: PhD candidates and recent PhDs (not more than five years since the awarding of the PhD) for work in the Gennadius Library.
**Eligibility**: PhD candidates and recent PhDs (up to five years) from a U.S. or Canadian institution. Candidates should demonstrate their need to work in the Gennadius Library.
**Level of Study**: Doctorate, Graduate, Postdoctorate, Postgraduate
**Type**: Fellowship
**Value**: Stipend of €11,500 plus room, board and waiver of School fees.
**Length of Study**: Academic year
**Frequency**: Annual
**Study Establishment**: American School of Classical Studies at Athens (ASCSA)
**Country of Study**: Greece
**Application Procedure**: Applicants must complete online applications. For guidelines and application visit www. ascsa.edu.gr.
**No. of awards offered**: 1
**Closing Date**: 15 January
**Funding**: Private
**No. of awards given last year**: 1
**No. of applicants last year**: 11

## Malcolm H. Wiener Laboratory Postdoctoral Fellowship

**Purpose**: To conduct research at the Malcolm H. Wiener Laboratory for Archaeological Science at the American

School of Classical Studies at Athens that addresses substantive problems pertaining to the ancient Greek world and adjacent areas through the application of interdisciplinary methods in the archaeological sciences. Laboratory facilities are especially well equipped to support the study of human skeletal biology, archaeobiological remains (faunal and botanical), environmental studies, and geoarchaeology (particularly studies in human-landscape interactions and the study of site formation processes). Research projects utilizing other archaeological scientific approaches are also eligible for consideration, depending on the strength of the questions asked and the suitability of the plan for access to other equipment or resources available elsewhere in Greece
**Eligibility**: The Post-Doctoral Fellowship is limited to individuals who have received their PhD within the last seven (7) years. Individuals who have received prior support as Pre-Doctoral Fellows must wait four (4) years before applying for a Post-Doctoral Fellowship. Former Research Associates must wait two (2) years before applying for a Post-Doctoral Fellowship.
**Level of Study**: Postdoctorate
**Type**: Fellowship
**Value**: €35,000 per year
**Length of Study**: 3 years
**Frequency**: Every 3 years
**Study Establishment**: Malcom H. Wiener Laboratory for Archaeological Science at the American School of Classical Studies at Athens (ASCSA)
**Country of Study**: Greece
**Application Procedure**: Submit cover sheet naming the applicant, current research interests, and title and brief summary of the proposed research project. Objectives, Significance and Background: Briefly describe the project's major goals and their impact on the state of the field and how the proposed work relates to the present state of knowledge and discuss the progress made on this research to date by the applicant.Research Description. Present a brief technical description of research plan for the overall research and a detailed presentation of what is to be accomplished during the tenure of the Research Associate appointment. Timeframe. A plan of how the research questions will be addressed throughout the proposed duration of the Research Associate appointment. Applicants should discuss how the tenure of this appointment will advance on-going research and include a plan of publication/dissemination of the results. Results of prior Wiener Laboratory Research. If the applicant has received Wiener Laboratory funding in the past, information on the prior award and its impact is required (half a page double spaced Times Roman 12pt).
**No. of awards offered**: 8
**Closing Date**: 15 January
**No. of awards given last year**: 1
**No. of applicants last year**: 8

**Additional Information**: www.ascsa.edu.gr/fellowships-and-grants/postdoctoral-and-senior-scholars

## For further information contact:

**Email**:  TKarkanas@ascsa.edu.gr

## Malcolm H. Wiener Laboratory for Archaeological Science Senior Fellowship

**Purpose**: To conduct research at the Malcolm H. Wiener Laboratory for Archaeological Science pertaining to the ancient Greek world and adjacent areas through the application of interdisciplinary methods in the archaeological sciences. Laboratory facilities are especially well-equipped to support the study of human skeletal biology, archaeobiological remains (faunal and botanical), environmental studies, and geoarchaeology (particularly studies in human-landscape interactions and the study of site formation processes)

**Eligibility**: Open to recent PhDs (at least 5 years) previous to application. Research projects utilizing other archaeological scientific approaches are also eligible for consideration, depending on the; strength of the questions asked and the suitability of the plan for access to other equipment or resources available elsewhere in Greece

**Level of Study**: Postdoctorate

**Type**: Fellowship

**Value**: Stipend of €15,000 (5-month term); stipend of €30,000 (10-month term)

**Length of Study**: 5–10 months with the next term beginning early September. It is expected that the applicant will maintain a physical presence at the Wiener Laboratory during the academic year (1 September to 1 June)

**Frequency**: Annual

**Country of Study**: Greece

**Application Procedure**: Applicants must complete online application. For guidelines and application, visit www.asca. edu.gr/index.php/wiener-laboratory/senior-instructions

**Closing Date**: 15 January

**Funding**: Private

**Additional Information**: www.ascsa.edu.gr/research/wiener-laboratory/fellowships-and-research-associate-appointments/research-associate-appointment

## For further information contact:

54 Souidias Street, GR-106 76 Athens, Greece.

**Tel**:       (30) 213 000 2400
**Fax**:      (30) 210 725 0584
**Email**:   ascsa_info@ascsa.edu.gr

## Malcolm H. Wiener Laboratory for Archaeological Science Research Associate Appointments

**Purpose**: To conduct short-term focused research at the Malcolm H. Wiener Laboratory for Archaeological Science of the American School of Classical Studies at Athens as part of a program of research that addresses substantive problems pertaining to the ancient Greek world and adjacent areas through the application of interdisciplinary methods in the archaeological sciences. Laboratory facilities are especially well equipped to support the study of human skeletal biology, archaeobiological remains (faunal and botanical), environmental studies, and geoarchaeology (particularly studies in human-landscape interactions and the study of site formation processes). Research projects utilizing other archaeological scientific approaches are also eligible for consideration, depending on the strength of the questions asked and the suitability of the plan for access to other equipment or resources available elsewhere in Greece

**Eligibility**: Individuals actively enrolled in a graduate program and individuals with a Masters or Doctorate in a relevant discipline. Applicants are welcome from any college or university worldwide. Independent scholars are also welcome to apply

**Level of Study**: Doctorate, Graduate, Postdoctorate, Postgraduate

**Type**: One fellowship

**Value**: Up to €7,000

**Length of Study**: Variable up to nine (9) months

**Frequency**: Annual

**Study Establishment**: ASCSA

**Country of Study**: Greece

**Application Procedure**: Link to Research Associate application instructions at: www.ascsa.edu.gr/index.php/wiener-laboratory/research-associate-appointment

**No. of awards offered**: 14

**Closing Date**: 15 January

**Funding**: Private

**Contributor**: ASCSA

**No. of awards given last year**: 1

**No. of applicants last year**: 14

**Additional Information**: www.ascsa.edu.gr/fellowships-and-grants/postdoctoral-and-senior-scholars

## For further information contact:

54 Souidias Street, GR-106 76 Athens, Greece.

**Tel**:       (30) 213 000 2400
**Fax**:      (30) 210 725 0584
**Email**:   application@ascsa.org

## National Endowment for the Humanities (NEH) Fellowships

**Subjects**: Archaeology, History, Classics, Medieval Studies.
**Purpose**: Postdoctoral Scholars and Professionals in the Humanities
**Eligibility**: Postdoctoral scholars and professionals in all fields relevant to the mission of the ASCSA who are US citizens, or foreign nationals who have lived in the US for the three years immediately preceding the application deadline. Applicants must already hold their PhD or have completed all requirements, except for the actual conferral of the degree, by the application deadline.
**Level of Study**: Postdoctorate, postgraduate
**Type**: Fellowship
**Value**: Montly stipend of €4,200 from a total pool of €75,600 per year
**Length of Study**: 4, 5, or 9-month duration
**Frequency**: Annual
**Study Establishment**: American School of Classical Studies at Athens (ASCSA)
**Country of Study**: Greece
**Application Procedure**: Applicants must complete online applications. For guidelines and application visit www. ascsa.edu.gr.
**No. of awards offered**: Two to Four
**Closing Date**: 31 October
**Funding**: National Endowment for the Humanities (NEH)
**No. of awards given last year**: 4
**No. of applicants last year**: 9

## Open Scholarship for Summer Sessions

**Purpose**: To attend ASCSA Summer Session
**Level of Study**: Postgraduate, Predoctorate, Professional development
**Type**: Scholarship
**Value**: €5,000
**Length of Study**: 6 weeks
**Study Establishment**: American School of Classical Studies at Athens (ASCSA)
**Country of Study**: Greece
**Application Procedure**: Applicants must complete online application. For guidelines and application visit www.ascsa. edu.gr
**No. of awards offered**: 65
**Closing Date**: 15 January
**No. of awards given last year**: 5
**No. of applicants last year**: 65

**For further information contact:**
**Email**: ssapplication@ascsa.org

## Open Scholarship for the Summer Session and Summer Seminars

**Subjects**: Archaeology, History, Classics, Medieval Studies
**Purpose**: To attend the ASCSA Summer Session or Summer Seminars
**Eligibility**: Catered towards graduate students enrolled in programs that focus on Greek and/or Latin languages and literature, ancient history, ancient philosophy or Classical art and archaeology. Funding is restricted to graduate students, who at the time of application, are enrolled at Cooperating Institutions of the American School of Classical Studies at Athens.
**Level of Study**: Postdoctorate, Postgraduate, Predoctorate, Graduate
**Type**: Scholarship
**Value**: All Fees
**Length of Study**: 6 weeks (Session) or 18 days (Seminar)
**Frequency**: Annual
**Study Establishment**: American School of Classical Studies at Athens (ASCSA)
**Country of Study**: Greece
**Application Procedure**: Applicants will be considered for this scholarship when they apply for the Summer Session and/or Summer Seminars. No additional forms are required. For guidelines and application visit www.ascsa.edu.gr.
**No. of awards offered**: 10
**Closing Date**: 10 January
**Funding**: Private
**No. of awards given last year**: 6
**No. of applicants last year**: 89

## Regular Member Fellowships

**Subjects**: Archaeology, History, Classics, Medieval Studies, Literature, Classical Philology
**Purpose**: Up to twelve fellowships available for the School's Regular Members.
**Eligibility**: Open to students at colleges or universities in the U.S. or Canada who have completed a B.A. but not a PhD, and who are preparing for an advanced degree in classical or ancient Mediterranean studies, or a related field.
**Level of Study**: Doctorate, Graduate
**Type**: Fellowship
**Value**: €11,500 stipend plus fees, room and partial board
**Length of Study**: 1 academic year

**Frequency**: Annual
**Study Establishment**: American School of Classical Studies at Athens (ASCSA)
**Country of Study**: Greece
**Application Procedure**: Applicants must complete online applications. For guidelines and application visit www.ascsa.edu.gr.
**No. of awards offered**: 12
**Closing Date**: 15 January
**Funding**: Private
**No. of awards given last year**: 12
**No. of applicants last year**: 27

## Samuel H Kress Joint Athens-Jerusalem Fellowship

**Purpose**: To enable students to conduct research in Greece and Israel in the same academic year and to promote better understanding of interrelationships between the cultures, languages, literature and history of the Aegean and the Near East
**Eligibility**: Open to any nationality but applicants must be at a college or university in the United States of America or Canada
**Level of Study**: Doctorate, Postgraduate, Predoctorate
**Type**: Fellowship
**Value**: A stipend of US$7,600 plus room and partial board at each of the two institutions
**Length of Study**: 1 academic year
**Frequency**: Annual
**Study Establishment**: The ASCSA and the W F Albright Institute of Archaeological Research in Jerusalem
**Country of Study**: Other
**Application Procedure**: Applicants must write for details or visit the website
**No. of awards offered**: 5
**Closing Date**: 25 October
**Funding**: Private
**No. of awards given last year**: 1
**No. of applicants last year**: 5
**Additional Information**: Further information can be found on the website

### For further information contact:

Albright Instituteco Department of Religious Studies, John Carroll University, 20,700 North Park Boulevard, University Heights, OH 44118, United States of America.

**Tel**: (1) 216 397 4705
**Fax**: (1) 216 397 4478
**Email**: spencer@jcu.edu

## The Paul Rehak Memorial Traveling Fellowship

**Subjects**: Graduate students/scholars in ancient studies, archaeology, classical studies, anthropology, Byzantine, post-Byzantine, Ottoman studies and modern Greek.
**Purpose**: To allow students in attendance at the School during the 2021-2022 academic year to travel in Greece or nearby lands including Magna Graeca, Asia Minor, and the Levant to conduct a research project during the academic year.
**Eligibility**: Regular Members and Student Associate Members currently in attendance at the School for the entire academic year.
**Level of Study**: Doctorate, Graduate
**Type**: Fellowship
**Value**: Up to US$1,000 and School fees waived.
**Length of Study**: Varied
**Frequency**: Annual
**Study Establishment**: American School of Classical Studies at Athens (ASCSA)
**Country of Study**: Greece and/or Italy
**Application Procedure**: Applicants must complete online applications. For guidelines and application visit www.ascsa.edu.gr.
**No. of awards offered**: 2
**Closing Date**: 1 March
**Funding**: Private
**No. of awards given last year**: 1
**No. of applicants last year**: 4

## Wiener Laboratory Predoctoral Fellowship

**Purpose**: To conduct research at the Malcolm H. Wiener Laboratory for Archaeological Science at the American School of Classical Studies at Athens that addresses substantive problems pertaining to the ancient Greek world and adjacent areas through the application of interdisciplinary methods in the archaeological sciences. Laboratory facilities are especially well equipped to support the study of human skeletal biology, archaeobiological remains (faunal and botanical), environmental studies, and geoarchaeology (particularly studies in human-landscape interactions and the study of site formation processes). Research projects utilizing other archaeological scientific approaches are also eligible for consideration, depending on the strength of the questions asked and the suitability of the plan for access to other equipment or resources available elsewhere in Greece.
**Eligibility**: The Post-Doctoral Fellowship is limited to individuals who have received their PhD within the last seven (7) years. Individuals who have received prior support as Pre-Doctoral Fellows must wait four (4) years before

applying for a Post-Doctoral Fellowship. Former Research Associates must wait two (2) years before applying for a Post-Doctoral Fellowship.

**Level of Study**: Predoctorate

**Type**: Fellowship

**Value**: Stipend of €35,000 for 12 months. School fees are waived for fellow. Fellow pays room and board.

**Length of Study**: 2 academic years

**Study Establishment**: Malcolm H. Wiener Laboratory for Archaeological Science at the American School of Classical Studies

**Country of Study**: Greece

**Application Procedure**: Applicants must complete online application. For guidelines and application visit www.ascsa.edu.gr

**Closing Date**: 15 January

**Additional Information**: www.ascsa.edu.gr/fellowships-and-grants/postdoctoral-and-senior-scholars

### For further information contact:

54 Souidias Street, GR-106 76 Athens, Greece.

**Tel**: (30) 213 000 2400
**Fax**: (30) 210 725 0584
**Email**: application@ascsa.org

## Wiener Laboratory Research Associate Appointment

**Purpose**: To conduct short-term focused research at the Malcolm H. Wiener Laboratory for Archaeological Science of the American School of Classical Studies at Athens as part of a program of research that addresses substantive problems pertaining to the ancient Greek world

**Eligibility**: PhD candidates and postdoctoral candidates worldwide

**Level of Study**: Postdoctorate, Predoctorate

**Type**: Research grant

**Value**: Up to €7,000

**Length of Study**: Up to 9 months

**Frequency**: Annual

**Study Establishment**: Malcolm H. Wiener Laboratory for Archaelogical Science at the American School of Classical Studies at Athens

**Country of Study**: Greece

**Application Procedure**: Applicants must complete online application. For guidelines and application visit www.ascsa.edu.gr

**No. of awards offered**: 5

**Closing Date**: 15 January

**No. of awards given last year**: 3

**No. of applicants last year**: 5

**Additional Information**: www.ascsa.edu.gr/fellowships-and-grants/postdoctoral-and-senior-scholars

### For further information contact:

54 Souidias Street, GR-106 76 Athens, Greece.

**Tel**: (30) 213 000 2400
**Fax**: (30) 210 725 0584
**Email**: TKarkanas@ascsa.edu.gr

## Wiener Laboratory Research Associate Appointments

**Subjects**: To conduct short-term, focused research at the Malcolm H. Wiener Laboratory for Archaeological Science of the American School of Classical Studies at Athens as part of a program of research that addresses substantive problems pertaining to the ancient Greek world, or adjacent areas, through the application of interdisciplinary methods in the archaeological sciences. Wiener Laboratory facilities are especially well equipped to support the study of human skeletal biology, archaeobiological remains (faunal and botanical), environmental studies, and geoarchaeology (particularly studies in human-landscape interactions and the study of site formation processes). Term is variable (up to 9 months) beginning early September 2021.

**Purpose**: To support research on studies from archaeology related to the ancient Greek world.

**Eligibility**: Individuals actively enrolled in a graduate program and individuals with a Masters or Doctorate in a relevant discipline. Applicants are welcome from any college or university worldwide. Independent scholars are also welcome to apply. Former Research Associates must wait two (2) years before applying for a Post- or pre- Doctoral Fellowship. Exceptions to these basic eligibility requirements will be granted only in extraordinary cases.

**Level of Study**: Doctorate, Graduate, Postdoctorate, Postgraduate

**Type**: Research Grant

**Value**: Variable amounts up to €7,000.

**Length of Study**: Term variuable, up to nine months

**Frequency**: Annual

**Study Establishment**: The Malcolm H. Wiener Research Laboratory for Archaeological Science, ASCSA

**Country of Study**: Greece

**Application Procedure**: Applicants must complete online applications. For guidelines and application visit www.ascsa.edu.gr.

**No. of awards offered**: 1

**Closing Date**: 15 January

**Funding**: Private
**No. of awards given last year**: 1
**No. of applicants last year**: 12

# American Schools of Oriental Research (ASOR)

656 Beacon Street, 5th Floor, Boston, MA 02215-2010, United States of America.

**Tel**:        (1) 617 353 6570
**Email**:    asor@bu.edu
**Website**:  www.asor.org
**Contact**:  Britta Abeln, Office Coordinator

The American Schools of Oriental Research's (ASOR) mission is to initiate, encourage and support research into, and public understanding of the people and cultures of the near East from the earliest times by fostering original research, archaeological excavations and explorations, by encouraging scholarship in the basic languages, cultural histories and traditions of the near Eastern world.

## Albright Institute of Archaeological Research (AIAR) Annual Professorship

**Purpose**: To support studies in Near Eastern archaeology, geography, history and biblical studies
**Eligibility**: Open to qualified applicants of any nationality. Citizens of the United States of America are eligible for the entire award. Non-United States of America citizens may apply but, by United States of America law, are only eligible for non-governmental funds
**Level of Study**: Postdoctorate
**Type**: Professorship
**Value**: A stipend of 30,000 new shekels. This consists of 14,200 new shekels plus 15,800 new shekels for room and half board for appointee and spouse at the Institute. The entire award is available via USIA for an appointee who is an citizen of the United States of America. Non-governmental funds for non United States of America citizens total 15,000 new shekels
**Length of Study**: 10 months
**Frequency**: Annual
**Study Establishment**: The W F Albright Institute of Archaeological Research (AIAR) in Jerusalem
**Country of Study**: Israel
**Application Procedure**: Applicants must write for details
**No. of awards offered**: 5
**Closing Date**: 15 October

**No. of awards given last year**: 1
**No. of applicants last year**: 5
**Additional Information**: The professorship period should be continuous, without frequent trips outside the country. Residence at the Institute is required

### For further information contact:

**Email**:    spencer@jcu.edu

## American Schools of Oriental Research Mesopotamian Fellowship

**Purpose**: To financially support field research in ancient Mesopotamian civilization carried out in Middle East
**Eligibility**: Open to applicants affiliated with an institution that is a corporate member of ASOR or who have an individual membership. See website for further details
**Level of Study**: Research
**Type**: Fellowship
**Value**: Amount of US$7,500 for one three-to-six month period of research
**Length of Study**: 3–12 months
**Frequency**: Annual
**Application Procedure**: Applicants need to submit cover sheet (with contact information, ASOR membership information, title of project, and brief abstract) and a short proposal. Applicants currently in graduate degree programs should provide three recommendations
**Closing Date**: 1 November
**Additional Information**: This fellowship is primarily intended to support field/research projects on ancient Mesopotamian civilization carried out in the Middle East, but other research projects such as museum or archival research related to Mesopotamian studies may also be considered www.asor.org/fellowships/mesopotamian-fellowship/

### For further information contact:

209 Commerce Street, Alexandria, VA 22314, United States of America.

**Tel**:       (1) 703 789 9229
**Email**:    programs@asor.org

## American Schools of Oriental Research W.F. Albright Institute of Archaeological Research/National Endowment of the Humanities Fellowships

**Purpose**: To financially support scholars holding a PhD or equivalent degree with a research project

**Eligibility**: Open to citizens of the United States or alien residents residing in the United States for the last 3 years. Please see the website for further details regarding eligibility

**Level of Study**: Doctorate

**Type**: Fellowships

**Value**: US$58,800 available for up to three awards from 4 to 6 months. The award is US$4,200 per month. Room and half-board at the Institute is US$1,200 per month and the remainder is stipend.

**Length of Study**: 4–12 months

**Frequency**: Annual

**Country of Study**: United States of America

**Application Procedure**: A completed application form must be sent

**No. of awards offered**: 3

**Closing Date**: 1 October

**Contributor**: National Endowment of the Humanities

**Additional Information**: Residence at the Institute in Jerusalem is preferred aiar.org/home/fellowships/available-fellowships/#associatefellowships

**For further information contact:**

Albright Fellowship Committee, Department of Art and Art History, Providence College, Providence, RI 02918, United States of America.

**Tel**: (1) 401 865 1789
**Fax**: (1) 401 865 2410
**Email**: jbranham@providence.edu

## Andrew W Mellon Foundation Fellowships

**Purpose**: To support Eastern European scholars

**Eligibility**: Open to Bulgarian, Czech, Hungarian, Polish, Romanian and Slovak scholars who have obtained a doctorate by the time the fellowship is awarded. Candidates should not be permanently resident outside the six countries concerned

**Level of Study**: Postdoctorate

**Type**: Fellowship

**Value**: IS$34,500 in total

**Length of Study**: 3 months

**Frequency**: Annual

**Study Establishment**: AIAR, Jerusalem

**Country of Study**: Israel

**Application Procedure**: Applicants must write for details

**No. of awards offered**: 15

**Closing Date**: 2 April

**No. of awards given last year**: 3

**No. of applicants last year**: 15

**Additional Information**: Fellows are expected to reside at the AIAR if room is available. The 3-month periods are

1 September – 30 November, 1 December – 29 February and 1 March – 31 May. The research period should be continuous without frequent trips outside the country

**For further information contact:**

**Email**: spencer@jcu.edu

## Council of American Overseas Research Centers (CAORC) Fellowships for Advanced Multi-Country Research

**Purpose**: The Council of American Overseas Research Centers Multi-Country Research Fellowship Program supports advanced regional or trans-regional research in the humanities, social sciences, or allied natural sciences for U.S. doctoral candidates and scholars who have already earned their PhD. Preference will be given to candidates examining comparative and/or cross-regional research. Scholars must carry out research for a minimum of 90 days in two or more countries outside the United States, at least one of which hosts a participating American overseas research center. Approximately eight awards of up to US$11,000 each will be given each year.

**Eligibility**: Be a U.S. citizen. Proof of citizenship (photocopy of passport) must be shown upon award notification. have a PhD or be a doctoral candidate who has completed all PhD requirements with the exception of the dissertation. Be engaged in the study of and research in the humanities, social sciences, and allied natural sciences. seek to conduct research of regional or trans-regional significance in two or more countries outside the United States, one of which must host a participating American overseas research center (ORC).

**Level of Study**: Doctorate

**Type**: Fellowship

**Value**: US$11,000

**Frequency**: Annual

**Study Establishment**: The W F Albright Institute of Archaeological Research in Jerusalem

**Country of Study**: Other

**Application Procedure**: Applicants must write for details

**Closing Date**: 23 January

**Additional Information**: Preference will be given to candidates examining comparative or cross-regional questions requiring research in two or more countries orcfellowships.fluidreview.com/res/p/orcfellowshipscaorc/

**For further information contact:**

Council of American Overseas Research Centers (CAORC), PO Box 37012, MRC 178, Washington, DC 20013, United States of America.

**Email**: siwp01.ic.bwack@ic.si.edu

## Samuel H Kress Joint Athens-Jerusalem Fellowship

**Purpose**: To support a joint fellowship for research

**Eligibility**: Open to predoctoral students who are United States citizens, or North American citizens studying at United States universities

**Level of Study**: Predoctorate

**Type**: Fellowship

**Value**: US$15,000. The stipend is US$7,600 and the remainder covers room and board at the two institutions

**Length of Study**: 10 months comprised of 5 months in Athens and 5 months in Jerusalem

**Frequency**: Annual

**Study Establishment**: The American School of Classical Studies in Athens and the W F Albright Institute of Archaeological Research in Jerusalem

**Country of Study**: Other

**Application Procedure**: Applicants must write for details and an application form

**No. of awards offered**: 4

**Closing Date**: 25 October

**No. of awards given last year**: 1

**No. of applicants last year**: 4

**Additional Information**: Residence at the Albright Institute is required. The research period should be continuous without frequent trips outside Greece and Israel

### For further information contact:

**Email**:    spencer@jcu.edu

## W. F. Albright Institute of Archaeological Research/National Endowment for the Humanities Fellowship

**Eligibility**: Open to scholars in Near Eastern studies holding a PhD, who are citizens of the United States of America or alien residents residing in the country for the last 3 years. Research projects must have a clear humanities focus

**Level of Study**: Postdoctorate

**Type**: Fellowship

**Value**: IS$40,000 for 1 year. A total of IS$60,000 is to be available for 1.5 awards

**Length of Study**: 4 months–1 year

**Frequency**: Annual

**Study Establishment**: The W F Albright Institute of Archaeological Research in Jerusalem

**Country of Study**: Israel

**Application Procedure**: Applicants must write for details

**No. of awards offered**: 8

**Closing Date**: 17 October

**Funding**: Government

**No. of awards given last year**: 2

**No. of applicants last year**: 8

**Additional Information**: The research period should be continuous, without frequent trips outside the country. Residence at the Institute is preferred

### For further information contact:

Department of Religious Studies, John Carroll University, 20,700 North Park Boulevard, University Heights, OH 44118, United States of America.

**Email**:    spencer@jcu.edu

## American Society for Engineering Education (ASEE)

1818 North Street NW, Suite 600, Washington, DC 20036 2479, United States of America.

**Tel**:         (1) 202 331 3500/3525/202 649 3834
**Email**:      sttp@asee.org
**Website**:    www.asee.org
**Contact**:    Mr Michael More, Projects Department

The American Society for Engineering Education (ASEE) is committed to furthering education in engineering and engineering technology by promoting excellence in instruction, research, public service and practice, exercising worldwide leadership, fostering the technological education of society and providing quality products and services to members.

## American Society for Engineering Education Air Force Summer Faculty Fellowship Program

**Purpose**: To enhance the research interests and capabilities of faculty and also to elevate the awareness in the United States academic community of Air Force research

**Eligibility**: Open to citizens or permanent residents of the United States and must hold a full-time appointment at a college or university located in the United States, preferably with a minimum of 2 years experience

**Level of Study**: Postgraduate, Research

**Type**: Fellowship

**Value**: A weekly stipend of up to US$1,650

**Length of Study**: 1 year

**Frequency**: Annual

**Country of Study**: United States of America

## American Society for Engineering Education Helen T Carr Fellowship Program

**Purpose**: To increase the number of engineering professors for the historically Black engineering colleges by providing financial aid for doctoral study in engineering

**Eligibility**: Open to African American faculty members, graduate students and other African Americans who have completed at least the equivalent of 1 academic year of full-time engineering graduate study. Candidates must be sponsored by the Dean of one of the historically Black engineering colleges at which they later intend to teach

**Level of Study**: Doctorate

**Value**: Up to US$10,000

**Length of Study**: 1 year, renewable as funding allows

**Frequency**: Annual

**Country of Study**: United States of America

**Application Procedure**: Applicants must first submit a letter to the Dean of a historically Black engineering college asking to be sponsored. Transcripts of undergraduate and graduate course credits and at least three references testifying to intellectual capacity and educational attainments, which give promise of satisfactory performance in advanced study, must then be submitted to the ASEE. A covering letter from the sponsoring Dean is required, and a single copy of each of these documents is to be sent to the committee through its secretary at ASEE headquarters

**Closing Date**: 15 May

**Funding**: Government, Commercial, Private

**Contributor**: The Allied-Signal Foundation, the AMOCO Foundation, AT&T-Bell Laboratories, El Dupont De Numours & Co., the Exxon Education Foundation, the General Electric Foundation, the IBM Corporation, the Mobil Oil Corporation, NASA, RCA and the Union Carbide

**Additional Information**: www.collegescholarships.com/scholarships/detail/86377

### For further information contact:

**Email**:   a.hicks@asee.org

## National Defense Science and Engineering Graduate Fellowship Program

**Purpose**: To increase the number of United States citizens and nationals trained in science and engineering disciplines of military importance

**Eligibility**: Must be a United States citizen or national. Applicants must be at or near beginning of graduate studies in one of the above-named fields. Applicants must be either enrolled in their final year of undergraduate studies or have completed no more than the equivalent of 2 year's of full-time graduate study in the field in which they are applying. Exceptional circumstances may qualify other applicants as being at the early stages of their graduate studies

**Level of Study**: Doctorate

**Type**: Fellowship

**Value**: US$34,000 annual stipend. Full tuition and required fees. Medical insurance coverage offered through the institution, up to a total value of US$1,000 per year

**Length of Study**: 3 years

**Frequency**: Annual

**Country of Study**: United States of America

**Application Procedure**: Apply online at www.asee.org/ndseg

**No. of awards offered**: 2000

**Closing Date**: 18 December

**Funding**: Government

**Contributor**: United States Department of Defense

**No. of awards given last year**: 200

**No. of applicants last year**: 2000

**Additional Information**: ndseg.asee.org/about_ndseg

### For further information contact:

**Email**:   ndseg@asee.org

## Naval Research Laboratory Post Doctoral Fellowship Program

**Purpose**: To increase the involvement of creative and highly trained scientists to scientific and technical areas of interest and relevance to the United States Navy

**Eligibility**: United States citizens and permanent residents

**Level of Study**: Doctorate, Postdoctorate

**Type**: Fellowship

**Value**: Up to a maximum of US$79,720

**Length of Study**: 1 year, renewable for a 2nd and 3rd year

**Frequency**: Annual

**Study Establishment**: Naval Research Laboratory

**Country of Study**: United States of America

**Application Procedure**: Apply online at www.asee.org/nrl

**Funding**: Government

**Contributor**: United States Navy

**No. of awards given last year**: 35

**Additional Information**: A group health insurance program is provided for participants (paid for by the fellowship) and optional for dependents (paid for by participant) nrl.asee.org/

### For further information contact:

**Email**:   postdocs@asee.org

## Office of Naval Research Summer Faculty Research Program

**Purpose**: Summer Faculty Research Program. The Summer Faculty Research Program provides science and engineering faculty members from institutions of higher education the opportunity to participate in research of mutual interest to the faculty member and peers at U.S. Navy laboratories for a 10-week period.

**Eligibility**: United States citizen or permanent resident, must hold teaching or research appointment at United States college or university

**Level of Study**: Postdoctorate

**Type**: Fellowship

**Value**: US$1,400–1,900 (US$1,400 per week at the Summer Faculty Fellow level, US$1,650 per week at the Senior Summer Faculty Fellow level, and US$1,900 per week at the Distinguished Summer Faculty Fellow level)

**Length of Study**: 10 weeks

**Frequency**: Annual

**Country of Study**: United States of America

**Application Procedure**: Apply online at www.asee.org/summer

**No. of awards offered**: 544

**Closing Date**: 15 March

**Funding**: Government

**No. of awards given last year**: 73

**No. of applicants last year**: 544

**Additional Information**: There are three levels of appointment: Summer Faculty Fellow, Senior Summer Faculty Fellow, and Distinguished Summer Faculty Fellow. Each fellow will be reimbursed for expenses incurred on an optional pre-program visit to the sponsoring laboratory and one round-trip encompassing travel to the sponsoring laboratory at the beginning of the program and travel back to their home residence at the end of the program www.onr.navy.mil/en/Education-Outreach/faculty/summer-faculty-research-program

### For further information contact:

**Email**:    anthony.c.smith1@navy.mil

## American Society for Microbiology (ASM)

1752 N Street North West, Washington, DC 20036-2904, United States of America.

**Tel**:         (1) 202 737 3600
**Email**:    awards@asmusa.org

**Website**:    www.asm.org/awards
**Contact**:    Ms Leah Gibbons, Program Assistant

The American Society for Microbiology (ASM) is the oldest and largest single life science membership organization in the world. With 43,000 members throughout the world. The ASM represents all disciplines of microbiological specialization including microbiology education. The ASM's mission is to promote research and research training in the microbiological sciences and to assist communication between scientists, policymakers and the public to improve health, the environment and economic well-being.

## American Society for Microbiology Microbe Minority Travel Awards

**Purpose**: The ASM Undergraduate Research Fellowship provides students an opportunity to conduct research and attend ASM Microbe to present their research results. Faculty have an opportunity to mentor students and receive stipend and travel support for their students to conduct research. It generally awards a limited number of travel awards to supports recipients and traval to ASM Microbe

**Eligibility**: To qualify for consideration the applicant must be: 1. A current ASM member at the time of ASM Microbe. 2. From one of the targeted groups. 3. Faculty from a Minority Serving Institution (MSI), such as Historically Black Colleges and Universities (HBCU), Hispanic Serving Institutions (HSI), and Tribal Colleges and Universities (TCU). Faculty from community colleges. 4. URM Faculty regardless of institutional type. 5. URM Postdoctoral Scholars. 6. URM Graduate Students

**Level of Study**: Graduate

**Type**: Travel award

**Value**: US$1,000 per awardee

**Frequency**: Annual

**Country of Study**: United States of America, Canada or Mexico

**Application Procedure**: The program requires a joint application from the student and the faculty research mentor, both parts must be completed by the deadline. The student's portion of the application includes: 1. ASM member number. 2. Letter of recommendation. 3. Personal statement

**Closing Date**: 24 January

**Funding**: Private

**Additional Information**: Each awardee will be offered up to US$1,000 to defray expenses associated with travel to the ASM Microbe www.asm.org/Travel-Award/ASM-Microbe-Minority-Travel-Award

### For further information contact:

**Email**:    services@asm.org

## American Society for Photogrammetry & Remote Sensing (ASPRS)

The Imaging and Geospatial Information Society 5410 Grosvenor Lane, Suite 210, Bethesda, MD 20814-2160, United States of America.

**Tel**: (1) 301 493 0290
**Email**: asprs@asprs.org
**Website**: www.asprs.org

The American Society for Photogrammetry and Remote Sensing (ASPRS) was founded in 1934. It is a scientific association serving over 7,000 professional members around the world whose mission is to advance knowledge and improve understanding of mapping sciences to promote the responsible applications of photogrammetry, remote sensing, geographic information systems and supporting technologies.

## American Society for Photogrammetry and Remote Sensing Robert N. Colwell Memorial Fellowship

**Purpose**: To encourage and commend college/university students or postdoctoral researchers who display exceptional interest, desire, ability and aptitude in the specified field and who have a special interest in developing practical uses of these technologies
**Eligibility**: Must be a postgraduate student. Must attend a university. Citizenship requirements: USA or Canada. Must not be attending high school currently. Must study full-time. Restricted to students studying Engineering/Technology, Geography. Must be affiliated with American Society for Photogrammetry and Remote Sensin
**Level of Study**: Doctorate, Postgraduate
**Type**: Fellowship
**Value**: US$6,000
**Frequency**: Annual
**Country of Study**: United States of America or Canada
**Application Procedure**: Applicants must include a listing of courses, transcripts, listing of internship, 3 letters of recommendation and statement of purpose along with a completed application form
**Closing Date**: 17 October
**Contributor**: ASPRS Foundation
**Additional Information**: Please see the website for further details www.asprs.org/Awards-and-Scholarships/Robert-N-Colwell-Memorial-Fellowship.html www.petersons.com/schol arship/robert-n-colwell-memorial-fellowship-111_172542. aspx

**For further information contact:**

Jesse Winch, Scholarship Administrator.

**Tel**: (1) 301 493 0290
**Email**: scholarships@asprs.org

## American Society for Quality (ASQ)

600 North Plankinton Avenue, Milwaukee, WI 53203, United States of America.

**Tel**: (1) 414 272 8575
**Email**: help@asq.org
**Website**: www.asq.org

The American Society for Quality (ASQ) is the world's leading authority on quality. With more than 100,000 individual and organizational members, this professional association advances learning, quality improvement and knowledge exchange to improve business results and to create better workplaces and communities worldwide.

## Ellis R. Ott Scholarship for Applied Statistics and Quality Management

**Purpose**: To encourage students to pursue a career in a field related to statistics and/or quality management
**Eligibility**: Open to candidates who are planning to enroll or are enrolled in a Master's degree or; higher level programme in the United States or Canada
**Level of Study**: Doctorate, Graduate, Postgraduate
**Type**: Scholarships
**Value**: US$5,000
**Length of Study**: 1 year
**Frequency**: Annual
**Country of Study**: United States of America
**Application Procedure**: Applicants can download the application form from the website. The completed application form along with curriculum vitae, academic transcripts and two letters of recommendation are to be submitted
**Closing Date**: 1 April
**Funding**: Foundation
**Additional Information**: studyabroad.shiksha.com/scholar ships/ellis-r-ott-scholarship-for-applied-statistics-and-quality-management

**For further information contact:**

55 Buckskin Path, Plymouth, MA 02360, United States of America.

**Tel**:        (1) 774 413 5268
**Email**:   lynne.hare@comcast.net

## American Society of Colon and Rectal Surgeons

### Career Development Award

**Subjects**: The pathophysiology or management of diseases of the colon, rectum, anus or small bowel.
**Purpose**: To provide young surgeons with the support necessary for the initiation and development of an academic career in colorectal surgery. The CDA focuses on career development and mentorship of the individual rather than solely on the research proposal. The award is intended for the academic investigator demonstrating significant creativity in research relevant to the pathophysiology or management of diseases of the colon, rectum, anus or small bowel.
**Eligibility**: Must be: Within 5 years of first full-time faculty appointment in the United States or Canadian government, public or private not-for-profit medical institution. United States or Canadian citizen having completed an approved colorectal surgery training program; if foreign national, then must have valid working visa at time of application for colorectal department/institution where work is proposed. ASCRS members only. Grant can support up to 10% of the of the NIH Cap salary (US$187,000 as of Jan. 2018). Applications should also include a letter of support from the department of surgery chair confirming at least 25% non-clinical time will be committed to the applicant. Applicant must not currently have or have previously received a career development award from another external funding source. If the applicant receives the Career Development Award from the Research Foundation of the ASCRS and is subsequently awarded another career development award from another external funding source with overlapping funding period, the applicant must return the residual funds to the Research Foundation of the ASCRS, or decline the funding from another source. The exception is a career development award from the NIH K-series award or funding from the applicants own institution.
**Type**: Award
**Value**: US$75,000 per year
**Length of Study**: Two years
**Frequency**: Annual
**Country of Study**: United States of America or Canada

**Application Procedure**: Apply online
**Closing Date**: 1 April
**Additional Information**: fascrs.org/my-ascrs/research-foundation/grants-awards#International%20Fellowship

### General Surgery Resident Research Initiation Grant

**Subjects**: Diseases of the colon, rectum and anus.
**Purpose**: To attract General Surgery Residents or recent graduates of such programs into the field of colon and rectal surgery by providing opportunities to engage in clinical or laboratory-based research focused on diseases of the colon, rectum and anus.
**Eligibility**: Must be General Surgical Residents or recent (within 2 years) Graduates of a US or Canadian approved General Surgery Training Program. Applicant must have designated time for research and no clinical responsibility. Preference is given to applicants with research or clinical career goals in the field of Colon & Rectal Surgery and whose research Mentor or Co-Investigator is a Fellow of ASCRS.
**Type**: Grant
**Value**: US$20,000
**Length of Study**: One year
**Frequency**: Annual
**Country of Study**: United States of America or Canada
**Application Procedure**: Research project applications to the Research Foundation of ASCRS are made on Public Health Service grant application form PHS 398. The PHS grant application process has had a long history of satisfactory operation. By using PHS 398, the process of renewal or extension to subsequent Research Foundation or NIH funding, if applicable, will be facilitated. The Research Committee of the Research Foundation will make every effort to perform a comprehensive review of your application in an expeditious manner. This review may require assignment of appropriate expertise from the scientific community outside of the colon and rectal surgical field.
**Closing Date**: 15 August
**Additional Information**: fascrs.org/my-ascrs/research-foundation/grants-awards#International%20Fellowship

### International Fellowship Grant

**Subjects**: Colon, rectum and anus diseases
**Purpose**: To provide support to research programs that are focused on diseases of the colon, rectum and anus that will ultimately impact how we treat these patients. This grant will focus on providing support to clinical investigators in the United States or Canada who would like to participate in

research outside the United States or Canada, including US investigator engagement in global health research projects focused in colorectal surgery.

**Eligibility**: Must be: ASCRS members only. ASCRS member must be co-principal investigator or principal investigator. The applicant must be pursuing a career in colorectal surgery. For Citizens of USA or Canada: The applicant must be currently enlisted in or a graduate of an accredited residency program in either general or colon and rectal surgery or be a recent graduate of a program approved by the Research Foundation. The applicant must be sponsored by a colon and rectal program director or ASCRS Fellow. For foreigners traveling to USA or Canada: The applicant must be sponsored by a clinician investigator who is an ASCRS member and board certified by the ABCRS with a research program.

**Type**: Grant
**Value**: US$12,500
**Length of Study**: One year
**Frequency**: Annual
**Country of Study**: United States of America or Canada
**Application Procedure**: Apply online
**Closing Date**: 15 August
**Additional Information**: fascrs.org/my-ascrs/research-foundation/grants-awards#International%20Fellowship

## Limited Project Grant (LPG)

**Subjects**: Colon and rectal surgery
**Purpose**: To provide investigators the opportunity to pursue research interest, specifically germane to the field of colon and rectal surgery. It is anticipated that successful research projects, initially funded through the Research Foundation's LPG mechanism, will ultimately secure funding from other national funding agencies.
**Eligibility**: The proposed research must be investigator-initiated, hypothesis-driven. The proposed research must be conducted within the United States or Canada. ASCRS members must be co-principal investigators or principal investigators. Prior to submitting your application, any proposed research that includes human or animal studies must have approval from the institutions appropriate review board.
**Type**: Grant
**Value**: Up to US$25,000
**Length of Study**: One year
**Frequency**: Annual
**Country of Study**: United States of America or Canada
**Application Procedure**: Research project applications to the Research Foundation of ASCRS are made on Public Health Service grant application form PHS 398. The PHS grant application process has had a long history of satisfactory operation. By using PHS 398, the process of renewal or extension to subsequent Research Foundation or NIH

funding, if applicable, will be facilitated. The Research Committee of the Research Foundation will make every effort to perform a comprehensive review of your application in an expeditious manner. This review may require assignment of appropriate expertise from the scientific community outside of the colon and rectal surgical field.
**Closing Date**: 1 April
**Additional Information**: fascrs.org/my-ascrs/research-foundation/grants-awards#International%20Fellowship

## Medical Student Research Initiation Grant

**Subjects**: Diseases of the colon, rectum and anus.
**Purpose**: To provide opportunities for Medical Students to participate in clinical or laboratory-based research focused on diseases of the colon, rectum and anus.
**Eligibility**: Must be a Medical Student in a US or Canadian Medical School. Applicant must have designated time for research and no competing clinical responsibility. Preference is given to individuals who will pursue or who are considering pursuit of a career in Colon and Rectal Surgery and whose project has a mentor or co-investigator who is a Fellow or Member of the American Society of Colon and Rectal Surgeons.
**Type**: Grant
**Value**: US$4,000
**Length of Study**: Two to three months dedicated to research during the academic year
**Frequency**: Annual
**Country of Study**: United States of America or Canada
**Application Procedure**: Research project applications to the Research Foundation of ASCRS are made on Public Health Service grant application form PHS 398. The PHS grant application process has had a long history of satisfactory operation. By using PHS 398, the process of renewal or extension to subsequent Research Foundation or NIH funding, if applicable, will be facilitated. The Research Committee of the Research Foundation will make every effort to perform a comprehensive review of your application in an expeditious manner. This review may require assignment of appropriate expertise from the scientific community outside of the colon and rectal surgical field.
**Closing Date**: 1 April
**Additional Information**: fascrs.org/my-ascrs/research-foundation/grants-awards#International%20Fellowship

## Research in Robotic Surgical Technology Grant

**Subjects**: Robotic surgical technology in the field of colon and rectal surgery

**Purpose**: The Research in Robotic Surgical Technology Grant provides an investigator the opportunity to pursue research interests, specifically germane to robotic surgical technology in the field of colon and rectal surgery. Innovative projects are encouraged. The Research Committee is particularly interested in fostering collaborative research. Proposals which include two or more institutions may be eligible for additional funding. This grant is supported by Intuitive Surgical Inc.

**Eligibility**: Proposed research must be investigator-initiated, hypothesis-driven. Proposed research must be conducted within the United States or Canada. ASCRS members must be co-principal investigators or principal investigators. Applicant submitting a proposal to this funding opportunity may not submit the same application to any other funding body at the same time. Prior to submitting your application, any proposed research that includes human or animal studies must have approval from the institutions appropriate review board.

**Type**: Grant

**Value**: US$50,000 for one year, or collaborative proposals may be funded up to US$100,000 for one year.

**Frequency**: Annual

**Country of Study**: United States of America or Canada

**Application Procedure**: Research project applications to the Research Foundation of the ASCRS are made on Public Health Service grant application form PHS 398. The PHS grant application process has had a long history of satisfactory operation. By using PHS 398, the process of renewal or extension to subsequent Research Foundation or NIH funding, if applicable, will be facilitated. The Research Committee of the Research Foundation will make every effort to perform a comprehensive review of your application in an expeditious manner. This review may require assignment of appropriate expertise from the scientific community outside of the colon and rectal surgical field.

**Closing Date**: 15 August

**Additional Information**: fascrs.org/my-ascrs/research-foundation/grants-awards#International%20Fellowship

### Training in Research Methodology Grant

**Subjects**: Research methodology

**Purpose**: This award provides an opportunity for a graduating CRS resident to attend training that will enhance their career. They may attend one of the following courses: the Career Development Course, Fundamentals of Surgical Research Course or the Early Career Development Course offered by the Association for Academic Surgery (AAS) or the American College of Surgeons (ACS) Health Services Research Methods Course.

**Eligibility**: Must be a graduating Colon and Rectal Surgeon resident or first year faculty with demonstrated interest in pursuing academic career in colon and rectal surgery. Applicant must be a Member or a Candidate member of ASCRS in good standing.

**Type**: Award

**Value**: Up to US$3,000 to be used for coach air travel, hotel accommodations, meals and registration for one of the following courses: AAS Fall Career Development Course, or AAS Fall Fundamentals of Surgical Research Course o ACS Health Services Research Methods Course

**Length of Study**: The length of one of three available courses

**Frequency**: Annual

**Country of Study**: Any country

**Application Procedure**: The Young Researchers Committee will review and score the applications and then submit their recommendation to the Research Committee for approval.

**Closing Date**: 1 April

**Additional Information**: fascrs.org/my-ascrs/research-foundation/grants-awards#International%20Fellowship

---

## American Society of Composers, Authors and Publishers Foundation

One Lincoln Plaza, New York, NY 10023-7142, United States of America.

| | |
|---|---|
| **Tel**: | (1) 212 621 6219 |
| **Email**: | info@ascapfoundation.com |
| **Website**: | www.ascapfoundation.org |
| **Contact**: | Michael Spudic |

The American Society of Composers, Authors and Publishers (ASCAP) is a membership association of over 260,000 composers, songwriters, lyricists and music publishers. It is dedicated to nurturing the music talent of tomorrow, preserving the legacy of the past and sustaining the creative incentive for today's creators through a variety of educational, professional and humanitarian programmes and activities which serve the entire music community. ASCAP's function is to protect the rights of its members by licensing and paying royalties for the public performances of their copyrighted works.

## American Society of Composers, Authors and Publishers Foundation Morton Gould Young Composer Awards

**Purpose**: To encourage talented young composers by providing recognition, appreciation and monetary awards

**Eligibility**: Open to United States citizens or permanent residents who have not reached their 30th birthday by 1 January in the year of competition. Original concert music of any style will be considered. However, works which have previously earned awards or prizes in any other national competition are ineligible. Arrangements are also ineligible. Open to all composers of Original Concert Music (classical)

**Level of Study**: Unrestricted

**Type**: Award

**Value**: The winning composers share over US$40,000 in ASCAP Foundation Awards

**Frequency**: Annual

**Application Procedure**: Applicants must complete an application form and other materials. For more information write to organization

**Closing Date**: 1 February

**Funding**: Private, Foundation

**Contributor**: The ASCAP Foundation's Jack and Amy Norworth Memorial Fund, the Leo Kaplan Fund and the Frank & Lydia Bergen Foundation

**No. of awards given last year**: 39

**Additional Information**: Each year the top award winner receives an additional cash prize, The ASCAP Foundation Leo Kaplan Award www.ascapfoundation.org/ascapfoundation/programs/awards/young-composer-awards

**For further information contact:**

The ASCAP Foundation/Morton Gould Young Composer Awards, 250 West 57th Street, New York, NY 10107, United States of America

**Email**: concertmusic@ascap.com

# American Society of Hematology

## ASH Scholar Award

**Subjects**: Hematology research

**Purpose**: Since 1985, the ASH Scholar Award has helped ease the difficult transition between completion of training and establishment of an independent career by providing partial salary or other support during that critical period required for completion of training and achievement of status as an independent investigator.

**Eligibility**: Applicants must meet the following criteria in order to qualify: Be a citizen of the United States or Canada. Both of which may now conduct work outside of the U.S. and Canada; Hold a visa or permanent resident status in the United States or Canada and plan to conduct his/her research within the U.S. or Canada (Individuals outside of the U.S. or Canada

should consider the Global Research Award); Be an ASH member in good standing at the time of the letter of intent deadline and plan to maintain membership for the duration of the award term; Have confirmation from the applicant's institution that at least 75 % of the applicant's full-time professional effort is devoted to research. If you have successfully competed for a substantial award (e.g. NIH R01 or equivalent grant) as the PI or co-PI before the application (not LOI) deadline, you are no longer eligible for the Scholar Award.

**Type**: Award

**Value**: Fellow Scholar Award provides up to US$100,000 over a two- to three-year period in equal quarterly payments over the award term. Fellow to Faculty Scholar Award provides up to US$125,000 over a two- to three-year period in equal quarterly payments over the award term. Junior Faculty Scholar Award provides up to US$150,000 over a two- to three-year period in equal quarterly payments over the award term.

**Length of Study**: Two to three years depending on the award

**Country of Study**: Any country

**Application Procedure**: The Scholar Award letter of intent (LOI) and the supporting documents outlined below must be submitted through the ASH online awards system. The LOI is mandatory and will be reviewed for eligibility to submit a full proposal. In addition to the letter of intent, the applicant must submit the following: Abstract of proposed project (350 words maximum). Applicant's NIH Biographical Sketch. Fellow to Faculty applicants will need to submit the Supplemental Budget Form. Please see the instruction in the online award system.

**Closing Date**: 1 May

**Additional Information**: www.hematology.org/awards/career-enhancement-and-training/scholar-award/apply#eligibility

# American Society of Interior Designers (ASID) Educational Foundation, Inc.

608 Massachusetts Avenue North East, Washington, DC 20002, United States of America.

**Tel**:　　　(1) 202 546 3480
**Email**:　　education@asid.org
**Website**:　www.asidfoundation.org
**Contact**:　Education Department

The American Society of Interior Designers (ASID) Educational Foundation represents the interests of more than 30,500 members including interior design practitioners, students and industry and retail partners. ASID's mission is to be the definitive resource for professional education and knowledge sharing, advocacy of interior designers' right to practice and expansion of interior design markets.

## The ASID Educational Foundation/Irene Winifred Eno Grant

**Country of Study**: Any country
**Additional Information**: www.asid.org/press-releases/asid-announces-2019-asid-foundation-scholarship-and-grant-recipients

### For further information contact:

**Email**:    schung@asid.org

# American Society of Mechanical Engineers (ASME International)

Two Park Avenue, New York, NY 10016-5990, United States of America.

**Tel**:            (1) 800 843 2763
**Email**:        CustomerCare@asme.org
**Website**:    www.asme.org/education/enged/aid
**Contact**:    Theresa Oluwanifise, Coordinator Educational Operations

Founded in 1880 as the American Society of Mechanical Engineers (ASME International), today ASME International is a non-profit educational and technical organization serving a worldwide membership.

## Elisabeth M and Winchell M Parsons Scholarship

**Purpose**: To assist ASME student members working towards a doctoral degree
**Eligibility**: Must be a U.S. citizen. Must be enrolled full time. Must be working toward a doctoral degree in engineering. Must major in mechanical engineering. This award is for U.S. students.
**Level of Study**: Doctorate
**Type**: Award
**Value**: US$3,000
**Frequency**: Annual
**Country of Study**: United States of America
**Application Procedure**: Application forms are available from the website
**No. of awards offered**: 2
**Closing Date**: 3 March

**No. of awards given last year**: 3
**No. of applicants last year**: 5
**Additional Information**: www.unigo.com/scholarships/by-major/engineering-scholarships/elisabeth-m-and-winchell-m-parsons-scholarship/1003462

### For further information contact:

2 Park Ave. New York, NY 10016, United States of America.

**Tel**:          (1) 212 591 8131; 212 591 7143
**Email**:      LefeverB@asme.org

## Marjorie Roy Rothermel Scholarship

**Purpose**: To assist students working towards a Master's degree
**Eligibility**: Selection is based on academic performance, character, need and ASME participation. Applicants must be citizens of the United States of America and must be enrolled in a United States school in an ABET-accredited mechanical engineering department. No student may receive more than one auxiliary scholarship or loan in the same academic year
**Level of Study**: Graduate
**Type**: Scholarship
**Value**: US$3,000
**Frequency**: Annual
**Country of Study**: United States of America
**Application Procedure**: Application forms are available from the website
**Closing Date**: 3 March
**Additional Information**: www.unigo.com/scholarships/by-major/engineering-scholarships/marjorie-roy-rothermel-scholarship/1003463

### For further information contact:

2 Park Ave., New York, NY 10016, United States of America.

**Tel**:          (1) 212 591 8131; 212 591 7143
**Email**:      LefeverB@asme.org

# American Society of Nephrology (ASN)

1510 H Street, NW, Suite 800, Washington, DC 20005, United States of America.

**Tel**:            (1) 202 640 4660
**Email**:        email@asn-online.org
**Website**:    www.asn-online.org
**Contact**:    Grants Co-ordinator

The American Society of Nephrology (ASN) was founded in 1967 as a non-profit corporation to enhance and assist the study and practice of nephrology, to provide a forum for the promulgation of research and to meet the professional and continuing education needs of its members.

## Carl W Gottschalk Research Scholar Grant

**Purpose**: To provide funding for young faculty to foster evolution to an independent research career and a successful application a National Institutes of Health (NIH) R01 grant or equivalent
**Eligibility**: Applicants must an active member of the ASN and hold an MD or PhD or equivalent degree. At the time of submission the applicant's membership must be current and their dues paid. Appointment to full-time faculty must be conformed in writing by the department chair
**Level of Study**: Postdoctorate, Postgraduate
**Type**: Grant
**Value**: US$100,000
**Length of Study**: 2 years
**Frequency**: Annual
**Country of Study**: United States of America
**Application Procedure**: Online application
**Closing Date**: 28 January
**Funding**: Foundation
**Contributor**: ASN Foundation for Kidney Research
**Additional Information**: Please visit the website for further details

### For further information contact:

**Email**:    grants@asn-online.org

## American University in Cairo (AUC)

PO Box 2511, 113 Kasr El Aini Street, Cairo 11511, Egypt.

**Tel**:        (20) 2 2794 2964
**Email**:     ocm@aucegypt.edu
**Website**:   www.aucegypt.edu/Pages/default.aspx
**Contact**:   Mrs Sawsan Mardini, Director of Graduate Students Services

The American University in Cairo (AUC) provides quality higher and continuing education for students from Egypt and the surrounding region. The University is an independent, non-profit, apolitical, non-sectarian and equal opportunity institution. English is the primary language of instruction. The University is accredited in the United States of America by the Commission of Higher Education of the Middle States Association of Colleges and Schools.

## African Graduate Fellowships

**Purpose**: The African Graduate Fellowship is a competitive fellowship program for bright, highly motivated African students interested in pursuing a master's degree at AUC
**Eligibility**: Non-Egyptian African nationals; Open to all disciplines of graduate studies; For new graduate degree-seeking students; full admission to one of the graduate programs in AUC, satisfying AUC graduate full admissions requirements. 1. Submit an International TOEFL iBT exam score or academic IELTS exam score as per the cut-off scores for AUC graduate admissions. 2. For continuing students; to retain the fellowship, the recipient must maintain a GPA of 3.2. 3. Financial need
**Level of Study**: Graduate
**Type**: Fellowship
**Value**: A waiver of tuition fee; student services and activities fees; a monthly stipend of LE 600 for 10 months
**Length of Study**: One semester and may be renewed for a maximum period of 2 years. The fellowship may cover a summer session
**Frequency**: Annual
**Country of Study**: Any country except India
**Application Procedure**: There are two steps which need to be followed to process the application. To Apply Step 1: Check how to apply and submit the online application Step 2: Submit the online fellowship application Application link is mentioned below:
**No. of awards offered**: 123
**Closing Date**: 16 February
**No. of awards given last year**: 18
**No. of applicants last year**: 123
**Additional Information**: For further information, refer the below link. ssb.aucegypt.edu:4444/PROD/twbkwbis.P_GenMenu?name=homepage www.aucegypt.edu/admissions/fellowships/listings/african-graduate

### For further information contact:

**Email**:    grad@aucegypt.edu

## American University of Beirut

American University of Beirut, 3 Dag Hammarskjold Plaza, 8th Floor, New York, NY 10017-2303, United States of America.

**Tel**:        (1) 212 583 7600
**Website**:   www.aub.edu.lb/main/about/Pages/index.aspx

AUB currently offers more than 120 programs leading to the bachelor's, master's, MD, and PhD degrees. The language of instruction is English (except for courses in the Arabic Department and other language courses).

## American University of Beirut Mediterranean Scholarships

**Purpose**: To strengthen capacity in implementation research on the neglected tropical diseases as well as malaria and tuberculosis. The American University of Beirut (AUB) is delighted to offer a number of scholarships for students from low- and middle-income countries

**Eligibility**: To be eligible, all candidates are expected to have good academic record in undergraduate education (and graduate education where relevant) in any discipline (health sciences, social sciences, nutrition, medicine, nursing, pharmacy, dentistry sciences or related discipline) and hold a bachelor's degree from AUB, or an equivalent degree from another recognized institution. Please note, all candidates must be a national of and resident in a low- or middle-income country of the Eastern Mediterranean region

**Level of Study**: Postgraduate

**Value**: The scholarships cover travel, tuition and living expenses for the duration of the program. English language training at AUB prior to enrolment is also covered for some students who need it

**Country of Study**: Any country

**Application Procedure**: The application should be made through the online system at: graduateadmissions.aub.edu.lb/

**Closing Date**: 1 April

**Funding**: Trusts

**Additional Information**: Place of Study – American University of Beirut (AUB), Lebanon scholarship-positions.com/american-university-of-beirut-aub-mediterranean-scholarships/2015/06/26/

### For further information contact:

**Email**:    GPHP@aub.edu.lb

## American Urological Association

### Research Scholar Awards

**Subjects**: Urology

**Purpose**: The AUA offers a portfolio of mentored research training awards to recruit outstanding young investigators into urologic research and foster their career success.

**Eligibility**: Must be either clinical and postdoctoral fellows who are no more than five years beyond completing

a doctorate or residency, or early career investigators who are in the first five years after beginning a faculty position

**Type**: Award

**Value**: US$40,000 per year

**Length of Study**: One and two years

**Frequency**: Annual

**Country of Study**: Any country

**Application Procedure**: Apply online

**Additional Information**: www.auanet.org/research/research-funding/aua-funding/research-scholar-awards

## American Water Works Association (AWWA)

6666 West Quincy Avenue, Denver, CO 80235, United States of America.

**Tel**:         (1) 303 794 7711
**Email**:      lmoody@awwa.org
**Website**:    www.awwa.org
**Contact**:    Administrative Assistant

The American Water Works Association (AWWA) is an international non-profit scientific and educational society dedicated to the improvement of drinking water quality and supply. The Association has more than 57,000 members who represent the full spectrum of the drinking water community, e.g. treatment plant operators and managers, scientists, environmentalists, manufacturers, academics, regulators and others who have a genuine interest in water supply and public health.

## American Water Works Association Abel Wolman Fellowship

**Purpose**: To encourage and support promising students from countries with AWWA sections to pursue advanced training and research

**Eligibility**: Open to candidates who anticipate completing the requirements for their PhD degree within 2 years of the award. Applicants must be citizens of a country that has an AWWA section, i.e. the United States of America, Canada or Mexico. Applicants will be considered without regard to colour, gender, race, creed or country of origin

**Level of Study**: Doctorate

**Type**: Fellowship

**Value**: US$30,000

**Length of Study**: Initially 1 year, renewable for 1 further year on submission of evidence of satisfactory progress and approval by a review committee

**Frequency**: Annual

**Country of Study**: United States of America, Canada or Mexico

**Application Procedure**: Applicants must submit an official application form, official transcripts of all university education, official copies of Graduate Record Examination scores, three letters of recommendation, a proposed curriculum of study and brief plans of dissertation research study

**No. of awards offered**: 17

**Closing Date**: 15 January

**Funding**: Private

**Additional Information**: www.awwa.org/Membership-Volunteering/Students-Young-Professionals/AWWA-Scholarships

**For further information contact:**

Tel:        (1) 303 347 6201
Email:      swheeler@awwa.org

---

## American Woman's Society of Certified Public Accountants

AWSCPA Administrative Offices, 136 South Keowee Street, Dayton, OH 45402, United States of America.

Tel:        (1) 937 222 1872
Email:      info@awscpa.org
Website:    www.awscpa.org

The American Woman's Society of CPA provides annual scholarships to women working towards an accounting degree as well as to those working towards their Certified Public Accountant License.

## Call for Nominations for Urdang Medal and Kremers Award

**Purpose**: The George Urdang Medal is awarded for an original and scholarly publication, or series of publications, pertaining primarily to historical or historico-social aspects of pharmacy. The Medal may also be awarded for popular works intended to achieve more widespread appreciation for, and better understanding of, pharmacy and its past among members of the pharmaceutical profession, allied professions, or the public. The Urdang Medal was established in 1952 in honor of Professor George Urdang, one of AIHP's founders and a renowned scholar of the history of pharmacy

**Eligibility**: 1. The Urdang Medal is awarded without restriction as to citizenship of the author or place of publication.

Evaluation is based on competence of research and skill of interpretation and presentation. 2. The nominee's age, total number of publications or previous honors is not given primary consideration

**Level of Study**: Professional development

**Type**: Award

**Frequency**: Annual

**Country of Study**: Any country

**Application Procedure**: In order to apply for the nominations for this award, kindly access the below link for the application form and procedures to be followed. networks.h-net.org/node/9782/discussions/3798798/call-nominations-2019-urdang-medal-and-kremers-award

**Closing Date**: 30 April

**Funding**: Private

**Additional Information**: networks.h-net.org/node/73374/announcements/3735293/call-nominations-2019-urdang-medal-and-kremers-award

**For further information contact:**

H-Net: Humanities & Social Sciences Online Old Horticulture 141H 506 East Circle Drive, East Lansing, MI 48824, United States of America.

Tel:        (1) 517 432 5134
Email:      aihp@aihp.org

---

## American-Scandinavian Foundation (ASF)

58 Park Avenue at 38th Street, New York, NY 10016, United States of America.

Tel:        (1) 212 779 3587
Email:      grants@amscan.org
Website:    www.amscan.org
Contact:    Director of Fellowships and Grants

The ASF is a publicity supported, non-profit organization that promotes international understanding through educational and cultural exchange between the United States and the Nordic countries.

## Awards for American Universities and Colleges to host Norwegian lecturers

**Purpose**: The American-Scandinavian Foundation (ASF) invites United States colleges and universities to apply for funding to host a visiting lecturer from Norway. The awards are for appointments of one semester, and should fall within an academic year

**Eligibility**: Terms of Award; 1. US$20,000 teaching/research stipend. 2. 5,000 travel stipend for lecture appearances outside home institution. Lectureships should be in the area of contemporary studies with an emphasis on one of five areas: 1. Public Policy. 2. Conflict Resolution. 3. Environmental Studies. 4. Multiculturalism. 5. Healthcare. Conditions of Award; 1. The lecturer must be a Norwegian citizen, and a scholar or expert in a field appropriate to the host department or program. 2. The ASF encourages consideration of the practitioner as well as the academic as a lectureship candidate. Responsibilities of the Host Institution; 1. The institution is responsible for selecting the lecturer it wishes to host. The ASF cannot assist in establishing contacts. 2. All pre-appointment communication with the lecturer, and arrangements for teaching, public presentations and housing during the lectureship appointment are the responsibility of the host institution. The host institution would be expected to provide support complementing the US$20,000 stipend. Additional support may be in the form of: 1. Subsidized faculty housing. 2. International Travel and insurance expenses. 3. Office and computer use. 4. Additional stipend support. Responsibilities of the Lecturer; 1. The selected lecturer is expected to teach one course (undergraduate or graduate level) and perform modest public activities (lectures, etc.) for which s/he will receive US$20,000. 2. The selected lecturer is expected to accept invitations to visit other academic institutions or conferences (including the NorTANA conference, the Swedish Teachers' conference, and the SASS conference) for which s/he will have US$5,000 available in travel funds

**Level of Study**: Unrestricted

**Type**: Lectureship/Prize

**Value**: US$25,000

**Length of Study**: One semester

**Frequency**: Annual

**Country of Study**: United States of America

**Application Procedure**: Complete online application - www. amscan.org/fellowships-grants/visiting-lectureships/

**Closing Date**: 15 February

**Funding**: Private

**No. of awards given last year**: 1

**Additional Information**: www.amscan.org/fellowships-grants/visiting-lectureships/

## Grants for Public Projects

**Purpose**: Through its public project grants, ASF funds a wide variety of programs that bring American and Scandinavian culture, art and thought to public audiences. The American-Scandinavian Foundation promotes the cultures of the Nordic

countries in the United States and American culture in the Nordic countries by encouraging programs that will enhance public appreciation of culture, art, and thought

**Eligibility**: Must be a non-profit organization and the project must be open to the public. ASF's funding priority has traditionally been to underwrite public programming and defined events. Awards are given to non-profit organizations only. Proof of an organization's non-profit status (as a 501(c)(3) in the United States or equivalent in Scandinavia) is required. ASF does NOT support: 1. Capital expenses. 2. Institutional overhead and other administrative fees. 3. Underwriting book, periodical or website publication. 4. Production of commercial CDs or cassettes. 5. Conference participation or conference registration for individuals. However, general conference expenses such as costs for special invitees/speakers can be supported. 6. Participation in studio residencies other than those with which ASF already has an ongoing affiliation. 7. Retroactive funding. Projects cannot begin before the decision announcement date. 8. The maximum award amount is US$5,000; however, average grants range between US$1,000 to US$2,000. ASF will only accept one application per organization per competition cycle and will grant only one award per organization per fiscal year in any one grant category

**Level of Study**: Unrestricted

**Type**: Project grant

**Value**: up to US$5,000

**Length of Study**: varies

**Frequency**: Twice a year

**Country of Study**: Scandinavian countries

**Application Procedure**: Complete online application - www. amscan.org/fellowships-and-grants/public-project-proposal-guidelines/

**Closing Date**: 15 February

**Funding**: Private

**Additional Information**: www.amscan.org/fellowships-grants/grants-for-organizations/

## Translation Competition

**Purpose**: ASF Translation Competition is an international competition for literary translations into English from any Nordic language and genre. Our annual competition recognizes outstanding translations of Scandinavian literature authored by a Scandinavian writer born after 1900

**Eligibility**: 1. The prizes are for outstanding English translations of poetry, fiction, drama or literary prose originally written in a Nordic language. 2. If prose, manuscripts must be no longer than 50 pages; if poetry, 25 (Do not exceed these limits). Manuscripts must be typed and double-spaced with numbered pages. 3. Translations must be from the writing of one author, although not necessarily from a single work.

Please include a one-paragraph description about the author. 4. An entry must consist of: One copy of the translation, including a title page and a table of contents for the proposed book of which the manuscript submitted is a part. One copy of the work(s) in the original language; please send the relevant pages. A CV containing all contact information, including email address, for the translator; and; A letter or other document signed by the author, the author's agent or the author's estate granting permission for the translation to be entered in this competition and published in Scandinavian Review. 5. Translator's names may not appear on any page of their manuscripts, including the title page. 6. The translation submitted in the competition may not have been previously published in the English language by the submission deadline. (If the translation being submitted to this competition is also under consideration by a publisher, you must inform us of the expected publication date.); 7. Translators may submit one entry only and may not submit the same entry in more than two competitions. 8. The Translation Prize cannot be won more than three times by the same translator

**Level of Study**: Unrestricted
**Type**: Translation prize
**Value**: US$2,000–US$2,500
**Frequency**: Annual
**Country of Study**: Any country
**Application Procedure**: Complete online application - www.amscan.org/fellowships-grants/translation-competition/
**Closing Date**: 15 June
**Funding**: Private
**No. of awards given last year**: 2
**Additional Information**: amscan.secure-platform.com/a/page/translation2020

## Analytics India

### University of Sydney: Data Science Scholarships

**Purpose**: The University of Sydney, one of Australia's premier universities is offering scholarships for international students for intake to high performing candidates
**Eligibility**: 1. Applicants must be a graduate of a quantitative degree program. A quantitative program includes Data Science, Computer Science, Mathematics, Statistics, Engineering, Physics, Economics and more. 2. Applicants must have achieved a minimum distinction average (equivalent to 75 at the University of Sydney) in their UG studies
**Level of Study**: Postgraduate
**Type**: Scholarship
**Value**: AU$6,000
**Frequency**: Annual
**Study Establishment**: University of Sydney

**Country of Study**: Australia
**Closing Date**: 30 April
**Funding**: Private
**Additional Information**: analyticsindiamag.com/8-scholarships-top-universities-data-science-2019/

**For further information contact:**

**Email**:    info@analyticsindiamag.com

## Anglo-Austrian Music Society

Richard Tauber Prize for Singers, 158 Rosendale Road, London, SE21 8LG, United Kingdom.

**Tel**:        (44) 20 8761 0444
**Email**:     info@aams.org.uk
**Website**:   www.aams.org.uk
**Contact**:   Jane Avery, Secretary

The Anglo-Austrian Music Society promotes lectures and concerts and is closely associated with its parent organization, the Anglo-Austrian Society, which was founded in 1944 to promote friendship and understanding between the people of the United Kingdom and Austria through personal contacts, educational programmes and cultural exchanges. AAMS awards the Richard Tauber prize for singers.

### Wigmore Hall/Independent Opera International Song Competition

**Purpose**: Wigmore Hall is responsible for the biennial International Song Competition
**Eligibility**: The Competition attracts singers and pianists of the highest calibre aged 33 or under, keen to pursue performing careers at the highest level
**Level of Study**: Graduate, Postgraduate, Undergraduate
**Type**: Competition
**Value**: It provides valuable opportunities for feedback from Jury members drawn from vocal artists of global stature; provides opportunities for participants to meet their peers from other countries and to exchange ideas on performance, technique and repertoire; and provides a vital public platform from which young singers and pianists can break into the world of professional performance at the highest level
**Frequency**: Every 2 years
**Country of Study**: Any country
**Application Procedure**: Application form and recording (MP3 or WAV files only) of prescribed repertoire plus application fee

**No. of awards offered**: 150 plus
**Closing Date**: 9 September
**Funding**: Private
**Contributor**: Independent Opera
**No. of awards given last year**: 6
**No. of applicants last year**: 150 plus
**Additional Information**: Please check at www.wigmore-hall.org.uk/song-competition wigmore-hall.org.uk/song-competition/wigmore-hall-independent-opera-international-song-competition

**For further information contact:**

Wigmore Hall/Independent Opera International Song Competition, Wigmore Hall, 36 Wigmore Street, Marylebone, London W1U 2BP, United Kingdom.

**Tel**:        (44) 20 7258 8244
**Email**:    songcompetition@wigmore-hall.org.uk

# Anglo-Danish Society

43 Maresfield Gardens, London, NW3 5TF, United Kingdom.

**Tel**:        (44) 1728 638 345
**Email**:    scholarships@anglo-danishsociety.org.uk
**Website**:  www.anglo-danishsociety.org.uk
**Contact**:  Mrs Margit Staehr, Administrator

The Anglo-Danish Society exists to promote closer understanding between the United Kingdom and Denmark by arranging lectures, outings, social gatherings and other events of interest for its members and their guests. The society administers scholarship funds which help Danish students visit the United Kingdom or British students visit Denmark, for the purpose of advanced or postgraduate studies.

## Denmark Liberation Scholarships

**Purpose**: To promote Anglo Danish relations
**Eligibility**: Open to graduates of British nationality only
**Level of Study**: Doctorate, Postdoctorate, Postgraduate, Professional development
**Type**: Scholarship
**Value**: One major award of £9,000 and others at £6,000 each
**Length of Study**: A minimum of 6 months
**Frequency**: Annual
**Study Establishment**: A Danish university or other approved institution

**Country of Study**: Denmark
**Application Procedure**: Applicants must complete an application form, available from the Secretary between 1 October and 31 December. Applicants should include a stamped addressed envelope or international reply coupons
**No. of awards offered**: 12
**Closing Date**: 30 June
**Funding**: Private
**No. of awards given last year**: 4
**No. of applicants last year**: 12
**Additional Information**: www.anglo-danishsociety.org.uk/scholarships

**For further information contact:**

**Email**:    scholars@anglo-danishsociety.org.uk

## Ove Arup Foundation Award

**Purpose**: Ove Arup Foundation and the Foundation's commitment to support and publicise any publication made as a result of the scholarship. For this reason, candidates who can demonstrate that their research is likely to result in publication will be favoured.
**Eligibility**: Open to graduates of British nationality only
**Level of Study**: Postdoctorate
**Type**: Scholarship
**Value**: £2,500
**Closing Date**: 30 June
**Additional Information**: www.anglo-danishsociety.org.uk/scholarships

**For further information contact:**

**Email**:    scholars@anglo-danishsociety.org.uk

## The ACE Foundation Scholarship

**Purpose**: The Anglo-Danish Society administers a special scholarship, together with the ACE Foundation.
**Eligibility**: Open to graduates of British nationality only
**Level of Study**: Postdoctorate
**Type**: Scholarship
**Value**: £2,500
**Closing Date**: 30 June
**Additional Information**: www.anglo-danishsociety.org.uk/scholarships

**For further information contact:**

**Email**:    scholars@anglo-danishsociety.org.uk

## William Charnley Anglo-Danish Scholarship

**Purpose**: As the award is for a British University postgraduate place, applicants should normally be Danish postgraduate students. However, British students who have taken their first degree or other postgraduate course in a Danish University will also be considered. Full details should be included in the Application.
**Eligibility**: Open to graduates of British nationality only
**Level of Study**: Postdoctorate
**Type**: Scholarship
**Value**: £2,500
**Closing Date**: 30 June
**Additional Information**: www.anglo-danishsociety.org.uk/scholarships

### For further information contact:

**Email**:    scholars@anglo-danishsociety.org.uk

## Anglo-Norse Society

Norwegian Embassy 25, Belgrave Square, London,  SW1X 8QD, United Kingdom.

**Tel**:         (44) 208 452 4843
**Email**:      Secretariat@anglo-norse.org.uk
**Website**:    www.anglo-norse.org.uk/

The Anglo-Norse Society in London is a registered charity for the purpose of promoting better understanding between Britain and Norway through learning about each other's country and way of life.

## The Anglo-Norse Dame Gillian Brown Postgraduate Scholarship

**Purpose**: To help towards the cost for a British student to undertake 1 year of postgraduate study in Norway in the fields of the humanities or social sciences
**Eligibility**: Any person holding a British passport and normally resident in the United Kingdom
**Level of Study**: Postgraduate
**Type**: Scholarship
**Value**: £2,000
**Length of Study**: Up to a year
**Frequency**: Annual
**Study Establishment**: University or equivalent, dependent on the nature of the research
**Country of Study**: Norway

**Application Procedure**: Students wishing to apply should request an application form which will ask for details of their degree results and the project for which they intend to use the scholarship, plus a letter of acceptance from the institution where they wish to pursue their research
**No. of awards offered**: 1
**Closing Date**: 31 March
**Contributor**: A bequest from Dame Gillian Brown and interest on capital built up by the Society
**No. of awards given last year**: 1
**No. of applicants last year**: 1
**Additional Information**: The Anglo-Norse Society also offers two annual grants of up to £500 each that may be used for travel or research related to Norway www.anglo-norse.org.uk/scholarships-grants

### For further information contact:

The Secretary, The Anglo-Norse Society, 25 Belgrave Square, London, SW1X 8QD, United Kingdom.

**Email**:    scholarships@anglo-norse.org.uk

## Appraisal Institute Education Trust

200 W. Madison, Suite 1500, Chicago, IL 60606, United States of America.

**Tel**:         (1) 312 335 4133
**Email**:      educationtrust@appraisalinstitute.org
**Website**:    www.aiedtrust.org

The Appraisal Institute is an international membership association of professional real estate appraisers, with more than 21,000 members and 99 chapters throughout the United States of America, Canada and abroad. Its mission is to support and advance its members as the choice for real estate solutions and uphold professional credentials, standards of professional practice and ethics consistent with the public good.

## Appraisal Institute Education Trust Minorities and Women Education Scholarship

**Purpose**: The Minority and Women Educational Scholarship is geared towards college students working towards a degree in real estate appraisal or a related field. The scholarship is to help offset the cost of tuition

**Eligibility**: Applicant must be a member of a racial, ethnic or gender group underrepresented in the appraisal profession and full- or part-time student enroled-in real estate related courses at a degree-granting college/university or junior college/university. Individuals must have proof a cumulative grade point average of no less than 2.5 on 4.0 scale and have demonstrated financial need. Scholarship award must be used in the same calendar year as awarded by the committee

**Level of Study**: Graduate, Postgraduate

**Type**: Scholarship

**Value**: US$1,000 per person

**Frequency**: Annual

**Country of Study**: United States of America

**Application Procedure**: An official student transcript for all college work completed to date. A 500-word written essay stating why applicant should be awarded the scholarship. Two letters of recommendation from previous employers and/or college professors. An attestation that the scholarship will be applied toward tuition/books expense as stated in the application. Optional: Applicants are asked to include a head and shoulders photograph as scholarship recipients may be profiled in Appraisal Institute newsletter/news releases

**Closing Date**: 15 April

**Funding**: Private

**Additional Information**: Applicants must visit the website www.aiedtrust.org www.appraisalinstitute.org/education/education-resources/scholarships/

## Arc of the United States

1825 K Street, NW, Suite 1200, Washington, DC 20006, United States of America.

**Tel**:        (1) 800 433 5255
**Email**:      info@thearc.org
**Website**:    www.thearc.org

The Arc of the United States advocates for the rights and full participation of all children and adults with intellectual and developmental disabilities. Together with our network of members and affiliation chapters, we improve systems of supports and services, connect families, inspire communities and influence public policy.

### Arc of the United States Research Grant

**Purpose**: To support research leading towards prevention, amelioration or cure of mental retardation

**Eligibility**: Open to United States nationals only

**Level of Study**: Unrestricted

**Type**: Research grant

**Value**: Various amounts up to US$25,000

**Length of Study**: 1 year, with the option of extension

**Frequency**: Annual

**Country of Study**: United States of America

**Application Procedure**: Applicants must submit project authorisation form, budget form, project summary, maximum of 15 double-spaced pages for narrative, and letters of support

**No. of awards offered**: 25

**Closing Date**: 1 April

**Funding**: Private

**No. of awards given last year**: 1

**No. of applicants last year**: 25

**Additional Information**: www.arc.gov/funding/GrantsandFunding.asp

### For further information contact:

Department of Research & Program Services, The Arc PO Box 1047, Arlington, Texas 76004, United States of America.

**Tel**:        (1) 817 261 6003
**Email**:      mwehmeye@metronet.com

## Archaeological Institute of America

### Anna C. & Oliver C. Colburn Fellowships

**Purpose**: To support studies undertaken at the American School of Classical Studies at Athens, Greece for no more than a year.

**Eligibility**: For members of the AIA at the time of application and until the end of the fellowship term. Applicant must be a citizen or permanent resident of the United States or Canada, must be at the pre-doctoral stage or have recently received a PhD (within five years of the date of the application).

**Level of Study**: Graduate

**Type**: Fellowship

**Value**: US$5,500

**Length of Study**: 1 year

**Frequency**: Every other year

**Country of Study**: United States of America or Canada

**Application Procedure**: Apply online: www.archaeological.org/programs/professionals/grants-awards/applications/aia-fellowships/

**No. of awards offered**: 2 Awards

**Closing Date**: 15 January

**Funding**: Foundation

**Additional Information**: www.archaeological.org/programs/professionals/grants-awards/

### For further information contact:

**Email**:   fellowships@archaeological.org

## Archaeology of Portugal Fellowship

**Purpose**: For archaeological research in Portugal, including the Autonomous Regions of the Azores and Madeira
**Eligibility**: Open to scholars of all nations.
**Level of Study**: Graduate
**Type**: Fellowship
**Value**: Varies, US$7,500 maximum
**Length of Study**: 1 year
**Frequency**: Annual
**Country of Study**: United States of America or Canada
**Application Procedure**: Apply online: www.archaeological.org/programs/professionals/grants-awards/applications/aia-fellowships/
**No. of awards offered**: 1 Award
**Closing Date**: 1 November
**Funding**: Foundation
**Additional Information**: www.archaeological.org/programs/professionals/grants-awards/

### For further information contact:

**Email**:   fellowships@archaeological.org

## C. Brian Rose AIA/DAI Exchange Fellowships

**Purpose**: The Archaeological Institute of America is pleased to announce a Fellowship for archaeologists employed by the Deutsches Archäologisches Institut (DAI), or project collaborators who have temporary contracts with the DAI. The purpose of the Fellowship is to encourage and support scholarship of the highest quality on various aspects of archaeology, and to promote contact between North American archaeologists and DAI scholars.
**Eligibility**: Applicants who are archaeologists must have a PhD degree; architects must have their diploma. Both must demonstrate professional competence in archaeology in their applications. Project collaborators must show proof of a long-time participation with a current DAI project by providing a letter of recommendation from a DAI project supervisor.
**Level of Study**: Postgraduate
**Type**: Fellowship
**Application Procedure**: 1. completed online application form. 2. a curriculum vitae, including a list of publications.

3. two references (please note that these are due by the November 1st application deadline). 4. a brief description of DAI project they are involved in, and the nature of their participation. 5. a letter of recommendation from a DAI project supervisor (also due by November 1st)
**Closing Date**: 1 November
**Additional Information**: www.archaeological.org/grant/aia-dai-exchange-fellowship-us/

### For further information contact:

**Tel**:       (1) 857 305 9360
**Email**:   fellowships@archaeological.org

## Harrietand Leon Pomerance Fellowship

**Purpose**: To support an individual project of a scholarly nature, related to Aegean Bronze Age Archaeology
**Eligibility**: For members of the AIA at the time of application and until the end of the fellowship term. Applicant must be a citizen or permanent resident of the United States or Canada, must be at the pre-doctoral stage or have recently received a PhD (within five years of the date of the application).
**Level of Study**: Graduate
**Type**: Fellowship
**Value**: US$5,000
**Length of Study**: 1 year
**Frequency**: annual
**Country of Study**: United States of America or Canada
**Application Procedure**: Apply online: www.archaeological.org/programs/professionals/grants-awards/applications/aia-fellowships/
**No. of awards offered**: 1 Award
**Closing Date**: 1 November
**Funding**: Foundation
**Additional Information**: www.archaeological.org/programs/professionals/grants-awards/

### For further information contact:

**Email**:   fellowships@archaeological.org

## Olivia James Traveling Fellowship

**Purpose**: For archaeological travel and research in Greece (the modern state), Cyprus, the Aegean Islands, Sicily, southern Italy (Campania, Molise, Apulia, Basilicata, and Calabria), Asia Minor (Turkey) or Mesopotamia (that is, the territory between the Tigris and Euphrates rivers, that is modern Iraq and parts of northern Syria and eastern Turkey).
**Eligibility**: For members of the AIA (see website). Applicant must be a citizen of the United States, must be at the

pre-doctoral stage or have recently received a PhD (within five years of the date of the application).
**Level of Study**: Graduate
**Type**: Fellowship
**Value**: US$24,000
**Length of Study**: 1 year
**Frequency**: Annual
**Country of Study**: United States of America
**Application Procedure**: Apply online: www.archaeological.org/programs/professionals/grants-awards/applications/aia-fellowships/
**No. of awards offered**: 1 Award
**Closing Date**: 1 November
**Funding**: Foundation
**Additional Information**: www.archaeological.org/programs/professionals/grants-awards/

**For further information contact:**

**Email**:    fellowships@archaeological.org


## Arctic Institute of North America (AINA)

The University of Calgary, 2500 University Drive North West, ES-1040, Calgary, AB T2N 1N4, Canada.

**Tel**:           (1) 403 220 7515
**Email**:        arctic@ucalgary.ca
**Website**:      www.arctic.ucalgary.ca
**Contact**:      Executive Director


Created in 1945, the Arctic Institute of North America (AINA) is a non-profit membership organization and a multidisciplinary research institute for the University of Calgary.


## Arctic Institute of North America Grants-in-Aid

**Purpose**: To support young investigators and provide funding to augment their research
**Eligibility**: enrolled in or affiliated with a scientist working at a U.S. or Canadian academic institution.
**Level of Study**: Postgraduate
**Type**: Grant
**Value**: Up to C$1,000 which can be used for travel, supplies, equipment and services but not salary or wages
**Length of Study**: Varies
**Frequency**: Annual
**Country of Study**: United States of America

**Application Procedure**: Applicants must submit proposals which must not exceed four double spaced pages. A title, introduction, objectives, methodology, anticipated results, period of performance and proposed use of the AINA award should be clearly stated. The total estimated budget for the project should be provided on a separate page and should clearly identify other anticipated and committed sources and amounts of funding
**Closing Date**: 7 February
**Additional Information**: A report to the committee will be required within one year following the award. Any report or publication resulting from the investigation should include acknowledgement of the AINA Grant-in-Aid programme. One copy of all publications should be sent to ASTIS at the AINA Calgary office for inclusion in the ASTIS database and AINA library arctic.ucalgary.ca/webform/aina-grant-aid-application

**For further information contact:**

Arctic Institute of North America Attn: AINA Grant-in-Aid University of Calgary 2500 University Drive N.W., ES-1040 Calgary, Alberta, Canada T2N 1N4.

**Email**:    arctic@ucalgary.ca


## Aristotle University of Thessaloniki

University Campus, GR-541 24, Thessaloniki, Greece.

**Tel**:        (30) 2310 99 4168, 99 6771
**Email**:      dps@auth.gr
**Website**:    www.auth.gr/services/admin/studies_department.en.php3
**Contact**:    Studies Department


### Summer Intensive Course in modern Greek Language Scholarship

**Subjects**: 4/weeks, 20h/week intensive summer course of modern Greek language classes, plus cultural program Each year mid August to mid September 3 levels (beginners, intermediate, advance) following the common European framework of reference for languages.
**Purpose**: Diffusion of Greek language & culture
**Eligibility**: Nationals of any country; priority given to students of Greek (language, history, art, etc.)
**Level of Study**: Unrestricted
**Type**: Studentship
**Value**: Tuition fee waiver (€324)
**Length of Study**: 4 weeks

**Frequency**: Annual
**Study Establishment**: Aristotle University of Thessaloniki, School of Modern Greek Language
**Country of Study**: Greece
**Application Procedure**: Application form and supporting documents to be sent to the Aristotle University Department of Studies by 28th February
**No. of awards offered**: Varies, decided each year by the Senate
**Closing Date**: 28 February
**Funding**: Government
**No. of awards given last year**: 18
**No. of applicants last year**: 54
**Additional Information**: While the application process, documents and deadline are standard each year, the type and number of awards are subject to change based on funds available and Senate's decision

### For further information contact:

Aristotle University of Thessaloniki, Department of Studies, University Campus, GR-541 24 Thessaloniki Hellas, Greece.

## Arizona Community Foundation

### George F. Wellik Scholarship

**Purpose**: George F. Wellik Scholarship was established to provide a college education for worthy and needy students from Wickenburg, Arizona.
**Eligibility**: High school student graduating from the greater Wickenburg area. Based on financial need and/or academic potential. Attending any 2 or 4 year, private or public college/university or vocational/trade school in the U.S. Open to any field of study. Minimum of 2.5 GPA.
**Level of Study**: Graduate
**Type**: Scholarship
**Value**: US$5,000
**Frequency**: Annual
**Country of Study**: United States of America
**Application Procedure**: Applications for the George F. Wellik Scholarship are available on the Arizona Community Foundation website. To apply, the applicant must register with the foundation. In addition to a completed application, the applicant must also submit the following: two letters of recommendation, one from his/her guidance counselor and one from a high school academic teacher, attesting to his/her academic strengths and determination to succeed at the university; a high school transcript through the seventh semester; a 500- to 700-word essay addressing the topic listed on the application; typed personal statements; verification of SAT and/or ACT test scores; and a Free Application for Federal Student Aid form (FAFSA). The FAFSA is available online at www.fafsa.ed.gov
**Closing Date**: 4 June
**Funding**: Foundation
**Additional Information**: azfoundation.academicworks.com/opportunities/4168

### For further information contact:

2201 E. Camelback Road, Suite 202, Phoenix, AZ 85016, United States of America.

**Tel**:       (1) 800 222 8221
**Email**:    scholarships@swe.org

## Arizona State University College of Business

PO Box 874906, Tempe, AZ 85287-4906, United States of America.

**Tel**:       (1) 602 965 3332
**Email**:    asu.mba@asu.edu
**Website**:  www.cob.asu.edu/mba
**Contact**:  MBA Admissions Officer

### Madbury Road Design Success Award Scholarship

**Purpose**: Madbury Road is offering a US$1,000 scholarship in support designers and architects of the future
**Eligibility**: This is an award that is only available for students currently enrolled at a university or college
**Level of Study**: Professional development
**Type**: Scholarship
**Value**: US$1,000
**Frequency**: Annual
**Country of Study**: Any country
**Application Procedure**: Your full name, telephone number and mailing address. The name of the college or university that you currently attend or will be attending. Proof that you have, either been accepted, or are currently attending the college or university that you specified. The area that you study.
**Closing Date**: 31 March
**Funding**: Private
**Additional Information**: www.madburyroad.com/scholarship/

### For further information contact:

**Email**:    scholarship@madburyroad.com

## The Ship Smart Annual Scholarship

**Purpose**: Ship Smart leads the industry in moving small amounts of high value goods and small shipments of household goods, electronics and artwork

**Eligibility**: Applicants must be current, full-time or part-time students of an accredited, non-accredited institute, truck driving school or other logistics program. They must have a minimum cumulative GPA of 3.0 to become eligible. There is no age requirement.

**Level of Study**: Graduate

**Type**: Scholarship

**Frequency**: Annual

**Country of Study**: United States of America

**Application Procedure**: To apply for the scholarship write a 1,000 word original essay or article, that may not have been posted anywhere on the internet, about an article related to our website. Some topics could be anything related to: 1. Shipping Furniture. 2. Small Moves. 3. Shipping Antiques. 4. Shipping Artwork. 5. Shipping Electronics. 6. Packing and Shipping

**Closing Date**: 12 April

**Funding**: Private

**Additional Information**: www.shipsmart.com/info/shipsmart-scholarship

### For further information contact:

**Email**:     scholarships@shipsmart.com

## Armenian International Women's Association

65 Main St, Watertown, MA 02472, United States of America.

## Armenian International Women

**Purpose**: AIWA annually awards scholarships in honor of Ethel Jaffarian Duffett, Agnes Missirian, Lucy Kasparian Aharonian

**Eligibility**: 1. Female of Armenian Descent. 2. Financial Need. 3. Full-Time Student. 4. Accredited University/College. 5. Junior, Senior, or Graduate Student. 6. 3.2 Minimum GPA. 7. Certified Copy of University/College Transcripts. 8. Two Letters of Recommendation, one from an academic instructor/advisor, one from a community representative. 9. Small (Passport Size) Photograph

**Level of Study**: Graduate

**Type**: Scholarship

**Frequency**: Annual

**Country of Study**: Any country

**Closing Date**: 17 April

**Funding**: Private

**Additional Information**: aiwainternational.org/scholarships-internships/

### For further information contact:

Armenian International Women's Association, Inc. 65 Main St., #3A Watertown, MA 02472, United States of America.

**Email**:     scholarships@aiwainternational.org

## Arthritis Research United Kingdom

Copeman House, St Mary's Court, St Mary's Gate, Chesterfield, S41 7TD, United Kingdom.

**Tel**:           (44) 12 4655 8033
**Email**:       info@arc.org.uk
**Website**:    www.arc.org.uk
**Contact**:    Mr Michael Patnick, Head of Research & Education Funding

The Arthritis Research Campaign (arc) is the fourth largest medical research charity in the United Kingdom, and the only charity in the country dedicated to finding the cause of and cure for arthritis, relying entirely upon voluntary donations to sustain its wide-ranging research and educational programmes.

## Clinical Research Fellowships

**Purpose**: Aim to provide an opportunity for training in clinical and/or laboratory research techniques in a project that demonstrates clear relevance to the aims of Arthritis Research United Kingdom in a centre of excellence in the United Kingdom

**Eligibility**: Open to medical graduates (including orthopaedic surgeons), usually during speciality training, who are expected to register for a higher degree, usually a PhD.

**Level of Study**: Doctorate, Professional development, Research

**Type**: Fellowship

**Value**: Salaries will be according to age and experience on the appropriate clinical salary scale. Applications may also be made for reasonable running costs although tuition fees will not generally be provided

**Length of Study**: 3 years

**Frequency**: Annual

**Study Establishment**: A university, hospital or recognized research institute
**Country of Study**: United Kingdom
**Application Procedure**: Applications for funding are available via an online system accessible from the website
**No. of awards offered**: 17
**Closing Date**: January
**Funding**: Private
**Contributor**: Voluntary charitable contributions
**No. of awards given last year**: 2
**No. of applicants last year**: 17

**For further information contact:**

**Email**:   cdftdr@who.int

## Artist Trust

1835, 12th Ave, Seattle, WA 98122, United States of America.

**Tel**:       (1) 2 064 678 734
**Email**:    info@artisttrust.org
**Website**:  www.artisttrust.org
**Contact**:  Zach Frimmel, Programs Assistant

Artist Trust is a non-profit organization whose sole mission is to support and encourage individual artists working in all disciplines in order to enhance community life throughout Washington state.

## Grants for Artist Projects (GAP)

**Purpose**: GAP awards provide support for artist-generated projects, which can include (but are not limited to) the development, completion or presentation of new work
**Eligibility**: Applicants must be a practicing artist, 18 years of age or older by application deadline date, a generative artist, and a resident of Washington State at the time of application and when the award is granted. Applicants may not be a graduate or undergraduate matriculated student enrolled in any degree program
**Level of Study**: Unrestricted
**Type**: Grant
**Value**: Up to US$1,400
**Frequency**: Annual
**Country of Study**: United States of America
**Application Procedure**: Complete application form, submit work samples, work sample description, resume and WA state ID

**No. of awards offered**: 698
**Closing Date**: February
**Funding**: Government, Commercial, Private, Corporation, Foundation, Individuals
**No. of awards given last year**: 58
**No. of applicants last year**: 698
**Additional Information**: philanthropynewsdigest.org/rfps/rfp10846-artist-trust-accepting-nominations-for-twining-humber-award-for-lifetime-artistic-achievement

**For further information contact:**

1835 12th Avenue, Seattle, WA 98122-2437, United States of America.

**Tel**:       (1) 206 467 8734
**Fax**:       (1) 206 467 9633
**Email**:    heatherjoy@srtisttrust.org

## Irving and Yvonne Twining Humber Award for Lifetime Artistic Achievement

**Purpose**: To reward a female visual artist over the age of 60 from Washington State
**Eligibility**: Artists must be nominated. Nominees must be female, over the age of 60, a Washington State resident and a visual artist who has been practicing for 25 years or more
**Level of Study**: Postgraduate, Unrestricted
**Type**: Award
**Value**: US$10,000
**Frequency**: Annual
**Country of Study**: Any country
**Application Procedure**: Nomination forms are available by mail or online
**No. of awards offered**: Approx. 50
**Closing Date**: 23 March
**Funding**: Government, Commercial, Private, Corporation, Foundation, Individuals
**Contributor**: Mrs Twining Humber
**No. of awards given last year**: 1
**No. of applicants last year**: Approx. 50
**Additional Information**: www.artscouncil.ie/Funds/Artist-in-the-community-scheme/

## Arts Council of Ireland

70 Merrion Square, Dublin 2, Ireland.

**Tel**:       (353) 1 661 1840
**Email**:    info@artscouncil.ie

**Website**:    www.artscouncil.ie
**Contact**:    Ms Tara Byrne, Artists' Support Executive

The Arts Council, the development agency for the arts in Ireland, exists to promote and support the arts. Its core

## Arts Council of Ireland Artist-in-the-Community Scheme

**Purpose**: To enable artists and community groups to work together on projects
**Eligibility**: Open to artists of Irish birth or residence and community groups. The artist must have evidence of having produced a body of work of recognised quality and significance, or in the case of individuals with less experience, demonstrable potential. They need to be able to show evidence of artistic developmental needs, evidence of financial need, including availability of other funding and a likelihood that an award will reach the desired effect. Applicants must be practising artists or arts workers but need not necessarily earn income from their arts practice. They must identify themselves and be recognised by their peers as practising artists
**Level of Study**: Professional development
**Type**: Grant
**Length of Study**: Varies
**Country of Study**: Ireland
**Application Procedure**: Applicants must contact CAFE for application information. Applications will be considered not eligible and returned if the eligibility criteria is not met, if all the support material specified is not included, if funding is requested for activities that have already occurred or will be completed before the closing date and also if the application or supporting documentation is late
**Closing Date**: 30 March
**Contributor**: CAFE

### For further information contact:

70 Merrion Square S, Saint Peter's, Dublin 2, D02 NY52, Ireland.

**Tel**:        (353) 1 473 66 00
**Email**:    support@create-ireland.ie

## Arts Council of Ireland Frameworks Animation Scheme

**Purpose**: To add to the range and scope of Irish animation and encourage new and established animation, which makes use of the medium and is primarily aimed at an adult audience

**Eligibility**: The artist must be an Irish national or permanent resident and have evidence of having produced a body of work of recognised quality and significance, or in the case of individuals with less experience, demonstrable potential. They need to be able to show evidence of artistic developmental needs, evidence of financial need, including availability of other funding and a likelihood that an award will reach the desired effect. Applicants must be practising artists or arts workers but need not necessarily earn income from their arts practice. They must identify themselves and be recognised by their peers as practising artists
**Value**: Approx. €25,000–32,000 to fund up to six animated shorts
**Country of Study**: Ireland
**Application Procedure**: Applicants must send completed applications to Bord Scannán na hÉireann. Applications will be considered not eligible and returned if the eligibility criteria is not met, if all the support material specified is not included, if funding is requested for activities that have already occurred or will be completed before the closing date and also if the application or supporting documentation is late
**Contributor**: The scheme is co-funded by RTÉ, Bord Scannán na hÉireann and The Arts Council
**Additional Information**: Information can be obtained from both the Arts Council and the Bord Scannán na hÉireann

### For further information contact:

70 Merrion Square S, Saint Peter's, Dublin 2, D02 NY52, Ireland.

**Tel**:        (353) 9 156 1398
**Fax**:        (353) 9 156 1405
**Email**:    info@filmboard.ie

## Arts Council of Wales

Museum Place, Cardiff, CF10 3NX, United Kingdom.

**Tel**:        (44) 29 2037 6500
**Email**:    info@artswales.org.uk
**Website**:    www.artswales.org.uk
**Contact**:    Angela Blackburn

The Arts Council of Wales is the national organization with specific responsibility for the funding and development of the arts in Wales. Most of its funds come from the National Assembly for Wales, but it also distributes National Lottery funds to the arts in Wales.

## Artists at Work

**Purpose**: To support businesses and artists to benefit from sharing their workplaces
**Eligibility**: Available for businesses that are interested in exploring the potential of creative collaboration and hosting an artist in residence and for artists keen to develop their practice through working in industry
**Type**: Grant
**Value**: Up to £6,000

### For further information contact:

11-12 Mount Stuart Square, Cardiff CF10 5EE, United Kingdom.

**Tel**: (44) 29 2048 9543
**Email**: info@cywaithcymru.org

## Arts Council of Wales Artform Development Scheme

**Purpose**: To support new talent and ideas in a range of activities eg. platforms of work in process or exploratory productions in mixed art-forms
**Type**: Grant
**Value**: £2,000–10,000
**Country of Study**: Wales
**Application Procedure**: Applicants must submit a completed application. These can be submitted at any time but early notice is needed for major projects. Applicants must contact Performing Arts at the Artform Development Division in Cardiff
**Closing Date**: March

### For further information contact:

**Email**: acw@wilsonarts.com

## Arts Council of Wales Awards for Career Development of Individual Visual Artists and Craftspeople

**Purpose**: Financial assistance for travel, research, the acquisition of new skills and collaboration which extends professional horizons
**Eligibility**: For individual professional visual artists and craftspeople at all stages of career development and whose work shows originality and excellence. For those who live and work in Wales for at least nine months of the year
**Level of Study**: Professional development
**Type**: Grant

**Country of Study**: Wales
**Application Procedure**: Applicants must contact Visual Arts and Craft, Artform Development Division, Cardiff office
**Additional Information**: Smaller awards of up to £500 are also available to emerging visual artists to help establish a studio, research contacts and potential markets

### For further information contact:

**Email**: acw@wilsonarts.com

## Arts Council of Wales Awards for Individual Visual Artists and Craftspeople

**Purpose**: To assist with research and developing skills to undertake a specific project or in developing new work in particular by releasing them from their normal commitments
**Eligibility**: For visual artists and individual craftspeople permanently living in Wales
**Level of Study**: Professional development
**Type**: Bursary
**Frequency**: Twice a year
**Country of Study**: Wales
**Application Procedure**: Applicants must contact Visual Arts and Craft, Artform Development Division, Cardiff office

### For further information contact:

**Email**: acw@wilsonarts.com

## Arts Council of Wales Barclays Stage Partners

**Purpose**: To enable the production and tour of a new theatrical production in Wales
**Type**: Grant
**Value**: Up to £53,000
**Country of Study**: Wales
**Application Procedure**: Applicants must contact the Arts Council for guidelines
**Funding**: Commercial

### For further information contact:

**Email**: acw@wilsonarts.com

## Arts Council of Wales Community Touring Night Out

**Purpose**: To support community-based organizations throughout Wales with access to suitable premises, who wish to promote occasional professional performing arts events for their locality

**Eligibility**: Eligibility for promoters of events is restricted to community organizations within Wales. Schools and colleges may participate if offering a service to the wider community that is beyond this normal educational role. Eligibility for performers governed by this ability to provide a professional service at an affordable price regardless of nationality and location

**Type**: Fees to performers

**Value**: Variable

**Country of Study**: Wales

**Application Procedure**: Applications may be submitted at any time to the Community Touring unit in Cardiff and must come from the local promoters of the event. The single-page application form is obtainable from the unit by post or may be found on the website at www.nightout.org.uk

**No. of awards offered**: 206

**Funding**: Government

**Contributor**: 51% from National Assembly of Wales, 49% box office supported by local authority guarantees

**No. of awards given last year**: 392

**No. of applicants last year**: 206

**Additional Information**: Community-based organizations dedicated to the arts who wish to plan more than five events in a year or more than 6 months ahead should seek advice from their local ACW office or the Community Touring Manager. This scheme assists community organizations by making professional performances available at a fraction of their real price. It covers all aspects of the performing arts

### For further information contact:

Community Touring Manager, Community Touring Unit, Arts Council of Wales, Museum Place, Cardiff, CF1 3NX, Wales, United Kingdom.

**Email**:    acw@wilsonarts.com

## Arts Council of Wales Music Projects Grants

**Purpose**: To help with either CD production of works by Welsh composers or books and journals concerned with Welsh music

**Type**: Grant

**Country of Study**: Any country

**Application Procedure**: Applications are invited from publishers and recording companies and should be sent to Performing Arts, Artform Development Division, Cardiff office

### For further information contact:

**Email**:    acw@wilsonarts.com

## Arts Council of Wales Performing Arts Projects

**Purpose**: To enable production by professional artists based in Wales working with a presenting organisation

**Eligibility**: Partnerships are a particular feature of this scheme and the involvement of a venue or presenter is essential. Applications may come from groups of artists, arts organisations or presenters

**Type**: Grant

**Value**: Grants range from £5,000–40,000. Quality, innovation and potential to enrich programming for the public will be priorities

**Country of Study**: Any country

**Application Procedure**: Applications should be sent to Performing Arts, Artform Development Division in Cardiff

**Closing Date**: 1 February

**Additional Information**: Venue commissions of artists may be one form of application

### For further information contact:

**Email**:    acw@wilsonarts.com

## Arts Council of Wales Pilot Training Grants Scheme

**Purpose**: Provides grants to arts organisations and owner managers in Wales for members of staff to attend or deliver training in IT, finance, marketing, management and other vocational skills

**Level of Study**: Professional development

**Type**: Grant

**Value**: The maximum grant awarded will be £5,000 and the scheme will provide a maximum of 45% of the total cost of attending or delivering training

**Country of Study**: Wales

**Application Procedure**: Applications must be submitted to Access Development Division, Cardiff Office

**Additional Information**: Training supported by this scheme must be completed and a monitoring report form submitted to ACW

### For further information contact:

**Email**:    acw@wilsonarts.com

## Community Dance Wales Grants

**Purpose**: To promote professional interest in community dance in Wales

**Level of Study**: Professional development

**Type**: Grant

**Value**: £25,342
**Frequency**: Annual
**Country of Study**: United Kingdom
**Funding**: Government

**For further information contact:**

**Tel**:      (44) 1495 224425
**Fax**:      (44) 1495 226457
**Email**:    roonem@caerphilly.gov.uk

## Cultural Enterprise Service Grant

**Purpose**: To provide financial assistance in the purchase of equipment, software and consultancy
**Level of Study**: Professional development
**Type**: Grant
**Value**: £10,000
**Frequency**: Annual
**Country of Study**: United Kingdom
**Application Procedure**: See the website
**Funding**: Government
**Contributor**: The Arts Council of Wales

**For further information contact:**

**Tel**:      (44) 29 2034 3205
**Fax**:      (44) 29 2034 5436
**Email**:    stephan@cultural-enterprise.com

## Good Ideas-Artist Led Projects

**Purpose**: To fulfil the needs of artists by providing funding for projects that develop their artistic practice and to help alleviate the associated administration
**Eligibility**: Open to artists who have project initiatives that involve community collaboration and that demonstrate innovative thinking and artistic practice
**Type**: Grant
**Value**: £6,000

**For further information contact:**

**Email**:    info@cywaithcymru.org

## International Opportunities Funding

**Purpose**: To encourage professional arts practitioners and presenters
**Type**: Funding support

**For further information contact:**

Wales Arts International, 28 Park place, Cardiff CF10 3Qe, United Kingdom.

**Tel**:      (44) 29 20393037
**Fax**:      (44) 29 20398779
**Email**:    Nikki.Morgan@wai.org.uk

## Vital Knowledge-Artists' Mentoring Scheme

**Purpose**: To encourage new applicants to gain experience and mentoring in all aspects of residency work
**Eligibility**: Open to candidates who would benefit from working alongside an artist in residence on one of the Cywaith Cymru
**Type**: Grant
**Value**: £500

**For further information contact:**

**Tel**:      (44) 29 2048 9543
**Email**:    info@cywaithcymru.org

## Wales One World Film Festival Grant

**Purpose**: To present audiences with the best in world cinema through the Festival
**Level of Study**: Professional development
**Type**: Grant
**Value**: £24,936
**Length of Study**: 2 years
**Frequency**: Annual
**Country of Study**: United Kingdom
**Application Procedure**: See the website
**Funding**: Government
**Contributor**: The Media Agency for Wales and the Arts Council of Wales

**For further information contact:**

**Tel**:      (44) 1239 615066
**Fax**:      (44) 1239 615066
**Email**:    sa3657@eclipse.co.uk

## Welsh Independent Dance Grant

**Purpose**: To develop a successful dance sector in Wales
**Level of Study**: Professional development
**Type**: Grant
**Length of Study**: £71,296

**Frequency**: Annual
**Country of Study**: United Kingdom
**Application Procedure**: See the website
**Funding**: Government
**Contributor**: The Arts Council of Wales
**Additional Information**: www.culturenet.hr/default.aspx?id=35969

**For further information contact:**

Tel:       (44) 29 2038 7314
Fax:       (44) 29 2038 7314
Email:     welshindance@btconnect.com

# Arts International

251 Park Avenue South, 5th Floor, New York, NY 10010-7302, United States of America.

Tel:       (1) 212 674 9744
Email:     info@artsinternational.org
Website:   www.artsinternational.org
Contact:   Mr Adam Bernstein, Director, Advised Funds & Regranting Programs

Arts International is an independent, non-profit, contemporary arts organization dedicated to global, cultural interchange. It carries out its work through developing global networks and partnerships, information services and grantmaking opportunities.

### Croatian Arts and Cultural Exchange Croatia

**Purpose**: FACE Croatia is designed to encourage tax deductible (for United States tax payers) donor advised contributions from private and public sources including individuals, private foundations, corporations and public sector donors. FACE Croatia maintains an active database of information on Croatian artists, arts and culture
**Eligibility**: FACE Croatia has two funding categories: Croatian Arts and Culture Projects, and United States/Croatian Cultural Exchange. 1. Croatian Arts and Culture Projects Grants. Any Croatian organization that qualifies as a charity under Croatian law is eligible (museums, galleries, theaters, etc.). 2. Croatian based non-governmental organizations (NGO's) engaged in arts and culture activity in Croatia are eligible to apply. 3. The program is open to any arts discipline and/or cultural activity. 4. Individual artists may not make

direct application to the program and must be sponsored by an eligible organization
**Level of Study**: Unrestricted
**Type**: Arts discipline or cultural activity
**Value**: Variable
**Length of Study**: Variable
**Study Establishment**: As approved. Typically museum, art gallery, theatre
**Country of Study**: United States of America and Croatia
**Application Procedure**: Proposals must include a narrative and budget, an organizational narrative and budget, evidence of non-profit status, and three letters of recommendation from professionals in the field
**Funding**: Private
**Contributor**: Heathcote Art Foundation

**For further information contact:**

CEC ArtsLink, 291 Broadway, 14th Floor, New York, NY 10007, United States of America.

Email:     al@cecartslink.org

# Arts NSW

Level 5, 323 Castlereagh Street, Sydney, NSW 2000, Australia.

Tel:       (61) 1800 358 594
Email:     arts.funding@arts.nsw.gov.au
Website:   www.arts.nsw.gov.au

Arts NSW is part of the NSW Department of the Arts, Sport and Recreation. Arts NSW advises the Minister for the Arts on all aspects of the arts and cultural activity. Arts NSW works closely with the state's 8 major cultural institutions, providing policy advice to Government on their operations. The institutions manage significant cultural heritage collections and provide services and programmes throughout the state and beyond.

### Asialink Residency Program

**Purpose**: To promote cultural understanding, information exchange and artistic endeavour between Australia and Asian countries
**Eligibility**: Open to Australian citizens or permanent residents who have at least 3 years professional experience in their field
**Level of Study**: Unrestricted

**Type**: Grant
**Value**: A travel grant of US$6,000–US$12,000 is provided to each resident to assist with residency-related expenses including airfares, accommodation, language lessons, living expenses, materials and production costs. The amount awarded is reflective of the residency period
**Length of Study**: 3 months
**Application Procedure**: Check website for further details
**Closing Date**: 1 March
**Contributor**: Arts NSW, in association with the Asialink Centre
**Additional Information**: adb.anu.edu.au/biography/landa-david-paul-paul-14142

## For further information contact:

Arts Program, The Asialink Centre, The University of Melbourne, Sidney Myer Asia Centre, Parkville VIC 3010, Australia.

**Tel**:    (61) 3 8344 4800
**Fax**:    (61) 3 9347 1768
**Email**:    arts@asialink.unimelb.edu.au

## David Paul Landa Memorial Scholarships for Pianists

**Eligibility**: Open to the Australian citizens currently residing in New South Wales or holding residence visas who have been residents of New South Wales for two consecutive years
**Level of Study**: Unrestricted
**Type**: Scholarship
**Value**: AU$25,000
**Frequency**: Every 2 years
**Application Procedure**: Applicants must forward the completed application form (and one copy of it), two copies of all written supporting material, single copies of other supporting material, the completed EFT authorization form and, if applicable, two copies of the completed RCTI to Program Support
**Additional Information**: Previous recipients of Arts NSW's fellowships and scholarships are ineligible to apply for the same award twice www.create.nsw.gov.au/uncategorized/indigenous-history-fellowship/

## For further information contact:

David Paul Landa Memorial Scholarship for Pianists, Musica Viva Australia, PO Box 1687, Strawberry Hills, NSW, 2012, Australia.

**Tel**:    (61) 2 8394 6666
**Fax**:    (61) 2 9698 3878
**Email**:    musicaviva@mva.org.au

## New South Wales Indigenous History Fellowship

**Purpose**: To assist a person living in New South Wales to research and produce a work on a subject of historical interest relating to New South Wales from an Indigenous point of view
**Eligibility**: Open to the candidates who may be independent historians, or historians working in conjunction with indigenous communities
**Level of Study**: Unrestricted
**Type**: Fellowship
**Value**: AU$20,000
**Length of Study**: 2 years
**Frequency**: Every 2 years
**Application Procedure**: Applicants must submit form with details of the proposal and their qualifications and experience details. Check website for further details
**Closing Date**: May
**Additional Information**: The fellowship will be administered by the History Council of New South Wales www.sl.nsw.gov.au/about-library/awards/nsw-premiers-history-awards/nsw-premiers-history-awards-nomination-form-and

## For further information contact:

History Council of New South Wales Inc., PO Box R1737, Royal Exchange, NSW 1225, Australia.

**Tel**:    (61) 2 9252 8715
**Fax**:    (61) 2 9252 8716
**Email**:    scholarship@sl.nsw.gov.au

## New South Wales Premier's History Awards

**Purpose**: To establish values and standards in historical research and publication and promote the excellence in the interpretation of history
**Eligibility**: Open only to the citizens of Australia
**Level of Study**: Unrestricted
**Type**: Award
**Value**: AU$15,000 each for 5 categories
**Frequency**: Annual
**Application Procedure**: Check website for further details
**Closing Date**: 8 April
**Additional Information**: Nominees may enter a published book or ebook in only one of the following categories: Australian History Prize; General History Prize; New South Wales Community and Regional History Prize; Young People's History Prize. Nominees may enter a non-print media work such as a film, television, or radio program, a DVD or website in one or both of the following categories (if appropriate): Young People's History Prize; Multimedia

History Prize. (Note: If entering into both categories, only one nomination form needs to be completed.) All works must have been first published, produced, performed or made publicly available between 1 April and 31 March belvoir.com.au/media-release/philip-parsons-fellowship-emerging-playwrights/

**For further information contact:**

Corner of Macquarie Street and Shakespeare Place, Sydney NSW 2000, Australia.

**Tel:** (61) 2 9273 1605 or (61) 2 9273 1582
**Email:** awards@sl.nsw.gov.au

## Philip Parsons Young Playwright's Award

**Purpose**: To honor a playwright living in NSW for an original and compelling theatrical voice
**Eligibility**: Writers must be under 35 years of age, based in NSW, and have had a play produced between 1 June and 31 May either in Australia or abroad. Shortlisted writers will be asked to submit a treatment of up to five pages for a proposed new work
**Level of Study**: Unrestricted
**Type**: Scholarship
**Value**: AU$12,500
**Frequency**: Annual
**Application Procedure**: Check website for further details
**Closing Date**: October
**Additional Information**: Please check website for more details

**For further information contact:**

18 & 25 Belvoir, St Surry Hills, NSW 2010, Australia.

**Tel:** (61) 2 8396 6242; 407 163 921
**Email:** elly@belvoir.com.au

## Western Sydney Artists

**Purpose**: To support the creative development of new work or professional development by Western Sydney artists
**Eligibility**: Open to professional artists working in music or literature who are the residents of, or whose practice is located primarily in, Western Sydney
**Level of Study**: Unrestricted
**Type**: Fellowship
**Value**: AU$5,000–25,000
**Country of Study**: Any country
**Application Procedure**: Check website for further details
**Closing Date**: 14 September

**Additional Information**: www.aaronsiskind.org/grant.html

**For further information contact:**

**Email:** mail@create.nsw.gov.au

# Artwork Archive

## Aaron Siskind Foundation - Individual Photographer's Fellowship

**Purpose**: The Aaron Siskind Foundation is offering a limited number of Individual Photographer's Fellowship grants of up to US$15,000 each, for artists working in photography and photo-based art
**Eligibility**: Work must be based on the idea of still-based photography, but can include digital imagery, installations, documentary projects, and photo-generated print media. Doctoral candidates considered on a case-by-case basis. 1. Applicants must be at least 21 years of age. Students enrolled in a college degree program are not eligible to apply. 2. Previous IPF recipients are not currently being considered for new awards
**Level of Study**: Postgraduate
**Type**: Fellowship
**Value**: US$15,000
**Frequency**: Annual
**Country of Study**: Any country
**Closing Date**: 31 May
**Funding**: Private
**Additional Information**: en.ashinaga.org/apply/aai/

**For further information contact:**

Aaron Siskind Foundation, c/o School of Visual Arts, MFA Photo Dept. 209 East 23rd Street, New York, NY 10010, United States of America.

**Email:** grant@aaronsiskind.org

# Ashinaga

## Ashinaga Scholarships

**Purpose**: Ashinaga is sponsoring scholarships to bereaved undergraduate Africans to Study in Japan, United States of America and the United Kingdom, Applicants are able to participate in the two Ashinaga preparatory programs before attending university

**Eligibility**: 1. Applicants should have a citizenship in any one of the countries listed below and pursued high school are eligible. 2. Applicants who have lost one or both parents (can submit an official document proving). 3. Applicants are able to participate in the two Ashinaga preparatory programs before attending university. 4. Students are willing to contribute to society in Africa after graduating from university and have no dependents who could interfere with academic progress and be in good condition of health and capable of studying abroad

**Level of Study**: Graduate

**Type**: Scholarship

**Frequency**: Annual

**Country of Study**: Any country

**Application Procedure**: 1. Have lost one or both parents. 2. Have completed secondary school and passed national secondary school examination (technical and vocational degrees not accepted) within the last two years (any date after 1st September 2017, including all of 2018 and 2019) or will have completed secondary school and received final exam results before February 28th. 3. Were born after 1st September. 4. Have an outstanding academic performance at high school and were amongst the top students in their class. 5. Be committed to returning home, or to Sub-Saharan Africa, and contribute to society in Sub-Saharan Africa after graduating from university.

**Closing Date**: August

**Funding**: Private

**Additional Information**: Citizens of the following Sub-Saharan African countries: a). English speaking: Uganda, Rwanda, Kenya, Ethiopia, Tanzania, Ghana, Namibia, Zimbabwe, Zambia, Malawi, Sudan, Botswana, South Africa, Lesotho, Swaziland, Mauritius, Somalia, Nigeria, The Gambia, Cape Verde, Mozambique, Guinea Bissau, Angola. b). French-speaking: Côte d'Ivoire, Senegal, Benin, Burundi, Gabon, Mali, Burkina Faso, Mauritania, DR Congo, Republic of Congo, Djibouti, Cameroon, Togo, Madagascar, Comoros www.arts ac.uk/study-at-ual/fees-and-funding/scholarships-search/ashley-family-foundation-scholarship

### For further information contact:

1-6-8 Hirakawa-cho, Chiyoda-Ku, Tokyo 102-8639, Japan.

**Email**: admissions.en@ashinaga.org

## Ashley Family Foundation

6 Trull Farm Buildings, Trull, Tetbury, GL8 8SQ, United Kingdom.

**Tel**: (44) 3030 401 005
**Email**: info@ashleyfamilyfoundation.org.uk

**Website**: www.ashleyfamilyfoundation.org.uk
**Contact**: The Administrator

The Ashley Family Foundation (formerly The Laura Ashley Foundation) is a United Kingdom registered charity, founded by Sir Bernard Ashley and his wife Laura Ashley following the success of the Laura Ashley brand.

## Ashley Family Foundation MA Photography Scholarship

**Eligibility**: To be eligible for the Ashley Family Foundation MA Photography Scholarship students must be: ordinarily resident in the United Kingdom; and considered Home status. Accepted on the full-time MA Photography course at London College of Communication, commencing January. A graduate, having already gained a first or 2:1 in a Bachelor's degree from a Higher Education institution, or an HE accredited Further Education institution able to demonstrate substantial equivalent and applicable experience

**Type**: Scholarship

**Value**: £10,890

**Frequency**: Annual

**Study Establishment**: London College of Communication

**Country of Study**: United Kingdom

**Closing Date**: 7 November

**Additional Information**: www.asianculturalcouncil.org/our-work/programs/fellowships-and-grants/individual-fellowship

### For further information contact:

Scholarships & Bursaries, SFS, University of the Arts London, 272 High Holborn, Holborn, London WC1V 7EY, United Kingdom.

**Tel**: (44) 20 7514 8080
**Email**: funding@arts.ac.uk

## Asian Cultural Council (ACC)

6 West 48th Street, 12th floor, New York, NY 10036-1802, United States of America.

**Tel**: (1) 2 524 5032, 2 524 5033/5024
**Email**: acc@accny.org
**Website**: www.asianculturalcouncil.org
**Contact**: Miho Walsh, Executive Director

The Asian Cultural Council (ACC) is a foundation that supports cultural exchange in the visual and performing arts between the United States and the countries of Asia. The emphasis of the ACC's programme is on providing individual fellowships to artists, scholars and specialists from Asia undertaking research, study and creative work in the United States. Grants are also made to United States citizens pursuing similar work in Asia.

## Asian Cultural Council Humanities Fellowship Program

**Purpose**: To assist American scholars, graduate students and specialists in the humanities to undertake research, training and study in Asia

**Eligibility**: 1. All nationalities. Meeting AIT's English Proficiency Requirement (i.e. IELTS-Academic or AIT EET score of 5.0 or above for Master and 5.5 for Doctoral program). 3. Having four-year Bachelor's degree from a recognized university. 4. Having a master's degree from recognized university for PhD applicants and should have a Cumulative GPA of 3.50 in their Master's degree and 2.75 in their undergraduate program from top universities.

**Level of Study**: Graduate, Postdoctorate, Postgraduate, Predoctorate, Professional development, Research, Unrestricted

**Type**: Fellowship or Grant

**Value**: Varies

**Length of Study**: 1–9 months

**Frequency**: Annual

**Country of Study**: United States of America or other countries if appropriate

**Application Procedure**: Applicants should send a brief description of the activity for which assistance is being sought to the Council

**No. of awards offered**: 49 (Humanities Program only)

**Closing Date**: 10 June

**Funding**: Government, Private, Foundation, Individuals

**Contributor**: The JDR 3rd Fund and the Andrew W. Mellon Foundation

**No. of awards given last year**: 11 (Humanities Program only)

**No. of applicants last year**: 49 (Humanities Program only)

**Additional Information**: The programme also supports American and Asian scholars participating in international conferences, exhibitions, visiting professorships and similar projects. Please see the website for further details www.asianculturalcouncil.org.hk/en/app/information_and_deadline www.ait.ac.th/admissions/scholarships/ait-fellowship/

### For further information contact:

AIT Admissions Office.

**Email**:    admissions@ait.ac.th

## Associated General Contractors of America (AGC)

2300 Wilson Boulevard, Suite 300, Arlington, VA 22201, United States of America.

**Tel**:        (1) 548 3118, 800 242 1767
**Email**:     info@agc.org
**Website**:   www.agc.org

The Associated General Contractors of America (AGC), the voice of the construction industry, is an organization of qualified construction contractors and industry-related companies dedicated to skill, integrity and responsibility. Operating in partnership with its chapters, the association provides a full range of services satisfying the needs and concerns of its members, thereby improving the quality of construction and protecting the public interest.

## Associated General Contractors of America The Saul Horowitz, Jr. Memorial Graduate Award

**Purpose**: To provide financial assistance to students who wish to pursue higher studies

**Eligibility**: Open to applicants enroled or planning to enroll, in a Master's or Doctoral level construction or civil engineering programme as a full-time student

**Level of Study**: Doctorate, Postgraduate

**Type**: Scholarship

**Value**: US$7,500. Paid in 2 installments of US$3,750

**Length of Study**: Up to 5 years

**Frequency**: Annual

**Country of Study**: United States of America

**Application Procedure**: Applications will only be accepted online. Apply online at scholarship.agc.org. Applicants must send an email to foundation@agc.org

**Closing Date**: 3 November

## Association for Canadian Studies in the United States

1317 F Street NW Suite 920, Washington, DC 20004-1151, United States of America.

**Tel**:        (1) 202 393 2580
**Email**:     info@acsus.org
**Website**:   www.acsus.org
**Contact**:   Publication Award Committee

## Distinguished Dissertation Award

**Purpose**: To recognize the best dissertation successfully defended in the two years prior to the Biennial conference that deals substantially or wholly with some aspect of Canada or Canadian Studies

**Eligibility**: Doctoral dissertations written at Universities in the United States within the two years before the Biennial conference at which the award will be made

**Level of Study**: Doctorate

**Type**: Cash prize

**Value**: US$500 and expenses to attend the Biennial conference

**Frequency**: Every 2 years

**Country of Study**: United States of America

**Application Procedure**: The nomination must be accompanied by two letters of support, one from the student's dissertation advisor and one from a second referee. The advisor and referee need not be members of ACSUS. Supporting Materials. Each nomination should be accompanied by a copy of the dissertation, a dissertation abstract not to exceed 500 words (typed, double-spaced), and a one-page resume of the nominee. The successful nominee's dissertation should represent original work that makes a significant contribution to the nominee's discipline and to the study of Canada. The dissertation must contain at least 50% content on Canada; the topic may, however, be comparative in nature. The dissertation will be judged on substantive and methodological quality, originality of thought, and clarity

**No. of awards offered**: 2

**Closing Date**: 1 August

**Funding**: Individuals

**Contributor**: Membership dues and royalties coming to the Association for Canadian Studies in the United States

**No. of awards given last year**: 1

**No. of applicants last year**: 2

**Additional Information**: www.acsus.org/programs/distinguished-dissertation-award

### For further information contact:

ACSUS Executive Director, 520 Park Hall, North Campus, University at Buffalo-SUNY, United States of America.

**Tel**: (1) 716 645 8440
**Fax**: (1) 716 645 2166

## Donner Medal in Canadian Studies

**Purpose**: The Donner Medal in Canadian Studies is presented biennially by The Association for Canadian Studies in the United States (ACSUS) for distinguished achievement, scholarship and program innovation in the area of Canadian Studies in the United States

**Eligibility**: The recipient is selected by a committee of members of the Association after nominations have been publicly solicited. Nominees can include a person in any field who has made a significant contribution to Canadian studies in the United States during a reasonable period of residence in the United States, even if no longer a resident. Current officers of ACSUS are ineligible for consideration. The primary criterion for selection is contribution to Canadian studies in the United States. The recipient shall have been active in and made contributions in at least one of the following categories: teaching, scholarship, administration, public affairs

**Level of Study**: Doctorate

**Type**: Honorific

**Frequency**: Every 2 years

**Country of Study**: United States of America

**No. of awards offered**: 1

**Closing Date**: 1 August

**Funding**: Government, Foundation, Individuals

**Contributor**: Individual membership dues and royalties from publications; some government grants; Donner Foundation

**No. of awards given last year**: 1

**No. of applicants last year**: 1

**Additional Information**: www.acsus.org/programs/donner-medal

### For further information contact:

**Tel**: (1) 716 645 8440
**Fax**: (1) 716 645 2166

## Association for Spina Bifida and Hydrocephalus (ASBAH)

ASBAH House, 42 Park Road, Peterborough, Cambridgeshire, PE1 2UQ, United Kingdom.

**Tel**: (44) 1733 555 988, 0845 450 7755
**Email**: info@asbah.org
**Website**: www.mencap.org.uk
**Contact**: Rylance

The Association for Spina Bifida and Hydrocephalus (ASBAH) is a voluntary organization that works for people with spina bifida and hydrocephalus. The charity lobbies for improvements in legislation and provides advisory and support services to clients and their families or carers, in addition to supplying information to professionals and sponsoring medical, social and educational research.

## Association for Spina Bifida and Hydrocephalus Research Grant

**Purpose**: To support research in an area directly related to spina bifida and/or hydrocephalus, and to explore ways of improving the quality of life for people with these conditions through medical, scientific, educational and social research

**Eligibility**: Applicants must be resident in the United Kingdom

**Level of Study**: Postgraduate

**Value**: Varies

**Length of Study**: Varies

**Frequency**: Dependent on funds available

**Study Establishment**: Varies

**Country of Study**: United Kingdom

**Application Procedure**: Applicants must make an initial enquiry to the Chief Executive. If the proposed research is considered to be interesting, the applicant will be asked to complete an application form. Applications must be submitted on time to the committees, which meet in February and September to October

**No. of awards offered**: 1

**Closing Date**: 1 August

**Funding**: Private, Trusts, Individuals

**Contributor**: Charitable donations

**No. of awards given last year**: 1

**No. of applicants last year**: 1

**Additional Information**: Award subjects: biology and life sciences; economics; medicine and surgery; social sciences; teacher training and education; theology and religious studies

## Association of American Geographers (AAG)

1710 16th Street NW, Washington, DC 20009-3198, United States of America.

**Tel**:        (1) 202 234 1450
**Email**:   cmannozzi@aag.org
**Website**:   www.aag.org
**Contact**:   Dr Patricia Solis, Director of Outreach and Strategic Initiatives

The Association of American Geographers (AAG) is a -non-profit organization founded in 1904 to advance professional studies in geography and to encourage the application of geographic research in business, education and government. The AAG was amalgamated with the American Society of Professional Geographers (ASPG).

## Association of American Geographers NSF International Geographical Union Conference Travel Grants

**Purpose**: To provide Travel Grants to the IGU conference

**Eligibility**: All scientists employed by United States agencies, firms and academic institutions may apply for support. All grantees must: be citizens or hold permanent residency in the United States of America, be registered for the main international congress or main regional conference even if their presentations are scheduled for a symposium or study group, and travel via a United States carrier in accordance with United States government regulations

**Level of Study**: Professional development

**Type**: Grant

**Value**: US$1,250 each to junior scholars, including graduate students and US$1,000 each to senior scholars

**Frequency**: Annual

**Country of Study**: As applicable

**Application Procedure**: Applications must be submitted digitally using the online application form provided in website

**Closing Date**: 31 May

**Contributor**: National Science Foundation

**Additional Information**: Please see the website for further details www.aag.org/cs/grantsawards/igutravel

### For further information contact:

**Email**:        psolis@aag.org

## Visiting Geographical Scientist Program

**Purpose**: To stimulate interest in geography

**Eligibility**: To qualify for the program, at least one-half of the institutions hosting a visiting scientist during the academic year must have active chapters of Gamma Theta Upsilon (an active chapter is one that has reported initiates in the past 2 years)

**Level of Study**: Professional development

**Type**: Grant

**Value**: US$100 per institutional visit to each visiting scientist and will reimburse the visitor up to US$600 for travel costs to and from the area of the institutions visited

**Frequency**: Annual

**Study Establishment**: Institution with an active chapter of Gamma Theta Upsilon

**Country of Study**: United States of America

**Application Procedure**: Applicants must write to Oscar Laron, VGSP Coordinator, at the main organization address at olarson@aag.org

**Contributor**: Gamma Theta Upsilon (GTU), the International Geographical Honor Society

**Additional Information**: The VGSP requires one scientist to visit two or more institutions over a one to three-day period. Please see the website for further details www.aag.org/cs/vgsp www.aag.org/vgsp

## Association of Anaesthetists of Great Britain and Ireland

9 Bedford Square, London, WC1B 3RA, United Kingdom.

**Tel**: (44) 20 7631 1650
**Email**: 100567.3364@compuserve.com
**Website**: www.ncl.ac.uk/2nanaes/aagbi.html
**Contact**: Honorary Secretary

The Association of Anaesthetists of Great Britain and Ireland encourages its members to participate in research to increase knowledge, to improve standards of anaesthesia and to enhance the standing of the speciality. It also aims to enable members to travel to centres of excellence throughout the world to increase their expertise in clinical work, teaching or research so that there may be benefit to members, trainees and patients at home.

## Baxter Travelling Fellowships, Research Grants, Travel Grants

**Eligibility**: Open to members in any category of the Association

**Level of Study**: Unrestricted

**Value**: Up to £2,500 (Baxter Travelling Fellowship), up to £5,000 (Research Grants), up to £500 (Travel Grants)

**Length of Study**: Unspecified duration

**Country of Study**: Other

**Application Procedure**: Application form is required

**Additional Information**: There are also special Travel Grants to Third World Countries. Travel Grants are not awarded for attendance at a meeting of a learned society, but may be considered for extensions of such a journey. They may be given for study or for assistance in undertaking an approved teaching tour. Recipients of Travel Fellowships are expected to prepare a report

### For further information contact:

**Email**: Education_Grants@baxter.com

## Association of Clinical Pathologists

189 Dyke Road, East Sussex, Hove, BN3 1TL, United Kingdom.

**Tel**: (44) 1273 775 700
**Email**: info@pathologists.org.uk
**Website**: www.pathologists.org.uk
**Contact**: Administrative Assistant

The Association of Clinical Pathologists promotes the practice of clinical pathology by running postgraduate education courses and national scientific meetings and has a membership of 2,000 worldwide.

## Student Research Fund

**Purpose**: To encourage undergraduates to undertake some research within laboratory medicine, to raise the profile of laboratory medicine within the minds of undergraduates and to aid in recruitment of young graduates

**Level of Study**: Graduate

**Type**: Scholarship

**Value**: Up to £150 per week for a maximum of six weeks (Funding of a small project), £5,000 maximum (Financial sponsorship to help support living expenses during their extra undergraduate year), up to £1,000 (Funding for the cost of consumables). See the website for details:

**Frequency**: Annual

**Country of Study**: Any country

**Application Procedure**: Applicants should complete the relevant application form, including a brief statement of not more than 400 words outlining their interest in laboratory medicine, and include a full curriculum vitae. Applications should include details of the work to be undertaken as part of the project or during the BSc and be supported in writing by the project supervisor, or by the Head of Department in which the student will be placed

**No. of awards offered**: 5

**Closing Date**: 12 April

**Contributor**: Association of Clinical Pathologists

**No. of awards given last year**: 3

**No. of applicants last year**: 5

**Additional Information**: Please return completed form by post to ACP Postgraduate Education Secretary, and also by email to rachel@pathologists.org.uk

### For further information contact:

**Email**: rachel@pathologists.org.uk

## Association of Flight Attendants

### Association of Flight Attendants Annual Scholarship

**Purpose**: This award is for United States high school seniors who are dependents of an Association of Flight Attendants member. Students must rank in the top 15% of their class, and must have or expect to have excellent SAT and ACT scores

**Eligibility**: 1. Must be a graduating high school senior at time of application. 2. Must be a United States citizen. 3. Must be ranked in the top 15% of his/her high school class. 4. Must be the dependent of an Association of Flight Attendants member. 5. Must have, or expect to have, excellent SAT or ACT scores. 6. This award is for United States students

**Level of Study**: Graduate

**Type**: Scholarship

**Value**: US$5,000

**Frequency**: Annual

**Country of Study**: United States of America

**Application Procedure**: Apply online: cdn.afacwa.org/docs/afa/afa-scholarship-application.pdf

**Closing Date**: 10 April

**Funding**: Foundation

#### For further information contact:

**Email**:    scholarships@swe.org

## Association of Management Development Institutions in South Asia (AMDISA)

University of Hyderabad Campus, Central University, Post Office Gachibowli, Hyderabad, Telangana 500 046, India.

**Tel**:          (91) 40 64545226, 40 64543774
**Email**:      amdisa@amdisa.org
**Website**:   www.amdisa.org
**Contact**:   Executive Director

Association of Management Development Institutions in South Asia (AMDISA) was established in 1988, with the initiative of leading management development institutions in the SAARC region. It is the only association that networks management development centres across 8 nations and promotes partnership between business schools, business leaders and policy administrators for enhancing the quality and effectiveness of management education in South Asia.

## Association of Management Development Institutions in South Asia Doctoral Fellowships

**Purpose**: To contribute to the development of South Asian academic perspectives, networks and communities in management and related areas

**Eligibility**: Open to citizens of any South Asian Commonwealth member country who are registered PhD scholars in a recognized university and are not more than 40 years of age

**Level of Study**: Doctorate

**Type**: Fellowship

**Value**: £1,500–4,500

**Country of Study**: Commonwealth countries

**Application Procedure**: Applications must have the applicant's name and contact co-ordinates, proof of registration as PhD scholar, curriculum vitae with list of publications and confidential recommendation letters

**Closing Date**: 31 December

#### For further information contact:

**Email**:    arifwaqif@amdisa.org

### Association of Management Development Institutions in South Asia Postdoctoral Fellowship

**Purpose**: To provide financial and academic-institutional assistance to PhD scholars and younger academics

**Eligibility**: Open to citizens of South Asian Commonwealth member country, not older than 50 years, who hold a PhD degree in management or related disciplines and are employed as a full-time teacher/researcher

**Level of Study**: Postdoctorate

**Type**: Fellowship

**Value**: £1,500–4,500

**Frequency**: Annual

**Application Procedure**: The application must contain proof of registration as PhD scholar, a curriculum vitae with list of publications

**Closing Date**: 30 April

#### For further information contact:

**Email**:    arifwaqif@amdisa.org

## Association of perioperative Registered Nurses Foundation

2170 South Parker Road, Suite 300, Denver, CO 80231, United States of America.

**Tel**:          (1) 800 755 2676
**Email**:      ibendzsa@aorn.org

**Website**:   www.aorn.org
**Contact**:   Ms Ingrid Bendzsa, Executive assistant

The AORN Foundation is a charitable and educational foundation created in 1992 by the Association of Perioperative Registered Nurses. Its mission is to secure resources and administer assets that provide support for the aim of preparing a new generation of surgical nurses.

## Association of perioperative Registered Nurses Scholarship Program

**Purpose**: The AORN Foundation supports your professional goals and helps you maintain evidence-based knowledge and competencies. We have awarded scholarships to more than 3,000 nurses working to earn a degree, achieve advanced certification, and complete continuing nurse education
**Eligibility**: Applicant must have been a member of AORN for 1 year and have a current licence to practice nursing
**Level of Study**: Doctorate
**Type**: Scholarship
**Frequency**: Annual
**Study Establishment**: Suitable accredited institution
**Country of Study**: United States of America
**Application Procedure**: Applicants must check the detailed guidelines on the website or obtain a copy from the Foundation's offices
**Closing Date**: 14 June
**Additional Information**: www.aorn.org/aorn-foundation/foundation-scholarships

### For further information contact:

**Tel**:       (1) 800 755 2676
**Email**:   foundation@aorn.org

## Association of Surgeons of Great Britain and Ireland

Association of Surgeons of Great Britain and Ireland, 35-43 Lincoln's Inn Fields, London, WC2A 3PE, United Kingdom.

**Tel**:       (44) 20 7973 0300
**Email**      admin@asgbi.org.uk
**Website**:   www.asgbi.org.uk

The founding objectives of the Association of Surgeons of Great Britain and Ireland, in 1920, were the advancement of the science and art of surgery and the promotion of friendship among surgeons. As other surgical specialities developed, the Association came to represent general surgery, encompassing breast, colorectal, endocrine, laparoscopic, transplant, upper gastrointestinal and vascular surgery.

## Moynihan Travelling Fellowship

**Purpose**: To enable specialist registrars or consultants to broaden their education, and to present and discuss their contribution to British or Irish surgery overseas
**Eligibility**: Open to either specialist registrars approaching the end of their higher surgical training or consultants in general surgery within 5 years of appointment after the closing date for applications. Candidates must be nationals of and residents of the United Kingdom or the Republic of Ireland, but need not be Fellows or affiliate Fellows of the Association. They may be engaged in general surgery or a sub-speciality thereof
**Level of Study**: Postdoctorate
**Type**: Fellowship
**Value**: £5,000
**Frequency**: Annual
**Country of Study**: Any country
**Application Procedure**: Applicants must submit 12 copies of an application, which must include a full curriculum vitae giving details of past and present appointments and publications, a detailed account of the proposed programme of travel, costs involved and the object to be achieved. Applications must be addressed to the Honorary Secretary at the Association of Surgeons. For further details contact Bhavnita Borkhatria at bhavnita@asgbi.org.uk
**No. of awards offered**: 6
**Closing Date**: 28 September
**Funding**: Private
**Contributor**: Charitable association funds
**No. of awards given last year**: 1
**No. of applicants last year**: 6
**Additional Information**: Shortlisted candidates will be interviewed by the Scientific Committee of the Association, which will pay particular attention to the originality, scope and feasibility of the proposed itinerary. The successful candidate will be expected to act as an ambassador for British and Irish surgery and should therefore be fully acquainted with the aims and objectives of the Association of Surgeons and its role in surgery. After the completion of the fellowship, the successful candidate will be asked to address the Association at its annual general meeting and to provide a written report for inclusion in the Executive Newsletter. A critical appraisal of the centres visited should form the basis of the report. Please see the website for further details www.asgbi.org.uk/en/awards_fellowships/moynihan_travelling_fellowship.cfm www.asgbi.org.uk/awards/moynihan-travelling-fellowship

### For further information contact:

**Email**:   bhavnita@asgbi.org.uk

# Association of Universities and Colleges of Canada (AUCC)

1710-350 Albert Street, Ottawa, ON K1R 1B1, Canada.

**Tel**:        (1) 613 563 1236
**Email**:    info@aucc.ca
**Website**: www.aucc.ca
**Contact**:  Mr Paul Davidson, President and CEO

The AUCC is a non-profit, non-governmental association that represents Canadian universities at home and abroad. The Association's mandate is to foster and promote the interests of higher education in the firm belief that strong universities are vital to the prosperity and wellbeing of Canada.

## Department of National Defence Postdoctoral Fellowships in Military History

**Eligibility**: Open to Canadian citizens or permanent residents who hold or will hold, prior to closing date of competition, a PhD degree or equivalent level of knowledge or experience in the field considered adequate by the Selection Committee
**Level of Study**: Postgraduate
**Type**: One fellowship
**Value**: C$24,000. Research expenses of up to C$1,500 may also be considered
**Frequency**: Annual
**Study Establishment**: for 1 year
**Country of Study**: Other
**Closing Date**: 1 February
**Additional Information**: Fellows may not concurrently hold any other awards whose cumulative value exceeds two thirds of the value of the fellowship accepted under this program. Upon completion of the fellowship, a manuscript resulting from research done should be submitted to AUCC

### For further information contact:

**Fax**:      (1) 613 563 9745
**Email**:   awards@aucc.ca

# Aston University

Aston University, Aston Triangle, Birmingham, B4 7ET, United Kingdom.

**Tel**:        (44) 121 204 3000
**Email**:    a.levey@aston.ac.uk

**Website**:   www.aston.ac.uk
**Contact**:   Alison Levey, Academic Registrar

Aston University is a long-established research – Centre for Executive Development (CED) university. It is known for its world-class teaching quality, strong links to industry, government & commerce, and its friendly and safe campus environment. Aston University is consistently featured in the top 30 universities in the country.

## Aston Dean

**Purpose**: To encourage students to pursue a PhD programme on a full-time basis
**Eligibility**: Scholarships are open to Home/European Union and Overseas applicants
**Level of Study**: Doctorate
**Type**: Scholarship
**Value**: £17,000 stipend and full fee waives
**Length of Study**: 3 years
**Frequency**: Annual
**Country of Study**: Any country
**Application Procedure**: Complete the online application form for entry to the programme: www.aston.ac.uk/study/postgraduate/apply/
**Closing Date**: August
**No. of awards given last year**: 7

## Computer Science Scholarship

**Purpose**: UK/EU students applying to study the Aston Masters MSc Computer Science.
**Eligibility**: 1. UK/EU citizen. 2. You must meet the entry requirements for MSc Computer Science. 3. Minimum three years' work experience.
**Level of Study**: Postgraduate
**Type**: Scholarship
**Value**: £2,500
**Application Procedure**: There is no need to submit a scholarship application as you will be assessed for the scholarship when you applly for the course. You must complete the work experience section of the course application form for us to be able to assess your eligiblity.
**Additional Information**: www2.aston.ac.uk/scholarships/stem-scholarship

## Ferguson Scholarships

**Purpose**: The School of Life & Health Sciences is offering 9 scholarships of £15,000 to students from Africa and South America

**Eligibility**: Hold a conditional or unconditional offer for one of the above courses. 1. Be a national from an African or South American country. 2. Hold a 2:1 degree or equivalent in a relevant subject for the course you are applying for. 3. Be a self-funded student. 4. Provide a strong personal statement when submitting your course application
**Level of Study**: Postgraduate (MSc)
**Type**: Scholarship
**Value**: £15,000
**Frequency**: As available
**Study Establishment**: Aston University
**Country of Study**: United Kingdom
**Application Procedure**: Submit an application for your chosen course via our online application form before the scholarship deadline
**Closing Date**: 31 March
**Funding**: Trusts
**Contributor**: Allan and Nesta Ferguson Charitable Trust
**Additional Information**: www2.aston.ac.uk/scholarships

## Global Excellence Scholarship

**Purpose**: Scholarships of up to £5,000 for well-qualified international students wishing to study at Aston
**Level of Study**: Graduate, Postgraduate
**Type**: Scholarship
**Value**: £3,000–£5,000
**Frequency**: As available
**Study Establishment**: Aston University
**Country of Study**: United Kingdom
**Closing Date**: 21 June
**Funding**: International office
**Additional Information**: www2.aston.ac.uk/scholarships

## Master of Business Administration Global Ambassador Scholarship

**Purpose**: Aston University has a proud network of Global Ambassadors, made up of international students who share their story and experience of studying at Aston with others around the world. Global Ambassadors represent Aston University in many different ways, such as attending events and Open Days, making videos and posting on social media, and speaking to people about what life is like as an international student at Aston.
**Eligibility**: MBA Global Ambassador Scholarship recipients will be awarded on merit to well-qualified applicants applying to study the MBA programme starting in January
**Level of Study**: MBA
**Type**: Scholarship
**Value**: £3,000
**Length of Study**: 1 year

**Frequency**: As available
**Study Establishment**: Aston Business School
**Country of Study**: United Kingdom
**Closing Date**: 31 March
**Funding**: International office
**Contributor**: Aston University
**Additional Information**: www2.aston.ac.uk/scholarships

### For further information contact:

Aston Business School, Aston University, Aston St, Birmingham B4 7ET, United Kingdom.

**Email**:   ask@aston.ac.uk

## Postgraduate Scholarships (ABS)

**Purpose**: To assist students with tuition fees
**Eligibility**: There are different eligibility criteria for each MSc scholarship. Please check website for complete and clear information
**Level of Study**: Postgraduate, MBA
**Value**: £1,000–5,000
**Frequency**: Annual
**Study Establishment**: Aston University
**Country of Study**: United Kingdom
**Application Procedure**: In order to be eligible to apply for a scholarship, candidates must hold an offer of a place. Notification of awards will be made at the end of July
**Funding**: International office
**Additional Information**: There are many MSc scholarships as well as Aston award scholarships

### For further information contact:

**Email**:   apply@aston.ac.uk

## School of Languages & Social Studies PhD Bursaries

**Purpose**: Financial support for PhD study
**Level of Study**: Doctorate
**Value**: Combination of fees only and fees plus maintenance offered
**Length of Study**: 3 years, full-time
**Frequency**: Annual
**Study Establishment**: Aston University
**Country of Study**: United Kingdom
**Application Procedure**: Please visit www.aston.ac.uk/study/postgraduate/apply/
**No. of awards offered**: 9
**Closing Date**: 29 February
**No. of awards given last year**: 4

**No. of applicants last year**: 9

**Additional Information**: Open to all nationals of any country; however, the bursaries only cover the HOME/European Union fees rate. Therefore those classified as overseas must pay the difference between the HOME and overseas fees rates

### For further information contact:

**Email**:    apply@aston.ac.uk

### School of Life and Health Sciences Postgraduate Masters Scholarships – Commonwealth Shared Scholarship Scheme

**Purpose**: These scholarships are for students from developing Commonwealth countries who would not otherwise be able to study in the United Kingdom

**Eligibility**: Applicants must hold an offer for MSc in molecular toxicology or MSc in psychology of health and illness; must hold an undergraduate Bachelor's degree at either First/Upper Second class or equivalent (work experience cannot be accepted as an alternative); must be a national of an eligible Commonwealth country and permanently living in that country; must have the minimum English language requirement for the programme as no funding will be given for pre-sessional language programmes; must not have studied for 1 year or more in a developed country previously; must not be employed by a national government or an organisation owned or part-owned by the government (parastatal organisation) – higher education institutions are exempted from this restriction

**Level of Study**: Postgraduate

**Type**: Scholarship

**Value**: These are fully funded scholarships and include living stipend

**Frequency**: Annual

**Study Establishment**: Aston University

**Application Procedure**: Application form is available on the website

**No. of awards offered**: 16

**Closing Date**: 18 December

**No. of awards given last year**: 2

**No. of applicants last year**: 16

**Additional Information**:  cscuk.dfid.gov.uk/apply/shared-scholarships/

### For further information contact:

Commonwealth Scholarship Commission in the UK, Woburn House 20-24 Tavistock Square, London WC1H 9HF, United Kingdom.

**Tel**:       (44) 207 380 6700
**Email**:    c.m.hoban@aston.ac.uk

### Vice-Chancellor's International Scholarship

**Purpose**: We are committed to offering the highest quality of teaching, based on cutting-edge research, and we aim to give our students the skills and knowledge they need to achieve career success.

**Eligibility**: International students from any country outside of the European Union can apply. This scholarship is available for applicants applying to all foundation, undergraduate and postgraduate programmes (except the MBChB in Medicine)

**Level of Study**: Postgraduate

**Type**: One scholarship

**Value**: £8,000

**Frequency**: As available

**Study Establishment**: Aston University

**Country of Study**: United Kingdom

**Application Procedure**: Online application form: www2.aston.ac.uk/scholarships/home-and-eu-scholarships/Vice-chancellors-international-scholarship/index

**Closing Date**: 31 March

**Funding**: International office

**Additional Information**: www2.aston.ac.uk/scholarships/home-and-eu-scholarships/Vice-chancellors-international-scholarship

### For further information contact:

**Email**:    ask@aston.ac.uk

## Ataxia United Kingdom

Lincoln House, Kennington Park, 1-3 Brixton Road, London, SW9 6DE, United Kingdom.

**Tel**:       (44) 20 7582 1444
**Email**:    research@ataxia.org.uk
**Website**:  www.ataxia.org.uk
**Contact**:  Mrs Julie Greenfield, Research Projects Manager

Ataxia United Kingdom is the leading charity in the United Kingdom working with and for people with ataxia. It will support research projects and related activities in order to enhance scientific understanding of ataxia, develop and evaluate therapeutic and supportive strategies and encourage wider involvement with ataxia research.

### Ataxia United Kingdom PhD Studentship

**Purpose**: To further research into causes of and treatments for progressive ataxias

**Eligibility**: Proposals are accepted from academic institutions, private sector research companies and suitably qualified individuals. There are no restrictions on age, nationality or residency

**Level of Study**: Postgraduate
**Type**: Studentship
**Value**: £5,000
**Length of Study**: Varies
**Frequency**: Annual, if funds are available
**Country of Study**: Any country
**Application Procedure**: Applicants must complete an application form available from Ataxia United Kingdom Research Projects Manager at research@ataxia.org.uk
**No. of awards offered**: 3
**Closing Date**: 1 June
**Funding**: Commercial, Private, Trusts, Individuals
**No. of applicants last year**: 3
**Additional Information**: There are a number of priority areas of research and these can be obtained from the Research Projects Manager www.ataxia.org.uk/News/apply-for-funding

### For further information contact:

**Tel**:    (44) 20 7582 1444

### Ataxia United Kingdom Research Grant

**Purpose**: To further research into causes of and treatments for progressive ataxias
**Eligibility**: Proposals are accepted from academic institutions, private sector research companies and suitably qualified individuals. There are no restrictions on age, nationality or residency
**Level of Study**: Unrestricted
**Type**: Project grant
**Value**  Varies
**Length of Study**: Varies
**Frequency**: Dependent on funds available
**Country of Study**: Any country
**Application Procedure**: Applicants must complete an application form available from Ataxia's Research Projects Manager at research@ataxia.org.uk
**No. of awards offered**: 16
**Funding**: Commercial, Private, Trusts, Individuals
**No. of awards given last year**: 1
**No. of applicants last year**: 16
**Additional Information**: There are a number of priority areas of research and these can be obtained from the Research Projects Manager www.ataxia.org.uk/News/apply-for-funding

### Ataxia United Kingdom Travel Grant

**Purpose**: To enable researchers to present their ataxia research at national and international conferences
**Eligibility**: Proposals are accepted from academic institutions, private sector research companies and suitably qualified individuals. There are no restrictions on age, nationality or residency, although preference will be given to events which could potentially benefit patients and researchers in the United Kingdom or Europe
**Level of Study**: Unrestricted
**Type**: Travel grant
**Value**: Dependent on the conference
**Length of Study**: Varies
**Frequency**: Dependent on funds available
**Country of Study**: Any country
**Application Procedure**: Applicants must complete an application form available from Ataxia's Research Projects Manager at research@ataxia.org.uk
**Funding**: Commercial, Private, Trusts, Individuals
**Additional Information**: There are a number of priority areas of research and these can be obtained from the Research Projects Manager www.ataxia.org.uk/News/apply-for-funding

### Athens State University

300 North Beaty Street, Athens, AL 35611, United States of America.

**Website**:    www.athens.edu
**Contact**:    Ms Helen Marks, Secretary, Financial Aid

### Athens State University Phi Theta Kappa Transfer Scholarship

**Purpose**: This scholarship is in the form of a tuition waiver only and will not pay in combination with any other ASU institutional scholarship
**Eligibility**: 1. Must be a new entering student with a minimum of 36 transfer credit hours and plan to enroll immediately in Athens State University in Alabama after completion of coursework at the two-year college level. 2. Students must not have more than six hours of coursework attempted at ASU by the end of the spring term of application year
**Level of Study**: Graduate
**Type**: Scholarship
**Frequency**: Annual
**Country of Study**: United States of America

**Application Procedure**: 1. Applications are available online at the Athens State University (ASU) website. 2. The student must submit a complete ASU application form, official transcripts from all prior colleges, two letters of recommendation from faculty members at transfer institutions, a letter verifying membership in Phi Theta Kappa from an adviser at transfer institution, and an essay outlining why the student feels he/she is deserving of the scholarship. 3. The student must submit his/her application to Student Financial Services before 4:30 p.m. EST by the deadline date

**Closing Date**: 31 March

**Funding**: Private

**Additional Information**: www.unigo.com/scholarships/by-state/alabama-scholarships/athens-state-university-phi-theta-kappa-transfer-scholarship/1000707

### For further information contact:

**Email**:    sarah.mcabee@athens.edu

## Auckland Medical Research Foundation

89 Grafton Road, Grafton, Auckland 1010, New Zealand.

**Tel**:         (64) 9 307 2886

**Contact**:    Secretary

### Auckland Medical Research Foundation Travel Grant

**Purpose**: To allow staff engaged in or associated with research projects to travel for a specific purpose

**Eligibility**: Open normally, but not exclusively, to staff associated with the Auckland Area Health Board, the School of Medicine in the University of Auckland, or to recipients of other grants from the Foundation. There are no requirements as to age, sex or citizenship

**Level of Study**: Postgraduate

**Type**: Varies

**Value**: Varies

**Study Establishment**: as approved

**Country of Study**: Any country

**Additional Information**: www.medicalresearch.org.nz/how-to-apply

### For further information contact:

**Email**:    amrf@medicalresearch.org.nz

## Auckland University of Technology University of Technology

55 Wellesley Street, Auckland 1010, New Zealand.

**Contact**:    Auckland University of Technology

Auckland University of Technology (AUT) is a university in New Zealand, formed on 1 January when a former technical college (originally established in 1895) was granted university status. It has five faculties across three campuses in Auckland: City, North, and South campuses, and an additional three specialist locations: AUT Millennium, Warkworth Radio Astronomical Observatory and AUT Centre for Refugee Education.

### AUT Doctoral Scholarships

**Purpose**: Auckland University of Technology (AUT) awards scholarships to high achieving candidates applying to an approved doctoral programme at AUT. AUT offers AUT Doctoral Scholarships in order to attract highly achieving doctoral research students to AUT and to encourage and stimulate doctoral studies in areas that enhance the University's research capability.

**Eligibility**: Applicants must meet English language proficiency requirements as stated in the Academic Calendar at the time of application. Applicants must meet the normal admission criteria for the doctoral programme. Recipients of this scholarship will have excellent academic record, strong academic references and have demonstrated the potential for high quality research.

**Type**: Scholarship

**Value**: NZ$25,000

**Length of Study**: 2 year

**Country of Study**: New Zealand

**Application Procedure**: In order for the application to be submitted applicants must complete all sections and request the required support statements. Incomplete applications will not be forwarded to the selection panel. The following documents or statements will need to be uploaded and submitted with the AUT Doctoral Scholarship On-line Application Form. Academic transcript(s) for any previous tertiary study that was completed at a university other than AUT. A brief C.V. (maximum three pages).

**No. of awards offered**: Various

**Closing Date**: 1 November

**Additional Information**: www.studyinnewzealand.govt.nz/how-to-apply/scholarship/details?scholarshipid=128068&institutionid=142314

## Access & Rural Women New Zealand Scholarship

**Purpose**: This is a scholarship for a health worker who wishes to further his/her studies in the health and/or disability fields, with a particular focus on the provision of services to the rural sector
**Type**: Scholarship
**Value**: NZ$3,000
**Length of Study**: 1 year
**Country of Study**: Any country
**Application Procedure**: For application procedure, please visit website www.aut.ac.nz/study/fees-and-scholarships/scholarships-and-awards-at-aut/scholarships-database/detail page?detailCode=802935&sessionID=27587614&source IP=&X_FORWARDED_FOR=
**Closing Date**: 1 July
**Additional Information**: For guidelines, application forms and more information about this award contact: Rural Women New Zealand, PO Box 12-021 Wellington, New Zealand; Email: enquiries@ruralwomen.org.nz www.aut.ac.nz/study/fees-and-scholarships/scholarships-and-awards-at-aut/scholarships-database/alphapage?letter=A&sessionID=34556024&sourceIP=&X_FORWARDED_FOR=

### For further information contact:

**Email**: enquiries@ruralwomen.org.nz

## Auckland University of Technology and Cyclone Computers Laptop and Tablet Scholarship

**Purpose**: The primary objectives of this award are to enhance the student learning experience and to increase study options for undergraduate and postgraduate students through the laptop scholarship programme
**Type**: Scholarship
**Value**: HP Elitebook or HP Elite X2 1,012 G2or AUT Optn A Macbook (A&D only)or devices of similar specification
**Country of Study**: Any country
**Closing Date**: 1 July
**Additional Information**: For guidelines, application forms and more information about this award contact: Auckland University of Technology, Phone: (64) 9 921 9837, Email: scholars@aut.ac.nz www.aut.ac.nz/study/fees-and-scholarships/scholarships-and-awards-at-aut/scholarships-database/detail page?detailCode=501009&sessionID=28545165&source IP=&X_FORWARDED_FOR=

### For further information contact:

**Email**: scholars@aut.ac.nz

## Auckland University of Technology Master of Human Rights Scholarship

**Purpose**: The purpose of this scholarship is to encourage and stimulate full-time students into the Master Human Rights, AUT will offer two AUT Master of Human Rights Scholarships to applicants wishing to enroll full-time into this Masters programme
**Eligibility**: IELTS (Academic) 6.5 overall with all bands 6.0 or higher; or equivalent
**Type**: Scholarship
**Length of Study**: 1 year full-time
**Frequency**: Annual
**Country of Study**: Any country
**Closing Date**: 13 July
**Additional Information**: www.aut.ac.nz/study/study-options/social-sciences-and-public-policy/courses/master-of-human-rights

### For further information contact:

**Tel**: (64) 9 921 9999
**Email**: contact@studyspy.ac.nz

## Auckland University of Technology Post Graduate Scholarships

**Purpose**: Auckland University of Technology offers AUT Postgraduate Scholarships - Equity (Maori and Pacific) to Maori and Pacific students for postgraduate study at AUT. UT Postgraduate Scholarship (coursework) is available to full-time students undertaking study at Level 8 or above (New Zealand Qualifications Framework) who have demonstrated the potential to achieve highly
**Eligibility**: Applicants must complete the online application available through the AUT Scholarships Database www.aut.ac.nz/scholarships. Applications will be open from 5 April
**Level of Study**: Postgraduate
**Type**: Scholarship
**Value**: Domestic full fees for 120pts
**Length of Study**: The scholarship is normally awarded for 12 months of full time study only
**Frequency**: Annual
**Country of Study**: New Zealand
**Application Procedure**: Application is through the AUT online scholarship portal accessed from the link above. Applications will open in October of the year preceding study for Semester 1 study or May for study in Semester 2. The following documentation must be received on or before the closing date. A one-page personal statement outlining the applicant's academic goals and career aspirations stating why they believe they merit the scholarship and provide an

outline of their Maori or Pacific cultural involvement. The personal statement should also attach an outline of recent leadership positions or responsibilities held within the University or community. A copy of the applicant's transcript will be added to the application by the Scholarships Office once grades have been finalized

**Closing Date**: 15 June

**Additional Information**: For guidelines, application forms and more information about this award contact: Auckland University of Technology; Phone: (64) 9 921 9837; Email: scholars@aut.ac.nz www.auckland.ac.nz/en/study/scholarships-and-awards/scholarship-types/postgraduate-scholarships.html

## Auckland University of Technology Vice Chancellor Doctoral Scholarship

**Purpose**: Auckland University of Technology (AUT) awards scholarships to high achieving candidates applying to an approved doctoral programme at AUT

**Type**: Scholarship

**Value**: Tuition fees (at the domestic rate) plus the compulsory student services fee; and an annual stipend of NZ$25,000 per annum

**Length of Study**: The scholarship is tenable for up to 3 years

**Country of Study**: New Zealand

**Application Procedure**: Applicants must meet the normal admission criteria for the doctoral programme. www.aut.ac.nz/study-at-aut/entry-requirements/postgraduate-and-graduate-admission-requirements

**Closing Date**: 1 December

**Additional Information**: www.aut.ac.nz/study/fees-and-scholarships/scholarships-and-awards-at-aut/scholarships-database/detailpage?detailCode=803262&sessionID=28550450&sourceIP=&X_FORWARDED_FOR=

### For further information contact:

**Tel**: (64) 9 921 9837
**Email**: scholars@aut.ac.nz

## Awarua Trust Scholarship

**Purpose**: To provide financial support to people in their pursuit of excellence

**Value**: Up to NZ$2,000 (or more by approval)

**Length of Study**: One year

**Country of Study**: Any country

**Closing Date**: 30 June

**Contributor**: The Awarua Trust

**Additional Information**: For guidelines, application forms and more information about this award contact: Gavin Haddon, (CA) trustee, The Awarua Trust, PO Box 388, Email: info@awaruatrust.org.nz www.awaruatrust.org.nz/page/scholarship-applications/

### For further information contact:

**Email**: info@awaruatrust.org.nz

## Betty Loughhead Soroptimist Scholarship Trust

**Purpose**: This scholarship provides financial support to women over the age of 25 who are studying to gain a further qualification to advance a careers in business, the professions, the arts

**Value**: NZ$3,000–NZ$5,000 (per award)

**Country of Study**: Any country

**Application Procedure**: Please ensure you provide 6 clean collated (stapled) copies (one for each trustee) of your application and references. "Emailed applications" cannot be accepted (and will not be considered).

**Closing Date**: 1 June

**Additional Information**: For guidelines, application forms and more information about this award contact: Hayley Denoual, Secretary, The Betty Loughhead Soroptimist Scholarship Trust, BLSST Secretary Sarnia, 52 Raukawa Street Strathmore Park, New Zealand; Phone: 04 388 2115; Email: retary@blsst.co.nz www.blsst.co.nz/

### For further information contact:

**Email**: secretary@blsst.co.nz

## Business, Economics & Law Postgraduate Academic Excellence Scholarship

**Purpose**: The purpose of the Business, Economics and Law Postgraduate Academic Excellence Scholarship is to encourage students with an excellent academic record to undertake postgraduate research in the Faculty of Business and Law

**Eligibility**: Applicants for this scholarship must complete an AUT Application for Enrolment (AFE) for the Bachelor of Business (Honours), the Master of Laws, the Master of Business or the Master of Philosophy

**Type**: Scholarship

**Value**: Tuition fees (up to 120 pts) and student levies

**Frequency**: Annual

**Country of Study**: New Zealand

**Application Procedure**: Application for this scholarship is via our AUT online scholarship application portal

**No. of awards offered**: 2

**Closing Date**: 1 June

**Additional Information**: For guidelines, application forms and more information about this award contact: Auckland University of Technology; Phone: (64) 9 921 9837; Email: scholars@aut.ac.nzscholarshipdb.net/scholarships-in-New-Zealand/Business-Economics-Law-Postgraduate-Academic-Excellence-Scholarship-Auckland-University-Of-Technology =C7FaW0Jq6BGUVQAlkGUTnw.html

**For further information contact:**

**Tel**: (64) 9 921 9837

**Email**: scholars@aut.ac.nz

## Colab PhD/MPhil Fees Scholarship

**Purpose**: Colab is the collaboratory for Design and Creative Technologies at the Auckland University of Technology (AUT), New Zealand. Our aim is to encourage researchers, students and stakeholders to imagine, construct, articulate and navigate rapidly changing social, economic, technological and career environments. To support innovative interdisciplinary research that reflects Colab's future focused aspirations in such areas as gaming, entrepreneurship, smart materials, wearable tech, making and digital civics Colab will offer fees scholarships for the doctoral programme and domestic equivalent fees Scholarships for the MPhil ptogramme

**Type**: Scholarship

**Value**: Full fees-PHD Domestic equivalent fees - MPhil

**Length of Study**: Up to 3 years for a PhD programme but will be reviewed annually

**Country of Study**: New Zealand

**Closing Date**: 14 December

**Additional Information**: For guidelines, application forms and more information about this award contact: Auckland University of Technology, Phone: (64) 9 921 9837, Email: scholars@aut.ac.nzstudyspy.ac.nz/scholarships/10389/colab-phd-mphil-fees-scholarship

**For further information contact:**

**Email**: scholars@aut.ac.nz

## Discrete Cosine Transform Mâori and Pacific Mature Student Doctoral Scholarship

**Purpose**: This scholarship is intended to provide support for Doctoral study completion, to Mâori and Pacific Island students who choose to undertake Doctoral studies later in life and who are making good progress towards PhD studies

**Eligibility**: All students nominated for this scholarship must be: 1. Of Maori and/or Pacific Island descent, and be NZ Citizens or permanent residents (Note: Pacific Island descent relates to one of the following Pacific countries, Cook Islands, Fiji, Kiribati, Nauru, Niue) Nominated by their PhD supervisor. Able to present a solid case for the scholarship to be awarded to them

**Type**: Scholarship

**Value**: An annual NZ$25,000 stipend, tuition fees

**Length of Study**: 2 years

**Country of Study**: New Zealand

**Closing Date**: 1 December

**Additional Information**: For guidelines, application forms and more information about this award contact: Auckland University of Technology, Phone: (64) 9 921 9837, Email: scholars@aut.ac.nz www.academicgates.com/job/detail/9d95 6ecd-e996-423f-b4af-e1348d5a15bb

**For further information contact:**

**Email**: scholars@aut.ac.nz

## Doctoral Fee Scholarships (Art & Design)

**Purpose**: The Doctoral Fee Scholarship (Art & Design) is offered to PhD candidates to nurture and support the research culture of the School of Art & Design

**Value**: Tuition fee and learner services levy

**Length of Study**: up to three years

**Country of Study**: Any country

**Application Procedure**: For application procedure, please visit website www.aut.ac.nz/study/fees-and-scholarships/ scholarships-and-awards-at-aut/scholarships-database/detailpa ge?detailCode=501191&sessionID=27587614&sourceIP =&X_FORWARDED_FOR=

**No. of awards offered**: Varies

**Closing Date**: 1 November

**Additional Information**: For guidelines, application forms and more information about this award contact: Auckland University of Technology; Phone: (64) 9 921 9837; Email: scholars@aut.ac.nzscholarshipdb.net/scholarships-in-New-Zealand/Aut-Doctoral-Scholarships-School-Of-Art-And-Des ign-Fees-Auckland-University-Of-Technology=RTdvIe6n6 RGUWgAlkGUTnw.html

**For further information contact:**

**Tel**: (64) 9 921 9837

**Email**: scholars@aut.ac.nz

## Fulbright New Zealand General Graduate Awards

**Purpose**: Fulbright New Zealand General Graduate Awards are for promising New Zealand graduate students to undertake postgraduate study or research at United States institutions in any field
**Type**: Award
**Value**: Up to NZ$31,000 plus travel expenses and insurance
**Length of Study**: 1 year
**Country of Study**: Any country
**Application Procedure**: For online application, please visit website apply.embark.com/student/fulbright/international/20/
**Closing Date**: 1 August
**Additional Information**: For guidelines, application forms and more information about this award contact: Shauna Mendez, Programme Manager, Fulbright New Zealand, PO Box 3465, Level 8, 120 Featherston Street, 6140 Wellington, New Zealand; Phone: (64) 4 494 1500; Email: shauna@fulbright.org.nz www.aut.ac.nz/study/fees-and-scholarships/scholarships-and-awards-at-aut/scholarships-database/detailpage?detailCode=100207&sessionID=34546231&sourceIP=&X_FORWARDED_FOR=

### For further information contact:

**Email**:     pip@fulbright.org.nz

## Kate Edger Educational Charitable Trust - Expenses / Class Materials Awards

**Purpose**: The main purpose of these awards is to assist women, who are studying undergraduate or post graduate degree or diploma courses which incur high materials' expenditure, with payment of essential costs
**Type**: Grant
**Value**: NZ$300–NZ$1,000 each
**Length of Study**: Each Expenses/Class Materials
**Frequency**: Annual
**Country of Study**: New Zealand
**Application Procedure**: Application forms for these awards are available from: www.academicdresshire.co.nz/Academic+Awards+Available/Postgraduate+Awards.html;
**Closing Date**: 16 March
**Additional Information**: For guidelines, application forms and more information about this award contact: Kate Edger Educational Charitable Trust, Private Bag 93208 Parnell, Email: enquiries@kateedgertrust.org.nz www.aut.ac.nz/study/fees-and-scholarships/scholarships-and-awards-at-aut/scholarships-database/detailpage?detailCode=500559&sessionID=34546231&sourceIP=&X_FORWARDED_FOR=

### For further information contact:

Kate Edger Educational Charitable Trust, Private Bag 93208, Parnell, New Zealand.

**Tel**:     (64) 9 358 1044
**Email**:     awards@kateedgertrust.org.nz

## Master of Arts Scholarship in Applied Language Studies or Professional Language Studies

**Purpose**: The purpose of this scholarship is to encourage and support postgraduate study in the area of Language Teaching or Applied Language Study AUT's language and culture programmes focus on language in its widest sense
**Eligibility**: Applicants must: 1. Be new students enrolling full-time into the Master of Professional Language Studies (Language Teaching) or the Master of Arts in Applied Language Studies. Applicants who have not applied for admission to the master's programme should commence this process as well. Information about these programmes is available from www.aut.ac.nz/study-at-aut/study-areas/language-culture/postgraduate-study/.2. Have demonstrated academic excellence in past tertiary study
**Type**: Scholarship
**Value**: NZ$8,000 towards fees
**Length of Study**: One year of full-time study only
**Country of Study**: New Zealand
**Application Procedure**: Information about these programmes is available from www.aut.ac.nz/study-at-aut/study-areas/language-culture/postgraduate-study/
**Closing Date**: September
**Additional Information**: For guidelines, application forms and more information about this award contact: Auckland University of Technology, Phone: +64 9 921 9837 www.aut.ac.nz/study/study-options/language-and-culture

### For further information contact:

Auckland University of Technology, 55 Wellesley Street East, Auckland CBD, Auckland 1010, New Zealand.

**Tel**:     (64) 9 921 9837
**Email**:     scholars@aut.ac.nz

## Master of Cultural & Creative Practice Scholarships (Art & Design)

**Purpose**: The Master of Cultural & Creative Practice (MCCP) is a one and a half year (full-time) taught degree aimed at developing expertise in cultural expression. Mixing live projects with coursework you can tailor your journey, choose to specialise or develop your existing skills and experience in a diverse array of subjects, for example; Arts Management, Cultural Production, Curatorial Practices, the Interarts, Interactive and Mixed Reality, Heritage Promotion and Cultural and Creative Production. Implementing creative strategies, whilst continuing to develop expertise related to your chosen field, you will contribute to a vibrant creative community critiquing notions of leadership and entrepreneurship in the cultural and creative sector. Considerate of cultural and ethical issues and their implications when working across cultural, social, and historical contexts you will be thoughtful and respectful in your research and production. Creative thinking will empower your decision-making and inform your professional encounters.

**Type**: Scholarship

**Value**: Tuition fees and learner services levy for the MCCP programme of study

**Length of Study**: The tenure of this scholarship is for up to three semesters of full-time study in the Master of Cultural & Creative Practice programme of study (180 points)

**Country of Study**: New Zealand

**Application Procedure**: For details, please visit website www.aut.ac.nz/study/fees-and-scholarships/scholarships-and-awards-at-aut/scholarships-database/detailpage?detailCode=501192&sessionID=27587614&sourceIP=&X_FORWARDED_FOR=

**Closing Date**: 1 June

**Additional Information**: For guidelines, application forms and more information about this award contact: Auckland University of Technology; Phone: (64) 9 921 9837; Email: scholars@aut.ac.nz www.aut.ac.nz/study/fees-and-scholarships/scholarships-and-awards-at-aut/scholarships-database/detailpage?detailCode=501192&sessionID=27587614&sourceIP=&X_FORWARDED_FOR=

**For further information contact:**

**Tel**:    (64) 800 288 864
**Email**:    pgartdes@aut.ac.nz

## Master of Professional Language Studies (Language Teaching) Scholarships

**Purpose**: The purpose of this scholarship is to encourage and support postgraduate study in the area of language teaching. The scholarship is open to domestic students only

**Type**: Scholarship

**Value**: Full fees and student levies up to 120 points of study

**Length of Study**: 1 year full-time / part-time available

**Country of Study**: Any country

**Application Procedure**: Applications are available from www.aut.ac.nz/study-at-aut/study-areas/language-culture/post graduate-study/master-of-professional-language-studies—language-teaching

**Closing Date**: 13 July

**Additional Information**: www.aut.ac.nz/study/study-options/language-and-culture/courses/master-of-professional-language-studies-language-teaching

**For further information contact:**

**Email**:    cdsouza@aut.ac.nz

## Ministry of Primary Industries/National Institute of Water and Atmospheric Research Masters Scholarships in Quantitative Fisheries Science

**Purpose**: To attract high performing New Zealand students into quantitative marine science; to encourage postgraduate students to contribute to priority research areas identified by the New Zealand Government; to train students at the postgraduate level by sharing and using the combined expertise of university academics, MPI and practising NIWA scientists; and to facilitate the professional development of postgraduate students by exposure to an applied commercial research environment

**Eligibility**: 1. Applicants need to be New Zealand citizens or permanent residents. 2. Study must be undertaken within New Zealand (with the possibility of some course work being undertaken through an Australian university). 3. You must be eligible to undertake an MSc at any New Zealand university. 4. You must undertake full-time study. 5. A suitable university supervisor and NIWA or Fisheries New Zealand technical advisor must be agreed prior to stage 2 of the application (organising a potential University supervisor is desirable but not necessary for stage 1). 6. There are no age restrictions. 7. Study must commence within 6 months of receiving this scholarship. 8. You may hold other scholarships but these must be disclosed to Fisheries New Zealand. Students are encouraged to apply for additional scholarships that cover the payment of fees.

**Value**: US$20,000

**Length of Study**: 2 years

**Country of Study**: Any country

**Application Procedure**: Application has to be processed using the link www.victoria.ac.nz/study/student-finance/scholarships

**Closing Date**: 7 December

**Additional Information**: niwa.co.nz/education-and-training/scholarships

**For further information contact:**

**Email**:    science.officer@mpi.govt.nz

## Peace and Disarmament Education Trust (PADET)

**Purpose**: The purpose of PADET is to advance education and promote international peace, arms control and disarmament. PADET funds not-for-profit projects and scholarship topics that support these objectives
**Type**: Scholarship
**Value**: Scholarships are awarded in two categories, depending on the individual's circumstances: up to NZ$14,000 for a full year's work is available for a Master's research thesis scholarship; up to NZ$21,000, plus up to NZ$5,000 for tuition fees, per year for up to three years is available for a PhD doctoral thesis scholarship
**Length of Study**: One year for a master
**Country of Study**: Any country
**Closing Date**: 29 July
**Additional Information**: For guidelines, application forms and more information about this award contact: Trust Advisor, Department of Internal Affairs, PO Box 805, Wellington 6140, New Zealand. Phone: (64) 800 824 824; Email: community.matters@dia.govt.nz www.aut.ac.nz/study/fees-and-scholarships/scholarships-and-awards-at-aut/scholarships-database/detailpage?detailCode=800035&sessionID=34546231&sourceIP=&X_FORWARDED_FOR=

### For further information contact:

Trust Advisor, Dept of Internal Affairs, PO Box 805, Wellington 6140, New Zealand.

**Tel**:      (64) 800 824 824
**Email**:    community.matters@dia.govt.nz

## Resource Management Law Association of New Zealand Masters Scholarship

**Subjects**: Masters Scholarship
**Purpose**: To encourage graduate students studying law, planning, engineering, geography, science, landscape architecture, urban planning and resource management, to focus their research theses or dissertations on topics related to the application of resource management in New Zealand
**Eligibility**: The scholarship is open to any graduate student in a University (New Zealand or Overseas) registered for a Masters (including an undergraduate Honours degree involving advanced levels of research and study at Masters degree level).
**Level of Study**: Masters
**Value**: NZ$5,000 per year
**Length of Study**: Any scholarship will be tenable for 1 year only. Awards may be made subject to acceptance into restricted courses. Any scholarship will be tenable for one

year only. Commencement may be delayed to coincide with an overseas University academic year. Tenure will be for a year in which thesis or dissertation work is the major academic activity. The RMLA may choose to pay the scholarship to the recipient in instalments.
**Frequency**: Every year
**Country of Study**: Any country
**Application Procedure**: To apply for an RMLA scholarship, simply download the RMLA Scholarship Application and post it to RMLA so it arrives before before 01 September. Selection will be based on relevance of the proposed thesis or dissertation topic to advancing excellence in resource management policy and process; and Resource management processes which are legally sound, effective and efficient and which produce high quality environmental outcomes
**No. of awards offered**: Up to three per annum
**Closing Date**: 1 September
**Funding**: From the Resource Management Law Association of New Zealand Inc.
**Additional Information**: For guidelines, application forms and more information about this award contact: Karol Helmink, Executive Officer, Resource Management Law Association, RMLA Scholarship Selection Committee, RMLA, PO Box 89187, Torbay, Auckland 0742, New Zealand www.rmla.org.nz/scholarships

### For further information contact:

RMLA, PO Box 89187, Torbay, Auckland 0742, New Zealand.

**Tel**:      (64) 272723960
**Email**:    Karol.helmink@rmla.org.nz

## The AUT Queen Elizabeth II Diamond Jubilee Doctoral Scholarship

**Purpose**: To develop an internationally aware, skilled future leader and establish enduring education and professional linkages. The Queen Elizabeth II Diamond Jubilee AUT Doctoral Scholarship marks the 60th anniversary of the accession of Her Majesty The Queen to the throne and will be awarded annually
**Type**: Scholarship
**Value**: NZ$25,000 annual stipend tuition fees and student services levies
**Length of Study**: One each year
**Country of Study**: New Zealand
**Closing Date**: 1 November

**Additional Information**: For guidelines, application forms and more information about this award contact: Auckland University of Technology, Phone: (64) 9 921 9837, Email: scholars@aut.ac.nz www.aut.ac.nz/study/fees-and-scholarships/scholarships-and-awards-at-aut/scholarships-database/detailpage?detailCode=500675&sessionID=32593825&sourceIP=&X_FORWARDED_FOR=

### For further information contact:

Auckland University of Technology, 55 Wellesley St E, Auckland 1010, New Zealand.

**Tel**:     (64) 9 921 9837
**Email**:     scholars@aut.ac.nz

## The Capstone Editing Conference Travel Grant for Postgraduate Research Students

**Purpose**: The purpose of attending the conference should be to assist with the student's research or professional development. The student does not necessarily have to be presenting a paper or poster at the conference to be eligible to apply for the grant, though it is preferred
**Eligibility**: For eligibility, please visit website www.aut.ac.nz/study/fees-and-scholarships/scholarships-and-awards-at-aut/scholarships-database/detailpage?detailCode=804076&sessionID=27587614&sourceIP=&X_FORWARDED_FOR=
**Type**: Grant
**Value**: Up to AU$3,000
**Country of Study**: Any country
**No. of awards offered**: 1
**Closing Date**: 20 May
**Additional Information**: For guidelines, application forms and more information about this award contact: Lisa Lines, Director and Head Editor, Capstone Editing, Tower A Level 5, 7 London Circuit, Canberra ACT 2601, Australia; Phone: (61) 1800 224 468; Email: lisa.lines@capstoneediting.com.au www.aut.ac.nz/study/fees-and-scholarships/scholarships-and-awards-at-aut/scholarships-database/detailpage?detailCode=804076&sessionID=34546231&sourceIP=&X_FORWARDED_FOR=

### For further information contact:

Lisa Lines, Director and Head Editor, Capstone Editing, Tower A Level 5/7 London Circuit, Canberra ACT 2601, Australia.

**Tel**:     (61) 1800 224 468
**Email**:     lisa.lines@capstoneediting.com.au

## The Capstone Editing Early Career Academic Research Grant for Women

**Purpose**: In offering this grant, Capstone Editing acknowledges the greater difficulties faced by female academics in developing and continuing their careers and seeks to ameliorate this situation with practical, financial support
**Eligibility**: You must be a woman. You must be employed as an academic staff member in a position that involves research at an Australian or New Zealand university (i.e. staff in teaching-only positions are not eligible). You may be employed on a continuing or fixed-term basis. (Casual staff are not eligible.) - You may be employed part time or full time. You must be an early career academic. This is defined as someone who has graduated from their PhD within the past six years or who has begun continuing or fixed-term employment in an academic position for the first time within the past two years. - The research project must be one intended to lead to publication. This is defined as a research project for which one of the expected outcomes is publication of a peer-reviewed journal article, book chapter or book. It is recognised that academic research is incredibly varied and that some research will result clearly and quickly in a publication while other research might not lead to a publication for some time. Part of the purpose of this grant is to assist women to overcome barriers to their career progression, and publication is crucial to this. That is why one of the goals of the research project should be publication. You can specify in your application the type of publication you are aiming for and how it is related to your research project. - Previous recipients of this grant may not apply again. - Previous unsuccessful applicants may reapply every year if they wish. - You cannot apply if you are an employee or contractor of Capstone Editing (or a family member of an employee or contractor).
**Value**: Up to NZ$5,000
**Country of Study**: New Zealand
**No. of awards offered**: 1
**Closing Date**: 3 June
**Additional Information**: www.aut.ac.nz/study/fees-and-scholarships/scholarships-and-awards-at-aut/scholarships-database/detailpage?detailCode=804074&sessionID=26750595&sourceIP=&X_FORWARDED_FOR=

### For further information contact:

Lisa Lines, Director and Head Editor, Capstone Editing, Tower A Level 5/7 London Circuit, Canberra ACT 2601, Australia.

**Tel**:     (61) 1800 224 468
**Email**:     lisa.lines@capstoneediting.com.au

## Todd Foundation Postgraduate Scholarship in Energy Research

**Purpose**: The purpose of the Todd Foundation Postgraduate Scholarship in Energy Research is to support students undertaking doctoral research in the field of energy, research which may have wide relevance and add value to New Zealand. This scholarship recognises the work of Sir Bryan Todd

**Eligibility**: Applicants must be New Zealand citizens or permanent residents. Applicants must hold an appropriate Bachelor's degree with first or second class honours or a Master's degree and have already demonstrated a capacity for research. Those currently in their final year of study for such a tertiary qualification are eligible to apply for the scholarship but any award made would be conditional upon the successful completion of that tertiary qualification.

**Level of Study**: Graduate
**Type**: Scholarship
**Value**: NZ$25,000 per year/plus one-off NZ$3,000
**Length of Study**: Up to 3 years
**Country of Study**: Any country
**Closing Date**: 1 September
**Funding**: Private
**Additional Information**: For guidelines, application forms and more information about this award contact: Scholarships, Universities New Zealand – Te Pôkai Tara, PO Box 11915, Wellington 6142; Phone: (64) 4 381 8510; Email: scholarships@universitiesnz.ac.nz www.aut.ac.nz/study/fees-and-scholarships/scholarships-and-awards-at-aut/scholarships-database/detailpage?detailCode=802361&sessionID=29519472&sourceIP=&X_FORWARDED_FOR=

**For further information contact:**

**Email**:    scholarships@universitiesnz.ac.nz

## Toloa Scholarships for Pacific STEM Scholars

**Purpose**: These scholarships are designed to motivate, celebrate and inspire Pacific people to study STEM courses and enter a career in STEM
**Type**: Scholarship
**Value**: NZ$25,000 each
**Length of Study**: Three years
**Country of Study**: New Zealand
**Application Procedure**: For application, visit website www.mpp.govt.nz/toloa-application-form-2018/
**No. of awards offered**: 8
**Closing Date**: 15 November
**Additional Information**: For guidelines, application forms and more information about this award contact: Ofania Ikiua, Ministry for Pacific Peoples, PO Box 833, New Zealand,

Phone: (64) 4 473 4493, Email: contact@mpp.govt.nz www.aut.ac.nz/study/fees-and-scholarships/scholarships-and-awards-at-aut/scholarships-database/detailpage?detailCode=803894&sessionID=33762433&sourceIP=&X_FORWARDED_FOR=

**For further information contact:**

Ofania Ikiua, Ministry for Pacific Peoples, PO Box 833, New Zealand.

**Tel**:         (64) 4 473 4493
**Email**:    contact@mpp.govt.nz

## Zonta Club of South Auckland Area Study Award

**Purpose**: To assist in women's education
**Value**: Up to NZ$5,000
**Application Procedure**: For further information and an application form see the website: www.zontasouthauckland.org.nz
**No. of awards offered**: 1
**Closing Date**: 16 August
**Additional Information**: www.aut.ac.nz/study/fees-and-scholarships/scholarships-and-awards-at-aut/scholarships-database/detailpage?detailCode=800997&sessionID=26786870&sourceIP=&X_FORWARDED_FOR=

**For further information contact:**

**Tel**:         (64) 9 299 8759
**Email**:    bev.pointon@gmail.com

## Zonta International Amelia Earhart Fellowships

**Purpose**: The Amelia Earhart Fellowship is awarded annually to women pursuing PhD/doctoral degrees in aerospace-related sciences and aerospace-related engineering
**Type**: Fellowship
**Value**: NZ$10,000
**Length of Study**: 1 year
**Country of Study**: New Zealand
**Application Procedure**: For application form, please visit website www.aut.ac.nz/study/fees-and-scholarships/scholarships-and-awards-at-aut/scholarships-database/detailpage?detailCode=100341&sessionID=26783186&sourceIP=&X_FORWARDED_FOR=
**Closing Date**: 15 November
**Additional Information**: For guidelines, application forms and more information about this award contact: Zonta International Foundation, 1211 West 22nd Street Suite 900 Oak Brook, United States, Phone: (1) 630-928-1400, Email: programs@zonta.org www.aut.ac.nz/study/fees-and-scholarships/

scholarships-and-awards-at-aut/scholarships-database/detailpage?detailCode=100341&sessionID=32593825&sourceIP=&X_FORWARDED_FOR=

**For further information contact:**

Email: zifoundation@zonta.org

---

## Australia Council for the Arts

372 Elizabeth Street, PO Box 788, Strawberry Hills, Surry Hills, NSW 2012, Australia.

Tel:      (61) 2 9215 9000
Email:   mail@australiacouncil.gov.au
Website: www.australiacouncil.gov.au

The Australia Council for the Arts is the Australian Government's arts funding and advisory body. Each year, the council delivers more than AU$160 million in funding for arts organisations and individual artists across the country. Individuals groups and organisations can apply to the Australia Council for funding. Individuals must be Australian citizens or have permanent resident status in Australia. All amounts are in Australian dollars.

### Aboriginal and Torres Strait Islander Arts Fellowship

**Purpose**: These grants provide financial support for two years to Aboriginal and Torres Strait Islander artists to enable them to undertake a major creative project or program in their artform
**Eligibility**: Open to practicing Aboriginal and Torres Strait Islander artists who are able to demonstrate at least 10 years experience as a practicing professional artist
**Level of Study**: Postgraduate
**Type**: Fellowship
**Value**: AU$100,000 up to two years for dance, emerging artforms and experimental practices
**Length of Study**: 2 years
**Frequency**: Annual
**Country of Study**: Australia
**Application Procedure**: Apply online. For further details mail to atsia@australiacouncil.gov.au
**Closing Date**: 19 November
**Funding**: Government
**Additional Information**: www.australiacouncil.gov.au/aboriginal-and-torres-strait-islander-arts/

**For further information contact:**

Level 5, 60 Union St Pyrmont NSW 2009 PO Box 576 Pyrmont NSW 2009, Australia.

Tel:      (61) 2 9215 9000
Email:   enquiries@australiacouncil.gov.au

### Aboriginal and Torres Strait Islander Arts Key Organisations Triennial

**Purpose**: To support a limited number of Aboriginal and Torres Strait Islander arts organisations to advance Aboriginal and Torres Strait Islander arts in Australia
**Eligibility**: Open to Aboriginal and Torres Strait Islander arts organisations only and must be outstanding organisations with a substantial record of achievement in their field
**Frequency**: Annual
**Country of Study**: Any country
**Application Procedure**: Application forms should include evidence of eligibility and the required support materials. Check website for further details
**Closing Date**: 15 July

**For further information contact:**

Email: stephanie.lord@sa.gov.au

### Aboriginal and Torres Strait Islander Arts Presentation and Promotion

**Purpose**: Presentation and Promotion grants support projects that promote Aboriginal and Torres Strait Islander artists and their work regionally, nationally and internationally through publications, recordings, performances, exhibitions and international export
**Eligibility**: Open to Aboriginal and Torres Strait Islander artists and community organisations and Aboriginal and Torres Strait Islander and non-indigenous arts organisations (including publishers)
**Type**: Grant
**Value**: Up to a maximum of AU$10,000 for CD/DVD recording projects involving writing, recording, production, manufacture, distribution and promotion
**Frequency**: Annual
**Country of Study**: Any country
**Application Procedure**: Apply online. Please mail to atsia@australiacouncil.gov.au
**Closing Date**: 18 November
**Additional Information**: Overseas applicants for international projects must provide written evidence of co-funding from the host country or organisation. All applicants are

encouraged to seek further funding support for the project from other sources

**For further information contact:**

**Email**:  vichealth@vichealth.vic.gov.au

## Aboriginal and Torres Strait Islander Arts Program

**Purpose**: To provide support towards the cost of an organisation wishing to employ an Aboriginal and Torres Strait Islander artworker or artist to organise, develop and initiate a programme or arts activities in their community or region
**Eligibility**: Open to Aboriginal and Torres Strait Islander arts organisations only
**Length of Study**: 1 year
**Frequency**: Annual
**Country of Study**: Any country
**Application Procedure**: Applications should include evidence of eligibility and required support materials. Check website for further details
**Closing Date**: 15 July

**For further information contact:**

**Email**:  stephanie.lord@sa.gov.au

## Aboriginal and Torres Strait Islander Arts Skills and Arts Development

**Purpose**: These grants support Aboriginal and Torres Strait Islander artists, groups, organisations and accredited non-Indigenous organisations to develop their ideas and skills such as: mentorship programs, arts workshops, professional development programs, conferences, seminars or planning and development programs
**Eligibility**: Applicants should be Aboriginal and Torres Strait Islander individuals, organisations or groups
**Type**: Grant
**Value**: Varies
**Country of Study**: Any country
**Application Procedure**: Apply online
**Closing Date**: 19 November
**Additional Information**: Applicants are encouraged to seek funding from a number of sources. Please mail to atsia@australiacouncil.gov.au

**For further information contact:**

**Email**:  stephanie.lord@sa.gov.au

## Aboriginal and Torres Strait Islander New Work Grant

**Purpose**: These grants support Aboriginal and Torres Strait Islander artists, groups, organisations and accredited non-Indigenous organisations to create new work with an expected public outcome
**Eligibility**: Open to Aboriginal and Torres Strait Islander artists who demonstrate artistic merit and innovation
**Level of Study**: Professional development
**Type**: Grant
**Value**: Varies
**Length of Study**: Up to 12 months
**Frequency**: Annual
**Country of Study**: Australia
**Application Procedure**: Apply online. For further information mail to atsia@australiacouncil.gov.au
**Closing Date**: 19 November
**Funding**: Government
**Additional Information**: All applicants are encouraged to seek further funding support for the project from other sources

## Community Cultural Development Category A

**Purpose**: To develop significant project ideas and/or extension of effective partnerships that enable future projects to take place
**Eligibility**: Open to individuals, groups and organisations and who have discussed their proposal with Community Partnerships staff
**Type**: Grant
**Value**: Up to AU$5,000 per grant
**Frequency**: Annual
**Country of Study**: Any country
**Application Procedure**: Applications should include required support materials. Check website for further details
**Closing Date**: 1 November

## Community Cultural Development Category B

**Purpose**: To support off community arts and culture projects which may have a public outcome and must involve a range of partners
**Eligibility**: Open to individuals, groups and organisations
**Type**: Grant
**Value**: Up to AU$20,000
**Frequency**: Annual
**Country of Study**: Any country
**Application Procedure**: Applications should include required support materials. Check website for further details
**Closing Date**: 1 July

## Community Cultural Development Category C

**Purpose**: To support one-off community arts and culture projects which have a public outcome and involve cross-sectoral partners
**Eligibility**: Open to individuals, groups and organisations who meet the general eligibility requirements
**Value**: AU$20,000–35,000
**Frequency**: Annual
**Country of Study**: Any country
**Application Procedure**: Applications should include required support materials. Check website for further details
**Closing Date**: 1 July

## Community Cultural Development Presentation and Promotion

**Purpose**: To support project that promote the value of community cultural development practice. This includes projects that create opportunities for practitioners to explore new ways of presenting the outcomes of existing best-practice models to new audiences
**Eligibility**: Open to individuals and organisations who meet the general eligibility requirements
**Type**: Grant
**Frequency**: Annual
**Country of Study**: Any country
**Application Procedure**: Applications should include required support materials. Check website for further details
**Closing Date**: 1 August

### For further information contact:

**Email**: arts.office@nt.gov.au

## Community Partnerships - Projects

**Purpose**: These grants provide funding for individuals, groups and organisations to develop and implement community arts and cultural development projects with a range of partners. These projects may or may not have a public outcome. Consideration of an evaluation strategy is recommended
**Eligibility**: Open to individuals, groups and organisations
**Type**: Grant
**Value**: Up to AU$20,000
**Length of Study**: Varies
**Frequency**: Annual
**Application Procedure**: Apply online
**Closing Date**: 5 September
**Additional Information**: Please mail to cp@australiacouncil.gov.au

### For further information contact:

**Tel**:      (61) 2 9215 9034
**Email**:   cp@australiacouncil.gov.au

## Dance New Work Creative Development

**Purpose**: To support the creation of new dance works
**Eligibility**: Open to individuals, groups, and organisations who meet the general eligibility requirements
**Level of Study**: Professional development
**Type**: Grant
**Value**: Varies
**Length of Study**: Varies
**Application Procedure**: Applications should include required support materials. Apply online. Check website for further details or contact Program Officer
**Closing Date**: 10 February
**Additional Information**: These are Projects Creative Development and Projects Presentation

### For further information contact:

**Tel**:      (61) 2 9215 9179
**Email**:   e.johnson@australiacouncil.gov.au

## Dance New Work Presentation

**Purpose**: To support public performance of a new work and any stages leading up to the production
**Eligibility**: Open to individuals who meet the general eligibility requirements. This can include final stage creative development and presentation/s and remounts of dance works. Applicants must provide information about presentation partner/s or presentation arrangements. Arrangements can include self presentation
**Value**: Varies
**Application Procedure**: Applications should include required support materials. Apply online. Check website for further details and contact Program Officer
**Closing Date**: 15 August

### For further information contact:

**Tel**:      (61) 2 9215 9179
**Email**:   e.johnson@australiacouncil.gov.au

## Festivals Australia

**Purpose**: These grants support regional, remote and community festivals to present quality arts projects which have not been presented before, and would not be possible without financial support

**Eligibility**: In order to apply you must be, or must apply through, a registered legal entity (with an ABN) or an incorporated organisation, which is able to produce an annual audited financial statement. Check website for complete details

**Type**: Grant

**Application Procedure**: Apply online

**Closing Date**: 29 August

**Additional Information**: Please mail to artsdevelopment@australiacouncil.gov.au

### For further information contact:

**Tel**:       (61) 2 9215 9176
**Email**:   T.Kita@australiacouncil.gov.au

## International Market Development Program

**Purpose**: International Pathways aims to assist with strategic international artistic and market development activities for Australian music and musicians

**Eligibility**: Applicants must have a commercially available CD, and touring experience

**Level of Study**: Professional development

**Type**: Grant

**Value**: AU$2,500–20,000

**Length of Study**: A maximum of 3 years

**Frequency**: Annual

**Country of Study**: Australia

**Application Procedure**: Contact the department

**Funding**: Government

### For further information contact:

**Tel**:       (61) 2 9215 9115
**Email**:   music@ozco.gov.au

## Literature Program

**Purpose**: These grants provide funding to established Australian organisations that support Australia's literary infrastructure

**Eligibility**: Open to Australian organisations which meet the eligibility requirements and provide the necessary support materials

**Value**: Covers production, program and/or operational costs

**Length of Study**: 1 year

**Frequency**: Annual

**Application Procedure**: Apply Online. Check website for further details. Applicant must provide evidence of his

eligibility and all required support material by the application closing date.

### For further information contact:

**Tel**:       (61) 2 9215 9057
**Email**:   l.byrne@australiacouncil.gov.au

## Music Presentation and Promotion

**Purpose**: To support one-off projects that present, publish, distribute and/or market quality music of any style within Australia

**Eligibility**: Open to individuals, performing groups/ensembles/bands and organisations which meet the eligibility requirements and provide the necessary support materials

**Value**: Up to AU$30,000 and associated expenses

**Length of Study**: Varies

**Application Procedure**: Application form should include the required supporting materials. Apply online. Check website for further details. For further details contact the Program Officer

**Closing Date**: 12 November

### For further information contact:

**Tel**:       (61) 2 9215 9108
**Email**:   p.keogh@australiacouncil.gov.au

## Music Program

**Purpose**: Supports organisations with a track record of achievement in presentation, service delivery, skills development or other relevant areas

**Eligibility**: Open to organisations which meet the eligibility requirements and provide the necessary support materials

**Value**: Up to AU$50,000

**Length of Study**: 1 year

**Frequency**: Annual

### For further information contact:

**Tel**:       (61) 2 9215 9301
**Email**:   m.collett@australiacouncil.gov.au

## Music Skills and Development

**Purpose**: To support skills development for professional artists and arts workers

**Eligibility**: Open to individuals and organisations which meet the eligibility requirements and provide the necessary support materials
**Type**: Grant
**Value**: Up to AU$10,000
**Frequency**: Every 2 years
**Application Procedure**: Apply online
**Closing Date**: 25 March
**Additional Information**: There are two subcategories: individuals and groups (established and emerging), and organisations (legally constituted). Please mail to music@australiacouncil.gov.au

**For further information contact:**

Tel:      (61) 2 9215 9108
Email:    p.keogh@australiacouncil.gov.au

## OZCO Community Cultural Development Fellowship

**Purpose**: To enhance the capacity of artists and artsworkers to provide leadership in the field
**Eligibility**: Applicants should have a solid record of achievement in community arts and culture, including community cultural development
**Level of Study**: Postgraduate, Professional development
**Type**: Fellowship
**Value**: AU$40,000
**Length of Study**: 2 years
**Frequency**: Annual
**Country of Study**: Australia
**Application Procedure**: Contact the department
**Closing Date**: 15 April
**Funding**: Government

**For further information contact:**

Tel:      (61) 2 9215 9029
Email:    ccd@ozco.gov.au

## OZCO Community Culture Development Grant Residency

**Purpose**: To afford an artist or arts worker the opportunity to take time out of project-based work and focus on professional development, reflection or individual arts practice
**Eligibility**: Artists applying require a driver's licence
**Level of Study**: Professional development
**Type**: Grant
**Value**: AU$14,000 and an AU$1,000 materials allowance
**Frequency**: Annual

**Study Establishment**: Hastings Council and Camden Haven Community College Inc
**Country of Study**: Australia
**Application Procedure**: Contact the department
**Closing Date**: 1 August
**Funding**: Government

**For further information contact:**

Tel:      (61) 2 9215 9034
Email:    m.martin@ozco.gov.au

## OZCO Dance Fellowship

**Purpose**: This grant is designed to support an established dance artist to undertake creative or professional development
**Eligibility**: This category is only open to individuals who are practising artists or arts workers. Applicant must meet the general eligibility requirements
**Level of Study**: Postdoctorate, Professional development
**Type**: Fellowship
**Value**: AU$50,000 per year
**Length of Study**: 2 years
**Frequency**: Annual
**Country of Study**: Australia
**Application Procedure**: Applicants are encouraged to apply online for this category
**Closing Date**: 31 July
**Funding**: Government
**Additional Information**: Please contact to dance@australiacouncil.gov.au

**For further information contact:**

Tel:      (61) 2 9215 9164
Email:    a.burnett@australiacouncil.gov.au

## OZCO Dance Grant Initiative: Take Your Partner

**Purpose**: To support young and emerging dance artists and art workers to forge a new relationship or build on an existing one through a specific project
**Level of Study**: Professional development
**Type**: Grant
**Value**: AU$15,000
**Frequency**: Annual
**Country of Study**: Australia
**Application Procedure**: Contact the department
**Closing Date**: June
**Funding**: Government

**For further information contact:**

**Tel**:      (61) 2 9215 9179
**Email**:    s.woo@ozco.gov.au

## OZCO Literature Fellowships

**Purpose**: To support excellence in Australian literature
**Eligibility**: Applications will only be accepted from individuals who have had a minimum of major works published or performed and have achieved substantial critical recognition
**Level of Study**: Postgraduate, Professional development
**Type**: Fellowship
**Value**: AU$100,000 over two years (paid in three instalments)
**Length of Study**: 2 years
**Frequency**: Annual
**Country of Study**: Australia
**Application Procedure**: Applicants are encouraged to apply online for this category. Duly filled application along with relevant supporting material, curriculum vitae, and one copy of two published books or performed plays in the genre of the project should be provided. For further details contact the Program Manager
**Closing Date**: 15 May
**Funding**: Government

**For further information contact:**

**Tel**:      (61) 2 9215 9057
**Email**:    literature@ozco.gov.au

## OZCO Literature Grants Initiative: Write in Your Face

**Purpose**: To support young writers using language in innovative ways
**Eligibility**: Applicant must be aged 30 years or under
**Level of Study**: Professional development
**Type**: Grant
**Value**: Up to AU$5,000
**Frequency**: Annual
**Country of Study**: Australia
**Application Procedure**: Contact the department. Apply online
**Closing Date**: 9 December

**For further information contact:**

**Tel**:      (61) 29215 9058
**Email**:    j.jones@ozco.gov.au

## OZCO Music Fellowship

**Purpose**: These two-year fellowship support outstanding, established music artists to produce new work and/or undertake professional development
**Eligibility**: This category is open to individuals who meet the general eligibility requirements. Fellowship recipients may not apply for a Project Fellowship where the start date of the Project Fellowship is less than five years after the end date of their Fellowship
**Level of Study**: Postdoctorate, Professional development
**Type**: Fellowship
**Value**: AU$100,000 (AU$50,000 per year for two years)
**Length of Study**: 2 years
**Frequency**: Annual
**Country of Study**: Australia
**Application Procedure**: Applicants are encouraged to apply online for this category
**Closing Date**: 31 July
**Funding**: Government
**Additional Information**: Fellowship recipients may apply for funding from other categories during the term of the Fellowship, with the exception of the project Fellowships initiative. Fellowships are granted only once in an artist's lifetime

**For further information contact:**

**Tel**:      (61) 2 9215 9115
**Email**:    music@australiacouncil.gov.au

## OZCO Music Project Fellowship

**Purpose**: These grants support mid-career and established artists to develop significant creative and/or developmental projects over a period of up to 12 months
**Eligibility**: Music artists working in music theatre and indigenous music artists are particularly encouraged to apply
**Level of Study**: Postgraduate, Professional development
**Type**: Fellowship
**Value**: AU$30,000
**Length of Study**: 1 year
**Frequency**: Annual
**Country of Study**: Australia
**Application Procedure**: Apply online
**Closing Date**: 31 July
**Funding**: Government
**Additional Information**: Please mail to music@australiacouncil.gov.au

**For further information contact:**

**Tel**:      (61) 2 9215 9108
**Email**:    music@ozco.gov.au

## OZCO New Media Residency

**Purpose**: To support hybrid and new media study abroad
**Level of Study**: Postdoctorate, Postgraduate
**Type**: Fellowship
**Length of Study**: 1 year
**Frequency**: Annual
**Study Establishment**: Banff Centre for the Arts
**Country of Study**: Canada
**Application Procedure**: Apply online
**Closing Date**: 1 November
**Funding**: Government

### For further information contact:

**Email**:    nma@ozco.gov.au

## OZCO Theatre Fellowship

**Purpose**: To financially support an individuals professional development
**Eligibility**: It is for artists with a record of outstanding achievement. Applicant must meet the general eligibility requirements and any specific eligibility requirements provided for this grant. In addition, applicant must be able to demonstrate at least 10 years' professional theatre experience
**Level of Study**: Postgraduate, Professional development
**Type**: Fellowship
**Value**: AU$45,000 per year over two years
**Length of Study**: 2 years
**Frequency**: Annual
**Country of Study**: Australia
**Application Procedure**: It is strongly recommended that you discuss your application with staff before applying. Applicants are encouraged to apply online for this category. Duly filled application along with relevant supporting material should be sent. For further details contact the Program Manager
**Closing Date**: 5 November
**Funding**: Government

### For further information contact:

**Tel**:    (61) 2 9215 9040
**Email**:    theatre@ozco.gov.au

## OZCO Visual Arts Fellowship

**Purpose**: To provide financial support to visual artists, craftspeople and specialist visual arts and craft writers of outstanding achievement to enable them to create new work and further develop their practice

**Eligibility**: This category is open to individual artists. Applications will be selected that best demonstrate: outstanding professional achievement; the artistic merit of the activities proposed for the fellowship period
**Level of Study**: Postgraduate
**Type**: Fellowship
**Value**: AU$120,000 over two years (in three instalments)
**Length of Study**: Up to 2 years
**Frequency**: Annual
**Country of Study**: Australia
**Application Procedure**: Applicants are encouraged to apply online for this category. Duly filled application along with relevant supporting material should be sent. For further details contact the Program Manager
**Closing Date**: 16 April
**Funding**: Government
**Additional Information**: Fellowships are granted only once in an artist's lifetime

### For further information contact:

**Tel**:    (61) 2 9215 9020
**Email**:    vac@ozco.gov.au

## Playing Australia: Regional Performing Arts Touring Fund

**Purpose**: These grants assist the touring of professionally produced performing arts across Australia, including regional and remote areas, where there is a demonstrated public demand and tours are otherwise not commercially viable
**Eligibility**: This category is open to organisations only
**Type**: Grant
**Value**: Varies
**Application Procedure**: Apply online
**Closing Date**: 1 December
**Additional Information**: Please mail to artsdevelopment@australiacouncil.gov.au

### For further information contact:

**Tel**:    (61) 2 9215 9176
**Email**:    T.Kita@australiacouncil.gov.au

## Projects – Creative Development

**Purpose**: These grants provide support for the research and creative development of new dance works
**Eligibility**: To be eligible, you must meet the general eligibility requirements and the specific eligibility requirements given below. This category is open to individuals, groups and

organisations. Dance Key Organisations are not eligible to apply to this category

**Type**: Grant

**Application Procedure**: You are encouraged to apply online for this grant

**Closing Date**: 16 August

**Additional Information**: Please mail to dance@australiacouncil.gov.au

**For further information contact:**

**Tel**:     (61) 2 9215 9179

**Email**:     k.morcombe@australiacouncil.gov.au

## Projects – Presentation

**Purpose**: The purpose of this grant is to provide support for dance works with a presentation outcome. This can include final stage creative development and presentation/s and remounts of dance works

**Eligibility**: To be eligible, you must meet the general eligibility requirements and the specific eligibility requirements given at the website. This category is open to individuals, groups and organisations. Key Organisations are not eligible to apply to this category

**Type**: Grant

**Value**: Up to AU$50,000

**Application Procedure**: You are encouraged to apply online for this grant

**Closing Date**: 15 August

**Additional Information**: Please mail to dance@australiacouncil.gov.au

**For further information contact:**

**Tel**:     (61) 2 9215 9179

**Email**:     k.morcombe@australiacouncil.gov.au

## The Dreaming Award

**Purpose**: This award supports a young artist aged 18–26 years to create a major body of work through mentoring and partnerships, either nationally or internationally

**Eligibility**: Open to First Nations Australian artists living here or overseas. Age open to 18-30. All artforms

**Type**: Award

**Value**: AU$20,000

**Country of Study**: Any country

**Application Procedure**: 1. Select 'Apply for a Grant' from the left panel menu. 2. From the list of opportunities select 'Apply' for the Dreaming Award. 3. Complete the fields and select answers with dropdown menus. 4. Upload any necessary support material. 5. Select 'Save' once complete. 6. If you are not ready to submit your application, you can return to it through 'Your Draft Applications' in the left panel menu at a later date. 7. Otherwise select 'Submit'.

**Closing Date**: 4 November

**Additional Information**: Please mail to atsia@australiacouncil.gov.au www.australiacouncil.gov.au/funding/funding-index/the-dreaming-award/

**For further information contact:**

**Tel**:     (61) 2 9215 9040

**Email**:     j.gillis@australiacouncil.gov.au

## The Red Ochre Award

**Purpose**: The Aboriginal and the Torres Strait Islander Arts Board established The Red Ochre Award in 1993 to pay tribute to an Aboriginal or Torres Strait Islander artist who, throughout their lifetime, has made outstanding contributions to the recognition of Aboriginal and Torres Strait Islander arts, both nationally and internationally

**Eligibility**: Nominations will be accepted from arts and community organisations and individuals. Nominations may only be made for living artists and individuals cannot nominate themselves. This award is not project based and, therefore is not given to assist any particular project, program or intended activity

**Type**: Award

**Value**: AU$50,000

**Country of Study**: Any country

**Application Procedure**: 1. Select 'Submit a Nomination' from the left panel menu. 2. Then under 'Awards' select 'Start a new award nomination'. 3. Ensure you select the correct award from the list of options. 4. Complete the fields and select answers with dropdown menus. 5. Upload any necessary support material. 6. Select 'Save' once complete. 7. If you are not ready to submit your nomination you can return to it through 'Your Draft Applications' in the left panel menu at a later date. 8. Otherwise select 'Submit'

**Closing Date**: 4 November

**Additional Information**: Please mail to atsia@australiacouncil.gov.au www.australiacouncil.gov.au/funding/travel-rights-and-translation-funds-for-literature-faqs/the-red-ochre-award-lifetime-achievement/

**For further information contact:**

**Tel**:     (61) 2 9215 9040

**Email**:     j.gillis@australiacouncil.gov.au

## Visions of Australia: Regional Exhibition Touring Fund

**Purpose**: Visions of Australia supports the development and touring of major public exhibitions of Australian cultural material throughout Australia, particularly into regional and remote areas

**Eligibility**: To be eligible, you must meet the general eligibility requirements and the specific eligibility requirements given at the website. This category is open to organisations only

**Type**: Funding support

**Value**: No maximum grant amount

**Application Procedure**: You are encouraged to apply online for this grant. To begin an online application, use the 'Apply online' button (www.australiacouncil.gov.au/grants/2013/visions-of-australia)

**Closing Date**: October

**Additional Information**: Please mail to artsdevelopment@australiacouncil.gov.au www.arts.gov.au/funding-and-support/visions-australia

### For further information contact:

The Program Officer, Visions of Australia, Department of Communications and the Arts, GPO Box 2154, Canberra ACT 2601, Australia.

**Tel**:        (61) 800 590 577
**Email**:   visions@arts.gov.au

## Visual Arts New Work

**Purpose**: To support the creation of new work by emerging and established craftspeople, designers, new media artists, visual artists, and arts writers

**Eligibility**: Open to individuals and groups that meet the eligibility requirements and provide the necessary support materials

**Value**: AU$10,000 for emerging and AU$20,000 for established craftspeople, designers, new media artists, visual artists and arts writers

**Frequency**: Annual

**Application Procedure**: Applications should include the required support materials. Apply online. Check website for further details. For further details contact the Program Officer

**Closing Date**: 16 April

**Contributor**: National Association for the Visual Arts (NAVA)

### For further information contact:

**Tel**:        (61) 2 9215 9020
**Email**:   s.saxon@australiacouncil.gov.au

## Visual Arts Presentation and Promotion

**Purpose**: To assist arts organisations to present and promote contemporary Australian craft, design, new media art and visual arts, to audiences in Australia and overseas

**Eligibility**: Open to organisations that meet the eligibility requirements and provide the necessary support materials

**Frequency**: Annual

**Application Procedure**: Applications should include the required support materials and apply online

**Closing Date**: 20 August

### For further information contact:

**Tel**:        (61) 2 9215 9131
**Email**:   v.lloyd@australiacouncil.gov.au

## Visual Arts Skills and Arts Development

**Purpose**: To enable professional development opportunities for craftspeople, designers, media artists, visual artists, arts writers and curators

**Eligibility**: Open to individuals and groups which meet the eligibility requirements and provide the necessary support materials

**Type**: Grant

**Value**: Supports artists to undertake professional development activities in Australia or overseas. AU$10,000 for Barcelona, Helsinki, Liverpool, London, New York, Paris, Rome or Tokyo; AU$25,000 for New York; AU$35,000 for Berlin residencies

**Length of Study**: More than 1 year (General). 3-month residency in Barcelona, Helsinki, Liverpool, London, New York, Paris, Rome or Tokyo; 6-month residency in New York; 12-month residency in Berlin

**Frequency**: Annual

**Application Procedure**: Apply online

**Closing Date**: 20 August

**Additional Information**: Please mail to visualarts@australiacouncil.gov.au

### For further information contact:

**Tel**:        (61) 2 9215 9336
**Email**:   r.petersen@australiacouncil.gov.au

## Australian Academy of Science

PO Box 783, Canberra, ACT 2601, Australia.

**Tel**:        (61) 2 6247 3966
**Email**:   io@science.org.au

**Website**:     www.science.org.au/internat
**Contact**:     International Programmes Officer

The Australian Academy of Science is an independent, non-profit organisation with a membership of 300 Fellows elected for making distinguished contributions in the area of natural sciences and their applications. The objectives of the Academy are to promote science and science education through a range of activities.

## Max Day Environmental Science Fellowship Award

**Purpose**: The Australian Academy of Science is inviting applications Max Day Environmental Science Fellowship Award. These fellowships are available to assist early stage PhD students or early career researchers with their research

**Eligibility**: 1. Applicants must be Australian citizens or permanent residents at the time of application. 2. be accepted to undertake a PhD (or equivalent research doctorate), have completed their confirmation and be enrolled in their first or second year of research (at the time of the award closing date). have held a PhD (or equivalent) for no more than 5 years at the time of the award closing date*

**Type**: Research

**Value**: The Max Day Environmental Science Fellowship Award is an annual award of up to AU$20,000 per awardee to assist early stage PhD students or early career researchers with their research. It provides funding support toward the costs of travel, courses or research expenses. Grants are GST exclusive

**Study Establishment**: Applicants must demonstrate a multi-disciplinary approach to their research work and conduct their research in one or more of the biological sciences relating to one or more of the following disciplines: Conservation of Australia's flora and fauna, Ecologically sustainable resource use, Environmental protection and Ecosystem services (either provisioning services, or habitat and supporting services)

**Country of Study**: Australia

**Application Procedure**: 1. A proposal summarising your chosen area of study/research and why the Max Day Fellowship will be of particular benefit to you. Please refer to the selection criteria section above for information outlining how the proposals are assessed. Maximum of two pages using size 12 font. 2. Itemised budget detailing eligible expenses with brief justification for each item, the names and details of funding already received (funding body, amount). Maximum of one page using size 12 font. The

applicant must show they have been recognised by one or more research institutions, such as their host institution, by the provision of some level of direct financial contribution towards their project (excluding salaries). 3. Brief CV including qualifications, summary of any professional/research experience and publications/presentations. A full publications list is not required. Maximum of three pages using size 12 font. 4. PhD students require a letter of reference from their supervisor confirming and commenting on their existing research. Maximum of one page using size 12 font. 5. Post-doctoral researchers must attach two referee reports to the application. The reports should be addressed to the Awards Committee and should indicate the referee's knowledge of the applicant's proposed Max Day Fellowship activities, and the potential benefits of these activities to the researcher and/or the research field. Maximum of one page using size 12 font per report.

**Closing Date**: 1 June

**Additional Information**: For more details please visit the website scholarship-positions.com/max-day-environmental-science-fellowship-award-australia/2018/02/22/ www.science.org.au/supporting-science/awards-and-opportunities/max-day-environmental-science-fellowship-award

### For further information contact:

**Email**:     awards@science.org.au

## Prostate Cancer Research Centre - NSW

**Purpose**: The objectives of the grant are: 1. to safeguard a prostate cancer biobank and databank through providing support for infrastructure and its maintenance for a period of up to six months. 2. establish a sustainability plan for future funding for the Australian Prostate Cancer Research Centre – NSW, Garvan Institute of Medical Research

**Eligibility**: The Australian Prostate Cancer Research Centre (APCRC) – NSW is the eligible organisation to apply for this Grant Opportunity

**Level of Study**: Postgraduate, Research

**Type**: Grant

**Frequency**: Annual

**Country of Study**: Any country

**Closing Date**: 21 January

**Funding**: Government

**Additional Information**:     www.cancer.nsw.gov.au/data-research/grants/grant-opportunities

### For further information contact:

**Email**:     Grant.ATM@health.gov.au

## Australian Academy of the Humanities (AAH)

3 Liversidge Street Acton, Canberra, ACT 2601, Australia.

| | |
|---|---|
| **Tel** | (61) 2 6125 9860 |
| **Email**: | enquiries@humanities.org.au |
| **Website**: | www.humanities.org.au |
| **Contact**: | Administration Officer |

The Australian Academy of the Humanities (AAH) was established under Royal Charter in 1969 for the advancement of the scholarship, interest in and understanding of the humanities. Humanities disciplines include, but are not limited to, history, classics, English, European languages and cultures, Asian studies, philosophy, the arts, linguistics, prehistory and archaeology and cultural and communications studies.

## Australian Academy of the Humanities Visiting Scholar Programmes

**Purpose**: To encourage scholarly contact with scholars from both Russia/the former USSR and Indonesia/South—East Asia and to assist scholars from those countries to obtain access to research materials held in Australia
**Eligibility**: Applicants must be identified as being appropriate representatives at Australia-based conferences
**Level of Study**: Doctorate, Postdoctorate
**Type**: Award
**Value**: AU$7,000 (for 2 scholars from Russia and the Former USSR) and AU$4,000 (for 2 scholars from Indonesia and South—East Asia)
**Frequency**: Annual
**Country of Study**: Australia
**Application Procedure**: Applicant (Australian host scholar) must send the Secretariat a brief explanation of the reason for the visit, a copy of the visiting scholar's curriculum vitae and a list of their most significant publications (in English), a provisional itinerary listing speaking engagements, potential contact with Australian scholars and research institutions to be visited and a provisional budget for the expenditure of the funds
**No. of awards offered**: 7
**Closing Date**: 31 July
**Funding**: Government
**No. of awards given last year**: 2
**No. of applicants last year**: 7
**Additional Information**: Eligible to nationals of: Russia and SE Asia www.humanities.org.au/opportunities/

### For further information contact:

| | |
|---|---|
| **Tel**: | (61) 2 6125 8950 |
| **Email**: | grants@humanities.org.au |

## The British Special Joint Project Funding Scheme

**Eligibility**: The principal applicant on the Australian side should be normally a resident of Australia. Other scholars associated with the project will normally be expected to be of postdoctoral status
**Level of Study**: Postdoctorate
**Type**: Award
**Value**: Up to £8,000 (if 1 award is given) or up to £4,000 per project (if 2 awards are given)
**Length of Study**: Up to 1 year
**Frequency**: Annual
**Country of Study**: United Kingdom and Australia
**Application Procedure**: Applicants from both sides must submit applications to the appropriate Academy. Australian scholars should apply through either the AAH or ASSA, depending on the nature of their project. Australian partners should consult the AAH or ASSA for application procedures. Equivalent information must be included on all application forms. All applications for Academy grants are considered in the light of referees comments
**No. of awards offered**: 22
**No. of awards given last year**: 2
**No. of applicants last year**: 22
**Additional Information**: www.humanities.org.au/opportunities/

### For further information contact:

| | |
|---|---|
| **Tel**: | (61) 2 6125 8950 |
| **Email**: | grants@humanities.org.au |

## Australian Bio Security-CRC (AB-CRC)

Building 76 Molecular Biosciences The University of Queensland, St Lucia, QLD 4072, Australia.

| | |
|---|---|
| **Tel**: | (61) 3346 8866 |
| **Email**: | corinna.lange@abcrc.org.au |
| **Website**: | www.abcrc.org.au |
| **Contact**: | Mrs Corinna Lange, Communications Manager |

The mission of the ABCRC is to protect Australia's public health, livestock, wildlife and economic resources through research and education that strengthens the national capability to detect, diagnose, identify, monitor, assess, predict and to respond to emerging infectious disease threats.

## AB-CRC Honours Scholarships

**Purpose**: To encourage students of high academic ability to take the first step in their career path as a researcher. To build research capacity in high priority areas related to biosecurity
**Eligibility**: Scholarships will be awarded preferentially to Australian residents and students from the Asia-Pacific region
**Level of Study**: Postgraduate
**Type**: Scholarship
**Value**: AU$5,000 per year (full-time) or AU$2,500 per year (part-time)
**Length of Study**: 1 or 2 years for a part-time scholarship
**Frequency**: Annual
**Study Establishment**: AB-CRC participating university
**Country of Study**: Australia
**Application Procedure**: Contact the scholarships Administrator officer
**Closing Date**: 31 October

### For further information contact:

**Tel**:      (61) 8 9266 1634
**Email**:    debra.gendle@abcrc.org.au

## AB-CRC Professional Development Scholarships

**Purpose**: To enhance linkages with research projects of relevance to the AB-CRC. To expand our capability to support the training of specialists. To provide students with access to the AB-CRC network and enhanced learning opportunities
**Eligibility**: PhD students enroled at AB-CRC partner organizations
**Level of Study**: Professional development
**Type**: Scholarship
**Value**: AU$2,000 per year
**Length of Study**: Varies
**Frequency**: Annual
**Study Establishment**: AB-CRC participating university
**Country of Study**: Australia
**Application Procedure**: Students must submit a Professional Development Plan. Contact the Scholarships Administration officer
**Closing Date**: 16 November
**Additional Information**: Candidates will be required to sign a confidentially agreement. Funding awarded in a Professional Development Scholarship will be on a sliding scale depending upon the student's enrolment date

### For further information contact:

**Email**:    debra.gendle@abcrc.org.uk

## The John Mulvaney Fellowship

**Purpose**: The Academy launched The John Mulvaney Fellowship in 2019. This award honours the outstanding contribution to Humanities scholarship, the Academy and the cultural life of the nation of one of our longest serving Fellows and former Academy Secretary John Mulvaney AO CMG FBA FSA FRAI FAHA.
**Eligibility**: 1. Applicants must be Aboriginal and/or Torres Strait Islander people. 2. The Fellowship is open to early career researchers (ECRs) and PhD students currently enrolled in an Australian institution. 3. Applicants must be Citizens or Permanent Residents of the Commonwealth of Australia, whose principal place of residence is Australia. 4. Applicants must be working in the Humanities, defined as those discipline areas by which the Academy is structured – Archaeology; Asian Studies; Classical Studies; English; European Languages and Cultures; History; Linguistics; Philosophy and the History of Ideas; Religion; Cultural and Communication Studies; and The Arts. Applicants working on projects in Indigenous Studies; Digital Humanities; and Environmental Humanities will also be eligible to apply. 5. Interdisciplinary work is encouraged, provided that it includes a substantial proportion of work in the Humanities. 6. Applications will be accepted from independent scholars holding a PhD as well as those working in institutional settings. 7. Early Career Researcher applicants must be in the early stages of their careers, which will be determined, inter alia, by how recently a PhD was conferred. In normal circumstances it should have been conferred no more than five years prior to the closing date for applications. 8. Recipients of a Humanities Travelling Fellowship offered by this Academy are ineligible. 9. Applicants must submit a complete application in order to be assessed for eligibility. 10. The decision of the Awards Committee upon the eligibility of an application is final.
**Level of Study**: Postgraduate
**Type**: Fellowship
**Value**: AU$4,000
**Study Establishment**: AB-CRC participating university
**Country of Study**: Australia
**Application Procedure**: 1. Rigour and significance of the research. 2. Likely impact within a specialist field. 3. Potential to engage and/or benefit the wider community. 4. Relevance of the project to their career development and be able to show evidence of this through either traditional or non-traditional research outputs.
**Closing Date**: 5 June
**Additional Information**: www.humanities.org.au/opportunities/mulvaney/

# Australian Catholic University (ACU)

Brisbane Campus (McAuley at Banyo), PO Box 456, Virginia, QLD 4014, Australia.

| | |
|---|---|
| **Tel** | (61) 2 9739 2305, 7 3623 7100 |
| **Email**: | studentcentre@mcauley.acu.edu.au |
| **Website**: | www.acu.edu.au |

Australian Catholic University (ACU) is a public university funded by the Australian Government and is open to students and staff of all beliefs. It has established a reputation for quality and innovative teaching and specialist tertiary education in health, education, business and informatics, arts, social sciences and theology.

## Adolescent Health and Performance Scholarship

**Purpose**: To attract a highly motivated postgraduate student who is interested in serially tracking the musculoskeletal health and performance of elite adolescent female athletes
**Eligibility**: Open to citizens or permanent residents of Australia between the ages of 22 and 30 to study in Australia. The candidate must have achieved First Class Honours or equivalent and have studied at or be currently studying at Australian Catholic University
**Level of Study**: Graduate
**Type**: Scholarship
**Value**: AU$25,627 per year
**Length of Study**: 3 years
**Study Establishment**: Australian Catholic University
**Country of Study**: Australia
**Application Procedure**: Candidates must apply directly to the Australian Catholic University
**Additional Information**: It is required that the study starts no earlier than 15 September and no later than 15 October

### For further information contact:

**Email**: robina.bamforth@acu.edu.au

## Co-op Bookshop Scholarship

**Purpose**: The Co-op Bookshop Scholarship has been established to assist high achieving students with financial costs associated with attending university.
**Eligibility**: Applicants must: be Australian citizens or permanent residents; be undergraduate students; be enrolled in Faculty of Law and Business or Faculty of Theology and Philosophy; and be in the first year of their course.

**Type**: Scholarship
**Value**: The scholarship is valued at US$2,500, paid in one lump sum.
**Length of Study**: 1 year
**Frequency**: Annual
**Country of Study**: Any country
**Closing Date**: March
**Additional Information**: www.australianuniversities.com. au/scholarships/guide/7886-co-op-bookshop-scholarship.html

## Council of Catholic School Parents (NSW) Indigenous Postgraduate Scholarship (IES)

**Purpose**: To encourage involvement of parents and the community in education
**Eligibility**: Open to Indigenous students enroled in a postgraduate course within the faculty of education at the Strathfield campus, and have a particular focus, interest, or understanding of the importance of parent and community involvement in education
**Type**: Scholarship
**Value**: AU$1,000 and a certificate
**Frequency**: Annual
**Study Establishment**: Strathfield campus
**Country of Study**: Australia
**Application Procedure**: Candidates can obtain further information from Yalbalinga Indigenous Unit, Strathfield campus. Online applications only
**Closing Date**: 18 March
**Contributor**: Council of Catholic School Parents (NSW)
**Additional Information**: Please check further information from Yalbalinga Indigenous Unit, Strathfield campus OR www.acu.edu.au/scholarships

### For further information contact:

**Email**: futurestudents@acu.edu.au

## International Postgraduate Research Scholarships (IPRS)

**Purpose**: To financially assist student to undertake full time postgraduate study who are otherwise unable to take up studies due to personal reasons (excluding employment)
**Eligibility**: Only international students are eligible for IPRS
**Level of Study**: Research
**Type**: Scholarship
**Value**: Full tuition fees (as approved by Common wealth Govt)
**Length of Study**: 2–3 years
**Frequency**: Annual
**Study Establishment**: Australian Catholic University (ACU)

**Country of Study**: Australia
**Application Procedure**: Application forms and further information on scholarships may be obtained by accessing the research services web site www.acu.edu.au/research
**Closing Date**: 31 October

**For further information contact:**

**Email**:    Res.Cand@patrick.acu.edu.au

## Pratt Foundation Bursary (IES)

**Purpose**: To make available a bursary to a suitably qualified Aboriginal and Torres Strait Islander student undertaking postgraduate study at ACU
**Eligibility**: 1. Citizenship: Australian Citizens. 2. Target group: Aboriginal and Torres Strait Islander. 3. Faculty: any. 4. Course: any ACU postgraduate degree. 5. Campus: any. 6. Year level: any
**Level of Study**: Graduate
**Type**: Bursary
**Value**: AU$2,500
**Frequency**: Annual
**Study Establishment**: Australian Catholic University (ACU)
**Country of Study**: Australia
**Application Procedure**: Candidates can obtain further information from Weemala Indigenous Unit, Brisbane campus. Online applications only
**No. of awards offered**: 1
**Closing Date**: 18 March
**Funding**: Foundation
**Contributor**: The Pratt Foundation
**Additional Information**: acu.fluidreview.com/p/a/110245/

**For further information contact:**

**Email**:    futurestudents@acu.edu.au

## Victorian International Research Scholarships

**Purpose**: The Victorian International Research Scholarship (VIRS) is offered in partnership between the Victorian Government and Victorian Universities. The Scholarship supports high-calibre international PhD scholars to undertake research in Victoria
**Eligibility**: Open to an international student; who accepted into a doctoral programme at ACU; intend to complete the majority of work related to the doctorate in Victoria; not have completed a degree equivalent to an Australian doctorate; willingness to act as an ambassador for the (VIRS) program
**Level of Study**: Doctorate
**Type**: Scholarship
**Value**: AU$90,000 over 3 years

**Length of Study**: Successful applicants will receive a scholarship of AU$90,000 for the duration of their PhD.
**Frequency**: Every 3 years
**Country of Study**: Any country
**Application Procedure**: Applicants must be a citizen of a country other than Australia
**Additional Information**: For further information, visit Study Melbourne, or email your application (MS Word document, 2.8 MB) to VIC.cand@acu.edu.au

## Australian Centre for Blood Diseases (ACBD)

6th Floor, Burnet Tower, 89 Commercial Road, Melbourne, VIC 3004, Australia.

**Tel**:        (61) 3 990 30122
**Email**:    acbd@med.monash.edu.au
**Website**:  www.acbd.monash.org

The Australian Centre for Blood Diseases (ACBD) brings together the skills and facilities of separate yet complementary organizations to enhance understanding of blood and its diseases. Its aim is to provide excellence in the diagnosis and treatment of blood conditions as well as play a leading role in the advancement of knowledge in this increasingly important area of medicine.

## Firkin PhD Scholarship

**Purpose**: To undertake a PhD programme at the ACBD or affiliated institutes comprising AMREP
**Eligibility**: Open to students interested in pursuing doctorate studies in cardiovascular disciplines, and who have the appropriate graduate qualifications
**Level of Study**: Graduate
**Type**: Scholarships
**Value**: AU$22,500 per year
**Length of Study**: 3 years
**Frequency**: Annual
**Application Procedure**: For further information, please contact Dr Robert Medcalf
**Additional Information**: www.monash.edu/medicine/ccs/blood-disease/education/firkin

**For further information contact:**

Australian Centre for Blood Diseases, Monash University, 6th Floor, Burnet Building, AMREP, Commercial Road, Melbourne, Victoria 3004, Australia.

**Email**:    Robert.Medcalf@med.monash.edu.au

## Australian Department of Science

PO Box 65, Belconnen, ACT 2616, Australia.

**Contact:**    Grants & Fellowships Branch

## Disability, Mental Health and Carers: National Disability Conference Initiative

**Purpose:** The Australian Government is inviting applications in an open process to apply to deliver services under the Disability, Mental Health and Carer: National Disability Conference Initiative in
**Eligibility:** To be eligible, applicants to the National Disability Conference Initiative (NDCI) must be one of the following entity types: 1. Indigenous Corporation. 2. Company. 3. Incorporated Association. 4. Cooperative. Applications from consortia are acceptable, as long as you have a lead applicant who is solely accountable to the Commonwealth for the delivery of grant activities
**Level of Study:** Graduate
**Type** Grant
**Value:** A maximum of AU$10,000 (GST exclusive) per conference is available for this grant opportunity
**Frequency:** Annual
**Country of Study:** Any country
**Application Procedure:** For further information on this grants, visit the website. www.communitygrants.gov.au/grants/disability-mental-health-and-carers-conference
**Closing Date:** 7 January
**Funding:** Government

### For further information contact:

**Tel:**    (61) 800 020 283
**Email:**    support@communitygrants.gov.au

## Australian Federation of University Women (AFUW)

School of Education, University of Ballarat, PO Box 663, Ballarat, VIC 3353, Australia.

**Tel:**    (61) 9557 2556
**Email:**    AFGW.Fellowships@gmail.com
**Website:**    www.afuw.org.au
**Contact:**    Dr Jacqueline Wilson, AFUW Vic Membership Secretary

Australian Federation of University Women (AFUW) Victoria was formed in 1922 as part of the international network of women Graduates for the benefit of women and society. AFUW Victoria is a member association of AFUW and serves a number of benefits both at personal and societal level in providing women with opportunities.

## Australian Federation of University Women - Western Australian -Foundation Bursary

**Eligibility:** Candidate should be women and must be a graduate members of the Australian Federation of University Women
**Level of Study:** Postdoctorate
**Type:** Bursary
**Value:** AU$2,500
**Frequency:** Annual
**Country of Study:** Any country
**Funding:** Private

### For further information contact:

Bursary Office, AFUW (WA), Inc., PO Box 48, Nedlands, WT 6009, Australia.

**Email:**    afuwwa@afuw.org.au

## Study in Australia - Northern Territory Scholarships

**Purpose:** This scholarship is provided to talented students from all over the world to study in Australia's Northern Territory. The scholarships recognize student's academic merit, leadership and community engagement
**Eligibility:** Applicants must: 1. have a demonstrated record of academic excellence, community engagement and leadership. 2. meet the Northern Territory education provider's academic and English entry requirement. 3. have applied and obtained an offer of admission to a Northern Territory education provider for study in the Northern Territory. i. Alana Kaye College. ii. Australian Careers College. iii. BCA National Training Group. iv. Charles Darwin University. v. Darwin High School. vi. International College of Advanced Education. vii. International House Darwin. viii. Navitas English Darwin. ix. Navitas Professional. x. The Essington International School Darwin. 4. reside in the Northern Territory. 5. not already be studying in the Northern Territory, or with a Northern Territory education provider. 6. not hold any other scholarship
**Level of Study:** Graduate
**Type:** Scholarship

**Value**: The scholarships are worth school (AU$10 000), English language (AU$5,000), vocational education and training (AU$7,500), Professional Year Program (AU$2,500) and higher education
**Frequency**: Annual
**Country of Study**: Australia
**Application Procedure**: For the complete information on the application methods, use the below link. studynt.nt.gov.au/file/923
**Closing Date**: 31 January
**Funding**: Private

### For further information contact:

**Email**:   StudyNT.nt.gov.au

## Women's Leadership and Development Program (WLDP) - Women's Economic Security Grant Guidelines

**Purpose**: The grant opportunity is to provide funding for one-off or small-scale projects that contribute towards achieving Women's Economic Security on a national scale within Australia
**Eligibility**: 1. A Company incorporated in Australia. 2. A Company incorporated by guarantee. 3. An Incorporated trustee on behalf of a trust. 4. A Publicly funded research organisation as defined in the Glossary. 5. An Aboriginal and/or Torres Strait Islander Corporation registered under the Corporations
**Level of Study**: Foundation programme
**Type**: Grant
**Frequency**: Annual
**Country of Study**: Any country
**Closing Date**: 25 January
**Funding**: Foundation

### For further information contact:

**Tel**:      (61) 2 6271 6074
**Email**:   WLDP17-18@pmc.gov.au

## Australian Government Research Training Scholarships

Flinders University is a public university in Adelaide, South Australia. The university is ranked within the world's top 400 institutions in the Academic Ranking of World Universities. Flinders University offers more than 160 undergraduate and postgraduate courses, as well as higher degree research supervision across all disciplines. Flinders University is renowned for world-class research and innovation that is relevant, of high quality, and has real impact.

## Australian Biological Resources Study (ABRS) National Taxonomy Research Grant Program

**Purpose**: The Australian Biological Resources Study (ABRS) provides research grants to Postdoctoral Fellows and established researchers to undertake research relevant to the taxonomy and systematics of the Australian biota
**Eligibility**: 1. All Research grants have a co-funding requirement. That is, applicants must have obtained a commitment for the applicable amount of co-funding for their application to be considered. 2. The ABRS will place no restrictions on the source of this contribution, but applicants will need to be aware of the rules of other granting agencies, which may limit how funds contributed by them may be used
**Level of Study**: Doctorate, Postdoctorate
**Type**: Research grant
**Value**: Research Grants of AU$10,000, AU$35,000, AU$70,000 or AU$90,000 per annum (excluding GST) are available, as well as a AU$90,000 per annum (excluding GST) Postdoctoral Fellowship grant
**Frequency**: Every 3 years
**Country of Study**: Any country
**Closing Date**: 22 November
**Funding**: Private
**Additional Information**: There are some funding agreement being meant for this funding scheme. All grant recipients who receive funding from the ABRS under the current and upcoming round, are subject to the terms and conditions set out in the ABRS Grant Funding Agreement. The Department of the Environment and Energy has developed standard funding agreements for grants. Applicants who are successful in receiving funding under the ABRS NTRGP are subject to the conditions set out in the following funding agreement templates. For further information towards the template, kindly visit our website. www.environment.gov.au/science/abrs/grants/research-grants www.communitygrants.gov.au/grants/national-taxonomy-research-grant-program

### For further information contact:

Business and Grants Manager Australian Biological Resources Study Department of the Environment and Energy GPO Box 787, Canberra ACT 2601, Australia.

**Email**:   abrs.grants@environment.gov.au

## Australian Security Intelligence Organisation Scheme

**Purpose**: It provides legal financial assistance for a person summoned by the Australian Security Intelligence Organisation (ASIO) to appear before a prescribed authority for questioning

**Eligibility**: At a minimum, you must: be a non-tax-exempt company, Australian University, Cooperative Research Centre (CRC) or Publicly Funded Research Agency (PRFA) have ownership, access to, or the beneficial use of any intellectual property necessary to carry out the projects under the JSF Program be able to match the value of funding dollar for dollar (co-contribution required) not be one of the companies engaged on the development of the Joint Strike Fighter (JSF)

**Level of Study**: Graduate

**Type**: Other

**Value**: complete value of the award is AU$3,316,000.00

**Frequency**: Annual

**Country of Study**: Any country

**Closing Date**: 7 September

**Funding**: Government

**Additional Information**: www.ag.gov.au/LegalSystem/Legalaidprogrammes/Commonwealthlegalfinancialassistance/Pages/Australian-Security-Intelligence-Organisation-scheme.aspx

## For further information contact:

**Tel**:  (61) 3 9268 7974

**Email**:  FinassGeneral@ag.gov.au

## Expensive Commonwealth Criminal Cases Fund (ECCCF)

**Purpose**: The Australian Government is inviting legal aid commissions to apply for reimbursement under the Expensive Commonwealth Criminal Cases Fund. This program, open to legal aid commissions, ensures that legal aid commissions have sufficient resources to provide a legal defence for people charged with serious Commonwealth criminal offences who cannot afford private legal representation

**Eligibility**: 1. Only legal aid commissions can apply for reimbursement under the ECCCF. 2. A legal aid commission is a statutory body established pursuant to legislation in the relevant state or territory to provide legal aid services

**Level of Study**: Graduate

**Type**: Funding support

**Frequency**: Annual

**Country of Study**: Any country

**Closing Date**: 28 November

**Funding**: Private

**Additional Information**: www.communitygrants.gov.au/grants/ecccf-2019-20

## For further information contact:

**Tel**:  (61) 800 020 283

**Email**:  support@communitygrants.gov.au

## National Disability Insurance Scheme Jobs and Market Fund Round 1

**Purpose**: The National Disability Insurance Scheme (NDIS) is a significant social and economic policy reform representing one of the largest job creation opportunities in Australia. Achieving choice and control for participants requires a well-functioning market of NDIS providers, from which empowered NDIS participants are able to choose quality services that meet their needs

**Eligibility**: To be eligible you must be one of the following entity types: 1. Indigenous Corporation. 2. Company. 3. Local Government. 4. Cooperative. 5. Incorporated Association. 6. Sole Trader. 7. Statutory Entity. 8. Partnership. 9. Trustee on behalf of a Trust

**Level of Study**: Graduate

**Type**: Scholarships

**Frequency**: Annual

**Country of Study**: Any country

**Closing Date**: 17 January

**Funding**: Government

**Additional Information**: This grant round is being administered by the Community Grants Hub, on behalf of the Department of Social Services www.communitygrants.gov.au/grants/ndis-jobs-and-market-fund-round-1

## For further information contact:

**Email**:  support@communitygrants.gov.au

## Volunteer Grants

**Purpose**: The Volunteer Grants program aims to support the efforts of Australia's Volunteers. They provide small amounts of money that organisations can use to help their volunteers. The grants form part of the Government's work to support the volunteers who help disadvantaged Australian communities and encourage inclusion of vulnerable people in community life

**Eligibility**: Eligible applicants must be Australian not-for-profit organisations or community groups; whose volunteers' work supports families and/or communities in Australia

**Level of Study**: Graduate

**Type**: Grants and studentships

**Value**: £5,000

**Frequency**: Annual

**Country of Study**: United Kingdom

**Closing Date**: 6 April

**Funding**: Private

**Additional Information**: www.communitygrants.gov.au/grants/volunteer-grants-activity-2019-20

**For further information contact:**

**Tel**:         (61) 800 020 283
**Email**:     support@communitygrants.gov.au

## Australian Institute of Aboriginal and Torres Strait Islander Studies (AIATSIS)

GPO Box 553, Canberra, ACT 2601, Australia.

**Tel**:         (61) 2 6246 1157
**Email**:     grants@aiatsis.gov.au
**Website**:   www.aiatsis.gov.au
**Contact**:   Mr Peter Veth, Research Administration Team

The Australian Institute of Aboriginal and Torres Strait Islander Studies (AIATSIS) is a federally funded organization devoted to Aboriginal and Torres Strait Islander research. Its principal function is to promote Australian Aboriginal and Torres Strait Islander studies. A staff of 90, directed by the Principal, engages in a range of services through the Research Programme, the Research Grants Programme, the archives and production team and the library.

## Australian Institute of Aboriginal and Torres Strait Islander Studies Conference Call for papers

**Purpose**: To promote research into Aboriginal and Torres Strait Islander studies. AIATSIS welcomes a variety of presentation and workshop formats (ranging from 30 mins to 1.5 hours) including:
**Eligibility**: Open to nationals of any country
**Level of Study**: Unrestricted
**Type**: Grant
**Value**: No pre-determined value
**Length of Study**: Up to 1 year
**Frequency**: Annual
**Country of Study**: Australia
**Application Procedure**: Applicants must complete an application form, available from the website
**No. of awards offered**: 101
**Closing Date**: 27 May
**Funding**: Government
**Contributor**: The Australian Federal Government
**No. of awards given last year**: 31
**No. of applicants last year**: 101
**Additional Information**: Permission to conduct research projects must be obtained from the appropriate Aboriginal

or Torres Strait Island community or organization aiatsis.gov.au/news-and-events/events/national-native-title-conference-2020

**For further information contact:**

Twin Towns Conference & Function Centre, 2 Wharf St, Tweed Heads, New Wales South 2485, Australia.

**Email**:     research@aiatsis.gov.au

## Australian Institute of Nuclear Science and Engineering (AINSE)

Private Mail Bag 1, Menai, NSW 2234, Australia.

**Tel**:         (61) 2 9717 3376
**Email**:     ainse@ansto.gov.au
**Website**:   www.ansto.gov.au
**Contact**:   Dr Dennis Mather, Scientific Secretary

Established in 1958, the Australian Institute of Nuclear Science and Engineering (AINSE) is a consortium of Australian universities and the University of Auckland

## Australian Institute of Nuclear Science and Engineering Awards

**Purpose**: Postgraduate Research Awards (PGRAs) are offered by AINSE Limited (the Australian Institute of Nuclear Science and Engineering) for suitably qualified persons wishing to undertake studies in AINSE's fields of interest for a higher degree at an AINSE member university
**Eligibility**: Open to member organizations of AINSE that are undertaking projects in an appropriate field
**Level of Study**: Unrestricted
**Type**: Grant
**Value**: Supplement stipend of AU$7,500 per annum and a generous travel and accommodation allowance to enable students to work at ANSTO facilities
**Length of Study**: 1 year
**Frequency**: Annual
**Study Establishment**: Lucas Heights Science and Technology Centre
**Country of Study**: Australia
**Application Procedure**: Applicants must contact the Scientific Secretary, AINSE or Research Office at member universities
**No. of awards offered**: 232

**Closing Date**: 15 April
**Funding**: Government
**No. of awards given last year**: 179
**No. of applicants last year**: 232

## For further information contact:

AINSE Ltd, Locked Bag 2001, Kirrawee DC NSW 2232, Australia.

**Tel**:    (61) 2 9717 3436
**Email**:    ainse@ainse.edu.au

# Australian National University (ANU)

Fees and Scholarships Office, Building X-005, Canberra, ACT 2601, Australia.

**Tel**:    (61) 2 6125 5111
**Email**:    research.scholarships@anu.edu.au
**Website**:    www.anu.edu.au

The Australian National University (ANU) was founded by the Australian Government in 1946 as Australia's only completely research-orientated university. It comprises of seven colleges and many research schools.

## Australian National University Doctoral Fellowships

**Purpose**: To help Doctoral students pursue research and dissertation writing
**Eligibility**: Open to candidates who have obtained their graduate degree from a university located in the United States
**Level of Study**: Doctorate
**Type**: Fellowships
**Value**: AU$1,600 per month, one round-trip economy class airfare and some funding for research
**Length of Study**: 3–9 months
**Frequency**: Annual
**Study Establishment**: Australian National University
**Country of Study**: Australia
**Application Procedure**: Applicants can download the application form from the website. The completed application form can be sent by post or electronically
**Closing Date**: 30 January
**Additional Information**: Fellows accompanied by their family and staying for 6 months or more at the ANU will be entitled to family support of up to AU$5,000, depending on

the number of family members and other circumstances www.anu.edu.au/study/scholarships/find-a-scholarship?&&&field_financial_sup_selection_tid%5B0%5D=105&combine=&sort_by=title&page=1#views-view-gateway-financial-support-option-panel-pane-1-container

## For further information contact:

**Email**:    hr.rspas@anu.edu.au

## Australian National University Excellence Scholarship Program

**Purpose**: To study full-time in postgraduate program at the Australian National University
**Value**: AU$5,000 in the first 12 months of study at ANU followed by 10% discount of tuition fees for years of study thereafter
**Country of Study**: Australia
**Closing Date**: 30 May
**Additional Information**: www.anu.edu.au/study/scholarships/find-a-scholarship?&&&field_financial_sup_selection_tid%5B0%5D=105&combine=&sort_by=title&page=1#views-view-gateway-financial-support-option-panel-pane-1-container

## For further information contact:

**Email**:    coursework.scholarships@anu.edu.au

## Australian National University-Study Canberra India Scholarship for Postgraduate and Undergraduates in Australia

**Purpose**: The objective of the award is to provide support for living costs to successful applicants who have achieved at an excellent level in their final years of schooling or university studies
**Eligibility**: Indian citizens are eligible to apply for this scholarship programme. Applicants whose first language is not English are usually required to provide evidence of proficiency in English at the higher level required by the University
**Type**: Postgraduate scholarships
**Value**: The Scholarship will be valued at AU$10,000. The first instalment of AU$2,500 will be paid to the student upon them enrolling in the first semester of their chosen undergraduate or postgraduate coursework program. The remaining funds will be paid after the census date of the first semester that the student is enrolled
**Study Establishment**: Scholarships are awarded in any of the subjects offered by the university

**Country of Study**: Australia

**Application Procedure**: The mode of application is online

**Closing Date**: 15 January

**Additional Information**: For more details please visit the website scholarship-positions.com/anu-study-canberra-india-scholarship-postgraduate-undergraduates-australia/2017/12/18/

**For further information contact:**

**Email**: international.recruitment@anu.edu.au

## College of Engineering and Computer Science: College Postgraduate International Award

**Eligibility**: The Scholarships are offered on the basis of offer of a place in the Master Degree by Coursework programs offered by the College of Engineering and Computer Science and other criteria as set out from time to time by the Program Authority. Eligible students will be automatically considered for the Scholarship on academic merit. The Scholarship is offered on the condition that the recipient is admitted to and continues to pursue a full-time postgraduate program of study at this University and in a program offered by the College of Engineering and Computer Science

**Type**: Award

**Value**: Stipend is AU$5,000, payable in two equal instalments of AU$2,500 at the beginning of each semester for one year. Scholars are required to meet all costs associated with their studies including travel, accommodation, books and incidental expenses. The scholar is responsible for paying International Tuition fees for the duration of the program

**Frequency**: Annual

**Additional Information**: A scholar may not hold concurrently another scholarship awarded by the University or another University College. A scholar must obtain permission from the College Coursework Scholarships Committee to hold any other scholarship or award concurrently with a College of Engineering and Computer Science Postgraduate Scholarship

**For further information contact:**

**Tel**: (61) 2 6125 0677

**Email**: student.services@cecs.anu.edu.au

## College of Engineering and Computer Science: College Postgraduate International Honours Award

**Type**: Award

**Value**: Stipend is AU$5,000, payable in two equal instalments of AU$2,500 at the beginning of each semester for one year

**Frequency**: Annual

**Additional Information**: The Scholarships are offered on the basis of offer of a place in the Master Degree by Coursework programs offered by the College of Engineering and Computer Science and other criteria as set out from time to time by the Program Authority

**For further information contact:**

Associate Dean (Education), ANU College of Engineering and Computer Science, Australia.

**Tel**: (61) 2 6125 0677

**Email**: student.services@cecs.anu.edu.au

## Full Tuition International Relations Scholarships

**Eligibility**: Scholarships are available for all students. There is no restriction or nationality criteria

**Value**: This scholarship will pay full tuition fees

**Length of Study**: Up to 4 full time semesters (24 months)

**Country of Study**: Australia

**Closing Date**: 31 October

**For further information contact:**

**Email**: info@InternationalRelationsEDU.org

## National Security College Entry Scholarship for Aboriginal and Torres Strait Islander Students

**Eligibility**: The Scholarship shall be available to an applicant who is of Australian Aboriginal and/or Torres Strait Islander descent; has completed a Bachelors degree; has been offered admission to the Graduate Certificate in National Security Policy or Master of National Security Policy; is not the recipient of a College sponsored place

**Type**: Scholarship

**Value**: The Scholarship covers the full domestic tuition fee for up to 24 units of College core courses. The Scholarship does not cover any necessary admissions and deposit fees, the payment of reading and study materials, living expenses, accommodation or any other costs associated with studying

**Country of Study**: Any country

**Application Procedure**: Please print and complete application form, available on the website

**Closing Date**: 20 July

**Additional Information**: The Scholarship is available in the first two semesters of study only. Please write to national.security.college@anu.edu.au

**For further information contact:**

**Email**: Crawford.degrees@anu.edu.au

## Research School of Accounting India Merit Scholarships

**Eligibility**: Students from India are eligible to apply
**Value**: The award will cover 50% of the awardees ANU International Student Fees per semester, for the standard full time duration of the degree in which the student is enrolled in
**Country of Study**: Australia
**Application Procedure**: Applications are called for with a closing date as set by the ANU CBE Scholarships Office. The application is submitted on the prescribed electronic form and supporting documentation forwarded to CBE by email
**Closing Date**: 18 May
**Additional Information**: Please visit scholarship-positions. com/research-school-of-accounting-india-merit-scholarships-australia/2018/03/31/

### For further information contact:

**Email**:    scholarships.cbe@anu.edu.au

## Tim and Margaret Bourke PhD Scholarships

**Purpose**: To support an ANU PhD student working in the area of pure (theoretical) mathematics, the advancement of women in the field of mathematics, and the teaching of mathematics at the Australian National University
**Eligibility**: A domestic or international student Enrolled or enrolling full-time in a program of study for the degree of Doctor of Philosophy at the Australian National University
**Type**: Scholarship
**Value**: AU$5,000 per annum
**Country of Study**: Australia
**No. of awards offered**: 1
**Closing Date**: 31 March
**Additional Information**: For further details, please visit www. scholarshipsupdates.com/australian-national-university-tim-and-margaret-bourke-phd-scholarships-2018/ www.anu.edu.au/study/scholarships/find-a-scholarship/tim-and-margaret-bourke-phd-scholarship

### For further information contact:

Kate Liesinger, MSI Administrative Officer John Dedman Building 27, Canberra ACT 2601, Australia.

**Tel**:    (61) 2 6125 0723
**Email**:    msi.hdr.sa@anu.edu.au

## Yuill Scholarship

**Purpose**: To support the International Court of Justice Traineeship Program

**Eligibility**: The scholarship applicant must be: a final year student in a Bachelor of Laws program in the ANU College of Law; or a final year student in a Juris Doctor program in the ANU College of Law; or enrolled in a Master of Laws program in the ANU College of Law; or a recent graduate of the Bachelor of Laws, Juris Doctor or Master of Laws program from the ANU College of Law. The Bachelor of Laws program may be undertaken as a single or a combined degree
**Type**: Scholarship
**Value**: AU$25,000
**Frequency**: Annual
**Country of Study**: Any country
**Additional Information**: The scholarship will apply for the duration of the traineeship (9 months in total). Application process and criteria is set out in the Conditions of Award. Applications can be sent electronically or in hard copy. Electronic applications can be sent to karen.heuer@anu.edu.au law.anu.edu.au/yuill-scholarship-application

### For further information contact:

**Email**:    scholarships.law@anu.edu.au

## Australian Research Council (ARC)

Level 2, 11 Lancaster Place, Canberra Airport, Canberra, ACT 2609, Australia.

**Tel**:        (61) 2 6287 6600
**Email**:    ncgp@arc.gov.au
**Website**:   www.arc.gov.au
**Contact**:   Dr Laura Dan, Chief Program Officer

The Australian Research Council (ARC) is a statutory authority within the Australian Government's Innovation, Industry, Science and Research portfolio. The ARC advises the Government on research matters, manages the National Competitive Grants Program, a significant component of Australia's investment in research and development, and has responsibility for the Excellence in Research for Australia initiative.

## Australia-India Strategic Research Fund (AISRF)

**Purpose**: The aim of Australia- India Strategic Research Fund is to 1. increase the uptake of leading science and technology by supporting collaboration between Australian and Indian researchers in strategically focused, leading-edge scientific research and technology projects. 2. strengthen strategic alliances between Australian and Indian researchers

**Eligibility**: To be eligible you must: 1. have an Australian Business Number (ABN) and be one of the following entities. 2. a company, incorporated in Australia. 3. an incorporated not for profit organisation. We can only accept applications: that have a primary Indian partner that has submitted, or is in the process of submitting, a corresponding application to India's Department of Science and Technology (DST) or the Department of Biotechnology (DBT)
**Level of Study**: Graduate
**Type**: Funding support
**Frequency**: Annual
**Country of Study**: Any country
**Closing Date**: 23 January
**Funding**: Government

### For further information contact:

**Email**:     enquiries@industry.gov.au

## Australian Sports Commission (ASC)

Australian Sports Commission, Leverrier Street, Bruce ACT 2617, PO Box 176, Belconnen, ACT 2616, Australia.

**Tel**:          (61) 2 6214 1111
**Email**:      recruitment@ausport.gov.au
**Website**:   www.ausport.gov.au

The Australian Sports Commission (ASC) is responsible for implementing the Australian Government's national sports policy, which is based on a sports philosophy of excellence and participation. It promotes an effective national sports system that offers improved participation in quality sports activities by all Australians and helps the talented and motivated to reach their potential excellence in sports performance. Its work is guided by the Australian Government's national sports policy, Building Australian Communities through Sport (BACTS).

### Biomechanics Postgraduate Scholarship (General Sports)

**Purpose**: To provide an opportunity for graduates with degrees with a major emphasis in biomechanics to have experience in the application of biomechanics to enhance elite sports performance
**Eligibility**: Applicants must have tertiary qualification in science, human movement, mathematics or a related area, should have an interest and/or understanding of research

principles and some knowledge of biomechanical systems and equipment
**Level of Study**: Graduate
**Type**: Scholarship
**Value**: AU$21,434 per year
**Length of Study**: 48 weeks
**Application Procedure**: Applicants must submit a covering letter, a statement of experience and curriculum vitae along with the application form
**Closing Date**: 29 September

### For further information contact:

**Tel**:     (61) 2 6214 1659

### Indigenous Sporting Excellence Scholarships

**Purpose**: To give indigenous sportspeople the opportunity to improve their sporting performance at an elite level
**Eligibility**: Applicants must be over 12 years of age, representing their state in national competition or Australia internationally within sport or the school sport system, a coach with level 1 or level 2 accreditation, a sports trainer with level 1 accreditation, a sports official with accreditation, competing in a sport that is recognized by the Australian Sports Commission
**Type**: Scholarship
**Value**: AU$500
**Country of Study**: Any country
**Application Procedure**: Check website for further details
**Closing Date**: 31 May
**Additional Information**: Athletes, coaches, sports trainers and officials who receive this scholarship are also eligible to apply for the Elite Indigenous Travel and Accommodation Assistance Program if they are selected for a state representative team attending national championships or an Australian team competing internationally

### For further information contact:

**Email**:     school.sport.victoria@edumail.vic.gov.au

### Performance Analysis Scholarship

**Purpose**: To provide performance analysis services to AIS sport programmes through coaches as directed and as required work on projects relating to enhancement of knowledge and coach education
**Eligibility**: Applicants must have a tertiary qualification in computer science, software engineering, information technology, human movement or a related area and an interest and/or understanding of research principles

**Type**: Scholarship
**Value**: AU$21,434 per year
**Length of Study**: 48 weeks
**Application Procedure**: Applicants must write a covering letter referencing the position title, prepare a thorough (but concise) statement that focuses on the relevant experience, curriculum vitae that summarize the qualifications including contact details for two referees and can be submitted by email
**Closing Date**: 29 September

### For further information contact:

**Tel**:　(61) 2 6214 1659

## PhD Scholarship Programs

**Eligibility**: Open to candidates who are keen to have a scholar carrying out innovative research specific to their needs
**Level of Study**: Doctorate
**Type** Scholarship
**Value**: AU$21,000 per year, with a further AU$3,000 per year set aside to cover routine expenses
**Country of Study**: Australia
**Application Procedure**: For application details, please visit the website, www.ausport.gov.au/jobs/index.asp
**Funding**: Government
**Contributor**: Australian Institute of Sports Medicine
**Additional Information**: Interested applicants need to visit the site regularly to watch for vacancies

### For further information contact:

**Email**:　john.williamsr@ausport.gov.au

## Postgraduate Scholarship Program–Physiology (Quality Control)

**Purpose**: To provide opportunity for a graduate whose primary role will be to assist in the area of quality control under the direction of the laboratory manager
**Eligibility**: Applicants must have a tertiary qualification in science or a related area, an interest and/or understanding of research principles and an experience in an administrative role and good computing skills
**Level of Study**: Graduate
**Type**: Scholarship
**Value**: AU$21,434 per year
**Length of Study**: 54 weeks
**Application Procedure**: Applicants must submit a covering letter, a statement of experience and curriculum vitae along with the application form
**Closing Date**: 29 September

**Contributor**: Australian Sports Commission
**Additional Information**: Terms and conditions are subject to change. Always confirm details with scholarship provider before applying www.postgraduatefunding.com/award-2363

### For further information contact:

**Tel**:　(61) 2 6214 1564

## Postgraduate Scholarship–Biomechanics (Swimming)

**Purpose**: To provide the opportunity for graduates of degrees with major emphasis in biomechanics and to have experience in the application of biomechanics to enhance elite sports performance
**Eligibility**: Applicants must have a degree in biomechanics or human movement sciences, an interest and/or understanding of research principles, experience in biomechanics services and knowledge of and experience in a competitive swimming environment
**Level of Study**: Graduate
**Type**: Scholarship
**Value**: AU$21,434 per year
**Length of Study**: 48 weeks
**Application Procedure**: Applicants must submit a covering letter, a statement of experience and curriculum vitae along with the application form
**Closing Date**: 29 September
**Additional Information**: www.postgraduatefunding.com/award-1736

### For further information contact:

PO Box 176, Belconnen, ACT, 2616, Australia.

**Tel**:　(61) 2 6214 1732

## Postgraduate Scholarship–Physiology (Biochemistry/Haematology)

**Purpose**: To provide an opportunity for a graduate whose primary role will be to assist in the area of biochemistry and haematology under the direction of the biochemistry/haematology manager
**Eligibility**: Applicants must have a degree in medical laboratory science or biological sciences and an interest and/or understanding of research principles, good computer skills
**Level of Study**: Postgraduate
**Type**: Scholarship
**Value**: AU$21,434 per year
**Length of Study**: 50 weeks

**Application Procedure**: Applicants must write a covering letter referencing the position title, prepare a thorough (but concise) statement that focuses on the relevant experience, curriculum vitae that summarize the qualifications including contact details for two referees and can be submitted by email
**Closing Date**: 29 September
**Additional Information**: www.postgraduatefunding.com/award-2362

### For further information contact:

PO Box 176, Belconnen, ACT 2616, Australia.

Tel:    (61) 2 6214 1111
Fax:    (61) 2 6251 2680, 2 6214 1836

## Sport Leadership Grants for Women Program

**Purpose**: To provide women with an opportunity to undertake sport leadership training
**Eligibility**: Applicants must be indigenous women, women in disability sport, women from culturally and linguistically diverse backgrounds and women in general sport leadership
**Type**: Grant
**Value**: Up to AU$5,000 for individuals and up to AU$10,000 for incorporated organizations
**Application Procedure**: Check website for further details
**Closing Date**: 29 April
**Funding**: Government
**Additional Information**: www.sportaus.gov.au/grants_and_funding/women_leaders_in_sport

### For further information contact:

Tel:    (61) 2 6214 7994
Email:    leadershipgrants@ausport.gov.au

## Sports Medicine Fellowship Program

**Eligibility**: Open to Australasian College of Sports Physicians (ACSP) trainees
**Level of Study**: Postgraduate
**Frequency**: Annual
**Study Establishment**: Australian Institute of Sports Science
**Country of Study**: Australia
**Application Procedure**: For application details, please visit the website, www.ausport.gov.au/jobs/sssmpostgrad.asp
**Funding**: Government

### For further information contact:

Tel:    (61) 2 6214 1578
Email:    jill.flanagan@ausport.gov.au

## Sports Physiology Postgraduate Scholarship– Fatigue and Recovery

**Purpose**: To offer an Honours graduate in science or a related field the opportunity to complete a scholarship in physiology (fatigue and recovery)
**Eligibility**: Applicants must have an Honours Degree in science or a related area, basic skills in conducting routine physiological testing procedures, good computing skills, outstanding organizational skills and a high level of initiative
**Level of Study**: Graduate
**Type**: Scholarship
**Value**: AU$19,890 per year
**Length of Study**: 1 year
**Application Procedure**: Applicants must submit a covering letter, a statement of experience and curriculum vitae along with the application form
**Closing Date**: 6 April
**Additional Information**: www.postgraduatefunding.com/award-2364

### For further information contact:

PO Box 176, Belconnen, ACT 2616, Australia.

Tel:    (61) 2 6214 1111
Fax:    (61) 2 6251 2680, 2 6214 1836
Email:    Recruitment@ausport.gov.au

## Austrian Academy of Sciences

Institute of Limnology, Mondseestrasse 9, AU-5310, Mondsee, Austria.

Tel:    (43) 623 240 79
Email:    ipgl.mondsee@oeaw.ac.at
Website:    www.ipgl.at
Contact:    Mr Regina Brandstätter, IPGL Officer

The Institute of Limnology of the Austrian Academy of Sciences performs ecological research on inland waters. The overall research goal is to understand the structure, function and dynamics of freshwater ecosystems. Although the Institute primarily conducts basic research, aspects of applied research are also considered. The Institute at Mondsee, located close to Salzburg, was established in 1981 and has a staff of 26, including 13 scientists. Currently, the Institute's main fields of research are tropic interactions and food-web structures in lakes.

## Austrian Academy of Sciences, 4-months Trimester at Egerton University, Kenya

**Purpose**: Postgraduate training of water experts of African countries: Ethiopia, Uganda, Kenya, Burundi, Tansania, Rwanda, Cape Verde, Burkina Faso, Senegal

**Eligibility**: Principal requirement for admission is a BSc degree or equivalent qualification in a relevant subject from a recognized university (e.g. BSc in botany, zoology, chemistry, agriculture, environmental science, aquaculture and fisheries, water resource management, environmental economics or engineering, etc.). Priority countries: Eastern Africa: Ethiopia, Uganda, Kenya, Burundi, Tanzania, Rwanda, Western Africa: Cape Verde, Burkina Faso, Senegal. Southern Africa: Mozambique

**Type**: Fellowship

**Value**: €450 monthly, to cover food, personal needs plus free tuition, health insurance, study material, equipment for lab work, field work and travelling expenses

**Length of Study**: 4 months

**Frequency**: Annual

**Study Establishment**: Egerton University, Kenya

**Country of Study**: Kenya

**Application Procedure**: Application forms are provided by Egerton University and IPGL Office within the Institute for Limnology of the Austrian Academy of Sciences

**No. of awards offered**: 2 qualified

**Closing Date**: 30 November

**Funding**: Government

**Contributor**: The Austrian Development Cooperation

**No. of awards given last year**: 2

**No. of applicants last year**: 2 qualified

**Additional Information**: No provisions are made for dependants. Country of study is Kenya

### For further information contact:

Egerton University, PO Box 536, Egerton 20115, Kenya.

**Email**:   info@egerton.ac.ke

## Austrian Academy of Sciences, MSc Course in Limnology and Wetland Ecosystems

**Purpose**: To understand the structure and functioning of aquatic and wetland ecosystems for the conservation of biodiversity and sustainable management of natural resources. To acquire skills for interacting with stakeholders, managers and policy makers in the development of best practices

**Eligibility**: Open to candidates from developing countries who are maximum 35 years of age, have a good working knowledge of English and have an academic degree in science, agriculture or veterinary medicine from a university or any other recognized Institute of Higher Education. Applicants should have 3 years practical experience in at least one special subject in their field of professional training. All applications are considered on their individual merits

**Level of Study**: Postgraduate

**Type**: Scholarship

**Value**: US$1,350 paid monthly to cover food, lodging and personal needs plus free tuition, health insurance, study material and equipment for laboratory work, field work and travelling expenses

**Length of Study**: 18 months

**Frequency**: Annual

**Study Establishment**: Institute for Limnology, Mondsee; Institute UNESCO-IHE, Delft, The Netherlands; Egerton University, Kenya; Czech Academy of Sciences, Trebon, Czech Republic; Austrian Universities and Federal Institutes in Austria

**Application Procedure**: Applicants must obtain application forms from the website. Filled application forms can be sent to Institute for Limnology of the Austrian Academy of Sciences

**No. of awards offered**: 90

**Closing Date**: January

**Funding**: Government

**Contributor**: The Austrian Development Co-operation

**No. of awards given last year**: 4

**No. of applicants last year**: 90

**Additional Information**: No provisions are made for dependants. It is strongly advised that dependants do not accompany fellows due to frequent moves during the course. Fellows must also provide their own transportation to and from Austria www.postgraduatefunding.com/award-1710

### For further information contact:

Institute of Limnology, Dr. Ignaz Seipel-Platz 2, A-1010, Vienna, Austria.

**Tel**:    (43) 6232 4079
**Fax**:    (43) 6232 3578

## Austrian Academy of Sciences, Short Course— Tropical Limnology

**Purpose**: To assist students studying the special characteristics of tropical river and lake ecosystems, its interactions with activities, processes in the watershed and relevant ecosystem services

**Eligibility**: Open to candidates from East African countries who have a good working knowledge of English and have an academic degree either in science, agriculture or veterinary medicine from a university or other recognised Institute of Higher Education. Applicants should have practical experience within at least one special subject in their field of professional training

**Level of Study**: Postgraduate

**Type**: Scholarship

**Value**: US$21 paid per day including accommodation, full board and US$2,500 d.s.a. plus free tuition, health insurance, study material and equipment for laboratory work, field work and travelling expenses

**Length of Study**: 3 weeks

**Frequency**: Annual

**Study Establishment**: Egerton University, Kenya, Sagana Fish Farm, Kenya

**Application Procedure**: Application forms are also available from the website

**No. of awards offered**: 75

**Closing Date**: 30 July

**Funding**: Government

**Contributor**: The Austrian Development Co-operation

**No. of awards given last year**: 10

**No. of applicants last year**: 75

**Additional Information**: No provisions are made for dependants. It is strongly advised that dependants do not accompany Fellows due to frequent moves during the course. Fellows must also arrange their own transportation to and from Kenya

### For further information contact:

Dept. of Zoology, Egerton University, PO Box 536, Egerton 20115, Kenya.

**Email**:     mathookoj@yahoo.com

## Austrian Exchange Service

Agency for International Co-operation in Education & Research Bureau for Academic Mobility Alserstrasse 4/1/15/7, A-1090, Vienna, Austria.

**Tel**:          (43) 142 772 8188
**Email**:      bamo@oead.ac.at
**Website**:   www.oead.ac.at
**Contact**:   Dr Lydia Skarits, Head of Office

### Austrian Academic Exchange Service Unilateral Scholarship Programs

**Purpose**: To enable postgraduates from developing countries to undertake professional training

**Eligibility**: Applicants must be postgraduates of natural scientific, technical, social and economic studies or medical doctors wishing to conduct professional training in Austria

**Level of Study**: Postgraduate, Professional development

**Type**: Scholarship

**Value**: Monthly scholarship payment, plus a possible additional payment for housing, as well as cover for accident and health insurance. After four months a start payment is granted. Under certain conditions there is the possibility of the coverage of travel costs

**Country of Study**: Austria

**Application Procedure**: Applicants can obtain information from the website or contact the Austrian Exchange Service

### For further information contact:

**Tel**:       (43) 142 772 8180
**Fax**:       (43) 142 772 8195
**Email**:    vbs@oead.ac.at

## Austrian Federal Ministry for Science and Research

Embassy of Austria, 12 Talbot Street, Forrest, ACT 2603, Australia.

**Tel**:          (61) 2 6295 1533
**Contact**:   Grants Management Officer

### Australia-India Strategic Research Fund (AISRF)

**Purpose**: Australia-India Collaborative Research Projects are funded by the Australia-India Strategic Research Fund (AISRF)

**Eligibility**: 1. A company, incorporated in Australia. 2. An incorporated not for profit organisation. 3. A publicly funded research organisation (PFRO) as defined in appendix A. 4. A Cooperative Research Centre. 5. An other Australian incorporated entity. 6. That have a primary Indian partner that has submitted, or is in the process of submitting, a corresponding application to India's Department of Science and Technology (DST) or the Department of Biotechnology (DBT)

**Level of Study**: Research

**Type**: Research grant

**Value**: AU$4,000,000.00

**Frequency**: Every 3 years

**Country of Study**: Any country

**Application Procedure**: Apply online

**Closing Date**: 23 January

**Funding**: Government

**Additional Information**: Business.gov.au provides information and advice to customers via a range of channels including phone (13 28 46), email and web chat. Contact us for assistance. Refer website www.business.gov.au/aisrf

**For further information contact:**

**Email**: enquiries@industry.gov.au

## Australian Prostate Centre - Victoria

**Purpose**: The purpose of the grant is to support prostate cancer research through the safeguarding of rare tissue and bioinformatics assets at the Australian Prostate Centre (Victoria)
**Eligibility**: The Australian Prostate Centre Victoria is the eligible organisation to apply for this Grant Opportunity
**Level of Study**: Research
**Type**: Grant
**Value**: AU$600,000.00
**Frequency**: Annual
**Country of Study**: Australia
**Closing Date**: 21 January
**Funding**: Government

**For further information contact:**

**Email**: grant.atm@health.gov.au

## Small and Medium Enterprises (SME) Export Hubs

**Purpose**: The Small and Medium Enterprises (SME) grant opportunity will support SME Export Hubs in the development of local, regional and Indigenous brands through business collaborations in the identified areas of competitive strength
**Eligibility**: 1. Incorporated association. 2. Company limited by guarantee. 3. Non-distributing co-operative. 4. Indigenous not for profit corporation. 5. Not-for-profit incorporated trustee on behalf of a trust. 6. Australian local government agency or body. 7. Australian state/territory government agency or body. 8. Regional Development Australia (RDA) committee
**Level of Study**: Professional development
**Type**: Grant
**Value**: AU$18,800,000.00
**Frequency**: Annual
**Country of Study**: Any country
**Closing Date**: 21 January
**Funding**: Government
**Additional Information**: Business.gov.au provides information and advice to customers via a range of channels including phone (13 28 46), email and web chat. Contact us for

assistance www.business.gov.au/Grants-and-Programs/Small-and-Medium-Enterprises-Export-Hubs

**For further information contact:**

**Email**: enquiries@industry.gov.au

## Austro-American Association of Boston

Austro-American Association of Boston, Inc. c/o Traude Schieber-Acker, President 67 Bridle Path, Sudbury, MA 01776, United States of America.

**Tel**: (1) 978 579 2191
**Email**: thansen@wellesley.edu
**Website**: www.austria-boston.org/

Membership of the Austro-American Association of Boston is open toany individual interested in any aspect of Austrian history, economy, culture, politics and tourism. The association conducts meetings and get togethers focusing on events and experiences related to Austria.

## A-AA Austrian Studies Scholarship Award

**Purpose**: Project areas may include history, literature, art, architecture, folk customs, music and contemporary life
**Eligibility**: All undergraduate and graduate students at New England colleges and Universities are eligible to apply
**Level of Study**: Graduate
**Type**: Award
**Value**: US$1,500
**Application Procedure**: There is no application form. Applicants should submit the following information: a detailed project proposal, including the reason for selecting it; curriculum vitae; and two confidential letters of support from faculty members who know the applicant well and can comment on the feasibility of the project
**Closing Date**: 1 March
**Additional Information**: Please feel free to email any or submissions or inquiries to the co-chair of the scholarship committee, Dr Johann Nittmann at Johann.Nittmann@cavium.comwww.austria-boston.org/scholar.asp

**For further information contact:**

Department of German, Wellesley College, 106 Central St, Wellesley, MA 02481, United States of America.

**Tel**: (1) 781 283 2255

## Austro-American Association of Boston Stipend

**Purpose**: To promote the understanding and dissemination of Austrian culture

**Eligibility**: Junior faculty members and students enroled in a college in New England

**Level of Study**: Unrestricted

**Type**: Stipendiary

**Value**: US$3,000

**Study Establishment**: Any in New England

**Country of Study**: United States of America

**Application Procedure**: Applicants must submit a detailed description of the project including the reasons for selecting it, a curriculum vitae and two letters of recommendation from faculty members who know the applicant well and can comment on the feasibility of the project

**No. of awards offered**: 1

**Closing Date**: 23 March

**Funding**: Private

**Contributor**: Association members

**No. of applicants last year**: 1

**Additional Information**: The award is limited to individuals living or studying in New England. Projects funded in the past have included the preparation of musical or dramatic performances, the facilitation of appropriate publications and research trips to Austria. Culture is defined to include the humanities and the arts. The recipient may be asked to present the results of the project at an event of the Austro-American Association. The award may not be used to pay tuition fees at a college or university in New England www.austria-boston.org/scholar.asp

### For further information contact:

Wellesley College, 106 Central St, Wellesley, MA 02481, United States of America.

**Email**:    scholarship@austria-boston.org

## Autism Speaks

### Postdoctoral Fellowship

**Subjects**: Autism research

**Purpose**: Autism Speaks is dedicated to promoting solutions, across the spectrum and throughout the life span, for the needs of individuals with autism and their families. We do this through advocacy and support; increasing understanding and acceptance of autism spectrum disorder; and advancing research into causes and better interventions for autism spectrum disorder and related conditions. The goal of our postdoctoral fellowships is to support well-qualified postdoctoral scientists pursuing training in autism.

**Eligibility**: The program is open to applicants from public or private institutions doing preclinical or clinical research.

**Type**: Fellowship

**Value**: Each fellowship includes both a competitive stipend and an US$11,000 annual allowance intended to cover professional conference travel, research costs and supplies, and/or fringe benefits. Indirect costs are not allowed. Stipend amounts based on years of experience since PhD can be found below, with the year 7 level being the maximum. The latest start year is 5 years.

**Length of Study**: Two years

**Country of Study**: Any country

**Application Procedure**: All proposals must be submitted online via Autism Speaks Science Grants System. Through its various user-friendly features, applicants and institutional officials can monitor the status of their applications and grants. System access instructions can be found in the RFAs.Electronic submissions are mandatory. No paper or e-mailed applications will be accepted.

**Closing Date**: Schedule to be confirmed

**Additional Information**: For queries contact research@autismspeaks.org. www.autismspeaks.org/scientific-research-grants-how-apply

# B

## Bath Spa University

Newton St Loe, Bath, BA2 9BN, United Kingdom.

**Website**: www.bathspa.ac.uk

Bath Spa University's vision is to be a leading educational institution in creativity, culture and enterprise. Through innovative teaching and research, the University provides a high quality student experience. Based in a world heritage city and connected to a network of international partners, Bath Spa University ensures that its graduates are socially engaged global citizens.

## International Partner Scholarship

**Purpose**: Bath Spa University's International Partner Scholarships celebrate our strong partnerships with leading universities across the world

**Eligibility**: Open to postgraduate taught Master's applicants from Bath Spa University partner institutions. Applications are welcome from international students who have completed undergraduate or postgraduate education at a partner institution; achieved high academic results; can demonstrate experience in university, community and society activities; can show future aspirations to become involved in university life at Bath Spa University; plus show ideas on how Bath Spa University can work with its partner institutions towards promoting global citizenship.

**Type**: Scholarship

**Value**: £3,000

**Frequency**: Annual

**Application Procedure**: Applications are made through the international scholarship application form. Applicants must hold an offer of admission for a Bath Spa University postgraduate taught degree programme that is full-time and taught on-campus, be a graduate of a Bath Spa University partner institution, and complete the International Scholarship Application Form

**Additional Information**: For further information, please check at www.bathspa.ac.uk/international-students/scholarships/international-partner-scholarship

**For further information contact:**

**Email**: international@bathspa.ac.uk

## Invertimos en el talento de los Colombianos (ICETEX) Artistas Jovenes Scholarships

**Purpose**: ICETEX's Artistas Jovenes Talentos programme is a unique programme that supports young Colombian artists and designers, filmmakers, performers and musicians, writers and poets. As the leading United Kingdom university for partner of ICETEX, and the top United Kingdom creative university, the ICETEX Artistas Jovenes Talentos is a perfect fit for applicants to Bath Spa University's programmes across art, design, film, writing, music and performance

**Eligibility**: Applications are open for candidates who meet the requirements of ICETEX application process. Full details of eligibility are available on the ICETEX website

**Level of Study**: Graduate, Postgraduate

**Type**: Scholarship

**Application Procedure**: (i) Eligible candidates must first have an offer of admission for the chosen programme, If you meet the entry criteria for the chosen course you will be sent a conditional offer of admission by email. You must meet all the academic conditions of offer, including submission of certificates and transcripts, translated copies, English Language requirement, passport copy, references. (ii) Once you have received an offer letter to the chosen programme of study you then complete the ICETEX Artistas Jovenes Talentos process

© Springer Nature Limited 2020
Palgrave Macmillan (ed.), *The Grants Register 2021*,
https://doi.org/10.1057/978-1-349-95988-4

**Additional Information**: Bath Spa University can provide individual help and advice on your application and has a dedicated office in Colombia

## For further information contact:

Bath Spa University, Newton Park, Newton St Loe Bath, BA2 9BN, United Kingdom.

**Tel**:       (44) 1 300 3710
**Email**:    BSUColombia@bathspa.ac.uk

## Invertimos en el Talento de los Colombianos (ICETEX) Scholarships

**Purpose**: The University of Salford is pleased to work with ICETEX to offer funding opportunities for Colombian students to study in the United Kingdom
**Eligibility**: Applications are open for candidates who meet the requirements of ICETEX application process. Full details of eligibility are available on the ICETEX website at
**Type**: Scholarship
**Value**: 50% tuition fee
**Frequency**: Annual
**Country of Study**: Any country
**Application Procedure**: Applicants must apply for the programme of study and then the scholarship via ICETEX. Applicants must also submit a completed Bath Spa University International Scholarship Application form and include the ICETEX reference number. Further application details are given in the website
**Closing Date**: 10 May
**Funding**: Private
**Additional Information**: Applications will be reviewed on submission of the relevant documentation to ICETEX and the Bath Spa University Application Form. The applications are reviewed within two weeks after the deadline by the University Committee. For further information, refer the website link below.    beta.salford.ac.uk/international/icetex-scholarships-colombia

## Latin America – Creative and Culture Scholarships

**Purpose**: Bath Spa University is the United Kingdom's leading university for creativity, culture and enterprise. To celebrate this excellence, and to support Bath Spa University's work in Latin America
**Eligibility**: Applicants must be nationals from Latin America who have applied for and hold an offer for any of the eligible programmes, have high academic results and can demonstrate a commitment to creativity, culture and enterprise in Latin America
**Level of Study**: Graduate, Postgraduate
**Type**: Scholarship
**Value**: £5,000 off tuition fees for your first year of study (two available)
**Application Procedure**: Please complete all the details, including your name, contact details, student number and qualifications. Applications with missing details will be automatically rejected. If you're awaiting your final results, you're still able to apply. Please state 'pending results' in the qualification section. You must submit your results when they're available. The scholarship essay question is very important. To answer this question you should include details that cover all the criteria: Academic achievement / results Involvement in activities at your previous university, community work and your contribution to society, Charity / volunteer work you've done, Information on your future aspirations, Examples on how you'll contribute to the social and economic development of your country. You should also give examples on how you intend to become involved in university life at Bath Spa.
**Closing Date**: 31 May
**Additional Information**: Applications are reviewed on submission of the International Scholarship Application Form. Particular attention is given to the scholarship essay. The applications are reviewed in the month after the deadline by the University Committee www.bathspa.ac.uk/students/student-finance/scholarships-and-funding/scholarships-latin-america/

## For further information contact:

**Tel**:       (44) 1225 875777
**Email**:    international@bathspa.ac.uk

## Postgraduate Overseas Scholarship

**Eligibility**: Open to applicants who have met the required entry qualification and been offered a place (conditional or unconditional) on a postgraduate taught Masters' programme. It is awarded on the basis of academic merit
**Type**: Scholarship
**Value**: £1,000
**Application Procedure**: Eligibility for the Overseas Scholarship is judged on the basis of the application to the chosen programme of study. There is no need to submit a separate application form. If you are selected for a Postgraduate Overseas Scholarship you will receive a confirmation letter at the time of your offer of admission

## For further information contact:

**Tel**:       (44) 1225 875 777
**Email**:    international@bathspa.ac.uk

## Vice Chancellor's International Scholarship

**Purpose**: The Bath Spa University Vice Chancellor's International Scholarship celebrates our commitment to internationalization and excellence in creativity, culture and enterprise

**Eligibility**: Applications are welcome from international students who have achieved high academic results and can demonstrate a commitment to creativity, culture and enterprise

**Level of Study**: Graduate, Postgraduate

**Type**: Scholarship

**Value**: £5,000

**Application Procedure**: Applicants must hold an offer of admission for a Bath Spa University postgraduate taught Master's degree programme that is full-time and taught on-campus, and complete the International Scholarship Application Form. Please complete all the details, including your name, contact details, student number and qualifications. Applications with missing details will be automatically rejected

**Closing Date**: 30 June

**Additional Information**: Please check details at www.bathspa.ac.uk/international-students/scholarships/vice-chancellors-international-scholarship

### For further information contact:

**Tel**:      (44) 1225 875 777
**Email**:    international@bathspa.ac.uk

## Bayer AG

Werk Leverkusen, D-51368 Leverkusen, Germany.

**Tel**:       (49) 214 3026672
**Email**:     gisela.dambach.gd@bayer-ag.de
**Website**:   www.aspirin.com
**Contact**:   Gisela Dambach, International Aspirin Award

## Bayer Foundation Scholarships

**Purpose**: Bayer Foundation supports students aspiring to study in Germany with five fellowship programmes in biology, medical science, agricultural science, non-academic professions, and chemistry

**Eligibility**: The project to be supported must be innovative and international. 1. Scholarships are granted to students and young professionals (up to 2 years after graduation) German student wishing to realize a study or research project abroad or Foreign students pursuing a project in Germany. 2. An innovative project plan. All applicants should have a high level of commitment, dedication and an innovative project plan. Scholarships are granted to students and young professionals (up to two years after graduation) from Germany wishing to realize a study or research project abroad or to foreign students/young professionals pursuing a project in Germany

**Level of Study**: Graduate

**Type**: Research grant

**Value**: Approximately €6,400 per year up to 2 years after graduation

**Frequency**: Annual

**Country of Study**: Any country

**Application Procedure**: The Bayer Science & Education Foundation supports students and young professionals that would like to study or work outside of their home country with the Bayer Foundation Fellowship Program, which consists of five scholarships. All applicants should have a high level of commitment, dedication and an innovative project plan. Scholarships are granted to students and young professionals (up to two years after graduation) from Germany wishing to realize a study or research project abroad or to foreign students/young professionals pursuing a project in Germany

**Closing Date**: 18 July

**Funding**: Private

### For further information contact:

**Email**:    info@global-opportunities.net

## Bayreuth International Graduate School of African Studies (BIGSAS)

University of Bayreuth, D-95440 Bayreuth, Germany.

**Email**:     bigsas@uni-bayreuth.de
**Contact**:   BIGSAS

The University of Bayreuth is a hub of international and interdisciplinary research. African Studies have been a priority at the University of Bayreuth since its foundation in 1975. The Bayreuth International Graduate School of African Studies (BIGSAS) brings together African and European academic networks and fosters partnership.

### Bayreuth International Graduate School of African Studies Sandwich Scholarship Programme

**Eligibility**: Applicants must have a very good Master's Degree in one of the disciplines represented at the Graduate

School. Applications may be sent in German, English or French; the working language of BIGSAS is English

**Level of Study**: Doctorate

**Type**: Programme grant

**Value**: €1,200 monthly

**Length of Study**: 3 years

**Frequency**: Annual

**Study Establishment**: The Bayreuth International Graduate School of African Studies

**Country of Study**: Germany

**Application Procedure**: For more information on your online application please refer to: www.bigsas.uni-bayreuth.de/en/phd_programme/application/index.html

**Closing Date**: 28 February

**Contributor**: German Research Foundation of the Excellence Initiative of the German Federal and State Governments

**Additional Information**: scholarship-fellowship.com/bigsas-sandwich-scholarship/

### For further information contact:

**Email**:     bigsas-application@uni-bayreuth.de

## Beinecke Scholarship Program

Box 125, Fogelsville, PA 18051-0125, United States of America.

**Tel**:          (1) 610 395 5560

**Email**:      BeineckeScholarship@earthlink.net

**Website**:   www.beineckescholarship.org

**Contact**:   Dr Thomas L. Parkinson, Program director

The Beinecke Scholarship Program, established in 1970, seeks to encourage and enable highly motivated students to take the fullest advantage of graduate opportunities available to them and be courageous in the selection of graduate study programmes.

### Beinecke Scholarship

**Purpose**: Established by the Board of Directors of The Sperry and Hutchinson Company, the Beinecke Scholarship Program awards substantial scholarships to students to support their graduate education in the arts, humanities and social sciences at any accredited institution.

**Eligibility**: junior at the time of application

**Level of Study**: Postgraduate

**Type**: Scholarship

**Value**: US$34,000

**Length of Study**: 1–5 years

**Study Establishment**: Any accredited university

**Application Procedure**: Request and submit a completed application form a curriculum vitae, a personal statement of 1,000 words and three letters of recommendation from faculty members

**Closing Date**: 12 February

**Funding**: Corporation

**Contributor**: The Sperry and Hutchinson Company

**Additional Information**: www.nyu.edu/academics/awards-and-highlights/global-awards/scholarships/beinecke-scholarship-program.html

### For further information contact:

**Email**:     scholarships@nyu.edu

## Beit Trust (Zimbabwe, Zambia and Malawi)

PO Box CH 76, Chisipite, Harare, Zimbabwe.

**Tel**:          (263) 4 496132

**Email**:      beitrust@africaonline.co.zw

**Website**:   www.beittrust.org.uk

### Beit Trust Postgraduate Scholarships

**Purpose**: To support postgraduate study or research

**Eligibility**: Open to persons under 30 years of age or 35 years for medical doctors, who are university graduates domiciled in Zambia, Zimbabwe or Malawi. Applicants must be nationals of those countries

**Level of Study**: Postgraduate

**Type**: Scholarship

**Value**: Fees and costs of tuition and related academic expenses are paid by the Trust direct to the universities. Payment of a personal allowance, index linked in accordance with guidance from an independent authority covering maintenance support. Other allowances are paid for arrival, a laptop and printing of a thesis, and return home. Economy Class air passages are provided by the Trust for the initial journey to the place of study, and for the return at the end of the course

**Length of Study**: A maximum of 3 years depending on course sought

**Frequency**: Annual

**Study Establishment**: Approved universities and other institutions in South Africa, Britain and Ireland

**Application Procedure**: Applicants must complete an application form

**No. of awards offered**: 400

**Closing Date**: 12 February

**Funding**: Private

**No. of awards given last year**: 8

**No. of applicants last year**: 400

**Additional Information**: Zambian applicants should contact the BEIT Trust United Kingdom office. Zimbabwe and Malawi applicants should contact the Zimbabwe office beittrust.org.uk/beit-trust-scholarships

## For further information contact:

The BEIT Trust, BEIT House, Grove Road, Woking, Surrey, GU21 5JB, United Kingdom.

**Tel**:      (44) 1483 772 575

**Fax**:      (44) 1483 725 833

**Email**:      africa@beittrust.org.uk

## Belgian American Educational Foundation (B.A.E.F.)

195 Church Street, New Haven, NH, 06510 United States of America.

**Email**:      Emile.Boulpaep@Yale.edu

**Website**:      www.baef.us

**Contact**:      Belgian American Educational Foundation, Inc

## Belgian American Educational Foundation (B.A.E.F.)

**Purpose**: For fellowships for advanced study or research

**Eligibility**: Applicants must be citizens or permanent residents of the United States. Knowledge of Dutch, or French, or German is optional

**Type**: Fellowship

**Value**: US$27,000 for Master

**Length of Study**: 1 year

**Frequency**: Annual

**Country of Study**: Any country

**Application Procedure**: Application forms can be downloaded from the B.A.E.F. website at: www.baef.us

**Closing Date**: 31 October

**Additional Information**: For additional information contact the Foundation at the above address or email: Emile. Boulpaep@Yale.edu www.baef.be/documents/fellowships-for-belgian-citizens/initial-master-degree-in-the-usa1.xml?lang=en

## For further information contact:

**Email**:      mail@baef.be

## Fellowships for study of research in Belgium

**Purpose**: Fellowships for advanced study or research during the academic year, at a Belgian university or institution of higher learning. The fellowships provide outright non-renewable grants carrying a stipend of US$28,000 for Master's or PhD students US$32,000 for Post-doctoral Fellows

**Eligibility**: Applicants must be citizens or permanent residents of the United States. Applicants must 1. Either at the time of application be registered in a PhD or equivalent degree program in the United States. 2. Or while holding the BAEF fellowship register in a graduate program (Master's or PhD) in Belgium. 3. Or hold a Master's, PhD, or equivalent degree. Post-doctoral applicants should by 1 July have no more than 2 years since obtaining their PhD degree

**Level of Study**: Doctorate, Graduate, Postdoctorate, Postgraduate, Predoctorate, Professional development, Research, MBA, Postgraduate (MSc)

**Type**: Ten fellowships

**Value**: $28,000 for Master's or PhD students, $32,000 for Post-doctoral Fellows

**Length of Study**: 12 months in Belgium. If the Fellow chooses to remain less than the full 12 months in Belgium, the stipend will be prorated accordingly. The minimum fellowship period is 6 months

**Frequency**: Annual

**Country of Study**: Belgium

**Application Procedure**: Applicants must be citizens or permanent residents of the United States Applicants must either at the time of application be registered in a PhD or equivalent degree program in the United States, or while holding the BAEF Fellowship register in a graduate program (Master's or PhD) in Belgium, or hold a Master's, PhD, or equivalent degree. Post-doctoral applicants should by July 1, 2020 have no more than 2 years since obtaining their PhD degree.

**No. of awards offered**: 40

**Closing Date**: 1 July

**Funding**: Foundation

**Contributor**: Foundation Endowment

**No. of awards given last year**: 10

**No. of applicants last year**: 40

**Additional Information**: Application forms can be downloaded from the B.A.E.F. website at: www.baef.us .www. baef.be/documents/fellowships-for-us-citizens/study-res-fellow.-for-us-citizen-.xml?lang=en

**For further information contact:**

Belgian American Educational Foundation, Inc., 195 Church Street, New Haven, CT 06510, United States of America.

**Email**:    emile.boulpaep@yale.edu

## Belgian Flemish University, VLIR-UOS

**Website**:    www.vliruos.be/6323.aspx

### VLIR-UOS Training and Masters Scholarships

**Purpose**: VLIR-UOS awards scholarships to students from 31 eligible countries in Africa, Asia and Latin-America, to follow an English-taught training or master programme at a Flemish university or university college in Belgium

**Eligibility**: You can only apply for a scholarship if you meet the following requisites: • Nationality and Country of Residence, A candidate should be a national and resident of one of the 31 countries of the VLIR-UOS country list for scholarships (not necessarily the same country) at the time of application. • Age. The maximum age for a Master programme candidate is 35 years for an initial masters and 40 years for an advanced masters. The candidate cannot succeed this age on January 1 of the intake year. • Professional background and experience, Priority is given to candidates who are employed in academic institutions, research institutes, governments, the social economy or NGOs, or who aim at a career in one of these sectors. However, master candidates employed in the profit sector or newly graduated candidates without any work experience can be eligible for the scholarship as well, depending on their motivation and profile. The training candidate should have relevant professional experience and a support letter confirming (re)integration in a professional context where the acquired knowledge and skills will be immediately applicable.

**Level of Study**: Postgraduate

**Type**: Scholarship

**Value**: VLIR-UOS only provides full scholarships for the total duration of the training or Master

**Frequency**: Annual

**Country of Study**: Belgium

**Application Procedure**: Via the university's website, you will have to apply for both admission to the programme as well as for the scholarship itself. When you apply for the programme, be sure to mention whether you wish to apply for a scholarship. The deadline varies and are determined by the programme but most deadlines are around 1 February or 1 March 2020 for Masters Programmes. The call of applications for training programmes will open at various times and can be monitored at this link. It is important to visit the official website and the websites of the specific Training or Master's Programme you have chosen for detailed information on how to apply for this scholarship.

**Closing Date**: 1 March

**Contributor**: Flemish university

**Additional Information**: For more information, please visit official scholarship website: www.vliruos.be/6323.aspx www.scholars4dev.com/2257/vlir-uos-masters-scholarships-for-developing-countries/

**For further information contact:**

**Email**:    scholarships@vliruos.be

## Belgian Technical Cooperation agency (BTC), Ghent University

BTC - Belgian Development Agency, Rue Haute, 147, B-1000 Brussels, Belgium.

**Tel**:        (32) 2 505 37 00

**Website**:    www.belspo.be/belspo/index_nl.stm

The Belgian Technical Cooperation agency (BTC) is the administrator and coordinator for scholarships awarded by the Belgian Directorate-General for Development Cooperation (DGDC). The BTC itself does not award grants. The BTC's Scholarship Unit implements the scholarship files, welcomes the students and provides them with guidance for the duration of their academic training and stay in Belgium.

### Belgian Technical Cooperation Scholarships

**Purpose**: The Belgian Technical Cooperation agency (BTC) is the administrator and coordinator for scholarships awarded by the Belgian Directorate-General for Development Cooperation (DGDC). The BTC itself does not award grants. The BTC's Scholarship Unit implements the scholarship files, welcomes the students and provides them with guidance for the duration of their academic training and stay in Belgium.

**Eligibility**: Candidates from one of the BTC partner countries

**Level of Study**: Postgraduate

**Type**: Scholarship

**Value**: The scholarships are awarded primarily to finance third– cycle (postgraduate) courses.

**Length of Study**: 1 or 2 academic years

**Country of Study**: Belgium

**Application Procedure**: Candidates interested in a scholarship should send their application form directly to the Attaché for Development Cooperation or to the Embassy of Belgium in the partner country

**Contributor**: Belgian Directorate-General

**Additional Information**: www.ugent.be/en/research/funding/devcoop/btc.htm

### For further information contact:

**Email**: development.cooperation@vub.ac.be

## Berkeley Graduate Division

### Conference Travel Grants

**Purpose**: Academic master's and all doctoral students may apply for funding to attend professional conferences or to participate in professional development activities

**Eligibility**: 1. Be registered for the term in which they are planning to attend the conference, which also includes payment of fees/tuitions. Note: students on filing fee are not eligible. 2. Be in good academic standing. 3. Be presenting a paper or poster at the conference.

**Level of Study**: Postgraduate

**Type**: Fellowship

**Value**: (up to US$600 within California, US$900 elsewhere in North America, including Canada and Mexico, and US$1,500 outside of North America)

**Additional Information**: grad.berkeley.edu/financial/fellowships/

### For further information contact:

318 Sproul Hall, Barrow Lane, Berkeley, CA 94704, United States of America.

**Tel**: (1) 510 642 0672

### Robert E. Thunen Memorial Scholarships

**Purpose**: These scholarships are for students who wish to study any and all fields of lighting (such as architectural, commercial, residential, airport, navigational, theatrical or television, agricultural, and vision)

**Eligibility**: They arrange for at least three letters of recommendation, at least one of which shall be from someone involved with lighting professionally or academically. The Thunen Scholars for each year will be announced in mid-May of each year

**Level of Study**: Graduate

**Type**: Scholarship

**Value**: US$2,500

**Frequency**: Annual

**Country of Study**: Any country

**Application Procedure**: Applications and letters of recommendation should be submitted before 1 April of each year

**Closing Date**: 1 April

**Funding**: Private

**Additional Information**: grad.berkeley.edu/news/funding/robert-thunen-memorial-scholarships/

### For further information contact:

Mary-Jane Lawless Thunen Scholarship Committee, IES San Francisco Section, 1201 Park Ave Ste 100, Emeryville, CA 94608, United States of America.

**Email**: mlaw@silvermanlight.com

## Berlin Graduate School Muslim Cultures and Societies

Altensteinstrasse 48, D-14195, Berlin, Germany.

**Tel**: (49) 30 838 53417

**Email**: office@bgsmcs.fu-berlin.de

**Website**: www.fu-berlin.de/en/

### Zentrum Moderner Orient and Berlin Graduate School of Muslim Cultures and Societies Visiting Research Fellowship

**Purpose**: We are interested in attracting outstanding researchers who are engaged in research projects that are relevant to the respective research profiles at ZMO and BGSMCS

**Eligibility**: The call is open for senior researchers and recent postdocs in the humanities and the social sciences. Applications by candidates from Africa, Asia and the Middle East are particularly encouraged

**Level of Study**: Postgraduate

**Value**: Successful applicants will receive a monthly stipend (€2,500, covering all expenses including travel and accommodation), and a period of stay that should normally last up to 3 months

**Country of Study**: Germany

**Closing Date**: 15 September

**Funding**: Trusts

**Additional Information**: mideast.unc.edu/zmo-bgsmc/

# Berlin Mathematical School

TU Berlin, Sekr. MA 2-2, Strasse des 17. Juni 136, D-10623 Berlin, Germany.

**Tel**: (49) 30 314 78611
**Email**: office@math-berlin.de
**Contact**: Berlin Mathematical School

The Berlin Mathematical School (BMS) is a joint graduate school of the mathematics departments of the three major Berlin universities, TU Berlin, FU Berlin, and HU Berlin. BMS invite excellent mathematics students from Berlin, Germany, Europe and all over the world to join BMS – and to make good use of the ample opportunities offered by the rich and diverse mathematics teaching and research environment.

## Dirichlet International Postdoctoral Fellowship at Berlin Mathematical School in Germany

**Purpose**: In 2012 the Berlin Mathematical School (BMS) implemented its Dirichlet Postdoctoral Fellowship Program. This program, advertised widely across the broad range of mathematical fields represented in Berlin, contributed to making the BMS even more visible internationally, and attracted outstanding applications from all around the world. This was evidenced by the many letters of recommendation from very prominent and international mathematicians.
**Eligibility**: International applicants are eligible to apply for this fellowship. For more details, please check the website
**Type**: Postdoctoral fellowship
**Value**: The competitive full-year salary includes health insurance
**Frequency**: Annual
**Study Establishment**: Fellowship is awarded to young mathematicians who want to pursue their own research in one of the eight research fields of mathematics offered by the Berlin Mathematical School
**Country of Study**: Germany
**Application Procedure**: Applications will be accepted via our online portal probably from 1 October to 1 December 2020
**Closing Date**: 1 December
**Additional Information**: For more details, please browse the below website. scholarship-positions.com/dirichlet-international-postdoctoral-fellowship-berlin-mathematical-school-germany www.math-berlin.de/bms-faculty/dirichlet-postdoctoral-program

### For further information contact:

**Email**: postdoc@math-berlin.de

# Beta Phi Mu Headquarters

PO Box 42139, Philadelphia, PA 19101, United States of America.

**Tel**: (1) 267 361 5018
**Email**: headquarters@betaphimu.org
**Website**: www.betaphimu.org
**Contact**: Isabel Gray, Program Director

Beta Phi Mu is a library and information studies honor society, founded in 1948, with over 35,000 graduates of the ALA-initiated accredited professional programmes. Beta Phi Mu was founded at the University of Illinois

## American Library Association Beta Phi Mu Award

**Purpose**: This award is given out on an annual basis
**Eligibility**: Library school faculty member or individual
**Type**: Award
**Value**: US$1,000
**Frequency**: Annual
**Country of Study**: Any country
**Application Procedure**: Guidelines and application available on the American Library Association website: www.ala.org/awardsgrants/awards/43/apply
**Closing Date**: 2 March
**Funding**: Trusts
**Contributor**: Beta Phi Mu International Library Science Honorary Society
**No. of awards given last year**: 1
**Additional Information**: www.ala.org/awardsgrants/beta-phi-mu-award

### For further information contact:

American Library Association 50 East Huron Street, Chicago, IL 60611-2795, United States of America.

**Tel**: (1) 312 944 6780
**Fax**: (1) 312 440 9374
**Email**: cmalden@ala.org

# Bibliographical Society of America (BSA)

PO Box 1537, Lenox Hill Station, New York, NY 10021, United States of America.

**Tel**: (1) 212 452 2710
**Email**: bsa@bibsocamer.org

**Website**: www.bibsocamer.org
**Contact**: Ms Michele Randall, Executive Director

The Bibliographical Society of America (BSA) invites applications for its annual short-term fellowships, which supports bibliographical inquiry as well as research in the history of the book trades and in publishing history.

## Bibilography Society of America -Harry Ransom Center Pforzheimer Fellowship in Bibliography

**Purpose**: Supports the bibliographical study of early modern books and manuscripts, 1455-1700, held in the Ransom Center's Pforzheimer Library and in related collections of early printed books and manuscripts, including the Pforzheimer Gutenberg Bible

**Eligibility**: For the 2020 Fellowship cycle, eligibility is limited to: US Citizens and Residents, Citizens of other nations without US residency who wish to conduct research outside of the United States only, This is a temporary restriction, and we are working to open our fellowships to all those who wish to apply in the 2021 cycle.

**Level of Study**: Unrestricted
**Type**: Fellowship
**Value**: US$3,000
**Frequency**: Annual
**Country of Study**: Any country
**Application Procedure**: Applications should include the following components: Applicant's curriculum vitae, project proposal of no more than 1,000 words, project budget, project timeline, Two letters of recommendation submitted via Kaleidoscope. The committee will not accept letters of recommendation by any other means.
**Closing Date**: 1 November
**Funding**: Private
**Contributor**: BSA-Harry Ransom Center Pforzheimer
**Additional Information**: www.hrc.utexas.edu/research/fellowships/bsa/ bibsocamer.org/awards/fellowships/

### For further information contact:

**Email**: bsafellowships@bibsocamer.org

## Justin G. Schiller Prize

**Purpose**: The Schiller Prize for Bibliographical Work on pre-twentieth century children's books is intended to encourage scholarship in the bibliography of historical children's books
**Eligibility**: Works put into nomination, which must be in English, may concentrate on any children's book printed before the year 1901 in any country or any language.

Submissions should involve research into bibliography and printing history broadly conceived and should focus on the physical book as historical evidence for studying topics such as the history of book production, publication, distribution, collecting, or reading. Studies of the printing, publishing, and allied trades, as these relate to children's books, are also welcome. Eligible scholarship may take the form of a published book or article, a master's thesis or doctoral dissertation that has been defended and approved, or research results distributed in another manner, such as on a website or a CD-ROM. Eligible scholarship must have been published, approved, or posted between 1 January and 1 October. Nominations, with copies of the monographs or links to articles and websites, must be completed by 15 November

**Level of Study**: Unrestricted
**Type**: Prize
**Value**: US$3,000
**Frequency**: Every 3 years
**Study Establishment**: pre-twentieth century children's books
**Country of Study**: Any country
**Application Procedure**: Applications must contain the following items: a letter of intent addressed to the "Schiller Prize Committee," a one-page curriculum vitae, any documentation regarding the approval of a thesis or a dissertation or confirming the date of a publication, if required. A hard copy of a published monograph or essay placed into nomination is encouraged, but a PDF is acceptable. If a copy is not submitted, a complete citation of the work must be included with the application. Authors of web-based or online resources should provide the URL for the full-text or submit a PDF. Web-based resources require free access to the website and instructions regarding its use, along with a statement regarding plans for maintaining ongoing access
**Closing Date**: 15 November
**Funding**: Individuals
**Contributor**: Endowed by Justin G. Schiller
**Additional Information**: Please also send an additional applications to this email - aimmel@Princeton.EDU bibsocamer.org/awards/justin-g-shiller-prize/

### For further information contact:

Department of Rare Books and Special Collections, Princeton University Library, 1 Washington Road, Princeton, NJ 08544-2098, United States of America.

**Tel**: (1) 609 258 1470

## St. Louis Mercantile Library Prize

**Purpose**: Encourage scholarship in the bibliography of American history and literature

**Eligibility**: Submissions for the Mercantile Library Prize should concentrate on some aspect of American history and culture in territories that now comprise the United States, or on literature by American authors, or literature intended for publication in territories that now comprise the United States. They should involve research in bibliography and printing history broadly conceived and focus on the book (the physical object) as historical evidence for studying topics such as the history of book production, publication, distribution, collecting, or reading. Studies of the printing, publishing, and allied trades, as these relate to American history and literature, are also welcome. Submissions may take the form of a published book or article, a master's thesis or doctoral dissertation defended and approved, or research results distributed in another manner, such as the website or CD-ROM. Submissions must have been published or, if a dissertation or thesis, approved the year of the deadline or in the three previous calendar years. If a publication has an incorrect nominal date disqualifying it for submission but an actual date of publication within the prize period, it may be nominated with a letter by the publisher or editor testifying to the actual date of publication. Unpublished dissertations and theses must be accompanied by a letter from the director attesting their approval. Scholars are eligible to apply for the Prize without regard to membership in the Bibliographical Society of America or any other society, and without regard to citizenship or academic affiliation, degree, or rank. The Prize will be awarded to the author of a particular work of scholarship without regard to the author's prolonged or repeated contributions to the field. Applications are encouraged from young or junior scholars who have not as yet published extensively. Applicants may nominate themselves or be nominated by others

**Level of Study**: Doctorate

**Type**: Prize

**Value**: US$2,000

**Frequency**: Every 3 years

**Study Establishment**: Bibliography of American History and Literature

**Country of Study**: United States of America

**Application Procedure**: Please send the following as separate PDF or Word (.doc or .docx) files to mercantile. prize@bibsocamer.org

**Closing Date**: 1 November

**Funding**: Private

**Contributor**: St. Louis Mercantile Library at the University of Missouri, St. Louis

**Additional Information**: If for any reason the cost of securing review copies is prohibitive to submitting a nomination, please contact Erin Schreiner, BSA Executive Director, by email at bsa@bibsocamer.org bibsocamer.org/awards/st-louis-mercantile-library-prize/

## The Bibilographic Society of America-Rare Book School Fellowship

**Purpose**: The BSA-Rare Book School Fellowship funds tuition for one course for one first-year attendee each year at the University of Virginia's Rare Book School

**Eligibility**: For the 2020 Fellowship cycle, eligibility is limited to: US Citizens and Residents, Citizens of other nations without US residency who wish to conduct research outside of the United States only, This is a temporary restriction, and we are working to open our fellowships to all those who wish to apply in the 2021 cycle.

**Level of Study**: Unrestricted

**Type**: Fellowship

**Value**: Tuition for 1 course and US$500 toward travel

**Length of Study**: 1 year

**Frequency**: Annual

**Country of Study**: United States of America

**Application Procedure**: Applications should include the following components: Applicant's curriculum vitae, Project proposal of no more than 1,000 words, Project budget, Project timeline, Two letters of recommendation submitted via Kaleidoscope. The committee will not accept letters of recommendation by any other means.

**Closing Date**: 1 November

**Funding**: Private

**Contributor**: Rare Book School University of Virgina

**Additional Information**: Candidates should consult the Rare Book School website and apply as there as directed. bibsocamer.org/awards/st-louis-mercantile-library-prize/

**For further information contact:**

**Email**:    bsafellowships@bibsocamer.org

## The Bibilographic Society of America Short-term Fellowships

**Purpose**: These fellowships support bibliographical research that focuses on the physical aspects of books or manuscripts as historical evidence. Books and manuscripts in any field and of any period are eligible for consideration. Projects may include studying the history of book or manuscript production, publication, distribution, collecting, or reading. Projects to establish a text are also eligible.

**Eligibility**: For the 2020 Fellowship cycle, eligibility is limited to: US Citizens and Residents, Citizens of other nations without US residency who wish to conduct research outside of the United States only This is a temporary restriction, and we are working to open our fellowships to all those who wish to apply in the 2021 cycle.

**Level of Study**: Unrestricted
**Type**: Fellowship
**Value**: US$3,000
**Frequency**: Varies
**Study Establishment**: Bibliographical research that focuses on the physical aspects of books or manuscripts as historical evidence
**Country of Study**: Any country
**Application Procedure**: Applications should include the following components: Applicant's curriculum vitae. Project proposal of no more than 1,000 words, Project budget, Project timeline, Two letters of recommendation submitted via Kaleidoscope. The committee will not accept letters of recommendation by any other means.
**Closing Date**: 1 November
**Funding**: Foundation
**Contributor**: The BSA
**Additional Information**: For more information, please contact Hope Mayo, Chair of the Fellowship Committee at bsafellowships@bibsocamer.org.          bibsocamer.org/awards/fellowships/

**For further information contact:**

**Email**:     bsafellowships@bibsocamer.org

## The Bibliographical Society of America - American Society for Eighteenth-Century Studies Fellowship for Bibliographical Studies in the Eighteenth Century

**Purpose**: Recipients must be a member of the American Society for Eighteenth-Century Studies at the time of the award
**Eligibility**: For the 2020 Fellowship cycle, eligibility is limited to: US Citizens and Residents, Citizens of other nations without US residency who wish to conduct research outside of the United States only, This is a temporary restriction, and we are working to open our fellowships to all those who wish to apply in the 2021 cycle.
**Type**: Fellowship
**Value**: US$3,000
**Frequency**: Annual
**Country of Study**: Any country
**Application Procedure**: Applications should include the following components: Applicant's curriculum vitae, Project proposal of no more than 1,000 words, Project budget, Project timeline, Two letters of recommendation submitted via Kaleidoscope. The committee will not accept letters of recommendation by any other means.
**Closing Date**: 1 November

**Funding**: Private
**Contributor**: American Society for Eighteenth-Century Studies
**Additional Information**: For more information, please contact Hope Mayo, Chair of the Fellowship Committee at bsafellowships@bibsocamer.org.          bibsocamer.org/awards/fellowships/

**For further information contact:**

**Email**:     bsafellowships@bibsocamer.org

## The Bibliographical Society of America - Pine Tree Foundation Fellowship in Culinary Bibliography

**Purpose**: Supports the bibliographical study of printed and manuscript cookbooks (once commonly known as receipt books); medical recipe books that also contain culinary recipes; other types of books, manuscript, and printed material that include a substantial body of culinary recipes; treatises on and studies of gastronomy; or memoirs, diary accounts, or descriptions of food and cooking. Projects may cover any period or country
**Eligibility**: US Citizens and Residents Citizens of other nations without US residency who wish to conduct research outside of the United States only This is a temporary restriction, and we are working to open our fellowships to all those who wish to apply in the 2021 cycle.
**Level of Study**: Unrestricted
**Type**: Fellowship
**Value**: US$3,000
**Frequency**: Annual
**Country of Study**: Any country
**Application Procedure**: Applications should include the following components: Applicant's curriculum vitae, Project proposal of no more than 1,000 words, Project budget, Project timeline, Two letters of recommendation submitted via Kaleidoscope. The committee will not accept letters of recommendation by any other means.
**Closing Date**: 1 November
**Funding**: Foundation
**Contributor**: BSA-Pine Tree Foundation
**Additional Information**: Links to the new Fellowship Application form will be available by 1 August. The application package and two supporting letters of recommendation must be received by 1 November. We regret that we cannot consider late or incomplete applications. Applicants are advised to request recommendation letters well in advance. For more information, please contact Hope Mayo, Chair of the Fellowship Committee at bsafellowships@bibsocamer.org bibsocamer.org/awards/fellowships/

**For further information contact:**

**Email**: bsafellowships@bibsocamer.org

## The Bibliographical Society of America - Pine Tree Foundation Fellowship in Hispanic Bibliography

**Purpose**: Supports the bibliographical study of printed and manuscript items 1) in the Spanish language produced during any period and in any country; or 2) in any language provided they were produced in Spain, or in its overseas dominions during the time of Spanish sovereignty; or 3) the bibliographical study of book and manuscript collections in Spain, or in its overseas dominions during the time of Spanish sovereignty; or 4) the bibliographical study of Spanish-language book and manuscript collections during any period and in any country

**Eligibility**: US Citizens and Residents Citizens of other nations without US residency who wish to conduct research outside of the United States only This is a temporary restriction, and we are working to open our fellowships to all those who wish to apply in the 2021 cycle.

**Level of Study**: Unrestricted

**Type**: Fellowship

**Value**: US$3,000

**Frequency**: Annual

**Country of Study**: Any country

**Application Procedure**: Applications should include the following components: Applicant's curriculum vitae, Project proposal of no more than 1,000 words, Project budget, Project timeline, Two letters of recommendation submitted via Kaleidoscope. The committee will not accept letters of recommendation by any other means.

**Closing Date**: 1 November

**Funding**: Foundation

**Contributor**: BSA- Pine Tree Foundation

**Additional Information**: Links to the new Fellowship Application form will be available by 1 August. The application package and two supporting letters of recommendation must be received by 1 November. We regret that we cannot consider late or incomplete applications. Applicants are advised to request recommendation letters well in advance. For more information, please contact Hope Mayo, Chair of the Fellowship Committee at bsafellowships@bibsocamer.org bibsocamer.org/awards/fellowships/

**For further information contact:**

**Email**: bsafellowships@bibsocamer.org

## The Bibliographical Society of America - St. Louis Mercantile Library Fellowship

**Purpose**: Supports research in North American bibliography, including studies in the North American book trade, production and distribution of North American Books, North American book illustration and design, North American collecting and connoisseurship, and North American bibliographical history in general. Non-traditional and innovative projects will be especially welcome and encouraged

**Eligibility**: US Citizens and Residents Citizens of other nations without US residency who wish to conduct research outside of the United States only This is a temporary restriction, and we are working to open our fellowships to all those who wish to apply in the 2021 cycle.

**Level of Study**: Unrestricted

**Type**: Fellowship

**Value**: US$3,000

**Frequency**: Annual

**Country of Study**: Any country

**Application Procedure**: Applications should include the following components: Applicant's curriculum vitae, Project proposal of no more than 1,000 words, Project budget, Project timeline, Two letters of recommendation submitted via Kaleidoscope. The committee will not accept letters of recommendation by any other means.

**Closing Date**: 1 November

**Funding**: Private

**Contributor**: St. Louis Mercantile Library

**Additional Information**: Links to the new Fellowship Application form will be available by 1 August. The application package and two supporting letters of recommendation must be received by 1 November. We regret that we cannot consider late or incomplete applications. Applicants are advised to request recommendation letters well in advance. For more information, please contact Hope Mayo, Chair of the Fellowship Committee at bsafellowships@bibsocamer.org bibsocamer.org/awards/fellowships/

**For further information contact:**

**Email**: bsafellowships@bibsocamer.org

## The Charles J. Tanenbaum Fellowship in Cartographical Bibliography

**Purpose**: Supports projects dealing with all aspects of the history, presentation, printing, design, distribution and reception of cartographical documents from Renaissance times to the present, with a special emphasis on eighteenth-century cartography

**Eligibility**: US Citizens and Residents Citizens of other nations without US residency who wish to conduct research outside of the United States only This is a temporary restriction, and we are working to open our fellowships to all those who wish to apply in the 2021 cycle.

**Level of Study**: Unrestricted

**Type**: Fellowship

**Value**: US$3,000

**Frequency**: Annual

**Country of Study**: Any country

**Application Procedure**: Applications should include the following components: Applicant's curriculum vitae, Project proposal of no more than 1,000 words, Project budget, Project timeline, Two letters of recommendation submitted via Kaleidoscope. The committee will not accept letters of recommendation by any other means.

**Closing Date**: 1 November

**Funding**: Foundation

**Contributor**: Pine Tree Foundation of New York

**Additional Information**: Links to the new Fellowship Application form will be available by 1 August. The application package and two supporting letters of recommendation must be received by 1 November. We regret that we cannot consider late or incomplete applications. Applicants are advised to request recommendation letters well in advance. For more information, please contact Hope Mayo, Chair of the Fellowship Committee at bsafellowships@bibsocamer.org bibsocamer.org/awards/fellowships/

**For further information contact:**

**Email**:	bsafellowships@bibsocamer.org

## The Fredson Bowers Award

**Purpose**: Major grant funded jointly with the Bibliographical Society of the UK

**Eligibility**: US Citizens and Residents Citizens of other nations without US residency who wish to conduct research outside of the United States only This is a temporary restriction, and we are working to open our fellowships to all those who wish to apply in the 2021 cycle.

**Level of Study**: Unrestricted

**Type**: Bursary

**Value**: £1,500

**Frequency**: Annual

**Country of Study**: United Kingdom or United States of America

**Application Procedure**: Applications for the Pantzer Fellowship and for major grants (including the Pantzer Scholarship) must be submitted, on the appropriate form (with no additional documentation). Two referees familiar with the applicant's work should be asked to email references to the Secretary to the Fellowships and Bursaries Sub-committee

**Closing Date**: 6 January

**Funding**: Private

**Contributor**: Bibliographical Society of America and Bibliographical Society of the United Kingdom

**Additional Information**: United Kingdom entries should follow application instructions located at this website www.bibsoc.org.uk/fellowships/application-procedure bibsocamer.org/awards/fellowships/

**For further information contact:**

**Email**:	acrd2002@aol.com

## The Katharine F. Pantzer Senior Fellowship in the British Book Trades

**Purpose**: To support the mission of the Society to foster the study of books and other textual artifacts in traditional and emerging formats, and in keeping with the value which the Society places on the field of bibliography as a critical interpretative framework for understanding such artifacts, the BSA funds a number of fellowships designed to promote bibliographical inquiry and research.

**Eligibility**: Supports research by a senior scholar engaged in bibliographical inquiry into the history of the book trades and publishing history in Britain during the hand-press period, as well as studies of authorship, reading and collecting based on the examination of British books published in that period, with a special emphasis on descriptive bibliography

**Type**: Fellowship

**Value**: US$6,000

**Frequency**: Varies

**Study Establishment**: Bibliographical research of the British Book Trades

**Country of Study**: Any country

**Application Procedure**: Applications are due 1 November of each year. Applications should include the following components: Application form; project proposal of no more than 1,000 words; Applicant's curriculum vitae; two signed letters of recommendation on official letterhead submitted independently by referees. The two letters of recommendation must be signed and submitted independently by referees (in PDF or MS Word format) via the BSA Fellowship recommendation submission form. No other documentation will be considered by the committee. - Please visit the website to download the form. The fellowship committee will match proposed projects to suitable fellowships, and the awards will be announced at the annual meeting of the Society in January of each year. All fellowships require a project report within one year of receipt of the award, and copies of any publications resulting from the project are to be sent to the BSA. Links to the new Fellowship Application form will be available by 1 August. The application package and two supporting letters of recommendation must be received by 1 November. We regret that we cannot consider late or incomplete applications. Applicants are advised to request recommendation letters well in advance. For more information, please contact Hope Mayo, Chair of the Fellowship Committee at bsafellowships@bibsocamer.org

**Closing Date**: 1 November

**Funding**: Individuals

**Contributor**: Katherine Panzer

**Additional Information**: Links to the new Fellowship Application form will be available by 1 August. The application package and two supporting letters of recommendation must be received by 1 November. We regret that we cannot consider late or incomplete applications. Applicants are advised to request recommendation letters well in advance. For more information, please contact Hope Mayo, Chair of the Fellowship Committee at bsafellowships@bibsocamer.org bibsocamer.org/awards/fellowships/

## The Katharine Pantzer Junior Fellowship in the British Book Trades

**Purpose**: Supports bibliographical inquiry into the history of the book trades and publishing history in Britain during the hand-press period, as well as studies of authorship, reading and collecting based on the examination of British books published in that period, with a special emphasis on descriptive bibliography

**Eligibility**: Supports bibliographical inquiry into the history of the book trades and publishing history in Britain during the hand-press period, as well as studies of authorship, reading and collecting based on the examination of British books published in that period, with a special emphasis on descriptive bibliography

**Level of Study**: Unrestricted

**Type**: Fellowship

**Value**: US$3,000

**Frequency**: Annual

**Country of Study**: Any country

**Application Procedure**: Applications are due 1 November of each year. Applications should include the following components: Application form; projectproposal of no more than 1,000 words; Applicant's curriculum vitae; two signed letters

of recommendation on official letterhead submitted independently by referees. The two letters of recommendation must be signed and submitted independently by referees (in PDF or MS Word format) via the BSA Fellowship recommendation submission form. No other documentation will be considered by the committee. Please visit the website to download the form. The fellowship committee will match proposed projects to suitable fellowships, and the awards will be announced at the annual meeting of the Society in January of each year. All fellowships require a project report within one year of receipt of the award, and copies of any publications resulting from the project are to be sent to the BSA. Links to the new Fellowship Application form will be available by 1 August. The application package and two supporting letters of recommendation must be received by 1 November. We regret that we cannot consider late or incomplete applications. Applicants are advised to request recommendation letters well in advance. For more information, please contact Hope Mayo, Chair of the Fellowship Committee at bsafellowships@bibsocamer.org

**Closing Date**: 1 November

**Funding**: Individuals

**Contributor**: Katherine Panzer

**Additional Information**: Links to the new Fellowship Application form will be available by 1 August. The application package and two supporting letters of recommendation must be received by 1 November. We regret that we cannot consider late or incomplete applications. Applicants are advised to request recommendation letters well in advance. For more information, please contact Hope Mayo, Chair of the Fellowship Committee at bsafellowships@bibsocamer.org bibsocamer.org/awards/fellowships/

## The Reese Fellowship for American Bibliography and the History of the Book in the Americas

**Purpose**: The fellowship may be awarded to any scholar, whether academic or independent, whose project explores the history of print culture in the Western Hemisphere

**Eligibility**: The fellowship may be awarded to any scholar, whether academic or independent, whose project explores the history of print culture in the Western Hemisphere

**Level of Study**: Unrestricted

**Type**: Fellowship

**Value**: US$3,000

**Frequency**: Annual

**Country of Study**: Any country

**Application Procedure**: Applications are due 1 November of each year. Applications should include the following components: Application form Project proposal of no more than 1,000 words Applicant's curriculum vitae Two signed letters of recommendation on official letterhead submitted independently by referees. The two letters of recommendation must be signed and submitted independently by referees (in PDF or MS Word format) via the BSA Fellowship recommendation submission form. No other documentation will be considered by the committee. The fellowship committee will match proposed projects to suitable fellowships, and the awards will be announced at the annual meeting of the Society in January of each year. All fellowships require a project report within one year of receipt of the award, and copies of any publications resulting from the project are to be sent to the BSA. Links to the new Fellowship Application form will be available by 1 August. The application package and two supporting letters of recommendation must be received by 1 November. We regret that we cannot consider late or incomplete applications. Applicants are advised to request recommendation letters well in advance. For more information, please contact Hope Mayo, Chair of the Fellowship Committee at bsafellowships@bibsocamer.org

**Closing Date**: 1 November
**Funding**: Corporation
**Contributor**: William Reese Company
**Additional Information**: Links to the new Fellowship Application form will be available by 01 August. The application package and two supporting letters of recommendation must be received by 1 November. We regret that we cannot consider late or incomplete applications. Applicants are advised to request recommendation letters well in advance. For more information, please contact Hope Mayo, Chair of the Fellowship Committee at bsafellowships@bibsocamer.org bibsocamer.org/awards/fellowships/

## Bielefeld University

Bielefeld Graduate School in History and Sociology, Postfach 10 01 31, D-33501 Bielefeld, Germany.

**Tel**:        (49) 521 106 6526
**Email**:     bghs@uni-bielefeld.de
**Website**:   www.uni-bielefeld.de/bghs

### Bielefeld Graduate School in History and Sociology Start-up Doctoral Scholarships

**Purpose**: The Bielefeld Graduate School in History and Sociology is inviting applications for six scholarships for international prospective doctoral researchers starting in 1 April
**Eligibility**: Applicants should hold a Master's degree or equivalent in sociology, history, political science, social anthropology or gender studies; applications from related disciplines are welcome. The university strongly encourages

women to apply. Graduates from abroad who wish to pursue a doctoral degree in history, sociology, anthropology or political science may apply for a start-up scholarship. We welcome applications from predoctoral researchers. Applicants should speak either German or English fluently
**Level of Study**: Doctorate, Postgraduate
**Type**: Scholarship
**Value**: A stipend of GE€1,200 per month. This amount will be supplemented by an allowance for children if applicable. Upon application, travel costs can also be covered by the Graduate School
**Length of Study**: 4 months
**Frequency**: Annual
**Study Establishment**: University of Bielefeld
**Country of Study**: Germany
**Application Procedure**: Applications should be submitted online (www.uni-bielefeld.de/(en)/bghs/bewerbung/startup/start-up.html)
**Closing Date**: 31 July
**Contributor**: University of Bielefeld
**Additional Information**: www.uni-bielefeld.de/(en)/bghs/neu/Ausschreibungen/startup_scholarships.html

## Bilkent University

Faculty of Business Administration, MBA Programme, Office of the Dean, TR-06800 Ankara, Turkey.

**Tel**:        (90) 312 290 1596
**Email**:     fba@bilkent.edu.tr
**Website**:   www.bilkent.edu.tr
**Contact**:   MBA Admissions Officer

Bilkent University is a non-profit research university. Courses are conducted in English. The University has more than 11,000 students and an international teaching staff of 1,000.

### Bilkent Industrial Engineering Fellowship

**Level of Study**: Doctorate

### For further information contact:

Bilkent University Department of Industrial Engineering, Main Campus Engineering Building Floor 3, Bilkent, TR-06800 Ankara, Turkey.

**Tel**:        (90) 312 290 1262
**Fax**:        (90) 312 266 4054
**Email**:     barbaros@bilkent.edu.tr

## Bilkent International Relations Fellowship

**Purpose**: To develop skills in international political analysis
**Eligibility**: Candidates are selected on the basis of past academic achievement and references
**Level of Study**: Doctorate
**Type**: Fellowship
**Value**: A monthly stipend and a tuition waiver
**Frequency**: Annual
**Study Establishment**: Bilkent University
**Country of Study**: Turkey
**Application Procedure**: Contact the Department of International Relations

### For further information contact:

**Tel**:      (90) 312 266 4195
**Fax**:      (90) 312 266 4326
**Email**:    ir@bilkent.edu.tr

## Bilkent Mathematics Fellowship

**Eligibility**: Preference is given to research proposals focused on non-linear differential equations and general relativity
**Level of Study**: Doctorate, Postdoctorate
**Type**: Fellowship
**Value**: A monthly stipend and a tuition fee waiver
**Frequency**: Annual
**Study Establishment**: Bilkent University
**Country of Study**: Turkey
**Application Procedure**: Contact the department

### For further information contact:

**Tel**:      (90) 312 266 4377
**Fax**:      (90) 312 266 4579
**Email**:    kocatepe@fen.bilkent.edu.tr

## Bilkent MIAPP Fellowship

**Purpose**: To fund International and European affairs and executives who, understand and can deal with the increasing complex problems of a rapidly changing world
**Level of Study**: Doctorate, Postdoctorate
**Type**: Fellowship
**Value**: A monthly stipend and a tuition fee waiver
**Length of Study**: 2 year
**Frequency**: Annual
**Study Establishment**: Bilkent University
**Country of Study**: Turkey
**Application Procedure**: Contact the Department

**Additional Information**: w3.bilkent.edu.tr/bilkent/gradstudents/master-of-international-affairs-and-public-policy/

### For further information contact:

**Tel**:      (90) 312 2901 249
**Fax**:      (90) 312 266 4960
**Email**:    muge@bilkent.edu.tr

## Bilkent Political Science Fellowship

**Purpose**: To provide a sophisticated conceptual framework and the analytical skills to specialize in a particular aspect of Turkish or comparative politics
**Eligibility**: Applicants are required to have an MA degree in Political Science, Public Administrator or International Relations
**Level of Study**: Doctorate
**Type**: Fellowship
**Value**: A monthly stipend and a tuition fee waiver
**Frequency**: Annual
**Study Establishment**: Bilkent University
**Country of Study**: Turkey
**Application Procedure**: Contact the department

### For further information contact:

**Tel**:      (90) 312 290 1931
**Fax**:      (90) 312 290 2792
**Email**:    cindoglu@bilkent.edu.tr

## Bilkent Turkish Literature Fellowship

**Purpose**: To enhance the standards of Turkish literary studies and universalize the field
**Eligibility**: Candidates will be required to take written and/or oral exams to prove their competence in Turkish, Ottoman and English
**Level of Study**: Doctorate
**Type**: Fellowship
**Value**: A monthly stipend and a tuition fee waiver
**Length of Study**: 3 years
**Frequency**: Annual
**Study Establishment**: Bilkent University
**Country of Study**: Turkey
**Application Procedure**: Contact the department

### For further information contact:

**Tel**:      (90) 312 290 2711
**Fax**:      (90) 312 266 4059
**Email**:    turkedeb@bilkent.edu.tr

# Biola University

The Financial Aid Office, 13800 Biola Avenue, La Mirada, CA 90639, United States of America.

**Tel**:        (1) 562 903 4742
**Email**:    finaid@biola.edu
**Website**:  www.biola.edu
**Contact**:  Financial Aid Officer

## Church Matching Scholarship

**Purpose**: Biola-funded match to church sponsorship
**Eligibility**: Students must meet the following eligibility requirements: Student must be enrolled at least half-time, Student must be enrolled in a traditional degree program. Student must demonstrate financial need based on FAFSA information. Student must receive financial sponsorship from a church. Special programs are not eligible.
**Level of Study**: Graduate
**Type**: Scholarship
**Value**: Up to US$1,300 per year
**Length of Study**: 1 year
**Frequency**: Annual
**Country of Study**: Any country
**Application Procedure**: Completed FAFSA (Biola listed), Complete the Church Matching Scholarship application, Church sponsorship check should be written out to Biola University and attached to the Church Matching Scholarship Application
**Closing Date**: 2 October
**Funding**: Private
**Additional Information**: This scholarship is not renewable. Student must reapply annually based on financial need and additional church sponsorship www.biola.edu/financial-aid/scholarships-and-aid/undergrad/biola- scholarships

### For further information contact:

13800 Biola Ave. La Mirada, CA 90639, United States of America.

**Tel**:      (1) 562 903 6000
**Email**:  business@biola.edu

# Biomedical Engineering Society (BMES)

## Career Development Awards

**Subjects**: Biomedical Engineering

**Purpose**: BMES is committed to inclusive excellence in building pathways to biomedical engineering careers and developing a diverse, technically and globally competent biomedical workforce. To that end, BMES has an award category to support travel to the BMES Annual Meeting for Graduate Students, Postdoctoral Fellows, and Early Career Professionals from underrepresented populations in biomedical engineering and/or involved in research and training focused on health disparities and minority health.Â.
**Eligibility**: Applicant must be: A Graduate Student, Postdoctoral Fellow, or Early Career Professional at a critical transition or re-entry point in their career from an underrepresented population that includes racial and ethnic minorities and/or involved in research or training focused on health disparities or minority health. Early Career Professional is defined as a junior professional, junior faculty, and young investigators who received a degree in biomedical engineering or a related science within three (3) years of the date of application. Groups identified as underrepresented in science and engineering include; Women, African Americans, Alaskan Natives, Hispanics, American Indians/Native Americans, and Pacific Islanders (Guam, Hawaii and American Samoa). A BMES Member in good standing who has not received BMES funding to attend the 2019 BMES Annual Meeting through any other BMES source.
**Type**: Award
**Value**: The award recipients will receive a complimentary registration to attend the meeting and a stipend in the amount of US$599 to assist with travel expenses to and from the meeting.
**Country of Study**: Any country
**Additional Information**: www.bmes.org/content.asp?admin=Y&contentid=594

## Diversity Lecture Award

**Subjects**: Biomedical Engineering
**Purpose**: The BMES Diversity Award honors an individual, project, organization, or institution for outstanding contributions to improving gender and racial diversity in biomedical engineering. The award is given for a broad range of activities, including research, education, and service improving diversity in the biomedical engineering industry and/or academia. The award seeks to recognize lifetime achievements as well as innovative and/or high impact activities.Â.
**Eligibility**: The nominee must be an individual, project, or organization/institution demonstrating outstanding contributions to improving gender and racial diversity in biomedical engineering. The nominee is not required to be a BMES member. The award recipient (individual or representative of the project or organization/institution) is expected to accept the award in person and deliver a 20-minute lecture at the 2020 BMES Annual Meeting in San Diego, California. The

recipient is expected to publish an article regarding aspects of the works recognized by the award in the Annals of Biomedical Engineering.

**Type**: Award

**Value**: This award consists of US$1,000 check, a crystal plaque, complimentary registration for the BMES Annual Meeting (for the individual or project/organization/institution)

**Frequency**: Annual

**Country of Study**: Any country

**Application Procedure**: The application, including CV and Nomination Summary on letterhead (not to exceed 3 pages), must be submitted by May 15.

**Closing Date**: 15 May

**Additional Information**: www.bmes.org/content.asp? admin=Y&contentid=593

## Robert A. Pritzker Distinguished Lecture Award

**Subjects**: Biomedical Engineering

**Purpose**: This prestigious award is given each year to recognize an individual's outstanding achievements and leadership in the science and practice of biomedical engineering.

**Eligibility**: The award recipient may have achieved excellence in biomedical engineering by contributions within the setting of the university, industry, or government. The awardee's contributions are not required to precede the award date by any specific period of time. Applicants must be a member of BMES in good standing.

**Type**: Award

**Value**: This recipient receives complimentary registration for the Annual Meeting, a crystal plaque, an honorarium of US$12,000 and travel expenses up to US$1,250.

**Frequency**: Annual

**Country of Study**: Any country

**Application Procedure**: Please complete the application form along with a letter describing the nominee's service to biomedical engineering, the nominee's Curriculum Vitae, and letter(s) of support (not to exceed 5 letters).

**Closing Date**: 15 May

**Additional Information**: www.bmes.org/content.asp? admin=Y&contentid=597

## Biotechnology and Biological Sciences Research Council (BBSRC)

Polaris House, North Star Avenue, Swindon, Wiltshire SN2 1UH, United Kingdom.

**Tel**:        (44) 1793 413 200
**Email**:   postdoc.fellowships@bbsrc.ac.uk
**Website**:  www.bbsrc.ac.uk

BBSRC is the United Kingdom's principal funder of basic and strategic biological research. It is a non-departmental public body, one of the seven Research Councils supported through the Science and Innovation Group of the Department for Innovation, Universities and Skills (DIUS). It supports research and research training in universities and research centres throughout the United Kingdom, including BBSRC-sponsored institutes, and promotes knowledge transfer from research to applications in business, industry and policy, and public engagement in the biosciences. It funds research in some exciting areas including genomics, stem cell biology, and bionanotechnology.

## David Phillips Fellowships

**Purpose**: The David Phillips Fellowship (DPF) provides support for researchers wishing to establish their first independent research group

**Eligibility**: DPF applicants are not eligible to apply to any additional 2020 BBSRC fellowship competitions or to the UK Research and Innovation Future Leaders Fellowship call in the same calendar year. Please see the Fellowship Handbook for further details on eligibility criteria.

**Level of Study**: Postdoctorate

**Type**: Fellowship

**Value**: value of up to £1 million (80% fEC)

**Length of Study**: 5 years

**Application Procedure**: Applicants should have considered their training needs (as detailed in the Career Development Plan), and the research environment should be supportive and the best place for the applicant to carry out their research project and advance their career.

**Closing Date**: 12 May

**Additional Information**: Fellowships are awarded under full economic costing (fEC). Further queries, please contact Postgraduate Training and Research Career Development Branch. Important: applicants should ensure proposals are submitted to their host institution's Je-S submitter/approval pool well in advance (a minimum of 5 working days) of the published deadline bbsrc.ukri.org/funding/filter/david-phillips/

### For further information contact:

**Email**:   postdoc.fellowships@bbsrc.ukri.org

## Institute Career Path Fellowships

**Eligibility**: Open to candidates who have a minimum of 3 years and no more than 10 years of active postdoctoral research experience

**Level of Study**: Doctorate, Postdoctorate

**For further information contact:**

**Email**:    fiona.tomley@bbsrc.ac.uk

## Institute Development Fellowships

**Purpose**: To enable BBSRC scientists to spend a period of collaborative work at another research organization and to provide a mechanism for the influx of new ideas and new skills in strategically important areas to enhance the quality of science in BBSRC sponsored institutes

**Eligibility**: Open to all BBSRC scientists at Band 5 and above on an open-ended contract, who have worked for a minimum of 5 years in their current or similar post

**Level of Study**: Research

**Type**: Fellowships

**Value**: To cover the costs associated with the proposed research development activities

**Length of Study**: 6–12 months

**Application Procedure**: All applications must be submitted online

**Closing Date**: 14 November

**Additional Information**: Further queries, please contact Postgraduate Training and Research Career Development Branch

## Professorial Fellowships

**Purpose**: To support world-class scientists with a proven track record of developing new and innovative directions of research and who have the potential to use a fellowship to open up dramatic and novel lines of work

**Eligibility**: Open to scientists who are already recognized at an international level as outstanding researchers with exceptional research and interpretative achievements

**Type**: Fellowships

**Value**: Grant to cover the costs of the research programme

**Length of Study**: 5 years

**Application Procedure**: Check website for further details

**Closing Date**: 14 November

**Additional Information**: Further queries, please contact Postgraduate Training and Research Career Development Branch

## Research Development Fellowships

**Purpose**: To support scientists wishing to undertake new directions in their research. Applicants seeking to develop interdisciplinary dimensions by integrating new techniques or methodologies into their research are particularly encouraged

**Eligibility**: Open to scientists who are full-time members of academic staff of a United Kingdom university who have worked for a minimum of 5 years in their current or similar post

**Type**: Fellowship

**Value**: To cover the costs associated with the proposed research development activities

**Length of Study**: 1–3 years

**Application Procedure**: Applications must be submitted online

**Closing Date**: 14 November

**Additional Information**: Further queries, please contact Postgraduate Training and Research Career Development Branch

## Birkbeck, University of London

Malet Street, Bloomsbury WC1E 7HX, United Kingdom.

Birkbeck, University of London, is a public research university located in Bloomsbury, London, United Kingdom, and a constituent college of the federal University of London

## Birkbeck International Merit Scholarships

**Eligibility**: Birkbeck is offering a number of merit scholarships to suitably qualified students from Japan, Russia, South Korea, Turkey, Latin America, South-East Asia (ASEAN) and Taiwan. Accepted International Student by the University; Excellent Academic and Leadership Achievements

**Type**: Scholarship

**Value**: Scholarship amount: £2,500–£5,000

**Country of Study**: United Kingdom

**Application Procedure**: 1. Initially, you will have to apply to Birkbeck, University of London. 2. Once you have received an offer from Birkbeck, you must email them an essay of no more than 500 words. The essay should detail why you are the ideal candidate to receive the International Merit Scholarship. Recipients will be chosen based on a combination of academic merit and financial need

**Closing Date**: 1 June

**Additional Information**: scholarship-positions.com/fully-funded-birkbeck-postgraduate-scholarships-international-students-uk/2017/11/15/

**For further information contact:**

**Email**:    international-office@bbk.ac.uk

## Bonnart Trust PhD Scholarship

**Purpose**: The scholarship will be awarded to an outstanding candidate whose research topic explores a theme concerned with either 'diversity and belonging' or 'minorities and social justice'

**Eligibility**: You should usually have an upper second-class undergraduate honours degree, or equivalent, and a Master's degree, or equivalent. You will need to be an outstanding candidate whose research topic explores a theme concerned with either diversity and belonging or minorities and social justice. We encourage applications from candidates who are able to draw connections between their doctoral research and contemporary concerns and practical outcomes beyond the university. We will only consider current Birkbeck students who are already enrolled on an MPhil/PhD degree within the School of Social Sciences, History and Philosophy under exceptional circumstances.

**Type**: Scholarship and award

**Value**: £1,000 per scholar

**Frequency**: Every 3 years

**Country of Study**: Any country

**Application Procedure**: For further information, check the following website. www.bbk.ac.uk/sshp/research/funding-for-research-students

**Closing Date**: 31 January

**Funding**: Private

**Contributor**: £1000 per scholar

**Additional Information**: If you have any questions about the Bonnart Trust PhD Scholarhip, please contact: sshp-studentships@bbk.ac.uk   www.bbk.ac.uk/student-services/financial-support/phd-funding/bonnart-trust-scholarship

### For further information contact:

School of Social Sciences, History and Philosophy, Birkbeck, University of London, 26 Russell Square London, United Kingdom.

**Email**:   sshp-studentships@bbk.ac.uk

## School of Arts Master's Bursaries and Studentships

**Purpose**: We are delighted to be able to offer up to twenty bursaries to Masters students coming into the School of Arts, Birkbeck. Please see details of each available award and application deadlines below. All applications should be made using the right application form which must be completed in addition to a College application.

**Eligibility**: 1. Level: Postgraduate Taught. 2. Fees: Home, EU or International. 3. Applicants should have an outstanding academic record and show excellent promise.

**Type**: Bursaries

**Value**: Up to £20,000

**Frequency**: 2 years

**Closing Date**: 29 May

**Additional Information**:   www.bbk.ac.uk/arts/research/research-bursaries-studentships-funding/arts-ma-bursaries

## Blakemore Foundation

1201 3rd Avenue, Suite 4900, Seattle, WA 98101-3099, United States of America.

**Tel**:          (1) 206 359 8778
**Email**:       blakemorefoundation@gmail.com
**Website**:     www.blakemorefoundation.org
**Contact**:     Eugene H. Lee, Trustee

## Blakemore Freeman Fellowships for Advanced Asian Language Study

**Purpose**: To permit American citizens or permanent residents of the United States to raise their language skills in Chinese, Japanese, Korean, Thai, Vietnamese, Indonesian, Khmer or Burmese to professional working proficiency

**Eligibility**: Pursuing a professional, business, technical or academic career that involves the regular use of Chinese, Japanese, Korean, Thai, Vietnamese, Indonesian, Khmer or Burmese. 1. By the start of the grant, have (at minimum) a college undergraduate degree. 2. Be at or near an advanced level in the language. By the start of the grant, applicants must have completed (at minimum) the equivalent of the third year of languages classes at the college level, either through classes taken in the United States or through a combination of study at the college level in the United States and intensive language study abroad programs. 3. Be able to devote oneself exclusively to full-time intensive language study during the term of the grant; grants are not made for part-time study or research. 4. Be a citizen or permanent resident of the United States of America

**Type**: A variable number of grants

**Value**: Full tuition at approved language schools in East & SE Asia plus stipend for travel, study & living expenses

**Length of Study**: 9–10 months

**Frequency**: Annual

**Study Establishment**: See website for list of approved language programs

**Country of Study**: Other

**Application Procedure**: To apply for a Blakemore Freeman Fellowship the applicant must complete an application form on our application portal at blakemorefoundation.communityforce.com

**No. of awards offered**: 139

**Closing Date**: 30 December

**Funding**: Foundation, Trusts

**Contributor**: Blakemore Foundation; The Freeman Foundation
**No. of awards given last year**: 14
**No. of applicants last year**: 139
**Additional Information**: Email address above is incorrect: The new email for the Foundation is contactus@ blakemore foundation.org einaudi.cornell.edu/opportunity/blakemore-foundation-blakemore-freeman-fellowships-advanced-asian-language-study

## Bond University

School of Business, c/o International Office, Gold Coast QLD 4229, Australia.

**Tel**: (61) 7 5595 1706
**Email**: international@bond.edu.au
**Contact**: MBA Admissions Officer

### Bond University United Kingdom Excellence Scholarship in Australia

**Purpose**: Bond University is now accepting applications from citizens of the United Kingdom for the United Kingdom Excellence Scholarship. Bond University aims to help identify future leaders and realize their full potential by providing access to an exceptional educational experience
**Eligibility**: To be considered applicants must: High achieving citizens of the United Kingdom who are currently residing outside of Australia are encouraged to apply; Applicants must have received an offer to study at Bond prior to applying. People studying in English as part of packaged offers at the Bond University College are still eligible to apply; Keep excellent academic qualifications; Students have already received a proposal from Bond University to start a bachelor or postgraduate degree; Examples of high academic achievement may include students with high achieving A Level or IB results; High achieving academic students applying for the undergraduate study who are not currently completing an Australian High School equivalent in the United Kingdom are also eligible to apply
**Level of Study**: Postgraduate
**Type**: Scholarship
**Value**: 25% tuition remission
**Frequency**: Annual
**Country of Study**: Australia, the United Kingdom, Europe or the United States of America
**Application Procedure**: To apply, students must complete the Bond University Online Application Form to receive their program offer before applying for this scholarship. 1. Once an offer has been received, students must download and complete the United Kingdom Excellence Scholarship

Application Form through the given link: Application Form. 2. Applicants must submit their complete application to international@bond.edu.au
**Closing Date**: 21 February
**Funding**: Private
**Contributor**: Bond University
**Additional Information**: Applications close on 24 May for students commencing in September semester bond.edu.au/intl/scholarship/uk-excellence-scholarship

### For further information contact:

14 University Drive, Robina, QLD 4226, Australia.

## Boren Awards

### Boren Scholarship

**Purpose**: Boren Scholars represent a vital pool of highly motivated individuals who wish to work in the federal national security arena. In exchange for funding, Boren Scholars commit to working in the federal government for at least one year after graduation
**Eligibility**: 1. A United States citizen at the time of application. 2. A high school graduate, or have earned a GED. 3. Matriculated in an undergraduate degree program located within the United States accredited by an accrediting body recognized by the United States Department of Education. Boren Scholars must remain matriculated in their undergraduate programs for the duration of the scholarship and may not graduate until the scholarship is complete. 4. Applying to a study abroad program that meets home institution standards in a country outside of Western Europe, Canada, Australia, or New Zealand. Boren Scholarships are not for study in the United States
**Level of Study**: Graduate
**Type**: Scholarship
**Value**: Up to US$20,000 for 25-52 weeks (preferred), US$10,000 for 12-24 weeks, US$8,000 for 8-11 weeks (STEM majors only)
**Frequency**: Annual
**Country of Study**: United States of America
**Closing Date**: 1 March
**Funding**: Private
**Additional Information**: www.borenawards.org/

### For further information contact:

1400 K Street, NW 7TH floor, Washington DC 20005, United States of America.

**Tel**: (1) 800 618 6737
**Email**: boren@iie.org

## Botswana Insurance Holdings Limited Trust

PO Box 336, Gaborone, BW, Botswana.

**Tel**:          (267) 3707400
**Email**:    webmaster@bihl.co.bw
**Website**:  www.bihl.co.bw/

BIHL Group is a leading financial services group, originally established in 1975. BIHL has been listed on the Botswana Stock Exchange and is the holding company for three subsidiaries and holds a stake in two associate companies.

## Botswana Insurance Holdings Limited Trust Thomas Tlou Scholarship for Master Programme

**Purpose**: The BIHL Trust Thomas Tlou Scholarship aims to benefit talented young Batswana with aspirations to pursue postgraduate studies in any discipline aimed at contributing to Botswana's socio-economic development
**Eligibility**: The scholarship is open to all citizens of Botswana who wish to pursue a master's programme in any discipline at a local reputable and recognized institution of higher learning on Botswana. The intended recipients must be aged between 18–35
**Level of Study**: Postgraduate
**Type**: Scholarship
**Value**: The Trust will spend a total of P 450,000
**Country of Study**: Any country
**Application Procedure**: Citizens of Botswana can apply for this scholarship
**Closing Date**: 30 June

### For further information contact:

BIHL Group, Plot 66458, Block A, 3rd Floor, Fairgrounds Office Park, Gaborone, Botswana.

**Fax**:       (267) 3973705
**Email**:  tkeepetsoe@bihl.co.bw

## Bournemouth University

Fern Barrow, Poole, Dorset, BH12 5BB, United Kingdom.

**Tel**:        (44) 1202 524111
**Email**:   enquiries@bournemouth.ac.uk

**Website**:   www.bournemouth.ac.uk
**Contact**:    Ms Karen Ward, Research Administrator

If you choose BU, you'll be learning from top academics in a community of academic excellence, with excellent industry links, accredited courses and placement opportunities, preparing you for professional practice. With a range of scholarships available, there's never been a better time to take charge of your own future with BU.

## Bournemouth University Dean

**Eligibility**: You will need to have a minimum of an upper second-class honours degree (2i). You cannot be in receipt of any other BU scholarship
**Type**: Scholarship
**Frequency**: Annual
**Study Establishment**: Bournemouth University
**Country of Study**: Any country
**Application Procedure**: Apply via online application form available on the BU website
**Closing Date**: 31 May
**Contributor**: Bournemouth University

## Bournemouth University Dean's Scholarship – The Media School

**Eligibility**: You will need to have a minimum of an upper second-class honours degree (2i), or overseas equivalent
**Level of Study**: Graduate, Postgraduate
**Value**: 50% tuition fee reduction
**Country of Study**: Any country
**Closing Date**: 31 July

## Bournemouth University Music Scholarships

**Purpose**: The scholarship supports young people with academic ability, leadership potential and a commitment to their community to achieve their full academic and leadership potential
**Eligibility**: Any UK, EU or international applicant applying for a full-time undergraduate or postgraduate course at BU
**Type**: Scholarship
**Value**: £600
**Frequency**: Annual
**Study Establishment**: Bournemouth University
**Country of Study**: United Kingdom

**Application Procedure**: Apply via online form available on the BU website. As part of your application, you will need to source two references. Referees can include your Director of Music, music teacher, instrumental/vocal coach, ensemble conductor etc, or any other person qualified to write about your musical abilities. They need to complete and submit the online reference form. Scholarships will be awarded for the first year of study and may be continued for subsequent years of study providing you continue to meet the criteria
**No. of awards offered**: 15
**Closing Date**: 31 August
**Contributor**: Bournemouth University
**No. of applicants last year**: 15
**Additional Information**: www.bournemouth.ac.uk/study/undergraduate/fees-funding/scholarships/ukeu-student-scholarships/bu-music-scholarships

### For further information contact:

**Tel**:    (44) 1202 961916

## Bournemouth University Vice-Chancellor's Scholarship – Most Promising Postgraduate Applicant

**Eligibility**: Any United Kingdom or European Union student who has completed an undergraduate degree at BU and who is applying for postgraduate study at BU
**Level of Study**: Graduate, Postgraduate
**Country of Study**: Any country

## Reham al-Farra International Scholarship in Journalism

**Purpose**: The Reham Al-Farra Memorial Journalism Fellowship is a unique opportunity for young journalists from developing countries and countries with economies in transition to cover the United Nations
**Eligibility**: The Reham al-Farra International Scholarship in Journalism is offered to an international applicant for MA Multimedia Journalism. You must be classed as an overseas student for fees purposes. You cannot be in receipt of any other BU scholarships
**Type**: Scholarship
**Value**: £3,000
**Frequency**: Annual
**Study Establishment**: Bournemouth University
**Country of Study**: Any country
**Application Procedure**: Apply via online form available on the BU website
**Closing Date**: 31 May

**Funding**: Private
**Contributor**: Bournemouth University
**Additional Information**: www.european-funding-guide.eu/scholarship/11272-reham-al-farra-international-scholarship-journalism

## The Business School Dean's Scholarship

**Eligibility**: You must be an applicant for a full-time taught Master's degree delivered by The Business School. Applicants will be considered based upon: 1. Academic achievement. 2. Work or voluntary experience relevant to the programme for which they have applied. 3. Any additional skills, experience or extra-curricular activities that will add value and indicate that they will make a significant contribution to the cohort on the programme or the Business School
**Level of Study**: Graduate, Postgraduate
**Type**: Scholarship
**Value**: up to £12,500
**Frequency**: Annual
**Country of Study**: Any country
**Application Procedure**: In order to apply for the scholarship, the following steps needs to be followed. To secure the scholarship award applicants must confirm acceptance of the award by the date stated on the scholarship offer email. Failure to confirm acceptance of the scholarship by this date may result in the applicant's right to the scholarship being removed and the scholarship being awarded to another applicant
**Closing Date**: 31 May
**Additional Information**: www.european-funding-guide.eu/scholarship/11270-business-school-dean%E2%80%99s-mba-scholarship

## Bradford Chamber of Commerce and Industry

Devere House, Vicar Lane, Little Germany, Bradford, Yorkshire BD1 5AH, United Kingdom.

**Tel**:        (44) 1274 772 777
**Email**:      info@bradfordchamber.co.uk
**Website**:    www.bradfordchamber.co.uk
**Contact**:    Julie Snook, Financial Controller

The Bradford Chamber of Commerce and Industry represents member companies in the Bradford and district area. It works with local partners to develop the economic health of the district and has a major voice within the British Chamber of

Commerce movement in order to promote the needs of local business on a national basis.

## John Speak Trust Scholarships

**Purpose**: To promote British trade abroad by assisting people in perfecting their basic knowledge of a foreign language
**Eligibility**: Open to British nationals intending to follow a career connected with the export trade in the United Kingdom. Applicants must be over 18 years of age with a sound, basic knowledge of at least one language
**Level of Study**: Professional development
**Type**: Scholarship
**Value**: 1. A financial Award ranging from £500 up to £2,000 towards living expenses. 2. Possible assistance with travel costs (up to £500) – individually assessed. 3. An opportunity to improve language skills and learn new customs. 4. Experience living abroad whilst studying a foreign language. 5. Gain valuable experience to assist in a chosen career. 6.n individually assessed application by the John Speak Committee
**Length of Study**: Between 3 months and 1 full academic year abroad depending on the circumstances and each candidate
**Frequency**: Annual
**Study Establishment**: A recognized college or university
**Country of Study**: Any country
**Application Procedure**: Applicants must complete an application form and undertake an interview
**No. of awards offered**: 14
**Closing Date**: 24 April
**Funding**: Private
**No. of awards given last year**: 10
**No. of applicants last year**: 14
**Additional Information**: www.johnspeaktrust.co.uk/new-applications-for-scholarships-are-invited-from-1st-sept-2017/

## Brain Research Institute

Florey Institute of Neuroscience and Mental Health, Melbourne Brain Centre - Austin campus, 245 Burgundy Street, Heidelberg, VIC 3084, Australia.

**Tel**:         (61) 3 9035 7000
**Email**:      BRI@brain.org.au
**Website**:    www.brain.org.au/

The Brain Research Institute (BRI) was established at Austin Health, Melbourne, Australia in 1996. It supports collaboration between specialities in order to develop a better understanding of how a healthy or diseased brain functions. It is an affiliated institution of The University of Melbourne

## Brain Research Institute PhD Scholarships

**Purpose**: To encourage competitive research in understanding the structure and function of the human brain
**Eligibility**: Open to candidates who have obtained Honours 1 or equivalent, or Honours 2a or equivalent
**Level of Study**: Doctorate
**Type**: Scholarship
**Value**: Varies
**Length of Study**: 3 years
**Frequency**: Annual
**Country of Study**: Australia
**Application Procedure**: Applicants must send a curriculum vitae, academic transcripts, expression of interest for area of research and details of two academic referees

### For further information contact:

**Email**:     scholarships@brain.org.au

## BrightFocus Foundation

22512 Gateway Center Drive, Clarksburg, MD 20871, United States of America.

**Tel**:       (1) 800 437 2423
**Email**:     info@brightfocus.org
**Website**:   www.brightfocus.org/
**Contact**:   Dr Kara Summers, Grants Coordinator

BrightFocus Foundation (formerly American Health Assistance Foundation [AHAF]) is a non-profit charitable organization that funds research and public education on age related and degenerative diseases including: Alzheimer's disease, macular degeneration, glaucoma.

## American Health Assistance Foundation Macular Degeneration Research

**Purpose**: To enable basic research on the causes of, or the treatment for, macular degeneration
**Eligibility**: The principal investigator must hold a tenure track or tenured position and the rank of assistant professor or higher
**Level of Study**: Research

**Type**: Grant
**Value**: maximum US$60,000 per year, payable over 2 years (total value US$120,000)
**Length of Study**: 2 year
**Frequency**: Annual
**Study Establishment**: Non-profit institutions and organizations
**Country of Study**: Any country
**Application Procedure**: Applicants must complete an application form. The current application form should be requested for each year or can be downloaded from the website
**No. of awards offered**: 81
**Closing Date**: July
**Funding**: Private
**No. of awards given last year**: 16
**No. of applicants last year**: 81
**Additional Information**: www.brightfocus.org/grants/request-proposal-fy20-macular-degeneration-research-program

**For further information contact:**

**Email**:    researchgrants@brightfocus.org

## British & Foreign School Society

Maybrook House, Godstone Road, Caterham, Surrey, CR3 6RE, United Kingdom.

**Tel**:         (44) 1883 331 177
**Website**:   www.bfss.org.uk
**Contact**:   Mr J Kidd ACIB, Director

## Global Professorships

**Purpose**: This programme aims to demonstrate and further enhance the UK's commitment to international research partnerships and collaboration as well as strengthen the UK's research capacity and capability in the humanities and the social sciences.
**Eligibility**: Applications must be submitted online using the British Academy's grants application system, Flexi-Grant. Be a world-class internationally-recognised mid-career to senior researchers who are currently employed outside the United Kingdom, on a permanent contract (which may be part-time or full-time) or, if temporary, would normally be on a contract that will not end during the course of the grant unless expressly agreed with the Academy prior to the application being submitted that such an application would be considered eligible, in any field of the humanities or the social sciences. Hold a doctoral degree (or have equivalent research

experience). Be available to take up an unpaid leave of absence, a long-term secondment or employment at an eligible United Kingdom host institution. Eligible institutions include but are not limited to the British International Research Institutes
**Level of Study**: Graduate, Postgraduate, Professional development, Research, Unrestricted
**Type**: Position (Employment)
**Value**: up to £187,500 per annum, and up to £750,000 over four years
**Length of Study**: For a period of 4 years
**Frequency**: Every 3 years
**Country of Study**: United Kingdom
**Application Procedure**: 1. Applications must be submitted online using the British Academy's grants application system, Flexi-Grant. 2.Application, reference, supporting statement and UK host institution application approval deadline: 17.00 (UK time) on Wednesday 19 February 2020.
**Closing Date**: 19 February
**Funding**: Government
**Additional Information**: All eligible proposals submitted in response to this funding call will be assessed by relevant British Academy peer reviewers and then considered by a final selection panel www.ucl.ac.uk/history/news/2019/oct/british-academy-funding-call-global-professorships-2020

**For further information contact:**

**Tel**:        (44) 20 7969 5220
**Email**:     internationalgrants@thebritishacademy.ac.uk

## The British & Foreign School Society

**Purpose**: We support charitable organisations that work to improve access to education or the quality of education for children and young people in remote or impoverished areas both in the UK and internationally. We do not have a particular geographic preference or focus.
**Eligibility**: 1. Organisations applying for funding should have UK charitable status or, in the case of schools, colleges, universities and Churches, "exempt charity" status. We do not fund non-UK based organisations, Community Interest Companies (CICs) or individuals. 2. Organisations should have continuous UK accounts for at least three years. 3. BFSS will only fund one project per charity at a time. If you are running a project with our funding, you cannot apply for a new grant until you have submitted your final project report. 4. BFSS focuses support on small to medium sized organisations who do not have ready access to much larger funding sources. We therefore do not usually fund charities with an average annual income above £2.5 million or below £5,000, except in exceptional circumstances. These restrictions do not apply to UK

based schools, colleges and other educational establishments. 5. Organisations should be directly involved in the provision of charitable services. We do not fund organisations whose primary purpose is fundraising. 6. We encourage close partnerships with local organisations. However, the applicant organisation must be willing to take full responsibility for the management, delivery, finances and integrity of the project.

**Application Procedure**: Applications from charitable organisations which meet the grant criteria are initially reviewed by the BFSS Grants Manager, and may then be submitted to the Grants Committee, which normally meets three times a year.

**Additional Information**: bfss.org.uk/grants/

## For further information contact:

7-14 Great Dover St, London, SE1 4YR, United Kingdom.

**Tel**:      (44) 20 7922 7814
**Email**:   grants@bfss.org.uk

## British Academy

10-11 Carlton House Terrace, London, SW1Y 5AH, United Kingdom.

**Tel**:      (44) 20 7969 5200
**Email**:   chiefexec@britac.ac.uk
**Website**: www.britac.ac.uk
**Contact**: Dr Ken Emond, Head of Research Awards

The British Academy is the premier national learned society in the United Kingdom devoted to the promotion of advanced research and scholarship in the humanities and social sciences.

## Browning Fund Grants

**Purpose**: To promote historical studies in the field of British history in the early modern period with particular reference to the 17th century
**Eligibility**: Applicants must be of postdoctoral status and ordinarily resident in the United Kingdom
**Level of Study**: Postdoctorate
**Type**: Research grant
**Value**: Up to £10,000
**Length of Study**: Up to 2 years

**Frequency**: Annual
**Country of Study**: Any country
**Application Procedure**: Application must be made to the BA/Leverhulme Small Research Grants Scheme via the BA's online e-GAP system at egap.britac.ac.uk
**No. of awards offered**: Part of a larger scheme
**Funding**: Private
**No. of awards given last year**: 1
**No. of applicants last year**: Part of a larger scheme
**Additional Information**: www.britac.ac.uk

## For further information contact:

**Email**:   bfi@brownfoundation.org

## Early Childhood Development Funding

**Purpose**: This programme is intended as the foundation for a wider research programme in subsequent years and thus aims to support a new generation of interlinked research and policy intervention that focuses on what works at scale in different contexts whilst building, and working with, local capacity to deliver effective research and change
**Eligibility**: 1. The Early Childhood Development Programme is open to researchers based at United Kingdom and overseas institutions. The main applicant must be based at a university or research institute and be of postdoctoral or above equivalent status. 2. The applicant must either be in a permanent position at the institution or have a fixed-term position for the duration of the award
**Level of Study**: Graduate
**Type**: Funding support
**Frequency**: Varies
**Country of Study**: Any country
**Closing Date**: 21 June
**Funding**: Private

## For further information contact:

10-11 Carlton House Terrace, London, SW1Y 5AH, United Kingdom.

**Email**:   ECD@britac.ac.uk

## Honor Frost Foundation Grants

**Purpose**: To provide support for research maritime archaeology and maritime cultural heritage
**Level of Study**: Postdoctorate
**Type**: Research grant
**Value**: Up to £10,000

**Length of Study**: Up to 2 years
**Frequency**: Annual
**Application Procedure**: Applications must be submitted via e-GAP2, the Academy's electronic grant application system, by applying for a BA/Leverhulme Small Research Grant
**No. of awards offered**: Part of a larger scheme
**Funding**: Private
**Contributor**: Honor Frost Foundation
**No. of awards given last year**: 2
**No. of applicants last year**: Part of a larger scheme
**Additional Information**: www.thebritishacademy.ac.uk/funding/honor-frost-foundation

### For further information contact:

**Email**: rebeccagould@honorfrostfoundation.org

## Newton International Fellowships

**Purpose**: The Newton International Fellowships aim to attract the most promising early career postdoctoral researchers from overseas in the fields of natural sciences, physical sciences, medical sciences, social sciences and the humanities. The Newton International Fellowships enable researchers to work for two years at a UK institution with the aim of fostering long-term international collaborations.
**Eligibility**: Applicants must have a PhD, have no more than 7 years of active full time postdoctoral experience, be working outside the UK, and not hold UK citizenship.
**Level of Study**: Postdoctorate
**Length of Study**: Up to 2 years
**Closing Date**: 8 April
**Additional Information**: www.thebritishacademy.ac.uk/funding/funding-opportunities

## Newton Mobility Grants

**Purpose**: Newton Mobility Grants provide support for international researchers based in a country covered by the Newton Fund to establish and develop collaboration with UK researchers around a specific jointly defined research project.
**Eligibility**: Both a UK-based applicant and an overseas-based applicant are required for this scheme. Both applicants must have a PhD or equivalent research experience and hold a permanent or fixed-term contract in an eligible university or research institute, which must span the duration of the project. Collaborations should focus on a single jointly defined research project involving (or lead by) the two applicants.
**Level of Study**: Research

**Type**: Grant
**Value**: maximum of £10,000
**Length of Study**: 1 year
**Frequency**: Annual
**Country of Study**: United Kingdom
**Application Procedure**: Applications must be submitted online using the British Academy's online grants management system, Flexi-Grant. For the assessment criteria please see the detailed scheme notes.
**Closing Date**: 5 September
**Funding**: Private
**Contributor**: Newton Fund
**Additional Information**: www.thebritishacademy.ac.uk/funding/newton-mobility-grants

### For further information contact:

10-11 Carlton House Terrace, London, SW1Y 5AH, United Kingdom.

**Tel**: (44) 207 969 5217
**Email**: newtonfund@thebritishacademy.ac.uk

## Sir Ernest Cassel Educational Trust Grants

**Purpose**: To enable early career researchers to travel overseas as part of a winter project supported under the BA/Leverhulme Small Research Grants Scheme
**Eligibility**: Applicants must be of postdoctoral status and ordinarily resident in the United Kingdom, and must be early career (within 5 years of the award or the doctorate)
**Level of Study**: Postdoctorate
**Type**: Research grant
**Value**: Normally not more than £1,000
**Length of Study**: Up to 2 years
**Frequency**: Annual
**Country of Study**: Any country
**Application Procedure**: Application must be made to the BA/Leverhulme small research Grants online e-GAP system at egap.britac.ac.uk
**No. of awards offered**: Part of a larger scheme
**Closing Date**: July
**Funding**: Private
**Contributor**: Sir Ernest Cassel Trust
**No. of awards given last year**: 11
**No. of applicants last year**: Part of a larger scheme
**Additional Information**: www.casseltrust.co.uk/

### For further information contact:

**Email**: casseltrust@btinternet.com

# British Association for American Studies (BAAS)

American Studies, School of Humanities, Keele University, Staffordshire, ST5 5BG, United Kingdom.

**Tel**:         (44) 1782 732000
**Email**:      jo.gill@baas.ac.uk
**Website**:    www.baas.ac.uk
**Contact**:    Dr Sue Currell, BAAS Chair

The British Association for American Studies (BAAS), established in 1955, promotes research and teaching in all aspects of American studies. The Association organizes annual conferences and specialist regional meetings for students, teachers and researchers. The publications produced are The Journal of American Studies with Cambridge University Press, BAAS Paperbacks with Edinburgh University Press and British Records Relating to America in Microform with Microform Publishing.

## British Association for American Studies Postgraduate and Early Career Short-Term Travel Awards

**Purpose**: To foster talent among the American Studies community in the United Kingdom. Fund travel to the United States of America for short-term research projects
**Eligibility**: Open to residents in the United Kingdom. Preference is given to young postgraduates and to members of BAAS. Successful candidates are required to provide a brief report of their research trip for publication in American Studies in Britain, and they are requested to acknowledge the assistance of BAAS in any other publication that results from research carried out during the tenure of the award
**Level of Study**: Doctorate, Postdoctorate, Postgraduate, Professional development
**Type**: Award
**Value**: £1,000
**Frequency**: Annual
**Country of Study**: United Kingdom or Australia
**Application Procedure**: Applicants must complete an application form
**No. of awards offered**: Classified
**Closing Date**: 10 December
**Funding**: Foundation
**Contributor**: American Embassy
**No. of awards given last year**: 6

**No. of applicants last year**: Classified
**Additional Information**: Successful candidates must write a report and acknowledge BAAS assistance in any related publication. Please contact at awards@baas.ac.uk www.baas. ac.uk/baas-postgraduate-short-term-travel-awards-2009/

### For further information contact:

**Email**:      awards@baas.ac.uk

# British Association for Canadian Studies (BACS)

UCL Institute of the Americas 51 Gordon Square, London, WC1H 0PN, United Kingdom.

**Tel**:         (44) 20 3108 9711
**Email**:      bacs@canadian-studies.org
**Website**:    www.canadian-studies.net
**Contact**:    Dr Tony McCulloch, President

In response to the growing academic interest in Canada, the British Association for Canadian Studies (BACS) was established in 1975. Its aim is to foster teaching and research on Canada and Canadian issues by locating study resources in Britain, facilitating travel and exchange schemes for professorial staff and ensuring that the expertise of Canadian scholars who visit the United Kingdom is put to effective use. Principal activities include the publication of The British Journal of Canadian Studies and the BACS Newsletter, and the organization of the Association's annual multidisciplinary conference, which attracts scholars from Canada and Europe as well as from the United Kingdom.

## Ontario Bicentennial Award

**Purpose**: To fund travel to Ontario to research topics concerned with that province in history or political science
**Eligibility**: Graduate students will normally only be considered in the final stages of their doctoral research, priority will be given to BACS members
**Level of Study**: Doctorate
**Type**: Travel grant
**Value**: C$500 approximately
**Length of Study**: Short visit
**Frequency**: Dependent on funds available
**Study Establishment**: University or library

**Country of Study**: Canada

**Application Procedure**: Application form, plus supporting letter, curriculum vitae, and the names of two referees must be submitted

**No. of awards offered**: 2

**Closing Date**: 1 May

**No. of awards given last year**: 1

**No. of applicants last year**: 2

**Additional Information**: Administered by BACS on behalf of the Foundation for Canadian Studies in the United Kingdom

# British Association for Japanese Studies

c/o Mrs Lynn Baird, BAJS Secretariat, University of Essex, Wivenhoe Park, Colchester, Essex, CO4 3SQ, United Kingdom.

**Tel**: (44) 7580 178 960

**Email**: bajs@bajs.org.uk

**Website**: www.bajs.org.uk

The Association was formed in 1974, with the 'aim to encourage Japanese studies in the United Kingdom, in particular by stimulating teaching and research'. With this in mind, the Association's first Conference was convened in Cambridge at Easter 1975, and since then the BAJS Conference has been an annual event.

## British Association for Japanese Studies Postgraduate Studentships

**Eligibility**: The studentships are open to postgraduate or prospective postgraduate students of all nationalities. Applicants must have been accepted onto a full-time or part-time course at a United Kingdom university at the time application. Their dissertation (or proposed dissertation) must be in the field of Japanese studies. For PhD students in particular, it will normally be expected that they will be using Japanese language materials in their research. They must use the award either to contribute towards their fees, maintenance, or extended fieldwork. Applicants must be a member of BAJS at the time of application

**Type**: Studentship

**Value**: Up to 5 individual scholarships of £4,000 will be granted for use in given academic year. No awards of less than £4,000 will be made

**Country of Study**: United Kingdom

**Application Procedure**: Application for BAJS Postgraduate Studentships is via the online application form. For detailed information, please visit www.bajs.org.uk/funding/bajs_studentship/

**Closing Date**: 15 May

**Additional Information**: Applicants will not be eligible to receive an award if they accept full scholarships from the AHRC, ESRC, or any other funding body (United Kingdom or overseas). Successful applicants will be expected to acknowledge the support of BAJS in their dissertations, presentations, and any subsequent publications; they will also be expected to submit a 500-word report on how they used the studentship to BAJS council by the end of November. Unsuccessful applicants will be considered for the BAJS Toshiba International Foundation studentship, provided they are eligible worldscholarshipforum.com/bajs-postgraduate-studentships-international-students-uk-2017/

### For further information contact:

**Email**: h.spurling@southampton.ac.uk

# British Association of Plastic Reconstructive and Aesthetic Surgeons (BAPRAS)

The Royal College of Surgeons, 35-43 Lincoln's Inn Fields, London, WC2A 3PE, United Kingdom.

**Tel**: (44) 20 7831 5161

**Email**: secretariat@bapras.org.uk

**Website**: www.bapras.org.uk

**Contact**: Ms Angela Rausch, Administrator

Founded in 1946 as British Association of Plastic Surgeons. The objective of the association is to relieve sickness and to protect and preserve public health by the promotion and development of Plastic Surgery. A name change to British Association of Plastic Reconstructive and Aesthetic Surgeons (BAPRAS).

## British Association of Plastic Reconstructive and Aesthetic Surgeons European Travelling Scholarships

**Purpose**: To enable Specialist Registrars from United Kingdom to visit any plastic surgical centre in Europe

**Eligibility**: Specialist Registrars (4–6) enrolled on a recognised training programme with the Specialist Advisory Committee in plastic surgery are eligible to apply. Preference will be given to trainees travelling abroad without other financial awards and those applying for funding prior travel. Candidates seeking funds to travel abroad in paid jobs are less preferred
**Type**: Scholarship
**Value**: Maximum value of one award is £5,000
**Frequency**: Annual
**Study Establishment**: Plastic Surgery Units
**Country of Study**: European Union
**Application Procedure**: Applicants should complete an application form, submit a proposed itinerary that should be detailed and give costs and the reasons for particular visits and a curriculum vitae (maximum length of two pages) to the Chairman of the Education and Research Sub-Committee, BAPRAS
**No. of awards offered**: 1
**Closing Date**: 10 December
**No. of awards given last year**: 1
**No. of applicants last year**: 1

### For further information contact:

**Email**:    bursaries@bapras.org.uk

### Travelling Bursaries for Presentation at Overseas Meetings

**Purpose**: To cover the expenses for overseas travel by a consultant or trainee to present papers at international meetings
**Eligibility**: Applicants must submit an application form to the Chairman of the Education and Research Sub-Committee, BAPRAS
**Type**: Travel award
**Value**: £600
**Frequency**: Annual
**Study Establishment**: Various
**Country of Study**: Any country
**Application Procedure**: Applicants must submit application form, abstract of paper to be presented and letter of acceptance to BAPRAS secretariat
**No. of awards offered**: 9
**Closing Date**: 10 December
**Contributor**: BAPRAS
**No. of awards given last year**: 5
**No. of applicants last year**: 9
**Additional Information**: www.bapras.org.uk/professionals/ training-and-education/prizes-grants-and-fellowships/travelling-bursaries-for-presentations-overseas

### For further information contact:

**Email**:    bursaries@bapras.org.uk

## British Broadcasting Corporation Writersroom

1st Floor, Grafton House, 379-381 Euston Road, London, NW1 3AU, United Kingdom.

**Email**:        writersroom@bbc.co.uk
**Website**:    www.bbc.co.uk/writersroom/opportunity

BBC Writersroom identifies and champions new writing talent and diversity across BBC Drama, Entertainment and Children's programmes. Writersroom is constantly on the lookout for writers of any age and experience who show real potential for the BBC. It invests in new writing projects nationwide and builds creative partnerships, including work with theatres, writer's organizations and film agencies across the country.

### Alfred Bradley Bursary Award

**Purpose**: The aim of the Award is to encourage new radio drama writing in the North of United Kingdom
**Eligibility**: Open to people who live in the North of United Kingdom and who have not had a previous network radio drama commission
**Level of Study**: Professional development
**Type**: Bursary
**Value**: Up to £5,000, writing bursary and the chance of a Radio 4 drama commission to Northern writers new to radio, and a 12 month mentorship with a Radio Drama producer
**Frequency**: Every 2 years
**Country of Study**: United Kingdom
**Application Procedure**: Applicants must send completed afternoon play scripts for consideration. Details published on www.bbc.co.uk/writersroom
**Closing Date**: 9 November
**Funding**: Private, Corporation
**Contributor**: BBC
**Additional Information**: There is a change of focus for each award, e.g. previous years have targeted comedy, drama, verse drama, etc.

### For further information contact:

**Email**:    admin@nawe.co.uk

# British Council

Bridgewater House, 58 Whitworth Street, M1 6BB, Manchester, M1 6BB, United Kingdom.

**Tel**: (44) 161 957 7755 ·
**Email**: general.enquiries@britishcouncil.org
**Website**: www.britishcouncil.org

The British Council is the United Kingdom's public diplomacy and cultural organization working in more than 100 countries, in arts, education, governance and science. The British Council promotes the diversity and creativity of British society and culture. The Foreign and Commonwealth Office provides The British Council with the core grant-in-aid

## Commonwealth Scholarships

**Purpose**: For students from the developed Commonwealth to study in the United Kingdom
**Eligibility**: Please check at
**Level of Study**: Doctorate
**Type**: Scholarship
**Value**: Student visas for the United Kingdom will be arranged gratis by the British Council
**Application Procedure**: See British Council website
**Closing Date**: 22 February
**Funding**: Government

### For further information contact:

Department of Higher Education, External Scholarship Division, ES.4 Section, West Block-1, Wing-6, 2nd Floor, R.K. Puram, New Delhi 110066, India.

**Tel**: (91) 11 26172491/26172492
**Email**: delhi.scholarship@in.britishcouncil.org

## Marshall Scholarships

**Purpose**: To finance young Americans of high ability to study for a degree in the United Kingdom
**Eligibility**: 1. Be citizens of the United States of America (at the time they apply for a scholarship); 2. (By the time they take up their scholarship ie September 2021) hold their first undergraduate degree from an accredited four-year college or university in the United States; 3. Have obtained a grade point average of not less than 3.7 on their undergraduate degree. (Applicants must have a GPA of 3.7 at the time of application). We do not accept rounded GPA's. 4. Have graduated from their first undergraduate college or university after April 2018. 5. Not have studied for, or hold a degree or degree-equivalent qualification from a British University or GCSE or A Levels taken at school in the UK.
**Type**: Scholarship
**Value**: University fees, cost of living expenses, annual book grant, thesis grant, research and daily travel grants, fares to and from the United States and, where applicable, a contribution towards the support of a dependent spouse
**Frequency**: Annual
**Country of Study**: United Kingdom
**Closing Date**: October
**Funding**: Government
**Contributor**: British Council
**No. of awards given last year**: 40
**Additional Information**: www.marshallscholarship.org/apply/criteria-and-who-is-eligible

### For further information contact:

11766 Wilshire Boulevard, Suite 1200, Los Angeles, CA 90025-6538, United States of America.

**Tel**: (1) 310 996 3028
**Email**: Losangeles@marshallscholarship.org

## The Goa Education Trust (GET) Scholarships

**Purpose**: To provide opportunities for dynamic young men and women of Goan origin who have demonstrated academic excellence and extra-curricular achievements to study or train in the United Kingdom
**Eligibility**: Open to Indian nationals, domiciled and resident in Goa or born of Goan parents, who are not more than 30 years of age at the time of applying for the scholarship and have an excellent academic track record. Candidates must have confirmed admission for any technical/vocational/academic course of study in the United Kingdom for up to 1 year
**Level of Study**: Postgraduate
**Type**: Scholarship
**Value**: Scholarships will fund young Indians to pursue a Masters in the United Kingdom and will cover part or full tuition fees not exceeding £15,000
**Length of Study**: 1 year
**Frequency**: Annual
**Country of Study**: United Kingdom
**Application Procedure**: A completed application form must be sent by post

**Closing Date**: 10 May
**Additional Information**: studyabroad.shiksha.com/scholar ships/goa-education-trust-scholarships

### For further information contact:

British Council Division, British Deputy High Commission, 901, 9th Floor, Tower1, One Indiabulls Centre, 841, Senapati Bapat Marg, Elphinstone Road (West), Mumbai 400 013, India.

**Tel**:        (91) 22 67486748
**Email**:    mumbai.enquiry@in.britishcouncil.org

## British Dental Association

64 Wimpole Street, London, W1G 8YS, United Kingdom.

**Tel**:        (44) 20 7935 0875
**Email**:    enquiries@bda.org
**Website**:  www.bda.org
**Contact**:  Miss Sarah Leithead, Marketing Executive

The British Dental Association (BDA) is the national professional association for dentists. With over 20,000 members, the Association strives to enhance the science, art and ethics of dentistry, improve the nation's oral health and promote the interests of its members.

### British Dental Association/Dentsply Student Support Fund

**Purpose**: To give financial assistance to students who are in severe financial hardship. Only open to 4th- and 5th-year BDS students or postgraduates
**Eligibility**: Open to BDA members only. All applicants must be registered students at a United Kingdom Dental School
**Level of Study**: Graduate, Postgraduate
**Type**: Scholarship/Hardship fund
**Value**: Varies
**Frequency**: Annual
**Country of Study**: United Kingdom
**Application Procedure**: Applicants must complete and submit application forms, accompanied by an academic reference or supporting letter. Application forms can be found in the student section of the BDA website
**No. of awards offered**: 30
**Closing Date**: 1 July
**Funding**: Commercial

**Contributor**: Dentsply United Kingdom Ltd
**No. of awards given last year**: 7
**No. of applicants last year**: 30
**Additional Information**: For BDS/Dental Students only

### For further information contact:

**Email**:    SSF@contacts.bham.ac.uk

## British Dietetic Association

The British Dietetic Association, 5th floor, Charles House, 148/9 Great Charles Street Queensway, Birmingham, B3 3HT, United Kingdom.

**Tel**:        (44) 1 2120 0802
**Email**:    info@bda.uk.com
**Website**:  www.bda.uk.com
**Contact**:  Mr Nula Marnell, Assistant to the Chief Executive

The British Dietetic Association (BDA) is the professional body for dietitians in the United Kingdom and provides grants for research into human nutrition and dietetic practice that advances the profession.

### Pace Award

**Purpose**: For the development or implementation of a nutrition education programme for staff addressing the problem of undernutrition
**Eligibility**: Applicants should be full members of the BDA and resident in the United Kingdom or Eire
**Level of Study**: Research
**Type**: Grant
**Value**: £500 to fund the development of the project and £300 worth of pace learning units for staff to use
**Country of Study**: Any country
**Application Procedure**: To apply, dietitians are to submit an outline of the proposed education programme that includes: which staff is targeted, subject area and level of the programme, which format will be taken, how the learner will be assessed, what effect it will have on nutritional care and how it will raise the profile of nutrition in your organization, potential benefits to employers and estimated cost of development and implementation. Four copies of the application are to be submitted
**Closing Date**: 28 January
**Funding**: Commercial

**Additional Information**: Applications should not exceed 1,000 words

**For further information contact:**

**Email**:    financial.aid@ohio.edu

## British Ecological Society (BES)

Charles Darwin House, 12 Roger Street, London, Wc1N 2JU, United Kingdom.

**Tel**:        (44) 20 7685 2500
**Email**:        grants@britishecologicalsociety.org
**Website**:        www.britishecologicalsociety.org

As a learned society and registered charity, the British Ecological Society (BES) is an independent organization receiving little outside funding. The aims of the Society are to promote the science of ecology through research, publications and conferences and to use the findings of such research to educate the public and to influence policy decisions that involve ecological matters. The BES is an active and thriving organization with something to offer anyone with an interest in ecology. Academic journals, teaching resources, meetings for scientists and policy makers, career advice and grants for ecologists are just a few of the societies areas of activity.

### Outreach Grant

**Purpose**: To promote ecological science to a wide audience
**Eligibility**: Awards are open to individuals and organizations to organize public engagement events in ecology. This includes, but is not limited to, members of the BES, researchers, schools, museums, libraries and community groups. Applications will not be considered for: staff salaries; Purchase of apparatus, including computers, cameras etc., unless these are integral to the application. Applications from museums and schools are welcome but projects must involve significant outreach beyond schools. Projects aimed solely at delivering curriculum to school children will not be considered
**Type**: Project grant
**Value**: £2,000
**Frequency**: Annual
**Country of Study**: Any country
**Application Procedure**: Applicants must complete an online application form through the BES website at www.britishecologicalsociety.org/grants-awards/outreach-grants
**No. of awards offered**: 113

**Closing Date**: 20 March
**Contributor**: British Ecological Society
**No. of awards given last year**: 11
**No. of applicants last year**: 113
**Additional Information**: Published papers and reports to other organizations should include an acknowledgement of the support from the BES. Other conditions may apply www.britishecologicalsociety.org/funding/outreach-grants/

**For further information contact:**

**Email**:    outreach@physoc.org

### Training & Travel Grants

**Purpose**: These grants help PhD students and postgraduate research assistants to meet the costs of specialist field training courses and to network and publicise their research by presenting their work at workshops and conferences.
**Eligibility**: 1. be a BES member. 2. have at least a B.Sc. or equivalent degree. 3. be a PhD student, postgraduate research assistant (within 3 years of completing relevant degree) or equivalent (Postdoc researchers are therefore not eligible to apply).4. work or study at a university or research institution (including field centres, NGOs, museums, etc.) that provide research facilities. 5. work in scientific areas within our remit (the science of ecology) and of relevance to the training course or meeting they are applying to attend. 6. give a presentation if attending a meeting. 7. no retrospective claims for funding will be considered. 8. no applicant may receive more than two Training & Travel Grants in any five year period. There must be at least three years between grants.
**Type**: Grants
**Value**: £1,000
**Closing Date**: September
**Additional Information**: www.britishecologicalsociety.org/funding/training-travel-grants/

## British Federation of Women Graduates (BFWG)

4 Mandeville Courtyard, 142 Battersea Park Road, London, SW11 4NB, United Kingdom.

**Tel**:        (44) 20 7498 8037
**Email**:        awards@bfwg.org.uk
**Website**:        www.bfwg.org.uk

The British Federation of Women Graduates (BFWG) provides opportunities to women in education and public life.

BFWG works as part of an international organization to improve the lives of women and girls, fosters local, national and international friendship and offers scholarships for third year doctorate research.

## American Association of University Women/ International Federation of University Women International Fellowships

**Purpose**: To assist study or research that demonstrates a continued interest in the advancement of women
**Eligibility**: Open to female members of the British Federation of Women Graduates (BFWG) or another national federation or association (NFA) of the International Federation of University Women (IFUW), who are not United States citizens, with acceptance by an institution in America at which the applicant proposes to undertake her work
**Level of Study**: Graduate, Postdoctorate, Postgraduate, Predoctorate, Research
**Type**: Fellowships
**Value**: Master's/first professional degree: US$18,000; Doctoral: US$20,000; Postdoctoral: US$30,000. These fellowships do not cover travel costs
**Length of Study**: 1 year
**Frequency**: Annual
**Study Establishment**: An Institute of Higher Education
**Country of Study**: United States of America
**Application Procedure**: Application material can be downloaded from AAUW's website
**Closing Date**: 1 December
**Funding**: Private
**Contributor**: AAUW members
**Additional Information**: A list of NFA's can be found on IFUW's website (www.ifuw.org www.scholars4dev.com/1877/aauw-international-fellowships-in-usa-for-women/)

### For further information contact:

AAUW Educational Foundation, International Fellowships, PO Box 4030, Iowa City, IA 52243-4030, United States of America.

**Email**:    aauw@act.org

## British Federation of Women Graduates Scholarships

**Purpose**: To assist final-year PhD research students
**Eligibility**: Academic excellence as evidenced by a proven ability to carry out independent research is the chief criterion. Open to female students, regardless of nationality, whose studies take place in Great Britain. Research students

should be entering into their final year of formal study towards a PhD degree. Taught Master's degrees do not count as research, although MPhil research students would need to be upgraded to a PhD during the close of the competition or thereabouts
**Level of Study**: Doctorate, Predoctorate, Research
**Type**: Scholarship
**Value**: The amounts offered in awards range upwards from GB£1,000 with the average award being around GB£3,000 and the maximum being GB£6,000
**Length of Study**: Student must be in her third year (or part time equivalent) at the time of giving out the awards (October each year)
**Frequency**: Annual
**Study Establishment**: A university or institution of university status in Britain
**Country of Study**: Great Britain
**Application Procedure**: Application materials can be downloaded from BFWG's website or www.bfwg.org.uk
**No. of awards offered**: 235
**Closing Date**: 18 March
**Funding**: Private
**Contributor**: BFWG members
**No. of awards given last year**: 7
**No. of applicants last year**: 235
**Additional Information**: Recipients must submit a written report within 6 months of being awarded their PhD

## French Association of University Women (AFFDU) Grants

**Purpose**: To assist those at doctoral or postdoctoral levels whose studies or research take place in France
**Eligibility**: Open to female members of the British Federation of Women Graduates (BFWG) or another national federation or association (NFA) of the International Federation of University Women (IFUW), who know the language of the country in which they plan to study
**Level of Study**: Doctorate, Postdoctorate, Postgraduate, Research
**Type**: Grant
**Value**: €1,000–1,500, should preferably cover a study or research project involving travelling to or outside of France
**Length of Study**: Up to 12 months
**Frequency**: Annual
**Study Establishment**: An Institute of Higher Education
**Country of Study**: France
**Application Procedure**: Applicants should be undergraduate or postgraduate students, should have applied for admission to the University for a full-time scheme and have satisfied the entry requirements
**Closing Date**: 30 April
**Funding**: Private

**Contributor**: AFFDU members

**Additional Information**: A list of NFA's can be found on IFUW's website (www.ifuw.org www.european-funding-guide.eu/scholarship/6992-affdu-grants-archaelogy-history-literature-physics-chemistry)

**For further information contact:**

AFFDU, Reid Hall, 4 rue de Chevreuse, F-75006 Paris, France.

**Email**: affdu@club-internet.fr

## French Association of University Women (AFFDU) Monique Fouet Grant

**Purpose**: To support a women postgraduate studying Political Science

**Eligibility**: Open to female members of the British Federation of Women Graduates (BFWG) or another National Federation of Association (NFA) of the International Federation of University Women (IFUW), who wish to undertake research on the AFFDU project site in Nabasdju Civol. Candidates must speak French

**Level of Study**: Postgraduate, Research

**Type**: Grant

**Value**: From €1,000–1,500. The award does not cover travel costs

**Length of Study**: Up to 1 year

**Frequency**: Annual

**Study Establishment**: A university or institution of university status

**Country of Study**: Any country

**Application Procedure**: Application materials can be downloaded from AFFDU's website or obtained via email

**Closing Date**: March

**Funding**: Private

**Contributor**: AFFDU members

**Additional Information**: A list of NFA's can be found on IFUW's website (www.ifuw.org)

**For further information contact:**

AFFDU, Reid Hall, 4 rue de Chevreuse, F-75006 Paris, France.

**Email**: affdu@club-internet.fr

## NKA Ellen Gleditsch Scholarship

**Purpose**: To assist independent research or advanced studies by women at the post-graduate or doctoral level

**Eligibility**: Open to female members of the British Federation of Women Graduates (BFWG) or another national federation or association (NFA) of the International Federation of University Women (IFUW) with acceptance by a Norwegian institution at which the applicant proposes to undertake her work and proof of adequate health insurance

**Level of Study**: Doctorate, Postgraduate, Research

**Type**: Scholarship

**Value**: NOK 40,000. The scholarship does not cover travel costs

**Length of Study**: 3–4 months

**Frequency**: Every 3 years

**Study Establishment**: A university or institution of university status

**Country of Study**: Norway

**Application Procedure**: Applicants studying in Great Britain must apply through BFWG. Application material and membership details can be downloaded from their website or for paper copies write to BFWG, 4 Mandeville Courtyard, 142 Battersea Park Road, London SW11 4NB, United Kingdom enclosing a C5 self-addressed stamped envelope

**Closing Date**: 1 September

**Funding**: Private

**Contributor**: NKA members

**Additional Information**: If studying outside Great Britain, candidates should check the list of NFAs on IFUW's website (www.ifuw.org)

**For further information contact:**

EGS, PO Box 251, N-5000 Bergen, Norway.

**Email**: elisabeth.haavet@hi.uib.no

## British Heart Foundation (BHF)

14 Fitzhardinge Street, London, W1H 6DH, United Kingdom.

**Tel**: (44) 20 7935 0185
**Email**: internet@bhf.org.uk
**Website**: www.bhf.org.uk
**Contact**: Ms Valerie Mason, Research Funds Manager

The British Heart Foundation (BHF) exists to encourage research into the causes, diagnosis, prevention and advances of cardiovascular disease, to inform doctors throughout the country of advances in the diagnosis, cure and treatment of heart diseases, and to improve facilities for the treatment of heart patients where the National Health Service is unable to help.

## British Heart Foundation-Daphne Jackson Fellowships

**Purpose**: To provide an opportunity for basic scientists to return to cardiovascular research at an established research institution in the United Kingdom after a career break of two years or more

**Eligibility**: Your eligibility and suitability are initially assessed using the information submitted to us in the CV and personal statement forms. If you do fit our eligibility criteria, one of our Fellowship Advisors will arrange an informal telephone interview with you to talk through your CV, your career break, your desire to retrain, your field of interest and assess your future employment prospects

**Type**: Fellowship

**Length of Study**: Up to three years

**Frequency**: Annual

**Country of Study**: Any country

**Application Procedure**: 1. Applicants will need to approach and agree a plan of work with a potential academic sponsor as part of the application process. We are particularly interested in supporting applicants working in interdisciplinary research, but applicants working in single disciplines will be considered equally. 2. The Elizabeth Blackwell Institute will half-sponsor the Fellowship and the remaining funding will be secured by the Daphne Jackson Trust from an additional sponsor

**Closing Date**: 18 February

**Funding**: Private

**Additional Information**: The fellowship will be part-time for a fixed term of up to three years daphnejackson.org/wp-content/uploads/2019/07/British-Heart-Foundation-Daphne-Jackson-Fellowship-2019.pdf

### For further information contact:

The Daphne Jackson Trust, Department of Physics, University of Surrey, Guildford, Surrey, GU2 7XH, United Kingdom.

**Email**:    djmft@surrey.ac.uk

## Career Re-entry Research Fellowships

**Purpose**: To provide an opportunity to re-establish a career in cardiovascular science in an established research institution in the United Kingdom, after a break of more than one year

**Eligibility**: 1. Successful post-doc returning after a career break of one or more years. 2. The candidate must have the support of a named senior investigator who will guarantee access to space and resources and provide scientific guidance

for the duration of their fellowship. This individual should be named on the application form as a 'Supervisor' and provide an appropriate letter of support as part of the application. 3. The fellowship may be taken up on a part-time employment basis, where appropriate, following discussion and agreement with us and the employing institution. For more information read about our Flexible working policies

**Level of Study**: Postdoctorate researcher

**Type**: Fellowship

**Value**: £500 per year

**Length of Study**: Up to 1 year full-time or up to 3 years part-time

**Frequency**: Varies

**Country of Study**: United Kingdom

**Application Procedure**: Application link for the grants are as follows:   gms.bhf.org.uk/Pages/Default.aspx?ReturnUrl=%252f_layouts%252fAuthenticate.aspx%253fSource%253d%252f&Source=%252f

**Funding**: Private

**Additional Information**: For further information, visit the website www.bhf.org.uk www.bhf.org.uk/for-professionals/information-for-researchers/what-we-fund/career-re-entry-research-fellowship

### For further information contact:

British Heart Foundation, Lyndon Place, 2096 Coventry Road, Sheldon, Birmingham, B26 3YU, United Kingdom.

**Tel**:        (44) 20 7554 0442
**Email**:    gmsqueries@bhf.org.uk

## Clinical Research Leave Fellowships

**Purpose**: To provide an opportunity for talented NHS staff to undertake dedicated PAs in research in a recognised United Kingdom centre of excellence in cardiovascular medicine

**Eligibility**: Awards may include: 1. Reimbursement of reasonable costs to cover relinquished PAs. 2. Research consumables directly attributable to the project

**Level of Study**: Graduate

**Type**: Fellowship

**Value**: £500 per year

**Length of Study**: Up to 1 year full-time or up to 3 years part-time

**Frequency**: Annual

**Country of Study**: Any country

**Application Procedure**: Candidates may be interviewed and a decision on this will be reached by the Fellowships Committee (four meetings a year) after it has considered external peer review reports

**Funding**: Private

**Additional Information**: www.bhf.org.uk/for-professionals/information-for-researchers/what-we-fund/clinical-research-leave-fellowship

### For further information contact:

180, Hampstead Road, London, NW1 7AW, United Kingdom.

**Tel**: 　(44) 20 7554 0442
**Email**: 　gmsqueries@bhf.org.uk

## Clinical Study Grants

**Purpose**: To provide an opportunity for talented NHS staff to undertake dedicated PAs in research in a recognised United Kingdom centre of excellence in cardiovascular medicine
**Eligibility**: 1. The principal investigator will be a senior researcher working in an established research institution in the United Kingdom. She/he must have a strong track record of grant support, usually from us, and an internationally recognised research profile. 2. Any multicentre interventional clinical trial, while remaining under the scientific control of the principal investigator, should usually be managed by a United Kingdom CRC-registered Clinical Trials Unit (CTU) and should usually include a member of the CTU as a co-applicant or principal investigator unless there are clearly justified reasons for not doing so
**Level of Study**: Graduate
**Type**: Fellowship or Grant
**Value**: £2,000 per year
**Length of Study**: Usually up to 5 years, with regular progress reports, initially annual reports
**Frequency**: Every 5 years
**Country of Study**: Any country
**Application Procedure**: Once a preliminary application is approved you should submit a full application: 1. Read the information in How to apply. 2. Read about the SoECAT form. 3. Also read: Costing a clinical study. Excess treatment costs. Costing a clinical research imaging scan. Clinical Trials Units. Clinical Study Guidelines. Patient and public involvement. 4. Log onto the online application form. Application has to be completed through online procedurals
**Closing Date**: 1 April
**Funding**: Private
**Additional Information**: www.bhf.org.uk/for-professionals/information-for-researchers/what-we-fund/clinical-study

### For further information contact:

180 Hampstead Road, London, NW1 7AW, United Kingdom.

**Tel**: 　(44) 20 7554 0442
**Email**: 　gmsqueries@bhf.org.uk

## Immediate Postdoctoral Basic Science Research Fellowships

**Purpose**: To provide an opportunity for the most promising newly qualified postdoctoral researchers to make an early start in developing their independent cardiovascular research careers in an established institution in the United Kingdom
**Eligibility**: Candidates should be in the final year of their PhD studies or have no more than two years of postdoctoral research experience from the date of the PhD viva. Candidates must be able to show, by publications or otherwise, evidence of exceptional research ability. The fellowship should not be held in the institution where the PhD was carried out. Residency requirements do not apply
**Level of Study**: Postgraduate
**Type**: Fellowship
**Value**: Travel funding of up to £500 per year & Housing contribution up to £3,000
**Length of Study**: 1.5 years
**Country of Study**: Any country
**Application Procedure**: The online application form must be completed by the applicant
**Funding**: Private
**Additional Information**: www.bhf.org.uk/for-professionals/information-for-researchers/what-we-fund/immediate-postdoctoral-basic-science-research-fellowship

### For further information contact:

**Tel**: 　(44) 20 7554 0442
**Email**: 　gmsqueries@bhf.org.uk

## Intermediate Clinical Research Fellowships

**Purpose**: To provide a career opportunity in an established research institution in the United Kingdom for individuals with an established research record who intend to become leaders in academic medical research
**Eligibility**: Successful PhD (or MD) plus NTN and at least two years completed specialist training, but usually no more than two years after CCT. NTN will be exchanged for NTN (A) on appointment, and the individual may progress to consultant level during the fellowship
**Level of Study**: Graduate
**Type**: Fellowships, operating grants
**Value**: Travel funding of up to £500 per year & Housing contribution up to £3,000
**Length of Study**: 5 years duration
**Frequency**: Annual
**Country of Study**: Any country
**Application Procedure**: 1. Read the information in How to apply. 2. Read our commitment to Improving Support for

Clinical Academics. If you are applying for funding for a clinical study, also read: 1. Costing a clinical study. 2. Costing a clinical research imaging scan. 3. Clinical Trials Units. 4. Clinical Study Guidelines. 5. Log onto the online application form. Complete all the sections of the online application form following the instructions in the GMS User Guide. The online application must be completed by the applicant. Shortlisted candidates may be interviewed

**Funding**: Government

**Additional Information**: www.bhf.org.uk/for-professionals/information-for-researchers/what-we-fund/intermediate-clinical-research-fellowships

### For further information contact:

Research Funds Department, British Heart Foundation, Greater London House, 180 Hampstead Road, London, NW1 7AW, United Kingdom.

**Tel**:      (44) 20 7554 0442
**Email**:   gmsqueries@bhf.org.uk

### New Horizon Grants

**Purpose**: To encourage scientists from outside traditional cardiovascular biology to engage in cardiovascular research and bring novel expertise to the field, and to develop new technologies, models or methodologies

**Eligibility**: 1. The principal investigator will be a senior researcher working in an established research institution in the United Kingdom. He/she must have a strong track record of project grant support and an internationally recognised research profile. 2. The principal investigator or co-applicant(s) should include researcher(s) with a strong track record of relevant cardiovascular research. 3. The principal investigator or co-applicant(s) should include researcher(s) from outside traditional cardiovascular biology, who do not have extensive existing collaborations with cardiovascular researchers

**Level of Study**: Graduate

**Type**: Grant

**Value**: Up to £300,000 and up to three years & Travel funding of up to £2,000 per year

**Frequency**: Every 3 years

**Country of Study**: Any country

**Application Procedure**: Kindly check the website for further information. www.bhf.org.uk/for-professionals/information-for-researchers/what-we-fund/new-horizon-grants

**Funding**: Private

**Additional Information**: You will be asked to attach a single PDF document to your online application form containing the following information: 1. For resubmissions, include an unedited copy of the original feedback followed by a detailed response, limited to 3 sides of A4, explaining how the revised application has changed from the original submission. 2. Abstract of the proposed investigation in 200 words or less. 3. Background to the project and pilot data. 4. Original hypothesis. 5. Experimental details and design of proposed investigation. 6. Power calculations. 7. Expected value of results. 8. List of references relevant to the proposed project www.bhf.org.uk/for-professionals/information-for-researchers/what-we-fund/new-horizon-grants

### For further information contact:

180 Hampstead Road, London, NW1 7AW, United Kingdom.

**Tel**:      (44) 20 7554 0442
**Email**:   gmsqueries@bhf.org.uk

### Non-Clinical PhD Studentships

**Purpose**: To allow talented students to complete a PhD in cardiovascular science in an established research institution in the United Kingdom

**Eligibility**: The application must be made by an established investigator who will be the supervisor and may be for a named or unnamed student. The primary supervisor must devote a minimum of 10% of their time to supervising the student and a second supervisor should also be included. Extra scrutiny will be given to applications from institutions in receipt of a BHF Research Excellence award or from supervisors named on a BHF 4 year PhD Scheme. These applications will require additional justification and should be for named students only. The BHF does not provide 'top-up' funding for existing PhD studentships supported by other grant giving organisations, which are incompletely funded

**Level of Study**: Graduate, Postgraduate

**Type**: Studentship and scholarship

**Value**: £10,000 per year

**Frequency**: Every 3 years

**Country of Study**: Any country

**Application Procedure**: Apply through online mode post registration on the below link. gms.bhf.org.uk/Pages/Default.aspx?ReturnUrl=%252f_layouts%252fAuthenticate.aspx%253fSource%253d%252f&Source=%252f

**Funding**: Private

**Additional Information**: www.bhf.org.uk/for-professionals/information-for-researchers/what-we-fund/phd-studentships

### For further information contact:

**Tel**:      (44) 20 7554 0442
**Email**:   gmsqueries@bhf.org.uk

## Research Training Fellowships for Nurses and Allied Health Professionals

**Purpose**: To provide a foundation in research training in an established research institution in the United Kingdom for nurses and allied health professionals, leading to the award of a PhD.

**Eligibility**: The named student should usually hold a good quality Masters degree or equivalent. 1. Students who have started a PhD (or equivalent) may be eligible to apply for a Research Training Fellowship, but the application must be received within 6 months of having registered for their PhD In these circumstances, the proposed start date for the Research Training Fellowship should also be no more than 12 months (or full-time equivalent) from the date of registration for the degree. 2. If the fellowship is taken up on a full-time research basis, we recognise that part of the time (ideally no more than 20% though sometimes more if it can be argued that the research directly involves their patients) may be spent on patient care. 3. The fellowship may be taken up on a part-time employment basis, where appropriate, following discussion and agreement with us and the employing institution. For more information, read about our Flexible working policies

**Level of Study**: Postgraduate
**Type**: Fellowship
**Value**: £10,000 per year
**Frequency**: 5 years
**Country of Study**: Any country
**Application Procedure**: Check through the website link. www.bhf.org.uk/for-professionals/information-for-researchers/what-we-fund/research-training-fellowships-for-nurses-and-allied-health-professionals
**Closing Date**: 22 April
**Funding**: Foundation
**Additional Information**: www.bhf.org.uk/for-professionals/information-for-researchers/what-we-fund/research-training-fellowships-for-nurses-and-allied-health-professionals

### For further information contact:

**Email**:    research@bhf.org.uk

## Travel Fellowships

**Purpose**: To enable a postdoctoral researcher to undertake a visit to a distinguished laboratory abroad, either for a short period of up to six months to acquire specialist knowledge or expertise, or for a longer period to carry out a research project that can not be done in United Kingdom
**Eligibility**: Usually more than three years postdoctoral experience, but applicants with less postdoctoral experience are also eligible to apply. Applicant must hold a post in the United Kingdom and a guaranteed post to return to after the fellowship
**Level of Study**: Postdoctorate
**Type**: Fellowship
**Frequency**: Annual
**Country of Study**: Any country
**Application Procedure**: 1. Read the information in How to apply. 2. Log onto the online application form. 3. Complete all the sections of the online application form following the instructions in the GMS User Guide. 4. Ensure the named Supervisor in the application form is your United Kingdom Supervisor
**Funding**: Private
**Additional Information**: www.bhf.org.uk/for-professionals/information-for-researchers/what-we-fund/travel-fellowships

### For further information contact:

**Email**:    research@bhf.org.uk

## British Institute at Ankara (BIAA)

10 Carlton House Terrace, London, SW1Y 5AH, United Kingdom.

| | |
|---|---|
| **Tel**: | (44) 20 7969 5204 |
| **Email**: | biaa@britac.ac.uk |
| **Website**: | www.biaa.ac.uk |
| **Contact**: | Claire McCafferty, London Administrator |

BIAA aims to support, promote, facilitate, and publish British research focused on Turkey and the Black Sea littoral in all academic disciplines within the arts, humanities, and social sciences and to maintain a centre of excellence in Ankara focused on the archaeology and related subjects of Turkey.

## British Institute at Ankara Research Scholarship

**Purpose**: To conduct their own research at doctoral level
**Eligibility**: Open to candidates who hold a Master's degree and have a demonstrable connection to United Kingdom academia
**Level of Study**: Postgraduate, Research
**Type**: Research scholarship
**Value**: £800 per month and the cost of one return flight between the United Kingdom and Turkey
**Length of Study**: 9 months
**Frequency**: Annual
**Country of Study**: Turkey

**Application Procedure**: Deadline for applications is mid-September. Check website for further details
**Closing Date**: September

## For further information contact:

British Institute at Ankara, Çankaya, Atatürk Blv No:154, 06690 Çankaya/Ankara, Turkey.

**Fax**:  (44) 20 7969 5401

## Martin Harrison Memorial Fellowship

**Purpose**: To assist junior Turkish archaeologists, who are not able to take advantage of travelling, working in any area of the archaeology of Anatolia from Prehistory to the Ottoman period, to visit the United Kingdom, especially Oxford, in connection with their research work
**Eligibility**: Open to Turkish citizens residing in Turkey who have completed at least 2 years of postgraduate research and at most held a doctorate for 5 years, working in any area of the archaeology of Anatolia (from the Prehistoric to the Ottoman period)
**Level of Study**: Doctorate, Postgraduate, Research
**Type**: Short-term fellowship
**Value**: £1,500 and travel expenses from and to Turkey
**Length of Study**: 6–13 weeks
**Frequency**: Annual
**Study Establishment**: University of Oxford
**Country of Study**: United Kingdom
**Application Procedure**: Completed applications, including a curriculum vitae, should be sent to the Turkey address
**Closing Date**: 31 March
**Funding**: Foundation
**Contributor**: Martin Harrison Fund for living expenses and British Institute at Ankara (BIAA) for travel
**Additional Information**: The selection will be made on the basis of the applicant's academic record, coherent research proposal, ability to benefit from libraries and scholars in Oxford, and a working knowledge of spoken and written English biaa.ac.uk/opportunities/item/name/martin-harrison-memorial-fund-fellowship

## For further information contact:

The British Institute at Ankara, 24 Tahran Caddesi, Kavaklidere, TR-06700 Ankara, Turkey.

**Tel**:    (90) 312 427 5487
**Fax**:    (90) 312 428 0159
**Email**:  ggirdivan@biaatr.org

## British Institute in Eastern Africa

British Institute in Eastern Africa, Laikipia Road, Kileleshwa, Nairobi, PO Box 30710 – 00100 GPO, Kenya.

**Tel**:     (254) 20 815 5186
**Email**:   office@biea.ac.uk
**Website**: www.biea.ac.uk
**Contact**: Dr David Anderson, Director

The British Institute in Eastern Africa (BIEA) exists to promote research in the humanities and social sciences. BIEA is based in Nairobi, but supports work across Eastern Africa, and is one of the schools and institutes supported by the British Academy.

## British Institute in Eastern Africa Minor Grants

**Purpose**: To assist with the costs of research projects in Eastern Africa
**Eligibility**: Open to applicants from United Kingdom and Eastern Africa
**Level of Study**: Postgraduate
**Type**: Grant
**Value**: Up to £1,000
**Study Establishment**: The British Institute in Eastern Africa
**Application Procedure**: Application forms can be downloaded from the BIEA website
**No. of awards offered**: 45
**Closing Date**: 31 January
**Funding**: Government
**Contributor**: British Academy
**No. of awards given last year**: 22
**No. of applicants last year**: 45
**Additional Information**: Applicants must contact the Director for further information on relevant topics likely to receive support. Those awarded grants will be required to keep the Institute regularly informed of the progress of their research, to provide a preliminary statement of accounts within 18 months of the award dates and to provide the Institute with copies of all relevant publications. They are encouraged to discuss with the Director the possibility of publishing their results in the Institute's journal, Azania. Results for the Minor Grants Award may be expected within 2 months of either 30 May or 30 November. Those awarded grants are required to become members of the BIEA www.biea.ac.uk/

## For further information contact:

**Email**:   pjlane@insightkenya.com

# British Medical Association (BMA)

BMA Research Grants, BMA House, Tavistock Square, London, WC1H 9JP, United Kingdom.

**Tel**:        (44) 20 7383 6341
**Email**:    info.sciencegrants@bma.org.uk
**Website**:  www.bma.org.uk

The BMA is a voluntary professional association with over two-thirds of practising United Kingdom doctors in membership and an independent trade union dedicated to protecting individual members and the collective interests of doctors.

## Helen H Lawson Research Grant

**Purpose**: To promote research into novel technologies and IT to assist in patient care, primary care or public health
**Eligibility**: Open to registered medical practitioners in the United Kingdom who are BMA members
**Level of Study**: Research
**Type**: Research grant
**Value**: £65,000
**Length of Study**: 3 years
**Frequency**: Annual
**Country of Study**: United Kingdom
**Application Procedure**: Applicants must complete an online application form. Applications that do not comply with all of the above terms and conditions will be rejected without exception
**No. of awards offered**: 10
**Closing Date**: 6 March
**Funding**: Trusts
**No. of awards given last year**: 1
**No. of applicants last year**: 10
**Additional Information**: Please check at bma.org.uk/ developing-your-career/portfolio-career/research-grants/rese arch-grants-details/research-grants-roscoe    www.bmafound ationmr.org.uk/media/1209/helen-h-lawson-2020.pdf

### For further information contact:

Corporate Development Directorate, British Medical Association, Tavistock Square, London, WC1H 9JP, United Kingdom.

**Tel**:        (44) 20 7383 6341
**Email**:    researchgrants@bma.org.uk

## Josephine Lansdell Research Grant

**Purpose**: To assist and support research into the field of heart diseases
**Eligibility**: Open to registered medical practitioners in the United Kingdom who are BMA members
**Level of Study**: Research
**Type**: Research grant
**Value**: £65,000
**Length of Study**: 3 years
**Frequency**: Annual
**Country of Study**: Any country
**Application Procedure**: Applicants must complete an online application form. Applicants are required to upload (PDF format) two references during the online application process. Please note each reference MUST bear the electronic (scanned) signature of the referee. For joint applications, each applicant requires two referees (these can be the same for both applicants)
**No. of awards offered**: 10
**Closing Date**: 6 March
**Funding**: Trusts
**No. of awards given last year**: 1
**No. of applicants last year**: 10
**Additional Information**: Please check at bma.org.uk/ developing-your-career/portfolio-career/research-grants/rese arch-grants-details/research-grants-lansdell    www.bmafound ationmr.org.uk/media/1210/josephine-lansdell-2020.pdf

### For further information contact:

Corporate Development Directorate, British Medical Association, Tavistock Square, London, WC1H 9JP, United Kingdom.

**Tel**:        (44) 20 7383 6341
**Email**:    researchgrants@bma.org.uk

## Vera Down Research Grant

**Purpose**: To assist and support research
**Eligibility**: Open to registered medical practitioners in the United Kingdom who are BMA members
**Level of Study**: Research
**Type**: Research grant
**Value**: £55,000
**Length of Study**: 3 years
**Frequency**: Annual
**Country of Study**: United Kingdom
**Application Procedure**: Applicants must complete an online application form
**No. of awards offered**: 10

**Closing Date**: 15 March
**Funding**: Trusts
**No. of awards given last year**: 1
**No. of applicants last year**: 10
**Additional Information**: Please check at bma.org.uk/
developing-your-career/portfolio-career/research-grants/rese
arch-grants-details/research-grants-down    bmafoundationmr.
org.uk/media/1143/vera-down-2019.pdf

## British School at Athens

52 Souedias Street, GR-10676 Athens, Greece.

**Tel**:          (30) 211 102 2800
**Email**:       admin@bsa.ac.uk
**Website**:    www.bsa.gla.ac.uk
**Contact**:    Dr Chryssanthi Papadopoulou, Assistant
                Director

The British School at Athens promotes research into the
archaeology, architecture, art, history, language, literature,
religion and topography of Greece in ancient, medieval and
modern times. It consists of the Library, Fitch Laboratory for
Archaeological Science, Archive, Museum, hostel and
a second base at Knossos for research and fieldwork.

### Hector and Elizabeth Catling Bursary

**Purpose**: To assist travel, maintenance costs and for the
purchase of scientific equipments. Its aim is to encourage
excellence in archaeological drawing, including the prepara-
tion of finished drawings for publication
**Eligibility**: Open to researchers of British, Irish or Common-
wealth nationality
**Level of Study**: Doctorate, Postdoctorate, Postgraduate,
Research
**Type**: Bursary
**Value**: £500 per bursary to assist with travel and maintenance
costs incurred in fieldwork, to pay for the use of scientific or
other specialized equipment in or outside the laboratory in
Greece or elsewhere and to buy necessary supplies
**Frequency**: Annual
**Study Establishment**: The British School at Athens
**Country of Study**: Any country
**Application Procedure**: 1. Applicants must submit
a curriculum vitae and state concisely the nature of the
intended work, a breakdown of budget, the amount requested
from the Fund and how this will be spent. 2. Applications
should include two sealed letters of reference. Bursary

holders must submit a short report to the Committee upon
completion of the project
**Closing Date**: 15 May
**Funding**: Private
**Additional Information**: The bursary is not intended for
publication costs, and cannot be awarded to an excavation
or field survey team www.bsa.ac.uk/awards/research-awards/
the-hector-and-elizabeth-catling-bursary/

### For further information contact:

**Email**:    assistant.director@bsa.ac.uk

### The Elizabeth Catling Memorial Fund for Archaeological Draughtsmanship

**Purpose**: To encourage excellence in archaeological drawing,
including the preparation of finished drawings for publication. It is hoped that awards will help individuals to improve
their standards of draughtsmanship and also enable the preparation of a larger number of drawings, of higher quality, than
might otherwise have been possible
**Eligibility**: Individual applicants must show that drawings are
an essential part of their research. Furthermore, although not
a precondition, it is hoped that they may be draughtsmen
themselves. Applications from project directors, who may
also apply during the course of a field campaign, are limited
to unexpected expenses that are not provided for in the project's budget, such as extra maintenance costs to enable
a draughtsman to draw unforeseen material and finds
**Level of Study**: Predoctorate
**Type**: Funding support
**Value**: £500
**Frequency**: Annual
**Application Procedure**: Candidates should submit letters of
application to the School's London office by post in four
copies or by email. Letters should not be longer than two
pages and should include a statement of the purposes of the
application and a budget and timetable for the proposed work,
together with the name and address of a referee whom the
awarding panel(s) may consult. Applications may be made for
but are not limited to, grants towards the maintenance costs of
longer stays at museums and other study centres so as to
achieve work that would not otherwise have been attempted.
Recipients of awards must have been admitted as Students of
the School for the appropriate Session before receiving their
grants, and must submit a short report on the use of the grant
to the London office
**Closing Date**: 24 April
**Additional Information**: The Fund does not support printing
expenses, or site drawings such as plans and sections, or
computer graphics www.bsa.ac.uk/awards/research-awards/

the-elizabeth-catling-memorial-fund-for-archaeological-draughtmanship/

## For further information contact:

British School at Athens, Senate House, Malet Street, London, WC1E 7HU, United Kingdom.

**Email**:   bsa@sas.ac.uk

## The John Morrison Memorial Fund for Hellenic Maritime Studies

**Purpose**: To further research into all branches of Hellenic maritime studies of any period
**Type**: Funding support
**Value**: £500
**Frequency**: Annual
**Application Procedure**: Candidates should submit letters of application to the School's London office by post in four copies or by email. Letters should not be longer than two pages and should include a statement of the purposes of the application and a budget and timetable for the proposed work, together with the name and address of a referee whom the awarding panel(s) may consult. Applications may be made for but are not limited to, grants towards the maintenance costs of longer stays at museums and other study centres so as to achieve work that would not otherwise have been attempted. Recipients of awards must have been admitted as Students of the School for the appropriate Session before receiving their grants, and must submit a short report on the use of the grant to the London office
**Closing Date**: 30 April
**Additional Information**: Grants may also be available from the Fund for buying maritime books and journals for the School's Library www.bsa.ac.uk/awards/research-awards/the-john-morrison-memorial-fund-for-hellenic-maritime-studies/

## For further information contact:

British School at Athens, Senate House, Malet Street, London, WC1E 7HU, United Kingdom.

**Email**:   assistant.director@bsa.ac.uk

## The Richard Bradford McConnell Fund for Landscape Studies

**Purpose**: To assist research in the interaction of place and people in Greece and Cyprus at any period(s)
**Type**: Funding support
**Value**: £400
**Frequency**: Annual

**Application Procedure**: Candidates should submit letters of application to the School's London office by post in four copies or by email. Letters should not be longer than two pages and should include a statement of the purposes of the application and a budget and timetable for the proposed work, together with the name and address of a referee whom the awarding panel(s) may consult. Applications may be made for but are not limited to, grants towards the maintenance costs of longer stays at museums and other study centres so as to achieve work that would not otherwise have been attempted. Recipients of awards must have been admitted as Students of the School for the appropriate Session before receiving their grants, and must submit a short report on the use of the grant to the London office
**Closing Date**: 24 April
**Contributor**: Richard Bradford Trust
**Additional Information**: www.bsa.ac.uk/awards/research-awards/the-richard-bradford-mcconnell-fund-for-landscape-studies/

## For further information contact:

British School at Athens, Senate House, Malet Street, London, WC1E 7HU, United Kingdom.

**Email**:   school.administrator@bsa.ac.uk

## To support research in the prehistory of the Aegean and its connections with the East Mediterranean

**Purpose**: To support research in the prehistory of the Aegean and its connections with the East Mediterranean
**Eligibility**: Preference may be given to younger Students
**Type**: Funding support
**Value**: £500 are available for the expenses (including, but not limited to, attending conferences to present papers, photography, and travel to museums and sites)
**Application Procedure**: Candidates should submit letters of application to the School's London office by post in four copies or by email. Letters should not be longer than two pages and should include a statement of the purposes of the application and a budget and timetable for the proposed work, together with the name and address of a referee whom the awarding panel(s) may consult. Applications may be made for but are not limited to, grants towards the maintenance costs of longer stays at museums and other study centres so as to achieve work that would not otherwise have been attempted. Recipients of awards must have been admitted as Students of the School for the appropriate Session before receiving their grants, and must submit a short report on the use of the grant to the London office

**Closing Date**: 1 April
**Additional Information**: Check website for more details

## For further information contact:

British School at Athens, Senate House, Malet Street, London, WC1E 7HU, United Kingdom.

**Email**:    bsa@sas.ac.uk

## Visiting Fellowships

**Purpose**: Visiting Fellowships at the British School at Athens are offered for 2-3 months for research in any branch of the arts or social sciences related to Greece. The Fellowship is non-stipendiary, but accommodation and airfare are provided
**Eligibility**: The Fellow is required to submit a report covering their research and their time at the School to the School's Council
**Level of Study**: Postgraduate
**Type**: Fellowship
**Frequency**: Annual
**Country of Study**: Any country
**Application Procedure**: The School Administrator, school. administrator@bsa.ac.uk
**Closing Date**: 19 April
**Funding**: Private
**Additional Information**: www.britishcouncil.in/study-uk/scholarships/charles-wallace-trust/visiting-fellows

## For further information contact:

The British School at Athens, 52 Souedias Street, GR-10676 Athens, Greece.

**Fax**:       (30) 211 102 2803
**Email**:    school.administrator@bsa.ac.uk

## British School at Rome (BSR)

The BSR at the British Academy, 10 Carlton House Terrace, London, SW1Y 5AH, United Kingdom.

**Tel**:          (44) 20 7969 5202
**Email**:      bsr@britac.ac.uk
**Website**:   www.bsr.ac.uk
**Contact**:   Natalie Arrowsmith, Communications Manager

The British School at Rome (BSR) is an interdisciplinary research centre for the humanities, visual arts and architecture. Each year, the School offers a range of awards in its principal fields of interest. These interests are further promoted by lectures, conferences, publications, exhibitions, archaeological research and an excellent reference library.

## Abbey Scholarship in Painting

**Purpose**: To give exceptionally promising early career painters the opportunity to work in Rome
**Eligibility**: offers one early-career artist a full academic year (October to June) at the British School at Rome
**Level of Study**: Doctorate, Graduate, Postdoctorate, Postgraduate
**Type**: Scholarship
**Value**: €800
**Length of Study**: 9 months
**Frequency**: Annual
**Study Establishment**: The British School at Rome
**Country of Study**: Italy
**Application Procedure**: We are now open for applications to the Abbey Fellowships and Scholarship until midday, 20th January 2020.
**Closing Date**: 20 January
**Funding**: Private
**Contributor**: The Abbey Council
**No. of awards given last year**: 1
**Additional Information**: Check website for more details abbey.org.uk/

## For further information contact:

Abbey Awards, 1 St Lukes Court, 136 Falcon Road, London, SW11 2LP, United Kingdom.

**Email**:    contact@abbey.org.uk

## Giles Worsley Travel Fellowship

**Purpose**: To enable an architect or architectural historian to spend 3 months in Rome studying an architectural topic of his choice
**Eligibility**: Open to those who are of British nationality or who have been living and studying in Britain for at least the last 3 years
**Level of Study**: Postdoctorate, Postgraduate, Professional development
**Type**: Fellowship
**Value**: Approx.€700 per month plus full board and lodging at the British School at Rome

**Length of Study**: 3 months
**Frequency**: Annual
**Study Establishment**: The British School at Rome
**Country of Study**: Italy
**Application Procedure**: Applicants must submit a curriculum vitae, a statement indicating the subject of their proposal and arrange for two references to be sent
**Closing Date**: February
**Funding**: Private
**No. of awards given last year**: 1
**Additional Information**: www.bsr.ac.uk/awards/architecture-awards-ii#giles

## Paul Mellon Centre Rome Fellowship

**Purpose**: To assist research on grand tour subjects or on Anglo-Italian cultural and artistic relations
**Eligibility**: Open to established scholars in the United Kingdom, United States or elsewhere. Applicants should be fluent in Italian
**Level of Study**: Doctorate, Graduate, Postdoctorate, Postgraduate, Professional development, Research
**Type**: Fellowship
**Value**: Full board at the British School at Rome. For independent scholars, the fellowship offers a stipend of €6,000 plus travel to and from Rome. For scholars in full-time university employment, the fellowship offers an honorarium of €2,000, travel to and from Rome and a sum of €6,000 towards replacement teaching costs for a term at the Fellow's home institution
**Length of Study**: 3 months
**Frequency**: Annual
**Study Establishment**: The British School at Rome
**Country of Study**: Italy
**Application Procedure**: Applicants must contact the Paul Mellon Centre for Studies in British Art for details
**Closing Date**: January
**Funding**: Private
**Contributor**: The Paul Mellon Centre for Studies in British Art
**No. of awards given last year**: 1
**Additional Information**: Please check website for more details www.bsr.ac.uk/paul-mellon-centre-rome-fellowship-deadline-approaching

### For further information contact:

The Paul Mellon Centre for Studies in British Art, 16 Bedford Square, London, WC1B 3JA, United Kingdom.

**Email**:    grants@paul-mellon-centre.ac.uk

## British Society for Antimicrobial Chemotherapy

British Society for Antimicrobial Chemotherapy, Griffin House, 53 Regent Place, Birmingham, B1 3NJ, United Kingdom.

**Tel**:          (44) 121 236 1988
**Website**:    www.bsac.org.uk
**Contact**:    Ms Tracey Guise, Executive Director

BSAC is an inter-professional organization with 40 years of experience and achievement in antibiotic education, research and leadership. It is dedicated to saving lives through appropriate use and development of antibiotics now and in the future.

## British Society for Antimicrobial Chemotherapy Overseas Scholarship

**Purpose**: Overseas Scholarships are to enable workers from other countries the opportunity to work in United Kingdom Departments for up to 6 months
**Level of Study**: Postgraduate, Professional development
**Type**: Scholarship
**Value**: £1,000 per calendar month for up to 6 months. The host institution will receive a consumables grant of £200 per calendar month for the duration of the scholarship. The Society will reimburse the cost of return air fares and travel via the most economical route. Candidates will be asked to seek approval of travel costs in advance
**Length of Study**: 6 months
**Frequency**: Annual
**Country of Study**: United Kingdom
**Application Procedure**: Successful applicants are required to submit a 500-word written report to the Secretary of the Grants Committee on completion of their project, and to forward details of any publications arising from the work undertaken. Applications for Overseas Scholarships should be made to the Society's HQ using the form provided on the BSAC website
**Closing Date**: 1 December
**Funding**: Foundation
**Additional Information**: Excludes applicants from United Kingdom www.bsac.org.uk/funding/overseas-scholarship/

### For further information contact:

**Email**:    tguise@bsac.org.uk

# British Society for Middle Eastern Studies

Institute for Middle Eastern & Islamic Studies, Durham University, Al-Qasimi Building, Elvet Hill Road, Durham, DH1 3TU, United Kingdom.

**Tel**:        (44) 191 33 45179
**Email**:    a.l.haysey@durham.ac.uk
**Website**:  www.brismes.ac.uk/

## Master's Scholarship

**Purpose**: BRISMES offers an annual Master's scholarship for taught Master's study at a United Kingdom institution. The Master's programme can be in any discipline but should include a majority component specifically relating to the Middle East
**Eligibility**: Preference will be given to candidates resident in the European Union, and to institutions who are members of BRISMES
**Level of Study**: Doctorate
**Type**: Scholarship
**Value**: £1,200
**Frequency**: Annual
**Country of Study**: United Kingdom
**Application Procedure**: Applications should be forwarded by the Director of the Master's programme concerned, to the BRISMES Administrative Office, and should include: a supporting statement from the course Director not exceeding 500 words; the programme syllabus; a statement by the candidate not exceeding 500 words; the candidate's curriculum vitae and transcript of previous academic results; two academic references. Applications should be sent to Institute for Middle Eastern & Islamic Studies
**Closing Date**: 31 March
**Funding**: Foundation
**Additional Information**: Please check website for more details    www.birmingham.ac.uk/postgraduate/funding/ BRISMES-Scholarships.aspx

### For further information contact:

**Email**:    a.l.haysey@dur.ac.uk

## The Abdullah Al-Mubarak Al-Sabah Foundation BRISMES Scholarships

**Purpose**: The purpose of the scholarships is to encourage more people to pursue postgraduate studies in disciplines related to the Middle East in British universities

**Eligibility**: To qualify you must be a paid-up member of BRISMES (student membership suffices) but the time you apply
**Level of Study**: Postgraduate
**Type**: Scholarship
**Value**: £2,000
**Length of Study**: 1 academic year
**Frequency**: Annual
**Country of Study**: United Kingdom
**Application Procedure**: To qualify applicants must fulfil the following conditions: 1. be registered at any UK university, 2. be a paid-up student member of BRISMES at the time of application, 3. submit an application of 600 - 1000 words, by E-mail to the BRISMES research committee This should include a sketch of the overall research topic, and a description of the purpose for which the grant would be used, 4. obtain a brief supporting statement from their supervisor
**Funding**: Foundation
**Additional Information**: www.brismes.ac.uk/student-area/the-abdullah-mubarak-brismes-scholarshp

### For further information contact:

**Email**:    a.l.haysey@dur.ac.uk

# British Veterinary Association

7 Mansfield Street, London, W1G 9NQ, United Kingdom.

**Tel**:        (44) 20 7636 6541
**Email**:    bvahq@bva.co.uk
**Website**:  www.bva.co.uk

The British Veterinary Association's chief interests are the standards of animal health and veterinary surgeons' working practices. The organization's main functions are the development of policy in areas affecting the profession, protecting and promoting the profession in matters propounded by government and other external bodies and the provision of services to members.

## Harry Steele-Bodger Memorial Travelling Scholarship

**Subjects**: Veterinary science and agriculture.
**Purpose**: To further the aims and aspirations of the late Harry Steele-Bodger.
**Eligibility**: Open to graduates of veterinary schools in the UK or the Republic of Ireland who have been qualified for not

more than 3 years, and to penultimate or final-year students at those schools.

**Level of Study**: Graduate, Postgraduate
**Type**: Scholarship
**Value**: Approx. £1,100
**Frequency**: Annual
**Study Establishment**: A veterinary or agricultural research institute or some other course of study approved by the governing committee
**Country of Study**: United Kingdom
**Application Procedure**: Applications can be submitted online www.bva.co.uk/Membership-and-benefits/Students/Travel-grants-for-students/
**No. of awards offered**: 1 or 2
**Closing Date**: 3 May
**Funding**: Private
**No. of awards given last year**: 1
**No. of applicants last year**: 5
**Additional Information**: www.bva.co.uk/membership/bva-student-membership/travel-grants-for-vet-students/

### For further information contact:

See online application.

**Tel**:     (44) 20 7908 6340
**Email**:   helenac@bva.co.uk

## Broadcast Education Association

613 Kane Street, Mount Pleasant, MI 48858, United States of America.

**Tel**:      (1) 989 773 9370
**Email**:    orlik1pb@cmich.edu
**Website**:  www.beaweb.org
**Contact**:  Dr Peter Orlik, Scholarship Chair

### Abe Voron Award

**Purpose**: Study for a career in radio at a BEA-member institution
**Eligibility**: 1. Must be a graduate student, 2. Must attend a university or a four-year college, 3. Must not be attending high school currently, 4. Must study full-time, 5. Restricted to students studying TV/Radio Broadcasting
**Level of Study**: Graduate, Undergraduate
**Type**: Scholarship
**Value**: US$3,000
**Length of Study**: One full academic year
**Frequency**: Annual

**Country of Study**: Any country
**Application Procedure**: The application MUST be typed to be considered. Keep an additional copy for your files. Remember to date and sign the form on the last page. Applications not typed and signed will be disqualified. Each copy of the application MUST be collated and securely stapled. The application asks for personal and academic data and transcripts, media and other experience, a written statement of goals, and supportive statements from two references, at least one of which must be an electronic media faculty member
**No. of awards offered**: 26
**Closing Date**: 12 October
**Funding**: Private
**Contributor**: Abe Voron Committee
**No. of awards given last year**: 3
**No. of applicants last year**: 26
**Additional Information**: www.petersons.com/scholarship/abe-voron-award-111_219381.aspx

### For further information contact:

613 Kane St, Mt. Pleasant, MI 48858, United States of America.

**Tel**:    (1) 989 773 9370

### John Bayliss Award

**Purpose**: Study toward a career in Radio at a Broadcast Education Association member institution.
**Eligibility**: 1. Must be a graduate student, 2. Must attend a university or a four-year college, 3. Must not be attending high school currently 4. Must study full-time, 5. Restricted to students studying TV/Radio Broadcasting
**Level of Study**: Graduate, Undergraduate
**Type**: Scholarship
**Value**: US$2,500
**Length of Study**: Full-time for one academic year
**Frequency**: Annual
**Country of Study**: Any country
**Application Procedure**: The application MUST be typed to be considered. Keep an additional copy for your files. Remember to date and sign the form on the last page. Applications not typed and signed will be disqualified. Each copy of the application MUST be collated and securely stapled. The application asks for personal and academic data and transcripts, media and other experience, a written statement of goals, and supportive statements from two references, at least one of which must be an electronic media faculty member
**No. of awards offered**: 26
**Closing Date**: 12 October
**Funding**: Private

**Contributor**: John Bayliss Foundation
**No. of awards given last year**: 1
**No. of applicants last year**: 26
**Additional Information**: www.petersons.com/scholarship/ john-bayliss-award-111_219383.aspx

## For further information contact:

613 Kane St, Mt. Pleasant, MI 48858, United States of America.

**Tel**:     (1) 989 773 9370

## Library of American Broadcasting Foundation Award

**Purpose**: Support for a graduate student focusing on the study of broadcast history
**Eligibility**: graduate student focusing on broadcast history
**Level of Study**: Graduate
**Type**: Scholarship
**Value**: US$3,000
**Length of Study**: One full academic year
**Frequency**: Annual
**Country of Study**: Any country
**Application Procedure**: see and fill out application found on BEA website www.beaweb.org
**No. of awards offered**: 5
**Closing Date**: 12 October
**Funding**: Foundation
**Contributor**: Library of American Broadcasting Foundation
**No. of awards given last year**: 1
**No. of applicants last year**: 5
**Additional Information**: www.beaweb.org/wp/?page_id=2431

## Peter B. Orlik Scholarship

**Purpose**: Study by juniors, seniors or graduate students at a BEA member institution
**Eligibility**: Any junior, senior or graduate student at a BEA member institution
**Level of Study**: Graduate, Undergraduate
**Type**: Scholarship
**Value**: US$3,000
**Length of Study**: One full academic year
**Frequency**: Annual
**Country of Study**: Any country
**Application Procedure**: See BEA website www.beaweb.org
**No. of awards offered**: 45
**Closing Date**: 12 October
**Funding**: Private
**Contributor**: Broadcast Education Association

**No. of awards given last year**: 1
**No. of applicants last year**: 45
**Additional Information**: bigfuture.collegeboard.org/scholar ships/peter-b-orlik-scholarship

## Richard Eaton Award

**Purpose**: Given for study of electronic media by juniors, seniors, and graduate students
**Eligibility**: Junior, senior or graduate student at a BEA member institution
**Level of Study**: Graduate, Undergraduate
**Type**: Scholarship
**Value**: US$2,500
**Length of Study**: 1 academic year – full-time
**Frequency**: Annual
**Country of Study**: Any country
**Application Procedure**: See and complete application on BEA website www.beaweb.org
**No. of awards offered**: 45
**Closing Date**: 12 October
**Funding**: Private
**Contributor**: Richard Eaton Foundation
**No. of awards given last year**: 1
**No. of applicants last year**: 45
**Additional Information**: www.unigo.com/scholarships/by-major/advertising-scholarships/richard-eaton-award/1004553

## Vincent T. Wasilewski Award

**Purpose**: For graduate study of electronic media at a BEA member institution
**Eligibility**: Any full-time graduate student at a BEA member institution
**Level of Study**: Graduate
**Type**: Scholarship
**Value**: US$4,000
**Length of Study**: One academic year
**Frequency**: Annual
**Country of Study**: Any country
**Application Procedure**: See and complete application found at BEA website www.beaweb.org
**No. of awards offered**: 20
**Closing Date**: 12 October
**Funding**: Private
**Contributor**: Patrick Communications
**No. of awards given last year**: 1
**No. of applicants last year**: 20
**Additional Information**: www.unigo.com/scholarships/by-major/advertising-scholarships/vincent-t-wasilewski-award/1004552

# Brunel University

Kingston Lane, Uxbridge, Middlesex, UB8 3PH, United Kingdom.

**Tel**: (44) 1895 274000
**Email**: admissions@brunel.ac.uk
**Website**: www.brunel.ac.uk
**Contact**: Professor Adrian Woods, Dean of the Graduate School

## Brunel Santander International Scholarship

**Purpose**: Brunel University London is pleased to offer a prestigious package of scholarships for International students. The Brunel Santander International Scholarship 2020/2021 is for self-funded students. Brunel University London offers candidates to help support international students.
**Eligibility**: 1. The candidate must for reasons related to fees, classified in the category "overseas" and financed from own resources (unfunded). 2. Applicants who are unsure of the status of their fees should note that Brunel uses the information provided in their application form to evaluate the fee status according to the rules established by the UK Government. 3. Applicants must have the opportunity to study in a post-graduate program or postdoctoral research program in September 2020 and must complete the corresponding fellowship application within the required timeframe. 4. Candidates must have accepted their course offer before the scholarship deadline.
**Level of Study**: Postgraduate
**Type**: Scholarship
**Value**: £3,000
**Length of Study**: 1 year
**Frequency**: Annual
**Country of Study**: Any country
**Application Procedure**: To apply for a Brunel Santander International Scholarship, candidates must fill out the application form, which requires a personal declaration within the prescribed deadlines. Supported Documents: As part of the application, the applicant must provide a personal statement.
**Closing Date**: 30 April
**Funding**: International office
**Additional Information**: worldscholarshipforum.com/brunel-santander-international-scholarship/

### For further information contact:

**Email**: scholarships@brunel.ac.uk

# Budapest International Music Competition

Philharmonia Budapest, Alkotmany u.31 1/2, H-1054 Budapest, Hungary.

**Tel**: (36) 1 266 1459, 302 4961
**Email**: liszkay.maria@hu.inter.net
**Contact**: Ms Maria Liszkay, Secretary

The Budapest Music Competition has been held since 1933. Competitions in different categories alternate annually.

## International Carl Flesch Violin Competition

**Purpose**: To promote European violinists
**Eligibility**: Competitors should possess at least 2 years of musical study in Europe and should be born on or after 1 January, 1980
**Type**: Competition
**Value**: €4,000 net (first prize), €3,000 net (second prize) and €2,000 net (third prize)
**Country of Study**: Hungary
**Application Procedure**: Application forms should contain brief curriculum vitae, certificate of musical qualification, letter of recommendation from a prominent musical personality, two recent photographs and a copy receipt about the transfer of the entry fee. For competitors outside Europe, a certificate of their European studies is required
**Closing Date**: 1 February
**Funding**: Private
**Contributor**: Philharmonia Budapest Concert Agency and Ms. Fejes Music Foundation
**Additional Information**: Special prizes will be offered to the winners

### For further information contact:

**Fax**: (36) 1 302 4962

# Bupa Foundation

Bupa House, 15-19 Bloomsbury Way, London, WC1A 2BA, United Kingdom.

**Tel**: (44) 20 7656 2591
**Email**: Bupafoundation@Bupa.com
**Website**: www.bupafoundation.co.uk
**Contact**: Lee Saunders, Registrar

The Bupa Foundation is an independent medical research charity that funds medical research to prevent, relieve and cure sickness and ill health.

## Bupa Foundation Annual Specialist Grant

**Eligibility**: The competition is open to those based in the United Kingdom, Australia, Denmark, Hong Kong, New Zealand, Saudi Arabia, Spain and Thailand. Entries must be compliant with the local health and safety legislation if applicable. The Foundation will seek peer reviews from the home country of each shortlisted entry. Researchers and health professionals working for public or private organisations may apply for Bupa Foundation specialist grants for United Kingdom-based projects.

### For further information contact:

**Tel**:        (36) 20 7656 2591
**Email**:    bupafoundation@bupa.com

## Bupa Foundation Medical Research Grant for Health at Work

**Purpose**: To support research into the feasibility and potential value of workplace conditions for health promotion and active management of employee health
**Eligibility**: Open to health professionals and health researchers
**Level of Study**: Doctorate, Postdoctorate, Postgraduate, Research
**Value**: Restricted by project need only
**Length of Study**: A maximum of 3 years
**Country of Study**: United Kingdom
**Application Procedure**: For all queries contact Lee Saunders, the Foundation's Registrar
**Funding**: Foundation

### For further information contact:

**Email**:    bupafoundation@bupa.com

## Bupa Foundation Medical Research Grant for Information and Communication

**Purpose**: To support research designed to enhance partnership between health professionals and public/patients
**Eligibility**: Open to health professional and health researchers
**Level of Study**: Doctorate, Postdoctorate, Postgraduate, Research

**Value**: Restricted by project needs only
**Length of Study**: Maximum of 3 years
**Country of Study**: United Kingdom
**Application Procedure**: For all queries contact Lee Saunders, the Foundation's Registrar
**Funding**: Foundation

### For further information contact:

**Email**:    bupafoundation@bupa.com

# Brandeis University

Brandeis University was founded in 1948 by the American Jewish community at a time when Jews and other ethnic and racial minorities, and women, faced discrimination in higher education. Brandeis' visionary founders established a nonsectarian research university that welcomed talented faculty and students of all backgrounds and beliefs. From the outset, Brandeis focused on undergraduate education, while building a pioneering research enterprise.

**Tel**:          (1) 781 736 2000
**Email**:      helleradmissions@brandeis.edu
**Website**:   www.brandeis.edu/
**Contact**:   415 South Street, Waltham, MA 02453, United States of America

## Sidney Topol Fellowship in Nonviolence Practice

**Purpose**: Practice honors the work of peace advocate, philanthropist, and entrepreneur, Sidney Topol, through the establishment of a full tuition scholarship to the Master's Degree program in Coexistence and Conflict (COEX) at the Heller School for Social Policy and Management at Brandeis University. This fellowship does not cover airfare, fees, health insurance, or housing. The Master's Degree in Coexistence and Conflict at Brandeis University trains students to recognize, understand and begin to heal the ethnic, religious and cultural fault lines that endanger our world. Through an approach that is equal parts theoretical and practical, graduate students investigate the root causes of violent conflict and they uncover effective means to prevent conflicts and to promote peaceful coexistence After a full year in residence at the Heller School, students take their knowledge into the field, working with a conflict prevention organization. They graduate with a firm grasp of the delicate role that peace professionals play in bringing antagonistic parties together and the leadership expertise to help communities build shared societies.

**Eligibility**: Applicants for the Sidney Topol Fellowship in Nonviolence Practice must prove that their community benefited from their personal commitment to nonviolent principles through prior volunteer or work projects and they must commit to returning to their community within the next 2 years after graduation from the COEX program, to establish projects in nonviolence.

**Level of Study**: postgraduate

**Type**: Scholarsip

**Value**: Full tuition scholarship. This fellowship does not cover airfare, fees, health insurance, or housing

**Country of Study**: US

**Application Procedure**: In addition to submitting a complete application to the Coexistence and Conflict program, fellowship applicants must submit the following materials; A personal essay which outlines their prior work in nonviolence, and their proposed work, and how completing the MA in Coexistence and Conflict will help them be successful in these endeavors; An interview either by phone or in person may be required. The deadline for applications for the fellowship is 15 April 2020. It is important to visit the official website (link found below) for detailed information on how to apply for this scholarship : apply.heller.brandeis.edu/register/TopolFellowshipsin Nonviolence

**Closing Date**: 15 April

**Additional Information**: apply.heller.brandeis.edu/register/ TopolFellowshipsinNonviolence

# C

## Camargo Foundation

1, Avenue Jermini, F-13260 Cassis, France.

| | |
|---|---|
| **Tel**: | (33) 4 4201 1311 |
| **Email**: | apply@camargofoundation.org |
| **Website**: | www.camargofoundation.org |
| **Contact**: | Cynthia A. Gehrig, President |

The Camargo Foundation is a residential center offering programming in the humanities and the arts.

### The Camargo Core Program

**Purpose**: The Camargo Foundation, located in Cassis, France, and founded by artist and philanthropist Jerome Hill, is a residential center offering programming in the Arts and Humanities. It offers time and space in a contemplative environment to think, create, and connect. The Foundation encourages the visionary work of artists, scholars, and thinkers in the Arts and Humanities. The Camargo Core Program is the historical and flagship program of the Camargo Foundation. Each year an international call is launched through which 18 fellows (9 artists and 9 scholars/thinkers) are selected. The Camargo Core Program offers time and space in a contemplative environment to think, create, and connect. By supporting ground-breaking research and experimentation, it contributes to the visionary work of artists, scholars and thinkers in the Arts and Humanities. By encouraging multidisciplinary and inter-disciplinary approaches, it intends to foster connections between research and creation

**Eligibility**: Scholars should be connected to the Arts and Humanities working on French and Francophone cultures, or cross-cultural studies that engage the cultures and influences of the Mediterranean region. To be eligible for a fellowship in the "Scholars" category, applicants are expected either to hold a PhD and a record of post-doctoral scholarship, or to be PhD candidates completing the final stages of research for, or writing of, their dissertation

**Level of Study**: Doctorate, Postdoctorate, Postgraduate, Professional development, Research, Foundation programme

**Type**: Residential fellowships

**Value**: A stipend of €250 per week is available, as is funding for basic transportation to and from Cassis for the Fellow for the residency. In the case of air travel, basic coach class booked far in advance is covered

**Frequency**: Annual

**Country of Study**: France

**Application Procedure**: The call for applications for the Camargo Core Program for the upcoming years will be open in summer years. More information will be available on www.camargofoundation.org

**No. of awards offered**: 1038

**Funding**: Government, Private, Foundation, Trusts, Individuals

**No. of awards given last year**: 18

**No. of applicants last year**: 1038

**Additional Information**: More information is available on camargofoundation.org/programs/camargo-core-program/

## Canada Council for the Arts

150 Elgin St., PO Box 1047, Ottawa, ON, K1P 5V8, Canada.

| | |
|---|---|
| **Tel**: | (1) 800 263 5588 or (1) 613 566 4414 |
| **Email**: | info@canadacouncil.ca |
| **Website**: | www.canadacouncil.ca |
| **Contact**: | Martin, Program Officer |

The Canada Council for the Arts is a national agency that provides grants and services to professional Canadian artists and art organizations in dance, media arts, music, theatre, writing and publishing, inter-arts and the visual arts.

© Springer Nature Limited 2020
Palgrave Macmillan (ed.), *The Grants Register 2021*,
https://doi.org/10.1057/978-1-349-95988-4

## John G. Diefenbaker Award

**Purpose**: The John G. Diefenbaker Award is funded by an endowment given to the Canada Council for the Arts by the Government of Canada. The endowment, announced by Prime Minister Brian Mulroney during his visit to Germany in the spring of 1991, honours the memory of former Prime Minister John G. Diefenbaker. The award is given annually, and it enables a distinguished German scholar to do research in Canada, which may include brief periods in the United States. The spirit of the award is to encourage exchange between scholarly communities in Canada and Germany

**Eligibility**: Candidates may not apply for this award: they must be nominated by a department within a host university or research institute in Canada. This award is open to German scholars who have demonstrated outstanding ability, especially through a substantial publication record over several years. The award is offered in support of research in any of the disciplines of the social sciences and humanities. Candidates must be German citizens with a contractual or working relationship with an academic institution in Germany. They must have a sound working knowledge of at least one of Canada's two official languages

**Value**: Up to US$95,000

**Country of Study**: Any country

**Application Procedure**: Check website for more details

**Closing Date**: 1 November

**Additional Information**: canadacouncil.ca/funding/prizes/john-g-diefenbaker-award

### For further information contact:

**Email**:    luiza.pereira@canadacouncil.ca

## John Hobday Awards in Arts Management

**Purpose**: Established through a donation of C$1,000,000 from The Samuel and Saidye Bronfman Family Foundation to the Canada Council for the Arts, the awards recognize outstanding established and mid-career arts managers in Canadian professional arts organizations. Arts managers from any artistic discipline supported by the Canada Council may apply for the awards, which are intended for professional development, mentoring and related purposes

**Eligibility**: Applicants should be a Canadian citizen or have permanent resident status, as defined by Citizenship and Immigration Canada. You do not need to be living in Canada when you apply. Applicants should have a minimum of 10 years' experience (not necessarily continuous years) as a professional arts manager

**Level of Study**: Postgraduate

**Type**: Cash prize

**Value**: Two awards of C$10,000 each may be given annually

**Frequency**: Annual

**Country of Study**: Canada

**Closing Date**: 30 September

**Additional Information**: canadacouncil.ca/funding/prizes/john-hobday-awards-in-arts-management

### For further information contact:

**Email**:    sarah.brown@canadacouncil.ca

## Killam Research Fellowships

**Purpose**: To support Canadian scholars of exceptional ability engaged in advanced research projects

**Eligibility**: Open to Canadian citizens or permanent residents of Canada. Killam Research Fellowships are aimed at established scholars who have demonstrated outstanding ability through substantial publications in their fields over a period of several years. Killam Research Fellows are expected to continue contributing to the Canadian research community after they have completed their fellowship project

**Level of Study**: Postgraduate

**Type**: Fellowship

**Value**: C$70,000 per year, paid to the university or research institution which employs the fellow

**Length of Study**: 2 years

**Frequency**: Annual

**Country of Study**: Any country

**Application Procedure**: There are no hard copy application forms: applicants must submit their requests through the Canada Council's online application system at killam.canadacouncil.ca

**Closing Date**: 15 May

**Funding**: Private

**Contributor**: Killam Trust

**Additional Information**: Please check at canadacouncil.ca/en/council/grants/find-a-grant        canadacouncil.ca/funding/prizes/killam-research-fellowships for further information

### For further information contact:

**Email**:    killam.canadacouncil.ca

## Musical Instrument Bank

**Purpose**: Every 3 years, talented Canadian classical musicians compete for the chance to borrow legendary instruments from the Canada Council's Musical Instrument Bank (MIB). The competition is intense and is decided by a jury of professional musicians and peers. Musicians who win the competition are often invited to perform with their instruments on some of the world's most celebrated stages. The MIB includes over 20 magnificent instruments worth a total of over C$41,000,000. These violins, cellos and bows, created by such master craftsmen as

Stradivari, Gagliano and Pressenda, have been donated or lent to the MIB since it was created in 1985

**Eligibility**: For eligibility criteria, the application form and further information on this competition, see the Canada Council's Musical Instrument Bank Guidelines and the Musical Instrument Bank website.

**Level of Study**: Doctorate

**Value**: C$100,000

**Length of Study**: 3 years

**Country of Study**: Canada

**Closing Date**: 1 April

**Additional Information**: canadacouncil.ca/funding/prizes/musical-instrument-bank

**For further information contact:**

**Tel**:    (1) 403 244 3074

## Prix de Rome in Architecture for Emerging Practitioners

**Purpose**: The Canada Council for the Arts Prix de Rome in Architecture for Emerging Practitioners is awarded to a recent graduate of a Canadian school of architecture who demonstrates exceptional potential in contemporary architectural design

**Eligibility**: Applicants must be a Canadian citizen or have Permanent Resident status, as defined by Citizenship and Immigration Canada

**Value**: The prize is C$34,000, to contribute towards the costs of the proposed program of work and related travels, and of the proposed public presentation

**Country of Study**: Any country

**Closing Date**: 1 October

**Additional Information**: Should have received a professional Bachelor or Master degree from a Canadian school of architecture that is certified by the Canadian Architectural Certification Board within 14 months prior to the deadline for submitting applications canadacouncil.ca/funding/prizes/prix-de-rome-in-architecture-for-emerging-practitioners

**For further information contact:**

**Email**:    sarah.brown@canadacouncil.ca

## Canadian Association of Broadcasters (CAB)

770-45 O'Connor St., Ottawa, ON K1P 1A4, Canada.

**Tel**:        (1) 613 233 4035

**Email**:    cab@cab-acr.ca

**Website**:    www.cab-acr.ca

**Contact**:    Vanessa Dawson, Special Events and Projects Co-ordinator

The Canadian Association of Broadcasters (CAB) is the collective voice of Canada's private radio and television stations and speciality services. The CAB develops industry-wide strategic plans, works to improve the financial health of the industry, and promotes private broadcasting's role as Canada's leading programmer and local service provider.

## Horatio Alger Association Canadian Scholarships

**Purpose**: Horatio Alger Association Canadian Scholarships are funded through the generosity of the Association's Members

**Eligibility**: 1. Be graduating high school (or be in the final year of CEGEP). 2. Exhibit a strong commitment to pursue and complete a bachelor's degree program at an accredited university 3. Demonstrate critical financial need (C$65,000 or less annual net income per family is required) 4. Be involved in co-curricular and community service activities 5. Display integrity and perseverance in overcoming adversity 6. Maintain a minimum grade percentage of 65. 7. Attend high school (or CEGEP) and reside in Canada 8. Be Canadian citizens

**Level of Study**: Graduate

**Type**: Scholarship

**Value**: C$5,000

**Frequency**: Annual

**Country of Study**: Canada

**Closing Date**: 25 October

**Funding**: Private

**Additional Information**: scholartree.ca/scholarship/horatio-alger-canadian-scholarships/ygaPZSxKV

**For further information contact:**

**Email**:    scholarships@horatioalger.org

## Canadian Blood Services (CBS)

1800 Alta Vista Drive, Ottawa, ON K1G 4J5, Canada.

**Tel**:        (1) 613 739 2300

**Email**:    onematch@blood.ca

**Website**:    www.bloodservices.ca

Canadian Blood Services (CBS) is a non-profit, charitable organization whose sole mission is to manage the blood system for Canadians. CBS collects approx. 900,000 units of blood annually and processes it into components and products that are administered to thousands of patients each year.

## Canadian Blood Services Graduate Fellowship Program

**Purpose**: To attract and support young investigators to initiate or continue training in the field of blood or blood products research
**Eligibility**: Open to graduate students who are undertaking full-time research training leading to a PhD degree. Students registering solely for a Master's degree will not be considered and only those demonstrating acceptance into a PhD programme will receive continued support. Candidates must have completed sufficient academic work to be admitted in good standing to a graduate school by the time the award is to take effect, or be already engaged in a PhD programme. Applicants possessing a medical degree but not licensed to practice medicine in Canada are eligible to apply for this award providing they meet the above criteria
**Level of Study**: Graduate
**Type**: Fellowship
**Value**: C$25,000 per annum with an additional travel allowance of C$1,000 per year
**Length of Study**: 4 years
**Country of Study**: Canada
**Application Procedure**: Candidates are required to submit a completed application form (GFP-01) that is available either from the website, from or the main address
**No. of awards offered**: 15
**Closing Date**: 15 November
**Funding**: Government
**No. of awards given last year**: 7
**No. of applicants last year**: 15
**Additional Information**: Please check at www.blood.ca/en/research/funding-programs blood.ca/en/research/our-research-activities/our-research-funding-opportunities/canadian-blood-services-graduate-fellowship-program

### For further information contact:

Program Assistant, R&D, Canadian Blood Services, 1800 Alta Vista Drive, Ottawa, ON K1G 4J5, Canada.

**Tel**:      (1) 613 739 2230
**Fax**:     (1) 613 739 2201
**Email**:   elaine.konecny@blood.ca

## Canadian Breast Cancer Research Alliance (CBCRA)

375 University Avenue, 6th Floor, Toronto, ON M5G 2JS, Canada.

**Tel**:      (1) 416 596 6598
**Email**:   pmacgregor@cbcra.ca

**Website**:   www.breast.cancer.ca
**Contact**:   Dr Pascale Macgregor, Research Program Director

Established in 1993, the Canadian Breast Cancer Research Alliance (CBCRA) is Canada's primary funder of breast cancer study. As a unique partnership of groups from the public, private and non-profit sectors, CBCRA is committed to reducing the incidence of breast cancer, increasing survival and enhancing the lives of those affected by the disease.

## Canadian Federation of University Women Bourse Georgette Lemoyne

**Purpose**: Award is for graduate study in any field at a Canadian university. The candidate must be studying in French and write the Statement of Intent essay (Section I) of the application in French
**Eligibility**: 1. Must be a graduate student 2. Must attend a university 3. Citizenship requirements: Canada 4. Restricted to female students 5. Must not be attending high school currently 6. Both full-time and part-time students 7. Restricted to residents of Alberta, British Columbia, Manitoba, New Brunswick, Newfoundland, Nova Scotia, Northwest Territories, Ontario, Prince Edward Island, Quebec, Saskatchewan, Yukon 8. Restricted to students studying in Alberta, British Columbia, Manitoba, New Brunswick, Newfoundland, Nova Scotia, Northwest Territories, Ontario, Prince Edward Island, Quebec, Saskatchewan, Yukon 9. Restricted to: Canadian
**Value**: C$5,000
**Country of Study**: Any country
**Closing Date**: 1 November
**No. of awards given last year**: 1
**Additional Information**: cfuwcharitabletrust.ca/cfuw-bourse-georgette-lemoyne-award-2019-2020/

### For further information contact:

331 Cooper Street, Suite 502, Ottawa, ON K2P 0G5, Canada.

**Tel**:      (1) 613 234 8252
**Email**:   fellowships@cfuw.org

## Canadian Bureau for International Education (CBIE)

220 Laurier West, Suite 1550, Ottawa, ON K1P 5Z9, Canada.

**Tel**:      (1) 613 237 4820
**Email**:   scholarships-bourses@cbie.ca
**Website**:   www.cbie.ca

The Canadian Bureau for International Education (CBIE) is a national non-profit association comprising educational institutions, organizations and individuals dedicated to internal education and intercultural training. CBIE's mission is to promote the free movement of learners and trainees across national borders.

## Canada-Asia-Pacific Awards

**Purpose**: To assist scholars in higher education institutions in Asia Pacific Region to undertake short-term research
**Eligibility**: Open to students from the Asia-Pacific region
**Level of Study**: Postgraduate
**Type**: Award
**Value**: C$5,000–10,000
**Frequency**: Annual
**Country of Study**: Canada
**Application Procedure**: A completed application form must be submitted
**Closing Date**: 30 September
**Funding**: Government
**Additional Information**: scholarshippositions.blogspot.com/2010/09/canada-asia-pacific-award-capa.html

### For further information contact:

**Email**:    charles.labrecque@asiapacific.ca

## Canada-Brazil Awards - Joint Research Projects

**Purpose**: The Canada-Brazil Awards - Joint Research Projects support exchanges of PhD students in the context of team based bilateral research projects. The projects must engage in collaborative research in key academic areas of bilateral cooperation leading to an eventual publication or collaborative research in line with the objectives of the Canada-Brazil Framework Agreement for Cooperation on Science, Technology and Innovation. Applicants must clearly explain the advantages of the partnership for both countries
**Eligibility**: This competition is open to research teams from Canadian and Brazilian universities. The coordination of the project will be the responsibility of both the Canadian and Brazilian Project Leads and the teams will consist of PhD students from both institutions. Canadian and Brazilian Project Members: Must be citizens or permanent residents of the country of their institution; Must be doctoral students - Master's students and post-doctoral researchers will not be considered; Must be enrolled full-time at a post-secondary institution in their country of origin and paying the tuition fees required by that institution for the full duration of the exchange; Must be proficient in the language of instruction at the Canadian institution (English or French). Students already participating in an exchange program in Canada or in Brazil are not eligible
**Level of Study**: Research
**Value**: C$9,700 for Canadian PhD students; for values for Brazilian students see: external link
**Length of Study**: 2 years
**Country of Study**: Any country
**Closing Date**: 3 July
**Funding**: Government
**Contributor**: Government of Canada, Foreign Affairs, Trade and Development Canada (DFATD)
**Additional Information**: www.educanada.ca/scholarships-bourses/can/institutions/brazil-cbjp-brezil.aspx?lang=eng

### For further information contact:

**Email**:    admin-scholarships-bourses@cbie.ca

## Canada-CARICOM Faculty Leadership Program

**Purpose**: To support international collaboration between Canadian post-secondary institutions and institutions in the CARICOM, through professional development opportunities for faculty and staff
**Eligibility**: This competition is open to research teams from Canadian and Brazilian universities. The coordination of the project will be the responsibility of both the Canadian and Brazilian Project Leads and the teams will consist of graduate project members from Canadian institutions and PhD project members from Brazilian institutions
**Value**: C$2,700 for faculty members for 2 to 3 weeks of course work or research as part of their professional development; C$2,700 for international directors, managers or administrators for 2 to 3 weeks of course work, or for a practicum in the area of internationalization of post-secondary institutions or student mobility as part of their professional development; or C$9,700 for faculty members for 5 to 6 months of study or research at the graduate level
**Country of Study**: Any country
**Closing Date**: 25 April
**Contributor**: Global Affairs Canada: the Department of Foreign Affairs, Trade and Development (DFATD)
**Additional Information**: Further information is available on the International Scholarships Canada Application Tool Help webpages. If institutions experience difficulty filling out or submitting the form, they should send an email to admin-scholarships-bourses@cbie.ca www.ub.edu.bs/wp-content/uploads/2020/01/2020-2021-Caricom-Faculty-Leadership-in-Canada-Call.pdf

### For further information contact:

**Email**:    admin-scholarships-bourses@cbie.ca

## Canada-CARICOM Leadership Scholarships Program

**Purpose**: The Canada-CARICOM Leadership Scholarships are facilitated through institutional collaborations and student exchange agreements between Canadian institutions and institutions in the CARICOM

**Eligibility**: Canadian institutions will disburse scholarship funds to the scholarship recipient to contribute to the following costs: 1. visa and/or study/work permit fees 2. airfare, for the scholarship recipient only, to Canada by the most direct and economical route and return airfare upon completion of the scholarship 3. health insurance 4. living expenses, such as accommodation, utilities and food 5. ground transportation expenses, including a public transportation pass and 6. books and supplies required for the recipient's study or research, excluding computers and other equipment.

**Value**: C$,200 for college, C$9,700 for graduate students, C$14,700 for undergraduate and college

**Length of Study**: 4 month, 5 or 6 months, 8 months of study or research

**Country of Study**: Any country

**Application Procedure**: The Canadian institution must apply on behalf of the candidate(s) by submitting the online application form and uploading all supporting documents prior to the deadline. The following documents must be uploaded and attached to the online application form in one of the following formats: .pdf, .jpg, .doc, .docx, .txt or .gif. Each document must be smaller than 5 MB in order for the application to upload successfully.

**Closing Date**: 3 March

**Contributor**: Canadian institutions

**Additional Information**: If institutions experience difficulty filling out or submitting the form, they should send an email to admin-scholarships-bourses@cbie.ca www.nationalmeritscholarships.com/canada-caricom-leadership-scholarships.html

## Canada-Chile Leadership Exchange Scholarship

**Purpose**: The Canada-Chile Leadership Exchange Scholarship program provides students and researchers from Chile with short-term exchange opportunities for study or research, in Canada, at the college, undergraduate and graduate levels

**Eligibility**: 1. Must be citizens of Chile. Must be enrolled full-time at a post-secondary institution in Chile and paying any tuition fees regulated by that institution for the full duration of the exchange. 2. People from Canadian institution can apply for this scholarship

**Value**: C$7,200 for college, undergraduate or graduate students (Master)

**Country of Study**: Any country

**Application Procedure**: Selected candidates are encouraged to: ensure that they fulfill the requirements of the Canadian institution including academic requirements and language proficiency; submit their visa application as early as possible and follow the procedures of Immigration, Refugees and Citizenship Canada as outlined by the Canadian institution (generally a study permit is required for course work and a work permit is required for research); initiate the process for the transfer of credits to their home institution as soon as their Canadian courses have been identified; and contact alumni of the program through their home institution for advice and a local perspective on the scholarship experience

**Closing Date**: 21 March

**Additional Information**: If institutions experience difficulty filling out or submitting the form, they should send an email to admin-scholarships-bourses@cbie.ca www.educanada.ca/scholarships-bourses/can/institutions/ccles-bdlcc.aspx?lang=eng

## Canadian Prime Minister's Awards for Publishing (CPMA)

**Purpose**: To increase the amount of published material related to Canada available in Japanese

**Eligibility**: Open to Japanese publishers who are likely to increase the knowledge and understanding of contemporary Canada

**Level of Study**: Postgraduate

**Type**: Scholarship

**Frequency**: Annual

**Application Procedure**: Further information available on the website

**Closing Date**: 15 November

**Funding**: Government

### For further information contact:

Academic Relations (CPMA), Public Affairs, Embassy of Canada, 7-3-38 Akasaka, Minato-Ku, Japan.

**Tel**: (81) 3 5412 6298
**Fax**: (81) 3 5412 6249
**Email**: tokyo.lib-bib@international.gc.ca

## Emerging Leaders in the Americas Program (ELAP)

**Purpose**: The Emerging Leaders in the Americas Program (ELAP) scholarships provide students and researchers from Latin America and the Caribbean with short-term exchange opportunities for study or research, in Canada, at the college, undergraduate and graduate levels

**Eligibility**: Candidates who have obtained Canadian citizenship or who have applied for permanent residency in Canada are not eligible; candidates who have already participating in an exchange scholarship program funded by the Government of Canada are not eligible; candidates who have already enrolled in a degree or diploma program at a Canadian university or college are not eligible; and the candidates must be enrolled full-time at a post-secondary institution in an eligible country and paying any tuition fees regulated by that institution for the full duration of the exchange
**Level of Study**: Postgraduate
**Type**: Scholarship
**Value**: C$7,200 for college, undergraduate or graduate students (Master)
**Length of Study**: 4 months to 1 academic year (master's and PhD)/ 5 to 6 months of study of research
**Country of Study**: Canada
**Application Procedure**: If institutions experience difficulty filling out or submitting the form, they should send an email to admin-scholarships-bourses@cbie.ca
**Closing Date**: 25 April
**Contributor**: Government of Canada
**Additional Information**: As part of the Emerging Leaders in the Americas Program, selected graduate-level recipients will be invited to participate in a study tour focused on Canadian democratic governance and civil society or other key priority areas www.educanada.ca/scholarships-bourses/can/institutions/elap-pfla.aspx?lang=eng

**For further information contact:**

**Email**:     admin-scholarships-bourses@cbie.ca

## International Council for Canadian Studies Graduate Student Scholarships

**Purpose**: To provide access to crucial scholarly information and resources in Canada in support of a thesis/dissertation
**Eligibility**: Open to students at the thesis or dissertation stage in the field of social sciences or humanities
**Type**: Scholarship
**Value**: C$3,500
**Frequency**: Annual
**Study Establishment**: Any accredited Canadian University
**Country of Study**: Canada
**Application Procedure**: A completed application form and all supporting materials should be submitted to the Canadian Studies Associations
**Closing Date**: 31 December
**Additional Information**: www.iccs-ciec.ca/graduate-student-scholarships.php

**For further information contact:**

**Tel**:       (1) 613 789 7834 ext. 242
**Email**:    csppec@iccs-ciec.ca

## Organization of American States (OAS) Fellowships Programs

**Purpose**: To fund education of Canadian residents and nationals in other American nations
**Eligibility**: Open to Canadian residents and nationals
**Level of Study**: Doctorate, Graduate, MBA
**Type**: Fellowship
**Value**: US$30,000 per academic year, which includes a round-trip economy-class airfare ticket; tuition fees and mandatory expenses for the academic program, a fixed monthly allowance, medical insurance, and a fixed annual book allowance
**Length of Study**: 1–2 years
**Frequency**: Annual
**Country of Study**: Any country
**Application Procedure**: A completed application form must be submitted on time. Please refer website for more information
**Closing Date**: 7 March
**Funding**: Government
**Additional Information**: Please check at www.cbie-bcei.ca/what-we-do/student-portal/scholarships/ www.educanada.ca/scholarships-bourses/can/oas-oea.aspx?lang=eng&view=d

**For further information contact:**

**Email**:     scholarships@oas.org

## Canadian Cancer Society Research Institute (CCSRI)

Suite 300, 55 St. Clair Avenue W, Toronto, ON M4V 2Y7, Canada.

**Tel**:       (1) 416 961 7223
**Email**:    research@cancer.ca
**Website**:  www.cancer.ca/research

The Canadian Cancer Society (CCS) is the largest non-government funder of cancer research in Canada. The CCS provides support for research and related programmes undertaken at Canadian universities, hospitals and other research institutions.

## Union for International Cancer Control American Cancer Society International Fellowships for Beginning Investigators (ACSBI)

**Purpose**: To provide funding for research that fosters a bi-directional flow of knowledge, experience, expertise and innovation to and from the United States of America

**Eligibility**: Candidates should be in the early stages of their career. Applications that are geared to the development of cancer control measures in developing central and east European countries are particularly encouraged

**Level of Study**: Postdoctorate, Professional development, Research

**Type**: Research grant

**Value**: Approx. US$35,000

**Length of Study**: 1 year

**Frequency**: Annual

**Country of Study**: Any country

**Application Procedure**: Applicants must write for details or refer to the website

**Closing Date**: 1 October

**Funding**: Private

**Contributor**: American Cancer Society

**Additional Information**: Results are available in April of the following year. Further information is available on the website www.uicc.org/news/acsbi-fellowship-call-proposals-now-open-0

### For further information contact:

UICC Fellowships Department 3 rue du Conseil-General, Geneva, CH-1205, Switzerland.

**Tel**:      (41) 22 809 1811
**Fax**:      (41) 22 809 1810
**Email**:    fellows@uicc.ch

## Union for International Cancer Control International Oncology Nursing Fellowships (IDNF)

**Purpose**: The NCIC financially supports the International Union Against Cancer (UICC) which administers a number of fellowships to qualified professionals

**Eligibility**: English speaking nurses who are actively engaged in the management of cancer patients and who come from the developing and East European countries

**Level of Study**: Professional development

**Type**: Fellowship

**Value**: US$2,800

**Length of Study**: 1–3 months

**Frequency**: Annual

**Application Procedure**: Applicants must request information

**Closing Date**: 1 November

**Additional Information**: Further information available on request or from the website

### For further information contact:

UICC Fellowships Department, 3 Rue de Conseil-Général, Geneva, CH-1205, Switzerland.

**Tel**:      (41) 22 809 1811
**Fax**:      (41) 22 809 1810
**Email**:    fellows@uicc.org

## Canadian Crafts Council

345 Lakeshore Road West, Oakville, ON L6K 1G3, Canada.

**Tel**:      (1) 905 845 5357
**Email**:    kingfish@spectranet.ca
**Contact**:  Ms Jan Waldorf

## Saidye Bronfman Award

**Purpose**: To recognise excellence in the crafts. The award is made to a craftsperson judged to be an outstanding practitioner in their field, shown by their output over a working life, and their current level of achievement

**Eligibility**: Open to Canadian citizens, or individuals who have had landed immigrant status for at least three years. The nominee must have made a significant contribution to the development of crafts in Canada over a significant period of time, usually more than ten years

**Level of Study**: Postgraduate

**Type**: Award

**Value**: C$25,000

**Frequency**: Annual

**Country of Study**: Any country

**Application Procedure**: Nominations are made through CCC member associations across Canada. Award recipients are selected by a committee of leading Canadian craftspersons, including the current President of the Canadian Crafts Council, a past recipient of the Award, a nominee of the Bronfman Foundation, a gallery or museum director, and a member of the CCC Board. Members are selected to represent all major disciplines and geographic areas of Canada

**Closing Date**: 15 June

**Additional Information**: canadacouncil.ca/funding/prizes/saidye-bronfman-award

## For further information contact:

**Tel**: (1) 613 556 4414
**Email**: jennifer.cherniack@canadacouncil.ca

# Canadian Embassy (United States of America)

501 Pennsylvania Ave. N.W., DC 20001-2114, Washington, United States of America.

**Tel**: (1) 202 682 1740
**Email**: enqserv@dfait-maeci.gc.ca
**Website**: www.canadianembassy.org

## Canadian Embassy (United States of America) Research Grant Program

**Purpose**: To assist individual scholars or a group of scholars in writing an article length manuscript of publishable quality and reporting their findings in scholarly publications
**Eligibility**: Open to full-time faculty members at accredited 4-year United States colleges and universities, as well as scholars at American research and policy planning institutes who undertake significant research projects concerning Canada, Canada and the United States, or Canada and North America. Recent PhD recipients who are citizens or permanent residents of the United States are also eligible to apply
**Level of Study**: Postgraduate
**Type**: Programme grant
**Value**: Up to US$15,000; applicants whose project focuses on the priority topics listed above and who can demonstrate matching funds from others sources may request funding up to US$20,000
**Frequency**: Annual
**Study Establishment**: An accredited 4-year college or university
**Country of Study**: United States of America
**Application Procedure**: Applicants must provide 6 copies of the following in this order: the completed application form, a concise proposal of 4-8 pages which will identify all members of the research team, if a team project, and specify each member's affiliation and role in the study, identify the key issues or the main theoretical problem, describe and justify the appropriate methodology, present a general schedule of research activities, indicate clearly both the nature and scope of the projects contribution to the advancement of Canadian Studies, include a detailed budget including all other funding sources and a description of anticipated expenditures. A curriculum vitae, and the names and addresses of two scholars from whom the applicants will solicit recommendations should also be included. Application forms are available on request
**Closing Date**: 1 November
**Funding**: Government
**Additional Information**: The Research Grant Program promotes research in the social sciences and humanities with a view to contributing to a better knowledge and understanding of Canada and its relationship with the United States or other countries of the world

## For further information contact:

**Tel**: (1) 202 682 7717
**Email**: daniel.abele@dfait-maeci.gc.ca

## Canadian Embassy Faculty Enrichment Program

**Purpose**: To provide faculty members with the opportunity to develop or redevelop courses with substantial Canadian content that will be offered as part of their regular teaching load, or as a special offering to select audiences in continuing or distance education
**Eligibility**: Open to full-time, tenured or tenure track faculty members at accredited 4-year United States colleges and universities. Candidates should be able to demonstrate that they are already teaching, or will be authorized to teach, courses with substantial Canadian content (33% or more). Team teaching applications are welcome. Applicants are ineligible to receive the same grant in 2 consecutive years or to receive two individual category Canadian Studies grants in the same grant period
**Type**: Programme
**Value**: Funding up to US$6,000; applicants may request an additional US$5,000 specifically to support student travel to Canada
**Frequency**: Annual
**Country of Study**: United States of America
**Application Procedure**: Applicants must contact the organization for an application form
**Closing Date**: 1 December
**Additional Information**: The Embassy especially encourages the use of new Internet technology to enhance existing courses, including the creation of instructional websites, interactive technologies and distance learning links to Canadian Universities grants.humanities.ufl.edu/2018/03/19/canadian-embassy-faculty-enrichment-course-development-program/

## For further information contact:

**Tel**: (1) 202 682 7717
**Email**: daniel.abele@dfait-maeci.gc.ca

## Canadian Embassy Graduate Student Fellowship Program

**Purpose**: To assist graduate students in conducting part of their doctoral research in Canada to acquire a better knowledge and understanding of Canada or its relationship with the United States and other countries of the world

**Eligibility**: Open to full-time doctoral students at accredited 4-year colleges and universities in the United States or Canada whose dissertations are related in substantial part to the study of Canada, Canada and the United States or Canada and North America. Candidates must be citizens or permanent residents of the United States and should have completed all doctoral requirements except the dissertation when they apply for a grant

**Level of Study**: Graduate

**Type**: Fellowship

**Value**: Fellowships carrying stipends of up to US$850 per month for up to 9 months

**Length of Study**: 9 months

**Frequency**: Annual

**Study Establishment**: An accredited 4-year college or university

**Country of Study**: Other

**Application Procedure**: Applicants must provide six copies of the following in the order listed: the completed application form, a concise letter of three to four pages which will explain clearly the present status of the candidate's doctoral studies, describe the candidate's study plans in Canada, list Canadian contacts such as Scholars, research institutes, academic institutions or libraries, state clearly the exact number of months for which financial support is needed, provide a complete and detailed budget, indicate what other funding sources are available, give the names and addresses of two referees, one of which must be the dissertation advisor, contain the dissertation prospectus which must identify the key issues or the main theoretical problem, justify the methodology and indicate clearly the nature of the dissertation's contribution to the advancement of Canadian Studies. An unofficial transcript of grades, a curriculum vitae and proof of United States citizenship or permanent residency must also be included. Application forms are available on request

**Closing Date**: October

**Funding**: Government

**Additional Information**: The Graduate Student Fellowship Program promotes research in the social sciences and humanities with a view to contributing to a better knowledge and understanding of Canada and its relationship with the United States or other countries of the world

### For further information contact:

**Tel**:        (1) 202 682 7727
**Email**:    daniel.abele@dfait-maeci.gc.ca

## Outreach Grant

**Purpose**: To encourage training and resource development

**Eligibility**: Open to all K-12 teacher who teach about Canada or Canada–United States relations

**Level of Study**: Professional development

**Type**: Grant

**Value**: Up to US$14,000

**Frequency**: Annual

**Country of Study**: United States of America

**Application Procedure**: Contact the academic relations officer

**Closing Date**: 30 June

**Funding**: Government

**Contributor**: Foreign Affairs Canada

### For further information contact:

**Email**:    outreach@physoc.org

## Canadian Federation of University Women (CFUW)

331 Cooper Street, Suite 502, Ottawa, ON K2P 0G5, Canada.

**Tel**:        (1) 613 234 8252 ext. 104
**Email**:    cfuwfls@rogers.com
**Website**:  www.cfuw.org
**Contact**:  Betty A Dunlop, CFUW Fellowships Program
               Manager

Found in 1919, the Canadian Federation of University Women (CFUW) is a voluntary, non-partisan, non-profit, self-funded bilingual organization of 9,000 women university graduates. CFUW members are active in public affairs, working to raise the social, economic, and legal status of women as well as to improve education, the environment, peace, justice and human rights.

## Dr. A. Vibert Douglas Fellowship

**Purpose**: The Fellowship is for a PhD thesis/project which focuses on advancing gender equality. The project must be led by women. The Fellowship is for a PhD thesis/project which focuses on advancing gender equality

**Eligibility**: If an applicant does not belong to an NFA of the GWI or to an organization that belongs to the IAW but meets the other criteria for the Fellowship they must make a US$10 donation that will be split between those two organizations

**Level of Study**: Postgraduate

**Type**: Fellowship

**Value**: US$8,000

**Frequency**: Annual
**Country of Study**: Any country
**Application Procedure**: Those who are interested in this fellowship will need to pay a US$60 application fee
**Closing Date**: 3 December
**Funding**: Private
**Additional Information**: For more information, visit fcfdu. fluidreview.com/ www.fcfdu.org/fellowshipsawards/dravib ertdouglasfellowship.aspx

## Canadian Foundation for the Study of Infant Deaths

Suite 308, 586 Eglinton Avenue East, Toronto, ON M4P 1P2, Canada.

**Tel**:        (1) 415 488 3260
**Email**:      sidsinfo@sidscanada.org
**Website**:    www.sidscanada.org
**Contact**:    Ravit Lasman, Executive Director

The Canadian Foundation for the Study of Infant Deaths is a federally incorporated charitable organization that was set up in 1973 to respond to the needs of families experiencing sudden and unexpected infant death. It is the only organization in Canada solely dedicated to finding the causes of Sudden Infant Death Syndrome, its effect on families and the education of the public.

## Cypress-Fairbanks Independent School District/ CIHR Doctoral and Postdoctoral Research Awards

### For further information contact:

The Canadian Institutes of Health Research, 440 Laurier Ave. 9th fl., Locator 4209A, Ottawa, ON K1A 0W9, Canada.

**Tel**:    (1) 613 954 1964
**Fax**:    (1) 613 941 1800
**Email**:  srobertson@cihr.ca

## Canadian Institute for Advanced Legal Studies

PO Box 43538, Leaside Post Office, 1601 Bayview Avenue, Toronto, ON M4G 4G8, Canada.

**Tel**:      (1) 416 429 3292
**Email**:    info@canadian-institute.com

**Website**:    www.canadian-institute.com
**Contact**:    Mr Randall J. Hofley, Vice-President

The Canadian Institute for Advanced Legal Studies conducts legal seminars for judges and lawyers in Cambridge, United Kingdom and Strasbourg, France.

## French Language Scholarship

**Purpose**: For graduate studies in law toward a second cycle or third cycle diploma (the equivalent of a Master's or Doctoral degree from a Canadian university), at a European university for a program of study that is conducted principally in the French language, to a person who has, in the four years before the candidate will commence the proposed studies been awarded a bachelor's degree in law from a Canadian university
**Eligibility**: An applicant must be accepted into a French-language European university for graduate studies in law in order to receive this Scholarship, although such acceptance need not be confirmed at the time of the application for the Scholarship or at the time that the Institute provides the candidate with notice that he or she has been selected to receive the Scholarship
**Level of Study**: Postgraduate
**Type**: Scholarship
**Value**: Full tuition fees payable by the recipient to a French-language European university and includes an allowance to cover a portion of living expenses and reasonable travel expenses to and from the European university, subject to any other awards received by the successful candidate. The Canadian Institute for Advanced Legal Studies shall determine each year the maximum amount of the scholarship, up to an amount of US$20,000 for the academic year, and in so doing will take into account the tuition fees as well as the anticipated living expenses and travel expenses of the successful candidate
**Length of Study**: 1 year
**Frequency**: Annual
**Study Establishment**: French Language European University
**Country of Study**: Europe, Germany
**Application Procedure**: Applications must include: Curriculum vitae; 1. A personal statement indicating why the applicant wishes to undertake graduate studies in law and why the applicant is suited to undertake such studies, as well as an undertaking that the proposed program study is conducted principally in the French language. 2. A copy of transcripts for undergraduate and graduate studies, for studies in law or for a Bar Admission Course, as applicable. 3. A maximum of three letters of reference. 4. A statement of tuition fees and anticipated living and travel expenses

**Closing Date**: 1 December
**Funding**: Trusts
**Contributor**: Canadian Institute for Advanced Legal Studies
**Additional Information**: www.canadian-institute.com/english/index.html

**For further information contact:**

Canadian Institute for Advanced Legal Studies, P.O.Box 43538, Leaside Post Office, 1601 Bayview Avenue, Toronto, ON M4G 4G8, Canada.

**Tel**:    (1) 416 429 3292
**Fax**:    (1) 416 429 9805

## The Right Honorable Paul Martin Sr. Scholarship

**Purpose**: To study for an LLM at the University of Cambridge
**Eligibility**: Open to graduates who have been awarded a law degree from a 3- or 4-year program at a faculty of law in a Canadian university in the 4 years before the candidate will commence his or her studies at the University of Cambridge (supported by The Right Honourable Paul Martin Sr. Scholarship). An applicant must be accepted into the University of Cambridge and a college of the University of Cambridge for graduate studies in law in order to receive this scholarship, although such acceptance need not be confirmed at the time of the application for the scholarship nor at the time that the Institute provides the candidate with notice that he or she has been selected to receive the scholarship
**Level of Study**: Postgraduate
**Type**: Scholarship
**Value**: £23,000
**Length of Study**: 1 year
**Frequency**: Annual
**Study Establishment**: The University of Cambridge
**Country of Study**: United Kingdom
**Application Procedure**: Applications must include curriculum vitae; a personal statement indicating why the applicant wishes to undertake graduate studies in law at the University of Cambridge and why the applicant is suited to undertake such studies; a copy of transcripts for undergraduate and graduate studies, for studies in law and for a Bar Admissions Course, as applicable; and a maximum of three letters of references
**No. of awards offered**: 25
**Closing Date**: 3 December
**Funding**: Private
**No. of awards given last year**: 2
**No. of applicants last year**: 25

**Additional Information**: The scholarship may be held with another small award as approved by the Institute. Please check at www.canadian-institute.com/english/index.html www.canadian-institute.com/english/index.html

**For further information contact:**

Canadian Institute for Advanced Legal Studies, P.O.Box 43538, Leaside Post Office, 1601 Bayview Avenue, Toronto, ON M4G 4G8, Canada.

**Fax**:    (1) 416 429 9805

## Canadian Institutes of Health Research

Canadian Institutes of Health Research; 160 Elgin Street, 9th Floor; Address Locator 4809A; Ottawa, ON K1A 0W9, Canada.

The Canadian Institutes of Health Research (CIHR) is Canada's federal funding agency for health research. Composed of 13 Institutes, we collaborate with partners and researchers to support the discoveries and innovations that improve our health and strengthen our health care system.

### Banting Postdoctoral Fellowships

**Eligibility**: Open to Canadian citizen, permanent resident of Canada, foreign citizens
**Level of Study**: Postdoctorate
**Type**: Award
**Value**: C$70,000 per year (taxable)
**Length of Study**: 2 years
**Country of Study**: Canada
**Closing Date**: April
**Additional Information**: For more details, visit website banting.fellowships-bourses.gc.ca/en/app-dem_guide.html

**For further information contact:**

**Email**:    banting@cihr-irsc.gc.ca

### Canadian Institutes of Health Research Gold Leaf Prizes

**Eligibility**: Open to Canadian citizen, permanent resident of Canada, foreign citizens
**Type**: Grant
**Value**: C$100,000

**Length of Study**: 2 years
**Frequency**: Every 2 years
**Country of Study**: Canada
**Additional Information**: For more details, please visit the Contact Centre: support@cihr-irsc.gc.ca cihr-irsc.gc.ca/e/27894.html

## For further information contact:

**Email**: support@cihr-irsc.gc.ca

## Foundation Grant Program

**Purpose**: Foundation grants are designed to support research leaders at any career stage to build and conduct programmes of health research across CIHR's mandate
**Eligibility**: Open to Canadian citizen, permanent resident of Canada, foreign citizens
**Type**: Grant
**Value**: Proportionate to the requirements of the research proposed and vary depending on the research field, research approach, and scope of programme activities
**Length of Study**: 5 to 7 years
**Country of Study**: Canada
**Application Procedure**: Please refer website www.cihr-irsc.gc.ca
**Closing Date**: 14 March
**Additional Information**: For more details, please visit the Contact Centre: support@cihr-irsc.gc.ca cihr-irsc.gc.ca/e/49798.html

## For further information contact:

**Email**: nbf@aabb.org

## Project Grant Program

**Purpose**: Project grants are designed to support researchers at any career stage to build and conduct health-related research and knowledge translation projects across CIHR's mandate
**Eligibility**: Open to Canadian citizen, permanent resident of Canada, foreign citizens
**Type**: Grant
**Country of Study**: Canada
**Application Procedure**: Your research proposal must include all crucial information (including tables, charts, figures and photographs) that a reviewer will need to read in order to assess your application. Reviewers are under no obligation to read other supplementary application materials that you may attach.
**Closing Date**: 15 May

**Additional Information**: For more details, please contact the Contact Centre: support@cihr-irsc.gc.ca cihr-irsc.gc.ca/e/49051.html

## For further information contact:

**Fax**: (1) 613 954 1968
**Email**: support-soutien@cihr-irsc.gc.ca

## Vanier Canada Graduate Scholarships

**Purpose**: The Vanier Canada Graduate Scholarships (Vanier CGS) was created to attract and retain world-class doctoral students and to establish Canada as a global centre of excellence in research and higher learning. The scholarships are towards a doctoral degree (or combined MA/PhD or MD/PhD).
**Eligibility**: 1. be nominated by only one Canadian institution, which must have received a Vanier CGS quota 2. be pursuing your first doctoral degree (including joint undergraduate/graduate research program such as: MD/PhD, DVM/PhD, JD/PhD - if it has a demonstrated and significant research component). Note that only the PhD portion of a combined degree is eligible for funding 3. intend to pursue, in the summer semester or the academic year following the announcement of results, full-time doctoral (or a joint graduate program such as: MD/PhD, DVM/PhD, JD/PhD) studies and research at the nominating institution Note that only the PhD portion of a combined degree is eligible for funding 4. not have completed more than 20 months of doctoral studies as of May 1. 5. have achieved a first-class average, as determined by your institution, in each of the last two years of full-time study or equivalent. Candidates are encouraged to contact the institution for its definition of a first-class average and 6. must not hold, or have held, a doctoral-level scholarship or fellowship from CIHR, NSERC or SSHRC to undertake or complete a doctoral degree.
**Level of Study**: Doctorate
**Type**: Scholarship
**Value**: C$50,000 per year
**Length of Study**: 3 years
**Frequency**: Annual
**Country of Study**: Canada
**No. of awards offered**: 166
**Closing Date**: 20 November
**Additional Information**: vanier.gc.ca/en/nomination_process-processus_de_mise_en_candidature.html

## For further information contact:

**Email**: vanier@cihr-irsc.gc.ca

## Canadian Library Association (CLA)

1150 Morrison Drive, Suite 400, Ottawa, ON K2H 8S9, Canada.

**Tel**: (1) 613 232 9625
**Email**: info@cla.ca
**Website**: www.cla.ca
**Contact**: Valoree McKay, Executive Director

The Canadian Library Association works to maintain a tradition of commitment to excellence in library education and to advance continuing research in the field of library and information science.

### Canadian Library Association Library Research and Development Grants

**Purpose**: To support members of the Canadian Library Association for theoretical and applied research in the related fields. To encourage and support research undertaken by practitionares in the field of library and information services. To promote research in the field of library and information services by and/or about Canadians
**Eligibility**: Open to personal members of the Canadian Library Association
**Level of Study**: Postgraduate
**Type**: Grant
**Value**: C$1,000
**Frequency**: Annual
**Country of Study**: Canada
**Application Procedure**: Applicants must submit grant applications via emails and MS word document in either French or English containing contact details, description of the research project, duration of the project, detailed assessment of costs and statement of other grants/awards received. Proposals should be submitted via email
**Closing Date**: February
**Additional Information**: Please check at www.cla.ca/AM/Template.cfm?Section=Grants&amp;Template=/CM/HTMLDisplay.cfm&amp;ContentID=12526 cla.ca/cla-at-work/cla-library-research-and-development-grants/

### For further information contact:

**Tel**: (1) 613 232 9625 ext 322
**Fax**: (1) 613 563 9895

## Canadian National Institute for the Blind (CNIB)

1929 Bayview Avenue, East York, Toronto, ON M4G 0A1, Canada.

**Tel**: (1) 800 563 2642, (1) 416 486 2500
**Email**: info@cnib.ca
**Website**: www.cnib.ca
**Contact**: Mr John M Rafferty, President and CEO

CNIB is a nationwide, community-based, registered charity committed to public education, research and the vision health of all Canadians. CNIB provides the services and support necessary to enjoy a good quality of life while living with vision loss. Founded in 1918, CNIB reaches out to communities across the country, offering access to rehabilitation training, innovative consumer products and peer support programs as well as one of the world's largest libraries for people with a print disability. CNIB supports research to advance knowledge in the field of vision health. Our research program funds projects that focus on ways to cure, treat and prevent eye disease, and improve the quality of life for people with vision loss.

### Canadian National Institute for the Blind Baker Applied Research Fund

**Purpose**: To promote non-medical applied research that will enhance the life of the blind or visually impaired
**Eligibility**: Open to residents of Canada enrolled in graduate study in Canada, and includes a co-applicant who is either a supervisor or mentor with an academic appointment in Canada, or a supervisory position at a healthcare facility. Refer to the website for complete details
**Level of Study**: Research
**Value**: Up to C$40,000 plus travel and publications costs up to C$2,000
**Length of Study**: One year
**Frequency**: Annual
**Country of Study**: Canada
**Funding**: Private
**Additional Information**: univrsapp.usask.ca/converis/publicweb/cfFund/5654?share=false&cntpers=false&reqst fulltxt=false&reports=false&lang=1

**For further information contact:**

Tel:     (1) 416 486 2500 ext. 7622
Fax:     (1) 416 480 7059
Email:   shampa.bose@cnib.ca

## Canadian National Institute for the Blind Baker Fellowship Fund

**Purpose**: CNIB's Baker Fellowships are awarded annually for post-graduate training in ophthalmic subspecialties
**Eligibility**: Open to Canadians for research or study in Canada, or abroad if returning to practice in Canada, with priority given to university teaching
**Level of Study**: Postgraduate, Professional development, Research
**Value**: Up to C$40,000
**Length of Study**: 1–2 years
**Frequency**: Annual
**Country of Study**: Any country
**Funding**: Private

**For further information contact:**

Tel:     (1) 416 486 2500 ext. 7622
Fax:     (1) 416 480 7059
Email:   shampa.bose@cnib.ca

## Canadian National Institute for the Blind Baker New Researcher Fund

**Purpose**: To provide one-year grants to encourage new investigations that may lead to the prevention of vision loss. It is intended to benefit new investigators (within 5 years after an academic faculty appointment) by giving them experience and results which can assist them in further grant applications and pilot investigations
**Eligibility**: Applicants must be residents of Canada and research must be conducted primarily in Canada
**Level of Study**: Postdoctorate, Professional development, Research
**Value**: Up to C$35,000
**Length of Study**: 1 year
**Frequency**: Annual
**Country of Study**: Canada
**Funding**: Private

**For further information contact:**

Tel:     (1) 416 486 2500 ext. 7622
Fax:     (1) 416 480 7059
Email:   shampa.bose@cnib.ca

## Canadian National Institute for the Blind Winston Gordon Award

**Purpose**: The award is presented to an individual or group who has made significant technological advances benefiting people with vision loss
**Eligibility**: The significant advances in, or application of, technology must have occurred within 10 years of nomination. The device or application must have a documented benefit to people who are blind or visually impaired. The award may be presented to an individual, group, or organization, including corporations and academic institutions
**Type**: Award
**Value**: The award consists of a cash prize of up to C$10,000
**Country of Study**: Any country
**Application Procedure**: To submit a nomination, please write a letter to the Winston Gordon Committee nominating the individual or group for its products or services, and explaining how the nominee meets or surpasses the eligibility criteria and matches the goals of the award
**Closing Date**: 16 January
**Funding**: Private
**Additional Information**: cnib.ca/en/about-us/awards/winston-gordon-award-excellence-accessible-technology?region=gta

**For further information contact:**

Winston Gordon Award Committee, CNIB, 1929 Bayview Avenue, East York, ON M4G 3E8, Canada.

Fax:     (1) 416 480 7000
Email:   shampa.bose@cnib.ca

## Gretzky Scholarship Foundation for the Blind Youth of Canada

**Purpose**: To provide scholarships to eligible blind and visually impaired students planning to study at the post-secondary level
**Eligibility**: All applicants must be blind or visually impaired, a graduate from secondary school entering their first year of post-secondary education, and a Canadian citizen. Candidates must be blind or living with vision loss. A secondary school graduate entering their first year of post-secondary education. A Canadian citizen or have held landed immigrant status for one year prior to date of application. Academic excellence, service to the community, financial need, superior leadership

**Type**: Scholarship
**Value**: C$3,000–5,000 each
**Frequency**: Annual
**Country of Study**: Canada
**Application Procedure**: All documents requested in the application form must be included with your application. Please send application and documents to Kim Kohler
**Closing Date**: 31 May
**Funding**: Private
**No. of awards given last year**: 23

### For further information contact:

955256 Canning Rd, Paris, ON N3L 3E2, Canada

| | |
|---|---|
| **Tel**: | (33) 519 458 8665 |
| **Fax**: | (33) 519 458 8609 |
| **Email**: | Kim.Kohler@cnib.ca |

## Ross Purse Doctoral Fellowship

**Purpose**: To encourage and support theoretical and practical research and studies at the postgraduate or doctoral level in the field of vision loss in Canada
**Eligibility**: Applications will be considered from persons studying at a Canadian University or college, or at a foreign University, where a commitment to work in the field of vision loss in Canada for at least 2 years can be demonstrated
**Level of Study**: Doctorate, Postgraduate
**Type**: Fellowship
**Value**: Up to C$12,500 to be paid in three equal installments
**Length of Study**: 2 years
**Frequency**: Annual
**Country of Study**: Any country
**Application Procedure**: Please send completed applications to Research Coordinator
**No. of awards offered**: 1
**Closing Date**: 30 June
**Funding**: Private
**Additional Information**: www.cnib.ca/en/about-us/awards/ross-c-purse-doctoral-fellowship?region=gta

### For further information contact:

CNIB, 1929 Bayview Avenue, East York, ON M4G 3E8, Canada.

| | |
|---|---|
| **Tel**: | (1) 416 486 2500 ext. 7622 |
| **Fax**: | (1) 416 480 7000 |
| **Email**: | cheryl-ann.ali@cnib.ca |

## The E. (Ben) & Mary Hochhausen Access Technology Research Award

**Purpose**: To encourage research in the field of access technology for people living with vision loss
**Eligibility**: Applications are accepted from any country in the world
**Level of Study**: Research
**Type**: Research award
**Value**: Up to C$10,000
**Country of Study**: International
**Application Procedure**: Please check at www.cnib.ca/en/research/funding/hochhausen/
**Closing Date**: 30 September
**Funding**: Private
**No. of awards given last year**: 1
**Additional Information**: www.cnib.ca/en/about-us/awards/ross-c-purse-doctoral-fellowship?region=gta

### For further information contact:

**Email**:    shampa.bose@cnib.ca

## Canadian Political Science Association

1 Stewart Street, Suite 205, University of Ottawa, Ottawa, ON K1N 6H7, Canada.

| | |
|---|---|
| **Tel**: | (1) 613 562 1202 |
| **Email**: | pip@csse.ca |
| **Contact**: | Grants Management Officer |

The Canadian Political Science Association was founded in 1913 with the aim of encouraging and developing political science and its relationship with other disciplines. To this end the Association holds conferences, meetings and exhibitions, gives grants, scholarships and fellowships and publishes journals, newspapers, books and monographs relating to political science.

## Canadian Parliamentary Internship Programme

**Purpose**: To give university graduates an opportunity to supplement their theoretical knowledge of Parliament with practical experience of the day to day work of the Members of Parliament and to provide back bench Members with highly qualified assistants
**Eligibility**: Open to Canadian university graduates

**Level of Study**: Postgraduate
**Type**: Scholarship
**Value**: An estimated stipend of C$16,500, plus travel subsidies
**Length of Study**: 10 months
**Frequency**: Annual, if funds are available
**Study Establishment**: The Canadian Parliament
**Country of Study**: Canada
**Application Procedure**: Applicants must submit the original and four copies of the completed application form, transcripts, letters of reference (two academic, one employer), and US$10 administrative fee cheque
**Closing Date**: January
**Funding**: Private
**Contributor**: The Social Sciences and Humanities Research council of Canada, Bank of Montreal, Canadian Airlines International, Canadian Bankers Association, Canadian Cable Television Association, The Canadian Life and Health Association, The Co-operators
**Additional Information**: Interns will be assigned specific responsibilities with Members of the House of Commons and will be required to attend seminars and prepare a paper analysing an aspect of parliamentary government in Canada

### For further information contact:

The Parliamentary Internship Programme, Room 1200, La Promenade Building, 151 Sparks Street, House of Commons, Ottawa, ON K1P 5E3, Canada.

**Tel**:     (44) 613 995 0764
**Fax**:     (44) 613 995 5357
**Email**:   cartwj@parl.gc.ca

## Ontario Legislature Internship Programme

**Purpose**: To provide university graduates with the opportunity to supplement their theoretical knowledge of the Legislature and its processes with practical experience of the day to day work of the members, and to provide back bench members with highly qualified assistants
**Eligibility**: Open to Canadian citizens only
**Level of Study**: Postgraduate
**Type**: Internship
**Value**: C$16,000
**Length of Study**: 10 months
**Frequency**: Dependent on funds available
**Country of Study**: Canada
**Application Procedure**: Applicants must complete an application form, available on request from the Program Officer
**No. of awards offered**: 97
**Closing Date**: January

**Funding**: Government, Commercial, Private
**No. of awards given last year**: 8
**No. of applicants last year**: 97

### For further information contact:

Department of Political Science, University of Waterloo, 200 University Ave W, Waterloo, ON N2L 3G1, Canada.

**Tel**:     (1) 519 888 4567 ext. 5682
**Fax**:     (1) 519 746 5622
**Email**:   olip@watarts.uwaterloo.ca

## Canadian Society for Chemical Technology

Chemical Institute of Canada, 222 Queen Street, Suite 400, Ottawa, ON K1P 5V9, Canada.

**Tel**:      (1) 613 232 6252 ext 223, (1) 888 542 2242
**Email**:    awards@cheminst.ca
**Website**:  www.cheminst.ca/about/cic/csct
**Contact**:  Gale Thirlwall, Awards Manager

The Canadian Society for Chemical Technology is the national technical association of chemical and biochemical technicians and technologists with members across Canada who work in industry, government or academia. The purpose of the Society is the advancement of chemical technology, the maintenance and improvement of practitioners and educators and the continual evaluation of chemical technology in Canada. The Society hopes to maintain a dialogue with educators, government and industry, to assist in the technology content of the education process of technologists, to attract qualified people into the professions and the Society, to develop and maintain high standards and enhance the usefulness of chemical technology to both the industry and the public.

## Canadian National Committee/IUPAC Travel Awards

**Purpose**: The purpose of these Awards is to help young Canadian scientists and engineers within 10 years of having gained their PhD who are currently working at a Canadian institution, present a paper at an IUPAC-sponsored conference outside of Canada.
**Eligibility**: A list of IUPAC-sponsored conferences for 2020 can be found on the IUPAC web-site (www.iupac.org/) and

also in Chemistry International, the IUPAC magazine. Awards are made to attend the conference identified in the application, and no changes are allowed without written permission from the Chair

**Level of Study**: Postdoctorate

**Value**: Up to US$2,500, paid in arrears after travel-expense receipts and a 150-word report on the conference have been received by the Secretary

**Country of Study**: Any country

**Application Procedure**: 1. a short Curriculum Vitae, 2. two Letters of Reference, including one from someone not at the applicant's university, research institution or company. 3. a cover letter outlining the name and location of the conference, a copy or link to the conference circular and the reasons why this particular conference fits your research goals.

**No. of awards offered**: 4

**Closing Date**: 16 October

**Funding**: Private

**Contributor**: Gendron Fund and CNC/IUPAC company associates

**No. of awards given last year**: 4

**Additional Information**: www.cnc-iupac.ca/awards_e.html

### For further information contact:

Steacie Institute for Molecular Sciences, NRC 100 Sussex Dr, Ottawa, ON K1A 0R6, Canada.

**Tel**: (1) 613 990 8326
**Email**: Homin.Shin@nrc-cnrc.gc.ca

## Canadian Society for Chemistry (CSC)

222 Queen Street, Suite 400, Ottawa, ON KIP 5V9, Canada.

**Tel**: (1) 613 232 6252 ext 223
**Email**: awards@cheminst.ca
**Website**: www.cheminst.ca/about/cic/csc
**Contact**: Gale Thirlwall, Awards Manager

The Canadian Society for Chemistry (CSC), one of three constituent societies of The Chemical Institute of Canada, is the national scientific and educational society of chemists. The purpose of the CSC is to promote the practice and application of chemistry in Canada.

## Award for Research Excellence in Materials Chemistry

**Purpose**: To recognize outstanding contribution to materials chemistry while working in Canada

**Eligibility**: Candidates must be within 15 years of their first independent appointment

**Level of Study**: Research

**Type**: Fellowship

**Value**: Up to US$1,000 travel costs for award tour, framed scroll

**Frequency**: Annual

**Application Procedure**: Please check website for details

**Closing Date**: 2 July

**Funding**: Private

**Additional Information**: Please check at www.cheminst.ca/awards/csc-awards www.cheminst.ca/wp-content/uploads/2019/04/Award20for20Research20Excellence20in20Materials20Chemistry20TofR.pdf

## Canadian Space Agency

John H. Chapman 6767 Route de l'Aéroport Saint-Hubert, Quebec J3Y 8Y9, Canada.

**Tel**: (1) 450 926 4800
**Email**: dave.kendall@space.gc.ca
**Website**: www.asc-csa.gc.ca
**Contact**: David Kendall, Director General, Space Science

The Canadian Space Agency (CSA) was established in 1989 by the Canadian Space Agency Act. The agency operates like a government department

## Canadian Space Agency Supplements Postgraduate Scholarships

**Purpose**: To foster advanced studies in space science by offering a supplement to the regular National Science and Engineering Research Council (NSERC) postgraduate scholarships

**Eligibility**: Open to graduate and permanent resident and citizen of Canada engaged in Masters or Doctoral studies in the natural sciences or engineering, or intend to pursue such studies in the following year, is successful in obtaining a NSERC postgraduate scholarship (PGS) or a Canada graduate scholarships (CGS-Master's)

**Level of Study**: Postgraduate

**Type**: Scholarship

**Value**: C$7,500 per year for one year for masters students and up to two years for doctoral students

**Length of Study**: 2 years

**Frequency**: Annual

**Country of Study**: Canada

**Application Procedure**: Candidates should apply to the NSERC postgraduate scholarship or Canada graduate scholarship programs by completing Form 200. After reviewing the forms, notification of award will be sent to the selected applicants

**Closing Date**: 1 May
**Funding**: Government
**Contributor**: National Science and Engineering Research Council
**Additional Information**: A candidate who is in receipt of a scholarship from federal sources other than NSERC will not be eligible for this supplement. Please check at www.asc-csa.gc.ca/eng/resources/gc/research.asp#recipients-2

### For further information contact:

**Email**:    sc-gc.centre.expertise@asc-csa.gc.ca

## Cancer Council N.S.W

153 Dowling Street, Woolloomooloo, NSW 2011, Australia.

**Tel**:        (61) 2 9334 1900
**Email**:    rong@nswcc.org.au
**Website**:  www.cancercouncil.com.au

The Cancer Council NSW is one of the leading cancer charity organizations in New South Wales. Its mission is to defeat cancer and is working to build a cancer-smart community. In building a cancer-smart community, the Council undertakes high-quality research and is an advocate on cancer issues, providing information and services to the public and raising funds for cancer programmes

## The Cancer Council NSW Research Project Grants

**Purpose**: To provide flexible support for cancer researchers
**Eligibility**: Open to researchers working in NSW institutions
**Level of Study**: Unrestricted
**Type**: Project grant
**Value**: up to AU$450,000
**Length of Study**: Up to 3 years
**Frequency**: Annual
**Study Establishment**: An approved institution in New South Wales
**Country of Study**: Australia
**Application Procedure**: Applicants must complete an application form available on request or from the website. Applications are submitted through the researcher's institution to NHMRC. Applicants must also complete a supplementary question form and a consumer review form
**No. of awards offered**: 106

**Closing Date**: 11 March
**Funding**: Private
**Contributor**: Community fund-raising
**No. of applicants last year**: 106
**Additional Information**: Further information is available from either the NHMRC Liaison Officer (National Cancer Research Grants Secretariat) or from Cancer Council NSW. Please check at www.cancercouncil.com.au/1221/research/research-funding-and-governance/funding-opportunities/new-grants/ www.cancercouncil.com.au/research/for-researchers/cancer-research-grants/project-grant-applications/

### For further information contact:

NHMRC, GPO Box 9848, Canberra ACT 2601, Australia.

**Tel**:        (61) 3 9635 5028
**Email**:    CancerCouncilGrants@cancervic.org.au

## Cancer Council South Australia

202 Greenhill Road, Eastwood, SA 5063, Australia.

**Tel**:        (61) 8291 4111
**Email**:    cc@cancersa.org.au
**Website**:  www.cancersa.org.au

The Cancer Council South Australia is a community-based charity independent of government control that has developed since 1928 with the support of South Australians. The Foundation's mission is to pursue the eradication of cancer through research and education on the prevention and early detection of cancer, thus enhancing the quality of life for people living with cancer.

## PhD Scholarships

**Purpose**: To support cancer researchers in South Australia through the provision of research and senior research fellowships
**Eligibility**: Applicant must be a student judged to be the best applicant from University of Adelaide, Flinders University or University of South Australia, who is commencing PhD studies. The applicant must not be currently enroled in a PhD, must be eligible for the Research Training Scheme and must not have been previously enroled for a Research Degree. Students are eligible to apply for the scholarship if they are enroled in the Faculty or Division of Health Sciences at their institution and if their PhD topic is in an area of cancer research
**Level of Study**: Postgraduate

**Type**: Scholarship
**Value**: Equivalent to the value of the stipend for an APA award
**Length of Study**: 3 years
**Frequency**: Annual
**Country of Study**: Australia
**Application Procedure**: Applicants must contact the relevant Scholarships Offices of The University of Adelaide, University of South Australia and Flinders University for further information and closing dates

**For further information contact:**

**Tel**:        (61) 8 8291 4297
**Email**:   npolglase@cancersa.org.au

## Cancer Immunotherapy

### National Cancer Institute Immunotherapy Fellowship

**Purpose**: This program allows the fellow to have exposure to multiple clinical immunotherapeutic approaches and key opinion leaders in the field of clinical immunotherapy. It helps to work with internationally recognized experts in immunotherapy
**Eligibility**: 1. Able to relocate to Bethesda, MD, for the duration of the fellowship. 2. Trained in Medical Oncology, Hematology, Pediatric Oncology, Radiation Oncology, or Surgical Oncology. 3. Interest in learning about immunotherapy. 4. Preference is given to those with an academic interest. 5. Open to United States and Non-United States trained physicians (the latter requires ECFMG certification)
**Level of Study**: Research
**Type**: Fellowships
**Value**: It is based on applicable laws, regulations, and policies
**Frequency**: Annual
**Country of Study**: Any country
**Application Procedure**: For further information, refer the below web link. www.sitcancer.org/funding/fellowships/2019/nci-immunotherapy-fellowship
**Closing Date**: 17 December
**Funding**: Private
**Additional Information**: www.sitcancer.org/funding/fellowships/2019/nci-immunotherapy-fellowship

**For further information contact:**

555 East Wells Street, Suite 1100, Milwaukee, WI 53202-2823, United States of America.

**Email**:   development@sitcancer.org

### Society for Immunotherapy of Cancer - Amgen Cancer Immunotherapy in Hematologic Malignancies Fellowship Award

**Purpose**: This cancer immunotherapy fellowship award aims to provide support for an individual who has a vested interest in furthering the research and translation of immunotherapeutic approaches for treating patients with hematologic malignancies
**Eligibility**: Candidature must follow the below eligibility to obtain the fellowship award. 1. Current SITC member. 2. Hold an MD or combined MD/PhD degree. 3. Currently hold a position at a leading academic cancer center as a postdoctoral fellow, resident, research scientist or comparable position. 4. Be within postdoctoral or postgraduate training, or no more than four years from completing such training. 5. Commit 75% of workday to research supported by the fellowship
**Level of Study**: Professional development
**Type**: Award/Grant
**Value**: US$100,000
**Frequency**: Annual
**Country of Study**: Any country
**Application Procedure**: The successful applicant will obtain the following benefits along with the award amount, omce they are eligible for the fellowship award. 1. Complimentary registration and travel for SITC's 34th Annual Meeting. 2. Recognition during the Award Ceremony at SITC's 34th Annual Meeting
**Closing Date**: 1 March
**Funding**: Private
**Additional Information**: www.sitcancer.org/funding/fellowships/2019/amgen-immunotherapy-hematologic-malignancies

**For further information contact:**

**Tel**:        (1) 414 271 2456
**Email**:   development@sitcancer.org

## Cancer Prevention and Research Institute of Texas - CPRIT

1701 North Congress Avenue, Austin, Suite 6-127, TX 78701, United States of America.

**Tel**:        (1) 512 463 3190
**Email**:   cprit@cprit.texas.gov
**Website**:   www.cprit.state.tx.us/

Texas voters overwhelmingly approved a constitutional amendment in 2007 establishing the Cancer Prevention and Research Institute of Texas (CPRIT) and authorizing the state to issue US$3 billion in bonds to fund groundbreaking cancer research and prevention programs and services in Texas. CPRIT's goal is to expedite innovation in cancer research and product development, and to enhance access to evidence-based prevention programs throughout the state. Under the guidance of its governing body, the Oversight Committee, CPRIT accepts applications and awards grants for a wide variety of cancer-related research and for the delivery of cancer prevention programs and services by public and private entities located in Texas. All CPRIT-funded research will be conducted in state by Texas-based scientists and reflect CPRIT's mission to attract and expand the state's research capabilities and create high quality new jobs in Texas.

## Individual Investigator Research Awards (IIRA)

**Purpose**: Supports applications for innovative research projects addressing critically important questions that will significantly advance knowledge of the causes, prevention, and/or treatment of cancer. Areas of interest include laboratory research, translational studies, and/or clinical investigations. Competitive renewal applications accepted.

**Eligibility**: The applicant must be a Texas-based institution of higher education or a component of a university system with appropriately accredited degree-granting training programs (if support is requested for training leading to a degree). 1. The Principal Investigator (PI) must have a doctoral degree, including MD, PhD, DDS, DMD, DrPH, DO, DVM, or equivalent, and must be a full-time resident of Texas during the time the research that is the subject of the grant is conducted. 2. An institution may submit only 1 new or renewal application under this RFA during this funding cycle. An exception will be made for institutions submitting applications for cancer prevention training; in this case, institutions may submit 1 prevention training program application and 1 additional application in another aspect of cancer research (new or renewal). 3. For the purposes of this RFA, an institution is defined as that component of a university system that has its own president. 4. There must be only 1 PI, but Co-PIs may direct individual components of the overall program described in the application. 5. An institution may apply for as many components of the training program as are appropriate for the institution. 6. An applicant is eligible to receive a grant award only if the applicant certifies that the applicant institution or organization, including the PI, any senior member or key personnel listed on the grant application, or any officer or director of the grant applicant's institution or organization (or any person related to 1 or more of these individuals within the second degree of consanguinity or affinity), has not made and will not make a contribution to CPRIT or to any foundation specifically created to benefit

CPRIT. 7. An applicant is not eligible to receive a CPRIT grant award if the applicant PI, any senior member or key personnel listed on the grant application, or any officer or director of the grant applicant's organization or institution is related to a CPRIT Oversight Committee member. CPRIT RFA R-21.1-RTA Research Training Awards Page 10 of 24 (Rev 1/31/20) 8. The applicant must report whether the applicant institution or organization, the PI, or other individuals who contribute to the execution of the proposed project in a substantive, measurable way, whether or not those individuals are slated to receive salary or compensation under the grant award, are currently ineligible to receive federal grant funds or have had a grant terminated for cause within 5 years prior to the submission date of the grant application. 9. CPRIT grants will be awarded by contract to successful applicants. Certain contractual requirements are mandated by Texas law or by administrative rules. Although applicants need not demonstrate the ability to comply with these contractual requirements at the time the application is submitted, applicants should make themselves aware of these standards before submitting a grant application. Significant issues addressed by the CPRIT contract are listed in section 10 and section 11. All statutory provisions and relevant administrative rules can be found at www.cprit.state.tx.us.

**Level of Study**: Masters

**Type**: Scholarships

**Value**: Award: Up to US$300,000 per year in total costs. Exceptions permitted if extremely well justified;

**Length of Study**: 3 years

**Country of Study**: US

**Application Procedure**: Each application must be accompanied by a letter of institutional support from the president or provost indicating support and commitment to the training program. The letter could include, but is not limited to, information about laboratory space, shared laboratory facilities and equipment, funds for curriculum development, support for additional trainees in the program, and initiatives to support recruitment of underrepresented minorities. A maximum of 3 pages may be provided. Applications that are missing 1 or more of these components, exceed the specified page, word, or budget limits, or that do not meet the eligibility requirements listed above will be administratively rejected without review. 8.3. Formatting Instructions Formatting guidelines for all submitted CPRIT applications are as follows: 1. Language: English. 2. Document Format: PDF only. 3. Font Type/Size: Arial (11 point), Calibri (11 point), or Times New Roman (12 point). 4. Line Spacing: Single. 5. Page Size: 8.5 x 11 inches. 6. Margins: 0.75 inch, all directions. 7. Color and High-Resolution Images: Images, graphs, figures, and other illustrations must be submitted as part of the appropriate submitted document. Applicants should include text to explain illustrations that may be difficult to interpret when printed in black and white. CPRIT RFA

R-21.1-RTA Research Training Awards Page 17 of 24 (Rev 1/31/20) 8. Scanning Resolution: Images and figures must be of lowest reasonable resolution that permits clarity and readability. Unnecessarily large files will NOT be accepted, especially those that include only text. 9. References: Applicants should use a citation style that includes the full name of the article and that lists at least the first 3 authors. Official journal abbreviations may be used. An example is included below; however, other citation styles meeting these parameters are also acceptable as long as the journal information is stated. Include URLs of publications referenced in the application. Smith, P.T., Doe, J., White, J.M., et al (2006). Elaborating on a novel mechanism for cancer progression. Journal of Cancer Research, 135: 45-67. 10. Internet URLs: Applicants are encouraged to provide the URLs of publications referenced in the application; however, applicants should not include URLs directing reviewers to websites containing additional information about the proposed research. 11. Headers and Footers: These should not be used unless they are part of a provided template. Page numbers may be included in the footer (see following point). 12. Page Numbering: Pages should be numbered at the bottom right corner of each page. 13. All attachments that require signatures must be filled out, printed, signed, scanned, and then uploaded in PDF format

**Closing Date**: 3 June

**Additional Information**: cpritgrants.org/

## Individual Investigator Research Awards for Cancer in Children and Adolescents (IIRACCA)

**Purpose**: Supports applications for innovative research projects addressing questions that will advance knowledge of the causes, prevention, progression, detection, or treatment of cancer in children and adolescents. Laboratory, clinical, or population-based studies are all acceptable. CPRIT expects the outcome of the research to reduce the incidence, morbidity, or mortality from cancer in children and/or adolescents in the near or long term. Competitive renewal applications accepted.

**Eligibility**: The applicant must be a Texas-based institution of higher education or a component of a university system with appropriately accredited degree-granting training programs (if support is requested for training leading to a degree). 1. The Principal Investigator (PI) must have a doctoral degree, including MD, PhD, DDS, DMD, DrPH, DO, DVM, or equivalent, and must be a full-time resident of Texas during the time the research that is the subject of the grant is conducted. 2. An institution may submit only 1 new or renewal application under this RFA during this funding cycle. An exception will be made for institutions submitting applications for cancer prevention training; in this case, institutions may submit 1 prevention training program application

and 1 additional application in another aspect of cancer research (new or renewal). 3. For the purposes of this RFA, an institution is defined as that component of a university system that has its own president. 4. There must be only 1 PI, but Co-PIs may direct individual components of the overall program described in the application. 5. An institution may apply for as many components of the training program as are appropriate for the institution. 6. An applicant is eligible to receive a grant award only if the applicant certifies that the applicant institution or organization, including the PI, any senior member or key personnel listed on the grant application, or any officer or director of the grant applicant's institution or organization (or any person related to 1 or more of these individuals within the second degree of consanguinity or affinity), has not made and will not make a contribution to CPRIT or to any foundation specifically created to benefit CPRIT. 7. An applicant is not eligible to receive a CPRIT grant award if the applicant PI, any senior member or key personnel listed on the grant application, or any officer or director of the grant applicant's organization or institution is related to a CPRIT Oversight Committee member. CPRIT RFA R-21.1-RTA Research Training Awards Page 10 of 24 (Rev 1/31/20) 8. The applicant must report whether the applicant institution or organization, the PI, or other individuals who contribute to the execution of the proposed project in a substantive, measurable way, whether or not those individuals are slated to receive salary or compensation under the grant award, are currently ineligible to receive federal grant funds or have had a grant terminated for cause within 5 years prior to the submission date of the grant application. 9. CPRIT grants will be awarded by contract to successful applicants. Certain contractual requirements are mandated by Texas law or by administrative rules. Although applicants need not demonstrate the ability to comply with these contractual requirements at the time the application is submitted, applicants should make themselves aware of these standards before submitting a grant application. Significant issues addressed by the CPRIT contract are listed in section 10 and section 11. All statutory provisions and relevant administrative rules can be found at www.cprit.state.tx.us.

**Level of Study**: Masters

**Type**: Scholarships

**Value**: Award: Up to US$300,000 per year in total costs. Applicants that plan on conducting a clinical trial as part of the project may request up to US$500,000 in total costs. Exceptions permitted if extremely well justified;

**Length of Study**: 4 years

**Country of Study**: US

**Application Procedure**: Each application must be accompanied by a letter of institutional support from the president or provost indicating support and commitment to the training program. The letter could include, but is not limited to, information about laboratory space, shared laboratory facilities and equipment, funds for curriculum development, support for additional trainees in the program, and initiatives to support recruitment of underrepresented minorities. A maximum of 3 pages may be provided. Applications that are missing 1 or more of these components, exceed the specified page, word, or budget limits, or that do not meet the eligibility requirements listed above will be administratively rejected without review. 8.3. Formatting Instructions Formatting guidelines for all submitted CPRIT applications are as follows: 1. Language: English. 2. Document Format: PDF only. 3. Font Type/Size: Arial (11 point), Calibri (11 point), or Times New Roman (12 point). 4. Line Spacing: Single. 5. Page Size: 8.5 x 11 inches. 6. Margins: 0.75 inch, all directions. 7. Color and High-Resolution Images: Images, graphs, figures, and other illustrations must be submitted as part of the appropriate submitted document. Applicants should include text to explain illustrations that may be difficult to interpret when printed in black and white. CPRIT RFA R-21.1-RTA Research Training Awards Page 17 of 24 (Rev 1/31/20) 8. Scanning Resolution: Images and figures must be of lowest reasonable resolution that permits clarity and readability. Unnecessarily large files will NOT be accepted, especially those that include only text. 9. References: Applicants should use a citation style that includes the full name of the article and that lists at least the first 3 authors. Official journal abbreviations may be used. An example is included below; however, other citation styles meeting these parameters are also acceptable as long as the journal information is stated. Include URLs of publications referenced in the application. Smith, P.T., Doe, J., White, J.M., et al (2006). Elaborating on a novel mechanism for cancer progression. Journal of Cancer Research, 135: 45-67. 10. Internet URLs: Applicants are encouraged to provide the URLs of publications referenced in the application; however, applicants should not include URLs directing reviewers to websites containing additional information about the proposed research. 11. Headers and Footers: These should not be used unless they are part of a provided template. Page numbers may be included in the footer (see following point). 12. Page Numbering: Pages should be numbered at the bottom right corner of each page. 13. All attachments that require signatures must be filled out, printed, signed, scanned, and then uploaded in PDF format

**Closing Date**: 3 June

**Additional Information**: cpritgrants.org/

## Individual Investigator Research Awards for Clinical Translation (IIRACT)

**Purpose**: Supports applications which propose innovative clinical studies that are hypothesis driven and involve patients enrolled prospectively on a clinical trial or involve analyses of biospecimens from patients enrolled on a completed trial for which the outcomes are known. Areas of interest include clinical studies of new or repurposed drugs, hormonal therapies, immune therapies, surgery, radiation therapy, stem cell transplantation, combinations of interventions, or therapeutic devices.

**Eligibility**: The applicant must be a Texas-based institution of higher education or a component of a university system with appropriately accredited degree-granting training programs (if support is requested for training leading to a degree). 1. The Principal Investigator (PI) must have a doctoral degree, including MD, PhD, DDS, DMD, DrPH, DO, DVM, or equivalent, and must be a full-time resident of Texas during the time the research that is the subject of the grant is conducted. 2. An institution may submit only 1 new or renewal application under this RFA during this funding cycle. An exception will be made for institutions submitting applications for cancer prevention training; in this case, institutions may submit 1 prevention training program application and 1 additional application in another aspect of cancer research (new or renewal). 3. For the purposes of this RFA, an institution is defined as that component of a university system that has its own president. 4. There must be only 1 PI, but Co-PIs may direct individual components of the overall program described in the application. 5. An institution may apply for as many components of the training program as are appropriate for the institution. 6. An applicant is eligible to receive a grant award only if the applicant certifies that the applicant institution or organization, including the PI, any senior member or key personnel listed on the grant application, or any officer or director of the grant applicant's institution or organization (or any person related to 1 or more of these individuals within the second degree of consanguinity or affinity), has not made and will not make a contribution to CPRIT or to any foundation specifically created to benefit CPRIT. 7. An applicant is not eligible to receive a CPRIT grant award if the applicant PI, any senior member or key personnel listed on the grant application, or any officer or director of the grant applicant's organization or institution is related to a CPRIT Oversight Committee member. CPRIT RFA R-21.1-RTA Research Training Awards Page 10 of 24 (Rev 1/31/20) 8. The applicant must report whether the applicant institution or organization, the PI, or other individuals who contribute to the execution of the proposed project in a substantive, measurable way, whether or not those individuals are slated to receive salary or compensation under the grant award, are currently ineligible to receive federal grant funds or have had a grant terminated for cause within 5 years prior to the submission date of the grant application. 9. CPRIT grants will be awarded by contract to successful applicants. Certain contractual requirements are mandated by Texas law or by administrative rules. Although applicants need not demonstrate the ability to comply with these contractual requirements at the time the application is submitted, applicants should make themselves aware of these standards before submitting a grant application. Significant issues addressed by the CPRIT contract are listed in section 10 and section 11. All statutory provisions and relevant administrative rules can be found at www.cprit.state.tx.us.

**Level of Study**: Masters

**Type**: Scholarships

**Value**: Award: Up to US$400,000 per year in total costs. Maximum duration: 3 years. Applicants that plan on conducting a clinical trial as part of the project may request up to US$600,000 in total costs and a maximum duration of 4 years. Exceptions permitted if extremely well justified.

**Length of Study**: 3-4 years

**Country of Study**: US

**Application Procedure**: Each application must be accompanied by a letter of institutional support from the president or provost indicating support and commitment to the training program. The letter could include, but is not limited to, information about laboratory space, shared laboratory facilities and equipment, funds for curriculum development, support for additional trainees in the program, and initiatives to support recruitment of underrepresented minorities. A maximum of 3 pages may be provided. Applications that are missing 1 or more of these components, exceed the specified page, word, or budget limits, or that do not meet the eligibility requirements listed above will be administratively rejected without review. 8.3. Formatting Instructions Formatting guidelines for all submitted CPRIT applications are as follows: 1. Language: English. 2. Document Format: PDF only. 3. Font Type/Size: Arial (11 point), Calibri (11 point), or Times New Roman (12 point). 4. Line Spacing: Single. 5. Page Size: 8.5 x 11 inches. 6. Margins: 0.75 inch, all directions. 7. Color and High-Resolution Images: Images, graphs, figures, and other illustrations must be submitted as part of the appropriate submitted document. Applicants should include text to explain illustrations that may be difficult to interpret when printed in black and white. CPRIT RFA R-21.1-RTA Research Training Awards Page 17 of 24 (Rev 1/31/20) 8. Scanning Resolution: Images and figures must be of lowest reasonable resolution that permits clarity and readability. Unnecessarily large files will NOT be accepted, especially those that include only text. 9. References: Applicants should use a citation style that includes the full name of the article and that lists at least the first 3 authors. Official journal abbreviations may be used. An example is included below; however, other citation styles meeting these parameters are also acceptable as long as the journal information is stated. Include URLs of publications referenced in the application. Smith, P.T., Doe, J., White, J.M., et al (2006). Elaborating on a novel mechanism for cancer progression. Journal of Cancer Research, 135: 45-67. 10. Internet URLs: Applicants are encouraged to provide the URLs of publications referenced in the application; however, applicants should not include URLs directing reviewers to websites containing additional information about the proposed research. 11. Headers and Footers: These should not be used unless they are part of a provided template. Page numbers may be included in the footer (see following point). 12. Page Numbering: Pages should be numbered at the bottom right corner of each page. 13. All attachments that require signatures must be filled out, printed, signed, scanned, and then uploaded in PDF format

**Closing Date**: 3 June

**Additional Information**: cpritgrants.org/

## Individual Investigator Research Awards for Computational Systems Biology of Cancer (IIRACSBC)

**Purpose**: Supports applications for innovative mathematical and/or computational research projects addressing questions that will advance current knowledge in the (a) mechanisms that tie altered gene expression and downstream molecular mechanisms to functional cancer phenotypes and/or (b) mechanisms that tie tumor morphology to functional cancer phenotypes, and/or (c) mechanisms that tie treatment sequence and combination to evolving functional cancer phenotypes (that emerge as a result of treatment selection). Broadly speaking, functional cancer phenotypes include migratory, proliferative, metabolic and resistant cancer cell phenotypes. Partnering of mathematical or computational scientists with cancer biologists or oncologists is highly recommended to form a truly interdisciplinary team that can both develop and validate models leading to a deeper integrated understanding of cancer progression and treatment.

**Eligibility**: The applicant must be a Texas-based institution of higher education or a component of a university system with appropriately accredited degree-granting training programs (if support is requested for training leading to a degree). 1. The Principal Investigator (PI) must have a doctoral degree, including MD, PhD, DDS, DMD, DrPH, DO, DVM, or equivalent, and must be a full-time resident of Texas during the time the research that is the subject of the grant is conducted. 2. An institution may submit only 1 new or renewal application under this RFA during this funding cycle. An exception will be made for institutions submitting applications for cancer prevention training; in this case, institutions may submit 1 prevention training program application and 1 additional application in another aspect of cancer research (new or renewal). 3. For the purposes of this RFA, an institution is defined as that component of a university system that has its own president. 4. There must be only 1 PI, but Co-PIs may direct individual components of the overall program described in the application. 5. An institution may apply for as many components of the training program as are appropriate for the institution. 6. An applicant is eligible to receive a grant award only if the applicant certifies that the applicant institution or organization, including the PI, any senior member or key personnel listed on the grant application, or any officer or director of the grant applicant's institution or organization (or any person related to 1 or more of these individuals within the second degree of consanguinity or affinity), has not made and will not make a contribution to CPRIT or to any foundation specifically created to benefit CPRIT. 7. An applicant is not eligible to receive a CPRIT grant award if the applicant PI, any senior member or key personnel listed on the grant application, or any officer or director of the grant applicant's organization or institution is related to a CPRIT Oversight Committee member. CPRIT RFA R-21.1-RTA Research Training Awards Page 10 of 24 (Rev 1/31/20) 8. The applicant must report whether the applicant institution or organization, the PI, or other individuals who contribute to the execution of the proposed project in a substantive, measurable way, whether or not those individuals are slated to receive salary or compensation under the grant award, are currently ineligible to receive federal grant funds or have had a grant terminated for cause within 5 years prior to the submission date of the grant application. 9. CPRIT grants will be awarded by contract to successful applicants. Certain contractual requirements are mandated by Texas law or by administrative rules. Although applicants need not demonstrate the ability to comply with these contractual requirements at the time the application is submitted, applicants should make themselves aware of these standards before submitting a grant application. Significant issues addressed by the CPRIT contract are listed in section 10 and section 11. All statutory provisions and relevant administrative rules can be found at www.cprit.state.tx.us.

**Level of Study**: Masters

**Type**: Scholarships

**Value**: Award: Up to US$400,000 per year in total costs. Exceptions permitted if extremely well justified

**Length of Study**: 3 years

**Country of Study**: US

**Application Procedure**: Each application must be accompanied by a letter of institutional support from the president or provost indicating support and commitment to the training program. The letter could include, but is not limited to, information about laboratory space, shared laboratory facilities and equipment, funds for curriculum development, support for additional trainees in the program, and initiatives to support recruitment of underrepresented minorities. A maximum of 3 pages may be provided. Applications that are missing 1 or more of these components, exceed the specified page, word, or budget limits, or that do not meet the eligibility requirements listed above will be administratively rejected without review. 8.3. Formatting Instructions Formatting guidelines for all submitted CPRIT applications are as follows: 1. Language: English. 2. Document Format: PDF

only. 3. Font Type/Size: Arial (11 point), Calibri (11 point), or Times New Roman (12 point). 4. Line Spacing: Single. 5. Page Size: 8.5 x 11 inches. 6. Margins: 0.75 inch, all directions. 7. Color and High-Resolution Images: Images, graphs, figures, and other illustrations must be submitted as part of the appropriate submitted document. Applicants should include text to explain illustrations that may be difficult to interpret when printed in black and white. CPRIT RFA R-21.1-RTA Research Training Awards Page 17 of 24 (Rev 1/31/20) 8. Scanning Resolution: Images and figures must be of lowest reasonable resolution that permits clarity and readability. Unnecessarily large files will NOT be accepted, especially those that include only text. 9. References: Applicants should use a citation style that includes the full name of the article and that lists at least the first 3 authors. Official journal abbreviations may be used. An example is included below; however, other citation styles meeting these parameters are also acceptable as long as the journal information is stated. Include URLs of publications referenced in the application. Smith, P.T., Doe, J., White, J.M., et al (2006). Elaborating on a novel mechanism for cancer progression. Journal of Cancer Research, 135: 45-67. 10. Internet URLs: Applicants are encouraged to provide the URLs of publications referenced in the application; however, applicants should not include URLs directing reviewers to websites containing additional information about the proposed research. 11. Headers and Footers: These should not be used unless they are part of a provided template. Page numbers may be included in the footer (see following point). 12. Page Numbering: Pages should be numbered at the bottom right corner of each page. 13. All attachments that require signatures must be filled out, printed, signed, scanned, and then uploaded in PDF format

**Closing Date**: 3 June

**Additional Information**: cpritgrants.org/

## Individual Investigator Research Awards for Prevention and Early Detection (IIRAP)

**Purpose**: Supports applications for innovative research projects addressing questions that will advance knowledge of the causes, prevention, early-stage progression, and/or early detection of cancer. Research may be laboratory-, clinical-, or population- based, and may include behavioral/intervention, dissemination or health services/outcomes research to reduce cancer incidence or promote early detection. Competitive renewal applications accepted.

**Eligibility**: The applicant must be a Texas-based institution of higher education or a component of a university system with appropriately accredited degree-granting training programs (if support is requested for training leading to a degree). 1. The Principal Investigator (PI) must have a doctoral degree, including MD, PhD, DDS, DMD, DrPH, DO, DVM, or equivalent, and must be a full-time resident of Texas during the time the research that is the subject of the grant is conducted. 2. An institution may submit only 1 new or renewal application under this RFA during this funding cycle. An exception will be made for institutions submitting applications for cancer prevention training; in this case, institutions may submit 1 prevention training program application and 1 additional application in another aspect of cancer research (new or renewal). 3. For the purposes of this RFA, an institution is defined as that component of a university system that has its own president. 4. There must be only 1 PI, but Co-PIs may direct individual components of the overall program described in the application. 5. An institution may apply for as many components of the training program as are appropriate for the institution. 6. An applicant is eligible to receive a grant award only if the applicant certifies that the applicant institution or organization, including the PI, any senior member or key personnel listed on the grant application, or any officer or director of the grant applicant's institution or organization (or any person related to 1 or more of these individuals within the second degree of consanguinity or affinity), has not made and will not make a contribution to CPRIT or to any foundation specifically created to benefit CPRIT. 7. An applicant is not eligible to receive a CPRIT grant award if the applicant PI, any senior member or key personnel listed on the grant application, or any officer or director of the grant applicant's organization or institution is related to a CPRIT Oversight Committee member. CPRIT RFA R-21.1-RTA Research Training Awards Page 10 of 24 (Rev 1/31/20) 8. The applicant must report whether the applicant institution or organization, the PI, or other individuals who contribute to the execution of the proposed project in a substantive, measurable way, whether or not those individuals are slated to receive salary or compensation under the grant award, are currently ineligible to receive federal grant funds or have had a grant terminated for cause within 5 years prior to the submission date of the grant application. 9. CPRIT grants will be awarded by contract to successful applicants. Certain contractual requirements are mandated by Texas law or by administrative rules. Although applicants need not demonstrate the ability to comply with these contractual requirements at the time the application is submitted, applicants should make themselves aware of these standards before submitting a grant application. Significant issues addressed by the CPRIT contract are listed in section 10 and section 11. All statutory provisions and relevant administrative rules can be found at www.cprit.state.tx.us.

**Level of Study**: Masters

**Type**: Scholarships

**Value**: Award: Up to of US$300,000 per year in total costs for up to 3 years for laboratory and clinical research; Up to US$500,000 per year in total costs for 4 years for population-based research, including implementation research designed to accelerate the adoption and deployment of sustainable, evidence-based cancer prevention and screening interventions at multiple levels and in different clinical and community settings. Exceptions permitted if extremely well justified

**Length of Study**: maximum duration: 3 years for laboratory and clinical research and 4 years for population-based research.

**Country of Study**: US

**Application Procedure**: Each application must be accompanied by a letter of institutional support from the president or provost indicating support and commitment to the training program. The letter could include, but is not limited to, information about laboratory space, shared laboratory facilities and equipment, funds for curriculum development, support for additional trainees in the program, and initiatives to support recruitment of underrepresented minorities. A maximum of 3 pages may be provided. Applications that are missing 1 or more of these components, exceed the specified page, word, or budget limits, or that do not meet the eligibility requirements listed above will be administratively rejected without review. 8.3. Formatting Instructions Formatting guidelines for all submitted CPRIT applications are as follows: 1. Language: English. 2. Document Format: PDF only. 3. Font Type/Size: Arial (11 point), Calibri (11 point), or Times New Roman (12 point). 4. Line Spacing: Single. 5. Page Size: 8.5 x 11 inches. 6. Margins: 0.75 inch, all directions. 7. Color and High-Resolution Images: Images, graphs, figures, and other illustrations must be submitted as part of the appropriate submitted document. Applicants should include text to explain illustrations that may be difficult to interpret when printed in black and white. CPRIT RFA R-21.1-RTA Research Training Awards Page 17 of 24 (Rev 1/31/20) 8. Scanning Resolution: Images and figures must be of lowest reasonable resolution that permits clarity and readability. Unnecessarily large files will NOT be accepted, especially those that include only text. 9. References: Applicants should use a citation style that includes the full name of the article and that lists at least the first 3 authors. Official journal abbreviations may be used. An example is included below; however, other citation styles meeting these parameters are also acceptable as long as the journal information is stated. Include URLs of publications referenced in the application. Smith, P.T., Doe, J., White, J.M., et al (2006). Elaborating on a novel mechanism for cancer progression. Journal of Cancer Research, 135: 45-67. 10. Internet URLs: Applicants are encouraged to provide the URLs of publications referenced in the application; however, applicants should not include URLs directing reviewers to websites containing additional information about the proposed research. 11. Headers and Footers: These should not be used unless they are part of a provided template. Page numbers may be included in the footer (see following point). 12. Page Numbering: Pages

should be numbered at the bottom right corner of each page. 13. All attachments that require signatures must be filled out, printed, signed, scanned, and then uploaded in PDF format
**Closing Date**: 3 June
**Additional Information**: cpritgrants.org/

## Research Training Awards (RTA)

**Purpose**: Supports applications for integrated institutional research training programs to support promising individuals who seek specialized training in the area of cancer research. Successful applicant institutions are expected to provide trainees with broad access to research opportunities across disciplinary lines and to maintain high standards for intellectual rigor and creativity.

**Eligibility**: The applicant must be a Texas-based institution of higher education or a component of a university system with appropriately accredited degree-granting training programs (if support is requested for training leading to a degree). 1. The Principal Investigator (PI) must have a doctoral degree, including MD, PhD, DDS, DMD, DrPH, DO, DVM, or equivalent, and must be a full-time resident of Texas during the time the research that is the subject of the grant is conducted. 2. An institution may submit only 1 new or renewal application under this RFA during this funding cycle. An exception will be made for institutions submitting applications for cancer prevention training; in this case, institutions may submit 1 prevention traininga program application and 1 additional application in another aspect of cancer research (new or renewal). 3. For the purposes of this RFA, an institution is defined as that component of a university system that has its own president. 4. There must be only 1 PI, but Co-PIs may direct individual components of the overall program described in the application. 5. An institution may apply for as many components of the training program as are appropriate for the institution. 6. An applicant is eligible to receive a grant award only if the applicant certifies that the applicant institution or organization, including the PI, any senior member or key personnel listed on the grant application, or any officer or director of the grant applicant's institution or organization (or any person related to 1 or more of these individuals within the second degree of consanguinity or affinity), has not made and will not make a contribution to CPRIT or to any foundation specifically created to benefit CPRIT. 7. An applicant is not eligible to receive a CPRIT grant award if the applicant PI, any senior member or key personnel listed on the grant application, or any officer or director of the grant applicant's organization or institution is related to a CPRIT Oversight Committee member. CPRIT RFA R-21.1-RTA Research Training Awards Page 10 of 24 (Rev 1/31/20) 8. The applicant must report whether the applicant institution or organization, the PI, or other individuals who contribute to the execution of

the proposed project in a substantive, measurable way, whether or not those individuals are slated to receive salary or compensation under the grant award, are currently ineligible to receive federal grant funds or have had a grant terminated for cause within 5 years prior to the submission date of the grant application. 9. CPRIT grants will be awarded by contract to successful applicants. Certain contractual requirements are mandated by Texas law or by administrative rules. Although applicants need not demonstrate the ability to comply with these contractual requirements at the time the application is submitted, applicants should make themselves aware of these standards before submitting a grant application. Significant issues addressed by the CPRIT contract are listed in section 10 and section 11. All statutory provisions and relevant administrative rules can be found at www.cprit.state.tx.us.

**Level of Study**: Masters
**Type**: Scholarships
**Value**: Up to US$800,000 per year in total costs
**Length of Study**: 5 years
**Country of Study**: US
**Application Procedure**: Each application must be accompanied by a letter of institutional support from the president or provost indicating support and commitment to the training program. The letter could include, but is not limited to, information about laboratory space, shared laboratory facilities and equipment, funds for curriculum development, support for additional trainees in the program, and initiatives to support recruitment of underrepresented minorities. A maximum of 3 pages may be provided. Applications that are missing 1 or more of these components, exceed the specified page, word, or budget limits, or that do not meet the eligibility requirements listed above will be administratively rejected without review. 8.3. Formatting Instructions Formatting guidelines for all submitted CPRIT applications are as follows: 1. Language: English. 2. Document Format: PDF only. 3. Font Type/Size: Arial (11 point), Calibri (11 point), or Times New Roman (12 point). 4. Line Spacing: Single. 5. Page Size: 8.5 x 11 inches. 6. Margins: 0.75 inch, all directions. 7. Color and High-Resolution Images: Images, graphs, figures, and other illustrations must be submitted as part of the appropriate submitted document. Applicants should include text to explain illustrations that may be difficult to interpret when printed in black and white. CPRIT RFA R-21.1-RTA Research Training Awards Page 17 of 24 (Rev 1/31/20) 1. Scanning Resolution: Images and figures must be of lowest reasonable resolution that permits clarity and readability. Unnecessarily large files will NOT be accepted, especially those that include only text. 2. References: Applicants should use a citation style that includes the full name of the article and that lists at least the first 3 authors. Official journal abbreviations may be used. An example is included below; however, other citation styles meeting these parameters are

also acceptable as long as the journal information is stated. Include URLs of publications referenced in the application. Smith, P.T., Doe, J., White, J.M., et al (2006). Elaborating on a novel mechanism for cancer progression. Journal of Cancer Research, 135: 45-67. 3. Internet URLs: Applicants are encouraged to provide the URLs of publications referenced in the application; however, applicants should not include URLs directing reviewers to websites containing additional information about the proposed research. 4. Headers and Footers: These should not be used unless they are part of a provided template. Page numbers may be included in the footer (see following point). 5. Page Numbering: Pages should be numbered at the bottom right corner of each page. 6. All attachments that require signatures must be filled out, printed, signed, scanned, and then uploaded in PDF format

**Closing Date**: 3 June

**Additional Information**: cpritgrants.org/

## Cancer Research Fund of the Damon Runyon-Walter Winchell Foundation

Fellowship Department, 131 East 36th Street, New York, NY 10016, United States of America.

**Tel**:        (1) 212 532 3888
**Email**:     drwwfellow@aol.com
**Contact**:   Ms Clare M Cahill, Assistant to the Director

### Cancer Research Fund of the Damon Runyon - Walter Winchell Foundation Research Fellowships for Physician Scientists

**Purpose**: To augment the training of a physician scientist who has demonstrated the motivation and potential to conduct original research under the supervision of a sponsor, thus, equipping the Fellow to become an independent investigator
**Eligibility**: Applicants must have completed at least one of the following degrees or its equivalent: MD, PhD, DDS, DVM, and have completed their residencies or clinical fellowship training within three years prior to the Scientific Advisory Committee meeting at which their applications are to be considered
**Level of Study**: Postdoctorate
**Type**: Fellowship
**Value**: US$46,500 stipend for the first year, US$47,500 for the second year and US$49,000 for the third year. In addition, US$2,000 expenses is awarded annually
**Length of Study**: 3 years, renewable annually

**Frequency**: 3 times each year
**Study Establishment**: An approved institution under a sponsor
**Country of Study**: Other
**Application Procedure**: Application form must be completed
**No. of awards offered**: 700
**Closing Date**: November
**No. of awards given last year**: 45
**No. of applicants last year**: 700

**For further information contact:**

**Email**:    awards@damonrunyon.org

### Damon Runyon Clinical Investigator Award

**Purpose**: The Damon Runyon Clinical Investigator Award supports early career physician-scientists conducting patient-oriented research. The goal of this innovative program is to increase the number of physicians capable of moving seamlessly between the laboratory and the patient's bedside in search of breakthrough treatments. Damon Runyon Clinical Investigators are eligible to apply for Continuation Grants in the final year of their award.
**Eligibility**: Applicants must have completed at least one of the following degrees or its equivalent: MD, PhD, DDS, DVM, and have completed their residencies or clinical fellowship training within three years prior to the Scientific Advisory Committee meeting at which their applications are to be considered
**Level of Study**: Postdoctorate
**Type**: Award
**Value**: US$46,500 stipend for the first year, US$47,500 for the second year and US$49,000 for the third year. In addition, US$2,000 expenses is awarded annually
**Closing Date**: November

**For further information contact:**

**Email**:    awards@damonrunyon.org

## Cancer Research Institute

681 Fifth Avenue, New York, NY 10022-2707, United States of America.

**Email**:     info@cancerresearch.org
**Website**:   www.cancerresearch.org
**Contact**:   Grants Enquiries

## Cancer Research Institute Irvington Postdoctoral Fellowship Program

**Purpose**: The CRI Irvington Postdoctoral Fellowship Program supports qualified young scientists at leading universities and research centers around the world who wish to receive training in fundamental immunology or cancer immunology

**Eligibility**: Applicants for the CRI Irvington Postdoctoral Fellowship Program must be working in areas directly related to immunology or cancer immunology. An eligible project must fall into the broad field of immunology with relevance to solving the cancer problem. Applicants must have a doctoral degree by the date of award activation and must conduct their proposed research under a sponsor who holds a formal appointment at the host institution. Applicants with 5 or more years of relevant postdoctoral experience are not eligible, with the exception of M.D. applicants, who should not include years of residency in this calculation. Only in exceptional circumstances will applicants who have already spent 3 or more years in a sponsor's laboratory by the start date of fellowship be considered for a fellowship award. The fellowship can be performed in the United States or abroad, but must take place at a non-profit institution. There are no citizenship restrictions. Only one fellow per sponsor may apply per application round, and faculty sponsors may not have more than three CRI-supported fellows at any time

**Level of Study**: Doctorate, Postdoctorate

**Type**: Fellowships

**Value**: US$175,500

**Length of Study**: 3 years

**Frequency**: Twice a year

**Country of Study**: Any country

**Application Procedure**: The application deadlines are April 1 and October 1; when those dates fall on the weekend, applications are due the following Monday. Applications are due by 5 p.m. Eastern Time on these dates. Applicants are notified of fellowship committee decisions within approximately 10–12 weeks of the application deadline. Fellowships can be activated three months after the application deadline but no later than one year following the deadline. Awards activate on the first of the month

**No. of awards offered**: 400

**Closing Date**: 1 April

**Funding**: Private, Individuals

**No. of awards given last year**: 35

**No. of applicants last year**: 400

**Additional Information**: www.biotecnika.org/2019/01/cancer-research-institute-irvington/

### For further information contact:

29 Broadway, 4th fl, New York, NY 10006, United States of America.

**Tel**: (1) 212 688 7515
**Email**: grants@cancerresearch.org

## Clinical and Laboratory Integration Program

**Purpose**: The Cancer Research Institute funds research aimed at furthering the development of immunological approaches to the diagnosis, treatment, and prevention of cancer. The Institute's mission is to bring effective immune system-based therapies to cancer patients sooner. To this end, CRI offers its Clinic and Laboratory Integration Program (CLIP) Grants to qualified scientists who are working to explore clinically relevant questions aimed at improving the effectiveness of cancer immunotherapies. The program supports pre-clinical and translational research that can be directly applied to optimizing cancer immunotherapy in the clinic

**Type**: Grant

**Country of Study**: Africa

**Additional Information**: researchfunding.duke.edu/clinic-and-laboratory-integration-program-clip

### For further information contact:

**Email**: grants@cancerresearch.org

## Lloyd J. Old STAR Program

**Purpose**: The Lloyd J. Old STAR Program provides grants of US$1.25 million over 5 years to mid-career scientists. This long-term funding will not be tied to a specific research project, but rather will aim to provide a degree of flexibility and freedom for investigators to explore out-of-the-box and disruptive avenues of research. Candidates selected for this award are expected to be future "stars" in the field of cancer immunology: Scientists Taking Risks

**Eligibility**: Mid-career scientists: tenure-track assistant professors (minimum 3 years) and associate professors (maximum 3 years)

**Level of Study**: Research

**Type**: Grant

**Value**: US$1,250,000

**Length of Study**: 5 years

**Frequency**: Annual

**Country of Study**: Any country

**Application Procedure**: The deadline for the receipt of applications is 1 March. Candidates will be notified in early May whether or not they have been invited to the Cancer Research Institute in New York City for an interview. All invited applicants must be available for an in-person interview with members of CRI's Scientific Advisory Council. The earliest an award can activate is 1 July. Awards must activate on the first of the month

**Closing Date**: 1 January

**Funding**: Private, Foundation, Individuals

**Additional Information**: researchfunding.duke.edu/lloyd-j-old-star-program

## Technology Impact Award

**Purpose**: The Cancer Research Institute Technology Impact Award provides seed funding of up to US$200,000 to be used over 12–24 months to address the gap between technology development and clinical application of cancer immunotherapies. These grants aim to encourage collaboration between technology developers and clinical cancer immunologists and to generate the proof-of-principle of a novel platform technology in bioinformatics, ex vivo or in silico modeling systems, immunological or tumor profiling instrumentation, methods, reagents and assays, or other relevant technologies that can enable clinician scientists to generate deeper insights into the mechanisms of action of effective or ineffective cancer immunotherapies

**Eligibility**: Applicants must hold a faculty appointment as a tenure-track assistant professor (or higher rank) at the time of award activation. The grant will be awarded to a scientist who describes an extraordinarily novel, yet practical research plan that is creative and technically sophisticated. Joint submissions from collaborators will also be considered. (The collaborators will share the award.) Each collaborator must meet the eligibility criteria

**Level of Study**: Research

**Type**: Grant

**Frequency**: Annual

**Country of Study**: Any country

**Application Procedure**: Letters of Intent describing the research plan will be submitted electronically by November 15. Selected applicants will be invited to submit a full research proposal with a submission deadline of March 15. Award winners will be announced on or around June 30. Successful applicants will have their project reviewed at 12 and 24 months

**No. of awards offered**: 100

**Closing Date**: 15 November

**Funding**: Private, Corporation, Foundation, Trusts, Individuals

**No. of awards given last year**: 5

**No. of applicants last year**: 100

**Additional Information**: www.cancerresearch.org/scientists/fellowships-grants/technology-impact-award

### For further information contact:

**Email**:    grants@cancerresearch.org

## Cancer Research United Kingdom

London Research Institute, PO Box 123, Lincoln's Inn Fields, London, WC2A 3PX, United Kingdom.

**Tel**:           (44) 20 7269 3609
**Website**:     www.cancerresearch.org
**Contact**:     Mrs Yvonne Harman, Graduate Programme Administrator

Cancer Research United Kingdom London Research Institute is part of CR-United Kingdom, which is a registered United Kingdom charity dedicated to saving lives through research into the causes, prevention, treatment and cure of cancer.

## Cancer Research United Kingdom LRI Graduate Studentships

**Purpose**: To enable research training

**Eligibility**: Open to candidates who have normally been resident in the United Kingdom for more than 3 years and have obtained, or are about to obtain, a First or Upper Second Class (Honours) Degree in science. Applicants must also be aged 25 years or younger. Non-residents are not excluded from consideration

**Level of Study**: Doctorate

**Type**: Studentship

**Value**: Approx. United Kingdom £13,701–14,821 per year, depending on location

**Length of Study**: 3 years

**Frequency**: Annual

**Study Establishment**: Cancer Research United Kingdom LRI laboratories

**Country of Study**: United Kingdom

**Application Procedure**: Applicants must refer to the advertisements that list procedure information.

### For further information contact:

**Email**:    eric.eve@hmc.ox.ac.uk

# Cancer Research United Kingdom Manchester Institute

The University of Manchester, Wilmslow Road, Manchester, M20 4BX, United Kingdom.

| | |
|---|---|
| **Tel**: | (44) 16 1446 3156 |
| **Email**: | enquiries@cruk.manchester.ac.uk |
| **Website**: | www.cruk.manchester.ac.uk |

The CRUK Manchester Institute is a leading cancer research institute within The University of Manchester

## 4-Year Studentship

**Purpose**: To support study towards a PhD.

**Eligibility**: Open to candidates who have obtained a First or Second Class (Honours) Bachelor of Science Degree. International First or 2.1 degree equivalent in biological science, medicine, or related subject

**Level of Study**: Doctorate, Postgraduate

**Type**: Studentship

**Value**: £19,000 as stipend per year, university fees and bench fees

**Length of Study**: 4 years

**Frequency**: Annual

**Study Establishment**: The University of Manchester

**Country of Study**: United Kingdom

**Application Procedure**: Please visit www.cruk.manchester.ac.uk

**No. of awards offered**: 343

**Funding**: Private

**Contributor**: Cancer Research United Kingdom

**No. of awards given last year**: 5

**No. of applicants last year**: 343

**Additional Information**: All positions are advertised on the website. Self-funded students are accepted subject to qualifications and 3-year funding. Please use application form, available at website wellcome.ac.uk/funding/schemes/four-year-phd-programmes-studentships-basic-scientists

### For further information contact:

Oglesby Building, 555 Wilmslow Rd, Manchester, M20 4G, United Kingdom.

| | |
|---|---|
| **Email**: | pgt@cruk.manchester.ac.uk |

# Canon Collins Trust

22 The Ivories, 6 Northampton Street, London, N1 2HY, United Kingdom.

| | |
|---|---|
| **Tel**: | (44) 20 7354 1462 |
| **Email**: | info@canoncollins.org.uk |
| **Website**: | www.canoncollins.org.uk |
| **Contact**: | Victoria Reed, Scholarships Officer |

We believe that southern Africa's development depends on strong leadership in key fields. Our scholars are outstanding academics and professionals who are dedicated to the development of their countries. We seek to invest in those who share our commitment to social justice and who can demonstrate their intention to return to their home countries after their study.

## Canon Collins Scholarship for Distance Learning Master of Laws (LLM)

**Purpose**: This scholarship allows the individual to study for the Postgraduate certificate, Post graduate diploma and Master of laws

**Eligibility**: Applicants for this scholarship must be a national of South Africa, Malawi, Zimbabwe or Zambia, normally resident in one of these four countries

**Frequency**: Annual

**Country of Study**: United Kingdom

**Application Procedure**: Check website for more details

**Closing Date**: 11 January

**Funding**: Trusts

**Additional Information**: scholarship-positions.com/canon-collins-scholarship-distance-learning-master-laws-llm-program-uk-2015/2015/05/13/

# Canterbury Christ Church, University College, Graduate School

North Holmes Road, Canterbury, CT1 1QU, United Kingdom.

| | |
|---|---|
| **Tel**: | (44) 1227 767 700 |
| **Email**: | research@cant.ac.uk |
| **Website**: | www.cant.ac.uk |
| **Contact**: | Miss Ashleigh Stuart, Research Secretary |

## Faculty PhD Scholarships

**Purpose**: Scholarships are available for doctoral projects which fall within the main research priorities of the University (healthcare and medicine; education; science and technology; creative and digital arts; business, the economy and policy) and within one of our four Faculties (Arts and Humanities, Education, Health and Wellbeing, Social and Applied Sciences).
**Level of Study**: Postgraduate
**Type**: Scholarship
**Value**: (a stipend of £13,000 p.a., tuition fee waiver for three years and an expense allowance of £500 p. a.).
**Length of Study**: 4 year
**Closing Date**: 17 April
**Additional Information**: www.canterbury.ac.uk/study-here/postgraduate-research/funding-for-research-degrees.aspx

### For further information contact:

**Email**:   lynn.revell@canterbury.ac.uk

## L.B. Wood Travelling Scholarship

**Purpose**: This scholarship is available to all graduates from any university in New Zealand, from any faculty providing that the application for the scholarship is made within three years from the date of graduation. The scholarship is offered as a supplement to some other postgraduate scholarships held for the purpose of study in Great Britain
**Eligibility**: 1. be graduates of or graduating from a New Zealand university 2. apply for the scholarship within three years from the date of their graduation 3. have applied for or been awarded another postgraduate scholarship.
**Level of Study**: Postgraduate
**Type**: Scholarship
**Value**: US$3,000
**Length of Study**: 3 year
**Frequency**: Annual
**Country of Study**: Any country
**Application Procedure**: 1. Check your eligibility. 2. Read the Regulations 3. Applications must be done online. A link to the application website is available here: universitiesnz. communityforce.com/
**Closing Date**: 1 April
**Funding**: Foundation
**Additional Information**: www.canterbury.ac.nz/scholarship search/ScholarshipDetails.aspx?ScholarshipID=6935.167

### For further information contact:

**Email**:   scholarships-cf@universitiesnz.ac.nz

## Lawson Robinson Hawke's Bay A&P Scholarship

**Purpose**: The Lawson Robinson Hawke's Bay A&P Scholarship aims to recognise outstanding academic and leadership qualities in a student currently enrolled in a full time land based programme. Applicants should have a familial association with Hawke's Bay
**Eligibility**: New Zealand Citizen or Permanent Resident Students
**Level of Study**: Postgraduate
**Type**: Scholarship
**Value**: US$3,000
**Length of Study**: 1 year
**Frequency**: Varies
**Country of Study**: Any country
**Application Procedure**: Apply online
**Closing Date**: 28 February
**Funding**: Foundation
**Additional Information**: www.wgtn.ac.nz/scholarships/current/lawson-robinson-hawkes-bay-a-and-p-scholarship

### For further information contact:

**Email**:   awards@showgroundshb.co.nz

## Canterbury Historical Association

History Department, University of Canterbury, Private Bag 4800, Christchurch 8140, New Zealand.

**Tel**:          (64) 3 364 2555
**Email**:      david.monger@canterbury.ac.nz
**Website**:   www.hums.canterbury.ac.nz/hist/
**Contact**:   Mrs Lynn McClelland, Director of Student Services and Communications

The Canterbury Historical Association (founded 1922, but in recess between 1940 and 1953) aims to foster public interest in all fields of history by holding meetings for the discussion of historical issues, and to promote historical research and writing through its administration of the J M Sherrard Award in New Zealand local and regional history.

## Anne Reid Memorial Trust Scholarship

**Purpose**: The scholarship commemorates Anne Reid of Blenheim/Christchurch/Singapore/Auckland who studied and taught at the University of Canterbury and The National University of Singapore. The purpose of this scholarship is to assist a graduate student from either the University of Canterbury or the University of Auckland overseas in an environment that encourages the completion of a course or work in progress, or the undertaking of further training in a recognised institution

**Level of Study**: Postgraduate
**Type**: Scholarship
**Value**: NZ$20,000
**Length of Study**: 1 year
**Frequency**: Annual
**Country of Study**: New Zealand
**Application Procedure**: Apply online
**Closing Date**: 30 April
**Funding**: Trusts
**Additional Information**: www.auckland.ac.nz/en/study/scholarships-and-awards/find-a-scholarship/anne-reid-memorial-trust-scholarship-408-cai.html

### For further information contact:

**Email**:    scholarships-cf@universitiesnz.ac.nz

## BayTrust Bruce Cronin Scholarship

**Purpose**: This scholarship has been established to recognise his service to the people of the Bay of Plenty
**Eligibility**: Applicants will be eligible if they were born in, or attended school in, or have whakapapa back to the area
**Level of Study**: Postgraduate
**Type**: Scholarship
**Value**: NZ$5,000
**Length of Study**: 1 year
**Frequency**: Annual
**Country of Study**: New Zealand
**Application Procedure**: Apply online universitiesnz.communityforce.com/
**Closing Date**: 1 February
**Funding**: Foundation
**Additional Information**: www.universitiesnz.ac.nz/scholarships/baytrust-bruce-cronin-scholarship

### For further information contact:

Level 1, 752 Cameron Road, Tauranga South, Tauranga 3112, New Zealand.

**Tel**:    (64) 7 578 6546
**Email**:   info@baytrust.org.nz

## Canterbury Scholarship

**Purpose**: These scholarships, tenable for study towards the degree of Doctor of Philosophy at the University of Canterbury, were established to recognise students of the highest calibre undertaking PhD research at the university
**Eligibility**: To apply for a Canterbury Scholarship, please use the UC Doctoral Scholarship application form. The very top ranked domestic applicants who apply for the UC Doctoral Scholarship will be awarded one of the limited number of Canterbury Scholarships available. Domestic students who do not receive a Canterbury Scholarship will be automatically considered for the UC Doctoral Scholarship.
**Level of Study**: Postgraduate
**Type**: Scholarship
**Value**: NZ$21,000
**Length of Study**: 3 year
**Frequency**: Annual
**Country of Study**: New Zealand
**Application Procedure**: See website address in additional information.
**Closing Date**: 15 May
**Funding**: Trusts
**Additional Information**: www.canterbury.ac.nz/scholarship search/ScholarshipDetails.aspx?ScholarshipID=6935.209

### For further information contact:

**Email**:    scholarships-cf@universitiesnz.ac.nz

## Clifford Wallace Collins Memorial Trust Scholarship

**Purpose**: The trust fund was established in 1980 to provide an annual award to support graduates of the University of Canterbury undertaking a course of study in Librarianship at a New Zealand university, and to commemorate the contribution made to the University and its library by Clifford Wallace Collins (1909–1979). Applications, addressing the selection criteria, must be made by letter to the Information Studies Programme Director of Victoria University of Wellington by 15 April
**Eligibility**: The trust fund was established in 1980 to provide an annual award to support graduates of the University of Canterbury undertaking a course of study in Librarianship at a New Zealand university, and to commemorate the contribution made to the University and its library by Clifford Wallace Collins (1909–1979). Mr Collins was Librarian to Canterbury University College and the University of Canterbury from 1934 to 1971
**Level of Study**: Postgraduate

**Type**: Scholarship
**Value**: NZ$750
**Length of Study**: 1 year
**Frequency**: Annual
**Country of Study**: New Zealand
**Application Procedure**: Apply online
**Closing Date**: 15 April
**Funding**: Trusts
**Additional Information**: www.canterbury.ac.nz/scholarship search/ScholarshipDetails.aspx?ScholarshipID=6935.101

**For further information contact:**

**Email**:     scholarships-cf@universitiesnz.ac.nz

## Marian D'Eve Memorial Scholarship

**Purpose**: This scholarship supports students studying, researching, or developing, resources for early-childhood special-needs education at the University of Canterbury. The scholarship was established in 2009 in memory of Marian D'Eve, an early-childhood education specialist and author of a handbook for teachers
**Level of Study**: Postgraduate
**Type**: Scholarship
**Value**: US$2,000
**Length of Study**: 1 year
**Frequency**: Annual
**Country of Study**: Any country
**Application Procedure**: Apply online
**Closing Date**: 31 March
**Funding**: Foundation
**Additional Information**: www.canterbury.ac.nz/scholarship search/ScholarshipDetails.aspx?ScholarshipID=6935.1061

**For further information contact:**

**Email**:     scholarships-cf@universitiesnz.ac.nz

## Roger Helm Scholarship in Pure Mathematics

**Purpose**: The scholarship supports students for study towards a research master's degree or a PhD degree in Pure Mathematics at the University of Canterbury. It was established in 2018 from a bequest by Roger Helm (1947-2015)
**Eligibility**: At the time of application, applicants must be enrolled in either a programme for a PhD degree in Pure Mathematics, or in Part II of a master's degree in Pure Mathematics. Applications are not accepted from candidates who already hold a research doctoral degree. Applications are not accepted from previous holders of the scholarship
**Level of Study**: Postgraduate
**Type**: Scholarship

**Value**: NZ$5,000
**Length of Study**: 1 year
**Frequency**: Annual
**Country of Study**: New Zealand
**Application Procedure**: Apply online
**Closing Date**: 15 May
**Funding**: Trusts
**Additional Information**: www.canterbury.ac.nz/scholarship search/ScholarshipDetails.aspx?ScholarshipID=6935.1764

**For further information contact:**

**Email**:     scholarships-cf@universitiesnz.ac.nz

## Susan Barnes Memorial Scholarship

**Purpose**: The scholarship supports students with a vision impairment in undertaking study at the University of Canterbury. It was established in 2016 by the Lighthouse Vision Trust
**Level of Study**: Postgraduate
**Type**: Scholarship
**Value**: NZ$10,000
**Length of Study**: 1 year
**Frequency**: Annual
**Country of Study**: New Zealand
**Application Procedure**: Apply online
**Closing Date**: 31 March
**Funding**: Foundation
**Additional Information**: www.canterbury.ac.nz/scholarship search/ScholarshipDetails.aspx?ScholarshipID=6935.1705

**For further information contact:**

**Email**:     scholarships-cf@universitiesnz.ac.nz

## The Auckland Medical Aid Trust Scholarship

**Purpose**: This scholarship was established in 2004 and is financed by the Auckland Medical Aid Trust to encourage research into social issues concerning being and becoming human, and provides funds for a doctoral candidate at a - New Zealand university
**Eligibility**: An applicant will be registered as a candidate or will be in the process of registering; as a candidate for a doctoral degree at a New Zealand university. (No award will be made to a candidate who has not successfully completed; registration for a doctoral degree.)
**Level of Study**: Postdoctorate
**Type**: Scholarship
**Value**: NZ$25,000
**Length of Study**: 3 year
**Frequency**: Annual

**Country of Study**: New Zealand
**No. of awards offered**: 1
**Closing Date**: 1 October
**Funding**: Foundation
**Additional Information**: scholarshipdb.net/scholarships-in-New-Zealand/The-Auckland-Medical-Aid-Trust-Scholarship-Auckland-University-Of-Technology=6BYuFpDl6RGUWgAlkGUTnw.html?r_id=162e16e8-e590-11e9-945a-00259065139f

### For further information contact:

PO Box 11915, Wellington 6142, New Zealand.

**Tel**:      (64) 4 381 8510
**Email**:   jon.winnall@universitiesnz.ac.nz

## Three Nations Conference Award

**Purpose**: This award assists Maori or Pasifika students, or students who are indigenous to states or territories of Australia, whose financial circumstances would otherwise preclude them from undertaking postgraduate study in the Department of Sociology and Anthropology at the University of Canterbury
**Eligibility**: Anthropology;Sociology
**Level of Study**: Postgraduate
**Type**: Award
**Value**: US$1,000
**Length of Study**: 1 year
**Frequency**: Annual
**Country of Study**: Any country
**Application Procedure**: Apply online
**Closing Date**: 31 March
**Funding**: Foundation
**Additional Information**: www.canterbury.ac.nz/scholarshipsearch/ScholarshipDetails.aspx?ScholarshipID=6935.136

### For further information contact:

**Email**:   scholarships-cf@universitiesnz.ac.nz

## University of Canterbury Mathematics and Statistics Scholarship

**Purpose**: These scholarships recognise and support high-achieving 200-, 300-, and 400-level students majoring in Mathematics, Statistics, Computational and Applied Mathematical Sciences, Data Science, Applied Data Science or Financial Engineering. The scholarships will be awarded in three categories, with the value of each category (NZ$1,000, NZ$2,500, NZ$5,000) reflecting the recipients' levels of achievement. Up to 45 scholarships will be available annually

**Eligibility**: By 31 March in the year of application, applicants must be enrolled full-time at the University in at least 60 points of 200-, 300-, or 400-level taught courses (not including any thesis course) for an undergraduate or postgraduate programme in: a. Applied Data Science; b. Computational and Applied Mathematical Sciences; c. Data Science; d. Financial Engineering; e. Mathematics; or f. Statistics.
**Level of Study**: Postgraduate
**Type**: Scholarship
**Value**: NZ$5,000 (Category A awards) NZ$2,500 (Category B awards) NZ$1,000 (Category C awards)
**Length of Study**: 1 year
**Frequency**: Annual
**Country of Study**: Any country
**Application Procedure**: Apply online
**Closing Date**: 31 March
**Funding**: Foundation
**Additional Information**: www.canterbury.ac.nz/scholarshipsearch/ScholarshipDetails.aspx?ScholarshipID=6935.1592

### For further information contact:

**Email**:   scholarships@canterbury.ac.nz

## Cardiff University

Deri House, 2-4 Park Grove, Cardiff, Wales, CF10 3PA, United Kingdom.

**Tel**:      (44) 29 2087 0084
**Email**:   graduate@cardiff.ac.uk
**Website**:   www.cardiff.ac.uk/postgraduate

Cardiff University is recognized in independent government assessments as one of the UK's leading teaching and research universities. Founded by Royal Charter in 1883, the University today combines impressive modern facilities and a dynamic approach to teaching and research with its proud heritage of service and achievement. Having gained national and international standing, Cardiff University's vision is to be recognized as a world-class university and to achieve the associated benefits for its students, staff and all other stakeholders.

## Cardiff Institute of Tissue Engineering and Repair (CITER) – EPSRC Studentship

**Purpose**: To support study on the MSc in Tissue Engineering at CITER

**Eligibility**: Applicants must be graduates in a biomedical/veterinary or other science subject or an engineering or clinical discipline from medicine or dentistry. United Kingdom or European Union students who have been resident in the United Kingdom for at least 3 years can apply. Other European Union participants may receive a fees only award
**Level of Study**: Postgraduate
**Type**: Studentship
**Value**: Fees and stipend at the current EPSRC rate
**Length of Study**: 1 year
**Application Procedure**: Check website for further details
**Closing Date**: 30 June

### For further information contact:

**Tel**:       (44) 29 2087 0129
**Email**:   HatchS@cardiff.ac.uk

## Cardiff School of Chemistry – Master's Bursaries

**Purpose**: To support study for the MSc in Molecular Modelling
**Eligibility**: Applicants must possess a 2:2 Honours Degree or equivalent in chemistry or a related discipline (e.g. physics, engineering, pharmacy, biosciences)
**Level of Study**: Postgraduate
**Type**: Bursary
**Value**: Cost of tuition fees at the United Kingdom/European Union rate
**Length of Study**: 1 year
**Country of Study**: United Kingdom
**Application Procedure**: Applicants must submit an application including two references for postgraduate study. Application forms can be downloaded from the website
**Closing Date**: 31 August

### For further information contact:

The Postgraduate Admissions Office, The Registry, Cardiff University, 30-36 Newport Road, Cardiff CF10 3AT, United Kingdom.

**Tel**:       (44) 29 2087 4950
**Email**:   platts@cardifff.ac.uk

## Cardiff School of Chemistry – MSc Studentships in Computing in the Physical Sciences

**Purpose**: To support study on a new MSc programme in Computing in the Physical Sciences

**Eligibility**: Applicants must be United Kingdom-resident European Union citizens. A minimum qualification of a 2ii degree or equivalent in a relevant scientific discipline is required
**Level of Study**: Postgraduate
**Type**: Studentship
**Length of Study**: 1 year
**Application Procedure**: Applicants must submit an application for postgraduate study along with two references
**Closing Date**: 31 August
**Contributor**: Schools of Computer Science and Mathematics

### For further information contact:

**Email**:   platts@cardiff.ac.uk

## Cardiff School of City and Regional Planning – Master's Bursaries

**Purpose**: To support study on the MSc in Transport and Planning
**Eligibility**: Applicants must have been offered and will have accepted a place on the MSc in Transport and Planning and must then be nominated for an award by the School. They must have a relevant honours degree at 2i or higher and they must be United Kingdom/European Union students intending to practice in the United Kingdom
**Level of Study**: Postgraduate
**Type**: Bursary
**Value**: Full United Kingdom/European Union fees and a maintenance stipend of £1,000 (by The Rees Jeffreys Road Fund Bursary) and £5,000 (by The Brian Largs Bursary Fund)
**Length of Study**: 1 year
**Application Procedure**: Check website for further details
**Closing Date**: 30 June
**Contributor**: The Rees Jeffreys Road Fund Bursary, The Brian Largs Bursary Fund

### For further information contact:

**Tel**:       (44) 29 2087 5294
**Email**:   Yewlett@cardiff.ac.uk

## Cardiff School of Mathematics – PhD Studentships

**Eligibility**: Applicants should hold a first or upper second class Honours degree (or overseas equivalent) in a relevant subject area or have appropriate professional experience.
**Level of Study**: Postgraduate

**Type**: Studentship
**Value**: UK and EU students: £9,700, Students from outside the EU : £21,950
**Length of Study**: 1 year
**Country of Study**: United Kingdom
**Application Procedure**: Applicants must submit an application for postgraduate study which can be downloaded from the website
**Closing Date**: 30 April
**Additional Information**: www.cardiff.ac.uk/study/postgraduate/taught/courses/course/mathematics-msc

## For further information contact:

Cardiff School of Mathematics, Senghennydd Rd, Cardiff CF24 4AG, United Kingdom.

**Tel**: (44) 29 2087 4813
**Email**: MScMaths@cardiff.ac.uk

## Cardiff School of Medicine – PhD Studentships

**Eligibility**: Applicants must be United Kingdom/European Union students. They must possess a First or at least Upper Second Class Honours in a subject of relevance to the project (preferably biological science)
**Level of Study**: Postgraduate
**Type**: Studentship
**Value**: Fees support at the United Kingdom/European Union level along with a maintenance stipend at the Research Council level (£12,600)
**Length of Study**: PhD 3-4 years
**Application Procedure**: Applicants must send a covering letter and an up-to-date curriculum vitae, including a breakdown of Year 2/Year 3 university grades, along with references
**Closing Date**: 30 June
**Contributor**: School and Research Council Funds
**Additional Information**: www.cardiff.ac.uk/study/postgraduate/research/programmes/programme/medicine

## For further information contact:

Institute of Medical Genetics, Cardiff University, Heath Park, 210 King George V Dr E, Cardiff CF14 4ER, United Kingdom.

**Tel**: (44) 29 2074 6716
**Fax**: (44) 29 2074 6551
**Email**: pgrmedic@cardiff.ac.uk

## Cardiff School of Medicine – PhD Studentships (Department of Surgery)

**Eligibility**: Applicants must be United Kingdom/European Union students and must possess (or be expected to obtain) a First or at least Upper Second Class Honours in a subject of relevance to the project
**Level of Study**: Postgraduate
**Type**: Studentship
**Value**: Fees support at the United Kingdom/European Union level plus £12,600
**Length of Study**: 3 years
**Application Procedure**: Applicants must send a covering letter and an up-to-date curriculum vitae along with references
**Closing Date**: 30 June

## For further information contact:

Department of Surgery, Cardiff School of Medicine, Cardiff University, Heath Park, Neuadd Meirionnydd, Cardiff CF14 4YS, United Kingdom.

**Tel**: (44) 29 2074 2895/2896
**Fax**: (44) 29 2076 1623
**Email**: JiangW@cardiff.ac.uk

## Cardiff School of Music – PhD Studentships

**Eligibility**: Applicants must have a good Honours Degree in Music (or be expecting to obtain one in the present year) and a Master's Degree is desirable. They should be United Kingdom/European Union citizens or have been resident in the United Kingdom/European Union for at least 3 years prior to starting their PhD.
**Level of Study**: Postgraduate
**Type**: Studentship
**Value**: One full studentship covering United Kingdom/European Union tuition fees and a maintenance stipend at the AHRC level (£12,300) and another, United Kingdom/European Union fees-only studentship
**Length of Study**: 3 years
**Application Procedure**: Applicants must complete and submit an application for postgraduate study. Application forms can be downloaded from the website
**Closing Date**: 30 June
**Additional Information**: www.cardiff.ac.uk/music/courses/postgraduate-research/postgraduate-research-scholarships

## For further information contact:

School of Music, Cardiff University, Corbett Road, Cardiff, CF10 3EB, United Kingdom.

**Tel**:        (44) 29 2087 4816
**Fax**:        (44) 29 2087 4379
**Email**:      musicschool@cardiff.ac.uk

## Cardiff School of Optometry and Vision Sciences – PhD Studentship

**Purpose**: To adopt a completely new approach to understanding the relationship between retinal structure and visual function in AMD
**Eligibility**: Applicants must possess a United Kingdom higher education Degree at First or Upper Second Class Honours or equivalent in a relevant discipline (optometry would be most suitable)
**Level of Study**: Postgraduate
**Type**: Studentship
**Value**: £12,600
**Length of Study**: 3 years
**Application Procedure**: Applicants must complete and submit a standard Cardiff University application form along with a curriculum vitae and covering letter. Application forms can be downloaded from the website
**Closing Date**: 1 November
**Additional Information**: The studentship is available to United Kingdom, European Union and overseas students, but will only cover tuition fees at the European Union/United Kingdom level

**For further information contact:**

**Email**:      BinnsAM@cardiff.ac.uk

## Cardiff University MSc/Diploma in Housing Studentship

**Purpose**: To fund a postgraduate course in housing
**Eligibility**: Studentships are available to United Kingdom applicants with a First or Upper Second Class (Honours) Degree only
**Level of Study**: Postgraduate
**Type**: Studentship
**Value**: University fees and maintenance grant
**Length of Study**: 2 years
**Frequency**: Annual
**Study Establishment**: Cardiff University
**Country of Study**: United Kingdom
**Application Procedure**: Applicants must contact the School of City and Regional Planning
**Closing Date**: June

**For further information contact:**

Cardiff School of City and Regional Planning, Glamorgan Building, King Edward VII Avenue, Cardiff, CF10 3WA, United Kingdom.

**Tel**:        (44) 29 2087 6092
**Email**:      cardpd@cardiff.ac.uk

## Cardiff University PhD Music Studentship

**Purpose**: To fund doctoral study in music
**Eligibility**: Applicants should have a good Honours degree in Music, be a United Kingdom or European Union citizen or have been a resident for at least 3 years for reasons other than education
**Level of Study**: Doctorate
**Type**: Studentship
**Value**: Tuition fees and maintenance
**Length of Study**: 3 years
**Frequency**: Annual
**Study Establishment**: Cardiff University
**Country of Study**: United Kingdom
**Application Procedure**: Applicants must contact the School of Music. They will need to have received an offer of a place to study before they can apply for financial support
**Closing Date**: June
**Additional Information**: www.cardiff.ac.uk/music/courses/postgraduate-research/postgraduate-research-scholarships

**For further information contact:**

School of Music, 31 Corbett Road, Cardiff, CF10 3EB, United Kingdom.

**Tel**:        (44) 29 2087 4816
**Fax**:        (44) 29 2087 4379
**Email**:      musicschool@cardiff.ac.uk

## Cardiff University PhD Social Sciences Studentship

**Purpose**: To fund PhD study in social sciences
**Eligibility**: Only United Kingdom and European Union students with a First or Upper Second Class (Honours) Degree can apply for a PhD studentship
**Level of Study**: Doctorate
**Length of Study**: 3-4 years
**Frequency**: Annual
**Study Establishment**: Cardiff University
**Country of Study**: United Kingdom

**Application Procedure**: Applicants must contact the School of Social Sciences. They will need to have received an offer of a place before they can apply for financial support
**Closing Date**: 9 June
**Additional Information**: www.cardiff.ac.uk/study/postgrad uate/research/programmes/programme/social-sciences

### For further information contact:

School of Social Sciences, Glamorgan Building, King Edward VII Avenue, Cardiff, CF10 3WT, United Kingdom.

**Tel**: (44) 29 2087 4972
**Fax**: (44) 29 2087 4436
**Email**: graduateoffice@cardiff.ac.uk

## Cardiff University PhD Studentship in European Studies

**Purpose**: To support students working towards a thesis in European Studies
**Eligibility**: All students accepted by the School of European Studies to study for a postgraduate research degree are automatically considered
**Level of Study**: Doctorate
**Type**: Studentship
**Value**: Full tuition fee plus stipend
**Frequency**: Annual
**Study Establishment**: Cardiff University
**Country of Study**: Wales
**Application Procedure**: Applicants must check the application guidelines available on the postgraduate webpages
**Closing Date**: 30 June

### For further information contact:

**Email**: business-phd@cardiff.ac.uk

## Economic & Social Research Council (1+3) Sociology Studentship

**Purpose**: To fund postgraduate training
**Eligibility**: Applicants must have a First or Upper Second Class (Honours) Degree
**Level of Study**: Postgraduate
**Type**: Studentship
**Length of Study**: 1 year for MSc and 3 years for PhD
**Frequency**: Annual
**Study Establishment**: Cardiff University
**Country of Study**: United Kingdom
**Application Procedure**: Applicants must contact the School of Social Sciences
**Closing Date**: June

## Engineering and Physical Sciences Research Council Studentships for Biophotonics

**Purpose**: To support study on the new MSc in Biophotonics
**Eligibility**: Applicants must be excellent candidates. Funding is available to United Kingdom and European Union students only
**Level of Study**: Postgraduate
**Type**: Studentship
**Value**: Fully funded studentships include a maintenance stipend
**Length of Study**: 1 year
**Application Procedure**: Applicants can apply via the standard Cardiff University postgraduate application form, which can be downloaded from the website
**Closing Date**: 31 July
**Contributor**: Cardiff School of Biosciences and Cardiff School of Physics and Astronomy

### For further information contact:

**Tel**: (44) 29 2087 0172
**Email**: mscbiophotonics@cardiff.ac.uk

## Fully-Funded PhD Studentship in Sustainable Place-Making

**Eligibility**: Residency: full awards (fees plus maintenance stipend) are open to United Kingdom nationals and European Union students without further restrictions. Academic criteria: successful applicants are likely to have a very good first degree (a first or upper second class BA or BSc Honours or equivalent), and an appropriate Masters degree in a relevant subject (e.g. social sciences; environmental studies; sustainable development; environmental psychology; sociology of technology/environment; human geography), with an average mark of at least 65
**Level of Study**: Postgraduate, Research
**Type**: Studentship
**Value**: Full United Kingdom/European Union tuition fees, as well as a doctoral stipend matching United Kingdom Research Council National minimum (£13,863 per year for current year, updated each year)
**Length of Study**: 3 years
**Country of Study**: United Kingdom
**Application Procedure**: (1) Submit a complete application form for admission to doctoral study in the School of Social Sciences, submitted to the Academic Registry via the online admissions portal (www.cardiff.ac.uk/regis/general/ applyonline/index.html)
**Closing Date**: 17 November
**Additional Information**: Cardiff University reserves the right to close applications early should sufficient applications be received

**For further information contact:**

**Tel:**      (44) 29 2087 0855
**Email:**   parkinva@cardiff.ac.uk

## International Engineering MSc Studentship

**Purpose**: To fund postgraduate study in areas of engineering
**Eligibility**: First or Upper Second Class (Honours) Degree
**Level of Study**: Postgraduate
**Type**: Studentship
**Value**: £1,500
**Length of Study**: 1 year
**Frequency**: Annual
**Study Establishment**: Cardiff University
**Country of Study**: United Kingdom
**Application Procedure**: Applicants must contact the School of Engineering
**Closing Date**: June
**Additional Information**: There is no need to apply seperately for scholarships as eligible applicants will be considered on the basis of their application forms

**For further information contact:**

Admission Office, Cardiff School of Engineering, Cardiff University, Cardiff, CF24 0YZ, United Kingdom.

**Tel:**      (44) 29 2087 4656
**Email:**   engineering-pg@cardiff.ac.uk

## Morgan E. Williams MRes Scholarship in Helminthology

**Eligibility**: English language proficiency is required. Applicants must have a undergraduate degree at level 2:2 (or higher) in a relevant biological, bio medical or bio-molecular science subject. For detailed information, please visit the website
**Level of Study**: Postgraduate
**Type**: Scholarship
**Value**: There is one scholarship offering a reduction of £2,500 off the tuition fees for MRes Biosciences
**Country of Study**: United Kingdom
**Application Procedure**: Applicants should submit a curriculum vitae and Covering Letter to Rachel Patterson, PatersonRJ@cardiff.ac.uk
**Closing Date**: May
**Contributor**: Cardiff School of Bio sciences
**Additional Information**: Scholarship is offered for 1 year armacad.info/cardiff-university-school-of-biosciences-morgan-e-williams-mres-scholarship-in-helminthology-uk

**For further information contact:**

**Email:**   BIOSI-MRes@cardiff.ac.uk

## PhD Studentship in Organisms and Environment at Cardiff University

**Eligibility**: Residency: full awards (fees plus maintenance stipend) are open to United Kingdom nationals and European Union students who can satisfy United Kingdom residency requirements. To be eligible for the full award, European Union nationals must have been in the United Kingdom for at least 3 years prior to the start of the course for which they are seeking funding, including for the purposes of full-time education. European Union nationals who do not meet the above residency requirement are eligible for a fees only award, provided that they have been ordinarily resident in the European Union for at least 3 years prior to the start of their proposed programme of study. Academic criteria: applicants for a studentship must have obtained, or be about to obtain, a 2.1 degree or higher in microbiology, ecology, biology or other relevant discipline. If you have a 2.2 degree, but have also obtained a Masters qualification, you are also eligible. If you do not have these qualifications but you have substantial relevant postgraduate experience please contact the department holding the studentship to find out if your relevant experience is sufficient
**Level of Study**: Doctorate, Postgraduate, Research
**Type**: Studentship
**Value**: This studentship consists of full United Kingdom/European Union tuition fees, as well as a Doctoral Stipend matching United Kingdom Research Council National Minimum
**Length of Study**: 3.5 years
**Frequency**: Annual
**Country of Study**: United Kingdom
**Application Procedure**: To apply, please email your curriculum vitae, 2 references and relevant academic qualifications along with a covering letter to Professor Lynne Boddy at BoddyL@cf.ac.uk
**Closing Date**: 15 January
**Additional Information**: Internal interviews will be conducted before the January 30th. Shortlisted candidates will then go on to an institutional interview which will take place between February 9th and 20th. Cardiff University reserves the right to close applications early should sufficient applications be received scholarship-positions.com/phd-studentship-in-organisms-and-environment-at-cardiff-university-in-uk-2015/2014/10/08/

**For further information contact:**

**Email:**   BoddyL@cf.ac.uk

## Postgraduate History and Archaeology Studentship

**Purpose**: To fund postgraduate training in history and archaeology

**Eligibility**: First or Upper Second Class (Honours) Degree. Those from the United Kingdom should apply for an award from the Arts and Humanities Research Board (AHRB)

**Level of Study**: Doctorate, Postgraduate

**Type**: Studentship

**Value**: Tuition fees and maintenance grant

**Length of Study**: 1 year for Masters, 3 years for PhD

**Frequency**: Annual

**Study Establishment**: Cardiff University

**Country of Study**: United Kingdom

**Application Procedure**: Applicants must submit an application form, which includes a research proposal and the names of two referees

**Closing Date**: 1 June

### For further information contact:

Cardiff School of History and Archaeology, Humanities Building, Colum Drive, Cardiff, CF10 3EU, United Kingdom.

**Tel**:      (44) 29 2087 4258
**Email**:   hisaroffice@cardiff.ac.uk

## The Beacon Scholarship

**Purpose**: The scholarship is awarded to students from Kenya, Tanzania, and Uganda looking to study a 3-4 year undergraduate course (excluding medicine)

**Eligibility**: To be eligible for this scheme, candidates must be able to demonstrate: 1. their normal residence is in Kenya, Tanzania or Uganda. 2. leadership capabilities: i. academic excellence. ii. achievement in sport, music or drama. iii. social influence and communication. iv. citizenship. 3. a capacity to study independently overseas. 4. financial need for study, ie annual gross household income not exceeding £80k (US$100k). 5. that they are aged 18-21. 6. a commitment to return to their home country within one month of degree completion

**Level of Study**: Postgraduate

**Type**: Scholarship

**Value**: Tuition and maintenance fees

**Length of Study**: 3-4 year

**Frequency**: Annual

**Country of Study**: Any country

**Funding**: Private

**Additional Information**: www.studyin-uk.in/profiles/university/cardiff/scholarships/523/

### For further information contact:

The Beacon Scholarship Sandells House Cliftons Lane Reigate, Surrey, RH2 9RA, United Kingdom.

**Email**:   delhi@studyin-uk.com

## Ursula Henriques Scholarships

**Purpose**: Scholarships are available for pursuing postgraduate taught and postgraduate research programme

**Eligibility**: For eligibility details, please visit website http://scholarship-positions.com/ursula-henriques-scholarships-uk-eu-international-students/

**Value**: Cardiff University received a gift of £100,000 from Professor Henriques (1,914–2,008), a former member of staff in the Department of History and Welsh History, University College Cardiff

**Frequency**: Annual

**Country of Study**: Any country

**Application Procedure**: The application form can be obtained by email. Completed forms should be returned electronically to the School Postgraduate Office

**Closing Date**: 18 May

**Contributor**: Cardiff University

**Additional Information**: For more details, please visit website www.cardiff.ac.uk/study/postgraduate/funding/view/Ursula-Henriques-Scholarship scholarship-positions.com/ursula-henriques-ma-phd-scholarship-cardiff-university-uk/2018/04/23/

### For further information contact:

**Email**:   share-pg@cardiff.ac.uk

## Carnegie Corporation of New York

437 Madison Avenue, Ne York, NY 10022, United States of America.

**Tel**:      (1) 212 371 3200
**Website**:   www.carnegie.org

Andrew Carnegie envisioned Carnegie Corporation as a foundation that would promote the advancement and diffusion of knowledge and understanding. In keeping with this mandate, our work incorporates an affirmation of our historic role as an education foundation but also honors Andrew Carnegie's passion for international peace and the health of our democracy.

## Next Gen Fellowship Program for Sub-Saharan African Countries

**Purpose**: This fellowship is available for pursuing PhD research level

**Eligibility**: All applicants must be citizens of and reside in a sub-Saharan African country while holding a current faculty position at an accredited college or university in Ghana, Nigeria, South Africa, Tanzania, or Uganda. Applicants for any of the funding opportunities offered through this program must have a master's degree and be working toward completion of the doctoral degree. The program seeks to promote diversity and encourages women to apply. To be eligible for the US$15,000 dissertation research fellowship, applicants must have an approved dissertation proposal but will not yet have undertaken research of 9 months or more. For detailed information, please visit website

**Level of Study**: Doctorate

**Type**: Fellowship

**Value**: The doctoral dissertation proposal fellowship supports short-term research costs of up to US$3,000 to develop a doctoral dissertation proposal. The doctoral dissertation completion fellowship supports a 1-year leave from teaching responsibilities and a stipend up to US$15,000 to permit the completion of a dissertation that advances research on peace, security, and development topics. The doctoral dissertation research fellowship supports 9–12 months of dissertation research costs of up to US$15,000 on a topic related to peace, security, and development

**Length of Study**: About 9–12 months

**Country of Study**: Africa

**Application Procedure**: The mode of applying is online. All applications must be submitted using the online application portal

**Closing Date**: 13 November

**Additional Information**: Citizens of and reside in a sub-Saharan African country while holding a current faculty position at an accredited college or university in Ghana, Nigeria, South Africa, Tanzania, or Uganda can apply for this PhD fellowship www.scholarshipsads.com/next-gen-fellowship-program-for-sub-saharan-african-countries/

### For further information contact:

**Email**:  nextgenafrica@ssrc.org

## Carnegie Trust

### Carnegie PhD Scholarships

**Purpose**: Candidates must have, or be on track to achieve, a first class Honours undergraduate degree from a Scottish institution of higher education

**Eligibility**: 1. You already hold, or are on track to graduate with a First Class Honours degree from one of the eligible host organisations in Scotland. 2. This undergraduate degree is in a subject related to the academic field of your proposed doctoral research. 3. You have been accepted on a doctoral programme at one of the eligible host organisations. 4. This doctoral programme will start in the coming academic year

**Level of Study**: Graduate

**Type**: Scholarship

**Value**: £16,800 for the academic year 2019-2020 and £3,000 for the whole tenure

**Length of Study**: 3 year

**Frequency**: Annual

**Country of Study**: Any country

**No. of awards offered**: 15-18 each year

**Closing Date**: 28 February

**Funding**: Foundation

**Additional Information**: www.carnegie-trust.org/award-schemes/carnegie-phd-scholarships/

### For further information contact:

Andrew Carnegie House, Pittencrieff St, Dunfermline KY12 8AW, United Kingdom.

**Tel**:   (44) 1383 724 990

### St Andrews Society of New York Scholarships

**Purpose**: The Carnegie Trust for the Universities of Scotland administers this scholarship programme for students in the United Kingdom who wish to apply for graduate study in the United States. Successful candidates are expected to be the highest caliber, both academically and in their wider personal interests

**Eligibility**: 1. Candidates must be Scottish by birth or descent, and have up-do-date knowledge of Scotland, Scottish current affairs and of the Scottish tradition generally. The Society expects its scholars to be good ambassadors for Scotland. 2. Either graduates of a Scottish university, Glasgow School of Art, Royal Conservatoire of Scotland, or of Oxford or Cambridge, who have completed their first degree course (so as to be qualified to graduate) not earlier than previous year. 3. Students of a Scottish university, Glasgow School of Art, Royal Conservatoire of Scotland, or of Oxford or Cambridge, who expect to complete their first degree course (so as to be qualified to graduate) in current year. 4. Preference is given to candidates who have no previous, or limited, experience of the United States and for whom a period of study in that country may provide a life-changing experience

**Level of Study**: Postgraduate

**Type**: Scholarship

**Value**: US$35,000
**Length of Study**: 1 year
**Frequency**: Annual
**Country of Study**: Any country
**Application Procedure**: Candidates apply directly to the university where they are studying in Scotland, Cambridge or Oxford. Under no circumstances should candidates apply directly to the trust.
**No. of awards offered**: 2 each year
**Closing Date**: 16 March
**Funding**: Private
**Additional Information**: www.carnegie-trust.org/award-schemes/st-andrews-society-of-new-york-scholarships/

### For further information contact:

Andrew Carnegie House, Pittencrieff St, Dunfermline KY12 8AW, United Kingdom.

**Tel**:        (44) 1383 724 990
**Email**:    office@standrewsny.org

## Casino Mucho

## Casinomucho Research Scholarship (CSR)

**Purpose**: This research scholarship provide an individual with a grant to shape up and change the face of online gambling industry within the next few years
**Eligibility**: 1. Full time student at college/university (preferred Marketing, Business or Communication courses). 2. No entry limit per contestant. 3. Casinomucho.com employees immediate families are not eligible. 4. 3,000–5,000 words essay on one of the given topic in Microsoft Word format with correct grammar, heading and punctuation. 5. The article must be plagiarism free
**Level of Study**: Postgraduate
**Type**: Scholarship
**Value**: £500
**Frequency**: Annual
**Country of Study**: United Kingdom
**Application Procedure**: 1. Students must submit their applications to scholarship [at] muchoent.com. 2. Applications should include: full name, date of birth, name or degree course, essay in Word format
**Closing Date**: 31 March
**Funding**: Private
**Additional Information**: casinomucho.com/scholarship/

### For further information contact:

**Email**:    scholarship@muchoent.com

## Catholic University of Louvain

1, Place de l'Université, B-1348 Louvain-la-Neuve, Belgium.

**Tel**:        (32) 10 472 111
**Website**:    www.uclouvain.be

## Hoover Fellowships for International Scholars

**Eligibility**: Candidates must be scholars from outside Belgium, who hold a doctorate or possess equivalent qualifications and are active in the field of economic or social ethics broadly conceived. Candidates for a full fellowship must have no professional income from other sources in the period concerned. Proficiency in either English or French is required, and at least a passive knowledge in both is desirable
**Type**: Fellowship
**Value**: One full Hoover fellowship of €2,000 per month (plus social security contributions) for a duration of 3 months. Several honorary Hoover fellowships for a duration of 1 to 6 months with a contribution to housing and travelling costs of up to €500 per month
**Frequency**: Annual
**Study Establishment**: UCL
**Country of Study**: Belgium
**Application Procedure**: Applications must reach Thérèse Davio by email (therese.davio@uclouvain.be)
**Closing Date**: 28 February
**Contributor**: UCL
**Additional Information**: For more information, please visit www.uclouvain.be/398682.html www.hoover.org/library-archives/about/fellowships

## CEC Artslink

291 Broadway, 12th Floor, New York, NY 10022, United States of America.

**Tel**:        (1) 212 643 1985
**Email**:    info@cecartslink.org
**Website**:    www.cecartslink.org

CEC Artslink is an international arts service organization. Our programmes encourage and support exchange of artists and cultural managers between the United States and Central Europe, Russia, and Eurasia. We believe that the arts are a society's most deliberate and complex means of communication.

## ArtsLink Independent Projects

**Purpose**: To provide funding to artists and arts managers who propose to undertake projects in the United States in collaboration with a United States non-profit arts organization
**Eligibility**: Candidates must be citizens of, and reside in, an eligible countries Albania, Armenia, Azerbaijan, Belarus, Bosnia and Herzegovina, Bulgaria, Croatia, Czech Republic, Estonia, Georgia, Hungary, Kazakhstan, Kosovo, Kyrgyzstan, Latvia, Lithuania, Macedonia, Moldova, Mongolia, Montenegro, Poland, Romania, Russia, Serbia, Slovak Republic, Slovenia, Tajikistan, Turkmenistan, Ukraine and Uzbekistan. There are no age limitations. Arts managers must be affiliated with an organization in the non-commercial sector
**Type**: Fellowship
**Value**: US$5,000
**Length of Study**: 1 year
**Frequency**: Annual
**Country of Study**: United States of America
**Application Procedure**: Complete online application form
**Closing Date**: December
**Funding**: Private, Trusts
**No. of awards given last year**: 5
**Additional Information**: Please check at www.cecartslink. org/grants/independent_projects/  www.transartists.org/air/ cec-artslink

### For further information contact:

CEC ArtsLink, 435 Hudson Street, 8th Floor, New York, NY 10014, United States of America.

**Email**:    al@cecartslink.org

## ArtsLink Projects

**Purpose**: To support United States artists, curators, presenters, and non-profit arts organizations undertaking projects in Eastern and Central Europe, Russia, Central Asia and the Caucasus
**Eligibility**: Open to citizens of eligible countries: Albania, Armenia, Azerbaijan, Belarus, Bosnia and Herzegovina, Bulgaria, Croatia, Czech Republic, Estonia, Georgia, Hungary, Kazakhstan, Kosovo, Kyrgyzstan, Latvia, Lithuania, Macedonia, Moldova, Mongolia, Montenegro, Poland, Romania, Russia, Serbia, Slovak Republic, Slovenia, Tajikistan, Turkmenistan, Ukraine and Uzbekistan
**Level of Study**: Postgraduate
**Type**: Fellowship
**Value**: Up to US$10,000
**Length of Study**: 1 year
**Frequency**: Annual

**Application Procedure**: Complete online application form
**Closing Date**: 15 January
**Funding**: Private, Trusts
**No. of awards given last year**: 10
**Additional Information**: Please check at www.cecartslink. org/grants/artslink_projects/  www.cecartslink.org/grants/ artslink_projects/

### For further information contact:

**Tel**:      (1) 212 643 1985
**Email**:   al@cecartslink.org

## ArtsLink Residencies

**Purpose**: To create opportunities for artists and communities across the United States to share artistic practices with artists and arts managers from abroad and engage in dialogue that advances understanding across cultures
**Eligibility**: Applicants must be the citizens of, and reside in, eligible countries: Afghanistan, Albania, Armenia, Azerbaijan, Belarus, Bosnia and Herzegovina, Bulgaria, Croatia, Czech Republic, Estonia, Georgia, Hungary, Kazakhstan, Kosovo, Kyrgyzstan, Latvia, Lithuania, Macedonia, Moldova, Mongolia, Montenegro, Poland, Romania, Russia, Serbia, Slovak Republic, Slovenia, Tajikistan, Turkmenistan, Ukraine and Uzbekistan
**Level of Study**: Postgraduate
**Type**: Fellowship
**Value**: offer artists and arts managers/curators from eligible overseas countries a six-week residency at an established, non-profit arts organization in the US
**Length of Study**: 6 weeks
**Frequency**: Annual
**Country of Study**: United States of America
**Application Procedure**: 1. A completed ArtsLink International Fellowship online application form. 2. Answers to the following questions: a. Describe the current issues in your work and explain how a residency in the United States will advance your professional development as an artist or arts manager. (300 words maximum) b. Please describe previous projects that have involved engagement or participation, and explain how you plan to engage with US artists and communities during your residency. (300 words maximum) c. Please list the most important types of activities and arts events you are hoping to take part in, keeping in mind that your residency may take place in any of the 50 states of the US. (300 words maximum) d. What prior experience or contact have you had with the United States (300 words maximum) e. Have you traveled outside your country of residence to pursue research or study If so, please indicate when and where you have traveled and in what capacity. (300 words maximum) g. How will you share your ArtsLink experience with your

home community (300 words maximum) 3. The most recent CV or résumé (only one-page PDF file) that lists your professional accomplishments in reverse chronological order starting from the most recent one. Only one-page documents will be submitted for panel review. 4. A letter of recommendation (only one-page PDF file) from a colleague or supervisor that explains how a residency in the United States will benefit you professionally and why it is an important endeavor at this time in your career. If written in a language other than English, please include an English translation. This letter can be submitted to mtumenev@cecartslink.org separately from your application, but it must arrive within two weeks of the application deadline. No emails will be accepted unless approved by ArtsLink staff. Letters without signatures will also not be accepted. 5. If you are applying as an arts manager / curator submit a one-page PDF file with description of your organization in English. Include information about staff size and resources.

**Closing Date**: 30 October

**Funding**: Private, Trusts

**Contributor**: ArtsLink Residencies are funded through public and private sources including CEC ArtsLink, the National Endowment for the Arts, the Trust for Mutual Understanding, the Ohio Arts Council, the Kettering Fund and the Milton and Sally Avery Arts Foundation with additional support from the Polish Cultural Institute and the Romanian Cultural Institute

**No. of awards given last year**: 16

**Additional Information**: Please check at www.cecartslink.org/grants/artslink_residencies/ www.cecartslink.org/grants/artslink_residencies/

### For further information contact:

291 Broadway, 14th Floor, New York, NY 10007, United States of America.

**Tel**: (1) 212 643 1985
**Fax**: (1) 212 643 1996

## Center for Creative Photography (CCP)

The University of Arizona 1030 North Olive Road, Tucson, AZ 210103, United States of America.

**Tel**: (1) 520 621 7970
**Email**: info@ccp.library.arizona.edu
**Website**: www.creativephotography.org/

The Center for Creative Photography (CCP) is an archive and research centre located on the University of Arizona campus.

## Center for Creative Photography Ansel Adams Research Fellowship

**Purpose**: To promote and support research on the Center's photograph, archive and library collections

**Eligibility**: Advanced scholars and researchers from any discipline are encouraged to apply. Pre-doctoral applicants must have completed coursework and preliminary examinations for the doctoral degree and must be engaged in dissertation research

**Level of Study**: Research

**Type**: Fellowship

**Value**: US$5,000

**Length of Study**: 2–4 weeks

**Frequency**: Annual

**Country of Study**: United States of America

**Application Procedure**: 1. Complete the application form. Please check back in Fall for new application form. 2. Include a 500-1,000 word statement detailing your research interests and project, and how they will be advanced by study of the Center's archives, library, and print collection 3. Attach a Curriculum Vitae of no more than four pages

**Closing Date**: 15 January

**Additional Information**: Please check at www.creativephotography.org/study-research/fellowships-internships ccp.arizona.edu/study-research/fellowships-internships/ansel-adams-research-fellowship-0

### For further information contact:

Center for Creative Photography, 1030 N. Olive Road, Tucson, AZ 85719, United States of America.

**Tel**: (1) 520 621 0050
**Fax**: (1) 520 621 9444
**Email**: peregoya@ccp.arizona.edu

## Center for Defense Information (CDI)

1100 G Street NW, Suite 500, Washington, DC 20005-3806, United States of America.

**Tel**: (1) 202 347 1122
**Email**: info@cdi.org
**Website**: www.cdi.org
**Contact**: Joe Newman, Director of Communications

The Center for Defense Information (CDI) provides responsible, non-partisan research and analysis on the social, economic, environmental, political and military components of national and global security, and aims to educate the public and inform policy makers about these issues. The organization is staffed by retired senior government officials and knowledgeable researchers and is directed by Dr Bruce G Blair.

## Center for Defense Information Internship

**Purpose**: To support the work of CDI's senior staff while gaining exposure to research, issues and communications related to national security and foreign policy
**Eligibility**: There are no eligibility restrictions. Paid internships are available for nationals of the United States and legal immigrants
**Level of Study**: Unrestricted
**Type**: Internship
**Value**: US$1,000 per month
**Length of Study**: 3–5 months
**Study Establishment**: CDI
**Country of Study**: Any country
**Application Procedure**: Applicants must submit a curriculum vitae, covering letter, brief writing sample, transcript and two letters of recommendation
**No. of awards offered**: 200
**Closing Date**: 15 October
**Funding**: Private
**No. of awards given last year**: 12
**No. of applicants last year**: 200

### For further information contact:

Center for Defense Information, 1779 Massachusetts Avenue, N.W., Washington, DC 20036, United States of America.

Fax:       (1) 202 462 4559
Email:    internships@cdi.org

## Central Queensland University

Building 5 Bruce Highway, Rockhampton, QLD 4702, Australia.

Tel:        (61) 7 4930 9000
Email:     research-enquiries@cqu.edu.au
Website:  www.cqu.edu.au

The Central Queensland University (CQU) is committed to excellence in research and innovation with a particular emphasis on issues that affect the region. CQU achieves relevance in its research goals through linkages with industry, business, government and the community and through collaboration with national and international researchers and research networks. CQU provides a range of exciting and relevant research opportunities for Masters and PhD candidates and is committed to excellence and quality in the research training experience of its candidates.

## CQUniversity Indigenous Australian Postgraduate Research Award

**Eligibility**: The applicant should be an Australian citizen and must be a Aborginal or Torres Strait Islander
**Level of Study**: Postgraduate, Research
**Type**: Scholarship
**Value**: AU$19,616 maximum 1 year
**Frequency**: Annual
**Study Establishment**: Central Queensland University
**Country of Study**: Australia
**Application Procedure**: For information on application procedure, check the website
**Closing Date**: 31 October
**Funding**: Government
**Additional Information**: This scholarship is paid fortnightly for the period of 2 years (Masters) or 3 years (PhD). Open for applications from June 30th www.cqu.edu.au/about-us/struc ture/governance/glossary/items/indigenous-australian-postgrad uate-research-award-iapra

### For further information contact:

Office of Research, Building 351, Central Queensland University, Rockhampton, QLD 4702, Australia.

Tel:        (61) 7 4923 2607
Fax:       (61) 7 4923 2600

## CQUniversity Womens Equal Opportunity Research Award

**Purpose**: To enable a woman to undertake full-time postgraduate research towards a PhD or Master's degree after having experienced a break in study
**Eligibility**: Open only to female candiates who are citizens or permanent residents of Australia and New Zealand
**Level of Study**: Doctorate, Postgraduate
**Type**: Research award
**Value**: AU$19,616 (maximum per year)
**Frequency**: Annual
**Study Establishment**: Central Queensland University

**Country of Study**: Australia
**Application Procedure**: Check website for further details
**Closing Date**: 31 October
**Funding**: Government
**Additional Information**: This scholarship is paid fortnightly for the period of 2 years (Masters) or 3 years (PhD). Open for applications from 1 July www.scholarshipcare.com/womens-equal-opportunity-postgraduate-research-award-upra-w/

## CQUniversity/Industry Collaborative Grants Scheme

**Purpose**: To encourage active research collaboration between the university and eligible industry partners
**Eligibility**: Open for candidates who are full-time members of staff (either individuals or teams) and are able to demonstrate through their track record that they have the capability to successfully complete the proposed project
**Type**: Grant
**Value**: Up to AU$10,000 is tenable for 1 year, commencing 1 January and ending 31 December
**Length of Study**: 12 months
**Study Establishment**: Central Queensland University
**Country of Study**: Australia
**Application Procedure**: Applications must be submitted on the current application form, in the required format with the required number of copies. One original application, and one identical copy must be submitted in hard copy, and one copy must be submitted electronically, either as a word or pdf document
**Closing Date**: 11 August

## For further information contact:

Bldg 351, Rockhampton (City) Campus, Rockhampton, QLD 4702, Australia.

**Tel**:     (61) 4923 2601
**Fax**:     (61) 4923 2600
**Email**:     l.walker@cqu.edu.au

## International Student Scholarship

**Purpose**: The International Student Scholarship is available to all new international undergraduate and postgraduate coursework students who meet the academic criteria at CQUniversity Australia. The Scholarship rewards successful applicants with up to the value of 20% of your tuition fees for the duration of their studies, subject to meeting terms and conditions.

**Eligibility**: 1. The International Student Scholarship is awarded, at the discretion of the University, to exceptional international students, undertaking on-campus, full-time degree study at CQUniversity Australia. 2. The International Student Scholarship is only available to students applying for undergraduate or postgraduate coursework. 3. The International Student Scholarship is only available for full degree courses (full bachelor or masters only). 4. The International Student Scholarship is only available to students new to CQUniversity Australia - it is not available to students who are currently studying at CQUniversity Australia. Students currently studying at CQUniversity and applying for Change of Course will also not be eligible for the International Student Scholarship. 5. The International Student Scholarship is not available in conjunction with any other CQUniversity Australia scholarship. 6. The International Student Scholarship is not available to any student who has been given entrance to CQUniversity Australia based on work experience. 7. The International Student Scholarship is not transferable to a third party or redeemable for cash. 8. The International Student Scholarship is calculated and applied on a per term basis.
**Level of Study**: postgraduate
**Type**: SCHOLARSHIP
**Value**: 20% of tuition fees
**Closing Date**: 31 December
**Additional Information**: www.cqu.edu.au/courses/future-students/scholarships/offerings/international-student-scholarship

## Merit Grants Scheme

**Purpose**: To provide opportunities for individuals or groups with well established or developing track records in research to initiate high quality research projects
**Eligibility**: Members of the full-time staff of the University with a proven research record 'relative to opportunity' are eligible to compete for Merit Research Grants. Candidates must not be absent for a period exceeding eight weeks during the proposed period of grant. A researcher may be in receipt of only one Merit Grant at any one time
**Type**: Grant
**Value**: AU$10,000–30,000
**Length of Study**: 1 year
**Study Establishment**: Central Queensland University
**Country of Study**: Australia
**Application Procedure**: Applications must be submitted on the current application form, in the required format, and with the required number of copies
**Funding**: Government
**Additional Information**: A researcher may be in receipt of only one Merit Grant at any one time

## Research Administration Assistants Postdoctoral Award

**Purpose**: To provide for the university's intellectual environment by facilitating mentoring, team building, and career development in areas of current or future research strength
**Eligibility**: The applicant must remain based on a Central Queensland University campus (excluding international campuses) for the duration of the award
**Level of Study**: Postdoctorate
**Type**: Award
**Value**: On-costs of 28% will be paid in addition to salary
**Frequency**: Annual
**Study Establishment**: Central Queensland University
**Country of Study**: Australia
**Application Procedure**: Applications must be submitted on the current application form, in the required format, and with the required number of copies
**Funding**: Government
**Additional Information**: Applicants may seek funding for 1, 2, or 3 years

## Seed Grants Scheme

**Purpose**: To provide seed funding to encourage new research-trained staff to undertake a funded research project
**Eligibility**: Open to newly trained researchers, who are currently within the first 5 years of academic or other research-related performance allowing uninterrupted, stable research development following completion of their postgraduate research training
**Level of Study**: Research
**Type**: Grant
**Value**: Up to AU$10,000
**Length of Study**: 1 year
**Study Establishment**: Central Queensland University
**Country of Study**: Australia
**Application Procedure**: Applications must be submitted on the current application form, in the required format, and with the required number of copies
**Closing Date**: 11 August
**Funding**: Government

## Centre de Recherches et d'Investigations Epidermiques et Sensorielles

20 rue Victor Noir, F-92200 Neuilly-sur-Seine, France.

**Tel**:        (33) 146 434 900
**Email**:      contact@ceries.com
**Website**:    www.ceries.com

CERIES (Centre de Recherches et d'Investigations Epidermiques et Sensorielles or Centre for Epidermal and Sensory Research and Investigation) is the healthy skin research centre of Chanel.

## Centre de Recherches et d'Investigations Epidermiques et Sensorielles Research Award

**Purpose**: To honour a scientific researcher for a fundamental or clinical research project in the field of healthy skin
**Eligibility**: There are no eligibility restrictions
**Level of Study**: Research
**Value**: €40,000
**Length of Study**: 1 year
**Frequency**: Annual
**Country of Study**: Any country
**Application Procedure**: Applicants must consult the website
**No. of awards offered**: 26
**Closing Date**: 1 June
**Funding**: Private
**Contributor**: Chanel
**No. of awards given last year**: 1
**No. of applicants last year**: 26
**Additional Information**: www.nature.com/naturecareers/events/event/8348

### For further information contact:

**Email**:    chanelrt.award@ruderfinnasia.com

## Centre De Science Humaines (CSH)

2 Aurangzeb Road, New Delhi 110011, India.

**Tel**:        (91) 11 30410070
**Email**:      direction@csh-delhi.com
**Website**:    www.csh-delhi.com

The Centre de Sciences Humaines (CSH), created in 1989, is a research centre funded by the French Ministry of Foreign Affairs

## Centre de Sciences Humaines Post-Doctoral Fellowship

**Purpose**: To question the status of India as an emerging power in the international scene

**Eligibility**: Open to candidates who hold a PhD in economics/economic geography/urban studies and are prefereable below 35 years of age
**Level of Study**: Postdoctorate
**Type**: Fellowship
**Value**: Indian Rupees 20,000–25,000 per month
**Length of Study**: 1 year
**Frequency**: Annual
**Country of Study**: India
**Application Procedure**: Applicants must send their curriculum vitae, 2 academic references letters, a synopsis of the PhD theses and a comprehensive research proposal
**Closing Date**: 31 January
**Additional Information**: calenda.org/203026

### For further information contact:

**Email**:    veronique.dupont@csh-delhi.com

## Centre for Clinical Research Excellence

Centre for Clinical Research Excellence - Infection and Bioethics in Haematological Malignancies, Level 3, ICPMR, Westmead Hospital, Institute Road, Westmead, NSW 2145, Australia.

**Tel**:    (61) 9845 6255
**Email**:    cjordens@med.usyd.edu.au
**Website**:    www.ccre-ibhm.org.au

The Centre for Clinical Research Excellence (CCRE) is multi-centre research collaboration with a special focus on bioethics, consisting of four research sites affiliated with the University of Sydney

## Postgraduate Scholarships for Interdisciplinary Bioethics Research

**Purpose**: To develop surveillance methods and interventions to improve infection-related outcomes in malignant haematology and bone marrow transplantation, with interdisciplinary bioethics research underpinning all major themes
**Eligibility**: Open to Australian citizens or permanent resident meeting the standard criteria for NHMRC scholarships, including full-time enrollment and status, as well as the criteria for admission to postgraduate study in the faculty of medicine or faculty of science at the University of Sydney
**Level of Study**: Graduate
**Type**: Scholarship
**Country of Study**: Australia
**Application Procedure**: Check website for further details

### For further information contact:

**Tel**:    (61) 434 07 07 88

## Centre for Environment Planning and Technology University

Kasturbhai Lalbhai Campus, University Road, Vasant Vihar, Navrangpura, Ahmedabad, Gujarat 380009, India.

**Contact**:    CEPT University

Centre for Environmental Planning and Technology University, formerly the Centre for Environmental Planning and Technology, is an academic institution located near university area in Ahmedabad, India offering postgraduate programmes in areas of the natural and developed environment of human society and related disciplines.

## Full-Tuition Fees Waiver for MPhil/PhD Students

**Purpose**: Scholarships are available for pursuing MPhil/PhD programme
**Eligibility**: Students from India are eligible to apply
**Type**: Grant
**Value**: The university offers full tuition fees waiver to MPhil/PhD students for their entire term of registration in the program. The university also offers a scholarship (Rs. 36,700 per month-subject to change) for the first six months (mandatory) of the coursework against teaching assignments (15–20 hours/week) as allocated by the respective faculty
**Country of Study**: India
**Application Procedure**: Go to the Centre for Environmental Planning and Technology(CEPT) website Click on the 'Admissions' button (on the header menu) at the top of the page. This will open a page with all the programs offered at CEPT University. Click on the program you wish to apply. This will open the tab with 'About' 'FAQ' & 'How to Apply'. Click on the 'How to Apply' button and you will be redirected to a page containing eligibility criteria, program details and the link to the admissions portal. For further information, kindly check the following link. cept.ac.in/2/37/faculty-of-architecture/479/fees-scholarship
**Closing Date**: 30 April
**Additional Information**: For detailed information, check with the below link. scholarship-positions.com/full-tuition-fees-waiver-mphil-phd-students-cept-university-india/ scholarship-positions.com/full-tuition-fees-waiver-mphil-phd-students-cept-university-india/2018/04/24/

**For further information contact:**

Harvard Square, Mifflin Pl, Cambridge, MA 02138, United States of America.

## Centre for Groundwater Studies (CGS)

GPO Box 2100, Adelaide, SA 5001, Australia.

**Tel**: (61) 8 8201 5632
**Email**: cgs@groundwater.com.au
**Website**: www.groundwater.com.au

Centre for Groundwater Studies (CGS) is an international leader in water and environmental research and education.

## Chinese Government Scholarship Water and Environmental Research Scholarships

**Purpose**: To assist students with research projects in the specified areas
**Eligibility**: Open to Australian citizens and permanent residents who have a background in science, mathematics or engineering
**Level of Study**: Postgraduate
**Type**: Scholarship
**Value**: AU$22,231
**Length of Study**: 1 year
**Frequency**: Annual
**Country of Study**: Australia
**Closing Date**: September
**Additional Information**: For additional information see the website

**For further information contact:**

**Email**: impt@scholars4dev.com

## Chandigarh University

NH-95 Chandigarh-Ludhiana Highway, Mohali, Punjab 140413, India.

**Contact**: Chandigarh University

A renowned university in India is offering scholarships for brilliant but less privileged students across the globe who have interest in studying in India.

## Chandigarh University Scholarships in India

**Purpose**: Chandigarh University offers undergraduate and post-graduate and doctorate courses in various disciplines including Engineering, Management, Computing, Education, Animation and Multimedia, Tourism, Pharma Sciences, Biotechnology, Architecture, Commerce and Legal Studies
**Eligibility**: Students outside India, Nepal and Bhutan can apply for these scholarships. Not Required but all academic documents are to be sent to micheal.africa-at-cumail.in for eligibility checking. Not required but the applicant must be able to read, write and understand the English Language
**Level of Study**: Graduate, Postgraduate
**Value**: It is between 15% and 50% (maximum) for tuition fees only
**Study Establishment**: Scholarships are awarded to study the subjects offered by the university
**Country of Study**: India
**Application Procedure**: Interested students can contact Mr. Michael on micheal.africa@cumail.in
**Closing Date**: July
**Additional Information**: For more details please contact the website scholarship-positions.com/chandigarh-university-scholarships-india/ www.shiksha.com/university/cu-chandigarh-university-45668/scholarships

**For further information contact:**

**Email**: micheal.africa@cumail.in

## Charles Babbage Institute (CBI)

211 Andersen Library, University of MN 222 21st Avenue South, Minneapolis, MN 55455, United States of America.

**Tel**: (1) 612 624 5050
**Email**: cbi@umn.edu
**Website**: www.cbi.umn.edu

The Charles Babbage Institute (CBI) is a research centre dedicated to promoting the study of the history of computing, its impact on society and preserving relevant documentation. CBI fosters research and writing in the history of computing by providing fellowship support, archival resources and information to scholars, computer scientists and the general public.

## Adelle and Erwin Tomash Fellowship in the History of Information Processing

**Purpose**: To advance the professional development of historians in the field

**Eligibility**: 1. Must be a graduate student or a postgraduate student 2. Must attend a university 3. Must not be attending high school currently 4. Must study full-time 5. Restricted to students studying Computer Science/Data Processing, Electrical Engineering/Electronics, Engineering/Technology, History, Humanities, Science, Technology, and Society

**Level of Study**: Doctorate

**Type**: Fellowship

**Value**: US$14,000

**Length of Study**: 1 year

**Frequency**: Annual

**Country of Study**: Any country

**Application Procedure**: 1. Recommendations or References 2. Other - Research proposal 3. Resume 4. Transcript

**No. of awards offered**: 1

**Closing Date**: 15 January

**Funding**: Private

**Additional Information**: Please check at www.cbi.umn.edu/research/tfellowship.html www.petersons.com/scholarship/adelle-and-erwin-tomash-fellowship-in-the-history-of-information-processing-111_150883.aspx

## For further information contact:

University of Minnesota 211 Elmer Andersen Library, 222-21st Avenue, South, Minneapolis, MN 55455, United States of America.

| | |
|---|---|
| **Tel**: | (1) 624 5050 |
| **Fax**: | (1) 612 625 8054 |
| **Email**: | cbi@tc.umn.edu |

## Charles Darwin University

Charles Darwin University 21 Kitchener Dr, Darwin City, NT 0800, Australia.

| | |
|---|---|
| **Tel**: | (61) 8 8946 6666 |
| **Website**: | www.cdu.edu.au/ |

Charles Darwin University is a new world university built on social justice, sustainability, creativity and collective effort.

## CDU Vice-Chancellor's International High Achievers Scholarships

**Purpose**: Charles Darwin University (CDU) offers the Vice-Chancellor's International High Achievers Scholarships to international students who have a record of academic excellence and high achievement and who are seeking to commence an Undergraduate or Postgraduate coursework degree at CDU.

**Eligibility**: Eligible applicants must: 1. Applicant must apply to commence study in 2020 2. Applicants must meet the University's academic and English language entry requirement for their chosen course; 3. Applicant must have a minimum overall score of 85% in their highest completed qualification; 4. Applicant must be an international student on a student visa; 5. Applicant must not hold another scholarship from an Australian or foreign sponsoring agency Please note: the VCIHAS scholarships are very competitive and meeting the minimum eligibility standards described above does not guarantee that you will be awarded a scholarship.

**Level of Study**: Bachelors/Masters Degree

**Type**: Scholarships

**Value**: 25% or 50% of the tuition fee. The tuition scholarships apply to the tuition fees for the full duration of the degree.

**Frequency**: annual

**Country of Study**: Australia

**Application Procedure**: To apply, you must complete the scholarship application form and submit it together with your application for admission to a degree program at CDU

**No. of awards offered**: Limited

**Closing Date**: 15 May

**Additional Information**: www.cdu.edu.au/international/future-students/scholarships

## Charles Darwin University (CDU)

Charles Darwin University Ellengowan Drive, Casuarina, NT 0811, Australia.

| | |
|---|---|
| **Tel**: | (61) 8 8946 6666 |
| **Email**: | scholarships@cdu.edu.au |
| **Website**: | www.cdu.edu.au |

The Charles Darwin University (CDU) offers programmes from certificate level to PhD, incorporating the full range of vocational education courses. CDU has a distinctive research profile, reflecting the priorities appropriate to its location. It is a participating member of several CRCs.

## Nanyang Technological University MBA Programme

**Length of Study**: 1 year, 18 months or 4 years

**Application Procedure**: Applicants must submit, with their application form, three recent passport sized photographs, official copies of degrees and professional qualifications, two references in sealed envelopes, evidence of finance, TOEFL and IELTS scores (overseas applicants only)

**For further information contact:**

**Tel**:     (61) 8 8946 6447
**Fax**:    (61) 8 8946 6777
**Email**:  busgrad@business.ntu.edu.au

## Vocational Education and Training (VET) Distinction Scholarship

**Purpose**: CDU Global offers a limited number of VET Distinction Scholarships to international students who come from China PRC, Indonesia or the Philippines and have a record of academic excellence and high achievement.
**Eligibility**: 1. Applicant must apply to study a Certificate III or higher VET qualification. 2. Applicant must be from China PRC, Indonesia or the Philippines. 3. Applicants must meet the University's academic and English language entry requirements for their chosen program. 4. Applicant must have a minimum overall score of 80% in their highest completed qualification. 5. Applicant must be classified as an International student on a student visa. 6. Applicant must be able to obtain a recommendation letter from a government sponsor, employer or partner institution of CDU. 7. Applicant should not hold another scholarship from an Australian or foreign sponsorship agency.
**Level of Study**: Postgraduate
**Type**: scholarship
**Value**: US$3,000
**Length of Study**: 1 year
**Application Procedure**: 1. Step 1: Submit your application to study with CDU in July through Studylink: student-cdu.studylink.com/ and make note of your application reference number. 2. Step 2: Complete and submit the online application form (this will be live as of the 24/3/20, please email: international@cdu.edu.au if you would like to be alerted when it is live). You will need to record your Studylink reference number and submit all the required items listed in the criteria at the time of completing your application.
**Closing Date**: 6 May
**Additional Information**: www.cdu.edu.au/international/how-apply/scholarships

## Charles Sturt University (CSU)

Charles Sturt University Boorooma Street, Locked Bag 588, Wagga Wagga, NSW 2678, Australia.

**Tel**:      (61) 2 6338 6077
**Email**:   inquiry@csu.edu.au
**Website**: www.csu.edu.au

CSU is one of the leading Australian universities for graduate employment and largest provider in distance education. Utilizing our expertise in distance education, CSU provides educational opportunities to students around the world. Around 36,000 students undertake their choice of study with CSU on one of our campuses, from home, their workplace or anywhere around the globe.

## Australian Postgraduate Awards

**Purpose**: To financially support postgraduate students of exceptional research promise in Master or Doctoral programs at Charles Sturt University
**Eligibility**: Awards will only be available to those who are Australian citizens and New Zealand citizens; have been granted permanent resident status by October 31st; have lived in Australia continuously for at least 12 months prior to October 31st; have completed at least 4 years of tertiary education studies at a high level of achievement; have obtained First Class Honours or equivalent results; will undertake a Master's (Honours) or Doctoral degree; are enroling as full-time students or, in exceptional circumstances, be granted approval by CSU for a part-time award; have had their enrolment into the proposed higher degree programme accepted by CSU
**Level of Study**: Postgraduate, Research
**Type**: Award
**Value**: US$32,500 per year
**Length of Study**: 2-3 years
**Frequency**: Annual
**Study Establishment**: Charles Sturt University
**Country of Study**: Australia
**Application Procedure**: Applicants must submit an application form
**Closing Date**: 31 October
**Funding**: Government
**Additional Information**: Please check at www.csu.edu.au/research/support/research-students/my-hdr/getting-started/scholarship-opportunities/main-round

**For further information contact:**

**Email**:    rgs@latrobe.edu.au

## Biology of Annual Ryegrass Scholarship

**Purpose**: To characterize annual ryegrass in Australian winter cropping areas
**Eligibility**: Open only for the citizens of Australia or permanent residents those who have a background in agriculture, biology, or plant science and achieved Honours 2a or equivalent
**Level of Study**: Graduate

**Value**: AU$24,616 (maximum per year) paid fortnightly for the period of 3 years
**Country of Study**: Australia

## For further information contact:

Charles Sturt University, Wagga Wagga, Boorooma St, North Wagga Wagga, NSW 2650, Australia.

**Tel**:        (61) 2 69 33 2862
**Email**:    jpratley@csu.edu.au

## Charles Sturt University Postgraduate Research Studentships (CSUPRS)

**Purpose**: To support high quality research students in Masters or Doctoral programs at Charles Sturt University
**Eligibility**: Open to the candidates who hold or expect to hold, at least a Bachelor degree with upper second class honours or a qualification deemed equivalent from CSU
**Level of Study**: Graduate, Research
**Type**: Studentship
**Value**: US$22,500 stipend plus allowances
**Frequency**: Annual
**Application Procedure**: Scholarship application form can be downloaded from the website. Send in the filled application to the center with original referee report and five copies of their report
**Closing Date**: 30 October
**Additional Information**: Offers of scholarships cannot be made to candidates until their enrolment as Research Higher Degree students has been approved by the Board of Graduate Studies. Please check at www.csu.edu.au/research/support/research-students/my-hdr/getting-started/scholarship-opportunities/main-round www.gooduniversitiesguide.com.au/scholarships/csu-postgraduate-research-scholarship-csuprs/charles-sturt-university/12142

## For further information contact:

Postgraduate Scholarships, Center for Research & Graduate Training, Charles Sturt University, Locked Bag 588, Wagga Wagga, NSW 2678, Australia.

**Tel**:        (61) 2 6933 4162
**Email**:    pgscholars@csu.edu.au

## Evidence-Based Approach to Improve Insulin Sensitivity in Horses, Using Dietary Ingredients

**Eligibility**: Open only for the citizens of Australia or permanent residents those who have achieved Honours 1 (Semester 1)

**Level of Study**: Graduate
**Value**: AU$19,231 (maximum per year) paid fortnightly for the period of 3 years and to be used for living expenses
**Country of Study**: Australia

## For further information contact:

Charles Sturt University, Locked Bag 588, Wagga Wagga, NSW 2678, Australia.

**Tel**:        (61) 2 6933 4242
**Email**:    gnoble@csu.edu.au

## Full-time scholarship (Australian Government's Research Training Program)

**Eligibility**: 1. Commencing a CSU HDR program, or currently enrolled. 2. Enrolling/enrolled as a full-time student. 3. Are enrolled concurrently in any other program, unless it is essential to the success of the HDR, or exceptional circumstances exist and are approved. 4. Are receiving another Commonwealth-funded postgraduate research scholarship.
**Level of Study**: Postgraduate
**Type**: scholarship
**Value**: This scholarship is valued at US$28,092 per annum, payable in fortnightly instalments.
**Length of Study**: 2 or 3 years
**Closing Date**: 1 May
**Additional Information**: research.csu.edu.au/study-with-us/scholarships/full-time-scholarship-agrtp

## Charlie Trotter Culinary Education Foundation

40 E. Chicago Avenue, Suite 418, Chicago, IL 60611, United States of America.

**Tel**:        (1) 312 600 9724
**Email**:    info@charlietrotters.com
**Website**: www.charlietrotters.com/about/foundation.asp

Charlie Trotter's is regarded as one of the finest restaurants in the world, dedicated to excellence in the culinary arts. It has been instrumental in establishing new standards for fine dining. Its main goal is to educate and expose youth to the great culinary arts in as many ways as possible. The Charlie Trotter Culinary Education Foundation, a non-profit organization, has been established to promote culinary arts among youth. The foundation is involved in awarding scholarships to students who are seeking careers in the culinary arts and working with Chicago-area youth to promote the enthusiastic quest for education as well as an interest in the cooking and food.

## Charlie Trotter's Culinary Education Foundation Culinary Study Scholarship

**Eligibility**: Open to an Illinois resident at the time of application
**Level of Study**: Professional development
**Type**: Scholarship
**Value**: US$5,000 cash scholarship for a pre-enroled student
**Length of Study**: 1 year
**Frequency**: Annual
**Country of Study**: United States of America
**Application Procedure**: Check website for further details
**Closing Date**: 1 March
**Funding**: Private, Foundation
**Contributor**: Charlie Trotter's
**Additional Information**: Please check website for more details

#### For further information contact:

The Culinary Trust Scholarship Program P.O. Box 273, New York, NY 10013, United States of America.

**Tel**:       (1) 646 224 6989
**Email**:    cholarships@theculinarytrust.com

## Chiang Ching Kuo Foundation for International Scholarly Exchange

13F, 65 Tun Hwa South Road, Section 2, 106-ROC, Taiwan, China.

**Tel**:       (886) 2 2704 5333
**Email**:    cckf@ms1.hinet.net
**Website**:  www.cckf.org

The Chiang Ching Kuo Foundation for International Scholarly Exchange is a non-profit organization headquartered in Taipei, the capital of the Republic of China. The Foundation was established in 1989 in honour of the late President Chiang Ching kuo. The main objective of the Foundation is to promote the study of Chinese culture and society, broadly defined.

## Chiang Ching Kuo Foundation Doctoral Fellowships

**Purpose**: To financially support Doctoral candidates while writing their dissertations
**Eligibility**: Open to applicants who have completed all other requirements for their PhD degree except the dissertation. Candidates must not be employed or receive grants from other sources
**Level of Study**: Doctorate
**Type**: Fellowships
**Value**: Up to US$15,000
**Length of Study**: 1 year
**Frequency**: Annual
**Application Procedure**: Applicants need to submit a 1 page summary of the proposed project, budget, curriculum vitae and detailed description of the proposed project along with the application form. Application forms are available online
**No. of awards offered**: 104
**Closing Date**: 15 October
**Funding**: Commercial, Private
**No. of awards given last year**: 28
**No. of applicants last year**: 104

## Chiang Ching Kuo Foundation for International Scholarly Exchange Eminent Scholar Lectureship

**Purpose**: To sponsor eminent foreign scholars to come to Taiwan to take up lectureships or positions as visiting scholars
**Eligibility**: Open to eminent scholars invited by universities or academic institutions of Taiwan
**Type**: Lectureship/Prize
**Value**: New Taiwan NT$2,000,000
**Length of Study**: 1 year
**Frequency**: Annual
**Study Establishment**: Universities or academic institutions in Taiwan
**Country of Study**: Taiwan
**Application Procedure**: Applicants must use the application forms provided by the Foundation. The application must be sent by registered mail to the Secretariat. Electronic version of all application materials must be enclosed on diskette or sent as email attachment to cckf@ms1.hinet.net with heading 'Application Materials from (Name)' in the header of the message. Applications are accepted from June 1st
**Closing Date**: 15 October
**Funding**: Foundation
**Additional Information**: Project directors who are currently receiving Foundation aid are ineligible to apply. Project directors may not submit more than one application

## Chiang Ching Kuo Foundation for International Scholarly Exchange Publication Subsidies

**Purpose**: To assist in the final stages of publishing academic works

**Eligibility**: Open to scholars in the final stages of publishing academic works. Applications from scholars affiliated with institutions in Taiwan must involve cooperation with one or more scholars from other countries. Applicants for publication subsidies must be affiliated with a university or other academic institution

**Type**: Grant

**Value**: Ranges between New Taiwan NT$5,000 and NT$10,000. Publication Subsidy Grants may only be used to cover editing, indexing, and other relevant publication costs. Translation and research-related expenses may not be included

**Application Procedure**: Applicants must use the application forms provided directly from the Foundation Secretariat. Three copies of the application and supporting documents must be submitted by registered mail to the Secretariat. In addition, electronic version of all application materials must be enclosed on diskette or sent as email attachment to cckf@ms1.hinet.net with heading 'Application Materials from (Name)' in the header of the message

**Closing Date**: 15 September

**Funding**: Trusts

**Additional Information**: Please check the website for more details

### For further information contact:

The Chiang Ching-kuo Foundation for International Scholarly Exchange, 8361 B Greensboro Dr. McLean, VA 22102, United States America.

**Email**: cckfnao@aol.com

## Doctoral Fellowships

**Purpose**: Supporting doctoral candidates for completing their dissertation in the last stage of their doctoral programs

**Eligibility**: Applicants should have completed all other requirements for their PhD degree. Applicants should be enroled in an accredited university in the United States, Canada, Mexico, and Central and Southern America

**Level of Study**: Doctorate

**Type**: Fellowship

**Value**: US$18,000

**Length of Study**: 1 year

**Frequency**: Annual

**Closing Date**: 15 October

**Funding**: Foundation

**Additional Information**: www.cckf.org/en/programs/american/doctoral-fellowships

## Junior Scholar Grants

**Purpose**: The Foundation provides grants for time off for research and writing to postdoctoral and assistant professors without tenure who are affiliated with an accredited American university and who have taught for no more than 6 years since receiving PhD degree

**Eligibility**: Junior Scholar Grants is only available for applicants who are affiliated with an American university

**Type**: Grant

**Value**: Up to US$30,000

**Frequency**: Annual

**No. of awards offered**: 80

**Closing Date**: 15 October

**Funding**: Foundation

**No. of awards given last year**: 20

**No. of applicants last year**: 80

## Scholar Grants

**Purpose**: To help replace half of the salary of faculty on sabbatical, or for time off for research and writing

**Eligibility**: Tenure faculty, including full professors and associate professor, in the accredited universities in the United States, Canada, Mexico, and Central and Southern America are eligible to apply for scholar grants

**Type**: Grant

**Value**: US$40,000 or US$35,000

**Frequency**: Annual

**No. of awards offered**: 42

**Closing Date**: 15 October

**No. of awards given last year**: 12

**No. of applicants last year**: 42

**Additional Information**: www.cckf.org/en/programs/american/scholar

## Chicago Tribune

435 North Michigan Avenue, Chicago, IL 60611, United States of America.

**Tel**:     (1) 312 222 3232
**Email**:     jwoelffer@tribune.com
**Website**:     www.chicagotribune.com

The Chicago Tribune is the Midwest's leading newspaper. The Chicago Tribune Literary Awards are part of a continued dedication to readers, writers and ideas.

## Nelson Algren Awards

**Purpose**: To award writers of short fiction
**Eligibility**: Each entrant must be at least 18 years old and a legal resident of the contest area (above) as of the date of entry
**Level of Study**: Unrestricted
**Type**: Award
**Value**: one grand prize winner (US$3,500) and five finalists (US$750)
**Frequency**: Annual
**Country of Study**: Any country
**Application Procedure**: Visit algren.submittable.com (the "Contest Page"), complete an entry form with the following required information: (a) name, (b) telephone number, (c) email address, (d) the title and word count of your submission, and submit it along with your short story (a "Story") (together with the entry form referred as an "Entry") that otherwise meets all Submission Requirements below. Entries will not be accepted through any other method
**Closing Date**: 17 February
**Funding**: Corporation
**Additional Information**: Please contact to Chicago Tribune for latest updates. Please check at articles.chicagotribune.com/2013-11-26/news/chi-2013-nelson-algren-award-official-rules-20120906_1_grand-prize-enter-or-win-chicago-tribune-company-llc www.chicagotribune.com/entertainment/books/literary-awards/ct-algren-contest-announcement-2019-20181121-story.html#nt=standard-embed

### For further information contact:

Chicago Tribune, Nelson Algren Awards, 435 N. TT200, Michigan Avenue, Chicago, IL 60611, United States of America.

**Email**:    printersrow@tribune.com

## Chilean International Cooperation Agency

### Chile: Nelson Mandela Scholarships

**Purpose**: The Chilean International Cooperation Agency (AGCI) is offering scholarships for accredited Spanish-taught Master's program at Chilean higher education institutions. The scholarships are offered to professionals who are citizens of South Africa, Mozambique and Angola

**Eligibility**: 1. Experience in the subjects they choose to pursue Master's studies in unconditional acceptance offer at a Chilean higher education institution. 2. 4-year university degree. 3. If employed already, you will need a letter of support, indicating that you will be released for the duration of your studies
**Level of Study**: Postgraduate
**Type**: Scholarship
**Value**: R$500
**Length of Study**: 4 year
**Frequency**: Annual
**Country of Study**: South Africa
**Application Procedure**: Apply online: www.agci.gob.cl
**Closing Date**: 31 October
**Funding**: Foundation

### For further information contact:

**Email**:    becasmandela@gmail.com

## China Scholarship Council

Level 13, Building A3 No.9 Chegongzhuang Avenue, 100044, Beijing, China.

**Tel**:         (86) 660 93900
**Email**:     webmaster@csc.edu.cn
**Website**:  www.csc.edu.cn

The China Scholarship council (CSC) is a non-profit institution, which is affiliated with the ministry of education. The main objective of the CSC is to develop the educational, scientific and technological, and cultural exchanges and economic and trade cooperation between China and other countries.

### K C Wong Postgraduate Scholarship Programme

**Purpose**: To support students who intend to study further at King's College London
**Eligibility**: Open to applicants who are citizens and permanent residents of People's Republic of china
**Type**: Scholarship
**Value**: Tuition fees at the international rate plus an annual stipend of £8,400
**Length of Study**: 3 years
**Frequency**: Annual
**Study Establishment**: King's College London
**Country of Study**: United Kingdom
**Application Procedure**: A completed application form, which is available online, must be sent

**Closing Date**: 1 February
**Funding**: Government
**Contributor**: K C Wong Education Foundation

### For further information contact:

Research & Graduate School Support Section King's College London, London WC2R 2LS, United Kingdom.

**Tel**: (44) 20 7848 3376
**Fax**: (44) 20 7848 3328
**Email**: graduateschool@kcl.ac.uk

## Chinese American Medical Society (CAMS)

41 Elizabeth Street, Suite 600, New York, NY 10013, United States of America.

**Tel**: (1) 212 334 4760
**Email**: jlove@camsociety.org
**Website**: www.camsociety.org
**Contact**: Dr H H Wang, Executive Director

The Chinese American Medical Society (CAMS) is a non-profit, charitable, educational and scientific society that aims to promote the scientific association of medical professionals of Chinese descent. It also aims to advance medical knowledge and scientific research with emphasis on aspects unique to the Chinese and to promote the health status of Chinese Americans. The Society makes scholarships available to medical dental students and provides summer fellowships for students conducting research in health problems related to the Chinese

## Chinese American Medical Society Scholarship Program

**Purpose**: In the early 1970's the Chinese American Medical Society went to considerable lengths to provide scholarships to outstanding medical students in need of financial assistance
**Eligibility**: 1. Must be a graduate student 2. Must attend a university 3. Must not be attending high school currently 4. Must study full-time 5. Restricted to students studying Health and Medical Sciences
**Level of Study**: Graduate, Postgraduate
**Type**: Programme grant
**Value**: US$5,000-US$20,000
**Frequency**: Annual
**Country of Study**: Any country

**Application Procedure**: The submission has to be made to the email address scholarship@camsociety.org Email is the preferred method of submission for applications. The committee asks that all applications and supporting materials be sent as a single PDF file and emailed to scholarship@camsociety.org
**Closing Date**: 30 March
**Funding**: Private
**Additional Information**: www.petersons.com/scholarship/chinese-american-medical-society-scholarship-111_150708.aspx

### For further information contact:

Scholarship Committee, 265 Canal Street, Suite 515, New York, NY 10013, United States of America.

**Tel**: (1) 212 334 4760
**Email**: scholarship@camsociety.org

## Chinook Regional Career Transitions for Youth

Room B310, 1701 - 5 Avenue South, Lethbridge, AB T1J 0W4, Canada.

**Tel**: (1) 403 328 3996
**Email**: mvennard@pallisersd.ab.ca
**Website**: www.careersteps.ca

The Chinook regional career transitions for youth aims to improve the school-to-work transitions for students, promoting lifelong learning and coordinating and implementing career development activities and programming for youth.

## Robin Rousseau Memorial Mountain Achievement Scholarship

**Purpose**: To bring about awareness of ways to improve safety in the mountains
**Eligibility**: Applicants must be Alberta residents and active in the mountain community; and plan to study in any recognized Mountain Leadership and Safety program
**Level of Study**: Professional development
**Type**: Scholarship
**Value**: Course fee
**Frequency**: Annual
**Application Procedure**: A completed application form must be sent
**Closing Date**: 30 January
**Additional Information**: myredkite.com/finaid/robin-rousseau-memorial-mountain-achievement-scholarship

**For further information contact:**

Alberta Scholarship Programs Box 28000 Stn Main, Edmonton, AB T5J 4R4, Canada.

**Tel**:      (1) 780 427 8640
**Fax**:     (1) 780 427 1288
**Email**:   scholarships@gov.ab.ca

## Toyota Earth Day Scholarship Program

**Purpose**: To encourage community service
**Eligibility**: Open to students who have achieved academic excellence and distinguished themselves in environmental community service and extracurricular and volunteer activities
**Level of Study**: Professional development
**Type**: Scholarship
**Value**: C$5,000
**Frequency**: Annual
**Application Procedure**: Application form available online
**Closing Date**: 15 February
**Additional Information**: ustpaul.ca/upload-files/Financial Aid/scholarships/Toyota_Earth_Day_Scholarship_Program %202010-En.pdf

**For further information contact:**

Toyota Earth Day Scholarship Program, III Peter St., Suite 503, Toronto, ON M5V 2H1, Canada.

**Email**:   scholarship@earthday.ca

## Choirs Ontario

Choirs Ontario A-1422 Bayview Avenue, Toronto, ON M4G 3A7, Canada.

**Tel**:      (1) 416 923 1144
**Email**:   info@choirsontario.org
**Website**: www.choirsontario.org
**Contact**: Melva Graham

Choirs Ontario is an arts service organization dedicated to the promotion of choral activities and standards of excellence. Established in 1971 as the Ontario Choral Federation, Choirs Ontario provides services to choirs, conductors, choristers, composers, administrators and educators as well as anyone who enjoys listening to the sound of choral music. Choirs Ontario operates with the financial assistance of the Ministry of Culture, the Ontario Arts Council, the Trillium Foundation, the Toronto Arts Council and numerous foundations, corporations and individual donors.

## Ruth Watson Henderson Choral Composition Competition

**Purpose**: To award new choral composition
**Eligibility**: Candidates must be Canadian citizens or landed immigrants who are permanent residents of Ontario
**Level of Study**: Postgraduate
**Type**: Prize
**Value**: C$1,000
**Country of Study**: Any country
**Application Procedure**: Further information available on the website
**Funding**: Private
**Additional Information**: fst.se/ruth-watson-henderson-choral-composition-competition

## Citizens United for Research in Epilepsy

### Taking Flight Award

**Subjects**: Medical and Health Sciences
**Purpose**: This award seeks to promote the careers of young epilepsy investigators to allow them to develop a research focus independent of their mentor(s).
**Type**: Fellowship
**Value**: Up to US$100,000
**Length of Study**: 1 year
**Frequency**: Annual, if funds are available
**Country of Study**: Any country
**Application Procedure**: Information at: www.cureepilepsy.org/the-cure-epilepsy-grant-program-and-grant-opportunities/
**No. of awards offered**: One
**Closing Date**: Varies by year but usually in March

## Citizens United in Research for Epilepsy (CURE)

### Taking Flight Award

**Subjects**: Basic mechanisms of epilepsy; Acquired epilepsies; Pediatric epilepsies; SUDEP; Treatment-resistant epilepsies; and Sleep & epilepsy.

**Purpose**: The award seeks to promote the careers of young epilepsy investigators to allow them to develop a research focus independent of their mentor(s).

**Eligibility**: You must fall into one of the following categories to be eligible for the Taking Flight Award: A senior postdoctoral fellow who has a minimum of 3 years postdoctoral experience; A clinical fellow who is a Neurology Resident in his/her Neurology training and considering Epilepsy Fellowships; Newly appointed faculty within one year of having completed postdoctoral training. International applicants are welcome; you do not have to be a US citizen or working in the US to apply for this award. All materials must be submitted in English.

**Type**: Award

**Value**: Requests may be made for up to US$100,000 for one year. Funding requests may include salary support for the PI, technical staff and/or collaborators; supplies, animal costs, publication fees etc.; and travel to an epilepsy-related conference if the PI is presenting his/her CURE-funded research. Funds are not to be used to purchase equipment. Indirect costs are not supported.

**Length of Study**: One year

**Country of Study**: Any country

**Application Procedure**: See website for further details.

**Closing Date**: 21 November

**Additional Information**: www.cureepilepsy.org/grants-program/#grant_opportunities

## The CURE Epilepsy Award

**Subjects**: Basic mechanisms of epilepsy; Acquired epilepsies; Pediatric epilepsies; SUDEP; Treatment-resistant epilepsies; and Sleep & epilepsy.

**Purpose**: The award reflects CURE's continued focus on scientific advances that have the potential to truly transform the lives of those affected by epilepsy, with prevention and disease modification as critical goals

**Eligibility**: This award is available to both established and early career investigators. Generally, early career investigators are university faculty at the assistant professor level (or hold an equivalent position in a non-university research organization) Established investigators are university faculty at the associate professor level or above. Researchers who serve on CURE's Scientific Advisory Council are ineligible to apply for or sponsor a grant for the duration of their term. International applicants are welcome. Postdoctoral fellows may not apply for this award. All materials must be submitted in English.

**Type**: Award

**Value**: Requests may be made for up to a total of US$250,000 paid over 2 years. Funding requests may include salary support for the Principal Investigator (PI), co-PIs, technical staff, supplies, animal costs, publication fees and travel to an epilepsy-related conference if the PI is presenting his/her CURE-funded research. Limited equipment purchases that are required to complete goals will be considered. Indirect costs are not supported.

**Length of Study**: Two years

**Country of Study**: Any country

**Application Procedure**: See website for further details.

**Closing Date**: 21 November

**Additional Information**: www.cureepilepsy.org/grants-program/#grant_opportunities

## Clara Haskil Competition

Case Postale 234, 31 rue du Conseil, CH-1800 Vevey, Switzerland.

| | |
|---|---|
| **Tel**: | (41) 21 922 6704 |
| **Email**: | info@clara-haskil.ch |
| **Website**: | www.regart.ch/clara-haskil |
| **Contact**: | Mr Patrick Peikert, Director |

The Clara Haskil Competition exists to recognize and help a young pianist whose approach to piano interpretation is of the same spirit that constantly inspired Clara Haskil, and that she illustrated so perfectly.

## Clara Haskil International Piano Competition

**Purpose**: To recognize and financially help a young pianist

**Eligibility**: Open to pianists of any nationality and either sex who are no more than 27 years of age

**Level of Study**: Postgraduate

**Type**: Prize

**Value**: CHF 25,000

**Frequency**: Every 2 years

**Country of Study**: Any country

**Application Procedure**: Applicants must pay an entry fee of CHF 200

**No. of awards offered**: Approx. 150

**Funding**: Corporation, Trusts, International office

**Contributor**: Fondation Nestlé pour l'Art

**No. of awards given last year**: 2

**No. of applicants last year**: Approx. 150

**Additional Information**: The competition is usually held during the last weeks of August or the beginning of September app.getaccepted.com/clarahaskil

**For further information contact:**

International Piano Competition, Concours Clara Haskil, CH-1800 Vevey, Switzerland.

**Tel**: (41) 21 922 67 04
**Fax**: (41) 21 922 67 34

## Clare Hall Cambridge

### Clare Hall Research Fellowships in the Arts and Social Sciences

**Purpose**: Research Fellowships are primarily intended to provide opportunities for scholars at an early stage of their academic careers to establish and pursue their research in a supportive academic environment
**Eligibility**: 1. During their tenure, Research Fellows have no college teaching duties other than to pursue their research. They are however members of the College Governing Body and may serve on other College committees. 2. Successful candidates are expected to be graduate students who have recently completed or who are about to complete their PhD 3. There is no restriction on age, sex or previous standing, except that candidates may not already have held a Research Fellowship at a college of either the University of Oxford or the University of Cambridge, and some preference may be given to candidates who are at a fairly early stage of their research career. 4. Research Fellows are required to live in Cambridge during Full Term, but leave may be granted to work away if necessary. Small grants for research expenses may be made available on application to the Senior Tutor
**Level of Study**: Research
**Type**: Fellowship
**Length of Study**: 3 years
**Frequency**: Annual
**Country of Study**: Any country
**Application Procedure**: Applications must be made online using the following link: app.casc.cam.ac.uk/fas_live/clh_arts.aspx
**Closing Date**: 13 March
**Funding**: Private
**Additional Information**: www.clarehall.cam.ac.uk/research-fellows

**For further information contact:**

Clare Hall, Herschel Road, Cambridge, CB3 9AL, United Kingdom.

**Email**: college.registrar@clarehall.cam.ac.uk

## Claude Leon Foundation

P.O. Box 30538, Tokai 7966, South Africa.

**Tel**: (27) 21 787 0418
**Email**: postdocadmin@leonfoundation.co.za
**Website**: www.leonfoundation.co.za

The Claude Leon Foundation is a South African Charitable Trust. resulting from a Bequest by Claude Leon (1884-1972), A prominent Johannesburg businessman. CLF funds a postdoctoral fellowship programme, now in it's 18th Year - It's goal is the building of research capacity in the faculties of Science, Engineering and Medical Sciences at South African Universities via awards to both South African and foreign postdoctoral scientists.

### Claude Leon Foundation Postdoctoral Fellowship

**Purpose**: To fund postdoctoral research
**Eligibility**: Open to South African and foreign nationals. Preference will be given to candidates who have received their doctoral degrees in the last 5 years, and to those who are currently underrepresented in South African tertiary institutions
**Level of Study**: Postdoctorate
**Value**: ZAR 235,000 PA for a 2-year fellowship plus travel grant up to a maximum of ZAR 45,000 to present a paper on poster at an international conference during the 2nd year of fellowship
**Length of Study**: 2 years on renewal after the first year
**Frequency**: Annual
**Study Establishment**: South African universities and some institutions.
**Country of Study**: South Africa
**Application Procedure**: Applications are not accepted directly from candidates. They must have been offered a postdoctoral position at a tertiary institution. The application should then be sent to the foundation by the institution not by the candidate
**No. of awards offered**: 400
**Closing Date**: 31 May
**Contributor**: The Claude Leon Foundation, South Africa
**No. of awards given last year**: 58
**No. of applicants last year**: 400
**Additional Information**: Applications should be sent to the foundation by the institution at which the candidate has secured a postdoctoral position, not by the candidate www.leonfoundation.co.za/postdoctoral.htm

**For further information contact:**

**Email**: billfrankel@kayacomm.com

# Coimbra Group

## Coimbra Group Scholarship Programme for Young Professors and Researchers from Latin American Universities

**Purpose**: It aims to increase cooperation amongst its members by enhancing special academic and cultural ties, and creating channels of information and exchange

**Eligibility**: To be a national of and currently resident in a Latin American country. Candidates already living and/or studying in Europe will not be considered. 1. To hold a university degree or equivalent. 2. To be linked as a professor or researcher to a Latin American University recognised as such by the authorities of the country. 3. To use the Coimbra Group Office electronic application process. Only one application per candidate will be accepted. 4. To submit online an Acceptance Letter/email from the tutor/ partner with whom the work programme will be undertaken in the host institution. This document is mandatory. 5. To be born on or after 1 January 1979. 6. Previously selected candidates can apply for a second grant, but they will not be prioritised

**Level of Study**: Graduate

**Type**: Scholarship

**Frequency**: Annual

**Country of Study**: Any country

**Application Procedure**: Kindly check the website for further information. www.coimbra-group.eu/wp-content/uploads/CALL-LA-2019-brochure-1.pdf

**Closing Date**: 31 March

**Funding**: Private

**Additional Information**: The Coimbra Group Office will contact all candidates and inform them about the result of their application by the end of May euraxess.ec.europa.eu/worldwide/brazil/coimbra-group-scholarship-programme-young-professors-and-researchers-latin

### For further information contact:

Egmontstraat, 11, rue d'Egmont, B-1000 Brussels, Belgium.

**Tel**:       (32) 2 513 83 32

**Email**:    Monteiro@coimbra-group.eu

## Coimbra Group Scholarship Programme for Young Researchers from the European Neighbourhood

**Purpose**: The main aim of this scholarship programme is to enable scholars to undertake research in which they are engaged in their home institution and to help them to establish academic and research contacts

**Eligibility**: Applicants must fulfil all the following criteria: 1. Be born before or after 1 January 1984. 2. Be nationals of and current residents in one Of the above-listed countries. 3. Be current academic staff members of a university or an equivalent higher education institution located in one of the above-listed countries and be of postdoctoral or equivalent status, although some institutions may offer opportunities to doctoral student

**Level of Study**: Graduate

**Type**: Programme grant

**Frequency**: Annual

**Country of Study**: Any country

**Application Procedure**: 1. Candidates may apply for one university only. Multiple applications will not be considered valid. 2. Only the universities listed in the table below are taking part in the current edition of the Coimbra Group Scholarship Programme. 3. Applicants will be able to fill in the on-line registration until 31 March midnight (Brussels time) on the Coimbra Group website: www.coimbra-group.eu/activities/scholarships

**Closing Date**: 31 March

**Funding**: Private

**Additional Information**: armacad.info/coimbra-group–2019-02-12–coimbra-group-scholarship-programme-2019-for-young-researchers-from-the-european-neighbourhood-europe

### For further information contact:

**Email**:    quici@coimbra-group.eu

## Coimbra Group Short Stay Scholarship Programme for Young Researchers

**Purpose**: It aims to increase cooperation amongst its members by enhancing special academic and cultural ties, and creating channels of information and exchange

**Eligibility**: Applicants should be: 1. Born on or after 1 January 1974. 2. Nationals of and current residents in a country in Sub-Saharan Africa. 3. Current staff members of a university or an equivalent higher education institution in Sub-Saharan Africa. 4. Of doctoral/postdoctoral or equivalent status. Eligible countries are all African countries except Algeria, Egypt, Libya, Morocco, and Tunisia applicants from these countries are eligible under the Scholarship Programme for Young Researchers from the European Neighbourhood

**Level of Study**: Graduate

**Type**: Scholarship

**Frequency**: Annual

**Country of Study**: Any country

**Application Procedure**: Online application form is available in the following link. There are two steps of application procedure to be followed. www.coimbra-group.eu/activities/scholarships

**Closing Date**: 31 March

**Funding**: Private

**Additional Information**: www.coimbra-group.eu/wp-content/uploads/CALL-Africa-2019-brochure.pdf

### For further information contact:

**Email**:    info@coimbra-group.eu

## Collegeville Institute for Ecumenical and Cultural Research

14027 Fruit Farm Road, Box 2000, Collegeville, MN 56321, United States of America.

**Tel**:          (1) 320 363 3366
**Email**:      staff@collegevilleinstitute.org
**Website**:   www.collegevilleinstitute.org
**Contact**:   Donald Ottenhoff, Executive Director

The Institute for Ecumenical and Cultural Research seeks to discern the meaning of Christian identity and unity in a religiously and culturally diverse nation and world and to communicate that meaning for the mission of the church and the renewal of human community. The Institute is committed to research, study, prayer, reflection and dialogue, in a place shaped by the Benedictine tradition of worship and work.

### Bishop Thomas Hoyt Jr Fellowship

**Purpose**: To provide the Institute's residency fee to a North American person of colour writing a doctoral dissertation, in order to help the churches to increase the number of persons of colour working in ecumenical and cultural research

**Eligibility**: Open to a North American, Canadian or Mexican person of colour writing a doctoral dissertation within the general area of the Institute's concern

**Level of Study**: Postgraduate

**Type**: Fellowship

**Value**: US$5,000 per year

**Length of Study**: 1 academic year

**Frequency**: Annual

**Study Establishment**: The Institute

**Country of Study**: United States of America

**Application Procedure**: Applicants must apply in the usual way to the Resident Scholars Programme (see separate listing). If invited by the admissions committee to be a Resident Scholar, the person will then be eligible for consideration for the Hoyt Fellowship

**No. of awards offered**: 1

**Closing Date**: 1 November

**Funding**: Private

**No. of awards given last year**: 1

**No. of applicants last year**: 1

### For further information contact:

**Tel**:          (1) 320 363 3367
**Email**:      dottenhoff@collegevilleinstitute.org

## Columbia College of Missouri

### Columbia College of Missouri Boone County Endowed Award

**Purpose**: This award is for Missouri high school seniors who are residents of Boone County and planning to attend Columbia College

**Eligibility**: Must be a graduating high school senior. Must be a resident of Boone County, MO. 1. Must be a United States citizen or permanent resident. 2. Must demonstrate community service/volunteer work. 3. Must enroll as a full-time student. 4. Must have a cumulative grade point average of 3.1 or higher. 5. Must have an ACT score of 22 or higher or the equivalent SAT score

**Level of Study**: Graduate

**Type**: Award

**Value**: US$1,000

**Frequency**: Annual

**Country of Study**: United States of America

**Application Procedure**: The scholarship is made possible through the support of more than 200 area businesses. Recipients of the award will be chosen by committee in April and will be notified appropriately. Application details are available in the form of pdf. www.ccis.edu/offices/financialaid/booneendowed/boonecountyendowedscholarshipday.pdf

**Closing Date**: 31 March

**Funding**: Private

**No. of awards given last year**: 5

**Additional Information**: www.unigo.com/scholarships/all/columbia-college-of-missouri-boone-county-endowed-award/1070

### For further information contact:

1001 Rogers St., Columbia, MO 65216, United States of America.

**Tel**:          (1) 573 875 7506
**Email**:      admissions@ccis.edu

# Columbia GSAS

## Foreign Language and Area Studies Fellowship

**Purpose**: Administered by the Title VI National Resource Centers at the University of Pennsylvania, the Foreign Language and Area Studies (FLAS) Fellowships program funding to Graduate and Undergraduate Students studying modern foreign languages and related area studies

**Eligibility**: Students receiving Academic Year Fellowships must be enrolled in full-time study for the duration of the FLAS award and must take one language course and one related area or international studies course each semester. 1. Fellows must be United States Citizens or permanent residents. 2. Academic Year Fellows must be admitted to or enrolled in undergraduate, graduate, or professional programs at the University of Pennsylvania. FLAS awards may be used in some cases for students participating in official overseas language programs and in very limited cases for dissertators

**Level of Study**: Postgraduate

**Type**: Fellowship

**Value**: US$5,000 and a US$2,500

**Frequency**: Annual

**Country of Study**: Any country

**Application Procedure**: You will need to create a free online Interfolio account and complete the application in that system. In addition to entering information into the account, you will need to upload: 1. A personal statement regarding your planned use of the FLAS fellowship. This is a one-page, single-spaced, essay describing why this language study is essential to realizing your study and career goals. 2. Your curriculum vitae. 3. Unofficial higher education transcript (s) of your most recent academic work, whether at the University of Pennsylvania or another university or college, in digital format. Transcripts may be verified during the review process. 4. Two letters of recommendation (you will request them through the system). When you ask the faculty members for a recommendation, tell them that all letters of recommendation must specifically address how a FLAS would contribute to your current program of study or would be integrated with it

**Closing Date**: 13 February

**Funding**: Private

**Additional Information**: gsas.columbia.edu/student-guide/financing-your-education/flas-fellowship-summer

### For further information contact:

Graduate School of Arts and Sciences, 107 Low Memorial Library, 535 West 116th Street, New York, NY 10027, United States of America.

**Email**:   gsas-fellowships@columbia.edu

## Graduate School of Arts and Sciences International Travel Fellowships

**Purpose**: Travel Fellowships provide funding for international travel (outside of the United States) that is necessary for the completion of the dissertation. Travel Fellowship funds may not be used for research in residence at Columbia

**Eligibility**: 1. Be a PhD student in an Arts and Sciences program 2. Have completed all requirements for the MPhil degree and passed the prospectus defense before September 1

**Level of Study**: Graduate

**Type**: Fellowships, operating grants

**Frequency**: Annual

**Country of Study**: Any country

**Application Procedure**: Applications must include the following items: 1. Completed GSAS online application form. 2. An up-to-date GSAS transcript (official PDF transcript from the Registrar's office). Note: The GSAS Fellowship application does not accept encrypted files for upload. Official Columbia transcript PDFs are encrypted; you may order a paper copy through SSOL or print the official transcript PDF you receive from Parchment, then scan and upload it. 3. A curriculum vitae (three pages maximum). 4. A statement of your language preparation for research abroad, specifying the language(s) needed to carry out your research and your proficiency in each (one page maximum). 5. A project proposal of no more than 1,500 words, which should include a justification of your need to travel and a specific discussion of your research plans during the fellowship period. Please do not submit a copy of the departmental dissertation prospectus. Proposals will be read by an inter-departmental faculty committee and should emphasize the potential of your research to make a contribution to the particular field and to scholarship in general. 6. A timetable for completion of research and writing (two pages maximum). Please be as specific as possible. Applicants can apply for only one of the following terms: academic year (fall and spring). 7. Two letters of recommendation. GSAS prefers that recommenders submit their letters of recommendation electronically to expedite processing. 8. A budget proposal

**Closing Date**: 26 February

**Funding**: Private

**Additional Information**: The terms of the GSAS Travel Fellowship prohibit grantees from holding teaching assignments or any other position concurrently gsas.columbia.edu/student-guide/dissertation/gsas-international-travel-awards

### For further information contact:

109 Low Memorial Library, MC 4306, 535 West 116th Street, New York, NY 10027, United States of America.

**Email**:   gsas-admissions@columbia.edu

# Columbia University

405 Low Library, MC 4335, 535 West 116th Street, New York, NY 10027, United States of America.

Tel:        (1) 212 854 3830
Email:    support@ei.columbia.edu
Website:  www.earth.columbia.edu

The Earth Institute at Columbia University brings together talent from throughout the University to address complex issues facing the planet and its inhabitants, with particular focus on sustainable development and the needs of the world's poor.

## Benjamin A. Gilman International Scholarship Program

Purpose: The United States Department of State's Benjamin A. Gilman International Scholarship is a grant program that enables students of limited financial means to study or intern abroad, thereby gaining skills critical to our national security and economic competitiveness
Eligibility: Gilman Scholarships are open to undergraduates in good academic standing at accredited United States colleges and universities who are United States citizens and who meet the following criteria: 1. They are receiving a federal Pell Grant or can provide proof that they will be receiving a Pell Grant at the time of application of during their term of study abroad. 2. They are applying to or have been accepted into a study abroad program eligible for credit at their home institution. 3. They are studying abroad for at least four consecutive weeks in one country. 4. They are studying abroad in any country except a country on the United States Department of State's current Travel Warning list
Level of Study: Postgraduate
Type: Scholarship
Value: Awards of up to US$5,000 for semester or academic year program
Frequency: Annual
Country of Study: Any country
Closing Date: 3 March
Funding: Private
Additional Information: urf.columbia.edu/fellowship/benjamin-gilman-international-scholarships

### For further information contact:

202 Hamilton Hall, MC 2811, 1130 Amsterdam Ave, New York, NY 10027, United States of America.

Tel:        (1) 212 853 2375
Fax:      (1) 212 854 2797
Email:    ugrad-urf@columbia.edu

## Knight-Bagehot Fellowships in Economics and Business Journalism at Columbia University

Purpose: To improve the quality of economics and business journalism through instruction to mid career journalists.
Eligibility: Open to professional journalists globally;
Level of Study: Graduate, Postgraduate, MBA
Type: Fellowship
Value: An approximately US$60,000 stipend to cover living expenses, plus tuition for the full academic year at Columbia University
Length of Study: 1 academic year
Frequency: Annual
Study Establishment: School of Journalism, Columbia University
Country of Study: United States of America
Application Procedure: Applicants must submit a completed application form, two 1,000 word essays, three letters of reference, and five work samples. journalism.columbia.edu/kb
No. of awards offered: 10 Fellows each year
Closing Date: 31 January
Funding: Corporation, Foundation, Trusts
Contributor: Knight Foundation
No. of awards given last year: 10
No. of applicants last year: 100
Additional Information: journalism.columbia.edu/kb

### For further information contact:

Graduate School of Journalism, Columbia University, 2950 Broadway, New York, NY 10027, United States of America.

Tel:        (1) 212 854 2711
Fax:      (1) 212 854 7837
Email:    ann.grimes@columbia.edu

## Marie Tharp Visiting Fellowships

Purpose: To provide an opportunity for women scientists to conduct research at one of the related departments within the Earth Institute
Eligibility: Open to women candidates who have obtained their PhD and are citizens of the United States
Level of Study: Doctorate, Research
Type: Fellowships
Value: US$25,000

**Length of Study**: 3 months
**Frequency**: Annual
**Country of Study**: United States of America
**Application Procedure**: Applicants must submit a 3-page proposal, a curriculum vitae, a proposed budget and complete contact information of 3 references
**Additional Information**: All application materials may be submitted by mail or by email www.earth.columbia.edu/sitefiles/file/Research/Marie_Tharp_Information_Packet.pdf

### For further information contact:

ADVANCE at The Earth Institute at Columbia University Lamont-Doherty Earth Observatory of Columbia University, 61 Rte 9W, Palisades, NY 10964, United States of America.

**Email**:   kdutt@ldeo.columbia.edu

## Commonwealth Eye Health Consortium

International Centre for Eye Health, London School of Hygiene & Tropical Medicine, Keppel Street, London, WC1E 7HT, United Kingdom.

**Tel**:       (44) 20 7636 8636
**Email**:     press@lshtm.ac.uk
**Contact**:   Commonwealth Eye Health Consortium

The Commonwealth Eye Health Consortium is a group of expert organizations working together to deliver a five-year programme of fellowships, research, and technology to strengthen eye health systems across the Commonwealth.

### CEHC Masters Scholarships in Public Health for Eye Care

**Purpose**: The Masters in Public Health for Eye Care at the London School of Hygiene & Tropical Medicine is a well-established course that aims to train leaders in the prevention of blindness and to strengthen research and academic capacity for eye care programmes and training facilities, particularly in low- and middle-income countries
**Eligibility**: See the website. Entrance Requirement : 1. Come from low or middle-income Commonwealth countries that are less represented in the alumni body of the MSc Public health for eye care. 2. Work in regions where there are severe constraints in human resources for eye health work in regions where there are no / limited training opportunities in

PHEC / community eye health. 3. Demonstrate previous involvement/commitment to community eye health activities or VISION2020 programmes Present a clear career plan in public health for eye care, which they will realistically. 4. Be able to follow on completion of the MSc. 5. Have experience in public health for eye care based research and/or training in eye care. 6. Fulfill the United Kingdom Border Agency English Language Requirement by passing the LSHTM English language requirement by 11 May
**Value**: Several scholarships are awarded each year. Each scholarship covers the following:All course feesTwo return flightsDissertation project fundLiving costsAccommodation with food at the International Students House in Central London. Find out more about the International Students House
**Study Establishment**: Scholarships are awarded to undertake MSc in Public Health for Eye Care
**Country of Study**: United Kingdom
**Application Procedure**: Apply to the London School of Hygiene & Tropical Medicine for a place on the course: if you have applied and been accepted to the academic year you must request to "be reconsidered" for the academic year. Please contact the LSHTM Registry to be asked to "be reconsidered" Once you have received an offer from the London School of Hygiene & Tropical Medicine here: CEHC; MSc Scholarships Application
**Closing Date**: 11 May
**Additional Information**: For more details please browse the website scholarship-positions.com/cehc-masters-scholarships-in-public-health-eye-care-uk/ iceh.lshtm.ac.uk/commonwealth-eye-health-consortium-cehc-scholarships-2018-19-for-msc-public-health-for-eye-care/

### For further information contact:

**Email**:   Romulo.Fabunan@Lshtm.ac.uk

## Commonwealth Fund

1 East 75th Street, New York, NY 10027, United States of America.

**Tel**:       (1) 212 606 3800
**Email**:     grants@cmwf.org
**Website**:   www.cmwf.org

The Commonwealth Fund of New York is a philanthropic foundation established in 1918. The Fund supports independent research on health and social issues and makes grants to improve healthcare practice and policy.

## Australian-American Health Policy Fellowship

**Purpose**: To enable Fellows to gain an in-depth understanding of the Australian health care system and policy process, recent reforms, and models for best practice, thus enhancing their ability to make innovative contributions to policymaking in the United States, to improve the theory and practice of health policy in Australia and the United States by stimulating the cross-fertilization of ideas and experience and to encourage ongoing health policy collaboration and exchange between Australia and the United States by creating a network of international health policy experts
**Eligibility**: Open to accomplished, mid-career health policy researchers and practitioners including academics, physicians, decision makers in managed care and other private organizations, federal and state health officials and journalists
**Level of Study**: Research
**Type**: Fellowship
**Value**: For a full 10-month stay in Australia, the fellowship awards up to AU$87,000 which includes a living allowance, relocation expenses, research related travel and conferences, etc. There is also a family supplement available (e.g. up to AU$26,000 for a partner and two children). Round trip airfares to Australia are also covered
**Length of Study**: Up to 10 months
**Frequency**: Annual
**Study Establishment**: Suitable establishment in Australia
**Country of Study**: Australia
**Application Procedure**: Please go to www.commonwealthfund.org/grants-and-fellowships/fellowships/australian-american-health-policy-fellowship/application-form to know complete procedure to apply for this program
**Closing Date**: 2 October
**Funding**: Government
**Additional Information**: In Australia: Director; International Strategies Branch Portfolio Strategies Division Department of Health and Ageing MDP 85, GPO Box 9848, Canberra ACT 2601, Australia; Tel: (61) 2 6289 4593; Fax: (61) 2 6289 7087. Australian-American Health Policy Fellowships is the successor of the Packer Policy Fellowship Program, which ran from 2003 to 2009. Email at packerpolicyfellowship@health.gov.au www.commonwealthfund.org/publications/newsletter-article/australian-american-health-policy-fellow ship-0

### For further information contact:

**Email**:   ro@cmwf.org

## Harkness Fellowships in Health Care Policy

**Purpose**: To build a network of policy orientated health care researchers whose multinational experience and outlook stimulate innovative policies and practices in the United States and other industrialised countries
**Eligibility**: Open to Australian, British, and New Zealand citizens. Applicants must be at postgraduate level or have equivalent experience
**Level of Study**: Postgraduate
**Type**: Fellowship
**Value**: Up to US$75,000
**Length of Study**: 4 months–1 year
**Frequency**: Annual
**Study Establishment**: A host institution which is normally, but not exclusively, of an intellectual kind, such as a university graduate school, a research institute or a 'think tank'
**Country of Study**: United States of America
**Application Procedure**: Applicants must write for details
**Additional Information**: www.commonwealthfund.org/fellowships/harkness-fellowships-health-care-policy-and-practice Applicants must be submitted via email

### For further information contact:

Harkness Fellowship in Health Care, Associate Professor & Directo, Center for Health Economics Research & Evaluation, University of Sydney, Mallett Street Campus, 88 Mallett Street Level 6 Building F, Camperdown, NSW 2050, Australia.

**Tel**:      (61) 2 9351 0900
**Fax**:     (61) 2 9351 0930
**Email**:   mf@cmwf.org

## Harkness Fellowships in Healthcare Policy and Practice

**Purpose**: To encourage the professional development of promising healthcare policy researchers and practitioners who will contribute to innovation in healthcare policy and practice in the United States of America and their home countries
**Eligibility**: Open to individuals who have completed a Master's degree or PhD in health services or health policy research. Applicants must also have shown significant promise as a policy-orientated researcher or practitioner, e.g. physicians or health service managers, journalists and government officials, with a strong interest in policy issues. Candidates should also be at the research Fellow to senior lecturer level, if academically based; be in their late 20s to early 40s, and have been nominated by their department chair or the director of their institution
**Level of Study**: Postgraduate, Professional development, Research
**Type**: Fellowship

**Value**: up to US$ 30,000 in support, with an additional family supplement (up to US$60,000 for a partner and two children up to age 18)
**Length of Study**: spend up to 12 months in the United States
**Frequency**: Annual
**Study Establishment**: An academic or other research policy institution
**Country of Study**: United States of America
**Application Procedure**: Applicants must complete a formal application available online at the website www.cmwf.org/fellowships
**Funding**: Private
**Contributor**: The Commonwealth Fund
**Additional Information**: www.commonwealthfund.org/fellowships/harkness-fellowships-health-care-policy-and-practice

**For further information contact:**

**Email**:    mf@cmwf.org

## The Commonwealth Fund Mongan Fellowship in Minority Health Policy

**Purpose**: To create physician-leaders who will pursue careers in minority health policy
**Eligibility**: Open to physicians who are citizens of the United States of America and who have completed their residency. Additional experience beyond residency is preferred. Applicants must demonstrate an awareness of, or interest and experience in dealing, with the health needs of minority populations, strong evidence of past leadership experience, as related to community efforts and health policy and the intention to pursue a career in public health practice, policy, or academia
**Level of Study**: Graduate, Postgraduate, Professional development, Research
**Type**: Fellowship
**Value**: US$60,000 stipend, full tuition, health insurance, books, travel, and related program expenses, including financial assistance for a practicum project
**Length of Study**: five one-year, degree-granting
**Frequency**: Annual
**Study Establishment**: Harvard Medical School
**Country of Study**: United States of America
**Application Procedure**: Applications available online at the website: www.cmwf.org/fellowships
**Closing Date**: 2 December
**Funding**: Foundation
**Additional Information**: For more information, please visit: mfdp.med.harvard.edu/cff/how-apply www.commonwealth fund.org/commonwealth-fund-fellowship-minority-health-policy-harvard-university

**For further information contact:**

Minority Faculty Development Program, Harvard Medical School, 164 Longwood Avenue, 2nd Floor, West Court, Boston, MA 02115, United States of America.

**Tel**:        (1) 617 432 2922
**Fax**:        (1) 617 432 3834
**Email**:    mfdp_cfhuf@hms.harvard.edu

## Commonwealth Scholarship and Fellowship Plan

Commonwealth Scholarship Commission in the United Kingdom, c/o Association of Commonwealth Universities, John Foster House, 36 Gordon Square, London, WC1H 0PF, United Kingdom.

The Plan was drawn up at the first Commonwealth Education Conference held in Oxford in 1959. It is a system of awards for men and women from all Commonwealth countries to study in countries other than their own. One of its guiding principles is that it be based on mutual co-operation

## Commonwealth Shared Scholarship Scheme at United Kingdom Universities

**Purpose**: Commonwealth Shared Scholarships are for candidates from least developed and lower middle income Commonwealth countries, for full-time Master's study on selected courses, jointly supported by United Kingdom universities. The scholarships do not cover undergraduate courses, PhD study, or any pre-sessional English language teaching
**Eligibility**: 1. Be a citizen of or have been granted refugee status by an eligible Commonwealth country, or be a British Protected Person. 2. Be permanently resident in a developing Commonwealth country. 3. Be available to start your academic studies in the United Kingdom by the start of the United Kingdom academic year in September/October. 4. By October, hold a first degree of at least upper second class (2:1) standard, or a second class degree and a relevant postgraduate qualification (usually a Master's degree). 5. Not have studied or worked for one (academic) year or more in a developed country. 6. Be unable to afford to study in the United Kingdom without this scholarship
**Level of Study**: Postdoctorate
**Type**: Scholarship
**Value**: £1,330
**Length of Study**: 1 year

**Frequency**: Annual
**Country of Study**: Any country
**Application Procedure**: Apply online
**Closing Date**: 14 March
**Funding**: Foundation
**Additional Information**: cscuk.dfid.gov.uk/apply/shared-scholarships/

**For further information contact:**

Woburn House, 20-24 Tavistock Square, London, WC1H 9HF, United Kingdom.

## Commonwealth Scholarship Commission in the United Kingdom

The Association of Commonwealth Universities, Woburn House, 20;24 Tavistock Square, London, WC1H 9HF, United Kingdom.

**Tel**:         (44) 20 7380 6700
**Email**:      info@cscuk.org.uk
**Website**:   www.dfid.gov.uk/cscuk
**Contact**:   Ms Natasha Lokhun, Communications Officer

The Commonwealth Scholarship Commission (CSC) in the United Kingdom is responsible for managing Britain's contribution to the Commonwealth Scholarship and Fellowship Plan (CSFP). The CSC makes available seven types of award and supports around 700 awards in total annually.

### Association of Commonwealth Universities Titular Fellowships

**Purpose**: To enable the universities of the commonwealth to develop the human resources of their institutions and countries through the interchanging of people, knowledge, skills and technologies. Not intended for degree courses, or for immediately postdoctoral programmes
**Eligibility**: Applicants must be on the staff of member universities under the ACU, the Commonwealth interuniversity organization or working in industry, commerce or public service in a Commonwealth country. Applicant must be within 28–50 years of age
**Level of Study**: Professional development
**Type**: Scholarship

**Value**: £5,000 for travel, board, insurance and fees where the approved programme includes a training programme
**Length of Study**: 6 months
**Frequency**: Annual
**Study Establishment**: ACU member university or in industry, commerce or public sector
**Country of Study**: Commonwealth countries
**Application Procedure**: Candidates must be nominated by executive heads of ACU member universities or by the chief executive officer of a Commonwealth interuniversity organization. Full application details on ACU website
**No. of awards offered**: 50
**Closing Date**: 30 April
**Contributor**: ACU
**No. of awards given last year**: 8
**No. of applicants last year**: 50

**For further information contact:**

**Email**:    acuawards@acu.ac.uk

## Community Foundation for Calderdale

Office 158, Dean Clough, Halifax, Yorkshire, HX3 5AX, United Kingdom.

**Tel**:         (44) 1422 349 700
**Email**:      enquiries@ccfound.co.uk
**Website**:   www.ccfund.co.uk
**Contact**:   Mr Mohammad Aslam, Director of the Board, Grants

### W.D. Farr Endowment Fund Grants

**Purpose**: The Greeley Rotary W. D. Farr Endowment Fund at the Community Foundation Serving Greeley and Weld County welcomes applications and considers grant requests from US$500 to US$2,500 for the benefit of the youth of Greeley, Colorado. The W.D. Farr Endowment Fund supports programs in the Greeley area that enhance
**Level of Study**: Graduate
**Type**: Grant
**Value**: US$500 to US$2,500
**Frequency**: Annual
**Country of Study**: Any country
**Application Procedure**: Attachment Checklist requires following information to process further proposal. 1. Cover letter. 2. Project budget sheet. 3. Board of Directors list

**Closing Date**: 31 January
**Funding**: Private

## For further information contact:

2425 35th Avenue. Suite 201, Greeley, CO 80634, United States of America.

**Email**: info@cfsgwc.org

## Concordia University

1455 De Maisonneuve Blvd. W., QC H3G 1M8, Montréal, Canada.

**Tel**: (1) 514 848 2424
**Website**: www.concordia.ca
**Contact**: Ms Patricia Verret, Graduate Awards Manager

Concordia University is the result of the 1974 merger between Sir George Williams University and Loyola College. The University incorporates superior teaching methods with an interdisciplinary approach to learning and is dedicated to offering the best possible scholarship to the student body and to promoting research beneficial to society

### Bank of Montréal Pauline Varnier Fellowship

**Purpose**: To support graduate students to acquire higher degree in the fields of business and commerce
**Eligibility**: Open to women with 2 years of cumulative business experience who are entering full-time studies in the MBA program at the John Molson School of Business. Candidates must be Canadian citizens or permanent residents
**Level of Study**: MBA
**Type**: Fellowship
**Value**: C$10,000 per year
**Length of Study**: 2 years
**Frequency**: Annual
**Study Establishment**: Concordia University
**Country of Study**: Canada
**Application Procedure**: Applicants must submit a completed application form, three letters of recommendation and official transcripts of all university studies by the closing date
**Closing Date**: 1 February

**Funding**: Private
**No. of awards given last year**: 1
**Additional Information**: Academic merit is the prime consideration in the granting of the awards

## For further information contact:

M.B.A. Program, Faculty of Commerce and Administration, Concordia University, 1455 Boulevard de Maisonneuve O, Montréal, QC H3G 1M8, Canada.

**Tel**: (1) 848 2424 ext 2717
**Email**: gradprograms@jmsb.concordia.ca

## Congressional Black Caucas Foundation

### Congressional Black Caucus Foundation Spouses Visual Arts Scholarship

**Purpose**: This award is for students with majors in the visual arts including, but not limited to, architecture, ceramics, drawing, fashion, graphic design, illustration, interior design, painting, photography, sketching, video production and other decorative arts
**Eligibility**: 1. Must be a full-time student. 2. Must be planning to pursue a degree in a field that will lead to a career in the visual arts. The visual arts include architecture, ceramics, drawing, fashion, graphic design, illustration, interior design, painting, photography, sketching, video production and other visual arts. Must have minimum GPA of 2.5 on a 4.0 scale. This award is for United States students
**Level of Study**: Postgraduate
**Type**: Scholarship
**Value**: US$3,000
**Frequency**: Annual
**Country of Study**: United States of America
**Application Procedure**: 1. The online application is available on the Congressional Black Caucus Foundations (CBC) website. During the online application process, the applicant must upload and/or complete the following forms. 2. A personal statement essay from the student (500–1,000 words) that addresses all four (4) of the topics listed on the application in one cohesive essay. 3. Two (2) letters of recommendation (Email addresses will be requested of each recommender for electronic submission of the letter. Hard copy letters will not be accepted.)
**Closing Date**: 31 March
**Funding**: Private

**Additional Information**: Late applications and materials will not be accepted www.petersons.com/scholarship/cbc-spouses-visual-arts-scholarship-111_182500.aspx

### For further information contact:

1720 Massachusetts Avenue NW, Washington, DC 20036, United States of America.

**Tel**:      (1) 202 263 2800
**Email**:    scholarships@cbcfinc.org

## Conseil Européen Pour la Recherche Nucléaire European Organization for Nuclear Research

CH-1211 Geneva 23, Switzerland.

**Tel**:        (41) 22 76 784 84
**Email**:      recruitment.service@cern.ch
**Website**:    www.cern.ch

CERN European Laboratory for Particle Physics is the world's leading laboratory in its field, that being the study of the smallest constituents of matter and of the forces that hold them together. The laboratory's tools are its particle accelerators and detectors, which are among the largest and most complex scientific instruments ever built

### Conseil Européen Pour la Recherche Nucléaire Summer Student Programme

**Purpose**: To awaken the interest of undergraduates in CERN's activities by offering them hands-on experience during their long summer vacation
**Eligibility**: 1. You are a Bachelor or Master student (not PhD) in the Fields of Physics, Engineering, Computer Science or Mathematics. 2. Should have completed, at least Three Years of Full-Time Studies at University Level. 3. You have a good knowledge of English (However, IELTS or TOEFL is Not Required). 4. Candidates of all nationalities are welcome to apply for this Summer Student Programme.
**Value**: A 90 CHF Per Day Allowance to Cover the Cost of Accommodation & Meals for a single person and A Round Airfare Tickets Travel Allowance to & From Geneva.
**Length of Study**: 8–13 weeks
**Study Establishment**: CERN
**Country of Study**: Switzerland
**Application Procedure**: You need to apply online

**Closing Date**: 31 January
**Additional Information**: Please check at home.web.cern.ch/students-educators/summer-student-programme opportunitiescorners.info/cern-summer-student-program-2020/

### For further information contact:

**Email**:    jkrich@umich.edu

### Conseil Européen Pour la Recherche Nucléaire-Japan Fellowship Programme

**Purpose**: To support young researchers who are interested in LHC data analysis and physics studies
**Eligibility**: Applicants should be nationals or permanent residents of Japan and have a doctorate for applicants in experimental or phenomenological physics and/or accelerator science. Candidates who are currently preparing a PhD are eligible to apply. However, they are expected to have obtained their PhD by the time they take up their appointment at CERN
**Level of Study**: Doctorate
**Type**: Fellowship
**Value**: Covers travel expense and insurance coverage
**Length of Study**: Up to 3 years
**Frequency**: Annual
**Application Procedure**: A completed electronic application form along with a curriculum vitae should be submitted
**Closing Date**: 1 December
**Contributor**: CERN
**Additional Information**: Please check at jobs.web.cern.ch/job/10941

### For further information contact:

**Email**:    recruitment.science@cern.ch

### Marie Curie Fellowships for Early Stage Training at CERN

**Purpose**: To offer structured scientific and/or technological training and to encourage participants to take up long-term research careers
**Eligibility**: Open to researchers in the first 4 years of their research activity. Persons who have obtained a doctorate are ineligible
**Study Establishment**: CERN
**Application Procedure**: Candidates should register and apply for the Marie Curie Fellowship programme using the CERN e-recruitment system
**Contributor**: European Comission

## Conservation Leadership Programme

Conservation Leadership Programme, Birdlife International, Wellbrook Court, Girton Road, Cambridge, CB3 0NA, United Kingdom.

| | |
|---|---|
| **Tel**: | (44) 12 2327 7318 |
| **Email**: | clp@birdlife.org |
| **Website**: | www.conservationleadershipprogramme.org |
| **Contact**: | The Programme Manager |

Since 1985, the Conservation Leadership Programme has supported and encouraged international conservation projects that address global conservation priorities at a local level. This is achieved through a comprehensive system of advice, training and awards. The programme is managed through a partnership between BP, FFI, CI, WCS and Birdlife International.

## Future Conservationist Awards

**Purpose**: To develop leadership capacity amongst emerging conservationists to address the most pressing conservation issues of our time
**Eligibility**: The project must address a globally recognized conservation priority, involve people, have host government approval, be run by teams of at least three people, be student-led, have over 50% students registered, last for less than 1 year and take place in Africa, Asia Pacific, Middle East, Eastern Europe, Latin America or the Caribbean
**Level of Study**: Doctorate, Graduate, Postgraduate
**Type**: Award
**Value**: Up to US$12,500
**Length of Study**: Projects should be less than 1 year in length
**Frequency**: Annual
**Country of Study**: This is a global programme
**Application Procedure**: Application forms are available from the website. Applications should be made electronically
**No. of awards offered**: 360
**Funding**: Private
**Contributor**: BP, BirdLife International, Conservation International, WildLife Conservation Society, and Fauna and Flora International
**No. of awards given last year**: 29
**No. of applicants last year**: 360
**Additional Information**: Please be sure to check at www. conservationleadershipprogramme.org/FutureConservatio nistAward.asp www.conservationleadershipprogramme.org/ grants/grant-overview/future-conservationist-award/

## Conservation Trust

National Geographic Society, 1145 17th Street NW, Washington, DC 20036-4688, United States of America.

| | |
|---|---|
| **Email**: | conservationtrust@ngs.org |
| **Website**: | www.nationalgeographic.com/conservation |

The objective of the Conservation Trust is to support conservation activities around the world as they fit within the mission of the National Geographic Society. The trust will fund projects that contribute significantly to the preservation and sustainable use of the Earth's biological, cultural, and historical resources.

## National Geographic Conservation Trust Grant

**Purpose**: To support cutting programmes that contribute to the preservation and sustainable use of the Earth's resources
**Eligibility**: Applicants must provide a record of prior research or conservation action. Researchers planning work in foreign countries should include at least one local collaboration as part of their research teams. Grants recipients are excepted to provide the National Geographic Society with rights of first refusal for popular publication of their findings
**Level of Study**: Research
**Type**: Research grant
**Value**: US$15,000–20,000
**Frequency**: Annual
**Application Procedure**: Apply online at www.national geographic.com/explorers/grants-programs/conservation-trust-application
**Funding**: Trusts
**Contributor**: National Geographic Society

### For further information contact:

Conservation Trust, National Geographic Society, 1145 17th Street NW, Washington, DC 20036, United States of America.

## Consortium for Advanced Research Training in Africa (CARTA)

Consortium for Advanced Research Training in Africa (CARTA), Nairobi, KE, Kenya.

| | |
|---|---|
| **Tel**: | (254) 20 4001000 |
| **Email**: | carta@aphrc.org |
| **Website**: | www.cartafrica.org/ |

CARTA's mission is to promote the health and development of African populations through high-quality research on policy-relevant priority issues. The initiative will foster the emergence of vibrant and viable multidisciplinary research hubs of locally-trained internationally recognized scholars.

## Consortium for Advanced Research Training in Africa PhD Fellowships

**Purpose**: CARTA offers an innovative model for doctoral training in sub-Saharan Africa to strengthen the capacity of participating institutions to conduct and lead internationally-competitive research
**Eligibility**: A Masters degree in a relevant field, Prior admission into a PhD program is not required for application but awards are contingent on such admission being obtained at one of the participating African universities, Male applicants must be under the age of 40 years and female applicants under the age 45 years
**Level of Study**: Postgraduate
**Type**: Fellowship
**Value**: Fellowships cover tuition fees, medical insurance and other university fees in special circumstances only
**Length of Study**: The fellowship runs for a maximum of 4 years
**Country of Study**: Africa
**Closing Date**: 30 April
**Funding**: International office
**Additional Information**: Please check website for more details www.opportunitiesforafricans.com/carta-phd-fellowships-2019-2020/

## For further information contact:

**Email**:     carta_fellowship@aphrc.org

## Consortium for Applied Research on International Migration

PO Box 616, NL-6200 MD, Maastricht, Netherlands.

**Email**:     secretariaat-carim@maaastrichtuniversity.nl

CARIM is one of the top institutes for translational cardiovascular research in Europe. It is among the world leaders in the fields of research into vascular and thrombotic disorders and atrial fibrillation as well as translational heart failure research. It has also made important international contributions to molecular imaging in the cardiovascular field.

## Consortium for Applied Research on International Migration Postdoctoral Talent Fellowship

**Purpose**: Purpose is to provide recently promoted top CARIM talent a chance to gain experience abroad and return to CARIM to perform excellent research
**Eligibility**: For eligibility details, please visit the website
**Level of Study**: Postdoctoral
**Type**: Fellowship
**Value**: The fellowship amounts to € 53,011 gross which is meant for a period of 12 months. Bench fees are not included in this fellowship. The fellowship includes one return flight to the host institute (based on economy fare)
**Country of Study**: Any country
**Application Procedure**: There will be one call a year, and the deadline for the "CARIM - Postdoctoral Talent Fellowship" is the 13th of May, 00.00 hours. To apply for the "CARIM - Postdoctoral Talent Fellowship", the applicants from within (or connected to) CARIM are invited to submit an application (by mail) to the CARIM office (secretariaat-carim-at-maastrichtuniversity.nl)
**Closing Date**: 30 May
**Additional Information**: www.nationalmeritscholarships.com/carim-postdoctoral-talent-fellowship.html

## For further information contact:

**Email**:     secretariaat-carim@maastrichtuniversity.nl

## Cooperative Research Centre for Water Quality and Treatment (CRCWQT)

Australia Water Quality Centre, Private Mail Bag 3, Salisbury, SA 5108, Australia.

**Tel**:         (61) 8 8259 0326
**Email**:     dennis.steffensen@sawater.com.au
**Website**:    www.waterquality.crc.org.au
**Contact**:    Professor Dennis Mulcahy, Training Leader

The Cooperative Research Centre for Water Quality and Treatment (CRCWQT) provides a national strategic research capacity for the Australian water industry and focuses on issues relating to water quality management and health risk reduction.

## Cooperative Research Center for Water Quality and Treatment Young Water Scientist of the Year Scholarship

**Purpose**: To provide support to PhD students for research done within the Water Forum CRC
**Eligibility**: Open to candidates who are in the final year of their PhD.
**Level of Study**: Doctorate
**Type**: Scholarship
**Value**: AU$2,500
**Length of Study**: 1 year
**Frequency**: Annual
**Country of Study**: Australia

**For further information contact:**

**Email**: detr@wmo.int

## Copenhagen Business School

Solbjerg Plads 3, DK-2000 Frederiksberg, Denmark.

**Tel**: (45) 3815 3815
**Email**: cbs@cbs.dk
**Website**: www.cbs.dk

## Copenhagen Business School PhD Scholarship on IT Management

**Eligibility**: To be considered, the candidate should have a basic training at the Masters level (similar to the 3 + 2 Bologna process). An educational background in the social sciences is necessary. The applicant must have successfully completed the Masters degree before commencing PhD at CBS. The applicants must be fluent in English
**Level of Study**: Doctorate, Research
**Type**: Scholarship
**Value**: The scholarships are fully salaried positions, according to the national Danish collective agreement. The scholarship includes the tuition fees, office space, travel grants, plus a salary, currently starting with per month approx. DKK 23,770 (approx. €3,160) up to DKK 28,964 (approx. €3,860) depending on seniority, plus a pension contribution totalling 17.1% of 85% of the base salary
**Length of Study**: 3 years
**Country of Study**: Denmark

**Application Procedure**: Application must be sent via the electronic recruitment system. The application must include a 5-page project description. This research proposal should contain a presentation of an original research question, a description of the initial theoretical framework and methodology, a presentation of the suggested empirical material as well as a work plan. In addition to the research proposal, the application must include copies of a Master's degree certificate or other certificates of a corresponding level, brief curriculum vitae, a list of papers and publications, and one copy of a selected written work (e.g. Master's thesis)
**Closing Date**: 28 February
**Contributor**: Copenhagen Business School
**Additional Information**: The scholarship requires the student to spend a minimum of 12 months of their PhD programme in a research institution in China. Countries of study are Denmark and China

**For further information contact:**

**Email**: dsi.msc@cbs.dk

## Core

3 St Andrew's Place, London, NW1 4LB, United Kingdom.

**Tel**: (44) 20 7486 0341
**Email**: info@corecharity.org.uk
**Website**: www.corecharity.org.uk
**Contact**: Alice Kington, Finance and Research Manager

## Core Fellowships and Grants

**Purpose**: To provide funding for gastroenterological research
**Eligibility**: Open to applicants resident within the United Kingdom. Fellowship projects must contain an element of basic science training
**Level of Study**: Doctorate, Postdoctorate, Postgraduate, Research
**Type**: Fellowship or Grant
**Value**: £50,000 per year salary and £10,000 per year consumables (Research Fellowships); £50,000 total (Development Grants)
**Length of Study**: 1–3 years
**Frequency**: Dependent on funds available
**Study Establishment**: Recognized and established research centres
**Country of Study**: United Kingdom

**Application Procedure**: Applicants must complete an application form for consideration in a research competition. Details are available from the website

**No. of awards offered**: Varies

**Funding**: Commercial, Private, Foundation, Trusts, Individuals

**Contributor**: Charitable donations

**No. of awards given last year**: 4

**No. of applicants last year**: Varies

**Additional Information**: Conditions are advertised on the core website www.corecharity.org.uk serb.gov.in/emr.php

### For further information contact:

**Email**: IAS_applications@ceu.edu

## Council of American Overseas Research Centers (CAORC)

PO Box 37012, MRC 178, Washington, DC 20013-7012, United States of America.

**Tel**: (1) 202 633 1599
**Email**: fellowships@caorc.org
**Website**: www.caorc.org

Council of American Overseas Research Centers (CAORC) serve as a base for virtually every American scholar undertaking research in the host countries. The members have centres in many locations across the world.

### Council of American Overseas Research Centers Andrew W. Mellon East-Central European Research Fellows

**Purpose**: To help scholars in the humanities and allied social sciences to carry out research at institutes of advanced study in other countries

**Eligibility**: Open to candidates who have obtained a PhD and are nationals of Bulgaria, Czech, Estonia, Hungary, Latvia, Lithuania, Poland, Romania or Slovakia

**Level of Study**: Research

**Type**: Fellowships

**Value**: Varies

**Length of Study**: Short-term residencies

**Frequency**: Annual

**Country of Study**: Any country

**Additional Information**: www.iwm.at/fellowships/former-fellowship-programs/andrew-w-mellon-east-central-european-research-visiting-fellowships/

### Council of American Overseas Research Centers Multi-Country Research Fellowship Program for Advanced Multi-Country Research

**Purpose**: To advance higher learning and scholarly research and to conduct research of regional or trans-regional significance

**Eligibility**: Applicants must have obtained a PhD or be established postdoctoral scholars. The candidate should be a citizen of the United States. Preference will be given to Candidates examining comparative and/or cross-regional research

**Level of Study**: Doctorate, Postdoctorate, Research

**Type**: Fellowships

**Value**: Up to US$10,500

**Frequency**: Annual

**Country of Study**: Any country

**Application Procedure**: The application can be downloaded from the website. To obtain hard copy of the application, please contact CAORC

**No. of awards offered**: 120

**Closing Date**: 20 January

**Contributor**: United States State Department

**No. of awards given last year**: 9

**No. of applicants last year**: 120

**Additional Information**: Scholars must carry out research in at least one of the countries that host overseas research centres. Please check website for further information einaudi.cornell.edu/opportunity/council-american-overseas-research-centers-multi-country-research-fellowship

### Council of American Overseas Research Centers Neh Research Fellowships

**Purpose**: The National Endowment for the Humanities (NEH) Senior Research Fellowship supports advanced research in the humanities. Fellowship awards are for four consecutive months

**Eligibility**: 1. Applicants must be United States citizens or foreign nationals who have resided in the United States for three years prior to the application deadline. 2. Applicants must be postdoctoral scholars. 3. Funding is not available for research conducted in the United States. 4. It is not required that you be affiliated with a United States academic institution to apply

**Level of Study**: Graduate
**Type**: Fellowship
**Value**: US$4,200
**Frequency**: Annual
**Country of Study**: Any country
**Closing Date**: 24 January
**Funding**: Foundation

## Council of Independent Colleges

One Dupont Circle, N.W, Suite 320, Washington DC 20036-1142, United States of America.

**Tel**:        (1) 202 466 7230
**Email**:      visitingfellows@cic.nche.edu
**Website**:    www.cic.org/projects_services/visitingfellows.asp
**Contact**:    Michelle Friedman, Program Manager

### Woodrow Wilson Visiting Fellows

**Purpose**: To encourage the flow of ideas between the academic and non-academic sectors of society
**Eligibility**: The program is available to all four-year public and private, non-profit colleges and universities in the United States as well as CIC International Member institutions. CIC member campuses participate at a discounted rate.
**Level of Study**: Postgraduate
**Type**: Fellowships
**Value**: STANDARD VISIT: CIC Non-Member Price: US$6,000, CIC Member Price: US$5,500 ABBREVIATED VISIT: CIC Non-Member Price: US$4,900, CIC Member Price: US$4,500
**Length of Study**: 1 year
**Frequency**: Annual
**Application Procedure**: If your campus is ready to start the process of hosting a Fellow, please complete this online form. The form should be completed by a campus-designated "campus coordinator" who will be CIC's point of contact throughout the planning and execution of the visit. Be prepared to provide a short list of preferred Fellows, preferred time to host a Fellow, preferred visit length, and a brief paragraph about the intended engagement of the Fellow on campus
**Closing Date**: 17 April
**Funding**: Private
**Contributor**: Lilly Endowment
**Additional Information**: www.cic.edu/member-services/woodrow-wilson-visiting-fellows

### For further information contact:

Visiting Fellows Program, 5 Vaughn Drive, Suite 300, Princeton, NJ 08540-6313, United States of America.

**Tel**:        (1) 609 452 7007 ext. 181
**Email**:      sanford@woodrow.org

## Council of Logistics Management

### George A. Gecowets Graduate Scholarship Program

**Subjects**: Logistics; all programs leading to careers in logistics management
**Purpose**: To grant scholarships solely on merit - academic achievement, work experience, leadership, and career commitment - rather than financial need.
**Eligibility**: A student is eligible to apply for this scholarship if they are already enrolled in the first year of a Master's degree program leading to a career in Logistics related graduate program.
**Type**: Scholarship
**Value**: US$1,000
**Country of Study**: United States of America
**Closing Date**: 1 April
**Additional Information**: phdstudents.smeal.psu.edu/scholarship-fellowship-opportunities/external-awards/gecowets.html

## Council of Supply Chain Management Professionals (CSCMP)

333 East Butterfield Road, Suite 140, Lombard, IL 60148, United States of America.

**Tel**:        (1) 630 574 0985
**Email**:      membership@cscmp.org
**Website**:    www.cscmp.org
**Contact**:    Kathleen Hedland, Director Education and Roundtable Services

The Council of Supply Chain Management Professionals (CSCMP) is a non-profit organization of business personnel who are interested in improving their logistics management skills. CSCMP works in co-operation with private industry and various organizations to further the understanding and development of the logistics concept. This is accomplished through a continuing programme of organized activities, research and meetings designed to develop the theory and understanding of the logistics process, promote the art and science of managing logistics systems, and foster professional dialogue and development within the profession.

## Council of Supply Chain Management Professionals Distinguished Service Award

**Purpose**: To provide honor to an individual for achievement in supply chain management

**Eligibility**: All individuals who have made contributions to the field of supply chain management are eligible for the DSA. This includes practitioners with responsibilities in a functional area of supply chain management, consultants and educators-anyone who has made a significant contribution to the advancement of supply chain management. Please check at cscmp.org/career/awards/distinguished-service-award-process for more detailed information

**Type**: Award

**Frequency**: Annual

**Application Procedure**: Nominations must be accompanied by a fully completed nomination form and should be emailed to Sue Paulson

**Closing Date**: 30 April

### For further information contact:

**Tel**:        (1) 630 645 3469
**Email**:     spaulson@cscmp.org

## Council of Supply Chain Management Professionals Doctoral Dissertation Award

**Purpose**: To encourage research leading to advancement of the theory and practice to supply chain management

**Eligibility**: Open to all candidates whose doctoral dissertation demonstrates signified originality and contributes to the logistics knowledge base. See cscmp.org/downloads/public/education/awards/dda-guidelines.pdf for details

**Level of Study**: Postdoctorate

**Type**: Award

**Value**: US$5,000

**Frequency**: Annual

**Closing Date**: May

**Additional Information**: cscmpedge.org/ehome/344812/awardsrecognitions/#DDA

### For further information contact:

**Email**:     kmcinerney@cscmp.org

## Supply Chain Innovation Award

**Purpose**: CSCMP's Research Strategies Committee (RSC) and Supply Chain Brain established the Supply Chain Innovation Award in 2005 to highlight and recognize the top players in the supply chain industry when it comes to innovative programs, projects and collaboration

**Eligibility**: The submitting company must be a CSCMP member. In addition, each member of your team must be registered for the annual conference by 1 August. All travel, accommodations, and related expenses are the responsibilities of the finalist teams

**Type**: Scholarship

**Frequency**: Annual

**Application Procedure**: While the finalist teams present their case studies, the panel of judges evaluates the session as it happens live in front of the audience of conference attendees

**Funding**: Private

**Contributor**: CSCMP's Research Strategies Committee (RSC) and Supply Chain Brain

**Additional Information**: Please check complete guidelines at cscmp.org/career/awards/supply-chain-innovation-award-competition-guidelines       www.eiseverywhere.com/eSites/219306/Guidelines

### For further information contact:

**Tel**:        (1) 630 645 3454
**Email**:     cscmpresearch@cscmp.org

# Council on Foreign Relations (CFR)

The Harold Pratt House, 58 East 68th Street, New York, NY 10065, United States of America.

**Tel**:        (1) 212 434 9400
**Email**:     fellowships@cfr.org
**Website**:   www.cfr.org
**Contact**:   Janine Hill, Director, Fellowship Affairs and Studies

The Council on Foreign Relations (CFR) is dedicated to increasing America's understanding of the world and contributing ideas to United States foreign policy. The Council accomplishes this mainly by promoting constructive debates and discussions, clarifying world issues and publishing Foreign Affairs, the leading journal on global issues.

## Council on Foreign Relations International Affairs Fellowship in Japan

**Purpose**: To cultivate the United State's understanding of Japan and to strengthen communication between emerging leaders of the two nations

**Eligibility**: 1. Applicants must be U.S. citizens. 2. Applicants must be mid-career professionals. 3. Applicants must have a strong record of professional achievement. 4. Applicants must have an interest in U.S.-Japan relations. 5. Applicants must hold at least a bachelor's degree. 6. Although the program is intended primarily for those without substantial prior experience in Japan, exceptions have been made when an applicant has demonstrated that the fellowship would add a significant new dimension to his or her career. 7. Knowledge of the Japanese language is not a requirement.

**Level of Study**: Professional development

**Type**: Fellowship

**Value**: Living expenses in Japan plus international transportation, health and travel insurance and necessary research expenses

**Length of Study**: 3-12 months

**Frequency**: Annual

**Country of Study**: Japan

**Application Procedure**: Application is primarily by invitation, on the recommendation of individuals in academic, government and other institutions who have occasion to know candidates particularly well suited for the experience offered by this fellowship. Others who inquire directly and who meet preliminary requirements may also be invited to apply without formal nomination. Those invited to apply will be forwarded application materials

**No. of awards offered**: 6

**Closing Date**: 31 October

**Funding**: Private

**Contributor**: Hitachi Limited

**No. of awards given last year**: 3

**No. of applicants last year**: 6

**Additional Information**: While the Fellow is not required to produce a book, article or report, it is hoped that some written output will result. Please check at www.cfr.org/thinktank/fellowships/iaf_japan.html www.cfr.org/fellowships/international-affairs-fellowship-japan

### For further information contact:

Fellowship Affairs, Council on Foreign Relations, 58 East 68th Street, New York, NY 10065, United States of America.

**Tel**:     (1) 212 434 9740
**Fax**:     (1) 212 434 9870

## Council on Library and Information Resources (CLIR)

1707 L Street, NW Suite 650, Washington, DC 20036, United States of America.

**Tel**:         (1) 202 939 4750/4751
**Email**:      abishop@clir.org
**Website**:    www.clir.org
**Contact**:    Alice Bishop, Senior Program Officer

CLIR is an independent, nonprofit organization that forges strategies to enhance research, teaching, and learning in collaboration with libraries, cultural institutions, and communities of higher learning.

## Council on Library and Information Resources Postdoctoral Fellowship

**Purpose**: The CLIR Postdoctoral Fellowship Program offers recent PhD graduates the chance to develop research tools, resources, and services while exploring new career opportunities. CLIR Postdoctoral Fellows work on projects that forge and strengthen connections among library collections, educational technologies, and current research. Host institutions benefit from fellows' field-specific expertise by gaining insights into their collections' potential uses and users, scholarly information behaviors, and current teaching and learning practices

**Eligibility**: Applicants must have received a PhD in a discipline no more than five years before applying; if a PhD has not yet been received, all work toward the degree (including dissertation defense and final dissertation editing) must be completed before starting the fellowship. Applicants can be citizens of any country but MUST be legally permitted to work in the United States and/or Canada

**Level of Study**: Postdoctorate

**Type**: Postdoctoral fellowship

**Value**: Varies by host institution

**Length of Study**: 2 years

**Frequency**: Annual

**Country of Study**: United States of America & Canada

**Application Procedure**: Complete an online application www.clir.org/fellowships/postdoc/applicants/

**No. of awards offered**: 115

**Closing Date**: 10 January

**Funding**: Private, Foundation

**Contributor**: Alfred P. Sloan Foundation, Andrew W. Mellon Foundation, individual host institutions

**No. of awards given last year**: 15

**No. of applicants last year**: 115
**Additional Information**: www.postdocs.ubc.ca/award/council-library-information-resources-postdoctoral-fellowship-program

## Craig H. Neilsen Foundation

16830 Ventura Boulevard, Suite 352, Encino, CA 91436, United States of America.

**Tel**:        (1) 818 925 1245
**Website**:   chnfoundation.org/

Established by Craig H. Neilsen in 2002 as a private foundation, the Craig H. Neilsen Foundation is dedicated to supporting both programs and scientific research to improve the quality of life for those affected by and living with spinal cord injury

### Neilsen SCIRTS Postdoctoral Fellowship Grants

**Purpose**: The Spinal Cord Injury Research on the Translational Spectrum (SCIRTS) portfolio supports research to improve the understanding of traumatic spinal cord injury and develop new approaches to alleviate the dysfunction and complications that follow. The scope of this portfolio is broad, encompassing mechanistic, preclinical modeling, translational and/or clinical research. These two-year Postdoctoral Fellowships encourage early-career training and specialization in the field of spinal cord injury research.
**Eligibility**: Applicants must have a doctoral degree or an equivalent terminal professional degree.
**Level of Study**: Postdoctoral
**Type**: Fellowships
**Value**: US$150,000
**Length of Study**: Two-year
**Frequency**: Annual
**Closing Date**: 5 November
**Additional Information**: chnfoundation.org/spinal-cord-injury-research-on-the-translational-spectrum/

## Craig H. Neilsen Foundation

### Pilot Grants

**Subjects**: Aging, caregiving, employment, health behaviors and fitness, independent living, self-management and technology access.

**Purpose**: This funding is intended to support pilot studies that lay essential groundwork, allow the applicant to test the feasibility of novel methods and procedures and/or collect new data that can lead to or enhance larger-scale studies. Proposed pilot projects should indicate how they will establish a new investigational program or take on 'risk' balanced by high potential impact.
**Eligibility**: Applicants must have a doctoral degree or other equivalent terminal professional degree, be beyond the post-doctoral level at the time of the FGA submission, and demonstrate appropriate experience to serve as an independent PI.
**Type**: Grant
**Value**: Funding for PSR Pilot grants is for up to two years, US$200,000 total costs
**Length of Study**: Two years
**Country of Study**: Any country
**Application Procedure**: See website for further details.
**Closing Date**: 25 March
**Additional Information**: chnfoundation.org/psychosocial-research/

### Postdoctoral Fellowships

**Subjects**: Spinal cord injury
**Purpose**: To encourage early-career mentored training to increase professional interest in the field and to encourage researchers from related health disciplines to undertake training in psychosocial research focused on spinal cord injury.
**Eligibility**: Fellows must have attained their doctoral degree or an equivalent terminal professional degree by the FGA submission deadline and have held that degree no longer than five years prior to the FGA submission deadline. For Fellows with an MD degree, the five-year period begins after completion of their residency program. Unique circumstances related to this criterion must be communicated to the Neilsen Foundation for approval prior to submission.
**Type**: Fellowship
**Value**: Funding for fellowships is US$75,000 per year, for up to two years; US$150,000 total costs.
**Length of Study**: Two years
**Country of Study**: Any country
**Application Procedure**: See website for further details.
**Closing Date**: 25 March
**Additional Information**: chnfoundation.org/psychosocial-research/

### Studies and Demonstration Projects

**Subjects**: Spinal cord injury
**Purpose**: This funding is intended to support substantive studies that fill important gaps in the SCI field, that open

new areas of SCI psychosocial research, or that develop and evaluate interventions to address psychosocial issues after SCI. Submissions in this category should facilitate, expand or improve the translation of knowledge and/or the adoption of interventions and practices that will have a positive impact for those living with SCI. Based within a psychosocial framework, PSR Studies and Demonstration Projects can range from SCI epidemiological studies to interventions that will enhance clinical treatment, rehabilitation, habilitation and/or other related quality of life outcomes.

**Eligibility**: Applicants must be independent investigators, actively employed at the grantee institution at the time of FGA submission, and can be at any stage of their research career. o Criteria for funding junior investigators include evidence of a research background that is relevant to the proposed study and the mission of the Neilsen Foundation. To establish independence, Applicants who hold a non-tenure track position (Instructor, Research Assistant, etc.) may include, with their Biosketch, a letter of support from the institution's Director or Department Chair at the LOI and FGA stage. Such a letter should confirm the Applicant's position as independent and that all needed space and equipment are available to this PI.

**Type**: Grant
**Value**: Funding for PSR Studies and Demonstration Projects is for up to three years, US$400,000 total costs
**Length of Study**: Three years
**Country of Study**: Any country
**Application Procedure**: See website for further details.
**Closing Date**: 25 March
**Additional Information**: chnfoundation.org/psychosocial-research/

## Cranfield University

School of Applied Sciences, Bedfordshire, MK43 OAL, United Kingdom.

**Tel**:       (44) 1234 754086
**Email**:     info@cranfield.ac.uk
**Website**:   www.cranfield.ac.uk/sas
**Contact**:   Vicky Mason, Online Marketing Manager

The School of Applied Sciences is recognized globally for its multidisciplinary approach to teaching and research in the key areas of manufacturing, materials, and environmental science and technology. Our focus is on fundamental research and its application, together with teaching, to meet the needs of industry and society.

## Cranfield Global Manufacturing Leadership Masters Scholarship

**Type**: Scholarship
**Value**: Tuition fee plus £1,000 cash
**Country of Study**: United Kingdom
**Application Procedure**: A number of Cranfield's full-time Manufacturing programme MSc courses are applicable to the Global Manufacturing Leadership (GML) Scholarships, please see the course list above. Applicants should submit a normal Cranfield application through the online application system. The online application forms part of the evaluation of academic achievement. Note the 6-digit online application number
**Closing Date**: 3 April
**Funding**: Private
**Additional Information**: www.cranfield.ac.uk/funding/funding-opportunities/cranfield-global-manufacturing-leadership-masters-scholarship

### For further information contact:

College Road, Cranfield, MK43 0AL, United Kingdom.

**Tel**:      (44) 1234758181
**Email**:    gmlscholarship@cranfield.ac.uk

## Cranfield Merit Scholarship in Leadership and Management

**Eligibility**: Sub-Saharan African countries are eligible
**Type**: Scholarship
**Value**: £4,000 for tuition fees
**Country of Study**: United Kingdom
**Application Procedure**: For application details, send an email to studysom@cranfield.ac.uk
**Closing Date**: 25 May
**Additional Information**: worldscholarshipforum.com/20182019-cranfield-merit-scholarship-leadership-management-cranfield-university-uk/

### For further information contact:

**Email**:    studysom@cranfield.ac.uk

## Cranfield Sub-Saharan Africa Merit Scholarship

**Purpose**: To commence full-time study in one of the eligible master courses for the current academic year
**Type**: Scholarship
**Value**: £4,000 for tuition fees
**Frequency**: Annual

**Country of Study**: Any country
**Closing Date**: 25 May
**Additional Information**: www.afterschoolafrica.com/25189/cranfield-sub-saharan-africa-merit-scholarship/

**For further information contact:**

**Email**:    studysom@cranfield.ac.uk

## Global Manufacturing Leadership Masters Scholarships

**Purpose**: The scholarships aim to contribute to the education of young professionals with the capabilities required to lead Manufacturing into the future
**Eligibility**: Applicants can be from any country. Please note Erasmus funded students are not eligible for this scholarship
**Type**: Scholarship
**Value**: The scholarship pays for the Cranfield Manufacturing Masters tuition fee and a £1,000 cash maintenance grant
**Country of Study**: Any country
**Application Procedure**: Applicants can be from any country. Please note Erasmus funded students are not eligible for this scholarship
**Closing Date**: 17 March
**Additional Information**: www.marj3.com/en/global-manufacturing-leadership-masters-scholarships-cranfield-university.html

**For further information contact:**

**Email**:    gmlscholarship@cranfield.ac.uk

## The Diamond Education Grant

**Purpose**: Its purpose is to provide grants to assist women to update their skills after employment breaks or to acquire new skills to improve their opportunities for employment and promotion
**Type**: Grant
**Value**: Small grants towards tuition fees and other study costs
**Frequency**: Annual
**Country of Study**: Any country
**Application Procedure**: Apply online at the Diamond Education Grant website
**Closing Date**: 15 April
**Contributor**: Soroptimist International
**Additional Information**: www.cranfield.ac.uk/funding/funding-opportunities/diamond-education-grant

**For further information contact:**

Soroptimist International Great Britain & Ireland (SIGBI) Ltd, 2nd Floor, Beckwith House, 1-3 Wellington Road North, Stockport, SK4 1AF, United Kingdom.

**Tel**:      (44) 161 480 7686
**Email**:    hq@sigbi.org

## The Lorch Foundation MSc Student Bursary

**Purpose**: To assist postgraduate study
**Eligibility**: Applicants should be United Kingdom citizens and possess a minimum 2:1 United Kingdom Honours degree in Engineering or Physical Sciences or related discipline, and have been offered a place on the 1-year full-time MSc in Water and Wastewater Engineering or Water and Wastewater Technology
**Level of Study**: Postgraduate
**Type**: Bursary
**Value**: £5,000 plus tuition fees
**Length of Study**: 1 year
**Frequency**: Annual
**Study Establishment**: Cranfield University, School of Applied Sciences
**Country of Study**: United Kingdom
**Application Procedure**: Applicants must apply directly to the university
**Closing Date**: 31 July
**Funding**: Foundation
**Contributor**: The Lorch Foundation
**No. of awards given last year**: 1
**Additional Information**: The bursary is provided by the Lorch Foundation, a charitable institution founded to support and promote education and research in the field of water purification and related sciences for the benefit of mankind. The successful applicant will undertake thesis research on processes of water purification and industrial effluent recycling as part of the MSc programme www.cranfield.ac.uk/funding/funding-opportunities/lorch-foundation-bursaries

**For further information contact:**

**Tel**:      (44) 1234758181
**Email**:    studentfunding@cranfield.ac.uk

## Water MSc Scholarship for Students from Malawi and Vietnam

**Purpose**: The aim of the scholarship is to recruit students across all of our areas of academic specialisms with expertise in a wide range of disciplines to pursue MSc programme

**Eligibility**: The scholarship is open to students from Malawi and Vietnam
**Value**: The Cranfield Water Scholarship provides funding of £6,000 towards tuition fees
**Country of Study**: Any country
**Closing Date**: 25 May
**Additional Information**: scholarship-positions.com/cranfield-water-msc-scholarship-students-malawi-vietnam-uk/2018/03/15/

**For further information contact:**

**Email**: studywater@cranfield.ac.uk

## Women as Cyber Leaders Scholarship

**Purpose**: For female students wishing to develop a career in Cyber
**Type**: Postgraduate scholarships
**Value**: £6,500 toward tuition fees
**Country of Study**: United Kingdom
**Application Procedure**: For eligibility and application details, please visit website www.cranfield.ac.uk/funding/funding-opportunities/women-as-cyber-leaders-scholarship
**Closing Date**: 30 June
**Contributor**: Cranfield Defence and Security
**Additional Information**: aseanop.com/women-cyber-leaders-scholarship-cranfield-university-uk/

**For further information contact:**

**Email**: cdsadmissionsoffice@cranfield.ac.uk

## Crohn's and Colitis Foundation of America

386 Park Avenue South, 17th Floor, New York, NY 10016, United States of America.

**Tel**: (1) 800 932 2423
**Email**: info@ccfa.org
**Website**: www.ccfa.org/

## Crohn's & Coltis Foundation Career Development Award

**Purpose**: To stimulate and encourage innovative research that is likely to increase our understanding of the aetiology, pathogenesis, therapy and preventive of Crohn's Disease and Ulcerative Clctis (IBD)

**Eligibility**: Candidates should hold an MD, must have 5 years of experience (with 2 years of research relevant to IBD)
**Level of Study**: Postdoctorate, Research
**Type**: Fellowship
**Value**: Not to exceed US$90,000 per year
**Length of Study**: 1–3 years
**Frequency**: Annual
**Study Establishment**: Approved research institute
**Country of Study**: United States of America
**Application Procedure**: See details at this link: www.crohnscolitisfoundation.org/sites/default/files/2019-06/CDAGuidelines2019.pdf
**Closing Date**: 1 July
**Funding**: Corporation, Foundation, Individuals
**Additional Information**: www.crohnscolitisfoundation.org/research/grants-fellowships/career-development-awards

**For further information contact:**

Crohn's & Colitis foundation of America, 386 park avenue south, 17th floor, New York, NY 10016, United States of America.

**Tel**: (1) 212 685 3440/800 932 2423
**Email**: info@icfa.org

## Crohn's & Coltis Foundation Research Fellowship Awards

**Level of Study**: Predoctorate, Research
**Funding**: Corporation, Foundation, Individuals
**Additional Information**: www.crohnscolitisfoundation.org/research/grants-fellowships/research-fellowship-awards

## Crohn's & Coltis Foundation Senior Research Award

**Purpose**: To stimulate and encourage innovative research that is likely to increase our understanding of the aetiology, pathogenesis, therapy and preventive of Crohnapos;s Disease and Ulcerative Clotis (IBD)
**Eligibility**: Applicants should be researchs who hold an MD, PhD or equivalent
**Level of Study**: Predoctorate, Research
**Type**: Research award
**Value**: Up to US$100,000 direct cost per year plus indirect cost of 15% of direct cost (or US$15,000, whichever is less)
**Length of Study**: Up to 2 years
**Frequency**: Annual
**Study Establishment**: Approved research institute
**Country of Study**: United States of America

**Application Procedure**: All completed applications must include one CD ROM or disk in PDF or word format, one master and four copies collected in order per check list. The complete application must be complied and saved as a single document
**Closing Date**: 1 July
**Funding**: Corporation, Foundation, Individuals
**Additional Information**: www.crohnscolitisfoundation.org/research/grants-fellowships/senior-research-awards

# Croucher Foundation

Suite 501, Nine Queen's Road Central, Hong Kong.

| | |
|---|---|
| **Tel**: | (852) 2 736 6337 |
| **Email**: | cfadmin@croucher.org.hk |
| **Website**: | www.croucher.org.hk |
| **Contact**: | Ms Elaine Sit, Administrative Officer |

Founded to promote education, learning and research in the areas of natural sciences, technology and medicine, the Croucher Foundation operates a scholarship and fellowship scheme for individual applicants who are permanent residents of Hong Kong wishing to pursue doctoral or postdoctoral research overseas. The Foundation otherwise makes grants to institutions only.

## Croucher Foundation PhD Scholarships and Postdoctoral Fellowships

**Purpose**: Our goal is to identify and support a group of talented Hong Kong students and early-career researchers who, through a process of intensive education and exposure to prominent academics in their respective fields, will develop independent and critical abilities and form enduring collaborative partnerships, to enable them to become next generation of leaders of science, technology and medicine in Hong Kong. Eligibility under the following programmes is restricted to permanent Hong Kong residents
**Eligibility**: 1. Fellows must be full-time research workers. 2. All applicants must disclose offers of financial support received, or likely to be received, from other sources. Applicants and Fellowship holders must keep the Foundation informed of the progress of applications for support from other sources. Croucher Fellowships are on occasion, and at the discretion of the Foundation as an exception, allowed to be held concurrently with other minor awards. 3. The Foundation occasionally gives approval for Fellows to be remunerated for a limited amount of teaching or research responsibilities but such Fellows must seek approval in advance from the Foundation which may in its absolute discretion modify the terms of the Fellowship
**Level of Study**: Doctorate, Postdoctorate
**Type**: Scholarships and fellowships
**Value**: an annual maintenance allowance has been set to US$48,240 per annum. one economy class single air fare and a one-off arrival allowance of US$1,000
**Length of Study**: six years of graduation with a doctoral degree
**Frequency**: Annual
**Country of Study**: Any country
**Closing Date**: 1 November
**Funding**: Foundation
**Additional Information**: For further inquiries, check the website croucher.org.hk/funding/study_awards/postdoctoral_fellowships croucher.org.hk/funding/study_awards/postdoctoral_fellowships

### For further information contact:

Croucher Foundation, Suite 501, Nine Queen's Road Central, Hong Kong.

**Fax**: (852) 2730 0742

## Croucher Science Communication Studentships

**Purpose**: These awards are intended for those engaged in full-time study leading to a Master's degree. Applicants must have obtained at least Second Class Honours Division One in their first degree. Otherwise they must obtain substantively a higher degree by September 2020 to become eligible. Students in their final year of first degree may also apply, but any offer of award will be conditional on their obtaining a suitable qualification upon their graduation by July 2020.
**Eligibility**: 1. an annual maintenance allowance which is set at US$22,400. 2. one economy class single air fare at both the beginning and end of the period of the award (if awards are tenable overseas); 3. tuition fees. 4. a one-off arrival allowance of US$1,000 to cover the costs of arriving in a new country during the first year of tenure (if awards are tenable overseas); 5. an academic development allowance of up to US$2,000 to allow Croucher Studentship recipients to attend conferences, workshops or courses during the tenure of their awards; 6. a medical insurance allowance of up to US$2,000 to cover medical insurance costs (if awards are tenable overseas);. 7. a family allowance of up to US$16,000 for the first child and up to US$6,800 for every additional child who resides with the scholar during the entire duration of the award; 8. a commencement award of US$2,500 to be offered towards the completion of the Master's degree to contribute towards the cost of travel expenses for family members to attend their graduation ceremonies. 9. a project allowance to

offer support to those award recipients particularly interested in designing and implementing activities and projects in schools and in the wider community during the tenure of the award and/or the period immediately following the award. Interested scholars are invited to submit proposals to the Foundation for consideration of a programme of activities designed to involve school students, teachers, families and/or other non-specialist audiences in dialogue and debate.

**Level of Study**: Postdoctorate
**Type**: Studentships
**Length of Study**: 1 year
**Closing Date**: May
**Additional Information**: croucher.org.hk/funding/croucher-science-communication-studentships

### For further information contact:

**Tel**:    (852) 2730 0742

## Culinary Trust

PO Box 5485, Portland, OR 10013, United States of America.

**Tel**:        (1) 97228 5485
**Email**:     scholarships@theculinarytrust.org
**Website**:   www.theculinarytrust.org/

The Culinary Trust has been the philanthropic partner to over 4,000 members of the International Association of Culinary Professionals (IACP) for over 20 years. The Trust solicits, manages and distributes funds for educational and charitable programmes related to the culinary industry in many areas.

## L'Academie de Cuisine Culinary Arts Scholarship

**Purpose**: To financially prospective students prospective students for the Culinary Arts Program each year
**Eligibility**: Open to a student pre-enroled for the 12 months, Culinary Arts or Pastry Arts Certificate Program
**Type**: Scholarship
**Value**: US$5,000
**Length of Study**: 1 year
**Application Procedure**: Check the website for further details
**Closing Date**: December
**Additional Information**: Scholarship is valid for enrollment during July or October only

### For further information contact:

**Tel**:    (1) 646 224 6989

## The Julia Child Endowment Fund Scholarship

**Purpose**: To support a career professional to conduct independent study and research in France, as it relates to French food, wine, history, culture and traditions. This programme also encourages, enables and assists aspiring students and career professionals to advance their knowledge of the culinary arts
**Eligibility**: Open to applicants who have 2 years of food service experience
**Level of Study**: Professional development
**Type**: Scholarship
**Value**: US$5,000
**Frequency**: Annual
**Country of Study**: France
**Application Procedure**: Applicants are required to include a three-page project proposal, an itemized budget detailing the use of this award, a tentative travel schedule with dates and locations, and provide a current curriculum vitae to qualify for this scholarship
**Closing Date**: 15 December
**Funding**: Trusts
**Additional Information**: Please check website for more details

### For further information contact:

**Email**:    foodwine@bu.edu

## Zwilling, J.A. Henckels Culinary Arts Scholarship

**Purpose**: To provide financial assistance to students from designated states who are interested in pursuing a degree in the culinary arts
**Eligibility**: Open to any pre-enroled student, currently enroled student or career professional toward any culinary arts degree or certificate program at any nationally accredited culinary school
**Level of Study**: Postgraduate
**Type**: Scholarship
**Value**: US$5,000
**Application Procedure**: Check the website for further details
**Closing Date**: 15 December
**Contributor**: Zwilling, J.A. Henckels Trust

## Cultural Vistas

440 Park Avenue South, 2nd Floor (between 29th and 30th Streets), New York, NY 10016, United States of America.

**Tel**:        (1) 212 497 3500
**Email**:     info@culturalvistas.org
**Website**:   www.culturalvistas.org/

CDS International, Inc. is a non-profit organization that administers work exchange programmes. CDS International's goal is to further the international exchange of knowledge and technological skills, and to contribute to the development of a pool of highly trained and interculturally experienced business, academic and government leaders.

## Robert Bosch Foundation Fellowship Program

**Purpose**: To support young Americans the opportunity to complete a high-level professional development program in Germany

**Eligibility**: 1. U.S. citizen 2. 40 years of age or younger at the application deadline 3. Minimum five years of relevant, full-time work experience in target fellowship field (excluding internships) 4. Graduate degree preferred 5. Evidence of outstanding professional performance 6. Sincere commitment to furthering the transatlantic relationship

**Level of Study**: Graduate, Unrestricted

**Type**: Fellowship

**Value**: Monthly stipend within the range of €3,200 to 3,700 starting in October; monthly summer stipend of 1.500 + free accommodations during July, August and September; exact amount of stipend dependent upon number of accompanying dependent family members

**Length of Study**: 9 months

**Frequency**: Annual

**Application Procedure**: 1. Complete application form 2. Resume 3. Official transcripts 4. 2 page personal statement 5. 2 letters of reference

**Closing Date**: 15 October

**Funding**: Private

**Additional Information**: culturalvistas.org/programs/abroad/robert-bosch-foundation-fellowship/

### For further information contact:

**Email**:    bosch@culturalvistas.org

## Curtin University

Kent Street, Bentley, Perth, WA 6102, Australia.

**Contact**:    Curtin University

Curtin University is an Australian public research university based in Bentley and Perth, Western Australia. The university is named after the 14th Prime Minister of Australia, John Curtin, and is the largest university in Western Australia, with over 58,000 students (as of 2016).

## Association of Firearm and Tool Mark Examiners Scholarship

**Purpose**: The scholarships listed here are offered to Curtin students by external organisations and individuals (Scholarship Providers) that are not affiliated with Curtin University. Curtin University cannot vouch for the accuracy of the information provided by these scholarship providers. All enquiries should be directed to the relevant scholarship provider

**Eligibility**: Scholarship is available for pursuing undergraduate and postgraduate degree program

**Level of Study**: Postgraduate

**Type**: Scholarship

**Value**: US$2,000

**Length of Study**: 3 year

**Frequency**: Annual

**Country of Study**: Any country

**Closing Date**: 1 April

**Funding**: International office

**Additional Information**: scholarship-positions.com/association-of-firearm-and-tool-mark-examiners-scholarship-for-international-students-in-australia/2019/03/12/

### For further information contact:

**Email**:    AFTEScholarship@gmail.com

## Three-year Fully Funded PhD Scholarship in Public Health

**Purpose**: Curtin University is offering three-year fully-funded PhD scholarship in Public Health. The scholarship is awarded to conduct health services research that focuses on health systems and implementation science at the School of Public Health

**Eligibility**: International students can apply for these scholarships. If English is not your first language then you will need to show that your English language skills are at a high enough level to succeed in your studies

**Value**: The successful candidate will receive a stipend of AU$27,082 per annum

**Study Establishment**: Scholarship is awarded to conduct health services research that focuses on health systems and implementation science at the School of Public Health

**Country of Study**: Australia

**Application Procedure**: The mode of applying is online

**Closing Date**: 9 April

**Additional Information**: For more details please visit our website scholarship-positions.com/three-year-fully-funded-phd-scholarship-public-health-australia/2018/02/27/

**For further information contact:**

**Email**: lynda.bergey@curtin.edu.au

## Curtin University of Technology

Office of Research and Development, GPO Box U1987, Perth, WA 6845, Australia.

**Tel**: (61) 8 9266 9266
**Email**: research_scholarships@curtin.edu.au
**Website**: www.curtin.edu.au/

Curtin University of Technology is a world class, internationally focused, culturally diverse institution. They foster tolerance and encourage the development of the individual. Their programmes centre around the provision of knowledge and skills to meet industry and workplace standards. A combination of first rate resources, staff and technology makes Curtin a forerunner in tertiary education both within Australia and internationally.

## American Planning Association(I) - Innovation, Competition and Economic Performance

**Purpose**: To encourage students to undertake a Higher Degree by Research within the the Centre for Research in Applied Economics (CRAE)
**Eligibility**: Candidates must be Australian citizens or permanent residents or New Zealand citizens, should hold or are expected to hold a First Class Honours Degree or its equivalent and must meet Curtin University of Technology's requirements for admission to a PhD.
**Level of Study**: Graduate
**Type**: Competition
**Value**: AU$25,118 per year
**Length of Study**: 3 years with the possibility of an extension of up to 6 months
**Application Procedure**: Candidates must forward the completed application for admission to a higher degree by research to the Centre for Research into Applied Economics (CRAE)
**Closing Date**: 31 March

**For further information contact:**

**Tel**: (61) 8 9266 2035
**Email**: H.Bloch@exchange.curtin.edu.au

## Australian Biological Resources Study Postgraduate Scholarship

**Purpose**: To foster research training compatible with ABRS and national research priorities
**Eligibility**: Applicants must be Australian citizens or permanent residents, must hold a First or Upper Second Class Honours or equivalent degree in an appropriate discipline and be enroled as a full-time student in a PhD degree at an Australian institution
**Level of Study**: Graduate
**Type**: Scholarship
**Value**: AU$22,500
**Country of Study**: Australia
**Application Procedure**: Applicants must submit the application to ABRS through the host institution. The application form will then be submitted to the ABRS Advisory Committee for consideration and assessment using the selection criteria. The individual selected as most worthy of funding will be awarded the scholarship
**Closing Date**: 26 October
**Additional Information**: scholarships.adelaide.edu.au/Scholarships/honours/faculty-of-sciences/australian-biological-resources-study-abrs-national

**For further information contact:**

Australian Biological Resources Study, GPO Box 787, Canberra, ACT 2601, Australia.

**Tel**: (61) 2 6250 9554
**Fax**: (61) 2 6250 9555
**Email**: abrs.grants@environment.gov.au

## Curtin Business School Doctoral Scholarship

**Purpose**: To enable doctoral (PhD, DBA) students to study at the Curtin Business School
**Eligibility**: Applicants must have completed at least 4 years of tertiary education studies at a high level of achievement and have First/Upper Second Class Honours or equivalent results. See scholarships.curtin.edu.au/scholarship.cfm?id=52 for more details
**Level of Study**: Postgraduate
**Type**: Scholarship
**Value**: US$25,000
**Length of Study**: Up to 3 years

**Frequency**: Annual
**Country of Study**: Any country
**Application Procedure**: Applicants can download the application form and obtain further information from the website
**Closing Date**: 31 December

### For further information contact:

**Tel**:     (61) 8 9266 4301
**Email**:   GRS.CurrentStudents@curtin.edu.au

## Curtin University Postgraduate Scholarship (CUPS)

**Purpose**: To assist with general living costs
**Eligibility**: Applicants must be Australian or New Zealand citizens or Australian permanent residents and must have completed 4 years of higher education studies at a high level of achievement and must hold, or are expected to obtain, First Class Honours or equivalent results; be enroled in or accepted to enrol in a Higher Degree by Research as a full-time student in the previous year in which the award is to be given
**Level of Study**: Graduate, Postgraduate
**Type**: Scholarship
**Value**: Varies, an annual living allowance of US$23,728 was given last year. This stipend is indexed annually and is tax-free unless taken on a part-time basis
**Length of Study**: 2 years for a Master by Research and 3 years, with a possible extension of up to 6 months, for a Doctoral degree
**Application Procedure**: Check website for further details
**Closing Date**: 31 October
**Additional Information**: www.australianuniversities.com.au/scholarships/guide/8014-curtin-university-postgraduate-scholarship-cups.html

### For further information contact:

**Tel**:   (1) 8 9266 4906
**Fax**:   (1) 8 9266 3793

## Establishing the Source of Gas in Australia's Offshore Petroleum Basins Scholarship

**Purpose**: To develop an isotopic method to analyse gases in fluid inclusions and to establish the source of gas in Australia's offshore petroleum basins
**Eligibility**: Applicants must have First Class Honours or equivalent science degree, preferably in chemistry/geology/geochemistry. Interests in analytical organic chemistry, laboratory skills in trace analysis, wet chemical methods, GC/GCMS or GC-IRMS instrumentation and awareness of stable isotopic concepts is desirable

**Level of Study**: Postgraduate
**Type**: Scholarship
**Value**: At least US$20,000 per year
**Application Procedure**: Check website for further details
**Closing Date**: 31 December
**Contributor**: The Stable Isotope and Molecular Biogeochemistry Research Group, Geoscience Australia, GFZ

### For further information contact:

Stable Isotope and Molecular Biogeochemistry Group, Centre for Applied Organic Geochemistry, Department of Applied Chemistry, Curtin University of Technology, GPO Box U1987, Perth, WA 6845, Australia.

**Tel**:   (61) 8 9266 2474
**Fax**:   (61) 8 9266 2300
**Email**:   K.grice@curtin.edu.au

## French-Australian Cotutelle

**Purpose**: To support the development of the double doctoral degree Cotutelle' between Australia and France
**Eligibility**: Applicants must be PhD students (of any nationality) enroled in a Cotutelle project between a French and an Australian university; should not have benefited from the French Embassy Cotutelle grant in previous years and should be registered with FEAST-France
**Level of Study**: Postgraduate
**Type**: Grant
**Value**: US$2,500
**Application Procedure**: Applicants must provide the French Embassy with the completed application form and a copy of the Cotutelle convention
**Closing Date**: 8 December

### For further information contact:

**Email**:   Stephane.GRIVELET@diplomatie.gouv.fr

## Hunter Postgraduate Scholarship

**Purpose**: To support a PhD student undertaking research in an area relevant to understanding the causes of Alzheimer's disease
**Eligibility**: Candidates must be PhD students undertaking research in an area relevant to understanding the causes of Alzheimer's disease
**Level of Study**: Postgraduate
**Type**: Scholarship
**Value**: Up to NZ$5,000 towards fees subject to funds available
**Length of Study**: 1 years

**Application Procedure**: Check website for further details
**Closing Date**: 31 October
**Additional Information**: www.wgtn.ac.nz/scholarships/current/hunter-postgraduate-scholarship

**For further information contact:**

**Tel**:   (61) 2 6254 7233
**Email**:   aar@alzheimers.org.au

## Masters Scholarship in Scotland

**Purpose**: The Scottish International Scholarship Programme is targeted at graduates in science, technology and the creative industries, and aims to create lasting connections between Scotland and industry leaders and entrepreneurs across the world
**Eligibility**: Open to Australian citizens who are presently studying science and technology
**Level of Study**: Postgraduate
**Value**: The Scotland Scholarship covers the tuition fee, airfare and a stipend for a taught masters course of up to 12 months duration at any Scottish Institution
**Length of Study**: Varies
**Frequency**: Annual
**Study Establishment**: Any Scottish institution
**Country of Study**: Scotland
**Application Procedure**: For more information including application forms please visit: www.gla.ac.uk/

**For further information contact:**

**Email**:   scholarships@glasgow.ac

## Scots Australian Council Scholarships

**Purpose**: To develop lasting links between young Scots and Australians by offering outstanding graduates and young professionals the opportunity to study at a Scottish university
**Eligibility**: Applicants must be Australian citizens or Australian permanent residents or New Zealand citizens or on permanent Humanitarian Visa. They must be indigenous or Torres Strait Islander students or students with a disability or students from rural or regional areas or mature students or sole parents or current students or prospective students
**Level of Study**: Postgraduate
**Type**: Scholarship
**Value**: £12,000
**Application Procedure**: Check website for further details
**Closing Date**: 14 January
**Contributor**: Scottish universities, Scottish business and industry, British Foreign and Commonwealth Office

**For further information contact:**

The Scots Australian Council, 19 Dean Terrace, Stockbridge, Edinburgh EH4 1NL, United Kingdom.

**Email**:   scholarships@scotsoz.org

## Sediment and Asphaltite Transport by Canyon Upwelling - Top Up Scholarship

**Purpose**: To investigate the role of upwelling currents in transporting material across the continental slope of the Morum Sub-Basin, southern Australia using an integrated geological, oceanographic, and organic geochemical approach
**Eligibility**: Applicants must be Australian and New Zealand residents, First Class Honours or equivalent science degree holders, preferably in chemistry/geology/geochemistry. Interests in analytical organic chemistry, laboratory skills in trace analysis, wet chemical methods, GC/GCMS or GC-IRMS instrumentation; awareness of stable isotopic concepts is desirable
**Level of Study**: Graduate
**Type**: Scholarship
**Value**: See the organization website
**Application Procedure**: Applicants must forward their interests, curriculum vitae and names of two referees to Stable Isotope and Molecular Biogeochemistry Group, Centre for Applied Organic Geochemistry, Department of Applied Chemistry
**Contributor**: The Stable Isotope and Molecular Biogeochemistry Research Group, Adelaide University, a petroleum industry partner

## The General Sir John Monash Awards

**Purpose**: To enable them to undertake postgraduate study abroad at the world's best universities, appropriate to their field of study
**Eligibility**: Applicants must be Australian citizens who have graduated from an Australian University with outstanding levels of academic achievement
**Level of Study**: Postgraduate Research
**Type**: Award
**Value**: AU$70,000 per annum
**Length of Study**: 3 years
**Frequency**: Annual
**Application Procedure**: 1. Be an Australian Citizen; 2. Have completed or be about to complete a full degree from an Australian university, and; 3. Be planning to undertake postgraduate study at an overseas university commencing in the calendar year following the year of application and selection;

it is not necessary to have already been accepted to the institution at the time of applying.

**No. of awards offered**: Between 15 and 20

**Closing Date**: 10 July

**Additional Information**: scholarships.adelaide.edu.au/ Scholarships/postgraduate-research/all-faculties/general-sir-john-monash-awards

### For further information contact:

The General Sir John Monash Foundation, Level 1, Bennelong House, 9 Queen Street, Melbourne, VIC 3000, Australia.

**Tel**:        (61) 613 9620 2428
**Email**:    peter.binks@monashawards.org

## Water Corporation Scholarship in Biosolids Research

**Purpose**: To investigate the potential impacts to soil and plants following the agricultural land application of alum-dosed wastewater sludge

**Eligibility**: Applicants must be Australian Citizens, Australian permanent residents or must hold an Australian permanent Humanitarian Visa. They must hold a relevant degree from a recognized University in the preferred fields of Agriculture, Environmental Science or the equivalent and demonstrate a high level in their Honours project or equivalent

**Level of Study**: Graduate, Postgraduate

**Type**: Scholarship

**Value**: US$23,400 per year

**Length of Study**: 3 years for a doctoral program and 2 years for a masters program

**Application Procedure**: Check website for further details

**Closing Date**: 31 October

### For further information contact:

**Email**:    D.Pritchard@curtin.edu.au

## Cystinosis Research Foundation

## Postdoctoral Research Fellowships

**Subjects**: Cystinosis research

**Purpose**: The ultimate goal of the Cystinosis Research Foundation is to find better treatments and a cure for cystinosis. Research and fellowship applications must take into consideration the mission and goals of the foundation in order to be considered.

**Eligibility**: First priority will be given to 'named' postdoctoral trainees. However, investigators who are already studying cystinosis can apply for a fellowship position with the expectation of attracting a suitable postdoctoral fellow within a year. Pre-doctoral students, who are already studying cystinosis, will be considered if funding is available.

**Type**: Fellowship

**Value**: Max. US$75,000 per year

**Length of Study**: One to two years

**Frequency**: Annual

**Country of Study**: Any country

**Application Procedure**: Maximum length is six one-sided pages, single-spaced, using a standard 12-point font with 1-inch margins (2.54 cm) on all sides including figures, diagrams and drawings. Cover sheet, documentation, budget and budget justification and curriculum vitae (CV limit is 5 pages maximum or a bio sketch) are not included in the 6-page limit. Longer applications will not be evaluated.

**Closing Date**: 20 April

**Additional Information**: Fellowship applications must provide a CV (maximum of 5 pages) of the proposed candidate and a statement outlining his/her career goals. Please discuss why this fellowship is important to the applicant. It should be clear who the fellow's mentor(s) will be. The mentor must provide a CV (maximum of 5 pages) or a bio sketch as well as a statement of the plan for training the fellow. www.cystinosis research.org/research/for-researchers/

## Research Proposals

**Subjects**: Cystinosis research

**Purpose**: The ultimate goal of the Cystinosis Research Foundation is to find better treatments and a cure for cystinosis. The Cystinosis Research Foundation is prepared to fund proposals to improve the immediate care of children and adults with cystinosis and to develop a new understanding and treatment of cystinosis in an effort to help these patients in the future.

**Eligibility**: No limitations to eligibility

**Type**: Research grant

**Length of Study**: One to two years

**Frequency**: Annual

**Country of Study**: Any country

**Application Procedure**: Maximum length is nine one-sided pages, single-spaced, using a standard 12-point font with 1-inch margins (2.54 cm) on all sides including figures, diagrams and drawings. Cover sheet, documentation, budget and budget justification and curriculum vitae (CV limit is 5 pages maximum or a bio sketch) are not included in the 9-page limit. Longer applications will not be evaluated.

**Closing Date**: 20 April

**Additional Information**: Applicants must submit the original completed application, nine (9) printed copies of each proposal and an electronic copy (PDF format if possible) www.cystinosisresearch.org/research/for-researchers/

# D

## Daiwa Anglo-Japanese Foundation

Daiwa Foundation Japan House 13-14 Cornwall Terrace, London, NW1 4QP, United Kingdom.

| | |
|---|---|
| **Tel**: | (44) 20 7486 4348 |
| **Email**: | grants@dajf.org.uk |
| **Website**: | www.dajf.org.uk |
| **Contact**: | Grants & Scholarships Office |

The Daiwa Anglo-Japanese Foundation aims to enhance the United Kingdom and Japan's understanding of each other's people and culture, enable British and Japanese students and academics to further their education through exchanges and co-operation and make grants available to individuals and organisations to promote links between the United Kingdom and Japan at all levels.

## Daiwa Foundation Awards

**Purpose**: Awards of £7,000–£15,000 are available for collaborative projects that enable British and Japanese partners to work together in the context of an institutional relationship. In order to fund as many applications as we possibly can, given our limited budget, we typically award an average of £7,000 to successful Award applications. Our funding rarely covers an application's budget in full, but is meant to be a "contribution" to the proposed project
**Eligibility**: Daiwa Foundation Awards cannot be used for: any project that does not involve both a British and a Japanese partner general appeals capital expenditure (eg, building refurbishment, equipment acquisition, etc) school, college or university fees research or study by an individual school/college/university student salary costs or professional fees commissions for works of art retrospective grants replacement of statutory funding commercial activities

**Type**: Award/Grant
**Value**: Between £7,000 and £15,000
**Frequency**: Twice a year
**Country of Study**: Japan
**Application Procedure**: Online: dajf.org.uk/grants-awards-prizes/daiwa-foundation-awards
**Closing Date**: 30 September
**Funding**: Foundation
**Additional Information**: dajf.org.uk/grants-awards-prizes/daiwa-foundation-awards

### For further information contact:

Daiwa Foundation Japan House, 13/14 Cornwall Terrace (Outer Circle), London, NW14QP, United Kingdom.

## Daiwa Foundation Small Grants

**Purpose**: Grants of £2,000–£7,000 are available to individuals, societies, associations or other bodies in the United Kingdom or Japan to promote and support interaction between the two countries
**Eligibility**: Those applying from the United Kingdom must be United Kingdom residents
**Type**: Grant
**Frequency**: Twice a year
**Country of Study**: Japan
**Application Procedure**: United Kingdom-based applicants can apply online. Applications from Japan should be posted to the Tokyo Office. dajf.org.uk/grants-awards-prizes/daiwa-foundation-small-grants
**Closing Date**: 30 September
**Funding**: Foundation
**Additional Information**: Daiwa Foundation Small Grants cannot be used for: general appeals capital expenditure (eg, building refurbishment, equipment acquisition, etc) consumables (eg, stationery, scientific supplies, etc) school, college or

© Springer Nature Limited 2020
Palgrave Macmillan (ed.), *The Grants Register 2021*,
https://doi.org/10.1057/978-1-349-95988-4

university fees research or study by an individual school/college/university student salary costs or professional fees commissions for works of art retrospective grants replacement of statutory funding commercial activities dajf.org.uk/grants-awards-prizes/daiwa-foundation-small-grants

### For further information contact:

Daiwa Foundation Japan House, 13/14 Cornwall Terrace (Outer Circle), London, NW14QP, United Kingdom.

## Daiwa Scholarships

**Purpose**: The Daiwa Scholarship is a unique 19-month programme of language study, work placement and homestay in Japan, following a month of Japanese language tuition in the United Kingdom. Daiwa Scholarships offer young and talented United Kingdom citizens with strong leadership potential, the opportunity to acquire Japanese language skills, and to access expertise and knowledge relevant to their career goals. No previous experience of Japan or Japanese is necessary. Daiwa Scholarships are provided by the Foundation to encourage better understanding between both countries
**Eligibility**: Candidates for the Daiwa Scholarships must be: 1. British citizens. 2. aged between 21 and 35 years of age by the time of departure. Candidates should be: 1. graduates or due to graduate by the time of departure. 2. equipped with a strong degree in any subject* or with a strong record of achievement in their field. 3. in possession of clear career objectives and a commitment to furthering United Kingdom-Japan links. *Graduates in Japanese language studies are not eligible to apply for Daiwa Scholarships but may wish to apply for support through the Daiwa Scholarships in Japanese Studies or the Foundation's grant schemes. Preference will normally be given to candidates no older than 30
**Type**: Scholarship/Bursary
**Value**: ¥ 260,000 per month
**Length of Study**: Japanese for 1 year followed by a 6-month work placement
**Frequency**: Annual
**Country of Study**: Japan
**Application Procedure**: Online: dajf.org.uk/scholarships/daiwa-scholarship/application-procedure
**No. of awards offered**: 155
**Closing Date**: 5 December
**Funding**: Foundation
**No. of awards given last year**: 7
**No. of applicants last year**: 155
**Additional Information**: www.worldartfoundations.com/daiwa-anglo-japanese-foundation-daiwa-scholarship/

### For further information contact:

**Email**:    scholarships@dajf.org.uk

## Daiwa Scholarships in Japanese Studies

**Purpose**: The Daiwa Scholarships in Japanese Studies, a postgraduate programme to support the study of Japanese Studies in either Japan or the United Kingdom. The Daiwa Anglo-Japanese Foundation gratefully acknowledges additional support for this programme from Daiwa Securities Group Inc. The intention is to support six individuals in any given year, of whom at least three must study full-time at a university in Japan
**Eligibility**: Candidates for the Daiwa Scholarships in Japanese Studies must be: United Kingdom citizens who hold or are completing a degree in Japanese Studies, defined as a course focussing primarily on the study of Japan, and containing a substantial Japanese language component. Applicants who hold (or are completing) combined honours courses where Japanese Studies accounts for at least 50% of the course are also eligible to apply. The Scholarship would be to cover a further course of study related to Japanese Studies. enrolled* or enrolling in a further course of study related to Japanese Studies in either Japan or the United Kingdom. *Please note that Scholarships will not be granted in arrears. Strong Japanese language ability will be a key selection criterion. Scholarships will not be awarded to former recipients of Daiwa Scholarships or to the same individual more than once
**Level of Study**: Doctorate, Postdoctorate, Postgraduate, Postgraduate (MSc)
**Type**: Bursary and scholarship
**Value**: We cover the tuition fee and award maintenance of £1,000 in the United Kingdom or ¥ 260,000 in Japan
**Length of Study**: Dependent on programme
**Frequency**: Annual
**Country of Study**: Japan
**Application Procedure**: Online application dajf.org.uk/scholarships/japanese-studies/application_procedure
**No. of awards offered**: 15
**Closing Date**: 28 January
**Funding**: Foundation
**No. of awards given last year**: 4
**No. of applicants last year**: 15
**Additional Information**: For study in the United Kingdom or Japan dajf.org.uk/scholarships/japanese-studies

### For further information contact:

**Email**:    scholarships@dajf.org.uk

## Dalai Lama Foundation

The Dalai Lama Foundation, 18579 Burke Ave N, Shoreline, WA 98133, United States of America.

**Email**:    scholarship@dalailamatrust.org
**Contact**:    Scholarship Committee

The Dalai Lama Foundation was founded in 2009 by His Holiness the XIVth Dalai Lama. The Foundation was established to support the advancement and welfare of the Tibetan people, the culture and heritage of the ancient civilization of Tibet, and the promotion of the deep rooted values associated with its culture and people.

## The Dalai Lama Foundation Graduate Scholarship Program

**Purpose**: The purpose of the scholarship program is to further the human capital development of Tibetan people by encouraging the pursuit of excellence among Tibetan students in a graduate field of study that has relevance and potential to contribute to the welfare of humanity and the Tibetan people in particular

**Eligibility**: Applicants must have already been enrolled in or be accepted to a full-time graduate degree program at a university in Australia, Europe or the Americas 1. Applicants must show proof of Tibetan heritage and continuity of Dhanglang Chatrel (Green Book) contribution. 2. Applicants are solely and directly responsible for obtaining the necessary visas to attend the university of their choice. 3. Eligible candidates must be pursuing graduate studies, whether at the master's or PhD level, or at a professional school. 4. All graduate programs should be at least one year or multi-year, full-time courses, offered by reputable and accredited universities

**Level of Study**: Doctorate, Postgraduate
**Type**: Scholarship
**Value**: US$10,000
**Frequency**: Annual
**Country of Study**: Any country
**Application Procedure**: For details, visit www.dalailamatrust.org/scholarship/127-scholarship
**Closing Date**: 30 April
**Funding**: Foundation
**Additional Information**: For further information, please contact: scholarship@dalailamatrust.org dalailamafoundation. org/scholarship/

## Davies Charitable Foundation

245 Alwington Place, Kingston, ON K7L 4P9, Canada.

**Tel**: (1) 613 546 4000
**Email**: daviesfoundation@cogeco.ca
**Website**: www.daviesfoundation.ca

The Davies Charitable Foundation is a registered, non-profit, charitable organization founded by Michael R.L. Davies,

former owner and publisher of the Kingston Whig Standard. The purpose of the Foundation is to support individuals and organizations within the local district in the areas of the arts, education, health and sports. Since its inception the Davies Charitable Foundation has donated over C$7,500,000 to over 400 individuals and institutions.

## The Davies Charitable Foundation Fellowship

**Purpose**: To support a native of the Kingston, Ontario, area at the peak of academic excellence
**Eligibility**: Open to candidates born in the Kingston area or have resided in the area for at least 5 years prior to their 20th birthday and must have been accepted into a postdoctoral or fellowship position at the university of their choice
**Level of Study**: Postdoctorate
**Type**: Fellowship
**Value**: C$10,000
**Length of Study**: 1 year
**Frequency**: Annual
**Country of Study**: Canada
**Application Procedure**: Application form can be downloaded from the website
**Closing Date**: 30 October
**Funding**: Foundation
**Contributor**: Davies Charitable Foundation
**Additional Information**: www.postdocs.ubc.ca/award/davies-charitable-foundation-research-foundation

### For further information contact:

The Davies Charitable Foundation, 245, Alwington Place, Kingston, ON K7L 4P9, Canada.

## De Montfort University

The Gateway, Leicestershire, Leicester, LE1 9BH, United Kingdom.

**Tel**: (44) 116 255 1551
**Email**: enquiry@dmu.ac.uk
**Website**: www.dmu.ac.uk
**Contact**: The Registrar

De Montfort University is a dynamic organization, formed from a diverse range of specialist institutions. Its long history of excellent teaching, learning and research is founded in the technical and trade education of the late 19th century. Today, the university has two campuses in Leicester, and special arrangements with more than 60 universities and colleges in 40 countries. It has approximately 20,000 students and 2,500 staff.

## De Montfort University Awards to Women for Final Year Doctoral Research

**Purpose**: To help women graduates with their living expenses (not fees) while registered for study or research at an approved institution of higher education in Great Britain
**Eligibility**: Open to students who are studying or intend to study in Great Britain at a postgraduate or postdoctoral level, there is no upper age limit to apply
**Level of Study**: Postdoctorate, Postgraduate
**Type**: Award/Grant
**Value**: Up to £2,500
**Frequency**: Annual
**Country of Study**: United Kingdom
**Funding**: Foundation

### For further information contact:

BFWG Charitable Foundation, 28 Great James Street, London, WC1N 3ES, United Kingdom.

**Tel**:      (44) 20 7404 6447
**Fax**:     (44) 20 7404 6505
**Email**:   BFWG.Charity@btinternet.com

## India GREAT Scholarship

**Purpose**: GREAT Scholarship awarded in partnership with the British Council to Indian students
**Eligibility**: 1. Applicants must be Indian passport holders and resident in India at the time of application. 2. Have an undergraduate degree that will enable you to gain entry onto a postgraduate programme at a UK university. 3. Meet the English language requirement of the UK Higher Education Institution. 4. Have an offer from one of the participating UK universities. 5. The course applied is starting in September 2020
**Value**: £4,000
**Country of Study**: United Kingdom
**Application Procedure**: For application, please visit www.dmu.ac.uk/international/en/fees-and-scholarships/india-great-scholarship.aspx
**Closing Date**: 31 July
**Additional Information**: For more details, visit website www.dmu.ac.uk/international/en/fees-and-scholarships/international-scholarships.aspx www.britishcouncil.in/study-uk/scholarships/great-scholarships

### For further information contact:

**Email**:    Greatedu.india@britishcouncil.org

## Leicester Castle Business School Full Postgraduate Scholarship

**Purpose**: Leicester Castle Business School is pleased to announce a full-fee postgraduate scholarship offering for those wishing to study in September
**Eligibility**: This scholarship is only available to students domiciled within the eligible areas (the continent of Africa, Russia, Taiwan, Thailand, United States of America)
**Value**: Our Full Postgraduate Scholarships which will cover the total value of the course fee. The scholarship also includes an additional £5,000 which can be used towards assistance with accommodation and living costs
**Length of Study**: 1 year
**Country of Study**: United Kingdom
**Application Procedure**: To apply, please complete the scholarship application web form
**Closing Date**: 31 July
**Additional Information**: For more details, please visit website lcbs.ac.uk/full-postgraduate-scholarships/ www.scholarshiproar.com/leicester-castle-business-school-postgraduate-scholarship/

### For further information contact:

**Email**:    enquiry@lcbs.ac.uk

## Leicester Castle Business School MBA Scholarship

**Purpose**: It is available to Global MBA students who have excelled academically and have an offer of admission for our full-time Global MBA programme
**Eligibility**: For eligibility, please refer website
**Value**: £2,500
**Country of Study**: United Kingdom
**Application Procedure**: To apply, please complete the scholarship application web form available at www.dmu.ac.uk/international/en/fees-and-scholarships/leicester-castle-business-school-scholarships.aspx?_ga=2.249885056.727537558.1523602564-1792966074.1523602564
**Closing Date**: 31 July
**Contributor**: Leicester Castle Business School
**Additional Information**: www.dmu.ac.uk/International/en/EU-fees-and-scholarships/EU-fees-and-scholarships.aspx

### For further information contact:

**Email**:    enquiry@lcbs.ac.uk

## Lesbian, Gay, Bisexual and Transgender+Allies Scholarship

**Purpose**: This scholarship will allow prospective students to study in a welcoming and inclusive environment to inspire and enhance continued activism during and after study, promoting LGBTQ+ rights worldwide

**Eligibility**: Eligible recipients should be domiciled outside the United Kingdom and EU area and have an offer of admission for any one year post-graduate taught programme

**Type** Postgraduate scholarships

**Value**: The scholarships also include an additional £1,015 (excluding any taxes) per month for the duration of the course, to assist with accommodation and living costs

**Length of Study**: 1 year

**Country of Study**: United Kingdom

**Closing Date**: 3 August

**Additional Information**: For details, visit website www.dmu.ac.uk/documents/international-documents/2018-scholarships-and-discounts/global-lgbtqallies-scholarship-tcs-final-v3.pdf

### For further information contact:

**Email**: campus@hrc.org

## Square Mile International Scholarship

**Purpose**: One Square Mile International Scholarship will be awarded to a student who demonstrates significant experience in engaging with their local community and a willingness to contribute to the DMU Square Mile Project

**Eligibility**: For eligibility details, please visit website

**Value**: Full tuition fees, a monthly bursary to cover living costs and one return flight to the United Kingdom

**Frequency**: Annual

**Country of Study**: United Kingdom

**Application Procedure**: To apply, please complete the scholarship application web form available at www.dmu.ac.uk/international/en/fees-and-scholarships/dmu-square-mile-international-scholarship.aspx

**Closing Date**: 29 June

**Contributor**: De Montfort University

**Additional Information**: scholarship-positions.com/dmu-square-mile-international-scholarship-uk/2016/06/14/

### For further information contact:

**Email**: ask.international@dmu.ac.uk

## Deakin University

221 Burwood Highway, Burwood, VIC 3125, Australia.

**Tel**:       (61) 3 9244 6100
**Email**:     enquire@deakin.edu.au
**Website**:   www.deakin.edu

Deakin University is one of Australia's largest universities providing all the resources of a major university to more than 32,000 award students. The University's reputation for excellent teaching and innovative course delivery has been recognized through many awards over the past few years.

## Deakin University Postgraduate Research Scholarships (DUPRS)

**Purpose**: Deakin University, this Higher Degree by Research (HDR) scholarship offers multiple awards to both domestic as well as international students.

**Eligibility**: Applicants must meet Deakin's PhD entry requirements, be enrolling full-time and hold an Honours degree (First Class) or a Master's degree with a substantial research component in a related field. Applicants applying for Research Masters or Research Doctorate must not hold an equivalent research qualification

**Level of Study**: Postgraduate

**Value**: A stipend of AU$26,682 per annum, a relocation allowance up to AU$1,500, tuition fee and overseas health coverage for international students for the duration of 4 years. Paid sick, maternity and parental leave are applicable

**Length of Study**: 3 years

**Country of Study**: Australia

**Application Procedure**: 1. click Website www.deakin.edu.au/research/become-a-research-student/how-to-apply-research-degrees. 2. The candidates applying in the areas of Arts and Education, Business and Law, Science, Engineering and Built Environment, and Frontier Materials need to submit an Expression of Interest (EOI) prior to formal application. 3. Refer to the guidelines specified for the application. 4. Prepare all relevant documents and follow the steps as specified.

**Closing Date**: 31 October

**Additional Information**: Applications can be made throughout the year except for Arts and Education. Arts and Education applications must be submitted before 31st October. Please contact the Deakin Research Scholarships Office: research-scholarships@deakin.edu.au       www.buddy4study.com/scholarship/deakin-university-postgraduate-research-scholarships-duprs

**For further information contact:**

HDR International Admissions Officer, Deakin Research, Building BC, Deakin University, 221 Burwood Highway, Burwood, VIC 3125, Australia.

**Email**:    research-scholarships@deakin.edu.au

## Marine Biotechnology PhD Studentship

**Purpose**: Candidates must carry out research that is relevant to marine biology. Projects on offer can be found on the list of available projects. Applicants are also invited to suggest their own projects; please visit our research pages for more information on our supervisors and their research areas.
**Type**: Scholarship
**Value**: AU$25,000 per annum
**Country of Study**: Australia
**Closing Date**: 7 January
**Contributor**: Jointly funded by Deakin University and Plant and Food Research, Nelson, NZ
**Additional Information**: Interested candidates please forward your CV and expression of interest to Professor Colin Barrow or Dr Susan Marshall www.zoo.cam.ac.uk/study/post graduate/phd-studentships-marine-biology

**For further information contact:**

**Email**:    graduate@zoo.cam.ac.uk

## Serendib Community Cultural Association Sri Lanka Bursary

**Purpose**: The Deakin University is awarding SCCA Sri Lanka Undergraduate Bursary in the field of Arts and Communication. The scholarship will cover 20% of the student contributions (tuition fees)
**Eligibility**: Applicants must: 1. be a prospective international student. 2. be a Sri Lankan citizen. 3. must meet eligibility criteria for their chosen Deakin degree. 4. have applied to study one of the following degrees: i. A353 Bachelor of Creative Arts (Animation); ii. A352 Bachelor of Creative Arts (Photography); iii. A359 Bachelor of Creative Arts (Visual Art); iv. A356 Bachelor of Creative Arts (Drama); v. A355 Bachelor of Creative Arts (Visual Communications Design); vi. A351 Bachelor of Creative Arts (Film & Television); vii. A331 Bachelor of Communications (Journalism); viii. A325 Bachelor of Communications (Public Relations); ix. A333 Bachelor of Communications (Digital Media); x. A743 Master of Communication

**Level of Study**: Graduate
**Type**: Bursary
**Value**: 20% of the student contributions (tuition fees)
**Frequency**: Annual
**Country of Study**: Australia, the United Kingdom, Europe or the United States of America
**Application Procedure**: The bursaries will automatically be offered to eligible students and will be awarded on a first come, first served basis. Strict quotas apply
**Closing Date**: July
**Funding**: Private
**Additional Information**: www.chevening.org/scholarship/sri-lanka/

**For further information contact:**

Deakin University, 221 Burwood Highway, Burwood VIC 3125, Australia.

**Email**:    deakin-int-scholarships@deakin.edu.au

# Denmark-America Foundation

Nørregade 7A, DK-1165 København K, Denmark.

**Tel**:         (45) 3532 4545
**Email**:       daf-fulb@daf-fulb.dk
**Website**:     www.wemakeithappen.dk
**Contact**:     Ms Marie Monsted, Executive Director

The Denmark-America Foundation was founded in 1914 as a private foundation, and today its work remains based on donations from Danish firms, foundations and individuals. The Foundation offers scholarships for studies in the United States of America at the graduate and postgraduate university level and also has a trainee programme.

## Denmark-America Foundation Grants

**Purpose**: To further understanding between Denmark and the United States of America
**Eligibility**: Open to Danes and Danish-American citizens
**Level of Study**: Graduate, Postdoctorate, Postgraduate, Professional development, Research, MBA
**Type**: Bursary
**Value**: Varies
**Length of Study**: 3–12 months
**Frequency**: Annual
**Country of Study**: United States of America

**Application Procedure**: Applicants must complete a special application form, available by contacting the secretariat
**No. of awards offered**: 250
**Funding**: Private
**No. of awards given last year**: 34–35
**No. of applicants last year**: 250
**Additional Information**: www.european-funding-guide.eu/scholarship/7822-crown-prince-frederik-foundation

## Department of Biotechnology

**Website**:    www.dbtindia.nic.in
**Contact**:    Department of Biotechnology

The Department of Biotechnology is an Indian government department, under the Ministry of Science and Technology responsible for administrating development and commercialization in the field of modern biology and biotechnology in India.

### National Bioscience Awards for Career Development (NBACD)

**Purpose**: Awards are given for pursuing research programme
**Eligibility**: Citizens of India are eligible to apply
**Type**: Award
**Value**: Each award carries a cash prize of Rs. 200,000 and a trophy along with a citation and a project research grant of Rs. 1,500,000 @ Rs. 500,000 per year for a period of 3 years for career development
**Country of Study**: India
**No. of awards offered**: up to 10 Awards
**Closing Date**: 15 April
**Additional Information**: www.nationalmeritscholarships.com/national-bioscience-awards-for-career-development.html

#### For further information contact:

**Email**:    jagadish.dora@nic.in

### Tata Innovation Fellowship

**Purpose**: Applications are invited for "Tata Innovation Fellowship", a highly competitive scheme instituted by the Department of Biotechnology, Ministry of Science & Technology, Govt. of India to recognize and reward scientists with outstanding track record in Biological sciences/Biotechnology to find innovative solutions to major problems in health care, agriculture, environment and other allied areas related to life sciences and biotechnology.

**Eligibility**: 1. The fellowship is open to Indian Nationals residing in India who are below the age of 55 years as 31-12-2019. The fellowship is co-terminus with the superannuation of fellow in his/her organization. 2. The applicant should possess a PhD degree in Life Sciences, Agriculture, Veterinary Science or a Master's degree in Medical Sciences, Engineering or an equivalent degree in Biotechnology/related areas. The applicant must have outstanding contribution and publication in the specific area. 3. The candidate must have a regular permanent position in a University/Institute/Organization and should be engaged in research and development. If he/she is availing any other fellowship, he/she will have to opt for only one of the fellowships. 4. The applicant should have spent at least 5 years in India before applying for the fellowship. 5. Evidence of outstanding track record and a deep commitment to find innovative solutions to major problems in health care, agriculture and other areas related to life sciences and biotechnology.
**Type**: Fellowship
**Value**: Rs. 25,000
**Frequency**: Varies
**Country of Study**: Any country
**Application Procedure**: Application could be processed through online mode or physical mode. Correspondence address is Dr. Kakali Dey Dasgupta, Scientist "E" Department of Biotechnology, Ministry of Science & Technology, Room No.814, 8 th Floor, Block-2, CGO Complex, Lodhi Road, New Delhi - 110 003, India.
**Closing Date**: 31 December
**Funding**: Government
**Additional Information**: www.noticebard.com/tata-innovation-fellowship-2019-20/

#### For further information contact:

Dr. Kakali Dey Dasgupta, Scientist "E", Department of Biotechnology, Ministry of Science & Technology, Room No.729, 7th Floor, Block-2, CGO Complex, Lodhi Road, New Delhi -110003, India.

**Email**:    epromis.dbt@nic.in

## Department of Education Services

22 Hasler Road, Osborne Park, Perth, WA 6017, Australia.

**Tel**:        (61) 8 9441 1900
**Email**:    des@des.wa.gov.au
**Website**:    www.des.wa.gov.au

The Department of Education Services provides policy advice to the Minister for Education and Training and supporting universities, non-government schools and international education providers and in some cases individual students and teachers through scholarship programmes in Western Australia.

## Western Australian Government Japanese Studies Scholarships

**Subjects**: Japanese studies.
**Purpose**: To provide students with the opportunity to spend 1 year studying at a tertiary institution in Japan
**Eligibility**: Candidates must have Australian citizenship, or evidence that Australian citizenship status will be approved prior to departure for Japan; be a student of a higher education institution in Western Australia, or an institution of equivalent standing, and have completed at least 2 years of full-time study (or equivalent of part-time study) in an appropriate Japanese language course; or be a graduate from a university, having a reasonable command of the Japanese language and developed an interest in Japan through employment or further studies.
**Level of Study**: Postgraduate
**Type**: Scholarship
**Value**: The scholarship includes a return economy airfare, an initial payment of AU$3,000 for fees and other expenses and a monthly maintenance allowance of ¥200,000
**Length of Study**: 1 year
**Frequency**: Annual
**Country of Study**: Japan
**No. of awards offered**: Two
**Closing Date**: July
**Funding**: Government
**Contributor**: Government
**Additional Information**: www.jtsi.wa.gov.au/trade-with-wa/buying-from-wa/education/japanese-studies-scholarships

### For further information contact:

Department of Jobs, Tourism, Science and Innovation.

**Email**:    diana.phang@jtsi.wa.gov.au

## Department of Foreign Affairs and Trade

**Website**:    www.dfat.gov.au/home.html
**Contact**:    Exchange Scholarship Programme

The Department is responsible for the Australian Government's international relations and trade and development assistance programs through its headquarters in Canberra and embassies, high commissions and consulates throughout the world.

## Australia Awards Scholarships

**Subjects**: Australia Awards Scholarships, formerly known as Australian Development Scholarships (ADS), provide opportunities for people from developing countries, particularly those countries located in the Indo-Pacific region, to undertake full time undergraduate or postgraduate study at participating Australian universities and Technical and Further Education (TAFE) institutions.
**Purpose**: They aim to contribute to the development needs of Australia's partner countries in line with bilateral and regional agreements
**Eligibility**: The Australian Government Scholarship is open to students of Asia, Middle East, Africa and Pacific. The Australia Awards Scholarship is fully funded scholarship and is administered by the Department of Foreign Affairs and Trade. To be eligible to receive an Australia Awards Scholarship, applicants must: 1. Be a minimum of 18 years of age on 1 February of the year of commencing the scholarship. 2. Be a citizen of a participating country (as listed on the Australia Awards website) and be residing in and applying for the scholarship from their country of citizenship. 3. Not be a citizen of Australia, hold permanent residency in Australia or be applying for a visa to live in Australia permanently. 4. Not be married to, engaged to, or a de facto of a person who holds, or is eligible to hold, Australian or New Zealand citizenship or permanent residency, at any time during the application, selection or mobilisation phases (note: residents of Cook Islands, Niue and Tokelau with New Zealand citizenship are eligible but must apply for a Student visa [subclass 500])
**Level of Study**: Postgraduate
**Type**: Scholarship
**Value**: full tuition fees, return air travel, establishment allowance, Contribution to Living Expenses (CLE), etc
**Frequency**: Annual
**Country of Study**: Australia
**Application Procedure**: Go to the Online Australia Scholarships Information System (OASIS). When you register online, you will be required to answer some questions to establish your eligibility. You will then be given a unique registration number, username and password. You do not need to submit your application immediately. You can set up a draft application form and update it, and your supporting documentation, until the designated closing date as on the relevant participating country profile
**Closing Date**: 30 April
**Funding**: Private

**Additional Information**: www.scholars4dev.com/3253/australia-awards-scholarships/

## For further information contact:

R.G. Casey Building John McEwen Crescent Barton, ACT 0221, Australia.

**Tel**: (61) 2 6261 1111

## Department of Innovation, Industry and Regional Development

GPO Box 4509, Melbourne, VIC 3001, Australia.

**Tel**: (61) 3 9651 9999
**Email**: innovation@diird.vic.gov.au
**Website**: www.diird.vic.gov.au

The Office of Science and Technology at the Department of Innovation, Industry and Regional Development, supports the ongoing development and advancement of a scientifically and technologically advanced Victoria.

## Victoria Fellowships

**Purpose**: To offer support and encouragement to aspiring students to broaden their experience and develop networks. The fellowship also provides an opportunity for recipients to develop commercial ideas
**Eligibility**: Open to candidates who are either currently employed or enroled in post-graduate studies in Victoria in a field relating to science, engineering or technology and Australian citizens or hold permanent residence in Australia and a current resident of Victoria
**Level of Study**: Postgraduate, Professional development
**Type**: Fellowships
**Value**: AU$3,500
**Length of Study**: 1 year
**Frequency**: Annual
**Country of Study**: Australia
**Application Procedure**: A completed application form should be submitted
**Closing Date**: April
**Funding**: Government
**Contributor**: Government of Victoria
**No. of awards given last year**: 6
**Additional Information**: www.veski.org.au/vicfellow

## For further information contact:

**Tel**: (61) 3 9864 0905/9655 1040
**Email**: vicprize.fellows@atse.org.au

## Department of Science and Technology and Indo-United States Science and Technology Forum (IUSSTF)

Indo-United States Science and Technology Forum, Fulbright House, 12, Hailey Road, New Delhi 110001, India.

**Tel**: (91) 11 2691700/716
**Email**: energy.fellowship@indousstf.org
**Website**: www.iusstf.org
**Contact**: Dr Nishritha Bopana

Recognizing that climate change, clean and efficient energy and environmental protection are among the biggest challenges facing India and the United States; the Department of Science and Technology, Govt. of India through its Solar Energy Research Initiative, and the Indo-United States Science and Technology Forum (IUSSTF) are committed to tackling these issues by building capacity in these frontier areas.

## Bhaskara Advanced Solar Energy (BASE) Fellowship Program

**Purpose**: The Department of Science and Technology, Government of India in partnership with Indo-US Science and Technology Forum (IUSSTF) invites applications from students who are pursuing or have completed their PhD in the field of Solar Energy for Bhaskara Advanced Solar Energy (BASE) Fellowship Program 2020. Through this fellowship programme, Indian students and scientists get an opportunity to gain exposure and access to world-class facilities in the leading US institutions and interact with their American peers. A monthly allowance, return air-fare and a contingency fund will be awarded to the selected fellows.
**Eligibility**: Indian citizens currently pursuing a PhD as full time scholars in the field of solar energy, in a public-funded R&D Laboratory/S&T institution (non-private)/recognized academic institute (University/College) in India
**Type**: Fellowship
**Value**: Monthly stipend, return air-fare, contingency allowance
**Length of Study**: Internship: Minimum 3 months and upto 6 months; Fellowship: Minimum 3 months and up to 1 year

**Frequency**: Annual
**Country of Study**: Any country
**Application Procedure**: 1. Register through the online application portal and make an account. 2. Verify account using the activation link sent on the email. 3. Login using the user id and password and fill in details in the application form. 4. Upload the supporting documents. 5. Submit the application form.
**Closing Date**: 31 January
**Additional Information**: For programe information contact: Dr. Nishritha Bopana, energy.fellowship@indousstf.org www.buddy4study.com/scholarship/bhaskara-advanced-solar-energy-base-fellowship-program

### For further information contact:

Dr. Nishritha Bopana, Indo-U.S. Science and Technology Forum, Fulbright House, 12, Hailey Road, New Delhi - 110001, India.

**Tel**:     (91) 11 42691700

## Deutsche Forschungsgemeinschaft (DFG)

Kennedyallee 40, D-53175 Bonn, Germany.

**Tel**:     (49) 228 885 1

The DFG is a central, self-governing research organization, which promotes research at universities and other publicity financial research institutions in Germany. The DFG serves all branches of science and the humanities by funding research projects and facilitating cooperation among researchers.

## Albert Maucher Prize

**Purpose**: To promote outstanding young scientists and scholars in the field of geosciences
**Eligibility**: Open to promising young scientists and scholars up to the age of 35 years who are German nationals or permanent residents of Germany
**Level of Study**: Postdoctorate
**Type**: Award
**Value**: €10,000 each
**Length of Study**: Varies
**Frequency**: Every 3 years
**Study Establishment**: Approved universities or research institutions

**Country of Study**: Germany
**Application Procedure**: Applicants must write for details or visit the website. Application is by nomination
**Contributor**: Professor Albert Maucher
**Additional Information**: www.dfg.de/en/research_funding/programmes/prizes/maucher_prize/

### For further information contact:

**Tel**:     (49) 228 885 2012
**Email**:   Kristian.Remes@dfg.de

## Bernd Rendel Prize in Geoscience

**Purpose**: For the young geoscientists who have graduated, but do not yet hold a doctorate, and who have demonstrated great potential in their scientific career. The award must be used for scientific purposes, e.g. enabling prizewinners to attend international conferences and congresses
**Eligibility**: Open to researchers from natural science-oriented fields in geoscience, researchers from humanities-oriented branches of geography are not eligible
**Level of Study**: Predoctorate
**Type**: Prize
**Value**: €1,000
**Frequency**: Annual
**Application Procedure**: Nominations may be submitted either by the researchers themselves, or by any researcher or academic working in a closely related field. Detailed information on the nominee's research to date (e.g. thesis, manuscripts, special publications) and future research plans, tabular curriculum vitae, list of publications, copies of certificates, statement on the proposed use of the prize money should be provided
**Closing Date**: 20 February
**Contributor**: The Bernd Rendel Foundation, which is administered by the Donors' Association for the Promotion of Sciences and Humanities in Germany
**Additional Information**: www.dfg.de/en/funded_projects/prizewinners/rendel_prize/index.html

### For further information contact:

**Tel**:     (49) 228 885 2328
**Email**:   Ismene.Seeberg-elverfeldt@dfg.de

## Communicator Award

**Purpose**: This personal award is presented to researchers who have communicated their scientific findings to the public with exceptional success
**Value**: €50,000
**Frequency**: Annual

**Application Procedure**: Proposals for candidates can be put forward by researchers who are capable of assessing both the communication effort and professional qualification of the nominee(s)
**Closing Date**: 20 March
**Additional Information**: www.communicatorawards.com/

**For further information contact:**

**Email**:    Jutta.hoehn@dfg.de

## Copernicus Award

**Purpose**: To promote young researchers to further advance research and contribute to the German–Polish research cooperation
**Eligibility**: Open to outstanding researchers in Germany and Poland who work at universities or research institutions
**Type**: Award
**Value**: €100.000 (donated in equal shares)
**Length of Study**: 5 years
**Frequency**: Every 2 years
**Application Procedure**: A completed application form along with the required documents should be submitted
**Contributor**: The Foundation for Polish Science and the DFG
**Additional Information**: www.dfg.de/en/research_funding/ programmes/prizes/copernicus_award/

**For further information contact:**

**Tel**:      (49) 228 885 2663
**Email**:    Philip.Thelen@dfg.de

## Deutsche Forschungsgemeinschaft Collaborative Research Centres

**Purpose**: To promote long-term co-operative research in universities and academic research
**Eligibility**: Universities (and institutions of equivalent status entitled to confer doctorates) in Germany; other research institutions which are to make essential contributions to the research programme can be integrated
**Level of Study**: Postdoctorate, Research
**Type**: Research grant
**Value**: Dependent on the requirements of the project
**Length of Study**: Up to 12 years
**Study Establishment**: Universities and academic institutions
**Country of Study**: Germany
**Application Procedure**: Applicants must write or visit the website for further information. Applications must be formally filed by the universities

**Additional Information**: A list of collaborative research centres is available in Germany only from the DFG www. dfg.de/en/research_funding/programmes/coordinated_program mes/collaborative_research_centres/

**For further information contact:**

**Tel**:      (49) 228 885 2312
**Email**:    petra.hammel@dfg.de

## Deutsche Forschungsgemeinschaft Mercator Programme

**Purpose**: The DFG offers the Mercator Programme to enable Germany's research universities to invite highly qualified scientists and academics working abroad to complete a DFG-funded stay at their institutes
**Eligibility**: Open to foreign scientists whose individual research is of special interest to research and teaching in Germany
**Level of Study**: Postdoctorate
**Type**: Fellowship
**Value**: Dependent on the duration of the stay
**Length of Study**: 3–12 months
**Frequency**: Annual
**Study Establishment**: German universities
**Country of Study**: Germany
**Application Procedure**: A proposal must be submitted by the university intending to host the guest professor
**Additional Information**: www.dfg.de/en/research_funding/ programmes/international_cooperation/mercator_fellows/

**For further information contact:**

**Tel**:      (49) 228 885 2232
**Email**:    cora.laforet@dfg.de

## Deutsche Forschungsgemeinschaft Research Training Groups

**Purpose**: To promote high-quality graduate studies at the doctoral level through the participation of graduate students recruited through countrywide calls in research programmes
**Eligibility**: Open to highly qualified graduate and doctoral students of any nationality
**Level of Study**: Postgraduate, Predoctorate
**Type**: Grant
**Length of Study**: Up to 9 years
**Frequency**: Annual
**Study Establishment**: Any approved university
**Country of Study**: Germany

**Application Procedure**: Applications should be submitted in response to calls. For further information applicants must visit the website

**Closing Date**: 1 October

**Additional Information**: A list of graduate colleges presently funded is available (in Germany only) from the DFG www.dfg.de/en/research_funding/programmes/coordinated_programmes/research_training_groups/

**For further information contact:**

**Tel**:       (49) 228 885 288
**Email**:    sebastian.granderath@dfg.de

## Emmy Noether Programme

**Purpose**: To give outstanding young scholars the opportunity to obtain the scientific qualifications needed to be appointed as a lecturer

**Eligibility**: Open to promising young postdoctoral scientists within 5 years of receiving their PhD, who are up to 30 years of age and who are German nationals or permanent residents of Germany

**Level of Study**: Postdoctorate

**Type**: Project grant

**Value**: For the 2 years of research spent abroad the candidate will receive a project grant in keeping with the requirements of the project including an allowance for subsistence and travel. For the 3 years of research spent at a German university or research institution the candidate will receive a project grant

**Length of Study**: 5 years

**Frequency**: Annual

**Study Establishment**: Universities or research institutions

**Country of Study**: Any country

**Application Procedure**: Applicants must complete an application form. For further information applicants must write or visit the website

**Closing Date**: 1 July

**Additional Information**: www.dfg.de/en/research_funding/programmes/individual/emmy_noether/

**For further information contact:**

**Tel**:       (49) 228 885 3008
**Email**:    Verfahren-Nachwuchs@dfg.de

## European Young Investigator Award

**Purpose**: To enable and encourage outstanding young researchers from all over the world, to work in an European environment for the benefit of the development of European

science and the building up of the next generation of leading European researchers

**Eligibility**: 1. Applicants must be practising paediatricians who are ESPE members. 2. Candidates should be still in training or no more than 5 years in a Senior (PI) role.

**Type**: Prize

**Value**: Up to €1,250,000

**Length of Study**: 5 years

**Application Procedure**: Applicants should provide a completed application form, letters of recommendation and the letter of support from the host institution to the DFG

**Closing Date**: 30 November

**Contributor**: The European Union Research Organizations Heads of Research Councils (EuroHORCS)

**Additional Information**: www.eurospe.org/grants-awards/awards/young-investigator-award/

**For further information contact:**

Bioscientifica Starling House, 1600 Bristol Parkway North, Bristol BS34 8YU, United Kingdom.

**Tel**:       (44) 1454 642246
**Email**:    espe@eurospe.org

## Excellence Initiative

**Purpose**: To promote top-level research and improve the quality of German universities and research institutions in general, thus making Germany a more attractive research location, and more internationally competitive and focussing attention on the outstanding achievements of German universities and the German scientific community

**Eligibility**: The precise conditions for receiving funding were defined in accordance with the criteria specified by the federal and state governments

**Level of Study**: Postgraduate

**Type**: Funding support

**Length of Study**: 5 years

**Frequency**: Annual

**Country of Study**: Any country

**Contributor**: German federal and state governments

**Additional Information**: The three funding lines of the initiative: graduate schools to promote young scientists, clusters of excellence to promote top-level research, institutional strategies to promote top-level university research. For more details log on to www.dfg.de/en/research_funding/programmes/excellence_initiative/ www.dfg.de/en/research_funding/programmes/excellence_initiative/

**For further information contact:**

**Tel**:       (49) 228 885 2254
**Email**:    internetredaktion@uni-konstanz.de

## Gottfried Wilhelm Leibniz Prize

**Purpose**: To promote outstanding scientists and scholars in German universities and research institutions
**Eligibility**: Open to outstanding scholars in German universities
**Level of Study**: Predoctorate, Research
**Type**: Research grant
**Value**: €2,500,000 per award
**Length of Study**: 5 years
**Frequency**: Annual
**Study Establishment**: Any approved university or research institution
**Country of Study**: Germany
**Application Procedure**: Applicants must write for details or visit the website. Application is by nomination. Nominations are restricted to selected institutions such as DFG member organizations or individuals, e.g. former prize winners or chairpersons of DFG review committees
**Additional Information**: A list of prize winners is available in Germany only from the DFG www.dfg.de/en/funded_projects/prizewinners/leibniz_prize/index.html

### For further information contact:

**Tel**: (49) 228 885 2726
**Email**: Ursula.Rogmans-Beucher@dfg.de

## Heinz Maier–Leibnitz Prize

**Purpose**: To promote outstanding young scientists at the doctorate level
**Eligibility** Open to promising young scholars up to 33 years of age, who are German nationals or permanent residents of Germany
**Level of Study**: Doctorate, Postdoctorate
**Type**: Consultancy
**Value**: €16,000 per award
**Length of Study**: Varies
**Frequency**: Annual
**Study Establishment**: Any approved university or research institution
**Country of Study**: Germany
**Application Procedure**: Applicants must write for details or visit the website. Application is by nomination
**Closing Date**: 31 August
**Funding**: Government
**Contributor**: The Federal Ministry of Education and Research
**Additional Information**: www.dfg.de/en/funded_projects/prizewinners/maier_leibnitz_prize/index.html

### For further information contact:

**Tel** (49) 228 885 2835
**Email**: Annette.Lessenich@dfg.de

## Heisenberg Programme

**Purpose**: To promote outstanding young and highly qualified researchers
**Eligibility**: Open to high-calibre young scientists up to the age of 35 years who are German nationals or permanent residents of Germany
**Level of Study**: Postdoctorate
**Type**: Scholarship
**Value**: Varies
**Length of Study**: 5 years
**Frequency**: Annual
**Study Establishment**: Any approved university or research institution
**Country of Study**: Germany
**Application Procedure**: Applicants must submit a research proposal, a detailed curriculum vitae, copies of degree certificates, a copy of the thesis, a letter explaining the choice of host institution, a list of all previously published material and a letter outlining financial requirements in duplicate. For further information applicants must contact the DFG
**Additional Information**: www.dfg.de/en/research_funding/programmes/individual/heisenberg/

### For further information contact:

**Tel**: (49) 228 885 2398
**Email**: paul.heuermann@dfg.de

## The Eugen and Ilse Seibold Prize

**Purpose**: To promote outstanding young scientists and scholars who have made significant contributions to the scientific interchange between Japan and Germany
**Eligibility**: Open to outstanding young German or Japanese scholars
**Level of Study**: Postdoctorate
**Type**: Prize
**Value**: €10,000
**Length of Study**: Varies
**Frequency**: Every 2 years
**Study Establishment**: Universities or research institutions
**Application Procedure**: Applicants must write for details or visit the website. Application is by nomination
**Closing Date**: 31 August
**Additional Information**: www.dfg.de/en/funded_projects/prizewinners/seibold_prize/index.html

### For further information contact:

**Tel**: (49) 228 885 2346
**Fax**: (49) 228 885 2550
**Email**: Joerg.Schneider@dfg.de

## The Von Kaven Awards

**Purpose**: The award is granted as a fellowship or as a support for research in the field of instrumental mathematics (including the von Kaven Prize and the von Kaven Research Award)

**Eligibility**: Persons who meet the general eligibility criteria stipulated by the DFG within the individual grants programme

**Level of Study**: Postgraduate

**Type**: Award

**Value**: €15,000 (€10,000 von Kaven Prize; €5,000 von Kaven Research Award)

**Frequency**: Annual

**Country of Study**: Africa

**Application Procedure**: Nominations for the von Kaven (Prize and) award may be made by the members of the mathematics review board, its previous chairs and other DFG committee members in the field of mathematics (such as senators and members of the senate committee working in the field of mathematics). It is not possible to apply directly for the von Kaven (Prize and) award

**Closing Date**: 31 January

**Funding**: Private

**Additional Information**: www.dfg.de/en/funded_projects/prizewinners/von_kaven_award/index.html

### For further information contact:

**Tel**:      (49) 228 885 2567
**Email**:   frank.kiefer@dfg.de

## Ursula M. Händel Animal Welfare Prize

**Purpose**: To award scientists who make, through research, a significant contribution to the welfare of animals

**Eligibility**: Open to scientists who aim at improving the welfare of animals through research

**Level of Study**: Postdoctorate

**Type**: Award

**Value**: €25,000

**Application Procedure**: A completed application form and required documents must be submitted

**Funding**: Trusts

**Contributor**: Mrs Ursula M. Händel

**Additional Information**: www.dfg.de/en/funded_projects/prizewinners/haendel_prize/index.html

### For further information contact:

**Tel**:      (49) 228 885 2658
**Email**:   Sonja.Ihle@dfg.de

## Deutscher Akademischer Austauschdienst

German Academic Exchange Service, 1 Southampton Place, London, WCIA 2DA, United Kingdom.

**Tel**:       (44) 20 7831 9511
**Email**:     info@daad.org.uk
**Website**:   www.daad.org.uk
**Contact**:   Ms Judie Cole

## Daad-Master Studies

**Purpose**: This scholarship programme offers you the opportunity to continue your academic education in Germany with a postgraduate course of study.

**Eligibility**: 1. Participation in a postgraduate programme after a first undergraduate course of study for the purpose of technical or scientific specialisation. 2. Specifically, the following is supported: a postgraduate or Master's degree programme completed at a state or state-recognised university in Germany.

**Level of Study**: Postdoctorate

**Type**: Scholarships

**Value**: €850 a month

**Length of Study**: 2-year

**Closing Date**: 1 October

**Additional Information**: www2.daad.de/deutschland/stipendium/datenbank/en/21148-scholarship-database/?detail=50026200

## Research Internships in Science and Engineering (RISE)

**Purpose**: To offer research internships to students in science and engineering

**Type**: Grant

**Value**: €650 per month

**Length of Study**: 1.5–3 years

**Frequency**: Annual

**Country of Study**: Germany

**Closing Date**: December

**Funding**: Government

**Additional Information**: Please visit www.daad.de/rise www.abroad.pitt.edu/RISE

### For further information contact:

**Email**:    a.olalde@pitt.edu

# Deutsches Museum

Museumsinsel 1, D-80538, Munich, Germany.

**Tel**: (49) 89 217 91, 89 217 9433
**Email**: information@deutsches-museum.de
**Website**: www.deutsches-museum.de/en

## Scholar-in-Residence Program

**Purpose**: The Fulbright Scholar-in-Residence (S-I-R) Program assists U.S. higher education institutions in expanding programs of academic exchange, by supporting non-U.S. scholars through grants for teaching at institutions that might not have a strong international component and/or serve minority audiences. Both the U.S. institution and the scholar grantee benefit from this experience.
**Eligibility**: 1. Minority Serving Institutions Asian American Native American Pacific Islander-Serving Institutions (AANAPISIs), American Indian and Alaskan Native-Serving Institutions (AIANSIs), Historically Black Colleges and Universities (HBCUs), Hispanic-Serving Institutions (HISs), Tribal Colleges and Universities (TCUs), and Predominately Black Institutions (PBIs). 2. Community Colleges. 3. Small Liberal Arts Colleges. 4. Rural Colleges and Universities.
**Level of Study**: Research
**Type**: Scholarship
**Value**: Predoctoral stipends: €7,500 (6 months) or €15,000 (full year). Postdoctoral stipends: €15,000 (6 months) or €30,000 (full year)
**Country of Study**: Germany
**Application Procedure**: Applicants should send their applications by post, including completed application form, curriculum vitae, project description (3–5 pages), two confidential references (can be sent directly by the referees)
**Closing Date**: 1 November
**Contributor**: Deutsches Museum
**Additional Information**: www.cies.org/program/fulbright-scholar-residence-program

### For further information contact:

**Email**: Scholars@iie.org

# Diabetes United Kingdom

Macleod House, 10 Parkway, London, NW1 7AA, United Kingdom.

**Tel**: (44) 20 7424 1000
**Email**: victoria.king@diabetes.org.uk
**Website**: www.diabetes.org.uk
**Contact**: Dr Victoria King, Research Manager

Diabetes United Kingdom's overall aim is to help and care for both people with diabetes and those closest to them, to represent and campaign for their interests and to fund research into diabetes. Diabetes United Kingdom continues to encourage research into all areas of diabetes.

## Endeavour Postgraduate Leadership Award

**Purpose**: The Endeavour Postgraduate Leadership Award provides financial support for international applicants to undertake a postgraduate qualification at a Masters or PhD level either by coursework or research in any field in Australia for up to 2 years for Masters and 4 years for PhD.
**Eligibility**: To participate in the ELP, individual applicants must: 1. not be undertaking their Leadership Activity in a country where they hold citizenship/dual citizenship or permanent residency (International Individual Endeavour Leaders must undertake their activity in Australia and not hold citizenship/dual citizenship or be a permanent resident of Australia.). 2. be aged 18 years or over at the commencement of their Leadership Activity. 3. not be in receipt of any other Australian Government sponsored mobility, scholarship or fellowship benefits
**Level of Study**: Postgraduate
**Type**: Award
**Length of Study**: 2 years for a Masters and up to 4 years for a PhD
**Frequency**: Annual
**Country of Study**: Any country
**Closing Date**: November
**Funding**: Private
**Additional Information**: internationaleducation.gov.au/Endeavour%20program/Scholarships-and-Fellowships/Pages/default.aspx www.scholars4dev.com/3710/endeavour-postgraduate-scholarship-awards/

### For further information contact:

**Email**: endeavour@education.gov.au

# Dominican College of San Rafael

School of Business & International Studies Graduate Program in Pacific Basin Studies, 50 Acacia Avenue, San Rafael, CA 94912-9962, United States of America.

**Tel**: (1) 415 257 1359
**Email**: pbsad@dominican.edu
**Contact**: MBA Admissions Officer

## Dominican College of San Rafael MBA in Strategic Leadership

**Length of Study**: 2 years
**Application Procedure**: All applicants must submit a completed application form, with official academic transcripts, a curriculum vitae, a statement of purpose (three-five pages), TOEFL score (if applicable), and a fee of US$40
**Additional Information**: www.gradschools.com/graduate-schools-in-united-states/california/dominican-university-california-san-rafael/mba-strategic-leadership-194144

### For further information contact:

Division of Liberal & Professional Studies MBA in Strategic Leadership, 50 Acacia Avenue, CA 94901, United States of America.

**Tel**:      (1) 415 485 3280
**Fax**:      (1) 415 485 3293
**Email**:   87pathways@dominican.edu

## Doshisha University

International Center, Office of International Students, Karasuma-Higashi-iru Imadegawa-dori, Kamigyo-ku, Kyoto 602-8580, Japan.

**Tel**:        (81) 75 251 3257
**Email**:     ji-intad@mail.doshisha.ac.jp
**Website**:   www.doshisha.ac.jp/english
**Contact**:   Chieko Toboku

Located in the heart of Kyoto, Doshisha University occupies 5 separate campuses and is home to over 29,000 students engaged in both undergraduate and graduate studies. As one of Japan's most highly esteemed educational institutions, Doshisha offers students a wide ranging liberal arts education as well as studies in business and science.

## Doshisha University Doctoral-Program Young Researcher Scholarship

**Purpose**: To support young researchers who hold future promise and display a strong passion toward academic research
**Eligibility**: Students with a passion for academic research who have received a recommendation from one of the graduate schools and match one of the following profiles: (1) Students enroled in doctoral programs at the Graduate Schools of

Theology Letters; Social Studies, Law, Economics, Commerce, Policy and Management, Culture and Information Science, Science and Engineering, Life and Medical Sciences, Health and Sports Science, Psychology and Global Studies, who are aiming to acquire a doctoral degree and are under 34 years of age at the time of admission. (2) Students enroled in an integrated program (master's and doctoral programs) (except the Graduate School of Brain Science) for a minimum of 2 years, who are aiming to acquire a doctoral degree and are under 32 years of age at the time of enrollment
**Level of Study**: Doctorate
**Type**: Scholarship
**Value**: Amount equivalent to annual school fees (including admission fees at the time of enrollment, tuition fee for educational support and lab/practical fees)
**Length of Study**: 1 year (renewable for up to the standard number of years required for graduation)
**Frequency**: Annual
**Study Establishment**: Doshisha University
**Country of Study**: Japan
**Application Procedure**: The scholarship is awarded on the basis of recommendations from the graduate schools and cannot be applied for individually
**Additional Information**: istc.doshisha.ac.jp/en/tuition/scholarship.html

### For further information contact:

**Email**:    ji-kosei@mail.doshisha.ac.jp

## Doshisha University Graduate School Reduced Tuition Special Scholarships for Self-Funded International Students

**Purpose**: To enable international students to concentrate on their studies free from financial concerns
**Eligibility**: Those who satisfy one of the following qualifications are eligible: 1. who have passed the entrance examination for international students and who hold a 'college student' visa prescribed in the, Emigration and Immigration Management and Refuge Recognition Law', at the time of enrollment. 2. who have passed the entrance examination for international students and who hold a 'Permanent Resident' visa etc. 3. who are enroled in Doshisha regardless of the type of admission (type of entrance examination) and who hold a 'College Student' visa
**Level of Study**: Doctorate, Postgraduate, MBA
**Type**: Scholarship
**Value**: Annual tuition fees
**Length of Study**: 2 years (renewable for up to the standard number of years required for graduation)
**Frequency**: Annual

**Study Establishment**: Doshisha University
**Country of Study**: Japan
**Application Procedure**: The Scholarship is awarded based on Doshisha's criteria without application

## Doshisha University Graduate School Scholarship

**Purpose**: To provide for students enroled in master's or doctoral programs experiencing difficulty meeting educational costs required for them to continue their academic research activities
**Eligibility**: Graduate students (regular students). Please note Law School, Business School, and Graduate School of Brain Science students may not apply. Students who have been enroled at school longer than the standard number of years for course completion (a leave of absence is not counted as) may not apply. Students selected to receive the following scholarships may not apply: Doshisha University Doctoral-Program Young Researcher Scholarship, Japanese Government (MEXT) Scholarship, Doshisha University Graduate School Reduced Tuition Special Scholarship for Self-Funded International Students
**Level of Study**: Doctorate, Postgraduate
**Type**: Scholarship
**Value**: Half of the total annual tuition fee
**Length of Study**: 1 year
**Frequency**: Annual
**Study Establishment**: Doshisha University
**Country of Study**: Japan
**Application Procedure**: Eligible applicants are required to submit an application to the Section for Scholarship by specified date
**No. of awards given last year**: 16
**Additional Information**: www.doshisha.ac.jp/scholarships/attach/page/SCHOLARSHIPS-PAGE-JA-8/111157/file/2019inshoISTC.pdf

### For further information contact:

**Email**: ji-kosei@mail.doshisha.ac.jp

## Doshisha University Reduced Tuition Scholarships for Self-Funded International Students

**Purpose**: To enable international students to concentrate on their studies free from financial concerns
**Eligibility**: Those who satisfy one of the following qualifications are eligible: 1. who have passed the entrance examination for international students and who hold a 'College Student' visa prescribed in the 'Emigration and Immigration

Management and Refuge Recognition Law', at the time of enrollment. 2. who have passed the entrance examination for international students and who hold a 'Permanent Resident' visa etc. 3. who are enroled in Doshisha regardless of the type of admission (type of entrance examination), and who hold a 'College Student' visa
**Level of Study**: Doctorate, Postgraduate, MBA
**Type**: Scholarship
**Value**: Equivalent to 50% of tuition, equivalent to 30% of tuition, to be made based on Doshisha's criteria
**Length of Study**: 2 years (renewable for up to the standard number of years required for graduation)
**Frequency**: Annual
**Study Establishment**: Doshisha University
**Country of Study**: Japan
**Application Procedure**: The scholarship is awarded based on Doshisha's criteria without application
**Additional Information**: Nationals of Japan are not eligible ois.doshisha.ac.jp/en/scholarships/reduced.html

## Graduate School of Brain Science Special Scholarship

**Eligibility**: Open to doctorate students with academic excellence and depending on the candidate's contribution to the field. Those who have passed the entrance examination at the Graduate School of Brain Science and are under the age of 32 (for 3rd-year transfer students under the age of 34) at the time of enrollment
**Type**: Scholarship
**Value**: Full-time fee: ¥8,850; Full-time fee: ¥23,500
**Length of Study**: 1 year (renewable for up to 5 years (for transfer students, for up to 3 years))
**Frequency**: Annual
**Study Establishment**: Doshisha University
**Country of Study**: Japan
**Application Procedure**: As the initial registration procedure, eligible applicants are required to remit the registration fee and submit an application for the 'Graduate School of Brain Science Special Scholarship' by specified date
**Additional Information**: www.gla.ac.uk/postgraduate/taught/brainsciences/#depositsterms&conditions, additionalfees, collegeofscienceandengineeringdeans'award, themartinniem%C3%B6llerscholarship(collegeofmedicalveterinaryandlifesciences), universityofglasgowafricanexcellencefeewaiver, pgtexcellencescholarship, universityofglasgowinternationalleadershipscholarship, cheveningscholarship

### For further information contact:

**Email**: mvls-brainsci@glasgow.ac.uk

# Duke University

2127 Campus Drive, PO Box 90065, Durham, NC 27708, United States of America.

**Tel**:        (1) 919 681 3257
**Email**:      grm@duke.edu
**Website**:    www.gradschool.duke.edu
**Contact**:    Co-ordinator

The Duke University ideally has a small number of superior students working closely with esteemed scholars. It has approximately 2,200 graduate students enroled there, working with more than 1,000 graduate faculty members.

## Frontier Research in Earth Sciences (FRES)

**Purpose**: The FRES program will support research in Earth systems from the core through the critical zone. The project may focus on all or part of the surface, continental lithospheric, and deeper Earth systems over the entire range of temporal and spatial scales. FRES projects should have a larger scientific scope and budget than those considered for funding by disciplinary programs in the Division of Earth Sciences (EAR). FRES projects may be interdisciplinary studies that do not fit well within EAR's disciplinary programs or cannot be routinely managed by sharing between disciplinary programs. Innovative proposals within a single disciplinary area with outcomes of potential broad relevance to Earth Science research are also encouraged. Investigations may employ any combination of field, laboratory, and computational studies with observational, theoretical, or experimental approaches. Projects should be focused on topics that meet the guidelines for research funded by the Division of Earth Sciences.

**Eligibility**: Institutions of Higher Education (IHEs) - Two- and four-year IHEs (including community colleges) accredited in, and having a campus located in the United States, acting on behalf of their faculty members. Special Instructions for International Branch Campuses of United States IHEs: If the proposal includes funding to be provided to an international branch campus of a United States of America institution of higher education (including through use of subawards and consultant arrangements), the proposer must explain the benefit(s) to the project of performance at the international branch campus, and justify why the project activities cannot be performed at the United States campus

**Level of Study**: Foundation programme
**Type**: Research grant
**Value**: US$3,000,000
**Frequency**: Annual

**Country of Study**: Any country
**Application Procedure**: Many of the projects will be collaborative research from multiple institutions. There is no upper or lower limit on award size, but investigators proposing projects with budgets of less than US$1,000,000 or more than US$3,000,000 are encouraged to contact a Program Officer before submitting a proposal
**Closing Date**: 5 February
**Funding**: Private
**Additional Information**: For-profit organizations: United States commercial organizations, especially small businesses with strong capabilities in scientific or engineering research or educationt researchfunding.duke.edu/frontier-research-earth-sciences-fres

### For further information contact:

**Email**:    mbenoit@nsf.gov

## The Prof. Rahamimoff Travel Grants Program

**Purpose**: The Prof. Rahamimoff Travel Grants Program is open to PhD students doing research that requires facilities or expertise not available in their home countries. Each trip will be for a maximum length of 2 months
**Eligibility**: 1. Applicants must be U.S. or Israeli citizens. 2. Applicants must be conducting supervised research towards a PhD in an accredited higher education institution, or in a non-profit research institution (government or other, including hospitals). 3. The BSF will only accept applications that are in the scientific fields it supports. 4. Applicants must be 35 years old or younger.
**Level of Study**: Graduate, Postdoctorate
**Type**: Grant
**Value**: US$4,000
**Frequency**: Annual
**Country of Study**: Any country
**Application Procedure**: Applications will be evaluated by a special committee on the basis of their merit in light of the overall aim of the program, and the qualifications of the candidates. In particular, the significance of the trip to the candidate's research will be estimated. One of the criteria frequently used by the panel is the stage of the research program. Trips planned very early or very late in the research program are often not approved
**Closing Date**: 7 May
**Funding**: Private
**Additional Information**: www.instrumentl.com/grants/afbsf-travel-grant-programme

### For further information contact:

**Email**:    fundopps@duke.edu

## Post-Doctoral Training in Genomic Medicine Research

**Purpose**: The Duke Center for Applied Genomics and Precision Medicine is pleased to announce a two-year post-doctoral training program in genomic medicine. This unique program will provide training in a fast-growing field marked by the advent of new technologies, increased use of clinical genomic medicine, and large-scale federally- and privately-funded research efforts. The Post-Doctoral Training Program in Genomic Medicine is supported by a Ruth L. Kirschstein Institutional National Research Service Award (T32).

**Eligibility**: 1. MDs who have completed clinical training in a non-genetics related discipline, such as internal medicine (with or without subspecialty training), pediatrics, surgery, etc., and are eligible for board certification in their discipline. 2. PhDs who have decided to focus their careers on clinical or translational research related to genomic medicine. 3. Postdoctoral trainees must have received, as of the beginning date of the appointment, a PhD, M.D., D.D.S., or comparable doctoral degree from an accredited domestic or foreign institution. Comparable doctoral degrees include, but are not limited to, the following: D.M.D., D.C., D.O., D.V.M., O.D., D.P.M., Sc.D., Eng.D., Dr. P.H., D.N.Sc., D.P.T., Pharm.D., N.D. (Doctor of Naturopathy), D.S.W., Psy.D, as well as a doctoral degree in nursing research. Documentation by an authorized official of the degree-granting institution certifying that all degree requirements have been met prior to the beginning date of the training appointment is acceptable. Individuals in postgraduate clinical training, who wish to interrupt their studies for a year or more to engage in full-time research training before completing their formal training programs, are also eligible. Applicants must be a U.S. Citizen, non-citizen national, or have permanent resident status.

**Level of Study**: Graduate, Postdoctorate
**Type**: Fellowship
**Study Establishment**: Duke University
**Closing Date**: 1 April
**Additional Information**: researchfunding.duke.edu/post-doctoral-training-genomic-medicine-research

## Durham University

### The Durham University Business School's Dean's Scholarship

**Purpose**: Durham University Business School Dean's Scholarship - awarded to an exceptional candidate who can demonstrate significant academic and extra-curricular achievements
**Eligibility**: Applicants will be considered based upon: Academic achievement Work or voluntary experience relevant to the programme for which they have applied Any additional skills, experience or extra-curricular activities that will add

value and indicate that they will make a significant contribution to the cohort on the programme or the Business School. Open to applicants for MSc Programmes (excluding MSc Business Analytics)
**Level of Study**: Postgraduate
**Type**: Scholarship
**Value**: Up to £12,500
**Frequency**: Annual
**Country of Study**: Any country
**Closing Date**: 31 May
**Funding**: Private
**Additional Information**: scholarship-positions.com/durham-university-business-school-deans-scholarship-for-international-students-in-uk/2019/01/10/

### For further information contact:

Durham University Business School, Mill Hill, Lane Durham, DH1 3LB, United Kingdom.

**Tel**: (44) 191 334 5200
**Email**: research.admissions@durham.ac.uk

## Dutch Ministry of Foreign Affairs

Bezuidenhoutseweg 67, The Hague, PO Box 20061, NL-2500 EB The Hague, Netherlands.

**Tel**: (31) 70 3486486
**Email**: dsi-my@minbuza.nl
**Website**: www.minbuza.nl
**Contact**: The Ministry of Foreign Affairs

Dutch foreign policy is driven by the conviction that international cooperation brings peace and promotes security, prosperity, and justice. It is bound by the obligation to promote Dutch interests abroad as effectively and efficiently as possible. To do so, the Netherlands needs a worldwide network of embassies, consulates, and permanent representations to international organizations. The activities, composition, and size of each mission depend on its host country and region. Embassies and consulates-bilateral missions-concern themselves with relations between the Netherlands and other countries.

## Netherlands Fellowship Programmes

**Purpose**: To support mid-career professionals nominated by their employers
**Eligibility**: Open to candidates who are employed by an organization other than a large industrial, commercial and/or multinational firm, must be nationals of one of the 57 selected

countries (see 'Eligible countries'), must declare that they will return to their home country immediately after they complete the master programme, must have gained admission to a TU/e master course, which is on the NFP course list and have sufficient mastery of the English language. Priority is given to female candidates and to candidates coming from sub-Saharan Africa

**Level of Study**: Postgraduate

**Type**: Fellowships

**Value**: Full-cost scholarship (including international travel, monthly subsistence allowance, tuition fee, books, and health insurance)

**Length of Study**: 2 years

**Frequency**: Annual

**Country of Study**: Netherlands

**Application Procedure**: Applicants must apply for an NFP fellowship through the Netherlands embassy or consulate in their own country by completing an NFP Application Form and submitting it together with all the required documents and information to the embassy or consulate. Then the Embassy checks and sends the forms to the Nuffic checks. Nuffic decides how many fellowships will be available for each program and sends TU/e the list of NFP candidates

**Funding**: Government

**Contributor**: Dutch Ministry of Foreign Affairs

**Additional Information**: Eligible countries: Afghanistan, Albania, Armenia, Autonomous Palestinian Territories, Bangladesh, Benin, Bhutan, Bolivia, Bosnia–Hercegovina, Brazil, Burkina Faso, Cambodia, Cape Verde, China, Colombia, Costa Rica, Cuba, Ecuador, Egypt, El Salvador, Eritrea, Ethiopia, Georgia, Ghana, Guatemala, Guinea–Bissau, Honduras, India, Indonesia, Iran, Ivory Coast, Jordan, Kenya, Macedonia, Mali, Moldova, Mongolia, Mozambique, Namibia, Nepal, Nicaragua, Nigeria, Pakistan, Peru, Philippines, Rwanda, Senegal, South Africa, Sri Lanka, Suriname, Tanzania, Thailand, Uganda, Vietnam, Yemen, Zambia, Zimbabwe. For a more detailed list of criteria, please check website www.scholars4dev.com/7672/netherlands-fellowship- program/

**For further information contact:**

**Tel**: (31) 40 247 4690
**Fax**: (31) 40 244 1692
**Email**: io@remove-this.tue.nl

# Deloitte Foundation

## Doctoral Fellowship Program

**Subjects**: Accounting
**Purpose**: To provide financial support to outstanding doctoral students in accounting as they complete their coursework and dissertations.

**Eligibility**: Any graduate student enrolled in and successfully pursuing a doctoral program in accounting at an accredited U.S. university who has completed two or more semesters (or the equivalent) of that program is eligible to apply for a Deloitte Foundation Fellowship. Applicants should have plans to teach at a U.S. college or university upon graduation. At some time during their doctoral studies Fellows are expected to teach or to prepare themselves for their teaching careers by participating in elective programs designed to enhance their teaching skills.

**Type**: Fellowship

**Value**: Each Fellow receives a grant of US$25,000, disbursed in four payments over two years, to help cover the Fellow's expenses during his or her final year of coursework and during the year immediately following, in which the Fellow is expected to complete the dissertation.

**Frequency**: Annual

**Country of Study**: United States of America

**No. of awards offered**: Up to ten

**Additional Information**: Prospective applicants and their PhD Program Coordinators should consider including any relevant materials (research papers, etc.) that could provide a comprehensive overview of the applicant's breadth and depth of qualifications. Selected award recipients may not accept other doctoral program financial assistance awards of US$10,000 or more from external sources (outside of applicant's school) while receiving payment from the Deloitte Foundation Doctoral Fellowship Program and must be a Ph.-D. student for at least two more years from the date of application. Additionally, since the grant's purpose is to encourage Fellows to devote themselves full-time to researching and writing their dissertations, Fellows are expected not to accept any employment outside of their university and are encouraged not to serve as teachers or research and teaching assistants during phase two of the fellowship program. Should a recipient complete his/her doctoral program prior to receiving all award payments, any monies not yet paid at the time a recipient has accepted and begun employment ('is on the payroll') at his/her new university, will be forfeited. www2.deloitte.com/content/dam/Deloitte/us/Documents/about-deloitte/us-dfdtn-doctoral-fellow ship-program-guidelines.pdf

# Defense Personnel Security Research Center

## Thesis, Dissertation and Institutional Research Awards

**Subjects**: The areas covered by this funding program include financial and credit, candidate screening and crime detection procedures, prescreening, background investigation, adjudication, continuing evaluation, employee assistance programs, security awareness, security education, and forensic psychophysiology.

**Purpose**: The purpose of the awards is to help fund research addressing issues pertinent to personnel security policy.

**Eligibility**: To be eligible for the thesis or dissertation award, applicants must be students enrolled in a graduate program at a university accredited by the Association of Colleges and Secondary Schools for their region and be sponsored by both their university and the chair of their thesis or dissertation committee. Candidates for a thesis award must also have satisfactorily completed at least 2/3 of the non-thesis credit hours required for graduation in their program. To receive a dissertation award candidates must be eligible to enter doctoral candidacy within six months from the date of their application. Prior to the dissertation award being granted, recipients must have completed all degree requirements except for the dissertation defense.

**Type**: Award

**Value**: The maximum award for master's degree thesis awards is US$5,000/student. The maximum award for dissertation grants is US$15,000/student. The maximum award for institutional awards is US$30,000/project. The maximum awards for forensic psychophysiology are US$5,000, US$15,000 and US$150,000 respectively. Institutions are eligible to receive multiple awards.

**Country of Study**: Any country

**Closing Date**: 15 July

# Doris Duke Charitable Foundation (DDCF)

## Physician Scientist Fellowship

**Subjects**: Physician science

**Purpose**: The Doris Duke Physician Scientist Fellowship program provides grants to physician scientists at the subspecialty fellowship level who are seeking to conduct additional years of research beyond their subspecialty requirement. The goal is to aid in the transition into a research faculty appointment.

**Eligibility**: The priority of the Physician Scientist Fellowship program is to fund outstanding individuals with excitement for clinical research careers, whose projects will address highly significant research questions and lead to career advancement. DDCF does not have funding priorities for this fellowship based on disease area or research type.

**Type**: Fellowship

**Value**: US$100,000 for annual direct costs plus US$10,000 for indirect costs

**Length of Study**: Two years

**Country of Study**: Any country

**Additional Information**: www.ddcf.org/what-we-fund/medical-research/goals-and-strategies/encourage-and-develop-clinical-research-careers/physician-scientist-fellowship/

# Doctoral New Investigator (DNI) Grants

## Doctoral New Investigator (DNI) Grants

**Subjects**: Chemical science; Chemical engineering

**Purpose**: Grants provide start-up funding for scientists and engineers in the United States who are within the first three years of their first academic appointment at the level of Assistant Professor or the equivalent.

**Eligibility**: Applicants must be: Regularly-appointed faculty members at U.S. academic institutions who are within the first three years of their first academic appointment at the rank of Assistant Professor or the equivalent are eligible to apply. In addition, applicants must meet the following criteria: The non-profit institution submitting the DNI proposal must certify that the individual listed as a principal investigator on the cover page qualifies as a principal investigator under the institution's policies. In view of the long-standing policy of The ACS Petroleum Research Fund to give priority to support of students (undergraduate, graduate, or postdoctoral), each principal investigator must be eligible to serve as the formal, official supervisor of graduate students in graduate degree programs. The terms of appointment of the principal investigator must promise reasonable continuity of service. The appointment should continue at least through the period of funding requested in the proposal.

**Level of Study**: Junior Faculty

**Type**: Grant

**Value**: US$110,000 over two years

**Length of Study**: Two years

**Country of Study**: United States of America

**No. of awards offered**: Approx. 75 each year

**Closing Date**: October

**Additional Information**: www.acs.org/content/acs/en/funding-and-awards/grants/prf/programs/dni.html

# David & Lucile Packard Foundation

## Packard Fellowships for Science and Engineering

**Subjects**: Science; engineering

**Purpose**: The program invites up to two nominations from selected institutions. The program supports the innovative research efforts of young faculty members in the natural and physical sciences or engineering.

**Eligibility**: Candidates must be faculty members in the first three years of their faculty careers.
**Level of Study**: Junior Faculty
**Type**: Fellowship
**Value**: US$875,000 over five years.
**Length of Study**: Five years

**Country of Study**: Any country
**No. of awards offered**: 20
**Closing Date**: 23 January
**Additional Information**: www.packard.org/what-we-fund/science/packard-fellowships-for-science-and-engineering/about-the-packard-fellowship-awards/

# E

## Earthwatch Institute

114 Western Avenue, Boston, MA 02134, United States of America.

| | |
|---|---|
| **Tel:** | (1) 978 461 0081 |
| **Email:** | research@earthwatch.org |
| **Website:** | www.earthwatch.org/research |
| **Contact:** | Gitte Venicx, Research Program Manager |

Earthwatch Institute supports diverse research projects of high scientific merit worldwide that address critical environmental and social issues at local, national and international levels. Researchers are given both funding and field assistance from layperson volunteers. Volunteers are recruited by Earthwatch, who pay for the opportunity to assist them in the field.

### Earthwatch Field Research Grants

**Purpose**: Earthwatch funds field-based scientific research that is rigorous, relevant, and impactful. Earthwatch-funded projects conduct research around the globe. All research must incorporate citizen-scientist participation in data collection. Citizen-scientist participants are recruited by Earthwatch. Requests for pre-proposals are distributed annually. Pre-proposals must be submitted by the PI. All PIs must have a PhD and an affiliation with a university, government agency, or science-focused NGO.
**Eligibility**: All proposals must be submitted by the Principal Investigator (PI). All PIs must have a PhD and an affiliation with a university, government agency, or NGO
**Level of Study**: Doctorate, Postdoctorate, Postgraduate, Research
**Type**: Grant
**Value**: US$20,000-80,000 annually

**Length of Study**: Successful proposals are funded for 3 years, subject to passing an annual performance review
**Frequency**: Annual
**Study Establishment**: Research sites
**Country of Study**: Any country
**Application Procedure**: Requests for proposals are distributed in the spring. Applicants must submit a pre-proposal for consideration. Please see the Earthwatch website (earthwatch.org) for more information
**Closing Date**: 31 December
**Funding**: Private, Corporation, Foundation
**Contributor**: Volunteers' contributions
**Additional Information**: For additional project requirements and information: earthwatch.org/research-funding www.archaeological.org/grant/field-research-grants/

## Ècole Normale Supérieure (ENS)

| | |
|---|---|
| **Tel:** | (33) 1 44 32 28 01 |
| **Email:** | ens-international@ens.fr |
| **Website:** | www.ens.fr/admission/selection-internationale/?lang=en |

Ècole Normale Supérieure (ENS) allows the most promising international students, either in Science or in Arts & Humanities, to follow a three-year Masters Degree at the University.

### Ècole Normale Supérieure International Selection Scholarships

**Level of Study**: Postgraduate
**Type**: Scholarship
**Value**: monthly grant of €1,000 for 3 years and accomodation facility provided

© Springer Nature Limited 2020
Palgrave Macmillan (ed.), *The Grants Register 2021*,
https://doi.org/10.1057/978-1-349-95988-4

**Length of Study**: 3 years
**Frequency**: Annual
**Country of Study**: France
**Application Procedure**: You must fill and validate the initial application form which will be available at the official website when the application opens. Within 2 days, you will receive an email to activate an account on Dematec, an application platform where you must upload the required documents
**Closing Date**: 31 October
**Contributor**: École Normale Supérieure in Paris, France
**Additional Information**: For more details, please visit official scholarship website: www.ens.fr/admission/selection-internationale/?lang=en    greatyop.com/ens-international-selection-scholarship/

**For further information contact:**

**Email**:    ens-international@ens.fr

## École Normale Supérieure de Lyon

**Website**:    www.ens-lyon.fr/en/grants-and-scholarships-2792 58.kjsp?RH=1440663599734&RF=1445867537 855

### Ampère & MILYON Excellence Scholarships for International Students

**Purpose**: The Ampère Scholarships of Excellence provide excellent international students with the opportunity to pursue one of the eligible Masters programs offered at ENS de Lyon
**Eligibility**: International students are eligible to apply for this scholarship. Host institution is ENS de Lyon
**Level of Study**: Graduate
**Type**: Scholarship
**Value**: Value is €1,000
**Length of Study**: 1-2 years
**Frequency**: Annual
**Country of Study**: France
**Application Procedure**: Check website
**Closing Date**: 8 January
**Funding**: Private
**Additional Information**: international.ens-lyon.fr/grants-and-scholarships-279258.kjsp?RH=TEMP-INTER    www.scholars4dev.com/10349/ampere-excellence-scholarships-for-international-students/

**For further information contact:**

**Email**:    ampere.scholarship@ens-lyon.fr

### Ampère Excellence Scholarships for International Students

**Purpose**: The Ampère Scholarships of Excellence provide excellent international students with the opportunity to pursue one of the eligible Masters programs offered at ENS de Lyon
**Eligibility**: You must be a foreign national. Candidate for admission in Masters Year 1: provide proof that you have obtained a License (equivalent to 180 ECTS European credits) or an equivalent diploma/level recognized by the ENS deLyon. Candidate for admission in Masters Year 2: provide proof that you have successfully reached Masters Year 1 level (equivalent to 240 ECTS European credits) or have attained an equivalent diploma/level recognized by the ENS de Lyon (e.g. MPhil)
**Level of Study**: Postgraduate
**Type**: Scholarship
**Value**: €1,000 per month for a duration of 1 year
**Frequency**: Annual
**Country of Study**: France
**Closing Date**: 12 January
**Funding**: Government
**Contributor**: ENS de Lyon, France
**Additional Information**: For more details, please visit official scholarship website: www.ens-lyon.fr/en/grants-and-scholarships-279258.kjsp?RH=1440663599734&amp;RF= 1445867537855    www.scholars4dev.com/10349/ampere-excellence-scholarships-for-international-students/

## École Normale Supérieure Paris-Saclay

The ENS Paris-Saclay is one of the most prestigious and selective French Grandes Ecoles.

### Monabiphot Masters Scholarships

**Purpose**: This masters course offers an original qualification in the highly innovative domain of molecular photonics for telecommunications and biology. Skills will be acquired at the strongly interdisciplinary level needed to master emerging technologies and to develop original concepts and applications aiming at novel technological breakthroughs in this domain
**Eligibility**:    Both    European    Union    students    and Non-European Union students are eligible to apply
**Level of Study**: Postgraduate
**Type**: Scholarship
**Value**: Non-European Union students: €23,500 per year, European Union students: €16,000 per year, Additional scholarships for specific regions: €47.000

**Country of Study**: France
**Closing Date**: 31 January
**Additional Information**: www.scholarshipsads.com/monabiphot-masters-scholarships-international-students-france-2017/

### For further information contact:

LPQM, ENS-Cachan 61, Avenue du President Wilson, F-94235 Cachan Cedex, France.

**Tel**:       (33) 1 47 40 55 60
**Email**:    ledoux@lpqm.ens-cachan.fr

## Ecole Polytechnique Federale de Lausanne

Route Cantonale, CH-1015 Lausanne, Switzerland.

**Tel**:       (41) 21 693 11 1
**Website**:   www.epfl.ch/

EPFL is Europe's most cosmopolitan technical university. It welcomes students, professors and collaborators of more than 120 nationalities. EPFL has both a Swiss and international vocation and focuses on three missions: teaching, research and innovation. EPFL collaborates with an important network of partners, including other universities and colleges, secondary schools and gymnasiums, industry and the economy, political circles and the general public, with the aim of having a real impact on society.

### Excellence Fellowships

**Purpose**: EPFL offers a limited number of fellowships at the Master's level to students with outstanding academic records. Some of the fellowships are financed by EPFL directly and others through partnerships with foundations or companies.
**Eligibility**: Anyone applying to an EPFL Master's Program is eligible for the scholarship. Anyone holding a Bachelor's degree (or the equivalent) in a related field from a recognized university can apply to one of the EPFL Masters Programs. The selection of candidates and the granting of the fellowships is done based solely on the evaluation of the academic records of the candidates.
**Level of Study**: Masters Degree
**Type**: Scholarships
**Value**: For external applicants, the scholarship includes CHF 16,000 per academic year split into monthly payments (CHF 32,000 for a two-year Master's or CHF 24,000 for a 1 1/2 year Master's) and reservation of a room in student's accommodation.
**Frequency**: annual
**Country of Study**: Switzerland
**Application Procedure**: The application is done via the same online form than your application to a Master's program. It is however necessary to tick a box indicating that your profile should also be considered for an excellence fellowship. Applications can be filled online from mid-November to the 15th of December, or from the 16th of December to the 15th of April. It is important to read the EPFL Fellowship guidelines and visit the official website (link found below) to access the application form and for detailed information on how to apply for this scholarship.
**Closing Date**: 15 April
**Additional Information**: www.epfl.ch/education/studies/en/financing-study/grants/excellence-fellowships/

### For further information contact:

**Email**:    student.services@epfl.ch

## Economic History Association (EHA)

Economic History Association Department of Economics University of Wisconsin-La Crosse, 1725 State St, La Crosse, WI 54601, United States of America.

**Phone**:    (1) 608 785 6863
**Email**:    mhaupert@uwlax.edu
**Website**:  www.eh.net/eha

The Economic History Association (EHA) was founded in 1940. Its mission is to stimulate interest in the study of economic history, to encourage research in economic history and ideas, to co-operate with societies devoted to the study of agricultural, industrial, technological or business history, and to collaborate with economists, historians, statisticians, geographers and all other students of economic change.

### Annual Meetings Travel and Hotel Subsidies

**Purpose**: Intended for disseminating preliminary results from graduate thesis work.
**Eligibility**: 1. Complimentary hotel rooms (double occupancy, shared with another graduate student) for up to 3 nights. 2. 60 % discount on the registration fee. 3. 80 % discount on the Saturday Presidential Banquet. 4. Free dinner with other graduate students Friday night.

**Level of Study**: Postdoctorate
**Type**: Travel
**Value**: up to US$500 for domestic flights or train fare, up to US$800 for international flights.
**Closing Date**: 20 May
**Additional Information**: eh.net/eha/grants-and-fellowships/

### For further information contact:

**Email**:    enw@economics.rutgers.edu

## Arthur H Cole Grants-in-Aid

**Purpose**: The Committee on Research in Economic History awards Arthur H. Cole grants-in-aid to support research in economic history, regardless of time period or geographic area.
**Eligibility**: Applicants must have completed a PhD and be members of the EHA
**Level of Study**: Postdoctorate
**Type**: Grant
**Value**: Up to US$5,000
**Frequency**: Annual
**Country of Study**: Any country
**Application Procedure**: The Committee on Research in Economic History awards Arthur H. Cole grants-in-aid to support research in economic history, regardless of time period or geographic area. Awards typically are in amounts up to US$5,000, although higher amounts may be awarded in exceptional cases. Applicants must be members of the Association and must hold the PhD degree. Preference is given to recent PhD recipients
**Closing Date**: 1 March
**Funding**: Private
**Contributor**: EHA members
**Additional Information**: Membership enquiries should be addressed to the office of the Executive Director or the website eh.net/eha/grants-and-fellowships/

### For further information contact:

**Email**:    tkd@hss.caltech.edu

## Edinburgh Napier University

219 Colinton Rd, Edinburgh, EH14 1DJ, United Kingdom.

**Tel**:       (44) 333 900 6040
**Contact**:   Edinburgh Napier University

Edinburgh Napier University is a public university in Edinburgh, Scotland. Napier Technical College, the predecessor of the university was founded in 1964, taking its name from Scottish mathematician John Napier.

## Brazil Scholarship

**Purpose**: The University has partial scholarships for self-funding students from Brazil.
**Eligibility**: 1. be living in Brazil at the time of application. 2. be self-funding your course. 3. be holding an unconditional offer to study a masters course. 4. have made your £3,500 deposit payment toward your fees.
**Level of Study**: Postgraduate
**Type**: Scholarship
**Value**: £4,000
**Application Procedure**: The scholarships will be awarded on a first-come, first-served basis when you meet the eligibility criteria.
**Closing Date**: September
**Additional Information**: www.napier.ac.uk/study-with-us/bursaries/brazil-scholarship

### For further information contact:

Rua Dr. Cesário Mota Junior, 369, Conj 52 – São Paulo, Brazil - 01221020, Brazil.

**Tel**:    (55) 11 3957 0488

## Data Visualisation Design, Ambiguity & Decision Making in Megaprojects: EPSRC Studentship

**Purpose**: Professor Paolo Quattrone has successfully been allocated a studentship for this project in collaboration with Costain
**Eligibility**: 1. United Kingdom/European Union Countries. 2. Applicants must meet EPSRC eligibility criteria. 3. Please note that international students are not eligible for this funding
**Level of Study**: Postgraduate
**Type**: Studentship
**Value**: £22,159
**Length of Study**: 4 year
**Frequency**: Annual
**Country of Study**: Any country
**Closing Date**: 31 May
**Funding**: International office
**Additional Information**: i3p.org.uk/2019/05/22/edinburgh-university-costain-sponsors-4-year-phd-scholarship-data-visualizations-governance-megaprojects/

### For further information contact:

**Email**:    phd@business-school.ed.ac.uk

## Gordon David Family Scholarship

**Purpose**: The Edinburgh Centre for Carbon Innovation (ECCI) is offering two scholarships for those undertaking research related to the work of ECCI
**Eligibility**: 1. An eligible MSc programme (see below). 2. PhD in a subject related to the work of the ECCI
**Level of Study**: Postgraduate
**Type**: Scholarship
**Value**: £8,000
**Length of Study**: 3 year
**Frequency**: Annual
**Country of Study**: Any country
**Closing Date**: 30 April
**Funding**: Foundation
**Additional Information**: www.ed.ac.uk/student-funding/postgraduate/uk-eu/humanities/law/georgedavidlaw

### For further information contact:

**Email**: phd@business-school.ed.ac.uk

## Improving Project Delivery: ESRC Studentship

**Purpose**: Professor Paolo Quattrone has successfully been allocated a studentship for the project 'Improving Project Delivery' in collaboration with the Infrastructure and Project Authority
**Eligibility**: 1. United Kingdom/European Union Countries. 2. Applicants must meet ESRC eligibility criteria. 3. Please note that international students are not eligible for this funding
**Level of Study**: Postgraduate
**Type**: Studentship
**Value**: £14,777
**Length of Study**: 3 year
**Frequency**: Annual
**Country of Study**: Any country
**Closing Date**: 31 May
**Funding**: International office
**Additional Information**: www.business-school.ed.ac.uk/scholarships/improving-project-delivery-esrc

### For further information contact:

University of Edinburgh Business School, 29 Buccleuch Place, Edinburgh, EH8 9JS, United Kingdom.

**Tel**: (44) 131 651 5337, (44) 131 651 5541
**Email**: paolo.quattrone@ed.ac.uk, phd@business-school.ed.ac.uk

## Institute for Particle and Nuclear Physics MSc Prize Scholarships

**Subjects**: We offer taught masters (MSc) programmes in Theoretical Physics and Mathematical Physics, and Particle & Nuclear Physics.
**Eligibility**: Applicants must have applied to study full-time on the MSc Particle and Nuclear Physics programme of study.
**Level of Study**: Postgraduate
**Type**: Scholarship
**Value**: £5,000
**Length of Study**: 1 year
**Frequency**: Annual
**Country of Study**: Any country
**Application Procedure**: The deadline for applying for this scholarship is 1 June, details on how to apply are found on the University's Scholarships and Student Funding pages. The online scholarship application form is located in EUCLID and can be accessed via MyEd our web based information portal at www.myed.ed.ac.uk
**No. of awards offered**: 6
**Closing Date**: 1 June
**Additional Information**: scholarship-positions.com/ipnp-msc-prize-scholarships-at-the-university-of-edinburgh-in-the-uk/2019/03/07/

### For further information contact:

www.myed.ed.ac.uk.

**Email**: msc.pnp@ph.ed.ac.uk

## Jean Kennoway Howells Scholarship

**Purpose**: One scholarship available for taught masters programmes offered by the Reid School of Music
**Eligibility**: The scholarship will be awarded to students who have applied for admission on a full-time basis for a postgraduate taught Masters programme of study within the Reid School of Music commencing in the academic year. To be eligible, applicants must have received an offer to study by the scholarship deadline
**Level of Study**: Postgraduate
**Type**: Scholarship
**Value**: £15,000
**Length of Study**: 1 year
**Frequency**: Annual
**Country of Study**: Any country
**Closing Date**: 2 March
**Funding**: Foundation

**Additional Information**: www.ed.ac.uk/student-funding/postgraduate/international/humanities/edinburgh-college-of-art/howells

### For further information contact:

**Email**: ecapgtdegrees@ed.ac.uk

## South Asian Scholarships at Edinburgh Napier University

**Purpose**: The Edinburgh Napier University is offering partial scholarships for self-funding students from Afghanistan, India, Pakistan, Bangladesh, Nepal or Sri Lanka. Scholarships are awarded to study a bachelor, masters or PhD course in September or January

**Eligibility**: Applicants whose native language is not English are required to demonstrate proficiency in English. The TOEFL is the most frequently submitted examination score that the University receives, however, the Admissions Office will use other measures upon the applicant's request. The IELTS, ACT, and SAT examinations may also be used

**Value**: The scholarships are merit-based ranging from £2,000 to £3,000

**Study Establishment**: Scholarships are awarded to study the subjects offered by the university

**Country of Study**: United Kingdom

**Application Procedure**: The scholarships will be awarded on a first-come, first-served basis. You will be automatically considered for the scholarship and be advised of the scholarship amount you are eligible for if you meet the following selection criteria: 1. You hold an unconditional offer to study on a full-time bachelors or masters course at Edinburgh Napier. 2. You meet the eligibility criteria detailed above. 3. You have made your £3,500 deposit payment towards your fees. There is no additional application process for this scholarship. You must self-funding your course holding an offer to study a bachelor, masters or PhD course in September or January

**Additional Information**: For more details please visit to the website scholarship-positions.com/south-asian-scholarships-edinburgh-napier-university-uk/2017/12/11/ www.napier.ac.uk/study-with-us/bursaries/south-asia-scholarship

### For further information contact:

**Tel**: (91) 40 4240 8800
**Email**: international@napier.ac.uk

## Edith Cowan University

270 Joondalup Drive, Joondalup, WA 6027, Australia.

**Tel**: (61) 8 6304 0000
**Email**: enquiries@ecu.edu.au
**Website**: www.ecu.edu.au
**Contact**: Edith Cowan University

The Edith Cowan University is an Australian public university located in Perth, Western Australia. It was named after the first woman to be elected to an Australian Parliament, Edith Cowan, and is the only Australian university named after a woman.

## Brett Lockyer Scholarship

**Purpose**: To enable the further development of jazz clarinet studies at ECU and to develop those specialist skills in a currently enrolled jazz clarinet student at WAAPA

**Eligibility**: Open for students studying jazz clarinet within the jazz programme

**Level of Study**: Postgraduate
**Type**: Scholarship
**Value**: Up to AU$5,000
**Application Procedure**: Check website for further details.

### For further information contact:

**Tel**: (33) 8 9370 6594
**Email**: j.hamilton@ecu.edu.au

## Luke Pen Fund-Honours Scholarships

**Purpose**: To encourage young people to be involved in the gaining of scientific knowledge of river characteristics

**Level of Study**: Graduate
**Type**: Scholarship
**Value**: AU$50,000
**Length of Study**: 1 year
**Frequency**: Annual
**Application Procedure**: Check website address for further details
**Closing Date**: 31 March
**Funding**: Trusts
**Contributor**: Luke Pen Scholarship Trust
**Additional Information**: www.mediastatements.wa.gov.au/Pages/Gallop/2004/03/The-inaugural-Luke-Pen-Scholarship.aspx

## For further information contact:

Department of Water, Drainage and Waterways Branch, PO Box K822, Perth, WA 6842, Australia.

**Email**:	james.mackintosh@water.wa.gov.au

## Merit International Postgraduate Scholarship

**Purpose**: The Edith Cowan University is inviting applications for Merit International Postgraduate Scholarship to study in Australia. This scholarship is available to students who can demonstrate high levels of academic achievement and English competency in their previous studies

**Eligibility**: 1. Your programme must commence at the University of Sheffield. 2. Distance learning courses are ineligible for a merit scholarship. 3. You must receive an offer for a course studied in full at the University of Sheffield. Masters programmes split between the University of Sheffield and a partner institution are not eligible to apply for a scholarship. 4. All Crossways courses and Erasmus Mundus courses are ineligible for a merit scholarship. 5. For tuition fee purposes you must be self-funded and required to pay the overseas tuition fee. 6. You must not be a sponsored student*. 7. For scholarship purposes all March programmes are considered as postgraduate taught programmes and are not eligible for undergraduate scholarships. 8. Anyone studying a Masters/integrated PhD programme is eligible for a merit scholarship in the Masters element of the programme only. 9.

**Type**: Postgraduate scholarships

**Value**: The scholarship offers a 10% reduction in your tuition fees for the duration of your course at ECU

**Study Establishment**: Scholarships are awarded to learn any of the courses offered by the university

**Country of Study**: Australia

**Application Procedure**: See the website

**Closing Date**: 4 May

**Additional Information**: For more details please visit the website scholarship-positions.com/merit-international-postgraduate-scholarship-edith-cowan-university-australia/2018/02/03/ www.sheffield.ac.uk/international/fees-and-funding/scholarships/postgraduate/international-merit-postgraduate-scholarship

## For further information contact:

The University of Sheffield, Western Bank, Sheffield, S10 2TN, United Kingdom.

**Tel**:	(44) 114 222 2000

## Postgraduate Petroleum Engineering Scholarship

**Purpose**: Petroleum Engineering has evolved into one of the well sought courses in universities. It is the field of engineering that deals with the exploration, extraction, and production of oil. It also increasingly deals with the production of natural gas.

**Eligibility**: 1. Be commencing study of a Graduate Diploma in Petroleum Engineering (J69); Master of Engineering (Petroleum Engineering specialization) (I59); or the Master of Technology (Petroleum Engineering) (J70). 2. Meet ECU's academic direct entry requirements for the course of your choice. 3. Not be in receipt of another scholarship or sponsorship. 4. Be an International student, not an Australian Citizen, Australian Permanent Resident, or New Zealand Citizen. 5. Intend to study a postgraduate degree. 6. Be studying at ECU Joondalup

**Level of Study**: Postgraduate

**Type**: Scholarship

**Frequency**: Annual

**Country of Study**: Any country

**Closing Date**: 31 July

**Funding**: International office

**Additional Information**: www.scholarshipsads.com/category/subject/petroleum-engineering/

## For further information contact:

**Email**:	international.parternships@ecu.edu.au

## Education and Research Foundation for the Society of Nuclear Medicine (SNM)

1850 Samuel Morse Drive, Reston, VA 20190, United States of America.

**Tel**:	(1) 703 708 9000
**Email**:	tpinkham@erfsnm.org
**Contact**:	Theresa Pinkham, Executive Director

The Society of Nuclear Medicine (SNM) is an international, scientific and professional organization founded in 1954 to promote the science, technology and practical application of nuclear medicine. Its 16,000 members are physicians, technologists and scientists specializing in the research and practice of nuclear medicine.

## Society of Nuclear Medicine Pilot Research Grants in Nuclear Medicine/Molecular Imaging

**Purpose**: To support Master's or PhD students to start research in nuclear medicine
**Eligibility**: Open to basic and clinical scientists in early stages of their career
**Level of Study**: Doctorate, Postgraduate
**Type**: Grant
**Value**: US$25,000
**Frequency**: Annual
**Study Establishment**: Society of Nuclear Medicine
**Country of Study**: United States of America
**Application Procedure**: Applicants must submit a completed application form along with abstract of project proposal and budget proposal
**Closing Date**: 20 February

### For further information contact:

SNM Development Office, 1850 Samuel Morse Drive, Reston, VA 20190, United States of America.

**Tel**:      (1) 703 652 6795
**Email**:   nmitchell@snm.org

## Education New Zealand (ENZ)

Level 5, Lambton House, 160 Lambton Quay, PO Box 12041, Wellington 6144, New Zealand.

**Tel**:        (64) 4 472 0788
**Email**:     info@educationnz.govt.nz
**Website**:   www.newzealandeducated.com/scholarships
**Contact**:   Scholarships Manager

Education New Zealand (ENZ) is the Government Agency responsible for promoting New Zealand education to the world. We create strategies and programmes alongside New Zealand's education sector, government agencies and governments overseas that increase and broaden our international education activities.

## Korea New Zealand Agricultural Cooperation Scholarships (KNZACS)

**Purpose**: To promote greater understanding between Korea and New Zealand, and strengthen the trade and economic relationship in veterinary or animal science or forestry sectors

**Level of Study**: Doctorate, Postgraduate
**Type**: Scholarship
**Value**: New Zealand university fees/levies and stipend of NZ$30,000 per year
**Length of Study**: 3 years in the case of PhD, and 2 years in the case of master
**Study Establishment**: Approved universities
**Country of Study**: New Zealand
**Application Procedure**: Please visit website to apply
**Closing Date**: 28 April
**Funding**: Government
**Additional Information**: Korea: Contact Sang-Hun Lee, EPIS International Cooperation Team, Manager sanghuni@epis.or.kr scholarshipdb.net/scholarships-in-New-Zealand/Korea-New-Zealand-Agricultural-Cooperation-Scholarships-Knzac-Massey-University=n0xfoMIX5hGUQg AlkGUTnw.html

### For further information contact:

**Email**:   scholarship@enz.govt.nz

## NZ-GRADS New Zealand Global Research Alliance Doctoral Scholarship

**Purpose**: The Global Research Alliance on Agricultural Greenhouse Gas Emissions is delighted to launch the new NZ-GRADS programme. If you are from a developing country and are ready to complete your PhD in science, you can do it in New Zealand for free.
**Eligibility**: 1. New Zealand University annual tuition fees and associated student levies up to a total of NZ$10,000 per year. 2. An annual living stipend of NZ$28,000 per year (tax free). 3. Medical insurance cover up to NZ$700 per year. 4. Visa application costs to a maximum of NZ$1,000. 5. Return flights to New Zealand up to a maximum of NZ$6,000. 6. Book and thesis preparation allowance of up to NZ$1,500.
**Level of Study**: Postgraduate
**Type**: Scholarship
**Value**: NZ$124,600 total value
**Length of Study**: 3 years
**Closing Date**: 1 June
**Additional Information**: www.studyinnewzealand.govt.nz/how-to-apply/scholarship/details?scholarshipid=138518&institutionid=378394

## Shirtcliffe Fellowship

**Purpose**: The purpose of the Shirtcliffe Fellowships is to assist students of outstanding ability and character who are graduates of a university in New Zealand, in the continuation of their studies in New Zealand or the Commonwealth.

**Eligibility**: New Zealand citizen, ordinarily resident in New Zealand. Must be a graduate of a New Zealand University, or about to graduate. Candidates must be enrolled, or plan to be enrolled in the year of tenure, as a Doctoral candidate in New Zealand or another Commonwealth country.

**Level of Study**: Doctorate
**Type**: Fellowship
**Value**: US$5,000 per annum
**Length of Study**: Up to three years
**Frequency**: Annual
**Country of Study**: New Zealand
**Application Procedure**: Apply online www.universitiesnz.ac.nz/scholarships/shirtcliffe-fellowship
**Closing Date**: 1 April
**Funding**: Private
**Additional Information**: www.universitiesnz.ac.nz/scholarships/shirtcliffe-fellowship

### For further information contact:

**Email**:     scholarships@universitiesnz.ac.nz

## Education.govt.nz

### Ngarimu VC and 28th (Maori) Battalion Memorial Scholarships

**Purpose**: These scholarships support high achieving tertiary students of Maori descent
**Eligibility**: 1. Applications for both scholarships will need to include a brief statement of up to 250 words, outlining the topic, the reasons for your interest in the subject area and your future expectations. 2. Preference will be given to applicants who are able to demonstrate that their studies aim to improve the social, economic and cultural wellbeing of Maori or are on Maori issues. Eligible applicants can apply for both scholarships
**Level of Study**: Research
**Type**: Scholarship
**Frequency**: Annual
**Country of Study**: Any country
**Application Procedure**: All applicants will need to include: 1. a form completed by a Kaumatua, Maori leader that certifies your whakapapa. 2. a form completed by someone who can endorse your academic achievement and suitability to study. 3. a Te Reo Maori statement that demonstrates your language capabilities. 4. a statement about the Nga Ahuatanga characteristics you possess that are similar to those identified as consistent with the 28th (Maori) Battalion soldiers

**Closing Date**: February
**Funding**: Private
**Additional Information**: www.education.govt.nz/further-education/information-for-students/scholarships/ngarimu-scholarships/

### For further information contact:

Matauranga House, Level 1, 33 Bowen Street, Wellington 6011, New Zealand.

**Tel**:       (64) 800 165 225
**Email**:     Ngarimu.Scholarship@education.govt.nz

## Educational Testing Service (ETS)

660 Rosedale Road, Princeton, NJ 08541-0001, United States of America.

**Tel**:       (1) 609 921 9000
**Email**:     ldelauro@ets.org
**Website**:   www.ets.org
**Contact**:   Ms Linda J DeLauro

The Educational Testing Service (ETS) is a non-profit organization whose goal is to help advance quality and equity in education by providing fair and valid assessments, research, and related services.

### Educational Testing Service Harold Gulliksen Psychometric Fellowship Program

**Purpose**: To increase the number of well-trained scientists in educational measurement, psychometrics, and statistics
**Eligibility**: At the time of application, candidates must be enrolled in a doctoral program, have completed all the coursework toward the doctorate, and be at the dissertation stage of their program. Dissertation topics in the areas of psychometrics, statistics, educational measurement or quantitative methods will be given priority. At the time of application, candidates will be asked to provide a statement describing any additional financial assistance such as assistantship or grant commitment that he/she will have during the fellowship period.
**Level of Study**: Predoctorate
**Type**: Fellowship
**Value**: US$20,000 (stipend), US$8,000 (tuition fees, and work-study program commitments), and a small grant for the purchase of equipment or software

**Length of Study**: 1 year
**Frequency**: Annual
**Country of Study**: United States of America or other countries if appropriate
**Application Procedure**: Submit all application materials via email with PDF attachments. Two applications have to be submitted for this program. Preliminary application requires letter of interest, statement describing finanical assistance, nomination letter and current curriculum vitae. Final application should contain the following information. Detailed project description (approximately 15 double-spaced pages) of the research the individual will carry out at the host university, including the purpose, goals and methods of the research Graduate academic transcripts (unofficial copies are acceptable) Evidence of scholarship (presentations, manuscripts, etc.)
**No. of awards offered**: 10
**Closing Date**: 15 February
**Funding**: Private
**Contributor**: ETS
**Additional Information**: Kindly refer the website for further information. www.ets.org/research/internship-fellowship/gulliksen www.ets.org/research/internship-fellowship/gulliksen/

### For further information contact:

**Email**:    internfellowships@ets.org

## Educational Testing Service Postdoctoral Fellowships

**Purpose**: To provide research opportunities to individuals who hold a doctorate in education and related fields, and to increase the number of women and minority professionals conducting research in educational measurement and related fields
**Eligibility**: Open to applicants who have received their doctoral degree within the past 3 years. Selections will be based on the candidate's scholarship, the technical strength of the proposed topic of research, and the explicit objective of the research and its relationship to ETS research goals and priorities
**Level of Study**: Postdoctorate
**Type**: Fellowship
**Value**: The amount is US$50,000 for the 1-year period. In addition, limited relocation expenses consistent with the ETS guidelines will be reimbursed. Renewal for a second year by mutual consent
**Length of Study**: Up to 2 years, renewable after the first year by mutual agreement
**Frequency**: Annual
**Country of Study**: United States of America

**Application Procedure**: Refer the ETS website for further details. All application materials should be sent electronically as attachments
**No. of awards offered**: 15
**Closing Date**: 1 January
**Funding**: Private
**Contributor**: ETS
**Additional Information**: www.iefa.org/scholarships/461/Educational_Testing_Service_Postdoctoral_Fellowship_Program

### For further information contact:

**Email**:    internfellowships@ets.org

## Educational Testing Service Summer Internship Program in Research for Graduate Students

**Purpose**: To provide research opportunities to individuals enroled in a doctoral program and to increase the number of women and underrepresented minority professionals conducting research in educational and related fields
**Eligibility**: Current full-time enrollment in a relevant doctoral program Completion of at least 2 years of coursework toward the PhD or EdD. prior to the program start date
**Level of Study**: Predoctorate
**Type**: Internship
**Value**: US$6,000 salary; Transportation allowance for relocating to and from the Princeton area; Housing will be provided for interns commuting more than 50 miles
**Length of Study**: June to July (8 weeks)
**Frequency**: Annual
**Country of Study**: United States of America
**Application Procedure**: 1. Choose up to two research areas in which you are interested and provide written statements about your interest in the particular area(s) of research. 2. Attach a copy of your curriculum vitae (preferably as a PDF). 3. Attach a copy of your graduate transcripts (unofficial copies are acceptable). 4. Download the recommendation form and share it with your recommenders. Recommendations should come from your academic advisor and/or major professors who are familiar with your work. ETS will only accept two recommendation forms. Recommendations should be sent electronically to internfellowships@ets.org and must be received by February 1. If you would like to download the recommendation form for sending to your recommenders before submitting your application, the option to save your application information for later is available.
**No. of awards offered**: 180
**Closing Date**: 1 February
**Funding**: Private

**Contributor**: ETS

**Additional Information**: Duration of Research Internship is eight weeks: 3 June-26 July www.ets.org/research/internship-fellowship/summer/

## For further information contact:

**Email**:    internfellowships@ets.org

## Educational Testing Service Summer Internships in Programme Direction

**Purpose**: To provide opportunities, especially for women and minority professionals, for a work and learning experience that will assist the participants in exploring career alternatives in the field of measurement and evaluation

**Eligibility**: Current full-time enrollment in a relevant doctoral program; Completion of at least two years of coursework toward the doctorate prior to the program start date

**Level of Study**: Doctorate, Postgraduate

**Type**: Internship

**Value**: Salary of US$6,000 with the transportation allowance and housing for interns who commute more than 50 miles

**Length of Study**: 8 weeks (3 June-26 July)

**Study Establishment**: ETS headquarters in Princeton

**Country of Study**: United States of America

**Application Procedure**: Application should include references and transcripts

**Closing Date**: 1 February

**Additional Information**: Applicants will be notified of selection decisions by 30 March www.ets.org/research/internship-fellowship/summer/

## Educational Testing Service Sylvia Taylor Johnson Minority Fellowship in Educational Measurement

**Purpose**: An award to a minority scholar who has received a doctorate degree within the past ten years. The fellow will conduct independent research under the mentorship of ETS researchers. The award is for a period of up to two years, renewable after the first year by mutual agreement. Applicant must have a commitment to education, particularly educational measurement.

**Eligibility**: Open to applicants who have received their doctoral degree within the past 10 years and who are citizens or permanent residents of the United States. Selections will be based on the applicant's record of accomplishment, and proposed topic of research. Applicants should have a commitment to education and an independent body of scholarship that signals the promise of continuing outstanding contributions to educational measurement

**Level of Study**: Postdoctorate

**Type**: Fellowship

**Value**: Salary is competitive. US$5,000 one-time relocation incentive for round-trip relocation expenses. In addition, limited relocation expenses, consistent with ETS guidelines, will be reimbursed

**Length of Study**: Up to 2 years, renewable after the first year by mutual agreement

**Frequency**: Annual

**Country of Study**: United States of America

**Application Procedure**: Refer the ETS website for further details. All application materials should be sent electronically as attachments

**No. of awards offered**: 15

**Closing Date**: 1 February

**Funding**: Private

**Contributor**: ETS

**Additional Information**: Through her research, extensive writings and service to the educational community as an educator, editor, counsellor, committee member and collaborator during her lifetime, Sylvia Taylor Johnson had a significant influence in educational measurement and assessment nationally. In honour of Dr Johnson's important contributions to the field of education, the ETS has established the Sylvia Taylor Johnson Minority Fellowship in educational measurement www.petersons.com/scholarship/sylvia-taylor-johnson-minority-fellowship-in-educational-measurement-111_169833.aspx

## For further information contact:

Rosedale Road, MS-19T, Princeton, NJ 08541-0001, United States of America.

**Tel**:       (1) 609 734 1806
**Fax**:      (1) 609 734 5410
**Email**:    internfellowships@ets.org

## Postdoctoral Fellowship Program

**Purpose**: Individuals who have earned their doctoral degree within the last three years are invited to apply for a rewarding fellowship experience which combines working on cutting-edge ETS research projects and conducting independent research that is relevant to ETS's goals. The fellowship is carried out in the ETS offices in Princeton, N.J.

**Eligibility**: 1. Doctorate in a relevant discipline within the past three years. 2. Evidence of prior independent research

**Level of Study**: Postdoctorate

**Type**: Fellowship

**Value**: US$5,000 one-time relocation incentive for round-trip relocation expenses

**Length of Study**: Upto 2 years and it is renewable

**Frequency**: Annual

**Country of Study**: Any country

**Application Procedure**: Two applications have to be submitted. Preliminary Application complete the electronic preliminary application form. On the application form: 1. Indicate your research area of interest. 2. Enter your statement of interest. 3. Enter an abstract about the independent research you propose to conduct while at ETS. 4. Attach a copy of your curriculum vitae. 5. Attach a copy of your graduate transcripts (student copy is acceptable). Final Application If your preliminary application is approved, you will be invited to submit the following materials: 1. a detailed proposal (approximately five double-spaced pages) describing the research that will be carried out at ETS and how it relates to current ETS research. 2. samples of published research. 3. names and email addresses of three individuals who are familiar with your work, and who are willing to complete a recommendation form that will be sent to them electronically

**Closing Date**: 15 April

**Funding**: Private

**Additional Information**: For more information on this internship program, contact internfellowships@ets.org www.usief.org.in/Fellowships/Fulbright-Nehru-Postdoctoral-Research-Fellowship.aspx

### For further information contact:

**Email**:    internfellowships@ets.org

## Eidgenössische Technische Hochschule Zurich

Patricia Heuberger-Meyer, HG E 68.1, Rämistrasse 101, CH-8092 Zürich, Switzerland.

**Tel**:       (41) 44 632 56 13

**Contact**:   ETH Zurich, Stab ETH Global

ETH Zurich is a science, technology, engineering and mathematics university in the city of Zürich, Switzerland.

### The Engineering for Development (E4D) Doctoral Scholarship Programme

**Purpose**: To promote doctoral research for the benefit of developing countries

**Level of Study**: Doctorate

**Type**: Scholarship

**Value**: CHF 175,000

**Length of Study**: 3 years

**Frequency**: Annual

**Country of Study**: Switzerland

**Application Procedure**: Please refer www.ethz.ch/content/dam/ethz/main/eth-zurich/global/r4d-netzwerk/E4D%20programme/Requirement%20criteria%20E4D_final_%202017.pdf

**Closing Date**: 30 November

**Contributor**: Sawiris Foundation for Social Development

**Additional Information**: Please send your complete concept note to patricia.heuberger@sl.ethz.ch scholarship-fellowship.com/engineering-for-development-e4d-doctoral-scholarship/

### For further information contact:

**Tel**:       (41) 44 632 11 11

**Email**:    e4d@sl.ethz.ch

## Electoral Commission New Zealand

Level 6, Greenock House 39, The Terrace, PO Box 3050, Wellington 6140, New Zealand.

**Tel**:       (64) 4 474 0670

**Email**:    helena@elections.govt.nz

**Website**:  www.elections.org.nz

The Electoral Commission New Zealand is an independent Crown entity, which registers political parties and party logos. It also receives registered parties annual returns of donations and returns of election expenses and allocates election broadcasting time and funds to eligible political parties. The Commission also encourages and conducts public education on electoral matters.

### Wallace Scholarships for Tertiary Student Research

**Purpose**: To encourage research work that will be useful in designing electoral education and information programmes and help raise public awareness of electoral issues

**Eligibility**: Scholarships are for research as part of a New Zealand university degree

**Level of Study**: Research

**Type**: Scholarships

**Value**: NZ$500-2,000

**Length of Study**: usually 1 year

**Frequency**: Annual

**Country of Study**: New Zealand

**Application Procedure**: Applicants must send a 1-page research proposal, letter of endorsement from an academic supervisor and contact details and enrollment qualifications

**No. of awards offered**: 6

**Closing Date**: 2 February

**Funding**: Government

**Additional Information**: All queries should be directed to Dr Helena Catt at catt@elections.govt.nz www.britishcouncil.in/study-uk/scholarships/charles-wallace-india-trust-scholarships

**For further information contact:**

**Email**:    Wellingtonorcatt@elections.govt.nz

# Embassy of France in Australia

6 Perth Avenue, Yarralumla, Canberra ACT 2600, Australia.

**Tel**:        (51) 2 6216 0100
**Email**:      education@ambafrance-au.org
**Website**:    www.ambafrance-au.org
**Contact**:    Higher Education Attaché

The Embassy of France in Australia supports the partnership between French and Australian Universities and offers grants and scholarships to help the students' mobility.

## Language Assistantships in France and New Caledonia

**Purpose**: To enable graduates who intend to teach French in the future or beginning teachers of French to improve their language skills

**Eligibility**: 1. Candidates must be Australian citizens or permanent residents. 2. Candidates must be enrolled at an Australian university or be recently graduated at the time of application. Candidates must have completed at least two years of university studies. 3. Candidates must be between 20 and 35 years of age at the time of taking up their positions (from 11 March). 4. Candidates must have a minimum Level B1 in French. 5. Candidates should preferably be single, as the salary of an assistant is not adequate to support dependents. 6. At the time of their visa appointment, candidates will be required to submit a National Police Check dated no older than three months.

**Level of Study**: Graduate

**Type**: Assistantship

**Value**: Net monthly allowance: €1,529.

**Length of Study**: 7 months

**Frequency**: Annual

**Study Establishment**: Any approved high school

**Country of Study**: Any country

**Application Procedure**: Application forms are available on the website of the French Embassy: www.ambafrance-au.org

**No. of awards offered**: 120

**Closing Date**: November

**Funding**: Government

**Additional Information**: These awards are organized by the higher education office of the Embassy of France in Australia. Successful applicants will conduct English conversation classes with small groups of students for 12 hours per week au. ambafrance.org/Become-an-English-Language-Teaching-Assistant-in-New-Caledonia

## Ministry of Foreign Affairs (France) International Teaching Fellowships

**Purpose**: To enable experienced teachers of French to spend time at a French primary school, a French college, or a French lycée

**Eligibility**: Open to Australian teachers of French employed by state education authorities

**Level of Study**: Professional development

**Type**: Fellowship

**Length of Study**: 1 year

**Frequency**: Annual

**Study Establishment**: A lycée, collège, primary school or Institut Universitaire de Formation de Maîtres (IUFM)

**Country of Study**: France

**Application Procedure**: Applicants must complete an application form, available from state departments of education and on the French Embassy website: www.ambafrance-au.org

**Closing Date**: 30 April

**Funding**: Government

**Additional Information**: These awards are organized by the higher education office of the Embassy of France in Australia (BCF)

**For further information contact:**

**Email**:    candidatures.eiffel@campusfrance.org

## Ministry of Foreign Affairs (France) Stage de la Réunion (One Month Scholarships)

**Purpose**: To enable school teachers of French to attend a course on the methodology specific to the teaching of French at primary or secondary level

**Eligibility**: Open to Australian teachers of French only

**Level of Study**: Professional development

**Type**: Scholarship

**Value**: All costs except travel costs between Australia and Réunion Island
**Length of Study**: 1 month
**Frequency**: Annual
**Study Establishment**: Cifept in Le Tampon
**Country of Study**: Other
**Application Procedure**: Applicants must write for details
**Closing Date**: 15 March
**Funding**: Government
**Additional Information**: These awards are organised by the Bureau de Co-opération pour le Francais of the Embassy of France in Australia (BCF)

### For further information contact:

**Email**:    candidatures.eiffel@campusfrance.org

## SAAFE Program

**Purpose**: The objective of the SAAFE program is to foster research collaborations between France and Australia in nuclear science and engineering in the field of human health, environment and nuclear fuel cycle.
**Eligibility**: 1. A PhD student currently enrolled in a French university or Australian AINSE-member university. 2. Enrolled in a PhD in collaboration between French and Australian institutions. 3. Hold a postdoctoral appointment at a French university or Australian AINSE-member university.
**Application Procedure**: Use the button below to download the SAAFE application form. Please review the guidelines within the form carefully.
**Closing Date**: 1 May
**Additional Information**: au.ambafrance.org/Grants-and-Opportunities-6980#Nicolas-Baudin-Travel-Grant

### For further information contact:

**Email**:    ainse@ainse.edu.au

## Embassy of the United States in Kabul

Humphrey Fellowship Program, Public Affairs Section, United States Embassy, Kabul, Afghanistan.

**Tel**:      (93) 20 230 0436
**Email**:    kabulwebmaster@state.gov

By providing future leaders and policy makers with experience in the United States society, culture and professional fields, the Embassy of the United States in Kabul provides a basis for lasting, productive, ties between Americans and their professional counterparts overseas.

## Ambassadors Fund for Cultural Preservation Small Grants Competition

**Eligibility**: 1. Full and complete Application for Federal Assistance (SF-424), including Budget Information for Non-Construction Programs (SF-424A), Assurances for Non-Construction Programs (SF-424B), Applicant Organizational Information Form, and, if applicable, Disclosure of Lobbying Activities (SF-LLL). 2. Project basics, including title, project dates, and AFCP focus area. 3. Project applicant information, including contact information, DUNS Number, and SAM registration status. 4. Project location. 5. Proof of official permission to undertake the project from the office, agency, or organization that either owns or is otherwise responsible for the preservation and protection of the site, object, or collection. 6. Project purpose that summarizes the project objectives and desired results. 7. Project activities description that presents the project tasks in chronological order (Note: If the proposed project is part of a larger effort involving multiple projects supported by other entities, the plan must present the full scope of the preservation effort and the place of the proposed project within that larger effort). 8. Project time frame or schedule that lists the major project phases and milestones with target dates for achieving them (Note: Applicants may propose project periods of up to 60 months [five years]; projects must begin before 30 September, and be completed no later than September 30, 2024). All submitted documents must be in English. 9. Project participant information, including resumes or CVs of the proposed project director and other primary project participants. For further information, refer website
**Level of Study**: Graduate
**Type**: Grant
**Frequency**: Annual
**Country of Study**: Any country
**Application Procedure**: The applicants will first be screened for technical eligibility based on the objectives, priorities, requirements, ineligible activities, and unallowable costs contained in this funding opportunity. The Embassy and its Washington office may deem applications ineligible if they do not fully adhere to the criteria stated
**Closing Date**: 28 November
**Funding**: Private
**Additional Information**: in.usembassy.gov/ambassadors-fund-for-cultural-preservation-afcp-2020-small-grants-competition-2/

## For further information contact:

United States Embassy New Delhi, Shantipath, Chanakyapuri, New Delhi 110021, India.

**Tel**:      (91) 11 2419 8000
**Email**:   Nd_GrantApplications@state.gov

## Hubert H. Humphrey Fellowship Program

**Purpose**: The Hubert H. Humphrey Fellowship Program, which is a Fulbright program, brings accomplished young and mid-career professionals from developing countries to the United States for ten months of non-degree graduate study and related practical professional experiences
**Eligibility**: Open to candidates who have completed a university degree programme, are proficient in written and spoken English, and also have 5 years of relevant professional experience
**Level of Study**: Postdoctorate
**Type**: Fellowship
**Length of Study**: 1 year
**Frequency**: Annual
**Country of Study**: United States of America
**Application Procedure**: Applicants should submit a curriculum vitae along with copies of university transcripts and degrees
**Closing Date**: 15 May
**Funding**: Government
**Contributor**: The United States Department of State Bureau of Educational and Cultural Affairs
**Additional Information**: www.usief.org.in/Hubert-H-Humphrey-Fellowship-Program.aspx

## For further information contact:

Senior Program Officer, Indian Program, USIEF, Fulbright House, 12 Hailey Road, New Delhi 110 001, India.

**Email**:   humphrey@usief.org.in

## Endeavour Research Fellowship

Department of Education and Training International Group International Mobility Branch Endeavour Scholarships and Fellowships, Canberra, ACT 2601 9880, Australia.

**Email**:      endeavour@education.gov.au
**Contact**:   Endeavour Research Fellowship

The Endeavour Scholarships and Fellowships are the Australian Government's competitive, merit-based scholarships and fellowships providing opportunities for Australians to undertake study, research or professional development overseas and for overseas citizens to do the same in Australia.

## Endeavour Research Fellowship for International Applicants

**Purpose**: The Endeavour Scholarships and Fellowships aim to build Australia's reputation for excellence in the provision of education and research, support the internationalisation of the Australian higher education and research sectors and offer high-achieving individuals from overseas and Australia opportunities to increase their productivity and expertise in their field
**Eligibility**: Be aged 18 years or over at the commencement of their program. Be a citizen and/or permanent resident of a participating country (section 8). Commence their proposed program after 1 January and no later than 30 November. Provide all relevant supporting documentation (section 9). Not currently hold or have completed, after 1 January, an Australian Government sponsored scholarship and/or fellowship (directly administered to recipients by the Australian Government). Not apply for a category in which they have already completed an Endeavour scholarship or fellowship
**Value**: All recipients will receive: travel allowance: AU$3,000 (provision to pay up to AU$4,500 under special circumstances); establishment allowance: AU$2,000 (fellowships) or AU$4,000 (scholarships); monthly stipend: AU$3,000 (paid up to the maximum category duration on a pro-rata basis)*; health insurance for the full category duration (OSHC for international recipients); travel insurance (excluding during programme for international recipients); Endeavour scholarship recipients will also receive tuition fees paid up to the maximum study/research duration on a pro-rata basis. Tuition includes student service and amenities fees
**Study Establishment**: Fellowships are awarded in any field of study
**Country of Study**: Australia
**Application Procedure**: Applications must be submitted using the Endeavour Online application system. Applicants are encouraged to commence their applications early and submit their application as early as possible during the application period due to the large volume of users on the system in the lead up to the closing date. Submitting early ensures that you will not have any last minute technical problems due to the large number of applications being submitted
**Closing Date**: 30 June
**Additional Information**: For more details please visit the website    scholarship-positions.com/endeavour-research-

fellowship-international-students-2014/2013/04/13/ www.
mladiinfo.eu/2018/10/05/endeavour-research-fellowship-
international-applicants/

## Engineering and Physical Sciences Research Council (EPSRC)

Polaris House, North Star Avenue, Wiltshire, Swindon, SN2
1ET, United Kingdom.

**Tel**:          (44) 17 9344 4239
**Email**:      jan.tucker@epsrc.ac.uk
**Website**:  www.epsrc.ac.uk
**Contact**:   Ms Jan Tucker, Peer Review Operations

The Engineering and Physical Sciences Research Council
(EPSRC) promotes and supports high quality, basic, strategic
and applied research and related postgraduate training in engineering and physical sciences. It aims to advance knowledge
and technology by providing trained scientists and engineers, in
order to meet the needs of users and beneficiaries, and thereby
contribute to economic competitiveness and quality of life.

### Daphne Jackson Fellowships

**Purpose**: To enable high-level scientists and engineers to
return to their professions after a career break for family
commitments
**Eligibility**: Promising engineers and scientists who have
taken a career break for family commitments, who have
obtained at least a first degree and who are normally resident
in the United Kingdom
**Level of Study**: Graduate, Postdoctorate, Research
**Type**: A variable number of fellowships
**Value**: Fixed to United Kingdom Research Council RA1A scale
**Length of Study**: 2 years (part-time possible)
**Frequency**: Dependent on funds available
**Study Establishment**: Universities or research institutions in
the United Kingdom that are convenient for the candidate
**Country of Study**: United Kingdom
**Application Procedure**: Applicants must complete an appli-
cation form. Further information can be found on the website
www.sst.ph.ic.ac.uk/trust
**No. of awards offered**: 69
**Funding**: Government, Commercial, Private
**Additional Information**: Daphne Jackson Fellowships are
sponsored by the Biotechnology and Biological Sciences
Research Council (BBSRC), the Particle Physics and Astronomy Research Council (PPARC) and the Natural Environ-
ment Research Council (NERC), together with charitable

foundations, learned societies, universities and industries
www.bristol.ac.uk/blackwell/funding/daphne-jackson-fellow
ships/

**For further information contact:**

The Daphne Jackson Memorial Fellowships Trust Department of Physics University of Surrey, Surrey, GU2 7XH,
United Kingdom.

**Tel**:       (44) 1483 689166
**Email**:   djmft@surrey.ac.uk

### Engineering and Physical Sciences Research Council Standard Research Studentships

**Purpose**: To enable training in the methods of research
**Eligibility**: Non European Union nationals must be settled in
the United Kingdom without being subject under immigration
law to any restriction for the period to which they remain.
European Union nationals may apply, provided their qualifi-
cations are equivalent to a British Upper Second Class
(Honours) Degree. Support will be fees only unless migrant
worker status has been established
**Level of Study**: Postgraduate
**Type**: Studentship
**Value**: £8,265 for students in London. £6,620 for students
elsewhere (1,999–2,000 rates). Values are reviewed annually.
In addition, other allowances are payable under certain condi-
tions. Approved tuition fees are paid directly to the institution
**Length of Study**: Maximum 3 years
**Frequency**: Annual
**Study Establishment**: Higher education institution
**Country of Study**: Other
**Application Procedure**: Applicants must be nominated by
departments of higher education institutes. Applications on
behalf of students should be directed to the relevant address.
Full information can be found on the web pages or from
academic institutions
**Closing Date**: 12 July
**Funding**: Government
**Additional Information**: epsrc.ukri.org/skills/students/

### Royal Society EPSRC BBSRC and Rolls Royce PLC Industry Fellowships

**Purpose**: To enhance the communication on science and technology between those in industry and those in universities or
similar institutions of higher education to the benefit of United
Kingdom firms, higher education institutions and the individual
scientist. The aim is to establish long-lasting personal and corporate linkages between the two sectors in the United Kingdom

**Eligibility**: Open to applicants of any nationality. Candidates should be at the mid-career level and have had significant achievement in their home organisations. Also a substantial career should be ahead of the candidate towards the end of the award, to build upon the contacts made during the fellowship. Candidates must hold a PhD or equivalent in their profession and a substantive post in a university or similar academic institution as a scientist, mathematician or engineer, or be employed as a scientist, mathematician or engineer in any industry, an industrial research organisation or a nationalised industry. Organisations partly or wholly supported by public funds may not act as the industrial partner for an award. Preference will be given to candidates showing evidence of previous contact with or interest in the other sector of employment

**Level of Study**: Postdoctorate

**Type**: Fellowship

**Value**: Payment of salary but not employers' National Insurance and pension contributions

**Length of Study**: Up to 2 years full–time. A part–time equivalent is available

**Country of Study**: Other

**Application Procedure**: Applicants must complete an application form available from the website. Details are available from the Royal Society Research Appointments Department

**Closing Date**: December

**Funding**: Government, Commercial, Private

**Additional Information**: The scheme provides opportunities for academic scientists, mathematicians and engineers to work in an industrial environment and undertake a project at any stage from fundamental science to industrial innovation, and for industrial scientists, mathematicians and engineers to undertake research or course development work in an institution of higher education

### For further information contact:

The Royal Society, Research Appointments Department, 6 Carlton House Terrace, London, SW1Y 5AR, United Kingdom.

| | |
|---|---|
| **Tel**: | (44) 20 7451 2547 |
| **Fax**: | (44) 20 7930 2170 |
| **Email**: | e-gap@royalsoc.ac.uk |

## Engineers Canada

180 Elgin Street Suite 1100, Ottawa, ON K2P 2K3, Canada.

| | |
|---|---|
| **Tel**: | (1) 613 232 2474 |
| **Email**: | awards@engineerscanada.ca |
| **Website**: | www.engineerscanada.ca |

Engineers Canada is the national organization of the provincial and territorial associations and order that regulate the practice of engineering in Canada.

## Engineers Canada's National Scholarship Program

**Purpose**: To reward excellence in the Canadian engineering profession and support advanced studies and research

**Eligibility**: Open to citizens or permanent residents of Canada who are registered as professional engineers in good standing with a provincial/territorial engineering association/order

**Level of Study**: Doctorate, Graduate, Postgraduate, Research, MBA

**Type**: Scholarships

**Value**: Canadian C$70,000 in total

**Frequency**: Annual

**Country of Study**: Canada and abroad

**Application Procedure**: Applicants must contact Marc Bourgeois for further details

**No. of awards offered**: Approx. 50-55

**Closing Date**: 1 March

**Contributor**: TD Insurance Meloche-Monnex Insurance and Manulife Financial

**Additional Information**: Postdoctoral Fellows are not eligible to apply engineerscanada.ca/awards-and-honours/scholarship-program

### For further information contact:

| | |
|---|---|
| **Tel**: | (1) 613 232 2474 ext. 238 |
| **Fax**: | (1) 613 230 5759 |
| **Email**: | marc.bourgeois@engineerscanada.ca |

## Engineers Canada-Manulife Scholarship

**Eligibility**: To be eligible for the scholarships program, candidates must be registered as an engineer (P.Eng./ing.) in good standing with one of the 12 regulators throughout the duration of their academic year.

**Level of Study**: Postgraduate

**Value**: C$12,500 each

**Frequency**: Annual

**No. of awards offered**: 1 Award

**Closing Date**: September

**Additional Information**: engineerscanada.ca/awards-and-honours/scholarships/engineers-canada-manulife-scholarship

## English-Speaking Union (ESU)

Dartmouth House, 37 Charles Street, London, W1J 5ED, United Kingdom.

**Tel**:          (44) 20 7529 1550
**Email**:      esu@esu.org
**Website**:   www.esu.org
**Contact**:    Head of Cultural Programmes

The English-Speaking Union (ESU) is an independent, non-political educational charity with members throughout the world, promoting international and human achievement through the worldwide use of the English language.

## English-Speaking Union Travelling Librarian Award

**Purpose**: To encourage United States and United Kingdom contacts in the library world and establish links between pairs of libraries
**Eligibility**: Open to professionally qualified United Kingdom and information professionals
**Level of Study**: Professional development
**Type**: Award
**Value**: Up to £3,000. Board and lodging and relevant flight costs
**Length of Study**: A minimum of 3 weeks
**Frequency**: Annual
**Country of Study**: United States of America
**Application Procedure**: Candidates must submit a curriculum vitae and a covering letter explaining why they are the ideal candidates for the award
**No. of awards offered**: 16
**Closing Date**: April
**Funding**: Commercial, Private
**Contributor**: The English-Speaking Union and The Chartered Institute of Library and Information Professionals
**Additional Information**: Candidates should contact the Librarian by telephone or email at library@esu.org www.sla.intexta.co.uk/blg-travelling-librarian-award.php

### For further information contact:

37 Charles Street, London, W1J 5ED, United Kingdom.

**Email**:   education@esu.org

## Entente Cordiale Scholarships

French Cultural Department, 23 Cromwell Road, London, SW7 2EN, United Kingdom.

**Tel**:          (44) 20 7073 1312
**Email**:      entente.cordiale@ambafrance.org.uk
**Website**:   www.ambascience.co.uk/entente-cordiale
**Contact**:    Administrative Officer

Launched by an agreement between the United Kingdom and French governments in 1995, the Entente Cordiale Scholarships enable outstanding British postgraduates to study or carry out research on the other side of the Channel, with a view to dispel preconceived ideas and promote good relations between the two countries.

## Bourses Scholarships

**Purpose**: To allow individuals to study or carry out research in France
**Eligibility**: Open to British citizens
**Level of Study**: Postgraduate
**Type**: Scholarship
**Value**: £8,000 for students living in Paris and £7,500 for those studying outside Paris for the 1-year award, £3,000 for 3 months, £6,000 for 6 months
**Length of Study**: 3 months, 6 months, or 1-year
**Frequency**: Annual
**Study Establishment**: Approved universities or grande écoles
**Country of Study**: France
**Application Procedure**: Applicants must complete an application form, available from the website
**No. of awards offered**: 60
**Closing Date**: 15 March
**Funding**: Private
**Contributor**: Blue Circle (Lafarge), BP, Kingfisher PLC, EDF Energy, UBS, Xerox, Paul Minet, Sir Patrick Sheehy Schlumberger, Vodafone, Rolls Royce, Parthenon Trust
**Additional Information**: Scholarships are also awarded to French postgraduates to study in the United Kingdom. Interested parties should contact the British Council in Paris

### For further information contact:

**Email**:   scholarships-bourses@cbie.ca

## Entomological Society of Canada (ESC)

393 Winston Ave, Ottawa, ON K2A 1Y8, Canada.

Tel:      (1) 613 725 2619
Email:    entos.can@bellnet.ca
Website:  www.esc-sec.ca
Contact:  Office Manager

The Entomological Society of Canada (ESC) is one of the largest and oldest professional societies in Canada. Founded in Toronto on April 16th, 1863, the Society was open to all students and lovers of entomology. ESC is a dynamic force in promoting research, disseminating knowledge of insects and encouraging the continued participation of all lovers of entomology in the most fascinating of all natural sciences. It is especially well known for its widely distributed and used publications.

## John H. Borden Scholarship

Purpose: To financially support students who are studying integrated pest management with an entomological emphasis
Eligibility: Open to postgraduate students of Integrated Pest Management
Level of Study: Postgraduate
Type: Scholarship
Value: Canadian C$1,000
Frequency: Every 2 years
Country of Study: Canada
Application Procedure: Applicants must submit their application form, curriculum vitae, transcripts and reference letters. Application forms are available online
Closing Date: 16 February
Additional Information: www.canadian-universities.net/Scholarships/J/John-H-Borden-Scholarship.html

### For further information contact:

Email:    Floate@agr.gc.ac

## Environmental Leadership Program

P.O. BOX 907, Greenbelt, MD 20768-0907, United States of America.

Email:    info@elpnet.org
Website:  www.elpnet.org

The Environmental Leadership Program (ELP) inspires visionary, action-oriented and diverse leadership to work for a just and sustainable future. ELP nurtures a new generation of environmental leaders characterized by diversity, innovation, collaboration and effective communications. ELP addresses the needs of relatively new environmental activists and professionals.

## Environmental Leadership Fellowships

Purpose: To build the leadership capacity of the environmental field's most promising and emerging practitioners
Eligibility: Open to citizens of the United States only
Level of Study: Postgraduate
Type: Fellowship
Value: US$750 which includes room and board for the 3 overnight retreats, participation in 10 days of training and community building and access to our network of over 480 Senior Fellows
Length of Study: 2 years
Frequency: Annual
Country of Study: United States of America
Closing Date: 2 April
Additional Information: naaee.org/eepro/opportunities/environmental-leadership-program

### For further information contact:

Email:    lori@elpnet.org

## Environmental Protection Agency

PO Box 3000, Johnstown Castle Estate, Wexford, Y35 W821, Ireland.

Website:  www.epa.ie/researchandeducation/research/epafunding/postgraduateprogrammes/
Contact:  Research Grants Programme

The mission of the Environmental Protection Agency is to protect human health and to safeguard the natural environment - air, water, and land - upon which life depends.

## Environmental Protection Agency-IRC Scholarship Scheme

Purpose: The EPA can also co-fund PhD Scholarships with Third Level Institutions. Proposal should be for innovative research aiming at supporting environmental policy in Ireland. The proposed Scholarship should provide evidence to identify pressures, inform policy and develop solutions

**Eligibility**: Under the EPA Co-funded Scholarships Scheme, funding is available for a small number of awards, as per the following: 48-month PhDs (indicative budget of €96,000); Limited to new and innovative projects; Co-funded by an Irish host research institution on a 50:50 basis; EPA is to be consulted in the drafting of the proposed PhD scope, as well as in the selection process of the candidate (i.e. interview panel); All co-funded PhDs would have to adhere to the EPA's funding rules and reporting requirements

**Level of Study**: Graduate

**Type**: Scholarship

**Value**: a stipend of €16,000 per annum a contribution to fees, including non-European Union fees, up to a maximum of €5,750 per annum eligible direct research expenses of €2,250 per annum

**Frequency**: Annual

**Country of Study**: Any country

**Funding**: Private

### For further information contact:

PO Box 3000, Johnstown Castle Estate, IRL Y35 W821, Wexford, Ireland.

**Tel**:      (353) 53 916 0600
**Email**:   research@epa.ie

## Escola Superior d'Administració i Direcció d'Empreses (ESADE)

MBA Office, Avenue d'Espluges 92–96, 08034 Barcelona, Spain.

**Tel**:        (34) 93 280 6162
**Email**:    mba@esade.edu
**Website**:  www.esade.edu
**Contact**:  Ms Jordi Mora Pintado, Financial Aid & Operations Director

ESADE is an independent nonprofit university institution, founded in 1958 in Barcelona when a group of entrepreneurs and Jesuit Society members joined forces. Since 1995, it has formed part of the Ramon Llull University. ESADE's academic activity takes place on its Barcelona, Madrid and Buenos Aires campuses. The three main areas it focuses on are education, research and social dialogue.

## Escola Superior d'Administració i Direcció d'Empreses (ESADE) MBA Scholarships

**Purpose**: To assist full-time MBA students with tuition fees award high potential candidates

**Eligibility**: Depending on the scholarship: enroled students: (Fellowships plus Impact); Admitted students: (Direct, Merit & Need-based Scholarships plus Excellence). Scholarships are awarded, restricted by merit achievement, geographical area, sector of activity and need based

**Level of Study**: MBA

**Type**: Scholarships

**Value**: Direct scholarships: up to 40 % of total tuition fees; Scholarship for excellence: up to 50 % of tuition fees; Merit & Need-based Scholarships: up to 50 % of tuition fees; Fellowships: variable; depending on length

**Length of Study**: 12, 15, or 18 months

**Frequency**: Annual

**Study Establishment**: ESADE Business School

**Country of Study**: Spain

**Application Procedure**: Send all required documents for your admittance to Admission Department, complete your Scholarship Application Form (Annex 1), include supporting documents, send all required documents in PDF format to mba@esade.edu

**No. of awards offered**: 250

**Closing Date**: 15 June

**Funding**: Foundation

**Contributor**: ESADE Foundation, ESCADE MBA scholarship fund

**Additional Information**: www.esade.edu/mba www.esade.edu/en/programmes/mba/full-time-mba/fees-financing/scholarships/full-time-mba-scholarships

### For further information contact:

ESADE Av. Pedralbes, 60-62, 08034 Barcelona, Spain.

**Email**:    financialaid@esade.edu

## ESMOD Berlin

**Email**:    j.hurley@esmod.de

The Hessnatur Foundation is a non-profit, independent foundation conducting research and development in the field of Applied Sustainability.

## Hessnatur Foundation Scholarship

**Eligibility**: 1. Candidates applying for Hessnatur Foundation Scholarship, must have applied successfully and received acceptance to the M.A. Sustainability in Fashion at ESMOD Berlin. 2. Applicants must be able to afford other expenses which include living costs and course related material costs. 3. Applicants of Hessnatur Foundation Scholarship, must possess the visas and insurances that are required to study in Germany by the start date of the course. 4. Scholarship holders are required to agree to allow ESMOD Berlin and the Hessnatur Foundation to use their images/other media and their works for educational and promotional purposes

**Level of Study**: Postgraduate
**Type**: Scholarship
**Value**: Tuition costs fully covered. Amount covered is €11,000
**Length of Study**: 1.6 years
**Study Establishment**: ESMOD Berlin
**Country of Study**: Germany
**Application Procedure**: Applications must be sent via email to j.hurley@esmod.de
**Closing Date**: 1 June
**Additional Information**: scholarship-fellowship.com/hessnatur-foundation-scholarship/

## Eta Sigma Phi

H-S Box 68, Hampden-Sydney, VA 23943-6244, United States of America.

**Tel**: (1) 804 223 6244
**Email**: waynet@tiger.hsc.edu
**Contact**: Professor C Wayne Tucker

It is Eta Sigma Phi's mission to promote scholarship in classics. The organisation awards scholarships for study abroad, publishes a newsletter, and holds annual translation and composition contests. A convention is also held in the spring of each year.

## Eta Sigma Phi Summer Scholarships

**Purpose**: To enable one member of Eta Sigma Phi to attend the summer session of the American Academy in Rome, Italy, another to attend the summer session of the American School of Classical Studies in Athens, Greece and a third to attend a session of the Vergilian Society at Cumae, Italy

**Eligibility**: Those eligible to apply are Eta Sigma Phi members and alumni who have received a Bachelor's degree since January 1st 1994, or shall have received it in or before June 2000, and who have not received a doctoral degree. For the Bedrick Scholarship at the Vergilian Society in Cumae, also eligible are Eta Sigma Phi members who will be rising juniors or seniors in the Summer of 2000, and preference for the scholarship will be given to such undergraduate members

**Level of Study**: Postgraduate
**Type**: Scholarship
**Value**: The scholarship to the American Academy in Rome will have a value of US$3,000, the Brent Malcolm Froberg Scholarship to the American School of Classical Studies at Athens will have a value of US$3,550 and the Theodore Bedrick Schoarship to the Virgilian Society at Cumae will have a value of US$2,540
**Length of Study**: 6 weeks
**Frequency**: Annual
**Study Establishment**: The American Academy in Rome, The American School of Classical Studies at Athens, and the Virgilian Society at Cumae
**Country of Study**: Other
**Application Procedure**: Applicants must submit an application form, an up to date transcript, letters of recommendation, and a 500 word statement which includes purpose for desiring the scholarship. Application information and forms are available by writing to Professor Caroline Perkins at the Eta Sigma Phi Scholarship Committee or by email: ruby@ezwv.com
**No. of awards offered**: 8
**Closing Date**: December
**Funding**: Private
**Contributor**: Investments, capital contributed by charitable gifts
**Additional Information**: The Chairman of the Scholarship Committee receives and sends the application material www.etasigmaphi.org/members/opportunities/

### For further information contact:

Eta Sigma Phi Scholarship Committee Department of Classical Studies Marshall University, United States of America.

**Email**: ruby@ezwv.com

## Ethnic Minority Foundation

Boardman House, 64 Broadway, Stratford, E15 1NG, United Kingdom.

**Tel**: (44) 208 432 0000 Free phone: 800 652 0390
**Email**: enquiries@emf-cemvo.co.uk

**Website**:　www.ethnicminorityfund.org.uk
**Contact**:　Grants Enquiries, Ethnic Minority Foundation

The EMF is a registered charity established in 1999 (Charity no 1077002). EMF is committed to building a secure base for Britain's minority ethnic communities and voluntary sector. It is dedicated to addressing some of the worst cases of social exclusion that affect and disadvantage minority ethnic communities living in the United Kingdom.

## Ethnic Minority Foundation Grants

**Purpose**: To provide long-term and short-term funding of minority ethnic voluntary and community organizations, and funding for other community needs such as education, health, women's and youth projects
**Type**: Grant
**Funding**: Foundation, Individuals
**Additional Information**: www.community-relations.org.uk/news-centre/201920-minority-ethnic-development-fund-now-open-applications

### For further information contact:

**Tel**:　(44) 208 432 0300, Free Phone: 800 652 0390
**Fax**:　(44) 208 432 0319

## Eugène Vinaver Memorial Trust

### Barron Bequest

**Subjects**: Any field of Arthurian studies
**Purpose**: To support postgraduate research in Arthurian studies
**Eligibility**: Open to graduates of any university of the United Kingdom and Ireland
**Level of Study**: Postgraduate research
**Type**: Grant
**Value**: £1,250, payment towards postgraduate fees
**Length of Study**: One year. Candidates may apply for further years on a basis of parity with those applying for the first time
**Frequency**: Annual
**Study Establishment**: Any university in United Kingdom or Ireland
**Country of Study**: United Kingdom, Republic of Ireland
**Application Procedure**: For application details, applicants must contact Professor Taylor at the address below

**No. of awards offered**: Varies, normally one or two per year
**Closing Date**: 30 April
**Funding**: Private
**Contributor**: The Eugène Vinaver Memorial Trust
**No. of awards given last year**: No awards made
**No. of applicants last year**: Two
**Additional Information**: www.science-community.org/en/node/150641 www.science-community.org/en/node/150641

### For further information contact:

Professor JHM Taylor, Garth Head, Penruddock, Penrith, Cumbria, CA11 0QU, United Kingdom

**Email**:　jane.taylor@durham.ac.uk or
　　　　　geoffreybromiley@btinternet.com

## European Association for the Study of Diabetes

Rheindorfer Weg 3, D-40591 Dusseldorf, Germany.

**Tel**:　(49) 211 758 4690
**Email**:　secretariat@easd.org
**Website**:　www.easd.org
**Contact**:　EASD Secretariat

## European Association for the Study of Diabetes-ADA Transatlantic Fellowships

**Purpose**: To encourage research into basic or clinical questions related to diabetes and its complications
**Eligibility**: Applicants should have completed their MD, PhD or equivalent within the previous 7 years and cannot be serving an internship or residency during the fellowship. European applicants must be EASD members and United States of America applicants should be ADA members
**Level of Study**: Research
**Type**: Fellowship
**Value**: US$50,000
**Length of Study**: 1 year
**Frequency**: Annual
**Country of Study**: United States of America
**Application Procedure**: Applications must be made on the forms provided. Two copies of the application forms should be submitted
**Closing Date**: 1 February

**Contributor**: EASD-Lilly Research Fund

**Additional Information**: Successful applicants will be notified of the award by 1 April. Funding begins on 1 July

# European Calcified Tissue Society

PO Box 337, Bristol, BS32 4ZR, United Kingdom.

**Tel**:　　(44) 14 5461 0255
**Email**:　　admin@actsoc.org
**Website**:　　www.ectsoc.org

The European Calcified Tissue Society is the major organization in Europe for researchers and clinicians working in the field of calcified tissues and related fields.

## European Calcified Tissue Society/Servier Fellowship

**Purpose**: To encourage the research involving pathophysiology of osteoporosis, particularly the coupling and uncoupling processes between bone formation and bone resorption and all related matters

**Eligibility**: Open for ECTS members who qualified PhD/MD within the last 10 years. Applications to include details of a preclinical or clinical research project on the pathophysiology of osteoporosis, particularly the coupling and uncoupling processes between bone formation and bone resorption and all related matters

**Level of Study**: Research

**Type**: Fellowship

**Value**: €80,000

**Length of Study**: 2 years

**Frequency**: Every 2 years

**Country of Study**: Any country

**Application Procedure**: Applicants should fill an application form. For further details log on to www.ectsoc.org

**No. of awards offered**: 20

**Closing Date**: November

**Funding**: Commercial

**Contributor**: Servier

**Additional Information**: www.asbmr.org/grants/detail. aspx?cid=067cfe7f-e71b-4ace-a2f4-6ea11e5abbb3

### For further information contact:

**Email**:　　ects@ectsoc.org

# European Committee for Treatment and Research in Multiple Sclerosis (ECTRIMS)

ECTRIMS Secretariat, Peter Merian-Strasse 80, CH-4002 Basel, Switzerland.

**Tel**:　　(41) 61 686 7779
**Email**:　　secretariat@ectrims.eu
**Website**:　　www.ectrims.eu

The committee works to facilitate communication, create synergies, and promote and enhance research and learning among professionals for the ultimate benefit of people affected by MS.

## European Committee for Treatment and Research in Multiple Sclerosis-MAGNIMS Fellowship in Magnetic Resonance Imaging in MS

**Purpose**: ECTRIMS and the European MAGNIMS (Magnetic Resonance Imaging in MS) network jointly support a postdoctoral fellowship to foster the development of young researchers in magnetic resonance imaging studies in MS. The goal of this programme is to achieve transfer and broadening of knowledge regarding the application of magnetic resonance to MS research and to promote the researcher's integration into the international scientific community

**Eligibility**: Applicants should be under 40 years and affiliated to an academic department which can guarantee a continuation of his or her research

**Type**: Fellowship

**Value**: €55,000

**Length of Study**: 1 year

**Frequency**: Annual

**Country of Study**: Any country

**Application Procedure**: Please check with the organization

**No. of awards offered**: 2

**Closing Date**: 1 February

**Additional Information**: Details about all ECTRIMS Fellowship Programmes and application material can be obtained from the ECTRIMS website: www.ectrims.eu/fellowships www.researchconnect.eu/archive/ectrims-magnims-2020-fellowship-open-for-application/

### For further information contact:

**Email**:　　chris.enzinger@medunigraz.at

# European Crohn's and Colitis Organisation

ECCO, Ungargasse 6/13, A-1030 Vienna, Austria.

**Tel**:     (43) 1 710 2242 0
**Email**:   ecco@ecco-ibd.eu

## ECCO GRANT

**Purpose**: Promote innovative scientific research in IBD in Europe
**Eligibility**: 1. Not be older than 40 years. If above 40 years, a certificate needs to be provided, proving that the candidate is being within 5 years after finishing GI training or PhD, graduation. 2. The principal investigator of the ECCO Grant application needs to be ECCO Member, (at the time of application). 3. ECCO Grant applicants are not limited to the ECCO Member Countries and can apply, from non-European countries; however, the impact of the project for the IBD, Community has to be clearly stated. 4. If your institute holds a current ECCO Grant, then another application for this period, is not possible. Therefore, an institute cannot apply for two ECCO Grants in, consecutive years. 5. Candidate can apply for one specific ECCO Research Award only. Several, applications with the same topic for different ECCO Research Awards will not be taken into account for review. 6. Recipients that have already been awarded with an ECCO Grant in the past cannot reapply.
**Level of Study**: Postgraduate
**Type**: Grant
**Value**: €80,000
**Length of Study**: 1
**No. of awards offered**: 8
**Closing Date**: 3 June
**Additional    Information**:    www.ecco-ibd.eu/science/
fellowships-and-grants.html

## European Crohn's and Colitis Organisation Fellowship

**Purpose**: The European Crohn's and Colitis Organisation (ECCO) offers Research Fellowships to encourage and support young individuals in their career and promote innovative scientific research in the area of Inflammatory Bowel Diseases (IBD) in Europe
**Eligibility**: 1. Not be older than 40 years or still in training at the time of application. 2. Submit an original research project

using the ECCO Fellowships and Grants Online Submission Pages. Incomplete applications will not be evaluated. 3. Have a hosting laboratory and/or department outside one's own country of practice, which has accepted to host and guide the Fellow under the supervision of a designated host for the duration of the Fellowship. The hosting institution is responsible, together with the Fellow, for the successful completion of the project. 4. At the time of the application as well as prior to the commencement of the Fellowship the candidate must not be involve/work in any research project at the future hosting institute. 5. If your hosting institute
**Level of Study**: Postgraduate
**Type**: Fellowships, operating grants
**Value**: €60,000 will be awarded per scholarship
**Frequency**: Annual
**Country of Study**: Any country
**Closing Date**: 3 June
**Funding**: Private
**Additional Information**: www.scholarshipportal.com/scholarship/ecco-fellowships-and-grants

### For further information contact:

European Crohn's and Colitis Organisation.

# European Molecular Biology Organization (EMBO)

PO Box 1022.40, D-69012 Heidelberg, Germany.

**Tel**:       (49) 622 188 910
**Email**:     embo@embo.org
**Website**:   www.embo.org
**Contact**:   Mr Yvonne Kaul, Communications Officer

The European Molecular Biology Organization (EMBO) was established in 1964 to promote biosciences in Europe. Today EMBO supports transnational mobility, training and exchange through initiatives such as fellowships, courses, workshops and its young investigator activities.

## European Molecular Biology Organisation Award for Communication in the Life Sciences

**Purpose**: To promote and reward public communication of the life sciences and their applications by practising scientists in Europe

**Eligibility**: Open to scientists working in active research in an area of life sciences at the time of nomination. Candidates must be working in Europe or Israel, and the criterion for consideration is excellence in public communication of science via any medium or activity

**Type**: Monetary award and medal

**Value**: €5,000 accompanied by a silver and gold medal inscribed with the winner's name

**Frequency**: Annual

**Application Procedure**: Applicants must apply using the forms available on the website

**No. of awards offered**: 27

**Closing Date**: 1 May

**Funding**: Private

**Contributor**: EMBO

**Additional Information**: For further information, email: Dr Andrew Moore at scisoc@embo.org

## For further information contact:

EMBO, Meyerhofstrasse 1, D-69117 Heidelberg, Germany.

**Tel**: (49) 622 188 91119
**Fax**: (49) 622 188 91200

## Long-Term Fellowship

**Purpose**: The EMBO Long-Term Fellowships are awarded for a period of up to two years and support post-doctoral research visits to laboratories throughout Europe and the world. International exchange is a key feature in the application process.

**Eligibility**: Applicants must hold a doctorate degree or equivalent at the start of the fellowship. Applicants who already hold a PhD degree at the time of application are eligible to apply only if they obtained their PhD degree during the two years prior to the date the application is complete. Applicants must have at least one first author publication accepted in or published in an international peer reviewed journal at the time of application. All applications must involve movement between countries (detailed information about mobility requirements is listed in guidelines).

**Level of Study**: doctorate

**Type**: Fellowships

**Value**: stipend & allowances over 2 years

**Length of Study**: 2 years

**Frequency**: Annual

**Closing Date**: 8 September

**Additional Information**: www.embo.org/funding-awards/fellowships/postdoctoral-fellowships#about

# European Science Foundation (ESF)

1 Quai Lezay Marnésia, F-67080 Strasbourg, France.

**Tel**:        (33) 3 88 76 71 25
**Email**:      sschott@esf.org
**Website**:    www.esf.org
**Contact**:    Ms Sabine Schott, Communication & Information Unit

The European Science Foundation (ESF) acts as a catalyst for the development of science by bringing together leading scientists and research funding agencies to debate, plan and implement pan-European initiatives.

## European Science Foundation Response of the Earth System to Impact Processes (IMPACT) Mobility Grants

**Purpose**: To initiate longer term research projects, encourage scientific exchanges, promote international and multi-disciplinary collaborations, and build strong ties between European institutions working on impact processes and their influence on the geological and biological evolution of the earth

**Eligibility**: Open to young scientists, graduate students or postdoctoral researchers. Established researchers can apply but must document that they do not have access to any other form of funding for this particular project. There are no restrictions regarding citizenship but applicants must be working in a European laboratory and applying for a stay in another European country

**Level of Study**: Graduate, Postdoctorate

**Type**: Other

**Country of Study**: Other

**Application Procedure**: Applicants must submit their personal details, institutional affiliation, brief curriculum vitae, a short invitation letter from the prospective host, a few keywords summarising the research, proposed investigation (maximum two printed pages in font size 12 or 600–1,000 words), significance of the investigation, justification of the collaborative research, and a detailed budget. One copy of the complete application must be sent to ESF and one to Dr Christian Koeberl at the University of Vienna

**Contributor**: The European Science Foundation

## For further information contact:

Institute of Geochemistry, University of Vienna, Althanstrae 14, A-1090, Vienna, Austria.

**Fax**:      (43) 131 336 7841
**Email**:    christian.koeberl@univie.ac.at

# European Society of Surgical Oncology (ESSO)

Avenue E. Mounier 83, B-1200 Brussels, Belgium.

**Tel**:       (32) 2 775 02 01
**Email**:     info@essoweb.org
**Website**:   www.esso-surgeonline.be
**Contact**:   Secretariat

ESSO was founded to advance the art, science and practice of surgery for the treatment of cancer. ESSO endeavours to ensure that the highest possible standard of surgical treatment is available to cancer patients throughout Europe by organizing congresses, granting fellowships and publishing the EJSO.

## European Society of Surgical Oncology Training Fellowships

**Purpose**: To provide young surgeons a chance to spend time in another specialist centre to either expand their experience or learn new techniques
**Eligibility**: Open to applicants who are specialists/specializing in surgery (or in any other medical discipline where cancer surgery is performed). Applicants must be less than 40 years of age. European applicants may choose to visit European or non-European units, while non-European applicants must choose to visit a European center
**Level of Study**: Postdoctorate
**Type**: Fellowship
**Value**: €2,000 for standard fellowships and €10,000 for the major international training fellowship
**Length of Study**: 1 to 3 months for standard fellowships and up to 1 year for the major training fellowship
**Frequency**: Annual
**Country of Study**: Any country
**Application Procedure**: Applicants must submit a full curriculum vitae with their application, together with a note of their career intentions. Applicants should also outline what they hope to gain from the training fellowship, including what specific experience is sought and how this will fit in with the applicant's career development. Applicants should provide details as to which institution they wish to visit, together with details of the clinical or research training opportunities that the department can offer. A letter of support from the applicant's head of department must be included and this can be in the form of a reference. A letter of support from the head of the department they wish to visit must also be supplied, indicating that the department to be visited will be in a position to provide the experience required by the applicant
**No. of awards offered**: 18
**Closing Date**: 31 October
**Additional Information**: Applicants must be or become ESSO members www.essoweb.org/fellowships/training-fellowships/

### For further information contact:

**Email**:     alberto.crespo@essoweb.org

# European Space Agency

8-10 rue Mario Nikis, Cedex 15, F-75738 Paris Cedex, France.

**Tel**:       (33) 153697654
**Email**:     ContactESA@esa.int
**Contact**:   European Space Agency

The European Space Agency (ESA) is Europe's gateway to space. Its mission is to shape the development of Europe's space capability and ensure that investment in space continues to deliver benefits to the citizens of Europe and the world.

## European Space Agency's Postdoctoral Internal Research Fellowship Programme

**Purpose**: ESA's postdoctoral Internal Research Fellowship programme (RIRF) aims to offer young scientists and engineers the possibility for two years to carry out research in a variety of disciplines related to space science, space applications or space technology
**Eligibility**: Applications are accepted from nationals of the ESA Member States and the European Cooperating States, together with Canada which has a cooperation agreement with ESA (see links on the right for details). Applicants must have recently completed their PhD in a field closely connected to space activities. The following requirements should be fulfilled in order for candidates to be qualified for the scholarship; Applications are accepted from nationals of the ESA Member States and the European Cooperating States, together with Canada which has a cooperation arrangement with ESA (see links on the right for information). Applicants needs to have just

recently finished their PhD in a field carefully linked to area activities

**Type**: Postdoctoral fellowship

**Value**: €3,000 to €3,800 per month depending on the location of the ESA Establishment

**Length of Study**: 2 years

**Study Establishment**: Space science, space applications or space technology

**Country of Study**: Any country

**Application Procedure**: Applications should be sent via the ESA online application form available in the 'how to apply' section of the opportunity. A cover letter, CV, and list of publications, with bibliographical references, should accompany the application, in one document (Word or PDF format). Each of the three referees named in the application form should send a reference letter to temp.htr-at-esa.int. No application sent after the closing date will be accepted

**Additional Information**: For more details please refer to the link scholarship-positions.com/esas-postdoctoral-internal-research-fellowship-programme/2017/09/23/

### For further information contact:

**Email**:   joerg.wehner@esa.int

## European Synchrotron Radiation Facility (ESRF)

6 rue Jules Horowitz, BP 220, F-38043 Grenoble Cedex, France.

**Tel**:        (33) 4 7688 2000
**Email**:    recruitment@esrf.fr
**Website**:  www.esrf.fr
**Contact**:  Ms Bénédicte Henry Canudas, Head of
              Recruitment

The European Synchrotron Radiation Facility (ESRF) supports scientists in the implementation of fundamental and applied research on the structure of matter in fields such as physics, chemistry, crystallography, Earth science, biology, medicine, surface science, and materials science.

## European Synchrotron Radiation Facility Postdoctoral Fellowships

**Purpose**: To enable postdoctoral fellows develop their own research programme and motivate them to collaborate with external users

**Eligibility**: Preference is given to PhD students who obtained their PhD less than 3 years ago

**Level of Study**: Postdoctorate

**Type**: Fellowship

**Value**: The annual gross salary is fixed at €40,910 for the first two years. This salary may be increased during the third year depending upon performance

**Length of Study**: 2-3 years

**Frequency**: Dependent on funds available

**Country of Study**: France

**Application Procedure**: Applicants must complete an application form, available on www.esrf.eu

**No. of awards offered**: 400

**Funding**: International office

**Contributor**: Public funds from 19 countries, mostly European

**Additional Information**: Member countries are Belgium, Denmark, Finland, France, Germany, Italy, the Netherlands, Norway, Spain, Sweden, Switzerland and the United Kingdom. New associated members are the Czech Republic, Israel, Portugal and the Republic of Hungary, Poland, Austria, and Slovakia www.esrf.eu/Jobs/Conditions/PostDocs

## European Synchrotron Radiation Facility Thesis Studentships

**Purpose**: To enable grant holders pursue a PhD at the ESRF and to enable young scientists acquire knowledge of the use of synchrotron radiation or its generation

**Eligibility**: Preference is given to member-country nationals, but other nationals may be accepted for the PhD's positions

**Level of Study**: Doctorate

**Value**: €2,280 per month. These amounts correspond to a gross remuneration and are subject to social charges and income tax in France

**Length of Study**: 2-3 years

**Frequency**: Dependent on funds available

**Study Establishment**: Universities

**Country of Study**: France

**Application Procedure**: Applicants must complete an application form, available on www.esrf.eu

**No. of awards offered**: 300

**Funding**: International office

**Contributor**: Public funds from 19 countries, mainly European

**Additional Information**: Member countries are Belgium, Denmark, Finland, France, Germany, Italy, the Netherlands, Norway, Spain, Sweden, Switzerland and the United Kingdom. Newly associated members are the Czech Republic, Israel, Portugal and the Republic of Hungary, Poland, Austria and Slovakia

# European University Institute (EUI)

Via dei Roccettini 9, I-50014 San Domenico di Fiesole, Italy.

**Tel**:        (39) 55 4685 373
**Email**:    lorenzo.ghezzi@eui.eu
**Website**: www.eui.eu
**Contact**: Mr Lorenzo GhezzI, Admissions officer

The European University Institute (EUI) is an international research institution set up by the Member States of the European Union. It focuses exclusively on doctoral and post-doctoral studies and offers a 4 year fully-funded PhD Programme in Economics, History and Civilization, Law and Political and Social Sciences and several Postdoctoral Fellowships opportunities.

## 150 Fully Funded PhD Degree Scholarships for International Students

**Purpose**: These scholarships are awarded in the field of Economics, Law, Political and Social Sciences and History
**Eligibility**: See the website
**Value**: These scholarships are fully funded
**Study Establishment**: Scholarships are awarded in the field of Economics, Law, Political and Social Sciences and History
**Country of Study**: Italy
**Application Procedure**: Applicants must submit an application and all required documents via the interactive online application form
**Closing Date**: 31 January
**Additional Information**: For more details please visit the website scholarship-positions.com/150-fully-funded-phd-scholarships-international-students-eui-italy/2016/10/22/scholarship-positions.com/fully-funded-phd-degree-scholarships-at-european-university-institute-italy/2020/01/21/

### For further information contact:

**Email**:    info@edu-active.com

## Doctor of Philosophy Scholarships in the Social Sciences

**Subjects**: The European University Institute (EUI) offers four-year fully-funded PhD programmes in Economics, History and Civilization, Law and Political and Social Sciences. Up to 150 scholarships are available for entry in September 2021, covering tuition and providing a monthly grant. The well-structured PhD programmes include closely supervised dissertation work, courses on methods and theory, topical workshops as well as academic and professional development training. Over 85% of EUI researchers successfully defend their thesis and more than 86% are either very satisfied or satisfied with their supervision. PhD researchers at the EUI enjoy: well-structured, fully funded PhD programmes; an academic environment that promotes research independence with close supervision, working groups, advanced training and courses; excellent research support facilities including an outstanding social science research Library, an on-site European Documentation Centre, and the Historical Archives of the European Union; a dynamic research community with visiting experts and high-level institutional and government actors from around the world; access to an international network of alumni holding posts in academia (60%), national-level institutions (7%), EU institutions (5%), international organisations (6%), the private sector (2%), law firms and NGOs (8.5%), and banks (1%)* (*Alumni Destination Survey 2018); an international, multi-lingual and culturally diverse campus near Florence, Italy. The European University Institute is an international postgraduate teaching and research institute. It offers advanced academic training for doctoral and postdoctoral researchers and fosters research in fields that are of particular interest for the development of Europe. The Institute is composed of four departments€"Economics, History and Civilization, Law, and Political and Social Sciences; the Robert Schuman Centre for Advanced Studies; the Max Weber Programme for Postdoctoral Studies; the School of Transnational Governance; and the Historical Archives of the European Union. Grants and tuition fees for PhD candidates are covered by the national grant-awarding authorities of our contracting states.
**Purpose**: Four-year fully-funded PhD programmes in History and the Social Sciences
**Eligibility**: Eligibility is determined by the national grant-awarding authorities of EUI contracting states. For more detailed information visit www.eui.eu/phd.
**Level of Study**: Doctorate
**Type**: Scholarship
**Length of Study**: Four years
**Frequency**: Annual
**Study Establishment**: European University Institute
**Country of Study**: Italy
**Application Procedure**: EUI's online application is open from early November to 31 January. For further information visit www.eui.eu/phd
**No. of awards offered**: Up to 150
**Closing Date**: 31 January
**Funding**: Government
**Contributor**: EUI contracting states and associate member states
**Additional Information**: The EUI community consists of over 900 academic staff and researchers from over 70 countries. www.eui.eu/phd

**For further information contact:**

European University Institute, Via della Badia dei Roccettini, 9. 50014 Fiesole FI, Italy.

## Evangelical Lutheran Church in America (ELCA)

Division for Ministry, 8765 West Higgins Road, Chicago, IL 60631-4195, United States of America.

| | |
|---|---|
| Tel: | (1) 773 380 2700 |
| Email: | pwilder@elca.org |
| Website: | www.elca.org |
| Contact: | Mr Pat Wilder, Executive Secretary |

## Evangelical Lutheran Church in America Educational Grant Program

**Eligibility**: Open to members of the Evangelical Lutheran Church in America who are enroled in an accredited graduate institution for study in a PhD, EdD, or ThD programme in a theological area appropriate to seminary teaching. Priority is given to women and minority students
**Level of Study**: Doctorate
**Type**: Grant
**Value**: Grants up to US$4,000 per individual, per year are awarded
**Length of Study**: Grants are awarded for a maximum of 4 years with a 5th-year award for the dissertation
**Frequency**: Annual
**Country of Study**: United States of America
**Application Procedure**: Applications are available online at www.elca.org/en/Our-Work/Leadership/Seminaries/Educational-Grant-Program in January. Two recommendations are required for each applicant
**No. of awards offered**: 72
**Closing Date**: 15 April
**Funding**: Private
**Additional Information**: www.elca.org/grants

## Evonik Foundation

Rellinghauserstrasse 1-11, D-45128 Essen, Germany.

| | |
|---|---|
| Tel: | (49) 201/177 4326 |
| Email: | info@evonik-stiftung.de |
| Contact: | Evonik Foundation |

The Evonik Foundation exclusively supports natural science students preparing master's, doctoral, and postdoctoral theses. Scholarships are only awarded for the scholarship focus defined for the year in question.

## Evonik Stiftung Scholarships

**Purpose**: The Evonik Foundation focuses on promoting education and science. The goal of Evonik Foundation is to sponsor talented up-and-coming researchers
**Eligibility**: Prerequisites for the award of a scholarship: The topic of your research project must coincide with one of the topics in our annual scholarship focus. 1. Your scientific research is being conducted in a well-known, chemically oriented working group at a German university or a non-university research institution. 2. You can provide proof of excellent academic performance. 3. You are unable to sufficiently fund your intended scientific study courses with means provided by you, your parents or other parties
**Value**: Bachelor's and master's theses: six months, €250-600 month Doctoral program: two years (option to extend), €1,400 month. In addition, applications can be submitted for funding of the purchase of research literature and attendance of scientific congresses. Postdoctoral studies: one year's funding is decided on a case-by-case basis
**Country of Study**: Germany
**Application Procedure**: Please check the website
**Closing Date**: 28 February
**Additional Information**: Please check the link for more details scholarship-positions.com/evonik-stiftung-scholarships-for-german-students/2018/01/23 www.research-in-germany.org/en/infoservice/newsletter/newsletter-2018/january-2018/evonik-foundation-scholarships.html

## EuroTech Universities Alliance

Square de Meeûs 23, 8th Floor B-1000 Brussels, Belgium.

| | |
|---|---|
| Email: | info@eurotech-universities.eu |
| Contact: | EuroTech Universities Alliance |

The EuroTech Universities Alliance is a strategic partnership of four leading European universities of science & technology: Technical University of Denmark (DTU)

## Collaborative Offline & Online Platform for Research EuroTechPostdoc Fellowships for International Students at European Universities

**Purpose**: The EuroTechPostdoc Programme is a postdoctoral fellowship programme for young experienced researchers who have already demonstrated excellence and potential in their field of research

**Eligibility**: Applicants of all nationalities are eligible. Please refer the website for more details

**Level of Study**: Postdoctorate

**Type**: Postdoctoral fellowship

**Value**: The fellowship consists of a monthly salary for the postdoctoral researcher based on the salary scale of the host institution and is granted for a period of twenty-four (24) months maximum. Prolongation of the fellowship is not possible

**Length of Study**: up to 24 months

**Frequency**: Annual, if funds are available

**Study Establishment**: Applicants may apply within one of the five focus research areas of the EuroTech Universities Alliance: Health & Bio Engineering Smart & Urban Mobility Data Science & Engineering High-Performance Computing Entrepreneurship & Innovation

**Country of Study**: Any country

**Application Procedure**: Please use the following templates for your application: 1. Project proposal template. 2. CV and publications template. 3. Ethics self-assessment

**No. of awards offered**: 87

**Closing Date**: 28 February

**Funding**: Government

**Contributor**: European Commission: This project has received funding from the European Union's Horizon research and innovation programme under the Marie Sklodowska-Curie grant agreement No 754462

**Additional Information**: For more details, please browse the below website, scholarship-positions.com/80-eurotechpost doc-fellowships-international-students-european-universities www.scholarshipsads.com/category/country/europe-scholar ships/

### For further information contact:

Arcisstrasse 21, D-80333, Munich, Germany.

**Tel**:     (49) 892 892 2813
**Email**:   postdoc@eurotech-universities.eu

## EuroTechPostdoc

**Purpose**: The EuroTech Universities Alliance invites highly talented experienced researchers to submit interdisciplinary collaborative research project proposals for one of the fellowships provided by the EuroTechPostdoc Programme. The Programme is a postdoctoral fellowship for young experienced researchers who have already demonstrated excellence and potential in their field of research. It provides its fellows exceptional international research and career development opportunities to promote their outstanding individual potential into a distinct, innovative and competitive profile of a researcher. The EuroTechPostdoc Programme is co-funded by the European Commission under its framework programme Horizon. All fellows of the EuroTechPostdoc programme will be Marie Sklodowska-Curie Fellows. Four of the six universities of the EuroTech Universities Alliance - Technical University of Denmark (DTU), Ecole Polytechnique Fédérale de Lausanne (EPFL), Eindhoven University of Technology (TU/e) and Technical University of Munich (TUM) - will grant 80 fellowships divided over two calls for experienced researchers. Per call, each university grants 10 fellowships for a 24-month period to collaborative and interdisciplinary research projects across the Alliance

**Eligibility**: Experience: Applicants must hold a PhD degree from a recognised university or plan to obtain a PhD degree by the time of employment or have at least four years of full-time equivalent research experience. Mobility: Researchers may not have resided or carried out their main activity (work, studies, etc.) in the country of the host university for more than twelve (12) months in the three (3) years immediately before the call deadline. Time spent as part of a procedure for obtaining refugee status under the Geneva Convention, compulsory national service and/or short stays such as holidays are not taken into account. Institutional Endorsement: Support from both the host and co-host. Please approach them early on. A standard process will be provided in the application portal. You will have to provide the email address of your supervisor and co-supervisor (please check spelling). The programme management office will approach host and co-host professors and ask them to provide the institutional endorsement. The Institutional endorsement comprises a confirmation of the availability of infrastructure, supervision and resources to successfully complete the project. Applicants must be able to carry out full time research during the fellowship period (parental leave, sick leave, military leave and care leave are accepted). Research direction follows the H2020 Ethics

**Type**: A variable number of fellowships

**Value**: complete salary covered (depending on country)

**Country of Study**: Other

**Application Procedure**: Applications to be supported via online participants portal by the respective deadline. Applications are assessed against criteria addressing the candidate's ability and commitment to research, the quality of the proposed research project as well as the synergy between the research proposed and the identified host and co-host, and the impact of the research project on the career development of the candidate. More information can be found here: postdoc. eurotech-universities.eu/for-applicants/#eval

**Closing Date**: 28 February

**Additional Information**: Please check our online presence: postdoc.eurotech-universities.eu/
postdoc.eurotech-universities.eu/

# F

## Fahs-Beck Fund for Research and Experimentation

### Doctoral Dissertation Grant Program (Fahs-Beck Scholars)

**Subjects**: Problems in the functioning or well being of children, adults, couples, families, or communities, or about interventions designed to prevent or alleviate such problems.
**Purpose**: To help support dissertation expenses of doctoral students in the United States and Canada whose studies have the potential for adding significantly to knowledge about problems in the functioning or well being of children, adults, couples, families, or communities, or about interventions designed to prevent or alleviate such problems.
**Eligibility**: Applicants must be enrolled in an accredited doctoral program in the United States or Canada. The sponsoring organization must agree to accept administrative responsibility for the project and submit required financial forms and reports to the Fund.
**Type**: Grant
**Value**: Up to US$5,000
**Country of Study**: United States of America or Canada
**Application Procedure**: Apply online
**Closing Date**: 1 April and 1 November
**Additional Information**: www.fahsbeckfund.org/grant_programs.html

## Fanconi Anemia Research Fund, Inc.

1301 Willamette Street, Suite 200, Eugene, OR 97401, United States of America.

**Tel**: (1) 541 687 4658
**Email**: info@fanconi.org

**Website**: www.fanconi.org
**Contact**: Ms Pamela Norr, Executive Director

To support research into effective treatments and a cure for Fanconi anemia.

### Fanconi Anemia Research Fund Award

**Purpose**: To support research into effective treatments and a cure for Fanconi anemia
**Eligibility**: There are no restrictions on eligibility in terms of nationality, residency, age, gender, sexual orientation, race, religion or politics
**Level of Study**: Doctorate, Postdoctorate
**Type**: Award
**Value**: range from US$25,000 - US$250,000
**Length of Study**: 1 to 2 years
**Country of Study**: Any country
**Application Procedure**: Applicants must email to obtain information and application forms
**No. of awards offered**: 29
**Closing Date**: 15 August
**Funding**: Foundation
**Additional Information**: The Internal Revenue Service has confirmed that the Fund is not a private foundation for the purposes of tax-exempt donations but a public charitable organization under 501(c) 3 of the Internal Revenue Code www.fanconi.org/explore/international-fa-support-grants

### For further information contact:

**Tel**: (1) 541 687 4658
**Email**: grants@fanconi.org

© Springer Nature Limited 2020
Palgrave Macmillan (ed.), *The Grants Register 2021*,
https://doi.org/10.1057/978-1-349-95988-4

# Federation University Australia

Vice-Chancellor's Office, P.O. Box 663, University Drive, Mt Helen, VIC 3350, Australia.

**Tel**:      (61) 5327 9000
**Website**:  federation.edu.au
**Contact**:  Sue Read

The University of Ballarat is Australia's only regional, multisector University acknowledged for its excellence in education, training, and research, committed to providing high quality services to students, the community, and the industry. It provides educational and training programs from apprenticeships, certificates and diplomas to postgraduate qualifications, masters, and doctorates by research. International students at the University come from over 25 different countries to participate in a diverse range of TAFE and higher education programmes. The University is proud of its track record in business innovation and entrepreneurship, research, consulting, and educational programs, and promoting new technology in products and services through scientific and industrial research.

## Australian Postgraduate Award

**Purpose**: To support postgraduate students undertaking research in either a Doctorate or Masters by Research program
**Eligibility**: Open to candidates who have a First Class (Honours) Degree or equivalent. The APA is open to candidates who have received a Masters by Research (for Doctorate applicants) and/or a Honours degree (First Class/H1A) or equivalent
**Level of Study**: Doctorate, Postgraduate, Research
**Type**: Scholarship
**Value**: AU$26,288 per year, Indexed annually
**Frequency**: Annual
**Study Establishment**: The University of Ballarat
**Country of Study**: Australia
**Application Procedure**: Application forms and further information about the Scholarships process can be found at federation.edu.au/research/research-degrees/scholarships
**No. of awards offered**: 130
**Closing Date**: 3 December
**Funding**: Government
**Additional Information**: It is required that the successful applicant commence studies in the year the scholarship was awarded for. Studies should commence no earlier than 1 February, and no later than 31 August

### For further information contact:

**Tel**:    (61) 3 5327 9508
**Fax**:    (61) 3 5327 9602
**Email**:  HDResearch@ballarat.edu.au

## Doctoral Research on Family Relationships

**Purpose**: To undertake doctoral research on family relationships
**Eligibility**: Open to Australian citizens or permanent residents who have achieved First Class (Honours) or equivalent
**Level of Study**: Postgraduate
**Type**: Scholarship
**Value**: AU$19,231
**Length of Study**: 3 years and 6 months
**Frequency**: Annual
**Study Establishment**: The University of Ballarat
**Country of Study**: Australia
**Application Procedure**: Check website for further details
Applications are open from 25 July
**Closing Date**: 30 November

### For further information contact:

**Tel**:    (61) 3 5327 9818
**Email**:  j.mcdonald@ballarat.edu.au

## International Excellence Scholarship

**Purpose**: The International Excellence scholarships commencing 2020 are equivalent to 16% of your tuition fees.
**Eligibility**: 1. A prospective international student. 2. Eligible to study in Australia with a student visa. 3. Not have accepted, or be in receipt of, any other FedUni scholarship or bursary, or any other reduced fee arrangements at the time of entry to the University (with the exception of Federation University Accommodation Scholarships). 4. Not be in receipt of credit transfers or exemptions. 5. Meet minimum academic English entry requirement and offered with no more than 10 weeks English pathway program (e.g. academic IELTS overall 5.5 with no band less than 5.5 for general programs);. 6. Enrolling in an eligible program. 7. Enrolling in a program at a higher level than your existing qualification. 8. Studying full-time at a home campus of Federation University Australia. Home campuses are located in Ballarat, Gippsland and Berwick.

These scholarships do not apply to students studying at a Federation University Partner Provider teaching location.

**Length of Study**: The scholarship will apply for the normal duration of your program.

**Closing Date**: 31 August

## University of Ballarat Part Postgraduate Research Scholarship

**Eligibility**: Open to citizens of Australia or permanent residents who have achieved First Class (Honours) or equivalent

**Level of Study**: Doctorate, Postgraduate, Research

**Type**: Scholarship

**Value**: AU$22,500

**Length of Study**: 3 years (PhD and Professional Doctorate) and 1.5 years (Masters)

**Frequency**: Annual

**Study Establishment**: University of Ballarat

**Country of Study**: Australia

**Application Procedure**: Check website for further details. Applications are open from 03 January

**Closing Date**: 31 October

**Funding**: Government, Commercial

**Additional Information**: The study should start no earlier than 1 February

### For further information contact:

**Tel**:       (61) 3 5327 9508
**Fax**:      (61) 3 5327 9602
**Email**:    s.murphy@ballarat.edu.au

## Fellowship Program in Academic Medicine

National Medical Fellowship, Inc., 254 West 31st Street, New York, NY 10001, United States of America.

**Contact**:    Awards Committee

## Akhtarali H. Tobaccowala Fellowship

**Purpose**: The fellowship was established in the memory of Akhtarali H. Tobaccowala who was a 1952 graduate of the Booth school

**Eligibility**: The fellowship which offer tuition support is available for students of Booth's full-time MBA program

**Level of Study**: Postgraduate

**Type**: Scholarship

**Value**: Upto US$25,000 per annum

**Frequency**: Annual

**Country of Study**: Any country

**Application Procedure**: There is no formal application process

**Funding**: Private

### For further information contact:

The Tobaccowala Foundation, 35. Printing House, Police Court Lane (Behind Handloom House) Fort, Mumbai, Maharashtra 400 001, India.

**Tel**:       (91) 22 22640386
**Email**:    tobaccowalafoundation@gmail.com

## Therla Drake Postgraduate Scholarships

**Purpose**: The scholarship is for postgraduate classical performance overseas study and application should be made in the year for which the project is planned. While the terms of the bequest are that preference be given to a piano student, other applicants will be considered. The scholarship is open to both domestic and international students

**Eligibility**: This scholarship is open to both domestic and international students. The scholarship may be held in; conjunction with other awards

**Level of Study**: Postgraduate

**Type**: Scholarship

**Value**: US$12,000 subject to funds availability

**Frequency**: Annual

**Country of Study**: Any country

**Application Procedure**: Applicants will complete the online application by the closing date. No late applications will be accepted. Applicants should provide the following supporting documentation: 1. A letter outlining the project and its benefit to your career plans. 2. A detailed budget. 3. Copies of any communication with the host person(s) or organisation (s) overseas. 4. A supporting statement from the principal supervisor. In order to proceed with the application, kindly check the below link. www.victoria.ac.nz/study/student-finance/scholarships

**Closing Date**: 31 March

**Funding**: Private

**Additional Information**: www.wgtn.ac.nz/scholarships/current/therle-drake-postgraduate-scholarship

**For further information contact:**

Scholarships Office, Victoria University of Wellington, PO Box 600, Wellington 6140, New Zealand.

**Email:**    scholarships-office@vuw.ac.nz

# Ferrari

Direzione e stablimento Abetone int. 4, ITA MO 41053, Maranello, Italy.

**Tel:**        (39) 536 949111
**Email:**     carrerservice@mip.polimi.it
**Website:**   www.ferrariworld.com

Born in 1947, Ferrari has always produced vehicles at its current site and has maintained its direction. It has progressively widened it range using visionary planning to both on a design level and on the quality of work produced.

## Ferrari Innovation Team Project Scholarship

**Purpose**: To create members of a new and innovative team for the new and innovative cars of the future
**Eligibility**: Knowledge of ergonomics will be considered a plus
**Level of Study**: Postgraduate, Professional development
**Type**: Scholarship
**Value**: €25,000 and all accommodation and training
**Length of Study**: 1 year
**Frequency**: Annual
**Study Establishment**: Ferrari Spa
**Country of Study**: Italy
**Closing Date**: 25 May
**Funding**: Commercial
**Contributor**: Ferrari

**For further information contact:**

**Email:**    cdozio@ferrari.it

# Fight for Sight

## Fight for Sight

**Purpose**: Fight for Sight is one of the leading United Kingdom charities dedicated to funding pioneering research to prevent sight loss and treat eye disease

**Eligibility**: Young (under 40) ophthalmologists and scientists working in the field of ophthalmology in the United Kingdom - awarded recognition of the completion of a significant piece of research completed within 18 months prior to the closing date
**Level of Study**: Postgraduate
**Type**: Grant
**Value**: £5,000
**Frequency**: Annual
**Country of Study**: Any country
**Closing Date**: February
**Funding**: Foundation
**Additional Information**: www.eyedocs.co.uk/ophthalmology-research-awards/1079-fight-for-sight-award

**For further information contact:**

**Email:**    training@rcophth.ac.uk

## PhD Studentships

**Purpose**: Fight for Sight's mission is to stop sight loss by funding the highest quality medical research. To help us achieve our goals we are committed to encouraging new and highly motivated graduates to take up and pursue a career in ophthalmic and vision research.
**Eligibility**: 1. Applications must be made by the potential PhD Supervisor(s). 2. Please note that Fight for Sight will only accept one PhD Studentship application from the same individual acting either as Supervisor or Co-Supervisor. 3. Supervisors must be affiliated with UK academic or medical institutions. 4. The Student must be attached to a UK institution but the research can be undertaken in the UK and/or overseas. 5. Supervisor(s) must have a contract which extends beyond the termination date of the PhD Studentship. 6. The Student appointed must not be medically or otherwise clinically qualified professionals. Clinically active individuals should consider the MRC / Fight for Sight Clinical Research Training Fellowships. 7. The scheme does not cover funding gaps for studentships already started. 8. The proposed project must aim to stop or reduce sight loss.
**Level of Study**: Postgraduate
**Type**: Studentship
**Value**: Up to £100,000
**Length of Study**: three years
**Closing Date**: 11 June
**Additional Information**: www.fightforsight.org.uk/apply-for-funding/funding-opportunities/phd-studentships/

**For further information contact:**

**Email:**    grants@fightforsight.org.uk

## Finnish National Agency for Education - EDUFI

Hakaniemenranta 6, P.O. Box 380, 00531 Helsinki, Finland.

Tel:          (358) 29 533 1000
Website:   www.oph.fi/

In Finland, the national administration of education and training has a two-tier structure. The Ministry of Education and Culture is the highest authority and is responsible for all publicly funded education in Finland. The Ministry is responsible for preparing educational legislation, all necessary decisions and its share of the state budget for the Government. The Finnish National Agency for Education is the national development agency responsible for early childhood education and care, pre-primary, basic, general and vocational upper secondary education as well as for adult education and training. Higher education is the responsibility of the Ministry of Education and Culture.

### EDUFI Fellowship

Purpose: The EDUFI Fellowships programme is open to young Doctoral level students and researchers from all countries and from all academic fields who wish to pursue their Doctorate (or Double Doctorate) at a Finnish university. Master's level studies or post-doctoral studies/research are not supported in the programme.
Eligibility: You can apply for the fellowship grant if 1. you work as a researcher or a teacher in a Finnish university department 2. you will be hosting the research fellow 3. you will commit to common objectives with the research fellow 4. you will offer facilities and equipment for the use of the research fellow 5. you will supervise the research. 6. You can apply for a fellowship for a non-Finnish post-graduate (post Master's degree) student or a young researcher that you will invite to Finland or who has been in Finland for a maximum of one year before applying for the fellowship. The EDUFI Fellowship is available to all foreign nationals and all fields of study.
Level of Study: Masters Degree
Type: Scholarships
Value: The scholarship period may vary from 3 to 12 months. The monthly allowance is €1,500. The scholarship is intended to cover living expenses in Finland for a single person. No additional allowance for housing is paid. Expenses due to international travel to and from Finland are not covered by EDUFI.
Frequency: Annual
Country of Study: Finland
Application Procedure: You can fill in the EDUFI Fellowship application form in Finnish, Swedish or English. The application form comes with instructions on how to fill it and a list of required annexes. Please post two copies of the form and annexes. Address: EDUFI, EDUFI Fellowship, P.O. Box 380, 00531 HELSINKI.
No. of awards offered: Not specified
Additional Information: www.oph.fi/en/development/edufi-fellowship

## Five Strong Scholarship Foundation

### 5 Strong Scholarship

Purpose: The 5 Strong Scholarship Foundation is a team of experienced educators that have over 30 years of experience helping minority students graduate from high school and get into college. We have teamed up to form a foundation that's going to be dedicated to building cohorts of 5 college ready scholars and placing them on the campuses of Historically Black Colleges and Universities
Eligibility: 1. Must be a graduating high school senior. 2. Have a minimum 2.5 GPA and a minimum ACT: 19/SAT: 980 (verbal and math only). 3. Must commit to attend all of the 5 Strong College Prep sessions (bi-monthly). 4. Must reside in the Metro Atlanta Area (Fulton, DeKalb, Cobb, Atlanta, Clayton Counties)
Level of Study: Graduate
Type: Scholarship
Value: US$50,000
Frequency: Annual
Country of Study: Any country
No. of awards offered: 20
Closing Date: 1 December
Funding: Foundation
Additional Information: www.scholarships.com/financial-aid/college-scholarships/scholarships-by-type/full-tuition-scholarships/5-strong-scholarship/

### For further information contact:

Andrew H. Ragland, 103 Pinegate Road, Peachtree City, GA 30269, United States of America.

Tel:          (1) 770 873 6621
Email:     5strongscholars@gmail.com

## Flinders University

GPO Box 2100, Adelaide, SA 5001, Australia.

Tel:          (61) 8 8201 3911
Email:     www.person@flinders.edu.au
Website:   www.flinders.edu.au

Flinders University is an integral part of Australia's respected higher education system and makes an important economic and social contribution to South Australia and to the nation. Flinders has a high research profile and consistently ranks among Australia's top universities on a per capita basis for research. It emphasizes innovation and excellence in its educational programs and researches across a wide range of disciplines.

## Advanced Community Care Scholarship

**Purpose**: To undertake a research project within the Faculty of Health Sciences related to the practical clinical, organizational and financial implications of home-based alternatives to hospital care

**Eligibility**: Applicants must be Australian citizens or permanent residents of Australia and have completed at least 4 years of tertiary education studies at a high level of achievement and have an appropriate Honours 1 or high 2A (or equivalent) undergraduate degree. They must enroll as full-time students (part-time awards are available in certain circumstances)

**Level of Study**: Postgraduate

**Type**: Scholarship

**Value**: AU$19,616 per year

**Length of Study**: 3 years

**Application Procedure**: Applicants must obtain the application kits from the Higher Degree Administration and Scholarships Office or can download it from the scholarships website

**Closing Date**: 31 October

**Contributor**: Advanced Community Care Association

### For further information contact:

**Tel**:      (61) 8 8201 3115
**Email**:    scholarships@flinders.edu.au

## Australian Health Inequities Program Research Scholarship

**Purpose**: To address health inequities, understand the social determinants of health and analyze policy and program strategies that aim to reduce inequities

**Eligibility**: Applicants should be Australian citizens, permanent residents of Australia or New Zealand citizens and have completed at least four years of tertiary education studies at a high level of achievement and have an appropriate Honours 1 or high 2A (or equivalent) undergraduate degree. They should enroll as full-time students (a part-time award may be available in certain circumstances) and should commence a Doctorate by research

**Level of Study**: Postgraduate

**Type**: Scholarship

**Value**: AU$19,616 per year

**Length of Study**: 3 years

**Application Procedure**: Applicants can obtain the application kits from the Higher Degree Administration and Scholarships Office or download it from Flinders University scholarships website

**Closing Date**: 31 October

### For further information contact:

Department of Public Health.

**Tel**:      (61) 8 8204 5983
**Email**:    fran.baum@flinders.edu.au

## Australian Health Inequities Program University Research Scholarship

**Purpose**: To address health inequities, to understand the social determinants of health and to analyze policy and program strategies that aim to reduce them

**Eligibility**: Applicants must be Australian citizens, permanent residents of Australia or New Zealand citizens and have completed at least 4 years of tertiary education studies at a high level of achievement and have an appropriate Honours 1 or high 2A (or equivalent) undergraduate degree. They should enroll as full–time students (a part–time award may be available in certain circumstances) and should commence a Doctorate by research

**Level of Study**: Postgraduate

**Type**: Scholarship

**Value**: AU$19,616 per year

**Length of Study**: 3 years

**Application Procedure**: Applicants can obtain the application kits from the Higher Degree Administration and Scholarships Office or download it from Flinders University scholarships website. It is essential to consult Prof. Baum or Dr. Newman before submitting an application

**Closing Date**: 31 October

### For further information contact:

Department of Public Health.

**Tel**:      (61) 8 8204 5983
**Email**:    fran.baum@flinders.edu.au

## Diamond Jubilee Bursary

**Purpose**: It is helpful for women, who are Australian citizens or permanent residents, enrolled in a postgraduate Masters degree (by research or including a thesis) at a South Australian university

**Eligibility**: Applicants: 1. Women students who are Australian citizens or permanent residents. 2. Must be studying at a South Australian University for a postgraduate award which is classified. 3. at Masters Degree level. This must be by research or include a thesis component. 4. Must have completed at least six months full time equivalent of their masters program. 5. Must have a good undergraduate academic record. 6. Must not be in full time paid employment or on fully paid leave during the tenure of the Scholarship. 7. Must not have received a scholarship or award in the same category

**Level of Study**: Postgraduate

**Type**: Bursary

**Value**: AU$4,000

**Length of Study**: 1 year

**Frequency**: Annual

**Country of Study**: Australia

**Application Procedure**: Application forms can be downloaded from the AFUW-SA website listed below. 1. Your application must reach the Trust Fund's secretarial service by 29 March. 2. Scholarship Type: postgraduate, academic merit, financial, commencing, continuing

**Closing Date**: 31 March

**Funding**: Private

**Additional Information**: Selection of winners is based primarily on academic merit, but also on the importance of the purpose for which the scholarship will be used to the progress or completion of the degree, on referees' report, on financial need as well as community activities and other interests www.afuwsa-trust.com.au/dj-scholarships/

### For further information contact:

The AFUW-SA Inc. Trust Fund, 213 Greenhill Road, Eastwood, SA 5063 Australia.

**Email**:     internationalapply@flinders.edu.au

## Faculty of Science and Engineering Research Awards (FSERA)

**Purpose**: To enable students to pursue a Masters Degree by research or Doctorate by research in the Faculty of Science and Engineering

**Eligibility**: Applicants should have achieved Honours 1 or equivalent, or Honours 2a or equivalent. Only citizens of Australia or New Zealand or permanent residents can apply

**Level of Study**: Graduate, Postgraduate

**Type**: Research award

**Value**: AU$19,616 per year

**Length of Study**: 2 years if masters or 3 years if PhD

**Country of Study**: Australia

**Application Procedure**: Applicants must apply directly to the university

**Closing Date**: 31 October

**Additional Information**: scholarship-positions.com/faculty-science-engineering-research-scholarships-fsera-flinders-university-australia/2017/05/26/

### For further information contact:

**Tel**:       (61) 8 8201 3115

**Fax**:      (61) 8 8201 5175

**Email**:    scholarships@flinders.edu.au

## Flinders University Research Scholarships (FURS)

**Purpose**: To enable suitably qualified applicants to proceed to a full-time Masters by research or Doctorate by research

**Eligibility**: Applicants must have achieved Honours 1 or equivalent, or Honours 2a or equivalent. Only citizens of Australia or New Zealand or permanent residents can apply

**Level of Study**: Postgraduate

**Type**: Scholarship

**Value**: AU$19,616

**Length of Study**: 2 years for masters or 3 years for PhD

**Frequency**: Annual

**Country of Study**: Australia

**Application Procedure**: Applicants must apply directly to the university

**Closing Date**: 31 October

**Additional Information**: www.australianuniversities.com.au/scholarships/guide/8495-flinders-university-research-scholarship-furs.html

### For further information contact:

**Tel**:       (61) 8 8201 3115

**Fax**:      (61) 8 8201 5175

**Email**:    scholarships@flinders.edu.au

## FMC Foundation Pink Ribbon Ball Committee Breast Cancer Research Scholarship

**Purpose**: To undertake a breast cancer biomedical research project within the Faculty of Health Sciences

**Eligibility**: Applicants must be Australian citizens or permanent residents of Australia and have completed at least 4 years of tertiary education studies at a high level of achievement and have an appropriate Honours 1 or high 2A (or equivalent) undergraduate degree. They must enroll as full-time students (part-time awards are available in certain circumstances) and must commence a Doctorate by research

**Level of Study**: Postgraduate

**Type**: Scholarship

**Value**: AU$25,000 plus up to AU$2,000 per year for conference travel and consumables

**Length of Study**: 3 years

**Frequency**: Annual

**Application Procedure**: Applicants can obtain the application kits from the Higher Degree Administration and Scholarships Office and can download it from the scholarship website

**Closing Date**: 31 October

**Contributor**: Flinders Medical Centre Foundation

**Additional Information**: breastcancernow.org/get-involved/social-events/pink-ribbon-ball-london

#### For further information contact:

**Tel**: (61) 8 8204 4100

**Email**: johnno.oliver@flinders.edu.au

### FMC Foundation Research Scholarship

**Purpose**: To undertake a health-related project within the Faculty of Health Sciences

**Eligibility**: Applicants should be Australian citizens or permanent residents of Australia and have completed at least 4 years of tertiary education studies at a high level of achievement and have an appropriate Honours 1 or high 2A (or equivalent) undergraduate degree. They should enroll as full-time students (part-time awards are available in certain circumstances) and should commence a Doctorate by research

**Level of Study**: Postgraduate

**Type**: Scholarship

**Value**: AU$25,000 plus up to AU$2,000 per year for conference travel and consumables

**Length of Study**: 3 years

**Frequency**: Annual

**Application Procedure**: Applicants can obtain application kits from the Higher Degree Administration and Scholarships Office or download from the scholarships website

**Closing Date**: 31 October

**Funding**: Foundation

**Contributor**: FMC Foundation

**Additional Information**: www.flinders.edu.au/scholarships-system/index.cfm/scholarships/display/a0502

#### For further information contact:

**Tel**: (61) 8 8204 4100

**Email**: johnno.oliver@flinders.edu.au

### Honours/Masters Scholarship for AI, User Interface or Robotics

**Purpose**: To enable students to undertake an Honours or Masters project in the Artificial Intelligence Laboratory in the School of Informatics and Engineering at Flinders University

**Eligibility**: Applicants must have Australian citizenship or permanent residence, plus distinction-level completion of the requirements of 3 years of undergraduate degree in cognitive science, computer science, mathematics, or engineering program

**Level of Study**: Graduate

**Type**: Scholarship

**Value**: AU$5,000

**Application Procedure**: Check website for further details

**Closing Date**: 15 November

#### For further information contact:

**Email**: David.Powers@flinders.edu.au

### Investigation of the Human Intestinal Nervous System

**Purpose**: To support investigation of the human intestinal nervous system

**Eligibility**: Applicants must be Australian citizens or permanent residents of Australia and have completed at least 4 years of tertiary education studies at a high level of achievement and have an appropriate undergraduate medical degree. They should enroll as full-time students and commence a Doctorate by research

**Level of Study**: Graduate

**Type**: Scholarship

**Value**: AU$29,172

**Length of Study**: 3 years

**Frequency**: Annual

**Application Procedure**: Applicants can obtain application kits from the Higher Degree Administration and Scholarships Office or can download from the scholarships website

**Closing Date**: 31 October

#### For further information contact:

**Tel**: (61) 8 8204 4253

**Email**: david.wattchow@flinders.edu.au

### May Mills Scholarship for Women

**Purpose**: The purpose of the scholarship is to encourage women who have experienced significant interruptions to their studies due to family responsibilities, to proceed to a research higher degree at Flinders University. The scholarship covers programs of study that will qualify women for admission to a research higher degree, such as honours, postgraduate coursework studies or bridging studies programs.

**Eligibility**: Applicants must be female citizens or permanent residents of Australia

**Level of Study**: Graduate, Postgraduate

**Type**: Scholarship

**Value**: Maximum AU$9,000 per year

**Length of Study**: 1 year

**Frequency**: Annual

**Country of Study**: Australia

**Application Procedure**: Applicants may consult the scholarship website

**Closing Date**: 31 January

**Contributor**: Flinders University

**Additional Information**: www.scholarshipcare.com/may-mills-scholarship-for-women/

### For further information contact:

Tel: (51) 8 82013143
Fax: (51) 8 8201 5175
Email: scholarships@flinders.edu.au

## Multi Scale Biomechanical Investigations of the Intervertebral Disc

**Purpose**: To undertake a challenging program of research that combines both analytical (finite element analysis) and experimental

**Eligibility**: Applicants must be Australian or international students who have completed at least 4 years of tertiary education studies at a high level of achievement and have an appropriate Honours 1 or high 2A (or equivalent) undergraduate degree in mechanical/biomedical/civil/chemical engineering or related fields

**Level of Study**: Postgraduate

**Type**: Scholarship

**Value**: AU$25,313

**Length of Study**: 3 years

**Frequency**: Annual

**Application Procedure**: Applicants can obtain the application kits from the Higher Degree Administration and Scholarships Office at Flinders University

**Closing Date**: 1 June

### For further information contact:

Tel: (61) 8 8275 1751
Email john.costi@rgh.sa.gov.au

## National Health and Medical Research Council Centre of Clinical Eye Research: PhD Scholarships

**Purpose**: To conduct clinical research in the major blinding diseases – cataract, glaucoma, diabetic retinopathy and corneal disease

**Eligibility**: Applicants must be Australian citizens, permanent residents of Australia or New Zealand citizens and have completed at least 4 years of tertiary education studies at a high level of achievement and have an appropriate Honours 1 or high 2A (or equivalent) undergraduate degree

**Level of Study**: Postgraduate

**Type**: Scholarship

**Value**: A stipend of AU$20,007–29,172 plus AU$2,000 for conference travel and consumables

**Length of Study**: 3 years

**Frequency**: Annual

**Application Procedure**: Applicants can obtain the application kits from the Higher Degree Administration and Scholarships Office or can download it from the scholarships website

**Closing Date**: 31 October

### For further information contact:

Tel: (61) 8 8204 4899
Email: Konrad.Pesudovs@flinders.edu.au

## National Health and Medical Research Council Medical and Dental Postgraduate Research Scholarships

**Purpose**: To provide full-time research experience to medical or dental graduates registered to practice in Australia

**Eligibility**: Applicants must be medical or dental graduates registered to practice in Australia. Graduates from overseas who hold permanent resident status and are currently resident in Australia are eligible to apply

**Level of Study**: Graduate

**Type**: Scholarship

**Value**: AU$29,172 per year plus AU$2,250 per year towards the cost of consumables and travel to approved conferences

**Length of Study**: 3 years

**Country of Study**: Australia

**Application Procedure**: Applicants can obtain application forms, instruction booklets, referee report pro formae and various attachments to the instructions from the NHMRC website

**Closing Date**: 25 July

### For further information contact:

Email: research@nhmrc.gov.au

## National Health and Medical Research Council Public Health Postgraduate Scholarships

**Purpose**: To encourage graduates to obtain formal training in public health research

**Eligibility**: Applicants must be Australian citizens who have already completed a degree in an area applicable in public health research at the time of submission of the application or graduates in areas applicable to public health who are from overseas, have permanent resident status and are currently residing in Australia. All candidates must enroll for a higher degree requiring full-time research

**Level of Study**: Graduate

**Type**: Scholarship

**Value**: AU$19,616 (Australian postgraduate award), AU$25,313 (nursing and allied health professionals) and AU$29,172 (medical/dental)

**Frequency**: Annual

**Country of Study**: Australia

**Application Procedure**: Applicants must submit the application forms to the Higher Degree Administration and Scholarships Office and should include one additional copy for University records. Application forms, instruction booklets, referee report pro formae and various attachments to the instructions are available from the NHMRC website

**Closing Date**: June

### For further information contact:

**Tel**:     (61) 2 8627 1444
**Email**:     research@nhmrc.gov.au

## National Health and Medical Research Council: Primary Health Care Postgraduate Research Scholarships

**Purpose**: To encourage graduates to obtain formal training in primary health care related research, with an emphasis on rural communities

**Eligibility**: Applicants must be Australian citizens or have permanent resident status, who are medical, dental or health-related graduates currently registered to practice within Australia or who have already completed a degree (or equivalent) at the time of submission of the application

**Level of Study**: Graduate

**Type**: Scholarship

**Value**: AU$19,616 (Australian postgraduate award), AU$25,313 (nursing and allied health professionals) and AU$29,172 (medical/dental) per year

**Country of Study**: Australia

**Application Procedure**: Applications must be submitted to the Higher Degree Administration and Scholarships Office

and should include one additional copy for University records. Application forms, instruction booklets, referee report pro formae and various attachments to the instructions are available from the NHMRC website

**Closing Date**: 25 July

### For further information contact:

**Email**:     research@nhmrc.gov.au

## PhD Scholarship for Vascular and Metabolic Research

**Purpose**: To focus on the relationship between obesity, adipose tissue distribution, endothelial function and cardiovascular risk in humans using established techniques such as liver MRI and spectroscopy, pulse-wave analysis, and forearm occlusion plethysmography

**Eligibility**: Applicants should be Australian citizens or permanent residents of Australia and have completed at least 4 years of tertiary education studies at a high level of achievement and have an appropriate undergraduate medical degree

**Level of Study**: Postgraduate

**Type**: Scholarship

**Value**: AU$20,007 per year

**Length of Study**: Up to 3 years

**Frequency**: Annual

**Study Establishment**: Faculty of Health Sciences, Flinders University

**Country of Study**: Australia

**Application Procedure**: Applicants can obtain the application kits from the Higher Degree Administration and Scholarships Office or can download it from the scholarships website

**Closing Date**: 31 October

### For further information contact:

**Tel**:     (61) 8 8204 5202
**Email**:     arduino.mangoni@flinders.edu.au

## Professor Lowitja O'Donoghue Indigenous Student Postgraduate Research Scholarship

**Purpose**: To enable suitably qualified applicants to proceed to a full-time Masters by research or Doctorate by research

**Eligibility**: Applicants must be Australian citizen, must have achieved Honours 1 or equivalent or Honours 2a or equivalent and must be an Aboriginal or Torres Strait Islander

**Level of Study**: Graduate

**Type**: Scholarship

**Value**: AU$25,627

**Length of Study**: 2 years if Masters and 3 years if PhD

**Frequency**: Annual
**Study Establishment**: Flinders University
**Country of Study**: Australia
**Application Procedure**: Applicants must apply directly to the university
**Closing Date**: 31 October

**For further information contact:**

Tel:      (61) 8 8201 3115
Fax:     (61) 8 8201 5175
Email:  scholarships@flinders.edu.au

## Reconciliation SA Aboriginal Education Leaders Fund Postgraduate Research Scholarship

**Purpose**: To foster leadership potential and skill development and to promote the vision of the Council for Aboriginal Reconciliation in South Australia
**Eligibility**: Applicants must have applied for admission to, or be enrolled in, a research higher degree on a full or part-time basis at Flinders University, University of Adelaide or University of South Australia and normally reside in South Australia and be of Australian Aboriginal or Torres Strait Islander descent and be identified and be accepted as an Australian Aboriginal or Torres Strait Islander by the community in which he or she lives or has lived
**Level of Study**: Graduate
**Type**: Scholarship
**Value**: AU$5,000
**Frequency**: Annual
**Application Procedure**: Applicants must contact the Yunggorendi First Nations Centre for Higher Education for further information and application forms
**Closing Date**: 31 January

**For further information contact:**

Email:  shane.carr@flinders.edu.au

## Repatriation General Hospital Department of Rehabilitation and Aged Care: Health Professionals Research Scholarship

**Purpose**: To undertake research in an area of rehabilitation (cerebral palsy, driving rehabilitation, hydrotherapy, multiple sclerosis rehabilitation, hip fracture recovery)
**Eligibility**: Applicants must normally be Australian citizens, permanent residents of Australia or New Zealand citizens, who hold a First Class or upper Second Class Honours Degree in an appropriate health-related discipline, or an equivalent qualification

**Level of Study**: Graduate
**Type**: Scholarship
**Value**: AU$25,000–29,172
**Length of Study**: 3 years
**Frequency**: Annual
**Application Procedure**: Applicants can obtain the application kits and further information from the scholarships web site or from the Higher Degree Administration and Scholarships Office
**Closing Date**: 7 January

**For further information contact:**

Tel:      (61) 8 8275 1103
Email:  maria.crotty@rgh.sa.gov.au

## Repatriation General Hospital Department of Rehabilitation and Aged Care: Medical Research Scholarship

**Purpose**: To join a world class research team and improve health care
**Eligibility**: Applicants must be medical graduates and normally Australian citizens, permanent residents of Australia or New Zealand citizens, who hold a First Class or upper Second Class Honours Degree in an appropriate health-related discipline, or an equivalent qualification
**Level of Study**: Graduate
**Type**: Scholarship
**Value**: AU$29,172
**Length of Study**: 3 years
**Application Procedure**: Applicants can obtain the application kits and further information from the scholarships web site or from the Higher Degree Administration and Scholarships Office
**Closing Date**: 31 October

**For further information contact:**

Tel:      (61) 8 8275 1103
Email:  maria.crotty@rgh.sa.gov.au

## Repatriation General Hospital Department of Rehabilitation and Aged Care: Nursing Research Scholarship

**Eligibility**: Applicants must be nursing graduates and normally Australian citizens, permanent residents of Australia or New Zealand citizens, who hold a First Class or upper Second Class Honours Degree in an appropriate health-related discipline, or an equivalent qualification
**Level of Study**: Graduate

**Type**: Scholarship
**Value**: AU$25,000–29,172 per year
**Length of Study**: 3 years
**Application Procedure**: Applicants can obtain the application kits and further information from the scholarships web site or from the Higher Degree Administration and Scholarships Office
**Closing Date**: 31 October

**For further information contact:**

**Tel**:     (61) 8 8275 1103
**Email**:   maria.crotty@rgh.sa.gov.au

## South Australian Department of Health Research Award

**Purpose**: To undertake a research project relevant to the health of South Australians, the South Australian health system, or the health-related targets in South Australia's Strategic Plan
**Eligibility**: Applicants must have achieved Honours 1 or equivalent, or Honours 2a or equivalent. Only citizens of Australia or permanent residents can apply
**Level of Study**: Postgraduate
**Type**: Scholarship
**Value**: AU$19,231 per year
**Length of Study**: 3 years
**Frequency**: Annual
**Country of Study**: Australia
**Application Procedure**: Applicants must apply directly to the university
**Closing Date**: 31 October

**For further information contact:**

**Tel**:     (61) 8 8201 3115
**Fax**:     (61) 8 8201 5175
**Email**:   scholarships@flinders.edu.au

## The Jack Loader Top-Up Scholarship

**Purpose**: To encourage research into dementia, in particular Alzheimer's Disease, and related disorders and/or the consequences of these diseases
**Eligibility**: Applicants must be Australian citizens or permanent residents of Australia and be enrolled full time in a research degree at one of the South Australian universities. Applicants should have received an Australian Postgraduate Award or equivalent University Scholarship
**Level of Study**: Graduate
**Type**: Scholarship

**Value**: AU$8,000
**Length of Study**: 12 months
**Frequency**: Annual
**Application Procedure**: Check website for further details
**Closing Date**: 31 October
**Funding**: Foundation
**Contributor**: The Rosemary Foundation for Memory Support Inc and Alzheimer's Australia South Australia

**For further information contact:**

**Email**:   jmck1279@bigpond.net.au

## University Hall Dean's Scholarship

**Eligibility**: Applicants must be resident in University Hall and enrolled in a degree course at the Flinders University at the time of application. Only citizens of Australia or New Zealand living in Australia over 1 year can apply
**Level of Study**: Graduate
**Type**: Scholarship
**Value**: AU$2,000 per year
**Length of Study**: 1 year
**Frequency**: Annual
**Country of Study**: Australia
**Application Procedure**: Applicants must apply directly to the scholarship provider
**Closing Date**: 20 October

**For further information contact:**

**Tel**:     (61) 8 8201 3115
**Fax**:     (61) 8 8201 5175
**Email**:   scholarships@flinders.edu.au

## University Hall Eurest Overseas Study Scholarship

**Purpose**: To enable full-time students residing in University Hall, who have demonstrated outstanding aptitude for research, to undertake a period of further study or research in approved universities or other institutions outside Australia
**Eligibility**: Applicants must have lived in University Hall for a period of not less than one academic year, have gained unqualified support for his/her supervisor for the proposed overseas visit, have gained approval from the overseas institution that he/she is acceptable for the proposed period of study and have demonstrated a suitable academic record in the previous academic year
**Level of Study**: Postgraduate
**Type**: Scholarship
**Value**: AU$2,500

**Length of Study**: 1 year

**Frequency**: Annual

**Application Procedure**: Applicants must contact the Higher Degree Administration and Scholarships Office and University Hall for application forms and further information

**Closing Date**: 20 October

### For further information contact:

**Email**:    flinders.housing@flinders.edu.au

## Winifred E. Preedy Postgraduate Bursary

**Purpose**: The scholarship may be used for conference attendance, the purchase or hire of equipment, fees incurred because of study commitments, short-term assistance with living expenses, or any other purpose that will assist with the completion of the postgraduate qualification

**Eligibility**: Applicants have the following selection criteria: 1. Women who are enrolled at an Australian university and are Australian citizens or permanent residents. 2. Must be enrolled in a Masters Degree or a PhD in dentistry or a related field. 3. Must be Australian citizens or permanent residents. 4. Must be past or present students in the Dental School at the University of Adelaide. 5. Must have completed at least one year of their postgraduate degree. 6. Must not be in full-time paid employment or on fully-paid leave during the tenure of the Bursary. 7. Must not have previously won the Winifred E. Preedy Postgraduate Bursary. Selection of winners is based primarily on academic merit, but also on the importance of the purpose for which the scholarship will be used to the progress or completion of the degree

**Level of Study**: Postgraduate

**Type**: Bursary

**Value**: Varies

**Frequency**: Annual

**Country of Study**: Australia

**Application Procedure**: Selection of winners is based primarily on academic merit, but also on the importance of the purpose for which the scholarship will be used to the progress or completion of the degree, on financial need as well as community activities and other interests

**Closing Date**: 29 March

**Funding**: Private

**Additional Information**: Funds are provided from the bequest of Winifred E. Preedy BDS (1901-1989), the second woman to graduate BDS in the University of Adelaide

### For further information contact:

Sturt Rd, Bedford Park, SA 5042, Australia.

**Email**:    internationalapply@flinders.edu.au

## Fogarty International Center

## African Association for Health Professions Education and Research

**Purpose**: The African Association for Health Professions Education and Research builds on the Medical Education Partnership Initiative (MEPI) and the Nursing Education Partnership Initiative (NEPI)

**Eligibility**: 1. Non-African partners may not be listed as Multiple Principal Investigators. 2. An international African consortium of committed institutions should submit an application together and form the basis for the founding network leadership. 3. Named participating institutions for the establishment of the Association must include at least one former MEPI awardee institution (programmatic, linked or pilot awards) and at least one former NEPI awardee institution; but are not limited to these institutions

**Level of Study**: Postgraduate

**Type**: Grant

**Frequency**: Annual

**Country of Study**: Any country

**Closing Date**: 28 March

**Funding**: Private

### For further information contact:

**Tel**:      (61) 301 402 9591

**Email**:    flora.katz@nih.gov

## Chronic, Noncommunicable Diseases and Disorders Research Training (NCD-Lifespan)

**Purpose**: The Chronic, Noncommunicable Diseases and Disorders Across the Lifespan: Fogarty International Research Training Award program supports collaborative research training between institutions in the United States and low-and middle-income countries (LMICs), defined by the World Bank classification system

**Eligibility**: 1. Applications from United States institutions must demonstrate collaborations with institutions in the low- and middle-income countries (LMICs), defined by the World Bank classification system, named in their application. 2. Foreign applications will only be accepted from LMIC institutions. 3. Only foreign LMIC institutions may apply for the D71 planning grant. 4. United States applicants must identify at least one scientist from each LMIC institution as the main foreign collaborator for that institution

**Level of Study**: Graduate

**Type**: Research grant

**Frequency**: Annual

**Country of Study**: Any country
**Closing Date**: 13 November
**Funding**: Private

### For further information contact:

Division of International Training and Research, Fogarty International Center, National Institutes of Health, Building 31, Room B2C39, Bethesda, MD 20892-2220, United States of America.

**Tel**:     (1) 301 496 1653
**Fax**:     (1) 301 402 0779
**Email**:   Kathleen.Michels@nih.gov

## Ernst Mach Grant for Young Researchers

**Purpose**: 1. The Ernst Mach grant is named after the famous Austrian physicist. Student and young researchers from foreign universities are invited to apply for this grant to come to Austria for research. 2. It promote research cooperation
**Eligibility**: 1. Very good knowledge of English/German
**Level of Study**: Graduate
**Type**: Grant
**Value**: For graduates with PhD degree the value is €1,150
**Frequency**: Annual
**Country of Study**: Any country
**Application Procedure**: 1. Applicants who seek admission to an university in Austria have to contact the institution of their choice. 2. The selection process for all grants is competitive, i.e., there is no legal claim to a grant even if all the application requirements are fulfilled. 3. Short-term grants (1-3 months) have a priority in the period from January to June. When applying for a short-term grant therefore consideration should be given primarily for a period of January to June
**Closing Date**: 30 September
**Funding**: Private

### For further information contact:

**Tel**:   (61) 1 534 080

## H3Africa Global Health Bioinformatics Research Training Program

**Purpose**: Through the Human Heredity and Health in Africa (H3Africa) Initiative, the Global Health Bioinformatics Research Training Program supports bioinformatics research training programs at low- and middle-income country (LMIC) institutions in Africa with significant genomics research capacity
**Eligibility**: H3Africa fosters genomic and epidemiological research in African scientific institutions

**Level of Study**: Postgraduate
**Type**: Programme grant
**Frequency**: Annual
**Country of Study**: Any country
**Application Procedure**: The training programs address the need for bioinformatics research expertise in the H3Africa Consortium, resulting in sustainable centers of bioinformatics research training relevant to global health research for the African continent
**Funding**: Private

### For further information contact:

**Tel**:     (1) 301 827 2227
**Fax**:     (1) 301 402 0779
**Email**:   laura.povlich@nih.gov

---

## Fondation des Etats-Unis

15 Boulevard Jourdan, F-75014 Paris, France.

**Tel**:       (33) 1 5380 6880
**Email**:     administration@feusa.org
**Website**:   www.feusa.org
**Contact**:   Mr Sophie Uasset, Director

For the past 75 years the Fondation des Etats-Unis has been welcoming American and International Students during their studies in Paris.

## Harriet Hale Woolley Scholarship

**Purpose**: To support the study of visual arts, music and psychiatry in Paris
**Eligibility**: Open to citizens of the United States of America, who are 21-30 years of age and have graduated with high academic standing from a United States college, university or professional school of recognized standing. Applicants should provide evidence of artistic or musical accomplishment. Applicants should have a good working knowledge of French, sufficient to enable the student to benefit from his or her study in France. Grants are for those studying painting, printmaking or sculpture and for instrumentalists, not for research in art history, musicology or composition, nor for students of dance or theatre. Successful candidates propose a unique and detailed project related to their study, which requires a 1-year residency in Paris
**Level of Study**: Doctorate, Graduate, Postgraduate, Predoctorate
**Type**: Scholarship

**Value**: A stipend of around US$10,000 (subject to fund earnings)
**Length of Study**: 1 academic year
**Frequency**: Annual
**Country of Study**: France
**Application Procedure**: For a complete description of the scholarship including a list of general requirements, an application checklist and an application form, please visit www. feusa.org/harriet-hale-woolley-scholarship
**Closing Date**: 31 January
**Funding**: Private

### For further information contact:

Fondation des Etats-Unis, 15 Boulevard Jourdan, F-75014 Paris, France.

**Tel**:      (33) 1 53 80 68 82
**Email**:    culture@feusa.org

## Fondation Fyssen

194 Rue de Rivoli, F-75001 Paris, France.

**Tel**:      (33) 1 42 97 53 16
**Email**:    secretariat@fondation-fyssen.org
**Website**:  www.fondation-fyssen.org
**Contact**:  Mrs Nadia Ferchal, Director

The aim of the Fyssen Foundation is to encourage all forms of scientific enquiry into cognitive mechanisms, including thought and reasoning, that underlie animal and human behaviour, their biological and cultural bases and phylogenetic and ontogenetic development.

### International Prize

**Purpose**: To encourage a scientist who has conducted distinguished research in the areas supported by the Foundation
**Eligibility**: Applicants are requested to visit the website
**Value**: €60,000
**Frequency**: Annual
**Country of Study**: Any country
**Application Procedure**: Candidates cannot apply directly but should be proposed by recognized scientists. Proposals for candidates should consist of (i) curriculum vitae, (ii) a list of publications, (iii) a summary (4 pages maximum) of the research. The proposal should be submitted in 14 copies to Secrétariat de la Fondation Fyssen
**Closing Date**: 6 November
**Funding**: Private

## Fondation Jeunesse Internationale, Ecole Franchaise d'Extreme-Orient

**Tel**:      (33) 1 53 70 18 60
**Email**:    contrats.postdocs@efeo.net
**Contact**:  Ms Evelise Bruneau

### Short-Term EFEO Postdoctoral Contracts

**Eligibility**: 1. Fellowships are offered in the fields of the Humanities and Social Sciences (Anthropology, Literature and Art Studies, History, Geography, Philosophy, Political Science, Sociology, etc.) 2. Applicants must have obtained a PhD following a viva voce examination held in or after 2013. There is no age limit. 3. Successful applicants must hold a bank account in France. 4. Applicants should have a good command of the language(s) required to successfully complete the research project. 5. The postdoctoral fellowships cannot be combined with any other full-time salaried employment
**Value**: €1,500
**Length of Study**: 3 to 6 months
**Country of Study**: France
**Application Procedure**: Applications may be submitted in French or English. Applications should be in PDF format (one document only) entitled NAME Surname Candidature Postdocs EFEO 2020
**Closing Date**: 14 October
**Additional Information**: For further information, please contact Ms. Evelise Bruneau (contrats.postdocs@efeo.net) www.efeo.fr/base.php?code=971

### For further information contact:

**Fax**:   (33) 1 53 70 18 60

## Ford Foundation

320 East 43rd Street, New York, NY 10017, United States of America.

**Tel**:      (1) 212 573 5000
**Website**:  www.fordfoundation.org

The Ford Foundation was established on 15 January, 1936, with an initial gift of US$25,000 from Edsel Ford, whose father Henry, founded the Ford Motor Company. During its early years, the foundation operated in Michigan under the leadership of Ford family members. Since the founding charter stated that resources should be used 'for scientific, educational and charitable purposes, all for the public welfare,' the foundation made grants to many kinds of organizations.

## Ford Foundation Predoctoral Fellowships for Research-Based PhD or ScD Programs in United States of America

**Purpose**: The fellowships are available for pursuing predoctoral level

**Eligibility**: All citizens, nationals, and permanent residents (holders of a Permanent Resident Card) of the United States, and individuals granted deferred action status under the Deferred Action for Childhood Arrivals Program, regardless of race, national origin, religion, gender, age, disability, or sexual orientation; individuals with evidence of superior academic achievement (such as grade point average, class rank, honors or other designations); individuals committed to a career in teaching and research at the college or university level; individuals enroled in or planning to enrol in an eligible research-based (dissertation-required), program leading to a PhD or ScD degree at a non-proprietary United States educational institution. For detailed information, please check website

**Level of Study**: Research

**Type**: Fellowship

**Value**: Annual stipend: US$20,000. Award to the institution in lieu of tuition and fees: US$2,000. Expenses paid to attend at least one Conference of Ford Fellows

**Length of Study**: 3 years

**Country of Study**: United States of America

**Application Procedure**: The mode of applying is online

**Closing Date**: 14 November

**Contributor**: Ford Foundation

### For further information contact:

**Email**:     fordapplications@nas.edu

## Foreign Affairs and International Trade Canada

Enquiries Service Foreign Affairs Canada, 125 Sussex Drive, Ottawa, ON K1A 0G2, Canada.

**Tel**:        (1) 613 944 4000
**Email**:     enqserv@dfait-maeci.gc.ca
**Website**:    www.dfait-maeci.gc.ca

Foreign Affairs and International Trade Canada supports Canadians abroad, helps Canadian companies succeed in global markets, promotes Canada's culture and values and works to build a more peaceful and secure world.

## Graduate Research Awards for Disarmament, Arms Control and Non-Proliferation

**Purpose**: To enhance Canadian graduate-level scholarship on disarmament, arms control and non-proliferation issues

**Eligibility**: Open to Master's and Doctoral candidates only

**Level of Study**: Doctorate, Postgraduate

**Value**: awards of C$5,000 are available to Canadian Master's

**Frequency**: Annual

**Country of Study**: Canada

**Closing Date**: 3 February

**Funding**: Government

**Additional Information**: For more information, please contact Elaine Hynes at The Simons Foundation by email to ehynes@thesimonsfoundation.ca www.thesimonsfoundation.ca/projects/graduate-research-awards-disarmament-arms-control-and-non-proliferation

### For further information contact:

**Email**:     simon.collard-wexlen@international.gc.ca

## Forgarty International Center

### Ecology and Evolution of Infectious Diseases Initiative (EEID)

**Purpose**: This joint National Institutes of Health (NIH) - National Science Foundation (NSF) initiative supports efforts to understand the underlying ecological and biological mechanisms that govern relationships between human-induced environmental changes and the emergence and transmission of infectious diseases

**Eligibility**: Check the website for further details.

**Level of Study**: Graduate

**Type**: Funding support

**Frequency**: Annual

**Country of Study**: Any country

**Closing Date**: 18 November

**Funding**: Private

### For further information contact:

Fogarty International Center, National Institutes of Health, Building 31, B2C39, Bethesda, MD 20892-2220, United States of America.

**Tel**:        (1) 301 496 1653
**Fax**:       (1) 301 402 0779
**Email**:     Christine.Jessup@nih.gov

## PhD Fellowship

**Purpose**: The Boehringer Ingelheim Fonds (BIF) awards PhD fellowships to European citizens working in Europe or overseas and to non-European citizens pursuing their PhD projects in Europe.

**Eligibility**: The basic monthly stipend amounts to €1,650. In most countries, fellows are paid an additional flat rate of €150 per month to cover minor research-related costs (books, travel expenses etc.). To adjust, e.g. for differences in living costs, country-related premiums may be added (in the United Kingdom, Austria, and the Netherlands currently €650, in the USA €1,175, in Switzerland €1,600, in Canada and Sweden €600, in Denmark and Belgium €700, and in Germany €200). Depending on the cost of living, most other countries are grouped into one of these categories. For example, an unmarried fellow working in Germany currently receives €2,000, in the USA €2,975, in the United Kingdom €2,450, and in Switzerland €3,400.

**Level of Study**: Postgraduate

**Closing Date**: 1 October

**Additional Information**: www.bifonds.de/fellowships-grants/phd-fellowships/who-can-apply-phd.html

## Forum Transregional Studies

Wallotstrae 14, D-14193, Berlin, Germany.
The Forum Transregional Studies in Berlin is a research organization on the content internationalization of the humanities and social sciences. The forum offers scope

## Forum Transregional Studies Postdoctoral Fellowships for International Students

**Purpose**: By creating a space of dialogue for university and museum scholars from all regions, it aims to discuss the potentials and contours of a plural history of art

**Eligibility**: International students are eligible to apply for this fellowship. Applicants whose first language is not English are usually required to provide evidence of proficiency in English at the higher level required by the University

**Type**: Postdoctoral fellowship

**Value**: In particular cases, shorter fellowship terms may be considered. Postdoctoral fellows will receive a monthly stipend of €2,500 plus supplements depending on their personal situation. Organizational support regarding visas, insurances, housing, etc. will be provided. Successful applicants become fellows of the program Art Histories and Aesthetic Practices at the Forum Transregionale Studien and are expected to take up residence in Berlin

**Country of Study**: Germany

**Application Procedure**: PDF files: 1. a curriculum vitae (in English). 2. a project description (no longer than five pages / in English). 3. a sample of scholarly work (about 20 pages of an article, conference paper, or dissertation chapter) names of two referees (including their e-mail addresses). The complete application should be submitted latest by 15 January and addressed to arthistories_application@trafo-berlin.de

**Closing Date**: 15 January

**Additional Information**: For more details please browse the link www.scholarshipsads.com/forum-transregional-studies-postdoctoral-fellowships-germany-2018-19/

### For further information contact:

**Email**: arthistories_application@trafo-berlin.de

## Foundation for Digestive Health and Nutrition

4930 Del Ray Avenue, Bethesda, MD 20814, United States of America.

**Tel**: (1) 301 222 4002
**Email**: awards@fdhn.org
**Website**: www.fdhn.org
**Contact**: Ms Wykenna S.C.Vailor, Research Awards Manager

The Foundation for Digestive Health and Nutrition is the foundation of the American Gastroenterological Association (AGA), the leading professional society representing gastroenterological and hepatologists worldwide. It is separately incorporated and governed by a distinguished board of AGA physicians and members of the lay public. The Foundation raises funds for research and public education in the prevention, diagnosis, treatment and cure of digestive diseases. Along with the AGA, it conducts public education initiatives related to digestive diseases. The Foundation also administers the disbursement of grants on the behalf of the AGA and other funders.

## American Gastroenterological Association - Elsevier Pilot Research Award

**Purpose**: To provide non-salary funds for new investigators to help them establish their research careers or to support pilot projects that represent new research directions for established investigators. The intent is to stimulate research in gastroenterology- or hepatology-related areas by permitting investigators to obtain new data that can ultimately provide the basis for subsequent grant applications of more substantial funding and duration

**Eligibility**: Applicants must possess an MD or PhD degree or equivalent and must hold faculty positions at accredited North American institutions. In addition, they must be AGA members at the time of application submission. Women and minorities are strongly encouraged to apply

**Level of Study**: Postdoctorate, Postgraduate, Predoctorate, Research

**Type**: Grant

**Value**: US$25,000

**Length of Study**: 1 year

**Frequency**: Annual

**Application Procedure**: Applications can be downloaded from the AGA Foundation website. The completed application, letters of support or commitment and other documents must be submitted as one PDF document, titled by the applicant's last name and first initial only. Hard copies are not permitted. For further information visit the AGA Foundation website

**No. of awards offered**: 22

**Closing Date**: 12 January

**Funding**: Private

**Contributor**: The AGA

### For further information contact:

**Tel**:    (1) 301 222 4012

## American Gastroenterological Association Fellowship to Faculty Transition Awards

**Purpose**: To prepare physicians for independent research careers in digestive diseases

**Eligibility**: Applicants must be MDs or MD/PhDs currently in a gastroenterology-related fellowship, at a North American institution and committed to academic careers. They should have completed at least 2 years of research training at the start of this award. Women and minority investigators are strongly encouraged to apply. Applicants must be AGA Trainee Members or be sponsored by an AGA Member at the time of application

**Level of Study**: Postgraduate

**Type**: Award

**Value**: US$40,000 per year

**Length of Study**: 2 years

**Frequency**: Annual

**Application Procedure**: Applications can be downloaded from the AGA Foundation website. The completed application, letters of support or commitment and other documents must be submitted as one PDF document, titled by the applicant's last name and first initial only. Hard copies are not

permitted. For further information visit the AGA Foundation website

**No. of awards offered**: 8

**Closing Date**: 31 August

**Funding**: Private

**Contributor**: The AGA

### For further information contact:

**Tel**:    (1) 301 222 4012

## American Gastroenterological Association R Robert and Sally D Funderburg Research Scholar Award in Gastric Cancer

**Purpose**: To support active, established investigators in the field of gastric biology who enhance the fundamental understanding of gastric cancer pathobiology in order to ultimately develop a cure for the disease

**Eligibility**: Applicants must hold faculty positions at accredited North American institutions and must have established themselves as independent investigators in the field of gastric biology. Women and minority investigators are strongly encouraged to apply. Applicants must be members of the AGA at the time of application submission

**Level of Study**: Postgraduate

**Type**: Award

**Value**: US$100,000

**Length of Study**: 2 years

**Frequency**: Annual

**Country of Study**: The United States of America, Canada or Mexico

**Application Procedure**: Applications can be downloaded from the AGA Foundation website. The completed application, letters of support or commitment and other documents must be submitted as one PDF document, titled by the applicant's last name and first initial only. Hard copies are not permitted. For further information visit the AGA Foundation website

**No. of awards offered**: 4

**Closing Date**: 21 August

**Contributor**: The AGA, the late R Robert and the late Sally D Funderburg

### For further information contact:

**Tel**:    (1) 301 222 4012

## American Gastroenterological Association Research Scholar Awards

**Purpose**: To enable young investigators to develop independent and productive research careers in digestive diseases by ensuring that a major proportion of their time is protected for research

**Eligibility**: Candidates must hold an MD, PhD, or equivalent degree and a full-time faculty positions at North American universities or professional institutes at the time of commencement of the award. They must be members of the AGA at the time of application submission. The award is for young faculty, who have demonstrated unusual promise and have some record of accomplishment in research. Candidates must devote at least 70% of their efforts to gastrointestinal tract or liver-related research. Women, minorities and physician/scientist investigators are strongly encouraged to apply

**Level of Study**: Graduate

**Type**: Research grant

**Value**: US$90,000 per year

**Length of Study**: 3 years

**Frequency**: Annual

**Country of Study**: United States of America

**Application Procedure**: Applications can be downloaded from the AGA Foundation website. The completed application, letters of support or commitment and other documents must be submitted as one PDF document, titled by the applicant's last name and first initial only. Hard copies are not permitted. For further information visit the AGA Foundation website

**No. of awards offered**: 40

**Closing Date**: 16 October

**Funding**: Private

**Additional Information**: The award provides salary support for additional full-time research training in basic science to acquire modern laboratory skills. The additional 2 years of research training provided by the award would broaden the scope of investigative tools available to the recipient, generally in basic disciplines such as cell or molecular biology, or immunology. A complete financial statement and scientific progress report are required annually and upon completion of the programme. All publications arising from work funded by this programme must acknowledge support of the award www.gastro.org/research-and-awards/research-awards/apply-for-awards/award/aga-research-scholar-award-rsa

**For further information contact:**

**Tel**:    (1) 301 222 4012

## American Gastroenterological Association/ American Gastroenterological Association-Eli & Edythe Broad Student Research Fellowship(s)

**Purpose**: To stimulate interest in research careers in digestive diseases by providing salary support for research projects

**Eligibility**: Applicants must be students at accredited North American institutions, may not hold similar salary support awards from other agencies. Women and minority students are strongly encouraged to apply

**Level of Study**: Graduate, Postgraduate, Professional development

**Type**: Award

**Value**: US$2,500 to 3,000 per year

**Length of Study**: 10 weeks

**Frequency**: Annual

**Application Procedure**: Applications can be downloaded from the AGA Foundation website. The completed application, letters of support or commitment and other documents must be submitted as one PDF document, titled by the applicant's last name and first initial only. Hard copies are not permitted. For further information visit the AGA Foundation website

**No. of awards offered**: 48

**Closing Date**: 1 June

**Funding**: Private

**Contributor**: The AGA

**For further information contact:**

**Tel**:    (1) 301 222 4012

# Foundation for Liberal and Management Education University

Gat No. 1270, Lavale, Off. Pune Bangalore Highway, Pune, Maharashtra 412115, India.

**Contact**:    Foundation for Liberal and Management Education University

FLAME University is a private, coeducational and fully residential university, anchored in liberal education located in Pune city in the state of Maharashtra. Earlier it was known as FLAME – Foundation for Liberal and Management Education.

## Foundation for Liberal and Management Education University Scholars Program

**Purpose**: The scholarship is designed to give students an opportunity to further their education at FLAME University

**Eligibility**: Students from India are eligible to apply

**Type**: Postgraduate scholarships

**Value**: FLAME University offers a range of scholarships that recognize the inherent excellence and distinctive attributes of students ensuring that FLAME attracts the brightest of minds. In addition, merit, need-based and special scholarships are provided with that may range from partial to full fee waivers

**Study Establishment**: Scholarships are awarded to study the students offered by the university

**Country of Study**: India

**Application Procedure**: To be considered for the scholarship, students need to email the supporting documents of achievements at admission-at-flame.edu.in. FLAME University's Scholarship Committee will evaluate your application and make the final decision

**Additional Information**: For more details please browse the website www.flame.edu.in/academics/flame-scholars-program

**For further information contact:**

Tel:       (61) 800 209 4567
Email:    enquiry@flame.edu.in

# Foundation for Science and Disability, Inc.

1700 SW 23rd Dr, Gainesville, FL 32608, United States of America.

Tel:          (1) 352 374 5774
Email:       richard.mankin@ars.usda.gov
Website:    stemd.org
Contact:     Dr Richard Mankin, Chair, Student Grants

The Foundation for Science and Disability aims to promote the integration of scientists with disabilities into all activities of the scientific community and of society as a whole, and to promote the removal of barriers in order to enable students with disabilities to choose careers in science.

## Foundation for Science and Disability Student Grant Fund

**Subjects**: Engineering, mathematics, medicine, natural sciences and computer science.

**Purpose**: To increase opportunities in science for graduate-level students who have disabilities.

**Eligibility**: Open to candidates from the USA.

**Level of Study**: Doctorate, Postgraduate

**Type**: Grant

**Value**: US$1,000

**Length of Study**: 1 year

**Frequency**: Annual

**Country of Study**: United States of America

**Application Procedure**: Applicants must submit a completed application form, copies of official college transcripts, a letter from the research or academic supervisor in support of the request and a second letter from another faculty member.

**No. of awards offered**: 1 to 3

**Closing Date**: 1 December

**Funding**: Private

**No. of awards given last year**: 1

**No. of applicants last year**: 8

**Additional Information**: The award may be used for an assistive device or instrument, or as financial support to work with a professor on an individual research project or for some other special need. www.stemd.org/

**For further information contact:**

Tel:       (1) 352 374 5774
Email:    Richard.Mankin@USDA.GOV

## Graduate Student Grant

**Purpose**: The Student Award Program of FSD helps to increase opportunities in science, engineering, mathematics, technology, and pre-medical/dental areas for graduate or professional students with disabilities. FSD has established a Science Graduate Student Grant Fund, which is available to fourth year undergraduates (who are disabled and have been accepted to a graduate or professional school in the sciences) and graduate science students who have a disability. Awards of US$1000 each are made to support research projects of qualified university students in any field of Mathematics, Science, Medicine, Technology, or Engineering

**Eligibility**: graduate students with a disability who have a research program in a science, technology, engineering or mathematics program

**Level of Study**: Doctorate, Graduate, Postgraduate (MSc)

**Type**: Award/Grant

**Value**: US$1,000

**Length of Study**: 1 year

**Frequency**: Annual

**Country of Study**: United States of America

**Application Procedure**: application form must be completed. Two letters of reference. Copy of passport or birth certificate

**No. of awards offered**: 11

**Closing Date**: 1 December

**Funding**: Foundation

**Contributor**: Foundation for Science and Disability

## Foundation of the American College of Healthcare Executives

Suite 1700, One North Franklin Street, Chicago, IL 60606-4425, United States of America.

Tel:         (1) 312 424 9388
Email:       membershipl@ache.org
Website      www.ache.org
Contact      The Membership Marketing Representative

It is the mission of the Foundation of the American College of Healthcare Executives to be the professional membership society for healthcare executives; to meet its members' professional, educational and leadership needs; to promote high ethical standards and conduct; and to advance healthcare leadership and management excellence.

### Albert W Dent Graduate Student Scholarship

**Purpose**: To help minority students better prepare themselves for a career in healthcare management
**Eligibility**: 1. You are a minority student enrolled full-time in a healthcare management graduate program - MHA, MPH, MBA in Healthcare Administration or similar. 2. You are entering your final year (fall/spring) of full-time study. 3. You expect to graduate between Sept. 1 and Aug. 31. 4. You are not required to be a Student Associate of the American College of Healthcare Executives. However, during the selection process, preference is given to applicants who are Student Associates of ACHE. 5. You can demonstrate financial need. 6. You are a U.S. or Canadian citizen. 7. You are not a previous recipient of this scholarship or the Foster G. McGaw Graduate Student Scholarship.
**Level of Study**: Graduate
**Type**: Scholarship
**Value**: Each scholarship is worth US$5,000
**Frequency**: Annual
**Country of Study**: United States of America or Canada
**Application Procedure**: Applications are accepted between Jan. 2 and March 31. All applicants will be notified about the status of their applications by letter in June: 1. Current resume or curriculum vitae 2. Official undergraduate and graduate transcripts 3. Three current letters of recommendation (one must be from your graduate program director)
**No. of awards offered**: 15
**Closing Date**: 31 March

### For further information contact:

Email:    membership@ache.org

## Foster G McGaw Graduate Student Scholarship

**Purpose**: To help students better prepare themselves for a career in healthcare management
**Eligibility**: 1. You are a student enrolled full-time in a healthcare management graduate program - MHA, MPH, MBA in Healthcare Administration or similar. 2. You are entering your final year (fall/spring) of full-time study. 3. You expect to graduate between Sept. 1 and Aug. 31. 4. You are not required to be a Student Associate of the American College of Healthcare Executives. However, during the selection process, preference is given to applicants who are Student Associates of ACHE. 5. You can demonstrate financial need. 6. You are a U.S. or Canadian citizen. 7. You are not a previous recipient of this scholarship or the Albert W. Dent Graduate Student Scholarship.
**Level of Study**: Graduate
**Type**: Scholarship
**Value**: Each scholarship is worth US$5,000
**Frequency**: Annual
**Country of Study**: United States of America or Canada
**Application Procedure**: Applications are accepted between Jan. 2 and March 31. All applicants will be notified about the status of their applications by letter in June. 1. Current resume or curriculum vitae 2. Official undergraduate and graduate transcripts 3. Three current letters of recommendation (one must be from your graduate program director)
**No. of awards offered**: 15
**Closing Date**: 31 March

### For further information contact:

Email:    contact@ache.org

## Foundation Praemium Erasmianum

Jan van Goyenkade 5, NL 1075 HN, Amsterdam, Netherlands.

Tel:         (31) 20 676 0222
Email:       spe@erasmusprijs.org
Website:     www.erasmusprijs.org
Contact:     Y C Goester, Secretary

The Foundation Praemium Erasmianum operates internationally in the fields of social studies and the arts and humanities, through the awarding of the Erasmus Prize and other activities.

## Foundation Praemium Erasmianum Study Prize

**Purpose**: To honour young academics who have written an excellent thesis in the field of humanities or social sciences
**Eligibility**: Open to students of Dutch universities
**Level of Study**: Postdoctorate
**Type**: Money prize
**Value**: €3,000
**Frequency**: Annual
**Country of Study**: Any country
**Application Procedure**: Relevant faculties or universities nominate candidates, from which the Foundation selects five winners
**No. of awards offered**: 21
**Closing Date**: 15 July
**Funding**: Private

### For further information contact:

**Email**: l.aalbers@erasmusprijs.org

## Freie Universitat Berlin and Peking University

No.5 Yiheyuan Road Haidian District, Beijing 100871, P.R.China.

**Email**: beate.rogler@fu-berlin.de
**Website**: www.fu-berlin.de
**Contact**: Freie Universitat Berlin and Peking University

### Free University of Berlin and Peking University Joint Postdoctoral Fellowship

**Purpose**: Applications are invited for Freie Universitat Berlin and Peking University Joint Postdoctoral Fellowship Program awarded for the duration of 24 months, starting 1 November. The fellowship is open to highly qualified researchers of all nationalities who received their PhD no more than three years prior to the deadline for this call
**Eligibility**: Applicants of all nationalities are eligible to apply. Applicants whose first language is not English are usually required to provide evidence of proficiency in English at the higher level required by the University
**Type**: Postdoctoral fellowship
**Value**: During their stay in Berlin, the Joint Postdoctoral Fellows will receive a monthly stipend of €1,853 and a one-time relocation allowance of €2,000. They are eligible for a monthly child allowance if travelling to Berlin with dependent children. All Fellows will furthermore have access to the Researcher Development Program of the Dahlem

Research School. During their stay at PKU, Joint Postdoctoral Fellows will receive a monthly stipend of RMB 15,000. They can receive an additional RMB 3,500 per month for self-organized accommodation or choose to live in a PKU postdoc flat. The Fellows are furthermore eligible to apply for travel funding. They will have access to China's Postdoctoral Funds or other national research funds upon registration at the Office of National Postdoctoral Affairs Management Committee
**Study Establishment**: Area Studies, Data Science & Mathematics, Each fellowship is awarded for 24 months, starting 1 November. It consists of two phases: Phase 1: 12 months of research at FUB (November to October) Phase 2: 12 months of research at PKU The Fellowship applicants must identify and secure the endorsement of two tenured faculty members, one at each university, who will serve as hosts. They will conduct their research projects under the
**Country of Study**: Any country
**Application Procedure**: Please refer the website
**Closing Date**: 22 February
**Additional Information**: Please browse the website for more details www.fu-berlin.de/en/sites/china/aktuelles/news/2017_11_FUB_PKU_Joint-Postdoc.html

### For further information contact:

**Email**: judith.winkler@fu-berlin.de

## French Ministry of Foreign Affairs

**Website**: www.campusfrance.org/en/eiffel

### Eiffel Scholarships in France for International Students

**Purpose**: The Eiffel Excellence Scholarship Programme was established by the French Ministry of Foreign Affairs and International Development to enable French higher education establishments to attract top foreign students to enroll in their master's and PhD courses
**Level of Study**: Doctorate, Postgraduate
**Type**: Scholarship
**Value**: For masters level studies, the Eiffel scholarship includes a monthly allowance of €1,181 (a maintenance allowance of €1,031 and a monthly stipend of €150) and can be awarded for 1 to 3 years. For PhD level studies, the Eiffel scholarship includes a monthly allowance of €1,400 and is awarded for a maximum of 10 months
**Length of Study**: 1 to 3 years
**Frequency**: Annual

**Study Establishment**: French Universities and Academic Institutions
**Country of Study**: France
**Application Procedure**: Only applications submitted by French higher education institutions are accepted
**Closing Date**: 9 January
**Contributor**: French Ministry of Foreign Affairs and International Development
**Additional Information**: Please visit Official Scholarship Website: www.campusfrance.org/en/eiffel-scholarship-program-of-excellence

### For further information contact:

Campus France - Programme Eiffel, 28 rue de la Grange-aux-Belles, F-75010 Paris, France.

**Email**: candidatures.eiffel@campusfrance.org

## Friends of Israel Educational Foundation

Academic Study Group, POB 42763, London, N2 0YJ, United Kingdom.

**Tel**: (44) 20 8444 0777
**Email**: info@foi-asg.org
**Website**: www.foi-asg.org
**Contact**: Mr John D A Levy

The Friends of Israel Educational Foundation and its sister operation, the Academic Study Group, aim to encourage a critical understanding of the achievements, hopes and problems of modern Israel, and to forge new collaborative working links between the United Kingdom and Israel.

## Friends of Israel Educational Foundation Academic Study Bursary

**Purpose**: To provide funding for British academics planning to pay a first research or study visit to Israel
**Eligibility**: Open to research or teaching postgraduates. The Academic Study Group will only consider proposals from British academics who have already linked up with professional counterparts in Israel and agreed terms of reference for an initial visit
**Level of Study**: Postdoctorate
**Type**: Bursary

**Value**: £300 per person
**Frequency**: Annual
**Country of Study**: Israel
**Application Procedure**: Applicants must contact the organization. There is no application form
**No. of awards offered**: Approx. 50
**Closing Date**: 15 March
**Funding**: Private
**Contributor**: Trusts and individual donations

## Fujitsu

1250 E. Arques Avenue, Sunnyvale, CA 94085-3470, United States of America.
Fujitsu is the Japanese global information and communication technology (ICT) company, offering a full range of technology products, solutions and services.

## Fujitsu Scholarship Program for Asia-Pacific Region

**Purpose**: Applications are invited for Fujitsu Scholarship program open to applicants of United States of America and Asia pacific region. The scholarship provides full financial assistance for postgraduate education and cross-cultural management training in the Global Leaders for Innovation and Knowledge program at JAIMS, the Japan-America Institute of Management Science in Hawaii, United States of America
**Eligibility**: A minimum TOEFL score of 577/233/90 (paper/computer/Internet), TOEIC score of 750, or IELTS (Academic) overall band test result of 6.5 or higher from a test taken within the last five years at the time of application
**Type**: Postgraduate scholarships
**Value**: See the website
**Study Establishment**: Scholarship is awarded for education and cross-cultural management training in the Global Leaders for Innovation and Knowledge program by Fujitsu-JAIMS Foundation
**Country of Study**: United States of America
**Application Procedure**: See the website
**Closing Date**: 7 March
**Additional Information**: For more details please visit the website scholarship-positions.com/fujitsu-scholarship-program-asia-pacific-region-usa/2013/12/07/

### For further information contact:

**Tel**: (33) 81 0 44 754 3413
**Email**: Dina.Tiongson@au.fujitsu.com

## Fulbright Commission (Argentina)

Viamonte 1653, 2 Piso, C1055 ABE, Buenos Aires Argentina.

Tel:         (54) 11 4814 3561
Email:      info@fulbright.com.ar
Website:    fulbright.edu.ar/en
Contact:    Melina Ginszparg, Educational Advisor

The Fulbright Programme is an educational exchange programme that sponsors awards for individuals approved by the J William Fulbright Board. The programme's major aim is to promote international co-operation and contribute to the development of friendly, sympathetic and peaceful relations between the United States and other countries in the world.

### Fulbright Commission (Argentina) Awards for United States Lecturers and Researchers

Purpose: To enable United States lecturers to teach at an Argentine university for one semester, and to enable United States researchers to conduct research at an Argentine institution for 3 months
Eligibility: Open to United States researchers and lecturers. Applicants must be proficient in spoken Spanish
Level of Study: Professional development
Value: Varies according to professional experience
Length of Study: 3 months
Frequency: Annual
Country of Study: Argentina
Closing Date: 31 July
Funding: Government
Contributor: The United States of America and the Argentine governments

### For further information contact:

The Council for International Exchange of Scholars, 3001 Tilden Street, Washington, DC 20008-3009, United States of America.

Tel:       (1) 202 686 4000
Email:    info@ciesnet.cies.org

### Fulbright Scholar-in-Residence

Purpose: To enable visiting scholars to teach in the United States about their home country or world region

Eligibility: Open to candidates with strong international interest and some experience in study abroad and exchange programmes
Level of Study: Professional development
Type: Grant
Value: Fulbright funding plus salary supplement and in-kind support from the host institution
Length of Study: 1 year
Frequency: Annual
Application Procedure: Candidates must submit a Fulbright visiting scholar application form and a brief project statement
Closing Date: 15 October

### For further information contact:

Tel:       (33) 1 481 435 61/62
Email:    info@fulbright.edu.ar

## Fulbright Foundation (United Kingdom)

Fulbright House, 62 Doughty Street, London, WC1N 2LS, United Kingdom.

Tel:        (44) 20 7404 6880
Contact:   Grants Management Officer

### British-American Chamber of Commerce Awards

Purpose: To fund postgraduate education between Britain and America
Eligibility: Open to graduates of any nationality
Level of Study: Postgraduate
Value: US$8,000
Frequency: Annual
Country of Study: United States of America
Application Procedure: Please write for details.

### For further information contact:

Email:    fulbrighttgc@irex.org

### Fulbright Scholarship Program for Nigerians

Purpose: The Fulbright Scholarship program for Nigerians is offering Scholarships to students of Nigeria who are interested in pursuing two years doctoral studies in United States of America, in the fields of natural and social sciences, arts, and humanities

**Eligibility**: Listed below are the supplementary documents which have to be added. Three academic and professional references. Curriculum Vitae academic transcripts from each post-secondary institution attended and writing sample english language certificates personal statement

**Level of Study**: Doctorate

**Type**: Scholarship

**Value**: It includes all related expenses

**Length of Study**: 2 years

**Frequency**: Annual

**Country of Study**: United States of America

**Application Procedure**: 1. To apply for the Fulbright Scholarship for Nigerians the applicants must be citizens or nationals of Nigeria, or permanent residents holding a valid passport issued by the government of Nigeria. 2. The applicants must be doctoral students who conducted research in their home institution, applicants must be at least two years into their doctoral program in any discipline that was related to the subjects offered by the university

**Closing Date**: June

**Funding**: Private

**Additional Information**: Young and talented scholars of Nigeria are invited to apply for Fulbright Scholarship Program for Nigerians to pursue doctoral studies in United States of America

### For further information contact:

**Email**:    professionalexchange@state.gov

## Fulbright United States Student Program

### Fulbright-National Geographic Digital Storytelling Fellowship

**Purpose**: The Fulbright-National Geographic Storytelling Fellowship, a component of the Fulbright United States Student Program, provides opportunities for United States citizens to participate in an academic year of overseas travel

**Eligibility**: Applications will be accepted for Fulbright-National Geographic Storytelling Fellowships in any country to which there is an active Fulbright United States Student Program with the exception of China

**Level of Study**: Postgraduate, Professional development

**Type**: Fellowship

**Frequency**: Annual

**Country of Study**: Any country

**Application Procedure**: Candidates must have completed at least an undergraduate degree by the commencement of the Fulbright awa Candidates from all fields are encouraged to apply. All application materials, including academic transcripts and letters of recommendation must be submitted in the Embark Online Application and Recommendation System by 9 October at 5pm Eastern Time

**Closing Date**: 9 October

**Funding**: Private

### For further information contact:

United States Student Programs Division, 809 United Nations Plaza, New York, NY 10017 3580, United States of America.

**Email**:    FBstudent.natgeo@iie.org

## Fund for Epilepsy

Ripponden Mill, Mill Fold, Ripponden, Halifax, H6 4DH, United Kingdom.

**Tel**:          (44) 1422 823508

**Email**:      ffe@epilepsyfund.org.uk

**Website**:   www.epilepsyfund.org.uk

**Contact**:   The Administrator

## Emergency Medicine Foundation Grants

**Purpose**: To aid various ethnic minority voluntary organizations

**Value**: Dependent, for 1–3 years

**Frequency**: Dependent on funds available

**Application Procedure**: Please write in to EMF, grants officer

**Funding**: Government, Individuals

### For further information contact:

**Tel**:       (44) 208 432 0000 Free phone : (44) 8000 652 0390

**Fax**:       (44) 208 432 0319

**Email**:    enquiries@emf-cemvo.co.uk

## Fundacion Educativa Carlos M. Castaneda

1925 Brickell Ave, FL 33129, Miami, United States of America.

**Email**:      fecmc@me.com

**Website**:   www.fecmc.org

## Carlos M. Castaeda Journalism Scholarship

**Purpose**: This award is for Spanish speaking students who are pursuing a graduate degree in journalism. Applicants must have a grade point average of 3.0 or higher

**Eligibility**: 1. Must be a graduate student 2. Must attend a university 3. Minimum 3.0 GPA 4. Must be at least 20 years old 5. Must not be older than 35 years old 6. Must study full-time 7. Restricted to students studying Communications, Journalism, Photojournalism/Photography 8. Restricted by ethnic heritage: Hispanic, Spanish

**Level of Study**: Graduate

**Type**: Scholarship

**Value**: US$7,000

**Frequency**: Annual

**Country of Study**: United States of America

**Application Procedure**: Applications and award information are available on the Carlos M. Castaeda Educational Foundation website at the address provided. In addition to the completed online application form, students must submit the following items: Official transcripts of all academic work completed; Proof of acceptance in an accredited graduate program; Recent 1,040 documents or equivalent information describing the student and his/her parents' financial status; Recent curriculum vitae describing the applicant's work history and activities; Three letters of reference in separately sealed envelopes; A portfolio showcasing three recently written works that have been published in the Spanish language

**Closing Date**: 15 April

**Funding**: Foundation

**No. of awards given last year**: 1

### For further information contact:

1925 Brickell Avenue D-1108, Miami, FL 33129, United States of America.

**Tel**:    (1) 305 283 4963

## Funds for Women Graduates

57 Alma Road, Leeds, LS6 2AH, United Kingdom.

**Tel**:           (44) 113 2747988
**Email**:       secretary@ffwg.org.uk
**Website**:    ffwg.org.uk/
**Contact**:    Mrs Sally Dowell, Co. Secretary

FFWG is the registered Trading Name for the BFWG Charitable Foundation. FfWG seeks to promote the advancement of education and the promotion of higher education of women graduates by offering grants to help women graduates with their living costs while registered for study or research at institutions in Great Britain.

## Emergency Grants

**Subjects**: Any subject

**Purpose**: FfWG offers Emergency Grants to graduate women who face an unforeseen financial crisis (not with their fees) whilst engaged in study or research at an approved institution of higher education in Great Britain. These grants will be offered twice a year, in May and November. Please see website for closing dates.

**Eligibility**: Please see website for details. www.ffwg.org.uk

**Level of Study**: Postgraduate

**Type**: Grant

**Value**: Up to £2,500

**Length of Study**: Any postgraduate course eligible

**Frequency**: Twice a year

**Study Establishment**: Any approved institution of higher education in Great Britain

**Country of Study**: England, Scotland and Wales

**Application Procedure**: Please see website for details. www.ffwg.org.uk

**No. of awards offered**: 15

**Funding**: Private

**Contributor**: Investment funds

**No. of awards given last year**: 30

**No. of applicants last year**: 140

## Emergency Grants for United Kingdom and International Women Graduates

**Purpose**: To allow a woman facing unexpected financial crises to continue in postgraduate study

**Eligibility**: Women graduates from Britain and overseas are eligible to apply. There is no upper age limit

**Type**: Grant

**Value**: These are one off payments to assist with the completion of an academic years work. No grant is likely to exceed £2,500. All grants are offered on a needs basis and therefore not all grants will be for £2,500

**Country of Study**: United Kingdom

**Application Procedure**: The mode of applying is by post. An application form for an Emergency Grant may be obtained by email only from the Grants Administrator at grants@ffwg.org.uk

**No. of awards offered**: 170

**Closing Date**: 5 October

**Funding**: Private

**Additional Information**: All grants are offered on a needs basis

**For further information contact:**

**Email**:   grants@ffwg.org.uk

## FfWG Foundation Grants

**Purpose**: To financially assist female graduates registered for study or research at an approved Institute of Higher Education within Great Britain

**Eligibility**: Open to female graduates who are in their final year or writing-up year of a PhD There is no restriction on nationality or age. Any subject

**Level of Study**: Doctorate, Postdoctorate, Postgraduate

**Type**: Grant

**Value**: Foundation Grants are up to £4,000 and Emergency Grants are up to £1,500. (these values are being reviewed)

**Length of Study**: Courses that exceed 1 year in length

**Frequency**: Annual

**Study Establishment**: Approved Institutes of Higher Education

**Country of Study**: Great Britain

**Application Procedure**: Applicants must complete an application form and submit it with two references and a brief summary of the thesis, if applicable. Requests for application forms must be made by email

**No. of awards offered**: 376

**Closing Date**: 31 May

**Funding**: Private

**Contributor**: Investment income

**Additional Information**: Closing dates are liable to change each year. Please refer to our website for details of the current year www.fundsforngos.org/global-fund-for-women/ffwgs-grants-helping-women-graduates/

**For further information contact:**

**Email**:   grants@ffwg.org.uk

## Foundation Grants

**Purpose**: FfWG offers Foundation Grants to help women graduates with their living expenses (not fees) while registered for study or research at an approved institution of higher education in Great Britain. The criteria are the proven needs of the applicant and her academic calibre. Foundation Grants will only be given for the final year of a PhD or DPhil. The closing date for applications for current and upcoming year is 5 March and the grants are awarded in July for the following academic year. Request for applications must be made by 28 February

**Eligibility**: For your application to be considered you must meet all the eligibility conditions which may be found on the 'Am I Eligible' (www.ffwg.org.uk/am-i-eligible-.html) page of the site. In brief, to be eligible you must be a woman postgraduate studying in Great Britain at an approved higher education institution (typically a university) and entering the final year for completing your PhD (or equivalent) thesis. Applications may only be made for financial support with living costs (not for fees) where there is genuine financial need to complete the course of study.

**Level of Study**: Doctorate

**Type**: Grant

**Value**: Up to £6,000

**Frequency**: Annual

**Study Establishment**: Any recognised university

**Country of Study**: United Kingdom, Scotland and Wales

**Application Procedure**: please see website for details www.ffwg.org.uk

**No. of awards offered**: 309

**Closing Date**: 5 March

**Funding**: Private

**Contributor**: Investment income

**Additional Information**: Please contact grants@ffwg.org.uk www.ffwg.org.uk/our-grants.html

**For further information contact:**

Sally Dowell, 57 Alma Road, Leeds, LS6 2AH, United Kingdom.

**Tel**:   (44) 113 2747988

## Theodora Bosanquet Bursary

**Subjects**: History or English Literature

**Purpose**: This Bursary is offered annually to women graduates whose research in History or English Literature requires a short residence in London in the summer. It provides accommodation in a hall of residence for up to 4 weeks between end of June and mid September. The closing date for applications is 31st October of the preceding year.

**Eligibility**: Please see website for details. www.ffwg.org.uk

**Level of Study**: Postgraduate

**Type**: Bursary

**Value**: Up to four weeks accommodation

**Frequency**: Once a year

**Country of Study**: England, Scotland and Wales

**Application Procedure**: Please see website for details. www.ffwg.org.uk

**No. of awards offered**: 2

**Funding**: Private
**Contributor**: Investment funds
**No. of awards given last year**: 1
**No. of applicants last year**: 1
**Additional Information**: Please contact grants@ffwg.org.uk for further details www.advance-africa.com/Theodora-Bosanquet-Bursary.html

## Fylde College

### Fylde College - Travel Award

**Purpose**: The scholarship is available to enable Fylde students to travel to: 1. Conferences or training. 2. Dissertation locations where costs exceed that normally expected as part of the degree course. 3. Undertake voluntary work in vacation time

**Eligibility**: For further information, refer the official website link
**Level of Study**: Postgraduate
**Type**: Travel award
**Value**: A total fund of US$1,500 is available
**Frequency**: Annual
**Country of Study**: Any country
**Application Procedure**: Please ask in the Fylde College office for an application form.
**Funding**: Private

**For further information contact:**

**Tel**:        (44) 1524 65201
**Email**:    fylde@lancaster.ac.uk

# G

## Garden Club of America

14 East 60th Street 3rd Floor, New York, NY 10022, United States of America.

| | |
|---|---|
| **Tel**: | (1) 212 753 8287 |
| **Email**: | judygow@comcast.net |
| **Website**: | www.gcamerica.org |
| **Contact**: | Judy Gow, Vice Chairman |

The Garden Club of America stimulates the knowledge and love of gardening, shares the advantages of association by means of educational meetings, conferences, correspondence and publications, and restores, improves and protects the quality of the environment through educational programmes and action in the fields of conservation and civic improvement.

### The Anne S. Chatham Fellowship

**Purpose**: To protect and preserve knowledge about the medicinal use of plants and thus prevent the disappearance of plants with therapeutic potential

**Eligibility**: Open to candidates who are currently enroled in PhD programmes or have obtained a PhD or a graduate degree

**Level of Study**: Doctorate, Postdoctorate

**Type**: Fellowship

**Value**: US$4,000

**Frequency**: Annual

**Application Procedure**: Applicants must submit an application letter, an abstract, a research proposal and a curriculum vitae

**Closing Date**: 1 February

**Contributor**: Garden Club of America

**Additional Information**: Contact Wendy Applequist for more information www.missouribotanicalgarden.org/plant-science/plant-science/william-l-brown-center/wlbc-resources/wlbc-awards/anne-s.-chatham-fellowship.aspx

### For further information contact:

Missouri Botanical Garden, PO Box 299, St Louis, MO 63166, United States of America.

| | |
|---|---|
| **Tel**: | (1) 314 577 9503 |
| **Email**: | wendy.applequist@mobot.org |

## Gates Cambridge Trust

PO Box 252, Cambridge CB2 1TZ, United Kingdom.

| | |
|---|---|
| **Tel**: | (44) 1223 338 467 |
| **Email**: | info@gates.scholarships.cam.ac.uk |
| **Website**: | www.gates.scholarships.cam.ac.uk |
| **Contact**: | Board of Graduate Studies |

### Gates Cambridge Scholarship

**Purpose**: The Gates Cambridge Scholarship programme was established in October 2000 by a donation of US$210m from the Bill and Melinda Gates Foundation to the University of Cambridge; this is the largest ever single donation to a United Kingdom university. Scholarships are awarded to outstanding applicants from countries outside the United Kingdom to pursue a full-time postgraduate degree in any subject available at the University of Cambridge. The selection criteria are: 1. outstanding intellectual ability. 2. leadership potential. 3. a commitment to improving the lives of others. 4. a good fit between the applicant's qualifications and aspirations and the postgraduate programme at Cambridge for which they are applying. While at Cambridge, Scholars pursue the full

© Springer Nature Limited 2020
Palgrave Macmillan (ed.), *The Grants Register 2021*,
https://doi.org/10.1057/978-1-349-95988-4

range of subjects available at the University and are spread across its departments and Colleges. The aim of the Gates Cambridge programme is to build a global network of future leaders committed to improving the lives of others

**Eligibility**: You can apply for a Gates Cambridge Scholarship if you are: 1. a citizen of any country outside the United Kingdom. 2. applying to pursue one of the following full-time residential courses of study at the University of Cambridge. PhD (three year research-only degree). MSc or MLitt (two year research-only degree). One year postgraduate course (e.g. MPhil, LLM, MASt, Diploma, MBA etc.). There is no age restriction for applications

**Level of Study**: Doctorate, Postgraduate, MBA, Postgraduate (MSc)

**Type**: Scholarship

**Value**: Tuition fees and maintenance allowance of £17,500

**Length of Study**: 12 months & PhD scholars the award is for up to 4 years

**Frequency**: Annual

**Study Establishment**: University of Cambridge

**Country of Study**: United Kingdom

**Application Procedure**: Complete relevant funding section of the University of Cambridge application form

**No. of awards offered**: circa 6,000

**Closing Date**: 7 January

**Funding**: Foundation

**Contributor**: Bill and Melinda Gates Foundation

**No. of awards given last year**: 90

**No. of applicants last year**: circa 6,000

**Additional Information**: Candidates must apply for a place at the University of Cambridge and for funding at the same time, using the University of Cambridge application portal - there is no separate Gates Cambridge application form except for MBA and MFin applicants who should consult the Cambridge Judge Business School website www.gatescambridge.org/apply-overview

### For further information contact:

The Warehouse, Ground Floor, 33 Bridge Street, Cambridge CB2 1UW, United Kingdom.

**Fax**:      (44) 1223 577004
**Email**:    info@gatescambridge.org

## General Social Care Council

Goldings House, 2 Hay's Lane, London SE1 2HB, United Kingdom.

**Tel**:      (44) 20 7397 5100
**Email**:    info@bursaries.gscc.org.uk

**Website**:    www.gscc.org.uk
**Contact**:    Administrative Officer

The General Social Care Council is the first ever regulatory body for the social care profession in United Kingdom. It was set up to establish codes of conduct and practice for social care workers, a register of practicing professionals and to regulate and support social work, education and training. It takes forwards some of the work of the Central Council for Education and Training in Social Work, which closed on September 28, 2001. Similar councils exist for Northern Ireland, Scotland and Wales.

## Social Work Bursary

**Purpose**: To support those seeking the qualifications required for social work

**Eligibility**: Open to graduates, who have ordinarily been resident in United Kingdom studying on an approved full-time postgraduate course. Amongst other eligibility criteria, students must also meet certain residency criteria. Please refer to the application packs for full eligibility criterion

**Level of Study**: Postgraduate

**Type**: Bursary

**Value**: Non-income-assessed grant of £2,500–2,900 and a contribution towards practice learning opportunity related expenses and tuition fees. It also includes a income-assessed maitenance grant and allowances to assist cost of living

**Length of Study**: 2 years

**Frequency**: Annual

**Study Establishment**: Accredited higher education institutions running a social work course approved by the General Social Care Council, the Scottish Social Services Council, the Care Council for Wales or the Northern Ireland Social Care Council

**Country of Study**: United Kingdom

**Application Procedure**: Application guide is available on the following link www.nhsbsa.nhs.uk/sites/default/files/2019-07/Your%20guide%20to%20Social%20Work%20Bursaries%202019-20%20%28V2%29%2007%202019.pdf

**No. of awards offered**: 2300

**Closing Date**: 1 February

**Funding**: Government

**Contributor**: The Department of Health

**No. of awards given last year**: 2100

**No. of applicants last year**: 2300

**Additional Information**: The bursary is a year-to-year funding arrangement. The bursary terms and conditions (including rates) may change from year-to-year www.gov.uk/social-work-bursaries

**For further information contact:**

NHS Business Services Authority, Sandyford House, Archbold Terrace, Newcastle Upon Tyne NE2 1DB, United Kingdom.

**Tel**: (44) 300 330 1343
**Email**: swb@ppa.nhs.uk

# GeneTex

## GeneTex Scholarship Program

**Purpose**: GeneTex believes in accelerating scientific advancement and the notion that the genesis of future discoveries begins with the support of young scientists today. The GeneTex Scholarship Program is intended for students that have declared a STEM major or are enrolled in a STEM graduate program
**Eligibility**: 1. Student in good standing and enrolled at an accredited college or university. 2. Declared STEM major. 3. Open to international students. 4. All accredited Universities are eligible
**Level of Study**: Postgraduate
**Type**: Programme grant
**Value**: US$2,000
**Frequency**: Annual
**Country of Study**: Any country
**Application Procedure**: See the website. www.genetex.com/Article/Company?param1=Scholarship
**Closing Date**: 21 December
**Funding**: Private
**Additional Information**: www.petersons.com/scholarship/genetex-scholarship-program-111_221336.aspx

**For further information contact:**

2456 Alton Parkway, Irvine, CA 92606, United States of America.

**Tel**: (1) 949 553 1900
**Email**: scholarship@genetex.com

# Geological Society of America (GSA)

3300 Penrose Place, PO Box 9140, Boulder, CO 80301-1806, United States of America.

**Tel**: (1) 303 357 1000
**Email**: awards@geosociety.org
**Website**: www.geosociety.org

**Contact**: Ms Program Manager, Grants, Awards and Recognition

Established in 1888, the GSA is a non-profit organization dedicated to the advancement of the science of geology. GSA membership is for the generalist and the specialist in the field of geology and offers something for everyone

## J. Hoover Mackin Award

**Purpose**: The award is given annually to an outstanding PhD student, on the basis of a research proposal submitted to the GSA student research grant program
**Eligibility**: 1. Eligibility is restricted to GSA members. 2. Applicants must be currently enrolled in a North American or Central American university or college in an earth science graduate degree program (with a geologic component). 3. The research focus can be any subject matter within the geological sciences, such as paleontology, karst, geochemistry, stratigraphy, geoscience education, petroleum geology, and more. 4. Students may receive a total of two GSA graduate student grants in their entire academic career, regardless of what program currently enrolled in.
**Level of Study**: Postgraduate
**Type**: Award
**Closing Date**: 1 February
**Additional Information**: community.geosociety.org/qggdivision/awards/mackin

**For further information contact:**

Geological Society of America, P.O. Box 9140, Boulder, CO 80301-9140, United States of America.

**Tel**: (1) 303 357 1025
**Email**: researchgrants@geosociety.org

## Marie Morisawa Award

**Purpose**: To support promising female MS and PhD graduate students pursuing a career in geomorphology
**Eligibility**: Female scientists in geomorphology currently enroled in a Masters or PhD program are encouraged to apply
**Level of Study**: Graduate, Research
**Type**: Fellowship
**Value**: US$1,000
**Frequency**: Annual
**Country of Study**: Any country
**Closing Date**: 1 February
**No. of awards given last year**: 1

**Additional Information**: Please check at rock.geosociety. org/qgg/M-H%20As.html community.geosociety.org/qgg division/awards/morisawa

### For further information contact:

Geological Society of America, P.O. Box 9140, Boulder, CO 80301-9140, United States of America.

**Tel**:       (1) 303 357 1025
**Email**:   researchgrants@geosociety.org

## George A and Eliza Gardner Howard Foundation

Brown University, Box 1867, 42 Charlesfield Street, Providence RI 02912, United States of America.

**Tel**:            (1) 401 863 2640
**Email**:        howard_foundation@brown.edu
**Website**:     www.brown.edu/divisions/graduate_school/
                 howard
**Contact**:    Ms Susan M Clifford, Co-ordinator


The George A and Eliza Gardner Howard Foundation was established in 1952 by Nicea Howard in memory of her grandparents. Although Miss Howard had a special interest in the arts, her stated purpose was to aid the personal development of promising individuals at the crucial middle stages of their careers.


### George A. and Eliza Gardner Howard Foundation

**Purpose**: Awards a limited number of fellowships each year for independent projects in selected fields, targeting its support specifically to early mid-career individuals, those who have achieved recognition for at least one major project. Our support is particularly intended to augment paid sabbatical leaves. In the case of independent artists or scholars, or those without paid leaves, we would expect that a Howard Fellowship would enable them to devote a substantial block of time to the proposed project. A total of eight fellowships of US$35,000 will be awarded in April 2020 for 2020-2021 in the fields of: Fiction, Poetry, and Playwriting and Theater Studies
**Eligibility**: In order to be eligible to apply for a Howard Fellowship, candidates should be able to answer "yes" to each of the following questions. If "no" is the correct answer to any of them, they are asked to explain on the application form what special circumstances might make them eligible

anyway, given the requirements for a Howard Fellowship. Can your current professional status appropriately be viewed as "early mid-career" as understood by the Howard Foundation? Appropriate candidates for a Howard Fellowship should have completed their formal studies within the past five to fifteen years of the application date and should also have successfully completed at least one major project beyond degree requirements that would be sufficient for the awarding of tenure at a research institution or for achieving comparable peer recognition, e.g., through publication or exhibition. Candidates who are already nationally and internationally recognized leaders in their fields as reflected by their promotion to full professor or by comparable recognition in their fields of endeavor are not normally eligible for a Howard Fellowship. Would a Howard Fellowship provide you with time off from other responsibilities to work on your proposed project? Our support is particularly intended to augment paid sabbatical leaves. In the case of independent artists or scholars, or those without paid leaves, we would expect that a Howard Fellowship would enable them to devote a substantial block of time to the proposed project. Are you, regardless of your citizenship, currently living and working in the United States or United States of America Territories?; Does your proposed project fall within one of the fields established for this year's round of applications? Given the limits of our resources, we must adhere strictly to the fields announced each year for project proposals
**Level of Study**: Doctorate, Postdoctorate, Postgraduate, Postgraduate (MSc)
**Type**: Fellowships
**Value**: US$35,000
**Length of Study**: 4 years
**Frequency**: Annual
**Country of Study**: United States of America
**Application Procedure**: Applications accepted through howardfoundation.fluidreview.com
**No. of awards offered**: 400
**Closing Date**: 1 November
**Funding**: Foundation
**No. of awards given last year**: 8
**No. of applicants last year**: 100-150
**Additional Information**: www.brown.edu/howard-foundation/ www.brown.edu/howard-foundation/george-and-eliza-gardner-howard-foundation

### For further information contact:

Brown University, Box 1857, Providence RI 02912, United States of America.

**Tel**:       (1) 401 863 2429
**Fax**:       (1) 401 863 1339
**Email**:   Howard_Foundation@brown.edu

## Gerber Foundation

### Novice Research Awards

**Subjects**: Pediatric research
**Purpose**: To provide funding for novice researchers studying pediatrics and related subjects
**Eligibility**: Organizations recognized as tax-exempt under Internal Revenue Code 501(c)(3) are eligible to apply for Foundation grants. Public governmental institutions such as universities are included in this definition. Organizations must also be determined not to be private foundations under Internal Revenue Code 509. No grants are made to individuals. With few exceptions, only organizations with principal operations in the United States and its territories are eligible for funding. Within the United States, there is no geographic limitation to the Foundation' grantmaking.
**Type**: Grant
**Value**: Max. US$20,000 in total
**Frequency**: Twice a year
**Country of Study**: Any country
**Application Procedure**: Apply online
**Closing Date**: 15 May and 15 November
**Additional Information**: www.gerberfoundation.org/how-to-apply/

## German Academic Exchange Service (DAAD)

### Dissertation Research Scholarship

**Subjects**: All
**Purpose**: Study scholarships are awarded to highly qualified graduate students to study in Germany or complete a post graduate or Master's degree course and obtain a degree at a German university or institution
**Eligibility**: Research grants are awarded primarily to highly qualified doctoral candidates as well as Master's degree holders and post-doc researcher for research or a course of study and training at universities or other institutes in Germany.
**Type**: Research grant
**Country of Study**: Germany
**Closing Date**: 15 November
**Additional Information**: Applicants should possess knowledge of the German language commensurate with the demands of their research project. The grant consists of a monthly maintenance allowance, international travel subsidy and health insurance www.daad.org

## German Historical Institute

1607 New Hampshire Avenue North West, Washington DC 20009-2562, United States of America.

**Tel**: (1) 202 387 3355
**Email**: fellowships@ghi-dc.org
**Website**: www.ghi-dc.org
**Contact**: Bryan Hart

The German Historical Institute is an independent research institute dedicated to the promotion of historical research in the Federal Republic of Germany and the United States of America. The Institute supports and advises German and American historians and encourages co-operation between them. It is part of the foundation Deutsche Geisteswissenschaftliche Institute im Ausland (DGIA).

### German Historical Institute Collaborative Research Program for Postdoctoral Scholars

**Purpose**: To support a research programme for postdoctoral scholars on the topic of continuity, change and globalization in postwar Germany and the United States of America
**Eligibility**: Open to German and United States of America postdoctoral students. Applications from women and minorities are especially encouraged
**Level of Study**: Postdoctorate
**Type**: Fellowship
**Value**: US$20,000–40,000, dependent on length of study
**Length of Study**: 6 months–1 year
**Frequency**: Dependent on funds available
**Country of Study**: United States of America
**Application Procedure**: Applicants must refer to the website for details
**Funding**: Government
**Contributor**: The National Endowment for Humanities
**No. of awards given last year**: 1
**Additional Information**: www.ghi-dc.org/fellowships-programs/programs-for-junior-scholars/collaborative-research-program-for-postdoctoral-scholars.html?L=0

### For further information contact:

**Email**: westermann@ghi-dc.org

### Summer Seminar in Germany

**Purpose**: To introduce students to German handwriting of previous centuries by exposing them to a variety of German archives, familiarizing them with major research topics in German culture and history and encouraging the exchange of ideas among the next generation of United States of America scholars

**Eligibility**: Open to United States of America doctoral students. Applications from women and minorities are especially encouraged

**Level of Study**: Doctorate

**Type**: Scholarship

**Value**: All transportation and accommodations

**Length of Study**: 2 weeks

**Frequency**: Annual

**Country of Study**: Germany

**Application Procedure**: Applicants must refer to the website for details

**Closing Date**: 31 January

**Funding**: Government

**No. of awards given last year**: Varies

**Additional Information**: Questions may be directed to Elisabeth Engel at engel@ghi-dc.org www.ghi-dc.org/fellowships-programs/programs-for-junior-scholars/archival-summer-seminar-in-germany.html?L=0

**For further information contact:**

**Email**: laurence.mcfalls@umontreal.ca

## Transatlantic Doctoral Seminar in German History

**Purpose**: To bring together young scholars from Germany and the United States of America who are nearing completion of their doctoral degrees. It provides an opportunity to debate doctoral projects in a transatlantic setting

**Eligibility**: Open to doctoral students in German history at North American and European Universities. Applications from women and minorities are especially encouraged

**Level of Study**: Doctorate

**Type**: Scholarship

**Value**: Travel and accommodation

**Length of Study**: 4 days

**Frequency**: Annual

**Country of Study**: Germany

**Application Procedure**: Applicants must refer to the website for details

**No. of awards offered**: Varies

**Closing Date**: 15 January

**Funding**: Government

**Contributor**: German Historical Institute Washington Georgetown University

**No. of awards given last year**: 16

**No. of applicants last year**: Varies

**Additional Information**: Questions may be directed to Dr Richard F. Wetzell at r.wetzell@ghi-dc.org www.ghi-dc.org/events-conferences/event-history/transatlantic-doctoral-seminar-in-german-history.html?L=0

**For further information contact:**

**Email**: mlist@ghi-dc.org

## German Marshall Fund of the United States (GMF)

1744 R Street NW, Washington DC 20009, United States of America.

**Tel**: (1) 202 683 2650
**Email**: info@gmfus.org
**Website**: www.gmfus.org
**Contact**: Lea Rosenbohm, Administrative Assistant

The German Marshall Fund (GMF) of the United States is an American institution that stimulates the exchange of ideas and promotes co-operation between the United States and Europe in the spirit of the post war Marshall Plan. GMF was created in 1972 by a gift from Germany as a permanent memorial to Marshall Plan Aid.

## German Marshall Fund Journalism Program

**Purpose**: To contribute to better reporting on transatlantic issues by both American and European journalist

**Eligibility**: Open to American and European journalists who have an outstanding record in reporting on foreign affairs

**Level of Study**: Postdoctorate, Professional development

**Type**: Fellowship

**Value**: US$2,000–25,000 and funds for travel

**Frequency**: Annual

**Application Procedure**: Applicants including a description of the proposed project, current curriculum vitae and samples of previous work must be sent

**Funding**: Foundation

**Contributor**: The German Marshall Fund

**For further information contact:**

**Email**: usoyez@gmfus.org

# German Studies Association

Kalamazoo College, 1200 Academy Street, Kalamazoo, MI 49006-3295, United States of America.

**Tel**: (1) 269 267 7585
**Email**: director@thegsa.org
**Website**: www.thegsa.org
**Contact**: David E. Barclay, Executive Director

The German Studies Association (GSA) is a non-profit educational organization that promotes the research and study of Germany, Austria and Switzerland. The GSA Endowment Fund provides financial support to Association projects, the annual conference, and general operations.

## Berlin Program Fellowship

**Purpose**: To support doctoral dissertation research as well as postdoctoral research leading to the completion of a monograph

**Eligibility**: Applicants for a dissertation fellowship must be full-time graduate students who have completed all coursework required for the PhD and must have achieved ABD status by the time the proposed research stay in Berlin begins. Also eligible are United States of America and Canadian PhDs who have received their doctorates within the past 2 calendar years

**Level of Study**: Doctorate, Postdoctorate

**Type**: Fellowship

**Value**: €1,100 per month for dissertation fellows, €1,400 per month for postdoctoral fellows

**Length of Study**: 10–12 months

**Frequency**: Annual

**Study Establishment**: Freie Universität Berlin

**Country of Study**: Germany

**Application Procedure**: Applicants must submit a single application packet consisting of completed application forms, a proposal, three letters of reference, language evaluation(s) and graduate school transcripts. Proposals should be no longer than 2,500 words or 10 pages, followed by a one- or two-page bibliography or bibliographic essay

**Closing Date**: 1 December

**Contributor**: Halle Foundation and the National Endowment for the Humanities

**Additional Information**: Please check at www.fu-berlin.de/en/sites/bprogram/application/index.html www.thegsa.org/blog/berlin-program-fellowship-due-dec-1

**For further information contact:**

Berlin Program for Advanced German and European Studies, Freie Universität Berlin, Garystrasse 45, D-14195 Berlin, Germany.

**Tel**: (49) 30 838 56671
**Fax**: (49) 30 838 56672
**Email**: bprogram@zedat.fu-berlin.de

# Getty Foundation

1200 Getty Center Drive, Suite 800, Los Angeles, CA 90049-1685, United States of America.

**Tel**: (1) 310 440 7320
**Email**: researchgrants@getty.edu
**Website**: www.getty.edu/grants
**Contact**: Grants Administration

The J Paul Getty Trust is a privately operating foundation dedicated to the visual arts and the humanities. The Getty supports a wide range of projects that promote research in fields related to the history of art, the advancement of the understanding of art and the conservation of cultural heritage.

## Postdoctoral Fellowships in Conservation Science

**Purpose**: To provide recent PhDs in chemistry or the physical sciences with experience in the GCI's Museum Research Laboratory

**Eligibility**: Open to scientists of all nationalities who are interested in pursuing a career in conservation science and have received a PhD in chemistry/physical science and have excellent written and oral communication skills

**Level of Study**: Research

**Type**: Fellowship

**Value**: US$29,300 per year

**Length of Study**: 2 years

**Application Procedure**: Applicants must complete and submit an online application which includes completing an online information form, and uploading a Statement of Interest in Conservation Science, Doctoral Dissertation Abstract, Curriculum Vitae, Writing Sample, and Degree Confirmation Letter. Applicants are also required to submit two confidential letters of recommendation in support of the their application

**Closing Date**: November

**Additional Information**: The successful candidate will have a record of scientific accomplishment combined with a strong interest in the visual arts www.getty.edu/conservation/publi cations_resources/newsletters/33_2/gcinews12.html

**For further information contact:**

Attn: Postdoctoral Fellowship in Conservation Science, The Getty Foundation, 1200 Getty Center Drive, Suite 800, Los Angeles CA 90049, United States of America.

**Tel**:    (1) 310 440 7374
**Fax**:    (1) 310 440 7703 (inquiries only)

## Ghent University

Ghent University, Campus Ufo, Rectorate, Sint-Pietersnieuwstraat 25, B-9000 Ghent, Belgium.

**Tel**:    (32) 9 331 01 01
**Email**:    info@ugent.be
**Website**:    www.ugent.be/en/

The Government of Flanders awards scholarships to academically outstanding students for master programmes in Flanders and Brussels.

## Master Mind Scholarships

**Purpose**: The Flemish Ministry of Education awards scholarships to outstanding students for Master programmes in Flanders and Brussels. The programme aims to promote Flanders and Brussels as a top study destination
**Eligibility**: • The applicant applies to take up a Master degree programme at a higher education institution in Flanders (hereafter 'Flemish host institution'). • The applicant should have a high standard of academic performance and/or potential. The student has a Grade Point Average of 3.5 out of 4.0 and has a good knowledge of the English language. • The student has to be accepted by the Host institution to be able to receive the scholarship. Even if the Host institution's decision to accept the student is taken after the selection of the Master Mind Scholarships programme, this criterion applies. • All nationalities can apply. The previous degree obtained should be from a higher education institution located outside Flanders. • Students who are already enrolled in a Flemish higher education institution cannot apply. See the full eligibility criteria at the 2020-2021 Master Mind Scholarship Guidelines (link found below)
**Level of Study**: Masters Degree
**Type**: Scholarships

**Value**: It is estimated that 30 international students (to be divided over the different Flemish higher education institutions) will be able to benefit from a Master Mind scholarship to start their studies in the academic year 2020-2021. For Ghent University this means approximately 6 students. The duration of mobility is one academic year for a Master programme of 60 ECTS and two academic years for a master programme of 120 ECTS. The incoming student is awarded a maximum scholarship of €8.000 per academic year. Ghent University will ask the applicant for a tuition fee that equals the lowest rate of the yearly tuition fee for a student who receives a study grant from the Flemish Government. The rate for the academic year 2020-2021 is €1,119. This rate may increase slightly from year to year.
**Frequency**: annual
**Country of Study**: Belgium
**Application Procedure**: Application procedure fully furnished @ www.ugent.be/prospect/en/administration/application/application-degree
**No. of awards offered**: 30
**Closing Date**: 1 March
**Additional Information**: www.ugent.be/en/research/funding/devcoop/grants-scholarships/master-mind

## Gilchrist Educational Trust (GET)

43 Fern Road, Storrington, Pulborough, West Sussex RH20 4LW, United Kingdom.

**Tel**:    (44) 1903 746 723
**Email**:    gilchrist.et@blueyonder.co.uk
**Website**:    www.gilchristgrants.org.uk
**Contact**:    Mrs J V Considine, Secretary

Gilchrist Educational Trust awards grants to: individuals who face unexpected financial difficulties, which may prevent completion of a degree or higher education course; organizations if it seems likely that a project for which funds to sought will fill an educational gap of an academic nature or make more widely available for a particular aspect of academic education or learning; British expeditions proposing to carry out research of a scientific nature abroad.

## Gilchrist Fieldwork Award

**Purpose**: To fund a period of fieldwork by established scientists or academics

**Eligibility**: Open to teams wishing to undertake a field season of over 6 weeks in relation to one or more scientific objectives. Teams should consist of not more than 10 members, most of whom should be British and holding established positions in research departments at universities or similar establishments. The proposed research must be original and challenging, achievable within the timetable and preferably of benefit to the host country or region

**Level of Study**: Research

**Type**: Grant

**Value**: £15,000

**Length of Study**: At least 6 weeks

**Frequency**: Every 2 years

**Country of Study**: Any country

**Application Procedure**: Send proposal to Secretary

**No. of awards offered**: 12

**Closing Date**: 21 February

**Funding**: Private

**No. of awards given last year**: 1

**No. of applicants last year**: 12

**Additional Information**: The award is competitive www.rgs. org/in-the-field/in-the-field-grants/research-grants/gilchrist-fieldwork-award/

### For further information contact:

RGS, 1 Kensington Gore, South Kensington, London SW7 2AR, United Kingdom.

**Email**:    grants@rgs.org

# Glasgow Caledonian University

Cowcaddens Road, Glasgow G4 0BA, Scotland, United Kingdom.

**Tel**:        (44) 1413 313 000
**Contact**:    Ms Irene Urquhart, MBA Admissions Officer

## Postgraduate Ambassador Studentship

**Purpose**: Glasgow Caledonian is the University for the Common Good. Our mission is to make a positive difference to the communities we serve and this is at the heart of all we do, especially in our social innovation teaching and research.

**Eligibility**: 1. Must hold an offer of study with GCU before applying or the application will be rejected. 2. You must be able to cover your living costs in line with the UKVI requirements when applying for a Visa. 3. All awards are non-transferable to any other programme or academic session if you are awarded

the scholarship. 4. Only applicants on a Full Time Taught Postgraduate Masters course are eligible to apply. 5. No late applications will be accepted. 6. Video Link must be submitted or application will be automatically be rejected.

**Level of Study**: Postgraduate

**Type**: Scholarship

**Value**: Full tuition fee Scholarship up to £15,000

## Scottish Power Masters Scholarships

**Purpose**: ScottishPower will provide scholarships for the academic year for postgraduate studies at universities in the United Kingdom

**Eligibility**: Students who are looking to study the following areas of knowledge: 1. Electrical/Mechanical/Civil Engineering. 2. Renewable/Sustainable Energy. 3. Onshore/Offshore Renewable Engineering. 4. Environmental Sciences /Climate Change. 5. Global Energy Management

**Level of Study**: Postgraduate

**Type**: Scholarship

**Value**: £1,200 per month

**Frequency**: Annual

**Country of Study**: Any country

**Application Procedure**: ScottishPower are looking for each scholar to: 1. Promote career opportunities available within the company. 2. Act as a STEM ambassador for the industry. 3. Introduce future scholarship applicants to the scheme

**Closing Date**: 29 March

**Funding**: Private

**Additional Information**: Kindly access the below link for processing the application. www.iberdrola.com/people-talent/international-scholarships-master-iberdrola/apply-scholarships-access www.scottishpower.com/pages/scottishpower_masters_scholarships.aspx

### For further information contact:

Glasgow Caledonian University, Cowcaddens Road, Glasgow G4 0BA, Scotland, United Kingdom.

**Email**:    ukroenquiries@gcu.ac.uk

# Goethe-Institut

Kundenmanagement, Goethestrasse 20, D-80336 München, Germany.

**Tel**:        (49) 89 159 21200
**Email**:      deutsch@goethe.de
**Contact**:    Goethe-Institut

The Goethe-Institut is a non-profit German cultural association operational worldwide with 159 institutes, promoting the study of the German language abroad and encouraging international cultural exchange and relations.

## Goethe-Institut Postdoctoral Fellowship for International Students

**Purpose**: The aim of the fellowship is to support promising and exceptional scholar for one academic year and shall concentrate on the research for a comprehensive exhibition project on the global art historical developments of the Postcolonial era covering the period 1955–1980

**Eligibility**: International applicants are eligible to apply for the fellowship. Applicants must have a doctorate degree in art history, museum studies or related fields. Applicants must be fluent in English

**Type**: Postdoctoral fellowship

**Value**: An overall remuneration package of €30.000 for the entire year. This includes any health care and tax payments. Accommodation is the responsibility of the successful candidate. Haus der Kunst will provide supplementary support to the scholar for accommodation in the amount of €300 per month. Haus der Kunst will support the fellow in organizing administrational paperwork such as limited residency, work permit, etc. Fellow will be provided with work area and full access to the infrastructure of Haus der Kunst and facilities in Munich

**Frequency**: Annual

**Study Establishment**: Fellowship is awarded for scholars whose research focuses on global perspectives on modern and contemporary art in the second half of the 20th century and the 21stcentury

**Country of Study**: Any country

**Application Procedure**: Interested scholars are invited to send their application via email. The application should be in English and include a CurriculumVitae, bibliography, reference letters and a cover letter explaining the motivation for the application

**Closing Date**: 14 January

**Additional Information**: For more details please check the website scholarship-positions.com/goethe-institut-postdoctoral-fellowship-international-students-haus-der-kunst-germany/2017/12/21/ mina7.net/en/grant/3671, goethe-institut-postdoctoral-fellowship-germany

### For further information contact:

**Email**: kredler@hausderkunst.de

# Google Sydney

Google headquarters, Google Inc., 1600 Amphitheatre Parkway, Mountain View, CA 94043, United States of America.

**Tel**:         (1) 650 253 0000
**Website**:   www.google.com

Google is a public and profitable company focused on search services. Google operates web sites at many international domains. Google is widely recognized as the "world's best search engine" because it is fast, accurate and easy to use. The company also serves corporate clients, including advertisers, content publishers and site managers with cost–effective advertising and a wide range of revenue generating search services. Google's breakthrough technology and continued innovation serve the company's mission of "organizing the world's information and making it universally accessible and useful".

## Lionel Murphy Endowment Postgraduate Scholarship

**Purpose**: A number of Australian and overseas postgraduate scholarships are awarded annually by the Lionel Murphy Foundation Endowment. These scholarships are known as the Lionel Murphy Endowment Postgraduate Scholarship. The number of scholarships awarded each year, and the method of payment, is recommended by the Advisory Committee.

**Eligibility**: This scholarship is applicable for candidates having the preference to study in any of the following areas. 1. The law and the legal system in a social context and their practical application; 2. Science and/or the law as a means of attaining social justice and human rights and as vehicles for change; 3. International law as a developing force for peace and as a means of achieving the rule of law in all nations. 4. Science as a tool for social benefit, particularly in meeting the needs of those most disadvantaged within society 5. Other disciplines, where the proposed nature and area of study are likely to promote the goals of social justice and benefit for the disadvantaged

**Level of Study**: Postgraduate

**Type**: Scholarship

**Value**: AU$40,000

**Length of Study**: 1 year

**Frequency**: Annual

**Country of Study**: Australia

**Application Procedure**: Check the website online. lionelmurphy.law.anu.edu.au/postgraduate-scholarship

**Closing Date**: 30 November

**Funding**: Private

**Additional Information**: lionelmurphy.law.anu.edu.au/postgraduate-scholarship

### For further information contact:

Lionel Murphy Foundation Endowment, c/- Secretariat Coordinator, ANU College of Law, Australian National University, Canberra, ACT 2601, Australia.

**Email**: lionelmurphy.law@anu.edu.au

## Government of the Punjab

### The Punjab Educational Endowment Fund

**Eligibility**: 1. Valid PhD admission offer from one of the Top 50 (Subject Wise) Universities of the World (QS ranking) in preferred subject areas. 2. Not less than 60% marks throughout the academic career. 3. Declared monthly family income (including self, spouse and parents) is equal to or less than PKR. 2,00,000/. 4. Maximum age of 35 years at the time of submission of application. 5. Not availed any foreign scholarship in the past. 6. Must take up the scholarship in the year for which it is offered and the scholarship shall not be deferred to the next year. 7. All Pakistani nationals, both males and females are eligible to apply

**Level of Study**: Postgraduate

**Type**: Award

**Frequency**: Annual

**Country of Study**: Any country

**Closing Date**: 22 April

**Funding**: International office

**Additional Information**: www.peef.org.pk/update.html

## Graduate Fellowships for Science, Technology, Engineering, and Mathematics Diversity

### Graduate Fellowships for Science, Technology, Engineering, and Mathematics Diversity

**Subjects**: Astronomy, Chemistry, Computer Science, Geology, Materials Science, Mathematical Sciences, Physics, and their subdisciplines, and related engineering fields: Chemical, Computer, Electrical, Environmental, Mechanical.

**Purpose**: GFSD's goal is to increase the number of American citizens with graduate degrees in STEM fields, emphasizing recruitment of a diverse applicant pool.

**Eligibility**: Any qualified U.S. citizen who has the ability to pursue graduate work at an GFSD univresity associate. Applicants at any stage of their graduate program may apply, as long as they will be available to accept two summers of paid internship. Those who already possess a doctoral degree are ineligible.

**Type**: Fellowship

**Value**: US$27,000 annually, of which US$20,000 is the fellow's expense allowance and US$7,000 is GFSD's fee to support its operations. The charge is subject to change at the discretion of the GFSD Board of Directors.

**Length of Study**: Initial support may be for two or three years, or for a full six years, depending on the employer-sponsor.

**Frequency**: Annual

**Country of Study**: United States of America

**No. of awards offered**: Varies yearly

**Closing Date**: December

**Additional Information**: Applicants must be accepted at a participating GFSD-member university or college and progress through a full-time study program leading to a graduate degree in the physical sciences or related engineering fields. Fellows must complete one or two summer internships, as the sponsoring employer requires. To continue in good standing, fellows must submit a transcript annually as well as any forms and information that GFSD requests. Fellows must perform satisfactorily in their summer internship and during the academic year. A fellow who switches his or her field of study to one not of interest to the sponsoring employer will likely have support terminated. stemfellowships.org/fellows/

## Greater Kansas City Community Foundation

1055 Broadway Blvd #130, Kansas City, MO 64105, United States of America.

**Website**: www.growyourgiving.org

### Ann Maly Davis Scholarship Fund

**Eligibility**: 1. Must attend Wahoo High School in Wahoo, Nebraska. 2. Must be a graduating high school senior. 3. Must have a grade point average of 3.0 or higher. 4. This award is for United States of America students

**Level of Study**: Graduate
**Type**: Scholarship
**Value**: US$500
**Frequency**: Annual
**Country of Study**: United States of America
**Closing Date**: 3 April
**Funding**: Foundation
**Additional Information**: gkccf.academicworks.com/opportunities/3061

**For further information contact:**

**Tel**:       (1) 816 627 3436
**Email**:   scholarships@growyourgiving.org

## Cheryl Barnett McLaughlin Wildcat Education Scholarship Fund

**Eligibility**: 1. Must be a graduating high school senior or undergraduate student at the time of application. 2. Must be a high school senior or previous graduate in the Shawnee Mission School District. 3. Must be enrolled at or planning to enroll at Kansas State University. 4. Must be majoring in education. 5. This award is for United States of America students
**Level of Study**: Graduate
**Type**: Scholarship
**Value**: US$500
**Frequency**: Annual
**Country of Study**: United States of America
**Application Procedure**: Application instructions and additional information about the CBM Wildcat Education Scholarship Fund are available online at the Greater Kansas City Community Foundation (GKCCF) website. In addition to the completed online application form, applicants for this scholarship must submit the following: proof of financial need; transcripts or other records of academic performance that include a current or recent grade point average; and additional information about any leadership roles, community service, or volunteer efforts that may be pertinent to the award. Completed applications with all supporting documents must be received no later than the deadline date. Late and incomplete submissions will not be considered
**Closing Date**: 15 April
**Funding**: Foundation
**Additional Information**: www.growyourgiving.org/scholarships/cbm-wildcat-education-scholarship-fund

**For further information contact:**

**Email**:   scholarships@growyourgiving.org

## Sam and Rosalee Scholarship Fund

**Purpose**: The purpose of the Fund shall be to provide scholarships to graduates of high schools in Bates County, Missouri, who plan to further their education at a four-year college or university and pursue a degree in either the educational field or medical field
**Eligibility**: The students eligible for assistance shall, 1. be graduating from a high school in Bates County, Missouri. 2. have at least a 3.0 cumulative high school GPA. 3. demonstrate financial need; and 4. be enrolling in a four-year college or university to pursue a degree in either the educational or medical fields
**Level of Study**: Graduate
**Type**: Scholarship
**Frequency**: Annual
**Country of Study**: Any country
**Application Procedure**: This award is managed and administered through the Greater Kansas City Community Foundation, a local area charity founded in 1978 with the mission of providing assistance and centralized resources for decentralized charitable causes and giving
**Closing Date**: 1 April
**Funding**: Private
**Additional Information**: For further information, www.growyourgiving.org/sites/default/files/scholarships/application.pdf   www.growyourgiving.org/scholarships/sam-and-rosalee-scholarship-fund

**For further information contact:**

**Email**:   scholarships@growyourgiving.org

## Starke-Blosser Memorial Scholarship Fund

**Purpose**: The Starke-Blosser Memorial Scholarship Fund is provided annually for graduating seniors at Higginsville High School, as well as undergraduate students who reside in Higginsville, Missouri
**Eligibility**: Applicants must demonstrate academic achievement, financial need, and participation in the community through service and other organizational involvement. Relatives of the Starke-Blosser family are also eligible to apply
**Level of Study**: Graduate
**Type**: Scholarship
**Value**: US$1,000 Funds may be used for tuition, books, and other educational fees
**Frequency**: Annual
**Country of Study**: Any country
**Application Procedure**: Students must submit the completed application form, as well as the following supporting

documents: two letters of recommendation as described in the application; a short personal statement; and verification of enrollment in or acceptance to an accredited college or university. Any late or incomplete submissions will not be considered

**Closing Date**: 1 April
**Funding**: Private
**Additional Information**: www.growyourgiving.org/scholarships/starke-blosser-memorial-scholarship-fund

### For further information contact:

**Tel**:        (1) 816 627 3436
**Email**:    scholarships@growyourgiving.org

## Greek Ministry of National Education and Religious Affairs

Greek Ministry of Education and Religious Affairs, Cultural and Sport, Directorate of International Relations in Education, Maroussi GR-15180 Maroussi, Greece.

**Tel**:        (30) 2103442469, 2103443129
**Email**:     des-a@minedu.gov.gr
**Website**:   www.minedu.gov.gr
**Contact**:   Directorate General of European and
               International Affairs

The Ministry's department of scholarships grants exclusively scholarships to students and PhD holders from developing countries through the OECD's D.A.C.

## Scholarships for a Summer Seminar in Greek Language and Culture

**Purpose**: To allow nationals from the Balkans, Eastern Europe, Asia and Africa to study Greek language
**Eligibility**: Applicants must be nationals of Albania, Armenia, Azerbaijan, Bosnia & Herzegovina, China, Egypt, Ethiopia, FYROM, Georgia, India, Indonesia, Iran, Iraq, Jordan, Kazakhstan, Korea, Lebanon, Moldove, Montenegro, Mongolia, Pakistan, Palestine, Russia, Serbia, Sudan, Syria, Thailand, Tunisia, Turkey, Ukraine, or Uzbekistan. Applicants should be foreign students/foreign professors of, Greek languages, or even foreign students/foreign professors of different fields who wish to improve their level of Greek language
**Type**: Scholarship

**Value**: The scholarships covers: accomodation, meals, tuition fees, small personal expenses, in case of an emergency medical care, visits to archaeological sites, museums, as well as instructive material
**Frequency**: Dependent on funds available
**Country of Study**: Greece
**Funding**: Government

### For further information contact:

**Email**:    foreigners@iky.gr

## Scholarships Granted by the GR Government to Foreign Citizens

**Purpose**: To support candidates who wish to study or conduct research project in Greek Universities, or summer seminars of Greek language and culture, postgraduate studies
**Eligibility**: Applicants must be nationals of China, Belgium, Bulgary France, Germany, Serbia, Syria, Turkey. Applicants should have an excellent knowledge of Greek or French or English language. Applicant must be of foreign nationality of Estonia, Israel, Croatia, Cyprus, Luxembourg, Mexico, Norway, Netherlands, Hungary, Poland, Romania, Slovakia, Slovenia, Czech Republic, and Finland
**Level of Study**: Doctorate, Graduate, Postdoctorate, Postgraduate, Predoctorate, Research, MBA
**Type**: Scholarship
**Value**: €550 per month, €500 lump sum for establishment expenses, €150 for transport expenses, exemption from tuition fees (only in selected master's degree) plus all expenses for summer seminars except travel expenses
**Length of Study**: Varies
**Frequency**: Annual
**Study Establishment**: Greek public universities
**Country of Study**: Greece
**Application Procedure**: Check with Ministry of Education or Ministry of Foreign Affairs in Individual country. Applicants must apply through their home countries. Find out about deadlines of their own countries but also refer to the website
**No. of awards offered**: 60
**Closing Date**: 31 March
**Funding**: Government
**Contributor**: Greek Ministry of Education and Religious Affairs, Culture and Sport
**No. of awards given last year**: 40
**No. of applicants last year**: 60
**Additional Information**: Information about eligible countries, number of scholarships and the way to apply is renewed every year and candidates can find next year's decision by the end of December at www.minedu.gov.gr

**For further information contact:**

Directorate of Studies and Student's Welfare, Greece.

**Tel**: (30) 2103443469, 2103443451
**Email**: foitmer.yp@minedu.gov.gr

# Greek Scholarships

## Atlantic Amateur Hockey Association Lou Manzione Scholarship

**Purpose**: The Atlantic Amateur Hockey Association is pleased to offer a scholarship program to students who plan to continue their education beyond the 12th grade. Scholarships are available, one to a New Jersey High School Senior and the second to a high school senior from Pennsylvania or Delaware

**Eligibility**: 1. The applicant must be pursuing education after the 12th grade. 2. The applicant should be a New Jersey High School Senior. 3. The applicant should be a high school senior from Pennsylvania or Delaware. 4. The applicant must be registered with USA Hockey.

**Level of Study**: Graduate
**Type**: Scholarship
**Value**: US$1,000
**Frequency**: Annual
**Country of Study**: United States of America
**Application Procedure**: 1. To be considered for this scholarship award, a candidate must complete a scholarship application form. 2. A candidate is required to submit an academic transcript from the previous semester. 3. He/she also needs to submit the ACT/SAT score report to determine academic achievement. 4. A student must provide a list of any participated High School Activities & Awards, List any awards or other forms of recognition that he/she has received. 5. A recipient must provide a letter of recommendation from the school's principal or guidance counselor, 6. Additionally, an applicant must write an essay that must give details about an applicant's background, interests, and future plans.
**No. of awards offered**: 2
**Closing Date**: 2 January
**Funding**: Private
**Additional Information**: www.thecollegemonk.com/scholarships/aaha-lou-manzione-scholarship

**For further information contact:**

Scholarship Committee, P.O. Box 213, Lafayette Hill, PA 19444, United States of America.

**Email**: info@aahahockey.org

## Cancer for College Carolinas Scholarship

**Purpose**: The Cancer for College Carolinas Scholarship is open to any cancer survivor who is enrolled in an accredited college or university in the United States

**Eligibility**: 1. The applicant must be a U.S. resident. 2. The applicant must be enrolled as a full-time student at an accredited institution. 3. The applicant must be from a state of North or South Carolina school.

**Level of Study**: Graduate
**Type**: Scholarship
**Value**: US$5,000
**Frequency**: Annual
**Country of Study**: Any country
**Application Procedure**: 1. The students applying for this grant must submit a Free Application for Federal Student Aid (FAFSA) application. 2. The initial two pages of the proper 2019 assessment form, If a candidate is under 25 and professing to be autonomous, should give your parent's profits to show that they don't guarantee you. 3. Two-years of Academic Transcripts (High School, College or Combination depending on your year in school), 4. Two Letters of Recommendation from two individuals OUTSIDE your family must be submitted by the candidates.
**Closing Date**: 31 January
**Funding**: Private
**Additional Information**: www.scholarships.com/financial-aid/college-scholarships/scholarships-by-type/cancer-scholarships/cancer-for-college-carolinas-scholarship/

**For further information contact:**

28465 Old Town Front Street, Suite 315, Temecula, CA 92590, United States of America.

**Tel**: (1) 760 599 5096
**Email**: applications@cancerforcollege.org

## Candice Sickle Cell Disease Scholarship

**Purpose**: Our goal is to help alleviate the financial pressures of college-bound students in the Tri-State Area (NY/NJ/CT) with sickle cell disease by providing three scholarships annually. These scholarships are awarded to assist scholarship recipients with their college education

**Eligibility**: Every scholarship winner is required to commit at least 5 hours minimum of their time towards one of the various Candice's Sickle Cell Fund activities during the year they receive their scholarship

**Level of Study**: Graduate
**Type**: Scholarship
**Value**: US$750-US$1,500

**Frequency**: Annual
**Country of Study**: Any country
**Application Procedure**: 1. Each applicant must submit a 250-word essay typewritten in double-spaced format to include how sickle cell disease has affected their life and education. 2. Each applicant should also include what their educational goals are and how they expect to achieve them, in addition, what person has been instrumental in their lives to help them persevere
**Closing Date**: 15 February
**Funding**: Private
**Additional Information**: www.washington.edu/doit/candices-sickle-cell-disease-scholarship

**For further information contact:**

Candice Young-Deler, P.O. Box 672237, Bronx, NY 10467-0237, United States of America.

**Tel**: (1) 646 436 0477
**Email**: cscfinc@gmail.com

## Dixie Youth Baseball Scholarship

**Purpose**: Scholarships are presented annually to deserving high school seniors who participated in the Dixie Youth Baseball program while age 12 and under.
**Eligibility**: 1. Must be an undergraduate student 2. Must attend a university, a four-year college, two-year college or a vocational-tech school 3. Citizenship requirements: US 4. Must currently be a high school student 5. Must study full-time 6. Restricted to residents of Alabama, Arkansas, Florida, Georgia, Louisiana, Mississippi, North Carolina, South Carolina, Tennessee, Texas, Virginia
**Level of Study**: Graduate
**Type**: Scholarship
**Value**: US$2,000-US$120,000
**Frequency**: Annual
**Country of Study**: Any country
**No. of awards offered**: 60
**Closing Date**: 15 March
**Funding**: Private
**Additional Information**: www.petersons.com/scholarship/dixie-youth-scholarship-program-111_165348.aspx

**For further information contact:**

PO Box 877, Marshall, TX 75671-0877, United States of America.

**Tel**: (1) 903 927 2255
**Email**: dyb@dixie.org

## Eileen Kraus Scholarship

**Purpose**: Mrs. Kraus is a past Chairman of the Board and currently a Trustee Emerita. She also served on the Board of Directors of Kaman Corporation for more than 20 years. This scholarship honours her achievement
**Eligibility**: Eligible applicants must be 1. Female students currently residing in Connecticut. 2. Recent high school graduates or in the final year of secondary school. 3. Intending to enroll in first year of college or university. 4. Able to attend the Connecticut Women's Hall of Fame Induction Ceremony in Hartford, CT for recognition
**Level of Study**: Graduate
**Type**: Scholarship
**Value**: US$5,000
**Length of Study**: 2 to 4 years
**Frequency**: Annual
**Country of Study**: Any country
**Closing Date**: 15 February
**Funding**: Private
**Additional Information**: www.petersons.com/scholarship/eileen-kraus-scholarship-111_216040.aspx

**For further information contact:**

Connecticut Women's Hall of Fame, 320 Fitch Street, B-3, New Haven CT 06515, United States of America.

**Tel**: (1) 203 392 9008
**Email**: scholarships@cwhf.org

## Environmental Professionals' Organization of Connecticut Environmental Scholarship Fund

**Purpose**: The purpose of the Scholarship Fund is to assist Connecticut residents, or an immediate family member (spouse or child) of an EPOC Member in good standing, who are attending an accredited college or university
**Eligibility**: Kindly contact sjm@epoc.org for further information
**Level of Study**: Graduate
**Type**: Funding support
**Frequency**: Annual
**Country of Study**: Any country
**Closing Date**: 30 April
**Funding**: Private
**Additional Information**: For further information about the EPOC Scholarship Fund, contact Seth Molofsky at (860) 537-0337 or Email: epoc@epoc.org www.epoc.org/epoc-news/7000206

## For further information contact:

P.O. Box 176, Amston, CT 06231-0176, United States of America.

**Tel**:        (1) 860 537 0337
**Fax**:       (1) 860 603 2075
**Email**:    epoc@epoc.org

## Islamic Scholarship Fund - Muslim Community Center Scholarship

**Purpose**: Islamic Scholarship fund supports Islamic organizations and mosques by planning and managing joint scholarships. ISF is honored to host the ISF-MCC Scholarship of the Muslim Community Center East Bay, MCC
**Eligibility**: Each Eligible Applicant Must Be: 1. An active member of the MCC. 2. Attending an accredited university in the United States of America. 3. Majoring in an ISF supported field of study. 4. Maintaining a minimum 3.0 Grade Point Average. 5. A Citizen or Permanent Resident of the United States of America. 6. An undergraduate (sophomore/junior/senior) or of graduate standing
**Level of Study**: Graduate
**Type**: Scholarship
**Value**: US$5,000
**Frequency**: Annual
**Country of Study**: Any country
**Closing Date**: 21 March
**Funding**: Private
**Additional Information**: islamicscholarshipfund.org/isf-mcc-scholarship/

## For further information contact:

Islamic Scholarship Fund, P.O. Box 802 Alamo, CA 94507, United States of America.

**Tel**:        (1) 650 995 6782
**Email**:    contact@islamicscholarshipfund.org

## Oregon-Idaho Conference Ethnic Leadership Award

**Purpose**: The Oregon-Idaho Conference Ethnic Leadership Award is for one undergraduate or graduate, ethnic student who is a member of an Oregon-Idaho Conference church
**Level of Study**: Graduate, Undergraduate
**Type**: Award
**Value**: US$750 - US$800

**Frequency**: Annual
**Country of Study**: Other
**Application Procedure**: Applicants are evaluated primarily on their leadership or potential leadership skills. Financial need is also considered. The scholarship may be used at any two- or four-year accredited institution of higher education
**Closing Date**: 1 March
**Funding**: Private
**Additional Information**: www.umoi.org/scholarships

## For further information contact:

Scholarship Committee, P.O. Box 340007, Nashville, TN 37203-0007, United States of America.

**Email**:    linda@umoi.org

## Teacher Education Assistance for College and Higher Education Grant

**Purpose**: You'll be able to teach in public or private elementary and secondary schools, as long as you sign on to teach in low-income areas in high-need fields. As a federal grant, you'll need to fill out a Free Application for Federal Student Aid, or FAFSA, to determine whether you're eligible for the TEACH Grant
**Eligibility**: 1. demonstrate financial need (for most programs). 2. be a United States of America citizen or an eligible noncitizen have a valid Social Security number (with the exception of students from the Republic of the Marshall Islands, Federated States of Micronesia, or the Republic of Palau). 3. be registered with Selective Service, if you're a male (you must register between the ages of 18 and 25). 4. be enrolled or accepted for enrollment as a regular student in an eligible degree or certificate program. 5. be enrolled at least half-time to be eligible for Direct Loan Program funds
**Level of Study**: Graduate
**Type**: Programme grant
**Value**: US$4,000 per year
**Frequency**: Annual
**Country of Study**: Any country
**Closing Date**: October
**Funding**: Private
**Additional Information**: studentaid.gov/understand-aid/types/grants/teach

## For further information contact:

**Tel**:        (1) 800 557 7394
**Email**:    HEAL@ed.gov

# Griffith University

Griffith University, Nathan Campus, 170 Kessels Road, Nathan, QLD 4111, Australia.

**Tel**:          (61) 7 3735 3870
**Email**:      scholarships@griffith.edu.au
**Website**:   www.gu.edu.au

In the pursuit of excellence in teaching, research and community service, Griffith University is committed to innovation, bringing disciplines together, internationalization, equity and social justice and lifelong learning, for the enrichment of Queensland, Australia and the international community.

## Master of Business Administration Programme

**Length of Study**: 1–2 years
**Application Procedure**: Applicants must complete an application form supplying Australian AU$50 fee, official transcripts, and TOEFL score

### For further information contact:

**Tel**:        (61) 7 3875 7111
**Fax**:       (61) 7 3875 3900
**Email**:    gsm_enquiry@gsm.gu.edu.au

## PhD Scholarship in Water Resources Management in Remote Indigenous Communities

**Purpose**: To utilize smart meters and loggers to gauge the degree of water savings attributable to the execution of various water conservation strategies
**Eligibility**: Open only to the citizens of Australia or New Zealand or permanent residents who have achieved Honours 1 or equivalent, Honours 2a or equivalent, or Masters or equivalent
**Level of Study**: Graduate, Postgraduate
**Type**: Scholarship
**Value**: The scholarship has an annual tax-free stipend of AU$30,000–35,000 per year
**Frequency**: Annual
**Study Establishment**: Griffith University
**Country of Study**: Australia
**Application Procedure**: Applicants must apply directly to the scholarship provider. Check the website for further details
**Closing Date**: 23 October

### For further information contact:

**Tel**:        (61) 7 3735 6596
**Email**:    M.Mitchell@griffith.edu.au

# Gypsy Lore Society

5607 Greenleaf Road, Cheverly, MD 20785, United States of America.

**Tel**:          (1) 301 341 1261
**Email**:      headquarters@gypsyloresociety.org
**Website**:   www.gypsyloresociety.org
**Contact**:   Ms Sheila Salo, Treasurer

The Gypsy Lore Society, an international association of persons interested in Gypsy Studies, was formed in the United Kingdom in 1888. The Gypsy Lore Society, North American Chapter, was founded in 1977 in the United States of America and since 1989, has continued as the Gypsy Lore Society. The Society's goals include the promotion of the study of the Gypsy peoples and analogous itinerant or nomadic groups, dissemination of information aimed at increasing understanding of Gypsy culture in its diverse forms and establishment of closer contacts among Gypsy scholars.

## Marian Madison Gypsy Lore Society Young Scholar's Prize

**Purpose**: To recognize outstanding work by young scholars in Romani (Gypsy) studies
**Eligibility**: Graduate students beyond the 1st year of study and PhD holders no more than 3 years beyond the degree. An unpublished paper not under consideration for publication is eligible for this award as well as self-contained scholarly articles of publishable quality that treat a relevant topic in an interesting and insightful way
**Level of Study**: Doctorate, Graduate, Postdoctorate
**Type**: Cash prize
**Value**: US$500
**Study Establishment**: Any
**Country of Study**: Any country
**Application Procedure**: Submission file format is rich text file (RTF, PDF, MS word compatible). Files bigger than 5 MB should be presented on CD to the postal address below. A cover sheet should be included with the title of the paper,

the author's name, affiliation, mailing, email address, telephone and fax number, date of entrance into an appropriate program or of awarding of the PhD, and United States of America social security number, if the author has one. The applicant's name should appear on the cover sheet only

**Closing Date**: 30 October
**Funding**: Corporation

**Contributor**: Gypsy Lore Society
**Additional Information**: www.gypsyloresociety.org/gypsy-lore-society-young-scholars-prize

**For further information contact:**

**Email**:    szahova@yahoo.com

# H

## Hague University of Applied Sciences

Johanna Westerdijkplein 75, NL-2521 EN Den Haag, Netherlands.

**Tel**: (31) 70 445 88 88
**Website**: www.thehagueuniversity.com/

Let's change. You. Us. The world. That's our message at The Hague University of Applied Sciences (THUAS). We want to empower our students to change and improve the world they live in, but this can only happen if we work together – if we evolve and change. We constantly need to apply new perspectives and solutions to resolve present and future challenges. We'll find the answers more quickly if we're prepared to share and apply each other's insights, skills and methods.

## World Citizen Talent Scholarship for International Students

**Purpose**: Each year, a maximum of three (one-time) scholarships each worth €5,000 are available to prospective master's degree students. The University is seeking young, intelligent, talented and ambitious people who view themselves as citizens of the world.
**Eligibility**: You are eligible for a World Citizen Talent Scholarship if you: 1. Come from outside The Netherlands and don't live in the Netherlands. 2. Are enrolling for the first time at The Hague University of Applied Sciences. 3. Have never applied for this scholarship before. 4. Have been conditionally accepted as a student (also-called offer of student position) on or before 31 March for the upcoming academic year.
**Level of Study**: Masters Degree
**Type**: Scholarships
**Value**: Each scholarship is worth Ne €5,000.
**Frequency**: Annual

**Country of Study**: Netherlands
**Application Procedure**: To apply for the scholarship, you must first apply to the Master programme of your choice and write an essay following the essay guidelines. Submit your essay by completing the scholarship application form between 1 November–31 March. It is important to visit the official website to access the application form and for detailed information on how to apply for this scholarship.
**No. of awards offered**: 3
**Closing Date**: 31 March
**Additional Information**: www.thehagueuniversity.com/study-choice/masters-professional-courses/scholarships/world-citizen-talent-scholarship

**For further information contact:**

**Email**: masters-admission@hhs.nl

## Harish-Chandra Research Institute

Chhatnag Road, Jhusi, Allahabad, Uttar Pradesh 211019, India.

**Tel**: (91) 532 256 9509
**Contact**: The Harish-Chandra Research Institute

## Postdoctoral Fellowships in Mathematics at Harish-Chandra Research Institute

**Purpose**: The Harish-Chandra Research Institute (HRI) welcomes applications to its active post-doctoral programme in mathematics. Post-doctoral fellows at HRI have the opportunity to work with the members of the mathematics group in diverse areas including Number Theory, Cryptography, Group Theory, Representation Theory, Harmonic Analysis, Algebraic Geometry and Differential Geometry.

© Springer Nature Limited 2020
Palgrave Macmillan (ed.), *The Grants Register 2021*,
https://doi.org/10.1057/978-1-349-95988-4

**Eligibility**: Covering letter, Curriculum Vitae, List of publications, A list of referees, A research plan for the next two years, PhD degree / Provisional certificate, if available, Document showing prior PDF experience, if any.
**Type**: Postdoctoral fellowship
**Length of Study**: Three years
**Closing Date**: 31 December
**Additional Information**: www.hri.res.in/academics/mathematics/pdf-fellowships/

**For further information contact:**

**Email**:    physvisit@hri.res.in

## Postdoctoral Fellowships in Physics at Harish-Chandra Research Institute

**Purpose**: The aim of the fellowships is to support Indian students and provide opportunities to researchers working in Astrophysics, Condensed Matter Physics, High Energy Phenomenology, Quantum Information & Computing, and String Theory
**Eligibility**: Applicants from India are eligible to apply for the fellowship. Applicants must be researchers
**Type**: Postdoctoral fellowship
**Value**: HRI offers opportunities to researchers working in Astrophysics, Condensed matter physics, High energy phenomenology, Quantum information & computing, and, String theory
**Study Establishment**: Fellowships are awarded in the field of Physics
**Country of Study**: India
**Application Procedure**: See the website
**Closing Date**: 31 December
**Additional Information**: For more details please visit the website at scholarship-positions.com/postdoctoral-fellowships-physics-harish-chandra-research-institute-india/2017/12/26/ www.hri.res.in/academics/physics/pdf-fellowships/

**For further information contact:**

**Email**:    physvisit@hri.res.in

## Harpo Foundation

**Tel**:         (1) 757 735 4269
**Website**:    www.harpofoundation.org/

The Harpo Foundation was established in 2006 to support emerging visual artists. The foundation seeks to stimulate creative inquiry and to encourage new modes of thinking about art. We view the definitions of art and artist to be open-ended and expansive. The Foundation's grant program awards 7–10 grants annually. Grants are made directly to artists to support their development and to non-profit organizations in support of new work by artists. The Foundation also supports two residency fellowship programs. The Native American Residency Fellowship program provides residency opportunities at the Vermont Studio Center to support the development of artists and the potential for inter-cultural dialog. The Emerging Artist Residency Fellowship program supports residency opportunities at the Santa Fe Art Institute for visual artists 25 years and older who need time and space to explore ideas and start new projects.

## Harpo Foundation Grants for Visual Artists

**Subjects**: Visual Arts
**Purpose**: The award provides direct support to under-recognized artists
**Eligibility**: 1. Self-defined under-recognized visual artist 21 years or older 2. United States citizen 3. Students who are enrolled in an undergraduate/graduate program are not eligible. 4. Not a previous recipient of a direct artist grant from Harpo. 5. Artists who have been supported by an organizational grant from Harpo in the past are eligible to apply for a direct grant.
**Level of Study**: Professional development
**Type**: Grant
**Value**: Up to US$10,000
**Length of Study**: 10-months
**Frequency**: Annual
**Country of Study**: United States
**Application Procedure**: To apply, a US$15 application fee is required. Fees are applied to grant administration and program development. Applicants must use the foundation's online application system to submit the following: 1. Artist resume 2. Artist statement (up to 200 words) 3. Work samples (up to 10)
**Closing Date**: 17 April
**Funding**: Foundation
**Additional Information**: www.harpofoundation.org/apply/grants-for-visual-artists/

**For further information contact:**

**Email**:    jdeamer@harpofoundation.org

## Harry S Truman Library Institute

500 West United States Highway 24, Independence, MO 64050, United States of America.

**Tel**:         (1) 816 268 8200
**Email**:       lisa.sullivan@nara.gov

**Website**: www.trumanlibrary.org
**Contact**: Lisa Sullivan, Grants Administrator

The Harry S Truman Library Institute is a non-profit partner of the Harry S Truman Library. The institute's purpose is to foster the Truman Library as a centre for research and as a provider of educational and public programmes.

## Harry S Truman Library Institute Dissertation Year Fellowships

**Purpose**: Dissertation Year Fellowships are intended to encourage historical scholarship of the public career of Harry S. Truman or the Truman era.
**Eligibility**: 1. Must be a graduate student 2. Must attend a university 3. Must not be attending high school currently 4. Must study full-time
**Level of Study**: Graduate, Postgraduate
**Type**: Fellowship
**Value**: US$16,000-US$32,000
**Length of Study**: 1 year
**Frequency**: Annual
**Country of Study**: United States of America
**Application Procedure**: Application forms are available from the website
**Closing Date**: 1 February
**Funding**: Private
**No. of awards given last year**: 2
**Additional Information**: Recipients will not be required to come to the Truman Library but will be expected to furnish the Library with a copy of their dissertation www.petersons.com/scholarship/harry-s-truman-library-institute-dissertation-year-fellowships-111_150880.aspx

### For further information contact:

Truman Library Institute, 5151 Troost Avenue, Suite 300, Kansas City, MO 64110, United States of America.

**Tel**: (1) 816 816 400 1212
**Fax**: (1) 816 268 8299
**Email**: lisa.sullivan@trumanlibraryinstitute.org

## Harry S Truman Library Institute Research Grant

**Purpose**: As part of our mission, Truman Library Institute grants are given for the purpose of supporting scholarship based on some aspect of the life and career of Harry S. Truman or of the public and foreign policy issues which were prominent during the Truman administration

**Eligibility**: 1. Must be a graduate student or a postgraduate student 2. Must attend a university or a four-year college 3. Must not be attending high school currently 4. Must study full-time 5. Restricted to students studying History, Political Science, Women's Studies
**Level of Study**: Research
**Type**: Research grant
**Value**: US$2,500 are awarded twice annually
**Length of Study**: 1-3 weeks
**Frequency**: Twice a year
**Country of Study**: Unrestricted
**Application Procedure**: Competitive proposals will evidence a clear understanding of the existing research in the field and how the proposed work adds significantly to that body of literature. Applicants are expected to demonstrate both an analytical and descriptive grasp of the project and its centrality to the Truman era. Application packages must include the following: completed Research Grant application; curriculum vitae (3 pages, maximum); project description and justification (5 pages, maximum); a list of specific files the candidate expects to access at the Harry S. Truman Library and Museum; and two letters of reference from persons familiar with the applicant's scholarly work, including one from the project advisor, if candidate is a graduate or postdoctoral student. Letters must be received by the deadline and mailed or emailed directly to the Grants Administrator by the referring individual
**No. of awards offered**: 25
**Closing Date**: 1 April
**Funding**: Foundation
**No. of awards given last year**: 15
**No. of applicants last year**: 25
**Additional Information**: Please visit trumanlibraryinstitute.org/research-grants/research-grants www.petersons.com/scholarship/harry-s-truman-library-institute-research-grants-111_152118.aspx

### For further information contact:

Truman Library Institute, 5151 Troost Avenue, Suite 300, Kansas City, MO 64110, United States of America.

**Tel**: (1) 816 816 400 1212
**Fax**: (1) 816 400 1213
**Email**: lisa.sullivan@trumanlibraryinstitute.org

## Harry S Truman Library Institute Scholar's Award

**Eligibility**: 1. Must be a postgraduate student 2. Must attend a university 3. Must not be attending high school currently 4. Must study full-time 5. Restricted to students studying History, Political Science, Women's Studies
**Level of Study**: Postdoctorate

**Type**: Award
**Value**: US$30,000
**Application Procedure**: Please check at trumanlibrar
yinstitute.org/research-grants/scholars-award
**Closing Date**: 15 February
**Funding**: Private
**Additional Information**: www.petersons.com/scholarship/harry-
s-truman-library-institute-scholars-award-111_150977.aspx

### For further information contact:

Truman Library Institute, 5151 Troost Avenue, Suite 300, Kansas City, MO 64110, United States of America.

**Tel**:        (1) 816 816 400 1212
**Fax**:        (1) 816 400 1213
**Email**:      lisa.sullivan@trumanlibraryinstitute.org

## Harvard Business School

### Harvard University Master of Business Administration Scholarship in the United States of America

**Subjects**: Business Administration
**Purpose**: Harvard MBA has been taught at one of the most prestigious universities in the world as one of the world's leading management programs. Once every two years, the Boustany MBA Harvard Bursary is awarded for a two-year program at Harvard Business School.
**Eligibility**: Candidates need an excellent academic background and a significant commitment. Even if the bursary can be granted to candidates from any country, the candidates from Lebanese origins will receive priority. Only upon receipt of an admission offer under the Harvard MBA program can applicants apply for a scholarship. During their Internship, students are required to work on a project which relates to one of the objectives of the Foundation. Students may also be required to work during their Internship with one of our partners.
**Type**: Scholarship
**Value**: US$95,000 (US$47,500 per year) towards tuition fees
**Length of Study**: Two years
**Frequency**: Every 2 years
**Study Establishment**: Harvard University
**Country of Study**: United States of America
**Application Procedure**: Send your copy of your curriculum vitae to admissions@boustany-foundation.org with a photograph, GMAT scores, and acceptance letter from the University.

## Harvard Travellers Club

PO Box 190, Canton, MA 02021, United States of America.

**Tel**:        (1) 781 821 0400
**Email**:      gpbdtes@shieldpdckdging.com
**Website**:    www.travellersfund.org
**Contact**:    George Bates

### Harvard Travellers Club Permanent Fund

**Purpose**: To support research involving travel from which results can be obtained of permanent scientific and educational value
**Eligibility**: 1. Must be an undergraduate student, a graduate student or a postgraduate student 2. Must attend a university or a four-year college 3. Must be at least 18 years old 4. Both full-time and part-time students
**Level of Study**: Doctorate, Graduate, Postdoctorate, Postgraduate, Predoctorate, Research, Unrestricted
**Type**: Grant
**Value**: US$1,000-US$5,000
**Frequency**: Annual
**Country of Study**: Worldwide
**Application Procedure**: Please check website for all details
**No. of awards offered**: 10
**Closing Date**: 31 March
**Funding**: Trusts
**Contributor**: Club membership contributions (no major contributor)
**No. of awards given last year**: 2
**No. of applicants last year**: 10
**Additional Information**: www.petersons.com/scholarship/
harvard-travellers-club-permanent-fund-111_151392.aspx

### For further information contact:

170 Hubbard St., Lenox, MA 01240, United States of America.

**Email**:      Jackdeary@harvardtravellersclub.org

## Health Canada

Applied Research & Analysis Directorate, Analysis & Connectivity Branch, 15th Floor, Jeanne Mance Building, Tunney's Pasture, Ottawa, ON K1A 1B4, Canada.

**Tel**:        (1) 613 954 8549
**Email**:      nhrdpinfo@isdicp3.hwc.ca
**Website**:    www.hc-sc.gc.ca
**Contact**:    Information & Resource Officer

The National Health Research and Development Programme (NHRDP) funds research with scientific merit to support the Federal Department of Health's mission and national health priorities, and researchers whose work will contribute to policy development and strategic planning. In general, the NHRDP funds research that relates to issues of concern to the federal government and to those that may be of concern to provincial and territorial health ministries pertaining to the health system and the promotion of population health.

## MSc Fellowships and PhD Fellowships

**Purpose**: To provide support to highly qualified students who wish to undertake full-time research training leading to an MSc degree (or equivalent) or a PhD degree (or equivalent)
**Eligibility**: Open to Canadian citizens or landed immigrants of high academic standing who hold an honours Bachelor's degree or a professional degree in a health field and are already engaged in a Master's or PhD program
**Level of Study**: Postgraduate
**Type**: A variable number of fellowships
**Value**: C$19,800 per year
**Frequency**: Annual
**Study Establishment**: at universities or affiliated institutions
**Country of Study**: Canada
**Closing Date**: 1 March
**Additional Information**: Prior to application, candidates should obtain a copy of the Training Awards Guide.

## For further information contact:

Extramural Research Programs Directorate, Health Programs & Services Branch, Health Canada, Ottawa, ON K1A 0S5, Canada.

**Fax:**    (1) 613 954 7363

## Health Research Board (HRB)

Research and Development for Health, 73 Lower Baggot Street, Dublin 2, Ireland.

**Tel**:      (353) 1 234 5000
**Email**:    hrb@hrb.ie
**Website**:  www.hrb.ie
**Contact**:  The Research Grants Manager

The Health Research Board (HRB) comprises 16 members appointed by the Minister of Health, with eight of the members being nominated on the co-joint nomination of the universities and colleges. The main functions of the HRB are to promote or commission health research, to promote and conduct epidemiological research as may be appropriate at national level, to promote or commission health services research, to liaise and co-operate with other research bodies in Ireland and overseas in the promotion of relevant research and to undertake such other cognate functions as the Minister may from time to time determine.

## Primary Care Training and Enhancement - Physician Assistant Program

**Purpose**: The purpose of the PCTE - PA Program is to increase the number of primary care physician assistants (PA), particularly in rural and underserved settings, and improve primary care training in order to strengthen access to and delivery of primary care services nationally
**Eligibility**: Eligible applicants must be academically affiliated PA training programs, accredited by the Accreditation Review Commission on Education for the Physician Assistant (ARC-PA). Domestic faith-based and community-based organizations, tribes and tribal organizations may apply for these funds, if otherwise eligible
**Level of Study**: Graduate
**Type**: Training award
**Value**: US$2,000,000
**Frequency**: Annual
**Country of Study**: Any country
**Application Procedure**: Links to the full announcement and online application process are available through grants.gov. check the website appropriately
**Closing Date**: 14 January
**Funding**: Private
**Additional Information**: Preference will be given to applicants that: 1. Demonstrate a high rate for placing graduates in practice settings having the principal focus of serving residents of Medically Underserved Communities. 2. Demonstrate a significant increase in the rate of placing graduates in Medically Underserved Community settings over the preceding 2 years. www.ruralhealthinfo.org/funding/4519

## For further information contact:

**Tel**:      (1) 301 443 7271
**Email**:    SCicale@hrsa.gov

## Research Leaders Awards

**Eligibility**: All applications must involve a partnership with at least one health-related partner organization involved in the delivery of health and social care and/or health and social care policy. Applications should be aligned with the strategic plans of the nominating organizations, and should reflect national priorities and strategies in health and social care

**Level of Study**: Doctorate, Postdoctorate

**Type**: Award

**Value**: Each Research Leader Award consists of a contribution to salary support for the nominee up to the grade of Associate Professor, an attractive discretionary research support package of up to €600,000 over the period of the award, and a contribution to overhead expenses

**Length of Study**: A maximum of 5 years

**Frequency**: Annual

**Country of Study**: Ireland

**Application Procedure**: All applications must be made online using the HRB GEMS. To access the application form the nominating Higher Education Institution must provide the HRB with the contact details of their nominated Principal Investigator. The HRB will then invite the nominated candidate to initiate the application form

**Closing Date**: 31 March

**Funding**: Government

**Additional Information**: Please check at www.hrb.ie/research-strategy-funding/grants-and-fellowships/hrb-grants-and-fellowships/grant/133 www.hrb.ie/fileadmin/2._Plugin_related_files/Funding_schemes/Research_Leader_Awards_2020_Guidance_Notes.pdf

**For further information contact:**

**Email**:    ferrism@queensu.ca

## Hearst Corporation

801 Texas Avenue, Houston, TX 77002, United States of America.

**Email**:    kenn.altine@chron.com
**Website**:    www.hearstfellowships.com

Hearst Corporation is one of the largest diversified communications companies.

## Hearst Fellowships

**Purpose**: To help develop excellent reporters, editors, photographers, designers and graphic artists

**Eligibility**: Open to candidates who are graduates and have experience or background in journalism or related fields

**Level of Study**: Professional development

**Type**: Fellowships

**Value**: Varies

**Length of Study**: 2 years

**Frequency**: Annual

**Country of Study**: Any country

**Application Procedure**: The applicants must download the application form from the website. The completed application form along with other enclosures is to be sent to Hearst Fellowships

**Closing Date**: 1 December

**For further information contact:**

**Email**:    fellowships@hearstnp.com

## Heart and Stroke Foundation

Suite 1402, 222 Queen Street, Ottawa, ON K1P 5V9, Canada.

**Tel**:        (1) 613 569 4361
**Email**:    research@hsf.ca
**Website**:    www.heartandstroke.ca

The Heart and Stroke Foundation is involved in eliminating heart disease and stroke and reducing their impact through the advancement of research and its application, and advocacy for the promotion of healthy living. It is a federation of 10 provincial foundations, led and supported by a force of more than 140,000 volunteers.

## Canada Doctoral Research Award

**Purpose**: To award highly qualified graduate students enrolled in a PhD program, undertaking full-time research training in the cardiovascular or cerebrovascular fields

**Eligibility**: Open to students enrolled in a PhD program and must be a full-time medical student

**Level of Study**: Doctorate, Research

**Type**: Research

**Value**: C$21,000

**Country of Study**: Canada

**Application Procedure**: Applicants must send the application form along with the transcript, essay references and a self-addressed stamped envelope

**Closing Date**: 1 November

**For further information contact:**

Research Department, Room 9A-27, Parklawn Building, 5600 Fishers Lane, Rockville, MD 20857, United States of America.

**Tel**: (1) 613 569 4361 ext. 327
**Fax**: (1) 613 569 3278
**Email**: lhodgson@hsf.ca

## Career Investigator Award

**Purpose**: To support established independent researchers who wish to make research their full-time career (Ontario applicants only)
**Eligibility**: Awards for individuals with an MD, PhD or equivalent degree working in the field of cardiovascular and/or cerebrovascular disease who wish to make their research a full-time career. Applicants must provide proof of national recognition
**Level of Study**: Postgraduate
**Type**: Scholarship
**Value**: Stipend C$81,500 per year, C$1,500 per year for travel, and minimum C$48,282 for scientific purpose
**Application Procedure**: Applicants must send the application form along with the transcript, essay references and a self-addressed stamped envelope and must provide proof of national recognition
**Closing Date**: 1 September
**Contributor**: Heart and Stroke Foundations of Ontario and British Columbia and the Yukon
**Additional Information**: For more details see website or contact the foundation.

## Dr Andres Petrasovits Fellowship in Cardiovascular Health Policy Research

**Eligibility**: Please visit the website
**Level of Study**: Postgraduate
**Type**: Fellowship
**Value**: C$70,000
**Length of Study**: 3 years
**Application Procedure**: Please contact the foundation for application form

## Grants-in-Aid of Research and Development

**Purpose**: To support researchers in projects of experimental nature in cardiovascular or cerebrovascular development
**Eligibility**: Open for full-time medical student
**Level of Study**: Postgraduate
**Type**: Grant
**Value**: Approx. C$33,000,000
**Frequency**: Every 3 years

**Application Procedure**: Applicants must send the application form along with the transcript, essay references and a self-addressed stamped envelope
**Closing Date**: 27 August
**Additional Information**: Please check website for more details.

## Heart and Stroke Foundation of Canada Doctoral Research Award

**Purpose**: To support individuals enroled in a PhD program and undertaking full-time research training in the stroke field
**Eligibility**: Applicants must be Canadians studying abroad or in Canada or for foreign visitors to Canada. The fellowship is open to citizens of United States
**Level of Study**: Postgraduate
**Type**: Fellowship
**Value**: Varies
**Country of Study**: Canada
**Application Procedure**: Applicants must send the application form along with the transcript, essay references and a self-addressed stamped envelope
**Closing Date**: 1 November

## For further information contact:

Heart and Stroke Foundation of Canada, 1037 Topsail Rd, Mount Pearl, NL A1N 5E9, Canada.

**Tel**: (1) 613 569 4361 ext. 268
**Fax**: (1) 613 569 3278
**Email**: anguyen@hsf.ca

## Heart and Stroke Foundation of Canada New Investigator Research Scholarships

**Eligibility**: 1. Must be a graduate student or a postgraduate student 2. Must attend a university 3. Citizenship requirements: Canada 4. Must not be attending high school currently 5. Must study full-time 6. Restricted to students studying Health and Medical Sciences
**Level of Study**: Postgraduate
**Type**: Scholarship
**Value**: Maximum C$30,000
**Application Procedure**: Applicants must send the application form along with the transcript, essay references and a self-addressed stamped envelope
**Closing Date**: 1 September
**Additional Information**: www.petersons.com/scholarship/heart-and-stroke-foundation-of-canada-new-investigator-111_151415.aspx

**For further information contact:**

1525 Carling Avenue, Suite 110, Ottawa, ON K1Z 8R9, Canada.

**Tel**:       (4041) 613 569 4361
**Email**:   research@heartandstroke.ca

## Heart and Stroke Foundation of Canada Nursing Research Fellowships

**Eligibility**: Applicants must possess a Nursing degree. For master's degree candidates, the programmes must include a thesis or project requirement
**Level of Study**: Postgraduate
**Type**: Fellowship
**Value**: Minimum C$18,570
**Country of Study**: Canada
**Application Procedure**: Applicants must send the application form along with the transcript, essay references and a self-addressed stamped envelope
**Closing Date**: 14 March
**Additional Information**: Please check website for more details.

**For further information contact:**

Research Department, 222 Queen Street, Suite 1402, Ottawa, ON K1P 5V9, Canada.

**Tel**:       (1) 613 569 4361 ext. 327
**Fax**:     (1) 613 569 3278
**Email**:   lhodgson@hsf.ca

## Heart and Stroke Foundation of Canada Research Fellowships

**Eligibility**: Applicants must possess a full-time degree for study towards an MSc or PhD.
**Level of Study**: Postgraduate
**Type**: Fellowship
**Value**: C$25,998 (minimum) and C$33,426 (maximum)
**Country of Study**: Canada
**Application Procedure**: Applicants must send the application form along with the transcript, essay references and a self-addressed stamped envelope
**Closing Date**: 1 November

## Heart Research United Kingdom

Suite 12D, Joseph's Well, Leeds, LS3 1AB, United Kingdom.

**Tel**:       (44) 11 3234 7474
**Email**:   mail@heartresearch.org.uk

**Website**:   www.heartresearch.org.uk
**Contact**:   Helen Wilson, Senior Research Officer

Heart Research United Kingdom funds pioneering medical research into the prevention, treatment and cure of heart disease. Heart Research United Kingdom is a visionary charity leading the way in funding ground-breaking, innovative medical research projects at the cutting edge of science into the prevention, treatment and cure of heart disease. There is a strong emphasis on clinical and surgical projects and young researchers. Heart Research United Kingdom encourages and supports original health lifestyle initiatives exploring novel ways of preventing heart disease in all sectors of the community.

## Heart Research United Kingdom Translational Research Project Grants

**Purpose**: To support ground-breaking, innovative medical research into prevention, treatment and cure of heart disease and related conditions
**Eligibility**: Graduates or those holding a suitable professional qualification. Research must be carried out in the United Kingdom at a university, hospital or other recognized research institution
**Level of Study**: Research, Unrestricted
**Type**: Project grant
**Value**: £200,000
**Length of Study**: Up to 3 years
**Frequency**: Annual
**Study Establishment**: Centres of health and educational establishments
**Country of Study**: United Kingdom
**Application Procedure**: Information and application forms available at heartresearch.org.uk/grants/translational-research-project-trp-grants
**No. of awards offered**: 45
**Closing Date**: 1 June
**Funding**: Private, Corporation, Foundation, Trusts, Individuals
**Contributor**: Voluntary funding from supporters and grant-making trusts
**No. of awards given last year**: 6
**No. of applicants last year**: 45
**Additional Information**: Please note that the HRUK office is closed on Saturdays and Sundays and therefore deliveries cannot be accepted at the weekend. heartresearch.org.uk/trp-apply/

**For further information contact:**

Heart Research UK, Suite 12D, Joseph's Well, Leeds, LS3 1AB, United Kingdom.

**Email**:   research@heartresearch.org.uk

# Heinrich Boll Foundation

Heinrich-Böll-Stiftung e.V. Schumannstr. 8, D-10117 Berlin, Germany.

**Tel**:        (49) 30 28 534 400
**Email**:      studienwerk@boell.de
**Website**:    www.boell.de/en

Fostering democracy and upholding human rights, taking action to prevent the destruction of the global ecosystem, advancing equality between women and men, securing peace through con–flict prevention in crisis zones, and defer-ding the freedom of individuals against excessive state and economic power – these are the objectives that drive the ideas and actions of the Heinrich Böll Foundation. We maintain close ties to the German Green Party (Alliance 90/The Greens) and as a think tank for green visions and projects, we are part of an international net–work encompassing well over 100 partner projects in approxi–mately 60 countries. The Heinrich Böll Foundation works independently and nurtures a spirit of intellectual openness. We maintain a world–wide network with currently 30 international offices. We co–operate closely with 16 state-level Böll Foundations in each of Germany's federal states, and we support talented, socio-politi–cally engaged undergraduate and graduate students in Germany and abroad. We gladly follow Heinrich Böll's exhortation for citizens to get involved in politics, and we want to inspire others to do the same.

## Heinrich Boll Scholarships in Germany for International Students

**Purpose**: The Heinrich Böll Foundation awards some schol-arships to international students who gained their university entrance qualification from a school outside of Germany who wish to study a Masters or PhD Degree in Germany.
**Eligibility**: International Master students who earned their university entrance qualification outside Germany: You may apply before commencing your Masters programme or at any time up to the end of the first semester of the Masters pro-gramme. Proof of first professional qualification must be provided, International Doctoral students who earned the university entrance qualification outside Germany: The appli-cant must have been accepted as a doctoral student by a state or state-recognised university in Germany. Proof of admis-sion, as a rule in Germany, must be included with the appli-cation. By the application date, preliminary work must have been completed and a valid timetable for completion must be submitted. PhD subjects related to focal points of the Foun-dation's activities will be given priority.

**Level of Study**: Masters Studies/ PhD Studies
**Type**: Scholarships
**Value**: Masters Studies: Non-EU students: €850 per month plus various individual allowances; tuition fees are in certain cases possible in Germany. EU students: varies, max. €649 plus €300 book money per month; tuition fees not possible in Germany but possible to a limited extent in other countries. The scholarship is awarded for the regular period of study, may be extended by one semester. PhD Studies: Non-EU students: €1,200 per month plus €100 mobility allowance per month, plus various individual allowances; tuition fees are not possible. EU students: €1,350 per month basic schol-arship plus €100 per month research costs allowance; tuition fees are not possible in Germany but possible to a limited extent in other countries. The scholarship is awarded for two years as a rule, may be extended twice at most by half a year.
**Frequency**: Annual
**Country of Study**: Germany
**Application Procedure**: For details of application require-ments and procedures, please consult information sheet A 1-1 ("scholarship application for undergraduate and graduate stu-dents", PDF) or A 2-1 ("scholarship application for doctoral studies"). The online application portal closes on 1 March at the latest. It is important to visit the official website (link found below) for details on how to apply for this scholarship.
**No. of awards offered**: Not specified
**Closing Date**: 1 March
**Additional Information**: www.boell.de/en/foundation/application.

# Helen Hay Whitney Foundation

## Postdoctoral Research Fellowship

**Subjects**: Biomedical sciences
**Purpose**: To attain its ultimate goal of increasing the number of imaginative, well-trained and dedicated medical scientists, the Foundation grants financial support of sufficient duration to help further the careers of young men and women engaged in biological or medical research.
**Eligibility**: Candidates who hold, or are in the final stages of obtaining a PhD, M.D., or equivalent degree and are seeking beginning postdoctoral training in basic biomedical research are eligible to apply for a fellowship. The Foundation accepts applications from candidates who have no more than one year of postdoctoral research experience at the time of the deadline for submitting the application (June 15), and who have received a PhD (or D.Phil. or equivalent) degree no more than two years before the deadline, or an M.D. degree no more than three years before the deadline. Fellowships may be awarded to US citizens planning to work in laboratories either in the US, Canada, or abroad and also to foreign citizens

for research in laboratories in the US only. We expect that most applicants will reside in North America at the time of application. Foreign Students will need to obtain appropriate visa documentation, as required by US Immigration. Applications from established scientists or advanced fellows will not be considered. The fellowships are for early postdoctoral training only. Clinical house-staff training does not count as postdoctoral laboratory training. The Foundation will not ordinarily consider applicants who plan tenure of the fellowship in the laboratory in which they have already received extensive predoctoral or postdoctoral training. The aim of the fellowship is to broaden postdoctoral training and experience, and a significant change of venue is advisable. Since the number of available fellowships is limited, the Foundation does not make more than one award per year for training with a given supervisor. It also does not support more than two fellows per laboratory at one time.

**Type**: Fellowship

**Value**: Up to US$54,000 in the first year; US$57,000 in the second and US$60,000 in the third, plus a US$1,500 annual research allowance. There is a Dependent Child Allowance of US$1,500 per annum for each child. There is no allowance for a spouse.

**Length of Study**: Three years

**Country of Study**: Any country

**Application Procedure**: Applications are to be filled out and submitted online at www.hhwf.org.

**Closing Date**: 15 June

**Additional Information**: Apply online. hhwf.org/research-fellowship/

---

# Hellenic Pasteur Institute

Vas Sofias Avenue 127, GR-11521 Athens, Greece.

**Tel**:       (30) 1 647 8800
**Website**:   www.pasteur.gr
**Contact**:   Dr S Tzartos

## W.D.E. Coulson & Toni M. Cross Aegean Exchange Program

**Purpose**: The purpose of these fellowships is to provide an opportunity for Greek scholars to meet with their Turkish colleagues, and to pursue research interests in the museum, archive, and library collections and at the sites and monuments of Turkey

**Eligibility**: The library at ARIT-Istanbul includes approximately 14,000 volumes and covers the Byzantine, Ottoman, and modern Turkish periods. Archives, libraries, sites, and museums in Turkey provide resources for research into many fields of study and geographical areas

**Level of Study**: Postdoctorate

**Type**: Fellowship

**Length of Study**: From two weeks to two months

**Frequency**: Annual

**Country of Study**: Any country

**Application Procedure**: 1. Stipend of US$250 is required. 2. Submit "Associate Membership with Fellowship" application online. 3. The application should include a curriculum vitae, statement of the project to be pursued during the period of grant (up to three pages, single-spaced in length), two letters of reference from scholars in the field commenting on the value and feasibility of the project

**Funding**: Private

**Additional Information**: ascsa.submittable.com/submit/ 115754/elizabeth-a-whitehead-distinguished-scholars-application-form hellenicstudies.gsu.edu/2019/01/21/w-d-e-coulson-toni-m-cross-aegean-exchange-program/

---

# Help Musicians United Kingdom

## Postgraduate Awards

**Purpose**: Help Musicians United Kingdom's postgraduate awards offer support to students who wish to complete their studies at the leading UK conservatoires and performing arts colleges. The charity has been making awards to postgraduate music students of between £1,000 and £5,000 since the 1970s. Previous winners of these awards include trumpeter Alison Balsom OBE, percussionist Dame Evelyn Glennie, violinist Clio Gould, cellist Guy Johnston, violinist Tasmin Little OBE and guitarist Miloš Karadaglic. The Postgraduate Awards were previously run on a nomination basis where Heads of Departments at select conservatoires and performing colleges put forward students who qualified for the grant. However, HMUK is now reviewing how accessible and inclusive the Programme is to ensure that any potential barriers there may be in applying for funding are removed. The new open and direct application process also aims to alleviate some of the administrative burden on the Heads of Department and empower the students to take control of their futures

**Level of Study**: Postgraduate

**Type**: Award

**Value**: Up to £5,000

**Length of Study**: Annual Awards

**Frequency**: Annual

**Country of Study**: United Kingdom

**Application Procedure**: Must have lived in United Kingdom for 3 consecutive years by Postgraduate start date. Applications made via online application form

**No. of awards offered**: 200

**Closing Date**: February

**Funding**: Private

**Contributor**: Help Musicians United Kingdom

**No. of awards given last year**: 125

**No. of applicants last year**: 200

**Additional Information**: Applications for musical theatre, opera, répétiteurs and popular music students open April of each year. (i.e. Mmus, MA, PGDip, Artist Diploma) Have lived in the United Kingdom for at least 3 consecutive years at the start of the academic year in which they will be supported by the award Be in financial need Demonstrate that they have the musical potential and ambition to create a successful and sustainable career within the music industry HMUK strongly encourages applications from students from underrepresented backgrounds, including those from BAME (Black, Asian and Minority Ethnic) backgrounds, D/deaf and disabled people; and those from lower socio-economic groups. Through our Postgraduate Awards, we are unable to fund: Non-music performance degrees such as composition, music technology, music education, music therapy, arts administration and music business Undergraduate courses PhDs, MPhil, DMus, Doctorates Study from the previous academic year

### For further information contact:

**Tel**: (44) 20 7239 9119

**Email**: creative@helpmusicians.org.uk

## Sybil Tutton Awards

**Purpose**: To assist students on advanced postgraduate opera courses

**Eligibility**: Nominees must be British or Irish or have lived in the United Kingdom for at least five consecutive years at the closing date

**Type**: Award

**Value**: £1,000–5,000

**Frequency**: Annual

**Country of Study**: Any country

**Application Procedure**: Application is by nomination only from head of voice at the United Kingdom conservatoires and the National Opera Studio

**Closing Date**: May

### For further information contact:

**Email**: awards@helpmusicians.org.uk

## Henry Moore Institute

The Headrow, Leeds, LS1 3AH, United Kingdom.

| | |
|---|---|
| **Tel**: | (44) 113 246 7467 |
| **Email**: | kirstie@henry-moore.org |
| **Website**: | www.henry-moore.org |
| **Contact**: | Kirstie Gregory, Research Programme Assistant |

The Henry Moore Institute is a world-recognized centre for the study of sculpture in the heart of needs an award-winning exhibitions venue, research centre, library and sculpture archive. The institute hosts exhibitions, conferences and lectures, as well as developing research to expand the understanding and scholarship of historical and contemporary sculpture.

## Henry Moore Institute Research Fellowships

**Purpose**: To enable scholars to use the Institute's facilities, which include the sculpture collection, library, archive and slide library, to assist them in researching their particular field

**Eligibility**: There are no restrictions

**Level of Study**: Doctorate, Postdoctorate, Postgraduate, Research

**Type**: Fellowship

**Value**: Accommodation, travel and daily living expenses

**Length of Study**: 1 month

**Frequency**: Annual

**Study Establishment**: The Henry Moore Institute

**Country of Study**: United Kingdom

**Application Procedure**: Applicants must send a letter of application, a proposal (maximum 1,000 words) and a curriculum vitae. Visit the website

**No. of awards offered**: 80

**Closing Date**: 12 January

**Funding**: Foundation

**Contributor**: The Henry Moore Foundation

**No. of awards given last year**: 4

**No. of applicants last year**: 80

**Additional Information**: www.henry-moore.org/grants/grants-programme/research-fellowships

## Henry Moore Institute Senior Fellowships

**Purpose**: Senior fellowships are intended to give established scholars (working on any aspect of sculpture) time and space to develop a research project free from their usual work commitments

**Level of Study**: Doctorate, Postdoctorate
**Type**: Fellowship
**Value**: Fellowships provide accommodation, travel expenses, and a per diem
**Length of Study**: 3–6 weeks
**Frequency**: Annual
**Study Establishment**: Henry Moore Institute
**Country of Study**: United Kingdom
**Application Procedure**: Full details are available from the website www.henry-moore.ac.uk
**No. of awards offered**: 15
**Closing Date**: 12 January
**Funding**: Foundation
**Contributor**: Henry Moore Foundation
**No. of awards given last year**: 1
**No. of applicants last year**: 15
**Additional Information**: Research fellowships are also available. The institute offers the possibility of presenting finished research in published form as a seminar or as a small exhibition

## Herb Society of America, Inc.

9019 Kirtland Chardon Road, Kirtland, OH 44094, United States of America.

| | |
|---|---|
| **Tel**: | (1) 440 256 0514 |
| **Email**: | herbs@herbsociety.org |
| **Website**: | www.herbsociety.org |
| **Contact**: | Ms Michelle Milks, Office Administrator |

The aim of the Herb Society of America Inc. is to promote the knowledge, use and delight of herbs through educational programmes, research and sharing the experience of its members with the community.

### Herb Society of America Research Grant

**Purpose**: To further the knowledge and use of herbs and to contribute the results of study and research to the records of horticulture, science, literature, history, art or economics
**Eligibility**: Open to persons with a proposed programme of scientific, academic or artistic investigation of herbal plants
**Level of Study**: Unrestricted
**Value**: Up to US$5,000
**Length of Study**: Up to 1 year
**Frequency**: Annual
**Country of Study**: Any country

**Application Procedure**: Applicants must submit an application clearly defining all their research in 500 words or less and a proposed budget with specific budget items listed. Requests for funds will not be considered unless accompanied by five copies of the application form and proposal. The application must be submitted in electronic form via email to herbs@herbsociety.org
**Closing Date**: 31 January
**Contributor**: Members
**Additional Information**: Finalists will be interviewed. In order to complete the application, use the below link. herbsocietyorg.presencehost.net/support/grants-scholarships/application-for-the-hsa-research-grant.html grad.uchicago.edu/fellowship/herb-society-of-america-research-grant/

## Heriot-Watt University

Postgraduate Admissions Office, Edinburgh, EH14 4AS, United Kingdom.

| | |
|---|---|
| **Tel**: | (44) 131 449 5111 |
| **Email**: | edu.liaison@hw.ac.uk |
| **Website**: | www.hw.ac.uk |
| **Contact**: | Fiona Watt, Wider Access Assistant |

Heriot-Watt University, one of the oldest higher education institutions in the United Kingdom, is Scotland's most international university. Our six academic schools and two postgraduate institutes offer research opportunities and postgraduate taught programmes in science and engineering, business, languages and design. We disburse over £6M in fee and stipend scholarships annually.

### Mexican Scholarships

**Purpose**: Financial assistance for Mexican students in science, engineering and technology
**Eligibility**: Mexican citizens
**Level of Study**: Postgraduate
**Type**: Scholarship
**Value**: Tuition fees and living costs
**Frequency**: Annual
**Study Establishment**: Heriot-Watt University
**Country of Study**: Scotland
**Application Procedure**: Contact Bob Tuttle
**Funding**: Government
**Contributor**: Heriot-Watt and CONACYT (Mexican National Council for Science and Technology)

## For further information contact:

Tel:     (44) 131 451 3746
Email:   b.tuttle@hw.ac.uk

## Music Scholarships

Purpose: To support musicians in obtaining a postgraduate qualification whilst developing their musical skills
Eligibility: All instrumentalists and vocalists who have been accepted for a course. The following criteria are taken into consideration: musical ability and potential, proof of exam results and membership of orchestras or choirs; a reference from your last vocal or instrumental teacher; in the case of the Archer Music Scholarships, a personal statement is also required; auditions will be held during Semester 1
Level of Study: Postgraduate, Research
Type: Scholarship
Value: free music tuition for talented singers and instrumentalists, up to a value of £400 per year and talented musician to receive music tuition up to a value of £500
Length of Study: 1 year
Frequency: Annual
Study Establishment: Heriot-Watt University
Country of Study: Scotland
Application Procedure: For an application form or more information please contact Steve King MBE, Director of Music
Additional Information: There will be a music scholar's concert in HWU in March each year at which all music scholars are all expected to participate. www.hw.ac.uk/news.htm

## For further information contact:

Tel:     (44) 131 451 3705
Email:   s.king@hw.ac.uk

## Overseas Research Students Awards Scheme (ORSAS)

Purpose: Assist international postgraduate research students with payment of tuition fees
Eligibility: Non-European Union research applicants
Level of Study: Research
Type: Scholarship
Length of Study: 3 years
Frequency: Annual
Study Establishment: Heriot-Watt University
Country of Study: Scotland
Application Procedure: Apply to School of Study
Closing Date: 30 November

Contributor: Heriot-Watt University
Additional Information: Successful applicants usually receive James Watt Scholarships for the remainder of their fees plus a maintenance contribution.

## For further information contact:

Email:   pgadmissions@glasgow.ac.uk

## Postgraduate Merit Award

Purpose: We aim to encourage well-qualified, ambitious students to study with us and we offer a wide variety of scholarships and bursaries to achieve this. Over £6 million worth of opportunities are available in fee and stipend scholarships, and more than 400 students benefit from this support.
Eligibility: 1. Domiciled in one of the countries listed above at the time of application and classified as an overseas student for fee purposes starting a full-time on-campus programme of study. 2. Self-funding your course. 3. Holding an offer to study a full-time postgraduate taught degree course starting in September 2020.
Level of Study: Postgraduate
Type: Scholarship
Value: £1,500 - £3,000
Frequency: Annual
Application Procedure: You will be automatically considered for the scholarship if you meet the academic criteria.
No. of awards offered: Multiple
Closing Date: September
Additional Information: www.hw.ac.uk/study/scholarships/postgraduate-merit-award.htm

## For further information contact:

Edinburgh, Scotland, EH14 4AS, United Kingdom.

Tel:     (44) 131 449 5111

## Higher & Education South Africa

## Africa: Mwalimu Julius Nyerere African Union Scholarship

Purpose: Mwalimu Julius Nyerere African Union Scholarship is intended to enable young Africans to study at reputable African universities with a binding agreement that scholarship beneficiaries will work in any African country for at least the same duration of the scholarship period after graduation. The scholarship aims to provide an opportunity to enhance knowledge, professional skills and capacity of refugees and displaced people, in order to streamline their integration to contribute towards sustainable development in Africa

**Eligibility**: 1. Applicants must be a citizen of an African Union Member State. 2. Must be a formally registered refugee/displaced person with a UNHCR registration number or be able to demonstrate confirmed refugee status in an African Union Member State. 3. Must be under the age of thirty five (35) years. 4. Must be a holder of a Bachelor's degree in the relevant field, at least at the level of Upper Second class Honours. The degree must be from a recognised university. 5. Must have demonstrated outstanding academic achievement as evidenced by academic transcripts, and academic awards if any. 6. Have proof of admission to undertake a full time Master's programme in a recognized university in an African Union Member State. 7. Be willing to commit to work in an African Union Member State on completion of studies for at least three (3) years

**Level of Study**: Postgraduate

**Type**: Scholarship

**Value**: Stipend to the value of ZAR500 monthly to cover accommodation, meals, utilities, local transport and medication, Travel allowance: once-off ZAR250, ZAR350 to assist with shipping and other terminal expenses, Computer allowance: ZAR1,000

**Frequency**: Annual

**Country of Study**: South Africa

**Application Procedure**: Apply online: www.edu-au.org/scholarshipg

**Closing Date**: 30 April

**Funding**: Foundation

### For further information contact:

Department of Human Resources, Science and Technology, African Union Commission, P O Box 3243, Addis Ababa, Ethiopia, Eastern Africa.

**Tel**:      (251) 11 551 77 00
**Fax**:      (251) 11 551 78 44
**Email**:      internationalscholarships@dhet.gov.za

## Africa: Next Einstein Forum (NEF) Fellows Programme

**Purpose**: The Next Einstein Forum (NEF) is an initiative of the African Institute for Mathematical Sciences (AIMS) in partnership with the Robert Bosch Stiftung. The NEF is a platform that connects science, society and policy in Africa and the rest of the world — with the goal to leverage science for human development globally. The Fellows Programme consists of Africa's most brilliant young scientists that the NEF showcases on the global stage. The Programme provides

Fellows with the opportunity to present their research and draw upon the vast networks of NEF members and participants for support, connections and advice to advance their work

**Eligibility**: 1. Africans from around the world — including those who currently reside in the Diaspora. 2. Hold a passport from an African country. 3. Hold a PhD in a field of science, Technology, Engineering, Mathematics or the social sciences. 4. Have a demonstrated track record of research/findings that have global impact. 5. You are passionate about raising Africa's profile in STEM globally. 6. Able to clearly present their work to an audience in English or French

**Level of Study**: Postgraduate

**Type**: Fellowship

**Frequency**: Annual

**Country of Study**: South Africa

**Closing Date**: 27 January

**Funding**: Foundation

**Additional Information**: www.afterschoolafrica.com/17391/next-einstein-forum-fellowship/

### For further information contact:

NEF Secretariat, c/o AIMS-NEI 590 KG ST Gasabo, Kigali, Rwanda.

**Email**:      info@nef.org

## Austria: Erasmus+ Master in Research and Innovation in Higher Education (MARIHE) Programme

**Purpose**: The Master in Research and Innovation in Higher Education (MARIHE) is supported by the Erasmus+ Programme of the European Union (EU) under the action of an Erasmus Mundus Joint Master Degree (EMJMD)

**Eligibility**: 1. Must hold a first university degree, this should be at least a Bachelor degree issued by a university, quantified as three years of studies corresponding. 2. Show a strong motivation and interest. 3. Have sufficient knowledge of English for academic purposes

**Level of Study**: Postgraduate

**Type**: Grant

**Frequency**: Annual

**Country of Study**: South Africa

**Application Procedure**: Apply online: www.marihe.eu/how-to-apply/application-process-and-timetable

**Closing Date**: 5 December

**Funding**: Private

### For further information contact:

**Email**:      marihe@donau-uni.ac.at

## Azerbaijan: Non-Aligned Movement (NAM) Scholarship

**Purpose**: The Government of the Republic of Azerbaijan is offering scholarships for Bachelor's, Master's and Doctoral programmes to the citizens of Non-Aligned Movement (NAM) countries (including South Africa)

**Eligibility**: 1. Citizen of Non-Aligned Movement (NAM) countries (this includes South Africa) 2. For undergraduate programmes applicants must be younger than 25 years old 3. For Master's programmes applicants must be younger than 30 years old 4. For doctoral programmes applicants must be younger than 40 years old

**Level of Study**: Postgraduate

**Type**: Scholarship

**Value**: Value of AZN 800

**Frequency**: Annual

**Country of Study**: South Africa

**Application Procedure**: Apply: www.internationalscholar ships.dhet.gov.za/Application%20form.pdf

**Closing Date**: 8 February

**Funding**: Foundation

**Additional Information**: www.internationalscholarships. dhet.gov.za/AZERBAIJANNon-AlignedMovement(NAM) Scholarship202021.html

#### For further information contact:

**Tel**: (994) 12 596 92 96

**Email**: scholars@mfa.gov.az

## Brunei Darussalam: Government of Brunei Darussalam Scholarship

**Purpose**: The Brunei Darussalam Ministry of Foreign Affairs invites applications for the Government of Brunei Darussalam Scholarship. The scholarship is tenable at higher education institutions in Brunei Darussalam and provides applicants with an opportunity to pursue Diploma, Bachelor's and Master's degrees

**Eligibility**: 1. Applicant must be citizen of Pakistan/AJK 2. Must be between the ages of 18-25 for undergraduate programmes 3. Age should not exceed from 35 years for candidates who are applying for Postgraduate programmes. 4. Applicants having 3rd division in their academic career are eligible to apply but NOT in the terminal degree. 5. The applicant must have completed HSSC/Intermediate or equivalent for application to 04 year Bachelor Program. 6. The applicant must have completed 16 years education or (04 years) Bachelors/equivalent Degree for application to Postgraduate Masters Program. 7. Certificates/Transcript/ Degrees to be attached must be attested by the attesting authorities such as IBCC and HEC. Equivalence of O & A level is mandatory by IBCC. 8. The applicant must provide Health certificate with his application. 9. IELTS/TOEFL scores are required, where applicable.

**Level of Study**: Postgraduate

**Type**: Scholarship

**Value**: BND250.00 to a country within the asean region; or BND500.00 to a country outside the asean region

**Frequency**: Annual

**Country of Study**: South Africa

**Application Procedure**: Apply online: www.ubd.edu.bn/ admission/scholarships.html

**No. of awards offered**: Several

**Closing Date**: 14 February

**Funding**: Foundation

**Additional Information**: www.afterschoolafrica.com/11428/ brunei-darussalam-government-scholarships/

#### For further information contact:

Assistant Director, Learning Opportunities Abroad (LOA), HRD Division, Higher Education Commission, Sector H-8, Islamabad, Pakistan.

**Tel**: (92) 51 111 119 432

**Email**: applyBDGS2020@mfa.gov.bn

## China: Chinese Government Scholarship

**Purpose**: The Chinese Government is offering scholarships for South African students to study at Chinese institutions. The Department of Higher Education and Training is responsible for nominations

**Eligibility**: Listed below are the eligibility factors for the scholarship: 1. South African citizens in good health (medical check will be required for successful applicants). 2. Strong academic record with a minimum 65% average in previous studies. 3. Demonstrated interest in China and commitment to the development of South Africa. 4. Applications in all fields of study except medicine will be considered. 5. Preference will be given to postgraduate applicants, previously disadvantaged applicants and applications in the following fields. The scholarship is offered for undergraduate (Bachelors) in the identified scarce skills, postgraduate (Masters or PhD) or non-degree Chinese language studies. Bachelor's degree scholarships are taught in Chinese and will only be awarded to applicants who already have the required level of Chinese proficiency (HSK 5 or above). Preference is given to applications for postgraduate studies

**Level of Study**: Postgraduate

**Type**: Scholarship

**Frequency**: Annual

**Country of Study**: South Africa
**Application Procedure**: Apply online: www.campuschina.org/universities/index.html
**Closing Date**: 15 March
**Funding**: Foundation

### For further information contact:

Level 13, Building A3 No. 9 Chegongzhuang St, Dong Wu Yuan, Xicheng Qu, CN 100738, Beijing Shi, China.

**Email**:    internationalscholarships@dhet.gov.za

## China: One Belt One Road Scholarship

**Purpose**: Peking University Guanghua School of Management is offering One Belt One Road Scholarship to pursue an MBA programme at Peking University. The International MBA programme is a full-time (2 years) English-taught programme
**Eligibility**: 1. Applicants must hold a non-Chinese citizenship and be citizens from Belt and Road Initiative (BRI) countries. 2. Must hold a Bachelor's degree equivalent to a Bachelor's degree in China. 3. Must have two or more years of relevant full-time work experience. 4. Must obtain a competitive score from the Guanghua MBA entrance exam. 5. Must have leadership quality
**Level of Study**: Postgraduate
**Type**: Scholarship
**Value**: Accommodation subsidy (RMB 4,000/person/month), Living allowance (RMB 3,000/person/month), edical insurance fee (RMB 800/person/year), Application fee of RMB 800 will be waived
**Length of Study**: 2 year
**Frequency**: Annual
**Country of Study**: South Africa
**Application Procedure**: Apply online: applymba.pku.edu.cn/ The One Belt One Road Scholarship will not only provide the opportunity to study at Peking University which is one of the most prestigious universities in China, and is ranked #1 in China and #2 in the Asia-Pacific region by Times Higher Education World University Rankings, but also a chance to become an expert in China affairs and gain a solid foothold in the China market
**Closing Date**: September
**Funding**: Private

### For further information contact:

Apply online: applymba.pku.edu.cn//

**Tel**:      (86) 15010 656 075
**Email**:    yul@gsm.pku.edu.cn

## China: Renmin University Master of Contemporary Chinese Studies Scholarship

**Purpose**: The Silk Road School at the Renmin University of China (Suzhou) offers scholarships to foreign students who wish to pursue a Master of Contemporary Chinese studies at Renmin University of China (Suzhou)
**Eligibility**: 1. Be foreign citizens who have interest in Belt and Road Initiative (BRI) and Chinese culture. 2. Have the ability to speak, read and write English at an equivalent score of IELTS 6.5 or TOEFL 90
**Level of Study**: Postgraduate
**Type**: Scholarship
**Frequency**: Annual
**Country of Study**: South Africa
**Application Procedure**: Apply online: www.rdcy.org/displaynewsen.php?id=45928
**Closing Date**: 10 June
**Funding**: Foundation
**Additional Information**: www.internationalscholarships.dhet.gov.za/china%20-%20Copy.html

### For further information contact:

**Tel**:      (86) 10 6251 6305
**Email**:    srsruc@ruc.edu.cn

## Embassy of France in South Africa Master Scholarship Programme

**Purpose**: The Embassy of France invites students who wish to continue their tertiary education at Master level in France for the academic year September apply for its scholarship programme
**Eligibility**: 1. Citizenship of South Africa or Lesotho. 2. Bachelor's or Honour's graduate (depending on the academic year to enrol for), completed or to be completed by the time the student would depart for France. 3. Acceptance from three selected French institutions of the candidate's choice. Students should apply for admission to these universities concurrently to the bursary application (admission letters or at least correspondence with the institutions will be required for complete applications). 4. Maximum academic fees (administration and tuition fees combined) financed with a full scholarship: €5,000. For academic fees higher than €5,000 co-financing options must be provided (personal savings and/or enterprise sponsorship). 5. Maximum academic fees (administration and tuition fees combined) financed with a full scholarship: €5,000. For academic fees higher than €5,000 co-financing options must be provided (personal savings and/or enterprise sponsorship). 6. No knowledge of French language required, depending on the availability of

study course in English. Courses relating to the French Language (i.e. translation, interpreting or French language teaching) must follow a different application process

**Level of Study**: Postgraduate

**Type**: Scholarship

**Value**: €5,000

**Length of Study**: 1 year

**Frequency**: Annual

**Country of Study**: Any country

**Closing Date**: 15 March

**Funding**: Foundation

**For further information contact:**

**Email**:   audrey.delattre@diplomatie.gouv.fr

## Embassy of France in South Africa PhD Grants

**Purpose**: The French Embassy scholarship programme offers grants to facilitate in the international academic and scientific mobility of South African and non-South African researchers to French Higher Education institutions. The programme offers the opportunity for doctoral students to integrate into French establishments for specified time periods in order to participate in collaborative research as part of their doctoral research project

**Eligibility**: 1. Registration for a PhD at a South African university. 2. A hosting agreement from the French institution. 3. Support letters from your South African supervisor and French co-supervisor, supporting the proposed research project. 4. Applications from all academic disciplines will be considered. 5. No knowledge of French language required, provided the student will be able to conduct research in English

**Level of Study**: Postgraduate

**Type**: Scholarship

**Value**: €1,065

**Frequency**: Annual

**Country of Study**: Any country

**Funding**: Foundation

**For further information contact:**

**Tel**:   (27) 12 343 6563

**Email**:   pretoria@campusfrance.org

## France: French Embassy and Saint-Gobain Master Scholarship

**Purpose**: Saint-Gobain and the Embassy of France in South Africa are offering scholarships to South Africans and Basotho graduates to pursue a Master's degree in Business studies or Engineering at public French universities

**Level of Study**: Postgraduate

**Type**: Scholarship

**Value**: €767 and annual tuition fees (€3,770) at public universities

**Frequency**: Annual

**Country of Study**: Any country

**Application Procedure**: Apply online: www.southafrica.campusfrance.org/page/campusfrance-south-africa-office

**Closing Date**: 30 March

**Funding**: Private

**Additional Information**: Contacts could be further established with the below link. www.southafrica.campusfrance.org/page/campusfrance-south-africa-office www.internationalscholarships.dhet.gov.za/FRANCEFrenchEmbassyandSaint-GobainMasterScholarship20192020.html

**For further information contact:**

**Email**:   pretoria.bourses@campusfrance.org

## France: French Embassy Masters and PhD Scholarship Programme

**Purpose**: The Embassy of France is offering scholarships to postgraduate South Africans who wish to pursue Master's and Doctoral studies at French higher education institutions

**Eligibility**: 1. Be a citizen and resident of South Africa. 2. Apply for university admission at three French universities concurrent to the scholarship application (admission letters or at least correspondence with the institutions will be required). Applications to French public universities are recommended since they have French government subsidised fees. 3. French proficiency is not required, provided they are pursuing a study course in English and have the ability to conduct research in English. 4. Courses relating to French language studies (i.e. translation, interpreting or French language teaching) must follow a different application process by contacting Audrey Delattre

**Level of Study**: Postgraduate

**Type**: Scholarship

**Frequency**: Annual

**Country of Study**: South Africa

**Application Procedure**: Apply online: www.southafrica.campusfrance.org/sites/locaux/files/PhD%20French%20Embassy%20application%20form%202019.pdf

**Closing Date**: 15 March

**Funding**: Foundation

**Additional Information**: www.internationalscholarships.dhet.gov.za/France%204-%20Copy.html

**For further information contact:**

**Email**:    pretoria@campusfrance.org

## France: ISAE-SUPAERO Scholarship Programmes

**Purpose**: The ISAE-SUPAERO Institute offers a wide range of science and engineering degree programs with a number of scholarships offered through industry support and the SUPAERO Foundation for pursuing studies towards a Master of Science in Aerospace Engineering degree. These scholarships cover tuition and part of living expenses
**Eligibility**: Applicants who hold a Bachelor's degree or the equivalent in Mechanical Engineering, Mechatronics, Aerospace, Electronics, Electrical Systems, Telecommunications or a French licence in Science and Engineering
**Level of Study**: Postgraduate
**Type**: Scholarship
**Value**: Tuition fees: €10,600, Living expenses: €8,000 to €10,000
**Frequency**: Annual
**Country of Study**: South Africa
**Application Procedure**: Apply online: www.isae-supaero.fr/en/academics/master-s-degree-msc/admissions/
**Funding**: Foundation
**Additional Information**: www.isae-supaero.fr/en/academics/ MSc/financing-144/financing/

**For further information contact:**

**Tel**:       (33) 561 338 027
**Email**:    philippe.galaup@isae-supaero.fr

## Hungary: Stipendium Hungaricum for South Africa

**Purpose**: The Hungarian Government is offering 100 scholarships to South African students to study at participating public university in Hungary. All courses available for South Africans are taught in English
**Eligibility**: 1. Be a South African citizen in good health. 2. Have a strong academic record. 3. An interest in studying in Hungary and demonstrated commitment to the development of South Africa. 4. Meet the entry criteria for their selected programme in Hungary. 5. Meet the minimum academic requirement for entry into a similar programme at a South African university
**Level of Study**: Postgraduate
**Type**: Grant
**Frequency**: Annual
**Country of Study**: South Africa

**Application Procedure**: Apply online: apply.stipendium hungaricum.hu/
**Closing Date**: 15 January
**Funding**: Foundation
**Additional Information**: www.internationalscholarships. dhet.gov.za/HUNGARY%20Stipendium%20Hungaricum%20for%20South%20Africa.html

**For further information contact:**

**Email**:    HungaryScholarshipApplications2019@dhet.gov.za

## India: Export-Import Bank of India BRICS Economic Research Award

**Purpose**: The Export-Import Bank of India (EXIM) has instituted the Export-Import Bank of India BRICS Economic Research Award. The award aims to encourage and stimulate advanced research on economics related topics of relevance to the member nations of Brazil Russia India China South Africa (BRICS). The EXIM Bank of India invites South African research scholars to apply for the Exim Bank of India BRICS Economic Research Award
**Eligibility**: Check online: www.eximbankindia.in/Assets/pdf/award/EXIM%20Bank%20BRICS%20Economic%20Research%20Award-%20Guidelines%20(English)%2015.04.2019.pdf
**Level of Study**: Postgraduate
**Type**: Award
**Value**: ZAR22 000
**Frequency**: Annual
**Country of Study**: South Africa
**Application Procedure**: Apply online: www.eximbankindia.in/awards
**Closing Date**: 15 April
**Funding**: Foundation
**Additional Information**: www.internationalscholarships. dhet.gov.za/INDIAExport-Import%20BankofIndiaBRICSEconomicResearchAward.html

**For further information contact:**

**Tel**:       (91) 22 2217 2701
**Email**:    rag@eximbankindia.in

## Indonesia: Kemitraan Negara Berkembang (Developing Countries Partnership) Scholarship

**Purpose**: The Kemitraan Negara Berkembang (KNB) Scholarship was first introduced by the Ministry of Education and Culture to embrace higher education globalization by providing financial assistance (scholarship) to the selected Indonesian Universities, to recruit potential international students to acquire Master's degrees in those universities. The KNB Scholarship program has expanded and is now offered to potential students from developing countries to acquire Bachelor's or Master's degrees at the prestigious universities in Indonesia. The Indonesian Government is offering 140 Master's and five Bachelor's degrees scholarships. All programmes are delivered in Bahasa Indonesia

**Eligibility**: 1. Applicants must not be older than 35 years of age. 2. Applicants must hold a Bachelor degree (Master's degree holder is not eligible to apply). 3. Applicants must have a TOEFL (or other certified English Proficiency) score of 500. 4. Applicants must be between the ages of 18-35 for Undergraduate and Diploma programmes

**Level of Study**: Postgraduate

**Type** Scholarship

**Frequency**: Annual

**Country of Study**: South Africa

**Application Procedure**: Apply online: www.knb.ristekdikti.go.id

**Closing Date**: 30 April

**Funding**: Foundation

**Additional Information**: www.internationalscholarships.dhet.gov.za/INDONESIAKemitraanNegaraBerkembang(Developing%20Countries%20Partnership)Scholarship.html

### For further information contact:

The Information and Socio-Cultural Section, The Embassy of the Republic of Indonesia, 949 Francis Baard Street, Arcardia 0083, South Africa.

**Tel**: (27) 12 342 3350
**Email**: info@indonesia-pretoria.org.za

## Ireland: Kader Asmal Fellowship Programme

**Purpose**: The Embassy of Ireland in South Africa in partnership with the Department of Higher Education and Training and the Canon Collins Trust invites applications for scholarships for one-year Master's degree study in Ireland commencing in September

**Eligibility**: 1. Be a South African citizen. 2. Have achieved the necessary standard to be accepted onto a postgraduate course in an institute of higher education in Ireland. 3. Be seeking funding for a full-time postgraduate programme in one of the above listed subject areas. 4. Be able to take up fellowship in the academic year. 5. Not have already applied for a course at an institution in Ireland - if you have already been admitted to a university you are not eligible

**Level of Study**: Postgraduate

**Type**: Fellowships, operating grants

**Frequency**: Annual

**Country of Study**: South Africa

**Application Procedure**: Apply online: www.canoncollins.org.uk/apply/scholarship/kader-asmal-fellowship

**Closing Date**: 31 December

**Funding**: Private

**Additional Information**: www.internationalscholarships.dhet.gov.za/IRELANDKaderAsmalFellowshipProgramme2020.html

### For further information contact:

**Email**: Rose.Machobane@dfa.ie

## Japan: MEXT Scholarships

**Purpose**: The Japanese Ministry of Education, Culture, Sports, Science, and Technology (MEXT) offers scholarships to foreign students who wish to study at Japanese universities under the Japanese Government Scholarship Program

**Eligibility**: see website: www.za.emb-japan.go.jp/itpr_en/MEXT_Scholarship.html

**Level of Study**: Postgraduate

**Type**: Scholarship

**Frequency**: Annual

**Country of Study**: South Africa

**Application Procedure**: Applications must be couriered or be hand delivered and addressed to: Cultural Section of the Embassy of Japan in South Africa: 259 Baines Street, Groenkloof, Pretoria, 0181

**Closing Date**: 8 June

**Funding**: Foundation

### For further information contact:

Cultural Section of the Embassy of Japan in South Africa, 259 Baines Street, Groenkloof, Pretoria 0181, South Africa.

**Email**: ryan.keet@pr.mofa.go.jp

## Jordan: Talal Abu-Ghazaleh University College for Innovation Scholarship

**Purpose**: Talal Abu-Ghazaleh University College for Innovation (TAGUCI) is offering a scholarship for a South African student who wishes to pursue a Master of Business Administration (MBA) degree at TAGUCI. Registration is now open for the semester

**Eligibility**: 1. Applicants must submit official Bachelor's degree transcripts and certificate, stamped by the Ministry of Higher Education and Scientific Research in Jordan.

2. English Language Equivalency exam mark of 65%. 3. Minimum of two years of work experience. 4. Written essay of up to 3,000 words. 5. Candidates must be prepared to fund any costs not covered by the scholarship

**Level of Study**: Postgraduate

**Type**: Scholarship

**Frequency**: Annual

**Country of Study**: Any country

**Application Procedure**: Apply online: www.taguci.edu.jo/RegistrationForm.aspx

**Closing Date**: 28 February

**Funding**: Foundation

**For further information contact:**

**Tel**:      (962) 65100 900

**Email**:   info@taguci.edu.jo

## Mauritius: Mauritius-Africa Scholarship Scheme

**Purpose**: As part of a commitment to promote capacity-building at high level across thecontinent, the Government of Mauritius is awarding scholarships to deserving students who are resident citizens of member states of the African Union or of African Commonwealth countries for full-time, on-campus undergraduate and postgraduate programmes tenable in public Higher Education Institutions (HEIs) in Mauritius

**Eligibility**: The Government of Mauritius is awarding scholarships to deserving students who are resident citizens of member states of the African Union or of African Commonwealth countries as per the following criteria: 1. For undergraduate programmes, applicants should be above 18 years of age and should not have reached their 26th birthday by the closing date of application. 2. For Master's programmes, applicants should not have reached 35 years and, for PhD programmes, applicants should not have reached 40 years by the closing date of application. 3. Applicants must have already applied for a full-time on-campus programme (Diploma, Degree, Master's or PhD) at a public Higher Education Institution in Mauritius (listed in Section 8 in the Guidelines for Applicants) for academic year starting in 2020. 4. The scholarship will be for a maximum duration as indicated in the table below or the minimum course duration whichever is lesser.

**Level of Study**: Postgraduate

**Type**: Scholarship

**Value**: Tuition fees and course-related costs of up to MUR 100,000; Monthly living allowance to the value of MUR 12,500

**Frequency**: Annual

**Country of Study**: South Africa

**Application Procedure**: Apply online: ministry-education.govmu.org/English/scholarships/Documents/2018/Application%20Form%20undergraduate%20MASS%2012Jan2018.pdf

**Closing Date**: 30 April

**Funding**: Foundation

**Additional Information**: opportunitydesk.org/2020/01/12/mauritius-africa-scholarship-scheme-2020/

**For further information contact:**

**Email**:    internationalscholarships@dhet.gov.za

## New Zealand: Scholarships for International Tertiary Students and Commonwealth Scholarship

**Purpose**: The New Zealand Aid Programme offers scholarships to potential applicants from eligible African countries (including South Africa) who are motivated to make a difference at home. Applications are now open for studies

**Level of Study**: Postgraduate

**Type**: Scholarship

**Frequency**: Annual

**Country of Study**: Any country

**Application Procedure**: All applications for the New Zealand Scholarship for International Tertiary Students must be submitted online. Please see the below links for more details on the process: All applications for the New Zealand Commonwealth Scholarship must be submitted on this application form. www.internationalscholarships.dhet.gov.za/Application Form 2019 Selection - Commonwealth.pdf

**Closing Date**: 31 March

**Funding**: Foundation

**Additional Information**: www.bursariesportal.co.za/bursary/new-zealand-scholarships-international-tertiary-students-and-commonwealth-scholarship-2021

**For further information contact:**

**Email**:    commonwealthscholarship@dhet.gov.za

## Romania: Romanian State Scholarships

**Purpose**: The Romanian Ministry of Foreign Affairs (MFA) and the Romanian Department of Public, Cultural and Scientific Diplomacy are offering 85 scholarship opportunities to foreign citizens, to study in Romania. This opportunity is open to students who wish to pursue studies in Bachelor's, Master's and PhD. Courses will be taught in Romanian language

**Eligibility**: 1. Applicants must be in good health and have a strong academic record. 2. Must present study papers issued by accredited / recognized educational institutions.

3. Applicants must not be older than 35 years of age for Bachelor's and Master's studies and 45 years respectively for Doctoral studies, by 31 December of the year in which they are nominated. 4. Candidates must be prepared to fund any costs not covered by the scholarship

**Level of Study**: Postgraduate

**Type**: Scholarship

**Value**: €85

**Length of Study**: 1 year

**Frequency**: Annual

**Country of Study**: South Africa

**Application Procedure**: Apply online: www.mae.ro/en/node/10251#null

**Closing Date**: 28 February

**Funding**: Foundation

### For further information contact:

**Email**: internationalscholarships@dhet.gov.za

## Romanian State Scholarships

**Purpose**: The Romanian Ministry of Foreign Affairs (MFA) and the Romanian Department of Public, Cultural and Scientific Diplomacy are offering 85 scholarship opportunities to foreign citizens, to study in Romania. This opportunity is open to students who wish to pursue studies in Bachelor's, Master's and PhD.

**Eligibility**: 1. Applicants must be in good health and have a strong academic record. 2. Must present study papers issued by accredited / recognized educational institutions. 3. Applicants must not be older than 35 years of age for Bachelor's and Master's studies and 45 years respectively for Doctoral studies, by 31 December of the year in which they are nominated. 4. Candidates must be prepared to fund any costs not covered by the scholarship

**Level of Study**: Postgraduate

**Type**: Scholarship

**Value**: €85

**Frequency**: Annual

**Country of Study**: South Africa

**Closing Date**: 28 February

**Funding**: Foundation

### For further information contact:

**Email**: internationalscholarships@dhet.gov.za

## Russia: Scholarships for South Africans

**Purpose**: The Russian Government offers annual scholarships for South Africans to study at Russian institutions. The scholarship is offered for Bachelor's, Masters and PhD degrees. Most programmes are taught in the Russian language. Scholarship recipients are required to undertake a preparatory course related to their field of study (including language training) for one year before pursuing their degree studies. Only after passing the examinations of the college preparatory course can they start their degree studies

**Eligibility**: 1. South African citizens in good health (medical test are required for successful applicants). 2. Have a strong academic record. 3. Demonstrated interest in Russia and commitment to the development of South Africa. 4. Applications in all fields of study except medicine will be considered. 5. Preference will be given to postgraduate applicants, previously disadvantaged applicants and applicants in the following fields

**Level of Study**: Postgraduate

**Type**: Scholarship

**Frequency**: Annual

**Country of Study**: South Africa

**Application Procedure**: Apply online: www.russia.study/en

**Closing Date**: 27 February

**Funding**: Foundation

**Additional Information**: www.internationalscholarships.dhet.gov.za/RUSSIA%20Scholarships%20for%20South%20Africans%202019.html

### For further information contact:

**Email**: Internationalscholarships@dhet.gov.za

## Spain: Student and Staff Exchange between South Africa and Spain

**Purpose**: Alianza 4 Universidades (A4U) is a consortium of four Spanish public universities. The consortium is funded by the Erasmus+ Programme of the European Union to enable student and staff exchange between universities members of the A4U and six South African partner universities

**Eligibility**: 1. Applicants from South African partner universities and A4U universities. South African partner universities include: University of Pretoria, University of the Witwatersrand, Stellenbosch University, University of Cape Town, University of the Western Cape and University of the Free State. 2. A4U Universities participating universities are Universitat Autònoma de Barcelona, Universidad Autónoma de Madrid, Universidad Carlos III de Madrid and Universitat Pompeu Fabra in Barcelona

**Level of Study**: Postgraduate

**Type**: Grant

**Frequency**: Annual

**Country of Study**: South Africa

**Application Procedure**: Apply online: alliance4universities.eu/en/mobility-scholarships/

**Closing Date**: December

**Funding**: Foundation
**Additional Information**: www.internationalscholarships.dhet.gov.za/SPAIN%20Student%20and%20staff%20exchange%20between%20South%20Africa%20and%20Spain.html

### For further information contact:

**Tel**:     (34) 935 422 079
**Email**:     coordinacion@a-4u.eu

## Sweden: Swedish Institute Scholarships for South Africa (SISSA)

**Purpose**: The Swedish Institute Scholarships for South Africa (SISSA) are being offered for South Africans to undertake Master's degrees at Swedish universities from September
**Eligibility**: 1. South African citizens in good health with a strong academic record. 2. Must have Bachelor's with Honours or equivalent, and should have performed well in his/her previous studies with minimum 65% average mark achieved. 3. Have applied for a Master's degree programme at a Swedish university on a full-time basis. 4. Intend to return to South Africa at the end of your studies. 5. Work and leadership experience is not a requirement but will be viewed favourably
**Level of Study**: Postgraduate
**Type**: Scholarship
**Frequency**: Annual
**Country of Study**: South Africa
**Application Procedure**: Apply online: si.se/en/apply/scholarships/swedish-institute-scholarships-for-south-africa/
**Closing Date**: 15 January
**Funding**: Foundation
**Additional Information**: opportunitydesk.org/2019/12/12/swedish-institute-scholarships-for-south-africa-2020/

### For further information contact:

**Email**:     Internationalscholarships@dhet.gov.za

## Switzerland: Swiss Government Excellence Scholarship for Foreign Students

**Purpose**: Through the Swiss Federal Commission for Scholarships for Foreign Students, the Swiss Government Grants foreign researchers, postgraduate scholarships at Swiss higher education institutions. The Swiss Government Excellence Scholarship are intended for highly motivated, competitive young researchers who have graduated from university. These scholarships will enable applicants to undertake research work in the fields in which the Swiss universities are particularly active.
**Eligibility**: 1. South African citizens. 2. Research fellowship applicants must have Master's degree or equivalent achieved and must be born after 31 December 1985. 3. PhD scholarship applicants must have a Master's degree or equivalent achieved and must be born after 31 December 1985. 4. Postdoctoral scholarship applicants must have a PhD degree achieved after 31 December 2016. 5. Applicants with admission letter from academic host institution. 6. Support letter from supervisor or academic host professor. 7. Research proposal including timeframe.
**Level of Study**: PhD, Post-doc and Research Fellow
**Type**: Scholarship
**Value**: CHF 1,920/month to CHF 3,500/month
**Length of Study**: 1 year-3 years
**Frequency**: Annual
**Study Establishment**: Swiss Confederation
**Country of Study**: Switzerland
**Application Procedure**: visit www.sbfi.admin.ch/scholarships_eng and click on South Africa. Request the application package at pre.vertretung@eda.admin.ch
**Closing Date**: 15 December
**Funding**: Foundation
**Contributor**: Swiss Confederation

### For further information contact:

**Tel**:     (27) 12 452 0660
**Email**:     pre.vertretung@eda.admin.ch

## Turkey: Türkiye Scholarships

**Purpose**: Türkiye Scholarships is a government-funded, competitive scholarship program, awarded to outstanding students to pursue full-time or short-term program at the top universities in Turkey. Applications will be open to applicants who wish to study at bachelor's, master's and doctoral levels.
**Eligibility**: 1. Applications for Türkiye Scholarships are open to citizens of all countries. 2. Applicants should not be older than 21 for Bachelor's, 30 for Master's and 35 for Doctoral studies. 3. For Undergraduate degree applications 70 %. 4. For Master's and Doctoral degree applications 75 %
**Level of Study**: Postgraduate
**Type**: Scholarship
**Value**: Bachelor: TRY 800 per month; Masters: TRY 1,100 per month; PhD: TRY 1,600 per month
**Length of Study**: 1. Undergraduate: 1 year Turkish Language course + 4-6 years (depending on the normal duration of the program) 2. Master's: 1 year Turkish Language course + 2 years 3. PhD: 1 year Turkish Language course + 4 years

**Frequency**: Annual
**Country of Study**: South Africa
**Application Procedure**: Apply online: www.turkiyeburslari.gov.tr
**Closing Date**: 20 February
**Funding**: Foundation
**Contributor**: Participating Universities in Turkey
**Additional Information**: www.turkiyeburslari.gov.tr/en/announcement/turkiye-scholarships-2020-applications-open

**For further information contact:**

**Email**: info@turkiyeburslari.org

## United Arab Emirates: Khalifa University Postgraduate Scholarships

**Purpose**: Khalifa University (KU) of Science and Technology is offering postgraduate scholarships to students who wish to pursue postgraduate studies in the field of Engineering Sciences in Abu Dhabi. Through these scholarships, the University aims to highlight the importance of investing in intellectual and human capital as well as its role in enhancing the performance of higher education system
**Eligibility**: Check website: www.ku.ac.ae/admissions/graduate-admissions/
**Level of Study**: Postgraduate
**Type**: Scholarship
**Frequency**: Annual
**Country of Study**: South Africa
**Application Procedure**: Apply online: admissions.kustar.ac.ae/pg/Account/Login
**Closing Date**: 30 April
**Funding**: Foundation
**Additional Information**: opportunitiescorners.info/khalifa-university-scholarship/

**For further information contact:**

**Email**: pgadmission@ku.ac.ae

## United States: Fulbright Foreign Student Program

**Purpose**: The Fulbright Foreign Student Program enables graduate students, young professionals and artists from abroad to study and conduct research in the United States at U.S. universities or other academic institutions.
**Eligibility**: All Foreign Student Program applications are processed by bi-national Fulbright Commissions/Foundations or U.S. Embassies. Therefore, foreign students must apply through the Fulbright Commission/Foundation or U.S. Embassy in their home countries. Deadline varies per country but is around February to October annually.
**Level of Study**: Postgraduate
**Type**: Studentship
**Value**: living stipend, and health insurance, etc
**Frequency**: Annual
**Country of Study**: South Africa
**Application Procedure**: In order to apply for this scholarship, you could use the following link. apply.iie.org/ffsp2020
**No. of awards offered**: Approximately 4,000 foreign students receive Fulbright scholarships each year.
**Closing Date**: February-October
**Funding**: Private
**Additional Information**: For further, kindly contact the organisation using the below link. za.usembassy.gov/education-culture/educational-exchanges/fulbright-flagship-programs/foreign-student-program-frequently-asked-questions/ www.scholarshiproar.com/fulbright-scholarships-usa/

## United States: Harvard South Africa Fellowship Program

**Purpose**: The HSAFP was initiated to provide educational enrichment for mid-career individuals in various occupations who have shown considerable skills and leadership in their chosen fields. Applications are invited for the Harvard South Africa Fellowship Program
**Eligibility**: 1. Fellows must be South African citizens. 2. Usually between 30 and 45 years of age. 3. Must not have just completed or not completed a Bachelor's degree, unless this degree has been pursued concurrently with or subsequent to experience in the workplace. 4. Applicants should determine well in advance whether if awarded a fellowship, they can be granted leave by their employers for Harvard's academic year
**Level of Study**: Postgraduate
**Type**: Fellowships, operating grants
**Frequency**: Annual
**Country of Study**: South Africa
**Application Procedure**: Apply onlline: africa.harvard.edu/south-africa-fellowship-program
**Closing Date**: 4 April
**Funding**: Foundation
**Additional Information**: www.internationalscholarships.dhet.gov.za/UNITED%20STATES%20Harvard%20South%20Africa%20Fellowship%20Program%202020-2021.html

**For further information contact:**

**Tel**: (27) 877 010 715
**Email**: AfricaOffice@Harvard.edu

## Hilda Martindale Educational Trust

Royal Holloway, University of London, Egham, Surrey, TW20 0EX, United Kingdom.

**Tel**:        (44) 17 8427 6158
**Email**:     hildamartindaletrust@rhul.ac.uk
**Contact**:   Miss Sarah Moffat, Administrator to the Trust

The Hilda Martindale Trust makes one-off awards to British women undertaking training or professional qualifications in areas in which women are underrepresented.

## Hilda Martindale Trust Awards

**Purpose**: To assist with the costs of training or professional qualifications in areas in which women are under represented
**Eligibility**: Open to women of the British Isles only. Assistance is not given to short courses, courses abroad, elective studies or access courses. Trust can only offer funding to women pursuing training/qualifications in areas in which women are under represented
**Level of Study**: Doctorate, Graduate, Postdoctorate, Postgraduate, Predoctorate, Professional development, MBA, Undergraduate, Postgraduate (MSc)
**Type**: Grant
**Value**: Up to £3,000
**Length of Study**: 1 year
**Frequency**: Annual
**Study Establishment**: Any establishment approved by the trustees
**Country of Study**: United Kingdom
**Application Procedure**: The application form and guidance for applicants are available from the website address below. In addition, requests for an application form can be made by email to Hildamartindaletrust@rhul.ac.uk
**No. of awards offered**: 55
**Closing Date**: 5 February
**Funding**: Private
**Contributor**: Private trust
**No. of awards given last year**: 16
**No. of applicants last year**: 55
**Additional Information**: Further information can be obtained via email at hildamartindaletrust@rhul.ac.uk www.royalholloway.ac.uk/studying-here/fees-and-funding/under graduate/scholarships-and-bursaries/scholarships/hilda-martin dale-trust-awards/

### For further information contact:

College Secretary's Office, RHUL, Egham, Surrey, TW20 0EX, United Kingdom.

**Email**:     HildaMartindaleTrust@royalholloway.ac.uk

## Hong Kong Baptist University

AAB703, Level 7, Academic and Administration Building, Baptist University Road Campus, Kowloon Tong, Hong Kong.

**Tel**:        (852) 3411 2188
**Contact**:   Hong Kong Baptist University

Hong Kong Baptist University (HKBU) is a publicly funded tertiary institution with a Christian education heritage.

### Fully Funded Master Scholarship at Hong Kong Baptist University

**Purpose**: The aim of the scholarship is to encourage the study of International Journalism
**Eligibility**: Vietnam, Philippines, India and Indonesia. Applicants must have a valid minimum TOEFL iBT 79 or IELTS 6.5
**Value**: HKBU Fully Funded International Postgraduate Scholarship
**Country of Study**: Any country
**Application Procedure**: The mode of applying is online
**Closing Date**: March
**Additional Information**: For more details please see the website scholarship-positions.com/fully-funded-master-scholar ship-hong-kong-baptist-university/2018/01/04/ worldscholar shipforum.com/hkbu-scholarship/

### For further information contact:

**Email**:     busd-external@hkbu.edu.hk

## Horowitz Foundation for Social Policy

PO Box 7, Rocky Hill, NJ 08553 0007, United States of America.

**Tel**:        (1) 732 445 2280
**Website**:   www.horowitz-foundation.org
**Contact**:   Ms Mary E. Curtis, The Chairman

The Horowitz Foundation for Social Policy was established to support the advancement of research and understanding in the social sciences including: psychology, anthropology, sociology, economics, and political science. The Foundation assists individual scholars at the early stages of their career who require small grants to complete their dissertations.

## Irving Louis Horowitz Award

**Purpose**: Awarded to the project that best represents the goals of the Horowitz Foundation in a specific award year

**Eligibility**: Open to nationals of any country. Candidates may solicit support for final work on a dissertation, including travel funds

**Level of Study**: Doctorate

**Type**: Award

**Value**: US$12,500 (US$10,000 initially and an additional US$2,500 upon receipt of a final report on a copy of the research)

**Length of Study**: 1 year

**Frequency**: Annual

**Country of Study**: Any country

**Application Procedure**: Applicants are not required to be United States citizens or United States residents. Candidates may propose new projects, and they may also solicit support for research in progress, including final work on a dissertation, supplementing research in progress, or travel funds. Awards are only open to aspiring PhDs at the dissertation level whose project has received approval from their appropriate department head/university. Grants are normally made for 1 year on a non-renewable basis. Awards will be made to individuals, not institutions, and if processed through an institution, a waiver for overhead is requested. A copy of the product of the research is expected no later than 1 year after completion. Upon receipt an additional US$2,500 will be paid Recipients are expected to acknowledge assistance provided by the Foundation in any publication resulting from their research. Awards are publicized in appropriate professional media and on the Foundation website

**No. of awards offered**: 300

**Closing Date**: 31 January

**Funding**: Private

**No. of awards given last year**: 15

**No. of applicants last year**: 300

**Additional Information**: The cover sheet in the application is most important, as it is the basis for the initial screening of prospects. www.horowitz-foundation.org/grant-info

## For further information contact:

**Email**: wagner.events@nyu.edu

## Refugee Study Awards

**Purpose**: The Refugee Study Awards are for women who are studying for a New Zealand tertiary qualification, and who have not been through the New Zealand school system. The awards are a one off grant to help with study and/or living expenses

**Eligibility**: To apply for the Refugee Study Awards you must meet all the following eligibility criteria: The applicant is a woman, who: 1. Is enrolled in a NZ approved tertiary qualification. 2. Is studying at diploma or degree level (NZQA level 5 or above). 3. Is a New Zealand citizen or holds a resident class visa, and lives in New Zealand. 4. Provides evidence of having arrived in New Zealand as a refugee - ID card or NZ Immigration Service refugee travel document. Has not previously received a NHWT:HK Award

**Level of Study**: Graduate

**Type**: Award

**Value**: NZ$3,000 - preference for an awardee from the Manawatu region. There is a second award of NZ$3,000 - preference for an awardee from the Wellington region

**Frequency**: Annual

**Country of Study**: Any country

**Application Procedure**: Please check the following website link for further details. www.newhorizonsforwomen.org.nz/awards/manawatu-charitable-trust-refugee/

**Closing Date**: 14 April

**Funding**: Private

**Additional Information**: One of these awards is sponsored by Graduate Women Manawatu Charitable Trust and preference will be given to applicants from Manawatu. The other award is sponsored by the Second Chance Group in Wellington and preference will be given to applicants from the greater Wellington region. Applications are welcome from women who are eligible from across the country.

## For further information contact:

New Horizons for Women Trust, PO Box 12498, Wellington, NZL 6144, New Zealand.

**Email**: enquiries@newhorizonsforwomen.org.nz

## The Horowitz Foundation for Social Policy

**Eligibility**: Awards are open only to PhD candidates whose project has received approval from their appropriate department head/university. Preference is given to projects that address contemporary issues in the social sciences and issues of policy relevance. Applicants are not required to be citizens or residents of the United States. Awards are based solely on merit, not to ensure a representative base of recipients or disciplines

**Level of Study**: Doctorate

**Type**: Grants and fellowships

**Value**: NZ$7,500—NZ$5,000 initially and an additional NZ$2,500 upon completion of the project. Criteria for completion include approval of the dissertation, acceptance of an article based on the research by a peer-reviewed journal, or an invitation to write a book chapter based on the research. Additional awards are given in certain suspect areas. The best overall project (as determined by the trustees) receives an additional NZ$5,000

**Frequency**: Annual

**Country of Study**: Any country

**Application Procedure**: Applications must be submitted through our online system which can be found on our website www.horowitz-foundation.org

**No. of awards offered**: 700

**Closing Date**: 1 December

**Funding**: Private

**No. of awards given last year**: 20

**No. of applicants last year**: 700

**Additional Information**: All submitted applications, letters, and documents must be in English. Applications are open 1 July through 1 December. Applicants are encouraged to apply as early as possible. Submitted materials become the property of the Foundation and will not be returned. Applicants should not send originals or other materials that cannot be replaced sociology.fas.harvard.edu/horowitz-foundation-social-policy-grant

**For further information contact:**

**Email**:   horowitz-foundation.org

## Hosei University

17-1 Fujimi 2 chome, Chiyoda-ku, Tokyo JP 102, Japan.

**Tel**:       (81) 3 3264 9564
**Email**:   ic@I.hosei.ac.jp
**Website**:  www.hosei.ac.jp/ic
**Contact**:  Ms Keiko Takahata, Executive Assistant

## Master of Business Administration Programme

**Application Procedure**: Applicants must complete an application form supplying official transcripts, passport sized photograph, curriculum vitae and a statement of financial support

**Closing Date**: 30 November

**For further information contact:**

Business Adminstration, 2-17-1 Fujimi, Tokyo 102, Japan.

**Tel**:      (81) 3 3264 9315
**Fax**:      (81) 3 3238 9873
**Email**:   ic@fujimi.hosei.ac.jp

## Howard Hughes Medical Institute (HHMI)

4000 Jones Bridge Road, Chevy Chase, MD 20815-6789, United States of America.

**Tel**:       (1) 301 215 8500
**Website**:   www.hhmi.org

HHMI is a science philanthropy whose mission is to advance biomedical research and science education for the benefit of humanity. We empower exceptional scientists and students to pursue fundamental questions about living systems.

## Howard Hughes Medical Institute Gilliam Fellowships for Advanced Study

**Purpose**: The goal of the Gilliam Fellowships for Advanced Study program is to ensure the development of a diverse and highly trained workforce is available to assume leadership roles in science, including college and university faculty, who have the responsibility to teach the next generation of scientists

**Eligibility**: Open to alumni of HHMI's Exceptional Research Opportunities Program (EXROP), regardless of country of origin or nationally, or students nominated by T32 predoctoral training grant principal investigators (PIs) supported by the National Institute for General Medical Sciences (NIGMS); each nominated student must be training grant eligible but does not need to have been a T32 trainee

**Type**: Fellowship

**Value**: US$46,000

**Length of Study**: Up to 3 years of their dissertation research, typically in years 3, 4, and 5 of their PhD studies

**Frequency**: Annual

**Country of Study**: United States of America

**Closing Date**: February

**Additional Information**: Please check details at www.hhmi.org/programs/gilliam-fellowships-for-advanced-study

**For further information contact:**

**Email**:   Gilliam@hhmi.org

## Postdoctoral Research Fellowships for Physicians

**Purpose**: To help increase the supply of well-trained physician-scientists, through fellowships for three years of training in fundamental research (basic biological processes or disease mechanisms)

**Eligibility**: Applicants must have gained their first degree within the last ten years, and must have had two years of postgraduate clinical training, and no more than two years of postdoctoral training in fundamental research

**Level of Study**: Postdoctorate

**Type**: Fellowship

**Value**: US$69,000–86,500 per year

**Length of Study**: 3 years

**Frequency**: Annual

**Study Establishment**: Academic or non-profit research institution

**Country of Study**: United States of America

**Application Procedure**: Application forms and instructions should be obtained from the address shown. Panels of scientists review applications, and the Institute makes the final selection

**No. of awards offered**: 255

**Closing Date**: December

**No. of awards given last year**: 30

**No. of applicants last year**: 255

**Additional Information**: Fellows must engage in full-time research. During the fellowship term, they may not be enrolled in a graduate degree program, nor hold a faculty appointment. The applicant is responsible for selecting a research mentor and making arrangements to work in that person's laboratory.

### For further information contact:

4000 Jones Bridge Road, Chevy Chase, MD 20815, United States of America.

| | |
|---|---|
| **Tel**: | (1) 301 215 8889 |
| **Fax**: | (1) 301 215 8888 |
| **Email** | fellows@hq.hhmi.org |

## Humane Research Trust

The Humane Research Trust, Brook House, 29 Bramhall Lane South, Bramhall, Stockport, Cheshire, SK7 2DN, United Kingdom.

| | |
|---|---|
| **Tel**: | (44) 161 439 8041 |
| **Email**: | info@humaneresearch.org.uk |
| **Website**: | www.humaneresearch.org.uk |
| **Contact**: | Jane McAllister, Trust Administrator |

The Humane Research Trust is a national charity, which funds a range of unique medical research programmes on human illness at hospitals and universities around the country. In keeping with the philosophy of the Trust, none of the research involves animals and much of it seeks to establish and develop pioneering techniques that will replace animal intensive experiments.

## The Humane Research Trust Grant

**Subjects**: Humane Research

**Purpose**: To encourage scientific programmes where the use of animals is replaced by other methods

**Eligibility**: Open to established scientific workers engaged in productive research. Nationals of any country are considered but for the sake of overseeing, projects should be undertaken in a UK establishment.

**Level of Study**: Unrestricted

**Type**: Grant

**Value**: Varies. Please note there is no set limit to either the duration of a project or funding amount. These points will be discussed if the application is successful, however you still need to include in your application the amount of funding you require and an estimate of the duration.

**Length of Study**: Varies

**Frequency**: Dependent on funds available

**Study Establishment**: Various

**Country of Study**: United Kingdom

**Application Procedure**: Applicants must complete an application form, available on the website www.humaneresearch.org.uk Please ensure you email all of the required documents, i.e. one fully complete application to info@humaneresearch.org.uk and post 10 hard copies to The Humane Research Trust.

**No. of awards offered**: Varies

**Closing Date**: Varies

**Funding**: Private

**Contributor**: Supporters and legacies

**No. of awards given last year**: 3

**No. of applicants last year**: 16

**Additional Information**: The Humane Research Trust is a registered charity and donations are encouraged.

### For further information contact:

The Humane Research Trust, 29 Bramhall Lane South, Bramhall, Stockport SK7 2DN, United Kingdom.

| | |
|---|---|
| **Tel**: | (44) 161 439 8041 |

# Humboldt University of Berlin

Office for Promotion of Young Researchers in the Excellence Initiative, D-10099 Berlin, Germany.

**Tel**:         (49) 30 2093 1795
**Contact**:    Humboldt Graduate School

## Humboldt Postdoc Scholarships

**Purpose**: To support young researchers in taking the next step in their academic career after acquiring their PhD.
**Eligibility**: Eligible to excellent researchers who either already hold a PhD from Humboldt-Universität or are about to complete their doctorate at Humboldt-Universität zu Berlin and who wish to conduct a postdoctoral research project. Half of the scholarships will be awarded to women
**Type**: Scholarship
**Value**: €1,500 per month is awarded for up to 6 months, additional family allowances are available, travel expenses may be covered. In exceptional cases, funding can be extended for up to an additional 6 months
**Study Establishment**: Humboldt-Universität
**Country of Study**: Germany
**Application Procedure**: Applications can be received only via an online application portal

### For further information contact:

**Email**:    hgs-grants@hu-berlin.de

# Imperial College of Science, Technology and Medicine

Exhibition Road, London, SW7 2AZ, United Kingdom.

**Tel**: (44) 20 7594 8023
**Email**: r.a.clay@ic.ac.uk
**Contact**: Ms R A Clay, Scholarships co-ordinator registry

The Imperial College of Science, Technology and Medicine is a college of the University of London and provides university education at first degree and postgraduate level in the fields of science, engineering and medicine.

## Stephen and Anna Hui Fellowship

**Purpose**: To facilitate postgraduate study or research
**Eligibility**: Open to graduates with a First or Upper Second Class (Honours) Degree from universities in China including Hong Kong and Taiwan
**Level of Study**: Doctorate, Postgraduate
**Type**: Fellowship
**Value**: It provide financial support to meet the full cost of tuition fees and an annual stipend equal to the College minimum (£15,863)
**Length of Study**: 3 years
**Study Establishment**: Imperial College
**Country of Study**: United Kingdom
**Application Procedure**: Applicants must complete an application form and submit this with two references and a transcript or academic record
**Closing Date**: 31 January
**Funding**: Private
**Contributor**: Stephen and Anna Hui Fellowship Trust Fund
**Additional Information**: Further information is available on request www.imperial.ac.uk/apex/apps/f?p=1007:201:0::

NO:201:P201_AWARD_INSTANCE_ID, P201_FEE_STATUS_ELIGIBILITY_TY, P201_PROGRAM_TYPE:2049, OVERSEAS, PHD

**For further information contact:**

**Email**: j.picken@imperial.ac.uk

## India Alliance

### Early Career Fellowship

**Purpose**: The proposed research should fall within the India Alliance's remit which is to support biomedical research that is relevant to human and animal welfare. If you are unsure if your research programme falls within our remit
**Eligibility**: The Early Career Fellowship (ECF) competition is open for basic science/veterinary researchers with -1 to 4 years of Post PhD research experience. This means that you must be in the final year of your PhD studies or have no more than four years of postdoctoral research experience from the date of your PhD viva to the full application submission deadline in order to be eligible for the competition. Applicant must have 0-4 years Post PhD Applicant in the final year of their PhD are also eligible. In line with the scheme's mandate to foster independence, Early Career Fellows are strongly encouraged to carry out their Fellowship project in a laboratory that is not their thesis laboratory or thesis environment. If you have compelling reasons to continue in or return to your thesis laboratory/environment, please present these appropriately in the preliminary application and arrange for a letter from the Fellowship Supervisor commenting on this decision
**Level of Study**: Postgraduate
**Type**: Fellowship
**Length of Study**: 4 years
**Frequency**: Annual

© Springer Nature Limited 2020
Palgrave Macmillan (ed.), *The Grants Register 2021*,
https://doi.org/10.1057/978-1-349-95988-4

**Country of Study**: Any country

**Application Procedure**: To complete a preliminary application use our online system, IASys. Refer to the IASys userguide for guidance on completing the application form and the submission process. Please ensure that the form is submitted by the published deadline. Your preliminary application is assessed and If successful, you will be invited to submit a full application. Your full application will be peer reviewed and considered by the appropriate Selection Committee and, if successful, you will be short-listed for interview. Short-listed candidates will be notified two weeks before the interview date. Applicants are not permitted to apply to multiple Fellowship schemes within the India Alliance in parallel. Only one application to one scheme will be entertained, at a time

**Closing Date**: 31 January

**Funding**: Private

**Additional Information**: www.indiaalliance.org/fellowships-at-a-glance

**For further information contact:**

**Email**:   info@indiaalliance.org

## India Habitat Centre

Visual Arts Galley, Lodhi Road, New Delhi 110003, India.

**Tel**:       (91) 11 246 820 01/05
**Email**:   info@indiahabitat.org
**Website**:   www.indiahabitat.org

The India Habitat Centre was conceived to provide a physical environment that would serve as a catalyst for a synergetic relationship between individuals and institutions working in diverse habitat related areas and, therefore, maximize their total effectiveness.

### India Habitat Centre Fellowship for Photography

**Purpose**: To promote photography as an art form

**Eligibility**: Open to Indian nationals who are between 21 and 40 years of age and who do not hold any other fellowship

**Level of Study**: Professional development

**Type**: Fellowship

**Value**: ₹120,000

**Frequency**: Annual

**Country of Study**: India

**Application Procedure**: Applicants must send a project summary, curriculum vitae and reference letters

**Closing Date**: 31 August

**Additional Information**: Entries with less/more than the required 12 images will be eliminated

**For further information contact:**

**Email**:   alkapande@indiahabitat.org

## Indian Council for Cultural Relations

Azad Bhavan, I.p. Estate, New Delhi 110002, India.

**Contact**:   Indian Council for Cultural Relations

The Indian Council for Cultural Relations (ICCR), is an autonomous organisation of the Government of India, involved in India's external cultural relations, through cultural exchange with other countries and their peoples. It was founded by Maulana Abul Kalam Azad, the first Education Minister of independent India.

### Indian Council for Cultural Relations Indian High Commission Bangladesh Scholarship Scheme

**Purpose**: The aim of the scholarship is to support meritorious Bangladeshi nationals who want to undertake engineering, graduate, post-graduate and PhD / post-doctoral course

**Eligibility**: 1. Applicants from Bangladesh are eligible to apply for the scholarship. 2. Candidates who wish to get scholarships must be proficient in English and have at least 60% marks in the passed examination or 3 in GPA 5. 3. Candidates will have to take part in 30-minute English proficiency test, whose time and place will be announced

**Level of Study**: Graduate

**Type**: Scholarship

**Value**: The Indian government has so far given ICCR education to nearly 3,000 Bangladeshi nationals

**Frequency**: Annual

**Study Establishment**: Scholarship is awarded in the subjects offered by the university

**Country of Study**: India

**Application Procedure**: To apply online for interested students, you need to create your own private login ID and password. The applicants are requested to apply online through the instructions. The applicant should keep the following points during the application process Those BE / B Tech. Must apply for the course, in their school-college syllabus must include Physics, Mathematics and Chemistry. The applicant's age must be 18 in July. All students must stay in the hostel. Cannot be outside without family and health reasons. The last date for submission of online application is 20 January, 5.00 pm on Saturday. Candidates will have to take part in 30-minute English proficiency test, whose time and place will be announced

**Closing Date**: 20 January

**Additional Information**: For more details please see the website scholarship-positions.com/iccr-indian-high-comm ission-bangladesh-scholarship-scheme-india/2018/01/08/

### For further information contact:

**Email**: admin@scholarship-positions.com

## Indian Council of Medical Research

V. Ramalingaswami Bhawan, Ansari Nagar, P.O. Box No. 4911, New Delhi 110029, India.

**Tel**:     (91) 11 265 888 95 / 11 265 889 80 / 11 265 897 94
**Email**:   icmrhqds@sansad.nic.in
**Website**: www.icmr.nic.in

The Indian Council of Medical Research (ICMR), New Delhi, the apex body in India for the formulation, coordination and promotion of biomedical research, is one of the oldest medical research bodies in the world.

## Indian Council of Medical Research Centenary-Postdoctoral Fellowship

**Purpose**: The aim of the fellowships is to giving research opportunities to promising fresh PhD/ MD/MS holders
**Eligibility**: Indian applicants are eligible for these fellowships. Entrance Requirement: Applicants must be PhDs/ MD/MS
**Type**: Postdoctoral fellowship
**Value**: ICMR Postdoctoral Fellows will be paid a consolidated fellowship of ₹50,000/- per month plus house rent allowance (HRA), Non-Practicing Allowance (NPA) as admissible and a contingency grant of ₹3.0 lakhs per annum. 25% of the contingency grant can be used for travel including per diem expenses
**Study Establishment**: These fellowships are awarded in cutting edge areas of basic science, communicable and non-communicable diseases, and reproductive health including nutrition
**Country of Study**: India
**Application Procedure**: See the website
**Closing Date**: 31 December
**Additional Information**: For more details please visit our website scholarship-positions.com/icmr-centenary-post-doctoral-fellowship-india/2017/06/06/

## Indian Education Department

Government of India, Ministry of Human Resource Department, Shastri Bhavan, New Delhi 110001, India.

**Tel**:     (91) 11 233 839 36
**Email**:   webmaster.edu@nic.in
**Website**: www.education.nic.in

The origin of the Indian Education Department, Government of India, dates back to pre-independence days when for the first time a separate Department was created in 1910 to look after education. However, soon after India achieved its independence, a full fledged ministry of Education was established.

## China Scholarships

**Eligibility**: Open to the Indian nationals below 40 years who have 2–3 year Cert/Dip in basic Chinese Language from a recognized Institution or University, have degree in fine arts with 60% and 60% for other subjects at postgraduate level with work research experience of 2 years
**Level of Study**: Graduate
**Type**: Scholarship
**Value**: The Chinese Government pays a sum of 2,000 per month to all senior advanced students, CNY 1,400 per month to ordinary graduate students and CNY 1,100 per month to undergraduate students. In addition, Government of India is paying supplementary grant of CNY 1,170 per month Government of China will also provide boarding, lodging, medical care and bear expenditure on tuition and other fees, etc
**Length of Study**: 1–4 years
**Country of Study**: Any country
**Application Procedure**: Applicants must send the application duly sponsored by the employers (if employed) furnishing particulars (as per notified format) by the prescribed date
**Closing Date**: 20 March
**Contributor**: Government of China in association with the government of India

**For further information contact:**

ES. 3 Section, Ministry of Human Resource Development, Department of Higher Education, External Scholarship Division, A1/w3, Curzon Road Barracks, KG Marg, New Delhi 110001, India.

**Email**: scholarship@dreamgo.com

## Erasmus Mundus Scholarship Programme

**Purpose**: For the benefit of Indian students
**Eligibility**: Open to Indian nationals who are graduates from recognized institutions or universities
**Level of Study**: Graduate
**Type**: Scholarships
**Value**: €9,000 (EU students) / 18,000 (non-EU students) including health insurance coverage 24 months
**Length of Study**: 1–2 years duration depending on the subject areas of study
**Application Procedure**: Applicants must apply directly to the universities/consortium of universities constituted under the Erasmus Mundus Programme
**No. of awards offered**: 3 Grants are available per year
**Closing Date**: 10 January
**Contributor**: European Union (EU)
**Additional Information**: www.euroculturemaster.eu/how-to-apply/erasmus-mundus-scholarship-programme

**For further information contact:**

**Email**: eac-info@cec.eu.int

## National Centre for Promotion of Employment for Disabled People (NCPEDP) Rajiv Gandhi Postgraduate Scholarship Scheme

**Purpose**: To enable disabled students with limited means to receive education or professional training at postgraduate and doctoral levels
**Eligibility**: Open to Indian nationals between 18 and 35 years of age. The scholarship may be awarded to students with the disabilities as recognized by N.C.P.E.D.P. The candidate should be either pursuing or should have gained admission to a full-time course in an Indian university established by law or in a recognized equivalent institution
**Level of Study**: Doctorate, Postgraduate
**Type**: Scholarship
**Value**: ₹1,200 per month
**Frequency**: Annual
**Application Procedure**: Applicants must apply to the National Centre for Promotion of Employment for Disabled People

**Funding**: Government
**Additional Information**: A scholarship will be provided for the entire duration of the approved course. Scholarship money will be released every 3 months. N.C.P.E.D.P. reserves the right to change the scheme and/or amend the rules without any notice. The income of the candidate or his parents/guardians should not exceed ₹5,000 per month. At the discretion of the awarding authority, a scholarship may also be awarded for a professional course of Indira Gandhi National Open University (IGNOU) or any other recognized Open University www.scholarships.net.in/1989.html

**For further information contact:**

National Centre for Promotion of Employment for Disabled People, A-77, South Extension, Part II, New Delhi 110 049, India.

**Tel**: (91) 11 262 656 47/48
**Email**: education@ncpedp.org

## Indian Institute of Management Ranchi

### Post-Doctoral Fellowship

**Purpose**: The Post-Doctoral Fellowship in Management (PDFM) is designed keeping in view IIM Ranchi's goal to create a high quality research environment in the institute. Its objective is to support high quality research by scholars with a doctoral degree and an outstanding academic record
**Eligibility**: 1. Contingency Grant: A contingency grant of ₹50,000 per annum will be provided to the post-doctoral research fellow for research purposes. 2. The IIM Ranchi would pay the expenses for a fellow to attend one conference abroad from an approved list of conferences if their joint paper with a resident faculty member is accepted for presentation at that conference. 3. Office space will be provided to post-doctoral research fellows along with a computer and printer. They will be issued special research library card, enabling them to borrow up to ten books from the library at a time. 4. A post-doctoral research fellow will be eligible for leave from the fellowship not exceeding 30 days in a year for each completed year of the fellowship. 5. The leave can be availed on a pro-rata basis for the duration (on a 6 months' basis) of the fellowship completed. The age limit for applicants for the Post-Doctoral Fellowship will be a maximum of 40 years (this limit may be relaxed by 5 years for women and reserved category)
**Level of Study**: Postgraduate
**Type**: Fellowship
**Value**: Contigency grants of ₹50,000 per annum will be provided

**Length of Study**: 2 years
**Frequency**: Annual
**Country of Study**: Any country
**Application Procedure**: 1. Selection will be based on demonstrated research skills and a fit with the research interests of resident faculty. Shortlisted candidates will be invited to campus to present their research before a final decision is made. 2. Past research I PhD thesis work demonstrating potential for scholarly work would facilitate the initial shortlist process. 3. The shortlisted candidates will be invited for on-campus presentation and interview. 4. The candidates selected for the PDFM will be attached to the given area and will be associated with a faculty member of the group who will essentially perform the role of a mentor and collaborator. 5. Selection will be based on demonstrated research skills and a fit with the research interests of resident faculty
**Closing Date**: 22 March
**Funding**: Private
**Additional Information**: www.iimranchi.ac.in/?page_id=11197

### For further information contact:

Indian Institute of Management Ranchi, Suchana Bhawan, 5th Floor, Audrey House Campus, Meur's Road, Ranchi, Jharkhand 834 008, India.

**Tel**:     (91) 65 1228 0113
**Fax**:    (91) 651 2280940
**Email**:  office.fpm@iimranchi.ac.in

## Indian Institute of Management, Calcutta

Diamond Harbour Road, Joka, Kolkata, West Bengal 700104, India.

**Contact**:    The Indian Institute of Management

Indian Institute of Management, Calcutta abbreviated as IIM Calcutta or IIM-C is a public business school located in Joka, Kolkata, India. It was the first Indian Institute of Management to be established.

## Postdoctoral Research Fellowship (PDRF)

**Purpose**: These fellowships are available for researchers who want to contribute to the theory and practice of management
**Eligibility**: Citizens of India are eligible to apply. These positions are open for candidates with 0-2 years of experience after obtaining PhD degree

**Level of Study**: Doctorate
**Type**: Fellowship
**Value**: Each fellowship will carry a stipend of ₹40,000/p.m. consolidated, depending on the level of prior experience of the chosen candidate. In addition, a contingency grant of ₹50,000/- per annum will be provided
**Length of Study**: 2 years
**Country of Study**: India
**Application Procedure**: Fellowships are negotiable up to 3 years. Under exceptional circumstances, tenure may be extended to a maximum of 5 years
**Closing Date**: 30 May
**Additional Information**: Please visit website scholarship-positions.com/postdoctoral-research-fellowships-iim-calcutta-india/2018/04/24/ indiabioscience.org/grants/post-doctoral-research-fellowship-pdrf

### For further information contact:

**Email**:   pgfunding@uct.ac.za

## Indian Institute of Science Bangalore (IISc)

The Registrar, Indian Institute of Science, Bangalore, Karnataka 560012, India.

**Tel**:       (91) 80 2360 0757
**Email**:    regr@admin.iisc.ernet.in
**Website**:  www.iisc.ernet.in
**Contact**:  The Registrar

The Indian Institute of Science (IISc) was started in 1909 through the pioneering vision of J N Tata. Since then, it has grown into a premier institution of research and advanced instruction, with more than 2,000 active researchers working in almost all frontier areas of science and technology.

## Indian Institute of Science Bangalore Kishore Vaigyanik Protsahan Yojana Fellowships

**Purpose**: To assist students in realizing their potential and to ensure that the best scientific talent is developed for research and growth in the country
**Eligibility**: Open to Indian citizens
**Level of Study**: Graduate, Postdoctorate, Postgraduate, Predoctorate, Research
**Type**: Fellowship
**Value**: ₹4,000–7,000 per month and contingency grants of ₹16,000–28,000

**Frequency**: Annual
**Study Establishment**: Indian Institute of Science, Bangalore
**Country of Study**: India
**Application Procedure**: Applicants can download the application form from the website
**Closing Date**: September
**Additional Information**: www.kvpy.iisc.ernet.in/main/index.htm

### For further information contact:

Indian Institute of Science, CV Raman Rd, Bengaluru, Karnataka 560012, India.

**Tel**:　　(91) 80 2360 1008/80 2293 2976
**Email**:　kvpy@admin.iisc.ernet.in

# Indian Institute of Technology (IIT)

Department of Computer Science and Engineering, Kanpur, Uttar Pradesh 208016, India.

**Tel**:　　　(91) 512 259 7338/7638
**Email**:　　pgadm@cse.iitk.ac.in
**Website**:　www.cse.iitk.ac.in
**Contact**:　Harish Karnick, Professor and Head

Indian Institute of Technology (IIT) imparts training to students to make them competent, motivated engineers and scientists. The Institute not only celebrates freedom of thought, cultivates vision and encourages growth, but also inculcates human values and concern for the environment and the society.

## Infosys Fellowship for PhD Students

**Purpose**: To support those interested in pursuing the PhD programme in the Department of Computer Science and Engineering at IIT Kanpur
**Eligibility**: Open to deserving students who have a MTech/ME in any branch of engineering and who have secured admission into the PhD programme
**Level of Study**: Postgraduate
**Type**: Fellowship
**Value**: ₹225,000 and ₹250,000 per year. Out of this grant, ₹180,000 (₹15,000 per month) will paid as stipend, remaining money can be utilized by the fellow for purchase of books, journals, payment of tuition fee, and travel for domestic and international conference attendance
**Length of Study**: 3.5–4 years

**Frequency**: Annual
**Study Establishment**: IIT Kanpur
**Country of Study**: India
**Application Procedure**: The applicant must submit a separate application form to the Department of Computer Science and Engineering. Please check at www.cse.iitk.ac.in
**Additional Information**: www.cse.iitm.ac.in/awards_details.php?arg=Nw==

# Indian Institute of Technology Kharagpur

## IT Kharagpur Post Doctoral Fellowship

**Purpose**: IIT Kharagpur is giving an excellent platform for the students possessing PhD degree with an excellent academic record by offering them IIT Kharagpur Post Doctoral Fellowship. The main objective of this fellowship is to give an opportunity to deserving scholars to carry out their research in the field of science and technology
**Eligibility**: 1. Must hold PhD Degree with the outstanding academic record. 2. Must have published research paper / patents on his/her name. 3. Age limit of a candidate is 35 years. 4. The candidates who are belonging to AICTE / UGC recognized teaching institution or sponsored by DISR recognized industrial organization they will get age relaxation up to 45 years of age
**Level of Study**: Postdoctorate
**Type**: Fellowship
**Value**: ₹25,000
**Frequency**: Annual
**Country of Study**: India
**Closing Date**: 31 December
**Funding**: Foundation
**Additional Information**: www.iitkgp.ac.in/academics-post-doc-fellowships

### For further information contact:

**Email**:　info@vidhyaa.in

# Indian Institute of Technology Ropar

Nangal Road, Rupnagar, Punjab 140001, India.

**Contact**:　Indian Institute of Technology Ropar

The Indian Institute of Technology Ropar (IIT Ropar) or IIT-RPR, is an engineering and technology higher education institute located in Rupnagar, Punjab, India. It is one of the eight newer Indian Institutes of Technology (IITs) established by the Ministry of Human Resource Development MHRD, Government of India under The Institutes of Technology (Amendment) Act.

## Indian Institute of Technology Ropar Institute Postdoctoral Fellowship

**Purpose**: The aim of the fellowship is to support Indian students and provide a contingency grant of ₹1,00,000/- per annum to the Post-Doctoral Fellow for research purposes. The unspent amount can be carried over to the next financial year
**Eligibility**: PhD degree holders are eligible to apply within five years after completion of their PhD Candidates completed PhD supervised/co-supervised by faculty members from IIT Ropar can apply after 3 years of completion of their PhD.
**Type**: Fellowship
**Value**: Between ₹45,000-55,000/- consolidated
**Length of Study**: 3 years
**Study Establishment**: Fellowship is awarded in the subjects offered by the university
**Country of Study**: Any country
**Application Procedure**: The application has to be submitted to the Department/Center in which the candidate intends to join as a Post Doctoral Fellow. Applicants can apply through the post and submit the application form to the Department/Center. Applicants can apply by rolling basis
**Additional Information**: For more information please browse the website scholarship-positions.com/iit-ropar-institute-post-doctoral-fellowship-for-indian-students/2017/11/11/ www.iitrpr.ac.in/institute-post-doctoral-fellowship

### For further information contact:

**Email**: admin@scholarship-positions.com

## Indian School of Business

Knowledge City, Sector 81, SAS Nagar, Mohali, Punjab 140 306, India.

**Tel**: (91) 172 459 0000
**Contact**: Indian School of Business

Indian School of Business is a private business school with campuses in Hyderabad, Telangana, India and Mohali, Punjab, India. The institute has various Management programs with the Post Graduate Program in Management as its flagship course.

## Indian Health Service Health Professions Scholarship Program

**Purpose**: The student must apply annually to request continued scholarship support until he/she has earned his/her degree and is eligible to pursue post-graduate clinical training or begin his/her Indian health career
**Eligibility**: 1. All applicants must intend to serve Indian people as a health professional in their chosen specialties. 2. They must also be willing to sign an IHS Scholarship Program Contract when accepting the scholarship. 3. By signing, the student agrees to fulfill a minimum two-year service commitment in full-time clinical practice at an Indian health facility in his/her chosen health profession after completing his/her academic or post-graduate clinical training. 4. The student must apply annually to request continued scholarship support until he/she has earned his/her degree and is eligible to pursue post-graduate clinical training or begin his/her Indian health career
**Level of Study**: Postgraduate
**Type**: Scholarship
**Value**: US$1,500
**Frequency**: Annual
**Country of Study**: Any country
**Application Procedure**: The IHS Scholarship Program awards scholarships based on a 100-point ranking system divided among three categories: academic performance, based on official transcripts (40 points); faculty/employer evaluations (30 points); and applicant essays (30 points)
**Closing Date**: 28 March
**Funding**: Private
**Additional Information**: www.unigo.com/scholarships/by-major/psychology-scholarships/ihs-health-professions-scholarship-program/1675

## Indian School of Business Funded Tuition Waivers at Indian School of Business

**Purpose**: The Post Graduate Programme in Management (PGP) is designed for those who want to transform their careers by expanding their existing thought process and refining their goals and objectives
**Eligibility**: Citizens of all nationalities are eligible to apply. Students whose first language is not English must demonstrate proficiency in English by submitting satisfactory scores from the Test of English as a Foreign Language (TOEFL)
**Type**: Postgraduate scholarships
**Value**: These waivers vary in amount from ₹5 Lakh to full tuition fee and are disbursed either on merit or need-based

criteria. These scholarships are awarded to candidates during admission or after enrolment, at the discretion of the AdCom or the corporate donor

**Study Establishment**: Scholarships are awarded in the field of Business

**Country of Study**: India

**Application Procedure**: These scholarships are awarded to candidates during admission or after enrolment, at the discretion of the AdCom or the corporate donor

**Closing Date**: 15 January

**Additional Information**: For more details please browse the website scholarship-positions.com/isb-funded-tuition-waivers-indian-school-business-india/2017/10/28/

**For further information contact:**

**Email**: admin@scholarship-positions.com

## Indian Veterinary Research Institute

Izatnagar, Bareilly, Uttar Pradesh 243122, India.

**Contact**: The Indian Veterinary Research Institute

The Indian Veterinary Research Institute (IVRI) is located at Izatnagar, Bareilly in Uttar Pradesh state. It is India's premier advanced research facility in the field of veterinary medicine and allied branches.

### Scholarships at Indian Veterinary Research Institute

**Purpose**: The Indian Veterinary Research Institute (IVRI) is offering scholarships for MVSc and PhD students. The duration of scholarship for MVSc course will be of two years and scholarship for the PhD course will be of three years

**Eligibility**: Students from India are eligible to apply. The candidates for admission to Master's programme must have Bachelor's Degree in Veterinary Science in the concerned discipline as specified by the Veterinary Council of India with a minimum of 60% marks in aggregate (55% for SC/ST or sponsored candidates) or equivalent CGPA

**Type**: Postgraduate scholarships

**Value**: The amount of the scholarship for Master's Degree programme is ₹7,560/- per month for 2 years with a contingent grant of ₹6,000/- per annum for two years and for Doctoral programme,

it is ₹13,125/- per month for three years with a contingent grant of ₹10,000/- per annum for three years

**Study Establishment**: Scholarships are awarded to study the subjects offered by the university

**Country of Study**: India

**Application Procedure**: See the website

**Additional Information**: For more details please visit our website scholarship-positions.com/scholarships-indian-veterinary-research-institute/2017/11/18/

**For further information contact:**

**Email**: sao_unitone@ivri.res.in

## Indira Gandhi Institute of Development Research

Film City Road, IGIDR, Nagri Niwara, Cooperative Housing Society, Goregaon East, Mumbai, Maharashtra 400065, India.

**Contact**: Indira Gandhi Institute of Development Research

Indira Gandhi Institute of Development Research (IGIDR) is an advanced research institute established and fully funded by the Reserve Bank of India for carrying out research on development issues from a multi-disciplinary point of view.

### Indira Gandhi Institute of Development Research-International Development Research Centre Scholarships and Fellowships for Asian Countries Students

**Purpose**: The aims and objectives of the Institute are to promote and conduct research on developmental issues from a broad inter-disciplinary perspective (economic, technological, social, political and ecological)

**Eligibility**: Scholarship is open for citizens of the following Asian countries: Afghanistan, Bangladesh, Bhutan, Cambodia, Indonesia, Malaysia, Maldives, Myanmar, Nepal, Philippines, Sri Lanka, Thailand and Vietnam

**Type**: Postdoctoral fellowship

**Value**: Selected scholar will be paid a scholarship of ₹100,000 per month, One round trip travel expense up to a maximum of ₹50,000, fixed medical coverage of ₹25,000, book grant of ₹50,000, research grant of ₹100,000, and conference travel support up to a maximum of ₹150,000

**Study Establishment**: Scholarships and fellowships are awarded in the field of labor market and industrial policy

**Country of Study**: India

**Application Procedure**: See the website

**Closing Date**: 30 April

**Additional Information**: For more details please browse the website scholarship-positions.com/igidr-idrc-scholarships-and-fellowships-asian-countries-students-2015/2014/12/27/ www.igidr.ac.in/igidr-idrc-scholarships-programs/

## For further information contact:

**Email**: asianhub@igidr.ac.in

## IndusInd Foundation

### IndusInd Foundation Scholarship for Postgraduate Students

**Purpose**: The IndusInd Foundation has invited applications from meritorious students studying in a degree course under the IndusInd Foundation Scholarship

**Eligibility**: 1. The student must have passed class 12 board or equivalent exam from an approved board/university with minimum 80% marks. 2. The student must have taken admission to any of regular degree courses in Science, Arts, Commerce, Eng., Medical, Computer, Mgt. etc. in an approved college/institute to any recognized university in India. 3. The student's family financial income should justify the grant of scholarship

**Level of Study**: Postdoctorate

**Type**: Scholarship

**Value**: Amount of Scholarship will range from ₹600/- to ₹2,200/- Actual Rate to be decided by the Foundation in each case

**Frequency**: Annual

**Country of Study**: Any country

**Closing Date**: 30 September

**Funding**: Foundation

**Additional Information**: www.scholarshiplives.com/indusind-foundation-scholarship/

## For further information contact:

The Trustee, IndusInd Foundation, Hinduja House, 171, Dr Annie Besant Road, Worli, Mumbai, 400018, India.

**Email**: info@vidhyaa.in

# Innovation and Entrepreneurship Development Centre Bled School of Management

Prešernova cesta 33, SI-4260 Bled, Slovenia.

| | |
|---|---|
| **Tel**: | (386) 457 92 500 |
| **Email**: | info@iedc.si |
| **Website**: | www.iedc.si |

The school is a center of excellence in management development and a business meeting point, where leaders and potential leaders come to learn and reflect. We offer a unique environment for developing leadership and management potential of international business executives at every stage of their careers.

## Innovation and Entrepreneurship Development Centre MBA Scholarship

**Purpose**: To finance an MBA programme for outstanding candidates from Moldova and Ukraine

**Eligibility**: Only outstanding candidates from Moldova and Ukraine will be considered

**Level of Study**: Professional development

**Value**: All tuition fees

**Length of Study**: 1 year

**Frequency**: Annual

**Study Establishment**: IEDC

**Application Procedure**: See website

**Closing Date**: 30 October

## For further information contact:

| | |
|---|---|
| **Tel**: | (386) 457 92 506 |
| **Email**: | emba@iedc.si |

## Trimo MBA Scholarship

**Purpose**: To finance an outstanding candidate from Serbia

**Eligibility**: The candidate must be from Serbia

**Level of Study**: Professional development

**Type**: Scholarship

**Value**: All tuition fees and agreed costs

**Length of Study**: 1 year

**Frequency**: Annual

**Study Establishment**: IEDC

**Application Procedure**: See website
**Closing Date**: 1 December
**Funding**: Corporation
**Contributor**: Trimo d.d. Slovenia
**Additional Information**: The successful candidate will be offered a position at Trimo Inženjering d.o.o Serbia

### For further information contact:

**Tel**:        (386) 457 92 506
**Email**:    emba@iedc.si

## Institut de Recherche Robert-Sauvé en Santé et en Sécurité du Travail (IRSST)

505, De Maisonneuve Ouest, Montréal, QC H3A 3C2, Canada.

**Tel**:          (1) 514 288 1551
**Email**:      grants@irsst.qc.ca
**Website**:   www.irsst.qc.ca

Institut de Recherche Robert-Sauvé en Santé et en Sécurité du Travail (IRSST), established in Quebec since 1980, is a scientific research organization known for the quality of its work and the expertise of its personnel. The Institute is a private, non-profit agency.

## Collaborative Research

**Purpose**: The Collaborative Research Grant Program covers work that may include studies, analyses, design or development carried out according to a scientific process and likely to contribute to the advancement of knowledge. This work is defined in collaboration with the IRSST and falls within the priority themes. Proposals for collaborative research studies are developed by researchers in collaboration with the research field leader, knowledge transfer advisor and research management advisor. First, the researchers are asked to send a brief summary of their proposed study, using the Summary page of the Letter of Intent form, to the research management advisor for the field concerned. This person coordinates the collaborative process. Once the process has been completed, the researcher may officially file his or her grant application by one of the periodically announced deadlines.
**Eligibility**: An applicant who files an application as a principal investigator must be a Canadian citizen or permanent resident of Canada, hold a doctorate or the equivalent, and hold a position as a professor or teacher in a Québec postsecondary educational or research establishment. The principal investigator is responsible for the intellectual direction of the proposed research, performs the administrative duties related to the grant, and acts as the contact person with the IRSST. Only one person may play this role.
**Value**: US$100,000 IRSST + US$30,000
**Additional Information**: www.irsst.qc.ca/en/grants/collaborative-research

### For further information contact:

**Tel**:        (1) 514 288 1551
**Email**:    subventions@irsst.qc.ca

## Competitive Research

**Purpose**: The Competitive Research Grant Program is intended exclusively for researchers affiliated with Québec universities or research centres who take the initiative of submitting occupational health and safety research proposals that the IRSST is likely to consider relevant, even if in some cases such projects go beyond the official bounds of the Institute's stated research priorities
**Eligibility**: An applicant who files an application as a principal investigator must be a Canadian citizen or permanent resident of Canada, hold a doctorate or the equivalent, and hold a position as a professor or teacher in a Québec postsecondary educational or research establishment. The principal investigator is responsible for the intellectual direction of the proposed research, performs the administrative duties related to the grant, and acts as the contact person with the IRSST. Only one person may play this role.
**Level of Study**: doctorate
**Value**: US$100,000 IRSST + US$30,000
**Additional Information**: www.irsst.qc.ca/en/grants/competitive-research

### For further information contact:

**Tel**:        (1) 514 288 1551
**Email**:    subventions@irsst.qc.ca

## Institut de Recherche Robert-Sauvé en Santé et en Sécurité du Travail Graduate Studies Scholarship and Postdoctoral Fellowship Program

**Purpose**: To support Master's and doctoral students who wish to acquire research training in the occupational health and safety field
**Eligibility**: Open to students who are registered full-time in a Master's or doctoral programme and have obtained a cumulative average of B+ for all of their undergraduate studies
**Level of Study**: Doctorate, Postgraduate

**Type**: Scholarship

**Value**: US$14,250 per year. In addition, a scholarship recipient whose training and research program is outside Canada is reimbursed for the amount exceeding the first US$750 in annual tuition fees; the cost of travelling to the training and research location, representing the cost of one round-trip economy airplane ticket or one round trip by car, for each year of the effective period of the scholarship (maximum of 2 years)

**Length of Study**: 2–3 years

**Frequency**: Annual

**Closing Date**: July

**Contributor**: The Commission des normes, de l'équité, de la santé et de la sécurité du travail provides most of the Institute's funding from the contributions it collects from the employers

**Additional Information**: Please check the website for further details

**For further information contact:**

**Tel**:      (1) 514 288 1551 ext. 377

**Email**:   bourses@irsst.qc.ca

## Institut Européen d'Administration des Affaires

Boulevard de Constance, F-77305 Fontainebleau Cedex, France.

**Tel**:       (33) 1 60 72 40 00

**Email**:    mba.europe@insead.edu

**Website**:  www.insead.edu/mba

**Contact**:  Ms Irina Schneider-Maunoury, Senior Manager, MBA Financing

INSEAD is widely recognized as one of the most influential business schools in the world. With its second campus in Asia to complement its established presence in Europe, INSEAD is setting the pace in globalizing the MBA. The 1-year intensive MBA programme is focused on international general management.

## Institut Européen d'Administration des Affaires Goldman Sachs Scholarship for African Nationals

**Purpose**: The Goldman Sachs scholarships for African nationals at INSEAD is designed to give candidates from African countries access to a world-class MBA education. The scholarship winners will be allocated a Goldman Sachs mentor throughout the 10-month MBA programme

**Eligibility**: The scholarship is open to all candidates from African countries studying at INSEAD on the Full-time MBA Programme. Successful candidates must demonstrate their desire to work in Africa and explain why building business in Africa is important to them

**Type**: Scholarship

**Value**: Up to €15,000 per class

**Frequency**: Annual

**Country of Study**: Any country

**Application Procedure**: For further information, kindly refer the official link. www.insead.edu/

**Additional Information**: Please check website for further information

## Institut Européen d'Administration des Affaires Jewish Scholarship

**Purpose**: An INSEAD alumnus offers scholarships to Jewish students admitted to the INSEAD MBA Programme; a limited number of small awards are made each year. In keeping with the spirit and tradition behind this award, the winners are encouraged to give back by making their own donation to scholarships at INSEAD through the Alumni Fund within a few years after graduation

**Eligibility**: Jewish students who can justify difficulty in raising sufficient finances for their living expenses

**Type**: Scholarship

**Value**: Up to €5,000

**Frequency**: Annual

**Country of Study**: Any country

**Additional Information**: Please check website for further information

## Institut Européen d'Administration des Affaires MBA Programme

**Length of Study**: 10 months

**Application Procedure**: Applicants must complete an application form supplying a €110 fee, photograph, essay, two letters of recommendation, transcripts of grades, Graduate Management Admission Test score, TOEFL score and self addressed acknowledgment card

**For further information contact:**

MBA Admissions Office Boulevard de Constance, Boulevard de Constance, F-77300 Fontainebleau, France.

**Tel**:     (33) 1 60 72 42 73

**Fax**:     (33) 1 60 74 55 30

**Email**:   mba.info@insead.fr

## Institut Européen d'Administration des Affaires Nelson Mandela Endowment Scholarships

**Purpose**: To honour the life and work of President Nelson Mandela of South Africa, the INSEAD MBA Class of 75 created the INSEAD Nelson Mandela Endowment Scholarships at their 30th Class Reunion to provide financial support for one or more African participants per year at INSEAD in perpetuity
**Eligibility**: To be eligible for the Nelson Mandela Endowed Scholarship, candidates must be a national of a sub-Saharan African country and have spent a substantial part of their lives and received part of their prior education in Africa. Preference will be given to candidates who require proven financial assistance
**Level of Study**: Postgraduate
**Type**: Scholarship
**Value**: Up to €20,000
**Country of Study**: Africa
**Closing Date**: 6 June
**Funding**: Government
**Contributor**: INSEAD
**Additional Information**: For more details, visit official scholarship website: mba.insead.edu/schlmgmt/dsp_schl_info.cfm?schlcode=AFR02

## Institut Français d'Amérique

Department of History, CB# 3195, Chapel Hill, NC 27599-3195, United States of America.

**Tel**:       (1) 919 962 2115
**Email**:    IFA@unc.edu
**Website**:  institut.unc.edu/
**Contact**:  Professor Jay Smith

The mission of the Institut Français de Washington is to promote the American study of French culture, language, history and society, and to encourage the work of teachers, scholars and students in these fields. The Institute also sponsors events to foster public understanding of French-American relations. The IFW provides funds for fellowships, prizes, and conferences that serve this mission.

## Edouard Morot-Sir Fellowship in French Studies

**Eligibility**: Open to those in the final stages of a PhD dissertation or who have held a PhD for no longer than 3 years before the application deadline
**Level of Study**: Doctorate, Postdoctorate
**Type**: Fellowship
**Value**: €1,500

**Length of Study**: At least 1 month
**Frequency**: Annual
**Country of Study**: France
**Application Procedure**: Applicants must write a maximum of two pages describing the research project and planned trip and enclose a curriculum vitae. A letter of recommendation from the dissertation director is required and a letter from a specialist in the field for assistant professors
**No. of awards offered**: 90
**Closing Date**: 15 January
**Funding**: Private, Foundation
**No. of awards given last year**: 3
**No. of applicants last year**: 90
**Additional Information**: Awards are for maintenance during research in France and should not be used for travel. Please check website institut.unc.edu/application/

## Gilbert Chinard Fellowships

**Eligibility**: Open to those in the final stages of a PhD dissertation or who have held a PhD for no longer than 3 years before the application deadline
**Level of Study**: Doctorate, Postdoctorate
**Type**: Fellowship
**Value**: €1,500
**Length of Study**: At least 1 month
**Frequency**: Annual
**Country of Study**: France
**Application Procedure**: Applicants must write a maximum of two pages describing the research project and planned trip and enclose a curriculum vitae. A letter of recommendation from the dissertation director is also required for PhD candidates and a letter from a specialist in the field for assistant professors
**No. of awards offered**: 28
**Closing Date**: 15 January
**Funding**: Private
**No. of awards given last year**: 1
**No. of applicants last year**: 28
**Additional Information**: Awards are for maintenance during research in France and should not be used for travel. Applications should be sent by email

## Harmon Chadbourn Rorison Fellowship

**Eligibility**: Open to those in the final stages of a PhD dissertation or who have held a PhD for no longer than 3 years before the application deadline
**Level of Study**: Doctorate, Postdoctorate, Postgraduate
**Type**: Fellowship
**Value**: US$1,500
**Length of Study**: At least 1 month
**Frequency**: Every 2 years

**Country of Study**: France

**Application Procedure**: Applicants must write a maximum of two pages describing the research project and planned trip and enclose a curriculum vitae. A letter of recommendation from the dissertation director is required for PhD candidates and a letter from a specialist in the field for assistant professors

**No. of awards offered**: 27

**Closing Date**: 15 January

**Funding**: Private, Foundation

**No. of awards given last year**: 1

**No. of applicants last year**: 27

**Additional Information**: Awards are for maintenance during research in France and should not be used for travel. Applications should be sent by email

## Institute for Advanced Studies in the Humanities

The Institute for Advanced Studies in the Humanities, The University of Edinburgh, Hope Park Square, Edinburgh, Scotland, EH8 9NW, United Kingdom.

**Tel**:       (44) 131 650 4671
**Email**:    iash@ed.ac.uk
**Contact**:  The Secretary

The Institute for Advanced Studies in the Humanities was established in 1969 to promote interdisciplinary research in the arts, humanities and social sciences at the University of Edinburgh. It provides an international, interdisciplinary and autonomous space for discussion and debate.

## Institute for Advanced Studies in the Humanities (The Institute for Advanced Studies in the Humanities)-SSPS (School of Social and Political Science) Research Fellowships

**Purpose**: The IASH-SSPS Research Fellowships are intended to encourage outstanding interdisciplinary research, international scholarly collaboration, and networking activities of visiting Research Fellows together with academics in the School of Social and Political Science (SSPS)

**Eligibility**: For eligibility criteria, please visit website

**Value**: Approximately £1,300-£3,900 as a contribution towards additional living costs, and/or travel grants of up to £500

**Country of Study**: Any country

**Application Procedure**: Applications received after that date will not be considered. Successful candidates will be notified by email with a formal letter of confirmation to follow; please ensure that you supply a valid email address so that you can be contacted quickly after decisions are made.

**Closing Date**: 28 February

**Contributor**: The Institute for Advanced Studies in the Humanities

**Additional Information**: For more details, visit www.iash.ed.ac.uk/iash-ssps-research-fellowships

### For further information contact:

The University of Edinburgh, Hope Park Square, Edinburgh, EH8 9NW, United Kingdom.

**Tel**:     (44) 131 650 4671

## Visiting Scholars Programme

**Purpose**: The Visiting Scholars Programme aims to encourage exceptional scholars working in areas relevant to our research strengths to spend a period of time—from one or two weeks to several months—conducting research and collaborating with scholars within the Institute. IASH aims to select a mixture of early, mid, and senior career scholars.

**Eligibility**: Applicants would normally have at least a PhD (or equivalent professional experience, research, and publications), and normally have an institutional affiliation to a University or to an equivalent research organisation. Students working to complete a research higher degree are not eligible to apply. International applicants are strongly encouraged. Visa documents, if required, are the responsibility of the applicant. The University of Queensland will provide a formal letter of invitation to successful applicants which may be used for visa purposes. While some financial support may be provided to some Visiting Scholars, all applicants will be responsible for their own financial costs during their stay in Brisbane

**Level of Study**: Postgraduate

**Value**: up to US$2,500

**Closing Date**: 31 May

**Additional Information**: iash.uq.edu.au/fellowships-and-scholarships/visiting-scholars-programme

## Institute for Advanced Studies on Science, Technology and Society (IAS-STS)

Kopernikusgasse 9, A-8010 Graz, Austria.

**Tel**:       (43) 316 813909 34
**Email**:    info@sts.tugraz.at
**Website**:  www.sts.tugraz.at
**Contact**:  Günter Getzinger, Acting Director

In 1999 the Inter University Research Centre for Technology, Work and Culture (IFZ) launched the IAS-STS in Graz, Austria. It promotes the interdisciplinary investigation of the links and interaction between science, technology and society as well as research on the development and implementation of socially and environmentally sound, sustainable technologies.

## Institute for Advanced Studies on Science, Technology and Society Fellowship Programme

**Purpose**: To give the students the opportunity to explore issues

**Eligibility**: Applicants must hold an academic degree

**Level of Study**: Doctorate, Postdoctorate, Postgraduate, Research

**Type**: Fellowships

**Value**: €940 per month

**Length of Study**: Up to 9 months

**Frequency**: Annual

**Study Establishment**: IAS-STS

**Country of Study**: Austria

**Application Procedure**: Application forms can be download from the website

**No. of awards offered**: 50

**Closing Date**: 30 April

**Funding**: Government

**Contributor**: Styrian Government

**No. of awards given last year**: 5

**No. of applicants last year**: 50

**Additional Information**: www.ifz.at/ias/IAS-STS/Application

### For further information contact:

Institute for Advanced Studies on Science, Technology and Society (IAS-STS), Attn. Günter Getzinger, Kopernikusgasse 9, A-8010 Graz, Austria.

**Tel**:     (43) 316/813909
**Email**:   office@sts.tugraz.at

## Institute for Advanced Study (IAS) Technical University of Munich

### Rudolf Diesel Industry Fellowship

**Purpose**: It is the Fellowship's purpose to enhance collaboration and knowledge-sharing between research units at TUM and company research laboratories. To increase international collaboration, TUM-IAS especially welcomes applications from companies from outside Germany

**Eligibility**: 1. a nomination letter including a description of the facilities provided for the Fellow by the TUM Host institute. 2. a CV including a list of publications. 3. a statement of purpose jointly signed by the candidate and the hosting professor, describing the content of the. 4. joint research, its innovative potential and the concrete implementation plans (budget), including any planned. 5. events to enhance the Institute's intellectual environment

**Level of Study**: Postgraduate

**Type**: Fellowship

**Value**: Up to €20,000

**Frequency**: Annual

**Country of Study**: Any country

**Application Procedure**: Please submit the following application documents: 1. a nomination letter including a description of the facilities provided for the Fellow by the TUM Host institute. 2. a CV (no more than 5 pages) and a list of publications. 3. a statement of purpose jointly signed by the candidate and the hosting professor, describing the content of the joint research, its innovative potential and the concrete implementation plans. This statement should also include. 4. a budget plan. 5. a time plan regarding the candidate's projected periods of stay at TUM. 6. an identification of possible additional (interdisciplinary) collaboration partners both within TUM-IAS and within TUM as well as a short explanation as to why this collaboration would be beneficial. 7. an outline for an international, ideally interdisciplinary workshop/colloquium, to be organized during the active Fellowship period. 8. a letter of nomination from the Dean of the hosting faculty or another member of the EHP or Board of Trustees

**Closing Date**: 24 October

**Funding**: Private

**Additional Information**: www.ias.tum.de/fellowship-program/rudolf-diesel-industry-fellowship/

### For further information contact:

Lichtenbergstrasse 2 a, D-85748 Garching, Germany.

**Tel**:     (49) 89 289 10550
**Email**:   info@ias.tum.de

## Institute for Labour Market Policy Evaluation (IFAU)

Box 513, S751-20 Uppsala, Sweden.

**Tel**:      (46) 184 717 070
**Email**:   ifau@ifau.uu.se
**Website**: www.ifau.se

The Institute for Labour Market Policy Evaluation (IFAU) is a research institute under the Swedish Ministry of industry, employment and communications. IFAU's objective is to promote, support and carry out evaluations of the effects of labour market policies, studies of the functioning of the labour market and evaluations of the labour market effects of measures within the educational system.

## Institute for Labour Market Policy Evaluation Post Doctoral Scholarship

**Purpose**: To evaluate measures motivated by labour market policy

**Eligibility**: Open to candidates who have recently obtained a PhD degree in economics or another social science and are EU nationals (not Sweden) or non-EU nationals if they have been resident in the EU (not Sweden) for more than 4 out of the last 5 years

**Level of Study**: Postdoctorate

**Type**: Scholarship

**Value**: €52,029 per year with a mobility allowance of €550 per month for single and €886 for researchers with a partner and/or children

**Length of Study**: 1 year

**Frequency**: Annual

**Application Procedure**: Applicants can download the application form from the website. The completed application form must be sent along with a curriculum vitae, names and addresses of 3 referees, a research paper (or link) and a research proposal (not more than 3 pages)

### For further information contact:

**Email**:     Cecilia.Andersson@ifau.uu.se

## Institute for South ASIA Studies UC Berkeley

### Berreman-Yamanaka Award for Himalayan Studies

**Purpose**: The Berreman-Yamanaka Fellowship for Himalayan Studies' provides for an annual award of up to US$1500 to UC Berkeley graduate students for research on topics related to Himalayan Studies across Bhutan, India, Nepal and Pakistan

**Level of Study**: Graduate

**Type**: Award

**Value**: US$1,500

**Frequency**: Annual

**Country of Study**: Any country

**Application Procedure**: In your application please include the following: 1. A cover letter stating the need for travel. (750 words or less, PDF format) 2. A 2-page project proposal. Which should include the proposed date of travel, as well as all other sources of funding available in the given summer or given AY. (double-spaced) (PDF format) 3. A budget (only for research) (PDF format) 4. A CV (PDF format) 5. One letter of support from your advisor (PDF, sent by the recommenders directly)

**Closing Date**: 15 April

**Funding**: Foundation

**Additional Information**: southasia.berkeley.edu/himalayan-studies-award

### For further information contact:

10 Stephens Hall (Rear Annex), University of California, Berkeley, Berkeley, CA 94720-2310, United States of America.

**Tel**:     (1) 510 642 3608
**Email**:   pkala@berkeley.edu

## Bhattacharya Graduate Fellowship

**Purpose**: The Bhattacharya Graduate Fellowship will award UC Berkeley graduate students competitive grants for topics related to contemporary India

**Level of Study**: Graduate

**Type**: Fellowship

**Value**: US$1,000 for research travel to India (a total of two will be awarded) and US$500 for domestic conference travel for presentations (a total of four will be awarded).

**Frequency**: Annual

**Country of Study**: Any country

**Closing Date**: 15 April

**Funding**: Foundation

**Additional Information**: southasia.berkeley.edu/bhattacharya-graduate-fellowship

### For further information contact:

10 Stephens Hall (Rear Annex), University of California, Berkeley, Berkeley, CA 94720-2310, United States of America.

**Tel**:     (1) 510 642 3608
**Email**:   pkala@berkeley.edu

## Bodha Pravaham Fellowship

**Purpose**: The Bodha Pravaham Undergraduate Fellowship for Tamil Studies, established with a generous contribution from Professor George Hart and Professor Kausalya Hart, both cornerstones of Tamil Studies at UC Berkeley, supports undergraduate students pursuing research projects focusing on Tamil studies

**Level of Study**: Graduate
**Type**: Fellowship
**Value**: US$900
**Length of Study**: 1 year
**Frequency**: Annual
**Country of Study**: Any country
**Application Procedure**: In your application for RESEARCH TRAVEL, please include the following: 1. A cover letter stating the need for travel (750 words or less) 2. A 2-page project proposal (double-spaced) (PDF format) 3. A budget (only for research) (PDF format) 4. A CV (PDF format) 5. One letter of support from your advisor (PDF, sent by the recommenders directly)
**Closing Date**: 15 April
**Funding**: Foundation
**Additional Information**: southasia.berkeley.edu/bodha-fund

### For further information contact:

10 Stephens Hall (Rear Annex), University of California, Berkeley, Berkeley, CA 94720-2310, United States of America.

**Tel**:       (1) 510 642 3608
**Email**:    pkala@berkeley.edu

## Hart Fellowship

**Purpose**: The Hart Fellowship for Tamil Studies, established with a generous contribution from Professor George Hart and Professor Kausalya Hart, both cornerstones of Tamil Studies at UC Berkeley, supports graduate students pursuing research projects focusing on Tamil studies
**Level of Study**: Graduate
**Type**: Fellowship
**Value**: US$2,000
**Length of Study**: 1 year
**Frequency**: Annual
**Country of Study**: Any country
**Closing Date**: 15 April
**Funding**: Foundation
**Additional Information**: southasia.berkeley.edu/hart-fund

### For further information contact:

10 Stephens Hall (Rear Annex), University of California, Berkeley, Berkeley, CA 94720-2310, United States of America.

**Tel**:       (1) 510 642 3608
**Email**:    pkala@berkeley.edu

## International Affairs Fellowship in India

**Purpose**: The Council on Foreign Relations International Affairs Fellowship (IAF) in India, sponsored by Bharti, seeks to strengthen mutual understanding and cooperation between rising generations of leaders and thinkers in the United States and India. The program provides for one to four mid-career United States professionals, who have had little or no substantial prior experience in India, the opportunity to spend three to twelve months conducting research and working in India. Fellows are drawn from academia, business, government, journalism, NGOs, and think tanks. While in India, fellows develop a new professional network as well as gain fresh insights and perspectives into the country and the opportunities and challenges that confront the region. CFR will work with its network of contacts to assist selected fellows in finding suitable host organizations that best match the fellow's proposed work in India. Possible placements include but are not limited to the CFR's local partner, the Centre for Policy Research; the Institute for Defense Studies and Analyses; or the Centre for Insurance and Risk Management
**Eligibility**: 1. Applicants must be United States citizens. 2. Applicants must be mid-career professionals. 3. Applicants must possess a strong record of professional achievement. 4. Applicants must hold at least a bachelor's degree
**Level of Study**: Graduate
**Type**: Fellowship
**Value**: US$90,000
**Length of Study**: 1 year
**Frequency**: Annual
**Country of Study**: Any country
**Closing Date**: 28 February
**Funding**: Foundation

### For further information contact:

**Email**:    fellowships@cfr.org

## International Studies Research Lab

**Purpose**: The Center for Global Studies at the University of Illinois, Urbana-Champaign, is pleased to announce funding to support the internationalization of community colleges nationwide. We invite applications from faculty, librarians, and administrators interested in expanding global studies curricula, instruction in less commonly taught languages, library collections, or international education programs at their home institutions. Projects for minority-serving institutions are particularly welcome. During their stay, Fellows can work one-on-one with international and area studies reference librarians and explore the unlimited print and online resources of the University of Illinois Library

**Eligibility**: Applicants must be faculty or administrators at 2-year community colleges or 4-year universities that offer associate degrees. The Center for Global Studies encourages applications particularly from minority-serving institutions. While fellowships that cover housing and parking will be reserved to applicants from outside of the Champaign-Urbana area, all participants will be eligible to receive research honoraria

**Level of Study**: Graduate

**Type**: Fellowship

**Frequency**: Annual

**Country of Study**: Any country

**Application Procedure**: Apply online: forms.illinois.edu/sec/5427515

**Closing Date**: 15 May

**Funding**: Foundation

**Additional Information**: emails.illinois.edu/newsletter/147164.html

## For further information contact:

Lynne Rudasill Global Studies Librarian, Center for Global Studies 306 International Studies Building, M/C 402 uiuc campus mail, IL 00001, United States of America.

**Email**: rudasill@illinois.edu

## Maharaj Kaul Memorial Trust

**Purpose**: UC Berkeley graduate students are invited to apply for competitive grants of up to US$1000 for research travel to South Asia (a total of two will be awarded), and up to US$500 for conference travel (a total of two will be awarded) made available through a gift from the Maharaj Kaul Memorial Fund to the Institute for South Asia Studies

**Level of Study**: Graduate

**Type**: Grant

**Value**: US$1,000

**Frequency**: Annual

**Country of Study**: Any country

**Application Procedure**: In your application for RESEARCH TRAVEL, please include the following: 1. A cover letter stating the need for travel (750 words or less) 2. A 2-page project proposal (double-spaced) (PDF format) 3. A budget (PDF format) 4. A CV (PDF format) 5. One letter of support from your advisor (PDF, sent by the recommenders directly) 6. Please Note: Two awards of upto US$1000 will be given for Research Travel to South Asia

**Closing Date**: 15 April

**Funding**: Foundation

**Additional Information**: southasia.berkeley.edu/maharaj-kaul-grants

## For further information contact:

10 Stephens Hall (Rear Annex), University of California, Berkeley, Berkeley, CA 94720-2310, United States of America.

**Tel**: (1) 510 642 3608

**Email**: pkala@berkeley.edu

## Outstanding Paper Prize

**Purpose**: The Subir and Malini Chowdhury Center for Bangladesh Studies welcomes submissions for the Outstanding Paper Prize in Bangladesh Studies. Submissions are welcome from any discipline, though preference will be given to papers in a social science field

**Eligibility**: 1. Full time UC Berkeley graduate students or undergraduates with upperclass standing. 2. Students must have been registered as a full time student at any accredited university. 3. Papers must be linked to a course for undergraduates, must be linked to a departmental thesis program

**Level of Study**: Graduate

**Type**: Grant

**Value**: US$500

**Frequency**: Annual

**Country of Study**: Any country

**Application Procedure**: 1. Only electronic submissions will be accepted. Please email all documents to chowdhury-center@berkeley.edu with subject heading: "Submission for Outstanding Bangladesh Paper Prize" 2. All documents should be in PDF format. 3. Please email copies of: 1) the paper, 2) the page with identifying information, and 3) the abstract attached as PDF fles. 4. Please send entries NO LATER THAN 5pm on, April 15

**Closing Date**: 15 April

**Funding**: Foundation

**Additional Information**: chowdhurycenter.berkeley.edu/paper-prize

**For further information contact:**

The Subir & Malini Chowdhury Center Institute for South Asia Studies UC Berkeley 10 Stephens Hall, Berkeley, CA 94720-2310, United States of America.

**Tel:** (1) 510 642 3608
**Email:** chowdhury-center@berkeley.edu

## South Asia Program Junior Fellowship

**Purpose:** The one-year, full-time fellowship will provide individuals with a unique opportunity to expand their knowledge of security issues in the subcontinent, engage the South Asia policy community in Washington and the region, and experience working at a dynamic think tank that provides close interaction with senior staff and researchers

**Eligibility:** 1. A strong background in: South Asian political, economic, or security issues; strategic studies; international relations theory; or economics. 2. Demonstrated analytical, research, and writing skills. 3. Ability to work independently and to collaborate with peers in a team environment. 4. Bachelor's degree. All applicants must be eligible to work in the United States for the full twelve months of the fellowship following graduation

**Level of Study:** Graduate
**Type:** Fellowship
**Value:** US$37,000
**Length of Study:** 1 year
**Frequency:** Annual
**Country of Study:** Any country
**Closing Date:** 21 February
**Funding:** Foundation
**Additional Information:** www.stimson.org/content/south-asia-program-junior-fellowship

**For further information contact:**

1. A one-page statement of interest laying out the candidate's research interests and career goals. Applicants should discuss how they can contribute to the mission and work of the Stimson South Asia Program and how the Stimson South Asia Junior Fellowship would contribute to their long-term professional growth. 2. A two-page curriculum vitae or resume including all educational qualifications, study abroad experience, and extracurricular activities, as well as any work experience to date. 3. Unofficial transcript (s) with academic record of undergraduate and Master's (if applicable) coursework and study abroad experience. 4. One or two letters of recommendation from a professor or former employer explaining what qualifications, skills, and experiences make the candidate a good fit for the

fellowship 5. A writing sample of no more than two pages on a topic related to South Asian political or security issues.

**Email:** southasiaadmin@stimson.org

# Institute for Supply Management (ISM)

2055 E. Centennial Circle, Tempe, AZ 85285-2160, United States of America.

**Tel:** (1) 480 752 6276
**Email:** ssturzl@ism.ws
**Website:** www.ism.ws
**Contact:** Valerie Gryniewicz, Manager, Education

The Institute for Supply Management (ISM) is a non-profit association that provides national and international leadership in purchasing and supply management research and education. ISM provides more than 40,000 members with opportunities to expand their professional skills and knowledge.

## Institute for Supply Management Professional Research Development Grant

**Purpose:** This program is designed to support assistants and young associate professor with terminal degree that are teaching in the field of a significant research track in supply management and associated areas. The goal is to help competitively selected faculty build a research and publication field and establish themselves in the profession (i.e. academic institutions, professional organisation, research fund granting bodies such as CAPS Research etc.). This would include CAPS research. Faculty selected will generally have 2 and 8 years of teaching and research experience and have successful publication experiments beyond the doctoral degree

**Eligibility:** Open to assistant professors, associate professors or equivalent who have demonstrated exceptional academic productivity in research and teaching. Candidates are chosen from those who can help produce useful research that can be applied to the advancement of purchasing and supply management. Candidates must be full-time faculty members within or outside the United States of America and be present or past members of ISM committees, groups, forums or affiliated organizations. An assistant professor should have 3 or more years of post-degree experience. Previous awardees are ineligible

**Level of Study**: Postdoctorate
**Type**: Grant
**Value**: US$10,000
**Frequency**: Annual
**Country of Study**: United States of America
**Application Procedure**: (1) Letter of application explaining qualifications of the grant. (2) Research proposal of no more than five pages, including problem statement or hypothesis; research methodology, with data sources, collection and analysis; and value to the field of supply management. (3) Curriculum vitae, including works in progress
**No. of awards offered**: 5–10
**Closing Date**: 30 January
**Funding**: Private
**Contributor**: ISM
**No. of awards given last year**: 1
**No. of applicants last year**: 5–10
**Additional Information**: It is expected that the recipients will present the results of their research at an ISM forum, e.g. research symposium, ISM Annual International Purchasing Conference and/or an ISM publication such as The Journal of Supply Chain Management

## For further information contact:

Robert A Kemp, PhD, CPM, Institute for Supply Management, P.O. Box 22160 Tempe, AZ 85285-2160, United States of America.

**Email**:    kempr@mchsi.com

## Institute of Advanced Legal Studies (IALS)

Institute of Advanced Legal Studies, Charles Clore House, 17 Russell Square, London, WC1B 5DR, United Kingdom.

**Tel**:         (44) 20 7862 5800
**Email**:     ials.administrator@sas.ac.uk
**Website**:  www.ials.sas.ac.uk
**Contact**:  Margaret Wilson, Institute Manager

The Institute of Advanced Legal Studies (IALS) plays a national and international role in the promotion and facilitation of legal research. It possesses one of the leading research libraries in Europe and organizes a regular programme of conferences, seminars and lectures. It also offers postgraduate taught and research programmes and specialized training courses.

## Institute of Advanced Legal Studies Visiting Fellowship in Law Librarianship

**Purpose**: To enable experienced law librarians, who are undertaking research in, appropriate fields, to relate their work to activities in which the Institutes own library is involved
**Eligibility**: Open to experienced law librarians from any country
**Level of Study**: Unrestricted
**Type**: Fellowship
**Value**: Fellowships can consist of or include a period working with Institute library staff or be a period of research based in a research carrel
**Length of Study**: Between 2 and 6 months
**Frequency**: Annual
**Study Establishment**: The IALS
**Country of Study**: United Kingdom
**Application Procedure**: Applicants must submit a full curriculum vitae, the names, addresses and telephone numbers of two referees and a brief statement of the research programme to be undertaken to the Administrative Secretary
**No. of awards offered**: 1
**No. of awards given last year**: 1
**No. of applicants last year**: 1
**Additional Information**: ials.sas.ac.uk/fellowships/institute-advanced-legal-studies-visiting-research-fellowship-programme/visiting/past

## Institute of Advanced Legal Studies Visiting Fellowship in Legislative Studies

**Purpose**: To enable individuals in the field to undertake research
**Eligibility**: Open to established academics and practitioners from any country. This award is not available for postgraduate research
**Level of Study**: Unrestricted
**Type**: Fellowship
**Value**: Non-stipendary
**Length of Study**: A minimum of 3 months and a maximum of 1 year
**Frequency**: Annual
**Study Establishment**: The IALS
**Country of Study**: United Kingdom
**Application Procedure**: Applicants must submit a full curriculum vitae, the names, addresses and telephone numbers of two referees and a brief statement of the research programme to be undertaken
**No. of awards offered**: 1
**Closing Date**: 30 January
**No. of applicants last year**: 1
**Additional Information**: ials.sas.ac.uk/fellowships/institute-advanced-legal-studies-visiting-research-fellowship-programme

**For further information contact:**

**Email**:     eliza.boudier@sas.ac.uk

## Institute of Behavioural Science (IBS), University of Colorado at Boulder

Department of Geography & Institute of Behavioural Science Campus Box 487, Boulder, CO 80309-0487, United States of America.

**Tel**:     (1) 303 492 1619
**Email**:     johno@colorado.edu
**Website**:     www.colorado.edu/IBS
**Contact**:     Mr John O'Loughlin

The Institute of Behavioural Science (IBS) provides a setting for interdisciplinary research on problems of societal concern. By engaging faculty from all of the social and behavioural sciences at the University of Colorado at Boulder, the Institute encourages work that transcends disciplinary boundaries, that illuminates the complexity of social behaviour and social life, and that has important implications for social policy.

### Master of Business Administration Programme

**Length of Study**: 1 year and 2 months
**Application Procedure**: Applicants must complete an application form supplying, TOEFL score, Graduate Management Admission Test score, plus personal and professional recommendations with career goals
**Closing Date**: 30 May

**For further information contact:**

Graduate School of Business Administration Campus Box 419, Boulder, CO 80309-0030, United States of America.

**Tel**:     (1) 303 492 1831
**Fax**:     (1) 303 492 1727
**Email**:     busgrad@colorado.edu

## Institute of Biology

20 Queensberry Place, London, SW7 2DZ, United Kingdom.

**Tel**:     (44) 20 7581 8333
**Email**:     info@iob.org

**Website**:     www.iob.org
**Contact**:     Ms Georgina Day, Education Officer

The Institute of Biology's mission is to promote biology and the biological sciences, to foster the public understanding of science, to enhance the status of the biology profession and to represent its members as a whole to government and other bodies worldwide. The Institute is the 'voice' of British biology.

### Dax Copp Travelling Fellowship

**Purpose**: To support overseas travel in connection with biological study, teaching or research and to aid those who would otherwise not have this opportunity
**Eligibility**: Open to students in the biological sciences studying in the United Kingdom
**Level of Study**: Unrestricted
**Type**: Fellowship
**Value**: £500
**Frequency**: Annual
**Application Procedure**: Applicants must complete an application form, available from the Expeditions Grants Manager. Applicants are also required to produce a reasoned statement of the purpose to which the fellowship will be put, supported by three referees
**No. of awards offered**: 20
**Closing Date**: January
**Funding**: Private
**Contributor**: Membership
**No. of awards given last year**: 1
**No. of applicants last year**: 20
**Additional Information**: Applicants receiving a fellowship will be expected to provide the Institute with a report within six months of the fellowship ending

### For further information contact:

Royal Geographical Society, 1 Kensington Gore, Kensington, London, SW7 2DZ, United Kingdom.

**Tel**:     (44) 20 7591 3073
**Email**:     grants@rsg.org

## Institute of Education

20 Bedford Way, London, WC1H 0AL, United Kingdom.

**Tel**:     (44) 20 7612 6000
**Email**:     info@ioe.ac.uk

**Website**: www.ioe.ac.uk
**Contact**: Josie Charlton, Head of Marketing and Development

Founded in 1902, the Institute of Education is a world-class centre of excellence for research, teacher training, higher degrees and consultancy in education and education-related areas of social science. Our pre-eminent scholars and talented students from all walks of life make up an intellectually rich and diverse learning community.

## Nicholas Hans Comparative Education Scholarship

**Purpose**: To assist a well-qualified student to study for a PhD in comparative education at the Institute of Education
**Eligibility**: Candidates must be registered Institute students not normally resident in the United Kingdom
**Level of Study**: Doctorate
**Type**: Scholarship
**Value**: Full-time tuition fees
**Length of Study**: 3–7 years
**Frequency**: Annual
**Study Establishment**: Institute of Education
**Country of Study**: United Kingdom
**Application Procedure**: Candidates are required to submit an extended essay of 25,000–30,000 words, based upon their research or proposed research, that exemplifies, extends or develops by critique the concerns of Nicholas Hans in comparative education
**Closing Date**: 1 June
**Funding**: Trusts
**Contributor**: Trust fund based upon money left in the will of Nicholas Hans' widow

### For further information contact:

**Email**: p.kelly@ioe.ac.uk

## Institute of Electrical and Electronics Engineers History Center

Samuel C. Williams Library, 3rd floor, 1 Castle point on Hudson, Hoboken, NJ 07030, United States of America.

**Tel**:      (1) 732 562 5450
**Email**:   ieee-history@ieee.org

**Website**: www.ieee.org/about/history_center/fellowship.html
**Contact**: Mr Robert Colburn, Research Co-ordinator

The mission of the IEEE History Center is to preserve, research and promote the history of information and electrical technologies.

## Charles LeGeyt Fortescue Fellowship

**Purpose**: The Charles LeGeyt Fortescue Scholarship was established in 1939 as a memorial to Charles LeGeyt in recognition of his valuable contributions to the field of electrical engineering
**Eligibility**: 1. To be eligible, the student must be a permanent resident of the United States, have majored in the field of electrical engineering, and have received a bachelor's degree from an engineering college of recognized standing. 2. The scholarship will be awarded to a first-year full-time graduate student only. In the event the college is conducting a combined BS and MS degree program, the student in the penultimate year would be eligible for the award, which would apply in the final year of the program
**Level of Study**: Postgraduate
**Type**: Fellowship
**Value**: US$24,000 per year
**Length of Study**: 1 year
**Frequency**: Every 2 years
**Study Establishment**: An engineering school of recognised standing
**Country of Study**: United States of America or Canada
**Application Procedure**: 1. Complete the entire application form. 2. Submit certified transcripts from all colleges/universities attended. 3. Provide letters of recommendation from three college/university professors who are familiar with your work. 4. The complete name, title, and address of the reference must be clearly noted on the letter. Letters of recommendation should address the following areas: the applicant's ability to perform graduate work; originality and creativity; character; diligence and social responsibility; ability to lead; ability to communicate; where the reference would rank the applicant among students he/she has known in this field in recent years. 5. All application documentation must be received by the first Monday after 30 April each year
**No. of awards offered**: 25
**Closing Date**: 4 May
**Funding**: Private
**No. of awards given last year**: 1

**No. of applicants last year**: 25
**Additional Information**: The Institute also offers many prize awards (service awards, field awards, and prize paper awards), and a number of medals www.ieee.org/education/awards/fortescue-scholarship.html

### For further information contact:

445 Hoes Lane, Piscataway, NJ 08854, United States of America.

## Institute of Electrical and Electronics Engineers Fellowship in the History of Electrical and Computing Technology

**Purpose**: To support graduate work in the history of electrical engineering
**Eligibility**: 1. Must be a graduate student or a postgraduate student 2. Must attend a university 3. Must not be attending high school currently 4. Must study full-time 5. Restricted to students studying Energy and Power Engineering, Engineering/Technology, Historic Preservation and Conservation, History, Science, Technology, and Society
**Level of Study**: Doctorate, Postdoctorate, Postgraduate
**Type**: Fellowship
**Value**: US$25,000 plus US$3,000 research budget
**Length of Study**: 1 year
**Frequency**: Annual
**Study Establishment**: A college or university of recognized standing
**Country of Study**: Any country
**Application Procedure**: Applicants must submit a completed application, transcripts, three letters of recommendation and a research proposal. Application materials can be downloaded from the website
**No. of awards offered**: 14
**Closing Date**: 1 February
**Funding**: Corporation
**No. of awards given last year**: 1
**No. of applicants last year**: 14
**Additional Information**: The fellowship is made possible by a grant from the IEEE Life Member Fund and is awarded by the IEEE History Committee. Application materials available on the website www.petersons.com/scholarship/ieee-life-members-fellowship-in-the-history-of-electrical-and-computing-technology-111_169647.aspx

### For further information contact:

**Tel**:     (1) 732 562 5450

## Institute of European Studies

**Tel**:     (32) 2 614 80 01

## Ana Hatherly Graduate Student Research Grant

**Purpose**: Cátedra Ana Hatherly promotes the work of one of the most important and multifaceted Portuguese poets, Ana Hatherly. In this context Camões, Instituto da Cooperação e da Língua and the Center for Portuguese Studies are pleased to announce a competition for 1 research grant of US$1000,00 each for Graduate Students in all areas of research at UC, Berkeley. Preference will be given to applicants interested in publishing research papers about Ana Hatherly's poetry, cinematography, and painting
**Level of Study**: Postgraduate
**Type**: Grant
**Value**: US$1,000
**Frequency**: Annual
**Country of Study**: Any country
**Closing Date**: 22 January
**Funding**: International office
**Additional Information**:    ies.berkeley.edu/ana-hatherly-graduate-student-research-grant

### For further information contact:

**Email**:     ies@berkeley.edu

## Regents' Junior Faculty Fellowships

**Purpose**: It is a pleasure to bring to the attention of junior faculty members the Regents' Junior Faculty Fellowships for the summer
**Eligibility**: Eligibility is limited to academic year appointees in the ranks of Assistant Professor, Acting Assistant Professor, Acting Associate Professor, and, in the School of Law, Acting Professor
**Level of Study**: Postgraduate
**Type**: Fellowship
**Value**: US$5,000
**Frequency**: Annual
**Country of Study**: Any country
**Closing Date**: 12 April
**Funding**: International office
**Additional Information**:        vpf.berkeley.edu/faculty-fellowships/regents-junior-faculty-fellowships

### For further information contact:

**Email**:     yasyavg@berkeley.edu

# Institute of Fundamental Sciences, Massey University

Institute of Fundamental Sciences, Massey University, Private Bag 11 222, Palmerston North, 4442, New Zealand.

**Tel:** (64) 6 350 5799 ext. 2909
**Email:** r.mclachlan@massey.ac.nz
**Website:** www.massey.ac.nz
**Contact:** Professor Robert McLachlan

Massey University has over 40,000 students, of which 19,000 study on three campuses, with the remaining 21,000 studying by correspondence. The five colleges of business, education, science, humanities and social sciences and design, fine arts and music provide a comprehensive range of undergraduate and graduate degrees and diplomas all tailored to meeting national and international needs.

## Massey Business School - PhD Scholarships

**Purpose:** The Massey Business School is seeking to strengthen its strategic research platforms
**Eligibility:** At a minimum, you must meet MU admission criteria: GPA of 7.5 or higher (on a 9 point scale). This is above an average grade of A- (an MBA is not a direct pathway to a PhD). Applicants should have a conditional or unconditional offer of place in a doctoral programme at Massey University. Full-time and part-time candidates are eligible to apply
**Level of Study:** Doctorate
**Type:** Scholarship
**Value:** NZ$25,000 per annum for a maximum of 3 years
**Length of Study:** 3 years
**Study Establishment:** Institute of Fundamental Sciences, Massey University
**Country of Study:** New Zealand
**Application Procedure:** you need to submit your academic CV, academic transcripts, a one-page research proposal and other supporting documents to the appropriate person listed: 1. School of Accountancy: Dr Lin Mei Tan L.M.Tan@massey.ac.nz
**Closing Date:** 30 April
**Additional Information:** www.massey.ac.nz/massey/learning/colleges/college-of-sciences/about/fundamental-sciences/phd-scholarships-and-jobs.cfm

### For further information contact:

**Tel:** (64) 6 350 5701
**Email:** contact@massey.ac.nz

## PhD Opportunity - Engineering

**Eligibility:** The successful candidate will likely have a background in physics or engineering and will provide evidence of well-developed mathematical skills and practical ability
**Level of Study:** Doctorate
**Value:** The project will be carried out with an industrial partner (Ravensdown) and a stipend is offered for a duration of 3 years
**Length of Study:** 3 years
**Study Establishment:** Institute of Fundamental Sciences, Massey University
**Country of Study:** New Zealand
**Application Procedure:** Applicants should provide their CV to Professor Clive Davies C.Davies@massey.ac.nz

### For further information contact:

**Email:** admissions@gcu.ac.uk

## PhD Scholarship (Drug Research Team, SHORE & Whariki Research Centre)

**Level of Study:** Doctorate
**Type:** Scholarship
**Value:** NZ$25,000 per annum (tax free) plus tuition fees
**Length of Study:** 3 year
**Frequency:** Annual
**Country of Study:** New Zealand
**Application Procedure:** To apply please send a covering letter, curriculum vitae and 3 recent examples of your written work via email to Dr. Chris Wilkins. If you would like to discuss this opportunity further please contact Dr. Chris Wilkins (c.wilkins@massey.ac.nz)
**Closing Date:** 20 March

### For further information contact:

**Email:** shore&amp;whariki@massey.ac.nz

## PhD Scholarship in Mathematics

**Eligibility:** Applicants should have or expect to receive a BSc (Hons) or MSc degree or equivalent in mathematics
**Level of Study:** Doctorate
**Type:** Scholarship
**Value:** The scholarship covers all tuition fees for international and domestic students and includes a tax-free stipend of NZ$25,000 per annum

**Study Establishment**: Institute of Fundamental Sciences, Massey University
**Country of Study**: New Zealand
**Application Procedure**: Applications including a CV, academic transcript and cover letter should be sent to Professor Robert McLachlan, Institute of Fundamental Sciences, Massey University, Palmerston North, New Zealand or by email to r.mclachlan@massey.ac.nz
**Additional Information**: See web site dynamics.massey.ac.nz for further information

### For further information contact:

**Email**:    jag.roberts@unsw.edu.au

## School of Engineering and Advanced Technology Scholarships

**Eligibility**: To be eligible you must hold a recognized entrance qualification
**Level of Study**: Doctorate
**Type**: Scholarship
**Value**: NZ$25,000 a year for 3 years, to cover fees and living expenses
**Length of Study**: 3 years
**Frequency**: Annual
**Study Establishment**: Institute of Fundamental Sciences, Massey University
**Country of Study**: New Zealand
**Application Procedure**: Initial applications should be on the Massey University form. Please send the form to Michele Wagner (m.wagner@massey.ac.nz)
**Closing Date**: Novermber

### For further information contact:

21 North Park Street, Madison, WI 53715, United States of America.

**Email**:    info@dcs.wisc.edu

## Institute of Museum and Library Services

## Accelerating Promising Practices for Small Libraries

**Purpose**: Accelerating Promising Practices for Small Libraries (APP) is a special initiative of the National Leadership Grants for Libraries Program. The goal of this initiative is to support projects that strengthen the ability of small and rural libraries and archives to serve their communities
**Eligibility**: See the Notice of Funding Opportunity for eligibility criteria for this program. To be eligible as an applicant for the Accelerating Promising Practices for Small Libraries Initiative, you must: 1. Be either a unit of State or local government or be a private, nonprofit institution that has nonprofit status under the Internal Revenue Code of 1954, as amended, and 2. Be located in one of the 50 States of the United States of America, the District of Columbia, the Commonwealth of Puerto Rico, the United States Virgin Islands, Guam, American Samoa, the Commonwealth of the Northern Mariana Islands, the Republic of the Marshall Islands, the Federated States of Micronesia, or the Republic of Palau. For further information, refer the below link. www.imls.gov/sites/default/files/fy19-ols-app-nofo.pdf
**Level of Study**: Postgraduate
**Type**: Grant
**Frequency**: Annual
**Country of Study**: Any country
**Closing Date**: 25 February
**Funding**: Private
**Additional Information**: The goal of this initiative is to support projects that strengthen the ability of small and rural libraries and archives to serve their communities. IMLS invites applications that focus on the following topics: transforming school library practice community memory digital inclusion www.imls.gov/grants/available/accelerating-promising-practices-small-libraries

### For further information contact:

955 L'Enfant Plaza North, SW, Suite 4000, Washington, DC 20024-2135, United States of America.

**Email**:    imlsinfo@imls.gov

## Native American Library Services: Enhancement Grants

**Purpose**: Native American Enhancement grants are competitive grants available to carry out activities, described in 20 U.S.C. 9141, that advance the programs and services of eligible
**Eligibility**: Indian tribes are eligible to apply for funding under the Native American Library Services Enhancement Grant program. See the Notice of Funding Opportunity for eligibility criteria for this program
**Level of Study**: Postgraduate
**Type**: Award
**Value**: US$10,000 to US$150,000
**Length of Study**: 2 years
**Frequency**: Annual

**Country of Study**: Any country
**Application Procedure**: Digital Services projects feature activities dedicated to the establishment and refinement of digital services and programs related to infrastructure, platforms, and technology, in general
**Closing Date**: 1 May
**Funding**: Private
**Additional Information**: www.imls.gov/grants/available/native-american-library-services-enhancement-grants

### For further information contact:

955 L'Enfant Plaza North, SW, Suite 4000, Washington, DC 20024-2135, United States of America.

**Tel**:    (1) 202 653 4716, (1) 202 653 4761
**Email**:    asmith@imls.gov, sboonie@imls.gov

## Institution of Engineering and Technology (IET)

Michael Faraday House, Six Hills Way, Stevenage, Hertfordshire, SG1 2AY, United Kingdom.

**Tel**:        (44) 1438 313 311
**Email**:      awards@theiet.org
**Website**:    www.theiet.org/awards
**Contact**:    J Tilley, Scholarships Coordinator

The IET is one of the world's largest engineering institutions with over 163,000 members in 127 countries. It is also the most interdisciplinary – to reflect the increasingly diverse nature of engineering in the 21st century. Energy, transport, manufacturing, information and communications, and the built environment: the IET covers them all.

## Hudswell International Research Scholarship

**Purpose**: To encourage excellence in engineering and technology research, with a preference for electrical, electronic or manufacturing engineering.
**Eligibility**: 1. You can apply for an award if you have a student loan, research grant, company bursary or similar, but you can't be a recipient of any other IET scholarship or bursary. 2. On the application form you'll need to include details of your referee. 3. The panel will consider you for all postgraduate awards where you meet the eligibility requirements. 4. If you're successful, you'll only be able to receive one IET Postgraduate Award during your PhD research.
**Type**: Scholarship

**Value**: £5,000
**Closing Date**: 2 April
**Additional Information**: www.theiet.org/impact-society/awards-scholarships/iet-postgraduate-research-awards/

## Institution of Engineering and Technology Postgraduate Scholarship for an Outstanding Researcher

**Purpose**: To assist IET members with research studies
**Eligibility**: Applicants should be members of the IET and must have commenced their studies prior to applying for this scholarship
**Level of Study**: Doctorate, Postgraduate, Research
**Type**: Scholarship
**Value**: £10,000
**Length of Study**: 1 year
**Frequency**: Annual
**Country of Study**: Any country
**Application Procedure**: Applicants should complete the online application form at www.theiet.org/postgradawards
**Closing Date**: April
**Funding**: Trusts
**Additional Information**: conferences.theiet.org/achievement/scholarships/postgraduate/index.cfm?

## Institution of Engineering and Technology Travel Awards

**Purpose**: To assist IET members undertaking international travel to attend conferences, participate in international research visits or projects
**Eligibility**: 1. Have been a member for a minimum of one year up to the date of application 2. Are IET members i.e. Student, Member, Fellow and some Associate categories. Lapsed members are not eligible 3. Reside in any country, as long as the travel is international
**Level of Study**: Unrestricted
**Type**: Travel grant
**Value**: We can award grants of up to £1,500 - a maximum of 75% of the total cost of the visit would be funded by the IET.
**Frequency**: Annual
**Country of Study**: Any country
**Application Procedure**: 1. You can apply for a grant at any time during the year 2. The travel should take place at least one month after the closing date for applications 3. You can't submit an application after an event has taken place 4. You can make up to two applications within a twelve-month period 5. If you have already received an IET Travel Award, a year must have passed before you can apply again 6. Please click the 'Apply' button above 7. You will be asked to attach

documentary evidence of the travel intention (e.g. invitation from the conference organiser) and confirmation that a visa has been sought (if required) 8. You will be requested to provide details of how any difference between the cost of the visit and the IET award will be funded 9. You'll need to provide contact details of your referee and send a request for a reference during the application

**Funding**: Trusts

**Additional Information**: If a successful applicant does not undertake the visit, or submit a report within 1 month of the visit, they must return the funding to the IET. Awards are available throughout the year for IET members who present a paper/poster at conferences around the world, or participate in international research visits or projects www.theiet.org/impact-society/awards-scholarships/travel-awards/

### Leslie H. Paddle Scholarship

**Purpose**: To encourage excellence in engineering and technology research, with a preference for electrical, electronic or manufacturing engineering.

**Eligibility**: 1. You can apply for an award if you have a student loan, research grant, company bursary or similar, but you can't be a recipient of any other IET scholarship or bursary. 2. On the application form you'll need to include details of your referee. 3. The panel will consider you for all postgraduate awards where you meet the eligibility requirements. 4. If you're successful, you'll only be able to receive one IET Postgraduate Award during your PhD research.

**Type**: Scholarship

**Value**: £5,000

**Closing Date**: 2 April

**Additional Information**: www.theiet.org/impact-society/awards-scholarships/iet-postgraduate-research-awards/

## Institution of Mechanical Engineers (IMechE)

1 Birdcage Walk, Westminster, London, SW1H 9JJ, United Kingdom.

**Tel**:         (44) 20 7222 7899
**Email**:      enquiries@imeche.org
**Website**:    www.imeche.org
**Contact**:    The Prizes and Awards Officer

The Institution of Mechanical Engineers (IMechE) was founded in 1847 by engineers. They formed an institution to promote the exchange of ideas and encourage individuals or groups in creating inventions that would be crucial to the development of the world as a whole. Now, over 150 years later, IMechE is one of the largest engineering institutions in the world, with over 88,000 members in 120 countries.

### James Clayton Lectures

**Purpose**: To provide for the expenses of the person presenting the lecture that is to take place at an ordinary meeting of the Institution on a subject relating to mechanical engineering science, research, invention or experimental work

**Level of Study**: Postgraduate

**Type**: Grant

**Value**: £500

**Frequency**: Annual

**Country of Study**: United Kingdom

**Application Procedure**: Applicants must write for details

**Funding**: Private

#### For further information contact:

**Email**:    eventenquiries@imeche.org

### Spencer Wilks Scholarship/Fellowship

**Purpose**: To promote or encourage the study of automobile engineering

**Level of Study**: Postgraduate

**Type**: Scholarship

**Value**: £10,000

**Frequency**: Annual

**Country of Study**: Any country

**Application Procedure**: Applicants must write for details

**Funding**: Private

#### For further information contact:

**Email**:    n.udovidchik03@imperial.ac.uk

## Intel Corporation

2200 Mission College Blvd, Santa Clara, CA 95054-1549, United States of America.

**Tel**:         (1) 408 765 8080
**Email**:      scholarships@intel.com
**Website**:    www.intel.com

Intel Corporation is committed to maintaining and enhancing the quality of life in the communities where the company has a major presence.

## Intel Public Affairs Russia Grant

**Purpose**: To support further study programmes with educational and technological components in Russia
**Eligibility**: Each request will be evaluated on the basis of the services offered and the programme's impact on the community and the potential for Intel employee involvement
**Type**: Grant
**Frequency**: Annual
**Country of Study**: Russia
**Application Procedure**: Apply online or contact the office
**Funding**: Corporation
**Contributor**: Intel Corporation

### For further information contact:

**Tel**:     (7) 831 296 94 44
**Email**:    paris@intel.com

## Interart Festival Center

PO Box 80 1051 Vörösmarty Tér 1, H-1366 Budapest, Hungary.

**Tel**:     (36) 1 317 9838
**Contact**:   Grants Management Officer

The Hungarian Television and Interart Festival Center has organised the International Conductors' Competition every third year since 1974. The goal of the competition is to discover gifted young conductors from Hungary and abroad, to introduce them to the possible audience and to stimulate public interest in musical performance, musical values and modes and possibilities of interpretation.

## International Glaucoma Award

**Purpose**: The International Glaucoma Association (IGA) is pleased to announce a grants programme in collaboration with The College of Optometrists and is pleased to offer Research Awards
**Eligibility**: Postgraduate research award. Multidisciplinary research teams are encouraged and should include a member/fellow of RCOphth but co-applicants (and project lead) may include hospital/community based optometrists and/or nurses undertaking glaucoma research in the United Kingdom and Ireland
**Level of Study**: Postgraduate
**Type**: Award
**Value**: £100,000
**Frequency**: Annual

**Country of Study**: Any country
**Closing Date**: 23 February
**Funding**: Foundation

## International Airline Training Fund (IATF)

33, Route de l'Aeroport PO Box 416, Gineva-15 Airport, CH-1215 Geneva, Switzerland.

**Tel**:     (41) 22 770 2525
**Email**:    iatf@iata.org
**Website**:   www.iata.org
**Contact**:   IATF Co-ordinator

The International Airline Training Fund's (IATF) mission is to provide vocational training opportunities for staff of IATA member airlines based in countries with developing economies. It does so by providing scholarships and other training opportunities to enable worthy candidates to follow vocational training courses conducted by the IATA Aviation Training & Development Institute, the Aviation MBA at Concordia University, as well as several other courses.

## International Airline Training Fund IATA Aviation Training and Development Institute (ATDI) Scholarships

**Purpose**: To enable staff of IATA member airlines based in countries with developing economies to follow short courses of specialist vocational training provided under the auspices of the IATA Aviation Training & Development Institute (ATDI)
**Eligibility**: Open to staff from IATA member airlines from countries with developing economies
**Level of Study**: Postgraduate
**Type**: Scholarship
**Value**: Please contact the organization
**Country of Study**: Switzerland, the United States of America or Singapore
**Application Procedure**: Applicants must channel applications through the human resources director of the IATA member airline which employs the applicant for an IATF-IATDI scholarship
**Funding**: Commercial, Private
**Contributor**: IATA member airlines and aviation industry suppliers
**Additional Information**: The scholarship committee meets quarterly to assess accumulated applications as of that date and to make awards. The ATDI seeks to offer skills training for managers, supervisors and other airline industry

specialist staff who wish to add to their professional knowledge and ability. The range of courses taught is wide, with courses in heavy demand being repeated during the course of the year

**For further information contact:**

**Email**: haroo@iata.org

## International Arctic Research Center Fellowships for Cancer Research

150 cours Albert-Thomas, F-69372 Lyon Cedex 08, France.

**Tel**: (33) 472 73 84 48
**Email**: fel@iarc.fr
**Contact**: Research on Cancer

### Postdoctoral Fellowships for Training in Cancer Research

**Purpose**: The IARC fellowships are intended for early career scientists wishing to complete their training in those aspects of cancer research related to the Agency's mission. Disciplines covered are: epidemiology (all disciplines included), biostatistics, bioinformatics, and areas related to, mechanisms of carcinogenesis including molecular and cell biology, molecular genetics, epigenetics, and molecular pathology
**Level of Study**: Research
**Type**: Fellowship
**Value**: The annual stipend with dependent allowance is competitive compared with other international fellowship schemes. The cost of travel for the Fellow, and in certain circumstances for dependants, will be met, and health insurance covered
**Length of Study**: 2 years
**Country of Study**: France
**Closing Date**: 30 November
**Additional Information**: For more details, please visit www.iarc.fr training.iarc.fr/education-and-training/

## International Association for the Study of Obesity

Charles Darwin House, 12 Roger Street, London, WCIN 2JU, United Kingdom.

**Tel**: (44) 20 7685 2580
**Email**: enquiries@iaso.org
**Website**: www.iaso.org

The International Association for the Study of Obesity (IASO) aims to improve global health by promoting the understanding of obesity and weight-related diseases through scientific research and dialogue whilst encouraging the development of effective policies for their prevention and management. IASO is the leading global professional organization concerned with obesity, operating in over 50 countries around the world.

## International Association for the Study of Obesity Per Björntorp Travelling Fellowship Award

**Purpose**: To provide travel grants to enable young researchers to attend the International Congress of Obesity
**Eligibility**: Applicants for this award must demonstrate their financial need for such support to attend the Congress. Applicants must be an IASO member. There is no age limit
**Level of Study**: Doctorate, Postdoctorate, Postgraduate, Predoctorate, Research
**Type**: Studentships and bursaries
**Value**: Up to US$2,000 of return economy flights, congress Registration and hotel accommodation at the International Congress of Obesity
**Study Establishment**: Any
**Country of Study**: Any country
**Application Procedure**: Download the application form from website
**Additional Information**: For further information about the IASO Travelling Fellowships Award please write to awards@iaso.org

### For further information contact:

28 Portland Place, Marylebone, London, W1B 1LY, United Kingdom.

**Tel**: (44) 20 7467 9610
**Fax**: (44) 20 7636 9258
**Email**: kate.baillie@iaso.org

## International Business Machines Corporation

1 New Orchard Road, Armonk, New York, NY 10504-1722, United States of America.

**Tel**: (1) 877 426 6006
**Email**: ews@us.ibm.com
**Website**: www.ibm.com

IBM stands today at the forefront of a worldwide industry that is revolutionizing the way in which enterprises, organizations and people operate and thrive. IBM strives to lead in the invention, development and manufacture of the industry's most advanced information technologies, including computer systems, software, storage systems, and microelectronics.

## International Business Machines Herman Goldstine Postdoctoral Fellowship

**Purpose**: To provide scientists of outstanding ability an opportunity to advance their scholarship as resident department members at the Research Center
**Eligibility**: Open to candidates who have obtained a PhD or expect to receive a PhD before the fellowship commences in the second half of current year
**Level of Study**: Research
**Type**: Fellowship
**Value**: The stipend is expected to be at least US$150,000
**Length of Study**: 1 year
**Frequency**: Annual
**Country of Study**: United States of America
**Application Procedure**: Applicants can download the application form from the website. The completed application form, curriculum vitae and abstract of PhD dissertation must be sent
**Closing Date**: 20 January
**Additional Information**: Applications shall be accepted through email at goldpost@watson.ibm.com scholarship-positions.com/ibm-herman-goldstine-postdoctoral-fellowships-mathematical-sciences/2016/01/07/

## International Business Machines PhD Fellowship Program

**Purpose**: To honour exceptional PhD students in an array of focus areas of interest to IBM and fundamental to innovation
**Eligibility**: Open to students nominated by a faculty member. They must be enroled full-time in a college or university PhD programme and they should have completed at least 1 year of study in their Doctoral programme at the time of their nomination
**Level of Study**: Doctorate
**Type**: Fellowships
**Value**: US$17,500
**Length of Study**: 3 years
**Frequency**: Annual
**Country of Study**: Any country
**Application Procedure**: All nominations for the IBM PhD Fellowship must be submitted by faculty electronically over the web on a standardized form. The nomination form will be available on the IBM PhD Fellowship nomination website from 19 September to 31 October
**Closing Date**: 31 October
**Additional Information**: Non-United States citizens who wish to participate in an internship in the United States must obtain work authorization under the specifics of their particular visa. For further information, see website at www.research.ibm.com/university/phdfellowship/#about

## International Centre for Education in Islamic Finance (INCEIF)

**Email**:        syarina@inceif.org
**Contact**:    Noorsyarina Mohd Sapiai

## Khazanah – INCEIF Scholarship

**Eligibility**: Information available on website: www.inceif.org/khazanah-inceif-scholarship-programme/
**Level of Study**: Doctorate, Postgraduate
**Value**: All applicable tuition fees and monthly allowances for the duration of the course
**Study Establishment**: INCEIF
**Country of Study**: Malaysia
**Application Procedure**: Kindly contact Ms Noorsyarina Mohd Sapiai at syarina@inceif.org
**Closing Date**: 16 March
**Additional Information**: Eligible to nationals of Malaysia. All communications will be done via email. Therefore please ensure the email address given is correct and active afterschool.my/scholarship/khazanah-inceif-scholarship-programme-2017

## International Centre for Genetic Engineering and Biotechnology (ICGEB)

AREA Science Park, Padriciano 99, I-34149 Trieste, Italy.

**Tel**:            (39) 40 375 71
**Email**:        fellowships@icgeb.org
**Website**:    www.icgeb.org
**Contact**:    Human Resources Unit

The International Centre for Genetic Engineering and Biotechnology (ICGEB) is an organization devoted to advanced research and training in molecular biology and biotechnology, with special regard to the needs of the developing world. The component host countries are Italy, India and South Africa. The full member states of ICGEB are Afghanistan, Algeria, Argentina, Bangladesh, Bhutan, Bosnia and Herzegovina, Brazil, Bulgaria, Burundi, Cameroon, Chile, China, Colombia, Costa Rica, Côte d'Ivoire, Croatia, Cuba, Ecuador, Egypt, Eritrea, FYR Macedonia, Hungary, Iran, Iraq, Jordan, Kenya, Kuwait, Kyrgyzstan, Liberia, Libya, Malaysia, Mauritius, Mexico, Montenegro, Morocco, Nigeria, Pakistan, Panama, Peru, Poland, Qatar, Romania, Russia, Saudi Arabia, Senegal, Serbia, Slovakia, Slovenia, Sri Lanka, Sudan, Syria, Tanzania, Trinidad and Tobago, Tunisia, Turkey, United Arab Emirates, Uruguay, Venezuela, and Vietnam.

## ICGEB Short-Term PhD Fellowships

**Purpose**: ICGEB offers Short-term fellowships for Pre-doctoral studies in ICGEB Component laboratories to fund ongoing collaborative research between scientists from ICGEB Member States and research groups at ICGEB laboratories in Trieste, Italy, New Delhi, India and Cape Town, South Africa, with the aim of facilitating access to the latest research techniques and to strengthen capacity building.

**Eligibility**: 1. Applicants must be nationals of an ICGEB Member State and may not apply for fellowships to be undertaken in their country of origin, unless working abroad at the time of application. 2. Degree requirements: applicants for ICGEB Trieste and Cape Town should hold a BSc (Honours) degree; applicants for ICGEB New Delhi should hold a MSc degree. 3. Candidates must have a good working knowledge of the English language, supported by a proficiency certificate (TOEFL, Cambridge Certificate, or equivalent). Not required when scholastic education has been undertaken in English.

**Level of Study**: Pre-doctoral
**Type**: Fellowship
**Value**: Trieste (Italy): €1,300, New Delhi (India): US$1,020, Cape Town (South Africa): SA$12,500.
**Length of Study**: 1 years
**Closing Date**: 15 April
**Additional Information**: www.icgeb.org/activities/fellow ship/short-term-phd-application/

## International Center for Genetic Engineering and Biotechnology Arturo Falaschi PhD and Postdoctoral Fellowships for Member Countries

**Purpose**: Funding opportunities are made available through the Collaborative Research Programme (CRP) – ICGEB Research Grants, which is a dedicated source of funding aimed at financing projects addressing original scientific

problems of particular relevance for the host country and of regional interest

**Eligibility**: Candidates must have a good working knowledge of the English language, supported by a proficiency certificate (TOEFL, Cambridge Certificate, or equivalent). Not required when scholastic education has been undertaken in English

**Type**: Fellowship
**Value**: See the website
**Study Establishment**: Fellowships are awarded in Life Sciences. The programme provides support for research projects in basic science, human healthcare, industrial and agricultural biotechnology and bioenergy
**Country of Study**: Any country
**Application Procedure**: The mode of application is online
**Closing Date**: 31 March
**Additional Information**: Please browse the website for more details scholarship-positions.com/icgeb-arturo-falaschi-phd-postdoctoral-fellowships-member-countries/2018/01/17/

## The Arturo Falaschi ICGEB Predoctoral Fellowships ICGEB Trieste International PhD Programme

**Purpose**: To enable promising young students to attend and complete the PhD programme at ICGEB Trieste in Italy. The programme is validated by the Open University, United Kingdom, and the University of Nova Gorica, Slovenia

**Eligibility**: 1. Applicants must be nationals of an ICGEB Member State. Nationals of India and South Africa, ICGEB Host Countries, are not eligible to apply for ICGEB Fellowships in their home country. 2. Degree requirements: applicants for ICGEB Trieste should hold a BSc (Honours) degree; applicants for ICGEB Cape Town and New Delhi should hold an MSc degree. 3. Candidates must have a good working knowledge of the English language, supported by a proficiency certificate (TOEFL, Cambridge Certificate, or equivalent). Not required when scholastic education has been undertaken in English. 4. Candidates for Trieste, Italy must be below the age of 32 years at the time of application (i.e. date of birth after 31/03/1988). There is no age limit for applications for ICGEB New Delhi and Cape Town.

**Level of Study**: Predoctorate
**Type**: Fellowship
**Value**: Trieste (Italy): €1,300, New Delhi (India): $1,020, Cape Town (South Africa): SA$12,500
**Length of Study**: 3 years PhD course with the possibility of 1-year extension
**Frequency**: Annual
**Study Establishment**: ICGEB laboratories in Trieste and Monterotondo (Rome)
**Country of Study**: Italy

**Application Procedure**: Applicants must refer to the website

**Closing Date**: 31 March

**Additional Information**: For more information on this programme please refer to the website www.icgeb.org/activities/fellowship/guidelines-and-application-form-arturo-falaschi-phd-fellowships/

### For further information contact:

**Email**:    admissions@cgebicgeb.res.in

## International Centre for Theoretical Sciences

Survey No. 151, Shivakote, Hesaraghatta Hobli, Bengaluru, Karnataka 560 089, India.

**Tel**:       (91) 80 6730 6000, 80 4653 6000
**Email**:    info@icts.res.in
**Contact**:  International Centre for Theoretical Sciences

International Centre for Theoretical Sciences (ICTS)contributes to research excellence in science in various ways. It has a high-quality faculty together with a large floating population comprising visitors, postdoctoral fellows and graduate students.

### International Centre for Theoretical Sciences S. N. Bhatt Memorial Excellence Research Fellowship

**Purpose**: The aim of the fellowship is to give an opportunity to master's students of Science and Engineering to work with faculty and post-doctoral fellows of the Centre and to participate in research at the frontiers of knowledge

**Eligibility**: Undergraduate students of science, mathematics and engineering, who are in their third, fourth or fifth year of the program are eligible to apply. Exceptional undergraduates in their second year may also apply. Masters degree students and those who have completed their undergraduate are also welcome to apply.

**Type**: Research

**Value**: This program offers a unique opportunity masters students of Science and Engineering to work with faculty and postdoctoral fellows of the Centre and to participate in research at the frontiers of knowledge

**Study Establishment**: The fellowship is awarded in the field of Science and Engineering

**Country of Study**: India

**Application Procedure**: Interested candidates should apply online with their CV and relevant details. The applicants also need to arrange at least two recommendation letters. Applications will be normally reviewed in February and results will be declared around early March every year.

**Closing Date**: 25 January

**Additional Information**: please visit our website for more information scholarship-positions.com/icts-s-n-bhatt-memorial-excellence-research-fellowship-india/2017/11/04/ icts.res.in/academic/summer-research-program

### For further information contact:

Survey No. 151, Shivakote, Hesaraghatta Hobli, Bengaluru - 560 089, India.

**Tel**:       (91) 80 4653 6000
**Email**:    summer.program@icts.res.in

## International Dairy-Deli-Bakery Association

IDDBA, 636 Science Drive, PO Box 5528, Madison, WI 53711-1073, United States of America.

**Tel**:       (1) 608 310 5000
**Email**:    iddba@iddba.org
**Website**:  www.iddba.org

Our mission is to expand our leadership role in promoting the growth and development of daily, deli, and bakery sales in the food industry. Our vision is to be the essential resource for relevant information and services that add value across all food channels for the dairy, deli and bakery categories.

### International Dairy-Deli-Bakery Association Graduate Scholarships

**Purpose**: To support employees of IDDBA-member companies

**Eligibility**: Applicants must be a current full- or part-time employee of an IDDBA-member company with an academic background in a food-related field and have a 2.5 grade-point average on a 4.0 scale, or equivalent

**Level of Study**: Postgraduate

**Type**: Scholarship

**Value**: US$250 to US$1,000

**Length of Study**: 1 year

**Frequency**: Annual
**Country of Study**: United States of America
**Application Procedure**: Contact the Education Information Specialist
**Closing Date**: 1 October
**Funding**: Foundation
**Contributor**: IDDBA
**Additional Information**: For additional information or enquiries contact organization and email at scholarships@iddba.org bigfuture.collegeboard.org/scholarships/scholarships/iddba-scholarship-for-growing-the-future

### For further information contact:

**Email**:   kpeckham@iddba.org

## International Education Specialist

### World Citizen Talent Scholarship

**Purpose**: We are seeking intelligent, talented and ambitious people who view themselves as citizens of the world
**Eligibility**: You are eligible to apply for the scholarship if you; 1. Come from outside The Netherlands and don't live in the Netherlands. 2. Are enrolling for the first time at The Hague University of Applied Sciences. 3. Have never applied for this scholarship before. 4. Have been conditionally accepted as a student (also-called offer of student position) on or before 31 March for the upcoming academic year
**Level of Study**: Postgraduate
**Type**: Scholarship
**Value**: €5,000
**Frequency**: Annual
**Country of Study**: Any country
**Application Procedure**: Applicants must submit the below documents to process further. 1. Outstanding Master's-level students can apply for these scholarships by submitting the application form including an essay of no more than 1,000 words, detailing their cultural background and contribution they wish to make to the university as global citizens. 2. Applications will be reviewed by an academic panel
**Closing Date**: 15 May
**Funding**: Private
**Additional Information**: www.scholars4dev.com/7275/one-world-citizen-talent-scholarship/

### For further information contact:

**Email**:   master-scholarship@hhs.nl

## International Federation of Library Associations and Institutions WLIC

### Chartered Institute of Library and Information Professionals International Library and Information Group Alan Hopkinson Award

**Purpose**: The Chartered Institute of Library and Information Professionals (CILIP) and its International Library and Information Group (ILIG) invite applicants from Europe to attend the International Federation of Library Associations and Institutions (IFLA) conference in Athens
**Eligibility**: 1. Applicants are required to write a reflective report of not more than 4,000 words within six months of their visit, and a version for publication in Focus on International Library and Information Work, the ILIG journal. 2. Applicants should submit a formal proposal in English of up to 500 words (equivalent to 1–2 pages of A4 paper) detailing how the visit will support their professional development within the context of their career to date and using the headings of 'Visit objectives' 'Planned approach and content' 'Application of learning post-visit'
**Level of Study**: Postgraduate
**Type**: Award
**Frequency**: Annual
**Country of Study**: Any country
**Closing Date**: 31 March
**Funding**: Private
**Additional Information**: 2019.ifla.org/2019-alan-hopkinson-award-cilip/

### For further information contact:

IFLA Headquarters IFLA P.O. Box 95312, NL-2509 CH The Hague, The Netherlands.

**Email**:   ilig@cilip.org.uk

### Dr. Shawky Salem Conference Grant

**Purpose**: The aim of the grant is to enable one expert in library and information sciences from the Arab Countries (AC) to attend the Annual IFLA Conference
**Eligibility**: 1. The grant is available to a librarian of Arab nationality, not exceeding 45 years. 2. Priority is given to applicants who are first-time attendees to the IFLA Congress. 3. The applicant should have at least 5 years of experience in

LIS profession. 4. The applicant must have the approval of his / her organization to attend the IFLA WLIC

**Level of Study**: Graduate, Professional development

**Type**: Grant

**Value**: US$1,900

**Frequency**: Annual

**Country of Study**: Any country

**Application Procedure**: Application has to b eprocessed physically. For further information, check the website. 2019. ifla.org/dr-shawky-salem-conference-grant-sscg-2019/

**Closing Date**: 31 March

**Funding**: Private

**Additional Information**: www.ifla.org/funds-grants-awards/ SSCG

### For further information contact:

**Email**:   grants@ifla.org

## International Federation of Library Associations and Institutions Green Library Award

**Purpose**: To create awareness of libraries' social responsibility and leadership in environmental education. Libraries of all types are encouraged to participate. To support the worldwide Green Library movement, concerned with 1. environmentally sustainable buildings. 2. environmentally sustainable information resources and programming conservation of resources and energy

**Eligibility**: They also focus on related services, activities, events, literature and projects, demonstrating the social role and responsibility of libraries as leaders in environmental sustainability. 1. Any type of library with an outstanding Green Library project, initiative or idea may apply for the IFLA Green Library Award. The project, initiative or idea may be presented in various ways (e.g. essay, video, poster, article, set of slides). 2. Applications must be written in one of the seven IFLA languages. 3. Applicants may also submit an English translation if they prefer. 4. Film and Video materials in languages other than English must have English subtitles. 5. The presentation of the project, initiative or idea should be submitted to the ENSULIB award reviewing committee

**Level of Study**: Postgraduate

**Type**: Grant

**Frequency**: Annual

**Country of Study**: Any country

**Application Procedure**: The quality and relevance of the project, initiative or idea will be evaluated by the ENSULIB committee in terms of applicability to the goals and the scope of ENSULIB. 2019.ifla.org/ifla-green-library-award-2019/

**Closing Date**: 1 April

**Funding**: Private

**Additional Information**: www.ifla.org/node/10159

### For further information contact:

P.O. Box 95312, NL-2509 CH The Hague, The Netherlands.

**Email**:   petra.hauke@hu-berlin.de

## International Federation of University Women (IFUW)

IFUW Headquarters, 10 rue de Lac, CH-1207 Geneva, Switzerland.

**Tel**:          (41) 22 731 2380

**Email**:      info@ifuw.org

**Website**:   www.ifuw.org

The International Federation of University Women (IFUW) is a non-profit, non-governmental organization comprising graduate women working locally, nationally and internationally to advocate the improvement of the status of women and girls at the international level, by promoting lifelong education and enabling graduate women to use their expertise to effect change.

## Canadian Federation of University Women/A. Vibert Douglas Fellowship

**Country of Study**: Any country

### For further information contact:

**Email**:   fellowships@cfuw.org

## Ida Smedley MacLean Fellowship

**Purpose**: To encourage advanced scholarship and original research relevant to IFUW's mission

**Eligibility**: Open to female applicants who are either members of one of IFUW's national federations or associations or, in the case of female graduates living in countries where there is not yet a national affiliate, independent members of

IFUW, or other applicants who pay a filing fee. Applicants should have completed at least the first year of a doctoral programme

**Level of Study**: Doctorate

**Type**: Fellowship

**Value**: CHF 8,000

**Length of Study**: More than 8 months

**Frequency**: Dependent on funds available

**Study Establishment**: An approved Institute of Higher Education

**Country of Study**: Worldwide

**Application Procedure**: Applicants must apply through their respective federation or association. A list of IFUW national federations and associations can be obtained from the IFUW website. IFUW independent members and others must apply directly to the IFUW headquarters in Geneva

**Funding**: Private

**Contributor**: British Federation of Women Graduates

**No. of awards given last year**: 1 of each fellowship

**Additional Information**: Please see the website for further details         www.ifuw.org/what-we-do/grants-fellowships/international-awards/

### The CFUW/A Vibert Douglas International Fellowship

**Purpose**: To encourage advanced scholarship and original research relevant to IFUW's mission

**Eligibility**: Open to female applicants who are either members of one of IFUW's national federations or associations or, in the case of female graduates living in countries where there is not yet a national affiliate, independent members of IFUW, or other applicants who pay a filing fee. Applicants should have completed at least the first year of a doctoral programme

**Level of Study**: Doctorate, Postdoctorate, Postgraduate

**Type**: Fellowship

**Value**: C$12,000

**Length of Study**: Requires 8–12 months' work in a country other than that in which the applicant was educated or habitually resides

**Frequency**: Dependent on funds available

**Study Establishment**: An approved Institute of Higher Education

**Country of Study**: Worldwide

**Application Procedure**: Applicants must apply through their respective federation or association. A list of IFUW national federations and associations can be obtained from the IFUW website. IFUW independent members and others must apply directly to the IFUW headquarters in Geneva

**Funding**: Private

**Contributor**: Canadian Federation of University Women

**Additional Information**: scwist.ca/cfuwa-vibert-douglas-fellowship/

## International Furnishings and Design Association Education Foundation

### Vercille Voss Scholarship

**Purpose**: The IFDA Illinois Chapter initiated the Vercille Voss Graduate Student Scholarship in memory of Vercille Voss, longtime chapter member and mentor to new members and students. The applicant must be enrolled as a part-time or full-time graduate student at an accredited university

**Eligibility**: 1. Must be a graduate student or a postgraduate student 2. Must attend a university or a four-year college 3. Both full-time and part-time students 4. Restricted to students studying Architecture, Interior Design, Industrial Design, Trade/Technical Specialties

**Level of Study**: Graduate

**Type**: Scholarship

**Value**: US$2,000

**Frequency**: Annual

**Country of Study**: Any country

**Application Procedure**: The IFDA Educational Foundation Board of Trustees will select the scholarship recipient based on the student's academic achievement, awards and accomplishments, future plans and goals, and letter of recommendation. All applicants must be graduate students and have completed four design courses in post-secondary education at the time of application and be majoring in Interior Design or a related field. For more information or to apply, please visit the scholarship provider's website

**Closing Date**: 31 March

**Funding**: Private

**No. of awards given last year**: 1

**Additional Information**: The application deadline date has not yet been finalized for this year, but is expected to remain the same as last year www.petersons.com/scholarship/vercille-voss-graduate-student-scholarship-111_157484.aspx

### For further information contact:

112 Hidden Lake, Canton, GA 30114, United States of America.

**Tel**:         (1) 770 378 7221
**Email**:     ef.ifda@tapestries.org

## International Human Frontier Science Program Organization (HFSP)

Bureaux Europe, 20 Place des Halles, F-67080 Strasbourg, France.

**Tel**:         (33) 3 88 21 51 12
**Email**:     info@hfsp.org

**Website:** www.hfsp.org
**Contact:** Mr Patrick Vincent, Director of Scientific Affairs and Communications

The International Human Frontier Science Program Organization (HFSP) promotes basic research into the complex mechanisms underlying the function of living organisms by supporting interdisciplinary and international collaboration. The programme only supports research that transcends national boundaries.

## Career Development Award

**Level of Study:** 3 years
**Value:** US$231,000
**Country of Study:** Any country
**Closing Date:** 15 October
**Additional Information:** professional.heart.org/profes sional/ResearchPrograms/UCM_495968_Career-Development-Award.jsp

### For further information contact:

**Email:** communications@hfsp.org

## Cross-Disciplinary Fellowships

**Purpose:** Cross-Disciplinary Fellowships (CDF) are for applicants with a PhD from outside the life sciences (e.g. in physics, chemistry, mathematics, engineering or computer sciences), who have had limited exposure to biology during their previous training
**Eligibility:** See application guidelines www.hfsp.org/funding/postdoctoral-fellowships/guidelines
**Level of Study:** Postdoctorate
**Type:** Fellowship
**Value:** About US$180,000 over three years (depending on host country)
**Length of Study:** 3 years
**Frequency:** Annual
**Country of Study:** Africa
**Application Procedure:** Online
**No. of awards offered:** 54
**Funding:** Government
**Contributor:** Australia, Canada, European Commission, France, Germany, India, Italy, Korea, Japan, New Zealand, Norway, Singapore, Switzerland, United Kingdom and United States of America
**No. of awards given last year:** 12
**No. of applicants last year:** 54

**Additional Information:** www.hfsp.org/sites/default/files/Sciences/fellows/2020%20Fellowship%20application%20guide lines.pdf

### For further information contact:

12 quai Saint Jean, F-67080 Strasbourg Cedex, France

## Long-Term Fellowships

**Purpose:** Long-Term Fellowships (LTF) are for applicants with a PhD in a biological discipline, who will broaden their expertise by proposing a project in the life sciences which is significantly different from their previous PhD or postdoctoral work. The HFSP fellowship program strongly supports frontier, potentially transformative ('out-of-the-box') proposals and encourages applications for high-risk projects. The projects should be interdisciplinary in nature and should challenge existing paradigms by using novel approaches and techniques. Scientifically, they should address an important problem or a barrier to progress in the field
**Eligibility:** See application guidelines www.hfsp.org/funding/postdoctoral-fellowships/guidelines
**Level of Study:** Postdoctorate
**Type:** Fellowship
**Value:** About US$180,000 over three years (depending on host country)
**Length of Study:** 3 years
**Frequency:** Annual
**Country of Study:** Any country
**Application Procedure:** Online
**No. of awards offered:** 534
**Funding:** Government
**Contributor:** Australia, Canada, European Commission, France, Germany, India, Italy, Korea, Japan, New Zealand, Norway, Singapore, Switzerland, United Kingdom and United States of America
**No. of awards given last year:** 79
**No. of applicants last year:** 534
**Additional Information:** www.hfsp.org/sites/default/files/Sciences/fellows/2020%20Fellowship%20application%20guide lines.pdf

## Program Grants

**Purpose:** Research grants are provided for teams of scientists from different countries who wish to combine their expertise in innovative approaches to questions that could not be answered by individual laboratories. Emphasis is placed on novel collaborations that bring together scientists preferably from different disciplines (e.g. from chemistry, physics, computer science, engineering) to focus on problems in the life sciences. Note, HFSPO funds only basic research. Applied applications, including medical research typically funded by national medical research bodies, will be deemed ineligible. Program Grants are awarded to teams of independent researchers at any stage of their careers. The research team is expected to develop new lines of research through the collaboration. Up to US$450,000 per grant per year may be applied for. Applications including independent investigators early in their careers are encouraged

**Eligibility**: See application guidelines www.hfsp.org/sites/ www.hfsp.org/files/webfm/Grants/LI%20Guidelines.pdf

**Level of Study**: Postdoctorate

**Type**: Grant

**Value**: A team of 2 investigators will receive US$250,000 and a team of 3 will receive US$350,000 per year and currently US$300,000 for a team of '2.5' and US$400,000 for '3.5' team members

**Length of Study**: 3 years

**Frequency**: Annual

**Country of Study**: Any country

**Application Procedure**: See application guidelines www. hfsp.org/sites/www.hfsp.org/files/webfm/Grants/LI%20Guidelines.pdf

**No. of awards offered**: 612

**Closing Date**: 30 March

**Funding**: Government

**Contributor**: Australia, Canada, European Commission, France, Germany, India, Italy, Japan, Republic of Korea, New Zealand, Norway, Singapore, Switzerland, United Kingdom, United States of America

**No. of awards given last year**: 23

**No. of applicants last year**: 612

**Additional Information**: www.hfsp.org/funding/hfsp-funding/ research-grants

### For further information contact:

12 quai Saint-Jean, F-67080 Strasbourg, France.

**Tel**:        (33) 3 88 21 51 23
**Email**:    grant@hfsp.org

### Young Investigator Grant

**Purpose**: Research grants are provided for teams of scientists from different countries who wish to combine their expertise in innovative approaches to questions that could not be answered by individual laboratories. Emphasis is placed on novel collaborations that bring together scientists preferably from different disciplines (e.g. from chemistry, physics, computer science, engineering) to focus on problems in the life sciences. Note, HFSPO funds only basic research. Applied

applications, including medical research typically funded by national medical research bodies, will be deemed ineligible. The research teams must be international. The principal applicant must be from one of the eligible countries. However, other participating scientists and laboratories may be situated anywhere in the world. Young Investigators' Grants are awarded to teams of researchers, all of whom are within the first five years after obtaining an independent laboratory (e.g. Assistant Professor, Lecturer or equivalent). Applications for Young Investigators' Grants will be reviewed in competition with each other independently of applications for Program Grants

**Eligibility**: See application guidelines: www.hfsp.org/ funding/postdoctoral-fellowships/guidelines

**Level of Study**: Postdoctorate

**Type**: Grant

**Value**: Teams will receive up to US$450,000 per year for the whole team depending on the size of the team

**Length of Study**: 3 years

**Frequency**: Annual

**Country of Study**: Any country

**Application Procedure**: See application guidelines: www. hfsp.org/sites/www.hfsp.org/files/webfm/Grants/LI%20Guidelines.pdf

**No. of awards offered**: 158

**Funding**: Government

**Contributor**: Australia, Canada, European Commission, France, Germany, India, Italy, Japan, Korea, New Zealand, Norway, Singapore, Switzerland, United Kingdom, United States

**No. of awards given last year**: 8

**No. of applicants last year**: 158

### For further information contact:

HFSPO, 12 quai Saint Jean, F-67080 Strasbourg, France

## International Institute for Management Development (IMD)

Chemin de Bellerive 23, PO Box 915, CH-1001 Lausanne, Switzerland.

**Tel**:        (41) 21 618 0298
**Email**:    mbainfo@imd.ch
**Website**:  www.imd.ch/mba
**Contact**:  Suzanne Laurent

The International Institute for Management Development (IMD), created by industry to serve industry, develops cutting-edge research and programmes that meet real world needs. Their clients include dozens of leading international companies and their experienced faculty incorporate new management practices into the small and exclusive MBA programme. With no nationality dominating, IMD is truly global, practical and relevant.

## International Institute for Management Development MBA Merit Scholarships

**Purpose**: To financially support applicants who consistently demonstrate exceptional qualities
**Eligibility**: Candidates who have already completed the IMD MBA application and admission process
**Level of Study**: MBA
**Type**: Scholarship
**Value**: CHF 10,000 towards tuition
**Length of Study**: 1 year
**Frequency**: Annual
**Study Establishment**: IMD
**Country of Study**: Switzerland
**Closing Date**: 30 September
**Funding**: Private
**No. of awards given last year**: 4
**Additional Information**: www.imd.org/news/updates/imd-mba-scholarship-program-a-commitment-to-diversity-and-impact/

### For further information contact:

**Email**:    MBAfinance@imd.org

## Stewart Hamilton Scholarship

**Purpose**: Financially support applicants who demonstrate an understanding of corporate governance and responsibility
**Eligibility**: Candidates who have already applied to the full-time IMD MBA program and who demonstrate financial need
**Level of Study**: MBA
**Type**: Scholarship
**Value**: CHF 15 000 payment each semester for the standard duration of the course
**Length of Study**: 1 year
**Frequency**: Annual
**Study Establishment**: IMD
**Country of Study**: Switzerland
**Application Procedure**: Applicants must complete and submit the IMD MBA application form for financial assistance and the MBA application form
**No. of awards offered**: 14
**Closing Date**: 10 March

**Funding**: Private
**No. of awards given last year**: 1
**No. of applicants last year**: 14
**Additional Information**: Scholarship essays or questions should be sent to mbafinance@imd.org www.imd.org/news/updates/the-imd-stewart-hamilton-scholarship-to-benefit-outstanding-women/

### For further information contact:

P.O. Box 915, CH-1001 Lausanne, Switzerland.

**Email**:    clientmarketdevelopmenteurope@imd.org

## International Institute for Population Sciences (IIPS)

Govandi Station Road Deonar, Bombay, Maharashtra 400088, India.

**Tel**:        (91) 22 2556 3254
**Email**:     diriips@bom8.vsnl.net.in
**Website**:   www.iipsindia.org
**Contact**:   Professor T K Roy, Director

The International Institute for Population Sciences (IIPS) is one of the few institutes set up solely for the purpose of studying demography. The only institute of its kind in the world, it was declared a deemed university on 15 August. The IIPS offers academic courses in population sciences and takes major initiatives to strengthen reproductive health, research and training programmes.

## International Institute for Population Sciences Diploma in Population Studies

**Purpose**: To train the recipient in obtaining basic knowledge in the field of population
**Eligibility**: Open to ESCAP and Pacific Region nationals who are already working in the fields of population and health. Applicants are required to be graduates
**Level of Study**: Professional development
**Type**: Fellowship
**Value**: Return air ticket plus US$6,000 per student per year as course fee and US$6,000 fellowship for students
**Length of Study**: 10 months
**Frequency**: Annual
**Country of Study**: India

**Application Procedure**: Applicants must make an application through UNFPA country directors or representatives in the applicant's own country

**No. of awards offered**: Unknown

**Closing Date**: 30 April

**Funding**: Private

**Contributor**: UNFPA

**No. of awards given last year**: 5

**No. of applicants last year**: Unknown

**Additional Information**: Further information on this programme is also available from the London School of Economics, on (44) 20 7405 7686 iipsindia.org/course/DPS%20Brochure.pdf

### For further information contact:

International Institute for Population Sciences (Deemed University) Govandi Station Road, Mumbai, Maharashtra 400088, India.

**Tel**: (91) 55 620 62
**Fax**: (91) 22 556 3257

## International Institute of Tropical Agriculture (IITA)

L W Lambourn & Co Ltd Carolyn House 26 Dingwall Road, Croydon, Surrey, CR9 3EE, United Kingdom.

**Email**: iita@cgnet.com
**Website**: www.cgiar.org/iita
**Contact**: Programme Leader

The International Institute of Tropical Agriculture (IITA) was founded in 1967 as an international agricultural research institute with a mandate for special food crops and with ecological and regional responsibilities to develop sustainable production systems in Africa.

### International Institute of Tropical Agriculture Research Fellowships

**Purpose**: To enable African postgraduate degree candidates to conduct research at the Institute or one of its satellites

**Eligibility**: Candidates should be residents of Sub Saharan Africa and be registered for a postgraduate degree at a university in Africa or abroad (generally a faculty of agriculture). Preference will be given to candidates of IITA stations - Nigeria, Cameroon, Uganda, Benin and Cote d'Ivoire

**Level of Study**: Doctorate, Postgraduate

**Type**: Fellowship

**Value**: Up to US$12,000 per year, includes board and lodging, various allowances for personal and other expenses, travel to and from the Institute, medical accident insurance, and all research costs. It also includes one round trip ticket for the student's university supervisor to IITA for PhD students

**Length of Study**: MSc is 1 year, the PhD is 2–3 years

**Frequency**: Annual

**Study Establishment**: IITA

**Country of Study**: Other

**Application Procedure**: Application form must be completed and submitted with a research proposal of no more than 10 pages and three letters of recommendation from the candidate's advisor at the university. Applications may be submitted by individuals. However it is preferred that all applications are made through the university. Candidate, advisor and university must accept a scientist from IITA as a supervisor of research while the Fellow is at IITA

**No. of awards offered**: 150

**Closing Date**: September

**Funding**: Government

**Contributor**: Donor agencies and the government

**No. of awards given last year**: 30

**No. of applicants last year**: 150

**Additional Information**: scholarshipstory.com/iita/

### For further information contact:

Head Training & Information Services, Oyo Road, PMB 5320, Ibadan, Nigeria.

**Tel**: (234) 2 241 2626
**Fax**: (234) 2 241 2221
**Email**: iita@cgiar.org

## International Mathematical Union (IMU)

International Mathematical Union, Office of the Secretariat, Zuse Institute Berlin, Takustrasse 7, D-14195 Berlin, Germany.

**Email**: secretary@mathunion.org
**Website**: www.mathunion.org
**Contact**: Martin Grötschel, Secretary

The International Mathematical Union (IMU) is an international, non-governmental and non-profit scientific organization, with the purpose of promoting international co-operation in mathematics. It belongs to the International Council of Scientific Unions (ICSU).

## International Mathematical Union Visiting Mathematician Programme

**Purpose**: To provide partial travel support for extended research visits in an advanced mathematical centre

**Eligibility**: Open to active mathematicians at PhD level with strong research possibilities. The programme is mainly intended for mathematicians working in a developing country to make an extended research visit to an advanced mathematical centre

**Level of Study**: Postdoctorate, Professional development

**Type**: Travel grant

**Value**: €4,400

**Length of Study**: 1 month

**Frequency**: Annual, if funds are available

**Study Establishment**: An advanced mathematical research centre

**Country of Study**: Any country

**Application Procedure**: 1. hold at the time of application a PhD in Mathematics, 2. be based in a developing country at the time of application 3. hold a position in a university/research institution 4. be in the early stages of their professional careers, more precisely: the applicants should 4. 1) not yet be of full professorial rank but have a working contract in a university/ college 4. 2) be under 40 years of age at the day of the application deadline.

**No. of awards offered**: 30

**No. of awards given last year**: 8

**No. of applicants last year**: 30

**Additional Information**: The host centre must commit itself to supporting local expenses www.mathunion.org/cdc/grantsresearch-travel-grants/abel-visiting-scholar-program

### For further information contact:

Mathematics Department Zuse Institute Berlin, D-14195 Berlin, Germany.

**Tel**:     (49) 801 581 5275
**Fax**:     (49) 801 581 4148
**Email**:   clemens@math.utah.edu

## International School of Crystallography, E Majorana Centre

Dip to Scienze Della Terra Geo Ambientoli, Piazza di Porta San Donato 1, I-40126 Bologna, Italy.

**Tel**:       (39) 51 209 4912
**Email**:     riva@geomin.unibo.it
**Website**:   www.geomin.unibo.it
**Contact**:   Professor L Riva Di Sanseverino

The International School of Crystallography is an international organizing committee that offers, once a year, short advanced courses of 9–11 days on frontier topics in crystallography, solid state chemistry, materials science, structure activity relationship, molecular biology and biophysics.

## International School of Crystallography Grants

**Purpose**: To enable postgraduates to attend short high-level courses held at Erice once a year

**Eligibility**: Open to all who have scientific interests related to the topic chosen each year at a PhD or postdoctoral level. English language proficiency is mandatory

**Level of Study**: Doctorate, Postdoctorate, Postgraduate

**Type**: Grant

**Value**: Fees, board and lodging during the course

**Length of Study**: 8–12 days

**Frequency**: Annual

**Study Establishment**: E Majorana Centre, Erice, Sicily, Italy

**Country of Study**: Italy

**Application Procedure**: Young applicants must submit a letter of recommendation stating their financial needs, personal data and details of scientific interests. Further details can be found at www.crystalerice.org

**No. of awards offered**: 250

**Closing Date**: Novermber

**Funding**: Government

**Contributor**: NATO, the European Commission and the Italian National Research Council

**No. of awards given last year**: 70

**No. of applicants last year**: 250

### For further information contact:

Department of Organic Chemistry, Via Francesco Marzolo, 135122 Padova PD, Italy.

**Tel**:     (39) 49 827 5275
**Fax**:     (39) 49 827 5239
**Email**:   paola.spadon@unipd.it

## International Society of Nephrology (ISN)

Avenue de Tervueren, 300, B-1150 Brussels, Belgium.

**Tel**:       (32) 2 743 1546
**Email**:     info@isn-online.org
**Website**:   www.nature.com/isn/about/index.html
**Contact**:   Professor John Feehally ISN Secretary General

The International Society of Nephrology (ISN) pursues the goal of worldwide advancement of education, science and patient care in nephrology. ISN achieves this through its journal Kidney International, organizing international congresses, symposia, specific programmes and fellowships. As a result, ISN helps to improve renal science and renal patient care worldwide, especially in emerging countries.

## International Society of Nephrology Fellowship Awards

**Purpose**: To offer training opportunities to young nephrologists in emerging countries with the ultimate goal of improving the standards of nephrology practice in their home institutions upon their return

**Eligibility**: Open to young nephrologists from emerging countries, as defined by World Bank criteria. Applicants must have received sufficient training in internal medicine or other fields to pass all host country examinations that are necessary for the care of patients. Fellowships are primarily offered for clinical training in nephrology, but in some circumstances research training may be allowed, priority can be considered for training in epidemiology

**Level of Study**: Postdoctorate, Predoctorate

**Type**: Fellowship

**Value**: The stipends are subject to indexation based on-the-cost-of-living in their host country; the top and bottom level grants are respectively US$26,000 and US$20,000 for 12 months of training. If the host country is contributing funds then this is subtracted from the standard fund

**Length of Study**: Short-term fellowships are for 3–6 months and long-term fellowships are for 12 months. Extensions are possible

**Frequency**: Annual

**Study Establishment**: Any suitable university, scientific institution or hospital

**Application Procedure**: Applicants must complete an application form, which is subjected to the review of an international committee. Applicants must provide evidence of a guaranteed position in a medical institution upon return to their home country. The applicant must agree to return to their home country upon completion of the training; if not, the recipient will have to refund the ISN fellowship in full

**Closing Date**: Novermber

**Funding**: Private, Foundation

**Contributor**: Offered in collaboration with sister societies and industry, the American Society of Nephrology, the National Kidney Research Fund in the United Kingdom, Fresenius Medical care in Germany and the European renal Association

**No. of awards given last year**: 44

**Additional Information**: The selection procedure has three parts: data verification, where information provided by applicants is verified and evaluated through correspondence; evaluation, where 7 members of the Committee, one from each Continent, score each application according to standard format; and finally, selection, which is largely based on the aforementioned scores but also considers the geographical balance, urgent needs in certain regions and the preference of certain sponsors

### For further information contact:

ISN Global Headquarters Av. Tervueren 300, B-1150 Brussels, Belgium.

**Email**:    an@associationhg.com

## International Society of Nephrology Travel Grants

**Purpose**: To encourage young physicians and scientists to attend conferences, especially those from emerging countries. Travel grants are offered to facilitate attendance at the ISN International Congress and the ISN Forefronts Commission Conference

**Eligibility**: Applicants must have training and experience in an area of research relevant to the conference and an infrastructure at their home institutions to allow the pursuit of techniques and approaches discussed at the conference. Young physicians and scientists are preferred as are ISN Fellows. A portion of the grants are reserved for applicants from emerging countries

**Level of Study**: Doctorate, Postdoctorate, Postgraduate, Research

**Type**: Travel grant

**Value**: The size of the grant is decided according to each conference and congress

**Length of Study**: Varies

**Application Procedure**: Applicants must complete an application form, which can be downloaded from the ISN website or requested from the ISN Secretary General a year prior to the Congress. Applications can also be obtained from the Directors of the ISN Forefront Programmes

**No. of awards offered**: 395

**Funding**: Private, Foundation

**Contributor**: Offered in collaboration with sponsors of ISN

**No. of awards given last year**: 120

**No. of applicants last year**: 395

### For further information contact:

ISN Secretary General, Cairo Kidney Centre, 3 Hussein El-Memar Street, Antikhana, PO Box 91, Bab El-Louk, Egypt.

**Tel**:    (20) 2 579 0267

**Email**:    lsn@rusys.eg.net

## International Society of Nephrology Visiting Scholars Program

**Purpose**: To improve the long-term quality of patient care, education and research in fields relevant to the kidney at the host institution, and enable senior physicians or scientists who are experts in nephrology and related disciplines to spend between 6 weeks and 3 months at an institution in the developing world

**Eligibility**: Applicants must focus primarily on hands-on activities that are the focus of this award, e.g. the establishment of a new clinical programme, research programme or laboratory technique. ISN visiting scholars should spend the duration of their study time at an institution in the developing world. Applicants must be experts in nephrology and related disciplines

**Level of Study**: Postdoctorate, Research

**Type**: Scholarship

**Value**: US$20,000, inclusive of travel and expenses, for 3 months or a pro rata amount for a shorter period of time

**Length of Study**: 6 weeks–3 months

**Application Procedure**: Applicants must send a description of the programme, its objectives, personal references and a letter of acceptance from the host institution to the ISN Secretary General. Applicants must be members of the ISN

**No. of awards offered**: 2

**Funding**: Private, Foundation

**No. of awards given last year**: 2

**No. of applicants last year**: 2

### For further information contact:

Cairo Kidney Centre, 3 Hussein El-Memar Street, Antikhana, PO Box 91, Bab El-Louk, Egypt.

**Tel**:     (20) 2 579 0267
**Email**:   isn@rusys.eg.net

## International Union for Vacuum Science and Technology (IUVSTA)

84 Oldfield Drive, Vicars Cross, Chester, CH3 5LW, United Kingdom.

**Tel**:       (44) 1244 34 2675, 771 34 03525
**Email**:     eisenmenger@ifp.tuwien.ac.at
**Website**:   www.iuvsta.org
**Contact**:   Dr Christoph Eisenmenger-Sittner, Secretary General

The International Union for Vacuum Science and Technology (IUVSTA) is a non-government organization whose member societies represent all vacuum scientists, engineers and technologists in their country.

## Welch Scholarship

**Purpose**: To encourage promising scholars who wish to study vacuum science, techniques or their application in any field

**Eligibility**: Open to applicants of any nationality who hold the minimum of a Bachelor's degree, although preference is given to those holding a doctoral degree

**Level of Study**: Doctorate, Postdoctorate, Postgraduate

**Type**: Scholarship

**Value**: US$15,000. The scholarship money is paid in three installments – one of US$7,500 at the beginning, another of US$7,000, 6 months after he/she has started work, and a third of US$500 upon delivery of a final report after completion of work

**Length of Study**: 1 year

**Frequency**: Annual

**Study Establishment**: An appropriate laboratory

**Country of Study**: Any country

**Application Procedure**: Applicants must complete and submit an application form with a research proposal, a curriculum vitae and two letters of reference. More information and application forms can be obtained from the website

**No. of awards offered**: 6

**Closing Date**: 15 April

**Funding**: Private

**Contributor**: IUVSTA

**No. of awards given last year**: 1

**No. of applicants last year**: 6

**Additional Information**: Researchers who applied unsuccessfully for previous Welch Scholarships may apply again. Applications for renewal of the Scholarship are not accepted iuvsta.org/welch-scholarship/

### For further information contact:

Canadian Photorics Fabrication Centre, Institute for Microstructural Sciences, National Research Council, 1200 Montreal Rd, Building M-50, Ottawa, ON K1A 0R6, Canada.

**Email**:    Frank.Shepherd@nrc-cnrc.gc.ca

## International Union of Biochemistry and Molecular Biology (IUBMB)

University of Calgary, Department of Biochemistry & Molecular Biology, 3330 Hospital Drive NW, HM G72B, Calgary, AB T2N 4N1, Canada.

**Tel**:      (1) 403 220 3021
**Email**:    walsh@ucalgary.ca

**Website**:     www.iubmb.org
**Contact**:     Professor Michael P Walsh, IUBMB General Secretary

IUBMB seeks to advance the international molecular life sciences community by: Promoting interactions across the diversity of endeavours in the molecular life sciences, creating networks that transcend barriers of ethnicity, culture, gender, and economic status, creating pathways for young scientists to fulfil their potential, providing evidence-based advice on public policy, promoting the values, standards, and ethics of science and the free and unhampered movement of scientists of all nations.

## Wood-Whelan Research Fellowships

**Purpose**: To provide financial assistance to young biochemists and molecular biologists to carry out research and training in a laboratory other than their own
**Eligibility**: Open to applicants who are residents of countries that are members of IUBMB and students or young researchers less than 35 years old. Retroactive applications will not be considered
**Level of Study**: Graduate, Postdoctorate, Postgraduate, Research
**Type**: Fellowship
**Value**: Up to US$4,000. It covers travel and incidental costs, as well as living expenses
**Length of Study**: 1–4 months
**Frequency**: Annual
**Application Procedure**: Applicants must submit a completed application form along with details of the research proposal, budget, curriculum vitae with a list of publications and letters of recommendation following the guidelines which can be found at website. The original application should be sent by the applicant by email as PDF files
**No. of awards offered**: 32
**Contributor**: The main sources of income for IUBMB are dues from adhering bodies (member societies) and revenue from publications
**No. of awards given last year**: 15
**No. of applicants last year**: 32
**Additional Information**: Travel should commence within 4 months of the award being made iubmb.org/guidelines-statutes/guidelines/wood-whelan-research-fellowships/

### For further information contact:

**Email**:     janet.macaulay@monash.edu

## Iota Sigma Pi

Microelectronics Technology, Lord Corporation, 110 Lord Drive, Cary, NC 27511, United States of America.

**Tel**:        (1) 919 468 5979
**Email**:      sara.paisner@lord.com
**Website**:    www.iotasigmapi.info
**Contact**:    Sara Paisner, Senior Scientist

Iota Sigma Pi, founded in 1902, is a National Honor Society that serves to promote the advancement of women in chemistry by granting recognition to women who have demonstrated superior scholastic achievement and high professional competence by election into Iota Sigma Pi.

## Agnes Fay Morgan Research Award

**Purpose**: To acknowledge research achievements in chemistry or biochemistry
**Eligibility**: Open to female applicants who are not more than 40 years of age
**Level of Study**: Postgraduate
**Type**: Award
**Value**: US$1,500
**Frequency**: Annual
**Study Establishment**: Any accredited institution
**Country of Study**: Any country
**Application Procedure**: The nomination dossier must be sent electronically (preferably as a pdf) to Dr Nancy Eddy Hopkins
**Closing Date**: 15 February
**Contributor**: Iota Sigma Pi
**Additional Information**: Please see the website for further details www.iotasigmapi.info/awards/professionalawards.html

### For further information contact:

**Tel**:        (1) 504 862 3162
**Email**:      nhopkin@tulane.edu

## Anna Louise Hoffman Award for Outstanding Achievement in Graduate Research

**Purpose**: To recognize outstanding achievement in chemical research
**Eligibility**: The candidate must be a full-time (as defined by the nominee's institution) woman graduate student who is a candidate for a graduate degree in an accredited institution.

The research presented by the candidate must be original research which can be described by one of the main chemical divisions (e.g., analytical, biochemical, inorganic, organic, physical, and/or ancillary divisions of chemistry). The nominee may be, but need not be, a member of Iota Sigma Pi

**Level of Study**: Postgraduate

**Type**: Award

**Value**: The award will be US$500, a certificate and a waiver of dues for 1 year

**Frequency**: Annual

**Study Establishment**: Any accredited institution

**Country of Study**: Any country

**Application Procedure**: The complete dossier must be sent electronically as a single file (pdf format is recommended) to Professor Jill Nelson Granger

**Closing Date**: 15 February

**Contributor**: Iota Sigma Pi

**Additional Information**: Please see the website for further details www.iotasigmapi.info/awards/studentawards.html#alh

### For further information contact:

Sweet Briar College, Department of Chemistry, Sweet Briar, VA 24595, United States of America.

**Tel**:     (1) 434 381 6166
**Email**:   granger@sbc.edu

## Gladys Anderson Emerson Scholarship

**Purpose**: To award excellence in chemistry or biochemistry

**Eligibility**: Open to applicants who are members of Iota Sigma Pi

**Level of Study**  Postgraduate

**Type**: Scholarship

**Value**: US$2,000 and a certificate

**Frequency**: Annual

**Study Establishment**: Any accredited institution

**Country of Study**: Any country

**Application Procedure**: The complete dossier must be sent electronically as a single file (pdf format is recommended) to Professor Jill Nelson Granger

**Closing Date**: 15 February

**Contributor**: Iota Sigma Pi

**Additional Information**: Please see the website for further details www.iotasigmapi.info/awards/studentawards.html#gae

## Iota Sigma Pi Centennial Award

**Purpose**: To award excellence in teaching chemistry, biochemistry or chemistry-related subjects

**Eligibility**: Holds a teaching position at an institution that does not have a graduate program in her department or holds a teaching position that is for teaching undergraduates >75% of her time at an institution that does have a graduate program in her department. The nominee may be, but need not be, a member of Iota Sigma Pi

**Level of Study**: Postgraduate

**Type**: Award

**Value**: US$500, a certificate and membership in Iota Sigma Pi with a waiver of dues for 1 year

**Frequency**: Annual

**Application Procedure**: One copy of the nomination dossier must be sent electronically (preferably as a pdf) to Dr Nancy Eddy Hopkins

**Closing Date**: 15 February

**Contributor**: Iota Sigma Pi

**Additional Information**: Please see the website for details

### For further information contact:

**Tel**:     (1) 504 862 3162
**Email**:   nhopkin@tulane.edu

## Iota Sigma Pi National Honorary Member Award

**Purpose**: To honour outstanding women chemists

**Eligibility**: Open to female candidate with exceptional achievements in chemistry. Applicants may or may not be members of Iota Sigma Pi

**Type**: Award

**Value**: US$1,500 a certificate and membership in Iota Sigma Pi with a lifetime waiver of dues

**Length of Study**: Every 3 years

**Frequency**: Every 3 years

**Application Procedure**: One copy of the nomination dossier must be sent electronically (preferably as a pdf) to Nancy Eddy Hopkins

**Closing Date**: 15 February

**Additional Information**: Please see the website for details

### For further information contact:

**Email**:   nhopkin@tulane.edu

## Violet Diller Professional Excellence Award

**Purpose**: To recognize significant accomplishments in academic, governmental or industrial chemistry

**Eligibility**: Open to female applicants who have contributed to the scientific community or society on a national level

**Level of Study**: Postgraduate

**Type**: Award

**Value**: US$1,000, a certificate and membership in Iota sigma Pi with a lifetime waiver of dues
**Frequency**: Every 3 years
**Application Procedure**: One copy of the nomination dossier must be sent electronically (preferably as a pdf) to Nancy Eddy Hopkins
**Closing Date**: 15 February
**Contributor**: Iota Sigma Pi
**Additional Information**: Please see the website for further details www.iotasigmapi.info/awards/professionalawards.html

**For further information contact:**

**Email**:    nhopkin@tulane.edu

## Iowa State University

Iowa State University, Ames, IA 50011, United States of America.

**Tel**:        (1) 515 2944111
**Email**:      online@iastate.edu
**Website**:    www.iastate.edu
**Contact**:    Dr James R Bloedell, Dean

Iowa State University of Science and Technology is a public band-grant institution serving the people of Iowa, the nation and the world.

### American Institute of Certified Public Accountants/Robert Half Student Scholarship Award

**Purpose**: AICPA and Robert Half offer the AICPA/Robert Half Student Scholarship Award to provide financial assistance to outstanding accounting students who demonstrate potential to become leaders in the CPA profession
**Eligibility**: Not eligible to students who have already gained their CPA
**Level of Study**: Postgraduate
**Type**: Scholarship
**Value**: US$2,500
**Length of Study**: 1 year
**Frequency**: Annual
**Study Establishment**: Iowa State University
**Country of Study**: United States of America
**Application Procedure**: When available, publication and application details for this award can be found at ThisWayToCPA.com
**Closing Date**: 1 March

**Funding**: Private
**Contributor**: AICPA
**Additional Information**: www.thiswaytocpa.com/education/scholarship-search/AICPA-RobertHalf-scholarship/

**For further information contact:**

AICPA/Accountemps Student Scholarship Program, AICPA-Team 331, 1211 Avenue of the Americas, New York, NY 10036-8775, United States of America.

**Email**:    scholarships@aicpa.org

## Iowa State University of Science and Technology

Institute of Social and Behavior Research, 2625 N Loop Drive Suite 500, Ames, IA 50010, United States of America.

**Email**:       rconger@iastate.edu
**Website**:     www.iastate.edu
**Contact**:     Mr Rand D Conger

### Acute Generalized Exanthematous Pustulosis Fellowship

**Purpose**: The primary goals of the ISU AGEP program are to (a) increase the number of underrepresented students obtaining graduate degrees in science, technology, engineering and mathematics (STEM)
**Eligibility**: You must meet the following requirements: 1. Member of an underrepresented ethnic group (African American, American Indian, Hispanic, Alaska Natives, and Native Hawaiian or Pacific Islander). 2. Admitted into a STEM (science, technology, engineering, mathematics) field. 3. United States citizenship (permanent residents are ineligible). 4. Enrolled as a first semester PhD student with a fall entry date
**Level of Study**: Graduate
**Type**: Fellowship
**Value**: The annual stipend is US$27,500
**Frequency**: Annual
**Country of Study**: Any country
**Application Procedure**: 1. The fellowship is for five (5) years from the term of entry. 2. Changing to another program of study may terminate the fellowship
**Funding**: Private

**For further information contact:**

1137 Pearson Hall 505 Morrill Rd, Ames, IA 50011, United States of America.

**Email**:    grad_college@iastate.edu

# Irish Research Council

First Floor, Brooklawn House, Crampton Avenue (off Shelbourne Road) Ballsbridge, Dublin 4, Ireland.

**Tel**:        (353) 1 231 5000
**Email**:    info@research.ie
**Website**:  www.research.ie

The Irish Research Council was formally launched by the Minister for Research and Innovation, Seán Sherlock TD, on 29 March. A sub-board of the Higher Education Authority, the Council was established through a merger of the Irish Research Council for Humanities and Social Sciences (IRCHSS) and the Irish Research Council for Science, Engineering and Technology (IRCSET).

## Employment-Based Postgraduate Programme

**Subjects**: All disciplines
**Purpose** Employment-based co-funded scholarships
**Level of Study**: Doctorate, Postgraduate
**Type**: Scholarship
**Value**: €24,000-€96,000
**Length of Study**: One to four years
**Frequency**: Annual
**Country of Study**: Republic of Ireland
**Application Procedure**: Online system
**Closing Date**: 20 February
**Funding**: Irish Research Council
**Contributor**: Employment Partner
**Additional Information**: www.research.ie

## Enterprise Partnership Scheme

**Subjects**: All disciplines
**Purpose**: Enterprise co-funded scholarships & fellowships
**Level of Study**: Doctorate, Postdoctorate, Postgraduate
**Type**: Fellowship/Scholarship
**Value**: €24,000-€96,000
**Length of Study**: One to four years
**Frequency**: Annual
**Country of Study**: Republic of Ireland
**Application Procedure**: Online system
**Closing Date**: 17 September
**Funding**: Irish Research Council
**Contributor**: Enterprise Partner
**Additional Information**: www.research.ie

**For further information contact:**
**Tel**:   (353) 1 231 5009
**Fax**:   (353) 1 231 5009

## Government of Ireland Postgraduate Scholarship Programme

**Subjects**: AHSS, STEM
**Purpose**: The programme provides outstanding students with the opportunity to direct their own research at the early-career stage, working with a supervisor, in their chosen area of interest.
**Eligibility**: Must have a first class or upper second-class honours bachelor's, or the equivalent, degree - Must be eligible to register for a Research Masters or PhD in a Higher Education Institution in Ireland. While the majority of scholarships will be awarded to applicants from the EFTA/EEA* member states a proportion of scholarships will also be made to exceptional applicants from non-EFTA/EEA countries. For more information see Terms and Conditions Document for eligibility criteria available on research.ie/funding/. *The European Free Trade Area (EFTA) and the European Economic Area (EEA)
**Level of Study**: Doctorate, Postgraduate
**Type**: Scholarship
**Value**: €24,000 per annum
**Length of Study**: One to four years
**Frequency**: Annual
**Study Establishment**: list of Eligible Higher Education Institutions (HEIs) and Research-Performing Organisations (RPOs) can be found on our website - research.ie/funding/eligible-higher-education-institutions-and-research-performing-organisations/
**Country of Study**: Ireland
**Application Procedure**: Online application system
**No. of awards offered**: 200
**Funding**: Government
**Additional Information**: research.ie/funding/goipg/

# Islamic Cooperation Organization (OIC)

## Islamic Cooperation Organization International Internship Program

**Purpose**: OIC Intern gives the opportunity for professional experience to young people through work ethic and teamwork experience
**Eligibility**: Equivalent, degree - Must be eligible to register for a Research Masters or PhD in a Higher Education Institution in Ireland.

**Level of Study**: Postgraduate
**Type**: Programme grant
**Frequency**: Annual
**Country of Study**: Any country
**Closing Date**: 24 March
**Funding**: Private
**Additional Information**: www.opportunitiesforafricans.com/oic-international-internship-program-2019/

## For further information contact:

P.O.Box 178, Jeddah 21411, Kingdom of Saudi Arabia.

**Tel**:  (966) 12 6515222
**Email**:  info@opportunitiesforafricans.com

## IT University of Copenhagen

Rued Langgaards Vej 7, DK-2300 Copenhagen S, Denmark.

**Tel**:  (45) 7218 5000
**Email**:  itu@itu.dk
**Website**:  en.itu.dk/

The IT University of Copenhagen (ITU) was established in 1999 and is Denmark's leading university focusing on IT research and education. We deliver state-of-the-art teaching and research within computer science, business IT and digital design. Our ambition is to create and share knowledge that is profound and leads to ground-breaking information technology and services for the benefit of humanity. The university collaborates closely with industry, the public sector and international researchers and is characterized by a strong entrepreneurial spirit among students as well as researchers. ITU's modern campus in central Copenhagen is designed by the world-renowned Danish architect Henning Larsen.

## IT University of Copenhagen State Scholarships

**Purpose**: The IT University of Copenhagen offers state scholarships to three or four exceptionally talented MSc applicants (full-degree students) from outside EU and EEA every year.
**Eligibility**: To be eligible for the scholarship, you must be admitted to a MSc Programme at IT University of Copenhagen. The scholarships will be offered to the applicants who achieve the best scores according to the criteria in the admission rules.
**Level of Study**: Masters Degree
**Type**: Scholarships
**Value**: Free tuition and partly covering of living expenses.
**Frequency**: Annual
**Country of Study**: Denmark
**Application Procedure**: Applicants cannot apply for the scholarships. The IT University considers all admitted MSc students for the scholarships and informs the students chosen for the scholarships in their letter of admission. Therefore, you must apply for admissions to be considered for the scholarship. Deadline for admissions is 1 April for September entry and 1 October for February entry. It is important to visit the official website (link found below) for detailed information on how to apply for this scholarshipOfficial Scholarship Website: en.itu.dk/Programmes/MSc-Programmes/Applying-to-a-MSc-Programme
**Closing Date**: 1 March
**Additional Information**: en.itu.dk/Programmes/MSc-Programmes/Applying-to-a-MSc-Programme

# J

## James Cook University

Graduate Research School, Townsville, QLD 4811, Australia.

| | |
|---|---|
| **Tel**: | (61) 7 4781 4575 |
| **Email**: | GRS@jcu.edu.au |
| **Website**: | www.jcu.edu.au |
| **Contact**: | Manager |

James Cook University prides itself on its international reputation for research and discovery and teaching that is enhanced and enlivened by that research activity.

## AIMS@JCU Scholarship

**Purpose**: The scholarships are provided to assist with the general living costs of the candidate.
**Eligibility**: Both domestic and international applicants
**Level of Study** Postgraduate, Research
**Type**: Scholarship
**Value**: AU$28,092pa in US$2,020 (living allowance paid fortnightly) + AU$5,000pa as living allowance or project expenses
**Length of Study**: 4 years
**Frequency**: Annual
**Application Procedure**: www.jcu.edu.au/__data/assets/pdf_file/0007/273670/2020-Scholarship-Scoring-Procedure-310519.pdf
**Closing Date**: 30 September

### For further information contact:

**Email**: grsapplications@jcu.edu.au

## Indigenous Research Training Program Scholarship (RTPSI)

**Purpose**: The scholarships are provided to assist with the general living costs of the candidate.
**Eligibility**: Applicants who identify as Australian Indigenous and/or Torres Strait Islander
**Level of Study**: Postgraduate, Research
**Type**: Scholarship
**Value**: AU$42,000 pa in AU$2,020 (living allowance paid fortnightly) + AU$10,000 one off for project expenses.
**Length of Study**: 3.5 years
**Frequency**: Annual
**Application Procedure**: wwww.jcu.edu.au/__data/assets/pdf_file/0007/273670/2020-Scholarship-Scoring-Procedure-310519.pdf
**Closing Date**: 30 September

### For further information contact:

**Email**: grsapplications@jcu.edu.au

## International Research Training Program Scholarship (IRTPS)

**Purpose**: The scholarships are provided to assist with the general living costs of the candidate.
**Eligibility**: Both domestic (RTPS) and international (IRTPS) applicants
**Level of Study**: Postgraduate, Research
**Type**: Scholarship
**Value**: AU$28,092pa in AU$2,020 (living allowance paid fortnightly) + Overseas Health Cover
**Length of Study**: 3.5 years
**Frequency**: Annual

© Springer Nature Limited 2020
Palgrave Macmillan (ed.), *The Grants Register 2021*,
https://doi.org/10.1057/978-1-349-95988-4

**Application Procedure**: www.jcu.edu.au/__data/assets/pdf_file/0007/273670/2020-Scholarship-Scoring-Procedure-310519.pdf
**Closing Date**: 30 September

### For further information contact:

**Email**:　grsapplications@jcu.edu.au

## James Cook University Postgraduate Research Scholarship

**Purpose**: To encourage full-time postgraduate research leading to a Master's or PhD degree
**Eligibility**: Open to any student who has attained at least an Upper Second Class (Honours) Bachelor's Degree
**Level of Study**: Postgraduate
**Type**: Scholarship
**Value**: AU$28,092 pa in AU$2,020 (living allowance paid fortnightly)
**Length of Study**: 3.5 years
**Frequency**: Annual
**Study Establishment**: James Cook University
**Country of Study**: Australia
**Application Procedure**: Details of how to apply can be found here: www.jcu.edu.au/graduate-research-school/candidates/prospective-students/how-to-apply
**Additional Information**: For further details visit the website www.jcu.edu.au/grs/scholarships/JCUDEV_014879.html www.jcu.edu.au/graduate-research-school/candidates/postgraduate-research-scholarships

### For further information contact:

**Fax**:　　(61) 7 4781 6204
**Email**:　grsapplications@jcu.edu.au

## Master of Business Administration Programme

**Length of Study**: 1 year
**Application Procedure**: Applicants must complete an application form supplying transcripts, a curriculum vitae, a one page essay, and referee reports
**Closing Date**: 15 June

### For further information contact:

Faculty of Arts Commerce & Economics MBA Programme Office of International Affairs.

**Tel**:　　(61) 7 7814 407
**Fax**:　　(61) 7 7815 988
**Email**:　InternationalAffairs@jcu.edu.aau

## Sustainable Tourism CRC – Climate Change PhD Scholarship

**Eligibility**: Open to the candidates who have achieved Honours 1 or equivalent
**Level of Study**: Postgraduate, Research
**Frequency**: 1
**Study Establishment**: 3 years
**Application Procedure**: AU$19,930 per year
**No. of awards given last year**: James Cook University

### For further information contact:

STCRC Education Program, Sustainable Tourism CRC.

**Tel**:　　(61) 7 5552 9063
**Email**:　Jane@crctourism.com.au

# James S. McDonnell Foundation

## Postdoctoral Fellowship Awards

**Subjects**: Brain sciences
**Purpose**: The program supports scholarship and research directed toward the discovery and refinement of theoretical and mathematical tools contributing to the continued development of the study of complex, adaptive, nonlinear systems. The program's emphasis is on the development and application of the theory and tools used in the study of complex research questions and not on particular fields of research per se. JSMF is also interested in projects attempting to apply complex systems approaches to coherently articulated questions where such approaches are not yet standard but could open up new paths to progress. The JSMF Fellowship is designed to provide students with opportunities to pursue postdoctoral training that might not be otherwise readily available. The Fellowships are intended to allow students to seek postdoctoral research opportunities aligned with the student's interest and desire to obtain additional skills and experience that will further their pursuit of careers in complex systems science.
**Eligibility**: The JSMF Fellowship is a unique opportunity for students with an interest in and an aptitude for complexity science who are in the final stages of completing their PhD and looking to make a significant change in direction for their first postdoctoral fellowship (field of study, model organism, theory vs experimental, etc.) that will either be difficult or impossible without an external source of funding.
**Type**: Fellowship
**Value**: US$200,000
**Length of Study**: Two to three years

**Frequency**: Annual
**Country of Study**: Any country
**Application Procedure**: Complete applications must be uploaded to the JSMF website.
**Closing Date**: 12 June
**Additional Information**: www.jsmf.org/apply/fellowship/

## Japan Society for the Promotion of Science (JSPS)

5-3-1 Kojimachi, Chiyoda-ku, Tokyo 102-0083, Japan.

**Tel**: (81) 3263 9094
**Email**: gaitoku@jsps.go.jp
**Website**: www.jsps.go.jp

The Japan Society for the Promotion of Science (JSPS) is an independent administrative institution, established for the purpose of contributing to the advancement of science in all fields of the natural and social sciences and the humanities. The JSPS plays a pivotal role in the administration of a wide spectrum of Japan's scientific and academic programmes.

## Japan Society for the Promotion of Science Postdoctoral Fellowships for North American and European Researchers (Short-term)

**Purpose**: To assist promising and highly qualified young foreign researchers wishing to conduct research in Japan
**Eligibility**: Be a citizen or permanent resident of an eligible country (the US, Canada, EU countries, Switzerland, Norway, and Russia). Candidates must have obtained their doctoral degree at a university outside Japan within 6 years of the date the fellowship goes into effect, or must be currently enroled in a doctoral course at a university outside Japan and scheduled to receive their PhD within 2 years
**Level of Study**: Postdoctorate, Predoctorate
**Type**: Fellowship
**Value**: Round-trip air ticket, monthly maintenance allowance of ¥362,000 for PhD holder and ¥200,000 for non-PhD holder, settling-in allowance of ¥200,000 and overseas travel insurance, research support allowance
**Length of Study**: 1 year but a minimum of 1 month
**Frequency**: Annual
**Study Establishment**: Universities and research institutions
**Country of Study**: Japan
**Application Procedure**: Applicants must write for details. Application must be submitted to JSPS by the host researcher in Japan

**Funding**: Government
**Additional Information**: Please see the website for further details www.jsps.go.jp/english/e-fellow/postdoctoral.html

### For further information contact:

**Email**: agneta.granlund@stint.se

## Research Fellowships for Young Researchers

**Purpose**: Awarded to excellent young researchers, these fellowships offer the fellows an opportunity to focus on a freely chosen research topic based on their own innovative ideas. Ultimately, the program works to foster and secure excellent researchers.
**Eligibility**: 1. Be a citizen of a country that has diplomatic relations with Japan. 2. Candidates must have obtained their doctoral degree within six years of the date the fellowship goes into effect. 3. Universities and inter-university research institutes. 4. MEXT-affiliated institutions engaged in research. 5. Colleges of technology. 6. Institutions designated by the Minister of MEXT.
**Level of Study**: Postdoctorate
**Type**: Fellowship
**Value**: Up to ¥1.5 million/year
**Length of Study**: 3 years
**Frequency**: Annual

### For further information contact:

5-3-1 Kojimachi, Chiyoda-ku, Tokyo 102-0083, Japan.

**Tel**: (81) 3 3263 3444
**Email**: postdoc-standardjsps.go.jp

## Japanese American Citizens League (JACL)

National Headquarters, 1765 Sutter Street, San Francisco, CA 94115, United States of America.

**Tel**: (1) 415 345 1075, 415 921 5225
**Email**: ncwnp@jacl.org
**Website**: www.jacl.org
**Contact**: Scholarships Officer

The Japanese American Citizens League (JACL) was founded in 1929 to fight discrimination against people of

Japanese ancestry. It is the largest and one of the oldest Asian American organizations in the USA. The JACL has over 24,500 members in 112 chapters located in 25 states, Washington, DC, and Japan. The organization operates within a structure of eight district councils, with headquarters in San Francisco, CA.

## Mike M. Masaoka Congressional Fellowship

**Purpose**: To financially support and develop leaders for public service

**Eligibility**: Candidates must be U.S. citizens who are graduating college seniors or students in graduate or professional programs and a member of the JACL. Preference will be given to those who have demonstrated a commitment to Asian American issues, particularly those affecting the Japanese American community. Communication skills, especially in writing, are important

**Level of Study**: Postgraduate, Professional development

**Type**: Fellowship

**Value**: US$2,200 to US$2,500 a month

**Length of Study**: 1 year

**Frequency**: Annual

**Country of Study**: United States of America

**Application Procedure**: Applicants must send a completed application form and a letter of reference to the JACL national headquarters

**Closing Date**: May

**Funding**: Foundation

**Additional Information**: Preference will be given to those who have demonstrated a commitment to Asian American issues, particularly those affecting the Japanese American community. Please see the website for further details at www.jacl.org/now-accepting-applications-for-mike-m-masaoka-congressional-fellowship/ jacl.org/about/jobs-at-jacl/mike-m-masaoka-congressional-fellowship/

### For further information contact:

Japanese American Citizens League Headquarters, Mike M. Masaoka Fellowship, 1850 M Street NW, Suite 1100, Washington, DC 20036, United States of America.

**Email**:    policy@jacl.org

## Norman Y. Mineta Fellowship

**Purpose**: To focus on public policy advocacy as well as programs of safety awareness in the Asian Pacific American (APA) community

**Eligibility**: Open to the members of the JACL with 4-year degree from an accredited college or university having excellent writing, analytical, and computer skills

**Level of Study**: Postgraduate

**Type**: Fellowship

**Value**: US$2,500 a month

**Length of Study**: 12 months

**Application Procedure**: Interested applicants should submit a curriculum vitae, a sample of writing, and names and contact information for two references to the Washington, DC office of the JACL at policy@jacl.org with 'Mineta Fellowship' in the subject line

**Closing Date**: 18 May

**Contributor**: State Farm Insurance

**Additional Information**: Candidates must have ability to take directions and follow through with assignments, must work well with others, and have good interpersonal skills. Please see the website for further details www.jacl.org/internships-and-fellowships/ jacl.org/internships-and-fellowships/

### For further information contact:

JACL, 1828 L Street, NW Suite 802, Washington, DC 20036, United States of America.

**Tel**:        (1) 202 223 1240
**Fax**:       (1) 202 296 8082
**Email**:    dc@jacl.org

## Jiamusi University

### Heilongjiang Provincial Government Scholarships

**Purpose**: the Jiamusi is the provincial key construction university with high level in Heilongjiang province, which is also a comprehensive university with a wide range of categories and medical specialties

**Eligibility**: For a Bachelors's degree, the candidate should have a high school degree with good marks/percentages. Also for a master's degree, you need to have a bachelor's degree with excellent grades. Similarly for PhD applicant needs a masters degree as well as an excellent percentage.

**Level of Study**: Postgraduate

**Type**: Scholarship

**Frequency**: Annual

**Country of Study**: Any country

**Closing Date**: 30 April

**Funding**: International office

**Additional Information**:    www.china-admissions.com/chinese-scholarships/heilongjiang-government-scholarship-international-students/

## For further information contact:

Room No. 209, the Admission Office of International Education College of Jiamusi University, No. 258 Xuefu Street, Jiamusi City, Heilongjiang Province, China.

**Tel**: (86) 454 8603918
**Fax**: (86) 454 8603918
**Email**: jmsuadmission@163.com

# John Carter Brown Library at Brown University

Box 1894, Brown University, Providence, RI 02912, United States of America.

**Tel**: (1) 401 863 2725
**Email**: JCBL_Information@Brown.edu
**Website**: www.jcbl.org

The John Carter Brown Library, an independently funded and administered institution for advanced research in history and the humanities, is located on the campus of Brown University. The Library supports research focused on the colonial history of the Americas, including all aspects of the European, African, and Native American involvement.

## Library Associates Fellowship

**Purpose**: The Hodson Trust - John Carter Brown Library Fellowship supports work by academics, independent scholars and writers working on significant projects relating to the literature, history, culture
**Type**: Fellowship
**Value**: The stipend is US$5,000 per month for a total of US$20,000
**Length of Study**: 2 Month
**Frequency**: Annual
**Closing Date**: 15 March
**Additional Information**: For more information on the fellowships and the sponsor institutions, please visit starrcenter. washcoll.edu and www.brown.edu/Facilities/John_Carter_ Brown_Library. jcblibrary.org/fellowships/apply

## For further information contact:

**Email**: jjohnson24@washcoll.edu OR applications_ starrcenter@washcoll.edu

## Norman Fiering Fund

**Purpose**: To support scholars in any area of research related to the Library's holdings
**Eligibility**: Open to scholars in any area of research related to the Library's holdings
**Type**: Funding support
**Value**: US$2,100 per month
**Length of Study**: 2–4 months
**Country of Study**: United States of America
**Closing Date**: 3 January

## For further information contact:

John Carter Brown Library, Box 1894, Providence, RI 02912, United States of America.

**Email**: JCBL_Fellowships@Brown.edu

## Ruth and Lincoln Ekstrom Fellowship

**Purpose**: To sponsor historical research
**Eligibility**: Open to scholars engaged in predoctoral, postdoctoral or independent research. Graduate students must have passed their preliminary or general examinations at the time of application
**Level of Study**: Postdoctorate, Predoctorate, Research
**Type**: Fellowship
**Value**: US$2,100 per month
**Length of Study**: 2–4 months
**Frequency**: Annual
**Country of Study**: United States of America
**Application Procedure**: Applicants must complete an application form. Candidates should write to, or email the Director
**Closing Date**: 15 December
**Funding**: Private
**No. of awards given last year**: 1

# John E Fogarty International Center (FIC) for Advanced Study in the Health Sciences

Building 31, 31 Center Drive, MSC 2220, Bethesda, MD 20892-2220, United States of America.

**Tel**: (1) 301 496 2075
**Email**: FICinfo@mail.nih.gov
**Website**: www.fic.nih.gov
**Contact**: Program Officer

The John E Fogarty International Center (FIC) for Advanced Study in the Health Sciences, a component of the National Institutes of Health (NIH), promotes international co-operation in the biomedical and behavioural sciences. This is accomplished primarily through long- and short-term fellowships, small grants and training grants. This compendium of international opportunities is prepared by the FIC with the hope that it will stimulate scientists to seek research enhancing experiences abroad.

## Global Health Research Initiative Program for New Foreign Investigators (GRIP)

**Purpose**: To assist well-trained young investigators to contribute to health care advances in their home countries
**Eligibility**: Open to all well-trained young investigators. To verify eligibility, new foreign investigators should review the answers to Frequently Asked Questions. Please contact Dr Xingzhu Liu by email at xingzhu.liu@nih.gov with questions
**Level of Study**: Postgraduate
**Type**: Grant
**Value**: US$50,000 per year
**Length of Study**: 5 years
**Frequency**: Annual
**Application Procedure**: Application form on request
**Funding**: Foundation
**Contributor**: Fugarty International Center
**Additional Information**: Please see the website for further details www.fic.nih.gov/programs/Pages/new-foreign-investigators.aspx www.fic.nih.gov/Programs/Info/Pages/grip-faqs.aspx

### For further information contact:

**Email**:   butrumb@mail.nih.gov

## John E Fogarty Foreign Funded Fellowship Programs

**Purpose**: To allow United States scientists to conduct collaborative research abroad
**Eligibility**: Open to scientists who are United States citizens or permanent residents invited by foreign host scientists to participate in research projects of mutual interest
**Level of Study**: Postdoctorate
**Type**: Fellowship
**Value**: To cover the visiting scientist's individual expenses abroad
**Length of Study**: Usually up to 1 year, possible extension in some countries
**Frequency**: Annual

**Country of Study**: Other
**Application Procedure**: Applicants must complete an application form, available on request or downloadable from www.avh.de
**Closing Date**: 5 December
**Additional Information**: Because fellowships are intended to support an individual's expenses abroad, the foreign host is expected to have the resources to support the research project. Types of activities in which Fellows engage include collaboration in basic or clinical research and familiarisation with or utilisation of special techniques and equipment not otherwise available to the applicant. The programmes do not provide support for activities which have as their principal purpose conducting brief observational visits, attending scientific meetings or formal training courses, or providing full-time clinical, technical or teaching services. Funding is provided by the Alexander von Humboldt Foundation (Germany), the Israeli Ministry of Health, the Japan Society for the Promotion of Science, the Japan Science and Technology Agency, the Swedish Medical Research Council, and the National Science Council of Taiwan. Candidates may apply to only one of these programmes during any given year

### For further information contact:

Alexander von Humboldt Foundation, US Liaison Office, 1055 Thomas Jefferson Street NW, Suite 2030, Washington, DC 20007, United States of America.

**Tel**:         (1) 202 296 2990
**Fax**:        (1) 202 833 8514
**Email**:    info@humboldtfoundation.org

## John F. Kennedy Library Foundation

Columbia Point, Boston, MA 02125, United States of America.

**Tel**:           (1) 866 514 1960
**Email**:      Kennedy.library@nara.gov
**Website**:   www.jfklibrary.org
**Contact**:    Fellowships Administrator

The John F. Kennedy Library Foundation is a non-profit organization that provides financial support, staffing and creative resources for the John F. Kennedy Presidential Library and Museum whose purpose is to advance the study and understanding of President Kennedy's life and career, and the times in which he lived and to promote a greater appreciation of America's political and cultural heritage, the process of governing and the importance of public service.

## Abba P. Schwartz Research Fellowship

**Purpose**: It is intended to support a scholar in the production of a substantial work in the areas of immigration, naturalization, or refugee policy, subjects of great personal and professional interest to Mr Schwartz

**Eligibility**: See award purpose

**Level of Study**: Postgraduate

**Type**: Fellowship

**Value**: A stipend of up to US$3,100

**Frequency**: Annual

**Country of Study**: United States of America

**Application Procedure**: Please submit the following documentation: (1) an application form (pdf) accompanied by a brief proposal (three to four pages) in the form of a letter describing the planned research, its significance, the intended audience, and expected outcome; (2) two letters of recommendation from academic or other appropriate references; (3) a sample of your writing (approx. 10 pages); (4) a project budget; and (5) a CV

**Closing Date**: 30 September

**Funding**: Foundation

**Contributor**: John F. Kennedy Library Foundation

**Additional Information**: The estimated per diem cost of accommodations, meals, and incidentals for Boston is US$250 Please see the website for further details www. jfklibrary.org/archives/research-fellowships-grants/schwartz-fellowship

### For further information contact:

**Tel**:     (1) 617 514 1630
**Fax**:    (1) 617 514 1625
**Email**:   Kennedy.Fellowships@nara.gov

## Arthur M. Schlesinger, Jr. Fellowship

**Purpose**: To financially support scholars in the production of substantial work on the foreign policy of the Kennedy years

**Eligibility**: Open to citizens of the US only

**Level of Study**: Postgraduate

**Type**: Fellowships

**Value**: Up to US$5,000

**Frequency**: Annual

**Country of Study**: United States of America

**Application Procedure**: Applicants must submit application form, financial need analysis, essay, reference letters, and curriculum vitae. Applicants are strongly encouraged to contact the Kennedy Library for information about its collections and holdings before applying

**Closing Date**: 15 August

**Funding**: Foundation

**Contributor**: Schlesinger Fund

**Additional Information**: Proposals are invited from all sources, but preference will be given to applicants specializing in the work on the foreign policy of the Kennedy years especially with regard to the western hemisphere, or on Kennedy domestic policy, especially with regard to racial justice and to the conservation of natural resources. Preference is also given to projects not supported by large grants from other institutions. Please see the website for further details www. jfklibrary.org/archives/research-fellowships-grants/schlesinger-fellowship

### For further information contact:

**Tel**:     (1) 617 514 1629
**Fax**:    (1) 617 514 1625

# John R. Mott Scholarship Foundation

## John R. Mott Scholarship

**Purpose**: This award is for Italian students from the Calabria region attending college. Awards are given based on academic achievement and financial need

**Eligibility**: 1. Students native to the region of Calabria, Italy. 2. Students enrolled and who will be attending university or graduate school in Fall 2020. 3. Students seeking an education leading to a degree or professional certification.

**Level of Study**: Graduate

**Type**: Scholarship

**Value**: US$10,000

**Frequency**: Annual

**Country of Study**: United States of America

**Application Procedure**: Applications are accepted between 9 February and 15 April. Applications will be available online from the John R. Mott Scholarship Foundation website. Applicants must complete the application online, and mail or fax the following materials to the foundation by the deadline: official transcript from university or official completion certification and academic performance document from high school, and ISEE-U certification attesting to the tax liability of the family

**Funding**: Foundation

**Additional Information**: mottscholarship.org/index.asp

### For further information contact:

1860 19th St., N.W. Washington, DC 20009, United States of America.

**Tel**:     (1) 202 483 2618
**Email**:   scholarships@swe.org

# Johns Hopkins University

615 N. Wolfe Street, Suite E1002, Baltimore, MD 21205, United States of America.

| | |
|---|---|
| **Tel:** | (1) 410 516 3400, 410 955 1680 |
| **Email:** | admiss@jhsph.edu |
| **Website:** | webapps.jhu.edu/jhuniverse/information_about_ hopkins/ |
| **Contact:** | Grants Co-ordinator |

The vision of the Johns Hopkins Center for Alternatives to Animal Testing is to be a leading force in the development and use of reduction, refinement and replacement alternatives in research, testing and education to protect and enhance the health of the public.

## Center for Alternatives to Animal Testing Grants Programme

**Purpose**: To promote and support research in the development of in vitro and other alternative techniques
**Eligibility**: No eligibility restrictions. Applicants' proposals must meet the goals of the CAAT Grants Program
**Level of Study**: Unrestricted
**Value**: For proposals relating to toxicology: up to US$25,000; proposals relating to developmental immunotoxicology: up to US$50,000.
**Length of Study**: 1 year
**Frequency**: Annual
**Country of Study**: United States of America
**Application Procedure**: Applicants must complete a preproposal. After review, selected applicants are invited to submit a full application
**No. of awards offered**: 30
**Closing Date**: 21 March
**Funding**: Private
**No. of awards given last year**: 12
**No. of applicants last year**: 30
**Additional Information**: Please see the website for further details caat.jhsph.edu/programs/grants/

### For further information contact:

615 N Wolfe St W7032, Baltimore, MD 21205, United States of America.

| | |
|---|---|
| **Fax:** | (1) 410 614 2871 |
| **Email:** | caat@jhsph.edu |

## Greenwall Fellowship Program

**Purpose**: To provide an unparalleled opportunity for fellowship and faculty development training in bioethics and health policy
**Eligibility**: Open to applicants who have Doctoral degrees in medicine, nursing, philosophy, law, public health, biomedical sciences, social sciences or a related field
**Level of Study**: Postdoctorate
**Type**: Fellowship
**Value**: US$122,003
**Length of Study**: 2 years
**Frequency**: Annual
**Study Establishment**: Johns Hopkins University
**Country of Study**: United States of America
**Application Procedure**: Applicants must send a cover letter, a personal statement describing why they want to be a Greenwall Fellow, a copy of their curriculum vitae, 3 reference letters, official copies of undergraduate and graduate/professional school transcripts and copies of their written and/or published work
**Closing Date**: 1 December

### For further information contact:

**Email:** fellows@ihsph.edu

## Joint Institute for Laboratory Astrophysics (formerly Joint Institute for Laboratory Astrophysics)

440 B, University of Colorado, Boulder, CO 80309, United States of America.

| | |
|---|---|
| **Tel:** | (1) 303 492 7789 |
| **Email:** | jilavf@jila.colorado.edu |
| **Website:** | www.colorado.edu |
| **Contact:** | Programme Assistant |

JILA's interests are at present research and applications in the fields of laser technology, optoelectronics, precision measurement, surface science and semiconductors, information and image processing, and materials and process science, as well as basic research in atomic, molecular and optical physics, precision measurement, gravitational physics, chemical physics, astrophysics and geophysical measurements. To provide an opportunity for persons actively contributing to these fields, JILA operates the Visiting Fellowship Programme as well as the Postdoctoral Research Associate Programme.

## Joint Institute for Laboratory Astrophysics Postdoctoral Research Associateship and Visiting Fellowships

**Purpose**: To support additional training beyond the PhD and sabbatical research
**Eligibility**: There are no restrictions other than those that might be required by the grant that supports the research
**Level of Study**: Postdoctorate, Professional development
**Type**: Fellowship
**Value**: Varies
**Length of Study**: Visiting fellowships are for 4–12 months and Postdoctoral Research Associateships are for 1 year or more
**Frequency**: Annual
**Country of Study**: United States of America
**Application Procedure**: Applicants should download an application form, complete it, and send it (along with requested supporting materials) to the Visiting Scientists Program Assistant. All materials may be submitted via email to secretary via email
**Closing Date**: 1 November
**Funding**: Government
**Contributor**: Varies
**Additional Information**: Please see the website for further details jila.colorado.edu/students-postdocs/postdocs

### For further information contact:

Visiting Scientists Program, 440 UCB, Boulder, CO 80309, United States of America.

**Tel**:      (1) 303 492 5749
**Email**:      secretary@jila.colorado.edu

## Juvenile Diabetes Foundation International/The Diabetes Research Foundation

26 Broadway, 14th Floor, New York, NY 10004, United States of America.

**Tel**:      (1) 1 800 533 CURE (2873)
**Email**:      info@jdrf.org
**Website**:      www.jdrf.org
**Contact**:      Grant Administrator

JDRF remains dedicated to finding a cure for type 1 diabetes as our highest priority. In addition to focusing on specific research challenges and gaps that will lead to curing, better treating, and preventing type 1 diabetes. JDRF works to decrease barriers to commercial development of products for type 1 diabetes.

## Strategic Research Agreement

**Purpose**: To support and fund research to find a cure for Type 1 diabetes
**Eligibility**: Required MD, DMD, DVM, PhD, or equivalent and faculty position or equivalent
**Level of Study**: Research
**Type**: Grant
**Value**: Varies
**Length of Study**: 3 years
**Closing Date**: 1 February
**Additional Information**: Please check website for further details

## Juvenile Diabetes Research Foundation - JDRF

Starting in the US in 1970, JDRF began in Australia in 1982 as a small group of parents who believed their children deserved better. Now, millions of people work with and support JDRF in over 20 countries. We connect the best people in every discipline, industry and organisation with a single focus on destroying T1D. 40 years of investment in the best researchers has created an exciting pipeline from academic research through to clinical trials and therapies requiring approval and financial support for people to access them.

**Tel**:      (61) 2 9020 6100
**Email**:      travelgrants@jdrf.org.au
**Website**:      jdrf.org.au/
**Contact**:      Grants Administration Officer on travelgrants@jdrf.org.au or 02 9020 6139.

JDRF has transformed the understanding of Type 1 Diabetes (T1D). We have been part of every breakthrough in T1D care in the last 40 years. We drive innovation, demand action and stand with everyone facing life with T1D. We know research is the key to destroy T1D.

## JDRF PhD Top-up Scholarships 2020

**Purpose**: The JDRF PhD Top-up scholarship is designed to support and encourage PhD students pursuing research in the field of type 1 diabetes in line with JDRF's mission - to treat, prevent and cure type 1 diabetes and its complications. The Top-Up will provide successful candidates with additional funding up to AU$6,000 per year, on top of their PhD Scholarship stipend, full-time or part-time, contingent on satisfactory progress.

**Eligibility**: The JDRF PhD Top-Up scholarship is available to domestic students in receipt of a Research Training Program Stipend (formerly Australian Postgraduate Award), NHMRC Postgraduate Award or University-funded scholarship. Students must be pursuing research relevant to JDRF's mission - to cure, treat and prevent type 1 diabetes and its complications. Applicants must be 1. Recipients of either a Research Training Program Stipend, NHMRC Postgraduate Award or a University-funded PhD scholarship 2. Not in receipt of any other PhD top-up funding 3. Pursuing research relevant to type 1 diabetes and its complications 4. Australian citizens or permanent residents currently residing in Australia

**Level of Study**: Postgraduate

**Type**: Scholarship

**Value**: The Top-Up will provide successful candidates with additional funding up to AU$6,000 per year, on top of their PhD Scholarship stipend, full-time or part-time, contingent on satisfactory progress.

**Frequency**: Annual

**Country of Study**: Australia

**Application Procedure**: The cut-off date for consideration of this scholarship is 5:00pm AEDT, 20th April. Applications must be submitted on the following application form with headings in order: 1. Details Summary - Please complete all fields within the application form. 2. Applicant Summary - Please complete all fields within the application form and adhere to the word limits of each question. 3. Letter confirming offer of a PhD Scholarship - Include a letter confirming your offer of a Research Training Program Stipend, NHMRC Postgraduate Award or a University-funded PhD scholarship. This should be pasted into the document. 4. Curriculum Vitae - 4 page limit. Please limit all information provided to that requested within the application form. 5. Academic transcript - Please provide a certified copy of your academic transcript. This should be pasted into the document. 6. NB: Please note that acceptable persons who may certify a document are listed in Schedule 2 of the 'Statutory Declarations Regulations 2018' located here. 7. Certification of both the Applicant and their Institution's Research Administration Office. 8. NB: Electronic signatures are acceptable. Letters of Recommendation - In addition to the above, two letters of recommendation must be sent by referees before 5:00pm AEDT, 20th April, directly to travelgrants@jdrf.org.au. Letters of recommendation should be e-mailed directly by the referee to maintain confidentiality. It is the applicant's responsibility to ensure that these letters are sent on time.

**Closing Date**: 20 April

### For further information contact:

Applications are to be submitted by your Institution's Research Administration Office as one document in PDF format with the naming convention of: "Surname_Firstname_Top-up.pdf" to travelgrants@jdrf.org.au.

# K

## Karnatak University

Dr. B. H. Nagoor, Coordinator, Dr. D. C. Pavate Foundation, C/o Department of Economics, Karnatak University, Dharwad, Karnataka 580003, India.

**Email**: nagoor_bh@yahoo.co.in

### Dr. D. C. Pavate Memorial Visiting Fellowship

**Eligibility**: To apply for the D. C. Pavate Memorial Visiting Fellowship, candidates must meet the following criteria: 1. Be below the age of 40 years as on January 1 of the academic year. 2. Secured a PhD or a masters degree or equivalent with a minimum of first class. 3. For fellowships valid for Karnataka candidates: A Karnataka candidate is any person who has studied at an educational institution in Karnataka or been employed in Karnataka for a minimum of 5 years continuously

**Level of Study**: Graduate

**Type**: Fellowship

**Frequency**: 3 times each year

**Country of Study**: Any country

**Application Procedure**: Application forms can be downloaded at www.kud.ac.in

**Closing Date**: 10 July

**Funding**: Private

**Additional Information**: www.indiaeducation.net/scholarships/dr-dc-pavate-memorial-fellowships.aspx

## Kay Kendall Leukaemia Fund

### Kay Kendall Leukaemia Fund Junior and Intermediate Research Fellowships

**Subjects**: Intermediate fellowships are awarded annually to scientists of outstanding potential allowing them to gain experience in an international centre of excellence prior to establishing an independent research group of their own. Applicants may be of any nationality and should be based currently in the UK and/or be planning to work in a recognised university or other equivalent department in a UK institution. A significant proportion of the fellowship (up to 3 years) may be spent in an appropriate institution outside the UK where this can be clearly demonstrated to be of significant benefit. The fellowship will cover the cost of the fellow's salary and may support one assistant together with consumable support in the UK, and travel costs where appropriate. Up to three junior fellowships are awarded annually and cover salary costs for three years and costs of laboratory consumables in the UK and travel costs where appropriate. They are made in the following categories: (i) Scientific fellowships are open to scientists who will usually have 1-4 years postdoctoral experience and be intending either to work at a recognised UK research institution or seeking a travel fellowship for relevant work abroad, with funding and administration via an appropriate UK institution. (ii) Clinical research fellow are open to clinicians seeking funding for a PhD in the field of leukaemia research, usually at a UK centre.

**Purpose**: Scientific Research and Clinical Research Fellowships on aspects of leukaemia and related haematological malignancies

**Eligibility**: Intermediate - Non-medical applicants will already have completed their PhD and will usually have 3-8 years of post-doctoral research experience. For medical graduates the Intermediate Fellowship is suitable for individuals who have obtained a PhD; in exceptional cases completion of clinical training during an Intermediate Fellowship may also be possible. Applicants for the Intermediate Fellowship will be expected to demonstrate their potential for achieving international status as researchers in leukaemia or a closely related field. Junior - Non-medical scientists who will usually have 1-4 years postdoctoral experience and are intending to work either at a recognised UK research institution or seeking a travel fellowship for relevant work abroad may apply for

© Springer Nature Limited 2020
Palgrave Macmillan (ed.), *The Grants Register 2021*,
https://doi.org/10.1057/978-1-349-95988-4

a scientific fellowship, with funding and administration via an appropriate UK institution. Clinicians seeking funding for a PhD in the field of leukaemia research, usually at a UK centre, may apply for a clinical research fellowship.

**Level of Study**: Postgraduate

**Type**: A variable number of fellowships

**Value**: Fellow's salary and consumable costs. Intermediate fellowships may include RA salary costs and Family Allowance if time is taken abroad.

**Length of Study**: Junior - 3 years; Intermediate - 4 years

**Frequency**: Annual

**Study Establishment**: UK university or research institution, or equivalent abroad (but to be administered by a UK university or research institution)

**Country of Study**: United Kingdom

**Application Procedure**: KKLF is spending out - the last year of making awards will be 2021/22. Calls for applications and relevant deadlines are advertised in the spring for Intermediate Fellowships and the summer for Junior Fellowships. Application is by application form available from KKLF. It must include a completed application form with all signatures, a scientific proposal, and a statement from the Departmental Chairman or Laboratory Director that he/she is prepared to make available all appropriate facilities if the applicant is successful. In addition it should include references, costings, and CV. Applications are triaged post-deadline to determine which will be sent out to review.

**No. of awards offered**: Junior 1-3; Intermediate 1

**Funding**: Trusts

**No. of awards given last year**: IF - 1: JF - 1

### For further information contact:

The Kay Kendall Leukaemia Fund, The Peak, 5 Wilton Road, London, SW1V 1AP, United Kingdom.

**Tel**:      (44) 207 410 0330
**Email**:   info@kklf.org.uk

## Keele University

Keele, Staffordshire, ST5 5BG, United Kingdom.

**Tel**:      (44) 1782 584002
**Email**:   aaa12@keele.ac.uk
**Website**: www.keele.ac.uk
**Contact**: Ms Joan Scrivener, Postgraduate Admissions Officer

Keele University is committed to provide high quality teaching and research, with particular emphasis on multidisciplinary and interdisciplinary studies, which are seen to be in the forefront of developments worldwide, promote networking, partnership and collaboration between disciplines and organisations at regional, national and international level, and develop the estate as a leading exemplar of a learning and working campus community of students, staff and business.

## Keele MBA Programme

**Length of Study**: 1 year full-time and 2 years part-time

**Application Procedure**: Applicants must complete an application form

### For further information contact:

**Tel**:      (44) 1782 583425
**Fax**:      (44) 1782 584272
**Email**:   mna09@keele.ac.uk

## Keio University

Garduate School of Business Administration, 2-1-1 Hiyoshi Honcho, Kohoku-ku, Yokohama 223-8523, Japan.

**Tel**:      (81) 9 3962 4436
**Contact**: MBA Admissions Officer

Keio University is the first private university in Japan, founded in 1858 by Yukichi Fukuzawa, who is often called the intellectual father of modern Japan. Since then Keio University has developed a brilliant history of producing distinguished personalities in every field of society.

## Joint Japan World Bank Graduate Scholarship Program

**Purpose**: The Joint Japan/World Bank Graduate Scholarship Program (JJ/WBGSP) is open to women and men from developing countries with relevant professional experience and a history of supporting their countries' development efforts who are applying to a master degree program in a development-related topic

**Eligibility**: The applicant must meet the following eligibility criteria: 1. Be a national of a World Bank member developing country (see above). 2. Not hold dual citizenship of a developed country. 3. Be in good health. 4. Hold a Bachelor (or equivalent) degree earned at least 3 years prior to the Application Deadline date. 5. Have 3 years or more of recent development-related experience after earning a Bachelor (or equivalent) degree. 6. Be employed in development-related work in a paid full-time position at the time of submitting the scholarship application. The only exception to this criterion is for developing country nationals from a country that will be on the updated list of Fragile and Conflict States provided to applicants in the Application Guidelines for each call for scholarships. 7. On or before the Scholarship Application Deadline date, be admitted unconditionally (except for funding) for the upcoming academic year to at least one of the JJ/WBGSP preferred university master's programs and located outside of the applicant's country of citizenship and country of residence listed at the time the call for scholarship applications open

**Level of Study**: Postgraduate

**Type**: Scholarship

**Length of Study**: 2 years

**Frequency**: Annual

**Country of Study**: Any country

**Application Procedure**: For scholarships to one of the preferred master's programs, you must first apply and be unconditionally accepted for admissions to one or more of the Preferred Program(s) to be considered for a JJ/WBGSP scholarship. The call for applications is open from 7 March to 11 April. For scholarships to one of the partner master's programs, you must apply for admission to one or more of the Partner Masters Degree Program(s). After reviewing submitted applications, each Partner Master Degree Program will identify a short list of eligible candidates who will then be invited by the JJ/WBGSP Secretariat to apply for a JJ/WBGSP scholarship

**Closing Date**: 11 April

**Funding**: Private

**Additional Information**: For further information, check the below website. www.ic.keio.ac.jp/en/study/jjwbgsp/index.html www.scholars4dev.com/2735/japan-world-bank-graduate-scholarships-for-development-related-studies/

## For further information contact:

**Email**: ic-scholarship@adst.keio.ac.jp

## Kennan Institute

Woodrow Wilson International Center for Scholars, One Woodrow Wilson Plaza, 1300 Pennsylvania Avenue North West, Washington, DC 20004-3027, United States of America.

**Tel**:     (1) 202 691 4100

**Email**:     kennan@wilsoncenter.org

**Website**:     www.wilsoncenter.org

**Contact**:     Scholar Programs

The Kennan Institute for Advanced Russian Studies sponsors advanced research on the successor states to the USSR and encourages Eurasian studies with its public lecture and publication programmes, maintaining contact with scholars and research centres abroad. The Institute seeks to function as a forum where the scholarly community can interact with public policymakers.

## Title VIII-Supported Summer Research Grant

**Purpose**: To support United States citizens whose research in the social sciences or humanities focuses on the former Soviet Union, and who demonstrate a particular need to use the resources of the Washington, DC area

**Eligibility**: Open to academic participants with a doctoral degree or those who have nearly completed their dissertation. For non-academic participants, an equivalent level of professional development is required. Applicants must be United States citizens

**Level of Study**: Doctorate, Postdoctorate, Postgraduate, Predoctorate, Professional development, Research

**Type**: Scholarship

**Value**: US$7,000 for 2 months

**Length of Study**: Up to 62 days

**Frequency**: Dependent on funds available

**Study Establishment**: The Kennan Institute

**Country of Study**: United States of America

**Application Procedure**: Applicants must submit a concise description of their research project of 700–800 words, a curriculum vitae, a statement of preferred dates of residence in Washington, DC, and two letters of recommendation specifically in support of the research proposal. No application form required

**No. of awards offered**: 25

**Closing Date**: 31 January

**Funding**: Government

**Additional Information**: Please email kennan@wilsoncenter.org or see our website with further details www.wilsoncenter.org/opportunity/kennan-institute-title-viii-supported-summer-research-scholarships

## For further information contact:

Applicants are required to submit the application form, a project proposal and title (not to exceed 1,000 words), curriculum vitae including publications, and two letters of recommendation specifically in support of the research to be conducted at the Institute.

# Kennedy Memorial Trust

3 Birdcage Walk, Westminster, London, SW1H 9JJ, United Kingdom.

**Tel**:            (44) 20 7222 1151
**Email**:        annie@kennedytrust.org.uk
**Website**:    www.kennedytrust.org.uk
**Contact**:    Ms Annie Thomas, Secretary

As part of the British national memorial to President Kennedy, the Kennedy Memorial Trust awards scholarships to British postgraduate students for study at Harvard University or the Massachusetts Institute of Technology. The awards are offered annually following a national competition and cover tuition costs and a stipend to meet living expenses.

## Kennedy Scholarships

**Subjects**: Kennedy Scholarships are tenable across the range of graduate programs offered at both Harvard University and the Massachusetts Institute of Technology.
**Purpose**: Kennedy Scholarships are the UK's living memorial to President Kennedy. They are offered annually to enable British citizens who are graduates of UK universities to take graduate programs at Harvard University and the Massachusetts Institute of Technology.
**Eligibility**: Applicants must be British citizens who are, or will be, graduates of a UK university by the time of taking up the award. Applicants must have commenced their undergraduate studies no earlier than ten years prior to September 1st of year in which their intended postgraduate studies will begin.
**Level of Study**: Doctorate, Graduate, Predoctorate, Professional development, Postgraduate (MSc)
**Type**: Scholarship
**Value**: Full tuition fees and health insurance plus a means-tested stipend for living expenses.
**Length of Study**: Typically one full academic year, starting in the Fall
**Frequency**: Annual
**Study Establishment**: Harvard University; Massachusetts Institute of Technology
**Country of Study**: United States of America
**Application Procedure**: Applications are made online and comprise a personal statement, an academic and professional history and the contact details for 2 referees who will be contacted automatically. See the website for full information.
**No. of awards offered**: 10
**Closing Date**: October
**Funding**: Private

**Contributor**: The Kennedy Memorial Trust is a British charity, dependent upon charitable donations
**No. of awards given last year**: 10
**No. of applicants last year**: 160
**Additional Information**: www.kennedytrust.org.uk/display.aspx?id=1848&pid=283

### For further information contact:

Kennedy Memorial Trust, 3 Birdcage Walk, London, SW1H 9JJ, United Kingdom.

**Tel**:            (44) 207 2221151
**Email**:        emily@kennedytrust.org.uk

# Kidney Health Australia

Level 1, 25 North Terrace, GPO Box 9993, Adelaide, SA 5001, Australia.

**Tel**:            (61) 8 8334 7555
**Email**:        research@kidney.org.au
**Website**:    www.kidney.org.au
**Contact**:    Medical Director's Office

Founded in 1968, the Australian Kidney Foundation's mission is to be recognized as the leading non-profit national organization providing funding for, and taking the initiative in, the prevention of kidney and urinary tract diseases.

## Australian Kidney Foundation Biomedical Scholarships

**Purpose**: To provide scholarships for individuals wishing to study full-time for the research degrees
**Eligibility**: Open to Australian applicants who are graduates, or proposing to graduate in the current academic year. Part-time students are not eligible
**Level of Study**: Doctorate, Postgraduate
**Type**: Scholarship
**Value**: AU$24,000 for science and AU$35,000 for medical
**Length of Study**: 2 or 3 years
**Frequency**: Annual
**Country of Study**: Any country
**Closing Date**: 31 August
**Contributor**: Kidney Health Australia

### For further information contact:

Kidney Health Australia, GPO Box 9993, Adelaide, SA 5001, Australia.

## Australian Kidney Foundation Medical Research Grants and Scholarships

**Purpose**: To support medical research
**Eligibility**: Open to Australian citizens who are graduates of Australian medical schools or overseas graduates who are eligible for Australian citizenship and for registration as medical practitioners in Australia
**Level of Study**: Doctorate, Postgraduate
**Type**: Scholarship
**Value**: Please contact the organization
**Length of Study**: Up to 3 years
**Frequency**: Annual
**Study Establishment**: Any approved medical centre, university or research institute
**Country of Study**: Australia
**Application Procedure**: See guidelines in website
**Closing Date**: 31 August
**Additional Information**: Please see the website for further details www.kidney.org.au/HealthProfessionals/MedicalResearchFunding/tabid/633/Default.aspx

## Investigator Driven Research Grants and Scholars

**Purpose**: To award investigators who have applied to the NHMRC for funding but have just missed the cut-off mark
**Eligibility**: Open to projects that are ranked as worthy of funding
**Type**: Scholarship
**Frequency**: Annual
**Country of Study**: Any country
**Contributor**: Kidney Health Australia

## Kidney Research United Kingdom

Nene Hall, Lynch Wood Park, Cambridgeshire, Peterborough, PE2 6FZ, United Kingdom.

**Tel**: (44) 300 303 1100
**Email**: grants@kidneyresearchuk.org
**Website**: www.kidneyresearchuk.org
**Contact**: Mrs Elaine Davies, Director of Research Operations

Kidney Research United Kingdom aims to advance and promote research into kidney and renal disease. These may include epidemiological, clinical or biological approaches to relevant problems. All research must be carried out in the United Kingdom.

## Allied Health Professional Fellowship (clinical)

**Purpose**: To enable nurses and allied health professionals to undertake a renal research study and obtain a higher degree (Masters, DPhil or PhD)
**Eligibility**: Open to nurses and allied health professionals to undertake a renal research study with the object of obtaining a higher degree (Masters, DPhil or PhD). Work and employment must be in the United Kingdom
**Level of Study**: Doctorate, Postdoctorate, Postgraduate
**Value**: The salary will be based on the appropriate NHS or university scale, and an allowance for consumables and higher degree fees is included
**Length of Study**: 3 years at full time or 5 years at part time
**Frequency**: Annual
**Country of Study**: Any country
**Application Procedure**: Applicants must complete an online application
**Closing Date**: November

## King's College London

King's College London, Strand, London, WC2R 2LS, United Kingdom.

**Email**: funding@kcl.ac.uk

### Bosco Tso & Emily Ng Scholarship

**Purpose**: The scholarship is intended to help support the winner with the cost of tuition fees and living expenses whilst studying
**Eligibility**: Eligible students must be: 1. be undertaking the 1 year LLM Law programme at King's. 2. be able to demonstrate a need for financial assistance. 3. have provided a written personal statement. 4. be willing to provide an end of year report and a letter of thanks to the donor. There are few more conditions being implied for the scholarship. The award of a scholarship to an offer-holder will be conditional upon: 1. the offer-holder accepting a place on the King's LLM programme and 2. the fulfilment by the offer-holder of all conditions, both academic and English Language, attached to his or her offer of a place at King's by 10 July
**Level of Study**: Graduate, Professional development
**Type**: Scholarship
**Value**: £22,500 (European Union/International) which intended towards tuition fees and others
**Frequency**: Annual
**Country of Study**: Any country

**Application Procedure**: Kindly access the application form with the below link. www.kcl.ac.uk/study/assets/pdf/fees-and-funding/postgraduate/bosco-tso-emily-ng-scholarship-2019.pdf

**Closing Date**: 12 April

**Funding**: Private

**Additional Information**: www.kcl.ac.uk/study/postgradu ate/fees-and-funding/student-funding/postgraduate-taught-funding/2019-20/bosco-tso-emily-ng-scholarship

### For further information contact:

King's College London, Strand, London, WC2R 2LS, United Kingdom.

## Claire Godfrey Postgraduate Fund

**Purpose**: The objective of the fund is to support postgraduate students at King's who are suffering unexpected, study-related, financial hardship

**Eligibility**: The fund is open to all home postgraduate students in financial hardship. All applicants will have to submit documentary evidence with their applications to verify their financial status

**Level of Study**: Postgraduate

**Type**: Funding support

**Frequency**: Annual

**Country of Study**: Any country

**Application Procedure**: To apply, you should download the form here. www.kcl.ac.uk/study/assets/pdf/fees-and-funding/postgraduate/claire-godfrey-postgraduate-fund.pdf

**Closing Date**: 30 April

**Funding**: Private

**Additional Information**: All applicants will be notified of the outcome of their application in May. The successful applicant will also receive payment at that time www.kcl.ac.uk/study/assets/pdf/fees-and-funding/postgraduate/claire-godfrey-postgraduate-fund.pdf

### For further information contact:

King's College London, Strand, London, WC2R 2LS, United Kingdom.

## King's China Council Scholarships

**Purpose**: King's College London and the China Scholarship Council (CSC) hold an agreement to jointly fund PhD students to pursue research degrees at King's College London.

**Type**: Scholarship

**Value**: Up to £100,000

**Closing Date**: 5 January

**Additional Information**: www.kcl.ac.uk/study/doctoral-studies/funding

## King's-HKU Joint PhD Scholarship

**Purpose**: King's College London ranked amongst some of the world's most prestigious universities. It is the research-intensive university with a global reputation for academic discovery and teaching. King's is in the top seven United Kingdom universities for research

**Eligibility**: 1. Be due to commence a full-time joint PhD programme run in collaboration between King's College London and the University of Hong Kong during the academic year. 2. Have applied to King's College London as the home institution. 3. Have submitted all the required application materials by the funding deadline

**Level of Study**: Postgraduate

**Type**: Scholarship

**Value**: £1,500

**Length of Study**: 4 year

**Frequency**: Annual

**Country of Study**: Any country

**Closing Date**: 31 May

**Funding**: International office

**Additional Information**: scholarship-positions.com/kings-hku-joint-phd-scholarship-for-international-students-in-the-uk/2019/03/11/

### For further information contact:

**Tel**:      (44) 20 7848 4568
**Email**:   doctoralstudies@kcl.ac.uk

## Norman Spink Scholarship

**Purpose**: The Norman Spink Scholarship Fund is a fund to help support all students who are able to demonstrate need of financial assistance, to undertake the one year LLM Law programme at King's specifically related to Tax Law

**Eligibility**: Eligible students must: 1. be undertaking the 1 year LLM Law programme at King's. 2. be undertaking the LLM (Tax Law Pathway). 3. be able to demonstrate a need for financial assistance. 4. have provided a written personal statement. 5. be willing to provide an end of year report and a letter of thanks to the estate of the donor. 6. Applicants must have a confirmed place to study the one year LLM Law programme at King's in September. 7. be willing to provide an end of year report and a letter of thanks to the estate of the donor

**Level of Study**: Postgraduate

**Type**: Scholarship

**Value**: £10,000 will be awarded for European Union students

**Frequency**: Annual

**Country of Study**: Any country

**Application Procedure**: Provided your application form has been accurately completed and the appropriate documentary evidence supplied, you will be notified of the decision during June. 1. The award of a scholarship to an offer-holder will be conditional upon: the offer-holder accepting a place on the King's LLM programme and. 2. the fulfilment by the offer-holder of all conditions, both academic and English Language, attached to his or her offer of a place at King's by 10 July

**Closing Date**: 12 April

**Funding**: Private

**Additional Information**: www.kcl.ac.uk/study/assets/pdf/fees-and-funding/postgraduate/norman-spink-scholarship-2019.pdf

### For further information contact:

**Tel**:   (44) 20 7848 4204

## Santander Masters Scholarship

**Purpose**: King's will be offering one scholarship per Faculty to an eligible international student starting a postgraduate taught programme in September. Students may be undertaking study in any discipline

**Eligibility**: Eligible applicants must meet the following criteria: 1. At the time of application, be a permanent resident of and ordinarily resident in one of the following Santander Network countries for at least 3 years prior to the start of the programme: Belgium, Italy, France, Germany, Poland, Portugal, Spain and the United Kingdom. 2. Be undertaking a full-time postgraduate taught Masters degree programme, commencing September. 3. Hold a conditional or unconditional offer of a place on the relevant programme. 4. Have applied to King's no later than 31 March. 5. Fulfil the relevant academic and English Language proficiency requirements set by King's. 6. Complete and submit the necessary scholarship application form and supporting documentation by the stated deadline of 15 May

**Level of Study**: Postgraduate

**Type**: Scholarship

**Value**: £5,000

**Length of Study**: 1 year

**Frequency**: Annual

**Country of Study**: Any country

**Application Procedure**: In order to be considered for an award, candidates must: 1. Submit a complete online admissions application (via apply.kcl.ac.uk/)

**No. of awards offered**: 4

**Closing Date**: 30 January

**Funding**: Private

**Additional Information**: www.st-andrews.ac.uk/study/fees-and-funding/postgraduate/scholarships/santander-taught/

### For further information contact:

King's College London Strand, London, WC2R 2LS, United Kingdom.

**Tel**:   (44) 1334 46 2254

## STEM Education Teacher Scholarship

**Purpose**: The STEM Education Teacher Scholarship is funded by Wipro Limited, a leading global information technology, consulting and business process services company

**Eligibility**: To be considered for a scholarship, on time of application, applicants MUST: 1. Work in a state-funded school in United Kingdom (e.g. comprehensive, academy, free school). Including, primary, secondary and FE-levels. 2. Be a specialist teacher in: Science, Mathematics, Computer Science or Geography. 3. Have completed, or is completing, their NQT year. 4. Have submitted an application for the MA in STEM Education

**Level of Study**: Professional development

**Type**: Scholarship

**Value**: 70% of the total fees

**Frequency**: Annual

**Country of Study**: Any country

**Closing Date**: 28 April

**Funding**: Private

**Additional Information**: www.kcl.ac.uk/study/postgraduate/fees-and-funding/student-funding/postgraduate-taught-funding/2019-20/stem-education-teacher-scholarship2019

### For further information contact:

King's College London, Strand, London, WC2R 2LS, United Kingdom.

## Kingdom of the Netherlands

### Small Scale Support Program and Accountability Fund

**Purpose**: It support projects in countries with which the Netherlands does not have a development cooperation relationship, such as India

**Eligibility**: The Embassy receives a large number of project applications whereas the budget available is sufficient to support only a limited number of projects. Check the website link for further communication.

**Level of Study**: Graduate
**Type**: Funding support
**Frequency**: Annual
**Country of Study**: Any country
**Application Procedure**: If your organization is working in India and provided that your project complies with the above mentioned criteria and is eligible to apply, please fill in the SSSP form. Organizations from Nepal and Bhutan, and projects in India with a focus on lobbying and advocacy have to use the Accountability form
**Closing Date**: 31 January
**Funding**: Private
**Additional Information**: www.netherlandsandyou.nl/your-country-and-the-netherlands/india/and-the-netherlands/small-scale-support-program

**For further information contact:**

**Email**:    NDE-Projects@minbuza.nl

# Kingston University

River House, 53–57 High Street, Kingston upon Thames, Surrey, KT1 1LQ, United Kingdom.

**Tel**:        (44) 20 8417 9000
**Contact**:   Kingston University

The university's aim is to be internationally recognized for a creative approach to education that has practical outcomes which benefit people and communities.

## Annual Fund Postgraduate Scholarships

**Purpose**: The aim is to encourage academic excellence and allow talented young graduates to continue to higher levels of learning and research, by offering a reduction in course fees for the most academically able applicants
**Eligibility**: Have already received an offer of a place to study at Kingston on an eligible course. Have first-class honours in a previous degree, or high 2:1 with additional evidence of academic excellence. Assessed as having Home/European Union fee status (not Overseas fee status). Students from outside the United Kingdom need to meet Kingston University's English language requirements – these depend on the course they are applying for
**Level of Study**: Postgraduate
**Type**: Scholarship

**Value**: The scholarship offers a £3,000 (full time) or £1,500 (part-time) reduction in annual course fees
**Length of Study**: Up to 2 years full time or 4 years part time
**Frequency**: Annual
**Study Establishment**: Kingston University
**Country of Study**: United Kingdom
**Application Procedure**: Completed application form 1. Academic letters of reference. 2. Copy of academic transcripts. 3. Copies of any certificates relevant to prizes or awards
**No. of awards offered**: 60
**Closing Date**: 26 July
**Funding**: Individuals
**Contributor**: Alumni of Kingston University
**Additional Information**: For more details, see the website: www.kingston.ac.uk/postgraduate/fees-and-funding/funding-your-course/scholarships/annual-fund-scholarship/

**For further information contact:**

**Tel**:        (44) 20 8417 3299
**Email**:    development@kingston.ac.uk

# Klynveld Peat Marwick Goerdeler Foundation

3 Chestnut Ridge Road, Montvale, NJ 07645, United States of America.

**Tel**:        (1) 201 307 7932
**Email**:    acenglish@kpmg.com
**Website**:   www.kpmgfoundation.org
**Contact**:   Anita C. English, Scholarship Administrator

## American Institute of Certified Public Accountants Fellowship for Minority Doctoral Students

**Purpose**: The AICPA Fellowship for Minority Doctoral Students ensures that CPAs of diverse backgrounds are visible in college and university classrooms. The program's goal is to increase the number of minority CPAs who serve as role models and mentors to young people in the academic environment and university classrooms
**Eligibility**: a) Applied to a PhD program and awaiting word on acceptance; b) been accepted into a PhD program; or c) already matriculated in a doctoral program and pursuing appropriate coursework; Earned a Master's Degree and/or completed at least 3 years of full-time experience in the accounting practice; 1. Minority student of Black or African American; Hispanic or Latino; or Native American ethnicity or Alaska Native; Native Hawaiian or Pacific Islander

ethnicity. 2. Attend school on a full-time basis and plan to remain enrolled full-time until attaining PhD 3. Agree not to work full-time in a paid position or accept responsibility for teaching more than one course per semester as a teaching assistant, or dedicate more than one quarter of my time as a research assistant

**Level of Study**: Doctorate
**Type**: Scholarship
**Value**: US$10,000 per year, renewable for a total of 5 years
**Length of Study**: Up to 5 years
**Frequency**: Annual
**Study Establishment**: A full-time AACSB-accredited university
**Country of Study**: United States of America
**Application Procedure**: Applicants must visit the website for further information and application forms
**Closing Date**: 15 May
**Funding**: Private
**Additional Information**: The awards are to be announced in May www.thiswaytocpa.com/education/scholarship-search/fellowship-minority-doctoral-students/

**For further information contact:**

**Email**:    academics@aicpa.org

# Korea Foundation

Fellowship Programme, 10th Floor, Diplomatic Center Building, 1376-1 Seocho-2-dong, Seocho-gu, Seoul 137-863, Korea.

**Tel**:        (82) 2 3463 5614
**Email**:     fellow@kf.or.kr
**Website**:   www.kf.or.kr
**Contact**:   Ms Bo Myung KIM, Programme Officer

The Korea Foundation seeks to improve awareness and understanding of Korea worldwide as well as to foster co-operative relationships between Korea and foreign countries through a variety of exchange programmes.

## Korea Foundation Fellowship for Field Research

**Purpose**: To promote Korean studies and support professional researchers in Korean studies by facilitating their research activities in Korea
**Eligibility**: Open to university professors and instructors, doctoral candidates, researchers and other professionals.

Candidates must be proficient in Korean or English. In the case of Korean nationals, only those with foreign residency status and regular faculty positions at foreign universities are eligible to apply. Fellows in this programme must concentrate on their research and may not enrol in any language courses or other university courses during the fellowship period. Candidates who are receiving support from other organizations or programmes administered by the Korea Foundation are not eligible to receive this fellowship at the same time
**Level of Study**: Doctorate, Postdoctorate, Professional development, Research
**Type**: Fellowship
**Value**: Monthly stipend of KRW 2,000,000 to KRW 3,000,000
**Length of Study**: 1 month-12month
**Frequency**: Annual
**Country of Study**: Korea
**Application Procedure**: Applicants must complete an application form. Application forms are available from the Foundation and the website
**No. of awards offered**: 30
**Closing Date**: 31 July
**Additional Information**: en.kf.or.kr/?menuno=3795

**For further information contact:**

**Email**:    hklee@kf.or.kr

## Korea Foundation Fellowship for Korean Language Training

**Purpose**: To provide foreign scholars and graduate students who need systematic Korean language education with the opportunity to enrol in a Korean language programme at a language institute affiliated to a Korean university
**Eligibility**: Candidates must have a basic knowledge of, and an ability to communicate in, the Korean language. In the case of Korean nationals, only those with foreign residency status are eligible to apply. Candidates who are receiving support from other organizations or programmes administered by the Korea Foundation are not eligible to receive this fellowship at the same time
**Level of Study**: Graduate, Postgraduate
**Type**: Fellowship
**Value**: (1) Living expenses (monthly basis), (2) Travel allowance: KRW 300,000 (one-time benefit)
**Length of Study**: 6 months
**Frequency**: Annual
**Study Establishment**: A language institute affiliated to a Korean university
**Country of Study**: Korea

**Application Procedure**: Applicants must complete an application form are available from the Korean Foundation. Applicants must request an application form by supplying their curriculum vitae along with details of their including Korean language ability and previous study of Korean

**No. of awards offered**: 40

**Closing Date**: 31 May

**Additional Information**: en.kf.or.kr/?menuno=3792

### For further information contact:

**Email**:   koreanstudies@isop.ucla.edu

## Korea Foundation Postdoctoral Fellowship

**Purpose**: To provide promising and highly qualified PhD recipients with the opportunity to conduct research at leading universities in the field of Korean studies so that they can further develop their scholarship as well as have their dissertations published as manuscripts

**Eligibility**: Open to non-Korean scholars who have received a PhD degree in a subject related to Korea within 5 years of their application, but do not currently hold a regular faculty position. Korean nationals with permanent resident status in foreign countries may apply. Candidates who are receiving support from other programmes administered by the Korea Foundation are not eligible to receive this fellowship at the same time

**Level of Study**: Postdoctorate

**Type**: Fellowship

**Value**: Stipend support for a 1-year period, of an amount to be determined based on the country, region and institution where the Fellow will conduct his or her research

**Length of Study**: 1 year

**Frequency**: Annual

**Country of Study**: Any country

**Application Procedure**: You will need to email a separate KI Korea Foundation application by the KI deadline, as well as, complete and submit the Korea Foundation application via the KF online portal by the Korea Foundation deadline. Be sure to verify and confirm the specific KF deadline by visiting the Korea Foundation website: Complete application form must have the following details. For further information, check with the below link. www.kf.or.kr/

**No. of awards offered**: 10

**Closing Date**: 7 January

**Additional Information**: en.kf.or.kr/?menuno=3794

### For further information contact:

CGIS South Building, Second Floor, 1730, Cambridge Street, Cambridge, MA 02138, United Kingdom.

**Tel**:   (44) 617 496 2141

**Email**:   cglover@fas.harvard.edu

## Kosciuszko Foundation

The Kosciuszko Foundation, Inc., 15 East 65th Street, New York, NY 10065, United States of America.

**Tel**:        (1) 212 734 2130
**Email**:     addy@thekf.org
**Website**:   www.thekf.org

The Kosciuszko Foundation, founded in 1925, is dedicated to promoting educational and cultural relations between the United States of America and Poland and increasing American awareness of Polish culture and history. In addition to its grants and scholarships, which total US$1,000,000 annually, the Foundation presents cultural programmes including lectures, concerts and exhibitions, promotes Polish culture in the United States of America and nurtures the spirit of multicultural co-operation.

## Jozef Tischner Fellowships

**Purpose**: To fund a Polish junior researcher in any academic discipline to work in Vienna on research projects of their choice related to one of the Institute for Human Sciences' (IWM) main research fields

**Eligibility**: Open to Polish citizens, permanent residents of Poland and Polish-American scholars with a recent PhD degree, not older than 35 years

**Level of Study**: Doctorate, Research

**Type**: Fellowship

**Value**: Fellowship and €8,000 stipend to cover accommodation, living expenses, travel, health insurance and incidentals during the stay

**Length of Study**: 6 months

**Frequency**: Annual

**Study Establishment**: The Institute for Human Sciences (IWM)

**Country of Study**: Austria

**Application Procedure**: Applicants must send the application by mail to address below

**Closing Date**: 1 December

**Additional Information**: www.iwm.at/fellowships/tischner/

### For further information contact:

**Fax**:     (1) 313 58 30
**Email**:   fellowships@iwm.at

## Polish National Alliance of Brooklyn, United States of America, Inc. Scholarship

**Purpose**: To fund qualified undergraduate students for full-time studies at accredited colleges and Universities in the United States

**Eligibility**: 1. Must be an undergraduate student 2. Must attend a university or a four-year college 3. Minimum 3.0 GPA 4. Citizenship requirements: US 5. Must study full-time 6. Restricted to residents of New York 7. Must be affiliated with Polish National Alliance 8. Restricted by ethnic heritage: Polish

**Type**: Scholarship

**Value**: US$2,000

**Frequency**: Annual

**Study Establishment**: At accredited colleges and universities in the United States

**Country of Study**: United States of America

**Application Procedure**: Submit application form, US$25 non-refundable application fee and supporting materials to the Kosciuszko foundation. E-mailed and faxed materials will not be considered

**Closing Date**: 15 January

**Funding**: Private

**No. of awards given last year**: 1

**Additional Information**: www.petersons.com/scholarship/polish-national-alliance-of-brooklyn-usa-inc-scholarship-111_172414.aspx

### For further information contact:

15 East 65th Street, New York, NY 10065, United States of America.

**Tel**:  (1) 212 734 2130

**Email**:  Addy@thekf.org

## Krist Law Firm, P.C

**Email**:  scholarship@houstoninjurylawyer.com

### The Krist Law Firm, P.C. National Scholarship

**Purpose**: Our Houston maritime lawyers are proud to announce that The Krist Law Firm, P.C. will be renewing our annual scholarship of US$10,000 to award an individual student the financial resources to accomplish their educational goals and prepare for future career aspirations!

**Eligibility**: 1. Be a United States citizen or permanent resident. 2. Be accepted to or currently enrolled in an accredited college, university, or graduate program within the United States. 3. Have a cumulative GPA of 3.0 or higher. 4. Demonstrate good character and high initiative

**Level of Study**: Graduate

**Type**: Scholarship

**Value**: US$10,000

**Frequency**: Annual

**Country of Study**: United States of America

**Closing Date**: 31 March

**Funding**: Foundation

## Kungliga Tekniska högskolan Royal Institute of Technology

S-100 44 Stockholm, Sweden.

**Tel**:  (46) 8 790 6000

**Contact**:  KTH Royal Institute of Technology

KTH Royal Institute of Technology is a university in Stockholm, Sweden, specializing in Engineering and Technology, it ranks highest in northern mainland Europe in its academic fields.

### Postdoctoral Scholarship in Solar Fuels at KTH

**Purpose**: A postdoctoral scholarship in Solar Fuels is available at the KTH Royal Institute of Technology

**Eligibility**: Students from Sweden can apply for this scholarship. If English is not your first language then you will need to show that your English language skills are at a high enough level to succeed in your studies

**Type**: Postdoctoral fellowship

**Value**: SEK 25,000 per month

**Country of Study**: Sweden

**Application Procedure**: Apply for this scholarship by e-mail

**Closing Date**: 26 February

**Funding**: Private

**Additional Information**: For more details please contact the website scholarship-positions.com/postdoctoral-scholarship-solar-fuels-kth-sweden/2018/02/19/

### For further information contact:

**Email**:  lichengs@kth.se

## Kurt Weill Foundation for Music

7 East 20th Street, New York, NY 10003, United States of America.

**Tel**:  (1) 212 505 5240

**Email**:  kwfinfo@kwf.org

**Website**:  www.kwf.org

**Contact**:  Ms Elizabeth Blaufox, Assoc. Director of Programs

The Kurt Weill Foundation for Music is a non-profit, private foundation chartered to preserve and perpetuate the legacies of the composer Kurt Weill (1900–1950) and his wife, singer and actress Lotte Lenya (1898–1981). The Foundation awards grants and prizes, sponsors print and online publications, maintains the Weill-Lenya Research Center and administers Weill's copyrights.

## Kurt Weill Prize

**Purpose**: To encourage distinguished scholarship in the disciplines of music, theater, dance, literary criticism and history addressing music theater since 1900 (including opera)
**Eligibility**: Open to nationals of any country
**Level of Study**: Unrestricted

**Type**: Prize
**Value**: US$5,000 for books, US$2,000 for articles
**Frequency**: Every 2 years
**Country of Study**: Any country
**Application Procedure**: Applicants must submit five copies of their published work. Works must have been published within the 2 years preceding the award year. Please visit www.kwf.org
**Closing Date**: 30 April
**Funding**: Private
**Additional Information**: www.kwf.org/pages/kurt-weill-prize.html

### For further information contact:

**Email**:    bsansone@kwf.org

# L

## La Trobe University

Research Services, Melbourne, VIC 3086, Australia.

| | |
|---|---|
| **Tel**: | (61) 3 9479 1976 |
| **Email**: | rgs@latrobe.edu.au |
| **Website** | www.latrobe.edu.au/rgso |
| **Contact** | Manager, Research Students |

La Trobe University is one of the leading research universities in Australia. The University has internationally regarded strengths across a diverse range of disciplines. It offers a detailed and broad research training programme and provides unique access to technology transfer and collaboration with end users of its research and training via its Research and Development Park.

## La Trobe Excellence Scholarships

**Value**: 25% reduction on course fees
**Country of Study**: Australia
**Application Procedure**: For application procedure, please visit www.latrobe.edu.au/contact
**Closing Date**: 1 July
**Additional Information**: www.kent.ac.uk/scholarships/search/FNADALUMNI02

### For further information contact:

**Email**: R.Lumley@latrobe.edu.au

## La Trobe – JSSAHER PhD Scholarship for Indian Students

**Purpose**: The aim of the project is to determine if the University and/or the Hospital have an effect on the microbial communities in the soils around them, including the amount and variation of multi-resistance organisms in the vicinity of the Hospital

**Eligibility**: 1. Indian students are eligible to apply for this scholarship programme. 2. Applicants should have a high level of achievement, including a first class honours degree or postgraduate degree or equivalent. 3. They will also need to fulfil the English language requirements at La Trobe University.
**Value**: La Trobe Research Scholarship for 3.5 years with a value of ₹25,000 per month in years 1 and 2, and ₹28,000 per month in year 3 and the first half of year 4 of candidature, to support your living costs. Opportunity to travel to La Trobe University, Australia for up to 6 months during your candidature, including accessing a travel grant of up to AU$15,000 (pro rata for six months) (upon prior approval)
**Length of Study**: 3.5 years
**Country of Study**: Any country
**Application Procedure**: For further details, please visit www.scholarshipsupdates.com/la-trobe-jssaher-phd-scholarship-for-indian-students-2018/
**Closing Date**: 15 March
**Additional Information**: career.webindia123.com/career/scholarships/scholarships_abroad/la-trobe-jssaher-phd-scholarship-in-life-science-for-indian-students/index.htm

### For further information contact:

Jagadguru Sri Shivarathreeshwara University, JSS Medical Institutions Campus, Sri Shivarathreeshwara Nagara, Mysuru - 570 015, Karnataka, India.

| | |
|---|---|
| **Tel**: | (91) 821 2548416/400 |
| **Fax**: | (91) 821 2548394 |
| **Email**: | admissions@jssuni.edu.in |

## La Trobe – JSSAHER PhD Scholarship in Life Science and Public Health

**Purpose**: The aim of the project is to determine if the University and/or the Hospital have an effect on the microbial communities

© Springer Nature Limited 2020
Palgrave Macmillan (ed.), *The Grants Register 2021*,
https://doi.org/10.1057/978-1-349-95988-4

in the soils around them, including the amount and variation of multi-resistance organisms in the vicinity of the Hospital

**Eligibility**: Indian students are eligible to apply for this scholarship programme. Applicants need to fulfil the English language requirements at La Trobe University

**Value**: La Trobe Research Scholarship for 3.5 years with a value of ₹25,000 per month in years 1 and 2, and ₹28,000 per month in year 3 and the first half of year 4 of candidature, to support your living costs Fee-relief scholarship (LTUFFRS) for up to four years (international candidates). Opportunity to travel to La Trobe University, Australia for up to six months during your candidature, including accessing a travel grant of up to AU$15,000 (pro rata for six months) (upon prior approval). Opportunities to work with outstanding researchers at La Trobe University and JSSAHER, and access to professional development programs through La Trobe's Research and Education Unit

**Study Establishment**: Scholarships are awarded in Life Science and Public Health. The focus of this research project is to analyze and monitor soil samples around JSSAHER and its JSS Hospital in Mysuru, India over the period of three years

**Country of Study**: Any country

**Application Procedure**: 1. Expression of Interest: Send your CV, transcripts, certificates and relevant publications (if any) in a pdf file by email by 29 March 2019. You will be notified of the outcome of your expression of interest by email. 2. Interview: If your expression of interest is successful, you will be invited to an interview with representatives of La Trobe on Skype and JSSAHER in person, separately, during April or early May 2019. Interviews will take place at the JSSAHER campus in Mysuru, India. 3. Invitation to apply: If you are shortlisted for the scholarship, you will be invited to formally apply for both the scholarship and for PhD candidature.

**Closing Date**: 31 March

**Additional Information**: For more details please visit the website scholarship-positions.com/la-trobe-jssaher-phd-scholarship-life-science-public-health-indian-students/2018/03/07/ www.latrobe.edu.au/scholarships/la-trobe-jssaher-phd-scholarship-in-public-health

### For further information contact:

**Email**:   admissions@jssuni.edu.in

## Lancaster University

Student Services, Lancaster University, Bailrigg, Lancaster, LA1 4YW, United Kingdom.

**Tel**:       (44) 1524 65201
**Email**:   studentfunding@lancaster.ac.uk

**Website**:   www.lancs.ac.uk/funding
**Contact**:   Craig Lowe

Lancaster University is a campus university dedicated to excellence in teaching and research, offering a wide range of nationally and internationally recognized postgraduate courses. For updated information on all the University's funding opportunities, please see our website www.lancs.ac.uk/funding

## Alumni Postgraduate Scholarships

**Eligibility**: 1. Hold, or be expected to hold a Bachelor's degree (1 or 2.1), or Master's degree (merit or distinction) from the University of Kent. 2. Hold an offer of a place for a full-time postgraduate research degree at University of Kent for the academic year 2020/21. 3. Demonstrate that they have made a contribution to the wider University community, for example, through Students' Union activities - societies, sports, volunteering - or acting as a student representative on University committees. 4. Have excellent written and oral communication skills and be able to: Explain their research clearly and without jargon to non-experts, Convey their passion for their research to a wider audience, Convince the panel of their research's wider value, Your supporting statement should be no more than two A4 pages. Any statement exceeding this limit will not be accepted. Act as 'ambassadors' for both the University and their subjects. Be prepared to attend an interview in person at Canterbury on Tuesday 5th May.

**Level of Study**: Postgraduate

**Type**: Studentship

**Value**: £1,000

**Frequency**: Annual

**Application Procedure**: In order to apply, you must complete an application form and submit your curriculum vitae and two references

**Closing Date**: 13 April

**Contributor**: Lancaster University Alumni

**Additional Information**: Please see the website for further details www.lums.lancs.ac.uk/masters/funding/ www.lancaster.ac.uk/student-and-education-services/money/funding/cartmel-college-postgraduate-studentship

### For further information contact:

Alumni & Development, Lancaster University, Bailrigg, Lancaster, LA1 4YW, United Kingdom.

**Tel**:       (44) 1524 592556
**Email**:   s.nelhams@lancaster.ac.uk

## Bowland College – Willcock Scholarships

**Purpose**: To provide financial assistance to undergraduate or postgraduate members of Bowland College who are in very good academic standing but who are facing long-term financial or other difficulties which are beyond their control and which jeopardise their continuing or commencing study at Lancaster University

**Eligibility**: All Bowland College students or alumni who would have difficulty achieving their full academic potential because of financial hardship may apply to the scholarship fund

**Level of Study**: Postgraduate

**Type**: Scholarship

**Value**: £2,500

**Frequency**: Annual

**Application Procedure**: Applications should be submitted to the Senior College Advisor

**Closing Date**: 27 April

**Additional Information**: Please see the website for further details www.lusi.lancaster.ac.uk/funding/Detail.aspx?Award ID=12 www.lancaster.ac.uk/student-and-education-services/money/funding/county-college-studentship

### For further information contact:

Bowland College Office, Lancaster University, Bailrigg, Lancaster, LA1 4YW, United Kingdom.

**Tel**:   (44) 1524 594 506
**Email**:   p.m.brown@lancaster.ac.uk

## Cartmel College Scholarships

**Purpose**: Each year, Cartmel College offers a limited number of awards to its present or alumni members who are unable to obtain adequate grants from other bodies

**Eligibility**: All applications will be considered on their merit

**Level of Study**: Postgraduate

**Type**: Scholarship

**Value**: £500

**Length of Study**: Awards are tenable for 1 year

**Frequency**: Annual

**Closing Date**: 1 June

**Additional Information**: www.lancaster.ac.uk/student-and-education-services/money/funding/donald–margot-watt-bursary-fund-fass-only

### For further information contact:

Cartmel College Manager, A22 Cartmel College.

**Email**:   cartmel@lancaster.ac.uk

## County College Scholarships

**Eligibility**: Members of the County College who have completed a Lancaster degree and are proposing to commence postgraduate study at the university are eligible to apply to this scholarship fund. Selections are on the basis of academic merit and financial need

**Level of Study**: Postgraduate

**Type**: Scholarship

**Value**: £1,000

**Length of Study**: Awards are tenable for 1 year

**Frequency**: Annual

**Closing Date**: 1 June

**Additional Information**: Please see the website for further details www.lancaster.ac.uk/linguistics/masters/

## County College Studentship

**Purpose**: To assist prospective students who are unable to obtain adequate grants from other bodies

**Eligibility**: Open to applicants who are past members of County College

**Level of Study**: Postgraduate

**Type**: Studentship

**Value**: £1,000 - two awards can be made each year

**Frequency**: Annual

**Study Establishment**: Lancaster University

**Country of Study**: United Kingdom

**Application Procedure**: Application available from Student Funding Service website

**Closing Date**: 1 June

**Funding**: Government

**Additional Information**: Please see the website for further details www.lancs.ac.uk/colleges/county/tutorial.html www.lancaster.ac.uk/student-and-education-services/money/funding/grizedale-college—travel-award

## Donald & Margot Watt Bursary Fund (FASS Only)

**Purpose**: This fund is to be used to support undergraduate students who run into financial difficulty whilst at University

**Eligibility**: Students will be expected to complete feedback on how the award has assisted them so the information can be used to encourage other donors to support Lancaster students. This fund is for Undergraduate students studying one of the following seven disciplines: Art, Design, English & Creative Writing, History, Philosophy, Religious Studies and Theatre Studies. (Those on joint degree schemes that include one of the specified subjects are also eligible)

**Level of Study**: Postgraduate

**Type**: Funding support
**Value**: Awards amounts of £500, £1,000, £1,500 or £2,000 depending on assessed financial need.
**Frequency**: Annual
**Country of Study**: Any country
**Application Procedure**: Please complete an Donald & Margo Watt Bursary Fund (FASS) application form and submit to The Base, University House. Application has to be processed in the physical format. Form detail is available on the official link. www.lancaster.ac.uk/student-based-services/money/funding/donald–margot-watt-bursary-fund-fass-only
**Funding**: Private
**Additional Information**: www.lancaster.ac.uk/lec/graduate-school/taught-masters/scholarships/

**For further information contact:**

Lancaster University, Bailrigg, Lancaster, LA1 4YW, United Kingdom.

**Tel**:     (44) 152 465 201
**Email**:   ugadmissions@lancaster.ac.uk

## FfWG - Foundation Grants for Women Graduates

**Purpose**: FfWG offers Foundation Grants to help women graduates with their living expenses (not fees) while registered for study or research at an approved institution of higher education in Great Britain. The criteria are the proven needs of the applicant and their academic calibre.
**Eligibility**: Grants are offered to British and overseas students alike at postgraduate level. Any subject or field of study will be considered. There is no upper age limit. Evidence of ability to pay fees is required. Grant holders must submit a written report on their year's work within six weeks of the end of their academic year. The grants will be a contribution only towards the living expenses of one year's academic study or research.
**Level of Study**: Postgraduate, Masters, Research
**Type**: Scholarship
**Value**: The grants are not likely to exceed £4,000. All our grants are offered on a needs basis and therefore not all grants will be for £4,000
**Length of Study**: 1 year
**Additional Information**: www.lancaster.ac.uk/student-and-education-services/money/funding/ffwg—foundation-grants-for-women-graduates

**For further information contact:**

**Email**:   jean.c@blueyonder.co.uk

## Geoffrey Leech Scholarships

**Purpose**: To mark the retirement of Professor Geoffrey Leech, the Department of Linguistics & English Language has established a scholarship fund in his honour
**Eligibility**: The Geoffrey Leech Scholarships are open to applicants who qualify to pay fees at the United Kingdom/European Union-fee rate. The scholarships will be awarded on a competitive basis; details of criteria applied may be found on the departmental website
**Level of Study**: Postgraduate
**Type**: Scholarship
**Value**: Covers the whole of the tuition fee at the appropriate rate
**Frequency**: Annual
**Application Procedure**: In order to be considered for these awards, applicants must write a formal request to be considered for the scholarship, in no more than 500 words to Postgraduate Secretary
**No. of awards offered**: 1
**Closing Date**: 28 February
**Additional Information**: www.lancaster.ac.uk/student-and-education-services/money/funding/the-peel-trust-studentship

**For further information contact:**

**Email**:   postgraduatelinguistics@lancaster.ac.uk

## Grizedale College Awards Fund

**Purpose**: Present and former undergraduate members of the college who wish to commence postgraduate study at Lancaster are eligible to apply for awards from this fund
**Eligibility**: The awards, in the form of grants, are made according to financial circumstances. The intended purpose of any grant awarded and any past or present contribution to college life are also taken into consideration
**Level of Study**: Postgraduate
**Type**: Award
**Value**: Up to £150 (depending on the number of applications received as there is a limit to the total funding available)
**Frequency**: Annual
**Closing Date**: 1 June
**Additional Information**: Please see the website for further details    www.lusi.lancs.ac.uk/funding/Detail.aspx?AwardID=29 lancaster.box.com/v/GrizedaleCollegeCATTravelAward www.lancaster.ac.uk/student-and-education-services/money/funding/lonsdale-college-travel-grant

**For further information contact:**

Grizedale College, Lancaster University, Lancaster, LA1 4YW, United Kingdom.

**Tel**: (44) 1524 592 190
**Email**: b.glass@lancaster.ac.uk

## Heatherlea Bursary

**Purpose**: Heatherlea, one of Britain's leading wildlife-holiday operators, offers one annual bursary of £1,000 to a student applying for and studying on either the MSc in ecology and environment or the MSc in conservation science
**Eligibility**: The Environment Centre will consider suitable candidates automatically so students do not need to apply separately. This award is a bursary and will be awarded on the basis of the financial background/need of the applicant
**Level of Study**: Postgraduate
**Type**: Bursary
**Value**: £1,500
**Frequency**: Annual
**Closing Date**: 31 July
**Additional Information**: Please see the website for further details www.jackierobinson.org/apply/

**For further information contact:**

Postgraduate Studies Office, Lancaster Environment Centre, Library Avenue, Lancaster University, Lancaster, LA1 4YQ, United Kingdom.

**Tel**: (44) 1524 593 478
**Email**: pgadmissions@lancaster.ac.uk

## Lancaster University Peel Studentship Trust

**Purpose**: The awards are available for the support of students for first or higher degrees, in any subject. The period of the award is one academic year, although students can apply each year. The value of the award is determined by the Trustees in each case.
**Eligibility**: A pre-condition of application to the Peel Studentship Trust is that the applicant must be aged 21 or over on the first day of the first term for which they are seeking assistance. Both United Kingdom and non-United Kingdom students can apply for a grant. Applications are assessed on the basis of both academic merit and financial need
**Level of Study**: Postgraduate
**Type**: Studentship
**Value**: Up to £2,500 and paid in three termly instalments dependent on satisfactory academic progression.

**Length of Study**: 1 year
**Frequency**: Annual
**Closing Date**: 22 May
**Contributor**: The Peel Studentship Trust
**Additional Information**: Please see the website for further details www.petersons.com/scholarship/culinary-trust-scholarship-program-for-culinary-study-and-research-111_153818.aspx

## Lonsdale College Travel Grant

**Purpose**: Lonsdale College offers Travel Awards to support undergraduate members of the College who propose to undertake an activity during the Summer vacation. Funds are awarded for voluntary activities which enhance or further your academic studies but which are not a compulsory part of your course. Please note that funds are not made available to final year students.
**Eligibility**: 1. These are cash grants available to assist Lonsdale students in travel projects where academic work would be advanced by such visits. 2. The visits must not be a compulsory part of the student's academic course. The grant will be considered a loan until a written report of 1,000 words has been completed and submitted to the college, no later than the fifth week of the following term
**Level of Study**: Postgraduate
**Type**: Travel grant
**Value**: Up to £250
**Frequency**: Annual
**Country of Study**: Any country
**Application Procedure**: Kindly contact Julie Shorrock for further information. For further information, refer the website link mentioned below. www.lancaster.ac.uk/student-based-services/money/funding/lonsdale-college-travel-grant
**Funding**: Private
**Additional Information**: www.instituteofmedicalethics.org/website/index.php?option=com_content&view=category&id=42&layout=blog&Itemid=17

**For further information contact:**

Julie Shorrock, Lonsdale College, Bailrigg, Lancaster, LA1 4YN, United Kingdom.

**Tel**: (44) 1542 92296

## Postgraduate Access Awards (United Kingdom-Fee Only)

**Purpose**: Lancaster University is intending to offer up to six Postgraduate Access Awards from the Access to Learning Fund

**Eligibility**: Applicants should normally hold at least a 2:1 Honours degree
**Level of Study**: Postgraduate
**Type**: Award
**Value**: £500. These awards are intended to help towards living costs associated with undertaking full-time or part-time postgraduate study (where part-time equals at least 50% of a full-time course). Awards are intended for students not otherwise in receipt of Government funding, but who are able to find finance for the remaining costs of their course
**Frequency**: Annual
**Closing Date**: July
**Contributor**: Access to learning fund
**Additional Information**: Please see the website for further details     www.heritage.edu/student-resources/financial-aid/scholarships/

## Robinson Scholarship

**Purpose**: The Jackie Robinson Foundation provides a multi-faceted experience designed to not only address the financial needs of minority students who aspire to attend college but also to guide them through the process of higher education.
**Eligibility**: As the scholarship will not cover all the costs associated with studying, applicants should explain carefully their financial circumstances. This explanation should cover two aspects. Firstly, why is it that you need funding? Secondly, how will you finance the rest of the cost of your stay in Lancaster?
**Level of Study**: Postgraduate
**Type**: Scholarship
**Value**: £5,000
**Frequency**: Annual
**Country of Study**: Any country
**Application Procedure**: Please see the application details at www.lancs.ac.uk/studentservices/download/forms/
**Closing Date**: 1 February
**Funding**: Private
**Additional Information**: Please see the website for further details  www.lums.lancs.ac.uk/masters/management-science/robinson/     mrc.ukri.org/skills-careers/fellowships/clinical-fellowships/clinical-research-training-fellowship-crtf/

### For further information contact:

Department of Management Science, Lancaster University Management School, Lancaster, LA1 4YX, United Kingdom.

**Email**:     g.rand@lancaster.ac.uk

## Le Cordon Bleu Australia

Days Road, Regency Park, SA 5010, Australia.

**Tel**:          (61) 618 8346 3700/61 8 8348 3000
**Email**:      australia@cordonbleu.edu
**Website**:  www.lecordonbleu.com

Le Cordon Bleu, a global leader hospitality education, provides professional development for existing executives.

## The Culinary Trust Scholarship

**Purpose**: Scholarships provides funds to qualified applicants for beginning, continuing, and specialty education courses at accredited culinary schools worldwide, as well as, independent study for research projects. Applicants must have at least, a minimum 3.0 GPA, must write an essay, submit two letters of recommendation
**Eligibility**: 1. Must be an undergraduate student, a graduate student or a postgraduate student. 2. Must attend a university, a four-year college, two-year college or a vocational-tech school. 3. Minimum 3.0 GPA. 4. Must be at least 18 years old. 4. Both full-time and part-time students. 5. Restricted to students studying Culinary Arts, Food Service/Hospitality, Food Science/Nutrition.
**Level of Study**: Postgraduate
**Type**: Partial scholarship
**Value**: AU$1,000, Low Amount Awarded; AU$5,000, High Amount Awarded; AU$90,000, Total Amount Awarded
**Length of Study**: 6 months
**Frequency**: Annual
**Study Establishment**: Le Cordon Bleu Australia, Adelaide
**Country of Study**: Australia
**Application Procedure**: Application form and full guidelines available from The Culinary Trust website
**Closing Date**: 1 March
**Funding**: Private
**Additional Information**: Scholarship is for partial tuition of the Graduate Certificate only and does not include other fees associated with commencing or continuing with the program www.leukaemia.org.au/research/current-funding-opportunities-2/phd-scholarships-program/

### For further information contact:

PO Box 273, New York, NY 10013, United States of America.

**Tel**:       (1) 888 345 4666
**Fax**:      (1) 888 345 4666
**Email**:   heather@theculinarytrust.org

## Leeds International Pianoforte Competition

Leeds International Piano Competition, The University of Leeds, Leeds, LS2 9JT, United Kingdom.

**Tel:** (44) 1132 446 586
**Email:** pianocompetition@leeds.ac.uk
**Website:** www.leedspiano.com

The Leeds International Pianoforte Competition is a member of the World Federation of International Music Competitions

## Henry Rudolf Meisels Bursary Awards

**Purpose** To award competitors accepted in the first stage of the competition
**Eligibility**: Open to candidates who are accepted to perform in the first stage of the competition
**Level of Study** Professional development
**Type**: Scholarships and fellowships
**Value**: £100
**Length of Study**: Every 3 years
**Frequency**: Every 3 years
**Study Establishment**: The University of Leeds
**Country of Study**: United Kingdom
**Application Procedure**: Entry by competitive audition. Application forms should be submitted by the closing date
**No. of awards offered**: 196
**Closing Date**: 1 February
**Contributor**: Henry Rudolf Meisels Bequest
**No. of awards given last year**: 71
**No. of applicants last year**: 196
**Additional Information**: A non-refundable entrance fee of United Kingdom £50 must be paid no later than 1 February librarycompany.org/academic-programs/fellowships/dissertation/

## Leiden University

Rapenburg 70, NL-2311 EZ Leiden, Netherlands.

**Tel:** (31) 71 527 27 27
**Website:** www.universiteitleiden.nl/

Leiden University was founded in 1575 and is one of Europe's leading international research universities. It has seven faculties in the arts, humanities and sciences, spread over locations in Leiden and The Hague. The University has over 6,700 staff members and 29,520 students. The motto of the University is 'Praesidium Libertatis' - Bastion of Freedom

## Leiden University Excellence Scholarships (LexS)

**Subjects**: All Masters programmes (with the exception of regular LLM (non-advanced) programmes) in the following Faculties: Archaeology, Humanities, Medicine/LUMC, Governance and Global Affairs, Law, Social and Behavioural Sciences, Science, Interfacultair Centrum voor Lerarenopleiding, Onderwijsontwikkeling en Nascholing (ICLON), African Studies Centre, International Institute for Asian Studies
**Purpose**: The Leiden University Excellence Scholarship Programme (LExS) is open to outstanding Non-EU/EEA students enrolling in a full-time master's degree programme at Leiden University.
**Eligibility**: Students must have achieved excellent study results in their previous education, this being relevant to the Master's programme for which they are applying. As an indication, the student is amongst the top 10% of graduates in his/her previous study programme. Note: proof of ranking is not required - this information is purely to indicate the level of competitiveness. Applicants must have a non EEA passport and may not be eligible for support under the Dutch system of study grants and loans (Studiefinanciering).
**Level of Study**: Masters Degree
**Type**: Scholarships
**Value**: The Leiden University Excellence Scholarship programme has 3 awards: 1. €10,000 of the tuition fee 2. €15,000 of the tuition fee 3. Total tuition fee minus the statutory tuition fee
**Frequency**: annual
**Country of Study**: Netherlands
**Application Procedure**: You must first apply online for admissions to a Master's programme at Leiden University. In your application, you must indicate clearly that you would like to apply for the LExS scholarship and upload your letter of motivation for the LExS scholarship on the scholarship page. The deadline for programmes starting in September is 1 February (exception - LLM Advanced Studies programmes: 1 March) while programmes starting in February has a deadline of 1 October. It is important to visit the official website (link found below) to access the online application form and for detailed information on how to apply for this scholarship
**No. of awards offered**: The number and type of award of the scholarship depends on the budget available for each Faculty department.

**Closing Date**: 1 March
**Additional Information**: www.universiteitleiden.nl/en/schol arships/sea/leiden-university-excellence-scholarship-lexs

### For further information contact:

**Email**:    studielijn@leidenuniv.nl

## Leo Baeck Institute (LBI)

15 West 16th Street (Between 5th & 6th Avenues), New York, NY 10011, United States of America.

**Tel**:         (1) 212 744 6400/212 294 8340
**Email**:      lbaeck@lbi.cjh.org
**Website**:    www.lbi.org
**Contact**:    Secretary

The Leo Baeck Institute (LBI) is a research, study and lecture centre, a library and repository for archival and art materials. It is devoted to the preservation of original materials pertaining to the history and culture of German-speaking Jewry.

### John A. S. Grenville PhD Studentship in Modern Jewish History and Culture

**Purpose**: The studentship is named after John A. S. Grenville (1928–2011), an eminent scholar of modern world history and German Jewish history
**Eligibility**: Check details on website
**Level of Study**: Doctorate
**Type**: Studentship
**Value**: The studentship amounts to £24,000 per year, from which tuition fees (Home/European Union students: £3,996 full-time/£1,998 part-time and non-European Union/overseas students: £12,600 full-time/£6,300 part-time) must be paid
**Length of Study**: 3 years
**Frequency**: Annual
**Country of Study**: United Kingdom
**Application Procedure**: Information on how to apply can be found    at    www.history.qmul.ac.uk/postgraduate/research-degrees/how-apply
**Additional Information**: The recipient of this scholarship will be enroled in the doctoral programme at the School of History, Queen Mary, University of London librarycompany. org/academic-programs/fellowships/postdoc/

### For further information contact:

**Email**:    d.wildmann@leobaeck.co.uk

## Lepra Health in Action

28 Middleborough, Essex, Colchester, CO1 1TG, United Kingdom.

**Tel**:         (44) 1206 216 700
**Email**:      lepra@lepra.org.uk
**Website**:    www.lepra.org.uk
**Contact**:    Programmes Department

LEPRA is a health development international organisation working to restore health, hope and dignity to people affected by leprosy and other diseases of poverty such as malaria, tuberculosis and HIV/AIDS, among others. LEPRA is currently working in India.

### Medical Elective Funding and Annual Essay Competition

**Purpose**: To encourage United Kingdom-based medical students wishing to undertake a leprosy assignment overseas
**Eligibility**: Students in the United Kingdom of any nationality. LEPRA would also like to encourage medical students to apply for the annual essay competition
**Level of Study**: Graduate, Postgraduate
**Type**: Grant
**Value**: Dependent on funds available and up to United Kingdom £1,000 fund for essay competition
**Length of Study**: Up to 3 years
**Frequency**: Annual, dependent on funds available
**Study Establishment**: As appropriate to the nature of the research or training
**Country of Study**: Any country
**Application    Procedure**:    Applicants    must    complete a research application pack, available on request. Applications must be submitted using the appropriate forms and should observe the time scales involved in the approval process
**No. of awards offered**: 5
**Funding**: Individuals
**No. of awards given last year**: 5
**No. of applicants last year**: 5
**Additional Information**: Occasionally also funded to physiotherapy students or students taking a BSc in nursing. Please check the website for more details pathwaystoscience.org/ programhub.aspx?sort=PDC-LifeSciences-Fellowship

### For further information contact:

**Email**:    deeptyh@leprahealthinaction.org

# LeTourneau University

2100 S. Mobberly Ave, Longview, TX 75602, United States of America.

| | |
|---|---|
| **Tel**: | (1) 903 233 3000 |
| **Email**: | admissions@james.letu.edu |
| **Contact**: | MBA Admissions Officer |

## Dual Credit Scholarship

**Purpose**: The Dual Credit scholarship cannot be combined with or stacked onto any previously awarded merit based scholarships from LeTourneau

**Eligibility**: 1. Have passed a minimum of one LETU Dual Credit course before graduating high school. 2. Classes offered the summer directly preceding attendance to LETU cannot be used to qualify for this scholarship. 3. Minimum score of 20 on the ACT or 1030 on the SAT. 4. Minimum cumulative high school GPA of 2.5 (on an unweighted 4.0 scale). 5. Enroll full-time in the residential program at the Longview campus

**Level of Study**: Postgraduate

**Type**: Scholarship

**Value**: US$16,000

**Length of Study**: Up to 4 years

**Frequency**: Annual

**Country of Study**: Any country

**Application Procedure**: Submit your online application for admission Send in your official high school transcript Send in your official test result (ACT or SAT) LETU ACT School Code: 4120 LETU SAT School Code: 6365 File your FAFSA to be considered for additional financial aid LETU FAFSA School Code: 003584

**Funding**: Private

**Additional Information**: Application link is as follows: www.letu.edu/admissions/index.html pathwaystoscience.org/programhub.aspx?sort=PDC-LifeSciences-Fellowship

## For further information contact:

| | |
|---|---|
| **Tel**: | (1) 903 233 4334 |
| **Email**: | SharleenHunt@letu.edu |

## Heritage Scholarship

**Purpose**: The Heritage Scholarship competition is designed to find students who will make an academic, spiritual, and personal impact on our campus from orientation through graduation and beyond. This "invitation only" event brings together the top students from all over the globe to LeTourneau University's Longview campus for a time of fun and competition

**Eligibility**: 1. The requirements to be invited to Heritage vary by the school at LeTourneau. 2. We are looking in the range of a 3.6+ GPA, and a score of 28+ composite on the ACT or 1260+ (critical reading plus math)

**Level of Study**: Postgraduate

**Type**: Scholarship

**Value**: US$100,000 over four years

**Length of Study**: Up to four years

**Frequency**: Annual

**Country of Study**: Any country

**Application Procedure**: With regard to the application procedure, kindly contact the director of admissions

**Funding**: Private

**Additional Information**: adastra.org.nz/scholarships/

## For further information contact:

| | |
|---|---|
| **Tel**: | (1) 509 865 8502 |
| **Email**: | financial_aid@heritage.edu |

# Leukaemia & Lymphoma Research

Leukaemia & Lymphoma Research, 39-40 Eagle Street, London, WC1R 4TH, United Kingdom.

| | |
|---|---|
| **Tel**: | (44) 2075 042 200 |
| **Email**: | info@llresearch.org.uk |
| **Website**: | www.llresearch.org.uk |

Leukaemia research is devoted exclusively to leukaemia, Hodgkin's disease and other lymphomas, myeloma, myelodysplastic syndromes, aplastic anaemia and the myeloproliferative disorders. We are committed to finding causes, improving and developing new treatments and diagnostic methods as well as supplying free information booklets and answering written and telephone enquiries.

## The Clinical Research Training Fellowship

**Purpose**: To train registrar grade clinicians in research and allow them to obtain a higher degree

**Eligibility**: Open to researchers of any nationality who work and reside in the United Kingdom

**Level of Study**: Research

**Type**: Fellowship

**Value**: £50,000–£100,000

**Length of Study**: 1–3 years

**Study Establishment**: Universities, medical schools, research institutes and teaching hospitals

**Country of Study**: United Kingdom
**Application Procedure**: Applicants must complete an application form
**Closing Date**: July
**Additional Information**: Please see the website for further details scholarshipdb.net/scholarships-in-New-Zealand/Australian-Institute-Of-Mining-And-Metallurgy-Scholarships-Lincoln-University=J3hEx8J06BGUVQAlkGUTnw.html

**For further information contact:**

**Tel**:       (44) 20 7405 0101
**Email**:    sdarling@lrf.org.uk

# Leukaemia Foundation

P.O.BOX 1025, Lutwyche, QLD 4030, Australia.

**Tel**:       (61) 3 9949 5831
**Email**:    jridge@leukaemia.org.au
**Website**:  www.leukaemia.org.au
**Contact**:  Jacinta Ridge, Mission and Vision Project Officer

The Leukaemia Foundation is the peak body for blood cancers and is dedicated to the care and cure of patients and families living with leukaemia, lymphoma, myeloma and related blood disorders.

## Leukaemia Foundation PhD Scholarships

**Purpose**: The Leukaemia Foundation is helping more medical and science graduates pursue a research career in blood cancer by combining resources and working in partnership with HSANZ to co-fund PhD scholarships.
**Eligibility**: Open to candidates who are citizens or permanent residents of Australia
**Level of Study**: Doctorate
**Type**: Scholarships
**Value**: AU$40,000
**Length of Study**: three-year
**Frequency**: Annual
**Study Establishment**: Research Institution in Australia
**Country of Study**: Australia
**Application Procedure**: Applicants can download the application forms from the website www.leukaemia.com/web/research/fellowships_phd.php
**No. of awards offered**: 22
**Closing Date**: 14 September
**Funding**: Foundation, Trusts

**Contributor**: Leukaemia Foundation
**No. of awards given last year**: 10
**No. of applicants last year**: 22
**Additional Information**: All queries should be directed to Dr Anna Williamson. Please see the website for further details www.leukaemia.com/web/research/researchgrants_applications.php study-uk.britishcouncil.org/scholarships/chevening-scholarship

**For further information contact:**

**Tel**:       1800 620 420
**Email**:    awilliamson@leukaemia.org.au

## Leukaemia Foundation Postdoctoral Fellowship

**Purpose**: To encourage and support young researchers and to foster cutting-edge research to improve the understanding of leukaemia and related malignancies and to benefit patients and families in the short-term or long-term
**Eligibility**: Open to candidates who have obtained a PhD no more than 3 years before the closing date for applications. Their PhD must be obtained by December of the year of application
**Level of Study**: Postdoctorate
**Type**: Fellowship
**Value**: AU$100,000 (75% salary plus 25% consumables) per year
**Frequency**: Annual
**Country of Study**: Australia
**Application Procedure**: Applicants can download the application form from the website
**Closing Date**: 27 July
**Funding**: Foundation
**Contributor**: Leukaemia Foundation
**Additional Information**: www.global-opportunities.net/scholarships-in-new-zealand/

**For further information contact:**

Advocacy and Patient Care, Leukaemia Foundation, National Research Program, PO Box 2126, Windsor, QLD 4030, Australia.

**Email**:    awilliamson@leukaemia.org.au

# Leukemia & Lymphoma Society

## Career Development Program - Fellow

**Subjects**: Leukemia and Lymphoma

**Purpose**: The Leukemia & Lymphoma Society (LLS) offers career development awards to postdoctoral fellows and instructors as well as early-career independent investigators, engaging in basic, clinical, or translational research to help understand and treat hematologic malignancies and relevant premalignant condicitons. Please verify in our Guidelines & Instructions which award is appropriate for your level of experience and apply to that category of the award.

**Eligibility**: You must be a promising investigator with less than 2.5 years of postdoctoral research training. This award encourages you to embark on an academic career involving basic or translational research in hematologic malignancies and/or relevant premalignant conditions under a research sponsor's direction. The proposal must be directly relevant to hematological malignancies and/or relevant pre-malignant conditions. In addition, your Sponsor(s) must be have the appropriate experience to mentor you as you engage in research of direct relevance to blood cancer.

**Type**: Fellowship

**Value**: US$60,000 per year

**Length of Study**: Three years

**Frequency**: Annual

**Country of Study**: Any country

**Application Procedure**: The CDP application will be completed in 3 phases: Eligibility, Abstracts, and Full Application. See online for details

**Closing Date**: 1 May

**Additional Information**: www.lls.org/research/career-development-program

## Career Development Program - Special Fellow

**Subjects**: Leukemia and Lymphoma

**Purpose**: The Leukemia & Lymphoma Society (LLS) offers career development awards to postdoctoral fellows and instructors, as well as early-career independent investigators, engaging in basic, clinical, or translational research to help understand and treat hematologic malignancies and relevant premalignant condicitons.

**Eligibility**: You must be a promising investigator with less than 2.5 years of postdoctoral research training. This award encourages you to embark on an academic career involving basic or translational research in hematologic malignancies and/or relevant premalignant conditions under a research sponsor's direction. The proposal must be directly relevant to hematological malignancies and/or relevant pre-malignant conditions. In addition, your Sponsor(s) must be have the appropriate experience to mentor you as you engage in research of direct relevance to blood cancer.

**Type**: Fellowship

**Value**: US$67,000 per year

**Length of Study**: Two or three years

**Frequency**: Annual

**Country of Study**: Any country

**Application Procedure**: The CDP application will be completed in 3 phases: Eligibility, Abstracts, and Full Application. See online for details.

**Closing Date**: 1 May

**Additional Information**: www.lls.org/research/career-development-program

---

# Leukemia Research Foundation (LRF)

Research Grants Administrator, Leukemia Research Foundation, 191 Waukegan Road, Suite 105, Northfield, IL 60091 1064, United States of America.

| | |
|---|---|
| **Tel**: | (1) 847 424 0600, 888 558 5385 |
| **Email**: | Linda@lrfmail.org |
| **Website**: | www.allbloodcancers.org |
| **Contact**: | Linda Kabot, Director of Programs |

The Leukemia Research Foundation (LRF) was established in 1946. It aims to conquer leukemia, lymphoma and myelodysplastic syndromes by funding research into their causes and cures and to enrich the quality of life of those touched by these diseases.

## Leukemia Research Foundation New Investigator Research Grant

**Purpose**: To enable an investigator to initiate and develop a project sufficiently to obtain continued funding from national agencies

**Eligibility**: Preference given to proposals that focus on leukemia, lymphoma and MDS. New Investigators are considered to be within seven years of their first independent position. Years as a resident physician, fellow physician, or post-doctoral fellow are considered to be training years. Questions regarding eligibility should be directed to our Research Grants Administrator. See the website for details regarding eligibility

**Level of Study**: Postgraduate

**Type**: Grant

**Value**: US$100,000

**Length of Study**: 1 year

**Frequency**: Annual

**Country of Study**: United States of America

**Application Procedure**: Applicants must submit application form, references, self-addressed stamped envelope and one paragraph abstract in lay terms

**No. of awards offered**: 73

**Closing Date**: 17 February
**Funding**: Private
**Contributor**: Leukaemia Research Foundation
**No. of awards given last year**: 10
**No. of applicants last year**: 73
**Additional Information**: Please see the website for further details    www.leukemia-research.org/page.aspx?pid=216 www.lincoln.ac.nz/Study/Qualifications/Qualification/scholar ships/?ScholarshipCode=Business+%26+Professional+Women+ Franklin+Tertiary+Study+Award&ScholarshipCode=Business+ %26+Professional+Women+Franklin+Tertiary+Study+Award

### For further information contact:

Leukemia Research Foundation, 820 Davis Street, Suite #420, IL 60201, United States of America.

**Tel**:       (1) 847 424 0600
**Fax**:      (1) 847 424 0606
**Email**:    Info@LRFMail.org

## Leverhulme Trust

Research Awards Advisory Committee, 1 Pemberton Row, London, EC4A 3BG, United Kingdom.

**Tel**:       (44) 2070 429 861
**Email**:    agrundy@leverhulme.ac.uk
**Website**:  www.leverhulme.ac.uk
**Contact**:  Miss Anna Grundy, Grants Manger

The Trust, established by the Will of William Hesketh Lever, makes awards for the support of research and education. The Trust emphasizes individuals and encompasses all subject areas.

### Study Abroad Studentship

**Purpose**: For students to study or undertake research at a centre of learning in any country except the UK or USA
**Eligibility**: Applicants must: have been resident in the UK for at least three years at the time of application hold an under-graduate degree (undergraduates are not eligible) hold a degree from a UK institution (this may be either the under-graduate degree or a further degree held by the applicant) either be a student at the time of application or have been registered as a student within the last eight years explain why their work requires residence overseas Wish to undertake study or research in any country except the United Kingdom or United States of America.

**Level of Study**: Doctorate, Graduate, Postdoctorate, Post-graduate, Predoctorate, Postgraduate (MSc)
**Type**: Studentship
**Value**: £21,000 for maintenance allowance plus fees, baggage and flight allowance
**Length of Study**: 12-24 months
**Frequency**: Annual
**Country of Study**: Worldwide
**Application Procedure**: The 2021 round of awards will open in early September. Closing date in early January.
**Funding**: Trusts
**Contributor**: The Leverhulme Trust
**No. of awards given last year**: 33
**No. of applicants last year**: 108
**Additional Information**: Further information available here www.leverhulme.ac.uk/study-abroad-studentships

### For further information contact:

The Leverhulme Trust 1 Pemberton Row.

**Tel**:    (44) 2070429862

## Library Company of Philadelphia

1314 Locust Street, Philadelphia, PA 19107, United States of America.

**Tel**:       (1) 215 546 3181
**Email**:    jgreen@librarycompany.org
**Website**:  www.librarycompany.org
**Contact**:  Fellowship Office

Founded in 1731, the Library Company of Philadelphia was the largest public library in America until the 1850s and contains printed materials on aspects of American culture and society in that period. It is a research library with a collection of 500,000 books, pamphlets, newspapers and periodicals, 75,000 prints, maps and photographs and 150,000 manuscripts.

### Library Company of Philadelphia Dissertation Fellowships

**Purpose**: To promote scholarship by offering long-term dissertation fellowships
**Eligibility**: The fellowship Supports dissertation research in the collections of the Library Company and other Philadelphia repositones

**Level of Study**: Doctorate
**Type**: Fellowship
**Value**: US$10,000–US$12,500
**Length of Study**: 4–5 months
**Frequency**: Annual
**Country of Study**: Any country
**Application Procedure**: Candidates are encouraged to enquire about the appropriateness of a proposed topic before applying. See website under fellowships
**No. of awards offered**: 45
**Closing Date**: 1 March
**Funding**: Private
**No. of awards given last year**: 6
**No. of applicants last year**: 45
**Additional Information**: Further Information can be found on the website, which also includes fellowships offered by the Library Company s programmes in early American economy and society and African American History www.growingnz.org.nz/charles-and-ella-elgar-trust-bursaries-scholarship_id-214.html

## Library Company of Philadelphia Postdoctoral Research Fellowship

**Purpose**: To promote scholarship by offering long-term post-doctoral and advanced research fellowships
**Eligibility**: The fellowship supports both postdoctoral and advanced research in the collections of the Library Company and often Philadelphia repositories. Applicants must hold a doctoral degree
**Level of Study**: Postdoctorate, Research
**Type**: Fellowship
**Value**: Stipend is around US$18,900–US$25,000
**Length of Study**: 4.5 months (1 semester)
**Frequency**: Annual
**Study Establishment**: An independent research library
**Country of Study**: United States of America
**Application Procedure**: Candidates are encouraged to enquire about the appropriateness of a proposed topic before applying. See website under fellowships
**No. of awards offered**: 57
**Closing Date**: 1 November
**Funding**: Government, Private
**Contributor**: National Endowment for the Humanities; Andrew W Mellon Foundation
**No. of awards given last year**: 8
**No. of applicants last year**: 57
**Additional Information**: Four of the fellowships are offered by the Library Company's programmes [etc]. Three are supported by the National Endowment for the Humanities www.universitiesnz.ac.nz/scholarships/edward-isabel-kidson-scholarship

**For further information contact:**

**Email**:   jgreen@librarycompany.org

## National Endowment for the Humanities Post-Doctoral Fellowships

**Purpose**: National Endowment for the Humanities Post-Doctoral Fellowships support research in residence at the Library Company on any subject relevant to its collections, which are capable of supporting research in a variety of fields and disciplines relating to the history of America and the Atlantic world form the 17th through the 19th centuries. NEH Fellowships are for individuals who have completed their formal professional training. Consequently, degree candidates and individuals seeking support for work in pursuit of a degree are not eligible to hold NEH-supported fellowships. Advanced degree candidates must have completed all requirements,
**Eligibility**: NEH Fellowships are for individuals who have completed their formal professional training. Consequently, degree candidates and individuals seeking support for work in pursuit of a degree are not eligible to hold NEH-supported fellowships. Advanced degree candidates must have completed all requirements, except for the actual conferral of the degree, by the application deadline
**Level of Study**: Postdoctorate
**Value**: US$5,000 per month
**Length of Study**: four to nine months
**Closing Date**: 1 November
**Additional Information**: librarycompany.org/academic-programs/fellowships/postdoc/

**For further information contact:**

**Tel**:      (1) 215 546 3181
**Email**:   jgreen@librarycompany.org

## Program in Early American Economy and Society (PEAES) Post-Doctoral Fellowships

**Purpose**: The fellowships provide scholars the opportunity to investigate the history of commerce, finance, technology, manufacturing, agriculture, internal improvements, economic policy making and other topics.
**Eligibility**: Applicants may be citizens of any country, and they must hold a PhD.
**Level of Study**: Postdoctorate
**Type**: Fellowships
**Value**: US$20,000
**Closing Date**: 1 September
**Additional Information**: librarycompany.org/academic-programs/fellowships/postdoc/

# Life Sciences Research Foundation (LSRF)

Lewis Thomas Laboratory, Princeton University, Washington Road, Princeton, NJ 08544, United States of America.

**Tel**:        (1) 410 467 2597
**Email**:    sdirenzo@princeton.edu
**Website**:  www.lsrf.org
**Contact**:  Susan DiRenzo, Assistant Director

The Life Sciences Research Foundation (LSRF) solicits monies from industry, foundations and individuals to support postdoctoral fellowships in the life sciences. The LSRF recognizes that discoveries and the application of innovations in biology for the public's good will depend upon the training and support of the highest quality young scientists in the very best research environments. The LSRF awards fellowships across the spectrum of life sciences: biochemistry, cell, developmental, molecular, plant, structural, organismic population and evolutionary biology, endocrinology, immunology, microbiology, neurobiology, physiology and virology.

## Life Sciences Research Foundation

**Purpose**: Three-year fellowships will be awarded on a competitive basis to graduates of medical and graduate schools in the biological sciences holding M.D., PhD, D.V.M. or D.D.S. degrees. Awards will be based solely on the quality of the individual applicant's previous accomplishments, and on the merit of the proposal for postdoctoral research. Persons doing a second postdoc are eligible only if they are transferring to a different supervisor's laboratory and embarking on a new project not connected to their previous research. All U.S. citizens are eligible to apply with no geographic restriction on the laboratory of their choice. Foreign applicants will be eligible for study in U.S. laboratories. LSRF fellows must carry out their research at nonprofit institutions. LSRF fellows may change projects, laboratories, and/or institutions during the fellowship as long as the eligibility rules listed here are not violated. A person holding a faculty appointment is not eligible to apply for an LSRF fellowship
**Eligibility**: Must be post-doctorals with less than five years from time of PhD awarded
**Level of Study**: Postdoctorate
**Type**: One fellowship
**Value**: US$58,000 stipend per year
**Length of Study**: 3 years
**Frequency**: Annual
**Country of Study**: Any country

**Application Procedure**: Application must be completed online
**No. of awards offered**: 800
**Closing Date**: 1 October
**Funding**: Foundation
**No. of awards given last year**: 27
**No. of applicants last year**: 800
**Additional Information**:    monashhealth.org/research/emerging-researcher-fellowships/

## Life Sciences Research Foundation Postdoctoral Fellowships

**Purpose**: Three-year fellowships will be awarded on a competitive basis to graduates of medical and graduate schools in the biological sciences holding M.D., PhD, D.V.M. or D.D.S. degrees. Awards will be based solely on the quality of the individual applicant's previous accomplishments, and on the merit of the proposal for postdoctoral research. Persons doing a second postdoc are eligible only if they are transferring to a different supervisor's laboratory and embarking on a new project not connected to their previous research. All U.S. citizens are eligible to apply with no geographic restriction on the laboratory of their choice. Foreign applicants will be eligible for study in U.S. laboratories. LSRF fellows must carry out their research at nonprofit institutions. LSRF fellows may change projects, laboratories, and/or institutions during the fellowship as long as the eligibility rules listed here are not violated. A person holding a faculty appointment is not eligible to apply for an LSRF fellowship.
**Eligibility**: Open to researchers of any nationality, who are graduates of medical or graduate schools in the biological sciences and who hold an MD or PhD degree. Awards will be based solely on the quality of the individual applicant's previous accomplishments and on the merit of the proposal for postdoctoral research
**Level of Study**: Postdoctorate
**Type**: Fellowship
**Value**: US$57,000 per year. The salary scale begins at US$43,000 for a first-year postdoctoral, US$45,000 for a second year, and US$47,000 thereafter. The fellow, not the advisor, will control expenditure of the remainder. It can be used for fringe benefits (up to US$2,000 per year), travel to the host institution, travel to visit the sponsor and to the LSRF annual meeting. However, its main purpose is to support the fellow
**Length of Study**: 3 years
**Frequency**: Annual
**Study Establishment**: Appropriate research institutions
**Country of Study**: Any country
**Application Procedure**: Electronic submission only. Please check website

**No. of awards offered**: 820
**Closing Date**: 1 October
**Funding**: Private
**No. of awards given last year**: 16
**No. of applicants last year**: 820
**Additional Information**: LSRF Fellows must carry out their research at non-profit institutions. The fellowship cannot be used to support research that has any patent commitment or other kind of agreement with a commercial profit-making company. Please see the website for further details www.lsrf.org/resources/resources-detail-view/LSRF-Awards-Postdoctoral-Fellowships www.lincoln.ac.nz/Study/Qualifications/Qualification/Scholarships/?ScholarshipCode=Environment,%20Society%20and%20Design%20Summer%20Scholarships&ScholarshipCode=Environment,%20Society%20and%20Design%20Summer%20Scholarships

## Linacre College

### Carolyn and Franco Gianturco Scholarship in Theoretical Chemistry

**Purpose**: The Department will select a scholarship holder from among all eligible students reading, or intending to read, for a Theoretical Chemistry degree (Theoretical and/or Computational Chemical Physics)
**Level of Study**: Graduate
**Type**: Scholarship
**Length of Study**: Period of fee liability
**Frequency**: Annual
**Country of Study**: Any country
**Funding**: Private
**Additional Information**: www.lincoln.ac.nz/Study/Qualifications/Qualification/Scholarships/?ScholarshipCode=Frank%20Sydenham%20Scholarship&ScholarshipCode=Frank%20Sydenham%20Scholarship

### For further information contact:

St. Cross Road, Oxford, OX1 3JA, United Kingdom.

**Tel**: (44) 1365 271 650
**Email**: support@linacre.ox.ac.uk

### Eldred Scholarship

**Purpose**: The Eldred Scholarship at Linacre College was established in 2012. It funds students from sub-Saharan Africa to study the MSc African Studies at Oxford
**Eligibility**: 1. You should be applying to start the MSc African Studies at Oxford and you must be ordinarily resident in sub-Saharan Africa. 2. You should be intending to return to your country of ordinary residence once your course is completed. Scholarships will be awarded on the basis of academic merit
**Level of Study**: Postgraduate (MSc)
**Type**: Scholarship
**Value**: £7,000. 100% of University and college fees, a grant for living costs and a return flight from your home country to United Kingdom
**Frequency**: Annual
**Country of Study**: Any country
**Application Procedure**: To apply this scholarship you don't need to provide a separated application for applying this scholarship. You are only required to apply the graduate study at the university
**Funding**: Private
**Additional Information**: No extra application necessary. Department will select a scholarship holder among all applicable students www.aut.ac.nz/study/fees-and-scholarships/scholarships-and-awards-at-aut/scholarships-database/detailpage?detailCode=500325&sessionID=26770340&sourceIP=&X_FORWARDED_FOR=

### For further information contact:

13 Bevington Rd, Oxford, OX2 6LH, United Kingdom.

**Email**: african.studies@africa.ox.ac.uk

## Lincoln Memorial University

School of Graduate Studies, Cumberland Gap Parkway, Harrogate, TN 37752, United States of America.

**Tel**: (1) 423 869 6374
**Email**: graduate@inetlmu.lmunet.edu
**Contact**: MBA Admissions Officer

### Fulbright - Platinum Triangle Scholarship in Entrepreneurship

**Purpose**: The Fulbright Platinum Triangle Scholarship in Entrepreneurship is for a talented New Zealander in a knowledge economy-related fields to complete a Masters degree in the United States of America
**Eligibility**: New Zealand Citizen or Permanent Resident Students
**Level of Study**: Postgraduate
**Type**: Award
**Length of Study**: 4 year
**Frequency**: Varies

**Country of Study**: Any country
**Application Procedure**: Apply online: www.fulbright.org.nz
**Closing Date**: 1 August
**Funding**: Foundation
**Additional Information**: www.canterbury.ac.nz/ scholarshipsearch/ScholarshipDetails.aspx?ScholarshipID =6935.1711

**For further information contact:**

**Email**:   info@fulbright.org.nz

## Sasakawa Young Leaders Fellowship Fund Research Scholarship - Masters and PhD

**Purpose**: Applicants must be New Zealand Citizens of Permanent residents and be studying in the fields of Humanities or Social Sciences (or other areas provided the research has a Humanities/Social Science angle)
**Eligibility**: New Zealand Citizen or Permanent Resident Students
**Level of Study**: Postdoctorate
**Type**: Scholarship
**Value**: NZ$25,000
**Frequency**: Annual
**Country of Study**: New Zealand
**Closing Date**: 1 October
**Funding**: Foundation
**Additional Information**: www.growingnz.org.nz/harwood %C2%A0farm-trust-scholarship-scholarship_id-156.html

**For further information contact:**

**Email**:   info@lincoln.ac.nz

## Zespri Innovation Scholarships

**Purpose**: The kiwifruit industry is New Zealand's largest horticultural exporter and Zespri is the leading global kiwifruit marketer. The Zespri Innovation Scholarships are offered to build awareness of the kiwifruit industry as an exciting career option, to encourage further research into kiwifruit and related fields and finally to encourage capability building
**Eligibility**: 1. New Zealand Citizen or Permanent Resident Students. 2. International Students
**Level of Study**: Postgraduate
**Type**: Scholarship
**Value**: Masters NZ$20,000pa (stipend) plus university fees PhD NZ$30,000pa (stipend) plus university fees
**Length of Study**: 1 year
**Frequency**: Annual

**Country of Study**: Any country
**Application Procedure**: Apply online: www.zespri.com/ Pages/InnovationScholarship.aspx
**Closing Date**: 31 July
**Funding**: Foundation
**Additional Information**: www.lincoln.ac.nz/Study/Qualifi cations/Qualification/scholarships/?ScholarshipCode=Heaton+ Rhodes+Scholarship&ScholarshipCode=Heaton+Rhodes Scholarship

**For further information contact:**

Innovation Coordinator, 400 Maunganui Road, PO Box 4043, Mount Maunganui, 3149, New Zealand.

**Email**:   corporate.communications@zespri.com

## Zonta International Canterbury Tertiary Education Scholarship

**Purpose**: In order to assist women for completion of tertiary course of study
**Eligibility**: It is available to New Zealand Citizen who is living in Canterbury or permanent residents
**Level of Study**: Graduate
**Type**: Grant
**Value**: NZ$3,000
**Frequency**: Annual
**Country of Study**: New Zealand
**Application Procedure**: Kindly send the application to the following address as mentioned in address field
**Closing Date**: 10 March
**Funding**: Private
**Additional Information**: Send the application to the secretary of the concern www.universitiesnz.ac.nz/scholarships/ henry-kelsey-scholarship

**For further information contact:**

Zonta International Canterbury Tertiary Education Scholarship, C/- Zonta Club of Christchurch South, PO Box 25196, Christchurch 8144, New Zealand.

**Email**:   info@lincoln.ac.nz

## Linnean Society of New South Wales

PO Box 137, Matraville, NSW 2036, Australia.

**Tel**:        (61) 2 9662 6196
**Email**:    linnsoc@acay.com.au

**Website**: www.acay.com.au/linnsoc
**Contact**: Grants Management Award

The Linnean Society of New South Wales is concerned with the publication of original scientific research papers and the encouragement of scientific research through grants and public lectures.

## The Betty Mayne Scientific Research Fund for Earth Sciences

**Purpose**: The Linnean Society seeks donations from individuals, institutions or organisations sympathetic to the purposes for which the fund is currently being used. All such donations, which are tax-deductible, will be gratefully received by the Linnean Society of New South Wales and used to support original scientific research in Australasia. Give yourself a tax break and help a struggling research student, as most of the funds go to students
**Level of Study**: Postgraduate
**Type**: Grant
**Value**: US$2,500
**Closing Date**: 1 March
**Additional Information**: linneansocietynsw.org.au//Mayne_Fund/Mayne_Fund.html

### For further information contact:

**Email**: secretary@linneansocietynsw.org.au

## The Joyce W. Vickery Research Fund

**Purpose**: Grants from the Joyce W. Vickery Research Fund are intended to support worthy research in those fields of the Biological Sciences that fall within the range of interests of the Society, especially natural history research within Australia.
**Level of Study**: postgraduate and Honours degree
**Type**: Fund
**Value**: Individual grants will not normally exceed US$2,500 for Members and US$1,500 for non-members
**Frequency**: Annual
**Application Procedure**: Applicants should email their signed applications
**Closing Date**: 1 March
**Additional Information**: linneansocietynsw.org.au/Vickery_Fund/Vickery_Fund.html

### For further information contact:

**Email**: secretary@linneansocietynsw.org.au

## Lock Heed Martin

### Lockheed Martin Corporation Scholarship for Freshmen

**Purpose**: Lockheed Martin has launched a new scholarship program to provide opportunities to students who want to build their talents and change the world
**Eligibility**: 1. Applicants must not be receiving full funding for education (tuition, fees, and books or equivalent) from their school or another organization (e.g. members of the Armed Services attending United States military academies, students receiving full reimbursement from an employer). 2. Applicants must be enrolled in a program accredited by ABET. Accreditation information for specific programs is available online at main.abet.org/aps/Accreditedprogramsearch.aspx
**Level of Study**: Graduate
**Type**: Award
**Value**: US$2,000. It Includes travel stipend for the SWE Annual Conference
**Frequency**: Annual
**Country of Study**: Any country
**Application Procedure**: This award is being provided by Society of Women Engineers (SWE). Applicants to the Lockheed Martin STEM Scholarship Program must meet the following eligibility requirements: 1. United States Citizens. 2. Current high school seniors with a cumulative 3.5 or above GPA, or current college freshmen or sophomores with a cumulative 3.0 or above GPA. 3. Planning to enroll full-time at an accredited four-year college or university in the United States
**Closing Date**: 12 March
**Funding**: Private

### For further information contact:

130 East Randolph Street, Suite 3500, Chicago, IL 60601, United States of America.

**Email**: community.relations@lmco.com

## London Goodenough Association of Canada

P.O. Box 5896, STN A, Toronto, ON M5W 1P3, Canada.

**Email**: admin@lgac.ca
**Website**: www.lgac.ca
**Contact**: Brian Cardie, Administrator

The London Goodenough Association of Canada (LGAC) is an association of Canadians who lived as graduate students at Goodebnough College in Mecklenburgh Square, London. The LGAC offers member events and provides a Scholarship Programme for Canadian graduate students studying in London and staying in London House or William Goodenough, the Goodenough College residence halls.

## London Goodenough Association of Canada Scholarship Program

**Purpose**: To support Canadian nationals who wish to pursue their higher studies in London
**Eligibility**: Open to candidates who are full-time students enroled in an accredited graduate programme in London or undertaking theses research in London while enroled elsewhere
**Level of Study**: Postgraduate, Research
**Type**: Scholarships
**Value**: £6,000
**Frequency**: Annual
**Study Establishment**: The London Goodenough Association of Canada
**Country of Study**: United Kingdom
**Application Procedure**: Application form can be downloaded from the website. Candidates must also arrange to have all post-secondary institution transcripts and 3 letters of reference sent to the address below
**Closing Date**: 25 January
**Funding**: Foundation, Individuals
**Additional Information**: For further information contact Dr Kathleen McCrone at the above address. Please see the website for further details www.lgac.ca/scholarships

### For further information contact:

The London Goodenough Association of Canada, Paul Zed, Chair, P.O. Box 5896, STN A, Toronto ON M5W 1P3, Canada.

## London Mathematical Society

De Morgan House, 57-58 Russell Square, London, WC1B 4HS, United Kingdom.

**Tel:** (44) 20 7637 3686
**Email:** lms@lms.ac.uk
**Website:** www.lms.ac.uk

The United Kingdom national learned society for the promotion and extension of mathematical knowledge, by means of publishing, grants, meetings and contribution to national debate on mathematics, research and education.

## Cecil King Travel Scholarship

**Purpose**: To enable a young mathematician of outstanding promise to spend a period of 3 months undertaking study or research overseas
**Eligibility**: Nationals of the United Kingdom or Republic of Ireland, having recently completed a doctoral degree at a United Kingdom. university
**Level of Study**: Postdoctorate, Postgraduate
**Type**: Scholarship
**Value**: £6,000
**Length of Study**: 3 months
**Frequency**: Annual
**Study Establishment**: University or research institute
**Country of Study**: Any country
**Application Procedure**: Application forms are available on request from the society or can be downloaded from the website. Applications should be returned by post or email to Duncan Turton
**No. of awards offered**: 5
**Closing Date**: 31 March
**Funding**: Trusts
**Contributor**: Cecil King Memorial Fund
**No. of awards given last year**: 1
**No. of applicants last year**: 5
**Additional Information**: Please see the website for further details www.lms.ac.uk/prizes/cecil-king-travel-scholarship

### For further information contact:

London Mathematical Society, De Morgan House, 57-58 Russell Square, Holborn, London WC1B 4HS, United Kingdom.

**Email:** ecr.grants@lms.ac.uk

## London Metropolitan University

London Metropolitan University, 166-220 Holloway Road, London, N7 8DB, United Kingdom.

**Tel:** (44) 20 7423 0000
**Email:** info@canoncollins.org.uk
**Website:** www.londonmet.ac.uk

London Metropolitan University is one of Britain's largest universities, which offers a wide variety of courses in a huge range of subject areas. The University aims to provide education and training that will help students to achieve their potential and London to succeed us a world city.

## Canon Collins Trust Scholarships

**Purpose**: The key aim of the Scholarships Programme is to help build the human resources necessary for economic, social and cultural development in the southern African region and to develop an educated and skilled workforce that can benefit the wider community. Canon Collins Trust scholarship holders are thus expected to use the knowledge, training and skills acquired through their studies to contribute positively to the development of their home country

**Eligibility**: Open to nationals of South Africa, Namibia, Botswana, Swaziland, Lesotho, Zimbabwe, Zambia, Malawi, Angola and Mozambique who have been offered admission to the University

**Level of Study**: Postgraduate

**Type**: Scholarship

**Value**: Full-fee or half-fee waiver and support in the form of stipend, fares and books

**Frequency**: Annual

**Study Establishment**: London Metropolitan University

**Country of Study**: United Kingdom

**Application Procedure**: Application should be sent to the Canon Collins Trust and the Trust will forward it to the university. Please see the website to know how to apply. Applications that have been emailed or faxed or those that have been received after the deadline will not be considered

**Closing Date**: 3 March

**Funding**: Trusts

**Contributor**: Cannon Collins Educational Trust and Department of Applied Social Sciences

**Additional Information**: Canon Collins Trust provides scholarships to students from South Africa, Namibia, Botswana, Swaziland, Lesotho, Zimbabwe, Zambia, Malawi, Angola and Mozambique who wish to pursue a postgraduate degree (mainly Master's degrees of one or two years) in either the United Kingdom or South Africa. Please see the website for details www.canoncollins.org.uk/scholarships.html

### For further information contact:

22 The Ivories, 6 Northampton Street, London, N1 2HY, United Kingdom.

**Tel**: (44) 20 7354 1462
**Fax**: (44) 20 7359 4875

## International Students House/London Metropolitan Scholarship Scheme

**Purpose**: To support international students from selected countries with tuition fees and accommodation

**Eligibility**: Open to students from Afghanistan, Armenia, Bhutan, Cameroon, Cuba, East Timor, Gambia, Iran, Indonesia, Jordan, Kazakhstan, Lebanon, Namibia, Nepal, Sri Lanka, Tanzania, Tibet, Uganda, Uzbekistan, Vietnam, and Zimbabwe who have been offered admission to the University

**Level of Study**: Postgraduate, MBA

**Type**: Scholarship

**Value**: Free tuition and accommodation

**Length of Study**: 1–2 years

**Study Establishment**: London Metropolitan University

**Country of Study**: United Kingdom

**Application Procedure**: Please see the website www.londonmet.ac.uk/scholarships

**Closing Date**: 31 October

**Funding**: International office

**Contributor**: International Students House (ISH) and London Metropolitan University

**No. of awards given last year**: 1–5

**Additional Information**: If applicants would like more information about International Students House, please access their website at www.ish.org.uk/

### For further information contact:

Scholarships International Office, London Metropolitan University, 166-220 Holloway Road, London N7 8DB, United Kingdom.

**Email**: scholarships@londonmet.ac.uk

## Savoy Educational Trust Scholarships

**Purpose**: To financially assist students wishing to pursue students in the field of Hospitality and Tourism

**Eligibility**: Open to applicants from any country in the world who have been offered admission to the University

**Level of Study**: Postgraduate

**Type**: Bursary

**Value**: Up to £9,000

**Frequency**: Annual

**Study Establishment**: London Metropolitan University

**Country of Study**: United Kingdom

**Application Procedure**: Please see the website www.londonmet.ac.uk/how

**Closing Date**: 31 October

**Funding**: Trusts

**Contributor**: Savoy Educational Trust

**For further information contact:**

Scholarship Department, c/o Student Recruitment Services, Room 210, London Metropolitan University, London N7 8DB, United Kingdom.

**Email**: epilepsy@savoy-foundation.ca

## The Katrina Mihaere Scholarship

**Purpose**: To honour the memory of Katrina Mihaere, a former London Metropolitan Women's Tennis team member
**Eligibility**: Open to all women tennis players who have been offered admission to the University, with an excellent track record in Women's sports
**Level of Study**: Postgraduate
**Type**: Scholarship
**Value**: Full tuition and accommodation
**Frequency**: Annual
**Study Establishment**: London Metropolitan University
**Country of Study**: United Kingdom
**Application Procedure**: Please see the website www. londonmet.ac.uk/how to apply. Applications that have been emailed or faxed or those that have been received after the deadline will not be considered
**Closing Date**: 31 October

**For further information contact:**

**Email**: i.jennings@londonmet.ac.uk

## The ODASS Scheme

**Purpose**: To financially assist students of high academic merit from developing Commonwealth countries
**Eligibility**: Open to students from developing Commonwealth
**Level of Study**: Postgraduate
**Type**: Scholarship
**Value**: Full tuition fees and living allowance
**Frequency**: Annual
**Study Establishment**: London Metropolitan Society
**Country of Study**: United Kingdom
**Application Procedure**: See the website
**Funding**: Government
**Contributor**: British Government's Aid Programme

**For further information contact:**

22 College Street Suite 300, Toronto. M5G 1K2. Canada.

**Email**: info@acu.ac.uk

# London School of Business & Finance

8/9 Holborn, London, EC1N 2LL, United Kingdom.

**Tel**: (44) 20 7823 2303
**Email**: admissions@lsbf.org.uk
**Website**: www.lsbf.org.uk

## Diversity Scholarship

**Purpose**: To ensure students originate from varied backgrounds creating an opportunity to form global corporate networks
**Eligibility**: Show a proven history of academic excellence. Meet the English requirements of the programme they are applying for. Provide proof of sufficient funds to pay the remaining course fees. Applicants must have already applied for a programme at LSBF. Applicants must be classified as an international student and not residing in the United Kingdom
**Level of Study**: Doctorate, Postgraduate, MBA
**Type**: Scholarship
**Value**: £1,000–8,000 (towards reducing tuition fees, not include a contribution to living costs, travel or other expenses)
**Study Establishment**: London School of Business & Finance
**Country of Study**: United Kingdom
**Closing Date**: 29 January
**Additional Information**: Size of awards vary according to each scholar's circumstances

**For further information contact:**

London School of Business and Finance, Postgraduate Admissions Office, 8/9 Holborn, London, EC1N 2LL, United Kingdom.

**Tel**: (44) 14168002204
**Fax**: (44) 20 7823 2302

## The Royal Bank of Scotland International Scholarship

**Purpose**: It aims at bridging international boundaries by providing Chinese business professionals with an opportunity to study a globally recognized degree in one of the world's financial centres
**Eligibility**: A national of the People's Republic of China, Hong Kong (SAR), Macau (SAR); a graduate with proven academic skills; committed to contribute to the socio-economic development of the People's Republic of China. Established in a career, with a track record of excellence and

achievement, and the prospect of becoming a leader in his/her chosen field; have good English Language skills, as most United Kingdom Higher Education Institutions require a minimum IELTS of 6.5 for admission onto Postgraduate courses; have sufficient funds to meet your tuition fees and living expenses, after taking account of the possible award of the Bank of Scotland International Scholarship

**Level of Study**: Doctorate, Postgraduate, MBA
**Type**: Scholarship
**Value**: Cover tuition fees
**Country of Study**: United Kingdom
**Application Procedure**: Application form available at www.lsbf.org.uk
**Closing Date**: 28 August
**Contributor**: Bank of Scotland

### For further information contact:

**Email**:    info@lsbf.org.uk

## London School of Economics and Political Science (LSE)

The London School of Economics and Political Science, Houghton Street, London, WC2A 2AE, United Kingdom.

**Tel**:        (44) 20 7405 7686
**Email**:    c.s.lee2@lse.ac.uk
**Website**:  www.lse.ac.uk

London School of Economics (LSE) was founded in 1895 by Beatrice and Sidney Webb. LSE has an outstanding reputation for academic excellence. LSE is a world class centre for its concentration of teaching and research across the full range of the social, political and economic sciences.

## CR Parekh Fellowship

**Purpose**: To encourage research that is of social, economic, political and constitutional concern to India
**Eligibility**: Open to established Indian scholars who are below 40 years of age and hold a PhD or comparable qualifications and experience. The fellowship is not intended for students registered for a degree or diploma, nor is it intended for senior academics
**Level of Study**: Doctorate, Research
**Type**: Fellowship
**Value**: £1,500 per month

**Length of Study**: 3 months
**Frequency**: Annual
**Country of Study**: United Kingdom
**Application Procedure**: Applications should include a curriculum vitae and an outline of proposed research and the names and addresses of 2 referees who are familiar with their work, to be contacted by the chairman
**Closing Date**: 13 January
**Additional Information**: Applications will not be accepted via email or fax

### For further information contact:

The Fellowships Selection Committee, Asia Research Center, London School of Economics & Political Science, Houghton Street, London, WC2A 2AE, United Kingdom.

**Email**:    arc@lse.ac.uk

## Sir Ratan Tata Postdoctoral Fellowship

**Purpose**: To encourage research on contemporary social and economic concerns of South Asia
**Eligibility**: Applicants should be scholars in the social sciences with experience of research on South Asia. They should hold a PhD.
**Level of Study**: Research
**Type**: Fellowship
**Value**: £1,750
**Length of Study**: Up to 8 months
**Frequency**: Annual
**Country of Study**: United Kingdom
**Application Procedure**: Applications should include a curriculum vitae and an outline of proposed research and the names and addresses of 2 referees who are familiar with their work, to be contacted by the Chairman. Applications should be addressed to The Fellowships Selection Committee
**Closing Date**: 27 April
**Additional Information**: The fellowship is not intended for students registered for a degree or diploma, nor is it intended for senior academics. Applications will not be accepted via email or fax. Please see the website for further details

### For further information contact:

The Fellowships Selection Committee, India Observatory, London School of Economics & Political Science, Houghton Street, London, WC2A 2AE, United Kingdom.

**Email**:    India.Observatory@lse.ac.uk

# London School of Hygiene & Tropical Medicine - LSHTM

The London School of Hygiene & Tropical Medicine is renowned for its research, postgraduate studies and continuing education in public and global health. We have an annual research income of more than £180 million and are one of the highest-rated research institutions in the UK.

**Tel**: (44) 20 7636 8636
**Website**: www.lshtm.ac.uk/
**Contact**: Keppel Street, London, WC1E 7HT, United Kingdom.

## Jeroen Ensink Memorial Fund Scholarship

**Purpose**: Jeroen Ensink was a Senior Lecturer in Public Health Engineering at the London School of Hygiene & Tropical Medicine (LSHTM) and a Programme Director for the MSc Public Health for Development between 2009 and 2015. Jeroen was passionately committed to a simple cause: improving access to water and sanitation in countries where children continue to die needlessly due to the lack of these basic services. As a researcher and educator, his career crossed many continents, living and working in Asian and African countries, collaborating with numerous universities and international agencies. He was a natural educator and immensely popular with students in whom he invested much time and energy. He provided support and inspiration in equal measure and many of his students are now successful researchers and public health professionals in their own right. Following his death on 29 December 2015, LSHTM established a Memorial Fund in his name to support students from sub-Saharan Africa and South Asia who are committed to improving public health in low- or middle- income countries and wish to undertake the MSc Public Health for Development programme.

**Eligibility**: Applicants for the scholarship must: 1. have been accepted onto the 2020-21 MSc Public Health for Development course; 2. have demonstrated a commitment to WASH (water, sanitation and hygiene); 3. be citizens of the ub-Saharan African or South Asian countries listed above; 4. have lived in one of the abovementioned developing countries and worked in activities related to public health for a minimum of 2 years; and 5. meet the LSHTM's minimum English language proficiency requirements.

**Level of Study**: Postgraduate
**Type**: Scholarsip
**Value**: A full scholarship covers: full-time overseas tuition fees for 2020-21 (including the mandatory field trip fee); flights from the student's home country to the United Kingdom, and return on expiry of the scholarship (to be booked by the Scholarships team in Registry); and a tax free stipend (living allowance) of £17,175.00.

**Country of Study**: UK

**Application Procedure**: Applicants should follow both steps outlined below by the scholarship deadline. Step 1 Submit an application for study for the MSc Public Health for Development, via the LSHTM Admissions portal. Please ensure that all the necessary supporting documents have been uploaded to your study application before the Scholarship deadline. Applicants are encouraged to communicate with their referees as early as possible in the application process, notifying them of this deadline. It is the responsibility of the applicant to ensure that their references have been submitted by the scholarship closing date. Due to the introduction of a GBP 50.00 application fee at LSHTM, applicants are advised to apply early to allow time for this payment to be processed. Until the payment is processed applicants will be unable to submit an application for study. We would therefore recommend that applicants for this funding apply for their study/programme by 15 March in order to ensure that there are no processing delays which could impact on meeting the scholarship deadline. Please note that if you are applying for admission to LSHTM and are accepted, you will be asked to pay a deposit within 28 days. If you are applying for a scholarship at LSHTM, please email the Admissions team within this 28 day period, specifying the name of this scholarship and the expected decision date. This must be repeated for every scholarship for which you are applying. The admissions team will then apply an extension to the deposit deadline to match the decision deadline of the scholarship. Step 2 Submit a Scholarship Application, via the LSHTM's Online Scholarship Application portal, indicating that you are applying for the 2020-21 Jeroen Ensink Memorial Fund Scholarship. As part of this application you should upload: a complete Curriculum Vitae (CV); and a statement of motivation of no more than 1,000 words. Your statement of motivation should address the following: a brief biography of your life and career, clarifying your commitment to WASH; your reasons for choosing the MSc Public Health for Development; and your future plans and ambitions in the field of public health. Applicants must submit both CV and the statement of motivation with their scholarship application to be considered for this funding, even though they may have already submitted a statement with their application for admission. Applicants may choose to tailor this statement for the funding (and therefore submit something different to their standard MSc programme application statement). Applicants should be aware that their application for this scholarship award may be considered alongside the documents submitted for their application to the MSc Public Health for Development programme. If you encounter any technical difficulties whilst using the online scholarships application form, in the first instance please try clearing your browser cache and ensure that you are using the latest version of Chrome, Firefox,

Internet Explorer or Safari. If this does not fix your technical issue, please contact the LSHTM's IT Services team, providing your full name; the scholarship that you are applying for; and the technical issue that you have encountered. Please also attach a screen shot where possible. servicedesk@lshtm.ac.uk. Application notes Each applicant should submit only one Jeroen Ensink MSc Scholarship application. We would therefore encourage applicants to check carefully their online application and attachment before submission, as the first application submitted will be the one considered and there will be no opportunity to upload a statement of motivation or CV after submission. Applicants who have already submitted a completed 2020-21 London-based MSc Public Health for Development application for study and/or have been made an Offer of Admission for the 2020-21 London-based MSc Public Health for Development programme should apply for the scholarship by completing the scholarship application (Step 2 above) and submitting this by the scholarship deadline. Incomplete applications will not be considered for this funding. Incomplete applications include those with missing supplementary documentation at either/both Steps 1 and 2 above. By submitting an application for this funding applicants agree to its terms and conditions.

**Closing Date**: 29 March

**Additional Information**: www.lshtm.ac.uk/study/fees-and-funding/funding-scholarships/2020-21-jeroen-ensink-memorial-fund-scholarship

## London South Bank University

103 Borough Road, London, SE1 0AA, United Kingdom.

**Tel**:      (44) 20 7815 7815
**Email**:    pgscholarships@lsbu.ac.uk
**Website**:  www.lsbu.ac.uk

## Vice-Chancellor's Scholarships

**Purpose**: This prestigious scholarship recognises applications from outstanding students who can demonstrate their skills and commitment to becoming future global leaders

**Eligibility**: 1. Be an international fee-paying undergraduate (including Level 0) or postgraduate taught degree offer holder, enrolling for the first time at Teesside University. 2. Start your course in September 2020. 3. Submit an application for consideration.

**Level of Study**: Graduate, Postgraduate

**Type**: Scholarship

**Value**: £5,000

**Frequency**: Annual

**Application Procedure**: You will be invited to apply online via email after you firmly accept your unconditional or conditional offer to study at LSBU. We recommend you apply for your place at LSBU as soon as possible to ensure you have been made an offer by the scholarship deadline of July

**Closing Date**: 30 April

**Funding**: Individuals

**Contributor**: Donations from alumni and other supporters

## Loren L Zachary Society for the Performing Arts

2250 Gloaming Way, Beverly Hills, CA 90210, United States of America.

**Tel**:       (1) 310 276 2731
**Email**:     info@zacharysociety.org
**Website**:   www.zacharysociety.org
**Contact**:   Mrs Nedra Zachary, President, Director of Competition

The Loren L Zachary Society for the Performing Arts was founded in 1972 by the late Dr Loren L Zachary, and Nedra Zachary. The purpose of the organization is to help further the careers of young opera singers by providing financial assistance and performance opportunities. The annual Loren L Zachary National Vocal Competition, now in its 46 year, has helped launch the International careers of many singers. For a complete list of winners and finalists visit the website.

## Loren L Zachary National Vocal Competition for Young Opera Singers

**Purpose**: To assist in the development of the careers of young opera singers through competitive auditions with monetary awards

**Eligibility**: Competition is open to applicants ages 21–35. Singers must be prepared to pursue a professional operatic stage career, be present for all phases of the Competition, and reside in the United States or Canada

**Level of Study**: Professional development

**Type**: Competition

**Value**: Ranges from US$10,000–US$12,000 for the top winner. US$50,000–US$55,000 is distributed among the finalists and the minimum award ranges from US$1,000 to US$2,000

**Frequency**: Annual

**Study Establishment**: Must be thoroughly trained and be ready to pursue a professional operatic career

**Country of Study**: Any country

**Application Procedure**: Applicants must complete an application form accompanied by a proof of age and an application fee of US$50. For application forms and exact dates, singers should refer to www.zacharysociety.org or send a stamped, self-addressed envelope with letter

**No. of awards offered**: 300

**Closing Date**: 28 February

**Funding**: Private, Trusts, Individuals

**No. of awards given last year**: 10

**No. of applicants last year**: 300

**Additional Information**: All applicants are guaranteed an audition provided application is completed correctly with application fee. Applicants must be present at all phases of the auditions. Recordings are not acceptable. Preliminary and semifinal auditions take place in New York in February, and in Los Angeles in April. The grand finals and awards distribution occurs on 20 May 2018 in Los Angeles, California

### For further information contact:

The Loren L. Zachary Society, 2250 Gloaming Way, Beverly Hills, CA 90210-1717, United States of America.

**Email**: infoz@zacharysociety.org

---

## Los Alamos National Laboratory (LANL)

PO Box 1663, MS P219, Los Alamos, NM 87545, United States of America.

**Tel**: (1) 505 667 4866
**Email**: bmontoya@lanl.gov
**Website**: www.lanl.gov

Los Alamos National Laboratory (LANL) is the largest institution in Northern New Mexico with more than 9,000 employees plus approximately 650 contractor personnel. From its origins as a secret Manhattan Project Laboratory, Los Alamos has attracted world-class scientists and applied their energy and creativity to solving the nation's most challenging problems.

### Los Alamos Graduate Research Assistant Program

**Purpose**: To provide students with relevant research experience while they are pursuing a graduate degree

**Eligibility**: Applicant must be a graduate

**Level of Study**: Doctorate, Research

**Type**: Research

**Value**: US$33,300–44,600, including benefits, travel and moving expenses

**Length of Study**: Year or less

**Frequency**: Annual

**Country of Study**: Any country

**Additional Information**: For further inquiries contact Brenda Montoya, 505/667 4866, bmontoya@lanl.gov

### For further information contact:

**Email**: errobinson@lanl.gov

---

## Loughborough University

Leicestershire LE11 3TU, United Kingdom.

**Tel**: (44) 1509 222 222
**Email**: international-office@lboro.ac.uk
**Website**: www.lboro.ac.uk

With 3,000 staff and 12,000 students Loughbrough, with its impressive 410 acre campus, is one of the largest university's in the United Kingdom. Our mission is to increase knowledge through research, provide the highest quality of educational experience and the widest opportunities for students, advance industry and the profession, and benefit society.

### Aziz Foundation Scholarships

**Purpose**: These scholarships aim to develop and empower graduates to bring positive change to British Muslim communites and beyond. They are designed to foster future leaders who aspire to make a positive contribution to society, raising aspirations and standards, and facilitating better representation of Muslim communities in civil society.

**Eligibility**: 1. have applied for a master's level programme (PGCE, PGDip and PGCert programmes are not considered) starting in the 2020/21 academic year. 2. dedicated to bettering Muslim communities and wider society. 3. experiencing financial barriers to pursing further study. 4. pursue a course that will benefit your career prospects and/or assist in the development of your current career geared towards community service. 5. willing to advocate on behalf of communities. 6. qualify for UK/EU tuition fee status.

**Level of Study**: Postgraduate

**Type**: Scholarship

**Value**: The Aziz Foundation is offering UK students 100% tuition fee scholarships for master's study at Loughborough University

**Study Establishment**: Loughborough University

**Country of Study**: United Kingdom

**Closing Date**: 1 June

**Additional Information**: www.lboro.ac.uk/study/postgradu ate/fees-funding/masters-funding/aziz-foundation-scholarships/

**For further information contact:**

**Email**: scholarships@azizfoundation.org.uk

## Daryl Jelinek Sporting Scholarship

**Purpose**: Daryl Jelinek studied at Loughborough University from 1980 to 1983, where he captained the rugby team as well as playing for England U23s. Daryl went on to play rugby for Blackheath, London Scottish, and the Anglo-Scots. When Daryl passed away in July 2018, the Daryl Jelinek Sporting Scholarship was established by Daryl's family and friends to create a legacy that will continue to help young people at Loughborough for many years to come.

**Level of Study**: Postgraduate

**Type**: Scholarship

**Value**: £2,000-£4,000

**Frequency**: Annual

**Closing Date**: 31 May

**Additional Information**: www.lboro.ac.uk/study/postgradu ate/fees-funding/masters-funding/daryl-jelinek-sporting-scholarship/

## Design School Scholarships

**Purpose**: To assist students financially who want to study in the department

**Eligibility**: Outstanding academic achievement

**Level of Study**: Postgraduate

**Type**: Scholarship

**Value**: £500

**Frequency**: Annual

**Study Establishment**: Loughborough University

**Country of Study**: United Kingdom

**Application Procedure**: If full supporting documentation is supplied with your application to study in the department, you will be automatically considered for a scholarship. No separate scholarship application is required

**Closing Date**: 29 February

**Additional Information**: Complete details of all available scholarships are given in the website

**For further information contact:**

**Email**: r.i.campbell@lboro.ac.uk

## Economic and Social Research Council Studentships

**Purpose**: To financially assist students to cover their living costs while undertaking a PhD.

**Eligibility**: Applicant must have been in full-time education in the United Kingdom throughout the 3 years preceding the start date of PhD course

**Level of Study**: Postgraduate

**Type**: Studentship

**Value**: The amount of funding is agreed each year by all the research councils and increase in line with inflation. Tuition fees are also paid

**Length of Study**: 1 year

**Frequency**: Annual

**Study Establishment**: Loughborough University

**Country of Study**: United Kingdom

**Application Procedure**: See website

**Closing Date**: 7 March

**Funding**: Government

**Contributor**: ESRC

**Additional Information**: Please see the website for further details www.lboro.ac.uk/departments/phir/pg-research/funding/

**For further information contact:**

**Email**: l.e.child@lboro.ac.uk

## Eli Lilly Scholarship

**Purpose**: To increase knowledge through research, provide the highest quality of educational experience and the widest opportunities for students, advance industry and the profession, and benefit society

**Eligibility**: Applicant must be a postgraduate in chemistry. See the website for details

**Level of Study**: Postgraduate

**Type**: Scholarships and fellowships

**Value**: £1,000

**Length of Study**: 1 year

**Frequency**: Annual

**Study Establishment**: Loughborough University

**Country of Study**: United Kingdom

**Application Procedure**: See website

**For further information contact:**

**Tel**: (44) 1509 263171

**Email**: l.e.child@lboro.ac.uk

## Jean Scott Scholarships

**Purpose**: To support best qualified Loughborough University students
**Eligibility**: Open to the best qualified Loughborough University students entering MSc programmes in the Department of Economics
**Level of Study**: Postgraduate
**Type**: Scholarship
**Value**: A maximum of £5,000
**Length of Study**: 1 year
**Frequency**: Annual
**Study Establishment**: Loughborough University
**Country of Study**: United Kingdom
**Application Procedure**: See website

### For further information contact:

**Email**:    msc.economics@lboro.ac.uk

## Loughborough Sports Scholarships

**Purpose**: To support elite athletes
**Eligibility**: Open to students who have excelled at least at junior international level (or equivalent) in their sport and have fulfilled the normal academic requirements for either undergraduate or postgraduate entry
**Type**: Scholarship
**Value**: Up to £5,000
**Frequency**: Annual
**Study Establishment**: Loughborough University
**Country of Study**: United Kingdom
**Application Procedure**: See website
**Closing Date**: 31 May
**Additional Information**: Please see the website for further details www.lboro.ac.uk/admin/ar/funding/university/sports_scholarships/

### For further information contact:

**Tel**:        (44) 1509 226108
**Email**:    sports-scholars@lboro.ac.uk

## Master of Business Administration Scholarships

**Purpose**: To support international Students who want to do MBA from University of Loughborough
**Eligibility**: Applicant may be a citizen of any country
**Level of Study**: MBA
**Type**: Scholarship
**Value**: Varies
**Length of Study**: Varies

**Frequency**: Annual
**Study Establishment**: Loughborough University
**Country of Study**: United Kingdom
**Application Procedure**: See website

### For further information contact:

**Email**:    exec.mba@lboro.ac.uk

## Mathematical Sciences Scholarship

**Level of Study**: Postgraduate
**Type**: Scholarship
**Value**: 25% of the programme tuition fee which will be credited to the student's tuition fee account
**Length of Study**: 1–3 years
**Frequency**: Annual
**Study Establishment**: Loughborough University
**Country of Study**: United Kingdom
**Application Procedure**: See website
**Additional Information**: Please see the website for further details

### For further information contact:

**Email**:    maths-admissions@lboro.ac.uk

## School of Art and Design Scholarships

**Level of Study**: Postgraduate
**Type**: Scholarship
**Value**: £1,000 (tuition fee)
**Length of Study**: 1–3 years
**Frequency**: Annual
**Study Establishment**: Loughborough University
**Country of Study**: United Kingdom
**Application Procedure**: See website

### For further information contact:

**Email**:    R.Turner@lboro.ac.uk

## School of Business and Economics Scholarships

**Purpose**: To assist financially the students who want to pursue a career in finance, international and marketing management
**Eligibility**: Applicants with a First Class Honours degree are eligible. A limited number of scholarships are available
**Level of Study**: Postgraduate

**Type**: Scholarship
**Value**: 50% of the tuition fee
**Length of Study**: 1 year
**Frequency**: Annual
**Study Establishment**: Loughborough University
**Country of Study**: United Kingdom
**Application Procedure**: See website
**Additional Information**: United Kingdom/European Union, self-funding, full-time or part-time where applicable

#### For further information contact:

**Tel**:      (44) 1509 228278, 228844, 223291
**Email**:    msc.management@lboro.ac.uk

## Loughborough University Business School

Ashby Road, Leicestershire, Loughborough, LE11 3TU, United Kingdom.

**Tel**:       (44) 1509 223 398
**Website**:   infc.lut.ac.uk.departments/bs
**Contact**:   Ms Gabriella Stenson, MBA Admissions Officer

### Dean's Award for Enterprise Scholarship

**Purpose**: The award will be given at the discretion of the Dean, with the support of the Senior Leadership Team. Applicants are asked to produce a one-page submission of their business idea; though students are encouraged to include images and media content to support their application
**Eligibility**: Shortlisted applicants will be asked to complete a short video interview to discuss their business idea in more detail
**Level of Study**: Graduate
**Type**: Scholarship
**Frequency**: Annual
**Country of Study**: Any country
**Closing Date**: 31 July
**Funding**: Private

#### For further information contact:

Epinal Way, Leicestershire, Loughborough, LE11 3TU, United Kingdom.

**Tel**:      (44) 1509 222 222
**Email**:    london@lboro.ac.uk

## Loyola Marymount University

1 Loyola Marymount University Dr, Los Angeles, CA 90045, United States of America.

**Tel**:      (1) 310 338 2700
**Contact**:  Fellowships Office

## Loyola Marymount University MBA Programme

**Length of Study**: 1–2 years
**Application Procedure**: Applicants must return a completed application form, two official undergraduate transcripts, a two page Statement of Intent, two letters of recommendation, test scores, and a fee of US$35

#### For further information contact:

**Tel**:      (1) 310 338 2848
**Fax**:      (1) 310 338 2899
**Email**:    mbapc@imumail.lmu.edu

## Ludwig-Maximilian University

Geschwister-Scholl-Platz 1, D-80539 Munich, Germany.

**Tel**:      (49) 89 2180 0
**Contact**:  Ludwig-Maximilians-Universität München

LMU is recognized as one of Europe's premier academic and research institutions. Since our founding in 1472, LMU has attracted inspired scholars and talented students from all over the world, keeping the University at the nexus of ideas that challenge and change our complex world.

### Liaoning Medical University Postdoctoral Fellowship for International Students at MCMP

**Purpose**: The Munich Center for Mathematical Philosophy (MCMP) seeks applications for two 3-year postdoctoral fellowships starting on 1 October 2018. International students are eligible to apply for this fellowship
**Eligibility**: International students are eligible to apply for this fellowship. The official language at the MCMP is English and fluency in German is not mandatory
**Type**: Postdoctoral fellowship

**Value**: The fellowships are remunerated with 1. 853 €/month (paid out without deductions for tax and social security). The MCMP also provides funds to cover costs to attend some workshops and conferences

**Study Establishment**: LMU is especially interested in candidates with research interests in at least one of the following fields: general philosophy of science, philosophy of physics, philosophy of the social sciences, philosophy of statistics, formal epistemology, formal philosophy of science, social epistemology, philosophy and psychology of reasoning and argumentation, agent-based modeling in philosophy, or decision theory

**Country of Study**: Any country

**Application Procedure**: Applications (including a cover letter that addresses, amongst others, one's academic background, research interests and the proposed starting date, a CV, a list of publications, a sample of written work of no more than 5,000 words, and a description of a planned research project of about 2,000 words) should be sent by email (in one PDF document) to office.hartmann-at-lrz.uni-muenchen.de by 15 April, 2018. Hard copy applications are not accepted. Additionally, two confidential letters of reference addressing the applicant's qualifications for academic research should be sent to the same email address from the referees directly

**Closing Date**: 15 April

**Additional Information**: For more details please see the website myschoolbeep.blogspot.in/2018/02/lmu-postdoctoral-fellowship-for.html

**For further information contact:**

**Email**: S.Hartmann@lmu.de

## Lung Cancer Research Foundation

### LCRF Research Grant on Disparities in Lung Cancer

**Subjects**: Lung cancer

**Purpose**: LCRF grant program provides funding for research into the prevention, diagnosis, treatment and cure of lung cancer.

**Eligibility**: Must be early- and mid-career investigators. icants from US-based and international institutions are eligible to apply and may hold any residency/citizenship status. Senior investigators with more than ten years experience since faculty appointment are generally not eligible for funding and are encouraged to mentor a junior team member through the application process. However, exceptions will be made for investigators with more than ten years experience in other disease areas or topics. Ineligible investigators with

these or other special circumstances may request review by contacting the LCRF grants office (see Inquiries section below). For full details about eligibility, see website.

**Type**: Grant

**Value**: Maximum of US$150,000

**Study Establishment**: US-based

**Country of Study**: United States of America

**Closing Date**: 1 May

**Additional Information**: www.lungcancerresearch foundation.org/research/funding-opportunities/

## Lupus Foundation of America

1300 Piccard Drive, Suite 200, Rockville, MD 20850, United States of America.

**Tel**: (1) 301 670 9292
**Contact**: Ms Arlise Davis, Executive Assistant

### Gary S. Gilkeson Career Development Award

**Purpose**: To facilitate the professional development of rheumatology, nephrology, and dermatology fellows in the U.S. and Canada who are interested in lupus research.

**Eligibility**: U.S. citizen or legal resident of the U.S. or Canada

**Type**: Grants

**Value**: Up to US$70,000 each

**Length of Study**: 2 years

**Frequency**: Annual

**Application Procedure**: Lupus Foundation of America, 2121 K Street, NW, Suite 200, Washington, DC 20037, United States of America

**No. of awards offered**: 4

**Closing Date**: 17 April

**Additional Information**: www.lupus.org/research/apply-for-funding

**For further information contact:**

**Tel**: (1) 202 349 1150
**Email**: marion@lupus.org

### Gina M. Finzi Memorial Student Summer Fellowship Program

**Purpose**: To foster an interest among students in the areas of basic, clinical, translational, epidemiological, or behavioral research relevant to lupus.

**Eligibility**: 1. The project must be in one of the following areas focused on lupus research: basic, clinical, translational, epidemiological, or behavioral research. 2. The applicant is responsible for identifying a supervising sponsor who is an established, tenure-track principal investigator who directs a laboratory dedicated at least in part to the investigation of lupus at an academic, medical, or research institution. 3. The institution where you re conducting your research must be in the U.S., Canada, or Mexico. 4. Undergraduates up to Medical Residents and/or PhDs' may apply. 5. Awards cannot be postponed for use in a later year or be carried out for two or more summers

**Level of Study**: Research

**Type**: Fellowships

**Value**: US$4,000

**Frequency**: Annual

**Application Procedure**: Lupus Foundation of America, 2121 K Street, NW, Suite 200, Washington, DC 20037

**No. of awards offered**: 6

**Closing Date**: 17 April

**Additional Information**: www.lupus.org/research/apply-for-funding

### For further information contact:

**Tel**: (1) 202 349 1150

**Email**: marion@lupus.org

## Lund University Global Scholarship

**Purpose**: The Lund University Global Scholarship programme seeks to recognise these students by awarding academic excellence grants. Scholarship recipients have a proven record of achieving consistently high grades in their previous studies and are assessed as being a good fit for our programmes

**Eligibility**: To be eligible to apply for a scholarship you must meet all of the following criteria: 1. You must be a citizen of a country from outside the European Union/EEA (and Switzerland) and are required to pay a tuition fee. 2. You have made a complete application for Bachelor's or Master's level studies at Lund University in a regular application round for a minimum of one semester of study (30 ECTS). Note that priority is given to students who have ranked a programme at Lund University as the first choice in their application at universityadmissions.se

**Level of Study**: Graduate

**Type**: Scholarship

**Value**: SEK 15 million (€1.4 million / US$1.7 million) will be awarded per annum

**Frequency**: Dependent on funds available

**Country of Study**: Any country

**Application Procedure**: The selection process for scholarships is undertaken in parallel with the programme/course selection process. Priority will be given to students with high academic performance, who are assessed as a good fit for the programme, who demonstrate a strong commitment and desire to study at Lund University and have selected a programme/course at Lund University as their first choice/choices when applying at www.universityadmissions.se

**Closing Date**: 27 February

**Funding**: Private

**Additional Information**: Note that the opening date for this proposal is February

### For further information contact:

Box 117, S-221 00 Lund, Sweden.

**Tel**: (46) 46 222 0000

**Fax**: (46) 46 222 4720

**Email**: maria.lindblad@er.lu.se

## Luton Business School University of Luton

MBA Programmes Putteridge Bury Hitchin Road, Luton, Bedfordshire, LU2 8LE, United Kingdom.

**Tel**: (44) 1582 482555

**Email**: faculty-of-business@luton.ac.uk

**Contact**: MBA Admissions Officer

### League of United Latin American Citizens National Educational Service Centers National Scholarship Fund

**Purpose**: Awards scholarships to Hispanic students who are enrolled or planning to enroll in accredited colleges or universities in the United States

**Eligibility**: Must be a full-time or part-time student. 1. Must be a Hispanic student. 2. Must be a United States citizen or permanent resident. 3. Must have a grade point average of 3.25 or higher. Must have applied to or be enrolled in a college, university, or graduate school, including two-year colleges or vocational schools that lead to an associate's degree

**Level of Study**: Graduate

**Type**: Funding support

**Value**: US$2,000

**Frequency**: Annual

**Country of Study**: Any country

**Application Procedure**: The applicants must send application and supporting materials to the LULAC council in his/her town. For a listing of participating councils, please visit: www.lnesc.org/index.asp?Type=B_BASIC&SEC=A9E53 D4E-6ADF-431B-A59A-E92DEDD44793

**Closing Date**: 31 March

**Funding**: Private

**For further information contact:**

2000 L St., N.W. Suite 610, Washington, DC 20036, United States of America.

**Email**:     mbosques@lnesc.org

# M

## Maastricht University

Minderbroedersberg 4-6, NL-6211 LK Maastricht, The Netherlands.

**Contact**: Maastricht University

Maastricht University (UM) is the most international university in the Netherlands and, with more than 16,000 students and 4,000 employees, is still growing. The university stands out for its innovative education model, international character and multidisciplinary approach to research and education.

### Orange Tulip Scholarship Scholarship for Indian Students

**Purpose**: The new Orange Tulip Scholarship India is now available for all Indian students who want to study at Maastricht University (UM) in the Netherlands
**Eligibility**: 1. You have the Indian nationality and you live in India. 2. You have a degree from a non-Dutch university. 3. You have not previously studied or worked in the Netherlands. 4. You have been admitted to a Master's programme at the Faculty of Law.
**Value**: 100% tuition fee. Please note no additional allowance towards living costs or visa costs
**Study Establishment**: At Maastricht University, an OTS grant is available at the Faculty of Law
**Country of Study**: Netherlands
**Application Procedure**: See the website
**Closing Date**: 1 April
**Additional Information**: For more details please visit our website at www.ru.nl/currentstudents/@1123620/orange-tulip-scholarship-india/ www.ru.nl/currentstudents/@1123620/orange-tulip-scholarship-india/

**For further information contact:**

**Email**: ots@nesoindia.org

## Macquarie University

Balaclava Road, North Ryde, NSW 2109, Australia.

**Tel**: (61) 2 9850 7111
**Email**: tgreen@ling.mq.edu.au
**Website**: www.mq.edu.au

Established in 1964, Macquarie attracts students from all walks of life, including large numbers from overseas. As the new millennium dawned, Macquarie had conferred some 58,000 degrees, diplomas and postgraduate certificates.

### Centre for Lasers and Applications Scholarships

**Purpose**: To enable holders to pursue a research programme leading to the degree of MSc or PhD in experimental and theoretical laser studies
**Eligibility**: Open to the Australian citizens, permanent residents, or citizens of overseas countries
**Level of Study**: Postgraduate, Research
**Type**: Scholarship
**Value**: AU$19,231 (maximum per year). This award is to be used for living expenses
**Length of Study**: 2 years (Masters) or 3 years (PhD)
**Frequency**: Annual
**Study Establishment**: Macquarie University
**Country of Study**: Australia
**Application Procedure**: Check website for further details
**Additional Information**: Please see the website for details

**For further information contact:**

**Tel**:     (61) 2 9850 8911, 2 9850 8645
**Fax**:    (61) 2 9850 8799
**Email**:   jpiper@ics.mq.edu.au

## Doctor of Philosophy Scholarship-Artificial Intelligence in Medicine and Healthcare

**Purpose**: The aim of this research program is to investigate the future role of AI in healthcare and its social, ethical and technical implications

**Eligibility**: Australian and international students can apply for these scholarships. If English is not your first language then you will need to show that your English language skills are at a high enough level to succeed in your studies

**Value**: The MQRTP full-time stipend rate is AU$27,082 per annum tax-exempt, for up to 3 years (indexed annually) The scholarship is comprised of a Tuition Fee Offset and a Living Allowance Stipend

**Study Establishment**: Scholarship is awarded to work on the project tiled, "Artificial Intelligence in Medicine and Healthcare"

**Country of Study**: Australia

**Application Procedure**: Applicants will need to complete an HDR Candidature and Scholarship Application Form and arrange for two academic referee reports to be submitted to the Higher Degree Research Office

**Closing Date**: 31 July

**Additional Information**: For more details please visit the website scholarship-positions.com/phd-scholarship-artificial-intelligence-medicine-healthcare/2018/01/06/

**For further information contact:**

**Email**:   annie.lau@mq.edu.au

## Macquarie University PhD Scholarship in Knowledge Acquisition and Cognitive Modelling

**Purpose**: To enable students to undertake research in related fields

**Eligibility**: Open to applicants who have completed, an Australian 4 year undergraduate degree with at least Second Class (Honours) division 1 in computing or a related field, or equivalent qualifications

**Level of Study**: Postdoctorate, Postgraduate

**Type**: Scholarships

**Value**: AU$19,231 plus AU$5,000 top-up per year tax exempt

**Length of Study**: 3 years

**Frequency**: Annual

**Study Establishment**: Macquarie University

**Country of Study**: Australia

**Application Procedure**: Applicants must download the form from the website

**Closing Date**: 31 May

**Additional Information**: Additional Information can be obtained from the Higher Degree Research Unit by phoning (61) 02 9850 7277, by emailing pgschol@mq.edu.au  or by downloading the form from the website

**For further information contact:**

Higher Degree Research Unit, Cottage C4C, Macquarie University, North Ryde, NSW 2109, Australia.

**Email**:   richards@mq.edu.au

## Macquarie Vice-Chancellor's International Scholarships

**Purpose**: The Macquarie University Vice-Chancellor's International Scholarship is awarded to recognise academic excellence for international students. This highly competitive scholarship is based on academic merit and awarded to future students

**Eligibility**: Applicants must: 1. Be a citizen of a country other than Australia or New Zealand. 2. Meet the University's academic and English requirements for the course (must hold a full offer of admission by the application deadline). 3. Achieved a minimum GPA equivalent of 5.0 out of 7.0 for Postgraduate applications; or a minimum ATAR equivalent of 90 out of 100 for Undergraduate applications. 4. Applied for a program that is longer than one session in duration. 5. Commence study in session and year indicated in the scholarship offer letter, and commencement may not be deferred

**Level of Study**: Postgraduate

**Type**: Scholarship

**Value**: AU$10,000

**Frequency**: Annual

**Country of Study**: Australia

**Closing Date**: 14 June

**Funding**: Private

**Additional Information**: www.mq.edu.au/study/why-study-here/scholarships/scholarships/details/vice-chancellors-international-scholarship

**For further information contact:**

**Email**:   scholarships@mq.edu.au

## Walter Heywood Bryan Scholarship for International Students in Australia

**Purpose**: The aim of the WH Bryan Scholarship is to advance the understanding of Queensland Earth Sciences by addressing a globally significant problem leading to impactful outcomes, with the supported project to be led by an outstanding PhD candidate

**Eligibility**: Australian and international students are eligible to apply. Students need to demonstrate that they have a good level of written and spoken English

**Value**: See the website

**Study Establishment**: Scholarship is awarded in the field of Earth Sciences

**Country of Study**: Australia

**Application Procedure**: The main written application is expected to be no more than 10 pages. Each application must be submitted from the host university

**Closing Date**: 30 April

**Additional Information**: For more details Please visit the website scholarship-positions.com/wh-bryan-scholarship-for-international-students-australia/2018/01/06

### For further information contact:

**Email**:     sef.hdrscholarships@qut.edu.au

## Magna Carta College

Milford House, 1A Mayfield Road, Summertown, Oxford, OX2 7EL, United Kingdom.

**Tel**:     (44) 1865 593 131
**Email**:     enquiries@magnacartacollege.org

Magna Carta College specializes in a range of business courses that can help you progress to university. Our programmes provide students with fast-track and alternative routes to achieving full degrees with work placement experience and scholarship opportunities available.

## Global Ambassador Scholarship Programme (GASPR)

**Purpose**: GASPR is a global annual rolling scholarship programme and aims to give financial support for those who are eager to improve their education

**Eligibility**: Applicant should be 18+ years old and can be citizen of any country in the world. Scholarships are only valid during the June intake. The difference in tuition fee for the entire programme must be paid in full before the commencement of studies. Students must cover all other related costs on their own (accommodation, meals, visa, medical insurance, etc.)

**Type**: Scholarship

**Value**: The scholarship provides discount on basic tuition fee

**Frequency**: Annual

**Country of Study**: United Kingdom

**Application Procedure**: Applicants should send the application form along with the required documents to the email address gaspr@magnacartacollege.org

**Closing Date**: 15 May

**Additional Information**: Successful scholarship candidates will not be able to apply for further College awards and payment plans: scholarships, discounts, installments, etc magnacartacollege.org/programme/gaspr

## Maine Restaurant Association

### Russ Casey Scholarship

**Purpose**: This scholarship is available for Maine undergraduate students who plan to pursue a career in culinary arts or hospitality. Culinary arts students will be given first consideration

**Eligibility**: 1. Must be a resident of Maine. 2. Must be a United States citizen or permanent resident. 3. Must be a high school senior or older to apply for this undergraduate award. 4. Must be planning to pursue a culinary arts or hospitality-oriented program. Culinary arts students will be given first consideration. 5. This award is for United States students

**Level of Study**: Graduate

**Type**: Scholarship

**Value**: US$1,000

**Frequency**: Annual

**Country of Study**: United States of America

**Application Procedure**: Applications are available on the Maine Restaurant Association (MRA) website by searching for "scholarship". In addition to a completed application, the student must submit the following: a high school transcript; three letters of reference (two from teachers or counselors, and one from a member of the Maine Restaurant Association); and a typed letter of not more than 300 words describing his/her affiliation with the hospitality industry, why he/she is applying for this scholarship, and his/her career goals. Applications and all supporting materials must be sent to the address provided, and must be received by the deadline date

**Closing Date**: 12 April

**Funding**: Foundation

**Additional Information**: www.unigo.com/scholarships/by-major/culinary-arts-scholarships/russ-casey-scholarship/1432

### For further information contact:

45 Melville Street, Augusta, ME 04330, United States of America.

**Email**:   becky@mainerestaurant.com

## Managed Care Organization

3000 Arlington Avenue, Toledo, OH 43199, United States of America.

**Contact**:   Dr Garry T Cole

### The James Madison Memorial Fellowship

**Purpose**: The James Madison Memorial Fellowship is a federal program that offers secondary level teachers (both pre-service and in-service) of history and government up to US$24,000 to complete a master's degree in history, political science, or related fields

**Eligibility**: To be eligible, 1. You must be, or plan to become, a teacher of American history, American government, or any other social studies class, teaching topics on the Constitution at the secondary school level (grades 7-12). 2. In addition, you must be a United States citizen and either possess a bachelor's degree, or plan to receive a bachelor's degree no later than August 31 of the year in which you are applying. 3. Fellows will have the unique opportunity to attend an intensive summer institute to strengthen their knowledge of the origins and development of American constitutional government. The Foundation plans to offer one fellowship per state per year

**Level of Study**: Graduate

**Type**: Fellowship

**Value**: US$24,000

**Frequency**: Annual

**Country of Study**: United States of America

**Application Procedure**: 1. Applicants compete only against other applicants from the states of their legal residence. 2. Applicants are evaluated on their demonstrated commitment to a career teaching American history, American government, or civics classes where you will teach topics on the Constitution at the secondary school level; demonstrated intent to pursue and complete a program of graduate study that emphasizes the Constitution and offers instruction in that subject; demonstrated devotion to civic responsibility. 3. Demonstrated capacity for study and performance as

classroom teachers, and their proposed courses of graduate study. 4. Applicants will be evaluated without regard to race, color, religion, sex, age, national origin, disability, political affiliation, marital status, sexual orientation or other non-merit factors

**Closing Date**: 9 March

**Funding**: Private

**Additional Information**: www.jamesmadison.gov/ www.jamesmadison.gov/

### For further information contact:

1613 Duke Street, Alexandria, VA 22314, United States of America.

**Email**:   Madison@scholarshipamerica.org

## Manipal University in India

Tiger Circle Road, Madhav Nagar, Manipal, Karnataka 576104, India.

**Tel**:          (91) 92437 77733
**Contact**:    Manipal University in India

Manipal Academy of Higher Education is synonymous with excellence in higher education. Over 28,000 students from 57 different nations live to learn and play in the sprawling University town, nestled on a plateau in Karnataka's Udupi district. It also has nearly 2,500 faculty and almost 10,000 other support and service staff, who cater to the various professional institutions in health sciences, engineering, management, communication and humanities which dot the Wi-Fi-enabled campus.

### Doctor TMA Pai PhD Scholarships for International Students at Manipal University

**Purpose**: The Manipal Academy of Higher Education is currently accepting applications for Dr. TMA Pai PhD scholarship program. Indian and Foreign students are eligible to apply for this scholarship

**Eligibility**: Indian and Foreign students are eligible to apply for this scholarship. Applicants whose first language is not English are usually required to provide evidence of proficiency in English at the higher level required by the University

**Value**: Scholarship amount per candidate: Six months Probationary period: ₹14,000 per monthFirst year: ₹16,000 per monthSecond year: ₹17,000 per monthThird year: ₹18,000 per month

**Study Establishment**: Atomic and Molecular Physics, Allied Health Science, Dentistry, Engineering, Life Science, Medicine, Nursing, Pharmacy, Science, Statistics, Regenerative Medicine, Public Health, Management, Information Science, Communication, Allied Hospitality Studies

**Country of Study**: India

**Application Procedure**: Candidates should download the application form, complete it in all respects and send it to Admissions Office, Manipal Academy of Higher Education, Manipal - 576104 along with a demand draft for ₹600 drawn in favour of 'Manipal Academy of Higher Education' payable at Manipal/Udupi and the following enclosures: Attested copy of the degree certificate of qualifying examinations. Attested copies of the marks cards of qualifying examinations. Any other relevant documents

**Closing Date**  31 March

**Additional Information**: For more details please browse the website  scholarship-positions.com/dr-tma-pai-phd-scholarships-international-students-manipal-university-india/2018/02/23/

**For further information contact:**

**Email**:  admin@scholarship-positions.com

## March of Dimes

1275 Mamaroneck Avenue, White Plains, NY 10605, United States of America.

**Tel**:  (1) 914 997 4488
**Email**:  researchgrantssupport@marchofdimes.com
**Website**:  www.marchofdimes.com/professionals
**Contact**:  Research and Grants Administration

Four major problems threaten the health of America's babies: birth defects, infant mortality, low birth weight and lack of prenatal care. The goal of the March of Dimes Birth Defects Foundation is to eliminate these problems so that all babies can be born healthy.

## Basil O'Connor Starter Scholar Research Award

**Purpose**: This award is designed to support young scientists just embarking on their independent research careers and is limited, therefore, to those holding recent faculty appointments. The applicants' research interests should be consonant with those of the Foundation

**Eligibility**: The Basil O'Connor Starter Scholar Research Award is intended to be an initial independent grant to young investigators. Eligibility is thus restricted. PhD applicants should be 4 to 8 years past their degree and must hold a full-time faculty position at their current institution. For MD or MD/PhD applicants, the same 4–8 year timeline applies, but begins upon completion of the last year of clinical training required for medical specialty board certification. Requests for exceptions (e.g. parental leave) should be directed to the Senior Vice President for Research & Global Programs

**Type**: Award/Grant

**Value**: Up to US$150,000 for 2 years

**Frequency**: Annual

**Application Procedure**: Deans, Chairs of Departments, or Directors of Institutes/Centers should submit nominations for this award addressed to the Senior Vice President for Research and Global Programs

**Closing Date**: 15 March

**Funding**: Private

**Additional Information**: These grants do not cover the recipient's salary, but do provide salary support for technical help. Please email any enquiries regarding award researchfunding.duke.edu/basil-o%E2%80%99connor-starter-scholar-research-award

**For further information contact:**

**Email**:  researchgrantsSupport@marchofdimes.com

## Marine Biological Association

Citadel Hill, Plymouth, Devon, PL1 2PB, United Kingdom.

**Tel**:  (44) 1752 633 341
**Contact**:  Dr A S Clare

## MarTERA Call

**Purpose**: The overall goal of the MarTERA Cofund is to strengthen the European Research Area (ERA) in maritime and marine technologies and Blue Growth

**Level of Study**: Graduate

**Type**: Research grant

**Frequency**: Annual

**Country of Study**: Any country

**Closing Date**: 27 March

**Funding**: Private

**Additional Information**: www.martera.eu/joint-calls www.martera.eu/joint-calls

**For further information contact:**

**Email**:  f.aslan@fz-juelich.de

## Peter Baker Fellowship

**Purpose**: The awards are intended for post-doctoral scientists interested in research in marine biology. Applications are particularly encouraged from those interested in physiological research.

**Level of Study**: Post-doctoral
**Type**: Fellowship
**Value**: Up to £3,000
**Application Procedure**: 1. Applications should be sent by e-mail to info@mba.ac.uk and one hard copy to the address shown below, to reach the MBA by 31st Januaryin any one year. 2. Applications will be reviewed by the Research Committee of the MBA Council at its April Council meeting. 3. Usually one Fellowship will be awarded each year. 4. On appointment the Fellow is expected to work at the Citadel Hill Laboratory, Plymouth, for a period of up to two months within a period of 2 years after appointment. 5. On completion of the award the Fellow is required to submit a Final Report. This will comprise a financial summary on how the award was used (max. one A4 page), a scientific report (max. one A4 page) summarising the research completed, its wider implications, outputs such as journal publications, and the synergies made with the MBA during the research visits.
**Closing Date**: 31 January
**Additional Information**: www.mba.ac.uk/research-top-3/awards-grants-and-training#b12

### For further information contact:

The Director, Marine Biological Association of the UK, The Laboratory, Citadel Hill, Plymouth, Devon, PL1 2PB, United Kingdom.

**Email**:  info@mba.ac.uk

## Marines' Memorial Association

609 Sutter Street, San Francisco, CA 94102, United States of America.

**Tel**:  (1) 415 673 6672
**Email**:  michaelallen@marineclub.com
**Website**:  www.marineclub.com

The Marines' Memorial Association is a non-profit veterans organization chartered to honor the memory of and commemorate the valour of Marines who have sacrificed in the nation's wars.

## The Marine Corps Scholarship

**Purpose**: To provide financial assistance to children of active and former members of the United States Marines Corps
**Eligibility**: Open to children of the MMA members scholastic aptitude, community involvement and civic spirit. Applicant must be Planning to attend an accredited undergraduate college or vocational/technical institution in the upcoming academic year. Applicant must have a maximum family adjusted gross income for the current tax year that does not exceed US$90,000. Non-taxable allowances are not included in determining adjusted gross income. Applicant must have A GPA of at least 2.0
**Level of Study**: Postgraduate
**Type**: Scholarship
**Value**: Varies
**Length of Study**: Renewable
**Frequency**: Annual
**Country of Study**: Any country
**Application Procedure**: See the website
**Closing Date**: 30 April
**Funding**: Foundation
**Contributor**: The Marine Corps Foundation
**Additional Information**: Please see the website for further details and if you have any questions, contact us by email or phone www.mcsf.org/ www.mcsf.org/

### For further information contact:

**Tel**:  (61) 415 673 6672 ext 293 or ext 215
**Email**:  Member@MarineClub.com

## Marketing Science Institute (MSI)

### Doctoral Dissertation Proposal Competition

**Subjects**: Marketing and Related Fields
**Purpose**: This competition recognizes marketing doctoral students who are working on research questions with important marketing, societal, and policy implications.
**Eligibility**: See website
**Type**: Research grant
**Value**: US$5,000
**Frequency**: Annual
**Country of Study**: Any country
**No. of awards offered**: Up to five
**Closing Date**: 31 July
**No. of awards given last year**: 2 winners
**Additional Information**: The competition is open to doctoral candidates in marketing and related fields (e.g., management, strategy, organizational behavior, consumer psychology, economics, etc.). The dissertation must be no more than fifty

percent completed at the time of submission. Proposals will be judged on importance and potential contribution of the subject to business and academia; quality of conceptual development; feasibility and appropriateness of methodology; fit of research with MSI priorities; and creativity. Design aspects will play a particularly important role in the evaluation process. www.msi.org

## Marshal Papworth

East of England Showground, Alwalton, Oundle Road, Peterborough, Cambridgeshire, PE2 6XE, United Kingdom.

**Tel**:      (44) 1733 363514
**Email**:    slauridsen@eastofengland.org.uk.
**Website**:  www.marshalpapworth.com

Marshal Papworth - the man behind the fund. Our Fund takes its name from our late founder, Marshal Papworth, a well-respected Huntingdonshire farmer, who played a key role in the agricultural community, as well as being a proactive member of the East of England Agricultural Society. Born in 1939 to parents who farmed in Huntingdonshire Marshal began his farming career as a tenant farmer on Lord de Ramsey's 270 acre Townsend Farm in Upwood. An adventurous and visionary man, Marshal travelled extensively to Africa and Asia. It was during these trips that he saw the plight that communities in developing countries faced on a daily basis in sourcing food and safe water. Witnessing these difficulties, Marshal recognised the benefits that such communities could gain at an over the counter from being given the opportunity to embrace sustainable farming practices and learn valuable agricultural and horticultural skills. Marshal's untimely death in a flying accident was a huge loss to his family and friends, and to the communities in which he was involved. However, through his sincere generosity, his legacy has been able to live on by way of our Fund by providing scholarship opportunities for students in developing countries. Marshal's vision - helping students develop skills they can take back to their homelands and use for the benefit of their own communities - stands as true today as it did while he was alive, and through our work, continues to enrich the lives of people from developing countries around the world.

### Marshal Papworth Scholarships in Agriculture for Developing Countries

**Purpose**: Marshal Papworth provides scholarships for students from developing countries for 1-year Masters degree programmes in agriculture or horticulture

**Eligibility**: Applicants should be nationals of and resident in developing countries (countries with a GNI per capita below US$11500), and scholarship candidates who fully meet the criteria for the courses will be shortlisted for the scholarships against 3 main criteria: academic excellence, professional experience (includes experience gained in a voluntary capacity) in community development and/or agricultural development, and the potential for contribution to development in their home country after completion of their degree programme. Applicants should be talented individuals who demonstrate that they have the potential, at the end of their Masters programme, to motivate people and communities in their home country towards positive change. Applicants must have a good command of the English Language
**Level of Study**: Masters Degree
**Type**: Scholarships
**Value**: £19,000
**Length of Study**: 1 year
**Frequency**: annual
**Country of Study**: UK
**Application Procedure**: Candidates for the Masters scholarships cannot apply directly to the Marshal Papworth Fund for the Masters programme. Rather, they have to apply directly to the participating universities. Once accepted into a course the university/college will select candidates they believe are eligible for a Marshal Papworth Scholarship and will forward the students application and CV onto the Marshal Papworth Fund directly for consideration. Applications for scholarships must be received from partnering universities/colleges no later than the end of the second week of April, or the last day before the Easter break, whichever is the former. To apply for the 10-week course at Harper Adams University starting in May, you must make an application through accredited organizations found at this link before their deadline. It is important to visit the official website (link found below) for detailed information on how to apply for this scholarship.
**No. of awards offered**: 15
**Closing Date**: April
**Additional Information**: www.marshalpapworth.com/our-scholarships/scholarship-details/

## Marshall Aid Commemoration Commission

Woburn House, 20-24 Tavistock Square, London, WC1H 9HF, United Kingdom.

**Tel**:      (44) 20 7380 6704/3
**Email**:    apps@marshallscholarship.org
**Website**:  www.marshallscholarship.org

The Marshall Aid Commemoration Commission is responsible for the selection and placement of recipients of Marshall scholarships from the United States to the United Kingdom. The first awards were presented in 1954.

## Marshall Scholarships

**Purpose**: To provide intellectually distinguished young Americans with the opportunity to study in the United Kingdom, and thus to understand and appreciate the British way of life

**Eligibility**: Open to citizens of the United States of America who have graduated with a minimum grade point average of 3.7 or A from an accredited United States college not more than 2 years previously.

**Type**: Scholarship

**Value**: University fees, cost of living expenses, annual book grant, thesis grant, research and daily travel grants, fares to and from the United States and, where applicable, a contribution towards the support of a dependent spouse

**Frequency**: Annual

**Country of Study**: United Kingdom

**Closing Date**: October

**Funding**: Government

**No. of awards given last year**: 37

**No. of applicants last year**: 900

**Additional Information**: Please see the website for further details www.marshallscholarship.org/apply

### For further information contact:

11766 Wilshire Boulevard, Suite 1200, Los Angeles, CA 90025-6538, United States of America.

**Tel**:     (1) 310 996 3028
**Email**:    Atlanta@marshallscholarship.org

## Marshall Sherfield Fellowships

**Purpose**: The aim of the Marshall Sherfield Fellowships is to introduce American scientists and engineers to the cutting edge of UK science and engineering

**Level of Study**: post-doctoral

**Type**: Fellowship

**Length of Study**: two academic years

**Frequency**: Annual

**Country of Study**: United Kingdom

**Closing Date**: October

**Additional Information**: www.marshallscholarship.org/marshall-sherfield

### For further information contact:

Marshall Aid Commemoration Commission, Woburn House, 20-24 Tavistock Square, London, WC1H 9HF, United Kingdom.

# Maryland Association of Certified Public Accountants

## Maryland Association of Certified Public Accountants Scholarship

**Purpose**: United States students who are Maryland residents enrolled full time in a college or university in Maryland with a grade point average of 3.0 or higher committed to pursuing careers as CPAs are eligible for this award. Students must have completed 60 hours of college credit at the time of award, with six or more of those hours in accounting courses

**Eligibility**: 1. Must attend a college or university in Maryland. 2. Must be a current college sophomore or older to apply for this undergraduate and graduate award. The applicant must have completed at least 60 total credit hours by the time of the award, of which at least six hours of credit are in accounting courses (including Accounting Principles I and II). 3. Must be a full-time student. 4. Must be a resident of Maryland. 5. Must be a United States citizen. 6. Must demonstrate commitment to pursuing a career as a certified public accountant. 7. Must have a grade point average of 3.0 or higher. 8. This award is for United States students

**Level of Study**: Graduate

**Type**: Scholarship

**Value**: US$1,000

**Frequency**: Annual

**Country of Study**: United States of America

**Application Procedure**: Applications are available online from the Maryland Association of Certified Public Accountants (MACPA) website. In addition to the completed application, the applicant must submit the following: a signed applicant's statement; a complete copy of the SAR (Student Aid Report) which is generated upon completion of the FAFSA (Free Application for Federal Student Aid); and an official, sealed transcript from the previous semester which shows cumulative grade point average, total credit hours completed and hours completed during the previous semester

**Closing Date**: 15 April

**Funding**: Foundation

**Additional Information**: www.unigo.com/scholarships/all/macpa-scholarship/1627

**For further information contact:**

901 Dulaney Valley Road, Suite 800, Townson, MD 21204-2683, United States of America.

**Tel**:     (1) 800 782 2036
**Email**:     scholarships@swe.org

---

# Massey University

Graduate Research School, Support, Private Bag 11-222, Palmerston North, 4442, New Zealand.

## Allan Kay Undergraduate Memorial Scholarship

**Purpose**: The Allan Kay Undergraduate Memorial Scholarship helps students obtain a university education, especially those facing financial difficulties
**Eligibility**: Applicants must be: 1. enrolled full time at Massey University for an undergraduate degree in agriculture or horticulture (mainly with paper prefixes of 112, 117, 119, 189, 283, 284 and 285). 2. New Zealand-born residents. 3. no older than 30 years in the year which the scholarship is initially allocated
**Level of Study**: Graduate
**Type**: Scholarship
**Value**: NZ$3,000
**Frequency**: Annual
**Country of Study**: Any country
**Application Procedure**: The scholarship is awarded by the Trustees of the estate of Grace Edith Meliora Kay on the recommendation of the Applied Academic Programmes Scholarships Committee
**No. of awards offered**: 6
**Closing Date**: 10 March
**Funding**: Private
**Additional Information**: www.massey.ac.nz/massey/admission/scholarships-bursaries-awards/other-scholarships/search-results/search-results_home.cfm?page=award_display&scholarship_id=166

**For further information contact:**

Massey University, Private Bag 11 222, Palmerston North, 4442, New Zealand.

**Email**:     K.Harrington@massey.ac.nz

## C. Alma Baker Postgraduate Scholarship

**Purpose**: To encourage students enroling in Master's or doctoral thesis programmes

**Eligibility**: Open to candidates who are graduates and citizens of New Zealand. Awards are available for those intending to undertake postgraduate research either in New Zealand or overseas. Scholarships will be based on academic achievement
**Level of Study**: Graduate, Postgraduate
**Type**: Scholarship
**Value**: Maximum NZ$13,000 a year for a Master's student and NZ$20,000 a year for a doctoral student
**Length of Study**: 1 year for Master's and up to 3 years for a Doctoral programme
**Frequency**: Dependent on funds available
**Country of Study**: New Zealand
**Application Procedure**: Applicants must apply on the prescribed form to the Secretary, C. Alma Baker Trust. A certified copy of Academic Record, birth certificate, passport, or other proof of citizenship, and an outline of proposed research (not more than one page) must be enclosed with the application
**Closing Date**: 1 February
**Funding**: Trusts
**Additional Information**: Do not send original documents as application and attachments will not be returned. Information provided will be used by the trust or its representatives only for awarding scholarships and may be subject to verification procedures as appropriate www.calmabakertrust.org/awards-grants-scholarships/postgraduate-scholarships

**For further information contact:**

C. Alma Baker Trust, c/o School of People, Environment & Planning Social Sciences Tower, Level 3, Massey University, Private Bag 11 222, Palmerston North, 4442, New Zealand.

**Email**:     Contact@massey.ac.nz

## Dreamfields Farm Agricultural Scholarship

**Purpose**: This scholarship was established in 2014, initially using money won by Bruce and Judy Woods from Dreamfields Farm in Bay of Plenty for the Ballance Farm Environment Award. It is designed to encourage students from their local secondary schools to study agriculture at Massey University
**Level of Study**: Graduate
**Type**: Scholarship
**Value**: NZ$1,000
**Length of Study**: 1 year
**Frequency**: Varies
**Country of Study**: Any country
**Application Procedure**: Apply online
**Closing Date**: 3 March

**Funding**: Trusts
**Additional Information**: www.growingnz.org.nz/dreamfields-farm-agricultural-scholarship-scholarship_id-25.html

**For further information contact:**

**Email**: K.Harrington@massey.ac.nz

## Horizons Regional Council Sustainable Land Use Scholarships - Year 1 & Year 2 Students

**Purpose**: Horizons Regional Council provides the scholarships to encourage students who are interested in a career in an environmental field, to undertake study in soil science and farm management as part of their undergraduate degree. Applicants are expected to have a solid interest in environmental management, soil, and land use mapping. The scholarships are considered to be a good entry point for year three and postgraduate Horizons Regional Council Sustainable Land Use Advanced Scholarships
**Level of Study**: Graduate
**Type**: Scholarship
**Value**: NZ$2,000
**Length of Study**: 3 year
**Frequency**: Varies
**Country of Study**: Any country
**Application Procedure**: Apply online
**No. of awards offered**: 1
**Closing Date**: 13 April
**Funding**: Trusts
**Additional Information**: www.horizons.govt.nz/about-our-region-and-council/grants-and-sponsorship/sustainable-land-use-scholarships

**For further information contact:**

Private Bag 11025 Manawatu Mail Centre, Palmerston North 4442, New Zealand.

**Tel**: (64) 508 800 800
**Email**: help@horizons.govt.nz

## Horticulture NZ Undergraduate Scholarships

**Purpose**: Horticulture New Zealand (HortNZ) and the Horticentre Trust has a number of scholarships available for undergraduate students studying towards a degree in areas of interest to the Horticulture Industry
**Level of Study**: Graduate
**Type**: Scholarship
**Value**: NZ$4,500
**Length of Study**: 1 year
**Frequency**: Varies

**Country of Study**: Any country
**Application Procedure**: Apply online
**Closing Date**: 20 March
**Funding**: Trusts
**Additional Information**: www.hortnz.co.nz/our-work/people/horticulture-scholarships/

**For further information contact:**

**Tel**: (4) 494 9978
**Email**: schols@hortnz.co.nz

## Hurley Fraser Postgraduate Scholarship

**Purpose**: To support postgraduate research in agriculture and horticulture
**Eligibility**: Applicants must have enroled for a full-time postgraduate degree or a diploma in one of the Applied Sciences. The award is based on the candidate's academic attainment
**Level of Study**: Graduate
**Type**: Scholarship
**Value**: Up to NZ$2,000 per year
**Study Establishment**: Massey University
**Country of Study**: New Zealand
**Application Procedure**: Applicants must apply to the Scholarships Office, Graduate Research School on forms (ASSC.3) available from Massey Contact or can be downloaded from the website
**Closing Date**: 10 March
**Contributor**: John Alexander Hurley Scholarship and the Edith Fraser Agricultural and Horticultural Research Fund
**Additional Information**: The award shall be paid in May. Applications will not be accepted more than 3 months in advance of the closing date studyspy.ac.nz/scholarships/10155/hurley-fraser-postgraduate-scholarship

**For further information contact:**

**Tel**: (64) 800 627 739
**Email**: Contact@massey.ac.nz

## Leonard Condell Farming Postgraduate Scholarship

**Purpose**: Candidates must be New Zealand born graduates in science, agriculture or related disciplines (e.g. horticulture, veterinary science, food technology, biotechnology) and must enter fields of research for the benefit of some branch of agriculture in New Zealand
**Eligibility**: There are two types of scholarships. (a) Postgraduate Scholarships: Candidates must be New Zealand born graduates in science, agriculture or related

disciplines (e.g. horticulture, veterinary science, food technology, biotechnology) and must enter fields of research for the benefit of some branch of agriculture in New Zealand. The emolument shall be up to NZ$3,000 per annum. (b) PhD Scholarships: Candidates must be New Zealand born graduates in science, agriculture or related disciplines (e.g. horticulture, veterinary science, food technology, biotechnology) and must enter fields of research for the benefit of some branch of agriculture in New Zealand. The emolument shall be up to NZ$4,000 per annum

**Level of Study**: Postgraduate

**Type**: Scholarship

**Value**: NZ$3,000

**Length of Study**: 1 year

**Frequency**: Annual

**Country of Study**: New Zealand

**Application Procedure**: All applications are acknowledged by email

**No. of awards offered**: 1

**Closing Date**: 10 March

**Funding**: Individuals

**Additional Information**: Specific criteria is being added to the concern. Applications will NOT be accepted more than 3 months in advance of the closing date www.massey.ac.nz/massey/admission/scholarships-bursaries-awards/other-scholarships/search-results/search-results_home.cfm?page=award_display&scholarship_id=70

### For further information contact:

Scholarships Office, (NSATS), Massey University, Private Bag 11-222, Palmerston North, 4442, New Zealand.

**Email**:    K.Harrington@massey.ac.nz

## Massey Doctoral Scholarship

**Purpose**: To fund research towards a PhD degree

**Eligibility**: Open to those with a minimum qualification of a First Class (Honours) Degree

**Level of Study**: Doctorate

**Type**: Scholarship

**Value**: The scholarship value for full-time recipients is a stipend of NZ$25,000 per annum plus tuition and non-tuition fees, for a maximum duration of 36 months. The value for part-time students is a stipend of NZ$15,000 per annum plus tuition and non-tuition fees, for a maximum duration of 60 months.

**Length of Study**: 3 years

**Frequency**: Annual

**Study Establishment**: Massey University

**Country of Study**: New Zealand

**Application Procedure**: Applicants must complete an application form, available from the University. Further details can be found on the website

**Closing Date**: 1 April

**Additional Information**: www.massey.ac.nz/massey/admission/scholarships-bursaries-awards/doctorate/doctorate_home.cfm

### For further information contact:

**Email**:    R.L.Izzard@massey.ac.nz

## Sir Alan Stewart Postgraduate Scholarships

**Purpose**: To encourage new postgraduate enrolments from other tertiary institutions and to assist Massey students to progress from undergraduate to postgraduate study

**Eligibility**: Applicant must be enroled or be intending to enrol full-time or part-time, in the year the award is to be made, in their initial year of a first postgraduate programme, undertaken either internally or extramurally and must be a New Zealand citizen or permanent resident who has completed an undergraduate degree at a New Zealand university

**Level of Study**: Graduate

**Type**: Scholarship

**Value**: NZ$4,000 per year for full-time students and pro-rated for part-time students

**Frequency**: Annual

**Study Establishment**: Any Massey University campus

**Country of Study**: New Zealand

**Application Procedure**: Check website for further details

**Closing Date**: 1 December

**Additional Information**: Consideration will normally only be given to students with a B+ average or better. Full-time students may hold the scholarship only once. Part-time students may re-apply to the maximum of NZ$4,000 in a period of 4 years from first enrolment in the postgraduate programme. Applications will NOT be accepted more than 3 months in advance of the closing date scholarshipdb.net/scholarships-in-New-Zealand/Sir-Alan-Stewart-Postgraduate-Scholarships-Massey-University=FABTZeXGB0K9zyX_mH3hhA.html

### For further information contact:

**Email**:    Contact@massey.ac.nz

## Sir John Logan Campbell Agricultural Scholarship

**Purpose**: Sir John Logan Campbell was a successful Auckland businessman who lived from 1817 to 1912. He made many donations to the people of Auckland, including Cornwall Park. This scholarship has resulted from money gifted in 1925 from his endowment fund to help set up an agricultural teaching course in Palmerston North. It will be used to encourage 1st Year students from urban areas such as Auckland to begin a course in agriculture

**Eligibility**: The John Logan Campbell Agricultural Scholarship shall have a value determined each year from the interest earned on the capital and be open to 1st Year Massey University students who are enrolled full-time for the Bachelor of AgriCommerce degree, or the agriculture major within either the Bachelor of AgriScience degree or the Bachelor of Science degree

**Level of Study**: Graduate

**Type**: Scholarship

**Value**: NZ$2,000

**Frequency**: Varies

**Country of Study**: Any country

**Application Procedure**: Apply online

**Closing Date**: 3 March

**Funding**: Trusts

**Additional Information**: www.massey.ac.nz/massey/admission/scholarships-bursaries-awards/other-scholarships/search-results/search-results_home.cfm?page=award_display&scholarship_id=672

**For further information contact:**

**Email**:    K.Harrington@massey.ac.nz

## Sydney Campbell Undergraduate Scholarship

**Purpose**: The Sydney Campbell Scholarships are provided under the Will of the late Mr Sydney Campbell, Riverside Farm, Masterton, and are tenable at Massey University

**Level of Study**: Graduate

**Type**: Scholarship

**Value**: NZ$1,000

**Length of Study**: 1 year

**Frequency**: Varies

**Country of Study**: Any country

**Application Procedure**: Apply online

**Closing Date**: 3 March

**Funding**: Trusts

**Additional Information**: www.massey.ac.nz/massey/admission/scholarships-bursaries-awards/other-scholarships/search-results/search-results_home.cfm?page=award_display&scholarship_id=57

**For further information contact:**

**Email**:    K.Harrington@massey.ac.nz

## Turners and Growers Undergraduate Scholarships

**Purpose**: These scholarships are offered annually by T&G (formerly Turners and Growers) to assist students of high academic calibre to undertake a degree that will provide them with the education and training to support the sustainable development of the New Zealand horticultural industry

**Level of Study**: Graduate

**Type**: Scholarship

**Value**: NZ$3,000

**Length of Study**: 3 year

**Frequency**: Varies

**Country of Study**: Any country

**Application Procedure**: Apply online

**No. of awards offered**: 1

**Closing Date**: 3 March

**Funding**: Trusts

**Additional Information**: www.massey.ac.nz/massey/admission/scholarships-bursaries-awards/other-scholarships/search-results/search-results_home.cfm?page=award_display&scholarship_id=1207

**For further information contact:**

**Email**:    K.Harrington@massey.ac.nz

# Materials Research Society

9800 McKnight Road, Pittsburgh, PA 15237, United States of America.

**Contact**:    Executive Director

## The Material Handling Education Foundation

**Purpose**: The Material Handling Education Foundation, Inc.

**Eligibility**: For the academic term, the following students are eligible to apply: 1. Students enrolled full time at a qualified four-year school in bachelors, masters or doctoral program that is on the target list of programs. Bachelors student must be classified as a junior or senior in the Fall term to be eligible. 2. Students from two-year, post-secondary schools (e.g., junior, community, or technical colleges) are eligible if the student has completed a minimum of two years of study and has been accepted as a transfer student to a target four-year baccalaureate program at a qualified school in the United States. 3. All applicants must be full-time students with a "B" grade point average in their major

**Level of Study**: Graduate

**Type**: Grants, work-study (not just grants)

**Frequency**: Annual
**Country of Study**: Any country
**Application Procedure**: The online application consists of three (3) letters of recommendation and all official transcripts must be received in the Foundation offices by 15 January. Official transcripts must be sent to the Foundation directly from the Registrar's office or equivalent office at the school
**Closing Date**: 31 March
**Funding**: Private
**Additional Information**: Kindly contact Ms. Donna Varner for further communication www.mhi.org/mhefi

### For further information contact:

**Tel**:        (1) 704 676 1190
**Email**:     dvarner@mhi.org

## Matsumae International Foundation (MIF)

### Matsumae International Foundation Research Fellowship Program

**Purpose**: Towards a greater understanding of Japan and a lasting world peace
**Eligibility**: 1. Applicants must obtain a Letter of Invitation from host institutions in Japan. 2. Applicants must hold a PhD (Doctorate) degree, or be recognized by MIF as possessing equivalent academic qualifications. 3. Applicants must be at the age of 49 years old or younger at the time when documents are submitted. 4. Applicants must have sufficient abilities in the English or Japanese languages. 5. Applicants should not have past or current experiences of staying in Japan. (Except for short-term stay. E.g. sightseeing, conferences). 6. Applicants should be in employment in their home countries, and must return to their countries upon completion of their MIF fellowship tenure
**Level of Study**  Postdoctorate
**Type**: Fellowship
**Length of Study**: Between 3 months to 6 months
**Frequency**: Annual
**Country of Study**: Japan
**Application Procedure**: Applications are evaluated by the Screening Committee of MIF on the basis of academic value and the degree of perfection of the research projects
**No. of awards offered**: 232
**Closing Date**: 30 June
**Funding**: Foundation
**Contributor**: Donations
**No. of awards given last year**: 30
**No. of applicants last year**: 232

**Additional Information**: www.mif-japan.org/fellowship/announcement/?hl=en www.mif-japan.org/fellowship/announcement/?hl=en

### For further information contact:

The Matsumae International Foundation, 4-14-46, Kamiogi, Suginami-ku, Tokyo 167-0043, Japan.

**Tel**:        (81) 333 017 600
**Email**:     contact@mif-japan.org

## Max Planck Institute

The Max Planck Society grants scholarships of various amounts in line with the academic qualifications of the applicant.

### Criminology Scholarships for Foreign Researchers in Germany

**Purpose**: To pursue research programme
**Eligibility**: Preference is given to those researchers whose work promotes and advances the goals of the research program and the research focuses of the Institute
**Level of Study**: Doctorate, Postdoctorate, Research
**Value**: Doctoral scholarships: €1,365 per month Postdoctoral scholarships: €2,100 per month Research scholarships: €2,300 per month
**Length of Study**: 2 to 4 months
**Country of Study**: Germany
**Closing Date**: 31 May
**Additional Information**: scholarship-positions.com/criminology-scholarships-foreign-researchers-germany/2017/02/02/

### Max Planck Institute for the History of Science Postdoctoral Fellowship in Germany

**Purpose**: The Max Planck Institute for the History of Science, Berlin is delighted to offer two postdoctoral fellows the opportunity to study in Germany starting on 1 September, for three years, with the employment contract
**Eligibility**: Candidates of all nationalities are invited to apply; applications from women are especially welcome. The Max Planck Society is committed to promoting handicapped individuals and encourages them to apply. Candidates should hold a doctorate in the history of science or related field at the time the position begins (PhD awarded in 2016 or later)

**Level of Study**: Postdoctorate
**Type**: Fellowship
**Frequency**: Annual
**Country of Study**: Any country
**Application Procedure**: Your application should contain:
1. Cover letter (indicating in which project you are interested).
2. Curriculum vitae including the list of publications.
3. Research prospectus (maximum 750 words). 4. Sample of writing. 5. Names and contact details of at least two referees
**Closing Date**: 15 November
**Funding**: Private
**Additional Information**: scholarship-positions.com/mpiwg-postdoctoral-fellowship-international-students-germany/2018/10/06/

**For further information contact:**

Max-Planck-Institut für Wissenschaftsgeschichte, Boltzmannstrasse 22, D-14195 Berlin, Germany.

## Max Planck Institute for Dynamics and Self-Organization

Am Faberg 17, D-37077 Göttingen, Germany.

**Tel**:      (49) 551 5176 0
**Email**:   info@ds.mpg.de
**Contact**: Max Planck Institute for Dynamics and Self-Organization

The Max Planck Institute for Dynamics and Self-Organization (MPIDS) belongs to the Max Planck Society

### Max Planck Institute-DS Gauss Postdoctoral Fellowships for International Students

**Purpose**: These prestigious positions are aimed at postdoctoral researchers who have shown exceptional promise in their doctoral or early postdoctoral work, which needs to be in a relevant field
**Eligibility**: International students are eligible to apply for this fellowship. The candidate should hold a PhD/DPhil degree with a background in theoretical physics, applied mathematics, or related fields, have prior experience with non-equilibrium statistical physics of biological systems and soft matter, and be fluent in the English language
**Type**: Postdoctoral fellowship
**Value**: The candidate should hold a PhD/DPhil degree with a background in theoretical physics, applied

mathematics, or related fields, have prior experience with nonequilibrium statistical physics of biological systems and soft matter, and be fluent in the English language. The Gauss fellowship is limited to two years with the possibility of extension. Salary is in accordance with the German state public service salary scale (E13 TVöD-Bund) and the corresponding social benefits. The earliest starting date is 1 March
**Study Establishment**: The MPI-DS has recently appointed Oxford University theoretical physicist Prof. Ramin Golestanian as a new Director, and he is currently in the process of establishing the Department of Living Matter Physics. The new department will engage in a wide range of theoretical research aimed at a multi-scale understanding of the dynamics of living systems from a physical perspective
**Country of Study**: Germany
**Application Procedure**: Please apply online on our application portal. Applications in writing will not be sent back. Please send your CV, publication list, a statement of research interest and at least two letters of reference. Your statement of research interest should be commensurate with the position you are applying to. In addition to the description of your proposed research if relevant (depending on the position you are applying to), it should also briefly describe your past and current research interests and why you are interested in joining our department. The positions are open until they are filled. Once a position is filled, all applicants will be informed about the final decisions
**Additional Information**: Please check the website for more details scholarship-positions.com/mpi-ds-gauss-postdoctoral-fellowships-international-students-germany/2017/12/26/ www.scholarshipsads.com/germany-mpi-ds-gauss-postdoctoral-international-fellowships-2018/

**For further information contact:**
**Email**:   ramin.golestanian@ds.mpg.de

## Max Planck Institute for European Legal History

Postfach 50 07 01, D-60395 Frankfurt, Germany.

**Tel**:       (49) 69 789 78
**Contact**: The Max Planck Institute for European Legal History

The Max Planck Institute for European Legal History (MPIeR) in Frankfurt is a world leader in researching the history of law in Europe and beyond. Its two research departments with more than 60 scholars, the unrivalled collections of its specialized library and its numerous national and international co-operations make it the central research hub for a global scientific community investigating the past, present and future of legal regimes.

## Postdoctoral and Research Scholarships at MPIeR in Germany

**Purpose**: The Max Planck Institute for European Legal History (MPIeR) invites scholars from Germany and abroad to apply for Postdoctoral and Research Scholarships. The Institute will be awarding several scholarships for a research stay at the MPIeR

**Eligibility**: Scholars from both Germany and abroad are eligible to apply. If English is not your first language then you will need to show that your English language skills are at a high enough level to succeed in your studies

**Type**: Research

**Value**: The amount of the scholarship awarded is dependent on the scholarship holder's level of qualification. Postdocs receive €2,100.00 per month and research scholarship holders receive €2,300.00 per month

**Study Establishment**: The main areas of research pursued at the Institute are: Department I - Professor Stefan Vogenauer (Legal transfer in the common law world, History of European Union Law, Fundamental issues concerning legal reception) and Department II - Professor Thomas Duve (Diversity, property and dependency regimes in Iberian Imperial territories (16th - 20th century), Legal history of the School of Salamanca, History of legal historiography: traditions of writing legal history)

**Country of Study**: Germany

**Application Procedure**: Applications should be complete (including CV, list of publications, and the form "Additional Application Details") and submitted via the online application system. Furthermore, we request PDF copies of three major publications the applicant has authored within the last five years as well as the contact details of two personal referees

**Closing Date**: 31 May

**Additional Information**: For more information, please see the website scholarship-positions.com/postdoctoral-and-research-scholarships-mpier-germany/2018/02/13/ www.scholarshipsads.com/postdoctoral-research-scholarships-mpier-germany-2019/

### For further information contact:

**Email**: ruether@rg.mpg.de

## Max Planck Institute for Human Cognitive and Brain Sciences

Stephanstrasse 1 a, D-04103 Leipzig, Germany.

**Tel**: (49) 341 9940 00
**Contact**: Max Planck Institute for Human Cognitive and Brain

The Max Planck Institute for Human Cognitive and Brain Sciences is located in Leipzig, Germany. The institute was founded in 2004 by a merger between the former Max Planck Institute of Cognitive Neuroscience in Leipzig and the Max Planck Institute for Psychological Research in Munich. It is one of 83 institutes in the Max Planck Society (Max Planck Gesellschaft).

## Max Planck Institute-CBS Postdoctoral Position in Neuroscience of Pain Perception in Germany

**Purpose**: The aim of this research project is to understand how the multifaceted experience of pain is constructed from the interaction of external noxious input and internal expectations and predictions about pain

**Eligibility**: International students are eligible to apply for the position. Applicants must have a PhD (or equivalent degree) in neuroscience, psychology, cognitive science or a related discipline (biology, physics, computer science, engineering, etc.)

**Type**: Postdoctoral fellowship

**Value**: Remuneration is based on the pay scale of the Max Planck Society. The Max Planck Society is committed to increasing the number of individuals with disabilities in its workforce and therefore encourages applications from such qualified individuals

**Study Establishment**: Position is awarded to understand how the multifaceted experience of pain is constructed from the interaction of external noxious input and internal expectations and predictions about pain

**Country of Study**: Germany

**Application Procedure**: To apply, please submit a cover letter stating personal qualifications, a curriculum vitae, contact information for two referees, a brief statement describing your research experience, your academic achievements and your motivation to apply for this position (1 page), and copies of up to three of your publications. Please submit your application via our online system

**Closing Date**: 20 January

**Additional Information**: For more details please refer to the website scholarship-positions.com/mpi-cbs-postdoctoral-position-neuroscience-of-pain-perception-germany/2018/01/03/

**For further information contact:**

**Email**:    eippert@cbs.mpg.de

## Max Planck Research Group Neural Mechanisms of Human Communication

Max-Planck-Institut für Kognitions- und Neurowissenschaften, Stephanstrasse 1a, D-04103 Leipzig, Germany.

**Tel**:        (49) 341 9940 2476
**Email**:    kriegstein@cbs.mpg.de
**Contact**:  Mrs Prof. Dr. Katharina von Kriegstein

The positions are funded by the ERC consolidator grant SENSOCOM. The aim of the SENSOCOM project is to investigate the role of auditory and visual subcortical sensory structures in analysing human communication signals and to specify how their dysfunction contributes to human communication disorders such as developmental dyslexia and autism spectrum disorders.

### Doctor of Philosophy and Postdoctoral Positions - Investigating Sensory Aspects of Human Communication

**Purpose**: The aim of the SENSOCOM project is to investigate the role of auditory and visual subcortical sensory structures in analysing human communication signals and to specify how their dysfunction contributes to human communication disorders such as developmental dyslexia and autism spectrum disorders

**Eligibility**: Applicants from Germany are eligible to apply
**Value**: Not Known
**Study Establishment**: Positions are awarded in Investigating Sensory Aspects of Human Communication
**Country of Study**: Germany
**Application Procedure**: To apply, please submit a CV, contact information of two references, a brief personal statement describing your qualifications and future research interests, copies of up to two of your publications. Please submit your application via our online system at tinyurl.com/yck4em3s
**Additional Information**: please visit the website for more information        scholarship-positions.com/phd-postdoctoral-positions-investigating-sensory-aspects-of-human-communi

cation/2018/02/19/ scholartechscience.com/2019/03/17/phd-and-postdoctoral-positions-investigating-sensory-aspects-of-human-communication-2018/

**For further information contact:**

**Email**:    katharina.von_kriegstein@tu-dresden.de

## Max Planck Society

Max-Planck-Institut für ausländisches und internationales Strafrecht - Stipendienstelle der Verwaltung, Günterstalstrasse 73, D-79100 Freiburg i. Br, Germany.

**Contact**:  Max-Planck-Institut für ausländisches und
              internationales Recht

### Max-Planck-Society Research Scholarships

**Purpose**: To foster individual research projects, the Max Planck Society offers foreign researchers the possibility of obtaining a scholarship
**Type**: Scholarship
**Value**: €1,365 per month for doctoral scholarships. €2,100 per month for post-doctoral scholarships and €2,300 per month for research scholarships
**Country of Study**: Any country
**Application Procedure**: For information concerning the application procedure, please email stipendien@mpicc.de
**Closing Date**: 31 May
**Additional Information**: Applications can be made either to the Department of Criminal Law (Prof. Dr. Dr. h.c. mult. Ulrich Sieber) or to the Department of Criminology (Prof. Dr. Dr. h.c. mult. Hans-Jörg Albrecht). Please clearly specify the chosen department in your application www.vergemagazine.com/program-search/funding/max-planck-institut-max-planck-society-research-scholarships.html

**For further information contact:**

**Email**:    stipendien@mpicc.de

## McGill University

845 Sherbrooke Street West, Montréal, QC H3A 0G4, Canada.

**Tel**:        (1) 514 398 4066/4455
**Email**:    graduate.admissions@mcgill.ca
**Website**:  www.mcgill.ca

McGill University is Canada's best known university, renowned internationally for the highest standards in teaching and research and the outstanding record of achievement of professors and students. In fields like neurosciences, pain, cancer research and public policy to name but a few McGill is at the forefront of achievement nationally and internationally.

## Boulton Fellowship

**Purpose**: To provide young scholars with an opportunity to pursue a major research project or to complete the research requirements for a higher degree

**Eligibility**: Open to candidates who have completed the residency requirements for a doctoral degree in law

**Level of Study**: Doctorate, Postdoctorate

**Type**: Fellowship

**Value**: C$50,000-55,000 per year

**Length of Study**: 1 year

**Frequency**: Annual

**Study Establishment**: McGill University

**Country of Study**: Canada

**Application Procedure**: Application details are listed on web page

**No. of awards offered**: 20

**Closing Date**: 1 February

**Funding**: Trusts

**No. of awards given last year**: 1

**No. of applicants last year**: 20

**Additional Information**: www.scholarshipdesk.com/boulton-fellowship-programs-at-mcgill-university-in-canada/

### For further information contact:

Boulton Fund Administrators, Faculty of Law, McGill University, 3644 Peel Street, Montreal, QC H3A 1W9, Canada.

**Email**: staffappointments.law@mcgill.ca

## Internal Studentships Past and Current Year

**Purpose**: Students who apply for a Faculty of Medicine Internal Studentship are automatically considered for every award for which they are eligible

**Eligibility**: To be eligible for the studentship competition: 1. Students must be registered full-time in a Faculty of Medicine graduate research training program. 2. At the time of application, student must be in MSc1 for Masters level students or between PhD1 and PhD4 for Doctoral level students. MSc 2 students must have already been accepted to fast-track

**Level of Study**: Graduate

**Type**: Studentship

**Value**: Faculty of medicine will award an amount of C$10,000 and C$12,000 for PhD students

**Frequency**: Annual

**Country of Study**: Any country

**Application Procedure**: Listed amenities are required to process the internal studentship. 1. Studentship Application Form. 2. Publication List. 3. All graduate and undergraduate transcripts. 4. CGPA calculation. 5. Supervisor biosketch form. 6. 2 letters of support

**Closing Date**: August

**Funding**: Private

**Additional Information**: www.mcgill.ca/medresearch/students-postdocs/graduate/funding/studentships

### For further information contact:

McIntyre Medical Building, 3655 Promenade Sir William Osler, Montreal, QC H3G 1Y, Canada.

**Email**: submitgrad.med@mcgill.ca

## McGill University PhD Studentships in Neurolinguistics

**Purpose**: To aid deserving students who wish to pursue a career in neuroscience

**Eligibility**: Open to applicants who possess a First class (Honours) degree in linguistics, psychology, communication disorders or a related discipline, preferably with courses in psycho or neuro linguistics

**Level of Study**: Postgraduate

**Type**: Studentship

**Value**: C$20,000 per year plus support for presenting work at research meetings

**Frequency**: Annual

**Study Establishment**: McGill University

**Country of Study**: Canada

**Application Procedure**: Applicants must send their curriculum vitae and a detailed cover letter describing their research interests and academic goals

**Closing Date**: 4 December

**Additional Information**: linguistlist.org/issues/17/17-2302.html

### For further information contact:

McGill University, SCSD 1266, Avenue des Pins Ouest, Montreal, QC H3A 1A3, Canada.

**Email**: marc.pell@mcgill.ca

## Media@McGill

**Website**:    mediaatmcgill.ahcs@mcgill.ca
**Contact**:    Media@McGill Postdoctoral Fellowship

Media@McGill is a hub of interdisciplinary research, scholarship and public outreach on issues in media, technology and culture, located in the Department of Art History and Communication Studies at McGill University in Montreal, Canada.

### Media@McGill Postdoctoral Fellowship

**Purpose**: Media@McGill's residential postdoctoral fellowships are awarded to scholars from the humanities and social sciences, working on any historical period
**Eligibility**: The Media@McGill Postdoctoral Fellowship is open to both national and international scholars who have completed their doctoral degree in a university other than McGill. Fluency in English is essential; working knowledge of French is an asset
**Value**: C$45,000 for 1 year
**Study Establishment**: Media@McGill
**Country of Study**: Canada
**Closing Date**: 3 February
**Additional Information**: For additional information, please contact mediaatmcgill.ahcs@mcgill.ca

### For further information contact:

840 Dr Penfield, Room 231, Montreal, QC H3A 0G2, Canada.

**Tel**:    (1) 514 398 1029

## Medical Library Association (MLA)

65 East Wacker Place, Suite 1900, Chicago, IL 60601-7246, United States of America.

**Tel**:        (1) 312 419 9094
**Email**:      grants@mlahq.org
**Website**:    www.mlanet.org
**Contact**:    Maria Lopez, CAE, Executive Director

The Medical Library Association (MLA) is organized exclusively for scientific and educational purposes, and is dedicated to the support of health sciences research, education and patient care. MLA fosters excellence in the professional achievement and leadership of health sciences libraries and information professionals to enhance the quality of healthcare, education and research.

### Eugene Garfield Research Fellowship

**Purpose**: To stimulate research into the history of information sciences to increase the underlying knowledge-base and enhance the current and future practice of the information professions, particularly health sciences librarianship and health informatics
**Eligibility**: Health sciences librarians and information scientists, health professionals, researchers, educators, and administrators are eligible. Applicants must have a master's or doctor's degree or be enroled in a program leading to such a degree and demonstrate a commitment to the health sciences
**Type**: Fellowship
**Value**: US$5,000
**Length of Study**: 1 year
**Frequency**: Annual
**Application Procedure**: Applicants must submit a complete application, curriculum vitae, a detailed research proposal, and letter(s) of support from the applicant's home institution
**Closing Date**: 1 December
**Funding**: Private
**Additional Information**: The fellowship is not designed to support research for a doctoral dissertation or master's thesis. For more information about any of MLA's grants or scholarships, contact Maria Lopez at (1) 312 419 9094 (x15) issi-society.org/awards/eugene-garfield-doctoral-dissertation-award/

### LA Doctoral Fellowship

**Purpose**: The MLA Doctoral Fellowship fosters and encourages superior students to conduct doctoral work in an area of health sciences librarianship or information sciences and to provide support to individuals who have been admitted to candidacy. The award supports research or travel applicable to the candidate's study within a twelve-month period. The award and may not be used for tuition.
**Eligibility**: 1. The applicant must be a member of MLA. 2. The applicant must be a graduate of an American Library Association-accredited school of library science or have equivalent graduate credentials in related information science disciplines (i.e., computer science, biomedical informatics). 3. The candidate must be a candidate in a doctoral program with an emphasis on biomedical and health-related information science. Preference will be given to applicants who have at least 75% of their course work completed and dissertation prospectus either approved or in the approval process. 4. The candidate must be a citizen of or have permanent residence status in the United States or Canada. 5. A past recipient of the MLA doctoral fellowship is ineligible.

**Type**: Fellowship
**Value**: US$2,000
**Length of Study**: 1 year
**Application Procedure**: 1. The completed online application and all additional documentation must be received by December 1. 2. Two letters of reference are required. One reference must be from the applicant's advisor for the doctoral program in which he or she is enrolled, and the other must be from a person recognized for special competence or expertise in the proposal field. 3. The candidate is required to submit an informative summary and detailed budget for the doctoral project along with the application. 4. Once the doctoral fellowship is awarded, no changes may be made in budget or plans without prior approval from MLA. 5. The MLA doctoral fellowship will pay US$2,000 in one payment toward: project expenses related travel expenses augmenting another larger, separately funded project relevant to health sciences librarianship and which is part of the requirements of a doctoral degree. 6. All publications and oral presentations by the grantee relevant to the project should acknowledge MLA support. 7. The period of disbursement will not exceed two years past the date of the MLA annual meeting at which the award is given. 8. Depending on the qualifications of the candidates, the jury may recommend that the fellowship not be awarded in a given year. 9. MLA will acknowledge applications upon receipt via email.
**Closing Date**: 1 December
**Additional Information**: www.mlanet.org/p/cm/ld/fid=310

# Medical Research Council (MRC)

David Phillips Building, Polaris House, North Star Avenue, Wiltshire, Swindon, SN2 1FL, United Kingdom.

**Tel**: (44) 20 7636 5422
**Email**: joanne.mccallum@headoffice.mrc.ac.uk
**Website**: www.mrc.ac.uk

The Medical Research Council (MRC) offers support for talented individuals who want to pursue a career in the biomedical sciences, public health and health services research. It provides its support through a variety of personal award schemes that are aimed at each stage in a clinical or non-clinical research career.

## Biomedical Catalyst: Developmental Pathway Funding Scheme (DPFS)

**Purpose**: To encourage clinicians to become involved in research and to promote research of relevance to the Royal College of Obstetricians and Gynaecologists

**Eligibility**: Open to members of the RCOG wishing to pursue research at PhD or MD level. Applicants must have a minimum of one year of experience in clinical obstetrics and gynaecology and hold part one membership of the college. Residence requirements apply
**Level of Study**: Postgraduate, Research
**Type**: Fellowship
**Value**: £50,000-100,000 (estimated total funds is £80,000). Predoctoral level-the award provides a competitive personal salary, up to Specialist Registrar but not including NHS Consultant level, a Research Training Support Grant of up to £10,000 per year (items must be detailed and justified), and an annual travel allowance of £450. Postdoctoral level-the fellowship provides a competitive personal salary, up to Specialist Registrar but not including NHS consultant level, research expenses, and travel costs at an appropriate level for the research, under full economic costs (FEC). For full details of what funding includes at each level please see their website
**Length of Study**: 1-3 years
**Frequency**: Annual
**Study Establishment**: A suitable university or similar institution
**Country of Study**: United Kingdom
**Application Procedure**: Applicants must contact the Fellowships Section, Research Career Awards of the MRC for details
**No. of awards offered**: 2
**Funding**: Government
**No. of awards given last year**: 2
**No. of applicants last year**: 2
**Additional Information**: Please see the website for further details mrc.ukri.org/funding/browse/biomedical-catalyst-dpfs/biomedical-catalyst-developmental-pathway-funding-scheme-dpfs-submission-deadlines/

### For further information contact:

**Tel**: (44) 20 7670 5485
**Email**: fellows@headoffice.mrc.ac.uk

## Medical Research Council Career Development Award

**Purpose**: The DPFS scheme is a key part of our Translational Research Strategy and supports the translation of fundamental discoveries toward benefits to human health. It funds the pre-clinical development and early clinical testing of novel therapeutics, devices and diagnostics, including "repurposing" of existing therapies
**Eligibility**: The following condition applies to this scheme, in addition to our normal rules: Individuals may be the principal investigator (the named, lead applicant) on one application per round. All costs towards the funding scheme should be

fully justified within a proposal and the Panel will assess value for money in the context of the proposed work

**Level of Study**: Graduate

**Type**: Funding support

**Frequency**: Annual

**Country of Study**: Any country

**Application Procedure**: Proposals are assessed in a two-stage process. 1. The first step involves review of an outline proposal (download the outline Case for Support form here). Successful outline applicants are invited to submit a full application, which undergoes external peer review before a further, more detailed, review by the Panel. 2. The total assessment time for an application submitted to MRC, from outline submission to full decision, is approximately 26 weeks. All applicants will receive feedback from the assessment process. Guidance for preparation of full proposals will be provided to successful applicants with the outline feedback

**Closing Date**: 21 March

**Funding**: Private

**Additional Information**: Fundamental or investigative research not linked to a development plan (supported by the Research Boards Clinical studies where the primary purpose is to investigate disease mechanism supported by the Research Boards Late-phase clinical trials supported by the MRC-NIHR Efficacy and Mechanism Evaluation Programme and the NIHR Health Technology Assessment Programme) mrc.ukri.org/skills-careers/fellowships/non-clinical-fellowships/career-development-award-cda-transition-to-independence/

**For further information contact:**

**Email**:    DPFSandDCS@mrc.ukri.org

## Medical Research Council Clinical Research Training Fellowships

**Purpose**: To award outstanding researchers who wish to consolidate and develop their research skills and make the transition from postdoctoral research and training to becoming independent investigators, but who do not hold established positions

**Eligibility**: It is expected that all applicants will hold a PhD or MPhil in a basic science and will have at least 3 years of postdoctoral research experience

**Level of Study**: Postdoctorate, Research

**Type**: Fellowship

**Value**: Competitive personal salary support plus research support staff at the technical level, research expenses, capital equipment and a travel allowance for attendance at scientific conferences

**Length of Study**: Maximum duration of upto 5 years

**Frequency**: Annual

**Study Establishment**: A suitable university department or similar institution

**Country of Study**: United Kingdom

**Application Procedure**: Applicants must submit a personal application. Forms and further details are available from the MRC

**No. of awards offered**: 86

**Closing Date**: 25 April

**Funding**: Government

**No. of awards given last year**: 13

**No. of applicants last year**: 86

**Additional Information**: Awards may occasionally be jointly funded with other bodies. Please contact the Fellowships Section at the MRC for further details. Please see the website for further details mrc.ukri.org/skills-careers/fellowships/clinical-fellowships/clinical-research-training-fellowship-crtf/

**For further information contact:**

**Email**:    fellows@headoffice.mrc.ac.uk

## Medical Research Council Clinician Scientist Fellowship

**Purpose**: To provide an opportunity for specialized or further research training leading to the submission of a PhD, DPhil, or MD

**Eligibility**: Open to hospital doctors, dentists, general practitioners, nurses, midwives and allied health professionals. Residence requirements apply

**Level of Study**: Postgraduate, Research

**Type**: Fellowship

**Value**: An appropriate clinical academic salary will be provided along with a fixed sum for research expenses and a travel allowance for attendance at scientific conferences

**Length of Study**: Up to 3 years

**Study Establishment**: A suitable university department or similar institution

**Country of Study**: United Kingdom

**Application Procedure**: Applicants must submit a personal application. Forms and further details are available from the MRC

**No. of awards offered**: 169

**Funding**: Government

**No. of awards given last year**: 39

**No. of applicants last year**: 169

**Additional Information**: In addition to this scheme, the MRC also offers Joint Training Fellowships with the Royal Colleges of Surgeons of United Kingdom and Edinburgh and the Royal College of Obstetricians and Gynaecologists. These awards are aimed at individuals whose long-term career aspirations involve undertaking academic clinical research. Fellowships may also be jointly funded with the MS Society or the Prior Group. Please contact the Fellowships Section at the MRC for further details and see the website mrc.ukri.org/skills-careers/fellowships/clinical-fellowships/clinician-scientist-fellowship-csf/

**For further information contact:**

**Email**:   validate@ndm.ox.ac.uk

## Medical Research Council Industrial CASE Studentships

**Purpose**: To provide an opportunity for outstanding clinical researchers who wish to consolidate their research skills and make the transition from postdoctoral research and training to becoming independent investigators
**Eligibility**: The scheme is open to hospital doctors, dentists, general practitioners, nurses, midwives and allied health professionals. All applicants must have obtained their PhD or MD in a basic science or clinical project, or expect to have received their doctorate by the time they intend to take up an award, and must not hold tenured positions
**Level of Study**: Postdoctorate, Research
**Type**: Fellowship
**Value**: Competitive personal salary support plus research support staff at the technical level, research expenses, capital equipment and a travel allowance for attendance at scientific conferences
**Length of Study**: Up to 4 years
**Frequency**: Annual
**Study Establishment**: A suitable university department or similar institution
**Country of Study**: United Kingdom
**Application Procedure**: Applicants must submit a personal application. Forms and further details are available from the MRC
**No. of awards offered**: 40
**Closing Date**: 10 January
**Funding**: Government
**No. of awards given last year**: 10
**No. of applicants last year**: 40
**Additional Information**: Please see the website for further details mrc.ukri.org/skills-careers/studentships/how-we-fund-studentships/industrial-case-studentships/

**For further information contact:**

**Email**:   fellows@headoffice.mrc.ac.uk

## Medical Research Council Senior Clinical Fellowship

**Purpose**: To enhance links between academia and industry in the provision of high-quality research training
**Eligibility**: Candidates should have graduated with a good Honours Degree from a United Kingdom academic institution in a subject relevant to the MRC's scientific remit. This should be an Upper Second Class (Honours) Degree or higher. The MRC will, however, consider qualifications or a combination of qualifications and experience that demonstrates equivalent ability and attainment, e.g. a Lower Second Class (Honours) Degree can be enhanced by a Master's degree. A copy of the regulations governing residence eligibility may be obtained from the Council
**Level of Study**: Postgraduate
**Value**: A tax-free maintenance stipend depending on United Kingdom location, university tuition fees up to the current DFEE recommended limit plus college fees, where applicable. Awards also include a fixed sum for conference travel expenses and a support grant to the university department to help cover incidental costs of students' training. As a measure of interest and involvement the industrial company is expected to make a financial contribution to the cost of the studentship
**Length of Study**: Up to 4 years
**Frequency**: Annual
**Study Establishment**: Universities, medical schools, industry and other academic institutions
**Country of Study**: United Kingdom
**Application Procedure**: The MRC does not make awards directly to students. Awards are made to industrial partners who apply for studentships by application. The individual or academic partner will then advertise for students to apply for their awards. Students who wish to apply for a studentship are advised to contact the department where they wish to study to see if it has an allocation of awards
**No. of awards offered**: 23
**Closing Date**: 10 July
**Funding**: Commercial
**No. of awards given last year**: 10
**No. of applicants last year**: 23
**Additional Information**: Applicants should ensure that they have read the MRC Industrial CASE Scheme Guidance Notes before completing their application. Please see the website for further details mrc.ukri.org/skills-careers/fellowships/clinical-fellowships/senior-clinical-fellowship-scf/

**For further information contact:**

**Email**:   students@headoffice.mrc.ac.uk

## Medical Research Council Senior Non-Clinical Fellowship

**Purpose**: Aim to develop outstanding medically and other clinically qualified professionals such that they become research leaders

**Eligibility**: Open to nationals of any country. Applicants are expected to have proven themselves to be independent researchers, be well qualified for an academic research career and demonstrate the promise of becoming future research leaders. The scheme is open to hospital doctors, dentists, general practitioners, nurses, midwives and allied health professionals. Applicants must hold a PhD or MD in a basic science or clinical project and have at least 3 years of post-doctoral research experience

**Level of Study**: Postdoctorate, Research

**Type**: Fellowship

**Value**: Competitive personal salary support is provided plus research support staff at the technical and postdoctoral level, research expenses, capital equipment and a travel allowance for attendance at scientific conferences

**Length of Study**: 5 years

**Frequency**: Annual

**Study Establishment**: A suitable university department or similar institution

**Country of Study**: United Kingdom

**Application Procedure**: Applicants must submit a personal application. Forms and further details are available from the MRC

**No. of awards offered**: 8

**Closing Date**: 9 April

**Funding**: Government

**No. of awards given last year**: 1

**No. of applicants last year**: 8

**Additional Information**: Please see the website for further details mrc.ukri.org/skills-careers/fellowships/non-clinical-fellowships/senior-non-clinical-fellowship-sncf/

### For further information contact:

**Email**:    information@psych.ox.ac.uk

## Medical Research Council Special Training Fellowships in Health Services and Health of the Public Research

**Purpose**: To provide support for non-clinical scientists of exceptional ability to concentrate on a period of research

**Eligibility**: Open to nationals of any country. Applicants are expected to have proven themselves to be independent researchers, be well qualified for an academic research career and demonstrate the promise of becoming future research

leaders. Applicants should normally hold a PhD or DPhil in a basic science project, have at least 6 years of relevant postdoctoral research experience and not hold a tenured position

**Level of Study**: Postdoctorate, Research

**Type**: Fellowship

**Value**: Competitive personal salary support is provided plus research support staff at the technical and postdoctoral level, research expenses, capital equipment and a travel allowance for attendance at scientific conferences

**Length of Study**: 7 years

**Frequency**: Annual

**Study Establishment**: A suitable university department or similar institution

**Country of Study**: United Kingdom

**Application Procedure**: Applicants must submit a personal application. Forms and further details are available from the MRC

**Closing Date**: 28 April

**Funding**: Government

**No. of awards given last year**: 3

**No. of applicants last year**: 24

**Additional Information**: Please see the website for further details mrc.ukri.org/skills-careers/fellowships/

### For further information contact:

**Email**:    fellows@headoffice.mrc.ac.uk

## Medical Research Council/RCOG Clinical Research Training Fellowship

**Purpose**: To provide support for researchers wishing to gain further training in multidisciplinary research to address problems of direct relevance to the health services within the United Kingdom

**Eligibility**: Open to non-medical graduates, hospital doctors, dentists, general practitioners, nurses, midwives and allied health professionals who are seeking a research career in health services and research

**Level of Study**: Postdoctorate, Research

**Type**: Fellowship

**Value**: An appropriate academic salary will be provided along with a fixed sum for research expenses and a travel allowance for attendance at scientific conferences

**Length of Study**: Up to 4 years

**Frequency**: Annual

**Study Establishment**: A suitable university department or similar institution

**Country of Study**: United Kingdom

**Application Procedure**: Applicants must submit a personal application. Forms and further details are available from the MRC

**No. of awards offered**: 52

**Closing Date**: October
**Funding**: Government
**No. of awards given last year**: 10
**No. of applicants last year**: 52
**Additional Information**: Some awards are jointly funded with the Department of Health www.rcog.org.uk/en/careers-training/academic-og/research-funding-opportunities/mrcrcog-clinical-research-training-fellowship/

**For further information contact:**

10-18 Union Street, London, SE1 1SZ, United Kingdom.

**Tel**:      (44) 20 7772 6200
**Fax**:      (44) 20 7723 0575
**Email**:    stephanie.worton@manchester.ac.uk

## Medical Research Scotland

Turcan Connell, Princes Exchange, 1 Earl Grey Street, Edinburgh, EH3 9EE, United Kingdom.

**Tel**:      (44) 131 659 8800
**Email**:    enquiries@medicalresearchscotland.org.uk
**Website**   www.medicalresearchscotland.org.uk
**Contact**   The Trust Administrator

Medical Research Scotland is comprehensive in its support and is not focused on research into any one disease or disorder. It supports the broad spectrum of medical research, all aimed at improving the understanding of basic disease mechanisms, diagnosis, treatment or prevention of disease or advances in medical technology.

## Doctor of Philosophy Studentship

**Purpose**: To provide fully funded four year PhD Studentships, delivered collaboratively by a recognized Scottish University/Research Institution and a company working in medically-relevant research, which incorporate enhanced and tailored academic and commercial training and experience
**Eligibility**: Open to Scottish universities/research institutions working in conjunction with a trading company involved in medically-relevant life sciences research, to deliver 4 high-quality PhD studentship for suitably highly-qualified and motivated graduates of any country
**Level of Study**: Postgraduate
**Type**: Studentship
**Value**: Approx. £115,000

**Length of Study**: 4 years
**Frequency**: Annual
**Study Establishment**: Scottish Universities, Higher Education or research institutions recognized as such
**Country of Study**: Scotland
**Application Procedure**: Applications must be submitted online, following the information available at  medicalresearchscotland.org.uk/
**Closing Date**: July
**Contributor**: Income from the original endowment fund, established when the charity came into being in 1953, invested and augmented by voluntary donations and bequests
**Additional Information**: Applications must be submitted by a university and an appropriate company and not by prospective students www.ntu.ac.uk/research/research-degrees-at-ntu/phd-studentships

**For further information contact:**

**Email**:    applications@medicalresearchscotland.org

## Medical Research Scotland Sponsored Daphne Jackson Trust Fellowships

**Purpose**: To provide three year part time fellowships for those wishing to return to medical research at a Scottish University or Research Institution after a career break of three years or more. Fellowships are awarded in conjunction with the Daphne Jackson Trust
**Eligibility**: 1. Have had a career break of at least two years', taken for family, caring or health reasons. 2. Have a good Honours degree in a science, technology, engineering or mathematics (STEM) subject. 3. Have a PhD or at least 3 years' research experience (academic or industrial) prior to the career break. 4. Have UK residency status/right to remain in the UK indefinitely. 5. have a good command of English (spoken and written). 6. Have appropriate computer skills.
**Level of Study**: Postdoctorate, Professional development
**Type**: Fellowship
**Value**: Approx. £115,000
**Length of Study**: 3 years
**Frequency**: Annual
**Study Establishment**: Scottish Universities, Higher Education or research institutions recognized as such
**Country of Study**: Scotland
**Application Procedure**: Applications must be submitted online, following the information available at medicalresearchscotland.org.uk/
**Contributor**: Income from the original endowment fund, established when the charity came into being in 1953, invested and augmented by voluntary donations and bequests
**Additional Information**: medicalresearchscotland.org.uk/daphne-jackson-fellowships/

**For further information contact:**

The Daphne Jackson Trust, Department of Physics, University of Surrey, Guildford, Surrey GU2 7XH, United Kingdom.

**Email:**   DJMFT@surrey.ac.uk

## Meet The Composer, Inc.

90 John Street, Suite 312, New York, NY 10038, United States of America.

**Tel:**        (1) 212 645 6949
**Email:**     mtc@meetthecomposer.org
**Website:**   www.newmusicusa.org

Meet The Composer's mission is to increase artistic and financial opportunities for American composers by fostering the creation, performance, dissemination and appreciation of their music.

## Commissioning Music/United States of America

**Purpose**: To support the commissioning of new works
**Eligibility**: Open to citizens of the United States of America only. Organizations that have been producing or presenting for at least 3 years are eligible and may be dance, chorus, orchestra, opera, theatre and music-theatre companies, festivals, arts presenters, public radio and television stations, internet providers, soloists and small performing ensembles of all kinds, e.g. jazz, chamber, new music, etc
**Level of Study**: Professional development
**Type**: Grant
**Value**: Up to US$10,000-20,000
**Frequency**: Annual
**Country of Study**: United States of America
**Application Procedure**: Individuals cannot apply on their own. Host organizations must submit completed application forms and accompanying materials
**No. of awards offered**: 150-200
**Closing Date**: 19 March
**Contributor**: Offered in partnership with the National Endowment for the Arts
**No. of awards given last year**: 20-30
**No. of applicants last year**: 150-200
**Additional Information**: Please see the website for further details www.newmusicusa.org/grants/commissioning-music-usa/

**For further information contact:**

**Tel:**        (1) 212 645 6040 ext 102
**Email:**     swinship@newmusicusa.org

## JP Morgan Chase Regrant Program for Small Ensembles

**Purpose**: To support small New York City-based ensembles and music organizations committed to performing the work of living composers and contemporary music
**Eligibility**: Open to organizations focused primarily or exclusively on new music and living composers, improvisers, sound artists or singer/songwriters
**Level of Study**: Professional development
**Type**: Grant
**Value**: US$1,000-5,000
**Frequency**: Annual
**Country of Study**: United States of America
**Application Procedure**: Applicants must contact the organization
**No. of awards offered**: 75-100
**Funding**: Commercial
**Contributor**: In partnership with JP Morgan Chase
**No. of awards given last year**: 15-20
**No. of applicants last year**: 75-100
**Additional Information**: jpmorganchaseco.gcs-web.com/static-files/3553e235-ead8-4320-bebe-8c4f5b5e7f65

**For further information contact:**

**Email:**     east.giving@jpmchase.com

## Melville Trust for Care and Cure of Cancer

Tods Murray LLP, Edinburgh Quay, 133 Fountain Bridge, Edinburgh, EH3 9AG, United Kingdom.

**Tel:**        (44) 131 656 2000
**Email:**     melvilletrust@todsmurray.com
**Contact:**   The Secretary

## Melville Trust for Care and Cure of Cancer Research Fellowships

**Purpose**: To fund innovative research work in the care or cure of cancer
**Eligibility**: Applicants, who need not necessarily hold a medical qualification or have experience of research, should

have formulated proposals for a research project which have been discussed with an established research worker in the field. The applicant should normally be under 30 years of age

**Level of Study**: Research

**Type**: Fellowship

**Value**: £2,000

**Length of Study**: 1-3 years

**Frequency**: Annual

**Study Establishment**: One of the clinical or scientific departments in Lothian, Borders, Fife or Dundee

**Application Procedure**: Applicants must complete an application form and then be interviewed

**No. of awards offered**: 4

**Closing Date**: 28 February

**Funding**: Private

**No. of awards given last year**: 1

**No. of applicants last year**: 4

**Additional Information**: blogs.cs.st-andrews.ac.uk/csblog/2019/07/03/the-melville-trust-for-the-care-and-cure-of-cancer-phd-award/

### For further information contact:

Melville Trust for Care and Cure of Cancer, c/o Tods Murray LLP, Edinburgh Quay 133 Fountain Bridge, Edinburgh EH3 9AG, United Kingdom.

## Melville Trust for Care and Cure of Cancer Research Grants

**Purpose**: To fund innovative research work in cure or care of cancer

**Eligibility**: Applicants need not necessarily hold a medical qualification or have experience of research. Research support by the Trust will be carried out in a clinical or scientific department in Lothians, Borders, Fife or Dundee, the head of which must signify his or her approval of the application

**Level of Study**: Research

**Type**: Grant

**Value**: Up to £25,000

**Length of Study**: 1-3 years

**Frequency**: Annual

**Study Establishment**: One of the clinical or scientific departments in Lothian, Borders, Fife or Dundee

**Application Procedure**: Applicants must complete an application form

**No. of awards offered**: 7

**Closing Date**: 28 February

**Funding**: Private

**No. of awards given last year**: 1

**No. of applicants last year**: 7

**Additional Information**: blogs.cs.st-andrews.ac.uk/csblog/2019/07/03/the-melville-trust-for-the-care-and-cure-of-cancer-phd-award/

## Memorial Foundation for Jewish Culture

50 Broadway, 34th Floor, New York, NY 10004, United States of America.

| | |
|---|---|
| **Tel**: | (1) 212 425 6606 |
| **Email**: | office@mfjc.org |
| **Website**: | www.mfjc.org |
| **Contact**: | Jeni S. Friedman, Executive Vice President |

The Memorial Foundation for Jewish Culture is committed to the creation, intensification, and dissemination of Jewish culture worldwide, the development of creative programs to meet the emerging needs of Jewish communities globally, and to serving as a central forum for identifying and supporting innovative programs to insure the continuation of creative Jewish life wherever Jewish communities exist.

## Ephraim Urbach Post Doctoral Fellowship

**Purpose**: To assist recent recipients of the PhD in a field of Jewish studies in publishing their first book, launching their scholarly career, and/or furthering research in their area of special interest

**Eligibility**: Graduates of a PhD programme in a field of Jewish studies who achieved superior grades, in graduate school, completed their dissertation with distinction, and who show promise of distinguished academic careers are eligible to apply

**Level of Study**: Postgraduate

**Type**: Fellowship

**Value**: Up to US$10,000

**Length of Study**: 1 academic year

**Frequency**: Annual

**Country of Study**: Any country

**Application Procedure**: Applicants must be nominated by the head of the department at which they completed their PhD and must have received their PhD within 3 years of the date of application. Applicants must write requesting an application

**Closing Date**: 31 March

**Additional Information**: www.jewish-studies.org/membership2_en.ehtml

### For further information contact:

**Email**:     office@mfjs.org

# Memorial University of Newfoundland (MUN)

Memorial University of Newfoundland, St. John's, PO Box 4200, St Johns, NL A1C 5S7, Canada.

| | |
|---|---|
| **Tel**: | (1) 709 737 8000 |
| **Email**: | info@mun.ca |
| **Website**: | www.mun.ca |

Located in Canada's most easterly province, Newfoundland and Labrador, Memorial University of Newfoundland (MUN) offers a diverse selection of Graduate programmes leading to diplomas, Master's and Doctoral degrees in the arts, sciences, professional and interdisciplinary areas of study. Their goal is to promote excellence in all aspects of Graduate education in order to assist students to fulfil their personal goals and to prepare for a productive career.

## School of Graduate Studies F. A. Aldrich Award

**Purpose**: To financially assist students with exceptional academic achievement to study further
**Eligibility**: Open to full-time Canadian students on the basis of exceptional academic achievement
**Level of Study**: Postdoctorate, Predoctorate
**Type**: Fellowship
**Value**: C$2,000
**Frequency**: Annual
**Study Establishment**: Memorial University of Newfoundland
**Country of Study**: Any country
**Additional Information**: Please see the website for details www.mun.ca/sgs/current/scholarships/internal_nominated.php#sgsaldrich   www.med.mun.ca/getdoc/359e8c84-8b04-48de-a8c4-f180bb039c61/School-of-Graduate-Studies-FA-Aldrich-Fellowship.aspx

## The Dr Ethel M. Janes Memorial Scholarship in Education

**Purpose**: To aid students who want to specialize in reading and language arts and to those who want to make a career in research and teaching in primary and elementary education
**Eligibility**: Must be a full-time graduate student (not working more than 24 hours per week) in the area of Language and Literacy Studies for the Fall and Winter semesters
**Level of Study**: Graduate

**Type**: Scholarship
**Value**: C$2,000
**Frequency**: Annual
**Country of Study**: Any country
**Application Procedure**: If you wish to be considered for this award please contact Darlene Flight (dflight@mun.ca)
**Closing Date**: 4 December
**Additional Information**: This scholarship will be awarded on the basis of academic standing in a first Memorial University of Newfoundland Education degree to a graduate student with a specialization in reading or language arts. In the event that in any given year no graduate student qualifies for the award, this scholarship will be awarded to an undergraduate student. Instalments of C$1,000.00 each will be awarded in two successive academic terms; and the scholarship is renewable for two years, provided first-class standing is maintained. Please see the website for details www.mun.ca/educ/grad/awards_scholarships.php   www.scholarshipscanada.com/Scholarships/6862/Dr.-Ethel-M.-Janes-Memorial-Scholarship-in-Education-(Undergraduate)

## Training Graduate PhD Salary Award (TGP)

**Purpose**: Salary awards are offered to graduate students who are undertaking full-time research training in an area of clear relevance to arthritis and the Arthritis Society's new Strategic Plan 2020-2025: Accelerating Impact - Research Strategy which aims to identify research avenues that focus on areas of highest priority to patients and achieve the highest levels of scientific excellence and rigour. Applications must focus on innovative research efforts in the following priority areas.
**Eligibility**: 1. Be engaged in full-time training in research in a Canadian graduate school program leading to a PhD 2. Be within the first three years of a PhD training program at the time of the application deadline. 3. Be working on a research project with clear relevance relevance to the research priority areas in the Arthritis Society's 2020-25.
**Level of Study**: Postgraduate
**Type**: Award
**Value**: 21,000
**Application Procedure**: All submissions will be screened for completeness and eligibility. Note that incomplete applications by the deadline will be deemed ineligible and withdrawn from the competition. It is the responsibility of the applicant to ensure that applications are complete at the time of submission.
**Closing Date**: 15 April
**Additional Information**: arthritis.ca/researchers-research-programs-awards/current-funding-opportunities/request-for-applications-training-graduate-phd-s

# Microsoft Research

One Microsoft Way, Redmond, WA 98052, United States of America.

**Tel:** (1) 300 642 7676
**Email:** latamint@microsoft.com
**Website:** www.research.microsoft.com

In 1991, Microsoft Corporation became the first software company to create its own computer science research organization. It has developed into a unique entity among corporate research laboratories, balancing an open academic model with an effective process for transferring its research to product development teams.

## Microsoft Fellowship

**Purpose**: To empower and encourage PhD students in the Asia-Pacific region to realize their potential in computer science-related research and to recognize and award outstanding PhD students

**Eligibility**: Open to candidates who specialize in computer science, electronic engineering, information technology or applied mathematics and are in their first or second year of PhD programme and is enroled as a PhD student by the time of the nomination and has spent 6-18 months working towards a PhD.

**Level of Study**: Research

**Type**: Fellowships

**Value**: 100% of the tuition and fees, a stipend to cover living expenses while in school (US$28,000), travel allowance to attend professional conferences or seminars (US$4,000). See the website for details

**Length of Study**: 2 years

**Frequency**: Annual

**Application Procedure**: Applicants must send the completed application form (downloaded from the website), 2 recommendation letters, curriculum vitae and a video or Power Point presentation with audio introduction (on compact disc), including statement of purpose, previous, on-going and future projects, research interests and accomplishments

**Closing Date**: 9 October

**Additional Information**: Previous Microsoft Fellows are excluded. Please see the website for further details www.microsoft.com/en-us/research/academic-program/phd-fellowship/

## For further information contact:

MS Fellow 2006 Committee Microsoft Research Asia 3F Beijing Sigma Center No 49 Zhichun Road, Beijing, China.

**Email:** msfellow@microsoft.com

## Microsoft Research European PhD Scholarship Programme

**Purpose**: To recognize and support exceptional students who show the potential to make an outstanding contribution to science

**Eligibility**: Applicant must have been accepted by a university in Europe to start a PhD or will have completed no more than 1 year of their PhD by October

**Level of Study**: Doctorate

**Type**: Scholarships

**Value**: €30,000 per year and a laptop with a range of software applications

**Length of Study**: 3 years

**Frequency**: Annual

**Closing Date**: 31 March

**Additional Information**: All queries should be sent via email and please see the website for further details www.microsoft.com/en-us/research/academic-program/phd-scholarship-europe-middle-east-africa/

## For further information contact:

**Email:** msrphd@microsoft.com

# Middlesex University London

**Website:** www.mdx.ac.uk
**Contact:** Scholarships office

## International Merit Award

**Purpose**: Middlesex University is renowned for offering unrivalled support to international students and gives out scholarships and merit awards to international students totalling around £1,000,000 each year

**Eligibility**: Open to any international postgraduate student in any subject

**Level of Study**: Graduate, Postgraduate

**Type**: Award

**Value**: Up to £2,000

**Frequency**: Annual
**Study Establishment**: Middlesex University London
**Country of Study**: United Kingdom
**Application Procedure**: There is no separate application for this award; international students should apply for their chosen course through the normal application process. Awards will be given on a case-by-case basis which will be dependent on your course and application
**Contributor**: Middlesex University London
**Additional Information**: Successful candidates will be notified at the point of offer for a programme of study and the award amount will be deducted from their tuition fees. NB: Research students are not eligible for the International Merit Award  studyabroad.shiksha.com/scholarships/international-merit-scholarship-master-of-engineering

## For further information contact:

**Tel**:      (61) 7 3138 8822
**Email**:    sef.enquiry@qut.edu.au

## Santander Formula Scholarship

**Eligibility**: Open to any undergraduate or postgraduate student from South America. Awarded to South American students demonstrating excellent academic potential. To be eligible students must: Hold an offer of a place for a one-year postgraduate taught masters at the University of Glasgow, Be a national of Argentina, Belgium, Brazil, Chile, China, Colombia Germany, Ghana, Mexico, Poland, Peru, Portugal, Puerto, Rico, Russia, Singapore, South Korea, Spain, United Arab Emirates, United Kingdom, Uruguay, Venezuela United States of America
**Level of Study**: Graduate, Postgraduate
**Type**: Scholarship
**Value**: £4,200 towards the students' fees
**Study Establishment**: Middlesex University London
**Country of Study**: United Kingdom
**Application Procedure**: Email the Americas and Caribbean regional office (info@mdxna.com)
**Contributor**: Middlesex University London
**Additional Information**: Please note that awards will be allocated based on application date so we encourage you to apply as soon as possible www.ufvinternational.com/en/santander-scholarships/formula-santander-international-scholarships/

## For further information contact:

**Email**:    support.team@postgraduatesearch.com

## Santander Mobility Scholarship

**Purpose**: The Santander Universities Mobility Scholarship is available for students from Edinburgh Napier University participating in a single trimester or full year overseas exchange programme. Awards will be made to students who would ordinarily be unable to participate in their exchange without support from the scholarship.
**Eligibility**: Open to any undergraduate or postgraduate exchange student. Available for exchange students resident within the United Kingdom and countries listed in the Santander Universidades scheme*
**Level of Study**: Graduate, Postgraduate
**Type**: Scholarship
**Value**: £1,000 each
**Study Establishment**: Middlesex University London
**Country of Study**: United Kingdom
**No. of awards offered**: 11
**Contributor**: Middlesex University London
**Additional Information**: *Countries involved in the Santander Universidades Scheme include; Argentina, Brazil, Belgium, Chile, China, Colombia, Germany, Ghana, Korea, Mexico, Poland, Portugal, Puerto Rico, Russia, Singapore, Spain, United States of America, United Kingdom, UAE, and Uruguay  www.becas-santander.com/en/program/santander-universities-mobility-scholarship

## For further information contact:

Dr Nosheen Rachel-Naseem, Student Exchange Manager.

**Tel**:      (44) 208 411 5962
**Email**:    N.Rachel-Naseem@mdx.ac.uk

## Santander Work Based Learning Scholarship

**Purpose**: This award is available to Work Based Learning students who have demonstrated academic excellence. You must have applied, or be currently enrolled on an undergraduate or postgraduate/doctoral programme within the Institute for Work Based Learning
**Eligibility**: Open to any Work Based Learning student who has demonstrated academic excellence. You must have applied, or be currently enroled on an undergraduate or postgraduate/doctoral programme within the Institute for Work Based Learning
**Level of Study**: Doctorate, Graduate, Postgraduate
**Type**: Scholarship
**Value**: £5,000
**Study Establishment**: Middlesex University London
**Country of Study**: United Kingdom

**Application Procedure**: To apply, please fill in our Scholarship application form
**Closing Date**: 28 August
**Contributor**: Middlesex University London
**Additional Information**: www.plymouth.ac.uk/study/fees/scholarships-bursaries-and-funding/santander-scholarships

### For further information contact:

**Tel**:  (44) 208 411 5415
**Email**:  scholarships@mdx.ac.uk

## Significant Achievement in Sport

**Purpose**: This is for talented sports performers, who are keen to continue their sporting endeavours and compete for the University.
**Eligibility**: Any undergraduate or postgraduate student demonstrating a significant achievement in sport.
**Level of Study**: Postgraduate
**Value**: Ranging from £200 to £1,000
**Closing Date**: 4 September
**Additional Information**: www.mdx.ac.uk/study-with-us/fees-and-funding/scholarships-and-bursaries

### For further information contact:

**Tel**:  (44) 208 411 5415
**Email**:  scholarships@mdx.ac.uk

## The Alumni Bursary

**Eligibility**: Available to United Kingdom/EU students who completed their first degree at Middlesex and have an offer for a further taught masters programme here. The bursary applies to self-financing students and students not eligible for funding from Student Finance United Kingdom. International (i.e. outside of the EU) alumni, not already receiving an International Merit Award or regional award, may be eligible to receive a 10% reduction in tuition fees when progressing to postgraduate study at Middlesex
**Level of Study**: Graduate, Postgraduate
**Type**: Bursary
**Value**: Up to 20% of the tuition fee
**Frequency**: Dependent on funds available
**Study Establishment**: Middlesex University London
**Country of Study**: United Kingdom
**Application Procedure**: Find out more from your nearest regional office
**Contributor**: Middlesex University London

**Additional Information**: Students already holding another Middlesex Scholarship (e.g. Academic Excellence Scholarship) are not entitled to the Alumni bursary london.ac.uk/applications/funding-your-study/alumni-bursary#terms-and-conditions-3425

### For further information contact:

The Burroughs, London, NW4 4BT, United Kingdom.

**Tel**:  (44) 20 8411 6286
**Email**:  scholarships@mdx.ac.uk

## The David Caminer Postgraduate Scholarship in Business Computing

**Eligibility**: Open to any first year MSc student in the School of Science and Technology. The scholarships will be available to students who have demonstrated excellent academic potential. Applications are welcome from students who have fulfilled the admission criteria and been offered a place to study for a postgraduate degree based in the School of Science & Technology
**Level of Study**: Graduate, Postgraduate
**Type**: Scholarship
**Value**: £5,000
**Frequency**: Annual
**Study Establishment**: Middlesex University London
**Country of Study**: United Kingdom
**Application Procedure**: To apply, please fill in the Scholarship application form (mdx.hobsons.co.uk/emtinterestpage.aspx?ip=scholarship)
**Closing Date**: August
**Contributor**: Middlesex University London
**Additional Information**: A student will only be entitled to one award during his/her period of study with Middlesex University scholarship-positions.com/david-caminer-postgraduate-scholarship-in-business-computing-middlesex-university-uk-2014/2014/07/23/

## Miles Morland Foundation

**Email**:  MMF@blakman.com
**Website**:  www.milesmorlandfoundation.com

The MMF was set up by Miles Morland after a career investing in Africa through two companies he founded, Blakeney Management and DPI (Development Partners International). In the course of this career Miles has been surprised, entertained, impressed, and humbled by the energy, wit, entrepreneurialism and talent of the Africans he has got to know.

## Miles Morland Foundation Writing Scholarship

**Purpose**: To help meet this need the MMF annually awards a small number of Morland Writing Scholarships, with the aim being to allow each Scholar the time to produce the first draft of a completed book. The Scholarships are open to anyone writing in the English language who was born in Africa, or both of whose parents were born in Africa

**Eligibility**: The Scholarships are open to anyone writing in the English language who was born in Africa, or both of whose parents were born in Africa. To qualify for the Scholarship a candidate must submit an excerpt from a piece of work of between 2,000 - 5,000 words, written in English that has been published and offered for sale,. This will be evaluated by a panel of readers and judges set up by the MMF. The work submitted will be judged purely on literary merit. It is not the purpose of the Scholarships to support academic or scientific research, or works of special interest such as religious or political writings. Submissions or proposals of this nature do not qualify.

**Type**: Scholarships

**Value**: £18,000, paid monthly

**Length of Study**: 12 Months

**Frequency**: Annual

**Closing Date**: 1 July

**Additional Information**: milesmorlandfoundation.com/about-2/

### For further information contact:

**Email**:    scholarships@milesmorlandfoundation.com

## Minerva Stiftung

Gesellschaft für die Forschung mbH, Hofgartenstrasse 8, D-80539 Munich, Germany.

**Tel**:        (49) 89 2108 1420
**Email**:    langegao@gv.mpg.de
**Website**:  www.minerva.mpg.de

### Minerva Short-Term Research Grants

**Purpose**: To fund scientific visits of Israeli scholars and scientists and to promote Israeli-German scientific co-operation

**Eligibility**: Open to applicants from all research facilities (in Israel-public or governmental research institutes) and universities in Germany and Israel. Applicants should not be older than 38 years. (Maternal leave will be taken into account with regard to the age limit)

**Level of Study**: Research

**Type**: Grant

**Value**: €300 per week for doctoral candidates and €425 per week for postdoctoral candidates. (Additional payments like travel grants and family allowances are possible, depending on the type of the fellowship/grant)

**Length of Study**: 1-8 weeks

**Study Establishment**: A German university or research institute

**Country of Study**: Germany

**Application Procedure**: Applications including letters of invitation and letters of recommendation must be sent by electronic mail and must reach the Minerva office by May 2nd

**Closing Date**: 2 November

**Additional Information**: Flights are covered by a lump sum of up to €700.00 www.minerva.mpg.de/16320/application

### For further information contact:

Minerva Foundation, Gesellschaft für die Forschung mbH, Hofgartenstraße 8, D-80539 München, Germany.

**Tel**:        (49) 89 2108 1258
**Fax**:       (49) 89 2108 1451
**Email**:    michael.nagel@gv.mpg.de

## Ministry of Education and Science Republic of Latvia (MESRL)

Valnuiela 2, LV-1050 Riga, Latvia.

**Tel**:        (371) 722 6209
**Email**:    info@izm.gov.lv
**Website**:  www.izm.gov.lv

The ministry was established immediately after the proclamation of the Latvian state on 18 November 1918. Today the Ministry of Education and Science is the leading public administration institution in the Republic of Latvia in the field of education and science, as well as in the areas of sports, youth and state language policies.

## Ministry of Education and Science of the Republic of Lithuania Scholarships for Studies and Research Work

**Purpose**: To encourage foreign students in studies and research work

**Eligibility**: Open to candidates from Belarus, The Czech Republic, Flanders, Greece, Estonia, Italy, China, Lithuania, Mongolia, Poland, Spain and Hungary
**Level of Study**: Research
**Type**: Scholarships
**Value**: Varies
**Length of Study**: 10 months
**Frequency**: Annual
**Application Procedure**: Applicants can download the application form from the website. The completed application form along with a curriculum vitae, letter of motivation, certified copies of education documents, letters of recommendation and photograph must be sent
**Closing Date**: 15 May
**Additional Information**: www.topuniversities.com/student-info/scholarships/international-scholarships-students-developing-countries

## For further information contact:

**Tel**:      (371) 704 7876
**Email**:   mara.katvare@izm.gov.lv

# Ministry of Fisheries

Pastoral House, 25 The Terrace, PO Box 2526, Wellington 6140, New Zealand.

**Tel**:        (64) 800 00 8333
**Email**:     info@fish.govt.nz
**Website**:   www.fish.govt.nz/en-nz/default.htm

## Ministry of Fisheries PG Scholarships in Quantitative Fisheries Science

**Purpose**: To allow graduate students to develop expertise in quantitative fisheries science and encourage postgraduate students to contribute to priority research areas identified by the New Zealand government
**Eligibility**: Open to applicants with majors or minors in mathematics, statistics, biology, economics or computer science
**Level of Study**: Postgraduate
**Type**: Scholarship
**Value**: NZ$30,000 per year for PhD and up to NZ$20,000 per year for Masters
**Length of Study**: 3 years (PhD) and up to 2 years (Masters)
**Frequency**: Annual
**Country of Study**: Any country
**Application Procedure**: Applicants should contact Rebecca Lawton for details

**Closing Date**: 20 September
**Contributor**: In collaboration with NIWA
**Additional Information**: Research is most likely to be carried out a NIWA facility. Preference will be given to New Zealand citizens docplayer.net/161463027-Ministry-of-fisheries-niwa-postgraduate-scholarships-in-quantitative-fisheries-science.html

## For further information contact:

**Tel**:      (64) 4 819 4251
**Email**:   rebecca.lawton@fish.govt.nz

# Ministry of Foreign Affairs

Piazzale della Farnesina, I-00135 Roma, Italy.

## Master Scholarships for International Students

**Purpose**: The aim of the Program is to foster cooperation among Italian Universities and Italian companies in order to promote their internationalization by sustaining higher education courses tailored to the needs of the labor market
**Eligibility**: Candidates should submit an English language certificate as proof of their proficiency in English. Candidates should hold at least a B2 level certificate within the Common European Framework of Reference for Languages (CEFR). Proof of proficiency in Italian is not mandatory but will be taken into consideration in the selection process
**Value**: Grantees will receive €888 monthly allowance every three months on their Italian bank account. The first instalment of the scholarship can only be received after the University enrollment according to the necessary administrative procedures. The last instalment of the scholarship can only be received after verification of conditions established under Article 6.2 of this Call. The scholarship only covers courses attended in Italy
**Study Establishment**: Scholarships are awarded to study the subjects offered by the university
**Country of Study**: Italy
**Application Procedure**: Candidates must complete and submit the online application form
**Closing Date**: 28 February
**Additional Information**: For more information please see the website scholarship-positions.com/master-scholarships-for-international-students-italy/2017/12/19

## For further information contact:

**Email**:   dgsp.iyt@esteri.it

## Ministry of Foreign Affairs and International Cooperation

Piazzale della Farnesina, 1, I-00135 Rome, Italy.

### Ministry of Foreign Affairs and International Cooperation Scholarships for Foreign and Italian Students

**Purpose**: The Ministry of Foreign Affairs and International Cooperation is inviting applications for grants for foreign citizens and Italian citizens living abroad awarded by the Italian Government

**Eligibility**: In order to apply for MAECI scholarships, candidates who enroll to courses held in Italian must possess an Italian language certificate level B2

**Type**: Scholarship

**Value**: €900 monthly allowance on a quarterly basis, which will be paid on their Italian bank account

**Country of Study**: Italy

**Application Procedure**: Applicants must complete and submit the online application form available upon registration at the following link: www.scholarshipsupdates.com/maeci-scholarships-for-foreign-and-italian-students-2018-2019/

**Closing Date**: 30 April

**Additional Information**: www.nationalmeritscholarships.com/maeci-scholarships-for-foreign-and-italian-citizens-in-italy.html

#### For further information contact:

Corso Duca degli Abruzzi, 24, I-10129 Torino, Italy.

**Email**:     admin@scholarship-positions.com

## Ministry of Foreign Affairs of the Republic of Indonesia

Directorate of Public Diplomacy, Tower Building, 12th Floor, Jl. Pejambon No. 6, Jakarta Pusat 10110, Indonesia.

**Tel**:          (62) 21 344 15 08
**Website**:    www.kemlu.go.id

### Indonesian Arts and Culture Scholarship

**Purpose**: The program serves to demonstrate Indonesia's commitment as an initiator of the establishment of South West Pacific Dialogue and as the originator member of ASEAN in advancing the social culture cooperation in the region. The program also has an objective to encourage better understanding amongst participants from member countries

**Eligibility**: The scholarship will cover: Tuition fee (including extra-curricular activities); A round trip economy class ticket; Accommodation (board and lodging); Local transportation during program; Health insurance (limited). All awardees are advised to have their own health insurance. Monthly allowance of Rp. 2,000.000

**Level of Study**: Postgraduate

**Type**: Scholarships and fellowships

**Frequency**: Annual

**Country of Study**: Any country

**Application Procedure**: 1. Candidates should be a single, between the ages of 21 to 27 years-old with at least a high school diploma. 2. Candidates should possess high interest and talent in arts. Arts students or those with an academic history on Indonesian culture are encouraged to apply. 3. Bearing in mind the intensity of the program, candidates are highly advised to ensure prime physical mentally psychologist conditions, particularly for female candidates to ensure that they do not conceive prior and during the program. 4. Participants must arrive in Indonesia a day before the Orientation Program. 5. Participants must follow the whole program, including orientation program and Indonesian Channel

**Closing Date**: 14 February

**Funding**: Private

**Additional Information**:     www.indonesia.cz/indonesian-arts-and-culture-scholarship/

#### For further information contact:

The Ministry of Foreign Affairs Directorate of Public Diplomacy Tower Building, 12th Floor, Jl. Taman Pejambon No. 6, Jakarta 10110, Indonesia.

**Tel**:          (62) 420 257 214 388
**Email**:      embassy@indonesia.cz

## Minnesota Historical Society (MHS)

345 Kellogg Boulevard West, St Paul, MN 55102, United States of America.

**Tel**:          (1) 651 297 4464
**Email**:      debbie.miller@mnhs.org
**Website**:    www.mnhs.org
**Contact**:    Ms Stacey Kennedy, Research Supervisor

The Minnesota Historical Society (MHS) is a private, non-profit educational and cultural institution established in

1849 to preserve and share Minnesota history. The Society collects, preserves and tells the story of Minnesota's past through interactive and engaging museum exhibits, extensive libraries and collections, 23 historic sites, educational programmes and book publishing.

## Minnesota Historical Society Research Grant

**Purpose**: To support original research and interpretative writing by academics, independent Scholars and professional or non professional writers
**Eligibility**: Open to applicants of any nationality with English reading and writing ability
**Level of Study**: Unrestricted
**Type**: Grant
**Value**: Varies. Up to US$1,500 for research that will result in an article, up to US$5,000 for research that will result in a book or up to US$1,000 for visiting Scholar grants
**Length of Study**: Varies
**Frequency**: Twice a year
**Country of Study**: Any country
**Application Procedure**: Applicants must complete an application form. Other documentation is also required. Guidelines and applications are available by writing to the given address, by sending an email or from the website
**No. of awards offered**: 45
**Closing Date**: 10 April
**Funding**: Government
**Contributor**: The state of Minnesota
**No. of awards given last year**: 22
**No. of applicants last year**: 45
**Additional Information**: www.mnhs.org/preservation/legacy-grants

### For further information contact:

**Email**: d@mhs.com

## Minnesota Ovarian Cancer Alliance (MOCA)

The Minnesota Ovarian Cancer Alliance funds research, provides support to women and families, educates the medical community and raises awareness.

**Tel**: (1) 612 822 0500
**Email**: info@mnovarian.org
**Website**: mnovarian.org/

**Contact**: Kathleen Gavin, Executive Director, Minnesota Ovarian Cancer Alliance, 4604 Chicago Avenue, Minneapolis, MN 55407, United States of America.

Formed in 1999 by a group of ovarian cancer survivors, MOCA is a statewide non-profit that serves women and families from throughout the Upper Midwest.

## National Early Detection of Ovarian Cancer Research Awards 2020

**Purpose**: The Minnesota Ovarian Cancer Alliance will award two grants in November 2020 to support research on early detection of ovarian cancer.
**Eligibility**: Research proposals may be for individual projects or part of a larger research project related to early detection of ovarian, primary peritoneal or fallopian tube cancer. Awards are available to researchers working anywhere in the U.S. Project funding is available for one year of activit
**Level of Study**: postgraduate
**Type**: Grant
**Value**: US$50,000
**Frequency**: Annual
**Country of Study**: United States of America
**Application Procedure**: Proposals must be paginated and include the following: Cover letter should include the grant title, the PI's name and direct contact information. Abstract of proposed research, including rationale of the study (you do not need to include an explanation of why ovarian cancer is worthy of being studied or basic statistics on ovarian cancer as these are very familiar to all our reviewers), significance of research, explanation as to why this is innovative (if it is), aims, and a brief overview of research design and methods. Summary of proposed research (one paragraph) which describes the proposed research in terms an educated layperson would understand and describes the significance of the research to the patient population. Research proposal, not to exceed 6 pages. Additional supporting information may be provided in addendum form if deemed essential. Budget should include category of expense and include a rationale for each budget item. MOCA funds can be used for PI salary, conference travel and publication costs as deemed necessary by PI. Salary costs should be detailed. MOCA funds cannot be used for indirect costs. Information about PI, including: Biographical statement of personal career goals of PI (one page) Contact information, including direct phone number and email address Curriculum vitae (resume), including education, honors, professional experience, publications, grants Biographical sketch format is acceptable Letter of recommendation from the relevant person overseeing the institution,

department, or lab where the research will be conducted. Project timeline detailing the expected chronological progress of research aims. Review of similar studies, including similar studies underway or pending which might influence subject accrual or funding.

**Closing Date**: 1 September

### For further information contact:

Kathleen Gavin, Executive Director, Minnesota Ovarian Cancer Alliance, 4604 Chicago Avenue, Minneapolis, MN 55407, United States of America.

**Email**:    kmicek@mnovarian.org

## Missouri Department of Higher Education

### Access Missouri Financial Assistance Program

**Purpose**: The Access Missouri Financial Assistance Program is a state program, administered through the Missouri Department of Higher Education, established to provide financial assistance to undergraduate student enrolled full-time at a participating Missouri school

**Eligibility**: The EFC is calculated by the United States Department of Education using information provided on the FAFSA. Students should contact his/her school or the MDHE for additional details regarding his/her eligibility status

**Level of Study**: Graduate

**Type**: Programme grant

**Value**: Award ranges US$300 and up to US$4,600 annually

**Frequency**: Annual

**Country of Study**: United States of America

**Application Procedure**: Submit your FAFSA each year by the deadlines in the Initial Students section under 'Am I Eligible'? The MDHE receives electronic FAFSA records for Missouri residents directly from the federal government. There is no state Access Missouri application to fill out

**Closing Date**: 1 April

**Funding**: Private

**Additional Information**:    dhewd.mo.gov/ppc/grants/accessmo.php

### For further information contact:

Missouri Department of Higher Education, 205 Jefferson Street, P.O. Box 1469, Jefferson City, MO 65102-1469, United States of America.

**Tel**:    (1) 573 751 2361
**Email**:    info@dhe.mo.gov

## Missouri State University

College of Business, Glass Hall 223, 901 South National Avenue, Springfield, MO 65897, United States of America.

**Tel**:        (1) 417 836 5616
**Email**:     MBAProgram@MissouriState.edu
**Website**:   www.mba.missouristate.edu
**Contact**:   Dr Elizabeth Rozell, MBA Program Director

Missouri State University's College of Business has earned the highest level of accreditation for its programs, ensuring you will be prepared for the regional, national and international job market. MBA students experience a program that is flexible, accessible, affordable and with a solid reputation for international excellence.

### The Robert W. and Charlotte Bitter Graduate Scholarship Endowment

**Purpose**: To assist a worthy graduate student in pursuing a master's of business administration or master's of accounting degree in College of Business

**Eligibility**: Awarded annually to a student seeking an MBA or MACC, be enroled in 12 hours or enroled in 6 hours or more each semester if the student is a graduate assistant, have a combined formula score (200 grade point average plus Graduate Management Admission Test score) of 1,100 or higher and minimum 3.3 graduate grade point average, have completed a minimum of 24 hours or 15 hours, if the student is a graduate assistant, and have completed all prerequisite courses or be currently enroled in final prerequisite courses

**Level of Study**: MBA

**Type**: Scholarship

**Value**: US$1,000

**Length of Study**: Varies

**Frequency**: Annual

**Study Establishment**: Missouri State University

**Country of Study**: United States of America

**Application Procedure**: Applicants must contact the organization for application details. Apply online (Check in November)

**No. of awards offered**: 121

**Closing Date**: 1 March

**Funding**: Private, Foundation

**Contributor**: The Robert W. and Charlotte Bitter Graduate Scholarship Endowment

**No. of awards given last year**: 1

**No. of applicants last year**: 121

**Additional Information**: Not renewable. Please contact the university for further information

## For further information contact:

**Email**: ammsi@uonbi.ac.ke

# Modern Language Association of America (MLA)

26 Broadway, 3rd Floor, New York, NY 10004-1789, United States of America.

| | |
|---|---|
| **Tel**: | (1) 646 576 5000 |
| **Email**: | awards@mla.org |
| **Website** | www.mla.org |
| **Contact** | Annie Reiser |

The Modern Language Association of America (MLA) is a non-profit membership organization that promotes the study and teaching of language and literature in English and foreign languages.

## James Russell Lowell Prize

**Purpose**: To recognize an outstanding literary or linguistic study, a critical edition of an important work or a critical biography
**Eligibility**: Open to books published the year preceding the year in which the award is due to be given. Authors must be current members of the MLA
**Level of Study**: Postdoctorate
**Type**: Prize
**Value**: Cash award and certificate
**Frequency**: Annual
**Country of Study**: Any country
**Application Procedure**: Applicants must send six copies of the work. For detailed information about specific prizes, applicants should contact the MLA
**Closing Date**: 1 March
**Funding**: Private
**Additional Information**: www.upress.umn.edu/press/press-releases/jonathan-p-eburne-will-receive-mlas-james-russell-lowell-prize

## Katherine Singer Kovacs Prize

**Purpose**: To recognize an outstanding book published in English or Spanish

**Eligibility**: Open to books published the year preceding the year in which the prize is given. Competing books should be broadly interpretative works that enhance the understanding of the interrelations among literature, the arts and society. Authors need not be members of the MLA
**Level of Study**: Postdoctorate
**Type**: Prize
**Value**: Cash award and certificate
**Frequency**: Annual
**Country of Study**: Any country
**Application Procedure**: Applicants must send six copies of the work. For detailed information about specific prizes, applicants should contact the MLA
**Closing Date**: 1 May
**Funding**: Private
**Additional Information**: einaudi.cornell.edu/opportunity/modern-language-association-katherine-singer-kovacs-prize

## For further information contact:

**Tel**: (1) 646 576 5141

## Modern Language Association Prize for a First Book

**Purpose**: To recognize an outstanding literary or linguistic study, or a critical biography
**Eligibility**: Open to books published in the year preceding the year in which the prize is given as the first book-length publication of a current MLA member
**Level of Study**: Postdoctorate
**Type**: Prize
**Value**: Cash award and certificate
**Frequency**: Annual
**Country of Study**: Any country
**Application Procedure**: Applicants must send six copies of the work. For detailed information about specific prizes, applicants should contact the MLA
**Closing Date**: 1 April
**Funding**: Private
**Additional Information**: www.upress.umn.edu/press/press-releases/jonathan-p-eburne-will-receive-mlas-james-russell-lowell-prize

## Modern Language Association Prize for Independent Scholars

**Purpose**: To encourage the achievements and contributions of independent scholars
**Eligibility**: Open to books published in the year preceding the year in which the prize is given. At the time of

publication of the book, the author must not be enroled in a programme leading to an academic degree or hold a tenured, tenure-accruing or tenure-track position in post-secondary education. Authors need not be members of the MLA

**Level of Study**: Postdoctorate

**Type**: Prize

**Value**: Cash award, certificate, and one-year membership in the association

**Frequency**: Annual

**Country of Study**: Any country

**Application Procedure**: Applicants must send six copies of the work. For detailed information about specific prizes, applicants should contact the MLA

**Closing Date**: 1 May

**Funding**: Private

## Monash Mount Eliza Business School

Level 4 27 Sir John Monash Drive, Caulfield, VIC 3145, Australia.

**Tel**: (61) 3 9215 1850
**Email**: genmba@mteliza.edu.au
**Website**: www.monash.edu.au/intoff
**Contact**: MBA Administration Assistant

### Monash Mt Eliza Business School Executive MBA Programme

**Purpose**: The Monash Global Executive MBA seeks to attract a cohort with gender, cultural, professional and sectoral diversity. A minimum of ten years' management experience is required. Applicants should be executives working in Australia, who can utilise program ideas in their roles and share their experiences in an executive-level peer-learning environment.

**Application Procedure**: Applicants must return a completed application form, a detailed curriculum vitae, full official academic transcripts, one passport photo, a reference from a sponsoring organisation, and an application fee of AU$495

**Closing Date**: 30 June

**Additional Information**: www.monash.edu/business/global-executive-mba/applications

#### For further information contact:

Kunyung Road, Mount Eliza, VIC 3930, Australia.

**Tel**: (61) 3 9215 1107
**Email**: cmccall@monashmteliza.edu.au

## Monash University

Monash Graduate Education, Chancellery Building, 26, Sports Walk, Clayton, VIC 3800, Australia.

**Tel**: (61) 3 9905 3009
**Email**: mge.apply@monash.edu
**Website**: www.monash.edu/graduate-research

Monash University is one of Australia's largest universities, with 10 faculties covering every major area of intellectual activity, 6 campuses in Australia and an increasing global presence. Research at Monash covers the full spectrum from fundamental to applied research and ranges across the arts and humanities, social, natural, health and medical sciences and the technological sciences. The University is determined to preserve its strength in fundamental research, which underpins its successes in applied research, and to continue to make a distinguished contribution to intellectual and cultural life.

## Corrosion Research Postgraduate Scholarships

**Eligibility**: Open only to the citizens of Australia or New Zealand or permanent residents who have achieved Honours 2a in Materials Engineering/Science, Metallurgy, Physics, Chemistry, Chemical Engineering, or Mechanical Engineering or equivalent

**Level of Study**: Postgraduate

**Type**: Scholarship

**Value**: AU$25,000 per year

**Length of Study**: 3 years

**Frequency**: Annual

**Study Establishment**: Monash University

**Application Procedure**: Applicants must apply directly to the scholarship provider. Check website for further details

**Contributor**: ARC Discovery and Linkage grants in association with Victorian State Government ETIS Program

**Additional Information**: www.academicgates.com/job/detail/00155d140103-11e8-c73c-375c16be-990b

#### For further information contact:

Department of Chemical Engineering, Monash University, Wellington Rd, Clayton, VIC 3800, Australia.

**Tel**: (61) 3 9905 3671
**Email**: raman.singh@eng.monash.edu.au

## Doctor of Philosophy APA(I) Police-Mental Health Scholarship

**Purpose**: To investigate the police-mental health interface
**Eligibility**: Open only to the citizens of Australia or New Zealand or permanent residents who have achieved Honours 1 or equivalent, or Honours 2a or equivalent with an HI or H2A Honours Degree in a social sciences discipline
**Level of Study**: Postgraduate, Research
**Value**: AU$25,118 per year
**Length of Study**: 3 years
**Frequency**: Dependent on funds available
**Study Establishment**: Monash University
**Application Procedure**: Applicants must apply directly to the scholarship provider

### For further information contact:

School of Psychology, Psychiatry, and Psychological Medicine.

**Email**:   Kathy.Avent@med.monash.edu.au

## Doctor of Philosophy Scholarship-Corrosion in Alumina Processing

**Eligibility**: Open only to the citizens of Australia or New Zealand or permanent residents who have achieved Honours 1 or equivalent, or Honours 2a or equivalent in chemical engineering/mechanical engineering/materials engineering/chemistry
**Level of Study**: Postgraduate, Research
**Type**: Scholarship
**Value**: AU$25,118 per year
**Length of Study**: 3 years
**Frequency**: Annual
**Study Establishment**: Monash University
**Application Procedure**: Applicants must apply direct to faculty. Check website for further details
**Contributor**: ARC

## Faculty of Law Masters International Scholarship

**Purpose**: At this university, candidates can study a broad range of subjects to shape a qualification that matches to their strengths and career interests. It helps the candidate with career planning, developing a CV and cover letters, interview skills, enhancing their employability skills
**Eligibility**: Scholarship is available for pursuing Undergraduate and Postgraduate

**Level of Study**: Postgraduate
**Type**: Scholarship
**Value**: Up to AU$20,000
**Length of Study**: 1 year
**Frequency**: Annual
**Country of Study**: Any country
**Closing Date**: 20 October
**Funding**: International office
**Additional Information**: scholarship-positions.com/faculty-of-law-masters-international-scholarship-at-monash-university-in-australia/2019/03/14/

# Montessori St Nicholas Centre

24 Prince's Gate, London, SW7 1PT, United Kingdom.

**Tel**:        (44) 207 584 9987
**Email**:    centre@montessori.org.uk
**Website**:  www.montessori.org.uk
**Contact**:  The Chief Executive

Montessori St Nicholas offer grants and awards under a scholarship scheme for Post Graduate Students carrying out research or training in Montessori teaching. Annual awards total £60,000 on average.

## The Birts Scholarship

**Purpose**: To recognise and encourage research into Montessori teaching
**Eligibility**: United Kingdom Citizens holding a United Kingdom recognised degree
**Level of Study**: Graduate
**Type**: Scholarship
**Value**: £4–6,000
**Length of Study**: 2 years
**Frequency**: Annual
**Country of Study**: United Kingdom
**Application Procedure**: By application form from the charity and interview
**No. of awards offered**: 12
**Closing Date**: 1 July
**Funding**: Private
**No. of awards given last year**: 1
**No. of applicants last year**: 12

### For further information contact:

**Email**:   reception@montessori.org.uk

# Morton Cure Paralysis Fund

## Morton Cure Paralysis Fund Research Grant

**Subjects**: Spinal cord injury and other disorders of the central nervous system

**Purpose**: The Morton Cure Paralysis Fund (MCPF) is committed to developing effective therapies (cures) for paralysis associated with spinal cord injury and other disorders of the central nervous system.

**Type**: Research grant

**Value**: Most research awards range from US$5,000 to US$75,000 and are based on one-year contracts

**Length of Study**: One or two years

**Frequency**: Annual

**Country of Study**: Any country

**Application Procedure**: Please provide the relevant information and send to info@mcpf.org

**Closing Date**: 30 April and 31 October

**Additional Information**: A second year may be considered contingent upon the grantee submitting a six-month progress report, a 12-month progress report and a continuation application that is favorably reviewed by MCPF's Grant Committee. www.mcpf.org/Pages/Resources.aspx

# Motor Neurone Disease Association

PO Box 246, Northamptonshire, Northampton, NN1 2PR, United Kingdom.

| | |
|---|---|
| **Tel**: | (44) 16 0461 1873 |
| **Email**: | research.grants@mndassociation.org |
| **Website**: | www.mndassociation.org |
| **Contact**: | Dr Sadie Vile, Research Grants Manager |

The Motor Neurone Disease Association supports research on fundamental aspects of motor neurone disease (MND) and on its management and alleviation. It provides information and advice to patients and carers, and runs a nationwide care service. MND paralyzes selectively or generally and is fatal, irreversible and at present, incurable.

## Motor Neurone Disease Association Non-Clinical Fellowship Awards

**Subjects**: Research on all aspects of Motor Neurone Disease in all relevant disciplines. These Fellowships are not open to clinicians.

**Purpose**: To allow Post-Doctoral Scientists with some experience of MND research to develop their career further.

Funded Fellowships will support research aimed at understanding the causes of MND,

**Eligibility**: Restricted to researchers at post-doctoral level to work at a suitable institute in the UK or Republic of Ireland. Applicants must be entitled to remain in the UK/Ireland for the whole period of the grant if awarded. For Junior Fellowships, applicants should have 2-6 years post-doc experience at the time of commencement of the grant. For Senior Fellowships, applicants should have 4-10 years post-doc experience at the time of commencement of the grant. In considering the periods, allowance is made for career breaks, family leave etc.

**Level of Study**: Postdoctorate, Professional development, Research

**Type**: Fellowship

**Value**: Junior Fellowships: Max £90,000 per year, for 3 years. Senior Fellowships: Max £110,000 per year, up to 4 years.

**Length of Study**: Up to 4 years

**Frequency**: Annual

**Study Establishment**: University and other suitable research institute

**Country of Study**: United Kingdom, Republic of Ireland

**Application Procedure**: Applicants must submit a summary of their proposal, which is first checked for eligibility and considered by three members of the research advisory panel (RAP). Full applications are invited thereafter and application forms are provided. Full applications will be considered by a minimum of two independent external referees and then by the Biomedical Research Advisory Panel (BRAP). Please see the website at www.mndassociation.org/research/forresearchers for full details of the application processes, together with grant guidelines and terms and conditions.

**No. of awards offered**: Usually 2, tyically one senior and one junior

**Closing Date**: 30 April

**Funding**: Trusts, Individuals

**No. of awards given last year**: 2 in 2018 (1 Junior Fellowship and 1 Senior Fellowship), only 1 award in 2019 as no suitable application for a Senior Fellowship

**No. of applicants last year**: 11 full applications in 2018, 4 full applications in 2019

**Additional Information**: The lead applicant should be the potential fellow, currently a post-doctoral scientist. The head of the proposed host laboratory should be a co-applicant www.mndassociation.org/research/for-researchers/apply-for-funding/

### For further information contact:

Motor Neurone Disease Association, Francis Crick House, 6 Summerhouse Road, Moulton Park, Northampton, NN3 6BJ, United Kingdom.

**Tel**:   (44) 1604 611846

## Motor Neurone Disease Association PhD Studentship Award

**Subjects**: Research on all aspects of Motor Neurone Disease in all relevant disciplines.

**Purpose**: To attract promising science graduates to develop a career in MND related research and to support research aimed at understanding the causes of MND, elucidating disease mechanisms and facilitating the translation of therapeutic strategies from the laboratory to the clinic.

**Eligibility**: Restricted to researchers based in laboratories in the United Kingdom and Republic of Ireland. Applicants must be entitled to remain in UK/Ireland for the whole period of the grant if awarded. The applicant should be the supervisor, not the potential student.

**Level of Study**: Doctorate, Graduate, Postgraduate, Research

**Type**: Studentship

**Value**: The Association will provide a student stipend of £16,000 per year (£17,000 in London), £8,000 per year for laboratory expenses and a total budget of £1,000, over 3 years, for conference attendance. The Association will also cover relevant tuition/bench fees at the rate payable by UK/European students.

**Length of Study**: 3 years

**Frequency**: Annual

**Study Establishment**: University and other suitable research institute

**Country of Study**: United Kingdom, Republic of Ireland

**Application Procedure**: Applicants must submit a summary of their proposal, which is first checked for eligibility and considered by three members of the research advisory panel (RAP). Full applications are invited thereafter and application forms are provided. Full applications are submitted to two or more independent referees and then to the RAP for consideration. Please see our research governance overview at www.mndassociation.org/research/for-researchers/apply-for-funding/ for information on our grant application processes. The summary application form will be available on our website from mid-March to be completed online.

**No. of awards offered**: Between 1 and 4

**Closing Date**: 30 April

**Funding**: Trusts, Individuals

**No. of awards given last year**: 5 awarded in 2019. This was exceptional as no studentships were awarded in 2018, so some budget was carried forward.

**No. of applicants last year**: 13 full applications were considered

**Additional Information**: The studentships are awarded on the basis of scientific merit and the value of research training offered. The applicant must be the potential supervisor not the student. www.mndassociation.org/research/for-researchers/apply-for-funding/

### For further information contact:

Motor Neurone Disease Association, Francis Crick House, 6 Summerhouse Road, Moulton Park, Northampton, NN3 6BJ, United Kingdom.

**Tel**: (44) 1604 611846

## Motor Neurone Disease Association Research Project Grants

**Subjects**: Research on all aspects of Motor Neurone Disease in all relevant disciplines.

**Purpose**: To understand and research the cause and effective treatments of MND. To fund research to the highest scientific merit and greatest clinical or translational relevance to MND.

**Eligibility**: Overseas applicants must have a project that is unique in concept or design and that involves significant aspect of collaboration with an institute in the United Kingdom or the Republic of Ireland. The applicant must be eligible to remain employed at the host research institution for the period of the grant if awarded.

**Level of Study**: Postdoctorate, Professional development, Research

**Type**: Project Grant

**Value**: £85,000 per year, maximum

**Length of Study**: Between 1 and 3 years

**Frequency**: Annual

**Study Establishment**: A research institution, including universities and hospitals

**Country of Study**: Any country

**Application Procedure**: Applicants must submit a summary of their proposal, which is first checked for eligibility and considered by three members of the research advisory panel (RAP). Full applications are invited thereafter and application forms are provided. Full applications are submitted to two or more independent referees and then to the RAP for consideration. Please see our research governance overview at www.mndassociation.org/research/for_researchers for information on our grant application processes. The summary application form for project grants will be available on our website from mid-September to be completed online.

**No. of awards offered**: Varies with quality of applications and availability of funds

**Closing Date**: 23 October

**Funding**: Trusts, Individuals

**No. of awards given last year**: 6

**No. of applicants last year**: 31 Full applications

**Additional Information**: The majority of grants are awarded to applicants based in the United Kingdom, Republic of Ireland, any country. However, overseas applicants may apply. Two of the grants awarded in 2016 are based outside the UK with appropriate UK collaboration. www.mndassociation.org/research/for-researchers/apply-for-funding/

**For further information contact:**

Motor Neurone Disease Association, Francis Crick House, 6 Summerhouse Road, Moulton Park, Northampton, NN3 6BJ, United Kingdom.

**Tel**:    (44) 1604 611846

## Mott MacDonald Charitable Trust

St Anne House, 20-26, Wellesley Road, Croydon, Surrey, CR9 2UL, United Kingdom.

**Tel**:             (44) 20 8774 2000
**Website**:    www.mottmac.com
**Contact**:    Secretary

### Mott MacDonald Charitable Trust Scholarships

**Purpose**: To enable a recipient to pursue studies and thus contribute to the advancement of engineering technology
**Eligibility**: Open to engineering students who wish to further their academic training at the postgraduate level. Students returning to academic training after a period of employment are preferred
**Type**: Scholarship
**Value**: Please consult the organization
**Frequency**: Annual
**Study Establishment**: Any university
**Country of Study**: United Kingdom
**Application Procedure**: Applicants must complete an application form, available on request from the main address
**No. of awards offered**: 129
**Closing Date**: 31 March
**Funding**: Commercial
**No. of awards given last year**: 4
**No. of applicants last year**: 129
**Additional Information**: www.imperial.ac.uk/news/28194/mott-macdonald-charitable-trust-award-2008/

**For further information contact:**

**Email**:    charitabletrust@mottmac.com

## MQ Mental Health

One in four people in the UK is living with a mental health condition. That's nearly 15 million people with an illness that affects their wellbeing, their relationships with family and friends, and their ability to work. For many the experience can be painful, exhausting and isolating. Despite extraordinary advances in treating physical health conditions, progress in understanding mental illness, and research into its causes, treatments and prevention, is nowhere near equal. In fact it falls woefully short, leaving millions of people worldwide without the help and support they need. We're here to change that. We are the leading charity funding much-needed scientific research to transform the lives of everyone affected by mental illness. And with our community of supporters and an international network of talented researchers we can make this a reality.

**Email**:       info@mqfoundation.org
**Website**:    www.mqmentalhealth.org/

The MQ Foundation was launched in 2018 by its founder and chairman, and noted philanthropist John Herrmann a longtime leader of mental health charities in New York. A member of the MQ: Transforming Mental Health Board of Trustees since 2017, John notes: "I was so impressed by MQ's direct approach to mental health research that I vowed to bring this organization to the attention of donors in the US as well... we must work together to achieve better treatments." The mission of the MQ Foundation is closely aligned with that of the preeminent UK-based organization, MQ: Transforming Mental Health (MQ). As the exclusive US partner of MQ the MQ Foundation is now poised to "promote, advance, foster and support mental health research into the nature, cause diagnosis, treatment, cure and prevention of all forms of mental illness and to promote public awareness and support for this research"

### MQ Fellows Awards 2020

**Purpose**: The Fellows Award supports talented researchers with bold ideas from across the globe, who aspire to be the next generation leaders in mental health research, as they establish their independence. MQ seeks to fund a diverse research portfolio that reflects a bio-psycho-social approach to mental health. The MQ Fellows Awards are open to researchers anywhere in the world and from all disciplines related to mental health research. Research may involve theoretical, experimental, social sciences or medical humanities approaches. Aligning with the work of our Brighter Futures Programme, applications to the 2020 MQ Fellows Award must have a focus on children and young people (which we define as from prenatal development up to 24 years of age). Projects should focus on genuine impact by charting, informing, developing and/or testing preventative or therapeutic interventions.

**Eligibility**: The MQ Fellows Award is designed to support early career researchers investigating questions that will ultimately improve the quality of life for people affected by mental illness. Applicants will have made an outstanding start to their research career as demonstrated by their research results and career track record to date. We are seeking applicants who are establishing their independence through their intellectual efforts and leadership. Researchers need to be fully committed to this path and at a career stage that demonstrates this commitment. Applicants will be able to demonstrate that they are either newly independent or will be independent by the time the awards are finalised in the summer of 2020. This award is not suitable for stand-alone 3-year post-doctoral research projects. Applicants must be early career researchers wishing to establish their independence: with a PhD, DPhil, DClinPsy, MBBS, MD or equivalent have accumulated 3-7 years by January 2020 through whole-time-equivalent research experience, equivalent in nature to post-doctoral research be able to show that this award will help to establish your independence relative to your current position

**Level of Study**: postgraduate

**Type**: grant

**Value**: £225,000

**Frequency**: Annual

**Country of Study**: UK

**Application Procedure**: The 2020 MQ Fellows Awards follow a 3-stage application process. Stage 1: Expression of Interest Applicants are required to complete and submit a Stage 1 Expression of Interest application form. This must be submitted through MQ's online application system by the deadline of Friday 3rd April at 17:00 BST (GMT +1). The Stage 1 Expression of Interest is comprised of a short application, an abbreviated curriculum vitae form, and a statement of support and signature from the applicant's Head of Department (HoD). Please ensure that sufficient time is left to obtain HoD authorisation before the relevant deadline. Applications will be reviewed by the MQ Research Team and the MQ Fellows Award Panel. Applications that do not meet the submission criteria will not be processed further. Applicants will be informed of the results of Stage 1 review by the end of May. Stage 2: Invited Proposal Shortlisted applicants will be invited to participate in Stage 2 of the process, by submitting a full application with a detailed scientific proposal including how PPI has been considered in the design of the project, along with a full budget. Applicants are asked to propose scientific mentor(s) for their project, who can be from any field, and whose research is pertinent to the proposed project. Deadline for invited proposals is Friday 3rd July at 17:00 BST (GMT+1) Applications must have the support of your Head of Department and be approved by grants or finance officer before the deadline. Stage 2 Invited Proposals will be further reviewed, scored and ranked by the MQ Fellows Award Panel, external and lay reviewers. Those successful at this stage will be invited attend an interview. Stage 3: Invited Interview Finalists will be interviewed by the MQ Fellows Award Panel the week commencing 21st September, in London, UK. By submitting a Stage 2 Invited Proposal, applicants verify their ability to participate in the interview process, and be able to accept an offer of funding under the highlighted terms and conditions associated with the Award, should an offer be made. Final decisions for the 2020 MQ Fellows Awards will be made by the MQ Fellows Award Panel in October, on the basis of applicant's Stage 2 Invited Proposal, external review and performance at interview.

**Closing Date**: 3 April

### For further information contact:

Application forms are to be submitted via the online system.

**Email**:    grants@mqmentalhealth.org

## Multiple Sclerosis Society of Canada (MSSC)

175 Bloor Street East, Suite 700, North Tower, Toronto, ON M4W 3R8, Canada.

**Tel**:         (1) 416 922 6065
**Email**:     jackie.munroe@mssociety.ca
**Website**:  www.mssociety.ca
**Contact**:  Ms Jackie Munroe, Research Grants Programme Manager

The mission of the MSSC is to be a leader in finding a cure for multiple sclerosis and enabling people affected by the disease to enhance their quality of life.

## Multiple Sclerosis Society of Canada Donald Paty Career Development Award

**Purpose**: To support the salary of an independent researcher whose research is relevant to MS

**Eligibility**: This award is open to those that hold a doctoral degree (PhD, MD or equivalent) and who have recently completed their training in research and are in the early stages of independent research relevant to MS. Applicants must hold a Canadian university faculty appointment and either holds an operating grant from the MSSOC or another funding agency

**Level of Study**: Postdoctorate

**Value**: The amount provided per year for the award is C$50,000

**Length of Study**: 3 years

**Frequency**: Annual

**Study Establishment**: A Canadian school of medicine/recognized institution

**Country of Study**: Canada

**Application Procedure**: All Applicants for regular research grants are required to use the website www.mscanadagrants.ca/ for the completion of their proposal. All components of the application must be submitted through the online system. No hard copies of any documentation will be accepted

**No. of awards offered**: 5

**Closing Date**: 1 October

**Funding**: Private

**No. of awards given last year**: 1

**No. of applicants last year**: 5

**Additional Information**: www.vchri.ca/i/pdf/MS_Canada_FundingOpportunities_2013.pdf

### For further information contact:

**Email**:    msresearchgrants@mssociety.ca

## Multiple Sclerosis Society of Canada Postdoctoral Fellowship Award

**Purpose**: To encourage research

**Eligibility**: Open to qualified persons holding an MD or PhD degree and intending to pursue research work relevant to multiple sclerosis and allied diseases. The applicant must be associated to an appropriate authority in the field he or she wishes to study

**Level of Study**: Postdoctorate

**Type**: Fellowship

**Value**: The amount provided per year for the award is C$39,000 for a PhD and C$48,500 for an MD

**Length of Study**: 1 year, with the opportunity for 2 renewals at 1 year each

**Frequency**: Annual

**Study Establishment**: A recognized institution which deals that problems relevant to multiple sclerosis

**Country of Study**: Other

**Application Procedure**: All Applicants for regular research grants are required to use the website www.mscanadagrants.ca/ for the completion of their proposal. All components of the application must be submitted through the online system. No hard copies of any documentation will be accepted

**No. of awards offered**: 26

**Closing Date**: 1 October

**Funding**: Private

**No. of awards given last year**: 31

**No. of applicants last year**: 26

**Additional Information**: mssociety.ca/information-for-researchers/funding-opportunities/endms-research-and-training-network-awards-and-programs/endms-postdoctoral-fellowships

### For further information contact:

**Email**:    msresearchgrants@mssociety.ca

## Murdoch University

Murdoch University is a public university in Perth, Western Australia with campuses also in Singapore and Dubai. University has more than 22,000 students and 2,000 staff from across 90 different countries with a desire to discover, use their imaginations and ultimately make a difference.

## International Postgraduate Research Studentship (IPRS) at Murdoch University in Australia

**Purpose**: The purpose is to undertake the degree of Doctor of Philosophy (PhD) and Doctor of Education (EdD) at Murdoch University in areas in which the University has specialized research strengths. Preference will be given to PhD candidates

**Eligibility**: An applicant must provide evidence of having achieved Murdoch University English language proficiency requirements. These requirements are IELTS Academic 6.5 - no individual band less than 6.0 or TOEFL iBT 90 - no individual band less than 20. Exceptions are Nursing, Education and Pharmacy with an IELTS requirement of 7.0

**Level of Study**: Doctorate

**Value**: The scholarships cover the research degree tuition fees and health insurance premiums

**Country of Study**: Singapore

**Application Procedure**: Visit website our.murdoch.edu.au/Research-and-Innovation/Resources-for-students/Future-research-students/Admission-and-scholarships/International-student-scholarships/IPRS/

**Closing Date**: 30 September

**Additional Information**: Applicants who have had sustained contact with a potential academic research supervisor at Murdoch University prior to submission of their application will be considered favourably scholarship-positions.com/international-postgraduate-research-studentship-iprs-murdoch-university-australia/2017/01/28/

### For further information contact:

**Email**:    admin@scholarship-positions.com

## International Welcome Scholarships (IWS)

**Purpose**: International Welcome Scholarships are open to eligible international students who choose to study a Murdoch University Bachelor, Honours or Postgraduate Coursework degree programme

**Eligibility**: Citizen of Bangladesh, Bhutan, China, India, Indonesia, Malaysia, Nepal, Pakistan or Sri Lanka can apply for these scholarships

**Type**: Postgraduate scholarships

**Value**: AU$10,000 for all Business and Governance eligible degree courses AU$11,000 for the Bachelor of Nursing course AU$7,000 for all other eligible degree courses

**Study Establishment**: Scholarships are available for all Business and Governance eligible degree courses and for all other eligible degree courses

**Country of Study**: Australia

**Application Procedure**: To be considered for a scholarship, applications for entry to an eligible course need to be submitted to the international admissions office at least two weeks prior to the start of the semester that the student intends to commence their studies at Murdoch

**Additional Information**: For more details please visit the website www.sofiri.com/blog/en/international-welcome-scholarship-iws-by-murdoch-university/?q=/blog/en/international-welcome-scholarship-iws-by-murdoch-university

### For further information contact:

**Email**: internationalscholarships@murdoch.edu.au

# N

## Nan Tien Institute

231 Nolan St, Unanderra, NSW 2526, Australia.

**Tel**:　　(61) 2 4272 0648
**Email**:　info@nantien.edu.au
**Website**:　www.nantien.edu.au

### Nan Tien Institute Postgraduate Scholarship

**Eligibility**: Open to Australian domestic students only
**Level of Study**: Graduate, Postgraduate
**Type**: Scholarship
**Value**: AU$13,800.00 covers tuition costs only (not text books, learning materials or accommodation) plus research supervision
**Length of Study**: Up to 3 years from commencement, unless otherwise agreed
**Frequency**: Annual
**Study Establishment**: Nan Tien Institute
**Country of Study**: Australia
**Application Procedure**: Complete and submit the application form, along with your application for admission form by the closing date
**Closing Date**: December
**Contributor**: Nan Tien Institute
**Additional Information**: Please check for more information at www.nantien.edu.au/content/nan-tien-institute-postgraduate-scholarship scholarshipdb.net/jobs-in-Australia/Nan-Tien-Institute-Postgraduate-Scholarship-Applied-Buddhist-Studies-Research-Pathway-Pgabssrp-Nan-Tien-Institute=Ox4iZhJ75RGUPAAlkGUTnw.html

### For further information contact:

**Tel**:　　(61) 4258 0700

## Nansen Fund

77 Saddlebrook Lane, Houston, TX 77024, United States of America.

**Tel**:　　(1) 713 686 3963
**Contact**:　Fellowships Office

### John Dana Archbold Fellowship

**Purpose**: To support educational exchange between the United States and Norway
**Eligibility**: Eligibility is limited to those aged between 20 and 35, in good health, of good character, and citizens of the United States of America, who are not recent immigrants from Norway
**Level of Study**: Postdoctorate, Postgraduate, Professional development
**Type**: Fellowship
**Value**: Grants vary, depending on costs and rates of exchange. The University of Oslo will charge no tuition and the Nansen Fund will pay up to US$10,000 for supplies, maintenance and travel. The maintenance stipend is sufficient to meet expenses in Norway for a single person. Air fare from the United States of America to Norway is covered
**Length of Study**: 1 year
**Frequency**: Every 2 years
**Study Establishment**: The University of Oslo
**Country of Study**: Norway
**Application Procedure**: Applicants must complete and submit an application form with references and transcripts
**Closing Date**: 31 January
**Additional Information**: Every other year the Norway-America Association, the sister organisation of the Nansen Fund, offers fellowships for Norwegian citizens wishing to study at a university in the United States of America. For

© Springer Nature Limited 2020
Palgrave Macmillan (ed.), *The Grants Register 2021*,
https://doi.org/10.1057/978-1-349-95988-4

further information please contact The Norway-America Association

## For further information contact:

The Norway-American Association, Drammensveien 20c, N-0271 Oslo, Norway.

| | |
|---|---|
| **Tel**: | (47) 2 244 7716 |
| **Fax**: | (47) 2 244 7716 |
| **Email**: | cg.newyork@mfa.no |

# Nanyang Technological University (NTU)

Nanyang Business School, Nanyang Avenue, 639798 Singapore.

| | |
|---|---|
| **Tel**: | (65) 6790 4803 |
| **Email**: | postgraduate@ntu.edu.sg |
| **Website**: | www.ntu.edu.sg |
| **Contact**: | Director |

The Nanyang Business School is one of Asia's top business schools. Its flagship programme is the Nanyang MBA, which has consistently been ranked one of the top in Asia and is ranked in the world top 100 by Economist intelligence unit, 2005.

## Asia Journalism Fellowship

**Eligibility**: At least five years of professional journalism experience, not including student journalism, who are currently working as a journalist. Freelancers are eligible, if journalism is their main activity. Applicants should be residing in Asia and should be able to operate in English which is the working language of the programme. Journalists working in non-English media are welcomed, but they will have to show their proficiency in English through a telephone interview. Permission is required from their employers to be away for the full three months of the Fellowship

**Type**: Fellowship

**Value**: Stipend of Singaporean S$1,500 per month for the duration of the three month programme. Travel to and from Singapore will also be covered. There is no extra funding for spouses and children to visit. Free accommodation is provided in service apartments. Two or three Fellows share one apartment with kitchen to cook meals. Fellows will have access to the library, computer, internet and athletic facilities of the NTU campus. NTU will apply for Training Employment Passes for the Fellows to come to Singapore. Any visiting family members must handle their own entry permit applications

**Country of Study**: Singapore

**Application Procedure**: The mode of applying is electronically send to applications@ajf.sg

**Closing Date**: 25 October

**Contributor**: Temasek Foundation and Nanyang Technological University

**Additional Information**: The Fellowship brings around 15 journalists from across Asia to Singapore for three months www.ajf.sg/applying/

## For further information contact:

**Email**: applications@ajf.sg

## Asian Communication Resource Centre (ACRC) Fellowship Award

**Purpose**: To encourage in-depth research, promote cooperation and support scholars who wish to pursue research in communication, information and ICT-related disciplines in Asia

**Eligibility**: All applicants should possess or be working towards a postgraduate degree from a reputable academic institution and Applicants should be working on a research project in communication, media, information or related areas that would be able to exploit the materials in the ACRC

**Level of Study**: Postgraduate, Research

**Type**: Fellowships

**Value**: Up to US$1,500 (economy class return air ticket), on-campus accommodation will be provided and weekly allowance of US$210 will be provided

**Length of Study**: 1–3 months

**Frequency**: Annual

**Application Procedure**: Applicants can download the application form from the website and send in their completed application form along with a copy of their latest curriculum vitae

**Closing Date**: 1 October

**Additional Information**: liskw.wordpress.com/page/57/?arch__That

## For further information contact:

| | |
|---|---|
| **Tel**: | (65) 6790 4577 |
| **Fax**: | (65) 6791 5214 |
| **Email**: | acrc_fellowship@ntu.edu.sg |

## Nanyang Technological University HASS International PhD Scholarship (HIPS) for Singaporean Students

**Purpose**: HIPS aims to encourage outstanding Singapore citizens and Singapore permanent residents to pursue an academic career in HASS by supporting their doctoral studies abroad

**Eligibility**: Under HIPS, the successful candidates will be employed as University staff. They will be granted paid leave to pursue a sponsored PhD programme in an approved overseas university or in NTU with an extended period of research in an approved overseas partner university. Upon successful completion of the PhD programme, they will be appointed as tenure-track Assistant Professors of the University

**Type**: Scholarship

**Frequency**: Annual

**Application Procedure**: Interested applicants should first get in touch with the relevant School and Division. Send all applications, through the respective Heads of Divisions/Groups and School Chairs, to: Dean's Office (or to the Dean's office). Applicants who wish to submit their documents electronically should email their application form and complete dossier to Ms Chan Bee Kwang email: BKCHAN@ntu.edu.sg

**Closing Date**: 31 December

**Additional Information**: All late and/or incomplete applications will not be considered. A check list is included in the application package cohass.ntu.edu.sg/Programmes/Pages/HIPS2020.aspx

### For further information contact:

**Email**:    wpseeto@ntu.edu.sg

## Singapore Education – Sampoerna Foundation MBA in Singapore

**Purpose**: To help Indonesian citizens below 35 years pursue their MBA studies

**Eligibility**: Applicant must be an Indonesian citizen under 35 years. hold a local Bachelor's degree from any discipline with a minimum GPA of 3.00 (on a 4.00 scale), have a minimum of 2 year full-time professional work experience after the completion of the undergraduate degree, currently not enroled in graduate or post-graduate program, or obtained a Master's degree or equivalent; not be a graduate from overseas tertiary institutions, unless was on a full scholarship, not receive other equivalent award or scholarship offering similar or other benefits at the time of the award

**Value**: Approx. US$70,000–150,000. This will cover GMAT and TOEFL/IELTS reimbursement, university application fee, student visa application fee, return airfares from Jakarta to the place of study, tuition fees for the duration of study, living allowance to support living costs during period of study and literature allowance to purchase textbooks required for study

**Country of Study**: Any country

**Closing Date**: 1 February

**Additional Information**: For further information see www.nanyangmba.edu.sg/Admissions/FinancialAid.asp

### For further information contact:

**Email**:    ella.cecilla@sampoernafoundation.org

## Singapore International Graduate Award Awards for International Students in Singapore

**Purpose**: Introducing a new Singapore International Graduate Award (or SINGA), for international students to do their PhD training in a multi-disciplinary environment in Singapore

**Eligibility**: International students with a passion for Science and Engineering research, excellent academic qualifications, good reports from academic referees, and fluency in English are encouraged to apply for this award. TOEFL, IELTS, and GRE are NOT required

**Value**: Stipends – S$2,000 per month (S$24,000 per annum), to be increased to S$2,500 per month (S$30,000 per annum) after passing qualifying examinations; one-time S$1,000 settling-in allowance; one-time airfare grant of S$1,500

**Length of Study**: 4 years

**Country of Study**: Singapore

**Application Procedure**: Applicants will need to complete and submit an online application form

**Closing Date**: 31 May

**Additional Information**: For more details, please visit the website wedushare.com/opportunity-detail/EXPT54EeMok7Ew4EQ/SINGA-Awards-for-International-Students-in-Singapore www.youthop.com/competitions/awards/singapore-international-graduate-award-singa-2019

### For further information contact:

**Email**:    singa_enquiries@hq.a-star.edu.sg

## Spring Management Development Scholarship (MDS)

**Purpose**: To nurture the next generation of leaders for the trailblazing companies of tomorrow

**Eligibility**: Those who are currently working in an SME or are interested to join one, are citizens or permanent residents of Singapore, have less than 5 years of working experience and successfully apply for one of the approved MBA programmes

**Value**: Full-time/Part-time MBA: SPRING will provide grant value of up to 70 % of tuition fees, and other related expenses for full-time MBA scholars up to a maximum qualifying cost of S$52,000
**Study Establishment**: Nanyang Business School
**Country of Study**: Singapore
**Application Procedure**: Applicants will have to go through a joint selection process by SPRING and the participating SME, serve a 3month internship in the SME prior to embarking on the approved MBA course (performance must be deemed satisfactory by the SME), and serve a bond of up to 2 years in the SME upon completion of studies. For more information on government assistance programmes, please contact the Enterprise One hotline at Tel: (65) 6898 1800 or email enterpriseone@spring.gov.sg or visit their website at www.spring.gov.sg/mds
**Contributor**: SPRING Singapore and small medium enterprises
**Additional Information**: For more information on government assistance programmes, please contact the Enterprise One hotline at Tel: (65) 6898 1800 or email enterpriseo ne@spring.gov.sg or visit their website at www.spring.gov. sg/mds scholarization.blogspot.com/2010/12/spring-management-development.html

### For further information contact:

**Tel**: (65) 6898 1800
**Email**: enquiry@enterprisesg.gov.sg

### The Lien Foundation Scholarship for Social Service Leaders

**Purpose**: To provide scholarships to support education and professional development
**Eligibility**: The scholarship is open to candidates with academic excellence, notable performance record and the potential to take up leadership positions in voluntary welfare organizations
**Type**: Scholarship
**Value**: The award includes tuition fees, maintenance allowance (for full-time studies), book allowance and any other compulsory fees
**Country of Study**: Any country
**Application Procedure**: For more information on the scholarship do visit the websites www.ncss.org.sg/lien
**Closing Date**: 22 June
**Additional Information**: becas.universia.net/beca/lien-foundation-scholarship-for-social-service-leaders-/253628

### For further information contact:

**Email**: socialservicescholarships@ncss.gov.sg

## Narotam Sekhsaria Foundation

1st Floor, Nirmal Building, Nariman Point, Mumbai, Maharashtra 400021, India.

**Tel**: (91) 22 6132 6200
**Email**: pgscholarship@nsfoundation.co.in
**Contact**: Narotam Sekhsaria Foundation

Narotam Sekhsaria Foundation is a non-profit initiative created to support enterprising individuals and innovative organizations.

## Narotam Sekhsaria Postgraduate Scholarship

**Purpose**: The aim of the scholarship is to help high achieving students to pursue postgraduate studies at prestigious Indian and international universities
**Eligibility**: Applicants must have sufficient knowledge of the language of instruction of the host university
**Type**: Postgraduate scholarships
**Value**: The award of scholarship is subject to securing admission
**Study Establishment**: The scholarship is awarded in the fields offered by the university
**Country of Study**: India
**Application Procedure**: Applicants can apply through the registration process given below the link of scholarship page
**Closing Date**: 28 March
**Additional Information**: For more details please see the website scholarship-positions.com/narotam-sekhsaria-postgraduate-scholarship-indian-students/2017/11/07/ pg.nsfoundation.co.in/programmes.html

### For further information contact:

**Tel**: (91) 22 61326200

## National Academies

500 5th Street NW, Washington, DC 20001, United States of America.

**Tel**: (1) 202 334 2000
**Email**: infofell@nas.edu
**Website**: www.nationalacademies.org

The National Academies perform an unparalleled public service by bringing together committees of experts in all areas of scientific and technological endeavour. These experts serve pro bono to address critical national issues and give advice to the federal government and the public.

## Christine Mirzayan Science & Technology Policy Graduate Fellowship Program

**Purpose**: To engage students in science and technology policy

**Eligibility**: Graduate students and postdoctoral scholars and those who have completed graduate studies or postdoctoral research within the last 5 years are eligible to apply

**Level of Study**: Postgraduate

**Type**: Fellowship

**Value**: The stipend for a 10-week program is US$5,300

**Length of Study**: 12 weeks

**Frequency**: Annual

**Country of Study**: Any country

**Application Procedure**: A completed application form must be submitted. Application forms are available on the website

**Closing Date**: September

**Additional Information**: mirzayanfellow.nas.edu/

### For further information contact:

**Email**: policyfellows@nas.edu

## Ford Foundation Dissertation Fellowships

**Purpose**: To achieve excellence in college and university teaching

**Eligibility**: Open to all citizens or nationals of the United States regardless of race, national origin, religion, gender, age, disability, or sexual orientation, individuals with evidence of superior academic achievement and committed to a career in teaching and research at the college or university level, PhD or ScD degree candidates studying in an eligible research-based discipline at a United States educational institution. Also individuals who have not earned a doctoral degree at any time, in any field

**Level of Study**: Doctorate

**Type**: Award

**Value**: Stipend: US$25,000 for 1 year. Expenses paid to attend one Conference of Ford Fellows. Access to Ford Fellow Liaisons, a network of former Ford Fellows who have volunteered to provide mentoring and support to current fellows

**Length of Study**: 9–12 months

**Frequency**: Annual

**Country of Study**: United States of America

**Application Procedure**: Applicants must register and establish a personal user ID and password. Check website for further details

**Closing Date**: 15 November

**Contributor**: The National Research Council

**Additional Information**: www.petersons.com/scholarship/ford-foundation-dissertation-fellowships-111_150501.aspx

### For further information contact:

**Tel**:  (1) 202 334 2872

## Ford Foundation Postdoctoral Fellowships

**Purpose**: For achieving excellence in college and university teaching and to increase the diversity of the nation's college and university faculties by increasing their ethnic and racial diversity, to maximize the educational benefits of diversity, and to increase the number of professors who can and will use diversity as a resource for enriching the education of all students

**Eligibility**: Open to all citizens or nationals of the United States regardless of race, national origin, religion, gender, age, disability, or sexual orientation, individuals with evidence of superior academic achievement and committed to a career in teaching and research at the college or university level. Individuals should hold a PhD or ScD degree in an eligible research-based field from a United States educational institution

**Level of Study**: Postdoctorate

**Type**: Fellowships

**Value**: One-year Stipend: US$45,000, Employing Institution Allowance: US$1,500 and expenses paid to attend one Conference of Ford Fellows

**Length of Study**: 9–12 months

**Application Procedure**: Applicants must register and establish a personal user ID and password. Check website for further details

**Closing Date**: 15 November

**Funding**: Government, Foundation

**Contributor**: National Research Council (NRC) on behalf of the Ford Foundation

**Additional Information**: Candidates demonstrating superior academic achievement according to the judgement panels will be awarded pathwaystoscience.org/programhub.aspx?sort=PDC-NationalAcademies-PostDoc

### For further information contact:

**Tel**:  (1) 202 334 2872

## Ford Foundation Predoctoral Fellowships

**Purpose**: For achieving excellence in college and university teaching and increasing the diversity of the nation's college and university faculties to maximize the educational benefits of diversity, and to increase the number of professors who can use diversity as a resource for enriching the education of all students

**Eligibility**: Open to all citizens or nationals of the United States regardless of race, national origin, religion, gender, age, disability, or sexual orientation, individuals with evidence of superior academic achievement and committed to a career in teaching and research at the college or university level, should enrol in or planning to enrol in an eligible research-based program leading to a PhD or ScD degree at a United States educational institution and who have not earned a doctoral degree at any time, in any field

**Level of Study**: Predoctorate

**Type**: Bursary and scholarship

**Value**: Annual stipend: US$24,000. Award to the institution in lieu of tuition and fees: US$2,000. Expenses paid to attend at least one Conference of Ford Fellows

**Length of Study**: 3 years

**Application Procedure**: Applicants must register and establish a personal user ID and password. Check website for further details

**Closing Date**: 19 November

**Funding**: Government, Foundation

**Contributor**: National Research Council on behalf of the Ford Foundation

**Additional Information**: Predoctoral fellows are required to enrol full-time in a program leading to a PhD or ScD degree in an eligible field of study www.petersons.com/scholarship/ford-foundation-predoctoral-fellowships–111_150500.aspx

### For further information contact:

**Tel**:    (1) 202 334 2872

## Jefferson Science Fellowship

**Purpose**: To offset the costs of temporary living quarters in the Washington, DC area

**Eligibility**: Applicants must be United States citizens and holding a tenured faculty position at a United States degree granting academic institution of higher learning. For terms and conditions as well as further details log on to the website

**Level of Study**: Postgraduate

**Value**: The Jefferson Science Fellow will be paid a per diem of up to US$50,000 by the United States Department of State and US$10,000 will be made available to the Fellow for travel associated with their assignment(s)

**Length of Study**: 1 year

**Frequency**: Annual

**Application Procedure**: A complete nomination/application package consists of nomination/application form in PDF format and in word format; curriculum vitae (limit 10 pages); statements of qualifications (limit 2 pages each); and at least 3, and no more than 5, letters of recommendation from peers of the nominee/applicant

**Closing Date**: 14 January

**Contributor**: National Academies supported through a partnership between American philanthropic foundations, the United States STE academic community, professional scientific societies, and the United States Department of State

**Additional Information**: Applicants should notify their institution while applying and encourage them to initiate a JSF/MOU as described on the website. Incomplete nomination/application packages, or those received after the deadline, will not be reviewed sites.nationalacademies.org/pga/jefferson/

### For further information contact:

**Tel**:       (1) 202 334 2643
**Fax**:       (1) 202 334 2759
**Email**:    jsf@nas.edu

## National Energy Technology Laboratory Methane Hydrates Fellowship Program (MHFP)

**Purpose**: To provide postgraduate and postdoctoral candidates opportunities for career development, largely of their own choice in the Methane Hydrates field that are compatible with the interests of the sponsoring laboratories and universities, and to contribute thereby to the overall efforts of NETL in their support in the development of Methane Hydrate Science

**Eligibility**: Open to candidates holding appropriate prior degree for the level of fellowship they intend to pursue. An applicant's training, professional experience, and research experience may be in any appropriate discipline or combination of disciplines required for the proposed project. Each Methane Hydrate Program fellow will be closely affiliated with a Research Adviser at the host venue

**Level of Study**: Doctorate, Postdoctorate, Postgraduate

**Type**: Fellowship

**Value**: Stipend Rates: Master's Level (Fellow) begins at US$30,000 with a maximum 2-year tenure, PhD Level (Fellow) begins at US$35,000 with a maximum 3-year tenure and Postdoctoral Level (Research Associate) begins at US$60,000 with a maximum 2-year tenure

**Length of Study**: 3 years

**Application Procedure**: Application must be submitted only in hard copy and sent by express delivery to the Associateship

Programs office. After completing the WebRAP application, you must also mail your supporting documents (transcripts and references) to the same address

**Closing Date**: 15 August

**Additional Information**: Please check the website for further details. Please direct all Application inquiries directly to the Research Associateship Programs at rap@nas.edu or by phone at 202 334 2760

### For further information contact:

**Tel**:     (1) 202 334 2707
**Email**:   ebasquest@nas.edu

## NRC Research Associate Programs (RAP)

**Purpose**: The National Academies of Sciences, Engineering, and Medicine administers competitive postdoctoral and senior research awards on behalf of U.S. federal research agencies and affiliated institutions with facilities at over 100 locations throughout the U.S. and abroad.

**Eligibility**: See Individual Agency restrictions

**Level of Study**: Postdoctoral

**Type**: Fellowships

**Value**: NRC Research Associates receive annual stipends ranging from US$45,000 to US$80,000 for recent doctoral recipients and are proportionally higher for Senior Associates.

**Length of Study**: more than 5 years

**Frequency**: Annual

**Closing Date**: 5 January

**Additional Information**: sites.nationalacademies.org/PGA/RAP/index.htm

## NRC Research Associateship Programs (RAP)

**Purpose**: The goal of these programs is to provide advanced training and collaborative research opportunities for highly qualified graduate postdoctoral and visiting scientists

**Eligibility**: Prospective applicants should carefully read the details and eligibility of the program to which they are applying. Some laboratories have citizenship restrictions (open only to U.S. citizens and permanent residents)

**Level of Study**: Postdoctoral

**Type**: Fellowship

**Length of Study**: 5 years

**Application Procedure**: an application is submitted through the NRC Research Associateship Programs online application system

**Closing Date**: 1 November

**Additional Information**: sites.nationalacademies.org/PGA/RAP/index.htm

### For further information contact:

NRC Research Associateship Programs, 500 Fifth Street, NW, Washington, DC 20001, United States of America.

**Tel**:     (1) 202 334 2760
**Email**:   rap@nas.edu

## The Optical Society, Foundation Fellowships

**Purpose**: The Optical Society of America Foundation inspires future optics innovators, supports career development for optics students, recent graduates, and young professionals and recognizes distinguished achievement in the field through the presentation of awards and honors. OSAF Fellowships are intended to provide career enhancing experiences to recent PhDs through postdoctoral research at an OSAF sponsoring company

**Eligibility**: Open to all nationalities; subject to visa requirements. Foreign nationals will be sponsored under a J-1 visa by the National Academy of Sciences.

**Level of Study**: Postgraduate

**Type**: Fellowship

**Value**: Stipend, health insurance allowance, relocation reimbursement, and funding for attendance and participation in OSA meetings and committees

**Length of Study**: One year with the possibility of renewal for additional year(s) based on adequate research progress and availability of funds

**Additional Information**: sites.nationalacademies.org/PGA/osaff/index.htm

### For further information contact:

The Optical Society, Foundation Fellowships, 500 Fifth Street NW, Keck 516, Washington, DC 2000, United States of America.

**Tel**:     (1) 202 334 3478
**Email**:   OSAFFellowships@nas.edu.

## National Aeronautics and Space Administration (NASA)

NASA Headquarters, Suite 5R30, Washington, DC 20546, United States of America.

**Tel**:       (1) 202 358 0001
**Email**:     hfinquiry@stsci.edu
**Website**:   www.nasa.gov
**Contact**:   Public Communications Office

## Hubble Fellowships for Postdoctoral Scientists

**Purpose**: The Hubble Fellowship Program provides an opportunity for highly qualified recent postdoctoral scientists to conduct independent research that is broadly related to the NASA Cosmic Origins scientific goals as addressed by any of the missions in that program: the Hubble Space Telescope, Spitzer Space Telescope, Stratospheric Observatory for Infrared Astronomy (SOFIA), the Herschel Space Observatory, and the James Webb Space Telescope. The research will be carried out at United States Host Institutions chosen by each Fellow
**Eligibility**: Applicants must have received a PhD or equivalent doctoral-level research degree in astronomy, physics, or a related discipline on or after 1 January (previous year). Graduate-student awardees who have not yet received their doctoral degree at the time of application must present evidence of having completed all requirements for the degree before commencing their Fellowships. Hubble Fellowships are open to citizens of the United States and to English-speaking citizens of other countries. Qualified applicants will receive consideration without regard to race, creed, color, age, gender, or national origin. Women and members of minority groups are strongly encouraged to apply. Incomplete applications and/or applications received after the deadline will not be considered
**Type**: Fellowship
**Value**: An annual stipend of approx. US$67,000 plus benefits, and an additional allowance of US$16,000 per year for travel and other research costs. Funding will be provided initially for the first year of the Fellowship. Renewals for the second and third years will depend on annual performance reviews
**Length of Study**: Up to 3 years
**Frequency**: Annual
**Country of Study**: United States of America
**Closing Date**: 6 November
**Additional Information**: The Hubble Fellowship Program is administered for NASA by the Space Telescope Science Institute (STScI), operated by the Association of Universities for Research in Astronomy, Inc., working in cooperation with astronomical institutions throughout the United States. Awards will be made to support each Hubble Fellow through a designated Host Institution www.stsci.edu/stsci-research/fellowships/nasa-hubble-fellowship-program

## National Air and Space Museum (NASM), Smithsonian Institution

600 Independence Ave SW, Washington, DC 20560, United States of America.

**Tel**: (1) 202 633 2471
**Email**: colette.williams@nasm.si.edu
**Website**: www.nasm.si.edu

The Smithsonian Institution's National Air and Space Museum (NASM) maintains the largest collection of historic air and spacecraft in the world. It is also a vital centre for research into the history, science and technology of aviation and spaceflight.

## A. Verville Fellowship

**Purpose**: The Verville Fellowship is a competitive nine- to twelve-month in-residence fellowship intended for the analysis of major trends, developments, and accomplishments in the history of aviation or space studies
**Level of Study**: Research
**Type**: Fellowship
**Value**: An annual stipend of US$55,000
**Length of Study**: 1 year
**Study Establishment**: NASM
**Closing Date**: 15 December
**Funding**: Private

### For further information contact:

**Email**: NASM-Fellowships@si.edu.

## Charles A Lindbergh Chair in Aerospace History

**Purpose**: To support senior scholars who are at work on, or anticipate being at work on, books on aerospace history
**Eligibility**: There are no eligibility restrictions
**Level of Study**: Research
**Type**: Fellowship
**Value**: US$100,000
**Length of Study**: 1 year
**Frequency**: Annual
**Study Establishment**: Smithsonian Institution
**Country of Study**: United States of America
**Application Procedure**: Applicants must complete an application form
**Closing Date**: 15 January
**Funding**: Private
**Contributor**: Smithsonian restricted funds
**Additional Information**: airandspace.si.edu/support/get-involved/fellowships/charles-lindbergh-chair-aerospace-history

### For further information contact:

**Email**: collette.williams@nasm.si.edu

## Guggenheim Fellowship

**Purpose**: Candidates are encouraged to pursue programs of research and writing that support publication of works that are scholarly

**Level of Study**: Postdoctoral
**Type**: Fellowship
**Value**: An annual stipend of US$30,000 for predoctoral candidates and US$45,000 for postdoctoral candidates will be awarded, with limited additional funds for travel and miscellaneous
**Study Establishment**: NASM
**Application Procedure**: All applicants must be able to speak and write fluently in English
**Closing Date**: 15 December
**Funding**: Private
**Additional Information**: airandspace.si.edu/support/get-involved/fellowships/guggenheim

**For further information contact:**

**Email**: NASM-Fellowships@si.edu.

## National Air and Space Museum Aviation/Space Writers Award

**Purpose**: To support research on aerospace topics. The product created as a result of the grant must be in any form suitable for potential public dissemination in print, electronic, broadcast, or other visual medium, including, but not limited to, a book manuscript, video, film script, or monograph
**Type**: Award
**Value**: US$5,000
**Frequency**: Annual
**Application Procedure**: 1. Maximum two-page, single-spaced proposal stating the subject of their research and their research goals 2. One- to two-page curriculum vitae 3. One-page detailed budget explaining how the grant will be spent.
**Closing Date**: March
**Additional Information**: airandspace.si.edu/support/get-involved/fellowships/aviation-space-writers-foundation-award

**For further information contact:**

National Air and Space Museum, Independence Ave at Sixth Street, SW, Rm 3313, MRC 312, P.O. Box 37012, Washington, DC 20013-7012, United States of America.

**Email**: NASM-Fellowships@si.edu

## Postdoctoral Earth and Planetary Sciences Fellowship

**Purpose**: To support scientific research
**Level of Study**: Postdoctorate
**Type**: Fellowship

**Value**: Stipend, compatible with National Research Council Awards
**Length of Study**: 1 or more years
**Frequency**: Dependent on funds available
**Study Establishment**: NASM
**Country of Study**: United States of America
**Application Procedure**: Applicants must complete an application form
**Closing Date**: 15 January
**Funding**: Private
**Contributor**: Smithsonian restricted funds
**Additional Information**: airandspace.si.edu/support/get-involved/fellowships/postdoctoral-earth-and-planetary-sciences

# National Association for Core Curriculum, Inc.

1640 Franklin Avenue, Suite 104, Kent, OH 44240-4324, United States of America.

**Tel**:      (1) 330 677 5008
**Email**:   gvarsnacc@aol.com
**Contact**: Dr Gordon F Vars, Executive Secretary & Treasurer

The National Association for Core Curriculum, Inc. has promoted integrative person centred education at all levels since 1953.

## Bossing-Edwards Research Scholarship Award

**Purpose**: To encourage research on core curriculum and other interdisciplinary or integrative approaches to education
**Eligibility**: Open to individuals who have previously been a core teacher for at least one year, and have been accepted on a graduate programme leading to a Master's, specialist's or doctor's degree at a university that has adequate resources for research in core curriculum
**Level of Study**: Doctorate, Postgraduate
**Type**: Scholarship
**Value**: Up to US$300
**Frequency**: Dependent on funds available
**Study Establishment**: An appropriate institution
**Country of Study**: United States of America
**Application Procedure**: Applicants should write explaining intended research and how they meet the criteria of eligibility
**No. of awards offered**: 5
**Closing Date**: 19 April
**No. of awards given last year**: 1
**No. of applicants last year**: 5

**For further information contact:**

**Email**: canada@berkeley.edu

# National Association for Gifed Children

## Davis Scholarship

**Purpose**: Lewis & Clark is pleased to announce its continuing commitment to the Davis United World College (UWC) Scholars program for the academic year
**Level of Study**: Postgraduate
**Type**: Scholarship
**Value**: US$20,000
**Length of Study**: 4 year
**Frequency**: Annual
**Country of Study**: Any country
**Closing Date**: 15 February
**Funding**: Foundation
**Additional Information**: www.lclark.edu/offices/international/financial_aid/davis_scholarship/

**For further information contact:**

Associate Dean of Students, Lewis & Clark College, 0615 SW Palatine Hill Road, Portland, OR 97219, United States of America.

**Tel**:      (1) 503 768 7305
**Fax**:     (1) 503 768 7301
**Email**:   iso@lclark.edu

## Distinguished Scholarship

**Purpose**: The National Association for Gifted Children (NAGC) annually presents the Distinguished Scholar Award to an individual who has made significant contributions to the field of knowledge regarding the education of gifted and talented individuals. This individual should have a continued record of distinguished scholarship and contributions to the field of gifted education for more than 10 years, and must show a record of ongoing scholarly productivity as recognized by experts in the field
**Eligibility**: 1. Evidence of research in the field of gifted and talented. 2. Evidence that the contributions reflect a continuous and noted record of involvement in the field of gifted and talented education. 3. Evidence of recognition by peers of the importance of the above-mentioned contributions
**Level of Study**: Postgraduate
**Type**: Scholarship
**Value**: US$30,000

**Length of Study**: 4 year
**Frequency**: Annual
**Country of Study**: Any country
**Closing Date**: 1 February
**Funding**: Foundation
**Additional Information**: www.nagc.org/about/awards-recognition/distinguished-scholar-award

## Goodrich Scholarship Program

**Purpose**: Goodrich students establish a dynamic presence on campus. They come hungry, ready to learn and eager to join the UNO community. Many recipients are the first in their families to attend college. They come from underrepresented populations and have earned an opportunity to continue their education
**Level of Study**: Postgraduate
**Type**: Scholarship
**Frequency**: Annual
**Country of Study**: Any country
**Funding**: Foundation

**For further information contact:**

UNO Campus, 6001 Dodge Street, CPACS 123, Omaha Nebraska, NE 68182, United States of America.

**Email**:   unogoodrich@unomaha.edu

## Paul Beck Memorial Scholarship

**Purpose**: The Faculty Senate of the University of Nebraska Omaha (UNO) has sponsored scholarships for students since 1970 when Paul L. Beck, a long-time member of the History Department, urged faculty and staff to go beyond the classroom to assist capable students in their educational pursuits at UNO
**Eligibility**: 1. Applications must include a one page letter describing how this scholarship will help further your educational needs. 2. Applications must include a letter of support from a UNO faculty member. This letter must be sent directly to the Faculty Senate office by the faculty member. 3. No application will be considered unless all documents listed above are on file in the Faculty Senate office by the deadline. 4. Only one application/category per student is permitted
**Level of Study**: Postgraduate
**Type**: Scholarship
**Value**: US$1,000
**Frequency**: Annual
**Country of Study**: Any country
**Closing Date**: 2 February

**Funding**: Foundation

**For further information contact:**

The Faculty Senate, University of Nebraska at Omaha, ASH 105, 6001 Dodge St., Omaha Nebraska, NE 68182, United States of America.

**Email**:    sbishop@unomaha.edu

## University of Nebraska Omaha Women's Club Scholarships

**Purpose**: A portion of the UNOWC treasury funds are transferred each year to the scholarship fund, as are memorials. Our Annual Membership Fundraiser Dinner gives members a chance to contribute individually and to meet the scholarship winners. These and other projects, carried out over the years with a lot of work and dedication from many members, continue to increase the UNOWC Scholarship Funds
**Level of Study**: Postgraduate
**Type**: Scholarship
**Value**: US$100
**Frequency**: Annual
**Country of Study**: Any country
**Closing Date**: 31 May
**Funding**: Foundation
**Additional Information**: www.unomaha.edu/womens-club/scholarships.php

**For further information contact:**

Gina Pearson/Elaine Allen, University of Nebraska Foundation, 2285 S. 67th St., Ste 200, Omaha Nebraska, NE 68106, United States of America.

**Email**:    uno.womens.club@gmail.com

## National Association of Teachers of Singing (NATS)

9957 Moorings Drive, Suite 401, Jacksonville, FL 32257, United States of America.

**Tel**:         (1) 904 992 9101; Toll Free: 888 262 2065
**Email**:      info@nats.org
**Website**:    www.nats.org

The National Association of Teachers of Singing (NATS) is now the largest association of teachers of singing in the world.

NATS offers a variety of lifelong learning experiences to its members, such as workshops, intern programmes, master classes, and conferences, all beginning at the chapter level and progressing to national events.

## National Association of Teachers of Singing Art Song Competition Award

**Purpose**: To stimulate the creation of quality vocal literature through the cooperation of singer and composer
**Eligibility**: Open to any composer whose submitted work is a song cycle, group of songs, or extended single song of approximately 15 minutes in length (13–17 minutes acceptable); for single voice and piano; to a text written in English, for which the composer has secured copyright clearance (only text setting permission necessary); composed within the last 2 years, and who pays the competition entry fee
**Type**: Cash prize
**Value**: US$2,000 plus the composer's expenses (US$500 airfare reimbursement plus hotel) and US$1,000, 2nd place
**Study Establishment**: Valdosta State University
**Country of Study**: United States of America
**Application Procedure**: check the website for further details
**Closing Date**: 1 December

**For further information contact:**

DepartmentofMusic,ValdostaStateUniversity,1500N.Patterson Street,Valdosta,GA31602,UnitedStatesofAmerica.

**Email**:    cmikkels@valdosta.edu

## National Breast Cancer Foundation (NBCF)

Level 9, 50 Pitt St, Sydney 2000, GPO Box 4129, Sydney, NSW 2001, Australia.

**Tel**:        (61) 2 8098 4800
**Email**:      info@nbcf.org.au
**Website**:    www.nbcf.org.au

The ultimate goal of the National Breast Cancer Foundation (NBCF) is to raise enough money to fund a cure for breast cancer. The NBCF supports and promotes research into breast cancer, facilitates consumer participation in all aspects of their work, acts as an advocate for breast cancer research, and provides opportunities for all Australians to contribute to breast cancer research.

## National Breast Cancer Foundation Doctoral Scholarship

**Purpose**: To provide outstanding graduates with a strong interest in breast cancer research with an opportunity to pursue full-time PhD studies at an Australian University
**Eligibility**: Open to applicants who are permanent residents of Australia
**Level of Study**: Doctorate, Postgraduate, Research
**Type**: Scholarship
**Value**: Scholars will receive a stipend of approx. AU$33,240
**Length of Study**: 3 years
**Frequency**: Annual
**Country of Study**: Australia
**Application Procedure**: The applications are judged under peer review by experts in the field for their scientific merit and contribution to either new knowledge or building on existing knowledge of breast cancer
**No. of awards offered**: 15
**Funding**: Foundation
**Contributor**: Australian community and corporate funding
**No. of awards given last year**: 4
**No. of applicants last year**: 15

### For further information contact:

**Email**:    lhan.gannon@nbcf.org.au

## Novel Concept Awards

**Purpose**: To provide investigators with the opportunity to pursue serendipitous observations and explore new, innovative, and untested ideas
**Eligibility**: Open to applicants undertaking research in the entire continuum of breast cancer research. Residing in Australia throughout the funding period. Must meet all eligibility criteria outlined in guidelines and application form. Please check at www.nbcf.org.au
**Level of Study**: Unrestricted
**Type**: Research grant
**Value**: Maximum value of AU$100,000 per grant per year
**Length of Study**: 1–2 years
**Country of Study**: Australia
**Application Procedure**: Please contact the Research Administrator or check the website for further details
**No. of awards offered**: 35
**Closing Date**: 20 June
**Funding**: Foundation, Trusts
**Contributor**: NBCF, Australian Community and Corporate
**No. of awards given last year**: 12

**No. of applicants last year**: 35
**Additional Information**: Each year NBCF board will decide when to call for application and closing dates in late February

## Pilot Study Grants

**Purpose**: To financially assist investigators to obtain preliminary data regarding methodology, effect sizes and possible findings relating to new research ideas relevant to breast cancer
**Eligibility**: Applicants must be Australian citizens, or be graduates from overseas with permanent Australian resident status, must reside in Australia throughout the funding period and not under bond to any foreign government
**Level of Study**: Research, Unrestricted
**Type**: Grant
**Value**: A maximum of AU$100,000 for up to 2 years
**Length of Study**: Up to 2 years
**Frequency**: Every 2 years
**Country of Study**: Australia
**Application Procedure**: Check website for further details
**No. of awards offered**: 76
**Closing Date**: 10 May
**Funding**: Foundation
**Contributor**: Australian Community and Corporate
**No. of awards given last year**: 3
**No. of applicants last year**: 76
**Additional Information**: NBCF Board will decide whether to offer this grant scheme again when they meet annual in late February researchfunding.duke.edu/pilot-study-grants

## National Bureau of Asian Research (NBR)

1414 NE 42nd Street, Suite 300, Seattle, WA 98105, United States of America.

**Tel**:       (1) 206 632 7370
**Email**:    nbr@nbr.org
**Website**:  www.nbr.org
**Contact**:  George F Russell

NBR is a nonprofit, nonpartisan research institution dedicated to informing and strengthening policy. NBR conducts advanced research on politics and security, economics and trade, and health and societal issues, with emphasis on those of interest to the United States.

## The Next Generation: Leadership in Asian Affairs Fellowship

**Purpose**: To further the professional development of Asian specialists in the year just after the completion of their Master's degree

**Eligibility**: Open to citizens or permanent residents of the United States who have obtained a Master's degree

**Level of Study**: Research

**Type**: Fellowships

**Value**: Each fellow will receive a US$32,500 fellowship award (with benefits), as well as a reimbursement for some relocation expenses

**Length of Study**: 1 year

**Frequency**: Annual

**Country of Study**: United States of America

**Application Procedure**: Candidates must submit an online cover letter, curriculum vitae, 750 word essay stating the purpose of applying and 3 written references

**Closing Date**: 15 January

**Funding**: Government, Corporation, Foundation

**No. of awards given last year**: 3

**Additional Information**: www.honorsociety.org/scholarships/next-generation-leadership-asian-affairs-fellowship

### For further information contact:

**Email**: nextgen@nbr.org

## National Cattleman Foundation

### Continuing Medical Education Beef Industry Scholarship

**Purpose**: Sponsored by CME Group & the National Cattlemen's Foundation, ten (10) scholarships of US$1,500 will be awarded to outstanding students who are pursuing careers in the beef industry

**Eligibility**: Must be enrolled as an undergraduate student in a two or four-year institution of higher education for the entire upcoming academic year. Proof of enrollment as a full-time student will be required to receive the scholarship money; 1. Write a one-page letter expressing/indicating your future career goals related to the beef industry. 2. Write an essay of 750 words or less describing an issue confronting the beef industry and offer your solution. 3. Obtain two (2) letters of reference from current or former instructors or industry professionals. 4. Applications must contain the Beef Industry scholarship cover page

**Level of Study**: Graduate

**Type**: Scholarship

**Length of Study**: 2- 4 years

**Frequency**: Annual

**Country of Study**: United States of America and Europe

**Closing Date**: 30 October

**Funding**: Private

**Additional Information**: www.nationalcattlemens foundation.org/scholarships/cme-beef-industry-scholarship

### For further information contact:

9110 East Nichols Ave., Suite #300, Centennial, CO 80112, United States of America.

**Email**: ncf@beef.org

## National Education Association (NEA) Foundation

1201 16th Street, North West, Washington, DC 20036, United States of America.

**Tel**: (1) 202 822 7840
**Email**: NEAFoundation@nea.org
**Website**: www.neafoundation.org

The NEA Foundation offers programs and grants that support public school educators' efforts to close the achievement gaps, increase student achievement, salute excellence in education and provide professional development.

### Student Achievement Grants

**Purpose**: To promote collaborative, innovative ideas that lead to student achievement of high standards

**Eligibility**: Open to teams of two or more practising United States public school teachers in grades K–12, public school education support personnel, public higher education faculty and staff. Preference will be given to National Education Association members, and to educators who serve economically disadvantaged and/or underserved students

**Level of Study**: Postgraduate

**Type**: Grant

**Value**: US$2,000 and US$5,000

**Length of Study**: 12 months

**Frequency**: Annual

**Country of Study**: United States of America

**Application Procedure**: Applicants must consult the organization for details

**Closing Date**: 15 October

**Additional Information**: www.neafoundation.org/for-educators/student-success-grants/

# National Endowment for the Humanities (NEH)

Division of Research, Room 318, 1100 Pennsylvania Avenue North West, Washington, DC 20506, United States of America.

| | |
|---|---|
| **Tel**: | (1) 202 606 8400 |
| **Email**: | research@neh.gov |
| **Website**: | www.neh.gov |
| **Contact**: | Programme Officer |

National Endowment for the Humanities' (NEH) Research Division facilitates research and original scholarship in the humanities through grants to universities, centres for advanced study and individual scholars. NEH uses the following definition of the humanities: 'The humanities include, but are not limited to, language, both modern and classical, linguistics, literature, history, jurisprudence, philosophy, archaeology, comparative religion, ethics, the history, criticism and theory of the arts, aspects of social sciences which have humanistic content and employ humanistic methods, and the study and application of the humanities to the human environment with particular attention to reflecting our diverse heritage, traditions and history and to the relevance of the humanities to the current conditions of national life'.

## National Endowment for the Humanities Fellowships

**Purpose**: To provide support for full-time research on projects that can be completed during the tenure of the award, as well as for work that is part of a long-term endeavour. Recipients usually produce scholarly articles, monographs on specialised subjects, books on broad topics, archaeological site reports, translations, editions or other scholarly tools

**Eligibility**: Open to faculty or staff members of colleges or universities, or of primary or secondary schools, or independent scholars or writers

**Level of Study**: Postdoctorate

**Type**: Fellowship

**Value**: US$24,000 for six–eight month tenure and US$40,000 for 9–12 month tenure

**Length of Study**: Varies

**Frequency**: Annual

**Country of Study**: Other

**Application Procedure**: Applicants must complete and submit an application form. Guidelines and application forms are posted on the NEH website

**Closing Date**: 1 May

**Funding**: Government

### For further information contact:

**Email**:   questions@neh.gov

# National Foundation for Infectious Diseases (NFID)

7201 Wisconsin Avenue, Suite 750, Bethesda, MD 20814, United States of America.

| | |
|---|---|
| **Tel**: | (1) 301 656 0003 |
| **Email**: | info@nfid.org |
| **Website**: | www.nfid.org |

The National Foundation for Infectious Diseases (NFID) is a non-profit, non-governmental organization whose mission is public and professional education and promotion of research on the causes, treatment and prevention of infectious diseases.

## National Foundation for Infectious Diseases Postdoctoral Fellowship in Nosocomial Infection Research and Training

**Purpose**: To encourage a qualified physician researcher to become a specialist and investigator in the field of nosocomial infections

**Eligibility**: Open to citizens of the United States

**Level of Study**: Postgraduate

**Type**: Fellowship

**Value**: US$40,000

**Frequency**: Annual

**Country of Study**: United States of America

**Application Procedure**: Applicants must submit their application form and curriculum vitae

**Closing Date**: 6 January

**Additional Information**: Contact Grants Manager. Priority will be given to Fellows in or entering into infectious diseases training www.neh.gov/grants/research/fellowships

### For further information contact:

**Email**:   nfid@aol.com

## National Health and Medical Research Council (NHMRC)

NHMRC, GPO Box 1421, Canberra, ACT 2601, Australia.

**Tel**:         (61) 2 6217 9000
**Email**:     grantnet.help@nhmrc.gov.au
**Website**:  www.nhmrc.gov.au
**Contact**:  Executive Director

The National Health and Medical Research Council (NHMRC) (Australia) consolidates within a single national organization the often independent functions of research funding and development of advice. One of its strengths is that it brings together and draws upon the resources of all components of the health system, including governments, medical practitioners, nurses and allied health professionals, researchers, teaching and research institutions, public and private programme managers, service administrators, community health organizations, social health researchers and consumers.

## National Health and Medical Research Council Equipment Grants

**Purpose**: To provide funding support for the purchase of items of equipment required for biomedical research
**Eligibility**: Open to individuals, groups or institutions which are normally eligible for NHMRC support. Grants will be made on the basis of scientific merit, taking into consideration factors including whether the applicants hold NHMRC grants, the institutional ranking of the application, and institutional or regional availability of major equipment
**Level of Study**: Unrestricted
**Type**: Grant
**Value**: AU$10 000 to cover the cost of equipment in excess of
**Frequency**: Annual
**Country of Study**: Australia
**Application Procedure**: Applicants must complete an application form
**Funding**: Government

### For further information contact:

MDP 33, Project Grants Office, GPO Box 9848, Canberra, ACT 2601, Australia.

**Tel**:       (61) 2 6289 8278
**Fax**:      (61) 2 6289 8617
**Email**:  jean.sewell@hhlgcs.ausgovhhcs.telememo.au

## National Health and Medical Research Council Public Health Travelling Fellowships

**Purpose**: To enable Fellows to make postgraduate study tours abroad or within Australia, which relate to their work and speciality and which will be of benefit to public health in Australia
**Eligibility**: Open to all personnel working in the field of public health, who are suitably qualified at a level appropriate for fulfilment of the objectives of the study and for implementation of its benefits. The applicant may be employed in government or industry, or may be self-employed. Preference will be given to those applicants who would not normally, in the course of their employment, have the opportunity, as part of their normal duties, for overseas travel and experience
**Level of Study**: Unrestricted
**Type**: Other
**Value**: Not exceeding AU$19,700, plus an agreed annual allowance to cover cost increases
**Length of Study**: 2–12 months
**Frequency**: Annual
**Country of Study**: Any country
**Application Procedure**: Please write for details
**No. of awards offered**: 18
**Closing Date**: 31 July
**Funding**: Government
**No. of awards given last year**: 8
**No. of applicants last year**: 18
**Additional Information**: Preference will be given to public health practitioners

### For further information contact:

Secretariat & Training Awards, GPO Box 9848, Canberra, ACT 2601, Australia.

**Tel**:       (61) 2 6289 7945
**Fax**:      (61) 2 6289 6957
**Email**:  trevorlord@hhlgcs.ausgovhhcs.telememo.au

## National Health and Medical Research Council Research Project Grants

**Purpose**: To provide support for work on problems which are likely to be capable of solution in a reasonably short period of time
**Eligibility**: Open to Australian researchers only
**Level of Study**: Unrestricted
**Type**: Grant
**Value**: To cover salary, equipment, maintenance and other specific expenses
**Frequency**: Annual
**Country of Study**: Australia

**Application Procedure**: Applicants must complete an application form
**No. of awards offered**: 1299
**Closing Date**: 6 March
**Funding**: Government
**No. of awards given last year**: 406
**No. of applicants last year**: 1299

### For further information contact:

Project Grants Office, GPO Box 9848, Canberra, ACT 2601, Australia.

Tel:       (61) 2 6289 6974
Fax:       (61) 2 6289 8617
Email:     elizabeth.hoole@hhlgcs.ausgovhhcs.telememo.au

## R Douglas Wright Awards

**Purpose**: To provide outstanding researchers at an early stage in their career with an opportunity for independent research together with improved security
**Eligibility**: Open to applicants who have completed postdoctoral research training or have equivalent experience, and are seeking to establish themselves in a career in medical research in Australia
**Level of Study**: Postdoctorate, Professional development
**Type**: Award
**Value**: Salary in the range of Senior Research Officer Level 1 to Senior Research Officer Level 4, with annual increments, plus an allowance of AU$10,000 per year
**Length of Study**: 4 years
**Frequency**: Annual
**Study Establishment**: Australian research institutions
**Country of Study**: Australia
**Application Procedure**: Applicants must complete an application form, available from Ms H Murray
**No. of awards offered**: 43
**Closing Date**: 30 April
**Funding**: Government
**No. of awards given last year**: 6
**No. of applicants last year**: 43
**Additional Information**: staff.unimelb.edu.au/mdhs/ research-development/research-collaboration-and-funding/ faculty-trust-fellowships/r-douglas-wright-research-fellowship

### For further information contact:

Fellowships Unit - Mail Drop Point, 33GPO Box 9848, Canberra, ACT 2601, Australia.

Tel:       (61) 2 6289 5034
Fax:       (61) 2 6289 1329
Email:     helen.murray@hhlgcs.ausgovhhcs.telememo.au

## Targeted Call for Research into Healthy Ageing of Aboriginal and Torres Strait Islander Peoples

**Purpose**: The aim of implementing this call is to provide funding for rigorous, culturally-informed research into improving the health and experiences of ageing in older Aboriginal and Torres Strait Islander peoples. Quality evidence generated from research will allow for better planning, funding and implementation of policies and services to achieve and support healthy ageing for Aboriginal and Torres Strait Islander peoples
**Eligibility**: Applications for NHMRC funding are subject to the general eligibility requirements set out in the NHMRC Funding Rules. Additional eligibility requirements are in scheme-specific funding rules. Institutions must be an NHMRC approved Administering Institution to be eligible to receive and administer NHMRC funding - refer to the NHMRC website for a list of approved Administering Institutions
**Level of Study**: Graduate
**Type**: Grant
**Value**: Total value available is AU$5,000,000
**Frequency**: Annual
**Country of Study**: Any country
**Application Procedure**: Official website to apply electronically for the grant application is www.nhmrc.gov.au/grants-funding-administering-grants
**Closing Date**: 15 August
**Funding**: Private
**Additional Information**: Applications must be submitted electronically using NHMRC's online Research Grants Management System (RGMS). Official link for the following grant is www.nhmrc.gov.au/grants-funding-administering-grants www.nhmrc.gov.au/funding/find-funding/targeted-call-research-healthy-ageing-aboriginal-and-torres-strait-islander-peoples

### For further information contact:

Email:     help@nhmrc.gov.au

## National Heart, Lung, and Blood Institute

### Immersive Training in the Glycosciences - Fellowship

**Subjects**: Glycosciences
**Purpose**: The ultimate goal of the program is to transform the study of glycoscience from a specialized domain into mainstream biology. This fellowship is expected to provide scholars with an unparalleled opportunity to participate in

cross-disciplinary research, obtain advanced knowledge, skills, and professional exposure within the glycosciences, as well as to develop a research portfolio from which to launch independent careers.

**Eligibility**: Scholars must be citizens or non-citizen nationals of the United States or have been lawfully admitted for permanent residence at the time of appointment. At the time of appointment scholars should hold an M.D. and/or PhD degree.

**Type**: Fellowship

**Value**: Salary support of up to US$100,000 per year (inclusive of benefits), research supplies, and travel. Rigorous training in the Glycosciences (didactic and technical) will be provided.

**Study Establishment**: John Hopkins University

**Country of Study**: United States of America

**Closing Date**: 30 July

**Additional Information**: glycocareers.cclinic.jhu.edu/styled/index.html

## National Institute for Health and Care Excellence (NICE)

Level 1A, City Tower, Piccadilly Plaza, Manchester, M1 4BT, United Kingdom.

**Tel**: (44) 300 323 0140
**Website**: www.nice.org.uk

The National Institute for Health and Care Excellence (NICE) provides national guidance and advice to improve health and social care. NICE was originally set up in 1999 as the National Institute for Clinical Excellence, a special health authority, to reduce variation in the availability and quality of NHS treatments and care.

## National Institute for Health and Care Excellence Scholarships

**Purpose**: NICE Scholarships are one-year opportunities for qualified health and social care professionals to find out about the inner workings of NICE and undertake a supported improvement project, related to NICE guidance, within their local organization

**Eligibility**: NICE Scholarships are typically awarded to specialist registrars, senior nurses, pharmacists and allied health professionals, service improvement leads, public health and social care specialists and health service managers. In addition to their project-based activities, NICE Scholars are expected to act as local ambassadors for clinical and public

health and social care excellence; promote the principles and the recommendations of NICE guidance-through teaching activities, for example

**Type**: Scholarship

**Value**: NICE Scholars are supported in their project via a series of workshops, access to a very experienced senior mentor and contact with the expert teams at NICE. NICE Scholars are not paid. NICE will, however, meet all reasonable expenses (e.g. travel, accommodation) incurred in the course of carrying out Scholarship activities

**Length of Study**: 1 year

**Frequency**: Annual

**Country of Study**: United Kingdom

**Application Procedure**: The mode of applying is by post

**Closing Date**: 1 November

**Additional Information**: Scholars are expected to devote approximately 7.5 hours per week to their Scholarship project. For detailed information, visit www.nice.org.uk/getinvolved/nice_fellows_and_scholars/scholars/NICEscholarships.jsp scientistsolutions.com/forum/jobs-clinicaldiagnostic/national-institute-health-and-care-excellence-scholarships

## National Institute of General Medical Sciences (NIGMS)

45 Center Drive, MSC 6200, Bethesda, MD 20892-6200, United States of America.

**Tel**: (1) 301 496 7301
**Email**: info@nigms.nih.gov
**Website**: www.nigms.nih.gov
**Contact**: Ms Jilliene Drayton, Information Development Specialist

The National Institute of General Medical Sciences (NIGMS) is one of the National Institutes of Health (NIH), the principal biomedical research agency of the United States Federal Government. NIGMS supports basic research that increases understanding of biological processes and lays the foundation for advances in disease diagnosis, treatment, and prevention.

## National Institute of General Medical Sciences Research Project Grants (R01)

**Purpose**: To support a discrete project related to the investigator's area of interest and competence

**Eligibility**: Research project grants may be awarded to non-profit organizations and institutions; governments and their agencies; occasionally, though rarely, to individuals who have access to adequate facilities and resources for conducting the research; and to profit-making organizations. Foreign institutions and international organizations are also eligible to apply for these grants

**Level of Study**: Postgraduate

**Type**: Grant

**Value**: These grants may provide funds for reasonable costs of the research activity, as well as for salaries, equipment, supplies, travel and other related expenses

**Frequency**: Annual

**Country of Study**: United States of America

**Application Procedure**: Applicants must contact the Office of Extramural Outreach for details

**Funding**: Government

**Additional Information**: www.grants.nih.gov/supportwww.nigms.nih.gov/Research/Mechanisms/Pages/ResearchProjectGrants.aspx

### For further information contact:

Office of Extramural Outreach, NIH 6701 Rockledge Drive Msc 7760, Bethesda, MD 20892-7760, United States of America.

**Tel**:      (1) 301 435 0714
**Email**:   grantsinfo@nih.gov

## National Road Safety Authority Individual Postdoctoral Fellowships (F32)

**Purpose**: NIGMS welcomes NRSA applications from eligible individuals who seek postdoctoral biomedical research training in areas related to the scientific programmes of the Institute

**Eligibility**: Open to applicants who have received the doctoral degree (domestic or foreign) by the beginning date of the proposed award

**Level of Study**: Postdoctorate

**Type**: Award

**Value**: NIGMS provides an annual stipend to postdoctoral fellows, and an institutional allowance to cover training-related expenses. The stipend, tuition/fees and institutional allowance are detailed at

**Length of Study**: Up to 3 years

**Frequency**: Annual

**Study Establishment**: The institutional setting may be domestic or foreign, public or private

**Country of Study**: Any country

**Application Procedure**: Applicants must write to the main address for details or telephone Dr Michael Sesma, at (1) 301 594 2772. Further details are also available from the website www.nigms.nih.gov

**Closing Date**: 8 April

**Funding**: Government

**Additional Information**: www.nigms.nih.gov/training/indivpostdoc/Pages/PostdocFellowshipDescription.aspx

---

## National Institutes of Health

900 Rockville Pike, Bethesda, MA 20892, United States of America.

**Website**:    www.nih.gov
**Contact**:    Dr Belinda Seto, Acting Deputy Director for Extramural Research

## Hitchings-Elion Postdoctoral Fellowships for United States Scientist

**Purpose**: The purpose of these fellowships is to promote scientific collaboration between British and American scientists for the conduct of biomedical and behavioral research

**Eligibility**: The applicant must be a United States citizen or permanent United States resident, hold a doctorate level degree in one of the medical or veterinary clinical, behavioral, or biomedical sciences, and be within ten years of the last doctoral degree

**Level of Study**: Research

**Type**: Fellowship

**Frequency**: Annual

**Country of Study**: Any country

**Application Procedure**: The administration of the program will be integrated into the administration of other Fogarty International Center fellowship activities and the application receipt processes of the Division of Research Grants, NIH. Applications must be sent to the Division of Research Grants, NIH. Special application forms must be used and are available, along with detailed instructions from International Research and Awards Branch. Fogarty International Center National Institutes of Health Building 31, Room B2C39

**Closing Date**: 10 September

**Funding**: Private

**Additional Information**: grants.nih.gov/grants/guide/pa-files/PA-92-030.html

### For further information contact:

Chief, International Research and Awards Branch, Fogarty International Center, Building 31, Room B2C21, Bethesda, MD 20892, United States.

**Tel**:    (1) 301 496 1653

## Ruth L. Kirschstein National Research Service Award (NRSA) Individual Postdoctoral Fellowship

**Purpose**: To support promising applicants during their mentored postdoctoral training under the guidance of outstanding faculty sponsors
**Level of Study**: Postdoctoral
**Type**: Fellowships
**Value**: stipend, allowance & tuition
**Frequency**: Annual
**Closing Date**: 8 April
**Additional Information**: grants.nih.gov/grants/guide/pa-files/PA-19-188.html

## National Library of Medicine (NLM)

8600 Rockville Pike Building 38A, Bethesda, MD 20894, United States of America.

**Tel**:      (1) 301 496 4221
**Email**:     dm99n@nih.gov
**Website**:   www.nlm.nih.gov
**Contact**:   Mr Dwight Mawrery, Grants Management Officer

As one of the nation's premier repositories of biomedical information, the National Library of Medicine (NLM) has a vital interest in information management and in the enormous utility of computers and telecommunications for improving storage, retrieval, access and use of biomedical information. The Library offers support for qualified investigators, be they individuals or institutions, in three separate but related programme areas: medical informatics, biotechnology information and health sciences library and information science.

## National Library of Medicine Fellowship in Applied Informatics

**Purpose**: To improve the American healthcare system by supporting health science professionals (including librarians) whose primary interest is to put informatics into practice, develop modern information systems in traditional organisations, use the new information techniques in a specific field and help disseminate promising programmes and systems
**Eligibility**: Open to individuals with a BA, BSc, MA, MSc or PhD in a field related to health, who are United States nationals or permanent residents of the United States of America

**Level of Study**: Doctorate, Graduate, Postdoctorate, Postgraduate
**Type**: Fellowship
**Value**: Up to US$58,000 per year, based on the salary or remuneration the individual would have been paid from their home institution
**Length of Study**: Varies
**Frequency**: Annual
**Study Establishment**: Universities, colleges, hospitals, laboratories, units of State and certain agencies of the Federal Government in the United States
**Country of Study**: United States of America
**Application Procedure**: Applications must be submitted by an organisation on behalf of the individual seeking the grant, on the standard grant application form PHS 416-1 (rev 8/95)
**Closing Date**: 5 December
**Additional Information**: The NLM encourages potential applicants to clarify any issues or questions. For enquiries regarding programmatic issues, please contact Mr Peter Clepper, Program Officer. For enquiries regarding Division of Nursing programmatic issues, please contact the Division of Nursing. For enquiries regarding fiscal matters, please contact Ms Shelley Carow, Grants Management Officer grants.nih.gov/grants/guide/pa-files/PA-92-090.html

### For further information contact:

Division of Nursing, Parklawn Building, Room 9-36, 5600 Fishes Lane, Rockville, MD 20852, United States of America.

**Tel**:   (1) 301 443 5786
**Fax**:   (1) 301 443 8586

## National Library of Medicine Investigator Initiated Project Grant

**Purpose**: To support individual investigators and their colleagues to pursue a discreet, circumscribed line of investigation to its logical conclusion
**Type**: Project grant
**Length of Study**: Up to 3 years
**Frequency**: 3 times each year
**Study Establishment**: United States universities or research institutions
**Country of Study**: United States of America
**Application Procedure**: Applications must be submitted on the PHS form 398 (ref 5/95)
**Closing Date**: 1 October
**Additional Information**: grants.nih.gov/grants/guide/pa-files/PA-96-001.html

**For further information contact:**

Division of Extramural Programmes, National Library of Medicine, Rockledge One Building, 6705 Rockledge Drive Suite 301, Bethesda, MD 20817, United States of America.

Tel:        (1) 301 594 4882
Fax:        (1) 301 402 2952
Email:    bean@nlm.nih.gov

## National Library of Medicine Postdoctoral Informatics Research Fellowships

**Purpose**: To promote researchers interested in informatics research training wishing to identify their own mentor and host institution
**Eligibility**: Open to applicants who have a PhD relevant to biomedicine or computer science or an equivalent degree from an accredited domestic or foreign institution
**Level of Study**: Postdoctorate
**Type**: Fellowship
**Value**: Based on established NIH schedules
**Frequency**: Annual
**Study Establishment**: United States universities or research institutions
**Country of Study**: United States of America
**Application Procedure**: Applicants must contact the organisation
**Additional Information**: For a complete list of NLM factsheets, please contact Factsheets, Office of Public Information

**For further information contact:**

Factsheets Office of Public Information National Library of Medicine, 8600 Rockville Pike, Bethesda, MD 20894, United States of America.

Fax:        (1) 301 496 4450
Email:    publicinfo@nlm.nih.gov

## National Library of Medicine Publication Grant Program

**Purpose**: To provide assistance for the preparation of book length manuscripts and, in some cases, the publication of important scientific information needed by United States health professionals
**Eligibility**: Open to public or private, non-profit institutions and individuals, who are involved in research

**Type**: Project grant
**Value**: US$35,000 direct costs per year over a period of three years maximum
**Length of Study**: 1–3 years
**Frequency**: 3 times each year
**Country of Study**: United States of America
**Application Procedure**: Applications must be submitted on the PHS FORM 398 (Rev 5/95) grant application ki
**Closing Date**: 1 October
**Additional Information**: Potential applicants are strongly encouraged to discuss projects early with the Program staff, who will discuss programme status and experience with them, provide additional information in response to specific application plans and review draft proposals for completeness if desired. For a complete list of NLM Factsheets, please contact Factsheets, Office of Public Information

**For further information contact:**

Tel:        (1) 301 594 4882
Fax:        (1) 301 402 2952
Email:    sparks@nlm.nih.gov

## National Multiple Sclerosis Society (MS)

National MS Society, P.O. Box 4527, New York, NY 10163, United States of America.

Tel:          (1) 800 344 4867
Website:    www.nationalmssociety.org/

The National Multiple Sclerosis Society (NMSS) is a non-profit organization based in New York City with chapters located throughout the United States. The organization funds research, advocates for social and political change, provides education, and sponsors services that help people with multiple sclerosis and their families.

## Career Transition Fellowships

**Purpose**: The Society's Career Transition Fellowship addresses this need by fostering the development and productivity of young scientists who have potential to make significant contributions to MS research and help ensure the future and stability of MS research. The Career Transition Fellowship targets current postdoctoral trainees who demonstrate both commitment and exceptional potential to conduct MS-related research.

**Eligibility**: Applicants must hold a doctoral degree (M.D., PhD or equivalent) and must be in a research-oriented post-doctoral training program. Individuals with less than two or more than five years of postdoctoral research experience at the time of application are ineligible for this award.

**Type**: Fellowships

**Value**: US$550,000

**Length of Study**: 5 years

**Frequency**: Annual

**Application Procedure**: The application process for this award involves two levels of review, preliminary and full applications. To submit a proposal for research support, investigators must first register with our Apply Online site (nmss. fluxx.io) and complete a pre-application. Staff will review the pre-applications and selected applicants will be invited to submit a full proposal.

**Closing Date**: 21 August

**Additional Information**: www.nationalmssociety.org/For-Professionals/Researchers/Society-Funding/Training-Grants-and-Fellowships/Career-Transition-Fellowships

### For further information contact:

**Email**: Douglas.Landsman@nmss.org

## National Research Council (NRC)

500 Fifth Street NW, Washington, DC 20001, United States of America.

**Tel**: (1) 202 334 2644

The National Research Council (NRC) was organized by the National Academy of Sciences in 1916 to associate the broad community of science and technology with the Academy's purposes of further knowledge and advising the federal government.

## Christine Mirzayan Science & Technology Policy Graduate Fellowship Program

**Country of Study**: Any country

**Additional Information**: mirzayanfellow.nas.edu/

### For further information contact:

**Email**: policyfellows@nas.edu

## National Research Foundation (NRF)

PO Box 2600, Pretoria 0001, South Africa.

**Tel**: (27) 12 481 4209
**Email**: haveline@nrf.ac.za
**Website**: www.nrf.ac.za
**Contact**: Ms HA Michau, Manager, Student Support

The National Research Foundation (NRF) is responsible for funding South African research and other expertise in the fields of the social, natural and applied sciences, humanities, engineering and technology. The NRF is funded by the government, but also pursues joint ventures and collaboration with industry and the international community to increase the impact of its activities.

## Innovation Masters and Doctoral Scholarships

**Eligibility**: Scholarships are open to South African citizens, South African permanent residents as well as a limited percentage of non-South African citizens registered at a South African public university

**Level of Study**: Postgraduate

**Value**: Masters scholarships worth ZAR 80,000 per annum and doctoral scholarships worth ZAR 110,000 per annum

**Country of Study**: South Africa

**Application Procedure**: Please check website for more details

**Closing Date**: 7 August

**Contributor**: Funded by Department of Science and Technology (DST) and managed by the National Research Foundation (NRF)

**Additional Information**: www.nrf.ac.za/document/innovation-masters-and-doctoral-scholarships-call-2015

### For further information contact:

**Email**: futurestudents@bournemouth.ac.uk

## National Research Foundation Fellowships for Postdoctoral Research

**Purpose**: To foster postdoctoral research in the natural and applied sciences, engineering, social sciences and the humanities

**Eligibility**: Open to any nationals who have received their PhD within the last 5 years

**Level of Study**: Postdoctorate

**Type**: Fellowship
**Value**: Up to ZAR 60,000 plus a contribution of ZAR 10,000 towards the running cost of the project
**Length of Study**: Up to 2 years
**Frequency**: Twice a year
**Study Establishment**: Any university, technikon or research institute for full-time research
**Country of Study**: South Africa
**Application Procedure**: Applicants must complete and submit an application form, full academic record and the names of referees. Forms are available from the bursary offices of universities and technikons or can be downloaded from the website
**No. of awards offered**: 150
**Closing Date**: 31 July
**Funding**: Government
**No. of awards given last year**: 50
**No. of applicants last year**: 150

### For further information contact:

**Email**:    fellowships@twas.org

## National Research Foundation Free-standing Masters and Doctoral Scholarships

**Eligibility**: Scholarships are open to South African citizens, South African permanent residents as well as a limited percentage of non-South African citizens registered at a South African public university. All applicants for full-time Masters or Doctoral studies in South Africa must be registered or intending to register at a South African public university. Applicants that already hold a degree at the level for which they are applying for funding are not eligible
**Level of Study**: Doctorate
**Value**: Masters scholarships worth ZAR 50,000 per year and doctoral scholarships worth ZAR 70,000 per year
**Frequency**: Annual
**Country of Study**: South Africa
**Application Procedure**: Applications must be submitted through an online application process to the NRF
**Closing Date**: 7 August
**Funding**: International office
**Additional Information**: www.opportunitiesforafricans.com/nrf-masters-and-doctoral-scholarships-2018-2019-for-young-south-africans/

### For further information contact:

**Email**:    CGSMSFSS-SEEMSBESC@cihr-irsc.gc.ca

## National Research Foundation Targeted Research Awards Competitive Industry Programme

**Purpose**: To support research in priority areas where expertise is lacking
**Eligibility**: Open to South African citizens only, who qualify for postgraduate support. Postdoctoral support is available for any nationality
**Level of Study**: Doctorate, Postdoctorate, Postgraduate
**Type**: Research grant
**Value**: From a total of approximately rand 20 million per year
**Frequency**: Annual
**Study Establishment**: Any tertiary educational institution in South Africa
**Country of Study**: Other
**Application Procedure**: Applicants must complete an electronic application form. For further information please contact Ms Jill Sawers
**No. of awards offered**: 200
**Closing Date**: 31 July
**Funding**: Government
**No. of awards given last year**: 181
**No. of applicants last year**: 200
**Additional Information**: Joint ventures and collaboration with industry are strongly encouraged

### For further information contact:

**Tel**:    (27) 12 481 4104
**Email**:    jill@frd.ac.za

## National Research Foundation Visiting Fellowships

**Purpose**: To strengthen areas of expertise needed in South Africa
**Eligibility**: Open to senior scientists of any nationality
**Level of Study**: Postdoctorate
**Type**: Fellowship
**Value**: To cover air fares and accommodation
**Length of Study**: Up to 3 months
**Frequency**: Annual, if funds are available
**Study Establishment**: Any South African university, technikon, museum or scientific society
**Country of Study**: South Africa
**Application Procedure**: Applications should be submitted by a South African counterpart attached to a South African university, technikon, museum or scientific society

**For further information contact:**

Meiring Naude Rd, Gauteng, Pretoria 0184, South Africa.

Tel:      (27) 12 481 4122
Email:    ferdi@frd.ac.za

## Vrije University Amsterdam-NRF Desmond Tutu Doctoral Scholarships

Eligibility: Be in possession of a research Master's degree, or be in the process of completing requirements for such a degree. Should be South African citizens or permanent residents
Level of Study: Postgraduate
Type: Scholarship
Value: ZAR 240,000
Length of Study: The VUA-NRF Desmond Tutu Training Programme provides funding for up to four (4) years of study, depending on satisfactory progress each year
Country of Study: South Africa
Application Procedure: Check website for more details
Closing Date: 17 July
Contributor: Vrije Universiteit Amsterdam (VUA)
Additional Information: scholarship-positions.com/vu-university-amsterdam-nrf-desmond-tutu-doctoral-scholarships-for-south-african-citizens-2015/2015/06/13/

**For further information contact:**

Email:    danielle.nel@nrf.ac.za

---

## National Science Foundation (NSF)

4201 Wilson Boulevard, Arlington, VA 22230, United States of America.

Tel:      (1) 703 292 5111
Email:    info@nsf.gov
Website:  www.nsf.gov
Contact:  Division Director

The National Science Foundation (NSF) supports research in the areas of geology, geophysics, geochemistry, paleobiology and hydrology, including interdisciplinary or multi-disciplinary proposals that may involve one or more of these disciplines.

## Cultural Anthropology Program Senior Research Awards

Purpose: The primary objective of the Cultural Anthropology Program is to support fundamental, systematic anthropological research and training to increase understanding of the causes, consequences, and complexities of human social and cultural variability
Eligibility: The categories of proposers eligible to submit proposals to the National Science Foundation are identified in the NSF Proposal & Award Policies & Procedures Guide
Level of Study: Graduate
Type: Grant
Frequency: Annual
Country of Study: Any country
Closing Date: 15 August
Funding: Foundation
Additional Information: The Cultural Anthropology Program cannot support research that takes as its primary objective improved clinical practice, applied policy, or other immediate application www.nsf.gov/funding/pgm_summ.jsp?pims_id=505513

**For further information contact:**

Email:    jmantz@nsf.gov

## Directorate for Education and Human Resources Core Research

Purpose: The ECR program places emphasis on the rigorous development of theory and accumulation of knowledge to inform efforts to address challenges in STEM interest, learning, and participation, for all groups and all ages in formal and informal settings. This emphasis includes research on advancing evaluative methodologies to support research efforts funded through ECR
Level of Study: Graduate
Type: Research
Frequency: Annual
Country of Study: Any country
Closing Date: 24 January
Funding: Foundation
Additional Information: 1. Level 1 and Level 2 proposals have a maximum grant duration of three years. 2. Level 3 proposals have a maximum grant duration of five years. ECR Proposals may fall within three levels of funding. Level 1 Proposals: have a maximum award size of US$5,00,000. Synthesis proposals may only be budgeted at Level 1 or 2. Level 2 Proposals: have a maximum award size of US$1,500,000.

Synthesis proposals may only be budgeted at Level 1 or 2. Level 3 Proposals: have a maximum award size of US$2,500,000 www.nsf.gov/funding/pgm_summ.jsp?pims_id=504924

**For further information contact:**

**Email**: ECR@nsf.gov

## Enabling Discovery through GEnomic Tools (EDGE)

**Purpose**: The Enabling Discovery through GEnomic Tools (EDGE) track was previously a component of the Division of Integrative Organismal Systems (IOS) Core Programs solicitation (NSF 16-505). Submission of letters of intent or preliminary proposals is not required. Only full proposals should be submitted in response to this solicitation. There is no annual limit to the number of proposals submitted per PI or co-PI in response to this solicitation

**Eligibility**: Institutions of Higher Education (IHEs) - Two- and four-year IHEs (including community colleges) accredited in, and having a campus located in the United States, acting on behalf of their faculty members. Special Instructions for International Branch Campuses of United States IHEs: If the proposal includes funding to be provided to an international branch campus of a United States institution of higher education (including through use of subawards and consultant arrangements), the proposer must explain the benefit(s) to the project of performance at the international branch campus, and justify why the project activities cannot be performed at the United States campus. Non-profit, non--academic organizations: Independent museums, observatories, research labs, professional societies and similar organizations in the United States associated with educational or research activities

**Level of Study**: Graduate

**Type**: Award

**Frequency**: Annual

**Country of Study**: Any country

**Application Procedure**: Step 1: Download a Grant Application Package and Application Instructions link and enter the funding opportunity number, (the program solicitation number without the NSF prefix) and press the Download Package button

**Closing Date**: 7 February

**Funding**: Private

**Additional Information**: For this solicitation, EDGE proposals do not require submission of a letter of intent or preliminary proposals. Additional merit review considerations and special review criteria can be found in section VI of this solicitation www.nsf.gov/pubs/2020/nsf20532/nsf20532.htm

**For further information contact:**

2415, Eisenhower Avenue., Alexandria, VA 22314, United States of America.

**Email**: nsfpubs@nsf.gov

## Faculty Early Career Development Program (CAREER)

**Purpose**: Each year NSF selects nominees for the Presidential Early Career Awards for Scientists and Engineers (PECASE) from among the most meritorious recent CAREER awardees. These awards foster innovative developments in science and technology, increase awareness of careers in science and engineering, give recognition to the scientific missions of the participating agencies, enhance connections between fundamental research and national goals

**Level of Study**: Foundation programme

**Type**: Fellowships, operating grants

**Frequency**: Annual

**Country of Study**: Any country

**Closing Date**: 17 July

**Funding**: Foundation

**Additional Information**: www.nsf.gov/funding/pgm_summ.jsp?pims_id=503214

## Macrosystems Biology and NEON-Enabled Science (MSB-NES)

**Purpose**: The Macrosystems Biology and NEON-Enabled Science (MSB-NES): Research on Biological Systems at Regional to Continental Scales program will support quantitative, interdisciplinary, systems-oriented research on biosphere processes and their complex interactions with climate, land use, and invasive species at regional to continental scales as well as training activities to enable groups to conduct Macrosystems Biology and NEON-Enabled Science research

**Eligibility**: Proposals may only be submitted by the following: Institutions of Higher Education (IHEs) - Two- and four-year IHEs (including community colleges) accredited in, and having a campus located in the United States, acting on behalf of their faculty members. Special Instructions for International Branch Campuses of United States IHEs: If the proposal includes funding to be provided to an international branch campus of a United States institution of higher education (including through use of subawards and consultant arrangements), the proposer must explain the benefit(s) to the project of performance at the international branch campus, and justify why the project activities cannot be performed at the United States campus. Non-profit, non-academic organizations: Independent museums, observatories, research labs, professional societies and similar organizations in the United States associated with educational or research activities

**Level of Study**: Graduate

**Type**: Award

**Value**: US$900,000

**Frequency**: Annual

**Country of Study**: Any country

**Closing Date**: 25 February

**Funding**: Private

**Additional Information**: www.nsf.gov/bfa/dias/policy/merit_review/ www.nsf.gov/funding/pgm_summ.jsp?pims_id=503425

**For further information contact:**

**Email**:     mbinford@nsf.gov

## National Science Foundation Research Traineeship (NRT) Program

**Purpose**: The NSF Research Traineeship (NRT) program is designed to encourage the development and implementation of bold and potentially transformative models for science, engineering and mathematics (STEM) graduate education training. The NRT program seeks proposals that explore ways for graduate students in research-based master's and doctoral degree programs to develop the skills, knowledge, and competencies needed to pursue a range of STEM careers

**Level of Study**: Graduate

**Type**: Grant

**Frequency**: Annual

**Country of Study**: Any country

**Closing Date**: 6 February

**Funding**: Foundation

**Additional Information**:     www.nsf.gov/funding/pgm_summ.jsp?pims_id=505015

**For further information contact:**

**Email**:     lregassa@nsf.gov

## Robert Noyce Teacher Scholarship Program

**Purpose**: The program invites creative and innovative proposals that address the critical need for recruiting and preparing highly effective elementary and secondary science and mathematics teachers in high-need local educational agencies

**Level of Study**: Graduate, Foundation programme

**Type**: Scholarship

**Frequency**: Annual

**Country of Study**: Any country

**Closing Date**: 27 August

**Funding**: Private

**Additional Information**: Capacity Building proposals are accepted from proposers intending to develop a future Track 1, 2, or 3 proposal www.nsf.gov/funding/pgm_summ.jsp?pims_id=5733

**For further information contact:**

**Email**:     rturley@nsf.gov

## Scalable Parallelism in the Extreme (SPX)

**Purpose**: The Scalable Parallelism in the Extreme (SPX) program aims to support research addressing the challenges of increasing performance in this modern era of parallel computing. This will require a collaborative effort among researchers in multiple areas, from services and applications down to micro-architecture

**Eligibility**: Proposals may only be submitted by the following: 1. Institutions of Higher Education (IHEs) - Two- and four-year IHEs (including community colleges) accredited in, and having a campus located in the United States, acting on behalf of their faculty members. 2. Non-profit, non-academic organizations: Independent museums, observatories, research labs, professional societies and similar organizations in the United States associated with educational or research activities

**Level of Study**: Graduate

**Type**: Grants, work-study (not just grants)

**Frequency**: Annual

**Country of Study**: Any country

**Closing Date**: 17 January

**Funding**: Private

**Additional Information**: This limit on the number of proposals per PI, co-PI or Senior Personnel applies only to this SPX program solicitation www.nsf.gov/pubs/2019/nsf19505/nsf19505.htm

**For further information contact:**

**Email**:     abanerje@nsf.gov

## National Sea Grant College

1315 East-West Highway, Silver Spring, MD 20910, United States of America.

**Tel**:          (1) 301 734 1066

**Email**:      sgfellow@ucsd.edu

**Website**:   www.seagrant.noaa.gov

**Contact**:   Jim Eckman, Director

Sea Grant is a nationwide network administered through the National Oceanic and Atmospheric Administration (NOAA) of 30 university-based programmes that work with coastal communities. The organizations research and programmes promote better understanding, conservation and use of America's coastal resources. In short, Sea Grant is science serving America's coasts.

## Sea Grant/NOAA Fisheries Graduate Fellowship

**Purpose**: To financially support and encourage qualified applicants to pursue careers in either population dynamics and stock assessment or in marine resource economics and also to increase available expertise related to these fields
**Eligibility**: Applicants have to be PhD students in population dynamics or marine resource economics or related disciplines concentrating on the conservation and management of living marine resources
**Level of Study**: Doctorate
**Type**: Fellowship
**Value**: US$43,500 per year
**Length of Study**: 2 years
**Frequency**: Annual
**Closing Date**: 26 January
**Funding**: Government

### For further information contact:

**Email**:    terry.smith@noaa.gov

## National Sun Yat-Sen University (NSYSU)

70 Lien-hai Road, Kaohsiung 804, Taiwan.

**Tel**:          (886) 7 525 2633
**Website**:    www.oia.nsysu.edu.tw

National Sun Yat-Sen University (NSYSU) was founded in 1924 and is located alongside the Hsitzu Bay of Kaohsiung city. It is the leading international academic institution in Southern Taiwan with a vision to provide diverse and comprehensive higher education.

## National Sun Yat-sen University International Fellowship

**Purpose**: To pursue academic excellence combining theory and practice

**Eligibility**: Open to candidates who are pursuing their Master's or Doctoral degrees
**Level of Study**: Doctorate, Postgraduate
**Type**: Fellowships
**Value**: Varies
**Length of Study**: 2–3 months
**Frequency**: Annual
**Application Procedure**: Applications along with a curriculum vitae, research proposal, name of the corresponding member in the Kuroshio Research Group and 2 letters of recommendation must be mailed
**Additional Information**: "Recommendation to Kuroshio Application" must appear as the subject line

### For further information contact:

**Email**:    keryea@mail.nsysu.edu.tw

## National Tax Association

### Tax Institute of America Doctoral Dissertations in Government and Taxation

**Subjects**: Finance
**Purpose**: To award original, innovative, clear and analytical dissertations written by scholars and practitioners of government finance.
**Eligibility**: The award will be granted to exceptional dissertations written by scholars and practitioners of government finance.
**Type**: Award
**Value**: The winning entry will receive US$2,000 and the opportunity to publish a paper based on the dissertation in the National Tax Journal. There will also be two honorable mentions of US$1,000 each for outstanding entries.
**Country of Study**: Any country
**Closing Date**: 15 June
**Additional Information**: www.ntanet.org

## National Tour Association

### National Tour Association (NTA) Luray Caverns Graduate Research Scholarship

**Purpose**: To aid graduate students who are conducting tourism-related research
**Eligibility**: 1. Applicants can be permanent residents of any country but must be enrolled at an accredited United States or Canadian four-year postsecondary institution. 2. They must be entering or returning graduate students who are conducting

research that focuses on tourism. They must have a proven commitment to the tourism industry, and must have a GPA of 3.0 or higher on a four-point scale. Selection is based on the strength of the research project

**Level of Study** Graduate

**Type**: Scholarship

**Frequency**: Annual

**Country of Study**: Any country

**Application Procedure**: Applications are available online. An application form, proof of residency, a personal essay, a resume, a research proposal, an official transcript and one letter of recommendation are required. Check the sponsor website for further information. www.tourismcares.org/academic-scholarships/

**Closing Date**: 3 April

**Funding**: Private

**Additional Information**: www.chegg.com/scholarships/national-tour-associationluray-caverns-graduate-research-scholarship-2345

### For further information contact:

**Email**: info@tourismcares.org

## National Union of Teachers (NUT)

Hamilton House, Mabledon Place, London, WC1H 9BD, United Kingdom.

**Tel**: (44) 20 7388 6191
**Email**: a.bush@nut.org.uk
**Website**: www.teachers.org.uk
**Contact**: Ms Angela Bush

## National Union of Teachers Page Scholarship

**Purpose**: To promote the exchange of educational ideas between Britain and America

**Eligibility**: Open to teaching members of the NUT aged 25–60 years, although 25–55 is preferred

**Level of Study**: Graduate

**Type**: Scholarship

**Value**: Each up to £1,700 pro rata daily rate with complete hospitality in the United States of America provided by the English- Speaking Union of the United States of America

**Length of Study**: 2 weeks. The scholarship must be taken during the American academic year, which is September–May

**Frequency**: Annual

**Country of Study**: United States of America

**Application Procedure**: Applicants must complete an application form. An outline and synopsis of the project must accompany the form along with a curriculum vitae and scholastic and personal testimonials

**No. of awards offered**: 100

**Funding**: Private

**No. of awards given last year**: 2

**No. of applicants last year**: 100

**Additional Information**: It is a discontinued award type. The scholarship is limited to the individual teacher and neither the spouse nor partner can be included in the travel, accommodation or study arrangements. Recipients are required to report on their visit to teacher groups and educational meetings in the United States and on their return home

### For further information contact:

**Tel**: (44) 1 812 277 9670
**Fax**: (44) 20 7388 6191

## National University of Ireland Galway

Postgraduate Admission Office, University Road, Galway, Ireland.

**Tel**: (353) 91 524 411
**Email**: info@it.nuigalway.ie
**Website**: www.nuigalway.ie
**Contact**: Mairead Faherty

## Charles Parsons Energy Research Award

**Purpose**: To focus on investigation and optimization of electron transfer reactions in biological fuel cells that can generate energy from diverse substrates. To focus the research on applications of pure- and mixed-culture microbial fuel cells, and biocatalytic enzyme-based fuel cells

**Eligibility**: Open to engineering graduates

**Level of Study**: Doctorate

**Type**: Research award

**Value**: Salary scale €55,000–80,486 per year for researchers, stipend of €18,000 per year plus tuition fees for PhD studentship and undergraduate engineering students €1,500 per month

**Application Procedure**: Applicants should include a curriculum vitae and the names of two academic referees

**Closing Date**: October

**Additional Information**: The research will involve liaison with international collaborators, bench research and reporting. To this end, good inter-personal, written communication and networking skills are advantageous

### For further information contact:

**Email**: donal.leech@nuigalway.ie

## Hardiman PhD Scholarships

**Eligibility**: 1. Successful applicants will be expected to have a first or upper second class honours primary degree or equivalent. 2. Applications will not be accepted from persons currently registered as PhD students. 3. English Language Requirements - please go to this webpage www.nuigalway.ie/international-students/entry-requirements/

**Level of Study**: Postgraduate

**Type**: Scholarship

**Value**: €16,000 p.a. plus fees

**Length of Study**: 4 years

**Application Procedure**: Applicants must read Applicant's Guide: (www.nuigalway.ie/media/hardiman/files/Applicants-Guide-2020.docx) prior to completing the application form

**Closing Date**: 14 February

**Additional Information**: www.nuigalway.ie/hardiman-scholarships/

### For further information contact:

**Email**:  hrscholar@nuigalway.ie

## PhD Student Scholarship in Atmospheric Science

**Purpose**: To study the effect of ambient relative humidity on aerosol radiative parameters: aerosol light scattering coefficient and aerosol absorption coefficient

**Eligibility**: Open to candidates who have obtained a good Honours Degree (grade 2.1 at least) in physics or in a cognate subject

**Level of Study**: Doctorate

**Type**: Scholarship

**Value**: stipend and tuition fees

**Length of Study**: 3 years

**Country of Study**: Ireland

**Application Procedure**: Applicants must submit a covering letter, curriculum vitae and the names of at least two referees

### For further information contact:

**Tel**:  (353) 91 492 704
**Fax**:  (353) 91 495 515
**Email**:  gerard.jennings@nuigalway.ie

## Student Research Scholarship in Occupational Hygiene

**Purpose**: To enhance GSK's exposure assessment strategy, to look at current occupational hygiene data collected from across all GSK sites and to apply Bayesian statistics to optimize the exposure assessment strategy

**Eligibility**: Open to candidates who have obtained an Honours Degree (2.1 minimum) in a science or engineering discipline. Ideally, the candidate should have a sound understanding of mathematics/statistics, combined with an understanding of exposure assessment

**Level of Study**: Postgraduate

**Type**: Scholarship

**Value**: Monthly stipend

**Country of Study**: Ireland

**Application Procedure**: Applicants must submit a covering letter, a curriculum vitae and the names of at least two referees

**Closing Date**: 31 August

**Contributor**: GlaxoSmithKline (GSK)

### For further information contact:

Department of Experimental Physics, National University of Ireland, University Road, Galway, Ireland.

**Email**:  marie.coggins@nuigalway.ie

## Taught Postgraduate Scholarships

**Purpose**: NUI Galway has established a Postgraduate Scholarship Scheme to support and facilitate students wishing to register for a Fulltime Taught Postgraduate Masters programme

**Eligibility**: In order to be eligible for the award of a scholarship, students must: 1. Have submitted a valid online scholarship application form by the deadline; 2. Be registered in Year 1 of a Fulltime Taught Masters programme for the academic year subsequent to the scholarship application (repeat students are not eligible to apply); 3. Have attained a first class honours (or equivalent) in a Level 8 primary degree.

**Level of Study**: Postgraduate

**Type**: Scholarship

**Value**: The total value of the Scholarship will be €1,500 per student

**Application Procedure**: Applications must be made using the online application form

**Closing Date**: 14 August

**Additional Information**: www.nuigalway.ie/media/registry/admissions/files/Scholarship_criteria.pdf

## National University of Ireland, Maynooth

Research Support Office, Auxilia House, North Campus, NUI, Maynooth, Co. Kildare, Ireland.

**Tel**:  (353) 17 086 000
**Email**:  research.support@nuim.ie
**Website**:  www.nuim.ie

Following two centuries of internationally renowned scholarly activity on the Maynooth campus, the National University of Ireland, Maynooth was established under the 1997 Universities Act as an autonomous member of the federal structure known as the National University of Ireland. With approximately 8,400 registered students, NUI, Maynooth has 26 academic departments which are organized into three Faculties: Arts, Celtic Studies and Philosophy; Science and Engineering; and Social Sciences. Building on a tradition of scholarship and excellence in all aspects of its teaching, learning, and research activities within the liberal arts and sciences tradition NUI, Maynooth is committed to being a first-class research-led centre of learning and academic discovery.

## John and Pat Hume Research Scholarships

**Purpose**: To build on excellence in areas across the arts, humanities, social sciences, sciences and engineering
**Eligibility**: Applicants must have a First or Upper Second-Class Honours Primary Degree (or equivalent) from Ireland, the European Union or from any overseas university and intend to pursue a PhD degree at the University. Those who have commenced a research degree at NUI Maynooth prior to application will not be eligible
**Level of Study**: Postgraduate, Research
**Type**: Scholarship
**Value**: €5,000 per year plus payment of fees at European Union level. In some cases an additional fund of €3,000 is also provided to the student researcher for activities undertaken in support of the Department including tutorials and laboratory demonstration
**Length of Study**: Up to 4 years
**Frequency**: Annual
**Study Establishment**: NUI Maynooth
**Country of Study**: Ireland
**Application Procedure**: Applicants must first make contact with a NUI Maynooth department or centre to discuss their suitability for a PhD programme. A list of departmental contacts is available on the website. Application for the scholarship can then be filed
**Closing Date**: May
**No. of awards given last year**: 30
**Additional Information**: Supplement the scholarship with an additional €3,000 for tutorial or demonstrating duties www.maynoothuniversity.ie/study-maynooth/postgraduate-studies/fees-funding-scholarships/john-and-pat-hume-doctoral-awards

### For further information contact:

**Tel**:      (353) 1 708 6018
**Fax**:      (353) 1 708 3359
**Email**:   pgdean@nuim.ie

## Maynooth University Teaching Studentships

**Purpose**: Funded student teaching assistant opportunities are offered across a range of disciplines at Maynooth University. Successful applicants will commence PhD Doctoral studies at Maynooth University in the Autumn semester and will have 5 years to complete their PhD
**Level of Study**: Postgraduate, PhD research
**Type**: Scholarship
**Value**: 1. Full annual tuition fees support (approximately €6,200 per annum); 2. A fixed stipend of €9,007 per annum
**Length of Study**: 5 years
**Additional Information**: www.maynoothuniversity.ie/study-maynooth/postgraduate-studies/fees-funding-scholarships/maynooth-university-teaching-studentship

## Taught Master's Scholarships

**Eligibility**: 1. 60 Taught Master's scholarships of €2000 each will be awarded to student across all disciplines in recognition of academic excellence. 2. All applicants must have achieved a minimum 2.1 honours undergraduate degree. 3. Open to both EU and Non-EU applicants. 4. Graduates or current students of PhD or Master's programmes are not eligible to apply. Prospective students interested in research programmes should apply instead for the Maynooth University John and Pat Hume Doctoral Research Awards.
**Level of Study**: Postgraduate, PhD research
**Type**: Scholarship
**Value**: US$2,000
**Application Procedure**: Apply online via www.maynoothuniversity.ie/study-maynooth/postgraduatestudies/fees-funding-scholarships
**Closing Date**: 15 June
**Additional Information**: www.maynoothuniversity.ie/study-maynooth/postgraduate-studies/fees-funding-scholarships/taught-masters-scholarships

### For further information contact:

**Tel**:      (353) 1708 3990
**Email**:   tmscholarships@mu.ie

## National University of Singapore (NUS)

21 Lower Kent Ridge Road, 119077 Singapore.

**Tel**:      (65) 6516 6666
**Email**:   gradenquiry@nus.edu.sg
**Website**: www.nus.edu.sg

NUS aspires to be a dynamic connected knowledge community imbued with a no walls culture that promotes the free flow of talent and ideas. Individual members of our community enjoy access to diverse opportunities for intellectual and professional growth and in twin add value to NUS becoming a global knowledge enterprise.

## Asian Development Bank-Japan Scholarship Program

**Purpose**: To find further study in public policy implementation

**Eligibility**: Open to residents of Asian Development Bank member countries currently enroled at NUS. Upon completion of their study programmes, scholars are expected to contribute to the economic and social development of their home countries. Check website for further details

**Level of Study**: Postgraduate

**Type**: Scholarship

**Value**: S$250 per semester (one-time book allowance), tuition, health insurance, examination and other approved fees. Cost of travel from home country to Singapore on award of the scholarship and from Singapore to home country on graduation

**Length of Study**: 2 years for Master in public policy

**Frequency**: Annual

**Study Establishment**: Lee Kuan Yew School of Public Policy, National University of Singapore

**Country of Study**: Singapore

**Application Procedure**: Application form with 3 photographs attached, certificate of citizenship (or a copy of your valid passport), research and/or work experience, two confidential letters of recommendation

**No. of awards offered**: 350

**Closing Date**: 12 July

**Funding**: Government

**Contributor**: Government

**No. of awards given last year**: 3

**No. of applicants last year**: 350

**Additional Information**: www.ait.ac.th/admissions/scholarships/asian-development-bank-japan-scholarship-program/

## Law/Faculty Graduate Scholarship (FGS)

**Purpose**: To reward an outstanding student of the faculty of Law

**Eligibility**: Outstanding applicants of any nationality (including Singapore citizens and permanent residents) may be awarded the FGS to pursue the LLM coursework degrees: LLM, LLM (Asian Legal Studies), LLM (Corporate & Financial Services Law), LLM (Intellectual Property & Technology Law), LLM (International & Comparative Law), LLM (Maritime Law)

**Level of Study**: Postgraduate

**Type**: Scholarship

**Value**: The scholarship will cover tuition fees

**Frequency**: Annual

**Study Establishment**: National University of Singapore

**Country of Study**: Singapore

**Additional Information**: Terms of award are subject to change without prior notice

## Lee Kuan Yew School of Public Policy Graduate Scholarships (LKYSPPS)

**Purpose**: To find further study in public policy and administration implementation

**Eligibility**: Open to all nationalities (except Singapore)

**Level of Study**: Postgraduate

**Type**: Scholarship

**Value**: A monthly stipend, a one-time book allowance, a one-time settling-in allowance, shared housing, tuition, health insurance, examination and other approved fees, cost of travel from home country to Singapore on award of the scholarship and from Singapore to home country on graduation

**Length of Study**: 1 year (for public administration) and 2 years (for public policy)

**Frequency**: Annual

**Study Establishment**: Lee Kuan Yew School of Public Policy, National University of Singapore

**Country of Study**: Singapore

**Application Procedure**: Apply online

**Funding**: Government

**Contributor**: Government

### For further information contact:

**Email**:     LKYSPPmpp@nus.edu.sg

## Master of Business Administration Programme

**Application Procedure**: Applicants must complete an application form supplying US$15 fee

**Closing Date**: 1 April

### For further information contact:

Graduate School of Business, MBA Programme, FBA2, Level 5, Room 6, 17 Law Link, 117592 Singapore.

**Tel**:      (65) 6874 6149
**Fax**:      (65) 6778 2681
**Email**:    fbagrad@nus.edu.sg

## National University of Singapore Design Technology Institute Scholarship

**Eligibility**: Open to all nationalities with good Bachelor's degree with Honours in Engineering or Science
**Level of Study**: Postgraduate
**Type**: Scholarship
**Value**: A monthly stipend S$1,500 with a possible monthly top-up of S$500 and all approved NUS fees
**Length of Study**: 2 years
**Frequency**: Annual
**Study Establishment**: National University of Singapore
**Country of Study**: Singapore
**Closing Date**: November
**Additional Information**: DTI Scholars who are international students will be required to serve a 2 years bond in Singapore upon graduation

### For further information contact:

**Tel**:       (65) 6374 1227
**Fax**:       (65) 6373 2175
**Email**:   dtibox@nus.edu.sg

## Singapore-MIT Alliance Graduate Fellowship

**Purpose**: The SMA Graduate Fellowship is established by the Singapore Ministry of Education in January 2009 to attract the best and most talented PhD students from Singapore, the region and beyond, and educate them to be future leaders in the areas of science and technology. The selection of candidates will take place twice a year, in time for the start of the semesters in August and January
**Eligibility**: The Scholarships are open to students of all nationalities who gain admission to any PhD programme at the University whose research interest fits within one or more of the projects currently being carried out in one of the SMART Interdisciplinary Research Groups (IRGs)
**Level of Study**: Graduate, Postgraduate
**Type**: Fellowship
**Value**: A monthly stipend of Singaporean S$3,200; Tuition fees at NUS; and Scholarship allowance of up to S$12,000 to help cover the expenses associated with a 6-month research residency at MIT
**Length of Study**: The award is tenable for 1 year in the first instance; but subject to the scholar's satisfactory progress, it may be renewed each semester. The maximum period of award is 4 years
**Frequency**: Annual
**Study Establishment**: National University of Singapore and Nanyang Technological University
**Country of Study**: Singapore

**Application Procedure**: Applicants must apply separately to both MIT and NUS/NTU for the dual degrees and only to NUS or NTU for direct PhD degree; applicants must also apply directly to SMA for an SMA Graduate Fellowship
**No. of awards offered**: 120
**Closing Date**: March
**Funding**: Government
**Contributor**: A*Star, Economic and Development Board (EDB), Ministry of Education (MOE), National University of Singapore (NUS) and Nanyang Technological University (NTU)
**No. of applicants last year**: 120
**Additional Information**: smart.mit.edu/fellowships/for-graduates-smart-graduates

### For further information contact:

**Tel**:       (65) 6516 4787
**Fax**:       (65) 6775 2920
**Email**:   smart@nus.edu.sg

## Natural Environment Research Council (NERC)

Polaris House, North Star Avenue, Wiltshire, Swindon, SN2 1EU, United Kingdom.

**Tel**:           (44) 17 9344 2644
**Email**:       stag@nerc.ac.uk
**Website**:   www.nerc.ac.uk/funding
**Contact**:   Studentships & Training Awards Group (STAG)

The Natural Environment Research Council (NERC) is one of the seven United Kingdom Research Councils that fund and manage research in the United Kingdom. NERC is the leading body in the United Kingdom for research, survey, monitoring and training in the environmental sciences. NERC supports research and training in universities and in its own centres, surveys and units.

## Natural Environment Research Council Independent Research Fellowships (IRF)

**Purpose**: To develop scientific leadership among the most promising early-career environmental scientists, by giving all Fellows 5 year's support, which will allow them sufficient time to develop their research programmes, and to establish international recognition
**Eligibility**: Open to any nationality, and may be held in any area of the NERC remit, but the fellowship must be based at

an eligible United Kingdom Research Organization. Applicants may not have a permanent academic position in a university or equivalent organization. Applicants must expect to submit their PhD thesis before the fellowship interview would take place (April following the closing date) and, if successful, would not be able to take up the fellowship until the intent to award the PhD has been confirmed by the awarding university. Applicants may have up to a maximum of 8 years of full-time postdoctoral research experience between the PhD certificate date and the closing date of the fellowship competition to which they are applying. The eight year window is based on full-time working. Where applicants have worked part-time or had research career breaks, the eight year window would be extended accordingly

**Level of Study**: Research
**Type**: Fellowship
**Value**: Includes 80% of the full economic cost (FEC) of the proposal. NERC will provide funding for the fellow
**Length of Study**: 5 years
**Frequency**: Annual
**Study Establishment**: Universities and other approved research institutes
**Country of Study**: United Kingdom
**Application Procedure**: Please refer to the Research Grants and Fellowships Handbook at www.nerc.ac.uk/funding/available/fellowships/apply/
**Closing Date**: October
**Funding**: Government
**No. of awards given last year**: 14
**Additional Information**: microsites.ncl.ac.uk/nubsstaffblog/2019/06/25/nerc-independent-research-fellowships/

### For further information contact:

**Email**:    Fellowships@nerc.ac.uk

## Natural Environment Research Council Research Grants

**Purpose**: To support a specific investigation in which the applicant will be engaged personally, to enter promising new or modified fields of research, or to take advantage of developments in apparatus offering improved techniques in promising lines of research already established
**Eligibility**: Open to research workers ordinarily resident in the United Kingdom who are also members of the academic staff of universities, colleges and similar institutions within the United Kingdom recognised by the NERC. Research assistants and technicians are not eligible to apply. Holders of Research Council Fellowships at an Institute of Higher Education are eligible to apply for research grants
**Level of Study**: Postdoctorate, Professional development

**Type**: Grant
**Value**: The Standard Research Grant offers amounts over £30,000, for periods not usually in excess of three years. The Small Research Grant offers a more rapid response for applications costing £2,000-30,000. Applications for less than £2,000 will not be accepted. The new investigator scheme offers up to the £50,000
**Frequency**: Throughout the year
**Study Establishment**: Any approved Institute of Higher Education in the United Kingdom
**Country of Study**: United Kingdom
**Application Procedure**: Applicants must complete an application form, available on request. Application forms and further information can be found on the NERC website
**Closing Date**: 1 October
**Funding**: Government
**No. of awards given last year**: 307

### For further information contact:

**Email**:    researchcareers@nerc.ac.uk

## Natural Hazards Center-University of Colorado

482 UCB, Boulder, CO 80309-0482, United States of America.

**Tel**:           (1) 303 492 6818
**Email**:      hazctr@colorado.edu
**Website**:  www.colorado.edu/hazards

The mission of the Natural Hazards Center at the University of Colorado at Boulder is to advance and communicate knowledge on hazards mitigation and disaster preparedness, response and recovery. Using an all hazards and interdisciplinary framework, the Center fosters information- sharing and integration of activities among researchers, practitioners and policy makers from around the world, supports and conducts research and provides educational opportunities for the next generation of hazards scholars and professionals.

## Dissertation Fellowship in Hazards, Risks, and Disaster

**Purpose**: To provide financial support for research that is crucial to advancing the knowledge in the hazards field, as well as ensure that the next generation of interdisciplinary hazards professional has a source of financial and academic support to foster sound development

**Eligibility**: Open to candidates who already have a dissertation at an institution in the United States. Non-United States citizens may apply as long as the Doctorate degree will be granted by a United States institution

**Level of Study**: Postgraduate

**Type**: Fellowships

**Value**: US$10,000

**Frequency**: Annual

**Country of Study**: United States of America

**Application Procedure**: The applicant must submit a curriculum vitae along with a dissertation summary

**Closing Date**: September

**Additional Information**: freestudiesabroad.blogspot.com/2006/06/dissertation-fellowship-in-hazards.html

**For further information contact:**

**Email**:   periship@riskinstitute.org

## Natural Sciences and Engineering Research Council of Canada (NSERC)

350 Albert Street, 16th floor, Ottawa, ON K1A 1H5, Canada.

**Tel**:        (1) 613 995 4273

**Email**:    claire.mcaneney@nserc-crsng.gc.ca

**Website**:  www.nserc.ca

**Contact**:  Corporate Account Executive

NSERC is Canada's instrument for promoting and supporting university research in the natural sciences and engineering, other than the health sciences. NSERC supports both basic university research through discovery grants and project, research through partnerships among universities, governments, and the private sector as well as the advanced training of highly qualified people.

## Aboriginal Ambassadors in the Natural Sciences and Engineering Award

**Purpose**: The Aboriginal Ambassadors in the Natural Sciences and Engineering (AANSE) award aims to engage Aboriginal students and fellows in promoting interest and participation in the natural sciences and engineering by visiting Canada's Aboriginal communities and schools and sharing their research and education experiences or participating in science promotion events and activities

**Eligibility**: Open to Canadian citizen or permanent resident of Canada

**Level of Study**: Postgraduate

**Type**: Award

**Value**: Up to C$5,000

**Country of Study**: Canada

**Application Procedure**: Applications must be submitted electronically using the Secure Submissions for NSERC's Innovative Collaborations and Science Promotion Programs (competitions.nserc-crsng.gc.ca/500001/default.aspx)

**Additional Information**: NSERC will notify you of the decision on your application within one month of receiving it. For more details, please mail to ambassadors@nserc-crsng.gc.ca www.nserc-crsng.gc.ca/Students-Etudiants/Aboriginal-Autochtones_eng.asp

**For further information contact:**

**Email**:   ambassadors@nserc-crsng.gc.ca

## Canada Graduate Scholarships – Michael Smith Foreign Study Supplements Program

**Purpose**: The Canada Graduate Scholarships – Michael Smith Foreign Study Supplements (CGS-MSFSS) Program supports high calibre Canadian graduate students in building global linkages and international networks through the pursuit of exceptional research experiences at research institutions abroad

**Eligibility**: Open to Canadian citizen or permanent resident of Canada

**Level of Study**: Postgraduate

**Type**: Award

**Value**: Up to C$6,000 for a period of research study abroad

**Length of Study**: 6 months

**Country of Study**: Canada

**Application Procedure**: Online application procedure. For details, contact schol@nserc-crsng.gc.ca

**Closing Date**: 10 October

**Additional Information**: For more information, contact CGSMSFSS@cihr-irsc.gc.ca www.nserc-crsng.gc.ca/Students-Etudiants/PG-CS/CGSForeignStudy-BESCEtudeEtranger_eng.asp

**For further information contact:**

**Email**:   cgsma@cihr-irsc.gc.ca

## Canada Graduate Scholarships-Master's (CGS M) Program

**Purpose**: The objective of the Canada Graduate Scholarships-Master's (CGS M) Program is to help develop research skills and assist in the training of highly qualified personnel by supporting students who demonstrate a high standard of achievement in undergraduate and early graduate studies

**Eligibility**: Open to Canadian citizen or permanent resident of Canada

**Level of Study**: Postgraduate

**Type**: Award

**Value**: C$17,500

**Length of Study**: 1 year

**Country of Study**: Canada

**Application Procedure**: Application/Canadian common CV

**Closing Date**: 1 December

**Additional Information**: Refer to the Tri-Agency Harmonization of the Canada Graduate Scholarships page www.nserc-crsng.gc.ca/Students-Etudiants/CGSHarmonization-HarmonizationBESC_eng.asp www.nserc-crsng.gc.ca/Students-Etudiants/PG-CS/CGSM-BESCM_eng.asp

### For further information contact:

**Email**:    Schol@nserc-crsng.gc.ca

## Canada Postgraduate Scholarships (PGS)

**Eligibility**: Open to a Canadian citizen or a permanent citizen of Canada, with a university degree in science or engineering, intending to pursue year full-time graduate study and research at the Master's or Doctorate level in one of the areas supported by NSERC with a first-class average in each of the last two completed years of study

**Level of Study**: Postgraduate

**Type**: Fellowship

**Value**: C$17,300 (Masters) per year for 1 year and C$21,000 (Doctoral) per year for a period of 2–3 years

**Length of Study**: 1 year

**Frequency**: Annual

**Country of Study**: Canada

**Application Procedure**: Check website for further details

**Closing Date**: 15 October

**Contributor**: Natural Sciences and Engineering Research Council of Canada (NSERC)

### For further information contact:

National Sciences and Engineering Research Council of Canada (NSERC), Scholarships and Fellowships Division, 350 Albert Street (for courier mailings, add 10th Floor), Ottawa, ON K1A 1H5, Canada.

**Fax**:     (1) 613 996 2589
**Email**:    schol@nserc.ca

## Defence Research and Development Canada Postgraduate Scholarship Supplements

**Purpose**: To encourage and support graduates to carry out research of interest to DRDC; to increase contact between DRDC researchers and those at Canadian universities; and to foster graduate training potential candidates for possible employment at DRDC

**Eligibility**: Open to candidates possessing a CGS, PGS or IPS award

**Level of Study**: Postgraduate

**Type**: Scholarship

**Value**: C$5,000 per year

**Length of Study**: 2 years

**Frequency**: Annual

**Country of Study**: Canada

**Application Procedure**: Applicants must submit a copy Notification of Award document from NSERC, a copy of successful scholarship application (Form 200), and a statement of interest in R&D for defence/national security. Check website for further details

**Closing Date**: 1 June

**Contributor**: Defence Research and Development Canada

### For further information contact:

DRDC Postgraduate Scholarship Supplements Program, Department of National Defence, 305 Rideau Street, Ottawa, ON K1N 5Y6, Canada.

**Tel**:     (1) 613 992 0563
**Fax**:     (1) 613 996 7063
**Email**:    hr-rh@drdc-rddc.gc.ca

## NSERC Postgraduate Scholarships-Doctoral program

**Purpose**: The NSERC Postgraduate Scholarships - Doctoral (PGS D) program provides financial support to high-calibre scholars who are engaged in an eligible doctoral program (see Eligibility Criteria for Students and Fellows) in the natural sciences or engineering. This support allows these scholars to fully concentrate on their studies and seek out the best research mentors in their chosen fields.

**Eligibility**: 1. be a Canadian citizen or a permanent resident of Canada, as of the application deadline date; 2. have completed no more than 24 months of full-time study in their doctoral program by December 31 of the year of application (no more than 36 months if transferred directly from Bachelors to a PhD or enrolled in a joint program, e.g., MD/PhD, MA/PhD); 3. submit only one doctoral award application in a given academic year. Nominations to the Vanier CGS program do not count towards this limit; 4. not have already received a doctoral-level scholarship or fellowship from CIHR, NSERC or SSHRC.

**Level of Study**: Postgraduate

**Type**: Scholarship

**Value**: C$21,000 per year

**Length of Study**: 3 years

**Country of Study**: Canada

**Application Procedure**: Refer to the CGS D program description for information on applying to the PGS D program: www.nserc-crsng.gc.ca/Students-Etudiants/PG-CS/CGSD-BESCD_eng.asp

**Closing Date**: 17 October

**Additional Information**: www.nserc-crsng.gc.ca/Students-Etudiants/PG-CS/BellandPostgrad-BelletSuperieures_eng.asp

### For further information contact:

**Email**:    ambassadors@nserc-crsng.gc.ca

---

## Netherlands Organization for Scientific Research (NWO)

Lann van Nieuw Oost Indie 300, PO Box 93138, NL-2509 The Hague AC, Netherlands.

**Tel**:         (31) 70 344 0640
**Email**:    nwo@nwo.nl
**Website**:  www.nwo.nl
**Contact**:  F.A.O. Grants Department

The Netherlands Organization for Scientific Research (NWO) is the central Dutch organization in the field of fundamental and strategic scientific research. NWO encompasses all fields of scholarship and consequently plays a key role in the development of science, technology and culture in the Netherlands. NWO is an independent organization that acts as the national research council in the Netherlands. NWO is the largest national sponsor of fundamental scientific research undertaken in the 13 Dutch universities and provides many types of funding for research driven by intellectual curiosity.

## Rubicon Programme

**Purpose**: To encourage talented researchers at Dutch Universities to dedicate themselves to a career in postdoctoral research

**Eligibility**: Open to researchers from all scientific disciplines engaged in PhD research or obtaining a PhD in the last 12 months

**Level of Study**: Postdoctorate

**Type**: Grant

**Value**: €5,300,000 a year

**Length of Study**: Up to 2 years

**Application Procedure**: A completed application form to be submitted via NOW's electronic submission system Iris

**Closing Date**: 28 November

**Contributor**: The Netherlands Ministry of Education, Culture and Science

**Additional Information**: Total amount for each (current year) Rubicon round is €2,900,000

### For further information contact:

**Tel**:       (31) 7034 405 65
**Email**:   rubicon@nwo.nl

## WOTRO DC Fellowships

**Purpose**: To support high-quality PhD and postdoctorate research projects

**Eligibility**: Open to project researchers with the appropriate degrees

**Level of Study**: Doctorate

**Value**: A contribution to personal living costs and research costs

**Length of Study**: 4 years for PhD research and 2 years for postdoctorate research

**Frequency**: Annual

**Application Procedure**: Applications must be formally submitted by a senior researcher employed at a Dutch research institution, together with a senior researcher from the home country as a co-applicant and as part of the supervising them

**Contributor**: WOTRO

### For further information contact:

**Tel**:       (31) 70 344 0945
**Email**:   dijk@nwo.nl

---

## New England Culinary Institute (NECI)

Admissions Office, 56 College Street, Montpelier, VT 05602, United States of America.

**Tel**:       (1) 877 223 324
**Website**:  www.neci.edu

New England Culinary Institute (NECI) is one of the leading culinary schools in the United States of America. It is located in Vermont, the Green Mountain State. Mr. Fran Voigt and Mr. John Dranow founded NECI in 1980.

## Cabot Scholarships

**Purpose**: To encourage and support students who are committed to furthering their education and enhancing their careers in the restaurant and food service industry
**Eligibility**: Open to candidates who are current resident of Vermont, New York, Maine, New Hampshire, Connecticut, Rhode Island or Massachusetts
**Level of Study**: Professional development
**Type**: Scholarship
**Value**: US$2,000
**Length of Study**: 1 year
**Frequency**: Annual
**Study Establishment**: New England Culinary Institute
**Country of Study**: United States of America
**Application Procedure**: Applicant must submit a complete application form to New England Culinary Institute

### For further information contact:

**Email**:    lindac@neci.edu

## New South Wales Architects Registration Board

NSW Architects Registration Board, Level 2, 156 Gloucester Street, Sydney, NSW 2000, Australia.

**Tel**:          (61) 2 9241 4033
**Email**:      mail@architects.nsw.gov.au
**Website**:   www.architects.nsw.gov.au
**Contact**:   Ms Mae Cruz, Deputy Registrar

## Client Service Excellence Award

**Purpose**: To encourage excellence in the professional services offered by architects
**Eligibility**: Open to all architects registered in New South Wales (NSW) who have completed projects in the last 2 years in NSW not exceeding AU$4 million
**Level of Study**: Unrestricted
**Type**: Award
**Value**: AU$5,000

**Frequency**: Annual
**Country of Study**: Any country
**Application Procedure**: For further information about the Client Service Excellence Award contact the Registrar of the NSW Architects Registration Board on (61) 2 9241 4033. Check website for further details
**Closing Date**: 28 September
**Contributor**: Victorian Architects Registration Board
**Additional Information**: Architect, architect corporations, and firms should have two nominations from clients

### For further information contact:

**Email**:    awards@rcsa.com.au

## New South Wales Ministry of the Arts

Level 9 St James Centre, 111 Elizabeth Street, PO Box A226, Sydney, NSW 1235, Australia.

**Tel**:          1800 358 594, (61) 2 8218 2222
**Email**:      mail@arts.nsw.gov.au
**Website**:   www.arts.nsw.gov.au

New South Wales Ministry of the Arts works closely with the State's 8 major cultural institutions, providing policy advice to Government on their operations.

## Western Sydney Artists Fellowship

**Purpose**: To encourage artists and students in the field of creative arts
**Eligibility**: Open to applicants who are residents of Western Sydney or whose practice is located primarily in Western Sydney
**Level of Study**: Postgraduate
**Type**: Fellowship
**Value**: AU$5,000–25,000
**Length of Study**: 1 year
**Frequency**: Annual
**Study Establishment**: New South Wales, Sydney Western Suburbs
**Country of Study**: Australia
**Closing Date**: September

### For further information contact:

**Email**:    mail@create.nsw.gov.au

# New York Foundation for the Arts (NYFA)

20 Jay Street, 7th floor, Brooklyn, NY 11201, United States of America.

**Tel**:        (1) 212 366 6900
**Email**:     fellowships@nyfa.org
**Website**:   www.nyfa.org

New York Foundation for the Arts (NYFA), founded in 1971, helps artists turn inspiration into art by giving more money and support to individual artists and arts organizations than any other comparable institution in the United States.

## Canadian Women Artists' Award

**Purpose**: The Canadian Women Artist's Award is open to emerging or early career artists in New York, New Jersey, and Connecticut. The C$5,000 award is designed to provide financial support to an emerging or early career artist working in any discipline, and can be used in any manner the recipient deems necessary to further their artistic goals. It is supported by funding granted to NYFA by the Canadian Women's Club (CWC) of New York as a way to continue its philanthropic work when it disbanded
**Eligibility**: The Canadian Women Artist's Award is open to women artists who meet the following requirements: Must be a Canadian citizen, and able to provide proof of citizenship with legal documentation upon receipt of the award; Must be between the ages of 21 and 35 before the application deadline; Must be a current resident of New York, New Jersey, or Connecticut; Must apply in only one of the eligible discipline categories; Must be the originators of the work, i.e. choreographers or playwrights; not awarded to interpretative artists such as dancers or actors; Must not be a previous recipient of the Canadian Women Artist's Award; Must not be a NYFA employee, member of the NYFA Board of Trustees or Artists' Advisory Committee, and/or an immediate family member of any of the previous
**Level of Study**: Unrestricted
**Type**: Award
**Value**: C$5,000
**Frequency**: Annual
**Country of Study**: Any country
**Application Procedure**: All applicants must apply online at apply.nyfa.org/submit. The application cycle runs through the Spring, opening in March and closing in May
**No. of awards offered**: 82

**Closing Date**: May
**Funding**: Private, Foundation
**Contributor**: The Canadian Women's Club (CWC) of New York
**No. of awards given last year**: 1
**No. of applicants last year**: 82
**Additional Information**: www.nyfa.org/Content/Show/Canadian-Women-Artists'-Award

## "Made in NY" Women's Film, TV and Theatre Fund

**Purpose**: The "Made in NY" Women's Film, TV and Theatre Fund provides grants to encourage and support the creation of film, television, digital, and live theatre content that reflects the voices and perspectives of all who identify as women
**Eligibility**: In addition to being made by, for, or about all who identify as women, projects are eligible if they feature a strong female perspective; and/or include a female director; and/or include a meaningful female producer credit; and/or include a meaningful female writing credit; and/or include a female protagonist(s). Projects must also meet the "Made in NY" criteria as described in the program guidelines
**Level of Study**: Unrestricted
**Type**: A variable number of grants
**Value**: US$20,000 - US$50,000
**Frequency**: Annual
**Country of Study**: Any country
**Application Procedure**: All applications must be submitted online at apply.nyfa.org/submit. Applications open in the summer, and close in the fall
**No. of awards offered**: 568
**Closing Date**: October
**Funding**: Government
**Contributor**: The City of New York Mayor's Office of Media and Entertainment (MOME)
**No. of awards given last year**: 60
**No. of applicants last year**: 568

## New York State Council on the Arts/New York Foundation for the Arts Artist Fellowship

**Eligibility**: 1. 25 years or older 2. Current residents of New York State and/or one of the Indian Nations located in New York State 3. Must have maintained New York State residency, and/or residency in one of the Indian Nations located therein, for at least the last two consecutive years (2018 & 2019) 4. Cannot be enrolled in a degree-seeking program of any kind 5. Are the originators of the work, i.e. choreographers or playwrights, not interpretive artists such as dancers or actors 6. Did not receive a NYSCA/NYFA Artist Fellowship in any discipline in the past five consecutive years: 2015, 2016, 2017, 2018, and 2019 7. Cannot submit any work samples that have been previously awarded a NYSCA/NYFA Artist Fellowship 8. While collaborating artists are eligible to apply, the total number of collaborators cannot exceed three 9. Are not a current NYFA employee or have been in the last 12 months, a member of the NYFA Board of Trustees or Artists' Advisory Committee, immediate family member of any of the aforementioned, or an immediate family member of a 2019-2020 panelist 10. Artists that have been awarded five NYSCA/NYFA Artist Fellowships receive Emeritus status and are no longer eligible for the award

**Type**: Fellowship
**Value**: US$7,000
**Length of Study**: Unrestricted
**Frequency**: Annual
**Closing Date**: 22 January
**Additional Information**: www.nyfa.org/content/Show/Artists'-Fellowships

## Rauschenberg Emergency Grants

**Purpose**: New York Foundation for the Arts (NYFA) is proud to partner with the Robert Rauschenberg Foundation to administer a new emergency grant program called Rauschenberg Emergency Grants. This marks the first phase of a program that will be in the tradition of Change, Inc., a non-profit foundation established in 1970 by Robert Rauschenberg to assist professional artists of all disciplines in need of emergency medical aid.

**Eligibility**: Open to visual and media artists and choreographers. If you aren't sure if your artistic discipline fits within these guidelines, please contact emergencyfunds@nyfa.org. 1. Open to artists who are U.S. citizens or permanent residents in the United States, District of Columbia, or U.S. Territories. 2. Applicants must demonstrate current and ongoing activity in artistic discipline/s. 3. Applicants cannot be enrolled in any degree-seeking program

**Type**: Grant
**Value**: Up to US$5,000
**Frequency**: Annual
**Application Procedure**: Apply online: apply.nyfa.org/submit/0696520d-f013-454d-8846-8da806d3920a/rauschenberg-emergency-grants
**Closing Date**: June
**Additional Information**: www.nyfa.org/Content/Show/Rauschenberg-Emergency-Grants

### For further information contact:

New York Foundation for the Arts, 20 Jay Street, Suite 740, Brooklyn, NY 11201, United States of America.

**Email**:    emergencyfunds@nyfa.org

## Recharge Foundation Fellowship for New Surrealist Art

**Purpose**: The New York Foundation for the Arts (NYFA) created the Recharge Foundation Fellowship for New Surrealist Art, a US$5,000 award for painters living in the United States and U.S. Territories who are working in the New Surrealist style, in 2019. The award program is administered by NYFA with funding provided by the Gu Family of the Recharge Foundation.

**Type**: Grant
**Value**: US$7,000
**Frequency**: Annual
**Application Procedure**: The JGS Fellowship for Photography is open to New York State photography artists, living and working anywhere in the following regions of New York State: Western New York, Finger Lakes, Southern Tier, Central New York, North Country, Mohawk Valley, Capital District, Hudson Valley, and Long Island. 1. Applicants must work in photography. 2. Applicants can work in traditional and experimental photography or any form in which photography or photographic techniques are pivotal, if not exclusive. 3. Applicants must be a current full-time resident of New York State and have lived full-time in one of the regions listed above for a minimum of 12 months at the time applications close. 4. Applicant must be at least 25 years of age at the time the application closes. 5. Students in bachelor's or master's degree programs of any kind are not eligible to apply. 6. All past recipients of any NYFA grant or Fellowship are eligible to apply. 7. NYFA employees, members of the NYFA Board of Trustees or Artists' Advisory Committee, and/or an immediate family member of any of the above cannot apply.

**Closing Date**: 15 May
**Additional Information**: www.nyfa.org/Content/Show/The-Recharge-Foundation-Fellowship-for-New-Surrealist-Art

---

## New York University

## Provost's Postdoctoral Fellowship Program

**Purpose**: NYU Provost's Postdoctoral Fellowship Program supports promising scholars and educators from diverse backgrounds whose life experience and research background will contribute significantly to academic excellence at NYU

**Eligibility**: 1. NYU Provost's Postdoctoral Fellowship Program is open to all areas of study represented at the University. Individuals who meet one of the following criteria are eligible to apply. 2. Individuals who have completed their dissertation within the last three years or who will have completed their dissertation by 1 September. 3. Professionals transitioning to academic careers in a field for which the doctorate is not the terminal degree

**Level of Study**: Postgraduate
**Type**: Fellowship
**Frequency**: Annual
**Country of Study**: Any country
**Application Procedure**: Required application materials include: 1. a curriculum vitae. 2. a statement of research and goals. 3. a personal statement detailing reasons for applying for the fellowship. 4. mentorship plan developed jointly with the proposed mentor (see below). 5. three letters of recommendation (with one of those letters to come from the proposed mentor at NYU). 6. one of the following: A dissertation abstract (postdoctoral applicants); or a statement of how your professional experience prepares you for a faculty position non-PhD terminal degree holders; and candidate information form
**Closing Date**: 15 January
**Funding**: Private
**Additional Information**: www.nyu.edu/faculty/faculty-diversity-and-inclusion/mentoring-and-professional-development/provosts-postdoctoral-fellowship-program.html

**For further information contact:**

383 Lafayette Street, New York, NY 10003, United States of America.

**Email**: admissions.ops@nyu.edu

## New York University Academic and Science

### Rangel Graduate Fellowship Program

**Purpose**: The Rangel Graduate Fellowship is a United States Department of State program, administered by Howard University, that seeks to attract and prepare outstanding young people for careers as Foreign Service Officers in the United States Department of State
**Eligibility**: 1. Applicants must be seeking admission to enter graduate school in the fall for a two-year program at a United States university in an area of relevance to the Foreign Service. They can be in their senior year of their undergraduate studies, graduating by June, or they can be college graduates. 2. Applicants must have a cumulative grade point average of 3.2 or higher on a 4.0 scale at the time of application. 3. Applicants must be United States citizen
**Level of Study**: Postgraduate
**Type**: Fellowship
**Value**: Up to US$37,500 annually toward tuition, fees and living expense
**Frequency**: Annual
**Country of Study**: United States of America

**Application Procedure**: The Rangel Program expects to award 30 fellowships each November for cohort. A panel of individuals with experience in the United States Foreign Service and academia makes selections for the Rangel Program. A candidate's community, academic, extracurricular, and leadership activities will be considered during the selection process. For further details, check the following link. rangelprogram.org/graduate-fellowship-program-application/
**Closing Date**: 17 September
**Funding**: Private
**Additional Information**: www.unigo.com/scholarships/minority/asian-scholarships/rangel-graduate-fellowship/1004264

**For further information contact:**

2218 6th Street NW, Washington, DC 20059, United States of America.

**Tel**: (1) 877 633 0002
**Email**: rangelprogram@howard.edu

## New Zealand Aid Programme

195 Lambton Quay, Private Bag 18 901, Wellington 6160, New Zealand.

**Tel**: (64) 4 439 8000
**Contact**: Ministry of Foreign Affairs and Trade

The purpose of New Zealand's aid is to develop shared prosperity and stability in the Pacific and beyond, drawing on the best of New Zealand's knowledge and skills. We support sustainable development in developing countries to reduce poverty and contribute to a more secure, equitable and prosperous world.

### New Zealand Pacific Scholarships

**Purpose**: A particular focus of NZPS is to increase the number of young pacific people studying in New Zealand and to build a new generation of Pacific leadership with strong links to New Zealand
**Type**: Scholarship
**Country of Study**: Any country
**Application Procedure**: For application procedure, please refer website www.mfat.govt.nz/en/aid-and-development/scholarships/how-to-apply/
**Closing Date**: 28 March

**Additional Information**: scholarship-positions.com/new-zealand-pacific-scholarships-for-pacific-countries/2011/06/11/

### For further information contact:

**Email**:    studentinfo@auckland.ac.nz

## Newberry Library

60 West Walton Street, Chicago, IL 60610-3380, United States of America.

**Tel**:          (1) 312 943 9090
**Email**:      research@newberry.org
**Website**:   www.newberry.org
**Contact**:   Research and Education

The Newberry Library, open to the public without charge, is an independent research library and educational institution dedicated to the expansion and dissemination of knowledge in the humanities. With a broad range of books and manuscripts relating to the civilizations of Western Europe and the Americas, the Library's mission is to acquire and preserve research collections of such material, and to provide for and promote their effective use by a diverse community of users.

## Associated Colleges of the Midwest/the Great Lakes Colleges Association Faculty Fellowships

**Purpose**: This fellowship supports faculty from the colleges of the Associated Colleges of the Midwest and the Great Lakes Colleges Association, Inc

**Eligibility**: Applicants can come from any of the colleges in ACM or GLCA, from any discipline

**Type**: Fellowship

**Value**: Fellows teach a small group of select undergraduate students in an advanced research seminar

**Application Procedure**: Potential applicants should contact Joan Gillespie at the ACM

**Closing Date**: 15 March

**Additional Information**: For more information, visit the Associated Colleges of the Midwest's call for proposals at www.acm.edu/programs/14/newberry/index.html

### For further information contact:

**Tel**:       (1) 312 263 5000
**Email**:    jgillespie@acm.edu

## Long-Term Fellowships

**Purpose**: Long-Term Fellowships are intended to support individual scholarly research and promote serious intellectual exchange through active participation in the Newberry's scholarly activities, including Fellows' Seminars and Weekly Colloquium.

**Eligibility**: For more information on eligibility, guidelines, and the application process, please visit: www.newberry.org/how-apply

**Level of Study**: Postgraduate

**Type**: Fellowships

**Value**: US$4,200 per month

**Length of Study**: 4 to 9 months

**Frequency**: Annual

**Study Establishment**: The Newberry Library

**Country of Study**: United States of America

**Application Procedure**: For more information on eligibility, guidelines, and the application process, please visit: www.newberry.org/how-apply

**Closing Date**: 1 November

**Funding**: Private

**Additional Information**: If you have any additional questions about the Newberry's Fellowship Program, please email research@newberry.org. www.newberry.org/long-term-fellowships

## Rudolph Ganz Fellowship

**Purpose**: The Rudolph Ganz Fellowship is a new opportunity at the Newberry Library. The fellowship is intended to support research using the Rudolph Ganz Papers and other late nineteenth- and early twentieth-century materials related to Chicago music in that period. The Rudolph Ganz Papers include the musical compositions of this world-renowned concert pianist, composer, conductor, and educator, as well as articles, speeches, lectures and essays by him, and two recordings. Also in the collection is correspondence to and from prominent musical figures, family correspondence, clippings, photographs, programs, and some artifacts

**Eligibility**: Applicants must demonstrate a specific need for the Newberry's collection. For additional information about eligibility requirements and application guidelines, please check the website: www.newberry.org/fellowships

**Type**: Scholarship

**Value**: Short-Term Fellowships are generally awarded for one continuous month in residence at the Newberry, with stipends of US$2,500 per month

**Country of Study**: United States of America

**Closing Date**: 15 December

**Additional Information**: networks.h-net.org/node/73374/announcements/85457/rudolph-ganz-fellowship

## Weiss/Brown Publication Subvention Award

**Subjects**: Music, theater, cultural studies, or French or Italian literature
**Purpose**: To subsidize the publication of scholarly book or books on European civilization before 1700 in the areas of music, theater, cultural studies, or French or Italian literature
**Type**: Grant
**Value**: Up to US$8,000
**Length of Study**: Doctorate, Postdoctorate
**Frequency**: Annual
**Country of Study**: United States of America
**Application Procedure**: For more information, please see www.newberry.org/how-apply
**Funding**: The Newberry Library
**Additional Information**: www.newberry.org/publication-subvention

## Newcastle University

Manager, Student Financial Support, Newcastle University, King's Gate, Newcastle upon Tyne NE1 7RU, United Kingdom.

| | |
|---|---|
| **Tel**: | (44) 191 208 3333 |
| **Email**: | scholarship.applications@ncl.ac.uk |
| **Website**: | www.ncl.ac.uk |
| **Contact**: | Mrs Rencesova Irena, Student Financial Support Officer |

The Newcastle University, established in Newcastle in 1834, is one of the United Kingdom's leading universities and is known for its quality of teaching, outstanding research, and works with the regional and local communities, business and industry.

## Advancing Women in Leadership Scholarship (MBA)

**Purpose**: We're committed to supporting innovative business women who aspire to higher levels of influence and professional development. Successful candidates will demonstrate a strong career trajectory, academic excellence and a wealth of professional experience
**Eligibility**: To be eligible for this partial-fee scholarship you must meet the following criteria: 1. complete the scholarship application form including submitting an essay of no more than 1,500 words in response to the question listed. Submissions need to be in English. 2. hold a conditional or unconditional offer of admission to the Full-time MBA programme entry. 3. have substantive managerial experience (normally 6 years or more, minimum 3 years). 4. preferably hold the equivalent of a United Kingdom 2:1 honours degree (however, applicants who do not meet this requirement but can demonstrate relevant work experience above the minimum plus significant career progression may also be considered). 4. perform well at interview across all competency areas. 5. hold an English language qualification of IELTS 6.5 or its equivalent with no subskill below 6.0 (if your first language is not English)
**Level of Study**: Postgraduate
**Type**: Scholarship
**Value**: A full fee award of £22,800, payable towards the cost of tuition fees
**Frequency**: Annual
**Study Establishment**: Newcastle University Business School
**Country of Study**: Any country
**Application Procedure**: Applications and essays will be reviewed by a panel of judges. Candidates need to complete the online application form. forms.ncl.ac.uk/view.php?id=2981403
**Closing Date**: 5 April
**Funding**: Private
**Contributor**: Newcastle University Business School
**Additional Information**: www.scholarshubafrica.com/34923/advancing-women-leadership-scholarship-mba-newcastle-university-uk/

### For further information contact:

| | |
|---|---|
| **Tel**: | (44) 191 208 1589 |
| **Email**: | mba@ncl.ac.uk |

## British Marshall Scholarships

**Purpose**: If you are an American graduate, and aged under 26, you may be eligible to apply for one of 40 competitive awards. The British Marshall Scholarships will finance two years of postgraduate and occasionally, undergraduate study in the United Kingdom
**Eligibility**: The scholarships cover: 1. fares to and from the United States. 2. university tuition fees. 3. cost of living expenses. 4. book, thesis, research and daily travel allowances and where applicable, a contribution towards the support of a dependent spouse
**Level of Study**: Postgraduate
**Type**: Scholarship
**Value**: Varies
**Length of Study**: Two years
**Frequency**: Annual

**Country of Study**: Any country

**Application Procedure**: For further information about the scholarship and details on eligibility and applications, contact the Marshall Aid Commemoration Commission. www.marshallscholarship.org/

**Funding**: Private

**Contributor**: The Marshall Aid Commemoration Commission

**Additional Information**: www.marshallscholarship.org/apply/criteria-and-who-is-eligible

### For further information contact:

**Tel**:       (44) 191 208 6000
**Email**:    apps@marshallscholarship.org

## European Excellence Scholarship (MBA)

**Purpose**: Our MBA provides an inclusive, diverse and collaborative learning community that educates and develops our students to be creative, innovative, enterprising and global in their outlook

**Eligibility**: To be eligible for this full-fee scholarship you must meet the following criteria: 1. completed the scholarship application form including submitting an essay of no more than 1,500 words in response to the question listed. Submissions need to be in English. 2. hold a conditional or unconditional offer of admission to the Full-time MBA programme entry. 3. have substantive managerial experience (minimum 3 years prior to starting the MBA) preferably hold the equivalent of a United Kingdom 2:1 honours degree (however, applicants who do not meet this requirement but can demonstrate relevant work experience above the minimum plus significant career progression may also be considered). 4. perform well at interview across all competency areas. 5. hold an English language qualification of IELTS 6.5 or its equivalent with no subskill below 6.0 (if your first language is not English). 6. be assessed as an European Union student for fee paying purposes

**Level of Study**: Postgraduate

**Type**: Scholarship

**Frequency**: Annual

**Country of Study**: Any country

**Application Procedure**: Applications and essays will be reviewed by a panel of judges. Candidates need to complete the online application form

**Closing Date**: 5 April

**Funding**: Private

**Additional Information**: www.ncl.ac.uk/business-school/courses/scholarships/mba/

### For further information contact:

**Tel**:       (44) 191 208 1589
**Email**:    mba@ncl.ac.uk

## Humanities and Social Sciences Postgraduate Scholarships

**Purpose**: The Faculty of Humanities and Social Sciences at Newcastle University is pleased to offer Humanities and Social Sciences Postgraduate scholarships to assist non-UK European Union nationals to study a postgraduate Master's degree.

**Eligibility**: To be considered for awards applicants must: 1. hold the equivalent of a first class UK honours degree 2. have an offer for an eligible, full time, taught postgraduate degree programme within the Faculty of Humanities and Social Sciences. Applicants applying to Newcastle University Business School are not eligible for these awards 3. must be non UK European Union nationals and must be classed as EU for fee paying purposes. 4. Eligible candidates will be assessed as part of their academic application.

**Level of Study**: Postgraduate

**Type**: Scholarship

**Value**: £2,000 tuition fee awards.

**Frequency**: Annual

**Country of Study**: United Kingdom

**Application Procedure**: Eligible candidates will automatically be considered for a Humanities and Social Sciences Postgraduate Scholarship as part of their academic course application.

**Closing Date**: September

**Funding**: Private

**Additional Information**: www.ncl.ac.uk//postgraduate/funding/sources/ukeustudents/hsspgs20.html

## Indonesia Endowment Fund for Education (LPDP)

**Purpose**: The Indonesia Endowment Fund (LPDP) provides funding for high achieving Indonesian students undertaking Master's or PhD study. It forms part of the Indonesian government's aim to nurture young talented individuals, enabling them to become future leaders

**Eligibility**: For detailed information about the eligiblity, check the website

**Level of Study**: Postgraduate

**Type**: Funding support

**Value**: The scholarship covers tuition fees and living expenses

**Frequency**: Annual

**Study Establishment**: Ministry of Finance and Minister of Research, Technology and Higher Education

**Country of Study**: Any country

**Application Procedure**: For detailed information grants, check the following link, www.lpdp.kemenkeu.go.id

**Closing Date**: October

**Funding**: Private

**Contributor**: Lembaga Pengelolaan Dana Pendidikan (LPDP)
**Additional Information**: www.ncl.ac.uk/postgraduate/funding/sources/internationalnoneustudents/lpdp19.html

**For further information contact:**

**Email**: cso.lpdp@kemenkeu.go.id

## International Family Discounts (IFD)

**Purpose**: We offer discounts to encourage relatives of our current international students, and past international graduates, to pursue their studies at Newcastle University
**Eligibility**: 1. This discount is only available to students studying at the Newcastle city campus. 2. The University offers partial discounts to close relatives (husband, wife, brother, sister, mother, father, son or daughter) of students and graduates, who have been assessed as International for fees purposes, and who wish to pursue their studies at Newcastle University in currently studying here. 3. Students may only apply for a discount if they are registered as a student at the University or after they have been offered a place to study on their chosen degree programme, and have been assessed as International for fees purposes
**Level of Study**: Postgraduate
**Type**: Funding support
**Value**: 10% of the tuition fee per year
**Frequency**: Annual
**Country of Study**: Any country
**Application Procedure**: Please complete the online International Family Discount application form in accordance with the IFD regulations. Further updates on regulatiobns and applications are available at: forms.ncl.ac.uk/view.php?id=12481
**Funding**: Private
**Additional Information**: www.ncl.ac.uk/postgraduate/funding/sources/internationalnoneustudents/ifd.html

**For further information contact:**

**Tel**: (44) 191 208 5537

## Master of Arts (Taught Masters) Scholarships in the School of Modern Languages

**Purpose**: The School of Modern Languages is offering competitive scholarships to outstanding applicants for the following programmes: MA programmes in Translating and Interpreting (Chinese) MA in Professional Translating for European Languages (French, German, Italian, Spanish) MA Film: Theory and Practice

**Eligibility**: Home, European Union and International Students are eligible to apply
**Level of Study**: Postgraduate
**Type**: Scholarship
**Value**: £5,000
**Frequency**: Annual
**Country of Study**: Any country
**Application Procedure**: In order to apply for the scholarship, check the website. www.ncl.ac.uk/sml/study/funding/#currentopportunities
**Closing Date**: 7 June
**Funding**: Private
**Contributor**: SML Postgraduate Officer

**For further information contact:**

**Tel**: (44) 191 208 5867
**Email**: modlang.pgadmin@ncl.ac.uk

## Master of Arts in Art Museum and Gallery Studies Scholarship

**Purpose**: The Art Museum and Gallery Studies MA provides students with the opportunity to develop skills as a curator or gallery educator in the fields of both historical and contemporary art
**Eligibility**: The studentships are open to United Kingdom, European Union and international applicants who hold, or expect to achieve a minimum of a 2.1 Honours degree (or international equivalent) in fine art or an art related subject. We welcome applications from all sections of the community regardless of race, ethnicity, gender or sexuality, and wish to encourage applications from traditionally underrepresented groups in United Kingdom higher education. International students If your first language is not English you must also meet our English language requirements
**Level of Study**: Professional development
**Type**: Scholarship
**Value**: £3,000
**Frequency**: Annual
**Country of Study**: Any country
**Application Procedure**: You must apply through the University's online postgraduate application system. To do this please 'Create a new account'. All relevant fields should be completed, but fields marked with a red asterisk must be completed. The following information will help us to process your application. You will need to: 1. insert the programme code 4138F in the programme of study section. 2. select 'MA Art Museum and Gallery Studies (full time)' as the programme of study. 3. insert the studentship code SAC025 in the studentship/partnership reference field. 4. attach a personal statement of no more than 500 words outlining. i. your preparedness to

undertake the Art Museum and Gallery Studies MA. ii. your aspirations for a career in the art museum and gallery sector

**Closing Date**: 30 April

**Funding**: Private

**Additional Information**: www.ncl.ac.uk/postgraduate/courses/degrees/art-museum-gallery-studies-ma-pgdip/#profile

### For further information contact:

**Email**:    gerard.corsane@ncl.ac.uk

## Master of Business Administration Business Excellence Scholarships

**Purpose**: The scholarship program will be awarded to a high caliber candidate with at least 5 years of work experience who can demonstrate achievement and impact in a business environment. Our MBA Business Excellence Scholarships will reward MBA candidates who are results orientated, customer focused, and can demonstrate emerging leadership qualities

**Eligibility**: To be eligible for this partial-fee scholarship you must meet the following criteria: 1. can demonstrate (through application and at interview) substantive managerial experience and good leadership potential for the future. 2. hold a conditional or unconditional offer of admission to the Full-time MBA programme entry. 3. have substantive managerial experience (normally 4 years or more, minimum 3 years) preferably hold the equivalent of a United Kingdom 2:1 honours degree (however, applicants who do not meet this requirement but can demonstrate relevant work experience above the minimum plus significant career progression may also be considered). Perform well at interview across all competency areas hold an English language qualification of IELTS 6.5 or its equivalent with no subskill below 6.0 (if your first language is not English)

**Level of Study**: Postgraduate

**Type**: Scholarship

**Frequency**: Annual

**Study Establishment**: Newcastle University Business School

**Country of Study**: Any country

**Application Procedure**: No application required. All candidates will be assessed at the point of interview for this Scholarship

**Closing Date**: 5 April

**Funding**: Private

**Additional Information**: studyabroad.shiksha.com/scholarships/newcastle-university-mba-business-excellence-scholarships

### For further information contact:

**Tel**:        (44) 191 208 1589

**Email**:    mba@ncl.ac.uk

## Newcastle University - English Language Excellence Scholarships (Business School Masters)

**Purpose**: Newcastle University Business School offers a number of partial scholarship awards to outstanding and high-quality Masters students each year to assist them to study for a Masters degree

**Eligibility**: You will be considered for an English Language Excellence Scholarship if you hold an unconditional offer for one of the following Masters courses: 1. Arts, Business and Creativity MA. 2. Innovation, Creativity and Entrepreneurship MSc. 3. Global Human Resource Management MSc. 4. International Economics and Finance MSc. 5. Banking and Finance MSc. 6. Finance MSc. 7. Quantitative Finance and Risk Management MSc. 8. International Business Management MSc. 9. International Marketing MSc. 10. Operations, Logistics and Supply Chain Management MSc. 11. Accounting, Finance and Strategic Investment MSc. 12. International Financial Analysis MSc. 13. E-Business MSc. 14. E-Business (Information Systems) MSc. 15. E-Business (E-Marketing) MSc

**Level of Study**: Postgraduate

**Type**: Scholarship

**Value**: Partial awards of £5,000 towards the cost of tuition fees

**Frequency**: Annual

**Country of Study**: Any country

**Application Procedure**: Regulations and application details are available on the below link, www.ncl.ac.uk/media/wwwnclacuk/postgraduate/funding/files/English%20Language%20Excellence%20Scholarships%20Regulations%202019%20Entry.pdf

**Funding**: Private

### For further information contact:

**Email**:    nubs@ncl.ac.uk

## Newcastle University - United States of America Athlete Scholarship

**Purpose**: Newcastle University offers partial scholarship awards to encourage United States of America athletes to undertake Master's level study

**Eligibility**: Applicants should ideally have NCAA D1- D3 playing experience in one of the following sports: Basketball, Lacrosse, Volleyball, Tennis, Golf, Women's Soccer, Waterpolo. They must also be: 1. registered at Newcastle University for the academic year. 2. registered for one of the following eligible courses Masters - MA; MBA; MClinRes; MEd; MMedEd; LLM; LLM (by research); MLitt; MMus; MPH; MRes; MSc. 3. defined as international for fee purposes. 4. resident in the United States of America. 5. registered to study at Newcastle University city centre campus

**Level of Study**: Graduate
**Type**: Scholarship
**Value**: 40% fee reduction, £5,000- £8,000 payable towards the first year of tuition fees and a comprehensive support package (see Overview for further details)
**Frequency**: Annual
**Country of Study**: Any country
**Application Procedure**: Complete the application form using the following link. www.ncl.ac.uk/nclsport/performance/scholarships/application.htm
**Closing Date**: 31 July
**Funding**: Private
**Contributor**: Newcastle University Performance Sport Team

**For further information contact:**

**Tel**: (44) 191 208 5230
**Email**: performance.sport@newcastle.ac.uk

## Newcastle University - Vice-Chancellor's Excellence Scholarships - Postgraduate

**Purpose**: Newcastle University is pleased to offer 40 Vice-Chancellor's Excellence Scholarships (VCES) for outstanding international applicants who apply to commence full-time Master's studies. There are 39 50% tuition fee scholarships and 2 100% tuition fee scholarship
**Eligibility**: To be considered for the 50% scholarships applicants must: be a national of one of the following countries: Algeria, Argentina, Brazil, Canada, Chile, China, Colombia, Ecuador, Egypt, India, Indonesia, Jordan, Lebanon, Malaysia, Mexico, Morocco, Peru, Thailand, Turkey, United States of America, Venezuela be assessed as international for fee purposes hold an offer for an eligible Master's degree programme at the University's Newcastle city centre campus for the academic year already have or expect to receive the equivalent of an upper second class United Kingdom honours degree or above
**Level of Study**: Postgraduate
**Type**: Scholarship
**Frequency**: Annual
**Study Establishment**: Newcastle University
**Country of Study**: Any country
**Application Procedure**: Online application form is available on the below web link path. app.geckoform.com/public/#/modern/FOEU01c3zJ6qAVgh
**Closing Date**: 28 June
**Funding**: Private
**Contributor**: Newcastle University
**Additional Information**: www.ncl.ac.uk/undergraduate/fees-funding/scholarships-bursaries/vc-excellence/

## Newcastle University International Postgraduate Scholarship (NUIPS)

**Purpose**: To provide a partial scholarship for international students
**Eligibility**: Candidates for scholarships must already have been offered a place to study at Newcastle University. See webpages: www.ncl.ac.uk/postgraduate/funding/search/list/nuips
**Level of Study**: Postgraduate
**Type**: Partial scholarship
**Value**: £2,000 per year
**Length of Study**: 1st year of study only
**Frequency**: Annual
**Study Establishment**: Newcastle University
**Country of Study**: United Kingdom
**Application Procedure**: All eligible applicants who are offered a place to study at Newcastle University are invited to apply for one of these scholarships. Applicants must check the website for details or contact the Student Financial Support Team
**No. of awards offered**: 800
**Closing Date**: 27 May
**Contributor**: Newcastle University
**No. of awards given last year**: 100
**No. of applicants last year**: 800
**Additional Information**: www.scholarshipsads.com/newcastle-university-international-postgraduate-scholarship-nuips-uk/

**For further information contact:**

**Email**: international-scholarships@ncl.ac.uk

## Newcastle University Overseas Research Scholarship (NUORS)

**Purpose**: Newcastle University is committed to offering support to the very best international students hoping to pursue a programme of research. We are pleased to offer a small number of University funded NUORS awards for outstanding international students who apply to commence PhD studies in any subject
**Eligibility**: 1. You could be eligible to apply for a NUORS award if. 2. you have been offered a place on a PhD research programme. 3. you have been assessed as international/overseas for fees purposes, and are wholly or partially self-financing. 4. you intend to register to start your studies during the academic year
**Level of Study**: Graduate
**Type**: Scholarship

**Value**: This award covers the difference between home and overseas fee rates (value approximately £11,490 to £17,700 per annum)

**Frequency**: Annual

**Country of Study**: Any country

**Application Procedure**: You must have already applied for and been offered a place to study at Newcastle University before you apply for a NUORS award. Please complete the online NUORS application form and in accordance with the NUORS regulations. You will also be required to provide details of an academic referee; the University will then contact your referee directly. Further details can be found in the NUORS Regulations 19-20? Please read these thoroughly before applying. forms.ncl.ac.uk/view.php?id=2526301

**Closing Date**: 26 April

**Funding**: Private

**Additional Information**: www.ncl.ac.uk/postgraduate/funding/sources/internationalnoneustudents/nuors.html

**For further information contact:**

**Tel**: (44) 191 208 5537/8107

## Newcastle University Scholarship – Thailand - GREAT

**Purpose**: This year, in partnership with the British Council and the GREAT Britain Campaign, Newcastle University is offering scholarships to students in Thailand applying for postgraduate taught courses listed below. This scholarship scheme is part of the "GREAT Scholarships - East Asia" campaign, which has been launched by the British Council together with 28 United Kingdom universities to support more students in East Asia to get access to the excellent United Kingdom higher education opportunities

**Eligibility**: To be considered for awards applicants must: 1. Must be passport holders of Thailand. 2. be assessed as international for fee purposes. 3. hold an offer for an eligible Master's degree programme listed below. 4. MSc Sustainable Chemical Engineering. 5. MSc REFLEX (Renewable Energy Flexible Training Programme)

**Level of Study**: Postgraduate

**Type**: Scholarship

**Value**: Full tuition fees

**Frequency**: Annual

**Study Establishment**: Newcastle University

**Country of Study**: Any country

**Application Procedure**: Applications must be submitted using the application form. Other applications will not be accepted. Application link is available below: app.geckoform.com/public/#/modern/FOEU01c3zJ6qAVgh

**Closing Date**: 30 April

**Funding**: Private

**Contributor**: British Council and Newcastle University

**Additional Information**: app.geckoform.com/public/#/modern/FOEU01c3zJ6qAVgh www.wemakescholars.com/scholarship/newcastle-university-great-scholarships-thailand

**For further information contact:**

**Email**: scholarship.applications@newcastle.ac.uk

## Newcastle Vice-Chancellor's Global Scholarships - Postgraduate

**Purpose**: Newcastle University is pleased to offer 5 Vice-Chancellor's Global Scholarships (VCGS) for outstanding international applicants who apply to commence full-time Master's studies

**Eligibility**: To be considered for the Vice-Chancellor's Global Scholarships applicants must: 1. be assessed as international for fee purposes. 2. hold an offer for an eligible Master's degree programme at the University's Newcastle city centre campus for the academic year. 3. already have or expect to receive the equivalent of an upper second class United Kingdom honours degree or above. 4. Applicants from the following countries are not eligible to apply for VCGS awards as the University offers specific schemes for these countries: Algeria, Argentina, Brazil, Canada, Chile, China, Colombia, Ecuador, Egypt, Ghana, India, Indonesia, Jordan, Kenya, Lebanon, Malaysia, Mexico, Morocco, Nigeria, Peru, Thailand, Turkey, United States of America, Uganda, Venezuela, Vietnam. 5. A scheme for postgraduate Master's applicants from Ghana, Kenya, Nigeria and Uganda will be launched in February

**Level of Study**: Postgraduate

**Type**: Scholarship

**Frequency**: Annual

**Country of Study**: Any country

**Application Procedure**: For further information about application process, refer the following link. www.ncl.ac.uk/media/wwwnclacuk/postgraduate/funding/files/VCGS%20postgraduate%20regulations%20(2019).pdf

**Closing Date**: 28 June

**Funding**: Private

## Postgraduate Masters Scholarships in the School of Geography, Politics and Sociology

**Purpose**: The scholarships are open to United Kingdom, European Union and international applicants who: Hold an offer of admission on one of the eligible programmes Hold, or expect to achieve, at least a 2.1 honours degree (or international equivalent), in a related discipline

**Eligibility**: The scholarships are open to United Kingdom, European Union and international applicants who: 1. Hold an offer of admission on one of the eligible programmes. 2. Hold, or expect to achieve, at least a 2.1 honours degree (or international equivalent), in a related discipline

**Level of Study**: Postgraduate

**Type**: Scholarship

**Value**: £7,410

**Frequency**: Annual

**Country of Study**: Any country

**Closing Date**: 7 June

**Funding**: Private

**Additional Information**: www.ncl.ac.uk/gps/about/funding/schoolfunding/#phdscholarships

**For further information contact:**

**Email**:   gps.pgr@ncl.ac.uk

## Postgraduate Master's Loan Scheme (Students from United Kingdom and non-United Kingdom European Union Countries)

**Purpose**: Student loans for full-time, part-time and distance learning Masters degrees in all subjects (taught or research)

**Eligibility**: 1. Taught and research Master's courses in all disciplines (online and campus-based) will normally be eligible, e.g. MA, MSc, MRes, MEd, MBA, LLM, MLitt, MFA. 2. You can receive a loan for an MPhil. However, this programme must lead to a standalone. Master's degree and not be part of a longer PhD programme. 3. You will not be entitled to receive the Postgraduate Loan if you are eligible to receive healthcare funding from any of the following organisations. i. National Health Service (NHS). ii. Department of Health (DOH). iii. Student Awards Agency Scotland (SAAS). iv. Doctoral degrees (eg PhD, EngD, Integrated PhDs), PG Certificates, PG Diplomas, PGCE's and Master's courses that are currently funded by the undergraduate support system, eg Master of Architecture (MArch), will not be eligible for the Loan. 4. You will not be eligible for the Postgraduate Loan if you are studying towards top-up credits to a gain a Master's qualification after studying a PG Certificate or PG Diploma

**Level of Study**: Postgraduate

**Type**: Award

**Value**: £10,906

**Frequency**: Annual

**Country of Study**: Any country

**Application Procedure**: The application cycle is still open. The quickest way to apply is online. www.gov.uk/masters-loan/apply

**Funding**: Private

**Additional Information**:   www.ncl.ac.uk/postgraduate/funding/sources/ukeustudents/mastersloan.html

**For further information contact:**

**Email**:   ltds@ncl.ac.uk

## Postgraduate Opportunity Scholarships

**Purpose**: The scholarships are available as part of Newcastle University's Postgraduate Support Scheme for Master's students. They have been designed to enable students from under-represented groups to progress to higher level study

**Eligibility**: Postgraduate Opportunity Scholarships are available only to students applying to Newcastle University who meet the following criteria: have been offered a place to study full time for one year or a maximum of two years part time on one of the University's eligible taught or research Master's courses commencing in September. are United Kingdom students progressing from undergraduate courses for which they were charged the higher tuition fee applying and falling into the following categories: 1. a student living in United Kingdom when they entered undergraduate study at any United Kingdom institution. 2. a student living in Scotland when they entered undergraduate study at any English, Northern Irish or Welsh institution. 3. a student living in Northern Ireland when they entered undergraduate study at any English, Scottish or Welsh institution

**Level of Study**: Postgraduate

**Type**: Scholarship

**Frequency**: Annual

**Country of Study**: Any country

**Application Procedure**: To apply for the Postgraduate Opportunity Scholarship, please complete the online application form. Check the following link. app.geckoform.com/public/#/modern/FOEU01c3RUfcdPr6%20

**Closing Date**: 28 June

**Funding**: Private

**Additional Information**: In order to be considered for a Postgraduate Opportunity Scholarship, you must have already applied to the University for an eligible taught or research Master's course and received an offer of a place by this date www.ncl.ac.uk/postgraduate/funding/sources/ukeustudents/pos20.html

**For further information contact:**

**Email**:   uk.postgraduate-scholarships@ncl.ac.uk

## Regional Impact Scholarship (MBA)

**Purpose**: To support aspiring and established leaders from the region to continue their professional development. The Regional Impact Scholarship is aimed at MBA candidates who can demonstrate their potential to the economy and society of the North East of United Kingdom

**Eligibility**: To be eligible for this full-fee scholarship you must meet the following criteria: 1. completed the scholarship application form including submitting an essay of no more than 1,500 words in response to the question listed. Submissions need to be in English. 2. hold a conditional or unconditional offer of admission to the Full-time MBA programme of current year entry. 3. have substantive managerial experience (minimum 3 years prior to starting the MBA). 4. preferably hold the equivalent of a United Kingdom 2:1 honours degree (however, applicants who do not meet this requirement but can demonstrate relevant work experience above the minimum plus significant career progression may also be considered). 5. perform well at interview across all competency areas hold an English language qualification of IELTS 6.5 or its equivalent with no subskill below 6.0 (if your first language is not English)

**Level of Study**: Postgraduate

**Type**: Scholarship

**Value**: A full fee award of £22,800, payable towards the cost of tuition fees

**Frequency**: Annual

**Country of Study**: United Kingdom

**Application Procedure**: Applications and essays will be reviewed by a panel of judges. Candidates need to complete the online application form. forms.ncl.ac.uk/view.php?id=2981068

**Closing Date**: 5 April

**Funding**: Private

**Additional Information**: www.ncl.ac.uk/business-school/courses/scholarships/mba/

**For further information contact:**

**Tel**:      (44) 191 208 1589
**Email**:      mba@ncl.ac.uk

---

# Newcastle University in the United Kingdom

Newcastle upon Tyne, Tyne and Wear NE1 7RU, United Kingdom.

**Tel**:      (44) 191 208 6000
**Contact**:      Newcastle University

Newcastle University officially, the University of Newcastle

## 40 Fully-Funded Postgraduate Scholarships at Newcastle University in the United Kingdom

**Purpose**: Students need a good level of English language to study at Newcastle University. English will be the main language you use socially and for study. If English is not their first language they will need to provide a recognised English language test or qualification

**Eligibility**: Citizens of China, United States of America, Canada, India, Indonesia, Malaysia, Thailand, Singapore, Jordan, Lebanon, Egypt, Turkey, Algeria, Morocco, India, Nigeria, Ghana, Kenya and Uganda are eligible to apply

**Type**: Postgraduate scholarships

**Value**: 50% or 100% of tuition fees

**Study Establishment**: Scholarships are awarded to study the subjects offered by the university

**Country of Study**: United Kingdom

**Application Procedure**: International preparation courses and graduate diplomas have a different application method. Students apply online through partner INTO. Applications must be submitted using the online application form

**Closing Date**: 29 June

**Additional Information**: For more details please browse the website scholarship-positions.com/fully-funded-postgraduate-scholarships-newcastle-university-uk/2017/11/14/

**For further information contact:**

**Email**:      scholarship.applications@ncl.ac.uk

---

# Newcomen Society of the United States

211 Welsh Pool Road, Suite 240, Exton, PA 19341, United States of America.

**Tel**:      (1) 610 363 6600
**Email**:      mstoner@newcomen.org
**Website**:      www.newcomen.org
**Contact**:      Ms Marcy J. Stoner, Executive Assistant

The Newcomen Society of the United States is a non-profit business educational foundation that studies and supports outstanding achievement in American business.

## Harvard/Newcomen Postdoctoral Award

**Purpose**: To improve the scholar's professional acquaintance with business and economic history, to increase his or her skills as they relate to this field, and to enable him or her to engage in research that will benefit from the resources of the Harvard Business School and the Boston scholarly community

**Eligibility**: Open to Scholars who have received a PhD in history, economics or a related discipline within the past

10 years, and who would not otherwise be able to attend Harvard Business School
**Level of Study**: Postdoctorate
**Type**: Fellowship
**Value**: US$46,000
**Length of Study**: 1 year
**Frequency**: Annual
**Study Establishment**: Harvard Business School in Cambridge, Massachusetts
**Country of Study**: United States of America
**Application Procedure**: Applicants must contact Harvard University for further details
**Closing Date**: 15 March

### For further information contact:

Straus Professor of Business History, Harvard University, Graduate School of Business Administration, Soldiers Field Road, Boston, MA 02163, United States of America.

| | |
|---|---|
| **Tel**: | (1) 6_7 495 6354 |
| **Email**: | tmccraw@hbs.edu |

## North Atlantic Treaty Organization (NATO)

Public Diplomacy Division, Office Nb 106, Boulevard Leopold III, B-1110 Brussels, Belgium.

| | |
|---|---|
| **Tel**: | (32) 2 707 4111 |
| **Email**: | natodoc@hq.nato.int |
| **Website**: | www.nato.int |
| **Contact**: | Academic Affairs Officer |

The North Atlantic Treaty was signed in Washington on 1 April, 1949, creating an alliance of 12 independent nations committed to each other's defence. Four more European nations later acceded to the Treaty between 1952 and 1982. On 12 March, 1999, the Czech Republic, Hungary and Poland were welcomed into the Alliance, which now numbers 19 members.

## Manfred Wörner Fellowship

**Purpose**: To honour the memory of the late Secretary General by focusing attention on his leadership in the transformation of the alliance, including efforts at extending NATO's relations with CEE countries and promoting the principles and image of the Transatlantic partnership

**Eligibility**: Open to applicants who are citizens of the EAPC countries with proven experience to carry out an important scholarly endeavour within the time limit of the Fellowship
**Level of Study**: Professional development
**Type**: Fellowship
**Value**: €5,000 (including all travel costs)
**Frequency**: Annual
**Country of Study**: Any country
**Application Procedure**: Application forms can be downloaded from the NATO website
**Closing Date**: 25 January
**Funding**: Government

### For further information contact:

| | |
|---|---|
| **Fax**: | (32) 2 707 5457 |
| **Email**: | academics@hq.nato.int |

## North Central College

Graduate Programs MBA Program, 30 North Brainard Street PO Box 3065, Naperville, IL 60566-7065, United States of America.

| | |
|---|---|
| **Tel**: | (1) 630 637 5840 |
| **Email**: | grad@noctrl.edu |
| **Website**: | www.noctrl.edu |
| **Contact**: | MBA Admissions Officer |

North Central College is a private, four year co-educational college located in Naperville, just 30 miles west of Chicago, Illinois. North Central offers over 50 undergraduate majors and six master's programmes.

## North Central Association for Counselor Education and Supervision Research Grant Awards

**Purpose**: The call for proposals is to fund studies that increase understanding of the counselor education profession (including research, teaching, supervision, leadership and advocacy). Research grant awards will be presented at the business meeting at the NCACES
**Eligibility**: Proposed topic is within the scope of this Research Award program. Need for the proposed topic is clearly outlined through review of the research. Objectives are clear and attainable in the proposed study. Methodology proposed is appropriate for the research questions. Outcomes are consistent with objectives and method. Research proposed

adheres to ACA/ACES ethical standards for research with human subjects

**Level of Study**: Graduate

**Type**: Study grant

**Value**: Three US$1,000 awards

**Frequency**: Annual

**Country of Study**: Any country

**Application Procedure**: The competition is open to both professional and student members of NCACES. The primary investigator must be an ACES/NCACES member at the time the application is submitted. Individuals may submit (or be part of a submission team) for only one proposal. ncaces.org/awards/general/gsubmit

**Closing Date**: 29 June

**Funding**: Private

## North Dallas Bank & Trust Company

P.O. Box 801826, Dallas, TX 75380-1826, United States of America.

**Tel**:          (1) 800 275 7966

**Email**:     scholarships@thetrustcompany.com.au

**Website**:  www.ndbt.com

The Trust Company is manager at a number high profile awards and scholarships made possible through Charitable bequests/trusts. These include the Miles Franklin Literary Award, Kathleen Mitchell Award (literary), Portia Geach Memorial Award (for female artists), the Sir Robert William Askin Operatic Travelling Scholarship (for male singers), the Lady Mollie Isabelle Askin Ballet Travelling Scholarship, and the Marten Bequest Travelling Scholarship.

### James W. Tyra Memorial Scholarship

**Purpose**: In 1994, the executive management established the James W. Tyra Scholarship, in honor of the bank's very first Community Reinvestment Act ("CRA") Officer. Mr. Tyra was committed to advancing the hopes and dreams of the local public, and tirelessly gave of himself for the benefit of the youth in the community

**Eligibility**: 1. Must be a high school senior at time of application. 2. Must be a United States citizen or permanent resident. 3. Must be attending a public high school inside the North Dallas Bank & Trust Company trade area (a list of eligible schools is available on the North Dallas Bank & Trust Company website). 4. Must be in the top 25 % of his/her graduating class. 5. Must have a grade point average of 3.0 or

higher. 6. the student must submit transcripts prior to the completion of each year of class, as failure to do so will result in loss of the scholarship

**Level of Study**: Graduate

**Type**: Scholarship

**Value**: US$1,000

**Frequency**: Annual

**Country of Study**: United States of America

**Application Procedure**: 1. Each student must complete the scholarship application available in the counselor's office of his/her high school. Each applicant must be recommended by his/her high school counselor or principal. 2. In addition to the completed application, each student must submit a current official transcript, two letters of recommendation (one from a high school teacher, counselor, or principal and one from a community member)

**Closing Date**: 1 April

**Funding**: Private

**Additional Information**: www.unigo.com/scholarships/all/james-w-tyra-memorial-scholarship/1559

### For further information contact:

12900 Preston Road, Suite 208, Dallas, TX 75230, United States of America.

**Tel**:          (1) 972 716 7299

**Email**:     scholarships@swe.org

## North West Cancer Research Fund

22 Oxford Street, Liverpool, L7 7BL, United Kingdom.

**Tel**:          (44) 15 1709 2919

**Email**:     nwcrf@btclick.com

**Website**:  www.cancerresearchnorthwest.co.uk

**Contact**:  Mr A W Renison, General Secretary

### North West Cancer Research Fund Research Project Grants

**Purpose**: To support fundamental research into the cause of cancers and the mechanisms by which cancers arise and exert their effects

**Eligibility**: Open to candidates undertaking cancer research studies at one of the universities named below in the Northwest. Grants are only available for travel costs associated with currently funded 3-year cancer research projects. No grants are awarded for buildings or for the development of drugs

**Level of Study**: Research

**Type**: Project
**Value**: Approx. £35,000 per year
**Length of Study**: Usually 3 years
**Frequency**: Dependent on funds available
**Study Establishment**: The University of Liverpool, Lancaster University and the University of Wales, Bangor
**Country of Study**: North West United Kingdom, North and Mid-Wales
**Application Procedure**: The NWCRF Scientific Committee meets twice a year. All applications are subject to peer review
**No. of awards offered**: 50
**Closing Date**: 1 October
**Funding**: Private, Individuals
**Contributor**: Voluntary donations
**No. of awards given last year**: 10
**No. of applicants last year**: 50

### For further information contact:

NWCRF Scientific Committee, Department of Medicine, Duncan Building, Daulby Street, Liverpool, L7 8XW, United Kingdom.

**Email**: ricketts@liverpool.ac.uk

## NWCR & Tenovus PhD Studentship Award

**Purpose**: We invite applications from principal investigators, with a track record of successful PhD supervision, to submit proposals for this jointly funded research award. NWCR and Tenovus Cancer Care (Tenovus) seek to fund a health services PhD research award which will aim to impact cancer policy or practice through the targeted area of psycho-social oncology.
**Level of Study**: Research
**Value**: Maximum funding budget of up to £75,000
**Length of Study**: 3 years
**Closing Date**: 22 June
**Funding**: Private, Individuals

## Northeast Florida Phi Beta Kappa Alumni Association

### Northeast Florida Phi Beta Kappa Alumni Association Scholarship

**Purpose**: The Fall Program provides a social and intellectual opportunity for members and their guests
**Eligibility**: Winners will be honored at the association's Spring Banquet. For further details, see the website.
**Level of Study**: Postgraduate

**Type**: Scholarship and Research award
**Value**: US$1,000
**Frequency**: Annual
**Country of Study**: Any country
**Application Procedure**: Application information is available online at the Phi Beta Kappa Alumni Association of Northeast Florida website
**Closing Date**: 1 March
**Funding**: Private

### For further information contact:

1606 New Hampshire Avenue NW, Washington, DC 20009, United States of America.

**Email**: mroberts@unf.edu

## Northeastern University

Graduate School of Business Administration, 350 Dodge Hall, 360 Huntington, Boston, MA 02115, United States of America.

**Tel**: (1) 617 373 2714
**Email**: gsba@neu.edu
**Contact**: MBA Admissions Officer

## National Robotics Initiative 2.0: Ubiquitous Collaborative Robots (NRI-2.0)

**Purpose**: The goal of the National Robotics Initiative (NRI) is to support fundamental research that will accelerate the development and use of robots in the United States that work beside or cooperatively with people
**Eligibility**: 1. An investigator may participate as PI, co-PI, or Senior Personnel in no more than two proposals submitted in response to this solicitation each year. 2. In the event that an individual exceeds this limit, proposals received within the limit will be accepted based on earliest date and time of proposal submission (i.e., the first two proposals received will be accepted and the remainder will be returned without review). No exceptions will be made. 3. The above limit applies only to proposals to the NRI-2.0 solicitation, not to the totality of proposals submitted to NSF
**Level of Study**: Graduate
**Type**: Grant
**Frequency**: Annual
**Country of Study**: Any country
**Closing Date**: 1 November
**Funding**: Private

**Additional Information**: www.nsf.gov/funding/pgm_summ.jsp?pims_id=503641

### For further information contact:

**Email**: k.drew@neu.edu

## Northumbria University

2 Ellison Pl, Newcastle upon Tyne NE1 8ST, United Kingdom.

**Contact**: Northumbria University

Northumbria University, officially the University of Northumbria at Newcastle, is a university located in Newcastle upon Tyne in the North East of United Kingdom. A former polytechnic, it was established as one of the new universities in 1992.

### Dean's Award Scholarship

**Purpose**: Scholarships are available for pursuing full-time or part-time LPC or LLM LPC programme
**Eligibility**: For eligibility details, please visit website
**Value**: £1,000 with 90% off tuition fees
**Country of Study**: Any country
**Application Procedure**: Applications must be must be sent via email
**Closing Date**: 31 July
**Contributor**: Northumbria University
**Additional Information**: For more details, please visit website www.northumbria.ac.uk/study-at-northumbria/fees-funding/pg-fees-funding/2018-deans-award-lpc/ www.northumbria.ac.uk/study-at-northumbria/fees-funding/pg-fees-funding/2018-deans-award-bptc/

### For further information contact:

**Email**: gradadms@mtu.edu

## Norway – the Official Site in the United States

2720 34th Street NW, Washington, DC 20008, United States of America.

**Tel**: (1) 202 333 6000
**Email**: cg.newyork@mfa.no

**Website**: www.norway.org
**Contact**: Grants and Scholarships Department

### Al Fog Bergljot Kolflats Stipendfond

**Purpose**: To provide a stipend for those who want to take a trip to the United States to get practical experience within their fields of interest
**Eligibility**: Open to Norwegian citizens only, especially for a Norwegian engineer or architect. The applicant must have worked for at least 3 years after graduation, and he/she must present a detailed plan for the trip when they apply. Also, a budget for the trip must be included as well as references
**Level of Study**: Postgraduate
**Value**: Up to NOK 30,000
**Closing Date**: 15 March

### For further information contact:

The Norway–America Association, Rådhusgaten 23B, N-0158 Oslo, Norway.

**Tel**: (47) 233 571 60
**Fax**: (47) 233 571 75
**Email**: info@noram.no

### American-Scandinavian Foundation Scholarships (ASF)

**Purpose**: To encourage Scandinavians to undertake advanced study and research programmes in the United States
**Eligibility**: Applicants must be citizens of Denmark, Finland, Iceland, Norway or Sweden and have completed their undergraduate degree. They should be fluent in English. Citizens of Finland, Iceland and Norway must apply through the sister-societies in their home country
**Level of Study**: Postgraduate
**Type**: Fellowship
**Value**: The American-Scandinavian Foundation (ASF) offers over US$500,000
**Length of Study**: 1 year
**Frequency**: Annual
**Country of Study**: United States of America
**Application Procedure**: Applicants must complete an application on ASF application forms. More information available on our website - www.amscan.org/fellowships-and-grants/fellowships-and-grants-for-advanced-study-or-research-in-the-usa/
**Funding**: Foundation
**Additional Information**: www.amscan.org/fellowships-and-grants/fellowshipsgrants-to-study-in-scandinavia/

**For further information contact:**

58 Park Ave, New York, NY 10016, United States of America.

| | |
|---|---|
| **Tel**: | (1) 212 879 9779 |
| **Fax**: | (1) 212 249 3444 |
| **Email**: | grants@amscan.org |

## John Dana Archbold Fellowship Program

**Purpose**: To support educational exchange between the United States and Norway

**Eligibility**: Open to citizens of the United States citizens aged 20–35, in good health and of good character. Qualified applicants must show evidence of a high level of competence in their chosen field, indicate a seriousness of purpose, and have a record of social adaptability. There is ordinarily no language requirement

**Level of Study**: Postdoctorate, Postgraduate, Professional development, Research

**Type**: Fellowship

**Value**: Up to US$5,000. Individual grants vary, depending on the projected costs. Note that there will be no tuition at the University of Oslo. The maintenance stipend is sufficient to meet expenses for a single person. The travel allowance covers round trip airfare to Oslo

**Length of Study**: 1 year

**Frequency**: Annual

**Study Establishment**: The University of Oslo

**Application Procedure**: Applicants must write to the Nansen Fund, Inc. for an application form

**Closing Date**: 1 February

**Funding**: Private

**Additional Information**: The University of Oslo International Summer School offers orientation and Norwegian languages courses 6weeks before the start of the regular academic year. For Americans, tuition is paid. Attendance is required. Americans visit Norway in even-numbered years and Norwegians visit the United States in odd-numbered years. For further information please contact the Nansen Fund, Inc grad.uchicago.edu/fellowship/john-dana-archbold-fellowship-in-norway/

**For further information contact:**

| | |
|---|---|
| **Tel**: | (1) 713 680 8255 |
| **Email**: | nacc@net1.net |

## Memorial Fund of 8 May

**Purpose**: To promote cultural exchange between foreign countries and Norwegian residential experiential colleges by providing scholarships for residence, and to help prepare young people for everyday life in the community

**Eligibility**: Open to candidates aged 18–22 years who do not have a permanent residence in Norway, and do not hold a Norwegian passport. Candidates must be planning to return to their home country after a year in Norway. Candidates must be aware of the kind of education the Memorial Fund bursaries cover, that being a year in a Norwegian residential colleges, not admission to education on a higher level, such as a university, or specialized training

**Type**: Scholarship

**Value**: The scholarship will cover board and lodging. In addition it is possible to apply for extra funds. Applicants from some countries may apply for required books and excursions arranged by the school. Also, extra support may be provided for short study trips and short courses before or after the school year. A fixed amount towards spending money may also be given. Normally the students must pay their own travelling expenses. The colleges do not charge tuition fees

**Length of Study**: 1 year

**Frequency**: Annual

**Study Establishment**: Norwegian residential experiential colleges

**Country of Study**: Norway

**Application Procedure**: Applicants must request more information and application forms from the Memorial Fund of 8 May or to the nearest Norwegian Embassy. Applicants who require a scholarship to attend a Norwegian college should not apply to a them directly. In this case, the Board will place successful applicants at a college school based on their hobbies and interest. Residence permits must be applied for by each individual student when a scholarship has been granted

**No. of awards offered**: 700

**Closing Date**: 1 November

**Funding**: Government

**No. of awards given last year**: 25

**No. of applicants last year**: 700

**Additional Information**: A residential experiential college is a 1-year independent residential school, primarily for young adults, offering many non-traditional subjects of study. Each college has its own profile, but as a group, the Norwegian colleges teach classes covering almost all areas, including history, arts, crafts, music, sports, philosophy, theatre, photography etc

**For further information contact:**

IKF, Grensen 9a, N-0159 Oslo, Norway.

| | |
|---|---|
| **Email**: | ikf@ikf.no |

## Norwegian Emigration Fund

**Purpose**: To support for advanced or specialized study in Norway

**Eligibility**: Open to citizens and residents of the United States of America. The fund may also give grants to institutions in the United States of America whose activities are primarily centred on the subjects mentioned

**Level of Study**: Doctorate, Graduate, Professional development

**Type**: Grant

**Value**: NOK 5,000–20,000

**Frequency**: Annual

**Country of Study**: Norway

**Application Procedure**: Applicants must complete an application form and return it clearly marked Emigration Fund to Nordmanns-Forbundet. Applications as well as enclosures will not be returned

**Closing Date**: 1 February

**Funding**: Government

### For further information contact:

**Email**:    norseman@online.no

## Norwegian Marshall Fund

**Purpose**: To provide financial support for Americans to come to Norway to conduct postgraduate study or research in areas of mutual importance to Norway and the United States, thereby increasing knowledge, understanding and strengthening the ties of friendship between the two countries

**Eligibility**: Open to citizens of the United States, who have arranged with a Norwegian sponsor or research institution to pursue a research project or programme in Norway. Under special circumstances, the awards can be extended to Norwegians for study or research in the United States

**Level of Study**: Graduate, Postgraduate

**Type**: Research grant

**Value**: US$1,500–4,500 or NOK 10,000–30,000

**Length of Study**: Varies

**Frequency**: Annual

**Study Establishment**: Norwegian universities

**Country of Study**: Norway

**Application Procedure**: Applicants must contact the Norway-America Association to receive an application. Application forms must be typewritten either in English or Norwegian and submitted in duplicate, including all supplementary materials. Each application must also be accompanied by a letter of support from the project sponsor or affiliated research institution in Norway. There is an application fee of NOK 350

**Closing Date**: 1 April

**Funding**: Private

### For further information contact:

**Tel**:    (47) 233 571 60
**Fax**:    (47) 233 571 75
**Email**:    info@noram.no

## The Norway-America Association Awards

**Eligibility**: Open to Norwegian who wish to study in the United States on the graduate level, must have completed their Bachelor's Degree before applying for these scholarships. The applicants must also be members of the Norway-America Association, and the membership fee is 200 NOK per year

**Level of Study**: Graduate, Research

**Type**: Award

**Value**: US$2,000–20,000

**Application Procedure**: Check website for further details

**Closing Date**: 22 September

**Additional Information**: Norwegians who reside in Norway and plan to return to Norway after graduation are given preference in the selection process, and they cannot have studied for four or more years in the United States Please contact the American-Scandinavian Foundation or the Norway-America Association directly in order to find the appropriate scholarship

### For further information contact:

**Tel**:    (47) 233 571 60
**Fax**:    (47) 233 571 75
**Email**:    info@noram.no

## The Norway-America Association Graduate & Research Stipend

**Purpose**: To give the student substantial financial support for 1 year of studies in the United States

**Eligibility**: Open to Norwegians and members of the Norway-America Association, and he/she must pay 250 NOK in administrative fees and are currently living in Norway, and intend to return to Norway after their graduation

**Level of Study**: Graduate, Research

**Value**: US$2,000–25,000

**Application Procedure**: Check website for further details

**Closing Date**: 22 September

### For further information contact:

**Tel**:    (47) 233 571 60
**Fax**:    (47) 233 571 75
**Email**:    info@noram.no

## The Professional Development Award

**Purpose**: To help established professionals with a higher education who want to study within their own field of interest
**Eligibility**: Open to Norwegian professionals who worked for at least 3 years after finishing his or her education as well as planning on doing special research or further study in their fields
**Level of Study**: Postgraduate
**Type**: Award
**Value**: The award amount can vary but there is a recommended minimum of US$250 and maximum of US$1,000 with only one award per student within a given academic year
**Frequency**: Annual
**Application Procedure**: Check website for further details
**Additional Information**: Candidates must be invited to apply for this award. There is also an administrative fee of 250 NOK, which must be deposited in bank account with number 7878.05.23025. Please contact the American-Scandinavian Foundation or the Norway-America Association directly in order to find the appropriate scholarship

### For further information contact:

**Tel**: (47) 233 571 60
**Fax**: (47) 233 571 75
**Email**: info@noram.no

## The Torskeklubben Stipend

**Purpose**: To promote Norwegian-American relations through helping Norwegians come to the United States to study
**Eligibility**: Open to Norwegians and must already be accepted at the Graduate School at the University of Minnesota before applying for the award
**Level of Study**: Graduate
**Value**: A stipend of US$15,000 for the academic year. For recipients without another source of tuition support, such as an assistantship, the Graduate School Fellowship Office will provide a Tuition Scholarship for full-time study for the academic year
**Frequency**: Annual
**Application Procedure**: Application forms are available upon request from the Norway-America Association and the Graduate School at the University of Minnesota or it can be downloaded from the website
**Closing Date**: 1 March

### For further information contact:

**Tel**: (47) 233 571 60
**Fax**: (47) 233 571 75
**Email**: info@noram.no

## Novo Nordisk A/S

Novo Alle, Bagsvaerd, DK -2880, Denmark.

**Contact**: Director

## National Fellowship and Scholarship for Higher Education of ST Students

**Purpose**: National Fellowship and Scholarship for Higher Education of ST Students is offered by Ministry of Tribal Affairs. This is a central sector scheme for the ST students who are selected for pursuing MPhil and PhD. The application form is available online and students can apply via the link given on this page. The scholarship has emerged as two different schemes i.e. Rajiv Gandhi National Fellowship for ST students and top class education for ST students. The fellowship covers under Rajiv Gandhi National Fellowship programme and scholarship is covered by top-class education
**Eligibility**: 1. Candidates must belong to ST category. 2. Candidates should get registered for the full-time Mphil and PhD course. 3. scholarship, the students must have taken admission in their notified institution. 4. Family income should not exceed more than 6 Lac P/A
**Level of Study**: Postdoctorate
**Type**: Scholarship
**Value**: ₹25,000
**Frequency**: Annual
**Country of Study**: Any country
**Closing Date**: 31 October
**Funding**: Foundation
**Additional Information**: vikaspedia.in/education/policies-and-schemes/scholarships/p-g-and-above-scholarships/national-fellowship-and-scholarship-for-higher-education-of-st-students

### For further information contact:

**Email**: info@vidhyaa.in

## Novo Nordisk Foundation

**Tel**: (45) 3527 6674
**Email**: KEKV@novo.dk
**Contact**: Kirsten Klüver, Grant Administrator

The Novo Nordisk United Kingdom Research Foundation is a charity to support research into diabetes by members of the medical and nursing professions Research fellowships.

## Postdoc Fellowship for Research Abroad

**Purpose**: The Novo Nordisk Foundation invites young, ambitious researchers in Denmark to apply for a post-doctoral fellowship to conduct research within bioscience or basic biomedicine outside of Denmark

**Eligibility**: The applicant must be employed by a research institution in Denmark for the entire fellowship period and this institution must administrate the project grant

**Type**: Fellowship

**Value**: The Novo Nordisk Foundation awards DKK 1 million per year, that is, for a total of up to DKK 4 million/fellowship

**Length of Study**: 4

**Frequency**: Annual

**Country of Study**: Denmark

**Application Procedure**: The application must be completed and submitted using the foundation's electronic application system

**Closing Date**: 1 February

**Contributor**: Novo Nordisk Foundation

**Additional Information**: For more information refer: novonordiskfonden.dk/sites/default/files/information_and_ guidelines_for_applicants_postdoc_fellowship_for_researc.pdf novonordiskfonden.dk/en/grants/postdoc-fellowship-for-rese arch-abroad-bioscience-and-basic-biomedicine/

### For further information contact:

**Email**:    info@novonordiskfonden.dk

## Nuffic

Kortenaerkade 11, 2518 AX Den Haag, PO Box 29777, NL-2502 LT The Hague, Netherlands.

**Tel**:          (31) 70 4260260
**Email**:      nuffic@nuffic.nl
**Website**:   www.nuffic.net

## Netherlands Organization for International Cooperation in Higher Education-Natural Family Planning Fellowships for PhD Studies

**Eligibility**: Candidate must be a national of one of 57 developing countries

**Level of Study**: Doctorate

**Country of Study**: Any country

**Additional Information**: www.european-funding-guide.eu/ other-financial-assistance/14452-nfp-fellowships-phd-studies

# O

## Office of International Affairs at Ohio State University (OIA)

300 Oxley Hall, 1712 Neil Avenue, Columbus, OH 43210-1219, United States of America.

**Tel**: (1) 614 292 4273
**Email**: ladman.1@osu.edu
**Website**: www.oia.osu.edu
**Contact**: Jerry Ladman, Associate Provost for International Affairs

Office of International Affairs at Ohio State University (OIA) is located in the Office of Academic Affairs, for the co-ordination, enhancement and development of Ohio State's international activities. It administers grants programmes for student travel, study and research, faculty travel and research and interdisciplinary lectures, seminars, workshops and conferences.

### Everett And Florence Drumright Scholarship

**Purpose**: The awarding of scholarships is based on a combination of academic merit and financial need. Students in all fields are eligible
**Eligibility**: Check the official website in the following link.
**Level of Study**: Graduate
**Type**: Scholarship
**Value**: US$1,000
**Frequency**: Annual
**Country of Study**: Any country
**Funding**: Private
**Additional Information**: oia.uic.edu/students/funding-resources/oia-and-uic-scholarships/everett-and-florence-drumright-scholarship/

### For further information contact:

509 University Hall (M/C 590), 601 South Morgan Street, Chicago, IL 60607-7128, United States of America.

**Tel**: (1) 312 996 5455
**Email**: oia@uic.edu

## Office of Research & Graduate Education Pfizer Inc

A-300 HSC, Box 35640, Washington DC, 20001–20098, United States of America.

**Tel**: (1) 800 201 1214
**Email**: info@psymark.com
**Website**: www.physicianscientist.com
**Contact**: Dr Albert Berger

Pfizer's Medical and Academic Partnerships provide support for researchers in a range of medical disciplines.

### Pfizer Scholar

**Purpose**: To support research bridging the basic science of epidemiology with clinical medicine
**Eligibility**: Applicants must have completed their clinical training and demonstrate the motivation and ability to conduct original research
**Level of Study**: Postgraduate
**Type**: Grant
**Value**: US$65,000 per year
**Length of Study**: 3 years

© Springer Nature Limited 2020
Palgrave Macmillan (ed.), *The Grants Register 2021*,
https://doi.org/10.1057/978-1-349-95988-4

**Frequency**: Annual
**Study Establishment**: A United States medical school
**Country of Study**: United States of America
**Application Procedure**: Online via the website
**Closing Date**: 9 January
**Funding**: Commercial
**No. of awards given last year**: 2
**Additional Information**: Grantees must plan to conduct their research at a United States academic institution with an experienced mentor www.collegescholarships.org/scholarships/companies/pfizer.htm

### For further information contact:

**Email**:    mzebrowski@metrohealth.org

## Pfizer Scholars Grants in Pain Medicine

**Purpose**: To support physician scientists who wish to pursue basic biomedical research in an academic setting
**Level of Study**: Postgraduate
**Type**: Scholarship
**Value**: US$65,000 per year
**Length of Study**: 2 years
**Frequency**: Annual
**Study Establishment**: United States academic medical institution
**Country of Study**: United States of America
**Application Procedure**: Online via the website
**Closing Date**: 9 January
**Funding**: Commercial
**Additional Information**: Applicants will be selected for the quality of their research proposals, mentioning program and potential for advancing pain medicine

### For further information contact:

**Email**:    mzebrowski@metrohealth.org

## Ohio Arts Council

30 E. Broad St., 33rd Floor, Columbus, OH 43215-3414, United States of America.

**Tel**:         (1) 614 466 2613
**Email**:      webmaster@oac.state.oh.us
**Website**:    www.oac.state.oh.us

The Ohio Arts Council is a state agency that funds and supports quality arts experiences to strengthen Ohio communities culturally, educationally and economically. It was created in 1965 to foster and encourage the development of the arts and assist the preservation of Ohio's cultural heritage.

## Ohio Arts Council Individual Excellence Awards

**Purpose**: To recognize and support the contributions of working artists to the cultural enrichment of the state
**Eligibility**: Open to residents of Ohio who have lived in the state continuously for 1 year before the deadline and continue to remain an Ohio resident during the term of the award. Applicants cannot be students enroled in any degree or certificate granting programme
**Level of Study**: Postgraduate
**Type**: Fellowship
**Value**: US$5,000
**Frequency**: Annual
**Country of Study**: United States of America
**Application Procedure**: Applicants must submit application form B and supporting documents. Guidelines and application forms are available on the OAC website or upon request by writing to the address. All forms must be submitted to the OAC in printed format, rather than electronically
**Closing Date**: 1 September
**Funding**: Government

## Omohundro Institute of Early American History and Culture

PO Box 8781, Williamsburg, VA 23187-8781, United States of America.

**Tel**:        (1) 757 221 1115
**Email**:     martha.howard@wm.edu
**Website**:   oieahc.wm.edu
**Contact**:   Ms Martha Howard, Assistant to the Director and Digital Editor

The Omohundro Institute of Early American History and Culture publishes books in its field of interest, the William and Mary Quarterly and a biannual newsletter, Uncommon Sense. It also sponsors conferences and colloquia and annually awards several predoctoral and postdoctoral fellowships. See www.oieahc.wm.edu for more information

## Omohundro Institute-NEH Postdoctoral Fellowship

**Purpose**: To provide receipt recipients of the PhD a chance to revise and refine their dissertation for eventual publication as a monograph. Fellows also get teaching experience at William & Mary

**Eligibility**: Applicants must meet the following requirements in order to be eligible. Applicants may not have previously published or have under contract a scholarly monograph. Applicants must have met all requirements for the doctorate, including a successful defense, by the application deadline. Foreign nationals must have been in continuous residence in the United States for the three years immediately preceding the date of application for the fellowship in order to be eligible for NEH funding

**Level of Study**: Postdoctorate

**Type**: Fellowship with stipend

**Value**: US$50,400 per year

**Frequency**: Annual

**Study Establishment**: Omohundro Institute

**Country of Study**: United States of America

**Application Procedure**: A principal criterion for selection is that the candidate's dissertation or other manuscript has significant potential as a distinguished, book-length contribution to scholarship. A substantial portion of the work must be submitted with the application. The Omohundro Institute holds first claim on publishing the appointed fellow's completed manuscript. See oieahc.wm.edu/fellowships/neh/ to begin the application process

**No. of awards offered**: 33

**Closing Date**: 1 November

**Funding**: Foundation

**Contributor**: Omohundro Institute and National Endowment of the Humanities

**No. of awards given last year**: 1

**No. of applicants last year**: 33

**Additional Information**: oieahc.wm.edu/fellowships/neh/announcement/

### For further information contact:

P.O. Box 8781, Williamsburg, VA 23186, United States of America.

**Tel**:      (1) 757 221 1114
**Fax**:     (1) 757 221 1047
**Email**:   oieahc@wm.edu

## Oncology Nursing Society Foundation (ONS)

125 Enterprise Drive, Pittsburgh, PA 15275, United States of America.

**Tel**:      (1) 412 859 6100
**Email**:   customer.service@ons.org

**Website**:   www.ons.org
**Contact**:   Director of Research

The mission of the Oncology Nursing Society (ONS) is to promote excellence in oncology nursing and quality cancer care. ONS works to fulfil this mission by providing nurses and healthcare professionals with access to the highest quality educational programmes, cancer care resources, research opportunities and networks for peer support.

## Doctoral Scholarships

**Purpose**: To provide scholarships to registered nurses who are interested in and committed to oncology nursing to continue their education by pursuing a research doctoral degree (PhD or DNSc) or clinical doctoral degree (DNP).

**Eligibility**: 1. The candidate must be currently enrolled in (or applying to) a PhD, DNSc or DNP nursing degree program for the 2020-2021 academic year. 2. The candidate must have a current license to practice as a registered nurse and must have an interest in and commitment to oncology nursing. 3. Two professional letters of support are required. One of these letters must address the applicant's ability to perform doctoral level work. 4. At the end of each year of scholarship participation, the nurse shall submit a summary describing the education activities in which he/she participated.

**Level of Study**: Doctoral

**Type**: Scholarship

**Value**: US$5,000 and US$7,500 annually

**Frequency**: Annual

**Country of Study**: Any country

**Application Procedure**: Apply Online

**Funding**: Private

**Additional Information**: www.onsfoundation.org/funding-for-nurses/education/doctoral-scholarships

### For further information contact:

**Tel**:      (1) 866 257 4667
**Email**:   info@onfgivesback.org

## Master's Scholarships

**Purpose**: To provide scholarships to registered nurses who are interested in and committed to oncology nursing to continue their education by pursuing a master's degree in nursing.

**Eligibility**: 1. The candidate must be currently enrolled in (or applying to) a masters nursing degree at an NLN or CCNE accredited School of Nursing and enrolled in the 2020-2021 academic year. 2. The candidate must have an interest in and commitment to oncology nursing.

**Type**: Scholarship
**Value**: Annually at US$5,000 each
**Frequency**: Annual
**Country of Study**: Any country
**Application Procedure**: Apply Online
**Closing Date**: 1 February
**Funding**: Private
**Additional Information**: www.closerware.com/intake/bo/grant/ApplicationEdit.do?ownerKey=onsf&intakeFormId=13&opportunityId=8459

**For further information contact:**

**Tel**:      (1) 866 257 4667
**Email**:    info@onfgivesback.org

## Oncology Doctoral Scholarships

**Purpose**: To provide scholarships to registered nurses who are interested in and committed to oncology nursing to continue their education by pursuing a research doctoral degree (PhD or DNSc) or clinical doctoral degree (DNP)
**Eligibility**: 1. The candidate must be currently enrolled in (or applying to) a PhD, DNSc or DNP nursing degree program for the current academic year. 2. The candidate must have a current license to practice as a registered nurse and must have an interest in and commitment to oncology nursing
**Level of Study**: Graduate
**Type**: Scholarship
**Value**: Between US$5,000 - US$7,000
**Frequency**: Annual
**Country of Study**: Any country
**Application Procedure**: Two professional letters of support are required. One of these letters must address the applicant's ability to perform doctoral level work. At the end of each year of scholarship participation, the nurse shall submit a summary describing the education activities in which he/she participated
**Closing Date**: July
**Funding**: Private
**Additional Information**: www.onsfoundation.org/funding-for-nurses/education/doctoral-scholarships

**For further information contact:**

**Email**:    info@onfgivesback.org

## Oncology Nursing Society Breast Cancer Research Grant

**Purpose**: To provide funding to support the ONS research agenda, which focuses on areas where gaps exist in the knowledge base for oncology nursing practice

**Eligibility**: Open to the principal investigator who is actively involved in some aspect of cancer patient care, education or research
**Level of Study**: Research
**Type**: Grant
**Value**: US$100,000 for 2 years for the research team
**Length of Study**: 2 years
**Frequency**: Annual
**Country of Study**: United States of America
**Funding**: Foundation
**Contributor**: ONS Foundation
**Additional Information**: Funding preference is given to projects that involve nurses in the design and conduct of the research activity www.onsfoundation.org/funding-for-nurses/community-advocacy/breast-cancer-community-education-grant

**For further information contact:**

125 Enterprise Drive, Pittsburgh, PA 15275, United States of America.

**Email**:    info@onfgivesback.org

## Oncology Nursing Society Foundation Research Grant Awards

**Purpose**: To financially support the principal investigator actively involved in some aspect of care, education or research for patients with cancer
**Eligibility**: The principal investigator must be actively involved in some aspect of cancer patient care, education, or research, and be PhD- or DNSc-prepared or a student working toward one of those research degrees. Funding preference is given to projects that involve nurses in the design and conduct of the research activity and that promote theoretically based oncology practice. Membership in ONS is not required for eligibility
**Level of Study**: Postgraduate
**Type**: Grant
**Value**: Up to US$25,000 each
**Frequency**: Annual
**Country of Study**: United States of America
**Funding**: Foundation
**Additional Information**: Preference is given to projects that involve nurses in the design and conduct of the research activity and that promotes theoretically based oncology practice. For more information, contact the ONS Foundation Research Department www.sigmanursing.org/advance-elevate/research/research-grants/oncology-nursing-society-foundation-grant

## Oncology Research Grant

**Purpose**: These grants support oncology nursing research. Research projects may include pilot or feasibility studies or the development of a new aspect of a program of research. Funding preference is given to research that addresses the ONS Research Priorities and/or the ONS Research Agenda
**Eligibility**: The principal investigator must be actively involved in some aspect of cancer patient care, education, or research, and be PhD- or DNSc-prepared. Funding preference is given to projects that involve nurses in the design and conduct of the research activity and that promote theoretically based oncology practice. Membership in ONS is not required for eligibility
**Level of Study**: Graduate
**Type**: Research grant
**Frequency**: Annual
**Country of Study**: Any country
**Closing Date**: 15 September
**Funding**: Private

### For further information contact:

**Tel**:     (1) 866 257 4667
**Email**:    info@onfgivesback.org

## Sandy Purl Mentorship Scholarship

**Purpose**: To support an additional ONS Chapter member to attend the ONS Chapter Leadership Workshop
**Eligibility**: 1. Must be a current ONS Chapter Board or committee member supported by a Chapter Leader Sponsor. (A Chapter Leader Sponsor is a current Chapter Board member that has agreed the applicant has the approval of the Chapter to attend). 2. Chapter Leaders Sponsors may support more than one individual however grant is restricted to support only one individual. 3. Applicant must share their goal for attending the Chapter Leadership Workshop and how they plan to use the information they gained by attending. Applicant must identify the other Chapter member that is attending the Chapter Leadership Workshop
**Level of Study**: Graduate
**Type**: Scholarship
**Value**: Up to US$1,000
**Frequency**: Annual
**Country of Study**: Any country
**Application Procedure**: 1. Applicant must share their goal for attending the Chapter Leadership Workshop and how they plan to use the information they gained by attending. Kindly view the following link for further details, www.onsfoundation.org/funding-nurses/chapter-funding/sandy-purl-mentorship-scholarship
**Closing Date**: 15 May

**Funding**: Private
**Additional Information**: www.onfgivesback.org/funding-nurses/chapter-funding/sandy-purl-mentorship-scholarship

### For further information contact:

**Email**:    info@onfgivesback.org

## Ontario Council on Graduate Studies (OCGS)

180 Dundas Street, West Suite 1100, Toronto, ON M5G 1Z8, Canada.

**Tel**:        (1) 416 979 2165 ext 212
**Email**:    kpanesar@cou.on.ca
**Website**:  ocgs.cou.on.ca

The Ontario Council on Graduate Studies (OCGS) is an affiliate of the Council of Ontario Universities (COU). OCGS strives to ensure quality research and education across Ontario. In order to achieve this, OCGS conducts quality reviews of research programmes that have been proposed for implementation in Ontario's universities. It also performs quality reviews of existing programmes on a 7-year cycle.

## Women's Health

**Purpose**: To financially support research in and study of women's health at Ontario universities
**Eligibility**: Open to students registered full-time in a Master's or Doctoral graduate programme at an Ontario university and sponsored and endorsed by a Dean of graduate studies at his or her university. For a postdoctoral award, applicants must be engaged in full-time research at an Ontario university at the time of taking up the award
**Level of Study**: Doctorate, Postdoctorate, Postgraduate
**Type**: Award
**Value**: Master's awards - C$25,000 plus C$1,000 research allowance; Doctoral awards - C$35,000 plus C$2,000 research allowance; Postdoctoral awards - C$50,000 plus C$5,000 research allowance
**Length of Study**: 2 year term for Master
**Frequency**: Annual
**Country of Study**: Canada
**Application Procedure**: Applicants must submit their application form, curriculum vitae, a statement of research to be undertaken during the period of graduate or postdoctoral study, transcripts and reference letters. Applications are

available from the Dean's office of Ontario universities or from the website

**Closing Date**: 31 January

**Funding**: Foundation

**Additional Information**: please see the website for further details cou.on.ca/about/awards/ontario-womens-health-scholars/

### For further information contact:

**Email**:     staceym.kwan@utoronto.ca

## Ontario Federation of Anglers & Hunters (OFAH)

4601 Guthrie Drive, PO Box 2800, Peterborough, ON K9J 8L5, Canada.

**Email**:     ofah@ofah.org
**Website**:     www.ofah.org

The Ontario Federation of Anglers & Hunters (OFAH), Canada's leading conservation organization, is a non-profit, registered charity, which is dedicated to protecting woodland and wetland habitat, conserving precious fish and wildlife stocks and promoting outdoor education.

### Oil Natural Air Forced/OFAF Zone 6 Wildlife Research Grant

**Purpose**: To financially support students who wish to pursue their research work in wildlife research

**Level of Study**: Research

**Type**: Fellowship

**Value**: C$2,000

**Frequency**: Annual

**Country of Study**: Canada

**Application Procedure**: 1. Applicants must submit a complete application form, research proposal consisting of abstract, introduction, methods, results anticipated, literature cited and budget, a curriculum vitae, transcripts. 2. Should submit letter from supervising professor supporting the intended research projects

### Ontario Federation of Anglers & Hunters/Oakville and District Rod & Gun Club Conservation Research Grant

**Purpose**: To financially support students who wish to pursue their research work in conservation research

**Level of Study**: Research

**Type**: Research grant

**Value**: C$2,000

**Frequency**: Annual

**Country of Study**: Canada

**Application Procedure**: Applicants must submit a completed application form, research proposal consisting of abstract, introduction, methods, research anticipated, literature cited and budget, curriculum vitae, transcripts and letter from supervising professor supporting the intended research project

**Closing Date**: 31 January

**Additional Information**: www.ofah.org/programs/ofah-student-research-grants/

### For further information contact:

Ontario Federation of Anglers & Hunters, PO Box 2800 / 4601 Guthrie Dr, Peterborough, ON K9J 8L5, Canada.

**Tel**:     (1) 705 748 9577 (6324)
**Fax**:     (1) 705 748 9577

## Ontario Ministry of Education and Training

Correspondence and Public Inquires Unit, 14th Floor, Mowat Block, 900 Bay Street, Toronto, ON M7A 122, Canada.

**Tel**:     (1) 325 2929
**Email**:     info@edu.gov.on.ca
**Website**:     www.edu.gov.on.ca
**Contact**:     OGS Officer

### Ontario Ministry of Education and Training Graduate Scholarship Programme

**Purpose**: To encourage excellence in graduate studies

**Eligibility**: Open to Canadian residents with an overall A-average or equivalent during the previous 2 years of study. 60 awards may be allocated to students holding a student authorization

**Level of Study**: Doctorate, Graduate, MBA

**Type**: Scholarship

**Value**: Approx. C$5,000 per term

**Length of Study**: 2 or 3 consecutive terms of full-time graduate study

**Frequency**: Annual

**Study Establishment**: A university in Ontario

**Country of Study**: Canada

**Application Procedure**: Applicants currently registered at a university in Ontario must submit their applications and supporting documentation through that institution
**Closing Date**: 15 November
**Funding**: Government
**Contributor**: The Ministry of Training, Colleges and Universities
**No. of awards given last year**: 2000
**No. of applicants last year**: 6500
**Additional Information**: Students may hold another award up to Canadian C$10,000 and may accept research assistantships or part-time teaching or demonstrating appointments, providing that the total amount paid to the scholar within the period of the award shall not interfere with their status as full-time graduate students. The total amount of time spent by the student in connection with such an appointment, including preparation, marking examinations, etc. must not exceed an average of 10 hours per week. Students must reapply each year and may receive a maximum of four awards osap.gov.on.ca/OSAPPortal/en/A-ZListofAid/PRDR019245.html

**For further information contact:**

**Email**:     edugrad@uwindsor.ca

## Ontario Student Assistance Program (OSAP)

PO Box 4500, 189 Red River Road, 4th Floor, Thunder Bay, ON P7B 6G9, Canada.

**Tel**:        (1) 807 343 7257
**Website**:   osap.gov.on.ca

Minister of Education and the Minister of Training, Colleges and Universities are responsible for the administration of laws relating to education and skills training in Ontario.

### Ontario Graduate Scholarship Program

**Purpose**: To encourage excellence in graduate studies at the Master's and Doctoral levels
**Eligibility**: Open to students who plan to be enrolled full-time in an approved graduate programme leading to a Master's or Doctoral degree. Candidates must be citizens or permanent residents of Canada
**Level of Study**: Doctorate, Postgraduate
**Type**: Scholarships
**Value**: C$5,000

**Length of Study**: 2 year
**Frequency**: Annual
**Study Establishment**: Some selected universities
**Country of Study**: Canada
**Application Procedure**: Applicants can send in paper or online application. For details see osap.gov.on.ca/eng/not_secure/ogsapply.htm
**Closing Date**: 3 June
**Funding**: Government
**Contributor**: Province of Ontario and the university
**Additional Information**: www.sgs.utoronto.ca/awards/ontario-graduate-scholarship/#section_2

**For further information contact:**

School of Graduate Studies, 63 St. George Street, Room 201, University of Toronto, Toronto, ON 416-946-0808, Canada.

**Tel**:        (1) 416 978 2205
**Email**:      ogs@utoronto.ca

## Open Society Foundation - Sofia

56 Solunska Street, BG-1000, Sofia, Bulgaria.

**Tel**:        (359) 2 930 6619
**Email**:      info@osf.bg
**Website**:    www.osf.bg
**Contact**:    Ms Iliana Bobova, Education Consultant

The goal of the Open Society Foundation network is to promote an open society. The concept of open society is based on the recognition that people act on the basis of imperfect knowledge and nobody is in possession of the ultimate truth. This leads to a respect for the rule of law, to a society which is not dominated by the state, to the existence of democratic government, to a market economy and, above all, to respect for minorities and minority opinions.

### Open Society Institute's Global Supplementary Grant Program (Grant SGP)

**Purpose**: To enable qualified students to pursue doctoral studies in the humanities and social sciences
**Eligibility**: Open to candidates from selected countries from Eastern and Central Europe and the former Soviet Union. Bulgarian nationals under the age of 40 who have been accepted into a full-time doctoral programme at an accredited

university in Western Europe, Asia, Australia or North America and have already been awarded partial or full tuition, room and board stipends or other types of financial aid are also eligible

**Level of Study**: Doctorate

**Type**: Grant

**Value**: 50% of tuition and fees or living expenses or additional expenses

**Length of Study**: Up to 1 year of study with the option to apply for a second year

**Frequency**: Annual

**Study Establishment**: Accredited universities

**Country of Study**: Other

**Application Procedure**: Applicants must complete an application form and provide the required supporting documents

**Closing Date**: 1 April

**Funding**: Private

**Contributor**: The Open Society Institute in New York

**No. of awards given last year**: 22

**Additional Information**: Programme availability and format are reviewed on an annual basis. Changes may occur from year to year. For the most up to date information please contact the Open Society Institute in New York www.european-funding-guide.eu/scholarship/12229-open-society-foundations%C2%A0-%E2%80%93-global-supplementary-grant-program

### For further information contact:

Open Society Institute, Network Scholarship Programs, 400 West 59th Street, New York, NY 10019, United States of America.

**Tel**:       (1) 212 548 0175
**Fax**:      (1) 212 548 4652
**Email**:   vjohnson@sorosny.org

## Oxford Colleges Hospitality Scheme for East European Scholars

**Purpose**: To enable overseas scholars to work in Oxford or Cambridge libraries or to consult Oxbridge specialists in their subjects

**Eligibility**: Open to Scholars from Eastern and Central Europe, who have a good knowledge of English and who are in the process of completing work for an advanced degree, or who are working on a book, or a new course of lectures

**Level of Study**: Professional development

**Type**: Scholarship

**Value**: Full scholarship

**Length of Study**: 1–3 months

**Frequency**: Annual

**Study Establishment**: The University of Oxford and the University of Cambridge

**Country of Study**: United Kingdom

**Application Procedure**: Applicants must submit a completed application form, a curriculum vitae, a list of publications and two recommendation letters

**No. of awards offered**: 45

**Closing Date**: November

**Funding**: Government, Private

**Contributor**: FCO, OSI-Budapest, University of Oxford

**No. of awards given last year**: 7

**No. of applicants last year**: 45

**Additional Information**: Programme availability and format are reviewed on an annual basis. Changes may occur from year to year. For the most up to date information please contact the Open Society Institute in Budapest www.eac.md/scholarships/soros/oxford_hospitality/index.html

### For further information contact:

Open Society Institute, Network Scholarship Programmes, Nador Utca 11, H-1051, Budapest, Hungary.

**Email**:    mariefergusonsmith@hotmail.com

## Organization for Autism Research (OAR)

The Organization for Autism Research (OAR) was created in December 2001 - the product of the shared vision and unique life experiences of OAR's seven founders. Led by these parents and grandparents of children and adults on the autism spectrum, OAR set out to use applied science to answer questions that parents, families, individuals with autism, teachers and caregivers confront daily.

**Tel**:        (1) 866 366 9710
**Email**:     info@researchautism.org
**Website**:   researchautism.org/
**Contact**:   2111 Wilson Boulevard, Suite 401 Arlington, VA 22201

## Applied Research Competition

**Purpose**: Since 2002, the Organization for Autism Research has proudly contributed more than US$4 million in research grants. OAR is currently accepting proposals for its 2020 Applied Research Competition. Through this competition,

OAR intends to promote evidence-based practices delivered from research in the following areas: The analysis, evaluation, or comparison of current models of assessment, intervention, or systems of service delivery, including policy analysis Applied aspects of educational, behavioral, or social/communicative intervention Effective intervention across the lifespan for individuals considered to be severely impacted by autism Adult issues such as continuing education, employment, residential supports, sexuality instruction, quality-of-life determinants, and "later intervention" Issues related to family support, social and community integration, assessment and intervention with challenging behavior, and the use of technology in support of learners with ASD

**Eligibility**: International researchers are eligible to apply. At least one member of the research team must hold a PhD, M.D., or equivalent degree and maintain a faculty position or equivalent at a college, university, medical school, or other research facility

**Level of Study**: postgraduate

**Type**: Grant

**Value**: OAR will consider awarding up to 8 grant awards for US$40,000 each

**Frequency**: Annual

**Country of Study**: United States of America

**Application Procedure**: OAR's Scientific Council and adjunct review panel will evaluate the proposals OAR receives for scientific and technical merit. Review criteria for the evaluation include: Significance - Does the study address an important problem or address the needs of a currently under-served cohort of individuals? How will the study advance scientific knowledge in the field? Can the outcomes be readily translated in support of evidence-based practice? Does it have the potential to impact public policy? Approach - Are the concepts, design, methods, and analyses adequate and appropriate? Are potentially confounding variables accounted for? Innovation - Does the project employ novel approaches or methods? Are its aims original? Does it have the potential to advance our understanding of ASD? Investigator - Is the investigator and/or research team appropriately trained and well-suited to carry out the research? Environment - Does the scientific environment in which the work will be done contribute to its probability of success? Does the work take advantage of any unique features of the environment or employ useful collaborative arrangements? Practical relevance - How relevant is the study and its outcomes to the everyday challenges posed by autism? Does it offer practical findings? Are they generalizable beyond the research setting? Can key components be readily replicated? OAR's Board of Directors makes grant awards based on these evaluations and the recommendations of the Scientific Council. OAR places special emphasis on studies that will likely produce outcomes that are meaningful to the autism community and have potentially broad application to the practical challenges autism presents. Competition. With this year's competition OAR will consider awarding up to 8 grant awards for US$40,000 each. Pre-proposals are due by March 30, at 11:59 PM ET. In June, OAR will invite selected applicants to submit full proposals, complete the final review in November, and announce grant recipients in December. OAR will notify all applicants of their status and offer to share feedback from the review panel after each round of the competition.

**No. of awards offered**: 8

**Closing Date**: 30 March

**Additional Information**: researchautism.org/research-grants/apply-for-a-grant/applied-research/

### For further information contact:

**Tel**:　　(1) 703 243 9762
**Email**:　research@researchautism.org

---

## Organization of American Historians

### Erik Barnouw Award

**Purpose**: To recognize outstanding reporting or programming on network television, cable television or in a documentary film, concerned with American history, the study of American history, and/or the promotion of history

**Level of Study**: Professional development

**Type**: Award

**Frequency**: Annual

**Country of Study**: Any country

**Application Procedure**: Applicants should visit the website for complete application requirements. There is no standard application form and no application fee. Companies are encouraged to enter one or more films in the competition

**No. of awards offered**: 16

**Closing Date**: 7 January

**Funding**: Private

**No. of awards given last year**: 1

**No. of applicants last year**: 16

**Additional Information**: Please check at www.oah.org/programs/awards/erik-barnouw-award/ www.oah.org/awards/uncategorized-awards/erik-barnouw-award/

### For further information contact:

112 North Bryan Avenue, PO Box 5457, Bloomington, IN 47408-5457, United States of America.

**Tel**:　　(1) 812 855 7311
**Email**:　khamm@oah.org

# Organization of American Historians (OAH)

**Tel**:     (1) 812 855 9852
**Email**:   khamm@oah.org
**Website**:  www.oah.org
**Contact**:  Kara Hamm

The Organization of American Historians (OAH) was founded in 1907 as the Mississippi Valley Historical Association and originally focused on the history of the Mississippi Valley. Now, national in scope and with approx. 11,000 members, it is a large professional organization created and sustained for the investigation, study and teaching of American history.

## Avery O. Craven Award

**Purpose**: For the most original book on the coming of the civil war, civil war years or the era of reconstruction, with the exception of works of purely military history
**Type**: Award
**Value**: US$500
**Frequency**: Annual
**Country of Study**: Any country
**Application Procedure**: Applicants must visit the website www.oah.org/activities
**No. of awards offered**: 50
**Closing Date**: 1 October
**Contributor**: OAH
**No. of awards given last year**: 1
**No. of applicants last year**: 50
**Additional Information**: The exception of works of purely military history recognizes and reflects the Quaker convictions of Avery Craven, President of the Organization of American Historians (1963-1964). Please check at www.oah.org/programs/awards/avery-o-craven-award/ for more information www.oah.org/awards/book-awards/avery-o-craven-award/

## China Residency Program

**Purpose**: Thanks to a generous grant from the Ford Foundation, the Organization of American Historians and the American History Research Association of China (AHRAC) are pleased to announce the third year of the teaching seminars in the People's Republic of China
**Eligibility**: The OAH International Committee seeks applications from OAH members with strong records of research and teaching excellence who are interested in leading an advanced seminar in the People's Republic of China, focused on one of the following three topics: constitutional history; cultural/gender history and history of the American West
**Level of Study**: Research
**Type**: Residency
**Length of Study**: 3 week-long intensive seminars
**Frequency**: Annual
**Country of Study**: United States of America
**Application Procedure**: The application consists of a short (3-5 pages) curriculum vitae, the name and contact information of 3 references who can speak to the applicant's teaching and scholarship, and an outline of the proposed intensive week-long seminar. Applications should be submitted electronically, in Microsoft Word format, to prizes@oah.org. Please indicate, China Residency Program in the subject line. If you do not receive an email confirmation that your application has been received within 3 days, please contact the OAH Committee Coordinator at khamm@oah.org or (1) 812 855 9650
**No. of awards offered**: 7
**Closing Date**: 1 October
**No. of awards given last year**: 3
**No. of applicants last year**: 7
**Additional Information**: Applicants are encouraged, if possible, to incorporate into their lectures a perspective of transnational/comparative history and place these topics in the context of American state- and nation-building processes www.artinresidence.it/china-international-artist-residency-program/

### For further information contact:

**Email**:   charlotte.brooks@baruch.cuny.edu

## David Montgomery Award

**Purpose**: For the best book on a topic in American labour and working-class history
**Eligibility**: Eligible works shall be written in English and deal with United States history in significant ways but may include comparative or transnational studies that fall within these guidelines
**Type**: Award
**Frequency**: Annual
**Country of Study**: Any country
**Application Procedure**: One copy of each entry, clearly labelled, David Montgomery Award Entry, must be mailed directly to the committee members listed below. Each committee member must receive all submissions by November 1st
**No. of awards offered**: 39
**Closing Date**: 1 October
**Contributor**: OAH with co-sponsorship by the Labor and Working-Class History Association (LAWCHA)

**No. of awards given last year**: 1
**No. of applicants last year**: 39
**Additional Information**: Each entry must be published during the period January 1st through December 31st. The final decision will be made by the David Montgomery Award Committee by February. The winner will be provided with details regarding the OAH Annual Meeting and awards presentation, where s/he will receive a cash award and a plaque www.oah.org/awards/book-awards/david-montgomery-award/

## For further information contact:

133 West 17th Street, Apartment 5D, New York, NY 10011, United States of America.

## David Thelen Award

**Purpose**: To expose Americanists to scholarship originally published in a language other than english, to overcome the language barrier that keeps scholars apart
**Type**: Award
**Value**: US$500 and the winning article will be printed in The Journal of American History
**Frequency**: Annual
**Country of Study**: Any country
**Application Procedure**: Please refer to the website www.oah.org/programs/awards/david-thelen-award/ The application must contain the following entries. The application should also include the following information: 1. Author's name. 2. Mailing address. 3. Institutional affiliation. 4. E-mail address. Language of submitted article
**No. of awards offered**: 5
**Closing Date**: 1 May
**No. of applicants last year**: 5
**Additional Information**: Please check at www.oah.org/programs/awards/david-thelen-award www.oah.org/awards/article-essay-awards/david-thelen-award/

## For further information contact:

Benjamin H. Irvin, Chair, 2022 David Thelen Award Committee, Executive Editor, Journal of American History, 1215 East Atwater Avenue, Bloomington, IN 47401, United States of America.

**Email**: jahms@oah.org

## Ellis W Hawley Prize

**Purpose**: For the best book-length historical study of the political economy, politics, or institutions of the United States in its domestic or international affairs, from the civil war to the present

**Eligibility**: Eligible works shall include book-length historical studies, written in English and published during a given calendar year
**Type**: Prize
**Value**: US$500
**Frequency**: Annual
**Country of Study**: Any country
**Application Procedure**: Applicants should visit the website for complete application requirements. There is no standard application form and no application fee
**No. of awards offered**: 91
**Closing Date**: 1 October
**No. of awards given last year**: 1
**No. of applicants last year**: 91
**Additional Information**: Please check at www.oah.org/programs/awards/ellis-w-hawley-prize/ www.oah.org/awards/book-awards/ellis-w-hawley-prize/

## Germany Residency Program

**Purpose**: Thanks to a generous grant from the Fritz Thyssen Foundation, the OAH International Committee is pleased to announce the continuation of the Residency Program in American History–Germany (Germany Residency Program) at the University of Tübingen
**Eligibility**: The committee seeks applications from OAH members who are established scholars affiliated with an American or Canadian University interested in leading an advanced undergraduate/graduate student seminar focusing on one aspect of United States History. The Residencies Program will provide round-trip airfare, housing for thirty days, a modest honorarium (around US$1,200), support by a graduate assistant, and office space
**Type**: Residency
**Value**: The Residency Program will provide round-trip airfare, housing for thirty days, a modest honorarium (US$1,500), a graduate assistant, and office space
**Frequency**: Annual
**Country of Study**: Any country
**Application Procedure**: The application process requires a short curriculum vitae, the name and contact information of one reference who can speak to an applicant's teaching and scholarship, and outline of the planned seminar at the University of Tübingen
**No. of awards offered**: 13
**Closing Date**: 1 October
**Funding**: Private
**Contributor**: OAH
**No. of awards given last year**: 1
**No. of applicants last year**: 13
**Additional Information**: You are also welcome to contact Professor Georg Schild georg.schild@uni-tuebingen.de newresidency.com/residency/germany-residency-program

**For further information contact:**

University of Colima, Mexico.

**Email**:    germanyresidency@oah.org

## Huggins-Quarles Award

**Purpose**: For graduate students of color at the dissertation research stage of their PhD programme
**Eligibility**: Open to minority graduate students at the dissertation research stage of their PhD.
**Level of Study**: Postgraduate
**Type**: Award
**Value**: US$1,500 for one award/US$750 each for two awards
**Frequency**: Annual
**Country of Study**: Any country
**Application Procedure**: Applicants should visit the website www.oah.org/activities for complete application requirements. There is no standard application form and no application fee
**No. of awards offered**: 20
**Closing Date**: 1 December
**No. of awards given last year**: 2
**No. of applicants last year**: 20
**Additional Information**: Please check at www.oah.org/programs/awards/huggins-quarles-award/ www.oah.org/awards/dissertation-awards/huggins-quarles-award/

**For further information contact:**

**Email**:    mwitgen@umich.edu

## James A Rawley Prize

**Purpose**: To reward a book dealing with the history of race relations in the United States
**Type**: Prize
**Value**: US$1,000
**Frequency**: Annual
**Country of Study**: Any country
**Application Procedure**: Applicants should visit the website www.oah.org/activities for complete application requirements. There is no standard application form and no application fee. Publishers are encouraged to enter one or more books in the competition
**No. of awards offered**: 76
**Closing Date**: 15 May
**No. of awards given last year**: 1
**No. of applicants last year**: 76
**Additional Information**: Please check at www.oah.org/programs/awards/organization-of-american-historians-oah-james-

a-rawley-prize/ www.historians.org/awards-and-grants/awards-and-prizes/james-a-rawley-prize

**For further information contact:**

400 A Street SE, Washington, DC 20003, United States of America.

**Tel**:      (1) 202 544 2422
**Email**:    awards@historians.org

## Japanese Residencies for United States of America Historians

**Purpose**: To strengthen international and comparative work, to enrich opportunities to engage significant research and to strengthen the study of United States history in Japanese universities
**Level of Study**: Research
**Type**: Residency
**Value**: The award covers round trip airfare to Japan, housing and modest daily expenses
**Frequency**: Annual, if funds are available
**Country of Study**: Japan
**Closing Date**: 15 December
**No. of awards given last year**: 3
**Additional Information**: These short-term fellowships are contingent on funding. Historians in residency are expected to enter into the life of their host university during the course of their brief visit by offering lectures or other public presentations, participating in symposia where appropriate, and consulting with faculty and students www.oah.org/awards/residencies/japan/

**For further information contact:**

**Tel**:      (1) 812 855 7345
**Email**:    john@oah.org

## John Higham Research Fellowship

**Purpose**: This fellowship is open to all graduate students writing doctoral dissertations for a PhD in American history. Applicants pursuing research in those fields most congenial to the research and writing interests of John Higham will receive special consideration
**Eligibility**: No specific eligibility terms
**Level of Study**: Graduate
**Type**: Fellowship
**Frequency**: Annual
**Country of Study**: Any country

**Application Procedure**: Applications are due by midnight (PST) on 3 December. Applications should include the following components: 1. Project proposal of no more than 1,000 words describing the applicant's research project and detailing how the funds will be used. 2. An updated curriculum vitae with a list of the names and addresses of references. 3. Two signed letters of recommendation on official letterhead submitted independently by referees. Letters in the form of a signed PDF should be e-mailed to the chair of the John Higham Research Fellowship Committee at the address listed below. We ask that recommenders use the subject line "Recommendation for [APPLICANT'S NAME]." Complete all application components (including project proposal, names and addresses of recommenders, and curriculum vitae), in a recent version of Microsoft Word or PDF (preferable), and e-mail the entire electronic file to the chair of the John Higham Research Fellowship Committee for the below listed e-mail

**Closing Date**: 2 December

**Funding**: Private

**Additional Information**: www.oah.org/awards/uncategorized-awards/john-higham-fellowship/

**For further information contact:**

Patrick Chung, University of Maryland, College Park, MD 20742, United States of America.; Julian Lim, Arizona State University. Phoenix, AZ 85004, United States of America.

**Tel**:      (1) 812 855 7311
**Email**:   jleroy@ucdavis.edu

## Lawrence W. Levine Award

**Purpose**: To recognize scholarly and professional achievement in the field of American cultural history

**Eligibility**: Open to applicants of any nationality

**Type**: Award

**Value**: US$1,000

**Frequency**: Annual

**Country of Study**: Any country

**Application Procedure**: Applicants must visit the website www.oah.org/activities for complete application requirements. There is no standard application form and no application fee. Publishers are encouraged to enter one or more books in the competition

**No. of awards offered**: 107

**Closing Date**: 1 October

**No. of awards given last year**: 1

**No. of applicants last year**: 107

**Additional Information**: Please check at www.oah.org/programs/awards/lawrence-w-levine-award  www.oah.org/awards/book-awards/lawrence-w-levine-award/

**For further information contact:**

112 N. Bryan Avenue, Bloomington, IN 47408-4141, United States of America.

**Tel**:      (1) 812 855 7311
**Email**:   oah@oah.org

## Louis Pelzer Memorial Award

**Purpose**: For the best essay in American history by a graduate student

**Type**: Award

**Value**: The winning essay will be published in The Journal of American History. The organization offers a prize of US$500

**Frequency**: Annual

**Country of Study**: Any country

**Application Procedure**: Applicants must visit the website www.oah.org/activities for complete application requirements. There is no standard application form and no application fee

**No. of awards offered**: 30

**Closing Date**: 2 December

**No. of awards given last year**: 1

**No. of applicants last year**: 30

**Additional Information**: Please check at www.oah.org/programs/awards/louis-pelzer-memorial-award for more information. The final decision will be made by the Louis Pelzer Memorial Award Committee by February. The winner will be provided with details regarding the OAH Annual Meeting and awards presentation www.oah.org/awards/article-essay-awards/louis-pelzer-memorial-award/

**For further information contact:**

1215 East Atwater Avenue, Bloomington, IN 47401, United States of America.

**Email**:   jahms@oah.org

## Mary Nickliss Prize in United States Women's and/or Gender History

**Purpose**: The Mary Nickliss Prize is given for "the most original" book in United States Women's and/or Gender History (including North America and the Caribbean prior to 1776). The best book recognizes the ideas and originality of the significant historical scholarship being done by historians of United States Women's and/or Gender History and makes a significant contribution to the understanding of United States Women's and/or Gender History

**Eligibility**: Each entry must be published during the calendar year preceding that in which the award is given. The prize will be presented at OAH Annual Meeting in Philadelphia, Pennsylvania, 4-6 April

**Level of Study**: Graduate
**Type**: Award
**Frequency**: Annual
**Country of Study**: Any country
**Application Procedure**: One copy of each entry, clearly labeled "Mary Nickliss Prize Entry" must be mailed directly to the committee members listed below. Each committee member must receive all submissions postmarked by 1 October. If a book carries a copyright date that is different from the publication date, but the actual publication date falls during the correct timeframe making it eligible, please include a letter of explanation from the publisher with each copy of the book sent to the committee members
**Closing Date**: 1 October
**Funding**: Private
**Additional Information**: www.oah.org/awards/book-awards/mary-nickliss-prize/

### For further information contact:

112 N. Bryan Avenue, Bloomington, IN 47408-4141, United States of America.

**Tel**:      (1) 812 855 7311
**Email**:   oah@oah.org

### Merle Curti Award in American Intellectual History

**Purpose**: To recognise books in the fields of american social, intellectual, and/or cultural history
**Type**: Award
**Value**: US$500
**Frequency**: Annual
**Country of Study**: Any country
**Application Procedure**: Applicants must send a copy of each entry to the committee members. Publishers are urged to enter one or more books in the competition. For further application details, candidates should visit the website
**No. of awards offered**: 73
**Closing Date**: 1 October
**Contributor**: OAH
**No. of awards given last year**: 1
**No. of applicants last year**: 73
**Additional Information**: www.oah.org/awards/book-awards/merle-curti-award-intellectual-history/

### For further information contact:

California Institute of Technology, Mail Code 228-77, Caltech Pasadena, CA 91125, United States of America.

### Merle Curti Intellectual History Award

**Purpose**: To recognize books in the fields of American social and intellectual history
**Level of Study**: Graduate
**Type**: Award
**Value**: US$500
**Frequency**: Annual
**Country of Study**: Any country
**Application Procedure**: Applicants must visit the website www.oah.org/activities for complete application requirements. There is no standard application form and no application fee. Publishers are encouraged to enter one or more books in the competition
**No. of awards offered**: 57
**Closing Date**: 1 October
**Funding**: Private
**Contributor**: OAH
**No. of awards given last year**: 1
**No. of applicants last year**: 57
**Additional Information**: Please check at www.oah.org/programs/ www.oah.org/awards/book-awards/merle-curti-award-intellectual-history/

### Merle Curti Social History Award

**Purpose**: One award is given annually to the author of the best book in American social history. Merle Curti was president of the OAH 1951-1952
**Level of Study**: Graduate
**Type**: Award
**Frequency**: Annual
**Country of Study**: Any country
**Application Procedure**: 1. One copy of each entry, clearly labeled "Merle Curti Social History Award Entry," must be mailed directly to the committee members listed below. Each committee member must receive all submissions postmarked by 1 October. 2. Bound page proofs may be used for books to be published after 1 October and before 1 January. If a bound page proof is submitted, a bound copy of the book must be received by each committee member postmarked no later than 7 January. (Please see "Submission Policy") 3. If a book carries a copyright date that is different from the publication date, but the actual publication date falls during the correct timeframe making it eligible, please include a letter of explanation from the publisher with each copy of the book sent to the committee members
**Closing Date**: 1 October
**Funding**: Private
**Additional Information**: The final decision will be made by the Merle Curti Social History Award Committee by February. The winner will be provided with details regarding

the OAH Annual Meeting and awards presentation www.oah. org/awards/book-awards/merle-curti-award-social-history/

## For further information contact:

Data Protection Officer, Organization of American Historians, 112 North Bryan Avenue, Bloomington, IN 47408-4141, United States of America.

**Email**: privacy@oah.org

## Presidents' Travel Fund

**Purpose**: The fund provides travel stipends of up to US$750 for up to five graduate students and recent PhDs in history (no more than four years from date of degree) whose papers or panels/sessions have been accepted by the OAH Program Committee for inclusion on the annual meeting program
**Eligibility**: For more details, check the website.
**Level of Study**: Graduate
**Type**: Other
**Value**: US$750 for five graduate students
**Frequency**: Annual
**Country of Study**: Any country
**Application Procedure**: Please e-mail your paper title or panel title, with an abstract and a CV (indicating your anticipated year of completion of the PhD or the year your PhD was granted), and a paragraph describing why it is important for you to attend the meeting (besides presenting your paper if you are doing so) For further information, check the websitre
**Closing Date**: 3 December
**Funding**: Private
**Additional Information**: www.oah.org/awards/travel-grants/presidents-travel-fund/

## For further information contact:

**Email**: presidentstravelfund@oah.org

## Ray Allen Billington Prize

**Purpose**: To award the best book in American frontier history, defined broadly so as to include the pioneer periods of all geographical areas and comparisons between American frontiers and others
**Type**: Award
**Value**: US$1,000
**Frequency**: Every 2 years
**Country of Study**: Any country
**Application Procedure**: Applicants must visit the website www.oah.org/activities for complete application requirements.

There is no standard application form and no application fees. Publishers are encouraged to enter one or more books in the competition
**No. of awards offered**: 89
**Closing Date**: 1 October
**Contributor**: OAH
**No. of awards given last year**: 1
**No. of applicants last year**: 89
**Additional Information**: Please check at www.oah.org/programs/awards/ray-allen-billington-prize/ www.oah.org/awards/book-awards/ray-allen-billington-prize/

## For further information contact:

Data Protection Officer, Organization of American Historians, 112 North Bryan Avenue, Bloomington, IN 47408-4141, United States of America.

**Email**: privacy@oah.org

## Richard W Leopold Prize

**Purpose**: To improve contacts and interrelationships within the historical profession where an increasing number of history-trained scholars hold distinguished positions in governmental agencies
**Eligibility**: Applicant must have been employed in a government position for at least five years
**Level of Study**: Professional development
**Type**: Prize
**Value**: US$1,500 (last year)
**Frequency**: Every 2 years
**Country of Study**: Any country
**Application Procedure**: Applicants must visit the website www.oah.org/activities for complete application requirements. There is no standard application form and no application fees. Publishers are encouraged to enter one or more books in the competition
**No. of awards offered**: 8
**Closing Date**: 1 October
**No. of awards given last year**: 1
**No. of applicants last year**: 8
**Additional Information**: Please check at www.oah.org/programs/awards/richard-w-leopold-prize/ www.oah.org/awards/book-awards/richard-w-leopold-prize/

## For further information contact:

400 J. L. Seehorn Road, Box 70672, Johnson City, TN 37614, United States of America.

**Email**: privacy@oah.org

## Tachau Teacher of the Year Award

**Purpose**: To recognize the contributions made by precollegiate and classroom teachers to improve history education

**Eligibility**: Precollegiate teachers engaged at least half time in United States history teaching, whether in history or social studies, are eligible. Successful candidates shall demonstrate exceptional ability in one or more of the following kinds of activities: 1. Initiating or participating in projects which involve students in historical research, writing, or other means of representing their knowledge of history. 2. Initiating or participating in school, district, regional, state, or national projects which enhance the professional development of history teachers. 3. Initiating or participating in projects to build bridges between precollegiate and collegiate history or social studies teachers

**Level of Study**: Professional development

**Type**: Award

**Value**: US$500, a one-year OAH membership, a one-year subscription to the OAH Magazine of History and a complimentary registration for the annual meeting. If the winner is an OAH member, the award will include a one-year renewal of membership in the awardee

**Frequency**: Annual

**Country of Study**: Any country

**Application Procedure**: Applicants must visit the website www.oah.org/activities for complete application requirements. There is no standard application form and no application fees. To nominate a teacher, please fill out the nomination form at www.oah.org/programs/awards/tachau-teacher-of-the-year-award/submission-form/

**No. of awards offered**: 2

**Closing Date**: 2 December

**No. of awards given last year**: 1

**No. of applicants last year**: 2

**Additional Information**: Please check at www.oah.org/programs/awards/tachau-teacher-of-the-year-award www.oah.org/awards/uncategorized-awards/tachau-teacher-of-the-year-award/

### For further information contact:

**Email**:  awards@oah.org

## The Japan Residencies Program

**Purpose**: To facilitate scholarly dialogue and contribute to the expansion of scholarly networks among students and professors of American history in America and Japan

**Eligibility**: Applicants must be members of the OAH, have a PhD and be scholars of American history

**Type**: Programme

**Value**: Round-trip airfare to Japan, housing (if the host university cannot offer housing, applicants are expected to pay hotel expenses from the daily stipend) and modest daily expenses

**Frequency**: Annual

**Country of Study**: Any country

**Application Procedure**: Please refer to the website oah.org/programs/residencies/index.html

**No. of awards offered**: 20

**Closing Date**: 1 October

**No. of awards given last year**: 2

**No. of applicants last year**: 20

**Additional Information**: Please check at www.oah.org/programs/residencies/japan www.oah.org/awards/residencies/japan/

### For further information contact:

Kumiko Noguchi, PhD, Associate Professor, Department of International Studies, Meiji Gakuin University, 1 Chome-2-37 Shirokanedai, Minato City, Tokyo 108-8636, Japan.

**Email**:  noguchik@k.meijigakuin.ac.jp

## Willi Paul Adams Award

**Purpose**: For the best book on American history published in a foreign language

**Eligibility**: This prize is not open to books whose manuscripts were originally submitted for publication in English or by people for whom English is their first language

**Type**: Award

**Value**: US$1,250

**Country of Study**: Any country

**Application Procedure**: Applicants must visit the website www.oah.org/activities for complete application requirements. There is no standard application form and no application fees. Publisher are encouraged to enter one or more books in the competition

**No. of awards offered**: 3

**Closing Date**: 1 May

**Contributor**: OAH

**No. of awards given last year**: 1

**No. of applicants last year**: 3

**Additional Information**: Please check at www.oah.org/programs/awards/willi-paul-adams-award/ www.oah.org/awards/book-awards/willi-paul-adams-award/

### For further information contact:

Willi Paul Adams Award Committee, c/o Organization of American Historians, 112 North Bryan Avenue, Bloomington IN 47408-4141, United States of America.

**Fax**:  (1) 812 855 0696

## Organization of American States (OAS)

1889 F Street North West, Washington, DC 20006-3897, United States of America.

| | |
|---|---|
| **Tel**: | (1) 202 458 3000 |
| **Email**: | porta@iacd.oas.org |
| **Website**: | www.oas.org |
| **Contact**: | Administrative Assistant |

### Stanton-Horton Award for Excellence in National Park Service History

**Purpose**: The award recognizes excellence in National Park Service historical efforts that make the NPS a leader in promoting public understanding of and engagement with American history. Please share with us exemplary projects that encourage civic dialogue in all areas of public history

**Level of Study**: Graduate

**Type**: Award

**Frequency**: Annual

**Country of Study**: Any country

**Application Procedure**: For further details on the application process, kindly check with the website. www.oah.org/programs/awards/stanton-horton-award/

**Closing Date**: 3 December

**Funding**: Private

### For further information contact:

**Email**:  saidenberg@gilderlehrman.org

## Oriel College

University of Oxford, Oxfordshire, Oxford, OX1 4EW, United Kingdom.

| | |
|---|---|
| **Tel**: | (44) 1865 276 520 |
| **Email**: | graduate.admissions@oriel.ox.ac.uk |
| **Contact**: | Tutor for Graduates |

### Oriel College: Oriel Graduate Scholarships

**Purpose**: Postgraduate students are an integral part of the Oriel community, and the College seeks to provide financial support and teaching opportunities to help students achieve their goals

**Eligibility**: Open to current graduate students at Oriel College

**Level of Study**: Postgraduate

**Type**: Scholarship

**Value**: Up to £2,500 per year and accommodation rights

**Frequency**: Annual

**Country of Study**: Any country

**Application Procedure**: Benefits of being a postgraduate scholar 1. Stipend. 2. High Table dining rights. 3. Entitlement to College accommodation

**Closing Date**: 31 January

**Funding**: Private

**Additional Information**: www.ianramseycentre.info/blog/Oriel-College-Graduate-Scholarship

### For further information contact:

Oriel College, Oxford, OX14EW, United Kingdom.

| | |
|---|---|
| **Tel**: | (44) 1865 276 555 |
| **Email**: | lodge@oriel.ox.ac.uk |

## Orthopaedic Research and Education Foundation (OREF)

### Grants Programs

**Subjects**: Orthopaedic research

**Purpose**: Orthopaedic Research and Education Foundation offers both Investigator-Initiated and Research Specific Grants. Read each program for details.

**Eligibility**: OREF invites applications for funding for qualified, clinically relevant orthopaedic research projects.

**Type**: Grant

**Value**: US$2,000

**Frequency**: Annual

**Country of Study**: Any country

**Closing Date**: 3 September

**Additional Information**: There are three cycles of funding: September, November or May. There are research-specific grants as well as investigator-initiated grants. See website for details. www.oref.org/grants-and-awards/grant-programs

### OREF Mentored Clinician-Scientist Grant

**Subjects**: Orthopaedic research

**Purpose**: The objective of this grant is to promote the development of new clinician-scientists who have demonstrated success as both a clinician and a researcher. This will allow the investigators to spend dedicated time in research for a period of up to five years to develop a long and productive career in academic surgery.

**Eligibility**: Eligible applicants are orthopaedic surgeons who have received recent K08 or K23 funding from the NIH, or equivalent mentored research funding.

**Level of Study**: Junior Faculty
**Type**: Grant
**Value**: US$20,000 annually, subject to annual review and available funds.
**Length of Study**: Renewable annually for up to five years
**Frequency**: Annual
**Country of Study**: Any country
**Application Procedure**: See website
**Closing Date**: September, November or May
**Additional Information**: www.oref.org/grants-and-awards/grant-programs/general-grants/oref-mentored-clinician-scientist-grant

## Otaru University of Commerce

Business Administration, 3-5-21 Midori, Otaru-shi, Hokkaido 047, Japan.

**Tel**:         (81) 1 3423 1101
**Contact**:   MBA Admissions Officer

### Bamforth Postgraduate Scholarship

**Purpose**: Doctoral scholarships are awarded by the University Council, on the recommendation of the Senate, to candidates proceeding to a course of supervised doctoral study at this University. These scholarships are normally available only to students seeking to obtain their first doctoral qualification. Candidates may be awarded one University of Otago doctoral scholarship only
**Eligibility**: In the case of an applicant for a doctoral scholarship who has completed a Master's degree by papers and thesis (at least 0.75 EFTS), the grades of all relevant advanced level papers counting towards the award of the degree and the thesis will be taken into account. An explanation of the time taken for completion of the thesis may be requested and considered by the Scholarships and Prizes Committee if the thesis has taken more than 2 EFTS (2 fulltime years) to complete
**Level of Study**: Postgraduate
**Type**: Scholarship
**Value**: NZ$27,000
**Length of Study**: 3 year
**Frequency**: Annual
**Country of Study**: New Zealand
**Funding**: Foundation
**Additional Information**: www.otago.ac.nz/study/scholarships/database/otago016138.html

### For further information contact:

**Email**:   scholarships@otago.ac.nz

## Ovarian Cancer Research Fund

### Ann and Sol Schreiber Mentored Investigator Award

**Subjects**: Ovarian cancer research
**Purpose**: The Ann and Sol Schreiber Mentored Investigator Award provides funding for trainees (post-doctoral fellows or clinical fellows) who are working under the supervision of a mentor who is a recognized leader in the field of ovarian cancer research.
**Eligibility**: Applicants must have an MD or a PhD degree.
**Type**: Award
**Value**: The award provides a total of US$75,000 to be used over one or two years
**Length of Study**: One or two years
**Country of Study**: Any country
**Closing Date**: August
**Additional Information**: ocrahope.org/grant/ann-schreiber-mentored-award/

## Oxford Brookes University, School of Business

Wheatley Campus, Wheatley, Oxfordshire, Oxford, OX33 1HX, United Kingdom.

**Tel**:         (44) 1865 485920
**Website**:   www.brookes.ac.uk
**Contact**:   MBA Admissions Officer

### Oxford Brookes University MBA Programme

**Length of Study**: 1 year for the full-time course. 2 years for the part-time course
**Country of Study**: Any country
**Application Procedure**: Applicants must submit an application form, four passport photos, and photocopies of any educational qualifications post 18 years. If candidates do not possess a required qualification, they should send official transcripts from previous colleges attended. Non native English speakers should provide evidence of proficiency in English, such as IELTS and TOEFL scores of 6+ and 550+ respectively. Two references (one academic, one professional) should be sent direct to the school from the referees
**Additional Information**: www.brookes.ac.uk/courses/postgraduate/oxford-brookes-mba/

# P

## Paloma O Shea Santander International Piano Competition

Calle Hernán Cortés 3, E-39003 Santander, Spain.

**Tel**:        (34) 94 231 1451
**Email**:      concurso@albeniz.com
**Website**:    www.concursodepianodesantander.com/
**Contact**:    A Kaufmann, Secretariat General

The Paloma O'Shea Santander International Piano Competition is one of the best rated competitions in the world. It provides an opportunity for exceptionally talented pianists to enhance their careers. The jury is composed of renowned musicians in order to ensure that grants are made in a fair and unbiased manner.

### Gold, Silver and Bronze Medals

**Subjects**: Musical instrument (piano)
**Purpose**: To give support to young pianists of Exceptional talents
**Eligibility**: Competition is open to all pianists born on 1st January, 1994 and after
**Level of Study**: Unrestricted
**Type**: Other
**Value**: Cash prizes totalling more than €90,000
**Frequency**: Varies
**Study Establishment**: ANY
**Country of Study**: Any country
**Application Procedure**: Online application for the 2022 competition www.santanderpianocompetition.com available from June
**No. of awards offered**: 7
**Closing Date**: November
**Funding**: Government, Commercial, Private, Foundation

**No. of applicants last year**: 241
**Additional Information**: Cash prizes totalling more than €90,000; concerts in Spain and abroad; CD recording; online promotion campaign

### For further information contact:

Calle Luis Martínez, 21, E-39005 Santander, Cantabria, Spain.

**Tel**:        (34) 942311451

## Paralyzed Veterans of America (PVA)

801, 18th Street NW, Washington, DC 20006-3517, United States of America.

**Tel**:        (1) 800 555 9140
**Email**:      info@pva.org
**Website**:    www.pva.org

The Paralyzed Veterans of America (PVA), a congressionally chartered veterans service organization founded in 1946, has developed a unique expertise on a wide variety of issues involving the special needs of the members-veterans of the armed forces who have experienced spinal cord injury or dysfunction.

### Paralyzed Veterans of America Fellowships in Spinal Cord Injury Research

**Purpose**: To provide support for research done in the United States or Canadian laboratories and improve the quality of life for individuals with spinal cord injury and spinal cord dysfunction and to find an eventual cure for paralysis

© Springer Nature Limited 2020
Palgrave Macmillan (ed.), *The Grants Register 2021*,
https://doi.org/10.1057/978-1-349-95988-4

**Eligibility**: Open to citizens of the United States
**Level of Study**: Postgraduate, Research
**Type**: Fellowship
**Value**: US$50,000
**Frequency**: Annual
**Country of Study**: United States of America
**Application Procedure**: Applicants must submit curriculum vitae and 10 copies of grant application. Application form, reference letters and budget are required
**Closing Date**: 1 April
**Additional Information**: pva.org/research-resources/research-foundation/

### For further information contact:

**Tel**:　　(1) 202 416 7611
**Email**:　LindsayP@pva.org

## Parapsychology Foundation, Inc.

PO Box 1562, New York, NY 10021-0043, United States of America.

**Tel**:　　　(1) 212 628 1550
**Email**:　　office@parapsychology.org
**Website**:　www.parapsychology.org
**Contact**:　Vice President

Established in 1951, the Parapsychology Foundation acts as a clearing house for information about parapsychology. Essentially an administrative organization, it maintains one of the largest libraries to do with parapsychology, the Eileen J Garret Library, as well as supporting various programmes that include the library, a grant and scholarship programme, a conference and lecture programme, and a speaker's bureau and publishing programme.

### Eileen J Garrett Scholarship

**Purpose**: To assist students attending an accredited college or university in pursuing the academic study of the science of parapsychology
**Eligibility**: 1. Must be an undergraduate student, a graduate student or a postgraduate student. 2. Must attend a university, a four-year college or two-year college. 3. Citizenship requirements: US. 4. Must not be attending high school currently. 5. Must study full-time. 6. Restricted to students studying Social Sciences.

**Level of Study**: Unrestricted
**Type**: Scholarship
**Value**: US$3,000
**Length of Study**: 1 year
**Frequency**: Annual
**Study Establishment**: An accredited college or university
**Country of Study**: Any country
**Application Procedure**: Applicants must submit samples of writings on the subject with an application form from the Foundation. Letters of reference are required from three individuals, familiar with the applicant's work and/or studies in parapsychology
**Closing Date**: 15 July
**Additional Information**: www.petersons.com/scholarship/eileen-j-garrett-scholarship-for-parapsychological-research-111_150558.aspx

### For further information contact:

PO Box 1562, New York, NY 10021-0043, United States of America.

**Tel**:　　(1) 212 628 1550
**Fax**:　　(1) 212 628 1559

## Paris School of International Affairs (PSIA)

27, Rue Saint-Guillaume, F-75007 Paris, France.

**Tel**:　　　(33) 1 4549 5050
**Website**:　www.sciencespo.fr/psia/

In keeping with Sciences Po's centennial tradition of excellence, PSIA offers a cutting-edge education to tomorrow's leaders in international affairs. With 1,300 students coming from 100 countries, taught by world-renowned professors and practitioners, PSIA rises as a vibrant global pulse in Europe and a primary platform for global debate, rooted in the academy.

### Kuwait Program at Sciences Po Excellence Scholarship for Arab Students and Kuwait Nationals

**Purpose**: The Kuwait Program at Sciences Po offers excellence scholarships to students with an interest in the Middle

East who are admitted to PSIA for the current year intake on the programs listed at the website

**Eligibility** These scholarships are awarded on a competitive basis, based on the candidate's excellent academic record and proposed project at Sciences Po. 1. This grant is applicable to the people residing at Gulf countries. 2. Applicants must be first-time degree seeking at France. 3. Applicants must have. i. Submitted a full application to Sciences Po (including all supporting documents and references). ii. Applied to any of the 7 graduate schools of Sciences Po, if any of the two-year Masters program

**Level of Study**: Postgraduate

**Type**: Scholarship

**Value**: Multiple scholarships of up to €10,000 per year will be awarded for the 2 years of study

**Frequency**: Annual

**Country of Study**: Any country

**Application Procedure**: Detailed information on this grant is available on the below file. www.sciencespo.fr/kuwait-program/wp-content/uploads/2018/10/Call-for-applications-2019-Kuwait-Excellence-Scholarship-for-Students-from-the-Arab-World.pdf

**Closing Date**: 16 February

**Additional Information**: The Kuwait Program at Sciences Po (KSP) is a partnership between the Kuwait Foundation for the Advancement of Sciences (KFAS) and Sciences Po, based at the Paris School of International Affairs www.sciencespo.fr/kuwait-program/student-activities/scholarship/

### For further information contact:

27, rue Saint Guillaume, F-75337 Paris Cedex 07, France.

**Tel**:      (33) 1 45 49 50 50
**Email**:    program.kuwait@sciencespo.fr

## Parkinson's United Kingdom

215 Vauxhall Bridge Road, London, SW1V 1EJ, United Kingdom.

**Tel**:      (44) 20 7932 1332
**Email**:    researchapplications@parkinsons.org.uk
**Website**:  www.parkinsons.org.uk
**Contact**:  Ms Bunia Gorelick, Research Grants Manager

Founded in 1969, Parkinson's UK is a charity that focuses on information and support, research, education and training and campaigning.

## Clinician Scientist Fellowship

**Purpose**: To support MDs and other health professionals studying for a PhD.

**Level of Study**: Doctorate

**Value**: Up to £250,000

**Length of Study**: 3 years

**Frequency**: Annual

**Country of Study**: United Kingdom

**Application Procedure**: Please see website

**Additional Information**: mrc.ukri.org/skills-careers/fellowships/clinical-fellowships/clinician-scientist-fellowship-csf/

### For further information contact:

**Email**:    cindy@cmscfoundation.org

## Paul & Daisy Soros Fellowships for New Americans

400 West 59th Street, 4th floor, New York, NY 10019, United States of America.

**Tel**:      (1) 212 547 6926
**Email**:    pdsoros_fellows@sorosny.org
**Website**:  www.pdsoros.org

## The Paul & Daisy Soros Fellowship for New Americans

**Purpose**: To provide opportunities for continuing generations of able and accomplished New Americans to achieve leadership in their chosen fields

**Eligibility**: Open to New Americans: resident aliens (Green Card Holders) naturalized United States citizens and/or children of 2 naturalized parents

**Level of Study**: Postdoctorate

**Type**: Fellowship

**Value**: US$25,000 up to US$20,000 in tuition support for each year

**Length of Study**: 2 years

**Study Establishment**: Any accredited graduate University in the United States

**Country of Study**: United States of America

**Application Procedure**: Apply online

**No. of awards offered**: 77

**Closing Date**: 12 November

**Funding**: Private

**Contributor**: Paul and Daisy Soros

**No. of awards given last year**: 30
**No. of applicants last year**: 77
**Additional Information**: pdsoros-fellowships.fluidreview. com/prog/2020_application/

**For further information contact:**

**Email**:    pdsoros@pdsoros.org

## Paul Lowin Prizes

Perpetual Trustees Australia Limited, 39 Hunter Street, Sydney, NSW 2000, Australia.

**Tel**:         (61) 2 9229 3951
**Email**:      lowinprizes@perpetual.com.au
**Website**:    www.paullowin.perpetual.com.au
**Contact**:    Charitable Planning Services Administration

The Paul Lowin Prizes are administered by the Perpetual Trustees Australia Limited, which is a public trustee company operating in all mainland states of Australia. It is the sole or co-trustee of 360 charitable trusts and foundations with a value of approximately AU$580 million. Income generated from investment of this capital is distributed annually to charitable organisations to fulfil the intent of the trusts under management.

### Paul Lowin Prizes - Song Cycle Prize

**Purpose**: To recognise original composition. For the purposes of the competition, a song cycle is music suitable for chamber performance
**Eligibility**: The composer must be at least 18 years of age and an Australian citizen or a resident of Australia for not less than three years prior to the closing date
**Level of Study**: Unrestricted
**Type**: Prize
**Value**: AU$15,000
**Frequency**: Every 2 years
**Country of Study**: Any country
**Application Procedure**: Applicants must refer to the website for details
**No. of awards offered**: 10
**Closing Date**: 30 June
**Funding**: Private
**No. of awards given last year**: 1
**No. of applicants last year**: 10
**Additional Information**: Works should use no more than one-eight independent vocal lines, which may be accompanied

by up to 10 instrumental players. The text of the work may have a unifying theme, and the composer and the author of the text may or may not be different people, but the author of the text is not eligible for the prize. The work may be no less than 15 minutes and no more than 60 in duration taitmemorialtrust. org/tag/paul-lowin-song-cycle-prize/

**For further information contact:**

Australian Music Centre, Level 4, The Arts Exchange, 18 Hickson Road, Dawes Point, NSW 2000, Australia.

**Email**:    info@australianmusiccentre.com.au

## Peninsula School of Medicine and Dentistry

The John Bull Building, Tamar Science Park, Research Way, Plymouth, PL6 8BU, United Kingdom.

**Tel**:         (44) 1752 437 474
**Email**:      info@psmd.ac.uk
**Website**:    www.pcmd.ac.uk

Peninsula Medical School and Peninsula Dental School have come together in The Peninsula College of Medicine and Dentistry, a partnership with the University of Exeter

### Peninsula College of Medicine and Dentistry PhD Studentships

**Purpose**: To attract PhD candidates of outstanding ability to join their exciting and rapidly expanding programme of internationally rated research
**Eligibility**: Open to the suitably qualified graduates
**Level of Study**: Doctorate
**Type**: Studentship
**Value**: £13,290 (Research Council Rate)
**Frequency**: Dependent on funds available
**Study Establishment**: Peninsula College of Medicine & Dentistry
**Country of Study**: United Kingdom
**Application Procedure**: Check website for the details
**Closing Date**: 8 November
**Contributor**: Various sources
**Additional Information**: scholarship-positions.com/student ship-peninsula-college-of-medicine-dentistry/2007/10/31/

## Penn State, College of Communications

### Call for Proposals: Narratives in Public Communications

**Purpose**: Organizational members use narratives to make sense of the organizational culture. The increased use of narratives in public communication calls for additional research that we hope will help shed new light on their applications and influences in these areas

**Eligibility**: This call therefore seeks grant proposals that will examine the uses and implications of stories and storytelling in public communications

**Level of Study**: Graduate

**Type**: Grant

**Frequency**: Annual

**Country of Study**: Any country

**Application Procedure**: Check the application procedure at the link below. The proposal requires the below information to process further. 1. Narrative (up to 5 pages). 2. Abstract (1 page). 3. Coversheet (1 page). 4. Budget (1 page). Curriculum Vitae or Professional Resume. bellisario.psu.edu/page-center/grants/legacy-scholar-grants/guidelines-for-grant-applications

**Closing Date**: 15 January

**Funding**: Private

**Additional Information**: bellisario.psu.edu/page-center/grants/legacy-scholar-grants/2019-call-for-grant-proposals

### For further information contact:

4 Carnegie Building, University Park, PA 16802, United States America.

**Email**: cuc15@psu.edu

## Perkins School of Theology

Southern Methodist University, PO Box 750133, Dallas, TX 75275-0133, United States of America.

**Tel**: (1) 214 768 8436
**Email**: theology@smu.edu
**Website**: www.smu.edu/perkins

Perkins School of Theology is one of the 13 seminaries of The United Methodist Church (and one of the only 5 university-related United Methodist theological schools), located in the heart of Dallas, Texas, with extension programmes in Houston/Galveston and San Antonio.

### Diaconia Graduate Fellowships

**Purpose**: To supplement the financial resources of United Methodist students

**Eligibility**: Open to consecrated diaconal ministers or ordained deacons and full-time Doctoral students

**Level of Study**: Doctorate

**Type**: Fellowships

**Value**: US$10,000

**Frequency**: Annual

**Application Procedure**: Request for application forms can be sent to theology@smu.edu

**Closing Date**: 31 December

**Contributor**: Section of Deacons and Diaconal Ministries, General Board of Higher Education and Ministry, The United Methodist Church

**Additional Information**: www.collegescholarships.com/scholarships/detail/110106

### For further information contact:

Diaconia Graduate Fellowships Section of Deacons and Diaconal Ministries, PO Box 340007, Nashville, TN 37203-0007, United States of America.

**Tel**: (1) 615 340 7375
**Fax**: (1) 510 649 1730
**Email**: finaid@gtu.edu

## Petro Jacyk Central & East European Resource Centre (PJRC)

University of Toronto, 27 King's College Circle, Toronto, ON M5S, Canada University of Toronto.

**Email**: jacyk.program@utoronto.ca
**Contact**: Petro Jacyk Program for the Study of Ukraine

The PJRC supports the activities of the centre for European, Russian and Eurasian studies, the Department of Slavic Languages and Literatures and the 5 research chairs connected with Estonian, Finnish, Hungarian, Polish History and Ukranian studies.

## Petro Jacyk Program

**Purpose**: The objective of the Post-Doctoral Fellowship is to support annually one of the most promising junior scholars studying contemporary Ukraine and thereby to advance academic understanding of Ukrainian politics, culture, and society

**Eligibility**: The Petro Jacyk Post-Doctoral Fellowship is available to junior scholars in the social sciences and humanities with a research and teaching focus on contemporary Ukraine. The fellowship is open to recently awarded PhDs (persons holding doctorates for no more than three years at the time of application)

**Level of Study**: Postdoctorate

**Type**: Fellowship

**Value**: C$40,000, which includes payment for teaching a - semester-long course, and separately an allowance of up to C$2,500 for research and travel expenses

**Length of Study**: 1 year

**Study Establishment**: University of Toronto

**Country of Study**: Canada

**Application Procedure**: Please send applications by email to: the Foundation at pjef@bellnet.ca and the Petro Jacyk Program for the Study of Ukraine at the University of Toronto at jacyk.program@utoronto.ca simultaneously

**Closing Date**: 1 February

**Contributor**: Petro Jacyk Education Foundation

**Additional Information**: For more information on the post-doctoral fellowship, please visit our website. sites.utoronto.ca/jacyk/postdoctoral www.science-community.org/en/node/161353

## Pfizer

Pfizer MAP Program, MedPoint Communications, 1603 Orrington Ave, Suite 1900, Evanston, IL 60201, United States of America.

| | |
|---|---|
| **Tel**: | (1) 877 254 6953 |
| **Email**: | MAPinfo@clinicalconnexion.com |
| **Website**: | www.pfizermap.com |
| **Contact**: | MAP Program Coordinator |

As a reflection of commitment to the advancement of healthcare, Pfizer Inc. supports medical innovation in a wide range of discipline through its Medical and Academic Partnership (MAP) grants and awards. The Fellowships and Scholar Grants, which offer career-building opportunities for academic researchers in basic, outcomes, and patient-oriented research, are key among these efforts. In addition, Pfizer Visiting Professorships continue to be a resource for in-depth, clinically focused exchange between medical scholars, host organizations and outside scholar-scientists.

## 2020 Acromegaly/Growth Hormone Excess Research

**Purpose**: Pfizer Global Medical Grants (GMG) supports the global healthcare community's independent initiatives (e.g., research, quality improvement or education) to improve patient outcomes in areas of unmet medical need that are aligned with Pfizer's medical and/or scientific strategies. Pfizer's GMG competitive grant program involves a publicly posted Request for Proposal (RFP) that provides detail regarding a specific area of interest, sets timelines for review and approval, and uses an external review panel (ERP) to make final grant decisions. Organizations are invited to submit an application addressing the specific gaps in research, practice or care as outlined in the specific RFP. For all Investigator Sponsored Research (ISRs) and general research grants, the grant requester (and ultimately the grantee) is responsible for the design, implementation, sponsorship, and conduct of the independent initiative supported by the grant, including compliance with any regulatory requirements. Pfizer must not be involved in any aspect of study protocol or project development, nor the conduct or monitoring of the research program.

**Eligibility**: The institution and principal investigator (PI) must be based in one of the eligible countries noted above. 1. Only organizations are eligible to receive grants, not individuals or medical practice groups. 2. The applicant (PI) must have a medical or postdoctoral degree (MD, PhD, or equivalent), an advanced nursing degree (BSN with a MS/PhD), or a degree in Pharmacy, Physiotherapy, or Social Work. 3. Applicant must be affiliated with a host institution 4. Both early career and experienced investigators are encouraged to apply and consideration will be given to all proposals meeting the selection criteria

**Level of Study**: Postgraduate

**Type**: Grant

**Value**: Individual projects requesting up to US$100,000 will be considered. Pfizer anticipates awarding up to 1 grant 1. The amount of the grant Pfizer will be prepared to fund for any project will depend upon the external review panel's evaluation of the proposal and costs involved, and will be stated clearly in the approval notification

**Frequency**: Annual

**Country of Study**: United States of America

**Application Procedure**: 1. Please go to www.cybergrants.com/pfizer/Research and sign in. First-time users should click "Create your password". Requirements for submission: 2. Select the following Competitive Grant Program Name:

2020 RD LAcromegaly/Growth Hormone Excess Research US 3. Complete all required sections of the online application. See Appendix A for additional details 4. If you encounter any technical difficulties with the website, please click the "Technical Questions" link at the bottom of the page

**No. of awards offered**: 1

**Closing Date**: 28 May

**Additional Information**: www.pfizer.com/purpose/independent-grants/competitive-grants

**For further information contact:**

**Email**: amanda.j.stein@pfizer.com

## 2020 Breast Cancer Competitive Research Grant Program

**Purpose**: Pfizer Global Medical Grants (GMG) supports the global healthcare community's independent initiatives (e.g., research, quality improvement or education) to improve patient outcomes in areas of unmet medical need that are aligned with Pfizer's medical and/or scientific strategies. Pfizer's GMG competitive grant program involves a publicly posted Request for Proposal (RFP) that provides detail regarding a specific area of interest, sets timelines for review and approval, and uses an external review panel (ERP) to make final grant decisions. Organizations are invited to submit an application addressing the specific gaps in research, practice or care as outlined in the specific RFP. For all Investigator Sponsored Research (ISRs), general research and medical education grants, the grant requester (and ultimately the grantee) is responsible for the design, implementation, sponsorship, and conduct of the independent initiative supported by the grant, including compliance with any regulatory requirements. Pfizer must not be involved in any aspect of study protocol or project development, nor the conduct or monitoring of the project.

**Eligibility**: The principal investigator (PI) and institution must be based in one of the eligible regions noted above. 1. The applicant (PI) must have a medical or postdoctoral degree (MD, PhD, or equivalent). 2. Applicant must be affiliated with a host institution. 3. Both early career and experienced investigators are encouraged to apply and consideration will be given to all proposals meeting the selection criteria. 4. If the project involves multiple departments within an institution and/or between different institutions/organizations/associations, all institutions must have a relevant role and the requesting organization must have a key role in the project.

**Level of Study**: Postgraduate

**Type**: Grant

**Value**: A total of US$3 million is allocated to this grants program. 1. Applications will be reviewed by an independent review panel. Up to 15 projects will be selected for funding. 2. The amount of the grant Pfizer will be prepared to fund for any project will depend upon the external review panel's evaluation of the proposal and costs involved, and will be stated clearly in the approval notification.

**Frequency**: Annual

**Country of Study**: United States of America

**Application Procedure**: Please go to www.cybergrants.com/pfizer/Research and sign in. Firsttime users should click "REGISTER NOW". Requirements for submission: 1. Select the following Competitive Grant Program Name: 2020 Breast Cancer Competitive Research for AfME, Asia, LatAm 2. Complete all required sections of the online application. See Appendix A for additional details. All applications must be in English. 3. If you encounter any technical difficulties with the website, please click the "Technical Questions" link at the bottom of the page

**Closing Date**: 7 April

**Additional Information**: www.pfizer.com/purpose/independent-grants/competitive-grants

**For further information contact:**

**Email**: Jessica.Romano@pfizer.com

## 2020 Growth Hormone Research

**Purpose**: Pfizer Global Medical Grants (GMG) supports the global healthcare community's independent initiatives (e.g., research, quality improvement or education) to improve patient outcomes in areas of unmet medical need that are aligned with Pfizer's medical and/or scientific strategies. Pfizer's GMG competitive grant program involves a publicly posted Request for Proposal (RFP) that provides detail regarding a specific area of interest, sets timelines for review and approval, and uses an external review panel (ERP) to make final grant decisions. Organizations are invited to submit an application addressing the specific gaps in research, practice or care as outlined in the specific RFP. For all Investigator Sponsored Research (ISRs) and general research grants, the grant requester (and ultimately the grantee) is responsible for the design, implementation, sponsorship, and conduct of the independent initiative supported by the grant, including compliance with any regulatory requirements. Pfizer must not be involved in any aspect of study protocol or project development, nor the conduct or monitoring of the research program.

**Eligibility**: The institution and principal investigator (PI) must be based in one of the eligible countries noted above. 1. Only organizations are eligible to receive grants, not individuals or medical practice groups. 2. The applicant (PI) must have a medical or postdoctoral degree (MD, PhD, or equivalent), an advanced nursing degree (BSN with a MS/PhD), or a degree in Pharmacy, Physiotherapy, or Social Work. 3. Applicant must be affiliated with a host institution 4. Both early career and experienced investigators are encouraged to apply and consideration will be given to all proposals meeting the selection criteria

**Level of Study**: Postgraduate

**Type**: Grant

**Value**: Individual projects requesting up to US$100,000 will be considered. Pfizer anticipates awarding up to 1 grant 1. The amount of the grant Pfizer will be prepared to fund for any project will depend upon the external review panel's evaluation of the proposal and costs involved, and will be stated clearly in the approval notification

**Frequency**: Annual

**Country of Study**: United States of America

**Application Procedure**: Please go to www.cybergrants.com/pfizer/Research and sign in. First-time users should click "Create your password". Requirements for submission: 1. Select the following Competitive Grant Program Name: 2020 RD LPediatric Growth Hormone Deficiency Research US 2. Complete all required sections of the online application. See Appendix A for additional details 3. If you encounter any technical difficulties with the website, please click the "Technical Questions" link at the bottom of the page

**No. of awards offered**: 1

**Closing Date**: 28 May

**Additional Information**: www.pfizer.com/purpose/independent-grants/competitive-grants

**For further information contact:**

**Email**:    amanda.j.stein@pfizer.com

## Global Hemophilia ASPIRE

**Purpose**: Projects that will be considered for Pfizer support will focus on the following areas in Gene Therapy for Hemophilia A or B: Basic Science of Gene Therapy for Hemophilia; Basic Science of TFPI & Anti-TFPI Monoclonal Antibodies; ross talk among regulators (e.g., Protein S being a co-factor for both Protein C and TFPI); AND Patients with MILD Hemophilia A or B.

**Eligibility**: The applicant (PI) must have a medical or postdoctoral degree (MD, PhD, or equivalent), an advanced nursing degree (BSN with a MS/PhD), or a degree in Pharmacy, Physiotherapy, or Social Work.

**Level of Study**: Postdoctoral

**Type**: Grants

**Value**: US$250,000

**Length of Study**: 1 to 2 year

**Frequency**: Annual

**Closing Date**: 31 August

**Additional Information**: pfe-pfizercom-prod.s3.amazonaws.com/Competitive%20Grant%20Program%20RFP_ Research_Hemophilia_GLOBAL.pdf

**For further information contact:**

**Email**:    amanda.j.stein@pfizer.com

## Pfizer Scholar

**Purpose**: To support cancer development in epidemiology

**Eligibility**: Open to individuals who are pursuing research in epidemiology relevant to human health

**Level of Study**: Postgraduate

**Type**: Grant

**Value**: US$130,000

**Length of Study**: 2 years

**Frequency**: Annual

**Country of Study**: Any country

**Application Procedure**: A completed application form must be submitted

**Closing Date**: 6 January

**Funding**: Commercial

**Additional Information**: www.collegescholarships.org/scholarships/companies/pfizer.htm

**For further information contact:**

**Email**:    mzebrowski@metrohealth.org

## Pfizer Scholars Grants in Clinical Epidemiology

**Purpose**: To support the career development of junior faculty

**Eligibility**: Citizens or permanent residents of the United States of America who have a doctoral degree, relevant research experience and postdoctoral clinical training appropriate for the proposed research are encouraged to apply. The applicant should hold a junior faculty position (with 2 years of appointment as an instructor, an assistant professor or an equivalent junior faculty rank) at an accredited academic medical institution

**Level of Study**: Professional development

**Type**: Grant

**Value**: US$195,000

**Length of Study**: 3 years

**Frequency**: Annual

**Country of Study**: United States of America

**Application Procedure**: Applicants must visit the website for full details on the application process
**Closing Date**: 5 January
**Funding**: Corporation
**Contributor**: Pfizer Inc

### For further information contact:

**Email**: mzebrowski@metrohealth.org


## Pfizer Scholars Grants in Clinical Psychiatry

**Purpose**: To support the development of junior faculty
**Eligibility**: Citizens or permanent residents of the United States of America who are junior faculty with a doctoral degree (with 2 years of appointment as an instructor, an assistant professor or an equivalent junior faculty rank) at an accredited academic medical institution are encouraged to apply
**Level of Study**: Professional development
**Type**: Grant
**Value**: US$130,000
**Length of Study**: 2 years
**Frequency**: Annual
**Country of Study**: United States of America
**Application Procedure**: Applicants must visit the website for full details
**Closing Date**: 5 January
**Funding**: Corporation
**Contributor**: Pfizer Inc

### For further information contact:

**Email**: mzebrowski@metrohealth.org


## Pfizer Scholars Grants in Clinical Rheumatology

**Purpose**: To support the career development of junior faculty
**Eligibility**: Citizens or permanent residents of the United States of America who have a doctoral degree, relevant research experience and postdoctoral clinical training appropriate for the proposed research are encouraged to apply. The applicant should hold a junior faculty position (with 2 years of appointment as an instructor, an assistant professor or an equivalent junior faculty rank) at an accredited academic medical institution
**Level of Study**: Professional development
**Type**: Grant
**Value**: Up to US$130,000
**Length of Study**: 2 years
**Frequency**: Annual
**Country of Study**: United States of America

**Application Procedure**: Applicants must visit the website for details on the application process
**Closing Date**: 24 February
**Funding**: Corporation
**Contributor**: Pfizer Inc
**Additional Information**: researchfunding.duke.edu/2020-rheumatology-fellowship-competitive-grant-program

### For further information contact:

**Email**: Amanda.solis@pfizer.com


## Pfizer Scholars Grants in Pain Medicine

**Purpose**: To support the career development of junior faculty
**Eligibility**: Citizens or permanent residents of the United States of America who have a doctoral degree, relevant research experience are encouraged to apply. The applicant should hold a junior faculty position (with 2 years of appointment as an instructor, an assistant professor or an equivalent junior faculty rank) at an accredited academic medical institution
**Level of Study**: Professional development
**Type**: Grant
**Value**: US$130,000
**Length of Study**: 2 years
**Frequency**: Annual
**Country of Study**: United States of America
**Application Procedure**: Applicants must visit the website for details on the application process
**Closing Date**: 5 January
**Funding**: Corporation
**Contributor**: Pfizer Inc

### For further information contact:

**Email**: mzebrowski@metrohealth.org


## Pfizer Visiting Professorships Program

**Purpose**: To create opportunities for selected institutions to invite a distinguished expert for three days of teaching
**Eligibility**: Open to accredited medical schools and/or affiliated teaching hospitals
**Level of Study**: Postgraduate
**Type**: Grant
**Value**: US$7,500 each
**Frequency**: Annual
**Country of Study**: Any country
**Application Procedure**: Applications available online
**Closing Date**: 12 February

**Additional Information**: researchfunding.duke.edu/pfizer-visiting-professorship-program

**For further information contact:**

**Email**: mzebrowski@metrohealth.org

## Transthyretin Amyloidosis (ATTR) Competitive Grant Program/ ASPIRE

**Subjects**: Transthyretin Amyloidosis (ATTR) including cardiomyopathy, peripheral neuropathy, and mixed phenotypes
**Purpose**: The intent of this Request for Proposal (RFP) is to improve the care of patients with ATTR by improving our understanding of disease epidemiology, pathophysiology, early diagnosis, prognosis, and emerging treatment paradigms.
**Eligibility**: Only organizations are eligible to receive grants, not individuals or medical practice groups. The principal investigator (PI) and institution must be based in one of the eligible countries noted above. The applicant (PI) must have a medical or postdoctoral degree (MD, PhD, or equivalent), an advanced nursing degree (BSN with a MS/PhD), or a degree in Pharmacy, Physiotherapy, or Social Work. Applicant must be affiliated with a host institution. Both early career and experienced investigators are encouraged to apply and consideration will be given to all proposals meeting the selection criteria
**Type**: Grant
**Value**: Up to US$75,000
**Country of Study**: United States of America
**Application Procedure**: Go to www.cybergrants.com/pfizer/Research and sign in. First-time users should click "REGISTER NOW"
**No. of awards offered**: Up to four
**Closing Date**: 17 May

## Phi Beta Kappa Society

1606 New Hampshire Avenue NW, Washington, DC 20009, United States of America.

**Tel**: (1) 202 265 3808
**Email**: info@pbk.org
**Website**: www.pbk.org

The Phi Beta Kappa Society has pursued its mission of fostering and recognizing excellence in the liberal arts and sciences since 1776.

## The Mary Isabel Sibley Fellowship

**Purpose**: To recognize female scholars who have demonstrated their ability to carry out original research
**Eligibility**: Candidates must be unmarried women 25–35 years of age who have demonstrated their ability to carry on original research. They must hold a doctorate or have fulfilled all the requirements for a doctorate except the dissertation, and they must be planning to devote full-time work to research during the fellowship year. The award is not restricted to members of Phi Beta Kappa or to United States citizens
**Level of Study**: Doctorate, Postdoctorate, Postgraduate
**Type**: Fellowship
**Value**: US$20,000
**Length of Study**: 1 year, non-renewable
**Frequency**: Annual
**Country of Study**: Any country
**Application Procedure**: Applicants must complete an application form, available from the website, and submit this with transcripts and references
**No. of awards offered**: 50
**Closing Date**: 15 January
**Funding**: Private
**No. of awards given last year**: 1
**No. of applicants last year**: 50
**Additional Information**: researchfunding.duke.edu/mary-isabel-sibley-fellowship-women-scholars-french-or-greek

**For further information contact:**

**Email**: awards@pbk.org

## PhRMA Foundation

### Postdoctoral Fellowship in Health Outcomes Research

**Subjects**: Health outcomes research
**Purpose**: This award supports individuals engaged in a research training program that will extend their credentials in health outcomes research.
**Eligibility**: Applicants (U.S. and non-U.S. citizens) attending schools of medicine, pharmacy, public health, nursing, and dentistry are eligible for this award. Applicants must 1) hold a PhD degree or appropriate terminal research doctorate in a field of study logically or functionally related to the proposed postdoctoral activities or 2) expect to receive the PhD before activating the award.
**Type**: Fellowship
**Value**: US$55,000 per year for stipend only
**Length of Study**: Two year
**Country of Study**: United States of America

**Closing Date**: 3 February
**Additional Information**: www.phrmafoundation.org/2018-awards/post-doctoral-fellowships/health-outcomes/

## Postdoctoral Fellowship in Translational Medicine

**Subjects**: Translational Medicine
**Purpose**: This award supports individuals engaged in multi-disciplinary/collaborative research training programs that will extend their credentials in Translational Medicine.
**Eligibility**: Eligible candidates (U.S. and non-U.S. citizens) will have doctoral degrees, e.g., PhD, D.Sc, D.Eng, MD, and seek to further develop and refine their skills and understanding of Translational Medicine through postdoctoral training. Applicants must write and submit a research plan and provide the mentor's research record, as well as a description of how the mentoring experience will enhance the applicant's career development in Translational Medicine. A key component of Translational Medicine involves collaborative programs that span non-clinical and clinical domains, potentially involving multiple laboratories, advisers, and institutions.
**Type**: Fellowship
**Value**: US$60,000 per year
**Length of Study**: Up to two years
**Frequency**: Varies
**Country of Study**: Any country
**Closing Date**: 3 February
**Additional Information**: www.phrmafoundation.org/2018-awards/post-doctoral-fellowships/translational-medicine/

## Pierre Elliott Trudeau Foundation

**Tel**: (1) 514 938 0001, extension 230
**Email**: competition@trudeaufoundation.ca
**Contact**: Josée St-Martin, Program Director, Doctoral Scholarships

## Pierre Elliott Trudeau Foundation Doctoral Scholarships

**Eligibility**: Open to Canadian citizen, permanent resident of Canada, foreign citizens; full-time first or second year students enrolled (or in the process of enrolling) in a doctoral programe in the humanities and social sciences
**Type**: Scholarship
**Value**: C$40,000 per year; C$20,000 per year for research and travel allowance
**Length of Study**: 3 years
**Country of Study**: Canada
**Closing Date**: November

**Contributor**: Pierre Elliott Trudeau Foundation
**No. of awards given last year**: 15
**Additional Information**: For more details, please visit the Contact Centre: support@cihr-irsc.gc.ca www.trudeaufoundation.ca/en/programs/scholarships/become-scholar

### For further information contact:

**Email**: scholarships@trudeaufoundation.ca

## Pine Tree State 4-H Foundation

### Azure Dillon 4-H Memorial Scholarship

**Eligibility**: The qualified candidate must be: 1. a current member of 4-H (enrolled by 31 December) who is currently active in 4-H activities and. 2. a graduating senior or an individual who has graduated from high school, but has delayed going to college for no more than one year. Candidates are only eligible to apply in the spring prior to entering college
**Level of Study**: Postgraduate
**Type**: Scholarship
**Value**: US$1,000
**Frequency**: Annual
**Country of Study**: Any country
**Application Procedure**: Scholarships are awarded based on a combination of demonstrated academic and 4-H excellence. Recipients will be requested to attend the foundation's annual meeting to receive their scholarship in person
**No. of awards offered**: 1
**Closing Date**: 2 March
**Funding**: Private
**Additional Information**: www.unigo.com/scholarships/by-state/maine-scholarships/azure-dillon-4-h-memorial-scholarship/1470

### For further information contact:

5741 Libby Hall, Room 103, Orono, ME 04469-5741, United States of America.

**Tel**: (1) 207 353 5550

## Plymouth University

Drake Circus, Plymouth, Devon PL4 8AA, United Kingdom.

**Tel**: (44) 1752 600 600
**Email**: prospectus@plymouth.ac.uk
**Website**: www.plymouth.ac.uk

## International Postgraduate Gaza Scholarships

**Purpose**: These scholarships will be awarded on a competitive basis to prospective masters students
**Eligibility**: 1. Be a citizen of Gaza. 2. Be self-funding and classified as overseas for tuition fee purposes. 3. Hold a conditional or unconditional offer from the University of Sheffield before Friday 25 May 2020 to study a full-time postgraduate taught Masters' course starting in September 2020.
**Type**: Scholarship
**Value**: Each scholarship will be for a fee discount of £5,000 on a masters programme at Plymouth University
**Country of Study**: United Kingdom
**Application Procedure**: Please send completed application form as an attachment to internationalscholarships@plymouth.ac.uk along with a copy of your offer letter; a copy of final transcript/marks sheet from undergraduate degree (if final transcript is not available at the time of application please send the most recent or provisional results); a reference letter, from a suitable source, supporting this scholarship application (please do not supply the same reference as that submitted with the postgraduate application). www.plymouth.ac.uk/uploads/production/document/path/5/5758/Gaza Scholarship2016.docx
**Closing Date**: 1 June
**Additional Information**: Please check at www1.plymouth.ac.uk/money/support13-14/Pages/international.aspx#PIS www.sheffield.ac.uk/international/fees-and-funding/scholarships/postgraduate/gaza

### For further information contact:

**Tel**:        (44) 114 222 1319
**Email**:    financialhelp@sheffield.ac.uk

## International Student Merit Scholarship

**Eligibility**: Applicants must have received a conditional offer of a place for a postgraduate taught programme commencing in September and be holding the equivalent of a United Kingdom university 1 class Bachelors degree in a relevant subject
**Type**: Scholarship
**Value**: £2,500
**Country of Study**: United Kingdom
**Application Procedure**: Applicants can apply via email. For detailed information, please visit website
**Closing Date**: 4 May
**Additional Information**: Please check at website www.sheffield.ac.uk/international/fees-and-funding/scholarships/undergraduate/international-undergraduate-merit-scholarship

### For further information contact:

The University of Sheffield, Western Bank, Sheffield, S10 2TN, England.

**Tel**:    (44) 114 222 2000

## International Student PGT Scholarship

**Purpose**: Scholarships are available for international students who wish to study postgraduate taught degree courses
**Eligibility**: Applicants should hold a conditional offer of a place on a postgraduate taught degree programme at Plymouth University. The University will automatically consider applicants with relevant Bachelor degree grades as stipulated in the list. Please note this eligibility criteria list is not exhaustive and graduates from all non-EU countries will be considered for these scholarships. The Bachelor's degree must be the equivalent of a United Kingdom Honours degree, as specified by United Kingdom NARIC. For detailed information, please visit
**Level of Study**: Postgraduate
**Type**: Scholarship
**Value**: £1,500
**Country of Study**: United Kingdom
**Application Procedure**: If the student has applied for a postgraduate taught degree programme, they will automatically be considered for this scholarship if their final transcript or marks sheet was submitted with their application.
**Additional Information**: studyabroad.shiksha.com/scholarships/school-of-management-pgt-scholarship-ma-international-development-management

### For further information contact:

**Tel**:        (44) 1274 236637
**Email**:    scholarships@bradford.ac.uk

## Poets Essayists Novelists American Center

588 Broadway, Suite 303, New York, NY 10012, United States of America.

**Tel**:        (1) 212 334 1660
**Email**:    pen@pen.org
**Website**:  www.pen.org
**Contact**:  Paul W Morris, Awards Director

PEN American Center is a fellowship of writers dedicated to advance literature, depend free expression and foster international fellowship. The American Center is the largest of 145 international PEN centers worldwide.

## The PEN Translation Fund Grants

**Purpose**: The fund seeks to encourage translators to undertake projects they might not otherwise have had the means to attempt

**Eligibility**: Book-length works that have not previously appeared in English in print or have appeared only in an outdated or flawed translation

**Level of Study**: Unrestricted

**Type**: Grant

**Value**: US$2,000–4,000

**Frequency**: Annual

**Country of Study**: Any country

**Application Procedure**: All applications must include the cover sheet and items outlined at www.pen.org/awards

**No. of awards offered**: 140

**Closing Date**: 1 June

**Funding**: Private

**No. of awards given last year**: 11

**No. of applicants last year**: 140

**Additional Information**: Anthologies with multiple translators, works of literary criticism and scholarly or technical texts do not qualify. Translators awarded grants by the fund are ineligible to reapply for 3 years after the year they receive a grant. Please check the website for more details pen.org/pen-heim-grants/

### For further information contact:

PEN Literary Awards, PEN Translation Fund, PEN American Center, 588 Broadway 303, New York, NY 10012, United States of America.

**Email**:   awards@pen.org

## Polycystic Kidney Disease Foundation

9221 Ward Parkway, Suite 400, Kansas City, MO 64114-3367, United States of America.

**Tel**:         (1) 816 931 2600
**Email**:    pkdcure@pkdcure.org
**Website**:  www.pkdcure.org
**Contact**:  Administrative Assistant

The PKD Foundation is the only organization worldwide solely devoted to promoting research into finding a cure for polycystic kidney disease (PKD) and to improving the care and treatment of those affected by it.

## Polycystic Kidney Disease Foundation Grant-In-Aid

**Purpose**: To encourage researchers to conduct research on PKD

**Eligibility**: Research Grants are open to basic and clinical principal investigators with quality projects relevant to finding a treatment and/or cure for PKD. Research Fellowships are open to promising postdoctoral researchers who have the potential to become productive, independent investigators in PKD research

**Level of Study**: Doctorate, Graduate, Postdoctorate, Predoctorate, Research

**Type**: Research grant or fellowship

**Value**: Research Grants: US$65,000 per year; fellowships: US$50,000 per year

**Length of Study**: Two years, renewable for a third year, pending scientific review and availability of funding

**Frequency**: Annual

**Country of Study**: Any country

**Application Procedure**: Application must not exceed a total of 18 pages; otherwise, it will be returned without review. Application guidelines will be available on the PKD foundation website after 1 April. Late applications will not be accepted. Please visit the website for complete application information

**No. of awards offered**: 71

**Closing Date**: 1 August

**Funding**: Private, Corporation, Foundation, Trusts, Individuals

**Contributor**: Individuals

**No. of awards given last year**: 46

**No. of applicants last year**: 71

### For further information contact:

**Email**:   research@pkdcure.org

## Population Council

Policy Research Division, One Dag Hammarskjold Plaza, New York, NY 10017, United States of America.

**Tel**:         (1) 212 339 0500
**Email**:    ssfellowship@popcouncil.org
**Website**:  www.popcouncil.org
**Contact**:  Fellowship Co-ordinator

The Population Council is an international non-profit, non-governmental institution that seeks to improve the well being and reproductive health of current and future generations around the world and to help achieve a humane, equitable and sustainable balance between people and resources. The Council conducts biomedical, social science and public health research and helps build research capacities in developing countries.

## Health and Population Innovation Fellowship Program

**Purpose**: To support mid-career individuals who have innovative ideas and the capacity to help shape public debate in the field of population, rights and reproductive health
**Level of Study**: Postdoctorate, Professional development
**Type**: Fellowship
**Length of Study**: 1 year
**Frequency**: Annual
**Study Establishment**: The Population Council, New Delhi
**Country of Study**: India
**Application Procedure**: Request application form
**Closing Date**: 15 September
**Funding**: Foundation
**Contributor**: John D. and Catherine T. MacArthur Foundation
**No. of awards given last year**: 12
**Additional Information**: nursing.duke.edu/centers-institutes/center-nursing-research/postdoctoral-fellowship-health-innovation

### For further information contact:

Zone 5A, Ground Floor India Habitat Centre, Lodi Road, New Delhi, Delhi 110003, India.

**Tel**:      (91) 11 2464 2901
**Fax**:      (91) 11 2464 2903
**Email**:    fellowships@pcindia.org

## Transmission of Immunodeficiency Viruses: Postdoctoral Research Position

**Additional Information**: www.niaid.nih.gov/about/postdoctoral-research-training

### For further information contact:

Center for Biomedical Research, Population Council, 1230 York Avenue, New York, NY 10065, United States of America.

**Tel**:      (1) 212 327 7794
**Fax**:      (1) 212 327 7764
**Email**:    mpope@popcouncil.org

## Prehistoric Society

Institute of Archaeology, University College London, 31-34 Gordon Square, London, WC1H 0PY, United Kingdom.

**Email**:       prehistoric@ucl.ac.uk
**Website**:    www.prehistoricsociety.org
**Contact**:    Ms Tessa Machling, Administrative Assistant

The Prehistoric Society is open to professionals and amateurs alike and has over 2,000 members worldwide. Its main activities are lectures, study tours and conferences and it publishes an annual journal (PPS) and a newsletter (PAST), which is published 3 times a year.

## Prehistoric Society Conference Fund

**Purpose**: It's aim is to further the development of prehistory as an international discipline. To offer funding to those who might not otherwise be able to travel to an international conference
**Eligibility**: There are no eligibility restrictions
**Level of Study**: Unrestricted
**Type**: Scholarship
**Value**: £200–300
**Frequency**: Annual
**Application Procedure**: Applications from both members and non-members will be considered. Applications may also be made by conference organisers, on behalf of attending scholars. Please check website for application: www.prehistoricsociety.org/grants/conference_fund/
**Closing Date**: 31 January
**Funding**: Private
**Additional Information**: www.prehistoricsociety.org/grants/conference_fund/

### For further information contact:

Administrative Assistant, Prehistoric Society, Institute of Archaeology, 31-34 Gordon Square, London, WC1H 0PY, UK.

## Research Fund

**Purpose**: The Research Grant aims to offer small 'pump-primer' grants to projects in their early stages. A further aim is to give preference to projects showing innovation in the field of prehistory research and to those scholars in the earliest stages of their research careers.
**Level of Study**: Unrestricted

**Type**: Award
**Value**: £100-£1,500 per award
**Frequency**: Annual
**Application Procedure**: Applications will only be considered from members of the society.
**Closing Date**: 31 January
**Funding**: Private
**Additional Information**: www.prehistoricsociety.org/grants/research_fund/

### For further information contact:

Administrative Assistant, Prehistoric Society, Institute of Archaeology, 31-34 Gordon Square, London, WC1H 0PY, UK.

**Email**:    prehistoric@ucl.ac.uk

## The John and Bryony Coles Bursary (Student Travel Award)

**Eligibility**: Applicants must be registered students of archaeology (either part or full time) in the later stages of undergraduate study or in the early years of postgraduate study, or other equivalent status, without restriction on age. All applicants must provide proof of their student status (i.e. a letter from their institution). Student cards will not be accepted.
**Level of Study**: Unrestricted
**Type**: Award
**Value**: £200 and £300 each are usually given each year
**Frequency**: Annual
**Application Procedure**: Applications will only be considered from members of the society.
**Closing Date**: 31 January
**Funding**: Private
**Additional Information**: www.prehistoricsociety.org/grants/the_john_and_bryony_coles_bursary_student_travel_award/

### For further information contact:

Administrative Assistant, Prehistoric Society, Institute of Archaeology, 31-34 Gordon Square, London, WC1H 0PY, UK.

**Email**:    prehistoric@ucl.ac.uk

## President's Commission on White House Fellowships

O.P.M-Sheila Coates, 1900 E.Street, NW, Room B431, Washington, DC 20415, United States of America.

**Tel**:          (1) 202 395 4522
**Email**:      comments@whitehouse.gov
**Website**:  www.whitehouse.gov/fellows
**Contact**:    White House Fellowships

## White House Fellowships

**Purpose**: To offer exceptional young men and women first-handed experience working at the highest levels of the federal government
**Eligibility**: Civilian employees of the Federal government are not eligible
**Level of Study**: Postgraduate
**Type**: Fellowship
**Value**: A full-time, paid assistantship to the Vice President, Cabinet Securities, and other top-ranking government officials
**Length of Study**: 1 year
**Frequency**: Annual
**Study Establishment**: The White House
**Country of Study**: United States of America
**Application Procedure**: Application instructions are available on the website
**Closing Date**: 1 February
**Additional Information**: Please check website for more details www.whitehouse.gov/get-involved/fellows/

### For further information contact:

**Email**:    whitehousefellows@who.eop.gov

## Prime Minister's Research Fellowship

Indian Institute of Technology Hyderabad, Kandi, Sangareddy, Telangana 502285, India.

**Contact**:    The Prime Minister's Research Fellowship

The Government of India is offering Prime Minister's Research Fellowship Scheme for Doctoral Studies (PhD) in IITs and IISc aimed at attracting the best talent.

## Prime Minister's Research Fellowship Scheme

**Purpose**: The Prime Minister's Research Fellowship (PMRF) scheme is aimed at attracting the talent pool of the country to doctoral (PhD) programs of Indian Institutes of Technology (IITs) and Indian Institute of Science (IISc) for carrying out research in cutting-edge science and technology domains, with focus on national priorities

**Eligibility**: Citizens of India are eligible to apply. The candidate should have a very good command of English language. Therefore, the application should be written in English

**Value**: Applicants who fulfill the eligibility criteria, and are finally selected through a selection process, will be offered admission to PhD program in one of IITs/IISc with a fellowship of ₹70,000/- per month for the first two years, ₹75,000/- per month for the 3rd year, and ₹80,000/- per month in the 4th and 5th years. Apart from this, a research grant of ₹2.00 lakh per year will be provided to each of the Fellows for a period of 5 years to cover their academic contingency expenses and for foreign/national travel expenses

**Country of Study**: Any country

**Application Procedure**: Apply online

**Closing Date**: 30 September

**Additional Information**: For more details please visit the website scholarship-positions.com/prime-minister-research-fellowship/2018/02/27/ vikaspedia.in/education/career-guidance/scholarships/prime-minister2019s-research-fellowship

### For further information contact:

**Email**: support@pmrf2018.iith.ac.in

## Prince Charles Hospital Foundation's

Rode Rd, Chermside West, QLD 4032, Australia.

**Tel**: (61) 3 9320 6888
**Website**: www.thecommongood.org.au
**Contact**: Prince Charles Hospital Foundation's

The Prince Charles Hospital is a major teaching hospital in Brisbane's northside with an emphasis in cardiac and respiratory medicine and cardiothoracic surgery. It also has geriatric and rehabilitation services, elective orthopaedic services and cardiothoracic services, an inpatient psychiatric unit and a 16-bed palliative care unit.

## Prince Charles Hospital Foundation's PhD Scholarship

**Purpose**: The aim of the scholarship is to support educational academic research and high-quality research training at TPCH or in the significant partnership with TPCH and its associated community programs. The scholarship provides the applicant with a living stipend to undertake research at or in significant association with, The Prince Charles Hospital

**Eligibility**: Applicants from Australia are eligible to apply for the scholarship. Applicants must be enrolled, or soon to be enrolled, full-time in a PhD program at an Australian University

**Value**: The scholarship will be valued at AU$27,082 per annum. The scholarship provides the applicant with a living stipend to undertake research at or insignificant association with, The Prince Charles Hospital

**Country of Study**: Australia

**Application Procedure**: See the website

**Closing Date**: 23 January

**Additional Information**: For more details please visit the website scholarship-positions.com/prince-charles-hospital-foundations-phd-scholarship-australia/2018/01/09/ www.studydriller.com/prince-charles-hospital-foundations-phd-scholarship-australia-2018/

### For further information contact:

**Email**: Stephanie.Yerkovich@tpchfoundation.org.au

# Q

## Qalaa Holdings Scholarship Foundation (QHSF)

Qalaa Holdings Scholarship Foundation, P.O Box: 29, Cairo EG 11516, Egypt.

**Tel**: (20) 2 2794 5553
**Email**: info@qalaascholarships.org
**Website**: www.citadelscholarships.org/index.html

In 2007, Qalaa Holdings established the Qalaa Holdings Scholarship Foundation (QHSF, previously known as the Citadel Capital Scholarship Foundation) as its flagship CSR project. The firm has endowed the Foundation to grant academic scholarships to talented young Egyptian men and women interested in pursuing Master's degrees and PhDs at international universities.

## Citadel Capital Scholarship

**Purpose**: The Citadel Capital Scholarship Foundation was created in 2007, out of a strong will to contribute to national development through creating high caliber professionals to help enhance Egypt's growth in all sectors
**Eligibility**: Students from Egypt can apply for this Citadel Capital Scholarship
**Level of Study**: Postgraduate
**Type**: Scholarship
**Value**: US$50,000
**Country of Study**: Any country
**Closing Date**: 30 April
**Additional Information**: www.bibalex.org/he_funding/Donors/Details.aspx?ID=54

### For further information contact:

P.O. Box 29, Cairo, 11516, Egypt.

**Tel**: (20) 2 27945553
**Fax**: (20) 2 27926783
**Email**: info@citadelscholarships.org

## Queen Elisabeth International Music Competition of Belgium

20 rue aux Laines, B-1000 Brussels, Belgium.

**Tel**: (32) 2 213 4050
**Email**: info@qeimc.be
**Website**: www.qeimc.be
**Contact**: Secretariat

The Queen Elisabeth International Music Competition of Belgium is a non-profit association, located in Brussels, whose principal aim is to organize major international competitions for music virtuosos. In this way, the competition participates in the Belgian and international music world, and gives its support to young musicians.

## Queen Elisabeth International Music Competition of Belgium

**Purpose**: To provide career support for young pianists, singers, violinists and cellists
**Eligibility**: Open to musicians of any nationality who are at least 17 years of age and not older than 30 years for violin, piano, singing and cellists. The competition is made up of a first round, a semi-final and a final round
**Level of Study**: Unrestricted
**Type**: Competition
**Value**: Prizes, awards and certificates along with cash prizes will be awarded
**Frequency**: Annual

© Springer Nature Limited 2020
Palgrave Macmillan (ed.), *The Grants Register 2021*,
https://doi.org/10.1057/978-1-349-95988-4

**Country of Study**: Any country

**Application Procedure**: Applicants must obtain an application form from the Secretariat of the Competition or via the website

**No. of awards offered**: Unrestricted

**Closing Date**: 10 January

**Funding**: Private

**No. of applicants last year**: Unrestricted

**Additional Information**: There are no master classes with jury members vere.fund/en/competitions/queen-elisabeth-international-violin-competition-of-belgium/

## Queen Margaret University

Queen Margaret University Drive, Musselburgh, Edinburgh, EH21 6UU, United Kingdom.

**Tel**:  (44) 131 474 0000
**Email**:  rilo@qmu.ac.uk
**Website**:  www.qmuc.ac.uk
**Contact**:  Professor Anthony Cohen, Principal

Queen Margaret University provides vocationally relevant education in business and enterprise; drama and creative industries; health, including international health; and social sciences, media and communication. Its internationally recognized research activity informs our teaching. With around 4,500 students, our small size allows us to offer students a highly supportive environment.

## Students Awards Agency for Scotland Postgraduate Students' Allowances Scheme (PSAS)

**Purpose**: International Health Scheme

**Eligibility**: United Kingdom and European Union nationals living in Scotland on the relevant date (conditions apply)

**Level of Study**: Postgraduate

**Value**: Up to £3,400 for full-time students and up to £1,700 for part-time students

**Length of Study**: 2 years, full-time

**Frequency**: Annual

**Study Establishment**: Queen Margaret University College

**Country of Study**: United Kingdom

**Application Procedure**: Applicants must complete an application and send it to the SAAS, once nominated by the institution

**Closing Date**: 31 March

**Funding**: Government

**Contributor**: Students Awards Agency for Scotland (SAAS)

**No. of awards given last year**: 2

**Additional Information**: Students cannot apply directly to the SAAS. They must have accepted an offer of a place and be nominated by the institution www.european-funding-guide.eu/scholarship/11778-saas-postgraduate-students-allowances-scheme-psas

## Queen Mary, University of London

Admissions and Research Student Office, Mile End Road, London, E1 4NS, United Kingdom.

**Tel**:  (44) 20 7882 5555
**Email**:  admissions@qmul.ac.uk
**Website**:  www.qmul.ac.uk
**Contact**:  Mr Peter Smith, Admissions Assistant

Queen Mary is the fourth largest college in the University of London. Located on an attractive campus, it has more than 8,000 students studying in four faculties plus St Bartholomew's and the Royal London School of Medicine and Dentistry. Of these, more than 1,600 are pursuing postgraduate courses or undertaking research.

## ANII Becas

**Purpose**: ANII and Queen Mary have formally partnered to fund Uruguayan Master's and Doctoral students to study at Queen Mary

**Level of Study**: Postgraduate

**Type**: Scholarships

**Value**: Up to US$20,000 per year. Queen Mary offer a 20% discount on Masters tuition fees and a 50% discount on PhD tuition fees for scholars with this funding

**Frequency**: Annual

**Country of Study**: United Kingdom

**No. of awards offered**: 5

**Closing Date**: 18 March

**Additional Information**: www.qmul.ac.uk/scholarships/items/anii-becas.html

### For further information contact:

Queen Mary University of London, Mile End Road, London E1 4NS, United Kingdom.

**Tel**:  (44) 20 7882 5555
**Email**:  scholarships@qmul.ac.uk

## Associate Alumni Bursary

**Eligibility**: 1. Must have studied on an Associate Student Programme since September 2015. 2. The scholarship is available for students applying for programmes running until September 2023. 3. Must have successfully completed their semester or year abroad at Queen Mary. 4. Must enrol on a postgraduate taught programme in the Faculty of Humanities and Social Sciences.
**Level of Study**: Postgraduate
**Type**: Scholarships
**Value**: 20% tuition fee discount
**Frequency**: Annual
**Country of Study**: All countries
**Application Procedure**: Students should submit an application for their programme of study using the following application link: www.qmul.ac.uk/postgraduate/taught/applyfortaughtprogrammes/
**No. of awards offered**: Unlimited
**Additional Information**: www.qmul.ac.uk/scholarships/items/associate-alumni-bursary.html

### For further information contact:

Queen Mary University of London, Mile End Road, London E1 4NS, United Kingdom.

**Tel:** (44) 20 7882 5555
**Email:** scholarships@qmul.ac.uk

## BASF (Ludwigshafen/Germany)

**Purpose** BASF (Ludwigshafen/Germany) are offering three fee waivers
**Level of Study**: Postgraduate
**Type**: Scholarships
**Value**: Value £9,150 each
**Frequency**: Annual
**Country of Study**: United Kingdom
**No. of awards offered**: 2
**Closing Date**: 1 May
**Additional Information**: For further information about the programme, and to apply, please visit: www.qmul.ac.uk/postgraduate/taught/coursefinder/courses/121436.html www.qmul.ac.uk/scholarships/items/basf-ludwigshafengermany-.html

### For further information contact:

Queen Mary University of London, Mile End Road, London E1 4NS, United Kingdom.

**Tel:** (44) 20 7882 5555
**Email:** r.goerner@qmul.ac.uk

## Business and Management Postgraduate Scholarships

**Purpose**: Awards for outstanding students enrolling on a full time Master's programme in the School of Business and Management
**Level of Study**: Postgraduate
**Type**: Scholarships
**Value**: £2,000
**Frequency**: Annual
**Country of Study**:United Kingdom
**Application Procedure**: There is no separate application for this scholarship. We will consider all applicants that have achieved a UK first class honours degree (or equivalent), and those who are on course to achieve a First. Applicants must be domiciled in one of the 15 eligible countries
**No. of awards offered**: 50
**Closing Date**: March
**Additional Information**: www.qmul.ac.uk/scholarships/items/business-and-management-postgraduate-scholarships.html

### For further information contact:

Queen Mary University of London, Mile End Road, London E1 4NS, United Kingdom.

**Tel:** (44) 20 7882 5555
**Email:** Scholarships@qmul.ac.uk

## Herchel Smith Scholarship in Intellectual Property

**Eligibility**: New PhD students undertaking full-time research in the area of Intellectual Property (IP) can apply for a Herchel Smith Scholarship to start in the academic year. Open to both United Kingdom and non-European Union applicants
**Type**: Scholarship
**Value**: The award will cover all tuition fees whether at the Home/European Union rate or the overseas rate. In addition, an award of around £15,000 per year (reviewed annually) will be paid to the recipient on a monthly basis throughout the calendar year starting from September
**Length of Study**: 3 years
**Frequency**: Annual
**Application Procedure**: Submit online application at www.law.qmul.ac.uk/postgraduate/funding/phd-ip/index.html
**Closing Date**: 1 June
**Additional Information**: www.scholarshiproar.com/intellectual-property-phd/

### For further information contact:

**Email:** g.skehan@qmul.ac.uk

## Historic Royal Palaces Heritage Scholarships

**Purpose**: Historic Royal Palaces (HRP) wishes to make careers in the heritage sector more accessible to people from UK-resident Black, Asian, and Minority Ethnic (BAME) communities to help ensure everyone feels the palaces are for them and make them accessible and relevant for all.

**Eligibility**: The scholarships will cover your part-time course fees

**Level of Study**: Postgraduate

**Type**: Scholarships

**Value**: £12,273 per annum

**Frequency**: Annual

**Country of Study**: United Kingdom

**Application Procedure**: Please read the full guidance notes and instructions on how to apply for the scholarship here: www.qmul.ac.uk/media/scholarships/documents/BAME-scholarships-application-procedure-guidance-and-information-(2020).docx

**No. of awards offered**: 2

**Closing Date**: 3 July

**Additional Information**: The part-time application form can be found via the www.qmul.ac.uk/postgraduate/taught/coursefinder/courses/heritage-management-ma/ www.qmul.ac.uk/scholarships/items/historic-royal-palaces-heritage-scholarships.html

### For further information contact:

Queen Mary University of London, Mile End Road, London E1 4NS, United Kingdom.

**Tel**:        (44) 20 7882 5555
**Email**:    john.davis@hrp.org.uk

## Marshall Scholarships

**Purpose**: The QMUL Marshall Scholarship offers support for candidates wishing to pursue up to two years of postgraduate study, on any Masters or PhD programme across the University. A third year of funding may be available for students engaged in doctoral degrees.

**Eligibility**: The award is open to US citizens

**Level of Study**: Postgraduate

**Type**: Scholarships

**Value**: Full tuition and living costs.

**Frequency**: Annual

**Country of Study**: United Kingdom

**Application Procedure**: Applications are made online directly to the: www.marshallscholarship.org/applications/apply

**No. of awards offered**: Up to 2 each year

**Additional Information**: www.qmul.ac.uk/scholarships/items/marshall-scholarships.html

### For further information contact:

Queen Mary University of London, Mile End Road, London E1 4NS, United Kingdom.

**Tel**:        (44) 207882 6484
**Email**:    scholarships@qmul.ac.uk

## Snowdon Masters Scholarship

**Purpose**: The scholarship has been designed to identify and accelerate talented disabled individuals through higher education.

**Level of Study**: Postgraduate

**Type**: Scholarships

**Value**: Up to £30,000

**Length of Study**: 1 year

**Frequency**: Annual

**Country of Study**: United Kingdom

**Application Procedure**: Apply online: forms.office.com/Pages/ResponsePage.aspx?id=DQSIkWdsW0yxEjajBLZtrQAAAAAAAAAAAFKIHENsu9UQUhaSllBTjYySTgySjhaTVMxMllUMERQQy4u

**Contributor**: Snowdon Trust

**Additional Information**: www.qmul.ac.uk/scholarships/items/snowdon-masters-scholarship.html

### For further information contact:

Queen Mary University of London, Mile End Road, London E1 4NS, United Kingdom.

**Tel**:        (44) 20 7882 5555

## Queen's Nursing Institute

3 Albemarle Way, London, EC1V 4RQ, United Kingdom.

**Tel**:          (44) 20 7549 1400
**Email**:      rosemary.cook@qni.org.uk
**Website**:  www.qni.org.uk
**Contact**:   Anne Pearson, Practice Development Manager

The Queen's Nursing Institute works to support and develop new and best nursing practice and innovation in primary care. Through this support we want to ensure that patients receive the highest standard of nursing in the community. Primary care has always been the highest priority and the Queen's Nursing Institute firmly believes in working in partnership with nurses to achieve its overall objectives.

## Queen's Nursing Institute Fund for Innovation and Leadership

**Purpose** Implementation of good practice, or a project or an idea, within the community
**Level of Study**: Graduate, Postgraduate
**Type**: A variable number of grants
**Value**: Up to £5,000
**Length of Study**: 1 year
**Frequency**: Annual
**Country of Study**: United Kingdom
**Closing Date**: 17 October
**No. of awards given last year**: 12

## Queen's University of Belfast

Postgraduate Office, Research and Regional Services, Lanyon North, Belfast, BT7 1NN, United Kingdom.

**Tel**:     (44) 28 9027 2585
**Email**:     pg.office@qub.ac.uk
**Website**:     www.qub.ac.uk
**Contact**:     Ms C Farrell

The Queen's University of Belfast has provided a stimulating environment for postgraduate students since the 1850s. It has a reputation as a centre of academic excellence, embracing the most effective technologies and techniques of the 21 century. It offers over 130 postgraduate courses and research opportunities in more than 60 different research areas.

## International Office Postgraduate Scholarship

**Purpose**: All new International students beginning their first year of full-time postgraduate taught study in Queen's University Belfast in September who meet the conditions of their academic offer will receive an International Office Postgraduate Taught Scholarship
**Eligibility**: 1. NI/EU/GB Undergraduate students. 2. NI/EU/GB Postgraduate Taught students. 3. International Undergraduate Students. 4. International Postgraduate Students
**Level of Study** Postgraduate
**Type**: Award
**Value**: £3,000
**Length of Study**: 1 year

**Frequency**: Annual
**Country of Study**: Any country
**Application Procedure**: Apply online
**Closing Date**: 14 March
**Funding**: International office
**Additional Information**: www.qub.ac.uk/International/International-students/International-scholarships/postgraduate-research-scholarships/international-office-postgraduate-research-scholarship/

### For further information contact:

**Email**:     internationalscholarships@qub.ac.uk

## International PhD Awards

**Purpose**: To pursue PhD programme
**Value**: Each award is valued at approximately £20,000
**Country of Study**: Any country
**Application Procedure**: For online application, please visit website dap.qub.ac.uk/portal/user/u_login.php
**Closing Date**: 1 May
**Additional Information**: uwaterloo.ca/graduate-studies-postdoctoral-affairs/awards/international-doctoral-student-award-idsa

### For further information contact:

**Email**:     G.ODonnell@qub.ac.uk

## Kyle Scholarship

**Type**: Residency
**Country of Study**: Any country
**Application Procedure**: For application procedure, please visit website scholarship-positions.com/kyle-scholarships-queens-university-belfast-uk/2018/04/14/. To apply for a programme, complete the online application for study form at: dap.qub.ac.uk/portal/ and receive an Offer of Study
**Closing Date**: 6 March
**Additional Information**: This award can be made in conjunction with other awards. The successful applicant must agree to produce a short report of their year to be shared with the donor at the end of their studies. During their studies, they must also deliver a presentation to students interested in taking an LLM at Queen's www.utrpro.com/kyle

### For further information contact:

4501 W. 38th Street, Indianapolis, IN 46254, United States of America.

**Email**:     law.office@qub.ac.uk

## Leverhulme (LINCS) PhD Scholarship

**Purpose**: To support pioneering research at the interface between the social sciences and electronic engineering and computer science
**Eligibility**: 1. Applicants must hold a minimum 2 Class Upper Degree (2:1) or equivalent qualification in a relevant Technology, Social Science or Humanities Based subject. 2. Applicants must be a United Kingdom or European Union citizen. 3. Applications from non-United Kingdom or non-European Union citizens may be accepted on an exceptional basis but additional funding to cover International student fees is not available and must be secured by the applicant prior to starting. 4. Applicants must be proficient in both writing and speaking in English
**Type**: Scholarship
**Value**: Full tuition fees at standard United Kingdom rates (currently £4,195 per annum) for 3 years; a maintenance award at the Research Councils United Kingdom national rate. £1,000 per annum research training and expenses to fund the costs of study abroad, conference attendance and fieldwork
**Frequency**: Annual
**Country of Study**: United Kingdom
**Closing Date**: 15 January
**Additional Information**: worldscholarshipforum.com/fully-funded-leverhulme-scholarship-queens-university-belfast-uk-20182019/

## Mary McNeill Scholarship in Irish Studies

**Purpose**: To fund one selected candidate for an MA in Irish Studies programme
**Eligibility**: Open to well-qualified United States of America or Canadian students enrolled in the MA (Irish Studies) programme
**Level of Study**: Postgraduate
**Type**: Scholarship
**Value**: £3,000
**Length of Study**: 1 year, full-time
**Frequency**: Annual
**Study Establishment**: Queen's University of Belfast
**Country of Study**: United Kingdom
**Application Procedure**: Applicants must contact the Institute of Irish Studies, for an application form
**Closing Date**: 31 May
**Additional Information**: For further information visit the website or contact the Institute of Irish studies www.qub.ac.uk/International/International-students/Your-Country/USA/Finance-fees-and-scholarships/mcneill-scholarship/

### For further information contact:

**Tel**:      (44) 28 9097 3386
**Email**:   irish.studiesequb.ac.uk

## PhD Studentships in Astrophysics Research Centre

**Purpose**: These scholarships are available for students wishing to undertake a PhD in the Astrophysics Research Centre
**Type**: Studentship
**Value**: £21,300
**Country of Study**: United Kingdom
**Application Procedure**: Applications for post-graduate studies must be made via the QUB portal
**Closing Date**: 9 February
**Contributor**: Queen's University Belfast
**Additional Information**: star.pst.qub.ac.uk/wiki/doku.php/public/phds2020

### For further information contact:

**Email**:    s.sim@qub.ac.uk

## Queen's Loyalty Scholarship

**Purpose**: The Queen's Loyalty Scholarship is a 20% reduction on first year gross tuition fees available to Exchange, Summer School and Study Abroad students paying International tuition rates progressing for a full duration undergraduate programme in September
**Eligibility**: Students must hold an offer of a place on a full-time and complete duration programme at the Queen's University Belfast campus, starting in the academic year and meet any academic and language conditions attached to their offer as stated in their offer letter. Students must be classified as international fee-paying students paying the international tuition fee rate in order to be considered for this discount. Students paying NI/GB/EU fees are not eligible for the Queen's Loyalty Scholarship. For further information check the website.
**Level of Study**: Graduate
**Type**: Scholarship
**Value**: 20% tuition fee reduction on year 1
**Country of Study**: Any country
**Closing Date**: 31 October
**Additional Information**: www.qub.ac.uk/International/International-students/International-scholarships/postgraduate-research-scholarships/queens-loyalty-scholarship/

### For further information contact:

Queen's University Belfast 2020, University Road, Belfast, BT7 1NN, Northern Ireland, United Kingdom.

**Tel**:      (44) 28 9024 5133
**Email**:   international@qub.ac.uk

## Vice-Chancellor's International Attainment Scholarship

**Purpose**: Two full tuition fee scholarships are available to exceptionally talented international students paying international tuition fee rates who will be starting their full- time Postgraduate Taught programme at Queen's University Belfast in September 2020

**Eligibility**: Students must hold an offer for a place on a full-time eligible postgraduate taught programme starting in the academic year 2020-21 at the Queen's University Belfast campus which has been confirmed as their FIRM choice, and prior to commencement of study have met any academic and language conditions attached to their offer as stated in their offer letter

**Level of Study**: Postgraduate

**Type**: Scholarship

**Value**: Full tuition fees paid for up to a maximum of two years

**Country of Study**: Any country

**Closing Date**: 12 May

**Additional Information**: Please follow the link below for further information on how to apply to study at Queen's: www.qub.ac.uk/International/International-students/Applying/

### For further information contact:

Queen's University Belfast 2020, University Road, Belfast, BT7 1NN, Northern Ireland, United Kingdom.

**Tel**:     (44) 28 9024 5133
**Email**:   internationalscholarships@qub.ac.uk

## Queensland University of Technology (QUT)

Research Students Centre, GPO Box 2434, Brisbane, QLD 4001, Australia.

**Tel**:     (61) 7 3138 4475
**Email**:   research.enquiries@qut.edu.au
**Website**: www.rsc.qut.edu.au

QUT provides a career-oriented education which helps graduates find employment in their chosen career, in an environment which uses the latest technology to make learning stimulating and enjoyable. It provides information for students, staff and visitors about the resources of the University, its facilities and processes.

## Australian Postgraduate Award Industry Scholarships within Integrative Biology

**Eligibility**: Open to citizens of Australia or permanent residents having Honours 1 Degree or equivalent

**Level of Study**: Postgraduate

**Type**: Scholarship

**Value**: AU$25,627

**Length of Study**: 3 years

**Frequency**: Annual

**Application Procedure**: Check website for further details

**Closing Date**: 2 March

**Additional Information**: scholarship-positions.com/australian- postgraduate-award-industry-apai-phd-scholarship/2009/03/31/

### For further information contact:

School of Integrative Biology, 286 Morrill Hall, MC-120 University of IL 505 S. Goodwin Ave., Urbana, IL 61801, United States of America.

**Email**:   susanne.schmidt@uq.edu.au

## Australian Research Council Australian Postgraduate Award Industry – Alternative Engine Technologies

**Purpose**: The multidisciplinary nature of the project will provide the student with a significant intellectual challenge, to assimilate the required background research and to integrate this knowledge to achieve the aims of the current project

**Eligibility**: Open to citizens of Australia or New Zealand or permanent residents who have achieved Honours 1 or equivalent, or Honours 2a or equivalent

**Level of Study**: Postdoctorate, Postgraduate

**Type**: Scholarship

**Value**: AU$26,140 per year

**Length of Study**: 3 years

**Frequency**: Annual

**Country of Study**: Australia

**Application Procedure**: Check website for further details

**Closing Date**: 28 September

**Additional Information**: Please check website for more details

### For further information contact:

**Tel**:     (61) 7 3138 5174
**Email**:   rong.situ@qut.edu.au

## Institute of Health and Biomedical Innovation Awards

**Purpose**: To support living expenses
**Eligibility**: Open for citizens of Australia or permanent residents who have achieved Honours 1 or equivalent, or Honours 2a or equivalent
**Level of Study**: Doctorate, Postgraduate
**Type**: Award
**Value**: AU$36,140
**Length of Study**: 2 years (Masters) or 3 years (PhD)
**Frequency**: Annual
**Country of Study**: Australia
**Application Procedure**: Check website for further details
**Closing Date**: 12 October

### For further information contact:

**Tel**:     (61) 7 3138 6056
**Fax**:     (61) 7 3138 6039
**Email**:    s.winn@qut.edu.au

## International Postgraduate Research Scholarship at Queensland University of Technology

**Eligibility**: Applicants should be applying to study a PhD, masters by research, or professional doctorate. They should have a minimum first class honours or equivalent. Applicants should not have previously held an Australian Government-funded research scholarship for more than 6 months
**Type**: Postgraduate scholarships
**Value**: It includes tuition fees and health-cover costs for the selected candidate and his/her dependents. Selected candidate may also be considered for an Australian Postgraduate Award living allowance scholarship
**Country of Study**: Australia
**Application Procedure**: Applicants should apply for admission to QUT during the Annual Scholarship Round. An indication should be provided on the application for admission that one wishes to be considered for a scholarship
**Closing Date**: 30 September
**Additional Information**: studentexp.cecs@anu.edu.au scholarship-positions.com/phd-scholarship-for-international-students-at-the-queensland-university-of-technology-in-australia-2020/2019/12/16/

# R

## Radboud University Nijmegen

Houtlaan 4, 6525 XZ Nijmegen, The Netherlands.

**Tel:** (31) 24 361 6161
**Website:** www.ru.nl/english

## Nijmegen

Houtlaan 4, NL-6525 XZ Nijmegen, The Netherlands.

**Tel:** (31) 24 361 61 61
**Email:** info@communicatie.ru.nl
**Website:** www.ru.nl/english

Radboud University Nijmegen was established on 17 October 1923 under the name Catholic University Nijmegen. With their own university, Dutch Catholics sought to promote the emancipation of Roman Catholics in the Netherlands, who at that time were strongly underrepresented in public administration, the legal profession, medicine and other sectors. The Radboud Foundation was the body behind this initiative. Today, Radboud University continues its commitment to the emancipation of certain groups. For example, the University has an above average percentage of female professors, compared to other Dutch universities. And of all the general universities, it has the highest relative number of students for whom neither parent had a university education (source: WO-instroommonitor, 1999-2000 t/m 2014-2015).

## Radboud Scholarship Programme

**Purpose:** The Radboud Scholarship Programme offers a select number of talented prospective non-EEA students the opportunity to receive a scholarship to pursue a complete English-taught Master's degree programme at Radboud University

**Eligibility:** You will only be eligible to obtain a Radboud Scholarship if you: 1. hold a non-EU/EEA passport. 2. are not eligible for the lower EEA tuition fee for other reasons. 3. have (will obtain) a Bachelor's degree achieved outside the Netherlands, have no degrees achieved in the Netherlands and did not receive any previous education in the Netherlands. 4. have a high level of language proficiency. 5. have been fully admitted to the English-taught Master's degree programme starting 01 September as stated in the formal letter of admission. 6. are able to comply with the conditions for obtaining a visa for the Netherlands

**Level of Study:** Graduate
**Type:** Scholarship
**Frequency:** Annual
**Country of Study:** Any country
**Application Procedure:** From the eligible candidates the Radboud Scholarship holders will be selected based on the following criteria: 1. Talent: this means that you must have outstanding study results in your present field of study. 2. You are expected to be a promising student in your desired field of study at Radboud University. 3. Proven academic quality and good results of your prior education for example through grades, test scores, publications. 4. Quality of the recommendations in the two reference letters. 5. Motivation: based on your motivation letter for the Master's progamme
**Closing Date:** 1 March
**Funding:** Private
**Additional Information:** www.ru.nl/english/education/masters-programmes/international-masters-students/financial-matters/scholarships-grants/read_more/rsprogramme/

### For further information contact:

Radboud University Houtlaan 4, NL-6525 XZ Nijmegen, The Netherlands.

**Tel:** (31) 24 361 61 61
**Email:** scholarships@ru.nl

© Springer Nature Limited 2020
Palgrave Macmillan (ed.), *The Grants Register 2021*,
https://doi.org/10.1057/978-1-349-95988-4

## Radboud Scholarship Programme for International Students

**Purpose**: The Radboud Scholarship Programme offers a selected number of talented prospective non-EEA students the opportunity to receive a scholarship to pursue a complete English-taught Master's degree programme at Radboud University.

**Eligibility**: You will only be eligible to obtain a Radboud Scholarship if you: hold a non-EU/EEA passport are not eligible for the lower EEA tuition fee for other reasons have (will obtain) a Bachelor's degree achieved outside the Netherlands, have no degrees achieved in the Netherlands and did not receive any previous education in the Netherlands have been fully admitted to the English-taught Master's degree programme starting 1 September 2020 as stated in the formal letter of admission are able to comply with the conditions for obtaining a visa for the Netherlands are enrolled at Radboud University as a full-time student for the academic year and Master's degree programme for which the scholarship will be awarded.

**Level of Study**: Masters Degree

**Type**: Scholarships

**Value**: The scholarship will be used to reduce the tuition fee to €2,143 and pays for costs for visa and insurance. For example: a grant holder in 2020/2021 will pay a tuition fee of only €2,143, instead of €11,471 or €12,645. In addition the Radboud Scholarship also covers costs such as those for visa, residence permit, health insurance and liability insurance (Insurance Passport for Students (IPS)). The Radboud Scholarship is not a full scholarship and does not include living costs. In the case of a two-year programme: to qualify for the grant during the second year, you need to have passed all courses in the first year.

**Length of Study**: 2 year

**Frequency**: Annual

**Country of Study**: Netherlands

**Application Procedure**: The application for admission and the application for the scholarship is fully integrated, there is no separate procedure for the scholarship. You apply for a Radboud Scholarship by indicating during your application for admission that you wish to apply for a Radboud Scholarship

**No. of awards offered**: About 30 each year

**Closing Date**: 1 March

**Additional Information**: www.ru.nl/english/education/masters/international-and-european-law/vm/scholarships-and-grants/scholarships/rsprogramme/

### For further information contact:

**Email**:    scholarships@ru.nl.

## Radboud Scholarships Programme for Masters Students

**Purpose**: The Radboud Scholarship Programme offers a select number of talented prospective non-EEA students the opportunity to receive a scholarship to pursue a complete English-taught Master's degree programme at Radboud University Nijmegen

**Eligibility**: Applicants will be eligible to obtain a Radboud Scholarship if they hold a non-EU/EEA passport; are not eligible for the lower EEA tuition fee for other reasons; have been fully admitted to the English-taught Master's degree programme as stated in the formal letter of admission; are able to comply with the conditions for obtaining a visa for the Netherlands; are enroled at Radboud University as a full-time student for the academic year and Master's degree programme for which the scholarship will be awarded

**Level of Study**: Graduate

**Type**: Scholarship

**Value**: The scholarship consists of a partial tuition waiver. The tuition fee will be waived to the level of an EEA student. In addition the Radboud Scholarship also covers costs such as those for visa, residence permit, health insurance and liability insurance. This amounts to about €700. For detailed information

**Country of Study**: The Netherlands

**Application Procedure**: The application for admission and the application for the scholarship is fully integrated, there is no separate procedure for the scholarship. Applicants must apply for a Radboud Scholarship by indicating during their application for admission that they wish to apply for a Radboud Scholarship. Applicants will then be requested to upload three additional documents including two recommendation letters and a curriculum vitae. Applicants also must have finalized their request for admission before the deadline

**Closing Date**: 1 April

**Additional Information**: For more information about the scholarship programme, contact the International Office on rsp@io.ru.nl www.ru.nl/english/education/masters-programmes/international-masters-students/financial-matters/scholarships-grants/read_more/rsprogramme/

### For further information contact:

**Email**:    rsp@io.ru.nl

## Radcliffe Institute for Advanced Study

Byerly Hall, 8 Garden Street, Cambridge, MA 02138, United States of America.

**Tel**:        (1) 617 495 8212
**Email**:    alison_ney@radcliffe.harvard.edu

**Website**:    www.radcliffe.edu
**Contact**:    Administrator of Fellowships

The Radcliffe Institute for Advanced Study is a scholarly community where individuals pursue advanced work across a wide range of academic disciplines, professions and creative arts. Within this broad purpose, the Radcliffe Institute sustains a continuing commitment to the study of women, gender and society.

## Radcliffe Institute Fellowship

**Purpose**: The Radcliffe Institute for Advanced Study at Harvard University awards 50 funded residential fellowships each year designed to support scholars, scientists, artists, and writers of exceptional promise and demonstrated accomplishment
**Eligibility**: For eligibility guidelines, please refer to our application portal
**Level of Study**: Postdoctorate
**Type**: Fellowship
**Value**: US$77,500
**Length of Study**: September-May
**Frequency**: Annual
**Country of Study**: Any country
**Application Procedure**: Please refer to our webpage for more information: www.radcliffe.harvard.edu/fellowship-program/how-apply
**Closing Date**: 12 September
**Funding**: Private, Individuals
**Additional Information**: radcliffe.onlineapplicationportal.com/

## Radiological Society of North America, Inc. (RSNA)

820 Jorie Boulevard, Oak Brook, IL 60523-2251, United States of America.

**Tel**:        (1) 630 571 2670
**Email**:     swalter@rsna.org
**Website**:   www.rsna.org/foundation
**Contact**:   Mr Scott Walter, Assistant Director, Grant Administration

The Research and Education Foundation of the Radiological Society of North America (RSNA) provides grant support to medical students, residents, Fellows and full-time faculty members of departments of radiology, radiation oncology and nuclear medicine.

## Medical Student Research Grant

**Purpose**: This R&E Foundation grant gives medical students the opportunity to gain research experience in medical imaging while they're still in school. Recipients will define objectives, develop research skills and test hypotheses,
**Eligibility**: 1. You must be an RSNA member to apply for the Medical Student Research Grant. If you're a non dues-paying member, your scientific advisor or your co-investigator must be a dues-paying member. You must also meet the following criteria. 2. You must be a full-time medical student at an accredited North American medical school. 3. You must commit to work full-time for at least 10 weeks on your research project. 4. Your research project must take place in a department of radiology, radiation oncology or nuclear medicine in a North American medical institution, but this doesn't have to be the same institution where you're enrolled as a student. 5. You cannot have been a principal investigator on a grant or contract totaling more than US$60,000 in a single year. This includes single and combined grants and contracts from government, private and commercial sources. 6. You and your principal investigators cannot be employed by any for-profit, commercial company in the radiologic sciences. 7. You cannot submit more than one grant application to the RSNA R&E Foundation a year, and cannot have a concurrent RSNA grant. 8. Funding from other grant sources must be approved by foundation staff if it wasn't described in the original research plan
**Level of Study**: Research
**Type**: Research grant
**Frequency**: Annual
**Country of Study**: Any country
**Application Procedure**: For detailed information, check the following link, ektron.rsna.org/uploadedFiles/RSNA/Content/R_and_E_Foundation/Grants_and_Awards/RMS_Policies Procedures.pdf
**Closing Date**: 1 February
**Funding**: Private
**Additional Information**: www.rsna.org/en/research/funding-opportunities/research-grants/medical-student-research-grant

### For further information contact:

820 Jorie Blvd., Suite 200 Oak Brook, IL 60523-2251, United States of America.

**Email**:     rmurray@rsna.org

## Radiological Society of North America Education Seed Grant

**Purpose**: To provide funding opportunities for individuals with an active interest in radiologic education

**Eligibility**: Applicants must hold a faculty position in a department of radiology, radiation oncology, or nuclear medicine within a North American, educational institution and must have completed advanced training and be certified by the American Board of Radiology (or equivalent), or on track for certification. Applicants must not have received grant/contract amounts totaling US$50,000 or more in a single calendar year as principal investigator

**Level of Study**: Research

**Type**: Grant

**Value**: Up to US$40,000 to support the preliminary or pilot phase of education projects, not to supplement major funding already secured. No salary support for the principal investigator will be provided

**Frequency**: Annual

**Country of Study**: Any country

**Application Procedure**: Application can be submitted online

**Closing Date**: 10 January

**Funding**: Foundation

**Additional Information**: www.rsna.org/en/research/funding-opportunities/research-grants/research-seed-grant

### For further information contact:

**Email**:    rmurray@rsna.org

## Radiological Society of North America Institutional Clinical Fellowship in Cardiovascular Imaging

**Purpose**: To provide opportunities for radiologists early in their careers to gain experience and expertise in cardiovascular imaging

**Eligibility**: Open to citizens or permanent residents of a North American country who have completed their residency training in the radiological sciences. Fellows must also hold an MD or the equivalent as recognized by the American Medical Association and must be ACGME-certified in radiology or be eligible to sit for such certification

**Type**: Fellowship

**Value**: US$50,000 per year paid to a department. The Foundation does not pay overhead or indirect costs

**Length of Study**: 3 years

**Frequency**: Annual

**Country of Study**: Any country

**Application Procedure**: Applications must be submitted by a department in preparation for the recruitment of a Fellow into an existing cardiovascular imaging training programme. Application forms are available from the website

**Closing Date**: 1 June

**Additional Information**: www.radiology.northwestern.edu/education/fellows/cardiovascular-imaging.html

### For further information contact:

Northwestern University Feinberg School of Medicine, Department of Radiology, Cardiovascular Imaging Fellowship Program, 676 N. Saint Clair St., Suite 800, Chicago, IL 60611, United States of America.

**Email**:    bcartalino@rsna.org

## Radiological Society of North America Medical Student Grant Program

**Purpose**: To make radiology research opportunities available for medical students early in their training and encourage them to consider academic radiology as a career option

**Eligibility**: Open to full-time medical students at an accredited North American medical school

**Level of Study**: Research

**Type**: Grant

**Value**: US$3,000 for an 10-week (minimum) research project, to be matched by the sponsoring department (US$6,000 total), as a stipend for the medical student

**Length of Study**: 1 year

**Frequency**: Annual

**Country of Study**: Any country

**Application Procedure**: Applicants must complete an application form available from the website rsna.org/foundation

**Closing Date**: 1 February

**Funding**: Foundation

**Contributor**: Individuals, private practice, corporate

**Additional Information**: www.rsna.org/en/research/funding-opportunities/research-grants/medical-student-research-grant

### For further information contact:

**Email**:    bcartalino@rsna.org

## Radiological Society of North America Research Resident Program

**Purpose**: To provide opportunities for individuals to gain further insight into scientific investigation, and to develop competence in research and educational techniques and methods

**Eligibility**: Open to citizens or permanent residents of a North American country. Applicants should be in residency training so that the award can occur during any year after the 1st year of training and should have an academic degree acceptable for a radiology residency

**Level of Study**: Postgraduate

**Type**: Grant

**Value**: US$30,000 designed to replace a portion of the resident

**Length of Study**: 1 year, non-renewable

**Frequency**: Annual

**Country of Study**: Any country

**Application Procedure**: Applicants must complete an application form, available from the website

**Closing Date**: 15 January

**Additional Information**: www.rsna.org/en/research/research-awards/roentgen-resident-fellow-research-award

### For further information contact:

820 Jorie Blvd., Suite 200, Oak Brook, IL 60523-2251 USA.

**Email**:    REfoundation@rsna.org

## Radiological Society of North America Research Resident/Fellow Program

**Purpose**: To provide young investigators not yet professionally established in the radiological sciences an opportunity to gain further insight into scientific investigation and to develop competence in research techniques and methods

**Eligibility**: Applicants must be a resident or fellow in a department of radiology, radiation oncology or nuclear medicine within a North American educational institutions at the time of application

**Level of Study**: Doctorate, Postdoctorate

**Type**: Fellowship

**Value**: US$30,000 for a 1-year Research Resident project or US$50,000 for a 1-year Research Fellow project, to be used for salary and/or non-personnel research expenses

**Length of Study**: 1 year

**Frequency**: Annual

**Country of Study**: Any country

**Application Procedure**: Applicants must complete an application form, available from the website rsna.org/foundation

**Closing Date**: 15 January

**Funding**: Foundation

**Contributor**: Individuals, private practice, corporate

**Additional Information**: www.rsna.org/en/research/research-awards/roentgen-resident-fellow-research-award

### For further information contact:

820 Jorie Blvd., Suite 200, Oak Brook, IL 60523-2251 USA.

**Email**:    REfoundation@rsna.org

## Radiological Society of North America Research Scholar Grant Program

**Purpose**: To support junior clinical faculty members and allow them to gain experience in research early in their academic careers

**Eligibility**: Applicants must be within 5 years of initial faculty appointment in a department of radiology, radiation oncology or nuclear medicine within a North American institution

**Level of Study**: Doctorate, Postdoctorate

**Type**: Award

**Value**: US$75,000 per year for 2 years (US$150,000 total), payable to the institution, to be used exclusively as a stipend for the scholar

**Length of Study**: 2 years

**Frequency**: Annual

**Country of Study**: Any country

**Application Procedure**: Scholar applicants must be nominated by their host institution. Applicants must complete an application form available from the website rsna.org/foundation

**Closing Date**: 15 January

**Funding**: Foundation

**Contributor**: Individuals, private practice, corporate

**Additional Information**: www.rsna.org/en/research/funding-opportunities/research-grants/research-scholar-grant

### For further information contact:

Radiological Society of North America, R&E Foundation 820 Jorie Boulevard, Oak Brook, IL 60523, United States of America.

**Email**:    kosley@rsna.org

## Research Scholar Grant

**Purpose**: This R&E Foundation grant supports junior faculty members who have completed resident and fellowship programs, but haven't been recognized as independent investigators

**Eligibility**: Any junior radiology faculty member may apply for the Research Scholar Grant, as long as you are an RSNA member and meet the following criteria: 1. You must hold a full-time faculty position in a department of radiology, radiation oncology or nuclear medicine within a North American educational institution. 2. You must have been hired within the last 5 years with an academic rank of instructor, assistant professor or an equivalent title. 3. You must have completed advanced training and be certified by either the American Board of Radiology (ABR), The Royal College of Physicians and Surgeons of Canada or are on track for certification. 4. You cannot have been a principal investigator on a grant or contract totaling more than US$60,000 in a single year. This includes single and combined grants and contracts from government, private and commercial sources. 5. You and your principal investigators cannot be employed by any for-profit, commercial company in the radiologic sciences. 6. You cannot submit more than one grant application to the RSNA R&E Foundation a year and cannot have a concurrent RSNA grant. 7. Funding from other grant sources must be approved by Foundation staff if it wasn't described in the original research plan

**Level of Study**: Research

**Type**: Grant for various aspects of field research and conservation projects in primate habitat countries

**Value**: US$75,000 will be awarded for a year

**Frequency**: Annual

**Country of Study**: Any country

**Application Procedure**: Elaborated information on grants will be available in the following link. www.rsna.org/research/funding-opportunities/research-grants/research-scholar-grant

**Closing Date**: 15 January

**Funding**: Private

**Additional Information**: www.rsna.org/en/research/funding-opportunities/research-grants/research-scholar-grant

### For further information contact:

Keshia Osley, Assistant Director, Grant Administration, Radiological Society of North America, R&E Foundation, 820 Jorie Boulevard, Oak Brook, IL 60523, United States of America.

**Email**:  kosley@rsna.org

## Research Seed Grant

**Purpose**: This R&E Foundation Research Seed Grant gives investigators around the world the chance to define objectives and test hypotheses in preparation for larger grant applications at corporations, foundations and government agencies

**Eligibility**: Any investigator from anywhere in the world with an academic appointment may apply for this grant, as long as you are an RSNA member. If you're a non dues-paying member, your scientific advisor or your co-investigator must be a dues-paying member. You must also meet the following criteria: All applicants; 1. You must hold a full-time faculty position in a radiology, radiation oncology or nuclear medicine department at an educational institution. 2. If you aren't currently a full-time faculty member, but will be by the time funding starts, a letter from the department chair must be included in your application. 3. You cannot have been a principal investigator on a grant or contract totaling more than US$60,000 in a single year. This includes single and combined grants and contracts from government, private and commercial sources. 4. You and your principal investigators cannot be employed by any for-profit, commercial company in the radiologic sciences. 5. Funding from other grant sources must be approved by foundation staff if it wasn't described in the original research plan

**Level of Study**: Professional development, Research

**Type**: Research grant

**Value**: Upto US$40,000 for a one-year project

**Length of Study**: 1

**Frequency**: Annual

**Country of Study**: Any country

**Application Procedure**: Applications should describe the unique nature of the research effort independent of existing research efforts. Our Research & Education Foundation provides a critical source of support for investigators. Since the Foundation's inception we've awarded over 1,450 grants. That's more than US$60 million in funding for radiology research and improving patient care

**Closing Date**: 15 January

**Funding**: Private

**Additional Information**: www.rsna.org/en/research/funding-opportunities/research-grants/research-seed-grant

### For further information contact:

Radiological Society of North America, R&E Foundation, 820 Jorie Boulevard, Oak Brook, IL 60523, United States of America.

**Email**:  kosley@rsna.org

## Ragdale

## Sybil Shearer Fellowship: Dancemakers

**Purpose**: The Ragdale Foundation and the Morrison-Shearer Foundation are pleased to announce a fellowship opportunity for dancemakers

**Eligibility**: Applications are reviewed by Ragdale's Curatorial Board and staff as well as Morrison-Shearer Foundation Trustees. We seek applicants who are pursuing new creativity in dance and movement. This may include both emerging and established practitioners

**Level of Study**: Postgraduate

**Type**: Fellowship

**Value**: Cash stipend US$500

**Frequency**: Annual

**Country of Study**: Any country

**Application Procedure**: Evaluations of work are based on the following criteria: 1. Work sample and statement show evidence of original, inventive and exciting new work. 2. Work sample demonstrates quality, technical proficiency, and is professionally presented. 3. Artist's statement and resumé show evidence that the applicant's work is reflective of continued, serious, and exceptional aesthetic investigation in the chosen medium. 4. Work plan demonstrates that the artist will maximize the benefits of a fellowship at Ragdale. 5. References reflect the artist's ability to work well in an artist community

**Closing Date**: 15 May

**Funding**: Private

**Additional Information**: inliquid.org/opportunity/sybil-shearer-fellowship-for-dancemakers/

### For further information contact:

1260 N. Green Bay Road, Lake Forest, IL 60045, United States of America.

**Tel**:  (1) 847 234 1063
**Email**:  info@ragdale.org

## Rebecca Skelton Fund

Dance Department Administrator, University of Chichester, Bishop Otter Campus, College Lane, Chichester, Sussex PO19 6PE, United Kingdom.

**Tel**:  (44) 12 4381 6485
**Email**:  rebeccaskeltonfund@chi.ac.uk
**Website**:  www.rebeccaskeltonfund.org
**Contact**:  The Rebecca Skelton Fund Administrator

The fund provides financial assistance towards the cost of postgraduate dance study in experiential/creative work to include dance improvization and those training methods such as Skinner Releasing Technique, Alignment Therapy, Feldenkrais Technique, Alexander Technique and other body-mind practices that focus on an inner awareness and use the proprioceptive communication system or an inner sensory mode.

## The Rebecca Skelton Scholarship

**Purpose**: To assist students to pursue a course of specific or advanced performance studies or an appropriate dance research and performance

**Eligibility**: Open to anyone pursuing dance studies at postgraduate level

**Level of Study**: Doctorate, Postdoctorate, Postgraduate, Professional development, Research

**Type**: Scholarships and fellowships

**Value**: £500

**Frequency**: Annual

**Country of Study**: United Kingdom

**Application Procedure**: Application form on request

**No. of awards offered**: 9

**Closing Date**: 12 January

**Funding**: Foundation

**Contributor**: The Rebecca Skelton Fund

**No. of awards given last year**: 5

**No. of applicants last year**: 9

**Additional Information**: www.theplace.org.uk/juice/rebecca-skelton-fund

### For further information contact:

**Email**:  artsresearch@chi.ac.uk

## Regent's Park College

### Regent's Park College: Aziz Foundation Scholarship

**Purpose**: In association with Regent's Park College, the Aziz Foundation is offering a scholarship worth up to £25,000 for a student who is undertaking, or has been accepted for, a Master's degree in the humanities, arts or social sciences at the University of Oxford

**Eligibility**: 1. Applicants should: be active within a Muslim community and their wider community, and demonstrate a desire to develop intellectual skills within a multi-faith and secular environment. 2. Applicants will be able to demonstrate long-term commitment to community/societal development and working for good relations through effecting public policy; and be eligible for Home

**Level of Study**: Postgraduate

**Type**: Scholarship

**Value**: Up to £25,000 per year

**Frequency**: Annual

**Country of Study**: Any country
**Closing Date**: 31 March
**Funding**: Private
**Additional Information**: www.rpc.ox.ac.uk/study-here/postgraduate-study/scholarships/

**For further information contact:**

Regent's Park College, Pusey Street, Oxford, OX1 2LB, United Kingdom.

**Email**: academic.administrator@regents.ox.ac.uk

## The Pamela Sue Anderson Studentship for the Encouragement of the Place of Women in Philosophy

**Purpose**: Regent's Park College is offering a postgraduate studentship who is currently engaged in or has been accepted for post graduate study in the University of Oxford
**Level of Study**: Postgraduate
**Type**: Studentship
**Frequency**: Annual
**Country of Study**: Any country
**Application Procedure**: 1. covering letter, explaining how the candidate's proposed research relates to the vision of the studentship; 2. current CV, including the names and contact details of two referees; 3. research proposal; 4. writing sample of no more than 5,000 words
**Closing Date**: 5 April
**Funding**: Private
**Additional Information**: www.theology.ox.ac.uk/article/pamela-sue-anderson-studentship

**For further information contact:**

Pusey Street, Oxford, OX1 2LB, United Kingdom.

**Email**: enquiries@regents.ox.ac.uk

## Regent's University London

Inner Circle, London, NW1 4NS, United Kingdom.

**Contact**: Regent's University London

Regent's University London is a private non-profit university located in London, United Kingdom. Regent's University is only the second institution in the United Kingdom to be granted the status of a private university.

## Greyfriars Postgraduate Scholarship

**Purpose**: In recognition of the historic commitment of the Greyfriars and of Regent's Park College to philanthropy and the inclusion of those whose life chances have been limited through no fault of their own, preference will be given to applicants whose financial needs are greatest and may otherwise prohibit their studies. The intention is that the Scholarship be applied to student fees.
**Level of Study**: Postgraduate
**Type**: Scholarship
**Value**: Up to £2,000
**Frequency**: Annual
**Country of Study**: Any country
**Application Procedure**: 1. covering letter, including an explanation of any special circumstances in relation to financial need that may otherwise prohibit or make it difficult to undertake postgraduate studies at Oxford University. Also state any other postgraduate grants or scholarships applied for and awarded; 2. current CV, including the names and contact details of two referees; 3. research proposal
**Closing Date**: 8 March
**Funding**: Private

**For further information contact:**

**Email**: academic.administrator@regents.ox.ac.uk

## Pakistan Fashion Journalism Scholarship

**Purpose**: An offer for students entering into MA programme
**Eligibility**: Pakistani students are eligible to apply for this scholarship. Scholarship can be taken in the United Kingdom. To enter the competition for the OK! Pakistan Fashion Journalism Scholarship, you should first meet all of the following criteria: You are a Pakistani national holding a Pakistani passport; You have achieved at least an upper second class (2:1) United Kingdom honours undergraduate degree (or its international equivalent from a recognised institution); You hold an offer of a place on the MA Fashion (Journalism) programme
**Type**: Scholarship
**Value**: £4,000 towards fees for one standard programme duration
**Country of Study**: United Kingdom
**Application Procedure**: For more details, visit www.regents.ac.uk/study/scholarships-funding-and-bursaries/ok-pakistan-fashion-journalism-scholarship
**Closing Date**: 30 June
**Funding**: Private

**Additional Information**: www.scholarshipsads.com/ok-pakistan-fashion-journalism-scholarship-regents-university-london-uk-2018-2019/

### For further information contact:

**Email**: enquiries@regents.ac.uk

## Robert McKee International Screenwriting Scholarships

**Level of Study**: Graduate
**Type**: Scholarship
**Value**: £7,000
**Country of Study**: Any country
**Closing Date**: 30 June
**Additional Information**: www.regents.ac.uk/study/scholarships-funding-and-bursaries/robert-mckee#overview

### For further information contact:

**Email**: contact@mckeestory.com

## The Dean of Humanities, Arts & Social Sciences Excellence Scholarship

**Purpose**: The Dean of the Faculty of Humanities, Arts & Social Sciences has established three scholarships that celebrate the University's independent, cosmopolitan and enterprising spirit
**Level of Study**: Graduate
**Type**: Scholarship and award
**Value**: The Scholarship award will cover a quarter of the tuition fees for the selected course
**Frequency**: Annual
**Country of Study**: Any country
**Application Procedure**: Applications must be emailed to: scholarships@regents.ac.uk
**No. of awards offered**: 3
**Closing Date**: 31 May
**Funding**: Private
**Additional Information**: For any queries, please contact: Regent's University London, Tel: (44) 20 7487 7505, Email: enquiries@regents.ac.uk www.regents.ac.uk/study/scholarships-funding-and-bursaries/the-dean-of-humanities-arts-social-sciences-excellence-scholarship

### For further information contact:

(44) 20 7487 7505

**Email**: scholarships@regents.ac.uk

## Regional Institute for Population Studies

University of Ghana, PO Box 96, Legon, Accra, Ghana.

**Tel**:      (233) 21 500 381 ext. 3418
**Email**:   rips@libr.ug.edu.gh
**Contact**: Director

The Regional Institute for Population Studies organises training courses leading to the award of MA, MPhil and PhD degrees, seminars and workshops. It also provides advisory services to member states on request, and facilities for students and research workers, as well as conducting research into population studies and related fields in the English speaking countries of Africa, focusing on level and trends of population growth, morbidity and mortality, reproduction, family formation, gender and the status of women, population structure and distribution, migration, and the interrelationship between population and development.

## Respective Government Fellowships

**Purpose**: To enable fellows to obtain advanced training through study or research leading to a Master of Arts, Master of Philosophy or PhD degree
**Eligibility**: Open to English speaking Sub-Saharan Africans, nominated by their governments, who are capable of pursuing a course of study or research using English as a medium of expression. Candidates should have a good first degree in population studies for the Master of Arts degree course or the Master of Population Studies degree, a Master of Arts in population studies or its equivalent for the Master of Philosophy degree, a Master of Philosophy in population studies or its equivalent for a PhD course
**Level of Study**: Doctorate, Postgraduate
**Type**: Fellowship
**Value**: Approx. US$13,840 per year including stipend, fees, costs for books, minor equipment and production of dissertations and theses
**Length of Study**: At least 1 year for Master of Arts, at least 18 months for MPhil and 36 months for PhD
**Frequency**: Annual
**Study Establishment**: Regional Institute for Population Studies at the University of Ghana
**Country of Study**: Ghana
**Application Procedure**: United Nations Fellows must complete an application form, available at any United Nations Development Programme Office in the capital city of each English speaking Sub Saharan African country, through

which all applications should be routed. Applications must be filled out in triplicate and submitted together with the relevant admission requirement through the government ministry responsible for recruiting candidates for the Institute. Non United Nation Fellows should send an application letter directly to the Director of the Institute. All seven students were sponsored through country programme budgets of governments of three of the member states of the Institute

**No. of awards offered**: 22

**Closing Date**: 30 June

**Funding**: Government

**No. of awards given last year**: 13

**No. of applicants last year**: 22

**Additional Information**: 20 of last year's candidates were sponsored directly by the Institute and 10 through country programme budgets of governments of four of the member states of the Institute www.mospi.gov.in/scheme-doctoral-fellowships

**For further information contact:**

| | |
|---|---|
| **Tel**: | (233) 21 773 8906 |
| **Fax**: | (233) 21 772 829 |
| **Email**: | fo.gha@undp.org |

# Religious Scholarships

## American Atheists Chinn Scholarships

**Purpose**: American Atheists is proud to award two Chinn Scholarships for LGBT Atheist Activism. These scholarships recognize activism in the area of LGBT equality. You do not have to be a member of the LGBT community to receive this scholarship; allies are encouraged to apply

**Eligibility**: 1. High school seniors or current college students. 2. Full-time graduate and law school students. 3. Applicants must be atheists. 4. Have a minimum cumulative GPA of at least 2.5

**Level of Study**: Graduate

**Type**: Scholarship

**Value**: NZ$500

**Length of Study**: 1 year

**Frequency**: Annual

**Country of Study**: New Zealand

**Application Procedure**: Apply online

**No. of awards offered**: 2

**Closing Date**: 3 February

**Funding**: Foundation

**Additional Information**: www.unigo.com/scholarships/by-type/religious-scholarships/american-atheists-chinn-scholarship/4504

**For further information contact:**

225 Cristiani St., Cranford, NJ 07016-3214, United States of America.

| | |
|---|---|
| **Tel**: | (1) 908 276 7300 |
| **Email**: | scholarship@atheists.org |

## American Atheists O'Hair Award

**Purpose**: The American Atheists awards a NZ$1,000 O'Hair Scholarship to an atheist student attending college or university. The award is given every year at the American Atheists National Convention. The Student Activist Scholarship program was founded by Life Members Barbara J. Baldock, Dr. Phillip Butler, Lillian B. Ramsden, Rice O'Dell and Irving Yablon

**Eligibility**: The scholarship can be used by a current college student or by high school student entering college the upcoming year. Additionally, full-time graduate and law school students are eligible for the scholarship. Applicants must be atheists and have a cumulative GPA of 2.5 or better. Applicants are judged based on their actions as atheists and activists

**Level of Study**: Graduate

**Type**: Award

**Value**: NZ$1,000

**Length of Study**: 1 year

**Frequency**: Annual

**Country of Study**: New Zealand

**Application Procedure**: Apply online

**No. of awards offered**: 8

**Closing Date**: 26 February

**Funding**: Foundation

**Additional Information**: www.scholarships.com/financial-aid/college-scholarships/scholarship-directory/religion/atheist/american-atheists-ohair-award

**For further information contact:**

P.O. Box 158, Cranford, NJ 07016, United States of America.

| | |
|---|---|
| **Tel**: | (1) 908 276 7300 |
| **Email**: | scholarships@atheists.org |

## Anna Schiller Scholarship

**Purpose**: To be eligible for the Anna Schiller Memorial Scholarship, you must be a Rockford Christian High School graduating senior who demonstrates a strong commitment to improving the quality of life for people in their school, community and/or world at large through their community service and demonstrates the same strong love for others that Anna exemplified through her life. Minimum GPA of 2.0/4.0 is required. For more information or to apply, please visit the scholarship provider's website

**Level of Study**: Graduate
**Type**: Scholarship
**Frequency**: Annual
**Country of Study**: New Zealand
**Closing Date**: 1 February
**Funding** Foundation
**Additional Information**: www.scholarships.com/financial-aid/college-scholarships/scholarships-by-grade-level/high-school-scholarships/anna-schiller-scholarship/

### For further information contact:

946 North Second Street, Rockford, IL 61107, United States of America.

**Tel**:      (1) 779 210 8209
**Email**:   cstahly@cfnil.org

## Associated Women for Pepperdine (AWP) Scholarship

**Purpose**: The Associated Women for Pepperdine (AWP) was established in 1958 and is the largest, most active women's group supporting colleges and universities in Southern California. For over 50 years members have been primary contributors to scholarships for Christian students and have forged a strong link between the University and the Churches of Christ across the country
**Eligibility**: Current, active member of a Church of Christ congregation. The Associated Women for Pepperdine (AWP) awards a number of scholarships annually on a renewable basis to active members from the Churches of Christ
**Level of Study**: Graduate
**Type**: Scholarship
**Value**: NZ$5,000
**Length of Study**: 1 year
**Frequency**: Annual
**Country of Study**: New Zealand
**Application Procedure**: Apply online
**Closing Date**: 15 February
**Funding**: Foundation
**Additional Information**: seaver.pepperdine.edu/admission/financial-aid/undergraduate/assistance/awp-scholarship-exception.htm

### For further information contact:

**Tel**:      (1) 310 506 4392
**Email**:   admission-seaver@pepperdine.edu

## Republic of South Africa

### Azerbaijan: Azerbaijan Diplomatic Academy University Scholarship

**Purpose**: The Government of the Republic of Azerbaijan and ADA University are offering scholarships to foreign students. The ADA University is committed to grooming world class leaders
**Eligibility**: Be South African citizens in good health, with a strong academic record. 1. Meet the entry criteria for their selected programme at the ADA University. 2. Meet the minimum academic requirement for entry into a similar programme at a South African university. 3. Applicants must be proficient in English
**Level of Study**: Postgraduate
**Type**: Scholarship
**Value**: offers tuition fees, travel expenses, medical benefits and monthly stipend
**Frequency**: Annual
**Country of Study**: Any country
**Application Procedure**: Information on the application process is available on the website. www.ada.edu.az/en-us/pages/admission_fellowships.aspx
**Closing Date**: 1 July
**Funding**: Private
**Additional Information**: allscholarshipforum.com/ada-university-in-azerbaijan-fully-funded-international-fellowship-2019/

### For further information contact:

**Email**:   admissions@ada.edu.az

## Research Corporation for Science Advancement

4703 E Camp Lowell Drive, Suite 201, Tucson, AZ 85712, United States of America.

**Tel**:      (1) 520 571 1111
**Email**:   awards@rescorp.org
**Website**:  www.rescorp.org
**Contact**:  Editor, Science Advancement Programme

The Research Corporation (United States of America) was one of the first United States foundations, and is the only one wholly devoted to the advancement of academic science. An endowed organization, it makes grants totalling

US$5,000,000–7,000,000 annually for independently proposed research in chemistry, physics and astronomy at United States and Canadian colleges and universities.

## Research Corporation (United States of America) Research Innovation Awards

**Purpose**: To assist innovative research programmes for faculty of PhD granting departments
**Eligibility**: Open to faculty members whose first tenure track position began in either the preceding or the current calendar year are eligible to apply
**Level of Study**: Doctorate
**Type**: Research grant
**Value**: US$35,000 for equipment and supplies, graduate stipends and some other expenses. The award does not cover overheads
**Frequency**: Annual
**Study Establishment**: Research universities with PhD granting departments of physics, chemistry and astronomy
**Country of Study**: United States of America or Canada
**Application Procedure**: Applicants must complete an application form. Guidelines and an application request forms are available from the website
**No. of awards offered**: 200
**Closing Date**: 1 May
**Funding**: Private
**Contributor**: Foundation endowment
**No. of awards given last year**: 45
**No. of applicants last year**: 200
**Additional Information**: Research proposals that transcend the ordinary and promise significant discoveries are sought after www.awa.asn.au/AWA_MBRR/About_AWA/Awards/Organ/Research_Innovation_Award.aspx

### For further information contact:

**Email**:    awards@ria.ie

## Research Council of Norway

Stensberggata 26, PO Box 2700, St Hanshaugen, N-0131 Oslo, Norway.

**Tel**:        (47) 2 203 7000
**Email**:    info@forskningsradet.no
**Website**:  www.forskningsradet.no

The Research Council of Norway is a strategic body for Norwegian research and a central advisory body to the government on issues concerning general research policy as well as the development of science and technology. The Council bears overall responsibility for national research strategy and manages nearly one third of the public sector research funding. One of the principal tasks of the Research Council is to promote co-operation and co-ordination among Norwegian academic institutions. Other important objectives include raising the general level of knowledge in society and encouraging innovation in industry and the public sector. The Research Council identifies important fields of research, allocates funds and evaluates research and development.

## Research Council of Norway Senior Scientist Visiting Fellowship

**Purpose**: To enable Norwegian research institutions to receive foreign scientists to participate in research groups, discuss research arrangements and give lectures within their special fields
**Eligibility**: Open to well established and internationally recognised scientists who are at a professional or equivalent level
**Level of Study**: Professional development
**Type**: Fellowship
**Value**: NOK 25,000 per month for the first two months, NOK 10,000 for each succeeding month. Travelling expenses may also be defrayed
**Length of Study**: 1–12 months
**Frequency**: Annual
**Study Establishment**: A Norwegian research institution
**Country of Study**: Norway
**Application Procedure**: Applications must be filed by Norwegian institutions, so individual scientists should contact the Norwegian research institution or university department of their choice
**Funding**: Government
**Additional Information**: The Research Council of Norway also administers the following: Research Programmes of the European Union (EU), Bilateral Scholarship Agreements, and the Nordic Scheme for the Baltic Countries and North West Russia www.timeshighereducation.com/news/senior-scientist-visiting-fellowship/179867.article

### For further information contact:

**Email**:    post@forskningsradet.no

## Reserve Bank of New Zealand

2 The Terrace, PO Box 2498, Wellington 6140, New Zealand.

**Tel**:        (64) 4 472 2029
**Email**:    rbnz-info@rbnz.govt.nz
**Website**:  www.rbnz.govt.nz

The Reserve Bank of New Zealand is New Zealand's central bank. They promote a sound and dynamic monetary and financial system. They work towards our vision by operating monetary policy to achieve and maintain price stability, assisting the functioning of a sound and efficient financial system, meeting the currency needs of the public, overseeing and operating effective payments systems and providing effective support services to the Bank.

## Reserve Bank of New Zealand Scholarships for International Students

**Purpose**: Scholarships are available for pursuing honours, master's or final year of PhD degree level at a New Zealand University
**Eligibility**: Applicants must be studying full time at a New Zealand University and be legally entitled to work in New Zealand. Students must have attained at least B+ average and be studying full time over the academic year (February to November). Applicants must have majoring in Economics, Finance or Banking and they should be entering their honours, Master's or final year of PhD study
**Type**: Scholarship
**Value**: The value of each scholarship will be NZ$10,000
**Country of Study**: New Zealand
**Application Procedure**: The mode of applying is by email
**Closing Date**: 15 January
**Contributor**: The Reserve Bank of New Zealand
**Additional Information**: Successful applicants will be asked to attend a half day interview process at the Bank in Wellington. This typically takes place in the beginning of February scholarship-positions.com/reserve-bank-of-new-zealand-scholarships-international-students/2013/07/12/

### For further information contact:

Northways Parade, 28 College Crescent, London NW3 5DN United Kingdom.

**Email**:   recruitment@rbnz.govt.nz

## Resuscitation Council (United Kingdom)

5th Floor, Tavistock House North, Tavistock Square, London WC1H 9HR, United Kingdom.

**Tel**:          (44) 20 7388 4678
**Email**:      enquiries@resus.org.uk
**Website**:   www.resus.org.uk
**Contact**:   Dr Sara Harris, Assistant Director

The Resuscitation Council (United Kingdom) is the expert advisory body on the training and practice of resuscitation in the United Kingdom. It also actively pursues and promotes research in the field of resuscitation medicine.

## Resuscitation Council (United Kingdom) Research & Development Grant

**Purpose**: To provide grants up to a maximum of £20,000 for capital costs, data analysis and administrative support for research into the science and practice of resuscitation medicine
**Type**: Grant
**Frequency**: Annual
**Country of Study**: Any country
**No. of awards offered**: 13
**Closing Date**: 31 May
**No. of awards given last year**: 5
**No. of applicants last year**: 13

## Rheumatology Research Foundation

2200 Lake Boulevard NE, Atlanta, GA 30319, United States of America.

**Tel**:          (1) 404 633 3777
**Email**:      foundation@rheumatology.org
**Website**:   www.rheumatology.org
**Contact**:   Sarah Barksdale, Senior Specialist, Awards and Grants

The American College of Rheumatology (ACR) is the professional organization of rheumatologists and associated health professionals who share a dedication to healing, preventing disability and curing more than 100 types of arthritis and related disabling and sometimes fatal disorders of the joints, muscles and bones.

## American College of Rheumatology REF Rheumatology Scientist Development Award

**Purpose**: To encourage qualified physicians without significant prior research experience to embark on careers in biomedical and/or clinical research in arthritis and rheumatic diseases
**Eligibility**: Candidates must be an ACR or ARHP member, have a doctoral level degree, must be clinician scientists
**Level of Study**: Doctorate, Postdoctorate, Professional development, Research

**Type**: Award
**Value**: US$50,000 for first year, US$75,000 for second year and US$100,000 for third year
**Length of Study**: 3 years
**Frequency**: Annual
**Country of Study**: United States of America
**Application Procedure**: Application forms are available on website
**No. of awards offered**: 12
**Closing Date**: 1 June
**Funding**: Foundation
**Contributor**: Centocor Inc
**Additional Information**: For any questions regarding eligibility, contact the REF www.rheumresearch.org/career-development-research-awards

**For further information contact:**

**Tel**: (1) 404 365 1373
**Email**: Foundation@rheumatology.org

## American College of Rheumatology/REF Arthritis Investigator Award

**Purpose**: To provide support to physicians and scientists in research fields related to arthritis for the period between the completion of postdoctoral fellowship training and establishment as an independent investigators
**Level of Study**: Research
**Type**: Award
**Value**: US$75,000 for the first 2 years and US$90,000 per year after renewal
**Length of Study**: 2–4 years
**Frequency**: Annual
**Country of Study**: United States of America
**Application Procedure**: Application forms are available on website
**Closing Date**: 1 September
**Funding**: Foundation
**Contributor**: The Arthritis Foundation

**For further information contact:**

**Email**: acrnominations@rheumatology.org

## Amgen Fellowship Training Award

**Purpose**: Ensure a more robust and highly-trained workforce is available to provide clinical care to people with rheumatic diseases
**Eligibility**: 1. Applicant (Program Director) must be an ACR or ARP member at the time of submission and for the duration of the award 2. Only Program Directors at ACGME-accredited institutionsin good standing may apply 3. The rheumatology fellowship training Program Director at the institution will be responsible for the overall direction, management and administration of the program 4. By submitting an application, the Program Director and sponsoring institution agree funds will be used ONLY for salary support of one fellow in their first orsecond year (or third year fellow in pediatric rheumatology) 5. Multiple applicationsfrom a single institution will not be permitted unless they are for separate training programs (e.g., adult and pediatric rheumatology) 6. Programs may not apply for the Amgen Fellowship Training Award and Fellowship Training Award for Workforce Expansion within the same application cycle. 7. Current recipients of the Fellowship Training Award for Workforce Expansion are not eligible to apply for this award. 8. Supported fellows do not need to be U.S. citizens or non-citizen nationals
**Type**: Award
**Value**: US$50,000
**Length of Study**: 1 year
**Frequency**: Annual
**Country of Study**: United States of America
**Application Procedure**: All applications must be submitted online by 5:00 PM ET on the deadline day through Zengine at: webportalapp.com/sp/fy2022fta
**Closing Date**: 1 May
**Funding**: Foundation
**Contributor**: Rheumatology Research Foundation
**Additional Information**: www.rheumresearch.org/file/FY22_Fellowship-Training-Award-PDM-Nelson_FINAL.pdf

**For further information contact:**

**Tel**: (1) 404 365 1373

## Career Development Bridge Funding Award: K Bridge

**Purpose**: Encourage junior investigators to continue conducting research into novel ideas while revising outstanding career development award applications
**Eligibility**: 1. All applicants must meet citizenship/permanent residentstatus and other eligibility requirements as outlined in the Awards and Grants policies. 2. Applicants must be ACR or ARPmembers with an MD, DO, PhD or equivalent doctoral level degree from an accredited institution. 3. The Foundation does not currently support non- MD/DO scientists working on basic science research. 4. Bridge funds are not intended to bridge the period between review and funding. 5. Previous recipients of this award are not eligible to apply. 6. In addition to an excellent application, applicantsmust be

capable of becoming independent researchers with a clear and firm institutional commitment to their career development, including a faculty position and other supporting resources.

**Level of Study**: Doctorate, Postdoctorate, Professional development, Research
**Type**: Award
**Value**: US$75,000
**Length of Study**: 1 year
**Frequency**: Annual
**Country of Study**: United States of America
**Application Procedure**: All applications must be submitted by 5:00 pm ET on the deadline day through Zengine at: webportalapp.com/sp/fy2021bfakb
**Closing Date**: 1 October
**Funding**: Foundation
**Contributor**: Rheumatology Research Foundation
**Additional Information**: www.rheumresearch.org/file/FY21-Career-Development-Bridge-Funding-Award_K-Bridge_FINAL.pdf

### For further information contact:

**Tel**: (1) 404 365 1373

## Career Development Bridge Funding Award: K Supplement

**Purpose**: Encourage junior investigators to expand promising research by providing additional support to cover research costs and help investigators become independent
**Eligibility**: 1. All applicants must meet citizenship/permanent resident status and other eligibility requirements as outlined in the Awards and Grants policies. 2. Applicants must be ACR or ARP members with an MD, DO, PhD or equivalent doctoral level degree from an accredited institution 3. The Foundation does not currently support non- MD/DO scientists working on basic science research. 4. In addition to an excellent application, applicants must be capable of becoming independent researchers with a clear and firm institutional commitment to their career development, including a faculty position and other supporting resources.
**Level of Study**: Doctorate, Postdoctorate, Professional development, Research
**Type**: Award
**Value**: US$100,000
**Length of Study**: 2 years
**Frequency**: Annual
**Country of Study**: United States of America
**Application Procedure**: All applications must be submitted by 5:00 pm ET on the deadline day through Zengine at: webportalapp.com/sp/fy2021bfaks
**Closing Date**: 3 August

**Funding**: Foundation
**Contributor**: Rheumatology Research Foundation
**Additional Information**: www.rheumresearch.org/file/FY21_Career-Development-Bridge-Funding-Award_K-Supplement_FINAL.pdf

### For further information contact:

**Tel**: (1) 404 365 1373

## Career Development Bridge Funding Award: R Bridge

**Purpose**: Support established independent investigators to continue conducting research into novel ideas while revising their outstanding NIH or equivalent grant applications
**Type**: Award
**Value**: US$200,000
**Length of Study**: 2 years
**Frequency**: Annual
**Country of Study**: United States of America
**Application Procedure**: All applications must be submitted by 5:00 pm ET on the deadline day through Zengine at this link: webportalapp.com/sp/fy2021bfarb
**Closing Date**: 1 October
**Funding**: Foundation
**Contributor**: Rheumatology Research Foundation
**Additional Information**: www.rheumresearch.org/file/FY21_Career-Development-Bridge-Funding-Award_R-Bridge_FINAL.pdf

### For further information contact:

**Tel**: (1) 404 365 1373

## Career Development in Geriatric Medicine Award

**Purpose**: To support career development for junior faculty in the early stages of their research career
**Eligibility**: To be eligible for the award, the candidate must: be a member of the ACR; have completed a rheumatology fellowship leading to certification by the ABIM and be within the first 3 years of his/her faculty appointment; and possess a faculty appointment at the time of the award. Award applicant must be a citizen or non-citizen national of the United States of America, or be in lawful possessions of a permanent resident card. Individuals on temporary (J1, H1) or student visas are not eligible
**Level of Study**: Doctorate, Professional development, Research
**Type**: Research award
**Value**: US$75,000 per year plus US$3,000 in travel grants

**Length of Study**: 2 years
**Frequency**: Annual
**Country of Study**: United States of America
**Application Procedure**: Application forms are available on website www.rheumatology.org/foundation/index.asp
**No. of awards offered**: 1
**Closing Date**: 1 August
**Funding**: Foundation
**Contributor**: Association of Subspecialty Professors
**No. of awards given last year**: 1
**No. of applicants last year**: 1
**Additional Information**: www.hrsa.gov/grants/find-funding/hrsa-19-007

**For further information contact:**

**Email**:  ysong@hrsa.gov

## Clinician Scholar Educator Award

**Purpose**: Enhance education in musculoskeletal and rheumatic diseases for future doctors and rheumatology health professionals
**Eligibility**: 1. Applicant must meet citizenship and other eligibility requirements as outlined in the Awards and Grants policies. 2. Applicant must be an ACR or ARP member at the time of submission and for the duration of the award. 3. Must propose educational projects related to rheumatic disease. 4. Applicant must be affiliated with an accredited graduate or medical school 5. Applicant must be able to devote at least 25 % full-time effort (including this project and other educational aendeavors) to educational and scholarly activity for the duration of the award. 6. Previous Clinician Scholar Educator awardees are not eligible to apply.
**Type**: Award
**Value**: US$180,000
**Length of Study**: 3 years
**Frequency**: Annual
**Country of Study**: United States of America
**Application Procedure**: All applications must be submitted online by 5:00 PM ET on the deadline day through Zengine at: webportalapp.com/sp/fy2022fta
**Closing Date**: 1 May
**Funding**: Foundation
**Contributor**: Rheumatology Research Foundation
**Additional Information**: www.rheumresearch.org/file/awards/04-education-and-training/FY22-Clinician-Scholar-Educator-Award_FINAL.pdf

**For further information contact:**

**Tel**:   (1) 404 365 1373

## Fellowship Training Award

**Purpose**: The purpose of this award is to provide support to fellows in rheumatology to help ensure that a diverse and highly trained workforce is available to provide competent care to those affected by rheumatic diseases
**Eligibility**: Only training directors at ACGME-accredited institutions in good standing may apply. The rheumatology fellowship training programme director at the institution will be responsible for the selection and appointment of trainees. Award applicant must be a citizen or non-citizen national of the United States of America, or be in lawful possession of a permanent resident card. Individuals on temporary (J1, H1) or student visas are not eligible
**Level of Study**: Doctorate
**Type**: Fellowship
**Value**: Recipients will receive US$50,000 to support the salary of any fellow. The award is paid directly to the sponsoring institution in 2 equal installments in July and January
**Length of Study**: 1 year
**Frequency**: Annual
**Country of Study**: United States of America
**Application Procedure**: www.rheumresearch.org/education-and-training-awards#AmgenFTA
**No. of awards offered**: 39
**Closing Date**: 1 May
**Funding**: Corporation, Foundation
**Contributor**: Amgen, Inc
**No. of awards given last year**: 23
**No. of applicants last year**: 39
**Additional Information**: www.rheumresearch.org/file/awards/2019/FY21-FTA-PDM-RFA_FINAL.pdf

**For further information contact:**

**Tel**:   (1) 404 365 1373

## Health Professional Online Education Grant

**Purpose**: Increase knowledge and skills of rheumatology health professionals so they are better equipped to meet the needs of a growing rheumatology patient population
**Eligibility**: 1. Applicants must meet citizenship and other eligibility requirements as outlined in the Awards and Grants Policies. 2. Applicants must be ARP members at the time of submission and for the duration of the award 3. Nurse practitioners, physician assistants, nurses, pharmacists, physical therapists, occupational therapists, social workers, psychologists, practice management staff, other licensed non-physician health professionals with an interest in rheumatology.
**Type**: Award

**Value**: Up to US$1,776 for the Advanced Rheumatology Courses or up to US$750 Fundamentals of Rheumatology Courses.

**Frequency**: Annual

**Country of Study**: United States of America

**Application Procedure**: All applications must be submitted online by 5:00 PM ET on the deadline day through Zengine at: webportalapp.com/sp/fy2022fta

**Closing Date**: 1 May

**Funding**: Foundation

**Contributor**: Rheumatology Research Foundation

**Additional Information**: www.rheumresearch.org/file/awards/04-education-and-training/FY21-Health-Professional-Online-Education-Grant_FINAL.pdf

### For further information contact:

**Tel**:    (1) 404 365 1373

## Innovative Research Award

**Purpose**: Encourage independent investigators to conduct novel studies that generate new insights into the cause, progression, treatment and outcomes of rheumatic diseases

**Eligibility**: To be eligible for this award, the applicant must: 1. Be a member of the ACR or ARP at the time of submission and for the duration of the award; 2. Hold a doctoral-level degree (MD, PhD, DO, MBBS or equivalent); 3. Have a faculty appointment (instructor, assistant professor, etc.) at an academic center or research institution at the time of application and for the duration of the award; 4. Must exhibit evidence of research independence, scientific productivity and career accomplishments; 5. Be able to devote a minimum of 20% full-time professional research effort to the project (see details below*); 6. Meet citizenship and other eligibility requirements as outlined in the Awards and Grants policies

**Level of Study**: Doctorate, Postdoctorate, Professional development, Research

**Type**: Award

**Value**: US$400,000

**Length of Study**: 2 years

**Frequency**: Annual

**Country of Study**: United States of America

**Closing Date**: 1 July

**Funding**: Foundation

**Contributor**: Rheumatology Research Foundation

**Additional Information**: www.rheumresearch.org/file/FY22-Innovative-Research-Award_FINAL.pdf

### For further information contact:

**Tel**:    (1) 404 365 1373

## Innovative Research Award for Community Practitioners

**Purpose**: Will help enable research that has the potential to improve treatment of rheumatic diseases, patient outcomes, and/or increase quality of care

**Eligibility**: To be eligible for this award, the applicant must: 1. Be a member of the ACR at the time of submission and for the duration of the award; 2. Hold a doctoral-level degree (MD, DO); 3. Have a current license to practice medicine and be in good medical standing; 4. Be employed in a community practice setting including: Solo practice, Single specialty group practice, Multi-specialty group practice, Hospital system-based practice 5. Have the ability to manage a grant award; administratively and fiscally. 6. Demonstrate certification of training in human subjects research and the ability to obtain human subjects research approval and oversight for the proposed research for the duration of the award;

**Level of Study**: Doctorate, Postdoctorate, Professional development, Research

**Type**: Award

**Value**: US$50,000 to US$200,000 per year

**Length of Study**: 2 years

**Frequency**: Annual

**Country of Study**: United States of America

**Application Procedure**: Applications should be submitted at: webportalapp.com/sp/fy2022iracp

**Closing Date**: 1 August

**Funding**: Foundation

**Contributor**: Rheumatology Research Foundation

**Additional Information**: www.rheumresearch.org/file/FY22-Innovative-Research-Awards-for-Community-Practitioners_FINAL.pdf

### For further information contact:

**Tel**:    (1) 404 365 1373

## Lawren H. Daltroy Health Professional Preceptorship

**Purpose**: Develop a more qualified and trained health professional workforce in order to improve patient-clinician interactions

**Eligibility**: Preceptee must meet citizenship requirements outlined by the Rheumatology Research Foundation Awards and Grants policies. Preceptee must be citizens or non-citizen nationals of the United States or in lawful possession of a permanent resident card. Other individuals on temporary (J1, H1) or student visas are not eligible. Preceptor must be an ARHP member. This award is not intended for physicians

**Level of Study**: Graduate, Postgraduate, Professional development

**Type**: Scholarship
**Value**: Up to US$12,000 for 1 year
**Length of Study**: 1 year
**Frequency**: Annual
**Country of Study**: United States of America
**Application Procedure**: Check the following document for further info. www.rheumresearch.org/file/awards/2018/Daltroy_RFA_FY20.pdf
**No. of awards offered**: 3
**Closing Date**: 1 May
**Funding**: Corporation
**Contributor**: Funding for this award is made possible through an endowment by Rheuminations, Inc
**No. of awards given last year**: 1
**No. of applicants last year**: 3
**Additional Information**: Please check website www.rheumresearch.org     www.rheumresearch.org/file/awards/2018/Daltroy_RFA_FY20.pdf

### For further information contact:

**Email**:     Foundation@rheumatology.org

## Medical and Graduate Student Preceptonship

**Eligibility**: Students enroled in LOME or AOA COCA accredited medical schools, undergraduate students who have been accepted into medical school, students enroled in an accredited graduate school, or undergraduate students who have been accepted into graduate school, are eligible to apply
**Level of Study**: Graduate, Postdoctorate, Postgraduate, Research
**Value**: US$2,000–4,000 plus complimentary registration and up to US$1,000 in travel expenses to attend the ACR/ARHP Annual Meeting
**Length of Study**: 1 academic year
**Frequency**: Annual
**Country of Study**: United States of America
**Application Procedure**: Only completed applications submitted online by the deadline will be accepted
**Closing Date**: 1 December
**Funding**: Foundation
**Contributor**: Rheumatology Research Foundation
**No. of awards given last year**: Up to 30
**Additional Information**:     www.rheumresearch.org/preceptorships

### For further information contact:

**Email**:     Foundation@rheumatology.org

## Mentored Nurse Practitioner/Physician Assistant Award for Workforce Expansion

**Purpose**: Increase the supply of rheumatology healthcare providers to better meet the needs of people with rheumatic diseases across the United States, particularly in geographically underserved areas.
**Eligibility**: 1. Eligible applicant ("Mentor") must be a board-certified rheumatologist employed in clinical rheumatology practice. The NP or PA does not have to be identified at the time of application but must be identified at the time of award contract. Eligible NP/PA must be new to the field of rheumatology (employed in a rheumatology practice setting for fewer than 18 months). 2. Mentor must meet citizenship and other eligibility requirements as outlined in the Awards and Grants policies. 3. Mentor must be an ACR member at the time of submission and for the duration of the award. 4. Mentor is eligible to receive the award multiple times; however, the mentor must work with a new NP or PA each time. The mentor may have only one active NP/PA award at a time. 5. NP or PA must be a graduate from a program accredited by either the Commission on Collegiate Nursing Education (CCNE) or the Accreditation Review Commission on Education for the Physician Assistant. 6. NP or PA must have current state licensure. 7. NP or PA must have national Board certification by one or more of the following: a. American Nurses Credentialing Center b. American Academy of Nurse Practitioners c. Pediatric Nursing Certification Board d. National Certification Corporation e. National Commission on Certification of Physician Assistants 8. NP or PA must be a member of the Association for Rheumatology Professionals for the duration of the award
**Type**: Award
**Value**: US$25,000
**Length of Study**: 1 year
**Frequency**: Annual
**Country of Study**: United States of America
**Application Procedure**: All applications must be submitted online by 5:00 PM ET on the deadline day through Zengine at: webportalapp.com/sp/fy2022fta
**Closing Date**: 2 March
**Funding**: Foundation
**Contributor**: Rheumatology Research Foundation
**Additional Information**:     www.rheumresearch.org/file/awards/04-education-and-training/FY22-Mentored-Nurse-Practitioner-Physician-Assistant-Award-for-Workforce-Expansion_FINAL.pdf

### For further information contact:

**Tel**:     (1) 404 365 1373

## Paula de Merieux Fellowship Training Award

**Purpose**: Ensure a diverse and highly-trained workforce is available to provide clinical care to people with rheumatic diseases

**Eligibility**: 1. Applicant (Program Director) must be an ACR or ARP member at the time of submission and for the duration of the award 2. Only Program Directors at ACGME-accredited institutionsin good standing may apply 3. The rheumatology fellowship training Program Director at the institution will be responsible for the overall direction, management and administration of the program 4. By submitting an application, the Program Director and sponsoring institution agree funds will be used ONLY for salary support of one fellow in their first orsecond year (or third year fellow in pediatric rheumatology) 5. Multiple applicationsfrom a single institution will not be permitted unless they are for separate training programs (e.g., adult and pediatric rheumatology) 6. Programs may not apply for the Amgen Fellowship Training Award and Fellowship Training AwardWorkforce Expansion within the same application cycle. 7. Current recipients of the Fellowship Training Award for Workforce Expansion are not eligible to apply for this award. 8. Supported fellows do not need to be U.S. citizens or non-citizen nationals

**Type**: Award

**Value**: US$50,000

**Length of Study**: 1 year

**Frequency**: Annual

**Country of Study**: United States of America

**Application Procedure**: All applications must be submitted online by 5:00 PM ET on the deadline day through Zengine at: webportalapp.com/sp/fy2022fta

**Closing Date**: 1 May

**Funding**: Foundation

**Contributor**: Rheumatology Research Foundation

**Additional Information**: www.rheumresearch.org/file/FY22_Fellowship-Training-Award-PDM-Nelson_FINAL.pdf

### For further information contact:

**Tel**: (1) 404 365 1373

## Rheumatology Future Physician Scientist Award

**Purpose**: Enhance the research training of promising students who are matriculated in a combined MD/PhD or DO/PhD dual-doctoral degree training program and who intend careers as physician-scientists

**Eligibility**: The Foundation encourages applications from students early in the research training phase of their dual degree training so that they can substantively benefit from the mentored research training opportunities. 1. Applicant must meet citizenship and other eligibility requirements as outlined in the Awards and Grants policies. 2. The applicant must have a baccalaureate degree, show evidence of high academic performance in the sciences, and commitment to a career as an independent physician-scientist. Applicants should demonstrate a strong interest in pursuing a career in rheumatology research. 3. This program is specifically designed to support combined, dual-degree training leading to award of both a health professional doctoral degree (MD, DO) that would make the awardee eligible for future training as a rheumatologist; and a research doctoral degree (PhD) from an accredited program. Thus, the applicant must be enrolled in an MD/PhD or DO/PhD program. The entirety of the award period must be devoted to full-time graduate research training leading to the doctoral research degree. This award will not support clinical training during the years of the MD/PhD or DO/PhD program. 4. To encourage timely completion of dual degree training, this award is generally not intended to support students after year 5 of their training program. Ideally, support will be for 2 years during years 3-6 of the dual degree program (after the initial 2 years of classwork but prior to the clinical rotations/medical training). 5. The applicant must have identified a dissertation research project and a primary mentor. The primary mentor must be a faculty member actively engaged in basic, translational, clinical or health services research with a strong record of peer-reviewed research relevant to rheumatology.

**Level of Study**: Doctorate, Postdoctorate, Professional development, Research

**Type**: Award

**Value**: Maximum US$60,000 over 2 years

**Length of Study**: 2 years

**Frequency**: Annual

**Country of Study**: United States of America

**Closing Date**: 1 July

**Funding**: Foundation

**Contributor**: Rheumatology Research Foundation

**Additional Information**: www.rheumresearch.org/file/FY22-Rheumatology-Future-Physician-Scientist-Award_FINAL.pdf

### For further information contact:

**Tel**: (1) 404 365 1373

## Scientist Development Award

**Purpose**: To provide a training programme to rheumatology fellows or rheumatologists in the early stages of their career on aspects of clinical investigations through a structured, formal training programme

**Eligibility**: Applicant must meet citizenship requirements outlined by the Rheumatology Research Foundations Awards and Grant policies, be an active member of the ACR or ARHP at the time of submission, have a doctoral level degree, and be affiliated with an accredited graduate or medical school. Applicant must be able to commit at least 75% full-time professional effort to research, career development and other scholarly activities. Candidates may not spend more than 25% effort in clinical and/or teaching activities. Former or current principal investigators of research grants (at the K level or higher, including institutional K) and past awardees of this or equivalent Foundation grants are NOT eligible to apply

**Level of Study**: Doctorate, Postdoctorate, Professional development, Research

**Type**: Award

**Value**: US$50,000 for first year, US$75,000 for second year and US$100,000 for third year

**Length of Study**: Up to 2 years

**Frequency**: Annual

**Country of Study**: United States of America

**Application Procedure**: www.rheumresearch.org/career-development-research-awards#SDA

**No. of awards offered**: 36

**Closing Date**: 1 July

**Funding**: Foundation

**Contributor**: Rheumatology Research Foundation

**No. of awards given last year**: 8

**No. of applicants last year**: 36

**Additional Information**: www.rheumresearch.org www.rheumresearch.org/file/Awards/SDA_RFA.pdf

### For further information contact:

**Email**:   apply@heart.org

# Rhode Island Foundation

## Cataract Fire Company #2 Scholarship

**Purpose**: This scholarship is open to residents of Warwick, Rhode Island, who are entering their first year of a two-year, four-year, or vocational/technical postsecondary institution. Students must demonstrate financial need

**Eligibility**: 1. Must be a high school senior who is entering his/her first year of a two-year, four-year, or vocational/technical postsecondary institution. 2. Must be a resident of Warwick, Rhode Island. 3. Must be a citizen of United States of America. 4. This award is for United States students

**Level of Study**: Graduate

**Type**: Scholarship

**Value**: US$1,458

**Frequency**: Annual

**Country of Study**: United States of America

**Application Procedure**: Applications are available on the Rhode Island Foundation website. The student must click on the "Scholarship/Fellowship Opportunities" link and then search for his/her desired scholarship to access the application. In addition to a completed application, the student must submit the following documents: a copy of his/her financial aid award letter; his/her official high school transcript; a resume or a list of activities in which he/she participates; a typed double-spaced essay of 300 words or less describing what he/she hopes to be doing in his/her professional life 10 years from now; and a copy of his/her final Student Aid Report (SAR), which is provided to the student after filing the FAFSA (Free Application for Federal Student Aid)

**Closing Date**: 5 April

**Funding**: Foundation

**Additional Information**: www.unigo.com/scholarships/all/cataract-fire-company-2-scholarship/1005829

### For further information contact:

34 Warwick Lake Ave., Warwick, RI 02889, United States of America.

**Tel**:          (1) 401 427 4011
**Email**:      rbogert@rifoundation.org

## Major Jeremiah P. Murphy Scholarship

**Purpose**: This scholarship is open to children of active, retired, or deceased Providence (RI) police officers who are or will be attending postsecondary institutions offering two-year associate's or four-year college degree

**Eligibility**: 1. Must be a resident of Rhode Island. 2. Must be a citizen of United States of America. 3. Must be attending or planning to attend a postsecondary institution offering a two-year associate's or a four-year college degree. 4. Must be the child of an active, retired, or deceased Providence, Rhode Island, police officer. 5. This award is for United States students

**Level of Study**: Graduate

**Type**: Scholarship

**Value**: US$2,500

**Frequency**: Annual

**Country of Study**: United States of America

**Application Procedure**: The application deadline date has not yet been finalized for this year, but is expected to remain the same as last year. The deadline date shown here is tentative based on last year's date. Please check back in November for a refreshed application deadline date. Applications are available on the Rhode Island Foundation website. The student must click on the "Scholarship/Fellowship Opportunities" link and then search for his/her desired scholarship to access the application. As part of the online application, the student must upload the following required documents: a completed 'Financial Information Worksheet' (accessible for download in the application); a copy of his/her SAR (Student Aid Report), which is generated after filing the FAFSA (Free Application for Federal Student Aid); the most recent version of his/her student transcript (unofficial accepted); an essay of one page or less on the topic listed on the application; proof of eligible parental employment

**Closing Date**: 6 April

**Funding**: Foundation

**Additional Information**: www.unigo.com/scholarships/by-type/government-scholarships/major-jeremiah-p-murphy-scholarship/1005833

## For further information contact:

1 Union Station, Providence, RI 02903, United States of America.

**Tel**: (1) 401 427 4011
**Email**: rbogert@rifoundation.org

## Rhodes College

2000 North Parkway, Memphis, TN 38112-1690, United States of America.

**Tel**: (1) 901 843 3000
**Email**: registrar@rhodes.edu
**Website**: www.rhodes.edu

Rhodes, founded in 1848, seeks to graduate students with a lifelong passion for learning, a compassion for others, and the ability to translate academic study and personal concern into effective leadership and action in their communities and world.

## Watson Fellowship

**Purpose**: To offer college graduates a year of independent study and travel outside the United States

**Eligibility**: Candidates must be graduating seniors to apply; United States citizenship NOT required

**Type**: Fellowship

**Value**: US$25,000

**Length of Study**: 1 year

**Frequency**: Annual

**Application Procedure**: A fellowship form along with a project application proposal and details in not more than 5 pages should be submitted electronically

**Closing Date**: October

**Contributor**: Thomas J. Watson Foundation

**Additional Information**: www.brynmawr.edu/fellowships/watson-fellowships

## For further information contact:

Watson Fellowship Program, 293 South Main Street, Providence, RI 02903, United States of America.

**Tel**: (1) 401 274 1952
**Fax**: (1) 401 274 1954
**Email**: tjw@watsonfellowship.org

## Rhodes Trust

### Rhodes Scholarship

**Purpose**: Rhodes's vision in founding the Scholarship was to develop outstanding leaders who would be motivated to 'fight the world's fight' and to 'esteem the performance of public duties as their highest aim', and to promote international understanding and peace

**Eligibility**: At the time of application, an applicant must be: a citizen of the United States OR a lawful permanent resident of the United States OR a U.S. resident with DACA status on April 15 in the year of application. Eligible to apply through one of the 50 states, the District of Columbia, or one of the U.S. territories: either in the state or territory where the applicant was legally resident on April 15 in the year of application, or where the applicant will have received at least two years of college training and a bachelor's degree before October 1 in the year following election. At least 18 but not yet 24 years of age (i.e., the applicant must still be 23 on October 1 in the year of application)

**Level of Study**: Postgraduate

**Type**: Scholarship

**Value**: Fees are paid directly by the Trust to the College and University

**Length of Study**: 2 year

**Frequency**: Varies

**Country of Study**: United Kingdom

**Application Procedure**: Apply online rhodes.embark.com/auth/login

**No. of awards offered**: 5

**Closing Date**: October
**Funding**: Foundation
**Additional Information**: admission.buddy4study.com/study-abroad/rhodes-scholarship

### For further information contact:

**Tel**: (64) 4 475 8403
**Email**: scholarships-cf@universitiesnz.ac.nz

---

## Rhodes University

PO Box 94, Grahamstown, 6139, South Africa.

**Tel**: (27) 46 603 8055
**Email**: research-admin@ru.ac.za
**Website**: www.ru.ac.za/research
**Contact**: John Gillam, Manager

Rhodes University is a small university campus in Grahamstown with one of the highest research outputs per capita in South Africa. The University offers excellent undergraduate and postgraduate education, and fosters personal development and leadership as well as team, social and communication skills amongst its diverse student body.

### Hobart Houghton Research Fellowship

**Purpose**: To promote work of scientific value relevant to the economic problems of the Eastern Cape Province, Republic of South Africa, that could contribute to the betterment of the people of the region
**Eligibility**: Open to English speakers who hold at least a Master's degree in economics and who exhibit successful research experience
**Level of Study**: Doctorate, Postdoctorate
**Type**: Fellowship
**Value**: ZAR 25,000
**Length of Study**: 2 months–1 year
**Frequency**: Annual
**Study Establishment**: Rhodes University, Grahamstown
**Country of Study**: South Africa
**Application Procedure**: Applicants must complete an application form, available from the Dean of Research or from the website
**No. of awards offered**: 4
**Closing Date**: 30 September
**Funding**: Commercial
**No. of awards given last year**: 1

**No. of applicants last year**: 4
**Additional Information**: www.ru.ac.za/economics/hobarthoughtonresearchfellowship/

### For further information contact:

**Email**: h.nel@ru.ac.za

### Ruth First Scholarship

**Purpose**: The scholarship is intended to support candidates whose research is in the spirit of Ruth First's life and work, poses difficult social questions, and links knowledge and politics and scholarship and action
**Eligibility**: For Masters or PhD study and black South African or Mozambican women candidates are particularly encouraged to apply
**Level of Study**: Doctorate, Postgraduate
**Type**: Scholarship
**Value**: ZAR 120,000 (PhD); ZAR 90,000 per year (Master's)
**Frequency**: Annual
**Study Establishment**: Rhodes University, Grahamsdown
**Country of Study**: South Africa
**Application Procedure**: Applicants to submit a letter of motivation (2 pages or more) as to why they would be a potentially suitable candidate for this award and how their proposed research will be within the spirit of Ruth First's work. In addition, an academic transcript, academic curriculum vitae and a copy of an identity document is required
**No. of awards offered**: 126
**Closing Date**: 4 March
**Funding**: Private
**Contributor**: Donor and Investments
**No. of awards given last year**: 1
**No. of applicants last year**: 126
**Additional Information**: www.dur.ac.uk/study/pg/finance/funding/bursaries/scholarships/ruthfirst/

### For further information contact:

**Tel**: (44) 191 334 3436
**Email**: m.p.thompson@durham.ac.uk

---

## Robert Wood Johnson Foundation

50 College Road East, Princeton, NJ 08540-6614, United States of America.

**Tel**: (1) 609 627 6000
**Website**: www.rwjf.org/

The Robert Wood Johnson Foundation (RWJF) is working alongside others to build a national Culture of Health that provides everyone in America a fair and just opportunity for health and well-being. We are facing many obstacles that pose challenges to this audacious vision-inequities in life expectancy across communities; high-cost health care but poorer quality of care and health; and more. That's why RWJF supports a number of leadership programs that aim to develop a generation of leaders who see that we need new approaches to these pressing problems. These programs support and connect leaders who are caring, curious, collaborative, and committed to taking risks and moving boldly toward real pathways to change and to achieving greater equity in communities across our country.

## Clinical Scholars

**Purpose**: Clinical Scholars is a three-year, team-based program for a wide variety of health professionals in community, clinical, or academic settings. By the end of the program, fellows will have gained the skills they need to appraise, synthesize, use the best evidence to guide practice and inform policy in addressing complex health problems in their teams, organizations, and communitie

**Eligibility**: Clinical Scholars is a team-based program for a wide variety of health professionals in community, clinical, or academic settings (e.g., audiologists, clinical counselors, dentists, dieticians, nurses, nurse practitioners, nutritionists, occupational therapists, pharmacists, physical therapists, physicians, physician assistants, psychologists, social workers, speech therapists, veterinarians). The team must be sponsored by an applicant organization that will manage the award.

**Level of Study**: Masters Degree

**Type**: Scholarships

**Value**: Number of fellows in the 2020 cohort: up to 35 (in teams of three to five) 1. Grant funds: Grant funding is awarded based on team size-ranging from up to US$315,000 for a three-person team to a maximum of US$525,000 for a five-person team-to support the ongoing participation of all team members for all three years, including salary support for leadership development and project time, project funding, and project travel. This "up to" amount does not include an optional administrative fee, which the applicant organization may include to support the administrative costs of managing the award. All travel expenses to participate in the program's on-site trainings are provided to fellows at no cost. Please note: The size of the team may not increase during the grant term. All grant funds will be paid to the applicant organization, which will be responsible for managing the grant budget. Recognizing that some team members may not be employees of the grantee, this may include subcontracts to other organizations to support the team members'

time. The number of grants awarded will vary depending on the selected applicant organizations' team sizes. The grantee organization must submit required reports, and team members must demonstrate satisfactory participation and progress toward the program's goals in order to continue receiving funding after the first year and each year thereafter. The grant opportunity outlined in this call for applications is contingent upon final funding confirmation from the Robert Wood Johnson Foundation for such grants.

**Country of Study**: United States of America

**Application Procedure**: Application procedure furnised @ www.rwjf.org/en/library/funding-opportunities/2020/clinical-scholars.html

**No. of awards offered**: 35

**Closing Date**: 11 March

**Additional Information**: my.rwjf.org/applyFromWebsite.do?cfp=2926

### For further information contact:

**Email**:     clinical.scholars@unc.edu

## Harold Amos Medical Faculty Development Program

**Purpose**: The Harold Amos Medical Faculty Development Program (AMFDP) offers four-year postdoctoral research awards to physicians, dentists, and nurses from historically disadvantaged backgrounds. Scholars should be committed to working toward eliminating health disparities by achieving senior rank in academic medicine, dentistry, or nursing.

**Eligibility**: To be eligible for this award, applicants must be physicians, dentists, or nurses who: are from historically disadvantaged backgrounds; are U.S. citizens, permanent residents at the time of application, or individuals granted Deferred Action for Childhood Arrivals (DACA) status by the U.S. Citizenship and Immigration Services at the time of application (changes in federal policy or law may necessitate that we consider adjustments in eligibility and grant terms); are completing or have completed their formal clinical training (we will give preference to those who have recently completed their formal clinical training or-in the case of nurses-their research doctorate); are not related by blood or marriage to any Officer or Trustee of the Robert Wood Johnson Foundation, or a descendant of its founder, Robert Wood Johnson. Federal, state, tribal, and local government employees who are not considered government officials under Section 4946 of the Internal Revenue Code are eligible to apply. Physicians must be Board-eligible to apply for this program. A dental applicant must be a general dentist with a master's degree or a PhD or have completed advanced dental education. Nurse applicants must be registered nurses with a research doctorate in nursing or a related discipline completed by the application deadline. Full eligibility criteria (including footnotes) are available in the CFA.

**Level of Study**: Masters Degree

**Type**: Scholarships

**Value**: RWJF will fund up to 10 four-year awards of up to US$420,000 each in this grant cycle. Scholars will receive an annual stipend of up to US$75,000 each, complemented by a US$30,000 annual grant to support research activities. As detailed above, additional awards are available through partnerships with the American Society of Hematology (ASH) and the American Heart Association (AHA)

**Country of Study**: United States of America

**Application Procedure**: Application procedure furnised @ www.rwjf.org/en/library/funding-opportunities/2020/harold-amos-medical-faculty-development-program.html

**Closing Date**: 18 March

**Additional Information**: www.rwjf.org/en/library/funding-opportunities/2020/harold-amos-medical-faculty-development-program.html

related by blood or marriage to any Officer or Trustee of the Robert Wood Johnson Foundation, or be a descendant of its founder, Robert Wood Johnson.

**Level of Study**: Masters Degree

**Type**: Scholarships

**Value**: Number of scholars in the 2020 cohort: up to 60 grant funds from RWJF will include: Stipend: US$30,000, per year for up to four years or until you complete your doctoral program (whichever is sooner). Administrative fee: Home Institutions may include an administrative fee of US$1,000 per year, US$4,000 in total to the grant amount to cover the administrative costs of managing the award.

**Country of Study**: United States of America

**Application Procedure**: Application procedure furnised @ http: www.rwjf.org/en/library/funding-opportunities/2020/health-policy-research-scholars.html

**No. of awards offered**: 60

**Closing Date**: 11 March

**Additional Information**: www.rwjf.org/en/library/funding-opportunities/2020/health-policy-research-scholars.html

## Health Policy Research Scholars

**Purpose**: Health Policy Research Scholars (HPRS) is a four-year national leadership development program for full-time doctoral students from nonclinical, academic disciplines-who want to improve health, well-being, and equity; challenge long-standing, entrenched systems; exhibit new ways of working; and collaborate across disciplines and sectors.

**Eligibility**: Applicants must be a full-time second or third year doctoral student as of fall 2020 at a degree-granting institution based in the United States or its territories; Applicants must have at least three (3) academic years remaining in their doctoral program and do not expect to graduate before spring/summer 2023; Applicants must be from populations underrepresented in specific doctoral disciplines and/or marginalized backgrounds. Examples of eligible individuals include, but are not limited to: first-generation college graduates; individuals from lower socioeconomic backgrounds; individuals from communities of color; and individuals with disabilities; Applicants cannot be a recipient of a national fellowship program that prohibits participation in additional programs, such as HPRS; Applicants must be at least 21 years old as of September 1, 2020; Federal, state, tribal and local government employees are eligible to apply unless they are considered government officials under Section 4946 of the Internal Revenue Code; Applicants must be U.S. citizens, permanent residents, or individuals granted Deferred Action for Childhood Arrivals (DACA) status by the U.S. Citizenship and Immigration Services at the time of application. As federal policy or laws change, we may need to consider adjustments in eligibility and grant terms; Applicants cannot be

## Interdisciplinary Research Leaders

**Purpose**: Interdisciplinary Research Leaders (IRL) is a three-year national leadership development program that aims to foster and support new interdisciplinary, action-oriented research collaborations that will help build the evidence base for effective community interventions to improve health for all. We'll support teams of mid-career individuals who come from diverse disciplinary backgrounds or scientific perspectives. The community-engaged partner on the team may work in a variety of organizational settings and have relevant expertise in the proposed research project.

**Eligibility**: The Interdisciplinary Research Leaders program is a team-based program; teams must be sponsored by an applicant organization. What are the requirements for teams? Teams must be: 1. Comprised of three mid-career individuals: 2. Two researchers: people with a terminal degree in their field (e.g., PhD) or extensive research or evaluation experience; and, 3. One community partner: individuals with close ties to a community of interest who do not regularly engage in research as a main function of their job; these individuals must have the potential to take action on the issue themselves or have relationships with entities that can take action; 4. Sponsored by an applicant organization. There are no strict rules for who is or is not mid-career, but we anticipate that mid-career applicants have approximately five years of high-quality experience and are not within 10 years of retirement. What are the requirements for individual team members? Researchers: 5. Should come from diverse disciplinary backgrounds or scientific perspectives; we are particularly interested in novel interdisciplinary partnerships (e.g., engineering and anthropology). 6. Do not need to be located in the same geographical area, but should articulate a plan for maintaining team cohesion as part of the application and selection process. 7. May hold academic appointments or positions in applied research firms or community organizations. Note: We especially encourage researchers who do not have prior direct experience in health research to apply. Community partners: 8. May work in a variety of organizational settings, as long as their experience and expertise are relevant to the proposed research project and the partner has authentic engagement with the community involved in the research project. May be community organizers, educators, leaders, local government workers, or any of a wide range of people working in the nonprofit and private sectors, whether health care-related or not. All team members must: 9. Be at least 21 years old as of September 1, 2020. 10. Be a U.S. citizen, permanent resident, or individual granted Deferred Action for Childhood Arrivals (DACA) status by the U.S. Citizenship and Immigration Services at the time of application. As federal policy or laws change, we may need to consider adjustments in eligibility and grant terms. The following individuals are not eligible to apply or be part of an Interdisciplinary Research Leaders team: 11. Federal, state, tribal and local government employees who are considered government officials1 under Section 4946 of the Internal Revenue Code. 12. Individual candidates who are related by blood or marriage to any Officer2 or Trustee of the Robert Wood Johnson Foundation, or be a descendant of its founder, Robert Wood Johnson. 13. Individuals who are receiving support from other research fellowships/traineeships; this includes NIH K award and similar training support.

**Level of Study**: Masters Degree

**Type**: Scholarships

**Value**: Number of grants: up to 15 grants (teams of three fellows) Total award: up to US$350,000 (plus an optional administrative fee explained below) per applicant organization supporting a team of three fellows for the duration of the three-year program; budget to include: up to US$25,000 per year per fellow is to be allocated to support the fellow's time in the program (approximately one day per week); this represents up to US$225,000 of the total award. a portion to be allocated to each team for research purposes; the total 24- to 30-month budget, including indirect costs/overhead for the project, will be up to US$125,000 (range US$25,000-US$125,000). This portion of the grant will support research activities only (e.g., purchasing data or supplies, support staff, IRL fellow research time, travel related to project execution). It is not intended to support intervention/program development or implementation. an optional administrative fee of US$3,000 per year, US$9,000 in total, to cover the applicant organization's administrative costs of supporting the fellow's time in the program.

**Country of Study**: US

**Application Procedure**: Application procedure furnished @ www.rwjf.org/en/library/funding-opportunities/2020/interdisciplinary-research-leaders.html

**No. of awards offered**: 15

**Closing Date**: 11 March

**Additional Information**: www.rwjf.org/en/library/funding-opportunities/2020/interdisciplinary-research-leaders.html

### For further information contact:

**Email**:     ResearchLeaders@umn.edu

## Roberta Sykes Indigenous Education Foundation

100 Botany Road, Alexandria, NSW 2015, Australia.

**Tel**:           (61) 2 9310 8400

**Contact**:     The Roberta Sykes Indigenous Education Foundation

The group began by publishing an Aboriginal community newspaper, Koori Bina, which later became AIM (Aboriginal and Islander Message). BWA taught students of the Aboriginal and Islander Dance Theatre the skills to publish a small community newspaper; literacy, reporting, creative writing, editing, lay-out and administration, which eventually lead to the students taking over its publication. Over time, BWA broadened its work and funded a number of small enterprises that were established by Aboriginal women.

## Roberta Sykes Bursary

**Purpose**: The Roberta Sykes Indigenous Education Foundation provides partial funding for Indigenous Australians to undertake short, executive education courses at leading overseas academic institutions

**Eligibility**: 1. Be of Aboriginal or Torres Strait Islander descent, identify as Aboriginal and/or Torres Strait Islander and be accepted as such by the community in which they live or have lived. 2. Provide Confirmation of Aboriginal or Torres Strait Islander descent through a signed statement (including common seal) from the Aboriginal or Torres Strait Islander Heritage Association, Aboriginal or Torres Strait Islander Corporation or Land Council of the country of your ancestors. If applicable, candidates are encouraged to provide a written statement from the Aboriginal or Torres Strait Islander Heritage Association, Aboriginal or Torres Strait Islander Corporation or Land Council of the community in which they live or have lived and/or are connected to. 3. Be accepted into an executive program at a recognised overseas academic institution. 4. Be able to demonstrate that their studies will be of benefit to their community upon their return to Australia.

**Type**: Bursary

**Value**: The value of the Bursary is up to AU$20,000

**Country of Study**: Australia

**Application Procedure**: Before applying for this scholarship, if any clarifications are required, contact the foundation using the link www.robertasykesfoundation.com/contact. html

**Closing Date**: 9 November

**Additional Information**: www.robertasykesfoundation. com/roberta-sykes-bursary.html

### For further information contact:

The Roberta Sykes Indigenous Education Foundation, 100 Botany Rd, Alexandria NSW 2015, Australia.

### Roberta Sykes Scholarship

**Purpose**: The Roberta Sykes Scholarship provides partial funding to Aboriginal and/or Torres Strait Islander postgraduate students who wish to undertake studies at recognised overseas universities

**Eligibility**: 1. Usually have an undergraduate degree with a strong academic record. 2. Be accepted into a postgraduate coursework or research degree at a recognised overseas university. 3. Be of Aboriginal and/or Torres Strait Islander descent, identify as Aboriginal and/or Torres Strait Islander and be accepted as such by the community in which they live or have lived. 4. Be able to demonstrate that alongside a Roberta Sykes Scholarship, they will have sufficient funds to support themselves during the course of their postgraduate degree (such as through another scholarship, private sponsorship or personal funds). 5. Be able to demonstrate that their studies will be of benefit to their community upon their return to Australia.

**Type**: Scholarship

**Value**: The value of the Scholarship is up to AU$30,000 per year

**Country of Study**: Australia

**Application Procedure**: In order to contact for the elaborate information about the application. check the below link. www.robertasykesfoundation.com/contact.html

**Closing Date**: 9 November

**Additional Information**: If you require further information or wish to discuss your application before submitting please contact the foundation at www.robertasykesfoundation.com/ contact.html www.robertasykesfoundation.com/roberta-sykes-scholarships.html

### For further information contact:

The Roberta Sykes Indigenous Education Foundation, 100 Botany Rd, Alexandria NSW 2015, Australia.

### The Annual Aurora Indigenous Scholars International Study Tour

**Purpose**: The Study Tour not only offers invaluable opportunities for students to gain insight into the realities of undertaking postgraduate study at these leading institutions but also provides the opportunity to travel with a group of like-minded students. The Study Tour involves meetings with key academics and administrators at each university, as well as current students in the areas of the participants' interest

**Eligibility**: 1. The Study Tour is open to applicants who have completed at least two years of their course of study and also to university graduates who wish to undertake further postgraduate study. 2. Each year, there is a competitive application process for the Study Tour. 3. The successful applicants will be chosen primarily on the basis of academic achievement

**Level of Study**: Postgraduate

**Type**: Scholarship

**Value**: Costs associated with travel, accommodation and meals are covered

**Frequency**: Annual

**Country of Study**: Australia

**Application Procedure**: To be considered, applicants must apply online via the Indigenous Scholarships Portal and upload the following documents: 1. A cover letter (including a personal statement about your background, career aspirations and reasons for wanting to go on the Tour). 2. A curriculum vitae. 3. An official transcript of all university results (including mid-year results, if available) Confirmation of Aboriginal or Torres Strait Islander descent through a signed written statement (including common seal if available) of an Aboriginal or Torres Strait Islander Heritage. 4. Association, Aboriginal or Torres Strait Islander Corporation or Land Council in the community where you live or have lived. 5. A high-resolution photo (headshot preferably) that could be used in promotional material, should you be selected to go on the Tour. 6. A scanned copy of your passport bio data page (if you have a valid passport)

**Closing Date**: 9 March

**Funding**: Private

**Additional Information**: For further information on the Study Tour, please please visit the Aurora Education Foundation website www.robertasykesfoundation.com/the-annual-aurora-indigenous-scholars-international-study-tour.html

### For further information contact:

**Email**:    scholarships@auroraproject.com.au

## The Roberta Sykes Harvard Club Scholarship

**Purpose**: The purpose of the award is to promote fellowship amongst alumni and to assist Australians wishing to study at Harvard

**Eligibility**: For eligibility details, please visit www.robertasy kesfoundation.com/roberta-sykes-scholarships.html. Usually have an undergraduate degree with a strong academic record; Be accepted into a postgraduate coursework or research degree at a recognised overseas university; Be of Aboriginal and/or Torres Strait Islander descent, identify as Aboriginal and/or Torres Strait Islander and be accepted as such by the community in which they live or have lived; Be able to demonstrate that alongside a Roberta Sykes Scholarship, they will have sufficient funds to support themselves during the course of their postgraduate degree (such as through another scholarship, private sponsorship or personal funds); Be able to demonstrate that their studies will be of benefit to their community upon their return to Australia

**Type**: Scholarship

**Value**: The value of the scholarship is up to AU$80,000 per annum to be paid over the course of the Scholar's study

**Country of Study**: Australia

**Application Procedure**: Before applying, prospective applicants should check the Harvard website (www.harvard.edu/admissions-aid)

**Contributor**: Roberta Sykes Harvard Club

**Additional Information**: For more information on the club and its programs, please visit www.harvardclub.org.au www.robertasykesfoundation.com/roberta-sykes-harvard-club-scholarship.html

### For further information contact:

**Email**: scholarships@auroraproject.com.au

## Rotterdam School of Management Erasmus University

**Tel**: (31) 10 408 2222
**Email**: info@rsm.nl
**Website**: www.rsm.nl
**Contact**: Denise Chasney van Dijk, Financial Aid Manager

As one of the world's top business schools, RSM is a centre of excellence and innovation for management education and research. Our goal is to empower individuals to succeed amid the complexities of modern international commerce and become the business leaders of tomorrow.

## Rotterdam School of Management Master of Business Administration Asia & Australia Regional Scholarship

**Purpose**: To assist candidates from the Asia & Australasia Region in financing their MBA study in the Netherlands

**Eligibility**: The scholarship is open to high potential candidates who are a citizen or hold permanent residence status in one of the following listed countries: Australia, Bangladesh, Bhutan, Brunei, Burma, Cambodia, China, Fiji, Hong Kong, India, Indonesia, Japan, Kiribati, Laos, Macau, Malaysia, Micronesia, Mongolia, Nepal, New Zealand, Palau, Papua New Guinea, Philippines, Samoa, Singapore, Solomon Islands, Sri Lanka, Thailand, Timor-Leste, Tonga, Tuvalu, Vietnam, Yemen

**Level of Study**: MBA

**Type**: Scholarship

**Value**: 20% tuition fee waiver

**Length of Study**: 12 months

**Frequency**: Annual

**Study Establishment**: Erasmus University

**Country of Study**: Netherlands

**Application Procedure**: Complete application form to be considered

**No. of awards offered**: 36

**Closing Date**: 30 September

**Funding**: Private

**Contributor**: RSM Erasmus University

**No. of awards given last year**: 1

**No. of applicants last year**: 36

**Additional Information**: Eligible to nationals of Asia and Australasia

## Rotterdam School of Management, Erasmus Graduate School of Business

PO Box 1738, Rotterdam, NL-3000 DR, Netherlands.

**Tel**: (31) 10 408 2222
**Email**: rsm@rsm.nl
**Website**: www.rsm.nl
**Contact**: Ms Connie Tai, Director of Recruiting & Admissions

## Holland Government Scholarship/Upcoming Year for School of Management

**Purpose**: The RSM scholarship will determine award recipient. The Holland Scholarship is financed by the Dutch Ministry of Education, Culture and Science

**Eligibility**: To be eligible, fulfill the following: 1. Your nationality is non-EEA. 2. You are a prospective student, starting your studies in the academic year. 3. You are applying for a full-time bachelor's or master's programme at RSM. 4. You meet the specific requirements of the programme you are applying for. 5. You do not have a degree from an educational institution in the Netherlands (excluding exchange programmes in the Netherlands). This content was originally published on After School Africa from www.afterschoolafrica.com/13953/netherlands-fellowship-programmes-nfp-developing-countries-phd-students/

**Level of Study**: Postgraduate

**Type**: Scholarship

**Value**: € 5,000 for maximum of 12 months

**Frequency**: Annual

**Country of Study**: Any country

**Application Procedure**: First Step is to register for the Bachelor International Business Administration programme. Required documents are : A scholarship application letter in OLAF of maximum 1 A4 size page, including the following information. 1. an explanation why you would need a scholarship, comprising a description of academic excellence and if application other merits. 2. a clear financial plan, of how you are going to finance year 2 and 4 of IBA programme. 3. If applicable, certified copies of the scholarship granted

**Closing Date**: 31 January

**Funding**: Private

**Contributor**: The Dutch Ministry of Education, Culture and Science

**Additional Information**: www.opportunitiesforafricans.com/holland-government-scholarship-2019-2020-for-study-at-rotterdam-school-of-management-erasmus-university/

# Royal Academy of Engineering

3 Carlton House Terrace, London SW1Y 5DG, United Kingdom.

| | |
|---|---|
| **Tel**: | (44) 20 7766 0600 |
| **Email**: | mark.bambury@raeng.org.uk |
| **Website**: | www.raeng.org.uk |
| **Contact**: | Dr Mark Bambury, Scheme Manager |

The Royal Academy of Engineering's objectives may be summarized as the pursuit, encouragement and maintenance of excellence in the whole field of engineering in order to promote the advancement of the science, art and the practice of engineering for the benefit of the public.

## ExxonMobil Excellence in Teaching Awards

**Purpose**: To encourage able young engineering and Earth science lecturers to remain in the education sector in their early years

**Eligibility**: Open to well-qualified graduates, preferably with industrial experience and full-time lecturing posts at Institutes of Higher Education in the United Kingdom. Applicants should have been in their current posts for at least 1 year. The post must include the teaching of chemical, petroleum or mechanical engineering to undergraduates through courses that are accredited for registration with professional bodies for qualifications such as chartered engineer. For applicants whose career path has been graduation at the age of 22, followed by academic or industrial posts, the age limit is generally 32 years (at the closing date). Older candidates who have taken time out, e.g. for industrial experience, parenthood or voluntary service, will also be considered. Applicants should preferably be chartered engineers, or of equivalent professional status, or should be making progress towards this qualification

**Level of Study**: Postdoctorate

**Type**: Fellowship

**Value**: A range of benefits in addition to the £10,000 prize

**Length of Study**: 12 months

**Frequency**: Annual

**Study Establishment**: The applicant's current university in the United Kingdom

**Country of Study**: United Kingdom

**Application Procedure**: Applicants must complete an application form

**Closing Date**: 31 October

**Funding**: Commercial

**Contributor**: Exxon Mobile

**Additional Information**: A brochure is available on request. Enquiries about Exxon mobile university contacts should be sent via email and please see the website for further details www.eng.ed.ac.uk/about/news/20130211/tina-d%C3%BCren-awarded-2012-exxonmobil-excellence-teaching-award

### For further information contact:

**Email**:    bowbricki@raeng.co.uk

## Royal Academy Engineering Professional Development

**Purpose**: To ensure that the stills and knowledge of employees reflect the very latest in technological advances

**Eligibility**: Open to United Kingdom citizens with a degree or HND/HNC in engineering or a closely allied subject. OND/ONC or City and Guilds Full Technological Certificate

or NVQ level III qualifications are acceptable provided the individual has substantial industrial experience
**Level of Study**: Professional development
**Type**: Grant
**Value**: £10,000 and £5,000 and prospective applicants should indicate for which level of award they are applying
**Length of Study**: 1 year
**Frequency**: Annual
**Country of Study**: United Kingdom
**Application Procedure**: For further information please contact the scheme manager Ian Bowbrick at the Academy
**Closing Date**: 24 October
**Additional Information**: Please see the website for further details

**For further information contact:**

**Email**: Ian.bowbrick@raeng.org.uk

## Royal Academy Sir Angus Paton Bursary

**Purpose**: To study water and environmental management
**Eligibility**: The bursary supports a suitably qualified engineer study a full-time Masters' degree course specifically related to water resources engineering or some other environmental technology
**Level of Study**: Postgraduate
**Type**: Bursary
**Value**: £8,000
**Length of Study**: 1 year
**Frequency**: Annual
**Country of Study**: United Kingdom
**Application Procedure**: For further information please contact the scheme manager Ian Bowbrick at the Academy
**Funding**: Private
**Contributor**: Sir Angus Paton

**For further information contact:**

**Email**: ian.bowbrick@raeng.org.uk

## Royal Academy Sir Henry Royce Bursary

**Eligibility**: Open to qualified engineers enrolled on part-time modular Master's courses
**Level of Study**: Postgraduate
**Type**: Bursary
**Value**: £1,000
**Length of Study**: 1 year
**Frequency**: Annual
**Country of Study**: United Kingdom

**Application Procedure**: For further information please contact the scheme manager Ian Bowbrick at the Academy
**Funding**: Foundation
**Contributor**: Sir Henry Royce Memorial Foundation
**Additional Information**: Each awardee will receive a commemorative certificate and, on successful completion of their studies and award of the degree, a medal from the Sir Henry Royce Memorial Foundation www.engagement.man chester.ac.uk/blog/?p=3667

**For further information contact:**

**Email**: ian.bowbrick@raeng.org.uk

## Sainsbury Management Fellowships

**Purpose**: The overall objective of the scheme is to improve the economic performance of UK engineering, manufacturing and construction businesses by providing a resource of highly-motivated engineers who have complemented their technical qualifications and skills with a first-class business education in an international environment
**Eligibility**: 1. Applicants must have a confirmed place on a full-time MBA programme at one of the 14 eligible business schools 2. You may apply before a place is confirmed but will not be invited to interview until a Business school place is confirmed 3. Applicants must have a first degree in an engineering, allied technology or science discipline, preferably a first or upper second class 4. Applicants must demonstrate a strong commitment to both UK engineering/business/industry and their respective engineering communities 5. Applicants must be a UK / EU / EEA citizen, normally domiciled in the United Kingdom 6. Applicants do not need to have Chartered Engineer status (or equivalent), however this qualification or progress towards it will be viewed favourably 7. Applicants would usually have 4-10 years professional experience post-degree
**Level of Study**: Postgraduate
**Type**: Fellowships
**Value**: £50,000
**Length of Study**: 4-10 years
**Frequency**: Annual
**Country of Study**: United Kingdom
**Application Procedure**: All applications must be submitted via the online system, available here: grants.raeng.org.uk
**Closing Date**: 1 June
**Additional Information**: www.raeng.org.uk/publications/ other/guidance-notes-sainsbury-management-fellowships

**For further information contact:**

**Email**: jacqueline.clay@raeng.org.uk

# Royal Agricultural University

Royal Agricultural University, Gloucestershire, Cirencester GL7 6JS, United Kingdom.

**Tel**:        (44) 1285 652531
**Website**:   www.rau.ac.uk/

The Royal Agricultural University has been at the forefront of agricultural education since 1845.

## Africa Land and Food Masters Fellowship

**Eligibility**: Fellowships are open to Africans from Sub-Saharan Africa who have experience in agriculture, agri-business, food or natural resource management; an interest in land reform; and a desire to make a strategic and sustainable contribution to Africa's development
**Level of Study**: Postgraduate
**Type**: Fellowship
**Value**: Since the Fellowship was launched in 2005, over £1,800,000 has been generously provided by the private sector, foundations and charities in support of the programme
**Country of Study**: United Kingdom
**Application Procedure**: Nationals from sub-Saharan Africa are invited to apply for a Fellowship
**Closing Date**: 31 October
**Funding**: International office
**Additional Information**: opportunitydesk.org/2015/07/07/africa-land-food-fellowship-in-uk/

### For further information contact:

**Email**:    african.fellowship-at-rau.ac.uk

## Royal College of Midwives

15 Mansfield Street, London W1G 9NH, United Kingdom.

**Tel**:        (44) 20 7312 3643
**Email**:     info@rcm.org.uk
**Website**:   www.rcm.org.uk
**Contact**:   S E MacDonald, Education and Research Manager

The Royal College of Midwives is the major professional organization for midwives in the United Kingdom, and aims to contribute to the art and science of midwifery knowledge and practice. The RCM awards and scholarships provide opportunities for the development of good practice ultimately improving the care provided to women, their babies and families.

## Royal College of Midwives Annual Midwifery Awards

**Purpose**: To recognize and celebrate innovation in midwifery practice, education and research
**Eligibility**: Applicants may be individuals or small groups but should meet the criteria of 1 of the 10 categories. Check the website for complete details: www.rcm.org.uk/college/annual-midwifery-awards/
**Level of Study**: Postgraduate, Professional development, Research
**Type**: Award
**Value**: Varies (up to £20,000 in total)
**Frequency**: Annual
**Application Procedure**: Applicants must apply in writing or email to the address given below. The application must be accompanied by a 500-word description of the project. Shortlisted candidates will be asked to attend an interview
**No. of awards offered**: 82
**Closing Date**: 1 November
**Funding**: Commercial
**Contributor**: Several
**No. of awards given last year**: 12 awards in 12 categories plus a midwife award
**No. of applicants last year**: 82

### For further information contact:

Gothic House, 3 The Green, Richmond, Surrey TW9 1PL, United Kingdom.

**Email**:    mail@chamberdunn.co.uk

## Ruth Davies Research Bursary

**Purpose**: To promote and develop midwifery research and practice
**Eligibility**: Open to practicing midwives who are RCM members, who have basic knowledge, skills and understanding of the research process, have access to research support in their trust or Institutes of Higher Education and who have been in practice for 2 years or more
**Level of Study**: Doctorate, Graduate, Postdoctorate, Postgraduate, Predoctorate, Professional development, Research
**Type**: Bursary

**Value**: £5,000 per bursary
**Length of Study**: 1 year
**Frequency**: Annual
**Country of Study**: United Kingdom
**Application Procedure**: Applicants must submit a succinct curriculum vitae covering the previous 5 years, a research proposal of no more than 2,500 words and letters of support from both employers and academics who are familiar with the applicant's work
**No. of awards offered**: 4 shortlisted
**Closing Date**: 30 July
**Funding**: Commercial
**Contributor**: Bounty
**No. of awards given last year**: 3
**No. of applicants last year**: 4 shortlisted
**Additional Information**: pdfslide.net/documents/ruth-davies-bursary-2010.html

### For further information contact:

**Tel**:       (44) 20 7312 3463
**Email**:   marlyn.gennace@rcm.org.uk

## Royal College of Nursing Foundation

20 Cavendish Square, London, W1G 0RN, United Kingdom.

**Tel**:        (44) 20 7647 3645
**Email**:    rcnfoundation@rcn.org.uk
**Website**:  www.rcnfoundation.org.uk
**Contact**:  Ms Grants Officer Awards Officer

The RCN Foundation is an independent charity supporting nursing to improve the health and well-being of the public.

## Mary Seacole Leadership and Development Awards

**Purpose**: To provide funding for a project, or other educational/development activity that benefits the health needs of people from black and minority ethnic communities
**Eligibility**: Open to nurses, midwives and health visitors in United Kingdom
**Level of Study**: Doctorate, Graduate, Postdoctorate, Postgraduate, Predoctorate, Professional development, Research
**Type**: Award
**Value**: £12,500, Development award £6,250
**Length of Study**: Unrestricted
**Frequency**: Annual

**Study Establishment**: Unrestricted
**Country of Study**: United Kingdom
**Application Procedure**: Applicants must send a stamped addressed envelope to the Royal College of Nursing (RCN) to obtain details and an application form
**No. of awards offered**: 16
**Closing Date**: 23 March
**Funding**: Government
**Contributor**: Department of Health
**No. of awards given last year**: 6
**No. of applicants last year**: 16
**Additional Information**: www.rcn.org.uk/professional-development/scholarships-and-bursaries/mary-seacole-awards

### For further information contact:

**Email**:    governance.support@rcn.org.uk

## Royal College of Obstetricians and Gynaecologists (RCOG)

27 Sussex Place, Regent's Park, London NW1 4RG, United Kingdom.

**Tel**:        (44) 20 7772 6200
**Email**:    mgoonewardene@rcog.org.uk
**Website**:  www.rcog.org.uk
**Contact**:  M Goonewardene, Awards Administrator

The Royal College of Obstetricians and Gynaecologists (RCOG) is dedicated to the encouragement of the study, and the advancement of science and practice of obstetrics and gynaecology.

## American Gyneocological Club/Gynaecological Visiting Society Fellowship

**Purpose**: Through generous funding from the American Gynecological Club and the Gynaecological Visiting Society of Great Britain, the RCOG can offer up to £1200 to an individual to visit and gain knowledge from a specific centre offering new techniques of clinical management within O&G
**Eligibility**: This award is open to Trainees in the United Kingdom and Republic of Ireland and their equivalents in the United States of America in alternating years. For the current year, only applicants from the United Kingdom are eligible. Applicants may make a submission to travel from the United Kingdom to the United States of America
**Level of Study**: Postgraduate

**Type**: Fellowship
**Frequency**: Annual
**Country of Study**: Any country
**Application Procedure**: Please ensure you read the guidance on submitting your application before entering any of the awards. current year Applications To apply, please send your application form (Word document) to the Awards Administrator awards@rcog.org.uk by midnight on Friday 31 May. Your application will be judged on the following criteria: Presentation and planning, Originality of elective, Evidence of student supervision and support, level of involvement and benefit of applicant
**Closing Date**: 31 May
**Funding**: Private
**Additional Information**: www.rcog.org.uk/en/careers-training/awards-grants-prizes/american-gynecological-clubgynaecological-visiting-society-fellowship/

### For further information contact:

**Email**:     awards@rcog.org

## Annual Academic Award

**Purpose**: The award recognises distinguished service to academic obstetrics and gynaecology.
**Eligibility**: 1. Outstanding contribution to the academic aspects of our speciality (scientific discovery, pre-clinical and clinical research, academic education and training) 2. UK RCOG Fellows or Members, RCOG Fellows ad eundem or others of equivalent academic distinction (professorial level), at the discretion of the Academic Board.
**Level of Study**: Postgraduate
**Type**: Award
**Frequency**: Annual
**Country of Study**: Any country
**Closing Date**: 24 April
**Funding**: Foundation
**Additional Information**: www.rcog.org.uk/en/careers-training/awards-grants-prizes/annual-academic-award/

### For further information contact:

**Email**:     academic@rcog.org.uk

## Bernhard Baron Travelling Fellowship

**Purpose**: The Bernhard Baron Charitable Trust has generously endowed to the RCOG two travel scholarships in obstetrics and gynaecology for Fellows and Members of the College worth up to £6000 each

**Eligibility**: 1. Travel must take place within 12 months of the award being made. 2. The award may only be used for the purpose outlined in your original application. 3. A detailed report (maximum 1,000 words), including pictures if necessary, must be submitted to the RCOG Awards Administrator within eight weeks after the elective
**Level of Study**: Postdoctorate
**Type**: Fellowships
**Value**: up to £6,000
**Length of Study**: 1 year
**Frequency**: Annual
**Country of Study**: Any country
**Closing Date**: 31 May
**Funding**: Foundation
**Additional Information**: www.rcog.org.uk/en/careers-training/awards-grants-prizes/bernhard-baron-travelling-fellowship/

### For further information contact:

27 Sussex Place Regent's Park London NW1 4RG, United Kingdom.

**Fax**:     (44) 20 7723 0575
**Email**:     awards@rcog.org.uk

## Bruggeman Postgraduate Scholarship in Classics

**Purpose**: Doctoral scholarships are awarded by the University Council, on the recommendation of the Senate, to candidates proceeding to a course of supervised doctoral study at this University. These scholarships are normally available only to students seeking to obtain their first doctoral qualification
**Level of Study**: Postgraduate
**Type**: Scholarship
**Value**: NZ$25,000
**Frequency**: Annual
**Country of Study**: New Zealand
**Funding**: Foundation
**Additional Information**: www.otago.ac.nz/graduate-research/scholarships/otago013798.pdf

### For further information contact:

**Email**:     scholarships@otago.ac.nz

## Calcutta Eden Hospital Annual Prize

**Purpose**: The Calcutta (Kolkata) Eden Hospital is notable because it is where the highly reputed Professor Green Armytage spent his professional career for 25 years at the turn of the 20th century. During his tenure, he designed 'uterine haemostatic forceps' which are still widely used around the world in caesarean sections

**Eligibility**: The prize is awarded for the best submission of an article that outlines your insight into any aspect of obstetrics and gynaecology undertaken during your training. Preference will be given to well-planned and presented applications

**Level of Study**: Postdoctorate

**Type**: Grant

**Value**: £350

**Frequency**: Annual

**Country of Study**: Any country

**Closing Date**: 31 May

**Funding**: Foundation

**Additional Information**: www.rcog.org.uk/en/careers-training/awards-grants-prizes/calcutta-eden-hospital-annual-prize/

**For further information contact:**

**Email**:  awards@rcog.org.uk

## Eden Travelling Fellowship in Obstetrics and Gynaecology

**Purpose**: Generously endowed by the late Mr Thomas Watts Eden, this fellowship is awarded to a medical graduate (who graduated within the last two years) currently undertaking a research project. The winner can use the funds to visit any other department(s) within O&G or a related discipline to gain additional knowledge and experience

**Eligibility**: This Fellowship is open to medical graduates (who graduated within the last 2 years) who are currently undertaking a research project. 1. Travel must take place within 12 months of the award being made in December. 2. The award may only be used for the purpose outlined in your original application. 3. A detailed report (maximum 1,000 words), including pictures if necessary, must be submitted to the RCOG Awards Administrator within eight weeks after the elective. 4. Applicants must declare that their project is entirely their own work and whether they have applied for other prizes for the same project

**Level of Study**: Postdoctorate, professional development

**Type**: Fellowship

**Value**: Up to £5,000

**Length of Study**: 2 year

**Frequency**: Annual

**Country of Study**: Any country

**Closing Date**: 31 May

**Funding**: Foundation

**Additional Information**: www.rcog.org.uk/en/careers-training/awards-grants-prizes/eden-travelling-fellowship-in-obstetrics-and-gynaecology/

**For further information contact:**

**Email**:  awards@rcog.org.uk

## Edgar Gentilli Prize

**Purpose**: Through the kind and generous bequest of the late Mr and Mrs Gilbert Edgar, the RCOG is delighted to offer this award of £750 plus £250 in book tokens to the candidate who submits the best piece of original work on the cause, nature, recognition and treatment of any form of cancer of the female genital tract

**Eligibility**: 1. The Edgar Gentilli Prize is open to both members and non-members of the RCOG. 2. Candidates for the prize should submit results of their research by way of an original manuscript, adequately referenced and written in a format comparable to that used for submission to a learned journal, or by means of a reprint of the published article. 3. A maximum of 2,000 words with a maximum of 10 references should be submitted. Applications that are over the word limit will be marked down

**Level of Study**: Graduate

**Type**: Prize

**Frequency**: Annual

**Country of Study**: Any country

**Application Procedure**: To apply, please send your application to the Awards Administrator awards@rcog.org.uk by midnight on Friday 31 May. Further procedure of the application is available on the below link. www.rcog.org.uk/en/careers-training/awards-grants-prizes/submitting-your-application/

**Closing Date**: 31 May

**Funding**: Private

**Additional Information**: www.rcog.org.uk/en/careers-training/awards-grants-prizes/edgar-gentilli-prize/

**For further information contact:**

**Email**:  awards@rcog.org.uk

## Elizabeth Garrett Anderson Hospital Charity Travelling Fellowship in Memory of Anne Boutwood

**Purpose**: Through the generosity of the EGA Hospital Charity, we award a prize of £5,000 to one United Kingdom trainee in the field of obstetrics and gynaecology in memory of Miss Anne Boutwood FRCOG

**Eligibility**: 1. Travel must take place within 12 months of the award being made. 2. The award may only be used for the purpose outlined in your original application. 3. A detailed report (maximum 1,000 words), including pictures if necessary, must be submitted to the RCOG Awards Administrator within eight weeks after the elective
**Level of Study**: Postgraduate
**Type**: Fellowship
**Value**: £5,000
**Frequency**: Annual
**Country of Study**: Any country
**Closing Date**: 31 May
**Funding**: Foundation
**Additional Information**: www.rcog.org.uk/en/careers-training/awards-grants-prizes/anne-boutwood-travelling-fellowship/

### For further information contact:

**Email**:    awards@rcog.org.uk

## Endometriosis Millenium Fund

**Purpose**: The RCOG is proud to support the Organising Committee of the World Congress of Endometriosis who, through a generous donation, have established the Endometriosis Millennium Fund
**Eligibility**: Applications are invited for the following: 1. To provide monies to fund a pilot project, clinical or laboratory based in the field of endometriosis, or to provide monies to fund an extension of an existing project researching endometriosis, or; 2. To provide a contribution towards a travelling fellowship to attend a recognised training centre, preferably overseas, to obtain surgical training in the management of cases of endometriosis, beyond the skills expected of core training
**Level of Study**: Postgraduate
**Type**: Funding support
**Frequency**: Annual
**Country of Study**: Any country
**Application Procedure**: To apply, please send your application form (Word document) to the Awards Administrator awards@rcog.org.uk
**Closing Date**: 31 May
**Funding**: Private
**Additional Information**: www.rcog.org.uk/en/careers-training/awards-grants-prizes/endometriosis-millennium-fund/

### For further information contact:

**Email**:    awards@rcog.org.uk

## Ethicon Foundation Fund Travelling Fellowship

**Purpose**: The objective of the Ethicon Foundation Fund Travelling Fellowship, established through the generosity of Ethicon Limited, is to promote international goodwill in medicine and surgery by means of grants to assist the overseas travel of surgeons
**Eligibility**: 1. Applicants must be MRCS(Glasg) or FRCS (Glasg) and in a higher training post in the United Kingdom, or equivalent elsewhere in the world. 2. The proposed work experience, research or other study should be of clear benefit to the individual's training and to the NHS- or equivalent- on return. 3. Periods abroad should generally be between 1-12 months. 4. Awards will not be given for the sole purpose of attending meetings, or conferences to present papers or for undertaking a series of brief visits to multiple centres
**Level of Study**: Postgraduate
**Type**: Travel grant
**Value**: Up to £900
**Frequency**: Annual
**Country of Study**: Any country
**Application Procedure**: Download and complete the application form and return the completed form to the address given. Make sure to include in your application: Your CV A signed letter of support from your current supervisor A signed letter from the centre you will be visiting confirming that you are welcome
**No. of awards offered**: 10
**Closing Date**: 30 April
**No. of awards given last year**: 6
**No. of applicants last year**: 10
**Additional Information**: Travel must take place within 6 months of the award being made rcpsg.ac.uk/awards-and-scholarships/ethicon-foundation-fund-travelling-fellowship

### For further information contact:

Royal College of Physicians and Surgeons of Glasgow, 232 - 242 St Vincent Street, Glasgow G2 5RJ, United Kingdom.

**Tel**:       (44) 141 221 6072
**Fax**:      (44) 141 221 1804
**Email**:    scholarships@rcpsg.ac.uk

## Ethicon Student Elective Award

**Purpose**: The RCOG, with the kind and generous support of Ethicon, was pleased to offer up to £500 of funding towards approved student medical electives in obstetrics and gynaecology taking place between autumn current and upcoming year
**Eligibility**: The successful applicant will have submitted well-planned and well-presented applications demonstrating

clear objectives and offering detailed information about the project they wish to undertake. Students wishing to pursue a career in obstetrics and gynaecology and undertaking their elective in a subject associated with this specialty in a low-resource country were particularly encouraged to apply. Successful applicants are required to provide a report on their elective. They will also be invited to receive their certificate at an RCOG event. 1. Travel must take place within 12 months of the award being made. Retrospective applications will not be accepted. 2. The award may only be used for the purpose outlined in your original application. 3. A detailed report (maximum 1,000 words), including pictures if necessary, must be submitted to the RCOG Awards Administrator within eight weeks after the elective

**Level of Study**: Postgraduate
**Type**: Award
**Value**: Up to £500
**Frequency**: Annual
**Country of Study**: Any country
**Application Procedure**: To apply, please send your application form (Word document) to the Awards Administrator awards@rcog.org.uk
**Closing Date**: 31 May
**Funding**: Private
**Additional Information**: www.rcog.org.uk/en/careers-training/awards-grants-prizes/ethicon-student-elective-award/

**For further information contact:**

**Email**:　awards@rcog.org.uk

## Florence and William Blair Bell Research Fellowship

**Purpose**: The funding has been donated in order to stimulate and encourage research (clinical or laboratory based) in the field of O&G. Clinicians are encouraged, with the use of funds, to acquire extra clinical or research skills to improve patient management or develop their postdoctoral research
**Eligibility**: 1. If the application is for travel funding, travel must take place within 12 months of the award being made. 2. The award may only be used for the purpose outlined in your original application. 3. A detailed report (maximum 1,000 words), including pictures if necessary, must be submitted to the RCOG Awards Administrator at the end of the grant period. 4. An undertaking must be given that the source of the grant will be acknowledged in any related publications
**Level of Study**: Postgraduate
**Type**: Fellowship
**Value**: Up to £5,000
**Frequency**: Annual
**Country of Study**: Any country

**Closing Date**: 31 May
**Funding**: Foundation
**Additional Information**: www.rcog.org.uk/en/careers-training/awards-grants-prizes/florence-and-william-blair-bell-research-fellowship/

**For further information contact:**

**Email**:　awards@rcog.org.uk

## Green-Armytage and Spackman Travelling Scholarship

**Purpose**: Through the generosity of the late Mr V B Green-Armytage and of the late Colonel W C Spackman, Council is able to award a biennial travelling scholarship up to £4,000 to a Fellow or Member of the College
**Eligibility**: Applicants should have shown a special interest in some particular aspect of obstetrical or gynaecological practice. The donors' wishes are that the awards should be used for the purpose of visiting centres where similar work is being carried out. Your application will be judged on the following criteria: 1. Presentation well planned and presented. 2. Relevance of project to career development in O&G. 3. Level of involvement. 4. References. 5. Value to the NHS/local community. 6. Value to personal development
**Level of Study**: Postgraduate
**Type**: Scholarship
**Value**: £4,000
**Frequency**: Annual
**Country of Study**: Any country
**Application Procedure**: Applicants must include information on qualifications, areas of interest and/or publications in a specified area, centres to be visited with confirmation from the head of that centre, estimated costs and the names of two referees
**Closing Date**: 24 May
**Funding**: Private
**Additional Information**: www.rcog.org.uk/en/careers-training/awards-grants-prizes/green-armytage-and-spackman-travelling-scholarship/

## Herbert Erik Reiss Memorial Case History Prize

**Purpose**: The prizes will be awarded to candidates who, in the opinion of the assessors, undertake the best presentation of a clinical case, including critical assessment and literature research, in a topic of obstetrics and gynaecology
**Eligibility**: Open to FY1 and FY2 doctors or Specialist Training Years 1 and 2 in the United Kingdom and the Republic of Ireland

**Level of Study**: Postgraduate
**Value**: First prize is £400 and second prize is £200
**Frequency**: Annual
**Country of Study**: Any country
**Application Procedure**: A maximum of 1,500 words with maximum of 10 references should be submitted. Please include a statement of contribution to the project and indicate the name and address of the supervisor. Only one submission per candidate is permitted
**No. of awards offered**: 20
**Closing Date**: 31 May
**No. of awards given last year**: 3
**No. of applicants last year**: 20
**Additional Information**: Please contact at mgoonewardene@rcog.org.uk www.rcog.org.uk/en/careers-training/awards-grants-prizes/green-armytage-and-spackman-travelling-scholarship/

For further information contact:

**Email**: awards@rcog.org.uk

## John Lawson Prize

**Purpose**: The prize will be awarded to a candidate who, in the opinion of the assessors, undertakes the best article on a topic of obstetrics or gynaecology derived from work carried out in Africa between the tropics of Capricorn and Cancer
**Eligibility**: Candidature is not restricted to fellows and members of the college
**Value**: £150
**Frequency**: Annual
**Country of Study**: Any country
**Application Procedure**: The record of the work can be submitted by way of an original manuscript, adequately referenced and written in a format comparable to that used for submission to a learned journal, or by means of a reprint of a published article
**No. of awards offered**: 8
**Closing Date**: 31 May
**No. of awards given last year**: 1
**No. of applicants last year**: 8
**Additional Information**: If joint authorship is involved then the candidate must identify his/her involvement in the publication www.rcog.org.uk/en/careers-training/awards-grants-prizes/john-lawson-prize/

## Malcolm Black Travel Fellowship

**Purpose**: The purpose of the fellowship is to enable a College Member of up to 5 years' standing or a Fellow at the time of application, to travel either to the British Isles or from the British Isles abroad, for a period of time to attend postgraduate training courses or to visit centres of research or of particular expertise within the specialty of obstetrics and gynaecology.
**Eligibility**: This Fellowship is open to college Members and Fellows
**Level of Study**: Postgraduate
**Type**: Fellowship
**Value**: This biennial travel fellowship awards up to £1,000 to RCOG Members and Fellows
**Length of Study**: 12 months
**Frequency**: Annual
**Additional Information**: For further guidance on how to submit your application, please see Oxford Abstracts' oxfordabstracts.freshdesk.com/support/solutions/articles/8000 072762-making-a-submission www.rcog.org.uk/en/careers-training/awards-grants-prizes/malcolm-black-travel-fellowship/

## Overseas Fund

**Purpose**: To allow individuals to travel to the United Kingdom for further training
**Eligibility**: Open to RCOG members or the equivalent, working overseas
**Level of Study**: Professional development
**Type**: Travel grant
**Value**: Up to £2,500
**Frequency**: Annual
**Country of Study**: Any country
**Application Procedure**: Applicants must see the website
**No. of awards offered**: 3
**Closing Date**: 31 May
**No. of awards given last year**: 1
**No. of applicants last year**: 3

## Peter Huntingford Memorial Prize

**Purpose**: The prize is for presenting the best case history, clinical audit or a report of a research project in any aspect of fertility control in which the applicant is directly involved
**Eligibility**: Open to doctors working in their foundation year or specialist training years 1 and/or 2 in the United Kingdom and the Republic of Ireland
**Type**: Grant
**Value**: First prize is £150 and second prize is £75
**Frequency**: Annual
**Country of Study**: Any country
**Application Procedure**: A submission of no more than 1,500 words outlining the research with reference to publications (if any) is required. Please include a statement of the

contribution to the project and indicate the name and address of the supervisor. Only one submission per candidate is permitted

**No. of awards offered**: 2
**Closing Date**: 31 May
**Contributor**: British Pregnancy Advisory Service (BPAS)
**No. of awards given last year**: 1
**No. of applicants last year**: 2
**Additional Information**: www.rcog.org.uk/en/careers-training/awards-grants-prizes/peter-huntingford-memorial-prize/

## Professor Geoffrey Chamberlain Award

**Purpose**: This award was established in memory of Professor Geoffrey Chamberlain who was a President of the College, Editor-in-Chief of BJOG and Head of the O&G Department at St George's Hospital London. The award consists of two separate awards.
**Eligibility**: 1. The first award is open to Trainees in the sub-continent: Nepal, Bhutan, Pakistan, India, Bangladesh or Sri Lanka. 2. The second award is open to all Trainees worldwide
**Level of Study**: Postgraduate
**Type**: Award
**Value**: First award: £1,000, Second award: £150
**Length of Study**: 3 years
**Frequency**: Annual
**Application Procedure**: Apply online: app.oxfordabstracts.com/stages/1748/submissions/new?behalf=false&fromDashboard=false&preview=true
**Funding**: Foundation
**Additional Information**: For further guidance on how to submit your application, please see Oxford Abstracts: oxfordabstracts.freshdesk.com/support/solutions/articles/8000072762-making-a-submission www.rcog.org.uk/en/careers-training/awards-grants-prizes/professor-geoffrey-chamberlain-award/

## Royal College of Obstetricians and Gynaecologists Edgar Research Fellowship

**Purpose**: To encourage research, especially into chorion carcinoma or other forms of malignant disease
**Eligibility**: Open to candidates of high academic standing either in obstetrics and gynaecology, or related fields
**Level of Study**: Postgraduate
**Type**: Fellowship
**Value**: Up to a maximum of £35,000
**Length of Study** Initially for 1 year's research but a further year's funding may be offered

**Frequency**: Annual
**Country of Study**: Any country
**Application Procedure**: Please contact the Research Administrator at the WellBeing address
**Closing Date**: December
**Additional Information**: In making the award the Council of the College will bear in mind the original intention of the fellowship, which was to encourage research into chorion carcinoma or other forms of malignant disease. Where applications of equal merit are received, priority will be given to the project most closely related to this condition. Fellows are required to submit a report on the work carried out as soon as the tenure of the fellowship is completed www.rcog.org.uk/en/careers-training/academic-og/research-funding-opportunities/mrcrcog-clinical-research-training-fellowship/

### For further information contact:

WellBeing 27 Sussex Place Regent's Park, London NW1 4SP, United Kingdom.

**Tel**:     (44) 20 7772 6338
**Fax**:     (44) 20 7724 7725
**Email**:   mary.stanton@wellbeing.org.uk

## Royal College of Obstetricians and Gynaecologists Research Training Fellowships

**Purpose**: To further the training of a young medical graduate in research techniques and methodology in a subject in a subject of direct or indirect relevance to obstetrics and gynaecology
**Eligibility**: Candidates will have had their basic training in obstetrics and gynaecology, preferably having passed their MRCOG. Candidates will be expected to enrol for a higher degree
**Type**: Fellowship
**Value**: Up to a maximum of three years salary
**Length of Study**: Up to 3 years
**Frequency**: Annual
**Application Procedure**: Enquiries about this award should be directed to The Research Administrator, WellBeing
**Closing Date**: October
**Additional Information**: www.rcog.org.uk/en/careers-training/academic-og/research-funding-opportunities/mrcrcog-clinical-research-training-fellowship/

### For further information contact:

WellBeing 27 Sussex Place Regent's Park, London NW1 4SP, United Kingdom.

**Tel**:     (44) 20 7772 6338
**Fax**:     (44) 20 7724 7725
**Email**:   mary.stanton@wellbeing.org.uk

## Royal College of Obstetricians and Gynaecologists WellBeing Grants

**Purpose**: To fund research into all aspects of Obstetrics and Gynaecology with emphasis on increasing safety of childbirth for mother and baby and prevention of handicap
**Eligibility**: Open to specialists in any obstetrics and gynaecology inter-related field
**Level of Study**: Professional development, Research
**Type**: Grant
**Value**: Maximum of £80,000 over three years, with not more than £45,000 in the first year
**Frequency**: Annual
**Application Procedure**: Applicants must write for details
**Funding**: Private
**Additional Information**: www.rcog.org.uk/en/careers-training/academic-og/research-funding-opportunities/

### For further information contact:

WellBeing 27 Sussex Place Regent's Park, London NW1 4SP, United Kingdom.

**Tel**:      (44) 20 7772 6338
**Fax**:      (44) 20 7724 7725
**Email**:      mary.stanton@wellbeing.org.uk

## Sims Black Travelling Proffesorship

**Purpose**: The purpose of the Sims Black Travelling Professorship is to: Contribute to postgraduate education by presenting lectures, participating in seminars, group discussions and clinical demonstrations (if appropriate)
**Eligibility**: Check for the eligibility through the below link.
**Level of Study**: Postgraduate
**Type**: Professorship
**Frequency**: Annual
**Country of Study**: Any country
**Closing Date**: 31 January
**Funding**: Private
**Additional Information**: www.rcog.org.uk/en/careers-training/awards-grants-prizes/sims-black-travelling-professorship/

### For further information contact:

10 -18 Union Street, London SE1 1SZ, UK.

**Tel**:      (44) 20 7772 6200
**Fax**:      (44) 20 7723 0575
**Email**:      awards@rcog.org.uk

## Target Ovarian Cancer Essay Prize

**Purpose**: The Target Ovarian Cancer essay prize is supported by The Royal College of Obstetricians and Gynaecologists. The prize is open to all undergraduate medical students across the United Kingdom. Its aim is to encourage students to read more widely on ovarian cancer, to think about some of the current issues and learn about recent research
**Level of Study**: Postgraduate
**Type**: Prize
**Value**: £500
**Frequency**: Annual
**Country of Study**: Any country
**Closing Date**: 30 June
**Funding**: Foundation
**Additional Information**: www.targetovariancancer.org.uk/health-professionals/target-ovarian-cancer-essay-prize

### For further information contact:

**Email**:      essay@targetovariancancer.org.uk

## Tim Chard Chase History Prize

**Purpose**: To award students showing the greatest understanding of a clinical problem in obstetrics and gynaecology
**Level of Study**: Professional development
**Type**: Prize
**Value**: 1st prize £500; 2nd prize £200
**Frequency**: Annual
**Country of Study**: United Kingdom, Northern Ireland and Republic of Ireland
**Application Procedure**: Applications should consist of one case history with discussion – max. of 1,500 words with 10 references
**Closing Date**: 15 February
**Funding**: Private
**Additional Information**: www.rcog.org.uk/en/careers-training/awards-grants-prizes/tim-chard-case-history-prize/

### For further information contact:

Royal College of Obstetricians and Gynaecologists, 27 Sussex Place, Regent's Park, London NW1 4RG, United Kingdom.

**Tel**:      (44) 20 7772 6263
**Fax**:      (44) 20 7772 6359
**Email**:      rdeshmukh@rcog.org.uk

## William Blair Bell Memorial Lecture

**Purpose**: The purpose of the lectureship is to allow a clinician or scientist who is at any stage of their career between award of an MD/PhD and the completion of their second year as a Senior Lecturer or its equivalent (e.g. Clinician Scientist), at the time of application, to give a lecture describing research in any area pertaining to Women's Health at the RCOG Annual Academic Meeting

**Eligibility**: 1. Clinician or scientist between the award of their MD/PhD thesis and completion of their second year as a Senior Lecturer or its equivalent. 2. Proposed lecture describes their personal research in any area pertaining to Women's Health

**Level of Study**: Postgraduate

**Type**: Grant

**Frequency**: Annual

**Country of Study**: Any country

**Closing Date**: 31 May

**Funding**: Foundation

**Additional Information**: www.rcog.org.uk/en/careers-training/awards-grants-prizes/william-blair-bell-memorial-lecture/

### For further information contact:

**Email**: awards@rcog.org.uk

## Women's Visiting Gynaecological Club Prize

**Purpose**: Through the generosity of the Women's Visiting Gynaecological Club, the RCOG is able to offer £500 towards an overseas elective in obstetrics and gynaecology to a medical student in the United Kingdom or Republic of Ireland

**Eligibility**: 1. The winner of this prize will be a medical student who presents an application that best articulates their reasoning and objectives for wanting to complete an overseas elective in a certain region. 2. The report submitted after this elective period is circulated to the members of the Women's Visiting Gynaecological Club

**Level of Study**: Postgraduate

**Type**: Prize

**Value**: £500

**Frequency**: Annual

**Country of Study**: Any country

**Closing Date**: 31 May

**Funding**: Foundation

**Additional Information**: www.rcog.org.uk/en/careers-training/awards-grants-prizes/womens-visiting-gynaecological-club-prize/

### For further information contact:

**Email**: awards@rcog.org.uk

## Royal College of Ophthalmologists

18 Stephenson Way, Euston, London NW1 2HD, United Kingdom.

**Tel**: (44) 20 7935 0702
**Email**: training@rcophth.ac.uk
**Website**: www.rcophth.ac.uk
**Contact**: Vanda Fadda, Deputy Head of Education and Training

The college is responsible for promoting high standards of professional practice, setting curricula and conducting examinations and providing professional support and advice for ophthalmologists. The college runs an annual scientific congress and seminars for ophthalmologists and publishes a range of clinical guidelines.

## Bayer Educational Grant Awards

**Purpose**: Supporting ophthalmologists to present work at educational meetings in the United Kingdom and overseas

**Eligibility**: Application from any grade of ophthalmologist working in the United Kingdom. Members and fellows of the Royal College of Ophthalmologists

**Level of Study**: Postgraduate

**Type**: Travel award

**Value**: Varies

**Country of Study**: United Kingdom

**No. of awards offered**: 37

**Closing Date**: November

**Funding**: Commercial

**Contributor**: Bayer HealthCare, Bayer plc

**No. of awards given last year**: 11

**No. of applicants last year**: 37

**Additional Information**: Please see the website for further details www.rcophth.ac.uk

### For further information contact:

**Email**: helen.sonderegger@rcophth.ac.uk

## Essay Prize for Foundation Doctors

**Purpose**: Entries are now invited to the Essay Prize for Foundation Doctors on the essay "Discuss the impact of multi professional working on eye care"
**Eligibility**: 1. The competition is open to all those currently in a United Kingdom Foundation Programme. (F1, F2) at the time of submission, as well as those who have completed the United Kingdom Foundation Programme but have not yet achieved an OST1 post. 2. Entries are invited on the essay "Discuss the impact of multi professional working on eye care"
**Level of Study**: Postgraduate
**Type**: Grant
**Frequency**: Annual
**Country of Study**: Any country
**Application Procedure**: Essays of up to 1,500 words should be submitted to education@rcophth.ac.uk
**Closing Date**: 7 October
**Funding**: Private
**Additional Information**: www.rcophth.ac.uk/wp-content/uploads/2019/02/Essay-prize-for-foundation-doctors-2019-1.pdf

### For further information contact:

18 Stephenson Way, Kings Cross, London NW1 2HD, United Kingdom.

**Email**:     education@rcophth.ac.uk

## Keeler Scholarship

**Purpose**: To enable the scholar to study, research or acquire special skills, knowledge or experience at a suitable location in the United Kingdom or elsewhere for a minimum period of 6 months
**Eligibility**: Applicants must be Fellows, Members or Affiliates of the Royal College of Ophthalmologists, those Fellows, Members and Affiliates being in good standing. Potential applicants who have received substantial (usually meaning amounts greater than the value of the scholarship) funding for their project are not eligible for the Keeler Scholarship. The trustees will give special consideration to candidates intending to make a career in ophthalmology in the United Kingdom. Applicants may apply retrospectively but should not be more than 3 months into the fellowship for which they are applying for support by 10 February (application closing date)
**Level of Study**: Postgraduate
**Type**: Scholarship
**Value**: Upto £30,000
**Length of Study**: 2 years
**Frequency**: Annual
**Country of Study**: Any country
**Application Procedure**: 5 copies each of the application form duly completed and the candidate's curriculum vitae should be submitted
**Closing Date**: 10 February
**Funding**: Private
**Contributor**: Keeler Ltd
**Additional Information**: Funds will be paid to the Scholar two months before the start date of the project or fellowship www.eyedocs.co.uk/ophthalmology-clinical-awards/1078-keeler-scholarship

### For further information contact:

The Royal College of Ophthalmologists Education and Training Department – Awards and Prizes, 18 Stephenson Way, Kings Cross, London NW1 2HD, United Kingdom.

## Patrick Trevor-Roper Undergraduate Award

**Purpose**: Applications are invited for the Patrick Trevor-Roper Award, which is open to all undergraduate medical students from the United Kingdom and Ireland who have an interest in the specialty. The money may be used to fund electives in Ophthalmology, and may be spent on traveling or subsistence
**Eligibility**: Medical Undergraduates
**Level of Study**: Postgraduate
**Type**: Award
**Value**: £550
**Frequency**: Annual
**Country of Study**: Any country
**Application Procedure**: Please post 4 hard copies of your application form and CV to: The Royal College of Ophthalmologists, Education and Training Department – Awards and Prizes, 18 Stephenson Way, NW1 2HD, London, United Kingdom
**Closing Date**: 31 May
**Funding**: Private
**Additional Information**: education@rcophth.ac.uk www.eyedocs.co.uk/undergraduate-ophthalmology-awards/1076-patrick-trevor-roper-award

### For further information contact:

The Royal College of Ophthalmologists, Education and Training Department – Awards and Prizes, 18 Stephenson Way, Kings Cross, London NW1 2HD, United Kingdom.

**Email**:     education@rcophth.ac.uk

# Royal College of Ophthalmologists-Bayer Research

## Royal College of Ophthalmologists-Bayer Research Award

**Purpose**: The Royal College of Ophthalmologists and Bayer have come together in a partnership to launch a grant to promote research in ophthalmology
**Eligibility**: Any Ophthalmic Specialist Trainee, Member or Fellow of The RCOphth with an interest in research
**Level of Study**: Postgraduate
**Type**: Award
**Value**: £8,000
**Frequency**: Annual
**Country of Study**: Any country
**Closing Date**: 30 March
**Funding**: Foundation

### For further information contact:

**Email**:    education@rcophth.ac.uk

# Royal College of Organists (RCO)

PO Box 56357, London SE16 7XL, United Kingdom.

**Tel**:       (44) 5600 767 208
**Email**:    admin@rco.org.uk
**Website**:  www.rco.org.uk
**Contact**:  Andrew McCrea, Director of Academic Development

The Royal College of Organists (RCO) is membership based. It promotes the art of organ playing as choral directing, and provides an organization with a library, events and examinations to further that object.

## Royal College of Organists Scholarships and Awards

**Purpose**: To assist organists with professional playing
**Eligibility**: Open to members of the College. Only in exceptional circumstances will awards be made to non members. Membership is open to all upon payment of an annual subscription
**Level of Study**: Unrestricted
**Type**: Grant

**Length of Study**: 2 year, renewable
**Frequency**: Annual
**Study Establishment**: Varies
**Country of Study**: Any country
**Application Procedure**: Applicants must write for an application form
**Closing Date**: 17 February
**Funding**: Private
**Contributor**: College trusts
**Additional Information**: www.rca.ac.uk/studying-at-the-rca/fees-funding/financial-help-/preentry-scholarships-and-awards/

### For further information contact:

**Tel**:       (44) 207 590 4108
**Email**:    scholarships@rca.ac.uk

## Royal College of Organists Various Open Award Bequests

**Purpose**: To assist students who are training to become organists
**Eligibility**: School and students in undergraduate and postgraduate education who are members of the college
**Level of Study**: Postgraduate, Professional development
**Type**: Award
**Value**: Between £100 and £400 each
**Frequency**: Annual
**Study Establishment**: Various
**Application Procedure**: Write for an application form
**Closing Date**: 18 April
**Funding**: Private

# Royal College of Physicians and Surgeons of Canada (RCPSC)

Office of Fellowship Affairs 774 Echo Drive, Ottawa, ON K1S 5N8, Canada.

**Tel**:       (1) 613 730 8177
**Email**:    awards@rcpsc.edu
**Website**:  rcpsc.medical.org/
**Contact**:  Dr James Hickey, FRCPC, Director

The Royal College of Physicians and Surgeons of Canada is a national organisation responsible for setting and maintaining the standards for postgraduate medical education, for the certification of specialist physicians and surgeons in Canada, and for promoting their continued education. The College benefits from the co-operation of its 30,000 members (Fellows), Canada's 16 faculties of medicine and national speciality societies.

## Canadian Research Awards for Specialty Residents (Medicine, Surgery)

**Purpose**: We serve patients, diverse populations and our Fellows by setting the standards in specialty medical education and lifelong learning, and by advancing professional practice and health care.
**Additional Information**: vascular.org/career-tools-training/awards-and-scholarships/resident-research-award

### For further information contact:

774 Echo Drive, Ottawa, ON K1S 0R4, Canada.

**Tel**:      (1) 613 730 8177
**Fax**:     (1) 613 730 8830
**Email**:   llocas@rcpsc.edu

## Royal College of Surgeons

### Ethicon Travel Award

**Purpose**: Ethicon Foundation Fund travel awards for overseas visits are awarded to fellows and members of the College who are in good standing
**Eligibility**: 1. The successful applicants will have submitted a well-articulated and well-planned application outlining the purpose and objectives of their trip. 2. It will provide detailed information about the work they would carry out during their placement to advance the practice and development of O&G. 3. The award may only be used for the purpose outlined in your original application. A detailed report (maximum 1,000 words), including pictures if necessary, must be submitted to the RCOG Awards Administrator within eight weeks after the elective. It supports the user by contributing to economy travel class upto the value £1,000
**Level of Study**: Graduate
**Type**: Award
**Value**: £500 payment will be awarded
**Frequency**: Annual
**Country of Study**: United Kingdom
**Application Procedure**: The successful applicant will be required to provide a report on their travelling fellowship
**Closing Date**: 14 March
**Funding**: Private

**Additional   Information**:   www.rcog.org.uk/en/careers-training/awards-grants-prizes/ethicon-travel-award/

### For further information contact:

The Royal College of Surgeons of United Kingdom, 35-43 Lincoln's Inn Fields, London WC2A 3PE, United Kingdom.

**Email**:   lslater@rcseng.ac.uk

## Royal College of Surgeons of United Kingdom

35-43 Lincoln's Inn Fields, London WC2A 3PE, United Kingdom.

**Tel**:        (44) 20 7869 6611
**Email**:     research@rcseng.ac.uk
**Website**:   www.rcseng.ac.uk
**Contact**:   Miss Bumbi Singh, Research Department

The Royal College of Surgeons of United Kingdom is an independent professional body committed to promoting and advancing the highest standards of surgical care for patients.

### Ethicon Foundation Fund

**Purpose**: The objective of the Ethicon Foundation Fund Travelling Fellowship, established through the generosity of Ethicon Limited, is to promote international goodwill in medicine and surgery by means of grants to assist the overseas travel of surgeons.
**Eligibility**: Open to Fellows of the Royal College of Surgeons of United Kingdom. Applicants should be sufficiently advanced in their training to benefit from such an experience or be within 1 year of their appointment as a consultant. Fellows, Members or Affiliate Members of the RCOphth who are travelling abroad for research or training
**Level of Study**: Professional development
**Type**: Grant
**Value**: £900
**Length of Study**: Varies
**Frequency**: Twice a year
**Country of Study**: Any country
**Application Procedure**: Applicants must send eight copies of the application form to the Research Department of the College and should include a letter of support from the head of department or consultant under whom the applicant is currently working and a letter of support from another

independent referee. Application forms are available from The Research Department at the main address

**Closing Date**: 30 April

**Additional Information**: rcpsg.ac.uk/awards-and-scholarships/ethicon-foundation-fund-travelling-fellowship

### For further information contact:

Shona McCall, Scholarship Committee Administrator, Royal College of Physicians and Surgeons of Glasgow, 232-242 St Vincent Street, Glasgow G2 5RJ, United Kingdom.

**Tel**:  (44) 141 221 6072
**Fax**:  (44) 141 221 1804
**Email**:  scholarships@rcpsg.ac.uk

## Royal Geographical Society (with the Institute of British Geographers)

1 Kensington Gore, London SW7 2AR, United Kingdom.

**Tel**:  (44) 20 7591 3000
**Email**:  grants@rgs.org
**Website**:  www.rgs.org/grants
**Contact**:  Juliette Scull, Grants Officer

The Royal Geographical Society (with the Institute of British Geographers) is the United Kingdom's learned society for geography and geographers and a professional body. It supports and promotes many aspects of geography including geographical research, education and teaching, field training and small expeditions, the public understanding and popularization of geography and the provision of geographical information.

## 30th International Geographical Congress Award

**Purpose**: To assist with the cost of attending an international geographical conference

**Eligibility**: Applicants must be United Kingdom/European Union nationals and must currently be employed by a United Kingdom Institute of Higher Education. Preference will be given to applicants within 6 years of completion of PhD Attendance at AAG, CAG, or the RGS-IBG Annual Conference is not eligible for support from this award

**Level of Study**: Research

**Type**: Award

**Value**: Up to £750

**Length of Study**: Unspecified

**Frequency**: Annual

**Country of Study**: Any country

**Application Procedure**: Applicants must download the guidelines and application form from the website www.rgs.org/grants or contact the grants officer

**No. of awards offered**: 12

**Closing Date**: 31 October

**No. of awards given last year**: 5

**No. of applicants last year**: 12

**Additional Information**: www.rgs.org/in-the-field/in-the-field-grants/research-grants/thirtieth-international-geographical-congress/

### For further information contact:

Royal Geographical Society (with the Institute of British Geographers), 1 Kensington Gore, London SW7 2AR, United Kingdom.

**Tel**:  (44) 20 7591 3000
**Fax**:  (44) 20 7591 3001

## Environment and Sustainability Research Grants

**Purpose**: To support researchers investigating some of the bigger issues in environmental sustainability

**Eligibility**: Please see www.rgs.org/grants

**Type**: Grant

**Value**: £15,000

**Frequency**: Annual

**Country of Study**: Any country

**Application Procedure**: Please see www.vgs.org

**Closing Date**: 22 February

**No. of awards given last year**: 4

**Additional Information**: www.rgs.org/in-the-field/in-the-field-grants/research-grants/environment-and-sustainability-research-grants/

### For further information contact:

Royal Geographical Society (with the Institute of British Geographers), 1 Kensington Gore, London SW7 2AR, United Kingdom.

**Tel**:  (44) 20 7591 3000
**Fax**:  (44) 20 7591 3001

## Geographical Club Award

**Purpose**: To support a postgraduate student (Masters or PhD) undertaking geographical fieldwork

**Eligibility**: Applicants must be United Kingdom/European Union nationals and must currently be registered for a Masters or PhD at a United Kingdom Institute of Higher Education. Students who receive full funding from a Research Council or comparable levels of support from other sources with support for fieldwork/data collection are not eligible to apply

**Level of Study**: Doctorate, Postgraduate
**Type**: Award
**Value**: £1,000
**Frequency**: Annual
**Country of Study**: United Kingdom or elsewhere
**Application Procedure**: Applicants must download the application guidelines from the website www.rgs.org/grants or contact the grants officer. There is no application form
**No. of awards offered**: 20
**Closing Date**: 23 November
**No. of awards given last year**: 2
**No. of applicants last year**: 20
**Additional Information**: www.rgs.org/in-the-field/in-the-field-grants/students/phd/geographical-club-award-(1)/

### For further information contact:

Royal Geographical Society (with the Institute of British Geographers), 1 Kensington Gore, London SW7 2AR, United Kingdom.

**Tel**:     (44) 20 7591 3000
**Fax**:    (44) 20 7591 3001

## Ray Y. Gildea Jr Award

**Purpose**: To support innovation in teaching and learning in higher and secondary education
**Eligibility**: The project should focus on innovation in teaching and learning of geography in higher education/college and/or secondary school level; including curriculum development, teaching and learning methods, and applications of new technology. 1. Projects that seek to research, develop and/or pilot innovations are eligible. 2. Outcomes should directly benefit students of geography. 3. Applicants must be currently employed in the higher education (college) sector and/or secondary school level, either in the United Kingdom or the United States of America and actively teaching students. 4. Applicants must be United Kingdom or United States of America nationals
**Type**: Grant
**Frequency**: Annual
**Country of Study**: Any country
**Application Procedure**: Please see www.rgs.org/grants
**Closing Date**: 30 November
**No. of awards given last year**: 1

**Additional Information**: www.rgs.org/schools/teacher-grants/ray-y-gildea-jr-award/

### For further information contact:

Royal Geographical Society (with the Institute of British Geographers), 1 Kensington Gore, London SW7 2AR, United Kingdom.

**Tel**:     (44) 20 7591 3000
**Fax**:    (44) 20 7591 3001

## Walters Kundert Fellowship

**Purpose**: To support field research within arctic or high mountain environments, with preference for field studies that advance the understanding of environmental change past or present.
**Eligibility**: Please see Website
**Type**: Grant
**Value**: £10,000
**Frequency**: Annual
**Country of Study**: Any country
**Closing Date**: 23 November
**Additional Information**: www.rgs.org/in-the-field/in-the-field-grants/research-grants/kundert-fellowship/

### For further information contact:

Royal Geographical Society (with the Institute of British Geographers), 1 Kensington Gore, London SW7 2AR, United Kingdom.

**Tel**:     (44) 20 7591 3000
**Fax**:    (44) 20 7591 3001

## Royal Holloway, University of London

Egham, Surrey TW20 0EX, United Kingdom.

**Tel**:        (44) 1784 443 399
**Email**:    liaison-office@rhul.ac.uk
**Website**:  www.rhul.ac.uk
**Contact**:  Ms Claire Collingwood, Schools & International Liaison Officer

All departments of Royal Holloway, University of London seek to provide taught programmes that reflect the latest developments and are responsive to the needs of students and society, together with research and scholarship, which contribute to the advancement of knowledge and the enhancement of public policy, wealth creation and the quality of life.

## American Foundation of RHBNC International Excellence Scholarship

**Purpose**: Two scholarships are available to students from the United States with outstanding academic ability studying any taught Masters course
**Eligibility**: You must be a US citizen applying for a full-time taught Masters course with a current grade average in the range of a First Class full-time Honours degree
**Level of Study**: Postgraduate
**Type**: Scholarships
**Value**: £3,250
**Frequency**: Annual
**Application Procedure**: You must apply via: admissions.royalholloway.ac.uk/#/login
**Closing Date**: 26 June
**Additional Information**: www.royalholloway.ac.uk/studying-here/fees-and-funding/postgraduate/scholarships/american-foundation-of-rhbnc-international-excellence-scholarship/

### For further information contact:

Royal Holloway, University of London Egham, Surrey TW20 0EX, United Kingdom.

**Tel**:     (44) 1784 414944
**Email**:  study@royalholloway.ac.uk

## Bedford Society Scholarship

**Purpose**: The scholarships are funded by the alumni and friends of Bedford College, one of the founding colleges of Royal Holloway and Bedford New College. Formed in 2013, the Bedford Society aims to ensure the spirit of Bedford College lives on by providing new scholars with access to financial support and opportunities for networking.
**Eligibility**: You must have achieved, or be on target to achieve, a First Class Honours degree
**Level of Study**: Postgraduate
**Type**: Scholarships
**Value**: Scholarships are offered as a tuition fee reduction of £7,000.
**Application Procedure**: You must apply via: admissions.royalholloway.ac.uk/#/login
**Closing Date**: 26 June

**Additional Information**: www.royalholloway.ac.uk/studying-here/fees-and-funding/postgraduate/scholarships/bedford-society-scholarships/

### For further information contact:

Royal Holloway, University of London Egham, Surrey TW20 0EX, United Kingdom.

**Tel**:     (44) 1784 414944
**Email**:  study@royalholloway.ac.uk

## Brian Harris Scholarship

**Purpose**: ravel costs. The scholarship was established by the donor Brian Harris so that those from lower-income backgrounds could stand out and have the opportunity to study an MA in History
**Eligibility**: You must be a full or part-time student from the UK applying
**Level of Study**: Postgraduate
**Type**: Scholarships
**Value**: Full tuition fee reduction plus £14,600 for living
**Frequency**: Annual
**Application Procedure**: You must apply via: admissions.royalholloway.ac.uk/#/login
**Closing Date**: 26 June
**Additional Information**: www.royalholloway.ac.uk/studying-here/fees-and-funding/postgraduate/scholarships/brian-harris-scholarship/

### For further information contact:

Royal Holloway, University of London Egham, Surrey TW20 0EX, United Kingdom.

**Tel**:     (44) 1784 414944
**Email**:  study@royalholloway.ac.uk

## RHBNC Trust Scholarship

**Purpose**: These scholarships provide a tuition fee reduction of £7,000 and are for new full-time or part-time taught Masters students with Home/EU fee status, studying for a postgraduate degree
**Eligibility**: You must have achieved, or be on target to achieve, a First Class Honours degree
**Level of Study**: Postgraduate
**Type**: Scholarships
**Value**: Tuition fee reduction of £7,000
**Frequency**: Annual

**Application Procedure**: You must apply via: admissions. royalholloway.ac.uk/#/login

**Closing Date**: 26 June

**Additional Information**: www.royalholloway.ac.uk/ studying-here/fees-and-funding/postgraduate/scholarships/ rhbnc-trust-scholarship/

### For further information contact:

Royal Holloway, University of London Egham, Surrey TW20 0EX, United Kingdom.

**Tel**:       (44) 1784 414944
**Email**:    study@royalholloway.ac.uk

## Royal Holloway, University of London MBA Programme

**Application Procedure**: Applicants must complete an application form

**Closing Date**: 30 June

**Additional Information**: studyabroad.shiksha.com/uk/uni versities/royal-holloway-university-of-london/mba-internati onal-management

### For further information contact:

School of Management Royal Holloway, University of London, Egham TW20 0EX, United Kingdom.

**Tel**:       (44) 1784 443 780
**Fax**:      (44) 1784 439 854
**Email**:    school-management@rhul.ac.uk

## Royal Horticultural Society (RHS)

80 Vincent Square, London SW1P 2PE, United Kingdom.

**Tel**:        (44) 845 260 5000
**Email**:     bursaries@rhs.org.uk
**Website**:   www.rhs.org.uk/courses/bursaries
**Contact**:   Secretary of RHS Bursaries Committee

The Royal Horticultural Society (RHS) is a membership charity holding a Royal Charter for horticulture. The Society promotes the science, art and practice of horticulture in all its branches through a wide range of educational, research and advisory activities. It also maintains some major gardens, shows and the internationally renowned Lindley Library.

## Blaxall Valentine Bursary Fund

**Purpose**: To help finance horticultural study tours and projects that will provide real benefits to horticulture.

**Eligibility**: Open to applicants worldwide, but preference is given to UK citizens. Financial sponsorship will be available to both professional and amateur horticulturists and consideration for an award is not restricted to RHS members. Proposals may be made by individuals or group of individuals.

**Level of Study**: Unrestricted

**Type**: Bursary

**Value**: Funds are limited. High-cost projects are expected to receive supplementary finance from other sources, including personal contributions

**Frequency**: Annual

**Country of Study**: Any country

**Application Procedure**: Applicants must complete an application form downloaded from the RHS website www.rhs.org. uk/bursaries.

**Closing Date**: 30 September

**Funding**: Private

**Additional Information**: Please contact at bursaries@rhs. org.uk for applying and deadline.

### For further information contact:

Royal Horticultural Society.

## Royal Horticultural Society Financial Awards

**Purpose**: To help finance horticulture-related projects and to further the interests of horticultural education along with horticultural work experience

**Eligibility**: Submissions are welcomed from applicants worldwide, but preference is given to United Kingdom and Commonwealth citizens. Applicants should preferably be within the age bracket of 20 and 35 years and satisfy the Society that their health enables them to undertake the project proposed. Financial sponsorship will be available to both professional and amateur horticulturists, and consideration for an award is not restricted to RHS members. Proposals may be made by individuals or groups

**Level of Study**: Unrestricted

**Type**: Bursary

**Value**: Funds are limited. High-cost projects are expected to receive supplementary finance from other sources, including personal contributions

**Frequency**: Annual

**Country of Study**: Any country

**Application Procedure**: Applicants must complete an application form, available on request. Candidates may be called for interview

**Closing Date**: 30 September

**Funding**: Private
**No. of awards given last year**: 6
**Additional Information**: Recipients must submit a brief factual report within 3 months of completion, along with an outline of achievements or difficulties, including any unusual problems, e.g. medical or political, and an account of expenses

## Royal Horticulture Society Bursary Scheme

**Purpose**: To broaden skills, increase knowledge and enhance career opportunities related to Horticulture
**Eligibility**: United Kingdom citizens may apply for projects worldwide. Others may only apply for projects based in the United Kingdom
**Level of Study**: Unrestricted
**Type**: Bursary
**Value**: Funds are limited. High-cost projects are expected to receive supplementary finance from other sources
**Frequency**: Annual
**Country of Study**: United Kingdom
**Application Procedure**: Applicants must complete an application form downloadable from the RHS website www.rhs. org.uk/bursarie
**Closing Date**: 15 December
**Funding**: Private
**Additional Information**: For further enquires on the bursary scheme, Please email bursanes@rhs.org.uk www.rhs.org.uk/ education-learning/bursaries-grants/rhs-bursaries/Apply-for-an-RHS-Bursary

### For further information contact:

RHS Garden, Wisley, Woking, Surrey GU23 6QB, United Kingdom.

**Email**:    bursanes@rhs.org.uk

## Royal Institution of Chartered Surveyors Education Trust

Royal Institution of Chartered Surveyors, RICS, Parliament Square, London SW1P 3AD, United Kingdom.

**Tel**:         (44) 24 7686 8555
**Email**:     contactrics@rics.org
**Website**:  www.rics-educationtrust.org

The Royal Institution of Chartered Surveyors (RICS) is the professional institution for the surveying profession.

## Royal Institution of Chartered Surveyors Education Trust Award

**Eligibility**: Open to chartered surveyors and others carrying out research studies in relevant subjects
**Level of Study**: Unrestricted
**Type**: Research grant
**Value**: Up to £7,500
**Country of Study**: Any country
**Application Procedure**: Applicants must complete an application form, available to download online at www.rics-educationtrust.org
**No. of awards offered**: 40
**Closing Date**: 6 March
**Funding**: Commercial
**Contributor**: RICS
**No. of awards given last year**: 20
**No. of applicants last year**: 40
**Additional Information**: www.rics.org/en-in/news-insight/ research/research-trust/

## Royal Irish Academy

19 Dawson Street, Dublin 2, D02 HH58, Ireland.

**Tel**:         (353) 1 676 2570
**Email**:     admin@ria.ie
**Website**:  www.ria.ie
**Contact**:   Ms Laura Mahoney, Assistant Executive Secretary

The Royal Irish Academy is the senior institution in Ireland for both the sciences and humanities. It publishes a number of journals and monographs. It is Ireland's national representative in a large number of international unions, and through its national committees runs conferences, lectures and workshops. It also manages a number of long-term research projects. The Academy participates in the Royal Society

## Royal Irish Academy Senior Visiting Fellowships

**Purpose**: To enable a new scientific research technique or development to be introduced into the Republic of Ireland
**Eligibility**: Open to senior researchers from member countries of the Organisation for Economic Co-operation and Development (OECD) only
**Level of Study**: Postdoctorate, Professional development
**Type**: Fellowship

**Value**: Varies
**Frequency**: Annual
**Country of Study**: Other
**Application Procedure**: Applicants must complete an application form
**Closing Date**: 15 October
**Funding**: Government
**No. of awards given last year**: 10
**Additional Information**: Senior Visiting Fellowships are made on behalf of the Irish government

### For further information contact:

**Email**: grants@ria.ie

## Royal Literary Fund RLF

3 Johnson's Court, London EC4A 3EA, United Kingdom.

**Tel**: (44) 20 7353 7160
**Email**: rlitfund@btconnect.com
**Website**: www.rlf.org.uk
**Contact**: Steve Cook, Fellowship Officer

The RLF has been continuously helping authors since it was set up in 1970. It is funded by requests and donations from writers who help other writers. Its committee members came from all walks of literary life and include novelists, biographers, poets, publishers, lawyers and agents.

### Royal Literary Fund Grant

**Purpose**: To support prolific writers suffering financial hardship
**Eligibility**: Open to applicants who have published several works for a general readership and are suffering financial hardship (books stemming from a parallel career as an academic or practitioner are not eligible)
**Level of Study**: Professional development
**Type**: Grant
**Value**: Funds are decided by the committee case by case
**Length of Study**: 1 year
**Frequency**: Annual
**Country of Study**: United Kingdom
**Application Procedure**: Contact the RLF General Secretary
**Contributor**: RLF
**No. of awards given last year**: 12
**Additional Information**: www.rlf.org.uk/

### For further information contact:

The Royal Literary Fund, 3 Johnson's Court, London EC4A 3EA, United Kingdom.

**Tel**: (44) 20 7353 7159
**Email**: egunnrlf@globalnet.co.uk

## Royal Melbourne Institute of Technology University

Info Corner - Office for Prospective Students, GPO Box 2476, Melbourne, VIC 3001, Australia.

**Tel**: (61) 3 9925 2260
**Email**: study@rmit.edu.au
**Website**: www.rmit.edu.au

RMIT University is one of Australia's original and leading educational institutions producing some of Australia's most employable graduates. RMIT has an international reputation for excellence in work-relevant education professional and vocational education, high quality research, and engagement with the needs of industry and community.

### Interior Design-Masters of Arts by Research

**Purpose**: To offer a space within which candidates develop and contribute to the knowledge and possibilities of interior design
**Eligibility**: Open to the candidates of any country who have a First Degree of RMIT with at least a credit average in the final undergraduate year or a deemed equivalent by RMIT to a First Degree of RMIT with at least a credit average in the final undergraduate year or evidence of experience
**Level of Study**: Postgraduate
**Length of Study**: 2 years full-time (Masters) and 4 years part-time (PhD)
**Application Procedure**: Check website for further details
**Closing Date**: 31 October
**Funding**: Government
**Contributor**: Commonwealth Government
**Additional Information**: Please check the website for more details

### For further information contact:

**Tel**: (61) 3 9925 2819
**Email**: suzie.attiwill@rmit.edu.au

## Royal Melbourne Institute of Technology PhD Scholarship in the School of Electrical and Computer Engineering

**Eligibility**: To be eligible for this scholarship you must: be enroled in a higher degree by research (HDR) at the RMIT School of Electrical and Computer Engineering; be a top ranking student using the RMIT University Scholarships Ranking Model; awarded an APA or RMIT PhD Scholarship and/or an RTS place; be aligned to one of the school's areas of strategic focus; not previously have held any Electrical and Computer Engineering (ECE) scholarship over the past 3 years (or more); demonstrate excellent academic results and research capability

**Type**: Scholarship

**Value**: AU$12,000

**Frequency**: Annual

**Country of Study**: Australia

**Application Procedure**: International applicants are expected to apply for the RMIT International PhD Scholarship. If successful, the school may supplement the scholarship stipend

**Additional Information**: Preference will be given to PhD students but high ranking Masters by Research students may also be eligible for the top-up scholarship www.rmit.edu.au/study-with-us/levels-of-study/research-programs/phd/phd-electrical–electronic-engineering-dr220

### For further information contact:

**Tel**:     (61) 3 9925 3174
**Email**:   elecengresearch@rmit.edu.au

## Royal Over-Seas League ARTS

Over-Seas House, Park Place, St James's Street, London SW1A 1LR, United Kingdom.

**Tel**:        (44) 20 7408 0214 ext 219
**Email**:      info@rosl.org.uk
**Website**:    www.rosl.org.uk
**Contact**:    Mandy Murphy, Administrative Assistant

The principal aim of the ROSL (Royal Over-Seas League) ARTS is to provide performance and exhibition opportunities for prize-winning artists and musicians early in their careers, bringing their work to the attention of the professional arts community, the media and the general public.

## Royal Over-Seas League Annual Music Competition

**Purpose**: To support and promote young Commonwealth musicians

**Eligibility**: Open to the citizens of the United Kingdom and Commonwealth, including former Commonwealth countries, for instrumentalists and singers up to and including the age of 30 as at the date of the final concert

**Level of Study**: Professional development

**Type**: Competition

**Value**: Over £60,000 in prizes, including a £10,000 gold medal and first prize and £10,000 for ensembles

**Frequency**: Annual

**Country of Study**: Any country

**Application Procedure**: Applicants must see the website: www.roslarts.org.uk

**No. of awards offered**: 500

**Closing Date**: 15 January

**Funding**: Commercial, Private, Trusts, Individuals

**No. of awards given last year**: 19

**No. of applicants last year**: 500

**Additional Information**: www.rosl.org.uk/events/rosl-events/event/1080-rosl-annual-music-competition-2020-season-ticket

### For further information contact:

Royal Over-Seas League, Over-Seas House, Park Pl, St James's St, London SW1A 1LR, United Kingdom.

**Email**:     head-conmus@uwa.edu.au

## Royal Over-Seas League Travel Scholarship

**Purpose**: To support and promote young United Kingdom and Commonwealth artists

**Eligibility**: Open to citizens of Commonwealth, including the United Kingdom, and former Commonwealth countries, who are up to 35 years of age, on year of application

**Level of Study**: Graduate, Postgraduate, Professional development, Unrestricted

**Value**: £3,000

**Frequency**: Annual

**Country of Study**: United Kingdom or Commonwealth

**Application Procedure**: Applicants must see the website: www.roslarts.co.uk

**No. of awards offered**: 450

**Closing Date**: 31 March

**Funding**: Commercial, Private, Trusts

**No. of awards given last year**: 5

**No. of applicants last year**: 450
**Additional Information**: Each artist may be represented by one recent work only, any medium. Works must not exceed 152 cm in their largest dimension, inclusive of frame www.student.uwa.edu.au/faculties/able/music-students/prizes/royal-over-seas-league-travel-scholarship

**For further information contact:**

**Email**:    Membership@rosl.org.uk

## Royal Scottish Academy (RSA)

The Mound, Edinburgh EH2 2EL, United Kingdom.

**Tel**:          (44) 131 225 6671
**Email**:       info@royalscottishacademy.org
**Website**:     www.royalscottishacademy.org
**Contact**:     Secretary

Founded in 1826, the RSA, Scotland's foremost body of artists, has promoted the works of leading contemporary painters, sculptors, printmakers and architects. It also gives practical and financial help to young artists through scholarships as well as the annual Student's Exhibition.

## The Barns-Graham Travel Award

**Purpose**: To provide a travel and research opportunity for graduating and postgraduate students
**Eligibility**: Entrants must be painters, printmakers or sculptors, entrants must either be graduating in the current academic year or currently studying at postgraduate level at one of the following art schools in Scotland – Aberdeen, Dundee, Edinburgh, Glasgow, and Moray
**Level of Study**: Postgraduate
**Type**: Scholarship
**Value**: £2,000
**Length of Study**: 3–6 months
**Frequency**: Annual
**Study Establishment**: Any of the main art colleges
**Country of Study**: Scotland
**Application Procedure**: Applications forms and regulations will be available to download at the end of February
**Closing Date**: 22 March
**Funding**: Private
**Contributor**: The Alastair Salvesen Trust
**No. of awards given last year**: 1

**Additional Information**: Please see the website for further details www.royalscottishacademy.org/artist/rsa-barns-graham-travel-award/

**For further information contact:**

**Email**:    opportunities@royalscottishacademy.org

## The Royal Scottish Academy John Kinross Scholarships to Florence

**Purpose**: For final year and postgraduate artists and architects to spend a period of 6 to 12 weeks in Florence to research and develop their practice
**Eligibility**: Art: Applications are invited from students in their Honours or post-graduate years of study at one of the following; art schools in Scotland (Aberdeen, Dundee, Edinburgh, Glasgow, and UHI). Architecture: Applicants must be RIBA Part 2 students in their final year, or currently attending a Masters programme,; at one of the six Scottish Schools of Architecture
**Level of Study**: Postgraduate, Undergraduate
**Type**: Scholarship
**Value**: £2,500
**Length of Study**: 6–12 weeks
**Frequency**: Annual
**Country of Study**: Italy
**Application Procedure**: Digital submissions accepted only, please see the opportunities section of our website for more details
**Closing Date**: 22 March
**Funding**: Private
**Contributor**: The Kinross Scholarship Fund, which is administered by the RSA
**No. of awards given last year**: 10
**Additional Information**: www.royalscottishacademy.org/artist/the-rsa-john-kinross-scholarships/

**For further information contact:**

**Email**:    opportunities@royalscottishacademy.org

## The Royal Scottish Academy William Littlejohn Award for Excellence and Innovation in Water-Based Media

**Purpose**: To provide young professional artists who are Scottish or have studied in Scotland, with a period for personal development and the exploration of new directions
**Eligibility**: Entrants must be working in water-based media (any pigment mixed with water), entrants must be born or have been resident in Scotland for at least 3 years, in the case

of students applying, entrants must either be graduating in current year or studying at postgraduate level at one of the following art schools in Scotland (Aberdeen, Dundee, Edinburgh, Glasgow, and Moray)

**Level of Study**: Postgraduate
**Type**: Residency
**Value**: £2,000
**Frequency**: Annual
**Study Establishment**: Hospitalfield House, Arbroath
**Country of Study**: Scotland
**Application Procedure**: Applicants must contact the RSA
**Closing Date**: 12 June
**Funding**: Private
**Contributor**: The Bequest Fund administered by the RSA
**Additional Information**: www.royalscottishacademy.org/artist/the-william-littlejohn-award/

**For further information contact:**

**Email**: opportunities@royalscottishacademy.org

## Royal Society

6-9 Carlton House Terrace, London SW1Y 5AG, United Kingdom.

**Tel**: (44) 20 7451 2500
**Email**: info@royalsoc.ac.uk
**Website**: www.royalsoc.ac.uk
**Contact**: Research Appointments Officer

### Charles Fleming Publishing Award

**Purpose**: To support the preparation of scientific books and relevant publications.
**Eligibility**: The fund will give preference to those who do not normally have access to funds through their place of employment for assisting with the writing and publication of their research or a review of a particular area of scientific endeavour.
**Level of Study**: Post graduate
**Type**: Grant
**Value**: NZ$8,000
**Frequency**: Annual
**Country of Study**: New Zealand
**No. of awards offered**: 1
**Closing Date**: 31 March
**Funding**: Foundation
**Additional Information**: www.royalsociety.org.nz/what-we-do/funds-and-opportunities/charles-fleming-fund/charles-fleming-publishing-award/

**For further information contact:**

**Email**: awards@royalsociety.org.nz

### Charles Fleming Senior Scientist Award

**Purpose**: To support the research of a senior scientist at a university, Crown Research Institute, polytechnic or other research organisation in New Zealand, and that of their research group.
**Level of Study**: Post Doctoral
**Type**: Grant
**Value**: NZ$10,000
**Frequency**: Annual
**Country of Study**: New Zealand
**No. of awards offered**: 1
**Closing Date**: 31 March
**Funding**: Foundation
**Additional Information**: www.royalsociety.org.nz/what-we-do/funds-and-opportunities/charles-fleming-fund/charles-fleming-senior-scientist-award/

**For further information contact:**

**Email**: awards@royalsociety.org.nz

### Global Challenges Research Fund Challenge-led Grants (GCRF)

**Purpose**: Generate excellent and novel research on global challenges directly and primarily relevant to developing countries that cuts across multiple thematic areas covered by the Sustainable Development Goals (SDGs).' Strengthen research capacity in developing countries through collaboration, sharing of knowledge and skills, and exchange of staff between research groups in the United Kingdom and their partners in developing countries
**Eligibility**: 1. Your proposed research must address two or more GCRF thematic areas. The proposal must ultimately benefit the economic development and welfare of developing countries (i.e. be compliant with the ODA guidelines). 2. Your proposal must fall within the remit of the United Kingdom academies and must be interdisciplinary. The consortia must consist of one United Kingdom research group and two research groups from developing countries
**Level of Study**: Graduate
**Type**: Grants, work-study (not just grants)
**Country of Study**: Any country
**Application Procedure**: Application should be submitted through the Royal Society's grants and awards management system (Flexi-Grant®). and weblink is grants.royalsociety.org/

**Closing Date**: 11 September
**Funding**: Private
**Additional Information**: www.thebritishacademy.ac.uk/funding/global-challenges-research-fund-challenge-led-grants

### For further information contact:

**Email**:    ChallengeGrants@royalsociety.org

## Hutton Fund

**Subjects**: Zoology, Botany, Geology
**Purpose**: To encourage research in New Zealand zoology, botany and geology.
**Eligibility**: Please note that funding is not available for fees, thesis production or conference attendance.
**Type**: Grant
**Value**: NZ$1,000
**Frequency**: Annual
**Country of Study**: New Zealand
**Closing Date**: 31 March
**Funding**: Foundation
**Additional Information**: www.royalsociety.org.nz/what-we-do/funds-and-opportunities/hutton-fund/

### For further information contact:

**Email**:    awards@royalsociety.org.nz

## Olga Kennard Research Fellowship Scheme

**Eligibility**: Applicants must be citizens of the EU, Norway, Israel or Switzerland. There are no UK residency requirements for this appointment. Applicants must have at least three years' postdoctoral experience and should be at least 26 but not have passed their 40th birthday on 1 October in the year of application
**Level of Study**: Postdoctorate
**Type**: Fellowship
**Value**: Salary with London allowance where appropriate, together with annual research expenses, travel expenses and a contribution to baggage costs for overseas applicants
**Length of Study**: 5 years
**Study Establishment**: Appropriate university departments
**Country of Study**: United Kingdom
**Application Procedure**: Applications can only be submitted online on the Royal Society's E-gap system. For further information on this scheme or the E-gap process, submit an enquiry to ukgrants@royalsoc.ac.uk
**No. of awards offered**: 1

**Additional Information**: Further information is available on the website vrijmetselaarsgilde.eu/Maconnieke%20Encyclopedie/RMAP~1/TRS/fell_okr.htm

### For further information contact:

**Tel**:       (44) 207 451 2547
**Email**:    ukresearch.appointments@royalsoc.ac.uk

## RHT Bates Postgraduate Scholarship

**Subjects**: Physical Sciences and Engineering
**Purpose**: For a PhD in the Physical Sciences and Engineering in a New Zealand university.
**Eligibility**: Applicants must have physical sciences or engineering as a significant part of their undergraduate degree. For the purposes of this scholarship, physical sciences shall be deemed to mean physics, chemistry and mathematical and information sciences. At the time of application students must be engaged in postgraduate studies (honours, masters or doctorate). Students in their final year of undergraduate study are ineligible to apply.
**Level of Study**: Postgraduate
**Type**: Grant
**Value**: NZ$6,000
**Frequency**: Annual
**Country of Study**: New Zealand
**No. of awards offered**: 1
**Closing Date**: 31 August
**Additional Information**: www.royalsociety.org.nz/what-we-do/funds-and-opportunities/r-h-t-bates-postgraduate-scholarship/

### For further information contact:

**Email**:    awards@royalsociety.org.nz

## Raewyn Good Study Award for Māori and Pasifika Social Science Research

**Subjects**: Social Science
**Purpose**: For Māori and Pasifika postgraduate student undertaking a Master's which involves social sciences research.
**Eligibility**: Māori and Pasifika postgraduate students at any New Zealand university/wānanga
**Level of Study**: Postgraduate
**Type**: Grant
**Value**: NZ$6,000
**Length of Study**: 1 year
**Frequency**: Annual
**Country of Study**: New Zealand
**No. of awards offered**: 1
**Closing Date**: 31 August

**Funding**: Foundation
**Additional Information**: www.royalsociety.org.nz/what-we-do/funds-and-opportunities/raewyn-good-study-award/

**For further information contact:**

**Email**: awards@royalsociety.org.nz

## Royal Society South East Asia Rainforest Research Project - Travel Grants

**Eligibility**: Open to scientists and nationals of European Union countries and South East Asia countries who are PhD or MSc students
**Level of Study**: Postgraduate
**Type**: Travel grant
**Value**: Economy air fare plus two weeks subsistence for European scientists travelling to South East Asia or three months subsistence for South East Asian scientists travelling to Europe
**Length of Study**: Varies
**Country of Study**: Other
**Application Procedure**: Applicants must apply for information, available on request from Programme Research Coordinator, Dr Stephen Sutton email sutton@hh.edi.co.uk
**Additional Information**: Further information available on request

**For further information contact:**

Department of Zoology, University of Cambridge, Downing Street, Cambridge CB2 3EJ, United Kingdom & Danum Valley Field Centre, PO Box 60282, 91112 Lahad Datu, Sabah, Malaysia.

**Fax**: (44) 8 983 4046
**Email**: ajdavis@pc.jaring.my

## Sir Henry Dale Fellowships

**Purpose**: This scheme is for outstanding post-doctoral scientists wishing to build their own UK-based, independent research career addressing an important biomedical question.
**Eligibility**: You can apply for a Small Grant if you're a humanities or social science researcher with a compelling research vision and you want to do one or more of the following: 1. Build your professional network. 2. Develop a new research agenda. 3. Increase the impact of your work
**Level of Study**: Postdoctorate, Research
**Type**: Research grant
**Value**: Value includes a basic salary, fellowship supplements. research and personal removal expenses. Check with website

**Frequency**: Every 5 years
**Country of Study**: Any country
**Closing Date**: 16 July
**Funding**: Private
**Additional Information**: royalsociety.org/grants-schemes-awards/grants/henry-dale/

**For further information contact:**

**Tel**: (44) 207 451 2500
**Email**: grants@royalsociety.org

## Skinner Fund

**Subjects**: History, art, culture, physical and social anthropology of the Māori and other Polynesian people
**Purpose**: To encourage research in the study of the history, art, culture, physical and social anthropology of the Māori and other Polynesian people
**Eligibility**: The results of research aided by grants from the fund, shall, where possible, be published in New Zealand, with due acknowledgement of the source of financial assistance, and one copy of any report stemming from such research shall be sent to the Society.
**Type**: Grant
**Value**: NZ$1,000
**Frequency**: Annual
**Country of Study**: New Zealand
**Closing Date**: 31 March
**Funding**: Foundation
**Additional Information**: www.royalsociety.org.nz/what-we-do/funds-and-opportunities/skinner-fund/

**For further information contact:**

**Email**: awards@royalsociety.org.nz

## The Sir Hugh Kawharu Masters Scholarship for Innovation in Science

**Subjects**: Sciences
**Purpose**: Supporting and encouraging masters level study by Māori in the sciences
**Eligibility**: To be eligible applicants must: be enrolled full-time in a one or two year masters degree in a science discipline; and be persons of Māori descent able to explain their tribal connections.
**Level of Study**: Masters
**Type**: Scholarship
**Value**: NZ$10,000
**Length of Study**: 1-2 Yeas
**Frequency**: Annual

**Country of Study**: New Zealand
**No. of awards offered**: 1
**Funding**: Foundation
**Contributor**: Sir Hugh Kawharu Foundation
**Additional Information**: www.royalsociety.org.nz/what-we-do/funds-and-opportunities/the-sir-hugh-kawharu-masters-scholarship-for-innovation-in-science/

**For further information contact:**

**Email**:    awards@royalsociety.org.nz

## Royal Society of Chemistry

Burlington House Piccadilly, London W1J 0BA, United Kingdom.

**Tel**:        (44) 20 7437 8656
**Email**:    langers@rsc.org
**Website**:  www.rsc.org
**Contact**:  Mr S S Langer

The Royal Society of Chemistry is the learned society for chemistry and the professional body for chemists in the United Kingdom with 46,000 members worldwide. The Society is a major publisher of chemical information, supports the teaching of chemistry at all levels, organizes hundreds of chemical meetings a year and is a leader in communicating science to the public. It is now the United Kingdom National Adhering Organization (NAO) to the International Union of Pure and Applied Chemistry (IUPAC).

## Royal Society of Chemistry Journals Grants for International Authors

**Purpose**: To allow international authors to visit other countries in order to collaborate in research, exchange research ideas and results, and to give or receive special expertise and training
**Eligibility**: Open to anyone with a recent publication in any of the Society's journals. Those from the United Kingdom or Republic of Ireland are excluded
**Level of Study**: Professional development
**Type**: Grant
**Value**: Up to £2,500 cover travel and subsistence (but not research related costs) and are available
**Length of Study**: Normally 1–3 months
**Country of Study**: Any country

**Application Procedure**: Candidates must apply for application forms, together with full details, from the International Affairs Officer
**No. of awards offered**: 107
**Closing Date**: 1 October
**No. of awards given last year**: 83
**No. of applicants last year**: 107
**Additional Information**: Please see the website for further details www.rsc.org/ScienceAndTechnology/Funding/Travel Grants/InternationalAuthors.asp    osc.universityofcalifornia.edu/for-authors/open-access-publishing-at-uc/publishing-discounts/royal-society-of-chemistry/

## Royal Society of Edinburgh

22-26 George Street, Edinburgh EH2 2PQ, United Kingdom.

**Tel**:        (44) 131 240 5000
**Email**:    afraser@royalsoced.org.uk
**Website**:  www.royalsoced.org.uk
**Contact**:  Anne Fraser, Research Awards Manager

The Royal Society of Edinburgh is Scotland's national academy of science and letters. It offers research and enterprise awards to candidates based in Scotland.

## Royal Society of Edinburgh Personal Research Fellowships

**Purpose**: To provide outstanding researchers, who have the potential to become leaders in their chosen field, with the opportunity to build an independent research career
**Eligibility**: Open to persons of all nationalities who have 2 to 6 years postdoctoral experience. They must also show that they have the capacity for innovative research and the potential to become leaders in their field
**Level of Study**: Doctorate
**Value**: Salary and research support costs for 5 years
**Length of Study**: 5 years
**Frequency**: Annual
**Study Establishment**: Any Higher Education Institution in Scotland
**Country of Study**: Scotland
**Application Procedure**: Applicants must complete an application form, available on the RSE website. Applicants should negotiate directly with their host institution
**No. of awards offered**: 53
**Closing Date**: 16 February

**Contributor**: Scottish Government, BP and Caledonian Research Fund
**No. of awards given last year**: 3
**No. of applicants last year**: 53
**Additional Information**: Successful applicants will be allocated a funding provider (BP, CRF or Scottish Government) according to their subject area. BP funding is available every 2nd year and is for candidates working in areas of interest to BP. CRF funding is for candidates in the biomedical sciences. Fellows are expected to devote their full time to research and are not allowed to hold any other paid appointments without the express permission of Council. Website: www.royalsoced.org.uk/549_RSEPersonalResearchFellowships.html www.rse.org.uk/awards/rse-personal-research-fellowships/

### For further information contact:

22-26 George Street, Edinburgh, EH2 2PQ, United Kingdom.

**Tel**:     (44) 131 240 5000
**Email**:   schooloffice-ls@dundee.ac.uk

# Royal Society of Medicine (RSM)

1 Wimpole Street, London W1G 0AE, United Kingdom.

**Tel**:        (44) 20 7290 3846
**Email**:     awards@rsm.dc.uk
**Website**:   www.rsm.ac.uk/awards
**Contact**:   Awards Manager, Alademic Department

The Royal Society of Medicine (RSM) provides academic services and club facilities for its members as well as publishing a monthly journal and an annual bulletin, and providing over 400 educational conferences and meetings per year. The RSM offers around 60 awards and prizes each year. The majority for medical doctors in training covering the majority of specialities in medicine and surgery.

## Adrian Tanner Prize

**Purpose**: To encourage surgical trainees submit the best clinical case reports
**Eligibility**: Open to all surgeons in training
**Value**: £250
**Frequency**: Annual
**Study Establishment**: Royal Society of Medicine–Surgery section
**Country of Study**: United Kingdom

**Application Procedure**: Applicants should download an application form from www.rsm.ac.uk/awards
**No. of awards offered**: 50
**Closing Date**: 12 July
**No. of awards given last year**: 1
**No. of applicants last year**: 50
**Additional Information**: www.rsm.ac.uk/prizes-and-awards/prizes-for-trainees/

### For further information contact:

**Email**:     surgery@rsm.ac.uk

## Alan Emery Prize

**Purpose**: To reward the best published research article in Medical Genetics in the past 2 years
**Eligibility**: Open to candidates in an accredited training or research post in the United Kingdom
**Type**: Prize
**Value**: £500 or £300 or 1 year membership of Royal Society of Medicine
**Frequency**: Annual
**Application Procedure**: Candidates must submit full copy of the article, curriculum vitae or covering letter explaining the significance of the publication
**No. of awards offered**: 7
**Closing Date**: 5 March
**No. of awards given last year**: 1
**No. of applicants last year**: 7

### For further information contact:

**Email**:     genetics@rsm.ac.uk

## Cardiology Section Presidents Prize

**Purpose**: To reward original work for specialist registrar in cardiology
**Eligibility**: Open to cardiology trainees who have received all or part of their training at recognized centres of excellence in the United Kingdom. The subject of the presentation should represent original work
**Level of Study**: Research
**Type**: Prize
**Value**: Commemoration medal and £1,000 (First prize); £500 (Second prize)
**Frequency**: Annual
**Study Establishment**: Recognized centres of excellence in United Kingdom
**Country of Study**: United Kingdom

**Application Procedure**: Candidates should submit an abstract of no more than 200 words
**Closing Date**: 31 March
**Contributor**: Cardiology Section Funds
**No. of awards given last year**: 2
**Additional Information**: www.rsm.ac.uk/prizes-and-awards/prizes-for-trainees/

**For further information contact:**

Cardiology Section, Royal Society of Medicine, 1 Wimpole Street, Marylebone, London W1G 0AE, United Kingdom.

**Email**:    cardiology@rsm.ac.uk

## Catastrophes & Conflict Forum Medical Student Essay Prize

**Eligibility**: Open to candidates who are enroled full-time at a United Kingdom medical school
**Level of Study**: Postgraduate
**Type**: Prize
**Value**: £250 plus encouragement and advice on submitting the essay for publication in the JRSM
**Frequency**: Annual
**Study Establishment**: Royal Society of Medicine
**Country of Study**: United Kingdom
**Application Procedure**: Candidates should submit an essay no longer than 1,500 words, emailed in Word format
**No. of awards offered**: 9
**Closing Date**: 1 March
**No. of awards given last year**: 2
**No. of applicants last year**: 9

**For further information contact:**

**Email**:    catastrophes@rsm.ac.uk

## Clinical Forensic and Legal Medicine Section Poster Competition

**Purpose**: To present a case or a poster in clinical studies
**Eligibility**: Undergraduate students who have been working as part of courses leading to primary qualifications such as Legal Medicine Special Study Modules and electives for MBBS
**Value**: £250
**Frequency**: Annual
**Application Procedure**: Please visit the website www.rsm.ac.uk/academ/awards/index

**Closing Date**: 15 December
**Additional Information**: www.rsm.ac.uk/prizes-and-awards/prizes-for-students/

**For further information contact:**

**Email**:    forensic@rsm.ac.uk

## Clinical Immunology & Allergy President's Prize

**Eligibility**: Open to training grade doctors and young scientists (not above Specialist Registrar, Grade B Clinical Scientist or equivalent grade) with an immunological or allergy component of their clinical research
**Level of Study**: Research
**Type**: Prize
**Value**: £300 (First prize); two prizes of £100 (Second prize)
**Frequency**: Annual
**Country of Study**: United Kingdom
**Application Procedure**: Check website for further details
**No. of awards offered**: 10
**No. of awards given last year**: 3
**No. of applicants last year**: 10
**Additional Information**: www.competitioninfo.com/opportunity/clinical-immunology-allergy-section-president-s-prize-123892

**For further information contact:**

**Email**:    immunology@rsm.ac.uk

## Clinical Neurosciences Gordon Holmes Prize

**Purpose**: To award a research prize in clinical neurosciences
**Eligibility**: Trainees in neurosciences, including neurology, neurosurgery, neurophysiology, neuropathology or neuroradiology
**Type**: Prize
**Value**: £300
**Frequency**: Every 2 years
**Application Procedure**: Please check the website www.rsm.ac.uk/prizes-awards/trainees.aspx
**Closing Date**: 12 January
**Additional Information**:    www.rsm.ac.uk/rsm-sections/clinical-neurosciences-section/

**For further information contact:**

**Email**:    cns@rsm.ac.uk

## Clinical Neurosciences President's Prize

**Purpose**: To encourage clinical case presentation
**Eligibility**: Open to trainees in neurosciences, including neurology, neurosurgery, neurophysiology, neuropathology, or neuroradiology
**Type**: Prize
**Length of Study**: £300
**Frequency**: Every 2 years
**Application Procedure**: Applicants must submit one A4 page (up to 500 words) summary of research carried out. Those considered to be the best will be asked to give a 15 minute presentation
**Additional Information**: www.bna.org.uk/mediacentre/events/the-royal-society-of-medicine-presidents-prize-meeting-and-neurology-in-africa/

**For further information contact:**

**Email**: cns@rsm.ac.uk

## Coloproctology John of Arderne Medal

**Purpose**: To award the presenter of the best paper presented at the short papers meeting of the section of coloproctology. Applicants have to submit an abstract for presentation at the meeting
**Eligibility**: Open to applicants of any nationality
**Level of Study**: Professional development
**Type**: Award
**Value**: Approx. £600
**Frequency**: Annual
**Study Establishment**: Varies
**Country of Study**: Any country
**Application Procedure**: Further details are available from the RSM administrator
**No. of awards offered**: 14–20
**Closing Date**: November
**Funding**: Private
**No. of awards given last year**: 1
**No. of applicants last year**: 14–20
**Additional Information**: www.thedukesclub.org.uk/2017/12/22/john-of-arderne-medal-royal-society-of-medicine/

**For further information contact:**

**Email**: coloproctology@rsm.ac.uk

## Dermatology Clinicopathological Meetings

**Eligibility**: Trainee Dermatologists
**Type**: Prize

**Value**: £150
**Frequency**: Annual
**Country of Study**: United Kingdom
**No. of awards offered**: 32
**Contributor**: Royal Society of Medicine
**No. of awards given last year**: 1
**No. of applicants last year**: 32
**Additional Information**: For more details, please refer the website: www.dermpath.com/news-events/calendar/practical-symposium-sharpen-your-dermatology-clinicopathologic-and-business www.rsm.ac.uk/events/dermatology/2019-20/den04/

**For further information contact:**

**Email**: dermatology@rsm.ac.uk

## Epidemiology & Public Health Young Epidemiologists Prize

**Purpose**: To reward outstanding papers
**Eligibility**: Any medical/non-medical epidemiologist or public health practitioner under the age of 40 years
**Level of Study**: Unrestricted
**Type**: Award
**Value**: £250
**Frequency**: Annual
**Country of Study**: United Kingdom
**Application Procedure**: Download the application form from website
**No. of awards offered**: 9
**Closing Date**: 27 November
**No. of awards given last year**: 1
**No. of applicants last year**: 9
**Additional Information**: www.rsm.ac.uk/rsm-sections/epidemiology-public-health-section/

**For further information contact:**

**Email**: epidemiology@rsm.ac.uk

## General Practice with Primary Healthcare John Fry Prize

**Purpose**: To award best examples of practice-based research involving members of the primary health and social community, demonstrating and promoting effective team work
**Eligibility**: Open to candidates currently working in primary healthcare in the United Kingdom excluding members of the RSM section of GP Council
**Level of Study**: Unrestricted
**Type**: Prize
**Value**: £300

**Frequency**: Annual
**Country of Study**: United Kingdom
**Application Procedure**: Application form must be completed in all respects
**No. of awards offered**: 4
**Closing Date**: 14 June
**Funding**: Private
**Contributor**: John Fry
**No. of awards given last year**: 1
**No. of applicants last year**: 4
**Additional Information**: www.rsm.ac.uk/rsm-sections/general-practice-with-primary-healthcare-section/

### For further information contact:

RSM, 1 Wimpole Street, Marylebone, London W1G 0AE, United Kingdom.

**Email**:   gp@rsm.ac.uk

## Laryngology & Rhinology Travel and Equipment Grants

**Purpose**: To assist with the cost of travel to overseas centres
**Eligibility**: Open to senior registrars or consultants of not more than 2 years standing, who must be members of the section of laryngology and rhinology of the RSM
**Level of Study**: Postdoctorate
**Type**: Scholarship
**Value**: £1,000
**Frequency**: Annual
**Country of Study**: Any country
**Application Procedure**: Applicants must submit a paper to the RSM section of laryngology and rhinology. Further details are available from the RSM administrator
**No. of awards offered**: 25
**Closing Date**: 15 April
**Funding**: Commercial
**Contributor**: Karl Storz Endoscopy Limited
**No. of awards given last year**: 1
**No. of applicants last year**: 25
**Additional Information**: The recipient will be required to submit a brief report on the visit within 3 months of his or her return

### For further information contact:

**Email**:   laryngology@rsm.ac.uk

## Military Medicine Colt Foundation Research Prize

**Purpose**: To recognize the best abstract by a serving military medical officer

**Eligibility**: Open to serving military officers in a training grade in general practice, a hospital or other speciality and are fellows of the RSM
**Level of Study**: Postgraduate
**Type**: Prize
**Value**: £200 (1st prize) and £100 each (2nd prize)
**Frequency**: Annual
**Study Establishment**: Royal Society of Medicine
**Country of Study**: United Kingdom
**Application Procedure**: Candidates should email the abstracts. The abstracts will be shortlisted by the panel and judged
**No. of awards offered**: 15
**Closing Date**: 6 November
**Funding**: Trusts
**Contributor**: Colt Foundation
**No. of awards given last year**: 1
**No. of applicants last year**: 15
**Additional Information**: www.imperial.ac.uk/events/107149/military-medicine-section-colt-foundation-research-meeting-and-prize/

### For further information contact:

**Email**:   united.services@rsm.ac.uk

## Nephrology Section Rosemarie Baillod Clinical Award

**Eligibility**: All doctors in training in nephrology and renal medicine at any grade
**Type**: Research award
**Value**: £200
**Frequency**: Annual
**Country of Study**: United Kingdom
**Application Procedure**: Please visit website for further details
**Closing Date**: 21 October
**Additional Information**: www.rsm.ac.uk/rsm-sections/nephrology-section/

### For further information contact:

**Email**:   nephrology@rsm.ac.uk

## Occupational Medicine Section Malcolm Harrington Prize

**Purpose**: To award the work that is most likely to advance the study of occupational medicine in its broadest sense
**Eligibility**: Open to occupational physician in training or within an year of achieving specialist accreditation
**Type**: Prize

**Value**: £250
**Frequency**: Annual
**Application Procedure**: Candidates should submit an abstract of their own work (no longer than 200 words)
**No. of awards offered**: 9
**Closing Date**: 9 March
**Funding**: Private
**Contributor**: Professor Harrington
**No. of awards given last year**: 1
**No. of applicants last year**: 9

**For further information contact:**

**Email**: occupational@rsm.ac.uk

## Oncology Section Sylvia Lawler Prize

**Purpose**: To encourage scientists and clinicians in training to present the best scientific paper and best clinical paper on oncology
**Eligibility**: All scientists and clinicians in training
**Level of Study**: Postgraduate
**Type**: Grant
**Value**: Two prizes of £50 to oral presenters and one prize of £50 voucher to poster presenter
**Frequency**: Annual
**Study Establishment**: Royal Society of Medicine
**Country of Study**: United Kingdom
**Application Procedure**: Applicants should download an application form from the website www.rsm.ac.uk/prizes-awards/trainees.aspx
**No. of awards offered**: 50
**Closing Date**: 26 April
**No. of awards given last year**: 1
**No. of applicants last year**: 50
**Additional Information**: www.rsm.ac.uk/rsm-sections/oncology-section/

**For further information contact:**

**Email**: oncology@rsm.ac.uk

## Ophthalmology Section Travelling Fellowships

**Purpose**: To enable British ophthalmologists to travel abroad with the intention of furthering the study or advancement of ophthalmology, or to enable foreign ophthalmologists to visit the United Kingdom for the same purpose
**Eligibility**: Open to ophthalmologists in the British Isles of any nationality who have not attained an official consultant appointment, nor undertaken professional clinical work or equivalent responsibility for any substantial period before or during the execution of original work

**Level of Study**: Professional development
**Type**: Fellowship
**Value**: £500–1,000
**Frequency**: Every 2 years
**Study Establishment**: Varies
**Country of Study**: Any country
**Application Procedure**: Applicants must apply to the academic administrator at RSM
**No. of awards offered**: 6
**Closing Date**: 1 May
**No. of awards given last year**: 4
**No. of applicants last year**: 6
**Additional Information**: www.eyedocs.co.uk/ophthalmology-travel-awards/1102-royal-society-of-medicine-travelling-fellowships

**For further information contact:**

**Email**: ophthalmology@rsm.ac.uk

## Orthopaedics Section President's Prize Papers

**Purpose**: To encourage research in the area of Orthopaedics
**Eligibility**: Open to all orthopaedic trainees
**Level of Study**: Postgraduate
**Type**: Prize
**Value**: Clinical paper prize – 1st prize of £300 and 2nd prize of £200
**Frequency**: Annual
**Study Establishment**: Royal Society of Medicine
**Country of Study**: United Kingdom
**Application Procedure**: Candidates should submit abstracts no longer than 200 words. The abstracts will be judged by a panel of experts, shortlisted and asked to be presented at a meeting
**No. of awards offered**: 10
**Closing Date**: 5 April
**No. of awards given last year**: 1
**No. of applicants last year**: 10
**Additional Information**: www.rsm.ac.uk/prizes-and-awards/prizes-for-trainees/

**For further information contact:**

**Email**: orthopaedics@rsm.ac.uk

## Otology Section Norman Gamble Grant

**Purpose**: To support specific research projects
**Eligibility**: British citizens, both lay and medical
**Level of Study**: Unrestricted
**Type**: Prize
**Value**: £100

**Frequency**: Annual
**Country of Study**: Any country
**Application Procedure**: Further details are available from the RSM administrator
**No. of awards offered**: 4
**Closing Date**: 26 January
**Funding**: Private
**No. of awards given last year**: 1
**No. of applicants last year**: 4
**Additional Information**: www.rsm.ac.uk/rsm-sections/otology-section/

**For further information contact:**

**Email**:   otology@rsm.ac.uk

## Paediatrics & Child Health Section Trainees Tim David Prize

**Purpose**: To encourage research in the area of Paediatrics & Child Health
**Eligibility**: Open to paediatric trainees
**Level of Study**: Postgraduate, Foundation programme
**Type**: Prize
**Value**: First prize £150, 1 year's subscription to the RSM (worth up to £200) and membership of the Council of the Section of Paediatrics and Child Health for 1 year. There will also be a second prize of £100
**Frequency**: Annual
**Application Procedure**: Candidates should submit abstracts
**No. of awards offered**: 12
**Closing Date**: 1 April
**Contributor**: Paediatrics & Child Health Section, RSM
**No. of awards given last year**: 2
**No. of applicants last year**: 12
**Additional Information**: www.rsm.ac.uk/events/paediatrics-and-child-health/2018-19/pdm11/

**For further information contact:**

**Email**:   paediatrics@rsm.ac.uk

## Palliative Care Section MSc/MA Research Prize

**Eligibility**: All students either currently studying, or within 18 months of completion, of MSc or MA in Palliative Medicine or an allied discipline, are eligible to apply
**Level of Study**: Postgraduate, Foundation programme
**Type**: Prize
**Value**: 1st prize of £250, 2nd prize of £100, and 3rd prize of £50

**Frequency**: Annual
**Closing Date**: 17 September
**Contributor**: Palliative Care Section
**Additional Information**: www.rsm.ac.uk/rsm-sections/palliative-care-section/

**For further information contact:**

**Email**:   palliative@rsm.ac.uk

## Psychiatry Section Mental Health Foundation Research Prize

**Purpose**: To award an outstanding published paper
**Eligibility**: Open to candidates practising medicine in the United Kingdom or the Republic of Ireland who are in training at any grade from senior house officer to senior registrar or equivalent. Applicants need not be members of RSM
**Type**: Prize
**Value**: £750 (1st prize); £100 (2nd prize)
**Frequency**: Annual
**Country of Study**: United Kingdom
**Application Procedure**: Full copy of the published article, curriculum vitae and covering letter explaining in their own words the significance of the publication to be submitted to the section of psychiatry
**No. of awards offered**: 1
**Closing Date**: 29 February
**Funding**: Private
**No. of applicants last year**: 1
**Additional Information**: www.rsm.ac.uk/rsm-sections/psychiatry-section/

**For further information contact:**

**Email**:   psychiatry@rsm.ac.uk

## Surgery Section Norman Tanner Prize and Glaxo Travelling Fellowship

**Purpose**: To encourage clinical registrars submit the best clinical paper
**Eligibility**: Open to all trainee oncologists
**Value**: £250 plus the Norman Tanner Medal. Runner up – £250 Glaxo Travelling Fellowship
**Frequency**: Annual
**Study Establishment**: Royal Society of Medicine
**Country of Study**: United Kingdom
**Application Procedure**: Applicants are requested to contact the Section Coordinator at oncology@rsm.ac.uk
**No. of awards offered**: 30

**Closing Date**: 1 September
**No. of awards given last year**: 12
**No. of applicants last year**: 30

### For further information contact:

**Email**:    surgery@rsm.ac.uk

## Trainees' Committee John Glyn Trainees' Prize

**Purpose**: The prize was established to promote best practise through high quality audit
**Eligibility**: Trainees from any hospital or primary care specialty
**Level of Study**: Graduate, Postgraduate, Research, Foundation programme
**Type**: Prize
**Value**: £300
**Frequency**: Annual
**No. of awards offered**: 40
**Closing Date**: 12 April
**Contributor**: Royal Society of Medicine
**No. of awards given last year**: 1
**No. of applicants last year**: 40
**Additional Information**: www.rsm.ac.uk/events/trainees/2018-19/trm04/

### For further information contact:

**Email**:    trainees@rsm.ac.uk

## Urology Professor Geoffrey D Chisholm CBE Communication Prize

**Purpose**: To reward the best abstract at the Short Papers Prize Meeting
**Eligibility**: Open to members of the Urology section
**Type**: Travel award
**Value**: Fully funded RSM travelling fellowship to the Urology Section's overseas winter scientific meeting in the next academic session
**No. of awards offered**: 30
**Closing Date**: 29 March
**No. of awards given last year**: 3
**No. of applicants last year**: 30
**Additional Information**: www.rsm.ac.uk/rsm-sections/urology-section/

### For further information contact:

**Email**:    urology@rsm.ac.uk

## Urology Section Professor John Blandy Essay Prize for Medical Students

**Purpose**: To enable the holder to enhance his or her knowledge and experience by visiting an overseas unit
**Eligibility**: Medical students
**Type**: Fellowship
**Value**: A bursary of £1,000 and an RSM award certificate
**Frequency**: Annual
**Closing Date**: 8 March
**Additional Information**: Candidates must be available on the May 16th for presentation of their short paper to be eligible for this prize www.baus.org.uk/professionals/sections/essay_competition.aspx

### For further information contact:

**Email**:    urology@rsm.ac.uk

## Urology Section Winter Short Papers Prize (Clinical Uro-Radiological Meeting)

**Purpose**: To reward the best clinicopathological short paper
**Eligibility**: Urological and radiological trainees
**Type**: Prize
**Value**: Fully funded RSM travelling fellowship to the Urology Section's overseas winter scientific meeting in the next academic session. Runner up prizes of a bursary towards the RSM overseas winter scientific meeting in the next academic session
**Frequency**: Annual
**Additional Information**: www.rsm.ac.uk/rsm-sections/urology-section/

### For further information contact:

**Email**:    urology@rsm.ac.uk

## Venous Forum Spring Meeting Prizes

**Purpose**: To recognize the best original paper by a non-consultant
**Eligibility**: Open to non-consultants
**Level of Study**: Postgraduate
**Type**: Prize
**Value**: £250 (1st prize); £200 (2nd prize); £150 (3rd prize); and £200 (Poster prize)
**Frequency**: Annual
**Study Establishment**: Royal Society of Medicine
**Country of Study**: United Kingdom
**Application Procedure**: Candidates should email abstracts. Shortlisted candidates will be invited to present their papers

**No. of awards offered**: 20
**Closing Date**: 27 March
**No. of awards given last year**: 1
**No. of applicants last year**: 20
**Additional Information**: www.rsm.ac.uk/rsm-sections/venous-forum/

### For further information contact:

**Email**:   venous@rsm.ac.uk

## Royal Town Planning Institute (RTPI)

41 Botolph Lane, London EC3R 8DL, United Kingdom.

**Tel**:       (44) 20 7929 9494
**Email**:   judy.woollett@rtpi.org.uk
**Website**: www.rtpi.org.uk/

The Royal Town Planning Institute (RTPI) was founded in 1914 and is a registered charity. Its aim is to advance the science and art of town planning in all its aspects, including local, regional and national planning for the benefit of the public. The Institute is primarily concerned with maintaining high standards of competence and conduct within the profession, promoting the role of planning within the country's social, economic and political structures, and presenting the profession's views on current planning issues.

### George Pepler International Award

**Purpose**: To enable young people of any nationality to visit another country for a short period to study. The George Pepler International Award is a bursary granted biennially to a person in their first ten years of post-qualification experience wishing to undertake a short period of study (3-4 weeks) on a particular aspect of spatial planning
**Eligibility**: Open to persons under 30 years of age of any nationality. Candidature must have the age limit of upto 30 years
**Level of Study**: Professional development, Research
**Type**: Fees to performers
**Value**: Up to £1,500
**Length of Study**: Short-term travel outside the United Kingdom for United Kingdom residents or for visits to the United Kingdom for applicants from abroad
**Frequency**: Every 2 years
**Country of Study**: Any country

**Application Procedure**: Applicants must submit a statement showing the nature of the study visit proposed, together with an itinerary. Application forms are available on request from the RTPI
**No. of awards offered**: 20
**Closing Date**: 31 March
**Funding**: Private
**Contributor**: Trust fund
**No. of awards given last year**: 1
**No. of applicants last year**: 20
**Additional Information**: At the conclusion of the visit the recipient must submit a report. Please see the website for further details www.rtpi.org.uk/events/awards/george-pepler-international-award/

### For further information contact:

The Royal Town Planning Institute, 41 Botolph Lane, London.

## Rural Health Information Hub

### National Board for Certified Counselors Minority Fellowship Program for Mental Health Counselors

**Purpose**: The purpose of the program is to ensure that the behavioral health needs of all Americans are met, regardless of language or culture, thereby reducing health disparities
**Eligibility**: Eligible applicants are United States citizens or permanent residents that are currently enrolled and in good standing in an accredited graduate level counseling program. Please check the website link for further details,
**Level of Study**: Graduate
**Type**: Programme grant
**Value**: US$10,000, plus travel expenses to participate in other program-related training
**Frequency**: Annual
**Country of Study**: Any country
**Closing Date**: 15 December
**Funding**: Private
**Additional Information**: For doctoral degree-level students: US$20,000, plus travel expenses to participate in other program-related training. www.nbccf.org/programs/scholarships/fellows

### For further information contact:

School of Medicine and Health Sciences, Suite E231, 1301 N. Columbia Road, Stop 9037, Grand Forks, ND 58202-9037, United States of America.

**Email**:   info@ruralhealthinfo.org

# Rural Maternity Care Research

Suite 530-1501 West Broadway, Vancouver, BC V6J 4Z6, Canada.

**Tel**: (1) 604 742 1796
**Email**: leslie@ruralmatresearch.net
**Website**: www.ruralmatresearch.net

Rural Maternity Care Research is a team of academic and community based researchers interested in rural maternity care. They believe their diversity of expertise, backgrounds and interests enhance their ability to comprehensively investigate the complexity of challenges and opportunities for rural maternity care in British Columbia.

## Rural Maternity Care Doctoral Student Fellowship

**Purpose**: To enable a motivated Doctoral student researcher to join the interdisciplinary team investigating rural maternity care in British Columbia
**Eligibility**: Open to citizens or permanent residents of Canada who are registered in a Doctoral programme in Canada
**Level of Study**: Doctorate
**Type**: Fellowship
**Value**: Up to C$45,000 (benefits included)
**Length of Study**: 18 months
**Frequency**: Annual
**Country of Study**: Canada
**Application Procedure**: Applicants must include the following documents in the application: cover letter, transcripts, curriculum vitae, contact information of 3 research referees and sample of the candidates writing preferably from an article published in a referred journal
**Closing Date**: 18 August
**Additional Information**: The fellow will be provided with office space in Vancouver, as well as access to and use of internet, printers and telephone and fax lines. Candidates from all academic disciplines are invited to apply. Candidates who may be completing coursework for their PhD programme, will be expected to contribute sufficient time to the RM-NET to develop a research focus area www.multicare.org/rural-fellowship/

### For further information contact:

**Email**: clin2@cw.bc.ca

# Ryerson University

## Autism Scholars Award

**Purpose**: With the support of the Ministry of Training, Colleges and Universities, a scholar awards program in autism has been established to ensure that Ontario attracts and retains pre-eminent scholars. The community of autism scholars fostered by this awards program will excel, according to internationally accepted standards of scientific excellence, in the creation of new knowledge concerning child autism, and its translation into improved health for children, more effective services and products for children with autism, and increase the province's capacity in diagnosis and assessment of autism and a strengthened treatment system
**Eligibility**: 1. a Canadian citizen or a permanent resident of Canada at the time of the application deadline (31 January). 2. registered as a full-time student in a master's or doctoral program at an Ontario university at the beginning of the award period (fall), and remain registered as a full-time student throughout the term of the award. 3. A master's student remains eligible until the end of the sixth term of full-time study. 4. A doctoral student remains eligible until the end of the 15th term of full-time study. 5. During the year an Autism Scholars Award is held, the recipient is precluded from holding any other award that offers financial support of more than US$20,000 for that same year (subject to the university's own policies)
**Level of Study**: Graduate
**Type**: Award
**Value**: US$20,000
**Frequency**: Annual
**Country of Study**: Any country
**Closing Date**: 31 January
**Funding**: International office
**Additional Information**: www.sgs.utoronto.ca/awards/autism-scholars-awards/

### For further information contact:

**Email**: SeniorDirectorQA@cou.on.ca

## C. Ravi Ravindran Outstanding Doctoral Thesis Award

**Purpose**: The C. Ravi Ravindran Outstanding Doctoral Thesis Award was established in 2008 (the 60th year of the creation of Ryerson as an educational institution) by his family in recognition of his long and distinguished industrial and academic career. He was the first winner of the Ryerson-

Sahota Faculty Research Award, Trustee of ASM International, and the first Ryerson faculty member elected as Fellow, and later President of the Canadian Academy of Engineering

**Eligibility**: 1. Registration as a graduate studies student in a program of study leading to a PhD 2. One student may be nominated by a program director from each PhD program. 3. A nominated student must have applied to graduate at the upcoming fall graduation convocation ceremonies or have already graduated at the spring graduation convocation ceremonies

**Level of Study**: Postgraduate

**Type**: Award

**Value**: US$1,000

**Length of Study**: 1 year

**Frequency**: Annual

**Country of Study**: Any country

**Closing Date**: 22 August

**Funding**: Foundation

### For further information contact:

**Email**:    grdadmit@ryerson.ca

## Canada's Distinguished Dissertation Awards

**Purpose**: The CAGS/ProQuest Distinguished Dissertation Awards recognize Canadian doctoral dissertations that make unusually significant and original contributions to their academic field. They were established in 1994 and are presented annually

**Eligibility**: 1. A dissertation in any discipline in engineering, medical sciences and natural sciences completed and accepted by the Graduate School. 2. A dissertation in any discipline in the fine arts, humanities and social sciences completed and accepted by the Graduate School between 1 January and 31 December

**Level of Study**: Graduate

**Type**: Award

**Value**: US$1,500

**Frequency**: Annual

**Country of Study**: Any country

**Closing Date**: 25 February

**Funding**: International office

**Additional Information**:    uwaterloo.ca/graduate-studies-postdoctoral-affairs/awards/cagsumi-distinguished-dissertation-awards

### For further information contact:

**Email**:    natasha.mills@ryerson.ca

## Doctoral Completion Award

**Purpose**: Funding amount is determined on a year-to-year basis and is a one-time-only award

**Eligibility**: 1. Satisfactory progress reports. 2. Comprehensive examination process. 3. Dissertation research proposal. 4. Those students who have a very high probability (ie. 90%) to complete in their 4th year

**Level of Study**: Graduate

**Type**: Award

**Value**: Up to US$10,000

**Frequency**: Annual

**Country of Study**: Any country

**Closing Date**: 19 November

**Funding**: International office

**Additional Information**:    www.sgs.utoronto.ca/awards/doctoral-completion-award-dca/

## Edward S. Rogers Sr. Graduate Student Fellowships

**Purpose**: The Edward S. Rogers Sr. Graduate School Fellowship, first awarded in 2001, was established by Ted and Loretta Rogers to honour the contributions of Edward S. Rogers Sr. to the Canadian communications industry

**Eligibility**: All Canadian PhD students in the Communication & Culture program

**Level of Study**: Graduate

**Type**: Fellowship

**Value**: US$20,000

**Frequency**: Annual

**Country of Study**: Any country

**Funding**: Foundation

**Additional Information**: www.ryerson.ca/graduate/future-students/financing-your-studies/scholarships-awards/rogers-graduate-student-fellowships/

### For further information contact:

**Email**:    grdadmit@ryerson.ca

## Fulbright Canada Scholarship

**Purpose**: The mandate of Fulbright Canada is to enhance mutual understanding between the people of Canada and the United States of America by providing support to outstanding graduate students, faculty, professionals, and independent researchers. These individuals conduct research, lecture, or enroll in formal academic programs in the other country. In doing so, Fulbright Canada aims to grow intellectual capacity, increase productivity, and assist in the shaping of future leaders in both countries

**Eligibility**: 1. Be a Canadian citizen (Permanent residence is not sufficient). 2. Hold a Bachelor's degree prior to the proposed start date of the grant. 3. Be proficient in English. 4. Be in compliance with all J. William Fulbright Foreign Scholarship Board (FFSB) guidelines. 5. Be in compliance with all governmental regulations regarding visas, immigration, travel and residence

**Level of Study**: Graduate
**Type**: Scholarship
**Value**: US$15,000
**Frequency**: Annual
**Country of Study**: Any country
**Closing Date**: 15 November
**Funding**: International office
**Additional Information**: www.ryerson.ca/graduate/future-students/financing-your-studies/scholarships-awards/fulbright-canada-scholarship/

**For further information contact:**

**Email**: grdadmit@ryerson.ca

## Governor General Gold Medal

**Purpose**: The Governor General Gold Medal (GGGM), Ryerson University's most prestigious academic award, is awarded annually to the graduate student who achieves the highest academic standing in a graduate degree program
**Eligibility**: All master's and doctoral program students, who are in their first Master's or Doctoral program respectively, are eligible for this award. The student must have completed his/her program within the normal time frame (as deemed by the Yeates School of Graduate Studies)
**Level of Study**: Graduate
**Type**: Grant
**Value**: No nominal value
**Frequency**: Annual
**Country of Study**: Any country
**Closing Date**: 15 August
**Funding**: International office
**Additional Information**: grad.uwo.ca/finances/external_funding/governor_general.html

**For further information contact:**

1151 Richmond Street, London, ON N6A 3K7, Canada.

**Tel**: (1) 519 661 2102
**Email**: natasha.mills@ryerson.ca

## Graduate Student Stipend

**Purpose**: A graduate student stipend provides financial support to a graduate student while completing their graduate studies. Normally the stipend is paid from the research funding of a faculty supervisor. Stipends are not payment for employment
**Level of Study**: Graduate
**Type**: Stipendiary
**Value**: Dollar amounts vary by program and/or discipline
**Frequency**: Annual
**Country of Study**: Any country
**Funding**: International office
**Additional Information**: gradschool.cornell.edu/financial-support/stipend-rates/

**For further information contact:**

**Email**: grdadmit@ryerson.ca

## John Charles Polanyi Prizes

**Purpose**: In honour of the achievement of John Charles Polanyi, recipient of the 1986 Nobel Prize in Chemistry, the Government of the Province of Ontario has established a fund to provide annually up to five (5) prizes to outstanding researchers in the early stages of their careers who are continuing to postdoctoral studies or have recently started a faculty appointment at an Ontario university. The John Charles Polanyi Prizes are available in the areas broadly defined as Physics, Chemistry, Physiology or Medicine, Literature and Economic Science
**Eligibility**: 1. Normally resident in Ontario and has completed or is near completion of doctoral studies in any recognized university in the world, or has completed or is nearing completion of doctoral studies in an Ontario university. 2. Has received the doctoral degree between 1 September and 30 April, or if the doctoral degree has not yet been awarded, will have completed all the requirements for the doctoral degree by 30 April. Applicants holding faculty appointments within these time limits may apply. 3. The prizes are awarded to assist the recipients in their research and professional development. 4. The prizes may be held along with any other financial support or research funds received by the winners. 5. It is hoped that the prizes will be conferred by September. No prize will be awarded without the successful applicant having completed all requirements for the doctoral degree
**Level of Study**: Graduate
**Type**: Grant
**Value**: US$20,000
**Frequency**: Annual

**Country of Study**: Any country
**Closing Date**: 1 December
**Funding**: International office
**Additional Information**: www.sgs.utoronto.ca/awards/john-charles-polanyi-prizes/

**For further information contact:**

**Email**:    natasha.mills@ryerson.ca

## Sandbox Student Grant Program

**Purpose**: The DMZ Sandbox Student Grant Program (also known as the "Grant Program") will financially support and provide eligible Ryerson led startups with the crucial grant funding and mentorship they need
**Eligibility**: The Sandbox Student Grant Program is open to Ryerson students registered in a; full-time academic program or a recent graduates (up to eight months after date of; graduation) from a full-time academic program who meet the following eligibility. requirements
**Level of Study**: Postgraduate
**Type**: Grant
**Value**: Up to US$15,000
**Length of Study**: 4 year
**Frequency**: Annual
**Country of Study**: Any country
**Closing Date**: 17 February
**Funding**: International office
**Additional Information**: startupheretoronto.com/partners/ryerson-university/sandbox-student-grant-program/

**For further information contact:**

**Email**:    sandbox@ryerson.ca

## Senior Women Academic Administrators of Canada Awards

**Purpose**: The Senior Women Academic Administrators of Canada (SWAAC), external link organization was founded in 1987 to provide a forum and a collective voice for women in senior administrative ranks in Canadian universities, colleges and technical institutes. The primary purpose of SWAAC is the promotion of female leadership in Canadian universities, colleges and technical institutes
**Eligibility**: Women registered in Master's or PhD programs at any Member Institution of Universities Canada within a designated region are eligible to be nominated. Regions and number of awards are defined as follows, and eligibility shall rotate among them; Ontario - 5 awards; Western

Provinces - 4 awards; Quebec - 4 awards; Atlantic Provinces - 4 awards
**Level of Study**: Graduate
**Type**: Award
**Value**: US$3,000
**Frequency**: Annual
**Country of Study**: Any country
**Closing Date**: 3 December
**Funding**: International office
**Additional Information**:    www.uwinnipeg.ca/graduate-studies/funding/masters-and-doctoral-awards/entrance-awards/index.html

**For further information contact:**

**Email**:    natasha.mills@ryerson.ca

## Social Sciences and Humanities Research Council Impact Awards

**Purpose**: SSHRC Impact Awards are designed to build on and sustain Canada's research-based knowledge culture in all research areas of the social sciences and humanities. The awards recognize outstanding researchers and celebrate their research achievements, research training, knowledge mobilization, and outreach activities funded partially or entirely by SSHRC
**Eligibility**: 1. Be a citizen or permanent resident of Canada at the time of nomination. 2. Be an active social sciences and humanities researcher or student. 3. Hold or have held SSHRC funding pertinent to the award category. 4. Be in good standing with SSHRC. 5. Be affiliated with an eligible institution
**Level of Study**: Graduate
**Type**: Award
**Value**: US$100,000
**Frequency**: Annual
**Country of Study**: Any country
**Application Procedure**: 1. Challenge—ambition and importance (25%): originality and significance of the body of work within the nominee's fields of research. 2. Achievements—impact and outcomes (75%): originality and significance of nominee's body of academic achievement and research, including quality of publications relative to stage of career; evidence of impact of the nominee's work within their fields of research and/or beyond the social sciences and humanities research community; nominee's ability and commitment to communicate research results within and/or beyond the academic community; level of nominee's engagement with, and quality of training and mentoring provided to, students, emerging scholars and participants, relative to the nominee's career level; and nominee's demonstrated potential for

leadership and societal contributions within and/or beyond the academic community

**Closing Date**: 1 April

**Funding**: Private

**Additional Information**: www.sshrc-crsh.gc.ca/funding-financement/programs-programmes/impact_awards-prix_impacts-eng.aspx

### For further information contact:

Research Training Portfolio, Social Sciences and Humanities Research Council, 350 Albert Street, P.O. Box 1610, Ottawa, ON K1P 6G4, Canada.

**Tel**:      (1) 613 943 7777
**Fax**:     (1) 613 943 1329
**Email**:   impactawards-priximpacts@sshrc-crsh.gc.ca

## The Dennis Mock Graduate Scholarship

**Purpose**: The Dennis Mock Graduate Scholarship is available annually to recognize the accomplishments of a first-year Master's student. This award was established in the name of Dennis Mock to honour his commitment to higher education, to recognize his leadership and dedication demonstrated during his 28 years at Ryerson, and to acknowledge his role in developing graduate studies at the university, as vice-president, academic. The funds have been provided by the Peter Bronfman Scholarship Program and the Ontario Student Opportunities Trust Fund

**Eligibility**: 1. Completion of an undergraduate degree program at Ryerson. 2. Full-time enrollment in the first year of a Master's program at Ryerson, with a course load of at least two graded, one-term courses in the fall term. 3. First time enrollment in a graduate program. 4. Canadian Citizen or Permanent Resident. 5. Must meet the Ontario Residency Requirement (see Application form for details). 6. Demonstrated financial need

**Level of Study**: Graduate

**Type**: Scholarship

**Value**: US$5,000

**Frequency**: Annual

**Country of Study**: Any country

**Closing Date**: 16 March

**Funding**: Foundation

**Additional Information**: www.ryerson.ca/graduate/future-students/financing-your-studies/scholarships-awards/dennis-mock-graduate-scholarship/

### For further information contact:

**Email**:   g2guerci@ryerson.ca

## The Dennis Mock Student Leadership Award

**Purpose**: The Dennis Mock Student Leadership Awards recognize graduating students who have made outstanding voluntary extracurricular contributions to their school or academic program department, their faculty, or to Ryerson University as a whole. The awards acknowledge and encourage student participation in university affairs

**Eligibility**: 1. Students who graduated in Fall or will be graduating in Spring. 2. In a full-time or part-time Ryerson degree program. 3. Clear academic standing at the time of nomination. 4 leadership on committees, or influence on student or university affairs. 5. improvement in the quality of life of students. 6. encouragement of fellow students to become involved in extracurricular activities; although external involvement is encouraged, activities should be focused on the Ryerson campus or community. 7. contribution to the sense of community at Ryerson.

**Level of Study**: Graduate

**Type**: Award

**Frequency**: Annual

**Country of Study**: Any country

**Closing Date**: 19 February

**Funding**: International office

**Additional Information**: www.ryerson.ca/graduate/future-students/financing-your-studies/scholarships-awards/dennis-mock-student-leadership-award/

### For further information contact:

**Email**:   grdadmit@ryerson.ca

## The Geoffrey F. Bruce Fellowship in Canadian Freshwater Policy

**Purpose**: Geoffrey F. Bruce was a distinguished Canadian, dedicated public servant and diplomat who devoted his career to advancing multilateral cooperation in pursuit of environmental protection and sustainable development practices. Geoffrey was passionate about the stewardship of Canadian water resources

**Eligibility**: 1. Aspects of freshwater as political, economic or strategic resource. 2. transboundary water governance. 3. water quality/quantity. 4. water security. 5. water export/sale. 6. water privatization.

**Level of Study**: Graduate

**Type**: Fellowship

**Value**: US$25,000

**Length of Study**: 2 year

**Frequency**: Annual

**Country of Study**: Any country

**Closing Date**: 30 September

**Funding**: Foundation

**Additional Information**: www.ryerson.ca/graduate/future-students/financing-your-studies/scholarships-awards/geoffrey-bruce-fellowship/

### For further information contact:

Selection Committee, Ryerson University, 350 Victoria Street, Toronto, ON M5B 2K3, Canada.

**Email**:    cjohns@ryerson.ca

## The Hydro One Aboriginal Award for Graduate Studies in Public Policy and Administration

**Purpose**: The Hydro One Aboriginal Award for Graduate Studies in Public Policy and Administration provides financial assistance and recognizes the academic achievement of an Aboriginal student entering the Master of Arts in Public Policy and Administration program at Ryerson University. It is awarded to up to two Aboriginal students entering the program. Funds are provided Hydro One Networks Inc. and the Ontario Trust for Student Support (OTSS)

**Eligibility**: 1. A four year degree with a least a B+ average in the last two years of study. 2. Demonstrated competence in the English Language. 3. Canadian citizenship or be a protected person. 4. Ontario residency (in accordance with OTSS requirements). 5. Demonstrated financial need as determined by Ryerson University

**Level of Study**: Graduate

**Type**: Award

**Value**: Up to US$10,000

**Frequency**: Annual

**Country of Study**: Any country

**Application Procedure**: 1. A one-page cover letter describing why they are an ideal candidate. The letter should address the applicant's reasons for pursuing graduate studies in this program, research interests which the applicant may wish to pursue, how the applicant's previous studies and experience have prepared him/her for the MA program, and the applicant's career objectives and how this program relates to them. 2. Three letters of support from both academic and community-based references. A student may substitute one letter from an employer for one of the academic references. A letter of recommendation from an Aboriginal community or organization supporting the applicant's future contributions may enhance the award application. 3. Resume. 4. OTSS budget form.

**Funding**: International office

**Additional Information**: www.ryerson.ca/graduate/future-students/financing-your-studies/scholarships-awards/hydro-one-aboriginal-award/

### For further information contact:

1 Dundas St. West (11th floor), Toronto, ON M5B 2K3, Canada.

**Tel**:      (1) 416 979 5365
**Email**:   grdadmit@ryerson.ca

## The Pierre Elliott Trudeau Foundation Scholarship

**Purpose**: The award supports interdisciplinary research and original fieldwork by providing a substantial yearly allowance for research and travel, enabling the Scholars to gain first-hand contact with the diverse communities that can enrich their studies. Moreover, each Scholar is paired with a distinguished Trudeau Mentor selected by the Foundation among the most eminent Canadian practitioners in all sectors of public life. The Scholarship also offers the opportunity to interact with an exceptional community of leaders and committed individuals in every field of the social sciences and humanities, to participate in events organized by the Foundation and to hold their own workshops, through available financial support

**Eligibility**: Be a Canadian citizen or landed immigrant applying to a doctoral program in the social sciences and humanities or registered full-time in the first or second year of such a program at a Canadian university OR Be a Canadian citizen applying to a doctoral program in the social sciences and humanities or registered full-time in the first or second year of such a program at a foreign university. OR 1. Be a foreign national [with a preference for candidates from the developing world] applying to a doctoral program in the social sciences and humanities or registered full-time in the first or second year of such a program at a Canadian university. 2. Present a research project linked to one of the Foundation's four themes (Human rights and dignity; Responsible citizenship; Canada in the world; People and their natural environment). 3. Be nominated by a university

**Level of Study**: Graduate

**Type**: Scholarship

**Value**: US$60,000

**Length of Study**: 3 year

**Frequency**: Annual

**Country of Study**: Any country

**Closing Date**: 3 December

**Funding**: International office

**Additional Information**: www.ryerson.ca/trudeau

### For further information contact:

Scholarships Liaison Officer, Yeates School of Graduate Studies, Ryerson University, Toronto, ON M5B 2K3, Canada.

**Tel**: (1) 416 979 5000 ext. 3648
**Email**: natasha.mills@ryerson.ca

## The W. L. Mackenzie King Scholarships

**Purpose**: The Mackenzie King Scholarships were established as an independent trust under the will of the late Rt. Hon. William Mackenzie King (1874-1950). Two classes of Mackenzie King Scholarship are available to graduates of Canadian universities: the Open Scholarship and the Travelling Scholarship. Both are to support graduate study
**Eligibility**: 1. The Mackenzie King Open Scholarship is open to graduates of any Canadian university who engage in (commence or continue) graduate study (mater's or doctoral) in any field, in Canada or elsewhere. One Open Scholarship is awarded annually. Its value has lately been US$8,500 but is subject to change. 2. The Mackenzie King Travelling Scholarship is open to graduates of any Canadian university who engage in (commence or continue) postgraduate study (mater's or doctoral) in the United States or the United Kingdom, of international relations or industrial relations (including the international or industrial relations aspects of law, history, politics and economics)
**Level of Study**: Graduate
**Type**: Scholarship
**Value**: US$10,500 - Travelling Scholarship US$8,500 - Open Scholarship
**Frequency**: Annual
**Country of Study**: Any country
**Closing Date**: 1 February
**Funding**: International office
**Additional Information**: www.grad.ubc.ca/awards/mackenzie-king-memorial-scholarships

### For further information contact:

**Email**: natasha.mills@ryerson.ca

# S

## Sacramento State

CSUS 6000 J Street, Sacramento, CA 95819, United States of America.

**Tel:** (1) 916 278 6011
**Email:** infodesk@csus.edu
**Website:** www.csus.edu
**Contact:** Timothy Hodson, Executive Director

Center for California Studies, CSU-Sacramento, California Legislature (CSUS) was founded in 1984. It is located on the capital campus of the California State University. Center for California Studies is a public service, educational support and applied research institute of CSUS. It is dedicated to promoting a better understanding of California's government, politics, people, cultures and history.

## California Senate Fellows

**Purpose:** To expose people with diverse life experiences and backgrounds to the legislative process and provide research and other professional staff assistance to the Senate
**Eligibility:** Open to candidates who have obtained a degree from a 4 year college or university
**Level of Study:** Professional development
**Type:** Fellowships
**Value:** A monthly stipend of US$2,627 plus full health, vision and dental benefits
**Length of Study:** 11 months
**Frequency:** Annual
**Country of Study:** United States of America
**Application Procedure:** Applicants can download the application form from the website
**Closing Date:** 8 February
**Funding:** Government

**Additional Information:** For further information please contact David Pacheco, the program director, at (1) 916 278 5408 (Sacramento State), (1) 916 651 4160 (Senate) or email to david.pacheco@sen.ca.gov sfela.senate.ca.gov/home

### For further information contact:

**Tel:** (1) 916 278 6906
**Email:** calstudies@csus.edu

## Jesse M. Unruh Assembly Fellowship Program

**Purpose:** To provide an opportunity for individuals of all ages, ethnic backgrounds and experiences to directly participate in the legislative process
**Eligibility:** Applicants must have completed a Bachelor's degree by the end of Summer of the fellowship year. There are no preferred majors
**Level of Study:** Professional development
**Type:** Fellowship
**Value:** US$1,972 per month and medical, dental and vision benefits
**Length of Study:** 11 months
**Frequency:** Annual
**Study Establishment:** Center for California Studies
**Country of Study:** United States of America
**Application Procedure:** Applicants must download the complete application form from the website. Applicants must furnish academic, employment and activities data, unofficial transcripts from colleges attended, a personal statement, a policy statement on a specific topic contained in the application and 3 references
**Closing Date:** 22 February
**Additional Information:** Individuals with advanced degrees or those in mid-career are encouraged to apply a70.asmdc.org/article/jesse-m-unruh-assembly-fellowship-program

© Springer Nature Limited 2020
Palgrave Macmillan (ed.), *The Grants Register 2021*,
https://doi.org/10.1057/978-1-349-95988-4

**For further information contact:**

Tel:      (1) 916 278 6906
Email:   calstudies@csus.edu

## Saint Louis University

John Cook School of Business MBA Program, 3674
Lindell Boulevard, St Louis, MO 63108, United States of
America.

Tel:        (1) 314 977 2013
Email:     mba@slu.edu
Website:   mba.slu.edu
Contact:   MBA Admissions Officer

## Saint Louis University International MBA Programme

**Length of Study**: More than 2 years
**Application Procedure**: Applicants must return a completed
application, with personal essays, a nonrefundable US$55
application fee, two letters of recommendation, official transcripts from all previously attended colleges and universities,
Graduate Management Admission Test score, and
a curriculum vitae. Overseas students must also provide evidence of financial support and a TOEFL score
**Closing Date**: 15 April

**For further information contact:**

Institute of International Business, International Option MBA.

Tel:      (1) 314 977 3630
Fax:      (1) 314 977 7188
Email:   biib@slu.edu

## Samuel H. Kress Foundation

174 East 80th Street, New York, NY 10075, United States of
America.

Tel:        (1) 212 861 4993
Email:     wyman.meers@kressfoundation.org
Website:   www.kressfoundation.org
Contact:   Wyman Meers, Program Administrator

The Samuel H. Kress Foundation, since its creation in 1929,
has devoted its resources almost exclusively to programmes

related to European art. The Foundation devotes its
resources to advancing the history, conservation, and enjoy-
ment of the vast heritage of European art, architecture, and
archaeology.

## Conservation Fellowships

**Purpose**: The purpose of the Kress Conservation Fellowship
program is to provide a wide range of post-graduate fellowship opportunities that will help develop the skills of emerging conservators.
**Eligibility**: Applications must be made by the museum
or conservation facility at which the fellowship will be
based. Prior to beginning the fellowship, fellows should
have completed a masters-level degree in conservation.
The fellowship candidate may be identified in advance
of application by the host institution or recruited
subsequently.
**Level of Study**: Postgraduate
**Type**: Fellowship
**Value**: US$32,000
**Frequency**: Annual
**Study Establishment**: Appropriate institutions
**Country of Study**: United States of America
**Application Procedure**: Application procedures and contact
information available at www.kressfoundation.org
**No. of awards offered**: Approx. 25–30
**Closing Date**: 22 January
**Funding**: Private
**No. of awards given last year**: 9
**No. of applicants last year**: Approx. 25–30
**Additional Information**: Emphasis is on hands-on training.
These grants are not for the completion of degree pro-
grammes. Enquiries should be directed to Wyman Meers
www.kressfoundation.org/fellowships/conservation/

**For further information contact:**

The Foundation of the American Institute for Conservation of
Historic and Artistic Works, 1156 15th St, NW; Suite 320, -
Washington, DC 20005, United States of America.

**Email**:   faicgrants@aic-faic.org

## History of Art Institutional Fellowships

**Purpose**: Institutional fellowships are intended to provide
promising young art historians with the opportunity to experience just this kind of immersion.
**Eligibility**: Restricted to pre-doctoral candidates in the history of art and related disciplines (such as archaeology,

architecture, or classics). Nominees must be U.S. citizens or individuals matriculated at an American university. Dissertation research must focus on European art from antiquity to the early 19th century. Candidates must be nominated by their academic department.

**Level of Study**: Predoctorate
**Type**: Fellowship
**Value**: US$30,000
**Frequency**: Annual
**Country of Study**: Any country
**Application Procedure**: Applicants must be nominated by their art history department. Limit of one applicant per department
**Closing Date**: 30 November
**Additional Information**: Enquiries should be directed to Lisa M Ackerman www.kressfoundation.org/fellowships/institutional/

### For further information contact:

174 East 80th Street, New York, NY 10075, United States of America.

**Tel**:      (1) 212 861 4993
**Email**:    info@kressfoundation.org

## Interpretive Fellowships at Art Museums

**Purpose**: The purpose of the Kress Interpretive Fellowship at Art Museums program is to provide a new kind of mentored professional development opportunity within American art museums
**Eligibility**: Application must be made by the art museum proposing to host a Kress Interpretive Fellow. These Interpretive Fellowships are intended as an opportunity for individuals who have completed a degree (B.A., M.A., or PhD) in art history, art education, studio art or museum studies and who are pursuing or contemplating graduate study or professional placement in these or related fields. The appropriate level of educational achievement will be determined by the host museum and be dependent upon the needs of the proposed fellowship project. The fellowship candidate may be identified in advance of application by the host institution or recruited subsequently.
**Type**: Fellowship
**Value**: US$30,000
**Length of Study**: 9-12 month
**Frequency**: Annual
**Country of Study**: Any country
**Application Procedure**: Applications must be submitted through the kressfoundation.fluxx.io/
**Closing Date**: 1 April

## San Antonio Nathan Shock Center

## Awards Supported by the San Antonio Nathan Shock Center

**Subjects**: Biomedical and Clinical; physiology; pharmacology; pathology
**Purpose**: #to support the research of any investigator who is developing a new project in the basic biology of aging.
**Eligibility**: Any investigator who is eligible to receive NIH grants according to the rules of their home institution.
**Type**: Research grant
**Value**: Contingent on the availability of funds
**Frequency**: Annual, if funds are available
**Study Establishment**: Any US Academic Institution
**Country of Study**: United States of America
**Application Procedure**: The projects should utilize one or more Cores of the Center. Projects that propose creative uses of more than one Core are encouraged. Center Cores and their capabilities are listed at nathanshock.barshop.uthscsa.edu Applications must include: One-page hypothesis and specific aims of your project. Include a title for your project. This can be very brief, sufficient for the reader to understand the importance of what is being proposed. Specifics such as numbers of animals, etc., are not initially needed because this will be determined in conjunction with the Core Leaders if the proposal is selected for further consideration. Please indicate which Cores of the Center will be needed for your studies. It is strongly suggested that you contact the Core Leaders (see above) in advance of submitting your proposal. If you have consulted with one or more Core Leaders during the development of your proposal, please so state in your application. Your NIH Biosketch and the Biosketches of any proposed collaborators. A budget is not initially required. If your proposal is selected for further consideration, a budget will be developed based on a power analysis of the number of samples, animals, etc., that will be needed for the successful development of your project. The budget will be used for internal planning purposes only. Costs of the entire project, including purchase of animals and their housing, will be borne by the San Antonio Shock Center. Some parts of the project may be more appropriately performed in the applicant's lab, in which case it will be expected that the PI will bear the cost of those studies.
**Closing Date**: 15 April

## San Francisco Foundation (SFF)

One Embarcadero Center, Suite 1400, San Francisco, CA 94111, United States of America.

**Tel**:      (1) 415 733 8500
**Email**:    info@sff.org
**Website**:  www.sff.org

The San Francisco Foundation (SFF) is a leading agent of Bay Area philanthropy. They rank 7th in grant making and assets among the nation's community foundations. They cultivate a family of donors who share a commitment to the Bay Area. They give millions of dollars a year to build on community assets, respond to community needs and elevate public awareness.

## Koshland Young Leader Awards

**Purpose**: It recognizes the next generation of leadership in community. Koshland Young Leaders are strongly motivated to achieve despite facing multiple challenges, such as economic and family responsibilities
**Eligibility**: San Francisco public high school juniors. The most competitive candidates have at least a 3.25 cumulative or continually improving GPA, are college-bound, and embrace a commitment to strengthening their families and communities despite facing formidable life challenges
**Level of Study**: Postgraduate
**Type**: Award
**Value**: US$7,000
**Length of Study**: 2 years
**Frequency**: Every 2 years
**Country of Study**: United States of America
**Closing Date**: January
**Contributor**: San Francisco Foundation
**Additional Information**: Each winter, we invite teachers and counselors to nominate outstanding San Francisco public high school juniors for this award. If you have questions, please email or call Joshua Jones sff.org/what-we-do/awards-programs/kyla/

### For further information contact:

**Tel**: (1) 415 733 8587
**Email**: akatz@sff.org

## San Francisco State University (SFSU)

1600 Holloway Avenue, San Francisco, CA 94132, United States of America.

**Tel**: (1) 415 338 2234/1111
**Email**: mritter@sfsu.edu
**Website**: www.sfsu.edu

San Francisco State University (SFSU) is one of the nation's leading public urban universities. SFSU helps create and maintain an environment for learning that promotes respect for and appreciation of scholarship, freedom, human diversity and the cultural mosaic of the City of San Francisco. SFSU also provides a higher education for residents of the region and state, as well as the nation and world.

## Robert Westwood Scholarship

**Purpose**: To assist SFSU students who are living with HIV and plan to make a contribution in any field to communities affected by HIV
**Level of Study**: Postgraduate
**Type**: Scholarship
**Value**: US$1,000
**Frequency**: Annual
**Study Establishment**: San Francisco State University
**Country of Study**: United States of America
**Application Procedure**: Applicants must submit a copy of the most recent SFSU academic transcript, along with a brief, typed essay discussing plans to incorporate academic work and degree at SFSU with service in the HIV community or in the area of HIV prevention
**Closing Date**: 7 May
**Additional Information**: Applicants must submit a verification from the physician sfsu.academicworks.com/opportunities/2089

### For further information contact:

**Tel**: (1) 415 338 7339

## Sanskriti Pratishthan

Head Office C-11 Qutab Institutional Area, New Delhi 110016, India.

**Tel**: (91) 11 2696 3226/2652 7077
**Email**: fellowships@sanskritifoundation.org
**Website**: www.sanskritifoundation.org

Sanskriti Pratishthan is a non-profit organization that was established in 1978. Sanskriti Pratishthan perceives its role as that of a catalyst, in revitalizing cultural sensitivity in contemporary times.

## Geddes Scholarship

**Purpose**: The scholarship has been instituted in the joint memory of Patrick Geddes and his son Arthur Geddes, both of whom had a long association with India
**Eligibility**: The scholarship is only open to Indian Nationals in the age group of 20 to 30. The applicant must be a student

of planning and architecture at a graduate/postgraduate/research level from a recognized university or institution and /or young practicing professionals. The applicants can be an individual or can be a collaborative work of a group of individuals.

**Level of Study**: Professional development
**Type**: Fellowships
**Value**: ₹45,000 will be given in two phases
**Length of Study**: 6 months
**Frequency**: Annual
**Funding**: Foundation
**Additional Information**: www.sanskritifoundation.org/Geddes-Fellowship.htm

### For further information contact:

Sanskriti Kendra / Sanskriti Museums, Anandagram, Mehrauli Gurgaon Road, New Delhi - 110047, Opposite Metro Pillar No. 165, Nearest Metro Station Arjangarh.

**Tel**: (91) 11 2696 3226, 2652 7077 / 8130968700

## Kalakriti Fellowship in Indian Classical Dance

**Purpose**: The purpose of the fellowship is to encourage young artists to develop their potential and enhance their skills through intensive practice and or incorporating different facets of their art.
**Eligibility**: The fellowship is only open to Indian Nationals in the age group of 25 to 40. While this fellowship specially encourages women applicants, all proposals that further the objectives of the program are welcome. The candidate should have at least ten years of initial training in Indian classical dance. The fellow would be required to have given at least 2-3 solo performances to his/her credit in recognized forums. The candidate will be required to take guidance from another senior guru and enhance the existing style. It would be a residency programme for a period of three months, which can be spread over the period of ten months. This will require the candidate to take consent from her current guru and the guru he/she would want to go to.
**Level of Study**: Professional development
**Type**: Fellowships
**Value**: ₹50,000
**Length of Study**: 10 months
**Frequency**: Annual
**Country of Study**: Any country
**Application Procedure**: Candidates should send their two page CV and a write up of approximately 500 words explaining their project. Full postal and telephonic contact details together with any e-mail id should be submitted to facilitate contact. Few samples of previous work, project or performances should be submitted. The names and contact addresses/telephones of two referees should also be sent. The application should bear the title 'Sanskriti - Kalakriti Fellowship' on the envelope when sent by post and in subject line if sent through email on fellowships@sanskritifoundation.org
**Funding**: Foundation
**Additional Information**: www.sanskritifoundation.org/Kalakriti-Fellowship.htm

### For further information contact:

Anandagram, Mehrauli Gurgaon Road, New Delhi - 110047, Opposite Metro Pillar No. 165, Nearest Metro Station Arjangarh.

**Tel**: (91) 11 2696 3226, 2652 7077 / 8130968700

## Madhobi Chatterji Memorial Fellowship

**Purpose**: The objective of the fellowship is to encourage promising young artists to develop their potential and perfect their skills by providing them the resources and time to dedicate to the art
**Eligibility**: The fellowship is open to Indian Nationals from any genre of Indian Classical Music (Vocal or Instrumental) or Dance (any form or choreography). Proposals that further the objectives of the program are welcome. The candidate should have at least some years of formal training in Indian classical Music or Dance. The fellow would be required to have given at least 2-3 solo performances to his/her credit.
**Level of Study**: Professional development
**Type**: Fellowships
**Value**: The grant of ₹100,000 will be given in two installments
**Length of Study**: 10 Months
**Frequency**: Annual
**Funding**: Foundation
**Additional Information**: www.sanskritifoundation.org/Madhobi-Chatterji-Memorial.htm

### For further information contact:

Sanskriti Kendra / Sanskriti Museums, Anandagram, Mehrauli Gurgaon Road, New Delhi - 110047, Opposite Metro Pillar No. 165, Nearest Metro Station Arjangarh.

**Tel**: (91) 11 2696 3226, 2652 7077 / 8130968700

## Mani Mann Fellowship

**Purpose**: This fellowship has been instituted to encourage promising young artists to advance in their field. This fellowship will enable the recipient to have the resources and time to dedicate to the art.

**Eligibility**: The fellowship is only open to Indian Nationals in the age group of 25 to 40. While this fellowship specially encourages women applicants, all proposals that further the objectives of the program are welcome. The applicant must hold a degree/diploma from a recognized university or institution in the field and/or the candidate should have at least ten years of initial training in Indian classical music. The fellow would be required to have given at least 2-3 solo performances to his/her credit in recognized forums. The candidate will be required to take guidance from another senior guru and enhance the existing style. It would be a residency programme for a period of three months, which can be spread over the period of one year.

**Level of Study**: Professional development

**Type**: Fellowships

**Value**: ₹100,000 will be given in two phases

**Length of Study**: 1 year

**Frequency**: Annual

**Application Procedure**: Candidates should send their two page CV and a write up of approximately 500 words explaining their project. Full postal and telephonic contact details together with any e-mail id should be submitted to facilitate contact. Few samples of previous work, project or performances should be submitted. The names and contact addresses/telephones of two referees should also be sent.

**Funding**: Foundation

**Additional Information**: www.sanskritifoundation.org/Mani-Mann-Fellowship.htm

### For further information contact:

Sanskriti Kendra / Sanskriti Museums, Anandagram, Mehrauli Gurgaon Road, New Delhi - 110047, Opposite Metro Pillar No. 165, Nearest Metro Station Arjangarh.

**Tel**:    (91) 11 2696 3226, 2652 7077 / 8130968700

## Prabha Dutt Fellowship

**Purpose**: The purpose of the fellowship is to encourage young mid career women journalists to develop their potential by pursuing meaningful projects without having to work under the pressures of short deadlines.

**Eligibility**: The fellowship is only open to women who are Indian Nationals in the age group of 25 to 40. It is exclusively for print journalists. The Fellows will be required to publish a stipulated number of articles in established publications.

The Fellow may work on a book or monograph for subsequent publication within the given time frame.

**Level of Study**: Professional development

**Type**: Fellowships

**Value**: ₹100,000 including travel expenses

**Length of Study**: 10 months

**Frequency**: Annual

**Application Procedure**: Candidates should send a two page CV and a write up of about 250 - 300 words explaining their project. Full postal and telephonic contact details together with any e-mail id should be submitted to facilitate contact. Five samples of work published. The names and contact addresses/telephones of two referees should also be sent.

**Funding**: Foundation

**Additional Information**:    www.sanskritifoundation.org/prabha-dutt-fellowship.htm

### For further information contact:

Sanskriti Kendra / Sanskriti Museums, Anandagram, Mehrauli Gurgaon Road, New Delhi - 110047, Opposite Metro Pillar No. 165, Nearest Metro Station Arjangarh.

**Tel**:    (91) 11 2696 3226, 2652 7077 / 8130968700

## Pt. Vasant Thakar Memorial Fellowship

**Purpose**: The objective of the fellowship is to recognize and provide a platform to excellent but lesser known artists and to bring them to larger audiences

**Eligibility**: The fellowship is open to Indian Nationals from any genre of Indian Classical Music (Vocal or Instrumental). Proposals that further the objectives of the program are welcome. The duration of the fellowship will be 10 months followed by a performance in Delhi.

**Level of Study**: Professional development

**Type**: Fellowships

**Value**: ₹100,000 will be given in two installments

**Length of Study**: 10 months

**Frequency**: Annual

**Funding**: Foundation

**Additional Information**: www.sanskritifoundation.org/Pt-Vasant-Thakar-Memorial-Fellowship.htm

### For further information contact:

Sanskriti Kendra / Sanskriti Museums, Anandagram, Mehrauli Gurgaon Road, New Delhi - 110047, Opposite Metro Pillar No. 165, Nearest Metro Station Arjangarh.

**Tel**:    (91) 11 2696 3226, 2652 7077 / 8130968700

## Sasakawa Fund

School of Economics, University of São Paulo 908, FEA 1, room D105, São Paulo, Buntantã, SP 055 (080) 10, Brazil.

**Tel**: (55) 11 3091 6075
**Email**: sylff@usp.br

Generally known as SYLFF, The Ryoichi Sasakawa young leaders fellowship fund established in 1987 aims to nurture future leaders who will transcend the geopolitical, religious, ethnic, and cultural boundaries and actively participate in the world community for peace and the well-being of humankind.

## Sasakawa Young Leader Fellowship (SYLFF) Program

**Purpose**: To provide grants for graduate students is social sciences areas
**Eligibility**: Open to postgraduate students from the university of Sao Paulo with research projects proposals that relate to approved subject areas and aim to assist Brazil in its global insertion
**Level of Study**: Postgraduate
**Type**: Fellowship
**Length of Study**: 2 years
**Frequency**: Annual
**Study Establishment**: São Paulo University
**Country of Study**: Brazil
**Funding**: Foundation
**Contributor**: The Tokyo Foundation
**No. of awards given last year**: 9
**Additional Information**: stanfordexeced.stanford.edu/lead-download-brochure/?campaignid=71700000059199127&adgroupid=58700005418275706&adgroup=LDC-NT+-+Leadership+-+Program+(b%2B)&creative=406588991184&kwid=43700049314447479&matchtype=b&feeditemid=&targetid=kwd-20128500519&cid=70131000001JEKkAAO&utm_source=GOOGLE&utm_medium=cpc&utm_campaign=LDC-NT+-+Leadership+(INTL)&utm_term=%2Bleadership+%2Bprogram&loc_physical_ms=9061916&loc_interest_ms=&network=g&adposition=1t1&target=&device=c&devicemodel=&gclid=EAIaIQobChMIuvickIfM5wIVViUrCh0ZTA-8EAAYASAAEgJBvD_BwE&gclsrc=aw.ds

## Savoy Foundation

230 Foch Street, St Jean Sur Richelieu, QC J3B 2B2, Canada.

**Tel**: (1) 450 358 9779
**Email**: epilepsy@savoy-foundation.ca
**Website**: www.savoy-foundation.ca
**Contact**: Vivian Downing, Assistant to Vice President/Secretary

The Savoy Foundation's main activity is to support and encourage research into epilepsy.

## Savoy Foundation International Grant

**Purpose**: To improve the situation of people with epilepsy where medical care is less available
**Eligibility**: Only available to clinicians and established scientists
**Level of Study**: Postdoctorate, Postgraduate, Research
**Type**: Research grant
**Value**: Up to C$30,000
**Length of Study**: 1 year
**Frequency**: Annual
**Study Establishment**: An affiliated University
**Country of Study**: Any country
**Application Procedure**: Applicants must contact the Foundation or visit the website for application forms and further information
**No. of awards offered**: 1
**Closing Date**: 15 January
**Funding**: Private
**Contributor**: The Savoy Foundation endowments
**No. of awards given last year**: 1
**No. of applicants last year**: 1
**Additional Information**: One grant is available per year. All applications are evaluated by the Medical Board of the Savoy Foundation for epilepsy mcgill.ca/research/files/research/savoy_foundation.pdf

## Savoy Foundation Postdoctoral and Clinical Research Fellowships

**Purpose**: To support a full-time research project in the field of epilepsy
**Eligibility**: Candidates must be scientists or medical specialists with a PhD or MD
**Level of Study**: Postdoctorate, Postgraduate, Research

**Type**: Research grant
**Value**: C$30,000
**Length of Study**: 1 year (non-renewable)
**Frequency**: Annual
**Country of Study**: Canada
**Application Procedure**: Applicants must contact the Foundation or visit the website for application forms and further information
**No. of awards offered**: 26
**Closing Date**: 15 January
**Funding**: Private, Foundation
**Contributor**: The Savoy Foundation endowments
**No. of awards given last year**: Five fellowships
**No. of applicants last year**: 26
**Additional Information**: gradfund.rutgers.edu/blog/awards/5109/

## Savoy Foundation Research Grants

**Purpose**: To support further research into epilepsy
**Eligibility**: Only available to clinicians and established scientists
**Level of Study**: Postdoctorate, Postgraduate, Research
**Type**: Research grant
**Value**: Up to C$25,000
**Frequency**: Annual
**Country of Study**: Canada
**Application Procedure**: Applicants must contact the Foundation or visit the website for application forms and further information
**No. of awards offered**: 20
**Closing Date**: 15 January
**Funding**: Private, Foundation
**Contributor**: The Savoy Foundation endowments
**No. of awards given last year**: 7 Research Grants
**No. of applicants last year**: 20
**Additional Information**: The grant is only available to Canadian citizens or for projects conducted in Canada www.ucalgary.ca/research/node/2407

## Savoy Foundation Studentships

**Purpose**: To support training and research in a biomedical discipline, the health sciences or social sciences related to epilepsy
**Eligibility**: Candidates must have a good university record, e.g. a BSc, MD or equivalent diploma and have ensured that a qualified researcher affiliated to a university or hospital will supervise his or her work. Concomitant registration in a graduate programme is encouraged. The awards are available to Canadian citizens or for projects conducted in Canada

**Level of Study**: Doctorate, Postgraduate, Predoctorate
**Type**: Studentship
**Value**: The stipend will be C$15,000 per year. An annual sum of C$1,000 will be allocated to the laboratory or institution as additional support for the research project. The student with the highest mark will receive the Van Gelder-Savoy award of an additional C$1,500. Also, in memory of the contribution made by Professor Laurent Descarries to the Savoy Foundation during his tenure as a member of the Research Committee, a new award of excellence has been created. The Descarries-Savoy award, in an amount of US$1,500, which will be granted to the student supported by the Foundation whom the committee decides has published the best paper during the year of the studentship
**Length of Study**: 1–4 years
**Frequency**: Annual
**Country of Study**: Canada
**Application Procedure**: Applicants must contact the Foundation or visit the website for application forms and further information
**No. of awards offered**: 17
**Closing Date**: 15 January
**Funding**: Private, Foundation
**Contributor**: The Savoy Foundation endowments
**No. of awards given last year**: 4 Studentships
**No. of applicants last year**: 17
**Additional Information**: webapps.cc.umanitoba.ca/gradawards/index.asp?WCI=SearchForm&WCE=browse&keywords=&criteria=any&category=0&citizen=0&range=0-1000000&tenable=0&byResearch=on&byAward=on&byEligibility=on&id=3481&letter=S

# Scholarship Foundation of the League of Finnish-American Societies

Mechelininkatu 10, Helsinki, FI-00100, Helsinki, Finland.

**Tel**:      (358) 9 4133 3700
**Email**:      sayl@sayl.fi
**Website**:      www.sayl.fi
**Contact**:      Ms Tuula Nuckols, Project Manager

## American Society of Naval Engineers (ASNE) Scholarship

**Purpose**: The American Society of Naval Engineers began its scholarship program in 1979 in order to promote the profession of naval engineering and to encourage college students to enter the field. Since the inception of the Scholarship Program, ASNE has since awarded more than 500 scholarships to undergraduate and graduate students interested in pursuing an education and career in naval engineering.

**Eligibility**: 1. Undergraduate candidates must be applying for support in their final year of an engineering program at an accredited undergraduate college or university. 2. Graduate candidates-May apply for support during one full year of a graduate program or co-op leading to an engineering or physical science degree at an accredited university.

**Level of Study**: Professional development

**Type**: Scholarship

**Value**: A combination of undergraduate scholarships (US$3,000 per year) and graduate scholarships (US$4,000 per year) are awarded each academic year.

**Frequency**: Annual

**Country of Study**: Any country

**Application Procedure**: Applications must have the below information. 1. The materials to be submitted with application form for American Society of Naval Engineers (ASNE) Scholarship. 2. Three letters of recommendations (letters of recommendation must be on college/university or business letterhead). 3. Official transcripts

**Closing Date**: March

**Funding**: Private

**Additional Information**: new.expo.uw.edu/expo/scholar ships/asne

### For further information contact:

Nancy Lackey, 1452 Duke Street, Alexandria, VA 22314, United States of America.

**Email**:     scholarships@navalengineers.org

## School of American Research

PO Box 2188, Santa Fe, NM 87504-2188, United States of America.

**Tel**:          (1) 505 982 3583
**Contact**:   Grants Management Officer

## Babe Ruth League College Scholarship

**Purpose**: Program to provide assistance to individuals (former Babe Ruth Baseball, Cal Ripken Baseball or Babe Ruth Softball players) who plan on furthering their education beyond high school. Outstanding student athletes will receive US$1000 each towards their college tuition.

**Eligibility**: 1. Must be an undergraduate student. 2. Must attend a university, a four-year college or two-year college.

3. Citizenship requirements: US. 4. Must currently be a high school student. 5. Both full-time and part-time students.

**Level of Study**: Graduate

**Type**: Scholarship

**Value**: US$1,000

**Frequency**: Annual

**Country of Study**: Any country

**Application Procedure**: Babe Ruth League College Scholarships are awarded based on an applicant's high school academic achievement, participating activities, community involvement and on the contents of the essay. The Babe Ruth League College Scholarship is a one-time award and cannot be combined with any other Babe Ruth League sponsored scholarship. Supporting documents required are: 1. Copy of your official high school transcript. 2. 200-word essay on the topic: how playing in the Babe Ruth league program has affected your life. 3. Verification of registration at an accredited two-year or four-year college or university, by June 30 of each year. www.baberuthleague.org/media/216298/Babe%20Ruth%20Combined%20Scholarship%20Program%20Applicaiton%20and%20Criteria.pdf

**Closing Date**: 1 September

**Funding**: Private

**Additional Information**: For further information, www.baberuthleague.org/media/216298/Babe%20Ruth%20Com bined%20Scholarship%20Program%20Applicaiton%20 and %20Criteria.pdf www.petersons.com/scholarship/babe-ruth-scholarship-program-111_179153.aspx

### For further information contact:

Babe Ruth League, 1670 Whitehorse-Mercerville Road, Hamilton, NJ 08619, United States of America.

**Tel**:       (1) 800 880 3142
**Fax**:      (1) 609 695 2505
**Email**:   info@baberuthleague.org

## School of Oriental and African Studies (SOAS)

University of London, Thornhaugh Street, Russell Square, London WC1H 0XG, United Kingdom.

**Tel**:          (44) 20 7637 2388
**Email**:      scholarships@soas.ac.uk
**Website**:   www.soas.ac.uk
**Contact**:   Miss Alicia Sales, Scholarships Officer, Registry

The School of Oriental and African Studies (SOAS) regards its role as advancing the knowledge and understanding of the cultures and societies of Asia and Africa and of the School's academic disciplines through high-quality teaching and research.

## Academy of Korean Studies Postgraduate Bursaries

**Eligibility**: Open to United Kingdom/European Union and overseas applicants. See the website for details
**Level of Study**: Postgraduate
**Type**: Bursary
**Value**: Up to £6,000 towards tuition fees
**Length of Study**: 1 year
**Frequency**: Annual
**Study Establishment**: SOAS
**Country of Study**: United Kingdom
**Application Procedure**: See website www.soas.ac.uk/scholarships
**Closing Date**: 24 May
**Funding**: Private
**Contributor**: Academy of Korean Studies
**No. of awards given last year**: 1
**Additional Information**: If you have any questions about the bursary application, please contact the Scholarships Officer

### For further information contact:

**Email**:　ak49@soas.ac.uk

## Arts and Humanities Research Council Studentships

**Purpose**: Up to 56 Arts and Humanities studentships available from CHASE Doctoral Training Partnership. CHASE Studentships are for PhD-level study only and successful applicants will have their fees paid, as well as receiving a stipend to cover living expenses (where eligible, see below) and access to further funds for skills training and research.
**Eligibility**: CHASE AHRC funding is only available to Home or EU students. Both Home and EU students must satisfy the standard research council eligibility criteria. Please see page 12 of the Research Councils Terms and Conditions for Training Grants to check eligibility. EU students not resident in the UK for three years prior to 30 September 2020 may be eligible for a fees-only award.
**Level of Study**: Doctorate, Postgraduate
**Type**: Scholarship
**Value**: Maintenance plus approved tuition fees
**Study Establishment**: SOAS

**Country of Study**: United Kingdom
**Application Procedure**: Scholarship application should be made on the appropriate scholarship application form which is available for download
**Closing Date**: 13 January
**Funding**: Government
**Additional Information**: There are two types of studentship awards – a full studentship award for United Kingdom. residents and a fees-only studentship award for European Union residents. Please see the website for further details www.kcl.ac.uk/study/postgraduate/fees-and-funding/student-funding/postgraduate-research-funding/arts-and-humanities-research-council-studentships

### For further information contact:

**Tel**:　(44) 20 7074 5088/5094/5091

## Bernard Buckman Scholarship

**Purpose**: The Bernard Buckman Scholarship was established in 1992 with generous support by Mrs Buckman in memory of her late husband who was a Governor of the School. There is one Bernard Buckman Scholarship available.
**Eligibility**: Open to those candidates who qualify to pay for home or European Union tuition fees. Applicants must possess a good Honours Degree from a United Kingdom university or its equivalent
**Level of Study**: Postgraduate
**Type**: Scholarship
**Value**: Home or European Union postgraduate fee
**Length of Study**: 1 year
**Frequency**: Annual
**Study Establishment**: SOAS
**Country of Study**: United Kingdom
**Application Procedure**: Candidates can apply for this scholarship via the online scholarship application form
**No. of awards offered**: 7
**Closing Date**: 9 January
**Funding**: Private
**No. of awards given last year**: 1
**No. of applicants last year**: 7
**Additional Information**: For enquiries, please contact Scholarships Officer www.soas.ac.uk/registry/scholarships/bernard-buckman-scholarship.html

### For further information contact:

Thornhaugh Street, Russell Square, London WC1H 0XG, United Kingdom.

**Tel**:　(44) 20 7074 5094/5091

# Brough Sanskrit Awards

**Purpose**: There are 3 awards of up to £1,200 for SOAS postgraduate research and master's students who use Sanskrit in their work and will use the funds for research activity such as fieldwork trips

**Eligibility**: 1. The funding is for students who use Sanskrit in their work. Evidence of this should be provided in your application. 2. We cannot normally hold an award over into the next academic year if a candidate does not make the trip or attend the conference or workshop when intended: a re-application has to be made. 3. For research degree applicants only 4. Any student accepting a Brough Sanskrit award for fieldwork, workshops and conference must be enrolled 5. The student must submit a brief report, signed by the supervisor, to the Scholarships Officer within one month of the end of the fieldwork visit, conference or workshop. 6. Retrospective applications for a Brough Sanskrit Award will be considered but will not be given priority. 7. If you have already had a Brough Sanskrit Award, you can be considered for another award in a different academic year. 8. For conference funding, priority may be given to students who have been invited to present a paper at the conference

**Level of Study**: Postgraduate
**Type**: Scholarship
**Value**: up to £1,200
**Length of Study**: 1 year
**Frequency**: Annual
**Study Establishment**: SOAS
**Country of Study**: United Kingdom
**Application Procedure**: Please apply online via the docs. google.com/forms/d/1QkSRSlcT0Fxq31RDMlsY4LiDEPHT X8hl2FgT-oFXTxA/edit
**No. of awards offered**: 3
**Closing Date**: 18 March
**Funding**: Foundation
**Additional Information**: www.soas.ac.uk/registry/scholar ships/brough-sanskrit-awards.html

## For further information contact:

SOAS University of London 10 Thornhaugh Street, Russell Square, London WC1H 0XG, United Kingdom.

**Tel**:      (44) 20 7637 2388

# CSJR Postgraduate Student Bursary

**Purpose**: The Centre for the Study of Japanese Religions offers a CSJR Postgraduate Student Bursary in Japanese Religions to be held at SOAS, University of London.
**Level of Study**: Postgraduate

**Type**: Scholarship
**Value**: £5,000
**Length of Study**: 1 year
**Frequency**: Annual
**Study Establishment**: SOAS
**Country of Study**: United Kingdom
**Application Procedure**: You must apply for this scholarship via the docs.google.com/forms/d/18fr_iN2K2UKbGCA7 ubI0IUv6SOPxSqRidLMiI9TS7no/closedform
**Closing Date**: 7 May
**Funding**: Foundation
**Additional Information**: www.soas.ac.uk/registry/scholar ships/csjr-postgraduate-student-bursary.html

## For further information contact:

SOAS University of London 10 Thornhaugh Street, Russell Square, London WC1H 0XG, United Kingdom.

**Tel**:      (44) 20 7074 5094/ 5091
**Email**:   scholarships@soas.ac.uk

# Felix Scholarship

**Purpose**: To support first class Indian students commencing a Master's programme or researching for a Doctoral degree at the School of Oriental and African Studies
**Eligibility**: Open to applicants of any full-time taught Master's or MPhil/PhD programme, under 30 years of age, able to demonstrate financial need and would return to work in their home country after completion of studies
**Level of Study**: Doctorate, Postgraduate
**Type**: Scholarship
**Value**: £12,316 per year plus tuition fees
**Length of Study**: 1–3 years
**Frequency**: Annual
**Study Establishment**: SOAS
**Country of Study**: United Kingdom
**Application Procedure**: A Felix Scholarship application form is available for download from the download box at the top right or can be obtained from Scholarships Officer
**Closing Date**: 31 January
**Funding**: Private
**Contributor**: Felix Scholarship Trust
**No. of awards given last year**: 6
**Additional Information**: One award is made each year to a non-Indian student from a developing country who demonstrates academic excellence and financial need. Please see the website for further details www.soas.ac.uk/registry/scholar ships/felix-scholarships.html www.ox.ac.uk/admissions/grad uate/fees-and-funding/fees-funding-and-scholarship-search/ felix-scholarships

**For further information contact:**

**Tel**:     (44) 20 7074 5094/5091

## Hong Kong and Shanghai Banking Corporation School of Oriental and African Studies Scholarships

**Purpose**: To support United Kingdom or European Union fee payers commencing a full-time master's course in Sinology or Chinese literature

**Eligibility**: Applicants must possess or be about to complete a good honours degree, preferably first class, from a United Kingdom institution or overseas equivalent

**Level of Study**: Postgraduate

**Type**: Scholarship

**Value**: £16,650 plus tuition fees at the home European Union rate

**Length of Study**: 1 year

**Frequency**: Annual

**Study Establishment**: SOAS

**Country of Study**: United Kingdom

**Application Procedure**: Candidates can apply for this scholarship via the online scholarship application form. For enquiries, please contact Scholarships Officer

**Closing Date**: 22 March

**Funding**: Trusts

**Contributor**: HSBC educational trust

**No. of awards given last year**: 2

**Additional Information**: www.soas.ac.uk/registry/scholar ships/hsbc-soas-scholarships.html

**For further information contact:**

**Tel**:     (44) 20 7074 5094/5091

## International Postgraduate Scholarships

**Purpose**: The International Postgraduate Scholarship is designed to award new entry 2020 Postgraduate students with outstanding academic performance.

**Eligibility**: 1. Have an offer to study a Full Time Postgraduate taught (on-campus) degree for September 2020 2. Overseas fee-paying student who is a national of China, Hong Kong, or Taiwan 3. Minimum UK upper second-class (2:1) or international equivalent

**Level of Study**: Postgraduate

**Type**: Scholarship

**Value**: £3,000 (fee waiver)

**Frequency**: Annual

**Study Establishment**: SOAS

**Country of Study**: United Kingdom

**Application Procedure**: Apply for the International Scholarship     docs.google.com/forms/d/e/1FAIpQLSd0uhFLoS8-FwcH6ii-3r5C7pZg4n68lr8DXeDDgZGcLRxfzQ/viewform?usp=sf_link

**No. of awards offered**: 10

**Closing Date**: 31 May

**Funding**: Foundation

**Additional Information**: www.soas.ac.uk/registry/scholar ships/international-pg-scholarships.html

**For further information contact:**

SOAS University of London 10 Thornhaugh Street, Russell Square, London WC1H 0XG, United Kingdom.

**Tel**:     (44) 20 7074 4700

**Email**:    study@soas.ac.uk

## Ouseley Memorial Scholarship

**Purpose**: The scholarships are for students entering the second or third year of the MPhil/PhD programme in 2020-21 (or part time equivalent). The Ouseley Memorial scholarships may be used towards tuition fees or living expenses.

**Eligibility**: Open to United Kingdom/European Union and overseas applicants. Applicants must refer to the organization website for detailed information

**Level of Study**: Doctorate, Postgraduate

**Type**: Scholarship

**Value**: £6,000 for 1 year only

**Frequency**: Annual

**Study Establishment**: SOAS

**Country of Study**: United Kingdom

**No. of awards offered**: 20

**Closing Date**: 7 May

**Funding**: Private

**No. of awards given last year**: 1

**No. of applicants last year**: 20

**Additional Information**: www.soas.ac.uk/registry/scholar ships/ouseley-memorial-scholarship.html

**For further information contact:**

**Tel**:     (44) 20 7074 5094/5091

## Shapoorji Pallonji Scholarships

**Purpose**: The Shapoorji Pallonji Scholarships will provide a contribution to fees and living costs calibrated according to merit and availability of funds.

**Level of Study**: Postgraduate

**Type**: Scholarship

**Length of Study**: The MPhil/PhD scholarship is paid for 3 years. The MA is paid for one year (or over two years if part-time)
**Frequency**: Annual
**Study Establishment**: SOAS
**Country of Study**: United Kingdom
**Closing Date**: 2 April
**Funding**: Foundation
**Additional Information**: www.soas.ac.uk/registry/scholar ships/shapoorji-pallonji-scholarships-.html

### For further information contact:

SOAS University of London 10 Thornhaugh Street, Russell Square, London WC1H 0XG, United Kingdom.

**Tel**: (44) 20 7074 5094/ 5091

## SOAS Master's Scholarship

**Purpose**: To provide financial assistance to study for a full-time taught Master's programme
**Eligibility**: 1. School of Law - any 12 months full-time master's programme. 2. Department of Politics & International Studies - any 12 months full-time master's programme. 3. School of Finance & Management - any 12 months full-time master's programme. 4. Department of Economics - any 12 months full-time master's programme. 5. Department of Development Studies - any 12 months full-time master's programme. 6. School of History, Religions and Philosophies - any 12 months full-time master's programme. 7. Department of Anthropology and Sociology - any 12 months full-time master's programme. 8. School of Arts - any 12 months full-time master's programme. 9. Department of East Asian Languages and Cultures - any 12 months full-time master's programme. 10. Interdisciplinary Studies (Centre of Development, Environment and Policy, Centre of Gender Studies, Centre of Global Media and Communications & Centre of International Studies and Diplomacy) - any 12 months full-time master's programme.
**Level of Study**: Postgraduate
**Type**: Scholarship
**Value**: £19,229
**Length of Study**: 1 year, non-renewable
**Frequency**: Annual
**Study Establishment**: SOAS
**Country of Study** United Kingdom
**No. of awards offered**: 350
**Closing Date**: 20 February
**Funding**: Government
**No. of awards given last year**: 11
**No. of applicants last year**: 350

**Additional Information**: www.soas.ac.uk/registry/scholar ships/soas-alumni-scholarship.html

### For further information contact:

**Tel**: (44) 20 7074 5094/5091

## SOAS Research Scholarship

**Purpose**: To support full-time research study at SOAS
**Eligibility**: Applicants must United Kingdom/European Union and overseas and must possess or expect to be awarded a distinction in their Master's degree from a United Kingdom university or its equivalent
**Level of Study**: Doctorate
**Type**: Scholarship
**Value**: £12,790
**Length of Study**: 3 years
**Frequency**: Annual
**Study Establishment**: SOAS
**Country of Study**: United Kingdom
**Application Procedure**: Applicants must complete and submit an application form that can be downloaded from the website
**Closing Date**: 31 January
**Funding**: Government
**No. of awards given last year**: 4
**Additional Information**: For enquiries, please contact Scholarships Officer www.afterschoolafrica.com/35577/ soas-research-studentships/

## SOAS Sanctuary Scholarship

**Purpose**: The SOAS Sanctuary scheme to support displaced people
**Eligibility**: 1. Any full time undergraduate degree of 3 years duration 2. Any full time one year or part time two year postgraduate taught Master's degree on campus (not distance learning) 3. In addition, a package of support will be provided to contribute towards the living costs (which includes accommodation, travel and study materials) for the student to take up their place.
**Level of Study**: Postgraduate
**Type**: Scholarship
**Value**: Full tuition fee waiver
**Frequency**: Annual
**Study Establishment**: SOAS
**Country of Study**: United Kingdom
**Closing Date**: 30 June
**Funding**: Foundation

**Additional Information**: www.soas.ac.uk/registry/scholarships/soas-sanctuary-scholarships-202021.html

### For further information contact:

SOAS University of London 10 Thornhaugh Street, Russell Square, London WC1H 0XG, United Kingdom.

**Tel**:    (44) 20 7074 5094

## Sochon Foundation Scholarship

**Purpose**: For a student undertaking a full-time postgraduate programme in Korean studies
**Eligibility**: 1. MA Korean Studies and Intensive Language (Korean). 2. MA History of Art and Archaeology of East Asia and Intensive Language (Korean). N.B. 90 credits (i.-e. 60 credit dissertation plus 30 others, of the non-language component) should be in Korea-related subjects. 3. MA History of Art and Archaeology (Korean). N.B. 75 credits (ie. 60 credit dissertation plus 15 credits on Korean art history). 4. MA History and Intensive Language (Korean). N.-B. 90 credits (i.e. 60 credit dissertation plus 30 others, of the non-language component) should be in Korea-related subjects. 5. MA Korean Studies. 6. Research Degrees (MPhil/PhD) in Japanese and Korean Studies. 7. Part-time programmes are not eligible.
**Level of Study**: Postgraduate
**Type**: Scholarship
**Value**: £6,000
**Length of Study**: 1 year
**Frequency**: Annual
**Study Establishment**: SOAS
**Country of Study**: United Kingdom
**Closing Date**: 2 April
**Funding**: Foundation
**No. of awards given last year**: 1
**Additional Information**: www.soas.ac.uk/registry/scholarships/sochon-foundation-scholarship.html

### For further information contact:

**Tel**:    (44) 20 7074 5091/5094

## Tibawi Trust Awards

**Purpose**: Dr Abdul-Latif Tibawi left a gift in his will to establish a Trust for a postgraduate award
**Eligibility**: Any postgraduate degree programme at SOAS.
**Level of Study**: Postgraduate
**Type**: Award
**Value**: Up to £1,300

**Frequency**: Annual
**Study Establishment**: SOAS
**Country of Study**: United Kingdom
**Application Procedure**: Late applications will not be considered
**No. of awards offered**: 2
**Closing Date**: 5 June
**Funding**: Foundation
**Additional Information**: www.soas.ac.uk/registry/scholarships/tibawi-trust-award.html

### For further information contact:

SOAS University of London 10 Thornhaugh Street, Russell Square, London WC1H 0XG, United Kingdom.

**Tel**:    (44) 20 7074 5094/ 5091

## VP Kanitkar Memorial Scholarship

**Purpose**: The V P Kanitkar Memorial Scholarships are available for postgraduates to support a taught masters in Religious Studies with reference to Hinduism and a taught masters in Anthropology with reference to Hindu culture in South Asia
**Level of Study**: Postgraduate
**Type**: Scholarship
**Value**: Each scholarship covers the cost of tuition fees and provides a maintenance
**Frequency**: Annual
**Study Establishment**: SOAS
**Country of Study**: United Kingdom
**Closing Date**: 2 April
**Funding**: Foundation
**Additional Information**: www.soas.ac.uk/registry/scholarships/soas-open-scholarship.html

### For further information contact:

SOAS, University of London, 10 Thornhaugh Street, Russell Square, London WC1H 0XG, United Kingdom.

**Tel**:    (44) 20 7074 5094/ 5091

## William Ross Murray Scholarship

**Purpose**: To support a student of high academic achievement from a developing country unable to pay overseas tuition fees and attending the full-time LLM degree at SOAS
**Eligibility**: 1. Must be domiciled in a developing country. 2. Possess a good honours degree, preferably first class, from a UK institution or overseas equivalent. 3. Have an unconditional offer of admission to pursue the full-time LLM at

SOAS by the scholarship application deadline. If your offer is conditional, please ensure you meet the conditions and receive an unconditional offer by the deadline.

**Level of Study**: Postgraduate

**Type**: Scholarship

**Value**: Overseas tuition fees. Free accommodation at International Student House and food vouchers

**Length of Study**: 1 year

**Frequency**: Annual

**Study Establishment**: SOAS

**Country of Study**: United Kingdom

**No. of awards offered**: 1

**Closing Date**: 20 February

**Funding**: Foundation

**No. of awards given last year**: 1

**Additional Information**: www.afterschoolafrica.com/159/william-ross-murray-scholarship/

## Science and Engineering Research Board

5 & 5A, Lower Ground Floor, Vasant Square Mall, Sector-B, Pocket-5, Vasant Kunj, New Delhi 110070, India.

| | |
|---|---|
| **Tel**: | (91) 11 40000398 |
| **Contact**: | Science and Engineering Research Board |

The Science and Engineering Research Board (SERB) is a statutory body established through an Act of Parliament. Supporting basic research in emerging areas of science and engineering are the primary and distinctive mandate of the Board. The Board structure, with both financial and administrative powers vested in the Board, enables quicker decisions on research issues, greatly improving thereby responsiveness to the genuine needs of the research scientists and the S&T system.

### J C Bose National Fellowship

**Subjects**: 1. Should be an active scientist with a record of outstanding performance apparent from the award of SS Bhatnagar prize and/or fellowship of science academies (including engineering, agriculture and medicine). 2. The scientist should be in service at the time of nomination to this fellowship. 3. The nominee should be an Indian national working in institutions/universities in India.

**Purpose**: The JC Bose fellowship is awarded to active scientists in recognition for their outstanding performance. The fellowship is scientist-specific and very selective.

**Level of Study**: Postgraduate

**Type**: fellowship

**Value**: ₹15,00,000 per annum

**Length of Study**: 5 years

**Frequency**: Annual

**Application Procedure**: Nominator should first register into the online website. www.serbonline.in/SERB/Registration

**Additional Information**: www.serb.gov.in/jcbn.php

### For further information contact:

Science and Engineering Research Board , 5 & 5A, Lower Ground Floor, Vasant Square Mall, Plot No. A, Community Centre, Sector-5, Pocket-5, Vasant Kunj, New Delhi-110070, India.

| | |
|---|---|
| **Tel**: | (91) 11 40000304 |
| **Email**: | monika@serb.gov.in |

### National Post Doctoral Fellowship (N-PDF)

**Purpose**: The SERB-National Post Doctoral Fellowship (N-PDF) is aimed to identify motivated young researchers and provide them support for doing research in frontier areas of science and engineering. The fellows will work under a mentor, and it is hoped that this training will provide them a platform to develop as an independent researcher

**Eligibility**: 1. The applicant should be an Indian citizen. 2. The applicant must have obtained PhD/M.D/M.S degree from a recognized University. Those who have submitted their PhD/M.D/M.S thesis and are awaiting award of the degree are also eligible to apply. However, such candidates, if selected, will be offered lower fellowship amount till they qualify the eligible degree. 3. The upper age limit for the fellowship is 35 years at the time of the submission of application, age will be calculated by taking the date of closure of the respective call. Age relaxation of 5 (five) years will be given to candidates belonging to SC/ST/OBC/Physically Challenged & Women candidates. 4. NPDF can be availed only once by a candidate in his/her career. 5. Mentor must hold a regular academic/research position in a recognized institution in India. Should hold PhD degree in Science or Engineering. 6. A mentor shall not have more than two SERB NPDF fellows at any given time. 7. Applicants of NPDF, SRG and EMR can submit their proposal only once in a calender year in any of these schemes.

**Type**: Fellowship

**Value**: Fellowship: ₹55,000 per month (consolidated) and ₹35,000 per month for candidates who have submitted the thesis but degree not awarded. Research Grant: ₹200,000 per annum. Overheads: ₹100,000 per annum

**Length of Study**: Initially for a period of 2 years. In exceptional cases, depending on the progress of research, the fellowship can be extended for 1 more year. There is no provision to extend the tenure beyond 3 years

**Country of Study**: Hungary

**Application Procedure**: The application form along with a research proposal highlighting the objectives of the research work to be undertaken should be submitted online through the website www.serbonline.in

**Additional Information**: The call for applications for SERB-N PDF will be notified twice a year through the websites www.serbonline.in and www.serb.gov.in. For details one may visit serbonline.in/SERB/npdf. www.serb.gov.in

### For further information contact:

**Email**: info@serbonline.in

## Prime Minister's Fellowship Scheme for Doctoral Research

**Purpose**: To conduct scientific and industrial research

**Level of Study**: Research

**Type**: Fellowship

**Value**: ₹6,00,000 per annum

**Length of Study**: 4 years

**Frequency**: Annual

**Country of Study**: India

**Application Procedure**: Application Performa is to be filled only through the web portal www.primeministerfellowshipscheme.com

**Funding**: Government

**Contributor**: Department of Science & Technology (DST) and Science & Engineering Research Board (SERB) with The Confederation of Indian Industry (CII)

**Additional Information**: For online applications, visit website: www.primeministerfellowshipscheme.com www.successcds.net/Scholarships/prime-minister-research-fellowships.html

### For further information contact:

**Email**: shalini.sharma@cii.in

## Ramanujan Fellowship

**Subjects**: Researchers scientists/engineers

**Purpose**: The scheme provides support to active researchers/scientists/engineers who want to return to India from abroad and contribute their work for the country.

**Eligibility**: 1. The fellowship is open to brilliant Indianscientists and engineers working abroad and are below the age of 40 years. 2. The nominee should possess a higher degree or equivalent, such as PhD in Science/ Engineering, Masters in Engineering or Technology/ MD in Medicine, etc. and have adequate professional experience. 3. These Fellowships are very selective and only those who have a proven/ outstanding track-record as evident from their research publications and recognition's would be eligible. 4. In case of selection of the candidate for regular position in the university/institute, the candidate will not be eligible for receiving grant under Ramanujan Fellowship 5. The fellowship is only for those scientists who are not holding any permanent/ tenuretrack/ contractual position in any Indian Institute/ University. 6. The Nominee should be working abroad at the time of nomination.

**Level of Study**: Postgraduate

**Type**: fellowship

**Value**: receive a research grant of ₹7,00,000 per annum and ₹60,000/- per annum as overhead charges

**Length of Study**: 5 years

**Frequency**: Annual

**Application Procedure**: Nominee need to register in SERB online portal, www.serbonline.in www.serbonline.in/SERB/Registration

**Additional Information**: www.serb.gov.in/rnf.php

### For further information contact:

Science and Engineering Research Board , 5 & 5A, Lower Ground Floor, Vasant Square Mall, Plot No. A, Community Centre, Sector-5, Pocket-5, Vasant Kunj, New Delhi-110070.

**Tel**:      (91) 11 40000304

**Email**:    monika@serb.gov.in

## S.N Bose Scholar Program

**Purpose**: S.N Bose Scholar Program is organized by the Science and Engineering Board (SERB), Department of science and technology (DST), Govt. of India, Indo–US Technology Forum and Win Step Forward. The scholarship envisages providing a world-class research platform in top US universities. It also aims at making Indo-US long-term collaboration in the field of research

**Eligibility**: 1. Students pursuing a Bachelor's or master's degree program from a recognized institution of India can apply for this scheme. 2. The disciplines of pursuing UG and PG degree are Atmospheric and Earth Sciences, Chemical Sciences, Engineering Sciences, Mathematical and Computational Sciences, and Physical Sciences. 3. Candidates who are studying PhD cannot apply

**Level of Study**: Postdoctorate

**Type**: Scholarship

**Length of Study**: 1 year

**Frequency**: Annual

**Country of Study**: Any country

**Closing Date**: May

**Funding**: Foundation

**Additional Information**: www.buddy4study.com/article/sn-bose-scholarship

### For further information contact:

Indo-US Science and Technology Forum, Fulbright House, 12, Hailey Road, New Delhi 110001, India.

Tel: (91) 11 42691712

Email: bose@indousstf.org

## Science and Engineering Research Board Distinguished Fellowship

**Purpose**: In order to support research of eminent scientists who do not hold any administrative roles and functions but are active and performing, SERB has instituted Distinguished SERB Fellowship Award

**Eligibility**: Superannuated scientist who is active in research. Must have received recognition for his/her work from National and/or International scientific bodies

**Level of Study**: Research

**Type**: Fellowship

**Value**: A research grant of ₹5,00,000 per annum and a fellowship amount of ₹60,000 per month will be given to each fellow

**Country of Study**: India

**Application Procedure**: Call for nomination is made from time to time. Nominations are accepted only when the call is made

**Closing Date**: 30 November

**Funding**: Government

**Additional Information**: www.scholarshipsinindia.com/fellowship/serb-distinguished-fellowship.html

### For further information contact:

Email: keerti.serb@gmail.com

## Science and Engineering Research Board Overseas Postdoctoral Fellowship (OPDF)

**Purpose**: SERB Overseas Postdoctoral fellowship (SERB-OPDF) aims to build national capacity in frontier areas of Science and Engineering, which are of interest to India by providing postdoctoral fellowship

**Eligibility**: The applicant should have completed PhD degree in science and engineering not earlier than the preceding 2 years from recognized institutions in India. For researchers who are in regular employment, the 2 years period may be relaxed

**Type**: Fellowship

**Length of Study**: 1 year, extendable to 1 more year subject to good performance

**Country of Study**: Any country

**Application Procedure**: The format, guidelines and other details of the SERB-OPDF Program details are also available at www.dst.gov.in

**Additional Information**: The programme admits candidates in identified areas and sends them to top institutions around the globe, other than United States of America and also to institutions where internationally acclaimed scientists are working www.serb.gov.in/opf.php

### For further information contact:

Email: opdf@serb.gov.in

## Science and Engineering Research Board Women Excellence Award

**Purpose**: SERB Women Excellence Award is a one-time award given to women scientists below 40 years of age and who have received recognition from any one or more of the following national academies such as Young Scientist Medal, Young Associate etc

**Level of Study**: Research

**Type**: Award

**Value**: ₹5,00,000 per annum

**Length of Study**: 3 years

**Country of Study**: Any country

**Application Procedure**: A copy of the proposal (in one file in PDF) may also be sent by email to: doyiltv@nic.in

**Funding**: Government

**Additional Information**: The call for proposals will be notified through the website annually. Women Scientists who have received the award earlier are not eligible to apply again www.serb.gov.in/wea.php

### For further information contact:

Email: doyiltv@nic.in

## Science and Technology Facilities Council (STFC)

Polaris House, North Star Avenue, Swindon SN2 1SZ, United Kingdom.

Tel: (44) 1793 442 000

Email: enquiries@stfc.ac.uk

Website: www.stfc.ac.uk

STFC is keeping the United Kingdom at the forefront of international science and tackling some of the most significant challenges facing society such as meeting our future energy needs, monitoring and understanding climate change, and global security. The Council has a broad science portfolio and works with the academic and industrial communities to share its expertise in materials science, space and ground-based astronomy technologies, laser science, microelectronics, wafer scale manufacturing, particle and nuclear physics, alternative energy production, radio communications and radar.

## Daphne Jackson Fellowships

**Purpose**: To enable high-level engineers and scientists to return to their professions after a career break for family or other reasons

**Eligibility**: Open to promising engineers and scientists who have taken a career break

**Level of Study**: Postdoctorate, Research

**Type**: Fellowship

**Value**: Fellowship will be financed by your sponsor and/or host institution. Please refer to the website for more details

**Length of Study**: 2 years

**Frequency**: Annual

**Study Establishment**: Any academic institution acceptable to the PPARC

**Country of Study**: United Kingdom

**Application Procedure**: Applicants must contact Jennifer Woolley, Trust Director, or Sue Smith, Fellowship Administrator, for application forms and further information

**Funding**: Government

**Additional Information**: Please refer to the website for more details: www.daphnejackson.org/fellowships/applicationprocess/ daphnejackson.org/about-fellowships/application-process/

### For further information contact:

The Daphne Jackson Trust, Department of Physics, University of Surrey, Guildford GU2 7XH, United Kingdom.

**Tel**:     (44) 1483 689166
**Email**:    djmft@surrey.ac.uk

## Ernest Rutherford Fellowship

**Purpose**: The Ernest Rutherford Fellowships will enable early career researchers with clear leadership potential to establish a strong, independent research programme

**Eligibility**: Ernest Rutherford Fellowships are intended for early career researchers who do not have a permanent academic position. You are not eligible if you currently hold a permanent academic position or the equivalent in institutions other than universities. Fellowships are open to applicants of any nationality

**Level of Study**: Research

**Type**: A variable number of fellowships

**Length of Study**: 5 years

**Frequency**: Annual

**Country of Study**: United Kingdom

**Application Procedure**: How to apply is detailed on STFC website:  stfc.ukri.org/funding/fellowships/ernest-rutherford-fellowship/

**No. of awards offered**: 160

**Closing Date**: September

**Funding**: Government

**No. of awards given last year**: 11

**No. of applicants last year**: 160

**Additional Information**:  stfc.ukri.org/funding/fellowships/ ernest-rutherford-fellowship/

## Industrial CASE Studentships

**Purpose**: Provides support for PhD students to work in collaboration with a non-academic partner on projects that aim to apply technologies or techniques developed within the programme into other areas

**Eligibility**: Organisations eligible to receive STFC grant funding

**Level of Study**: Postgraduate

**Type**: Studentship

**Value**: Stipend, fees, research training and fieldwork travel

**Length of Study**: 3.5 years

**Frequency**: Annual

**Country of Study**: United Kingdom

**Application Procedure**: Call opens in August. Applications must be submitted by the academic partner through the Je-S system. Proposals may be led by either the academic supervisor at an eligible United Kingdom University or research institute or supervisor/supervisors at the non-academic partner organisation, but the application process must be completed by the academic partner, who will then be the recipient of the award

**Closing Date**: October

**Funding**: Commercial

**Additional Information**: Please check at www.mrc.ac.uk/ skills-careers/studentships/how-we-fund-studentships/industrial-case-studentships/

## Industrial CASE-Plus Studentship

**Purpose**: Provides support for PhD students to work in collaboration with a non-academic partner on projects that aim to apply technologies or techniques developed within the programme into other areas. The student would spend a further year working full time on the premises of the non-academic partner as an employee

**Eligibility**: Organisations eligible to receive STFC grant funding
**Level of Study**: Postgraduate
**Type**: Studentship
**Value**: Stipend, fees, research training and fieldwork travel
**Length of Study**: 3.5 years
**Frequency**: Annual
**Study Establishment**: Science and Technology Facilities Council
**Country of Study**: United Kingdom
**Application Procedure**: The call opens May. Proposals may be submitted up to the closing date of July for awards to start in October. Proposals should be submitted by a supervisor from a Research Organization eligible to be the academic partner through the Je-S system
**Funding**: Commercial
**Additional Information**: Please check STFC website for more information - stfc.ukri.org/funding/studentships/industrial- case-studentships/

## PPARC Communications/Media Programme

**Purpose**: To support students undertake communications training
**Level of Study**: Postgraduate
**Type**: Bursary
**Value**: All tuition fees
**Length of Study**: 1 academic year
**Frequency**: Annual
**Study Establishment**: Any approved university
**Country of Study**: United Kingdom
**Application Procedure**: Contact the PPARC Science and Society team
**Closing Date**: 13 October
**Additional Information**: www.lse.ac.uk/study-at-lse/Graduate/Degree-programmes-2020/MSc-Media-and-Communications

### For further information contact:

**Tel**:      (44) 1793 442030
**Email**:   pr.pus@pparc.ac.uk

## PPARC Royal Society Industry Fellowships

**Purpose**: To enhance interaction between those in industry and the research base, to the benefit of United Kingdom industry

**Eligibility**: Open to senior academic scientists and industrial employees with a project proposal central to their own research programme for which a collaborative effort would bring benefits
**Level of Study**: Postdoctorate, professional development
**Type**: Fellowship
**Value**: Varies
**Length of Study**: 6 months–2 years full-time, or part-time over a period of up to 4 years
**Frequency**: Annual
**Study Establishment**: An appropriate academic institution or position in the industry
**Country of Study**: United Kingdom
**Application Procedure**: Applicants must find a suitable industrial or academic partner to host their project before submitting an application. Applications and further information are available from the Research Appointments Department of The Royal Society
**Closing Date**: December
**Funding**: Commercial, Private
**Contributor**: The Royal Society, EPSRC, BBSRC, Rolls-Royce and PPARC
**Additional Information**: Apart from the Royal Society Fellowships Programme the following fellowship programmes are administered by the PPARC in collaboration with other partners: The European Organisation for Nuclear Research (CERN) Fellowships, The European Space Agency (ESA) Fellowships, The Anglo-Australian Postdoctoral Research Fellowships, and the Daphne Jackson Fellowships. Further information on these programmes is available on the PPARC website royalsociety.org/grants-schemes-awards/grants/industry-fellowship/

### For further information contact:

Research Appointments Department, The Royal Society, 6 Carlton House Terrace, St. James's, London SW1Y 5AR, United Kingdom.

**Tel**:      (44) 20 7451 2542
**Email**:   ukresearch.appointments@royalsoc.ac.uk

## PPARC Standard Research Studentship

**Purpose**: To enable promising scientists and engineers to continue training
**Eligibility**: Advice on eligibility should be sought from the Registrar's Office
**Level of Study**: Postgraduate
**Type**: Studentship
**Value**: Tuition fees only
**Length of Study**: 1–3 years

**Frequency**: Annual
**Country of Study**: United Kingdom
**Application Procedure**: Contact the PPARC
**Closing Date**: 31 March

### For further information contact:

**Tel**:        (44) 1793 442026
**Email**:    steve.cann@pparc.ac.uk

## Science and Technology Facilities Council Postgraduate Studentships

**Subjects**: Particle physics, accelerator science, nuclear physics, particle astrophysics, solar system science and astronomy.
**Purpose**: STFC postgraduate studentships are awarded to enable promising scientists and engineers to continue training beyond a first degree.
**Eligibility**: Open to postgraduates from the UK and EU countries. All studentship projects supported through STFC funding must fall within STFC remit.
**Level of Study**: Postgraduate
**Type**: Studentship
**Value**: Stipend (excluding fees only students), approved fees, research training support grant, conference and U.K. fieldwork element, fieldwork expenses, long term attachments, other allowances (where applicable).
**Length of Study**: 3.5 years
**Frequency**: Annual
**Country of Study**: United Kingdom
**Application Procedure**: If you are interested in applying for an STFC-funded PhD, please contact the institution at which you wish to undertake a research degree directly.
**No. of awards offered**: Approx. 220
**Funding**: Government
**Additional Information**: Please check at www.stfc.ac.uk/funding/studentships/types-of-postgraduate-studentship/ for more information. stfc.ukri.org/funding/studentships/

### For further information contact:

**Email**:    Studentships@stfc.ukri.org

## University of Canterbury Pasifika Doctoral Scholarship

**Purpose**: This scholarship supports Pasifika students for study towards a research doctoral degree at the University of Canterbury
**Eligibility**: 1. Candidates must be Pasifika. 2. Intending students who already hold a research doctoral degree4 are not eligible for the scholarship. 3. Students may not take up the

scholarship until any non-academic requirements for the qualifying degree have been completed and credited. Offers of scholarships to candidates whose qualifying degree is the BE (Hons) are conditional on the completion and crediting of ENGR 200 no later than 12 months after the formal offer of a place in a doctoral programme has been accepted.
**Level of Study**: Doctorate
**Type**: Scholarship
**Value**: Up to US$21,000 per annum plus tuition fees at domestic rate
**Length of Study**: Up to 3 years
**Frequency**: Annual
**Country of Study**: Any country
**Application Procedure**: You may apply through this webpage approximately 8 weeks before applications close. If it's possible to apply on-line for this scholarship there will be a link above to the on-line system. If the link is not provided, please download and complete the application form located below. However, if the scholarship is managed by Universities NZ or another department of the University an External Website link will appear below and application instructions will be available through that link. Apply through online link. www.canterbury.ac.nz/scholarshipsearch/ScholarshipDetails.aspx
**No. of awards offered**: 2
**Closing Date**: 15 May
**Funding**: Private
**Additional Information**: www.canterbury.ac.nz/scholarshipsearch/ScholarshipDetails.aspx www.canterbury.ac.nz/scholarshipsearch/ScholarshipDetails.aspx?ScholarshipID=6935.1640

### For further information contact:

**Email**:    info@canterbury.ac.nz

## Science Foundation Ireland

Wilton Park House, Wilton Place, Dublin 2, Ireland.

**Tel**:           (353) 1 607 3200
**Email**:      info@sfi.ie
**Website**:   www.sfi.ie
**Contact**:   Professor Mark W. J. Ferguson, Director

Science Foundation Ireland funds oriented basic and applied research in the areas of science, technology, engineering and mathematics (STEM), which promotes and assists the development and competitiveness of industry, enterprise and employment in Ireland. SFI will build and strengthen scientific and engineering research and its infrastructure in the areas of greatest strategic value to Ireland's long-term competitiveness and development.

## President of Ireland Young Research Award (PIYRA)

**Purpose**: The purpose of the PIYRA programme is to recruit and retain outstanding early career investigators with leadership potential. Its aim is to enable those at an earlier career stage who already hold permanent academic positions to advance their careers and build up their research teams and activities; to allow researchers in temporary positions to advance their careers and provide them with enhanced opportunities to move into a permanent academic position; to enable the award holder, together with his/her team, to carry out their work in Ireland's public research bodies; to offer funding opportunities that help third-level institutions attract and develop researchers and their careers; to allow earlier-career investigators of all nationalities to enhance their experience in Irish HEIs and to allow those employed outside of Ireland to return to work in an Irish HEI

**Eligibility**: The lead applicant must have completed a minimum of 36 months of active postdoctoral research. The lead applicant must have been awarded a PhD or MD within the last 8 years, in the normal case, or up to a maximum of 12 and a half years for applicants who have taken documented eligible leave, as described below. The lead applicant has an exceptional record of internationally recognized independent research accomplishments for their career stage. The lead applicant must be an individual who will be recognized by the research body upon receipt of the SFI grant as an independent investigator who will have an independent office and research space at the host research body for which he/she will be fully responsible for at least the duration of the SFI grant

**Level of Study**: Research

**Type**: Grant

**Value**: Up to €1,000,000 of total value (inclusive of the host institution contribution) in direct costs

**Length of Study**: Up to 5 years

**Frequency**: Annual

**Study Establishment**: Host Research Bodies must be situated in the Republic of Ireland. Research Bodies will include Universities, Institutes of Technology and independent not-for-profit public research organizations that receive a significant share of their total funding from public sources

**Country of Study**: Ireland

**Application Procedure**: Applicants are invited to submit the following documentation: expression of Interest and if invited to do so after the Expression of Interest evaluation stage; full proposal. Application must be submitted via an eligible research body. Application must be submitted online via SESAME

**Closing Date**: December

**Funding**: Government

**Contributor**: Science Foundation Ireland

**Additional Information**: www.sfi.ie/funding/funding-calls/sfi-president-of-ireland/

## Science Foundation Ireland Career Development Award (CDA)

**Purpose**: The SFI Career Development Award (CDA) aims to support early- and mid-career researchers who already hold a salaried, independent research post and who are looking to expand their research activities. Its aims is to support excellent scientific research that has potential economic and societal impact; to enable those at an earlier career stage who already hold permanent academic positions to advance their careers and build up their research teams and activities; to allow researchers in temporary positions to advance their careers and provide them with enhanced opportunities to move into a permanent academic position; to provide the support and infrastructure to carry out novel research in areas that underpin SFI's legal remit; to enable the award holder, together with his/her team, to carry out their work in Ireland's public research bodies, including Universities and Institutes of Technology; to offer funding opportunities that help third-level institutions attract and develop researchers and their careers; to allow earlier-career investigators of all nationalities to enhance their experience in Irish HEIs

**Eligibility**: The applicant will be a researcher with 3–15 years of relevant experience beyond the award of their doctoral degree, who at the time of application will be either in a permanent, full-time academic position (either within the institution at which they wish to base their CDA-funded research or another elsewhere in Ireland or overseas), or employed on a temporary (fixed-term) contract where it is evident that the role being carried out is an independent research position (i.e., Postdoctoral Research Associates (or equivalent) or Research Fellows working under the guidance of a supervisor and who have never held an independent position are not eligible to apply to the CDA Programme)

**Level of Study**: Research

**Type**: Award

**Value**: Between €300,000 and €500,000 direct costs

**Length of Study**: 4 years

**Frequency**: Every 2 years

**Study Establishment**: Host Research Bodies must be situated in the Republic of Ireland. Research Bodies will include Universities, Institutes of Technology and independent not-for-profit public research organizations that receive a significant share of their total funding from public sources

**Country of Study**: Ireland

**Application Procedure**: Application must be submitted via an eligible research body. Application must be submitted online via SESAME (www.sfi.ie/funding/award-management-system)

**Closing Date**: 10 December

**Funding**: Government

**Contributor**: Science Foundation Ireland

**No. of awards given last year**: 20

**Additional Information**: Please write to cda@sfi.ie www.sfi.ie/funding/funding-calls/sfi-career-development-award/

## Science Foundation Ireland Investigator Programme

**Purpose**: To fund scientific research projects of excellence in focused areas. To build capacity, expertise and relationships so as to enable researchers to compete in future SFI Research Centre Programmes or in other funding programmes such as ERC and Horizon 2020. To encourage researchers to build capacity, expertise, collaborations and relationships in areas of strategic economic importance through themed calls. To facilitate partnerships with other agencies. To support collaborations and partnerships between academia and industry

**Eligibility**: The lead applicant and any co-applicant(s) must hold a PhD/MD or equivalent for at least 5 years by the proposal deadline. The lead applicant and any co-applicant (s) are required to have demonstrated that they are each senior author on at least 10 international peer reviewed articles. The lead applicant and any co-applicant(s) are required to have demonstrated research independence through securing at least one independent research grant as a lead investigator or as co-investigator

**Level of Study**: Research

**Type**: Grant

**Value**: €400,000–2,500,000 per year

**Length of Study**: 3–5 years

**Frequency**: Annual

**Study Establishment**: Host Research Bodies must be situated in the Republic of Ireland. Research Bodies will include Universities, Institutes of Technology and independent not-for-profit public research organizations that receive a significant share of their total funding from public sources

**Country of Study**: Ireland

**Application Procedure**: Application must be submitted via an eligible research body. Application must be submitted online via SESAME (www.sfi.ie/funding/award-management-system)

**Closing Date**: 26 June

**Funding**: Government

**Contributor**: Science Foundation Ireland

**No. of awards given last year**: 40

**Additional Information**: www.sfi.ie/funding/funding-calls/sfi-investigators-programme/

## For further information contact:

**Email**:    investigators@sfi.ie

## Starting Investigator Research Grant (SIRG)

**Purpose**: The SIRG programme supports excellent postdoctoral researchers who wish to take steps towards a fully independent research career. Aims: to support excellent scientific research that has potential economic and societal impact. To enable those at an early career stage to establish themselves as independent researchers; to provide the support and infrastructure to carry out novel research in areas that underpin SFI's legal remit; to gain important experience towards a full-time academic position, including the supervision of the postgraduate student supported by the award; to enable the award holder, together with his/her postgraduate student, to carry out their work in Ireland's public research bodies, including Universities and Institutes of technology; to offer funding opportunities that help third-level institutions attract and develop researchers and their careers; to allow early-career investigators of all nationalities to enhance their experience in Irish HEIs; to allow early-career investigators who have been employed outside of Ireland to return to work in an Irish HEI

**Eligibility**: The applicant will be a researcher with between 3 and 8 years of relevant experience beyond the award of their doctoral, who is currently employed as a Postdoctoral Research Associate (or equivalent) or a Research Fellow under the guidance of a named supervisor, and who has never previously held an independent research position of any kind where they were primarily responsible for a research team and its financial support. Allowances will be made for documented leave, including maternity leave, paternity leave, parental leave, military service, sick/disability leave and carer's leave

**Level of Study**: Research

**Type**: Grant

**Value**: Up to €400,000 direct costs

**Length of Study**: 4 years

**Study Establishment**: Host Research Bodies must be situated in the Republic of Ireland. Research Bodies will include Universities, Institutes of Technology and independent not-for-profit public research organizations that receive a significant share of their total funding from public sources

**Country of Study**: Ireland

**Application Procedure**: Application must be submitted via an eligible research body. Application must be submitted online via SESAME

**Closing Date**: 26 November

**Funding**: Government
**Contributor**: Science Foundation Ireland
**No. of awards given last year**: 20
**Additional Information**: www.sfi.ie/funding/funding-calls/sirg/

### For further information contact:

**Email**:  sirg@sfi.ie

## Sciences Po

rue Saint Guillaume, F-75337 Paris, France.

**Tel**:        (33) 1 45 49 50 50
**Contact**:  Sciences Po - 27

### David Gritz Scholarship

**Purpose**: the David Gritz Scholarship is meant to attract undergraduate and graduate Israeli citizens who wish to study at Sciences Po
**Eligibility**: The scholarship is awarded every year to 1 Israeli citizen. The candidates must be admitted to an undergraduate or a masters programme or have submitted an application for admission to Sciences Po
**Level of Study**: Postgraduate
**Type**: Scholarship
**Value**: €15,000 per year
**Length of Study**: 1 year
**Country of Study**: France
**Application Procedure**: Applicants must send the forms to caterina.sabbatini@sciencespo.fr
**Closing Date**: 1 June
**Contributor**: Sciences Po Foundation
**Additional Information**: For more details contact Caterina Sabbatini-Clec'h, caterina.sabbatini@sciencespo.fr www.sciencespo.fr/students/en/finance/financial-aid/bourse-david-gritz.html

### For further information contact:

**Tel**:        (33) 1 45 49 55 46
**Email**:  lea.albrieux@sciencespo.fr

### Emile Boutmy Scholarships

**Purpose**: Sciences Po created the Emile Boutmy Scholarships after the founder of Sciences Po in order to attract the very best international students from outside of the European Union who are first time applicants and who have been admitted to an undergraduate or master's programme offered at the University
**Eligibility**: Non-EU international students. This scholarship is awarded based on factors of excellence and according to the type of profile sought for this programme. Social criteria are also taken into account
**Level of Study**: Postgraduate
**Type**: Scholarship
**Value**: From €5,000 to €10,000 for complete 2 years of the master's programme
**Length of Study**: 2 years
**Frequency**: Annual
**Country of Study**: France
**Application Procedure**: It is important to visit the official website to access the application form and for detailed information on how to apply for this scholarship. Students must indicate that they are applying for the Emile Boutmy scholarship in their Sciences Po application
**Closing Date**: 8 April
**Contributor**: Science Po Foundation
**Additional Information**: For more details, please visit official scholarship website: formation.sciences-po.fr/en/contenu/the-emile-boutmy-scholarship www.sciencespo.fr/students/en/fees-funding/financial-aid/emile-boutmy-scholarship.html

### For further information contact:

**Tel**:        (33) 1 45 49 50 82
**Email**:  isabelle.karcher@sciencespo.fr

### KSP Excellence Scholarship for Least Developed Countries

**Purpose**: The KSP Excellence Scholarship for Least Developed Countries is directed to outstanding students, covering full tuition
**Level of Study**: Postgraduate
**Type**: Scholarship
**Value**: Each recipient is awarded full tuition each year
**Frequency**: Annual
**Country of Study**: France
**Application Procedure**: To apply, please send the following materials by email to program.kuwait@sciencespo.fr with 'KSP Excellence Scholarship LDC Application' in the subject line
**Closing Date**: 10 January
**Contributor**: Sciences Po and the Kuwait Foundation for the Advancement of Sciences (KFAS)

**Additional Information**: www.opportunitiesforafricans.com/kuwait-program-at-sciences-po-ksp-excellence-scholarship-2016-for-least-developed-countries/

**For further information contact:**

**Email**: program.kuwait@sciencespo.fr

## KSP Fund for Innovative Projects

**Purpose**: The KSP Fund for Innovative Projects supports extra-curricular student-led initiatives taking place in countries of the Arab World and the Gulf Region. It is aimed at fostering innovation and providing funding for the realization of creative ideas benefiting the region in all sectors
**Level of Study**: Postgraduate
**Value**: €5,000–€10,000
**Country of Study**: Any country
**Application Procedure**: To apply, please send the following materials with 'KSP Fund for Innovative Projects' in the subject line, by email to the Kuwait Program Assistant fatima.iddahamou@sciencespo.fr
**Closing Date**: 28 February
**Additional Information**: Proposed projects must take place in a country of the Arab World or the Gulf Region. For further details, please contact Kuwait Program Assistant, Fatima Iddahamou: fatima.iddahamou@sciencespo.fr

**For further information contact:**

**Email**: kancelaria@ksplegal.pl

## KSP Joint Research Projects

**Purpose**: KSP Joint Research Projects are funded by the Kuwait Program at Sciences Po to foster research links between faculty members at Sciences Po and in Kuwait, in the interest of building a unique scholarly network
**Level of Study**: Research
**Value**: Up to €50,000
**Length of Study**: 1 year
**Country of Study**: Any country
**Application Procedure**: Application files should be sent to the Kuwait Program Manager at: mariezenaide.jolys@sciencespo.fr
**Closing Date**: 31 October
**Funding**: Foundation
**Contributor**: Sciences Po and the Kuwait Foundation for the Advancement of Sciences (KFAS)
**Additional Information**: For details, please check the website: www.sciencespo.fr/psia/kuwait-program www.cnr.it/en/joint-research-projects

**For further information contact:**

**Email**: info@itsr.ir

## KSP Mobility Grant – Spring

**Purpose**: The KSP Mobility Grant programme supports projects of Sciences Po students in countries of the Arab World and the Gulf Region with the objective of enhancing their experience in the region
**Eligibility**: Sciences Po students of all nationalities may apply. Student projects must take place in a country of the Arab World or the Gulf Region
**Level of Study**: Postgraduate, Research
**Type**: Grant
**Value**: Up to €5,000 per year
**Frequency**: Annual
**Country of Study**: Any country
**Application Procedure**: To apply, please send the following materials to the Kuwait Program Assistant, Fatima Iddahamou, at: fatima.iddahamou@sciencespo.fr with 'KSP Mobility Grant Application Spring' in the subject line
**Closing Date**: 31 October
**Additional Information**: For details, please contact Kuwait Program Assistant, Fatima Iddahamou: fatima.iddahamou@sciencespo.fr www.european-funding-guide.eu/scholarship/7175-ksp-mobility-grant

**For further information contact:**

**Email**: fatima.iddahamou@sciencespo.fr

## KSP Visiting Faculty program

**Purpose**: The KSP Visiting Faculty program offers 1-semester teaching opportunities at the Paris School in International Affairs of Sciences Po (PSIA) for leading specialists of the Arab World and the Gulf Region
**Eligibility**: This opportunity is open to both professors and practitioners, specialists of the Arab World and the Gulf Region. Individuals of all nationalities may apply
**Value**: €20,000 and travel allowance of up to €1,500
**Country of Study**: Any country
**Application Procedure**: To apply, please send the application in English to the Kuwait Program Manager by email at: mariezenaide.jolys@sciencespo.fr
**Closing Date**: 31 January
**Additional Information**: For more information, please visit the Kuwait Program website or contact the Kuwait Program Manager by email at: mariezenaide.jolys@sciencespo.fr mideast.unc.edu/kuwait-program-at-sciences-po-ksp-visiting-faculty-program-20152016/

**For further information contact:**

**Email:**   mariezenaide.jolys@sciences-po.fr

## Kuwait Excellence Scholarship for Arab students and Kuwait Nationals

**Purpose**: The KSP Excellence Scholarship for Arab students intends to support the next generation of leaders and experts coming from the Arab World and the Gulf Region who specialize in the broad field of international affairs. The current call for applications is dedicated to graduate students admitted to the Paris School of International Affairs of Sciences Po (PSIA)
**Type**: Scholarship
**Value**: 2-year masters
**Country of Study**: France
**Application Procedure**: To apply, please send the following materials by email to program.kuwait@sciencespo.fr with 'KSP Excellence Scholarship Application' in the subject line
**Closing Date**: 17 February
**Funding**: Private
**Additional Information**: www.sciencespo.fr/kuwait-program/wp-content/uploads/2018/05/Kuwait_Excellence_Scholarship_2018.pdf

## Scope

6 Market Road, London N7 9PW, United Kingdom.

**Tel:**       (44) 20 7619 7100
**Email:**     richard.parnell@scope.org.uk
**Website:**   www.scope.org.uk
**Contact:**   Mr Richard Parnell, Research & Public Policy Manager

## Charles Pick Fellowship

**Purpose**: The Charles Pick Fellowship seeks to give support to the work of a new and, as yet, unpublished writer of fictional or non-fictional prose its purpose is to give promising writers time to devote to the development of his/her talents
**Eligibility**: Applicants for the fellowship must be writers of fictional or non-fictional prose in English who have not yet published a book. (please note that for the purposes of this Fellowship non-fiction prose includes, for example, biography, memoir and travel writing. But not critical or historical monographs based on academic research). During the residential period, the fellow will be required to submit written work to a nominated mentor and take part in Creative Writing Research Seminars

**Level of Study**: Graduate
**Type**: Fellowship
**Frequency**: Annual
**Country of Study**: Any country
**Closing Date**: 31 January
**Funding**: Private
**Additional Information**: Duration of this fellowship is 6 months. The fellow will be a member of the School of Literature and Creative Writing. And it is necessary to reside at the University of East Anglia, Norwich, United Kingdom www.advance-africa.com/Charles-Pick-Fellowship.html

**For further information contact:**

**Email:**   charlespickfellowship@uea.ac.uk

## Seoul National University

1 Gwanak-ro, Gwanak-gu, Seoul 151 742, Korea.

**Tel:**       (82) 822 880 6971, 6977
**Email:**     snuadmit@snu.ac.kr
**Website:**   www.useoul.edu
**Contact:**   MBA Admissions Officer

## Korea Foundation Fellowship

**Eligibility**: Preference is given to Korean nationals residing abroad
**Level of Study**: Postdoctorate, Postgraduate, Research
**Type**: Fellowship
**Value**: To be determined by the review committee
**Length of Study**: 1 academic year
**Frequency**: Annual
**Study Establishment**: Seoul National University
**Country of Study**: Korea
**Application Procedure**: Contact the Office of international Affairs
**Closing Date**: January
**Funding**: Foundation
**Contributor**: The Korean Foundation
**Additional Information**: scholarship-positions.com/korea-foundation-fellowship-korean-language-training-program/2015/08/08/

**For further information contact:**

**Tel:**       (82) 2 880 8635
**Fax:**       (82) 2 880 8632
**Email:**     yss@snu.ac.kr

## Korea-Japan Cultural Association Scholarship

**Eligibility**: Japanese students enroled in undergraduate programs who are not in 1st-year
**Level of Study**: Postdoctorate, Postgraduate, Research
**Type**: Scholarship
**Value**: KRW 3,500,000
**Length of Study**: 1 academic year
**Frequency**: Annual
**Study Establishment**: Seoul National University
**Country of Study**: Korea
**Application Procedure**: Contact the Office of International Affairs
**Closing Date**: March
**Funding**: Foundation
**Contributor**: Korea-Japan Cultural Association
**Additional Information**: en.saitama-u.ac.jp/news/scholarship-for-privately-financed-students-in-saitama-university-japan-korea-culture-association/

### For further information contact:

The Office of International Affairs, Korea.

**Tel**:      (82) 2 880 8638
**Fax**:     (82) 2 880 8632
**Email**:   sjlim@snu.ac.kr

## Overseas Koreans Scholarship

**Purpose**: To support students with an outstanding academic record
**Eligibility**: Preference is given to Korean students with majors related to Korean studies, in particular: language, literature, medicine, education or IT, which are beneficial to the development of Korea. Overseas Korean students who wish to take graduate degrees at SNU.
**Level of Study**: Postdoctorate, Postgraduate, Research
**Type**: Scholarship
**Value**: KRW 800,000, full tuition exemption for 8 months, airfare for one economic round trip, medical insurance, Korean language training
**Length of Study**: 1 year
**Frequency**: Annual
**Application Procedure**: Contact the Overseas Korean Foundation
**Closing Date**: March
**Additional Information**: For further details, please refer to the website: www.useoul.edu/apply/under/scholarships/before-application  oia.snu.ac.kr/page/scholarships-OKS.php

### For further information contact:

Education Department, Overseas Korean Foundation, Seocho 2-dong, Seocho-gu, South Korea.

**Tel**:      (82) 64 786 0274
**Fax**:     (82) 2 3415 0118
**Email**:   scholarship@okf.or.kr

## Shastri Indo-Canadian Institute

Room 1402 Education Tower, 2500 University Drive NW Calgary, AL T2N-1N4, Canada.

**Tel**:      (1) 403 220 7467
**Email**:   sici@ucalgary.ca
**Website**: www.ucalgary.ca
**Contact**:   Programme Officer India Studies

The Shastri Indo-Canadian Institute was originally founded to promote studies in the arts, literature, culture, social sciences and the humanities. However, the Institute's mandate now incorporates a rich diversity of disciplines. Today, Shastri Indo-Canadian Institute builds knowledge and understanding between Canada and India by sponsoring academic activities.

## Shastri Indo-Canadian Institute Doctoral Research Fellowships

**Purpose**: It helps the scholars in the following ways. 1. Excursion rate return air ticket between India and Canada by the most direct route, and 2. a suitable living and accommodation allowance
**Eligibility**: 1. Candidates must able to work at least 6 months on doctoral dissertation in Canada. Preference will be given to thesis work on policies related Canada and its foreign policy. 2. Topics may include Democracy & Rule of Law, Economic Development, Environment, Managing Diversity, North American Partnership, Peace and Security, Education and Bilateral ties. Proposals in Comparative studies with substantial Canadian content. 3. To apply for SICI Doctoral Research Fellowships interested candidates must be enrolled in Doctoral program and must have successfully completed non-thesis requirements of the PhD by the time the tenure of the award commences. Proficiency in English and or French is necessary. 4. Only Indian nationals are eligible to apply
**Level of Study**: Graduate
**Type**: Fellowship
**Frequency**: Annual

**Country of Study**: Canada

**Application Procedure**: Apply online. Refer the website link. www.sici.org.in. To apply for SICI Doctoral Research Fellowships interested candidates must be enrolled in Doctoral program and must have successfully completed non-thesis requirements of the PhD by the time the tenure of the award commences

**Closing Date**: 15 October

**Funding**: Private

**Additional Information**: www.indiaeducation.net/scholarships/sici-doctoral-research-fellowships.aspx

**For further information contact:**

The Executive Centre, Level 6, Tower A, Business Bay, Airport Road, Yerwada, Pune 411006, India.

**Email**:    sciapplications@sici.org.in

## Shastri Institutional Collaborative Research Grant (SICRG)

**Purpose**: This grant is to support and encourage Institutional collaboration in R&D for a period of two years in the areas in which Institutions from SICI's Indian and Canadian Member Council can benefit. This grant intends to fill information gaps for policy makers and others influencing the policy-making process

**Eligibility**: 1. Proposed SICRG projects must involve a - bi-national research initiative in any of the fields mentioned above. 2. Faculty members/academics/researchers of Canadian and Indian member institutions are eligible to apply for this grant. 3. The applicant and co-applicant should be a full-time faculty member of a Canadian or Indian member institution. 4. The receipt of the award is a faculty from an Institution of good standing either from India or Canada who are in the Member Council of SICI. 5. Applicant must involve young faculty/research scholars/students in the proposed project.

**Level of Study**: Graduate

**Type**: Grant

**Value**: ₹1,000,000 (disbursement of grant will be in two equal installment of ₹5,000,00 each year)

**Frequency**: Annual

**Country of Study**: Any country

**Application Procedure**: Apply online at GMS portal www.sicigms.org/login

**Closing Date**: 17 December

**Funding**: Private

**Additional Information**: Contact our organisation with the following link. shastriinstitute.org/contact-us www.shastriinstitute.org/Shastri-institutional-collaborative-research-grant

**For further information contact:**

5 Bhai Vir Singh Marg, New Delhi 110001, India.

**Tel**:      (91) 11 2374 6417
**Email**:    siciapplications@sici.org.in

## Sher-Gil-Sundaram Arts Foundation

3/9, Sector 3, Shanti Niketan, New Delhi 110021, India.

**Tel**:      (91) 96813 65997
**Email**:    contact@ssaf.in
**Website**:  www.ssaf.in

## Sher-Gil Sundaram Arts Foundation: Installation Art Grant

**Purpose**: The SSAF Installation Art Grant is premised on the fact that Indian art has been energized since the 1990s by what is broadly termed installation art, but that there is, till today, limited infrastructural and institutional support for such projects

**Eligibility**: 1. Individuals of Indian origin residing in India, or collectives whose members are Indian nationals residing in India. 2. Artists who currently do not have a grant or a residency where the proposed project has been developed

**Level of Study**: Postgraduate

**Type**: Grant

**Frequency**: Annual

**Country of Study**: Any country

**Closing Date**: 28 March

**Funding**: Foundation

**Additional Information**: concoursn.com/applications-open-for-sher-gil-sundaram-arts-foundation-installation-art-grant-2019/

**For further information contact:**

**Email**:    ssaf.installationart@gmail.com

## Shorenstein Asia-Pacific Research Center (APARC)

Encina Hall, Room E301, 616 Serra Street, Stanford University, Stanford, CA 94305-6055, United States of America.

**Tel**:      (1) 650 723 9741
**Email**:    sishi@stanford.edu
**Website**:  www.aparc.stanford.edu

Shorenstein Asia-Pacific Research Center (APARC) is an important Stanford venue where faculty and students, visiting scholars and distinguished business and government leaders meet and exchange views on contemporary Asia and United States involvement in the region.

## Shorenstein Fellowships in Contemporary Asia

**Purpose**: To financially support research and writing on Asia
**Eligibility**: Open to candidates who have obtained a PhD.
**Level of Study**: Doctorate, Postdoctorate
**Type**: Fellowships
**Value**: US$54.000 + research funds
**Length of Study**: 10 months
**Frequency**: Annual
**Country of Study**: Asia
**Application Procedure**: Applicants should submit via email brief research statement (not to exceed five typed pages), which describes the research and writing to be undertaken during the fellowship period as well as the proposed publishable product; curriculum vitae and three letters of recommendation
**No. of awards offered**: 75+
**Closing Date**: 20 December
**Funding**: Private
**No. of awards given last year**: 2
**No. of applicants last year**: 75+
**Additional Information**: fundit.fr/en/calls/shorenstein-post doctoral-fellowships-contemporary-asia

### For further information contact:

**Tel**:        (1) 650 723 2408
**Email**:    shorensteinfellowships@stanford.edu

## Shuttleworth Foundation Trust

12 Plein St, Durbanville, Cape Town 7550, South Africa.

**Website**:    www.shuttleworthfoundation.org

## Feminist Criminology Graduate Research Scholarship

**Purpose**: The Division on Women and Crime of the American Society of Criminology is now accepting applications for the Feminist Criminology Graduate Research Scholarship, which is designed to recognize an exceptional graduate student in the field of gender and crime

**Level of Study**: Graduate, research
**Type**: Scholarship
**Value**: US$5,000
**Frequency**: Annual
**Country of Study**: Any country
**Application Procedure**: Winners will be notified by May. Applicants and their research projects may be based anywhere in the world. Applications must be in English
**Closing Date**: 1 April
**Contributor**: The scholarship is funded by the royalties from Feminist Criminology, an innovative journal that is dedicated to research related to women, girls, and crime within the context of a feminist critique of criminology
**Additional Information**: Feminist Criminology is published quarterly by SAGE Publications as the official journal of the Division on Women and Crime (DWC) of the American Society of Criminology. This international publication focuses on research and theory that highlights the gendered nature of crime. For more information, please visit fcx. sagepub.com/ www.praeventionstag.de/nano.cms/daily-prev ention-news/details/2721

## Sickle Cell Disease Foundation of California

5110 Woodleaf Cir 150, Los Angeles, CA 90056-1298, United States of America.

**Tel**:        (1) 323 299 3600
**Email**:    scdfc@aol.com
**Website**:    www.scdrf.org
**Contact**:    Ms Deborah Jones, Managing Director

## Single-Molecule Sensors and NanoSystems International Conference

**Purpose**: Sensor systems have emerged that exhibit extraordinary sensitivity for detecting physical, chemical, and biological entities at the micro/nanoscale. This conference will bring together researchers in the rapidly advancing field of Single Molecule Sensors and nanoSystems
**Eligibility**: The programme includes research presentations and interactive sessions of esteemed external and ColOpt speakers and a young scientist workshop with talks from rising stars
**Level of Study**: Graduate
**Type**: Grant
**Frequency**: Annual
**Country of Study**: Any country

**Application Procedure**: You could proceed with the following application link as mentioned below. www.colopt.eu/winterschool-2019

**Closing Date**: 14 January

**Funding**: Private

**Additional Information**: Micro- and nanosensors by virtue of their small interaction length probe molecules over a dynamic range often inaccessible by other techniques conferencealerts.com/show-event?id=218232

**For further information contact:**

**Email**:    s3ic2019@premc.org

## Sidney Sussex College

Cambridge University, Sidney Street, Cambridge CB2 3HU, United Kingdom.

**Tel**:        (44) 1223 338800
**Email**:     gradtutor@sid.cam.ac.uk
**Website**:  www.sid.cam.ac.uk
**Contact**:  Sidney Sussex College Tutor for Graduate Students

Founded in 1596, Sidney Sussex College admits men and women as undergraduates and graduates. The college presently has approximately 200 graduate students, including about 100 working for the PhD degree. The college has excellent sporting, dramatic and musical facilities.

### Evan Lewis-Thomas Law Studentships

**Purpose**: To support students carrying out research or taking advanced courses

**Eligibility**: There are no eligibility restrictions. Candidates must have shown proficiency in Law and Jurisprudence, normally by obtaining a university degree in Law by August, and they must be or become candidates for the PhD Degree, the Diploma in Legal Studies, the Diploma in International Law, the MPhil Degree (1 year course) in Criminology, or the LLM Degree. Students from other Cambridge Colleges may apply, but if successful they would be expected to transfer their membership to Sidney Sussex College. In the competition for the studentship, no preference will be given to candidates who nominate Sidney Sussex College as their college of first or second choice on their application form

**Level of Study**: Doctorate, Postgraduate

**Type**: Scholarship

**Value**: Up to £12,000 to match with funds administered centrally by the UCAM

**Length of Study**: 1–3 years

**Study Establishment**: The University of Cambridge

**Country of Study**: United Kingdom

**Application Procedure**: Sidney Sussex is implementing a new online application process. Please refer to the website www.sid.cam.ac.uk/postgrads/scholarships

**Closing Date**: 1 April

**Funding**: Private

**Contributor**: Sidney Sussex College

**Additional Information**: For further information contact the Tutor for Graduate Students at gradtutor@sid.cam.ac.uk www.sid.cam.ac.uk/current/postgrads/scholarships/lewisthomas

**For further information contact:**

Sidney Street, Cambridge CB2 3HU, United Kingdom.

**Tel**:        (44) 1223 338800
**Email**:     graduate.funding@admin.cam.ac.uk

### The Gledhill Research Studentship

**Purpose**: To provide full support for research leading to a PhD degree

**Eligibility**: Applicants must apply for a postgraduate place at the University of Cambridge. Students from other Cambridge colleges may apply, but if successful they would be expected to transfer their membership to Sidney Sussex College. In the competition for the studentship, no preference will be given to candidates who nominate Sidney Sussex as their college of first or second choice on their application form

**Level of Study**: Doctorate

**Type**: Studentship

**Value**: Up to £12,000 to match with funds administered centrally by the UCAM

**Length of Study**: 3 years

**Frequency**: Dependent on funds available, every 3 years

**Study Establishment**: The University of Cambridge

**Country of Study**: United Kingdom

**Application Procedure**: Sidney Sussex is implementing a new online application process. Please see the college's website www.sid.cam.ac.uk/postgrads/scholarships

**No. of awards offered**: 2

**Closing Date**: 1 April

**Funding**: Private

**Contributor**: Sidney Sussex College

**Additional Information**: For further information contact the Tutor for Graduate Students. Check website: www.sid.cam.ac.uk/current/postgrads/scholarships www.student-funding.cam.ac.uk/gledhill-research-studentship-202021

# Sievert Larsson Foundation

Box 23415, CY-1683 Nicosia, Cyprus.

**Email**: info@sievertlarssonscholarships.org
**Contact**: The Sievert Larsson Scholarship Foundation

The Sievert Larsson Scholarship Foundation's primary purpose is to facilitate the education of promising students from disadvantaged backgrounds. The Foundation will also facilitate the education of a few high calibre students that have exhibited excellence through their academic achievements.

## The Sievert Larsson Scholarship

**Purpose**: To support students who come from financially vulnerable homes and who would not otherwise have the opportunity to study in Sweden
**Level of Study**: Postgraduate
**Type**: Scholarship
**Value**: Version 1: Full tuition fee waiver (covers 100% of the tuition fees) during the 2-year programme (4 semesters). Version 2: Full tuition fee waiver (covers 100% of the tuition fees) and SEK 230,000 for costs of living during the 2-year programme (4 semesters)
**Length of Study**: 2 years
**Study Establishment**: Chalmers University of Technology
**Country of Study**: Thailand
**Application Procedure**: Applications for the Sievert Larsson Scholarship are made online via the Chalmers scholarship application form
**Closing Date**: 16 January
**Contributor**: The Sievert Larsson Foundation
**Additional Information**: www.chalmers.se/en/education/fees-finance/Pages/The-Sievert-Larsson-Scholarship.aspx

### For further information contact:

**Email**: charlotte.salmenius@chalmers.se

# Sigma Theta Tau International

550 West North Street, Indianapolis, IN 46202, United States of America.

**Tel**: (1) 888 634 7575
**Email**: research@stti.iupui.edu

**Website**: www.nursingsociety.org
**Contact**: Tonna M.Thomas, Grants Coordinator

Sigma Theta Tau International exists to promote the development, dissemination and utilization of nursing knowledge. It is committed to improving the health of people worldwide through increasing the scientific base of nursing practice. In support of this mission, the society advances nursing leadership and scholarship, and furthers the utilization of nursing research in healthcare delivery as well as in public policy.

## Sigma Theta Tau International/Association of Operating Room Nurses Foundation Grant

**Purpose**: To encourage nurses to conduct research related to perioperative nursing practice and contribute to the development of perioperative nursing science
**Eligibility**: The principal investigator should be a registered nurse with a current license in the perioperative setting and have received a Master's degree in nursing. Membership of either funding organisation is acceptable but not required
**Level of Study**: Predoctorate
**Value**: US$10,000
**Frequency**: Annual
**Country of Study**: Any country
**Application Procedure**: Applicants should submit a completed application package for the relevant institution for that year
**Closing Date**: 1 April
**Funding**: Private
**No. of awards given last year**: 1
**Additional Information**: www.sigmanursing.org/advance-elevate/research/research-grants/association-of-perioperative-registered-nurses-(aorn)-grant

### For further information contact:

Association of Operating Room Nurses, 2170 South Parker Road, Suite 300, CO 80231, United States of America.

**Tel**: (1) 800 755 2676 ext. 277
**Fax**: (1) 303 750 2927
**Email**: sbeyea@aorn.org

## Sigma Theta Tau International/Association of Perioperative Registered Nurses Foundation Grant

**Purpose**: To encourage nurses to conduct research related to perioperative nursing practice and contribute to the development of perioperative nursing science

**Eligibility**: Applicants must be a registered nurse with a current license in the perioperative setting, or a registered nurse who demonstrates interest in or significant contributions to nursing practice. The principal investigator must have, as a minimum, a Master's degree in nursing. Applicants must submit a completed Association of Perioperative Registered Nurses (AORN) research application. Membership of either organization is acceptable, but not required
**Level of Study**: Doctorate, Postdoctorate, Postgraduate, Predoctorate
**Type**: Research grant
**Value**: US$5,000. Allocation of funds is based on the quality of the research, the future promise of the applicant and the applicant's research budget
**Frequency**: Annual
**Country of Study**: Any country
**Application Procedure**: Applicants must write to the AORN for an application form and general instructions
**Closing Date**: 1 April
**Funding**: Private, Foundation
**Contributor**: The Association of Perioperative Registered Nurses and Sigma Theta Tau International
**No. of awards given last year**: 1
**Additional Information**: July is the funding month. Please check at website for more information www.sigmanursing. org/advance-elevate/research/research-grants/association-of-perioperative-registered-nurses-(aorn)-grant

### For further information contact:

Association of Perioperative Registered Nurses (AORN), 2170 South Parker Road, Suite 400, CO 80231, United States of America.

**Tel**:     (1) 800 755 2676 ext. 207
**Fax**:    (1) 303 750 2927
**Email**:  lspruce@aorn.org

### Sigma Theta Tau International/Rehabilitation Nursing Foundation Grant

**Purpose**: The Sigma Theta Tau International/Rehabilitation Nursing Foundation (RNF) Grant encourages research related to rehabilitation nursing.
**Eligibility**: The applicant must be a registered nurse in rehabilitation or a registered nurse who demonstrates interest in and significantly contributes to rehabilitation nursing. Proposals that address the clinical practice, educational or administrative dimensions of rehabilitation nursing are requested. Quantitative and qualitative research projects will be accepted for review. The principal investigator must have a Master's

degree in nursing and an ability to complete the project within 2 years of initial funding
**Level of Study**: Doctorate, Postdoctorate, Postgraduate, Predoctorate
**Type**: Research grant
**Value**: Up to US$4,500
**Length of Study**: 1 year
**Frequency**: Annual
**Country of Study**: Any country
**Application Procedure**: Applicants must write to the Rehabilitation Nursing Foundation for details
**Closing Date**: 1 March
**Funding**: Private, Foundation
**Contributor**: The Rehabilitation Nursing Foundation and Sigma Theta Tau International
**Additional Information**: The funding month is the following January    www.sigmanursing.org/advance-elevate/research/research-grants/rehabilitation-nursing-foundation-grant-(rna)

### For further information contact:

Rehabilitation Nursing Foundation, 4700 West Lake Avenue, Glenview, IL 60025, United States of America.

**Tel**:     (1) 800 229 7530
**Fax**:    (1) 847 375 4710
**Email**:  info@rehabnurse.org

## Silicon Valley Community Foundation

2440 West El Camino Real, Suite 300, Mountain View, CA 94040, United States of America.

**Tel**:     (1) 650 450 5400
**Email**:   donorservices@siliconvalleycf.org
**Website**: www.siliconvalleycf.org

### Western Digital Scholarship Program

**Purpose**: The Western Digital Scholarship Program is available for underprivileged and under-represented students who are majoring in STEM as well as the children and legal dependents of Western Digital Employees. Applicants must have a grade point average of 3.0 or higher
**Eligibility**: 1. Undergraduate student enrolled on a full-time basis at a four-year accredited University located in the countries where scholarships are being offered. 2. Majoring in Computer Science (B.S. programs only), Engineering, Mathematics or Science (excluding agricultural sciences, health and other life sciences). 3. Minimum grade average of 3.0

on a 4.0 scale or equivalent. 4. Demonstrated financial need or hardship. 5. Traditionally under-represented populations in the STEM disciplines, including females and individuals of African-American or Latino descent in the United States. 6. This award is for United States and international students

**Level of Study**: Graduate

**Type**: Scholarship

**Value**: US$5,000

**Frequency**: Annual

**Country of Study**: United States of America

**Application Procedure**: Applications are available on the Silicon Valley Community Foundation website. In addition to a completed application, the applicant must also submit the following: two letters of recommendation (the letters must be from the people listed on the application); an official transcript of grades; a personal statement addressing the topics listed on the application; evidence of financial need as described on the application; and proof of United States citizenship (photocopy of birth certificate, passport or naturalization papers). The complete application packet must be completed online by the deadline date

**No. of awards offered**: Up to 500 one-time scholarships

**Closing Date**: 2 April

**Funding**: Foundation

**Additional Information**: www.siliconvalleycf.org/scholarships/westerndigital

### For further information contact:

**Tel**:        (855) 670 ISTS (4787)

**Email**:    contactus@applyISTS.com

## Simon Fraser University

8888 University Drive, Burnaby, BC V5A 1S6, Canada.

**Tel**:        (1) 604 291 5310

**Email**:    pchhina@sfu.ca

**Website**:  www.business.sfu.ca

**Contact**:  Ms Preet Virk, Manager, Donor Relations

Named after explorer Simon Fraser, SFU opened on September 9, 1965. Taking only 30 months to grow from the idea stage into an almost-completed campus with 2,500 52 Silicon Valley Community Foundation students it was dubbed the 'Instant University'. The original campus has grown into three vibrant campuses in Burnaby, Vancouver and Surrey and SFU's reputation has grown into one of the innovative teaching, research, and community outreach.

## Natural Sciences and Engineering Research Council of Canada - Postdoctoral Fellowship Program

**Purpose**: The Postdoctoral Fellowships (PDF) Program provides support to a core of the most promising researchers at a pivotal time in their careers

**Eligibility**: Open to any graduate student in Simon Fraser University (SFU) using mathematics in their research. You can hold your fellowship at the following institutions. 1. Canadian institutions. 2. Provincial research institutions in Canada. 3. Other appropriate research laboratories in Canada. 4. Institutions and research institutions abroad

**Level of Study**: Doctorate, Graduate, Postgraduate

**Type**: Scholarship

**Value**: C$45,000

**Length of Study**: Up to 2 years

**Frequency**: Annual

**Study Establishment**: Simon Fraser University (SFU)

**Country of Study**: Canada

**Application Procedure**: You can apply for a PDF by completing and submitting form 201, and attaching supporting documents if necessary. For further information, check with the below link., www.nserc-crsng.gc.ca/students-etudiants/pd-np/pdf-bp_eng.asp#apply

**Closing Date**: 15 October

**Additional Information**: www.nserc-crsng.gc.ca/Students-Etudiants/PD-NP/PDF-BP_eng.asp

### For further information contact:

350 Albert Street, 16th Floor, Ottawa, ON K1A 1H5, Canada.

**Email**:    schol@nserc-crsng.gc.ca

## Natural Sciences and Engineering Research Council of Canada Industrial Post-Graduate Scholarships (IPS)

**Purpose**: To encourage scholars to consider research careers in industry

**Eligibility**: Open to highly qualified science and engineering graduates

**Level of Study**: Graduate

**Type**: Scholarship

**Value**: C$15,000 per year for up to 2 years plus company contribution of C$6,000 minimum per year

**Length of Study**: Up to 2 years

**Frequency**: Annual

**Country of Study**: Canada

**Application Procedure**: Check website for further details

**Additional Information**: uwaterloo.ca/graduate-studies-postdoctoral-affairs/awards/nserc-industrial-postgraduate-scholarships-ips

### For further information contact:

Office of the Dean of Graduate Studies, Canada.

**Email**: dcoburn@sfu.ca

## Winter Pilot Award

**Purpose**: The goal of the Pilot Award is to provide early support for exploratory ideas, particularly those with novel hypotheses

**Eligibility** All applicants and key collaborators must hold a PhD, MD or equivalent degree and have a faculty position or the equivalent at a college, university, medical school or other research facility

**Level of Study**: Graduate

**Type**: Award

**Value**: The total budget of a Pilot Award is US$300,000 or less

**Frequency**: Annual

**Country of Study**: Any country

**Application Procedure**: Applications must be completed electronically and submitted using forms provided at proposalCENTRAL. Please log in as an applicant, go to the "Grant Opportunities" tab, scroll to Simons Foundation and click "Apply Now" for the SFARI Pilot Award program. Application link is www.sfari.org/grant/pilot-awards-request-for-applications/

**Closing Date**: 14 September

**Funding**: Foundation

**Additional Information**: To that end, the initiative is seeking applications from individuals positioned to conduct bold, imaginative, rigorous, and relevant research www.sfari.org/grant/pilot-awards-request-for-applications/

### For further information contact:

**Email**: grants@simonsfoundation.org

## Simons Foundation

## Bridge to Independence Award Program

**Subjects**: Autism research

**Purpose**: SFARI is invested in supporting the next generation of top autism researchers. The Bridge to Independence Award program engages talented early-career scientists in autism research by facilitating their transition to research independence and providing grant funding at the start of their professorships at a U.S. or Canadian research institution.

**Eligibility**: Applicants must hold a PhD, M.D. or equivalent degree. Applicants must have fewer than six (6) years of postdoctoral or otherwise mentored training. Applicants must be currently in non-independent, mentored, training positions, as recognized by their institution. Applicants must be actively seeking a tenure-track position at a U.S. or Canadian institution of higher education during the 2020-2021 academic year. Applicants are not eligible if they are recipients of other career development awards with similar budgetary scopes as the SFARI Bridge to Independence Award. Applicants must not have accepted a formal offer for a tenure-track faculty position.

**Type**: Award

**Value**: US$495,000 over three years

**Length of Study**: Three years

**Country of Study**: United States of America or Canada

**Application Procedure**: See website.

**Closing Date**: 2 March

**Additional Information**: www.sfari.org/grant/bridge-to-independence-award-request-for-applications/

## Singapore-MIT Alliance for Research and Technology

## Singapore-MIT Alliance for Research and Technology Scholars Programme for Postdoctoral Research

**Purpose**: These awards will provide a unique opportunity for recent or soon to be PhD graduates to participate in the Singapore-MIT Alliance for Research and Technology (SMART) Centre in Singapore, and to become members of an alumni network that we anticipate will continue to evolve

**Eligibility**: The fellowship recipient would be able to conduct research of his/her own choice in Singapore within, but not necessarily tied closely to, a current project in one of the SMART Interdisciplinary Research Groups

**Level of Study**: Research

**Type**: Research grant

**Value**: US$120,000 per year

**Frequency**: Annual

**Country of Study**: Any country

**Closing Date**: 12 April

**Funding**: Private

**Additional Information**: For further information on the research grant, check the website link. smart.mit.edu/fellowships/for-post-doctoral-smart-scholars www.mladiinfo.eu/2019/03/06/smart-scholars-programme-postdoctoral-research/

**For further information contact:**

**Email:**     smart_scholar@smart.mit.edu

## Sir Richard Stapley Educational Trust

PO Box 839, Richmond, Surrey TW9 3AL, United Kingdom.

**Email:**     admin@stapleytrust.org
**Website:**     www.stapleytrust.org
**Contact:**     The Administrator

The Sir Richard Stapley Educational Trust awards grants to graduates studying for higher degrees in the United Kingdom without subject restriction, and to graduates studying medicine as a second degree. The grants are to cover shortfall incurred by the payment of tuition fees.

### Sir Richard Stapley Educational Trust Grants

**Purpose**: To support postgraduate study
**Eligibility**: Open to graduates holding a First Class (Honours) degree or a good Second Class (Honours) degree (65% or above, or its overseas equivalent, or a Masters or PhD) and who are more than 24 years of age on October 1st of the proposed academic year. Students in receipt of a substantial award from local authorities, the NHS Executive, Industry, Research Councils, the British Academy or other similar public bodies will not normally receive a grant from the Trust. Courses not eligible include electives, diplomas, placements, professional training and intercalated degrees. The Trust does not support students for full-time PhD studies beyond year 3, or part-time PhD studies beyond year 6. Applicants must already be resident in the United Kingdom at the time of application
**Level of Study**: Postgraduate
**Type**: Grant
**Value**: £500 and £1,500
**Length of Study**: Grants are awarded for 1 full academic year in the first instance
**Frequency**: Annual
**Study Establishment**: Any appropriate University
**Country of Study**: United Kingdom
**Application Procedure**: Electronic applications are available in early January. The trust will consider either the first 300 complete applications or all applications received on or before deadline
**No. of awards offered**: 300
**Closing Date**: 29 February
**Funding**: Trusts

**No. of awards given last year**: 133
**No. of applicants last year**: 300
**Additional Information**: Please check at www.stapleytrust.org/wp/about www.birmingham.ac.uk/postgraduate/funding/The-Sir-Richard-Stapley-Educational-Trust.aspx

## Sir William Lister/Dorey Bequest

18 Stephenson Way, London NW1 2HD, United Kingdom.

### Sir William Lister/Dorey Bequest

**Purpose**: To provide personal travel expenses to members and Fellows of the Royal College of Ophthalmologists who are travelling abroad for research or training
**Eligibility**: Ophthalmologists in training who are citizens of the United Kingdom as well as Members and Fellows of the RCOphth in good standing. Applications are invited for the Sir William Lister and Dorey Bequest Travel Awards
**Level of Study**: Postgraduate
**Type**: Grant
**Value**: £300 – £600
**Frequency**: Annual
**Country of Study**: Any country
**Application Procedure**: 1. Successful applicants will submit a report to the Education Committee on completion of the period of training or research for which the award is granted. 2. The number and value of the awards will be determined by the state of the funds and the candidate's requirement
**Closing Date**: 28 September
**Funding**: Private
**Additional Information**: www.eyedocs.co.uk/ophthalmology-travel-awards/1110-dorey-bequest-and-sir-william-lister-travel-awards

**For further information contact:**

**Email:**     vanna.fadda@rcophth.ac.uk

## Smeal College of Business

### Edward & Susan Wilson Graduate Scholarship in Business

**Subjects**: Business
**Purpose**: The purpose of this program is to identify and honor full-time graduate students enrolled or planning to enroll in Smeal College of Business.

**Eligibility**: Consideration for this scholarship shall be given to all full-time graduate students who are currently enrolled or are planning to enroll in Smeal College of Business and have achieved superior academic standing.

**Type**: Scholarship

**Value**: The amount of the awards will depend on the performance of the endowment.

**Study Establishment**: Smeal College of Business, The Pennsylvania State University

**Country of Study**: United States of America

**Application Procedure**: Nominations should be made by the Department Chair (attach copy of transcript and resume) and send to Hans Baumgartner, 483-A Business Building.

**Closing Date**: 1 May

## Jeanne and Charles Rider Graduate Fellowship

**Subjects**: Business

**Purpose**: The purpose of this fellowship shall be to recognize and support outstanding graduate students enrolled or planning to enroll in The Smeal College of Business

**Eligibility**: Selection is based on academic merit.

**Type**: Fellowship

**Value**: To be determined

**Length of Study**: One academic year and may be renewed for subsequent years providing the recipient continues to meet the conditions of eligibility and funds are available.

**Study Establishment**: Smeal College of Business, The Pennsylvania State University

**Country of Study**: United States of America

**Application Procedure**: Nominations should be made by Department Chair to Hans Baumgartner, PhD Director. Recipient shall be selected by the Graduate Fellowship Committee.

**No. of awards offered**: To be determined

**Closing Date**: 1 May

## Ossian R. MacKenzie Teaching Award

**Subjects**: Business Administration

**Purpose**: The purpose of this program is to identify and honor an exceptional doctoral candidate who demonstrates a high degree of promise toward making significant teaching contributions in business administration.

**Eligibility**: Be an exceptional doctoral candidate with demonstrable experience working towards a career teaching business administration.

**Type**: Award

**Value**: The amount of each award shall be determined by a selection committee and shall depend upon the amount of income earned by the Ossian R. MacKenzie Doctoral Award Fund.

**Length of Study**: One academic year

**Frequency**: Annual

**Study Establishment**: Smeal College of Business, The Pennsylvania State University

**Country of Study**: United States of America

**Application Procedure**: To nominate a graduate student, faculty are encouraged to send their letters of recommendation to 351 Business Building.

**Closing Date**: 1 May

## Peter E. Liberti and Judy D. Olian Scholarship

**Subjects**: Business

**Purpose**: The purpose of this scholarship shall be to provide recognition and financial assistance to outstanding PhD students enrolled or planning to enroll in The Smeal College of Business.

**Eligibility**: Selection is based on superior academic records or who manifest promise of outstanding academic success.

**Type**: Scholarship

**Value**: To be determined.

**Length of Study**: One academic year and may be renewed for subsequent years providing the recipient continues to meet the conditions of eligibility and funds are available.

**Frequency**: Annual

**Study Establishment**: Smeal College of Business, The Pennsylvania State University

**Country of Study**: United States of America

**Application Procedure**: Nominations should be made by Department Chair to Hans Baumgartner, PhD Director. Recipient shall be selected by the Graduate Fellowship Committee.

**No. of awards offered**: Two

**Closing Date**: 1 May

## Smithsonian Environmental Research Center (SERC)

Smithsonian Institution, PO Box 28, 647 Contees Wharf Road, Edgewater, MD 21037-0028, United States of America.

| | |
|---|---|
| **Tel:** | (1) 443 482 2217 |
| **Email:** | gustafsond@si.edu |
| **Website:** | serc.si.edu/fellowships |
| **Contact:** | Daniel E Gustafson, Jr, Professional Training & Volunteer Coordinator |

Smithsonian Environmental Research Center (SERC) is the world's leading research center for environmental studies of the coastal zone. For over 40 years, SERC has been involved in critical research, professional training for young scientists and environmental education.

## Smithsonian Environmental Research Center Graduate Student Fellowship

**Subjects**: Global climate change, marine invasion biology, forest and wetland ecology, trace element and nutrient cycling, solar UV radiation, water quality, food web dynamics, coastal and upland ecosystems, and plant-herbivore interactions.
**Purpose**: To financially support student research at Smithsonian facilities or research stations.
**Eligibility**: Students must be formally enroled in a graduate program of study at a degree granting institution must have completed at least one full-time semester. Intended for students who have not yet been advanced to candidacy if in a doctoral program.
**Level of Study**: Graduate
**Type**: Fellowship
**Value**: US$6,500
**Length of Study**: 10 weeks
**Frequency**: Annual
**Country of Study**: Any country
**Application Procedure**: Need to use Smithsonian online academic appointment system.
**Closing Date**: 1 November
**Funding**: Smithsonian Instution
**No. of awards given last year**: 3
**No. of applicants last year**: 6
**Additional Information**: serc.si.edu/fellowships

### For further information contact:

solaa.si.edu/solaa/#/public.

**Tel**:   (1) 443 482 2217

## Smithsonian Institution-National Air and Space Museum

PO Box 37012, MRC 010, Washington, DC 20013-7012, United States of America.

**Tel**:       (1) 202 633 2648
**Email**:     NASM-Fellowships@si.edu
**Website**:   www.airandspace.si.edu
**Contact**:   Ms Collette Williams, Fellowships Programme Coordinator

## Charles A Lindbergh Chair in Aerospace History

**Eligibility**: Open to senior scholars with distinguished records of publication who are at work on, or anticipate being at work on, books in aerospace history
**Type**: Fellowship
**Value**: Replacement of salary and benefits up to a maximum of US$100,000 a year. Research expenses and relocation are negotiable
**Length of Study**: 12 months
**Closing Date**: 15 January
**Additional Information**: For more information, please contact David DeVorkin DeVorkinD@si.edu airandspace.si.edu/support/get-involved/fellowships/charles-lindbergh-chair-aerospace-history

### For further information contact:

**Email**:   PisanoD@si.edu

## The Aviation Space Writers Foundation Award

**Purpose**: The product created as a result of the grant must be in any form suitable for potential public dissemination in print, electronic, broadcast, or other visual medium, including, but not limited to, a book manuscript, video, film script, or monograph. Potential topics might be contemporary aviation or space events that are of interest to the general public; significant persons, historical events, or trends that illuminate the history of human flight in air and space; records; or compendia of aerospace source material.
**Type**: Grant
**Value**: US$5,000
**Frequency**: Every 2 years
**Application Procedure**: Candidates should submit the online Aviation Space Writers Foundation Award Application form, including 1. a maximum two-page, single-spaced proposal stating the subject of their research and their research goals; 2. a one to two-page curriculum vitae; and 3. a one-page detailed budget explaining how the grant will be spent
**Closing Date**: 15 January
**Additional Information**: Award winners are required to provide a summary report in the form of a memorandum to Ms Collette Williams that outlines how the grant was used to accomplish the goals of the project airandspace.si.edu/support/get-involved/fellowships/aviation-space-writers-foundation-award

### For further information contact:

National Air and Space Museum, Independence Ave at Sixth Street, SW, Rm 3313, MRC 312, P.O. Box 37012, Washington, DC 20013-7012, United States of America.

# Smithsonian National Air and Space Museum

**Website**: airandspace.si.edu/
**Contact**: Miss Collette Williams

## A. Verville Fellowship

**Purpose**: To pursue programs of research and writing professional in tone and substance, but addressed to an audience with broad interests
**Value**: US$55,000 per year
**Length of Study**: 9 months to 1 year
**Country of Study**: United States of America
**Application Procedure**: All applications for the Verville Fellowships must be submitted electronically through the Smithsonian Online Academic Appointment System (SOLAA)
**Closing Date**: 1 November
**Additional Information**: For any further queries, please contact NASM-Fellowships@si.edu airandspace.si.edu/support/get-involved/fellowships/verville

### For further information contact:

**Email**: NASM-Fellowships@si.edu

## Charles A. Lindbergh Chair in Aerospace History

**Purpose**: The Charles A. Lindbergh Chair in Aerospace History is a competitive 12-month fellowship open 15 October, to senior scholars with distinguished records of publication who are at work on, or anticipate being at work on, books in aerospace history
**Eligibility**: The Lindbergh Chair is open to established and recognized senior scholars with distinguished records of publication who are at work on, or anticipate being at work on, books in aerospace history
**Value**: US$100,000 per year
**Length of Study**: 1 year
**Frequency**: Annual
**Country of Study**: United States of America
**Application Procedure**: All applications for the Lindbergh Fellowships must be submitted electronically through the Smithsonian Online Academic Appointment System (SOLAA)
**Closing Date**: 15 January
**Funding**: Private
**Additional Information**: For more information, please contact Layne Karafantis in the Aeronautics Department karafantisl@si.edu airandspace.si.edu/support/get-involved/fellowships/charles-lindbergh-chair-aerospace-history

### For further information contact:

**Tel**: (1) 202 633 2648
**Email**: kinneyj@si.edu, neufeldm@si.edu

## Engen Conservation

**Purpose**: This fellowship is intended to contribute to the education of recent graduates by allowing them to continue research into traditional historic objects and delve into the complexities of working with modern composite materials
**Eligibility**: Must have master's degree in conservation from a recognized programme and be able to conduct research independently
**Value**: US$43,000 per year in addition to US$3,000 for medical insurance
**Length of Study**: 1 year
**Country of Study**: United States of America
**Application Procedure**: Applications are submitted through the Smithsonian Online Academic Appointment System (SOLAA)
**Closing Date**: 15 February
**Additional Information**: For further queries, please contact CollumM@si.edu airandspace.si.edu/collections/conservation/fellowships

### For further information contact:

**Email**: HorelickL@si.edu

## Guggenheim Fellowships

**Purpose**: To pursue programs of research and writing that support publication of works that are scholarly in tone and substance and intended for publication as articles in peer-reviewed journals or in book form from a reputable publisher (in the case of post postdoctoral applicants) or in a doctoral dissertation (in the case of pre-docs)
**Level of Study**: Doctorate, Postdoctorate
**Value**: US$30,000 for predoctoral candidates and US$45,000 for postdoctoral candidates
**Length of Study**: 1 year
**Country of Study**: United States of America
**Application Procedure**: All applications for the Guggenheim, Verville and Lindbergh Fellowships must be submitted electronically through the Smithsonian Online Academic Appointment System (SOLAA)
**Closing Date**: 15 January

**Additional Information**: If you have any further questions, please contact NASM-Fellowships@si.edu www.gf.org/applicants/

### For further information contact:

John Simon Guggenheim Memorial Foundation, 90 Park Avenue, New York, NY 10016, United States of America.

## National Air and Space Museum

**Purpose**: To support research on aerospace topics
**Value**: US$5,000
**Frequency**: Every 2 years
**Country of Study**: United States of America
**Closing Date**: 15 January
**Additional Information**: airandspace.si.edu/visit

### For further information contact:

Aeronautics Department, MRC 312, National Air and Space Museum, Smithsonian Institution, Washington, DC 20013-7012, United States of America.

**Tel**:      (1) 202 633 2214
**Email**:    karafantisl@si.edu

## Smithsonian Tropical Research Institution (STRI)

Roosvelt Avenue, Tupper Building 401, Balboa, Ancón, Panamá, República de Panamá, Washington, DC 20521-9100, United States of America.

**Tel**:      (1) 507 212 8000
**Email**:    fellows@si.edu
**Website**:   www.stri.org

The Smithsonian Tropical Research Institution (STRI) in Panama is a bureau of the Smithsonian Institution based outside of the United States and it is dedicated to understanding biological diversity. STRI's facilities provide a unique opportunity for long-term ecological studies in the tropics, and are used extensively by some 900 visiting scientists from academic and research institutions in the United States and around the world every year. STRI aims to offer research facilities that allow staff scientists, fellows, and visiting scientists to achieve their research objectives. STRI's Center for Tropical Forest Science uses large, fully enumerated forest plots to monitor tree demography in 14 countries located in

Africa, Asia and the Americas. More than 3,000,000 individual trees representing 6,000 species are being studied.

## STRI Postdoctoral Research in Hydrology

**Eligibility**: Open to applicants with a PhD in spatial analysis applied to soils or hydrology, hands-on programming skills, fluency in English and Spanish
**Level of Study**: Postdoctorate
**Type**: Research grant
**Value**: Minimum salary of US$40,000
**Length of Study**: 2 years
**Frequency**: Annual
**Application Procedure**: Applicants should send an electronic copy of the current curriculum vitae, statement of research accomplishments and goals, names and contact information of three references, and reprints to Helmut Elsenbeer. Review of applications begins by July 15th
**Additional Information**: stri.si.edu/academic-programs/fellowships

### For further information contact:

**Email**:    ElsenbeerH@si.edu

## STRI Tropical Forest/Restoration Ecologist

**Purpose**: To support a long-term study to understand the ecosystem services provided by forests within the Panama Canal Watershed
**Eligibility**: Open to applicants with a PhD in forestry, forest ecology, restoration ecology, or a closely related field, a proven ability to develop research programs and publish in scientific journals, ability to work well in teams, and preferred with Spanish language skills
**Level of Study**: Doctorate
**Value**: US$40,000 per year
**Frequency**: Annual
**Application Procedure**: Applicants should send a letter detailing qualifications and interest in the position, curriculum vitae, and contact information for three references to Adriana Sautu. For questions related to the position, please contact Jefferson Hall (hallje@si.edu)
**Closing Date**: 1 August
**Additional Information**: The successful candidate will work in a multidisciplinary team to design landscape treatments and the vegetation monitoring program for focal research catchments. She will synthesize data from the Native Species Reforestation Project (PRORENA) growth trials to inform species selection for native species reforestation treatments and for publication. The Research Fellow will be expected to

develop his/her own research program in association with this project

**For further information contact:**

**Email**: sautua@si.edu

## Social Science Research Council (SSRC)

One Pierrepont Plaza, 15th Floor, 300 Cadman Plaza West, Brooklyn, NY 11201, United States of America.

**Tel**: (1) 212 377 2700
**Email**: info@ssrc.org
**Website**: www.ssrc.org
**Contact**: Director

Founded in 1923, the Social Science Research Council (SSRC) is an independent, non-governmental, non-profit international association devoted to the advancement of inter-disciplinary research in the social sciences. The aim of the organization is to improve the quality of publicly available knowledge around the world.

### African Peacebuilding Network (APN) Residential Postdoctoral Fellowship Program

**Purpose**: To support independent African research and its integration into regional and global policy communities
**Eligibility**: Applicants must be African citizens currently residing in an African country. Researchers based in conflict-affected African countries or those recently emerging from conflict are especially encouraged to apply. Applicants must hold a faculty or research position at an African university and have completed their PhD within 7 years of the application deadline
**Level of Study**: Research
**Type**: Fellowships
**Value**: A maximum of US$20,000
**Frequency**: Annual
**Application Procedure**: All applications must be uploaded through our online portal. For enquiries or technical questions pertaining to the portal, please contact APN staff (apn@ssrc.org)
**Closing Date**: December
**Additional Information**: If you have questions, please contact APN program staff by telephone at (1) 212 377 2700 or by email at apn@ssrc.org www.ssrc.org/programs/compo nent/apn/residential-postdoctoral-fellowships/

**For further information contact:**

**Email**: apn@ssrc.org

### Berlin Program Fellowship

**Purpose**: To support doctoral dissertation research as well as postdoctoral research leading to the completion of a monograph
**Eligibility**: Applicants for a dissertation fellowship must be full-time graduate students who have completed all coursework required for the PhD and must have achieved ABD status by the time the proposed research stay in Berlin begins. Also eligible are United States of America and Canadian PhD's who have received their doctorates within the past two calendar years
**Level of Study**: Postdoctorate
**Value**: €1,100 per month for dissertation fellows, €1,400 per month for postdoctoral fellows
**Length of Study**: 10 months–1 year
**Frequency**: Annual
**Study Establishment**: Freie Universität Berlin
**Country of Study**: Germany
**Closing Date**: 25 March
**Additional Information**: grad.uchicago.edu/fellowship/ berlin-program-for-advanced-german-and-european-studies-fellowship/

**For further information contact:**

Berlin Program for Advanced German and European Studies, Freie Universität Berlin, Kaiserswerther Str. 16-18, 14195 Berlin, Germany.

**Tel**: (49) 30 838 56671
**Fax**: (49) 30 838 56672
**Email**: bprogram@zedat.fu-berlin.de

### ESRC/SSRC Collaborative Visiting Fellowships

**Purpose**: To encourage communication and cooperation between social scientists in Great Britain and the Americas
**Eligibility**: Open to PhD scholars in the Americas, ESRC-supported centres, and holders of large grants awards or professorial fellowships in Britain
**Level of Study**: Doctorate, Research
**Type**: Fellowship
**Value**: Up to US$9,500
**Length of Study**: 1–3 months
**Frequency**: Annual
**Application Procedure**: Check website for further details
**Closing Date**: 16 April

**Additional Information**: www.scholarshipsinindia.com/esrc-ssrc.html

**For further information contact:**

**Email**:  international@esrc.ac.uk

## Eurasia Program Fellowships

**Purpose**: To allow advanced graduate students to devote to the intellectual development of their projects and to write-up the results of their research

**Eligibility**: Applicants for Dissertation Write-up Fellowships must have attained ABD status (must have completed all requirements for the PhD degree except for the dissertation) by the fellowship start date. They must be citizens or permanent residents of the United States of America. The Fellow's home institution is expected to make a cost-sharing contribution of no less than 10% of the fellowship award. Detailed information on eligibility criteria and conditions of awards will be available in the application materials

**Level of Study**: Doctorate, Graduate

**Type**: Fellowship

**Value**: Up to US$25,000

**Length of Study**: Up to 1 year

**Frequency**: Annual

**Application Procedure**: Awards are made on the basis of evaluations and recommendations by the Title VIII Program Committee, an interdisciplinary committee composed of scholars of the region. The committee rewards proposals with clarity of argument, purpose, theory and method, written in a style accessible to readers outside the applicant's discipline. Applicants must submit a completed application, a narrative statement, transcripts, a course list and language evaluation form, and references. Full information is available online

**No. of awards offered**: Approx. 40

**Funding**: Government

**Contributor**: United States Department of State under the Program for Research and Training on Eastern Europe and the Independent States of the Former Soviet Union (Title VIII)

**No. of awards given last year**: 4

**No. of applicants last year**: Approx. 40

**Additional Information**: No funding is available for research on the Baltic States www.youthop.com/fellowships/fully-funded-osf-eurasia-programme-fellowships-2019-2020-at-the-university-of-tartu-in-estonia

**For further information contact:**

**Email**:  eurasia@ssrc.org

## Japan Society for the Promotion of Science (JSPS) Fellowship

**Purpose**: To provide qualified researchers with the opportunity to conduct research at leading universities and other research institutions in Japan

**Eligibility**: Applicants must be United States citizens or permanent residents at the time of application and submit proof of affiliation with an eligible host research institution in Japan as part of the application packet. Permanent residents must provide a copy of a permanent resident card. Citizens of other countries are eligible for the short-term fellowship (1–12 months) if they have completed a Master's or PhD course at an institution of higher education in the United States and, upon completing the course, have for at least three continuous years conducted high-level research at a university in the United States. Applicants for long-term (12–24 months) fellowships must submit a copy of a PhD diploma dated no more than 6 years prior to applying. Check website for further details

**Level of Study**: Doctorate, Postdoctorate, Research

**Type**: Fellowship

**Value**: Round-trip airfare, insurance coverage for accidents and illness, a monthly stipend and settling-in allowance. Applicants will also be eligible for additional funds annually for research expenses for stays of 1–2 years and a domestic travel allowance for stays of 3–12 months

**Length of Study**: 1 month to 2 years

**Frequency**: Annual

**Study Establishment**: An approved institution

**Country of Study**: Japan

**Application Procedure**: Applications are available on www.ssrc.org/fellowships/jsps-fellowships

**No. of awards offered**: 25–40

**Closing Date**: 1 December

**Funding**: Government

**Contributor**: The Japan Society for the Promotion of Science

**No. of awards given last year**: 10–20

**No. of applicants last year**: 25–40

**Additional Information**: Fellows are selected by the Japan Society for the Promotion of Science based on nominations made by the SSRC Japan Advisory Board. Applicants will be notified of their nomination status by the following March. Successful applicants will be notified directly by JSPS in the summer www.ssrc.org/fellowships/view/jsps-fellowship/

**For further information contact:**

**Tel**:      (1) 212 377 2700

**Email**:  japan@ssrc.org

## Mellon Mays Predoctoral Research Grants

**Purpose**: The Graduate Initiatives Program offers three predoctoral grant opportunities: the Graduate Studies Enhancement Grant (GSE), the Predoctoral Research Development Grant (PRD), and the Dissertation Completion Grant (DCG)

**Eligibility**: Applicants must be a Mellon fellow enroled in a doctoral program. Applicants must have been selected as Mellon Mays Fellows as undergraduates. Fellows may apply for one grant per year and must be enroled in a doctoral program in one of the fields listed in the website or have filed a petition for inclusion of another field

**Type**: grant

**Value**: Total of US$5,000 in GSE and PRD funds; DCG grant money is not applied towards this total

**Country of Study**: Any country

**Application Procedure**: Applicants should use the online application portal to apply. For detailed information, please visit: www.ssrc.org/fellowships/mellon-mays-predoctoral-research-grants/

**No. of awards offered**: 1

**Closing Date**: 1 November

**Additional Information**: If accepted, grants take 5–6 weeks to process www.ssrc.org/fellowships/view/mellon-mays-predoctoral-research-grants/

## Social Science Research Council Abe Fellowship Program

**Purpose**: To encourage international multidisciplinary research on topics of pressing global concern and to foster the development of a new generation of researchers who are interested in policy-relevant topics of long-range importance and who are willing to become key members of a bilateral and global research network built around such topics

**Eligibility**: Open to citizens of Japan and the United States of and to other nationals who can demonstrate serious and long-term affiliations with research communities in Japan or the United States. Applicants must hold a PhD or have attained an equivalent level of professional experience. Applications from researchers in non-academic professions are welcome

**Level of Study**: Postdoctorate

**Type**: Fellowship

**Value**: Research and travel expenses as necessary for the completion of the research project in addition to limited salary replacement

**Length of Study**: Up to 1 year

**Frequency**: Annual

**Study Establishment**: An appropriate institution

**Country of Study**: United States of America

**Application Procedure**: Applicants must submit an online application along with a writing sample, letter of reference and an optional language evaluation form

**No. of awards offered**: 60–100

**Closing Date**: 1 September

**Funding**: Foundation

**Contributor**: The Japan Foundation Center for Global Partnership

**No. of awards given last year**: 14

**No. of applicants last year**: 60–100

**Additional Information**: In addition to working on their research projects, Fellows will attend annual conferences and other events sponsored by the program, which will promote the development of an international network of scholars concerned with research on contemporary policy issues. Funds are provided by the Japan Foundation Center for Global Partnership www.jpf.go.jp/cgp/e/fellow/abe/index.html

### For further information contact:

Japan Foundation Center for Global Partnership, 4-16-3 Yotsuya, Shinjuku-ku Tokyo 160-0004, Japan.

**Tel**:    (81) 3 5369 6085
**Fax**:    (81) 3 5369 6142
**Email**:    abe@ssrc.org

## Social Science Research Council Eurasia Program Postdoctoral Fellowships

**Purpose**: To support research and/or publication records and to further the recipients academic career

**Eligibility**: Applicants for Postdoctoral Fellowships must have the PhD in hand at the time of application (ABDs will not be considered), and must have received the degree no more than 5 years prior to the application deadline. They must be citizens or permanent residents of the United States of America. Detailed information on eligibility criteria and conditions of awards will be in the application materials

**Level of Study**: Doctorate, postdoctorate

**Type**: Fellowship

**Value**: Up to US$20,000

**Length of Study**: 18–24 months

**Frequency**: Annual

**Application Procedure**: Awards are made on the basis of evaluations and recommendations by the Title III Program Committee, an interdisciplinary committee and composed of scholars of the region. The committee rewards proposals with clarity of argument, purpose, theory, and method, written in a style accessible to readers outside the applicant's discipline.

Applicants must submit a completed application, a narrative statement, a curriculum vitae and references. Full information is available online

**No. of awards offered**: Approx. 30

**Closing Date**: 13 November

**Funding**: Government

**Contributor**: United States Department of State under the Program for Research and Training on Eastern Europe and the Independent States of the Former Soviet Union (Title VIII)

**No. of awards given last year**: Approx. 3

**No. of applicants last year**: Approx. 30

**Additional Information**: No funding is available for research on the Baltic States www.ssrc.org/programs/view/eurasia-program/

**For further information contact:**

**Email**:    eurasia@ssrc.org

## Social Science Research Council Eurasia Program Predissertation Training Fellowships

**Purpose**: To provide graduate students with the opportunity to enhance their research skills in the field of Eurasian Studies

**Eligibility**: Applicants for Predissertation Training Fellowships must be enrolled in a doctoral programme in the social sciences or humanities or equivalent degree, but not yet advanced to the PhD candidacy. ABD's are not eligible for these fellowships. They must be citizens or permanent residents of the United States of America. Detailed information on eligibility criteria and conditions of awards will be available in the application materials

**Level of Study**: Doctorate, Graduate

**Type**: Fellowship

**Value**: Up to US$7,000

**Length of Study**: Up to 9 months

**Frequency**: Annual

**Country of Study**: United States of America

**Application Procedure**: Awards are made on the basis of evaluations and recommendations by the Title VIII Program Committee, an interdisciplinary committee composed of scholars of the region. The committee rewards proposals with clarity of argument, purpose, theory, and method, written in a style accessible to readers outside the applicant's discipline. Applicants must submit a completed application, a narrative statement, transcripts, a course list and language evaluation form and references. Full information is available online

**No. of awards offered**: Approx. 20

**Closing Date**: 13 November

**Funding**: Government

**Contributor**: United States Department of State under the Program for Research and Training on Eastern Europe and the Independent States of the Former Soviet Union (Title VIII)

**No. of awards given last year**: 2

**No. of applicants last year**: Approx. 20

**Additional Information**: No funding is available for research on the Baltic States www.ssrc.org/programs/view/eurasia-program/

**For further information contact:**

**Email**:    eurasia@ssrc.org

## Social Science Research Council Eurasia Program Teaching Fellowships

**Purpose**: To encourage and support faculty members at all career levels in their efforts to impart their own knowledge and expertise to their students

**Eligibility**: Applicants for the Teaching Fellowships must have the PhD in hand and currently be teaching full-time in an accredited United States of America university, and the must be citizens or permanent residents of the United States of America. The home institution of the teaching fellowship recipient is expected to provide a letter of intent stating that the institution or relevant department intends to support the implementation of the Fellow's new course into the offered curriculum at least once within a period of no more than 2 years. Detailed information on eligibility criteria and conditions of awards will be available in the application materials

**Level of Study**: Postdoctorate

**Type**: Fellowship

**Value**: US$10,000

**Length of Study**: Maximum 2 years

**Frequency**: Annual

**Country of Study**: United States of America

**Application Procedure**: Awards are made on the basis of evaluations and recommendations by the Title III Programme Committee, an interdisciplinary committee and composed of scholars of the region. The committee rewards proposals with clarity of argument, purpose, theory, and method, written in a style accessible to readers outside the applicant's discipline. Applicants must submit a completed application, a narrative statement, a curriculum vitae and references. Full information is available online

**No. of awards offered**: 15

**Closing Date**: 1 November

**Funding**: Government

**Contributor**: United States Department of State (Title VIII)

**No. of awards given last year**: 3

**No. of applicants last year**: 15

**Additional Information**: www.ssrc.org/programs/view/eurasia-program/

**For further information contact:**

**Email**: eurasia@ssrc.org

## Social Science Research Council International Dissertation Research Fellowship

**Purpose**: To support distinguished graduate students in the humanities and social sciences conducting dissertation research outside the United States

**Eligibility**: Open to full-time graduate students in the humanities and social sciences regardless of citizenship enroled in doctoral programs in the United States. Applicants must complete all PhD requirements except on-site research by the time the fellowship begins

**Level of Study**: Doctorate

**Type**: Fellowship

**Value**: Approx. US$20,000

**Length of Study**: 9–12 months

**Frequency**: Annual

**Application Procedure**: Applications are available on SSRC website

**Closing Date**: 3 November

**Funding**: Private

**Contributor**: The Andrew W Mellon Foundation

**Additional Information**: Applicants must contact the programme for further information by emailing www.ssrc.org/fellowships/view/idrf-fellowship/

**For further information contact:**

**Email**: idrf@ssrc.org

## Social Science Research Council Summer Institute on International Migration

**Purpose**: To enable attendance at a workshop/conference training young scholars in the field of migration studies

**Eligibility**: Open to advanced doctoral candidates currently involved in research or writing for their dissertations and recent PhDs revising their dissertations for publication or initiating new research

**Level of Study**: Postdoctorate, Postgraduate, Predoctorate

**Type**: Award

**Value**: Flights, meals and lodging necessary for participation in the institute are fully subsidized

**Length of Study**: 1 Week

**Frequency**: Dependent on funds available

**Study Establishment**: The University of California at Irvine

**Country of Study**: United States of America

**Application Procedure**: Applicants must download the application form from the website www.cri.uci.edu

**No. of awards offered**: 250

**Closing Date**: 18 February

**Funding**: Private

**Contributor**: UCT and SSRC

**No. of awards given last year**: 20

**No. of applicants last year**: 250

**Additional Information**: The Institute is a collaboration between the SSRC and the Center for Research on Immigration, Population and Public Policy (CRI) at the University of California, Irvine www.ssrc.org/programs/view/migration-program/

**For further information contact:**

Center for Research on International Migration, United States of America.

**Tel**: (1) 949 824 1361

**Email**: cbramle@uci.edu

## SSRC/ACLS Eastern European Program Dissertation Fellowships

**Purpose**: To fund dissertation research

**Eligibility**: Open to United States citizens or permanent legal residents

**Level of Study**: Postgraduate

**Type**: Varies

**Value**: Up to US$15,000 plus expenses

**Length of Study**: 1 academic year

**Frequency**: Annual, if funds are available

**Study Establishment**: Any university or institution

**Country of Study**: Other

**Application Procedure**: Applicants must contact the American Council of Learned Societies (ACLS) for further information

**Closing Date**: November

**Additional Information**: The product of the proposed work must be disseminated in English www.ssrc.org/programs/view/eurasia-program/

**For further information contact:**

ACLS Office of Fellowships & Grants, 228 East 45th Street, New York, NY 10017, United States of America.

**Tel**: (1) 212 377 2700

**Email**: grants@acls.org

## Social Sciences and Humanities Research Council of Canada (SSHRC)

350 Albert Street, PO Box 1610, Ottawa, ON K1P 6G4, Canada.

**Tel**:        (1) 613 995 2694
**Email**:      award@sshrc-crsh.gc.ca
**Website**:    www.sshrc-crsh.gc.ca

The Social Sciences and Humanities Research Council of Canada (SSHRC) is the federal agency responsible for promoting and supporting research and research training in the social sciences and humanities in Canada. SSHRC supports research on the economic, political, social and cultural dimensions of the human experience.

## Aid to Scholarly Journals

**Purpose**: To promote the sharing of research results by assisting the publication of individual works that make an important contribution to the advancement of knowledge
**Eligibility**: Applicants must consult the Canadian Federation for the Humanities and Social Sciences website for eligibility requirements
**Level of Study**: Postdoctorate, Research
**Type**: Grant
**Value**: Up to US$30,000 per year
**Length of Study**: 3 years
**Frequency**: Annual
**Application Procedure**: Applicants must refer to the website or email the Humanities and Social Sciences Federation of Canada
**Closing Date**: 2 June
**Funding**: Government
**Additional Information**: The program is administered on behalf of SSHRC by the Humanities and Social Sciences Federation of Canada www.sshrc-crsh.gc.ca/news_room-salle_de_presse/latest_news-nouvelles_recentes/2018/aid_to_scholarly_journals-aide_aux_revues_savantes-eng.aspx

### For further information contact:

The Humanities and Social Sciences Federation of Canada, 151 Slater Street, Ottawa, ON, Canada.

**Tel**:        (1) 613 238 6112 ext 350
**Email**:      scholarlyjournals@sshrc-crsh.gc.ca

## Canadian Forest Service Graduate Supplements

**Purpose**: To promote Canadian doctoral research into forestry, to encourage the use of Canadian Forest Service (CFS) centres and to increase contacts between CFS researchers and Canadian universities
**Eligibility**: Open to SSHRC Doctoral Fellows who are conducting research in an area related to forestry in Canada and who are in the 3rd or 4th year of their programme. Candidates must have at least one CFS scientist on their supervisory committee and must carry out all or part of their research at a CFS forestry centre
**Level of Study**: Doctorate, Predoctorate, Research
**Type**: Supplement or Fellowship
**Value**: C$5,000 supplement to the C$20,000 doctoral fellowship
**Length of Study**: Up to 2 years
**Frequency**: Annual
**Application Procedure**: Applicants must visit the website
**Funding**: Government, Foundation
**Contributor**: The Canadian Forest Service

### For further information contact:

Canadian Forest Service Graduate Supplements, Science Branch, Natural Resources Canada, 580 Booth Street, Ottawa, ON K1A 0E4, Canada.

**Tel**:        (1) 613 947 8992
**Fax**:        (1) 613 947 9090
**Email**:      mlamarch@nrcan.gc.ca

## Canadian Tobacco Control Research Initiative Planning Grants

**Purpose**: To support investigators in developing strong proposals for grants in tobacco control research
**Eligibility**: Open to experts in programme and policy development as well as researchers
**Level of Study**: Research
**Type**: Grant
**Value**: Up to C$30,000
**Length of Study**: Up to 1 year
**Frequency**: Dependent on funds available
**Country of Study**: Canada
**Application Procedure**: Applicants must complete an application form available with instructions on the National Cancer Institute of Canada website www.ncic.cancer.ca
**Closing Date**: 1 March
**Funding**: Government, Private
**No. of awards given last year**: 6

**Additional Information**: www.idrc.ca/en/funding

### For further information contact:

Research Programs Department National Cancer Institute of Canada (NCIC) 10 Alcorn Avenue Suite 200, Toronto, ON, Canada.

**Tel**:      (1) 416 961 7223
**Email**:   mwosnick@cancer.ca

## Society for Academic Emergency Medicine Foundation

### Education Research Grant

**Subjects**: Emergency medicine
**Purpose**: The SAEMF Education Research Grant strives to foster innovation in teaching, education, and educational research in emergency medicine for faculty-, fellow-, resident- and medical student-level learners. The mission of the grant is to develop the academic potential of the selected fellow by providing support for a dedicated two-year training period, including pursuit and preferably completion of an advanced degree in education.
**Eligibility**: An applicant for the Education Research Grant must: Be a member of SAEM in good standing at application deadline and during the entire award period. Be board eligible or certified by the American Board of Emergency Medicine or American Board of Osteopathic Emergency Medicine and practicing in an emergency care setting. Senior/final year residents (3rd or 4th year, as applicable to the applicant's residency program) in good standing to graduate from an ACGME accredited emergency medicine residency program may also apply but must complete their residency program before the start of the award period. Not have completed more than one year of an education fellowship at the start of the award period. Not have received an Education Research Grant (formerly Education Fellowship grant) previously. Express and, if possible, provide evidence of a commitment to leadership in emergency medicine education in his/her current or prior work, or show potential for serving as a future leader in emergency medicine education. Demonstrate a sustained interest in and commitment to emergency medicine education and an education career. This demonstrated commitment may include previous participation in educational activities related to emergency medicine or another field, peer-reviewed publications, current or previous educational research, presentations of educational scholarly activity at scientific meetings, and engagement in local, regional, national and international activities focused on research and emergency medicine-focused education. Applicants will be judged and scored according to their expressed and demonstrated commitment to these areas. Greater consideration and potentially higher scores will be given to applicants who can demonstrate this commitment. Demonstrate evidence of involvement in SAEM activities and functions. Demonstrated involvement includes number of years as a member of SAEM and participation in SAEM activities and functions (e.g., SAEM presentations and committee membership). Applicants will be judged and scored according to their expressed and demonstrated commitment to SAEM. Greater consideration and potentially higher scores will be given to applicants who can demonstrate this commitment.
**Type**: Grant
**Value**: Up to US$50,000 per year for two years
**Length of Study**: Two years
**Frequency**: Annual
**Country of Study**: Any country
**Closing Date**: 1 August
**Additional Information**: www.saem.org/saem-foundation/grants/funding-opportunities/what-we-fund/education-fellowship-grant

### Research Training Grant

**Subjects**: Emergency medicine
**Purpose**: The SAEM Foundation, in partnership with SAEM, provides grants to national and international universities and medical schools to help fund innovative research and education initiatives in the field of emergency medicine. The SAEMF Research Training Grant is intended to provide funding to support the development of a scientist in emergency medicine.
**Eligibility**: Applicants should: Be a member of SAEM in good standing at application deadline and during the entire award period. Have an advanced/doctoral or terminal educational degree (e.g., MD, DO, PhD, PharmD, DSc or equivalent). Hold a university appointment (e.g., faculty, fellow, or similar) in or be actively involved (e.g., have an adjunct appointment) with a department or division of emergency medicine or pediatric emergency medicine at the start of the Research Training Grant award period. Emergency medicine residents in their final year of residency may apply for the Research Training Grant, subject to the same stipulation of holding a university appointment at the start of the Research Training Grant award period. The applicant may work as a clinician at an institution other than the host institution or the institution at which the project will be conducted. Not have previously received a SAEMF Research Training Grant, an Emergency Medicine Foundation (EMF) Research

Fellowship grant or other EMF grant with similar purpose as the SAEMF Research Training Grant, a federally funded individual career development award (K-series or VA CDA), or a similar research training grant from another entity, prior to the start of the Research Training Grant period. If an applicant has received funding for an institutional training grant (K12, KL2 or similar), he/she should provide a detailed description of the currently funded project and any similarities or overlap with the SAEMF application.

**Type**: Grant

**Value**: The Research Training Grant will provide a total of up to US$150,000 per year for two years, contingent on the availability of funds from the SAEMF. The SAEMF Research Training Grant funds only may be used for the applicant's salary. Fringe benefits are permissible in addition to salary, but the total of salary and fringe benefits may not exceed US$150,000 per year for two years. No additional costs, such as project costs, tuition, travel, and indirect costs, are supported by SAEMF; any other costs are the responsibility of the fellow's host institution or another group specified in the application.

**Length of Study**: Two years

**Frequency**: Annual

**Country of Study**: Any country

**Additional Information**: www.saem.org/saem-foundation/grants/funding-opportunities/what-we-fund/research-training-grant

## Society for Promotion of Roman Studies

Roman Society, Room 252, South Block, Senate House, Malet Street, London WC1E 7HU, United Kingdom.

**Tel**:           (44) 20 7862 8727
**Email**:        office@romansociety.org
**Website**:      www.romansociety.org
**Contact**:      Dr Fiona Haarer, Secretary of Society

The Society for the Promotion of Roman Studies aims to promote the study of history, architecture, archaeology, language, literature and the art of Italy and the Roman Empire, including Roman Britain, from the earliest times to about 700 AD.

### Hugh Last Fund and General Fund

**Purpose**: To assist in the undertaking, completion, or publication of works relating to the general scholarly purposes of the Roman Society, excluding expenses in connection with archaeological projects. The Hugh Last Fund also excludes travelling, hotel, conference, or other living expenses of scholars

**Level of Study**: Graduate, Postdoctorate, Postgraduate, Research

**Type**: Funding support

**Value**: Varies £100–1,000

**Frequency**: Annual

**Country of Study**: Any country

**Application Procedure**: Applications should be made using the application form – the completed application should not exceed two sides of A4. Applicants should give a concise and clear outline of the project, including publication plans if relevant, and itemise the costs requested. They must declare any other applications being made for the same project. Completed applications should be sent to the Secretary by email: office@romansociety.org

**Closing Date**: 31 January

**Additional Information**: Individuals may not make more than one application in any year www.romansociety.org/Grants-Prizes/Hugh-Last-Fund-General-Fund

## Society for the Arts in Religious and Theological Studies (SARTS)

United Theological Seminary of the Twin Cities, 3000 5th Street NW, New Brighton, MN 55112, United States of America.

**Tel**:           (1) 651 255 6117, 651 255 6190
**Email**:        wyates@unitedseminary-mn.org
**Website**:      www.artsmag.org
**Contact**:      Wilson Yates

The Society for the Arts in Religious and Theological Studies (SARTS) was organized to provide a forum for scholars and artists interested in the intersections between theology, religion and the arts to share thoughts, challenge ideas, strategize approaches in the classroom and to advance the discipline in theological and religious studies.

### Luce Fellowships

**Purpose**: To enhance and expand the conversation on theology and art

**Eligibility**: Open to candidates teaching theology as a faculty member at an accredited postsecondary educational institution or graduate students

**Level of Study**: Graduate, Research
**Type**: Fellowships
**Value**: Awards are up to US$3,000 each
**Length of Study**: 1 year
**Frequency**: Annual
**Application Procedure**: Applicants must submit an information sheet, curriculum vitae, a project abstract, a formal proposal, a budget and 2 letters of recommendation
**Closing Date**: 20 February
**Additional Information**: ahf.usc.edu/fellowships/luce/

### For further information contact:

University of St Thomas, Mail JRC 153 2115 Summit Avenue, MN 55105, United States of America.

**Email**:    office@societyarts.org

## Society for the Psychological Study of Social Issues (SPSSI)

SPSSI Central Office, 208 I Street NE, Washington, DC 20002-4340, United States of America.

**Tel**:          (1) 202 675 6956
**Email**:      spssi@spssi.org
**Website**:   www.spssi.org
**Contact**:   Alex Ingrams, Administrative Assistant

The Society for the Psychological Study of Social Issues (SPSSI) is an interdisciplinary, international organization of over 3,000 social scientists who share an interest in research on the psychological aspects of important social issues. The Society's goals are to increase the understanding of social issues through research and its dissemination and to support policy efforts consistent with such research.

## Society for the Psychological Study of Social Issues Grants-in-Aid Program

**Purpose**: To support scientific research in social problem areas related to the basic interests and goals of SPSSI
**Eligibility**: Applicant must be a member of SPSSI. Applicants may submit only one application per deadline. If applied to the Clara Mayo Grant in the same award year he/she is not eligible for GIA. Individuals may submit a joint application
**Level of Study**: Doctorate, Graduate, Postdoctorate, Postgraduate
**Type**: Grant

**Value**: Up to US$2,000 for postdoctoral work and up to US$1,000 for graduate student research that must be matched by the student's university
**Country of Study**: Any country
**Application Procedure**: The Application should include: 1. A cover sheet with the applicant's name, address, phone number, email address and title of the proposal. 2. An abstract of 100 words or less summarizing the proposed research. 3. Project purposes, theoretical rationale, and research methodology and analytical procedures to be employed. 4. Relevance of research to SPSSI goals and Grants-in-Aid criteria. 5. Status of human subjects review process (which must be satisfactorily completed before grant funds can be forwarded). 6. Curriculum vitae of investigator (a faculty sponsor's recommendation must be provided if the investigator is a graduate student; support is seldom awarded to students who have not yet reached the dissertation stage). 7. Specific amount requested, including a budget. For co-authored submissions, please indicate only one name and institution to which a check should be jointly issued if selected for funding
**No. of awards offered**: Approx. 18
**Closing Date**: 15 October
**Funding**: Private
**Contributor**: The Sophie and Shirley Cohen Memorial Fund and membership contributions
**No. of awards given last year**: Approx. 10
**No. of applicants last year**: Approx. 18
**Additional Information**: Late applications may be held until the next deadline. Proposals for highly timely and event-oriented research may be submitted at any time during the year to be reviewed within 1 month of receipt on an ad hoc basis. If yours is a time-sensitive application, please indicate that on the outside of the envelope www.apa.org/about/awards/gia-program

### For further information contact:

**Email**:    awards@spssi.org

## The Clara Mayo Grants

**Purpose**: The Clara Mayo Grant program was set up to support masters' theses or pre-dissertation research on aspects of sexism, racism, or prejudice, with preference given to students enrolled in a terminal master's program.
**Eligibility**: Individuals who are SPSSI members and who have matriculated in graduate programs in psychology, applied social science, and related disciplines. A student who is applying for a Grants-In-Aids may not apply for the Clara Mayo award in the same award year. Applicants may submit only one Clara Mayo grant application per calendar year.

**Type**: Grant
**Value**: US$1,000
**Country of Study**: Any country
**No. of awards offered**: 6
**Closing Date**: 10 December
**Funding**: Private
**Additional Information**: www.spssi.org/index.cfm?fuseaction=page.viewpage&pageid=727

### For further information contact:

**Email**:    awards@spssi.org.

## Society for the Scientific Study of Sexuality (SSSS)

881 Third Street, Suite B-5, Whitehall, PA 18052, United States of America.

**Tel**:    (1) 610 443 3100
**Email**:    thesociety@sexscience.org
**Website**:    www.sexscience.org
**Contact**:    Mr David L Fleming, Executive Director

The Society for the Scientific Study of Sexuality (SSSS) is an international organization dedicated to the advancement of knowledge about sexuality. The Society brings together an interdisciplinary group of professionals who believe in the importance of both production of quality research and the clinical, educational and social applications of research related to all aspects of sexuality.

### Society for the Scientific Study of Sexuality Student Research Grants

**Purpose**: The purpose of the research can be a master's thesis or doctoral dissertation, but this is not a requirement
**Eligibility**: Applicants must be a member of the SSSS
**Level of Study**: Doctorate, Postgraduate
**Type**: Scholarship
**Value**: US$1,000
**Length of Study**: 1 year
**Frequency**: Annual
**Application Procedure**: Contact the society or check website for details
**Closing Date**: 1 August
**Funding**: Foundation
**Contributor**: The Foundation for the Scientific study of sexuality

**Additional Information**: phd.northeastern.edu/opportunity/society-for-the-scientific-study-of-sexuality-ssss-graduate-research-grant/

### For further information contact:

**Email**:    mlpeters@sexscience.org

## Society of Apothecaries of London

Black Friars Lane, London, EC4V 6EJ, United Kingdom.

**Tel**:    (44) 20 7236 1189
**Email**:    clerk@apothecaries.org
**Website**:    www.apothecaries.org
**Contact**:    Wallington Smith, Clerk

### Gillson Scholarship in Pathology

**Purpose**: To encourage original research in any branch of pathology
**Eligibility**: Open to candidates under 35 years of age who are either licenciates or freemen of the Society, or who will obtain the licence or the freedom within 6 months of election to the scholarship
**Level of Study**: Postgraduate
**Type**: Scholarship
**Value**: £1,800 in total. Payments are made twice annually for the duration of the scholarship
**Length of Study**: 3 years, renewable for a second term of 3 years
**Frequency**: Every 3 years
**Country of Study**: Any country
**Application Procedure**: Applicants must submit two testimonials and present evidence of their attainments and capabilities as shown by any papers already published, and a detailed record of any pathological work already done. Candidates should also state where the research will be undertaken
**Closing Date**: 1 December
**Funding**: Private
**Additional Information**: Preference is given to the candidate who is engaged in the teaching of medical science or in its research. Scholars are required to submit an interim report at the end of the first 6 months of tenure, and a complete report 1 month prior to the end of the 3rd year. Any published results should also be submitted to the Society

### For further information contact:

**Email**:    admin@scholarship-positions.com

# Society of Architectural Historians (SAH)

1365 North Astor Street, Chicago, IL 60610, United States of America.

| | |
|---|---|
| **Tel**: | (1) 312 573 1365 |
| **Email**: | info@sah.org |
| **Website**: | www.sah.org |

SAH is an international not-for-profit membership organization that promotes the study and preservation of the built environment worldwide. The society serves scholars, professionals in allied fields and the interested general public.

## American Council of Learned Societies Digital Extension Grants

**Purpose**: ACLS invites applications for ACLS Digital Extension Grants, made possible by the generous assistance of The Andrew W. Mellon Foundation. This program supports digitally based research projects in all disciplines of the humanities and related social sciences. It is hoped that these grants will advance humanistic scholarship by enhancing established digital projects and extending their reach to new communities of users

**Eligibility**: The project must be hosted by an institution of higher education in the United States. The project's principal investigator must be a scholar in a field of the humanities and the; humanistic social sciences. The principal investigator must have a PhD degree conferred prior to the application; deadline. (An established scholar who can demonstrate the equivalent of the PhD in; publications and professional experience may also qualify.)

**Level of Study**: Graduate

**Type**: Grant

**Length of Study**: 12 – 18 months

**Frequency**: Annual

**Country of Study**: Any country

**Application Procedure**: 1. Applicants must list current and past funding sources for their projects; in the case of joint funding sources for the project. 2. Applicants should indicate clearly in their budget plans how each source of project funding will be used during the ACLS grant period. 3. Awards provide funding of up to US$150,000 for project costs. A portion of grant funds must go towards collaborations with new project partners who could benefit from access to the infrastructure at the project's host site or from substantive participation in the development of the project. 4. Grants may be used to cover salary replacement, staffing, equipment, and other costs. 5. Tenure: 12–18 months, to be initiated between 1 July and 31 December

**Closing Date**: 31 December

**Funding**: Private

**Additional Information**: www.acls.org/programs/digital extension/

### For further information contact:

**Email**:     fellowships@acls.org

## Edilia and François-Auguste de Montequin Fellowship in Iberian and Latin American Architecture

**Purpose**: To fund travel for research into Spanish, Portuguese and Ibero American architecture

**Eligibility**: Open to SAH members who are junior Scholars, including graduate students

**Level of Study**: Doctorate, Postdoctorate, Postgraduate

**Type**: Fellowship

**Value**: US$2,000 for junior scholars awarded each year and US$6,000 for senior scholars offered every 2 years

**Country of Study**: Any country

**Application Procedure**: Applicants must complete an application form, available on request by writing to SAH for guidelines or visiting the SAH website

**No. of awards offered**: 5

**Closing Date**: 16 October

**Funding**: Private

**No. of awards given last year**: 1

**No. of applicants last year**: 5

**Additional Information**: eahn.org/2017/08/fellowship-edilia-and-francois-auguste-de-montequin-fellowship/

### For further information contact:

**Email**:     vnelson@unm.edu

## Sally Kress Tompkins Fellowship

**Purpose**: To enable an architectural history student to work as an intern on an Historic American Buildings Survey project, during the summer

**Eligibility**: Open to architectural history and historic preservation students

**Level of Study**: Doctorate, Postdoctorate, Postgraduate

**Type**: Fellowship

**Value**: US$10,000

**Length of Study**: 12 weeks

**Frequency**: Annual

**Country of Study**: United States of America

**Application Procedure**: Applicants must submit an application including a sample of work, a letter of recommendation from a faculty member, and a United States Government Standard Form 171, available from HABS or most United States government personnel offices. Applications should be sent to the Sally Kress Tompkins Fellowship. Applicants not selected for the Tomkins Fellowship will be considered for other HABS Summer employment opportunities. For more information, please contact Lisa P. Davidson, HABS/HAER Co-ordinator

**Closing Date**: 31 December

**Funding**: Government

**No. of awards given last year**: 1

**Additional Information**: researchfunding.duke.edu/sally-kress-tompkins-fellowship

### For further information contact:

The Sally Kress Tompkins Fellowship, c/o HABS/HAER, National Park Service, 1201 Eye Street, 7th floor NW, Washington, DC 20005, United States of America.

**Tel**:        (1) 202 354 2179
**Fax**:       (1) 202 371 6473
**Email**:   lisa.davidson@nps.gov

## Society of Naval Architects and Marine Engineers

### John W. Davies Scholarship

**Subjects**: Marine transportation, development of offshore resources, eco-systems interaction with development of Arctic/cold ocean resources, climate change impact in marine cold regions, or special areas of research for Arctic/cold ocean environments.

**Purpose**: The competition is open to any full time graduate student at a recognized University in Canada or the US State of Alaska whose research will assist in providing solutions to problems encountered in the Arctic or in cold ocean environments.

**Eligibility**: The competition is open to any full time graduate student at a recognized University in Canada or the US State of Alaska

**Type**: Scholarship

**Value**: C$3,000

**Study Establishment**: Any recognized University in Canada or the US State of Alaska

**Country of Study**: United States of America or Canada

**Application Procedure**: An abstract of approximately 500 words is to be submitted explaining the objectives of the research being undertaken, progress to date, and how this research is to be applied in the Arctic or to cold ocean environments. Applicants are also encouraged to describe how their research is placed within the context of broader Arctic issues. In addition, the selection panel will require a resume, a transcript of marks, sent by the university directly to the Awards Committee (for the most recent degree completed and degree in progress), and three letters of reference, two of which being former or current professors, to be sent by the referees directly to the Awards Committee.

**Closing Date**: 26 June

**Additional Information**: www.sname.org/arcticsection/home

## Society of Women Engineers (SWE)

203 N. La Salle Street, Suite 1675, Chicago, IL 60601, United States of America.

**Tel**:          (1) 877 793 4636
**Email**:     hq@swe.org
**Website**:  www.swe.org
**Contact**:   Ms Karen Horting, Executive Director

The Society of Women Engineers (SWE) was founded in 1950, and is a non-profit educational service organization. SWE is the driving force that establishes engineering as a highly desirable career aspiration for women. SWE empowers women to succeed and advance in those aspirations and be recognized for their life-changing contributions and achievements as engineers and leaders.

### Society of Women Engineers Past Presidents Scholarships

**Eligibility**: Open only to women majoring in engineering or computer science in a college or university with an ABET accredited programme. United States of America citizenship is required

**Level of Study**: Doctorate, Graduate, Postgraduate

**Type**: Scholarship

**Value**: US$2,000

**Frequency**: Annual

**Country of Study**: United States of America

**Application Procedure**: Application forms are available from the website

**Closing Date**: 1 February

**Funding**: Private

**No. of awards given last year**: 2

**Additional Information**: www.collegexpress.com/scholar ships/swe-past-presidents-scholarship/5002472/

## For further information contact:

**Email**: hg@swe.org

## Södertörn University

SE-141 89 Huddinge, Sweden.

**Contact**: Södertörn University Registrator

Södertörn University is a public university located in Flemingsberg, which is located in Huddinge Municipality, and the larger area called Södertörn, in Stockholm County, Sweden. In 2013, it had about 13,000 full-time students.

## Södertörn University Tuition Fee Waive

**Purpose**: Södertörn University is offering tuition fee waiver for pursuing master's programme studies
**Eligibility**: Students who have applied for a one or two-year Master's programme at Södertörn University may submit an application for a tuition fee waiver
**Level of Study**: Postgraduate
**Length of Study**: 1 to 2 years
**Country of Study**: Sweden
**Application Procedure**: Send the application form along with necessary supporting documents to the following email address: registrator@sh.se
**Closing Date**: 10 March
**Additional Information**: scholarship-fellowship.com/sodertorn-university-tuition-fee-waiver/

## For further information contact:

**Email**: studentservice@sh.se

## Soil and Water Conservation Society (SWCS)

945 SW Ankeny Road, Ankeny, IA 50023, United States of America.

**Tel**:       (1) 515 289 2331
**Email**:    swcs@swcs.org
**Website**:  www.swcs.org

The Soil and Water Conservation Society (SWCS) fosters the science and the art of soil, water and related natural resource management to achieve sustainability. The SWCS promotes and practices an ethic recognizing the interdependence of people and the environment.

## The Kenneth E. Grant Scholarship

**Purpose**: To actively promote multi-disciplinary research
**Eligibility**: An applicant for the research scholarship must: be a member of SWCS for at least 1 year by the scholarship due date, as recognized by headquarters; have demonstrated integrity, ability, and competence to complete the specified study topic; be eligible for graduate work at an accredited institution; and show reasonable need for financial assistance
**Level of Study**: Postgraduate
**Type**: Scholarship
**Value**: US$1,300
**Length of Study**: 1 year
**Frequency**: Annual
**Application Procedure**: The scholarship application can be filled out and submitted electronically at swcs.formstack.com/forms/2015_kenneth_e_grant_research_scholarship_application
**Closing Date**: 12 February
**Additional Information**: www.unigo.com/scholarships/by-major/science-scholarships/kenneth-e-grant-research-scholarship/1965

## For further information contact:

**Email**:    awards@swcs.org

## South African Association of Women Graduates (SAAWG)

SAAWG NATIONAL OFFICE, Suite 329, Rondebosch, 7701, South Africa

**Tel**:       (27) 11 883 4847
**Email**:    medwards@netactive.co.za
**Website**:  www.ifuw.org/southafrica
**Contact**:  Miss Margaret Edwards, National President

The South African Association of Women Graduates (SAAWG) promotes the tertiary education of women and their self-development over their life span. It seeks and facilitates equity for women graduates, cross-cultural insights and co-operation and societal advancement. Its great underlying purpose is world peace, brought about through education and international friendship. SAAWG is affiliated to the International Federation of University Women (IFUW) and is a member of the Federation of University Women of Africa (FUWA).

## Hansi Pollak Scholarship

**Purpose**: To assist postgraduate study or research devoted to the practical purpose of ameliorating social conditions in South Africa
**Eligibility**: Open to South African women graduates of all races who are, or have become, members of the Association
**Level of Study**: Doctorate, Postgraduate
**Type**: Scholarship
**Value**: ZAR 6,000 paid in 6-month installments
**Length of Study**: 2 years, non-renewable
**Frequency**: Every 2 years
**Study Establishment**: Any recognized university
**Country of Study**: Any country
**Application Procedure**: Applicants must write for application forms
**No. of awards offered**: 50
**Closing Date**: 25 March
**Funding**: Private
**No. of awards given last year**: 1
**No. of applicants last year**: 50
**Additional Information**: Fellows must spend at least 2 years in South Africa after completing a Master's or doctoral degree, in order to put into practice the results of the research www.instrumentl.com/grants/south-african-association-of-women-graduates-hansi-pollak-fellowship

### For further information contact:

Post Suite 329, Private Bax X18, South Africa.

**Email**: hbowen@telkomsa.net

## Isie Smuts Research Award

**Purpose**: To assist postgraduate women in research
**Eligibility**: 1. For a female applicant undertaking postgraduate studies/research in any field. 2. Applicants must be studying in South African Universities or Universities of Technology. 3. There is option for renewal of scholarship.
**Level of Study**: Postgraduate
**Type**: Award
**Value**: Rand 1,300
**Frequency**: Annual
**Study Establishment**: Any university

**Country of Study**: South Africa
**Application Procedure**: Applicants must write to Miss V Henley
**Closing Date**: 25 March
**Funding**: Private
**No. of awards given last year**: 1
**Additional Information**: www.instrumentl.com/grants/south-african-association-of-women-graduates-isie-smuts-award

### For further information contact:

**Email**: fellowships@saawg.org

## South African Association of Women Graduates International Fellowship

**Purpose**: To assist women, who wish to study in South Africa
**Eligibility**: Open to members of the International Federation of University Women, foreign students enrolled at a South African university for at least one year for postgraduate research
**Level of Study**: Postgraduate
**Type**: Fellowship
**Value**: At least ZAR 1,000
**Length of Study**: Not less than 6 months
**Frequency**: Every 3 years
**Study Establishment**: A university
**Country of Study**: South Africa
**Application Procedure**: Applicants must write for application forms
**Closing Date**: 25 March
**Funding**: Private
**Additional Information**: The award is made when a suitable applicant applies www.saawg.org/Bursaries.html

### For further information contact:

**Email**: fellowships@saawg.org

## South African Council for English Education (SACEE)

Post Net Suite 141, Private Bag X0001, IFAFI, N. W. Province 0260, South Africa.

| | |
|---|---|
| **Tel**: | (27) 12 259 1429 |
| **Email**: | sacee12@telkomsa.net |
| **Website**: | www.sacee.org.za |
| **Contact**: | Ms Patricia Bootland, Administrative Secretary |

The South African Council for English Education's (SACEE) mission statement is to support the teaching, learning and appreciation of English. They have branches throughout South Africa, and major national projects are the English Alive publication, English Olympiad, language challenge and plays festival.

## South African Council for English Education's EX-PCE Bursary

**Purpose**: To assist teachers in service who wish to improve their qualifications and to assist those who wish to take up postgraduate study specializing in the English language
**Eligibility**: Applicants who are not normally resident in the Pretoria area will not be considered for an award. Such applications will not be acknowledged
**Level of Study**: Postgraduate
**Type**: Bursary
**Value**: Varies, depending upon type of course taken
**Length of Study**: Varies
**Frequency**: Annual
**Study Establishment**: Any academic institution
**Country of Study**: South Africa
**Application Procedure**: An application form must be completed. Interview by a local (Pretoria) selection committee may be required. Application can be sent through post, fax or email
**No. of awards offered**: 3
**Closing Date**: 31 July
**Funding**: Private
**No. of awards given last year**: 1
**No. of applicants last year**: 3
**Additional Information**: sastudy.co.za/article/south-african-council-for-english-education-ex-pce-bursary/

### For further information contact:

**Email**:     sacee@iburst.co.za

## South African Institute of International Affairs (SAIIA)

Jan Smuts House, PO Box 31596, Johannesburg, Braamfontein 2017, South Africa.

**Tel**:          (27) 11 339 2021
**Email**:        info@saiia.org.za
**Website**:      www.saiia.org.za
**Contact**:      Mr Jonathan Stead, Director of Operations

The South African Institute of International Affairs (SAIIA) is an independent, non-governmental foreign policy think tank, whose purpose is to encourage wider and more informed interest in international affairs and public education and to focus on policy-relevant research.

## South African Institute of International Affairs Konrad Adenauer Foundation Research Internship

**Purpose**: To enable research interns to enrol at the University of Witwatersrand for a Master's degree by coursework while simultaneously working at SAIIA
**Eligibility**: Open to South African citizens under 30 years of age
**Level of Study**: Postgraduate
**Type**: Internship
**Value**: Full bursary for tuition fees and a monthly stipend to cover living costs and accommodation
**Length of Study**: 10 months
**Frequency**: Annual
**Study Establishment**: SAIIA and the University of Witwatersrand
**Country of Study**: South Africa
**Application Procedure**: Applicants must send a curriculum vitae, names and contact details of three referees, letter of motivation, outline of research interests in the field of international relations, three written references, June results and academic transcripts of previous degree and one example of written work not exceeding 3,000 words on a topic of choice
**No. of awards offered**: 32
**Closing Date**: 8 October
**Funding**: Foundation
**Contributor**: Konrad Adenauer Foundation
**No. of awards given last year**: 2
**No. of applicants last year**: 32
**Additional Information**: www.kas.de/en/web/suedafrika/kas-stipendienprogramm-in-suedafrika1

### For further information contact:

**Email**:     grobbelaarn@saiia.wits.ac.za

## Southern African-Nordic Center (SANORD)

SANORD Central Office, University of the Western Cape, Private Bag x17, Bellville, ZA 7535, South Africa.

**Website**:     www.sanord.net/

The Southern African-Nordic Centre is a non-profit membership organization of institutions of higher education and research for all Nordic countries and southern Africa.

## Brain O'Connell (BOC) Partial Scholarship

**Purpose**: SANORD is making available partial scholarship opportunities for students from the Southern Africa institutions of higher education and research
**Eligibility**: Enrolled for mainly Master's degrees at a SANORD member, Southern African institution. Must be willing to enhance their knowledge in order to make a contribution toward the development of Southern Africa. The applicant must liaise with the SANORD Coordinator at the host university and provide a written communication of acceptance from a host university
**Level of Study**: Postgraduate
**Length of Study**: Successful students will be required to spend 3 to 5 months at a Nordic (Norway, Sweden, Finland, Iceland or Denmark) SANORD member institution in order to engage in activities that will support the completion of the students' Master's degree
**Country of Study**: Any country
**Application Procedure**: Please check website for more details
**Closing Date**: 15 August
**Additional Information**: www.opportunitiesforafricans. com/brian-o-connell-boc-scholarship-programme-2019/

### For further information contact:

**Email**:    sanordcentraloffice@gmail.com

## Southern Cross University

Graduate Research College, PO Box 157, Lismore, NSW 2480, Australia.

**Tel**:        (61) 2 6620 3705
**Email**:    jrussell@scu.edu.au
**Website**:  www.scu.edu.au
**Contact**:  Mr John Russell, Administrative Officer

Southern Cross University is one of Australia's most modern, creative and innovative universities founded on traditions of academic excellence, with national and international industry links. The University's courses emphasize real-world skills and vocational training, and are designed to give graduates a competitive edge in today's demanding employment market.

## Master of Business Administration Programme

**Length of Study**: Please contact the Organisation
**Application Procedure**: Applicants must complete the application form, supply evidence of any previous academic qualifications, as well as a curriculum vitae and a letter of support from your employer
**Closing Date**: 30 November

### For further information contact:

**Tel**:      (61) 2 6620 3876
**Fax**:      (61) 2 6620 3227
**Email**:    intoff@scu.edu.au

## Space Environment Research Centre (SERC)

Brisbane St Lucia, QLD 4072, Australia.

**Tel**:        (61) 7 3365 1111
**Contact**:  The University of Queensland

## Space Environment Research Centre Scholarships

**Purpose**: The CRC for Space Environment Management (SEMCRC), managed by the Space Environment Research Centre (SERC) has been established to build on Australian and international expertise. Students can receive additional support and opportunities provided by the Space Environment Research Centre. Successful scholarship candidates will also have the opportunity to apply for exciting short-term placements in space research centres internationally and within Australia
**Eligibility**: Consideration of all candidates will be given based on academic merit, relevance of studies to SERC objectives and potential for long-term contribution to research outcomes. Priority is given to students with first class honours (or equivalent) from participating countries, currently Australia, Japan and the United States of America
**Level of Study**: Graduate, Postgraduate
**Country of Study**: Australia
**Application Procedure**: To apply please visit: serc.org.au/ students
**Closing Date**: 31 December
**Additional Information**: The applicant is or will be enrolled in academic studies at a reputable Australian University. In the case of an international applicant, the applicant is required to have a valid passport, appropriate visa and may not be from

a country subject to Trade Controls www.scholarshipsads. com/space-environment-research-centre-scholarships-internat ional-students-australia-2017/

**For further information contact:**

**Email**:   admissions@gradschool.uq.edu.au

---

# Spencer Foundation

875 North Michigan Avenue, Suite 3930, Chicago, IL 60611-1803, United States of America.

**Tel**:         (1) 312 337 7000
**Website**:   www.spencer.org
**Contact**:   Fellowships Office

The Spencer Foundation is a private foundation that grants funds to support research which contributes to the understanding of education and improvement of its practice.

## Research Grants on Education: Small

**Purpose**: The Small Research Grants Program supports education research projects that will contribute to the improvement of education, broadly conceived, with budgets up to US$50,000 for projects ranging from one to five years
**Eligibility**: 1. Proposals to the Research Grants on Education program must be for academic research projects that aim to study education. Proposals for activities other than research, or proposals for research studies focused on areas other than education, are not eligible. 2. Principal Investigators (PIs) and Co-PIs applying for a Small Research Grant on Education must have an earned doctorate in an academic discipline or professional field, or appropriate experience in an education research-related profession. While graduate students may be part of the research team, they may not be named the PI or Co-PI on the proposal. Proposals to the Research Grants on Education program must be for academic research projects that aim to study education. Proposals for activities other than research, or proposals for research studies focused on areas other than education, are not eligible. While graduate students may be part of the research team, they may not be named the PI or Co-PI on the proposal
**Level of Study**: Postgraduate
**Type**: Grant
**Frequency**: Annual
**Country of Study**: Any country
**Application Procedure**: The application process begins with a full proposal; there is no requirement to submit a letter of intent or intent to apply form. Full proposals for a Small Research Grant on Education are due by 2:00pm central time, 1 July. Full Proposal Guidelines Small Grant proposals must be submitted through an online application form following the guidelines below. Step 1 - Registration. Step 2 - My Profile. Step 3 - Start a Proposal. Step 4 - Small Grant Proposal Elements. Step 5 - Proposal Summary. Application could be processed as follows. spencer.smartsimple.us/s_Login.jsp
**Closing Date**: 3 November
**Funding**: Private
**Additional Information**:   www.spencer.org/grant_types/small-research-grant

**For further information contact:**

The Spencer Foundation, 625 N Michigan Ave, Suite 1600, Chicago, IL 60611, United States of America.

**Email**:   smallgrants@spencer.org

## Spencer Foundation Dissertation Fellowship Program

**Purpose**: To encourage a new generation of scholars from a wide range of disciplines and professional fields to undertake research relevant to the improvement of education
**Eligibility**: Applicants need not be citizens of the United States; however, they must be candidates for a doctoral degree at a graduate institution within the U.S. The fellowship is not intended to finance data collection or the completion of doctoral coursework but rather to support the final analysis of the research topic and the writing of the dissertation. For this reason, all applicants must confirm via the online application that they will have completed all pre-dissertation requirements by June 1, 2020 and must provide a clear and specific plan for completing the dissertation within a one or two-year time frame.
**Level of Study**: Doctorate
**Type**: Fellowship
**Value**: US$25,000
**Frequency**: Annual
**Country of Study**: United States of America
**Application Procedure**: Applicants must apply online. In addition to the completed application form they must submit a list of publications/presentations, a dissertation abstract, a narrative discussion of the dissertation, a work plan, 2 letters of recommendation and a graduate transcript
**Closing Date**: 3 October
**Additional Information**: Please see the website for further details www.spencer.org/content.cfm/fellowship-awards naeducation.org/naedspencer-dissertation-fellowship-program-faqs/

**For further information contact:**

**Email**:    fellows@spencer.org

---

## Spinal Research

80 Coleman St, London, EC2R 5BJ, United Kingdom.

**Tel**:          (44) 20 7653 8935
**Email**:      info@spinal-research.org
**Website**:   www.spinal-research.org

### International Spinal Research Trust

**Purpose**: Healthcare Innovations that could have a significant impact on bladder, bowel and sexual function. The aim of the call is to support high-quality clinical research that develops and tests innovative ways to recover bladder, bowel or sexual function after spinal cord injury.
**Eligibility**: Any application is expected to have direct relevance to the fields of research discussed in the following published articles on the ISRT Research Strategy, copies are available: Adams et al. International Spinal Research Trust Research Strategy: a discussion document. Spinal Cord (2007) 45: 2-14.
**Level of Study**: Graduate
**Type**: Grant
**Value**: Upto £250,000
**Length of Study**: 3 years
**Frequency**: Annual
**Country of Study**: Any country
**Closing Date**: 8 May
**Funding**: Private

#### For further information contact:

International Spinal Research Trust, 80 Coleman Street, London EC2R 5BJ, United Kingdom.

**Email**:    research@spinal-research.org

### Solomon Awards

**Purpose**: We are pleased to announce the first of what we plan will be an annual call for proposals, in the name of a generous benefactor, to help support quality experimental medicine, translational and reverse translational research in the United Kingdom within the field of spinal cord injury
**Eligibility**: Proposals should be limited to the following areas: - Biomedical research - Experimental medicine -

Clinical studies - Suitably justified case for travel/sabbatical to enable the transfer of best practice or research methodology to the United Kingdom
**Level of Study**: Graduate
**Type**: Award
**Frequency**: Annual
**Country of Study**: Any country
**Funding**: Private

#### For further information contact:

**Tel**:    (44) 20 7653 8935

---

## St Cross College

61 St. Giles', Oxford OX1 3LZ, United Kingdom.

**Tel**:          (44) 1865 278490
**Website**:   www.stx.ox.ac.uk

### HAPP MSc Scholarship in the History of Science

**Purpose**: The successful scholar and will be expected to engage with the termly activities of the St Cross Centre for the History and Philosophy of Physics (HAPP).
**Eligibility**: To be considered for these scholarships, applicants must have applied to study for an MSc in History of Science, Medicine and Technology
**Level of Study**: Postgraduate
**Type**: Scholarship
**Value**: £10,000
**Length of Study**: 1 year
**Frequency**: Annual
**Country of Study**: Any country
**Application Procedure**: No separate application is required and all eligible offer-holders will be considered for these awards.
**Closing Date**: 10 January
**Funding**: Private
**Additional Information**:    www.stx.ox.ac.uk/happ-msc-scholarship-in-the-history-of-science

### Lorna Casselton Memorial Scholarship in Plant Sciences

**Purpose**: St Cross College, jointly with the Department of Plant Sciences, invites applications for the Lorna Casselton Memorial Scholarship from successful Home/European

Union applicants who will begin studying at the University of Oxford

**Level of Study**: Postgraduate

**Type**: Scholarship

**Frequency**: Annual

**Country of Study**: Any country

**Application Procedure**: For the detailed information, visit the following site. www.stx.ox.ac.uk/prospective-students/funding-support/lorna-casselton-memorial-scholarship-plant-sciences

**Closing Date**: 22 March

**Funding**: Private

**Additional Information**: www.plants.ox.ac.uk/lorna-casselton-memorial-scholarship-plant-sciences

### For further information contact:

**Email**:  admissions-academic@stx.ox.ac.uk

## Mabel Churn Scholarship in Ophthalmology

**Purpose**: St Cross College invites applications for the Mabel Churn Scholarship from successful applicants normally resident in the United Kingdom or the European Union,

**Eligibility**: Applicants must list St Cross College as their first choice college on their Graduate Admissions application form in order to be eligible to apply for this scholarship

**Level of Study**: Postgraduate

**Type**: Scholarship

**Value**: up to £500

**Frequency**: Annual

**Country of Study**: Any country

**Closing Date**: 1 May

**Funding**: Private

**Additional Information**: www.stx.ox.ac.uk/mabel-churn-scholarship-in-ophthalmology

### For further information contact:

61 St Giles, Oxford OX1 3LZ, United Kingdom.

**Email**:  master@stx.ox.ac.uk

## Mabel Churn Scholarship in Ophthalmology

**Purpose**: St Cross College invites applications for the Mabel Churn Scholarship from successful applicants normally resident in the UK or the European Union studying at the University of Oxford for a DPhil research degree in the Nuffield Department of Clinical Neurosciences (NDCN) in any area of retinal research and who are studying for a DPhil in Clinical Neurosciences (course code RD_CU1)

**Eligibility**: To be considered for this scholarship, applicants must have applied to study for a Clinical Neurosciences

**Type**: Scholarship

**Value**: Up to £500 per annum for travel and research expenses

**Frequency**: Annual

**Country of Study**: Any country

**Application Procedure**: No separate application is required and all eligible offer-holders will be considered for these awards.

**Closing Date**: 1 May

**Funding**: Private

**Additional Information**: www.stx.ox.ac.uk/mabel-churn-scholarship-in-ophthalmology

## MPhil Scholarships in the Humanities and Social Sciences

**Purpose**: St Cross College offers two MPhil Scholarships for students studying at the University of Oxford for an MPhil degree in any of the humanities and social science disciplines or for the BPhil degree in Philosophy

**Eligibility**: To be considered for these scholarships, applicants must have applied to study for a Master's-level course

**Level of Study**: Postgraduate

**Type**: Scholarship

**Value**: £4,000 per annum

**Length of Study**: 2 years

**Frequency**: Annual

**Country of Study**: Any country

**Application Procedure**: No separate application is required and all eligible offer-holders will be considered for these awards.

**Closing Date**: January

**Funding**: Private

**Additional Information**: www.stx.ox.ac.uk/mphil-scholarships-in-the-humanities-and-social-sciences

## St Cross Divisional Scholarships

**Purpose**: St Cross College is delighted to offer four Divisional Scholarships for applicants who apply to a one-year Master's course in one of the four University Divisions (Humanities; Mathematical, Physical & Life Sciences; Medical Sciences and Social Sciences) with one Scholarship being awarded per Division.

**Eligibility**: To be considered for these scholarships, applicants must have applied to study for a Master's-level course

**Level of Study**: Postgraduate

**Type**: Scholarship

**Value**: Value of £10,000

**Length of Study**: 1 year

**Frequency**: Annual
**Country of Study**: Any country
**Application Procedure**: No separate application is required and all eligible offer-holders will be considered for these awards.
**Closing Date**: January
**Funding**: Private
**Additional Information**: www.stx.ox.ac.uk/st-cross-divisional-scholarships

## St Cross Worldwide Scholarships

**Purpose**: St Cross College is pleased to offer six scholarships to Master's-level students who have successfully applied and being accepted to St Cross College
**Eligibility**: To be considered for these scholarships, applicants must have applied to study for a Master's-level course
**Level of Study**: Postgraduate
**Type**: Scholarship
**Value**: value of £10,000
**Frequency**: Annual
**Country of Study**: Any country
**Closing Date**: January
**Funding**: Private
**Additional Information**: www.stx.ox.ac.uk/st-cross-worldwide-scholarships

## St John's College

St Johns Street, Cambridge CB2 1TP, United Kingdom.

**Tel**:       (44) 1223 338600
**Email**:   graduate-office@joh.cam.ac.uk

### The Louis Cha Scholarship

**Purpose**: St John's College, Cambridge is delighted to announce that the noted writer, press editor, and philanthropist Dr Louis Cha has made a very generous donation to support graduate research on dynastic China at St John's. Dr Cha, internationally renowned for his novels on the Chinese past
**Eligibility**: 1. St John's College therefore proposes to award a Louis Cha Scholarship commencing in October, to enable a student to undertake research in the University of Cambridge in the literature, history, and culture of early and dynastic China (pre-1912). 2. The successful applicant will be selected from those who have obtained a place at St John's College Cambridge to read for the MPhil or PhD degree in a relevant subject

**Level of Study**: Postgraduate
**Type**: Scholarship
**Value**: £15,000 per annum
**Length of Study**: 3 years
**Frequency**: Annual
**Country of Study**: Any country
**Application Procedure**: 1. Candidates should apply to the University of Cambridge through the University's Graduate Admissions Office at the Board of Graduate Studies for admission as a graduate student, specifying St John's as their first choice of College For further information
**Closing Date**: 30 November
**Funding**: Private
**Additional Information**: www.joh.cam.ac.uk/louis-cha-scholarship

### For further information contact:

The Graduate Office, St John's College Cambridge CB2 1TP, U.K.

**Tel**:       (44) 1223 338600
**Email**:   arts@hku.hk

## St. Baldricks Foundations

In the 1950s, almost all kids diagnosed with cancer died. Because of research, today about 90% of kids with the most common type of cancer will live. But for many other types, progress has been limited, and for some kids there is still little hope for a cure.

**Tel**:        (1) 626 792 8247
**Website**:   www.stbaldricks.org
**Contact**:   1333 South Mayflower Avenue, Suite 400, Monrovia, CA 91016, United States of America.

### Research Grants

**Purpose**: The St. Baldrick's Foundation is a volunteer and donor powered charity committed to supporting the most promising research to find cures for childhood cancers and give survivors long and healthy lives. It started with a friendly dare: would you shave your head to raise money for kids' cancer research? What happened next would change the world. This bold act of baldness has gained major momentum, since its start in 2000. Today, we have more than 1,000 head-shaving events taking place around the world at pubs, restaurants, schools, churches, parks, firehouses, military bases - you name it. It is our constituents' way of changing the world, in a meaningful way. Since the Foundation's first grants as an independent charity in 2005, St. Baldrick's has invested more than US$279 million in childhood cancer research grants worldwide. It's about collaboration. It's about powerful ideas, big and small. It's about never giving up until we have cures for all kids with cancers

**Eligibility**: Applicants need not be American citizens; however, they must work at an academic, medical, or research institution within the United States. 1. A program/institution is defined as an entity essentially operating under one management. Any questions or questionable situations will be reviewed by a subset of the Scientific Advisory Board of St. Baldrick's. Questions can be emailed to Grants@Stbaldricks.org, please include a copy of the potential Scholar's biosketch. 2. Institutions that are actively involved in (sponsor, promote, or participate in) non-St. Baldrick's head-shaving fundraising events are not eligible to apply for St. Baldrick's funding. 3. St. Baldrick's funds may not be used for human embryonic stem cell research. 4. All awards will be payable to the Scholar's academic institution, non-profit research institution, or laboratory. 5. Applicants should hold a PhD, M.D., or D.O. degree in a field of research specialty by the date the award becomes effective. 6. Applicants must currently hold (for no longer than 7 years at the time the award begins), or will hold by start of the award, a title that is considered by the institution to be a fulltime faculty position. Situations may occur where the institutions definition of "faculty" may differ from the Foundation's definition, this should be fully explained in the Scholar Applicant Checklist (required at LOI stage). 7. This is an early-career award. The Scholar award is intended to develop the independent pediatric cancer research careers of highly qualified investigators, not to support well established or senior investigators. 8. Scholars may receive funding from other sources to support their research. However, no other comparable or higher (monetary value) career development award may be held prior to or at the time the award begins. Scientific or budgetary overlap with other funded projects is not allowed. o In the event of comparable or higher (monetary value) career development funding after the LOI has been approved, the Scholar must give up the remainder of their St. Baldrick's award, unless otherwise approved by the St. Baldrick's Foundation. 9. Applicants holding or awarded R01s at the time of the LOI are not eligible to apply. Applicants cannot hold a NIH K-award at the time that they apply (institutional K12 funding is allowable). See "Conditions of Award" below regarding other awards received after the LOI is approved. 10. Applicants must have an appropriate Sponsor who provides supervision, facilities, and research support. If appropriate for the project, applicants may have more than one (1) Sponsor. 11. Research projects must have direct applicability and relevance to pediatric cancer. They may be in any discipline of basic, clinical, translational, or epidemiological research.

**Level of Study**: Postgraduate

**Type**: Grant

**Value**: This award is granted for three years with an opportunity to apply for an additional two years of funding based upon the demonstration of significant accomplishment. (Years 4- 5, if funded, will be up to US$115,000/year).

**Frequency**: Annual

**Country of Study**: US

**Application Procedure**: Category/Cycle specific LOI Instructions/Requirements are available in ProposalCENTRAL upon starting the LOI and on the St. Baldrick's website (stbaldricks.org/for-researchers). 1. LOI, application, and required documents must be submitted by the Principal Investigator, in English, online through ProposalCENTRAL (proposalcentral.altum.com) before 5 p.m. EST on the deadline. 2. All application instructions and templates/requirements will be available in ProposalCENTRAL upon approval of an LOI. 3. Applicants can enable other users to access their proposal (e.g., department or grants administrators) in the full proposal section of ProposalCENTRAL. 4. It is the responsibility of the applicant to ensure and to verify that the application is received by the deadline date and that the application is complete and correct prior to submission. 5. Eligible current St. Baldrick's Scholars applying for extended funding will be contacted by the St. Baldrick's Foundation Grants Administration staff with instructions for applying. Applications will be submitted via ProposalCENTRAL and reviewed for progress. Grantees can email Grants@StBaldricks.org with further questions about the optional funding. Applications are due before 5 p.m. EST on March 29, 2019. 1. St. Baldrick's Foundation funds biomedical research to better understand the causes of pediatric cancers and to advance its prevention, treatment, and cure. The main output of this research is new knowledge. To ensure this knowledge can be accessed, read, applied, and built upon in fulfillment of our goals, St. Baldrick's Foundation encourages researchers to share data with the research community in accordance with the NIH policy on data sharing and expects its grantees to publish their findings, including but not limited to publication in peer reviewed journals. Applicants will be asked about data sharing plans as part of the application. 2. All application evaluations are considered confidential and are available to scientific reviewers, the Foundation's Board of Directors, and the administrative personnel of the St. Baldrick's Foundation only. 3. Resubmissions: Applicants with resubmissions have the option to check a box in ProposalCENTRAL on the title page of the application stating that it is a resubmission. Resbumissions are not marked in the Letter of Intent stage. You may mention it is a resubmission in your LOI. Applicants with a resubmission are asked to address the reviewer comments in the appendix. Be sure that the document addressing previous reviewer comments is listed in the table of contents for your appendix. Resubmission applicants will not have all three of the same reviewers. St. Baldrick's does ask at least one of the previous reviewers to re-review the resubmission. Once marked as a resubmission in ProposalCENTRAL, new reviewers will have access to the past reviewer comments. Resubmissions are still required to go through limited submission decisions per the institution.

**Closing Date**: 27 March

**Additional Information**: www.stbaldricks.org/for-researchers

### For further information contact:

**Tel**:        (1) 626 792 8247 (ext. 236)

**Email**:    Laura@StBaldricks.org

## St. Baldrick's International Scholars

**Purpose**: The St. Baldrick's Foundation is a volunteer and donor powered charity committed to supporting the most promising research to find cures for childhood cancers and give survivors long and healthy lives. It started with a friendly dare: would you shave your head to raise money for kids' cancer research? What happened next would change the world. This bold act of baldness has gained major momentum, since its start in 2000. Today, we have more than 1,000 head-shaving events taking place around the world at pubs, restaurants, schools, churches, parks, firehouses, military bases - you name it. It is our constituents' way of changing the world, in a meaningful way. Since the Foundation's first grants as an independent charity in 2005, St. Baldrick's has invested more than US$279 million in childhood cancer research grants worldwide. It's about collaboration. It's about powerful ideas, big and small. It's about never giving up until we have cures for all kids with cancers

**Eligibility**: Applicants need not be American citizens; however, they must work at an academic, medical, or research institution within the United States. 1. A program/institution is defined as an entity essentially operating under one management. o Any questions or questionable situations will be reviewed by a subset of the Scientific Advisory Board of St. Baldrick's. Questions can be emailed to Grants@Stbaldricks.org, please include a copy of the potential Scholar's biosketch. 2. Institutions that are actively involved in (sponsor, promote, or participate in) non-St. Baldrick's head-shaving fundraising events are not eligible to apply for St. Baldrick's funding. 3. St. Baldrick's funds may not be used for human embryonic stem cell research. 4. All awards will be payable to the Scholar's academic institution, non-profit research institution, or laboratory. 5. Applicants should hold a PhD, M.D., or D.O. degree in a field of research specialty by the date the award becomes effective. 6. Applicants must currently hold (for no longer than 7 years at the time the award begins), or will hold by start of the award, a title that is considered by the institution to be a fulltime, faculty position. o Situations may occur where the institutions definition of "faculty" may differ from the Foundation's definition, this should be fully explained in the Scholar Applicant Checklist (required at LOI stage). 7. This is an early-career award. The Scholar award is intended to develop the independent pediatric cancer research careers of highly qualified investigators, not to support well established or senior investigators. 8. Scholars may receive funding from other sources to support their research. However, no other comparable or higher (monetary value) career development award may be held prior to or at the time the award begins. Scientific or budgetary overlap with other funded projects is not allowed. o In the event of comparable or higher (monetary value) career development funding after the LOI has been approved, the Scholar must give up the remainder of their St. Baldrick's award, unless otherwise approved by the St. Baldrick's Foundation. 10. Applicants holding or awarded R01s at the time of the LOI are not eligible to apply. Applicants cannot hold a NIH K-award at the time that they apply (institutional K12 funding is allowable). See "Conditions of Award" below regarding other awards received after the LOI is approved. 11. Applicants must have an appropriate Sponsor who provides supervision, facilities, and research support. If appropriate for the project, applicants may have more than one (1) Sponsor. 12. Research projects must have direct applicability and relevance to pediatric cancer. They may be in any discipline of basic, clinical, translational, or epidemiological research.

**Level of Study**: Postgraduate

**Type**: Grant

**Value**: This award is granted for three years with an opportunity to apply for an additional two years of funding based upon the demonstration of significant accomplishment. (Years 4- 5, if funded, will be up to US$115,000/year).

**Frequency**: Annual

**Country of Study**: US

**Application Procedure**: Category/Cycle specific LOI Instructions/Requirements are available in ProposalCENTRAL upon starting the LOI and on the St. Baldrick's website (stbaldricks.org/for-researchers). 1. LOI, application, and required documents must be submitted by the Principal Investigator, in English, online through ProposalCENTRAL (proposalcentral.altum.com) before 5 p.m. EST on the deadline. 2. All application instructions and templates/requirements will be available in ProposalCENTRAL upon approval of an LOI. 3. Applicants can enable other users to access their proposal (e.g., department or grants administrators) in the full proposal section of ProposalCENTRAL. 4. It is the responsibility of the applicant to ensure and to verify that the application is received by the deadline date and that the application is complete and correct prior to submission. 5. Eligible current St. Baldrick's Scholars applying for extended funding will be contacted by the St. Baldrick's Foundation Grants Administration staff with instructions for applying. Applications will be submitted via ProposalCENTRAL and reviewed for progress. Grantees can email Grants@StBaldricks.org with further questions about the optional funding. Applications are due before 5 p.m. EST on March 29, 2019. 1. St. Baldrick's Foundation funds biomedical research to better understand the causes of pediatric cancers and to advance its prevention, treatment, and cure. The main output of this research is new knowledge. To ensure this knowledge can be accessed, read, applied, and built upon in fulfillment of our goals, St. Baldrick's Foundation encourages researchers to share data with the research community in accordance with the NIH policy on data sharing and expects its grantees to publish their findings, including but not limited to publication in peer reviewed journals. Applicants will be asked about data sharing plans as part of the application. 2. All application evaluations are considered confidential and are available to scientific reviewers, the Foundation's Board of Directors, and the administrative personnel of the St. Baldrick's Foundation only. 3. Resubmissions: Applicants with resubmissions have the option to check a box in ProposalCENTRAL on the title page of the application stating that it is a resubmission. Resbumissions are not marked in the Letter of Intent stage. You may mention it is a resubmission in your LOI. Applicants with a resubmission are asked to address the reviewer comments in the appendix. Be sure that the document addressing previous reviewer comments is listed in the table of contents for your appendix. Resubmission applicants will not have all three of the same reviewers. St. Baldrick's does ask at least one of the previous reviewers to re-review the resubmission. Once marked as a resubmission in ProposalCENTRAL, new reviewers will have access to the past reviewer comments. Resubmissions are still required to go through limited submission decisions per the institution.

**Closing Date**: 27 March

**Additional Information**: www.stbaldricks.org/for-researchers

### For further information contact:

**Tel**:     (1) 626 792 8247 (ext. 236)
**Email**:    Laura@StBaldricks.org

## St. Baldrick's Scholars

**Purpose**: The St. Baldrick's Foundation is a volunteer and donor powered charity committed to supporting the most promising research to find cures for childhood cancers and give survivors long and healthy lives. It started with a friendly dare: would you shave your head to raise money for kids' cancer research? What happened next would change the world. This bold act of baldness has gained major momentum, since its start in 2000. Today, we have more than 1,000 head-shaving events taking place around the world at pubs, restaurants, schools, churches, parks, firehouses, military bases - you name it. It is our constituents' way of changing the world, in a meaningful way. Since the Foundation's first grants as an independent charity in 2005, St. Baldrick's has invested more than US$279 million in childhood cancer research grants worldwide. It's about collaboration. It's about powerful ideas, big and small. It's about never giving up until we have cures for all kids with cancers

**Eligibility**: Applicants need not be American citizens; however, they must work at an academic, medical, or research institution within the United States. 1. A program/institution is defined as an entity essentially operating under one management. o Any questions or questionable situations will be reviewed by a subset of the Scientific Advisory Board of St. Baldrick's. Questions can be emailed to Grants@Stbaldricks.org, please include a copy of the potential Scholar's biosketch. 2. Institutions that are actively involved in (sponsor, promote, or participate in) non-St. Baldrick's head-shaving fundraising events are not eligible to apply for St. Baldrick's funding. 3. St. Baldrick's funds may not be used for human embryonic stem cell research. 4. All awards will be payable to the Scholar's academic institution, non-profit research institution, or laboratory. 5. Applicants should hold a PhD, M.D., or D.O. degree in a field of research specialty by the date the award becomes effective. 6. Applicants must currently hold (for no longer than 7 years at the time the award begins), or will hold by start of the award, a title that is considered by the institution to be a fulltime, faculty position. o Situations may occur where the institutions definition of "faculty" may differ from the Foundation's definition, this should be fully explained in the Scholar Applicant Checklist (required at LOI stage). 7. This is an early-career award. The Scholar award is intended to develop the independent pediatric cancer research careers of highly qualified investigators, not to support well established or senior investigators. 8. Scholars may receive funding from other sources to support their research. However, no other comparable or higher (monetary value) career development award may be held prior to or at the time the award begins. Scientific or budgetary overlap with other funded projects is not allowed. o In the event of comparable or higher (monetary value) career development funding after the LOI has been approved, the Scholar must give up the remainder of their St. Baldrick's award, unless otherwise approved by the St. Baldrick's Foundation. 9. Applicants holding or awarded R01s at the time of the LOI are not eligible to apply. Applicants cannot hold a NIH K-award at the time that they apply (institutional K12 funding is allowable). See "Conditions of Award" below regarding other awards received after the LOI is approved. 10. Applicants must have an appropriate Sponsor who provides supervision, facilities, and research support. If appropriate for the project, applicants may have more than one (1) Sponsor. 11. Research projects must have direct applicability and relevance to pediatric cancer. They may be in any discipline of basic, clinical, translational, or epidemiological research.

**Level of Study**: Postgraduate
**Type**: Grant
**Value**: This award is granted for three years with an opportunity to apply for an additional two years of funding based upon the demonstration of significant accomplishment. (Years 4- 5, if funded, will be up to US$115,000/year).
**Frequency**: Annual
**Country of Study**: US
**Application Procedure**: Category/Cycle specific LOI Instructions/Requirements are available in ProposalCENTRAL upon starting the LOI and on the St. Baldrick's website (stbaldricks.org/for-researchers). 1. LOI, application, and required documents must be submitted by the Principal Investigator, in English, online through ProposalCENTRAL (proposalcentral.altum.com) before 5 p.m. EST on the deadline. 2. All application instructions and templates/requirements will be available in ProposalCENTRAL upon approval of an LOI. 3. Applicants can enable other users to access their proposal (e.g., department or grants administrators) in the full proposal section of ProposalCENTRAL. 4. It is the responsibility of the applicant to ensure and to verify that the application is received by the deadline date and that the application is complete and correct prior to submission. 5. Eligible current St. Baldrick's Scholars applying for extended funding will be contacted by the St. Baldrick's Foundation Grants Administration staff with instructions for applying. Applications will be submitted via ProposalCENTRAL and reviewed for progress. Grantees can email Grants@StBaldricks.org with further questions about the optional funding. Applications are due before 5 p.m. EST on March 29, 2019. 1. St. Baldrick's Foundation funds biomedical research to better understand the causes of pediatric cancers and to advance its prevention, treatment, and cure. The main output of this research is new knowledge. To ensure this knowledge can be accessed, read, applied, and built upon in fulfillment of our goals, St. Baldrick's Foundation encourages researchers to share data with the research community in accordance with the NIH policy on data sharing and expects its grantees to publish their findings, including but not limited to publication in peer reviewed journals. Applicants will be asked about data sharing plans as part of the application. 2. All application evaluations are considered confidential and are available to scientific reviewers, the Foundation's Board of Directors, and the administrative personnel of the St. Baldrick's Foundation only. 3. Resubmissions: Applicants with resubmissions have the option to check a box in ProposalCENTRAL on the title page of the application stating that it is a resubmission. Resbumissions are not marked in the Letter of Intent stage. You may mention it is a resubmission in your LOI. Applicants with a resubmission are asked to address the reviewer comments in the appendix. Be sure that the document addressing previous reviewer comments is listed in the table of contents for your appendix. Resubmission applicants will not have all three of the same reviewers. St. Baldrick's does ask at least one of the previous reviewers to re-review the resubmission. Once marked as a resubmission in ProposalCENTRAL, new reviewers will have access to the past reviewer comments. Resubmissions are still required to go through limited submission decisions per the institution.

**Closing Date**: 27 March
**Additional Information**: www.stbaldricks.org/for-researchers

### For further information contact:

**Tel**: (1) 626 792 8247 (ext. 236)
**Email**: Laura@StBaldricks.org

## St. Catherine's College - University of Oxford

Manor Rd, Oxford OX1 3UJ, United Kingdom.

**Tel**: (44) 1865 271 700
**Email**: admissions@stcatz.ox.ac.uk
**Website**: www.stcatz.ox.ac.uk
**Contact**: Mrs Ben Nicholas, Graduate Funding Administrator

## Berlinski-Jacobson Graduate Scholarship (Humanities & Social Sciences)

**Eligibility**: For students who in October will be reading for any Oxford University graduate degree in the Arts (Humanities Division and Social Science Division) for which St Catherine's admits graduate students
**Level of Study**: Graduate
**Type**: Scholarship
**Length of Study**: £4,000 will worth per annum
**Frequency**: Every 3 years
**Country of Study**: United Kingdom
**Closing Date**: 8 March
**Funding**: Private
**Additional Information**: studyqa.com/scholarships/view/257

**For further information contact:**

**Email**: development.office@stcatz.ox.ac.uk

## St. Mary's University

Waldegrave Rd, Twickenham TW1 4SX, United Kingdom.

**Tel**: (44) 20 8240 4000
**Email**: scholarships@stmarys.ac.uk
**Website**: www.stmarys.ac.uk

### Centre for Bioethics and Emerging Technologies PhD Funding

**Purpose**: The Centre for Bioethics and Emerging Technologies (CBET) at St Mary's University, Twickenham, offers a fully funded, full-time three year PhD programme commencing in October to support the successful applicant's research in bioethics

**Eligibility**: 1. The successful applicant would also expected to be involved with CBET activities, including conference organization and undergraduate teaching after a mandatory induction course. A major conference is being considered for 2020, together with the Centre for the Study of Modern Slavery based at the University. 2. The successful candidate may if they wish, carry out work with the Catholic Bishops' Conference of England and Wales. 3. It is also highly desirable that the successful applicant be located within the Greater London area during their studies

**Level of Study**: Graduate

**Type**: Funding support

**Value**: Provide full-time PhD fees at the current home/European Union rate of £4,375 p.a. and a bursary of £13,000 p.a

**Length of Study**: Up to 3 years

**Frequency**: Annual

**Country of Study**: Any country

**Application Procedure**: To apply, download and complete a full registration PhD application and send it together with your 3,000-4,000 word research proposal, two academic references from your chosen referees, copies of your Master's qualification(s), a current CV and a covering letter stating the reasons you wish to be considered for the bursary to the physical address mentioned below

**Closing Date**: 26 April

**Funding**: Private

**For further information contact:**

**Email**: maggie.mayer@stmarys.ac.uk

## Stanford University

450 Serra Mall, Stanford, CA 94305–2004, United States of America.

**Tel**: (1) 650 723 2300
**Website**: www.stanford.edu

Stanford University, located between San Francisco and San Jose in the heart of California's Silicon Valley, is one of the world's leading teaching and research universities. Since its opening in 1891, Stanford has been dedicated to finding solutions to big challenges and to preparing students for leadership in a complex world.

### School of Medicine Dean's Postdoctoral Fellowship

**Purpose**: The School of Medicine Dean's Postdoctoral Fellowships encourage and support young investigators in the first two years of their postdoctoral (PhD or MD) research training at the School of Medicine and who are under the mentorship of faculty in the School of Medicine. With the goal to support current postdocs and to facilitate the recruitment of new scholars, support of a Dean's Fellowship is often used as "seed" money while outside funds are sought

**Eligibility**: 1. Applicants must be postdoctoral scholars at the School of Medicine at the time the award begins. If applicant is not a postdoc at the application deadline, additional documents must be submitted with application (see below). 2. Faculty sponsors must be appointed in the School of Medicine. Acting, consulting, and courtesy appointees are ineligible. 3. Awardees cannot be enrolled in a degree-granting program while funded. 4. Applicants in the first one or two years of postdoctoral research training are preferred. 5. Foreign fellows must have visas that allow stipend support (typically a J-1 & F-1 OPT). H1-B and TN visa holders are ineligible. Citizenship is not a selection factor. 6. This is a one-year fellowship and applications for a second year of funding will not be reviewed.

**Level of Study**: Postgraduate

**Type**: Fellowship

**Value**: Stipend is US$31,350

**Frequency**: Annual

**Country of Study**: Any country

**Application Procedure**: Complete applications must be submitted online by the deadline. Start applications early to allow enough time for the system to solicit the required form from your faculty mentor which is due at the same time as your application. Applications due by 11:59 PM PST on deadline date.

**Closing Date**: 8 April

**Funding**: Foundation
**Additional Information**: postdocs.stanford.edu/current/fellowship/deans

### For further information contact:

Medical School Office Building (MSOB), 1265 Welch Rd., Suite 100, Stanford, CA 94305-5402, United States of America.

## Stanford Postdoctoral Recruitment Initiative in Sciences and Medicine (PRISM)

**Purpose**: We invite all graduate students, and especially those from backgrounds underrepresented in the sciences, to apply for the Stanford Postdoctoral Recruitment Initiative in Sciences and Medicine (PRISM) postdoc interview opportunity. Underrepresented groups include, but are not limited to: African Americans, Latinos, Native Americans, Pacific Islanders, those with disabilities or from disadvantaged backgrounds. Stanford PRISM enables students who might not typically consider a postdoc at Stanford the opportunity to see firsthand if Stanford would be a good match for them
**Eligibility**: 1. Eligible for NIH T-32 training grants, which are limited to US Citizens or Permanent Residents, by the time they will begin their postdoctoral appointment. 2. Currently at any institution in the US. Applications from students in Canada, Mexico, Puerto Rico, etc., may also be considered, pending funding availability. Travel funds are not available for those currently located overseas. 3. Intend to complete their PhD within 15 months of PRISM, though later graduation dates may be considered, at the discretion of the faculty or program.
**Level of Study**: Postgraduate
**Type**: Grant
**Frequency**: Annual
**Country of Study**: Any country
**Closing Date**: 2 March
**Funding**: Foundation
**Additional Information**: postdocs.stanford.edu/PRISM

### For further information contact:

Medical School Office Building (MSOB), 1265 Welch Rd., Suite 100, Stanford, CA 94305-5402, United States of America.

**Email**:   stanfordprism@stanford.edu

## The Helena Anna Henzl-Gabor Young Women in Science Fund for Postdoctoral Scholars Travel Grant

**Purpose**: The Helena Anna Henzl-Gabor Young Women in Science Fund for Postdoctoral Scholars Travel Grant is open to currently appointed Stanford postdoctoral scholars in the School of Medicine and School of Humanities & Sciences who have demonstrated a positive attitude through professional teamwork and collaborations of men and women. The Henzl-Gabor Travel Grant supports travel (airline tickets, accommodations, and registration expenses) for participation at scientific conferences. These travel grants are meant to help defray the costs of attending a national or international meeting for travel taking place during the period of December 1 - November 30
**Eligibility**: Applicants must have completed an MD or PhD degree within the past six years of fund application submission. Awards may be given in amounts up to US$2,000 based on the detailed expenses submitted. Total awards given and funding levels may vary depending on the size and strength of the applicant pool
**Level of Study**: Postgraduate
**Type**: Grant
**Frequency**: Annual
**Country of Study**: Any country
**Closing Date**: 22 October
**Funding**: Foundation
**Additional Information**: postdocs.stanford.edu/current/fellowship/henzlgabor

### For further information contact:

Medical School Office Building (MSOB), 1265 Welch Rd., Suite 100, Stanford, CA 94305-5402, United States of America.

## The Katharine McCormick Advanced Postdoctoral Scholar Fellowship to Support Women in Academic Medicine

**Purpose**: The Katharine McCormick Advanced Postdoctoral Fellowships are for advanced postdoctoral scholars who are pursuing faculty careers in academic medicine. The program aims to provide a bridge of the gap of support for advanced postdoctoral trainees who are competitive, yet have not yet been selected, for faculty positions
**Eligibility**: Eligibility requirements:; Only individuals who are currently appointed as Postdoctoral Scholars at Stanford University are eligible to apply. Instructors and Research Associates may not apply. The applicant may be a United States citizen, permanent resident, or foreign national. Foreign scholar applicants must be a holder of a J1 visa or an F1 visa in OPT status. Applicants who hold H1B, TN, J2, O-1 or other visas are ineligible. The scholar's faculty mentor must have a primary appointment in the School of Medicine. Acting, consulting and courtesy faculty are not eligible. Commitment on the part of the applicant and his/her faculty mentor to hold monthly mentorship meetings with a focus on topics related to the job search process and starting out as an assistant professor. Candidate's willingness to make a presentation

of their work to a large scientific audience. A progress report is required at the end of the fellowship

**Level of Study**: Graduate

**Type**: Fellowship

**Frequency**: Annual

**Country of Study**: Any country

**Application Procedure**: Application Process: Complete online application Applicant's NIH Biosketch (uploaded by applicant online) Applicant's complete curriculum vitae (uploaded by applicant online) Research proposal: (uploaded by applicant online): Two page limit, including any graphics or charts. The research proposal must be written by the fellow and reviewed by the faculty sponsor. These two pages should include a brief statement of proposed investigation in the following sections: Background, Goals, Hypothesis, and Experimental methods. If the applicant chooses to include references in the two pages, the reference should include enough information to allow the reviewer to look up the paper. Three letters of reference. One letter is required from the faculty sponsor (mentor) at Stanford. Two letters are required from other faculty, at Stanford or elsewhere, who are familiar with the candidate's work and will likely serve as references for the candidate's anticipated job search. Letters will be submitted online by the reference writer directly to the application. Letters are due the s

**Closing Date**: 10 June

**Funding**: Private

**Additional Information**: postdocs.stanford.edu/current/fellowship/katharine-mccormick-advanced-postdoctoral-scholar-fellowship-support-women

### For further information contact:

Medical School Office Building (MSOB), 1265 Welch Rd., Suite 100, Stanford, CA 94305-5402, United States of America.

**Email**:  postdocaffairs@stanford.edu

## The Walter V. and Idun Berry Postdoctoral Fellowship Program

**Purpose**: The fellowships aims to enhance research which utilizes the most advanced technologies and methodologies available to improve the health and wellness of children, including the latest opportunities in molecular and genetic medicine

**Eligibility**: 1. The applicant must be appointed as a postdoctoral scholar at the Stanford University School of Medicine at the time the award begins. If the applicant is not an appointed postdoctoral scholar at the time of the application deadline, additional documents must be submitted with the application (see application checklist below). Instructors and Research Associates may not apply. 2. Applicants must also hold an MD, PhD and/or a DVM/VMD degree(s); selection preference will be given to physician scientists. 3. The faculty mentor/sponsor must be appointed in the School of Medicine. Acting, consulting and courtesy appointees are not eligible. 4. Foreign scholars may have J-1 or F-1 OPT (receiving stipends), or H1B visas (receiving the award as salary). Citizenship is not a selection factor. 5. Applicants must be available for an interview on the interview date listed on this website

**Level of Study**: Postgraduate

**Type**: Fellowship

**Frequency**: Annual

**Country of Study**: Any country

**Application Procedure**: 1. Complete online application form (application visible only when application period is open). 2. Applicant's NIH Biosketch (uploaded by applicant online). 3. Research Proposal: (two page limit, including any graphics, charts or references). The research proposal must be written by the postdoc and reviewed by the faculty sponsor. These two pages should include a brief statement of proposed investigation in the following sections: Background, Goals, Hypothesis, and Experimental methods. Formatting guidelines require at least 1-inch margins at the top, bottom, left and right; and 12 point or larger font Times New Roman, Times Roman, Arial, Helvetica, or Verdana. Include title of project and your name on both pages and number pages. If the applicant choses to include references, the reference should include enough information to allow the reviewer to look up the paper. 4. Three letters of recommendation: one from the sponsoring Faculty Mentor at Stanford, and two additional letters from other recommenders. Letters are due the same day as the application, so please request these letters at the beginning of the application process via the online application

**Closing Date**: 31 August

**Funding**: Private

**Additional Information**: postdocs.stanford.edu/current/fellowship/walter-v-and-idun-berry-postdoctoral-fellowship-program

### For further information contact:

**Email**:  postdocaffairs@stanford.edu

## Stanley Smith (United Kingdom) Horticultural Trust

Cambridge University Botanic Garden. Cory Lodge, 1 Brookside, Cambridge CB2 1JE, United Kingdom.

**Tel**:  (44) 12 2333 6299

**Email**:  jc240@cam.ac.uk

**Contact**:  Dr James Cullen, Director

The Stanley Smith (UK) Horticultural Trust supports projects that contribute to the development of the art and science of horticulture, i.e. garden conservation and restoration, education and training, research, publications and travel.

## Stanley Smith (UK) Horticultural Trust Awards

**Eligibility**: Open to institutions and individuals. All projects are judged entirely on merit and there are no eligibility requirements, but grants are not awarded for students to take academic or diploma courses of any kind
**Level of Study**: Unrestricted
**Type**: Varies
**Value**: Varies
**Length of Study**: Dependent on the nature of the project
**Country of Study**: Any country
**Application Procedure**: Applicants must apply to the Trust. Trustees allocate awards in Spring and Autumn
**No. of awards offered**: 200
**Closing Date**: 15 August
**Funding**: Private
**Contributor**: Donations
**No. of awards given last year**: 30
**No. of applicants last year**: 200
**Additional Information**: www.fundingforall.org.uk/funds/stanley-smith-uk-horticultural-trust/

### For further information contact:

**Email**:     tdaniel@calacademy.org

## State Secretariat for Education, Research and Innovation SERI

Einsteinstrasse 2, CH-3005 Bern, Switzerland.

**Email**:      sgs@sbfi.admin.ch
**Website**:   www.sbfi.admin.ch

## Swiss Government Excellence Scholarships for Foreign Scholars and Artists

**Purpose**: The Swiss government, through the Federal Commission for Scholarships for Foreign Students (FCS), awards various postgraduate scholarships to foreign scholars and researchers
**Eligibility**: These scholarships provide graduates from all fields with the opportunity to pursue doctoral or postdoctoral research in Switzerland at one of the public funded universities or recognised institutions
**Level of Study**: Doctorate, Postdoctorate
**Type**: Scholarship
**Frequency**: Annual
**Country of Study**: Any country
**Additional Information**: Please check www.sbfi.admin.ch/scholarships_eng    www.sbfi.admin.ch/sbfi/en/home/education/scholarships-and-grants/swiss-government-excellence-scholarships.html

### For further information contact:

**Tel**:       (41) 446326161
**Email**:    exchange@ethz.ch

## Statistical Society of Canada

210 - 1725 St. Laurent Blvd., Ottawa, ON K1G 3V4, Canada.

**Tel**:         (1) 613 733 2662
**Email**:     info@ssc.ca
**Website**:   www.ssc.ca
**Contact**:   Sudhir Paul, Chair, Pierre Robillard Award

The Statistical Society of Canada provides a forum for discussion and interaction among individuals involved in all aspects of the statistical sciences. It publishes a newsletter, Liaison as well as a scientific journal, The Canadian Journal of Statistics. The Society also organizes annual scientific meetings and short courses on professional development.

## Pierre Robillard Award

**Purpose**: To recognize the best PhD thesis defended at a Canadian university and written in a field covered by the Canadian Journal of Statistics
**Eligibility**: Open to all postgraduates who have made a potential impact on the statistical sciences
**Level of Study**: Doctorate
**Type**: Award
**Value**: A certificate, a monetary prize of C$1,000 and 1 year's membership of the Society
**Frequency**: Annual
**Country of Study**: Canada
**Application Procedure**: Applicants must submit four copies of the thesis together with a covering letter from the thesis supervisor

**No. of awards offered**: 8
**Closing Date**: 31 January
**No. of awards given last year**: 1
**No. of applicants last year**: 8
**Additional Information**: The committee may decide that none of the submitted theses merits the award ssc.ca/en/award/pierre-robillard-award

### For further information contact:

Department of Mathematical and Statistical Sciences, University of Alberta 632 Cab, AB, Canada.

**Tel**:      (1) 780 492 4230
**Fax**:     (1) 780 492 6826
**Email**:   kc.carriere@ualberta.ca

## Stellenbosch University

Private Bay XI, Matieland 7602, South Africa.

**Tel**:      (27) 21 808 9111
**Email**:   info@sun.ac.za
**Website**: www.sun.ac.za

The raison d'être of the chemistry of Stellenbosch is to create and sustain, in commitment to the academic ideal of excellent scholarly and scientific practice, an environment within which knowledge can be discovered, shared and applied for the benefit of the community.

## Harry Crossley Doctoral Fellowship

**Purpose**: To reward academically above-average students
**Eligibility**: Individuals are not eligible who will be employed for more than 20 hours per week in 2020; who will register for part-time courses, the 4th year of an undergraduate degree, the LLB, postgraduate certificates and postgraduate diplomas and who will register for degrees in disciplines in Religious Studies and Political Studies
**Level of Study**: Doctorate
**Type**: Fellowship
**Value**: ZAR 80,000
**Length of Study**: 2 years
**Frequency**: Annual
**Study Establishment**: Stellenbosch University
**Country of Study**: South Africa
**Application Procedure**: Request application

**No. of awards offered**: 350
**Closing Date**: 29 September
**Funding**: Foundation
**Contributor**: Harry Crossley Foundation
**No. of awards given last year**: 50
**No. of applicants last year**: 350
**Additional Information**: www.validate-network.org/event/the-harry-crossley-foundation-research-fellowships-2020

### For further information contact:

Level 3, Otto Beit Building, Upper Campus Rondebosch, 7700, South Africa.

**Tel**:      (27) 21 650 3622
**Fax**:     (27) 21 808 2739
**Email**:   pgfunding@uct.ac.za

## Harry Crossley Master

**Purpose**: To reward academically above-average students
**Eligibility**: To full-time students registered at Stellenbosch University in any postgraduate degree programme except theology and political science
**Level of Study**: Doctorate, Postgraduate
**Type**: Bursary
**Value**: R 75,000 (Honours), R 80,000 (Master)
**Length of Study**: 1 year
**Frequency**: Annual
**Study Establishment**: Stellenbosch University
**Country of Study**: South Africa
**No. of awards offered**: 500
**Closing Date**: December
**Funding**: Foundation
**Contributor**: Harry Crossley Foundation
**No. of awards given last year**: 30
**No. of applicants last year**: 500
**Additional Information**: Please see the website further details www.scholarshubafrica.com/41257/harry-crossley-foundation-research-fellowship-uct-south-africa/

### For further information contact:

**Tel**:      (27) 21 808 4208
**Fax**:     (27) 21 808 3799
**Email**:   usbritz@sun.ac.za

## Stellenbosch Fellowship in Polymer Science

**Purpose**: To fund further study in Polymer Science and synthetic Polymer chemistry

**Eligibility**: Open to students with a PhD in Polymer Science or Environmental Engineering and experience in membranes, membrane operations, polymer brushes, grafts and other nano particles
**Level of Study**: Postdoctorate
**Type**: Fellowship
**Length of Study**: 1 year
**Frequency**: Annual
**Study Establishment**: University of Stellenbosch
**Country of Study**: South Africa
**Application Procedure**: Request application.

### For further information contact:

Department of Chemistry, Division of Polymer Science University of Stellenbosch, Private Bag X1, Matieland, 7602, South Africa.

**Email**:   rds@sun.ac.za

## Stellenbosch Merit Bursary Award

**Purpose**: To reward academically above-average students
**Eligibility**: Available to full-time students registered at Stellenbosch University in any postgraduate degree programme
**Level of Study**: Postgraduate
**Type**: Bursary
**Value**: R 4,100–34,700
**Length of Study**: Up to 2 years
**Frequency**: Annual
**Study Establishment**: Stellenbosch University
**Country of Study**: South Africa
**Application Procedure**: Students must submit an application and a certified copy of a complete, official academic record
**No. of awards offered**: Approx. 700
**Closing Date**: 6 December
**Contributor**: Stellenbosch University
**No. of awards given last year**: 340
**No. of applicants last year**: Approx. 700
**Additional Information**: www.sun.ac.za/english/learning-teaching/undergraduate-bursaries-loans/su-funding/merit-bursaries

### For further information contact:

Office for postgraduate student funding, Postgraduate and International Office, Wilcocks Building, Room 3015, Stellenbosch Central, Stellenbosch, 7600, South Africa.

**Tel**:        (27) 21 808 4208
**Fax**:      (27) 21 808 3799
**Email**:    postgradfunding@sun.ac.za

## Stellenbosch Postdoctoral Research Fellowship in Geology

**Purpose**: To finance a student interested in Archaen tectonics and applied structural geology of high-grade metamorphic granite-gneiss terrains
**Eligibility**: Open to students with a PhD in geology obtained within the past 5 years, with a background in regional mapping and structural geology
**Level of Study**: Postdoctorate
**Type**: Fellowship
**Value**: ZAR 60,000 per annum
**Length of Study**: 2 years
**Frequency**: Annual
**Study Establishment**: University of Stellenbosch
**Country of Study**: South Africa
**Application Procedure**: Submit a covering letter, curriculum vitae and all research outputs
**Closing Date**: 21 March
**Additional Information**: www.researchersjob.com/research-fellowship/

### For further information contact:

**Fax**:      (27) 21 808 3129
**Email**:    akister@sun.ac.za

## Stellenbosch Rector's Grants for Successing Against the Odds

**Purpose**: To award students who have achieved exceptional success despite difficult circumstances
**Eligibility**: Open to candidates who satisfy the admission requirements of the University and who can provide proof of exceptional achievement despite handicaps and/or specific physical, educational or social challenges
**Level of Study**: Postgraduate
**Type**: Grant
**Value**: R 60,000
**Length of Study**: Up to 3 years
**Frequency**: Annual
**Study Establishment**: Stellenbosch University
**Country of Study**: South Africa
**Application Procedure**: Students must submit a complete application form accompanied by a curriculum vitae and 2 references
**No. of awards offered**: 100
**Closing Date**: 10 September
**Funding**: Foundation
**Contributor**: Andrew Mellon Foundation
**No. of awards given last year**: 3
**No. of applicants last year**: 100

**For further information contact:**

Tel:      (27) 21 8084208
Fax:      (27) 21 808 2739
Email:    beursnavrae_nagraads@sun.ac.za

## Stockholm School of Economics

PO Box 6501, SE-11383 Stockholm, Sweden.

Tel:      (46) 8 736 9000
Email:    info@hhs.se
Website:  www.hhs.se

An international higher educational institution on a comparatively small scale with a dynamic international learning environment to further economic and business study.

### Consejo Nacional de Ciencia y Tecnologia (CONACYT) Scholarships

Eligibility: Open to Mexican students only
Level of Study: MBA
Type: Scholarship
Value: All agreed fees
Length of Study: 1 year
Frequency: Annual
Country of Study: Sweden
Application Procedure: Contact the Foundation
Funding: Foundation
Contributor: CONACYT
Additional Information: www.sussex.ac.uk/study/phd/doc toral/funding-support-international/conacyt

**For further information contact:**

Email:    ochoa@buzon.main.conacyt.mx

### Petra Och Kail Erik Hedborgs Stiftelse Scholarship

Level of Study: MBA
Type: Scholarship
Value: All tuition fees and travel costs
Length of Study: 1 year
Frequency: Annual
Country of Study: Sweden
Application Procedure: Contact the institute
Funding: Private
Additional Information: www.pkhedborg.com/english.html

**For further information contact:**

Tel:      (46) 8 765 6327
Email:    info@pkhedborg.com

## The Swedish Foundation for International Cooperation in Research and Higher Education (STINT) Scholarship

Eligibility: Open to Brazilian nationals only
Level of Study: MBA
Type: Scholarship
Length of Study: 1 year
Frequency: Dependent on funds available
Country of Study: Sweden
Application Procedure: Contact the institute
Funding: Government
Contributor: STINT
Additional Information: www.european-funding-guide.eu/ scholarship/5175-initiation

**For further information contact:**

STINT, Wallingatan 2, SE-111 60 Stockholm, Sweden.

Tel:      (46) 46 8662 7690
Fax:      (46) 46 8661 9210
Email:    info@stint.se

## Strathclyde University

16 Richmond Street, Glasgow, G1 1XQ, United Kingdom.

Tel:      (44) 141 552 4400
Website:  www.strath.ac.uk

Based in the heart of the City of Glasgow, Strathclyde University is a leading technological university with around 23,000 students from more than 100 nations. With an international reputation for teaching excellence, the university has a five-star Overall Rating in the QS Stars University Ratings, and seven Times Higher Education awards in as many years.

### Strathclyde Prestige Award for Excellence in Business Translation & Interpreting

Purpose: Strathclyde University is a major international technical university situated in Glasgow, Scotland. The mission of the university is socially progressive and brings positive change in the life of its students for society and the world

**Eligibility**: 1. Be available to commence their academic studies in the United Kingdom by the start of the academic year in September. 2. Hold a first degree at first class or upper second class honours, or equivalent. 3. Hold an academic offer to study MSc Business Translation & Interpreting. 4. Provide a 300-word essay demonstrating their ability to contribute to the field of Business Translation & Interpeting

**Level of Study**: Postgraduate

**Type**: Award

**Value**: £5,000

**Length of Study**: 1 year

**Frequency**: Annual

**Country of Study**: Any country

**Closing Date**: 31 May

**Funding**: International office

**Additional Information**: www.eafinder.com/strathclyde-prestige-international-award-for-excellence-in-business-translation-interpreting-in-uk-2019/

### For further information contact:

**Tel**:  (44) 141 444 8600
**Email**:  hass-pg-enquiries@strath.ac.uk

## Stroke Association

Stroke House, 240 City Road, London EC1V 2PR, United Kingdom.

**Tel**:  (44) 20 7566 1543
**Email**:  research@stroke.org.uk
**Website**:  www.stroke.org.uk
**Contact**:  Rachael Sherrington, Research Awards Officer

The Stroke Association funds research into stroke prevention, treatment, rehabilitation, and long term care. It also helps stroke patients and their families directly through community services. It campaigns, educates and informs to increase knowledge of stroke at all levels of society and it acts as a voice for everyone affected by stroke.

## Priority Programme Awards

**Purpose**: This new funding stream is aimed at addressing the gaps in research in the following areas

**Type**: Award

**Value**: Up to the amount of £450,000

**Length of Study**: 3–5 years

**Frequency**: Annual

**Country of Study**: Any country

**Closing Date**: January

**Additional Information**: These awards will be made in July. Please contact research@stroke.org.uk www.stroke.org.uk/research/our-funding-schemes/priority-programme-awards

## The Stroke Association Research Project Grants

**Purpose**: To advance research into stroke

**Eligibility**: 1. Stroke Association Awards must be carried out at Universities, NHS Trusts, Statutory Social Care Organisations or other Research Institutions within Great Britain and Northern Ireland. 2. The lead applicant must be a senior researcher holding a PhD (or equivalent) with a track record of managing grants, delivering research studies and a strong publication record. 3. The salary of the lead applicant has to be guaranteed for the duration of the proposed programme; the Lead applicant's salary cannot be requested in the budget. 4. For this funding call masters, PhD studentships, and clinical fellowships are not eligible to be included in the budget.

**Level of Study**: Research

**Type**: Project grant

**Value**: Up to £250,000

**Length of Study**: 3–5 years

**Frequency**: Annual

**Study Establishment**: A suitable university or hospital in the United Kingdom

**Country of Study**: United Kingdom

**Application Procedure**: Application forms are available from the website

**No. of awards offered**: 20

**Closing Date**: 4 February

**Funding**: Private, Trusts

**Contributor**: Donations

**No. of awards given last year**: 3

**No. of applicants last year**: 20

**Additional Information**: Please visit www.stroke.org.uk/research/looking-funding/project-grants www.stroke.org.uk/research/our-funding-schemes/project-grants

### For further information contact:

**Tel**:  (44) 20 7566 1543

## Sugar Research Australia - SRA

SRA invests in and manages a portfolio of research, development and adoption projects that drive productivity, profitability and sustainability for the Australian sugarcane industry. An industry-owned company, we are funded by a statutory levy paid by growing and milling businesses. The SRA levy payers' stakeholder investment is also supported by the Commonwealth Government co-investment and grants from the Queensland Government and other bodies. We know and understand the issues our members and levy payers face. We tackle these issues to find research solutions and new and better ways of doing things on-farm and at the mill.

**Tel**:       (61) 7 3331 3333
**Website**:   sugarresearch.com.au/
**Contact**:   50 Meiers Road, Indooroopilly QLD 4068 PO Box 86, Indooroopilly QLD 4068, Australia.

Sugar Research Australia invests in and manages a portfolio of research, development and adoption projects that drive productivity, profitability and sustainability for the Australian sugarcane industry.

## Sugar Industry Postgraduate Research Scholarships (SPRS)

**Purpose**: Sugar Research Australia (SRA) invests in and manages a portfolio of research, development and adoption (RD&A) projects that drive productivity, profitability and sustainability for the Australian sugarcane industry. SRA also invests significantly in industry capability with the ongoing future success of the sugar industry dependent upon improving the capability of existing industry employees. With respect to research funding and encouraging young scientists into our industry, SRA makes available a number of SPRS awards every year, tenable at Australian universities and institutions, for postgraduate research study. The purpose of these awards is to enable qualified graduates to undertake Research Doctorate or Research Masters study and to facilitate research and training in areas of value to the Australian sugarcane industry.

**Eligibility**: The purpose of the SPRS is to enable high calibre students to undertake a Masters or PhD research degree in disciplines relevant to the future of the Australian sugar industry. Scholarships are available for three years for PhD studies and two years for Research Masters studies and are awarded on the basis of academic excellence. Applicants should consult the SRA Strategic Plan document available on the SRA website and focus on inventive projects that address at least one of the following eight key focus areas of investment: 1. Optimally-adapted varieties, plant breeding and release 2. Soil health, nutrient management and environmental sustainability 3. Pest, disease and weed management 4. Farming systems and harvesting 5. Milling efficiency and technology 6. Product diversification and value addition 7. Knowledge and technology transfer and adoption 8. Collaboration and capability development To be eligible for a full SPRS or a top-up scholarship, the candidate must be a citizen or permanent resident of Australia and must have acceptance at a recognised research institution. The principal supervisor for the postgraduate study program must provide evidence that the host organisation supports the project and the applicant's candidature for the relevant study program. Awards are tenable at Australian universities/institutions; however for applicants of proven ability who are undertaking a PhD, training at overseas institutions may be approved where benefits will return to the Australian sugar industry and where overseas supervision will confer additional benefit. Awards are conferred on the student based on merit, with the evaluation criteria set out within this document. Generic applications from prospective supervisors requesting support for postgraduate research projects without identifying a specific candidate will not be considered. The SPRS award offers supplementary or full scholarships, the number and value of which are at the discretion of SRA. For a higher probability of success, the applicant is encouraged to also apply for a Research Training Program (RTP) scholarship or equivalent through their host university. Preference will be given to applicants who receive an RTP or equivalent scholarship. Successful applicants not holding an RTP scholarship or any other base scholarship will be provided a tax-free stipend of AU$32,000 per annum (exclusive of GST). Successful applicants with an RTP scholarship will be provided a tax free top-up set at a maximum of 75% of the RTP stipend rate which is determined by the Australian Government Department of Education and Training each year. All successful applicants will also be provided with an additional budget of AU$10,000 (excluding GST) per year to support research project operating expenses.

**Level of Study**: postgraduate
**Type**: Scholarship
**Value**: AU$32,000
**Frequency**: Annual
**Country of Study**: Australia
**Application Procedure**: The SRA SugarNet online submission system must be used for all SPRS applications. This can be accessed at sugarnet.sugarresearch.com.au. Applications will not be considered to be complete until the curriculum vitae (CV), certified copies of the academic record and academic transcript, letters of reference from at least two referees and proof of nationality or permanent residence visa are uploaded through SugarNet to accompany the application. The project title needs to be a concise statement of the aim of the proposed research project. The title, objectives and outcomes expected from the project may be published in the SRA Annual Report. Candidates are encouraged to consult their Principal Supervisor when completing this section of the online submission form. No additional information or

attachments (such as images, diagrams, flow-charts, tables etc.) should be included unless a prior arrangement has been made with SRA

**Closing Date**: 31 October

**Additional Information**: www.worldwidecancerresearch. org/for-researchers/our-funding-criteria/

### For further information contact:

**Tel**:     (61) 7 3331 3333
**Email**:  fundingunit@sugarresearch.com.au.

## Swansea University

Singleton Park, Swansea, SA2 8PP Wales, United Kingdom.

**Tel**:       (44) 1792 205 678
**Email**:    sro@swansea.ac.uk
**Website**:  www.swan.ac.uk
**Contact**:  Dr Mark Skippen, Senior Postgraduate
              Recruitment Officer

Swansea University is a United Kingdom top 30 institution for research excellence (REF2014) that has been providing the highest quality postgraduate teaching since 1920. Our campuses are situated on the stunning sandy beach of Swansea Bay. We have taught and research postgraduate funding for United Kingdom, European Union and international students: www.swansea.ac.uk/postgraduate/scholarships

### Computer Science: Fully Funded EPSRC PHD Scholarship

**Purpose**: The Department of Computer Science is part of the Computational Foundry, a world-class centre for computational research, part-funded by the European Regional Development Fund through the Welsh Government

**Eligibility**: 1. Candidates must have a first or upper second class honours or a Master's degree with Merit (or equivalent), in a relevant discipline. 2. For candidates whose first language is not English, we require IELTS 6.5 (with 6.0 in each component) or equivalent. Please visit our website for a list of acceptable English language tests. 3. We prefer candidates to have already met the English Language requirements at the point of application, although this is not a requirement

**Level of Study**: Graduate

**Type**: Scholarship

**Value**: annual stipend of £15,009 per annum

**Frequency**: Annual

**Country of Study**: Any country

**Application Procedure**: To apply, please complete and return the following documents to the College of Science: 1. College of Science PGR Scholarship Application. 2. Academic References – all scholarship applications require two supporting references to be submitted. Please ensure that your chosen referees are aware of the funding deadline, as their references form a vital part of the evaluation process. Please either include these with your scholarship application or ask your referees to send them directly to science-scholarships@ swansea.ac.uk

**Closing Date**: 23 March

**Funding**: Private

**Additional Information**: The Computational Foundry has dedicated research labs, runs specialised seminar series, frequently hosts international guest researchers from academia and industry, and is involved in large United Kingdom- and European Union-funded research projects that provide opportunities for additional training and research visits at partner universities

### For further information contact:

**Email**:    science-scholarships@swansea.ac.uk

### International Excellence Scholarships

**Eligibility**: Awards are available to postgraduate applicants from outside the EU. Other eligibility criteria may apply. Please contact us for details

**Level of Study**: Postgraduate

**Type**: Scholarship

**Value**: Approx. £4,000

**Length of Study**: 1 year (Masters)

**Frequency**: Annual

**Study Establishment**: Swansea University

**Country of Study**: United Kingdom

**Application Procedure**: Complete application form, available online at website

**Closing Date**: 22 May

**Additional Information**: Please contact at international@swansea.ac.uk studyabroad.shiksha.com/scholarships/international-excellence-scholarship-masters

### For further information contact:

**Tel**:     (44) 1245 493131
**Email**:   scholarships@brunel.ac.uk

### MRes Scholarships

**Type**: Scholarship

**Value**: Each scholarship is worth £2,500, to be used towards the cost of tuition fees

**Country of Study**: Any country
**Application Procedure**: To apply please complete and return the following application form to science-scholarships@swansea.ac.uk
**Closing Date**: 20 July
**Additional Information**: www.bournemouth.ac.uk/study/postgraduate-research/fees-funding/studentships-scholarships/mres-scholarships

## For further information contact:

Macquarie University, NSW 2109, Australia.

**Email**: hdrcotutelle@mq.edu.au

## PhD Fees-only Bursaries

**Eligibility**: Open to good Master's graduates from the United Kingdom/European Union who will be commencing PhD studies at Swansea University
**Type**: Scholarship
**Value**: Covers United Kingdom/European Union tuition fees
**Length of Study**: 3 years
**Frequency**: Annual
**Study Establishment**: Swansea University
**Country of Study**: United Kingdom
**Application Procedure**: Please contact us for an application form
**No. of awards given last year**: 10

## For further information contact:

**Email**: admissions-enquiries@swansea.ac.uk

## Swansea University Masters Scholarships

**Eligibility**: Open to students from the United Kingdom/European Union who will be starting an eligible master's course at Swansea University for the first time in September
**Level of Study**: Postgraduate
**Type**: Scholarship
**Value**: £1,500 towards tuition fees
**Length of Study**: 1 year full time or 2–3 years part-time
**Frequency**: Annual
**Study Establishment**: Swansea University
**Country of Study**: United Kingdom
**Application Procedure**: Eligible students are sent an application form when offered a place on a course
**Closing Date**: 17 July
**No. of awards given last year**: 100

**Additional Information**: www.swansea.ac.uk/science/postgraduatescholarships/swansea-science-masters-scholarships/

## For further information contact:

Postgraduate Admissions Office, Swansea University, Singleton Park, Sketty, Swansea SA2 8PP, United Kingdom.

**Email**: science-scholarships@swansea.ac.uk

## Swansea University PhD Scholarships

**Eligibility**: Open to good Master's graduates from the United Kingdom/European Union who will be commencing PhD studies at Swansea University
**Level of Study**: Doctorate, Postgraduate
**Type**: Scholarship
**Value**: Annual stipend at Rcuk level (approx. £14,000)
**Length of Study**: 3 years
**Frequency**: Annual
**Study Establishment**: Swansea University
**Country of Study**: United Kingdom
**Application Procedure**: Please see individual scholarship listings on our website: www.swansea.ac.uk/postgraduate/scholarships/research
**No. of awards given last year**: 15

## For further information contact:

Postgraduate Admissions Office, Swansea University, Singleton Park, Sketty, Swansea SA2 8PP, United Kingdom.

**Email**: postgraduate.admissions@swansea.ac.uk

## Swansea University Research Excellence Scholarship

**Purpose**: The project aims to create novel approaches to contemporary challenges in theoretical and applied ecological and evolutionary biosciences
**Type**: Scholarship
**Value**: The scholarship covers the full cost of United Kingdom/European Union tuition fees, plus an annual stipend of £14,553 (in line with the RCUK stipend amount) for 3 years. There will also be £1,000 per annum available for research expenses such as travel, accommodation, field trips and conference attendance
**Country of Study**: United Kingdom
**Closing Date**: 8 January
**Contributor**: Swansea University
**Additional Information**: To apply please complete and return the following documents to Dr Vivienne Jenkins (pgrsures-at-swansea.ac.uk) using the quote reference COS2

www.postgrad.com/news/Applications-open-for-Swansea-University-Research-Excellence-Scholarships-SURES/2563/

### For further information contact:

**Email**: pgrsures@swansea.ac.uk

## The James Callaghan Scholarships

**Eligibility**: Research students from Commonwealth member countries are eligible to apply. Awards are available for full-time or part-time MPhil or PhD studies
**Level of Study**: Doctorate, Predoctorate
**Type**: Scholarship
**Value**: £1,700 (full-time) and £850 (half-time)
**Length of Study**: 1 year (MPhil) and 3 years (PhD)
**Frequency**: Annual
**Study Establishment**: Swansea University
**Country of Study**: United Kingdom
**Application Procedure**: Please contact us for an application form
**Closing Date**: 1 June
**Additional Information**: www.advance-africa.com/The-James-Callaghan-Scholarships.html

### For further information contact:

Postgraduates Admissions Office, Swansea University, Singleton Park, Sketty, Swansea SA2 8PP, United Kingdom.

**Email**: postgraduate.admissions@swansea.ac.uk

## Swedish Institute

Slottsbacken 10, Box 7434, SE-103 91 Stockholm, Sweden.

**Tel**: (46) 8 453 7800
**Email**: si@si.se
**Contact**: The Swedish Institute

SISS is the Swedish government's international awards scheme aimed at developing global leaders. It is funded by the Ministry for Foreign Affairs of Sweden and administered by the Swedish Institute (SI). The programme offers a unique opportunity for future leaders to develop professionally and academically, to experience Swedish society and culture, and to build a long-lasting relationship with Sweden and with each other.

## Swedish Institute Scholarships for Global Professionals (SISGP)

**Purpose**: The Swedish Institute (SI) is now launching the Swedish Institute Scholarships for Global Professionals (SISGP), a new scholarship programme which replaces Swedish Institute Study Scholarships (SISS)
**Eligibility**: Work experience; You must have minimum of 3,000 hours of demonstrated employment. Read more about the criteria for work experience Leadership experience; You must have demonstrated leadership experience from your current or previous employment. Read more about the leadership experience criteria University admissions; You must be liable to pay tuition fees to Swedish universities, have followed the steps of university admission, and be admitted to one of the eligible master's programmes by 4 April
**Level of Study**: Graduate
**Type**: Scholarship
**Value**: Living expense of SEK 10,000 and travel allowance of SEK 15,000
**Length of Study**: One academic year (2 sememsters)
**Frequency**: Varies
**Country of Study**: Any country
**Application Procedure**: A complete application must consist of: 1. A completed motivation letter. 2. A CV. 3. Two valid and completed letters of reference. 4. Valid and completed proof of work and leadership experience. 5. A copy of your valid passport
**Closing Date**: 20 February
**Funding**: Private
**Additional Information**: For further information on application process, visit the website. si.se/en/apply/scholarships/swedish-institute-scholarships-for-global-professionals/ www.opportunitiesforafricans.com/swedish-institute-scholarships-for-global-professionals-sisgp-2020-2021/

### For further information contact:

Swedish Institute, Slottsbacken 10, SE-111 30 Stockholm, Sweden.

## Swedish Institute Scholarships for the Western Balkans Programme

**Purpose**: The SI Scholarships for the Western Balkans Programme aims at supporting advanced level studies and research within the field of social sciences in order to forge closer links between the Western Balkans and the European Union, and to contribute to strengthened democracy in the region
**Eligibility**: The scholarships are intended for PhD students and postdoctoral researchers from Albania, Bosnia-Herzegovina, Kosovo, Macedonia (FYROM), Montenegro and Serbia

conducting part of their studies/research in Sweden within the field of social sciences
**Level of Study**: Doctorate, Postdoctorate
**Type**: Scholarship
**Value**: SEK 15,000 per month for PhD students, and SEK 18,000 per month for postdoctoral researchers and senior scientists
**Length of Study**: 1 year
**Frequency**: Annual
**Country of Study**: Sweden
**Application Procedure**: Online application portal
**Closing Date**: 10 January
**Contributor**: Ministry for Foreign Affairs of Sweden and administered by the Swedish Institute (SI)
**Additional Information**: Please contact sischolarships@si.se

### For further information contact:

**Email**: sischolarships@si.se

## Swedish-Turkish Scholarship Programme for PhD Studies and Postdoctoral Research

**Purpose**: The Swedish-Turkish Scholarship Programme aims at supporting advanced level studies and research in order to forge closer links between Turkey and the European Union, and to contribute to strengthened democracy and a greater respect for human rights
**Eligibility**: The scholarships are intended for PhD students and postdoctoral researchers from Turkey conducting part of their studies/research in Sweden within the field of social sciences. You should not be a resident for more than 2 year in Sweden
**Level of Study**: Doctorate, Postdoctorate
**Type**: Scholarship
**Value**: SEK 15,000 per month for PhD students, and SEK 18,000 per month for postdoctoral researchers and senior scientists
**Length of Study**: 1 year
**Country of Study**: Sweden
**Closing Date**: 1 November
**Contributor**: Ministry for Foreign Affairs of Sweden and administered by the Swedish Institute (SI)
**Additional Information**: Please contact sischolarships@si.se scholarization.blogspot.com/2010/07/swedish-turkish-scholarship-program.html

## The Swedish Institute Study Scholarships (SISS)

**Purpose**: SISS is the Swedish government's international awards scheme aimed at developing global leaders

**Eligibility**: Applicants must be from an eligible country and have at least 3,000 hours of experience from full-time/part-time employment, voluntary work, paid/unpaid internship, and/or position of trust. Applicants must display academic qualifications and leadership experience. In addition, applicants should show an ambition to make a difference by working with issues which contribute to a just and sustainable development in their country, in a long term perspective. The travel grant is a one-time payment of SEK 15,000
**Level of Study**: Foundation programme
**Type**: Scholarship
**Value**: The scholarship covers both tuition fees (paid directly to the Swedish university/university college by the Swedish Institute) and living expenses to the amount of SEK 10,000 per month. There are no additional grants for family members
**Length of Study**: The scholarship is intended for full-time master's level studies of one or two years, and is only awarded for programmes starting in the autumn semester. The scholarship covers the whole duration of the master's programme
**Country of Study**: Any country
**Closing Date**: 20 February
**Funding**: Government
**Contributor**: Ministry for Foreign Affairs of Sweden
**Additional Information**: www.opportunitiesforafricans.com/swedish-institute-study-scholarships-siss-2020-2021/

## The Swedish Institute Study Scholarships for South Africa

**Purpose**: The programme offers a unique opportunity for future leaders to develop professionally and academically, to experience Swedish society and culture, and to build a long-lasting relationship with Sweden and with each other
**Type**: Scholarship
**Value**: The scholarship covers both tuition fees (paid directly to the Swedish university/university college by the Swedish Institute) and living expenses to the amount of SEK 9,000 per month. The travel grant is a one-time payment of SEK 15,000
**Length of Study**: Whole duration of the master's programme
**Country of Study**: Sweden
**Application Procedure**: Online application
**Closing Date**: 15 January
**Contributor**: Ministry for Foreign Affairs of Sweden and administered by the Swedish Institute (SI)
**Additional Information**: opportunitydesk.org/2019/12/12/swedish-institute-scholarships-for-south-africa-2020/

## Visby Programme Scholarships

**Purpose**: The aim of the Visby Programme is to support individual mobility, thereby contributing to increased contacts and collaborations between actors in Sweden and countries in the EU Eastern Partnership and Russia. The goal is to build an integrated, knowledge-based and research-intense region, centred on the Baltic Sea while also including EU Eastern Partnership countries and Russia

**Eligibility**: 1. PhD student, applying for a part of his/her ongoing PhD studies to be carried out in Sweden (1 year maximum). 2. Postdoctoral researcher, with priority given to holders of a PhD degree. 3. Senior scientist - holders of a PhD degree obtained before 2012 (6 months maximum)

**Level of Study**: Doctorate, Postdoctorate

**Type**: Scholarship

**Value**: SEK 15,000 per month for PhD students, and SEK 18,000 per month for postdoctoral researchers and senior scientists. The scholarship cannot be prolonged or extended

**Country of Study**: Any country

**Application Procedure**: Applications are evaluated by the Swedish Institute (SI) and an academic board. Online application form

**Closing Date**: 14 February

**Additional Information**: Please contact sischolarships@si.se www.youthop.com/scholarships/swedish-institute-visby-programme-scholarships

### For further information contact:

**Email**:    markus.boman@si.se

## Swedish Natural Science Research Council (NFR)

Box 7142, SE-10387 Stockholm, Sweden.

**Tel**:          (46) 85 464 400
**Email**:      vetenskapsradet@vr.se
**Website**:   www.nfr.se
**Contact**:   Grants Management Officer

### NFR FRN Grants for Scientific Equipment

**Purpose**: To assist researchers

**Eligibility**: Open to individuals holding a research grant from any Swedish research council

**Level of Study**: Research

**Type**: A variable number of grants

**Value**: Up to SEK 10,000,000

**Length of Study**: Dependent on the requirements of the projects

**Frequency**: Annual

**Study Establishment**: Universities

**Country of Study**: Sweden

**Application Procedure**: Applicants must contact the organisation for details

**Funding**: Government

### For further information contact:

**Tel**:        (46) 84 544 254
**Email**:    lars@nfr.se

### NFR Travel Grants

**Purpose**: To give financial support to researchers attending conferences or wishing to undertake short-term research abroad

**Eligibility**: Open to Swedish researchers and foreign national researchers who have completed their PhD at a Swedish university and have embarked on postdoctoral studies

**Level of Study**: Postdoctorate, Research

**Type**: Travel grant

**Value**: Travelling expenses and subsistence

**Length of Study**: Up to 2 months

**Frequency**: Throughout the year

**Study Establishment**: Universities or academic institutions abroad

**Country of Study**: Any country

**Application Procedure**: Applicants must complete an application form

**Closing Date**: 15 August

**Funding**: Government

### For further information contact:

**Tel**:        (46) 84 544 229
**Email**:    elisa@nfr.se

## Swinburne University of Technology

PO Box 218, Hawthorn, VIC 3122, Australia.

**Tel**:          (61) 3 9214 8000
**Email**:      webmaster@swin.edu.au
**Website**:   www.swinburne.edu
**Contact**:   MBA Admissions Officer

It provides career-orientated education and as a university with a commitment to research. The University maintains a strong technology base and important links with industry, complemented by a number of innovative specialist research centres which attract a great deal of international interest.

A feature of many Swinburne undergraduate courses is the applied vocational emphasis and direct industry application through Industry Based Learning (IBL) programs. Swinburne was a pioneer of IBL program which places students directly in industry for vocational employment as an integral part of the course structure. Swinburne is committed to the transfer of lifelong learning skills. It is heavily involved in international initiatives and plays a significant part in the internationalization of Australia's tertiary education system.

## Chancellor's Research Scholarship

**Purpose**: To award students of exceptional research potential to undertake a higher degree by research (HDR)
**Eligibility**: Open to a local or an international student undertaking a higher degree by research (HDR) with Bachelor Degree with First Class Honours. For further details, please check the website
**Level of Study**: Doctorate
**Type**: Research scholarship
**Value**: An annual stipend of US$30,000, an Establishment Grant of up to US$3,000 and up to US$5,000 for a 6-month overseas placement
**Length of Study**: 3 years
**Frequency**: Annual
**Application Procedure**: Check website for further details
**Additional Information**: Please refer website for details: www.swinburne.edu.au/study/options/scholarships/215/chancellors-research-scholarship-/

### For further information contact:

Building 60Wm. Level 7, 60 William Street, Hawthorn Campus, VIC 3122, Australia.

**Tel**:       (61) 9214 5547 or 9214 8744
**Email**:   ehill@swin.edu.au

## PhD in Mechatronics

**Purpose**: To provide full time scholarships to undertake the degree of Doctor of Philosophy (PhD) at the Faculty of Engineering and Industrial Sciences of Swinburne University of Technology
**Eligibility**: Applicants should have completed an undergraduate course in engineering preferably in mechatronics or electrical engineering. Candidates with a Masters Degree in a related area or with previous research experience will be given priority
**Level of Study**: Doctorate

**Type**: Scholarship
**Value**: AU$19,616 per year
**Length of Study**: 3 years
**Application Procedure**: Check website for further details
**Closing Date**: 20 July

### For further information contact:

Swinburne University of Technology, PO Box 218, VIC 3122, Australia.

**Tel**:       (61) 61 3 9214 5659
**Email**:   arad@swin.edu.au

## Swinburne University Postgraduate Research Award (SUPRA)

**Purpose**: To assist with general living costs
**Eligibility**: Open to domestic or an international student undertaking a higher degree by research. Hold a bachelor's degree with first-class honours or equivalent. Please check the website for further details
**Level of Study**: Doctorate, Research
**Type**: Research award
**Value**: A non-taxable indexed stipend of around US$23,728 per year and a tuition fee scholarship (total value around US$49k per year)
**Length of Study**: 3 years (Research Doctorate)
**Country of Study**: Any country
**Application Procedure**: Complete an application for admission to research higher degree candidature and scholarship and mail/courier or you can scan your application forms in and email them
**Closing Date**: October
**Additional Information**: www.swinburne.edu.au/study/options/scholarships/221/swinburne-university-postgraduate-research-award/

### For further information contact:

**Tel**:       (61) 9214 5547 or 9214 8744
**Email**:   ehill@swin.edu.au

## Vice Chancellor's Centenary Research Scholarship (VCRS)

**Purpose**: To assist with general living costs
**Eligibility**: Open to domestic or an international student who have completed a Bachelor degree with First Class Honours and are of exceptional research potential undertaking a higher degree by research (HDR). For further details, please check the website

**Level of Study**: Research

**Type**: Research scholarship

**Value**: The value of the VCRS will be up to US$35,000 (tax-exempt) over a maximum period of up to 3.5 full-time years, payable at the rate of US$5,000 per year for the 1st year and US$12,000 per year for the remaining 2.5 years

**Length of Study**: 3 years

**Application Procedure**: Check website for further details

### For further information contact:

Building 60Wm, Level 7, 60 William Street, Hawthorn Campus, VIC 3122, Australia.

**Tel**:       (61) 9214 5547 or 9214 8744
**Email**:   ehill@swin.edu.au

## Swiss National Science Foundation (SNSF)

Wildhainweg 20, PO Box CH-3001 Berne, Switzerland.

**Tel**:            (41) 31 308 2222
**Website**:    www.snf.ch
**Contact**:    Dr Benno G Frey, Office for Fellowship Programmes

The Swiss National Science Foundation (SNSF) supports scientific research at Swiss universities and other scientific institutions and awards fellowships to Swiss scientists or scientists living in Switzerland. The SNSF was established in 1952 as a private foundation entrusted with the promotion of basic non commercial research. While the SNSF supports research through grants given to established or promising researchers, it does not maintain its own research institutions. The main objectives of the SNSF are to support basic research in all areas of academic research and to support young scientists and researchers, with the intent of ensuring the continuing high quality of teaching and research in Swiss higher education. In addition to the general research funding, the SNSF is responsible for the National Research Programmes (NRP).

## Swiss National Science Foundation Fellowships for Prospective Researchers

**Purpose**: To promote holders of MA or PhD degrees, who have had at least one year's experience in active research after the completion of their degree

**Eligibility**: Open to promising young Scholars under the age of 33 who are Swiss nationals or permanent residents of Switzerland, hold an MA or PhD and can demonstrate at least one year's experience in active research. An exception to the age restriction (to a maximum of two years) can be made for candidates from clinical disciplines, or candidates who have interrupted their scientific careers due to family obligations. The main condition for such an exception is that the candidate has reached a high scientific level and will in the future pursue an active career in science and research. A high priority will be given to candidates who plan to return to Switzerland

**Level of Study**: Postdoctorate, Predoctorate

**Type**: A variable number of fellowships

**Value**: Varies

**Length of Study**: Varies

**Frequency**: Annual

**Study Establishment**: Universities worldwide

**Country of Study**: Any country

**Application Procedure**: Applicants must complete an application form, available from the Local Research Commission. Candidates with a degree from a Swiss university should contact the Research Commission of their institution. Candidates with Italian as their native language, who have completed their studies in a foreign country should contact the Research Commission for the Italian speaking part of Switzerland. Swiss candidates who are residents of foreign countries, hold a degree from a foreign university, but who intend to return to Switzerland should contact the Swiss scientific academy responsible for their area of research

**Additional Information**: For further information please contact Benno Frey or Laurence at the Office for Fellowship Programmes, or refer to the website www.snf.ch/SiteCollec tionDocuments/stip_ang_weisungen_mySNF_e.pdf

## Syracuse University

900 South Crouse Ave, Syracuse, NY 13244, United States of America.

**Tel**:         (1) 315 443 1870
**Email**:    grad@syr.edu
**Website**:  www.syr.edu

Syracuse University is a non-profit, private student research university. Its mission is to promote learning through teaching, research, scholarship, creative accomplishment and service.

## Syracuse University Executive MBA Programme

**Length of Study**: 2 years
**Application Procedure**: Applicants must return a completed 'Independent Study MBA' application form
**Closing Date**: 7 May
**Additional Information**: onlinebusiness.syr.edu/mba/

### For further information contact:

School of Management, Suite 100, Crouse-Hinds School of Management, Syracuse, NY 13244, United States of America.

**Tel**:     (1) 315 443 3006
**Fax**:     (1) 315 443 5389
**Email**:   grad@gwmail.syr.edu

## Syracuse University MBA

**Purpose**: All Syracuse MBA scholarships are awarded based on merit and the qualifications shown on a student's admission application. Applicants are not required to apply separately for merit-based scholarships
**Eligibility**: To be eligible for the MBA admission, listed below are the requirements. 1. A United States bachelor's degree or its equivalent from an accredited college or university Completed application. 2. Recommended minimum GPA is 3.0 on a 4.0 scale. 4. GMAT or GRE exam. 5. Recommended minimum GMAT score is 600. The 2016 entering class average was 623. 6. For those with GRE scores you can convert them to GMAT through the website www.ets.org/gre/institutions/about/mba/comparison_tool. 7. Program code for GMAT is NG0-SB-40. 8. Institution code for GRE is 2823. 9. English exam (for international students). 10. Minimum total score for TOEFL is 100, IELTS 7.0, PTE 68. 11. Preferred speaking score for TOEFL is 24, IELTS 7.5, PTE 65. 12. Institution code for TOEFL is 2823, department code is 02 if required. 13. PTE Academic program code is 5LD-BQ-15. 14. IELTS: Whitman downloads IELTS scores that have been transmitted to our e-download account
**Length of Study**: 1–2 years
**Country of Study**: Any country
**Application Procedure**: Applicants must complete the application form (including the specified number of photocopies) with official academic transcripts, two letters of recommendation, personal essays, requested financial documents, Graduate Management Admission Test and TOEFL (if applicable) scores, and a fee of US$50. Applications may be fully completed online

**Additional Information**: whitman.syr.edu/programs-and-academics/programs/whitman-mba-experience/fulltime-mba-experience/index.aspx

### For further information contact:

Syracuse University, School of Management, Suite 100, Crouse-Hinds School of Management, Syracuse, NY 13244, United States of America.

**Tel**:      (1) 315 443 4492
**Fax**:      (1) 315 443 3423
**Email**:   lescis@syr.edu

## System for Analysis Research and Training (START)

International START Secretariat, 2000 Florida Avenue NW Suite 200, Washington, DC 20009, United States of America.

**Tel**:        (1) 202 462 2213
**Email**:     START@agu.org
**Website**:   www.start.org
**Contact**:   Professor Roland Fuchs, Director

The global change SysTem for Analysis, Research and Training (START), provides an international framework for capacity building. It fosters regional networks of collaborating scientists and institutions in developing countries to conduct research on regional aspects of environmental change, assess impacts and vulnerabilities to such changes and provide information to policy makers.

## Start/Norad Fellowship for Doctoral Research and Dissertation on Global Environmental Change

**Purpose**: To financially support outstanding young African scientists in their research
**Eligibility**: Open to candidates who are not more than 35 years of age and are currently enrolled in a graduate degree programme leading to a PhD degree in an African university. The applicant must have obtained a Master's degree
**Level of Study**: Doctorate
**Type**: Fellowship
**Value**: Varies
**Length of Study**: 2 years

**Frequency**: Annual
**Study Establishment**: Any accredited university
**Country of Study**: Africa
**Application Procedure**: Applicants must submit a completed programme application form, a detailed proposal, a curriculum vitae and a letter of recommendation
**Closing Date**: 15 August

**Additional Information**: Application materials can be sent electronically or faxed scholarship-positions.com/doctoral-dissertation-research-fellowship-in-the-united-states/2019/12/21/

**For further information contact:**

**Email**:     cskauffman@agu.org

# T

## Tante Marie's Cooking School

271 Francisco Street, San Francisco, CA 94133, United States of America.

**Tel**: (1) 415 788 6699
**Email**: peggy@tantemarie.com
**Website**: www.tantemarie.com

Tante Marie's Cooking School, located in San Francisco was founded as a full-time school in 1979. It is one of the first schools of fine cooking offering all-day, year-round classes for people who are serious about cooking well. Graduates from Tante Marie's have interesting and varied careers. In addition to offering professional courses for people wanting to begin a career in culinary or pastry, Tante Marie's welcomes interested avocational students in the Evening Series, Weekend Workshops, One-Day Workshops and Cooking Vacations. There are also cooking parties on weekend evenings where groups of up to 30 people cook together. The emphasis at Tante Marie's is in building confidence in the kitchen.

## The Absolute Taste Scholarship

**Purpose**: To make candidates learn cooking professionally
**Eligibility**: All prospective students ordinarily resident in the British Isles who are at least 16 years of age and under 25 years of age on commencement of the course
**Level of Study**: Unrestricted
**Type**: Scholarship
**Value**: Up to 100 % of the course fee
**Frequency**: Annual
**Country of Study**: United States of America
**Application Procedure**: Check website for further details
**Closing Date**: 7 June
**Funding**: Private

**Additional Information**: Please refer to the website for details

**For further information contact:**

**Email**: info@tantemarie.co.uk

## Tanzania Communications Regulatory Authority (TCRA)

Tanzania Communications Regulatory Authority (TCRA), Mawasiliano Towers, 20 Sam Nujoma Road, Dar Es Salaam, Tanzania.

**Tel**: (255) 22 219 9760 8; 22 241 2011 2
**Email**: dg@tcra.go.tz
**Website**: www.tcra.go.tz

The Tanzania Communications Regulatory Authority (TCRA) is a quasi-independent Government body responsible for regulating the communications and broadcasting sectors in Tanzania. It was established under the TCRA Act no. 12 of 2003 to regulate the electronic communications, and postal services, and management of the national frequency spectrum in the United Republic of Tanzania.

## Tanzania Communications Regulatory Authority ICT Scholarship

**Purpose**: The scholarship offers Tanzania students the opportunity to obtain degrees in the Information and Communication Technologies (ICT) and related areas
**Eligibility**: The scholarship will be awarded on the basis of academic merit and an interview to be conducted by the Scholarship Panel

**Level of Study**: Postgraduate
**Type**: Scholarship
**Length of Study**: All scholarships are provided for the specified duration of a particular degree course
**Country of Study**: Tanzania
**Closing Date**: 20 July
**Funding**: International office
**Additional Information**: Tanzanian students can apply for these ICT scholarships www.tcra.go.tz/images/headlines/ScholarshipAdvertReadvertisement2015-16.pdf

## Tata Trusts

### Lady Meherbai D. TATA Education Trust

**Purpose**: The Lady Meherbai D Tata Education Trust awards scholarships to Indian women graduates of recognised universities to pursue higher education abroad, towards the tuition fee
**Eligibility**: Indian women graduates from a recognised university. 1. Should have a consistently remarkable academic record. 2. Must have applied for admission / secured admission to reputed accredited universities or institutions in the United States, United Kingdom or Europe for the current academic year. 3. Preference will be given to candidates with a minimum of 2 years of work experience in the requisite fields of study
**Level of Study**: Graduate
**Type**: Grant
**Value**: Scholarship amount of ₹600,000 per student is awarded, depending on the performance of candidate
**Frequency**: Annual
**Country of Study**: Any country
**Application Procedure**: Applications have to be processed through mailing process. Application forms will be emailed to the students on request from 11 March to 19 April. Application forms will be emailed to the applicants upon submission of a neatly typed letter / email giving details of: 1. The course they wish to pursue. 2. The university they will be attending. 3. The course fee required. 4. Sources of funding. 5. Their current profile along with documents for the same
**Closing Date**: 26 April
**Funding**: Private
**Additional Information**: Students shortlisted for the interviews and scholarships awarded would be solely at the discretion of the Trustees of the Lady Meherbai D Tata Education Trust www.tatatrusts.org/upload/scholarship-announcement-2019-2020.pdf

### For further information contact:

Bombay House, 24, Homi Mody Street, Mumbai, Maharashtra 400 001, India.

**Tel**:         (91) 22 6665 8282
**Email**:     igpedulmdtet@tatatrusts.org

## Te Pôkai Tara Universities New Zealand

PO Box 11915, Manners Street, Wellington 6142, New Zealand.

**Tel**:         (64) 404 381 8500
**Email**:     kiri@nzvcc.ac.nz
**Website**:  www.nzvcc.ac.nz
**Contact**:   Kiri Manuera, Scholarships Manager

The New Zealand Vice Chancellors Committee (NZVCC) was established by the Universities Act 1961, which replaced the federal University of New Zealand with separate institutions. Today the Committee represents the interests of New Zealand's 8 universities. The NZVCC represents the interests of the New Zealand university system to government, its agencies and the public through a range of forums and communications from joint consultative groups to electronic and print publications.

### William Georgetti Scholarships

**Purpose**: To encourage postgraduate study and research in a field that is important to the social, cultural or economic development of New Zealand
**Eligibility**: Applicants must: a) have resided in New Zealand for a period of at least five years immediately preceding the year of selection; b) be of good moral character and repute; c) be of good health; d) hold a degree of a university in New Zealand or elsewhere or any other academic qualification of a university or other institution of learning (in New Zealand or elsewhere) reasonably equivalent in the opinion of the Scholarship Board to a degree of a university in New Zealand.
**Level of Study**: Postgraduate
**Type**: Scholarship
**Value**: Up to US$45,000 per annum
**Length of Study**: 3 year
**Frequency**: Annual
**Study Establishment**: Suitable universities
**Country of Study**: Any country
**Application Procedure**: You may apply through the website approximately 8 weeks before applications close.
**Closing Date**: 1 February

**Funding**: Private
**Contributor**: The Georgetti Trust
**Additional Information**: Further information is available on request. universitiesnz.communityforce.com/ www.universitiesnz.ac.nz/scholarships/william-georgetti-scholarship

**For further information contact:**

**Email**:   scholarshipscf@universitiesnz.ac.nz

## Technical University of Denmark (DTU)

Anker Engelunds Vej 1 Bygning 101A, DK 2800 Lyngby, Denmark.

**Tel**:        (45) 45 25 11 56
**Email**:      oerstedpostdoc@adm.dtu.dk
**Contact**:   COFUND secretariat

### H.C. Ørsted Fellowships for International Researchers

**Purpose**: The Programme will contribute to the researcher's career development, broadening and be deepening individual competencies through exposure to an international and multidisciplinary environment. Eligibility: The programme is open for young talented researchers from all over the world. 1. Level of Study: Research. 2. Type: Fellowships 3. Value: The grant will cover the salary for the postdoc fellow for up to 2 years
**Length of Study**: 2 years
**Country of Study**: Denmark
**Application Procedure**: Applications must be submitted as one compiled PDF file containing all material via DTU's online submission form at www.dtu.dk/english/career
**Closing Date**: 23 February
**Contributor**: Marie Sklodowska-Curie Actions
**Additional Information**: For any queries please contact oerstedpostdoc@adm.dtu.dk www.scholarshipsads.com/16-dtu-h-c-orsted-fellowships-international-researchers-2017/

## Technische Universiteit Delft (TUD)

Post bus 5, NL 2600 AA Delft, Netherlands.

**Tel**:        (31) 15 278 9111
**Email**:      info@tudelft.nl
**Website**:   www.tudelft.nl/msc

Founded in 1842, the Delft University of Technology is the oldest, largest, and most comprehensive technical university in the Netherlands. It is an establishment of both national importance and significant international standing. Renowned for its high standard of education and research, TU Delft collaborates with other educational establishments and research institutes, both within and outside of the Netherlands. TU Delft aims at being an, interactive partner' to social issues, committed to answering its multifaceted demands and initiating changes to benefit people in the future.

## The Shell Centenary Scholarship Fund, Netherlands

**Purpose**: To give students the opportunity to study at the TUD and gain skills that will make a long-term contribution to the further development of their countries
**Eligibility**: Open to candidates who are nationals of and resident in any country other than the ones listed in, the additional information section below and aged 35 or under, intending to study a subject that will be of significant value in aiding the sustainable development of their home country, fluent in spoken and written English, and neither a current nor former employee of the Royal Dutch/Shell Group of companies
**Level of Study**: Postgraduate
**Type**: Scholarship
**Value**: Full-cost scholarship including tuition fees, international travel, living allowances and health insurance
**Length of Study**: 2 years
**Frequency**: Annual
**Country of Study**: Netherlands
**Application Procedure**: Applicants must have been admitted to a MSc programme of TU Delft, the International Office will subsequently send you the application form by email, the International Office will check your application on the basis of the Royal Dutch/Shell criteria
**Closing Date**: 15 December
**Contributor**: TUD with support from The Shell Centenary Scholarship Fund (TSCSF)
**Additional Information**: Countries not eligible: Australia, Austria, Belgium, Canada, Cyprus, Czech Republic, Denmark, Estonia, Finland, France, Germany, Greece, Hungary, Iceland, Ireland, Italy, Japan, Latvia, Lithuania, Luxembourg, Malta, The Netherlands, New Zealand, Norway, Poland, Portugal, Slovenia, Slovakia, Spain, Sweden, Switzerland, United Kingdom, and United States

**For further information contact:**

**Tel**:      (31) 15 278 5690
**Email**:   msc2@tudelft.nl

# Tel Aviv University (TAU)

PO Box 39040, Tel Aviv 6997801, Israel.

**Tel**: (972) 3 640 8111
**Email**: tauinfo@post.tau.ac.il
**Website**: www.tau.ac.il

Tel Aviv University (TAU) was founded in 1956 and is located in Israel's cultural, financial and industrial heartland, TAU is the largest university in Israel and the biggest Jewish university in the world. TAU offers an extensive range of programmes in the arts and sciences.

## Tel Aviv University Scholarships

**Purpose**: To encourage innovative and interdisciplinary research that cuts across traditional boundaries and paradigms
**Eligibility**: Open to candidates who have registered for their Doctoral or Postdoctoral degree
**Level of Study**: Doctorate, Postdoctorate
**Type**: Scholarships
**Value**: Minimum award amount is US$500
**Frequency**: Annual
**Application Procedure**: Applicants can download the application form from the website. The completed application form along with a curriculum vitae and a description of research project with a list of publications is to be sent
**Closing Date**: 30 April
**Additional Information**: Applications if sent by email, must be directed to ddprize@post.tau.ac.il international.tau.ac.il/scholarship_programs

### For further information contact:

The Lowy School for Overseas Students, Center Building, Tel-Aviv University, Israel.

**Email**: scholarship@tauex.tau.ac.il

# Texas LBJ School

## Barbara Jordan Baines Report Fellowship Fund

**Purpose**: The Barbara Jordan Baines Report Fellowship Fund is available to students interested in gaining skills in policy writing and storytelling, as well as exercising leadership through managing the student-run publication

**Eligibility**: The Baines Report Fellowship supports a master's student pursuing skills in writing about public policy and experience in news media and content creation. Preference will be given to applicants with prior writing or journalism experience. All currently enrolled full-time LBJ School Master's students who are in good academic standing are eligible to apply
**Level of Study**: Graduate
**Type**: Funding support
**Value**: Students are eligible up to US$750 fund and US$500 toward travel funds
**Frequency**: Annual
**Country of Study**: Any country
**Application Procedure**: Apply using the common Current Student Endowed Fellowship Application form, located on the right side of this page. Students must also submit a current resume, a letter of interest, two writing samples and one well-planned story idea. Final candidates may be interviewed. For further details, check the following link: lbj.utexas.edu/sites/default/files/BJBREligCriteria.pdf
**Funding**: Private
**Additional Information**: In addition, both the fall and spring fellowship awards provide US$500 towards travel to attend the Journal of Public and International Affairs (JPIA) reading weekend in February, contingent on JPIA's invitation. JPIA provides main meals and lodging lbj.utexas.edu/lbj-school-fellowships#Baines%20Report

### For further information contact:

Lyndon B. Johnson School of Public Affairs, The University of Texas at Austin, P.O. Box Y, Austin, TX 78713-8925, United States of America.

**Tel**: (1) 512 471 3200
**Email**: lbjdeansoffice@austin.utexas.edu

## Elspeth D. Rostow Memorial Graduate Fellowship

**Purpose**: The LBJ Foundation is supporting the LBJ School of Public Affairs through the Elspeth Rostow Memorial Fellowship Fund.
**Eligibility**: To be considered for this fellowship, applicants must be degree-seeking master's students who have completed one year of full-time study at the LBJ School with a cumulative GPA of 3.0 or above. There are no exceptions to these requirements
**Level of Study**: Graduate
**Type**: Fellowship
**Value**: US$3,000.
**Frequency**: Annual
**Country of Study**: Any country

**Application Procedure**: 1. Complete the Elspeth D. Rostow Memorial Graduate Fellowship application. 2. Submit a one-page statement describing your public service related commitments since enrolling in the LBJ School. Your statement should describe the needs of the community served, how the project pursued addressed those needs, the role you personally played in the public service activities, and the time commitment of the activity. 3. A current resume.

**Closing Date**: November

**Funding**: Private

**Additional Information**: lbj.utexas.edu/sites/default/files/RostowCriteria.pdf

**For further information contact:**

**Email**:  lbjdeansoffice@austin.utexas.edu

## Michael and Alice Kuhn Summer Fellowships

**Purpose**: The Kuhn Fellowship grant, made possible by the Michael and Alice Kuhn Foundation, awards each grantee US\$6,000 to cover living expenses during their summer internship

**Eligibility**: 1. A selection committee will review applications on a rolling basis and recommend applicants with demonstrated commitment to the goals of the Kuhn Summer Fellowship Program: to promote social justice and fight poverty. 2. Students with diverse backgrounds receive priority consideration. 3. The selection committee may make requests in addition to the online application, such as official UT transcripts and/or interviews. 4. The selection committee will make its recommendations to the LBJ School leadership. Final selection is at the discretion of school leadership

**Level of Study**: Graduate

**Type**: Fellowship

**Frequency**: Annual

**Country of Study**: Any country

**Application Procedure**: The student's summer work must be done for a nonprofit organization in Central Texas or the United States whose mission is related to social justice and alleviating poverty. There is an interest in supporting students whose placements involve leadership opportunities in the areas of public and legislative advocacy, program-related management, as well as opportunities to work with executive team members on strategic priorities and projects. Students will be asked to link to a Google Drive PDF copy of their: 1. Resume. 2. Relevant three- to five-page writing sample from school or professional setting. 3. Offer letter from the nonprofit confirming the internship and description of work

**Closing Date**: 30 April

**Funding**: Commercial, Private

**Additional Information**:  lbj.utexas.edu/michael-and-alice-kuhn-summer-fellowships

**For further information contact:**

**Email**:  LBJFellowships@austin.utexas.edu

## Terrell Blodgett Fellowship for Government Services in Urban Management and Finance

**Purpose**: The Blodgett Fellowship is awarded annually on a competitive basis as part of the internship fellowship process

**Eligibility**: The Blodgett Fellowship is awarded annually on a competitive basis as part of the internship fellowship process. First-year master's students pursuing an internship in local government and/or city management are eligible to apply. To be considered for this fellowship, applicants must be degree-seeking master's stundents

**Level of Study**: Graduate

**Type**: Fellowship

**Frequency**: Annual

**Country of Study**: Any country

**Application Procedure**: To apply, students must complete the LBJ internship fellowship application and submit it along with their approved internship request form, a letter from the agency supervising the internship, a one-page essay on career goals, and a current resume. Using the following link for further information. www.blodgettfellows.org/

**Closing Date**: April

**Funding**: Private

**Additional Information**:  lbj.utexas.edu/sites/default/files/Blodgett%20Criteria%20PDF.pdf

**For further information contact:**

**Email**:  lbjwriting@austin.utexas.edu

## The Community Foundation of South Alabama

### Harry & Lula McCarn Nurses Scholarship

**Subjects**: Nursing Administration or other field of nursing

**Purpose**: To offer financial assistance to a student pursuing a Master's degree in Nursing Administration or a related field.

**Eligibility**: For a student living in Mobile or Baldwin Counties and pursuing a Master's degree in Nursing Administration or other field of nursing in the USA. Applicants must have a minimum 3.0 GPA.

**Type**: Scholarship

**Study Establishment**: University of South Alabama
**Country of Study**: United States of America
**Additional Information**: www.communityfoundationsa.org/apply-for-a-scholarship

## The Foundation for Advancement of Diversity in IP Law

### AIPLEF Sidney B. Williams Scholarship

**Subjects**: Law
**Purpose**: The Foundation for Advancement of Diversity in IP Law is a charitable organization whose mission is to increase the diversity of the IP bar by providing scholarships and mentoring to underrepresented minority law school students pursuing careers in IP law.
**Eligibility**: Be enrolled as an entering law school (1L) student. Have proven academic performance at the undergraduate, graduate, and law school levels (if applicable). Have a financial need. Have record of leadership, community activities, and/or special accomplishments. Demonstrate intent to engage in the full-time practice of patent law. Are currently enrolled in or have been accepted to an ABA-accredited law school.
**Type**: Scholarship
**Value**: Students will be selected to receive a three-year scholarship of up to US$30,000 (US$10,000 per academic year, US$5,000 per semester, which can only be applied to verifiable costs associated with average tuition and usual fees).
**Length of Study**: Three years
**Country of Study**: United States of America
**Additional Information**: The curriculum of law school as it relates to intellectual property law is not considered in awarding scholarships. Applicants related to a trustee of AIPLEF, a council member of the ABA-IPL Section, Officer or member of the Board of Directors of the AIPLA, or a member of the AIPLEF Scholarship Committee are ineligible to apply. Scholarship recipients are required to attend law school, day or evening, on either a full-time or part-time enrollment basis, and to maintain a grade point average of "B" (3.0) or better. Scholarship recipients are required to join and maintain membership in AIPLA.

## The Gerda Henkel Foundation

### Lost Cities Funding Programme

**Subjects**: Abandoned cities
**Purpose**: The aim of the program is to describe the tangible cultures of interpretation, knowledge and perception within these different contexts. Lost Cities are part of a distinct culture of memory, for example, which serves for the negotiation of identities, the preservation of knowledge cultures, the formulation of criticism of progress, or the construction of mythical or sacral topographies as part of a veritable "ruin cult". On this basis, the focus here should not be on the question of which factors led to the city's abandonment. Rather, it is the abandoned cities themselves that are of particular interest, as well as the different forms of their interpretation, instrumentalization and coding in various cultures and time frames.
**Eligibility**: Eligible to apply are post-doctoral researchers based in a university and working in the area of the humanities and the social sciences. Funding can be provided for projects with a thematic focus being addressed by a group of researchers. The Foundation uses the term "group of researchers" to mean associations of at least two researchers actively involved in the project work which is to be funded by means of scholarships from the Foundation and who are carrying out research into the same issues. Applications can only be made for PhD or research scholarships. Applications for a research scholarship by the applicant (project leader) are also possible. A maximum total of three scholarships per group of researchers can be applied for, as well as funds for travel and materials. A fundamental prerequisite for a grant is that project staff conduct their own research, which is published under their name. Other contributors who are not financed by scholarships can also be involved in the project. Scholarship applications made by individual researchers outside of the group are not accepted. The funding programme also provides for the project partners to participate in a public "workshop discussion on Lost Cities" organised by the Foundation.
**Type**: Grant
**Value**: €2,300 monthly scholarship, plus a bonus €400 grant for one child and €100 for each further child
**Length of Study**: 36 months
**Country of Study**: Any country
**Closing Date**: 2 June
**Additional Information**: The Foundation generally accepts applications for research projects made by universities, other research institutes or comparable institutions as well as by one or several Postdocs or scholars with Post Doctoral Lecture Qualification. www.gerda-henkel-stiftung.de/en/lost_cities

## The Lynde and Harry Bradley Foundation

### Grant

**Subjects**: Projects may address any arena of public life economics, politics, culture or civil society. As such, support is provided to schools of business, economics, public policy and more for activities including research, general operating expenses, graduate and post-graduate fellowships, seminars and speakers programs.

**Purpose**: Supports projects that "nurture a solid foundation of competent, self-governing citizens, who are capable of and responsible for making the major political, economic and moral decisions that shape their lives."

**Eligibility**: See website.

**Type**: Grant

**Value**: Varies

**Country of Study**: Any country

**Application Procedure**: The application process proceeds in two stages. First, brief letters of inquiry are required. If the foundation determines the project to be within its policy guidelines, the applicant will receive a brochure with further application instructions.

**Closing Date**: 1 March; 1 July; 1 September; 1 December

**Additional Information**: www.bradleyfdn.org

# The Marfan Foundation

Marfan syndrome is a genetic disorder that affects the body's connective tissue. Connective tissue holds all the body's cells, organs and tissue together. It also plays an important role in helping the body grow and develop properly. Connective tissue is made up of proteins. The protein that plays a role in Marfan syndrome is called fibrillin-1. Marfan syndrome is caused by a defect (or mutation) in the gene that tells the body how to make fibrillin-1. This mutation results in an increase in a protein called transforming growth factor beta, or TGF-$\beta$. The increase in TGF-$\beta$ causes problems in connective tissues throughout the body, which in turn creates the features and medical problems associated with Marfan syndrome and some related conditions. Because connective tissue is found throughout the body, Marfan syndrome can affect many different parts of the body, as well. Features of the disorder are most often found in the heart, blood vessels, bones, joints, and eyes. Some Marfan features - for example, aortic enlargement (expansion of the main blood vessel that carries blood away from the heart to the rest of the body) - can be life-threatening. The lungs, skin and nervous system may also be affected. Marfan syndrome does not affect intelligence.

**Tel**:        (1) 516 883 8712
**Email**:      research@marfan.org
**Website**:    www.marfan.org/
**Contact**:    Josephine Grima, PhD Chief Science Officer The Marfan Foundation 22 Manhasset Avenue Port Washington, NY 11050, United States of America

The Marfan Foundation's mission is to save lives and improve the quality of life of individuals with Marfan syndrome and other genetic aortic conditions. Our values in our mission to save and improve lives, we hold a number of core beliefs and values that drive everything we do: We put families at the heart of what we do. Marfan syndrome and related conditions affect not only individuals but also the people who love them. We stand with and for the whole community.

## Faculty Grant Program

**Purpose**: The Marfan Foundation is requesting proposals to the Faculty Grant Program which supports two-year grants for basic, translation or clinical research. The grant program is designed to provide financial support for senior faculty members studying any or all disciplines involved in Marfan syndrome, EDS, LDS, and other related disorders. Grant awards are based on proposal evaluation by The Marfan Foundation Scientific Advisory Board with the approval of the Board of Director. The Marfan Foundation will award up to three 2-year US$100,000 grants. We are pleased to announce that one faculty grant will be funded by the Loeys-Dietz Foundation for studies dedicated to Loeys-Dietz syndrome vasculature or TGFBeta.

**Eligibility**: The principal investigator must hold an MD, DO, PhD, ScD, DDS, DVM or equivalent degree. The investigator must have proven ability to pursue independent research as evidenced by original research publications in peer-reviewed journals and should hold a position of Associate Professor or above. Faculty members with less experience who have obtained an NIH R-01 grant are also eligible for the faculty grant award. Work can be performed in the U.S. or internationally and non U.S. appointments are acceptable.

**Level of Study**: postgraduate

**Type**: grant

**Value**: The Marfan Foundation will award up to three 2-year US$100,000 grant

**Frequency**: Annual

**Country of Study**: US

**Application Procedure**: The application must be submitted electronically, including the application forms, additional pages, and appendices, as a single PDF file, via The Marfan Foundation website, marfan.org. Please name your application using the following format: FacultyGrant_Lastname_FirstName.pdf Example: FacultyGrant_Smith_Jane.pdf The application forms may be completed by using the free Adobe Reader program. If you do not already have it, you can download it at www.adobe.com/products/reader.html. The Title Page form requires dated signatures; you may either insert a digital signature and date or print the form and then scan it to include in your application PDF. Additional pages should be typed single-spaced using a font size of at least a 10 points and with one inch margins. Pages should be numbered at the bottom. Appendices should not be used to subvert the page limitation on the grant, however, figures, tables, diagrams and photographs can be placed in the appendices. Please present the proposal in the order that follows: THE MARFAN FOUNDATION FACULTY GRANT GUIDELINES 5 1. Title Page: 1 page Application form provided 2. Table of Contents: 1 page Application form provided 3. Project Abstract and Lay Person Summary: 1 page each On a single page, describe precisely and clearly the nature, objective, methods of procedure and significance of the proposed research project, and how it relates to the goal of providing a better understanding of Marfan syndrome, EDS, LDS, and other related disorders and/or improving the treatment or diagnosis of Marfan syndrome, EDS, LDS, and other related disorders (limit 300 words). Rewrite the abstract in abbreviated form in terms suitable for presentation to lay persons (limit 500 words). 4. Research Plan: 3 pages a. Include Goals and Objectives; Rationale; Methodology; Evaluation. (Figures may be placed in appendix if needed). b. Please comment upon the importance of funding: i. Will this funding allow you to pursue studies that would otherwise not be performed? Is funding meant to supplement other sources of support? ii. Do you anticipate that this funding will increase your competitiveness for other funding sources? c. Please comment upon the significance of the work that you propose: i. Is it similar to or a direct extension of work that has been or is being performed elsewhere? ii. Does the work complement or extend other studies that are being performed at your institution? iii. How novel are the studies that you describe? iv. Would such a proposal be competitive for NIH funding in its current form, or would you require additional preliminary data? v. Do you anticipate that the support would lead to the generation of physical resources that might be useful to other investigators in the field? vi. If so, would you be willing to make them widely available? 5. Budget and Justification List full budget with amount requested. Include: a. Names, titles, time/percentage effort of all participants, requested salaries and fringe benefits and total amount required. b. Statement that the institution or other funding sources will absorb indirect costs. c. A written budget justification. 6 The budget justification should be suited to the proposal. It is important that the investigators match the dollar award with the actual project. If funding from other sources is being used to cover certain parts of the study, please elaborate on what parts of the budget will not be completed with Foundation funding and what the approximate costs of the full project would be. No overhead or indirect costs will be considered. List the additional sources of funding if budget exceeds proposal amount. 6. Other Support: 2 pages List other support received by principal and co-investigators for any projects (include yearly and total budget and duration of any grants): a. Current b. Pending c. Description (in a paragraph, describe each current or pending grant and whether it has scientific or budgetary overlap with the present proposal). 7. Biographical Sketches: 5 pages each Using the supplied form, please provide biographical sketches for key personnel. Indicate the total number of publications in each of the (2) categories: referenced articles and invited works. If you prefer, you may use the NIH biosketch form instead. 8. Facilities Description: 1 page Describe the research facilities (laboratory space, clinical population, etc) available for the project. 9. Appendix a. Figures, tables etc. b. Literature cited c. Human subjects experimental approval d. Vertebrate animal experimental approval Letters of support

**Closing Date**: 3 April

### For further information contact:

The application must be submitted electronically, including the application forms, additional pages, and appendices, as a single PDF file, via The Marfan Foundation website, marfan.org.

## The National Academies of Sciences, Engineering and Medicine

### Gulf Research Program Science Policy Fellowships

**Subjects**: Science policy

**Purpose**: Science Policy Fellowships will contribute to leadership development and capacity building by providing recipients with a valuable educational experience at the science-policy interface. Fellows will spend one year on the staff of a state environmental, natural resources, oil and gas, or public health agency; or regional offices of relevant federal agencies in the Gulf region.

**Eligibility**: Applicants must: Be currently enrolled in a doctoral program or hold an eligible degree, including MA/MS, MPH/MSPH, PhD, ScD, EngD, MD, DrPH, and DVM. For applicants not currently enrolled in a doctoral program, eligible degrees must be completed by August 15, 2020, and conferred by December 31, 2020. Applicants currently enrolled in a doctoral program must take a leave of absence for the duration of the fellowship. Come from an area of research including social and behavioral sciences, health sciences and medicine, engineering and physical sciences, earth and life sciences, and interdisciplinary scientific fields relevant to the charge of the Gulf Research Program to focus on "human health and environmental protection including issues relating to offshore oil drilling and hydrocarbon production and transportation in the Gulf of Mexico and on the

United States" outer continental shelf. Be a U.S. citizen, U.S. national, or lawful permanent resident. Not be currently employed by the U.S. federal government. Full-time, paid, permanent federal employees are not eligible for the fellowship.

**Type**: Fellowship

**Value**: Fellows who have completed an MA, MS, or MPH degree or who are currently enrolled in a doctoral program will receive an annual stipend of US$45,000. Fellows who have completed a PhD, ScD, MD, or DVM will receive an annual stipend of US$55,000. Stipends will be paid directly to the fellow in monthly disbursements.

**Frequency**: Annual

**Country of Study**: Any country

**Application Procedure**: Applications submitted through the online application system.

**Closing Date**: 4 March

**Additional Information**: www.nationalacademies.org/gulf/fellowships-and-grants/science-policy-fellowship

# The National GEM Consortium

## MS Engineering Fellowship Program

**Subjects**: Engineering

**Purpose**: The objective of this program is to promote the benefits of a masters degree within industry.

**Eligibility**: Must be studying disciplines including, but not limited to: Aeronautical Engineering, Aerospace, Agricultural Engineering, Analytical Chemistry, Anatomy, Automotive, Biochemistry, Bioengineering, Biology, Biomedical Engineering, Chemical Engineering, Chemistry, Civil Engineering, Computer Science, Electrical Engineering, Environmental Engineering, Environmental Science, Industrial Engineering, Information Systems, Inorganic Chemistry, Manufacturing Engineering, Materials Engineering, Materials Science, Mathematics, Mechanical Engineering, Metallurgical Engineering, Nuclear Engineering, Operations Research, Organic Chemistry, Petroleum Engineering, Physics, Structural Engineering, Systems Engineering

**Type**: Fellowship

**Value**: US$4,000 living stipend per full-time semester up to 4 semesters (US$8K per academic year 3 quarters); up to two paid summer internships with a GEM Employer Member; full tuition and fees provided by a GEM University Member

**Country of Study**: United States of America

**Application Procedure**: See website.

**Closing Date**: 15 November

**Additional Information**: www.gemfellowship.org/students/gem-fellowship-program/

## PhD Engineering Fellowship

**Subjects**: Engineering

**Purpose**: The objective of this program is to offer doctoral fellowships to underrepresented minority students who have either completed, are currently enrolled in a master's in engineering program, or received admittance into a PhD program directly from a bachelor's degree program.

**Eligibility**: Fellowships will be awarded to underrepresented minority students who have either completed, are currently enrolled in a master's in engineering program, or received admittance into a PhD program directly from a bachelor's degree program.

**Type**: Fellowship

**Value**: During the first academic year of being awarded the GEM Fellowship, the GEM Consortium remits a stipend and a cost of instruction grant to the institution where the fellow is enrolled. Thereafter, up to the fifth year of the doctoral program, continued financial support of the GEM Fellow is borne by the GEM University through alternative sources of funding such as institutional awards, assistantships or other external fellowships. Fellows recieve US$16,000 stipend in the first academic year of the GEM Fellowship; GEM Member University provides a living stipend up to the 5th year of PhD program, equivalent to other funded doctorate students in the department; a minimum of one paid summer internship with a GEM Employer Member; full tuition and fees at a GEM University Member

**Country of Study**: Any country

**Application Procedure**: See website.

**Closing Date**: 15 November

**Additional Information**: Continued support from the GEM University will be contingent upon the GEM Fellow remaining in good academic standing and making satisfactory progress in their graduate program. Fellows are provided a paid graduate level summer work experience through the Employer Member for at least one summer. www.gemfellowship.org/students/gem-fellowship-program/

## PhD Science Fellowship

**Subjects**: Chemistry, physics, earth sciences, mathematics, biological sciences, and computer science.

**Purpose**: The goal of this program is to increase the number of minority students who pursue doctoral degrees in the natural science disciplines

**Eligibility**: Applicants to this program are accepted as early as their senior undergraduate year, as well as candidates currently enrolled in a Master's of Engineering program and working professionals.

**Type**: Fellowship

**Value**: During the first academic year of being awarded the GEM Fellowship, the GEM Consortium remits a stipend and a cost of instruction grant to the institution where the fellow is enrolled. Thereafter, up to the fifth year of the doctoral program, continued financial support of the GEM Fellow is borne by the GEM University through alternative sources of funding such as institutional awards, assistantships or other external fellowships. Fellows recieve US$16,000 stipend in the first academic year of the GEM Fellowship; GEM Member University provides a living stipend up to the 5th year of PhD program, equivalent to other funded doctorate students in the department; a minimum of one paid summer internship with a GEM Employer Member; full tuition and fees at a GEM University Member

**Country of Study**: Any country

**Application Procedure**: See website.

**Closing Date**: 15 November

**Additional Information**: Fellowships offered through this program are portable and may be used at any participating GEM Member University where the GEM Fellow is admitted. www.gemfellowship.org/students/gem-fellowship-program/

## The National Hispanic Scholarship Fund

### HSF Scholarship

**Subjects**: All

**Purpose**: The HSF Scholarship is designed to assist students of Hispanic heritage obtain a university degree.

**Eligibility**: Must be of Hispanic heritage. Minimum of 2.5 GPA on a 4.0 scale (or equivalent) for graduate students. Must plan to enroll full-time in an accredited, not-for-profit graduate school, in the US. Must complete FAFSA or state based financial aid application (if applicable).

**Type**: Scholarship

**Value**: Awards are based on merit; amounts range from US$500 to US$5,000, based on relative need, among the Scholars selected.

**Country of Study**: United States of America

**Additional Information**: www.hsf.net

## The Thomas R. Pickering Foreign Affairs Fellowship Program

### The Thomas R. Pickering Foreign Affairs Fellowship

**Subjects**: Public policy, international affairs, public administration, business, economics, political science, sociology, or foreign languages

**Purpose**: Prepares outstanding young people for Foreign Service careers in the U.S. Department of State. It welcomes the application of members of minority groups historically underrepresented in the State Department, women, and those with financial need.

**Eligibility**: Must be seeking admission to a two-year, full-time, on-campus, master's degree program at a U.S.-based graduate institution in an academic field relevant to the work of the Foreign Service. Must have a cumulative grade point average of 3.2 or higher on a 4.0 scale.

**Type**: Fellowship

**Value**: US$37,500 annually for a two-year period for tuition, room, board, books, and mandatory fees for completion of two-year master's degrees. This includes up to US$21,500 per year for tuition and mandatory fees and an academic year stipend of US$16,000.

**Length of Study**: Two years

**Frequency**: Annual

**Study Establishment**: Howard University

**Country of Study**: United States of America

**No. of awards offered**: 30

**Closing Date**: September

**Additional Information**: Law degrees do not satisfy this requirement. Fellows are expected to maintain a cumulative GPA of 3.2 throughout their period of study. Applicants apply to two-year graduate programs at U.S.-based universities simultaneously with their application to the Pickering Program. pickeringfellowship.org/

## The White House

### Fellowship

**Subjects**: All

**Purpose**: The White House Fellowship is a highly competitive opportunity to participate in and learn about the Federal Government from a unique perspective.

**Eligibility**: See website.

**Type**: Fellowship

**Value**: The work assignment provides the Fellow the opportunity to observe closely the process of public policy development and to come away with a sense of having participated in the governmental process as well as having made an actual contribution to the business of government.

**Country of Study**: Any country

**Closing Date**: 1 February

**Additional Information**: Fellows typically spend a year working as full-time, paid special assistants to senior White House Staff, the Vice President, Cabinet Secretaries and other top-ranking government officials. Fellows also participate in an education program consisting of roundtable discussions with renowned leaders from the private and public sectors, and trips to study U.S. policy in action both domestically and internationally.

# Third World Academy of Sciences (TWAS)

TWAS Executive Director ICTP Enrico Fermi Building, Room 108. Via Beirut 6, 34151 Trieste Italy.

**Tel**:          (39) 40 2240 327
**Email**:       edoffice@twas.org
**Website**:    www.twas.org
**Contact**:    Professor Romain Murenzi, Executive Director

The Third Word Academy of Sciences (TWAS) is an autonomous international organization that promotes and supports excellence in scientific research and helps build research capacity in the South.

## Council of Scientific and Industrial Research/ TWAS Fellowship for Postgraduate Research

**Purpose**: To enable scholars from developing countries (other than India) who wish to pursue postgraduate research to undertake research in laboratories or institutes of the CSIR

**Eligibility**: Candidates must have a Master's or equivalent degree in science or engineering and should be a regular employee in a developing country (other than India) and be holding a research assignment

**Level of Study**: Postgraduate

**Type**: Fellowship

**Value**: Monthly stipend to cover for living costs, food and health insurance

**Length of Study**: Up to 4 years

**Frequency**: Annual

**Study Establishment**: CSIR research laboratories or institutes

**Country of Study**: India

**Application Procedure**: One copy of the application should be sent to TWAS and three copies to CSIR. Application forms are available on request or from the website

**Closing Date**: 11 May

**Funding**: Government

**Contributor**: CSIR (India), the Italian Ministry of Foreign Affairs and the Directorate General for Development Co-operation

**No. of awards given last year**: 8

**Additional Information**: CSIR is the premier scientific organization of India, and has a network of research laboratories covering wide areas of scientific and industrial research twas.org/opportunity/twas-csir-postgraduate-fellowship-programme

## For further information contact:

International S&T Affairs Directorate, Council for Scientific and Industrial Research (CSIR), Anusandhan Bhavan, 2 Rafi Marg, New Delhi, Delhi 110001, India.

**Tel**:          (39) 040 2240 314, (91) 11 2331 6751
**Fax**:         (91) 11 2371 0618, (39) 040 2240 689
**Email**:       fellowships@twas.org, jaipal@csir.res.in

## OWSD PhD Fellowships for Women Scientists

**Purpose**: The PhD fellowship for women scientists from Science and Technology Lagging Countries (STLCs) supports them to undertake PhD research in the Natural, Engineering and Information Technology sciences at a host institute in the South.

**Eligibility**: The OWSD PhD Fellowship is offered only to women candidates. 1. Candidates must confirm that they intend to return to their home country as soon as possible after completion of the fellowship.

**Level of Study**: Postgraduate

**Type**: Fellowship

**Length of Study**: Up to 4 years

**Frequency**: Annual

**Closing Date**: 31 May

## The Council of Scientific and Industrial Research/ TWAS Fellowship for Postdoctoral Research

**Purpose**: To enable scholars from developing countries (other than India) who wish to pursue postdoctoral research to undertake research in laboratories or institutes of the CSIR

**Eligibility**: The minimum qualification requirement is a PhD degree in science or technology. Applicants must be regular employees in a developing country (but not India) and should hold a research assignment. Be a maximum age of 45 years on December 31st of the application year

**Level of Study**: Postdoctorate

**Type**: Fellowship

**Value**: Monthly stipend to cover for living costs, food and health insurance

**Length of Study**: Up to 12 months

**Frequency**: Annual

**Study Establishment**: CSIR research laboratories or institutes

**Country of Study**: India

**Application Procedure**: Applicants must complete an application form, available on request or from the website

**Closing Date**: 11 May

**Funding**: Government

**Contributor**: CSIR (India), the Italian Ministry of Foreign Affairs and the Directorate General for Development Co-operation

**No. of awards given last year**: 4

**Additional Information**: CSIR is the premier civil scientific organization of India, which has a network of research laboratories covering wide areas of industrial research twas.org/opportunity/twas-csir-postdoctoral-fellowship-programme

### For further information contact:

**Tel**:      (39) 040 2240 314, (91) 11 2331 6751
**Fax**:      (91) 11 2371 0618, (39) 040 2240 689
**Email**:    fellowships@twas.org, jaipal@csir.res.in

## TWAS-SN Bose Postgraduate Fellowship Programme

**Eligibility**: 1. be a maximum age of 35 years on 31 December of the application year; 2. be nationals of a developing country (other than India); 3. must not hold any visa for temporary or permanent residency in India or any developed country; 4. hold a Masters Degree in physics, mathematics or physical chemistry. S/He must have completed at least a total 5 years of undergraduate and postgraduate studies in a recognized university or institute. 5. provide evidence of proficiency in English, if medium of education was not English; 6. provide evidence that s/he will return to her/his home country on completion of the fellowship; 7. not take up other assignments during the period of her/his fellowship; 8. be financially responsible for any accompanying family members.

**Level of Study**: Postgraduate
**Type**: Fellowship
**Length of Study**: 5 years
**Frequency**: Annual
**Study Establishment**: S.N. Bose National Centre for Basic Sciences
**Closing Date**: 1 June

### For further information contact:

**Tel**:      (91) 33 2335 5706
**Fax**:      (91) 33 2335 3477
**Email**:    deanap@bose.res.in, studentsprogramme@boson.bose.res.in

## Thomson Foundation

37 Park Place, Cardiff, CF10 3BB, United Kingdom.

**Tel**:      (44) 29 2035 3060
**Email**:    enquiries@thomfound.co.uk

**Website**:   www.thomsonfoundation.co.uk
**Contact**:   Mr Gareth Price

The Thomson Foundation provides practical, intensive training both in the United Kingdom and abroad, along with a wide range of consultancies to journalists, managers, technicians and production staff in television, radio and the press.

## Thomson Foundation Scholarship

**Purpose**: To enable recipients to attend Thomson Foundation training courses in Britain

**Eligibility**: Open to professional journalists and broadcasters with at least 3 years of full-time experience

**Level of Study**: Professional development
**Type**: Scholarship
**Value**: Varies
**Length of Study**: Varies, usually a 12-week Summer course or a shorter 4-week course
**Study Establishment**: The Thomson Foundation
**Country of Study**: United Kingdom
**Application Procedure**: Applicants must complete an application form, available from the Foundation, for the courses they wish to apply for
**No. of awards offered**: 20
**Closing Date**: 15 April
**Funding**: Government, Private
**Contributor**: The British Foreign Office Chevening Scholarship Scheme
**No. of awards given last year**: 6
**No. of applicants last year**: 20
**Additional Information**: Annual 3-month courses in television, radio and press journalism run from June to September Webpage not open

### For further information contact:

**Email**:    enquiries@thomsonfoundation.org

## Thurgood Marshall College Fund (TMCF)

901 F Street NW, Suite 300, Washington, DC 20004, United States of America.

**Tel**:      (1) 202 507 4851
**Email**:    info@tmcfund.org
**Website**:   www.thurgoodmarshallfund.org

The Thurgood Marshall College Fund (TMCF) was established in 1987 to carry on Justice Marshall's legacy of equal access to higher education by supporting exceptional merit scholars attending America's public historically Black colleges and universities. More than 5,000 Thurgood Marshall Scholars have graduated and are making valuable contributions to science, technology, government, human service, business, education and various communities

## Center for Advancing Opportunity Doctorial Fellowship

**Subjects**: Education, criminal justice, and entrepreneurship
**Purpose**: CAO supports faculty and students at Historically Black Colleges and Universities (HBCUs) and other post-secondary institutions to develop research-based solutions to the most challenging issues. Our constituency is people living in fragile communities and they are members of all races, ethnicities, and religions.
**Eligibility**: Must be a current doctoral student at an accredited college or university. Must have received a four-year under-graduate degree from an HBCU, have a current cumulative grade point average of 3.0 or higher, be able to demonstrate leadership abilities and be able to demonstrate a financial need.
**Type**: Fellowship
**Value**: Scholars will be selected to receive a scholarship up to US$15,000 for the academic school year (US$7,500 per semester which can only be applied to verifiable costs associated with average tuition and usual fees).
**Study Establishment**: A Historically Black College and University (HBCU).
**Country of Study**: United States of America
**No. of awards offered**: Up to five

## CVS Health Pharmacy Scholarship

**Purpose**: To offer financial assistance to outstanding students attending one of the three pre-selected publicly-supported Historically Black College and University (HBCU) and Pre-dominantly Black Institution (PBI) Pharmacy Schools within the TMCF 47 member-school network.
**Eligibility**: Must be enrolled as a full-time graduate or doctoral student. Must have a current grade point average of 3.0 or higher. Must demonstrate outstanding financial need and must demonstrate leadership ability through a variety of measures.
**Type**: Scholarship
**Value**: One-year scholarship up to US$5,000 for the 2020 Spring and 2020 Fall semester which will be used to cover the costs of tuition and fees, on-campus room and board, and required textbooks purchased from member schools.

**Study Establishment**: Florida A & M University, Pharmacy School; University of Maryland Eastern Shore, Pharmacy School; and Texas Southern University, Pharmacy School.
**Country of Study**: United States of America
**Additional Information**: The recipient must be willing to apply for a CVS Health Summer internship.

## Thurgood Marshall College Fund Scholarships

**Purpose**: To financially support outstanding students
**Eligibility**: Open to candidates who are academically exceptional in the creative and performing arts requiring financial help
**Type**: Scholarship
**Value**: Varies
**Frequency**: Annual
**Application Procedure**: Completed applications must be submitted along with the required attachments
**Closing Date**: 30 March
**Funding**: Foundation
**Additional Information**: Refer to the website for details: tmcf.org/our-scholarships/current-scholarships www.tmcf. org/students-alumni/scholarship/tmcf-all-around-scholarship/

## For further information contact:

AIPLEF Scholarship, 80 Maiden Lane, Suite 2204, New York, NY 1138, United States of America.

**Email**: jessica.barnes@tmcfund.org

## WGRG Foundation Terri Grier Memorial Scholarship

**Subjects**: Public policy, public administration, political science, community engagement or other advocacy disciplines.
**Purpose**: To offer financial aid towards books, tuition and/or other college expenses.
**Eligibility**: Must be a member of an ethnic minority group: African-American (Black), Asian and Pacific Islanders, Hispanic/Latin (Black, White or Asian), Indians (Western and Eastern). Must be a high school senior and/or enrolled in an accredited college or university in the year of the award; demonstrate a 3.0 or higher GPA; demonstrate leadership skills through participation in community/public service, issue advocacy, research, extracurricular, and/or other activities; demonstrate the courage of conviction, persistence, and determination in the pursuit of his or her goals; and demonstrate a commitment to a career in government or the non-profit and advocacy sectors.
**Type**: Scholarship

**Value**: At least US$5,000.00 towards your books, tuition and/or other college expenses.

**Country of Study**: United States of America

**Application Procedure**: Must: complete the online application form; select one individual to complete a reference survey to be submitted by either an educator/college professor, administrator, counselor, employer, or individual with significant knowledge of the applicant's experience and public service engagement; provide an official and recent academic transcript with cumulative grade point average and a class standing/rank; submit a personal essay - in your essay, please answer the question directly in the application.

# Toxicology Education Foundation (TEF)

626 Admiral Drive, Ste. C, PMB 221, Annapolis, MD 21401, United States of America.

**Tel**:       (1) 443 321 4654
**Email**:    tefhq@toxedfoundation.org
**Website**:  www.toxedfoundation.org

The mission of TFE is to encourage, support and promote charitable and educational activities that increase the public understanding of toxicology.

## Alleghery-ENCRC Student Research Award

**Purpose**: To support a student's thesis, dissertation and summer research project in toxicology and to encourage them to formulate and conduct meaningful research

**Eligibility**: Open to students who are members in good standing of AE-SOT. The student's advisor must also be a member in good standing and submit a letter concerning availability

**Level of Study**: Graduate

**Type**: Award

**Value**: Up to US$1,000

**Frequency**: Annual

**Country of Study**: United States of America

**Application Procedure**: Applicants must send four copies of completed application form along with a project description and budget

**Closing Date**: 30 May

### For further information contact:

CDC/NIOSH MS 2015, 1095 Willowdale Road, Morgantown, WV 26505, United States of America.

**Email**:    LBattelli@cdc.gov

## Colgate-Palmolive Grants for Alternative Research

**Purpose**: To identify and support efforts that promote, develop, refine or validate scientifically acceptable animal alternative methods to facilitate the safety assessment of new chemicals and formulations

**Level of Study**: Research

**Type**: Research grant

**Value**: Plaque and maximum award of US$40,000

**Frequency**: Annual

**Country of Study**: United States of America

**Application Procedure**: Application is available online. A research plan, budget, curriculum vitae and a letter from the institution must be sent

**Closing Date**: 9 October

**Funding**: Private

**Contributor**: Colgate-Palmolive

**No. of awards given last year**: 5

**Additional Information**: www.toxicology.org/awards/sot/awards.aspx?AwardID=79

## Food Safety SS Burdock Group Travel Award

**Purpose**: To cover travel expenses for a student to attend the Annual Meeting

**Eligibility**: Open to full-time graduate students with research interests in toxicology. Students in their early graduate training, who have not attended any SOT Annual Meeting are encouraged to apply

**Level of Study**: Graduate

**Value**: Up to US$500

**Frequency**: Annual

**Country of Study**: United States of America

**Application Procedure**: Applicants must send a letter of request indicating that he/she is enroled in good standing in a doctoral training programme. The applicant must also state how the research and training relate to food safety

**Closing Date**: 24 February

### For further information contact:

**Email**:    rmatulka@burdockgroup.com

## Regulation and Safety SS Travel Award

**Purpose**: To help defray the costs of travel to the SOT meeting

**Eligibility**: Open to students submitting a poster or making a presentation at the SOT meeting

**Type**: Travel award

**Value**: US$1,500 each

**Frequency**: Annual

**Country of Study**: United States of America
**Application Procedure**: Applicants must fill an application form and an abstract of work preserved
**Closing Date**: 15 December

### For further information contact:

**Email**:   jtmacgror@earthlink.net

## Robert L. Dixon International Travel Award

**Purpose**: To financially assist students studying in the area of reproductive toxicology
**Eligibility**: Open to applicants enroled full-time in a PhD programme studying reproductive toxicology and are student members of SOT
**Level of Study**: Doctorate, Graduate
**Type**: Award
**Value**: Includes a stipend of US$2,000 for travel costs to enable students to attend the International Congress of Toxicology meeting
**Frequency**: Every 3 years
**Country of Study**: United States of America and abroad
**Application Procedure**: Applicants must submit a completed application form, reference letter, graduate transcripts and lists of complete citations of the original work
**Closing Date**: 9 October
**Contributor**: Toxicology Education Foundation
**Additional Information**: toxedfoundation.org/travel-awards/

## Transport Research Laboratory

Old Wokingham Road, Crowthorne, Berkshire, RG11 6AU, United Kingdom.

**Contact**:   Research Division

## A Master of Science Degree Scholarship

**Purpose**: To financially support postgraduate study
**Eligibility**: Open to part-time self-financing students only. Applicants must have applied for a place for graduate study at UCL
**Level of Study**: Postgraduate
**Type**: Scholarship
**Value**: United Kingdom/European Union tuition fees
**Length of Study**: Full time: 1 year , Part time: 2-3 years
**Frequency**: Annual
**Study Establishment**: University College London
**Country of Study**: United Kingdom

**Application Procedure**: Applicants should contact the department. If the applicants have not applied to UCL they complete a graduate application form and enclose it with the scholarship application

### For further information contact:

**Tel**:     (44) 20 7288 3548
**Fax**:    (44) 20 7288 3322
**Email**:   p.taylor@chime.ucl.ac.uk

## Tropical Agricultural Research and Higher Education Center (CATIE)

7170 Cartago, Turrialba 30501, Costa Rica.

**Tel**:       (506) 2558 2000
**Email**:    posgrado@catie.ac.cr
**Website**:  www.catie.ac.cr
**Contact**:  Dean of the Graduate School

The Tropical Agricultural Research and Higher Education Center (CATIE) is an international, non-profit, regional, scientific and educational institution. Its main purpose is research and education in agricultural sciences, natural resources and related subjects in the American tropics, with emphasis on Central America and the Caribbean.

## Scholarship Opportunities Linked to CATIE

**Purpose**: To develop specialized intellectual capital in clean technology, tropical agriculture, natural resources management and human resources in the American tropics
**Eligibility**: Priority is given to citizens of Belize, Guatemala, El Salvador, Honduras, Nicaragua, Panama, Costa Rica, Mexico, Venezuela, Colombia, the Dominican Republic, Bolivia and Paraguay
**Level of Study**: Doctorate, Postgraduate
**Type**: Scholarship
**Value**: Tuition and fees
**Length of Study**: 2 years for a Master
**Frequency**: Annual
**Country of Study**: Costa Rica
**Application Procedure**: Applicants must undertake an admission process that constitutes 75% for curricular evaluation and 25% for a domiciliary examination. Please refer to the CATIE website for full instructions
**No. of awards offered**: 350
**Funding**: Government, Private, Foundation, International office

**Contributor**: ASDI, OAS, CATIE, DAAD, CONACYT (Mexico), Ford Foundation, Kellogg Foundation, Joint/Japan World Bank. USAID provided the original donation for the endowment financing the Scholarship-Loan Program, SENACYT and Belgium Cooperation

**No. of awards given last year**: 32 in the Scholarship-Loan Program. Over 25 students received funding from alternative sources

**No. of applicants last year**: 350

## Trust Company

Level 15, 20 Bond Street, GPO Box 4270, New South Wales, Sydney, NSW 2001, Australia.

### Miles Franklin Literary Award

**Purpose**: To reward the novel of the year that is of the highest literary merit and presents Australian life in any of its phases

**Eligibility**: Refer to the application form. The novel must have been first published in any country in the year preceding the award. Biographies, collections of short stories, children's books and poetry are not eligible. All works must be in English

**Level of Study**: Unrestricted

**Type**: Award

**Value**: AU$60,000

**Frequency**: Annual

**Country of Study**: Any country

**Application Procedure**: Applicants must complete an application form and send six copies of their novel

**Funding**: Trusts

**Contributor**: The estate of the late Miss SMS Miles Franklin

**No. of awards given last year**: 1

**Additional Information**: If there is no novel worthy of the prize, the award may be given to the author of a play. Please refer to the website for further details: www.milesfranklin.com.au/

### For further information contact:

**Email**:    trustawards@thetrustcompany.com.au

## Tu Delft

### Justus & Louise van Effen Excellence Scholarships

**Purpose**: The Foundation Justus & Louise van Effen was established with the aim of stimulating excellent international

MSc students and financially supporting them in their wish to study at TU Delft

**Eligibility**: Excellent international applicants (conditionally) admitted to one of the 2-year Regular TU Delft's MSc programmes. With a cumulative grade point average (GPA) of 80% or higher of the scale maximum in the bachelor's degree from an internationally renowned university outside The Netherlands

**Level of Study**: Graduate

**Type**: Scholarship

**Value**: €30.000 per year for Non-EU students and €11.500 per year for EU/EFTA students

**Frequency**: Annual

**Country of Study**: Any country

**Application Procedure**: Apply it online. Check with the below link for further information. www.tudelft.nl/en/education/admission-and-application/msc-international-diploma/1-admission-requirements/

**Closing Date**: 1 December

**Funding**: Private

**Additional Information**: Membership to the Scholarship club giving access to personal development, workshops, seminars, etc www.tudelft.nl/en/education/practical-matters/scholarships/justus-louise-van-effen-excellence-scholarships/

### For further information contact:

Postbus 5, NL 2600 AA Delft, Netherlands.

**Tel**:      (31) 15 27 89111
**Email**:    info@tudelft.nl

## Turkiye Scholarships Burslari

### Turkey Government Scholarships

**Purpose**: Winning this Turkish scholarship gives the chance to experience a 4-year undergraduate, master or doctoral program at the partner Turkish Universities and that too in English

**Eligibility**: 1. There is also a strict criterion when it comes to the age of the applicant. 2. For the undergraduate degree, the candidates should not be born earlier than January 1997. 3. While for Master's degree the candidates must not be born before January 1988. For PhDs the date is January 1983 and for Research program the applicants should be born before January 1973. 4. 70% marks required for the application of an undergraduate program. 5. 75% marks required for the application of PhD and Masters. 6. 90% marks required for the application of Medical School programs. 7. Anyone holding Turkish citizenship or having previously held Turkish citizenship cannot apply for the program. 8. Students who are already studying in Turkey are not able to apply for the Scholarship. 9. Students who are selected must present their documents if they are asked otherwise they will not be entertained

**Level of Study**: Doctorate

**Type**: Scholarship

**Value**: Free Accomodation, No tuition fees, Health expense, Travel Expenses, Language Course Requirement.

**Frequency** Annual

**Country of Study**: Any country

**Application Procedure**: Turkey scholarship will be applied with the following terms. 1. University Entrance Exam Grade. 2. Diploma Grade. 3. Average Grades. 4. High School Graduation. 5. International Test Score. 6. CGPA

**Closing Date**: 20 February

**Funding**: Private

**Additional Information**: Türkiye Scholarships applications will be received in one period, and applications will be open between 15 January- 20 February for international students from all countries www.turkiyeburslari.gov.tr/en/announcement/turkiye-scholarships-2020-applications-open

**For further information contact:**

**Email**:    intoffice@agu.edu.tr

# U

## UHasselt University

Hasselt University, Martelarenlaan 42, B-3500 Hasselt, Belgium.

**Tel**:     (32) 11 268 111
**Website**:  www.uhasselt.be/

Civic university UHasselt is more than its seven faculties, four research institutes, three research centres, 6,500 students and 1,400 researchers and staff. As civic university we are strongly committed to the Region and the world. Better through education, research and technology transfer.

## Master Mind Scholarships

**Purpose**: The Flemish Ministry of Education awards scholarships to outstanding students for Master programmes in Flanders and Brussels. The programme aims to promote Flanders and Brussels as a top study destination

**Eligibility**: The applicant should have a high standard of academic performance: - a Grade Point Average of 3.5 out of 4.0: www.foreigncredits.com/resources/gpa-calculator/ - a sufficient knowledge of the English language: an overall band score of min. 7.0 on the IELTS test; a min. total score of 94 on a TOEFL test; a C1 level on the Certificate in Advanced English (CAE); or similar results in another official English language test. Hasselt University will perform an academic check of the student's file. Therefore, we advise students to check our admission requirements before applying. Please note that the host institution can ask the applicant for a tuition fee that equals the rate of the yearly tuition fee for a student from who receives a study grant from the Flemish Government. Important: - only students who are currently not enrolled at a Flemish higher education institution are eligible.

The only exception is made for international students who are enrolled in a preparatory programme only in order to start a master's programme in September 2020. - students who enrol for only a preparatory programme, a bridging programme or a distance learning programme are not eligible. - all nationalities can apply, but the previous degree obtained should be from a higher education institution located outside Flanders. - students can not combine this scholarship with another scholarship from the Flemish government or an Erasmus Mundus scholarship.

**Level of Study**: Masters Degree
**Type**: Scholarships
**Value**: The Flemish Ministry of Education awards scholarships of €8.000 per academic year to outstanding students for master programmes in Flanders. A number of scholarships are reserved for students from certain countries: Japan (3), Mexico (3), Palestine (2) and USA (5). More information about the study programmes offered by Hasselt University can be found on our website (UHasselt - Study Programmes).
**Frequency**: Annual
**Country of Study**: Belgium
**Application Procedure**: UHasselt screens all applicants and submits a shortlist of max. 20 candidates for the scholarship. The Flemish Government makes the final selection on the basis of this shortlist. To apply for the Master Mind scholarship, students need to complete the following steps: Step 1: Submit a completed application file (including all the mandatory documents) for the relevant Master programme at UHasselt (see application procedure) before the deadline of the specific master programme. Step 2: Complete this Master Mind application form by 15 March. Please note that you need to upload the following documents in the application form: - 2 recommendation letters from professors of your (previous) Home university, University or recent employer written in English. Please merge the 2 letters in 1 PDF document and upload the document

Palgrave Macmillan (ed.), *The Grants Register 2021*, https://doi.org/10.1057/978-1-349-95988-4

here. - Students applying for Master of Management or Master of Transportation Sciences also have to upload their admission letter from Hasselt University. Please make sure you have completed step 1 first and on time (before the application deadline of your specific master programme) in order to be eligible for this scholarship. Potential candidates will be screened by the selection committee of the relevant master programme and will be contacted in the first half of April to complete the Master Mind online application. The Flemish selection commission will announce the selection results in June

**Closing Date**: 15 March

**Additional Information**: www.uhasselt.be/scholarships

# Union College

## Union College Board of Trustees Scholarship

**Purpose**: This scholarship is worth full tuition

**Eligibility**: 1. Must attend a college or university in the state of Nebraska. 2. Must be an incoming freshman. 3. Must enroll full time. 4. Must have a grade point average of 3.9 or higher (or a GED score of 750 or higher). 5. Must have an ACT score of 32 or higher OR an SAT score of 1,500 or higher

**Level of Study**: Graduate

**Type**: Scholarship

**Value**: US$21,250

**Length of Study**: Varies. addition of years is possible

**Frequency**: Annual

**Country of Study**: Any country

**Application Procedure**: 1. Admissions information is available on the Union College website by clicking on the 'Admissions Policy' link. Admissions applications are available in online and PDF formats. 2. In addition to a completed application, each student must submit an official high school transcript and ACT/SAT scores. 3. Students whose first language is not English must also submit TOEFL (Test of English as a Foreign Language) scores. 4. Admissions applications are available in online and PDF formats. In addition to a completed application, each student must submit an official high school transcript and ACT/SAT scores

**Closing Date**: 1 April

**Funding**: Private

**Additional Information**: www.unigo.com/scholarships/all/union-college-board-of-trustees-scholarship/1005990

### For further information contact:

3800 S. 48th St., Lincoln, NE 68506-4386, United States of America.

**Tel**:        (1) 402 486 2600
**Email**:    enroll@ucollege.edu

# United Nations Educational, Scientific and Cultural Organization (UNESCO)

7 place de Fontenoy, F-75352 Paris, France.

**Tel**:         (33) 1 45 68 10 00 ext. 81507
**Contact**:    Ms F Abu-Shady, Director, Equipment & Fellowships Division

As early as 1951, a programme to promote and develop youth exchange for educational purposes has existed in UNESCO. The Organization continued its action under the Fellowships Programme to respond to the needs of Member States in the field of human resources development and capacity building. This programme has up to date enabled more than 52,000 fellows from around the world to study in different countries contributing to intellectual solidarity, international cooperation and mutual understanding.

## United Nationals Educational Scientific Cultural Organization Individual Fellowships

**Purpose**: To provide opportunities to further primarily higher education or research generally abroad, and to acquire international experience in fields of study for which appropriate facilities are not available in the country of origin

**Eligibility**: Open to nationals of UNESCO member states and associate members

**Level of Study**: Doctorate, Postdoctorate, Postgraduate, Professional development

**Type**: Fellowship

**Value**: Monthly allowance usually based on UN stipend scale, plus travel, tuition, books and small equipment costs

**Length of Study**: No more than 9 months

**Frequency**: Dependent on funds available

**Country of Study**: Other

**Application Procedure**: Application through national authorities specially designated by UNESCO member states (usually National Commission for UNESCO or appropriate Ministry). Direct applications will not be considered.

## United Nations Educational, Scientific and Cultural Organization(UNESCO)/International Sustainable Energy DeISEDC Co-Sponsored Fellowships Programme

**Purpose**: To enhance the capacity-building and human resources development in the area of sustainable and renewable energy sources in developing countries and countries in transition

**Eligibility**: Holder of at least a BSc degree or BA in Economics; proficient in English language; not more than 35 years of age

**Length of Study**: This is a four weeks fellowship programme

**Country of Study**: Any country

**Application Procedure**: All applications should be endorsed by the National Commission for UNESCO and must be duly completed in English or French

**Closing Date**: 3 April

**Contributor**: UNESCO/ISEDC

**Additional Information**: For more details, please visit the website www.opportunitiesforafricans.com/unesco-isedc-co-sponsored-fellowships-programme-2018-fully-funded-to-moscow-russia/

### For further information contact:

**Email**: info@oppurtunitydesk.org

## United Nations International School of Hanoi

G9 Ciputra Lac Long Quan Road, Tay Ho District, Vietnam.

**Tel**:  (84) 4 3758 1551
**Email**: info@unishanoi.org
**Website**: www.unishanoi.org

United Nations International School of Hanoi's mission is to encourage students to be independent, lifelong learners who strive for excellence and become responsible stewards of our global society and natural environment, achieved within a supportive community that values diversity and through a programme reflecting the ideals and principles of the United Nations.

### United Nations International School (UNIS) Hanoi Scholarship Programme for Vietnamese Students in Vietnam

**Purpose**: Students may apply to the UNIS Hanoi Scholarship Programme for entry to Grade 8, Grade 9 and Grade 10. The students will graduate with the International Baccalaureate Diploma

**Eligibility**: The Students applying for the Scholarship Programme at UNIS Hanoi must hold or be eligible to hold a Vietnamese passport and should have permanent residence no more than one hour of transport from UNIS Hanoi. Applicants are required to provide a copy of Household registration

book. Graduate from Grade 12 at UNIS Hanoi before their 20th Birthday. Vietnamese students are eligible to apply for this scholarship. For detailed information, please visit website

**Type**: Scholarship

**Value**: The UNIS Hanoi Scholarship Programme gives the opportunity for students to enter UNIS Hanoi with a full (100%) fee waiver until graduation

**Country of Study**: Vietnam

**Application Procedure**: Applicants should use the Application Checklist in the Application Package to ensure they have a complete application. All applicants are strongly encouraged to submit applications well before deadline. Completed applications with supporting documents and a recent passport style photo should be handed in to the school at the main gate addressed

**Closing Date**: 31 December

**Contributor**: United Nations International School of Hanoi

**Additional Information**: Shortlist finalists are invited to UNIS Hanoi for interview and testing in the week of May 20th

### For further information contact:

**Email**: scholarships@unishanoi.org

## United Nations University - Institute for the Advanced Study of Sustainability (UNU - IAS)

UNU-IAS is one of 13 institutes and programmes, located in 12 different countries, which together comprise the United Nations University (UNU)-a global think tank and postgraduate teaching organization, headquartered in Tokyo. The mission of UNU is to contribute, through collaborative research and education, to efforts to resolve the pressing global problems of human survival, development and welfare that are the concern of the United Nations, its Peoples and Member States.

**Tel**:  (81) 3 5467 1212
**Website**: ias.unu.edu/
**Contact**: 5-53-70 Jingumae, Shibuya-ku, Tokyo 150-8925, Japan.

### PhD in Sustainability Science

**Purpose**: The Japan Foundation for UNU (JFUNU) Scholarship is available for outstanding applicants from developing countries who can demonstrate a need for financial assistance and who are granted admissions to the PhD

Programme in Sustainability Science at United Nations University Institute for the Advanced Study of Sustainability (UNU-IAS).

**Eligibility**: Applicants for the PhD in Sustainability Science are required to have met ALL of the following requirements by the application deadline in order to be considered: 1. Strong interest in sustainability studies; 2. Demonstrated commitment to study and understand global issues; 3. A completed Master's degree in disciplines related to sustainability studies and a minimum of 2 years of practical field experience related to UNU-IAS research themes OR Two completed Master's degrees, at least one of which must be in disciplines related to sustainability studies; 4. A GPA of 3.5 or above on a 4.0 scale on at least one of the Master's degrees earned; and 5. English language proficiency Eligibility Requirements for the scholarships: Applicants must be from developing countries* who can demonstrate a need for financial assistance. Applicants who are currently living in Japan under a working visa are NOT eligible for the scholarship. Applicants who want to pursue a second PhD degree at UNU-IAS are not eligible for the scholarship.

**Level of Study**: Postgraduate

**Type**: Scholarsip

**Value**: The scholarship provides a monthly allowance of ¥120,000 for living expenses for a maximum of 36 months. Travel costs to and from Japan, visa handling fees, and health/accident insurance costs must be covered by the student. The tuition fees are fully waived for the scholarship recipients

**Country of Study**: Japan

**Application Procedure**: It is important to visit the official website (link found below) to access the application form and for detailed information on how to apply for this scholarship. ias.unu.edu/en/admissions/degrees/phd-in-sustainability-science-2020.html#overview

**Closing Date**: 10 April

**Additional Information**: ias.unu.edu/en/admissions/degrees/phd-in-sustainability-science-2020.html#overview

## United States Center for Advanced Holocaust Studies

United States Holocaust Memorial Museum, 100 Raoul Wallenberg Place South West, Washington, DC 20024-2126, United States of America.

**Tel**:        (1) 202 488 0400 / 202 314 7802
**Email**:    vscholars@ushmm.org
**Website**:  www.ushmm.org
**Contact**:  Ms Jo-Ellyn Decker, Program Coordinator

The United States Holocaust Memorial Museum is the United State's national institution for the documentation, study and interpretation of Holocaust history, and serves as the country's memorial to the millions of people murdered during the Holocaust. The Center for Advanced Holocaust Studies fosters research in Holocaust and genocide studies.

## Joyce and Arthur Schechter Fellowship

**Purpose**: To provide for a Scholar to be in residence at the Museum for a period of six weeks to three months to conduct research using the vast resources of the Museum

**Eligibility**: Applicants must hold a PhD or be an advanced PhD candidate (ABD) by the application deadline. Those candidates with equivalent professional or terminal degrees or recognised professional standing may also apply

**Type**: Fellowship

**Value**: A stipend of US$5,000 to cover housing, living, and international or domestic travel expenses. The Joyce and Arthur Schechter Fellow will also be provided with office space, postage, and access to a computer, telephone, facsimile machine, and photocopier. Cost sharing by the applicants home institution is welcome

**Frequency**: Annual

**Country of Study**: United States of America

**Application Procedure**: Applicants must submit a completed application form and supporting material for fellowship consideration. To request an application form or additional information please contact Renee Taft, Director, Visiting Scholars Program, at the Center for Advanced Holocaust Studies

**Closing Date**: 31 October

**Funding**: Private

**Additional Information**: The Schechter Fellow is encouraged to participate in the Museum's broad array of scholarly and other programmes

### For further information contact:

**Tel**:     (1) 202 314 0378
**Fax**:     (1) 202 479 9726
**Email**:   rtaft@ushmm.org

## United States Center for Advanced Holocaust Studies Dissertation Award

**Purpose**: To encourage the work of exceptional new scholars in the area of the holocaust and genocide studies. The fellowship also provides an opportunity for a new PhD to work at the Center on a conversion of the dissertation into a monograph or on a new post dissertation holocaust related research topic

**Eligibility**: Open to all PhD candidates completing their dissertations after January 1st 1998 and before the application deadline

**Level of Study**: Postdoctorate

**Type**: Award

**Value**: A stipend of up to US$15,000 for residence at the Center. The museum will also provide office space, postage, and access to a computer, telephone, facsimile machine, and photocopier

**Length of Study**: 1 semester or more

**Frequency**: Annual

**Study Establishment**: United States Center for Advanced Holocaust Studies

**Country of Study**: United States of America

**Application Procedure**: Applicants must contact Renee Taft, Director, Visiting Scholars Programme, or Betsy Anthony, Programme Assistant, Visiting Scholar Programme for more information and application forms. Dissertations should be nominated by the author's university department chair and accompanied by a letter of acceptance for the degree and a 250 word abstract of the dissertation's subject matter. Three copies of the dissertation should be submitted. A statement must be included giving the United States Holocaust Memorial Museum permission to produce the dissertation for copying purposes

**Closing Date**: 15 March

**Funding**: Private

**Additional Information**: The Center's historian, Fellows in residence, and publications staff will be available to assist the successful applicant

### For further information contact:

**Tel**:       (1) 202 314 0378
**Fax**:      (1) 202 479 9726
**Email**:   rtaft@ushmm.org

## United States Commission on International Religious Freedom (USCIRF)

732 N. Capitol Street, N.W., Suite A714, Washington, DC 20401, United States of America.

**Tel**:        (1) 202 523 3240
**Email**:    communications@uscirf.gov
**Website**:  www.uscirf.gov

United States Commission on International Religious Freedom is an independent, bipartisan United States of America federal government commission, the first of its kind in the world, that monitors the universal right to freedom of religion or belief abroad. USCIRF reviews the facts and circumstances of religious freedom violations and makes policy recommendations to the President, the Secretary of State, and Congress. USCIRF Commissioners are appointed by the President and the Congressional leadership of both political parties.

## United States of America Commission on International Religious Freedom Internships

**Eligibility**: Currently enroled undergraduates (sophomores, juniors and seniors) and graduate students (including JD and LLM candidates) with minimum 2.5 GPA are eligible for internships with USCIRF. Students of United States of America can apply (or otherwise authorized to intern with the United States of America government). For detailed information, visit website

**Type**: Internship

**Value**: All United States Commission on International Religious Freedom (USCIRF) internships are paid; however, course credit may be available

**Country of Study**: United States of America

**Application Procedure**: The mode of applying is via email, fax, or mail (applicants should specify the internship and semester they are applying for in their cover letter and the subject line of an emailed application). Policy Department: Regional Policy Analysis Intern should specify what region they are applying for in their cover letter and the subject line of an emailed application. Application requirements: cover letter explaining qualifications and why one would like to intern at USCIRF; resume; 3–5 page writing sample; 2–3 letters of reference

**Closing Date**: 1 April

**Contributor**: United States of America Commission on International Religious Freedom (USCIRF)

**Additional Information**: Internships can be full-time or part-time for a minimum of 8 weeks. Internships are available year-round, and applications are accepted on a rolling basis www.heysuccess.com/opportunity/USCIRF-Internships-(United-States-Commission-on-International-Religious-Freedom)-19798

### For further information contact:

**Email**:    internship@uscirf.gov

# United States Institute of Peace (USIP)

2301 Constitution Avenue, NW, Washington, DC 20037, United States of America.

**Tel**: (1) 202 457 1700
**Email**: grant_program@usip.org
**Website**: www.usip.org
**Contact**: Ms Cornelia Hoggart, Senior Programme Assistant

The United States Institute of Peace (USIP) is mandated by the Congress to promote education and training, research and public information programmes on means to promote international peace and resolve international conflicts without violence. The Institute meets this mandate through an array of programmes, including grants, fellowships, conferences and workshops, library services, publications and other educational activities.

## Jennings Randolph Program for International Peace Dissertation Fellowship

**Purpose**: To support dissertations that explore the sources and nature of international conflict, and strategies to prevent or end conflict and to sustain peace
**Eligibility**: Open to applicants of all nationalities who are enroled in an accredited college or university in the United States of America. Applicants must have completed all requirements for the degree except the dissertation by the commencement of the award
**Level of Study**: Doctorate
**Type**: Fellowships
**Value**: Stipends of up to US$20,000 per academic year
**Length of Study**: 1 year
**Frequency**: Annual
**Study Establishment**: The student's home university or site of fieldwork
**Country of Study**: United States of America
**Application Procedure**: Application Applications must be submitted through the FLUXX online application system. On the application form, please indicate the scholarship for which you would like to be considered: the USIP Peace Scholar fellowship only; Minerva Research Initiative Peace and Security Fellowship only; or no preference. 1. Both fellowships have the same application form, deadline, award amount, and selection process; the only difference between the USIP and Minerva Fellowships is the source of funding. 2. Three letters

of recommendation must be attached to your application in the FLUXX system. One letter must be from your dissertation advisor and two from current professors.
**Closing Date**: 15 October
**Funding**: Government
**No. of awards given last year**: 10
**Additional Information**: The programme does not support work involving partisan political and policy advocacy or policy making for any government or private organization www.usip.org/grants-fellowships/fellowships/jennings-randolph-peace-scholar-dissertation-fellowship-program

**For further information contact:**

**Tel**: (1) 202 429 3853
**Email**: jrprogram@usip.org

## Jennings Randolph Program for International Peace Senior Fellowships

**Purpose**: To use the recipient's existing knowledge and skills towards a fruitful endeavour in the international peace and conflict management field, and to help bring the perspectives of this field into the Fellow's own career
**Eligibility**: Open to outstanding practitioners and scholars from a broad range of backgrounds. The competition is open to citizens of any country who have specific interest and experience in international peace and conflict management. Candidates would typically be senior academics, but applicants who hold at least a Bachelor's degree from a recognized university will also be considered
**Type**: Fellowship
**Value**: A stipend, an office with computer and voicemail and a part-time research assistant
**Length of Study**: Up to 10 months
**Frequency**: Annual
**Study Establishment**: USIP
**Country of Study**: United States of America
**Application Procedure**: Applicants must complete a web-based application form, available on request from the Institute or from the website
**No. of awards offered**: 136
**Closing Date**: January
**Funding**: Government
**No. of awards given last year**: 10
**No. of applicants last year**: 136
**Additional Information**: www.usip.org/grants-fellowships/fellowships/jennings-randolph-senior-fellowship-program

**For further information contact:**

**Tel**:       (1) 202 429 3886
**Email**:    jrprogram@usip.org

# United States-India Educational Foundation (USIEF)

Fulbright House 12 Hailey Road, New Delhi, Delhi 110001, India.

**Tel**:        (91) 11 2332 8944/48
**Email**:     info@fulbright-india.org
**Website**:   www.fulbright-india.org
**Contact**:   Programme Officer

The activities of the United States Educational Foundation in India (USEFI) may be broadly categorized as the administration of the Fulbright Exchange Fellowships for Indian and United States of America scholars and professionals, and the provision of educational advising services to help Indian students wishing to pursue higher education in the United States. USEFI also works for the promotion of dialogue among fulbrighters and their communities as an outgrowth of educational exchange.

## Fulbright Distinguished Awards in Teaching Program for International Teachers

**Purpose**: It is part of the overall Fulbright Program, named in honor of Senator J. William Fulbright, which promotes mutual understanding among people of the United States and other countries

**Eligibility**: 1. Be a citizen of India and reside in India at the time of application. 2. Live and teach in the states of Arunachal Pradesh, Assam, Bihar, Jharkhand, Manipur, Meghalaya, Mizoram, Nagaland, Sikkim, Tripura, West Bengal, Chandigarh, Delhi, Haryana, Himachal Pradesh, Jammu and Kashmir, Ladakh, Punjab, Rajasthan, Uttarakhand and Uttar Pradesh; 3. Hold at least a bachelor's degree. A teacher training degree is preferred. 4. Be a full-time teacher teaching any subject at any level (primary, middle, secondary or senior secondary). 5. Have completed at least five years of full-time teaching experience at the program start. 6. Primary and secondary level library media specialists, guidance counselors, curriculum specialists, special education coordinators, and administrators who spend at least fifty percent of their

time teaching or working directly with students may also apply to the program. 7. Teacher trainers are eligible to apply. 8. Demonstrate good English language competence. 9. Demonstrate a commitment to continue teaching or working in their field after completion of the program. Candidates should be planning to continue working in elementary or secondary education for at least five years after the conclusion of the program.

**Type**: Award
**Frequency**: Annual
**Country of Study**: Any country
**Application Procedure**: 1. Fellows will be selected through a merit-based open competition. After the application deadline, a screening committee will review all eligible applications. 2. Short listed candidates will be interviewed by a committee in New Delhi which will select nominees whose names will be forwarded to Washington, D.C. for further consideration. Nominees will be required to take the iBT TOEFL examination in May. 3. All candidates will be notified of their status in September
**Closing Date**: 2 March
**Funding**: Private
**Additional Information**: Click for www.usief.org.in/uploadip/ip2021-22/2020%20FDAI%20Online%20form%20instructions.doc on completing the online application www.usief.org.in/Distinguished-Fulbright-Awards-Teaching-Program.aspx

**For further information contact:**

**Tel**:       (91) 33 39846310
**Email**:    usiefkolkata@usief.org.in

## Fulbright Indo-American Environmental Leadership Program

**Purpose**: To provide funding for Indian environment professionals to explore future links between American and Indian organisations with common agendas
**Eligibility**: Open to all Indian mid-level environment professionals with at least five years of professional experience in the respective field and a Master's or professional degree of at least four years duration. Applicants will preferably be under 50 years of age. Special attention will be given to applicants who can demonstrate involvement in cooperative efforts between academia, research institutions, government, industry and non governmental organisations to make practical contributions to environmental policies and programmes
**Level of Study**: Postdoctorate, Professional development

**Type**: Internship
**Value**: Round-trip travel from India to the United States of America, a monthly stipend, professional allowance, settling-in allowance plus health insurance. No allowance or travel is provided for dependants
**Length of Study**: 4 and 8 weeks
**Frequency**: Annual
**Study Establishment**: Selected Fellows will be placed at environmental public, private, non governmental organisations, academic institutions, research centres or environment related government agencies
**Country of Study**: United States of America
**Application Procedure**: Applicants must obtain an application form either in person from USEFI offices or by sending a stamped addressed envelope to the nearest local USEFI office. The envelope should be superscribed USEFI-IAELP. Application forms can also be downloaded from the website or requested via email specifying the relevant fellowship category. Although USEFI does not require applicants to have a letter of affiliation from a United States institution at the time of applying, it encourages all applicants to correspond, in advance, with potential host institutions
**Closing Date**: 15 July
**Additional Information**: If the applicant is successful but unable to arrange an affiliation or name an institution in the United States of America with which to be affiliated, USEFI will help secure placement. The programme will combine short-term practical training/internship with opportunities for networking with American counterpart organisations

**For further information contact:**

**Email**:    lakshmi@fulbright-india.org


## Fulbright-Nehru Doctoral Research Fellowships

**Purpose**: The Fulbright-Nehru Academic and Professional Excellence Fellowships aim to provide Indian faculty, researchers, and professionals the opportunity to teach, conduct research, or carry out a combination of teaching and research at a U.S. institution
**Eligibility**: 1. faculty/researchers must have a PhD degree or equivalent published work with at least five years of relevant teaching/research experience; 2. professionals outside academe must have a master's degree or equivalent published work with recognized professional standing and at least five years relevant experience; 3. the applicant should upload a recent significant publication (copy of paper/article) in the online application; and 4. If the applicant is employed, s/he must follow the instructions carefully regarding Letter of Support from Home Institution. The employer must indicate

that leave will be granted for the fellowship period. The applicant must obtain the endorsement from the appropriate administrative authority on the Letter of Support from Home Institution. The applicant can download the Letter of Support from Home Institution from the USIEF website.
**Type**: Fellowship
**Value**: See website for details
**Length of Study**: 4 to 6 months
**Frequency**: Annual
**Country of Study**: United States of America
**Application Procedure**: Applications must be submitted online at: apply.iie.org/fvsp2021
**Closing Date**: 15 July
**Additional Information**: www.usief.org.in/Fellowships/Fulbright-Nehru-Academic-Professional-Excellence-Fellowships.aspx


## Fulbright-Nehru Master's Fellowships

**Purpose**: The Fulbright-Nehru Master's Fellowships are designed for outstanding Indians to pursue a master's degree program at select United States of America colleges and universities in the areas of Arts and Culture Management including Heritage Conservation and Museum Studies; Environmental Science/Studies; Higher Education Administration; International Legal Studies;
**Eligibility**: In addition to the General Prerequisites, the applicants should: 1. must have completed an equivalent of a U.-S. bachelor's degree from a recognized Indian university with at least 55% marks. Applicants must either possess a four-year bachelor's degree; or a completed master's degree, or a full-time postgraduate diploma from a recognized Indian institution, if the bachelor's degree is of less than four years' duration; 2. must have at least three years' full-time (paid) professional work experience relevant to the proposed field of study by the application deadline; 3. should demonstrate experience in leadership and community service; 4. must not have another degree from a U.S. university or be enrolled in a U.S. degree program; and 5. if employed, should follow the instructions carefully regarding employer's endorsement. If applicable, obtain the endorsement from the appropriate administrative authority on the FNMasters Employer's Endorsement Form. The employer must indicate that leave will be granted for the fellowship period.
**Type**: Fellowship
**Frequency**: Annual
**Country of Study**: Any country
**Application Procedure**: Applications must be submitted online at: apply.iie.org/ffsp2021
**Closing Date**: 15 May
**Funding**: Private
**Additional Information**: IMPORTANT: 1. You can apply for only ONE Fulbright-Nehru fellowship category during

a competition cycle. 2. Plagiarism in the application will lead to disqualification. 3. Unless otherwise specified, Fulbright-Nehru applications are to be submitted online. 4. Applications received after the deadline will NOT be considered. 5. Extensions and Transfer of visa sponsorship will not be permitted. www.usief.org.in/Fulbright-Nehru-Fellowships.aspx

**For further information contact:**

**Email**: masters@usief.org.in

## Fulbright-Nehru Postdoctoral Research Fellowships

**Purpose**: These fellowships are designed for Indian faculty and researchers who are in the early stages of their research careers in India

**Eligibility**: In addition to the General Prerequisites: 1. the applicant must have a PhD or a DM degree within the past four years. S/he must have obtained PhD degree between July 16, 2016 and July 15, 2020. The applicant is required to upload his/her PhD or DM degree/provisional certificate on the online application; 2. the applicant must be published in reputed journals and demonstrate evidence of superior academic and professional achievement. S/he must upload a recent significant publication (copy of paper/article) on the online application; and 3. If applicant is employed, please follow the instructions carefully regarding Letter of Support from Home Institution. If applicable, please obtain the endorsement from the appropriate administrative authority on the FNPostdoc Letter of Support from Home Institution. The employer must indicate that leave will be granted for the fellowship period. The applicant can download the FNPostdoc Letter of Support from Home Institution from the USIEF website. Candidates working under government-funded projects are also required to get endorsement from their affiliating institutions in India.

**Level of Study**: Postgraduate
**Type**: Fellowship
**Frequency**: Annual
**Country of Study**: Any country
**Application Procedure**: Applications must be submitted online at: apply.iie.org/fvsp2021
**Closing Date**: 15 July
**Funding**: Private
**Additional Information**: www.usief.org.in/Fellowships/Fulbright-Nehru-Postdoctoral-Research-Fellowship.aspx

**For further information contact:**

**Email**: postdoc@usief.org.in

## United States-India Educational Foundation (USIEF) Fulbright-CII Fellowships for Leadership in Management

**Purpose**: To enable business managers to attend a management programme in the United States
**Eligibility**: Open to Indian business managers. Age limit, preferably not above 40, Nationality: Indian, Designed for: Mid-level Managers in Indian Industries
**Level of Study**: Professional development
**Type**: Fellowship
**Value**: See website for details
**Length of Study**: 10 weeks
**Frequency**: Annual
**Study Establishment**: Carnegie Mellon University
**Country of Study**: United States of America
**Application Procedure**: Applicants must complete an application form, available from the CII
**No. of awards offered**: 49
**Closing Date**: 15 February
**Funding**: Corporation, Foundation
**Contributor**: USEFI and employers of selected Managers
**No. of awards given last year**: 8
**No. of applicants last year**: 49
**Additional Information**: For further information contact the Confederation of Indian Industry (CII). Please check the website www.usief.org.in/Fulbright-Nehru-CII-Fellowships-Leadership-Management.aspx scholarship-positions.com/fulbright-nehru-cii-fellowships-for-leadership-in-management-in-usa-2015-2016/2011/09/10/

**For further information contact:**

Confederation of Indian Industry, Mantosh Sondhi Centre, 23, Institutional Area, Lodi Road, New Delhi, Delhi 110003, India.

**Tel**: (91) 2462 9994 7 ext. 367
**Fax**: (91) 2460 1298, 2462 6149
**Email**: sudarsan@usief.org.in

## United States-United Kingdom Fulbright Commission

188 Kirtling Street, London SW8 5BN, United Kingdom.

**Tel**: (44) 2074 046 880
**Email**: programmes@fulbright.co.uk
**Website**: www.fulbright.co.uk
**Contact**: Mr Michael Scott-Kline, Director

The United States-United Kingdom Fulbright Commission has a programme of awards offered annually to citizens of the United Kingdom and United States of America.

## The Fulbright-Edinburgh University Award

**Purpose**: To enable a United States citizen to pursue postgraduate study in the United Kingdom at the University of Bristol

**Eligibility**: Applicant must be a United States citizen (resident anywhere but the United Kingdom), and a graduating senior, holding a BS/BA degree, master's or doctoral degree candidate, young professional or artist

**Level of Study**: Doctorate, Graduate, Postgraduate

**Type**: Award/Grant

**Value**: Up to £20,000, limited sickness and accident benefit coverage, as well as participation in a number of Fulbright Scholar events including the Fulbright Forum in January are also included

**Frequency**: Annual

**Study Establishment**: University of Edinburgh

**Country of Study**: United Kingdom

**Application Procedure**: Please visit the website us. fulbrightonline.org/applynow.html

**Closing Date**: 18 October

**Additional Information**: For more information, visit www. ed.ac.uk/studying/postgraduate

### For further information contact:

**Tel**:        (44) 131 651 4221
**Email**:    Robert.Lawrie@ed.ac.uk

## Universities Canada

**Tel**:          (1) 613 563 3961 ext. 259
**Email**:      tanaka@univcan.ca
**Contact**:   Gabrielle Leblanc, Program Officer

Universities Canada manages government-funded international partnership programs and more than 130 scholarship programs on behalf of private sector companies.

## ConocoPhillips Canada Centennial Scholarship Program

**Purpose**: To support young Canadian visionaries who have a drive to make a difference in the future. The scholarship programme encourages individuals with academic excellence and demonstrated leadership

**Eligibility**: Canadian citizens or permanent residents of Canada

**Type**: Scholarship

**Value**: Up to C$5,000 per year for college studies and up to C$10,000 per year for university studies

**Length of Study**: 2 years

**Country of Study**: Canada

**Closing Date**: 30 May

**Additional Information**: For more information, please contact awards@univcan.ca www.scholarshipdesk.com/cono cophillips-canada-centennial-scholarship/

### For further information contact:

**Email**:     ucawards@ucalgary.ca

## Fessenden-Trott Scholarship

**Eligibility**: 1. Be entering the second year of their first bachelor degree on a full-time basis in September 2019. 2. Have Canadian citizenship or permanent residency by June 14th in the year of application. 3. Have completed the first year of their first bachelor degree program in a Canadian educational institution. 4. Have attained a high academic standing as defined by the nominating institution. 5. Be nominated by a Canadian educational institution where the first year of the first bachelor degree studies has been completed.

**Type**: Scholarship

**Value**: C$9,000

**Length of Study**: 3 years

**Country of Study**: Canada

**Closing Date**: 1 April

**Additional Information**: For more information, please contact awards@univcan.ca scholartree.ca/scholarship/fessen den-trott-scholarship-program/0WPlIx3yy

### For further information contact:

**Tel**:      (1) 613 563 1236
**Email**:   awards@aucc.ca

## Multiple Sclerosis Society of Canada Scholarship Programs: John Helou Scholarship

**Purpose**: To encourage academic excellence and the pursuit of higher education among students who are directly affected by Multiple Sclerosis

**Eligibility**: Candidates must be female Canadian citizens or permanent residents

**Type**: Fellowship

**Value**: C$5,250 per academic year
**Length of Study**: 4 years
**Country of Study**: Canada
**Application Procedure**: Applicants must submit their own application electronically through the online platform: www.fwis.fr
**Closing Date**: 31 March
**Additional Information**: For additional information, please contact awards@univcan.ca

### For further information contact:

**Email**: lindsay.gulin@mssociety.ca

## Tanaka Fund Program

**Purpose**: The Tanaka Fund Program provides institutional support for the enhancement of Japanese language study opportunities at Canadian universities. It aspires to promote and help improve Japanese language education, and to support institutional program development
**Type**: Grant
**Value**: US$50,000 is available for this year's awards and Grants up to a maximum of US$10,000 are available
**Length of Study**: 3 Months
**Country of Study**: Canada
**Closing Date**: 7 January
**Additional Information**: For further details, please contact tanaka@univcan.ca www.univcan.ca/programs-and-scholarships/tanaka-fund-program/

## Universities Federation for Animal Welfare (UFAW)

The Old School, Brewhouse Hill, St Albans AL4 8AN, United Kingdom.

**Tel**: (44) 15 8283 1818
**Email**: ufaw@ufaw.org.uk
**Website**: www.ufaw.org.uk

The Universities Federation for Animal Welfare (UFAW), the international animal welfare science society, is a United Kingdom registered scientific and educational charity that brings together the animal welfare science community, educators, veterinarians and all concerned about animal welfare worldwide in order to achieve advances in the well-being of farm, companion, laboratory and captive wild animals, and for those animals with which we interact in the wild.

## Universities Federation for Animal Welfare Student Scholarships

**Purpose**: To encourage students to develop their interests in animal welfare and their abilities for animal welfare research
**Eligibility**: Applications are welcome from individuals studying at universities or colleges in the United Kingdom or an overseas institution at which there is a UFAW University Links representative. Students will usually be undertaking courses in the agricultural, biological, medical, psychological, veterinary or zoological sciences. Applicants need a nominated supervisor to oversee the project
**Level of Study**: Postgraduate
**Type**: Scholarship
**Value**: £170 subsistence and £30 departmental expenses for each week of study
**Length of Study**: Funding provided for a maximum of 8 weeks (although project duration may be longer)
**Frequency**: Annual
**Country of Study**: Any country
**Application Procedure**: Applicants must complete a UFAW Animal Welfare Student Scholarship application form available for download from the UFAW website www.ufaw.org.uk
**Closing Date**: 28 February
**Funding**: Private
**Additional Information**: Successful applicants must submit a written report to UFAW by November of the year in which the project was undertaken. Please see the website for further details www.ufaw.org.uk www.ufaw.org.uk/animal-welfare-student-scholarships/animal-welfare-student-scholarships

### For further information contact:

Wendy Goodwin, UFAW, The Old School, Brewhouse Hill, Wheathampstead, Hertfordshire, AL4 8AN, United Kingdom.

**Tel**: (44) 1582 831818
**Email**: goodwin@ufaw.org.uk

## University College Birmingham

Summer Row, Birmingham B3 1JB, United Kingdom.

**Tel**: (44) 12 1604 1000
**Email**: Registry@bcftcs.ac.uk
**Website**: www.ucb.ac.uk
**Contact**: Student Scholarships

## Target Recruitment Partial Fee Waiver

**Purpose**: To reduce tuition fee for new international students

**Eligibility**: Applicants must refer to the website for details
**Level of Study**: Postgraduate
**Type**: Scholarships
**Value**: Up to £1,000
**Length of Study**: 1 year
**Frequency**: Annual
**Study Establishment**: University College Birmingham
**Country of Study**: United Kingdom
**Additional Information**: Applications can be considered for entry in Semester 1 (Late September/Early October) or Semester 2 (Late January/Early February). Applications should be made at least 2 months prior to the entry date. No applications are necessary. Partial Fee Waivers will be noted in all offer letters sent to applicants from relevant countries. For more information contact the International Student Office on international

**For further information contact:**

**Email**:    international@ucb.ac.uk

## University College London

Gower Street, London WC1E 6BT, United Kingdom.

**Tel**:        (44) 20 7679 2000
**Website**:    www.ucl.ac.uk

Just 175 years ago, the benefits of a university education in United Kingdom were restricted to men who were members of the Church of United Kingdom; University College London (UCL) was founded to challenge that discrimination. UCL was the first university to be established in United Kingdom after Oxford and Cambridge, providing a progressive alternative to those institutions social exclusivity, religious restrictions and academic constraints. UCL is the largest of over 50 colleges and institutes that make up the federal University of London.

## A C Gimson Scholarships in Phonetics and Linguistics

**Purpose**: To financially support MPhil/PhD research
**Eligibility**: United Kingdom, European Union and overseas students are eligible to apply
**Level of Study**: Doctorate, Postgraduate, Research
**Type**: Scholarship
**Value**: £1,000
**Frequency**: Annual
**Study Establishment**: University College London

**Country of Study**: United Kingdom
**Application Procedure**: Applicants should write indicating their intention to compete for the bursaries to the department
**Closing Date**: 1 June

**For further information contact:**

**Tel**:        (44) 20 7679 4245
**Email**:    n.wilkins@ucl.ac.uk

## A J Ayer-Sumitomo Corporation Scholarship in Philosophy

**Purpose**: To financially support MPhil/PhD research
**Eligibility**: This scholarship is open to candidates from any country however candidates need to apply to a graduate programme in Philosophy by the relevant deadline to be eligible
**Level of Study**: Doctorate, Postgraduate, Research
**Type**: Scholarship
**Value**: Up to £800
**Length of Study**: 1 year
**Frequency**: Annual
**Study Establishment**: University College London
**Country of Study**: United Kingdom
**Application Procedure**: No separate application is required for the AJ Ayer-Sumitomo Corporation. All who are admitted to research programmes in Philosophy will be invited to apply, and decisions regarding these awards will be made in September.
**Additional Information**: For further details on how to apply please visit: www.ucl.ac.uk/prospective-students/scholarships/graduate/deptscholarships/philosophy www.scholarshipeye.com/2018/01/06/aj-ayer-sumitomo-corporation-scholarship/

**For further information contact:**

**Tel**:        (44) 20 7679 4451
**Email**:    r.madden@ucl.ac.uk

## Alfred Bader Prize in Organic Chemistry

**Purpose**: To financially support MPhil/PhD research
**Eligibility**: Applicants must contact the department
**Level of Study**: Doctorate, Postgraduate, Research
**Type**: Scholarship
**Value**: £1,000
**Frequency**: Annual
**Study Establishment**: University College London
**Country of Study**: United Kingdom
**Application Procedure**: Applicants must contact the department

**Closing Date**: 1 May

**Additional Information**: The award will be announced in October www.universitystory.gla.ac.uk/award/?id=487&l=

### For further information contact:

**Tel**: (44) 20 7679 4650
**Fax**: (44) 20 7679 7463
**Email**: m.l.jabore@ucl.ac.uk

## Amelia Zollner IPPR/UCL Internship Award

**Purpose**: The Amelia Zollner IPPR/UCL Internship Award was founded in 2007 in memory of University College London's (UCL) student Ameial Zollner. IPPR and UCL co-fund an annual, approximately 3-month London-based IPPR internship reserved for a recent UCL graduate – as a stepping stone to working in policy or politics. The internship will normally run from October through December, but can take place at any time of the year

**Eligibility**: (1) Applicants must be final year UCL students, about to graduate (Bachelors, Masters or Research degree) in any area, interested in and passionate about policy and politics, current affairs and social justice, and the work of IPPR, as well as enthusiastic about political research. (2) Applicants can come from any country, but must be able to work in the United Kingdom (United Kingdom/European Union nationals or holders of valid work permit). (3) Applicants should have some research skills, and need to be committed to the aims of IPPR of wanting to build a fair, more democratic and environmentally sustainable world

**Level of Study**: Graduate, Postgraduate, Research

**Type**: Award

**Value**: £5,000 or the equivalent of the current IPPR salary for the duration of the internship. Check with website

**Length of Study**: 3 months

**Frequency**: Annual

**Country of Study**: United Kingdom

**Application Procedure**: Applications should be made direct to IPPR and submitted preferably by email to intern@ippr.org

**No. of awards offered**: 4–8

**Closing Date**: 30 January

**No. of applicants last year**: 4–8

**Additional Information**: Please refer website for further information www.ucl.ac.uk/prospective-students/scholarships/undergraduate/zollner_ippr_internship www.european-funding-guide.eu/other-financial-assistance/13920-amelia-zollner-ippruel-internship-award

### For further information contact:

**Tel**: (44) 20 7470 6133
**Email**: k.simony@ippr.org

## Archibald Richardson Scholarship for Mathematics

**Purpose**: To financially support students to pursue MPhil/PhD research

**Eligibility**: United Kingdom, European Union and overseas applicants are eligible to apply. All applicants who firmly accept a place for MPhil/PhD research in pure Mathematics department will be considered

**Level of Study**: Doctorate, Postgraduate, Research

**Type**: Scholarship

**Value**: £3,000

**Frequency**: Annual

**Study Establishment**: University College London

**Country of Study**: United Kingdom

**Application Procedure**: All applicants who firmly accept a place for MPhil/PhD research in pure mathematics will be considered automatically

**Closing Date**: 15 May

**Additional Information**: www.european-funding-guide.eu/other-financial-assistance/14077-archibald-richardson-scholarship-mathematics%C2%A0

### For further information contact:

**Tel**: (44) 20 7679 2839
**Fax**: (44) 20 7383 5519
**Email**: h.higgins@ucl.ac.uk

## Arnold Hugh William Beck Memorial Scholarship

**Purpose**: To financially support research Master's and MPhil/PhD students

**Eligibility**: Applicants should have applied for a place for graduate study at University College London. A past or current holder of the scholarship may apply again for the scholarship but such applications will be considered in open competition with other applicants. No individual may hold the scholarship for more than three years in total

**Level of Study**: Doctorate, Postgraduate, Research

**Type**: Scholarship

**Value**: £6,500

**Frequency**: Annual

**Study Establishment**: University College London

**Country of Study**: United Kingdom

**Application Procedure**: Applicants should send an academic curriculum vitae and a letter of more than 500 words describing their areas of interest in the discipline to the address given below. If the applicant has not applied to UCL, they must complete a graduate application form and enclose it with the scholarship application

**Closing Date**: 15 August

**Additional Information**: www.european-funding-guide.eu/other-financial-assistance/14156-ahw-beck-memorial-scholarship

**For further information contact:**

Tel: (44) 20 7679 7306
Email: p.johnson@ee.ucl.ac.uk

## Bentham Scholarships

**Purpose**: To financially support prospective LLM students
**Eligibility**: Applicants must be overseas students from outside the European Union. An applicant must have accepted an offer (either conditional or unconditional) to read for the LLM at UCL to be eligible
**Level of Study**: Postgraduate
**Type**: Scholarship
**Value**: £16,000
**Length of Study**: 4 years
**Frequency**: Annual
**Study Establishment**: University College London
**Country of Study**: United Kingdom
**Application Procedure**: There is no application procedure. All eligible students will automatically be considered if they have firmly accepted their offer of admission by May 31st
**Closing Date**: 30 April
**Additional Information**: The scholarships will be based on academic merit. The faculty will only consider these applicants who have firmly accepted their offer of admission to the LLM by May 31st www.ucl.ac.uk/political-science/study/post-graduate-research/funding-opportunities/departmental-scholarships

**For further information contact:**

Tel: (44) 20 7679 1441
Fax: (44) 20 7209 3470
Email: polsci.admissions@ucl.ac.uk

## Bioprocessing Graduate Scholarship

**Purpose**: To financially support study leading to an MPhil/PhD.
**Eligibility**: Open to students resident outside the United Kingdom and pursuing the MSc or MPhil or PhD research in the department of biomedical engineering
**Level of Study**: Doctorate, Postgraduate
**Type**: Scholarship
**Value**: Up to a maximum of £11,000 per year. This sum can be set against tuition fees and/or be received as maintenance allowance payable in quarterly installments
**Length of Study**: Maximum of 4 calendar years
**Frequency**: Annual

**Study Establishment**: University College London
**Country of Study**: United Kingdom
**Application Procedure**: Applicants must contact the department at the address given below
**No. of awards offered**: 8
**Closing Date**: 15 February
**Funding**: Trusts
**No. of applicants last year**: 8
**Additional Information**: www.scholarshipsads.com/category/subject/bioprocessing/

**For further information contact:**

Tel: (44) 20 7679 3796
Email: nigelth@ucl.ac.uk

## Brain Research Trust Prize

**Purpose**: To financially support MPhil/PhD research students
**Eligibility**: Open to United Kingdom, European Union and overseas students. Overseas fee-paying students should be aware that only home tuition fee (European Union rates) is included in the award
**Level of Study**: Doctorate, Postgraduate, Research
**Type**: Studentship
**Value**: Stipend, tuition fees at United Kingdom/European Union rate and travel budget
**Length of Study**: Up to 3 years
**Frequency**: Annual
**Study Establishment**: University College London Institute of Neurology
**Country of Study**: United Kingdom
**Application Procedure**: Applicants should contact the UCL Institute of Neurology. Please submit full curriculum vitae, references and statement of research interests indicating how these would complement projects on offer
**Funding**: Government, Trusts
**Contributor**: The Brian Research Trust

**For further information contact:**

Cell Signalling Laboratory, Institute of Neurology, UCL, 1 Wakefield Street, London WC1N 1PJ, United Kingdom.

Tel: (44) 20 7679 4031
Email: phdstudentship@ion.cl.ac.uk

## British Chevening/University College London (UCL) Israel Alumni/Chaim Herzog Award

**Purpose**: To financially support masters study

**Eligibility**: Candidates will need to return to Israel for at least 3 years after completion. Preference will be given to candidates between 25 and 40; Israeli nations currently living in Israel; applicants who have never studied in the United Kingdom; applicants who are graduates of an Israeli university/students who obtained 1st degree by summer. Please contact the University for updated information
**Level of Study**: Postgraduate
**Type**: Scholarship
**Value**: Tuition fees, return airfare and living expenses
**Frequency**: Annual
**Study Establishment**: University College London
**Country of Study**: United Kingdom
**Additional Information**: scholarship-positions.com/british-chevening-ucl-israel-alumni-chaim-herzog-award-israeli-nationals-2/2013/10/26/

### For further information contact:

The British Council, PO Box 10304, 3 Shimshom Street, Jerusalem 91102, Israel.

**Email**: scholarships@britishcouncil.org.il

## Child Health Research Appeal Trust Studentship

**Purpose**: To fund graduate students for MPhil/PhD research
**Eligibility**: Open to committed individuals wishing to do research in a clinical context, who expect to graduate with a United Kingdom first class or upper second class honours degree or equivalent from abroad
**Level of Study**: Doctorate, Postgraduate
**Type**: Studentship
**Value**: Tuition fees at the United Kingdom/European Union student rate, a stipend equivalent to MRC levels and £3,000 towards research costs
**Length of Study**: 3 years
**Frequency**: Annual
**Study Establishment**: UCL Institute of Child Health
**Country of Study**: United Kingdom
**Application Procedure**: Studentships are advertised on the department's vacancy website between November–January each year. Applicants should refer to www.ich.ucl.ac.uk/ich/humanresources/
**Closing Date**: January
**Funding**: Trusts
**No. of awards given last year**: Up to 4

### For further information contact:

**Email**: chratapps@ich.ucl.ac.uk

## Civil and Environmental Engineering Graduate Scholarship

**Purpose**: To financially support MPhil/PhD study
**Eligibility**: Applicants should hold or except to obtain a First Class (Honours) Degree or equivalent. Applicants should have been offered a place at UCL and should firmly have accepted that offer or be intending to do so. They can be from any country outside the European Union
**Level of Study**: Doctorate, Postgraduate
**Type**: Scholarship
**Value**: £5,000 per year
**Length of Study**: 3 years
**Frequency**: Annual
**Study Establishment**: University College London
**Country of Study**: United Kingdom
**Application Procedure**: Applicants should write indicating their intention to compete for the scholarship to the department
**Closing Date**: 31 July
**Additional Information**: If the applicant has not already applied to UCL, please complete a graduate application form and enclose it with the scholarship application

### For further information contact:

**Tel**: (44) 20 7679 7994
**Fax**: (44) 20 7380 0986
**Email**: m.khraisheh@ucl.ac.uk

## Common Wealth Shared Scholarship Scheme (CSSS)

**Purpose**: To financially help students of high academic ability from developing Commonwealth countries
**Eligibility**: Candidates must be from a developing Commonwealth country, must not have undertaken studies lasting a year or more or be currently studying in a developed country. They should hold or expect to attain, a United Kingdom First Degree (Bachelor's degree) with at least Upper Second Class (Honours) Degree or equivalent and have accepted an offer of place at the development planning unit
**Level of Study**: Postgraduate
**Type**: Scholarship
**Value**: Tuition fees, maintenance costs, some study expenses and return airfare
**Length of Study**: 1 year
**Frequency**: Annual
**Study Establishment**: University College London
**Country of Study**: United Kingdom
**Application Procedure**: Application forms are available from the Development Planning Unit

**Closing Date**: 31 March
**Contributor**: Department for International Development (DFID) and UCL
**No. of awards given last year**: 3
**Additional Information**: Preference is given to candidates unable to afford the cost of studying abroad by themselves. Candidates are expected to return to their home countries to work or study as soon as the award ends www.ucl.ac.uk/scholarships/commonwealth-shared-scholarship-scheme

### For further information contact:

**Tel**:        (44) 20 7679 1111
**Fax**:        (44) 20 7679 1112
**Email**:      dpu@ucl.ac.uk

## Dawes Hicks Postgraduate Scholarships in Philosophy

**Purpose**: To financially support postgraduate research
**Eligibility**: United Kingdom, European Union and overseas students are eligible to apply
**Level of Study**: Postgraduate, Research
**Type**: Scholarship
**Value**: Up to £5,000
**Frequency**: Annual
**Study Establishment**: University College London
**Country of Study**: United Kingdom
**Application Procedure**: No separate application is required. All who are admitted to research programmes in philosophy will automatically be considered for the scholarship. Any queries should be directed to the department
**Additional Information**: Decisions regarding this award will be made in September www.european-funding-guide.eu/other-financial-assistance/14159-dawes-hicks-postgraduate-scholarships-philosophy

### For further information contact:

**Tel**:        (44) 20 7679 4451
**Email**:      r.madden@ucl.ac.uk

## Department of Communities and Local Government (formally Office of the Deputy Prime Minister)

**Purpose**: To financially support full-time study
**Eligibility**: Open to candidates who take up full time study only with residence restrictions, already holding or offer for the MSC spatial planning or MSC international planning, 2:1 or equivalent (except in exceptional circumstances)
**Level of Study**: Postgraduate

**Type**: Bursary
**Value**: Tuition fees at United Kingdom/European Union rate plus (For United Kingdom/European Union nationals only) along with a monthly stipend of £500
**Length of Study**: 1 year
**Frequency**: Annual
**Study Establishment**: University College London
**Country of Study**: United Kingdom
**Application Procedure**: Applications are available from www.esrc.ac.uk (ESRC) and should be sent to the department. Potentially eligible candidates will be contacted by the department
**No. of awards offered**: 16
**Funding**: Government
**Contributor**: Department of Communities and Local Government
**No. of awards given last year**: 7
**No. of applicants last year**: 16

### For further information contact:

**Tel**:        (44) 20 7679 7501
**Email**:      j.hillmore@ucl.ac.uk

## Edwin Power Scholarship

**Purpose**: To support a graduate student to the Department of Mathematics for Master's study or PhD research in Applied Mathematics
**Eligibility**: Applicant must be a graduate student admitted to the Department of Mathematics for Master's study or MPhil/PhD research in applied mathematics
**Level of Study**: Postgraduate, Research
**Type**: Scholarship
**Value**: £400, subject to annual renewal based on satisfactory progress
**Length of Study**: 3 years
**Frequency**: Annual
**Study Establishment**: University College London
**Country of Study**: United Kingdom
**Application Procedure**: Candidates wishing to apply for the Scholarship must send written notice of their intention to apply for the Scholarship to the Head of the Department of Mathematics at UCL
**Closing Date**: 15 August
**Additional Information**: www.scholarshipsads.com/edwin-power-scholarships-at-university-college-london-in-uk-2019/

### For further information contact:

**Tel**:        (44) 20 7679 2839
**Fax**:        (44) 20 7383 2839
**Email**:      h.higgins@ucl.ac.uk

## Eleanor Grove Scholarships for Women Students

**Purpose**: To promote and encourage study and proficiency in German

**Eligibility**: Candidate must be a female student of the college. The scholarship will be awarded to assist a student who is reading for a higher degree, or, in special cases, to enable a BA student to study German abroad. Candidates must have completed at least five terms of study with UCL's Arts and Humanities faculty

**Type**: Scholarship

**Value**: £950

**Frequency**: Annual

**Study Establishment**: University College or elsewhere approved by the Faculty of Arts and Humanities

**Country of Study**: United Kingdom

**Application Procedure**: Contact the Graduate Tutor

**No. of awards offered**: 2

**Closing Date**: 25 May

**No. of applicants last year**: 2

**Additional Information**: This scheme is currently under process, please check for the availability of scheme from the college

### For further information contact:

The Graduate Tutor, Department of German, London, UCL WC1E 6BT, United Kingdom.

**Email**: german@ucl.ac.uk

## English Heritage Scholarships

**Purpose**: To financially support postgraduate study

**Eligibility**: Applicants need a minimum of 2 years work experience in British archaeology

**Level of Study**: Postgraduate

**Type**: Scholarship

**Value**: Up to £13,210

**Frequency**: Annual

**Study Establishment**: University College London

**Country of Study**: United Kingdom

**Application Procedure**: Applicants must contact the department

**Closing Date**: July

### For further information contact:

**Tel**:    (44) 20 7679 7495
**Fax**    (44) 20 7383 2572
**Email**:  k.thomas@ucl.ac.uk

## Fielden Research Scholarship

**Purpose**: To financially support MPhil/PhD study

**Eligibility**: Applicants must have applied for MPhil/PhD research in German language and literature

**Level of Study**: Doctorate, Graduate, Postgraduate

**Type**: Scholarship

**Value**: £500

**Frequency**: Annual

**Study Establishment**: University College London

**Country of Study**: United Kingdom

**Application Procedure**: Applicants must contact the department

**No. of awards offered**: 1

**Closing Date**: 25 May

**No. of awards given last year**: 1

**No. of applicants last year**: 1

**Additional Information**: www.european-funding-guide.eu/it/supporto_finanziario/13993-Fielden-Research-Scholarship

### For further information contact:

School of European Languages, Culture and Society, University College London, Gower Street, London WC1E 6BT, United Kingdom.

**Email**:    joseph.tilley@ucl.ac.uk

## Follett Scholarship

**Purpose**: To financially support MPhil/PhD research

**Eligibility**: United Kingdom, European Union and overseas students are eligible to apply

**Level of Study**: Doctorate, Postgraduate, Research

**Type**: Scholarship

**Value**: Up to £13,000 towards fees and/or maintenance

**Frequency**: Annual

**Study Establishment**: University College London

**Country of Study**: United Kingdom

**Application Procedure**: No separate application is required. Applicants who are admitted to research programmes in philosophy will automatically be considered for the scholarship. Any queries should be directed to the department

**Additional Information**: www.european-funding-guide.eu/other-financial-assistance/14161-follett-scholarship

### For further information contact:

**Tel**:    (44) 20 7679 4451
**Fax**:    (44) 20 7679 3336
**Email**:    r.madden@ucl.ac.uk

## Franz Sondheimer Bursary Fund

**Purpose**: To financially support MPhil/PhD research
**Eligibility**: Preference is given to overseas applicants
**Level of Study**: Doctorate, Postgraduate, Research
**Type**: Scholarship
**Value**: Approx. £2,000
**Study Establishment**: University College London
**Country of Study**: United Kingdom
**Application Procedure**: Applicants must contact the department
**No. of awards offered**: 2
**Closing Date**: 1 May
**No. of awards given last year**: 1
**No. of applicants last year**: 2
**Additional Information**: www.european-funding-guide.eu/other-financial-assistance/14181-franz-sondheimer-bursary-fund

### For further information contact:

**Tel**:        (44) 20 7679 4650
**Fax**:        (44) 20 7679 7463
**Email**:      m.l.jabore@ucl.ac.uk

## Gaitskell MSc Scholarship

**Purpose**: To financially support full-time Master's study in the Department of Economics
**Eligibility**: Open to candidates who have applied for a place for graduate study at UCL and are not already receiving full financial support from other sources for fees and living costs
**Level of Study**: Postgraduate
**Type**: Scholarship
**Value**: £5,000
**Frequency**: Annual
**Study Establishment**: University College London (UCL)
**Country of Study**: United Kingdom
**Application Procedure**: Applications not needed. All applicants to the department are automatically considered
**Additional Information**: www.european-funding-guide.eu/other-financial-assistance/14086-gaitskell-msc-scholarships

### For further information contact:

**Tel**:        (44) 20 7679 5861
**Fax**:        (44) 20 7616 2775
**Email**:      d.fauvrelle@ucl.ac.uk

## Gay Clifford Fees Award for Outstanding Women Students

**Purpose**: To financially support postgraduate study
**Eligibility**: Open to prospective female Master's degree students in the faculties of Arts and Humanities and Social and

Historical Sciences with a First Class (Honours) undergraduate degree or equivalent
**Level of Study**: Postgraduate
**Type**: Scholarship
**Value**: £2,500 (deducted from tuition fees)
**Length of Study**: 1 year
**Frequency**: Annual
**Study Establishment**: University College London
**Country of Study**: United Kingdom
**Application Procedure**: Applicants should refer to the website for further information about the application procedures and deadlines
**No. of awards given last year**: 4
**Additional Information**: This scholarship is under review. To be notified of any updates follow us on Twitter@ucl_studentfund    www.european-funding-guide.eu/other-financial-assistance/14100-gay-clifford-fees-awards-outstanding-women-students

### For further information contact:

**Tel**:        (44) 20 7679 2005/4167
**Email**:      studentfunding@ucl.ac.uk

## Harold and Olga Fox Overseas Postgraduate Prize Studentship

**Purpose**: To provide financial assistance to prospective overseas students intending to pursue a full-time programme of research leading to MPhil/PhD degree in the Department of Biology at UCL
**Eligibility**: Applicants should contact the Department of Biology for full details on eligibility
**Level of Study**: Postgraduate, Research
**Type**: Scholarship
**Value**: £15,000
**Application Procedure**: Applicants should contact the Department of Biology for further information
**Additional Information**: www.european-funding-guide.eu/scholarship/2175-harold-and-olga-fox-scholarship-ukeu-students

### For further information contact:

**Email**:      k.rowlinson@ucl.ac.uk

## Health Risk Resources International (HRRI) Scholarship

**Purpose**: To financially support postgraduate study
**Eligibility**: Applicants must have applied for a place for graduate study at UCL
**Level of Study**: Postgraduate

**Type**: Scholarship
**Value**: United Kingdom/European Union tuition fees
**Frequency**: Annual
**Study Establishment**: University College London
**Country of Study**: United Kingdom
**Application Procedure**: Applicants should contact the department. If the applicants have not applied to UCL they must complete a graduate application form and enclose it with the scholarship application

### For further information contact:

**Tel**: (44) 20 7288 3366
**Fax**: (44) 20 7288 3322
**Email**: m.jacks@chime.ucl.ac.uk

## Ian Karten Charitable Trust Scholarship (Hebrew and Jewish Studies)

**Purpose**: To financially support postgraduate study
**Eligibility**: Applicants must have applied for a place for graduate study at UCL in the Department of Hebrew and Jewish Studies
**Level of Study**: Graduate, Postgraduate
**Type**: Scholarship
**Value**: £1,000 each
**Frequency**: Annual
**Study Establishment**: University College London
**Country of Study**: United Kingdom
**Application Procedure**: Applicants should contact the department. If the applicants have not applied to UCL they must complete a graduate application form and enclose it with the scholarship application
**Closing Date**: 1 June
**Funding**: Trusts

### For further information contact:

**Tel**: (44) 20 7679 3028
**Fax**: (44) 20 7209 1026
**Email**: n.f.lochery@ucl.ac.uk

## Ian Karten Charitable Trust Scholarship (Microbiology)

**Purpose**: To financially support postgraduate study
**Eligibility**: Applicants must be United Kingdom nationals aged 30 years or under at the start of their intended academic year of study
**Level of Study**: Postgraduate
**Type**: Scholarship
**Value**: £2,500
**Frequency**: Annual

**Study Establishment**: University College London
**Country of Study**: United Kingdom
**Application Procedure**: Applicants should contact the department

### For further information contact:

**Email**: t.mchugh@rfc.ucl.ac.uk

## Ian Karten Charitable Trust Scholarship (Neuroscience)

**Purpose**: To financially support postgraduate study in neuroscience
**Eligibility**: Applicants must be United Kingdom nationals aged 30 years or under on October 10th in the intended year of entry
**Level of Study**: Postgraduate
**Type**: Scholarship
**Value**: £2,750
**Frequency**: Annual
**Study Establishment**: University College London
**Country of Study**: United Kingdom
**Application Procedure**: Applicants must contact the department

### For further information contact:

Department of Anatomy and Developmental Biology, Gower St, Bloomsbury, London, United Kingdom.

**Tel**: (44) 20 7679 7740
**Fax**: (44) 20 7679 7349
**Email**: anatpgenquires@anatomy.ucl.ac.uk

## Institute of Education, University of London Centenary Masters Scholarships

**Purpose**: For 2020/21, IOE is offering Centenary Masters Scholarships for students who plan to work either in their home country, or another, to improve the circumstances of disadvantaged, excluded or underachieving citizens.
**Eligibility**: 1. Be citizens and residents of a low or middle income country with a GNI not higher than US$8000 per capita (as per the World Bank GNI per capita classification tables) 2. Have an offer to study a full time masters degree in London at the UCL Institute of Education (September/October 2020 start). 3. Not have studied or lived in the UK before.
**Level of Study**: Postdoctorate
**Type**: Scholarship
**Value**: US$8,000
**Length of Study**: 1 year

**Frequency**: Annual
**Country of Study**: Any country
**Application Procedure**: To be eligible for the scholarship, you must have an offer to study a full time masters degree in London at the UCL Institute of Education. If you fulfill all the criteria, please email IOEinternational[at]ucl.ac.uk to request a scholarship application form. Please include in your email your student ID number. The deadline to apply for these scholarships is 4 May (5pm London time).
**Closing Date**: 4 May
**Funding**: Foundation
**Additional Information**: www.scholars4dev.com/10515/ioe-ish-centenary-masters-scholarships-for-international-students/

**For further information contact:**

**Email**:    international@ucl.ac.uk

## Jacobsen Scholarship in Philosophy

**Purpose**: To financially support MPhil/PhD research
**Eligibility**: Open to United Kingdom, European Union and overseas students
**Level of Study**: Doctorate, Postgraduate, Research
**Type**: Scholarship
**Value**: Up to £9,500
**Frequency**: Annual
**Study Establishment**: University College London
**Country of Study**: United Kingdom
**Application Procedure**: No separate application is required. Applicants who are admitted to research programmes in philosophy will automatically be considered for the scholarship. Any queries should be directed to the department
**Additional Information**: Decisions regarding this award will be made in September www.european-funding-guide.eu/other-financial-assistance/14162-jacobsen-scholarship-philosophy

**For further information contact:**

**Tel**:      (44) 20 7679 7115
**Email**:   r.madden@ucl.ac.uk

## James Joseph Sylvester Scholarship

**Purpose**: To financially support MPhil/PhD research
**Eligibility**: United Kingdom, European Union and overseas students are eligible to apply
**Level of Study**: Doctorate, Postgraduate, Research
**Type**: Scholarship
**Value**: Up to £3,000
**Frequency**: Annual
**Study Establishment**: University College London
**Country of Study**: United Kingdom

**Application Procedure**: Applicants must contact the department
**Closing Date**: 15 May

**For further information contact:**

Department of Mathematics, University College London, Gower Street, London, WC1E 6BT, United Kingdom.

**Tel**:      (44) 20 7679 2839
**Fax**:      (44) 20 7383 5519
**Email**:   h.higgins@ucl.ac.uk

## Jevons Memorial Scholarship in Economic Science

**Purpose**: To financially support MPhil/PhD study
**Eligibility**: Candidates must have graduated or be a candidate for graduation in the term in which the award is made. Previous tenure of the scholarship does not debar candidate from competing on a second occasion. Normally the scholar elected must pursue a course of study and research for a higher degree at UCL
**Level of Study**: Doctorate, Postgraduate
**Type**: Scholarship
**Value**: £55
**Frequency**: Annual
**Study Establishment**: University College London
**Country of Study**: United Kingdom
**Application Procedure**: Applicants should send particulars of the research work they intend to pursue plus an academic curriculum vitae to the department. If the applicant has not applied to UCL, they must complete a graduate application form and enclose it with the scholarship application
**Closing Date**: 15 May

**For further information contact:**

**Tel**:      (44) 20 7679 5861
**Fax**:      (44) 20 7916 2775
**Email**:   d.fauvrelle@ucl.ac.uk

## John Carr Scholarship for Students from Africa and the Caribbean

**Purpose**: To financially support prospective LLM students
**Eligibility**: Applicants must be overseas students from Africa and the Caribbean. An applicant must have accepted an offer (either conditional or unconditional) to read for the LLM at UCL to be eligible
**Level of Study**: Postgraduate
**Type**: Scholarship
**Value**: £2,000
**Frequency**: Annual

**Study Establishment**: University College London
**Country of Study**: United Kingdom
**Application Procedure**: There is no application procedure. All eligible students who have accepted the offer of admission by March 31st will automatically be considered
**Closing Date**: 2 March
**Additional Information**: The scholarships will be based on academic merit. The faculty will only consider those applicants who have firmly accepted their offer of admission to the LLM by May 31st www.european-funding-guide.eu/other-financial-assistance/14064-john-carr-scholarship-students-africa-and-caribbean

**For further information contact:**

Tel:      (44) 20 7679 1441
Fax:     (44) 20 7209 3470
Email:   graduatelaw@ucl.ac.uk

## John Hawkes Scholarship

**Purpose**: The primary purpose is to support third year study in pure mathematics but a secondary purpose when there is no suitable candidate or candidates for the whole sum available, is to support a graduate research student
**Eligibility**: United Kingdom, European Union and overseas students are eligible to apply
**Level of Study**: Doctorate, Postgraduate, Research
**Type**: Scholarship
**Value**: Up to £12,000 per annum
**Length of Study**: 3 years
**Frequency**: Annual
**Study Establishment**: University College London
**Country of Study**: United Kingdom
**Application Procedure**: All students registered or accepted for MPhil/PhD research in Pure Mathematics will be considered for the scholarship.
**Closing Date**: 1 May
**Additional Information**: www.scholarshipdesk.com/john-hawkes-scholarships/

**For further information contact:**

Tel       (44) 20 7679 2839
Fax:     (44) 20 7383 5519
Email:   h.higgins@ucl.ac.uk

## John Stuart Mill Scholarship in Philosophy of Mind and Logic

**Purpose**: To financially support MPhil/PhD research
**Eligibility**: Open to United Kingdom, European Union and overseas applicants

**Level of Study**: Doctorate, Postgraduate, Research
**Type**: Scholarship
**Value**: Up to £1,400
**Frequency**: Annual
**Study Establishment**: University College London
**Country of Study**: United Kingdom
**Application Procedure**: No separate application is required. All who are admitted to research programmes in philosophy will automatically be considered for the scholarship. Any queries should be directed to the department
**Additional Information**: Decision regarding this award will be made in September www.scholarshipeye.com/2018/01/06/john-stuart-mill-scholarship-in-philosophy-of-mind-and-logic/

**For further information contact:**

Tel:      (44) 20 7679 4451
Email:   r.madden@ucl.ac.uk

## Joseph Hume Scholarship

**Purpose**: To financially support LLM students or MPhil/PhD research
**Eligibility**: For all LLM or MPhil/PhD research students in the Department of Laws
**Level of Study**: Doctorate, Postgraduate, Research
**Type**: Scholarship
**Value**: £1,600
**Frequency**: Annual
**Study Establishment**: University College London
**Country of Study**: United Kingdom
**Application Procedure**: There is no application procedure. All eligible students will automatically be considered
**Closing Date**: 23 March
**Additional Information**: Please check the website for further details www.laws.ucl.ac.uk/study/graduate/applying/funding-scholarships/ www.european-funding-guide.eu/other-financial-assistance/14068-joseph-hume-scholarship

**For further information contact:**

Tel:      (44) 20 7679 1441
Fax:     (44) 20 7209 3470
Email:   graduatelaw@ucl.ac.uk

## Keeling Scholarship

**Purpose**: To financially support MPhil/PhD research
**Eligibility**: United Kingdom, European Union and overseas students are eligible to apply
**Level of Study**: Doctorate, Postgraduate, Research
**Type**: Scholarship
**Value**: Up to £1,000

**Length of Study**: 3 years
**Frequency**: Annual
**Study Establishment**: University College London
**Country of Study**: United Kingdom
**Application Procedure**: No separate application is required. Applicants who are admitted to research programmes in philosophy will automatically be considered for the scholarship. Any queries should be directed to the department
**Closing Date**: 30 January
**Additional Information**: For more information on eligibility please check www.ucl.ac.uk/philosophy/keeling/scholarship www.ucl.ac.uk/philosophy/keeling/scholarship

### For further information contact:

**Tel**: (44) 20 7679 7115
**Email**: r.madden@ucl.ac.uk

## Liver Group PhD Studentship

**Purpose**: To financially support students to pursue MPhil/PhD research
**Eligibility**: Open to United Kingdom and European Union applicants holding a relevant First or Upper Second Class
**Level of Study**: Doctorate, Postgraduate, Research
**Type**: Scholarship
**Value**: Home student fees plus a maintenance allowance (1st year approx. £14,500)
**Length of Study**: 3 years
**Frequency**: Dependent on funds available
**Study Establishment**: Royal Free and University College Medical School, UCL-Hampstead campus
**Country of Study**: United Kingdom
**Application Procedure**: Applicants should contact the department
**Funding**: Foundation
**Contributor**: The Liver Group Charity
**No. of awards given last year**: 1

### For further information contact:

Centre for Hepatology, Department of Medicine (Royal Free Campus), Royal Free and University College Medicine School, Rowland Hill Street, Hampstead, London, NW3 2PF, United Kingdom.

**Tel**: (44) 20 7433 2854
**Fax**: (44) 20 7433 2852
**Email**: c.selden@rfc.ucl.ac.uk

## Margaret Richardson Scholarship

**Purpose**: To financially support MPhil/PhD study
**Eligibility**: This scholarship is open to candidates from any country however candidates must have an upper second-class degree or equivalent in German or a related field of study to enable them to undertake research work in this subject.
**Level of Study**: Doctorate, Postgraduate
**Type**: Scholarship
**Value**: £5,000 but may be split into two awards of £2,500 (1 year)
**Length of Study**: 1 years
**Frequency**: Annual
**Study Establishment**: University College London
**Country of Study**: United Kingdom
**Application Procedure**: Applicants should contact the department. If the applicant has not applied to UCL, they must complete a graduate application form and enclose it with the scholarship application. The application must give particulars of the research work which they intend to pursue in the event of the scholarship being awarded to them
**No. of awards offered**: 2
**Closing Date**: 25 May
**Additional Information**: www.scholarshipeye.com/2018/01/06/margaret-richardson-scholarship/

### For further information contact:

School of European Languages, Culture and Society, University College Gower Street, London, WC1E 6BT, United Kingdom.

**Email**: joseph.tilley@ucl.ac.uk

## Master of the Rolls Scholarship For Commonwealth Students

**Purpose**: To financially support prospective LLM students
**Eligibility**: Applicants must be overseas students from the Commonwealth countries. An applicant must have accepted an offer (either conditional or unconditional) to read for the LLM at UCL
**Level of Study**: Postgraduate
**Type**: Scholarship
**Value**: £2,000
**Frequency**: Annual
**Study Establishment**: University College London
**Country of Study**: United Kingdom
**Application Procedure**: There is no application procedure. All eligible students who firmly accept the offer of admission by May 31st will be automatically considered

**No. of awards given last year**: 1

**Additional Information**: The scholarships will be based on academic merit. The faculty will only consider those applicants who have firmly accepted their offer of admission to the LLM by May 31st www.european-funding-guide.eu/other-financial-assistance/14063-master-rolls-scholarship-commonwealth-students

### For further information contact:

**Tel**: (44) 20 7679 1441
**Fax**: (44) 20 7209 3470
**Email**: graduatelaw@ucl.ac.uk

## Master's Degree Awards in Archaeology

**Subjects**: Archaeology.
**Purpose**: To financially support MA and MSc programmes in the Institute of Archaeology.
**Eligibility**: Open to students on MA and MSc programmes in UCL's institute of archaeology.
**Level of Study**: Postgraduate
**Type**: Scholarship
**Value**: Approx. £1,000
**Length of Study**: 1 year Full Time, 2 years Part Time
**Frequency**: Annual
**Study Establishment**: University College London
**Country of Study**: United Kingdom
**Application Procedure**: Applicants must contact the department.
**No. of awards offered**: 10
**Closing Date**: March
**No. of applicants last year**: 46
**Additional Information**: www.ucl.ac.uk/archaeology/study/graduate-taught-programmes

### For further information contact:

Institute of Archaeology.

**Tel**: (44) 020 7679 7499
**Email**: l.daniel@ucl.ac.uk

## Master's Degree Awards in Biochemical Engineering

**Purpose**: To financially support postgraduate study
**Eligibility**: Open to United Kingdom/European Union resident applicants only
**Level of Study**: Postgraduate

**Type**: Scholarship
**Value**: A full award amounts to £9,000 plus tuition fees
**Frequency**: Annual
**Study Establishment**: University College London
**Country of Study**: United Kingdom
**Application Procedure**: Applicants must contact the department at the address given below or the British Council Office in Colombo
**Closing Date**: 1 July
**Additional Information**: The scholarships may be partly or fully funded

### For further information contact:

**Tel**: (44) 20 7679 3796
**Email**: nigelth@ucl.ac.uk

## Member Scholarship in Statistics

**Purpose**: To financially support full-time graduate study and research
**Eligibility**: Applicants should have graduated from UCL or be a candidate for graduation in the term in which the award is made. United Kingdom, European Union and overseas students are eligible to apply
**Level of Study**: Postgraduate, Research
**Type**: Scholarship
**Value**: £55
**Frequency**: Annual
**Study Establishment**: University College London
**Country of Study**: United Kingdom
**Application Procedure**: Applicants should write to the department indicating their intention to compete for the scholarship

### For further information contact:

**Tel**: (44) 20 7679 1872
**Fax**: (44) 20 7383 4703
**Email**: marion@stats.ucl.ac.uk

## Monica Hulse Scholarship

**Purpose**: This Scholarship, founded in 2004, is funded from a regular lifetime gift from Dr Paul Hulse, alumnus of UCL, in memory of his mother, Monica Hulse (1934-1999). One scholarship is awarded annually to a prospective graduate student from any country admitted to the Department of Mathematics for full-time Master's study or MPhil/PhD research

**Eligibility**: 1. University College London - Monica Hulse Scholarships in UK, 2019 is available to candidates from all nationalities. 2. Candidates intending to pursue their masters or PhD studies can apply. 3. The applicants of University College London - Monica Hulse Scholarships in UK, 2019 must be enrolled in a full-time program in the Department of Mathematics at UCL. 4. Candidates are not permitted to receive any other special funding
**Level of Study**: Doctorate, Postgraduate, Research
**Type**: Scholarship
**Value**: £1,000
**Length of Study**: 1 year
**Frequency**: Annual
**Country of Study**: Any country
**Application Procedure**: Candidates wishing to apply for the Scholarship must send written notice of their intention to apply for the Scholarship, along with an academic CV, to the Graduate Tutor in the Department of Mathematics. Applicants should not normally be in receipt of any other special funding (other than in exceptional circumstances).
**Closing Date**: 31 May
**Funding**: Private
**No. of awards given last year**: 1
**Additional Information**: Application link for the following grant is www.ucl.ac.uk/prospective-students/scholarships/graduate/deptscholarships/mathematics www.scholarshipdesk.com/monica-hulse-scholarship/

**For further information contact:**

**Email**: h.higgins@ucl.ac.uk

## National Health Service Bursaries

**Purpose**: To financially support postgraduate study
**Eligibility**: Open to United Kingdom and European Union applicants only who have applied for a place for graduate study at UCL
**Level of Study**: Postgraduate
**Type**: Bursary
**Value**: United Kingdom/European Union tuition fees. United Kingdom residents will also normally be eligible for a means tested bursary
**Frequency**: Annual
**Study Establishment**: University College London
**Country of Study**: United Kingdom
**Application Procedure**: There is no separate bursary application form. Application procedure is an automatic process once an offer of a place has been made
**Additional Information**: When an offer of a place has been made, the NHS Student Grants unit will contact the applicant directly

**For further information contact:**

**Tel**: (44) 20 7679 4202
**Email**: n.wilkins@ucl.ac.uk

## Nederlandse Taalunie Scholarship

**Purpose**: To financially support postgraduate study
**Eligibility**: Applicants must have applied for a place for graduate study at UCL
**Level of Study**: Postgraduate
**Type**: Scholarship
**Value**: £2,500
**Frequency**: Annual
**Study Establishment**: University College London
**Country of Study**: United Kingdom
**Application Procedure**: Applicants should contact the department. If the applicant has not applied to UCL, they must complete a graduate application form and enclose it with the scholarship application
**Closing Date**: 15 July

**For further information contact:**

**Tel**: (44) 20 7679 3117
**Fax**: (44) 20 7616 6985
**Email**: t.hermans@ucl.ac.uk

## Perren Studentship

**Purpose**: To financially support graduate study and research
**Eligibility**: United Kingdom, European Union and overseas applicants are eligible to apply
**Level of Study**: Postgraduate, Research
**Type**: Studentship
**Frequency**: Every 2 years
**Study Establishment**: University College London
**Country of Study**: United Kingdom
**Application Procedure**: Applicants should provide particulars of their academic record and of the work that they intend to pursue to the department
**Closing Date**: 15 May
**Funding**: Trusts
**Contributor**: Perren Fund

**For further information contact:**

**Tel**: (44) 20 7679 473
**Email**: lahauestar@ucl.ac.uk

## R B Hounsfield Scholarship in Traffic Engineering

**Purpose**: To financially support MPhil/PhD research in Traffic Engineering in the Department of Civil and Environmental Engineering
**Eligibility**: Candidates should hold or expect to obtain a First Class (Honours) Degree or equivalent and should have been offered a place at UCL and have firmly accepted that offer or be intending to do so
**Level of Study**: Doctorate, Postgraduate, Research
**Type**: Scholarship
**Value**: Not less than £120
**Frequency**: Dependent on funds available
**Study Establishment**: University College London
**Country of Study**: United Kingdom
**Application Procedure**: Enquiries should be directed to the department
**Closing Date**: 15 May
**Additional Information**: If the applicant has not already applied to UCL, please complete a graduate application form and enclose it with the scholarship application

### For further information contact:

**Tel**:    (44) 20 7679 2710
**Fax**:    (44) 20 7380 0986
**Email**:    civeng.admissions@ucl.ac.uk

## Research Degree Scholarship in Chemical Engineering

**Purpose**: To financially support MPhil/PhD research
**Level of Study**: Doctorate, Postgraduate, Research
**Type**: Scholarship
**Value**: £2,000
**Frequency**: Annual
**Study Establishment**: University College London
**Country of Study**: United Kingdom
**Application Procedure**: Applicants must contact the department

### For further information contact:

**Tel**:    (44) 20 7679 3835
**Fax**:    (44) 20 7383 2348
**Email**:    h.mahgerefteh@ucl.ac.uk

## Research Degree Scholarships in Anthropology

**Purpose**: To financially support research in the field of anthropology

**Eligibility**: Please contact the Department of Anthropology for details
**Level of Study**: Doctorate, Postgraduate, Research
**Type**: Scholarship
**Value**: United Kingdom/European Union tuition fees
**Frequency**: Annual
**Study Establishment**: University College London
**Country of Study**: United Kingdom
**Application Procedure**: Applicants must contact the department
**No. of awards offered**: 12
**Closing Date**: 30 April
**No. of awards given last year**: 4
**No. of applicants last year**: 12

### For further information contact:

**Tel**:    (44) 20 7679 8622
**Fax**:    (44) 20 7679 8632
**Email**:    ucsapga@ucl.ac.uk

## Richard Chattaway Scholarship

**Purpose**: To financially support MPhil/PhD study
**Eligibility**: This scholarship is open to candidates from any country however candidates need to apply to a graduate programme in History by the relevant deadline to be eligible
**Level of Study**: Doctorate, Postgraduate
**Type**: Scholarship
**Value**: £2,000
**Length of Study**: 1 year
**Frequency**: Annual
**Study Establishment**: University College London
**Country of Study**: United Kingdom
**Application Procedure**: Applicants must contact the department. If the applicants have not already applied to UCL they must complete a graduate application form and enclose it with the scholarship application. Applicants must include particulars of the research work they intend to pursue in the event of the scholarship being awarded to them
**Closing Date**: 15 May
**Funding**: Individuals
**Contributor**: Private donation in honour of Richard Chattaway
**No. of awards given last year**: 1
**Additional Information**: www.scholarshipeye.com/2018/01/06/richard-chattaway-scholarship/

### For further information contact:

**Email**:    n.miller@ucl.ac.uk

## Royal National Orthopaedic Hospital Special Trustees Research Training Scholarship

**Purpose**: To give orthopaedic specialists of the future an early exposure to the first-class research culture at Stanmore
**Eligibility**: Open to students enrolled in the MSc in Surgical Sciences programme undertaking a research project at the Royal National Orthopaedic Hospital/Institute of Orthopaedic and Musculoskeletal Science
**Level of Study**: Postgraduate
**Type**: Scholarship
**Value**: A stipend, tuition and bench fees
**Frequency**: Annual
**Study Establishment**: Royal National Orthopaedic Hospital, Stanmore
**Country of Study**: United Kingdom
**Application Procedure**: Once students have been accepted by a supervisor, they should contact the R&D office, Royal National Orthopaedic Hospital. Applicants will be asked to send an outline of the research project and their curriculum vitae. Applicant should contact the department at the address given below
**Funding**: Private
**Contributor**: The RNOH Special Trustees and the R&D Subcommittee
**Additional Information**: Recipients of the scholarships must present their research findings at a symposium to be held at the RNOH. The R&D Director and the Non-Executive Director for research will review applications www.european-funding-guide.eu/other-financial-assistance/14163-keeling-scholarship

### For further information contact:

Royal National Orthopaedic Hospital, Brockley Hill, Stanmore, Middlesex HA7 4LP, United Kingdom.

**Tel**:      (44) 20 8909 5752
**Email**:   lphilpots@rnoh.nhs.uk

## Score Africa/Allan & Nesta Ferguson Charitable Trust Scholarship

**Purpose**: To financially assist African nationals to undertake MSc/PhD studies at the Centre for International Health and Development (CIHD) at UCL
**Eligibility**: Applicants should refer to the website for full details on eligibility
**Level of Study**: Postgraduate
**Type**: Scholarship
**Value**: Partial payment towards tuition fees
**Frequency**: Annual

**Application Procedure**: Applicants should refer to the website for further information on application procedures, forms and deadlines
**Additional Information**: www.scholarshiproar.com/allan-nesta-ferguson-charitable-trust-scholarships/

### For further information contact:

**Email**:    cihdsc@ich.ucl.ac.uk

## Shell Petroleum Development Company Niger Delta Postgraduate Scholarship

**Purpose**: To provide opportunities for postgraduate study in the United Kingdom for young students and professionals, who demonstrate both academic excellence and the potential to become leading professionals in the oil and associated industries
**Eligibility**: The applicant must: 1. have obtained a degree of at least an equivalent standard to a United Kingdom Upper Second Class (Honours Degree); 2. be neither a current nor former employee (who have left employment less than 5 years before) of SPDC, the Royal Dutch Shell Group of Companies or Wider Perspectives Limited, or current employee's relatives; 3. not already have had the chance of studying in the United Kingdom or another developed country; 4. be aged between 21 and 28 years; 5. originate from one of the Niger Delta States in Nigeria, namely Rivers, Delta or Bayelsa and currently reside in Nigeria
**Level of Study**: Postgraduate
**Type**: Scholarship
**Value**: Full tuition fee funding, maintenance allowance, return airfares and arrival allowance
**Frequency**: Annual
**Study Establishment**: University College London
**Country of Study**: United Kingdom
**Additional Information**: www.european-funding-guide.eu/other-financial-assistance/14013-spdc-niger-delta-scholarship

### For further information contact:

Student Funding Office, UCL, Gower Street, WC1E 6BT, London, United Kingdom.

**Email**:    studentfunding@ucl.ac.uk

## Sir Frederick Pollock Scholarship for Students from North America

**Purpose**: To financially support prospective LLM students
**Eligibility**: Applicants must be overseas students from North America. An applicant must have accepted an offer (either conditional or unconditional) to read for the LLM at UCL to be eligible
**Level of Study**: Postgraduate

**Type**: Scholarship
**Value**: £2,000
**Frequency**: Annual
**Country of Study**: United Kingdom
**Application Procedure**: There is no application procedure. All eligible students will be automatically considered
**Closing Date**: 2 March
**Additional Information**: The scholarships will be based on academic merit. The faculty will only consider those applicants who have firmly accepted their offer of admission to the LLM by May 31st www.european-funding-guide.eu/other-financial-assistance/14065-sir-frederick-pollock-scholarship-students-north-america

**For further information contact:**

Tel:     (44) 20 7679 1441
Fax:     (44) 20 7209 3470
Email:   jane.ha@ucl.ac.uk

## Sir George Jessel Studentship in Mathematics

**Purpose**: To financially support MPhil/PhD research
**Eligibility**: A candidate must have been an undergraduate student of UCL, and must have graduated, or be a candidate for graduation in the term in which the award is made. The studentship may also be awarded to someone who has held it in the previous year.
**Level of Study**: Doctorate, Postgraduate, Research
**Type**: Studentship
**Value**: £1,800
**Frequency**: Annual
**Study Establishment**: University College London
**Country of Study**: United Kingdom
**Application Procedure**: Applicants must contact the department
**Closing Date**: 15 May
**Additional Information**: Please refer the website for further details www.ucl.ac.uk/prospective-students/scholarships/graduate/deptscholarships/mathematics www.scholarshipdesk.com/sir-george-jessel-studentship/

**For further information contact:**

Tel:     (44) 20 7679 2839
Fax:     (44) 20 7383 5519
Email:   h.higgins@ucl.ac.uk

## Sir James Lighthill Scholarship

**Purpose**: To financially support MPhil/PhD research
**Eligibility**: United Kingdom, European Union and overseas students are eligible to apply. All applicants who firmly accept

a place for MPhil/PhD research in the Mathematics Department will be considered
**Level of Study**: Doctorate, Postgraduate, Research
**Type**: Scholarship
**Value**: £500 per year
**Frequency**: Annual
**Study Establishment**: University College London
**Country of Study**: United Kingdom
**Application Procedure**: Applicants must contact the department
**Additional Information**: www.educationprogram.scholarshipcare.com/sir-james-lighthill-scholarship/

**For further information contact:**

Tel:     (44) 20 7679 2839
Email:   h.higgins@ucl.ac.uk

## Sir John Salmond Scholarship for Students from Australia and New Zealand

**Purpose**: To financially support prospective LLM students
**Eligibility**: Applicants must be overseas students from Australia and New Zealand. An applicant must have accepted an offer (either conditional or unconditional) to read for the LLM at UCL to be eligible
**Level of Study**: Postgraduate
**Type**: Scholarship
**Value**: £2,000
**Frequency**: Annual
**Study Establishment**: University College London
**Country of Study**: United Kingdom
**Application Procedure**: There is no application
**Additional Information**: The scholarships will be based on academic merit. The faculty will only consider these applicants who have firmly accepted their offer of admission to the LLM by May 31st

**For further information contact:**

Tel:     (44) 20 7679 1441
Fax:     (44) 20 7209 3470
Email:   jane.ha@ucl.ac.uk

## Sully Scholarship

**Purpose**: To financially support MPhil/PhD research
**Eligibility**: Open to the most outstanding candidate in the second year of their PhD research programme
**Level of Study**: Doctorate, Postgraduate, Research
**Type**: Scholarship
**Value**: £2,200
**Frequency**: Annual

**Study Establishment**: University College London
**Country of Study**: United Kingdom
**Application Procedure**: There is no separate application and the award is given to an outstanding student who is registered in the department's PhD programme and is in the second year of study
**No. of awards given last year**: 1

### For further information contact:

**Tel**:       (44) 20 7679 5332
**Fax**:       (44) 20 7430 4276
**Email**:    psychology-pg-enquiries@ucl.ac.uk

## Teaching Assistantships (Economics)

**Purpose**: To financially support MPhil/PhD students
**Eligibility**: MPhil/PhD students who have successfully completed their 1st year in the department
**Level of Study**: Doctorate
**Type**: Assistantship
**Value**: £11,000
**Frequency**: Annual
**Study Establishment**: University College London
**Country of Study**: United Kingdom
**Application Procedure**: Contact the Department of Economics for details

### For further information contact:

**Email**:    d.fauvrelle@ucl.ac.uk

## Thames and Hudson Scholarship

**Purpose**: To financially support postgraduate study
**Level of Study**: Postgraduate
**Type**: Scholarship
**Value**: A scholarship up to a maximum value of £15,000 or up to 4 scholarships totalling that value
**Frequency**: Annual
**Study Establishment**: University College London
**Country of Study**: United Kingdom
**Application Procedure**: Applicants must contact the department for details
**Closing Date**: July

### For further information contact:

**Tel**:       (44) 20 7679 7495
**Fax**:       (44) 20 7383 2572
**Email**:    k.thomas@ucl.ac.uk

## The George Melhuish Postgraduate Scholarship

**Purpose**: To financially support postgraduate research
**Eligibility**: Open to United Kingdom, European Union and overseas applicants
**Level of Study**: Postgraduate, Research
**Type**: Scholarship
**Value**: Up to £3,700
**Frequency**: Annual
**Study Establishment**: University College London
**Country of Study**: United Kingdom
**Application Procedure**: No separate application is required. Applicants who are admitted to research programmes in philosophy will automatically be considered for the scholarship. Any queries should be directed to the department
**No. of awards given last year**: 2
**Additional Information**: Decision regarding this award will be made in September www.european-funding-guide.eu/other-financial-assistance/14165-george-melhuish-postgraduate-scholarships

### For further information contact:

**Tel**:       (44) 20 7679 4451
**Email**:    r.madden@ucl.ac.uk

## The Lloyd's Register Scholarship for Marine Engineering and Naval Architecture

**Purpose**: To financially support an MSc in marine engineering or naval architecture
**Eligibility**: Any country students are eligible to apply. All students must apply in writing. Consideration will be given to those with low financial means
**Level of Study**: Postgraduate
**Type**: Scholarship
**Value**: £10,000
**Frequency**: Annual
**Study Establishment**: University College London
**Country of Study**: United Kingdom
**Application Procedure**: Applicants should write indicating their interest in being considered for this scholarship to the department
**Closing Date**: 1 June
**Funding**: Commercial
**Contributor**: Lloyd's Register
**No. of awards given last year**: 1
**Additional Information**: Only one award is currently available

**For further information contact:**

**Tel**: (44) 20 7679 3907
**Fax**: (44) 20 7388 0180
**Email**: info@meng.ucl.ac.uk

## The Professor John Scales Award in Biomedical Engineering

**Purpose**: To financially support postgraduate study
**Eligibility**: Applicants should hold a First or Upper Second Class (Honours) Degree in engineering, material science or biology
**Level of Study**: Postgraduate
**Type**: Scholarship
**Value**: £6,500
**Length of Study**: 3 years
**Frequency**: Every 3 years
**Study Establishment**: University College London
**Country of Study**: United Kingdom
**Application Procedure**: Applicants should send a curriculum vitae along with a covering letter to the address given below
**Funding**: Private
**Additional Information**: Overseas students would have to pay their own fees www.ucl.ac.uk/surgery/news/2014/oct/john-scales-prize-award-ceremony

**For further information contact:**

**Tel**: (44) 20 8954 0636
**Email**: a.bartram@ucl.ac.uk

## University College London Department Awards for Graduate Students

**Purpose**: To financially support Master's and MPhil/PhD programmes
**Eligibility**: United Kingdom, European Union and overseas students are eligible to apply
**Level of Study**: Doctorate, Postgraduate
**Type**: Scholarship
**Value**: £500
**Frequency**: Annual
**Study Establishment**: University College London
**Country of Study**: United Kingdom
**Application Procedure**: Applicants must contact the department
**Closing Date**: 15 May

**For further information contact:**

**Tel**: (44) 20 7679 3262
**Fax**: (44) 20 7383 4108
**Email**: s.anyadi@ling.ucl.ac.uk

## University College London-AET Undergraduate International Outreach Bursaries

**Eligibility**: Applicants must be a national of any African country (including Madagascar), currently living in an African country, and have one or both parents living in an African country, or are orphaned
**Additional Information**: www.advance-africa.com/University-College-London-Undergraduate-International-Outreach-Bursaries.html

**For further information contact:**

**Email**: m.omona@africaeducationaltrust.org

## University College of London Hong Kong Alumni Scholarships

**Purpose**: To provide financial aid for studies at UCL
**Eligibility**: 1. Be domiciled in Hong Kong; 2. hold a valid UCL Student Number; 3. Hold a valid UCAS Personal ID (not UCAS Registration number); 4. Be in financial need; 5. Hold an offer of admission to UCL to study for a full-time undergraduate or postgraduate Master's degree for the 2020/21 intake (commencing in September 2020); or 6. Be currently enrolled at UCL on an undergraduate or postgraduate Master's programme.
**Level of Study**: Postgraduate
**Type**: Scholarship
**Value**: £5,000 (towards tuition fee for one year)
**Length of Study**: 1 year
**Frequency**: Annual
**Study Establishment**: United College London
**Country of Study**: United Kingdom
**Application Procedure**: Completed UG HK application form should be submitted along with required documentation as detailed in the form to UCL Scholarships
**No. of awards offered**: 13
**Closing Date**: 8 May
**Funding**: Foundation
**No. of awards given last year**: 1
**No. of applicants last year**: 13
**Additional Information**: Interviews will be held in Hong Kong and applicants invited for interview will be required to present themselves for interview in Hong Kong at applicants'

own expense www.ucl.ac.uk/scholarships/ucl-hong-kong-scholarships-fund

## For further information contact:

**Tel**: (44) 20 7679 0004
**Email**: studentfunding@ucl.ac.uk

## William Blake Trust Bursary

**Purpose**: To financially support postgraduate or MPhil/PhD study
**Eligibility**: Applicants must have applied for a place for graduate study at UCL
**Level of Study**: Doctorate, Postgraduate
**Type**: Bursary
**Value**: £2,000
**Frequency**: Annual
**Study Establishment**: University College London
**Country of Study**: United Kingdom
**Application Procedure**: Applicants must contact the department. If the applicants have not already applied to UCL they must complete a graduate application form and enclose it with the scholarship application
**Closing Date**: 15 May

## For further information contact:

**Tel**: (44) 20 7679 7546
**Fax**: (44) 20 7916 5939
**Email**: d.dethloff@ucl.ac.uk

## William Moore Gorman Graduate Research Scholarship

**Purpose**: To financially support students entering the first year of the MPhil/PhD degree in department of Economics
**Eligibility**: Open to candidates who have applied for a place for graduate study at University College London
**Level of Study**: Doctorate, Postgraduate
**Type**: Scholarship
**Value**: £16,200
**Length of Study**: 1 year
**Frequency**: Annual
**Study Establishment**: University College London
**Country of Study**: United Kingdom
**Application Procedure**: Students must indicate why they wish to be considered for this scholarship on their admission application form (section 26)

**No. of awards given last year**: 9
**Additional Information**: The scholarship will be awarded to students who are not already receiving full financial support from other sources for fees and living costs, and will be, awarded on the basis of academic merit www.ucl.ac.uk/economics/study/postgraduate/funding/funding/w-m-gorman-graduate-research-scholarships

## For further information contact:

**Tel**: (44) 20 7679 5861
**Fax**: (44) 20 7916 2775
**Email**: d.fauvrelle@ucl.ac.uk

## University Commission for Development Academy of Research and Higher Education Scholarships

Rue Royale 180, B-1000 Brussels, Belgium.

**Website**: www.ares-ac.be/en/cooperation-au-developpement/bourses/masters-et-stages-en-belgique
**Contact**: ARES

## Academy of Research and Higher Education Scholarships

**Level of Study**: Postgraduate
**Value**: The scholarship covers international travel expenses, living allowance, tuition fees, insurance, housing allowance
**Country of Study**: Any country
**Application Procedure**: To apply for the scholarship, complete the single form scholarship application and admission to one of the French-speaking universities of Belgium
**Closing Date**: 9 February
**Additional Information**: The scholarships are for nationals of: Benin, Bolivia, Burkina Faso, Burundi, Cambodia, Cameroon, Cuba, Ecuador, Ethiopia (only for courses in English), Haiti, Madagascar, Morocco, Niger, Peru, Philippines, DR Congo, Rwanda, Senegal, Vietnam. For more details, please visit official scholarship website: www.ares-ac.be/en/cooperation-au-developpement/bourses/masters-et-stages-en-belgique

## For further information contact:

**Email**: scholarships-cooperation@ares-ac.be

## University Institute of European Studies

Via Maria Vittoria 26, I-10123 Turin, Italy.

**Tel**: (39) 11 839 4660
**Email**: info@iuse.it
**Website**: www.iuse.it
**Contact**: Ms Maria Grazia Goiettina, Course Secretariat

The University Institute of European Studies promotes international relations and European integration by organizing academic activities. The Institute has a comprehensive library in international law and economics. Since 1952 the Institute has been a European Documentation Centre (EDC), thus receiving all official publications of European institutions.

## LLM in International Trade Law – Contracts and Dispute Resolution – Scholarships

**Eligibility**: Applicants must have successfully completed a first level university degree of at least 3 years' duration, either in law, economics, political sciences, business administration or equivalent
**Level of Study**: Postgraduate
**Funding**: Government, Private, Foundation, Individuals

### For further information contact:

**Tel**: (39) 11 69 36 945
**Fax**: (39) 11 69 36 369
**Email**: tradelaw@itcilo.org

## University of Aarhus

Nordre Ringgade 1, Bygning 327 3, DK-8000 Aarhus, Denmark.

**Tel**: (45) 8942 1111
**Email**: au@au.dk
**Website**: www.au.dk
**Contact**: Faculty of Social Sciences

The University of Aarhus was founded in 1928 as Universitetsundervisningen i Jylland – University Teaching in Jutland in classrooms rented from the Technical College and a teaching corps consisting of 1 Professor of philosophy and 4 Readers of Danish, English, German and French. However, today the University has 20,000 students with 5,000 staff.

## Doctor of Philosophy Scholarship in Globalisation and International Economics

**Purpose**: To enable students to take up research in the related fields
**Eligibility**: Open to applicants who have a Master's degree or to students who expect to obtain their Master's degree in the near future
**Level of Study**: Postgraduate, Research
**Type**: Scholarship
**Value**: Approx. salary of €2,700
**Length of Study**: 3 years
**Frequency**: Annual
**Study Establishment**: Aarhus School of Business
**Country of Study**: Denmark
**Application Procedure**: Application forms can be downloaded from the Aarhus website. The form should be sent with a curriculum vitae and an outline of a research project including a description of the proposed theory and methods
**Closing Date**: 19 February
**Contributor**: Danish Social Science Research Council

### For further information contact:

**Tel**: (45) 89 486 482/392
**Email**: pje@asb.dk

## University of Aarhus PhD Scholarships

**Purpose**: To provide financial support and encourage research work
**Eligibility**: Open to candidates who have obtained a Danish university Master's degree or an examination at an equivalent level
**Level of Study**: Doctorate
**Type**: Scholarship
**Value**: US$42,000; US$44,000 per year
**Length of Study**: 3 years
**Frequency**: Annual
**Country of Study**: Denmark
**Application Procedure**: Applicants may download the application form from the website. The completed application form along with project description, plan for the course, budget and copy of degree certificate(s) must be submitted

**Closing Date**: 16 June
**Additional Information**: Further information may be obtained from Administrator Henrik Friis Bach, The Faculty of Social Sciences Secretariat, Tel: (45) 8942 1546

**For further information contact:**

**Email**:    socialsciences@au.dk

## University of Aberdeen

University Office, King's College, Aberdeen AB24 3FX, United Kingdom.

**Tel**:        (44) 12 2427 3506
**Email**:     ptgoff@abdn.ac.uk
**Website**:   www.abdn.ac.uk
**Contact**:   The Postgraduate Registry

The University of Aberdeen is the fifth oldest in the United Kingdom. Aberdeen is an international university serving one of the most dynamic regions of Europe with over 13,000 students and over 3,000 staff, and is at the forefront of teaching and research in medicine and the humanities and sciences.

### Aberdeen International Masters Scholarship

**Value**: £2,000 tuition fee discount
**Country of Study**: United Kingdom
**Application Procedure**: You will be awarded your scholarships as tuition fee discount and the value of the scholarship will be included in your CAS letter.
**Additional Information**: Students cannot receive a cash alternative for scholarship www.abdn.ac.uk/study/funding/341

**For further information contact:**

**Email**:    study@abdn.ac.uk

### Arts Humanities Research Council Collaborative Doctoral Partnership PhD Studentship

**Purpose**: The Collaborative Doctoral Partnership scheme gives non-higher education institutions with a proven track record in postgraduate research the opportunity to manage PhD students, with a minimum of three studentships per year
**Eligibility**: 1. Residency: Students from the EU are normally eligible for a fees-only scholarship, unless they have been ordinarily resident in the UK for three or more years directly prior to the start of the studentship (with some further constraint regarding residence for education). 2. Projects: These awards are attached to specific projects. Only students chosen by the project supervisors can apply.
**Value**: £15,009+ per annum, plus £550 enhancement, plus tuition fees
**Length of Study**: 3 years
**Country of Study**: Any country
**Application Procedure**: You could use the website link: www.ahrc-cdp.org
**No. of awards offered**: 8
**Closing Date**: 29 January
**Additional Information**: www.york.ac.uk/study/postgraduate-research/funding/ahrc-collaborative-doctoral-awards/

**For further information contact:**

**Email**:    Lucie.Connors@ahrc.ukri.org

### China Scholarship Council (CSC) Scholarship

**Purpose**: The CSC Scholarship is a scholarship programme for Chinese PhD students, who will take a full PhD at the University of Aberdeen
**Eligibility**: 1. To be eligible to apply for this scholarship in China, candidates must submit with their application, a conditional scholarship offer letter from Curtin University. 2. To ensure interested candidates meet the China Scholarship Council application deadline in March each year, Curtin University strongly encourage students submit their online e-application for admissions latest by 31 January of the applying year to avoid missing the deadline. 3. Scholarship Recipients must hold a conditional offer of enrolment subject to the CSC award and also fulfil the entry requirements of Curtin University, including a high level of English language proficiency
**Type**: Scholarship
**Country of Study**: Any country
**Application Procedure**: Applications for the CSC Scholarship should be submitted online at: apply.csc.edu.cn/csc/main/person/login/index.jsf
**Additional Information**: If you have any further questions, please contact Catriona Milne, International Officer for China, via email: catriona.milne@abdn.ac.uk graduate school.nd.edu/admissions/international-students/china-scholarship-council/

**For further information contact:**

**Email**:    catriona.milne@abdn.ac.uk

## Common Data Access MSc Petroleum Data Management Scholarships

**Purpose**: To pursue MSc programme
**Value**: Each scholarship is valued at £5,000 for the duration of the MSc Petroleum Data Management degree and will contribute towards the programme tuition fees
**Country of Study**: Any country
**Closing Date**: 31 May

### For further information contact:

**Email**:   info@cdal.com

## Elphinstone PhD Scholarships

**Type**: Scholarship
**Value**: Cover tuition fees for the duration of their supervised study
**Country of Study**: Any country
**Additional Information**: www.european-funding-guide.eu/scholarship/10782-elphinstone-phd-scholarship

### For further information contact:

**Email**   infohub@abdn.ac.uk

## Principal

**Level of Study**: Unrestricted
**Type**: Scholarship
**Study Establishment**: University of Aberdeen
**Country of Study**: United Kingdom

### For further information contact:

**Email**:   studentfunding@ed.ac.uk

## University of Adelaide

Graduate School of Management, 3rd Floor Security House, 233 North Terrace, Adelaide, SA 5005, Australia.

**Tel**:        (61) 8 3035 525
**Email**:     cmchugh@gsm.adelaide.edu.au
**Website**:   www.gsm.adelaide.edu.au
**Contact**:   MBA Admissions Officer

## Adelaide Postgraduate Coursework Scholarships

**Eligibility**: Open only to the citizens of Australia or permanent residents who have achieved Honours 1 or equivalent
**Level of Study**: Postgraduate
**Type**: Scholarship
**Value**: Covers 50% of the tuition fee costs
**Length of Study**: 2 years
**Frequency**: Annual
**Study Establishment**: University of Adelaide
**Country of Study**: Australia
**Application Procedure**: Applicants must apply directly to the scholarship provider. Check website for further details

### For further information contact:

Adelaide Graduate Centre, Adelaide University, Adelaide, SA 5005, Australia.

**Tel**:        (61) 8 8313 4455
**Fax**:        (61) 8 8223 3394
**Email**:     adrienne.gorringe@adelaide.edu.au

## Adelaide Scholarships International

**Purpose**: To attract high quality overseas postgraduate students to areas of research strength in the University of Adelaide to support its research effort
**Eligibility**: Open only to the citizens of Australia or permanent residents who have achieved Honours 1 or equivalent
**Level of Study**: Postgraduate
**Type**: Scholarships
**Value**: AU$28,092 (2020 rate)
**Length of Study**: 2 years (Masters) or 3 years (PhD)
**Frequency**: Annual
**Study Establishment**: University of Adelaide
**Country of Study**: Australia
**Application Procedure**: Candidates must apply directly to the university. Check the website for further details
**Closing Date**: 10 July
**Contributor**: Adelaide University
**Additional Information**: scholarships.adelaide.edu.au/Scholarships/postgraduate-research/all-faculties/adelaide-scholarships-international

### For further information contact:

**Email**:   student.centre@adelaide.edu.au

## Adelaide Scholarships International (ASI)

**Purpose**: The University of Adelaide offers a number of Adelaide Scholarships International to outstanding international graduates from any country to commence their education via a Masters or Doctorate degree by research.

**Eligibility**: Applicants must be international students who are acceptable to commence a Masters or Doctorate by research degree at the University of Adelaide. 1. Citizens and Permanent Residents of Australia, and citizens of New Zealand are ineligible. 2. Applicants who have applied for Australian permanent residency status, but have not yet received an outcome, can apply. 3. Successful recipients are required to apply and enrol in their intended program of study at The University of Adelaide as 'international students' to retain their scholarship. Applicants are required to provide evidence of meeting the University of Adelaide's minimum English language proficiency requirements for direct entry by the application deadline. Applicants with a qualification in progress will not be eligible for consideration until the qualification has been satisfactorily completed (and acceptable evidence provided), or evidence of withdrawal has been provided. Applicants are required to have successfully completed at least the equivalent of a First Class Australian Honours degree. (In Australia an Honours degree is generally a one year qualification taken after an undergraduate degree and involves further study in a particular discipline area. In some areas, Honours is available as part of the final year of a four year undergraduate degree. It is recognised as a prestigious qualification that further develops research, writing and organisational skills. It also demonstrates an ability to undertake high-level study. Achievement of a First Class Honours degree indicates that the recipient performed at the highest academic level and indicates that they have had an introduction to independent research.) International applicants must not hold a research qualification regarded by the University of Adelaide to be equivalent to an Australian Research Doctorate degree or, if undertaking a Research Masters degree, not hold a research qualification regarded by the University of Adelaide to be equivalent to or higher than an Australian Research Masters degree.

**Level of Study**: Masters/PhD Degree

**Type**: Scholarships

**Value**: The scholarship includes course tuition fees, annual living allowance (AU$28,092 in 2020), overseas student health cover plus relocation and publication expenses. The scholarship is awarded for two years for a Masters degree by Research and three years (with a possible 6 month extension) for a Doctoral research degree.

**Frequency**: annual

**Country of Study**: Australia

**Application Procedure**: The prerequisite for applying is that the visiting researcher must have established contacts with a Finnish host university - please see the section 'Doctoral Admissions' for further information (you'll find links to the universities' Doctoral Admissions pages there). You are also advised to visit the Finnish universities' own websites for info on Doctoral level study and research options. If a Finnish university is willing to host you, then the Finnish university department wishing to host you can apply to EDUFI for the grant on your behalf. In other words, only the hosting Finnish university can act as an "applicant" in the EDUFI Fellowship programme. There are no annual application deadlines in the EDUFI Fellowship programme. Applications may be considered at all times. However, please note that applications should be submitted at least 5 months before the intended scholarship period.

**No. of awards offered**: Limited

**Closing Date**: 10 July

**Additional Information**: scholarships.adelaide.edu.au/Scholarships/postgraduate-research/all-faculties/adelaide-scholarships-international

## Arts Start Up Scholarships at University of Adelaide in Australia

**Purpose**: The Faculty of Arts at the University of Adelaide is inviting applications for Arts Start Up Scholarships. The scholarships are available to international students from India, Sri Lanka, Vietnam, Indonesia, Malaysia, United Kingdom and Hong Kong who are seeking entry into a Faculty of Arts postgraduate coursework program

**Eligibility**: Citizens of India, Sri Lanka, Vietnam, Indonesia, United Kingdom, Malaysia and Hong Kong are eligible to apply. If English is not your first language then you will need to show that your English language skills are at a high enough level to succeed in your studies

**Type**: Postgraduate scholarships

**Value**: The scholarship provides a one-off AU$4,000 payment for travel and living expenses. The scholarship will be paid to the recipient following confirmation of enrolment after the census date for the semester they commenced in

**Study Establishment**: Scholarships are awarded within the Faculty of Arts

**Country of Study**: Australia

**Application Procedure**: When offered admission to The University of Adelaide, you will need to accept the offer within 20 business days. This will automatically be your application for the scholarship

**Additional Information**: Please check the website for more details        scholarship-positions.com/arts-start-scholarships-university-adelaide-australia/2018/02/06/

### For further information contact:

**Email**:     admin@scholarship-positions.com

## Asia Pacific Institute of Information Technology_IT PhDs in Grid Computing

**Purpose**: To enable high performance numerical computing on service-oriented architectures
**Eligibility**: Open only to the citizens of Australia and New Zealand or permanent residents who have achieved Honours 2a or equivalent
**Level of Study**: Postgraduate
**Type**: Scholarship
**Value**: AUS24,650 per year
**Length of Study**: 3 years and 6 months
**Frequency**: Annual
**Study Establishment**: The Australian National University, The University of Adelaide
**Country of Study**: Australia
**Application Procedure**: Check website for further details
**Closing Date**: 21 September
**Contributor**: Adelaide University and The Australian National University

### For further information contact:

**Email**: Peter.Strazdins@cs.anu.edu.au

## Australian Building Codes Board Research Scholarship

**Purpose**: The ABCB runs the Student Research Scholarship Program to encourage undergraduate and postgraduate research in the field of building regulatory reform in Australia, which can contribute to the ABCB fulfilling its charter
**Eligibility**: To be eligible for the scholarship, applicants must be students currently undertaking undergraduate or postgraduate studies in building, building surveying, fire engineering, architecture, construction, plumbing, hydraulic design or similar at an Australian educational institution; and research that forms a component of a program or course at an educational institution (e.g. tertiary), such as a research project, thesis or dissertation
**Level of Study**: Graduate
**Type**: Scholarship
**Value**: Up to AU$5,000 one off payment
**Length of Study**: 1 year
**Country of Study**: Australia
**Application Procedure**: To apply for the scholarship, applicants are asked to submit an ABCB Research Scholarship Application Form together with a resume and academic transcript to date to the Research Scholarship Project Officer at abcb.scholarship@abcb.gov.au

**Additional Information**: For more information on the Student Research Scholarship Program, please contact the Research Scholarship Project Officer at abcb.scholarship@abcb.gov.au scholarshipdb.net/scholarships-in-Australia/Australian-Building-Codes-Board-Research-Scholarship-University-Of-South-Australia=_6naSSb-5hGUSwAlk GUTnw.html

### For further information contact:

**Email**: abcb.scholarship@abcb.gov.au

## Ferry Scholarship – UniSA

**Purpose**: To promote study and research into the scientific fields of physics and chemistry
**Eligibility**: Open only to the citizens of Australia below the age of 25 who have achieved Honours 1 or equivalent
**Level of Study**: Postgraduate
**Type**: Scholarship
**Value**: AU$7,500 per year
**Length of Study**: 1 year
**Frequency**: Annual
**Study Establishment**: Flinders University, The University of Adelaide, University of South Australia
**Country of Study**: Australia
**Application Procedure**: Applicants must apply directly to the university. Check the website for further details
**Closing Date**: 31 March
**Funding**: Individuals
**Contributor**: Late Cedric Arnold Seth Ferry

### For further information contact:

**Tel**: (61) 8302 3967
**Email**: jenni.critcher@unisa.edu.au

## Joint Postgraduate Scholarship Program

**Eligibility**: Open to applicants who are citizens and permanent residents of the People's Republic of China at the time of application; are less than 35 years old at the time of application (this is a CSC eligibility requirement); are a university student completing a master's degree, or enrolled as a first year PhD student, or new graduates from their university at the time of application; agree to return to China upon completion of their studies and/or research; hold an unconditional offer of enrolment at the University of Adelaide, which is subject to the applicant also being successful in applying for a CSC award. They must therefore fulfil the relevant academic entry requirements set by the University of Adelaide for all international scholarship holders, including a high level of English language proficiency; English is the language of instruction at the University of Adelaide and proficiency in speaking, listening to, reading and writing English is essential. The IELTS (International English Language Testing System) is the preferred English language proficiency although TOEFL scores are also accepted. Applicants who have not provided evidence that they have met the university's minimum English Language Proficiency requirements by the closing date are not eligible for a CSC scholarship. CSC applicants are not permitted to undertake Pre-Enrolment English programs as the CSC will not award scholarships to applicants who have not met the university's minimum ELP requirements for direct entry. The Scholarships will give priority to graduates of the Chinese universities listed as "985 Project" Universities. Eligible candidates will be assessed by the University of Melbourne and Karlsruhe Institute of Technology on the basis of their academic transcripts and their research work

**Type**: Scholarship

**Value**: Australia

**Country of Study**: Any country

**Application Procedure**: The mode of applying is electronically. For detailed information, please visit website

**Closing Date**: 31 March

**Contributor**: The China Scholarship Council (CSC) and The University of Adelaide (UA)

**Additional Information**: The students of China can apply for these scholarships

## Scholarships in Plant Cell Physiology

**Purpose**: To improve the nutritional qualities of crop plants allowing the fortification of animal and human diets without adversely affecting crop plant

**Eligibility**: Open only to the citizens of Australia who have achieved Honours 1 or equivalent, or Honours 2a or equivalent

**Level of Study**: Postgraduate

**Type**: Scholarship

**Value**: AU$27,500 per year

**Length of Study**: 3 years

**Frequency**: Annual

**Study Establishment**: The University of Adelaide

**Country of Study**: Australia

**Application Procedure**: Applicants must apply directly to the university. Check website for further details

**Closing Date**: 31 August

**Contributor**: Adelaide University

### For further information contact:

**Tel**:      (61) 8 8303 8145
**Email**:   matthew.gillam@adelaide.edu.au

# University of Alabama

## Alumni Heritage Graduate Scholarship (AHGS)

**Subjects**: All

**Purpose**: To recruit children and grandchildren of graduates of The University of Alabama. To send a clear signal to our graduates that want your children. To provide a tangible Alumni Association membership benefit for UA graduates.

**Eligibility**: One time only (non-renewable) scholarship for first-year graduate students who are Alabama residents and who are children or grandchildren of a University of Alabama graduate. The scholarship is for the student's first term of graduate enrolment. Parent or grandparent must be a degree holder (undergraduate, graduate, or law degree) from The University of Alabama. The qualifying parent or grandparent must be an active member of the National Alumni Association for three of the past five years. (Parent or grandparent cannot write check for all three years in one year.) The student must be admitted to a graduate degree program at UA and may be enrolled part-time or full-time. Please note: students admitted to the Graduate School through special program such as the University Scholars Program or any Honor Program will be considered undergraduates for the purpose of this scholarship until the bachelor's degree is awarded.

**Type**: Scholarship

**Value**: The award will be equal to $500 towards the cost of in-state tuition of graduate level course work. (Subject to a maximum of actual in-state tuition not covered by other awards, whichever is lower).

**Frequency**: Annual

**Study Establishment**: University of Alabama

**Country of Study**: United States of America

**Application Procedure**: Submit online scholarship form

**Closing Date**: 15 July, for students entering Fall Semester. 30 November, for students entering Spring Semester. 1 May, for students entering Summer Semester.

**Additional Information**: graduate.ua.edu/prospective-students/graduate-school-scholarships-fellowships/

## Graduate Council Fellowships

**Subjects**: All

**Purpose**: To award University of Alabama Graduate School students.

**Eligibility**: Prospective and current University of Alabama students are nominated by their departments for our fellowships, so it is important that you are talking to the Graduate Program Director for your program. Prior to nomination, nominees who are prospective students must have been offered admission.

**Type**: Fellowship

**Value**: Stipend of $20,000 for the academic year (fall and spring semesters). A limited number of David A. Francko Fellowships are available for our top applicants. This highly selective fellowship includes a stipend of $25,000/year for a maximum of 5 years. This fellowship is only awarded from the pool of nominees submitted for the January 16 deadline. For new UA students the prospective department may add up to $2,000 to the stipend, which will be matched by the Graduate School (for a total stipend of up to $24,000). For doctoral students awarded this supplement, the prospective department will commit to a departmental assistantship in year 2, and continuation of the supplement in year 2.

**Length of Study**: One year

**Frequency**: Annual

**Study Establishment**: University of Alabama

**Country of Study**: United States of America

**Additional Information**: graduate.ua.edu/prospective-students/graduate-school-scholarships-fellowships/

## McNair Graduate Fellowships

**Subjects**: All

**Purpose**: McNair Graduate Fellowships are specifically for entering graduate students who have either completed a McNair Undergraduate Scholars program or who are McNair eligible.

**Eligibility**: Low income (as defined by the US Department of Education) AND a first-generation college student or a member of a group traditionally underrepresented in graduate education (i.e. Hispanic, African American, Native American, Native Hawaiian, Pacific Islander). Although any prospective or current graduate student may be nominated for this fellowship, preference is given to students who have completed a McNair program and have been accepted into a Doctoral program at The University of Alabama. Exceptional current University of Alabama students may also be considered for this fellowship.

**Type**: Fellowship

**Value**: The stipend for the McNair Graduate Fellowship is US$20,000 for the academic year (fall and spring semesters).

**Length of Study**: One year

**Frequency**: Annual

**Study Establishment**: University of Alabama

**Country of Study**: United States of America

**Additional Information**: For students in doctoral programs the fellowship lasts two years and is followed by a minimum of two years of support through a departmental assistantship or equivalent. For students in masters programs the fellowship lasts one year and is followed by a minimum of one year of support through a departmental assistantship or equivalent. graduate.ua.edu/prospective-students/graduate-school-scholarships-fellowships/

## University of Alaska Fairbanks (UAF)

School of Management PO Box 756080, Fairbanks, AK 99775-6080, United States of America.

**Tel**:       (1) 907 474 6511
**Email**:     famba@som.uaf.edu
**Website**:   www.uaf.edu/som/mba
**Contact**:   MBA Admissions Officer

## Rasmuson Fisheries Research Center Fellowships

**Purpose**: This fellowship is especially interested in seeing proposals on applied topics aligned with the research priorities and needs of the North Pacific Fishery Management Council [PDF]

**Eligibility**: 1. Awards will be made to support excellence in graduate student research. The award is not a Research Assistantship, but a Fellowship in recognition of scholastic excellence. Awards are open to any full-time or prospective CFOS graduate student. 2. Research should produce findings with a potential for continued development as a scientific or applied initiative. 3. Projects should be distinctive and make an original contribution to existing knowledge. 4. Projects should have potential economic value to the fishing industry and contribute to long-term benefits for Alaska. 5. Awards may be contingent on receipt of research funding from other sources. The award cannot be used for research expenses. See item #6, "Current and Pending," under "Format of Proposals" below. 6. Proposals should be submitted by the graduate student with faculty advisor endorsement as described in item #8 below. 7. Awards are renewable. Master's students can be funded for a maximum of two (2) years and PhD students for a maximum of three (3) years. Continuation requests require a satisfactory progress report

**Level of Study**: Postgraduate

**Type**: Fellowship

**Value**: Fellowship award of US$35,000

**Length of Study**: Master's students can be funded for a maximum of two (2) years and PhD students for a maximum of three (3) years.

**Frequency**: Annual

**Country of Study**: Any country

**Application Procedure**: Complete format of proposals are available in the below link. www.uaf.edu/cfos/research/major-research-programs/rasmuson-fisheries-resear/rfc-fellowships/

**Closing Date**: 22 January

**Funding**: Private

**Additional Information**: www.uaf.edu/cfos/research/major-research-programs/rasmuson-fisheries-resear/rfrc-fellowships/

**For further information contact:**

**Tel**:      (1) 907 474 2619
**Email**:   clsutton3@alaska.edu

# University of Alberta

Faculty of Graduate Studies & Research, Killam Centre for Advanced Studies, 2-29 Triffo Hall, University of Alberta, Edmonton, AB T6G 2E1, Canada.

**Tel**:      (1) 780 492 3499
**Email**:   grad.services@ualberta.ca
**Website**:  www.ualberta.ca/gradstudies

Opened in 1908, the University of Alberta has a long tradition of scholarly achievements and commitment to excellence in teaching, research and service to the community. It is one of Canada's five largest research-intensive universities, with an annual research income from external sources of more than C\$3,000,000,000. It participates in 18 of 21 of the Federal Networks of Centres of Excellence, which link industries, universities and governments in applied research and development.

## Canadian Initiatives For Nordic Studies (CINS) Graduate Scholarship

**Purpose**: To provide financial assistance to students who wish to pursue higher studies
**Eligibility**: Open to Canadian citizens or landed immigrants, who have completed a Bachelor's degree from a Canadian university or college with high scholastic achievement. Applicants must be in residency at the Nordic destination for a minimum of 6 months and provide a written report to CINS no later than 6 months after completing the proposed programme of study
**Level of Study**: Postgraduate
**Type**: Scholarship
**Value**: C\$5,000
**Frequency**: Annual
**Application Procedure**: Applicants should include the following in their application: contact details, citizenship status, social insurance number and date of birth, current academic status with formal transcripts, written acceptance from the host Nordic institution and reference letters
**Closing Date**: 15 February
**Additional Information**: Applicants can study at any recognized institution granting earned degrees at the postbaccalaureate level in the applicant's field of study and located in one of the Nordic countries: Denmark, Finland, Iceland, Norway, Sweden, the Faroe Islands and Greenland

**For further information contact:**

**Tel**:      (1) 780 492 3111
**Email**:   chale@ualberta.ca

## Izaak Walton Killam Memorial Scholarship

**Purpose**: It will be offered to outstanding students registered in, or admissible to, a doctoral program. No restrictions on citizenship
**Eligibility**: Offered to outstanding students registered in, or admissible to, a doctoral program. No restrictions on citizenship. All fields are eligible for funding. Applicants must have completed at least one year of graduate work (master's or doctoral level) before start of tenure; tenure may begin on 1 May or 1 September. Additional information regarding eligibility criteria can be found in the Applicant Instructions document below. Please note that the GPA is calculated over the current graduate program graded course work
**Level of Study**: Graduate
**Type**: Scholarship
**Value**: 1. C\$35,000 per year for up to 2 years 2. A one-time research grant of C\$2,000
**Length of Study**: 2 years
**Frequency**: Annual
**Country of Study**: Any country
**Application Procedure**: Students complete the Izaak Walton Killam Memorial Scholarship application form and submit supporting documents to their department to be considered for both the Izaak Walton Killam Memorial Scholarship and the Dorothy J Killam Memorial Graduate Prizes. A complete Izaak Walton Killam Memorial Scholarship Application includes: For Applicants: Izaak Walton Killam Memorial Scholarship Applicant Instructions 1. Izaak Walton Killam Memorial Scholarship Application Form. 2. Two Letter of Reference to Support Application for Graduate Awards. 3. Transcripts (copies of official transcripts for all post-secondary study are required to support an application. Your home department may have copies in your department file. If your department does not have these transcripts, you are required to submit new transcripts. Unofficial copies of University of Alberta transcripts are acceptable)
**Closing Date**: 31 January
**Funding**: Private
**Additional Information**: www.buddy4study.com/scholarship/izaak-walton-killam-memorial-scholarship

## For further information contact:

School of Library and Information Studies, 7-104 Education North, University of Alberta, Edmonton, AB T6G 2R3, Canada.

**Tel**:    (1) 780 492 7625
**Email**:    slis@ualberta.ca

## University of Alberta MBA Programme

**Length of Study**: 20 months; 72 months
**Application Procedure**: Applicants must complete and return the form, with two official academic transcripts, Graduate Management Admission Test scores, three letters of recommendation, a two page statement of intent, a detailed curriculum vitae, an application deposit of C$60 (US$45), and a TOEFL score (if applicable) of 550+
**Closing Date**: 30 April

## For further information contact:

**Tel**:    (1) 780 492 3946
**Fax**:    (1) 780 492 7825
**Email**:    mba.programs@ualberta.ca

# University of Amsterdam

The University of Amsterdam is a public university located in Amsterdam, The Netherlands.

## Amsterdam Excellence Scholarships (AES)

**Purpose**: The Amsterdam Excellence Scholarships (AES) awards scholarships to exceptionally talented students from outside Europe to pursue eligible Master's Programmes offered at the University of Amsterdam
**Eligibility**: Non-European Union students from any discipline who graduated in the top 10% of their class may apply. Selection is on the basis of academic excellence, ambition and the relevance of the selected Master's programme to a student's future career
**Level of Study**: Postgraduate
**Type**: Scholarship
**Value**: €25,000 per annum
**Length of Study**: 1 year
**Frequency**: Annual
**Study Establishment**: University of Amsterdam
**Country of Study**: Netherlands
**Application Procedure**: Applications are made through the Admissions Offices of the Graduate Schools

**Closing Date**: 15 January
**Additional Information**: For more details, please visit official scholarship website: www.uva.nl/en/education/master-s/scholarships–tuition/scholarships-and-loans/amsterdam-excellence-scholarship/amsterdam-excellence-scholarship.html www.uva.nl/en/education/master-s/scholarships–tuition/scholarships-and-loans/amsterdam-excellence-scholarship/amsterdam-excellence-scholarship.html?1581921251233

## For further information contact:

P.O. Box 19268, NL-1000 GG Amsterdam, The Netherlands.

**Email**:    servicedesk-ac@uva.nl

## Amsterdam Science Talent Scholarship (ASTS)

**Purpose**: Scholarship is available for pursuing the masters degree programme at the University of Amsterdam
**Eligibility**: Non-Dutch talented students from the European Union / European Economic Area can apply
**Value**: €12,500 (covering tuition and living expenses)
**Length of Study**: 2 years
**Country of Study**: Any country
**Application Procedure**: To be eligible, an applicant must: 1. Be an international student 2. Be registered or admissible to a full-time doctoral program 3. Have completed at least one year of graduate work (master or doctoral level) 4. Have an intellect complemented by a sound character
**Closing Date**: 1 March
**Additional Information**: For more details, please visit the website scholarship-positions.com/fully-funded-science-talent-scholarship-university-amsterdam-netherlands gss.uva.nl/scholarships/amsterdam-talent-scholarship/amsterdam-science-talent-scholarship.html?1581921289624

## For further information contact:

**Email**:    master-science@uva.nl

## MacGillavry Fellowships

**Purpose**: These fellowships are available in the field of Biological Science and Biomedical Science, Earth Sciences (Physical Geography), Informatics and Logic, Physics, Chemistry, Astronomy, Mathematics, and Statistics
**Eligibility**: Eligibility for the Scholarship: 1. A PhD degree in one of the scientific disciplines of their Faculty. 2. A scientific profile that links to one of the research fields eligible for application. 3. A publication record in international, high quality, peer-reviewed journals. 4. A few years of postdoctoral experience, preferably at the international level. 5. Well-

developed organizational and communication skills. 6. Affinity for teaching at the undergraduate and graduate level

**Level of Study**: Postgraduate

**Type**: Fellowship

**Value**: The annual salary range for an assistant professor, including annual holiday allowance and the bonus is between €50,755 and €78,935 (before tax), depending on experience and past performance

**Frequency**: Annual

**Country of Study**: Any country

**Application Procedure**: To apply for the MacGillavry Fellowship you are invited to use the application form on the MacGillavry website of the Faculty of Science. www.uva.nl/en/faculty/faculty-of-science/macgillavry-fellowship/macgillavry-fellowship.html

**Closing Date**: 4 February

**Funding**: Private

**Additional Information**: www.uva.nl/en/about-the-uva/organisation/faculties/faculty-of-science/working-at-the-faculty/macgillavry-fellowship/macgillavry-fellowship.html

### For further information contact:

**Email**:    servicedesk-icts@uva.nl

---

# University of Antwerp

Prinsstraat 13, B-2000 Antwerp, Belgium.

**Tel**:          (32) 3 265 41 11
**Email**:      internationalstudents@uantwerpen.be
**Website**:   www.uantwerpen.be/en/

The Flemish Ministry of Education awards scholarships to outstanding students for Master programmes in Flanders and Brussels. The Master Mind programme aims to promote Flanders and Brussels as a top study destination. The call for the next round of applications (academic year 2020-2021) has now been launched. It is estimated that 30 international students can benefit from the Master Mind Scholarships 2020-2021. Students cannot apply directly. Applications need to be submitted by the Flemish host institution. The deadline for applications to the University of Antwerp is 1 March 2020. Applications have to be done online through Mobility Online.

## Master Mind Scholarships

**Purpose**: The Flemish Ministry of Education awards scholarships to outstanding students for Master programmes in Flanders and Brussels. The programme aims to promote Flanders and Brussels as a top study destination

**Eligibility**: The applicant applies to take up a Master degree programme at the University of Antwerp. The applicant should have a high standard of academic performance and/or potential. This means: The student has a Grade Point Average (GPA) of 3.5 out of 4.0. You can find the GPA calculator here. The student has a good knowledge of the English language, proven by one of the following situations: an overall band score of minimum 7.0 on the IELTS test; a minimum total score of 94 on a TOEFL test; a C1 level of the Common European Framework of Reference; a similar result in another official language test; or an exemption provided by the Master programme Selection Committee. Additionally, the University of Antwerp will consider the following aspects when evaluating candidates: Academic performance Motivation Attitude and maturity Relevant work experience The student has to be accepted by the University of Antwerp to be able to receive the scholarship. Even if the university's final decision is taken after awarding the scholarship to the student. All nationalities can apply. The previous degree obtained should be from a higher education institution located outside Flanders. Students who are already enrolled in a Flemish higher education institution cannot apply. The only exception is made for international students who, at the moment of their application in the spring of 2020, are already enrolled in a preparatory programme in order to start a Master programme in September 2020. Students who enroll for the following programmes for the academic year 2020-2021 are not eligible for a Master Mind scholarship: preparatory programmes distance learning programmes Student mobility during the master programme is allowed. However, at least half of the credits of the master programme must be obtained at the University of Antwerp.

**Level of Study**: Masters Degree

**Type**: Scholarships

**Value**: The incoming student is awarded a maximum scholarship of €8,000 per academic year

**Frequency**: annual

**Country of Study**: Belgium

**Application Procedure**: The University of Antwerp screens all applicants and submits a shortlist of 20 candidates for the scholarship. The Flemish Government makes the final selection on the basis of this shortlist. To apply for the Master Mind scholarship, students need to complete the following steps: Complete your application and upload all documents for the relevant Master programme at the University of Antwerp. Click here to read more about the Admission and enrolment procedure. Please do not forget to upload your English test scores! During your application indicate that you would also like to apply for the Master Mind Scholarship. In your motivation text, clearly specify why you are applying for the Master Mind scholarship and why you should be selected.

Please address every selection criterium. In addition, specify your GPA score. Applications without a motivation text will not be considered. Application process for candidates who do not need to submit a Master application in Mobility Online (previous degree from Wallonia, Netherlands or Luxembourg) or those currently enrolled in a preparatory or bridge programme at the University of Antwerp: Please submit your application directly to the Master programme you are applying for. See programme links above for the contact details. Your application should include a motivation letter addressing the selection criteria and clearly specifying your language test and GPA scores.

**No. of awards offered**: 20

**Closing Date**: 1 March

**Additional Information**: www.uantwerpen.be/en/study/international-mobility/scholarships/master-mind/

# University of Auckland

Private Bag 92019, Auckland 1000, New Zealand.

**Tel**:       (64) 9 373 7599
**Email**:    appointments@auckland.ac.nz
**Website**:  www.auckland.ac.nz
**Contact**:  Ms S Codhersides, HR Manager

## Anne Bellam Scholarship

**Purpose**: To assist students to further their musical education overseas

**Eligibility**: The candidate must be under 30 years of age and a citizen of New Zealand, must have completed or will complete in the year of application any degree or diploma in performance or any postgraduate music degree at the University of Auckland

**Level of Study**: Postgraduate

**Type**: Scholarship

**Value**: Up to NZ$30,000 for study overseas and up to NZ$10,000 for study at the University of Auckland

**Length of Study**: 1 year

**Frequency**: Annual

**Study Establishment**: University of Auckland

**Country of Study**: New Zealand

**Application Procedure**: The candidate must supply, one week in advance of examination, an outline of his proposed study plans and itinerary

**Funding**: Government

**Additional Information**: www.auckland.ac.nz/en/study/scholarships-and-awards/find-a-scholarship/anne-bellam-scholarship-68-ca.html

## For further information contact:

Faculty of Creative Arts and Industries, School of Music, University of Auckland, Private Bag 92019, Auckland 1000, New Zealand.

**Email**:    scholarships@auckland.ac.nz

## Arthington Davy Scholarship

**Purpose**: To study and research in areas which will significantly contribute to the development of Tonga

**Eligibility**: The candidate must be a Tongan citizen, born to Tongan parents and possess a first University degree

**Level of Study**: Research

**Type**: Scholarship

**Value**: The Arthington Davy Scholarship may cover the cost of part of the cost of a postgraduate study or research programme

**Study Establishment**: Trinity College

**Country of Study**: United Kingdom

**Application Procedure**: The candidate must submit a complete curriculum vitae and academic record, proof of Tongan origin, details of the intended postgraduate study preferably with a letter of conditional acceptance from the University concerned, full details of tuition fees and living expenses and of finances available from the student's own resources or elsewhere and the names of two academic referees

**Closing Date**: 31 May

**Funding**: Commercial, Private, Foundation, Individuals

**Additional Information**: www.auckland.ac.nz/en/study/international-students/scholarships-loans-and-funding/country-specific-scholarships-and-funding0/tonga/arthington-davy-scholarship.html

## For further information contact:

**Email**:    hf202@hermes.cam.ac.uk

## Asian Development Bank Japan Scholarship

**Eligibility**: 1. Be a national of an ADB borrowing member. 2. Have gained admission to an approved masters at an approved academic institution. 3. Have a bachelors degree or its equivalent with a superior academic record. 4. Have at least two years of full-time professional work experience (acquired after a university degree) at the time of application. 5. Be proficient in oral and written English communication skills to be able to pursue studies. 6. Be under 35 years old at the time of application. In exceptional cases, for programmes which are appropriate for senior officials and managers, the age limit is 45 years. 7. Be in good health. 8. Agree to return to your home country after completing the programme.

**Level of Study**: Postgraduate

**Type**: Scholarship

**Value**: Tuition fee at the University of Auckland, Airfare from his or her home country to Auckland, New Zealand, Basic cost of living in Auckland, Health and medical insurance in New Zealand, and Airfare from Auckland, New Zealand, to the scholar's home country at the conclusion of his or her course of study

**Study Establishment**: University of Auckland

**Country of Study**: New Zealand

**Application Procedure**: 1. Completed ADB-JSP Information Sheet 2. Completed ADB-JSP Application Form 3. Copy of your offer letter to the University of Auckland 4. Academic documentation - both academic transcripts and degree certificates 5. Certificate of Employment for the duration of employment issued by the company 6. Certificate of Income issued by the company 7. Certificate of Family Income issued by the company. Must be either your parents or spouses annual/monthly income. 8. Copy of your Passport 9. Valid IELTS test

**Closing Date**: 19 July

**Funding**: Government, Private

**Contributor**: Asian Development Bank and Government of Japan

**Additional Information**: www.auckland.ac.nz/en/study/international-students/scholarships-loans-and-funding/development-scholarships/asian-development-bank-japan-scholarship-program.html

### For further information contact:

**Email**:    information@adbj.org

## Auckland Council Research Scholarship in Urban Economics

**Purpose**: The purpose of this scholarship is to encourage and support postgraduate research into urban economics that has particular relevance to local government in New Zealand

**Eligibility**: 1. At the time of application candidates must be enrolled or planning to enrol in a postgraduate programme at a New Zealand university (applicants may be enrolled as full time students). 2. The postgraduate programme must be in the area of urban economics. Universities NZ and Auckland Council reserve the right to determine the eligibility of a particular area of study. 3. A thesis, dissertation, or research report must be a requirement of the postgraduate programme

**Level of Study**: Postgraduate

**Type**: Scholarship

**Value**: NZ$3,000 or NZ$1,500

**Frequency**: Annual

**Country of Study**: Any country

**Application Procedure**: Candidates must complete an application using the Universities NZ scholarships application website universitiesnz.communityforce.com/ Each year Auckland Council may grant one scholarship with an award of NZ$3,000. For candidates who are enrolled on a part time basis the value of the award will be NZ$1,500

**Closing Date**: 1 February

**Funding**: Private

**Additional Information**: Application link to fill the basic information is universitiesnz.communityforce.com/Login.aspx www.universitiesnz.ac.nz/scholarships/auckland-council-research-scholarship-urban-economics

### For further information contact:

**Email**:    scholarships-cf@universitiesnz.ac.nz

## Commonwealth Scholarship

**Purpose**: The scholarships are available to students to be enroled at the University of Auckland for the Degree of Doctor of Philosophy; another approved Doctorate or a Master's degree

**Eligibility**: The candidate must be a citizen of Commonwealth of Nations, including Australian, British and Canadian citizens. The candidate must be tenable for a maximum of 36 months for a PhD candidate or 21 months for a Master's candidate

**Level of Study**: Doctorate, Postgraduate

**Type**: Scholarship

**Value**: Up to NZ$25,000 per year plus health insurance and fees at the domestic rate

**Study Establishment**: University of Auckland

**Country of Study**: New Zealand

**Application Procedure**: The candidate must send the application for UA Commonwealth Scholarships must be made through the appropriate organization in the scholar's home country on the Commonwealth Scholarship application form

**Closing Date**: 31 July

**Funding**: Government

**Additional Information**: www.auckland.ac.nz/en/study/scholarships-and-awards/find-a-scholarship/university-of-auckland-commonwealth-scholarship-266-all.html

### For further information contact:

Scholarships Office, Student Administration, The University of Auckland, Private Bag 92019, Auckland Mail Centre, Auckland 1142, New Zealand.

**Tel**:       (64) 9 373 7599 ext 87494

**Fax**:      (64) 9 308 2309

**Email**:    scholarships@auckland.ac.nz

## Doctoral Scholarships

**Purpose**: To assist and encourage students to pursue doctoral studies at The University of Auckland

**Eligibility**: The candidate must be a citizen or a permanent resident of New Zealand. New Māori and domestic3 Pacific doctoral applicants with a GPA of 7.50 or above, from their most recent qualifying programme, will be guaranteed a scholarship provided the qualifying programme was completed at a New Zealand university

**Level of Study**: Doctorate

**Type**: Scholarship

**Value**: NZ$27,900 plus fees, with the possibility of a six-month extension. There will be an annual cost-of-living adjustment to the doctoral stipend

**Length of Study**: 3 years

**Frequency**: Annual

**Study Establishment**: University of Auckland

**Country of Study**: New Zealand

**Application Procedure**: The candidate must fill the application form and send it to the Scholarships office. The selection will be made on the basis of merit

**Funding**: Government

**Additional Information**: www.auckland.ac.nz/en/study/scholarships-and-awards/scholarship-types/postgraduate-scholarships/doctoral-scholarships.html#schol-regs

### For further information contact:

**Email**: c.tuu@auckland.ac.nz

## Fulbright Scholarship

**Purpose**: To encourage and facilitate study for approved postgraduate degrees at the University of Auckland by candidates already selected to hold Fulbright Awards

**Eligibility**: The candidate must be a citizen of the United States of America and intending to take up Fulbright Awards to study in New Zealand and should enrol for a full-time at the University of Auckland for an approved Master's or Doctoral degree

**Level of Study**: Doctorate, Postgraduate

**Type**: Scholarship

**Value**: NZ$15,000 per year plus research/tuition fees

**Frequency**: Annual

**Study Establishment**: University of Auckland

**Country of Study**: New Zealand

**Application Procedure**: The candidate must send the completed application form to the Scholarships office

**Funding**: Government

**Additional Information**: www.auckland.ac.nz/en/study/scholarships-and-awards/find-a-scholarship/university-of-auckland-fulbright-scholarship-293-all.html

## Hope Selwyn Foundation Scholarship

**Purpose**: The HOPE Selwyn Foundation is a registered charitable trust established in 1996 to assist the funding of research and education essential to the health and welfare of older people in New Zealand

**Eligibility**: 1. The purpose of the scholarships is to support or partially support the salaries of young scientists (the definition of "young" being reasonably flexible) who are in the early stages of their careers. 2. Candidates undertaking a Masters or doctoral thesis will be considered for support. Candidates will normally be working under supervision in a recognised research environment with a senior research leader. 3. HOPE Sewlyn Foundation scholarships may be held with any other bursary or award unless the candidate's other awards preclude this

**Level of Study**: Postgraduate

**Type**: Scholarship

**Value**: NZ$6,000

**Length of Study**: 4 years

**Frequency**: Annual

**Country of Study**: New Zealand

**Closing Date**: 31 October

**Funding**: Foundation

### For further information contact:

The University of Auckland, Private Bag 92019, Auckland 1142, New Zealand.

**Email**: pc.dasilva@auckland.ac.nz

## International College of Auckland PhD Scholarship in Plant Sciences

**Purpose**: To assist eminent Chinese scholars from nominated areas of China to study plant sciences at the University of Auckland and to promote links between China and New Zealand in the field of plant sciences

**Eligibility**: The candidate must possess a PhD in the field of plant science and who has paid the fees, or arranged to pay the fees, for full–time enrolment in the School of Biological Sciences

**Level of Study**: Postdoctorate

**Type**: Scholarship

**Value**: NZ$20,000 per year. The scholarship's emolument will be paid as a tuition/compulsory fees credit and the balance as a fortnightly stipend

**Length of Study**: 3 years

**Frequency**: Annual

**Study Establishment**: University of Auckland

**Country of Study**: New Zealand

**Application Procedure**: The candidate must submit the completed application form along with the curriculum vitae and at least two academic reference letters
**Closing Date**: 1 October
**Funding**: Government
**Contributor**: The International College of Auckland

### For further information contact:

**Email**:   scholarships@auckland.ac.nz

## Maori and Pacific Graduate Scholarships (Masters/Honours/PGDIP)

**Purpose**: The Scholarship is offered each semester to Māori students enrolled in any Masters or postgraduate level Bachelors (Honours) degree, or any Postgraduate Diploma
**Eligibility**: The University assesses your eligibility when you submit an Application for Admission. You will be advised of your eligibility once we have received your final grades and you have a firm offer of place for your chosen programme. 1. Maori students who are citizens or permanent residents of New Zealand with a grade point average (GPA) of 7.50 or higher in their qualifying programme from a recognised university. 2. Applying for an honours degree, a postgraduate diploma or a masters degree at the University of Auckland.
**Level of Study**: Postgraduate
**Type**: Scholarship
**Value**: Tax-free stipend of US$13,390 plus the cost of your compulsory fees
**Length of Study**: 1 year
**Frequency**: Annual
**Country of Study**: New Zealand
**No. of awards offered**: Varies
**Funding**: University of Auckland
**Additional Information**: www.auckland.ac.nz/en/study/scholarships-and-awards/scholarship-types/postgraduate-scholarships/maori-postgraduate-scholarships.html

### For further information contact:

**Email**:   scholarships@auckland.ac.nz

## Masters/Honours/PGDIP Scholarships

**Eligibility**: The candidate must be a citizen or a permanent resident of New Zealand. In case of a Master's degree, the candidate must be tenable until the date for completion of the requirements for the degree as specified in the General Regulations – Masters degrees
**Level of Study**: Graduate, Postgraduate
**Type**: Scholarship
**Value**: Up to NZ$10,000 per year plus compulsory fees

**Length of Study**: 1 year
**Frequency**: Annual
**Study Establishment**: University of Auckland
**Country of Study**: New Zealand
**Application Procedure**: The candidate must fill the application form and send it to the Scholarships office. Selection will be made on the basis of merit
**Closing Date**: 1 November
**Funding**: Government
**Additional Information**: www.auckland.ac.nz/en/study/scholarships-and-awards/find-a-scholarship/faculty-of-arts-masters-honours-pgdip-scholarship-50-art.html

## New Zealand Agency for International Development Scholarship (NZDS) – Open Category

**Eligibility**: The candidate must possess minimum English language requirements for entry into the University of Auckland postgraduate study. IELTS (International English Language Testing System Certificate) with an overall score of 6.5 and no band less than 6.0 or a TOEFL (Test of English as a Foreign Language) paper based 575 with a TWE of 4.5 or computer based 233
**Level of Study**: Postgraduate
**Type**: Scholarship
**Value**: Tuition, enrollment/orientation fees, return economy fare travel, medical insurance and provision for students to meet course and basic living costs
**Study Establishment**: University of Auckland
**Country of Study**: New Zealand
**Application Procedure**: Application form can be downloaded from the website
**Closing Date**: 1 June
**Funding**: Government
**Contributor**: New Zealand Agency for International Development and the Ministry of Foreign Affairs

### For further information contact:

**Tel**:      (64) 9 373 7599 ext 87556
**Fax**:     (64) 9 373 7405
**Email**:   rfatialofa.patolo@auckland.ac.nz

## New Zealand International Doctoral Research (NZIDRS) Scholarship

**Purpose**: To provide financial support for postgraduate students from designated countries seeking doctoral degrees by research in New Zealand universities
**Eligibility**: The candidate must hold an A' average or equivalent in their studies, meet the requirements for entry into a research-based doctoral degree programme at a New Zealand university

**Level of Study**: Doctorate, Research
**Type**: Research scholarship
**Value**: Living allowance (NZ$25,000 per year), a travel allowance (NZ$2,000), a health insurance allowance (NZ$500), and a book and thesis allowance (NZ$800)
**Length of Study**: 3 years
**Study Establishment**: University of Auckland
**Country of Study**: New Zealand
**Application Procedure**: The candidate must complete the application form in English and attach supporting documents as stipulated in the application form
**Closing Date**: 16 July
**Funding**: Government
**Contributor**: Government of New Zealand
**Additional Information**: scholarshipdb.net/scholarships-in-New-Zealand/New-Zealand-International-Doctoral-Research-Scholarships-Nzidrs-Auckland-University-Of-Technology=u2NUb6tF6BGUVQAlkGUTnw.html

## For further information contact:

**Tel**:  (64) 4 472 0788
**Fax**:  (64) 4 471 2828
**Email**:  scholarships@educationnz.org.nz

## Property Institute of New Zealand Postgraduate Scholarship

**Purpose**: To promote postgraduate study in the field of real property
**Eligibility**: The candidate must possess a Master's degree or full-time PhD candidate and has the paid the fees, or arranged to pay the fees, for study in the Department of Property at Lincoln University, Massey University or The University of Auckland
**Level of Study**: Doctorate
**Type**: Scholarship
**Value**: NZ$1,500
**Length of Study**: 1 year
**Frequency**: Annual
**Study Establishment**: University of Auckland
**Country of Study**: New Zealand
**Closing Date**: 31 March
**Funding**: Government
**Contributor**: Property Institute of New Zealand
**Additional Information**: www.auckland.ac.nz/en/study/scholarships-and-awards/find-a-scholarship/property-institute-of-new-zealand-postgraduate-award-369-bus.html

## For further information contact:

**Tel**:  (64) 9 373 7599 ext 87494
**Fax**:  (64) 9 308 2309
**Email**:  scholarships@auckland.ac.nz

## Reardon Postgraduate Scholarship in Music

**Purpose**: To honour and in memory of Daniel Patrick Reardon and Kathleen Mary Reardon
**Eligibility**: The candidate must possess a degree or diploma with a specialization in Performance in the year of the award
**Level of Study**: Postgraduate
**Type**: Scholarship
**Value**: NZ$4,500
**Length of Study**: 1 year
**Frequency**: Annual
**Study Establishment**: University of Auckland
**Country of Study**: New Zealand
**Closing Date**: 30 September
**Funding**: Government
**Contributor**: Reardon Memorial Music Trust
**Additional Information**: www.auckland.ac.nz/en/study/scholarships-and-awards/find-a-scholarship/reardon-postgraduate-scholarship-in-music-74-cai.html

## Senior Health Research Scholarships

**Purpose**: To attract health professionals to return to the University to study full-time for a PhD in a health-related field
**Eligibility**: The candidate must be a citizen or a permanent resident of New Zealand and who have worked for 3 years as a health professional
**Level of Study**: Doctorate
**Value**: NZ$40,000 plus compulsory fees
**Length of Study**: 3 years
**Frequency**: Annual
**Study Establishment**: University of Auckland
**Country of Study**: New Zealand
**Application Procedure**: The candidate must submit an application form and send it to the Scholarships office. Selection shall be made on the basis of merit
**Closing Date**: 1 November
**Funding**: Government
**Additional Information**: indiabioscience.org/grants/senior-and-intermediate-fellowships-in-basic-biomedical-research

## The AUT Queen Elizabeth II Diamond Jubilee Doctoral Scholarship

**Purpose**: AUT Doctoral Scholarship AUT aims to: Develop an internationally-aware, skilled future leader Establish enduring education and professional linkages
**Eligibility**: 1. The scholarship will be awarded annually to a doctoral student who is a citizen, and resident in, one of the following Pacific countries; Cook Islands, Fiji, Kiribati, Nauru, Niue, Papua New Guinea, Samoa, Solomon Islands, Tokelau, Tonga and Vanuatu to carry out doctoral study at

AUT University. 2. Applicants must be a citizen and resident of one of the eligible countries. Applicants may not have citizenship or permanent residence status of New Zealand or any other developed country. Applicants who are New Zealand citizens from the Cook Islands, Niue, Tokelau and dual citizens of Samoa are exempt from this requirement; however, they must reside in the Cook Islands, Nuie, Tokelau or Samoa or another eligible country. Preference may be given to those applicants who have also been schooled in an eligible country. 3. The recipients of this scholarship will have strong academic references plus a strong academic record and/or have demonstrated the potential for quality research. Previous study should include research methodologies papers and an independent research project, including the writing of a report on that research

**Level of Study**: Postgraduate
**Type**: Scholarship
**Value**: NZ$25,000
**Length of Study**: 1 year
**Frequency**: Annual
**Country of Study**: Any country
**Application Procedure**: Application will be via the online scholarship application portal available from the link. It is not possible to submit incomplete scholarship applications through the online application process. In order for the application to be submitted all requested documentation must be included. The following documents or statements must be completed and uploaded in the application portal by the closing date. Incomplete applications will not be forwarded to the selection panel. 1. AUT Queen Elizabeth II Diamond Jubilee Doctoral Scholarship on-line application form. 2. Academic transcript(s) if any previous tertiary study has been completed at a university other than AUT. 3. A certified copy of the applicant's birth certificate or passport. 4. Two referee's reports are required. Applicants must not submit referee's reports directly. Nominated referees will be sent a request directly by the on-line application system. Please advise your referees that they will be receiving an email requesting a reference statement and that this must be submitted by the closing date or your application will be ineligible. If the referee declines to provide a reference before the closing date you will be able to nominate another referee. 5. A two page statement (maximum 1,000 words) outlining the applicant's research proposal using the template provided with the online application form. Please note this must be two pages only (plus one page for references). If a longer document is provided you will be asked to rewrite it. 6. Written support from the proposed primary supervisor if they have not acted as one of the referees above. 7. A brief C.V. (maximum three pages)

**Closing Date**: 1 November
**Funding**: Private

**Additional Information**: www.aut.ac.nz/study/fees-and-scholarships/scholarships-and-awards-at-aut/scholarships-database/detailpage?detailCode=500675&sessionID=32 593825&sourceIP=&X_FORWARDED_FOR=

### For further information contact:

55 Wellesley St E, Auckland 1010 New Zealand.

**Tel**:      (64) 9 921 9837
**Email**:   scholars@aut.ac.nz

## The University of Auckland International Doctoral Fees Bursary

**Purpose**: To assist international students from all countries who wish to pursue doctoral studies
**Eligibility**: Permanent citizens and residents of Australia and New Zealand are not eligible for the scholarship
**Level of Study**: Doctorate
**Type**: Bursary
**Value**: NZ$25,000
**Frequency**: Annual
**Study Establishment**: University of Auckland
**Country of Study**: New Zealand
**Application Procedure**: The application form can be obtained from the Scholarships Office, University of Auckland
**Closing Date**: 1 August
**Funding**: Government

## University of Auckland International Doctoral Scholarship

**Purpose**: To assist international students from all countries who wish to pursue doctoral studies
**Eligibility**: The scholarship is available to international students from all countries who wish to pursue Doctoral studies on a full-time basis. Permanent citizens and residents of Australia and New Zealand are not eligible for the scholarship
**Level of Study**: Doctorate
**Type**: Scholarship
**Value**: NZ$25,000, in the form of a fortnightly stipend
**Frequency**: Annual
**Study Establishment**: University of Auckland
**Country of Study**: New Zealand
**Application Procedure**: The application form can be obtained from the Scholarships Office, University of Auckland
**Funding**: Government

## University of Auckland Business School

School of Business & Economics, Private Bag 92019, Auckland, New Zealand.

| | |
|---|---|
| **Tel**: | (64) 9 373 7599 |
| **Email**: | execpro@auckland.ac.nz |
| **Website**: | www.business.auckland.ac.nz |
| **Contact**: | Dr Gary Cayton, Director MBA |

### Kupe Leadership Scholarships

**Purpose**: The Kupe Leadership Programme will involve a three-day Orientation in early March; two two-day workshops held during each mid-semester break; a one-day workshop in the inter-semester break and a concluding day-long workshop in November

**Eligibility**: The Kupe Leadership alumni will develop a reputation for embodying these values and for contributions they make, nationally and possibly internationally

**Level of Study**: Postgraduate

**Type**: Scholarship

**Frequency**: Annual

**Country of Study**: Any country

**Closing Date**: 24 August

**Funding**: Private

**Additional Information**: www.auckland.ac.nz/en/study/scholarships-and-awards/scholarship-types/postgraduate-scholarships/kupe-leadership-scholarships.html

#### For further information contact:

The University of Auckland, Private Bag 92019, Auckland, 1142, New Zealand.

| | |
|---|---|
| **Tel**: | (64) 800 61 62 63 |
| **Email**: | pc.dasilva@auckland.ac.nz |

### University of Auckland Executive MBA Programme

**Eligibility**: 1. Have a relevant bachelors degree with a GPA of 5.0 or higher in at least 90 points in the most advanced courses OR 2. Have completed the Postgraduate Diploma in Business (in Administration OR in Maori Development) with a GPA of 5.0 or higher OR 3. Have a bachelor degree and completed the Postgraduate Certificate in Business from this University with a GPA of 5.0 or higher AND 4. Have at least three years' relevant management experience 5. Have successfully completed all application requirements (see domestic application Checklist and Reference form)

**Length of Study**: More than 2 years

**Application Procedure**: Applicants must return a completed form. A deposit of AU$250 is payable on acceptance. Foreign students may be required to sit a test of English proficiency

**Closing Date**: 1 February

**Additional Information**: www.mba.auckland.ac.nz/our-mba-programme/domestic-students/

#### For further information contact:

Business Administration International Students Office, Private Bag 92019, Auckland 1142, New Zealand.

| | |
|---|---|
| **Tel**: | (64) 9 373 7513 |
| **Fax**: | (64) 9 373 7405 |
| **Email**: | international@auckland.ac.nz |

## University of Bath

Claverton Down, Bath BA2 7AY, United Kingdom.

| | |
|---|---|
| **Tel**: | (44) 1225 388388 |
| **Website**: | www.bath.ac.uk |
| **Contact**: | University of Bath |

The University of Bath received its Royal Charter in 1966 and is now firmly established as a top ten United Kingdom university with a reputation for research and teaching excellence.

### United Kingdom-India Year of Culture Great Postgraduate Scholarships

**Purpose**: The University of Bath is currently accepting applications for United Kingdom-India Year of Culture GREAT Scholarships. This scholarship is available to the international fee-paying student from India studying a full-time taught postgraduate masters programme

**Eligibility**: Indian students are eligible to apply for this scholarship. For most programmes, the requirement for non-native English speakers is 6.5 in the IELTS Academic English test, with no less than 6.0 in any element

**Type**: Postgraduate scholarships

**Value**: If you are an international fee-paying student you could be eligible for one of ten United Kingdom-India Year of Culture GREAT Scholarships each worth £5,000

**Study Establishment**: Scholarships are awarded in the Faculty of Humanities and Social Sciences, Faculty of Engineering and Design and scholarship in the Faculty of Science
**Country of Study**: United Kingdom
**Application Procedure**: If you are eligible for the scholarship scheme we will let you know and invite you to apply. Queries for MSc students should be addressed to msc-mn-at-bath.ac.uk and for MBA students to mbaapps-at-management.bath.ac.uk
**Closing Date**: 1 June
**Additional Information**: For more details please see the website scholarship-positions.com/uk-india-year-of-culture-great-postgraduate-scholarships-university-bath-uk/2018/01/27/

### For further information contact:

**Email**: mbaapps-at-management.bath.ac.uk

## University of Bern

Hochschulstrasse 4, CH-3012 Bern, Switzerland.

**Tel**: (41) 31 631 81 11
**Email**: info@imd.unibe.ch
**Website**: www.unibe.ch/eng/

The University of Bern offers top quality teaching, special recognition in leading–edge disciplines, and a campus environment intimately linked to the social, economic, and political life of the city. The university's comprehensive offering includes 8 faculties and some 160 institutes with 12,500 students. Its academic and research organization prides itself on its interdisciplinarity. The university is actively involved in a wide range of European and worldwide research projects.

## Excellence Scholarships for Postgraduate Study

**Purpose**: Scholarship for international students
**Eligibility**: Applicants must, by end of July, have graduated with at least a Bachelor's degree in the same field of study as the selected Master's programme and must be residing in their home country. The criteria for selection are previous academic excellence and the potential of the candidate
**Level of Study**: Graduate
**Type**: Scholarship
**Value**: CHF 1,600 per month for the entire duration of the course
**Frequency**: Annual
**Application Procedure**: Check website for specific details

**Closing Date**: 21 December
**Funding**: Commercial

### For further information contact:

**Tel**: (41) 31 631 80 49
**Email**: claudine.rossi@int.unibe.ch

## UniBE International 2021

**Purpose**: To support for young researchers and to the university's internationalization
**Level of Study**: Doctorate, Postgraduate
**Length of Study**: 3 years
**Study Establishment**: University of Bern
**Country of Study**: Switzerland
**Application Procedure**: Please email your application including any related documents as one pdf to lenka.fehrenbach@entwicklung.unibe.ch
**Closing Date**: 17 May
**Contributor**: Swiss National Fund (SNF)

### For further information contact:

**Email**: sandro.stauffer@uls.unibe.ch

## University of Bologna

Via Zamboni, 33, I-40126 Bologna Italy.

**Tel**: (39) 51 2088101
**Website**: www.unibo.it/

The origins of the University of Bologna go way back, and it is considered to be the oldest university in the Western world. Its history is intertwined with that of the great names of science and literature, it is a keystone and a point of reference for European culture.

## University of Bologna Study Grants for International Students

**Purpose**: The University of Bologna awards study grants and full tuition fee waivers to deserving international students who wish to register for First, Single, and Second Cycle Degree Programmes at the University of Bologna for A.Y. 2020/2021.
**Eligibility**: Application is open exclusively to candidates who: 1. Possess qualifications for admission to the chosen First, Single, or Second Cycle degree programme issued by an

institution outside of the Italian education system or in an Italian institute outside Italy, after at least two years of attendance. If the qualification for admission is a one-year title, the prior qualification will be considered too. Qualifications issued by institutions of the Republic of San Marino do not satisfy this condition. The applicant's citizenship is not considered; 2. Meet the admission requirements for the chosen degree programme or will meet such requirements at the time of registration; 3. Are not current students at the University of Bologna for First, Single or Second Cycle degree programmes. Important! Those whose student career (First, Single or Second Cycle degree programme) ended within A.Y. 2018-19 for any reason are not considered students. Withdrawals from studies must have been completed before the publication of this call; 4. Have not already benefited from the Unibo Action 2 study grant or from the Unibo Action 1 waiver; 5. Are not 30 years or older as of the deadline of the call.

**Level of Study**: Bachelors/Masters Degree

**Type**: Scholarships

**Value**: Each Unibo Action 2 study grants are awarded for one academic year only and amounts to a total of €11.059, gross of all charges for the beneficiary's account. Each Unibo Action 1 full tuition waivers are awarded for one academic year only. Students who are awarded the waivers must pay €157.64 in regional taxes, the duty stamp and insurance premium (amount subject to change).

**Frequency**: annual

**Country of Study**: Italy

**Application Procedure**: Applications must be submitted by 31 March (Second Cycle Programmes) or 30 April (First or Single Cycle Programmes), exclusively through Studenti Online, as explained in the call for applications. It is important to read the 2020/21 Call for Applications (GRE) or 2020/21 Call for Applications (SAT) and visit the official website (link found below) to access the online application system and for detailed information on how to apply for this scholarship.

**No. of awards offered**: 1. 5 study grants worth €11.059 each (Unibo Action 2) and full tuition fee waivers for a total amount of €16.000 (Unibo Action 1) for First Cycle and Single Cycle degree programmes 2. 17 study grants worth €11.059 each (Unibo Action 2) and full tuition fee waivers for a total amount of €100.000 (Unibo Action 1) for Second Cycle degree programmes Target group

**Closing Date**: 30 April

**Additional Information**: www.unibo.it/en/services-and-opportunities/study-grants-and-subsidies/exemptions-and-incentives/unibo-actions-1-2-study-grants-and-tuition-fee-waivers-for-international-students/Unibo-actions-1-and-2-study-grants-and-tuition-fee-waivers-for-international-students

### For further information contact:

**Email**:    internationaldesk@unibo.it

## University of Bristol

Student Funding Office, Senate House (Ground Floor), Tyndall Avenue, Bristol BS8 1TH, United Kingdom.

**Tel**:         (44) 11 7928 9000
**Email**:      student-funding@bris.ac.uk
**Website**:    www.bristol.ac.uk
**Contact**:    Ms Penny Rowe, Student Funding Advisor

The University of Bristol is committed to providing high-quality teaching and research in all its designated fields.

## Global Accounting and Finance Scholarship

**Purpose**: The Department of Accounting and Finance is offering eight scholarships worth £5,000 each to eligible international students studying for a postgraduate qualification in Accounting and Finance

**Eligibility**: You can apply for a University of Bristol Global Accounting and Finance Scholarship if you: 1. are classed as an overseas student for fee purposes AND. 2. have applied to start one of the qualifying Accounting and Finance MSc programmes at the University of Bristol in September. To be eligible for the University's Postgraduate scholarships, students must: 1. Be an applicant to any one year, full-time postgraduate programme at the University of Bristol. 2. Start their postgraduate programme in September. 3. Be classed as an overseas student for fee paying purposes. 4. Not already be in receipt of other funding which would equate to more than the full cost of tuition fees alongside a Bristol scholarship

**Level of Study**: Postgraduate

**Type**: Scholarship

**Value**: 1. Eight scholarships worth £5,000 each. 2. The awards can only be used as fee waivers towards the cost of tuition fees

**Frequency**: Annual

**Country of Study**: Any country

**Application Procedure**: You can submit an application for the Global Accounting and Finance Scholarship using the International Scholarships online application form

**Closing Date**: 10 July

**Funding**: Private

**Additional Information**: www.bristol.ac.uk/fees-funding/awards/global-accounting-finance/

### For further information contact:

**Tel**:     (44) 117 928 9000
**Email**:   funding@bristol.ac.uk

## Global Economics Postgraduate Scholarship

**Purpose**: The Department of Economics is offering five scholarships worth £5,000 each to eligible international students studying for a postgraduate qualification in Economics
**Eligibility**: Kindly check the terms and conditions for the scholarship under the following link,
**Level of Study**: Postgraduate
**Type**: Scholarship
**Value**: 1. Five scholarships worth £5,000 each. 2. The awards can only be used as fee waivers towards the cost of tuition fees
**Frequency**: Annual
**Country of Study**: Any country
**Application Procedure**: There are two rounds of scholarships to avail. Round One Deadline: 31 March. Successful applicants will be informed via email by 26 April. Round Two Deadline: 30 June. Successful applicants will be informed via email by 19 July
**Closing Date**: 30 June
**Funding**: Private
**Additional Information**: www.bristol.ac.uk/fees-funding/awards/global-economics-pg/

### For further information contact:

University of Bristol, Senate House, Tyndall Avenue, Bristol, BS8 1TH, United Kingdom.

**Tel**:      (44) 117 331 1223
**Email**:   iro@bristol.ac.uk

## International Postgraduate Scholarships – Taught Master's Programmes

**Purpose**: This programme provides plenty of offers for future research postgraduate researchers with access to studentships, supervision from world-class experts and excellent facilities on our PhD and doctoral programmes
**Eligibility**: Open to candidates holding an offer for a 1 year taught postgraduate programme at the University of Bristol
**Level of Study**: Postgraduate
**Type**: Scholarship (MSc)
**Value**: £2,000
**Length of Study**: 1 year
**Frequency**: Annual
**Study Establishment**: University of Bristol
**Country of Study**: United Kingdom
**Application Procedure**: Check website for further details
**Closing Date**: 30 June
**Funding**: Private

### For further information contact:

International Recruitment Office, University of Bristol Union, Queens Road, Clifton, Bristol BS8 1ND, United Kingdom.

**Email**:    iro@bristol.ac.uk

## Phyllis Mary Morris Bursaries

**Purpose**: Phyllis Mary Morris née Doidge graduated with a degree in Geography in 1930
**Eligibility**: You can apply for a Phyllis Mary Morris Bursary if you: 1. are classed as an overseas student for fee purposes AND. 2. have applied to start a qualifying one-year, full-time taught postgraduate programme at the University of Bristol in September
**Level of Study**: Postgraduate
**Type**: Bursary
**Value**: 1. Six bursaries worth £2,000 each. 2. The awards can be used towards living costs.
**Frequency**: Annual
**Country of Study**: Any country
**Closing Date**: 10 July
**Funding**: Private
**Additional Information**: www.bristol.ac.uk/geography/courses/postgraduate/pmmbursaries.html

### For further information contact:

University of Bristol, Beacon House, Queens Road, Bristol, BS8 1QU, United Kingdom.

**Tel**:      (44) 117 928 9000
**Email**:    graduation-office@bristol.ac.uk

## Think Big Postgraduate Scholarships

**Subjects**: Any full-time Undergraduate programme (except Medicine, Dentistry and Veterinary Science) or any one-year, full-time taught postgraduate programme offered at the University
**Purpose**: Helping and nurturing global talent to produce the future leaders of tomorrow.
**Eligibility**: You can apply for a Think Big Postgraduate Scholarship if you: are classed as an overseas student for fee purposes AND have applied to start a one-year, full-time taught postgraduate programme at the University of Bristol in September 2020
**Level of Study**: Bachelors/Masters Degree

**Type**: Scholarships
**Value**: A number of awards valued at £5,000 and £10,000 are available to Undergraduate students for September 2020 entry. A number of awards valued at £5,000, £10,000 and £20,000 are available to Postgraduate students for September 2020 entry. The awards can only be used as fee waivers towards the cost of tuition fees.
**Frequency**: annual
**Country of Study**: UK
**Application Procedure**: You can submit an application for the Think Big Undergraduate and Postgraduate Scholarship using the International Scholarships online application form. The deadline for undergraduate scholarships is 29 March. There are two rounds of applications for postgraduate scholarships: 1. The deadline for the first round is 29 March. 2. The deadline for the second round is 14 June. It is important to visit the official website (link found below) to access the application form and for detailed information on how to apply for this scholarship.
**Closing Date**: 29 March
**Additional Information**: www.bristol.ac.uk/fees-funding/awards/think-big-postgraduate/

# University of British Columbia (UBC)

2329 West Mall, Vancouver, BC V6T 1Z2, Canada.

**Tel**: (1) 604 822 2211
**Email**: graduate.awards@ubc.ca
**Website**: www.ubc.ca
**Contact**: Ms Jiffin Arboleda, Awards Administrator

The University of British Columbia (UBC) is one of North America's major research universities. The Faculty of Graduate Studies has 6,500 students and is a national leader in interdisciplinary study and research, with 98 departments, 18 interdisciplinary research units, 9 interdisciplinary graduate programmes, 2 graduate residential colleges and 1 scholarly journal.

## Izaak Walton Killam Predoctoral Fellowships

**Purpose**: To assist doctoral students with full-time studies and research
**Eligibility**: Open to students of any nationality, discipline, age or sex. This award is given at the PhD level only and is strictly based on academic merit. Students must have a First Class standing in their last 2 years of study

**Level of Study**: Doctorate
**Type**: Fellowship
**Value**: C$22,000 per year and C$1,500 travel allowance for the duration of the award
**Frequency**: Annual
**Study Establishment**: UBC
**Country of Study**: Canada
**Application Procedure**: Top ranked students are selected from the University Graduate Fellowship competition. Application forms can be obtained from individual departments, the Faculty of Graduate Studies or the website. Students must submit their applications to the departments, not to the Faculty of Graduate Studies
**No. of awards offered**: 200
**Funding**: Private
**No. of awards given last year**: 12
**No. of applicants last year**: 200

### For further information contact:

**Email**: gsaward@ucalgary.ca

## University of British Columbia Graduate Fellowship (UGF)

**Purpose**: To assist graduate students with their studies and research
**Eligibility**: Academic Standing 1. A progress report evaluated as satisfactory by the College of Graduate Studies based on established, articulated criteria Number of Months of Study 1. Master's students must have completed, as of April 30 of the adjudication year, no more than 24 months of study in the program for which they are requesting funding 2. PhD students must have completed, as of April 30 of the adjudication year, no more than 48 months of study in the program for which they are requesting funding
**Level of Study**: Masters and Doctoral
**Type**: Fellowship
**Value**: Awarded in a minimum base unit of US$3,000 to a maximum of C$24,000
**Frequency**: Annual
**Study Establishment**: UBC
**Country of Study**: Canada
**Application Procedure**: Annual progress reports must be completed and signed by both the student and supervisor/advisor, reviewed by the program coordinator, and submitted to the College of Graduate Studies by June 1 of each year to qualify for the fellowship
**No. of awards offered**: Approx. 2,500
**Closing Date**: 1 June

**Funding**: Government
**No. of awards given last year**: 460
**No. of applicants last year**: Approx. 2,500
**Additional Information**: Please check for internal departmental deadlines gradstudies.ok.ubc.ca/resources/award-opportunities/university-graduate-fellowship/

### For further information contact:

Okanagan Campus, EME2121 - 1137 Alumni Ave, Kelowna, BC V1V 1V7, Canada.

**Tel**:    (1) 250 807 8772
**Fax**:    (1) 250 807 8799
**Email**:    graduateawards.ok@ubc.ca

## University of California at Los Angeles (UCLA) Center for India and South Asia

Department of History, 11387 Bunche Hall, Los Angeles, CA 90095-1487, United States of America.

**Tel**:    (1) 310 206 2654
**Email**:    subrahma@history.ucla.edu
**Website**:    www.international.ucla.edu
**Contact**:    Professor Sanjay Subrahmanyam, Chair of Indian History

The main thrust behind the creation of the UCLA Center for India and South Asia is to raise the profile of South Asia on campus and more generally in southern California. The organization aims at transforming UCLA into one of the leading poles of integrated research activity on India and South Asia in the country.

## University of California, Los Angeles (UCLA) Sardar Patel Award

**Purpose**: To award the best dissertation submitted at any American university on the subject of modern India
**Eligibility**: Open to candidates who have written their dissertations while being enrolled at any accredited university in the United States
**Level of Study**: Research
**Type**: Award
**Value**: US$10,000
**Frequency**: Annual
**Application Procedure**: Applicants must submit 2 hard copies of their dissertation, 7 copies of abstract, a copy of their curriculum vitae and a letter from the dissertation supervisor

**Closing Date**: 15 October

### For further information contact:

**Email**    cisa@international.ucla.edu

## University of California Berkeley - Haas School

S440 Student Services Building, Suite 1902, Berkeley, CA 94720-1902, United States of America.

**Tel**:    (1) 510 642 1405
**Website**:    www.haas.berkeley.edu
**Contact**:    MBA Admissions Officer

## Hellman Fellows Fund

**Purpose**: The purpose of the Hellman Fellows Fund is to support substantially the research of promising assistant professors who show capacity for great distinction in their research
**Eligibility**: In determining the allocation of awards, the Chancellor will seek the counsel of a panel of faculty comprised of tenured Hellman Fellows and a member of the Academic Senate Committee on Research, chaired by the Vice Provost for the Faculty. Applications should therefore include an introductory description which is accessible to someone who is not an expert in the given field
**Level of Study**: Postgraduate
**Type**: Funding support
**Value**: Maximum value of up to US$60,000
**Frequency**: Annual
**Country of Study**: Any country
**Application Procedure**: 1. Applications should be brief, no more than 3 pages, and written with the understanding that they will be reviewed by a panel of faculty from the sciences and humanities that may not include specialists in the field of study. 2. Applications should therefore include an introductory description which is accessible to someone who is not an expert in the given field
**Closing Date**: May
**Funding**: Private

### For further information contact:

Vice Provost for the Faculty, 200 California Hall, MC 1500 Berkeley, CA 94720-1500, United States of America.

**Tel**:    (1) 510 642 6474
**Email**:    yasyavg@berkeley.edu

## Western Center for Agricultural Health and Safety

**Purpose** The overarching goal of the WCAHS Small Grant Program is to encourage the development of creative research projects while nurturing researchers – particularly early-career researchers – interested in improving agricultural health and safety for the Western United States

**Eligibility**: 1. Faculty with PI eligibility in the Western region (AZ, CA, HI, NV). 2. PhD students or postdoctoral scholars in the Western region. 3. Applicants from AZ, HI, and NV are encouraged to apply

**Level of Study**: postdoctoral

**Type**: Grant

**Value**: Graduate students and postdoctoral scholars may request up to US$10,000. Faculty may request up to US$30,000

**Frequency**: Annual

**Country of Study**: Any country

**Application Procedure**: For further information, check the website aghealth.ucdavis.edu/

**Closing Date**: 27 July

**Funding** Private

**Additional Information**: aghealth.ucdavis.edu/small-grant-program aghealth.ucdavis.edu/funding/small-grant-program

### For further information contact:

**Email**:   aghealth@ucdavis.edu

## University of California, Berkeley

Graduate Services, Graduate Fellowships Office, 318 Sproul Hall #5900, Berkeley, CA 94720-5900, United States of America.

**Tel**:   (1) 510 642 6000
**Email**:   gradappt@berkeley.edu
**Website**:   www.berkeley.edu

Founded in the wake of the gold rush by the leaders of the newly established 31st state, the University of California's flagship campus at Berkeley has become one of the preeminent universities in the world. Its early guiding lights, charged with providing education (both 'practical' and 'classical') for the state's people, gradually established a distinguished faculty (with 20 Nobel laureates to date), a stellar research library, and more than 350 academic programs.

## Conference Travel Grants

**Purpose**:   To allow students to attend professional conferences

**Eligibility**: Applicants must be registered graduate students in good academic standing. They must be in the final stages of their graduate work and planning to present a paper on their dissertation research at the conference they are attending

**Level of Study**: Doctorate, Graduate

**Type**: Grant

**Value**: Amount of the grant depends upon the location of conference (i.e. up to US$400 within California; US$600 elsewhere in North America, including Mexico or Canada; and US$1,000 outside North America)

**Frequency**: Dependent on funds available

**Study Establishment**: University of California, Berkeley

**Country of Study**: United States of America

**Application Procedure**: Applicants must submit an application form and one letter of support from their graduate advisor attesting to the academic merit of the trip. Applications can be obtained from the website

### For further information contact:

**Email**:   aips@pakistanstudies-aips.org

## University of California, Los Angeles (UCLA) Center for 17th and 18th Century Studies and the William Andrews Clark Memorial Library

10745 Dickson Plaza, 310 Royce Hall, Los Angeles, CA 90095-1404, United States of America.

**Tel**:   (1) 310 206 8552
**Email**:   c1718cs@humnet.ucla.edu
**Website**:   www.c1718cs.ucla.edu/
**Contact**:   Fellowship Co-ordinator

University of California, Los Angeles (UCLA) Center for 17th and 18th century Studies provides a forum for the discussion of central issues in the field of early modern studies, facilitates research and publication, supports scholarship and encourages the creation of interdisciplinary, cross-cultural programmes that advance the understanding of this important period. The William Andrews Clark Memorial Library, administered by the Center, is known for its collections of rare books and manuscripts concerning 17th and 18th-century Britain and Europe,

Oscar Wilde and the 1890s, the history of printing, and certain aspects of the American West.

## Clark-Huntington Joint Bibliographical Fellowship

**Purpose**: To support bibliographical research
**Level of Study**: Postdoctorate, Professional development
**Type**: Fellowship
**Value**: US$5,000
**Length of Study**: 2 months
**Frequency**: Annual
**Study Establishment**: The Clark Library and the Huntington Library
**Country of Study**: United States of America
**Application Procedure**: Applicants must submit an application form, a curriculum vitae, a proposal statement, a bibliography and three letters of reference
**No. of awards offered**: 15
**Closing Date**: 1 February
**Funding**: Private
**No. of awards given last year**: 1
**No. of applicants last year**: 15

### For further information contact:

**Email**:    ortiz@humnet.ucla.edu

## University of California, Los Angeles (UCLA) Institute of American Cultures (IAC)

1237 Murphy Hall, Box 951419, Los Angeles, CA 90095-1419, United States of America.

**Tel**:    (1) 310 206 2557
**Email**:    iaccoordinator@gdnet.ucla.edu
**Website**:    www.gdnet.ucla.edu/iacweb/iachome.htm
**Contact**:    Dr N Cherie Francis, Co-ordinator

The UCLA Institute of American Cultures (IAC) is committed to advancing knowledge, strengthening and integrating interdisciplinary research and enriching instruction on African Americans, American Indians, Asian Americans and Chicanos. Since 1969, the IAC has been responsible for developing and expanding graduate studies, research and training in ethnic studies and is a major contributor to the academic and intellectual life of the University.

## University of California at Los Angeles Institute of American Culture (IAC) Postdoctoral/Visiting Scholar Fellowships

**Purpose**: To enable PhD scholars wishing to work in association with the American Indian Studies Center, the BUNCHE Center for African American Studies, the Asian American Studies Center and the Chicano Studies Research Center, to conduct research and publish books or manuscripts relating to ethnic studies and interdisciplinary instruction
**Eligibility**: Open to citizens of the United States of America and permanent residents
**Level of Study**: Postdoctorate
**Type**: Fellowship
**Value**: US$29,000; US$34,000 stipend plus health benefits and up to US$4,000 in research support
**Length of Study**: Up to 1 year
**Frequency**: Annual
**Country of Study**: United States of America
**Application Procedure**: Applicants must complete an application form, available from one of the ethnic studies centres, the IAC, or from the website
**Closing Date**: 31 December
**No. of awards given last year**: 4
**Additional Information**: Further information is available on request or from the in dashbord

### For further information contact:

**Tel**:    (1) 310 825 7315
**Fax**:    (1) 310 206 7060
**Email**:    aisc@ucla.edu

## University of Cambridge

The Old Schools, Trinity Lane, Cambridge CB2 1TN, United Kingdom.

**Tel**:    (44) 12 2333 7733
**Email**:    dmh14@cam.ac.uk
**Website**:    www.admin.cam.ac.uk
**Contact**:    Hugo Hocknell, Student Registry

The University of Cambridge is a loose confederation of faculties, colleges and other bodies. The colleges are mainly concerned with the teaching of their undergraduate students through tutorials and supervisions and the academic support of both graduate and undergraduate students, while the

University employs professors, readers, lecturers and other teaching and administrative staff who provide the formal teaching in lectures, seminars and practical classes. The University also administers the University Library.

## Arthington-Davy Grants for Tongan Students for Postgraduate Study

**Eligibility**: 1. Hold a first University degree, 2. Have applied for admission, or already received an offer of admission, for a post-graduate study course at any University in the world, and 3. Be of Tongan origin

**Level of Study**: Postgraduate

**Type**: Grant

**Value**: Graduate Course Fees, and maintenance allowance, less any financial support received from elsewhere

**Length of Study**: For minimum further period required to complete PhD

**Frequency**: Annual

**Country of Study**: Any country

**Application Procedure**: A completed application form should be sent together with the following: Proof of Tongan origin academic transcripts details of the intended postgraduate study, preferably with a letter of conditional acceptance from the University concerned 1. Clear and precise details of tuition fees, living expenses and finances available from the student's own resources and/or from other institutions. 2. Names and email addresses of two academic referees. 3. CV

**Closing Date**: 31 May

**Funding**: Private

**Additional Information**: For full details on how to apply please visit: www.trin.cam.ac.uk/postgraduate/graduate-funding-awards/ www.scholarshipeye.com/2018/01/06/arthington-davy-grants-for-tongan-students-for-postgraduate-study/

### For further information contact:

**Email**:  grad.tutor@trin.cam.ac.uk

## Dorothy Hodgkin Postgraduate Award

**Eligibility**: Applicants must have already applied for and been accepted for a PhD place at the University of Cambridge, must be a national of one of the eligible countries (Russia plus all countries on the DAC List of ODA Recipients), must be intending to start their PhD that coming October and must hold a high-grade qualification, at least the equivalent of a United Kingdom First Class (Honours) Degree, from a prestigious academic institution

**Type**: Award

**Value**: Approx. £12,300 per year (university composition plus college fees and maintenance stipend)

**Length of Study**: 3 years

**Frequency**: Annual

**Application Procedure**: There is no separate application form for this competition

**Closing Date**: 15 December

**Contributor**: The United Kingdom Research Councils and Industrial Partners

**Additional Information**: Each DHPA is jointly sponsored by both a Research Council partner and a private sector company partner. Further details can be found on the Research Councils United Kingdom website www.european-funding-guide.eu/awardprize/11552-dorothy-hodgkin-postgraduate-awards-dhpa

### For further information contact:

**Email**:  kfw20@admin.cam.ac.uk

## Evans Fund

**Purpose**: To support research

**Eligibility**: Open to graduates of any university who intend to engage in research in a suitable field

**Level of Study**: Doctorate, Postdoctorate, Postgraduate

**Type**: Fellowship

**Value**: Up to £6,000 per year

**Length of Study**: 1 or 2 years in the first instance, up to a maximum of 3 years

**Frequency**: Annual

**Study Establishment**: The University of Cambridge

**Country of Study**: Any country

**Application Procedure**: Applicants must obtain an application form from the Secretary, which must be returned together with an outline of the applicant's proposed scheme of travel and research, a curriculum vitae and the names and addresses of two referees

**No. of awards offered**: 8

**Closing Date**: 7 March

**Funding**: Private

**Contributor**: Legacy

**No. of awards given last year**: 5

**No. of applicants last year**: 8

**Additional Information**: It is expected that the successful candidate will either be based in Cambridge, or will spend a substantial period of time in Cambridge during or after their period of research www.socanth.cam.ac.uk/about-us/funding/research-funding/evans-fund

## For further information contact:

Department of Social Anthropology, University of Cambridge, 2 Free School Lane, Cambridge CB2 3QA, United Kingdom.

**Tel**:       (44) 12 2333 4599
**Fax**:       (44) 12 2333 5993
**Email**:   ms127@hermes.cam.ac.uk

## Fitzwilliam College Charlton Studentships

**Purpose**: Part-cost award for masters students
**Eligibility**: Fitzwilliam must be the applicant's first choice on university application form, and must have received a conditional offer from the university by the closing date for receipt of applications
**Level of Study**: Graduate
**Type**: Scholarship
**Value**: £3,000 to £10,000
**Length of Study**: 1 year
**Frequency**: Annual
**Study Establishment**: Fitzwilliam College
**Country of Study**: United Kingdom
**Application Procedure**: Apply online at www.fitz.cam.ac.uk/academic/scholarships-prizes/graduate-scholarships
**No. of awards offered**: 45
**Closing Date**: 31 March
**Funding**: Individuals
**Contributor**: Fitzwilliam College
**No. of awards given last year**: 2
**No. of applicants last year**: 45
**Additional Information**: Does not include PhD, MBA, MFin or PGCE.

## For further information contact:

Graduate officer, Fitzwilliam College, Cambridge CB3 0DG, United Kingdom.

**Email**:   graduate.officer@fitz.cam.ac.uk

## Fitzwilliam College Graduate Scholarship

**Eligibility**: Open to candidates who have applied for admission to Cambridge University through the Board of Admission of Graduate Studies and subsequently satisfied the conditions of admission. Preference is given to those studying arts subjects
**Level of Study**: Postgraduate
**Type**: Fellowship
**Value**: £1,250

**Length of Study**: A maximum of 3 years. Candidates must reapply annually
**Frequency**: Annual
**Study Establishment**: Fitzwilliam College, University of Cambridge
**Country of Study**: United Kingdom
**Application Procedure**: Applicants must write for details
**No. of awards offered**: 15
**Closing Date**: 31 August
**Funding**: Private
**No. of awards given last year**: 1
**No. of applicants last year**: 15
**Additional Information**: Preference is given to candidates conducting research in an arts subject www.student-funding.cam.ac.uk/fitzwilliam-college-graduate-scholarship-202021

## For further information contact:

**Tel**:       (44) 12 2333 2035
**Fax**:       (44) 12 2333 2082
**Email**:   grad.scholarships@fitz.cam.ac.uk

## Fitzwilliam College Hirst-Player Studentship

**Purpose**: To support students who need assistance with payment of fees and who would otherwise be unable to read for a degree in Cambridge
**Eligibility**: Open to graduates of any university. The awards are only available to candidates who have applied for admission to the University through the Board of Graduate Studies and subsequently satisfied the conditions of admission made by the Board. Preference is given to those intending to take holy orders in a Christian church
**Level of Study**: Postgraduate
**Type**: Studentship
**Value**: £2,000 per year. The award is designed to supplement other funds
**Length of Study**: 1 year
**Frequency**: Annual
**Study Establishment**: Fitzwilliam College, University of Cambridge
**Country of Study**: United Kingdom
**Application Procedure**: Applicants must complete the application form, available on request. Candidates should also place Fitzwilliam College as first preference on the form
**Closing Date**: 1 October
**Funding**: Private
**No. of awards given last year**: 1
**Additional Information**: www.student-funding.cam.ac.uk/fitzwilliam-college-hirst-player-studentship-201920

## For further information contact:

**Email**:   grad.scholarships@fitz.cam.ac.uk

## Fitzwilliam College J R W Alexander Studentship in Law

**Eligibility**: Open to graduates from a British university who will have graduated by the time they come into residence
**Level of Study**: Postgraduate
**Type**: Studentship
**Value**: £350. The award is designed to supplement funding from other sources
**Length of Study**: 1 year
**Frequency**: Annual
**Study Establishment**: Fitzwilliam College, University of Cambridge
**Country of Study**: United Kingdom
**Application Procedure**: Applicants must have applied for admission to the University through the Board of Graduate Studies and subsequently satisfied the conditions of admission made by the Board. Candidates should also place Fitzwilliam College as their first preference on their application
**No. of awards offered**: 2
**Closing Date**: 25 September
**Funding**: Private
**No. of awards given last year**: 1
**No. of applicants last year**: 2
**Additional Information**: www.student-funding.cam.ac.uk/fitzwilliam-college-j-r-w-alexander-law-book-grants-201920

### For further information contact:

**Email**: graduate.office@fitz.cam.ac.uk

## Fitzwilliam College Leathersellers

**Purpose**: To support students who wish to undertake research
**Eligibility**: Open to home graduates from any United Kingdom university who have been admitted to a course of research in one of the appropriate faculties
**Level of Study**: Postgraduate
**Type**: Scholarship
**Value**: £3,500
**Length of Study**: 3 years, subject to an annual review
**Frequency**: Annual
**Study Establishment**: Fitzwilliam College, University of Cambridge
**Country of Study**: United Kingdom
**Application Procedure**: Please apply using the application form on the College website - www.fitz.cam.ac.uk/academic/scholarships-prizes/graduate-scholar
**No. of awards offered**: 6
**Closing Date**: 13 May
**Funding**: Commercial
**No. of awards given last year**: 1

**No. of applicants last year**: 6
**Additional Information**: www.student-funding.cam.ac.uk/fitzwilliam-college-leathersellers-graduate-scholarship-202021

### For further information contact:

**Tel**: (44) 1223 332035
**Email**: graduate.office@fitz.cam.ac.uk

## Fitzwilliam College Research Fellowship

**Purpose**: To enable scholars to carry out a programme of new research
**Eligibility**: Open to candidates who are carrying out research for a PhD at any United Kingdom or Irish university, or who have recently (normally defined as less than 1 year before the date of application) completed their course of study for this degree
**Level of Study**: Doctorate
**Type**: Fellowship
**Value**: Varies. Non-stipendiary funding is also offered (candidates are expected to apply for the appropriate grants for the support of their research on their own initiative)
**Frequency**: Annual
**Study Establishment**: Fitzwilliam College, University of Cambridge
**Country of Study**: United Kingdom
**Application Procedure**: Applicants must write for details
**No. of awards offered**: 161
**Closing Date**: January
**No. of awards given last year**: 1
**No. of applicants last year**: 161
**Additional Information**: Fellowships are awarded for new research only and not to enable candidates to complete their PhD dissertation www.fitz.cam.ac.uk/sites/default/files/2019-10/Junior%20Research%20Fellowships%202020.pdf

### For further information contact:

**Email**: jmw65@cam.acuk

## Fitzwilliam College Shipley Studentship

**Purpose**: To enable graduates to undertake research
**Eligibility**: Open to graduates of any university. The awards are only available to candidates who have applied for admission to the University through the Board of Graduate Studies and subsequently satisfied the conditions of admission made by the Board. Candidates should also place Fitzwilliam College as their first preference in their application
**Level of Study**: Postgraduate
**Type**: Studentship

**Value**: £1,250 per year. The award is designed to supplement other funds
**Length of Study**: 1 year
**Frequency**: Annual
**Study Establishment**: Fitzwilliam College, University of Cambridge
**Country of Study**: United Kingdom
**Application Procedure**: Applicants must complete an application form, available on request
**No. of awards offered**: 5
**Closing Date**: 1 October
**Funding**: Private
**No. of awards given last year**: 1
**No. of applicants last year**: 5
**Additional Information**: www.student-funding.cam.ac.uk/ fitzwilliam-college-shipley-studentship-201920

**For further information contact:**

**Email**:      graduate.office@fitz.cam.ac.uk

### Fitzwilliam College: E D Davies Scholarship

**Eligibility**: Candidates should be already registered for, or applying for, a research degree course, at Fitzwilliam College
**Level of Study**: Graduate
**Type**: Scholarship
**Value**: £1,250 per year
**Length of Study**: 1–3 years, yearly re-application required
**Frequency**: Annual
**Country of Study**: United Kingdom
**Application Procedure**: Submit online application form
**No. of awards offered**: 25
**Closing Date**: 25 September
**No. of awards given last year**: 2
**No. of applicants last year**: 25
**Additional Information**: www.student-funding.cam.ac.uk/ fitzwilliam-college-e-d-davies-scholarship-201920

### Fitzwilliam College: Gibson Scholarship

**Eligibility**: Intention to work towards a doctorate in New Testament Studies required
**Level of Study**: Graduate, Postgraduate
**Type**: Scholarship
**Value**: £1,000 per year
**Length of Study**: 1–3 years
**Frequency**: Annual
**Country of Study**: United Kingdom
**Application Procedure**: Submit online application form

**No. of awards offered**: 8
**Closing Date**: 25 September
**No. of awards given last year**: 1
**No. of applicants last year**: 8

**For further information contact:**

**Email**:      graduate.office@fitz.cam.ac.uk

### Fitzwilliam College: Hirst-Player Scholarship

**Eligibility**: Students needing assistance with fees, who would otherwise be unable to study at Cambridge, eligible only. Students having intention to take Holy Orders in a Christian Church preferred. Students must be studying as a member of Fitzwilliam College during the period of the award
**Level of Study**: Postgraduate
**Type**: Scholarship
**Value**: £2,000 maximum
**Length of Study**: 1–2 years
**Frequency**: Annual
**Country of Study**: United Kingdom
**Application Procedure**: Submit online application form
**Closing Date**: 25 September
**No. of awards given last year**: 2
**Additional Information**: www.student-funding.cam.ac.uk/ fitzwilliam-college-hirst-player-studentship-201920

**For further information contact:**

**Email**:      graduate.office@fitz.cam.ac.uk

### Fitzwilliam College: Leathersellers

**Eligibility**: Only home graduates from a British University are eligible. Physical or biological sciences or mathematics students also eligible. Studying as a member of Fitzwilliam College during the period of the award
**Level of Study**: Doctorate
**Type**: Scholarship
**Value**: £3,000 per year
**Length of Study**: 1–3 years, subject to the approval of the Tutorial Committee
**Frequency**: Annual
**Country of Study**: United Kingdom
**Application Procedure**: Application form available from college graduate admissions office gradadmissions@fitz. cam.ac.uk
**No. of awards offered**: 8
**Closing Date**: 13 June

**No. of awards given last year**: 1
**No. of applicants last year**: 8
**Additional Information**: www.student-funding.cam.ac.uk/fitzwilliam-college-leathersellers-graduate-scholarship-201920

## Fitzwilliam College: Shipley Scholarship

**Eligibility**: Applicant must be studying as a member of Fitzwilliam during the period of the award
**Level of Study**: Postgraduate
**Type**: Scholarship
**Value**: £1,460
**Length of Study**: 1 year
**Frequency**: Annual
**Country of Study**: United Kingdom
**Application Procedure**: Submit online application form
**No. of awards offered**: 1
**Closing Date**: 31 August
**No. of awards given last year**: 1
**Additional Information**: www.student-funding.cam.ac.uk/fitzwilliam-college-shipley-studentship-202021

### For further information contact:

**Tel**:       (44) 1223 332035
**Email**:   graduate.office@fitz.cam.ac.uk

## Fitzwilliam Society JRW Alexander Law Book Grants

**Eligibility**: All Fitzwilliam students on the LLM degree course are eligible
**Level of Study**: Postgraduate
**Type**: Grant
**Value**: £100
**Length of Study**: 1 year
**Frequency**: Annual
**Country of Study**: United Kingdom
**Application Procedure**: No application is necessary
**No. of awards offered**: 3
**Closing Date**: 30 September
**No. of awards given last year**: 3
**No. of applicants last year**: 3
**Additional Information**: www.student-funding.cam.ac.uk/fitzwilliam-college-j-r-w-alexander-law-book-grants-202021

### For further information contact:

**Tel**:       (44) 1223 332035
**Email**:   graduate.office@fitz.cam.ac.uk

## Fitzwilliam Studentship: Peter Wilson Estates Gazette Scholarships

**Purpose**: It was established to encourage expertise in Land Economy that will be put to good use in the wider world in the future
**Eligibility**: Applying to a course 1. Must have a conditional offer from the University for a place on the course by 31 March 2. Must have Fitzwilliam College membership agreed for this course by 31 March 3. To achieve both of the above it is recommended that the University application is submitted by the funding deadlines for the course
**Level of Study**: Postgraduate Master of Philosophy
**Type**: Scholarship
**Value**: £4,000 Fees and living costs
**Length of Study**: 1 year
**Frequency**: Annual
**Country of Study**: All Countries
**Application Procedure**: Apply using separate College application form, available on Fitzwilliam College website. www.fitz.cam.ac.uk/academic/scholarships-prizes/graduate-scholar
**Funding**: Fitzwilliam College
**Additional Information**: www.student-funding.cam.ac.uk/fitzwilliam-college-peter-wilson-estates-gazette-scholarship-202021

### For further information contact:

**Tel**:       (44) 1223 332035
**Email**:   grad.scholarships@fitz.cam.ac.uk

## Girton College Graduate Research Scholarship

**Eligibility**: A first-class degree is almost always required and election will be conditional on the candidate being granted Graduate Student status by the University of Cambridge. The holder must become a member of the college and either be a candidate for a masters or a PhD degree
**Level of Study**: Doctorate, Postgraduate, MBA
**Type**: Scholarship
**Value**: The value of the award for this year is likely to be approximately £27,000
**Frequency**: Annual
**Study Establishment**: University of Cambridge
**Country of Study**: United Kingdom
**Application Procedure**: Application should be made online via www.girton.cam.ac.uk/graduates/research-awards
**No. of awards offered**: 200
**Closing Date**: 27 March
**No. of awards given last year**: 3
**No. of applicants last year**: 200

**Additional Information**: www.girton.cam.ac.uk/prospective-students/graduate/graduate-research-awards/

**For further information contact:**

**Email**:    graduate.office@girton.cam.ac.uk

## Girton College Overseas Bursaries

**Eligibility**: A first-class degree is almost always required and election will be conditional on the candidate being granted Graduate Student status by the University of Cambridge. The holder must become a member of the college
**Level of Study**: Doctorate, Graduate, Postgraduate, MBA
**Type**: Bursary
**Value**: £200–£1,000 per year
**Frequency**: Dependent on funds available
**Study Establishment**: University of Cambridge
**Country of Study**: United Kingdom
**Application Procedure**: Application forms can be downloaded from www.girton.cam.ac.uk/graduates/research-awards or may be obtained from the Graduate Secretary, Girton College, Cambridge, CB3 0JG, United Kingdom (email: graduate.office@girton.cam.ac.uk)
**Closing Date**: 28 March

**For further information contact:**

**Email**:    graduate.office@girton.cam.ac.uk

## Girton College: Doris Woodall Studentship

**Eligibility**: A first-class degree is almost always required and election will be conditional on the candidate being granted Graduate Student status by the University of Cambridge. The holder must become a member of the college
**Level of Study**: Doctorate, Postgraduate, MBA
**Type**: Studentship
**Value**: £6,400
**Length of Study**: 1 year
**Frequency**: Annual
**Study Establishment**: University of Cambridge
**Country of Study**: United Kingdom
**Application Procedure**: Application should be made online via www.girton.cam.ac.uk/graduates/research-awards
**No. of awards offered**: 1
**Closing Date**: 27 March
**Additional Information**: www.student-funding.cam.ac.uk/doris-woodall-studentship-201920-202021

**For further information contact:**

**Email**:    graduate.office@girton.cam.ac.uk

## Girton College: Ida and Isidore Cohen Research Scholarship

**Eligibility**: Open to students working in modern Hebrew studies. A first-class degree is almost always required and election will be conditional on the candidate being granted Graduate Student status by the University of Cambridge. The holder must become a member of the college
**Level of Study**: Doctorate, Graduate, Postgraduate
**Type**: Scholarship
**Value**: Between £3,000 and £5,000
**Frequency**: Annual
**Study Establishment**: University of Cambridge
**Country of Study**: United Kingdom
**Application Procedure**: Application forms can be downloaded from external link or may be obtained from the Graduate Secretary, Girton College, Cambridge, CB3 0JG, United Kingdom
**Closing Date**: 28 March

**For further information contact:**

**Email**:    graduate.office@girton.cam.ac.uk

## Girton College: Irene Hallinan Scholarship

**Eligibility**: A first-class degree is almost always required and election will be conditional on the candidate being granted Graduate Student status by the University of Cambridge. The holder must become a member of the college and either be a candidate for a masters or a PhD degree
**Level of Study**: Doctorate, Postgraduate, MBA
**Type**: Scholarship
**Value**: £4,900
**Length of Study**: 1 year
**Frequency**: Annual
**Study Establishment**: University of Cambridge
**Country of Study**: United Kingdom
**Application Procedure**: Application should be made online via www.girton.cam.ac.uk/graduates/research-awards
**No. of awards offered**: 200
**Closing Date**: 27 March
**No. of awards given last year**: 3
**No. of applicants last year**: 200
**Additional Information**: www.student-funding.cam.ac.uk/irene-hallinan-scholarship-202021

## For further information contact:

**Email**: graduate.office@girton.cam.ac.uk

## Girton College: Maria Luisa de Sanchez Scholarship

**Eligibility**: Applicants must be of Venezuelan nationality. A first-class degree is almost always required and election will be conditional on the candidate being granted Graduate Student status by the University of Cambridge. The holder must become a member of the college

**Level of Study**: Doctorate, Graduate, Postgraduate, MBA

**Type**: Scholarship

**Value**: University and college fees, and some proportion of maintenance costs

**Frequency**: Annual

**Study Establishment**: University of Cambridge

**Country of Study**: United Kingdom

**Application Procedure**: Application forms can be downloaded from www.girton.cam.ac.uk/graduate/research-awards or may be obtained from the Graduate Secretary, Girton College, Cambridge, CB3 0JG, United Kingdom (email: graduate.office@girton.cam.ac.uk)

**Closing Date**: 28 March

**No. of awards given last year**: 1

**Additional Information**: Eligible to nationals of Venezuela www.student-funding.cam.ac.uk/maria-luisa-de-sanchez-sch olarship-201920

## For further information contact:

**Email**: graduate.office@girton.cam.ac.uk

## Girton College: Ruth Whaley Scholarship

**Eligibility**: Open to outstanding students of non-European Union citizenship seeking admission to Girton. It is open to students following arts subjects. A first-class degree is almost always required and election will be conditional on the candidate being granted Graduate Student status by the University of Cambridge. The holder must become a member of the college

**Level of Study**: Doctorate, Postgraduate

**Type**: Scholarship

**Value**: £3,400

**Frequency**: Annual

**Study Establishment**: University of Cambridge

**Country of Study**: United Kingdom

**Application Procedure**: Application forms can be downloaded from www.girton.cam.ac.uk/graduates/research-awards or may be obtained from the Graduate Secretary

**Closing Date**: 27 March

**No. of awards given last year**: 1

**Additional Information**: For further details, please refer to the website www.girton.cam.ac.uk/students/graduate-scholarships/ www.student-funding.cam.ac.uk/ruth-whaley-scholarship-202021

## For further information contact:

Girton College, Huntingdon Rd, Girton, Cambridge CB3 0JG, United Kingdom.

**Email**: graduate.office@girton.cam.ac.uk

## Girton College: Sidney and Marguerite Cody Studentship

**Purpose**: Period of travel and study in continental Europe of up to 12 months and normally of not less than 6 months

**Eligibility**: Open to graduate members of any faculty except English who have completed less than nine terms in residence. A first-class degree is almost always required and election will be conditional on the candidate being granted Graduate Student status by the University of Cambridge. The holder must become a member of the college

**Level of Study**: Doctorate, Graduate, Postgraduate

**Type**: Studentship

**Value**: Up to £3,000

**Frequency**: Annual

**Study Establishment**: University of Cambridge

**Country of Study**: United Kingdom

**Application Procedure**: Application should be made online via www.girton.cam.ac.uk/graduates/research-awards

**Closing Date**: 28 March

**No. of awards given last year**: 1

**Additional Information**: www.student-funding.cam.ac.uk/sidney-and-marguerite-cody-studentship

## For further information contact:

**Email**: graduate.office@girton.cam.ac.uk

## Girton College: Stribling Award

**Eligibility**: Open to Girton students who are already members of the College, namely undergraduates coming into graduate status or current MPhil students who are going on to a PhD A first-class degree is almost always required and election will be conditional on the candidate being granted Graduate Student status by the University of Cambridge

**Level of Study**: Doctorate, Postgraduate

**Type**: Award

**Value**: £1,000, normally in addition to a studentship or any other funding for fees and maintenance
**Length of Study**: 1 year
**Frequency**: Annual
**Study Establishment**: University of Cambridge
**Country of Study**: United Kingdom
**Application Procedure**: Application should be made online via www.girton.cam.ac.uk/graduates/research-awards
**No. of awards offered**: 2
**Closing Date**: 28 March
**No. of awards given last year**: 2
**Additional Information**: Award only available to Girton College Students www.student-funding.cam.ac.uk/stribling-award-202021

### For further information contact:

**Email**:     graduate.office@girton.cam.ac.uk

## Girton College: Travel Grant

**Level of Study**: Postgraduate
**Type**: Grant
**Value**: Contribution to academic travel and
**Frequency**: Every 2 years
**Country of Study**: Any country
**Application Procedure**: Application should be made online via www.girton.cam.ac.uk/graduates/research-awards
**Closing Date**: 24 April
**Additional Information**: Please note this is a strict dead-line, no allowance can be made for late applications or reference letters        www.girton.cam.ac.uk/girton-community/travel-awards/

### For further information contact:

**Email**:     ns714@cam.ac.uk

## Gonville and Caius College Gonville Bursary

**Purpose**: To help outstanding students from outside the European Union to meet the costs of degree courses at the University of Cambridge
**Eligibility**: Open to candidates who have been accepted by the College through its normal admissions procedures, and who are classified as overseas students for fees purposes. A statement of financial circumstances is required
**Level of Study**: Doctorate, Postgraduate
**Type**: Bursary
**Value**: Reimbursement of college fees
**Length of Study**: Up to 3 years, with a possibility of renewal, dependent on satisfactory progress

**Frequency**: Annual
**Study Establishment**: Gonville and Caius College, the University of Cambridge
**Country of Study**: United Kingdom
**Application Procedure**: Applicants must contact the Admissions Tutor for further information. There are no application forms

### For further information contact:

Gonville and Caius College, Trinity Street, Cambridge CB2 1TA, United Kingdom.

**Tel**:        (44) 12 2333 2447
**Fax**:        (44) 12 2333 2456
**Email**:     admissions@cai.cam.ac.uk

## Gonville and Caius College Michael Miliffe Scholarship

**Subjects**: All Subjects
**Eligibility**: Applicants must apply to the University of Cambridge in the regular way and must have a first class/high second class (Honours) degree or equivalent. Must be under 26 years.
**Level of Study**: Post Graduate
**Type**: Scholarship
**Value**: £5,000 is awarded
**Length of Study**: 2 years
**Frequency**: Annual
**Country of Study**: United Kingdom
**Funding**: University of Cambridge
**Additional Information**: www.cai.cam.ac.uk/undergraduate/overseas

### For further information contact:

**Email**:     admissions@cai.cam.ac.uk

## Gonville and Caius College W M Tapp Studentship in Law

**Purpose**: To encourage the study of law
**Eligibility**: Open to candidates who are not already members of the College, but who propose to register as graduate students at the University of Cambridge. Candidates must be under 30 years of age as of October 1st of the studentship year and be graduates or expect to be graduates no later than August of the same year. Preference is given to applicants nominating Gonville and Caius College as their first choice when applying under the Cambridge Intercollegiate Graduate Application Scheme

**Level of Study**: Doctorate, Postgraduate
**Type**: Studentship
**Value**: A stipend similar to that of a state studentship for research, plus fees and certain allowances, a dependent allowance, an allowance for a period of approved postgraduate experience, a travelling contribution for foreign students and a research allowance for research students
**Length of Study**: 1 year, renewable for up to a maximum of 3 years
**Frequency**: Annual
**Study Establishment**: Gonville and Caius College, University of Cambridge
**Country of Study**: United Kingdom
**Application Procedure**: Applicants must complete an application form, available from the Admissions Tutor
**Closing Date**: 15 January
**Additional Information**: www.student-funding.cam.ac.uk/w-m-tapp-studentships-law-college-studentship-llm-students-202021

## Kings College: Stipendiary Junior Research Fellowships

**Purpose**: To support gifted young researchers
**Level of Study**: Postdoctorate, Research
**Type**: Fellowship
**Value**: Permit complete freedom to carry out research within the academic environment of the college
**Length of Study**: 4 years
**Frequency**: Annual
**Study Establishment**: University of Cambridge, King's College
**Country of Study**: United Kingdom
**Closing Date**: October

### For further information contact:

King's College, King's Parade, Cambridge CB2 1ST, United Kingdom.

**Tel**: (44) 1223 331 100
**Email**: info@kings.cam.ac.uk

## Lucy Cavendish College: Becker Law Scholarships

**Eligibility**: Open to women accepted to read for the LLM and MCL by the law Faculty at the University of Cambridge
**Level of Study**: Postgraduate
**Type**: Scholarship
**Value**: At least £1,000 per year

**Length of Study**: Up to 3 years, conditional on satisfactory academic progress
**Frequency**: Annual
**Study Establishment**: Lucy Cavendish College, University of Cambridge
**Country of Study**: United Kingdom
**Application Procedure**: Please contact to the Secretary of the Studentship and Bursary Committee
**Closing Date**: 30 June
**Additional Information**: llm-guide.com/scholarships/becker-law-scholarships-257

### For further information contact:

Lucy Cavendish College, Lady Margaret Rd, Cambridge, CB3 0BU, United Kingdom.

**Tel**: (44) 1223 332 190
**Fax**: (44) 1223 332 178
**Email**: st420@cam.ac.uk

## Lucy Cavendish College: Dorothy and Joseph Needham Studentship

**Purpose**: For studies in Natural Sciences
**Eligibility**: Check website or contact organisation for updates
**Level of Study**: Postgraduate
**Type**: Studentship
**Value**: £1,000 per year
**Length of Study**: Up to 3 years, conditional on satisfactory academic progress
**Frequency**: Annual
**Study Establishment**: Lucy Cavendish College, University of Cambridge
**Country of Study**: United Kingdom
**Application Procedure**: Please contact to the Secretary of the Studentship and Bursary Committee
**Closing Date**: 30 June
**Additional Information**: studyabroad.shiksha.com/scholarships/dorothy-and-joseph-needham-scholarship

## Lucy Cavendish College: Enterprise Studentship

**Eligibility**: Open to women accepted on the MBA course and on the MPhil in Bioscience Enterprise. One is open to any student the other is only available to nationals of United States of America and Canada
**Level of Study**: Postgraduate, MBA
**Type**: Studentship
**Value**: £1,000 per year
**Frequency**: Annual

**Study Establishment**: Lucy Cavendish College, University of Cambridge
**Country of Study**: United Kingdom
**Application Procedure**: Please contact to the Secretary of the Studentship and Bursary Committee
**Closing Date**: 30 June

## Lucy Cavendish College: Evelyn Povey Studentship

**Subjects**: French Studies
**Purpose**: The Evelyn Povey Studentship for French Citizens and the Evelyn Povey Studentship in French Studies
**Eligibility**: The Evelyn Povey Studentship for French Citizens
**Type**: Studentship
**Value**: value of around £4,500
**Frequency**: Annual
**Closing Date**: 28 February
**Funding**: Lucy Cavendish College
**Contributor**: Lucy Cavendish College
**Additional Information**: www.lucy.cam.ac.uk/study-us/post graduates/studentships-and-awards

### For further information contact:

**Tel**:      (44) 1223 322190
**Email**:    development@lucy.cam.ac.uk

## Lucy Cavendish College: Isaac Newton – Dorothy Emmet Research Fellowships Positions in Arts and Humanities

**Purpose**: To assist research in the arts and humanities, with a preference for law and English
**Eligibility**: Open to women who hold PhDs for research in the arts and humanities, with a preference for law and English
**Level of Study**: Postdoctorate
**Type**: Fellowships
**Value**: Stipend for each of these Research Fellowships will be £17,111 per year
**Length of Study**: The appointments will be for one year in the first instance from October and will be renewable annually
**Frequency**: Annual
**Application Procedure**: Please contact to the Secretary of the Studentship and Bursary Committee
**Closing Date**: 31 May
**Additional Information**: scholarization.blogspot.com/2011/02/isaac-newton-dorothy-emmet-research.html

### For further information contact:

**Email**:    lcc-admin@lists.cam.ac.uk

## Lucy Cavendish College: Lord Frederick Cavendish Studentship

**Purpose**: The Lord Frederick Cavendish Studentship, open to any student
**Eligibility**: Applying to a course
**Level of Study**: postgraduate
**Type**: Studentship
**Value**: Value around £4,500
**Frequency**: Annual
**Country of Study**: All Countries
**Closing Date**: 28 February
**Funding**: Lucy Cavendish College
**Contributor**: Lucy Cavendish College
**Additional Information**: www.lucy.cam.ac.uk/study-us/post graduates/studentships-and-awards

### For further information contact:

**Tel**:      (44) 1223 322190
**Email**:    development@lucy.cam.ac.uk

## Lucy Cavendish College: Mastermann-Braithwaite Studentship

**Subjects**: PhD applicants in any subject, and MPhil applicants intending to embark on further research study.
**Eligibility**: Applying to a course
**Level of Study**: postgraduate
**Type**: Studentship
**Value**: Value up to £6,000
**Frequency**: Annual
**Country of Study**: All Countries
**No. of awards offered**: 2
**Closing Date**: 28 February
**Funding**: Lucy Cavendish College
**Contributor**: Lucy Cavendish College
**Additional Information**: www.lucy.cam.ac.uk/study-us/post graduates/studentships-and-awards

### For further information contact:

**Tel**:      (44) 1223 322190
**Email**:    development@lucy.cam.ac.uk

## Lucy Cavendish College: Research Fellowships

**Purpose**: To support post-doctoral research
**Eligibility**: Female, right to work in United Kingdom, holder of PhD or equivalents
**Level of Study**: Postdoctorate

**Type**: Research fellowship
**Value**: tbc
**Length of Study**: 3 years
**Frequency**: Every 3 years
**Study Establishment**: Lucy Cavendish College, University of Cambridge
**Country of Study**: As applicable
**Application Procedure**: see notices when advertised
**No. of awards offered**: 110
**Funding**: Private
**No. of awards given last year**: 1
**No. of applicants last year**: 110

**For further information contact:**

**Email**:    registrar@lucy-cav.cam.ac.uk

## Nabil Boustany Scholarships

**Purpose**: To enable a Lebanese national to attend the Cambridge MBA on a full scholarship
**Eligibility**: Open to candidates of all nations although priority given to Lebanese nationals, who have obtained a good Honours Degree from a recognized university and have at least 3 years of full-time, real-world experience. Candidates will need to demonstrate a high intellectual potential, practical common sense and the ability to put ideas into action. They also need to be highly motivated with a strong desire to learn. Applicants will be asked to take the Test of English as a Foreign Language (TOEFL) where applicable and the Graduate Management Admission Test (GMAT)
**Level of Study**: MBA
**Type**: Scholarship
**Value**: £30,000
**Length of Study**: 2 years
**Frequency**: Every 2 years
**Study Establishment**: Judge Business School, University of Cambridge
**Country of Study**: United Kingdom
**Application Procedure**: Applicants must email their curriculum vitae to admissions@boustany-foundation.org
**No. of awards offered**: 4
**Closing Date**: 15 May
**Funding**: Foundation
**Contributor**: The Nabil Boustany Foundation
**No. of awards given last year**: 1
**No. of applicants last year**: 4
**Additional Information**: The scholarship recipient is normally required to spend a summer internship, carrying no salary, within a Lebanese organization. Applicants must be accepted into the Cambridge MBA programme

**For further information contact:**

1 avenue des Citronniers, F-06800 Cagnes-sur-Mer, France.

**Fax**:      (44) 77 93 15 05 56
**Email**:    info@boustany-foundation.org

## Newnham College: Moody-Stuart Scholarships in Turkish Studies

**For further information contact:**

Newnham College, Sidgwick Avenue, Cambridge CB3 9DF, United Kingdom.

**Tel**:      (44) 1223 335 700
**Fax**:      (44) 1223 357 898
**Email**:    enquiries@newnham.cam.ac.uk

## Osborn Research Studentship

**Purpose**: To support students carrying research or taking advanced courses
**Level of Study**: Postdoctorate, Postgraduate
**Type**: Studentship
**Value**: Up to £12,000 to match with funds administered centrally by the UCAM
**Length of Study**: 1–3 years
**Frequency**: Every 3 years
**Study Establishment**: The University of Cambridge
**Country of Study**: United Kingdom
**Application Procedure**: For further details, please check website www.sid.cam.ac.uk/current/postgrads/scholarships
**Closing Date**: 1 April
**Funding**: Private
**Contributor**: Sidney Sussex College
**Additional Information**: www.sid.cam.ac.uk/current/post grads/scholarships/osborn

**For further information contact:**

**Email**:    graduate.funding@admin.cam.ac.uk

## Pembroke College: College Research Studentships

**Eligibility**: Preference in awarding these studentships will be given to candidates who intend to register for a PhD degree at Pembroke. However, candidates registering to study for an MPhil will also be considered for an award if they are intending to carry on to a PhD after they have finished their MPhil
**Level of Study**: Postgraduate

**Type**: Studentship
**Value**: College/University fees plus a maintenance allowance of £12,000 per year
**Frequency**: Annual
**Study Establishment**: Pembroke College
**Country of Study**: United Kingdom
**Application Procedure**: All applicants for any of these awards must apply in the first instance to the Board of Graduate Studies for their University place. Candidates should indicate that they are applying for a Pembroke College award. In making awards preference will be given to those who nominate Pembroke as their college of first choice. All candidates are expected to apply for Research Council funding where appropriate, and for University CHESS funding, if they are eligible. The College will take into account candidates' income from other sources when making awards
**Closing Date**: 6 January
**Additional Information**: Applicants should also complete a Pembroke Studentship form. This can be completed online, downloaded or obtained from the Graduate Secretary. The awards are conditional on the selected students being admitted as a registered Graduate Student by the Board of Graduate Studies with effect from October 1st each academic year. Early application is recommended

### For further information contact:

Pembroke College, Cambridge CB2 1RF, United Kingdom.

**Tel**:     (44) 1223 338 100
**Fax**:     (44) 1223 338 163
**Email**:   tut@pem.cam.ac.uk

## Pembroke College: Graduate Studentships in Arabic and Islamic Studies (including Persian)

**Eligibility**: Preference in awarding these studentships will be given to candidates who intend to register for a PhD degree at Pembroke. However, candidates registering to study for an MPhil will also be considered for an award if they are intending to carry on to a PhD after they have finished their MPhil
**Level of Study**: Postgraduate
**Type**: Studentship
**Value**: Covers University and College fees (at the Home/European Union rate) for three years
**Frequency**: Annual
**Study Establishment**: Pembroke College
**Country of Study**: United Kingdom
**Application Procedure**: All applicants for any of these awards must apply in the first instance to the Board of

Graduate Studies for their University place. Candidates should indicate that they are applying for a Pembroke College award. In making awards preference will be given to those who nominate Pembroke as their college of first choice. All candidates are expected to apply for Research Council funding where appropriate, and for University CHESS funding, if they are eligible. The college will take into account candidates' income from other sources when making awards
**Additional Information**: Applicants should also complete a Pembroke Studentship form. This can be completed online, downloaded or obtained from the Graduate Secretary. The awards are conditional on the selected students being admitted as a registered Graduate Student by the Board of Graduate Studies with effect from October 1st each academic year. Early application is recommended.

## Pembroke College: MPhil Studentship for Applicants from the Least Developed Countries

**Purpose**: The College is offering this one-year studentship to enable the winner to study for an MPhil degree, or equivalent, at the University of Cambridge
**Eligibility**: Eligibility is confined to nationals of the fifty 'Least Developed Countries' as defined by the United Nations. The other is for nationals of the fifty 'Least Developed Countries' as defined by the United Nations.
**Level of Study**: Postgraduate
**Type**: Studentship
**Value**: University fees at least at the standard rate for Home/European Union students, plus college fees and a maintenance of £10,465
**Frequency**: Annual
**Study Establishment**: Pembroke College, University of Cambridge
**Application Procedure**: All applicants for any of these awards must apply in the first instance to the Board of Graduate Studies for their University place. Candidates should indicate that they are applying for a Pembroke College award. In making awards preference will be given to those who nominate Pembroke as their College of first choice. All candidates are expected to apply for Research Council funding where appropriate, and for University CHESS funding, if they are eligible. The College will take into account candidates' income from other sources when making awards
**Additional Information**: Applicants should also complete a Pembroke Studentship form. This can be completed online, downloaded or obtained from the Graduate Secretary. The awards are conditional on the selected students being admitted as a registered Graduate Student by the Board of Graduate Studies with effect from October 1st each academic year. Early application is recommended

## Pembroke College: The Bethune-Baker Graduate Studentship in Theology

**Eligibility**: Open to candidates who intend to register for the PhD degree at the University of Cambridge
**Level of Study**: Postgraduate
**Type**: Studentship
**Value**: College and university fees for three years
**Frequency**: Annual
**Study Establishment**: University of Cambridge
**Country of Study**: United Kingdom
**Application Procedure**: All applicants for any of these awards must apply in the first instance to the Board of Graduate Studies for their University place. Candidates should indicate that they are applying for a Pembroke College award. In making awards preference will be given to those who nominate Pembroke as their college of first choice. All candidates are expected to apply for Research Council funding where appropriate, and for University CHESS funding, if they are eligible. The College will take into account candidates' income from other sources when making awards
**Contributor**: HM the Sultan of Oman and Professor E.G. Browne
**Additional Information**: Applicants should also complete a Pembroke Studentship form. This can be completed online, downloaded or obtained from the Graduate Secretary. The awards are conditional on the selected students being admitted as a registered Graduate Student by the Board of Graduate Studies with effect from October 1st each academic year. Early application is recommended

## Pembroke College: The Bristol-Myers Squibb Graduate Studentship in the Biomedical Sciences

**Eligibility**: Open to candidates who intend to register for a PhD degree at the University of Cambridge
**Level of Study**: Postgraduate
**Type**: Studentship
**Value**: The studentship will have a value sufficient to pay college fees for three years
**Frequency**: Annual
**Country of Study**: United Kingdom
**Application Procedure**: All applicants for any of these awards must apply in the first instance to the Board of Graduate Studies for their University place. Candidates should indicate that they are applying for a Pembroke College award. In making awards preference will be given to those who nominate Pembroke as their college of first choice. All candidates are expected to apply for Research Council funding where appropriate, and for University CHESS funding, if they are eligible. The College will take into account candidates' income from other sources when making awards

**Additional Information**: Applicants should also complete a Pembroke Studentship form. This can be completed online, downloaded or obtained from the Graduate Secretary. The awards are conditional on the selected students being admitted as a registered Graduate Student by the Board of Graduate Studies with effect from October 1st each academic year. Early application is recommended

## Pembroke College: The Grosvenor-Shilling Bursary in Land Economy

**Eligibility**: Applicants must normally reside in Australia and hold a qualification from an Australian tertiary institution. There is no restriction as to the academic field
**Level of Study**: Postgraduate
**Type**: Scholarship
**Value**: £500
**Frequency**: Annual
**Application Procedure**: All applicants for any of these awards must apply in the first instance to the Board of Graduate Studies for their University place. Candidates should indicate that they are applying for a Pembroke College award. In making awards preference will be given to those who nominate Pembroke as their college of first choice. All candidates are expected to apply for Research Council funding where appropriate, and for University CHESS funding, if they are eligible. The College will take into account candidates' income from other sources when making awards
**Additional Information**: Applicants should also complete a Pembroke Studentship form. This can be completed online, downloaded or obtained from the Graduate Secretary. The awards are conditional on the selected students being admitted as a registered Graduate Student by the Board of Graduate Studies with effect from October 1st each academic year. Early application is recommended

## Pembroke College: The Lander Studentship in the History of Art

**Purpose**: The College is very pleased to be able to offer one studentship for an outstanding art historian, supported by the estate of Professor J.R. Lander
**Eligibility**: Candidates must be applying to study for a PhD degree in the History of Art at the University of Cambridge, with Pembroke as first-choice college
**Level of Study**: Postgraduate
**Type**: Studentship
**Value**: The studentship will, if necessary, pay university and college fees, at the home rate, plus a maintenance allowance (approx. £10,140 a year), for a maximum of 3 years

**Frequency**: Annual
**Study Establishment**: Pembroke College, University of Cambridge
**Country of Study**: United Kingdom
**Application Procedure**: All applicants for any of these awards must apply in the first instance to the Board of Graduate Studies for their University place. Candidates should indicate that they are applying for a Pembroke College award. In making awards preference will be given to those who nominate Pembroke as their College of first choice. All candidates are expected to apply for Research Council funding where appropriate, and for University CHESS funding, if they are eligible. The College will take into account candidates' income from other sources when making awards
**Closing Date**: 10 January
**Additional Information**: Applicants should also complete a Pembroke Studentship form. This can be completed online, downloaded or obtained from the Graduate Secretary. The awards are conditional on the selected students being admitted as a registered Graduate Student by the Board of Graduate Studies with effect from October 1st each academic year. Early application is recommended

## Pembroke College: The Monica Partridge Studentship

**Purpose**: To offer a graduate studentship for a student from South-East Europe to study at Pembroke
**Eligibility**: Open to the students of the nationals of Albania, Bosnia and Herzegovina, Bulgaria, Croatia, Greece, Kosovo, Macedonia, Montenegro and Serbia. Applications from students from Romania, Slovenia and Turkey will be considered if there is no suitable candidate from the countries listed above. Preference will be given to fund students studying for a PhD, but MPhil applicants intending to continue to a PhD will also be considered
**Level of Study**: Postgraduate
**Type**: Studentship
**Value**: The studentship will have a value sufficient to cover college fees (£2,229) and maintenance (£10,140) for three years for a PhD student or, in the case of an MPhil student, one year
**Frequency**: Annual
**Study Establishment**: Pembroke College, University of Cambridge
**Country of Study**: United Kingdom
**Application Procedure**: All applicants for any of these awards must apply in the first instance to the Board of Graduate Studies for their University place. Candidates should indicate that they are applying for a Pembroke College award. In making awards preference will be given to those who nominate Pembroke as their college of first choice. All candidates are expected to apply for Research Council funding where appropriate, and for University CHESS funding, if they are eligible. The College will take into account candidates' income from other sources when making awards
**Closing Date**: 31 January
**Additional Information**: Applicants should also complete a Pembroke Studentship form. This can be completed online, downloaded or obtained from the Graduate Secretary. The awards are conditional on the selected students being admitted as a registered Graduate Student by the Board of Graduate Studies with effect from October 1st each academic year. Early application is recommended

## Pembroke College: The Nahum Graduate Studentship in Physics

**Eligibility**: Preference in awarding these studentships will be given to candidates who intend to register for a PhD degree at Pembroke. However, candidates registering to study for an MPhil will also be considered for an award if they are intending to carry on to a PhD after they have finished their MPhil
**Level of Study**: Postgraduate
**Type**: Studentship
**Value**: The studentship will have a value sufficient to pay College fees for three years. Moreover, additional awards, of up to the equivalent of University fees for a Home student (£3,465), may be made to individual applicants, depending on need and the availability of funds
**Frequency**: Annual
**Study Establishment**: Pembroke College
**Country of Study**: United Kingdom
**Application Procedure**: All applicants for any of these awards must apply in the first instance to the Board of Graduate Studies for their University place. Candidates should indicate that they are applying for a Pembroke College award. In making awards preference will be given to those who nominate Pembroke as their college of first choice. All candidates are expected to apply for Research Council funding where appropriate, and for University CHESS funding, if they are eligible. The College will take into account candidates' income from other sources when making awards
**Closing Date**: 31 January
**Additional Information**: Applicants should also complete a Pembroke Studentship form. This can be completed online, downloaded or obtained from the Graduate Secretary. The awards are conditional on the selected students being admitted as a registered Graduate Student by the Board of Graduate Studies with effect from October 1st each academic year. Early application is recommended

## Pembroke College: The Pembroke Australian Scholarship

**Eligibility**: Applicants must normally reside in Australia and hold a qualification from an Australian tertiary institution. There is no restriction as to the academic field
**Level of Study**: Postgraduate
**Type**: Scholarship
**Value**: £500
**Frequency**: Annual
**Application Procedure**: All applicants for any of these awards must apply in the first instance to the Board of Graduate Studies for their University place. Candidates should indicate that they are applying for a Pembroke College award. In making awards preference will be given to those who nominate Pembroke as their College of first choice. All candidates are expected to apply for Research Council funding where appropriate, and for University CHESS funding, if they are eligible. The College will take into account candidates' income from other sources when making awards
**Closing Date**: 31 January
**Additional Information**: Applicants should also complete a Pembroke Studentship form. This can be completed online, downloaded or obtained from the Graduate Secretary. The awards are conditional on the selected students being admitted as a registered Graduate Student by the Board of Graduate Studies with effect from October 1st each academic year. Early application is recommended

## Pembroke College: The Thornton Graduate Studentship in History

**Eligibility**: Preference in awarding these studentships will be given to candidates who intend to register for a PhD degree at Pembroke. However, candidates registering to study for an MPhil will also be considered for an award if they are intending to carry on to a PhD after they have finished their MPhil
**Level of Study**: Postgraduate
**Type**: Studentship
**Value**: The studentship will have a value sufficient to pay College fees for three years. Moreover, additional awards, of up to the equivalent of University fees for a Home student (£3,465), may be made to individual applicants, depending on need and the availability of funds
**Frequency**: Annual
**Study Establishment**: Pembroke College
**Country of Study**: United Kingdom
**Application Procedure**: All applicants for any of these awards must apply in the first instance to the Board of Graduate Studies for their University place. Candidates should indicate that they are applying for a Pembroke College award. In making awards preference will be given to those who nominate

Pembroke as their college of first choice. All candidates are expected to apply for Research Council funding where appropriate, and for University CHESS funding, if they are eligible. The College will take into account candidates' income from other sources when making awards
**Closing Date**: 31 January
**Additional Information**: Applicants should also complete a Pembroke Studentship form. This can be completed online, downloaded or obtained from the Graduate Secretary. The awards are conditional on the selected students being admitted as a registered Graduate Student by the Board of Graduate Studies with effect from October 1st each academic year. Early application is recommended

## Pembroke College: The Ziegler Graduate Studentship in Law

**Eligibility**: Preference in awarding studentships is given to candidates who intend to register for a PhD degree at Pembroke
**Level of Study**: Postgraduate
**Type**: Studentship
**Value**: Covers university and college fees (at the Home/European Union rate)
**Frequency**: Annual
**Study Establishment**: Pembroke College
**Country of Study**: United Kingdom
**Application Procedure**: All applicants for any of these awards must apply in the first instance to the Board of Graduate Studies for their University place. Candidates should indicate that they are applying for a Pembroke College award. In making awards preference will be given to those who nominate Pembroke as their college of first choice. All candidates are expected to apply for Research Council funding where appropriate, and for University CHESS funding, if they are eligible. The College will take into account candidates' income from other sources when making awards
**Closing Date**: 31 January
**Additional Information**: Applicants should also complete a Pembroke Studentship form. This can be completed online, downloaded or obtained from the Graduate Secretary. The awards are conditional on the selected students being admitted as a registered Graduate Student by the Board of Graduate Studies with effect from October 1st each academic year. Early application is recommended

## Peterhouse: Research Studentships

**Eligibility**: Open to prospective PhD candidates
**Level of Study**: Postgraduate

**Type**: Studentship
**Value**: varies
**Frequency**: Annual
**Study Establishment**: Peterhouse College
**Country of Study**: United Kingdom
**Application Procedure**: Please contact at graduates@pet. cam.ac.uk
**No. of awards offered**: 57
**Closing Date**: January
**No. of awards given last year**: 5
**No. of applicants last year**: 57
**Additional Information**: Number of awards varies from year to year

**For further information contact:**

Peterhouse, Trumpington Street, Cambridge CB2 1RD, United Kingdom.

**Email**:    graduates@pet.cam.ac.uk

## Principal's Studentship

**Purpose**: To support an MPhil or PhD student
**Level of Study**: Graduate
**Type**: Studentship
**Value**: Approx. Between £3,000 and £12,000 per year
**Length of Study**: 1–3 years
**Frequency**: Dependent on funds available
**Study Establishment**: Newnham College, University of Cambridge
**Country of Study**: United Kingdom
**Closing Date**: 3 April
**Funding**: Private

**For further information contact:**

**Email**:    studentfunding@ed.ac.uk

## Ramanujan Research Studentship in Mathematics

**Purpose**: The Ramanujan Studentship is normally awarded for nine months in the first instance, while the student takes the course leading to the MASt in Mathematics
**Eligibility**: For students from India hoping to do research for a PhD degree in Cambridge. Students of any University or comparable institution in India who have not already begun residence in Cambridge and who hold a First Class Honours degree or its equivalent, or are likely to do so by the time of entry, are eligible to apply
**Level of Study**: Research
**Type**: Studentship

**Value**: £45,650
**Length of Study**: 1 year
**Frequency**: Annual
**Country of Study**: United Kingdom
**Closing Date**: 10 January
**Additional Information**: Shortlisted applicants will be invited to submit a full application by 4 February www. student-funding.cam.ac.uk/ramanujan-research-studentship-mathematics-202021

**For further information contact:**

**Tel**:    (44) 1223 761893
**Email**:    gradfunding-at-trin.cam.ac.uk

## Ramanujan Research Studentship in Mathematics at Trinity College, Cambridge

**Purpose**: Trinity College, University of Cambridge is offering Ramanujan Research Studentship for students who wish to undertake research in Mathematics. Student should hold a first class honours degree or its equivalent from any university or comparable institution in India
**Eligibility**: Indian students can apply for this studentship. Applicants from outside the home country will often need to meet specific English language/other language requirements in order to be able to study there
**Type**: Research
**Length of Study**: 1 year
**Study Establishment**: Studentship is awarded in the field of Pure or Applied Mathematics of Cambridge
**Country of Study**: Any country
**Application Procedure**: Completed Preliminary Application Forms must be returned by post or email
**No. of awards offered**: 1
**Closing Date**: 10 January
**Additional Information**: For more details please browse the website       scholarship-positions.com/ramanujan-research-studentship-mathematics-trinity-college-cambridge-uk/2015/ 11/14/ www.student-funding.cam.ac.uk/ramanujan-research-studentship-mathematics-202021

**For further information contact:**

**Email**:    gradfunding-at-trin.cam.ac.uk

## Robinson College: Lewis Graduate Scholarship

**Purpose**: The College expects to award one Lewis Scholarship to a graduate student applying to read for a PhD degree in the humanities

**Eligibility**: Open to all applicants who name Robinson College as their college of first choice on the Board of Graduate Studies Application Form for Admissions as a Graduate student, or are prepared to change college if offered the scholarship. The scholarship is conditional on the candidate being offered a place at the University
**Level of Study**: Postgraduate
**Type**: Scholarship
**Value**: varies
**Length of Study**: The scholarship is tenable for up to 3 years, subject to satisfactory academic progress
**Study Establishment**: University of Cambridge
**Country of Study**: United Kingdom
**Application Procedure**: Applicants should send a curriculum vitae and details of their intended programme of research including no more than one A4 page describing their proposed research project, together with details of other grant applications. Applications must be submitted by post to the Graduate Admissions Tutor
**Additional Information**: Please check website for latest updates

### For further information contact:

Robinson College, Grange Rd, Cambridge CB3 9AN, United Kingdom.

| | |
|---|---|
| **Tel**: | (44) 1223 339 100 |
| **Fax**: | (44) 1223 351 794 |
| **Email**: | graduate-admissions@robinson.cam.ac.uk |

## St John's College Benefactors' Scholarships for Research

**Purpose**: To fund candidates for PhD and MPhil degrees
**Eligibility**: Open to candidates of any nationality with a First Class (Honours) Degree or equivalent
**Level of Study**: Postgraduate
**Type**: Scholarship
**Value**: £9,000, plus approved college and university fees, a Scholar's Book Grant of up to £100 and other expenses
**Length of Study**: Up to 3 years
**Frequency**: Annual
**Study Establishment**: St John's College, University of Cambridge
**Country of Study**: United Kingdom
**Application Procedure**: Applicants must see the Cambridge University Graduate Studies prospectus for particulars
**Closing Date**: 1 May
**No. of awards given last year**: 3
**Additional Information**: www.student-funding.cam.ac.uk/nodefield-er-awardtitle-201920-4

### For further information contact:

St John's College, St John's Street, Cambridge CB2 1TP, United Kingdom.

| | |
|---|---|
| **Tel**: | (44) 12 2333 8612 |
| **Fax**: | (44) 12 2376 6419 |
| **Email**: | graduate_admissions@joh.cam.ac.uk |

## Trinity College: Studentships in Mathematics

**Purpose**: The Trinity Studentship in Mathematics is a one-year studentship intended for students who wish to undertake research in Mathematics at the University of Cambridge but who are required by the Faculty of Mathematics to take, in the first instance, the course leading to the Master of Advanced Study (MASt)
**Eligibility**: Eligible candidates must; 1. Have applied for admission, or already received an offer of admission, to the University of Cambridge for the MASt degree. 2. Not yet have been members of the University of Cambridge as an undergraduate or graduate student
**Level of Study**: Postgraduate
**Type**: Studentship
**Value**: £25,000 - £45,000
**Length of Study**: 1 year of study
**Frequency**: Annual
**Country of Study**: Any country
**No. of awards offered**: 4
**Closing Date**: 10 January
**Funding**: Private
**Additional Information**: Please visit the website for more information www.student-funding.cam.ac.uk/trinity-studentship-mathematics-202021

### For further information contact:

| | |
|---|---|
| **Tel**: | (1) 1223 761893 |
| **Email**: | gradfunding@trin.cam.ac.uk |

## Westminster College Lewis and Gibson Scholarship

**Purpose**: To enable Scholars to study for a theology degree at the University of Cambridge as an integral part of his or her training for the ministry of a church in the reformed tradition which has a Presbyterian order
**Eligibility**: Open to graduates of a recognised university who are members of the United Reformed Church in the United Kingdom or of any church not established by the state which is a member of the World Alliance of Reformed Churches and has a Presbyterian form of government. Applicants must have

been recognised by their churches as candidates for the Ministry of Word and Sacrament, but should not yet have been ordained

**Level of Study**: Postgraduate
**Type**: Scholarship
**Value**: One scholarship of £6,000 or two scholarships of £3,000 approx
**Length of Study**: 1 year, renewable for up to 2 further years
**Study Establishment**: The University of Cambridge
**Country of Study**: United Kingdom
**Application Procedure**: If it is the intention to study at the postgraduate level, an application should be made at the same time to the Board of Graduate Studies of the university. The Scholar will normally study for one of the following degrees: BA or MPhil in theology, or PhD. He or she will be a member of both Westminster College and one of the University's constituent colleges
**Closing Date**: 24 December
**Funding**: Private
**Contributor**: A legacy controlled by the United Reformed Church
**No. of awards given last year**: 2
**Additional Information**: Scholars from outside the United Reformed Church have usually been theology graduates and have used the scholarship for postgraduate work

### For further information contact:

Westminster College, Madingley Rd, Cambridge CB3 0AA, United Kingdom.

**Tel**:     (44) 1223 741 084
**Fax**:    (44) 1223 300 765
**Email**:  jp225@cam.ac.uk

## William Wyse Studentship in Social Anthropology

**Purpose**: To support study
**Eligibility**: Open to all students who wish to study for the degree of PhD The Studentships are open to any person who is admitted to the University of Cambridge by the Board of Graduate Studies and intends to do research in Social Anthropology leading to the PhD Degree, regardless of whether they are liable for fees at the Home or Overseas rate. It is a condition of the Studentships that United Kingdom and European Union students are eligible for ESRC or Vice-Chancellor's Awards and that overseas students fulfil the eligibility criteria for Cambridge International Scholarships
**Level of Study**: Doctorate
**Type**: Studentship
**Value**: Varies
**Length of Study**: 3 years

**Frequency**: Annual
**Study Establishment**: The University of Cambridge
**Country of Study**: United Kingdom
**Application Procedure**: Applicants should contact the admissions secretary for details
**No. of awards offered**: 8
**Closing Date**: 11 January
**Funding**: Private
**No. of awards given last year**: 5 grants
**No. of applicants last year**: 8
**Additional Information**: For further details, refer the website link mentioned below. www.socanth.cam.ac.uk/about-us/funding/william-wyse-funding/william-wyse-stud entship www.student-funding.cam.ac.uk/william-wyse-studentship-201920

### For further information contact:

**Email**:    enquiries@socanth.cam.ac.uk

## Wood Whistler Prize and Medal

**Purpose**: To reward an outstanding student
**Level of Study**: Graduate
**Type**: Prize
**Value**: Approx. £2,500
**Frequency**: Annual
**Study Establishment**: Newnham College, University of Cambridge
**Country of Study**: United Kingdom
**Application Procedure**: There is no application form. Names are put forward by the English faculty of the University of Cambridge
**Funding**: Private

### For further information contact:

**Email**:    tutorial.office@newn.cam.ac.uk

## University of Cambridge (Cambridge Commonwealth Trust, Cambridge Overseas Trust, Gates Cambridge Trust, Cambridge European Trust and Associated Trusts)

Cambridge Trusts, Trinity College, Trinity Street, Cambridge, CB2 1TQ, United Kingdom.

**Tel**:      (44) 1223 351 449
**Email**:    info@overseastrusts.cam.ac.uk
**Website**:  www.admin.cam.ac.uk

The Cambridge Commonwealth Trust and the Cambridge Overseas Trust (formerly the Chancellor's Fund) were established in 1982 by the University of Cambridge under the Chairmanship of his Royal Highness the Prime of Wales to provide financial assistance for students from overseas who, without help, would be unable to take up their places at Cambridge. Since 1982, the Cambridge Commonwealth Trust has brought 6,600 students from 51 countries to Cambridge, the Cambridge Overseas trust 4,252 students from 76 countries.

## British Chevening Cambridge Scholarships for Postgraduate Study (Indonesia)

**Purpose**: To financially support those undertaking postgraduate study
**Eligibility**: Applicants must be citizens of Indonesia
**Level of Study**: Postgraduate
**Type**: Scholarship
**Value**: The University Composition Fee at the overseas rate, approved college fees, a maintenance allowance sufficient for a single student and a contribution towards return economy airfare
**Length of Study**: 1 year
**Frequency**: Annual
**Study Establishment**: The University of Cambridge
**Country of Study**: United Kingdom
**Application Procedure**: Applicants must apply directly to the British Embassy in Indonesia
**Contributor**: Offered in collaboration with the Malaysian Commonwealth Studies Centre and the Foreign and Commonwealth Office (FCO)
**Additional Information**: Further information is available on request www.scholars4dev.com/3299/british-chevening-scholarships/

### For further information contact:

**Email**:   cambridge.trust@admin.cam.ac.uk

## British Chevening Malaysia Cambridge Scholarship for PhD Study

**Purpose**: To financially support study towards a PhD
**Eligibility**: Open to students from Malaysia. Applicants must apply to the University of Cambridge and be offered a place at Cambridge in the normal way. All applicants must have a First Class or High Second Class (Honours) Degree or equivalent and normally be under 26. They must be successfully nominated for an Overseas Research Student (ORS) award

**Level of Study**: Doctorate
**Type**: Scholarship
**Value**: The University Composition Fee at the appropriate rate, approved college fees, a maintenance allowance sufficient for a single student and a contribution towards return economy airfare
**Length of Study**: Up to 3 years
**Frequency**: Annual
**Study Establishment**: The University of Cambridge
**Country of Study**: United Kingdom
**Application Procedure**: Applicants must complete a preliminary application form, which can be obtained from local universities, offices of the British Council or the Trust. Completed forms must be returned to the main address. Shortlisted candidates will be sent forms for admission to the University of Cambridge. The preliminary application form can also be downloaded from www.admin.cam.ac.uk/offices/gradstud/admissions/forms/
**Contributor**: Offered in collaboration with the Foreign and Commonwealth Office (FCO)
**Additional Information**: www.youthop.com/scholarships/british-chevening-scholarship-for-international-student-2019-2020-in-uk

### For further information contact:

**Email**:   cambridge.trust@admin.cam.ac.uk

## British Petroleum Research Bursaries for PhD Study

**Purpose**: To celebrate the Centenary for BP and New Hall College
**Eligibility**: For citizens of Russia, Ukraine, Countries of the former Soviet Union, China, The Middle East (particularly Egypt), Southern Africa, or South Asia
**Level of Study**: Doctorate
**Type**: Bursary
**Value**: £2,000 annually
**Frequency**: Annual
**Study Establishment**: BP and New Hall College, The University of Cambridge
**Country of Study**: United Kingdom
**Application Procedure**: Applicants for a place to do a PhD should apply for an ORS award and should normally be successfully nominated for an ORS award or an ORS equivalent award, which meets the difference between the higher overseas rate and the lower domestic rate of the University Composition Fee

### For further information contact:

**Email**:   enquiry@bpgraduates.co.uk

## British Petroleum Research Bursaries for Postgraduate Study

**Purpose**: To celebrate the Centenary for BP and New Hall College

**Eligibility**: For citizens of Russia, Ukraine, Countries of the former Soviet Union, China, The Middle East (particularly Egypt), Southern Africa, or South Asia

**Level of Study**: Doctorate

**Type**: Bursary

**Value**: £2,000 annually

**Length of Study**: 1 year

**Frequency**: Annual

**Study Establishment**: BP and New Hall College, The University of Cambridge

**Country of Study**: United Kingdom

### For further information contact:

**Email**:    enquiry@bpgraduates.co.uk

## Charles Wallace India Trust

**Purpose**: To financially assist postgraduate study for applicants who are not successful in winning a scholarship

**Eligibility**: This scholarship is only available for citizens of India. Applicants for a place to do a PhD should apply for an ORS award and should be successfully nominated for an ORS award or an ORS equivalent award, which meets the difference between the higher overseas rate and the lower domestic rate of the University Composition Fee

**Type**: Bursary

**Value**: Varies

**Frequency**: Annual

**Study Establishment**: The University of Cambridge

**Country of Study**: Any country

**Contributor**: Charles Wallace India Trust

**Additional Information**: www.successcds.net/Scholarships/charles-wallace-india-trust-scholarships.html

### For further information contact:

**Email**:    cwit@in.britishcouncil.org

## China Scholarship Council Cambridge Scholarships

**Purpose**: To financially assist study towards a PhD

**Eligibility**: Applicants must be from China, and have a first-class honours degree, and preferably, a Masters degree or its equivalent from a recognised university in China

**Level of Study**: Doctorate

**Type**: Scholarship

**Value**: The University Composition Fee at the appropriate rate, approved College fees, a maintenance allowance sufficient for a single student, contribution towards an economy return airfare

**Frequency**: Annual

**Study Establishment**: The University of Cambridge

**Country of Study**: United Kingdom

**Application Procedure**: Applicants for a place to do a PhD should apply for an ORS award and should normally be successfully nominated for an ORS award or an ORS equivalent award, which meets the difference between the higher overseas rate and the lower domestic rate of the University Composition Fee

**Contributor**: In collaboration with the China Scholarship Council

### For further information contact:

**Email**:    cambridge.trust@admin.cam.ac.uk

## Corpus Christi Research Scholarship

**Purpose**: To financially assist study towards a PhD

**Eligibility**: Applicants must be from India, and already hold a degree equivalent to a first-class or a high upper second from a United Kingdom university

**Level of Study**: Doctorate

**Type**: Scholarship

**Value**: Varies

**Study Establishment**: Corpus Christi College, The University of Cambridge

**Country of Study**: United Kingdom

**Application Procedure**: Applicants for a place to do a PhD should apply for an ORS award and should normally be successfully nominated for an ORS award or an ORS equivalent award, which meets the difference between the higher overseas rate and the lower domestic rate of the university composition fee

**Contributor**: In collaboration with the Corpus Christi College

### For further information contact:

**Email**:    research-fellowships@corpus.cam.ac.uk

## David M. Livingstone (Australia) Scholarship

**Purpose**: To support students to undertake 1-year postgraduate degree course at the University of Cambridge

**Eligibility**: The scholarship is only available for citizens of Australia. Scholars must specify Jesus College as their first choice college

**Level of Study**: Postgraduate

**Type**: Scholarship

**Value**: University composition fee and college fee
**Length of Study**: 1 year
**Frequency**: Annual
**Closing Date**: 31 March
**Contributor**: Jesus College
**Additional Information**: scholarshipdb.net/scholarships-in-Australia/University-Of-Cambridge-David-M-Livingstone-Australia-Scholarship-Non-Australian-Institutions-Non-Austr alian-Institutions=ZAiKwlhnjEyXXwt_1S5kCw.html

### For further information contact:

**Tel**:	(44) 1223 760 606
**Fax**:	(44) 1223 338 723
**Email**:	admissions@gradstudies.cam.ac.uk

## Developing World Education Fund Scholarships for PhD Study

**Purpose**: To financially support study towards a PhD
**Eligibility**: For citizens from Bangladesh, China, India, Pakistan, Sri Lanka or Zambia. Applicants must apply to the University of Cambridge and be offered a place at Cambridge in the normal way. All applicants must have a degree equivalent to a First Class from a United Kingdom university, and normally be under 26
**Level of Study**: Doctorate
**Type**: Scholarships and fellowships
**Value**: The University Composition Fee at the appropriate rate, approve College fees, a maintenance allowance sufficient for a single student, contribution towards an economy return airfare
**Study Establishment**: The University of Cambridge
**Country of Study**: United Kingdom
**Application Procedure**: Applicants for a place to do a PhD should apply for an ORS award and should normally be successfully nominated for an ORS award or an ORS equivalent award, which meets the difference between the higher overseas rate and the lower domestic rate of the University Composition Fee

### For further information contact:

**Email**:	joe@advance-africa.com

## International Club of Boston College Cambridge Scholarship

**Purpose**: To financially support those undertaking postgraduate study
**Eligibility**: Open to students from Chile
**Level of Study**: Postgraduate
**Type**: Scholarships and fellowships

**Value**: The University composition fee at the overseas rate, approved college fees, a maintenance allowance sufficient for a single student, contribution towards an economy return airfare
**Length of Study**: 1 year
**Frequency**: Annual
**Study Establishment**: The University of Cambridge
**Country of Study**: United Kingdom
**Application Procedure**: Apply directly to the British Council in Chile. Applicants are reminded that they will also need to apply to the Cambridge Trusts on the Scholarship Application Form (SAF) in the usual way
**Contributor**: Offered in collaboration with the Instituto Chileno Britanico de Cultura, the British Council, Chile and Cambridge Assessment (formerly the Local Examinations Syndicate), University of Cambridge

### For further information contact:

**Email**:	internationalstudents@admin.cam.ac.uk

## Jawaharlal Nehru Memorial Trust Commonwealth Shared Scholarships

**Purpose**: To offer financial support
**Eligibility**: Open to citizens from India. All applicants must be under the age of 35 on October 1st with priority given to those candidates under the age of 30. They must not be employed by a national or local government department or by a parastatal organization, nor at present be living or studying in a developed country and not have undertaken studies lasting a year or more in a developed country. Priority will be given to candidates wishing to pursue a study related to the economic and social development of their country
**Level of Study**: Postgraduate
**Type**: Scholarship
**Value**: The University Composition Fee, approved college fees, annual stipend sufficient for a single student and contribution towards travel costs
**Length of Study**: 1 year
**Frequency**: Annual
**Study Establishment**: The University of Cambridge, Trinity College
**Country of Study**: United Kingdom
**Application Procedure**: Applicants may obtain further details and a preliminary application form by writing before August 16th of the year before entry to the Joint Secretary of the Nehru Trust for Cambridge University, giving details of their academic qualifications
**Closing Date**: 28 February
**Contributor**: Offered in collaboration with the Jawaharlal Nehru Memorial Trust and the Commonwealth Scholarship Commission

**For further information contact:**

The Nehru Trust for Cambridge University, Teen Murti House, Teen Murti Marg 53 - 54 Sidney Street, Cambridge, CB2 3HX, United Kingdom.

**Email**:    cambridge.trust@admin.cam.ac.uk

## Ministry of Education (Malaysia) Scholarships for Postgraduate Study

**Purpose**: To financially support those undertaking postgraduate study

**Eligibility**: Applicants must be from Malaysia, and must be nominated by the Ministry of Education. Applicants must apply to the University of Cambridge and be offered a place at Cambridge in the normal way. They must have a First Class or High Second Class (Honours) Degree or equivalent and normally be under 26

**Level of Study**: Postgraduate

**Type**: Scholarship

**Value**: The University Composition Fee at the overseas rate, approved college fees, a maintenance allowance sufficient for a single student and a contribution to return economy airfare

**Length of Study**: 1 year

**Frequency**: Annual

**Study Establishment**: The University of Cambridge

**Country of Study**: United Kingdom

**Application Procedure**: Applicants must complete a preliminary application form, which can be obtained from local universities, offices of the British Council or the Trust. Completed forms must be returned to the main address. Shortlisted candidates will be sent forms for admission to the University of Cambridge. The preliminary application form can also be downloaded from www.admin.cam.ac.uk/offices/gradstud/admissions/forms/

**Closing Date**: 28 February

**Contributor**: Offered in collaboration with the Malaysian Commonwealth Studies Centre and the Ministry of Education, Government of Malaysia

**For further information contact:**

**Email**:    education.intoday@gmail.com

## Ministry of Science, Technology and the Environment Scholarships for Postgraduate Study (Malaysia)

**Purpose**: To financially support those undertaking postgraduate study

**Eligibility**: Applicants must be from Malaysia, and must be nominated by the Ministry of Science, Technology and the Environment. Applicants must apply to the University of Cambridge and be offered a place at Cambridge in the normal way. They must have a First Class or High Second Class (Honours) Degree or equivalent and normally be under 26

**Level of Study**: Postgraduate

**Type**: Scholarship

**Value**: The University Composition Fee at the overseas rate, approved college fees, a maintenance allowance sufficient for a single student and a contribution to return economy airfare

**Length of Study**: 1 year

**Frequency**: Annual

**Study Establishment**: The University of Cambridge

**Country of Study**: United Kingdom

**Application Procedure**: Applicants must complete a preliminary application form, which can be obtained from local universities, offices of the British Council or the Trust. Completed forms must be returned to the main address. Shortlisted candidates will be sent forms for admission to the University of Cambridge. The preliminary application form can also be downloaded from www.admin.cam.ac.uk/offices/gradstud/admissions/forms/

**Closing Date**: 28 February

**Contributor**: Offered in collaboration with the Malaysian Commonwealth Studies Centre and the Ministry of Science, Technology and the Environment, Government of Malaysia

**For further information contact:**

**Email**:    international_scholar@mohe.gov.my

## Nehru Trust for the Indian Collections V&A Cambridge DFID Scholarship

**Purpose**: To financially support those undertaking postgraduate study

**Eligibility**: Applicants must be from India, and must be under the age of 35 on October 1st with priority given to those candidates under the age of 30. Applicants must not be employed by a national or local government department or by a parastatal organization, nor at present be living or studying in a developed country. Priority will be given to candidates wishing to pursue a course of study related to the economic and social development of their country

**Level of Study**: Postgraduate

**Type**: Scholarship

**Value**: The University Composition Fee at the overseas rate, approved college fees, a maintenance allowance sufficient for a single student and a contribution to return economy airfare. In addition a supplementary allowance to cover a short period of practical training at the Victoria and Albert Museum, or other approved institution, will be given

**Length of Study**: 1 year

**Frequency**: Annual

**Study Establishment**: The University of Cambridge
**Country of Study**: United Kingdom
**Application Procedure**: Applicants may obtain further details and a preliminary application form by writing before August 16th of the year before entry to the Joint Secretary at the address given below with details of academic qualifications
**Closing Date**: 28 February
**Contributor**: Offered in collaboration with the Nehru Trust for the Indian Collections at the Victoria and Albert (V&A) Museum and the Department for International Development (DFID)

## Oxford and Cambridge Society of Bombay Cambridge DFID Scholarship

**Purpose**: To financially support those undertaking postgraduate study
**Eligibility**: Open to a resident of Bombay City or the State of Maharashtra whose application is supported by the Oxford and Cambridge Society of Bombay. All applicants must be under the age of 35 on October 1st with priority given to those candidates under the age of 30. They must not be employed by a national or local government department or by a parastatal organization, nor at present be living or studying in a developed country. Priority will be given to candidates wishing to pursue a study related to the economic and social development of their country
**Level of Study**: Postgraduate
**Type**: Scholarship
**Value**: The University Composition Fee at the overseas rate, approved college fees, a maintenance allowance sufficient for a single student and a contribution to return economy airfare
**Length of Study**: 1 year
**Frequency**: Annual
**Study Establishment**: The University of Cambridge
**Country of Study**: United Kingdom
**Application Procedure**: Applicants may obtain further details and a preliminary application form by writing before August 16th of the year before entry to the Joint Secretary at address given below with details of academic qualifications
**Closing Date**: 28 February
**Contributor**: Offered in collaboration with the Department for International Development (DFID)

## Pok Rafeah Cambridge Scholarship

**Purpose**: To financially support study towards a PhD
**Eligibility**: Applicants must be from Malaysia. The Trusts cannot admit students to the University or any of its colleges. Applicants for awards from the Trusts must therefore also apply to the University of Cambridge and be offered a place at Cambridge in the normal way. All applicants must have a First Class or High Second Class (Honours) Degree or equivalent and normally be under 26. Applicants for scholarships for study towards the degree of PhD must be successfully nominated for an Overseas Research Student (ORS) award, which covers the difference between the home and overseas rate of the University Composition Fee
**Level of Study**: Doctorate, Postgraduate, Predoctorate
**Type**: Scholarship
**Value**: The University Composition Fee at the approved rate, approved college fees, a maintenance allowance sufficient for a single student and a contribution to a return economy airfare
**Length of Study**: Up to 3 years for PhD study, and 1 year for postgraduate study
**Frequency**: Annual
**Study Establishment**: The University of Cambridge
**Country of Study**: United Kingdom
**Application Procedure**: Applicants must complete a preliminary application form, which can be obtained from local universities, offices of the British Council or the Trust. The preliminary application form can be downloaded from www.admin.cam.ac.uk/univ/gsprospectus/c7/overseas/schemes.html
**Contributor**: Offered in collaboration with the Pok Rafeah Foundation
**Additional Information**: Further information is available on request

### For further information contact:

**Email**: cambridge.trust@admin.cam.ac.uk

## University of Cambridge, Judge Business School

Trumpington Street, Cambridge, CB2 1AG, United Kingdom.

**Tel**: (44) 1223 339 700
**Email**: enquiries@jbs.cam.ac.uk
**Website**: www.jims.cam.ac.uk
**Contact**: Mrs Natacha Wilson

The Judge Business School is the University of Cambridge's business school. Founded in 1990, it offers a portfolio of management programmes, including the Cambridge MBA. Accredited by AMBA and EQUIS, the business school now hosts one of the largest concentrations of interdisciplinary business and management research activity in Europe.

## Browns Restaurant Scholarships

**Purpose**: To provide funds for United Kingdom citizens with a strong interest in the hospitality and tourism industries to study for an MBA

**Eligibility**: Open to candidates with at least three years of experience in the hospitality or tourism industries. Candidates must show evidence of a career plan showing how they would use the skills and knowledge gained on the MBA course to develop their career within the hospitality or tourism industries. Where an applicant opts for the two year integrated version of the MBA course, arrangements should be in place for the placement year to be in an organisation in the hospitality or tourism industries. Applicants must be United Kingdom citizens

**Level of Study**: MBA

**Type**: Scholarship

**Value**: One scholarship of £20,000 to cover fees and two scholarships of £10,000 to cover roughly half the fees

**Length of Study**: 1 year

**Frequency**: Annual

**Study Establishment**: Judge Institute of Management, University of Cambridge

**Country of Study**: United Kingdom

**Application Procedure**: Applicants must complete and submit an application form, together with a covering letter indicating that they would like to apply for a Browns Restaurant Scholarship, to the Judge Institute of Management

**Closing Date**: March

**Funding**: Commercial

**Contributor**: Browns Restaurants Limited

### For further information contact:

**Email**:    financial_aid@brown.edu

## University of Canberra

The scholarship is funded under the Australian government Research Training Program (RTP) scheme and is available for future and current international students in all research disciplines. The University of Canberra is proudly the university of Australia's capital. UC is one of Australia's top universities for getting a job.

## Australian Government Research Training Program (AGRTP) Stipend Scholarship

**Purpose**: Scholarships are offered in diverse fields to help students in upgrading their education

**Eligibility**: To be eligible to apply for this scholarship you must: 1. Be an international student. 2. Be seeking to enrol, or enrolled, as a full-time Doctor of Philosophy (PhD) candidate. 3. Have a minimum first-class honours (H1) or be regarded by the University as having an equivalent level of attainment. 4. Not have previously held an Australian Government-funded research scholarship for more than 6 months

**Level of Study**: Postgraduate

**Type**: Scholarship

**Value**: AU$26,682 for 2017, tax-free

**Length of Study**: 3 years

**Frequency**: Annual

**Country of Study**: Australia

**Application Procedure**: The mode of applying is online

**Closing Date**: 31 October

**Additional Information**: www.biotecnika.org/2018/06/australian-government-research-training-program-agrtp-scholarship-international/

### For further information contact:

The Australian National University, Canberra, ACT 0200, Australia.

**Tel**:        (61) 2 6125 5111
**Email**:     student@anu.edu.au

## University of Canterbury

College of Arts, University of Canterbury, Private Bag 4800, Christchurch 8140, New Zealand.

**Tel**:        (64) 3 364 2426 (ext: 6426)
**Email**:     erin.hird@canterbury.ac.nz
**Website**:   www.canterbury.ac.nz
**Contact**:   Ms Erin Hird, Human Resource Administrator

The University of Canterbury offers a variety of subjects in a few flexible degree structures, namely, first and postgraduate degrees in arts, commerce, education, engineering, fine arts, forestry, law, music and science. At Canterbury, research and teaching are closely related, and while this feature shapes all courses, it is very marked at the postgraduate level.

## Dow Agrosciences Bursary in Chemical Engineering

**Purpose**: In 1990, DowElanco (NZ) Limited took over the bursary, formerly offered by Ivon Watkins-Dow Limited, for tenure in the Department of Chemical Engineering. In January 1998, DowElanco (NZ) Limited changed its name to Dow AgroSciences (NZ) Limited

**Eligibility**: Must be a full time student who is enrolled for a BE(Hons) in Chemical & Process Engineering. The applicant must have completed, or been exempted from, the First Professional examination

**Type**: Bursary

**Value**: NZ$2,500

**Length of Study**: 1 year

**Frequency**: Annual

**Country of Study**: Any country

**Application Procedure**: You may apply through the webpage approximately 8 weeks before applications close. If it's possible to apply on-line for this scholarship there will be a link to the on-line system. If the link is not provided, please download and complete the application form. However, if the scholarship is managed by Universities NZ or another department of the University an External Website link will appear and application instructions will be available through that link

**Closing Date**: 31 March

**Funding**: Private

**Additional Information**: www.studyinnewzealand.govt.nz/how-to-apply/scholarship/details?scholarshipid=84159

**For further information contact:**

0800 Varsity, New Zealand.

**Tel**:  (64) 800 827 748
**Email**:  enrol@canterbury.ac.nz

## Freyberg Scholarship

**Purpose**: Freyberg Scholarships are awarded to encourage graduate study into areas relevant to national security. Study should be undertaken at a recognised institution in New Zealand or an Asia-Pacific country, including Canada and the United States

**Eligibility**: Applicants must be New Zealand citizens or permanent residents who meet the following academic requirements: they should normally have obtained at least second class honours, division A, or equivalent in their qualifying degree and have completed academic studies in political science, history, economics or some other discipline that may be considered an appropriate foundation for such study

**Level of Study**: Graduate

**Type**: Scholarship

**Value**: NZ$70,000 will be made annuallyfor the award of one or more scholarship

**Frequency**: Annual

**Country of Study**: New Zealand

**Application Procedure**: Apply online. check the below link for further information. www.universitiesnz.ac.nz/scholarships/freyberg-scholarship

**Closing Date**: 1 October

**Funding**: Private

**Additional Information**: www.universitiesnz.ac.nz/scholarships/freyberg-scholarship

**For further information contact:**

**Email**:  scholarships-cf@universitiesnz.ac.nz

## Gordon Watson Scholarship

**Purpose**: The general purpose of the scholarship is to enable New Zealanders to study international relationships or social and economic conditions at a university overseas. Candidates will be planning to study at Masters or PhD level

**Eligibility**: 1. Graduated with or be graduating with an Honours or Masters degree in arts, science, commerce, law or divinity from a New Zealand university. 2. New Zealand citizens or permanent residents

**Level of Study**: Postgraduate

**Type**: Scholarship

**Value**: NZ$12,000

**Length of Study**: 3 years

**Country of Study**: New Zealand

**Application Procedure**: Apply online: www.universitiesnz.ac.nz/scholarships/gordonwatson

**Closing Date**: 1 April

**Funding**: Private

**Additional Information**: Please note that to be eligible a planned Masters degree must have a substantial research component, i.e. at least half www.studyinnewzealand.govt.nz/how-to-apply/scholarship/details?scholarshipid=25581&institutionid=142318

**For further information contact:**

**Tel**:  (64) 3 369 3999
**Email**:  info@canterbury.ac.nz

## Kitchener Memorial Scholarship

**Purpose**: The Kitchener Memorial Scholarship Fund offers scholarships to past or present members of the Armed Forces or their children, who are undertaking an agricultural course of study at a New Zealand university

**Eligibility**: Applicants must be either; 1. Past or present members of the Armed Forces or children of past or present members of the Armed Forces who have seen active service and who, at the time of enlistment, were domiciled in New Zealand, whether actually resident there or not, or. 2. Past or present members of the Armed Forces or their children to whom the above does not apply, or. 3. People resident in New Zealand for a period of not less than three years immediately before the award of the scholarship

**Level of Study**: Graduate

**Type**: Scholarship

**Value**: NZ$500

**Frequency**: Annual

**Country of Study**: Any country

**Closing Date**: 1 December

**Funding**: Private

**Additional Information**: www.scholarshipdesk.com/gordon-watson-scholarship-program/

## Lighthouse Vision Trust Scholarship

**Purpose**: The scholarships support students with a vision impairment in undertaking study at the University of Canterbury. It was established in 2016 by the Lighthouse Vision Trust

**Eligibility**: Applicants must have a vision impairment that qualifies them to register with the Blind Foundation. By the closing date for applications, an applicant must have registered with the University's Disability Resource Service as a student with a vision impairment. Applicants must be citizens of New Zealand or holders of New Zealand residence class visas. Applicants must be enrolled, full-time or part-time, at the University at either undergraduate or postgraduate level.

**Level of Study**: Postgraduate

**Type**: Scholarship

**Value**: Up to NZ$10,000 can be received as total value

**Length of Study**: 1 year

**Frequency**: Annual

**Country of Study**: Any country

**Application Procedure**: 1 Applications must be made online at the Scholarships website by 31 March. 2 Applicants will be considered for both scholarships, and the decision on which of the top candidates will be offered which of the two scholarships will be made randomly. 3 A previous recipient of Lighthouse Vision Trust Scholarship or a Susan Barnes Memorial Scholarship may re-apply for the scholarship that they held, and a previous recipient of one of the scholarships may apply for the other scholarship in another year. However, no student may hold one of the scholarships or a combination of the two scholarships over a total period of more than three years

**Closing Date**: 31 March

**Funding**: Private

**Additional Information**: www.canterbury.ac.nz/scholarshipsearch/ScholarshipDetails.aspx?ScholarshipID=6935.1709

**For further information contact:**

**Email**:    enrol@canterbury.ac.nz

## Marian D Eve Memorial Scholarship

**Purpose**: This scholarship supports students studying, researching, or developing, resources for early-childhood special-needs education at the University of Canterbury

**Eligibility**: Recipients must be undergraduate or postgraduate students who are enrolled full-time at the University and studying, researching, or developing, in any discipline, resources for early-childhood special-needs education

**Level of Study**: Postgraduate

**Type**: Scholarship

**Value**: NZ$2,000

**Frequency**: Annual

**Country of Study**: Any country

**Application Procedure**: You may apply through the webpage approximately 8 weeks before applications close. If it's possible to apply on-line for this scholarship there will be a link above to the on-line system. Apply through online link. www.studyinnewzealand.govt.nz/how-to-apply/scholarship/details?scholarshipid=25668&institutionid=142318

**Closing Date**: 31 March

**Funding**: Private

**Additional Information**: www.studyinnewzealand.govt.nz/how-to-apply/scholarship/details?scholarshipid=25668&institutionid=142318

**For further information contact:**

**Email**:    scholarships@canterbury.ac.nz

## McKelvey Award

**Purpose**: This award supports master's and PhD students in the New Zealand School of Forestry at the University of Canterbury. Normally, the award is available to assist students to present a paper at a relevant conference. However, in the absence of suitable applications, the applications may be opened to eligible students seeking support to meet other costs associated with their study

**Eligibility**: This award supports master's and PhD students in the New Zealand School of Forestry at the University of Canterbury. Normally, the award is available to assist students to present a paper at a relevant conference. However, in the absence of suitable applications, the applications may be opened to eligible students seeking support to meet other costs associated with their study. Students enrolled in a programme for a master's or PhD degree in the New Zealand School of Forestry

**Level of Study**: Postgraduate
**Type**: Scholarship
**Value**: NZ$1,000
**Frequency**: Annual
**Country of Study**: Any country
**Application Procedure**: Apply online: www.fore.canterbury.ac.nz/people/index.shtml
**No. of awards offered**: 1
**Closing Date**: 1 April
**Funding**: Foundation
**Additional Information**: www.studyinnewzealand.govt.nz/how-to-apply/scholarship/details?scholarshipid=128787&institutionid=142318

### For further information contact:

**Email**:     scholarships-cf@universitiesnz.ac.nz

## Park and Paulay Scholarship

**Purpose**: This scholarship acknowledges and rewards a top performer in the first two Professional years of the programme for a Bachelor of Engineering (Honours) degree in Civil Engineering at the University of Canterbury
**Eligibility**: Full-time students in the Third Professional Year of the programme for the Bachelor of Engineering (Honours) degree in Civil Engineering (BE(Hons)(Civil)) at the University of Canterbury, who are enrolled in at least four courses related to Structural or Geotechnical or Earthquake Engineering
**Level of Study**: Graduate
**Type**: Scholarship
**Value**: NZ$2,500
**Length of Study**: 1 year
**Frequency**: Annual
**Country of Study**: Any country
**Application Procedure**: You may apply through the webpage approximately 8 weeks before applications close. If it's possible to apply on-line for this scholarship there will be a link above to the on-line system. If the link is not provided, please download and complete the application form located below. Closing dates are yet to be released for the same
**No. of awards offered**: 1
**Closing Date**: 31 March
**Funding**: Private
**Additional Information**: www.studyinnewzealand.govt.nz/how-to-apply/scholarship/details?scholarshipid=131215&institutionid=142318

### For further information contact:

**Tel**:     (64) 3 369 4900
**Email**:     scholarships@canterbury.ac.nz

## Wood Technology Research Centre – Postgraduate Scholarships

**Purpose**: To develop a computer model to simulate energy flow and energy efficiency in wood and wood product processing industry
**Level of Study**: Postgraduate
**Type**: Scholarship
**Value**: NZ$24,000 per year for PhD and NZ$18,000 per year for ME
**Length of Study**: 3 years for PhD and one and half year for ME
**Application Procedure**: To apply or for further information on the above scholarships, please contact Dr Shusheng Pang
**Contributor**: University of Canterbury
**Additional Information**: Case studies will be conducted for manufacturing of Laminated Veneer Lumber (LVL) and Medium Density Fibreboard (MDF). The project will be conduced in collaboration with the University of Otago and a wood processing company

### For further information contact:

Wood Technology Centre, Department of Chemical and Process Engineering, University of Canterbury, Christchurch, 8041, New Zealand.

**Tel**:     (64) 3 364 2538
**Fax**:     (64) 3 364 2063
**Email**:     shusheng.pang@canterbury.ac.nz

# University of Canterbury, Department of Management

Private Bag 4800, Christchurch, 8140, New Zealand.

**Tel**:     (64) 3 364 2808
**Email**:     s.worrall@mang.canterbury.ac.nz
**Website**:     www.regy.canterbury.ac.nz.home.html
**Contact**:     Mrs Suzanne Worrall, MBA Programme Director

## Auckland Council Chief Economist's Research Scholarship in Economics

**Purpose**: The purpose of this scholarship is to encourage and support postgraduate research into urban economics that has particular relevance to local government in New Zealand
**Eligibility**: 1. At the time of application candidates must be enrolled or planning to enrol in a postgraduate programme at a New Zealand university. 2. The postgraduate programme

must be in the area of urban economics. Universities NZ and Auckland Council reserve the right to determine the eligibility of a particular area of study. 3. A thesis, dissertation, or research report must be a requirement of the postgraduate programme

**Level of Study**: Postgraduate

**Type**: Scholarship

**Value**: Each year Auckland Council may grant one scholarship with an award of NZ$4,000 or two scholarships with an award of NZ$2,000 each

**Length of Study**: 1 year

**Frequency**: Varies

**Country of Study**: Any country

**Application Procedure**: Apply online: universitiesnz. communityforce.com/

**No. of awards offered**: 3

**Closing Date**: 1 February

**Funding**: Foundation

**Additional Information**: For candidates who are enrolled on a part time basis the value of the award will be NZ$1,500. The award is intended to help with tuition fees and research costs (e.g. data costs), and to contribute towards living costs www. studyinnewzealand.govt.nz/how-to-apply/scholarship/details? scholarshipid=116825&institutionid=142318

**For further information contact:**

**Email**:    scholarships-cf@universitiesnz.ac.nz

## Barbara Mito Reed Award

**Purpose**: The award was established in memory of Dr Barbara Mito Reed (1955-1990), a graduate in Japanese of the University of Canterbury, by her husband, Mr T. Mito, her family and her friends. It was established to help outstanding graduate students of Japanese, whose native language is not Japanese, to further their studies towards a higher degree in a field of Japanese language and/or culture

**Eligibility**: The scholarship is open to graduates of the University of Canterbury enrolled, or intending to enrol, in a postgraduate programme in a field of Japanese studies at the University of Canterbury or at a university in Japan. Normally, the programme will be for a BA(Hons), master's or doctoral degree. The scholarship is open to citizens or Permanent Residents of New Zealand, excluding native speakers of Japanese

**Level of Study**: Postgraduate

**Type**: Scholarship

**Value**: NZ$1,000

**Length of Study**: 1 year

**Frequency**: Annual

**Country of Study**: Any country

**Application Procedure**: Apply online universitiesnz. communityforce.com/

**Closing Date**: 31 March

**Funding**: Foundation

**Additional Information**: www.canterbury.ac.nz/scholarship search/ScholarshipDetails.aspx?ScholarshipID=6935.135

**For further information contact:**

**Tel**:       (64) 3 369 4900

**Email**:    scholarships@canterbury.ac.nz

## BayTrust Bruce Cronin Scholarship

**Purpose**: This scholarship has been established to recognise his service to the people of the Bay of Plenty

**Eligibility**: Applicants will be eligible if they were born in, or attended school in, or have whakapapa back to the area

**Level of Study**: Postgraduate

**Type**: Scholarship

**Value**: NZ$5,000

**Length of Study**: 1 year

**Frequency**: Annual

**Country of Study**: Any country

**Application Procedure**: Apply online

**Closing Date**: 1 February

**Funding**: Foundation

**Additional Information**: www.universitiesnz.ac.nz/scholar ships/baytrust-bruce-cronin-scholarship

**For further information contact:**

Level 9, 142 Lambton Quay, Wellington, PO Box 11915, Wellington 6142, New Zealand.

**Tel**:       (64) (04) 381 8500

**Email**:    info@baytrust.org.nz

## Christchurch City Council Antarctic Scholarship

**Purpose**: The Christchurch City Council offers a NZ$10,000 one-year scholarship for a University of Canterbury student to carry out Antarctic or Southern Ocean research at master's or PhD level. The scholarship includes one season of logistical support provided by Antarctica New Zealand

**Eligibility**: A candidate who, during the tenure of the scholarship, is studying for a PhD or is in the thesis year of a master's degree at the University of Canterbury in an Antarctic-related topic

**Level of Study**: Postgraduate

**Type**: Scholarship
**Value**: NZ$10,000
**Length of Study**: 1 year
**Frequency**: Varies
**Country of Study**: Any country
**Application Procedure**: Apply online through link www.antarcticanz.govt.nz/scholarships-and-fellowships
**Closing Date**: 12 March
**Funding**: Foundation
**Additional Information**: www.studyinnewzealand.govt.nz/how-to-apply/scholarship/details?scholarshipid=54787&institutionid=142318

### For further information contact:

International Antarctic Centre, 38 Orchard Road, Christchurch 8053, New Zealand.

**Email**:    adrian.mcdonald@canterbury.ac.nz

## Deutscher Akademischer Austauschdienst (German Academic Exchange Service) Scholarships

**Purpose**: The DAAD supports over 100,000 German and international students and researchers around the globe each year – making it the world's largest funding organisation of its kind
**Eligibility**: Graduates of all disciplines can apply for a scholarship to complete a postgraduate or Master's degree course at a German higher education institution and to gain a degree in Germany (Master's/Diploma)
**Level of Study**: Postgraduate
**Type**: Scholarship
**Value**: €750
**Length of Study**: 10-24 Months
**Frequency**: Annual
**Country of Study**: Any country
**Application Procedure**: See Website: www.universitiesnz.ac.nz/scholarships/daad
**Closing Date**: 15 October
**Funding**: Trusts
**Additional Information**: www.canterbury.ac.nz/scholarshipsearch/ScholarshipDetails.aspx?ScholarshipID=6935.239

### For further information contact:

Embassy of the Federal Republic of Germany, PO Box 1687, Wellington, 6011, New Zealand.

**Email**:    daad@auckland.ac.nz

## Ernest William File Scholarship

**Purpose**: The purpose of the scholarship is to support the sons and daughters of members of the Rail and Maritime Transport Union (RMTU) in their first year of degree study at a New Zealand university
**Eligibility**: 1. Sons or daughters of financial members of the RMTU. 2. Enrolled or planning on enrolling in their first year of full time study for an undergraduate degree at a - New Zealand university. Applications will not be accepted from anyone who already has a qualification from a tertiary institution in New Zealand or overseas
**Level of Study**: Graduate
**Type**: Scholarship
**Value**: The value of the scholarship is NZ$2,000 per year for one
**Frequency**: Annual
**Country of Study**: New Zealand
**Application Procedure**: See Website: www.universitiesnz.ac.nz/scholarships/ernest-william-file-scholarship
**Closing Date**: 1 April
**Funding**: Private
**Additional Information**: www.canterbury.ac.nz/scholarshipsearch/ScholarshipDetails.aspx?ScholarshipID=6935.481

## Francis Martin Baillie Reynolds Scholarship in Law to Oxford

**Purpose**: The purpose of the scholarship is to assist New Zealand Law graduates to commence postgraduate study in Law at the University of Oxford. It has been established to recognise the support that Emeritus Professor Francis Reynolds, Worcester College, Oxford, has provided to New Zealand Law students at the University of Oxford for over 40 years
**Eligibility**: 1. A New Zealand citizen or permanent resident. 2. Has completed the requirements for a LLB degree from a New Zealand University. 3. The date of application has applied for a place in a postgraduate programme in Law at the University of Oxford
**Level of Study**: Postgraduate
**Type**: Scholarship
**Value**: NZ$10,000
**Length of Study**: 1 year
**Frequency**: Annual
**Country of Study**: Any country
**Application Procedure**: Apply online through link universitiesnz.communityforce.com
**Closing Date**: 28 February
**Funding**: Trusts

## Frank Knox Memorial Fellowships at Harvard University

**Purpose**: Annie Reid Knox set up these scholarships to honour her late husband and asked that future scholars be selected on the basis of future promise of leadership, strength of character, keen mind, a balanced judgement and a devotion to the democratic ideal

**Eligibility**: 1. New Zealand citizens at the time of application, normally resident in New Zealand. 2. Have completed or will complete a first or higher degree at a New Zealand university. 3. Studying for a first or higher degree; or have completed a first or higher degree and graduated no earlier than 2014

**Level of Study**: Postgraduate

**Type**: Fellowship

**Length of Study**: 2 year

**Frequency**: Annual

**Country of Study**: Any country

**Application Procedure**: Apply online through the link universitiesnz.communityforce.com

**Closing Date**: 1 November

**Funding**: Trusts

### For further information contact:

**Email**:    rbauerlock@fas.harvard.edu

## G B Battersby-Trimble Scholarship in Computer Science

**Purpose**: The income from the trust fund is added to an annual grant from Trimble Navigation N Z Ltd. The Trimble grant has been given in recognition of the long service provided by the late Dr Battersby to the University and to the computing profession

**Eligibility**: Enrolled in final-year Honours, Master's or PhD level study at Canterbury, for advancing study in Computer Science that will be of benefit to NZ

**Level of Study**: Postgraduate

**Type**: Scholarship

**Value**: 1. US$2,000 for honours students and master's students doing courses. 2. US$7,000 for master's thesis students. 3. US$8,000 for PhD thesis students

**Length of Study**: 1 year

**Frequency**: Annual

**Country of Study**: Any country

**Application Procedure**: Apply online: universitiesnz. communityforce.com

**Closing Date**: 31 March

**Funding**: Trusts

**Additional Information**: www.canterbury.ac.nz/scholar shipsearch/ScholarshipDetails.aspx?ScholarshipID=6935.11

### For further information contact:

**Email**:    scholarships@canterbury.ac.nz

## Gateway Antarctica's Ministry of Foreign Affairs and Trade Scholarship in Antarctic and Southern Ocean Studies

**Purpose**: The Ministry of Foreign Affairs and Trade (MFAT) Scholarship was founded in 2001 in support of research and teaching in Antarctic Studies in recognition of Antarctica as a continent devoted to peace and research

**Eligibility**: PhD or master's thesis students are eligible. The scholar is required to undertake research concerning a matter of importance to the understanding of Antarctica or the Southern Ocean

**Level of Study**: Postgraduate

**Type**: Scholarship

**Value**: NZ$5,000

**Length of Study**: 1 year

**Frequency**: Varies

**Country of Study**: Any country

**Application Procedure**: Apply online

**Closing Date**: 28 February

**Funding**: Foundation

**Additional Information**: www.studyinnewzealand.govt.nz/ how-to-apply/scholarship/details?scholarshipid=128786& institutionid=142318

## Geography Students Conference Fund

**Purpose**: The fund was raised by Geography graduates, associates and the Canterbury Branch of the New Zealand Geographical Society to commemorate the golden jubilee of the Department of Geography in 1987

**Eligibility**: The fund provides grants-in-aid to research students in the Department of Geography to assist with expenses involved in attending conferences. Priority will be given to conferences of the New Zealand Geographical Society

**Level of Study**: Postgraduate

**Type**: Scholarship

**Value**: NZ$500

**Length of Study**: 1 year

**Frequency**: Varies

**Country of Study**: Any country

**Application Procedure**: Apply online: universitiesnz. communityforce.com

**Closing Date**: 31 March

**Funding**: Trusts

**Additional Information**: www.canterbury.ac.nz/scholar shipsearch/ScholarshipDetails.aspx?ScholarshipID=6935.40

## Gertrude Ardagh Holmes Bursary Fund

**Purpose**: The bursaries shall be for the purpose of assisting students of ability and good character to commence or to continue their studies at the University of Canterbury, who would otherwise by reason of their financial circumstances be unable to do so or be seriously handicapped in doing so. Preference shall be given to students who desire to undertake a medical course. Assistance may be continued to such students after they have proceeded to a medical or dental school in another New Zealand university

**Eligibility**: Grants are for students to commence or continue study at the University of Canterbury and who face financial hardship. Preference will be given to those who wish to pursue a medical course

**Level of Study**: Postgraduate

**Type**: Scholarship

**Value**: NZ$600

**Frequency**: Varies

**Country of Study**: Any country

**Application Procedure**: Apply online: universitiesnz. communityforce.com

**Closing Date**: 31 March

**Funding**: Foundation

**Additional Information**: www.canterbury.ac.nz/scholar shipsearch/ScholarshipDetails.aspx?ScholarshipID=6935.26

**For further information contact:**

**Email**: scholarships@canterbury.ac.nz

## Grant Lingard Scholarship

**Purpose**: These scholarships were established by the estate of Peter Lanini in memory of Grant Lingard (1961-1995), a graduate of the School of Fine Arts

**Level of Study**: Graduate

**Type**: Scholarship

**Value**: Full-time tuition fees at the New Zealand domestic rate

**Length of Study**: 1 year

**Frequency**: Annual

**Country of Study**: New Zealand

**Application Procedure**: You may apply through this webpage approximately 8 weeks before applications close. If it's possible to apply on-line for this scholarship there will be a link above to the on-line system. If the link is not provided, please download and complete the application form located below. Please check the website with the following link. scholarshipscanterbury.communityforce.com

**Closing Date**: 31 October

**Funding**: Private

**Additional Information**: www.canterbury.ac.nz/scholar shipsearch/ScholarshipDetails.aspx?ScholarshipID=6935.223

**For further information contact:**

0800 Varsity, New Zealand.

**Tel**: (64) 800 827 748, (64) 3 369 4900

**Email**: scholarships@canterbury.ac.nz

## Henry Kelsey Scholarship

**Purpose**: The purpose of the scholarship is to provide funds for individuals to undertake research towards a PhD at a - New Zealand university or research institution, studying muscular function, including the causes and treatment of muscular dysfunction

**Eligibility**: Applicants will be New Zealand citizens or permanent residents, and will have a Bachelor degree or equivalent, with honours where they are awarded, in a field appropriate to their intended doctoral study at a New Zealand university

**Level of Study**: Postgraduate

**Type**: Scholarship

**Value**: NZ$10,000

**Length of Study**: 3 year

**Frequency**: Varies

**Country of Study**: Any country

**Application Procedure**: Apply online: universitiesnz. communityforce.com

**Closing Date**: 1 October

**Funding**: Trusts

**Additional Information**: www.universitiesnz.ac.nz/scholar ships/henry-kelsey-scholarship

**For further information contact:**

Level 9, 142 Lambton Quay, Wellington, PO Box 11915, Wellington 6142, New Zealand.

**Tel**: (64) (04) 381 8500

## Joan Burns Memorial Scholarship in History

**Purpose**: This scholarship recognises and supports academic excellence by honours and master's students in History at the University of Canterbury. It was established from a 1995 bequest from Joan Mary Burns

**Eligibility**: Applicants must be enrolled full-time or part-time in a Bachelor of Arts with Honours degree programme or in Part 1 of a Master of Arts degree programme

**Level of Study**: Postgraduate

**Type**: Scholarship
**Value**: Stipend equivalent to domestic tuition fees
**Length of Study**: 1 year
**Frequency**: Annual
**Country of Study**: Any country
**Application Procedure**: Apply online: universitiesnz. communityforce.com
**Closing Date**: 31 March
**Funding**: Private
**Additional Information**: www.canterbury.ac.nz/scholar shipsearch/ScholarshipDetails.aspx?ScholarshipID=6935.14

## Kia Ora Foundation Patricia Pratt Scholarship

**Purpose**: The purpose of the Kia Ora Foundation Patricia Pratt Music Scholarship is to assist outstanding New Zealand musical performers, who have completed the equivalent of an honours degree in musical performance in New Zealand, to continue their musical development at a renowned international music school or conservatorium
**Eligibility**: Applicants will be New Zealand citizens. Applicants may apply from outside New Zealand but must have resided in New Zealand for at least three of the last five years immediately preceding the year of selection. Applicants will have recently completed the requirements for an honours degree in musical performance at a New Zealand university (or an equivalent musical qualification)
**Level of Study**: Postgraduate
**Type**: Scholarship
**Value**: Funds available for the scholarship are up to NZ$ 70,000 per annum
**Length of Study**: 1 year
**Frequency**: Annual
**Country of Study**: Any country
**Application Procedure**: Apply online: universitiesnz. communityforce.com
**Closing Date**: 1 March
**Funding**: Foundation
**Additional Information**: www.canterbury.ac.nz/scholar shipsearch/ScholarshipDetails.aspx?ScholarshipID=6935.1778

## Kiwi Music Scholarship

**Purpose**: The purpose of the scholarship is to assist outstanding New Zealand musical performers or conductors who have completed or are completing an honours or master's degree in musical performance in New Zealand to continue their musical development either overseas or in New Zealand
**Eligibility**: Applicants will have completed or are completing an honours or masters degree in musical performance

(including vocal performance) or conducting at a New Zealand university, or an equivalent musical qualification
**Level of Study**: Postgraduate
**Type**: Scholarship
**Value**: NZ$50,000–NZ$60,000
**Length of Study**: 3 year
**Frequency**: Varies
**Country of Study**: Any country
**Application Procedure**: Apply online universitiesnz. communityforce.com
**Closing Date**: 1 March
**Funding**: Trusts
**Additional Information**: www.universitiesnz.ac.nz/scholar ships/kiwi-music-scholarship

## L B Wood Travelling Scholarship

**Purpose**: The LB Wood Traveling Scholarship is awarded to supplement some other postgraduate scholarship held by the scholar supporting their studies in Britain. The scholarship can only be awarded for postgraduate study at a university or institution of university rank in Britain
**Eligibility**: Applicants must be graduates of a New Zealand university. No distinction is made regarding subject, disciple or faculty
**Level of Study**: Postgraduate
**Type**: Scholarship
**Value**: NZ$3,000
**Length of Study**: 3 years
**Frequency**: Annual
**Country of Study**: Any country
**Application Procedure**: Apply online universitiesnz. communityforce.com/Login.aspx
**Closing Date**: 1 April
**Funding**: Foundation
**Additional Information**: www.studyinnewzealand.govt.nz/ how-to-apply/scholarship/details?scholarshipid=25582& institutionid=142318

### For further information contact:

**Tel**:  (64) 3 369 3999
**Email**:  info@canterbury.ac.nz

## LB Wood Scholarship

**Purpose**: 1. The LB Wood Traveling Scholarship is awarded to supplement some other postgraduate scholarship held by the scholar supporting their studies in Britain. 2. The scholarship can only be awarded for postgraduate study at a university or institution of university rank in Britain

**Eligibility**: Applicants must be graduates of a New Zealand university. No distinction is made regarding subject, disciple or faculty

**Level of Study**: Postgraduate

**Type**: Scholarship

**Value**: NZ$3,000

**Length of Study**: 3 year

**Frequency**: Varies

**Country of Study**: Any country

**Application Procedure**: Apply online: universitiesnz. communityforce.com

**No. of awards offered**: 1

**Closing Date**: 1 March

**Funding**: Trusts

**Additional Information**: www.aut.ac.nz/study/fees-and-scholarships/scholarships-and-awards-at-aut/scholarships-database/detailpage?detailCode=100049&sessionID=267 50595&sourceIP=&X_FORWARDED_FOR=

## Master of Business Administration Programme

**Length of Study**: 1 to 5 years

**Application Procedure**: Applicants must complete an application form, a self-evaluation essay, supply an original transcript or a certified copy of grades and provide two references

### For further information contact:

**Tel**: (64) 3 364 2657

**Fax**: (64) 3 364 2925

**Email**: international@regy.canterbury.ac.nz

## New Zealand Law Foundation Ethel Benjamin Scholarship (for Women)

**Purpose**: To support postgraduate research in Law that encompasses the wider objectives of the NZ Law Foundation, in particular research that will protect and promote the interests of the public in relation to legal matters in New Zealand

**Eligibility**: 1. A New Zealand citizen or permanent resident. 2. The holder of a New Zealand university law degree. 3. Accepted into a postgraduate course in law at either a - New Zealand or an overseas university acceptable to the Selection Committee

**Level of Study**: Postgraduate

**Type**: Scholarship

**Value**: NZ$20,000- NZ$50,000

**Length of Study**: 3 years

**Frequency**: Annual

**Country of Study**: Any country

**Application Procedure**: Apply online universitiesnz. communityforce.com

**Closing Date**: 1 March

**Funding**: Trusts

**Additional Information**: www.universitiesnz.ac.nz/scholar ships/new-zealand-law-foundation-ethel-benjamin-scholarship-women

## Prince of Wales' Cambridge International Scholarship

**Purpose**: Each year the Cambridge Commonwealth, European & International Trust www.cambridgetrust.org/ offers several prestigious awards to enable graduates of high academic ability to study at Cambridge University

**Eligibility**: These scholarships are open to graduates who are New Zealand citizens and who wish to pursue a course of research leading to the degree of PhD at Cambridge University

**Level of Study**: Postgraduate

**Type**: Scholarship

**Length of Study**: 3 years

**Frequency**: Varies

**Country of Study**: Any country

**Application Procedure**: Apply online: universitiesnz. communityforce.com

**Closing Date**: 1 October

**Funding**: Trusts

**Additional Information**: www.canterbury.ac.nz/scholar shipsearch/ScholarshipDetails.aspx?ScholarshipID=6935.1593

### For further information contact:

**Email**: cambridge.trust@admin.cam.ac.uk

## Pukehou Poutu Scholarship

**Purpose**: The money for this scholarship has been made available by a bequest from the estate of Edith Fraser who wished that it be used for an award in agricultural or silvicultural sciences

**Eligibility**: Applicants must be graduates of a New Zealand university and be New Zealand citizens

**Level of Study**: Postgraduate

**Type**: Scholarship

**Value**: NZ$10,000

**Length of Study**: 1 year

**Frequency**: Annual

**Country of Study**: New Zealand

**Application Procedure**: Apply online universitiesnz. communityforce.com

**Closing Date**: 1 October
**Funding**: Foundation
**Additional Information**: www.canterbury.ac.nz/scholarshipsearch/ScholarshipDetails.aspx?ScholarshipID=6935.194

### For further information contact:

**Tel**:      (64) 3 369 3999
**Email**:    info@canterbury.ac.nz

## Roland Stead Postgraduate Scholarship in Biology

**Purpose**: This scholarship supports Master's research students of biology with an interest in ecology, freshwater fisheries and the Canterbury region
**Eligibility**: The scholarship will be available to full-time students in the School of Biological Sciences who are engaged in research in Part II of the Master of Science degree programme
**Level of Study**: Postgraduate
**Type**: Scholarship
**Value**: NZ$5,000
**Length of Study**: 1 year
**Frequency**: Annual
**Country of Study**: Any country
**Application Procedure**: Apply online: myuc.canterbury.ac.nz/sso
**Closing Date**: 10 March
**Funding**: Foundation
**Additional Information**: www.canterbury.ac.nz/scholarshipsearch/ScholarshipDetails.aspx?ScholarshipID=6935.1578

### For further information contact:

**Email**:    scholarships@canterbury.ac.nz

## Sir Douglas Myers Scholarship

**Purpose**: The Scholarship provides an opportunity for students who have already distinguished themselves academically to attend one of the most prestigious universities in the world
**Eligibility**: Candidates for the Scholarship must: 1. Be entered for the Year 13 senior school examination (for example, NCEA Level 3, Cambridge exams, etc.) or equivalent senior school exam in the year of application. 2. Have a record of achievement sufficient to satisfy the academic criteria for entry to Cambridge University and Gonville and Caius College. 3. Be New Zealand citizens or permanent residents. 4. Normally have completed their five years of secondary schooling in New Zealand
**Level of Study**: Graduate

**Type**: Scholarship
**Value**: One scholarship is awarded each year and provides tuition fees and a living allowance
**Frequency**: Annual
**Country of Study**: Any country
**Application Procedure**: See website: www.universitiesnz.ac.nz/scholarships/douglasmyers
**Closing Date**: 1 December
**Funding**: Private
**Additional Information**: www.canterbury.ac.nz/scholarshipsearch/ScholarshipDetails.aspx?ScholarshipID=6935.234

### For further information contact:

**Tel**:      (64) 3 369 3999
**Email**:    info@canterbury.ac.nz

## The Claude McCarthy Fellowships

**Purpose**: Claude McCarthy Fellowships (Category A) are available to candidates who are graduates of a New Zealand university and who are enrolled in a PhD programme at a New Zealand university
**Eligibility**: 1. A graduate of a New Zealand university. 2. Registered for a doctoral degree at a New Zealand university. 3. Have been registered for their doctoral degree for at least one year at the closing date for applications
**Level of Study**: Postgraduate
**Type**: Scholarship
**Value**: NZ$5,000
**Length of Study**: 1 year
**Frequency**: Annual
**Country of Study**: Any country
**Application Procedure**: See Website: www.universitiesnz.ac.nz/scholarships/claudemccarthy
**Funding**: Trusts
**Additional Information**: www.canterbury.ac.nz/scholarshipsearch/ScholarshipDetails.aspx?ScholarshipID=6935.191

### For further information contact:

**Tel**:      (64) 3 369 3999
**Email**:    info@canterbury.ac.nz

## The Dick and Mary Earle Scholarship in Technology

**Purpose**: The purpose of the scholarship is to provide funds for individuals to undertake research towards a masterate or doctorate degree at a New Zealand university or research institution in one or both of these fields: 1. Innovation and product development. 2. Bioprocess technology

**Eligibility**: 1. Applicants will be New Zealand citizens or permanent residents who have resided in New Zealand for at least three years immediately preceding the year of selection. 2. Applicants will have completed the requirements for a BTech, BEng, BE degree or equivalent, with honours where they are awarded, at a New Zealand university and in a field appropriate to their intended postgraduate study

**Level of Study**: Postgraduate

**Type**: Scholarship

**Value**: Up to NZ$17,000 per annum at Masters level and NZ$25,000 per annum at PhD level

**Length of Study**: 3 year

**Frequency**: Varies

**Country of Study**: Any country

**Application Procedure**: See Website: www.universitiesnz. ac.nz/scholarships/dick-and-mary-earle

**Closing Date**: 1 September

**Funding**: Trusts

**Additional Information**: www.canterbury.ac.nz/scholar shipsearch/ScholarshipDetails.aspx?ScholarshipID=6935.172

**For further information contact:**

Tel:      (64) 3 369 3999
Email:   info@canterbury.ac.nz

## The Edward & Isabel Kidson Scholarship

**Purpose**: The purpose of the scholarships is to enable a graduate of a New Zealand university, who is of good character and who has shown an ability in physics or a combination of physics and mathematics, to undertake further advanced study or research in meteorology, either in New Zealand or elsewhere

**Eligibility**: Applicants should be graduates of a New Zealand university, be of good character and have shown ability in physics or a combination of physics and mathematics. 1. Past pupils of Nelson Boys' College. 2. Graduates of the University of Canterbury

**Level of Study**: Postgraduate

**Type**: Scholarship

**Value**: NZ$6,000

**Length of Study**: 3 year

**Frequency**: Annual

**Country of Study**: Any country

**Application Procedure**: See Website: www.universitiesnz. ac.nz/scholarships/edward-and-isabel-kidson

**Closing Date**: 1 October

**Funding**: Trusts

**Additional Information**: www.canterbury.ac.nz/scholar shipsearch/ScholarshipDetails.aspx?ScholarshipID=6935.185

**For further information contact:**

Tel:      (64) 3 369 3999
Email:   info@canterbury.ac.nz

## The Judith Clark Memorial Fellowships

**Purpose**: The Judith Clark Memorial Fellowships have been established to assist music graduates undertake a special short-term project that will have long term benefits for their future professional careers as musicians

**Eligibility**: Applicants must hold New Zealand citizenship or permanent residency and must have recently graduated, or expect to graduate in the year of application, with an Honours degree, or equivalent, in music from a New Zealand university

**Level of Study**: Postgraduate

**Type**: Fellowship/Scholarship

**Value**: NZ$15,000

**Length of Study**: 1 year

**Frequency**: Varies

**Country of Study**: Any country

**Application Procedure**: See website: www.universitiesnz. ac.nz/JudithClark

**Closing Date**: 15 August

**Funding**: Foundation

**Additional Information**: There are two application rounds available Round 1 : Principally to the support the cost of attending auditions in the November to February period. Round 2: Principally to support attendance at a summer school or summer academy in the May to August period www.canterbury.ac.nz/scholarshipsearch/ScholarshipDetails. aspx?ScholarshipID=6935.1627

**For further information contact:**

Tel:      (64) 3 369 3999
Email:   info@canterbury.ac.nz

## The Kia Ora Foundation Patricia Pratt Music Scholarship

**Purpose**: The purpose of the Kia Ora Foundation Patricia Pratt Music Scholarship is to assist outstanding New Zealand musical performers, who have completed the equivalent of an honours degree in musical performance in New Zealand, to continue their musical development at a renowned international music school or conservatorium

**Eligibility**: Applicants will be New Zealand citizens. Applicants may apply from outside New Zealand but must have resided in New Zealand for at least three of the last five years immediately preceding the year of selection. Applicants will have recently completed the requirements for an honours degree in musical performance at a New Zealand university (or an equivalent musical qualification)

**Level of Study**: Postgraduate
**Type**: Scholarship
**Value**: NZ$70,000
**Length of Study**: 2 years
**Frequency**: Varies
**Country of Study**: Any country
**Application Procedure**: See Website: www.universitiesnz. ac.nz/scholarships/kia-ora-foundation-patricia-pratt-scholarship
**Closing Date**: 1 March
**Funding**: Trusts
**Additional Information**: For further details and application instructions, refer to the www.universitiesnz.ac.nz/scholar ships/kia-ora-foundation-patricia-pratt-scholarship www.can terbury.ac.nz/scholarshipsearch/ScholarshipDetails.aspx? ScholarshipID=6935.1778

**For further information contact:**

**Tel**:       (64) 3 369 3999
**Email**:    info@canterbury.ac.nz

## University of Canterbury Doctoral Scholarship

**Purpose**: These scholarships support students for study towards a research doctoral degree at the University of Canterbury. Approximately 60 scholarships are available each year, over two annual application rounds
**Eligibility**: The scholarships are tenable by full-time and part-time students engaged in study for a research doctoral degree at UC. An applicant must have completed an appropriate qualification at a level judged to be equivalent to a bachelor's or master's degree with first-class honours at UC (equivalent to a UC GPA of at least 7.0)
**Level of Study**: Postgraduate
**Type**: Scholarship
**Value**: NZ$21,000 per 120 points of thesis enrolment
**Frequency**: Every 3 years
**Country of Study**: Any country
**Application Procedure**: Apply online thro below link. www. canterbury.ac.nz/scholarships/
**Closing Date**: 15 May
**Funding**: Private
**Additional Information**: www.canterbury.ac.nz/scholar shipsearch/scholarshipdetails.aspx?ScholarshipID=6935.127

**For further information contact:**

**Tel**:       (64) 3 369 4900
**Email**:    scholarships@canterbury.ac.nz

## Woolf Fischer Scholarship

**Purpose**: The Woolf Fisher Trust offers up to three Scholarships each year tenable at the University of Cambridge for three or four years of postgraduate research leading to a doctoral degree or equivalent
**Eligibility**: The Scholarships are open to New Zealand citizens who: a. are under the age of 30 in the year of application. b. attended a secondary school in New Zealand. c. have graduated or are expected to graduate with a first-class honours degree from a university in New Zealand. No application will be considered from a student already living outside of New Zealand and no award will be made for post-doctoral study
**Level of Study**: Graduate
**Type**: Scholarship
**Value**: Approximately NZ$100,000 per annum
**Length of Study**: 3 years
**Frequency**: Every 3 years
**Country of Study**: New Zealand
**Application Procedure**: You may apply through this webpage approximately 8 weeks before applications close. If it's possible to apply on-line for this scholarship there will be a link above to the on-line system. For further details, visit the website. www. universitiesnz.ac.nz/scholarships/woolf-fisher-scholarship
**Closing Date**: 1 August
**Funding**: Private
**Additional Information**:    www.canterbury.ac.nz/scholar shipsearch/ScholarshipDetails.aspx?ScholarshipID=6935.215

**For further information contact:**

**Tel**:       (64) 3 369 3999
**Email**:    info@canterbury.ac.nz

## University of Cape Town

University of Cape Town, Private Bag X3, Rondebosch, 7701, South Africa.

**Tel**:       (27) 21 650 3622
**Email**:    pgfunding@uct.ac.za

University of Cape Town (UCT) is very similar to the city of Cape Town: it has a vibrant, cosmopolitan community. It is a cultural melting pot where each person contributes their unique blend of knowledge and thinking. Our staff and students come from over 100 countries in Africa and the rest of the world. The university has also built links, partnerships and exchange agreements with leading African and international institutions that further enrich the academic, social and cultural diversity of our campus.

## University of Cape Town Masters Scholarships in Public Health

**Purpose**: To support the training of eye health professionals with strong public health skills, the Consortium offers scholarships for candidates from low- and middle-income African Commonwealth countries who have been accepted to study for a Masters Public Health, Community Eye Health at the University of Cape Town, South Africa
**Eligibility**: Applicants must come from a low- or middle-income African Commonwealth country to apply. Funding is available for postgraduate studies only. The bursaries are awarded on a yearly basis
**Level of Study**: Postgraduate
**Country of Study**: South Africa
**Application Procedure**: Check website for more details
**Closing Date**: 31 July
**Funding**: Trusts

## University of Delaware

Department of History, Newark, DE 19716, United States of America.

| | |
|---|---|
| **Tel**: | (1) 302 831 8226 |
| **Email**: | dianec@udel.edu |
| **Website**: | www.udel.edu |
| **Contact**: | Ms Diane Clark, Administrative Assistant |

The Department of History offers MA and PhD programmes in American and European history and more limited graduate study Ancient, African, Asian, Latin American, and Middle Eastern history. In conjunction with these, it offers special programmes in the history of industrialization, material culture studies, American Civilization, and museum studies.

## Executive MBA Programme

**Length of Study**: 1 year; 3 years
**Application Procedure**: Applicants must complete an application form supplying US$45 fee, transcripts, Graduate Management Admission Test score, TOEFL score and two letters of recommendation

### For further information contact:

| | |
|---|---|
| **Tel**: | (1) 302 831 2221 |
| **Fax**: | (1) 302 831 3329 |
| **Email**: | E-MBA@strauss.udel.edu |

## University of Derby

Kedleston Rd, Derby DE22 1GB, United Kingdom.

| | |
|---|---|
| **Tel**: | (44) 1332 590 500 |
| **Website**: | www.derby.ac.uk |
| **Contact**: | University of Derby |

The University of Derby is a public university in the city of Derby, United Kingdom. It traces its history back to the establishment of the Derby Diocesan Institution for the Training of Schoolmistresses in 1851 and gained university status in 1992 as one of the new universities.

## International Scholarships at University of Derby

**Purpose**: The University of Derby is offering international scholarships for the academic year. These scholarships are available to apply for once you have received an offer on a course from the University
**Eligibility**: These scholarships are available to apply for once you have received an offer on a course from the University. International students are eligible to apply
**Type**: Postgraduate scholarships
**Value**: Varies
**Study Establishment**: Scholarships are awarded to study the subjects offered by the university
**Country of Study**: United Kingdom
**Application Procedure**: The mode of applying is online
**Closing Date**: 14 January
**Additional Information**: For more details please visit the website scholarship-positions.com/international-scholarships-university-derby-uk/2017/09/29/

### For further information contact:

| | |
|---|---|
| **Email**: | iadmissions@derby.ac.uk |

## University of Dundee

Nethergate, Dundee DD1 4HN, United Kingdom.

| | |
|---|---|
| **Tel**: | (44) 13 8234 5028 |
| **Email**: | j.e.nicholson@dundee.ac.uk |
| **Website**: | www.dundee.ac.uk |
| **Contact**: | Postgraduate Office |

The University of Dundee is one of United Kingdom's leading universities, named Scottish University of the Year 2004/

2005 (Sunday Times) and ranked top for teaching quality in 2005 (THES). It is internationally recognised for its expertise across a range of disciplines including science, medicine, engineering and art and graduates more people into the professions than any other university in Scotland.

## Al-Maktoum College Humanitarian Scholarship in Islamic Finance

**Subjects**: Business (Accountancy / Economics / Finance / International Business)
**Eligibility**: 1. Have firmly accepted their offer of entry for the Postgraduate MSc Islamic Finance programe, starting in September 2020 or January 2021. This can be a conditional or unconditional offer. 2. Have International, Home/EU or RUK fee status, as verified by the University of Dundee. 3. Applicants who can evidence their refugee status will be considered as a priority group, however we may invite additional students to apply.
**Level of Study**: Postgraduate
**Type**: Scholarship
**Value**: Full tuition fee and stipend
**Length of Study**: 1 year only
**Closing Date**: 31 March
**Additional Information**: www.dundee.ac.uk/scholarships/2020-21/al-maktoum-college/

### For further information contact:

**Email**:    contactus@dundee.ac.uk

## Al-Maktoum College Living Support Scholarship

**Subjects**: Business (Accountancy / Economics / Finance / International Business)
**Eligibility**: The University of Dundee is pleased to announce scholarship opportunities, in conjunction with Al-Maktoum College Dundee. In order to be eligible to apply for the scholarship, applicants must: 1. Have firmly accepted their offer of entry for the Postgraduate MSc Islamic Finance programe, starting in September 2020 or January 2021. This can be a conditional or unconditional offer. 2. Have International fee status, as verified by the University of Dundee. 3. Have already been awarded the University of Dundee Global Excellence Postgraduate Taught Scholarship 2020/21.
**Level of Study**: Postgraduate
**Type**: Scholarship
**Value**: £5,000
**Length of Study**: 1 year only
**Additional Information**: www.dundee.ac.uk/scholarships/2020-21/al-maktoum-college-living-support/

### For further information contact:

**Email**:    admissions@almcollege.ac.uk Or contactus@dundee.ac.uk.

## Alumni Scholarship

**Eligibility**: 1. Have applied to study a full (180 credit) postgraduate taught programme starting in September 2020 or January 2021. If you are returning to study an Undergraduate programme, a Postgraduate taught programme which is less than 180 credits, a Distance Learning Programme, or a Postgraduate Research Programme then unfortunately you are not eligible - please read out Key Facts Document for more information on this. 2. Have graduated from the University of Dundee, having previously completed a full undergraduate or postgraduate taught degree, OR; 3. If you have not graduated from the University of Dundee, but an immediate family member has, then you are eligible to apply for this scholarship. Please read the "Do I have to apply?" section below for further information.
**Level of Study**: Postgraduate
**Type**: Scholarship
**Value**: Up to £3,000
**Length of Study**: 1 year
**Additional Information**: www.dundee.ac.uk/scholarships/2020-21/alumni-scholarship/

### For further information contact:

**Email**:    contactus@dundee.ac.uk

## Commonwealth Infection Prevention and Control Scholarship

**Subjects**: Nursing and Health Sciences
**Eligibility**: In order for candidate applications to be eligible for consideration, candidates will need the following: 1. Copy of valid passport or national ID card showing photograph, date of birth, and country of citizenship - uploaded to the online application system 2. At least one reference - submitted directly by the referee to the online application system. Referees will be sent an email request however applicants are responsible for seeking permission from their referees in advance of submitting their application; for ensuring that their referees are available to complete the reference by the deadline; and that the referees have received the reference request email. 3. An offer letter to start chosen course of study in the 2019-2020 academic year - uploaded to the online application system 4. Full transcripts detailing all higher education qualifications (with certified translations if not in English) - uploaded to the online application system 5. The

CSC will not accept supporting documentation submitted outside the online application system.

**Level of Study**: Postgraduate

**Type**: Scholarship

**Application Procedure**: You can apply directly to the CSC cscuk.dfid.gov.uk/apply/distance-learning/

**Closing Date**: 13 April

**Additional Information**: www.dundee.ac.uk/scholarships/2020-21/commonwealth-ipc-scholarship/

## GREAT Scholarships

**Eligibility**: The University of Dundee is pleased to announce we have 2 scholarship opportunities, in conjunction with the British Council. In order to be eligible to apply for the scholarship, the applicant must: 1. Have a Conditional or Unconditional Offer to study at the University of Dundee in September 2020. This can be any full time (180 credits), postgraduate taught, on campus programme. 2. Have International fee status as verified by the University of Dundee. 3. Hold a Chinese passport, from mainland China only

**Level of Study** Postgraduate

**Type**: Scholarship

**Value**: £10,000

**Length of Study**: 1 year

**Additional Information**: www.dundee.ac.uk/scholarships/2020-21/great-scholarships-china/

### For further information contact:

**Email**: contactus@dundee.ac.uk

## Humanitarian Scholarship - The University of Dundee

**Level of Study**: Postgraduate

**Type**: Scholarship

**Value**: Up to £38,500

**Length of Study**: 1 year

**Study Establishment**: The University of Dundee is pleased to announce the 2020/21 Humanitarian Scholarship. Applicants who are eligible to apply for this scholarship will be invited to apply by the University. In order to be considered, applicants must: 1. Hold an academic offer of entry for a postgraduate taught programme in any of our academic schools, beginning in September 2020 or January 2021. The programe must be a full 180 credit, 12 month programme. 2. Have Refugee Status or Humanitarian Protection, recognised by the 1951 UN Convention on the Status of Refugees.

**Additional Information**: www.dundee.ac.uk/scholarships/2020-21/humanitarian-scholarship/

### For further information contact:

**Email**: contactus@dundee.ac.uk

## Humanitarian Scholarship - The University of Dundee 2020/21

**Purpose**: The University of Dundee is offering 8 Humanitarian Scholarships to students on refugee or humanitarian protection status who are applying to study 1-year full-time Masters degree programmes at the University in AY 2020/2021. Studies could be in any field, at any of the University's academic schools.

**Eligibility**: Applicants must hold an academic offer of entry for a postgraduate taught programme in any of the University's academic schools, beginning in September 2020 or January 2021. The programme must be a full 180 credit, 12 month programme. They can be from anywhere in the world, but they must have Refugee Status or Humanitarian Protection, as recognised by the 1951 UN Convention on the Status of Refugees. See the Official Website for list of all countries who are eligible.

**Level of Study**: postgraduate

**Type**: Scholarsip

**Value**: The Scholarship will provide a full tuition fee waiver for the year of study, plus a monthly stipend and accommodation costs. The value of the scholarship is up to £38,500.

**Country of Study**: UK

**Application Procedure**: Applicants who are eligible to apply for this scholarship will be invited to apply by the University. The University will identify candidates who are eligible to apply and an application form will be emailed to those applicants. The deadline to submit the application form and any supporting evidence is 31 March. It is important to visit the official website (link found below) for detailed information on how to apply for this scholarship. www.dundee.ac.uk/scholarships/2020-21/humanitarian-scholarship/

**No. of awards offered**: 8

**Closing Date**: 31 March

**Additional Information**: www.dundee.ac.uk/scholarships/2020-21/humanitarian-scholarship/

### For further information contact:

**Tel**: (44) 1382 38 19 00

## Master of Business Administration Programme

**Length of Study**: 2 years; 5 years

**Application Procedure**: Applicants must complete an application form supplying £25 fee, two academic references, official transcripts and evidence of English Language proficiency if applicable

**For further information contact:**

**Tel**:        (44) 1382 344300
**Fax**:       (44) 1382 228578
**Email**:     cepmlp@dundee.ac.uk

## RTPI Future Planners Bursary

**Subjects**: Architecture and Urban Planning
**Level of Study**: Postgraduate
**Type**: Scholarship
**Value**: £2,000
**Length of Study**: 1 year
**Study Establishment**: The RTPI Future Planners Bursary is available to students studying MSc Spatial Planning courses only. This bursary is available to postgraduate students after enrolment. You could qualify for the Future Planners bursary if you: 1. are eligible to work in the UK or Ireland after graduation 2. have a First or Upper 2nd class undergraduate degree3. can show that you are interested in a career in town planning 4. have applied for a fully accredited Planning Master's degree at a university in England, Scotland or Northern Ireland.
**Additional Information**: www.dundee.ac.uk/scholarships/2020-21/rtpi-future-planners-bursary/

## University of East Anglia (UEA)

Faculty of Arts and Humanities, School of Literature and Creative Writing, Norwich NR4 7TJ, United Kingdom.

**Tel**:        (44) 16 0345 6161
**Website**:   www.uea.ac.uk/lit/fellowships
**Contact**:   Fellowship Administrator

The University of East Anglia (UEA) is organized into 23 schools of study encompassing arts and humanities, health, sciences and social sciences. These are supported by central service and administration departments.

## Global Talent Fellowships

**Purpose**: The UEA GCRF Global Talent Fellowships provide the opportunity for international researchers
**Eligibility**: Applicants must currently be based in an institution outside of the UK, with established or prospective research links to UEA researchers (a letter of recommendation from the host supervisor from UEA, as well as approval from the Head of School or Departmentare both required). To meet the funding conditions of the GCRF, the proposed impact of this research must also comply with requirements for Official Development Assistance (ODA)
**Level of Study**: Research
**Type**: FELLOWSHIPS
**Value**: £637,000
**Length of Study**: 3 year
**Frequency**: Annual
**Additional Information**: www.uea.ac.uk/research/fellowships/uea-gcrf-qr-allocation

**For further information contact:**

**Email**:     rin.international@uea.ac.uk

## University of East Anglia International Development Scholarships

**Purpose**: The University of East Anglia is offering one full fee scholarship for international students towards Masters Degree courses offered by the School of International Development
**Eligibility**: The scholarships are awarded on the basis of academic excellence (e.g. first class degree) and their personal statement. All applicants are expected to have met the School's English language requirements and been offered and accepted a place on the course by the deadline
**Level of Study**: Postgraduate
**Type**: Scholarship
**Value**: Full fees for masters degree programme
**Frequency**: Annual
**Study Establishment**: University of East Anglia
**Country of Study**: United Kingdom
**Application Procedure**: It is important to visit the official website for detailed information on how to apply for this scholarship
**Closing Date**: 31 March
**Funding**: Corporation

**For further information contact:**

**Email**:     admissions@uea.ac.uk

## University of Edinburgh

Old College South Bridge, Edinburgh EH8 9YL, United Kingdom.

**Tel**:        (44) 131 650 2159
**Email**:     postgrad@ed.ac.uk
**Contact**:   Grants Management Officer

## Alice Brown PhD Scholarships

**Purpose**: The Alice Brown Scholarship is a new 6-year PhD scholarship offering a programme of advanced study, ongoing research, professional training and development
**Eligibility**: Citizens of United Kingdom, European Economic Area and Switzerland are eligible to apply. A first class honours degree (or equivalent) in a subject relevant to the studentship OR a taught MSc degree at distinction level in a subject relevant to the studentship. Conditional offers can be made to applicants currently enrolled in a degree programme on the basis of anticipated results. 1. As comprehensive research training is integrated into the programme of this PhD, there will be no automatic preference given to those holding MSc qualifications covering research training. 2. Applications are encouraged from those nearing the end of an undergraduate degree in a subject relevant to the scholarship. 3. Due to constraints on part-time study for international students on visas, this award is only open to nationals of the United Kingdom, countries of the European Economic Area, or Switzerland
**Level of Study**: Postgraduate
**Type**: Scholarship
**Value**: The scholarship covers full payment of PhD tuition fees and provides an annual stipend of £10,000 each year
**Length of Study**: 6-year PhD programme
**Country of Study**: United Kingdom
**Application Procedure**: Applicants are invited to submit a current CV, a short research proposal/idea (max. 1,000 words) and a personal statement of up to 500 words explaining their suitability for the scholarship in the field to which they are applying
**Closing Date**: 3 February
**Contributor**: University of Edinburgh
**Additional Information**: For more details, please visit scholarship-positions.com/alice-brown-phd-scholarships-university-edinburgh-uk/2018/02/27/ www.sps.ed.ac.uk/gradschool/prospective/funding/alice_brown_phd_scholarships

### For further information contact:

**Email**:   pgresearch.sps@ed.ac.uk

## Clinical Management of Pain Scholarship

**Value**: Each scholarship provides a one-off payment of £815 towards tuition fees
**Country of Study**: Any country
**Application Procedure**: In order to gain access to the scholarship application system applicants must have applied for admission to the University of Edinburgh. Please note that, following the submission of an application for admission, it can take up to five working days for all system checks to be completed and for access to be granted. The online scholarship application form is located in EUCLID and can be accessed via MyEd our web based information portal at www.myed.ed.ac.uk
**Closing Date**: 31 July
**Additional Information**: www.ed.ac.uk/student-systems/support-guidance www.ed.ac.uk/student-funding/postgraduate/e-learning/painnew

### For further information contact:

**Email**:   studentfunding@ed.ac.uk

## Commonwealth Online Global Health Scholarships at University of Edinburgh

**Purpose**: The University's Global Health Academy has been awarded 10 fully funded studentships across five online Masters programmes within the domain of Global Health
**Eligibility**: The scholarships will be awarded to a candidate who is accepted for admission on to an eligible programme (see above) and who is a citizen of and resident in one of the following developing Commonwealth countries
**Level of Study**: Postdoctorate
**Type**: Scholarship
**Frequency**: Annual
**Country of Study**: Any country
**Closing Date**: 22 March
**Funding**: Foundation
**Additional Information**: www.scholars4dev.com/18289/commonwealth-online-global-health-scholarships-at-university-of-edinburgh/

## Edinburgh Global Online Distance Learning Masters Scholarship

**Value**: Each scholarship will cover full tuition fees and will be tenable for the normal duration of the programme of study
**Length of Study**: Three years
**Country of Study**: Any country
**Application Procedure**: The online scholarship application form is located in EUCLID and can be accessed via MyEd our web based information portal at www.myed.ed.ac.uk
**Closing Date**: 1 June
**Additional Information**: www.ed.ac.uk/student-funding/postgraduate/international/global/distance-learning

### For further information contact:

**Email**:   studentfunding@ed.ac.uk

## Edinburgh Global Online Distance Learning Scholarships

**Purpose**: The University of Edinburgh will offer a number of scholarships for distance learning Master's programmes offered by the University

**Eligibility**: 1. Scholarships will be available for students commencing in session 2020-21 in any distance learning Masters programme offered by the University. Applicants must be nationals of the eligible countries. 2. Applicants should already have been offered a place at the University of Edinburgh and should have firmly accepted that offer or be intending to do so.

**Level of Study**: Postdoctorate

**Type**: Scholarship

**Length of Study**: 3 years

**Frequency**: Annual

**Country of Study**: Any country

**Application Procedure**: Eligible applicants should complete an online scholarship application. The scholarship deadline is 1 June.

**No. of awards offered**: 12

**Closing Date**: 1 June

**Funding**: Private

**Contributor**: University of Edinburgh

**Additional Information**: www.scholars4dev.com/2719/distance-learning-scholarships-at-university-of-edinburgh/

### For further information contact:

**Email**:    family.medicine@ed.ac.uk

## Edinburgh Global Research Scholarship

**Purpose**: These awards are designed to attract high quality overseas research students to the University of Edinburgh

**Eligibility**: The awards are open to overseas nationals commencing a PhD in any field of study

**Type**: Scholarship

**Value**: Each scholarship will cover the difference between the tuition fee for a United Kingdom/European Union postgraduate student and that chargeable to an overseas postgraduate student. The awards do not cover maintenance expenses

**Length of Study**: Three years

**Country of Study**: United Kingdom

**Closing Date**: April

**Additional Information**: For more details on this award please contact Scholarships and Student Funding Services. Work: (44) 131 651 4070; Email: studentfunding@ed.ac.uk www.ed.ac.uk/student-funding/postgraduate/international/global/research

### For further information contact:

**Tel**:       (44) 131 651 4070

**Email**:    studentfunding@ed.ac.uk

## Glenmore Medical Postgraduate Scholarship

**Purpose**: Two scholarships are available for postgraduate full-time one year Masters study for eligible Human Medical programmes offered by the University in the upcoming academic session

**Eligibility**: The scholarship will be awarded on the basis of academic merit. Candidates must have, or expect to obtain, the overseas equivalent of a United Kingdom first-class honours degree

**Level of Study**: Postgraduate

**Type**: Scholarship

**Value**: Each scholarship will cover full overseas tuition fees for eligible programmes, and will be tenable for one academic year.

**Length of Study**: One academic year

**Frequency**: Annual

**Country of Study**: United Kingdom

**Application Procedure**: Please check website for more details: www.ed.ac.uk/student-funding/pgt-application

**Closing Date**: 29 May

**Additional Information**: www.ed.ac.uk/student-funding/postgraduate/international/medicine-vet-medicine/glenmore

### For further information contact:

The University of Edinburgh, Old College, South Bridge, Edinburgh, EH8 9YL, United Kingdom.

**Tel**:       (44) 131 651 4070

**Email**:    studentfunding@ed.ac.uk

## Haywood Doctoral Scholarship

**Purpose**: To offer Haywood Doctoral Scholarship to an outstanding doctoral research candidate in History of Art

**Type**: Scholarship

**Value**: As an international student, you will receive a reduction in tuition fees equivalent to the Home European Union rate if successful

**Country of Study**: United Kingdom

**Closing Date**: 2 March

**Additional Information**: www.scholarshipsads.com/haywood-doctoral-scholarship-international-applicants-uk-2018/

**For further information contact:**

Tel:     (44) 1214 143 344
Email:   calpg-research@contacts.bham.ac.uk

## Institute for Advanced Studies in the Humanities-School of Social and Political Science Visiting Fellowships

**Purpose**: The IASH-SSPS Visiting Fellowships are intended to encourage outstanding interdisciplinary research, international scholarly collaboration, and networking activities of Visiting Research Fellows together with SSPS academics

**Eligibility**: Kindly check the below steps for further instructions. 1. Fellows are expected to be resident in Edinburgh throughout the tenure of their Fellowship and to play a full part in the activities of the Institute. The Institute will be pleased to help with finding suitable accommodation in Edinburgh but is unable to pay accommodation costs. 2. The minimum tenure for a Fellowship is two months; applications for less than two months will not be considered. 3. Only fully completed applications will be considered. It is the responsibility of each applicant to ensure that all documentation is complete, and that referees submit their reports to the Institute by the closing date. Applications may include a copy of any one article or publication that is thought to be specially relevant to the research proposal and Fellowship submission

**Level of Study**: Graduate
**Type**: Fellowship
**Frequency**: Annual
**Country of Study**: Any country
**Application Procedure**: The next closing date for the receipt of applications will be Thursday 28 February. Applications received after that date will not be considered. Successful candidates will be notified by email with a formal letter of confirmation to follow; please ensure that you supply a valid email address so that you can be contacted quickly after decisions are made. The application form can be completed online. Check with the below link. www.sps.ed.ac.uk/research/academic_visitors/iash-ssps_visiting_fellowships
**Closing Date**: 28 February
**Funding**: Commercial, Private
**Additional Information**: www.iash.ed.ac.uk/iash-ssps-research-fellowships

**For further information contact:**

The University of Edinburgh, Hope Park Square, Edinburgh, EH8 9NW. United Kingdom.

Tel:     (44) 131 650 4671
Email:   iash@ed.ac.uk

## National Health Service Education for Scotland Primary Care Ophthalmology Scholarship

**Eligibility**: The scholarships will be awarded to students who are accepted for admission on to the online distance learning MSc in Primary Care Ophthalmology at the University of Edinburgh. Applicants should already have been offered a place at the University of Edinburgh and should have firmly accepted that offer or be intending to do so
**Type**: Scholarship
**Value**: The scholarship will have a total value of 50% of the course fees
**Country of Study**: United Kingdom
**Closing Date**: 27 July
**Additional Information**: For further information, please contact Scholarships and Financial Support Team. Work: (44) 131 651 4070; Email: studentfunding@ed.ac.uk Notfound in dash bord

**For further information contact:**

Email:   studentfunding@ed.ac.uk

## Perfect Storms: Leverhulme Doctoral Scholarships

**Level of Study**: Doctorate
**Value**: Full fees, living and research costs
**Length of Study**: 3 years
**Frequency**: Annual
**Study Establishment**: University of Edinburgh
**Country of Study**: Scotland
**Contributor**: The Leverhulme Trusts
**No. of awards given last year**: 5

**For further information contact:**

Email:   studentfunding@ed.ac.uk

## PhD Social Work Scholarship at University of Edinburgh in United Kingdom

**Purpose**: This award is available to students intending to commence PhD Social Work study in September on either a full-time or part-time basis
**Eligibility**: Citizens of all nationalities are eligible to apply. If English is not your first language then you will need to show that your English language skills are at a high enough level to succeed in your studies
**Value**: One award covering tuition fees at the Home/European Union fee rate, a maintenance stipend of £14,000 and a research grant of £500 is on offer to applicants for PhD Social Work in the School of Social and Political Science

**Study Establishment**: Social Work study
**Country of Study**: Any country
**Application Procedure**: The online scholarship application form is located in EUCLID and can be accessed via MyEd our web-based information portal. www.myed.ed.ac.uk/
**Closing Date**: 1 March

### For further information contact:

**Email**:   GradSchool.HCA@ed.ac.uk

## Polish School of Medicine Memorial Fund Scholarships

**Purpose**: The scholarship enables medical scientists at the outset of their careers to undertake a period of further study or research at the University's Medical School and return to Poland
**Eligibility**: The programme is open to Polish doctors and postgraduate medical scientists: 1. in their early career (usually within 10 years of their medical graduation - MB ChB equivalent) 2. working in Polish Medical Academies/ Universities and Research Institutes 3. with excellent mastery of English; and 4. who are committed to the further development of medical research expertise in Poland.
**Value**: Allowance for a period of up to 1 year
**Length of Study**: One year
**Country of Study**: Any country
**Application Procedure**: Eligible applicants should complete an online scholarship application
**Closing Date**: 28 May
**Additional Information**: www.ed.ac.uk/student-funding/ postgraduate/uk-eu/medicine-vet-medicine/polish

### For further information contact:

The University of Edinburgh, Old College, South Bridge, Edinburgh, EH8 9YL, United Kingdom.

**Tel**:   (44) 131 651 4070
**Email**:   studentfunding@ed.ac.uk

## Principal Career Development PhD Scholarship

**Purpose**: To attract the best and brightest PhD students, the University seeks to offer not only unparalleled research facilities and superb supervision, but also to provide development opportunities which will support our research students as they progress beyond their PhD, through an innovative programme of integrated research, training, and career development
**Type**: Scholarship
**Value**: Each scholarship covers the United Kingdom/European Union rate of tuition fee as well as a stipend of £15,000

**Country of Study**: United Kingdom
**Closing Date**: 1 February
**Additional Information**: For further information, please contact Scholarships and Financial Support Team, phone :0131 651 4070, email: studentfunding@ed.ac.uk www.ed. ac.uk/student-funding/postgraduate/uk-eu/university-scholar ships/development

### For further information contact:

**Tel**:   (44) 131 651 4070
**Email**:   studentfunding@ed.ac.uk

## Shell Centenary Scholarships and Shell Centenary Chevening Scholarships at Edinburgh

**Eligibility**: Students from countries that are not present or applicant members of the Organization for Economic Co-operation and Development (OECD). Candidates should normally be aged 20–35, be resident in one of the non-OECD countries and be intending to return to the country concerned at the end of the period of study. They should normally already hold a degree equivalent to a United Kingdom First Class (Honours) Degree or be expecting to obtain such a degree before the start of their proposed course
**Level of Study**: Postgraduate
**Type**: Scholarship
**Value**: The scholarships covers tuition fees, accommodation, maintenance costs and a return airfare for the scholarship holder
**Length of Study**: 1 year
**Frequency**: Annual
**Study Establishment**: University of Edinburgh
**Country of Study**: Scotland
**Application Procedure**: Applicants must apply separately for admission to the University of Edinburgh making a clear statement that they wish to be considered for a Shell Scholarship
**Closing Date**: 1 March
**No. of awards given last year**: 6

### For further information contact:

**Email**:   scholarships@ed.ac.uk

## The Anne Rowling Clinic Regenerative Neurology Scholarships

**Purpose**: Masters scholarships for applicants commencing Stem Cells and Translational Neurology programmes in the academic year
**Type**: Scholarship

**Value**: One International Anne Rowling Clinic Regenerative Neurology Scholarship will cover 60 credits towards your module fees. Two Anne Rowling Clinic Regenerative Neurology Scholarships will cover 30 credits worth of course fees
**Country of Study**: United Kingdom
**Application Procedure**: Eligible applicants should complete an online scholarship application. Website link is www.ed.ac.uk/student-funding/postgraduate/e-learning/regenerative-neurology
**Closing Date**: 20 August
**Funding**: Private
**Additional Information**: For further information, please visit www.ed.ac.uk/student-funding/postgraduate/e-learning/regenerative-neurology www.ed.ac.uk/student-funding/postgraduate/e-learning/regenerative-neurology

**For further information contact:**

**Email**:    studentfunding@ed.ac.uk

## The Edinburgh Online Family Medicine Scholarships Fund

**Purpose**: Through the generous donations of a benefactor in India who is committed to improving healthcare in rural regions this full scholarship award will allow a student from South Asia to study the online Masters of Family Medicine
**Type**: Scholarship
**Frequency**: Annual
**Country of Study**: Any country
**Application Procedure**: Applications should be made to Michelle Hart at family.medicine@ed.ac.uk
**Closing Date**: 1 July
**Additional Information**: scholarship-positions.com/edinburgh-online-family-medicine-scholarships-fund-uk/2018/05/22/

**For further information contact:**

**Email**:    family.medicine@ed.ac.uk

## The Garden Scholarship in Surgical Sciences

**Type**: Scholarship (grant-in-aid)
**Value**: £1,000
**Country of Study**: Any country
**Additional Information**: www.ed.ac.uk/student-funding/postgraduate/e-learning/garden

**For further information contact:**

**Email**:    studentfunding@ed.ac.uk

## The Kirby Laing International Scholarships

**Value**: The scholarships will cover tuition fees and provide a maintenance allowance of £12,000
**Length of Study**: 1 year
**Country of Study**: United Kingdom
**Closing Date**: 2 April
**Additional Information**: For further information, please contact School of Divinity, Work: 044 1316 508 900, Email: Divinity.PG@ed.ac.uk www.ed.ac.uk/student-funding/postgraduate/international/humanities/divinity/kirby-laing

**For further information contact:**

**Email**:    Divinity.PG@ed.ac.uk

## The Lt. Col Jack Wishart Scholarship

**Value**: £500 per year toward tuition fees
**Length of Study**: Two academic years
**Country of Study**: Any country
**Application Procedure**: The online scholarship application form is located in EUCLID and can be accessed via MyEd our web based information portal at www.myed.ed.ac.uk
**Closing Date**: 30 September
**Additional Information**: www.ed.ac.uk/student-funding/postgraduate/e-learning/wishart

**For further information contact:**

**Email**:    studentfunding@ed.ac.uk

## The Rev Dr Norma P Robertson Scholarship

**Type**: Scholarship
**Value**: The scholarship will have a maximum value of £7,500
**Country of Study**: Any country
**Additional Information**: www.ed.ac.uk/student-funding/postgraduate/e-learning/wishart

**For further information contact:**

**Email**:    studentfunding@ed.ac.uk

## The Sanders Scholarship in Clinical Ophthalmology

**Purpose**: University of Edinburgh is offering twenty four scholarships for online distance learning. Scholarships are available for pursuing online distance learning masters degree programmes

**Eligibility**: The scholarships will be awarded to students who are accepted for admission on to the online distance learning MSc in Primary Care Ophthalmology and the ChM in Clinical Ophthalmology at the University of Edinburgh. Applicants must be medical or surgical trainees registered with the General Medical Council and working in a recognised training programme in the Scottish NHS, and be resident in Scotland. Applications from other health professionals involved in delivering eye care (except optometrists) in the Scottish NHS may be considered on an individual basis
**Level of Study**: Graduate
**Type**: Scholarship
**Value**: £1,000
**Country of Study**: United Kingdom
**Application Procedure**: Complete an online EUCLID application for the MSc in Primary Care Ophthalmology or the ChM (Master of Surgery) in Clinical Ophthalmology – instructions on full application process can be found on the University's degree finder pages for the MSc PCO and the ChM CO. Wait for decision on application via EUCLID. If eligible to join the course, you will be given a conditional or unconditional offer, which you must accept prior to applying for a scholarship. Email a personal statement to declare your wish to apply for a scholarship to: chm.info@ed.ac.uk
**Closing Date**: 27 July
**Funding**: Private
**Additional Information**: For further details, please contact Scholarships and Financial Support Team, Work: 0131 651 4070, Email: studentfunding@ed.ac.uk www.ed.ac.uk/student-funding/postgraduate/e-learning/sanders

**For further information contact:**

**Email**:     sarah.jones@ed.ac.uk

## University of Edinburgh - KU Leuven PhD Studentship

**Eligibility**: The studentships will be awarded competitively and are open to UK, EU and overseas students applying to start their PhD programme of study in 2020-2021.
**Level of Study**: PhD
**Type**: Studentship
**Value**: Full tuition fees, a stipend and provision of research costs
**Length of Study**: 4 years
**Frequency**: Annual
**Study Establishment**: The University of Edinburgh

**No. of awards offered**: 3
**Closing Date**: 26 March
**Additional Information**: www.ed.ac.uk/student-funding/postgraduate/international/humanities/cross-disciplinary/ku-leuven

**For further information contact:**

**Email**:     pgawards@ed.ac.uk

## Wellcome Trust 4-Year PhD Programme Studentships

**Eligibility**: Students should be from a life sciences background and should hold, or expect to obtain, at least an Upper Second Class (Honours) Degree
**Level of Study**: Doctorate
**Type**: Studentship
**Value**: Tuition fees, research costs and maintenance allowance
**Length of Study**: 4 years
**Frequency**: Annual
**Study Establishment**: The University of Edinburgh
**Country of Study**: Scotland
**Application Procedure**: Please see the website www.wcb.ed.ac.uk/phd
**Closing Date**: 10 December
**No. of awards given last year**: 5
**Additional Information**: wellcome.ac.uk/funding/schemes/four-year-phd-programmes-studentships-basic-scientists

**For further information contact:**

**Email**:     karen.traill@ed.ac.uk

## University of Essex

Graduate Admissions Office, University of Essex, Wivenhoe Park, Colchester C04 3SQ, United Kingdom.

**Tel**:          (44) 12 0687 2719
**Email**:      pgadmit@essex.ac.uk
**Website**:   www.essex.ac.uk
**Contact**:   V Bartholomew, CRM Operations Manager

The University of Essex is one of the United Kingdom's leading academic institutions, ranked 10th nationally for research and 7th for teaching. It offers degrees and research opportunities across 19 academic departments (including government and sociology, which both have 6-star research ratings) and numerous research centres of world renown.

## Academic Excellence International Masters Scholarship

**Purpose**: University of Essex is inviting applications for academic excellence international masters scholarship
**Eligibility**: Applicants must meet the necessary language proficiency requirements of the host institution
**Value**: The scholarship worth up to £5,000, paid as a discount on tuition fee
**Frequency**: Annual
**Study Establishment**: Scholarships are awarded in the fields offered by the university
**Country of Study**: United Kingdom
**Application Procedure**: If applicants meet all the eligibility criteria and firmly accept the offer of your place by 30 September then you will automatically be awarded this scholarship. Applicants will be notified of your award by the end of October. You don't need to complete an application form
**Closing Date**: 30 September
**Additional Information**: For more details please visit the website scholarship-positions.com/academic-excellence-international-masters-scholarship-uk-2017/2015/11/16/ www1.essex.ac.uk/fees-and-funding/masters/scholarships/academic-excellence.aspx

### For further information contact:

**Email**: enquiries@essex.ac.uk

## Arts and Humanities Research Council Department of Sociology Studentships

**Purpose**: To support students on a research programme
**Eligibility**: Open to United Kingdom or European Union applicants
**Level of Study**: Postgraduate
**Type**: Scholarship
**Value**: UK students - fees plus maintenance; European Union students - fees
**Frequency**: Annual
**Study Establishment**: University of Essex
**Country of Study**: United Kingdom
**Contributor**: AHRC

### For further information contact:

**Email**: pgeduc@leeds.ac.uk

## Arts and Humanities Research Council Research Preparations Masters Award for Literature, Film, and Theatre Studies

**Purpose**: To support students undertaking a research preparations in the department
**Eligibility**: Open to postgraduates offered a place to study in the department
**Level of Study**: Postgraduate
**Type**: Award
**Value**: £10,600 per year maintenance grant
**Length of Study**: 1 year
**Frequency**: Annual
**Study Establishment**: University of Essex
**Country of Study**: United Kingdom
**Application Procedure**: Applicants must contact the department concerned

### For further information contact:

**Email**: graduateschool@gold.ac.uk

## Dowden Scholarship

**Purpose**: To help highly able students who otherwise would not be able to study at postgraduate level
**Eligibility**: Applicant must have settled status in the United Kingdom; been 'ordinarily resident' in the United Kingdom for the 3 years before the start of their studentship; not been residing in the United Kingdom wholly or mainly for the purpose of full-time education (United Kingdom and European Union nationals are exempt from this requirement). The Vera Dowden Baldwin Scholarship awards financial assistance to a resident of Dowden Hall who demonstrates financial need. The fund is named in honor of the late Vera Dowden Baldwin '34, whose connection with the University spanned more than seventy years
**Level of Study**: Postgraduate
**Type**: Scholarship
**Value**: Up to £5,000
**Frequency**: Annual
**Study Establishment**: University of Essex
**Country of Study**: United Kingdom
**Application Procedure**: Indicate on application for doctoral course
**Additional Information**: Please contact the university for more information

## Drake Lewis Graduate Scholarship for Art History

**Purpose**: To support new MA students in art history
**Eligibility**: Open to postgraduate applicants
**Level of Study**: Postgraduate
**Type**: Scholarship
**Value**: £5,000
**Frequency**: Annual
**Study Establishment**: University of Essex
**Country of Study**: United Kingdom
**Funding**: Private
**Contributor**: Drake Lewis
**Additional Information**: Please check website for further information

### For further information contact:

**Email**:    scholarships@essex.ac.uk

## Drake Lewis Graduate Scholarship for Health and Human Sciences

**Purpose**: To support students on full-time masters in public health or health studies
**Eligibility**: Open to postgraduate applicants
**Level of Study**: Postgraduate
**Type**: Scholarship
**Value**: £5,000
**Frequency**: Annual
**Study Establishment**: University of Essex
**Country of Study**: United Kingdom
**Application Procedure**: Applicants must contact the department concerned
**Funding**: Private
**Contributor**: Drake-Lewis
**Additional Information**: Please check website for further information

### For further information contact:

**Email**:    scholarships@essex.ac.uk

## Economic and Social Research Council 1+3 Department of Sociology Studentships

**Purpose**: To support students on a 1 year research training programme
**Eligibility**: Open to United Kingdom or European Union applicants who have not completed a programme of research training
**Level of Study**: Postgraduate
**Type**: Scholarship

**Value**: UK students – fees plus maintenance; European Union students – fees
**Frequency**: Annual
**Study Establishment**: University of Essex
**Country of Study**: United Kingdom
**Application Procedure**: See website
**Closing Date**: March
**Contributor**: ESRC

### For further information contact:

**Email**:    fass-pg@lancaster.ac.uk

## Santander Masters Scholarship

**Purpose**: To support students from Santander network countries to undertake further study
**Eligibility**: Open to graduates residing in one of the Santander network countries who have an offer to study at Masters level
**Level of Study**: Postgraduate
**Type**: Scholarships
**Value**: £5,000
**Frequency**: Annual
**Study Establishment**: University of Essex
**Country of Study**: United Kingdom
**Application Procedure**: Please check website
**Funding**: Corporation
**Contributor**: Santander
**Additional Information**: www1.essex.ac.uk/fees-and-funding/masters/scholarships/santander-apply.aspx

### For further information contact:

**Email**:    pgtaught@lboro.ac.uk

## Tinson Fund Scholarship for Law

**Purpose**: To support students from the former Soviet Bloc interested in studying postgraduate law
**Eligibility**: Open to students from former Soviet Bloc countries, who have an offer on an LLM programme
**Level of Study**: Postgraduate
**Type**: Scholarship
**Value**: Tuition fees
**Frequency**: Annual
**Study Establishment**: University of Essex
**Country of Study**: United Kingdom
**Application Procedure**: See website for details
**Closing Date**: 31 May
**No. of awards given last year**: 1
**Additional Information**: www.essex.ac.uk/departments/law/scholarships-and-funding

**For further information contact:**

**Email:** law.gtadmin@essex.ac.uk

## University of Essex Centre for Psychoanalytic Studies Scholarship

**Purpose**: To support postgraduate study within the centre
**Eligibility**: Open to postgraduates within the centre for psychoanalytic studies
**Level of Study**: Postgraduate
**Type**: Scholarship
**Value**: Depends on funds available
**Length of Study**: 1 year
**Frequency**: Annual
**Study Establishment**: University of Essex
**Country of Study**: United Kingdom
**Application Procedure**: Applicants must contact the centre concerned
**Contributor**: University of Essex

## University of Essex Silberrad Scholarship

**Purpose**: To support graduates to pursue PhD study
**Eligibility**: Open to applicants holding a degree from or about graduate from University of Essex who have an offer place at the University of Essex and are eligible to pay Home/European Union tuition fees
**Level of Study**: Postgraduate, Research
**Type**: Scholarship
**Value**: Home/European Union tuition fee and bursary element towards living costs
**Length of Study**: Up to 1 year
**Frequency**: Annual
**Study Establishment**: University of Essex
**Country of Study**: United Kingdom
**Application Procedure**: Please check website
**Funding**: Trusts
**Contributor**: Silberrad Estate
**Additional Information**: www1.essex.ac.uk/fees-and-funding/documents/research/silberrad-2018.pdf

## University of Exeter

Postgraduate Administration Office, Northcote House, The Queen's Drive, Exeter EX4 4QJ, United Kingdom.

**Tel:** (44) 1392 723 044
**Email:** pg-ad@exeter.ac.uk
**Website:** www.exeter.ac.uk/postgraduate/money/funding/
**Contact:** Mrs Julie Gay, Scholarships Secretary

## Full-Fee Master's Scholarships

**Purpose**: Full fee waiver offered to students who best demonstrate the potential to progress to doctoral study
**Eligibility**: Applicants who demonstrate exceptional academic ability such as a first class honours or direct equivalent, and the potential to progress to doctoral study based on a submitted research proposal and personal statement will be considered
**Level of Study**: Graduate, Postgraduate
**Type**: Scholarship
**Value**: Full fee waiver of the taught Master's programme irrespective of fee status
**Length of Study**: 1 year
**Frequency**: Annual
**Study Establishment**: The University of Exeter
**Country of Study**: United Kingdom
**Application Procedure**: Application forms can be downloaded from the website www.exeter.ac.uk/scholarships/post graduate/fullmasters
**No. of awards offered**: 185
**Closing Date**: 31 March
**Funding**: Corporation
**No. of awards given last year**: 15
**No. of applicants last year**: 185
**Additional Information**: Applications will only be considered from students who have received an offer of a place on a taught Master's programme at the University

**For further information contact:**

Scholarship Administrator, Admissions Office, Laver Building, North Park Road, Exeter EX4 4QE, United Kingdom.

**Email:** admissions-scholarships@exeter.ac.uk

## University of Exeter Alumni Scholarship

**Eligibility**: In order to be eligible for the scholarship, you must obtain the necessary academic and English language entry requirements for your chosen postgraduate programme.
**Type**: Scholarship
**Value**: 10% reduction in first year tuition fee
**Length of Study**: 1 year
**Frequency**: Annual
**Application Procedure**: This award is applied automatically to University of Exeter alumni; you do not need to make seperate scholarship application. Submit your postgraduate application, remembering to complete the relevant section to indicate your previous Exeter study, by 31 August at the latest in order to be eligible.
**Closing Date**: 31 August
**Contributor**: University of Exeter

**Additional Information**: www.exeter.ac.uk/studying/funding/award/?id=2492

## University of Exeter Chapel Choir Choral and Organ Scholarship

**Purpose**: Annual scholarships offered to choral and organ practitioners to aid in recitals on behalf of the chapel choir

**Eligibility**: Based on audition. The Director of Chapel Music will invite for competitive audition on the basis of applications demonstrating a high level of competence and experience plus details of two referees familiar with the applicant's ability

**Level of Study**: Doctorate, Graduate, Postgraduate, Research, MBA

**Type**: Scholarship

**Value**: £400 per year for choral scholars, £700 per year for senior organ scholars, £300 per year for junior organ scholars

**Length of Study**: 1 year initially but may be renewed for the duration of study, where appropriate

**Frequency**: Annual

**Study Establishment**: The University of Exeter

**Country of Study**: United Kingdom

**Application Procedure**: Applicants can contact the Director for more information and request an application form

**No. of awards offered**: 60

**Closing Date**: 13 February

**Funding**: Corporation, Trusts, Individuals

**No. of awards given last year**: 10

**No. of applicants last year**: 60

**Additional Information**: From the 10 choral scholarships available, 4 are offered to sopranos, 2 each for other voice parts of alto (male and female), tenor and bass. The award for senior organ scholarship status will require recipients to direct the choir when required

### For further information contact:

**Email**:    a.j.musson@exeter.ac.uk

## World Class Business School International Scholarship

**Eligibility**: A scholarship will be awarded to the most talented international students who have had an application accepted to one of The Business School MSc programmes. Applicants must be resident in one of the following: Africa, Asia, and the Commonwealth of Independent States including students resident in Azerbaijan, Kazakhstan, Norway, Russia, Ukraine and Turkey

**Type**: Scholarship

**Value**: £10,000

**Length of Study**: 1 year

**Frequency**: Annual

**Country of Study**: United Kingdom

**Application Procedure**: Please apply at www.exeter.ac.uk/studying/funding/apply/step1/?award=1039

**Closing Date**: 31 March

**Contributor**: University of Exeter

**Additional Information**: www.exeter.ac.uk/postgraduate/money/fundingsearch/awarddetails/?id=956

### For further information contact:

**Email**:    business-school-admissions@ex.ac.uk

---

# University of Geneva

University of Geneva, Geneva, Switzerland.

**Email**:        Excellence-Master-Sciences@unige.ch

**Contact**:    Dean of the Faculty of Science

The University of Geneva is a public research university located in Geneva, Switzerland. It was founded in 1559 by John Calvin as a theological seminary and law school.

## University of Geneva Excellence Masters Fellowships

**Purpose**: The Faculty of Science of the University of Geneva, in collaboration with several sponsors, has established an Excellence Fellowship Program to support outstanding and highly motivated candidates who intend to pursue a Master of Science in any of the disciplines covered by the Faculty

**Eligibility**: The fellowships are open to students from any university with very good performance in their studies (belonging to the best 10% of their bachelor's programme) and that have completed the Bachelor degree or expect to complete it within 6 months. Selection of the applicants will be based on excellence

**Level of Study**: Doctorate, Postgraduate

**Type**: Fellowship

**Value**: CHF 10,000 to CHF 15,000 per year

**Country of Study**: Switzerland

**Application Procedure**: You must submit the application form and supporting documents as a unique PDF file by e-mail to the Dean of the Faculty of Science

**Closing Date**: 15 March
**Additional Information**: Please visit official website for more details: www.unige.ch/sciences/Enseignements/Formations/Masters/ExcellenceMasterFellowships_en.html www.scholars4dev.com/13822/university-of-geneva-excellence-masters-fellowships/

**For further information contact:**

24 rue du Général-Dufour, CH-1211 Genève 4, Switzerland.

**Tel**: (41) 22 379 71 11
**Email**: Sciences@unige.ch

## University of Glasgow

Postgraduate Research Office, Research and Enterprise, University of Glasgow, Glasgow G12 8QQ, United Kingdom.

**Tel**: (44) 1413 301 989
**Email**: s.rait@enterprise.gla.ac.uk
**Website**: www.gla.ac.uk
**Contact**: Shirley Rait

The University of Glasgow is a major research led university operating in an international context, which aims to provide education through the development of learning in a research environment, to undertake fundamental, strategic and applied research and to sustain and add value to Scottish culture, to the natural environment and to the national economy.

## Alexander and Dixon Scholarship (Bryce Bequest)

**Eligibility**: Open to the citizens of United Kingdom or a European Union national
**Level of Study**: Doctorate
**Type**: Scholarship
**Value**: Fee waiver (Home/EU fees) for 1 year of full time study or 2 years of part time study.
**Length of Study**: 3 years
**Application Procedure**: The application should consist of a 500-word case for support and a brief covering letter, including the proposed title of the thesis, the name(s) of the proposed supervisor(s), and give the applicant's email and other contact details
**Closing Date**: 21 June
**Additional Information**: www.gla.ac.uk/scholarships/alexanderanddixonscholarshipbrycebequest/

**For further information contact:**

Department Office, Department of English Literature, University of Glasgow, Glasgow G12 8QQ, United Kingdom.

**Email**: critstudies-pgscholarships@glasgow.ac.uk

## Alexander and Margaret Johnstone Postgraduate Research Scholarships

**Eligibility**: Open to students intending a research degree in the faculty of arts in a department rated 5 or 5* in the research assessment exercise
**Level of Study**: Doctorate
**Type**: Research scholarship
**Value**: Tuition fees at the Home/European Union student rate, plus stipend of between £6,000 and £7,000
**Length of Study**: 3 years
**Application Procedure**: Check website for further details
**Funding**: Government

**For further information contact:**

**Tel**: (44) 141 330 6828
**Email**: e.queune@admin.gla.ac.uk

## Bellahouston Bequest Fund

**Eligibility**: Open to postgraduate students undertaking a Masters Degree course in the faculty of arts
**Level of Study**: Postgraduate
**Type**: Scholarship
**Value**: £1,000
**Length of Study**: 1 year
**Frequency**: Annual
**Application Procedure**: The candidate must contact the clerk of the faculty of arts. Check website for further information
**Closing Date**: 31 July
**Additional Information**: Preference will be given to the Glaswegians

**For further information contact:**

**Tel**: (44) 141 330 2000
**Email**: ugs@archives.gla.ac.uk

## British Federation of Women Graduates (BFWG)

**Purpose**: To encourage applicants to become members of the Federation to help promote better links between female graduates throughout the world

**Eligibility**: Open to female graduate with academic excellence. Doctoral students of all nationalities who will be studying in the United Kingdom are eligible for the scholarship
**Level of Study**: Postgraduate
**Type**: Scholarship and award
**Value**: £1,000–6,000
**Length of Study**: Four years
**Frequency**: Annual
**Country of Study**: United Kingdom
**Application Procedure**: Check website for further details
**Closing Date**: 22 February
**Funding**: Private
**No. of awards given last year**: 6
**Additional Information**: Male graduates and female undergraduates are not eligible bfwg.org.uk/bfwg2/

**For further information contact:**

Tel:      (44) 20 7498 8037
Fax:     (44) 20 7498 5213
Email:   awardsqueries@bfwg.org.uk

## Clark Graduate Bursary Fund for International Students at University of Glasgow

**Purpose**: The aim of the bursary is to support graduates of the University of Glasgow or Strathclyde studying for, or applying to study for, a subsequent degree at a university in the United Kingdom or abroad
**Eligibility**: Applicants can either be graduates of the University of Glasgow or Strathclyde studying for, or applying to study for, a subsequent degree at a university in the United Kingdom or abroad. Applicants must be fluent in English
**Type**: Postgraduate scholarships
**Value**: The value of the bursary normally between £500 and £1,500
**Study Establishment**: Bursary is awarded in the field offered by the university
**Country of Study**: United Kingdom
**Application Procedure**: There is an annual application process. Applications can be submitted between 1st March and 1st October each year. Applications must be submitted online. Interviews of candidates selected for consideration are held in Glasgow at a Governors' meeting during November. Interviewees will usually be notified within a week of the interviews whether they will receive an award. Awards are normally paid to successful applicants before the end of the year
**Closing Date**: 15 September
**Additional Information**: For more details please visit the website scholarship-positions.com/clark-raduate-bursary-fund-international-students-university-of-glasgow-uk/2017/12/20/ scholarship-positions.com/clark-raduate-bursary-fund-internationl-students-university-of-glasgow-uk/2017/12/20/

**For further information contact:**

Email:   clarkmileendfund@gmail.com

## Glasgow Educational & Marshall Trust Award

**Purpose**: To offer financial support to those who have lived, or are currently living within the Glasgow Municipal Boundary
**Eligibility**: Open to the candidates who are above 18 years of age and a resident of Glasgow within one of the following post code areas: G1–5, G11/12, G14/15, G20, G22/23, G31, G34, G40–42, G45, 51
**Level of Study**: Doctorate, Graduate, Postdoctorate, Postgraduate, Predoctorate, Research, MBA
**Type**: Studentships and bursaries
**Value**: £50-1,000
**Length of Study**: 1 year
**Study Establishment**: Glasgow Educational and Marshall Trust
**Country of Study**: United Kingdom
**Application Procedure**: Check website for further details
**Closing Date**: 30 April
**Contributor**: Glasgow Educational and Marshall Trust
**Additional Information**: www.itpt.co.uk/glasgow-educational-marshall-trust/

**For further information contact:**

Tel:      (44) 141 4334449
Fax:     (44) 141 424 1731
Email:   sloanea@hutchesons.org

## Henry Dryerre Scholarship in Medical and Veterinary Physiology

**Eligibility**: Open to candidates holding a degree of a Scottish University with first class honours or, if in their final year, to be expected to achieve first class honours
**Level of Study**: Postgraduate
**Type**: Scholarships and fellowships
**Value**: Varies
**Frequency**: Every 3 years
**Country of Study**: Any country
**Application Procedure**: The candidate must submit the application form through a member of staff on the appropriate Henry Dryerre Nomination Form

**For further information contact:**

Email:   scholarships@glasgow.ac.uk

## Lord Kelvin/Adam Smith Postgraduate Scholarships

**Purpose**: To enable the University to recruit outstanding postgraduate research students to a range of innovative, boundary-crossing research developments
**Eligibility**: Open to postgraduate students
**Level of Study**: Postgraduate
**Type**: Scholarship
**Value**: Stipend of £13,590. The project will benefit from £5,300 per year research costs
**Length of Study**: 4 years
**Frequency**: Annual
**Application Procedure**: Check website for further details
**Funding**: Trusts
**Additional Information**: www.gla.ac.uk/scholarships/lordkelvinadamsmithlkasinterdisciplinaryphdscholarships/

### For further information contact:

**Email**: lauren-currie@enterprise.gla.ac.uk

## R. Harper Brown Memorial Scholarship

**Purpose**: To honour the late R. Harper Brown and to assist in defraying the cost of an American (United States) college student's study at a university in Scotland
**Eligibility**: Open to the candidates who are graduating seniors in high school with an acceptance and intention to attend university in Scotland or a student in an accredited American (United States) college or university looking for a study-abroad experience
**Level of Study**: Graduate
**Type**: Scholarship
**Application Procedure**: Check website for further details
**Closing Date**: 31 March
**Funding**: Private
**Contributor**: The Illinois Saint Andrew Society
**Additional Information**: www.fastweb.com/college-scholarships/scholarships/145173-r-harper-brown-memorial-scholarship

### For further information contact:

**Tel**: (44) 847 967 2725
**Email**: dforlow@yahoo.com

## Royal Historical Society: Postgraduate Research Support Grants

**Purpose**: To assist postgraduate students in the pursuit of advanced historical research
**Eligibility**: The candidate must be a postgraduate student registered for a research degree at United Kingdom Institute of Higher Education
**Level of Study**: Graduate, Research
**Type**: Award/Grant
**Country of Study**: United States of America
**Application Procedure**: Check website for further details
**Closing Date**: 12 November
**Contributor**: Royal Historical Society

### For further information contact:

**Email**: m.ransom@royalhistsoc.org

## Saint Andrew's Society of the State of New York Scholarship Fund

**Eligibility**: Open to candidates who are either graduates of a Scottish university or of Oxford or Cambridge and have completed their first Degree course
**Level of Study**: Postgraduate
**Type**: Scholarship
**Value**: Each scholarship currently provides funds of US$20,000 to US$30,000 to be used initially against tuition
**Length of Study**: 1 academic year
**Frequency**: Annual
**Country of Study**: United States of America
**Application Procedure**: The candidate must arrange for references from two academic referees to be submitted in the appropriate referee forms
**Closing Date**: 1 December
**Funding**: Trusts
**Contributor**: Saint Andrew's Society of the State of New York
**Additional Information**: www.st-andrews.ac.uk/study/fees-and-funding/postgraduate/scholarships/new-york/

### For further information contact:

**Tel**: (44) 141 330 6063
**Email**: c.omand@admin.gla.ac.uk

## Stevenson Exchange Scholarships

**Purpose**: To promote friendly relations between the students of Scotland, Germany, France and Spain
**Eligibility**: Open to current or recent students of French, German or Spanish universities who intend to study at any university in Scotland
**Level of Study**: Postdoctorate
**Type**: Scholarship
**Value**: £250–2,000
**Application Procedure**: Check website for further details

**Closing Date**: 31 January
**Additional Information**: www.ed.ac.uk/student-funding/current-students/study-abroad/undergraduate/stevenson-exchange

### For further information contact:

1 The Square, University of Glasgow, Glasgow, United Kingdom.

**Tel**:      (44) 141 330 4241
**Fax**:     (44) 141 330 4045
**Email**:   delc@ed.ac.uk

### The Catherine Mackichan Trust

**Eligibility**: Open to applications from academic centres worldwide, schools, colleges and individuals or groups
**Level of Study**: Research
**Type**: Award
**Value**: £500
**Length of Study**: 1 year
**Frequency**: Annual
**Country of Study**: Any country
**Application Procedure**: Check website for further details
**Closing Date**: 15 April
**Funding**: Trusts
**Contributor**: The Catherine Mackichan Trust
**Additional Information**: grants-search.turn2us.org.uk/grant/the-catherine-mackichan-trust-13908

### For further information contact:

**Email**:   peter.mcghee@vaslan.org.uk

### William and Margaret Kesson Award for Postgraduate Study

**Purpose**: To enable a student to undertake study leading to a postgraduate degree in the faculty of arts
**Eligibility**: Open to candidates of Scottish or English nationality possessing a graduate degree
**Level of Study**: Graduate
**Type**: Scholarship
**Length of Study**: 3 years
**Country of Study**: Any country
**Application Procedure**: Check website for further details
**Closing Date**: 1 May

### For further information contact:

**Email**:   e.queune@admin.gla.ac.uk

### William Ross Scholarship

**Purpose**: To encourage the extraction of Scottish material from archives outside Scotland relating to all aspects of the history of Scotland, the Scottish people and Scottish influence abroad
**Eligibility**: Open to candidates possessing a degree in MLitt
**Level of Study**: Research
**Type**: Scholarships and fellowships
**Value**: £1,000
**Length of Study**: 1 year
**Frequency**: Annual
**Application Procedure**: The candidate must submit a letter outlining a dissertation research proposal including the planned topic and archival research plans
**Closing Date**: 1 July
**Contributor**: Trustees of the Ross Fund

### For further information contact:

**Email**:   c.leriguer@arts.gla.ac.uk

### Wingate Scholarships

**Purpose**: To support creative or original work of intellectual, scientific, artistic, social or environmental value
**Eligibility**: Open for mature candidates and those from non-traditional academic backgrounds without any upper age limit
**Level of Study**: Unrestricted
**Type**: Scholarship
**Value**: £6,500–10,000 in any 1 year
**Length of Study**: 1 year
**Frequency**: Annual
**Country of Study**: Any country
**Application Procedure**: Check website for further details
**Closing Date**: 1 February
**Additional Information**: www.soas.ac.uk/registry/scholarships/william-ross-murray-scholarship.html

### For further information contact:

**Email**:   emma@shrimsley.com

### University of Göttingen

Project management, Equal Opportunities Office, Gosslerstrasse 9, D-37073 Göttingen, Germany.

**Tel**:      (49) 551/39 33959
**Email**:   nina.guelcher@zvw.uni-goettingen.de
**Contact**: Mrs Nina Gülcher

The University of Göttingen is a public research university in the city of Göttingen, Germany.

## Dorothea Schlozer Postdoctoral Scholarships for Female Students

**Purpose**: The University of Göttingen is inviting female postdocs from Germany to apply for Dorothea Schlozer Postdoctoral Scholarships. These scholarships are available to conduct a research project at the Georg-August-University
**Eligibility**: Female postdocs from Germany are eligible to apply. The candidate should have a very good command of English language. Therefore, the application should be written in English
**Value**: There will be 3 positions (TV-L 13, 100%, term of 2 years), one of which at the University Medical Center (UMG)
**Length of Study**: 2 years
**Country of Study**: Germany
**Application Procedure**: Applications will only be accepted through the online portal. After submitting your application you will receive an automatic confirmation of receipt via e-mail
**Closing Date**: 8 April
**Additional Information**: For more details, please visit the website www.uni-goettingen.de/de/122481.html scholarship-positions.com/dorothea-schlozer-postdoctoral-scholarships-female-students-germany/2018/02/20/

### For further information contact:

**Email**:  admin@scholarship-positions.com

---

## University of Graz

Universitätsplatz 3, A-8010 Graz, Austria.

**Contact**:  University of Graz

The University of Graz (German: Karl-Franzens-Universität Graz), located in Graz, Austria, is the largest and oldest university in Styria, as well as the second-largest and second-oldest university in Austria.

## Ida Pfeiffer Scholarships

**Purpose**: This program is designed to give applicants the opportunity to submit an application for a waiver of tuition fees
**Eligibility**: For details, visit website www.european-funding-guide.eu/other-financial-assistance/14286-ida-pfeiffer-scholarships. Successful completion of at least two semesters at the

University of Graz. Minimum age of 19 years and maximum age of 35 years, in exceptional cases (late start of studies, concurrent employment
**Type**: Scholarship
**Length of Study**: 1 year
**Country of Study**: Austria
**Application Procedure**: Eligibility requirements are as follows: 1. Successful completion of at least 2 semesters at the University of Graz. 2. Minimum age of 19
**Closing Date**: 13 April
**Funding**: Private
**Additional Information**: Please visit website international.uni-graz.at/de/stud/outgoing/s-out-mprog/ida-pfeiffer-stipendium/www.european-funding-guide.eu/other-financial-assistance/14286-ida-pfeiffer-scholarships

### For further information contact:

**Email**:  maren.leykauf@uni-graz.at

## Marie Sklodowska-Curie Actions Postdoctoral Fellowships

**Purpose**: Fellowship is available to pursue Postdoctoral programme
**Eligibility**: Please visit www.scholarshipsupdates.com/university-of-graz-marie-curie-individual-postdoctoral-fellowship-in-austria-2018/ for eligibility criteria
**Value**: Receive up to €400 for your travel costs to Austria
**Country of Study**: Austria
**Closing Date**: 1 May
**Contributor**: University of Graz
**Additional Information**: Please visit www.unica.it/unica/it/news_avvisi_s1.page?contentId=AVS93045 www.ersnet.org/professional-development/fellowships/marie-curie-postdoctoral-research-fellowships-respire

---

## University of Guelph

University Centre, Room 437, 50 Stone Road East, Guelph, ON N1G 2W1, Canada.

**Tel**:  (1) 519 824 4120
**Email**:  immccorki@uoguelph.ca
**Website**:  www.uoguelph.ca
**Contact**:  Linda McCorkindale, Associate Registrar

The University of Guelph is renowned in Canada and around the world as a research-intensive and learner-centred institution and for its commitment to open learning, internationalism and collaboration. Their vision is to be Canada's leader in creating, transmitting and applying knowledge to improve the social, cultural and economic quality of life of people in Canada and around the world.

## The Brock Doctoral Scholarship

**Purpose**: To financially support Doctoral students to attain a high level of academic achievement and to make significant teaching and research contributions

**Eligibility**: Open to students with sustained outstanding academic performance, evidence of strong teaching and research skills, demonstrated outstanding communication skills and excellent potential for research and teaching as assessed by the College Dean

**Level of Study**: Doctorate

**Type**: Scholarship

**Value**: Up to C$120,000 (C$10,000 per semester for up to 12 semesters)

**Length of Study**: 6 years

**Frequency**: Annual

**Study Establishment**: University of Guelph

**Country of Study**: Canada

**Application Procedure**: Students entering a Doctoral programme should apply to their College Dean by 1 February with a curriculum vitae, which must then be forwarded to Graduate Program Services by February 15th, with the Dean's written assessment of the candidate's research and teaching potential attached

**Closing Date**: 15 February

**Additional Information**: The Brock Doctoral Scholarship is one of the most prestigious Doctoral awards available at the University. It is hoped that award holders will be mentors for future Brock Doctoral Scholarship winners graduatestudies. uoguelph.ca/Brock

### For further information contact:

Office of Registrarial Services, University of Guelph.

**Email**: sinclair@registrar.uoguelph.ca

## University of Hertfordshire

College Lane, Hatfield, Hertfordshire AL10 9AB, United Kingdom.

**Tel**: (44) 1707 284 800

## Yaasa Scholarship

**Purpose**: The Yaasa Scholarships are available to all high school juniors and seniors as well as all students currently registered in any accredited post-secondary institution

**Level of Study**: Graduate, Postgraduate

**Type**: Scholarship

**Value**: C$1,000

**Frequency**: Annual

**Country of Study**: Any country

**Application Procedure**: The winner(s) of this annual scholarship will receive their award within 2 weeks of the listed deadline. All applicants should include their full name and mailing address with their submissions as well as the school they are currently attending

**Closing Date**: 14 June

**Additional Information**: Students who are successfully awarded the UH Graduate Scholarship are still eligible for the £500 tuition fee discount if they pay in full at registration. Please check at www.herts.ac.uk/international/fees/scholarships-for-international-students/uh-family-scholarships

### For further information contact:

**Email**: scholarships@yaasa.com

## University of Illinois

225 DKH, 1407 West Gregory, Urbana, IL 61801, United States of America.

**Tel**: (1) 217 333 8153

**Website**: www.uiuc.edu

**Contact**: Ms Diane Carson, Graduate Advising Office

## Master of Business Administration Programme

**Length of Study**: 2 years

**Application Procedure**: Applicants must complete an application form supplying US$50 fee, official transcripts, TOEFL score, statement of financial support and a personal statement

### For further information contact:

**Tel**: (1) 217 244 8019

**Email**: mba@uiuc.edu

# University of Kent

Admissions and Partnership Services, The Registry, Canterbury, Kent CT2 7NZ, United Kingdom.

| | |
|---|---|
| **Tel**: | (44) 1227 764 000 |
| **Email**: | scholarships@kent.ac.uk |
| **Website**: | www.kent.ac.uk |

The University of Kent is a United Kingdom higher education institution funded by the Higher Education Funding Council for United Kingdom (HEFCE). The university provides education of excellent quality characterized by flexibility and inter disciplinarily and informed by research and scholarship, meeting the lifelong needs of diversity students.

## Ian Gregor Scholarship

**Purpose**: To support a candidate registered for a taught MA programme in English

**Eligibility**: Candidates are expected to hold at least an Upper Second Class (Honours) Degree or equivalent. Candidates should also have applied for an external scholarship, such as AHRC

**Level of Study**: Graduate, Postgraduate

**Type**: Scholarship

**Value**: Home fees and a £500 bursary for 1 year's full-time study

**Length of Study**: 1 year

**Frequency**: Annual

**Study Establishment**: The University of Kent

**Country of Study**: United Kingdom

**Application Procedure**: See webpages at www.kent.ac.uk/english/postgraduate/fund.htm

**Closing Date**: 28 June

**Funding**: Trusts

**No. of awards given last year**: 1

**Additional Information**: www.kent.ac.uk/scholarships/search/FN03IANGRE02

### For further information contact:

| | |
|---|---|
| **Email**: | englishpg@kent.ac.uk |

## Kent Law School Studentships and Bursaries

**Purpose**: To provide funding for 1 year in the first instance, extended to a maximum of 3 years (for registered students only) based on satisfactory progress (including upgrading to a PhD). The retention of the posts will be subject to a review of progress and performance in both research and teaching after the 1st year

**Eligibility**: Candidates should hold an Upper Second Class (Honours) Degree or a good postgraduate taught degree in law

**Level of Study**: Doctorate, Postgraduate, Research

**Type**: Studentship

**Value**: £13,863 and tuition fees paid at the Home/European Union rate (up to £3,900 last year)

**Length of Study**: 1–3 years

**Frequency**: Annual

**Study Establishment**: The University of Kent

**Country of Study**: United Kingdom

**Application Procedure**: Applicants must submit to the University's recruitment and admissions office a research proposal, curriculum vitae and covering letter with an application for their chosen research degree. They should also ensure that the recruitment and admissions office receives two referees' reports by the closing date for applications. Applications are available at records.kent.ac.uk/external/admissions/pg-application.php

**No. of awards offered**: 20–30

**Closing Date**: 31 January

**Funding**: Private

**Contributor**: Kent Law School

**No. of awards given last year**: 2

**No. of applicants last year**: 20–30

**Additional Information**: Holders of the studentships will be expected to teach for a maximum of 4 hours per week in term time on an undergraduate law module, at the direction of the head of department. For further information contact the Kent Law school at kls-pgoffice@kent.ac.uk www.kent.ac.uk/scholarships/search/FN37LSSTUD02

### For further information contact:

| | |
|---|---|
| **Tel**: | (44) 1227 827949 |
| **Email**: | m.drakopoulou@kent.ac.uk |

## Language Lector Scholarships

**Purpose**: To support research

**Eligibility**: The scholarship is open to candidates who have made an application for any one of the taught MA programmes (except programmes taught in Paris or Athens) in SECL in an area related to the language they will be teaching. Candidates must hold a First Class or Upper Second Class Undergraduate Degree in a relevant subject (or have reached an appropriate point in their University education to be accepted onto a United Kingdom Master's degree). Candidates must be a native speaker of French, German, Spanish,

Catalan or Portuguese. Candidates must have excellent communication skills, both written and oral and ideally some experience of language teaching. This scholarship is open to United Kingdom, European Union and overseas fee-paying students

**Level of Study**: Postgraduate, Research

**Type**: Studentship

**Value**: 100% of tuition fees at the Home/European Union rate for a postgraduate programme within the School of European Culture and Languages (SECL) and combined maintenance grant and salary

**Length of Study**: 3 years

**Frequency**: Annual

**Study Establishment**: The University of Kent

**Country of Study**: United Kingdom

**Application Procedure**: Application is via School of European Culture and Language website www.kent.ac.uk/secl/postgraduate/funding.html?tab=language-lector-scholarships

**Funding**: Government

**Additional Information**: Candidates may be interviewed over the telephone as appropriate. Language Lectors teach for at least 20 of these 24 weeks and will be expected to teach 10 hours a week

### For further information contact:

**Email**:    seclpgadmin@kent.ac.uk

## Postgrad Solutions Study Bursaries

**Purpose**: Kent University- Kent offers well-structured and ambitious. It provides a comprehensive package of skills development training programs, careers advice, and volunteering and paid work opportunities to enhance your career prospects in a global workplace.

**Eligibility**: Scholarship is available for pursuing Postgraduate degree program

**Level of Study**: Postgraduate

**Type**: Bursary

**Value**: £500

**Frequency**: Annual

**Country of Study**: Any country

**Closing Date**: 14 September

**Funding**: International office

**Additional Information**:   www.kent.ac.uk/scholarships/search/FNADPGSOLU02

### For further information contact:

The University of Kent, Canterbury, Kent CT2 7NZ, United Kingdom.

**Tel**:    (44) 1227 764000

## School of Economics Funding

**Purpose**: To support research

**Eligibility**: All applicants for a scholarship should have completed a Master's degree in Economics or a closely-related subject. In order to be eligible for this scholarship, you must have applied for and accepted a place to study at the University

**Level of Study**: Doctorate, Postgraduate, Research

**Type**: Bursary

**Value**: Tuition fees at the Home/European Union rate and a maintenance grant, usually up to a similar rate to an ESRC grant (£13,590 for last year)

**Length of Study**: 1 year in the 1st instance, renewable for a maximum of 3 years subject to satisfactory academic performance

**Frequency**: Dependent on funds available

**Study Establishment**: The University of Kent

**Country of Study**: United Kingdom

**Application Procedure**: To apply for a scholarship, please send a curriculum vitae, including the names of two referees, a brief research proposal, transcripts of your previous degrees and a covering letter to the Postgraduate Co-ordinator, Katie Marshall at econpg@kent.ac.uk

**Closing Date**: 15 April

**Funding**: Government

**Additional Information**: Candidates should note that 4–6 hours of teaching per week and acceptable progress in the programme of study will be expected of the student. The bursary will be subject to review each year www.kent.ac.uk/economics/prospective/research/funding.html

### For further information contact:

The University of Kent, Canterbury, Kent CT2 7NZ, United Kingdom.

**Tel**:    (44) 1227 764000

**Email**:    Y.Zhu-5@kent.ac.uk

## School of English MA Scholarships for International Students at University of Kent in United Kingdom

**Purpose**: The purpose of the scholarships is to award candidates with the strongest academic records. The School of English reserves the right to distribute the scholarships amongst candidates in a way that will honour that commitment

**Eligibility**: Please check details at

**Level of Study**: Doctorate, Postgraduate

**Type**: Scholarship

**Value**: The scholarships are worth £8,000 towards the cost of tuition fees
**Length of Study**: Up to 3 years
**Frequency**: Annual
**Study Establishment**: The University of Kent
**Country of Study**: United Kingdom
**Application Procedure**: All students who have made an application to study on an MA programme in the School of English by the deadline will automatically be considered for a scholarship
**Closing Date** 31 May
**Funding**: Government, Commercial
**No. of awards given last year**: 5
**Additional Information**: www.kent.ac.uk/scholarships/search/FNADINTAMA02

**For further information contact:**

The University of Kent, Canterbury, Kent CT2 7NZ, United Kingdom.

**Tel**: (44) 1227 764000
**Email**: international@kent.ac.uk

## South East ESRC DTC Funding

**Purpose**: To support research studies
**Level of Study**: Postgraduate, Research
**Type**: Studentship
**Value**: The funding will typically cover yearly maintenance (£13,863 for last year) and fees for one of the following: +3 programme or 1+3
**Length of Study**: 3 years
**Frequency**: Annual
**Study Establishment**: The University of Kent
**Country of Study**: United Kingdom
**Application Procedure**: Applicants must complete an application form
**No. of awards offered**: 30–40
**Closing Date**: 2 February
**Funding**: Private
**Contributor**: South-East ESRC DTC
**No. of awards given last year**: 2
**No. of applicants last year**: 30–40
**Additional Information**: Studentships will be awarded on the basis of the academic excellence of both the candidate and the research proposal

**For further information contact:**

**Tel**: (44) 1227 823085
**Email**: rsg@kent.ac.uk

## University of Kent Anthropology Bursaries

**Purpose**: To support both research and taught programmes
**Eligibility**: Candidates are expected to hold an Upper Second Class (Honours) Degree
**Level of Study**: Doctorate, Postgraduate, Research
**Type**: Bursary
**Value**: Home fees only
**Length of Study**: 3 years
**Frequency**: Dependent on funds available
**Study Establishment**: The University of Kent
**Country of Study**: United Kingdom
**No. of awards given last year**: 2

**For further information contact:**

**Email**: n.a.kerry-yoxall@ukc.ac.uk

## University of Kent at Canterbury Second English Scholarship

**Purpose**: To support research
**Eligibility**: Candidates are expected to hold at least an Upper Second Class (Honours) Degree or equivalent. Candidates should also have applied for an external scholarship, such as AHRB
**Level of Study**: Postgraduate
**Type**: Research grant
**Value**: Home tuition fees up to £3,500 bursary per year for up to three years full-time study. Some undergraduate teaching or research assistance will be expected from the successful candidate
**Frequency**: Annual
**Study Establishment**: The University of Kent
**Country of Study**: United Kingdom
**Application Procedure**: Candidates must complete the postgraduate application form, indicating in the appropriate section that they are interested in being considered for departmental scholarships. A covering letter supporting the scholarship application should be attached
**Closing Date**: 30 May

## University of Kent Department of Electronics Studentships

**Purpose**: To enable well-qualified students to undertake research programmes within the department
**Eligibility**: Candidates are expected to hold an Upper Second Class (Honours) Degree or equivalent in an appropriate subject, and be nationals of one of the European Union countries
**Level of Study**: Doctorate, Postgraduate, Research
**Type**: Studentship

**Value**: Research Council studentships are at a fixed rate determined annually by EPSRC. Departmental bursaries depend on individual circumstances
**Length of Study**: 3 years
**Frequency**: Annual
**Study Establishment**: The University of Kent
**Country of Study**: United Kingdom
**Application Procedure**: Applicants should contact the Department of Electronics
**No. of awards offered**: 10
**Closing Date**: June
**Funding**: Government
**Contributor**: EPSRC
**No. of awards given last year**: 5
**No. of applicants last year**: 10

### For further information contact:

**Email**:    ee-admissions-pg@kent.ac.uk

## University of Kent Law School Studentship

**Purpose**: To support research
**Eligibility**: Applicants should normally have obtained, or be about to obtain an undergraduate degree of at least Upper Second Class Honours level (2:1 or equivalent from other countries), or a postgraduate degree
**Level of Study**: Doctorate, Postgraduate
**Type**: Scholarships
**Value**: Maintenance grant equivalent to that offered by ESRC (£13,863 in last year) and tuition fees paid at the Home/European Union rate (£3,900 in last year)
**Length of Study**: Up to 3 years
**Frequency**: Annual
**Study Establishment**: University of Kent
**Country of Study**: United Kingdom
**Application Procedure**: Applications to be filled electronically at www.kent.ac.uk/law/postgraduate/research/entryreq-research.html
**Closing Date**: 31 January
**Funding**: Government, Commercial
**No. of awards given last year**: 8
**Additional Information**: See website for further details: www.kent.ac.uk/law/postgraduate/research/KLS_research_funding.html    www.kent.ac.uk/scholarships/search/FN37 LSSTUD02

### For further information contact:

The University of Kent, Canterbury, Kent CT2 7NZ, United Kingdom.

**Tel**:      (44) 1227 764000
**Email**:    m.drakopoulou@kent.ac.uk

## University of Kent School of Drama, Film and Visual Arts Scholarships

**Purpose**: To support research
**Eligibility**: Candidates are expected to hold an Upper Second Class (Honours) Degree and be a citizen of one of the European Union countries
**Level of Study**: Postgraduate, Research
**Value**: To cover home fees only
**Length of Study**: The bursary is 1 year
**Frequency**: Annual
**Study Establishment**: The University of Kent
**Country of Study**: United Kingdom
**Application Procedure**: Applicants must indicate their interest on the postgraduate application form
**Closing Date**: 31 July
**Additional Information**: Some teaching or research assistant work may be required

### For further information contact:

**Email**:    k.j.goddard@kent.ac.uk

## University of Kent School of Mathematics, Statistics and Actuarial Science Scholarships

**Purpose**: To support research
**Eligibility**: Candidates should hold a good (first or upper second) Honours degree, or a Master's degree in a relevant subject
**Level of Study**: Doctorate, Postgraduate
**Type**: Scholarship
**Value**: Home fees and maintenance stipend
**Length of Study**: Up to 3 years
**Frequency**: Annual
**Study Establishment**: University of Kent
**Country of Study**: United Kingdom
**Application Procedure**: See webpages at www.kent.ac.uk/
**Closing Date**: 20 April
**Funding**: Government, Commercial
**No. of awards given last year**: 5

## University of Kent School of Politics and International Relations Scholarships

**Purpose**: To support research
**Eligibility**: These scholarships are available to Home/European Union/Overseas students who have been made an offer by Kent for MPhil/PhD study
**Level of Study**: Doctorate, Postgraduate
**Type**: Scholarship
**Value**: Home fees and maintenance stipend

**Length of Study**: Up to 3 years
**Frequency**: Annual
**Study Establishment**: University of Kent
**Country of Study**: United Kingdom
**Application Procedure**: See webpages at www.kent.ac.uk/scholarships/postgraduate/departmental/politicsandir.html
**Closing Date**: April
**Funding**: Government, Commercial
**No. of awards given last year**: 2

## University of Kent School of Psychology Scholarships

**Purpose**: To support research
**Eligibility**: Candidates must hold a good Honours degree (first class or 2i) or a Master's degree at merit or distinction in Psychology. Non-British qualifications will be judged individually; we will generally require an overall result in the top two grading categories
**Level of Study**: Doctorate, Postgraduate
**Type**: Scholarship
**Value**: Home fees and maintenance stipend
**Length of Study**: Up to 3 years
**Study Establishment**: University of Kent
**Country of Study**: United Kingdom
**Application Procedure**: Please check at www.kent.ac.uk/scholarships/postgraduate/departmental/psychology.html
**Closing Date**: April
**Funding**: Government, Commercial
**No. of awards given last year**: 5

## University of Kent School of Social Policy, Sociology and Social Research Scholarships

**Purpose**: To support research
**Eligibility**: Candidates should hold a good (First or Upper Second Class) Honours degree or equivalent, in a relevant discipline
**Level of Study**: Doctorate, Postgraduate
**Type**: Scholarship
**Value**: The School will award up to three £3,000 scholarships (as contribution to tuition fees) on a competitive basis.
**Length of Study**: Up to 3 years
**Frequency**: Annual
**Study Establishment**: University of Kent
**Country of Study**: United Kingdom
**Application Procedure**: See webpages at www.kent.ac.uk/sspssr/studying/scholarships-and-bursaries/index.html
**Closing Date**: 26 June
**Funding**: Government, Commercial
**No. of awards given last year**: 3

**Additional Information**: This scholarship will be in addition to any Kent scholarships and discounts (such as the £1,000 Graduate School Scholarship, 10% Loyalty Discount and the School £500 discount for high performing students) www.kent.ac.uk/scholarships/search/FN40SAM00002

### For further information contact:

**Email**: K.Glezakou@kent.ac.uk

## University of KwaZulu-Natal

Westville Campus, Private Bag X54001, Durban, South Africa.

**Email**: heard@ukzn.ac.za
**Website**: www.heard.org.za/

HEARD is a leading applied research centre with a global reputation for its research, education programmes, technical services, partnerships and networks, devoted to addressing the broad health challenges of Africa. HEARD was established in 1998 and is based at the University of KwaZulu-Natal, South Africa.

## Health Economics and HIV/AIDS Research Division PhD Scholarships

**Purpose**: Under the supervision of Professor Nana Poku and with the generous support of Sida/NORAD, HEARD is offering up to four full-time PhD Research Scholarships in any of the following key areas of strategic focus: Sexual and Reproductive Health; Health Systems Strengthening and Economics of Critical Enablers in HIV Programming
**Eligibility**: Applicant must have the below criteria. 1. Hold a Master's Degree in a pertinent subject or a first or upper second class degree together with a track record of professional experience in a health o health-related field. 2. Have demonstrable research experience. 3. Undertake to register for a PhD dissertation (full time) at the University of KwaZulu–Natal (UKZN). 4. Make a commitment to remain on the African continent for at least TWO years after graduation
**Value**: The value of each scholarship is ZAR 540,000 paid over three years
**Length of Study**: Scholarships will be paid in tranches over 3 years. Tranche payments will be conditional on research progress
**Country of Study**: South Africa
**Application Procedure**: 1. A letter of motivation and CV. 2. An eight to ten page concept note on one of HEARD's key

thematic research areas: Sexual & Reproductive Health & Rights; Gender, Equality & Health; Health Governance & Finance; and Health Systems Strengthening. 3. Certified copies of both your academic qualifications and your full academic records. If qualifications were obtained from non-English speaking countries please ensure that an official English translation is included. 4. A certified copy of your ID/passport. 5. Two letters of reference, at least one of which must be academic. The second can be from an individual of professional standing

**Closing Date**: 30 January

**Funding**: Private

**Additional Information**: www.afterschoolafrica.com/43874/university-of-kwazulu-natal-health-economics-and-hiv-aids-research-division-heard-phd-scholarships-2020-for-african-students/

### For further information contact:

**Email**: Hedderwick@ukzn.ac.za

---

# University of Leeds

Postgraduate Scholarships, Research Student Administration, Leeds LS2 9JT, United Kingdom.

**Tel**: (44) 113 343 4077 ext 34077
**Email**: pg_scholarships@leeds.ac.uk
**Website**: www.scholarships.leeds.ac.uk
**Contact**: Erika Smith, Senior Clerk

The University of Leeds aims to promote excellence and to achieve and sustain international standing in higher education teaching, learning and research, and to serve a wide range of student constituencies, social and professional communities and industrial, commercial and government agencies, locally, nationally and internationally.

## Beit Trust Postgraduate Scholarships

**Purpose**: To support Postgraduate Study or research at Masters' level (MSc/MA)

**Eligibility**: Open to persons under 30 years of age, or 35 years for medical doctors, who are university graduates domiciled in Zambia, Zimbabwe or Malawi. Applicants must be nationals of those countries, and have an Honours degree at undergraduate level

**Level of Study**: Postgraduate

**Type**: Scholarship

**Value**: Academic fees, living expenses, other allowances, economy return airfares and allowance toward laptops

**Length of Study**: a maximum of 2 years at a South African University or 1 year at a United Kingdom University

**Frequency**: Annual

**Study Establishment**: The University of Leeds

**Country of Study**: United Kingdom

**Application Procedure**: Please see the Beit Trust website on 1 April for the new Scholarship application process. Applicants from Zimbabwe and Malawi should contact the Harare office at: africa@beittrust.org.uk

**No. of awards offered**: 720

**Closing Date**: 12 February

**Funding**: Private

**No. of awards given last year**: 19

**No. of applicants last year**: 720

**Additional Information**: Zambian applicants should contact the Beit Trust United Kingdom office at: scholarships@beittrust.org.uk beittrust.org.uk/beit-trust-scholarships

### For further information contact:

**Tel**: (44) 1483 772575
**Email**: scholarships@beittrust.org.uk

## Canon Collins Trust-FCO Chevening-University of Leeds Scholarships

**Purpose**: To provide awards to students of high academic calibre, who demonstrate both academic excellence and the potential to become leaders, decision makers and opinion formers in their own countries

**Eligibility**: Open to candidates from Angola, Botswana, Lesotho, Malawi Mozambique, Namibia, South Africa, Swaziland, Zambia or Zimbabwe. Applicants must already hold a degree of equivalent standard to a United Kingdom upper second class honours degree. An adequate standard of English is required

**Level of Study**: Postgraduate

**Type**: Scholarship

**Value**: Academic fees, living expenses, other allowances, economy return airfares

**Length of Study**: 1 year

**Frequency**: Annual

**Study Establishment**: The University of Leeds

**Country of Study**: United Kingdom

**Application Procedure**: Applicants must complete an application form available on request from the Canon Collins Trust

**No. of awards offered**: Not known

**Closing Date**: 28 February

**Funding**: Government, Private

**No. of awards given last year**: 10

**No. of applicants last year**: Not known

**For further information contact:**

**Email**: info@canoncollins.org.uk

## Derek Fatchett Memorial Scholarships (Palestine)

**Purpose**: To provide awards to students of high academic calibre

**Eligibility**: Open to candidates who have obtained or are about to obtain the equivalent of a United Kingdom First or Second Class (Honours) Degree. Candidates must be nationals of Palestine

**Level of Study**: Postgraduate

**Type**: Scholarship

**Value**: Academic fees, living expenses, books, equipment, arrival and departure allowance, economy return airfares and the production of a dissertation

**Length of Study**: 1 year

**Frequency**: Annual

**Study Establishment**: The University of Leeds

**Country of Study**: United Kingdom

**Application Procedure**: Application procedures are now handled by the British Council offices in Ramallah and East Jerusalem

**No. of awards offered**: Not known

**Closing Date**: 31 May

**Funding**: Private

**No. of applicants last year**: Not known

**For further information contact:**

**Email**: Lmec@Lmec.org.uk

## Frank Parkinson Scholarship

**Purpose**: To provide postgraduate scholarships for United Kingdom research students of high calibre

**Eligibility**: Candidates must be commencing PhD study for the first time and hold at least a United Kingdom upper second class honours degree or equivalent. Candidates must have British parents who have been domiciled in Yorkshire for a period of not less than 10 years

**Level of Study**: Doctorate

**Type**: Scholarship

**Value**: Fees at the United Kingdom rate plus a maintenance allowance

**Length of Study**: Up to 3 years, subject to satisfactory progress

**Frequency**: Annual

**Study Establishment**: University of Leeds

**Country of Study**: United Kingdom

**Application Procedure**: An application form must be completed and returned to the Postgraduate Scholarships Office by the relevant date

**No. of awards offered**: 39

**Closing Date**: 1 June

**Funding**: Private

**No. of awards given last year**: 2

**No. of applicants last year**: 39

**For further information contact:**

**Email**: fbsgrad@leeds.ac.uk

## Frank Stell Scholarship

**Purpose**: To provide postgraduate scholarships for United Kingdom research students of high calibre

**Eligibility**: Candidates must be commencing PhD study for the first time and hold at least a United Kingdom Upper Second Class Honours degree or equivalent. Candidates should be resident, or have parents resident within the former administrative area of the County Council of the West Riding of Yorkshire

**Level of Study**: Doctorate

**Type**: Scholarship

**Value**: Fees at the University of Leeds standard United Kingdom/European Union rate plus a maintenance allowance

**Length of Study**: Up to 3 years, subject to satisfactory progress

**Frequency**: Dependent on funds available

**Study Establishment**: University of Leeds

**Country of Study**: United Kingdom

**Application Procedure**: Details provided on website www. scholarships.leeds.ac.uk

**Additional Information**: The scholarship is subject to funding and will only be advertised on www.scholarships. leeds.ac.uk

**For further information contact:**

**Email**: fbsgrad@leeds.ac.uk

## Henry Ellison Scholarship

**Purpose**: To provide postgraduate scholarships for United Kingdom and European Union research students of high calibre

**Eligibility**: Candidates must be from the United Kingdom or an European Union country (or eligible to pay fees at the United Kingdom rate) and be commencing PhD study for the first time. Candidates must hold at least a United Kingdom

Upper Second Class Honours degree or equivalent and be a University of Leeds graduate

**Level of Study**: Doctorate

**Type**: Scholarship

**Value**: Fees at the University of Leeds standard United Kingdom/European Union rate plus a maintenance allowance

**Length of Study**: Up to 3 years, subject to satisfactory progress

**Frequency**: Dependent on funds available

**Study Establishment**: University of Leeds

**Country of Study**: United Kingdom

**Application Procedure**: Details provided on website www. scholaships.leeds.ac.uk

**Additional Information**: The award is available within the School of Physics and Astronomy. The scholarship is subject to funding and will only be advertised on scholarships.leeds. ac.uk scholarization.blogspot.com/2011/02/henry-ellison-scholarship-at-university.html

### For further information contact:

**Email**:   maps.pgr.admissions@leeds.ac.uk

### John Henry Garner Scholarship

**Purpose**: To provide postgraduate scholarships for United Kingdom and European Union research students of high calibre

**Eligibility**: Candidates must be from the United Kingdom or an European Union country (or eligible to pay fees at the United Kingdom rate) and be commencing PhD study for the first time. Candidates must hold at least a United Kingdom Upper Second Class Honours degree or equivalent

**Level of Study**: Doctorate

**Type**: Scholarship

**Value**: A maintenance grant at the standard UKRI rate of £14,000 for 3 years (full-time), or £8,400 for 5 years (part-time)

**Length of Study**: Full-time (3 years) or part-time (5 years)

**Frequency**: Dependent on funds available

**Study Establishment**: University of Leeds

**Country of Study**: United Kingdom

**Application Procedure**: Details provided on website www. scholarships.leed.ac.uk

**Closing Date**: 1 June

**Additional Information**: For further information please contact the www.leeds.ac.uk/info/130500/faculties phd.leeds.ac. uk/funding/24-john-henry-garner-scholarship-2020

### For further information contact:

**Tel**:   (44) 113 343 34077

### Marks and Spencer - Leeds University- FCO Chevening Scholarships

**Purpose**: To provide postgraduate scholarships to students of high academic calibre

**Eligibility**: Open to candidates from Hong Kong who have obtained, or are about to obtain, a first degree of a similar standard to a United Kingdom good Upper Second Class (Honours) Degree. An adequate standard of English language is required

**Level of Study**: Postgraduate

**Type**: Scholarship

**Value**: Full tuition fees, maintenance allowance, books, equipment and production of dissertation

**Length of Study**: 1 year

**Frequency**: Annual

**Study Establishment**: The University of Leeds

**Country of Study**: United Kingdom

**Application Procedure**: By application form and acceptance onto taught course. Both application forms are available from the University and British Council (Hong Kong)

**Funding**: Government, Commercial

**No. of awards given last year**: 1

**Additional Information**: The address for the British Council in Hong Kong is: The Education Exchange Unit, 255 Hennessey Road, Wanchai, Hong Kong

### For further information contact:

**Email**:   scholarships@gcu.ac.uk

### Mary and Alice Smith Memorial Scholarship

**Purpose**: To provide postgraduate scholarships for United Kingdom research students of high calibre

**Eligibility**: Candidates must be British and be commencing PhD study for the first time. Candidates must hold at least a United Kingdom Upper Second Class Honours degree or equivalent

**Level of Study**: Doctorate

**Type**: Scholarship

**Value**: A maintenance grant at the standard UKRI rate of £14,000 for 3 years (full-time), or £8,400 for 5 years (part-time)

**Length of Study**: Full-time (3 years) or part-time (5 years)

**Frequency**: Dependent on funds available

**Study Establishment**: University of Leeds

**Country of Study**: United Kingdom

**Application Procedure**: Details provided on www.scholar ships.leeds.ac.uk

**Closing Date**: 1 June

**Additional Information**: For further information please contact the www.leeds.ac.uk/info/130500/faculties phd.leeds.ac.uk/funding/43-mary-and-alice-smith-memorial-scholarship-2020

**For further information contact:**

Tel:     (44) 113 343 34077
Email:  pg_scholarships@ac.uk

## Stanley Burton Research Scholarship

**Purpose**: To provide postgraduate scholarships for United Kingdom/European Union research students of high calibre
**Eligibility**: Candidates must be from United Kingdom or an European Union country and be commencing PhD study for the first time. Candidates must hold at least a United Kingdom upper second class honours degree or equivalent
**Level of Study**: Doctorate
**Type**: Scholarship
**Value**: A maintenance grant at the standard UKRI rate of £14,000 for 3 years (full-time), or £8,400 for 5 years (part-time)
**Length of Study**: Full-time (3 years) or part-time (5 years)
**Frequency**: Dependent on funds available
**Study Establishment**: University of Leeds
**Country of Study**: United Kingdom
**Application Procedure**: Details provided on www.scholarships.leeds.ac.uk
**Closing Date**: 1 June
**Additional Information**: The award is available within the School of Music. This scholarship is subject to funding and will only be advertised on scholarships.leeds.ac.uk phd.leeds.ac.uk/funding/23-stanley-burton-research-scholarship-2020

**For further information contact:**

Tel:   (44) 113 343 34077

## University of Leeds International Fee Bursary (Vietnam)

**Purpose**: To provide scholarships to students of high academic calibre
**Eligibility**: Open to nationals of Vietnam who have obtained a degree equivalent to a good Second Class (Honours) Degree. An adequate standard of English is required
**Level of Study**: Postgraduate
**Type**: Scholarship
**Value**: Academic fees

**Length of Study**: 1 year
**Frequency**: Annual
**Study Establishment**: The University of Leeds
**Country of Study**: United Kingdom
**Application Procedure**: Applicants must address a letter of application to the School of Computing
**Closing Date**: 10 June
**Funding**: Private
**No. of awards given last year**: 1

## University of Leeds International Fee Bursary (Vietnam) - for Subject Areas Listed below Leeds

**Purpose**: To provide scholarships to students of high academic calibre in the School of Computing, Politics and International Studies and Leeds University Business School
**Eligibility**: Open to nationals of Vietnam who have obtained a degree equivalent to a good Second Class (Honours) Degree. An adequate standard of English is required
**Level of Study**: Postgraduate
**Type**: Scholarship
**Value**: Academic fees
**Length of Study**: 1 year
**Frequency**: Annual
**Study Establishment**: The University of Leeds
**Country of Study**: United Kingdom
**Application Procedure**: Applicants must make an application in letter format to the Taught Postgraduate Secretary in the school they intend to study
**No. of awards offered**: Not known
**Closing Date**: 29 May
**Funding**: Private
**No. of awards given last year**: 4
**No. of applicants last year**: Not known

**For further information contact:**

Email:   info@lubs.leeds.ac.uk

## University of Leeds International Fee Bursary (Vietnam) - Information Systems/Multimedia Systems

**Purpose**: To provide scholarships to students of high academic calibre who wish to study in the school of computing
**Eligibility**: Applicants must be nationals of Vietnam and must already have obtained a good Second Class (Honours) Degree. An adequate standard of English is also required
**Level of Study**: Postgraduate
**Type**: Scholarship

**Value**: Academic fees
**Length of Study**: 1 year
**Frequency**: Annual
**Study Establishment**: The University of Leeds
**Country of Study**: United Kingdom
**Application Procedure**: Applicants must make an application in letter form to the Taught Postgraduate Secretary in the School of Computing
**Closing Date**: 11 June
**Funding**: Private
**No. of awards given last year**: 1

### For further information contact:

International office, University of Leeds, Leeds LS2 9JT, United Kingdom.

**Email**: info@lubs.leeds.ac.uk

## University of Leicester

University Road, Leicester LE1 7RH, United Kingdom.

**Tel**: (44) 162 522 522
**Email**: upim@admin.le.ac.uk
**Website**: www.le.ac.uk
**Contact**: Mr K J Julian, Registrar and Secretary

## Central United Kingdom NERC Training Alliance (CENTA) PhD Studentships for European Union Students

**Purpose**: Studentships are available to pursue PhD research programme
**Type**: Award
**Value**: CENTA has been awarded £4.9 million from the Natural Environment Research Council (NERC)
**Length of Study**: 5 years
**Country of Study**: United Kingdom
**Closing Date**: 22 January

### For further information contact:

**Email**: communications@ukri.org

## College of Science and Engineering Postgraduate Scholarship Scheme

**Purpose**: University of Leicester's aim is to be a world-class research-intensive university and deliver teaching and facilitate learning of the highest quality

**Eligibility**: Applicants must be classified as an international (non-European Union) student for fee purposes. The fee discount will be calculated on the basis of the standard tuition fee, excluding components for 'with industry' degrees. In accordance with scholarship guidelines, students are allowed to hold only one University of Leicester scholarship, awarded either centrally or by a department. If you are awarded more than one scholarship, you will therefore receive only the higher value award. The scholarship is only valid for entry in September. If you currently have a conditional offer of a place at the University, you will still need to fulfil any conditions stated on your offer letter. The scholarship is only available for campus-based courses
**Type**: Postgraduate scholarships
**Value**: Scholarship worth up to £5,600 per year of full
**Study Establishment**: Scholarships are awarded in the field of Chemistry, Engineering, Geography, Informatics, Mathematics and Physics and Astronomy
**Country of Study**: United Kingdom
**Application Procedure**: Academic qualifications and transcripts Personal statement/research proposal Two completed references (one must be academic) OR names and contact details of two people from whom references can be requested (one must be an academic referee). Proof of English language competency (if your first language is not English)
**Additional Information**: please browse the website for more details scholarship-positions.com/college-of-science-engineering-postgraduate-scholarship-scheme-uk/2017/12/18/ le.ac.uk/study/postgraduates/fees-funding/scholarships-discounts/scieng-pg

### For further information contact:

The University of Leicester, University Road, Leicester LE1 7RH, United Kingdom.

**Email**: scholarships@le.ac.uk

## PhD Studentships in Computer Science

**Purpose**: To support research organizations attract the best people into postgraduate research and training and to provide doctoral training grant support
**Eligibility**: Please check at EPSRC website at www2.le.ac.uk/study/research/funding/epsrc-computing
**Level of Study**: Doctorate
**Type**: Studentship
**Value**: The successful applicants will receive an annual stipend of at least £13,863 together with a conference allowance and training support grant worth £600 each year
**Length of Study**: 3 years
**Frequency**: Dependent on funds available

**Study Establishment**: University of Leicester, Computer Science Department

**Country of Study**: United Kingdom

**Application Procedure**: Please refer to the University of Leicester website at www2.le.ac.uk/study/research/funding/epsrc-computing. Our PhD superiors have a range of interests and the aim is to align you with someone with expertise in your field. Details of our research themes are on the website

**Funding**: Government

**Contributor**: EPSRC (DTG)

**Additional Information**: Applications are considered throughout the year. Refer to advertisement on website

**For further information contact:**

**Email**:     fdv1@mcs.le.ac.uk

## PhD Studentships in Mathematics

**Eligibility**: United Kingdom and European Union PhD students, who have been residents in the United Kingdom for 3 years prior to application, and fees-only funding for other European Union students

**Level of Study**: Doctorate, Research

**Type**: Studentship

**Value**: £14,057 in the first year, rising in successive years, and full tuition fees

**Length of Study**: 3.5 years

**Country of Study**: United Kingdom

**Application Procedure**: Applications can be made online and submitted to admissions office. Information on how to apply and what supporting documents needed can be found at www2.le.ac.uk/research/degrees/phd/maths/supervision

**For further information contact:**

**Email**:     pgresearch@maths.ed.ac.uk

## President's Postgraduate Scholarship Scheme

**Purpose**: This is a postgraduate scholarship that enables international students to get a chance to study in University of Leicester, United Kingdom

**Eligibility**: 1. This scholarship is for new international (non-EU) students on a full-time, taught, campus-based Masters course starting in September 2020 or January 2021. 2. This scholarship is open to applicants who already have an offer (conditional or unconditional) to study for a Masters degree programme at the University. 3. If you receive your offer to study by 10 March 2020, please submit your scholarship application by the first deadline of 30 March 2020. If you receive your offer to study after 10 March 2020, please apply by the second deadline of 13 July 2020. 4. You cannot combine this scholarship with a full scholarship (for tuition fees and living costs) from any other source. You are able to receive only one partial scholarship from the University. If you have a partial scholarship from other sources you will still be considered for the President's Postgraduate Scholarship. 5. This scholarship is not available for distance learning courses.

**Value**: Value of Scholarship: £3,000 in the form of reduction in tuition fees

**Length of Study**: 1 to 2 years

**Country of Study**: Any country

**Application Procedure**: Send your completed application by email to scholarships@le.ac.uk

**No. of awards offered**: 100

**Closing Date**: 31 July

**Additional Information**: le.ac.uk/study/postgraduates/fees-funding/scholarships-discounts/presidents-pg

**For further information contact:**

**Tel**:     (44) 141 331 3000

**Email**:     ukroenquiries@gcu.ac.uk

## University of Limerick

Kemmy Business School, Limerick, Ireland.

**Tel**:     (353) 61 202 116
**Email**:     elaine.kirwan@ul.ie
**Website**:     www.ul.ie
**Contact**:     Elaine Kirwan

## Kemmy Business School: PhD Scholarship

**Purpose**: The competition is open to prospective students, as well as those who have registered in the current calendar year, and will cover fees and a stipend of €1,000 per month for years one to four of a full time traditional or structured PhD programme

**Eligibility**: Applicants should have first or upper second class degree (Level 8 – National Qualifications Authority of Ireland or equivalent) or a Master's degree in economics, statistics, demography, mathematics, computer science or cognate discipline. They should have strong econometric skills, computer programming skills and demonstrated experience in at least one high-level language, such as R or Matheamatica. Applicants should have strong verbal and written communication skills and should have the ability to write concise and accessible reports for both specialist and non-specialist audiences. Non-European Union citizens are eligible for this international PhD scholarship

**Level of Study**: Doctorate

**Type**: PhD scholarship
**Value**: The value of the scholarship is €14,000 per year plus European Union fees for a maximum of 3 years (the final year fee will have to be paid by the student)
**Frequency**: Every 3 years
**Country of Study**: Ireland
**Application Procedure**: The mode of applying is electronically. Completed application forms should be submitted electronically to michelle.cunningham@ul.ie
**Closing Date**: 10 May
**Contributor**: Kemmy Business School at the University of Limerick
**Additional Information**: The duration is of maximum 3 years www.ul.ie/business/news/2012/04/kbs-phd-scholarships

**For further information contact:**

**Email**:    rebecca.gachet@ul.ie

# University of Lincoln

Brayford Pool, Lincoln LN6 7TS, United Kingdom.

**Tel**:          (44) 1522 882 000
**Website**:   www.lincoln.ac.uk
**Contact**:   University of Lincoln

Lincoln is ranked 11th in the United Kingdom for student satisfaction in the National Student Survey (NSS) 2016. The University is committed to developing enterprising graduates, with Lincoln students enjoying good graduate prospects and many going on to start their own successful businesses. The University of Lincoln is producing world-leading research across many subject areas.

## Academic Excellence Scholarship

**Purpose**: For programmes commencing in January / February and September, the university invites applications for Academic Excellence Scholarships from students from around the world. Students from China, India, Malaysia, Norway, Nigeria, Saudi Arabia, Thailand, Vietnam and the United States are eligible to apply for these scholarships
**Eligibility**: The University invites applications from students in the following countries: China, India, Malaysia, Norway, Nigeria, Saudi Arabia, Thailand, Vietnam and the United States. Applicants must have their previous degree. Applicants must meet the programmes general English language requirements

**Type**: Postgraduate scholarships
**Value**: £5,000 which will be deducted from your tuition fees during the first year of enrolment
**Study Establishment**: Scholarships are awarded to learn in any of subjects offered by the university
**Country of Study**: United Kingdom
**Application Procedure**: To apply for an Academic Excellence Scholarship, you will need to complete an Academic Excellence Scholarship Application Form and submit to intscholarships-at-lincoln.ac.uk
**Closing Date**: 22 June
**Additional Information**: For more details please visit the website          scholarship-positions.com/academic-excellence-scholarship-university-lincoln-uk/2017/01/05/     afterschool.my/scholarship/university-lincoln-academic-excellence-scholarship

## Egypt Scholarship

**Purpose**: To offer Egypt Scholarships to high achieving postgraduate applicants
**Eligibility**: Be an Egyptian citizen
**Level of Study**: Postgraduate
**Type**: Scholarship
**Value**: This scholarship is valued at £5,000
**Country of Study**: United Kingdom
**Application Procedure**: Submit application to intscholarships@lincoln.ac.uk
**Additional Information**: For further information, please contact the international@lincoln.ac.uk
www.lincoln.ac.uk/home/studywithus/scholarshipsandbursaries/

**For further information contact:**

**Email**:    international@lincoln.ac.uk

## Ghana Scholarship

**Purpose**: The University of Lincoln are delighted to offer Ghana Scholarships to high achieving applicants
**Type**: Scholarship
**Value**: £5,000
**Country of Study**: Any country
**Application Procedure**: Submit the application to intscholarships@lincoln.ac.uk
**Closing Date**: 22 June

**For further information contact:**

**Email**:    international@lincoln.ac.uk

## Global Postgraduate Scholarship

**Purpose**: To be eligible for the scholarship, students must hold a recognised Bachelor degree with a minimum grade of 2:2 or equivalent. Please note that this scholarship is not available for MPhil/PhD programmes.

**Eligibility**: 1. University of Lincoln International Scholarships take the form of a tuition fee reduction upon enrolment. 2. University of Lincoln International Scholarships are non-transferable and are not valid in conjunction with each other; only one Scholarship per student per course will be applied. 3. The University of Lincoln reserves the right to withdraw any University of Lincoln International Scholarship at any point and without notice. 4. Students who are sponsored by an organisation such as an external funding body, Government, or employer are not eligible to receive a University of Lincoln International Scholarship.

**Level of Study**: Postgraduate

**Type**: Scholarship

**Value**: Valued at £2,000

**Frequency**: Varies

**Country of Study**: Any country

**Application Procedure**: You do not need to apply for this scholarship. You will automatically be considered for a Global Postgraduate Scholarship once you have submitted your course application.

**Funding**: Trusts

**Additional Information**: For further information, please contact the international@lincoln.ac.uk www.lincoln.ac.uk/home/studywithus/scholarshipsandbursaries/

### For further information contact:

**Email**:    international@lincoln.ac.uk

## India Scholarship

**Purpose**: The Lincoln India Scholarship is aimed at supporting high-achieving postgraduate students from across India.

**Eligibility**: 1. University of Lincoln International Scholarships take the form of a tuition fee reduction upon enrolment. 2. University of Lincoln International Scholarships are non-transferable and are not valid in conjunction with each other; only one Scholarship per student per course will be applied. 3. The University of Lincoln reserves the right to withdraw any University of Lincoln International Scholarship at any point and without notice. 4. Students who are sponsored by an organisation such as an external funding body, Government,

or employer are not eligible to receive a University of Lincoln International Scholarship.

**Level of Study**: Postgraduate

**Type**: Scholarship

**Value**: £5,000

**Length of Study**: 1 year

**Frequency**: Varies

**Country of Study**: Any country

**Funding**: Trusts

**Additional Information**:    www.lincoln.ac.uk/home/studywithus/scholarshipsandbursaries/

### For further information contact:

**Email**:    intscholarships@lincoln.ac.uk

## Indonesia Scholarship

**Purpose**: The University of Lincoln Indonesia Scholarship is aimed at supporting high-achieving postgraduate students from across Indonesia

**Eligibility**: 1. University of Lincoln International Scholarships take the form of a tuition fee reduction upon enrolment. 2. University of Lincoln International Scholarships are non-transferable and are not valid in conjunction with each other; only one Scholarship per student per course will be applied. 3. The University of Lincoln reserves the right to withdraw any University of Lincoln International Scholarship at any point and without notice. 4. Students who are sponsored by an organisation such as an external funding body, Government, or employer are not eligible to receive a University of Lincoln International Scholarship

**Level of Study**: Postgraduate

**Type**: Scholarship

**Value**: This scholarship is valued at £5,000

**Frequency**: Varies

**Country of Study**: Any country

**Funding**: Trusts

**Additional Information**:    www.lincoln.ac.uk/home/studywithus/scholarshipsandbursaries/

### For further information contact:

**Email**:    intscholarships@lincoln.ac.uk

## Lincoln Alumni Master of Architecture Scholarship

**Purpose**: This scholarship is available to Home/European Union students holding a University of Lincoln degree when enrolling on the Master of Architecture programme (MArch)

**Eligibility**: 1. You will have previously completed an undergraduate degree (or equivalent qualification that leads to postgraduate study), Graduate Certificate or Graduate Diploma at the University of Lincoln, confirmed by a University of Lincoln Board of Examiners 2. You are subject to tuition fees of £9,250 per year for Home/EU or £14,600 for International (pro-rata for part-time studies) 3. You will be enrolled on the University's Student Management System on either the MSc Nursing with Registered Nurse (Adult/Child/Mental Health), MSc Physiotherapy (Pre-registration) or MSc Occupational Therapy (Pre-registration) programme 4. All tuition fees and payments due to the University in relation to any previous study have been paid in full.

**Level of Study**: Postgraduate

**Type**: Scholarship

**Value**: £1,000 will be paid directly to the student for each year of study for each completed academic year of study, with part-time students eligible for a pro-rata payment.

**Country of Study**: United Kingdom

**Application Procedure**: No procedure is required. Eligible students will receive this scholarship upon enrolling for the Master of Architecture programme

**Funding**: Private

**Additional Information**: Please contact admissions@lincoln.ac.uk for further details. www.lincoln.ac.uk/home/studywithus/scholarshipsandbursaries/

**For further information contact:**

**Email**:    intscholarships@lincoln.ac.uk

## Master of Science Sport Science: Applied Sport Science Bursary

**Purpose**: Up to three Applied Sport Science Bursaries will be offered to exceptional students enrolling on MSc Sport Science program

**Level of Study**: Postgraduate

**Type**: Bursary

**Value**: £1,500

**Frequency**: Varies

**Country of Study**: Any country

**Application Procedure**: Apply online

**Closing Date**: 19 September

**Funding**: Trusts

**For further information contact:**

**Tel**:      (44) 1522 886651

**Email**:    swillmott@lincoln.ac.uk

## Nigeria Scholarship

**Purpose**: The University of Lincoln Nigeria Scholarship is aimed at supporting high-achieving postgraduate students from across Nigeria

**Eligibility**: Be a Nigerian citizen. Already hold a conditional or unconditional offer from the University of Lincoln for a full-time postgraduate taught or Master's by Research programme commencing in September

**Type**: Scholarship

**Value**: The scholarship is valued at £5,000

**Country of Study**: United Kingdom

**Application Procedure**: Submit applications to intscholarships@lincoln.ac.uk

**Funding**: Private

**Additional Information**: For further information, please contact the International Office

**For further information contact:**

**Email**:    intscholarships@lincoln.ac.uk

## Thai Scholarship

**Purpose**: For programmes commencing in 2019, the University of Lincoln are delighted to offer Thai Scholarships to high achieving postgraduate applicants.

**Eligibility**: 1. University of Lincoln International Scholarships take the form of a tuition fee reduction upon enrolment. 2. University of Lincoln International Scholarships are non-transferable and are not valid in conjunction with each other; only one Scholarship per student per course will be applied. 3. The University of Lincoln reserves the right to withdraw any University of Lincoln International Scholarship at any point and without notice. 4. Students who are sponsored by an organisation such as an external funding body. Government, or employer are not eligible to receive a University of Lincoln International Scholarship

**Level of Study**: Postgraduate

**Type**: Scholarship

**Value**: £5,000

**Frequency**: Varies

**Country of Study**: Any country

**Funding**: Trusts

**Additional Information**: For further information, please contact the international@lincoln.ac.uk www.lincoln.ac.uk/home/studywithus/scholarshipsandbursaries/

**For further information contact:**

**Email**:    intscholarships@lincoln.ac.uk

## Thailand Scholarship

**Purpose**: The University of Lincoln Thai Scholarship is aimed at supporting high-achieving postgraduate students from across Thailand
**Eligibility**: Be a Thai citizen. Already hold a conditional or unconditional offer from the University of Lincoln for a full-time postgraduate taught or Master's by Research programme commencing in September
**Type**: Scholarship
**Value**: £5,000
**Application Procedure**: For details, please visit intscholarships@lincoln.ac.uk

### For further information contact:

**Email**:    intscholarships@lincoln.ac.uk

## The Lincoln 50% Global Scholarship

**Purpose**: The University of Lincoln are delighted to offer 50% Global Scholarships to international applicants who demonstrate the highest levels of excellence in academia, extracurricular and personal endeavour.
**Eligibility**: 1. University of Lincoln International Scholarships take the form of a tuition fee reduction upon enrolment. 2. University of Lincoln International Scholarships are non-transferable and are not valid in conjunction with each other; only one Scholarship per student per course will be applied. 3. The University of Lincoln reserves the right to withdraw any University of Lincoln International Scholarship at any point and without notice. 4. Students who are sponsored by an organisation such as an external funding body. Government, or employer are not eligible to receive a University of Lincoln International Scholarship.
**Level of Study**: Postgraduate
**Type**: Scholarship
**Frequency**: Varies
**Country of Study**: Any country
**Funding**: Trusts
**Additional Information**: For further information, please contact the international@lincoln.ac.uk www.lincoln.ac.uk/home/studywithus/scholarshipsandbursaries/

### For further information contact:

**Email**:    intscholarships@lincoln.ac.uk

## University of Lincoln India Scholarships

**Value**: £5,000
**Country of Study**: Any country
**Application Procedure**: The mode of applying is online
**Closing Date**: September

### For further information contact:

**Email**:    intscholarships@lincoln.ac.uk

## Uruguay PhD Scholarship

**Purpose**: To conduct PhD studies in Life Sciences has recently been agreed between the University of Lincoln and the Uruguay National Agency for Research and Innovation (ANII - Agencia Nacional de Investigación e Innovación)
**Type**: Scholarship
**Value**: The scholarship covers university fees and a subsistence bursary
**Country of Study**: United Kingdom
**Application Procedure**: 1. Must be a citizen of Uruguay 2. Have already obtained a BSc (or equivalent) degree in an area relevant to the research fields described above. A minimum of a UK equivalent to a 2:1 award is required to enter the application process 3. The applications must include a copy of the applicant's CV and a one page research statement describing research interests, ambition and briefly outline a research project 4. The deadline for submissions is 18 March, at 14:00 (UYT) 5. Full details are available www.anii.org.uy/apoyos/formacion/9/maestrias-y-doctorados-en-el-exterior-en-areas-estrategicas/
**Closing Date**: 18 March
**Additional Information**: For additional information regarding this scholarship please contact: Prof. Fernando Montealegre-Zapata www.lincoln.ac.uk/home/studywithus/scholarshipsandbursaries/

### For further information contact:

**Tel**:    (44) 1522 835460
**Email**:    fmontealegrez@lincoln.ac.uk

## Vietnam Merit Scholarship

**Purpose**: The University of Lincoln Vietnam Merit Scholarship is aimed at supporting high achieving postgraduate students from across Vietnam
**Value**: Tuition fees and are valued at £5,000
**Country of Study**: Any country
**Application Procedure**: Submit applications to intscholarships@lincoln.ac.uk
**Additional Information**: For further information, please contact the international@lincoln.ac.uk www.lincoln.ac.uk/home/studywithus/scholarshipsandbursaries/

### For further information contact:

**Email**:    intscholarships@lincoln.ac.uk

## University of Liverpool

Liverpool L69 3BX, United Kingdom.

The University of Liverpool is a public university based in the city of Liverpool, United Kingdom. Founded as a college in 1881, it gained its royal charter in 1903 with the ability to award degrees and is also known to be one of the six original "red brick" civic universities. It comprises three faculties organized into 35 departments and schools. It is a founding member of the Russell Group, the N8 Group for research collaboration and the University Management school is AACSB accredited.

## Commonwealth Shared Scholarship Scheme

**Purpose**: Commonwealth Shared Scholarships, offered in partnership with United Kingdom universities, are for developing country students who would not otherwise be able to undertake master's level study in the United Kingdom
**Eligibility**: The scholarship has certain eligibility criteria and other requirements, which include: 1. Students who hold a first degree at either first class or upper second-class level are eligible for the award 2. The university confirms candidates are sufficiently fluent in written and oral English to pursue their proposed studies immediately 3. Scholarships are applicable to the nationals of commonwealth developing countries, who are not at present living or studying in a developed commonwealth country. 4. Students must return to their home country as soon as the award comes to an end.
**Type**: Scholarship
**Value**: Covers tuition fees, living costs and return flights to the United Kingdom
**Country of Study**: United Kingdom
**No. of awards offered**: 5
**Closing Date**: 1 April
**Additional Information**: www.univariety.com/scholarship/Commonwealth-Shared-Scholarship-Scheme-University-of-Liverpool/6670280b

## For further information contact:

**Tel**:      (44) 3806700
**Email**:   irro@liverpool.ac.uk

## FIDERH Award

**Eligibility**: You must be a Mexican national
**Type**: Award
**Value**: 20% reduction in tuition fees for postgraduate taught and research programmes

**Country of Study**: United Kingdom
**Closing Date**: 28 February
**Additional Information**: Please apply for funding through FIDERH. Students who are awarded a FIDERH Graduate Loan and register at the University of Liverpool will automatically receive the award www.liverpool.ac.uk/study/postgraduate-taught/finance/scholarships/scholarships/fiderh-award/

## Hodgson Law Scholarship

**Purpose**: The Trustees wish Hodgson Law Scholars to benefit from education in Liverpool with a view to encouraging the intellectual growth of promising law students and the nurturing of close links with the City of Liverpool and the Liverpool City Region
**Eligibility**: 1. Procedure 2: Application for an LLM place at University Applicants should apply for, and hold an offer of place, for a full-time postgraduate taught degree in law (LLM) at the University of Liverpool or Liverpool John Moores University to be eligible for the Hodgson Law Scholarship
**Value**: The Scholarship includes full tuition fees for a full-time postgraduate taught degree in law (LLM), and a stipend of £9,135
**Country of Study**: United Kingdom
**Application Procedure**: You will need to complete and submit the Hodgson Law Scholarship application form electronically to the Hodgson Selection Committee by email to hodgscho@liverpool.ac.uk
**Closing Date**: 1 May
**Additional Information**: For enquiries please contact Dr Gregory Messenger, Hodgson Scholarship Liaison. www.liverpool.ac.uk/law/study/masters/ www.liverpool.ac.uk/study/postgraduate-taught/finance/scholarships/scholarships/hodgson-law-scholarship/

## For further information contact:

**Email**:   hodgscho@liverpool.ac.uk

## John Lennon Memorial Scholarships

**Purpose**: The award is intended to support students from Merseyside who might be in financial need and enhance, among other things, awareness of global problems and environmental issues. The John Lennon Memorial Scholarships were set up by a trust fund endowed in the University for the provision of scholarships in the memory of John Lennon
**Type**: Scholarship
**Length of Study**: Three years
**Country of Study**: Any country

**Application Procedure**: You will need to complete and submit the form by email to the Secretary to the Scholarships Sub-Committee by email to seschol@liverpool.ac.uk

**Closing Date**: 5 April

**Additional Information**: www.liverpool.ac.uk/study/postgraduate-taught/finance/scholarships/scholarships/john-lennon-memorial-scholarship/

**For further information contact:**

**Email**: seschol@liverpool.ac.uk

## Liverpool International College (LIC) Excellence Award

**Eligibility**: Students who achieve an average of 75% or above in their LIC Pre-Master's programme

**Type**: Award

**Value**: £2,500 tuition fee reduction

**Country of Study**: United Kingdom

**Additional Information**: No application necessary. The award will automatically be awarded to those who meet criteria www.liverpool.ac.uk/study/postgraduate-taught/finance/scholarships/scholarships/lic-excellence-award/

**For further information contact:**

**Email**: irro@liverpool.ac.uk

## Liverpool Law School LLM Bursaries

**Purpose**: Awards will help students with their tuition fees. They are offered to encourage the best students, from the United Kingdom, Europe and internationally, to join the expanding LLM programme

**Eligibility**: Home, European Union and international students studying a LLM programme. Liverpool Law School LLM Bursaries will be awarded on the basis of merit. Academic performance in earlier degrees they have taken, as well as any other practical or intellectual achievements, will be taken into account

**Type**: Bursary

**Value**: 1. Two bursaries worth £500 each for Home/EU students 2. Two bursaries wroth £1,000 each for international students

**Country of Study**: United Kingdom

**Application Procedure**: Students do NOT need to make an extra application for the Liverpool Law School LLM Bursaries. All students who have registered for the LLM will be considered automatically. The decision of Liverpool Law School on the award of the bursaries is final

**Additional Information**: www.liverpool.ac.uk/study/postgraduate-taught/finance/scholarships/scholarships/liverpool-law-school-llm-bursaries/

**For further information contact:**

**Email**: irro@liverpool.ac.uk

## Marshall Scholarships

**Purpose**: To enable intellectually distinguished young Americans, their country's future leaders, to study in the United Kingdom. 1. To help Scholars gain an understanding and appreciation of contemporary Britain

**Eligibility**: To qualify, candidates should: 1. Be citizens of the United States of America normally resident in the United States of America. 2. Hold a doctorate in a science or engineering subject by the time they take up their Fellowship

**Type**: Scholarship

**Value**: Full tuition fee waiver for a master

**Country of Study**: United Kingdom

**Closing Date**: 30 September

**Additional Information**: Apply via: www.marshallscholarship.org/applications/apply www.marshallscholarship.org/apply

**For further information contact:**

**Email**: apps@marshallscholarship.org

## Santander Awards

**Purpose**: Santander International Postgraduate Scholarships reward international students who demonstrate academic excellence. The awards are available to international students entering onto postgraduate taught programmes at the University of Liverpool in September

**Value**: £5,000 tuition fee reduction for 1 year only

**Country of Study**: United Kingdom

**Closing Date**: 15 June

**For further information contact:**

**Email**: santander.universities@santander.co.uk

## University of Liverpool Commonwealth Postgraduate Bursary

**Purpose**: The University of Liverpool Commonwealth Postgraduate Bursary fee reduction for students from Commonwealth countries new to studying at the University of Liverpool on master's programmes

**Type**: Bursary
**Value**: £2,500 fee reduction for Commonwealth students studying Engineering, Electrical Engineering and Electronics, and Computer Science programmes; £1,500 fee reduction for Commonwealth students studying all other subjects
**Country of Study**: Any country
**Additional Information**: No application necessary, automatically awarded to those who meet criteria www.liverpool.ac.uk/study/postgraduate-taught/finance/scholarships/scholarships/university-of-liverpool-commonwealth-postgraduate-bursary/

### For further information contact:

**Email**:    irro@liverpool.ac.uk

## University of Liverpool Management School Academic Award

**Purpose**: The University of Liverpool Management School is delighted to offer range of generous scholarships and study awards to help cover the cost of MBA tuition fees
**Eligibility**: HEU/OSI applicants on the Liverpool MBA and the Football Industries MBA* programmes with an excellent academic profile and excellent work experience, or combination of very high standards in both of the above. It is an on-campus programme
**Type**: Award
**Value**: £2,000
**Country of Study**: United Kingdom

### For further information contact:

**Email**:    ulmsmba@liverpool.ac.uk

## University of Manchester

Oxford Road, Manchester M13 9PL, United Kingdom.

**Tel**:        (44) 161 306 6000
**Email**:    hr@manchester.ac.uk
**Website**:  www.manchester.ac.uk

## Indian Excellence Scholarship Award

**Purpose**: Scholarships are available for pursuing undergraduate degree programme
**Eligibility**: This scheme applies to any undergraduate degree programme within the Faculty of Science and Engineering at The University of Manchester. Each scholarship will be awarded on the basis of a student demonstrating high performance in their International Baccalaureate or Standard XII examinations and the academic reference on their UCAS form. Applicants must be Indian nationals or permanently domiciled in India. Applicants must have applied through UCAS for a place on an undergraduate degree programme in FSE for entry in September. Applicants must have accepted a programme in FSE as their firm choice by the end of June
**Type**: Scholarship
**Value**: £3,000 per annum
**Country of Study**: Any country
**Closing Date**: June
**Additional Information**: Application for courses in this School should be made online through the Universities and Colleges Admissions Service (UCAS) www.eee.manchester.ac.uk/study/undergraduate/fees-and-funding/

### For further information contact:

**Email**:    app.req@ucas.ac.uk

## Institute for Development Policy and Management Taught Postgraduate Scholarship Scheme

**Eligibility**: Bachelors degree with Second Class Honours, Upper Division or above, or Overseas equivalent (please contact School for details of equivalencies). Applicants whose first language is a language other than English must achieve 7.0 or above in IELTS or an equivalent test (TOEFL)
**Level of Study**: Postgraduate
**Type**: Scholarship
**Value**: £2,000
**Frequency**: Annual
**Application Procedure**: Check website for further details www.manchester.ac.uk/postgraduate/funding/search/display/?id=00000177
**Closing Date**: 30 June

### For further information contact:

**Email**:    paul.arrowsmith@manchester.ac.uk

## Manchester-China Scholarship Council Joint Postgraduate Scholarship Programme

**Purpose**: To provide scholarships to the nationals of PR China who wish to pursue their PhD at the University of Manchester
**Eligibility**: Open to students who are citizens and permanent residents of PR China and who hold a Master's degree from one of the 38 Chinese universities under 985 Programme

**Level of Study**: Doctorate, Postgraduate
**Type**: Scholarships
**Value**: Tuition fees and annual stipend of approx. £4,800
**Length of Study**: 3 years
**Frequency**: Annual
**Study Establishment**: University of Manchester
**Country of Study**: United Kingdom
**Application Procedure**: Applicants must complete the standard postgraduate application form and return it together with: Academic transcripts, English language qualification, 2 reference letters and a research proposal
**Closing Date**: 12 February
**Additional Information**: For enquires to the China Scholarship Council, please contact Miss Zou Dongyun www.bmh. manchester.ac.uk/study/research/financial-support/csc-scholarship/

**For further information contact:**

**Tel**:     (86) 10 6609 3977
**Email**:   dyzou@csc.edu.cn

## President's Doctoral Scholar Award

**Type**: Scholarship
**Value**: an annual maintenance stipend at £15,000 per annum
**Length of Study**: 3 years
**Country of Study**: United Kingdom
**Application Procedure**: For further information, please visit the PDS website
**Closing Date**: 27 February
**Additional Information**: www.bmh.manchester.ac.uk/study/research/financial-support/presidents-doctoral-scholar-awards/

**For further information contact:**

**Email**:   EPSGradEd@manchester.ac.uk

## School of Social Sciences - Manchester Master

**Purpose**: The bursaries are aimed at widening access to master's courses by removing barriers to postgraduate education for students from underrepresented groups, so applicants need to meet a number of criteria to be eligible. Last year, there were more eligible applications than places, so meeting the criteria is no guarantee of an award
**Eligibility**: 1. Eligible courses include LLM, MA, MEd, MBA, MEnt, MPhil, MRes, MSc, MSc by Research, MusM. 2. Courses can be studied full-time for one or two academic years or part-time for a maximum of two academic years. 3. You must be a home student paying home level tuition fees, and have been resident in the United Kingdom for at least three years prior to starting your undergraduate course for a purpose other than study. 4. You must be commencing your degree course in September. 5. You must not hold a master's qualification or higher. 6. You must have commenced your undergraduate course. 7. Intercalating medical students taking a master's course are eligible to apply. Medical students should note that if they plan to intercalate and take a master's course between Years 2 and 3, they will not be eligible for UG loans in Year 3. However, there will be no interruption to funding if they intercalate between Years 3 and 4, and they will be eligible for the postgraduate loan
**Level of Study**: Postgraduate
**Type**: Bursary
**Value**: £3,000
**Length of Study**: 1 year
**Frequency**: Annual
**Country of Study**: Any country
**Closing Date**: 30 May
**Funding**: International office
**Additional Information**: www.socialsciences.manchester.ac.uk/study/masters/applying/ www.socialsciences.manchester.ac.uk/study/masters/applying/

**For further information contact:**

Postgraduate Admissions Team, School of Social Sciences.

**Tel**:     (44) 161 275 4471 or (44) 161 275 1296
**Email**:   pg-soss@manchester.ac.uk

---

# University of Massachusetts Amherst

## Refractique (Lensball World) Photography Innovation & Excellence Scholarship

**Purpose**: We provide a premium offering and pride ourselves on our products - enjoying this fun creative photography ourselves initially before enabling others to learn more about this wonderful hobby
**Eligibility**: studying an Arts Degree (or relevant photography course)
**Level of Study**: Postgraduate
**Type**: Scholarship
**Value**: US$2,000 (occurs on a twice yearly basis with a US$1,000 per scholarship eligible)
**Frequency**: Annual
**Country of Study**: Any country
**Application Procedure**: 1. Prepare a refraction photography submission and send to support@refractique.com
**Closing Date**: 30 June
**Funding**: Private

**Additional Information**: For further information, refer the website link. lensballs.com/pages/social-support

**For further information contact:**

**Email**:    support@refractique.com

# University of Melbourne

Scholarships Office, Melbourne, Melbourne, VIC 3010, Australia.

**Tel**:        (61) 3 8344 4000
**Email**:    pg-schools@unimelb.edu.au
**Website**: www.unimelb.edu.au

## Dairy Postgraduate Scholarships and Awards

**Purpose**: To enable students for research contributing to the technical areas relevant to dairy farming and dairy manufacturing operations
**Eligibility**: Open to citizens or permanent residents of Australia
**Level of Study**: Postgraduate
**Type**: Scholarship
**Value**: AU$25,000 stipend plus AU$3,000 per year
**Frequency**: Annual
**Country of Study**: Australia
**Application Procedure**: To apply for this scholarship one must apply direct to the faculty
**Closing Date**: 20 October

**For further information contact:**

**Tel**:      (61) 3 9694 3810
**Fax**:      (61) 3 9694 3701
**Email**:    research@dairyaustralia.com.au

## PhDs in Bio Nanotechnology

**Eligibility**: Open to those who have achieved Honours 2a or equivalent
**Level of Study**: Postgraduate, Research
**Type**: Scholarship
**Value**: AU$19,616 per year
**Length of Study**: 2 years (Masters) and 3 years (PhD)
**Frequency**: Annual
**Study Establishment**: University of Melbourne
**Country of Study**: Australia
**Application Procedure**: Applicants must apply directly to the scholarship provider. Check website for further details

**Closing Date**: 21 July
**Contributor**: University of Melbourne

**For further information contact:**

**Email**:    fcaruso@unimelb.edu.au

## Rae and Edith Bennett Travelling Scholarship

**Purpose**: To enable students and graduates of the University of Melbourne to undertake postgraduate study or research in the United Kingdom
**Eligibility**: Open to students and graduates of the University of Melbourne who can demonstrate outstanding academic merit and promise
**Level of Study**: Postgraduate
**Type**: Scholarship
**Value**: up to AU$90,000
**Frequency**: Annual
**Country of Study**: Australia
**Application Procedure**: Please see the website www.services.unimelb.edu.au/scholarships/research/local/available/travelling/rae
**No. of awards offered**: 6
**Closing Date**: 31 May
**Funding**: Private
**Contributor**: Rae and Edith Bennett Travelling Scholarship Fund
**Additional Information**: scholarships.unimelb.edu.au/awards/rae-and-edith-bennett-travelling-scholarship

**For further information contact:**

**Email**:    gsa@gsa.unimelb.edu.au

## Sir Arthur Sims Travelling Scholarship

**Purpose**: To enable graduates of Australian universities to undertake postgraduate study or research in United Kingdom
**Eligibility**: Open to graduates of Australian universities who can demonstrate outstanding academic merit and promise. Applicants must be born in Australia or have parents who have been Australian residents for 7 years or more
**Level of Study**: Postgraduate, Research
**Type**: Scholarship
**Value**: Living allowance, tuition fees (approx. US$20,000 per year)
**Length of Study**: 1–3 years
**Country of Study**: United Kingdom
**Application Procedure**: Check website www.services.unimelb.edu.au/scholarships/research/local/available/travelling/sims
**Closing Date**: 30 June

**Funding**: Private
**Contributor**: Sir Arthur Sims Traveling Scholarship Fund
**Additional Information**: scholarships.unimelb.edu.au/awards/sir-arthur-sims-travelling-scholarship

### For further information contact:

**Email**: 13melb@unimelb.edu.au

## Sir Thomas Naghten Fitzgerald Scholarship

**Purpose**: This scholarship is to support further surgical training in Australia or Overseas
**Eligibility**: Open to candidates studied or currently studying at The University of Melbourne
**Level of Study**: Postgraduate
**Type**: Scholarship
**Value**: Approx. AU$12,000
**Length of Study**: 1 year
**Frequency**: Annual
**Study Establishment**: University of Melbourne
**Country of Study**: Australia
**Application Procedure**: Check website www.research.mdhs.unimelb.edu.au/fitzgerald-scholarship
**Closing Date**: 31 October
**Funding**: Government
**Additional Information**: scholarships.unimelb.edu.au/awards/the-sir-thomas-naghten-fitzgerald-scholarship

### For further information contact:

**Email**: jyv@unimelb.edu.au

## The Helen Macpherson Smith Scholarships

**Purpose**: To establish special scholarships for outstanding women who are entering graduate study
**Eligibility**: To be eligible for this scholarship, you need to: 1. Be an Australian citizen or permanent resident 2. Have applied for and meet the entry requirements for a graduate research degree at the University of Melbourne 3. Have not already completed a research qualification at the same or higher level as the course for which a scholarship is sought 4. Intend to study as a full-time student unless there are compassionate or compelling circumstances that prevent full-time study 5. Not have previously received a graduate research scholarship with similar benefits
**Level of Study**: Postgraduate
**Type**: Scholarship
**Value**: Up to AU$5,000
**Frequency**: Annual
**Country of Study**: Australia

**Application Procedure**: If you have applied for a Master by research or Doctorate by research degree by 31 October for commencement in the following year, you will be automatically considered for this scholarship.
**No. of awards offered**: 2
**Closing Date**: 31 October
**Funding**: Trusts
**Contributor**: Helen Macpherson Smith Trust
**Additional Information**: scholarships.unimelb.edu.au/awards/helen-macpherson-smith-scholarship

### For further information contact:

**Email**: gsa@gsa.unimelb.edu.au

## University of Melbourne Graduate Research Scholarships

**Purpose**: Established by the University of Melbourne, this scholarship is available to high achieving domestic and international students undertaking a Master by research degree or Doctoral degree.
**Eligibility**: To be eligible for this scholarship, you need to have applied for and meet the entry requirements for a graduate research degree at the University of Melbourne, or be currently enrolled in a graduate research degree at the University of Melbourne.
**Level of Study**: Masters/PhD Degree
**Type**: Scholarships
**Value**: 1. Full fee offset for up to two years for students undertaking a Masters by Research degree or up to four years for students undertaking a doctoral degree 2. Living allowance of US$30,600 per year pro rata (2,019 full-time study rate) for up to two years for students undertaking a Masters by Research degree or up to 3.5 years for students undertaking a doctoral degree. 3. Relocation grant of US$2,000 for students moving from States or Territories other than Victoria or US$3,000 for students moving from outside Australia. 4. Overseas Student Health Cover (OSHC) Single Membership for international students who require a student visa to study in Australia
**Frequency**: annual
**Country of Study**: Australia
**Application Procedure**: If you are a new student and have applied for a graduate research course by the application closing date for that course, you will be automatically considered for the Graduate Research Scholarships. It is important to visit the official website to access the application form for detailed information on how to apply for this scholarship.
**No. of awards offered**: About 600
**Additional Information**: scholarships.unimelb.edu.au/awards/graduate-research-scholarships

## Viola Edith Reid Bequest Scholarship

**Purpose**: This scholarship is to support postgraduate study in any discipline of Medicine
**Eligibility**: To be eligible for this scholarship, you need to: 1. Be an outstanding graduate research applicant, or enrolled graduate researcher, of the Melbourne Medical School within the Faculty of Medicine, Dentistry and Health Sciences 2. Be a medical graduate 3. Satisfy faculty entry requirements for PhD.
**Level of Study**: Postgraduate, Research
**Type**: Scholarship
**Value**: Up to AU$15,300
**Length of Study**: 1 year
**Frequency**: Annual
**Study Establishment**: University of Melbourne
**Country of Study**: Australia
**Application Procedure**: Check website www.research. mdhs.unimelb.edu.au/viola-edith-reid-bequest
**No. of awards offered**: 4
**Closing Date**: 31 October
**Funding**: Government
**Additional Information**: scholarships.unimelb.edu.au/awards/ viola-edith-reid-bequest-scholarship

### For further information contact:

**Tel**:      (61) 8344 4019
**Fax**:      (61) 9347 7854
**Email**:   mdhs-scholarships@unimelb.edu.au

## University of Montevallo

75 College Dr, Montevallo, AL 35115, United Statesof America.

**Tel**:   (1) 205-665-6000

## Graduate Honors Scholarship

**Subjects**: English
**Purpose**: To award prospective English students at the University of Montevallo.
**Eligibility**: Note: In order to be eligible for consideration, each student must have a minimum overall GPA of 3.5 on a 4.0 scale, and a minimum of 1100/old format or 302/new format on the verbal and quantitative portions of the GRE, a minimum of 407 on the MAT, or a 550 on the GMAT (for MBA students). Please note that the selection of scholarship recipients and amount of the award is made in each department and is based upon scholarship money available to that department. A student who meets all scholarship requirements is not guaranteed an award and receiving the scholarship one semester does not guarantee an award for future semesters. Only students who have been admitted to a graduate program may be considered for the scholarship.
**Type**: Scholarship
**Value**: Varies
**Frequency**: Annual
**Study Establishment**: University of Montevallo
**Country of Study**: United States of America
**Application Procedure**: Applicants must supply: a completed application; Official transcripts sent from all institutions attended; Graduate Record Examination (GRE); Miller Analogies Test (MAT), or GMAT (for MBA students) scores sent; a letter of professional intent, including a statement of career goals; three letters of recommendation covering academic ability, personal qualities, and professional qualifications
**Closing Date**: 1 July
**Additional Information**: Renewal requests are no longer required for students currently enrolled in graduate courses as completed scholarship packets are processed and sent to department chairs for review each semester. However, students who change programs or plan to apply to another program after graduation should reapply for the scholarship. www.montevallo.edu/academics/colleges/college-of-arts-sci ences/department-of-english-foreign-languages/programs/ english-m-a/scholarships-and-deadlines/

## Minority Educators Scholarship

**Subjects**: English
**Purpose**: The shortage of minority teachers in Alabama and across the nation has been linked to multiple educational, social, and economic issues. The University of Montevallo College of Education recognizes this shortage and established The Minority Educators Scholarship Program to increase the number of minority students completing teacher education programs.
**Eligibility**: Graduate students who received this scholarship as undergraduates are not eligible to re-apply. Eligibility requirements include a minimum MAT score of 388 or a minimum of 290 on the GRE and a minimum grade point average of 2.5 earned in undergraduate work or 2.75 earned in college work. Recipients must maintain a 3.0 or better grade point average on graduate work, must maintain "full-time" status, and must complete the Alternative Master's Degree Program within two years of admission. Recipients must grant an exit interview upon leaving the program.
**Type**: Scholarship
**Value**: Varies
**Frequency**: Annual
**Study Establishment**: University of Montevallo
**Country of Study**: United States of America
**Closing Date**: 1 March
**Additional Information**: www.montevallo.edu/academics/ colleges/college-of-arts-sciences/department-of-english-foreign-languages/programs/english-m-a/scholarships-and-deadlines/

## Ronald E. McNair Post-Baccalaureate Achievement Program

**Subjects**: English
**Purpose**: Designed to provide effective preparation for doctoral study for low-income, first generation, and underrepresented undergraduate students.
**Eligibility**: Low-income, first generation, and underrepresented undergraduate students.
**Type**: Scholarship
**Value**: Varies
**Frequency**: Annual
**Study Establishment**: University of Montevallo
**Country of Study**: United States of America
**Additional Information**: Selection as a McNair Scholar is the result of a competitive process to participate in a program that prepares them for success in graduate school. The scholarship is awarded annually to graduate students who successfully participated in the McNair Scholars Program and are in good academic standing. Scholarship awards may be renewed annually for a maximum of 2 years. www.montevallo.edu/academics/colleges/college-of-arts-sciences/department-of-english-foreign-languages/programs/english-m-a/scholarships-and-deadlines/

## University of Nevada, Las Vegas (UNLV)

Graduate College, 4505 Maryland Parkway, Box 451010, Las Vegas, NV 89154-1017, United States of America.

| | |
|---|---|
| **Tel**: | (1) 702 895 3011 |
| **Email**: | gradcollege@unlv.edu |
| **Website**: | www.unlv.edu |
| **Contact**: | Administrative Officer |

## University of Nevada, Las Vegas Alumni Association Graduate Scholarships

**Purpose**: To reward outstanding graduate students
**Eligibility**: Students must have completed any degree at UNLV, with a 3.5 GPA or better and be a member of the UNLV Alumni Association. Students must enrol in a graduate program at least half-time (6 credits/semester), and must maintain a cumulative and semester GPA of 3.5
**Level of Study**: Graduate, MBA
**Type**: Scholarship
**Value**: US$1,500
**Length of Study**: 1 year
**Frequency**: Annual
**Study Establishment**: UNLV

**Country of Study**: United States of America
**Application Procedure**: Please check the website www.financialaid.unlv.edu/apps/ScholarshipSearch/index.asp?action=detail&s=466
**Closing Date**: 3 March
**Additional Information**: Student may receive the scholarship for a maximum of two (2) years, or four (4) semesters

### For further information contact:

**Email**:    unlvscholarships@unlv.edu

## University of Nevada, Las Vegas James F Adams/GPSA Scholarship

**Purpose**: To recognize the academic achievements of graduate students
**Eligibility**: Applicant must be a master's-level or specialist student. He/she must have completed at least 12 credits of graduate study at UNLV (by the end of the current spring semester). Have a minimum graduate GPA of 3.5. Enroll in six or more credits in each semester of the scholarship year
**Level of Study**: Graduate, MBA
**Type**: Scholarship
**Value**: US$1,000
**Length of Study**: Varies
**Frequency**: Annual
**Study Establishment**: UNLV
**Country of Study**: United States of America
**Application Procedure**: Please see the website www.financialaid.unlv.edu/apps/ScholarshipSearch/index.asp?action=detail&s=419
**Closing Date**: 3 March

### For further information contact:

**Email**:    eric.lee@unlv.edu

## University of New England (UNE)

Research Grants Office, Armidale, NSW 2351, Australia.

| | |
|---|---|
| **Tel**: | (61) 2 6773 3333 |
| **Email**: | research@une.edu.au |
| **Website**: | www.une.edu.au |

UNE is internationally recognized as one of the best teaching and research universities. Yearly, the university offers students more than AU$2,500,000 in scholarships, prizes, and bursaries and more than AU$18,000,000 for staff and students involved in research. It provides distance education for the students. Its scholars and scientists have established international reputations through their contributions in areas such as rural science, agricultural economics, educational administration, linguistics and archaeology.

## A S Nivison Memorial Scholarship

**Eligibility**: To be eligible, candidates should domestic students who are pursuing research program in one of the fields mentioned above.
**Level of Study**: Doctorate, Postgraduate
**Type**: Scholarship
**Value**: AU$5,000
**Length of Study**: 1 year
**Frequency**: Annual
**Country of Study**: Australia
**Application Procedure**: Check website for further details: www.une.edu.au/research/research-services/hdr/hdr-scholar ships/a-s-nivison-memorial-scholarship
**Closing Date**: 30 April
**Funding**: Private
**Contributor**: Nivison family
**Additional Information**: www.scholarshipdesk.com/s-nivison-memorial-scholarship-at-the-university-of-new-england-australia/

### For further information contact:

**Tel**:       (61) 2 6773 3745
**Email**:   pgscholarships@une.edu.au

## Cooperative Research Centre Programme Spatial Information PhD Scholarship

**Purpose**: To produce long-lasting outcomes relating to understanding how complex decision-making processes can be improved using spatial and other data
**Eligibility**: Applicants must hold a Class 1 or 2A Honours (or equivalent) Degree in a suitable discipline, and be a citizen or permanent resident of Australia. A valid driver's licence is also a necessary requirement
**Level of Study**: Doctorate
**Type**: Scholarship
**Value**: Please check website
**Frequency**: Annual
**Study Establishment**: University of New England
**Country of Study**: Australia
**Application Procedure**: Applicants should send a letter outlining suitability for the position, accompanied by a brief

curriculum vitae (including contact details of two referees) and a copy of academic transcripts
**Funding**: Government

### For further information contact:

**Tel**:       (61) 2 6773 2436
**Email**:   jim.scott@une.edu.au

## Cotton Research and Development Corporation Postgraduate Scholarship

**Purpose**: To enhance the environmental, economic and social performance of the Australian cotton industry
**Eligibility**: These scholarships are open to anyone who is an Australian resident, studying at an Australian university and interested in working in the Australian cotton industry to pursue postgraduate studies relating to the cotton industry or its related activities
**Level of Study**: Postgraduate
**Type**: Scholarship
**Value**: AU$30,000
**Length of Study**: 3 years
**Frequency**: Annual
**Study Establishment**: University of New England
**Country of Study**: Australia, New Zealand or South Africa
**Application Procedure**: Check with the website for further details
**Closing Date**: January
**Funding**: Government
**Contributor**: Cotton Research and Development Corporation (CRDC)
**Additional Information**: Projects may relate to any field of cotton-related research

### For further information contact:

Cotton Research and Development Corporation, 2 Lloyd Street, Narrabri, NSW 2390, Australia.

**Tel**:       (61) 2 6792 4088
**Fax**:      (61) 2 6792 4400
**Email**:   research@crdc.com.au

## PhD Scholarship in Animal Breeding

**Purpose**: To investigate aspects of sow feed intake and its impact on reproductive performance and longevity
**Eligibility**: Applicants should be well versed in statistics and/or animal breeding units at a tertiary level and computing and data analysis skills is highly desirable
**Level of Study**: Doctorate

**Type**: Scholarship
**Value**: AU$23,000 per year
**Length of Study**: 3 years
**Frequency**: Annual
**Study Establishment**: University of New England
**Country of Study**: Australia
**Application Procedure**: Please check with the website
**Closing Date**: 30 June
**Contributor**: Australian Pork CRC

**For further information contact:**

**Tel**:      (61) 2 6773 3788
**Email**:   kburter2@une.edu.au

## PhD Scholarship: Molecular Factors in Plant-Microbe Associations

**Purpose**: To study the molecular aspect of the interaction between the fungal pathogen and the plant
**Eligibility**: Applicants must hold a Class 1 or 2A Honours (or equivalent) Degree in a suitable discipline, and be a citizen or permanent resident of Australia
**Level of Study**: Doctorate
**Type**: Scholarship
**Value**: AU$26,000 per year (tax free)
**Length of Study**: 3 years
**Frequency**: Annual
**Study Establishment**: University of New England
**Country of Study**: Australia
**Application Procedure**: Applicants should send a letter outlining their suitability for the position, accompanied by a brief curriculum vitae (including contact details of two referees) and a copy of their academic transcripts
**Funding**: Government

**For further information contact:**

**Tel**:      (61) 2 6773 2708
**Fax**:      (61) 2 6773 3267
**Email**:   lperegge@une.edu.au

## PhD Scholarship: Weed Ecology

**Purpose**: To manage the species through a series of field and controlled environment experiments on emergence, growth, reproduction and spread of environment experiments on emergence, growth, reproduction and spread of fleabane species
**Eligibility**: Applicants must hold a Class 1 or 2A Honours (or equivalent) Degree in a suitable discipline, and be an citizen or permanent resident of Australia
**Level of Study**: Doctorate

**Type**: Scholarship
**Value**: AU$26,000 per year (tax free)
**Length of Study**: 3 years
**Study Establishment**: University of New England
**Country of Study**: Australia
**Application Procedure**: Applicants should send a letter outlining their suitability for the position accompanied by a brief curriculum vitae (including contact details of two referees) and a copy of their academic transcripts
**Closing Date**: 27 April
**Funding**: Government

**For further information contact:**

School of Rural Science and Agriculture, University of New England, Armidale, NSW 2351, Australia.

**Tel**:      (61) 2 6773 3238
**Email**:   bsindel@une.edu.au

## University of New England Research Scholarship

**Eligibility**: Applicants must have achieved Honours 1 or equivalent, or Masters or equivalent
**Level of Study**: Doctorate, Postgraduate
**Type**: Scholarship
**Value**: AU$19,231
**Length of Study**: 3 years (PhD) and 2 years (Masters)
**Frequency**: Annual
**Study Establishment**: University of New England
**Country of Study**: Australia
**Application Procedure**: Contact the university for details
**Closing Date**: December
**Funding**: Government

**For further information contact:**

**Tel**:      (61) 6773 3571
**Fax**:      (61) 6773 3543
**Email**:   aharris@une.edu.au

## University of New England Equity Scholarship for Environmental and Rural Science

**Eligibility**: Applicants must be citizens of Australia or New Zealand and be an Aboriginal or Torres Strait Islander, non-English speaking background person, student with a disability or woman from non-traditional area
**Level of Study**: Postgraduate, Research
**Type**: Scholarship
**Length of Study**: 2 years (Masters) or 3 years (PhD)

**Frequency**: Annual
**Study Establishment**: University of New England
**Country of Study**: Australia, New Zealand or South Africa
**Application Procedure**: Check website for further details
**Funding**: Government

### For further information contact:

University of New England, Armidale, NSW 2351, Australia.

**Email**:     aharris@une.edu.au

## University of New South Wales

Sydney NSW 2052, Australia.

**Tel**:          (61) 2 93851000
**Website**:    www.unsw.edu.au/a

UNSW Scholarships is responsible for the administration of all undergraduate and postgraduate coursework scholarships offered at UNSW and is the point of contact for any questions relating to these scholarships. Scholarships are offered in a variety of categories and are funded by the University with the support of many generous donors and organisations. Merit Scholarships are available to recognise your academic and other achievements (such as leadership, community involvement, commitment to a program of study). Equity Scholarships provide assistance to students that may experience educational disadvantage or are from low socio-economic backgrounds, and to support access and diversity. UNSW Scholarships is home to the Elite Athlete Support Program and Sports Scholarships, including the Ben Lexcen Sports Scholarship. We also provide information on Prestigious Programs for UNSW students to undertake graduate study at overseas institutions, and manage the Australian selection process for the Robertson Scholars Leadership Program Scholarship to study at Duke University/UNC in the United States. Please search for a scholarship program that may suit you and check the eligibility, selection criteria and closing dates. Scholarships are competitive and there are less scholarships than applicants. UNSW Scholarships allows you to apply for as many scholarships as you are eligible for.

### UNSW International Scholarships

**Purpose**: UNSW offers a wide range of Scholarships and Awards to support International undergraduate and postgraduate coursework students commencing full-time study at UNSW

**Eligibility**: 1. an International student 2. be commencing full-time studies in Term 3, 2020; and 3. Must have received an offer of admission and be commencing in any UNSW undergraduate or postgraduate coursework degree program by Friday, 31 July 2020. This must include one of the following: 4. Undergraduate or Postgraduate Letter of Offer (unconditional) 5. Undergraduate or Postgraduate English Package Offer (UEEC) - students must be enrolled in the UNSW Institute of Languages and successfully complete the program prior to commencing studies.
**Level of Study**: Bachelors/Masters Degree
**Type**: Scholarships
**Value**: The scholarships may provide full or partial tuition fee payment, while others provide a stipend to assist with the costs associated with your studies.
**Frequency**: annual
**Country of Study**: Australia
**Application Procedure**: Applications open 1 May. By applying for the Term 3 2020 - UNSW International Scholarships Application, you may be considered for the scholarships. You must have received an offer of admission by 31 July.
**No. of awards offered**: Not specified
**Closing Date**: 31 July
**Additional Information**: www.scholarships.unsw.edu.au/scholarships/id/1431

## University of New South Wales (UNSW)

Scholarships and Financial Support, Sydney, NSW 2052, Australia.

**Tel**:          (61) 2 9385 1000
**Email**:      scholarships@unsw.edu.au
**Website**:    www.unsw.edu.au

University of New South Wales (UNSW) is one of Australia's leading research and teaching universities. UNSW takes great pride in the broad range and high quality of teaching programmes. UNSW's teaching gains strength, vitality and currency both from their research activities and from their international nature.

### Association of Professional Academic Institutions Scholarship in Metallurgy/Materials

**Purpose**: To undertake blast furnace research in collaboration with industry
**Eligibility**: This scholarship requires candidates to have achieved Honours 1 or equivalent, or Honours 2a or equivalent

**Level of Study**: Doctorate, Postgraduate
**Type**: Scholarship
**Value**: Stipend of AU$25,000 per year
**Length of Study**: 3–3.5 years
**Frequency**: Annual
**Study Establishment**: School of Materials Science and Engineering
**Application Procedure**: Check website for further details
**Closing Date**: 31 October

**For further information contact:**

**Email**:   a.yu@unsw.edu.au

## College of Fine Arts Research Scholarship

**Purpose**: To support students with outstanding research potential who are ineligible for an APA/UPA
**Eligibility**: Students with an offer to commence a full-time PhD at COFA, or students currently enroled full-time in a PhD at COFA
**Level of Study**: Doctorate
**Type**: Scholarship
**Value**: AU$22,500 per year
**Length of Study**: Up to 3 years
**Frequency**: Annual
**Study Establishment**: University of New South Wales
**Country of Study**: Australia
**Application Procedure**: Application forms are available at the COFA Student Centre on the UNSW Scholarships website www.cofa.unsw.edu.au/about-us/scholarships/cofa-research-scholarship/
**Closing Date**: 31 January

**For further information contact:**

COFA Students Centre.

**Tel**:   (61) 2 9385 0684
**Email**:   chad.roberts@unsw.edu.au

## PhD Scholarship – Metal Dusting

**Purpose**: To support research on metal dusting
**Eligibility**: Open to citizens of Australia or permanent residents holding high Honours Degree in science
**Level of Study**: Postgraduate, Research
**Type**: Scholarship
**Value**: AU$25,000–30,000 per year (tax free)
**Length of Study**: 3–3.5 years
**Frequency**: Annual
**Study Establishment**: University of New South Wales

**Country of Study**: Australia
**Application Procedure**: Check website for further details
**Closing Date**: 28 February

**For further information contact:**

**Tel**:   (61) 93 854 322
**Fax**:   (61) 93 855 956
**Email**:   d.young@unsw.edu.au

## PhD Scholarships in Environmental Microbiology

**Purpose**: To attract the nation's strongest candidates capable of pursuing PhD studies in the genomics of environmental microorganisms
**Eligibility**: This scholarship is for study in Australia for those who have achieved Honours 1 or equivalent, or Masters or equivalent. There are no restrictions on citizenship
**Level of Study**: Doctorate, Postgraduate, Research
**Type**: Scholarship
**Value**: AU$35,000
**Application Procedure**: Check website www.emi.science.unsw.edu.au/recruitment.html
**Closing Date**: 31 March

**For further information contact:**

**Email**:   r.cavicchioli@unsw.edu.au

## Postdoctoral Fellow Positions in Computational Mathematics

**Purpose**: Applications are sought for two Postdoctoral Fellow positions in Computational Mathematics in the School of Mathematics and Statistics, UNSW Sydney.
**Eligibility**: Australian citizens are eligible to apply.
**Type**: Postdoctoral fellowship
**Value**: Australian AU$89K – Australian AU$96K per year (plus up to 17% superannuation and leave loading)
**Frequency**: Annual
**Study Establishment**: Positions are awarded in Computational Mathematics in the School of Mathematics and Statistics, UNSW Sydney
**Country of Study**: Australia
**Application Procedure**: Applicants should submit the following documents to ims@shanghaitech.edu.cn
**Closing Date**: 1 February
**Additional Information**: For more details please visit the website scholarship-positions.com/postdoctoral-fellow-positions-computational-mathematics-unsw-australia/2018/03/06/

**For further information contact:**

**Email**:    ims@shanghaitech.edu.cn

## Vida Rees Scholarship in Pediatrics

**Purpose**: To support Australian students to undertake research in paediatrics
**Eligibility**: To be eligible for a Scholarship an applicant must be an Australian citizen or permanent resident undertaking an Honours project or Postgraduate Research in Paediatrics. Recipients may not concurrently hold any other scholarship or award (except for Youth Allowance) except with the permission of the UNSW Selection Committee
**Level of Study**: Postgraduate, Research
**Type**: Scholarship
**Value**: AU$1,000
**Length of Study**: 1 year
**Frequency**: Annual
**Study Establishment**: University of New South Wales
**Country of Study**: Australia
**Application Procedure**: Completed application forms and any supporting documentation should be scanned and emailed (preferably as a single pdf document) to the Graduate Research School. For more details please see the website
**No. of awards offered**: 1
**Additional Information**: www.scholarships.unsw.edu.au/scholarships/id/563

**For further information contact:**

**Email**:    domestic.grs@unsw.edu.au

## Viktoria Marinov Award in Art

**Purpose**: To financially assist female artists under the age of 35 years who are proposing to undertake the Master of Art or Master of Fine Arts course
**Eligibility**: Female students who are under 35 years old completing the Master of Fine Arts (by research). Must be Australian citizens or permanent residents
**Level of Study**: Postgraduate
**Type**: Award
**Value**: AU$7,500
**Length of Study**: 1 year
**Frequency**: Annual
**Study Establishment**: New South Wales, Sydney City Central and Eastern Suburbs
**Country of Study**: Australia
**Application Procedure**: Applicants need to provide at least 6 images of their work, including information on the dimensions and materials of each work. These images can be supplied either electronically on DVD/CD or as attached printed images (no larger than A4). Applicants must include a personal statement addressing the selection criteria as part of their application. Please see the website for more applications related details: www.cofa.unsw.edu.au/about-us/scholarships/the-viktoria-marinov-award-in-art/
**No. of awards offered**: 2
**Closing Date**: 30 September
**Additional Information**: www.gooduniversitiesguide.com.au/scholarships/viktoria-marinov-award-in-art/unsw-australia/9241

**For further information contact:**

**Tel**:       (61) 2 9385 0684
**Email**:    chad.roberts@unsw.edu.au

## University of Newcastle

Research Division, University of Newcastle, Callaghan, NSW 2308, Australia.

**Tel**:       (61) 2 4921 5000
**Email**:    research@newcastle.edu.au
**Website**:  www.newcastle.edu.au/research/rhd/
**Contact**:  Office of Graduate Studies

## Chemical Engineering Scholarship

**Purpose**: To develop models capable of simulating temporal and spatial characteristics of rainfall fields over large river basins using novel approaches to hierarchical modelling, storm clustering, advection and calibration. The models will provide continuous simulation support for the design and assessment of water-related infrastructure
**Eligibility**: Open only to the postgraduates who are the citizens of Australia or the permanent residents of Australia
**Level of Study**: Postgraduate
**Type**: Scholarship
**Value**: A living allowance of AU$24,653 per year
**Length of Study**: 2 years (Masters) and 3 years (PhD)
**Frequency**: Annual
**Country of Study**: Australia
**Application Procedure**: Application form and the Research Higher Degree prospectus from can be downloaded from the website
**Closing Date**: 31 October

**For further information contact:**

**Tel**:       (61) 2 4921 6038
**Email**:    George.Kuczera@newcastle.edu.au

## PhD Scholarship in Coal Utilization in Thermal and Coking Applications

**Purpose**: To undertake research on particular coal properties which determine its utilization potential
**Eligibility**: Open to the engineering and the science graduates who have an Honours Degree in chemical or mechanical engineering or chemistry
**Level of Study**: Doctorate, Postgraduate
**Type**: Scholarship
**Value**: AU$19,616 per year
**Length of Study**: 3 years
**Application Procedure**: Check website for further details
**Closing Date**: 1 March

**For further information contact:**

**Tel**:     (61) 2 49 21 6179
**Email**:   Terry.Wall@newcastle.edu.au

## PhD Scholarship in Immunology of Kidney Stone Diseases

**Purpose**: This project aims to improve our understanding of how our immune system protects against stone recurrence and its role in preventing long-term consequences such as impaired kidney function
**Eligibility**: This scholarship is for domestic and international students. If English is not your first language then you will need to show that your English language skills are at a high enough level to succeed in your studies
**Type**: Scholarship
**Value**: Scholarship Value: AU$26,682 p.a., indexed in January each year. The scholarship is for a period of three years and a half years. This Scholarship is linked to the Dr Starkey ARC DECRA fellowship
**Frequency**: Annual
**Study Establishment**: Scholarships are awarded to work on the project titled, "Immunology of kidney stone diseases"
**Country of Study**: Australia
**Application Procedure**: To enable us to assess your application, candidates will be expected to submit an email expressing their interest including: 1. Academic transcripts. 2. A brief statement of research interests. 3. Full CV including previous degrees, grades, research experience, employment, papers published, and any grants obtained. Applicants are automatically considered for the scholarship on acceptance to University College
**Closing Date**: 1 April
**Additional Information**: For more details please visit the website scholarship-positions.com/phd-scholarship-immun ology-kidney-stone-diseases-australia/2018/02/01/

## Postgraduate Research Scholarship in Physics

**Eligibility**: Open to the residents of Australia and New Zealand or the permanent residents of Australia who have an Honours 1 or 2A or a Masters Degree
**Level of Study**: Postgraduate, Research
**Type**: Scholarship
**Value**: AU$17,071 per year
**Length of Study**: 3 years
**Frequency**: Annual
**Application Procedure**: Check website for more details
**Closing Date**: 1 July
**Contributor**: ARC Discovery-projects

**For further information contact:**

School of Mathematical and Physical Sciences.

**Tel**:     (61) 2 4921 6653
**Fax**:     (61) 2 4921 6907
**Email**:   vicki.keast@newcastle.edu.au

## University of Newcastle Postgraduate Research Scholarship (UNRS Central)

**Eligibility**: Open to the residents of Australia and New Zealand or permanent residents who have achieved Honours 1 or equivalent and have completed at least 4 years of undergraduate study
**Level of Study**: Postgraduate, Research
**Type**: Scholarship
**Value**: AU$23,728 per year full-time stipend, AU$12,898 part time stipend
**Length of Study**: 2 years (Masters) and 3 years (PhD)
**Frequency**: Annual
**Country of Study**: Australia
**Application Procedure**: Check website for further details
**Closing Date**: 31 October

**For further information contact:**

Research Higher Degrees, The Chancellery Eastern Wing, University Drive, 905 University Dr., State College, PA 16801, United States of America.

**Tel**:     (61) 2 4921 6537
**Fax**:     (61) 2 4921 6908

## University of Newcastle, Australia MBA Programme

**Application Procedure**: Applicants must return a completed application form, with original or certified copies of official academic transcripts (not to be returned), Graduate

Management Admission Test and TOEFL (if applicable) scores, the names of two referees

## For further information contact:

Business Administration International Students Office University Drive, 905 University Dr., State College, PA 16801, United States of America.

**Tel**: (61) 4 9216 595
**Fax**: (61) 4 9601 766
**Email**: io@newcastle.edu.au

# University of Notre Dame

1124 Flanner Hall, Notre Dame, IN 46556, United States of America.

**Tel**: (1) 574 631 1305
**Email**: ndias@nd.edu
**Website**: www.nd.edu
**Contact**: Brad S Gregory, Director of the Notre Dame Institute for Advanced Study

The University of Notre Dame provides a distinctive voice in higher education that is at once rigorously intellectual, unapologetically moral in orientation, and firmly embracing of a service ethos.

## Break Travel and Research Grants for Sophomores and Juniors

**Purpose**: The Break Travel and Research Grant provides seed funding for educational and research projects in European studies. The grant is intended to support well-focused, short-term exploratory trips conducted over fall, winter, or spring break
**Eligibility**: Applicants must be enrolled as a sophomore or junior at the University of Notre Dame and scheduled to return the following semester
**Level of Study**: Postgraduate
**Type**: Grant
**Value**: US$2,500. Funds are typically paid at one-time sum
**Frequency**: Annual
**Country of Study**: Any country
**Closing Date**: 4 February
**Funding**: Private

## For further information contact:

**Tel**: (1) 574 631 8326
**Email**: cstump@nd.edu

## Templeton Fellowships for United States of America and International Scholars at NDIAS

**Purpose**: With grant support from the John Templeton Foundation, the NDIAS will help chart a new course for future scholarship by offering Templeton Fellowships that encourage scholars to return to reflection on the broad questions that link multiple areas of inquiry and to do so in a manner that embraces a value-oriented interpretation of the world
**Eligibility**: Distinguished senior scholars with extensive records of academic accomplishment and who have had a considerable impact on their discipline are encouraged to apply. Outstanding junior scholars with academic records of exceptional promise and whose research agendas align with the purpose and parameters of the program are also invited to apply
**Type**: Fellowship
**Value**: These distinctive fellowships offer an extraordinary measure of scholarly support, including: a stipend of up to US$100,000; fully furnished faculty housing (for those who reside outside of the Michiana area); up to US$3,000 in research expenditures; a private office at the NDIAS, with a personal desktop computer and printer; etc. Check detailed information on the website
**Frequency**: Annual
**Country of Study**: United States of America
**Application Procedure**: Please see ndias.nd.edu/fellowships/templeton/application-instructions/
**Closing Date**: 15 October
**Additional Information**: For more information, please check at ndias.nd.edu/fellowships/templeton/

## For further information contact:

**Email**: csherman@nd.edu

# University of Notre Dame: College of Arts and Letters

Office of the Dean, 100 O'Shaughnessy Hall, Notre Dame, IN 46556, United States of America.

**Tel**: (1) 574 631 7085
**Email**: aldean@nd.edu
**Website**: al.nd.edu

University of Notre Dame: College of Arts and Letters offers one of the finest liberal arts educations in the nation. Its Division of the Humanities was recently ranked 12th among private universities, while the social sciences continue their ascent in the national rankings. College of Arts and Letters is the largest and oldest of the University's 4 colleges.

## The Erskine A. Peters Dissertation Year Fellowship at Notre Dame

**Purpose**: To provide an opportunity for African American scholars at the beginning of their academic careers to experience life at a major Catholic research university

**Eligibility**: Open to African American Doctoral candidates who have completed all degree requirements with the exception of the dissertation

**Level of Study**: Postgraduate, Research

**Type**: Fellowship

**Value**: US$30,000 stipend and US$2,000 research budget

**Length of Study**: 10 months

**Frequency**: Annual

**Country of Study**: United States of America

**Application Procedure**: Applicants may apply online

**Closing Date**: December

**No. of awards given last year**: 3

### For further information contact:

**Tel**: (1) 574 631 5628
**Fax**: (1) 574 631 3587
**Email**: astudies@nd.edu

## University of Nottingham

University of Nottingham, University Park, Nottingham NG7 2RD, United Kingdom.

**Tel**: (44) 115 846 8400
**Email**: graduate-school@nottingham.ac.uk
**Website**: www.nottingham.ac.uk/gradschool
**Contact**: Ms Nicola Pickering, Process Manager Funding

The University of Nottingham is a community of students and staff dedicated to bringing out the best in all of its members. It aims to provide the finest possible environment for teaching, learning and research and has a world class record of success.

## Developing Solutions Masters Scholarship

**Purpose**: The aim of the Developing Solutions Masters Scholarship is to enable and encourage academically able students from Africa, India or one of the countries of the Commonwealth

**Eligibility**: Students who are a national of (or permanently domiciled in) Africa, India, or one of the countries of the Commonwealth countries. You can apply for this scholarship if you: are a national of (or permanently domiciled in) Africa, India, OR one of the other Commonwealth countries AND are classed as an overseas student for fee purposes AND have not already studied outside of your home country

**Value**: 30 × 100% tuition fee; 75 × 50% of tuition fees

**Country of Study**: Any country

**Application Procedure**: Apply online

**Closing Date**: 22 March

**Additional Information**: For more details, visit www.nottingham.ac.uk/studywithus/international-applicants/scholarships-fees-and-finance/scholarships/masters-scholarships/dev-sol-masters.aspx www.nottingham.ac.uk/pgstudy/funding/developing-solutions-masters-scholarship

### For further information contact:

**Tel**: (44) 115 951 5247
**Email**: scholarship-assistant@nottingham.ac.uk

## High Achiever Foundation Prize for Africans

**Purpose**: Prizes are available for pursuing foundation courses at University of Nottingham

**Eligibility**: Candidates can apply if they are a national of (or permanently domiciled in) Africa, they are classed as an overseas student for fee purposes, already hold an offer to start a full-time foundation program at Nottingham in September

**Type**: Prize

**Value**: 3 undergraduate high achiever prizes of £2,000 towards tuition fees

**Country of Study**: United Kingdom

**Application Procedure**: The mode of applying is online

**Closing Date**: 15 April

**Additional Information**: Successful applicants will be notified of the outcome within 6 weeks of the closing date www.opportunitiesforafricans.com/2015-high-achiever-foundation-prize-undergraduate-scholarships-for-africans-to-study-in-the-united-kingdom-2000-towards-tuition-fees/

### For further information contact:

**Email**: scholarship-assistant@nottingham.ac.uk

## Japan Masters Scholarships at University of Nottingham in United Kingdom

**Purpose**: The aim of the scholarship is strengthen the bond of Japan and United Kingdom

**Eligibility**: 1. National of (or permanently domiciled in) Japan. 2. Classed as an overseas student for fee purposes. 3. Already have, or expect to receive, a final CGPA of no less than 3.2/grade B or 70%. 4. Already hold an offer to start a full-time master degree programme, including MRes, at Nottingham in September, any subject area

**Level of Study**: Postgraduate

**Type**: Scholarship

**Value**: These scholarships will cover 25% each towards tuition fees for students from Japan

**Country of Study**: Any country

**Application Procedure**: Applications must complete online application form to apply for scholarships. www.nottingham. ac.uk/international/_online_forms/scholarships/_sships_app form_p1.php

**Closing Date**: 18 May

### For further information contact:

**Email**: scholarship-assistant@nottingham.ac.uk

## Nottingham Developing Solutions Scholarships

**Purpose**: The Developing Solutions Scholarships are designed for international students who want to pursue a Master's Degree in the University of Nottingham and make a difference to the development of their home country

**Eligibility**: 1. Are a national of (or permanently domiciled in) Africa, India or one of the countries of the Commonwealth. 2. Are classed as an overseas student for fee purposes. 3. Have not already studied outside of your home country. 4. Are not currently studying at a University of Nottingham campus or are not a University of Nottingham graduate

**Level of Study**: Postdoctorate

**Type**: Scholarship

**Frequency**: Annual

**Country of Study**: Any country

**Closing Date**: 22 March

**Funding**: Foundation

**Additional Information**: www.nottingham.ac.uk/pgstudy/funding/developing-solutions-masters-scholarship

## Nottingham University Business School MBA Programme

**Length of Study**: 1 year full-time or 2;4 years part-time

**Country of Study**: Any country

**Application Procedure**: Applicants must complete an application form, and provide transcripts or copies of professional qualifications together with two references (ideally, one should be from an academic source, the other from an employer or business contact). All language test scores must be submitted for International students. Note that the school may ask for further individual details to support an application

**Additional Information**: www.nottingham.ac.uk/business/programmes/mba/index.aspx

### For further information contact:

**Tel**:     (44) 115 551 5500
**Fax**:     (44) 115 551 5503
**Email**:     business-enquiries@nottingham.ac.uk

## University of Oklahoma

College of Business Administration, Adams Hall Room 105K, Norman, OK 73019, United States of America.

**Tel**:     (1) 405 325 4107
**Email**:     awatkins@ou.edu
**Contact**:     MBA Admissions Officer

## Ben Barnett Scholarship

**Purpose**: Any full-time Art majors admitted to either the MA or MFA degree program

**Eligibility**: Applicant must be a full-time student in the School of Art and have a minimum 3.0 GPA and an outstanding portfolio

**Level of Study**: Postgraduate

**Type**: Scholarship

**Value**: Maximum of US$1,000 will be given as scholarship amount

**Frequency**: Annual

**Country of Study**: Any country

**Application Procedure**: Contact Director, School of Art University of Oklahoma 520 Parrington Room 202 Normak, OK 73019 United States Phone: (405) 325-2691

**Closing Date**: 1 March

**Funding**: Private

**Additional Information**: Visit the official website for further info: www.ou.edu www.collegexpress.com/scholarships/ben-barnett-scholarship/6650/

### For further information contact:

**Email**: art@ou.edu

## University of Ontario

Graduate Finance and Administration, 2000 Simcoe Street North, London, ON L1H 7K4, Canada.

**Email**:     pmenzies@uwo.ca
**Contact**:     Office of Graduate Studies Manager,

The University of Ontario Institute of Technology is a public research university located in Oshawa, Ontario, Canada.

## The Ontario Trillium Scholarships (OTS)

**Purpose**: To attract top international students to Ontario for PhD studies

**Eligibility**: An eligible applicant must have achieved a minimum of 80% in each of the last 2 most recently completed years of full-time university study, or equivalent to full-time study. Eligibility averages for competitive scholarship are rounded ONLY to the nearest decimal place

**Type**: Scholarship

**Value**: C$40,000 annually

**Length of Study**: 4 years

**Frequency**: Annual

**Country of Study**: Any country

**Application Procedure**: Submit a complete UOIT application with supporting documentation to the Office of Graduate Studies

**Closing Date**: April

**Additional Information**: Submit the PDF nomination to SGPS pmenzies@uwo.ca uwaterloo.ca/graduate-studies-postdoctoral-affairs/awards/ontario-trillium-scholarship-ots

## University of Oregon

1585E, 13th Ave, Eugene, OR 97403, United States of America.

**Tel**: (1) 541 346 1000

**Website**: www.uoregon.edu

## Center for AIDS Prevention Studies, Small Professional Grants for Graduate Students

**Purpose**: Awards will be made for the following purposes: travel to conferences to present papers, travel to library, museum, and archival collections; and expenses related to book and article production and publication

**Eligibility**: The Center for Asian and Pacific Studies is offering awards of up to US$500 in support of the professional activities of UO graduate students studying Asia. Awards will be made for the following purposes: travel to conferences to present papers, travel to library, museum, and archival collections; and expenses related to book and article production and publication

**Level of Study**: Postgraduate

**Type**: Grant

**Frequency**: Annual

**Country of Study**: Any country

**Application Procedure**: 1. To submit a proposal, please click here to complete the online application form. 2. A brief letter of support from your advisor explaining how this activity is central to your research interests is also required. This letter can be emailed directly to Holly Lakey at lakey@uoregon.edu

**Closing Date**: 10 April

**Funding**: Private

**Additional Information**: caps.uoregon.edu/2010/11/03/caps-small-professional-grants-for-graduate-students/

### For further information contact:

1246 University of Oregon, Eugene, OR 97403, United States of America.

**Tel**: (1) 541 346 5068

**Email**: lakey@uoregon.edu

## Jeremiah Lecture Series Support

**Purpose**: The Center for Asian and Pacific Studies is accepting proposals from UO faculty for speakers to visit the UO and deliver a public lecture on campus

**Level of Study**: Postgraduate

**Type**: Award

**Frequency**: Annual

**Country of Study**: Any country

**Application Procedure**: For a hardcopy version of the application form, please contact Holly Lakey at lakey@uoregon.edu

**Closing Date**: 10 April

**Funding**: Private

**Additional Information**: caps.uoregon.edu/2010/10/15/proposals-for-the-jeremiah-fund-lecture-series/

### For further information contact:

**Email**: lakey@uoregon.edu

## University of Oslo

Problemveien 7, N-0315 Oslo, Norway.

**Contact**: University of Oslo

The University of Oslo, until 1939 named the Royal Frederick University, is the oldest university in Norway, located in the Norwegian capital of Oslo.

## PhD Research Fellowship in Ecotoxicology

**Purpose**: The purpose of the PhD Fellowship is research training leading to the successful completion of a PhD degree
**Eligibility**: International students are eligible to apply for the fellowship. Applicants must have a Master's degree or equivalent in toxicology or marine ecology, relevant to this PhD project. A good command of English is required of all students attending the University of Oslo
**Type**: Fellowship
**Value**: NOK 436,900–490,900 per year
**Country of Study**: Norway
**Application Procedure**: Please visit www.scholarshipsads.com/norway-university-oslo-phd-fellowship-exotoxicology-2018/#gs.wOqf5y0
**Closing Date**: 1 February
**Additional Information**: The project combines knowledge from ecotoxicology, ecology, and environmental chemistry. The successful candidate will design and conduct extensive field studies, analyze contaminants and dietary descriptors, and deal with large datasets scholarship-positions.com/phd-research-fellowship-in-ecotoxicology-university-of-oslo-norway/2018/01/04/

### For further information contact:

**Email**: nina.holtan@mn.uio.no

## PhD Research Fellowships in Energy Informatics

**Purpose**: Fellowships are available to pursue PhD Research programme. The aim of providing the scholarship is to achieve a balanced gender composition in the organisation and to recruit people with ethnic minority backgrounds
**Eligibility**: For eligibility details, please visit
**Type**: Research fellowship
**Value**: NOK 436,900–490,900 per year. Attractive welfare benefits and a generous pension agreement, in addition to Oslo's family-friendly environment with its rich opportunities for culture and outdoor activities
**Length of Study**: 3 years
**Country of Study**: Norway
**Application Procedure**: The mode of applying is online
**Closing Date**: 15 November
**Contributor**: University of Oslo
**Additional Information**: www.successcds.net/Scholarships/phd-research-fellowships-in-energy-informatics-university-of-oslo.html

### For further information contact:

**Email**: yanzhang@ifi.uio.no

## Postdoctoral Fellowships in Educational Assessment and Measurement

**Purpose**: The main purpose of the fellowships is to qualify researchers for work in higher academic positions within their disciplines
**Eligibility**: For eligibility, please visit
**Level of Study**: Professional development
**Type**: Fellowship
**Value**: Salary NOK 499,600–569,000
**Length of Study**: 4 years
**Frequency**: Annual
**Country of Study**: Norway
**Application Procedure**: For online application, visit website www.jobbnorge.no/en/available-jobs/job/149727/1-2-four-year-postdoctoral-fellowships-in-educational-assessment-and-measurement
**Closing Date**: 15 May
**Additional Information**: www.mladiinfo.eu/2018/04/03/postdoctoral-fellowships-educational-assessment-measurement-university-oslo/

### For further information contact:

**Email**: rolfvo@cemo.uio.no

## Postdoctoral Fellowships in Political Philosophy or Legal Theory

**Purpose**: Fellowships are available to pursue postdoctoral programme
**Eligibility**: For eligibility, please visit
**Type**: Postdoctoral fellowship
**Value**: NOK 552 800 to 615 900
**Country of Study**: Any country
**Closing Date**: 30 January
**Additional Information**: stilling.forskning.no/job-ads-oslo-og-akershus-postdocpostdoktor/postdoctoral-fellowships-in-political-philosophy-or-legal-theory-on-the-legitimacy-of-international-courts-and-tribunals/1581825

### For further information contact:

**Email**: siri.johnsen@jus.uio.no

# University of Otago

Advanced Business Programme, PO Box 56, Dunedin, 9054, New Zealand.

**Tel**: (64) 3 479 8046
**Email**: mbainfo@commerce.otago.ac.nz

**Website**: www.otago.ac.nz

**Contact**: MBA Admissions Officer

## Aarhus University PhD Fellowships Program

**Purpose**: Aarhus University PhD Fellowships Program, Denmark are fully funded fellowships offered to the students of Denmark to pursue PhD fellowships and research training supplements, both research and PhD fellowships are funded by the Faculty of Health Science at Aarhus University, the scholarships are developed with an aim to develop international cooperation in the areas of teaching and research, university is a modern, academically diverse and research-intensive university with a strong commitment to high-quality research and education and the development of society existed around the world

**Eligibility**: The candidates who are interested to apply for the Aarhus University scholar apply for a 3-year PhD study programme students must have completed a relevant Master's degree, the Master's study has to be equivalent to a Danish Master's degree of 120 ECTS, all applications will be evaluated based on the submitted material using the following criteria, the time for research experience after the qualifying exam is taken into consideration, all applicants must document English language qualifications comparable to an 'English B level' in the Danish upper secondary school, if the candidate has any doubt about the criteria they can submit your diplomas for an assessment via graduateschoolhealth-at-au.dk

**Level of Study**: Postgraduate

**Type**: Fellowship

**Length of Study**: 3 year

**Frequency**: Annual

**Country of Study**: New Zealand

**Closing Date**: February

**Funding**: Foundation

**Additional Information**: scholarship-positions.com/health-scholarships-international-phd-students-aarhus-university-denmark/2017/04/07/

### For further information contact:

**Tel**: (45) 8715 0000

**Email**: housing@au.dk

## Alliance Group Postgraduate Scholarship

**Eligibility**: 1. Obtaining their first doctoral qualification 2. Domestic students 3. Undertaking research related to the improvement of livestock

**Level of Study**: Postgraduate

**Type**: Scholarship

**Value**: NZ $27,500 per annum plus domestic tuition fees waiver (excludes student services fee)

**Frequency**: Annual

**Country of Study**: New Zealand

**No. of awards offered**: Varies

**Funding**: Foundation

**Additional Information**: www.otago.ac.nz/study/scholarships/database/otago016137.html

### For further information contact:

**Tel**: (64) 800 80 80 98

**Email**: scholarships@otago.ac.nz

## Angus Ross Travel Scholarship in History

**Purpose**: Established by the family of Angus Ross in 2010, the Angus Ross Travel Scholarship in History is intended to assist PhD candidates studying history with the costs associated with off-campus field and archival research

**Eligibility**: Applications are open to current University of Otago PhD candidates who, as part of their PhD studies: 1. are conducting historically-focused research (preference will be given to candidates primarily based in the Department of History and Art History); 2. will be conducting off-campus field or archival research in the year for which the scholarship is awarded (the year following application). Note that this scholarship is not intended to support travel to a conference. Previous recipients are not eligible to apply for the scholarship in subsequent years.

**Level of Study**: Postgraduate

**Type**: Scholarship

**Value**: NZ$1,000

**Frequency**: Annual

**Country of Study**: New Zealand

**Application Procedure**: Every applicant must submit to the Doctoral and Scholarships Office by 1 November. 1. A brief Curriculum Vitae; 2. A description of the work to be conducted with the assistance of the scholarship, and the significance this work will have for their PhD research (no more than 500 words); 3. A budget of costs associated with the work to be conducted with the assistance of the scholarship; 4. A letter of support from their PhD supervisor. The University may also access academic transcripts and evidence of PhD progress in assessing this award. In exceptional circumstances applicants may be required to attend an interview either in person or by teleconference.

**Closing Date**: 1 November

**Funding**: Foundation

**Additional Information**: www.otago.ac.nz/graduate-research/scholarships/otago0055091.pdf

## Brenda Shore Award for Women

**Purpose**: Brenda Shore was an enthusiastic, enterprising person famous for her energy and passion. Over the course of 35 years Brenda became a prominent figure in the University of Otago Botany Department, both as a researcher and teacher, until her retirement in 1983. Leading by example Brenda Shore established this fund to help support women who have that same passion and energy for the natural sciences, particularly where their research relates to the Otago, Southland or Antarctic region

**Eligibility**: 1. University of Otago women graduates. 2. Women graduates carrying out research related to the Otago, Southland and Antarctic area. 3. Women graduates carrying out research for a postgraduate degree at the University of Otago

**Level of Study**: Postgraduate

**Type**: Award

**Value**: Up to NZ$15,000

**Length of Study**: 1 year

**Frequency**: Annual

**Country of Study**: New Zealand

**No. of awards offered**: Varies

**Closing Date**: 28 February

**Funding**: Foundation

**Additional Information**: www.otago.ac.nz/study/scholar ships/database/otago014683.html

## Bruggeman Postgraduate Scholarship in Classics

**Eligibility**: 1. Obtaining their first Master's or Doctoral qualification 2. Domestic students 3. Undertaking research in the field of Classics

**Level of Study**: Postgraduate

**Type**: Scholarship

**Value**: NZ $15,000 stipend per annum (Master's); NZ $27,000 stipend per annum (PhD) plus domestic tuition fee waiver (excludes student services fee)

**Frequency**: Annual

**Country of Study**: New Zealand

**No. of awards offered**: Varies

**Funding**: Foundation

**Additional Information**: www.otago.ac.nz/study/scholar ships/database/otago016143.html

### For further information contact:

**Tel**:        (64) 800 80 80 98
**Email**:    scholarships@otago.ac.nz

## China Scholarship Council and Griffith University PhD Scholarships

**Purpose**: China Scholarship Council and Griffith University PhD Scholarships are offering scholarships to the students of China who are interested to pursue PhD degree programme at the Griffith university which is based in the United Kingdom, through this scholarship the students develops the research opportunities with an environment that collaborates the students

**Eligibility**: The participants should meet all the necessary requirements, polices and the rules that are offered by the China Scholarship Council and Griffith University, this scholarship program is extended to all research programs where, The applicants of the China Scholarship Council and Griffith University PhD scholarships should meet the academic entry requirements which also include the level of English language Proficiency with good communication skills and the student must be certified or held with a bachelor degree with a first class or second-class honors which come under the Division A or the Master's degree or its equivalent incorporating a significant research component, from a recognised institution or its equivalent, Candidates are selected based on the criteria that was instructed by China Scholarship Council

**Level of Study**: Postgraduate

**Type**: Scholarship

**Length of Study**: 4 year

**Frequency**: Annual

**Country of Study**: New Zealand

**Closing Date**: January

**Funding**: Foundation

## Demand Response in the Agricultural Sector PhD Scholarship

**Purpose**: The Centre for Sustainability calls for expressions of interest in a PhD scholarship focusing on "Demand response in the agricultural sector – a socio-technical study". The research will examine farmer interest in electricity demand response, examine the barriers that farmers face in engaging in demand response, and identify solutions to improve adoption of demand response strategies. Candidates with a background in socio-technical studies would be ideal, although those with a background in social or physical sciences will be considered if they have an interest in extending their theoretical and methodological scope. The scholarship is funded by Science for Technological Innovation, a National Science Challenge and the successful candidate will be based at the Centre for Sustainability, University of Otago

**Level of Study**: Postgraduate
**Type**: Scholarship
**Value**: NZ$27,500
**Length of Study**: 3 year
**Frequency**: Annual
**Country of Study**: New Zealand
**Closing Date**: 22 February
**Funding**: Foundation, International office
**Additional Information**: www.otago.ac.nz/study/scholar ships/database/otago634665.html

### For further information contact:

**Email**: janet.stephenson@otago.ac.nz

## Diane Campbell-Hunt Memorial Award

**Purpose**: Diane Campbell-Hunt was a PhD candidate in the Department of Geography, funded by a Tertiary Education Commission Top Achiever Doctoral scholarship. She had completed two-thirds of her PhD programme at the time of her death. Her project looked at the long-term sustainability of fenced sanctuaries in New Zealand in a multi-disciplinary analysis: ecological, economic, social, and governmental
**Eligibility**: 1. Be enrolled and confirmed in a PhD programme in any Department or School at the University of Otago. 2. Have had accepted a peer-reviewed academic paper (conference or journal) that contributes to New Zealand conservation (as defined above), and in which they are the lead author. 3 Not have previously been awarded the award
**Level of Study**: Postgraduate
**Type**: Award
**Value**: NZ$1,000
**Frequency**: Annual
**Country of Study**: New Zealand
**Closing Date**: 30 June
**Funding**: Foundation
**Additional Information**: www.otago.ac.nz/geography/study/scholarships/otago091040.pdf

## Douglass D Crombie Award in Physics

**Purpose**: Established by the University of Otago Council in memory of Mr Douglass D Crombie. This award has been made possible by a generous bequest from the late Mr Crombie for the purpose of encouraging postgraduate research in Physics. This award will be offered to an outstanding University of Otago Physics graduate intending to undertake a PhD in Physics at an overseas university

**Eligibility**: 1. Were born in New Zealand. 2. Graduated or will soon graduate from the University of Otago with a degree in Physics. 3. Are intending to pursue doctoral-level studies in Physics. 4. Are intending to undertake their studies at an English speaking University in an English speaking country (excluding New Zealand). 5. Have displayed outstanding academic ability
**Level of Study**: Postgraduate
**Type**: Award
**Value**: NZ$7,000
**Frequency**: Annual
**Country of Study**: New Zealand
**Application Procedure**: 1. be born in New Zealand 2. have graduated or will soon graduate from the University of Otago with a degree in Physics 3. be intending to pursue doctoral-level studies in Physics 4. be intending to undertake their studies at an English speaking University in an English speaking country (excluding New Zealand) 5. have displayed outstanding academic ability
**No. of awards offered**: 1
**Funding**: Foundation
**Additional Information**: www.otago.ac.nz/study/scholar ships/database/otago040266.html

### For further information contact:

Scholarships Office, Graduate Research School, PO Box 56, Dunedin 9054, New Zealand.

**Tel**: (64) 3 479 7000
**Email**: scholarships@otago.ac.nz

## Dr Sulaiman Daud 125th Jubilee Postgraduate Scholarship

**Purpose**: This scholarship was established in 1994 to mark the 125th Anniversary of the foundation of the University of Otago, New Zealand's oldest university. The purpose of the scholarship is to assist an exceptional postgraduate research student from Malaysia to attend the University
**Eligibility**: 1. Unless otherwise stated in these conditions or within the schedule, doctoral and Masters' scholarships are open only to Domestic Fee Paying Students. International candidates studying for professional doctorates are eligible to apply but if awarded a scholarship the tuition fee waiver will be capped at the domestic rate. 2. In the case of applicants for a doctoral scholarship, confirmation of the scholarship is dependent on approval of their application for admission to the relevant doctoral programme and completion of the enrolment procedure. 3. In the case of applicants for a Master's

scholarship, confirmation of the scholarship is dependent on approval of their application to register as a Master's candidate and completion of the enrolment procedure

**Level of Study**: Postgraduate

**Type**: Scholarship

**Value**: Establishment allowance of NZ$575; domestic tuition fee waiver (excludes student services fee); health insurance to the value of NZ$600; NZ$27,000 per annum stipend; educational allowance of NZ$550

**Length of Study**: 1 year

**Frequency**: Annual

**Country of Study**: New Zealand

**No. of awards offered**: 1

**Funding**: Foundation

**Additional Information**: www.otago.ac.nz/study/scholarships/database/otago020604.html

### For further information contact:

P.O. Box 514070, Milwaukee, WI 53203-3470, United States of America.

**Email**:    scholarships@otago.ac.nz

## Elizabeth Jean Trotter Postgraduate Research Travelling Scholarship in Biomedical Sciences

**Purpose**: Established by the University of Otago Council from a generous donation in memory of Elizabeth Jean Trotter

**Eligibility**: 1. Be enrolled for a PhD or in the research year of a Master's programme with primary supervision in the Otago School of Medical Sciences (OSMS). 2. Be undertaking research in a Biomedical Sciences field

**Level of Study**: Postgraduate

**Type**: Fellowships

**Value**: Up to NZ$5,000

**Length of Study**: 1 year

**Frequency**: Annual

**Country of Study**: New Zealand

**Application Procedure**: Every application for the scholarship must be submitted to the University of Otago Scholarships Office by the closing date. Every applicant must submit: 1. A completed application form detailing the purpose of, and benefits expected to result from, the proposed travel. 2. A letter of support from the candidate's primary supervisor, addressing the candidate's work to date and the value of the chosen conference, workshop, or laboratory visit, to the candidate. 3. A brief Curriculum Vitae. 4. Title of proposed oral presentation or poster at the chosen conference (if applicable)

**No. of awards offered**: Varies

**Closing Date**: 1 November

**Funding**: Foundation

**Additional Information**: www.otago.ac.nz/study/scholarships/database/otago622380.html

### For further information contact:

**Tel**:    (64) 3 479 7000

## Elman Poole Travelling Scholarship

**Purpose**: Dr Elman Poole and the University of Otago are pleased to be able to offer this award to promote, encourage and facilitate research by providing grants to PhD students of the University of Otago to study overseas during their PhD, for a period normally not less than three months and not more than six months to gain experience or to use facilities not normally available at Otago and to further their subsequent work or career at Otago

**Eligibility**: 1. Enrolled full-time for a Doctor of Philosophy (PhD) at the University of Otago. 2. Majoring in one of following areas: Physical or Biological Sciences, Health Sciences or music. 3. Intending to engage in study in the second or third year of his/her PhD outside of New Zealand. 4. New Zealand citizen or New Zealand permanent resident. 5. under 35 years of age on the first day of February in the year of application

**Level of Study**: Postgraduate

**Type**: Scholarship

**Value**: Maximum NZ$20,000, plus up to NZ$5,000 additional expenses

**Length of Study**: 2 year

**Frequency**: Annual

**Country of Study**: New Zealand

**Application Procedure**: 1. Enrolled full-time in PhD study at the University of Otago majoring in one of the following areas: physical or biological sciences, health sciences or music 2. Intending to engage in study outside of New Zealand in their second or third year of PhD study 3. New Zealand citizens or New Zealand permanent residents 4. Under the age of 35 on 1 February in the year of application; Preference will be given to candidates who were born in Otago or Southland.

**No. of awards offered**: Varies

**Closing Date**: 1 June

**Funding**: Foundation

**Additional Information**: www.otago.ac.nz/study/scholarships/database/otago014682.html

### For further information contact:

St David II Building, University of Otago, PO Box 56, Dunedin 9054, New Zealand.

## Freemasons Scholarships

**Purpose**: The Freemasons Scholarships are provided annually by Freemasons New Zealand and are administered by the Freemasons Charity

**Eligibility**: 1. Have a good academic report. 2. Be a New Zealand citizen or permanent resident. 3. Demonstrate good citizenship. 4. Show leadership potential. 5. Have proven community commitment

**Level of Study** Postgraduate

**Type**: Scholarship

**Value**: NZ$10,000

**Frequency**: Annual

**Country of Study**: New Zealand

**Closing Date**: 1 July

**Funding**: Foundation

**Additional Information**: freemasonsnz.org/charity/freemasons-university-scholarships/

### For further information contact:

**Email**: info@lincoln.ac.nz

## Fully Funded PhD Scholarships

**Purpose**: Fully Funded PhD Scholarships, University of Sheffield, United Kingdom are offered to international students who attract the administration panel with their academic performance to pursue PhD programme. The candidates should have the knowledge in the English language and candidates from non-English countries should meet the abilities of the university by attaining the IELTS and other related tests. Annually the university offers five scholarships

**Eligibility**: 1. Eligible Countries: Overseas participants are eligible. 2 Acceptable Course or Subjects: The program will be awarded for the PhD degree in Quantitative Biology 3. Admissible Criteria: To be eligible, the applicants must meet all the given criteria: 4. Applicants must have a master's degree in a relevant area. There are three types of PhD students can apply for this grant: 5. Students with a life science degree, interested in working in an experimental lab, but with a high degree of motivation to learn the fundamentals of computational biology, and to develop quantitative skills to analyze data more effectively 6. Students with a life science degree interested in working in a dry computational lab, keen to deepen their quantitative skills and broaden their horizon in terms of experimental and computational techniques 7. Students with a non-biological background (e.g. computer science, maths, physics), who are highly motivated to transition to Life Sciences

**Level of Study**: Postgraduate

**Type**: Scholarship

**Frequency**: Annual

**Country of Study**: New Zealand

**Application Procedure**: Aspirants are suggested to take part in a PhD degree program at the university. And then apply for the grants through completing the career5.successfactors.eu/sfcareer/jobreqcareer?jobId=14879&company=universitdP

**No. of awards offered**: 15

**Funding**: Foundation

**Additional Information**: scholarship-positions.com/15-fully-funded-phd-studentsnational-students-in-switzerhips-for-interland/2019/09/27/

## Future Global Leaders Fellowship Program

**Purpose**: Future Global Leaders Fellowship Program is an international program designed for Freshmen students who are interested to pursue research and fellowship training, where the fellowship program is an internationally competitive program which is intended for granting first generation and low-income students entry into the Fortis Society, which is the world's first private network for diverse leaders, The main objective of the program is to gather students from world's top most universities which includes-Harvard University, the University of Oxford, Sciences Po, and Peking University

**Eligibility**: Applicants must be first-year university students and must fit the following eligibility criteria: 1. First-Generation or Low-Income University Student – students who do not have a family history of higher education, or who come from a low-income background. 2. Track Record of Academic Excellence – throughout high school and during the first months of the current school year. 3. Proven Leadership Abilities – through self-started initiatives and ventures, or leadership in their schools or communities

**Level of Study**: Postgraduate

**Type**: Fellowship

**Frequency**: Annual

**Country of Study**: New Zealand

**Closing Date**: 31 January

**Funding**: Foundation

**Additional Information**: opportunitydesk.org/2018/11/07/future-global-leaders-fellowship-2019/

## Gilbert M Tothill Scholarship in Psychological Medicine

**Purpose**: Doctoral scholarships are awarded by the University Council, on the recommendation of the Senate, to candidates proceeding to a course of supervised doctoral study at this University. These scholarships are normally available only to students seeking to obtain their first doctoral qualification

**Eligibility**: In the case of an applicant for a doctoral scholarship who has completed a Master's degree by papers and thesis (at least 0.75 EFTS), the grades of all relevant2 advanced level papers counting towards the award of the degree and the thesis will be taken into account. An explanation of the time taken for completion of the thesis may be requested and considered by the Scholarships and Prizes Committee if the thesis has taken more than 2 EFTS (2 fulltime years) to complete

**Level of Study**: Postgraduate

**Type**: Scholarship

**Value**: NZ$10,000

**Length of Study**: 3 year

**Frequency**: Annual

**Country of Study**: New Zealand

**Funding**: Foundation

**Additional Information**: www.otago.ac.nz/study/scholarships/database/otago089208.html

### For further information contact:

**Email**:    scholarships@otago.ac.nz

## Helen Rosa Thacker Scholarship in Neurological Research

**Purpose**: The Helen Rosa Thacker Scholarship in Neurological Research was established by Helen Rosa Thacker in 2012 to support research and teaching in the field of neurology at the University of Otago. The scholarship aims to recognise, reward and inspire a particularly good PhD student. This scholarship can be held alongside an existing scholarship. This scholarship will be awarded for one year, with a chance of extension to a second year due to outstanding progress

**Eligibility**: 1. A full time PhD student in neurological research at the University of Otago. 2. A male scholar holding a New Zealand birth certificate. 3. Available to receive the scholarship in person and provide updates on the progress of their research

**Level of Study**: Postgraduate

**Type**: Scholarship

**Value**: NZ$5,000

**Length of Study**: 1 year

**Frequency**: Annual

**Country of Study**: New Zealand

**Application Procedure**: 1. A full time PhD student in neurological research at the University of Otago 2. A male scholar holding a New Zealand birth certificate 3. Available to receive the scholarship in person and provide updates on the progress of their research

**Closing Date**: 26 October

**Funding**: Foundation

**Additional Information**: www.otago.ac.nz/study/scholarships/database/otago055663.html

### For further information contact:

Jane Reynolds, Administrative Assistant, Brain Health Research Centre, C/- Department of Anatomy, PO Box 56, Dunedin 9054, New Zealand.

**Tel**:    (64) 3 479 7612

**Email**:    bhrc@otago.ac.nz

## James Park Scholarship in Geology

**Purpose**: Masters' scholarships are awarded by the University Council, on the recommendation of the Senate, to candidates in the first year of their thesis research for a Master's degree which constitutes entry to the PhD course at this University. These scholarships are available only to students seeking to obtain their first research-based Master's qualification

**Eligibility**: 1. Unless otherwise stated in these conditions or within the schedule, doctoral and Masters' scholarships are open only to Domestic Fee Paying Students. International candidates studying for professional doctorates are eligible to apply but if awarded a scholarship the tuition fee waiver will be capped at the domestic rate. 2. In the case of applicants for a doctoral scholarship, confirmation of the scholarship is dependent on approval of their application for admission to the relevant doctoral programme and completion of the enrolment procedure. 3. In the case of applicants for a Master's scholarship, confirmation of the scholarship is dependent on approval of their application to register as a Master's candidate and completion of the enrolment procedure

**Level of Study**: Postgraduate

**Type**: Scholarship

**Value**: NZ$15,000 stipend per annum (Master's); NZ$27,000 stipend per annum (PhD); domestic tuition fee waiver (excludes student services fee)

**Frequency**: Annual

**Country of Study**: New Zealand

**No. of awards offered**: Varies

**Funding**: Foundation

**Additional Information**: For further information about the application, please contact the Scholarships Office at the University of Otago email scholarships@otago.ac.nz www.otago.ac.nz/study/scholarships/database/otago020608.html

### For further information contact:

Educational Credential Evaluators, Inc., P.O. Box 514070, Milwaukee, WI 53203-3470, USA.

**Tel**:    (1) 414 289 3400

**Email**:    scholarships@otago.ac.nz

## Macandrew-Stout Postgraduate Scholarship in Economics

**Purpose**: Established from funds made available by public subscription in memory of the late James Macandrew, member of the Council and one of the founders of the University and in 1920 by Sir Robert Stout, KCMG, Chief Justice of New Zealand

**Eligibility**: 1. Unless otherwise stated in these conditions or within the schedule, doctoral and Masters' scholarships are open only to Domestic Fee Paying Students. International candidates studying for professional doctorates are eligible to apply but if awarded a scholarship the tuition fee waiver will be capped at the domestic rate. 2. In the case of applicants for a doctoral scholarship, confirmation of the scholarship is dependent on approval of their application for admission to the relevant doctoral programme and completion of the enrolment procedure. 3. In the case of applicants for a Master's scholarship, confirmation of the scholarship is dependent on approval of their application to register as a Master's candidate and completion of the enrolment procedure

**Level of Study** Postgraduate

**Type**: Scholarship

**Value**: NZ$15,000 stipend per annum (Master's); NZ$27,000 stipend per annum (PhD); domestic student fee waiver (excludes student services fee)

**Frequency**: Annual

**Country of Study**: New Zealand

**Funding**: Foundation

**Additional Information**: For further information about the application, please contact the Scholarships Office at the University of Otago email scholarships@otago.ac.nz www.otago.ac.nz/study/scholarships/database/otago020612.html

### For further information contact:

Educational Credential Evaluators, Inc., P.O. Box 514070, Milwaukee, WI 53203-3470, USA.

**Tel**: (1) 414 289 3400
**Email**: scholarships@otago.ac.nz

## Neuropsychology Scholarships

**Purpose**: To investigate how visual information is used by humans in the learning of new skills

**Eligibility**: Open to applicants with an undergraduate qualification and a background or interest in cognitive science or neuropsychology. The project would suit a self-motivated person who is able to work well with participants and patients and other members on the study team. A working knowledge of the software package MATLAB and experience in programming with its language, is highly desirable

**Level of Study**: Postgraduate

**Type**: Scholarship

**Value**: NZ$12,000 per year for 2 years maximum, plus a maximum of NZ$4,000 per year towards tuition fees

**Application Procedure**: Applicants must enquire in the first instance to the director of the Cognitive Science programme

**Contributor**: Marsden Fund of the Royal Society of New Zealand

### For further information contact:

**Tel**: (64) 3 479 5269
**Fax**: (64) 3 479 8335
**Email**: lfranz@psy.otago.ac.nz

## Nga Pae O Te Maramatanga Doctoral Scholarships

**Purpose**: Fostering Te Pa Harakeke – understanding, achieving and maintaining 'healthy and prosperous families of mana' and the lessons this may hold for New Zealand families overall. Understanding what 'Te Pa Harakeke' is, enabling it to be achieved and addressing the barriers

**Eligibility**: For Maori or indigenous students who are currently enrolled or in the process of enrolling in a recognised doctoral programme of study and research at a tertiary institution. Applicants must not work more than 10 hours per week in paid employment while in receipt of this scholarship

**Level of Study**: Postgraduate

**Type**: Scholarship

**Value**: NZ$25,000

**Length of Study**: 3 year

**Frequency**: Annual

**Country of Study**: New Zealand

**Closing Date**: 30 September

**Funding**: Foundation

**Additional Information**: www.otago.ac.nz/study/scholarships/database/otago021502.html

## Noni Wright Scholarship

**Purpose**: Established by the University Council in association with the Guardian Trust in 2011 to provide support for Theatre Studies students to pursue postgraduate study. The scholarship was made possible by a generous endowment from the late Mrs Eleanor Wright, to honour the memory of her daughter Noni Wright, who was well known in drama circles, and had appeared on programmes for the BBC

**Eligibility**: The scholarship is open to both domestic and international students. Applicants must be currently enrolled or intending to enrol for full-time study at the University of Otago in the year following the closing date, for the degree of

MA or MFA in Theatre Studies, or for a PhD researching a topic in Theatre Studies
**Level of Study**: Postgraduate
**Type**: Scholarship
**Value**: NZ$5,000
**Length of Study**: 1 year
**Frequency**: Annual
**Country of Study**: New Zealand
**Closing Date**: 1 November
**Funding**: Foundation
**Additional Information**: www.otago.ac.nz/study/scholar ships/database/otago030561.html

**For further information contact:**

**Email**:     scholarships@otago.ac.nz

## Patricia Pratt Scholarships in Musical Performance

**Purpose**: The purpose of the scholarship is to assist outstanding New Zealand musical performers who have completed an honours degree in musical performance in New Zealand to continue their musical development at a renowned international music school or conservatorium. The scholarship will be awarded for classical music performance including vocal or instrumental performance or conducting
**Eligibility**: 1. Be New Zealand citizens with preference given to students who have resided in New Zealand for at least three years immediately preceding the year of selection. 2. Hold an honours degree in music performance from a New Zealand University
**Level of Study**: Postgraduate
**Type**: Scholarship
**Value**: Up to NZ$45,000
**Frequency**: Annual
**Country of Study**: New Zealand
**Closing Date**: 1 March
**Funding**: Foundation
**Additional Information**: www.universitiesnz.ac.nz/scholar ships/kia-ora-foundation-patricia-pratt-scholarship

## Postgraduate Tassell Scholarship in Cancer Research

**Purpose**: Doctoral scholarships are awarded by the University Council, on the recommendation of the Senate, to candidates proceeding to a course of supervised doctoral study at this University. These scholarships are normally available only to students seeking to obtain their first doctoral qualification

**Eligibility**: 1. Unless otherwise stated in these conditions or within the schedule, doctoral and Masters' scholarships are open only to Domestic Fee Paying Students. International candidates studying for professional doctorates are eligible to apply but if awarded a scholarship the tuition fee waiver will be capped at the domestic rate. 2. In the case of applicants for a doctoral scholarship, confirmation of the scholarship is dependent on approval of their application for admission to the relevant doctoral programme and completion of the enrolment procedure. 3. In the case of applicants for a Master's scholarship, confirmation of the scholarship is dependent on approval of their application to register as a Master's candidate and completion of the enrolment procedure
**Level of Study**: Postgraduate
**Type**: Scholarship
**Value**: NZ$27,000
**Frequency**: Annual
**Country of Study**: New Zealand
**Closing Date**: Applicants can apply anytime
**Funding**: Foundation
**Additional Information**: www.otago.ac.nz/study/scholar ships/database/otago035878.html

**For further information contact:**

**Email**:     scholarships@otago.ac.nz

## Ramboll Masters Scholarship for International Students

**Purpose**: Ramboll Masters Scholarship for International Students provides scholarships to the students all over the world who are pursuing masters degree and diploma in engineering in all related fields of Engineering, Natural Science, Political Science, Economics or Architecture, the candidates are selected based on the academic merit considering their projects and profile, the Ramboll offers opportunities to the students by providing inspirational and longstanding solutions that strengthen the ideas of candidate and enhance the nature and future
**Eligibility**: To be eligible to be granted a Ramboll Scholarship the applicant should meet necessary criteria such as the candidate is currently studying Engineering, Natural Science, Political Science, Economics or Architecture subjects as one of their course studies, and are going to study abroad outside of Denmark, to be eligible to apply the applicant should be a Diploma Engineer on semester 4 – 7 or studying on a Master's level, and must agree to send Ramboll two travel updates during their stay abroad
**Level of Study**: Postgraduate
**Type**: Scholarship
**Value**: NZ$25,000

**Frequency**: Annual
**Country of Study**: New Zealand
**Closing Date**: 8 May
**Funding**: Foundation
**Additional Information**: scholarship-fellowship.com/ramboll-masters-scholarship-for-international-students/

## Senior Smeaton Scholarship in Experimental Science

**Purpose**: Masters' scholarships are awarded by the University Council, on the recommendation of the Senate, tocandidates in the first year of their thesis research for a Master's degree which constitutes entry to the PhD course at this University. These scholarships are available only to students seeking to obtain their first research-based Master's qualification
**Eligibility**: 1. Unless otherwise stated in these conditions or within the schedule, doctoral and Masters' scholarships are open only to Domestic Fee Paying Students. 3 International candidates studying for professional doctorates are eligible to apply but if awarded a scholarship the tuition fee waiver will be capped at the domestic rate. 2. In the case of applicants for a doctoral scholarship, confirmation of the scholarship is dependent on approval of their application for admission to the relevant doctoral programme and completion of the enrolment procedure. 3. In the case of applicants for a Master's scholarship, confirmation of the scholarship is dependent on approval of their application to register as a Master's candidate and completion of the enrolment procedure
**Level of Study**: Postgraduate
**Type**: Scholarship
**Value**: NZ$27,000
**Frequency**: Annual
**Country of Study**: New Zealand
**Funding**: Foundation
**Additional Information**: www.otago.ac.nz/study/scholarships/database/otago020614.html

### For further information contact:

Educational Credential Evaluators, Inc. P.O. Box 514070, Milwaukee, WI 53203-3470, USA.

**Tel**: (1) 414 289 3400
**Email**: scholarships@otago.ac.nz

## The Dr Stella Cullington Postgraduate Scholarship in Ophthalmology

**Purpose**: Established in 2014 by the Faculty of Medicine, from a generous donation from Dr Stella Cullington.

Dr Cullington is a medical graduate and practised as a GP in United Kingdom and New Zealand. The Dr Stella Cullington Postgraduate Scholarship in Ophthalmology was created to support the sustainability and development of Ophthalmology Research within the academic discipline
**Eligibility**: 1. Be a NZ citizen or NZ permanent resident. 2. Hold a Bachelor of Medicine and Bachelor of Surgery degrees (MBChB) or an equivalent medical degree. 3. Demonstrate proof of potential academic research ability through (i) successful completion of a research Master's degree, or (ii) appropriate and equivalent prior research experience. 4. Be enrolled or intending to enrol for a MOphth or PhD at the University of Otago
**Level of Study**: Postgraduate
**Type**: Scholarship
**Value**: up to NZ$5,000
**Length of Study**: 1 year
**Frequency**: Annual
**Country of Study**: New Zealand
**No. of awards offered**: 1
**Funding**: Foundation
**Additional Information**: www.otago.ac.nz/study/scholarships/database/otago597632.html

## The Eamon Cleary Trust Postgraduate Study Scholarship

**Purpose**: Established in 2016 by the University of Otago Council from a generous donation by the Eamon Cleary Trust. The Eamon Cleary Trust Postgraduate Study Scholarship was created to support University of Otago students undertaking postgraduate research in Irish Studies. The scholarship may be used for expenses associated with postgraduate study, such as tuition fees, research expenses or travel associated with their research programme
**Eligibility**: 1. Be intending to enrol in a Doctoral or Research Masters programme in Irish Studies or a Coursework Masters programme in Irish Studies with a research component greater than or equal to 60 points at the University of Otago for the year of the award. 2. Have made contact to discuss satisfactory supervisory arrangements with the Eamon Cleary Professor of Irish Studies prior to submission of the application
**Level of Study**: Postgraduate
**Type**: Scholarship
**Value**: Between NZ$15,000 to NZ$25,000
**Frequency**: Annual
**Country of Study**: New Zealand
**Closing Date**: 1 November
**Funding**: Foundation
**Additional Information**: www.otago.ac.nz/study/scholarships/database/otago616894.html

## The Joan, Arthur & Helen Thacker Aboriginal and/or Torres Strait Islander Postgraduate Scholarship

**Purpose**: Established by the University of Otago Council in 2014, through the provision of funding from Helen R Thacker, this scholarship aims to support students of Aboriginal and/or Torres Strait Islander descent to undertake postgraduate studies in the field of Health Sciences at the University of Otago. The purpose of the fund is to support research and training in health sciences subjects that may have a future benefit to Aboriginal and/or Torres Strait Islander communities

**Eligibility**: 1. Aboriginal and/or Torres Strait Islander descent. 2. Australian citizens and residing in Australia at the time of application. 3. Planning to enrol in a postgraduate course of study in either Dental Technology, Dentistry, Oral Health, Medicine, Neuroscience, Pharmacy or Radiation Therapy at the University of Otago. 4. Planning to undertake study/research that is likely to be of future benefit to their Aboriginal and/or Torres Strait Islander community. 5. Intending to return to work in Australia after their course of study

**Level of Study**: Postgraduate

**Type**: Scholarship

**Value**: NZ$30,000

**Frequency**: Annual

**Country of Study**: New Zealand

**Closing Date**: 1 October

**Funding**: Foundation

**Additional Information**: www.otago.ac.nz/study/scholarships/database/otago106285.html

## The Robinson Dorsey Postgraduate Scholarship

**Purpose**: The Robinson Dorsey Postgraduate Scholarship was created to support postgraduate students who are returning to university study after a break, and/or who through their personal circumstances, are not eligible for usual scholarships

**Eligibility**: 1. A NZ citizen or NZ permanent resident. 2. Enrolled or intending to enrol in a postgraduate diploma, honours degree, Master of Science or PhD degree in Physiology or Human Nutrition at the University of Otago. 3. Returning to university study after a break, and/or who through their personal circumstances are not eligible for usual scholarships

**Level of Study**: Postgraduate

**Type**: Scholarship

**Value**: NZ$25,000 full time PhD study or NZ$13,000 full time Masters', Postgraduate Diploma or Honours Study

**Frequency**: Annual

**Country of Study**: New Zealand

**Closing Date**: 28 February

**Funding**: Foundation

**Additional Information**: www.otago.ac.nz/study/scholarships/database/otago664753.html

### For further information contact:

Post to Student Administration (Scholarships), St David II Building, University of Otago, PO Box 56, Dunedin 9054, New Zealand.

**Email**: scholarships@otago.ac.nz

## University of Helsinki Masters Scholarships

**Purpose**: University of Helsinki Masters Scholarships are offered to the students of international arena who are interested to pursue masters degree from the university, the scholarships offered are fully funded which includes full tuition fees, eligible candidates are selected by the committee not only based on academic criteria the committee will also consider the variety and diversity of the applicants and grant the scholarships to those coming from different backgrounds and fields of studies, the main aim hidden under the scholarship program is to create a rich and diverse learning environment at the University of Helsinki, candidates should receive an offer from the university to apply for the scholarship

**Eligibility**: All candidates must meet the following requirements: 1. You are eligible for the Master's programme at the University of Helsinki 2. The country of your nationality is outside the EU/EEA and you meet the requirements for obtaining an entry visa and residence permit for Finland. More information at the Studyinfo. 3. You have obtained excellent results in your previous studies and can prove this in your application.

**Level of Study**: Postgraduate

**Type**: Scholarship

**Value**: Tuition fees range from €13,000 to €18,000

**Length of Study**: 2 years

**Frequency**: Annual

**Country of Study**: Finland

**Application Procedure**: The scholarship application will be filled out in the same application system and simultaneously with your online application to the University of Helsinki English language Master's programmes. The possible scholarship-related documents should be delivered with the other enclosed documents of your degree application.

**Closing Date**: 10 January

**Funding**: Private

**Additional Information**: Tuition fee will range from €13,000 to €18,000. For further information on the scholarship, refer the below link. www.helsinki.fi/en/admissions/

scholarship-programme www.afterschoolafrica.com/17865/university-helsinki-masters-scholarships/

## University of Otago Academic General Practitioner Registrar PhD Scholarship

**Purpose**: Established in 2013 by the Faculty of Medicine, the University of Otago Academic General Practitioner Registrar PhD Scholarship was created to support the sustainability and development of the Primary Health Care and General Practice academic discipline. The scholarship aims to help establish research capability among a new generation of General Practitioners by supporting the achievement of a Doctoral degree (PhD) at the University of Otago as well as vocational registration as a Fellow of the Royal New Zealand College of General Practitioners (RNZCGP)

**Eligibility**: 1. A NZ citizen or NZ permanent resident. 2. Hold a Bachelor of Medicine and Bachelor of Surgery degrees (MBChB) or an equivalent medical degree. 3. Demonstrate a formal commitment to a General Practice career by having successfully completed either (i) the General Practice Education Programme first year (GPEP1) with an above average pass in the Primary Membership Examination (PRIMEX) or (ii) a RNZCGP Fellowship. 4. Have successfully completed either the 'Health Sciences Research Methods' paper (HASX417) or the 'Research Methods in General Practice' paper (GENX821), or an alternative 30 point postgraduate research methods paper with a minimum B+ grade. 5. Demonstrate proof of potential academic research ability through (i) successful completion of a research Master's degree, or (ii) appropriate and equivalent prior research experience

**Level of Study**: Postgraduate
**Type**: Scholarship
**Value**: NZ$25,000 per year for full-time study or NZ$12,500 per year for part-time study plus a tuition fee waiver for the PhD thesis paper for the period of tenure
**Frequency**: Annual
**Country of Study**: New Zealand
**Closing Date**: 15 September
**Funding**: Foundation
**Additional Information**: www.otago.ac.nz/study/scholarships/database/otago049881.html

## University of Otago China Scholarship Council Doctoral Scholarship

**Purpose**: Masters' scholarships are awarded by the University Council, on the recommendation of the Senate, to candidates in the first year of their thesis research for a Master's degree which constitutes entry to the PhD course at this University. These scholarships are available only to students seeking to obtain their first research-based Master's qualification

**Eligibility**: 1. Unless otherwise stated in these conditions or within the schedule, doctoral and Masters' scholarships are open only to Domestic Fee Paying Students. International candidates studying for professional doctorates are eligible to apply but if awarded a scholarship the tuition fee waiver will be capped at the domestic rate. 2. In the case of applicants for a doctoral scholarship, confirmation of the scholarship is dependent on approval of their application for admission to the relevant doctoral programme and completion of the enrolment procedure. 3. In the case of applicants for a Master's scholarship, confirmation of the scholarship is dependent on approval of their application to register as a Master's candidate and completion of the enrolment procedure

**Level of Study**: Postgraduate
**Type**: Scholarship
**Frequency**: Annual
**Country of Study**: New Zealand
**Closing Date**: Applicants can apply anytime
**Funding**: Foundation
**Additional Information**: www.otago.ac.nz/study/scholarships/database/otago049881.html

### For further information contact:

**Email**:   scholarships@otago.ac.nz

## University of Otago City of Literature PhD Scholarship

**Purpose**: Masters' scholarships are awarded by the University Council, on the recommendation of the Senate, to candidates in the first year of their thesis research for a Master's degree which constitutes entry to the PhD course at this University. These scholarships are available only to students seeking to obtain their first research-based Master's qualification

**Eligibility**: 1. Unless otherwise stated in these conditions or within the schedule, doctoral and Masters' scholarships are open only to Domestic Fee Paying Students. 3 International candidates studying for professional doctorates are eligible to apply but if awarded a scholarship the tuition fee waiver will be capped at the domestic rate. 2. In the case of applicants for a doctoral scholarship, confirmation of the scholarship is dependent on approval of their application for admission to the relevant doctoral programme and completion of the enrolment procedure. 3. In the case of applicants for a Master's scholarship, confirmation of the scholarship is dependent on approval of their application to register as a Master's candidate and completion of the enrolment procedure

**Level of Study**: Postgraduate
**Type**: Scholarship
**Value**: NZ$27,000
**Frequency**: Annual
**Country of Study**: New Zealand
**Closing Date**: 30 September
**Funding**: Foundation
**Additional Information**: www.otago.ac.nz/study/scholarships/database/otago624693.html

**For further information contact:**

**Email**:     scholarships@otago.ac.nz

## University of Otago Doctoral Scholarships

**Purpose**: To fund research towards a PhD degree at the University of Otago
**Eligibility**: Open to applicants of any country but must be primarily resident in New Zealand during study
**Level of Study**: Doctorate, Research
**Type**: Scholarship
**Value**: NZ$27,000 stipend per annum plus a domestic tuition fees waiver for 36 months (excludes student services fee and insurance) Professional Doctorates (DClinDent, DMA, DBA, EDd) - NZ$27,000 stipend per annum plus a tuition fee waiver for up to 36 months capped at the domestic rate (excludes student services fee and insurance).
**Length of Study**: 3 years
**Frequency**: Annual
**Study Establishment**: The University of Otago
**Country of Study**: New Zealand
**Application Procedure**: Please visit www.otago.ac.nz/applynow
**No. of awards offered**: 200
**No. of awards given last year**: 180
**Additional Information**: www.otago.ac.nz/study/scholarships/database/otago014687.html

**For further information contact:**

**Tel**:       (64) 800 80 80 98
**Email**:     scholarships@otago.ac.nz

## University of Otago Doctorate in Medical Education Scholarship

**Purpose**: Established with funding from the Otago Medical School, this scholarship is intended to provide support for clinically qualified health care professionals with an interest in medical education to undertake research at PhD level. The research must be applicable to the enhancement of the Otago MB ChB programme. The scholarship will be awarded for a three-year period; part-time PhDs will be considered. The participants will perform medical educational research in their own educational setting at University of Otago campuses in Dunedin, Christchurch or Wellington, but associated sites e.g. Invercargill, Nelson, Palmerston North, Hawkes Bay will be considered provided satisfactory supervisory arrangements can be made
**Eligibility**: 1. Normally be a NZ citizen or NZ permanent resident. 2. Hold a clinical health care discipline degree. Non-clinically qualified people with a strong background in Education may be considered but priority will be given to applicants from the first category. 3. Provide confirmation that this is their first doctoral qualification. 4. Be enrolled or intending to enrol for a PhD.
**Level of Study**: Postgraduate
**Type**: Scholarship
**Value**: NZ$25,000 stipend per annum plus a domestic tuition fees waiver
**Frequency**: Annual
**Country of Study**: New Zealand
**Closing Date**: 20 February
**Funding**: Foundation
**Additional Information**: www.otago.ac.nz/study/scholarships/database/otago634374.html

## University of Otago International Master's Scholarship

**Purpose**: To assist international students in their master's thesis year of studies at the University of Otago
**Eligibility**: Open to all international applicants intending to study at the University of Otago who would normally be charged international fees
**Level of Study**: Postdoctorate, Research
**Type**: Scholarship
**Value**: NZ$13,000, International tuition fees (excluding insurance and student services fees)
**Frequency**: Annual
**Country of Study**: Any country
**Funding**: Private
**Additional Information**: scholarship-positions.com/university-of-otago-international-masters-research-scholarship-in-new-zealand/2019/09/28/

**For further information contact:**

Doctoral and Scholarships Office, PO Box 56, Dunedin, 9054, New Zealand.

**Email**:     university@otago.ac.uk

## University of Otago Maori Doctoral Scholarship

**Purpose**: Doctoral scholarships are awarded by the University Council, on the recommendation of the Senate, tocandidates proceeding to a course of supervised doctoral study at this University. These scholarships are normally available only to students seeking to obtain their first doctoral qualification

**Eligibility**: 1. Unless otherwise stated in these conditions or within the schedule, doctoral and Masters' scholarships are open only to Domestic Fee Paying Students. 3 International candidates studying for professional doctorates are eligible to apply but if awarded a scholarship the tuition fee waiver will be capped at the domestic rate. 2. In the case of applicants for a doctoral scholarship, confirmation of the scholarship is dependent on approval of their application for admission to the relevant doctoral programme and completion of the enrolment procedure

**Level of Study**: Postgraduate

**Type**: Scholarship

**Value**: NZ$27,000 stipend per annum plus a domestic tuition fees waiver for 36 months

**Frequency**: Annual

**Country of Study**: New Zealand

**No. of awards offered**: Varies

**Funding**: Foundation

**Additional Information**: www.otago.ac.nz/study/scholarships/database/otago014684.html

### For further information contact:

**Email**: scholarships@otago.ac.nz

## University of Otago Postgraduate Scholarship in Obstetrics and Gynaecology

**Purpose**: The Scholarship is intended to provide support for Obstetrics and Gynaecology trainees to carry out research in Obstetrics, Gynaecology and Women's Health whilst enrolled at the University of Otago for a graduate research degree, such as a Master of Medical Science (MMedSc) or Doctor of Philosophy (PhD). It is desirable, but not compulsory, that the research be carried out at the University of Otago

**Eligibility**: 1. Medical graduates (normally Registrars enrolled in the Royal Australian and New Zealand College of Obstetrics and Gynaecology Integrated Training Programme, or Members or Fellows of the College). 2. Enrolled in, or intending to enrol in a research Master's degree or PhD, normally towards a topic in the field of Obstetrics and Gynaecology or Women's Health

**Level of Study**: Postgraduate

**Type**: Scholarship

**Value**: NZ$25,000

**Frequency**: Annual

**Country of Study**: New Zealand

**Closing Date**: 17 November

**Funding**: Foundation

**Additional Information**: www.otago.ac.nz/study/scholarships/database/otago115047.html

## University of Otago Special Health Research Scholarship

**Purpose**: The University of Otago Special Health Research Scholarship provides funding to support outstanding doctoral students who are contemplating a career in Health Research.

**Eligibility**: 1. seeking to obtain their first doctoral qualification 2. studying, or planning to study, full-time 3. undertaking health related research

**Level of Study**: Postgraduate

**Type**: Scholarship

**Value**: NZ $27,000 stipend per annum plus domestic tuition fees waiver (excludes student services fee and insurance)

**Frequency**: Annual

**Country of Study**: New Zealand

**No. of awards offered**: 1

**Funding**: Foundation

**Additional Information**: www.otago.ac.nz/study/scholarships/database/otago016136.html

### For further information contact:

**Tel**: (64) 800 80 80 98

**Email**: scholarships@otago.ac.nz

## Waddell Smith Postgraduate Scholarship

**Purpose**: Masters' scholarships are awarded by the University Council, on the recommendation of the Senate, to candidates in the first year of their thesis research for a Master's degree which constitutes entry to the PhD course at this University. These scholarships are available only to students seeking to obtain their first research-based Master's qualification

**Eligibility**: 1. Unless otherwise stated in these conditions or within the schedule, doctoral and Masters' scholarships are open only to Domestic Fee Paying Students. International candidates studying for professional doctorates are eligible to apply but if awarded a scholarship the tuition fee waiver will be capped at the domestic rate. 2. In the case of applicants for a doctoral scholarship, confirmation of the scholarship is dependent on approval of their application for admission to the relevant doctoral programme and completion of the enrolment procedure. 3. In the case of applicants for a Master's scholarship, confirmation of the scholarship is dependent on approval of their application to register as a Master's candidate and completion of the enrolment procedure

**Level of Study**: Postgraduate
**Type**: Scholarship
**Value**: NZ$7,750 per annum
**Frequency**: Annual
**Country of Study**: New Zealand
**No. of awards offered**: Varies
**Funding**: Foundation
**Additional Information**: www.otago.ac.nz/study/scholarships/database/otago020616.html

### For further information contact:

Educational Credential Evaluators, Inc., P.O. Box 514070, Milwaukee, WI 53212, United States of America.

**Email**:    graduate@balliol.ox.ac.uk

### Williamson Medical Research PhD Scholarship

**Purpose**: The scholarship may be held by PhD candidates studying towards a PhD in the field of medical research. Applicants must have previously completed a medical degree and be New Zealand citizens (preference will be given to New Zealand–born applicants). The scholarship shall be awarded by the University of Council on the recommendation of the Faculty of Medicine
**Eligibility**: 1. Unless otherwise stated in these conditions or within the schedule, doctoral and Masters' scholarships are open only to Domestic Fee Paying Students. 3 International candidates studying for professional doctorates are eligible to apply but if awarded a scholarship the tuition fee waiver will be capped at the domestic rate. 2. In the case of applicants for a doctoral scholarship, confirmation of the scholarship is dependent on approval of their application for admission to the relevant doctoral programme and completion of the enrolment procedure. 3. In the case of applicants for a Master's scholarship, confirmation of the scholarship is dependent on approval of their application to register as a Master's candidate and completion of the enrolment procedure
**Level of Study**: Postgraduate
**Type**: Scholarship
**Value**: NZ$25,000
**Length of Study**: 3 year
**Frequency**: Annual
**Country of Study**: New Zealand

**Funding**: Foundation
**Additional Information**: www.otago.ac.nz/study/scholarships/database/otago046608.html

### For further information contact:

**Email**:    scholarships@otago.ac.nz

## University of Oxford

University Offices, Wellington Square, Oxford OX1 2JD, United Kingdom.

### Alan Turing Doctoral Studentships

**Eligibility**: Open to all graduate applicants for a variety of doctoral graduate courses related to data science. Please see website for further details and eligible subjects, including how to apply
**Level of Study**: Doctorate
**Type**: Studentship
**Value**: Studentships include a generous tax-free stipend of £20,500 per annum, a travel allowance and tuition fees (home/European Union rate) for a period of 3.5 years. A limited number of studentships include fully funded international tuition fees or a partial contribution towards international tuition fees
**Length of Study**: 3.5 years
**Country of Study**: Any country
**Additional Information**: Please visit the website: www.turing.ac.uk/opportunities/studentships/ www.birmingham.ac.uk/postgraduate/pgr/funding/alan-turing-phds.aspx

### For further information contact:

**Email**:    hr@turing.ac.uk

### Archaeology: AHRC

**Purpose**: Archaeology
**Eligibility**: Open to United Kingdom applicants for DPhils in Archaeology and Classical Archaeology. Other European Union nationals are eligible for a fees-only award. All eligible applicants will be automatically considered
**Level of Study**: Doctorate
**Type**: Scholarship
**Value**: University fee, college fee and full living expenses. Fees-only awards for non-United Kingdom, European Union students
**Length of Study**: Up to 3 years

**Country of Study**: Any country

**Closing Date**: 20 January

**Additional Information**: Please visit the website: www. humanities.ox.ac.uk/prospective_students/graduates/ahrc

### For further information contact:

**Email**: hca-research@ed.ac.uk

## Archaeology: Edward Hall Awards

**Purpose**: Archaeological Science

**Eligibility**: Open to all applicants for the MSc/MSt in Archaeological Science. All applicants to course will be automatically considered

**Level of Study**: Postgraduate

**Type**: Award

**Value**: £8,120

**Length of Study**: 1 year

**Country of Study**: Any country

**Closing Date**: 20 January

**Additional Information**: Please visit the website: www.arch. ox.ac.uk/graduate-archaeological-science.html www.european-funding-guide.eu/other-financial-assistance/13823-edward-hall-memorial-fund

### For further information contact:

**Email**: webofficer@arch.ox.ac.uk

## Area Studies: FirstRand Laurie Dippenaar Scholarship

**Purpose**: African Studies

**Eligibility**: Open to South African graduate applicants for the MSc African Studies

**Level of Study**: Postgraduate

**Type**: Scholarship

**Value**: value of R850,000

**Length of Study**: Period of fee liability

**Frequency**: Annual

**Study Establishment**: Wadham College

**Country of Study**: South Africa

**Application Procedure**: Please see website for further details, including how to apply

**Closing Date**: 20 February

**Additional Information**: Please visit the website: www. firstrand.co.za/csi/Pages/laurie-dippenaar-scholarship.aspx bursaries.firstrand.co.za/Bursary/FirstRandLaurieDippenaar Scholarship?AspxAutoDetectCookieSupport=1

## Atmospheric, Oceanic & Planetary Physics: STFC Studentships

**Eligibility**: Open to Home and European Union graduate applicants to the DPhil Atmospheric, Oceanic and Planetary Physics. To be eligible for consideration for these scholarships, applicants must be successful in being offered a place on their course after consideration of applications received by the relevant January deadline for the course

**Level of Study**: Doctorate

**Type**: Studentship

**Value**: Tuition and college fees, and a tax free stipend. Fees-only award for European Union students who have not been resident in the United Kingdom for the previous 3 years

**Length of Study**: 3 years

**Frequency**: Annual

**Country of Study**: Any country

**Closing Date**: 20 January

**Additional Information**: Please visit the website: www2. physics.ox.ac.uk/study-here/postgraduates/atmospheric-oceanic-and-planetary-physics/funding

### For further information contact:

**Email**: F.Y.Ogrin@exeter.ac.uk

## Balliol College: Balliol Economics Scholarship

**Eligibility**: Open to all graduate applicants to MPhil or MPhil +DPhil 2+2 in Economics. Students of any nationality applying to read for the MPhil in economics

**Type**: Scholarship

**Value**: Up to £6,500. When offered in conjunction with Clarendon funding this will create a combined award covering university and college fee and full living expenses

**Length of Study**: Up to 3 years

**Application Procedure**: Please see website for how to apply and more details

**Closing Date**: 22 January

**Additional Information**: www.balliol.ox.ac.uk/sites/default/files/balliol_economics_scholarship_2015_entry.pdf

### For further information contact:

**Email**: graduate.admissions@balliol.ox.ac.uk

## Balliol College: Brassey Italian Scholarship

**Eligibility**: Open to all applicants to postgraduate degrees in Modern Languages where Italian is the principal subject of study. Please see website for more details

**Level of Study**: Postgraduate, Research

**Type**: Scholarship
**Value**: College fee
**Length of Study**: Duration of fee liability
**Application Procedure**: Please see website for how to apply and more details
**Closing Date**: 22 January
**Additional Information**: www.balliol.ox.ac.uk/sites/default/files/brassey_italian_2014.pdf

**For further information contact:**

**Email**:    graduate.admissions@balliol.ox.ac.uk

## Balliol College: Eddie Dinshaw Scholarship

**Eligibility**: Open to all graduate applicants from India for relevant areas of study
**Level of Study**: Postgraduate, Research
**Type**: Scholarship
**Value**: Full living expenses
**Length of Study**: Up to 3 years
**Frequency**: Annual
**Application Procedure**: Please see website for more details and how to apply
**Closing Date**: 18 January
**Additional Information**: Eligible to nationals of India. Please check at www.balliol.ox.ac.uk/graduate-admissions/scholarships www.balliol.ox.ac.uk/sites/default/files/eddie_dinshaw_2020.pdf

**For further information contact:**

**Email**:    graduate.admissions@balliol.ox.ac.uk

## Balliol College: Foley-Bejar Scholarships

**Eligibility**: Open to all graduate applicants who a) were born in or who have one parent born in Mexico, Spain, or the Republic of Ireland, or who have a strong connection with Northern Ireland; and b) are ordinarily resident in Mexico, Spain or the Republic of Ireland. Please see website for more details
**Type**: Scholarship
**Value**: Stipend
**Length of Study**: Period of fee liability up to 4 years
**Country of Study**: Any country
**Application Procedure**: Please see website for more details and how to apply
**Closing Date**: 23 January
**Additional Information**: Please check at www.balliol.ox.ac.uk/graduate-admissions/scholarships www.balliol.ox.ac.uk/sites/default/files/foley_bejar_2017_0.pdf

**For further information contact:**

**Email**:    graduate@balliol.ox.ac.uk

## Balliol College: IKOS Half Bursary

**Eligibility**: Open to candidates of any nationality who have expressed an intention to pursue an academic, vocational or public-service oriented career following their degrees
**Level of Study**: Postgraduate, Research
**Type**: Bursary
**Value**: Up to £6,000 per year
**Length of Study**: Up to 3 years
**Application Procedure**: Applicants must apply to the University of Oxford for admission by the University's second deadline in January, and must apply for any University scholarship, including the Clarendon, for which they are eligible
**Closing Date**: 24 January
**Additional Information**: Please check at www.balliol.ox.ac.uk/graduate-admissions/scholarships www.balliol.ox.ac.uk/admissions/graduate-admissions/scholarships

**For further information contact:**

**Email**:    graduate.admissions@balliol.ox.ac.uk

## Balliol College: Jason Hu Scholarship

**Eligibility**: Open to all graduate applicants from Asia with preference for candidates from Taiwan and China
**Level of Study**: Postgraduate, Research
**Type**: Scholarship
**Value**: £10,000 per year
**Length of Study**: Up to 3 years
**Frequency**: Annual
**Application Procedure**: Please see website for more details and how to apply
**Closing Date**: 18 January
**Additional Information**: It is awarded in conjunction with Clarendon Fund or other award or scholarship. Four scholarships can only be offered to students from Taiwan and China as a whole, one can be offered to candidates from any Asian country www.balliol.ox.ac.uk/sites/default/files/jason_hu_2020.pdf

**For further information contact:**

**Email**:    graduate.admissions@balliol.ox.ac.uk

## Balliol College: McDougall Scholarship

**Eligibility**: Open to graduate applicants to Law
**Level of Study**: Graduate, Postgraduate

**Type**: Scholarship
**Value**: Combined with Research Council award will cover university fee, college fee and full living expenses
**Length of Study**: Up to 3 years
**Frequency**: Annual
**Application Procedure**: Please see website for how to apply and more details
**Closing Date**: 22 January
**Additional Information**: www.balliol.ox.ac.uk/sites/default/files/mcdougall_2020.pdf

**For further information contact:**

**Email**:    graduate.admissions@balliol.ox.ac.uk

## Balliol College: Peter Storey Scholarship

**Eligibility**: Open to all applicants to Master's degrees in History. May be awarded as a fully-funded scholarship in partnership with an AHRC award or as a standalone award of £10,000 per year. Please see website for more details
**Level of Study**: Postgraduate, Research
**Type**: Scholarship
**Value**: A minimum of £10,000 per year
**Length of Study**: Period of fee liability
**Application Procedure**: Please see website for more details and how to apply
**Closing Date**: 22 January
**Additional Information**: Scholarship will be awarded to a candidate with AHRC Funding www.balliol.ox.ac.uk/sites/default/files/storey_masters_2018_entry.pdf

**For further information contact:**

**Email**:    graduate.admissions@balliol.ox.ac.uk

## Balliol College: Snell Scholarship

**Purpose**: The College seeks to elect one Scholar who has gained an offer of admission to read for a higher degree at Balliol College after completing a degree at the University of Glasgow
**Eligibility**: Honours graduates or in their final Honours year, applicants must have a connection with Scotland by birth (either themselves or one parent), domicile (at least three years) or education at a school in Scotland (at least three years) before admission to the University of Glasgow. Graduates of the University of Glasgow. Please see website for more details including how to apply
**Type**: Scholarship
**Value**: Up to £10,000. When offered in conjunction with RCUK funding this will create a combined award covering university and college fee, and full living expenses

**Length of Study**: Up to 3 years
**Country of Study**: Any country
**Closing Date**: 22 January
**Additional Information**: Please check at www.balliol.ox.ac.uk/graduate-admissions/scholarships www.balliol.ox.ac.uk/sites/default/files/snell_2015_2.pdf

**For further information contact:**

**Email**:    outreach@balliol.ox.ac.uk

## Blavatnik School of Government: Africa Governance Initiative Scholarship

**Eligibility**: Open to all Master of Public Policy applicants who are ordinarily resident in Africa. Scholarships are awarded on the basis of outstanding academic ability, commitment to public service, a capacity to lead, an interest in and experience of improving governance in Africa, a commitment to completing their summer project on some aspect of governance in Africa, and a commitment to return to Africa after their time at the School to continue their work on governance there
**Level of Study**: Postgraduate
**Type**: Scholarship
**Value**: University fee, college fee and full living expenses
**Length of Study**: Period of fee liability
**Frequency**: Annual
**Country of Study**: Any country
**Application Procedure**: To apply, applicants must provide a supporting statement. Please see website for more details
**Closing Date**: 20 January
**Additional Information**: opportunitydesk.org/2019/08/01/africa-initiative-for-governance-scholarships-2020-2021/

**For further information contact:**

**Email**:    inquiries@aigafrica.org

## Blavatnik School of Government: African Initiative for Governance Scholarships

**Purpose**: Public Policy
**Eligibility**: Open to all Master of Public Policy applicants who are ordinarily resident in Nigeria and Ghana (and other West African nations). Scholarships are awarded on the basis of exceptional academic and leadership merit and/or potential. Applicants will usually hold an undergraduate degree from an African university. They should also intend to return to work in public service in Qualifying country for at least three years after completing their studies
**Level of Study**: Postgraduate
**Type**: Scholarship

**Value**: University fee, college fee and full living expenses
**Length of Study**: Period of fee liability
**Frequency**: Annual
**Country of Study**: Any country
**Application Procedure**: To apply, applicants must provide a supporting statement. Please see website for more details
**Closing Date**: 20 January
**Additional Information**: Please visit the website: www.bsg. ox.ac.uk/study/mpp/bsg-funding-options www.aigafrica.org/ Our-initatives/AIG-Scholarships

**For further information contact:**

**Email**:     enquiries@bsg.ox.ac.uk

## Blavatnik School of Government: Public Service Scholarship

**Purpose**: Public Policy
**Eligibility**: Open to all Master of Public Policy applicants. Scholarships are awarded on the basis of unwavering dedication to public service, shown through an exceptional academic and professional record
**Level of Study**: Postgraduate
**Type**: Scholarship
**Value**: University fee, college fee and full living expenses
**Length of Study**: Period of fee liability
**Frequency**: Annual
**Country of Study**: Any country
**Application Procedure**: To apply, applicants must provide a supporting statement. Please see website for more details
**Closing Date**: 10 January
**Additional Information**: Please visit the website: www.bsg. ox.ac.uk/study/mpp/bsg-funding-options ssc.govt.nz/assets/ SSC-Site-Assets/Workforce-and-Talent-Management/Diversity-Inclusion/Blavatnik-School-of-Govt-brochure.pdf

**For further information contact:**

**Email**:     enquiries@bsg.ox.ac.uk

## Blavatnik School of Government: The Lemann Fellows Scholarships

**Eligibility**: Open to all Master of Public Policy applicants that are ordinarily resident in Brazil. Scholarships are awarded on the basis of exceptional academic merit and a commitment to social change in Brazil. To apply applicants must provide a supporting statement
**Level of Study**: Postgraduate
**Type**: Scholarship
**Value**: University fee, college fee and full living expenses

**Length of Study**: Period of fee liability
**Country of Study**: Any country
**Application Procedure**: Please see the website for full details, including how to apply
**Closing Date**: 20 January
**Additional Information**: Please check at www.bsg.ox.ac.uk/ study/mpp/bsg-funding-options www.european-funding-guide.eu/other-financial-assistance/13898-university-college-blavatnik-school-government-scholarships

**For further information contact:**

**Email**:     enquiries@bsg.ox.ac.uk

## Blavatnik School of Government: The Walter Kwok Scholarships

**Eligibility**: Open to all Master of Public Policy applicants that are ordinarily resident in Hong Kong or China. Scholarships are awarded on the basis of exceptional academic merit and a commitment to change in the HKSAR region. Interviews may be held as part of the selection process
**Type**: Scholarship
**Value**: University fee, college fee and full living expenses
**Length of Study**: Period of fee liability
**Country of Study**: Any country
**Application Procedure**: Please see website for more details and how to apply
**Closing Date**: 31 March
**Additional Information**: Please check at www.bsg.ox.ac.uk/ study/mpp/bsg-funding-options kwokscholars.org/graduate-study-at-the-university-of-oxford-scholarship.html

**For further information contact:**

**Email**:     enquiries@bsg.ox.ac.uk

## Brasenose College: Senior Fiddian

**Eligibility**: Open to graduates who are former members of Monmouth School or Haberdashers Monmouth School for Girls
**Level of Study**: Graduate, Postgraduate
**Type**: Grant
**Value**: £3,000
**Length of Study**: Period of fee liability
**Study Establishment**: Brasenose College
**Country of Study**: Any country
**Application Procedure**: Please see website for more details
**Additional Information**: For more information, please check at www.bnc.ox.ac.uk/prospective-students/graduate-admissions/fees-funding

## For further information contact:

Brasenose College Radcliffe Square Oxford OX1 4AJ, United Kingdom.

**Email**:  college.office@bnc.ox.ac.uk

## Brasenose Hector Pilling Scholarship

**Purpose**: For graduates of Commonwealth countries
**Eligibility**: Open to graduates of any Commonwealth university, excluding the United Kingdom
**Level of Study**: Postgraduate
**Type**: Scholarship
**Value**: Fees and maintenance to be determined by the administrators of the Clarendon Fund Scholarships
**Frequency**: Annual
**Study Establishment**: Brasenose College, University of Oxford
**Country of Study**: United Kingdom
**Application Procedure**: Applicants must write for details
**No. of awards offered**: 1
**Funding**: Private
**Contributor**: In conjunction with the Clarendon Fund Studentship Scheme
**No. of awards given last year**: 1
**No. of applicants last year**: 1
**Additional Information**: This scholarship is offered in conjunction with the Clarendon Fund Studentship Scheme

## For further information contact:

**Email**:  international.office@admin.ox.ac.uk

## Brasenose Joint Commonwealth Studentship

**Eligibility**: Open to all applicants from Commonwealth countries. Please see website for more details
**Level of Study**: Graduate, Postgraduate
**Value**: University fee, college fee, and living expenses (of which £13K funded by BNC)
**Length of Study**: One year
**Study Establishment**: Brasenose
**Country of Study**: United Kingdom
**Application Procedure**: For more information, please check website: www.bnc.ox.ac.uk/prospective-students/graduate-admissions/fees-funding
**Closing Date**: 22 January
**Additional Information**: cscuk.dfid.gov.uk/apply/shared-scholarships/

## For further information contact:

**Email**:  lawfac@law.ox.ac.uk

## Business School (Saïd): Registrar's University of Oxford Scholarship

**Purpose**: To assist graduate students with fees and a living allowance
**Eligibility**: A portion of the scholarships will be available to candidates who have shown strong career progression and excellent career potential. Candidates should have strong communication skills, strong leadership ability or potential, and a readiness and enthusiasm to become a strong ambassador for the School whilst on the programme and beyond. A further portion of these scholarships will be awarded on the basis of academic excellence demonstrated through degree results, GMAT or GRE score, previous university prizes and awards, and other academic achievements. Candidates should also demonstrate good leadership skills and strong professional experience.
**Level of Study**: Postgraduate, MBA
**Type**: Scholarship
**Value**: No fixed value. We offer a range of partial awards, contributing towards course fees
**Length of Study**: 2 years
**No. of awards offered**: 40
**Additional Information**: www.sbs.ox.ac.uk/oxford-experience/scholarships-and-funding/oxford-pershing-square-scholarship

## For further information contact:

**Email**:  Diana.Hulin@admin.ox.ac.uk

## Chevening Scholarships

**Eligibility**: Eligibility varies by country
**Level of Study**: Graduate
**Type**: Scholarship
**Value**: University fee, college fee, and full living expenses
**Length of Study**: 1 year
**Country of Study**: Any country
**Application Procedure**: Please see website for more details and how to apply
**Closing Date**: 5 November
**Additional Information**: Please check at www.fco.gov.uk/en/about-us/what-we-do/scholarships/chevening/how-to-apply/ study-uk.britishcouncil.org/scholarships/chevening-scholarship

**For further information contact:**

**Email**:    international@lincoln.ac.uk

## Christ Church Senior Scholarship

**Purpose**: To enable graduate scholars to undertake training or a definite course of literary, educational, scientific or professional study

**Eligibility**: Open to candidates who will have been reading for a higher degree at the University of Oxford for at least 1 year, but not more than 2 years, by October 1st of the year in which the award is sought

**Level of Study**: Postgraduate

**Type**: Scholarship

**Value**: Varies

**Length of Study**: 2 years, with a possibility of renewal for a further year

**Frequency**: Annual

**Study Establishment**: Christ Church, University of Oxford

**Country of Study**: United Kingdom

**Application Procedure**: Applicants must write for details. Applications should be made in February

**No. of awards offered**: 102

**Closing Date**: 1 April

**No. of awards given last year**: 2

**No. of applicants last year**: 102

**Additional Information**: Normally, the scholarship is held in conjunction with an award from a government agency that pays the university fees www.ccgs.wa.edu.au/community/giving/the-students-scholarship

## Commonwealth Shared Scholarship Scheme (CSSS)

**Purpose**: To support students from developing Commonwealth countries who would not otherwise be able to study in the United Kingdom

**Eligibility**: Open to new students from developing Commonwealth countries. Candidates should normally be under 35 at the time the award begins. This scholarship is not available to those living or studying in a developed country, employees of government departments or parastatal organisations

**Level of Study**: Postgraduate

**Value**: University and college fees; full grant for living costs; return air travel to the United Kingdom

**Length of Study**: 1 year

**Country of Study**: Any country

**Application Procedure**: Candidates must apply to Oxford by completing the Graduate Application Form by Application Deadline 2. They must complete the CSSS application form and submit this to Student Funding Services by email or post by March 13th

**Closing Date**: 13 March

**Additional Information**:    www.ucl.ac.uk/scholarships/commonwealth-shared-scholarship-scheme

## Comparative Philology: Joint Christ Church Linguistics Graduate Scholarship

**Purpose**: To assist graduate students with fees and maintenance

**Eligibility**: Open to all

**Level of Study**: Postgraduate, Research

**Type**: Scholarship

**Value**: College fees and maintenance allowance of £2,000

**Length of Study**: Up to 3 years

**Closing Date**: 16 January

**For further information contact:**

**Email**:    kate.dobson@ling-phil.ox.ac.uk

## Computer Science: Department Studentships

**Purpose**: To develop practical methods, algorithms, and tools for a use-case driven approach to system-level hardware/software formal co-verification. A key objective, and the foundation for the methodology, will be the invention of a systematic abstraction framework that closes the gap, currently unaddressed, between a system and implementation levels in co-verification

**Eligibility**: Open to all applicants applying for a DPhil in Computer Science

**Level of Study**: Doctorate

**Type**: Studentship

**Value**: Course fee, college fee and stipend

**Length of Study**: 3 years

**Country of Study**: Any country

**Closing Date**: 10 March

**Additional Information**: Please visit the website: www.cs.ox.ac.uk/aboutus/vacancies/studentship.html

**For further information contact:**

**Email**:    enquiries@cs.ox.ac.uk

## Computer Science: Engineering and Physical Sciences Research Council (EPSRC) Doctoral Training Partnership Studentships

**Purpose**: Computer Science

**Eligibility**: Open to applicants applying for a DPhil in Computer Science. Home students and European Union students who have studied in the United Kingdom for the previous 3 years are eligible for full studentship. European Union students who have studied elsewhere in the European Union are eligible for fees only award

**Level of Study**: Doctorate

**Type**: Studentship

**Value**: Course fee, college fee and stipend (if eligible). Home students and European students who have studied in the United Kingdom for the previous 3 years are eligible for full studentship. European Union students who have studied elsewhere in the European Union are eligible for fees only award

**Length of Study**: Up to 3.5 years

**Country of Study**: Any country

**Closing Date**: 30 March

**Additional Information**: Please visit the website: www.cs. ox.ac.uk/aboutus/vacancies/studentship.html www.brunel. ac.uk/research/Research-degrees/PhD-Studentships/Student ship?id=a2efbe35-b0b9-46a7-b284-3fd40ff05174

## Continuing Education: MSc Programme Scholarship

**Eligibility**: Open to all applicants for the MSc in Sustainable Urban Development who apply by the Late-January deadline

**Level of Study** Postgraduate

**Type**: Scholarship

**Value**: Course fee

**Length of Study**: Duration of programme

**Frequency**: Annual

**Country of Study**: Anywhere

**Application Procedure**: Through Graduate Admissions website (www.ox.ac.uk/admissions/graduate/courses/msc-sustainable-urban-development)

**Closing Date**: 21 January

**Additional Information**: Please visit the website: www. conted.ox.ac.uk/about/msud-programme-scholarship for more information. www.conted.ox.ac.uk/about/msc-in-sustainable-urban-development

### For further information contact:

**Tel**: (44) 1365 286952

**Email**: sud@conted.ox.ac.uk

## Corpus Christi College: A E Haigh English Studentship

**Eligibility**: Open to all graduate applicants in English

**Level of Study**: Postgraduate, Research

**Type**: Studentship

**Value**: £7,500 per year towards college fee and contribution towards living expenses

**Length of Study**: Period of fee liability

**Country of Study**: Any country

**Application Procedure**: Please see website for details of how to apply

**Additional Information**: Please check at www.ccc.ox.ac.uk/

### For further information contact:

**Email**: jane.sherwood@admin.ox.ac.uk

## Crystal Clinical Scholarships

**Type**: Scholarship

**Value**: Scholarship funds will be used for travel and associated expenses

**Length of Study**: 1 year

**Country of Study**: Any country

### For further information contact:

**Email**: info@onfgivesback.org

## Department of Education: Talbot Scholarship

**Eligibility**: Open to all applicants for DPhil in Education. Please visit website for more details

**Level of Study**: Doctorate

**Type**: Partial scholarship

**Value**: £15,000 per annum contribution towards fees and living expenses 35% reduction of tuition fee

**Length of Study**: 3 years

**Frequency**: Every 3 years

**Country of Study**: Any country

**Closing Date**: 20 January

**Additional Information**: Please visit the website: www.edu cation.ox.ac.uk/courses/d-phil/funding-opportunities/

## Donald Tovey Memorial Prize

**Purpose**: To assist in the furtherance of research or in the publication of work already done, in the fields of philosophy, history or understanding of music

**Eligibility**: Open to men or women, without regard to nationality, age or membership of a university

**Level of Study**: Postdoctorate

**Type**: Prize

**Value**: £1,000

**Frequency**: Dependent on funds available

**Study Establishment**: Unrestricted

**Country of Study**: Any country

**Application Procedure**: Applications should be addressed to the Heather Professor of Music at the address shown

**Closing Date**: June

**Funding**: Private

**Contributor**: Donal Tovey Memorial Fund

**Additional Information**: If for furtherance of research, applicants need to demonstrate that the programme falls within the scope of the award, and produce testimonials or other written evidence of previous attainment which demonstrate the researcher's fitness to undertake it. If to assist in publication of work already completed, the applicant must submit one copy of work with an explanation of why the Prize is needed to ensure publication. The Prize is generally awarded for postdoctoral or advanced research www.music.ox.ac.uk/donald-tovey-memorial-prize/

### For further information contact:

Faculty of Music, St Aldate's, Oxford OX1 1DB, United Kingdom.

**Tel**:     (44) 1865 276 125
**Fax**:     (44) 1865 276 128
**Email**:   musicfac@sable.ox.ac.uk

### Duke of Cambridge Scholarship at University of Oxford

**Purpose**: Public Policy

**Eligibility**: Open to applicants who are ordinarily resident in the United Kingdom and who are applying to the Master of Public Policy (MPP). Please see website for more details

**Level of Study**: Postgraduate

**Type**: Scholarship

**Value**: University fee, college fee, and full living expenses of about £14,553

**Length of Study**: Period of fee liability

**Country of Study**: Any country

**Closing Date**: 20 January

**Additional Information**: The scholarship is only tenable at University College. Please visit the website: www.ox.ac.uk/admissions/graduate/fees-and-funding/fees-funding-and-scholar ship-search/scholarships-1#duke www.scholarshubafrica.com/19991/duke-cambridge-scholarship-university-oxford/

### For further information contact:

**Tel**:     (44) 1865 614 343
**Email**:   admin@scholarship-position.com

### Economic and Social Research Council (ESRC) Quota Award

**Purpose**: To assist graduate students with fees and maintenance

**Eligibility**: Open to all graduate applicants in Economics

**Level of Study**: Doctorate, Research

**Type**: Award

**Value**: University fee, college fee, and full living expenses

**Length of Study**: Up to 4 years

**Application Procedure**: Applicants are strongly advised to submit their application for consideration at the first application deadline of January 18th. Places on the second application deadline will be limited

**Closing Date**: 18 January

**Additional Information**: Please visit website for more details and how to apply www.economics.ox.ac.uk/index. php/graduate warwick.ac.uk/fac/arts/history/prospective/postgraduate/pgfunding/esrcquota/

### For further information contact:

**Tel**:     (44) 1865 281 162
**Email**:   econgrad@economics.ox.ac.uk

### Economic and Social Research Council (ESRC): Social Policy & Intervention

**Eligibility**: Open to applicants to MSc/MPhil comparative social policy, MSc/MPhil evidence based social intervention and policy evaluation and DPhil social policy/social intervention. Candidates apply at the same time as they apply for admission to their postgraduate programme at the University of Oxford, using the same application form

**Level of Study**: Postgraduate

**Value**: University fee, college fee and living expenses. Fees-only award for European Union applicants

**Length of Study**: Period of fee liability

**Country of Study**: Any country

**Application Procedure**: Please apply using the standard graduate application form, and confirm with the Department that you wish to be considered for an ESRC studentship

**Closing Date**: 22 January

**Additional Information**: Please check at www.spi.ox.ac.uk/study-with-us/funding.html www.spi.ox.ac.uk/oxford-institute-of-social-policy

### For further information contact:

**Email**:   erzsebet.bukodi@spi.ox.ac.uk

## Economic and Social Research Council: Interdisciplinary Area Studies

**Eligibility**: Candidates need to apply by the January admissions deadline to their postgraduate programme at the University of Oxford, using the statement of purpose form, which requires candidates to write an indicative research proposal for DPhil level study
**Level of Study**: Graduate
**Value**: University fee, college fee, and living expenses. Fees-only award for European Union applicants
**Length of Study**: Period of fee liability
**Country of Study**: Any country
**Application Procedure**: Please visit website for more details and how to apply
**Closing Date**: 20 January
**Additional Information**: Please check at www.area-studies. ox.ac.uk/scholarships-sias

### For further information contact:

**Email**:    f.ciuta@ucl.ac.uk

## Economic and Social Research Council: Socio-Legal Studies

**Eligibility**: Open to all prospective students applying for the 1 +3 MSt Socio-Legal Studies and DPhil Socio-Legal Studies, or just for the latter
**Level of Study**: Postgraduate
**Type**: Scholarship
**Value**: University fee, college fee, and living expenses. Fees-only award for European Union applicants
**Length of Study**: Period of fee liability
**Frequency**: Annual
**Country of Study**: United Kingdom
**Application Procedure**: Please contact the pathway representitive Professor Richard Sparks before applying: r.sparks@ed.ac.uk
**Closing Date**: 20 January
**Funding**: Trusts
**Additional Information**: Please see website: www.law. ox.ac.uk/postgraduate/scholarships.php  www.ed.ac.uk/student-funding/postgraduate/uk-eu/humanities/law/esrc-socio-legal

### For further information contact:

**Email**:    r.sparks@ed.ac.uk

## Economics: Doctoral Studentship

**Purpose**: Economics
**Eligibility**: Open to Home/Eu/Overseas. DPhil in economics. Please note this is only available to those who will have DPhil status in MT 2012
**Type**: Studentship
**Value**: £11,126
**Length of Study**: 2 years
**Application Procedure**: Applicants are strongly advised to submit their application for consideration at the first application deadline of January 20th. Places on the second application deadline will be limited
**Closing Date**: 24 January
**Additional Information**: All applicants accepted by the Department will be offered a place at a college. You may indicate on your application form which college you would like to be considered for; if you have no preference Graduate Admissions will make a selection for you. Students do not necessarily get accepted by their first choice. Please check at www.economics.ox.ac.uk/index.php/graduate  www.york.ac.uk/economics/postgrad/funding/phd-studentships/#tab-1

### For further information contact:

**Tel**:       (44) 1865 281 162
**Email**:    econgrad@economics.ox.ac.uk

## Education: Economic and Social Research Council (ESRC)

**Eligibility**: Open to all Home/European Union applicants for both DPhil in Education and MSc Education (Research Design and Methodology). Please visit website for more details
**Level of Study**: Doctorate, Postgraduate
**Type**: Studentship
**Value**: University fee, college fee and full living expenses
**Length of Study**: Period of fee liability
**Country of Study**: Any country
**Closing Date**: 20 January
**Additional Information**: Please visit the website: www.education.ox.ac.uk/courses/d-phil/funding-opportunities/

### For further information contact:

**Email**:    eddev@esrc.ukri.org

## Engineering and Physical Sciences Research Council (EPSRC) Centre for Doctoral Training in Autonomous Intelligent Machines and Systems

**Purpose**: To develop in-depth knowledge, understanding and expertise in autonomous intelligent systems
**Eligibility**: Open to United Kingdom and European Union applicants for DPhil in Engineering. European Union applicants may only be eligible for a fees-only award, depending on residency requirements. Please visit website for more details
**Level of Study**: Doctorate
**Type**: Scholarship
**Value**: University fee, college fee and full living expenses
**Length of Study**: 4 years
**Country of Study**: Any country
**Closing Date**: 20 January
**Additional Information**: Please visit the website: www.ox.ac.uk/admissions/graduate/courses/autonomous-intelligent-machines-and-systems  eng.ox.ac.uk/aims-cdt/

### For further information contact:

**Tel**:      (44) 1865 270 000
**Email**:   aims-cdt@robots.ox.ac.uk

## Engineering and Physical Sciences Research Council (EPSRC) Doctoral Training Programme Studentships

**Eligibility**: Open to United Kingdom and European Union applicants for DPhil in Statistics. European Union applicants may only be eligible for a fees-only award, depending on residency requirements
**Level of Study**: Postgraduate
**Value**: University fee, college fee and full living expenses
**Length of Study**: Three and a half years maximum
**Frequency**: Annual
**Country of Study**: United Kingdom
**Closing Date**: 20 January
**Funding**: Trusts
**Additional Information**: For more information, please visit website: www.stats.ox.ac.uk/study_here/research_degrees epsrc.ukri.org/skills/students/dta/

### For further information contact:

**Email**:   phdfunding-salc@manchester.ac.uk

## Engineering and Physical Sciences Research Council CDT in Industrially Focussed Mathematical Modelling

**Eligibility**: Four studentships will be available to applicants regardless of nationality. The remaining studentships are restricted to United Kingdom/European Union nationals
**Level of Study**: Postgraduate
**Type**: Scholarship
**Value**: University fee, college fee and full living expenses (minimum £14,296 per year for 4 years)
**Length of Study**: 4 years
**Frequency**: Annual
**Country of Study**: Any country
**Application Procedure**: We will automatically assign students to funding and no separate application for funding is required
**Closing Date**: 10 March
**Funding**: Trusts
**Additional Information**: For more information, please visit the website: www.maths.ox.ac.uk/study-here/postgraduate-study/industrially-focused-mathematical-modelling-epsrc-cdt

### For further information contact:

**Email**:   infomm@maths.ox.ac.uk

## English Faculty: AHRC Doctoral Training Partnership Studentships

**Eligibility**: Open to all Home/European Union's graduates applying to undertake research degrees in the Faculty of English. Please see website for more details
**Level of Study**: Postgraduate
**Type**: Studentship
**Value**: University fee, college fee, and full living expenses. Fees-only awards for non-United Kingdom, European Union students
**Length of Study**: Period of fee liability
**Frequency**: Annual
**Country of Study**: United Kingdom
**Closing Date**: 20 January
**Additional Information**: For more information, please check website:      www.humanities.ox.ac.uk/prospective_students/graduates/funding/ahrc      www.humanities.ox.ac.uk/ahrc-doctoral-training-partnership#collapse395456

### For further information contact:

**Email**:   FASS-PhD-Applications@open.ac.uk

## English Faculty: Asian Human Rights Commission (AHRC) Doctoral Training Partnership Studentship (Master)

**Eligibility**: Open to all Home/European Union applicants to MSt and MPhil degrees offered by the Faculty of English. Please see website for more details
**Level of Study**: Postgraduate
**Type**: Studentship
**Value**: University fee, college fee, and living expenses (pro-rata for courses less than 1 year). Fees-only awards for non-United Kingdom, European Union students
**Length of Study**: Period of fee liability
**Frequency**: Annual
**Country of Study**: United Kingdom
**Closing Date**: 20 January
**Funding**: Trusts
**Additional Information**: For more information, please visit: www.humanities.ox.ac.uk/prospective_students/graduates/funding/ahrc www.humanities.ox.ac.uk/ahrc-doctoral-training-partnership#collapse395456

### For further information contact:

**Email**: ahrcdtp@admin.ox.ac.uk

## English Faculty: Cecily Clarke Studentship

**Eligibility**: Open to all applicants to English Medieval Studies, with preference to Middle English Philology. All students applying for English graduate courses will automatically be considered
**Level of Study**: Postgraduate
**Type**: Studentship
**Value**: £12,000 per year
**Length of Study**: Up to 2 years
**Country of Study**: Any country
**Closing Date**: 18 January
**Additional Information**: All students applying for English graduate courses will automatically be considered. Candidates apply at the same time as they apply for admission to their postgraduate programme at the University of Oxford, using the same application form. To be considered candidates must apply by the January deadline. Please check at www.english.ox.ac.uk www.european-funding-guide.eu/scholarship/13407-cecily-clark-studentship

### For further information contact:

**Tel**: (44) 1865 270 000

## Exeter College Usher-Cunningham Senior Studentship

**Purpose**: To support graduate study
**Eligibility**: History is open to graduates of Irish universities only. Medicine is open to all
**Level of Study**: Postgraduate
**Type**: Studentship
**Value**: Home level fees plus maintenance up to the equivalent of a Research Council Award
**Length of Study**: Usually awarded for up to 3 years
**Frequency**: Every 3 years
**Study Establishment**: Exeter College, University of Oxford
**Country of Study**: United Kingdom
**Application Procedure**: Applicants must address enquiries to the Academic Administrator
**Funding**: Private
**Contributor**: An endowment
**Additional Information**: www.exeter.ox.ac.uk/wp-content/uploads/2018/12/Usher-Cunningham-Medicine-2019.pdf

### For further information contact:

**Email**: admissions@exeter.ox.ac.uk

## Exeter College: Exonian Graduate Scholarship

**Eligibility**: Exeter College is pleased to offer a studentship covering college fees to two DPhil students, linked to a United Kingdom Research Council award covering university fees
**Level of Study**: Postdoctorate
**Type**: Fellowship
**Value**: College fee only
**Length of Study**: Up to 3 years
**Country of Study**: United Kingdom
**Application Procedure**: Applicants must address enquiries to the Academic Administrator
**Closing Date**: January
**Funding**: Private
**Additional Information**: www.exeter.ox.ac.uk/wp-content/uploads/2019/09/Exonian-2020.pdf

### For further information contact:

Exeter College, Turl St, Oxford OX1 3DP, United Kingdom.

**Email**: academic.administrator@exeter.ox.ac.uk

## Exeter College: Nicholas Frangiscatos Scholarship in Byzantine Studies

**Eligibility**: For a DPhil student in the field of Byzantine studies
**Level of Study**: Doctorate, Postdoctorate
**Type**: Fellowship
**Value**: Up to £10,000 per year
**Length of Study**: Up to 3 years
**Frequency**: Every 3 years
**Country of Study**: United Kingdom
**Application Procedure**: Please see website for how to apply
**Closing Date**: 12 March
**Funding**: Private
**Additional Information**: Please check at www.exeter.ox.ac. uk/currentstudents/finance/scholarships www.exeter.ox.ac. uk/wp-content/uploads/2018/12/Nicholas-Frangiscatos-2019.pdf

### For further information contact:

**Email**:    admissions@exeter.ox.ac.uk

## Exeter College: Senior Scholarship in Theology

**Purpose**: To support a graduate who wishes to read for the Final Honour School of Theology or Philosophy and Theology
**Eligibility**: Applicants must hold at least a Second Class (Honours) Degree by the time of admission in a subject other than theology
**Level of Study**: Postgraduate
**Type**: Scholarship
**Value**: University and college fees at Home/European Union rate, maintenance grant £5,000 per year
**Length of Study**: 3 years
**Frequency**: Every 3 years
**Study Establishment**: Exeter College, the University of Oxford
**Country of Study**: United Kingdom
**Application Procedure**: Applicants must apply in writing to the Academic Administrator or see the website www.exeter. ox.ac.uk
**Closing Date**: 1 May
**Funding**: Private
**Contributor**: Endowment
**No. of awards given last year**: 1
**Additional Information**: The College proposes to elect a graduate to a Senior Scholarship in Theology from October 1st. The Scholar is to study for the Final Honour School of either Theology or Philosophy & Theology (2nd BA)

## Faculty of Medieval and Modern Languages: Heath Harrison DPhil Award

**Eligibility**: Open to graduate students accepted to read for a DPhil in Medieval and Modern Languages. Please visit the website for more details
**Level of Study**: Postgraduate
**Type**: Scholarship
**Value**: University fee, college fee, and full living expenses
**Length of Study**: Three years
**Frequency**: Annual
**Country of Study**: United Kingdom
**Application Procedure**: For more information, please check the website: grad.mml.ox.ac.uk/funding_fees
**Closing Date**: 22 January
**Funding**: Trusts

### For further information contact:

**Email**:    office@mod-langs.ox.ac.uk

## Freshfields Bruckhaus Deringer Scholarships (Law)

**Purpose**: To assist graduate students with fees and a living allowance
**Eligibility**: Varies
**Level of Study**: Doctorate, Postgraduate, Research
**Type**: Scholarships
**Value**: To be confirmed
**Length of Study**: 1 year
**Country of Study**: Any country
**Closing Date**: 22 January
**Additional Information**: www.freshfields.com/en-gb/about-us/responsible-business/freshfields_stephen_lawrence_scholarship/

### For further information contact:

**Email**:    ContactFSLScheme@freshfields.com

## Frost Scholarship Programme (Israel)

**Purpose**: The Frost Scholarship Programme (Israel) funds current students of Israeli universities to study one-year, full-time master's courses in science, technology, engineering and mathematics ('STEM' subjects) at the University of Oxford
**Eligibility**: Open to Israeli residents currently studying at an Israeli university, who have not previously been enrolled on a full degree programme at an institution outside of Israel.

You must be applying for a one-year, full-time Master's course in a STEM subject (Science, Technology, Engineering and Mathematics). Four awards will be made each year. Closing date varies according to course
**Level of Study**: Postgraduate
**Type**: Scholarship
**Value**: University fee, college fee, and full living expenses
**Length of Study**: Period of fee liability
**Frequency**: Annual
**Country of Study**: Any country
**Closing Date**: January
**Funding**: Trusts
**Additional Information**: Please see website: www.graduate. ox.ac.uk/frostisrael www.scholarshipdesk.com/frost-scholarship-programme-for-israel-students/

## Geography and the Environment: Andrew Goudie Bursary

**Eligibility**: Open to all applicants for MSc in Environmental Change and Management
**Level of Study**: Postgraduate
**Type**: Scholarship
**Value**: Up to £5,000
**Length of Study**: 1 year
**Country of Study**: Any country
**Closing Date**: 20 January
**Additional Information**: Please visit the website: www.eci. ox.ac.uk/msc/funding.html

### For further information contact:

**Email**:     support@linacre.ox.ac.uk

## Geography and the Environment: Boardman Scholarship

**Eligibility**: Open to all applicants for MSc in Environmental Change and Management
**Level of Study**: Postgraduate
**Type**: Scholarship
**Value**: Up to £5,000
**Length of Study**: 1 year
**Country of Study**: Any country
**Closing Date**: 20 January
**Additional Information**: Please visit the website: www.eci. ox.ac.uk/msc/funding.html

### For further information contact:

**Email**:     socialsciences@devoff.ox.ac.uk

## Geography: Sir Walter Raleigh Postgraduate Scholarship

**Eligibility**: Open to all applicants for MSc Environmental Change and Management. The award is tenable only at Oriel College
**Level of Study**: Postgraduate
**Type**: Scholarship
**Value**: £3,500
**Length of Study**: 1 year
**Frequency**: Annual
**Application Procedure**: Any person wishing to be considered for this award should follow the application procedure for admission to the degree of Master of Science in Environmental Change and Management at Oxford University, nominating Colleges of preference as detailed in the application procedure. They must, additionally, download (from website) and complete the application form and return it to the address given below
**Additional Information**: Please note that Oriel College only offers a small number of places per year to applicants for the MSc in Environmental Change and Management, and one of these places will be reserved for the applicant who has been awarded the Sir Walter Raleigh Scholarship

### For further information contact:

**Tel**:     (44) 1865 276 520
**Fax**:     (44) 1865 286 548
**Email**:     admissions@oriel.ox.ac.uk

## Goodger and Schorstein Research Scholarships in Medical Sciences

**Eligibility**: Open to postdoctoral researchers from any department/institute of the Medical Sciences Division. Applicants must have completed their DPhil (at any Higher Education Institution) at the time of application and are required to work primarily in units run by the University of Oxford
**Type**: Scholarship
**Value**: Typically in the range between £2,000 and £25,000
**Length of Study**: Up to 1 year
**Country of Study**: Any country
**Application Procedure**: Please see the website for more details. Enquires may be sent by email to Aga. Bush@medsci.ox.ac.uk
**Closing Date**: 13 February
**Additional Information**: Please visit the website: www.med sci.ox.ac.uk/research/internal/funding-directory/goodger-and-schorstein-scholarship canvas.ox.ac.uk/courses/22105/pages/goodger-and-schorstein-research-scholarships-in-medical-sciences

**For further information contact:**

**Email:**    Aga.Bush@medsci.ox.ac.uk

## Graduate Scholarship in Medieval and Modern Languages with Keble College

**Purpose**: To assist graduate students with fees, maintenance and accommodation
**Eligibility**: All eligible doctoral applicants submitting applications before the third gathered field will automatically be considered, irrespective of choice of college, provided that they have applied for other funded awards (if eligible)
**Level of Study**: Research
**Type**: Scholarship
**Value**: £10,145
**Length of Study**: 4 years
**Country of Study**: Any country
**Closing Date**: 3 March
**Additional Information**: www.ox.ac.uk/admissions/graduate/courses/dphil-medieval-and-modern-languages?wssl=1

**For further information contact:**

**Tel:**    (44) 1865 270751
**Email:**    graduate.studies@mod-langs.ox.ac.uk

## Graduate Scholarship in Medieval and Modern Languages with Merton College

**Purpose**: To assist graduate students with fees and a living allowance
**Eligibility**: All eligible doctoral applicants submitting applications before the third gathered field will automatically be considered, irrespective of choice of college, provided that they have applied for other funded awards (if eligible)
**Level of Study**: Research
**Type**: Scholarship
**Value**: University fee at United Kingdom/European Union rate; allowance of £5,000 to assist with college fees and/or maintenance
**Length of Study**: Up to 3 years
**Country of Study**: Any country
**Closing Date**: 22 January

**For further information contact:**

**Email:**    trish.long@keble.ox.ac.uk

## Graduate Scholarship in Medieval and Modern Languages with Somerville College

**Purpose**: To assist graduate students with fees, maintenance and accommodation
**Eligibility**: All eligible doctoral applicants submitting applications before the third gathered field will automatically be considered, irrespective of choice of college, provided that they have applied for other funded awards (if eligible)
**Level of Study**: Research
**Type**: Scholarship
**Value**: University fee at United Kingdom/European Union rate; maintenance grant of £6,000. Additional benefits include some dining rights and guaranteed accommodation in 1st year
**Length of Study**: Up to 3 years
**Country of Study**: Any country
**Closing Date**: 22 January

**For further information contact:**

**Email:**    trish.long@keble.ox.ac.uk

## Green Moral Philosophy Scholarship

**Eligibility**: Open to all graduate applicants for DPhil courses in the Faculty of Philosophy. All applicants who receive a place on any graduate course automatically considered
**Type**: Scholarship
**Value**: The value of the scholarship is to be determined by the Board of Graduate Admissions. The scholarship may not be offered on a yearly basis
**Length of Study**: 1 year
**Country of Study**: Any country
**Closing Date**: 4 January
**Additional Information**: Please check website for more information

**For further information contact:**

**Email:**    jane.sherwood@admin.ox.ac.uk

## Green Templeton College: GTC-Medical Sciences Doctoral Training Centre Scholarship

**Purpose**: Green Templeton College is pleased to be able to offer a top-up award for overseas students who have been awarded a Studentship for study at the Medical Sciences Doctoral Training Centre beginning in October month
**Eligibility**: Open to all applicants to the Medical Sciences Doctoral Training Centre with Overseas fee status
**Level of Study**: Doctorate
**Type**: Scholarship

**Value**: £1,000
**Length of Study**: Up to 4 years
**Country of Study**: Any country
**Closing Date**: 11 January
**Additional Information**: Please visit the website: www.gtc.ox.ac.uk/admissions/scholarships-and-awards   www.gtc.ox.ac.uk/students/how-to-apply/scholarships-bursaries/

**For further information contact:**

**Email**:   enquiries@msdtc.ox.ac.uk

## Green Templeton College: GTC-SBS DPhil Scholarship

**Eligibility**: Open to all applicants to the DPhil in Management Studies
**Level of Study**: Doctorate, Graduate
**Type**: Scholarship
**Value**: £15,009
**Length of Study**: 4 years
**Study Establishment**: Green Templeton College
**Country of Study**: Any country
**Application Procedure**: Please see website: www.gtc.ox.ac.uk/admissions/scholarships-and-awards
**Closing Date**: 11 January
**Additional Information**: Restrictions: New DPhil students in Management Studies only (includes both Management Research and Financial Economics routes) www.gtc.ox.ac.uk/students/how-to-apply/scholarships-bursaries/gtc-sbs-dphil-scholarships/

## Green Templeton College: Rosemary Stewart Scholarship

**Eligibility**: DPhil students with research interests in the area of health care organization and management
**Level of Study**: Doctorate
**Type**: Scholarship
**Value**: £5,000 per annum
**Length of Study**: Up to 3 years
**Study Establishment**: Green Templeton College
**Country of Study**: Any country
**Application Procedure**: Please see website for more details and how to apply
**Closing Date**: 1 May
**Additional Information**: Please visit the website: www.gtc.ox.ac.uk/admissions/scholarships-and-awards   www.gtc.ox.ac.uk/students/how-to-apply/scholarships-bursaries/rosemary-stewart-scholarship/

**For further information contact:**

**Tel**:       (44) 1865 274 770
**Email**:    admissions@gtc.ox.ac.uk

## Hertford - English Graduate Scholarship in Irish Literature

**Eligibility**: Open to Home/European Union students applying to undertake a DPhil in Irish Literature. Applicants are automatically considered for the scholarship by the English Faculty. Please visit the website for more details
**Level of Study**: Postgraduate
**Type**: Scholarship
**Value**: University fee, college fee and full living expenses
**Length of Study**: Period of fee liability
**Frequency**: Annual
**Country of Study**: United Kingdom
**Application Procedure**: For more information, please visit the website: www.english.ox.ac.uk
**Closing Date**: 8 January
**Funding**: Trusts

**For further information contact:**

**Email**:    college.office@hertford.ox.ac.uk

## Hertford College Archaeology Award

**Eligibility**: Open to all graduate students pursuing the MSt in Archaeology. Please see the website for more details
**Level of Study**: Postgraduate
**Type**: Scholarship
**Value**: £10,000 towards course fees, college fees and living costs where appropriate
**Length of Study**: One year
**Frequency**: Annual
**Study Establishment**: Hertford
**Country of Study**: United Kingdom
**Application Procedure**: For more information, please check the website: www.hertford.ox.ac.uk/discover-hertford/graduates/graduate-scholarships
**Closing Date**: 11 March
**Funding**: Trusts
**Additional   Information**:   www.hertford.ox.ac.uk/news/university-prizes-for-hertfordians

**For further information contact:**

**Email**:    communications@hertford.ox.ac.uk

## Hertford College Law Award

**Eligibility**: Open to all graduate students pursuing the BCL or Mjur. Please see the website for more details
**Level of Study**: Postgraduate
**Type**: Scholarship
**Value**: £10,000 towards course fees, college fees and living costs where appropriate
**Length of Study**: One year
**Frequency**: Annual
**Study Establishment**: Hertford
**Country of Study**: United Kingdom
**Application Procedure**: For more information, please check the website: www.hertford.ox.ac.uk/discover-hertford/gradu ates/graduate-scholarships
**Closing Date**: 11 March
**Funding**: Trusts
**Additional Information**: www.hertford.ox.ac.uk/study-here/graduates/finance/senior-scholarships

### For further information contact:

**Email**:    graduate.admissions@hertford.ox.ac.uk

## Hertford College Pharmacology Award

**Eligibility**: Open to all graduate students pursuing a DPhil in Pharmacology. Please see the website for more details, including how to apply
**Level of Study**: Postgraduate
**Type**: Scholarship
**Value**: £6,500 towards course fees, college fees and living costs where appropriate
**Length of Study**: Three years
**Frequency**: Annual
**Study Establishment**: Hertford
**Country of Study**: United Kingdom
**Application Procedure**: For more information, please visit the website: www.pharm.ox.ac.uk/gso/dphil-in-pharmacology
**Closing Date**: 8 January
**Funding**: Trusts
**Additional Information**: www.hertford.ox.ac.uk/news/university-prizes-for-hertfordians

### For further information contact:

**Email**:    communications@hertford.ox.ac.uk

## Hertford College Senior Scholarships

**Eligibility**: Restricted to students who are about to commence a new research degree course or those about to upgrade their current course

**Level of Study**: Postgraduate
**Type**: Scholarship
**Value**: £1,000 per year, plus priority for housing and some dining rights
**Length of Study**: 2 years
**Frequency**: Annual
**Study Establishment**: Hertford College, University of Oxford
**Country of Study**: United Kingdom
**Application Procedure**: Applicants must write to the College for further details
**Additional Information**: www.hertford.ox.ac.uk/study-here/graduates/finance/senior-scholarships

### For further information contact:

**Email**:    graduate.admissions@hertford.ox.ac.uk

## Hertford College: Baring Senior Scholarship

**Eligibility**: Open to all graduate students pursuing research in any area of study
**Level of Study**: Postgraduate
**Type**: Scholarship
**Value**: £5,000 per year with certain associated dining rights
**Length of Study**: Two years
**Frequency**: Annual
**Study Establishment**: Hertford
**Country of Study**: United Kingdom
**Application Procedure**: For more information, please visit the website: www.hertford.ox.ac.uk/discover-hertford/gradu ates/graduate-scholarships
**Closing Date**: 11 March
**Funding**: Trusts
**Additional Information**: www.hertford.ox.ac.uk/study-here/graduates/finance/senior-scholarships

### For further information contact:

**Email**:    graduate.admissions@hertford.ox.ac.uk

## Hertford College: Vaughan Williams Senior Scholarship

**Purpose**: The Vaughan Williams Fund supports medical students with a £300 award per student towards stethoscopes and 'on the ward' textbooks
**Eligibility**: Open to all graduate students pursuing research in any area of study. Please see website for more details, including how to apply
**Level of Study**: Postgraduate

**Type**: Scholarship
**Value**: £5,000 per year with certain associated dining rights
**Length of Study**: Two years
**Frequency**: Annual
**Study Establishment**: Hertford
**Country of Study**: United Kingdom
**Application Procedure**: For more information, please visit : www.hertford.ox.ac.uk/discover-hertford/graduates/graduate-scholarships
**Closing Date**: 11 March
**Funding**: Trusts

**For further information contact:**

**Email**:    communications@hertford.ox.ac.uk

## Hertford College: Worshipful Company of Scientific Instrument Makers Senior Scholarship

**Eligibility**: Open to DPhil applicants in all subjects. Please note: applicants are expected to be involved in the design of instrumentation
**Level of Study**: Doctorate, Graduate
**Type**: Scholarship
**Value**: £4,000 per year with certain associated dining rights
**Length of Study**: 2 years
**Country of Study**: Any country
**Application Procedure**: Please see website for details of how to apply
**Additional Information**: Please check at www.hertford.ox.ac.uk/advertised-posts

**For further information contact:**

**Email**:    college.office@hertford.ox.ac.uk

## Hong Kong Jockey Club Graduate Scholarships

**Purpose** To students who combine outstanding academic performance with a strong commitment to serving the community
**Eligibility**: Open to applicants who are ordinarily resident in Hong Kong and who are applying to a full-time master's or full-time DPhil course at Oxford. Please note that DPhil courses with four years of fee liability are not eligible. Please see website for more details
**Level of Study**: Doctorate, Postgraduate
**Type**: Scholarship
**Value**: University fee, college fee, and full living expenses
**Length of Study**: Period of fee liability
**Country of Study**: Any country

**Closing Date**: January
**Funding**: Trusts
**Additional Information**: Please visit the website: www.ox.ac.uk/admissions/graduate/fees-and-funding/fees-funding-and-scholarship-search/scholarships-1#hkjc

**For further information contact:**

**Email**:    hkjcscholarships@hkjc.org.hk

## International Development: QEH Scholarship

**Eligibility**: Open to all graduate applicants for MPhil in Development Studies with a preference for those from Sub-Saharan Africa. Please visit departmental website for more details
**Level of Study**: Predoctorate
**Type**: Scholarship
**Value**: University fee, college fee, and £13,000 towards living expenses
**Length of Study**: 21 months
**Country of Study**: Any country
**Closing Date**: 20 January
**Additional Information**: Please visit the website: www.qeh.ox.ac.uk/content/fees-funding

**For further information contact:**

**Email**:    jane.sherwood@admin.ox.ac.uk

## Ioan and Rosemary James / Mathematical Institute Scholarship

**Eligibility**: Open to applicants for the DPhil in Mathematics, or CDT in Mathematical Institute only
**Value**: University fees (at either the Home/European Union or Overseas student rate as applicable), College fees and a maintenance stipend at the United Kingdom research council rate
**Country of Study**: Any country
**Application Procedure**: Duration of full-fee liability; 3 years for DPhil and 4 years for CDT. For non-CDT students, the Mathematical Institute will provide an additional 6 months of funding from its own funds for maintenance
**Closing Date**: January
**Additional Information**: For more details, please visit website www.sjc.ox.ac.uk www.sjc.ox.ac.uk/study/undergraduate/

**For further information contact:**

**Email**:    sarah.jones@sjc.ox.ac

## James Fairfax - Oxford-Australia Fund Scholarships

**Eligibility**: Applicants should normally be under 30 on January 1st in the year in which the scholarship is to be taken up, and must have a bachelor's degree with first or upper second class honours or equivalent from a recognized university

**Level of Study**: Graduate, Postgraduate

**Type**: Scholarship

**Value**: University fees at the home and European Union rate, college fees and a living allowance of the order of AU$12,000 per year

**Length of Study**: Oxford-Australia Fund scholarships are for 2 years, or in the case of DPhil for 3 years, and James Fairfax scholarships are generally of 2 years duration

**Frequency**: Annual

**Study Establishment**: University of Oxford

**Country of Study**: United Kingdom

**Application Procedure**: Applicants must write for details or visit the website at www.admin.ox.edu.au/io

**Closing Date**: 21 February

**Funding**: Private, Individuals

**Contributor**: Australian scholars who have studied at Oxford and, in particular, Mr James Fairfax

**Additional Information**: rsc.anu.edu.au/~oxford/2017%20JFOA%20Nov%2017.pdf

### For further information contact:

**Tel**:      (61) 2 6125 3578/3761

**Email**:   jww@rsc.anu.edu.au

## Jesus College: Joint Law Faculty-Jesus College BCL Scholarship

**Eligibility**: Open to all graduate applicants to the BCL (Bachelor of Civil Law). Please see website for further details

**Level of Study**: Graduate

**Type**: Scholarship

**Value**: £10,000

**Length of Study**: Period of fee liability

**Frequency**: Annual

**Study Establishment**: Jesus College

**Country of Study**: Any country

**Closing Date**: 20 January

**Additional Information**: Please visit the website: www.jesus.ox.ac.uk/current-students/scholarships-prizes-awards?field_subject_target_id=20&field_type_value=Graduate

### For further information contact:

**Email**:   lodge@jesus.ox.ac.uk

## Kalisher Trust-Wadham Student Scholarship

**Purpose**: The scholarships are intended to encourage and assist those intending to practise at the Criminal Bar who demonstrate 'exceptional promise but modest means'

**Eligibility**: Applications are invited from United Kingdom residents who can demonstrate: 1. Intellectual ability – demonstrated by academic performance, past work, activities and other experience. 2. Motivation to succeed at the Criminal Bar – including steps taken to acquire the personal skills required of a Barrister, and a demonstration of the will to succeed. 3. Potential as an advocate – both in oral and written skills. 4. Personal qualities – including self-reliance, independence, integrity, reliability and humanity. 5. Financial need - candidates will be asked to supply to the interview panel, in confidence, information demonstrating financial need

**Level of Study**: Graduate

**Type**: Scholarship

**Frequency**: Annual

**Country of Study**: Any country

**Application Procedure**: In particularly to discuss their motivation to succeed at the Criminal Bar. This statement should be no more than 800 words

**Closing Date**: 27 November

**Funding**: Private

**Additional Information**: www.law.ox.ac.uk/sites/files/oxlaw/kalisher_trust_scholarship.pdf

### For further information contact:

The Faculty of Law, University of Oxford, St Cross Building, St Cross Road, Oxford OX1 3UL, United Kingdom.

**Email**:   tracy.kaye@crim.ox.ac.uk

## Keble College Gosden Graduate Scholarship

**Eligibility**: Open to students intending to seek ordination in a church in communion with the Church of England. Candidates must be either ordained or be able to show clear evidence of desire for ordination in the Church of England or a church in communion therewith, and be already at or intending to be registered for a postgraduate degree at Keble College, University of Oxford

**Level of Study**: Postgraduate

**Type**: Scholarship

**Value**: Up to £5,000 per year

**Length of Study**: Up to 3 years

**Frequency**: Dependent on funds available

**Study Establishment**: Keble College, University of Oxford

**Country of Study**: United Kingdom

**Application Procedure**: Applicants must contact the Deputy Academic Administrator at Keble College in the first instance

**No. of awards offered**: 4

**Closing Date**: 24 January

**No. of awards given last year**: 2

**No. of applicants last year**: 4

**Additional Information**: www.keble.ox.ac.uk/admissions/graduates/scholarships/

**For further information contact:**

Keble College, Oxford OX1 3PG, United Kingdom.

**Email**:    college.office@keble.ox.ac.uk

## Keble College Gwynne-Jones Scholarship

**Eligibility**: Open to nationals of Sierra Leone or the Yoruba-speaking people of Nigeria

**Level of Study**: Postgraduate

**Type**: Scholarship

**Value**: £10,127

**Length of Study**: Up to 3 years

**Frequency**: Varies

**Study Establishment**: Keble College, University of Oxford

**Country of Study**: United Kingdom

**Application Procedure**: Applicants must write for details

**Closing Date**: 24 January

**Funding**: Private

**Additional Information**: www.keble.ox.ac.uk/admissions/graduates/scholarships/

**For further information contact:**

**Email**:    college.office@keble.ox.ac.uk

## Keble College Ian Palmer Graduate Scholarship in Information Technology

**Eligibility**: Applicants must write for details

**Level of Study**: Postgraduate

**Type**: Scholarship

**Value**: £3,130

**Length of Study**: Up to 3 years

**Frequency**: Dependent on funds available

**Study Establishment**: Keble College, University of Oxford

**Country of Study**: United Kingdom

**Application Procedure**: Applicants must write for details

**Closing Date**: 24 January

**Funding**: Private

**Additional Information**: www.keble.ox.ac.uk/admissions/graduates/scholarships/

**For further information contact:**

**Email**:    college.office@keble.ox.ac.uk

## Keble College Ian Tucker Memorial Bursary

**Eligibility**: Candidates must demonstrate sporting prowess principally in the field of rugby football, together with qualities that will make a contribution to both the College and University

**Level of Study**: Graduate

**Type**: Bursary

**Value**: £6,000

**Length of Study**: 1 year

**Frequency**: Annual

**Study Establishment**: Keble College, University of Oxford

**Country of Study**: United Kingdom

**Application Procedure**: Applicants must contact the Tutor for Graduates at Keble College for an application form

**No. of awards offered**: 6

**Closing Date**: 24 January

**No. of awards given last year**: 2

**No. of applicants last year**: 6

**Additional Information**: www.keble.ox.ac.uk/admissions/graduates/scholarships/

**For further information contact:**

**Email**:    college.office@keble.ox.ac.uk

## Keble College Keble Association Open Graduate Scholarship

**Eligibility**: Open to research students and 2nd BM applicants

**Level of Study**: Postgraduate, Research

**Type**: Scholarship

**Value**: £2,000

**Length of Study**: Up to 3 years

**Frequency**: Annual

**Study Establishment**: Keble College, University of Oxford

**Country of Study**: United Kingdom

**Application Procedure**: Applicants must write to request an application form

**No. of awards offered**: 19

**Closing Date**: May

**Funding**: Private

**No. of awards given last year**: 2

**No. of applicants last year**: 19

## Keble College Paul Hayes Graduate Scholarship

**Eligibility**: Candidates must demonstrate sporting excellence
**Level of Study**: Doctorate, Graduate
**Type**: Scholarship
**Value**: Up to the value of college fees
**Length of Study**: Up to 3 years
**Study Establishment**: Keble College, the University of Oxford
**Country of Study**: United Kingdom
**Application Procedure**: Applicants must contact the Deputy Academic Administrator at Keble College
**Closing Date**: May

## Keble College Water Newton Scholarship

**Eligibility**: Open to students intending to seek ordination in a church in communication with the Church of United Kingdom
**Level of Study**: Postdoctorate, Research
**Type**: Scholarship
**Value**: £10,000
**Length of Study**: Up to 3 years
**Frequency**: Dependent on funds available
**Study Establishment**: Keble College, University of Oxford
**Country of Study**: United Kingdom
**Application Procedure**: Applicants must contact the Deputy Academic Administrator
**Closing Date**: 24 January
**Funding**: Private
**Additional Information**: www.keble.ox.ac.uk/admissions/graduates/scholarships/

**For further information contact:**

**Email**:     college.office@keble.ox.ac.uk

## Keble College: Delia Bushell Graduate Scholarship

**Eligibility**: Open to graduate applicants to study for a postgraduate degree in the History Faculty in the University of Oxford, or be presently registered for a postgraduate degree in the History Faculty in the University of Oxford
**Level of Study**: Postgraduate
**Type**: Scholarship
**Value**: Up to £6,250 per year towards living expenses
**Length of Study**: 1 year
**Study Establishment**: Keble College
**Country of Study**: Any country
**Application Procedure**: Please see website for more details, including how to apply

**Closing Date**: 24 January
**Additional Information**: Please visit the website: www.keble.ox.ac.uk/admissions/graduate/graduate-scholarships www.keble.ox.ac.uk/admissions/graduates/scholarships/

**For further information contact:**

**Email**:     college.office@keble.ox.ac.uk

## Keble College: James Martin Graduate Scholarship

**Eligibility**: Open to Home/European Union students, who can demonstrate that they are in financial need. Applicants must be intending to study for a MSc in the MPLS (Mathematical, Physical and Life Sciences) Division, Medical Sciences Division or Geography and the Environment department
**Level of Study**: Postgraduate
**Type**: Scholarship
**Value**: £9,000, for one year only
**Length of Study**: 1 year
**Study Establishment**: Keble College
**Country of Study**: Any country
**Application Procedure**: Please see website for further details, including how to apply
**Closing Date**: 24 January
**Additional Information**: Please visit the website: www.keble.ox.ac.uk/admissions/graduate/graduate-scholarships www.keble.ox.ac.uk/admissions/graduates/scholarships/

**For further information contact:**

**Email**:     college.office@keble.ox.ac.uk

## Kellogg College: Naji DPhil Scholarship in the Public Understanding of Evidence-Based Medicine

**Eligibility**: Open to applicants for the DPhil in Primary Health Care whose research directly addresses public understanding of evidence for health claims
**Level of Study**: Doctorate
**Type**: Scholarship
**Value**: University fee, college fee, and full living expenses
**Length of Study**: Period of fee liability
**Study Establishment**: Kellogg College
**Country of Study**: Any country
**Application Procedure**: Please see website for more details, including how to apply
**Closing Date**: 6 January

**Additional Information**: Please visit the website: www.kellogg.ox.ac.uk/study/scholarships-2017/naji-dphil-scholarship-in-the-public-understanding-of-evidence-based-medicine/

**For further information contact:**

**Tel**:　(44) 1865 612 000

## Kellogg College: Oxford-McCall MacBain Graduate Scholarship

**Purpose**: The scholarship is only tenable at Kellogg College. All eligible applicants will be considered for the scholarship
**Eligibility**: All eligible applicants will be considered for the scholarship, regardless of which college (if any) you state as your preference on the graduate application form. However, successful applicants will be transferred to Kellogg College in order to take up the scholarship
**Level of Study**: Graduate
**Type**: Scholarship
**Value**: The scholarship covers course fees and provides a study support grant
**Frequency**: Annual
**Country of Study**: Any country
**Closing Date**: 1 March
**Funding**: Private
**Additional Information**: Initially the MMF operated on a regional-based approach, with a strategy to develop and encourage best practices and policies in multiple areas related to improving the human condition scholarscareers.com/2019/02/16/oxford-mccall-macbain-graduate-scholarship/

**For further information contact:**

Kellogg College, 60-62 Banbury Road, Oxford OX2 6PN, United Kingdom.

**Email**:　enquiries@kellogg.ox.ac.uk

## Lady Margaret Hall Talbot Research Fellowship

**Purpose**: To provide an opportunity for academic postdoctoral research
**Eligibility**: Open to qualified persons who hold or will have obtained a postdoctoral or equivalent degree by the start of tenure
**Level of Study**: Postgraduate
**Type**: Fellowship
**Value**: Please contact the college for details
**Length of Study**: 3 years, not renewable
**Frequency**: Every 3 years

**Study Establishment**: Lady Margaret Hall, the University of Oxford
**Country of Study**: United Kingdom

**For further information contact:**

Lady Margaret Hall Norham Gardens, Oxford OX2 6QA, United Kingdom.

**Tel**:　(44) 1865 274 300
**Fax**:　(44) 1865 511 069
**Email**:　college.office@lmh.ox.ac.uk

## Lady Margaret Hall: Ann Kennedy Graduate Scholarship in Law

**Eligibility**: Open to graduate applicants for the BCL, MJur, MSt in Legal Research or MPhil in Law at Lady Margaret Hall. The award will be made on the basis of academic excellence
**Level of Study**: Graduate, Postgraduate, Predoctorate
**Type**: Scholarship
**Value**: The award covers college fees and a contribution to the university fees. It is awarded for one year for an amount of up to £14,000. It is not intended to contribute to living expenses
**Length of Study**: 1 year
**Study Establishment**: Lady Margaret Hall
**Country of Study**: Any country
**Closing Date**: 20 January
**Additional Information**: Please visit the website: www.law.ox.ac.uk/admissions/scholarships-index/college-awards-specific-law-postgraduates-index

**For further information contact:**

**Email**:　enquiries@lmh.ox.ac.uk

## Lady Margaret Hall: Gavin Cameron Graduate Scholarship in Economics

**Level of Study**: Graduate
**Type**: Scholarship
**Value**: Free accommodation in new Graduate accommodation
**Length of Study**: Three years
**Study Establishment**: Lady Margaret Hall
**Country of Study**: Any country
**Application Procedure**: Open to all graduate applicants in Economics with a preference for, but not restricted to, applicants who put LMH as their first choice College
**Closing Date**: January

**Additional Information**: Please visit the website: www.lmh. ox.ac.uk/prospective-students/Graduates/Scholarship-oppor tunities.aspx    www.lmh.ox.ac.uk/sites/default/files/docu ments/2017-07/LMH_DF_FPs%202017_0.pdf

**For further information contact:**

**Email**:    stassistant@lmh.ox.ac.uk

## Lady Margaret Hall: Open Residential Scholarships

**Eligibility**: Open to all graduate applicants with a preference for, but not restricted to, applicants who put LMH as their first choice college. Please see website for details of how to apply
**Level of Study**: Postgraduate
**Type**: Scholarship
**Value**: £5,000 plus additional benefits including an option on accommodation and limited dining rights
**Length of Study**: 1 year
**Frequency**: Annual
**Study Establishment**: Lady Margaret Hall
**Country of Study**: Any country
**Closing Date**: January
**Additional Information**: Please check the website: www. lmh.ox.ac.uk

**For further information contact:**

**Email**:    graduate.admissions@lmh.ox.ac.uk

## Latin American Centre-Latin American Centre Scholarship

**Eligibility**: Open to all graduate applicants to the MSc in Latin American Studies from one of the CAF shareholder countries. Applicants must send an email to the Admissions Secretary requesting to be considered
**Level of Study**: Postgraduate
**Type**: Scholarship
**Value**: University and college fees (not living expenses)
**Length of Study**: 1 year (Non-renewable)
**Country of Study**: Any country
**Application Procedure**: Please visit website for more details and how to apply
**Closing Date**: 10 March
**Additional Information**: For more information, please check the websites: www.lac.ox.ac.uk/funding
www.educationprogram.scholarshipcare.com/lac-caf-scholar ships/

**For further information contact:**

**Email**:    laclib@bodleian.ox.ac.uk

## Law Faculty: David and Helen Elvin Scholarship

**Eligibility**: Open to all graduate applicants for the BCL and MJur. Award holders will become members of Hertford College. Please see website for more information
**Level of Study**: Graduate, Postgraduate
**Type**: Scholarship
**Value**: £10,000 towards course fees, college fees and living costs where appropriate
**Length of Study**: 1 year
**Study Establishment**: Hertford College
**Country of Study**: Any country
**Closing Date**: 20 January
**Additional Information**: Please visit the website: www.law. ox.ac.uk/postgraduate/scholarships.php

**For further information contact:**

**Email**:    lawfac@law.ox.ac.uk

## Law Faculty: Des Voeux Chambers

**Eligibility**: Open to all graduate applicants to the BCL. Preference may be shown for candidates with an interest in pursuing a career at the Hong Kong Bar. Please see website for more information
**Level of Study**: Postgraduate
**Type**: Scholarship
**Value**: £10,000
**Length of Study**: 1 year
**Frequency**: Annual
**Country of Study**: United Kingdom
**Closing Date**: 20 January
**Funding**: Trusts
**Additional Information**: Please check the website: www. law.ox.ac.uk/postgraduate/scholarships.php

**For further information contact:**

**Email**:    pupillage@dvc.com.hk

## Law Faculty: James Bullock Scholarship

**Purpose**: The James Bullock Scholarship is restricted to students taking the MSc in Taxation and provides an award of £5,000 which will be paid in two instalments
**Eligibility**: Open to all applicants for the MSc in Taxation

**Level of Study**: Postgraduate
**Type**: Scholarship
**Value**: £2,500 per year
**Length of Study**: 2 years
**Country of Study**: Any country
**Closing Date**: 10 March
**Additional Information**: Please visit the website: www.law. ox.ac.uk/postgraduate/scholarships.php www.law.ox.ac.uk/content/james-bullock-scholarship

## For further information contact:

**Email**: lawfac@law.ox.ac.uk

## Law Faculty: The Peter Birks Memorial Scholarship

**Purpose**: To assist graduate students with fees
**Eligibility**: Open to all graduate applicants to BCL/MJur, MSc in Law and Finance, MSt Legal Research, MPhil Or DPhil Law. Please see website for further information
**Level of Study**: Graduate, Postgraduate
**Type**: Scholarship
**Value**: £7,500 per year
**Length of Study**: 1 year
**Frequency**: Annual
**Country of Study**: Any country
**Closing Date**: 20 January
**Additional Information**: Please check the website: www. law.ox.ac.uk/postgraduate/scholarships.php www.law.ox.ac. uk/admissions/scholarships-index/law-faculty-awards-study-any-college-index/peter-birks-memorial

## For further information contact:

**Email**: lawfac@law.ox.ac.uk

## Linacre College: Applied Materials MSc Scholarship

**Purpose**: To assist graduate students with fees and a living allowance
**Eligibility**: Open to all
**Level of Study**: Postgraduate
**Type**: Scholarship
**Length of Study**: 1 year

## For further information contact:

School of Geography and the Environment, University of Oxford, South Parks Road, Oxford OX1 3QY, United Kingdom.

**Tel**:      (44) 1865 285 070
**Email**:   enquiries@ouce.ox.ac.uk

## Linacre College: David Daube Scholarship

**Purpose**: The David Daube Law Scholarship is available to a student reading or intending to read for a DPhil in law, and who is liable to pay fees
**Eligibility**: Open to all graduate applicants for the BCL and MJur
**Level of Study**: Postgraduate
**Type**: Scholarship
**Value**: College fee
**Length of Study**: Period of fee liability
**Country of Study**: Any country
**Closing Date**: 12 March
**Additional Information**: Applicants should first secure a place on the Oxford BCL or MJur course and mark Linacre College as their chosen College. Please check at www.linacre. ox.ac.uk/Admissions/Scholarships

## For further information contact:

**Email**:   ben.nicholson@admin.ox.ac.uk

## Linacre College: EPA Cephalosporin Scholarship

**Purpose**: To assist graduate students with fees
**Eligibility**: Open to all graduate students
**Level of Study**: Postgraduate, Research
**Type**: Scholarship
**Value**: College fees
**Length of Study**: Up to 2 years depending on fee liability
**Additional Information**: www.linacre.ox.ac.uk/prospective-students/scholarships/epa-cephalosporin-scholarship

## For further information contact:

Sir William Dunn School of Pathology.

**Email**:   administration@path.ox.ac.uk

## Linacre College: Hicks Scholarship

**Purpose**: With the initial support of several Old Members, a fund is being established to provide a College fee scholarship to a Linacre student studying for a degree in Economics
**Eligibility**: Open to students reading, or intending to read for a DPhil in Economics who are liable to pay fees
**Level of Study**: Doctorate, Postgraduate

**Type**: Scholarship
**Value**: £80,000. 1st 3 years scholarship paid out = £6,486
**Length of Study**: Period of fee liability
**Study Establishment**: Linacre College
**Country of Study**: Any country
**Closing Date**: 21 April
**Funding**: Private
**Additional Information**: Please visit the website: www.lina cre.ox.ac.uk/prospective-students/scholarships www.linacre. ox.ac.uk/prospective-students/scholarships/hicks-scholarship-economics

**For further information contact:**

Linacre College, St. Cross Road, Oxford OX1 3JA, United Kingdom.

**Tel**:        (44) 1865 271 650
**Email**:     development@linacre.ox.ac.uk

## Linacre College: Hitachi Chemical Europe Scholarship

**Eligibility**: Preference given to applicant from China or Central/South America
**Level of Study**: Postgraduate
**Type**: Scholarship
**Value**: £9,000 and lasts one year
**Length of Study**: 1 year
**Application Procedure**: Eligible candidates are automatically considered for this scholarship
**No. of awards offered**: 1
**Closing Date**: 24 January
**Additional Information**: Please check at www.linacre.ox.ac. uk/extras/scholarships    www.linacre.ox.ac.uk/prospective-students/scholarships/hitachi-chemical-environmental-scholar ship

**For further information contact:**

Oxford University Centre for the Environment, Environmental Change Institute, South Parks Road, Oxford OX1 3QY, United Kingdom.

**Email**:     thomas.thornton@ouce.ox.ac.uk

## Linacre College: John Bamborough MSc Scholarship

**Eligibility**: Open to all graduate applicants for MSc courses in the Humanities division
**Level of Study**: Postgraduate

**Type**: Scholarship
**Value**: 100% university and college fees. £3,205
**Length of Study**: One year
**Study Establishment**: Linacre College
**Country of Study**: Any country
**Application Procedure**: Please see website for more details, including how to apply
**Closing Date**: 19 April
**Additional Information**: Please visit the website: www.lina cre.ox.ac.uk/prospective-students/scholarships scholarship-positions.com/john-bamborough-msc-scholarships-humanities-linacre-college-uk/2018/04/10/

**For further information contact:**

**Email**:     scholarships@linacre.ox.ac.uk

## Linacre College: Linacre Rausing Scholarship (English)

**Level of Study**: Research
**Type**: Scholarship
**Value**: £3,300
**Length of Study**: Up to 3 years
**Country of Study**: Any country
**Application Procedure**: Eligible candidates are automatically considered for this scholarship
**No. of awards offered**: 1
**Additional Information**: www.linacre.ox.ac.uk/prospective-students/scholarships/rausing-scholarship-english

**For further information contact:**

**Email**:     english.office@ell.ox.ac.uk

## Linacre College: Mary Blaschko Graduate Scholarship

**Purpose**: To enable European students to carry out research for 1 year in the department of pharmacology or the MRC anatomical neuropharmacology unit
**Eligibility**: Open to all graduate applicants for research degrees in the Humanities division
**Level of Study**: Postgraduate, Research
**Type**: Scholarship
**Value**: £3,300
**Length of Study**: Period of fee liability
**Study Establishment**: Linacre College
**Country of Study**: Any country
**Application Procedure**: Please see website for more details, including how to apply
**No. of awards offered**: 2

**Additional Information**: Please visit the website: www.lina cre.ox.ac.uk/prospective-students/scholarships www.linacre. ox.ac.uk/prospective-students/scholarships/mary-blaschko-scholarship

**For further information contact:**

**Email**:    scholarships@linacre.ox.ac.uk

## Linacre College: Rausing Scholarship in Anthropology

**Eligibility**: Open to all graduate applicants in Anthropology
**Level of Study**: Research
**Type**: Scholarship
**Value**: College fee plus £2,000 towards living expenses
**Length of Study**: Period of fee liability
**Country of Study**: Any country
**Application Procedure**: There is no application form. Applications should consist of a detailed doctoral proposal of 3–4 pages, a curriculum vitae and two letters of reference, one of which should be provided by the student's current or prospective supervisor for the doctorate. Applications should be sent to the Director of Graduate Studies. Please see website for details of how to apply
**Additional Information**: Please check at www.linacre.ox.ac. uk/Admissions/Scholarships www.linacre.ox.ac.uk/ prospective-students/scholarships/rausing-scholarship-anthro pology

**For further information contact:**

**Email**:    ben.nicholson@admin.ox.ac.uk

## Linacre College: Rausing Scholarship in English

**Eligibility**: Open to all graduate applicants for any course in the English Faculty
**Level of Study**: Doctorate
**Type**: Scholarship
**Value**: £3,300
**Length of Study**: Two years in first instance, possible third
**Study Establishment**: Linacre College
**Country of Study**: Any country
**Application Procedure**: Please see website for more details, including how to apply
**Additional Information**: Please visit the website: www.lina cre.ox.ac.uk/prospective-students/scholarships www.lina cre.ox.ac.uk/prospective-students/scholarships/rausing-scholar ship-english

**For further information contact:**

**Email**:    support@linacre.ox.ac.uk

## Linacre College: Raymond and Vera Asquith Scholarship

**Eligibility**: Open to suitably qualified students who were born in the United Kingdom, reading or intending to read for a DPhil in Humanities who are liable to pay fees and have AHRC funding
**Level of Study**: Doctorate, Postgraduate
**Type**: Scholarship
**Value**: College fee
**Length of Study**: Period of fee liability
**Country of Study**: Any country
**Application Procedure**: Please see website for details of how to apply
**Additional Information**: Please check at www.linacre.ox.ac. uk/Admissions/Scholarships www.linacre.ox.ac.uk/raymond-vera-asquith

**For further information contact:**

**Email**:    ben.nicholson@admin.ox.ac.uk

## Linacre College: Ronald and Jane Olson Scholarship

**Eligibility**: Open to all graduate applicants for the MSc in Refugee and Forced Migration Studies
**Level of Study**: Postgraduate
**Type**: Scholarship
**Value**: College fee, plus a maintenance grant of £2,500
**Length of Study**: 1 year
**Study Establishment**: Linacre College
**Country of Study**: Any country
**Closing Date**: 20 January
**Additional Information**: Please visit the website: www.lina cre.ox.ac.uk/prospective-students/scholarships www.lina cre.ox.ac.uk/prospective-students/scholarships/ronald-and-jane-olson-scholarship-refugee-studies

**For further information contact:**

**Email**:    rsc-msc@qeh.ox.ac.uk

## Linacre College: Women in Science Scholarship

**Eligibility**: Open to all graduate applicants for the DPhil in Materials who are liable to pay fees

**Level of Study**: Doctorate
**Type**: Scholarship
**Value**: College fee
**Length of Study**: Period of fee liability
**Study Establishment**: Linacre College
**Country of Study**: Any country
**Closing Date**: 21 April
**Additional Information**: Please visit the website: www.lina cre.ox.ac.uk/prospective-students/scholarships www.lina cre.ox.ac.uk/alumni-friends/funds-campaigns/50th-anniversary-campaign/women-science-scholarship-fund

**For further information contact:**

**Email**:    support@linacre.ox.ac.uk

## Lincoln College: Berrow Foundation Lord Florey Scholarships

**Eligibility**: Open to all graduate applicants for courses in Medical, Chemical or Biochemical Sciences of Swiss or Lichtenstein nationality who are students at, or have recently graduated from, any Swiss university, including ETHZ and EPFL, and who must not be more than five years beyond graduation from their first degree at one of these institutions (except for candidates in medicine, for whom the five years limit dates from obtaining the Federal Diploma in Medicine). Up to two awards available. Please see website for full details and application form
**Level of Study**: Postgraduate, Research
**Type**: Scholarship
**Value**: £15,900 per annum
**Length of Study**: Up to 3 years
**Frequency**: Annual
**Study Establishment**: Lincoln
**Country of Study**: Any country
**Application Procedure**: Please see website for details of how to apply
**Closing Date**: 24 January
**Funding**: Foundation
**Additional Information**: Please check the website: www. lincoln.ox.ac.uk/funding-and-awards-for-graduates www. lincoln.ox.ac.uk/berrow-foundation-scholarships-_for-swis

**For further information contact:**

**Email**:    rectors.office@lincoln.ox.ac.uk.

## Lincoln College: Berrow Foundation Scholarships

**Eligibility**: Open to all graduate applicants of Swiss or Lichtenstein nationality who are students at, or have recently graduated from, selected Swiss universities. Up to four awards available. Please see website for full details and application form
**Level of Study**: Postgraduate, Research
**Type**: Scholarship
**Value**: University fee (at the United Kingdom level), college fee, and living expenses equivalent to Rhodes Scholarship stipend
**Length of Study**: Up to 3 years
**Frequency**: Annual
**Study Establishment**: Lincoln
**Country of Study**: Any country
**Closing Date**: 24 January
**Funding**: Foundation
**Additional Information**: Please check the website: www. lincoln.ox.ac.uk/funding-and-awards-for-graduates www. lincoln.ox.ac.uk/berrow-foundation-scholarships-_for-swis

**For further information contact:**

**Email**:    rectors.office@lincoln.ox.ac.uk.

## Lincoln College: Crewe Graduate Scholarships

**Eligibility**: Students, in any subject, ordinarily resident in the Dioceses of Durham and Newcastle; Northallertonshire (in North Yorkshire); Howdenshire (in Humberside); Leicestershire; Northamptonshire; and the Diocese of Oxford. Applicants must hold an offer of a place to read for a graduate degree course at an Oxford college before applying. Successful applicants holding an offer of a place at another College will be required to migrate to Lincoln College in order to take up the award.
**Level of Study**: Graduate, Postgraduate, MBA
**Type**: Scholarship
**Value**: £7,000
**Length of Study**: One year, with the possibility of renewal on applying
**Frequency**: Annual
**Study Establishment**: Lincoln College, University of Oxford
**Country of Study**: United Kingdom
**Application Procedure**: A combined application form is available www.lincoln.ox.ac.uk/uploads/files/Scholarship% 20application%20form%202020.docx.
**Closing Date**: 6 June
**Funding**: Trusts
**No. of awards given last year**: 6
**Additional Information**: www.lincoln.ox.ac.uk/funding-and-awards-for-graduates#Crewe%20GA

**For further information contact:**

**Email**:    admissions@lincoln.ox.ac.uk

## Lincoln College: Hartley Bursary

**Eligibility**: New or current graduate students of Lincoln College, ordinarily resident in the UK, who are studying for a degree in any humanities subject and who are in financial need
**Level of Study**: Graduate
**Type**: Scholarship
**Value**: £1,200
**Length of Study**: 1 years
**Study Establishment**: Lincoln College
**Country of Study**: Any country
**Application Procedure**: A combined application form is available www.lincoln.ox.ac.uk/uploads/files/Scholarship%20application%20form%202020.docx.
**No. of awards offered**: 1
**Closing Date**: 6 June
**Additional Information**: Please visit the website: www.lincoln.ox.ac.uk/funding-and-awards-for-graduates www.lincoln.ox.ac.uk/funding-and-awards-for-graduates#Hart

### For further information contact:

**Email**:  admissions@lincoln.ox.ac.uk

## Lincoln College: Jermyn Brooks Graduate Award

**Eligibility**: Open to graduate students of the college (other new or continuing) who are studying in the humanities, with a preference for modern languages
**Level of Study**: Postgraduate
**Type**: Scholarship
**Value**: £1,000
**Length of Study**: One year
**Frequency**: Annual
**Study Establishment**: Lincoln College, University of Oxford
**Country of Study**: United Kingdom
**Application Procedure**: Application form available from Admissions Office at Lincoln College
**Closing Date**: August
**Funding**: Private
**Additional Information**: www.scholarshipslab.com/lincoln-college-university-of-oxford-the-jermyn-brooks-graduate-award-in-uk-2019/

### For further information contact:

The Admissions Office Lincoln College.

**Email**:  info@lincoln.ox.ac.uk

## Lincoln College: Kenneth Seward-Shaw Scholarship

**Eligibility**: Candidates must be graduate students in the area of Law, History, English, or Politics. They should have attained a high standard in their previous academic work. The candidate who is selected for this award will be expected to give a presentation on their work to members of the Middle and Senior Common Room at a joint seminar during their first year at Lincoln. There will be a reward of an additional £500 for doing so.
**Level of Study**: Postgraduate
**Type**: Scholarship
**Value**: £1,500 (+£500)
**Length of Study**: 1 year
**Frequency**: Annual
**Study Establishment**: Lincoln College, University of Oxford
**Country of Study**: United Kingdom
**Application Procedure**: A combined application form is available www.lincoln.ox.ac.uk/uploads/files/Scholarship%20application%20form%202020.docx.
**Closing Date**: 6 June
**Funding**: Private
**Additional Information**: www.lincoln.ox.ac.uk/funding-and-awards-for-graduates#Shaw

### For further information contact:

**Email**:  admissions@lincoln.ox.ac.uk

## Lincoln College: Lord Crewe Graduate Scholarship in Medical Sciences (Clarendon-Linked)

**Eligibility**: Students, in any subject, ordinarily resident in the Dioceses of Durham and Newcastle; Northallertonshire (in North Yorkshire); Howdenshire (in Humberside); Leicestershire; Northamptonshire; and the Diocese of Oxford. Applicants must hold an offer of a place to read for a graduate degree course at an Oxford college before applying. Successful applicants holding an offer of a place at another College will be required to migrate to Lincoln College in order to take up the award.
**Level of Study**: Postgraduate, Research
**Type**: Scholarship
**Value**: £7,000
**Length of Study**: 1 year
**Country of Study**: Any country
**Application Procedure**: A combined application form is available www.lincoln.ox.ac.uk/uploads/files/Scholarship%20application%20form%202020.docx.
**No. of awards offered**: 2

**Closing Date**: 6 June

**Additional Information**: www.lincoln.ox.ac.uk/funding-and-awards-for-graduates#Crewe

### For further information contact:

**Email**:    admissions@lincoln.ox.ac.uk

## Lincoln College: Lord Crewe Graduate Scholarship in Social Sciences (Clarendon-Linked)

**Eligibility**: Applicants must nominate Lincoln as their College of Preference and be considered for a Clarendon Fund Scholarship

**Level of Study**: Postgraduate, Research

**Type**: Scholarship

**Value**: All university and college fees and a generous living allowance (Clarendon-linked)

**Length of Study**: Period of Fee liability

**Frequency**: Annual

**Country of Study**: Any country

**Closing Date**: 20 January

**Additional Information**: Please check at www.clarendon.ox.ac.uk/partnership/ www.lincoln.ox.ac.uk/funding-and-awards-for-graduates#Crewe

### For further information contact:

**Email**:    info@lincoln.ox.ac.uk

## Lincoln College: Lord Crewe Graduate Scholarships in the Humanities

**Eligibility**: Open to graduates of any United Kingdom university for all courses within the Humanities

**Level of Study**: Postgraduate, Research

**Type**: Scholarship

**Value**: £18,000 per year

**Length of Study**: Period of fee liability

**Country of Study**: Any country

**Application Procedure**: Please see website for details of how to apply

**Closing Date**: 18 January

**Additional Information**: Please check at www.lincoln.ox.ac.uk/

### For further information contact:

**Email**:    info@lincoln.ox.ac.uk

## Lincoln College: Lord Crewe Graduate Scholarships in the Social Sciences

**Eligibility**: Open to graduates of any United Kingdom university for all courses within the Social Sciences

**Level of Study**: Postgraduate, Research

**Type**: Scholarship

**Value**: £18,000 per year

**Length of Study**: Period of fee liability

**Country of Study**: Any country

**Application Procedure**: Please see website for details of how to apply

**Closing Date**: 18 January

**Additional Information**: Please check at www.lincoln.ox.ac.uk/

### For further information contact:

**Email**:    info@lincoln.ox.ac.uk

## Lincoln College: Menasseh Ben Israel Room

**Eligibility**: Open to all graduate applicants who have graduated from an Israeli university. Preference will be shown to graduates of the Hebrew University, Jerusalem. Applicants must hold a place, or an offer of a place, at Lincoln College before making an application. Please see website for full details and application form

**Level of Study**: Graduate, Postgraduate

**Type**: Scholarship

**Value**: Free accommodation for one academic year (37 weeks) as occupant of the Menasseh Ben Israel Room in college

**Length of Study**: 1 year

**Country of Study**: Any country

**Application Procedure**: Please see website for full details and application form

**Closing Date**: 1 June

**Additional Information**: Please check at www.lincoln.ox.uk/funding-and-awards-for-graduates    testbig.com/article_items/menasseh-ben-israel-room-scholarship-israeli-students-lincoln-college-uk-2013

### For further information contact:

**Email**:    info@lincoln.ox.ac.uk

## Lincoln College: Overseas Graduate Entrance Scholarship

**Eligibility**: All non-European Union nationals

**Type**: Scholarship
**Value**: £2,300
**Length of Study**: 1 year
**Country of Study**: Any country
**Closing Date**: 1 June
**Additional Information**: Successful candidates will show evidence of both academic merit and financial need. Applicants must hold a place, or an offer of a place, at Lincoln College before applying. Eligible to the nationals of Overseas

**For further information contact:**

**Email**:    info@lincoln.ox.ac.uk

## Lincoln College: Polonsky Foundation Grants

**Eligibility**: Open to all overseas graduate applicants who show evidence of financial need, academic merit and potential for good college citizenship
**Type**: Grant
**Value**: Approx. £5,300 per year
**Length of Study**: Up to 3 years
**Study Establishment**: Lincoln
**Country of Study**: Any country
**Application Procedure**: Applicants must hold a place, or an offer of a place, at Lincoln College before making an application. Please see website for full details and application form
**Closing Date**: 3 June
**Additional Information**: Candidates may be new or current students and must be citizens of countries not in the European Union. Please check the website: www.lincoln.ox.ac.uk/funding-and-awards-for-graduates www.scholarshipsads.com/polonsky-foundation-scholarships-international-graduate-students-lincoln-college-uk/

**For further information contact:**

**Email**:    info@lincoln.ox.ac.uk

## Lincoln College: Sloane Robinson Foundation Graduate Awards

**Purpose**: To fund those intending to pursue research programmes at Oxford
**Eligibility**: Any DPhil candidates in the Social Sciences
**Level of Study**: Graduate, Postgraduate, Research, MBA
**Type**: Award
**Value**: Fees and Stipend
**Length of Study**: 3 to 4 years
**Frequency**: Annual

**Study Establishment**: Lincoln College, University of Oxford
**Country of Study**: United Kingdom
**Application Procedure**: There is no application form for these awards. All eligible candidates are considered by the Departmental Scholarship panels
**No. of awards offered**: 1
**Closing Date**: 1 June
**Funding**: Foundation
**Additional Information**: Successful candidates will show evidence of both academic merit and financial need. Applicants must hold a place, or an offer of a place, at Lincoln College before applying www.lincoln.ox.ac.uk/funding-and-awards-for-graduates

**For further information contact:**

**Email**:    info@lincoln.ox.ac.uk

## Lincoln College: Supperstone Law Scholarship

**Eligibility**: Open to candidates reading for the BCL or the MJuris, with an emphasis or special interest in European or public law. Applicants must have an offer of a college place at Lincoln College
**Level of Study**: Postgraduate
**Type**: Scholarship
**Value**: £650
**Length of Study**: 1 year
**Frequency**: Annual
**Study Establishment**: Lincoln College, University of Oxford
**Country of Study**: United Kingdom
**Application Procedure**: Applicants must contact the Admissions Office at Lincoln College
**Funding**: Trusts

## Lingyin Graduate Scholarship in Buddhist Studies

**Purpose**: Oriental Studies
**Eligibility**: Open to current and incoming Master's or DPhil students whose study or research focuses on Buddhist Studies (including all areas, historical periods, and aspects of this field). Eligible incoming students will be considered automatically, but current students need to submit a Lingyin application form. Three scholarships available. Please see website for more details
**Level of Study**: Postgraduate
**Type**: Scholarship

**Value**: £8,000 tenable only for one year at a time. Students holding the scholarship who would wish to reapply for it for the following year would be required to submit a new application for that year, which would be considered competitively alongside other applications for that year
**Length of Study**: One year
**Frequency**: Annual
**Country of Study**: United Kingdom
**Application Procedure**: For more information, please visit the website: www.orinst.ox.ac.uk/administration/grants/index.html
**Closing Date**: 22 January
**Funding**: Trusts
**Additional Information**: www.orinst.ox.ac.uk/article/lingyin-graduate-scholarship-in-buddhist-studies

**For further information contact:**

**Email**:    Buddhist-studies@email.arizona.edu

## Magdalen College: Perkin Research Studentship

**Eligibility**: Open to all graduate applicants from Commonwealth countries for Chemistry
**Level of Study**: Research
**Type**: Studentship
**Value**: £7,000 per year
**Length of Study**: Period of fee liability
**Country of Study**: Any country
**Application Procedure**: Please see website for details of how to apply
**Additional Information**: Please check at www.magd.ox.ac.uk/admissions_graduate/scholarships.shtml

**For further information contact:**

**Email**:    jane.sherwood@admin.ox.ac.uk

## Magdalen College: Student Support Fund Graduate Grants

**Eligibility**: Graduate students already studying at Magdalen
**Level of Study**: Postgraduate, Research
**Type**: Grant
**Value**: According to individual circumstances
**Length of Study**: 1 year, renewable after review
**Country of Study**: Any country
**Additional Information**: www.magd.ox.ac.uk/alumni-friends/supporting-magdalen/priorities/student-support/

**For further information contact:**

**Email**:    senior.tutor@magd.ox.ac.uk

## Magdalen Hong Kong Scholarship

**Eligibility**: Open to students who are ordinarily resident in Hong Kong and are citizens of the People's Republic of China (PRC). Candidates should be intending to return to Hong Kong or the PRC on completion of their studies
**Level of Study**: Postgraduate
**Type**: Scholarship
**Value**: Maximum of £26,250 per year as a contribution towards college and university tuition fees and living expenses
**Length of Study**: Up to 4 years
**Application Procedure**: Please see the website for further details
**Closing Date**: 22 January
**Additional Information**: Please visit www.magd.ox.ac.uk/studying-here/as-a-graduate/scholarships-and-awards-2 www.magd.ox.ac.uk/hongkongscholarship/

**For further information contact:**

**Email**:    admissions@magd.ox.ac.uk

## Mansfield College: Adam von Trott Scholarship

**Eligibility**: Open to German nationals applying to the two year MPhil in Politics. Please see website for more details
**Level of Study**: Postgraduate, Research
**Type**: Scholarship
**Value**: University fee, college fee, living expenses up to €20,000 per annum
**Length of Study**: Duration of fee liability
**Country of Study**: Any country
**Closing Date**: 6 January
**Additional Information**: Please check the website: www.mansfield.ox.ac.uk/prospective/postgrad/scholarships.html www.politics.ox.ac.uk/materials/degrees/testimonials/David_Hageboelling_Study_Report_2014-15.pdf

**For further information contact:**

**Email**:    avt.committee@outlook.com

## Mansfield College: Elfan Rees Scholarship

**Purpose**: To commencing studies towards a higher degree in the field of theology
**Eligibility**: Open to students on the MSt, MPhil, MLitt or DPhil in any branch of theology
**Level of Study**: Postdoctorate, Postgraduate, Research
**Type**: Scholarship
**Value**: £3,000 maintenance, college fee waiver, matching Faculty award up to £5,000

**Length of Study**: Up to 2 years
**Country of Study**: Any country
**Closing Date**: October
**Additional Information**: Please check at www.mansfield.ox. ac.uk/current/prizes-scholarships.html www.mansfield.ox. ac.uk/graduate-scholarships

### For further information contact:

**Email**:    lodge@mansfield.ox.ac.uk

## Medical Sciences Doctoral Training Centre: British Heart Foundation Studentship in Cardiovascular Science

**Eligibility**: Open to all applicants to the DPhil in Cardiovascular Science. All applicants are automatically considered for these awards
**Level of Study**: Doctorate
**Type**: Studentship
**Value**: Course fee, college fee, living expenses
**Length of Study**: 4 years
**Country of Study**: Any country
**Closing Date**: 6 January
**Funding**: Foundation
**Additional Information**: Please visit the website: www. medsci.ox.ac.uk/study/graduateschool/courses/dtc-structured-research-degrees/cardiovascular-science

### For further information contact:

**Email**:    Graduate.School@medsci.ox.ac.uk

## Medical Sciences Doctoral Training Centre: Wellcome Trust Fellowship in Biomedical and Clinical Sciences

**Eligibility**: Open to all applicants to the DPhil in Biomedical and Clinical Sciences. All applicants are automatically considered for these awards
**Level of Study**: Doctorate
**Type**: Fellowship
**Value**: Course fee, college fee, living expenses
**Length of Study**: 3 years
**Country of Study**: Any country
**Closing Date**: 6 January
**Funding**: Trusts
**Additional Information**: Please visit the website: www. medsci.ox.ac.uk/study/graduateschool/courses/dtc-structured-research-degrees/doctoral-training-fellowship-scheme-for-clinicians

### For further information contact:

**Email**:    christopher.buckley@kennedy.ox.ac.uk

## Medical Sciences Doctoral Training Centre: Wellcome Trust Studentship in Chromosome and Developmental Biology

**Purpose**: To provide students with training and supporting infrastructure to apply advanced biological imaging/super resolution microscopy, high-throughput sequencing method (and computational genomics for data analysis), advanced proteomics, and state of the art genome engineering
**Eligibility**: Open to all applicants to the DPhil in Chromosome and Developmental Biology. All applicants are automatically considered for these awards
**Level of Study**: Doctorate
**Type**: Studentship
**Value**: Course fee, college fee, living expenses
**Length of Study**: 4 years
**Country of Study**: Any country
**Closing Date**: 6 January
**Funding**: Trusts
**Additional Information**: Please visit the website: www. medsci.ox.ac.uk/study/graduateschool/courses/dtc-structured-research-degrees/chromosome-and-developmental-biology

### For further information contact:

**Email**:    enquiries@msdtc.ox.ac.uk

## Medical Sciences Doctoral Training Centre: Wellcome Trust Studentship in Genomic Medicine and Statistics

**Purpose**: Trains future scientific leaders who will work at the cutting edge of genomics in biomedical research and enable effective delivery into the clinic
**Eligibility**: Open to all applicants to the DPhil in Genomic Medicine and Statistics. All applicants are automatically considered for these awards
**Level of Study**: Doctorate
**Type**: Studentship
**Value**: Course fee, college fee, living expenses
**Length of Study**: 4 years
**Country of Study**: Any country
**Closing Date**: 6 January
**Funding**: Trusts
**Additional Information**: Please visit the website: www. medsci.ox.ac.uk/study/graduateschool/courses/dtc-structured-research-degrees/genomic-medicine-and-statistics

**For further information contact:**

**Email**:	enquiries@msdtc.ox.ac.uk

## Medical Sciences Doctoral Training Centre: Wellcome Trust Studentship in Infection, Immunology and Translational Medicine

**Purpose**: Provides integrated training in infection and immunology, and how fundamental research can be translated into benefits for human health
**Eligibility**: Open to all applicants to the DPhil in Infection, Immunology and Translational Medicine. All applicants are automatically considered for these awards
**Level of Study**: Doctorate
**Type**: Studentship
**Value**: Course fee, college fee, living expenses
**Length of Study**: 4 years
**Country of Study**: Any country
**Application Procedure**: Applicants are suggested to select St Edmund Hall as their college choice. Please see the website for more details
**Closing Date**: 6 January
**Funding**: Trusts
**Additional Information**: Please visit the website: www.medsci.ox.ac.uk/study/graduateschool/courses/dtc-structured-research-degrees/infection-immunology-and-translational-medicine

**For further information contact:**

**Email**:	Graduate.School@medsci.ox.ac.uk

## Medical Sciences Doctoral Training Centre: Wellcome Trust Studentship in Ion Channels and Disease

**Purpose**: Trains the student in a range of multidisciplinary approaches and embraces all aspects of ion channel and membrane transport research from protein structure, genetics and cell physiology to animal behaviour and human disease
**Eligibility**: Open to all applicants to the DPhil in Ion Channels and Disease. All applicants are automatically considered for these awards
**Level of Study**: Doctorate
**Type**: Studentship
**Value**: Course fee, college fee, living expenses
**Length of Study**: 4 years
**Country of Study**: Any country
**Application Procedure**: Applicants who have no strong preference for a college are suggested to consider Green Templeton College or The Queen's College as their choice

**Closing Date**: 6 January
**Funding**: Trusts
**Additional Information**: Please visit the website: www.medsci.ox.ac.uk/study/graduateschool/courses/dtc-structured-research-degrees/ion-channels-and-membrane-transport-in-health-and-disease-oxion

**For further information contact:**

**Email**:	enquiries@msdtc.ox.ac.uk

## Medical Sciences Doctoral Training Centre: Wellcome Trust Studentship in Neuroscience

**Purpose**: Provides a wide range of skills training in experimental and theoretical methods that is intended to enable you to ask questions and tackle problems that transcend the traditional disciplines from which this field has evolved
**Eligibility**: Open to all applicants to the Wellcome Trust combined MSc and DPhil in Neuroscience. All applicants are automatically considered for these awards
**Level of Study**: Doctorate
**Type**: Studentship
**Value**: Course fee, college fee, living expenses
**Length of Study**: 4 years
**Country of Study**: Any country
**Closing Date**: 6 January
**Funding**: Trusts
**Additional Information**: Please visit the website: www.medsci.ox.ac.uk/study/graduateschool/courses/dtc-structured-research-degrees/neuroscience

**For further information contact:**

University of Oxford, Wellington Square, Oxford OX1 2JD, United Kingdom.

**Tel**:	(44) 1865 270000
**Email**:	enquiries@msdtc.ox.ac.uk

## Medical Sciences Doctoral Training Centre: Wellcome Trust Studentship in Structural Biology

**Purpose**: Provides training in structural biology and related biochemical, genetic and cell biological approaches to understand molecular and cellular function
**Eligibility**: Open to all applicants to the DPhil in Structural Biology. All applicants are automatically considered for these awards
**Level of Study**: Doctorate
**Type**: Studentship
**Value**: Course fee, college fee, living expenses

**Length of Study**: 4 years
**Country of Study**: Any country
**Closing Date**: 6 January
**Funding**: Trusts
**Additional Information**: Please visit the website: www.medsci.ox.ac.uk/study/graduateschool/courses/dtc-structured-research-degrees/cellular-structural-biology

**For further information contact:**

**Email**: enquiries@msdtc.ox.ac.uk

## Merton College Leventis Scholarship

**Eligibility**: Open to citizens of Greece or the Republic of Cyprus only
**Level of Study**: Graduate
**Type**: Scholarship
**Value**: Fees and maintenance
**Length of Study**: Up to 4 years depending on programme of study
**Frequency**: Every 2 years
**Study Establishment**: Merton College, University of Oxford
**Country of Study**: United Kingdom
**Application Procedure**: Further particulars and application forms are available from the Merton College website www.merton.ox.ac.uk/vacancies
**No. of awards offered**: 10
**Closing Date**: January
**Funding**: Private
**No. of applicants last year**: 10
**Additional Information**: Prospective applicants should refer to the college website www.merton.ox.ac.uk

**For further information contact:**

Merton College Merton Street, Oxford OX1 4JD, United Kingdom.

**Email**: julie.gerhardi@merton.ox.ac.uk

## Merton College: Barton Scholarship

**Eligibility**: Open to British graduate applicants for the BCL. Awarded with the Law Faculty. No separate application required
**Level of Study**: Graduate, Postgraduate
**Type**: Scholarship
**Value**: £5,000 per year
**Length of Study**: 1 year
**Country of Study**: Any country
**Application Procedure**: No separate application required

**Closing Date**: 22 January
**Additional Information**: Please check at www.merton.ox.ac.uk/graduate/graduate-scholarships-2015

**For further information contact:**

**Email**: jane.sherwood@admin.ox.ac.uk

## Merton College: Chemistry Scholarship

**Eligibility**: Open to Home/European Union applicants for any graduate Chemistry programme of study normally considered by the College. Please see website for more details
**Level of Study**: Graduate
**Type**: Scholarship
**Value**: Course fees, college fees, full maintenance award (at RCUK rate)
**Length of Study**: Duration of fee liability
**Study Establishment**: Merton College
**Country of Study**: Any country
**Closing Date**: January
**Additional Information**: Please visit the website: www.merton.ox.ac.uk/graduate/graduate-scholarships

**For further information contact:**

**Tel**: (44) 1865 276 310

## Merton College: Merton Lawyers

**Eligibility**: Open to graduate applicants for the BCL/MJur. No separate application required. Please see website for more details
**Level of Study**: Graduate, Postgraduate
**Type**: Scholarship
**Value**: £5,000 from each of the Faculty and College
**Length of Study**: 1 year
**Frequency**: Annual
**Study Establishment**: Merton
**Country of Study**: Any country
**Closing Date**: 20 January
**Additional Information**: Please check the website: www.merton.ox.ac.uk/graduate/graduate-scholarships

## Merton College: Peter J Braam Global Wellbeing Graduate Scholarship

**Eligibility**: Open to Home/European Union applicants for any graduate Biochemistry programme of study normally considered by the College. Please see website for more details
**Level of Study**: Doctorate

**Type**: Scholarship
**Value**: Course fees, college fees, full maintenance award (at RCUK rate)
**Length of Study**: Duration of fee liability
**Country of Study**: Any country
**Application Procedure**: Applicants wishing to be considered for this scholarship should apply for the DPhil in Biochemistry and state how their research addresses a problem related to global wellbeing
**Closing Date**: January
**Additional Information**: Please visit the website: www.merton.ox.ac.uk/graduate/graduate-scholarships www.devex.com/jobs/peter-j-braam-junior-research-fellowship-in-global-wellbeing-561725

### For further information contact:

**Email**:    graduate.admissions@admin.ox.ac.uk

## Merton College: Two Merton Domus B Scholarships

**Purpose**: To enable United Kingdom/European Union students pursue studies at Merton College
**Eligibility**: Home/European Union applicants
**Level of Study**: Graduate, Postgraduate, Research
**Type**: Scholarship
**Value**: All fees plus maintenance award of £11,500
**Length of Study**: Up to 4 years
**Frequency**: Annual
**Study Establishment**: Merton College, University of Oxford
**Country of Study**: United Kingdom
**Application Procedure**: Further particulars and application forms are available from the Merton College website www.merton.ox.ac.uk/vacancies/index.htm
**Closing Date**: 20 January

### For further information contact:

**Email**:    julie.gerhardig@merton.ox.ac.uk

## New College: The Yeotown Scholarship in Science

**Eligibility**: Open to all Home/European Union applicants to a research degree in Computer Science. The scholarship covers living costs and will be offered in conjunction with a departmental scholarship covering University and college fees. Please see website for more details
**Level of Study**: Postgraduate
**Type**: Scholarship
**Value**: Tuition and college fee plus maintenance stipend
**Length of Study**: Period of fee liability
**Frequency**: Annual

**Study Establishment**: New College
**Country of Study**: United Kingdom
**Application Procedure**: For more information, please check the website: www.new.ox.ac.uk/scholarships-0
**Closing Date**: 8 January
**Funding**: Trusts

### For further information contact:

**Email**:    thenewcollege600014@gmail.com

## North American Electric Reliability Corporation (NERC) Studentships in Earth Sciences

**Purpose**: To assist graduate students with fees and maintenance
**Eligibility**: Open to Home or European Union candidates usually with a 2.1 degree or higher
**Level of Study**: Research
**Type**: Studentship
**Value**: £5,000 per year
**Length of Study**: Duration of fee liability
**Frequency**: Annual
**Country of Study**: Any country
**Application Procedure**: 1. Upload a transcript from your current or previous study, a CV and any other documents that you feel would support your application (within 24 hours of submitting your online application you will receive a link allowing you to upload additional supporting documents). 2. Ask your referees to submit a reference for you by 29 April at the very latest. Note: when you submit your application, an email will automatically be sent to your referees requesting a reference for you. This email will contain a secure link for your referee to upload a reference for you. 3. View the available projects. 4. Make an initial project enquiry by contacting supervisors directly
**Closing Date**: January
**Additional Information**: The Department will have a number of NERC studentships, to be confirmed. An European Union national who has studied for an undergraduate degree at a United Kingdom university during the 3 years leading up to the application may be classed as a United Kingdom resident

### For further information contact:

**Email**:    researchcareers@nerc.ac.uk

## Nuffield College Funded Studentships

**Purpose**: To assist students in a postgraduate degree course
**Eligibility**: Open to persons with at least an Upper Second Class (Honours) Degree or equivalent

**Level of Study**: Postgraduate
**Type**: Studentship
**Value**: Maximum £14,500 (home and European Union students) £19,500 (overseas students), usually partial awards only
**Length of Study**: For the length of the course, subject to satisfactory progress up to 4 years
**Frequency**: Annual
**Study Establishment**: Nuffield College, University of Oxford
**Country of Study**: United Kingdom
**Application Procedure**: All students offered a place at Nuffield College will automatically be considered for a studentship without the need for further application, other than the University of Oxford Graduate Admissions application form
**Additional Information**: Requests for information should be addressed to the Academic Administrator www.nuffield.ox.ac.uk/study-here/funding-your-studies/

### For further information contact:

Nuffield College, New Rd, Oxford OX1 1NF, United Kingdom.

**Email**:    academic.administrator@nuffield.ox.ac.uk

## Nuffield College Guardian Research Fellowship

**Purpose**: To support research on projects directly related to the media
**Eligibility**: Open to journalists or management staff members from fields of newspaper press, periodicals and broadcasting
**Level of Study**: Professional development
**Type**: Fellowship
**Value**: Varies according to the fellow's financial circumstances and proposed research
**Length of Study**: 1 academic year
**Frequency**: Every 2 years
**Study Establishment**: Nuffield College, the University of Oxford
**Country of Study**: United Kingdom
**Application Procedure**: Applicants are required to submit CV, research proposal, and names and addresses of three referees when the post is advertised
**Closing Date**: January
**Funding**: Commercial
**Contributor**: The Scott Trust
**Additional Information**: Preference will be given to proposals directly related to the applicant's experience of working in the media. The fellow will be asked to give the annual Guardian Lecture to members of the university and the public at some time during tenure. Requests for information should

be addressed to the Warden's Secretary www.nuffield.ox.ac.uk/media/2407/srf_britishpolicy_fp.pdf

### For further information contact:

**Tel**:      (44) 1865 278 520
**Fax**:     (44) 1865 278 676
**Email**:   marion.rogers@nuf.ox.ac.uk

## Nuffield College Gwilym Gibbon Research Fellowships

**Purpose**: To support the study of problems of government, especially by co-operation between academic and non academic persons
**Eligibility**: Preference will be given to candidates with experience in some form of public service
**Level of Study**: Postdoctorate, Postgraduate, Professional development
**Type**: Fellowship
**Value**: To cover accommodation, necessary travel costs and some secretarial and other assistance
**Length of Study**: 1 year
**Frequency**: Annual
**Study Establishment**: Nuffield College, the University of Oxford
**Country of Study**: United Kingdom
**Application Procedure**: Write for application form
**Closing Date**: April
**No. of awards given last year**: 1
**Additional Information**: It is hoped that the results of the research will be published or made available in some way to interested persons. Requests for information should be addressed to the Student Administrator. Please note that the 1998-9 competition was suspended and that it is possible that it may not run in subsequent years. For further information please consult the Warden of the College

### For further information contact:

**Tel**:      (44) 1865 278 515
**Fax**:     (44) 1865 278 621
**Email**:   glynis.baleham@nuf.ox.ac.uk

## Nuffield College ODA Shared Scholarship

**Eligibility**: Graduates from developing countries of the Commonwealth are eligible to apply
**Level of Study**: Postdoctorate
**Type**: Studentship
**Value**: Fees and maintenance
**Length of Study**: Up to 3 years
**Frequency**: Annual

**Study Establishment**: Nuffield College, the University of Oxford

**Country of Study**: United Kingdom

**Application Procedure**: Applicants must submit a list of publications, a curriculum vitae, a synopsis of the proposed research and the names and addresses of three referees when the post is advertised

### For further information contact:

**Email**:    marion.rogers@nuf.ox.ac.uk

## Nuffield College Postdoctoral Prize Research Fellowship

**Subjects**: Currently 3 separate competitions in economics, politics, and sociology. Subjects are broadly constructed to include, for example, economic history, political history, political theory, international relations, social and medical statistics, and social policy.

**Purpose**: To allow scholars who have recently completed, or who are close to the completion of, a doctorate, to engage in independent scholarly research in the social sciences.

**Eligibility**: Check post job descriptions

**Level of Study**: Postdoctorate, Postgraduate

**Type**: Fellowship

**Value**: £32,150 p.a.

**Length of Study**: 3 years

**Frequency**: Annual

**Study Establishment**: Nuffield College, University of Oxford

**Country of Study**: United Kingdom

**Application Procedure**: Check post job descriptions

**No. of awards offered**: 3 to 6

**No. of awards given last year**: 6

**Additional Information**: www.nuffield.ox.ac.uk/the-college/jobs-and-vacancies/

### For further information contact:

Nuffield College.

**Email**:    pprf@nuffield.ox.ac.uk

## Nuffield Department of Clinical Medicine: LICR Studentship (Ludwig Institute for Cancer Research)

**Eligibility**: Minimum 2:1 or above, higher level English language test. Open to United Kingdom, European Union and Overseas Students

**Type**: Studentship

**Value**: All University and College fees plus stipend £16,500 per year

**Length of Study**: 3-4 years

**Country of Study**: Any country

**Additional Information**: Please check at www.ludwig.ox.ac.uk/ www.ndm.ox.ac.uk/ludwig-institute-for-cancer-research

### For further information contact:

**Email**:    webmaster@ox.ac.uk

## Nuffield Department of Orthopaedics, Rheumatology and Musculoskeletal Sciences: Kennedy Trust Prize Studentships

**Purpose**: To provide world-class scientific training in a supportive and collaborative environment

**Eligibility**: Both European Union and Overseas applicants for the DPhil in Molecular and Cellular Medicine are eligible for this award. Interested applicants should have or expect to obtain a first or upper second class BSc degree or equivalent, and will also need to provide evidence of English language competence at time of application

**Level of Study**: Doctorate

**Type**: Studentship

**Value**: £22,000 per annum

**Length of Study**: 4 years

**Frequency**: Annual

**Country of Study**: Any country

**Additional Information**: Please visit the website: www.ndorms.ox.ac.uk/graduate-courses/kennedy-trust-prize-studentships www.ndorms.ox.ac.uk/graduate-courses/kennedy-trust-prize-studentships/how-to-apply

### For further information contact:

**Email**:    reception@kennedy.ox.ac.uk

## Nuffield Department of Population Health: NDPH Scholarship

**Eligibility**: The department aims to provide up to two fully funded scholarships for the MSc each year. All applicants for the MSc in Global Health Science are eligible for this; the highest ranked applicants in the department are shortlisted for funding

**Level of Study**: Postgraduate

**Type**: Scholarship

**Value**: Course fee, College fee, living expenses at RCUK rate

**Length of Study**: 1 year

**Frequency**: Annual

**Country of Study**: Any country

**Closing Date**: 6 January
**Additional Information**: Please visit the website: www. ndph.ox.ac.uk/study/for-postgraduates/fees-and-funding armacad.info/university-of-oxford–2019-05-27–nuffield-department-of-population-health-fellowship-programs-2019-university-of-oxford-uk

### For further information contact:

**Email**:    enquiries@ndph.ox.ac.uk

## Nuffield Department of Primary Care Health Science: NIHR School for Primary Care Research DPhil Studentship

**Purpose**: The Health Sciences Research Group invites applications for 2011 NIHR School for Primary Care Research (NSPCR) PhD studentships
**Eligibility**: The award can only be taken up by a student enrolled on the DPhil in Primary Health Care programme in a non-clinical area
**Level of Study**: Doctorate
**Type**: Studentship
**Value**: Course fee up to Home/European Union level, college fee, stipend. Annual tax-free stipend of £18,000
**Length of Study**: 3 years
**Frequency**: Annual
**Country of Study**: Any country
**Closing Date**: 11 January
**Additional Information**: www.phc.ox.ac.uk/study/dphil-and-msc-by-research/postgrad-study-info

### For further information contact:

Radcliffe Observatory Quarter, Woodstock Road, Oxford OX2 6GG, United Kingdom.

**Tel**:    (44) 1865 289 300

## Ooni Adeyeye Enitan Ogunwusi Scholarships

**Purpose**: The scholarship is funded by the Imperial Majesty Oba Adéyeyè Enitan Ògúnwùsì and aims to provide funding to exceptional candidates pursuing postgraduate study of Africa
**Eligibility**: Open to graduate applicants who are ordinarily resident in Nigeria and applying to a full- time one-year master's course within the African Studies Centre at Oxford
**Level of Study**: Postgraduate
**Type**: Scholarship
**Value**: Course fee and a grant for living expenses of at least £ 14,777 per year

**Frequency**: Annual
**Country of Study**: Any country
**Application Procedure**: For further information, check the below link. www.ox.ac.uk/admissions/graduate/fees-and-funding/fees-funding-and-scholarship-search/scholarships-2#ooni
**Closing Date**: January
**Funding**: Private
**Additional Information**: www.opportunitiesforafricans. com/ooni-adeyeye-enitan-ogunwusi-scholarships-2019/

### For further information contact:

University of Oxford, University Offices, Wellington Square, Oxford OX1 2JD, United Kingdom.

**Tel**:    (44) 1865 270 000
**Email**:    joe@advance-africa.com

## Oriel College: Oriel Graduate Scholarships

**Eligibility**: Open to all current graduate students at the college. Please see website for more details, including how to apply
**Level of Study**: Postgraduate, Research
**Type**: Scholarship
**Value**: Approximately £2,500 per year and accommodation rights
**Length of Study**: Period of fee liability
**Country of Study**: Any country
**Closing Date**: 29 January
**Additional Information**: Scholars are entitled to dine free of charge at High Table once per week during term time. Please contact to Academic Assistant at academic.office@oriel.ox. ac.uk

### For further information contact:

**Email**:    jane.sherwood@admin.ox.ac.uk

## Oriel College: Paul Ries Collin Graduate Scholarship

**Eligibility**: Open to current graduate students at Oriel
**Level of Study**: Postgraduate, Research
**Type**: Scholarship
**Value**: Annual stipend equivalent to college fee; guaranteed college room at usual charge
**Length of Study**: 1 year, renewable for second or third
**Frequency**: Annual
**Country of Study**: Any country
**Closing Date**: 27 January

**Additional Information**: Scholars are entitled to dine free of charge at High Table once a week during term-time

### For further information contact:

Oriel College, Oriel Square, Oxford OX1 4EW, United Kingdom.

**Email**:    academic.office@oriel.ox.ac.uk

## Oriel College: Sir Walter Raleigh Scholarship

**Purpose**: To assist a student studying at the Environmental Change Institute for an MSc degree in Environmental Change and Management
**Eligibility**: Open to all applicants to the MSc in Environmental Change and Management. Please see website for more details, including how to apply
**Level of Study**: Postgraduate
**Type**: Scholarship
**Value**: £4,000
**Length of Study**: 1 year
**Frequency**: Annual
**Country of Study**: Any country
**Application Procedure**: Applicants can download an application form from the website www.ox.ac.uk/admissions/index.html or obtain one from the Academic Office or the Environmental Change Institute
**Closing Date**: 30 April
**Additional Information**: The successful applicant will be expected to transfer their application to Oriel College if they have already been accepted by another college. Please check the website for further details www.oriel.ox.ac.uk/content/financial-support-postgraduates     www.eci.ox.ac.uk/msc/funding.html

### For further information contact:

**Email**:    admissions@oriel.ox.ac.uk

## Oriental Studies: H.H. Sheikh Hamad bin Khalifa Al Thani Graduate Studentship in Contemporary Islamic Studies

**Purpose**: Contemporary Islamic Studies
**Eligibility**: Open to applicants to the DPhil in Oriental Studies. The award is intended for any postgraduate student pursuing doctoral research in any field of Contemporary Islamic Studies. Please see website for more information
**Level of Study**: Doctorate
**Type**: Studentship

**Value**: University fee, college fee, and maintenance grant. The award is tenable from October for 1 year in the first instance, renewable for up to a maximum of 3 years subject to receipt of a satisfactory report from the supervisor(s)
**Length of Study**: Up to 4 years
**Country of Study**: Any country
**Closing Date**: 31 March
**Additional Information**: Please visit the website: www.orinst.ox.ac.uk/administration/grants/index.html    weblearn.ox.ac.uk/access/content/group/a55c44d3-9f21-4dec-b48c-2dc6fa4e4bee/Grants/H.H.%20Sheikh%20Hamad%20bin%20Khalifa%20Al%20Thani%20Graduate%20Studentship%20in%20Contemporary%20Islamic%20Studies.pdf

### For further information contact:

62 Woodstock Road, Oxford OX2 6JF, United Kingdom.

## Oriental Studies: KS Scholarship in Chinese Art

**Eligibility**: Open to applicants to graduate degrees at the University in any field of Chinese Art History, with a preference for Chinese painting. Please see website for more details and how to apply
**Level of Study**: Postgraduate
**Type**: Scholarship
**Value**: University fee, college fee and living expenses
**Length of Study**: Period of fee liability
**Frequency**: Annual
**Country of Study**: United Kingdom
**Application Procedure**: For more information, please check the website: www.orinst.ox.ac.uk/administration/trust_funds/ks_scholarship_in_chinese_art.html
**Closing Date**: 22 January
**Funding**: Trusts

### For further information contact:

**Email**:    orient@orinst.ox.ac.uk

## Oriental Studies: Sasakawa Fund

**Eligibility**: Open to all graduate applicants in Oriental Studies, or United Kingdom applicants whose work will require some time spent in Japan
**Level of Study**: Postgraduate, Research
**Type**: Award
**Value**: £5,000 per year
**Length of Study**: Period of fee liability
**Application Procedure**: An application form is available at www.orinst.ox.ac.uk/general/grants/sasakawa_fund.html
**Closing Date**: 18 January

**Additional Information**: www.nissan.ox.ac.uk/sasakawa-fund-travel-grant-at-the-faculty-of-oriental-studies

### For further information contact:

Tel:     (44) 1865 278 225
Fax:    (44) 1865 278 190
Email:  chris.williams@orinst.ox.ac.uk

## Other Studentships in Earth Sciences

**Eligibility**: Applicants must have 2.1 degree or higher. United Kingdom students are eligible for full support, and a range of support is available for European Union and international students
**Level of Study**: Research
**Type**: Studentship
**Value**: University and college fees and maintenance allowance
**Length of Study**: Normally 3 years, which can be extended in some cases
**Frequency**: Dependent on funds available
**Application Procedure**: Candidates are advised to apply directly to the department as advertised on the website
**Closing Date**: 20 January
**Additional Information**: The department occasionally has studentship funding associated with grants or industrial funding www.earth.ox.ac.uk/teaching/graduates/funding/

### For further information contact:

Email:  emmab@earth.ox.ac.uk

## Oxford Research in the Scholarship and Humanities of Africa Studentships

**Purpose**: To support postgraduate study of Africa in the humanities
**Eligibility**: Open to candidates for admission, or those already registered as graduate students. The successful applicant, if not already a member of an Oxford College, may be offered a place at St Antony's College or St Cross College
**Level of Study**: Postgraduate
**Type**: Studentship
**Value**: Varies, however it will cover college and University fees plus maintenance allowance. University fees will normally be covered at the home rate, although in exceptional circumstances supplemental grants may be made in order to meet, or to go some way towards meeting, the difference between the home and overseas fee
**Length of Study**: 2 years with the possibility of extension for 3 and occasionally 4 years

**Frequency**: Annual
**Study Establishment**: University of Oxford
**Country of Study**: United Kingdom
**Application Procedure**: Refer to the website www.africanstudies.ox.ac.uk/orisha
**Additional Information**: www.earth.ox.ac.uk/teaching/graduates/funding/

### For further information contact:

Email:  african.studies@africa.ox.ac.uk

## Oxford University Theological Scholarships (Eastern and Central Europe)

**Purpose**: To enable students to pursue further studies in the University's Faculty of Theology
**Eligibility**: Open to candidates aged 22–40, who already have, or expect to obtain, a theological degree from a recognized university or theological college. Applications are invited from citizens of Russia, the Ukraine and any other countries of the former Soviet Union (apart from the Baltic States), Croatia, Serbia, Montenegro, Bosnia, Macedonia, Bulgaria, Albania and Romania
**Level of Study**: Graduate
**Type**: Scholarship
**Value**: Fees, a maintenance allowance and, where necessary, a return airfare
**Length of Study**: Up to 1 year
**Frequency**: Annual
**Study Establishment**: The Faculty of Theology, University of Oxford
**Country of Study**: United Kingdom
**Application Procedure**: Applicants must contact Mrs Elizabeth Macallister for further information
**Funding**: Government, Private
**Contributor**: Member churches of the Council of Churches for Britain and Ireland, the Foreign and Commonwealth Office and Oxford University
**Additional Information**: Scholarships are open to members of any Christian denomination. Applicants must be sponsored by a recognised church authority in their home country

### For further information contact:

Email:  elizabeth.macallister@admin.ox.ac.uk

## Oxford-A G Leventis Graduate Scholarship

**Eligibility**: Open to all applicants applying for a DPhil in history, specialising in Byzantine studies
**Type**: Scholarship

**Value**: University fee, college fee and full living expenses
**Length of Study**: Period of fee liability
**Country of Study**: Any country
**Application Procedure**: Please visit the website for application details
**Closing Date**: 22 January
**Additional Information**: Please check at www.graduate.ox. ac.uk/ogs oxfordbyzantinesociety.files.wordpress.com/2011/ 05/leventis-graduate-scholarship.pdf

**For further information contact:**

**Email**:     peter.frankopan@worc.ox.ac.uk

## Oxford-Aidan Jenkins Graduate Scholarship

**Eligibility**: Open to applicants who are applying to any full-time course in the Faculty of English Language and Literature. Tenable at Merton College only. Please see website for more details
**Type**: Scholarship
**Value**: University fee, college fee, and full living expenses
**Length of Study**: Duration of fee liability
**Study Establishment**: Merton College
**Country of Study**: Any country
**Closing Date**: 20 January
**Additional Information**: Please visit the website: www.ox. ac.uk/admissions/graduate/fees-and-funding/fees-funding-and-scholarship-search/scholarships-2#aidanjenkins www.european-funding-guide.eu/scholarship/13585-oxford-aidan-jenkins-graduate-scholarship

## Oxford-Bellhouse Graduate Scholarship

**Eligibility**: Open to applicants who are ordinarily resident in the EEA or Switzerland and who are applying to the full-time DPhil in Engineering Sciences, specialising in Biomedical Engineering. The scholarship is only tenable at Magdalen College. Please see website for more details
**Level of Study**: Doctorate
**Type**: Scholarship
**Value**: University fee, college fee, and full living expenses
**Length of Study**: Period of fee liability
**Study Establishment**: Magdalen College
**Country of Study**: Any country
**Closing Date**: 20 January
**Additional Information**: Please visit the website: www.ox. ac.uk/admissions/graduate/fees-and-funding/fees-funding-and-scholarship-search/scholarships-2#bellhouse www.european-funding-guide.eu/scholarship/13586-oxford-bellhouse-graduate-scholarship

**For further information contact:**

**Email**:     accommodation@linacre.ox.ac.uk

## Oxford-Brunsfield Association of Southeast Asian Nations (ASEAN) Human Rights Graduate Scholarships

**Eligibility**: Open to applicants who are nationals of and ordinarily resident in Brunei Darussalam, Cambodia, Indonesia, Laos, Malaysia, Myanmar (Burma), Philippines, Singapore, Thailand or Vietnam and who are applying to the part-time MSt in International Human Rights Law. Please see website for more details
**Level of Study**: Postgraduate
**Type**: Scholarship
**Value**: University fee, college fee, and study support grant
**Length of Study**: Period of fee liability
**Country of Study**: Any country
**Closing Date**: 31 March
**Additional Information**: Please visit the website: www.ox. ac.uk/admissions/graduate/fees-and-funding/fees-funding-and-scholarship-search/scholarships-2#brunsfield www.devwise. com/opps/brunsfield-oxford-asean-human-rights-scholarships-at-university-of-oxford/

**For further information contact:**

**Email**:     iphumrts@conted.ox.ac.uk

## Oxford-Calleva Scholarship

**Purpose**: It is intended to make available three scholarships for entry in October to applicants ordinarily resident in the European Union applying to the DPhil History (including History of Science and Medicine, and Economic and Social History), the DPhil Experimental Psychology, or the DPhil Anthropology
**Eligibility**: Each DPhil student will develop their own project within their respective discipline that explores childhood experiences and the impact of adversity and inequalities, using either psychological or modern British historical evidence
**Level of Study**: Doctorate
**Type**: Scholarship
**Frequency**: Annual
**Country of Study**: Switzerland
**Application Procedure**: The scholarship is only tenable at Linacre College. All eligible applicants will be considered for this scholarship, regardless of which college (if any) you state as your preference on the graduate application form
**Closing Date**: 1 January

**Funding**: Private

**Additional Information**: www.magd.ox.ac.uk/the-oxford-calleva-scholarship/

### For further information contact:

**Email**: lucy.bowes@psy.ox.ac.uk

## Oxford-Hoffmann Graduate Scholarships

**Purpose**: Fondation Hoffmann is a Swiss-based grant making institution supporting the emergence and expansion of concrete projects which address global problems in today's societies

**Eligibility**: Open to applicants who are applying to any full or part-time course within the Medical Science Division. Tenable at Jesus College only

**Level of Study**: Graduate

**Type**: Scholarship

**Value**: 100% of course fees and a grant for living costs (at least £14,777)

**Length of Study**: Duration of fee liability

**Frequency**: Annual

**Study Establishment**: Jesus College

**Country of Study**: Any country

**Closing Date**: April

**Additional Information**: Please visit the website: www.ox.ac.uk/admissions/graduate/fees-and-funding/fees-funding-and-scholarship-search/scholarships-2#hoffmann www.ox.ac.uk/admissions/graduate/fees-and-funding/fees-funding-and-scholarship-search/weidenfeld-hoffmann-scholarships-and-leadership-programme

## Oxford-Jerry Hausman Graduate Scholarship

**Eligibility**: Open to all applicants applying for any graduate course in the departments of Economics, Politics, and Sociology. Tenable at Nuffield College only. Please see website for more details

**Level of Study**: Postgraduate

**Type**: Scholarship

**Value**: University fee, college fee, and full living expenses

**Length of Study**: Period of fee liability

**Frequency**: Annual

**Study Establishment**: Nuffield College

**Country of Study**: United Kingdom

**Application Procedure**: For more information, please check the website: www.ox.ac.uk/admissions/graduate/fees-and-funding/fees-funding-and-scholarship-search/scholarships-2#jerryhausman

**Closing Date**: 22 January

**Funding**: Trusts

**Additional Information**: One full scholarship is available for applicants who are applying to any full-time or part-time graduate course in the departments of Economics, Politics and International Relations and Sociology; preference will be given to applicants for Economics courses under Oxford-Jerry Hausman Graduate Scholarship

### For further information contact:

**Email**: information@anthro.ox.ac.uk

## Oxford-John and Pat Cuckney Graduate Scholarship

**Eligibility**: Open to applicants who are ordinarily resident in EEA or Switzerland and who are applying to the full-time DPhil in Particle Physics. Tenable at Lincoln College only

**Level of Study**: Doctorate

**Type**: Scholarship

**Value**: University fee, college fee, and a grant for living costs of £14,553 towards the tenable year

**Length of Study**: Duration of fee liability

**Study Establishment**: Lincoln College

**Country of Study**: Any country

**Closing Date**: 20 January

**Additional Information**: Please visit the website: www.ox.ac.uk/admissions/graduate/fees-and-funding/fees-funding-and-scholarship-search/scholarships-2#cuckney www2.physics.ox.ac.uk/study-here/postgraduates/condensed-matter-physics/sources-of-funding

### For further information contact:

**Email**: dtcenquiries@dtc.ox.ac.uk

## Oxford-Keith Lloyd Graduate Scholarship

**Eligibility**: Open to applicants ordinarily resident in sub-Saharan Africa (excluding South Africa), and who is studying for an MSc course in the School of Geography and the Environment. The scholarship is only tenable at Linacre College

**Level of Study**: Postgraduate

**Type**: Scholarship

**Value**: University fee, college fee, and a grant for living costs

**Length of Study**: 1 year

**Study Establishment**: Linacre College

**Country of Study**: Any country

**Closing Date**: 20 January

**Additional Information**: Please visit the website: www.ox.ac.uk/admissions/graduate/fees-and-funding/fees-funding-and-scholarship-search/scholarships-3#keithlloyd www.linacre.ox.ac.uk/prospective-students/scholarships/norman-and-ivy-lloyd-scholarshipcommonwealth-shared-scholarship

**For further information contact:**

**Email**:    shared.scholarships@cscuk.org.uk

## Oxford-Mary Jane Grefenstette Graduate Scholarship

**Eligibility**: Open to all applicants applying for a DPhil in Computer Science or Philosophy, specialising in the cross-over between the subjects. Tenable at Hertford College only. Please see website for more details
**Level of Study**: Postgraduate
**Type**: Scholarship
**Value**: University fee, college fee, and full living expenses
**Length of Study**: Period of fee liability
**Frequency**: Annual
**Study Establishment**: Hertford
**Country of Study**: United Kingdom
**Application Procedure**: For more information, please check the website: www.ox.ac.uk/admissions/graduate/fees-and-funding/fees-funding-and-scholarship-search/scholarships-3#grefenstette
**Closing Date**: 22 January
**Funding**: Trusts

**For further information contact:**

**Email**:    enquiries@cs.ox.ac.uk

## Oxford-Mitsui & Co. Europe PLC Graduate Scholarships

**Purpose**: Two full scholarships are available for applicants ordinarily resident in Africa, and who are applying for the full-time MSc in African Studies
**Eligibility**: Open to applicants ordinarily resident in Africa, applying for the full-time MSc in African Studies. You are applying to start a new graduate course;; You submit your course application by the relevant January admissions deadline;; You are subsequently offered a place after consideration of applications received by the deadline;; Your application is not placed on a waiting list or held back after the January admissions deadline to be re-evaluated against applications received by the March admissions deadline; and You meet the eligibility criteria. This content was originally published on After School Africa from www.afterschoolafrica.com/17003/oxford-mitsui-scholarships/
**Level of Study**: Postgraduate

**Type**: Scholarship
**Value**: Covers course fees, college fees and a grant for living costs of at least £14,553
**Length of Study**: Period of fee liability
**Frequency**: Annual
**Study Establishment**: University of Oxford
**Country of Study**: Any country
**Closing Date**: May
**Funding**: Trusts
**Additional Information**: For more information, please check the website: www.ox.ac.uk/admissions/graduate/fees-and-funding/fees-funding-and-scholarship-search/scholarships-3#mitsui www.scholarshipdesk.com/oxford-mitsui-co-europe-plc-full-graduate-scholarships-uk/

**For further information contact:**

**Email**:    webmaster@ox.ac.uk

## Oxford-Nizami Ganjavi Graduate Scholarships

**Purpose**: The University of Oxford is home to a dedicated centre for the study of Azerbaijan, the Caucasus and Central Asia, thanks to generous philanthropic support from the British Foundation for the Study of Azerbaijan and the Caucasus (BFSAC)
**Eligibility**: Open to applicants applying for any full or part-time DPhil or Master's course offered by the Humanities or Social Sciences Division where the course content relates to the study of the history, languages and cultures of Azerbaijan, the Caucasus and Central Asia. Please see the website for further details, including how to apply
**Level of Study**: Graduate
**Type**: Scholarship
**Frequency**: Annual
**Country of Study**: Any country
**Closing Date**: January
**Funding**: Private
**Additional Information**: www.scholarshipdesk.com/oxford-mitsui-co-europe-plc-full-graduate-scholarships-uk/

**For further information contact:**

**Tel**:    (44) 1865 270 000
**Fax**:    (44) 1865 270 708

## Oxford-Oak Foundation Clinical Medicine

**Eligibility**: Open to applicants who are applying to the full-time DPhil in Clinical Medicine, specializing in Tropical Medicine and Global Health, with a preference for the candidates to be ordinarily resident in Nepal, Zimbabwe, Kenya and Vietnam

**Level of Study**: Doctorate
**Type**: Scholarship
**Value**: University fee, college fee, and full living expenses
**Length of Study**: Duration of fee liability
**Country of Study**: United Kingdom
**Closing Date**: 5 January
**Additional Information**: Please visit the website: www.ox. ac.uk/admissions/graduate/fees-and-funding/fees-funding-and-scholarship-search/scholarships-3#oak scholarship-positions. com/oak-foundation-clinical-medicine-scholarships-university-oxford-uk/2016/12/29/

## Oxford-Particle Physics Graduate Scholarship

**Purpose**: The scholarship has been made possible through the support of an anonymous donor, with the aim of supporting an outstanding thinker of tomorrow undertaking research in the field of experimental particle physics.
**Eligibility**: Open to applicants who are applying to the full-time DPhil Particle Physics course
**Level of Study**: Doctorate
**Type**: Scholarship
**Value**: University fee, college fee, and full living expenses
**Length of Study**: Duration of fee liability
**Country of Study**: Any country
**Closing Date**: April
**Additional Information**: Please visit the website: www.ox. ac.uk/admissions/graduate/fees-and-funding/fees-funding-and-scholarship-search/scholarships-3#particlephysics www.ox.ac. uk/admissions/graduate/courses/dphil-particle-physics?wssl=1

### For further information contact:

**Email**:    contact@physics.ox.ac.uk

## Oxford-Percival Stanion Graduate Scholarship in Biochemistry

**Eligibility**: Open to applicants who are applying to the DPhil Biochemistry or MSc by Research Biochemistry. Tenable at Pembroke College only. Please see the website for more details
**Level of Study**: Doctorate, Postgraduate
**Type**: Scholarship
**Value**: University fee, college fee, and a grant for living costs
**Length of Study**: Period of fee liability
**Study Establishment**: Pembroke College
**Country of Study**: Any country
**Closing Date**: 6 January

**Additional Information**: Please visit the website: www.ox. ac.uk/admissions/graduate/fees-and-funding/fees-funding-and-scholarship-search/scholarships-3#percivalstanion www.pmb. ox.ac.uk/oxford-percival-stanion-graduate-stories

### For further information contact:

St Aldate's, Oxford OX1 1DW, United Kingdom.

**Tel**:    (44) 1865 276444
**Fax**:    (44) 1865 276418
**Email**:    ioannis.vakonakis@bioch.ox.ac.uk

## Oxford-Qatar-Thatcher Graduate Scholarships

**Purpose**: The Oxford-Qatar-Thatcher Graduate Scholarship has been created as a result of a £3 million donation by the Qatar Development Fund, which supports international education, health and economic development causes.
**Eligibility**: Candidates who have been accepted to study at the University of Oxford on a graduate course offered by the Faculty of English Language and Literature, Department of Engineering Science or Faculty of Law. There is a preference for students ordinarily resident in Algeria, Bahrain, Egypt, Iraq, Jordan, Kuwait, Lebanon, Libya, Morocco, Oman, Palestine, Qatar, Saudi Arabia, Sudan, Syria, Tunisia, United Arab Emirates or Yemen
**Level of Study**: Postgraduate
**Type**: Scholarship
**Value**: Tuition fees, college fees and a grant for living costs
**Length of Study**: Period of fee liability
**Frequency**: Annual
**Study Establishment**: Somerville College
**Country of Study**: Any country
**No. of awards offered**: 4
**Closing Date**: January
**Funding**: Trusts
**Additional Information**: Please visit the website: www. some.ox.ac.uk/studying-here/fees-funding/thatcher-scholarships/ www.afterschoolafrica.com/16550/oxford-thatcher-graduate-scholarships/

### For further information contact:

**Email**:    academic.office@some.ox.ac.uk

## Oxford-Robert and Soulla Kyprianou Graduate Scholarship

**Purpose**: The University of Oxford is currently accepting applications for the Oxford-Robert and Soulla Kyprianou

Program. This fully-funded scholarship is exclusively open to students from Republic of Cyprus

**Eligibility**: Open to applicants ordinarily resident in the Republic of Cyprus, applying for any full- or part-time master's or DPhil course offered by Brasenose College. This scholarship is open to applicants who are ordinarily resident in the Republic of Cyprus and who are applying for a full- or part-time master's or DPhil course, within the range accepted by Brasenose College

**Level of Study**: Doctorate, Postgraduate

**Type**: Scholarship

**Value**: £14,296

**Length of Study**: Period of fee liability

**Study Establishment**: Brasenose College

**Country of Study**: United Kingdom

**Closing Date**: January

**Additional Information**: The scholarship is only tenable at Brasenose College. Please check the website: www.ox.ac.uk/admissions/graduate/fees-and-funding/fees-funding-and-scholarship-search/scholarships-3#kyprianou www.scholarshipdesk.com/oxford-robert-and-soulla-kyprianou-full-scholarships/

## For further information contact:

**Email**:    contact@scholarshipdesk.com

## Oxford-Rothermere American Institute Graduate Scholarship

**Eligibility**: Open to applicants who are ordinarily resident in the EEA and who are applying to a full- or part-time DPhil in History, specialising in American History. The scholarship is ordinarily tenable at University College. Please see website for more details

**Level of Study**: Doctorate

**Type**: Scholarship

**Value**: University fee, college fee, and full living expenses

**Length of Study**: Period of fee liability

**Study Establishment**: University College

**Country of Study**: Any country

**Closing Date**: 20 January

**Additional Information**: Please visit the website: www.ox.ac.uk/admissions/graduate/fees-and-funding/fees-funding-and-scholarship-search/scholarships-3#rothermere www.european-funding-guide.eu/scholarship/13600-oxford-rothermere-american-institute-clarendon-graduate-scholarship

## For further information contact:

**Email**:    enquiries@rai.ox.ac.uk

## Oxford-Sir Anwar Pervez Graduate Scholarships

**Purpose**: The scholarship is funded by the Imperial Majesty Oba Adéyeyè Enitan Ògúnwùsì and aims to provide funding to exceptional candidates pursuing postgraduate study of Africa

**Eligibility**: 1. Open to applicants ordinarily resident in Pakistan, who have not previously studied for an HE qualification outside of Pakistan. 2. Candidates can be applying for any graduate course. Scholars to be selected on the basis of academic merit and financial need. Please see the website for further details

**Level of Study**: Postgraduate

**Type**: Scholarship

**Value**: University fee, college fee, and full living expenses of at least £14,777

**Length of Study**: Period of fee liability

**Frequency**: Annual

**Country of Study**: United Kingdom

**Application Procedure**: For more information, please check the website: www.ox.ac.uk/admissions/graduate/fees-and-funding/fees-funding-and-scholarship-search/scholarships-3#pervez

**Closing Date**: April

**Funding**: Trusts

**Additional Information**: www.ox.ac.uk/admissions/graduate/fees-and-funding/fees-funding-and-scholarship-search/scholarships-a-z-listing?wssl=1

## For further information contact:

**Tel**:       (44) 1865 611 530

**Email**:    enquiries@devoff.ox.ac.uk

## Oxford-Sir David Weatherall Graduate Scholarship

**Eligibility**: Open to applicants who are applying to a full-time DPhil in Medical Sciences, based at the Weatherall Institute of Molecular Medicine. The scholarship is only tenable at Green Templeton College

**Level of Study**: Doctorate

**Type**: Scholarship

**Value**: University fee, college fee, and full living expenses

**Length of Study**: Duration of fee liability

**Study Establishment**: Green Templeton College

**Country of Study**: Any country

**Closing Date**: 6 January

**Additional Information**: Please visit the website: www.ox.ac.uk/admissions/graduate/fees-and-funding/fees-funding-and-scholarship-search/scholarships-3#weatherall www.gtc.ox.ac.uk/news-and-events/news/profile-spencer-tong-dphil-oxford-sir-david-weatherall-scholar/

**For further information contact:**

**Email**: development@gtc.ox.ac.uk

## Oxford-Swire Graduate Scholarship

**Purpose**: The Swire Scholarship has allowed me to pursue my goal of improving the educational outcomes of disadvantaged learners in secondary classrooms in China and internationally. In my DPhil, I will explore the classroom interactions, teachers and students perceptions on teaching and learning processes in secondary classrooms, and their language challenges and copying strategies.

**Eligibility**: Open to all applicants for any full- or part-time master's and DPhil courses in the Faculty of History, within the range accepted by University College

**Level of Study**: Doctorate, Postgraduate

**Type**: Scholarship

**Value**: University fee, college fee, and full living expenses

**Length of Study**: Period of fee liability

**Country of Study**: Any country

**Closing Date**: 9 March

**Additional Information**: The scholarship is only tenable at University College. Please check the website: www.ox.ac.uk/admissions/graduate/fees-and-funding/fees-funding-and-scholarship-search/scholarships-3#swire www.sant.ox.ac.uk/prospective-students/fees-and-funding/scholarships-new-students/swire

**For further information contact:**

**Email**: swirescholarships@jsshk.com

## Oxford-TrygFonden Graduate Scholarship

**Purpose**: One full scholarship is available for applicants who are ordinarily resident in Denmark and who are applying for one of the following courses (preference will be given to courses in the order listed): MSc Evidence-Based Social Intervention and Policy Evaluation; MSc Education, with a speciality in Research Training

**Eligibility**: Open to applicants ordinarily resident in Denmark who are applying to various master's courses. One full scholarship is available for applicants who are ordinarily resident in Denmark and who are applying for one of the following courses (preference will be given to courses in the order listed): MSc Evidence-Based Social Intervention and Policy Evaluation; MSc Education, with a speciality in Research Training

**Level of Study**: Postgraduate

**Type**: Scholarship

**Value**: It covers the expenditure of about £14,777 (students on part-time courses will receive a study support grant instead)

**Length of Study**: Period of fee liability

**Frequency**: Annual

**Country of Study**: Any country

**Application Procedure**: 1. The eligibility criteria will be applied automatically, using the details you provide in the relevant sections of the graduate application form (for example, your country of ordinary residence and your previous education institutions), to determine whether you are eligible. 2. Selection is based on academic merit, unless specified otherwise. Some of the scholarships are only tenable at specific colleges. Unless specified otherwise, you do not need to select that college as your preference on the graduate application form. All eligible applicants will be considered, regardless of which college (if any) you state as your preference. However, successful applicants will be transferred to the relevant college in order to take up the scholarship

**Closing Date**: April

**Funding**: Private

**Additional Information**: Please check the website: www.ox.ac.uk/admissions/graduate/fees-and-funding/fees-funding-and-scholarship-search/scholarships-3#trygfonden www.ox.ac.uk/admissions/graduate/fees-and-funding/fees-funding-and-scholarship-search/scholarships-a-z-listing?wssl=1#trygfonden

**For further information contact:**

**Tel**: (44) 1865 270 000
**Fax**: (44) 1865 270 708

## Oxford-Urquhart-RAI Graduate Scholarship

**Eligibility**: Open to applicants who are ordinarily resident in the EEA or Switzerland and who are applying to a DPhil in Politics, specializing in American Politics

**Value**: University fee, college fee and full living expenses

**Length of Study**: Period of fee liability

**Country of Study**: Any country

**Closing Date**: 6 January

**Additional Information**: For more details, please visit www.ox.ac.uk/admissions/graduate/fees-and-funding/fees-funding-and-scholarship-search/scholarships-3#urquhart

**For further information contact:**

**Email**: enquiries@rai.ox.ac.uk

## Oxford-Wadham Graduate Scholarships for Disabled Students

**Purpose**: Scholarships are awarded to applicants who have demonstrated excellent academic ability, who will contribute to the University's ground-breaking research, and who will go on to contribute to the world as leaders in their field, pushing the frontiers of knowledge

**Eligibility**: Open to all applicants applying to any full- and part-time master's courses offered by Wadham College, who have a disability as defined by the Equality Act and determined by the University's Disability Advisory Service
**Level of Study**: Postgraduate
**Type**: Scholarship
**Value**: University fee, college fee, and a grant for living costs
**Length of Study**: Period of fee liability
**Frequency**: Annual
**Study Establishment**: Wadham College
**Country of Study**: Any country
**Closing Date**: May
**Funding**: Trusts
**Additional Information**: The scholarship is only tenable at Wadham College. For more information, please check the website: www.ox.ac.uk/admissions/graduate/fees-and-funding/fees-funding-and-scholarship-search/scholarships-3#wadham www.wadham.ox.ac.uk/students/graduate-students/graduate-finance/graduate-scholarships

### For further information contact:

**Email**:    graduate.admissions@wadham.ox.ac.uk

## Oxford-Weidenfeld and Hoffmann Scholarships and Leadership Programme

**Purpose**: The Oxford-Weidenfeld and Hoffman Scholarship and Leadership Programme supports outstanding students from transition and emerging economies throughout Africa,
**Eligibility**: Open to applicants from selected countries to selected courses. Please see website for more details and how to apply, including closing dates
**Level of Study**: Postgraduate
**Type**: Scholarship
**Value**: 100% of university fee, college fee, and full living expenses. Average cost of at least £15,009 being covered
**Length of Study**: Period of fee liability
**Frequency**: Annual
**Country of Study**: Any country
**Closing Date**: May
**Funding**: Trusts
**Additional Information**: For more information, please check the website: www.graduate.ox.ac.uk/weidenfeld-oxford www.ox.ac.uk/admissions/graduate/fees-and-funding/fees-funding-and-scholarship-search/weidenfeld-hoffmann-scholarships-and-leadership-programme

### For further information contact:

Weidenfeld-Hoffmann Trust, Saïd Business School, Park End Street, Oxford OX1 1HP, United Kingdom.

**Email**:    info@whtrust.org

## Oxford-Wolfson-Ancient History Graduate Scholarship

**Eligibility**: Open to applicants ordinarily resident in the EEA or Switzerland, applying for any graduate course in Ancient History, preferably with a focus on economics and banking. Tenable at Wolfson College only. Please see website for more details
**Level of Study**: Postgraduate
**Type**: Scholarship
**Value**: University fee, college fee, and full living expenses
**Length of Study**: Period of fee liability
**Frequency**: Annual
**Study Establishment**: Wolfson
**Country of Study**: United Kingdom
**Application Procedure**: For more information, please check the website: www.ox.ac.uk/admissions/graduate/fees-and-funding/fees-funding-and-scholarship-search/scholarships-3#wolfsonancienthistory
**Closing Date**: 22 January
**Funding**: Trusts

### For further information contact:

Wolfson College, Linton Road, Oxford OX2 6UD, United Kingdom.

## Oxford-Wolfson-Min Sunshik Graduate Scholarship in Modern Korean Literature

**Eligibility**: Open to applicants who are ordinarily resident in the EEA or Switzerland and who are applying to the full-time MSt Korean Studies. Preference will be given to applicants focussing on Modern Korean Literature and Translation Studies
**Level of Study**: Postgraduate
**Type**: Scholarship
**Value**: University fee, college fee, and a grant for living expenses
**Length of Study**: Period of fee liability
**Frequency**: Annual
**Study Establishment**: Wolfson College
**Country of Study**: Any country
**Closing Date**: 20 January
**Funding**: Trusts
**Additional Information**: he scholarship is only tenable at Wolfson College. For more information, please check the website: www.ox.ac.uk/admissions/graduate/fees-and-funding/fees-funding-and-scholarship-search/scholarships-3#minsunshik www.britishkoreansociety.org.uk/uncategorized/oxford-wolfson-min-sunshik-graduate-scholarship-in-modern-korean-literature/

## Pembroke College Jose Gregorio Hernandez Award of the Venezuelan National Academy of Medicine

**Eligibility**: Open to nationals of Venezuela. Students must be nominated by the Venezuelan National Academy of Medicine and then accepted by the General Medical Council
**Level of Study**: Postgraduate
**Type**: Stipendiary
**Value**: Full fees and maintenance
**Length of Study**: 1 year, renewable for a further year
**Frequency**: Dependent on funds available
**Study Establishment**: Pembroke College, University of Oxford
**Country of Study**: United Kingdom
**Application Procedure**: Applicants must write or email the Admissions Secretary for details
**Funding**: Private

### For further information contact:

Pembroke College, Cambridge, CB2 1RF, United Kingdom.

**Email**: admissions@pmb.ox.ac.uk

## Pembroke College: Gordon Aldrick Scholarship

**Purpose**: To assist scholars in Chinese cultural studies
**Eligibility**: Open to candidates beginning a two or three-year research degree at Oxford
**Level of Study**: Research
**Type**: Scholarship
**Value**: £5,000 per year towards college fee and contribution towards living expenses
**Length of Study**: Tenable for up to three years whilst the recipient is liable to pay University and College fees. Automatically renewed each year if satisfactory academic progress is made
**Frequency**: Annual
**Country of Study**: Any country
**Application Procedure**: Intending candidates should apply in Section L of the Oxford University graduate application form or notify the Admissions & Access Officer at Pembroke
**Closing Date**: 1 May

### For further information contact:

**Email**: jane.sherwood@admin.ox.ac.uk

## Pembroke College: Tokyo Electric Power Company (TEPCO) Scholarship

**Eligibility**: Open to all graduate applicants specialising in studies of Japanese literature, art or history. Please see website for details of how to apply at

**Level of Study**: Research
**Value**: £5,000 per year towards college fee and contribution towards living expenses
**Length of Study**: Period of fee liability
**Country of Study**: Any country
**Closing Date**: 3 May

### For further information contact:

**Email**: ben.nicholson@admin.ox.ac.uk

## Philosophy Faculty-Wolfson College Joint Scholarship

**Eligibility**: Open to Home/European Union graduate applicants to DPhil courses in the Faculty of Philosophy. Eligible applicants for these courses are automatically considered. Please see website for more information
**Level of Study**: Postgraduate
**Type**: Scholarship
**Value**: University fee, college fee, and living expenses
**Length of Study**: Period of fee liability
**Frequency**: Annual
**Study Establishment**: Wolfson
**Country of Study**: United Kingdom
**Application Procedure**: For more information, please check the website: www.philosophy.ox.ac.uk/admissions/graduate/graduate_funding
**Closing Date**: 8 January
**Funding**: Trusts
**Additional Information**: www.ox.ac.uk/admissions/graduate/colleges/wolfson-college?wssl=1

### For further information contact:

**Email**: graduatestudies@mml.cam.ac.uk

## Physics: Engineering and Physical Sciences Research Council (EPSRC) and Doctoral Training Grant Studentships

**Eligibility**: United Kingdom residents are eligible for full awards, including fees and maintenance; European Union residents are eligible for awards covering fees only. European Union Students who have studied in the United Kingdom for the previous 3 years are eligible for a full award. The Department automatically considers all eligible applicants who have been offered places and who have applied by the January deadline
**Type**: Studentship
**Value**: University fee, college fee, and living expenses (European Union fee-only awards)
**Length of Study**: Period of fee liability

**Country of Study**: Any country

**Application Procedure**: Please visit the website for application details

**Closing Date**: 22 January

**Additional Information**: Please check at www2.physics.ox. ac.uk/study-here/postgraduates/fees-and-funding  www.epsrc. group.cam.ac.uk/DTP

## Pirie-Reid Scholarships

**Purpose**: To enable persons who would otherwise be prevented by lack of funds to begin a course of study at Oxford

**Eligibility**: Preference will be given to candidate's who have lived in or been educated in Scotland, who are applying from other universities (i.e. not already studying at Oxford)

**Level of Study**: Doctorate, Postgraduate

**Type**: Scholarship

**Value**: University and college fees normally at the home rate plus maintenance grant, subject to assessment of income from other sources

**Length of Study**: Renewable from year to year, subject to satisfactory progress and continuance of approved full-time study

**Frequency**: Annual

**Study Establishment**: University of Oxford

**Country of Study**: United Kingdom

**Application Procedure**: Candidates must apply for admission to the University through the Graduate Admissions Office (www.admin.ox.ac.uk/gsp)

**Closing Date**: 1 May

**Funding**: Private

**Additional Information**: Preference will be given to candidates domiciled or educated in Scotland. Candidates not fulfilling these criteria are unlikely to be successful scholarship-positions.com/2012-pirie-reid-scholarship-for-graduate-studies-at-oxford-university-uk/2011/10/03/

### For further information contact:

**Email**:    student.funding@admin.ox.ac.uk

## Politics and International Relations: ESRC DTC +3 Studentships (Doctoral Awards)

**Eligibility**: Open to all United Kingdom applicants for DPhil Politics and DPhil International Relations. Other European Union nationals are eligible for a fees-only award

**Level of Study**: Graduate, Postdoctorate

**Type**: Studentship

**Value**: University fee, college fee and full living expenses

**Length of Study**: Period of fee liability

**Country of Study**: Any country

**Application Procedure**: Please visit website for more details and how to apply

**Closing Date**: 9 January

**Additional Information**: Please check at www.politics.ox. ac.uk/index.php/student-funding/student-funding.html

### For further information contact:

**Email**:    r.llewellyn@bbk.ac.uk

## Radcliffe Department of Medicine: RDM Scholars Programme

**Eligibility**: Open to basic science applicants of any nationality applying for projects based within the Radcliffe Department of Medicine. Please see additional information on personal statement on the RDM webpage

**Value**: All fees and living expenses of £18,000 per annum

**Length of Study**: 4 years

**Country of Study**: Any country

**Closing Date**: 6 January

**Additional Information**: For more details, please visit www. rdm.ox.ac.uk/rdm-scholars-programme          www.european-funding-guide.eu/other-financial-assistance/13805-rdm%C2% A0scholars-programme

### For further information contact:

**Email**:    graduate.enquiries@rdm.ox.ac.uk

## Radiation Oncology & Biology: Departmental Studentships

**Purpose**: To provide comprehensive preparation for a career in research or industry, whether in radiobiology, protection or the advancement of cancer treatments

**Eligibility**: Open to home/European Union and overseas students

**Level of Study**: Postgraduate, Research

**Type**: Studentship

**Value**: University and college fees at the home/European Union rate, stipend, research expenses and support with travel to conferences

**Length of Study**: Up to 4 years

**Frequency**: Annual

**Closing Date**: 10 January

**Contributor**: Cancer Research United Kingdom(United Kingdom) or Medical Research Council(MRC)

**Additional Information**: The Medical Research Council (MRC) awards have residency requirements www.ox.ac.uk/admissions/graduate/courses/msc-radiation-biology?wssl=1

**For further information contact:**

**Tel**: (44) 1865 617410
**Email**: graduate.studies@oncology.ox.ac.uk

## Regent's Park College: Eastern European Scholarship

**Eligibility**: Open to new or continuing graduate in theology from Central and Eastern Europe. Preference is shown for members of the Baptist denomination
**Level of Study**: Postgraduate, Research
**Type**: Scholarship
**Value**: Up to the amount of the College Fee each year
**Length of Study**: Up to 3 years
**Frequency**: Annual
**Application Procedure**: Please visit website for more details and how to apply
**Closing Date**: 1 February
**Additional Information**: Please check at www.rpc.ox.ac.uk/index.php?pageid=272&tln=Courses

**For further information contact:**

Regent's Park College, Pusey Street, Oxford OX1 2LB, United Kingdom.

**Tel**: (44) 1865 288 120
**Fax**: (44) 1865 288 121
**Email**: enquiries@regents.ox.ac.uk

## Regent's Park College: Ernest Payne Scholarship

**Eligibility**: Open to all new and continuing United Kingdom graduate students of theology. Preference is shown for those preparing for the Baptist ministry
**Level of Study**: Postgraduate, Research
**Type**: Scholarship
**Value**: Up to the amount of the College Fee each year
**Length of Study**: 2 years initially
**Application Procedure**: Please visit website for more details and how to apply
**Closing Date**: 1 May
**Additional Information**: Scholarship is awarded over 2 years, extendable in proportion for a 3rd year. Please check at www.rpc.ox.ac.uk/index.php?pageid=272&tln=Courses

## Regent's Park College: Henman Scholarship

**Eligibility**: Open to all graduate applicants in Theology
**Level of Study**: Postgraduate, Research
**Type**: Scholarship
**Value**: Up to the amount of the College Fee each year
**Length of Study**: Period of fee liability
**Application Procedure**: Please see website for details of how to apply
**Closing Date**: 1 May
**Additional Information**: Eligible to overseas nationals. Please check the website www.rpc.ox.ac.uk

**For further information contact:**

**Email**: larry.kreitzer@regents.ox.ac.uk

## Regent's Park College: J W Lord Scholarship

**Eligibility**: Open to all graduate applicants in Theology that are preparing to serve Christian churches in India, Hong Kong or China, or otherwise in Asia, Africa, Central and South America and the Caribbean
**Type**: Scholarship
**Value**: Up to the value of the college fee each year
**Length of Study**: Up to 3 years
**Frequency**: Annual
**Application Procedure**: Please see website for details of how to apply
**Closing Date**: 1 May
**Additional Information**: Eligible to overseas countries. Please check the website www.rpc.ox.ac.uk/index.php?pageid=272&tln=Courses

## Roche-Law Faculty Scholarship

**Eligibility**: Open to all graduate applicants to BCL/MJur, MSc in Law and Finance, MSt Legal Research, MPhil or DPhil Law. Award holders will become members of New College. Please see website for more information
**Level of Study**: Doctorate, Graduate, Postgraduate, Research
**Type**: Scholarship
**Value**: £10,000
**Length of Study**: Dependent on fee liability
**Study Establishment**: New College
**Country of Study**: Any country
**Closing Date**: 20 January
**Additional Information**: Please visit the website: www.law.ox.ac.uk/postgraduate/scholarships.php www.law.ox.ac.uk/admissions/graduate-scholarships/new-college-roche-scholarship

**For further information contact:**

**Email**: student.finance@new.ox.ac.uk

## Sasakawa Fund Scholarships

**Eligibility**: Candidates must be Japanese nationals or students from countries other than Japan whose course at the University of Oxford requires some period of study in Japan
**Level of Study**: Doctorate, Graduate, Postgraduate
**Type**: Scholarship
**Value**: Up to £5,000
**Length of Study**: 1 year in the first instance, with the possibility of renewal for a maximum of 3 years, subject to satisfactory progress
**Frequency**: Annual
**Study Establishment**: University of Oxford
**Country of Study**: United Kingdom
**Application Procedure**: Applicants must complete the relevant section of the graduate admission form available at www. admin.ox.ac.uk/gsp Applicants from the United Kingdom should contact the Secretary of the Sasakawa Fund
**Closing Date**: 1 March
**Additional Information**: Applicants must either have been accepted by the University of Oxford to undertake a research degree as a probationer research or DPhil student, or be currently undertaking such a course www.wmujapan.net/concept.html

### For further information contact:

**Tel**:       (44) 1865 278 225
**Fax**:      (44) 1865 278 190
**Email**:    sasakawa@massey.ac.nz


## Sasakawa Postgraduate Studentship in Japanese Studies

**Eligibility**: The Nissan Institute of Japanese Studies, University of Oxford invites applications for up to three Sasakawa Postgraduate Studentships in Japanese Studies, with the generous support by the Nippon Foundation and the Great Britain Sasakawa Foundation. The studentship consists of £10,000 for either MSc or MPhil course in Japanese studies or DPhil research which focuses on any aspect of Japan
**Level of Study**: Doctorate, Postgraduate, Research
**Type**: Studentship
**Value**: £10,000
**Length of Study**: 1 year
**Country of Study**: Any country
**Application Procedure**: Please see website for more details, including how to apply
**Closing Date**: 7 February
**Additional Information**: Please check the website: www. nissan.ox.ac.uk/sasakawa-japanese-studies-postgraduate-studentships-0 scholarship-positions.com/sasakawa-japanese-studies-postgra duate-studentship-for-international-students-in-the-uk/2020/01/04/

### For further information contact:

**Email**:    erica.baffelli@manchester.ac.uk


## School of Anthropology and Museum Ethnography: Peter Lienhardt/Philip Bagby Travel Awards

**Eligibility**: Open to new and current Anthropology students who are hoping to fund research/travel. Please see website for more details, including closing dates and how to apply
**Level of Study**: Postgraduate
**Type**: Scholarship
**Value**: Up to £1,000 for travel/small research projects only
**Length of Study**: Ad hoc
**Frequency**: Annual
**Country of Study**: United Kingdom
**Application Procedure**: For more information, please check the website:   www.anthro.ox.ac.uk/prospective-students/funding/travel-grants/
**Closing Date**: 22 January
**Funding**: Trusts

### For further information contact:

**Email**:    information@anthro.ox.ac.uk


## Sir William Dunn School of Pathology: Departmental PhD Prize Studentships

**Eligibility**: Open to applicants for the DPhil in Molecular Cell Biology in Health and Disease with a minimum 2.1 degree in relevant area. Relevant research experience required and must apply for one of the advertised projects. Please see website for more details
**Value**: Full fees, a stipend of £16,000 pa, and research and travel costs of £5,300 pa
**Length of Study**: 4 years
**Frequency**: Annual
**Country of Study**: Any country
**Closing Date**: 6 January
**Additional Information**: For more details, please visit www. path.ox.ac.uk/ www.path.ox.ac.uk/content/competition-now-closed-oct-2020-applications

### For further information contact:

**Tel**:       (44) 1865 275 500
**Email**:    finance@path.ox.ac.uk

## Social & Cultural Anthropology: Economic and Social Research Council

**Eligibility**: Open to United Kingdom applicants for Social Anthropology. Other European Union nationals are eligible for a fees-only award
**Level of Study**: Graduate
**Type**: Grant
**Value**: University fee, college fee and full living expenses
**Length of Study**: Period of fee liability
**Country of Study**: Any country
**Application Procedure**: Please visit website for more details and how to apply
**Closing Date**: 23 January
**Additional Information**: Please check at www.isca.ox.ac.uk/prospective-students/funding/

### For further information contact:

**Email**:    enquiries@sociology.ox.ac.uk

## Social Policy and Intervention: Barnett House-Nuffield Joint Scholarship

**Eligibility**: Open to all applicants applying for the DPhil Social Policy at the Department of Social Policy and Intervention and Nuffield College
**Value**: Course fee, college fee, maintenance
**Length of Study**: 3 years
**Country of Study**: Any country
**Closing Date**: October
**Additional Information**: For more details, please visit www.spi.ox.ac.uk/study-with-us/funding.html   www.spi.ox.ac.uk/departmental-scholarships#collapse401546

### For further information contact:

**Tel**:    (44) 1865 280734
**Email**:    admissions(at)spi.ox.ac.uk

## Social Policy and Intervention: Barnett Scholarship

**Purpose**: The scholarship is open to all students applying for a DPhil (both new students and those already in the department studying for an MSc or MPhil), and is awarded on the basis of academic merit, assessed on both academic track record and potential.
**Eligibility**: Open to all applicants applying for a DPhil at the Department of Social Policy and Intervention

**Value**: £25,000
**Length of Study**: 3 years or 2 years for MPhil applicants applying for 2 year DPhil study
**Country of Study**: Any country
**Closing Date**: 20 January
**Additional Information**: For more details, please visit www.spi.ox.ac.uk/study-with-us/funding.html   www.spi.ox.ac.uk/departmental-scholarships#collapse401536

### For further information contact:

**Tel**:    (44) 1865 280734
**Email**:    scholarships@spi.ox.ac.uk

## Social Policy and Intervention: Centenary Scholarship

**Eligibility**: Open to all applicants applying for a DPhil at the Department of Social Policy and Intervention
**Level of Study**: Graduate
**Type**: Scholarship
**Value**: £25,000
**Length of Study**: 3 years or 2 years for MPhil applicants applying for 2 year DPhil study
**Country of Study**: Any country
**Closing Date**: 20 January
**Additional Information**: For more details, visit website www.spi.ox.ac.uk/study-with-us/funding.html   www.spi.ox.ac.uk/departmental-scholarships#collapse401541

### For further information contact:

Department of Social Policy and Intervention, 32 Wellington Square, OX1 2ER, United Kingdom.

**Tel**:    (44) 1865 280734
**Email**:    scholarships@spi.ox.ac.uk

## Somerville College Janet Watson Bursary

**Eligibility**: Open to graduates from the United States of America who are in need of financial assistance
**Level of Study**: Postgraduate
**Type**: Bursary
**Value**: £2,000, £3,500 p.a
**Length of Study**: 1 year, with possibility of renewal for second year
**Study Establishment**: Somerville College, the University of Oxford
**Country of Study**: United Kingdom

**Application Procedure**: Applicants must contact the Assistant College Secretary
**Funding**: Private

### For further information contact:

**Email**:    sara.kalim@some.ox.ac.uk

## Soudavar Fund

**Purpose**: The Soudavar Fund provides small grants to assist students from Iran who are studying for a degree at the University of Oxford and who are facing financial difficulty
**Eligibility**: The Soudavar Fund provides small grants of up to £2,500 to assist students from Iran at the University of Oxford and who are facing genuine financial difficulty. The award is open to students who have started their degree at Oxford
**Type**: Funding support
**Value**: Up to £2,500
**Length of Study**: 1 year
**Frequency**: Annual
**Application Procedure**: Application forms can be obtained from the International Office
**Additional Information**: Eligible to nationals of Iran. The Soudavar Fund assists students from Iran who are facing genuine financial difficulty. Applicants must be able to show how they are connected to Iran, e.g. through citizenship, residence etc. Soudavar Fund scholarships are made in conjunction with the Clarendon Fund to support Iranian graduate students

### For further information contact:

**Email**:    international.office@admin.ox.ac.uk

## St Antony's College - Swire Scholarship

**Purpose**: The Swire Scholarships at St Antony's are generously funded by the Swire Charitable Trust, founded by John Swire & Sons. These scholarships are available to graduate students demonstrating exceptional academic merit
**Eligibility**: The scholarships are open to applicants who are permanent residents of Japan, China or Hong Kong and have completed the majority of their formal education in their country of permanent residency. The Scholarships will be awarded primarily on academic merit, although financial need may be taken into account. Applicants must apply for admission to a full-time graduate course of study that is offered by St Antony's College to start in current and upcoming year
**Level of Study**: Graduate
**Type**: Scholarship
**Value**: 100% of the university fees, a grant for living costs of £17,442 per year

**Frequency**: Annual
**Country of Study**: Japan
**Closing Date**: 9 March
**Funding**: Private
**Additional Information**: www.sant.ox.ac.uk/prospective-students/fees-and-funding/scholarships-new-students/swire

### For further information contact:

**Email**:    scholarships@jsshk.com

## St Antony's College Ali Pachachi Scholarship

**Purpose**: To assist candidates pursue doctoral study in any discipline in the humanities or social sciences with a primary focus on the social and political issues confronting the modern Middle East
**Eligibility**: St Antony's doctoral students
**Level of Study**: Doctorate, Research
**Value**: £7,500 towards fees and maintenance
**Length of Study**: One year
**Application Procedure**: Please check the website for further details
**Additional Information**: scholarshipandinternship.blogspot.com/2011/10/st-antonys-college-scholarships.html

### For further information contact:

The Director, Middle East Centre, St Antony's College, 62 Woodstock Rd, Oxford OX2 6JF, United Kingdom.

**Email**:    mec@sant.ox.ac.uk

## St Antony's College Wai Seng Senior Research Scholarship

**Level of Study**: Doctorate
**Type**: Scholarship
**Value**: Fees and maintenance
**Length of Study**: 2 years
**Frequency**: Every 2 years
**Study Establishment**: St Antony's College, University of Oxford
**Country of Study**: United Kingdom
**Application Procedure**: See www.sant.ox.ac.uk
**Funding**: Individuals
**Additional Information**: Available in even-numbered years only www.sant.ox.ac.uk/prospective-students/fees-and-funding/scholarships-new-students/wai-seng-senior-research-scholarship

### For further information contact:

**Email**:    asian@sant.ox.ac.uk

## St Catherine's College Glaxo Scholarship

**Purpose**: To assist graduates who are, or will be registered for the Oxford University 2nd BM or the accelerated graduate entry medicine course
**Eligibility**: Open to graduates who have a confirmed place in the Oxford University 2nd BM or the accelerated graduate entry medicine course
**Level of Study**: Graduate
**Type**: Scholarship
**Value**: £3,300 per year
**Length of Study**: Up to 2 years whilst the recipient is liable for university and college fees
**Frequency**: Annual
**Study Establishment**: St Catherine's College, University of Oxford
**Country of Study**: United Kingdom
**Application Procedure**: See www.stcatz.ox.ac.uk
**Closing Date**: 13 March
**Additional Information**: www.stcatz.ox.ac.uk/prospective-students/postgraduate-admissions/student-finance-and-scholarships/

### For further information contact:

St Catherine's College, Manor Rd, Oxford OX1 3UJ, United Kingdom.

**Tel**: (44) 1865 271 768
**Email**: college.office@stcatz.ox.ac.uk

## St Catherine's College: College Scholarship (Arts)

**Purpose**: 1. A completed Graduate Scholarship Application Cover Form including the names and addresses of two referees. 2. A personal statement. 3. A research outline accessible to non-specialists (up to 1,200 words). For taught courses, applicants may provide a statement of their academic interests and motivation for undertaking their course in place of a research outline. Alternatively, applicants for taught courses may provide a two-page personal statement in place of a one-page personal statement and research outline. 4. A full curriculum vitae.
**Eligibility**: Open to DPhil, MLitt, and MSc by Research applicants and students in the Humanities and Social Sciences Divisions
**Level of Study**: Doctorate, Postgraduate, Research
**Type**: Scholarship
**Value**: £3,300 per annum
**Length of Study**: Period of fee liability (up to 3 years)
**Frequency**: Annual

**Study Establishment**: St Catherine's College, University of Oxford
**Country of Study**: United Kingdom
**Application Procedure**: Please see website for full details including how to apply
**Closing Date**: 13 March
**Funding**: Private
**Additional Information**: Please check the website: www.stcatz.ox.ac.uk/Scholarships-and-bursaries/Postgraduate www.stcatz.ox.ac.uk/prospective-students/postgraduate-admissions/student-finance-and-scholarships/

### For further information contact:

**Fax**: (44) 1865 271 700
**Email**: college.office@stcatz.ox.ac.uk

## St Catherine's College: College Scholarship (Sciences)

**Eligibility**: Open to DPhil and MSc by research applicants and students in the Mathematical, Physical and Life Sciences Division and Medical Sciences Division
**Level of Study**: Doctorate, Postgraduate, Research
**Type**: Scholarship
**Value**: £3,300 per annum
**Length of Study**: Period of fee liability (up to 3 years)
**Frequency**: Annual
**Study Establishment**: St Catherine's College, University of Oxford
**Country of Study**: United Kingdom
**Application Procedure**: Please see website for full details including how to apply
**Closing Date**: 13 March
**Funding**: Private
**Additional Information**: Please check the website: www.stcatz.ox.ac.uk/Scholarships-and-bursaries/Postgraduate www.stcatz.ox.ac.uk/prospective-students/postgraduate-admissions/student-finance-and-scholarships/

### For further information contact:

**Email**: college.office@stcatz.ox.ac.uk

## St Catherine's College: Ghosh Graduate Scholarship

**Eligibility**: Open to BPhil, MFA, MSt, MSc by Coursework or MPhil in the Humanities Division. Please see website for full details including how to apply
**Level of Study**: Postgraduate, Predoctorate
**Type**: Scholarship

**Value**: £5,000 per annum
**Length of Study**: Period of fee liability (up to 2 years)
**Study Establishment**: St Catherine's College, University of Oxford
**Country of Study**: United Kingdom
**Closing Date**: 13 March
**Funding**: Private
**Additional Information**: Please see check the website: www.stcatz.ox.ac.uk/Scholarships-and-bursaries/Postgradu ate www.stcatz.ox.ac.uk/prospective-students/postgraduate-admissions/student-finance-and-scholarships/

### For further information contact:

**Email**:    college.office@stcatz.ox.ac.uk

## St Catherine's College: Leathersellers' Company Scholarship

**Eligibility**: Open to DPhil and MSc by Research applicants and students in the MPLS Division and Department of Biochemistry who have studied at a European (including United Kingdom) university
**Level of Study**: Doctorate, Postgraduate, Research
**Type**: Scholarship
**Value**: £3,000 per annum
**Length of Study**: Period of fee liability (up to 3 years)
**Frequency**: Annual
**Study Establishment**: St Catherine's College, University of Oxford
**Country of Study**: United Kingdom
**Closing Date**: 13 March
**Funding**: Private
**Additional Information**: Please check the website: www.stcatz.ox.ac.uk/Scholarships-and-bursaries/Postgraduate www.stcatz.ox.ac.uk/prospective-students/postgraduate-admis sions/student-finance-and-scholarships/

### For further information contact:

**Email**:    college.office@stcatz.ox.ac.uk

## St Catherine's College: Overseas Scholarship

**Purpose**: To assist students who are, or will be reading for an Oxford University DPhil, MLitt or MSc by research degree
**Eligibility**: Open to overseas DPhil, MLitt and MSc by research applicants and students
**Level of Study**: Doctorate, Postgraduate, Research
**Type**: Scholarship

**Value**: £3,300 per year plus additional benefits including guaranteed accommodation at the current room charge rate and dining rights
**Length of Study**: Up to 3 years while student is liable for fees
**Frequency**: Annual
**Study Establishment**: St Catherine's College, University of Oxford
**Country of Study**: United Kingdom
**Application Procedure**: Please refer to the website www. stcatz.ox.ac.uk
**Closing Date**: 13 March
**Funding**: Private
**Additional Information**: Eligible to the overseas countries www.stcatz.ox.ac.uk/prospective-students/postgraduate-admis sions/student-finance-and-scholarships/

### For further information contact:

**Email**:    college.office@stcatz.ox.ac.uk

## St Catherine's College: Poole Scholarship

**Purpose**: To assist students who are or will be reading for an Oxford University DPhil, MLitt or MSc by research degree
**Eligibility**: British nationals of good character studying for a DPhil. Limited SCR dining rights and guaranteed 2 years' single accommodation at current room rate
**Level of Study**: Graduate, Research
**Type**: Scholarship
**Value**: £2,500 per annum
**Length of Study**: Up to 3 years while student is liable for fees
**Frequency**: Dependent on funds available
**Study Establishment**: St Catherine's College, University of Oxford
**Country of Study**: United Kingdom
**Application Procedure**: See www.stcatz.ox.ac.uk

### For further information contact:

**Fax**:       (44) 1865 271 768
**Email**:    academic.registrar@stcat2.ox.ac.uk

## St Cross College: E.P. Abraham Scholarships

**Purpose**: St Cross College is a graduate college of the University of Oxford. It offers an outstanding academic environment dedicated to the pursuit of excellence within the Collegiate University

**Eligibility**: Open to all graduate applicants for research degrees in the chemical, biological/life and medical sciences. Please visit website for more details, including how to apply

**Level of Study**: Postgraduate

**Type**: Scholarship

**Value**: £10,000 per year towards college fee with the remainder towards living expenses

**Length of Study**: Up to three years

**Frequency**: Annual

**Study Establishment**: St Cross College

**Country of Study**: United Kingdom

**Application Procedure**: For more information, please check the website: www.stx.ox.ac.uk/prospective-students/funding-support/ep-abraham-scholarships-chemical-biologicallife-and-medical

**Closing Date**: 18 May

**Funding**: Trusts

**Additional Information**: armacad.info/2017-11-28–st-cross-college-e-p-abraham-scholarship-in-the-chemical-biolog ical-life-and-medical-sciences-2018-uk

## For further information contact:

**Email**: master.pa@stx.ox.ac.uk

## St Cross College: Graduate Scholarship in Environmental Research

**Purpose**: St Cross College, jointly with the Oxford NERC Doctoral Training Program in Environmental Research, offers the following scholarship for students in this Doctoral Training Programme (DTP) at the University of Oxford - the DTP recruits to three subject streams: The Physical Climate; Biodiversity, Ecology & Evolutionary Processes and the Dynamic Earth - Surface Processes and Natural Hazards.

**Eligibility**: St Cross College, jointly with the Oxford NERC Doctoral Training Program in Environmental Research, offers this scholarship for Home/European Union students who will be studying for a DPhil in this Doctoral Training Programme (DTP). Please visit website for more details including how to apply

**Value**: University fee, college fee and living expenses. Fees-only awards for European Union residents

**Length of Study**: Up to 3 years

**Country of Study**: Any country

**Closing Date**: 18 January

**Additional Information**: For more details, please visit website www.stx.ox.ac.uk/prospective-students/funding-support/graduate-scholarship-environmental-research www.stx.ox.ac.uk/graduate-scholarship-in-environmental-research

## For further information contact:

61 St Giles, Oxford OX1 3LZ, United Kingdom.

**Email**: bursar@stx.ox.ac.uk

## St Cross College: HAPP MPhil Scholarship in the History of Science

**Eligibility**: Open to applicants for the MPhil in History of Science, Medicine and Technology. Preference will be given to candidates with an interest in the history of physics for their MPhil dissertation topic. Please see website for further details, including how to apply

**Value**: £10,000 per annum to cover the annual college fee and an annual stipend

**Length of Study**: Tenable for 2 years coterminous with college fee liability

**Country of Study**: Any country

**Closing Date**: 10 January

**Additional Information**: For more details, please visit www.stx.ox.ac.uk/prospective-students/funding-support/happ-mphil-scholarship-history-science scholarship-positions.com/st-cross-college-happ-mphil-scholarship-history-of-science/2018/08/02/

## For further information contact:

**Email**: admissions-academic@stx.ox.ac.uk

## St Cross College: MPhil Scholarships in the Humanities and Social Sciences

**Purpose**: St Cross College offers two MPhil Scholarships for students studying at the University of Oxford for an MPhil degree in any of the humanities and social science disciplines or for the BPhil degree in Philosophy.

**Eligibility**: Open to all applicants for MPhil degrees in the Humanities and the Social Sciences or for the BPhil degree in Philosophy. The scholarships are tenable at St Cross College only

**Level of Study**: Predoctorate

**Type**: Scholarship

**Value**: £4,000

**Length of Study**: 2 years

**Study Establishment**: St Cross College

**Country of Study**: United Kingdom

**Application Procedure**: Please visit website for more details, including how to apply

**Closing Date**: 10 March

**Additional Information**: Please check the website: www.stx. ox.ac.uk/prospective-students/funding-support/mphil-scholar ships-humanities-and-social-sciences      www.stx.ox.ac.uk/ mphil-scholarships-in-the-humanities-and-social-sciences

### For further information contact:

St Cross College, St Giles, Oxford OX1 3LZ, United Kingdom.

**Tel**:       (44) 1865 278 458
**Fax**:      (44) 1865 278 484
**Email**:    admissions-academic@stx.ox.ac.uk

## St Cross College: ORISHA DPhil Scholarship in Area Studies

**Eligibility**: Applicants applying to study for the DPhil in Area Studies
**Level of Study**: Doctorate
**Type**: Scholarship
**Value**: University fee, college fee, maintenance stipend of £12,910
**Length of Study**: 3 years
**Study Establishment**: St Cross College
**Country of Study**: Any country
**Closing Date**: 25 January
**Additional Information**: Please visit the website: www.stx. ox.ac.uk/prospective-students/funding-support/orisha-dphil-scholarship-area-studies www.stx.ox.ac.uk/graduate-scholar ship-in-archaeology

### For further information contact:

**Email**:    master@stx.ox.ac.uk

## St Cross College: Oxford-Ko Cheuk Hung Graduate Scholarship

**Eligibility**: Open to applicants who are ordinarily resident in the EEA or Switzerland and who are applying for the full-time MSt Chinese Studies
**Level of Study**: Postgraduate
**Type**: Residency
**Value**: Tuition fees, college fees and a grant towards living expenses
**Length of Study**: Period of fee liability
**Frequency**: Annual
**Study Establishment**: St Cross
**Country of Study**: United Kingdom
**Application Procedure**: For more information, please check the website: www.ox.ac.uk/admissions/graduate/fees-and-

funding/fees-funding-and-scholarship-search/scholarships-3#kocheukhung
**Closing Date**: March
**Funding**: Trusts
**Additional Information**: www.ox.ac.uk/admissions/gradu ate/fees-and-funding/fees-funding-and-scholarship-search/ scholarships-a-z-listing?wssl=1

### For further information contact:

**Tel**:       (44) 1865 278 490
**Email**:    master@stx.ox.ac.uk

## St Cross College: SBFT Scholarship in the Humanities

**Eligibility**: Open to applicants who will be studying for a doctoral degree in the Humanities Division at the University of Oxford in the academic year. The scholarship is open to applicants who are students or academic staff members at a university, other higher education institution or vocational training institution in China. Please see website for further details, including how to apply
**Value**: £15,000 per annum. The successful scholar will also be guaranteed to have a room in College accommodation (at the standard rent) for the first year of their course
**Length of Study**: Three fee-liability years of the doctoral course
**Country of Study**: Any country
**Closing Date**: 20 January
**Additional Information**: For more details, visit website www.stx.ox.ac.uk/prospective-students/funding-support/st-cross-sbft-scholarship-humanities www.mod-langs.ox.ac. uk/news/2016/11/10/scholarship-humanities-dphil-entry-2017-2018

### For further information contact:

**Email**:    master@stx.ox.ac.uk

## St Cross College: The Harun Ur Rashid Memorial Scholarship

**Eligibility**: Open to applicants (who are normally resident in Bangladesh) for MPhil degrees in the Humanities and the Social Sciences or for the BPhil degree in Philosophy. Please visit website for more details including how to apply
**Value**: £3,000
**Length of Study**: 2 years
**Country of Study**: Any country
**Closing Date**: 9 June

**Additional Information**: For more details, visit website www.stx.ox.ac.uk/prospective-students/funding-support/harun-ur-rashid-memorial-scholarship www.scholarshipcare.com/scholarship/the-harun-ur-rashid-memorial-scholarship/

**For further information contact:**

**Email**: master@stx.ox.ac.uk

## St Cross College: The Robin & Nadine Wells Scholarship

**Purpose**: To provide financial assistance to an academically meritorious graduate student who has been accepted into both an accredited one year's Masters programme at the University of Oxford and St Cross College and are unable to secure funding elsewhere
**Eligibility**: Open to all applicants for one-year Master's courses who are unable to secure funding from elsewhere
**Level of Study**: Postgraduate
**Type**: Scholarship
**Value**: £10,000
**Length of Study**: 1 year
**Frequency**: Annual
**Study Establishment**: St Cross College
**Country of Study**: United Kingdom
**Application Procedure**: Please visit website for more details, including how to apply
**Closing Date**: 16 June
**Additional Information**: Please note that this scholarship is not open to students who have already been accepted by another Oxford college. Please check the website: www.stx.ox.ac.uk/prospective-students/funding-support/robin-nadine-wells-scholarship www.nissan.ox.ac.uk/the-robin-and-nadine-wells-scholarship-for-the-academic-year-2018-19

## St Cross College: Unilever Graduate Scholarship in Sciences

**Purpose**: To assist graduate students with fees
**Eligibility**: Open to graduate students
**Level of Study**: Postgraduate, Research
**Type**: Scholarship
**Value**: £2,208 per year
**Length of Study**: Up to 3 years of study, depending on college fee liability
**Country of Study**: Any country
**Closing Date**: 13 March
**Additional Information**: www.afterschoolafrica.com/18614/unilever-graduate-scholarship-uk/

**For further information contact:**

**Email**: jane.sherwood@admin.ox.ac.uk

## St Edmund Hall William R Miller Graduate Awards

**Level of Study**: Postgraduate
**Type**: Scholarship
**Value**: £6,000
**Length of Study**: 1 year with possible extension for a further year
**Frequency**: Annual
**Study Establishment**: St Edmund Hall, University of Oxford
**Country of Study**: United Kingdom
**Application Procedure**: Application forms are available from the website www.seh.ox.ac.uk or from the Registrar at the address below. Forms are available from around the beginning of February
**No. of awards offered**: 50
**Closing Date**: 1 May
**Funding**: Private
**Contributor**: William R Miller
**No. of awards given last year**: 4 (1 new award, 3 extended for a further year)
**No. of applicants last year**: 50
**Additional Information**: www.seh.ox.ac.uk/study/postgraduate/postgraduate-scholarships

**For further information contact:**

Queen's Lane, Oxford OX1 4AR, United Kingdom.

**Tel**: (44) 1865 279000
**Email**: admissions@seh.ox.ac.uk

## St Edmund Hall: Graduate Scholarships

**Purpose**: To assist graduate students with fees and a living allowance
**Eligibility**: Open to all
**Level of Study**: Postgraduate, Research
**Type**: Scholarship
**Country of Study**: Any country

**For further information contact:**

**Email**: lodge@seh.ox.ac.uk

## St Edmund Hall: Peel Award

**Eligibility**: Open to all students applying for Master of Fine Art at the Ruskin School

**Level of Study**: Postgraduate
**Type**: Scholarship
**Value**: £5,000
**Length of Study**: 1 year
**Frequency**: Annual
**Study Establishment**: St Edmund Hall
**Country of Study**: Any country
**Closing Date**: 20 January
**Additional Information**: Please visit the website: www.seh.ox.ac.uk/admissions/scholarships www.seh.ox.ac.uk/study/postgraduate/postgraduate-scholarships

**For further information contact:**

**Email**:    lawfac@law.ox.ac.uk

## St Edmund Hall: William Asbrey BCL Studentship

**Purpose**: The William Asbrey scholarship is worth £10,000, is jointly funded by St Edmund Hall and the Law Faculty, and is available to all BCL applicants. There is no separate application procedure.
**Eligibility**: Open to all graduate applicants to the BCL
**Value**: £10,000
**Length of Study**: 1 year
**Country of Study**: Any country
**Closing Date**: 20 January
**Additional Information**: For more details, visit website www.law.ox.ac.uk/admissions/graduate-scholarships www.seh.ox.ac.uk/study/postgraduate/postgraduate-scholarships

**For further information contact:**

Queen's Lane, Oxford OX1 4AR, United Kingdom.

**Tel**:    (44) 1865 279000
**Email**:    lodge@seh.ox.ac.uk

## St Edmund Hall: William R. Miller Postgraduate Award

**Purpose**: To assist graduate students with fees and accommodation
**Eligibility**: A rent-free college room for one academic year offered to a student entering the first or second year of a research degree (DPhil or MRes)
**Level of Study**: Postgraduate, Research
**Type**: Award
**Value**: £6,000
**Length of Study**: 1 year
**Frequency**: Annual
**Country of Study**: Any country

**Application Procedure**: Please see website for more details, including how to apply
**Closing Date**: 20 January
**Additional Information**: Please check the website: www.seh.ox.ac.uk/admissions/scholarships www.seh.ox.ac.uk/study/postgraduate/postgraduate-scholarships

**For further information contact:**

Queen's Lane, Oxford OX1 4AR, United Kingdom.

**Tel**:    (44) 1865 279000
**Email**:    jane.sherwood@admin.ox.ac.uk

## St Hilda's College: New Zealand Bursaries

**Eligibility**: Open to all graduate applicants from New Zealand
**Level of Study**: Postgraduate
**Type**: Scholarship
**Value**: Up to £2,000 per year
**Length of Study**: 1 year with the possibility of renewal
**Frequency**: Annual
**Application Procedure**: Please see website for details of how to apply

**For further information contact:**

**Tel**:    (44) 1865 276 884
**Fax**:    (44) 1865 276 816
**Email**:    college.office@st-hildas.ox.ac.uk

## St John's College North Senior Scholarships

**Purpose**: The College proposes to elect from October 2020 two North Senior Scholars from among its current graduate students
**Eligibility**: Open to graduates normally with United Kingdom degrees, who have already begun research and who are aged under 25
**Level of Study**: Postgraduate
**Type**: Scholarship
**Value**: £1,000
**Length of Study**: Usually 2 years
**Study Establishment**: St John's College, the University of Oxford
**Country of Study**: United Kingdom
**Application Procedure**: Applicants must contact the Secretary to the Tutor for Graduates in the first instance
**Closing Date**: 27 May
**Additional Information**: www.sjc.ox.ac.uk/current-students/grants-scholarships-and-prizes/financial-support-graduates/

**For further information contact:**

| | |
|---|---|
| **Tel**: | (44) 1865 277 428 |
| **Fax**: | (44) 1865 277 640 |
| **Email**: | graduate.admissions@sjc.ox.ac.uk |

## St John: Ioan & Rosemary James Undergraduate Scholarships

**Eligibility**: The scholarship is available to any graduate student embarking upon a DPhil in Mathematics or joining a CDT in the Mathematical Institute. Please see website for further details
**Value**: University fees (at either the Home/European Union or Overseas student rate as applicable), College fees and a maintenance stipend at the United Kingdom research council rate
**Length of Study**: Duration of full-fee liability; 3 years for DPhil and 4 years for CDT
**Country of Study**: Any country
**Closing Date**: 12 February
**Additional Information**: For more details, please visit www.sjc.ox.ac.uk www.sjc.ox.ac.uk/current-students/grants-scholarships-and-prizes/

**For further information contact:**

| | |
|---|---|
| **Email**: | sarah.jones@sjc.ox.ac.uk |

## St Peter's College Bodossaki Graduate Scholarship in Science

**Purpose**: To assist Greek or Cypriot citizens under the age of 30, based on merit and financial need
**Eligibility**: Applicants should be Greek or Cypriot citizens under the age of 30. Award made on the basis of academic merit and financial need
**Level of Study**: Research
**Type**: Scholarship
**Value**: Up to £13,000 per annum; may be used for university & college fees, and maintenance
**Length of Study**: Up to 3 years, subject to satisfactory academic progress
**Frequency**: Annual
**Study Establishment**: St Peter's College, the University of Oxford
**Country of Study**: United Kingdom
**Application Procedure**: Applicants must contact the College Secretary at St Peter's College in the first instance, or see www.spc.ox.ac.uk
**Closing Date**: 30 January
**Funding**: Foundation
**Contributor**: The Bodossaki Foundation

**For further information contact:**

| | |
|---|---|
| **Email**: | college.secretary@spc.ox.ac.uk |

## Standard Bank Derek Cooper Africa Scholarship

**Eligibility**: Open to applicants who are ordinarily resident in one of the following countries: Angola, Botswana, Cote d'Ivoire, Democratic Republic of the Congo, Ghana, Kenya, Lesotho, Malawi, Mauritius, Mozambique, Namibia, Nigeria, South Africa, South Sudan, Swaziland, Tanzania, Uganda, Zambia or Zimbabwe. Preference will be given to nationals of Angola, Ghana, Kenya, Mozambique, Nigeria, South Africa and South Sudan. You must also be applying to start any full-time, 1 year taught master's course within the Mathematical, Physical and Life Sciences, Social Sciences, or Humanities Divisions
**Level of Study**: Postgraduate
**Type**: Scholarship
**Value**: University fee, college fee and a grant for living costs
**Length of Study**: Period of fee liability
**Frequency**: Annual
**Country of Study**: United Kingdom
**Closing Date**: 27 April
**Funding**: Trusts
**Additional Information**: For more information, please check the website: www.ox.ac.uk/admissions/graduate/fees-and-funding/fees-funding-and-scholarship-search/scholarships-4 www.lse.ac.uk/study-at-lse/Graduate/fees-and-funding/standard-bank-derek-cooper-africa-scholarships

**For further information contact:**

| | |
|---|---|
| **Tel**: | (44) 20 7405 7686 |
| **Email**: | graduates@standardbank.co.za |

## Statistical Science (EPSRC and MRC Centre for Doctoral Training) Studentships

**Eligibility**: Open to United Kingdom and European Union applicants for Statistical Science (EPSRC and MRC CDT)
**Level of Study**: Doctorate, Research
**Type**: Studentship
**Value**: University fee, college fee and full living expenses
**Length of Study**: 4 years
**Frequency**: Annual
**Country of Study**: Any country
**Closing Date**: 20 January
**Funding**: Trusts

**Additional Information**: For more information, please check the website: www.stats.ox.ac.uk/study_here/research_degrees

### For further information contact:

**Email**:    ri@fgv.br

## Synthetic Biology Doctorate Training Centre EPSRC/ BBSRC Studentships

**Eligibility**: Open to United Kingdom applicants for all MPLS subjects. Other European Union nationals are eligible for a fees-only award. It is recommended that students submit a CV directly to us prior to making a full application. Please visit website for more information
**Level of Study**: Postgraduate
**Type**: Scholarship
**Value**: University fee, college fee and full living expenses for home students. University and college fees only for European Union
**Length of Study**: Four years
**Frequency**: Annual
**Country of Study**: United Kingdom
**Application Procedure**: For more information, please check the website: www.dtc.ox.ac.uk/
**Funding**: Trusts

### For further information contact:

**Email**:    dtcenquiries@dtc.ox.ac.uk

## Templeton College Barclay DPhil Scholarship

**Level of Study**: Doctorate
**Type**: Scholarship
**Value**: £5,000
**Length of Study**: Up to 3 year
**Frequency**: Annual
**Study Establishment**: Templeton College, University of Oxford
**Country of Study**: United Kingdom
**Application Procedure**: Applicants must apply to the Graduate Services Manager, Templeton College and should visit the website www.templeton.ox.ac.uk
**Funding**: Private
**Additional Information**: scholarship-positions.com/barclay-scholarship-social-sciences-gtc-oxford-university-uk-201415/2013/11/01/

### For further information contact:

Templeton College, Wellington Square, Oxford OX1 2JD, United Kingdom.

**Email**:    admissions@templeton.ox.ac.uk

## Templeton College Leyland Scholarships

**Level of Study**: Postgraduate
**Type**: Scholarship
**Value**: Up to £1,500
**Length of Study**: 1 year
**Frequency**: Annual
**Study Establishment**: Templeton College, University of Oxford
**Country of Study**: United Kingdom
**Application Procedure**: Applicants must contact the Academic Administrator for further information

### For further information contact:

**Email**:    thc@eastern.edu

## Templeton College MBA Scholarship

**Level of Study**: MBA
**Type**: Scholarship
**Value**: Up to £5,000
**Length of Study**: 1 year
**Frequency**: Annual
**Study Establishment**: Templeton College, the University of Oxford
**Country of Study**: United Kingdom
**Application Procedure**: Applicants must contact the Academic Administrator

### For further information contact:

**Email**:    admissions@templeton.ox.ac.uk

## The Christopher Welch Scholarship in Biological Sciences

**Eligibility**: Open to all DPhil applicants applying for a project falling within the broad topic of Biological Sciences in Departments in the Medical Science, the Department of Plant Sciences and the Department of Zoology. Enquires may be sent by email to ga.Bush@medsci.ox.ac.uk.
**Level of Study**: Graduate
**Value**: University fee (Home/European Union level), college fee, full living expenses and a research support and training grant
**Length of Study**: 3 years
**Country of Study**: Any country
**Closing Date**: January
**Additional Information**: Check on the following weblink for application www.medsci.ox.ac.uk/study/medicine www.medsci.ox.ac.uk/study/graduateschool/application-process/funding/the-christopher-welch-scholarship-in-biological-sciences

**For further information contact:**

**Email**:    ga.Bush@medsci.ox.ac.uk

## The John Brookman Scholarship

**Purpose**: The Brookman Fund may also be able to help with certain expenses such as instrumental tuition or hire of a piano

**Eligibility**: The Scholarship is open to those reading for, and those who have applied to read for, a graduate degree at the University of Oxford in any subject, and who as John Brookman Scholar will participate in the musical life of the College

**Level of Study**: Graduate

**Type**: Scholarship

**Value**: £3,206

**Frequency**: Annual

**Country of Study**: Any country

**Application Procedure**: 1. Please email graduate.admissions@wadham.ox.ac.uk a full CV detailing: your academic and musical qualifications and experience; the graduate course that you are following or to which you have applied; and the names of two referees. 2. Applicants should also ask their referees to email their references to the Graduate Administrator (on the email above) by this same date. 3. The successful candidate will take up their scholarship from 1 October. For further information on selection process, kindly check the following link. www.wadham.ox.ac.uk/students/graduate-students/graduate-finance/graduate-scholarships

**Closing Date**: 22 March

**Funding**: Private

**Additional Information**: scholarship-positions.com/john-brookman-graduate-scholarship-university-oxford-uk/2018/01/31/

## The Khazanah Asia Scholarship in Collaboration with Ancora Foundation

**Purpose**: Initiated through a generous benefaction from Mr. Gita Irawan Wirjawan, this scholarship provides one year's tuition, fees, and expenses,

**Eligibility**: Applicants should have; (a) a confirmed acceptance at the Environmental Change Institute, Oxford University; (b) an excellent academic record with a first degree equivalent to a good Second Class (Upper) Honors or a GPA of at least 3.5; (c) a very good command of the English language; (d) a commercial or industrial background and a deep interest in the environment; (e) assessed to have outstanding potential for leadership in government, business, or civil society after graduation

**Level of Study**: Graduate

**Type**: Scholarship

**Value**: Up to £28,500

**Frequency**: Varies

**Country of Study**: Any country

**Application Procedure**: Each fellowship is tenable for one-year only for full-time students on the Master of Science in Environmental Change and Management program. The successful candidate is expected to complete his/her studies within the tenable period. Each scholarship will cover the following: Tuition and other compulsory fees (as specified by Oxford University); Monthly stipend; and Return air-ticket (economy class)

**Closing Date**: 6 December

**Funding**: Private

**Additional Information**: www.heysuccess.com/opportunity/Khazanah-Asia-Scholarship-Programme-21462

**For further information contact:**

Equity Tower, 41st Floor Sudirman Central Business District (SCBD), Jl. Jend. Sudirman Kav. 52-53, Lot 9, Jakarta 12190, Indonesia.

**Email**:    inquiry@ancorafoundation.com

## Theology and Religion: AHRC Doctoral Training Partnership Studentships

**Level of Study**: Graduate

**Value**: University fee, college fee and full living expenses. Fees-only awards for non-United Kingdom, European Union students

**Length of Study**: Period of fee liability

**Country of Study**: Any country

**Application Procedure**: Open to all graduate applicants for the DPhil degree offered by the Faculty of Theology and Religion. Please see website for more details

**Closing Date**: 20 January

**Additional Information**: For more details, please visit www.humanities.ox.ac.uk/prospective_students/graduates/funding/ahrc www.humanities.ox.ac.uk/ahrc-doctoral-training-partnership#collapse395446

**For further information contact:**

**Email**:    theo.pgresearchadmissions@durham.ac.uk

## Theology and Religion: Faculty Graduate Studentships

**Level of Study**: Graduate

**Value**: At least £1,000

**Length of Study**: Period of fee liability

**Country of Study**: Any country

**Application Procedure**: Open to all graduate applicants and continuing graduate students in Theology and Religion. Please see website for more details, including how to apply

**Closing Date**: 20 January

**Additional Information**: For more details, please visit website www.theology.ox.ac.uk/ www.theology.ox.ac.uk/funding

### For further information contact:

**Email**:     theo.pgresearchadmissions@durham.ac.uk

## Trinity College Birkett Scholarship in Environmental Studies

**Eligibility**: Open to any graduate accepted for the MSc

**Level of Study**: Postgraduate

**Type**: Scholarship

**Value**: £2,400

**Length of Study**: 1 year

**Frequency**: Annual

**Study Establishment**: Trinity College, University of Oxford

**Country of Study**: United Kingdom

**Application Procedure**: Applicants must contact the Academic Administrator for details

### For further information contact:

Trinity College, Broad St, Oxford OX1 3BH, United Kingdom.

**Email**:     jane.sherwood@admin.ox.ac.uk

## Trinity College Junior Research Fellowship

**Purpose**: To promote and encourage research among those at the start of an academic career

**Eligibility**: Open to suitably qualified candidates having some research experience (e.g. a completed doctoral thesis)

**Level of Study**: Doctorate, Postdoctorate

**Value**: Approx. £20,000 p.a

**Length of Study**: 3 years, non renewable

**Frequency**: Annual

**Study Establishment**: Trinity College, University of Oxford

**Country of Study**: United Kingdom

**Application Procedure**: Please see application form on Trinity College website www.trinity.ox.ac.uk

**Additional Information**: www.trin.cam.ac.uk/vacancies/junior-research-fellowships/

## Trinity College: Michael and Judith Beloff Scholarship

**Purpose**: To assist graduate students with fees

**Eligibility**: Open to all graduate applicants for the BC-L. Preference given those intending to practise at the Bar of United Kingdom and Wales

**Level of Study**: Postgraduate

**Type**: Scholarship

**Value**: £8,000

**Length of Study**: 1 year

**Frequency**: Annual

**Country of Study**: Any country

**Application Procedure**: Please note interest on application form. Please see website for details of how to apply

**Closing Date**: October

**Additional Information**: Please check at www.trinity.ox.ac.uk/pages/admissions/loans-grants-and-bursaries.php www.trinity.ox.ac.uk/postgraduate-study/postgraduate-application/postgraduate-scholarships/

## University College: Chellgren

**Purpose**: Applicants must have a place on a postgraduate programme at University College, Oxford. Scholarships can be awarded to students embarking on any postgraduate programme. However, prospective economics students are given preference

**Eligibility**: Open to all graduate applicants in Economics. Applicants must have a place on a postgraduate programme at University College, Oxford

**Level of Study**: Postgraduate

**Type**: Scholarship

**Value**: £4,000 per year

**Length of Study**: Up to 3 years

**Frequency**: Annual

**Study Establishment**: University

**Country of Study**: United Kingdom

**Application Procedure**: Please see website for more details, including how to apply

**Closing Date**: January

**Funding**: Trusts

**Additional Information**: For more information, please check the website: www.univ.ox.ac.uk/postgraduate/financial_1/scholarships_and_studentships/

## University College: Henni-Mester Scholarship

**Eligibility**: Open to all graduate applicants to the Nuffield Department of Orthopaedics, Rheumatology and Musculoskeletal Sciences. Please see website for more details

**Level of Study**: Postgraduate
**Type**: Scholarship
**Value**: University fee, college fee and full living expenses
**Length of Study**: Period of fee liability
**Frequency**: Annual
**Study Establishment**: University
**Country of Study**: United Kingdom
**Application Procedure**: For more information, please check the website: www.univ.ox.ac.uk/postgraduate/financial_1/scholarships_and_studentships/
**Closing Date**: 8 January
**Funding**: Trusts

### For further information contact:

**Email**:    lodge@univ.ox.ac.uk

## University College: Loughman

**Eligibility**: Open to graduates who have been offered a place at University College, who are outstanding in their academic field and who, in addition, can demonstrate that they will make significant contributions to College life through the quality of their extra-academic pursuits (sports, arts, community service, etc.)
**Level of Study**: Postgraduate
**Type**: Scholarship
**Value**: £4,000 per year
**Length of Study**: Up to 3 years
**Frequency**: Annual
**Study Establishment**: University
**Country of Study**: United Kingdom
**Closing Date**: January
**Funding**: Trusts
**Additional Information**: For more information, please check the website: www.univ.ox.ac.uk/postgraduate/financial_1/scholarships_and_studentships/

### For further information contact:

**Email**:    john.loughman@ucd.ie

## University Hardship Fund

**Purpose**: The University Hardship Fund aims to assist students who experience unexpected financial difficulties due to circumstances which could not have been predicted at the start of their course
**Eligibility**: Students can apply to the University Hardship Fund (UHF) if they are experiencing unexpected and unforeseeable financial difficulties
**Level of Study**: Graduate

**Type**: Funding support
**Value**: £6,000
**Frequency**: Annual
**Country of Study**: Any country
**Application Procedure**: Students should contact their college hardship officer to request an application form and discuss their application. The hardship officer varies across colleges but could be your Senior Tutor, Bursar or Academic Administrator. Complete application forms should be submitted by the student or their college to Student Fees and Funding as soon as possible and by the appropriate deadline listed below. The form includes sections for the student, tutor or supervisor and college hardship officer to complete, and applications will only be considered when all sections and evidence have been received
**Closing Date**: 1 May
**Funding**: Trusts
**Additional Information**:    www.ox.ac.uk/students/fees-funding/assistance/hardship/uhf?wssl=1

### For further information contact:

**Email**:    graduatefunding@admin.cam.ac.uk

## Wadham College - David Richards Scholarship in Chemistry

**Purpose**: Applicants for postgraduate research courses offered by the Department of Chemistry. The scholarship is open to home,
**Eligibility**: To be eligible for consideration for this scholarship, applicants must be successful in being offered a place on their course after consideration of applications received by the relevant January deadline for the course. Course applications which are held over after the January deadline to be re-evaluated against applications received by the March deadline or course applications which have been put on a waiting list are not eligible for scholarship consideration
**Level of Study**: Graduate
**Type**: Scholarship
**Value**: 100% of course fees and a grant for living costs (at least £14,777) for the duration of the course
**Frequency**: Annual
**Country of Study**: Any country
**Application Procedure**: Scholarships are awarded to applicants who have demonstrated excellent academic ability, who will contribute to the University's ground-breaking research, and who will go on to contribute to the world as leaders in their field, pushing the frontiers of knowledge. The Richards family bequest contributes 60% of the funds for these scholarships, with the remaining 40% being contributed by the University of Oxford

**Closing Date**: January
**Funding**: Private
**Additional Information**: www.wadham.ox.ac.uk/students/
graduate-students/graduate-finance/graduate-scholarships

**For further information contact:**

**Email**:    graduate.admissions@wadham.ox.ac.uk

## Wadham College: Beit Scholarship

**Value**: University fee, college fee, and full living expenses
**Length of Study**: 1 year
**Country of Study**: Any country
**Application Procedure**: Open to graduate applicants for 1-year Masters courses who are ordinarily resident in Malawi, Zambia or Zimbabwe. Please see website for further details, including how to apply
**Closing Date**: January
**Additional Information**: For more details, please visit website www.wadham.ox.ac.uk/students/graduate-students/graduate-finance/graduate-scholarships

**For further information contact:**

**Email**:    graduate.admissions@wadham.ox.ac.uk

## Wadham College: Donner Canadian Foundation Law Scholarship

**Purpose**: The Donner Canadian Scholarship is awarded to Canadian graduates intending to undertake the BCL or MJur at the University of Oxford as a member of Wadham College. This prize is available on an annual basis and is awarded on the basis of academic excellence and aptitude
**Eligibility**: Open to any graduate applicant to the BCL or MJur who is ordinarily resident in Canada. Please see website for more details
**Level of Study**: Postgraduate
**Type**: Scholarship
**Value**: £20,000 towards University and college fees or living expenses
**Length of Study**: One year
**Frequency**: Annual
**Country of Study**: Any country
**Application Procedure**: For more information, please check the    website:    www.wadham.ox.ac.uk/students/graduate-students/graduate-finance/graduate-scholarships
**Closing Date**: 22 January
**Funding**: Trusts

**Additional Information**: www.wadham.ox.ac.uk/students/
graduate-students/graduate-finance/graduate-scholarships

**For further information contact:**

Tutor for Graduates, Wadham College, Parks Road, Oxford OX1 3PN, United Kingdom.

**Email**:    senior.tutor@wadh.ox.ac.uk

## Wadham College: Hackney BCL Scholarship

**Value**: £15,009
**Length of Study**: 1 year
**Country of Study**: Any country
**Application Procedure**: Open to all graduate applicants for the BCL
**Closing Date**: April
**Additional Information**: For more details, please visit website www.wadham.ox.ac.uk/students/graduate-students/graduate-finance/graduate-scholarships

**For further information contact:**

**Email**:    graduate.admissions@wadham.ox.ac.uk

## Wadham College: John Brookman Scholarship

**Purpose**: To assist an organisation scholar who has been given admission to read for a higher degree in the university
**Eligibility**: Open to any graduate student who wishes to play a role in the musical life of the college
**Level of Study**: Postgraduate, Research
**Type**: Scholarship
**Value**: Equivalent to college fee
**Length of Study**: Duration of fee liability
**Frequency**: Annual
**Study Establishment**: Wadham College, University of Oxford
**Country of Study**: United Kingdom
**Application Procedure**: Applicants should send a full curriculum vitae detailing: their academic and musical qualifications and experience; the graduate course that they are following, or to which they have applied; and the names of two referees, either by post to the Tutor for Graduates. Applicants should also request referees to submit their references (using the same contact details as listed above) by the same date. A successful candidate will take up his/her scholarship from October 1st
**Closing Date**: 23 April
**Funding**: Trusts

**Contributor**: Endowed by late E.W.M. Brookman, an old member of the college, in memory of his son, John M. Brookman (1926–1980)
**Additional Information**: www.wadham.ox.ac.uk/students/graduate-students/graduate-finance/graduate-scholarships

**For further information contact:**

**Email**:    admissions@wadh.ox.ac.uk

## Wadham College: Oxford-Richards Scholarship in Chemistry

**Eligibility**: Open to a graduate applying for one of the DPhil courses offered by the Chemistry Department. Please see website for details
**Level of Study**: Postgraduate
**Type**: Scholarship
**Value**: University fee, college fee, and full living expenses
**Length of Study**: Duration of fee liability
**Frequency**: Annual
**Study Establishment**: Wadham
**Country of Study**: United Kingdom
**Application Procedure**: For more information, please check the website: www.ox.ac.uk/admissions/graduate/fees-and-funding/fees-funding-and-scholarship-search/scholarships-3#richards
**Closing Date**: 22 January
**Funding**: Trusts

**For further information contact:**

**Email**:    graduate.admissions@wadham.ox.ac.uk

## Wadham College: Oxford-Richards Scholarship in Economics

**Eligibility**: Open to a graduate applying for the DPhil in Economics. Please see website for details
**Level of Study**: Postgraduate
**Type**: Scholarship
**Value**: University fee, college fee, and full living expenses
**Length of Study**: Duration of fee liability
**Frequency**: Annual
**Study Establishment**: Wadham
**Country of Study**: United Kingdom
**Application Procedure**: For more information, please check the website: www.ox.ac.uk/admissions/graduate/fees-and-funding/fees-funding-and-scholarship-search/scholarships-3#richards
**Closing Date**: 22 January
**Funding**: Trusts

**For further information contact:**

**Email**:    graduate.admissions@wadham.ox.ac.uk

## Wadham College: Oxford-Richards Scholarships in Climate Science

**Eligibility**: Open to a graduate applying for a DPhil in Atmospheric, Oceanic and Planetary Physics. Please see website for more details
**Level of Study**: Postgraduate
**Type**: Scholarship
**Value**: University fee, college fee, and full living expenses
**Length of Study**: Duration of fee liability
**Frequency**: Annual
**Study Establishment**: Wadham
**Country of Study**: United Kingdom
**Application Procedure**: For more information, please check the website: www.ox.ac.uk/admissions/graduate/fees-and-funding/fees-funding-and-scholarship-search/scholarships-3#richards
**Closing Date**: 8 January
**Funding**: Trusts

**For further information contact:**

**Email**:    domestic.bursar@wadham.ox.ac.uk

## Wadham College: Oxford-Richards Scholarships in History

**Eligibility**: Open to a graduate applying for one of the DPhil courses offered by the History Faculty. Please see website for more details
**Level of Study**: Postgraduate
**Type**: Scholarship
**Value**: University fee, college fee, and full living expenses
**Length of Study**: Duration of fee liability
**Frequency**: Annual
**Study Establishment**: Wadham
**Country of Study**: United Kingdom
**Application Procedure**: For more information, please check the website: www.ox.ac.uk/admissions/graduate/fees-and-funding/fees-funding-and-scholarship-search/scholarships-3#richards
**Closing Date**: 22 January
**Funding**: Trusts

**For further information contact:**

**Email**:    graduate.admissions@wadham.ox.ac.uk

## Wadham College: Peter Carter Graduate Scholarship in Law

**Level of Study**: Graduate
**Value**: £10,000 towards course and college fees or living expenses
**Length of Study**: Duration of fee liability
**Country of Study**: Any country
**Application Procedure**: Open to all graduate applicants for the BCL, MJur, MPhil in Law or DPhil in Law
**Closing Date**: 20 January
**Additional Information**: For more details, please visit website www.wadham.ox.ac.uk/students/graduate-students/graduate-finance/graduate-scholarships llm-guide.com/scholarships/peter-carter-graduate-scholarship-in-law-318

### For further information contact:

**Email**:    study@ox.ac.uk

## Wadham College: Peter Carter Taught Graduate Scholarship in Law

**Purpose**: The Taught Graduate Scholarship in Law is available to graduate students of exceptional academic merit embarking on the BCL or MJur at Wadham College and is available to law graduates of any university
**Eligibility**: Open to all graduate applicants for the BCL or MJur. Please see website for details
**Level of Study**: Graduate, Postgraduate
**Type**: Scholarship
**Value**: £12,500 towards course and college fees or living expenses
**Length of Study**: 1 year
**Study Establishment**: Wadham College
**Country of Study**: Any country
**Application Procedure**: Please visit the website: www.wadham.ox.ac.uk/students/graduate-students/graduate-finance/graduate-scholarships
**Closing Date**: 20 January
**Additional Information**: Please visit the website: www.wadham.ox.ac.uk/students/graduate-students/graduate-finance/graduate-scholarships for more information. The scholarship can be used to defray in part University fees, College fees and/or maintenance of the Scholar during their period of study. It does not cover all fees so you will have to demonstrate sufficient funds for additional costs llm-guide.com/scholarships/peter-carter-taught-graduate-scholarship-in-law-201

### For further information contact:

**Email**:    admissions@wadh.ox.ac.uk

## Wadham College: Philip Wright Scholarship

**Eligibility**: Open to any graduate student who is a former student of Manchester Grammar School
**Level of Study**: Postgraduate, Research
**Type**: Scholarship
**Value**: University and college fee (to a maximum of £10,000) plus £8,000 per year stipend or, where recipient receives financial support from another source (i.e. RCUK), payment of the college fee
**Length of Study**: 1 year, possible renewal
**Application Procedure**: Application forms are available at www.wadham.ox.ac.uk/student-life/scholarships/the-philip-wright-scholarship.html either in Word or PDF format. Please send the completed form, a full Curriculum Vitae and (for graduates applying for research work) a one page summary of your research proposal, either by post to the Tutor for Graduates
**Closing Date**: 23 April
**Funding**: Trusts
**Contributor**: Philip Wright Fund
**Additional Information**: www.european-funding-guide.eu/other-financial-assistance/13742-philip-wright-scholarship

## Wakeham Humanities Scholarship (History or Literature)

**Purpose**: All of these scholarships, apart from the Light Senior Scholarships, are open to new graduate students commencing graduate study at Oxford in October
**Eligibility**: Students at other colleges are eligible to apply for all of these scholarships apart from the Light Senior Scholarships, but would need to migrate to St Catherine's to take up the scholarship if their application was successful
**Level of Study**: Graduate
**Type**: Scholarship
**Value**: Check the website for further details
**Frequency**: Every 2 years
**Country of Study**: Any country
**Application Procedure**: Applications for Graduate Scholarships should be sent by email to college.office@scatz.ox.ac.uk
**Closing Date**: 10 May
**Funding**: Private
**Additional Information**: www.ox.ac.uk/admissions/graduate/colleges/st-catherines-college

### For further information contact:

Manor Road, Oxford OX1 3UJ, United Kingdom.

## Weatherall Institute of Molecular Medicine: WIMM Prize Studentship

**Level of Study**: Graduate
**Value**: All fees and living expenses of £18,000 per annum
**Length of Study**: 4 years
**Country of Study**: United Kingdom
**Application Procedure**: Open to applicants of any nationality applying for projects advertised on the WIMM website. Applicants must quote scholarship reference code H816027
**Closing Date**: 1 June
**Additional Information**: For more details, visit website www.imm.ox.ac.uk/wimm-prize-studentship-2017 www.rdm.ox.ac.uk/study-with-us/funding-options/wimm-prize-student ships

### For further information contact:

University of Oxford Level 6, West Wing John Radcliffe Hospital Headington Oxford OX3 9DU, United Kingdom.

**Email**:   graduate.enquiries@rdm.ox.ac.uk

## Weidenfeld-Hoffmann Scholarships and Leadership Programme

**Purpose**: The Weidenfeld-Hoffmann Scholarships and Leadership Programme cultivates the leaders of tomorrow by providing outstanding university graduates and professionals from developing and emerging economies with the opportunity to pursue fully-funded graduate studies at the University of Oxford, combined with a comprehensive programme of leadership development, long-term mentoring and networking.
**Eligibility**: You must be applying to start a new graduate course at Oxford. Please visit the website to see the complete list of eligible courses and country of residence
**Level of Study**: Postgraduate
**Type**: Scholarship
**Value**: University fee, college fee, and full living expenses
**Length of Study**: Period of fee liability
**Frequency**: Annual
**Country of Study**: United Kingdom
**Application Procedure**: Please see website for more details, including how to apply
**Closing Date**: May
**Funding**: Trusts
**Additional Information**: For more information, please check the website: www.graduate.ox.ac.uk/weidenfeld-hoffmann www.ox.ac.uk/admissions/graduate/fees-and-funding/fees-funding-and-scholarship-search/weidenfeld-hoffmann-scholar ships-and-leadership-programme

### For further information contact:

**Email**:   info@whtrust.org

## Wolfson College: Lorne Thyssen Scholarship

**Level of Study**: Graduate
**Value**: University fee, college fee, and living expenses
**Length of Study**: Period of fee liability
**Country of Study**: Any country
**Application Procedure**: Open to new Home/European Union applicants to DPhil courses within the range accepted by Wolfson College, and who are specializing in Ancient World Studies. Please see website for more details
**Closing Date**: January
**Additional Information**: For more details, please visit www.wolfson.ox.ac.uk/scholarships/lorne-thyssen www.wolfson.ox.ac.uk/lorne-thyssen-scholarship

### For further information contact:

**Email**:   ancient.world@wolfson.ox.ac.uk

## Wolfson College: Mougins Museum Ashmolean Scholarship

**Eligibility**: Open to Home/European Union and Overseas. The applicant's thesis should fall within the field of 'Greek material culture from 700 to 30 BC' and will ideally focus on the archaeological and/or numismatic collections within the Ashmolean. The Mougins Museum itself holds important collections which can be made available for study
**Level of Study**: Research
**Type**: Scholarship
**Value**: £20,000 per year for 3 years towards university fees, college fees and maintenance
**Length of Study**: Up to 3 years
**Frequency**: Annual
**Application Procedure**: Select the 'Mougins Scholarship's box in the University of Oxford Scholarships section of the Application Form for Graduate Study. Applicants are encouraged to include a statement explaining how their proposed research relates to the Scholarship. Preference may be given to those who list Wolfson as their first choice college
**Closing Date**: 22 January
**Additional Information**: Graduate scholarship in Greek material culture of the archaic, classical or Hellenistic periods. Please check at www.wolfson.ox.ac.uk/mougins-museum-ashmolean-scholarship-2015-16

### For further information contact:

**Email**:   susan.walker@ashmus.ox.ac.uk

## Worcester College: C. Douglas Dillon Scholarship

**Eligibility**: Open to graduate applicants for 1 year or 2-year courses in the fields of Politics, Diplomacy, Governance and International Relations. Please see website for more details, including eligible courses and how to apply
**Level of Study**: Graduate
**Value**: £10,000
**Length of Study**: 1 or 2 years
**Country of Study**: Any country
**Closing Date**: 6 March
**Additional Information**: For more details, visit website www.worc.ox.ac.uk/applying/graduates/graduate-scholarships www.worc.ox.ac.uk/sites/default/files/ad_c_douglas_dillon_scholarship_2020-21.pdf

### For further information contact:

**Tel**: (44) 1865 278300
**Email**: graduate.enquiries@worc.ox.ac.uk

## Worcester College: Drue Heinz Scholarship

**Level of Study**: Graduate
**Value**: £10,000
**Length of Study**: 1 year
**Country of Study**: Any country
**Application Procedure**: Open to graduate applicants in the Humanities. Preference given to international applicants. Please see website for more details, including how to apply
**Closing Date**: 6 March
**Contributor**: Worcester
**Additional Information**: For more details, please visit website: www.worc.ox.ac.uk/applying/graduates/graduate-scholarships www.worc.ox.ac.uk/sites/default/files/ad_drue_heinz_scholarship_2020-21.pdf

### For further information contact:

**Email**: graduate.enquiries@worc.ox.ac.uk

## Worcester College: Law Faculty Graduate Scholarship

**Eligibility**: Open to applicants who are applying for the Bachelor of Civil Law or Magister Juris. Award holders will become members of Worcester College. Please see website for more information
**Level of Study**: Graduate, Postgraduate
**Type**: Scholarship
**Value**: £10,000
**Length of Study**: 1 year

**Study Establishment**: Worcester College
**Country of Study**: Any country
**Closing Date**: January
**Additional Information**: Please visit the website: www.worc.ox.ac.uk/applying/graduates/graduate-scholarships

### For further information contact:

**Tel**: (44) 1865 278 300
**Email**: lodge@worc.ox.ac.uk

## Worcester College: Martin Senior Scholarship

**Eligibility**: Open to graduate applicants to research degrees from the United Kingdom or European Union who are current or previous members of Worcester College
**Level of Study**: Postgraduate, Research
**Type**: Scholarship
**Value**: £4,000
**Length of Study**: Duration of student's fee liability
**Frequency**: Annual
**Study Establishment**: Worcester College
**Application Procedure**: Please see college website for details of how to apply
**Closing Date**: 1 March
**Additional Information**: Please check the website: www.worc.ox.ac.uk/applying/graduates/graduate-scholarships

### For further information contact:

**Email**: graduate.enquiries@worc.ox.ac.uk

## Worcester College: Ogilvie Thompson Scholarships

**Purpose**: To assist graduate students with fees
**Eligibility**: Open to incoming graduates who have been undergraduates at Worcester within the last two years and have not undertaken any graduate work at Oxford or elsewhere
**Type**: Scholarships
**Value**: Up to £6,000
**Length of Study**: 1 year
**Country of Study**: Any country
**Closing Date**: 6 March
**Additional Information**: www.worc.ox.ac.uk/sites/default/files/ad_ogilvie_thompson_2020-21.pdf

### For further information contact:

**Tel**: (44) 1865 278300
**Email**: graduate.enquiries@worc.ox.ac.uk

## University of Paris-Saclay

**Website:** www.universite-paris-saclay.fr/en/universite-paris-saclay-international-masters-scholarship

The University of Paris-Saclay is a French federal research university which is currently under development with the aim to become a world top-10 university.

## Université Paris-Saclay International Master's Scholarships

**Purpose:** The Université Paris-Saclay would like to promote access to its master's (nationally-certified degree) programs to international students, taught in its member establishments, and to make it easier for highly-qualified foreign students to attend its university especially those wishing to develop an academic project through research up to the doctoral level
**Eligibility:** Newly arrived international students, aged 30 and under during the course of the selection year. - International students living in France for less than a year, taking language classes (type FFL or the like). - Students enrolled in a Université Paris-Saclay Master's programme and whose institution of administrative enrolment is one of the following: AgroParisTech, CentraleSupelec, ENS Paris-Saclay, INSTN-CEA, IOGS, UVSQ, UEVE, UPSud
**Level of Study:** Postgraduate
**Value:** €10,000 per year
**Frequency:** Annual
**Study Establishment:** Université Paris-Saclay, France
**Country of Study:** France
**Application Procedure:** To be considered for the scholarships, students must first be admitted to a Master's Programme offered at Université Paris-Saclay
**Closing Date:** 6 May
**Funding:** Government
**Additional Information:** For more details visit official scholarship website: www.universite-paris-saclay.fr/en/universite-paris-saclay-international-masters-scholarship-programme-academic-year-2017-2018 www.universite-paris-saclay.fr/en/admission/scholarships-and-financial-aid/bourses-internationales-de-master/international-masters

## University of Pretoria

Private Bag X20, Hatfield 0028, South Africa.

**Tel:** (27) 12 420 3111
**Website:** www.up.ac.za/

## Commonwealth PhD Scholarships

**Purpose:** Commonwealth PhD Scholarships are for candidates from low and middle income Commonwealth countries, for full-time doctoral study at a United Kingdom university. Commonwealth PhD Scholarships are for candidates from low and middle income Commonwealth countries, for full-time doctoral study at a United Kingdom university
**Eligibility:** 1. Applicants should be citizens of Commonwealth countries (excluding South African students). 2. Applicants must conduct their studies at the University of Pretoria. 3. They must have completed the degree that will give them admission to a doctoral programme a maximum of 3 years prior to their application for the University of Pretoria Commonwealth Doctoral Scholarship. 4. They must not be older than 35 years of age at the time of application. Masters students currently registered at the University of Pretoria are not eligible for the Doctoral Scholarship
**Level of Study:** Doctorate
**Type:** Scholarship
**Value:** The value of the Doctoral Scholarships will be ZAR 120,000. This amount must be used to cover accommodation and living cost, medical aid and books/stationery. For detailed information, please visit website
**Country of Study:** South Africa
**Application Procedure:** The mode of applying is electronically or by post
**Closing Date:** 30 August
**Contributor:** University of Pretoria
**Additional Information:** For further information, kindly check the following pdf link. cscuk.dfid.gov.uk/wp-content/uploads/2019/02/terms-conditions-phd-scholarships-low-middle-income-countries-2019-FINAL._.pdf cscuk.dfid.gov.uk/apply/phd-scholarships-least-developed-countries-and-fragile-states/

### For further information contact:

**Email:** eas@cscuk.org.uk

## University of Pune

Institute of Bioinformatics & Biotechnology (IBB), Ganeshkhind, Pune, Maharashtra 411007, India.

**Tel:** (91) 20 2569 2039
**Email:** director@bioinfo.ernet.in
**Website:** www.unipune.ernet.in
**Contact:** Director

The University stands for humanism and tolerance, for reason for adventure of ideas and for the search of truth. It stands for the forward march of the human race towards even higher objectives. If the universities discharge their duties adequately then it is well with the nation and the people–Jawaharlal Nehru.

## Department of Biotechnology (DBT) Junior Research Fellowship

**Purpose**: To support candidates pursuing research in areas of biotechnology and applied biology
**Eligibility**: Open to candidates from the centres supported by the DBT, New Delhi
**Level of Study**: Research
**Type**: Fellowship
**Value**: INR 30,000 per fellow per year
**Length of Study**: 3–5 years
**Frequency**: Annual
**Study Establishment**: University of Pune
**Country of Study**: India
**Application Procedure**: A written application along with application fee of INR 500 in the form of a DD in favour of Registrar, University of Pune
**Contributor**: Government of India
**Additional Information**: career.webindia123.com/career/scholarships/scholarships_india/dbt-junior-research-fellowship/index.htm

### For further information contact:

Department of Biotechnology, University of Pune, Pune, Maharashtra 411007, India.

**Tel**:       (91) 20 2569 4952, 2569 2248
**Email**:   jkpal@unipune.ernet.in

## University of Queensland

Research and Postgraduate Studies, Cumbrae-Stewart Building, Brisbane, St Lucia, QLD 4072, Australia.

**Tel**:        (61) 7 3365 1111
**Email**:    scholarships@research.uq.edu.au
**Website**:  www.uq.edu.au

The University of Queensland has an outstanding profile in the Australian and international research community. It maintains a world-class, comprehensive programme of research and research training, underpinned by state-of-the-art infrastructure and a commitment to rewarding excellence. As one of Australia's premier universities, UQ attracts researchers and students of outstanding calibre.

## Dr Rosamond Siemon Postgraduate Renal Research Scholarship

**Purpose**: To support a research higher degree candidate to undertake multidisciplinary, collaborative research into renal disease, repair and regeneration
**Eligibility**: Open to candidates who are enroled or intend to enrol in a research higher degree at the University of Queensland and who demonstrate a high level of academic achievement and ability
**Level of Study**: Postgraduate
**Type**: Scholarship
**Value**: AU$30,000 per year (a stipend of AU$25,000 and a direct research cost allowance of AU$5,000)
**Length of Study**: 3 years and 6 months
**Frequency**: Annual
**Country of Study**: Australia
**Application Procedure**: Applicants must send a proposed research project description, certified copies of academic transcripts, academic curriculum vitae, including publications and 3 letters of recommendation
**Closing Date**: 31 August
**Funding**: Individuals
**Contributor**: Dr Rosamond Siemon
**Additional Information**: Research Scholarships Referee Report Form can be used. This can be accessed from www.uq.edu.au/grad-school/scholarship-forms

### For further information contact:

Research Scholarships, Office of Research and Postgraduate Studies, The University of Queensland, St Lucia, QLD 4072, Australia.

**Email**:    postgrad-office@imb.uq.edu.au

## Global Archaeological Science Scholarships

**Purpose**: The University of Queensland Archaeology Program is offering four PhD studentships for international and domestic students to start for archaeological science projects in Africa, Europe and Australia.
**Eligibility**: Australian and international students are eligible to apply. Students whose first language is not English must demonstrate proficiency in English by submitting satisfactory scores from the Test of English as a Foreign Language (TOEFL).

**Type**: Postgraduate scholarships
**Value**: AU$27,082 (old rate) indexed annually, tuition fees, Overseas Student Health Cover (OSHC)
**Study Establishment**: Scholarships are awarded for archaeological science projects in Africa, Europe and Australia
**Country of Study**: Australia
**Application Procedure**: See the website
**Closing Date**: 17 January
**Additional Information**: For more details please visit the website scholarship-positions.com/global-archaeological-science-scholarships-university-queensland-2018/2017/12/29/

### For further information contact:

**Email**: a.crowther@uq.edu.au

## Herdsman Fellowship in Medical Science

**Purpose**: The fellowship is open to graduates in medicine or related health sciences enroled full-time for a PhD on a topic related to the medical problems of the aged
**Eligibility**: Applicants must be graduates in medicine or related health sciences, enrol full-time for a PhD, and be undertaking a research topic related to the medical problems of the aged
**Level of Study**: Postgraduate
**Type**: Fellowship
**Value**: AU$22,860 per year
**Length of Study**: Fellowship shall initially be for 1 year but may be extended by the committee for further terms of 1 year up to a total of 3 years
**Country of Study**: Australia
**Application Procedure**: Applications must consist of: covering letter addressing the Herdsman Fellowship Rules, in particular point 2, academic curriculum vitae, 2 referee reports. No strict format is required; however the Research Scholarships generic Referee Report may be used
**No. of awards offered**: 1
**Closing Date**: 31 August
**Contributor**: Maintained by the income from a bequest of AU$2,60,000 from Mrs Rose Herdsman
**No. of awards given last year**: 1
**No. of applicants last year**: 1
**Additional Information**: scholarships.uq.edu.au/files/448/sched-a-pg-research-scholarships.pdf

### For further information contact:

Faculty of Health Sciences, University of Queensland, St Lucia, QLD 4072, Australia.

**Email**: s.tett@pharmacy.uq.edu.au

## PhD Scholarship in Immunology and Immunogenetics

**Purpose**: To provide the foundations for the development of treatments based on the genetic findings
**Eligibility**: Open to a dynamic, intelligent and diligent PhD candidate (Australian or international) with either a clinical or a relevant basic science background to take forward the project
**Level of Study**: Doctorate
**Type**: Scholarship
**Value**: AU$25,000 per year
**Length of Study**: 3 years
**Frequency**: Annual
**Study Establishment**: The University of Queensland
**Country of Study**: Australia
**Application Procedure**: Candidates must contact Prof. Brown for more information
**Closing Date**: 3 September
**Additional Information**: International applicants must cover tuition fees (AU$27,000 per year)

### For further information contact:

**Tel**: (61) 7 3240 2870
**Email**: matt.brown@qut.edu.au

## R.N. Hammon Scholarship

**Purpose**: To assist Australian Aboriginal and/or Torres Strait Island students for further studies
**Eligibility**: Open to Australian Aboriginal and/or Torres Strait Island students who have successfully completed at least 1 year of an undergraduate or postgraduate program and are enroling on a full-time basis for a subsequent year of that program, or for a further program
**Level of Study**: Postgraduate
**Type**: Scholarship
**Value**: AU$3,500
**Frequency**: Annual
**Study Establishment**: The University of Queensland, Queensland University of Technology, University of Southern Queensland, Central Queensland University, or Queensland Colleges of TAFE
**Country of Study**: Australia
**Application Procedure**: Candidates can download the application form and referee report form from the website
**Closing Date**: 2 March
**Additional Information**: The Selection Committee shall take into account the academic merit or technical excellence, any other scholarship, bursary, award or benefit, whether governmental or otherwise, to which the applicant is entitled;

and social and economic need scholarships.uq.edu.au/scholar ship/rn-hammon-scholarship

**For further information contact:**

**Tel**:     (61) 7 33651984
**Email**:   ugscholarships@uq.edu.au

## Sustainable Tourism CRC Climate Change PhD

**Purpose**: To develop a tourism consumer decision-making model that focuses on climate change as a driver of consumer choice and apply it to Australian tourism market
**Eligibility**: Open to candidates who have achieved First Class (Honours) Degree or equivalent
**Level of Study**: Postgraduate, Research
**Type**: Scholarship
**Value**: AU$19,930 per year
**Length of Study**: 3 years
**Frequency**: Annual
**Study Establishment**: The University of Queensland
**Country of Study**: Australia
**Application Procedure**: Candidates must contact Jane Malady for application forms
**Contributor**: Sustainable Tourism CRC and University of Queensland
**Additional Information**: For further information on topic and research proposal contact Prof. Ballantyne at r.ballantyne@uq.edu.au

**For further information contact:**

**Tel**:     (61) 7 5552 9063
**Email**:   Jane@crctourism.com.au

## The Constantine Aspromourgos Memorial Scholarship for Greek Studies

**Purpose**: To assist a research higher degree student studying at least 1 area of Greek studies
**Eligibility**: Open to candidates who have obtained their Bachelors or Masters degrees and are undertaking a postgraduate programme involving studies which pertain to at least one area of Greek studies
**Level of Study**: Postgraduate
**Type**: Scholarship
**Value**: Approx. AU$4,000
**Length of Study**: 1 year
**Frequency**: Annual
**Country of Study**: Australia
**Application Procedure**: Applicants must send a completed application form

**Closing Date**: 22 March
**Funding**: Individuals
**Additional Information**: The Scholarship is also open to candidates who are undertaking the programme as a student of another university acceptable to the committee, or this university, provided that some part of the programme involves studies at another university scholarships.uq.edu. au/scholarship/constantine-aspromourgos-memorial-scholar ship-greek-studies#qt-scholarship_tabs-foundation-tabs-1

**For further information contact:**

Faculty of Arts, Forgan Smith Building, The University of Queensland, St Lucia, QLD 4072, Australia.

**Tel**:     (61) 7 3365 1333
**Email**:   arts@uq.edu.au

## University of Queensland PhD Scholarships for International Students

**Purpose**: Students must have achieved an entry level OP minimum of 11 or the equivalent if originating from another Australian state or territory or for continuing students has a GPA of at least 4.0.
**Eligibility**: Australian and Permanent Residents or NZ citizens and International students are eligible to apply. Applicants must meet the university's English language proficiency requirements apply. A postgraduate degree of at least one year full-time equivalent with an overall GPA (grade point average) equivalent to 5.0 on the 7-point UQ scale, together with demonstrated research experience equivalent to honors IIA will be considered for PhD entry on a case by case basis.
**Value**: A Base stipend of AU$27,082 per annum (old rate), indexed annually, tuition fees, Overseas Student Health Cover (OSHC)
**Study Establishment**: View projects by area Agribusiness, Agriculture, Environment, and Science Engineering, Architecture and Planning, and Information Technology Health Humanities, Education, Psychology, and Music Business, economics, and law (coming soon)
**Country of Study**: Australia
**Application Procedure**: See the website.
**Closing Date**: 31 December
**Additional Information**: For more details please visit the website scholarship-positions.com/uq-phd-scholarships-inter national-students-australia/2018/03/06/

**For further information contact:**

**Email**:   graduateschool@uq.edu.au

## Walter and Eliza Hall Scholarship Trust Opportunity Scholarship for Nursing

**Purpose**: Awarded to a financially disadvantaged student studying the Bachelor of Nursing or Bachelor of Nursing/ Bachelor of Midwifery program

**Eligibility**: The scholarship is open to students who: 1. Are domestic students in accordance with The University's Fee Policy; and; 2. Are enrolled full-time in the Bachelor of Nursing program or the dual Bachelor of Nursing/Bachelor of Midwifery program; and; 3. Have completed at least 16 units towards their program; and do not hold another similar scholarship

**Level of Study**: Graduate

**Type**: Scholarship

**Value**: AU$10,000

**Length of Study**: 2nd - 4th year

**Frequency**: Annual

**Country of Study**: Any country

**Application Procedure**: The Scholarship will be awarded on the basis of: I. academic merit. II. financial disadvantage. III. a personal statement. The Scholarship will be awarded by a selection committee consisting of members nominated by the Deputy Vice Chancellor (Registrar) or their nominated delegate

**Closing Date**: 4 March

**Funding**: Private

**Additional Information**: The recipient must demonstrate financial need, and also have performed satisfactorily in the program to date. Grade point averages will be considered; however, the grade point average will not be the sole determinant in satisfactory progress – the applicants' behaviour, class attendance, dedication to the program and career aspirations are also a part of the selection process sydney.edu.au/ scholarships/c/walter-eliza-hall-trust-opportunity-scholarship-nursing.html

### For further information contact:

Brisbane, St Lucia, QLD 4072, Australia.

**Email**: nmsw scholarship@uq.edu.au

---

## University of Reading

Whiteknights, PO Box 217, Reading RG6 6AH, United Kingdom.

**Tel**: (44) 1189 875 123
**Email**: student.recruitment@reading.ac.uk
**Website**: www.rdg.ac.uk
**Contact**: Student Financial Support Office

The University of Reading offers postgraduate taught and research degree courses in all the traditional subject areas except medical sciences. Vocational courses are also offered. Research work in many areas is of international renown.

## British Property Federation Lord Samuel of Wych Cross Memorial Award

**Purpose**: To assist students who would otherwise be unable financially to follow the MSc course

**Eligibility**: Open to candidates who hold a 1st degree and are, at the time of the award, ordinarily resident in the United Kingdom

**Level of Study**: Postgraduate

**Type**: Scholarship

**Value**: £1,000 - £2,000

**Length of Study**: 1 year

**Frequency**: Annual

**Study Establishment**: The University of Reading

**Country of Study**: United Kingdom

**Application Procedure**: Applicants must submit a curriculum vitae by invitation to the Director of the Full-Time Postgraduate Real Estate Programme

**Closing Date**: May

**Funding**: Private

**No. of awards given last year**: 3

**Additional Information**: Scholars must intend to remain resident in the United Kingdom after the term of the scholarship has ended

### For further information contact:

**Tel**: (44) 1183 786 336
**Email**: n.s.french@reading.ac.uk

## Otway Cave Scholarship

**Purpose**: To assist students who would otherwise be unable financially to follow the MSc course in Land Management

**Eligibility**: Open to candidates who hold a first degree and are, at the time of the award, ordinarily resident in the United Kingdom

**Level of Study**: Postgraduate

**Type**: Scholarship

**Value**: £1,000 (but may be higher)

**Length of Study**: 1 year

**Frequency**: Annual

**Study Establishment**: The University of Reading

**Country of Study**: United Kingdom

**Application Procedure**: Applicants must submit curriculum vitaes by invitation

**No. of awards offered**: 20
**Funding**: Private
**No. of awards given last year**: 1
**No. of applicants last year**: 20
**Additional Information**: Scholars must intend to remain resident in the United Kingdom after the term of the scholarship has ended. Awarded only to students accepted to study MSc Land Management

### For further information contact:

**Tel**:      (44) 1734 318 182
**Fax**:      (44) 1734 316 658
**Email**:      n.samman@reading.ac.uk

## University International Research Studentships

**Subjects**: All subject areas are eligible
**Eligibility**: Open to nationals of countries outside of the UK/EU
**Level of Study**: PhD
**Type**: Studentship
**Value**: All tuition fees and a grant for living costs
**Length of Study**: Up to 3 years
**Frequency**: Annual
**Study Establishment**: University of Reading
**Country of Study**: United Kingdom
**Application Procedure**: Contact Jonathan Lloyd at the University Graduate School
**No. of awards offered**: Varies
**Closing Date**: 10 January
**Funding**: University of Reading
**Contributor**: University of Reading
**Additional Information**: www.reading.ac.uk/graduate school/funding-and-fees/gs-studentships-international.aspx

### For further information contact:

**Tel**:      (44) 118 378 6839
**Email**:      j.d.lloyd@reading.ac.uk

## University of Reading Dorothy Hodgkin Postgraduate Award

**Eligibility**: Open to nationals of either India, Mainland China, Hong Kong, Russia or a country in the developing world only
**Level of Study**: Postgraduate
**Type**: Scholarship
**Value**: All tuition fees and a grant for living costs
**Length of Study**: 1 year; 3 years
**Frequency**: Annual

**Study Establishment**: University of Reading
**Country of Study**: United Kingdom
**Application Procedure**: Contact the Jonathan Lloyd at the faculties of science and life science
**Closing Date**: 6 May
**Additional Information**: www.european-funding-guide.eu/awardprize/11552-dorothy-hodgkin-postgraduate-awards-dhpa

### For further information contact:

**Tel**:      (44) 1183 788 341
**Email**:      j.d.lloyd@reading.ac.uk

## University of Reading MSc Intelligent Buildings Scholarship

**Eligibility**: In order to be considered for this Scholarship you must hold the offer of a place on the MSc Intelligent Buildings course
**Level of Study**: Postgraduate
**Type**: Scholarship
**Value**: £3,000
**Length of Study**: 1 year
**Frequency**: Annual
**Study Establishment**: University of Reading
**Country of Study**: United Kingdom
**Application Procedure**: Contact Gulay Ozkan, Programme Coordinator at the School of Construction Management and Engineering
**No. of awards offered**: 1
**Closing Date**: 30 August
**Contributor**: The Happold Trust
**No. of awards given last year**: 1
**No. of applicants last year**: 1

### For further information contact:

**Tel**:      (44) 1183 786 254
**Email**:      g.ozkan@rdg.ac.uk

## University of Reading Music Scholarship

**Purpose**: To support excellence in music
**Eligibility**: In order to be considered for this scholarship you must already hold an offer of a place at the university
**Level of Study**: Postgraduate
**Type**: Scholarship
**Value**: All tuition fees
**Length of Study**: 1 year
**Frequency**: Annual
**Study Establishment**: University of Reading
**Country of Study**: United Kingdom

**Application Procedure**: Apply online
**Closing Date**: 1 March
**Additional Information**: Students must be available for audition on 21 March

**For further information contact:**

**Email**:  music@rdg.ac.uk

## University of Regina

### Master of Indigenous Education

**Purpose**: The Master of Indigenous Education degree aims to: 1. Prepare students as leaders in pedagogical practice in Indigenous Education. 2. Provide students with the required skills, knowledge, and competencies needed to become effective Indigenous educators. 3. Prepare students to conduct research with Indigenous peoples
**Eligibility**: Below details should be mandatorily available to process the application for the grant. 1. Personal information. 2. Proxy or Third-Party information (if you want to designate a proxy or third party to act on your behalf). 3. Educational history of all higher post-secondary institutions attended, and dates attended. This includes institutions that you attended but no degree was awarded, and degrees that are in progress and have not yet been awarded. 4. English Proficiency test scores (if applicable). 5. Names and e-mail addresses of your references. 6. Personal statement of interest. Please review "Most Common Mistake Applicants Make" before submitting your personal statement. 7. Resumé or CV. 8. Valid credit card (MasterCard, VISA, or American Express). Pre-paid credit cards and MasterCard Debit, VISA Debit or American Express Debit are not acceptable methods of payment. 9. Valid e-mail address
**Level of Study**: Postgraduate
**Type**: Funding support
**Frequency**: Annual
**Country of Study**: Any country
**Application Procedure**: 1. The online application takes about 30 minutes to complete. 2. The first time you access the online application, you will be asked to create a Login ID and PIN. For security reasons, it is important that you choose a unique (hard-to-guess) PIN number. Please make a note of your login information, as you will need it later. 3. Once you have started your application, you may choose to finish at a later date. You can return to the application at any time by re-entering your Login ID and PIN number. However, you must complete it prior to the application deadline for your program
**Closing Date**: 15 October
**Funding**: Private

**Additional Information**:  www.uregina.ca/education/Programs1/Graduate-Degree-Programs/Masters_Degree/mied.html

**For further information contact:**

**Tel**:  (44) 3065 854 502
**Email**:  Grad.Studies@uregina.ca

## University of Sheffield

85 Wilkinson Street, Sheffield S10 2GJ, United Kingdom.

**Tel**:  (44) 1142 221 404
**Website**:  www.shef.ac.uk
**Contact**:  Graduate Office

The University of Sheffield is a research led university offering research supervision, taught courses and professional training in engineering and physical sciences, biologies, environmental sciences, humanities, social sciences, medical and health sciences. Many departments have funding council accreditation and scholarships and bursaries may be available.

### Allan & Nesta Ferguson Charitable Trust

**Purpose**: The Allan & Nesta Ferguson Charitable Trust was set up to promote their particular interests in education, international friendship and understanding, and the promotion of world peace and development
**Eligibility**: Applications for either a gap year or PhD grant should be made as soon as possible, either before the beginning of the proposed gap year or at least three months before the start of the final year of a PhD course
**Level of Study**: Graduate
**Type**: Varies
**Value**: £13,320
**Frequency**: Annual
**Country of Study**: Any country
**Application Procedure**: 1. The Trust prefer where possible that you complete and submit the on-line application form on this website and email it to us. Alternatively you may download and print out the application form, complete it and send it by letter post. 2. Please do not extend the length of the forms, or add any attachments. Applications MUST NOT exceed 3 pages. Please use text size 12. 3. If you are applying for more than one project, please use a separate form for each project. All applications by email will be acknowledged and a decision will usually be given within three months of the application

**No. of awards offered**: 2
**Closing Date**: 3 February
**Funding**: Private
**Additional Information**: scholarship-positions.com/allan-and-nesta-ferguson-charitable-trust-scholarships-at-university-of-leeds-in-uk/2019/11/07/

### For further information contact:

John St, Royston SG8 9BG, United Kingdom.

**Email**:   internationalscholarships@sheffield.ac.uk

## Allan & Nesta Ferguson Charitable Trust Masters Scholarships at University of Sheffield

**Purpose**: The University of Sheffield, in collaboration with the Allan and Nesta Ferguson Charitable Trust and the Sheffield Institute for International Development, is now able to offer 10 scholarships (over 3 years) targeted at international students from developing countries for a number of courses that are affiliated with the Sheffield Institute for International Development

**Eligibility**: 1. Must be between the ages of 23-32 at the time of submitting his/her application. 2. Must have obtained or be on the verge of completing their undergraduate degree with a Baccalaureate from an accredited college/university, or its equivalent. 3. Must have a minimum cumulative GPA of 3.0 or higher on a 4.0 rating system, or its equivalent. 4. Must be matriculated at an accredited university for the upcoming academic year starting August/September, and must maintain full-time status for the duration of the Master's Degree

**Level of Study**: Postgraduate
**Type**: Scholarship
**Frequency**: Annual
**Study Establishment**: University of Sheffield
**Country of Study**: Any country
**Application Procedure**: You will be automatically considered for the scholarship if you receive an offer to study one of the eligible courses and you are a national of, or permanently domiciled in, one of the eligible countries or territories. Your course application will be assessed by a panel of academic judges to decide whether you will progress to the final stage of the application process. Please use our postgraduate online application system to submit your application for an eligible course. For further information, check the website link. www.sheffield.ac.uk/international/money/fergusonscholarship
**Closing Date**: 25 May
**Funding**: Private
**Contributor**: University of Sheffield
**Additional Information**: www.sheffield.ac.uk/international/fees-and-funding/scholarships/postgraduate/ferguson

### For further information contact:

The University of Sheffield, Western Bank, Sheffield S10 2TN, United Kingdom.

**Email**:   internationalscholarships@sheffield.ac.uk

## Economic and Social Research Council (ESRC) White Rose Doctoral Training Partnership (DTP) and Faculty Scholarships

**Purpose**: The University is part of the ESRC White Rose Doctoral Training Partnership - a collaboration between the Universities of Leeds, Sheffield, York, Sheffield Hallam, Hull, Bradford and Manchester Metropolitan University - and offers a range of ESRC Postgraduate Scholarships
**Eligibility**: Our Faculty scholarships are open to applicants of any nationality and in any discipline within the Faculty of Social Sciences. Most ESRC White Rose DTP scholarships are open to United Kingdom and European Union applicants; there may be limited opportunities for overseas students, and all applicants should check ESRC White Rose DTP guidance before making an application
**Level of Study**: Graduate, Postgraduate
**Type**: Scholarship
**Value**: Tuition Fees, an annual stipend and research training support grant
**Frequency**: Annual
**Study Establishment**: University of Sheffield
**Country of Study**: Any country
**Funding**: Private
**Additional Information**: www.sheffield.ac.uk/postgraduate/phd/scholarships/esrc

### For further information contact:

**Email**:   pgr-scholarships@sheffield.ac.uk

## Edward Bramley Excellence Postgraduate Scholarship

**Purpose**: The University of Sheffield is pleased to offer the Edward Bramley Excellence Postgraduate Scholarship to support an outstanding United Kingdom or European Union law student, based on academic excellence
**Eligibility**: 1. Be a UK/EU student for fee purposes. 2. Achieve a first-class honours degree at undergraduate Bachelors or Masters level. 3. Have an academic offer from us to study the full-time LLM (includes Sheffield LLM, LLM Corporate and Commercial Law and LLM International Law and Global Justice pathways) scheduled to commence

in September 2020. 4. have an application number. 5. provide a personal statement to evidence excellence.

**Type**: Scholarship

**Value**: University has one full fee waiver with £4,000 towards living costs for the outstanding student

**Country of Study**: United Kingdom

**Closing Date**: 12 June

**Contributor**: Edward Bramley Excellence

**Additional Information**: www.sheffield.ac.uk/law/postgrad uate/scholarships-and-fees

**For further information contact:**

**Email**:    law@sheffield.ac.uk

## Hossein Farmy Scholarship

**Purpose**: The Hossein Farmy Scholarship was founded by the late Hossein Farmy, a graduate of the University's former Department of Mining. It is available for students pursuing research related to mining. This includes the geological, engineering, scientific and technological aspects of mining, and the archaeological, economic, historical, legal and social aspects of mining and the mining industry.

**Eligibility**: 1. You should be intending to pursue a course of research related to mining. 2. You should have, or expect to achieve, a first or upper second class UK honours degree or equivalent qualifications gained outside the UK in an appropriate area of study. 3. You should be registering on your first year of doctoral study with the University for 2019-20. 4. Awards are open to UK applicants only.

**Value**: £15,009

**Country of Study**: United Kingdom

**Closing Date**: 30 April

**Funding**: Private

**Additional Information**: If you have any questions about the Hossein Farmy Scholarship please email pgr-scholarships@ sheffield.ac.uk www.sheffield.ac.uk/postgraduate/phd/schol arships/hossein-farmy

**For further information contact:**

**Email**:    pgr-scholarships@sheffield.ac.uk

## International Merit Postgraduate Scholarship

**Purpose**: Each scholarship is a competitive award worth 25% of the original tuition fee for a postgraduate taught programme starting in September 2020. The scholarships are available to all new international (non-EU) students who meet the eligibility criteria

**Value**: 50% of the annual postgraduate tuition fee

**Country of Study**: Any country

**Application Procedure**: Please visit website www.sheffield. ac.uk/international/enquiry/money/pgtmerit

**Closing Date**: 22 May

**Additional Information**: www.sheffield.ac.uk/international/ fees-and-funding/scholarships/postgraduate/international-merit-postgraduate-scholarship

**For further information contact:**

**Email**:    l.a.tarrant@sheffield.ac.uk

## Postgraduate Taught Sheffield Scholarship

**Purpose**: To offer the Postgraduate Taught Sheffield Scholarship to international students starting a taught masters programme in September

**Eligibility**: 1. To be eligible for the scholarship, applicants must be a national of or permanently domiciled in one of the following. 2. Your taught masters programme must be scheduled to commence at the University of Sheffield. 3. You must accept your offer for your course before 16:00 (UK time) on 15 June 2020 to receive this award. 4. Subject to meeting the eligibility and award criteria the International Postgraduate Taught Sheffield Scholarship 2020 will be awarded automatically - no application is required.

**Type**: Scholarship

**Value**: £2,000 if your tuition fees are between £16,800 and £18,900 and £2,500 if your tuition fees are £18,901 and upwards

**Country of Study**: United Kingdom

**Application Procedure**: Subject to meeting the eligibility and award criteria the Postgraduate Taught Sheffield Scholarship will be awarded automatically – no application is required

**Closing Date**: 15 June

**Additional Information**: www.sheffield.ac.uk/international/ fees-and-funding/scholarships/postgraduate/international-post graduate-taught-scholarship

**For further information contact:**

**Email**:    eurec@sheffield.ac.uk

## Sheffield Postgraduate Scholarships

**Purpose**: The scholarships are for students who meet at least one of our widening participation criteria and/or students who achieve a first in their undergraduate degree. If your application is successful you can use the scholarship towards fees or living expenses, the choice is yours

**Eligibility**: You can apply for a scholarship if you meet the following four criteria: Studying a taught postgraduate course full-time or part-time for a maximum of four years. Domiciled in the United Kingdom (United Kingdom) or European Union (European Union) and not charged international rate fees. Not already qualified at masters level, or higher. Must be self funding - courses fully funded by the NHS or the Initial Teacher Training bursary, or courses that are eligible for undergraduate funding such as integrated masters are not eligible

**Type**: Scholarship

**Value**: £10,000 each

**Country of Study**: United Kingdom

**Application Procedure**: A selection panel consisting of senior academic and professional services staff, will consider your scholarship application. The panel will look at personal circumstances of those who meet widening participation criteria and take into account achievements of the academic merit applicants. All applications are anonymised and the decision of the panel is discretionary and final

**Closing Date**: 11 May

**Additional Information**: If you have any questions or would like to talk to someone about the awards, please contact the Financial Support Team on 0114 222 1319 or sheffieldscholars@sheffield.ac.uk www.sheffield.ac.uk/postgraduate/taught/funding/sps#

### For further information contact:

**Tel**:       (44) 1142221319

**Email**:   funding@sheffield.ac.uk

## University Prize Scholarships

**Purpose**: Each year the University offers a small number of University Prize Scholarships to the very best PhD applicants

**Type**: Scholarship

**Value**: Full tuition fees (United Kingdom, European Union or overseas), an annual, tax-free maintenance stipend of £20,000, a Research Training Support Grant of £2,500 per year for study visits, conferences, books, consumables and equipment

**Country of Study**: United Kingdom

**Closing Date**: 23 January

**Additional Information**: If you have any questions about University Prize Scholarships please email pgr-scholarships@sheffield.ac.uk www.sheffield.ac.uk/postgraduate/phd/scholarships/prize

### For further information contact:

**Email**:   pgr-funding@sheffield.ac.uk

## White Rose Studentships

**Purpose**: Collaborative research networks within the three White Rose Universities

**Eligibility**: 1. These scholarships are only available to applicants to Sheffield Institute of Education (SIoE) and the Centre for Regional Economic and Social Research (CRESR). 2. UK applicants will be eligible for a full award (paying fees and maintenance at standard UKRI rates). EU applicants are normally eligible for a fees only award, unless they have been resident in the UK for 3 years immediately preceding the date of the award. These awards are not open to applicants who are liable to pay tuition fees at the International fee rate. 3. For 1 +3 and +3 awards, applicants must hold at least a UK upper second class honours degree or equivalent. 4. Where English is not your first language, you must show evidence of English language ability to the following minimum level of proficiency: an overall IELTS score of 7.0 or above, with at least 7.0 in each component or an accepted equivalent. Please note that your test score must be current, i.e. within the last two years. 5. Please note that students must be resident close to the University at which they are registered and we would expect there to be direct contact between the student and supervisor. This applies to full-time and part-time students.

**Level of Study**: Postgraduate, Research

**Type**: Studentship

**Value**: £15,009

**Length of Study**: 3 years

**Frequency**: Annual

**Study Establishment**: One of the three White Rose Universities

**Application Procedure**: Candidates can check the website for further details

**Closing Date**: 29 January

**Additional Information**: International applicants are only eligible if they can show sufficient funds to cover the difference between the United Kingdom and international students tuition fee www.shu.ac.uk/research/degrees/phd-scholarships/white-rose-dtp-scholarships

### For further information contact:

**Email**:   fdsresearch@shu.ac.uk

## University of South Australia

GPO Box 2471, Adelaide, SA 5001, Australia.

**Tel**:       (61) 8 8302 6611/3615

**Email**:   research.international@unisa.edu.au

**Website**:   www.unisa.edu.au

The University of South Australia is an innovative and successful institution with a distinctive profile. It is committed to educating professionals, creating and applying knowledge and serving the community.

## Division of Business Student Mobility Scholarships

**Purpose**: To assist business students undertaking an international exchange (via the UniSA International Student Exchange Program) at a partner university
**Eligibility**: Open to both undergraduate and postgraduate coursework students enroled in a Division of Business program and are participating in exchange for the first time
**Level of Study**: Postgraduate
**Type**: Scholarship
**Value**: AU$5,000 for Institutional Partner Scholarships; AU$2,500 for Student Mobility Scholarships
**Frequency**: Annual
**Application Procedure**: For extended criteria and application details, please contact: Ms Sarah Oolyer-Braham
**Closing Date**: 30 January
**Additional Information**: i.unisa.edu.au/students/scholarships/postgraduate-scholarships/unisa-business-school/

**For further information contact:**

**Tel**:     (61) 8 8302 0880
**Email**:   sarah.collyer-braham@unisa.edu.au

## Donald Dyer Scholarship – Public Relations & Communication Management

**Purpose**: To encourage research of an original nature leading to the advancement of knowledge in public relations and communication
**Eligibility**: Open to candidates who have achieved First Class (Honours) or equivalent. Candidates from discipline areas such as public relations, communication, marketing or advertising are encouraged to apply
**Level of Study**: Postgraduate, Research
**Type**: Scholarship
**Value**: AU$22,000 per year (tax-free) plus one return travel airfare between the candidate's home location and Adelaide, and organized by the University
**Frequency**: Annual
**Study Establishment**: University of South Australia
**Country of Study**: Australia
**Application Procedure**: Check website for further details
**Closing Date**: 29 October
**Contributor**: Bequest from the estate of the Late Sylvia Dyer

**For further information contact:**

**Tel**:     (61) 8 8302 4493
**Fax**:     (61) 8 8302 4745
**Email**:   david.brittan@unisa.edu.au

## Ferry Scholarship

**Purpose**: Promoting study and research in physics and chemistry
**Eligibility**: Open to Australian citizens under the age of 25 years on January 1st of the year of the award, who have completed at least 4 years of tertiary education studies, have a First Class (Honours) (or equivalent undergraduate degree), and have enroled as full–time students for a Master's Degree or Doctorate by research in chemistry or physics
**Level of Study**: Postgraduate
**Type**: Scholarship
**Value**: AU$7,500 per year
**Length of Study**: Up to 3 years (Doctorate) and 2 years (Masters Degree)
**Frequency**: Annual
**Application Procedure**: Applications can be filled online
**Closing Date**: 31 January
**Contributor**: Bequest from the late Cedric Arnold Seth Ferry
**Additional Information**: publictrustee.sa.gov.au/content/uploads/2018/10/2019-Scholarship-Application-form.pdf

**For further information contact:**

**Tel**:     (61) 8302 3967
**Email**:   jenni.critcher@unisa.edu.au

## Lewis O'Brien Scholarship

**Purpose**: To assist and encourage Aboriginal and Torres Strait Islander people in postgraduate study in a field of particular relevance and potential benefit to the Indigenous Australian community
**Eligibility**: Open to Aboriginal and Torres Strait Islander people eligible to undertake a postgraduate program in the division of education, arts and social sciences
**Level of Study**: Postgraduate
**Type**: Scholarship
**Value**: Maximum AU$10,000 per year (AU$2,500 will be paid on commencement and the remainder will be paid in instalments during the year subject to certification by the supervisor of satisfactory progress)
**Frequency**: Annual
**Country of Study**: Australia
**Application Procedure**: Candidates must contact Ms Jillian Mille for further information

**Closing Date**: 11 February
**Contributor**: Division of Education, Arts and Social Sciences
**Additional Information**: lc.academicworks.com/opportunities/790

### For further information contact:

**Tel**:        (61) 8 8302 9151
**Fax**:        (61) 8 8302 7034
**Email**:      jillian.miller@unisa.edu.au

## Margaret George Award

**Purpose**: To encourage and facilitate use of National Archives collection by promoting archival research in Australia and encouraging scholarly use of its holdings
**Eligibility**: Open to postgraduate degree holders, historians, academics, independent researchers, or journalists with a talent for research
**Level of Study**: Postgraduate
**Type**: Award
**Value**: AU$10,000
**Frequency**: Annual
**Country of Study**: Australia
**Application Procedure**: Check website for further details
**Closing Date**: 30 June
**Additional Information**: Successful applicants may undertake their award at any time from the date of the announcement of the award until June 30th the following year

### For further information contact:

**Tel**:        (61) 2 6212 3986
**Fax**:        (61) 2 6212 3699
**Email**:      derina.mclaughlin@naa.gov.au

## Research Training Program International Scholarships in Australia (RTPI)

**Purpose**: To offer Research Training Program international (RTPi) Scholarships
**Eligibility**: Generally, an applicant must have first-class Honours or equivalent to gain a scholarship at the University of South Australia. An awardee must be enrolled on a full-time basis as a candidate for a Masters by Research or PhD at the University of South Australia. An awardee shall be enrolled as an internal candidate at the University of South Australia
**Level of Study**: Research
**Type**: Scholarship
**Value**: At least AU$26,682 per annum for 3 years, with the possibility of one 6-month extension
**Length of Study**: 3 years

**Country of Study**: Any country
**Closing Date**: 31 August
**Funding**: Government
**Additional Information**: An RTPi scholarship will cover your tuition fees and your Overseas Student Health Cover (OSHC), and provide a stipend (living allowance), but will not pay for travel expenses. A thesis allowance is funded to cover the cost of printing and binding the thesis

### For further information contact:

**Email**:      research.degrees@unisa.edu.au

## Synchrotron Microprobe Analysis of Nickel Laterites Scholarship

**Purpose**: To enable deserving students to pursue a career in the related fields
**Eligibility**: Open to citizens or permanent residents of Australia or New Zealand who have achieved an Honours Degree or equivalent
**Level of Study**: Postgraduate
**Type**: Scholarship
**Value**: AU$4,000 per year
**Frequency**: Annual
**Study Establishment**: University of South Australia
**Country of Study**: Australia
**Application Procedure**: Applicants must write to the faculty
**Closing Date**: 30 September
**Contributor**: South Australian Premier's Science and Research Fund grant with matching funding from Rio Tinto and BHP-Billiton

### For further information contact:

**Email**:      andrea.gerson@unisa.edu.au

## Trevor Prescott Memorial Scholarship

**Purpose**: To help youth in the South Australian community to advance their careers through further postgraduate studies
**Eligibility**: Open to students between 20 and 30 years of age who desire to do further postgraduate studies or equivalent
**Level of Study**: Unrestricted
**Type**: Scholarship
**Value**: Up to AU$25,000 and may be divided between more than 1 recipient
**Frequency**: Annual
**Application Procedure**: Check website for further details
**Closing Date**: 30 June
**Funding**: Foundation
**Contributor**: The Masonic Foundation Inc

**Additional Information**: Preference is not given to a Freemason or to a member of the family for the scholarship freemasonsfoundation.com.au/pdf/trevor%20prescott.pdf

### For further information contact:

**Tel**:     (61) 8 8443 9909
**Fax**:    (61) 8 8443 9928
**Email**:  masfound@senet.com.au

## University of South Wales

Pontypridd, Wales NP18 3YG, United Kingdom.

**Tel**:     (44) 8455 767 778
**Email**:  enquiries@southwales.ac.uk
**Website**:  www.southwales.ac.uk

The University of Wales, Newport, has been involved in higher education for more than 80 years, and its roots go back even further to the first Mechanics Institute in the town, which opened in 1841.

### University of Wales Postgraduate Studentship

**Purpose**: To support a student with a First Class (Honours) Degree at the university to progress to postgraduate research
**Level of Study**: Doctorate, Doctorate
**Type**: Scholarship
**Frequency**: Annual
**Study Establishment**: University of Wales
**Country of Study**: Wales
**Application Procedure**: Applicants must check with the website or the University
**Funding**: Private, Private
**Contributor**: Private benefactions
**Additional Information**: www.wales.ac.uk/en/AboutUs/Alumni/Benefits/Scholarships.aspx

### For further information contact:

**Email**:  shelley.doolan@uwtsd.ac.uk

## University of Southampton

University of Southampton, University Road, Southampton SO17 1BJ, United Kingdom.

**Tel**:     (44) 238 059 5000
**Email**:  admissns@soton.ac.uk

**Website**:  www.soton.ac.uk
**Contact**:  Student Marketing Office

The University of Southampton was granted its Royal Charter. Today, the University is one of the United Kingdom's top ten research universities, offering a wide range of postgraduate taught and research courses in engineering, science, mathematics, law, arts, social sciences, medicine and health and life sciences.

### Honor Frost Foundation Masters and/or Doctoral Awards in Maritime Archaeology

**Purpose**: The Foundation's mission is to promote the advancement and research, including publication, of maritime archaeology with particular focus on the eastern Mediterranean
**Eligibility**: 1. The successful candidate must demonstrate a genuine interest in maritime archaeology and would be expected to develop the subject in their home country upon their return. 2. The successful candidate will also be required to submit annual reports on their progress to the Honor Frost Foundation and contribute towards the Foundation's activities during the duration of their studies, including supporting the annual lecture. 3. The MA Scholarship requires: a good 2:1 honours degree (or equivalent) in either archaeology or a related discipline. You must be a citizen of Cyprus, Lebanon, Egypt or Syria
**Level of Study**: Postgraduate
**Type**: Award
**Value**: an annual stipend of £15,000 with an additional travel fund of £1,000
**Frequency**: Annual
**Country of Study**: Any country
**Application Procedure**: The MA Scholarship requires: a good 2:1 honours degree (or equivalent) in either archaeology or a related discipline. You must be a citizen of Cyprus, Lebanon, Egypt or Syria. The MA scholarship is tenable for one year, commencing September, at an annual stipend of £15,000 with an additional travel fund of £1,000, which can be drawn as required during your study. Tuition fees will also be paid directly to the University at the appropriate fee rate. There may also be the opportunity to continue to PhD, fully funded, for a further 3 years on completion of the MA/MSc. Application for this studentship is by CV; a sample of written work (4,000 words, max); and a personal statement of up to 800 words explaining why you feel you are suitable for the MA or PhD scholarship. Please also arrange for two academic references to be sent independently by the deadline
**Closing Date**: 15 May
**Funding**: Private

**Additional Information**: educaloxy.com/honor-frost-foundation-masters-andor-doctoral-awards-in-maritime-archaeology,i6125.html

**For further information contact:**

**Email**:    lkb@soton.ac.uk

## University of Southern California (USC)

College of Letters, Arts and Sciences, University Park, Mail Code 4012, Los Angeles, CA 90089, United States of America.

**Tel**:          (1) 213 740 2531
**Website**:   www.usc.edu/schools/college
**Contact**:   Mr Richard Tithecott, Assistant Administrative Director

Located near the heart of Los Angeles, the University of Southern California (USC) is a private research university. It maintains a tradition of academic strength at all levels, from the earliest explorations of the undergraduate to the advanced scholarly research of the postdoctoral Fellow.

## Master of Business Administration/Master of Science in Industrial and Systems Engineering (MSISE) Programme

**Application Procedure**: Please contact the organisation for details

**For further information contact:**

**Tel**:          (1) 213 740 4893
**Fax**:          (1) 213 740 1120
**Email**:      gradapp@enroll1.usc.edu

## University of Stirling

University of Stirling, Stirling FK9 4LA, United Kingdom.

**Email**:      international@stir.ac.uk
**Website**:   www.stir.ac.uk

The University of Stirling is a United Kingdom research intensive campus university founded by Royal charter in 1967 in Stirling, Scotland. It is ranked among the top 60 universities in the world that are under 50 years old by the Times Higher Education World University Rankings.

## Postgraduate Awards for International Students at University of Stirling in United Kingdom

**Purpose**: The University, via its awards, aims to be at the forefront of research and learning that helps to improve lives
**Level of Study**: Postgraduate
**Type**: Award
**Value**: Each award has a value of £3,000
**Country of Study**: Scotland
**Application Procedure**: Students from eligible countries will automatically be assessed for an International Postgraduate Award as part of the admissions process; there is no separate application required for this award. Students who qualify for award will be notified by admissions, once academic offer conditions have been met
**Closing Date**: 31 August
**Additional Information**: For details, contact international@stir.ac.uk   www.scholarshipportal.com/scholarship/postgraduate-awards-for-international-students-at-univer sity-of-stirling-in-uk-2017

**For further information contact:**

**Email**:      graduate.admissions@stir.ac.uk

## University of Strasbourg

**Contact**:    Dr Stéphanie Loison, Scientific coordinator

Strasbourg has a long tradition of scientific excellence, in particularly in chemistry, built through the ages by renowned scientists such as Louis Pasteur, Charles Gerhardt and Nobel Laureates Adolf von Baeyer, Emil Fischer, Hermann Staudinger, Jean-Marie Lehn and more recently Martin Karplus (2013) and now Jean-Pierre Sauvage (2016). The result is that Strasbourg has always been a center of excellence in molecular science, with its top 20 worldwide ranking.

## PhD Fellowships in Chemistry

**Purpose**: To pursue PhD
**Eligibility**: Foreign students can apply for these PhD fellowships, as well as French national students, who wish to pursue

their PhD research study in Strasbourg from September or October

**Length of Study**: 3 years
**Country of Study**: France
**Closing Date**: 15 November
**Funding**: Foundation
**Contributor**: Ernest Solvay Fund and the FRC Foundation

### For further information contact:

**Email**:  admir.@scholarship-positions.com

## University of Strathclyde

McCance Building, 16 Richmond Street, Glasgow G1 1XQ, United Kingdom.

**Tel**:  (44) 14 1548 2387
**Email**:  r.livingston@mis.strath.ac.uk
**Website**:  www.strath.ac.uk

### Department of Chemical and Process Engineering PhD Studentship

**Eligibility**: Candidates should be highly motivated and have a First Class Honours degree in chemical engineering, physics or chemistry. An MSc/MEng in science or engineering and previous experience in the field of chemistry of materials would be an advantage. Students will engage in the Department's research seminar programme, and will have opportunities to attend national and international conferences. Other generic skills and courses are open to students, including scientific writing, presentation and careers workshops. International students must be proficient in English language (the University's entry requirements are IELTS 6.5, TOEFL 600 including the test of written English, TOEFL 250 computer based test or TOEFL 90–95 internet based test)
**Level of Study**: Doctorate
**Type**: Studentship
**Value**: The award will cover United Kingdom/European Union tuition fees and will pay a stipend of £13,863 per year (for 3 years). International students would have to pay the difference between the Home/European Union and international fee
**Length of Study**: 3 years
**Frequency**: Annual
**Study Establishment**: University of Strathclyde
**Country of Study**: Scotland

**Application Procedure**: Please send your curriculum vitae and a covering letter, indicating your previous experience and fields of interest and include the details of at least two academic referees to Dr S. V. Patwardhan
**Closing Date**: 30 May
**Additional Information**: www.surrey.ac.uk/postgraduate/chemical-and-process-engineering-research-phd

### For further information contact:

**Tel**:  (44) 141 548 5786
**Email**:  Siddharth.Patwardhan@strath.ac.uk

### Fraser of Allander Institute Scholarships for MSc Applied Economics

**Purpose**: Scholarships are available to join the MSc Applied Economics programme
**Value**: Each scholarship worth £6,000
**Country of Study**: United Kingdom
**Application Procedure**: Candidates interested in applying should provide a maximum 1,000 word statement demonstrating, through their ideas, experience and future career plans (including their reasoning for joining the MSc Applied Economics) why they should be awarded this scholarship. Candidates will also be considered on the overall quality of their application and financial need. The mode of applying is online. Please visit website www.sbs.strath.ac.uk/apps/scholarships/economics/applied-economics.asp
**Closing Date**: 30 January
**Additional Information**: For more details, please visit the website www.strath.ac.uk/studywithus/scholarships/strathclydebusinessschoolscholarships/economicsscholarships/fraserofallanderinstitutefaihomeeuscholarshipsformscappliedeconomics/

### For further information contact:

**Email**:  sbs.admissions@strath.ac.uk

### International Marketing Bursaries

**Purpose**: To assist applicants who are seeking sources of financial assistance to pursue full-time postgraduate study in international marketing
**Eligibility**: A limited number of departmental bursaries are available to well qualified candidates
**Level of Study**: Postgraduate
**Type**: Departmental bursaries
**Value**: £3,000
**Length of Study**: 1 year

**Frequency**: Annual
**Study Establishment**: University of Strathclyde
**Country of Study**: United Kingdom
**Application Procedure**: Applicants must contact the Department of Marketing
**Contributor**: Department of Marketing, Strathclyde University

### For further information contact:

**Tel**:       (44) 141 548 3451
**Email**:    mscim.helpdesk@strath.ac.uk

## International Strathclyde Prestige Award for Excellence in Business Translation and Interpreting in United Kingdom

**Purpose**: Scholarship is available for pursuing Postgraduate degree program
**Eligibility**: To be eligible, the applicants must meet all the following criteria: 1. To apply for this scholarship, the applicants must be available to commence their academic studies in the United Kingdom. By the start of the academic year in September. 2. The candidates must hold a first degree at first class or upper second class honors, or equivalent
**Level of Study**: Postgraduate
**Type**: Award
**Value**: £5,000 with tuition fees
**Frequency**: Annual
**Country of Study**: United Kingdom
**Application Procedure**: 1. Applications must be processed with the below link. r1.dotmailer-surveys.com/432p4736-ae3nzoab
**Closing Date**: 31 May
**Funding**: Private
**Additional Information**: For further information, check the following link: r1.dotmailer-surveys.com/432p4736-ae3nzoab scholarship-positions.com/international-strathclyde-prestige-award-for-excellence-in-business-translation-interpreting-in-uk/2019/03/12/

### For further information contact:

**Email**:    hass-pg-enquiries@strath.ac.uk

## John Mather Scholarship

**Purpose**: To encourage potential rising stars in the business world, selected on the basis of academic merit
**Eligibility**: Open to students from the vicinity of the former Strathclyde Region area enrolled in postgraduate instructional courses

**Level of Study**: Postgraduate
**Type**: Scholarship
**Value**: £5,000
**Length of Study**: 1 year
**Frequency**: Annual
**Study Establishment**: Strathclyde Business School
**Country of Study**: United Kingdom
**Application Procedure**: Applicants must be nominated by their Head of Department on forms available from the Faculty Officer
**No. of awards offered**: 10
**Closing Date**: 23 July
**Funding**: Trusts
**Contributor**: John Mather Charitable Trust
**No. of awards given last year**: 4
**No. of applicants last year**: 10
**Additional Information**: spacegrant.org/programs/john-mather/

### For further information contact:

**Email**:    e.leiper@mis.strath.ac.uk

## Mac Robertson Travelling Scholarship

**Purpose**: To provide funding that will enrich and further the award holder's academic experience and research achievements
**Eligibility**: Applicants should be postgraduate research students currently registered at Strathclyde or Glasgow Universities
**Level of Study**: Postgraduate, Research
**Type**: Scholarship
**Value**: £2,000–3,000
**Length of Study**: 1 year
**Frequency**: Annual
**Study Establishment**: University of Strathclyde
**Country of Study**: United Kingdom
**Application Procedure**: Application forms can be downloaded from the website www.strath.ac.uk
**No. of awards offered**: 20
**Closing Date**: 4 May
**Funding**: Individuals
**Contributor**: Mac Robertson
**No. of awards given last year**: 11
**No. of applicants last year**: 20
**Additional Information**: The aim of the scheme is to provide funding which will enrich and further the award holder's experience and research achievements www.strath.ac.uk/studywithus/scholarships/macrobertsontravellingscholarship/

### For further information contact:

**Email**:    cathy.bonner@mis.strath.ac.uk

## University of Strathclyde and Glasgow Synergy Scholarships

**Purpose**: To assist applicants and students who are seeking sources of financial assistance to pursue full-time postgraduate research study at the University of Strathclyde
**Eligibility**: Applicants should be PhD candidates of outstanding academic merit
**Level of Study**: Doctorate
**Type**: Scholarship
**Value**: £12,600 per year
**Length of Study**: Up to 3 years
**Frequency**: Annual
**Study Establishment**: University of Strathclyde
**Country of Study**: United Kingdom
**Application Procedure**: Applicants seeking nomination for the awards should contact the department they wish to join. Existing research students should contact their head of department or supervisor
**Funding**: International office
**Contributor**: University
**Additional Information**: For more information, visit the website www.strath.gla.ac.uk/synergy www.strath.ac.uk/studywithus/scholarships/

### For further information contact:

**Email**: synergy@gla.ac.uk

## University of Surrey

University of Surrey, Guildford GU2 7XH, United Kingdom.

**Tel**: (44) 148 386 050
**Email**: maphdinfo@surrey.ac.uk
**Website**: www.maths.surrey.ac.uk

## Studentship in Physical Sciences

**Purpose**: The aim of this project is to determine the microscopic length scales that control the macroscopic rheology using novel magnetic resonance imaging and optical light scattering techniques in combination with conventional tools
**Eligibility**: To be eligible for this studentship, you are required to have a First, 2:1 or merit in a masters degree in a physical sciences subject. If English is not your first language you are required to have an IELTS of 6.5 or above. United Kingdom and European Union candidates are eligible to apply. Activities at the Cambridge centre focus on the

development of new science and technology for well construction, with an emphasis on drilling and automation
**Level of Study**: Graduate
**Type**: Studentship
**Frequency**: Annual
**Country of Study**: Any country
**Application Procedure**: In order to apply for this studentship, kindly contact Noelle Hartley, Centre Manager for the EPSRC CDT in MiNMaT Greater understanding of the hierarchy of relevant structural lengths from the nanoscale to the macroscale will enable the design of improved complex fluid formulations with predictable rheological properties. N.Hartley@surrey.ac.uk
**Closing Date**: 30 April
**Funding**: Private

### For further information contact:

**Tel**: (44) 1483 683467
**Email**: N.Hartley@surrey.ac.uk

## University of Sussex

Postgraduate Office, Sussex House, Falmer, Brighton BN1 9RH, United Kingdom.

**Tel**: (44) 1273 606 755
**Email**: information@sussex.ac.uk
**Website**: www.sussex.ac.uk
**Contact**: Mr Terry O'Donnell

The University of Sussex is one of the United Kingdom's foremost research institutions. The University boasts a distinguished faculty that includes 17 Fellows of the Royal Society and four Fellows of the British Academy. The University has around 12,000 students, 25% of whom are postgraduates.

## Chancellor's International Scholarship

**Purpose**: Applications are invited for University of Sussex to international postgraduate students who can demonstrate academic excellence
**Value**: 50% tuition fee reduction
**Length of Study**: 2 years
**Country of Study**: Any country
**Application Procedure**: Apply online. For application procedures, please visit website www.sussex.ac.uk/study/money/apply-chancellors-international-scholarship
**Closing Date**: May

**Contributor**: University of Sussex
**Additional Information**: www.sussex.ac.uk/study/fees-funding/masters-scholarships/view/1005-Chancellor%E2%80%99s-International-Scholarship

## PhD Studentships in Mathematics

**Eligibility**: Applicants must hold, or expect to hold, a Bachelor degree at first or upper second class, and/or a Masters degree, in Mathematics, or equivalent non United Kingdom qualifications. United Kingdom and European Union residents are eligible. Overseas (ex-European Union) students may also apply, but applicants should note that the awards waive the fees at United Kingdom/European Union rates only, of £3,900 per year. Ex-European Union students must state in their application how they would fund the remaining fees. (Overseas fees will be £13,000 per year in total, so additional funding of £9,100 will be needed)
**Level of Study**: Doctorate
**Type**: Studentship
**Value**: £15,009
**Length of Study**: Scholarships will be offered for 3.5 years
**Country of Study**: United Kingdom
**Application Procedure**: The mode of applying is online
**Closing Date**: 31 January
**Contributor**: University of Sussex, United Kingdom
**Additional Information**: www.ed.ac.uk/student-funding/postgraduate/international/science-engineering/mathematics/maths

### For further information contact:

**Email**:    pgresearch@maths.ed.ac.uk

## Sussex Malaysia Scholarship

**Purpose**: The aim of the Sussex Master Scholarship is to enable and encourage academically able students from Malaysia
**Eligibility**: Listed are the eligibility requirements. 1. Be a Malaysian national. 2. Be classified as overseas for fee purposes. 3. Be self-financing. 4. Have accepted an offer to study an eligible Masters course at Sussex
**Type**: Scholarship
**Value**: £3,500 towards your tuition fee when you register on your Masters at Sussex
**Length of Study**: 2 years
**Country of Study**: United Kingdom
**Application Procedure**: Register your interest in the scholarship through the postgraduate application system when you accept our offer of a place on an eligible Masters course. To submit the registration, use the below link. www.sussex.ac.uk/study/masters/apply/log-into-account
**Closing Date**: 1 August
**Contributor**: University of Sussex
**Additional Information**: www.sussex.ac.uk/study/fees-funding/masters-scholarships/view/970-Sussex-Malaysia-Scholarship

### For further information contact:

**Email**:    scholarships@sussex.ac.uk

## University of Sussex Chancellor's International Scholarships

**Purpose**: University of Sussex Chancellor's International Scholarships are available in the majority of Sussex Schools, and are awarded on the basis of academic performance and potential to non-EU international students who have applied for and been offered a place for eligible full-time Postgraduate Taught degrees at the University of Sussex.
**Eligibility**: 1. be classified as overseas for fee purposes. 2. have accepted a place on a full time eligible Masters, commencing at the University of Sussex in September 2020. 3. have excellent grades (UK first class or equivalent) 4. have clear and specific goals with defined links to your course. As there are limited scholarships available, this scholarship is extremely competitive (for 2019 entry, the University received more than 1,000 applications for only 25 awards).
**Level of Study**: Masters Degree
**Type**: Scholarships
**Value**: 50% reduction of the overseas tuition fee
**Frequency**: annual
**Country of Study**: UK
**Application Procedure**: To be considered for the Chancellors International Scholarship, you need to have received and accepted an offer of a place on an eligible Masters at Sussex. To apply, you must complete the online application form. The deadline is 1 May 23:59 GMT. It is important to visit the official website (link found below) to access the online application form and for detailed information on how to apply for this scholarship.
**No. of awards offered**: 25
**Closing Date**: 1 May
**Additional Information**: www.sussex.ac.uk/study/fees-funding/masters-scholarships/view/1094-Chancellor%E2%80%99s-International-Scholarship

### For further information contact:

**Email**:    study@sussex.ac.uk

# University of Sydney

Scholarships and Financial Support Service, Jane Foss Russell Building, G02, Sydney, NSW 2006, Australia.

| | |
|---|---|
| **Tel**: | (61) 2 8627 8112 |
| **Email**: | scholarships.officer@sydney.edu.au |
| **Website**: | www.sydney.edu.au |
| **Contact**: | Manager |

## Alexander Hugh Thurland Scholarship

**Eligibility**: Open to the graduates from other universities with relevant degree

**Level of Study**: Doctorate, Postgraduate, Research

**Type**: Scholarship

**Value**: AU$24,653 per year

**Length of Study**: 2 years for Masters by research candidates and 3 years with a possible 6-month extension for research doctoral candidates

**Frequency**: Dependent on funds available

**Study Establishment**: The University of Sydney

**Country of Study**: Australia

**Application Procedure**: Check website www.sydney.edu.au/agriculture

**Funding**: Trusts

### For further information contact:

| | |
|---|---|
| **Tel**: | (61) 2 8627 1002 |
| **Fax**: | (61) 2 8627 1099 |
| **Email**: | pg@agric.usyd.edu.au |

## Dean's International Postgraduate Research Scholarships

**Purpose**: Scholarships are available to undertake a research doctorate degree (PhD) programme

**Eligibility**: To be eligible, the applicants must meet all the given criteria: 1. have an offer of admission for full-time studies in a master's by research or doctor of philosophy (PhD) 2. be currently enrolled either a. the final year of at least a four-year bachelor's degree in science or relevant discipline area, b. an equivalent degree at a non-Australian university, with at least 25% of the final year of the degree being a research component 3. have achieved a minimum weighted average mark (WAM) equivalent to a grade of 85 not be an Australian citizen or permanent resident, or a New Zealand citizen 4. apply for a Research Training Program (RTP) Fee Offset and Stipend scholarship

**Level of Study**: Postgraduate

**Value**: The scholarship consists of the full cost of academic tuition fees plus a stipend equivalent to an Australian Postgraduate Award indexed annually (RTP stipend rates for 2016 are AU$26,288 for full-time students)

**Length of Study**: 3 years

**Study Establishment**: Faculty of Science

**Country of Study**: Australia

**Application Procedure**: International students (except Australia or New Zealand) can apply for these postgraduate research scholarships. An annual stipend allowance equivalent to the Research Training Program (RTP) stipend rate indexed annually

**Closing Date**: 30 April

**Additional Information**: For more details, visit website scholarship-positions.com/deans-international-postgraduate-research-scholarships-in-australia-2015-2016/2015/03/03/ scholarship-positions.com/deans-international-postgraduate-research-scholarship-at-the-university-of-sydney-australia/2019/02/01/

## Dr Abdul Kalam International Postgraduate Scholarships

**Eligibility**: 1. Be an international student 2. Have an unconditional offer of admission for a master's by coursework in the Faculty of Engineering 3. Have achieved a minimum WAM of 75 in your undergraduate studies 4. Be commencing your degree in the same semester and year the scholarship is offered.

**Level of Study**: Postgraduate

**Type**: Scholarship

**Value**: Half of tuition fees

**Frequency**: Annual

**Country of Study**: United States of America

**Application Procedure**: Applicants must complete an online scholarship application (sydney.edu.au/engineering/scholarships/postgraduate/dr-kalam.shtml)

**Closing Date**: April

**Additional Information**: Please check at sydney.edu.au/engineering/scholarships/postgraduate/future-coursework.shtml sydney.edu.au/scholarships/b/dr-abdul-kalam-international-scholarship.html

### For further information contact:

| | |
|---|---|
| **Tel**: | (61) 2 8627 1444 |
| **Fax**: | (61) 2 9351 7082 |
| **Email**: | engineering.scholarships@sydney.edu.au |

## International Postgraduate Research Scholarships (IPRS) Australian Postgraduate Awards (APA)

**Purpose**: To support candidates with exceptional research potential

**Eligibility**: Open to suitably qualified graduates eligible to commence a higher degree by research. Australia and New Zealand citizens and Australian permanent residents are not eligible to apply

**Level of Study**: Doctorate, Postgraduate, Research

**Type**: Scholarship

**Value**: Tuition fees for IPRS, and an Australian Postgraduate Award for AU$24,653 per year

**Length of Study**: 2 years for the Master's by research candidates, and 3 years with a possible 6-month extension for PhD candidates

**Frequency**: Annual

**Study Establishment**: The University of Sydney

**Country of Study**: Australia

**Application Procedure**: Applicants must complete an application form for admission available from the International Office

**Closing Date**: 15 December

**Funding**: Government

**Contributor**: Australian Government and University of Sydney

**No. of awards given last year**: 34

### For further information contact:

**Tel**:       (61) 2 8627 8358
**Fax**:      (61) 2 8627 8387
**Email**:   infoschol@io.usyd.edu.au

## Master of Business Administration Programme

**Length of Study**: 1 year

**Application Procedure**: Applicants must complete an application form supplying official transcripts and a Graduate Management Admission Test score

**Closing Date**: 31 October

### For further information contact:

**Tel**:       (61) 2 9351 0038
**Fax**:      (61) 2 9351 0099
**Email**:   gsbinfo@gsb.usyd.edu

## PhD Scholarship Healthcare Services for Older People

**Purpose**: To investigate the effectiveness of transition care services for older people

**Eligibility**: Open only to permanent residents and the citizens of Australia or New Zealand who have Honours Degree, or equivalent, in health–related discipline to undertake research studies

**Level of Study**: Postgraduate

**Type**: Scholarship

**Value**: AU$22,000 per year

**Length of Study**: 3 years

**Frequency**: Annual

**Study Establishment**: University of Sydney

**Application Procedure**: Applicants must send their curriculum vitae, copy of academic transcript, names and contact details of at least 2 referees to Prof Cameron (preferably by email)

**Closing Date**: 14 August

### For further information contact:

**Tel**:       (61) 2 9808 9236
**Fax**:      (61) 2 9809 9037
**Email**:   ianc@mail.usyd.edu.au

## PhD Scholarship to Advance Aquaculture in Australasia

**Purpose**: To improve the productivity and profitability of smallholder shrimp farms in Indonesia

**Eligibility**: Open only to the citizens of Australia or permanent residents

**Level of Study**: Postgraduate, Research

**Type**: Scholarship

**Value**: AU$25,000 per year

**Length of Study**: 3 years

**Frequency**: Annual

**Application Procedure**: Applicants must mail their curriculum vitae, copy of academic transcript, proof of citizenship or permanent residency, names and contact details of at least 2 referees to Dr Toribio

**Closing Date**: 17 August

### For further information contact:

**Tel**:       (61) 612 9351 1609
**Fax**:      (61) 612 9351 1618
**Email**:   jennyt@camden.usyd.edu.au

## University of Tasmania

Private Bag 45, Hobart, TAS 7001, Australia.

**Tel**:       (61) 3 6226 2999
**Email**:   scholarships@research.utas.edu.au

**Website**: www.utas.edu.au
**Contact**: Graduate Research Unit

The University of Tasmania was officially founded on January 1st 1890, by an Act of the Colony's Parliament and was only the fourth university to be established in 19th century Australia. The university represents areas of significant research strengths and substantial teaching endeavours.

## Across PhD – Bio Analytical Research – Pharmacokinetics and Drug Metabolism Scholarship

**Purpose**: To promote research on retention mechanisms, breakthrough, and recovery for the model analytes together with appropriate characterization of the monolithic phase
**Eligibility**: Open to applicants who have achieved Honours 2a or equivalent
**Level of Study**: Postgraduate, Research
**Type**: Scholarship
**Value**: AU$20,000 for living expenses
**Length of Study**: 3 and a half years
**Frequency**: Annual
**Application Procedure**: Applicants should send a curriculum vitae directly to Prof Paul Haddad. Check website for further details
**Contributor**: Pfizer Analytical Research Centre (PARC)

### For further information contact:

**Tel**:     (61) 3 6226 2179
**Email**:   paul.haddad@utas.edu.au

## Across PhD Scholarship; Analytical Chemistry; Rock Lobster Aquaculture

**Eligibility**: Open to applicants who have achieved Honours 2a or equivalent
**Level of Study**: Postgraduate, Research
**Type**: Scholarship
**Value**: AU$25,118 for living expenses
**Length of Study**: 3 and a half years
**Frequency**: Annual
**Application Procedure**: Applicants should send a curriculum vitae directly to Prof Paul Haddad. Check website for further details

### For further information contact:

**Tel**:     (61) 3 6226 2179
**Email**:   paul.haddad@utas.edu.au

## Across PhD, High Performance Ion Exchange Chromatography Scholarship

**Purpose**: To investigate the feasibility of using HP-IEC for the separation and detection of small to medium MW organic acids and bases
**Eligibility**: Open to applicants who have achieved Honours 2a or equivalent
**Level of Study**: Postgraduate, Research
**Type**: Scholarship
**Value**: AU$20,000 for living expenses
**Length of Study**: 3 and a half years
**Frequency**: Annual
**Country of Study**: Australia
**Application Procedure**: Applicants should send a curriculum vitae directly to Prof Paul Haddad. Check website for further details
**Contributor**: Pfizer Analytical Research Centre (PARC)

## Cancer Council Honours Scholarship

**Purpose**: To fund honours student to undertake research on cancer
**Eligibility**: Open to a full-time student undertaking honours in any area that focuses on cancer control
**Level of Study**: Research
**Type**: Scholarship
**Value**: AU$10,000 (AU$7,000 for living allowance and AU$3,000 for research costs)
**Length of Study**: 1 year
**Frequency**: Annual
**Application Procedure**: Check website for further details
**Closing Date**: 31 October
**Additional Information**: www.cancerwa.asn.au/cancer-research/i-am-a-cancer-researcher/funding/honours-masters-scholarships/

### For further information contact:

**Tel**:     (61) 3 6226 4832
**Email**:   g.m.woods@utas.edu.au

## Cardiac Rehabilitation UTAS Exercise Physiology Graduate Research Scholarship

**Purpose**: To investigate the effectiveness of provision of an exercise physiology service as part of a cardiac rehabilitation program, as well as identifying the optimal modality and intensity of exercise undertaken by patients as part of the program

**Eligibility**: Open to applicants who have achieved Honours 2a or equivalent. Only citizens of Australia or permanent residents can apply
**Level of Study**: Postgraduate, Research
**Type**: Scholarship
**Value**: AU$19,616
**Length of Study**: 3 years
**Frequency**: Annual
**Study Establishment**: University of Tasmania
**Country of Study**: Australia
**Application Procedure**: Check website for further details
**Closing Date**: 30 June
**Additional Information**: www.utas.edu.au/exercise-phys iology-clinic/cardiac-rehabilitation

### For further information contact:

**Tel**:      (61) 3 6324 5487
**Email**:   Andrew.Williams@utas.edu.au

## Centre of Excellence in Ore Deposits PhD Scholarships

**Purpose**: For students to study within one of the five major programs of the centre: location, formation, discovery, recovery or technology
**Eligibility**: Open to students undertaking PhD research in the specified fields. Applicants require either an MSc in geology/geophysics or a first or upper second–class honours degree. Some experience in the minerals industry is preferred but not essential
**Level of Study**: Postgraduate
**Value**: AU$20,000 - AU$30,000 depending on qualifications and experience
**Length of Study**: 3 and a half years
**Additional Information**: www.utas.edu.au/codes/available-rhd-projects

### For further information contact:

**Tel**:      (61) 3 6226 2892
**Email**:   j.mcphie@utas.edu.au

## Master of Business Administration Programme

**Length of Study**: Varies
**Application Procedure**: Applicants must contact The University of Tasmania Graduate School of Management for an application form

### For further information contact:

**Tel**:      (61) 2 2078 37
**Fax**:     (61) 2 2078 62
**Email**:   International.Office@admin.utas.edu.au

## Menzies Research Institute Honours Scholarship

**Purpose**: To support vital work in epidemiology, and diseases which affect the community
**Eligibility**: Open to a student eligible to undertake an honours research program in any area of research undertaken by the Institute
**Level of Study**: Research
**Type**: Scholarship
**Value**: AU$5,000
**Length of Study**: 1 year
**Frequency**: Annual
**Country of Study**: Any country
**Application Procedure**: Applicants can apply through the Tasmania Honours Scholarship application form downloaded from the website. All potential honours students should contact the Honours Co-ordinator in their discipline to discuss interests and options
**Closing Date**: 31 October
**Additional Information**: menzies.utas.edu.au/education/study-at-menzies/scholarships-and-awards/honours-scholar ships-at-menzies

### For further information contact:

**Email**:   enquiries@menzies.utas.edu.au

## North Hobart Football Club Peter Wells Scholarships

**Purpose**: To support North Hobart players while at UTAS
**Eligibility**: One scholarship available to a north-western/northern student and one to a southern student with good academic records and who are available to play for the NHFC while studying at UTAS
**Type**: Scholarship
**Value**: AU$3,000 and AU$2,000
**Length of Study**: 1 year
**Frequency**: Annual
**Country of Study**: Any country
**Contributor**: The late Peter Wells

### For further information contact:

**Email**:   International.Scholarships@utas.edu.au

## Qantas Tasmanian Devil Research Scholarship

**Purpose**: To assist research into the facial tumour disease affecting devil populations
**Eligibility**: Open to researchers in facial tumour diseases
**Level of Study**: Research
**Type**: Scholarship
**Value**: Up to APA level, additional research funding may be available
**Length of Study**: 3 and a half years
**Frequency**: Annual
**Country of Study**: Any country
**Application Procedure**: Check website for further details
**Contributor**: Qantas
**Additional Information**: www.cnaviationplane.com/news/0/981.html

### For further information contact:

**Email**:    devil.appeal@utas.edu.au

## Quantitative Marine Science PhD Scholarships

**Purpose**: To offer specialized graduate-level coursework in quantitative marine science (QMS)
**Eligibility**: Open to students who hold at least an upper second-class honours degree, or equivalent, and have a major in mathematics, physical sciences, life sciences, geomatics or Engineering
**Level of Study**: Doctorate
**Type**: Scholarship
**Value**: AU$32,000 per annum. and production costs will also be provided
**Length of Study**: Up to 3 years
**Frequency**: Annual
**Country of Study**: Any country
**Application Procedure**: Application forms, conditions of awards and program information on Graduate Research Scholarships can be downloaded from the website
**Funding**: Private
**Contributor**: Commonwealth Scientific and Industrial Research Organisation (CSIRO) in partnership with the University of Tasmania
**Additional Information**: For further information on all Graduate Research Scholarships please contact the Graduate Research Office on (3) 6226 2766

### For further information contact:

CSIRO-UTAS Joint PhD Program in Quantitative Marine Science, Private Bag 129, Hobart, TAS 7001, Australia.

**Tel**:    (61) 3 6226 2108
**Email**:    Peter.Strutton@utas.edu.au

## Riawunna Postgraduate Scholarship

**Purpose**: To encourage an Aboriginal or Torres Strait Islander student to undertake honours or postgraduate coursework study at the University and committed to the advancement of knowledge about Aboriginal and Torres Strait Islander cultures and societies
**Eligibility**: Open to an Aboriginal or Torres Strait Islander student who undertake honours or postgraduate coursework study at the University
**Level of Study**: Postgraduate
**Type**: Scholarship
**Value**: AU$3,000
**Length of Study**: 1 year
**Frequency**: Annual
**Country of Study**: Any country
**Contributor**: Riawunna
**Additional Information**: www.utas.edu.au/riawunna/scholarships

### For further information contact:

**Email**:    scholarships.referee@utas.edu.au

## Sir Victor Burley Scholarship in Music

**Purpose**: The family of Victor Burley has endowed this scholarship to encourage the development of advanced music skills, especially in the classical music area
**Eligibility**: Open to student eligible to enter a postgraduate music course at the Conservatorium of Music preferably studying in a classical area of music
**Level of Study**: Postgraduate
**Type**: Scholarship
**Value**: AU$1,000
**Length of Study**: 1 year
**Frequency**: Annual
**Country of Study**: Australia
**Contributor**: The family of the late Sir Victor Burley
**Additional Information**: info.scholarships.utas.edu.au/Award Details.aspx?AwardId=218

### For further information contact:

**Email**:    Scholarships.Referee@utas.edu.au

## Tasmania Honours Scholarships

**Purpose**: To encourage excellent students to continue their study at honours level
**Eligibility**: Open to students with excellent academic achievement in their undergraduate courses who wish to

study at honours level. Additional benefits may be available to students who obtain a first-class honours degree and continue on to a research program at UTAS

**Level of Study**: Postgraduate

**Type**: Scholarship

**Value**: AU$4,500; AU$9,000 include a living allowance, course fees, support with accommodation and establishment fees and a return airfare to Tasmania if you live interstate

**Length of Study**: 1 year (full-time study)

**Frequency**: Annual

**Country of Study**: Any country

**Application Procedure**: Applicants can apply through the Tasmania Honours Scholarship application form from the website. All potential honours students should contact the Honours Co-ordinator in their discipline to discuss interests and options

**Closing Date**: 31 October

**Additional Information**: Six of the 10 awards will target students commencing study at the University of Tasmania info.scholarships.utas.edu.au/AwardDetails.aspx?AwardId=41

**For further information contact:**

**Email**:     Scholarships.Referee@utas.edu.au

## Tasmania University Cricket Club Scholarship

**Purpose**: To support cricketers at UTAS

**Eligibility**: Available to a commencing or current student who can demonstrate a talent and commitment to cricket. Selection will based on the following five criteria: 1. Cricket skill i.e. representative levels and success at those levels. 2. Academic achievement and potential to succeed at university. 3. Leadership skills and experiences. 4. Cricket involvement e.g. coaching. 5. Community involvement. The selected student must be playing for, or be able to play for, the TUCC in the coming season. Potential applicants may also wish to visit the Cricket website

**Type**: Scholarship

**Value**: AU$3,000

**Length of Study**: 1 year

**Frequency**: Annual

**Country of Study**: Any country

**Application Procedure**: Apply online prior to closing date. Applications cannot be submitted after closing date. As applicants will be assessed on the quality of application, all questions should be answered in full. Please ensure care is taken with spelling and grammar. info.scholarships.utas.edu.au/AwardDetails.aspx?AwardId=281

**Closing Date**: 31 October

**Contributor**: Supporters and past players of the Tasmania University Cricket Club

**Additional     Information**:     info.scholarships.utas.edu.au/AwardDetails.aspx?AwardId=281

**For further information contact:**

**Email**:     chas.rose@gmail.com

## Tasmanian Government Mining Honours Scholarships

**Purpose**: To encourage geological research at CODES on topics that are relevant to the Tasmanian minerals industry

**Eligibility**: Open to students undertaking research in the field of geology, with relevance to the Tasmanian minerals industry. Specialization in one or more of: ore deposit geology, igneous petrology, volcanology, structure, sedimentology, geochemistry or geophysics. Applicants require at least a credit average in geology units at the second or third year levels

**Level of Study**: Research

**Type**: Scholarship

**Value**: AU$5,000; AU$8,000 depending on qualifications and experience

**Length of Study**: 1 year

**Frequency**: Annual

**Application Procedure**: Applicants can apply through the Tasmania Honours Scholarship application form downloaded from the website

**Closing Date**: 31 October

**Contributor**: Mineral Resources Tasmania

**For further information contact:**

**Tel**:       (61) 3 6226 2815

**Email**:     garry.davidson@utas.edu.au

## Tasmanian Government Mining PhD Scholarship

**Purpose**: To encourage geological research undertaken at the ARC Centre of Excellence in Ore Deposits (CODES) on topics relevant to the Tasmanian minerals industry

**Eligibility**: The following eligibility criteria apply to this scholarship: 1. The scholarship is open to domestic (Australian and New Zealand) and international candidates. 2. The Research Higher Degree must be undertaken on a full-time basis. 3. Applicants must already have been awarded a First Class Honours degree or hold equivalent qualifications or relevant and substantial research experience in an appropriate sector. 4. Applicants must be able to demonstrate strong research and analytical skills

**Level of Study**: Doctorate, Research

**Type**: Scholarship

**Value**: AU$18,000–25,000 depending on qualifications and experience
**Length of Study**: 3 and a half years
**Frequency**: Annual
**Country of Study**: Any country
**Contributor**: Mineral Resources Tasmania

**For further information contact:**

**Tel**: (61) 3 6226 2819
**Email**: anita.parbhakar@utas.edu.au

---

## University of Technology Sydney (UTS)

PO Box 123 Broadway, Ultimo, NSW 2007, Australia.

**Tel**: (61) 2 9514 1659
**Email**: clg.postgraduate@uts.edu.au
**Contact**: UTS Institute for Public Policy and Governance

The University of Technology Sydney (UTS) is a thriving university located in the centre of Sydney, one of the world's most desirable and multicultural cities.

### University of Technology Sydney Institute for Public Policy and Governance Postgraduate Scholarship in Australia, 2017

**Purpose**: To support commencing University of Technology Sydney (UTS) Master of Local Government students by assisting them financially.
**Eligibility**: Australian or New Zealand citizen, or the holder of an Australian permanent resident visa or permanent humanitarian visa; and must have submitted an application and met the entry requirements for admission to the UTS Institute for Public Policy and Governance Master of Local Government degree by coursework degree; and must be commencing the UTS Institute for Public Policy and Governance Master of Local Government program; and must not have completed any study under any other postgraduate courses within the UTS Institute for Public Policy and Governance; and intend to enroll in a minimum of 12 credit points/session in the session immediately following the Scholarship selection; and all candidates must apply using the online UTS online Scholarship Application form to be eligible.
**Level of Study**: Postgraduate
**Type**: Scholarship
**Value**: The maximum value of this scholarship is AU$5,000 for each recipient

**Length of Study**: 1 year
**Frequency**: Annual
**Country of Study**: Any country
**Application Procedure**: Please note that Scholarship applicants must first submit an application for the UTS Master of Local Government to be considered for the Scholarship. To apply for the Master course, please request an application form from the Institute at postgraduate-at-uts.edu.au or on (61) 2 9514 1659.
**Closing Date**: 6 March
**Funding**: Government
**Additional Information**: The UTS Institute for Public Policy and Governance (UTS:IPPG) Postgraduate Scholarship was designed to support local government professionals seeking to broaden their knowledge and skills through postgraduate study and to recognize the diverse pathways to a local government career armacad.info/university-of-technology-sydney-institute-for-public-policy-and-governance-postgraduate-scholarship-2017-australia

**For further information contact:**

**Email**: Alan.Morris@uts.edu.au

---

## University of Texas

School of Public Health Health, Science Center, PO Box 20186, Houston, TX 77225, United States of America.

**Contact**: Mr Robert E Roberts

### Harry Ransom Center: Research Fellowships

**Purpose**: The fellowships are awarded for projects that require substantial on-site use of its collections
**Eligibility**: All applicants, with the exception of dissertation fellowship applicants, must have a PhD or be an independent scholar with a substantial record of achievement; if the PhD is in-progress, the proposal and letters of recommendation must clearly indicate a June 1st, completion in order to be eligible for fellowships. Dissertation fellowship applicants must be doctoral candidates engaged in dissertation research by the time of application. United States of America citizens and foreign nationals are eligible to apply. Previous recipients of Ransom Center fellowships are eligible to reapply after two full academic years have passed. All things being equal, however, preference is given to applicants who have not previously held a Ransom Center fellowship
**Type**: Research fellowship
**Value**: stipends of US$3,500 per month

**Frequency**: Annual
**Country of Study**: United States of America
**Application Procedure**: Fellowships must be submitted electronically through an online fellowship account on the Ransom Center's website
**Closing Date**: 31 March
**Additional Information**: Please visit at www.hrc.utexas.edu/ research/fellowships/ www.hrc.utexas.edu/fellowships/#prog ram-guidelines

### For further information contact:

**Email**: ransomfellowships@utexas.edu

## Mobility Scooters Direct Scholarship Program

**Purpose**: Mobility Scooters Direct provides a US$1,500 scholarship each year to selected students who apply to the program
**Eligibility**: 1. Must be enrolled in a minimum of 6 hours undergraduate or 3 hours graduate at an accredited University or College. 2. Must have taken at least 40 undergraduate credit hours or 10 graduate credit hours. 3. Must have proof of a declared major. 4. Must demonstrate involvement on campus or in the community of attended University or College. 5. Must attach one letter of recommendation on official letterhead. 6. You must be at least 18 years of age to apply. 7. You must be currently enrolled at your college or university during the time of submission. 8. You must have a 3.0 GPA or higher
**Level of Study**: Graduate
**Type**: Programme grant
**Value**: US$1,500
**Frequency**: Annual
**Country of Study**: Any country
**Application Procedure**: The below details have to be included in the application. 1. Your first & last name, ph. number & email address(s). 2. Statement or transcript of your Grade Point Average (GPA). Letter of recommendation should have the below entities. 1. All applicants must meet certain criteria outlined below and submit an application via email or United States mail. 2. Applicants are also required to provide a letter of recommendation from a teacher, professor or counselor from the school being attended by the applicant
**Closing Date**: 10 December
**Funding**: Private
**Additional Information**: blogs.uw.edu/gfis/2019/11/08/ mobility-scooters-direct-scholarship-program/

### For further information contact:

4135 Dr. M.L. King Jr Blvd. Store D21, Ft. Myers, FL 33916, United States of America.

**Email**: orders@mobilityscootersdirect.com

## University of Tokyo

9-7-3, Akasaka TK 107-0052, Japan.

**Tel**: (81) 3 6271 4368
**Contact**: Fujixerox Co., Ltd., Kobayashi Fund, c/o Fuji Xerox

The University of Tokyo aims to be a world-class platform for research and education, contributing to human knowledge in partnership with other leading global universities. The University of Tokyo aims to nurture global leaders with a strong sense of public responsibility and a pioneering spirit, possessing both deep specialism and broad knowledge.

## Kobayashi Research Grants

**Purpose**: Grants are available to pursue research programme
**Eligibility**: International students from Asia, Oceania countries/regions. 1. Note the Asia-Pacific countries and regions as referred to here, it shows the following countries and regions
**Type**: Grant
**Value**: Maximum of ¥1,200,000 /person
**Country of Study**: Japan
**Application Procedure**: Please download the application documents and instructions for sending at the following link: www.fujixerox.com/eng/company/social/pdf/1.pdf
**Closing Date**: 28 February
**No. of awards given last year**: 39
**Additional Information**: research.nd.edu/our-services/ funding-opportunities/faculty/internal-grants-programs/kobay ashi-travel-fund/

### For further information contact:

International Liaison Office Room 120, Environmental Studies Building 5-1-5 Kashiwanoha, Kashiwa, Chiba 277-8563, Japan.

## Kobayashi Research Grants in Humanities and Social Sciences

**Eligibility**: Scholarships are offered in diverse fields to help students in upgrading their education
**Type**: Research
**Value**: Maximum ¥1,200,000 per grantee will be available to approximately 30 grantees. An amount from ¥320,000 to ¥1,200,000 per grantee was provided to 32 grantees for the program. (Depending upon the results of the Grantee

Screening Committee's assessment, the actual amount for some grantees could be less than the originally requested amount.)

**Study Establishment**: Grants shall be conferred for individual research (not group research) in the field of Humanities (Cultural Science) or Social Sciences, with special emphasis on themes that help deepen the researcher's understanding and awareness of Japanese or Asian/Oceanian society and culture and enhance international interchanges among them in the future

**Country of Study**: Japan

**Application Procedure**: The mode of applying is online

**Closing Date**: 28 February

**Additional Information**: For more details please visit to the website scholarship-positions.com/kobayashi-research-grant-humanities-social-sciences-university-tokyo-japan/2017/01/24/myhealthbasics.site/kobayashi-research-grants-humanities-social-sciences-university-tokyo-japan-2017/

---

## University of Twente

Universiteit Twente, Drienerlolaan 5, NL-7522 Enschede, Netherlands.

| | |
|---|---|
| **Tel**: | (31) 53 489 9111 |
| **Email**: | info@utwente.nl |
| **Website**: | www.utwente.nl/en |

### ASML Henk Bodt Scholarship

**Purpose**: The ASML Henk Bodt Scholarship supports a talented technical student who has completed (or is about to complete) the Bachelor of Science programme, and who is further motivated to pursue a 2 years full-time Master of Science degree in technical and scientific disciplines at the University of Twente

**Eligibility**: To qualify for a ASML Henk Bodt Scholarship, candidates must at least fulfill the following basic requirements: Bachelor of Science diploma, academic transcripts of each academic year from the BSc programme, cumulative Grade Point Average of at least 80% of the scale maximum of all courses of the BSc program, MSc programme admission letter from the University of Twente, up-to-date curriculum vitae

**Type**: Scholarship

**Value**: The scholarship will provide financial support for the entire duration of the Master's degree (2-year period) which covers the full tuition fee and living expenses, approx. €22,000 per year

**Length of Study**: 2 years

**Frequency**: Annual

**Country of Study**: Any country

**Closing Date**: 1 March

**Additional Information**: Check details at www.utwente.nl/internationalstudents/scholarshipsandgrants/all/asml_henk_bodt_scholarship/ www.utwente.nl/en/news/2015/4/41467/asml-technology-scholarships

### For further information contact:

| | |
|---|---|
| **Tel**: | (81) 40 268 6572 |
| **Email**: | scholarships@asml.com |

### Holland Scholarship

**Purpose**: The Holland Scholarship is a scholarship for excellent students from non-European Union/EEA countries, applying for a Bachelor or Masters programme at the University of Twente

**Eligibility**: Open to non-European Union/EEA countries. In order to be eligible for a Holland Scholarship, you should meet all the requirements as follows: your programme starts in the current academic year; you have not studied in the Netherlands before for a full degree (e.g. a Bachelor's or Master's degree); you are from a non-European Union/EEA country; you are an excellent student (i.e. CGPA of 7.5 (out of 10)); etc. Please check complete eligibility criteria at

**Type**: Scholarship

**Value**: US$5,000

**Country of Study**: Any country

**Application Procedure**: In order to apply for this scholarship, you already need to be (provisionally) admitted to one of the qualifying Bachelor or Master programmes

**Closing Date**: 1 May

**Additional Information**: Outcomes will be communicated by 15 May. Please note: if you apply for a Holland Scholarship without meeting all the requirements, your application will not be considered. www.studyinholland.nl/scholarships/holland-scholarship www.studyinholland.nl/finances/scholarships/highlighted-scholarships/holland-scholarship

### Kipaji Scholarship

**Purpose**: University Twente Scholarships (UTS) are scholarships for excellent students from both EU/EEA and non-EU/EEA countries, applying for a graduate programme (MSc) at the University of Twente.

**Eligibility**: In order to be eligible for a the University of Twente Scholarship, you should meet all the requirements below Application for an UT scholarship is a procedure separate from the application for course entry at the University of Twente. Regardless of funding, you will need to gain an admission letter first. You have been (provisionally) admitted to one of the qualifying UT Master programmes starting in the academic year 2020/2021 (September). Please note: After completion of your application, it may take up to 8 weeks before you receive the results. You must have a studentnumber. You have not graduated from a UT (under) graduate programme; You comply with the conditions for obtaining an entry visa in the Netherlands (if applicable); You comply with the general English language test requirement Academic IELTS 6.5 (or TOEFL iBT of 90) and an additional 6.0 (TOEFL iBT 20) on the subscore of speaking skills You are not eligible for a Dutch study loan; The University Twente Scholarship is a scholarship for excellent students. Typically this means that you belong to the best 5 to 10 % of your class

**Level of Study**: Masters Degree

**Type**: Scholarships

**Value**: The scholarship value ranges from €3,000 - €25,000 for one year. In case of a two-year study programme, students can receive an additional UTS of an amount equal to that in the first year when they meet the process requirements for the UTS

**Length of Study**: 2 year

**Frequency**: annual

**Country of Study**: Netherlands

**Application Procedure**: You have to apply for a Master's programme first. Once you applied for a Master's programme and received a (conditional) admission letter, you can apply for the scholarship with your student number. UTS is not available for Dutch and/or current UT students. This programme is also not available for Master's programmes at the Faculty of Geo-Information Science and Earth Observation (ITC).

**No. of awards offered**: Approximately 50

**Closing Date**: 1 May

**Additional Information**: www.utwente.nl/en/education/scholarship-finder/university-of-twente-scholarship/#application-deadlines-details

### For further information contact:

**Email**:    study@utwente.nl;

## Orange Tulip Scholarship (OTS) China

**Purpose**: The Orange Tulip Scholarship (OTS) offers talented students from China the opportunity to obtain a Masters degree at the University of Twente. The scholarship programme is highly selective, offering two scholarships for the current academic year

**Level of Study**: Graduate

**Type**: Scholarship

**Value**: €24,000. The scholarship consists of a reduction of the institutional tuition fee for non-EEA students (to €2,083)

**Country of Study**: Any country

**Application Procedure**: Applications should be submitted to the Netherlands Education Support Office (NESO) China. Visit their website for more information about the requirements for the Orange Tulip Scholarship (OTS), or send an email to ots@nesochina.org

**Closing Date**: 1 April

**Additional Information**: www.ru.nl/currentstudents/during-your-studies/@924838/orange-tulip-scholarship-china/

## Orange Tulip Scholarship (OTS) Indonesia

**Purpose**: The Orange Tulip Scholarship (OTS) offers talented students from Indonesia the opportunity to obtain a Master degree at the University of Twente

**Level of Study**: Graduate

**Type**: Scholarship

**Value**: Tuition fee of €4,450

**Country of Study**: Any country

**Application Procedure**: Applications should be submitted to the Netherlands Education Support Office (NESO) Indonesia. Visit their website for more information about the requirements for the Orange Tulip Scholarship (OTS), or send an email to ots@nesoindonesia.or.id

**Closing Date**: 15 April

**Additional Information**: Please visit www.utwente.nl/internationalstudents/scholarshipsandgrants/all/ots-indonesia/scholarship-positions.com/orange-tulip-scholarship-program-in-indonesia/2019/12/05/

## Orange Tulip Scholarship (OTS) Mexico

**Purpose**: The Orange Tulip Scholarship (OTS) offers talented students from Mexico the opportunity to obtain a Master degree at the University of Twente. The scholarship programme is highly selective, offering one scholarship for the current academic year

**Level of Study**: Graduate

**Type**: Scholarship

**Value**: €24,000

**Frequency**: Annual

**Country of Study**: Any country

**Application Procedure**: Visit the website of NESO Mexico. Applications should be submitted to the Netherlands Education Support Office (NESO) Mexico. Visit their website for more information about the requirements for the Orange Tulip Scholarship (OTS), or send an email to ots@nesomexico.org

**Closing Date**: 1 April

**Additional Information**: Check information at www.utwente.nl/internationalstudents/scholarshipsandgrants/all/ots-mexico/ www.studyinholland.nl/finances/scholarships/find-a-scholarship/orange-tulip-scholarship-programme-neso-mexico

## Professor de Winter Scholarship.

**Purpose**: Professor de Winter and Mrs. de Winter were highly involved in UT programmes and with 'their' students. Their heirs continue to be involved in their honour by awarding a scholarship of €7,500 to an excellent female student. The Professor de Winter Scholarship is provided by the inheritors of Professor de Winter and his wife. Professor de Winter was one of the founders of the research and education department of the 'Technische Hogeschool Twente' - which later became the University of Twente.

**Eligibility**: The student must have obtained an average grade of 7 (out of 10) at the end of the third quartile of the first year of the programme; The student must have obtained at least 50% of European Credits at the end of the third quartile of the first year programme; The student must have obtained 90% of European Credits before start of the second year programme.

**Level of Study**: Masters Degree

**Type**: Scholarships

**Value**: €7,500 per year for the full duration of your Master's programme.

**Length of Study**: 2 year

**Frequency**: annual

**Country of Study**: Netherlands

**Application Procedure**: You cannot apply for a Professor de Winter scholarship yourself. You need to be nominated by your faculty, after you have applied for the University of Twente Scholarship (UTS)

**Closing Date**: 1 May

**Additional Information**: www.utwente.nl/en/education/scholarship-finder/professor-de-winter-scholarship/#eligible-programmes-and-countries

### For further information contact:

**Email**: study@utwente.nl;

## University of Ulster

Research Office, Cromore Road, Coleraine, Co. Londonderry BT52 1SA, Northern Ireland.

**Tel**: (44) 28 7032 4729
**Email**: hj.campbell@ulster.ac.uk
**Website**: www.ulster.ac.uk
**Contact**: Mrs H Campbell, Administrative Officer

The University of Ulster is a dynamic and innovative institution, which is very proud of its excellent track record in the education and training of researchers. Our doctoral graduates can demonstrate outstanding achievements in advancing knowledge and making breakthroughs of relevance to the economic, social and cultural development of society.

## University Studentships/Vice-Chancellor's Research Studentships (VCRS)

**Subjects**: Arts, Humanities, Social Sciences, Computing, Engineering, Built Environment, Business, Life and Health Sciences

**Purpose**: From time to time the University makes funding available to support University Studentships. The awards for for UK, European Union and overseas students. Applicants should indicate in the appropriate area on their University application form that they wish to apply for a University Studentship/VCRS award.

**Eligibility**: These awards are open to applicants who hold or, expect to obtain, a first or upper second class honours degree and provide for payment of fees and maintenance allowance.

**Level of Study**: Doctorate

**Type**: Scholarships

**Length of Study**: Up to 3 years subject to satisfactory progress

**Frequency**: Annual

**Country of Study**: United Kingdom

**Application Procedure**: www.ulster.ac.uk/doctoralcollege/postgraduate-research/apply

**Closing Date**: February

**Funding**: Government

**No. of awards given last year**: 30

**No. of applicants last year**: 1000

**Additional Information**: www.ulster.ac.uk/__data/assets/pdf_file/0010/429940/VCRS-Terms-and-Conditions-201920.pdf

### For further information contact:

Ulster University.

**Email**: researchstudent@ulster.ac.uk

## Vice Chancellor

**Subjects**: Computing, engineering and Built Environment

**Purpose**: To assist candidates of a high academic standard to complete research degrees (PhD)

**Eligibility**: Applicants must have or expect to obtain the minimum of an upper second class Honours degree in a specific research area (as advertised). Applications are invited from United Kingdom, European Union and overseas students. Only candidates who are new applicants to PhD will be eligible

**Level of Study**: Doctorate, Postgraduate
**Type**: Scholarship
**Value**: Fees and maintenance grant
**Length of Study**: Up to 3 years
**Frequency**: Annual
**Study Establishment**: Ulster University
**Country of Study**: United Kingdom
**Application Procedure**: Applicants must apply online research.ulster.ac.uk/info/prospective/funding.html
**Funding**: Private
**No. of awards given last year**: 30
**No. of applicants last year**: 800
**Additional Information**: Applications are invited from United Kingdom, European Union and Overseas students. Further information is available on the website www.ulster.ac.uk/research www.ulster.ac.uk/about/people/vice-chancellor

**For further information contact:**

**Email**:    research.support@sydney.edu.au

## University of Verona

Via S. Francesco, 22, I-37129 Verona, Italy.

**Tel**:        (39) 45 802 8588
**Contact**:    University of Verona

The University of Verona is a university located in Verona, Italy. It was founded in 1982 and is organized in 12 Departments.

## Invite Doctoral Programme

**Subjects**: Life and Health Sciences
**Purpose**: The INVITE doctoral programme aims to encourage each student's intellectual curiosity and support the acquisition of critical thinking skills by training them in the use of innovative theoretical tools and practical methods
**Value**: Living allowance: €2,000/month for 36 months, mobility allowance: €600/month for 36 months, family allowance: €150/month for 36 months
**Country of Study**: Italy
**Closing Date**: 16 April
**Additional Information**: www.timeshighereducation.com/unijobs/minisites/university-of-verona/the-invite-doctoral-programme/

**For further information contact:**

**Email**:    invite@ateneo.univr.it

## University of Waikato

Private Bag 3105, Hamilton, New Zealand.

**Tel**:        (64) 7 856 2889 ext. 6723
**Email**:      scholarships@waikato.ac.nz
**Website**:    www.waikato.ac.nz/asd/groups/scholarships.shtml
**Contact**:    Ms Maureen Phillips, Assistant Manager, Scholarships

The Mission of the University of Waikato is to be the New Zealand leader in the business of knowledge. The business of knowledge includes the development of new knowledge, the transmission and dissemination of knowledge, and the assembling and structuring of knowledge.

## Acorn Foundation Eva Trowbridge Scholarship

**Subjects**: Business
**Purpose**: To support the people of Tauranga and the Western Bay of Plenty community
**Eligibility**: Adult students (25 years and over) studying at the University of Waikato's Tauranga campus and residing in the areas administered by Tauranga City Council or Western Bay of Plenty District Council are eligible for the award
**Type**: Scholarship
**Value**: NZ$3,000 per year
**Length of Study**: 1 year
**Frequency**: Annual
**Country of Study**: New Zealand
**Closing Date**: 31 August
**Contributor**: Acorn Foundation
**Additional Information**: The Scholarship will be paid in one lump sum to the successful applicant www.waikato.ac.nz/scholarships/s/acorn-foundation-eva-trowbridge-scholarship

**For further information contact:**

**Tel**:    (64) 7 838 4964 or 7 858 5195

## Alan Turing Prize

**Purpose**: To encourage students to develop strong joint interests in Computer Science and Mathematics

**Eligibility**: Open to students who have strong interest in computer science and mathematics
**Level of Study**: Research
**Type**: Prize
**Length of Study**: 3 years
**Frequency**: Annual
**Country of Study**: Any country
**Application Procedure**: Check website for further details
**Contributor**: Council of the University of Waikato

### For further information contact:

**Email**: info@waikato.ac.nz

## Alumini Master's Scholarship

**Purpose**: To support a student who has graduated with a degree of the University of Waikato and is enroled for a Masters Degree at this University in the year of tenure
**Eligibility**: Open to New Zealand citizens or permanent residents who have qualified for a First Degree from the University of Waikato and be enroled full-time for a Masters Degree at the University of Waikato in the year of tenure. The candidate must be in their final year of study for the degree
**Level of Study**: Postgraduate
**Type**: Scholarship
**Value**: NZ$5,500 plus actual tuition fees up to a maximum of NZ$4,000
**Length of Study**: 1 year
**Frequency**: Annual
**Application Procedure**: Check website for further details
**Closing Date**: 31 October
**Additional Information**: The Scholarship will be awarded to a student who demonstrates academic merit; who is active in University affairs and who contributes to the activities of the School or Faculty in which they are enroled; who demonstrates willingness to maintain an active relationship with the Alumni programme; who demonstrates willingness to attend Alumni functions and promotional activities; who is considered to be a good ambassador for the University of Waikato and the Alumni Association studyabroad.shiksha.com/scholarships/alumni-scholarship

## Chamber of Commerce Tauranga Business Scholarship

**Purpose**: For the benefit of members of the Tauranga Chamber of Commerce to assist the recipient to undertake study at postgraduate level
**Eligibility**: Open to citizens or permanent residents of New Zealand having a tertiary or relevant professional qualification; must have a minimum of 5 years' relevant work experience; must own or be employed by a business or organization which is a member of the Tauranga, Chamber of Commerce; must have the support of his/her employer and currently not enroled in a Postgraduate Diploma in Management Studies with the Waikato, Management School, University of Waikato. Check website for further details
**Level of Study**: Postgraduate
**Type**: Scholarship
**Value**: The value of the scholarship is usually equivalent to 1 year's fees (a total of four papers)
**Length of Study**: Above 2 years
**Frequency**: Annual
**Application Procedure**: Check website for further details
**Closing Date**: 30 November
**Additional Information**: www.tauranga.org.nz/business-services-2/waikato-university-business-scholarship/

## Evelyn Stokes Memorial Doctoral Scholarship

**Eligibility**: Open to candidates enroled or intending to enrol in an approved full-time programme of study at the University of Waikato in the years of tenure of the scholarship. Applicants who have undertaken study outside the University of Waikato must supply a full verified copy of their academic transcript(s) from their previous institution(s)
**Level of Study**: Doctorate
**Type**: Scholarship
**Value**: NZ$5,000 per year
**Length of Study**: 3 years
**Frequency**: Annual
**Study Establishment**: University of Waikato
**Country of Study**: New Zealand
**Application Procedure**: Check website for further details
**Closing Date**: 4 February
**Funding**: Private
**Additional Information**: The Scholarship will end on the completion of doctoral study, or after 3 years, whichever is the earlier date, provided that the candidate is enroled during this time in an appropriate programme of studies. Completion takes place when the postgraduate studies committee has accepted the report of the examiners and recommends the awarding of the degree www.waikato.ac.nz/scholarships/s/evelyn-stokes-memorial-doctoral-scholarship

### For further information contact:

Te Mata Kairangi School of Graduate Research, The University of Waikato, Private Bag 3105, Hamilton 3240, New Zealand.

**Tel**: (64) 7 858 5096

## Lee Foundation Grants

**Eligibility**: 1. Applicable to students who are pursuing a full-time undergraduate degree programme at the Institute. 2. Singapore Citizens or Permanent Residents. 3. Preference will be given to applicants who are hindered by financial difficulties where a lack of financial assistance will result in a discontinuation of their studies
**Type**: Grant
**Value**: NZ$500
**Application Procedure**: Application dates & submission instructions can be found www.singaporetech.edu.sg/fees/bursaries-study-grants
**Additional Information**: Grants are awarded on the basis of above average academic performance www.singaporetech.edu.sg/lee-foundation-study-grant

### For further information contact:

10 Dover Drive Singapore 138683.

**Tel**:    (65) 6592 1189
**Fax**:    (65) 6592 1190

## Priority One Management Scholarship

**Eligibility**: Open to citizens or permanent residents of New Zealand who have a tertiary or relevant professional qualification with a minimum of 5 years relevant work experience, own or be employed by a business or organization which is a member of Priority One, have the support of his/her employer, must not already be enroled in a Postgraduate Diploma in Management Studies with the Waikato, Management School, University of Waikato, not have been a previous recipient of any Waikato Management School, University of Waikato
**Level of Study**: Postgraduate
**Type**: Scholarship
**Value**: Equivalent to 1 year's fees
**Length of Study**: 2 years
**Frequency**: Annual
**Application Procedure**: Check website for further details
**Closing Date**: 30 November

## Tauranga Campus Research Masters Scholarship

**Purpose**: At this university, candidates can study a broad range of subjects to shape a qualification that matches to their strengths and career interests. It helps the candidate with career planning, developing a CV and cover letters, interview skills, enhancing their employability skills.
**Eligibility**: For students who have applied to enrol full-time in a thesis of 90-points or more as part of their first master's degree at the University of Waikato and will be based at the Tauranga campus. International applicants must have completed one full academic year (120-points) at a NZ university to be eligible to apply. If you do not meet this criteria, please do not submit an application.
**Level of Study**: Postgraduate
**Type**: Scholarship
**Value**: Up to NZ$23,000
**Frequency**: Annual
**Country of Study**: Any country
**Closing Date**: 30 April
**Funding**: International office
**Additional Information**: www.waikato.ac.nz/scholarships/s/tauranga-campus-research-masters-scholarship

### For further information contact:

Te Mata Kairangi School of Graduate Research, The University of Waikato, Private Bag 3105, Hamilton 3240, New Zealand.

**Tel**:    (64) 7 858 5096

## Ted Zorn Waikato Alumni Award For Management Communication

**Purpose**: To provide an opportunity for peer recognition of graduates of the department who have, since their graduation, distinguished themselves in a field of management communication
**Eligibility**: Open to candidates holding a responsible position in an organization or in a project, sustainability and/or workplace well being; must know the use of creativity and initiative in performing the responsibilities of the position. Check website for further details
**Level of Study**: Postgraduate
**Type**: Award
**Value**: NZ$1,000
**Frequency**: Annual
**Application Procedure**: Check website for further details
**Closing Date**: 31 December

### For further information contact:

**Email**:    jbeaton@waikato.ac.nz

## University of Waikato Masters Research Scholarships

**Purpose**: To encourage research at the University, principally by assisting with course-related costs

**Eligibility**: For students intending to enrol full-time in a 500-level thesis of 90 points or more as part of their first master's degree at the University of Waikato. International students must have completed at least 120 points of study at a - New Zealand university in order to be eligible for this Scholarship.

**Level of Study**: Postgraduate

**Type**: Research grant

**Value**: Tier 1 - US$15,000 for 120-point theses (or more), Tier 2 - US$12,000 for 90-point theses, or Tier 3 - US$5,500 towards the tuition fees of the master's programme

**Length of Study**: 1 year

**Frequency**: Annual

**Closing Date**: 30 April

**No. of awards given last year**: 65

**Additional Information**: Should a student also hold another fees scholarship, the University of Waikato Masters Research Scholarship will pay the balance of any fees (up to NZ$3,500) www.waikato.ac.nz/scholarships/s/university-of-waikato-research-masters-scholarship

### For further information contact:

Te Mata Kairangi School of Graduate Research, The University of Waikato, Private Bag 3105, Hamilton 3240, New Zealand.

**Tel**: (64) 7 858 5096

## University of Waikato MBA Programme

**Value**: US$38,000

**Length of Study**: 18 months (international students) or 24-36 months (domestic students)

**Application Procedure**: All applicants must return a complete application form. Candidates may be required to sit a Graduate Management Admission Test or TOEFL exam

**Additional Information**: www.waikato.ac.nz/study/qualifications/master-of-business-administration

### For further information contact:

**Tel**: (64) 7 838 4833

**Email**: execed@waikato.ac.nz

## University of Wales, Bangor (UWB)

Bangor North Wales, Bangor, Wales, Gwynedd LL57 2DG, United Kingdom.

**Tel**:        (44) 12 4838 2025/18

**Email**:     admissions@bangor.ac.uk

**Website**:   www.bangor.ac.uk

**Contact**:   The Student Recruitment Unit

The University of Wales, Bangor (UWB) is the principal seat of learning, scholarship and research in North Wales. It was established in 1884 and is a constituent institution of the Federal University of Wales. The University attaches considerable importance to research training in all disciplines and offers research studentships of a value similar to those of other United Kingdom public funding bodies.

## Bangor University Merit Scholarships for International Students

**Eligibility**: All international students will be automatically considered for these scholarships. These scholarships are not open to United Kingdom/European Union applicants

**Type**: Scholarship

**Value**: £2,500 (Bangor campus); £2,000 (London centre). Candidates who are fully sponsored by a third party will not be entitled to these Scholarships

**Frequency**: Annual

**Country of Study**: Any country

**Application Procedure**: All applicants will be automatically considered for these scholarships. No additional scholarship application needed

**Additional Information**: Please check at www.bangor.ac.uk/international/future/merit_scholarships.php#ug scholarship-positions.com/bangor-university-country-scholarships-for-international-students-in-uk/2019/06/20/

### For further information contact:

**Email**:     international@bangor.ac.uk

## Gold and Silver Scholarships

**Purpose**: To provide financial support to full-time students on all MSc, MBA and MA programmes

**Eligibility**: Open to applicants who wish to apply for a postgraduate MBA or MA degree programme included in the scholarship scheme

**Level of Study**: Postgraduate, MBA

**Type**: Scholarship

**Value**: Gold Scholarship £5,000 per year. Silver Scholarship £2,000 per year

**Length of Study**: 1 year

**Frequency**: Annual

**Study Establishment**: Bangor University

**Country of Study**: United Kingdom

**Application Procedure**: There is no application form for scholarships. Candidates who wish to be considered for the awards should include a letter listing their main academic and personal achievements together with a short essay on why they have chosen to study at Bangor and a curriculum vitae. For further information contact at law.pg@bangor.ac.uk

**Closing Date**: 1 December

**Funding**: Government

**Additional Information**: PLEASE NOTE: your application form will NOT be accepted without a CV www.bangor.ac.uk/business/study-with-us/postgraduate-funding/en

**For further information contact:**

Tel:        (44) 1248 382 644
Fax:        (44) 1248 383 228
Email:      b.hamilton@bangor.ac.uk

## MSc Bursaries

**Eligibility**: Open to applicants with good second class honours degree in sports science or health and to students with a 2:2 degree or a degree from a different academic area will also be considered

**Level of Study**: Postgraduate

**Type**: Bursary

**Value**: £2,500 (United Kingdom/European Union students); £3,500 (non-European Union international students)

**Length of Study**: 1 year (full-time); 2 years (part-time); 30 weeks full-time (diploma)

**Frequency**: Dependent on funds available

**Study Establishment**: Bangor University

**Country of Study**: United Kingdom

**Application Procedure**: Complete a Postgraduate Application Form with a four page (maximum) curriculum vitae or resumé. Refer to the website for further details or mail to postgraduate@bangor.ac.uk

**Closing Date**: 30 June

**Contributor**: Bangor University

**Additional Information**: £1,000 internal bursaries to former SHES (or related disciplines) students (who have 1st class undergraduate degree). £1,000 internal assistantships in addition to the other bursaries aimed at the very best students

**For further information contact:**

Tel:        (44) 1248 383 493
Email:      mscsport@bangor.ac.uk

## Open PhD Studentships

**Eligibility**: Open to candidates who have applied unsuccessfully to a United Kingdom funding council (e.g. the AHRC or the ESRC) to study at Bangor

**Level of Study**: Doctorate

**Type**: Studentship

**Value**: Fees plus maintenance grant

**Frequency**: Dependent on funds available

**Application Procedure**: Applicants must submit a scholarship application form along with a summary of your proposed research project in up to 500 words

**For further information contact:**

Email:      s.lee@bangor.ac.uk

## Santander Taught Postgraduate Scholarships

**Purpose**: The Santander Group awards a number of 1 year undergraduate and taught postgraduate scholarships to current Bangor University students

**Eligibility**: The scholarship fund aims to reward the most academically gifted students from countries that are supported by the Santander Universidades scheme. The award will be given to students from the following 11 countries: Argentina, Brazil, Chile, Colombia, Mexico, Portugal, Puerto Rico, Spain, Uruguay and Venezuela. To be eligible for the postgraduate scholarship you will have to have studied within a University which is part of the Santander Universidades Scheme

**Type**: Scholarship

**Value**: £5,000

**Length of Study**: 1 year

**Application Procedure**: Application forms and guidance notes for the Santander Scholarship Scheme are available on the University website www.bangor.ac.uk/scholarships/santander.php.en

**No. of awards offered**: 4

**Closing Date**: 29 January

**Additional Information**: For further information or if you have any questions about the scheme, please contact Academic Registry www.st-andrews.ac.uk/study/fees-and-funding/postgraduate/scholarships/santander-taught/

**For further information contact:**

University of St Andrews, St Katharine's West, The Scores, St Andrews KY16 9AX, United Kingdom.

**Tel**:        (44) 1334 46 2254
**Fax**:        (44) 1334 46 2254
**Email**:        admissions@st-andrews.ac.uk

## University of Wales (Bangor) MBA in Banking and Finance

**Length of Study**: 1 year
**Country of Study**: Any country
**Application Procedure**: Applicants must submit an application form, together with two references and copies or transcripts of previous qualifications. Where necessary TOEFL and IELTS scores must be included
**Additional Information**: www.bangor.ac.uk/courses/post graduate/banking-and-finance-mba#overview

**For further information contact:**

Bangor University, Bangor, Gwynedd, LL57 2DG, United Kingdom.

**Tel**:        (44) 1248 382028
**Fax**:        (44) 1248 370 769
**Email**:        international@bangor.ac.uk

## University of Warwick

**Tel**:        (44) 2476 523 523
**Website**:        www.warwick.ac.uk
**Contact**:        Project Officer, Postgraduate Scholarships

The University of Warwick offers an exciting range of doctoral, research-based and taught Master's programmes in the humanities, sciences, social sciences and medicine. In the 2001 Research Assessment Exercise, Warwick was ranked 5th in the United Kingdom for research quality. Postgraduate students make up around 35% of Warwick's 18,000 students. The University is located in the heart of United Kingdom, adjacent to the city of Coventry and on the border with Warwickshire.

## Argentina Chevening Scholarship

**Eligibility**: Applicants should be nationals of Argentina not currently registered at the University
**Level of Study**: Postgraduate

**Type**: Scholarship
**Value**: UK cost of Academic fee and maintenance
**Length of Study**: 1 year
**Study Establishment**: University of Warwick
**Country of Study**: United Kingdom
**Application Procedure**: Applicants must complete an application form, available from the British Council
**Closing Date**: August
**Contributor**: University of Warwick, Foreign and Commonwealth office
**Additional Information**: www.chevening.org/scholarship/argentina/

**For further information contact:**

**Email**:        info@britishcouncil.org

## College of Continuing Professional Studies Doctoral Scholarship

**Purpose**: Scholarship is available for pursuing doctoral degree level at the University of Warwick
**Eligibility**: To be eligible for the scholarship, candidates must have received an unconditional offer for entry to CCPS MPhil/PhD programme by January 31st. The scholarship scheme is open to both European Union and Overseas candidates
**Level of Study**: Doctorate
**Type**: Scholarship
**Value**: The value of the scholarship will be around £18,000 per year. The precise amount will be confirmed at the time of the offer
**Study Establishment**: Drury University
**Country of Study**: United Kingdom
**Application Procedure**: The mode of applying is online
**Closing Date**: 31 January
**Contributor**: Centre for Cultural Policy Studies
**Additional Information**: The successful candidate will be notified before the end of February www.fundsforngos.org/developing-countries-2/cambodia/centre-cultural-policy-studies-doctoral-scholarship-program/

**For further information contact:**

**Email**:        drury@drury.edu

## Colombia Postgraduate Awards (Warwick Manufacturing Group/Colfuturo)

**Purpose**: To support Master's Columbian students at WMG
**Eligibility**: Applicants should be nationals of Columbia, not currently registered on a postgraduate course at the University, and should have received an offer of a place from

WMG. Only students who have been awarded a COLFUTURO scholarship-loan are eligible
**Level of Study**: Postgraduate
**Type**: Scholarship
**Value**: full tuition fees
**Length of Study**: 1 year
**Frequency**: Dependent on funds available
**Study Establishment**: University of Warwick United Kingdom
**Country of Study**: United Kingdom
**Application Procedure**: Applicants must apply via COLFUTURO
**Funding**: Private
**Contributor**: WMG/COLFUTURO
**Additional Information**: Non-renewable, for taught masters only

### For further information contact:

**Email**:    yosoyfuturo@colfuturo.com

## Colombia Postgraduate Awards (Warwick/ Foundation for the Future of Colombia - Colfuturo)

**Purpose**: To support Columbian students on postgraduate courses at Warwick
**Eligibility**: Applicants should be nationals of Columbia and classed as an international fee-payer. Applicants can be registered on an Undergraduate course at the University of Warwick, but should have received a place on a Postgraduate Taught Master's course at Warwick. Only students who have been awarded a COLFUTURO scholarship-loan are eligible
**Level of Study**: Postgraduate
**Type**: Scholarship
**Value**: Tuition fees
**Length of Study**: 1 year
**Frequency**: Dependent on funds available
**Study Establishment**: University of Warwick
**Country of Study**: United Kingdom
**Application Procedure**: Application should be submitted via COLFUTURO
**Funding**: International office
**Contributor**: Foundation for the Future of Colombia Colfuturo (COLFUTURO)
**Additional Information**: Non-renewable, for taught masters only

### For further information contact:

**Email**:    yosoyfuturo@colfuturo.com.co

## Karim Rida Said Foundation Postgraduate Award (KRSF/Warwick)

**Purpose**: To support students from the Middle Eastern region on Postgraduate courses at Warwick
**Eligibility**: Applicants should be Jordanian, Iraqi, Lebanese, Palestinian or Syrian nationals and be resident in the Middle East. Applicants should meet all other eligibility criteria as set by KRSF and awards will only be offered to applicants who already hold an offer of a place at Warwick
**Level of Study**: Postgraduate
**Type**: Scholarship
**Length of Study**: 1 year
**Study Establishment**: University of Warwick
**Country of Study**: United Kingdom
**Application Procedure**: Applications are submitted via KRSF website www.krsf.org/whatwedo/masters
**Funding**: International office
**Contributor**: KRSF
**No. of awards given last year**: 2
**Additional Information**: Non-renewable, for taught masters only www.saidfoundation.org/pages/9-said-foundation-scholarships-programme

### For further information contact:

**Tel**:      (44) 24 7652 2469
**Email**:    j.c.inegbedion@warwick.ac.uk

## Mexico Postgraduate Award (Chevening/ Brockmann/Warwick)

**Purpose**: To support Mexican students on a postgraduate course at Warwick
**Eligibility**: Applicants should be nationals of Mexico, not currently registered at the University of Warwick and should have received an offer of a place at Warwick
**Level of Study**: Postgraduate
**Type**: Scholarship
**Value**: Full tuition fees plus maintenance
**Length of Study**: 1 year
**Study Establishment**: University of Warwick
**Country of Study**: United Kingdom
**Application Procedure**: Applicants must complete an application
**Closing Date**: August
**Funding**: Government
**Contributor**: The Foreign and Commonwealth Office and the Brockmann Foundation
**No. of awards given last year**: 1
**Additional Information**: Non-renewable www.chevening.org/scholarship/mexico/

**For further information contact:**

Tel: (44) 24 7657 2686
Email: ana_delcarmen@hotmail.com

## School of Law - Brazil Postgraduate Award

**Purpose**: To support students from Brazil on LLM programme at Warwick
**Eligibility**: Open to prospective full-time postgraduate students in any postgraduate degree within the Law School. Applicants can be registered on Undergraduate courses at the University of Warwick, but should have received a place for taught master courses at Warwick Law School
**Level of Study**: Postgraduate
**Type**: Scholarship
**Value**: 50% towards tuition fees
**Length of Study**: 1 year
**Frequency**: Dependent on funds available
**Study Establishment**: University of Warwick
**Country of Study**: United Kingdom
**Application Procedure**: Applicants must complete an online application form
**Closing Date**: 31 May
**Contributor**: Warwick Law School
**Additional Information**: Non-renewable, deducted from tuition fees, for taught masters only

**For further information contact:**

Email: paula nascimento@britishcouncil.org.br

## Sociology Departmental MA Scholarship

**Purpose**: 10 awards of £5,000 are available for students commencing MA study in the Sociology department in Autumn. The award will automatically be deducted from the winners' tuition fees.
**Eligibility**: 1. Open to applicants on all Sociology taught Masters programmes. 2. Candidates must apply to the university and have paid their application fee no later no later than 26 April. You must submit your application to the MA programme before submitting your scholarship application. 3. Successful candidates must obtain an offer from the university before taking up the award. 4. Candidates may apply concurrently to other funding sources; however, successful candidates who receive major tuition funding elsewhere will be disqualified.
**Level of Study**: Postgraduate
**Type**: Scholarship

**Value**: £2,500
**Length of Study**: 2 year
**Frequency**: Annual
**Country of Study**: Any country
**Closing Date**: 26 April
**Funding**: Foundation
**Additional Information**: warwick.ac.uk/fac/soc/sociology/prospective/pgtstudy/feesfunding/mascholarship/

**For further information contact:**

Social Sciences Building, The University of Warwick, Coventry CV4 7AL, United Kingdom.

Email: m.j.wolfe@warwick.ac.uk

## Warwick Postgraduate Research Scholarships

**Eligibility**: Open to Home, European Union and Overseas students from all disciplines at Warwick. For more details, please refer to the website
**Level of Study**: Doctorate
**Type**: Scholarship
**Value**: £3,390 for full-time students for the payment of academic fees at the Home/European Union rate. A maintenance grant, in line with the United Kingdom Research Council stipend, of £13,290 for full-time award holders
**Country of Study**: United Kingdom
**Application Procedure**: Please refer to the website www2.warwick.ac.uk/services/academicoffice/gsp/scholarship/apply/pgr_guidelines_2015-16.pdf
**Closing Date**: 12 January
**Additional Information**: Students and applicants who wish to apply for an AHRC doctoral award should apply to the WPRS competition and will automatically be considered for both competitions

**For further information contact:**

Email: aci@mrc.ac.za

## University of Washington

School of Business Administration, 110 Mackenzie Hall Box 353200, Seattle, WA 98195, United States of America.

Tel: (1) 206 543 4661
Email: mba@u.washington.edu
Contact: MBA Admissions Officer

## African American Heritage Endowed MBA Scholarship

**Purpose**: This scholarship is available for African-American MBA students who are attending the Foster Business school at the University of Washington in Seattle

**Eligibility**: 1. Must be an African American student. 2. Must be an MBA candidate at the time of application. 3. Must be enrolled at the Foster Business School at the University of Washington in Seattle. 4. This award is for United States of America students

**Level of Study**: Graduate

**Type**: Scholarship

**Value**: US$10,000

**Frequency**: Annual

**Country of Study**: United States of America

**Application Procedure**: Applications and information about the African American Heritage Endowed MBA Scholarship are available online at the University of Washington Foster School of Business website. To apply for this award, students must first be accepted to the MBA program at the University of Washington in Seattle. Eligible students who are interested in this award should contact the Michael G. Foster School of Business for further information about the admissions and scholarship application process. All applications must be completed online by the deadline date

**Closing Date**: 15 April

**Funding**: Foundation

**Additional Information**: www.unigo.com/scholarships/by-state/washington-scholarships/african-american-heritage-endowed-mba-scholarship/1004476

### For further information contact:

124 Mackenzie Hall Box 353200, Seattle, WA 98195-3200, United States.

**Email**:    scholarships@swe.org

---

## University of Waterloo

200 University Avenue West, Waterloo, ON N2L 3G1, Canada.

**Email**:    rchild@uwaterloo.ca

## International Research Partnership Grants (IRPG)

**Purpose**: The International Research Program Grants (IRPG) programs are internal seed grants aimed to provide Waterloo researchers with incentives to develop new or existing international research collaborations with leading institutions known for high quality research and global ranking

**Eligibility**: Projects should involve a group of Waterloo researchers and international partners. Preference will be given to projects with multiple Waterloo faculties/departments and a network of partner institutions;; 1. Preference will be given to projects that have not received IRPG funding for a previous project with the same international partners. 2. Preference is given to applications where matching cash contribution is from a new source or one that is outside of University of Waterloo, instead of existing research funds

**Level of Study**: Graduate

**Type**: Grants and fellowships

**Value**: Up to C$20,000, 50% of the costs

**Frequency**: Annual

**Country of Study**: Any country

**Application Procedure**: You could refer to the following pdf for further instructions. uwaterloo.ca/research/sites/ca.research/files/uploads/files/irpg_program_guidelines-30-nov-2018.pdf

**Closing Date**: 1 November

**Funding**: Private

### For further information contact:

200 University Avenue West, Waterloo, ON N2L 3G1, Canada.

## Mitacs Accelerate Fellowship

**Purpose**: The Mitacs Accelerate Fellowship provides a long-term funding and internship option for master's and PhD students. Recipients can also access professional development training that helps them ensure project success and gain in-demand career skills

**Level of Study**: Graduate

**Type**: Fellowship

**Value**: C$40,000 per year

**Length of Study**: 18 months

**Frequency**: Annual

**Country of Study**: Any country

**Application Procedure**: Interested applicants can apply for the Accelerate Fellowship at any time. All other Accelerate program guidelines apply. 1. Review the following information when you begin writing your proposal. Eligible research and adjudication criteria 1. Writing Your Proposal guide Policies. 2. Submit Cover Sheet to Office of Research contact below, with a copy of the draft proposal. 3. Get feedback on the proposal from all participants and the Mitacs Program contact below. 4. Collect all required signatures: intern(s), professor(s), partner representative and the Office of Research contact below. 5. Email your proposal package to your Mitacs

Program contact below Additional Information available on the Mitacs website
**Funding**: Private
**Additional Information**: uwaterloo.ca/research/mitacs-accelerate-fellowship

### For further information contact:

**Tel**:      (1) 519 888 4567
**Email**:    accelerate@mitacs.ca

## University of West London

### International Ambassador Scholarships at University of West London

**Purpose**: The International Ambassador Scholarship recognises and provides financial support for outstanding students who wish to act as ambassadors for the University of West London
**Eligibility**: Applicants must be: 1. An offer holder for an undergraduate or postgraduate course at UWL, to commence study in September 2020. This means that you must have already applied for a course of study at this university and you must have already received an official offer from one of our admissions officers. 2. A self-funded overseas full fee-paying paying student (please note: EU applicants are not eligible). The International Ambassador Scholarship will be awarded on a competitive basis to candidates who demonstrate enthusiasm and the ability to be an excellent international student ambassador.
**Level of Study**  Graduate
**Type**: Scholarship
**Frequency**: Annual
**Country of Study**: Any country
**Application Procedure**: To be considered for the scholarship, you must have been offered a place to study on a full-time undergraduate or postgraduate course at the University of West London
**No. of awards offered**: 100
**Closing Date**: 1 July
**Funding**: Private
**Contributor**: University of West London
**Additional Information**: Official Scholarship Website: www.uwl.ac.uk/courses/undergraduate-study/fees-and-funding/bursaries-and-scholarships www.scholars4dev.com/8119/international-ambassador-scholarships-university-west-london/

### For further information contact:

**Tel**:      (44) 20 8231 2914
**Email**:    int.app@uwl.ac.uk

## University of Western Australia

35 Stirling Highway, Crawley, WA 6009, Australia.

**Tel**:        (61) 8 9380 2490, 8 6488 6000
**Email**:      general.enquiries@uwa.edu.au
**Website**:    www.uwa.edu.au

Since its establishment in 1911, the University of Western Australia has helped to shape the careers of more than 75,000 graduates. Their success reflects the UWA's balanced coverage of disciplines in the arts, sciences and professions.

### Advanced Consumer Research PhD Scholarship

**Purpose**: To study the effectiveness of Commonwealth, State and Territory consumer protection laws in relation to information disclosure
**Eligibility**: Open to those who have completed an undergraduate degree in law with honours or equivalent research qualifications
**Level of Study**: Postgraduate
**Type**: Scholarship
**Value**: AU$25,000 per year
**Length of Study**: 3 years and 6 months
**Frequency**: Annual
**Study Establishment**: The University of Western Australia
**Application Procedure**: Check website for further details
**Closing Date**: 3 August

### For further information contact:

**Tel**:      (61) 8 6488 2947
**Email**:    eileen.webb@uwa.edu.au

### Health Effects of Air Pollution (Top-Up)

**Purpose**: To support various projects in the School of Population Health
**Eligibility**: Open to those doing research in Australia
**Level of Study**: Postgraduate
**Type**: Scholarship
**Value**: AU$10,000, plus Australian Dollar; AU$2,500 for relocation costs
**Frequency**: Annual
**Study Establishment**: University of Western Australia
**Country of Study**: Australia

**Application Procedure**: Candidates must apply direct to the faculty. Check website for further details
**Closing Date**: 1 December

### For further information contact:

**Tel**:      (61) 8 6488 7804
**Email**:   Angus.Cook@uwa.edu.au

## Master of Business Administration Programme

### For further information contact:

**Tel**:      (61) 9 3803 939
**Fax**:      (61) 9 3824 071
**Email**:   icweb@acs.edu.au

## Natural Gas/LNG Production Scholarships

**Purpose**: To use the research outcomes to improve the design of LNG production trains and to treat contaminated gas reserves
**Eligibility**: Open to candidates who have achieved Second Class (Honours) or equivalent
**Level of Study**: Postgraduate
**Type**: Scholarship
**Value**: AU$31,118 per year
**Length of Study**: 3 years
**Frequency**: Annual
**Country of Study**: Australia
**Application Procedure**: Check website for further details
**Closing Date**: 17 December
**Additional Information**: www.nlng.com/Our-CSR/Pages/Scholarships.aspx

### For further information contact:

**Tel**:      (61) 6488 2954
**Fax**:      (61) 6488 1964
**Email**:   Eric.May@uwa.edu.au

## The Science & Innovation Studentship Award

**Purpose**: To promote innovation in areas of key technologies
**Eligibility**: Open to citizens of Australia or permanent residents who have completed 2 years, or more, full-time study in a science degree at a recognized Western Australian University
**Level of Study**: Postgraduate
**Type**: Studentship
**Value**: AU$7,000 per year

**Frequency**: Annual
**Study Establishment**: Curtin University of Technology, Edith Cowan University, Murdoch University, The University of Notre Dame, The University of Western Australia
**Country of Study**: Any country
**Application Procedure**: Check website for further details
**Closing Date**: 14 September

### For further information contact:

100 Plain Street, Perth, WA 6004, Australia.

**Tel**:      (61) 8 9222 3333
**Fax**:      (61) 8 9222 3862
**Email**:   rchapman@wellesley.edu

## Water and Health Scholarships

**Purpose**: To position graduates favourably with respect to future employment opportunities through research projects in the area of public health impacts of recycled water use
**Eligibility**: Open to Australian candidates with a broad range of backgrounds
**Level of Study**: Postgraduate
**Type**: Scholarship
**Value**: AU$30,000 per year
**Length of Study**: 3 years
**Frequency**: Annual
**Study Establishment**: The University of Western Australia
**Country of Study**: Australia
**Application Procedure**: Check website for further details
**Closing Date**: 6 July
**Additional Information**: Applications are open from 13 June

### For further information contact:

**Tel**:      (61) 8 6488 7804
**Email**:   Angus.Cook@uwa.edu.au

## Western Australian CSIR University Postgraduate Scholarships

**Purpose**: To enhance research into minerals and energy exploration, extraction and processing
**Eligibility**: Open to citizens of Australia enrolling for postgraduate research
**Level of Study**: Postgraduate
**Type**: Scholarship
**Value**: AU$25,000 per year
**Length of Study**: 3 years
**Country of Study**: Australia

**Application Procedure**: Check website for further details
**Additional Information**: www.csiro.au/en/Careers/Student
ships/Postgraduate-scholarships

**For further information contact:**

**Tel**:      (61) 8 6488 3027
**Email**:    campbell.thomson@uwa.edu.au

## University of Western Sydney

Office of Research Services, Hawkesbury Campus, Building
H3, Locked Bag 1797, Penrith South DC, NSW 1797,
Australia.

**Tel**:       (61) 2 4570 1463
**Email**:     t.mills@uws.edu.au
**Website**:   www.uws.edu.au
**Contact**:   Ms Tracey Mills, Research Scholarships
               Development Officer

## Master of Business Administration Programme

**Length of Study**: 1–5 years
**Application Procedure**: Applicants must complete an appli-
cation form supplying a TOEFL score
**Closing Date**: January
**Additional Information**: www.uwa.edu.au/study/courses/
master-of-business-administration-intensive

**For further information contact:**

**Tel**:      (61) 2 9685 9297
**Fax**:      (61) 2 9685 9298
**Email**:    international@uws.edu.au

## University of Westminster

Scholarships Department, Cavendish House, 101 New Cavendish Street, London W1W 6XH, United Kingdom.

**Tel**:       (44) 20 7911 5000 Exts 66257, 66258, 66259
**Email**:     scholarships@westminster.ac.uk
**Website**:   www.westminster.ac.uk

The University of Westminster is proud of its generous scholarship programme, which benefits both United Kingdom and
international students. Full details are available on our
website www.westminster.ac.uk/scholarships

## Brian Large Bursary Fund

**Purpose**: To provide financial support to United Kingdom
students that are studying full time on the Transport and
Planning MSc
**Eligibility**: Applicants must have been accepted for a full
time Masters course in transport for 2019/20. While no min-
imum level of first degree is required, the Trustees expect
young graduates to have at least a 2.2, preferably a 2.1.
However, they are willing to relax that requirement for out-
standing mature students.
**Type**: Funding support
**Value**: £8,000
**Country of Study**: United Kingdom
**Application Procedure**: If you are interested in applying for
one of these bursaries please contact Dr. Enrica Papa, the
Course Leader of MSc Transport Planning at:
papa@westminster.ac.uk
**Closing Date**: 12 July
**Additional Information**: For more information, visit the:
www.blbf.co.uk/services environment.leeds.ac.uk/dir-record/
scholarships/665/the-brian-large-bursary-fund

## Fully Funded Master Scholarship

**Purpose**: To study a full-time master degree in a subject
within the School of Media, Arts and Design at the university
**Type**: Scholarship
**Value**: Full tuition fee award, accommodation, living
expenses, flights to and from London
**Country of Study**: Any country
**Application Procedure**: For application, please visit website
www.westminster.ac.uk/about-us/faculties/westminster-school-
of-media-arts-and-design/departments
**Closing Date**: 31 October
**Additional Information**: www.afterschoolafrica.com/624/
university-of-westminster-international/

**For further information contact:**

**Email**:    graduate.admissions@cs.ox.ac.uk

## Fully Funded University of Westminster Master's Scholarship for Developing Countries

**Purpose**: The Westminster Vice-Chancellor's Scholarships,
is one of the University's most prestigious award, it is aimed

at fully funding a student from a developing country to study a full-time Master's degree at the University

**Eligibility**: The main requirement of this scholarship is that the candidates must hold an offer for a full-time Master's degree at University of Westminster. In addition, the applicant should have First Class Honours degree, financial need and development potential

**Level of Study**: Postgraduate

**Type**: Award

**Value**: The winner of this scholarship may expect to receive full tuition fee waivers, accomodation and flights to and from London

**Frequency**: Annual

**Country of Study**: Any country

**Application Procedure**: 1. A copy of the letter/email from the University of Westminster confirming your conditional or unconditional offer of a place on your chosen course. 2. An official copy of your transcript from your chosen course. 3. A reference letter written specifically in support of your scholarship application. This should be written by a previous tutor, professor, academic or employer and cannot be the same reference provided as part of your admission application

**Closing Date**: 31 May

**Funding**: Private

**Additional Information**: oyaop.com/opportunity/scholar ships-and-fellowships/fully-funded-scholarship-at-the-univer sity-of-westminster/

### For further information contact:

**Tel**:       (44) 20 7911 5000
**Email**:   course-enquiries@westminster.ac.uk

## Higher Education Scholarship Palestine (HESPAL) Scholarships

**Purpose**: The University of Westminster is working in partnership with the British Council to provide a Higher Education Scholarship for a Palestinian (HESPAL); that is, to support a junior academic at a Palestinian University wishing to study a one-year masters programme or a three-year PhD research programme in the United Kingdom

**Eligibility**: For eligibility and other details visit how to apply page www.westminster.ac.uk/study/fees-and-funding/scholar ships/before-you-apply

**Value**: Full tuition fee award, pre-departure briefing from the British Council, arrival allowances, thesis allowances and a monthly allowance to cover living expenses

**Country of Study**: Any country

**Application Procedure**: Applications are made through the British Council in the Palestinian Territories. Find out more on the British Council website

**Closing Date**: 23 January

**Additional Information**: www.britishcouncil.ps/en/study-uk/scholarships/hespal

### For further information contact:

**Email**:   tom.sperlinger@bristol.ac.uk

## Politics and International Relations PhD Scholarships

**Purpose**: Scholarships are available for pursuing PhD programme

**Eligibility**: Candidates should normally have a minimum classification of a 2.1 in their BA, or equivalent, and preferably a Master's degree

**Value**: One fee waiver (Home/European Union rate applications are invited for the following awards which are tenable for up to 3 years for full-time study:) and £16,000 per year for 3 years. Up to two fee waivers (Home/European Union rate) and £5,000 per year for 3 years

**Length of Study**: 3 years

**Country of Study**: United Kingdom

**Application Procedure**: Apply online. Please visit the website www.westminster.ac.uk/study/postgraduate/research-degrees/research-areas/social-sciences-and-humanities/how-to-apply

**Closing Date**: 27 April

**Contributor**: University of Westminster

**Additional Information**: For more details, visit website www.westminster.ac.uk/news/2018/call-for-applications-poli tics-and-international-relations-2018-phd-scholarships blogs. kent.ac.uk/aspirations/2019/11/19/politics-international-relat ions-phd-scholarships/

### For further information contact:

**Tel**:       (44) 20 7911 5000
**Email**:   robert.elgie@dcu.ie

## Rees Jeffrey Road Fund

**Purpose**: To support financially for education, research and physical road transport-related projects in accordance with the founding Trust Deed

**Type**: Bursary

**Value**: This fund provides a bursary of up to £10,000 towards financial support for education, research and physical road transport-related projects

**Country of Study**: Any country

**Application Procedure**: Expressions of interest should in the first instance be directed to Dr. Enrica Papa, the Course Leader of Transport Planning MSc at: E.papa@westminster. ac.uk

**Closing Date**: June
**Additional Information**: For more information visit the Rees Jeffreys website environment.leeds.ac.uk/dir-record/scholarships/666/rees-jeffreys-road-fund-bursaries

### For further information contact:

**Email**: brianmurrell@reesjeffreys.org

## Westminster Full-Fee Masters Scholarships for International Students

**Purpose**: The Westminster University offers full tuition fee scholarships to prospective postgraduate applicants from any country
**Eligibility**: You must hold an offer for a full-time Masters Program at the University of Westminster. The main scholarship criteria are: equivalent to a United Kingdom First Class Honours degree and financial need
**Level of Study**: Doctorate, Postgraduate
**Type**: Scholarship
**Value**: Full tuition fee award only
**Country of Study**: United Kingdom
**Application Procedure**: You should only apply for a scholarship once you have applied for admission and successfully been offered a place (either conditional or unconditional) on the course you wish to study. To apply for a scholarship, you will need to download and complete the relevant scholarship application form and submit it together with supporting documents by post
**Closing Date**: 13 October
**Additional Information**: For more details visit official scholarship Website: www.westminster.ac.uk/study/prospective-students/fees-and-funding/scholarships/international-postgraduate-scholarships/westminster-full-fee-scholarship www.scholars4dev.com/8785/full-tuition-fee-waivers-international-students-westminster-university/

### For further information contact:

**Email**: course-enquiries@westminster.ac.uk

## Westminster School of Media, Arts and Design Scholarship

**Purpose**: To pursue a full-time master degree in a subject within the School of Media, Arts and Design at the university
**Value**: Full tuition fee award, accommodation, living expenses and flights to and from London
**Frequency**: Annual
**Country of Study**: Any country

**Application Procedure**: For application forms, please visit website www.westminster.ac.uk/study/fees-and-funding/scholarships/westminster-school-of-media-arts-and-design-scholarship
**Closing Date**: 31 May
**Contributor**: Westminster School of Media, Arts and Design
**Additional Information**: www.scholarshubafrica.com/23116/westminster-school-media-arts-design-masters-scholarship-uk/

## Westminster Vice-Chancellor's Scholarships

**Purpose**: The Westminster Vice-Chancellor's Scholarships, the university's most prestigious award, is aimed at fully funding a student from a developing country to study a full-time masters degree at the University
**Eligibility**: You must be an international student from a developing country and hold an offer for a full-time Undergraduate degree at University of Westminster. The main criteria are: United Kingdom First Class Honours degree, financial need and development potential
**Level of Study**: Postgraduate
**Type**: Scholarship
**Value**: Full tuition fee waivers, accommodation, living expenses and flights to and from London
**Frequency**: Annual
**Study Establishment**: University of Westminster
**Country of Study**: United Kingdom
**Application Procedure**: It is important to visit the official website to access the application form and for detailed information on how to apply for this scholarship
**Closing Date**: 31 May
**Additional Information**: For more details, please visit official scholarship website: www.westminster.ac.uk/study/prospective-students/fees-and-funding/scholarships/international-postgraduate-scholarships/vice-chancellor-scholarship www.scholarshiproar.com/westminster-vice-chancellors-scholarships/

# University of Winnipeg

## The University of Winnipeg Manitoba Graduate Scholarships (MGS)

**Purpose**: Applications are open for the University of Winnipeg Manitoba Graduate Scholarships (MGS) organized by the University of Winnipeg. These scholarships are open to the students who are enrolled or plan to enroll as a full-time student in a master's program at the University of Winnipeg
**Eligibility**: 1. Have achieved a minimum GPA of 3.75 in the last 60 credits hours of study. 2. Be in a pre-master's program and/or entering the first or second year of an eligible master's

program as of May or September of the current year or January of the upcoming year. 3. Be enrolled in or plan to enroll in as a full-time student in a master's program.

**Level of Study**: Postdoctorate
**Type**: Scholarship
**Value**: US$15,000
**Length of Study**: 1 year
**Frequency**: Annual
**Country of Study**: Any country
**Application Procedure**: Apply online: www.uwinnipeg.ca/graduate-studies/docs/uwmgs-application+checklist-revised jan2019-2.pdf
**Closing Date**: 1 March
**Funding**: Foundation
**Additional Information**: www.uwinnipeg.ca/graduate-studies/funding/uw-fgs-awards/the-mgs/index.html

## For further information contact:

**Email**:    gradstudies@uwinnipeg.ca

## University of Wisconsin-Milwaukee

University of Wisconsin-Milwaukee, PO Box 413, Milwaukee, WI 53201, United States of America.

**Tel**:         (1) 414 229 1122
**Email**:    fellowship@uwm.edu
**Website**:  www.uwm.edu

The University of Wisconsin-Milwaukee (UWM) is located just a few blocks from Lake Michigan in one of Milwaukee's most attractive residential areas, and offers research and teaching programmes extending to 148 different degree programmes that serve nearly 26,000 students. UWM focuses on approaches to education that are inclusive, multidisciplinary and marked by excellent research and outstanding teaching.

## University of Wisconsin-Milwaukee Graduate School Dissertation Fellowships

**Purpose**: To fund dissertation-level graduate students at the University of Wisconsin-Milwaukee
**Eligibility**: Applicants must have completed all coursework, passed preliminary examinations, completed PhD residency requirements and obtained dissertator status. No other award may be held concurrently (with the exception of the Chancellor's Graduate Student Award). Current or previous awardees are not eligible

**Level of Study**: Doctorate
**Type**: Fellowship
**Value**: US$14,000, in addition to full coverage of resident instructional fees (approx. US$1,740), a remission of the out-of-state portion of the tuition, low-cost comprehensive health insurance and other benefits
**Length of Study**: 1 academic year
**Frequency**: Annual
**Study Establishment**: University of Wisconsin-Milwaukee
**Country of Study**: United States of America
**Application Procedure**: Applicants must check the website for details
**Closing Date**: 21 January

## For further information contact:

**Tel**:    (1) 414 229 6276

## University of Wollongong (UOW)

Northfields Ave, Wollongong, NSW 2522, Australia.

**Tel**:         (61) 2 4221 3555
**Email**:    scholarships@uow.edu.au
**Website**:  www.uow.edu.au

The University of Wollongong (UOW) is a university of international standing with an enviable record of achievement in teaching and research. It enjoys a significant international research profile, attracting more Australian Research Council funding per student that any other Australian university. Over 850 postgraduate students are enrolled of which 30% are overseas students.

## Marketing Research Innovation Centre PhD Scholarship

**Purpose**: To conduct research in the area of qualitative and quantitative methods, market segmentation, brand image studies and advertising experiments
**Eligibility**: Open to applicants who have an excellent tertiary track record, experience with conducting academic research
**Level of Study**: Postgraduate, Research
**Type**: Scholarship
**Value**: AU$20,000 per year
**Length of Study**: 3 years
**Frequency**: Annual
**Country of Study**: Australia

**Application Procedure**: Candidates can check the website for further details

**For further information contact:**

Tel:     (44) 20 7000 7000
Fax:     (44) 2 4221 3862
Email:   housing@london.ac.uk

## University of Wollong (UOW) Work-Integrated Learning Scholarship

**Purpose**: To reward outstanding academic achievements
**Eligibility**: Open to students with outstanding academic achievements
**Level of Study**: Postgraduate
**Type**: Scholarship
**Value**: AU$3,000; AU$9,300
**Frequency**: Annual
**Study Establishment**: University of Wollongong
**Country of Study**: Australia
**Application Procedure**: Apply online
**Closing Date**: October
**Additional Information**: Scholarship holders are required to undertake a period, usually 6-10 weeks of professional work experience each year with an appropriate sponsor organization    scholarships.uow.edu.au/scholarships/search?scholarship=603

**For further information contact:**

Tel:     (61) 1300 367 869
Fax:     (61) 2 4221 3233
Email:   uniadvice@uow.edu.au

## University of Wollongong Sydney Business School Bursary Scheme

**Purpose**: The University of Wollongong (UOW) is offering Sydney Business School Bursary Scheme for students commencing master's courses. The bursaries offer a 15% reduction of the tuition fee per trimester of the study of applied
**Eligibility**: The bursary will apply to the following citizenships only: India, Nepal, Vietnam, Pakistan, Indonesia, Sri Lanka, Bangladesh, Thailand, Iran, Kenya, Mongolia, Nigeria, Cambodia, Zimbabwe, Myanmar and Ghana
**Value**: The bursaries offer a 15% reduction of the tuition fee per trimester of the study of applied
**Study Establishment**: Bursaries are awarded to study the subjects offered by the university
**Country of Study**: Australia

**Application Procedure**: You do not have to make a separate application for a bursary, as it will be awarded automatically when you receive an offer for an eligible course and meet scholarship requirements. Applicants will receive a bursary notification and Terms and Conditions of their bursary at the same time as their offer of admission into their course
**Additional Information**: For more details please visit the website scholarship-positions.com/uow-sydney-business-school-bursary-scheme-australia/2017/07/27/    sydneybusinessschool.edu.au/content/groups/public/@web/@gsb/documents/doc/uow 247217.pdf

**For further information contact:**

Email:   business-enquiries@uow.edu.au

## University of Wollongong In Dubai (UOWD)

Blocks 5 & 15, Knowledge Village, PO Box 20183, Dubai United Arab Emirates.

Tel:     (971) 4 367 2400
Email:   info@uowduabi.ac.ae

The UOWD in Dubai, established in 1993, is one UAE's oldest and most prestigious universities. The university strives to provide a fertile environment for bright young minds to flourish, and maintains a long and proud tradition of excellence in education.

## University of Wollongong In Dubai Postgraduate Scholarships

**Purpose**: To reward the academically outstanding postgraduates
**Eligibility**: Open to all outstanding postgraduate students enrolled at the university
**Level of Study**: Postgraduate
**Type**: Scholarship
**Value**: Payment of tuition fees
**Frequency**: Annual
**Study Establishment**: University of Wollongong in Dubai
**Country of Study**: United Kingdom
**Application Procedure**: Contact the University
**No. of awards offered**: 2
**Closing Date**: 9 January
**No. of awards given last year**: 1

**Additional Information**: For further information regarding UOWD Scholarships you can contact Student Recruitment on +9714 278 1800 or info@uowdubai.ac.ae www.uowdubai.ac.ae/postgraduate-programs/scholarships-new-students

## For further information contact:

**Tel**:       (971) 4 278 1800
**Fax**:     (971) 4367 8047
**Email**:   info@uowdubai.ac.ae

## University of York

Graduate Schools Office, Heslington, York Y010 5DD, United Kingdom.

**Tel**:          (44) 1904 432 143
**Email**:      graduate@york.ac.uk
**Website**:   www.york.ac.uk/admin/gso/gsp
**Contact**:   Mr Philip Simison

The University of York offers postgraduate degree courses in archaeology, art history, biology, biochemistry, chemistry, communication studies, computer science, economics, educational studies, electronics, English, environment, health sciences, history, language and linguistics, management, mathematics, medieval studies, music, philosophy, physics, politics, psychology, social policy, social work, sociology and women's studies.

## China Scholarships Council Joint Research Scholarships

**Purpose**: The scholarships are open to Chinese nationals intending to begin a PhD in the current and upcoming academic year. They will be awarded on the basis of academic merit and CSC priorities
**Eligibility**: 1. You must be a citizen and permanent resident of the People's Republic of China at the time of application. 2. You must hold an unconditional offer* for a full-time PhD degree programme at the University of York commencing in Autumn. 3. You must fulfil any English language requirements of your offer by 15 February. 4. You must satisfy the eligibility and selection criteria set out by the CSC
**Level of Study**: Postgraduate
**Type**: Scholarship
**Value**: 100% of tuition fees for the full duration of the CSC funding period, a grant and uk visa fees
**Frequency**: Annual

**Country of Study**: Any country
**Application Procedure**: Check the details online. www.york.ac.uk/study/postgraduate-research/funding/china-scholarships/
**No. of awards offered**: 10
**Closing Date**: 1 March
**Funding**: Private
**Additional        Information**:        www.york.ac.uk/study/postgraduate-research/funding/china-scholarships/

## For further information contact:

**Tel**:       (44) 1904 323534
**Email**:   international@york.ac.uk

## Overseas Continuation Scholarship (OCS)

**Purpose**: For current University of York Masters students who are progressing to PhD studies at the University of York
**Eligibility**: Students must be outstanding academically and have the support of their chosen department at York. You must hold an offer for PhD study and be a current University of York Masters student to be eligible to apply
**Level of Study**: Doctorate
**Type**: Scholarship
**Value**: The scholarship is worth £5,000 in the first year of study as a deduction from tuition fees
**Application Procedure**: Please visit www.york.ac.uk/study/international/fees-funding/scholarships/
**Closing Date**: 30 April
**Additional Information**: Please email international@york.ac.uk

## For further information contact:

**Email**:   international@york.ac.uk

## Overseas Research Scholarship (ORS)

**Purpose**: For applicants commencing PhD study at the University of York. Applicants must be liable to pay the overseas rate of tuition fee
**Eligibility**: Students must be outstanding academically and have the support of their chosen department at York. You must hold an offer for PhD study to be eligible to apply
**Level of Study**: Doctorate
**Type**: Scholarship
**Value**: The scholarship will pay the full overseas tuition fee and a stipend of £5,000 per year for each year of successful study
**Application Procedure**: Please visit www.york.ac.uk/study/international/fees-funding/scholarships/
**Closing Date**: 30 April

**Additional Information**: Please email international@york.ac.uk www.ucl.ac.uk/scholarships/overseas-research-scholarships

For further information contact:

**Email**:    international@york.ac.uk

## Scholarship for Overseas Students

**Subjects**: All subjects except MBBS (Medicine), GEMMA, CASPPER and Mundus MAPP.

**Purpose**: For applicants commencing study of any taught subject (excluding students applying to the Hull York Medical School) at any level as a full-time student at the University of York. Applicants must be liable to pay the overseas rate of tuition fee.

**Eligibility**: This is a competitive scholarship based on academic merit and financial need. You must hold an offer for academic study to be eligible to apply.

**Level of Study**: Postgraduate

**Type**: Scholarship

**Value**: The scholarship is worth one-quarter (25%) of the overseas tuition fee for each year of successful study

**Frequency**: Annual

**Application Procedure**: Please visit www.york.ac.uk/study/international/fees-funding/academic-excellence-scholarships/

**Closing Date**: 30 April

**Additional Information**: Please email international@york.ac.uk for further information.

For further information contact:

**Email**:    international@york.ac.uk

## White Rose University Consortium Studentships

**Purpose**: Each year York collaborates with the Universities of Leeds and Sheffield to be able to offer a number of studentships in each of the three universities

**Eligibility**: In order to be eligible you must: have applied for a place on a full time PhD programme in the relevant Department. Have or expect to obtain a first or upper second class honours degree or equivalent prior to commencing the PhD degree

**Level of Study**: Doctorate

**Type**: Studentship

**Value**: A full Research Council equivalent stipend: £14,057. Rates for current year were not set at time of publication. A fee waiver at the Home/European Union rate (Overseas candidates are welcome to apply but would need to fund the difference between Home/European Union fee rate and international fee rate.). A Research Support Grant: £900

**Frequency**: Annual

**Application Procedure**: Please visit www.york.ac.uk/study/postgraduate/fees-funding/research/white-rose-studentships/

**Closing Date**: 30 April

**Additional Information**: Contact research-student-admin@york.ac.uk

For further information contact:

**Email**:    research-student-admin@york.ac.uk

## Wolfson Foundation Scholarships

**Purpose**: The University is delighted to be offering Wolfson Scholarships in the Humanities for the second year as part of a national Arts funding scheme

**Eligibility**: The Wolfson Postgraduate Scholarships in the humanities will be awarded to outstanding students who demonstrate the potential to make an impact on their chosen field. Wolfson Scholarships will be awarded solely on academic merit. In order to be eligible you must: have applied for and be in receipt of an offer of a place on a full time PhD programme in the relevant department (some departments may be able to accept applications on the basis of a programme application without an offer, please speak to your prospective department to confirm). Expect to begin your PhD studies in October. Have or expect to obtain a first or upper second class honours degree or equivalent prior to commencing the PhD Have completed a masters level qualification before commencing the PhD.

**Level of Study**: Doctorate

**Type**: Scholarship

**Value**: The scholarships are worth £26,000 per year for up to 3 years of PhD study. Each scholarship offers a stipend of £17,750 per year for up to 3 years of PhD study. Each scholarship will contribute to fees (up to £10,000). Any funds remaining after payment of the stipend and fees will be kept as a Research Training and Support Grant to be accessed by the award holder on request to support the work of the PhD.

**Country of Study**: Any country

**Application Procedure**: Please visit www.york.ac.uk/study/postgraduate/fees-funding/postgraduate/wolfson/

**Closing Date**: 1 February

**Additional Information**: www.st-andrews.ac.uk/study/fees-and-funding/postgraduate/scholarships/wolfson-postgraduate/

For further information contact:

**Tel**:      (44) 1334 46 2254

**Email**:    admissions@st-andrews.ac.uk

## Uppsala University

**Website**: www.uu.se/en/admissions/scholarships/uppsala-university/

Uppsala University is a research university in Uppsala, Sweden, and is the oldest university in Sweden and all of the Nordic countries, founded in 1477.

### Uppsala IPK Scholarships for International Students

**Purpose**: Uppsala University awards several scholarships for fee-paying students applying for Master's programmes commencing in the autumn. One of these scholarship programs is the Uppsala IPK Scholarships

**Eligibility**: 1. Citizens of a country outside the European Union/EEA and Switzerland. 2. Applicants must demonstrate academic talent and show interest in belonging to an educational milieu. 3. Students can only be awarded an IPK scholarship for their first priority programme at Uppsala University. 4. You must meet the entrance requirements for the programme you applied to and application fee and supporting documents must have been received before deadline to University Admissions

**Type**: Scholarship

**Value**: Scholarships will cover the cost of tuition but not living expenses

**Country of Study**: Any country

**Application Procedure**: You must then submit an online scholarship application form on which you will note your application ID from www.universityadmissions.se

**Closing Date**: 20 January

**Contributor**: The Uppsala University in Sweden

**Additional Information**: For more details, visit official scholarship website: www.uu.se/en/admissions/scholarships/uppsala-university/

#### For further information contact:

**Email**:    tuitiongrants@uadm.uu.se

## US Department of Energy

### Department of Energy Computational Science Graduate Fellowship Krell Institute

**Subjects**: Engineering and the physical, computer, mathematical or life sciences

**Purpose**: To help ensure a supply of scientists and engineers trained to meet workforce needs; to make Department of Energy laboratories available to fellows for work experiences; to strengthen ties between the national academic community and Department of Energy laboratories; and to make computational science careers more visible.

**Eligibility**: Applicants should either be undergraduate seniors, applicants with no more than B.S. or B.A. degrees who are not enrolled in graduate school, first-year graduate students (M.S. degree or PhD students without an M.S. degree), enrolled M.S. degree students beyond their first year provided that they plan full-time, uninterrupted study toward a PhD at: 1) a different academic institution, OR 2) in a different academic department, applicants with no more than M.S. degrees who are not currently enrolled AND who will not have been enrolled in graduate school for two years prior to resuming graduate studies, first-year PhD students with an M.S. degree provided that they 1) completed the M.S. degree within two years at a different academic institution, 2) completed the M.S. degree within two years in a different academic department, OR 3) prior to current enrollment, they had not been enrolled in graduate school for at least two years

**Type**: Fellowship

**Value**: Yearly stipend of $37,000, payment of full tuition and required fees during the appointment period (at any accredited U.S. university), a $5,000 academic allowance in the first fellowship year and a $1,000 allowance each renewed year (to be used for the purchase of a computer workstation or for research/professional development expenses), and more

**Length of Study**: 4 years, but must be renewed annually

**Frequency**: Annual

**Country of Study**: United States of America

**Additional Information**: www.krellinst.org/csgf/

### Nuclear Security Administration Stewardship Science Graduate Fellowship

**Purpose**: To ensure a continuous supply of highly trained scientists and engineers in areas of study related to high energy density physics, nuclear science, and materials under extreme conditions and hydrodynamics; to give DOE NNSA SSGF recipients opportunities to do research at DOE defense laboratories; to assemble a national meeting where fellows, university faculty and laboratory scientists share research advancements; to give fellows opportunities to work with some of the nation's most sophisticated and powerful experimental and computational facilities; to make graduating fellows aware of employment opportunities within the Department of Energy and its laboratory system; and to build the next generation of leaders with expertise in stewardship science in support of national defense.

**Eligibility**: Senior undergraduate students and first- and second-year graduate students. Recipients must be enrolled as full-time graduate students at an accredited U.S. college or university and must study and research within the fellowship's goals. During the summer, fellows should conduct full-time research related to completing their degree, enroll in classes or take a practicum assignment at one of the DOE NNSA laboratories.

**Type**: Fellowship

**Value**: Yearly stipend of $36,000, payment of full tuition and required fees during the appointment period (at any accredited U.S. university), a $5,000 academic allowance in the first fellowship year and a $1,000 allowance for research or professional development expenses

**Length of Study**: Four years, but must be renewed annually

**Frequency**: Annual

**Country of Study**: United States of America

**Closing Date**: January

**Additional Information**: www.krellinst.org/ssgf/

## The Energy Efficiency and Renewable Energy (EERE) Science and Technology Policy (STP) Fellowships

**Subjects**: Engineering; Physical Sciences

**Purpose**: The Energy Efficiency and Renewable Energy (EERE) Science and Technology Policy (STP) Fellowships serve as a next step in the educational and professional development of scientists and engineers by providing opportunities to participate in policy-related projects at DOE's Office of Energy Efficiency and Renewable Energy in Washington, D.C. Participants will become part of a group of highly-trained scientists and engineers with the education, background, and experience to be part of the workforce that supports the DOE's mission in the future.

**Eligibility**: Advanced degree in engineering or physical sciences; Knowledge of energy efficiency concepts, technologies and RD&D programs, specifically those related to HVAC, refrigeration, refrigerants, and/or building energy efficiency

**Type**: Fellowship

**Value**: Selected candidates will receive a stipend as support for their living and other expenses during this appointment. Stipend rates are determined by EERE officials and are based on the candidate's academic and professional background. Relocation expenses, not to exceed $5,000, incurred in relocating from the participant

**Length of Study**: Varies

**Study Establishment**: Office of Energy Efficiency and Renewable Energy (EERE) Building Technologies Office (BTO)

**Country of Study**: United States of America

**Application Procedure**: Via website at: www.zintellect.com/Account/ApplicantRegister/4347; A complete application consists of: An application Transcript(s) - For this opportunity, an unofficial transcript or copy of the student academic records printed by the applicant or by academic advisors from internal institution systems may be submitted. Selected candidate may be required to provide proof of completion of the degree before the appointment can start. A current resume/curriculum vitae (CV) The resume/CV must include the following: Basic applicant Information: Name, address, phone, email, and other contact information. Work & Research Experience: List all work and research experiences beginning with current or most recent. Include the name of the employer, location, position held, and time period involved. Leadership Experience: List experiences (e.g., work, civic, volunteer, research) that demonstrate your leadership skills. Detail your role, type of experience, organization, location, and duration. Educational History: List all institutions from which you received or expect to receive a degree, beginning with current or most recent institution. Include the name of the academic institution, degree awarded or expected, date of awarded or expected degree, and academic discipline. Honors & Awards: List in chronological order (most recent first) any awards or public recognitions. Include the name of awarding institution, title of the award or honor, and date of award or honor. All documents must be in English or include an official English translation.

**Additional Information**: Quote reference code in all correspondence: DOE-EERE-STP-BTO-2018-1202 www.zintellect.com/Opportunity/Details/DOE-EERE-STP-BTO-2018-1202

## Utrecht University

Domplein 29, NL-3512 JE Utrecht, Netherlands.

**Tel**: (31) 30 253 26 70
**Email**: studievoorlichting@uu.nl
**Website**: www.uu.nl

Utrecht University stands for broad and interdisciplinary education. Students at Utrecht University learn to look beyond the boundaries of their fields of study and work together in interdisciplinary projects. The education programmes are modern and innovative. Students and high-ranking scientists work together on a better future.

## Utrecht Excellence Scholarships for International Students

**Eligibility**: To be eligible for an Utrecht Excellence Scholarship, you must: 1. Belong to the top 10% of your graduating class. 2. Hold a non-European Union/EEA passport and not be eligible for support under the Dutch system of study grants and loans. 3. Have completed your secondary school and/or Bachelor degree outside the Netherlands. 4. Have applied for an eligible international master's programme with a start date of 1 September

**Level of Study**: Graduate, Postgraduate

**Type**: Scholarship

**Value**: tuition fees plus €11.000 living expenses

**Frequency**: Annual

**Country of Study**: Any country

**Application Procedure**: Your application for a scholarship will only be processed if you have submitted an application for a Master's programme as well. After submitting an application for the Master's programme, non-European Union/ EEA students will have the option to submit an application for an Utrecht Excellence Scholarship. Prospective students who wish to be considered for the scholarship must apply before 1 February. Please note that in some cases you may need to apply before 1 December; check the 'When to apply' section under Admission and application of your master's programme. It is important to visit the official website (link found below) for detailed information on how to apply for this scholarship. Application has to be processed online. E-mail is not required

**No. of awards offered**: 25

**Closing Date**: 31 January

**Funding**: Private

**Additional Information**: Official Scholarship Website: www. uu.nl/masters/en/general-information/international-students/ financial-matters/grants-and-scholarships/utrecht-excellence-scholarships www.uu.nl/masters/en/general-information/international-students/financial-matters/grants-and-scholarships/ utrecht-excellence-scholarships

### For further information contact:

**Email**:      study@uu.nl

# V

## Vascular Cures

### Wylie Scholar Program

**Subjects**: Vascular health

**Purpose**: Vascular Cures, Wylie Scholar Program is building a pipeline of innovators in vascular health. We provide 3-year career development grants to outstanding young vascular surgeon-scientists who combine active patient care with academic research. The award supports crucial research that enables them to compete for future research funding. Wylie Scholars become North America's world-class vascular surgeon-scientists; many are now chiefs at major academic centers, prominent leaders in the field, and play a key role in our programs. Four Wylie Scholars are on our Scientific Advisory Board and another is leading Project Voice.

**Eligibility**: Candidates must hold a full-time faculty appointment as a vascular surgeon with active privileges at a medical school accredited by the Liaison Committee on Medical Education in the United States or the Committee for the Accreditation of Canadian Medical Schools in Canada. Only one nomination per institution per year will be considered. The following conditions also must be met: The candidate must hold a valid and current certification from the American Board of Surgery, or the Royal College of Physicians and Surgeons of Canada, in general surgery or vascular surgery. The candidate must be an active, practicing clinical vascular surgeon. The candidate must present convincing evidence of rigorous research training and significant research accomplishments to date. The candidate must not be currently funded by a career development award from the National Institutes of Health, Veterans Affairs, American Heart Association, or similar extramural funding agencies. Concomitant awards similar in size to the Wylie Scholar (e.g. from professional societies such as the American College of Surgeons) must be disclosed and will be considered on an individual basis. The candidate must prepare and present a challenging research plan to be completed during the term of the award. The candidate must have a research mentor who will be an additional resource for his or her research. The Chairman of the Department of Surgery must guarantee that the candidate will have 40% protected time available to devote to the research investigation, as well as facilities, equipment and resources to execute the proposed studies. The candidate is expected to participate in the Vascular Cures Wylie Scholar award event each year during their research grant tenure. This includes participating in a scientific interchange with Vascular Cures Board of Directors and donors. Up to C$1,800 of the annual stipend may be used for travel expenses and one night of lodging.

**Level of Study**: Junior Faculty

**Type**: Grant

**Value**: C$150,000

**Length of Study**: 3 years

**Country of Study**: United States of America or Canada

**Application Procedure**: Apply online

**Closing Date**: 2 March

**Additional Information**: vascularcures.org/wylie-scholar-program-2/

## Victoria University

PO Box 14428, Melbourne, VIC 8001, Australia.

| | |
|---|---|
| **Tel**: | (61) 9919 4659 |
| **Email**: | lesley.birch@vu.edu.au |
| **Website**: | www.vu.edu.au |
| **Contact**: | Ms Lesley Birch |

Victoria University is one of Australia's leading universities, where challenging conventional thinking is not only encouraged but also expected. It has 11 campuses and sites, 46,000 enrolled students, 7,900 international students from over 30 countries, 700 courses in higher education and TAFE.

© Springer Nature Limited 2020
Palgrave Macmillan (ed.), *The Grants Register 2021*,
https://doi.org/10.1057/978-1-349-95988-4

## Victoria University Research Scholarships

**Purpose**: To support students undertaking Master's research and research Doctorates
**Eligibility**: Open to citizens or permanent residents of Australia who have achieved Honours 1 or equivalent having studied at or currently studying at Victoria University of Technology
**Level of Study**: Postgraduate
**Type**: Scholarship
**Value**: AU$22,500
**Length of Study**: 1 year
**Frequency**: Annual
**Study Establishment**: Victoria University
**Country of Study**: Australia
**Closing Date**: 31 October

### For further information contact:

**Tel**:      (61) 3 9688 4659
**Fax**:     (61) 3 9688 4559
**Email**:   Lesley.Birch@vu.edu.au

## Victoria University of Wellington

PO Box 600, Wellington 6140, New Zealand.

**Tel**:          (64) 4 463 5113, 4 472 1000
**Email**:      scholarships-office@vuw.ac.nz
**Website**:   www.vuw.ac.nz
**Contact**:   Scholarship Office

Victoria University of Wellington is New Zealand's most research intensive university, located in New Zealand's compact vibrant capital city. It is one of the oldest universities in New Zealand. Victoria has produced Nobel prize winning scholars and a Booker Prize winner. Victoria provides excellent supervision, facilities and financial support for postgraduate research. Scholarships are available in all disciplines.

## Therle Drake Postgraduate Scholarship

**Purpose**: The scholarship is for postgraduate classical performance overseas study and application should be made in the year for which the project is planned. While the terms of the bequest are that preference be given to a piano student, other applicants will be considered
**Eligibility**: The project will normally involve the student attending a short course (up to four weeks), or attending and/or participating in concerts and/or masterclasses in Europe, North America or Australia. The project should be complementary to the current postgraduate course of study at the NZSM and create minimal disruption to any structured course work.
**Level of Study**: Postgraduate
**Type**: Scholarship
**Value**: Approximately US$12,000, subject to funds available
**Length of Study**: 1 year
**Frequency**: Annual
**Country of Study**: Any country
**No. of awards offered**: Varies
**Closing Date**: 1 November
**Funding**: Private
**Additional Information**: www.scholarshipsads.com/therle-drake-postgraduate-scholarship-for-international-students-in-new-zealand-2019/

### For further information contact:

**Tel**:        (64) 4 463 5557
**Email**:   scholarships-office@vuw.ac.nz, pg-research@vuw.ac.nz, summer-research@vuw.ac.nz

## Vice-Chancellor's Strategic Doctoral Research Scholarships

**Eligibility**: Applicants are expected to have the equivalent of a New Zealand First Class Honours Degree and skills and research experience appropriate for the topic
**Level of Study**: Doctorate, Research
**Type**: Scholarship
**Value**: NZ$20,000 per year
**Frequency**: Annual
**Study Establishment**: Victoria University
**Country of Study**: New Zealand
**Application Procedure**: Application forms must be forwarded to the scholarships manager. Topics are advertised at www.ac.nz/scholarships from 1 March each year
**No. of awards offered**: 35
**Closing Date**: 15 May
**Contributor**: Victoria University
**No. of awards given last year**: 10
**No. of applicants last year**: 35

### For further information contact:

Scholarships Office, Office of Research and Postgraduate Study, Victoria University of Wellington, PO Box 600, Wellington 6140, New Zealand.

**Tel**:        (64) 4 463 5113 or 4 463 7493
**Email**:   Scholarships-Office@vuw.ac.nz

## Victoria Hardship Fund Equity Grants for International Students in New Zealand

**Purpose**: These grants are to encourage students who are facing financial hardship to continue in their studies at Victoria University. The Grants are intended to assist with ongoing costs related to study. They are not intended for tuition fees
**Eligibility**: Scholarships are open to all students who are studying at Victoria University of Wellington including domestic, international, undergraduate, postgraduate, part-time and full-time students. The Victoria University has a tradition of fostering strong global links in teaching and research and program of national significance and international quality. Applicants must be enrolled in the trimester they are applying for e.g. students who apply for round 1 must be enrolled in trimester 1 of the same year. The grants will be awarded on the basis of financial need and satisfactory academic commitment and progress. Factors taken into consideration when assessing financial need could include - high course costs, high transport costs, medical conditions or disability preventing part-time work, family to support, any other relevant circumstances
**Level of Study**: Graduate
**Type**: Grant
**Value**: Scholarship upto NZ$2,000 will be provided
**Frequency**: Annual
**Country of Study**: Any country
**Application Procedure**: Application can be processed through online mode with the below link. www.victoria.ac.nz
**Closing Date**: 18 February
**Funding**: Private
**Additional Information**: scholarship-positions.com/victoria-hardship-fund-equity-grants-international-students-new-zealand/2018/12/20/

### For further information contact:

Victoria University of Wellington, PO Box 600, Wellington 6140, New Zealand.

**Tel**:      (64) 4 463 5557
**Email**:   info@victoria.ac.nz

## Victoria Tongarewa Scholarship

**Purpose**: Scholarships for study in the following year will be awarded competitively on the basis of academic excellence. Scholarships will be credited to tuition fees. Shortlisted candidates may be requested to undertake a skype interview
**Eligibility**: Scholarship is available for pursuing Undergraduate and postgraduate degree
**Level of Study**: Postgraduate
**Type**: Scholarship

**Value**: US$10,000
**Length of Study**: 1 year
**Frequency**: Annual
**Country of Study**: Any country
**Closing Date**: 31 October
**Funding**: International office
**Additional Information**: www.scholarshipsads.com/victoria-tongarewa-scholarship-at-victoria-university-of-wellington-in-new-zealand-2019/

### For further information contact:

**Tel**:      (64) 4 463 5557

## Wellington Graduate Award

**Purpose**: The Wellington Graduate Award encourages undergraduate students to proceed to graduate study and to research degrees
**Eligibility**: Applicants are expected to have achieved a minimum A grade average (GPA 8.0) at 300-level or above however, the number offered are based on the funds available determining the final minimum GPA requirement in any one year.
**Level of Study**: Postgraduate
**Type**: Scholarship
**Value**: Value of US$5,000
**Length of Study**: 1 year
**Frequency**: Annual
**Study Establishment**: Victoria University
**Country of Study**: Any country
**No. of awards offered**: Varies
**Closing Date**: 1 November
**Contributor**: Victoria University
**Additional Information**: www.wgtn.ac.nz/scholarships/scholarships-office

### For further information contact:

Scholarships Office, Office of Research and Postgraduate Study, Victoria University of Wellington, PO Box 600, Wellington 6140, New Zealand.

**Tel**:      (64) 4 463 5557
**Email**:   scholarships-office@vuw.ac.nz, pg-research@vuw.ac.nz

## Wellington Master's by Thesis Scholarship

**Purpose**: To encourage postgraduate research at Victoria University of Wellington, the University offers scholarships to students about to begin a full-time, research-focussed Master's degree

**Eligibility**: Applications are sought from those who are eligible at the time of application, or who will have become eligible at the start of Trimester 2 the following year, to enrol for a Master's degree by thesis worth 90 points or more. In some cases this will be Part 2 of a two-year Master's degree and will usually have the course code 591. Applicants undertaking a 180 point Master's degree will not be eligible for this scholarship. Applicants would normally be expected to have completed a Bachelor's degree or Master's degree Part 1 demonstrating academic achievement equivalent to a First-Class Honours degree from a New Zealand University. Scholarships will be awarded solely on the basis of academic merit by the University Research Scholarships Committee, a sub-committee of the University Research Committee.

**Level of Study**: Postgraduate
**Type**: Scholarship
**Value**: US$15,000 tax free stipend
**Length of Study**: 1 year
**Frequency**: Annual
**Study Establishment**: Victoria University
**Country of Study**: Any country
**No. of awards offered**: Varies
**Closing Date**: 1 November
**Contributor**: Victoria University
**Additional Information**: www.wgtn.ac.nz/scholarships/current/victoria-masters-by-thesis-scholarship

### For further information contact:

Scholarships Office, Office of Research and Postgraduate Study, Victoria University of Wellington, PO Box 600, Wellington 6140, New Zealand.

**Tel**:        (64) 4 463 5557
**Email**:    scholarships-office@vuw.ac.nz, pg-research@vuw.ac.nz

## Villa I Tatti and the Museo Nacional del Prado

Florence, Italy and Madrid, Spain.

**Email**:      fellowships@itatti.harvard.edu
**Website**:   itatti.harvard.edu/

Villa I Tatti - The Harvard University Center for Italian Renaissance Studies (Florence, Italy) and the Museo Nacional del Prado (Madrid, Spain)

## I Tatti/Museo Nacional del Prado Joint Fellowship

**Subjects**: These fellowship are for scholars specializing in art history, with preference given to advanced research projects that address the relationship between Spain and Italy (including transnational connections and dialogues with Latin America) during the Renaissance, broadly understood historically to include the period from the 14th to the 17th century.

**Purpose**: A fellowship designed to support early and mid-career scholars in the field of art history, with preference given to advanced research projects that address the relationship between Spain and Italy (including transnational connections and dialogues with Latin America) during the Renaissance, broadly understood historically to include the period from the 14th to the 17th century.

**Eligibility**: Applicants must have their PhD certificate by the time they apply. They must be conversant in English and Spanish and have at least a reading knowledge of Italian, with a solid background in Italian and/or Spanish and Latin American studies. Each successful candidate must be approved by both the Museo Nacional del Prado and Villa I Tatti and will spend the fall term (mid-September - mid-December) at the Museo del Prado in Madrid supported by Centro de Estudios de Europa Hispánica and the spring term (January-June) at Villa I Tatti in Florence. During both terms, it must be possible for Fellows to carry out most of their research with the resources available in the city where they are resident. Priority will be given to applicants with no previous association with either I Tatti or the Museo del Prado.

**Level of Study**: Postdoctorate
**Type**: Residential Fellowship
**Value**: The stipend for the autumn semester in Madrid is €3,000 per month, supported by the Centro de Estudios de Europa Hispánica. The stipend for the spring semester in Florence is US$4,000 per month, plus a one-time supplement (maximum US$1,500) towards relocation expenses. An additional US$1,000 per month will be offered to offset rental costs, if applicable.

**Length of Study**: One academic year
**Frequency**: Annual
**Country of Study**: Fellows will spend the fall tsemester (September - December) in Madrid and the spring semester (January-June) in Florence.
**No. of awards offered**: 1
**Closing Date**: 15 November
**Contributor**: The semester at the Prado in Spain is made possible with the support of the Centro de Estudios de Europa Hispánica (CEEH)
**Additional Information**: itatti.harvard.edu/fellowships

### For further information contact:

itatti.harvard.edu/i-tattimuseo-nacional-del-prado-joint-fellowship.

## Villa I Tatti and the Warburg Institute School of Advanced Study

Florence, Italy and London, England.

**Email**:     fellowships@itatti.harvard.edu
**Website**:   itatti.harvard.edu/
                warburg.sas.ac.uk/

Villa I Tatti - The Harvard University Center for Italian Renaissance Studies (Florence, Italy) and the Warburg Institute School of Advanced Study at the University of London, England.

### Warburg - I Tatti Joint Fellowship

**Subjects**: A joint, residential fellowship for scholars in the field of history, with preference given to advanced research projects that address the history of science and knowledge related to early modern Italy, including transnational connections between Italy and other cultures. Scholars can also apply to work on the transmission and circulation of ideas, objects, and people during the Renaissance, into and beyond the Italian peninsula, or on the historiography of the Italian Renaissance, including the rebirth of interest in the Renaissance in later periods.
**Purpose**: Villa I Tatti - The Harvard University Center for Italian Renaissance Studies in Florence, Italy, and the Warburg Institute School of Advanced Study at the University of London offer a joint, residential fellowship for early and mid-career scholars in the field of history, with preference given to advanced research projects that address the history of science and knowledge related to early modern Italy, including transnational connections between Italy and other cultures. Scholars can also apply to work on the transmission and circulation of ideas, objects, and people during the Renaissance, into and beyond the Italian peninsula, or on the historiography of the Italian Renaissance, including the rebirth of interest in the Renaissance in later periods.
**Eligibility**: Scholars must have a PhD to apply and may not may not be working on a second doctorate at the time of application. Applicants must be conversant in English and have at least a reading knowledge of Italian, with a solid background in Italian Renaissance Studies. Each successful candidate must be approved by both the Warburg Institute and Villa I Tatti and will spend the fall term (September - December) at the Warburg Institute in London and the spring term (January-June) at Villa I Tatti in Florence. During both terms, It must be possible for Fellows to carry out most of

their research with the resources available in the city where they are resident for the fellowship. Priority will be given to applicants with no previous association with either I Tatti or the Warburg Institute. Applications will not be accepted from candidates proposing to revise their doctoral dissertation for publication.
**Level of Study**: Postdoctorate
**Type**: Residential Fellowship
**Value**: The stipend for the autumn semester at the Warburg is £1,500 per month. The stipend for the spring semester at I Tatti is US$4,000 per month, plus a one-time supplement (maximum US$1,500) towards relocation expenses. An additional US$1,000 per month will be offered to offset rental costs, if applicable.
**Length of Study**: One academic year
**Frequency**: Annual
**Country of Study**: Fellows will spend the fall term (September - December) at the Warburg Institute in London and the spring term (January-June) at Villa I Tatti in Florence.
**No. of awards offered**: 1
**Closing Date**: 15 November
**Additional Information**: itatti.harvard.edu/fellowships

#### For further information contact:

itatti.harvard.edu/warburgi-tatti-joint-fellowship.

## Villa I Tatti: The Harvard University Center for Italian Renaissance Studies

Florence, Italy.

**Email**:     fellowships@itatti.harvard.edu
**Website**:   itatti.harvard.edu/
**Contact**:   Angela Lees, Administrative Assistant

Villa I Tatti is the Harvard University Center for Italian Renaissance Studies in Florence, Italy.

### Berenson Fellowship

**Subjects**: Post-doctoral reasearch on "Italy in the World." Projects should address the transnational dialogues between Italy and other cultures (e.g. Latin American, Mediterranean, African, Asian etc.) during the Renaissance, broadly understood historically to include the period from the 14th to the 17th century.

**Purpose**: A fellowship to support post-doctoral research of scholars who explore "Italy in the World." Projects should address the transnational dialogues between Italy and other cultures (e.g. Latin American, Mediterranean, African, Asian etc.) during the Renaissance, broadly understood historically to include the period from the 14th to the 17th century.

**Eligibility**: At the time of application, scholars must have a PhD They may not be working on a second PhD at the time of application. Applicants must be conversant in English and have familiarity with Italian. Priority will be given to early and mid-career scholars. I Tatti welcomes applications from scholars from all nations and gives special consideration to candidates without regular access to research materials and facilities in Italy.

**Level of Study**: Postdoctorate
**Type**: Residential Fellowship
**Value**: NZ$4,200 per month, plus a one-time supplement (maximum, NZ$1,500) towards relocation expenses. When possible, a one-bedroom apartment will be set aside for the Fellow's use, rent free, but with charges for utilities. If an apartment is not available, NZ$1,000 per month will be offered to help offset rental costs.
**Length of Study**: 4-6 months
**Frequency**: Annual
**Country of Study**: Italy
**No. of awards offered**: Up to 4
**Closing Date**: 15 November
**Contributor**: The Berenson Fellowship is made possible by The Lila Wallace - Reader's Digest Fund
**Additional Information**: itatti.harvard.edu/fellowships

**For further information contact:**

itatti.harvard.edu/berenson-fellowship.

## Craig Hugh Smyth Fellowship

**Subjects**: The Craig Hugh Smyth Fellowship is designed for curators and conservators pursuing advanced research in any aspect of the Italian Renaissance.
**Purpose**: A fellowship designed for curators and conservators pursuing advanced research in any aspect of the Italian Renaissance.
**Eligibility**: Applicants should be scholars who work for an educational or cultural institution as a curator or conservator. They may apply to carry out research on behalf of their home institution, or propose projects relating to their personal research interests. Applicants must be conversant in English and have familiarity with Italian. Priority will be given to early and mid-career scholars. It must be possible for applicants to carry out most of their research in Florence. I Tatti welcomes applications from scholars from all nations and

gives special consideration to candidates without regular access to research materials and facilities in Italy.
**Type**: Residential Fellowship
**Value**: US$4,200 per month, plus a one-time supplement (maximum, US$1,500) towards relocation expenses. When possible, a one-bedroom apartment will be set aside for the Fellow's use, rent free, but with charges for utilities. If an apartment is not available, US$1,000 per month will be offered to help offset rental costs.
**Length of Study**: 4-6 months
**Frequency**: Annual
**Country of Study**: Italy
**No. of awards offered**: 2
**Closing Date**: 15 November
**Additional Information**: itatti.harvard.edu/fellowships

**For further information contact:**

itatti.harvard.edu/craig-hugh-smyth-fellowship.

## David and Julie Tobey Fellowship

**Subjects**: This fellowship supports research on drawings, prints, and illustrated manuscripts from the Italian Renaissance, and especially the role that these works played in the creative process, the history of taste and collecting, and questions of connoisseurship. Proposals on a variety of subjects with a substantive component of research on drawings, prints, and illustrated manuscripts done on paper or parchment types are welcome.
**Purpose**: A fellowship to support post-doctoral research on drawings, prints, and illustrated manuscripts from the Italian Renaissance, and especially the role that these works played in the creative process, the history of taste and collecting, and questions of connoisseurship.
**Eligibility**: Scholars must have a PhD to apply and may not may not be working on a second doctorate at the time of application. They must be conversant in English and have familiarity with Italian. Priority will be given to early and mid-career scholars. It must be possible for applicants to carry out most of their research in Florence. I Tatti welcomes applications from scholars from all nations and gives special consideration to candidates without regular access to research materials and facilities in Italy.
**Level of Study**: Postdoctorate
**Type**: Residential Fellowship
**Value**: US$4,200 per month, plus a one-time supplement (maximum, US$1,500) towards relocation expenses. When possible, a one-bedroom apartment will be set aside for the Fellow's use, rent free, but with charges for utilities. If an apartment is not available, US$1,000 per month will be offered to help offset rental costs.

**Length of Study**: 4-6 months
**Frequency**: Annual
**Country of Study**: Italy
**No. of awards offered**: 1
**Closing Date**: 15 November
**Additional Information**: itatti.harvard.edu/fellowships

**For further information contact:**

itatti.harvard.edu/david-and-julie-tobey-fellowship.

## Fellowship in the Digital Humanities

**Subjects**: Projects can address any aspect of the Italian Renaissance, broadly understood historically to include the period from the 14th to the 17th century, and geographically to include transnational dialogues between Italy and other cultures (e.g. Latin American, Mediterranean, African, Asian, etc.). Projects should apply digital technologies such as mapping, textual analysis, visualization, or the semantic web to topics in fields such as art and architecture, history, literature, material culture, music, philosophy, religion, and the history of science.
**Purpose**: A fellowship to support research of scholars in the humanities or social sciences, librarians, archivists, and data science professionals whose research interests or practice cut across traditional disciplinary boundaries and actively employ technology in their work.
**Eligibility**: Applicants must be conversant in English and have familiarity with Italian. At the time of application, a PhD is required for scholars in the humanities and social sciences. A Master's degree is required for librarians, archivists, and data science professionals. A background in programming, library sciences, computer graphics, computational linguistics, or other fields relevant to digital humanities research is highly desirable. Candidates should possess the technical skills to carry out their project at the time of application, and it must be possible for applicants to carry out most of their research in Florence. Priority will be given to early and mid-career scholars. I Tatti welcomes applications from scholars from all nations and gives special consideration to candidates without regular access to research materials and facilities in Italy.
**Level of Study**: A PhD is required for scholars in the humanities and social sciences. A Master's degree is required for librarians, archivists, and data science professionals.
**Type**: Residential Fellowship
**Value**: US$4,200 per month, plus a one-time supplement (maximum, US$1,500) towards relocation expenses. When possible, a one-bedroom apartment will be set aside for the Fellow's use, rent free, but with charges for utilities. If an apartment is not available, US$1,000 per month will be offered to help offset rental costs.
**Length of Study**: 4-6 months
**Frequency**: Annual
**Country of Study**: Italy
**No. of awards offered**: Up to 4
**Closing Date**: 15 November
**Contributor**: The Fellowship in the Digital Humanities is generously supported in part by the Samuel H. Kress Foundation.
**Additional Information**: itatti.harvard.edu/fellowships

**For further information contact:**

A link to the application will be available at itatti.harvard.edu/fellowship-digital-humanities.

## I Tatti Fellowship

**Subjects**: Post-doctoral research in any aspect of the Italian Renaissance, broadly understood historically to include the period from the 14th to the 17th century and geographically to include transnational dialogues between Italy and other cultures (e.g. Latin American, Mediterranean, African, Asian etc.).
**Purpose**: A Fellowship to support post-doctoral research in any aspect of the Italian Renaissance.
**Eligibility**: Scholars must hold a PhD, dottorato di ricerca, or an equivalent degree. They must be conversant in either English or Italian and able to understand both languages. They should be in the early stages of their career, having received a PhD between 2010-2020 and have a solid background in Italian Renaissance studies. Candidates may not be working on a second PhD at the time of application. In the event that a candidate holds two doctoral degrees, the eligibility dates (PhD certificate dated between January 1, 2010 and December 31, 2020, inclusive) apply to the more recent degree.
**Level of Study**: Postdoctorate
**Type**: Residential Fellowship
**Value**: US$60,000, plus relocation supplement and housing or housing supplement
**Length of Study**: 1 year
**Frequency**: Annual
**Country of Study**: Italy
**No. of awards offered**: 15
**Closing Date**: 15 October
**Additional Information**: itatti.harvard.edu/fellowships

**For further information contact:**

itatti.harvard.edu/i-tatti-fellowship.

## Mellon Fellowship in Digital Humanities

**Eligibility**: A PhD is required for scholars in the humanities and social sciences; in exceptional cases, applications from advanced PhD (ABD) students will be considered. A Master's degree is required for librarians, archivists, and data science professionals. A background in programming, library sciences, computer graphics, computational linguistics, or other fields relevant to digital humanities research is highly desirable. Candidates should possess the technical skills to carry out their project at the time of application

**Type**: Residential fellowships

**Value**: Up to US$4,000 per month plus a one-time supplement (Max: US$1,500)

**Length of Study**: 4 to 6 months

**Frequency**: Annual

**Country of Study**: Italy

**Application Procedure**: Please check at itatti.harvard.edu/mellon-fellowship-digital-humanities

**Closing Date**: 14 December

**Funding**: Foundation

**Contributor**: Andrew W. Mellon Foundation

**Additional Information**: www.sas.rochester.edu/humanities/fellowships/mellon.html

### For further information contact:

**Tel**:      (1) 585 275 9025
**Email**:    morris.eaves@rochester.edu

## Villa I Tatti - Bogaziçi University Joint Fellowship

**Subjects**: This fellowship focusses on the interaction between Italy and the Byzantine Empire (ca. 1300 to ca. 1700) and aims to foster the development of research on Late Byzantine-Italian relations by supporting early-career scholars whose work explores Byzantium's cross-cultural contacts in the late medieval and early modern Mediterranean world through the study of art, architecture, archaeology, history, literature, material culture, music, philosophy, religion, or science.

**Purpose**: Villa I Tatti - The Harvard University Center for Italian Renaissance Studies (VIT, Florence) and the Byzantine Studies Research Center of Bogaziçi University (BSRC, Istanbul) offer a joint, residential fellowship to support research on the interaction between Italy and the Byzantine Empire (ca. 1300 to ca. 1700). This collaboration aims to foster the development of research on Late Byzantine-Italian relations by supporting early-career scholars whose work explores Byzantium's cross-cultural contacts in the late medieval and early modern Mediterranean world through the study of art, architecture, archaeology, history, literature, material culture, music, philosophy, religion, or science.

**Eligibility**: The VIT-BSRC Joint Fellowship is offered for candidates who have received a PhD in or after 2010. Candidates must be conversant in English and have at least a reading knowledge of Italian. They must have a solid background in Italian Renaissance and/or Byzantine Studies. Each successful candidate must be approved by both the BSRC and VIT and will spend the fall term (September - December) at Bogaziçi University in Istanbul and the spring term (January-June) at Villa I Tatti in Florence. During both terms, it must be possible for Fellows to carry out most of their research with the resources available in the city where they are resident. Priority will be given to applicants with no previous association with VIT or BSRC.

**Level of Study**: The VIT-BSRC Joint Fellowship is offered for candidates who have received a PhD in or after 2010.

**Type**: Residential Fellowship

**Value**: The stipend for the autumn semester in Istanbul is US$1,800 per month, plus a one-time supplement (maximum US$1,500) towards airfare to/from Istanbul. The stipend for the spring semester in Italy is US$4,200 per month plus a one-time supplement (maximum US$1,500) towards relocation expenses. An additional US$1,000 per month will be offered to offset rental costs, if applicable.

**Length of Study**: One academic year.

**Frequency**: Annual

**Country of Study**: Fellows will spend the fall term (September - December) in Istanbul and the spring term (January - June) in Florence.

**No. of awards offered**: 1

**Closing Date**: 15 November

**Additional Information**: itatti.harvard.edu/fellowships

### For further information contact:

itatti.harvard.edu/i-tatti-bogazici-joint-fellowship.

## Wallace Fellowship

**Subjects**: Post-doctoral research on historiography and impact of the Italian Renaissance in the Modern Era (19th-21st centuries). Projects can address the historiography or impact of the Renaissance on any field, including art and architecture, landscape architecture, history, literature, material culture, music, philosophy, religion, and science.

**Purpose**: A Fellowship to support post-doctoral research on the historiography and impact of the Italian Renaissance in the Modern Era (19th-21st centuries).

**Eligibility**: At the time of application, scholars must have a PhD They may not be working on a second PhD at the time of application. Applicants must be conversant in English and have familiarity with Italian. Priority will be given to early and mid-career scholars. It must be possible for applicants to carry out most of their research in Florence. I Tatti welcomes applications from scholars from all nations and gives special consideration to candidates without regular access to research materials and facilities in Italy.

**Level of Study**: Postdoctorate

**Type**: Residential Fellowship

**Value**: US$4,200 per month, plus a one-time supplement (maximum, US$1,500) towards relocation expenses. When possible, a one-bedroom apartment will be set aside for the Fellow's use, rent free, but with charges for utilities. If an apartment is not available, US$1,000 per month will be offered to help offset rental costs.

**Length of Study**: 4-6 months

**Frequency**: Annual

**Country of Study**: Italy

**No. of awards offered**: Up to 4

**Closing Date**: 15 November

**Contributor**: The Wallace Fellowships are made possibly by a generous grant from The Lila Wallace - Reader's Digest Fund.

**Additional Information**: itatti.harvard.edu/fellowships

### For further information contact:

itatti.harvard.edu/wallace-fellowship.

## Vinaver Trust

45 Albert Street, Western Hill, Durham DH1 4RJ, United Kingdom.

| | |
|---|---|
| **Tel**: | (44) 19 1386 8898 |
| **Email**: | geoffreybromiley@btinternet.com |
| **Contact**: | Dr G.N. Bromiley, Secretary-Treasurer |

The Eugène Vinaver Memorial Trust exists to promote research into Arthurian studies, as defined by the International Arthurian Society. It offers subventions to publishers to facilitate the publication of scholarly works; it also offers grants to postgraduate students pursuing research in the Arthurian field.

## Barron Bequest

**Subjects**: Any field of Arthurian studies

**Purpose**: To support postgraduate research in Arthurian studies

**Eligibility**: Open to graduates of any university of the United Kingdom and Ireland

**Level of Study**: Postgraduate research

**Type**: Grant

**Value**: £1,250, payment towards postgraduate fees.

**Length of Study**: One year. Candidates may apply for further years on a basis of parity with those applying for the first time

**Frequency**: Annual

**Study Establishment**: Any university in United Kingdom or Ireland

**Country of Study**: United Kingdom, Republic of Ireland

**Application Procedure**: For application details, applicants must contact Professor Taylor at the address below

**No. of awards offered**: Varies, normally one or two per year

**Closing Date**: 30 April

**Funding**: Private

**Contributor**: The Eugène Vinaver Memorial Trust

**No. of awards given last year**: No awards made

**No. of applicants last year**: 2

**Additional Information**: www.science-community.org/en/node/150641

### For further information contact:

Professor JHM Taylor, Garth Head, Penruddock, Penrith, Cumbria CA11 0QU, United Kingdom.

| | |
|---|---|
| **Email**: | jane.taylor@durham.ac.uk or |
| | geoffreybromiley@btinternet.com |

## Vinod & Saryu Doshi Foundation

58, Nariman Bhavan, Nariman Point, Mumbai, Maharashtra 400021, India.

| | |
|---|---|
| **Tel**: | (91) 6117 9000 |
| **Contact**: | Vinod & Saryu Doshi Foundation |

The Vinod & Saryu Doshi Foundation is a non-profit charitable trust that supports initiatives in the fields of Art & Culture, Education and Community. It seeks to embody the lifelong passions and values of Vinod and Saryu Doshi, who believed that the mind is enriched through education and the spirit through art and culture. They have spent a considerable part of their lives supporting these causes. The Vinod & Saryu Doshi Foundation initiated these Fellowships to assist Indian nationals who have received acceptance in a University abroad to pursue their post-graduate studies (Masters, Postgraduate diploma/certificate or doctorate) in the field of Liberal Arts & Sciences. This includes the Humanities, Social Sciences, the Natural Sciences and Mathematics.

### Vinod & Saryu Doshi Foundation Postgraduate Fellowships

**Purpose**: The main aim of the fellowship program is to enhance the higher education by giving an opportunity to academically bright students who have the drive to succeed but are unable to do so due to their financial challenges. This is a need-based merit Fellowship and abides by the Equal Opportunity and Affirmative Action policy. The maximum amount of the Fellowship will be up to ₹3 lakhs per fellow, which will be payable as a one-time amount

**Eligibility**: Indian Nationals only

**Type**: Postgraduate scholarships

**Value**: Up to ₹3 lakh

**Study Establishment**: Liberal Arts and Social Sciences

**Country of Study**: Any country

**Application Procedure**: Fill in the application form and send the hard copy to Vinod & Saryu Doshi Foundation

**Closing Date**: 7 May

**Additional Information**: For more details please visit the website scholarship-positions.com/vinod-saryu-doshi-found ation-postgraduate-fellowships-liberal-arts-sciences-2017/2017/02/20/

## For further information contact:

**Email**: ericadesouza@vsdf.org

## Volkswagen Foundation

Kastanienallee 35, D-30519 Hannover, Germany.

**Tel**: (49) 511 8381 0
**Email**: info@volkswagenstiftung.de
**Contact**: VolkswagenStiftung

The Volkswagen Foundation (VolkswagenStiftung) is dedicated to the support of the humanities and social sciences as well as science and technology in higher education and research. It funds research projects in path-breaking areas and provides assistance to academic institutions for the improvement of the structural conditions for their work. In particular, the Foundation perceives its mission in supporting aspiring young researchers and in promoting interdisciplinary and international collaboration.

## Volkswagen Foundation Freigeist Fellowships

**Purpose**: The Freigeist funding initiative aims to encourage exceptional research personalities to embark on visionary, risk-taking research projects at the intersections between established field of research

**Eligibility**: Anyone can apply who identifies with the goals of a "Freigeist" Fellowship and whose proposed research projects fits in with the aims pursued by the Freigeist initiative

**Level of Study**: Doctorate, Postdoctorate

**Value**: Up to €3,500,000

**Length of Study**: 4 years

**Frequency**: Annual

**Country of Study**: Germany

**Application Procedure**: Applications can be submitted online via the Electronic Application System of the Volkswagen Foundation. Instructions are found online

**Closing Date**: 15 October

**Additional Information**: scholarships.unimelb.edu.au/awards/volkswagen-foundation-freigeist-fellowships

# W

## W.F. Albright Institute of Archaeological Research

### Sean W. Dever Memorial Prize

**Purpose**: The W.F. Albright Institute of Archaeological Research in Jerusalem announces the Sean W. Dever Memorial Prize call for papers. This prize provides US$750 for the best article published or paper presented at a conference that treats a topic in the field of Syro-Palestinian or Biblical Archaeology

**Eligibility**: Authors must be PhD candidates in the semester in which the winner is announced. They may be of any nationality, but the article or paper must be in English. Co-written or co-presented pieces may be submitted if all the authors or presenters are doctoral candidates; the prize, if awarded, will be divided equally among authors or presenters. All submissions must be in PDF format only

**Level of Study**: Postgraduate

**Type**: Prize

**Frequency**: Annual

**Country of Study**: Any country

**Application Procedure**: The submission of conference papers must include images (if used in the presentation) in PDF format (either as a separate document or embedded within the text of the paper), and full citations and bibliographic references. Kindly submit the initial documents through the following link. aiarfellowships.fluidreview.com

**Closing Date**: 31 December

**Funding**: Private

**Additional Information**: aiar.org/sean-w-dever-memorial-prize-2018/

### For further information contact:

P.O. Box 19096, Jerusalem 9119002, Israel.

**Tel**:     (972) 2 628 8956
**Email**:     albrightinstitute@aiar.org

## Wageningen University

### Wageningen University & Research Africa Scholarship Program

**Purpose**: Applications are open for the Wageningen University & Research Africa Scholarship Program. The Africa Scholarship Program (ASP) has been initiated by Wageningen University & Research to give talented and motivated students from Africa the opportunity to study at the university in Wageningen. With this programme, Wageningen wants to support capacity building in Africa by attracting excellent students for a 2-years master's program. Wageningen University & Research is a collaboration between Wageningen University and the Wageningen Research foundation

**Eligibility**: 1. African students who want to start their study in September may be eligible for the scholarship. 2. Excellent students with a GPA of 80% or higher in a bachelor degree, and admitted to a Wageningen University MSc Program

**Level of Study**: Postgraduate

**Type**: Scholarship

**Frequency**: Annual

**Country of Study**: Any country

**No. of awards offered**: 7

**Closing Date**: 1 February

**Funding**: Foundation

**Additional Information**: For More Information: www.wur.nl/en/Education-Programmes/master/Scholarships/Africa-Scholarship-Programme.htm www.opportunitiesforafricans.com/wageningen-university-research-2020-africa-scholarship-programme/

### For further information contact:

**Email**:     wufp@wur.nl

© Springer Nature Limited 2020
Palgrave Macmillan (ed.), *The Grants Register 2021*,
https://doi.org/10.1057/978-1-349-95988-4

# Wal-Mart Foundation

## Walmart Dependent Scholarship

**Purpose**: This award is for graduating high school seniors who are dependents of actively employed Walmart associates within any division of Walmart for at least six consecutive months as of the application deadline. Students must have a grade point average of 2.0 or higher and must demonstrate financial need

**Eligibility**: 1. Must be a high school or home school senior graduating or earning a GED between 1 August, and 31 July. 2. Must be a United States citizen or a United States permanent legal resident. 3. Must be the dependent of an actively employed Walmart associate (employee) within any division of Walmart for at least six consecutive months as of the application deadline date. 4. Must have a cumulative high school grade point average of 2.0 or higher on a 4.0 scale. 5. This award is for United States students

**Level of Study**: Graduate

**Type**: Scholarship

**Value**: US$13,000 - US$6,448,000

**Frequency**: Annual

**Country of Study**: Any country

**Application Procedure**: Apply online: aim.applyISTS.net/WALDEPS

**Closing Date**: 1 April

**Funding**: Foundation

**No. of awards given last year**: 496

**Additional Information**: www.petersons.com/scholarship/walmart-dependent-scholarship-111_190313.aspx

### For further information contact:

702 SW 8th Street, Bentonville, AR 72716, United States of America.

**Tel**:      (1) 877 333 0284
**Fax**:      (1) 479 273 6850
**Email**:    W.Mschol@wal-mart.com

# Warsaw Agricultural University The International Institute of Management and Marketing in Agri-Business (IZMA)

Nowoursynowska 166, PL-02 787 Warsaw Poland.

**Tel**:      (48) 22 873 8501
**Email**:    izma@sggw.waw.pl
**Contact**:  MBA Admissions Officer

# Warsaw Agricultural University MBA in Agribusiness Management

**Length of Study**: 2–5 years

**Application Procedure**: Applicants must supply an application form together with the following: transcripts from previous institutions, a leaving school certificate, three passport photos, a certificate of physical fitness, relevant identification documents. All documents must be translated into Polish by an official translator

### For further information contact:

**Tel**:      (48) 22 843 9751
**Fax**:      (48) 22 843 1877
**Email**:    majewski@alpha.sggw.waw.pl

# Washington Conservation Guild

## Smithsonian Post-Graduate Paintings Conservation Fellowship with NMAAHC and MCI

**Purpose**: The fellow will be invited to participate in the survey, treatment, and exhibition of paintings and will be invited to participate in the preventive care in painting storage at NMAAHC's Visual Art Collection and conduct technical

**Level of Study**: Postgraduate

**Type**: Fellowship

**Value**: US$40,000

**Length of Study**: 1 year

**Frequency**: Annual

**Application Procedure**: Applications for this opportunity are being accepted through the solaa.si.edu/solaa/SOLAAHome.html

**Closing Date**: 31 May

**Additional Information**: washingtonconservationguild.org/2020/02/06/2020-smithsonian-post-graduate-paintings-conservation-fellowship-nmaahc-mci/

### For further information contact:

**Fax**:      (1) 301 238 1231
**Email**:    andersonrs@si.edu, tsangj@si.edu

## National Air and Space Museum - Engen Conservation Fellowship

**Purpose**: Fellows will be encouraged to develop a research project while at NASM. The independent research will be derived from the diverse collection of materials and may be related to evaluations of treatment procedures, ethical considerations, or technical studies

**Eligibility**: 1. The ideal candidate will have a Master's degree in conservation from a recognized program and be able to conduct research independently. The candidate should have knowledge of ethical and professional principles and concepts related to the preservation of objects in a wide variety of media. 2. They should also understand the theories, principles, techniques, practices, and methodologies used to examine, study, treat, analyze and preserve historic objects. 3. Applicants should have a proven record of research, writing ability, and verbal communication skills

**Level of Study**: Graduate, Postgraduate
**Type**: Fellowship
**Frequency**: Annual
**Country of Study**: Any country
**Closing Date**: 15 January
**Funding**: Private
**Additional Information**: washingtonconservationguild.org/2017/11/05/nasm-engen-conservation-fellowship/

**For further information contact:**

Washington Conservation Guild, P.O. Box 553, Kensington, MD 20895, United States of America.

**Email**:    Horelickl@si.edu

# Washington University

Graduate School of Arts and Sciences, Box 1186, 1 Brookings Drive, St. Louis, MO 63130-4899, United States of America.

**Tel**:        (1) 314 935 5000
**Email**:    graduateartsci@wustl.edu
**Contact**:    Dr Nancy P. Pope, Associate Dean

Washington University has a diverse offering of events, disciplines, people, and resources that create unlimited possibilities for discovery and growth. The Graduate School of Arts and Sciences signals a curriculum and place, a core of teaching, learning, and discovery at Washington University.

## Olin School of Business Washington University MBA Programme

**Length of Study**: 2 years
**Application Procedure**: Applicants must have Graduate Management Admission Test scores and TOEFL scores if applicable sent directly to the University, and submit an application form and US$80, before attending a personal interview. International applicants may be invited to participate in a telephone interview. Also necessary are two references and original transcripts from previous colleges both in sealed envelopes, a work history form and a curriculum vitae. Applications can also be made through www.embark.com

**For further information contact:**

John M. Olin School of Business, MBA Program, 1 Brookings Drive, St. Louis, MO 63130, United States of America.

**Tel**:        (1) 314 935 7301
**Fax**:        (1) 314 935 6309
**Email**:    mba@olin.wustl.edu

## Washington American Indian Endowed Scholarship

**Purpose**: The award is based on the financial need of the student. Recipients are selected on the basis of academic merit and a commitment to serve the American Indian community in Washington

**Eligibility**: Recipients are selected on the basis of academic merit and a commitment to serve the American Indian community in Washington. Scholarships are awarded from the interest earnings of an endowment established from funds appropriated by the Washington State Legislature with matching contributions from tribes, individuals, and organizations

**Level of Study**: Graduate
**Type**: Scholarship
**Value**: US$500 to US$2,000
**Frequency**: Annual
**Country of Study**: Any country
**Application Procedure**: Scholarships are awarded from the interest earnings of an endowment established from funds appropriated by the Washington State Legislature with matching contributions from tribes and organizations
**Closing Date**: 1 February
**Funding**: Private
**Additional Information**: www.unigo.com/scholarships/by-major/dance-scholarships/washington-american-indian-endowed-scholarship/1905

**For further information contact:**

917 Lakeridge Way SW, Olympia, WA 98502, United States of America.

**Email**:    aies@wsac.wa.gov

# Wellcome Trust

215 Euston Road, London NW1 2BE, United Kingdom.

**Tel**: (44) 20 7611 2020
**Email**: grantenquiries@wellcome.ac.uk
**Website**: www.wellcome.ac.uk

The Wellcome Trust's mission is to foster and promote research with the aim of improving human and animal health. The Trust funds most areas of biomedical research and funds research in the history of medicine, biomedical ethics, public engagement of science.

## Arts Awards

**Purpose**: Arts Awards support imaginative and experimental arts projects that investigate biomedical science
**Eligibility**: The scheme is open to a wide range of people including, among others, artists, scientists, curators, film-makers, writers, producers, directors, academics, science communicators, teachers, arts workers and education officers. Applicants are usually affiliated to organizations, but can apply as individuals. Organizations might include: museums and other cultural attractions; arts agencies; production companies; arts venues; broadcast media; schools; local education authorities; universities and colleges; youth clubs; community groups; research institutes; the NHS; and science centres. Partnership projects (between different people and organizations, e.g. scientists and ethicists, educators and artists) are welcomed. If this is the first time an organization is applying to the Wellcome Trust an eligibility assessment will be carried out. For this assessment, the following documentation from the applying organization should be submitted: articles of association; audited accounts from the previous 2 years; details of similar projects/grant funding received; confirmation that no funding has been received or is scheduled to be received from any tobacco company
**Level of Study**: Research
**Type**: Award
**Value**: Funding can be applied for at two levels: (1) Small to medium-sized projects (up to and including £40,000). This funding can either be used to support the development of new project ideas, deliver small-scale productions or workshops, investigate and experiment with new methods of engagement through the arts, or develop new collaborative relationships between artists and scientists and (2) Large projects (above £40,000). This funding can be used to fund full or part production costs for large-scale arts projects that aim to have significant impact on the public's engagement with biomedical science. We are also interested in supporting high-quality, multi-audience, multi-outcome projects. Applicants can apply for any amount within the above boundaries, for projects lasting a maximum of 3 years
**Frequency**: Annual
**Application Procedure**: Application form for awards up to and including £40,000, preliminary application form for awards over £40,000
**Funding**: Trusts
**Additional Information**: Applicants must be based in the United Kingdom or the Republic of Ireland and the activity must take place in the United Kingdom or the Republic of Ireland

### For further information contact:

**Tel**: (44) 20 7611 5757
**Email**: PEgrants@wellcome.ac.uk

## Broadcast Development Awards

**Purpose**: To support the development of broadcast proposals in any genre that engages the audience with issues around biomedical science in an innovative, entertaining and accessible way
**Eligibility**: The proposal must primarily be aimed at a mainstream United Kingdom and/or Republic of Ireland audience in the first instance but the subject matter can be international. Applicants are usually affiliated to organizations, but can apply as individuals. The scheme is open to broadcast professionals and other organizations or individuals working on broadcast projects. Partnership between broadcasters and other professionals such as scientists, ethicists, educators etc. are especially welcomed
**Level of Study**: Research
**Type**: Award
**Value**: Up to £10,000, for a maximum of 1 year
**Length of Study**: 1 year
**Application Procedure**: Candidates should complete and submit an application form by the published deadline
**Funding**: Trusts
**Additional Information**: Applicants must be based in the United Kingdom or the Republic of Ireland, although other members of the project team can be based overseas

### For further information contact:

**Tel**: (44) 20 7611 5757
**Email**: PEgrants@wellcome.ac.uk

## Career Re-Entry Fellowships

**Purpose**: This scheme is for postdoctoral scientists who have recently decided to recommence a scientific research career after a continuous break of at least 2 years

**Eligibility**: The awards are open to individuals with a relevant connection to the European Economic Area (EEA). You should be a research scientist with at least 2 years' postdoctoral experience and intend to be based in a United Kingdom or Republic of Ireland organization. You must have had a continuous career break of at least 2 years and should have either a strong research track record (if applying for up to 4 years' support) or demonstrated the potential for a strong research career prior to your break (if applying for 2 years' support). A 2-year fellowship should provide sufficient training support to consolidate your potential. The proposed research should fall within the Wellcome Trust's normal funding remit. Resubmissions are not normally encouraged. If your application has been unsuccessful, please contact the Office for advice. You must have an eligible sponsoring laboratory in the United Kingdom or Republic of Ireland that will administer the fellowship for the duration of the award

**Level of Study**: Professional development

**Type**: Fellowship

**Value**: It provides support that includes the fellow's salary, as determined by the host institution with an additional Trust enhancement, and Research expenses (consumables, animals, travel support to attend scientific meetings)

**Length of Study**: 2–4 years

**Application Procedure**: A preliminary application form (Word 92kB) should be completed and submitted by the published deadline. It should be sent electronically (as a Word document), with the requested accompanying information, to the appropriate funding stream at the Trust (see website). If successful, you will be shortlisted for interview

**Funding**: Trusts

**Additional Information**: For further information visit www. wellcome.ac.uk/Funding/Biomedical-science/Funding-schemes/Fellowships/Basic-biomedical-fellowships/wtd004380.htm wellcome.ac.uk/funding/schemes/research-career-re-entry-fellowships

### For further information contact:

**Tel**:     (44) 20 7611 5757
**Email**:   sciencegrants@wellcome.ac.uk

## Clinical PhD Programmes

**Purpose**: This is a flagship scheme aimed at supporting the most promising medically qualified clinicians who wish to undertake rigorous research training

**Eligibility**: You should have demonstrated the potential to pursue a career as an academic clinician. It is anticipated that many applicants will have already commenced their specialist training, but this is not essential

**Level of Study**: Postgraduate, Research

**Type**: Grant

**Value**: The duration may vary from Programme to Programme, but each provides a clinical salary, PhD registration fees at United Kingdom/EU student rate, research expenses, contribution towards travel and contribution towards general training costs

**Frequency**: Annual

**Country of Study**: African countries

**Application Procedure**: Students are recruited annually by the individual Programmes. Recruitment begins in the preceding January. If you are interested in applying you should contact the relevant Programme directly. Please see website for more details

**Closing Date**: 6 March

**Funding**: Trusts

**Additional Information**: www.sanger.ac.uk/about/study/phd-programmes/clinical-phd-programme

### For further information contact:

**Email**:     clinicalphd@wellcome.ac.uk

## Doctoral Studentships

**Purpose**: This scheme enables scholars to undertake up to 3 years of full-time research on a history of medicine topic leading to a doctoral degree at a university in the United Kingdom or Republic of Ireland

**Eligibility**: You should hold a Master's in the history of medicine or a Master's with strong emphasis on the history of medicine. The proposed project must be on a history of medicine topic. If specialist language skills are essential to undertake the research, a Master's in the language required may be acceptable (classical languages, Arabic, Chinese, etc.). Your application must be sponsored by a senior member of the department, unit or institute, or History of Medicine grantholder (current or former), who would supervise you if an award were made. Applications must be submitted through the host institution

**Level of Study**: Postgraduate, Research

**Value**: Support is provided for up to 3 years, and includes: the student's stipend; a set amount to cover conference travel, research expenses and, where justified, the cost of overseas fieldwork; all compulsory university and college fees at the United Kingdom/Irish/Dutch home postgraduate student level; fees at the overseas rate will not be provided; institutions sponsoring candidates are expected to provide laptops and PCs as part of their postgraduate research-training infrastructure

**Length of Study**: 3 years

**Application Procedure**: Preliminary applications should be made by email or post by the published deadline, and should include: a brief curriculum vitae with details of the Master's degree held; details of the research proposed (maximum of one page); a letter of support from the head of the department in which you will be working (this can be sent under separate cover); a letter of support from the supervisor

**Closing Date**: 16 March

**Funding**: Trusts

**Additional Information**: wellcome.ac.uk/funding/schemes/doctoral-studentships

### For further information contact:

**Tel**:      (44) 20 7611 5757
**Email**:    MHgrants@wellcome.ac.uk

## Four-year PhD Studentship Programmes

**Purpose**: This is a flagship scheme aimed at supporting the most promising students to undertake in depth postgraduate training. Supporting specialized training provided in a range of important biomedical research areas: (1) developmental biology and cell biology; (2) genetics, statistics and epidemiology; (3) immunology and infectious disease; (4) molecular and cellular biology; (5) neuroscience; (6) physiological sciences; (7) structural biology and bioinformatics

**Eligibility**: You should be a student who has, or expects to obtain, a first- or upper-second-class honours degree or equivalent

**Level of Study**: Postgraduate, Research

**Value**: A stipend, PhD registration fees at United Kingdom/EU student rate, contribution towards laboratory rotation expenses in the first year, research expenses for years two to four, contribution towards travel and contribution towards transferable-skills training

**Length of Study**: Support provided for 4 years

**Application Procedure**: Students are recruited annually by the individual Programmes for uptake in October each year. Recruitment begins in the preceding December. If you are interested in applying you should contact the relevant Programme directly. Please see website for details

**Closing Date**: October

**Funding**: Trusts

**Additional Information**: wellcome.ac.uk/funding/schemes/four-year-phd-programmes-studentships-basic-scientists

### For further information contact:

**Email**:    4yrphd@wellcome.ac.uk

## Innovator Awards

**Purpose**: These awards support researchers who are transforming great ideas into healthcare innovations that could have a significant impact on human health.

**Eligibility**: 1. Innovator Awards are open to researchers who are developing healthcare innovations that could have a major and measurable impact on human health. 2. Individuals and teams from not-for-profit and commercial organisations can apply. 3. Organisations can be of any size, based anywhere in the world (apart from mainland China).

**Level of Study**: Research

**Type**: Award

**Value**: Up to £500,000, or up to £750,000 for multi-disciplinary collaborations

**Length of Study**: 2 year

**Frequency**: Annual

**Application Procedure**: You must submit your application through the Wellcome Trust Grant Tracker (WTGT).

**Funding**: Trusts

### For further information contact:

Gibbs Building, 215 Euston Road, London NW1 2BE, United Kingdom.

**Tel**:      (44) 20 7611 5757
**Email**:    innovations@wellcome.ac.uk

## Intermediate Clinical Fellowships

**Purpose**: This scheme is for medical, dental, veterinary or clinical psychology graduates who have had an outstanding start to their research career. It will enable successful candidates to continue their research interests at a postdoctoral level in an appropriate unit or clinical research facility

**Eligibility**: The award is open to individuals with a relevant connection to the EEA. You should have previously undergone a period of research training and will have completed, or be about to complete, a higher degree. You should have completed general professional training as defined by the relevant college. (1) Medical and dental candidates should either have a National Training Number (NTN) or Certificate of Completion of Specialist Training (CCST) or equivalent. (2) Veterinary candidates should have a degree in veterinary medicine (e.g. BVSc, BVM&S, BVMS, BVetMed, VetMB) and some experience in clinical practice and will have completed, or be about to complete, a higher research degree (preferably a PhD). (3) GPs are advised to contact the office to clarify their eligibility. (4) Clinical Psychologists must have obtained a professional Doctorate-level qualification in Clinical Psychology accredited by the British Psychological Society

**Level of Study**: Postgraduate, Research
**Type**: Fellowship
**Value**: Fellowships are for up to 4–5 years, depending on situation. They provide research expenses (consumables, travel, support to attend scientific meetings) and the fellow's salary, set by the host institution according to age and experience. Requests for specific items of equipment, where relevant, may be considered, and research or technical assistance may be requested. However, a laboratory appropriate to the research proposed should be selected, and the necessary facilities required for the proposed research must be available to the candidate. Funding for a period of research abroad may be requested if scientifically justified, and we provide appropriate allowances for fellows based overseas
**Frequency**: Annual
**Application Procedure**: A preliminary application form should be completed and submitted at any time before the appropriate deadline. It should be sent electronically (as a Word document) to the appropriate funding stream at the Trust (see website). If your preliminary application is successful, you will be invited to submit a full application by the published deadline. This will be peer reviewed and considered by the relevant Funding Committee. Shortlisted candidates will subsequently be invited to attend for interview at the Trust
**Funding**: Trusts
**Additional Information**: wellcome.ac.uk/funding/schemes/intermediate-clinical-fellowships

### For further information contact:

**Tel**: (44) 20 7611 5757
**Email**: sciencegrants@wellcome.ac.uk

## Intermediate Fellowships in Public Health and Tropical Medicine

**Purpose**: This scheme enables high-calibre, mid-career researchers from low- and middle-income countries to establish an independent research programme. Fellows must be based primarily in a low- and middle-income country. Research projects should be aimed at understanding and controlling diseases (either human or animal) of relevance to local, national or global health. This can include laboratory based molecular analysis of field or clinical samples, but projects focused solely on studies in vitro or using animal models will not normally be considered under this scheme
**Eligibility**: Applications are only accepted in the Public Health and Tropical Medicine Interview Committee remit. This covers research on infectious and non-communicable diseases within the fields of public health and tropical medicine that is aimed at understanding and controlling diseases (either human or animal) of relevance to local, national or global health. You must be a national or legal resident of a low- and middle-income country and should be either: (1) A graduate in a subject relevant to public health or tropical medicine (e.g. biomedical or social science, veterinary medicine, physics, chemistry or mathematics) with a PhD and 3–6 years' postdoctoral experience, or (2) A medical graduate with a higher qualification equivalent to membership of the United Kingdom Royal Colleges of Physicians (i.e. qualified to enter higher specialist training) or recognized as a specialist within a relevant research area, with 3–6 years' research experience. You must have a relevant high-quality publication record and show potential to become a future scientific leader. Applicants who do not have a PhD but who are educated to first degree or Master's level and have extensive research experience, as evidenced by their publication record, may be considered
**Level of Study**: Postgraduate, Research
**Type**: Fellowship
**Value**: Fellowships are for up to 5 years (non-renewable) and provide support that includes: a basic salary for the fellow; research expenses (e.g. consumables, equipment, collaborative travel, research assistance, technical support); training costs where appropriate and justified; an inflation/flexible funding allowance and support to attend scientific meetings. Contributions to costs of the project which are directly incurred by the overseas institution may be provided
**Application Procedure**: You must complete and submit a preliminary application form by the published deadline. The form should be emailed to phatic@wellcome.ac.uk
**Funding**: Trusts
**Additional Information**: For complete details please check the link www.wellcome.ac.uk/Funding/Biomedical-science/Funding-schemes/Fellowships/Public-health-and-tropical-medicine/wtd025883.htm www.successcds.net/Scholarships/wellcome-trust-training-fellowships-in-public-health-and-tropical-medicine.html

### For further information contact:

**Tel**: (44) 20 7611 5757
**Email**: sciencegrants@wellcome.ac.uk

## International Engagement Awards

**Purpose**: To provide funding for innovative public or community engagement projects that explore biomedical research or health in Africa and Asia and to ensure science can be enjoyed and experienced as part of culture, entertainment and everyday life

**Eligibility**: The scheme is open to a wide range of people, including media professionals, educators, science communicators, health professionals and researchers in bioscience, health, bioethics and history. Partnership projects (between different people and organizations, e.g. scientists and media professionals, ethicists and community workers) are welcomed. Applicants must be based in listed low- and middle-income countries or in the United Kingdom working with partners in the low- and middle-income countries. The activity must primarily take place in one or more low- and middle-income countries and the primary goal must be to involve participants or engage audiences located in low- and middle-income countries. Applicants from listed restructuring countries in Europe and Asia are not eligible. We can only accept applications in the English language but we welcome projects that bring together people from different backgrounds who speak diverse languages. All projects must involve engagement with health research. Projects dealing purely with development research not related to health are not eligible. Please note also, that the scheme is not intended to support standard delivery of health education and promotion which does not focus on health research or involve health researchers. Applicants must be affiliated to organizations or institutions. Organizations might include: media organizations, research centres or research groups, community-based development organizations, education organizations. The International Engagement Awards will not fund traditional scientist-led health research. We may consider an application for participatory health research. This is research in which participants are supported to own and shape a research process, setting their own research questions and directing the research process. This type of research should not look like a consultatory exercise or health education but should aim to be collaborative process of enquiry in which the analysis is conducted and findings can be used by all participating parties. This could lead into circular processes of research and action

**Level of Study**: Research

**Type**: Award

**Value**: Up to £30,000 for projects lasting a maximum of 3 years

**Application Procedure**: Please contact the International Engagement Awards office well in advance of the deadline to request an application form and to confirm the eligibility of your project

**Closing Date**: 19 August

**Funding**: Trusts

**Additional Information**: wellcome.ac.uk/what-we-do/directories/international-engagement-awards-people-funded

### For further information contact:

**Tel**:      (44) 20 7611 5757
**Email**:   PEgrants@wellcome.ac.uk

## International Training Fellowships

**Purpose**: This scheme offers nationals of low- and middle-income countries the opportunity to receive training at postgraduate or postdoctoral level.

**Eligibility**: 1. You're a national of a low- or middle-income country 2. Your proposed research focuses on a health priority in a low- or middle-income country 3. You have sponsorship from an eligible host organisation in a low- or middle-income country apart from mainland China. 4. You must want to undertake a guided period of research so that you can consolidate your existing experience and explore new areas of research. 5. You must have a PhD and be an early-career researcher or have a degree in a relevant subject and some initial research experience or be a clinically qualified doctor (and be qualified to enter higher specialist training), vet, dentist or clinical psychologist, and have some initial research experience.

**Level of Study**: Postgraduate, Postdoctoral

**Type**: Fellowship

**Value**: Usually £15,000 to £300,000 for salary, fees and research expenses

**Length of Study**: 3 year

**Frequency**: Annual

**Application Procedure**: You must submit your application through the Wellcome Trust Grant Tracker (WTGT).

**Closing Date**: 9 July

**Funding**: Trusts

### For further information contact:

Gibbs Building, 215 Euston Road, London NW1 2BE, United Kingdom.

**Tel**:    (44) 20 7611 5757

## Investigator Awards

**Purpose**: To support world-class researchers who are no more than 5 years from appointment to their first academic position, but who can already show that they have the ability to innovate and drive advances in their field of study

**Eligibility**: To be eligible for an Investigator Award you must be based at an eligible higher education or research institution in the United Kingdom, Republic of Ireland or a low- or middle-income country. You should be employed in an established academic post: a permanent, open-ended or long-term rolling contract, salaried by your host institution. You are also eligible if you have a written guarantee of an established academic post at your host institution, which you will take up by the start of the award. If you are based in a low- or middle-income country in sub-Saharan Africa, South-east

Asia or South Asia (with the exception of India - see below), you are eligible to apply if you fulfil the above eligibility criteria and are working within the Trust's broad science funding remit

**Level of Study**: Research

**Type**: Award

**Value**: Awards may be small or large, typically up to £3,000,000, and lasting up to 7 years. The duration and costs you request should be clearly justified by your proposed research. Also, you should ensure that the scope of your proposal and the associated resources are appropriate for your career stage and research experience. The award covers the direct costs of carrying out the research, such as: research expenses; this may include research assistance, animals, equipment, fieldwork costs and funding for collaborative activity; travel and subsistence for scientifically justified visits; overseas allowances where appropriate

**Length of Study**: Flexible duration, up to 7 years

**Frequency**: Annual

**Application Procedure**: The key stages of the application process are: submission of an Investigator Award application form; scientific peer review by one of the Trust's Expert Review Groups, which shortlist the candidates for interview; written peer review of shortlisted applications by external specialist referees, who will include members of the Trust's Peer Review College; selected unattributed referee comments will be fed back to candidates before interview; interview of shortlisted candidates by our Interview Panel. Application forms are available on eGrants, our electronic application system. Please refer to the Additional information for completing the Investigator Award form on eGrants, which provides an overview to help guide you through the application process

**Closing Date**: 27 February

**Funding**: Trusts

**Additional Information**: The Trust has combined its New Investigator and Senior Investigator Award schemes to create a single type of Investigator Award, providing all who hold established posts in eligible organizations with the same opportunity to obtain funding wellcome.ac.uk/funding/schemes/investigator-awards-science

### For further information contact:

**Email**: sciencegrants@wellcome.ac.uk

## Learned Society Curation Awards

**Purpose**: These awards support learned society publishers who want to explore new ways of signalling the significance of published research outputs in an open and transparent manner.

**Level of Study**: Research

**Type**: Award

**Value**: Up to £200,000

**Length of Study**: 3 year

**Frequency**: Annual

**Application Procedure**: You must submit your application through the Wellcome Trust Grant Tracker (WTGT).

**Closing Date**: 20 April

**Funding**: Trusts

### For further information contact:

Gibbs Building, 215 Euston Road, London NW1 2BE, United Kingdom.

**Tel**:     (44) 20 7611 5757

**Email**:    openresearch@wellcome.ac.uk

## Master's Awards

**Purpose**: This scheme enables scholars to undertake basic training in research and methods through a 1-year Master's course in medical history and humanities

**Eligibility**: You should have a minimum of an excellent upper-second-class honours degree (or equivalent) in a relevant subject. Applications will not be considered from those who have already received support for their postgraduate studies from another funding body

**Level of Study**: Postgraduate, Research

**Type**: Award

**Value**: The award is for 1 year, and includes: the student's stipend; all compulsory university and college fees at the United Kingdom home postgraduate student level. Fees at the overseas rate will not be provided

**Frequency**: Annual

**Application Procedure**: All enquiries about Master's Awards should be made directly to the relevant institution

**Closing Date**: 1 May

**Funding**: Trusts

### For further information contact:

**Tel**:     (44) 20 7611 5757

**Email**:    MHgrants@wellcome.ac.uk

## Master's Fellowships in Public Health and Tropical Medicine

**Purpose**: This scheme strengthens scientific research capacity in low- and middle-income countries, by providing support for junior researchers to gain research experience and high-quality research training at Master's degree level.

Research projects should be aimed at understanding and controlling diseases (either human or animal) of relevance to local, national or global health. This can include laboratory based molecular analysis of field or clinical samples, but projects focused solely on studies in vitro or using animal models will not normally be considered under this scheme

**Eligibility**: You should be: 1. A national or legal resident of a low- and middle-income country, and hold a first degree in subject relevant to tropical medicine or public health (clinical or non-clinical). 2. At an early stage in your career, with limited research experience, but have a demonstrated interest in or aptitude for research

**Level of Study**: Postdoctorate, Postgraduate, Research

**Type**: Fellowship

**Value**: This fellowship normally provides up to 30 months' support. A period of 12 months should normally be dedicated to undertaking a taught Master's course at a recognized centre of excellence, combined with up to 18 months to undertake a research project. While undertaking a Master's course, fellows will receive a stipend in accordance with the cost of living in the country in which he/she will be studying; travel costs and support for approved tuition fees. Master's training by distance learning is acceptable. Master's course fees will be paid according to the rate charged by the training institution

**Application Procedure**: A completed application form should be submitted by the sponsor by the published deadline. The form should be emailed to phatic@wellcome.ac.uk

**Closing Date**: 2 March

**Funding**: Trusts

**Additional Information**: For complete details go to address www.wellcome.ac.uk/Funding/Biomedical-science/Funding-schemes/Fellowships/Public-health-and-tropical-medicine/wtd025881.htm

#### For further information contact:

**Tel**:        (44) 20 7611 5757
**Email**:    sciencegrants@wellcome.ac.uk

## Pathfinder Awards

**Purpose**: This scheme, offering pilot funding to catalyse innovative early-stage applied research and development projects in areas of unmet medical need, has been expanded. It now funds discrete projects from applicants in the United Kingdom and Republic of Ireland as well as partnerships between academia and industry based anywhere in the world

**Eligibility**: Applications are welcome from academic and commercial organizations based in the United Kingdom or the Republic of Ireland. Applications from organizations and companies overseas will only be considered when applying in partnership. Check website for complete details

**Level of Study**: Research

**Type**: Grant

**Value**: The average award amount is envisaged to be in the region of £100,000, but up to £350,000 will be considered in exceptional circumstances

**Length of Study**: 18 months

**Frequency**: Dependent on funds available

**Application Procedure**: You should contact us to confirm that your proposed application (and partnership, if appropriate), is eligible before submitting a full application form. After confirming that your application is eligible, you should complete the full application form (see 'Forms and guidance') and send it to innovations@wellcome.ac.uk

**Closing Date**: February

**Funding**: Trusts

**Additional Information**: wellcome.ac.uk/funding/schemes/pathfinder-awards

#### For further information contact:

**Email**:    innovations@wellcome.ac.uk

## Postdoctoral Research Training Fellowships for Clinicians

**Purpose**: This is a flexible fellowship scheme to enable individuals to engage with areas of research that are new to them. It is for candidates who either undertook a PhD early in their career and now wish to refresh their research skills, or have recently completed a successful PhD and wish to explore a new research field or environment, to gain the skills that will help them answer their longer-term research vision

**Eligibility**: The scheme may be suitable for clinicians who: are due to complete their higher degree or are no more than 2 years from the date of their PhD viva by the full application deadline; graduated with a MB/PhD qualification or have achieved a high-quality PhD in a relevant subject, either during or prior to commencing their initial medical, veterinary or dental degree

**Level of Study**: Postgraduate, Research

**Type**: Fellowship

**Value**: Awards are for 2–4 years, depending on whether or not you are planning to reintegrate into your clinical training programme. The total cost of a Fellowship would typically range from £250,000 to £400,000

**Frequency**: Annual

**Application Procedure**: A preliminary application form should be completed and submitted at any time before the published deadline. It should be sent electronically (as a Word document) to Dr Lucy Bradshaw (see website for contact details). If your preliminary application is successful, you will be invited to submit a full application. This will be reviewed and if successful you will be shortlisted for interview

**Funding**: Trusts

**Additional Information**: For more details see www. wellcome.ac.uk/Funding/Biomedical-science/Funding-schemes/ Fellowships/Clinical-fellowships/wtp052588.htm wellcome.ac. uk/funding/schemes/postdoctoral-research-training-fellow ships-clinicians

### For further information contact:

**Tel**:      (44) 20 7611 5757
**Email**:   sciencegrants@wellcome.ac.uk

## Principal Research Fellowships

**Purpose**: This is the most prestigious of our personal awards and provides long-term support for researchers of international standing. Successful candidates will have an established track record in research at the highest level

**Eligibility**: You should have an established track record in research at the highest level. This award is particularly suitable for exceptional senior research scientists currently based overseas who wish to work in the United Kingdom or Republic of Ireland

**Level of Study**: Postgraduate, Research

**Type**: Fellowship

**Value**: Awards are for 7 years in the first instance, and provide both a personal salary and research programme funding in full. After the first period of award, the fellowship will be subject to a competitive scientific review, which will subsequently occur on a rolling basis every 5 years

**Length of Study**: 7 years

**Application Procedure**: If you intend to apply you should contact us with a full curriculum vitae, preferably 18 months in advance of the desired award date. You may not apply for more than one Wellcome Trust fellowship scheme at any one time

**Funding**: Trusts

**Additional Information**: The maximum duration of the awards is 3 years. The awards are full-time but can be tenable on a part-time basis if a case can be made that personal circumstances require this wellcome.ac.uk/funding/schemes/ principal-research-fellowships

### For further information contact:

**Tel**:      (44) 20 7611 5757
**Email**:   sciencegrants@wellcome.ac.uk

## Research and Development for Affordable Healthcare in India

**Purpose**: The objective of this initiative is to fund translational research projects that will deliver safe and effective healthcare products for India, and potentially other markets, at affordable costs. A key feature of the scheme is that it encourages innovations that bring together researchers from both the public and private sectors to extend access to care to the greatest numbers of beneficiaries, without compromising on quality

**Eligibility**: Awards will be agreed by Committee and governed by the terms and conditions, including Wellcome Trust Grant Conditions, funding terms for Affordable Healthcare. In addition there will be additional terms and conditions that will be negotiated under the funding agreement for the award with the applicant

**Level of Study**: Research

**Type**: Award

**Value**: Awards will be made by way of funding agreements that will be negotiated on a case-by-case basis. The principles of the Wellcome Trust Grant Conditions will apply. The terms and conditions of funding will be discussed with applicants individually. Typically, the agreements will contain a provision for the appropriate sharing of benefits. The funds available will be ring-fenced for the specified programme of work. Neither working capital nor building or refurbishment expenditure will be provided. Funding will be released in tranches against the attainment of pre-agreed project milestones

**Application Procedure**: In the first instance interested applicants should contact Dr Shirshendu Mukherjee to discuss their interest in funding via the Affordable Healthcare Initiative. Alternatively, applicants may complete a concept note and mail this directly to Dr Shirshendu Mukherjee

**Closing Date**: 31 January

**Funding**: Trusts

### For further information contact:

**Email**:   s.mukherjee@wellcome.ac.uk

## Research Career Development Fellowships in Basic Biomedical Science

**Purpose**: To provide support for outstanding postdoctoral scientists based in academic institutions in the United Kingdom and Republic of Ireland (RoI)

**Eligibility**: You should have a relevant connection to the European Economic Area. You are expected to have science or veterinary qualifications and, at the preliminary application stage, should normally have between three and 6 years' research experience from the date of your doctoral degree (PhD viva). Due allowance will be given to those whose career has been affected for personal reasons. You must have made intellectual contributions to research that have been published in leading journals, and be able to demonstrate your potential to carry out independent research. The proposed research should fall within our normal funding remit. Resubmissions are not normally encouraged. If your application has been unsuccessful, please contact the Office for advice. You must have an eligible sponsoring host institution in the United Kingdom or Republic of Ireland (RoI) and an eligible sponsor who can guarantee space and resources for the tenure of any award

**Level of Study**: Postdoctorate, Research

**Type**: Fellowship

**Value**: 1. A basic salary, as determined by the host institution, with an additional Wellcome Trust enhancement. 2. Research expenses, including research assistance if required (normally a graduate research assistant or technician; requests for additional research staff may be considered where fieldwork or clinical studies in a low- or middle-income country are proposed). 3. Overseas allowances where appropriate. 4. Travel and subsistence for scientifically justified visits of up to 1 year

**Length of Study**: 5 years

**Frequency**: Annual

**Application Procedure**: A preliminary application form should be completed and submitted by the published deadline. It should be sent electronically (as a Word document), with the requested accompanying information, to the appropriate funding stream at the Trust (see website). If successful, you will be invited to submit a full application

**Closing Date**: 12 May

**Funding**: Trusts

**Additional Information**: wellcome.ac.uk/funding/schemes/research-career-development-fellowships

### For further information contact:

**Tel**:       (44) 20 7611 5757
**Email**:   sciencegrants@wellcome.ac.uk

## Research Fellowships

**Purpose**: Due to the multidisciplinary nature of research on the social and ethical aspects of biomedicine and healthcare, Research Fellowships may provide postdoctoral researchers with support to enable them to obtain research training, either in a new discipline or in a new aspect of their own field, e.g. a humanities scholar who wishes to be trained in social science. In such cases, the requested training must form a substantial component of the proposed research and should not normally be available via the standard funding routes, e.g. by learning new skills as a postdoctoral researcher on a project grant. The requested training should also include methodologies and skills that are new to the applicant. Research training provision can include participation in taught courses, and periods spent in other research groups gaining practical, technical or other skills for introduction to the sponsor's or individual's own group

**Eligibility**: You are eligible to apply if you are a postdoctoral scholar who is not in a tenured or otherwise long-term established post. Fellowships must be held at a United Kingdom, Irish or low- or middle-income country institution. You will also be expected to have been awarded your PhD before you are eligible to apply. Applications from candidates who are still awaiting their viva by the time of the full application will not normally be accepted

**Level of Study**: Research

**Type**: Fellowship

**Value**: An award will not normally exceed £250,000, exclusive of any standard Wellcome Trust allowances. Fellowships provide a salary, plus appropriate employer's contributions. Essential research expenses, including travel and fieldwork, are available, as is a set amount for travel to conferences, seminars and other meetings of a scholarly nature

**Length of Study**: 3 years

**Application Procedure**: Preliminary applications should be made in writing, and include: a brief curriculum vitae and full publication list; details of research proposed (maximum of 1 page); a letter of support from the head of department in which you will be working; the approximate cost of the proposal, broken down into equipment and project running expenses

**Funding**: Trusts

### For further information contact:

**Tel**:       (44) 20 7611 5757
**Email**:   MHgrants@wellcome.ac.uk

## Research Fellowships in Humanities and Social Science

**Purpose**: This scheme supports postdoctoral researchers in health-related humanities and social sciences who do not hold established academic posts.

**Level of Study**: postdoctoral

**Type**: Fellowship

**Value**: Salary and research expenses covered

**Length of Study**: 3 year

**Frequency**: Annual

**Application Procedure**: You must submit your application through the Wellcome Trust Grant Tracker (WTGT).

**Closing Date**: 10 September

**Funding**: Trusts

### For further information contact:

Gibbs Building, 215 Euston Road, London NW1 2BE, UK.

**Tel**:       (44) 20 7611 5757
**Email**:   hss@wellcome.ac.uk.

## Research Training Fellowships

**Purpose**: Provide support for medical, dental, veterinary and clinical psychology graduates who have little or no research training, but who wish to develop a long-term career in academic medicine

**Eligibility**: The fellowship is open to individuals with a relevant connection to the European Economic Area (EEA) for fellowships to be held in a United Kingdom or Republic of Ireland institution. Non-United Kingdom candidates should contact the office for advice before submitting an application. 1. Medical graduates must have passed the relevant exam for their specialty, e.g. MRCP, MRCS, MRCOphth/FRCOphth Part 1, MRCPsych, MRCOG Part 1, MRCPCH, FRCA Part 1. GPs are advised to contact the office to clarify their eligibility. 2. Dental candidates must have obtained MFD, MFDS, MGDS, MFGDP or equivalent. 3. Veterinary candidates should have a degree in veterinary medicine (e.g. BVSc, BVM&S, BVMS, BVetMed, VetMB) and some experience in clinical practice. An intercalated degree is desirable, but not essential. 4. Clinical psychology candidates must have obtained a professional Doctorate-level qualification in Clinical Psychology accredited by the British Psychological Society before taking up the award. Candidates are advised to contact the office to clarify their eligibility. You are expected to undertake a high-quality research project that balances the provision of training with the opportunity to advance knowledge in a given area. A project based solely on a systematic review of a particular area is not suitable, unless it includes a significant element of methodological innovation

**Level of Study**: Postgraduate, Research

**Type**: Fellowship

**Value**: Fellowships are normally for 2–3 years. In exceptional cases a fellowship may be for up to 4 years for those who wish to undertake a relevant Master's training or diploma course. All training requests must be fully justified in the application. Fellowships provide research expenses (consumables, travel, and support to attend scientific meetings) and a fellow's salary, set according to age, experience and our policy on enhancement

**Length of Study**: 2–3 years

**Application Procedure**: Application form is available from the website

**Funding**: Trusts

### For further information contact:

**Tel**: (44) 20 7611 5757
**Email**: sciencegrants@wellcome.ac.uk

## Science Media Studentships

**Purpose**: We aim to increase the crossover between science and the media and to enable bright, articulate and motivated scientists to explore a career in the broadcast industry

**Eligibility**: Applicants should be PhD-level biomedical scientists wishing to explore a career in the broadcast, games and film industries. Applicants must have a PhD or equivalent, some experience of science communication, and a demonstrable aptitude for working with TV, radio, film or games

**Level of Study**: Postdoctorate, Research

**Type**: Studentship

**Value**: Awards will pay for tuition costs plus a grant to cover basic living expenses for the duration of the studentship

**Frequency**: Annual

**Application Procedure**: Application is through the Imperial College website

**Closing Date**: 26 February

**Funding**: Trusts

**Additional Information**: wellcome.ac.uk/news/science-media-studentships-call-applications-open

### For further information contact:

**Tel**: (44) 20 7594 8753
**Email**: liam.watson@imperial.ac.uk

## Seeding Drug Discovery

**Purpose**: To facilitate early-stage small-molecule drug discovery. The awards help applicants with a potential drug target or new chemistry embark on a programme of compound discovery and/or lead optimization

**Level of Study**: Research

**Type**: Award

**Value**: Early-stage drug discovery projects are able to apply for funding for up to 2 years to facilitate screening of chemical compounds to identify one or more lead series of molecules. Late-stage projects, where a lead compound has already been identified, are able to apply for funding for up to 4 years, to support lead optimization and preclinical development through to clinical trials

**Application Procedure**: A preliminary application form should be completed and returned to Technology Transfer by the published deadline. Applications will be considered at one of the two Seeding Drug Discovery Committee meetings in each 12-month period. Successful applicants will be shortlisted and invited to complete a full application

**Funding**: Trusts

**Additional Information**: wellcome.ac.uk/what-we-do/directories/seeding-drug-discovery-projects-funded

### For further information contact:

**Tel**: (44) 20 7611 5757
**Fax**: (44) 20 7611 8857
**Email**: innovations@wellcome.ac.uk

## Senior and Intermediate Research Fellowship for International Students

**Purpose**: The aim of the fellowship is to supports outstanding researchers of any nationality, either medically qualified or science graduates, who wish to pursue a research career in an academic institution in India

**Eligibility**: Applicants of any nationality are eligible to apply for the fellowship. Applicants must be a basic science/veterinary researchers with 4 -15 years of post-PhD research experience. Applicants must be fluent in English

**Type**: Research

**Value**: The fellowship has the tenure of five years and provides: The Fellow's personal support. Research expenses, including research assistance if required (normally funding for four research staff may be requested). The total award for a Senior Fellowship typically includes the costs requested by the applicant as well as the set contributions by the India Alliance. For further details, see costing policies. Costs requested by the applicant must be commensurate with their research proposal and should be fully justified in the full application. Inadequate justifications may result in costs being revised. Time permitted for non-research related activity during the fellowship is normally restricted to a maximum of eight hours each week

**Study Establishment**: Fellowship is awarded to support biomedical research that is relevant to human and animal welfare

**Country of Study**: India

**Application Procedure**: See the website

**Closing Date**: 15 January

**Additional Information**: For more details please visit the website scholarship-positions.com/senior-intermediate-research-fellowship-for-international-students-india/2018/01/02/ www.scholarshipsads.com/india-senior-intermediate-research-fellowship-international-students-2018/

### For further information contact:

**Email**:   info@wellcomedbt.org

## Senior Fellowships in Public Health and Tropical Medicine

**Purpose**: This scheme supports outstanding researchers from low- and middle-income countries to establish themselves as leading investigators at an academic institution in a low- and middle-income country location. This fellowship is the most senior of a series of career awards aimed at building sustainable capacity in areas of research that have the potential for increasing health benefits for people and their livestock in low- and middle-income countries. Research projects should be aimed at understanding and controlling diseases (either human or animal) of relevance to local, national or global health

**Eligibility**: Candidate must be a graduate in a subject relevant to public health or tropical medicine (for example; biomedical or social science, veterinary medicine, physics, chemistry or mathematics) with a PhD and at least 5 years' postdoctoral experience, or a medical graduate with a higher qualification equivalent to membership of the United Kingdom Royal College of Physicians (i.e. qualified to enter higher specialist training), or be recognized as a specialist within a relevant research area, and have at least 5 years' research experience

**Level of Study**: Postgraduate, Research

**Type**: Fellowship

**Value**: A basic salary; research expenses (e.g. consumables, equipment, collaborative travel, research assistance, technical support), training costs where appropriate and justified; an inflation/flexible funding allowance and support to attend scientific meetings; and contributions to costs of the project that are directly incurred by the overseas institution may also be provided

**Length of Study**: Up to 5 years

**Application Procedure**: You are required to complete and submit a preliminary application form by the published deadline. The form should be emailed to phatic@wellcome.ac.uk

**Funding**: Trusts

**Additional Information**: Overseas allowances will be provided for periods of training or collaborative research spent outside the home institution country, where appropriate. Research-dedicated costs (excluding salary costs) should not exceed £100,000 per year www.advance-africa.com/Fellowships-in-Public-Health-and-Tropical-Medicine.html

### For further information contact:

**Tel**:        (44) 20 7611 5757
**Email**:    sciencegrants@wellcome.ac.uk

## Senior Research Fellowships in Basic Biomedical Science

**Purpose**: To provide support for outstanding postdoctoral scientists based in academic institutions in the United Kingdom and Republic of Ireland (RoI)

**Eligibility**: The fellowship is open to individuals with a relevant connection to the EEA. You should have between 5 and normally 10 years' research experience (from the date of your viva to the date of your preliminary application) at postdoctoral level, or veterinary equivalent, and have a substantial record of publications in your chosen area of research in leading international journals. Candidates that do not hold an established post may apply to remain in their current laboratory, to return to one where they have worked before or to move to a new laboratory in the United Kingdom or Republic of Ireland. Candidates that hold an established post are not eligible to apply for a fellowship to be held at their current employing institution. However, we are willing to consider a preliminary application where a candidate wishes to move institution and is able to make an appropriate justification for the move. The Trust does not normally accept resubmissions of full applications for its fellowships. Please contact the Office for further advice. You must have an eligible sponsor and host institution in the United Kingdom or Republic of Ireland who can guarantee space and resources for the tenure of the award

**Level of Study**: Postdoctorate, Research

**Type**: Fellowship

**Value**: The fellowship is for 5 years in the first instance, and provides a basic salary, as determined by the host institution (normally up to £55,000 per year) with an additional Trust supplement of £12,500 per year; the essential costs of the research programme (e.g. consumables, equipment, research assistance, overseas allowances, collaborative travel and subsistence); an inflation and Flexible Funding Allowance; and support to attend scientific meetings

**Frequency**: Annual

**Application Procedure**: A preliminary application form should be completed and submitted electronically (as a Word document) to the relevant funding stream (see website) no later than the published deadline. Full application forms will usually be sent to shortlisted candidates within 1 month of the preliminary deadline. In the full application, if invited, the host institution will be required to confirm that it will support a successful renewal of the fellowship under the shared funding arrangement for the full period of any renewal

**Funding**: Trusts

**Additional Information**: Refer to the website www.wellcome.ac.uk/funding/biomedical-science/funding-schemes/fellowships/basic-biomedical-fellowships/wtd004442.htm

### For further information contact:

**Tel**:      (44) 20 7611 5757

**Email**:   sciencegrants@wellcome.ac.uk

## Senior Research Fellowships in Clinical Science

**Purpose**: This scheme provides support for clinical investigators to further develop their research potential and to establish themselves as leading investigators in clinical academic medicine

**Eligibility**: You must have a relevant connection to the EEA. If you are a non-United Kingdom candidate, please contact the Office for advice before submitting a preliminary application. You should be a clinical scientist

with a medical, dental, veterinary or clinical psychology qualification and will normally have no more than 15 years' clinical and research experience from the date of your first medical, dental, veterinary or British Psychological Society-accredited psychology qualification. (Due allowance will be given to those whose career has been affected by a late start or interruption for personal/family reasons.) Successful candidates will have made significant progress towards establishing themselves as independent clinical investigators. A research degree (PhD/MD), together with evidence of advanced (postdoctoral) research training (typically at least 3–5 years), is expected. They will have published consistently in their chosen area of research, placing substantive papers in leading journals. Candidates will not normally hold a tenured academic post in a university in the United Kingdom or Republic of Ireland, or a consultant post in the NHS

**Level of Study**: Postgraduate, Research

**Type**: Fellowship

**Value**: The fellowship is for 5 years in the first instance, and provides: a basic salary, as determined by the host institution; research expenses; an inflation allowance and support to attend scientific meetings; provision for public engagement cost

**Frequency**: Annual

**Application Procedure**: A preliminary application form should be completed and submitted by the published deadline. It should be sent electronically (as a Word document), with the requested accompanying information, to the appropriate funding stream at the Trust (see website). Incomplete or incorrectly completed forms will not be accepted. Faxed applications will not be accepted. Please do not send any additional material. You will be notified in writing of your success, or otherwise, in reaching the next round of the competition. In some instances, we may recommend that candidates apply for an Intermediate Clinical Fellowship

**Funding**: Trusts

### For further information contact:

**Tel**:      (44) 20 7611 5757

**Email**:   sciencegrants@wellcome.ac.uk

## Short-term Research Leave Awards for Clinicians and Scientists

**Purpose**: This scheme enables clinicians, scientists and other healthcare professionals to undertake up to 6 months (FTE) of research at a centre or department with academic expertise in medical humanities, to explore the wider determinants and contexts of their own medical and scientific work

**Eligibility**: You should be a scientist, clinician or healthcare professional holding an established post to which you would return on completion of the award. You must be resident in the United Kingdom or Republic of Ireland. You should have a record of publication in medical or scientific journals

**Level of Study**: Research

**Type**: Award

**Value**: We will provide the salary of a locum or replacement lecturer for the duration of the award, and a set amount for travel to conferences

**Length of Study**: Up to 6 months

**Application Procedure**: You should submit a preliminary application in writing, including: a brief curriculum vitae, a full publication list and confirmation that your personal support is from the Higher Education Funding Council; details of the research proposed (maximum one page); details of hours spent on teaching and administration; the approximate cost of the proposal, broken down into staff salaries, equipment and running expenses

**Closing Date**: 23 January

**Funding**: Trusts

### For further information contact:

**Tel**: (44) 20 7611 5757
**Email**: MHgrants@wellcome.ac.uk

## Sir Henry Wellcome Postdoctoral Fellowships

**Purpose**: To provide a unique opportunity for the most promising newly qualified postdoctoral researchers to make an early start in developing their independent research careers, working in the best laboratories in the United Kingdom and overseas

**Eligibility**: These awards are open to individuals with a relevant connection to the European Economic Area. You must be in the final year of your PhD studies or have no more than 1 year of postdoctoral research experience from the date of your PhD viva to the full application submission deadline (e.g. if the full deadline is in February, your viva should not have occurred prior to last February). Time spent outside the research environment will be taken into consideration. You must have an eligible sponsoring institution in the United Kingdom or Republic of Ireland that will administer the fellowship for the full duration of the award

**Level of Study**: Postdoctorate, Research

**Type**: Fellowships

**Value**: 4 year full-time fellowship. Provides an award of £250,000

**Length of Study**: 4 years

**Frequency**: Annual

**Application Procedure**: You should complete and submit a preliminary application form by the published deadline. It should be sent electronically (as a Word document), with the requested accompanying information, to the relevant funding stream at the Trust. Your preliminary application will be assessed within 4 weeks of the submission deadline. If successful, you will be invited to submit a full application. Your full application will be peer reviewed by the relevant Funding Committee and, if successful, you will be shortlisted for interview

**Funding**: Trusts

**Additional Information**: wellcome.ac.uk/funding/schemes/sir-henry-wellcome-postdoctoral-fellowships

### For further information contact:

**Tel**: (44) 20 7611 5757
**Email**: sciencegrants@wellcome.ac.uk

## Strategic Awards in Biomedical Science

**Purpose**: Strategic awards provide flexible forms of support to excellent research groups with outstanding track records in their field

**Eligibility**: Applications will be considered from principal applicants who meet our eligibility criteria and are recognized international leaders in their field

**Level of Study**: Research

**Type**: Award

**Value**: It provides equipment, support staff, consumables, training programmes, networking, biological, clinical or epidemiological research resources. Limited capital building or refurbishment essential to the programme can also be requested

**Length of Study**: Awards are normally for 5 years

**Application Procedure**: You (prospective applicant) are required to submit a preliminary application, which should include the following information: 1. your track record, you must complete the curriculum vitae pages (these are questions 14 and 15 from the standard project grant application form); 2. high-level aims and objectives, and how the proposal addresses the strategic challenges in the Wellcome Trust's Strategic Plan (maximum of two pages); 3. key targets, milestones and management structures, if appropriate (maximum of two pages); 4. duration of support requested and outline costings broken down into main headings (e.g. staff, equipment); 5. a statement from the head of the institution, indicating how the proposal fits within the context of the institution's strategic vision and what financial commitment the institution will make to the group if the application is successful. If your preliminary application is successful, you will be invited to submit a full application. The relevant form will be provided at this time

**Funding**: Trusts

**Additional Information**: wellcome.ac.uk/what-we-do/direc tories/science-strategic-awards-people-funded

### For further information contact:

**Tel**: (44) 20 7611 5757
**Email**: sciencegrants@wellcome.ac.uk

## The Hub Award

**Purpose**: The Hub Award brings researchers and creative professionals together at Wellcome Collection to work as a collaborative residency.
**Type**: Award
**Value**: Flexible funding, up to £1 million
**Length of Study**: 1 to 2 year
**Frequency**: Annual
**Application Procedure**: You must submit your application through the Wellcome Trust Grant Tracker (WTGT).
**Closing Date**: 20 February
**Funding**: Trusts

### For further information contact:

Gibbs Building, 215 Euston Road, London NW1 2BE, United Kingdom.

**Tel**: (44) 20 7611 5757

## Training Fellowships in Public Health and Tropical Medicine

**Purpose**: This scheme provides researchers from low- and middle-income countries–who are at an early stage in the establishment of their research careers–with opportunities for research experience and high-quality research training in public health and tropical medicine. Research projects should be aimed at understanding and controlling diseases (either human or animal) of relevance to local, national or global health. This can include laboratory-based molecular analysis of field or clinical samples, but projects focused solely on studies in vitro or using animal models will not normally be considered under this scheme
**Eligibility**: Applications are only accepted in the Public Health and Tropical Medicine Interview Committee remit. This covers research on infectious and non-communicable diseases within the fields of public health and tropical medicine that is aimed at understanding and controlling diseases (either human or animal) of relevance to local, national or global health. You must be a national or legal resident of a low- and middle-income country and should be either: 1. a graduate in a subject relevant to public health or tropical medicine (e.g. biomedical or social science, veterinary medicine, physics, chemistry or mathematics) with a PhD and no more than 3 years' postdoctoral experience, or 2. a medical graduate with a higher qualification equivalent to membership of the United Kingdom Royal Colleges of Physicians (i.e. qualified to enter higher specialist training) and some initial research experience. Applicants may also apply if they do not have a PhD, but have a clinical, basic or Master's degree and some initial research experience, with the expectation that they will register for a PhD.
**Level of Study**: Postgraduate, Research
**Type**: Fellowship
**Value**: Usually £15,000 to £300,000 for salary, fees and research expenses
**Length of Study**: 3 years
**Application Procedure**: You are required to complete and submit a preliminary application form by the published deadline. The form should be emailed to phatic@wellcome.ac.uk
**Closing Date**: 9 July
**Funding**: Trusts
**Additional Information**: www.scholarshipportal.com/schol arship/wellcome-trust-training-fellowships-in-public-health-and-tropical-medicine

### For further information contact:

**Tel**: (44) 20 7611 5757
**Email**: sciencegrants@wellcome.ac.uk

## Translation Fund

**Purpose**: Translation Awards are response-mode funding designed to bridge the funding gap in the commercialisation of new technologies in the biomedical area
**Eligibility**: Projects must address an unmet need in healthcare or in applied medical research, offer a potential new solution, and have a realistic expectation that the innovation will be developed further by the market. Institutions: eligible institutions are not-for-profit research institutions, including those funded by the Medical Research Council, Cancer Research United Kingdom, and Biotechnology and Biological Sciences Research Council, in the United Kingdom. Institutions are normally required to sign up to a short funding agreement and the Grant Conditions. Companies: we are able to use our charitable monies to fund commercial companies to meet our charitable objectives through programme-related investment (PRI). For further details please refer to our policy on PRI. Companies will normally be expected to sign up to specific terms relating to the scheme. Overseas organizations: United Kingdom organizations may contract or collaborate with overseas organizations. Although overseas organizations are not eligible for Translation Awards, some proposals may

be invited for consideration as a Strategic Translation Award (including Seeding Drug Discovery). Overseas organizations should contact Technology Transfer staff about their proposed project in the first instance. Principal applicants and coapplicants: applicants should normally hold a position of responsibility within the eligible organization and be able to sign up to or comply with the conditions or terms of an award. In addition, postdoctoral research assistants–whether seeking their own salary as part of the grant proposal, funded by the Wellcome Trust on another grant, or funded by another agency–are eligible for coapplicant status if they make a significant contribution to a research proposal and have agreement from their funding agency. Other eligibility information: Disciplines outside biomedicine – researchers from disciplines outside biomedicine can apply providing the application of research is designed to facilitate or meet a need in healthcare. For example, the application of physics, chemistry, computing, engineering and materials science to the development of medical products is entirely appropriate. Healthcare need in an area that is not commercially attractive. We are committed to the translation of research into practical healthcare benefits across the full spectrum of disease. Disease areas neglected by industry because of the lack of a return on investment pose a particular problem, but imaginative ways forward can sometimes be developed (e.g. public-private partnerships such as the Medicines for Malaria Venture). Intellectual property rights (IPR)/publications – if there are any restrictions on IPR or publications arising from your research, you must provide a written statement that details them. Restrictions on intellectual property may affect your eligibility to apply to the Trust. Please refer to our Grant Conditions

**Level of Study**: Research

**Type**: Award

**Value**: The important criterion is to develop the innovation to the point at which it can be adopted by another party. Providing it is adequately justified, modest equipment purchase and maintenance costs may be included in a Translation Award application. Building or refurbishment expenditure will not normally be considered. Applications may not include requests for academic institutional overheads. If you hold a tenured university post, you may not re-charge your salary (in full or part) to a Translation Award

**Application Procedure**: A preliminary application form must be completed and sent to Technology Transfer by the published deadline. Preliminary applications are subject to a triage for shortlisting for the full application stage. Applications will be considered by the Technology Transfer Challenge Committee (TTCC), which meets twice a year. Full applications will be invited following the triage meeting. Shortlisted applicants will be invited to submit a full application and will be subject to international peer review and due diligence. Applicants will be expected to make a presentation on their proposal to the TTCC. Unless otherwise advised, this will be at the next scheduled meeting of the TTCC

**Funding**: Trusts

**Additional Information**: erc-online.eu/financial-support/translation-fund/

### For further information contact:

**Tel**: (44) 20 7611 5757
**Fax**: (44) 20 7611 8857
**Email**: innovations@wellcome.ac.uk

## Translational Medicine and Therapeutics Programmes

**Purpose**: This flagship scheme established four high-quality integrated research training programmes for clinicians in translational medicine and therapeutics. The programmes have been developed around a unique partnership between academic and industrial partners. Support for the programmes has been provided to the host institutions by GlaxoSmithKline, Wyeth Research, Roche, AstraZeneca, Sanofi-Aventis, Sirtris Pharmaceuticals and PTC Therapeutics

**Eligibility**: You should have demonstrated the potential to pursue a career as an academic clinician. It is anticipated that many applicants will have already commenced their specialist training, but this is not essential

**Level of Study**: Postgraduate, Research

**Value**: Includes a clinical salary, PhD registration fees at United Kingdom/EU rate, research expenses, contribution towards travel, and a contribution towards training costs

**Length of Study**: Support varies

**Frequency**: Annual

**Application Procedure**: If you are interested in applying you should contact the relevant programme. Please see website for details

**Closing Date**: October

**Funding**: Trusts

### For further information contact:

**Email**: j.williams@wellcome.ac.uk

## University Awards

**Purpose**: This scheme allows universities to attract outstanding research staff by providing support for up to 5 years, after which time the award holder takes up a guaranteed permanent post in the university. A monograph and other substantial publications are expected to result from an award, so teaching and other non-research commitments are expected to be minimal during the period of full Wellcome Trust support

**Eligibility**: You must be nominated by your prospective head of department and have an undertaking from the head of the institution, vice-chancellor, principal or dean that your personal support will be taken over by the institution at the end of the award. Support is normally available only at lecturer level, although in exceptional cases awards to senior-lecturer level may be possible

**Level of Study**: Research

**Type**: Award

**Value**: Up to 5 years' support is available, providing your full salary for 3 years, 50% in the fourth year and 25% in the fifth year. Travel expenses to attend meetings are provided for 5 years, but research expenses are provided for the first 3 years of the award only

**Application Procedure**: Initial enquiries about the scheme may be made by you (the potential candidate) or a department in an institution. These enquiries should be followed by a preliminary application from you by email or post including an explicit statement from the head of the institution, vice-chancellor or dean demonstrating the institution's commitment to the history of medicine field, and a statement confirming that the institution will provide 50% salary costs in year four, 75% in year 5 and full salary thereafter; curriculum vitae and full publication list; an outline of no more than two pages of the proposed project; a letter of support from the head of department, including a statement on your expected teaching/administrative load for the 5-year period (this can be sent by separate cover); the approximate cost of the proposal, broken down into your salary, equipment and project running costs

**Funding**: Trusts

**Additional Information**: studentaffairs.ku.edu/university-awards

### For further information contact:

**Tel**:  (44) 20 7611 5757
**Email**:  MHgrants@wellcome.ac.uk

## Wellcome Trust and NIH Four-Year PhD Studentships

**Purpose**: This scheme provides opportunities for the most promising postgraduate students to undertake international, collaborative four-year PhD training based in both a United Kingdom/Republic of Ireland (RoI) academic institution and the intramural campus of the National Institutes of Health at Bethesda (Maryland, United States of America)

**Eligibility**: You should be a United Kingdom/European Economic Area (EEA) national with (or be in your final year and expected to obtain) a first- or upper-second-class honours degree or an equivalent EEA graduate qualification. You must have: (1) a suitable doctoral supervisor at an eligible academic host institution in the United Kingdom or Republic of Ireland. The host institution must be able to confer doctoral degrees; (2) a suitable supervisor at a NIH institute. The NIH supervisor should hold a tenured or tenured-track position for the proposed period of the award and should be willing to provide funding for the student whilst at the NIH

**Level of Study**: Doctorate, Research

**Type**: Studentship

**Value**: The studentship is awarded for 4 years with support provided by the Wellcome Trust (in the United Kingdom/ Republic of Ireland) and the NIH (in the United States of America). Our funding will provide support for the student's stipend, PhD fees, college fees (if required) and a contribution towards research costs

**Length of Study**: 4 year

**Frequency**: Annual

**Application Procedure**: The application form should be completed and submitted by the closing date. An electronic copy (as a Word document) should be emailed to wtnih@wellcome.ac.uk

**Funding**: Trusts

### For further information contact:

Wellcome Trust-NIH PhD Studentships, Wellcome Trust, Gibbs Building, 215 Euston Road, Bloomsbury, London, NW1 2BE, United Kingdom.

**Email**:  wtnih@wellcome.ac.uk

## Wellcome Trust-POST Fellowships in Medical History and Humanities

**Purpose**: This scheme enables a PhD student or junior fellow funded through the Wellcome Trust Medical History and Humanities (MHH) programme to undertake a 3-month fellowship at the Parliamentary Office of Science and Technology (POST)

**Eligibility**: Applicants should be in the second or third year of their PhD or in the first year of a fellowship funded by the MHH Programme. POST is a strictly non-partisan organization. Wellcome Trust-POST Fellows will be required to abstain from any lobbying or party political activity, and generally uphold the principles of parliamentary service, including a commitment to confidentiality, during their time with the Office. All provisionally selected candidates must sign a declaration to this effect. They must also receive security clearance from the parliamentary security authorities as a condition of finally taking up the fellowship

**Level of Study**: Postdoctorate, Research

**Type**: Fellowship

**Value**: The successful applicant will receive a fully funded 3-month extension to their PhD or fellowship award. While placements typically last 3-months, they may be extended under exceptional circumstances. If the successful applicant is not within reasonable daily travelling distance to POST in London, the Wellcome Trust will consider paying travel and accommodation costs up to a maximum of £2,000

**Frequency**: Annual

**Application Procedure**: An application should include the application form, your curriculum vitae, a letter of support from your sponsor/supervisor and a summary of a proposed topic for a POST publication. The summary should be no longer than 1,000 words and should demonstrate: why you think this subject would be of particular parliamentary interest; how the training you have received and your research to date will enable you to carry out this work; your ability to write in a style suitable for a parliamentary (rather than an academic) audience

**Closing Date**: 23 November

**Funding**: Trusts

**Additional Information**: Check website for more details

### For further information contact:

**Tel**:      (44) 20 7611 5757
**Email**:   MHgrants@wellcome.ac.uk

## Wells Mountain Foundation

### Woodcock-Munoz Foundation Empowerment Through Education Scholarships

**Purpose**: The Foundation believes in the power and importance of community service; therefore, all scholarship participants are required to volunteer for a minimum of 100 hours a year

**Eligibility**: WMF's ideal candidate is a student, male or female, from a country in the developing world, who: 1. Successfully completed a secondary education, with good to excellent grades. 2. Will be studying in their country or another country in the developing world. 3. Plans to live and work in their own country after they graduate. 4. Has volunteered prior to applying for this scholarship and/or is willing to volunteer while receiving the WMF scholarship

**Level of Study**: Graduate

**Type**: Scholarship

**Value**: Average of US$1,400 for tuition and fee, books and materials

**Frequency**: Annual

**Country of Study**: Any country

**Application Procedure**: You must submit a complete application via the online scholarship application portal (preferred method) or via postal mail to the Foundation's office Kindly check the below site for further details. www.wellsmountain foundation.org/our-programs/scholarships/

**Closing Date**: 1 April

**Funding**: Private

**Additional Information**: scholarshipfellow.com/wmf-empower ment-through-education-in-is-now-accepting-applications/

### For further information contact:

**Email**:    info@scholars4dev.com

## Wells Mountain Initiative

### Westmead Millennium Institute Micro-Grants

**Purpose**: The WMI Micro-Grants Program is open exclusively to all WMI Graduate Scholars. Preference is given to Graduates who are actively involved in Fellowship groups if present within their nation and participation in WMI's Scholar Journey opportunities

**Eligibility**: Graduate Scholars are eligible to apply for a maximum of two grants. There is a required two-year wait time before applying for a second award

**Level of Study**: Graduate

**Type**: Grant

**Value**: US$100 to US$1,000

**Frequency**: Annual

**Country of Study**: Any country

**Application Procedure**: To enhance professional growth with all aspects of program development and grant writing skills, WMI provides all Graduate Scholars with individualised application coaching. After submitting your first round proposal, the review committee will provide direct feedback for each qualifying application. With this feedback, Graduate Scholars will have one month to continue developing their proposals by creating more detailed processes, conducting research and community outreach, revising budgets and timelines, etc. A final revised application will be submitted online and a funding decision will be made

**Closing Date**: 15 April

**Funding**: Private

**Additional Information**: You could also write to tyhe following contact address: info@wellsmountaininit ative.org www.wellsmountaininitiative.org/micro-grant-program/

### For further information contact:

Wells Mountain Initiative, 25D Main Street, Bristol, NY 05443, United States of America.

**Email**:    nicole@wellsmountain.com

# Wenner-Gren Foundation for Anthropological Research

The Fellowships Office, 470 Park Avenue South, 8th Floor, New York, NY 10016, United States of America.

| | |
|---|---|
| **Tel**: | (1) 212 683 5000 |
| **Email**: | inquiries@wennergren.org |
| **Website**: | www.wennergren.org |
| **Contact**: | Victoria Malkin, Anthropologist |

The Wenner-Gren Foundation for Anthropological Research supports research, conferences, training, archiving and collaboration in all branches of anthropology, including cultural and social anthropology, ethnology, biological and physical anthropology, archaeology and anthropological linguistics, and in closely related disciplines concerned with human origins, development and variation.

## Hunt Postdoctoral Fellowships

**Purpose**: To support the writing-up of already completed research

**Eligibility**: Applicants must have a PhD or equivalent at the time of application and must have received a PhD or equivalent within 10 years of the application deadline. Qualified scholars are eligible without regard to nationality, institutional, or departmental affiliation although preference is given to applicants who are untenured or do not yet have a permanent academic position

**Level of Study**: Postdoctorate

**Type**: Fellowship

**Value**: Up to US$40,000

**Frequency**: Annual

**Country of Study**: Any country

**Application Procedure**: Applications can be downloaded from the website and must be submitted online

**No. of awards offered**: 89

**Closing Date**: 1 May

**No. of awards given last year**: 9

**No. of applicants last year**: 89

**Additional Information**: Qualified scholars are eligible without regard to nationality or institutional affiliation www.wennergren.org/programs/hunt-postdoctoral-fellowships

# Wharton School

University of Pennsylvania MBA Admissions & Financial Aid, 102 Vance Hill, Philadelphia, PA 19104-6361, United States of America.

| | |
|---|---|
| **Tel**: | (1) 215 898 6182 |
| **Email**: | mba.admissions@wharton.upenn.edu |
| **Website**: | www.wharton.upenn.edu/mba/catalog |
| **Contact**: | MBA Programme |

## Wharton Executive MBA Programme

**Length of Study**: 2 years

**Application Procedure**: Applicants may apply online or contact Wharton for information

### For further information contact:

Executive MBA Programme, The Wharton School, University of PA 224 Steinberg Conference Centre, 255 South 38th Street, Philadelphia, PA 19104-6359, United States of America.

| | |
|---|---|
| **Tel**: | (1) 215 898 5887 |
| **Fax**: | (1) 215 898 2598 |
| **Email**: | wemba-admissions@wharton.upenn.edu |

# Whitehall Foundation, Inc.

PO Box 3423, Palm Beach, FL 33480, United States of America.

| | |
|---|---|
| **Tel**: | (1) 561 655 4474 |
| **Email**: | email@whitehall.org |
| **Website**: | www.whitehall.org |
| **Contact**: | Ms Catherine Thomas, Corporate Secretary |

The Whitehall Foundation, Inc. through its programme of grants and grants-in-aid, assists scholarly research in the life sciences. It is the Foundation's policy to assist those dynamic areas of basic biological research that are not heavily supported by federal agencies or other foundations with specialized missions.

## Whitehall Foundation Grants-in-Aid

**Purpose**: To better understand behavioural output or brain mechanisms of behaviour

**Eligibility**: Open to researchers at the assistant professor level who have experienced difficulty in competing for research funds as they have not yet become firmly established. Senior scientists may also apply

**Level of Study**: Research

**Type**: Research grant one year

**Value**: Up to US$30,000

**Length of Study**: 1 year
**Frequency**: Annual
**Country of Study**: United States of America
**Application Procedure**: Applicants must contact the Foundation
**Funding**: Private
**Additional Information**: For up to date policy, application information and important calendar deadlines please refer to the website www.whitehall.org/applying/

## Whitehall Foundation Research Grants

**Purpose**: To better understand behavioural output or brain mechanisms of behaviour
**Eligibility**: Open to established scientists of all ages working at accredited institutions in the United States of America. The principal investigator must hold no less than the position of assistant professor, or the equivalent, in order to make an application. The Foundation does not award funds to investigators who have substantial existing or potential support
**Level of Study**: Research
**Type**: Research grant one year
**Value**: US$30,000–US$75,000 per year
**Length of Study**: Up to 3 years
**Frequency**: Annual
**Country of Study**: Any country
**Application Procedure**: Please visit web-site @ www.white hall.org
**Funding**: Private
**Additional Information**: For up to date policy, application information and important calendar deadlines, please refer to the website www.whitehall.org/grants/

## Wilfrid Laurier University

75 University Avenue West, Waterloo, ON N2L 3C5, Canada.

**Tel**: (1) 519 884 1970
**Email**: webmaster@wlu.ca
**Website**: www.wlu.ca
**Contact**: Mr Al Hecht, International Relations

Wilfrid Laurier University is well known for offering an extremely high quality academic experience as well as for cultivating a closely-knit undergraduate and graduate student population. Wilfrid Laurier University is committed to continuing to provide the educational experiences and environment that foster such development and nurture what can best be described as the 'Laurier spirit'.

## Viessmann/Marburg Travel Scholarship

**Purpose**: To assist students wanting to study in Germany
**Level of Study**: Postgraduate
**Type**: Scholarship
**Value**: €767
**Length of Study**: 1 year
**Frequency**: Annual
**Study Establishment**: An approved place of study in Marburg
**Country of Study**: Germany
**Application Procedure**: Contact University
**Closing Date**: 2 July

## Wilfrid Laurier University President

**Purpose**: To reward significant contribution to the community as a volunteer or to the discipline as a scholar
**Eligibility**: Full-time undergraduate students entering year 1. Minimum overall average of 95% in best six Grade 12 U and/or Grade 12 M courses or Ontario Academic Credits (OACs) (or equivalent)
**Level of Study**: Postgraduate
**Type**: Scholarship
**Value**: C$23,000 (C$3,000 1st year; renewable based on academic performance for up to 4 years at C$5,000 per year) 4th year of renewal eligibility for approved 5-year undergraduate programs only
**Length of Study**: 1 year
**Frequency**: Annual
**Study Establishment**: Laurier University
**Country of Study**: Canada
**Application Procedure**: Apply online
**Funding**: Trusts
**Contributor**: Dr Neale H. Taylor

**For further information contact:**

**Email**: fgps@wlu.ca

## Wingate Scholarships

2nd Floor, 20-22 Stukeley Street, London WC2B 5LR, United Kingdom.

**Email**: enquiries@wingate.org.uk
**Website**: www.wingatescholarships.org.uk
**Contact**: Ms Sarah Mitchell, Administrator

Wingate Scholarships are awarded to individuals for creative or original work of intellectual, scientific, artistic, social or environmental value of great potential or proven excellence, and to outstanding musicians for advanced training in music performance.

## Wingate Scholarships

**Purpose**: To fund creative or original work of intellectual, scientific, artistic, social or environmental value and advanced music study

**Eligibility**: Open to United Kingdom, Commonwealth, former Commonwealth, Israeli. Also open to European Union and Council of Europe country citizens provided that they are and have been resident in the United Kingdom for at least 3 years at start of award. Applicants must be over 24 years of age. No upper age limit is prescribed. No academic qualifications are necessary. Applications must be made in United Kingdom from a valid United Kingdom address

**Level of Study**: Doctorate, Postdoctorate, Postgraduate, Research

**Type**: Scholarship

**Value**: Costs of a project, which may last for up to 3 years, to a maximum of United Kingdom £10,000 in any 1 year

**Length of Study**: 1–3 years

**Frequency**: Annual

**Study Establishment**: Any approved institute or independent research

**Country of Study**: Any country

**Application Procedure**: Applicants must be living in United Kingdom during the period of application. Applications from a valid United Kingdom address only are acceptable. Applicants must complete online application form from the website. Applicants must be able to satisfy the Scholarship Committee that they need financial support to undertake the work projected, and show why the proposed work (if it takes the form of academic research) is unlikely to attract Research Council, British Academy or any other major agency funding if they are United Kingdom applicants. All applications require two references to be submitted independently. Guidance is available on the website

**No. of awards offered**: 228

**Closing Date**: 1 February

**Funding**: Foundation

**Contributor**: HHW Foundation

**No. of awards given last year**: 39

**No. of applicants last year**: 228

**Additional Information**: The scholarships are not awarded for professional qualifications, taught courses or electives, or in the following subject areas: performing arts, fine art, business studies. Practising musicians (not composers) are eligible for advanced training, but apart from that, all applicants must have projects that are personal to them and involve either creative or original work. Only postgraduate students in their final two years can apply for scholarships to enable them to undertake field work, or in exceptional circumstances where an award has been withdrawn or closed, to complete a PhD. Applications for studies or projects undertaken post doctorally are eligible, but not postdoctoral fellowship posts per se. Applicant must be based in United Kingdom when applying www.tau.ac.il/acad-sec/grantsite/abroad/britania%20wingate.htm

### For further information contact:

**Email**: emma@shrimsley.com

## Winston Churchill Foundation of the United States of America

600 Madison Avenue, Suite 1601, New York, NY 10022-1737, United States of America.

| | |
|---|---|
| **Tel**: | (1) 212 752 3200 |
| **Email**: | info@churchillscholarship.org |
| **Website**: | www.churchillscholarship.org |
| **Contact**: | Mr Michael Morse, Executive Director |

The Winston Churchill Foundation of the United States was established in 1959 as an expression of American admiration for one of the great leaders of the free world. The foundation enables outstanding American students to attend graduate school at the University of Cambridge.

## Churchill Scholarship

**Purpose**: The Churchill Scholarship provides funding to American students for a year of Master's study at the University of Cambridge, based at Churchill College. The program was set up at the request of Sir Winston Churchill in order to fulfill his vision of United States–United Kingdom scientific exchange with the goal of advancing science and technology on both sides of the Atlantic, helping to ensure our future prosperity and security

**Eligibility**: An applicant for the Churchill Scholarship must be a citizen of the United States, either native born or naturalized, and must be a senior who is enrolled in one of the institutions participating in the Scholarship Program or a student who has graduated from one of those institutions within the past 12 months. Upon taking up the Churchill Scholarship, a Churchill Scholar must hold a bachelor's degree or an equivalent, and may not have attained a doctorate

**Type**: Fellowship/Scholarship

**Value**: US$55,000
**Length of Study**: 1 year
**Frequency**: Annual
**Country of Study**: United Kingdom
**Application Procedure**: Must be nominated by undergraduate institution
**No. of awards offered**: 105
**Closing Date**: November
**Funding**: Foundation
**No. of awards given last year**: 15
**No. of applicants last year**: 105
**Additional Information**: www.churchillscholarship.org/apply.html

### For further information contact:

Winston Churchill Foundation, 600 Madison Avenue, Suite 1601, New York, NY 10022, United States of America.

## Winston Churchill Memorial Trust

### Winston Churchill Memorial Trust (United Kingdom) Travelling Fellowships

**Subjects**: Churchill Fellowships explore the whole spectrum of challenges facing the UK. We focus them around eight universal themes in society: Arts and culture, Community and citizenship, Economy and enterprise, Education and skills, Environment and resources, Health and wellbeing, Governance and public provision, Science and technology.
**Purpose**: The Winston Churchill Memorial Trust runs the Churchill Fellowships, a unique programme of overseas practical research grants. These support UK citizens from all parts of society to travel the world in search of innovative and practical solutions for today's most pressing problems.
**Eligibility**: Open to all UK citizens resident in the UK aged 18 and above. We do not fund gap year activities, courses, volunteering, academic studies, degree placements, internships, medical electives or post-graduate studies.
**Level of Study**: Unrestricted
**Type**: Fellowship
**Length of Study**: 4 - 8 weeks
**Frequency**: Annual
**Country of Study**: Any country
**Application Procedure**: Applicants must complete an online application form which can be accessed via our website: www.wcmt.org.uk
**No. of awards offered**: Up to 150 each year
**Funding**: Private
**No. of applicants last year**: 1409

**Additional Information**: Please sign up for application alerts via our website to be notified when the next round of applications open. www.wcmt.org.uk/application-alerts www.wcmt.org.uk

### For further information contact:

South Door, Church House, 29 Great Smith Street, London, SW1P 3BL, England, United Kingdom.

**Email**: office@wcmt.org.uk

## Winterthur

Winterthur Museum, Garden and Library, 5105 Kennett Pike, Winterthur, DE 19735, United States of America.

**Tel**: (1) 800 448 3883
**Email**: tourinfo@winterthur.org
**Website**: www.winterthur.org
**Contact**: Thomas A. Guiler, Manager and Instructor, Academic Programmes

Founded by Henry Francis du Pont, Winterthur is the premier museum of American Decorative Arts, reflecting both early America and the du Pont family's life here. Its 60-acre naturalistic garden is among the country's best, and its research library serves scholars from around the world.

### Winterthur Dissertation Research Fellowships

**Purpose**: To encourage the use of Winterthur's collections for critical inquiry that will further the understanding of American history and visual and material culture
**Level of Study**: Research
**Type**: Fellowship
**Value**: US$7,000 per semesters
**Length of Study**: 1–2 semesters
**Frequency**: Annual
**Country of Study**: United States of America
**Application Procedure**: Applicants can download application form from the website
**Closing Date**: 15 January
**Funding**: Foundation
**Contributor**: Winterthur
**No. of awards given last year**: 4
**Additional Information**: www.winterthur.org/education/academic-programs/research-fellowships/fellowships-available/

## For further information contact:

Winterthur Museum, Garden & Library, 5105 Kennett Pike, Winterthur, DE 19735, United States of America.

**Tel:** (1) 800 448 3883
**Email:** tguiler@winterthur.org.

## Winterthur Postdoctoral Fellowships

**Purpose**: To encourage the use of Winterthur's collections for critical inquiry that will further the understanding of American history and visual and material culture
**Eligibility**: Open to scholars who hold the PhD degree, pursuing advanced research
**Level of Study**: Postdoctorate, Research
**Type**: Fellowships
**Value**: up to US$4,200 per month.
**Length of Study**: 4 months
**Frequency**: Annual
**Country of Study**: United States of America
**Application Procedure**: Applicants can download the application form from the website
**Closing Date**: 15 January
**Funding**: Foundation
**Contributor**: Winterthur
**No. of awards given last year**: 2
**Additional Information**: www.winterthur.org/education/academic-programs/research-fellowships/fellowships-available/

## For further information contact:

Winterthur Museum, Garden & Library, 5105 Kennett Pike, Winterthur, DE 19735, United States of America.

**Tel:** (1) 800 448 3883
**Email:** tguiler@winterthur.org.

## Winterthur Research Fellowships

**Purpose**: To encourage the use of Winterthur's collections for critical inquiry that will further the understanding of American history and visual and material culture
**Eligibility**: Open to scholars pursuing advanced research
**Level of Study**: Research
**Type**: Fellowship
**Value**: US$1,750 per month
**Length of Study**: 1–3 months
**Frequency**: Annual
**Country of Study**: United States of America
**Application Procedure**: Applicants can download the application form from the website

**Closing Date**: 15 January
**Funding**: Foundation
**Contributor**: Winterthur
**No. of awards given last year**: 21

## For further information contact:

**Email:** researchapplication@winterthur.org

## Wolf Blass Wines International

97 Sturt Highway, Nuriootpa, Adelaide, SA 5355, Australia.

**Tel:** (61) 8 8568 7311
**Email:** cellardoor@wolfblass.com.au
**Website:** www.wolfblass.com.au/brands/wolfblass/index.asp

Wolf Blass Wines International is public listed company and one of the Australia's top sellers of red and white wine. It is one of the best Australian wine-producing company. As they have for almost 30 years, Wolf Blass wines continue to delight wine lovers all over the world.

## Wolf Blass Australian Winemaking Independent Study Scholarship

**Purpose**: To support independent study related to winemaking in Australia
**Eligibility**: Open to culinary professional to conduct research and writing related to Australian winemaking and culinary traditions
**Type**: Scholarship
**Value**: AU$5,000
**Country of Study**: Australia
**Application Procedure**: All applicants are required to include a project proposal, an itemized budget detailing the use of this award and a tentative travel schedule with dates and locations. Check website for further details
**Additional Information**: Applicant is additionally required to provide a current resume to qualify for this scholarship

## For further information contact:

304W, Liberty Street, Suite 201, Louisville, KY 40202, United States of America.

**Tel:** (1) 800 928 4227 Ext 264
**Fax:** (1) 502 589 3602
**Email:** tgribbins@hqtrs.com

# Wolfsonian-Florida International University

1001 Washington Avenue, Miami Beach, FL 33139, United States of America.

| | |
|---|---|
| **Tel**: | (1) 305 531 1001 |
| **Email**: | research@thewolf.fiu.edu |
| **Website**: | www.wolfsonian.org |
| **Contact**: | Mr Jonathan Mogul, Fellowship Co-ordinator |

The Wolfsonian-Florida International University is a museum and research centre that promotes the examination of modern material culture. Through exhibitions, publications, scholarships, educational programmes and public presentations, the Wolfsonian strives to enhance the understanding of objects as agents and reflections of social, cultural, political and technological change. The collection includes works on paper, furniture, paintings, sculpture, glass, textiles, ceramics, books and many other kinds of objects.

## Wolfsonian-FIU Fellowship

**Purpose**: To conduct research on the Wolfsonian's collection of objects and library materials from the period 1885 to 1945, including decorative arts, works on paper, books and ephemera

**Eligibility**: The programme is open to holder of Master's or doctoral degrees, PhD candidates, and to other who have a record of significant professional achievement in relevant fields

**Level of Study**: Doctorate, Postdoctorate, Professional development

**Type**: Fellowship

**Value**: Fellowships include a stipend, accommodations, and round-trip travel

**Length of Study**: 3–5 weeks

**Frequency**: Annual

**Study Establishment**: The Wolfsonian-Florida International University

**Country of Study**: United States of America

**Application Procedure**: Applicants must complete an application form and submit this with three letters of recommendation. Contact the Fellowship Co-ordinator for details and application materials. Applicants may also download programme information and an application form from the website www.wolfsonian.fiu.edu/education/research

**No. of awards offered**: 26

**Closing Date**: 31 December

**No. of awards given last year**: 5

**No. of applicants last year**: 26

**Additional Information**: networks.h-net.org/node/73374/announcements/2914100/wolfsonian-fiu-fellowship-program

**For further information contact:**

**Tel**:    (1) 305 535 2613

---

# Women's Studio Workshop (WSW)

722 Binnewater Lane, PO Box 489, Rosendale, NY 12472, United States of America.

| | |
|---|---|
| **Tel**: | (1) 845 658 9133 |
| **Email**: | info@wsworkshop.org |
| **Website**: | www.wsworkshop.org |
| **Contact**: | Ms Ann Kalmbach, Executive Director |

The Women's Studio Workshop (WSW) is an artist-run workshop with facilities for printmaking, papermaking, photography, book arts and ceramics. WSW supports the creation of new work through studio residency and annual book arts grant programmes and an ongoing subsidized fellowship programme. WSW offers studio-based educational programming in the above disciplines through its annual Summer Arts Institute.

## Artists Fellowships at WSW

**Purpose**: To provide a time for artists to explore new ideas in a dynamic and co-operative community of women artists in a rural environment

**Eligibility**: Open to women artists only

**Level of Study**: Unrestricted

**Type**: Fellowship

**Value**: The award includes on-site housing and unlimited access to the studios. Cost to artists will be US$200 per week, plus their own material

**Length of Study**: Each fellowship is 3–6 weeks long. Fellowship opportunities are from September to June

**Frequency**: Annual

**Study Establishment**: WSW

**Country of Study**: United States of America

**Application Procedure**: Applicants must complete an application form, available on request or online at the website. One-sentence summary plus half-page description of proposed project, resume, 10 slides plus slide script, self addressed stampe envelope for return of materials

**No. of awards offered**: 100

**Closing Date**: 15 October
**Funding**: Government, Private
**Contributor**: Private foundations
**No. of awards given last year**: 25
**No. of applicants last year**: 100

## Women's Studio Workshop Internships

**Purpose**: To provide opportunities for young artists to continue development of their work in a supportive environment, while learning studio skills and responsibilities
**Eligibility**: Open to emerging and established female artists
**Level of Study**: Unrestricted
**Type**: Internship
**Value**: A private room in our onsite housing and a stipend of US$250/month
**Length of Study**: 2–6 months
**Frequency**: Annual
**Study Establishment**: WSW
**Country of Study**: United States of America
**Application Procedure**: Applicants must submit a curriculum vitae, 10 slides with slide list, 3 current letters of reference, a letter of interest that addresses the question of why an internship at WSW would be important and a stamped addressed envelope. Arts administration: 3 work samples, i.e. press releases, design samples, etc
**No. of awards offered**: 150
**Funding**: Government, Private
**Contributor**: Private foundations
**No. of awards given last year**: 6
**No. of applicants last year**: 150
**Additional Information**: wsworkshop.org/residencies/studio-internship/

## Woodrow Wilson National Fellowship Foundation

P O Box 5281, Princeton, NJ 08543-5281, United States of America.

**Tel**:  (1) 609 452 7007
**Email**:  marrero@woodrow.org
**Website**:  www.woodrow.org
**Contact**:  Ms Frances Micklow, Communications Associate

The Woodrow Wilson National Fellowship Foundation identifies and develops the best minds for the nation's most important challenges. The fellowships are awarded to enrich human resources, work to improve public policy, and assist organizations and institutions in enhancing practice in the United States and abroad.

## The Millicent C. McIntosh Fellowship

**Purpose**: These fellowships are specifically intended for recently tenured faculty who would benefit from additional time and resources
**Level of Study**: Postgraduate
**Type**: Fellowship
**Value**: A US$15,000 stipend
**Length of Study**: 1 year
**Frequency**: Annual
**Application Procedure**: Contact the Foundation
**Closing Date**: 31 March
**Funding**: Private
**Contributor**: Gladys Krieble Delmas Foundation

### For further information contact:

**Tel**:  (1) 609 452 7007 ext. 301
**Email**:  mcintoshfellowship@woodrow.org

## Woodrow Wilson MBA Fellowship in Education Leadership

**Purpose**: To address the United States' twin educational achievement gaps–the one between the nation's lowest performing and its best schools, as well as the one between the nation's best schools and their top international competitors. The Fellowship seeks both to prepare leaders who can bring all American schools up to world-class levels of performance and to develop a new gold standard for preparing education leaders
**Eligibility**: Fellows commit to serve for 3 years in approved school or district leadership positions within their states
**Level of Study**: Postgraduate
**Type**: Fellowship
**Value**: Fellows will receive a stipend to cover tuition for the MBA program and other expenses
**Length of Study**: The program will require 13–15 months of full-time study, depending on the institution–two summers and an academic year
**Frequency**: Annual
**Country of Study**: Any country
**Application Procedure**: Fellows must be nominated by a local education leader/colleague before they are eligible to apply. Contact information buntrock@woodrow.org
**Closing Date**: December

**Additional Information**: If you have already been nominated, see the respective pages for the WW MBA Fellowship at MSOE www.msoe.edu/community/academics/business/page/2311/mba-in-education-leadership-overview woodrow.org/mobile/fships/ww-ed-mba/

### For further information contact:

**Email**:    buntrock@woodrow.org

## Woodrow Wilson Teaching Fellowship

**Eligibility**: The Woodrow Wilson Teaching Fellowship seeks to attract talented, committed individuals with science, technology, engineering, and mathematics (STEM) backgrounds – including current undergraduates, recent college graduates, midcareer professionals, and retirees – into teaching in high-need secondary schools. A qualified applicant should demonstrate a commitment to the program and its goals; have United States citizenship or permanent residency; have attained, or expect to attain by 30 June, a bachelor's degree from an accredited United States college or university; have majored in and/or have a strong professional background in an STEM field; have achieved a cumulative undergraduate grade point average (GPA) of 3.0 or better on a 4.0 scale (negotiable for applicants from institutions that do not employ a 4.0 GPA scale). Note: Prior teaching experience does not exclude a candidate from eligibility. All applications are considered in their entirety and selection is based on merit

**Level of Study**: Graduate

**Type**: Fellowship

**Value**: US$30,000-US$32,000 stipend, with tuition arrangements varying by campus in Georgia, Indiana, and New Jersey. (Once Fellows are certified teachers at the end of the first year, they obtain salaried employment in high-need schools.)

**Length of Study**: 12–18 months plus 3-year teaching commitment

**Frequency**: Annual

**Study Establishment**: Fellowship is only available for use at specific schools in Indiana (Ball State University, Indiana University-Purdue University Indianapolis, Purdue University, and the University of Indianapolis); Michigan (Eastern Michigan University, Grand Valley State University, Michigan State University, University of Michigan, Wayne State University, Western Michigan University); and Ohio (John Carroll University, Ohio State University, University of Akron, and University of Cincinnati)

**Application Procedure**: Online application procedure and supporting documents. See www.wwteachingfellowship.org

**No. of awards offered**: 1690

**Funding**: Government, Private, Foundation

**Contributor**: Ohio STEM, Lilly Endowment Inc., W K Kellogg Foundation, Choose Ohio First

**No. of awards given last year**: 260

**No. of applicants last year**: 1690

**Additional Information**: University of Dayton and University of Toledo are also included in study establishment woodrow.org/fellowships/ww-teaching-fellowships/

### For further information contact:

**Tel**:      (1) 609 452 7007 ext. 141
**Email**:    wwteachingfellowship@woodrow.org

# Woods Hole Oceanographic Institution (WHOI)

266 Woods Hole Road, Woods Hole, MA 02543-1050, United States of America.

**Tel**:      (1) 508 548 1400
**Email**:    information@whoi.edu
**Website**:   www.whoi.edu/education
**Contact**:   Janet Fields, Coordinator

The Woods Hole Oceanographic Institution is a private, independent, non-profit corporation dedicated to research and higher education at the frontiers of ocean science. Its primary mission is to develop and effectively communicate a fundamental understanding of the processes and characteristics governing how the oceans function and how they interact with the Earth as a whole.

## Postdoctoral Scholar Program

**Purpose**: Eighteen-month Postdoctoral Scholar awards are offered to recipients of new or recent doctorates in the fields of chemistry, engineering, geology, geophysics, mathematics, meteorology, physics, and biology as well as oceanography. The awards are designed to further the education and training of the applicant with primary emphasis placed on the individual's research promise.

**Eligibility**: In order to be eligible for one of these awards, applicants must have received their doctoral degree within the past 2-3 years

**Level of Study**: Postdoctoral

**Type**: Fellowship

**Value**: US$61,200 per year

**Length of Study**: 18 month

**Frequency**: Annual

**Study Establishment**: Woods Hole Oceanographic Institution

**Country of Study**: United States of America

**Closing Date**: 1 December

## Woods Hole Oceanographic Institution Postdoctoral Awards in Marine Policy and Ocean Management

**Eligibility**: Open to Scholars and practitioners from relevant fields in the social sciences, natural sciences, law and management who are interested in applying their disciplinary training and experience to investigations which require a significant component of marine research. Applicants must have completed their doctorate degree or possess equivalent professional qualifications through career experience
**Level of Study**: Postdoctorate
**Value**: Please contact the organization
**Length of Study**: 1 year
**Frequency**: Annual
**Study Establishment**: Woods Hole Oceanographic Institution
**Country of Study**: United States of America
**Additional Information**: Award recipients in the programme have pursued such studies as the implications of oil exploration along the North eastern coast of the United States of America, problems of international law created by new developments in aquaculture and fish farming, economic benefits of some oceanographic research, a perceptual study of United Kingdom fishermen, and oceanic waste disposal

## Woods Hole Oceanographic Institution Postdoctoral Fellowships in Ocean Science and Engineering

**Purpose**: To further the education and training of recent recipients of doctoral degrees in engineering science or with interests in marine science
**Eligibility**: Open to United States citizens and foreign nationals who have earned a PhD degree in biology, physics, microbiology, molecular biology, chemistry, geology, geophysics, oceanography, meteorology, engineering or mathematics. Scientists with more than three years of postdoctoral experience are not eligible
**Level of Study**: Postdoctorate
**Type**: Fellowship
**Value**: Please contact the organization
**Length of Study**: 1 year
**Frequency**: Annual
**Study Establishment**: Woods Hole Oceanographic Institution
**Country of Study**: United States of America
**Application Procedure**: Applicants must complete and submit an application form with transcripts, reference letters, complete transcripts of undergraduate and graduate records, and a concise statement describing research interests. Further information and application forms may be obtained from the postdoctoral section of the website

**Funding**: Government, Private
**Additional Information**: Award holders work in the laboratory under the general supervision of an appropriate member of the staff, but are expected to work independently on research problems of their own choice

### For further information contact:

**Email**: postdoc@whoi.edu

## Worcester College

### Drue Heinz Scholarship

**Purpose**: Open to all graduate applicants for courses in the Humanities in which Worcester College admits students and who specify Worcester College as their first choice College
**Eligibility**: All applicants for courses in the Humanities
**Level of Study**: Graduate
**Type**: Scholarship
**Value**: Up to £10,000 per annum towards full cost of fee
**Frequency**: Annual
**Country of Study**: Any country
**Application Procedure**: Requirements for the application is: 1. a completed application cover sheet. i. an up-to-date Curriculum Vitae. ii. a covering letter stating their reasons for applying for the particular course and providing information about applications they have made to relevant funding bodies
**Funding**: Private
**Additional Information**: www.worc.ox.ac.uk/sites/default/files/ad_drue_heinz_scholarship_2020-21.pdf

### For further information contact:

Porters' Lodge, Worcester College, Oxford OX1 2HB, United Kingdom.

**Tel**: (44) 1865 278300
**Email**: graduate.enquiries@worc.ox.ac.uk

## World Bank Institute

1818 H Street NW, Washington, DC 20433, United States of America.

**Tel**: (1) 202 473 1000
**Email**: pic@worldbank.org
**Website**: www.worldbank.org
**Contact**: Communications Officer

One of the largest sources of funding and knowledge for transition and development councils; The World Bank uses its financial resources, staff and extensive experience to help developing countries reduce poverty, increase economic growth and improve their quality of life.

## World Bank Grants Facility for Indigenous Peoples

**Purpose**: To support sustainable and culturally appropriate development projector planed and implemented by and for Indigenous People

**Eligibility**: Applicant must be an Indigenous People's community or not-for-profit/non-governmental Indigenous People's organization, must be legally registered in the country of grant implementation, the country must be eligible to borrow from the World Bank (IBRD and/or IDA). Applicant should have an established bank account in the name of the applicant organization and should demonstrate internal controls to govern the use of funds. Applicant should not have received a grant from the Grants Facility for Indigenous Peoples in the previous 2 years

**Level of Study**: Professional development, Research

**Type**: Grant

**Value**: Proposed project budget requests should range between US$10,000 and US$30,000 and include a minimum contribution of 20% of the total project cost

**Frequency**: Annual

**Application Procedure**: A complete application, not more than 10 pages, should be submitted

**Closing Date**: 15 November

**Contributor**: The World Bank

**Additional Information**: siteresources.worldbank.org/INTINDPEOPLE/948158-1113428433802/20662536/english call.pdf

### For further information contact:

**Fax**:      (1) 202 522 1669
**Email**:    indigenouspeoples@worldbank.org

## World Bank Scholarships Program

**Purpose**: The World Bank Scholarships Program contributes to the World Bank Group's mission of forging new dynamic approaches to capacity development and knowledge sharing in the developing world. It is an important component of the Bank Group's efforts to promote economic development and shared prosperity through investing in education

**Eligibility**: Eligibility criteria has been mentioned in elaborated way as follows. 1. Be a national of a World Bank member developing country. 2. Not hold dual citizenship of any developed country. 3. Be in good health. 4. Hold a Bachelor's (or equivalent) degree earned at least 3 years prior to the Application Deadline date

**Level of Study**: Graduate, Postgraduate

**Type**: Programme grant

**Frequency**: Annual

**Country of Study**: Any country

**Application Procedure**: Applicants can apply for scholarships to both Preferred and Partner Programs. The process to apply to a Preferred Program and to a Partner Program differs: 1. See our Announcements posted on the right side of this website for upcoming calls for scholarship applications for developing country nationals to study at one of our partner master programs, as these calls are announced on a rolling basis throughout the calendar year. 2. Those seeking a JJ/WBGSP Partner Program scholarship (.xlsx 5 KB) must first apply for admission to one or more of the Partner Master's Degree Program(s). 3. Announcements from a JJWBGSP Partner Program on when to apply for admission to their program is often posted on the right-side margin of this website. Inquiries on how to submit an admission application to a partner program should be submitted to the respective university

**Closing Date**: 11 April

**Funding**: Private

**Additional Information**: www.worldbank.org/en/programs/scholarships

### For further information contact:

**Tel**:      (1) 202 473 1000
**Email**:    support@wizehive.com

## World Federation of International Music Competitions

104, rue de Carouge, CH-1205 Genéve, Switzerland.

**Tel**:      (41) 22 321 3620
**Email**:    info@beethoven-comp.at
**Website**:  www.beethoven-comp.at

## International Beethoven Piano Competition Vienna

**Purpose**: To encourage the artistic development of young pianists

**Eligibility**: Open for pianists born between January 1, 1981 and December 31, 1996

**Level of Study**: Unrestricted

**Type**: Competition
**Value**: The first prize is €8,000, a Boesendorfer Model 200 piano and engagements, the second prize is €6,000, the third prize is €4,500, and there are three further prizes of €2,000. All information subject to change
**Country of Study**: Austria
**Application Procedure**: Apply online through the website www.beethoven-comp.at
**No. of awards offered**: 207
**Closing Date**: 15 October
**Funding**: Government, Private
**No. of awards given last year**: 6 plus special prizes
**No. of applicants last year**: 207
**Additional Information**: Please refer to the website for more details

#### For further information contact:

Competition Office, University of Music and Performing Arts, Anton-von-Webern Platz 1, A-1030 Wien, Austria.

**Tel**: (43) 1 711 55/5113
**Fax**: (43) 1 711 55/5199

## World Learning

School for International Training (SIT), Kipling Road, PO Box 676, Brattleboro, VT 05302, United States of America.

**Tel**: (1) 802 258 3510
**Email**: admissions@sit.edu
**Website**: www.worldlearning.org
**Contact**: Enrollment Services

The School for International Training (SIT) at World Learning educates leaders capable of bridging differences between people and nations in an effort to build a more peaceful and sustainable world. Accredited by the New United Kingdom Association of Schools and Colleges, SIT offers Master's degrees in international and intercultural fields, as well as continuing education opportunities, management development courses and peace and conflict transformation training.

### School for International Training (SIT) Master of Arts in Teaching Program

**Purpose**: To prepare language teachers committed to professional development and service in their field

**Eligibility**: Open to persons of any nationality who are preparing for a language teaching career. Awards are available only to students studying at the School for International Training
**Level of Study**: Graduate
**Type**: Scholarship
**Value**: Varies
**Length of Study**: A period that includes a time of student teaching and homestay. The programme is offered in a 1 year or 2 Summer format designed for working professionals
**Frequency**: Annual
**Study Establishment**: SIT
**Country of Study**: Any country
**Application Procedure**: Applicants must complete an institutional financial aid application and should contact the Financial Aid Office for further details, by email at finaid@sit.edu
**Additional Information**: Students master technical teaching methodologies through language classroom practice, on campus coursework and a supervised teaching internship. Further information is available on the website www.sit.edu/mat

#### For further information contact:

**Email**: tesol@rennert.com

## Worshipful Company of Musicians

6th Floor, 2 London Wall Buildings, London EC2M 5PP, United Kingdom.

**Tel**: (44) 20 7496 8980
**Email**: deputyclerk@wcom.org.uk
**Website**: www.wcom.org.uk
**Contact**: Ms Margaret Alford, Clerk

The Worshipful Company of Musicians supports young musicians particularly in the wilderness years between graduating and setting out on their musical careers.

### Carnwath Scholarship

**Purpose**: Open to any person permanently resident in the United Kingdom and 21-25 years of age. The scholarship is intended only for the advanced student who has successfully completed a solo performance course at a college of music
**Eligibility**: Open to any person permanently resident in the United Kingdom and 21–25 years of age. The scholarship is intended only for the advanced student who has successfully completed a solo performance course at a college of music

**Level of Study**: Postgraduate
**Type**: Scholarship
**Value**: £4,150 per year
**Length of Study**: Up to 2 years
**Frequency**: Annual
**Country of Study**: United Kingdom
**Application Procedure**: 1. Applicants must be nominated by principals of the Royal Academy of Music, the Guildhall School of Music, the Royal Northern College of Music, the Royal Scottish Academy of Music, Trinity College of Music, London College of Music, the Welsh College of Music, the Birmingham School of Music or the Royal College of Music. 2. No application should be made directly to the Worshipful Company of Musicians
**Closing Date**: 30 April
**Funding**: Private
**Additional Information**: Website link error

**For further information contact:**

**Email**:    clerk@wcom.org.uk

---

# Writtle University College

Lordship Road, Writtle, Chelmsford CM1 3RR, United Kingdom.

**Tel**:          (44) 1245 424 200
**Contact**:   Writtle University

Writtle University College is one of the largest land-based university colleges in the United Kingdom; it is also one of the oldest. Set in the Essex countryside on a 220 hectare estate, Writtle, previously known as Writtle College, provides FE and HE programmes.

## Elinor Roper Scholarship 2020

**Eligibility**: To be considered for a Writtle University College Elinor Roper Scholarship award, students must be Home students and must apply by completing the ERS application form. This application must include a written statement of between 500 - 800 words detailing the value the applicant expects to gain from study on the Master's programme and the way in which they anticipate using the experience after graduation to further their chosen career. If you have a "conditional offer" the scholarship will only be awarded if the conditions are met. Any applicant who defers entry will have to submit a new application for the academic year their studies will commence. Current Writtle University College

students are not eligible to apply. The value of the scholarship will be deducted from the tuition fee invoice. It will be a condition of the scholarship that the successful applicant agrees to provide a student profile detailing their experience on the programme to be used in publications for the purpose of marketing Writtle University College and/or inclusion in the "University College Alumni Association" publication.
**Level of Study**: Postgraduate
**Type**: Scholarship
**Value**: £1,000 tuition fee
**Length of Study**: 1 year
**Frequency**: Annual
**Country of Study**: Any country
**Closing Date**: 31 August
**Contributor**: Writtle University
**Additional Information**: writtle.ac.uk/pdfs/Scholarships/ 2020/3/ERS2020_Form.pdf

**For further information contact:**

Student Finance, Writtle University College, Writtle, Chelmsford, Essex CM1 3RR, United Kingdom.

**Tel**:          (44) 1245 424200
**Email**:     student.finance@writtle.ac.uk

## Postgraduate International Scholarships

**Purpose**: Scholarships are available for pursuing postgraduate programme
**Eligibility**: The scholarship is only available to new postgraduate Writtle University College students. Applicants whose first language is not English are usually required to provide evidence of proficiency in English at the higher level required by the University
**Value**: For taught MA/MSc courses, the award will be worth £1,000; for MA conversion students the award will be delivered within the conversion year ONLY, as per the terms and conditions set out below
**Length of Study**: 2 years
**Frequency**: Annual
**Country of Study**: Any country
**Application Procedure**: Applications to be sent via email. For more details, please refer website: scholarship-positions. com/writtle-university-college-postgraduate-international-scholarships-uk/2017/10/23/
**Closing Date**: 31 August
**Contributor**: Writtle University
**Additional Information**: writtle.ac.uk/scholarships.cfm? Scholarship=62&nohead=1&nofooter=1

**For further information contact:**

**Email**:     student.recruitment@glasgow.ac.uk

# X

## Xavier Labor Relations Institute -Xavier School of Management

MDP Office, CH Area (East), Jamshedpur, Jharkhand 831001, India.

**Tel**:　(91) 657 398 3329, 3330

XLRI – Xavier School of Management is a management school founded in 1949 by the Society of Jesus and based in Jamshedpur, Jharkhand, India.

### Fellow Programme in Management (FPM) at Xavier Labor Relations Institute

**Purpose**: The programme aims to train prospective scholars to become highly skilled and innovative researchers and teachers in various aspects of management. It primarily aims at preparing students for careers as faculty members at premier academic institutions and for position outside academics requiring advanced research and analytical capabilities
**Eligibility**: Citizens of India
**Study Establishment**: Fellowship is available for pursuing full-time, residential doctoral programme
**Country of Study**: India
**Application Procedure**: See the website
**Additional Information**: For more details please see the website scholarship-positions.com/fellow-programme-in-management-fpm-at-xlri-in-india/2017/08/17/

### For further information contact:

**Email**:　satellitecoord@xlri.ac.in

## Xerox Foundation

6th Floor/PO Box 4505, 45 Glover Avenue, Norwalk, CT 06856-4505, United States of America.

**Tel**:　　　(1) 800 275 9376
**Email**:　　D.Garvin.Byrd@xerox.com
**Website**:　www.xerox.com
**Contact**:　Dr Joseph M. Cahalan

Xerox Foundation is a US$15.7 billion technology and services enterprise that helps businesses deploy Smarter Document Management strategies and find better ways to work. Its intent is to constantly lead with innovative technologies, products and services that customers can depend upon to improve business results.

## Xerox Technical Minority Scholarship

**Purpose**: To provide funding to minority students enroled in one of the technical sciences or engineering disciplines
**Eligibility**: Open to citizens of the United States or visa-holding permanent residents of African American, Asian, Pacific Island, Native American, Native Alaskan or Hispanic descent. Applicants must have grade point average of 3.0 or better
**Level of Study**: Postgraduate
**Type**: Scholarship
**Value**: Scholarships amount vary from US$1,000–US$10,000
**Frequency**: Annual
**Country of Study**: United States of America

**Application Procedure**: Applicants must submit the completed application form along with a curriculum vitae

**Closing Date**: 30 September

**Additional Information**: worldscholarshipforum.com/xerox-technical-minority-scholarship/

**For further information contact:**

Xerox Technical Minority Scholarship Programme office.

**Email**:   xtmsp@rballiance.com

# Y

## Yale Center for British Art

Public Information, Education and Programs, 1080 Chapel Street, PO Box 208280, New Haven, CT 06520-8280, United States of America.

**Tel**: (1) 203 432 2850
**Email**: bacinfo@yale.edu
**Website**: www.yale.edu/ycba
**Contact**: Ms Mary Beth Graham, Acting Programme Co-ordinator

The Yale Center for British Art houses the most comprehensive collection of English paintings, prints, drawings, rare books and sculpture outside the United Kingdom. Given to Yale University by Paul Mellon, the Center's resources illustrate British life and culture from the 16th century to the present.

### Andrew W Mellon Fellowship

**Purpose**: To promote the study of British art
**Eligibility**: Open to foreign students enrolled for a higher degree at a British or other non-American university
**Level of Study**: Postgraduate
**Type**: Fellowship
**Value**: US$15,000 plus return airfare from London, health benefits and travel expenses up to US$1,000
**Length of Study**: 1 year
**Frequency**: Annual
**Study Establishment**: The Yale Center for British Art
**Country of Study**: United States of America
**Application Procedure**: There is no application form. Please submit name, address, telephone number, CV listing professional experience, education and publications, three page outline of research proposal, and two confidential letters of recommendation

**No. of awards offered**: 2
**Closing Date**: 15 January
**Funding**: Private
**No. of awards given last year**: 1
**No. of applicants last year**: 2

**For further information contact:**

**Email**: bacinfo@minerva.cis.yale.edu

## Yale School of Management (SOM)

135 Prospect Street, Box 208200, New Haven, CT 06520-8200, United States of America.

**Tel**: (1) 203 432 5932
**Email**: admissions@admin.som.yale.edu
**Contact**: MBA Admissions Officer

### Arthur Liman Public Interest Law Fellowship

**Purpose**: The Arthur Liman Public Interest Law Summer Fellowship Program supports the work of law students, law school graduates, and students from six universities, all of whom work to respond to problems of inequality and to improve access to justice
**Eligibility**: The Liman Fellowship program supports Harvard College undergraduates who perform domestic summer fellowships in public interest law at a 501(c)(3) nonprofit organization. Students who perform fellowships in the following fields are eligible for consideration: 1. Client-oriented, direct service case work and litigation, both civil and criminal. 2. Enforcement work and other litigation for governmental agencies. 3. Alternative dispute resolution, such as negotiation, mediation, and arbitration. 4. Policy-making legislative and regulatory reform. 5. Policy-oriented class action and impact legislation

© Springer Nature Limited 2020
Palgrave Macmillan (ed.), *The Grants Register 2021*,
https://doi.org/10.1057/978-1-349-95988-4

**Level of Study**: Graduate
**Type**: Fellowship
**Frequency**: Annual
**Country of Study**: Any country
**Application Procedure**: At the time of application, students need not have identified a specific project. The Liman advisor at Brown will help with placements, including at organizations with Liman Fellows. However, if students are interested in specific substantive areas or projects, they should describe them in their application. The Review Committee will evaluate applications with preference toward applications that: 1. Focus on public service work that has a clear and significant legal flavor. All else being equal, the more fully the summer fellowship engages the legal system, the more favorably the committee will view the application. 2. Demonstrate the applicant has carefully researched the summer fellowship site. 3. Demonstrate the applicant has thoughtfully considered how the summer fellowship would support the applicant's academic and career interests
**Closing Date**: 11 January
**Funding**: Private
**Contributor**: The Liman Summer Fellowships at Brown are funded by the generous support of Arthur Liman's son, the filmmaker Doug Liman and the Liman Foundation
**Additional Information**: Summer Fellows have worked on issues such as immigrant's rights, worker's rights, prison conditions, educational equity, juvenile justice and marriage equality

## For further information contact:

**Email**:     tlovett@fas.harvard.edu

# Yanshan University

438 Hebei Street West Section, Haigang Qu, Qinhuangdao Shi, Hebei Sheng, China.

**Contact**:     Yanshan University

The Yanshan University is a university in Qinhuangdao, Hebei, China under the provincial government. It has a student population of 39,000 and a staff population of 3,200. It is a national key school and runs state key labs on its campus.

## China Scholarship Council Scholarships

**Purpose**: The scholarship is awarded only to PhD candidates
**Eligibility**: For eligibility refer website www.cscscholar ships.net/yanshan-university-csc-scholarships-ranking-agency-number-and-faculty.html

**Value**: Registration fee, tuition fee, and accommodation fee for dormitory on campus, monthly allowance: ¥1,400 for 12 months/year, one-off settlement subsidy: ¥2,000
**Length of Study**: 3 to 4 years
**Country of Study**: China
**Application Procedure**: For application procedure, please refer website www.cscscholarships.net/yanshan-university-csc-scholarships-ranking-agency-number-and-faculty.html
**Closing Date**: May

## For further information contact:

**Email**:     scholarships@cscscholarship.com

## Chinese Government Scholarship Program

**Purpose**: Chinese Government Scholarship Program is established by the Ministry of Education of P.R. China in accordance with educational exchange agreements or understandings reached between the Chinese government and the governments of other countries, organizations, education institutions and relevant international organizations to provide both full scholarships and partial scholarships to international students and scholars
**Eligibility**: For eligibility, please visit website
**Type**: Scholarship
**Value**: Master's degree students and general scholars: ¥1,700; doctoral degree students and senior scholars: ¥2,000. Exempt from registration fee, tuition fee, fee for laboratory experiment, fee for internship, fee for basic learning materials; and accommodation fee for dormitory on campus
**Length of Study**: 1 to 2 years for both post graduate and doctorate degrees
**Country of Study**: China
**Application Procedure**: Please visit website english.ysu.edu.cn/info/2345/1095.htm
**Contributor**: Yanshan University
**Additional Information**: The CSC Online Application System for Study in China is available on laihua.csc.edu cn english.ysu.edu.cn/info/2345/1095.htm

## For further information contact:

**Email**:     zizhu2@csc.edu.cn

## Yanshan University Doctoral Scholarships

**Purpose**: The aim of the scholarships is to provide financial help to the students who are coming to study in China
**Eligibility**: Non-Chinese citizens are eligible to apply for this scholarship programme
**Type**: Scholarships

**Value**: Registration fee, tuition fee, and accommodation fee for dormitory on campus. Monthly allowance of ¥1,400 for 12 months, one-off settlement subsidy ¥2,000
**Country of Study**: Any country
**Application Procedure**: Please visit website www.cscscholar ships.org/yanshan-university-doctoral-scholarships.html
**Closing Date**: 20 May
**Contributor**: Yanshan University
**Additional Information**: Please visit website english.ysu. edu.cn/info/2345/1092.htm www.chinesescholarshipcouncil. com/yanshan-university-doctoral-scholarships.html

### For further information contact:

**Email**:  study@ysu.edu.cn

## Yanshan University Scholarship Program for International Students

**Purpose**: Scholarships are available for pursuing master degree programme
**Eligibility**: Non-Chinese citizens are eligible to apply. For more details, visit website
**Value**: First class scholarship covers the following: registration fee, tuition fee, and accommodation fee for dormitory on campus. The second class scholarship covers the following: registration fee and tuition fee
**Country of Study**: China
**Application Procedure**: The mode of applying is online. Email application to study@ysu.edu.cn
**Closing Date**: 20 May

### For further information contact:

**Email**:  study@ysu.edu.cn

## Yidisher Visnshaftlekher Institut Institute for Jewish Research

15 West 16th Street, New York, NY 10011-6301, United States of America.

**Tel**:  (1) 212 246 6080
**Email**:  pglasser@yivo.cjh.org
**Website**:  www.yivoinstitute.org
**Contact**:  Dr Paul Glasser, Dean, Senior Research Associate

YIVO Institute for Jewish Research was founded in 1925, in Vilna, Poland as the Yiddish Scientific Institute, the YIVO Institute for Jewish Research is dedicated to the history and culture of Ashkenazi Jewry and to its influence in the Americas.

## Abraham and Rachela Melezin Fellowship

**Purpose**: To support doctoral and postdoctoral research on Jewish educational networks in Lithuania, with emphasis on pre-war Vilna and the Vilna region
**Level of Study**: Doctorate, Postdoctorate
**Type**: Fellowship
**Value**: US$1,500
**Length of Study**: 1–3 months
**Frequency**: Annual
**Study Establishment**: YIVO Library and Archives
**Country of Study**: United States of America
**Application Procedure**: Applicants must send a covering letter, curriculum vitae, research proposal and 2 letters of support through regular mail, fax or email
**Closing Date**: 31 December
**Additional Information**: A written summary of one's research is required; a public lecture is optional www. petersons.com/scholarship/abraham-and-rachela-melezin-fellowship-111_153684.aspx

## Abram and Fannie Gottlieb Immerman and Abraham Nathan and Bertha Daskal Weinstein Memorial Fellowship

**Purpose**: To support travel for PhD dissertation research in archives and libraries of the Baltic states with preference given to research on the Jews of Courland and Latvia
**Eligibility**: For those engaged in PhD dissertation research in archives and libraries of the Baltic states with preference given to research on the Jews of Courland and Latvia
**Level of Study**: Doctorate, Research
**Type**: Fellowship
**Value**: US$2,000
**Frequency**: Every 2 years
**Application Procedure**: Applicants must send a cover letter, curriculum vitae, research proposal and 2 letters of support through regular mail, fax or email. A written summary of one's research is required
**Closing Date**: 31 December
**Funding**: Private
**Additional Information**: www.petersons.com/scholarship/ abram-and-fannie-gottlieb-immerman-and-abraham-nathan-and-bertha-daskal-weinstein-memorial-fellowship-111_182 517.aspx

### For further information contact:

YIVO Institute for Jewish Research, 15 West 16 Street, New York, NY 10011, United States of America.

## Aleksander and Alicja Hertz Memorial Fellowship

**Purpose**: To encourage research on Jewish-Polish relations and Jewish contributions to Polish literature and culture in the modern period
**Level of Study**: Doctorate, Postdoctorate
**Type**: Fellowship
**Value**: US$1,500
**Length of Study**: 1–3 months
**Frequency**: Annual
**Country of Study**: United States of America
**Application Procedure**: Applicants must send their curriculum vitae, research proposal and 2 letters of support through regular mail, fax or email. A written summary of one's research is required
**Closing Date**: 31 December
**Additional Information**: www.petersons.com/scholarship/aleksander-and-alicja-hertz-memorial-fellowship-111_153683.aspx

## Dina Abramowicz Emerging Scholar Fellowship

**Purpose**: To support a significant scholarly publication that may encompass the revision of a doctoral dissertation
**Eligibility**: Applicants are required to give a public lecture
**Level of Study**: Postdoctorate
**Type**: Fellowship
**Value**: US$3,000
**Length of Study**: 1–3 months
**Frequency**: Annual
**Application Procedure**: Applicants must send their curriculum vitae, a research proposal and 2 letters of support through regular mail, fax or email
**Closing Date**: 31 December
**Additional Information**: Please check website for more details www.petersons.com/scholarship/dina-abramowicz-emerging-scholar-fellowship-111_153681.aspx

## Dora and Mayer Tendler Fellowship

**Purpose**: To support graduate research in Jewish studies with preference given to research in YIVO collections
**Eligibility**: Graduate applicants must carry out original research in the field of Jewish studies and give a written summary of the research carried out
**Level of Study**: Doctorate, Graduate
**Type**: Fellowship
**Value**: US$3,000
**Frequency**: Annual
**Study Establishment**: YIVO collections
**Country of Study**: United States of America

**Application Procedure**: Applicants must send a cover letter, curriculum vitae, research proposal and 2 letters of support through regular mail, fax or email
**Closing Date**: 31 December
**Additional Information**: A public lecture at the end of the tenure of the Fellowship is optional www.petersons.com/scholarship/dora-and-mayer-tendler-fellowship-111_169669.aspx

### For further information contact:

**Email**:     eportnoy@yivo.cjh.org

## Joseph Kremen Memorial Fellowship

**Purpose**: To financially assist researchers at the YIVO Archives and Library
**Eligibility**: A written summary of one's research is required
**Level of Study**: Postgraduate, Research
**Type**: Fellowship
**Value**: US$2,000
**Frequency**: Annual
**Application Procedure**: Applicants must send their curriculum vitae, research proposal and 2 letters of support by regular mail, fax or email
**Closing Date**: 31 December
**Additional Information**: www.petersons.com/scholarship/joseph-kremen-memorial-fellowship-111_175652.aspx

## Maria Salit-Gitelson Tell Memorial Fellowship

**Purpose**: To support original doctoral or postdoctoral research in the field of Lithuanian Jewish history, the city of Vilnus in particular, at the YIVO Library and Archives
**Eligibility**: Applicants must carry out original doctoral or postdoctoral research in the field of Lithuanian Jewish history and give a public lecture at the end of the tenure of the Fellowship
**Level of Study**: Doctorate, Postdoctorate
**Type**: Fellowship
**Value**: US$1,500
**Length of Study**: 1–3 months
**Frequency**: Annual
**Study Establishment**: YIVO Library and Archives
**Country of Study**: United States of America
**Application Procedure**: Applicants must send a cover letter, curriculum vitae, research proposal and 2 letters of support through regular mail, fax or email
**Closing Date**: 31 December
**Additional Information**: www.petersons.com/scholarship/maria-salit-gitelson-tell-memorial-fellowship-111_153686.aspx

## Natalie and Mendel Racolin Memorial Fellowship

**Purpose**: To support original doctoral or postdoctoral research in the field of East European Jewish history at the YIVO Library and Archives
**Eligibility**: Applicants must carry out original doctoral or postdoctoral research in the field of East European Jewish history and give a public lecture at the end of the tenure of the Fellowship
**Level of Study**: Doctorate, Postdoctorate
**Type**: Fellowship
**Value**: US$1,500
**Length of Study**: 1–3 months
**Frequency**: Annual
**Study Establishment**: YIVO Library and Archives
**Country of Study**: United States of America
**Application Procedure**: Applicants must send a cover letter, curriculum vitae, research proposal and 2 letters of support through regular mail, fax or email
**Closing Date**: 31 December
**Additional Information**: www.petersons.com/scholarship/natalie-and-mendel-racolin-memorial-fellowships-111_153685.aspx

## Professor Bernard Choseed Memorial Fellowship

**Purpose**: To financially support doctoral and postdoctoral students who conduct research
**Eligibility**: Applicants are required to give a public lecture
**Level of Study**: Doctorate, Postdoctorate
**Type**: Fellowship
**Value**: US$7,500
**Length of Study**: 1–3 months
**Frequency**: Annual
**Country of Study**: United States of America
**Application Procedure**: Applicants must submit a curriculum vitae, a research proposal and 2 letters of support through regular mail, fax or email
**Closing Date**: 31 December
**Additional Information**: www.petersons.com/scholarship/professor-bernard-choseed-memorial-fellowship-111_153138.aspx

## Rose and Isidore Drench Memorial Fellowship

**Purpose**: To encourage research in American Jewish history
**Eligibility**: Applicants are required to give a public lecture
**Level of Study**: Doctorate, Postdoctorate
**Type**: Fellowship
**Value**: US$2,500
**Length of Study**: 1–3 months

**Frequency**: Annual
**Application Procedure**: Applicants must submit their curriculum vitae, a research proposal and 2 letters of support through regular mail, fax or email
**Closing Date**: 31 December
**Additional Information**: www.petersons.com/scholarship/rose-and-isidore-drench-memorial-fellowships-111_151729.aspx

## Samuel and Flora Weiss Research Fellowship

**Purpose**: To support research on the destruction of Polish Jewry or on Polish-Jewish relations during the Holocaust period
**Eligibility**: Applicants must carry out original research on the destruction of Polish Jewry or on Polish-Jewish relations during the Holocaust period and give a written summary of the research carried out. The research should result in a scholarly publication
**Level of Study**: Doctorate
**Type**: Fellowship
**Value**: US$2,500
**Frequency**: Annual
**Country of Study**: Any country
**Application Procedure**: Applicants must send a cover letter, curriculum vitae, research proposal and 2 letters of support through regular mail, fax or email
**Closing Date**: 31 December
**Additional Information**: A public lecture at the end of the tenure of the Fellowship is optional www.petersons.com/scholarship/samuel-and-flora-weiss-research-fellowship-111_175653.aspx

### For further information contact:

**Tel**:     (1) 212 294 613
**Email**:   pglasse@yivo.cjh.org

## Vivian Lefsky Hort Memorial Fellowship

**Purpose**: To support original doctoral or postdoctoral research in the field of Yiddish literature
**Eligibility**: Applicants must carry out original doctoral or postdoctoral research in Yiddish literature and give a public lecture at the end of the tenure of the Fellowship
**Level of Study**: Doctorate, Postdoctorate
**Type**: Fellowship
**Value**: US$2,000
**Length of Study**: 1–3 months
**Frequency**: Annual
**Study Establishment**: YIVO Library and Archives
**Country of Study**: United States of America

**Application Procedure**: Applicants must send a cover letter, curriculum vitae, research proposal and 2 letters of support through regular mail, fax or email

**Closing Date**: 31 December

**Additional Information**: www.petersons.com/scholarship/vivian-lefsky-hort-memorial-fellowship-111_151730.aspx

## Vladimir and Pearl Heifetz Memorial Fellowship in Eastern European Jewish Music

**Purpose**: To assist undergraduate, graduate and postgraduate researchers defray expenses connected with research in YIVO's music collection at the YIVO Archives and Library

**Eligibility**: Undergraduate, graduate and postgraduate researchers who will carry on research in YIVO's music collection at the YIVO Archives and Library

**Level of Study**: Graduate, Postgraduate

**Type**: Fellowship

**Value**: US$1,500

**Frequency**: Annual

**Study Establishment**: YIVO's music collection

**Country of Study**: United States of America

**Application Procedure**: Applicants must send a cover letter, curriculum vitae, research proposal and 2 letters of support through regular mail, fax or email

**Closing Date**: 31 December

**Funding**: Foundation

**Additional Information**: A written summary of one's research is required; a public lecture is optional gradfund.rutgers.edu/blog/awards/2485/

## Workmen's Circle/Dr Emanuel Patt Visiting Professorship

**Purpose**: To support postdoctoral research at the YIVO Library and Archives

**Level of Study**: Postdoctorate

**Type**: Fellowship

**Value**: US$5,000

**Length of Study**: 3 months

**Frequency**: Annual

**Study Establishment**: YIVO Library and Archives

**Country of Study**: United States of America

**Application Procedure**: Applicants must send a covering letter, curriculum vitae, research proposal and 2 letters of support through regular mail, fax or email

**Closing Date**: 31 December

**Additional Information**: The visiting faculty member should give a public lecture at the end of the award's tenure www.petersons.com/scholarship/workmens-circledr-emanuel-patt-visiting-professorship-in-eastern-european-jewish-studies-111_169668.aspx

# AGRICULTURE, FORESTRY AND FISHERY

General
Agricultural business
Agricultural economics
Agriculture and farm management
Agronomy
Animal husbandry
    Sericulture
Crop production
Fishery
    Aquaculture
Food science
    Brewing
    Dairy
    Fish
    Harvest technology
    Meat and poultry
    Oenology
Forestry
    Forest biology
    Forest economics
    Forest management
    Forest pathology
    Forest products
    Forest soils
Horticulture and viticulture
Soil and water science
    Irrigation
    Soil conservation
    Water management
Tropical agriculture
Veterinary science

# ARCHITECTURE AND TOWN PLANNING

General
Architectural and environmental design
Architectural restoration
Landscape architecture
Regional planning
Rural planning
Structural architecture
Town planning

# ARTS AND HUMANITIES

General
Archaeology
Classical languages and literatures
    Classical Greek
    Latin
    Sanskrit
Comparative literature
History
    Ancient civilisations
    Contemporary history
    Medieval studies
    Modern history
    Prehistory
Linguistics
    Applied linguistics
    Grammar
    Logopedics
    Phonetics
    Psycholinguistics
    Semantics and terminology
    Speech studies
Modern languages
    African Languages
    Afrikaans
    Altaic languages
    Amerindian languages
    Arabic
    Austronesian and oceanic languages
    Baltic languages
    Celtic languages

© Springer Nature Limited 2020
Palgrave Macmillan (ed.), *The Grants Register 2021*,
https://doi.org/10.1057/978-1-349-95988-4

Chinese
Danish
Dutch
English
Eurasian and North Asian languages
European languages (others)
Finnish
Fino Ugrian languages
French
German
Germanic languages
Hebrew
Hungarian
Indian languages
Indic languages
Iranic languages
Italian
Japanese
Korean
Modern Greek
Norwegian
Portuguese
Romance languages
Russian
Scandinavian languages
Slavic languages (others)
Spanish
Swedish
Native language and literature
Philosophy
    Ethics
    Logic
    Metaphysics
    Philosophical schools
Translation and interpretation
Writing (authorship)

## BUSINESS ADMINISTRATION AND MANAGEMENT

General
Accountancy
Business and commerce
Business computing
Business machine operation
Finance, banking and investment
Human resources
Institutional administration
Insurance
International business
Labour/industrial relations
Management systems
Marketing
    Public relations
MBA

Personnel management
Private administration
Public administration
Real estate
Secretarial studies

## EDUCATION AND TEACHER TRAINING

General
Adult education
Continuing education
Educational science
    Curriculum
    Distance education
    Educational administration
    Educational and student counselling
    Educational research
    Educational technology
    Educational testing and evaluation
    International and comparative education
    Philosophy of education
    Teaching and learning
Higher education teacher training
Nonvocational subjects education
    Education in native language
    Foreign languages education
    Humanities and social science education
    Literacy education
    Mathematics education
    Physical education
    Science education
Pre-school education
Primary education
Secondary education
Special education
    Bilingual/bicultural education
    Education of foreigners
    Education of natives
    Education of specific learning
      disabilities
    Education of the gifted
    Education of the handicapped
    Education of the socially disadvantaged
Staff development
Teacher trainers education
Vocational subjects education
    Agricultural education
    Art education
    Commerce/business education
    Computer education
    Health education
    Home economics education

Industrial arts education
Music education
Technology education

## ENGINEERING

General
Aeronautical and aerospace engineering
Agricultural engineering
Automotive engineering
Bioengineering and biomedical engineering
Chemical engineering
Civil engineering
Computer engineering
Control engineering (robotics)
Electrical and electronic engineering
Energy engineering
Engineering drawing/design
Environmental and sanitary engineering
Forestry engineering
Hydraulic engineering
Industrial engineering
Marine engineering and naval architecture
Materials engineering
Measurement/precision engineering
Mechanical engineering
Metallurgical engineering
Mining engineering
Nanotechnology
Nuclear engineering
Petroleum and gas engineering
Physical engineering
Production engineering
Safety engineering
Sound engineering
Surveying and mapping science

## FINE AND APPLIED ARTS

General
Art criticism
Art history
    Aesthetics
Art management
Cinema and television
Dance
Design
    Display and stage design
    Fashion design
    Furniture design
    Graphic design
    Industrial design

Interior design
    Textile design
Drawing and painting
Handicrafts
Music
    Conducting
    Jazz and popular music
    Music theory and composition
    Musical instruments
    Musicology
    Opera
    Religious music
    Singing
Photography
Religious art
Sculpture
Theatre

## HOME ECONOMICS

General
Child care/child development
Clothing and sewing
Consumer studies
House arts and environment
Household management
Nutrition

## LAW

General
Air and space law
Canon law
Civil law
Commercial law
Comparative law
Criminal law
European community law
History of law
Human rights
International law
Islamic law
Justice administration
Labour law
Maritime law
Notary studies
Private law
Public law
    Administrative law
    Constitutional law
    Fiscal law

## MASS COMMUNICATION AND INFORMATION SCIENCE

General
Communication arts
Documentation techniques and archiving
Journalism
Library science
Mass communication
Media studies
Museum management
Museum studies
Public relations and publicity
Radio/television broadcasting
Restoration of works of art

## MATHEMATICS AND COMPUTER SCIENCE

General
Actuarial science
Applied mathematics
Artificial intelligence
Computer science
Statistics
Systems analysis

## MEDICAL SCIENCES

General
Acupuncture
Biomedicine
Chiropractic
Dental technology
   Prosthetic dentistry
Dentistry and stomatology
   Community dentistry
   Oral pathology
   Orthodontics
   Periodontics
Forensic medicine and dentistry
Health administration
Homeopathy
Medical auxiliaries
Medical technology
Medicine
   Anaesthesiology
   Cardiology
   Dermatology
   Endocrinology
   Epidemiology
   Gastroenterology

   Geriatrics
   Gynaecology and obstetrics
   Haematology
   Hepathology
   Nephrology
   Neurology
   Oncology
   Ophthalmology
   Otorhinolaryngology
   Paediatrics
   Parasitology
   Pathology
   Plastic surgery
   Pneumology
   Psychiatry and mental health
   Rheumatology
   Tropical medicine
   Urology
   Venereology
   Virology
Midwifery
Nursing
Optometry
Osteopathy
Pharmacy
Podiatry
Public health and hygiene
   Dietetics
   Social/preventive medicine
   Sports medicine
Radiology
Rehabilitation and therapy
Traditional eastern medicine
Treatment techniques

## NATURAL SCIENCES

General
Astronomy and astrophysics
Biological and life sciences
   Anatomy
   Biochemistry
   Biology
   Biophysics and molecular biology
   Biotechnology
   Botany
   Embryology and reproduction biology
   Genetics
   Histology
   Immunology
   Limnology
   Marine biology

Microbiology
Neurosciences
Parasitology
Pharmacology
Physiology
Plant pathology
Toxicology
Zoology
Chemistry
    Analytical chemistry
    Inorganic chemistry
    Organic chemistry
    Physical chemistry
Earth sciences
    Geochemistry
    Geography (scientific)
    Geology
    Geophysics and seismology
    Mineralogy and crystallography
    Palaeontology
    Petrology
Marine science and oceanography
Meteorology
    Arctic studies
    Arid land studies
Physics
    Atomic and molecular physics
    Nuclear physics
    Optics
    Solid state physics
    Thermal physics

## RECREATION, WELFARE, PROTECTIVE SERVICES

General
Civil security
Criminology
Environmental studies
    Ecology
    Environmental management
    Natural resources
    Waste management
    Wildlife and pest management
Fire protection science
Leisure studies
Military science
Parks and recreation
Peace and disarmament
Police studies
Social welfare and social work
    Social and community services

Sports
    Sociology of sports
    Sports management
Vocational counselling

## RELIGION AND THEOLOGY

General
Church administration (pastoral work)
Comparative religion
Esoteric practices
History of religion
Holy writings
Religious education
Religious practice
Religious studies
    Agnosticism and atheism
    Ancient religions
    Asian religious studies
    Christian religious studies
    Islam
    Judaic religious studies
Sociology of religion
Theology

## SERVICE TRADES

General
Cooking and catering
Cosmetology
Hotel and restaurant
Hotel management
Retailing and wholesaling
Tourism

## SOCIAL AND BEHAVIOURAL SCIENCES

General
    Econometrics
    Economic and finance policy
    Economic history
    Economics
    Industrial and production economics
    International economics
    Taxation
Ancient civilisations (egyptology, assyriology)
Anthropology
    Ethnology
    Folklore

Cognitive sciences
Cultural studies
   African American
   African studies
   American
   Asian
   Canadian
   Caribbean
   East Asian
   Eastern European
   European
   Hispanic American
   Indigenous studies
   Islamic
   Jewish
   Latin American
   Middle Eastern
   Native American
   Nordic
   North African
   Pacific area
   South Asian
   Southeast Asian
   Subsahara African
   Western European
Demography and population
Development studies
Geography
Heritage preservation
International relations
Political science and government
   Comparative politics
Psychology
   Clinical psychology
   Development psychology
   Educational psychology
   Experimental psychology
   Industrial and organisational psychology
   Personality psychology
   Psychometrics
   Social psychology
Rural studies
Sociology
   Comparative sociology
   Futurology
   History of societies
   Social institutions
   Social policy
   Social problems
Urban studies
Women's studies

## TRADE, CRAFT AND INDUSTRIAL TECHNIQUES

General
Building technologies
Electrical and electronic equipment and maintenance
Food technology
Graphic arts
   Printing and printmaking
   Publishing and book trade
Heating, and refrigeration
Laboratory techniques
Leather techniques
Mechanical equipment and maintenance
Metal techniques
Optical technology
Paper and packaging technology
Textile technology
Wood technology

## TRANSPORT AND COMMUNICATIONS

General
Air transport
Marine transport and nautical science
Postal services
Railway transport
Road transport
Telecommunications services
Transport economics
Transport management

## ANY SUBJECT

*Any Country*

# AGRICULTURE, FORESTRY AND FISHERY

## GENERAL

STRI Postdoctoral Research in Hydrology, 790

**Australia**

Chinese Government Scholarship Water and Environmental Research Scholarships, 278

Water Corporation Scholarship in Biosolids Research, 316

## WATER MANAGEMENT

**Any Country**

The Geoffrey F. Bruce Fellowship in Canadian Freshwater Policy, 749

Luke Pen Fund-Honours Scholarships, 344

**Australia**

PhD Scholarship in Water Resources Management in Remote Indigenous Communities, 413

**New Zealand**

PhD Scholarship in Water Resources Management in Remote Indigenous Communities, 413

## TROPICAL AGRICULTURE

**African Nations**

International Institute of Tropical Agriculture Research Fellowships, 480

## VETERINARY SCIENCE

**Any Country**

Early Career Fellowship, 443

Harry Steele-Bodger Memorial Travelling Scholarship, 222

Intermediate Clinical Fellowships, 1142

International Training Fellowships, 1144

Research Training Fellowships, 1149

Senior Research Fellowships in Clinical Science, 1151

**Asian Countries**

Korea New Zealand Agricultural Cooperation Scholarships (KNZACS), 346

Scholarships at Indian Veterinary Research Institute, 450

**New Zealand**

Korea New Zealand Agricultural Cooperation Scholarships (KNZACS), 346

## ARCHITECTURE AND TOWN PLANNING

## GENERAL

**Any Country**

American School of Classical Studies at Athens Advanced Fellowships, 88

American School of Classical Studies at Athens Summer Sessions, 90

Client Service Excellence Award, 620

Edilia and François-Auguste de Montequin Fellowship in Iberian and Latin American Architecture, 801

Giles Worsley Travel Fellowship, 220

Lincoln Alumni Master of Architecture Scholarship, 973

Madbury Road Design Success Award Scholarship, 119

Ramboll Masters Scholarship for International Students, 1002

Resource Management Law Association of New Zealand Masters Scholarship, 146

Robert E. Thunen Memorial Scholarships, 183

University Studentships/Vice-Chancellor's Research Studentships (VCRS), 1105

Vice Chancellor, 1105

**European Union**

Asia Pacific Institute of Information Technology_IT PhDs in Grid Computing, 885

Australian Building Codes Board Research Scholarship, 885

**Canada**

Prix de Rome in Architecture for Emerging Practitioners, 231

**New Zealand**

Asia Pacific Institute of Information Technology_IT PhDs in Grid Computing, 885

**North American Countries**

Samuel H Kress Joint Athens-Jerusalem Fellowship, 100

**United Kingdom**

British Property Federation Lord Samuel of Wych Cross Memorial Award, 1081

The Royal Scottish Academy John Kinross Scholarships to Florence, 732

**United States of America**

A-AA Austrian Studies Scholarship Award, 175

American Association of University Women Selected Professions Fellowships, 45

## ARCHITECTURAL AND ENVIRONMENTAL DESIGN

**Any Country**

Sally Kress Tompkins Fellowship, 801

**South Africa**

Air-Conditioning, Heating, and Refrigeration Institute MSc Scholarship, 18

## LANDSCAPE ARCHITECTURE

**Any Country**

Max Brauer Award, 21

## REGIONAL PLANNING

**European Union**

Cardiff School of City and Regional Planning – Master's Bursaries, 264

## ARCHAEOLOGY

## ANCIENT CIVILISATIONS

## NATIVE LANGUAGE AND LITERATURE

*Any Country*
Herb Society of America Research Grant, 426

## PHILOSOPHY

*Any Country*
American Council of Learned Societies Humanities Program in Belarus, Russia and Ukraine, 55
Business, Economics & Law Postgraduate Academic Excellence Scholarship, 142
Commonwealth Scholarship, 892
Donald & Margot Watt Bursary Fund (FASS Only), 513
Donald Tovey Memorial Prize, 1015
Exeter College: Senior Scholarship in Theology, 1020
Frank Chapman Sharp Memorial Prize, 84
International Postgraduate Research Studentship (IPRS) at Murdoch University in Australia, 582
A J Ayer-Sumitomo Corporation Scholarship in Philosophy, 862
John G. Diefenbaker Award, 261
Liaoning Medical University Postdoctoral Fellowship for International Students at MCMP, 537
Oxford-Mary Jane Grefenstette Graduate Scholarship, 1050
*African Nations*
Respective Government Fellowships, 691
*Australia*
Co-op Bookshop Scholarship, 161
*European Union*
Philosophy Faculty-Wolfson College Joint Scholarship, 1055
*New Zealand*
Elman Poole Travelling Scholarship, 998

## TRANSLATION AND INTERPRETATION

*Any Country*
The PEN Translation Fund Grants, 671
Translation Competition, 112
*European Countries*
Oxford-Wolfson-Min Sunshik Graduate Scholarship in Modern Korean Literature, 1054

## WRITING (AUTHORSHIP)

*Any Country*
Donald & Margot Watt Bursary Fund (FASS Only), 513
Invertimos en el talento de los Colombianos (ICETEX) Artistas Jovenes Scholarships, 177
*African Nations*
Miles Morland Foundation Writing Scholarship, 570
*Australia*
OZCO Literature Grants Initiative: Write in Your Face, 154

## BUSINESS ADMINISTRATION AND MANAGEMENT

### GENERAL

*Any Country*
Acorn Foundation Eva Trowbridge Scholarship, 1106
Advancing Women in Leadership Scholarship (MBA), 625
American Association of University Women (AAUW) International Fellowships, 43
Blakemore Freeman Fellowships for Advanced Asian Language Study, 196
Business and Management Postgraduate Scholarships, 677
Business, Economics & Law Postgraduate Academic Excellence Scholarship, 142
The Business School Dean's Scholarship, 199
Center for Advancing Opportunity Doctorial Fellowship, 845
China: One Belt One Road Scholarship, 430
Council of Supply Chain Management Professionals Distinguished Service Award, 304
Council of Supply Chain Management Professionals Doctoral Dissertation Award, 304
Dean's Award for Enterprise Scholarship, 537
Division of Business Student Mobility Scholarships, 1087
Edward & Susan Wilson Graduate Scholarship in Business, 786
European Excellence Scholarship (MBA), 626
France: French Embassy and Saint-Gobain Master Scholarship, 431
France: French Embassy Masters and PhD Scholarship Programme, 431
George A. Gecowets Graduate Scholarship Program, 303
Gold and Silver Scholarships, 1109
Harvard University Master of Business Administration Scholarship in the United States of America, 418
HKBU Fully Funded International Postgraduate Scholarship, 15
Jeanne and Charles Rider Graduate Fellowship, 787
Jordan: Talal Abu-Ghazaleh University College for Innovation Scholarship, 433
LLM in International Trade Law – Contracts and Dispute Resolution – Scholarships, 881
Massey Business School - PhD Scholarships, 465
Master of Business Administration Business Excellence Scholarships, 628
Master of Business Administration Programme, 413, 806
Master of Business Administration Scholarships, 536
Nabil Boustany Scholarships, 915
Olin School of Business Washington University MBA Programme, 1139
Ossian R. MacKenzie Teaching Award, 787
Peter E. Liberti and Judy D. Olian Scholarship, 787

## ACCOUNTANCY

## BUSINESS AND COMMERCE

## BUSINESS COMPUTING

## BUSINESS MACHINE OPERATION

## FINANCE, BANKING AND INVESTMENT

## HUMAN RESOURCES

*New Zealand*
Charles Fleming Senior Scientist Award, 733

## EDUCATIONAL TECHNOLOGY

*Russia*
Intel Public Affairs Russia Grant, 469

## EDUCATIONAL TESTING AND EVALUATION

*Any Country*
Educational Testing Service Harold Gulliksen Psychometric
    Fellowship Program, 347

## INTERNATIONAL AND COMPARATIVE EDUCATION

*Any Country*
Nicholas Hans Comparative Education Scholarship, 463

## TEACHING AND LEARNING

*Any Country*
College of Science and Engineering Postgraduate Scholarship
    Scheme, 970
Fulbright-Nehru Doctoral Research Fellowships, 858
*United States of America*
James Bryant Conant Award in High School Chemistry
    Teaching, 53

## HIGHER EDUCATION TEACHER TRAINING

*Any Country*
Fulbright-Nehru Master's Fellowships, 858
Lady Meherbai D. TATA Education Trust, 834
Robinson Scholarship, 516
Snowdon Masters Scholarship, 678
United Nationals Educational Scientific Cultural Organiza-
    tion Individual Fellowships, 852
*Asian Countries*
Brunei Darussalam: Government of Brunei Darussalam
    Scholarship, 429
Fellow Programme in Management (FPM) at Xavier Labor
    Relations Institute, 1169
*Canada*
Multiple Sclerosis Society of Canada Scholarship Programs:
    John Helou Scholarship, 860
*United Kingdom*
Ray Y. Gildea Jr Award, 726
*United States of America*
Access Missouri Financial Assistance Program, 574
Ray Y. Gildea Jr Award, 726

## NONVOCATIONAL SUBJECTS EDUCATION

HUMANITIES AND SOCIAL SCIENCE EDUCATION
*Any Country*
Associate Alumni Bursary, 677

Foundation Praemium Erasmianum Study Prize, 390
Global Professorships, 201
Lost Cities Funding Programme, 838
Short-Term EFEO Postdoctoral Contracts, 383
*African Nations*
Zentrum Moderner Orient and Berlin Graduate School of
    Muslim Cultures and Societies Visiting Research Fellow-
    ship, 183
*Asian Countries*
Zentrum Moderner Orient and Berlin Graduate School of
    Muslim Cultures and Societies Visiting Research Fellow-
    ship, 183
*Middle East*
Zentrum Moderner Orient and Berlin Graduate School of
    Muslim Cultures and Societies Visiting Research Fellow-
    ship, 183

## SECONDARY EDUCATION

*United Kingdom*
Ray Y. Gildea Jr Award, 726
*United States of America*
Ray Y. Gildea Jr Award, 726
Woodrow Wilson Teaching Fellowship, 1164

## SPECIAL EDUCATION

*United States of America*
Alliance for Clinical Research Excellence and Safety Teacher
    Scholarship Award, 57

## EDUCATION OF THE GIFTED

*Any country*
Distinguished Scholarship, 594

## STAFF DEVELOPMENT

*Any Country*
American Council on Education Fellows Program, 56
Fowler-Merle Smith Summer Scholarship for Teachers, 91
Scholar-in-Residence Program, 331
*United Kingdom*
De Montfort University Awards to Women for Final Year
    Doctoral Research, 320
*United States of America*
Oregon-Idaho Conference Ethnic Leadership Award, 412

## VOCATIONAL SUBJECTS EDUCATION

*Any Country*
Balliol College: IKOS Half Bursary, 1010
*Asian Countries*
Vocational Education and Training (VET) Distinction Schol-
    arship, 280

## AERONAUTICAL AND AEROSPACE ENGINEERING

## AUTOMOTIVE ENGINEERING

## BIOENGINEERING AND BIOMEDICAL ENGINEERING

## CHEMICAL ENGINEERING

## ART HISTORY

## ART MANAGEMENT

## JOURNALISM

## LIBRARY SCIENCE

## MEDIA STUDIES

## MUSEUM STUDIES

## PUBLIC RELATIONS AND PUBLICITY

## RADIO/TELEVISION BROADCASTING

## MATHEMATICS AND COMPUTER SCIENCE

### GENERAL

## APPLIED MATHEMATICS

## ARTIFICIAL INTELLIGENCE

## COMPUTER SCIENCE

## STATISTICS

# MEDICAL SCIENCES

## GENERAL

## ANAESTHESIOLOGY

## CARDIOLOGY

## DERMATOLOGY

## ENDOCRINOLOGY

## EPIDEMIOLOGY

## ASTRONOMY AND ASTROPHYSICS

## BIOLOGICAL AND LIFE SCIENCES

## SOCIAL AND BEHAVIOURAL SCIENCES

### GENERAL

# Index of Awards

© Springer Nature Limited 2020
Palgrave Macmillan (ed.), *The Grants Register 2021*,
https://doi.org/10 1057/978-1-349-95988-4

# Index of Awarding Organisations

© Springer Nature Limited 2020
Palgrave Macmillan (ed.), *The Grants Register 2021*,
https://doi.org/10.1057/978-1-349-95988-4